Let's Go

Let's Go writers travel on your budget.

"Guides that penetrate the veneer of the holiday brochures and mine the grit of real life."

—The Economist

"The writers seem to have experienced every rooster-packed bus and lunar-surfaced mattress about which they write."

—The New York Times

"All the dirt, dirt cheap."

—People

Great for independent travelers.

"The guides are aimed not only at young budget travelers but at the independent traveler; a sort of streetwise cookbook for traveling alone."

—The New York Times

"A guide should tell you what to expect from a destination. Here *Let's Go* shines."

—The Chicago Tribune

"An indispensible resource, *Let's Go*'s practical information can be used by every traveler."

—The Chattanooga Free Press

Let's Go is completely revised each year.

"A publishing phenomenon...the only major guidebook series updated annually. *Let's Go* is the big kahuna."

—The Boston Globe

"Unbeatable: good sight-seeing advice; up-to-date info on restaurants, hotels, and inns; a commitment to money-saving travel; and a wry style that brightens nearly every page."

—The Washington Post

All the important information you need.

"*Let's Go* authors provide a comedic element while still providing concise information and thorough coverage of the country. Anything you need to know about budget traveling is detailed in this book."

—The Chicago Sun-Times

"*Let's Go* guidebooks take night life seriously."

—The Chicago Tribune

Let's Go Publications

Let's Go: Alaska & the Pacific Northwest 2002
Let's Go: Amsterdam 2002 **New Title!**
Let's Go: Australia 2002
Let's Go: Austria & Switzerland 2002
Let's Go: Barcelona 2002 **New Title!**
Let's Go: Boston 2002
Let's Go: Britain & Ireland 2002
Let's Go: California 2002
Let's Go: Central America 2002
Let's Go: China 2002
Let's Go: Eastern Europe 2002
Let's Go: Egypt 2002 **New Title!**
Let's Go: Europe 2002
Let's Go: France 2002
Let's Go: Germany 2002
Let's Go: Greece 2002
Let's Go: India & Nepal 2002
Let's Go: Ireland 2002
Let's Go: Israel 2002
Let's Go: Italy 2002
Let's Go: London 2002
Let's Go: Mexico 2002
Let's Go: Middle East 2002
Let's Go: New York City 2002
Let's Go: New Zealand 2002
Let's Go: Paris 2002
Let's Go: Peru, Ecuador & Bolivia 2002
Let's Go: Rome 2002
Let's Go: San Francisco 2002
Let's Go: South Africa with Southern Africa 2002
Let's Go: Southeast Asia 2002
Let's Go: Southwest USA 2002 **New Title!**
Let's Go: Spain & Portugal 2002
Let's Go: Turkey 2002
Let's Go: USA 2002
Let's Go: Washington, D.C. 2002
Let's Go: Western Europe 2002

Let's Go *Map Guides*

Amsterdam
Berlin
Boston
Chicago
Dublin
Florence
Hong Kong
London
Los Angeles
Madrid
New Orleans
New York City
Paris
Prague
Rome
San Francisco
Seattle
Sydney
Venice
Washington, D.C.

Let's Go SOUTHEAST ASIA 2002

Gautam Bhan editor
Megha M. Doshi associate editor
Kiri J. Mah associate editor
Gretchen C. Puttkamer associate editor

researcher-writers

Cutler Cook
Olivia Cowley
Lisa Frenchik
Christian Fung
Philip Hodges
Alisa Sakai
Brooke Scelza
Maya Sen
Allie Thompson
Ben Wilkinson
Jason D. Williams
Jonathan Williams
Michael Wheeler

Julia A. Stephens map editor

Marly Ohlsson managing editor

Macmillan

HELPING LET'S GO If you want to share your discoveries, suggestions, or corrections, please drop us a line. We read every piece of correspondence, whether a postcard, a 10-page email, or a coconut. Please note that mail received after May 2002 may be too late for the 2003 book, but will be kept for future editions. **Address mail to:**

Let's Go: Zembla
67 Mount Auburn Street
Cambridge, MA 02138
USA

Visit Let's Go at **http://www.letsgo.com,** or send email to:

feedback@letsgo.com
Subject: "Let's Go: Zembla"

In addition to the invaluable travel advice our readers share with us, many are kind enough to offer their services as researchers or editors. Unfortunately, our charter enables us to employ only currently enrolled Harvard students.

Published in Great Britain 2002 by Macmillan, an imprint of Pan Macmillan Ltd.
20 New Wharf Road, London N1 9RR
Basingstoke and Oxford
Associated companies throughout the world
www.panmacmillan.com

Published in the United States of America by St. Martin's Press.

ISBN: 0-333-90598-9
First edition
10 9 8 7 6 5 4 3 2 1

Let's Go: Zembla is written by Let's Go Publications, 67 Mount Auburn Street, Cambridge, MA 02138, USA.

Printed in the USA on recycled paper with biodegradable soy ink.

ADVERTISING DISCLAIMER All advertisements appearing in Let's Go publications are sold by an independent agency not affiliated with the editorial production of the guides. Advertisers are never given preferential treatment, and the guides are researched, written, and published independent of advertising. Advertisements do not imply endorsement of products or services by Let's Go, and Let's Go does not vouch for the accuracy of information provided in advertisements.

If you are interested in purchasing advertising space in a Let's Go publication, contact: Let's Go Advertising Sales, 67 Mount Auburn St., Cambridge, MA 02138, USA.

ABOUT LET'S GO

FORTY-TWO YEARS OF WISDOM

For over four decades, travelers crisscrossing the continents have relied on *Let's Go* for inside information on the hippest backstreet cafes, the most pristine secluded beaches, and the best routes from border to border. *Let's Go: Europe*, now in its 42nd edition and translated into seven languages, reigns as the world's bestselling international travel guide. In the last 20 years, our rugged researchers have stretched the frontiers of backpacking and expanded our coverage into the Americas, Australia, Asia, and Africa (including the new *Let's Go: Egypt* and the more comprehensive, multi-country jaunt through *Let's Go: South Africa & Southern Africa*). Our new-and-improved City Guide series continues to grow with new guides to perennial European favorites Amsterdam and Barcelona. This year we are also unveiling *Let's Go: Southwest USA*, the flagship of our new outdoor Adventure Guide series, which is complete with special roadtripping tips and itineraries, more coverage of adventure activities like hiking and mountain biking, and first-person accounts of life on the road.

It all started in 1960 when a handful of well-traveled students at Harvard University handed out a 20-page mimeographed pamphlet offering a collection of their tips on budget travel to passengers on student charter flights to Europe. The following year, in response to the instant popularity of the first volume, students traveling to Europe researched the first full-fledged edition of *Let's Go: Europe*. Throughout the 60s and 70s, our guides reflected the times—in 1969, for example, we taught you how to get from Paris to Prague on "no dollars a day" by singing in the street. In the 90s we focused in on the world's most exciting urban areas to produce in-depth, fold-out map guides, now with 20 titles (from Hong Kong to Chicago) and counting. Our new guides bring the total number of titles to 57, each infused with the spirit of adventure and voice of opinion that travelers around the world have come to count on. But some things never change: our guides are still researched, written, and produced entirely by students who know first-hand how to see the world on the cheap.

HOW WE DO IT

Each guide is completely revised and thoroughly updated every year by a well-traveled set of nearly 300 students. Every spring, we recruit over 200 researchers and 90 editors to overhaul every book. After several months of training, researcher-writers hit the road for seven weeks of exploration, from Anchorage to Adelaide, Estonia to El Salvador, Iceland to Indonesia. Hired for their rare combination of budget travel sense, writing ability, stamina, and courage, these adventurous travelers know that train strikes, stolen luggage, food poisoning, and marriage proposals are all part of a day's work. Back at our offices, editors work from spring to fall, massaging copy written on Himalayan bus rides into witty, informative prose. A student staff of typesetters, cartographers, publicists, and managers keeps our lively team together. In September, the collected efforts of the summer are delivered to our printer, who turns them into books in record time, so that you have the most up-to-date information available for your vacation. Even as you read this, work on next year's editions is well underway.

WHY WE DO IT

We don't think of budget travel as the last recourse of the destitute; we believe that it's the only way to travel. Our books will ease your anxieties and answer your questions about the basics—so you can get off the beaten track and explore. Once you learn the ropes, we encourage you to put *Let's Go* down and strike out on your own. You know as well as we that the best discoveries are often those you make yourself. When you find something worth sharing, please drop us a line. We're Let's Go Publications, 67 Mount Auburn St., Cambridge, MA 02138, USA (feedback@letsgo.com). For more info, visit our website, www.letsgo.com.

CHINA
Guangzhou
Macau
Kowloon
HONG KONG
MYANMAR
Mandalay
Red River
Hanoi
Haiphong
Luang Prabang
LAOS
Chiang Mai
Vientiane
Gulf of Tonkin
Hainan Island
Yangon
Mekong River
Khon Kaen
Sukhothai
THAILAND
Hue
Da Nang
Chao Phraya River
Nakhon Ratchasima
Ayutthaya
Andaman Sea
Bangkok
Siem Reap
VIETNAM
CAMBODIA
SOUTH CHINA SEA
Phnom Penh
Nha Trang
Ho Chi Minh City (Saigon)
Gulf of Thailand
Can Tho
Phuket
Banda Aceh
Balabac Strait
Kota Bharu
Georgetown
Kota Kinabalu
Bandar Seri Bagawan
BRUNEI DARUSSALAM
SABAH
Medan
Strait of Melaka
Kuala Lumpur
MALAYSIA
Melaka
SINGAPORE
SARAWAK
Kuching
Pulau Nias
SUMATRA
Riau Islands
BORNEO
Padang
KALIMANTAN
Jambi
Karimata Strait
Bangka
Palembang
Makassar Strait
Bandar Lampung
Jakarta
INDO
Java Sea
Bandung
Surabaya
Yogyakarta
JAVA
BALI
LOMBOK
Denpasar
SUMBAWA
INDIAN OCEAN

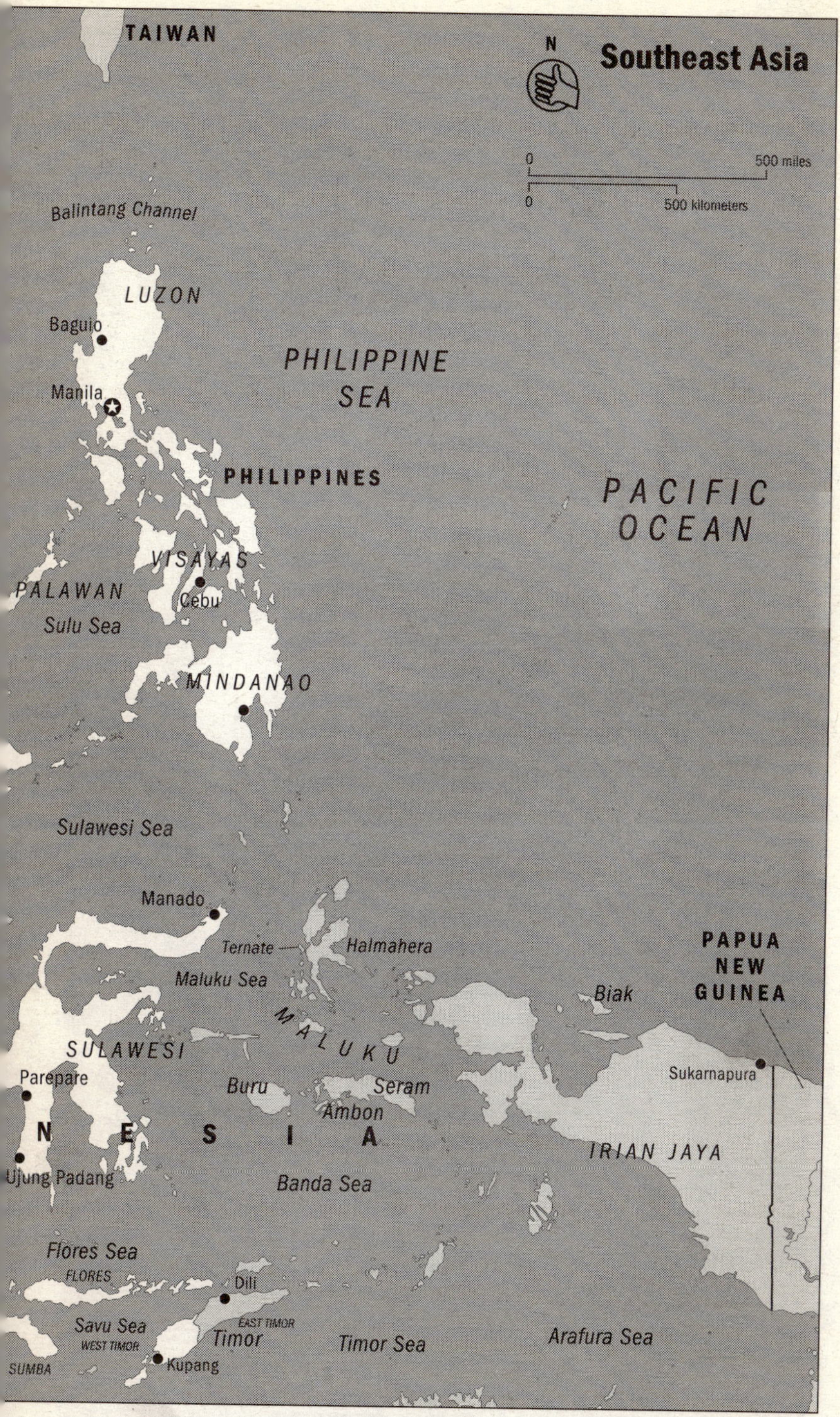

Southeast Asia
N
0
500 miles
0
500 kilometers
TAIWAN
Balintang Channel
LUZON
Baguio
Manila
PHILIPPINE SEA
PHILIPPINES
PACIFIC OCEAN
VISAYAS
PALAWAN
Cebu
Sulu Sea
MINDANAO
Sulawesi Sea
Manado
Ternate
Halmahera
Maluku Sea
MALUKU
PAPUA NEW GUINEA
Biak
SULAWESI
Parepare
Buru
Seram
Ambon
Sukarnapura
NESIA
Ujung Padang
IRIAN JAYA
Banda Sea
Flores Sea
FLORES
Dili
EAST TIMOR
Savu Sea
WEST TIMOR
Timor
Timor Sea
Arafura Sea
SUMBA
Kupang

CONTENTS

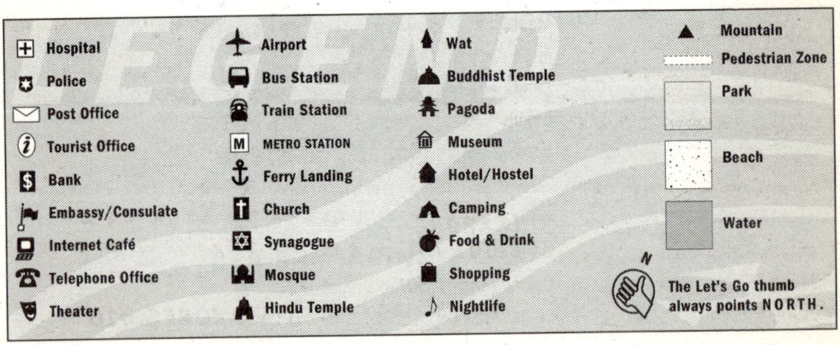
Hospital
Police
Post Office
Tourist Office
Bank
Embassy/Consulate
Internet Café
Telephone Office
Theater
Airport
Bus Station
Train Station
METRO STATION
Ferry Landing
Church
Synagogue
Mosque
Hindu Temple
Wat
Buddhist Temple
Pagoda
Museum
Hotel/Hostel
Camping
Food & Drink
Shopping
Nightlife
Mountain
Pedestrian Zone
Park
Beach
Water
N
The Let's Go thumb always points NORTH.

MAPS

RESEARCHER-WRITERS

Cutler Cook *Sumatra and Jakarta*

Seemingly unable to stop traveling, our Eton-trained warrior earned his four middle names battling Indonesian squat toilets. Scoffing at the idea of "rest days," he set Sumatra on fire in his search for tea and crumpets, all the while managing to send immaculate "CCTC" emblazoned copy to us like clockwork. Sorry to make you cover Jakarta after 50 days of travel, Cuttlefish and chips, but no one could have done it with your flavour. And no, that ain't no typo. Long live the Queen.

Olivia Cowley *Ho Chi Minh City*

Our dame in shining Armani, Olivia added one more tango to her already extensive Let's Go dance card—she was a researcher for *Let's Go: Peru and Ecuador 1999*, the editor of *Let's Go: Spain, Portugal, and Morocco 2000*, and a managing editor in 2001—and took a twirl around HCMC to help us in our hour of need. The only person we know who just "happens to be in Vietnam," our Superwoman reminded us what keeps *Let's Go* going.

Lisa Frenchik *Bali, Lombok, Flores, Sumbawa, Sumba*

Picture this: a girl born with the chic of the independent film maker she's soon to become sits in an open-top jeep as she hauls ass through the beaches of Bali, yawning at the tasks we set out for her. With enough girl power to make Xena blush, Lisa tore through her itinerary at record speed but still found time to teach surfer dudes in Bali how to be cool, cabaret boys in Senggigi how to truly get down, and us back in the office how to write copy for travelin' divas. We want your biceps, Lisa. We really do.

Christian Fung *Vietnam*

There are about seven gay men in Hanoi. Christian found them all. Having been to more countries than the entire bookteam put together, this intrepid traveler set off to trace the Vietnamese coastline from Hanoi to Ho Chi Minh City, running away from the beaten path to find the Vietnam hidden behind the package tours. Handwriting that had us crying with joy documented immaculately researched copy; no price fluctuated in all of Vietnam without Christian knowing about it. We're sorry, babe, but your plant died. Apparently, plants don't like vodka.

Philip Hodges *Java, Sulawesi*

Taking time off from filming a Pakistani cigarette commercial, Phil explored every inch of Java, from ditches that left him smelling like cheese to the summit of Mt. Bromo. Stuffing his 194cm. into minibuses across the land, we're glad that he realized that we weren't serious about the 79hr. bus trip at the end of his route. Sorry you searched for four hours for that rock that didn't quite exist, P-diddy, but we're glad you found every techno club east of Jakarta. Oh, and thanks for the Viagra tea. If we have it everyday, can we be like you too?

Alisa Sakai *Singapore, Peninsular Malaysia, Southern Thailand*

One of only two researchers to be entrusted with an entire chapter, Alisa came through big time. Sometimes it seems like half of Southeast Asia drove (or wanted to drive) her around as she traversed the urban meccas of Singapore and Kuala Lumpur before proving that a wild time could be had in the islands of Southern Thailand, even in the low season. This is our wedding present to you, A., enjoy it, thanks, and congratulations!

Brooke Scelza *Peninsular Malaysia, Sabah, Sarawak, Brunei*

Who'd have guessed that little Brooke was so hardcore. This world traveler caught us all off guard with her impeccable organization, unmatched stamina, and handwriting clearer than the waters in which she snorkeled. Neither scary terrorists nor nasty illnesses kept Brooke "8 times an hour" Scelza from foraging through national parks or climbing Gunung Kinabalu. We don't know how you did it all, Brooke, but we're sure glad you did.

Maya Sen *Central and Southern Thailand*

We have bones to pick with Maya—she made us work. Not only did she have 8 million ideas for how each Thai island should be organized, they all made perfect sense, leaving us no choice but to put them all in. Who does that?!? Breaking down the myths of Thailand's sun and sands, Maya used the beach sense she gained as the editor of *Let's Go: Mexico 2000* and told it like it is, using adjectives in ways that taught us all a thing or two. We surrender, Ms. Sen.

Allie Thompson *Laos, Cambodia, and the Mekong Delta*

The baby of the SEAS family, Allie shrugged off all doubters and set off to explore Laos and Cambodia. Though at times hindered by the fact that roads ceased to exist in the monsoon, she managed to reach every nook, cranny, and pub in the region, proving that with skills like hers, there's a way to research everything. We're not jealous at all, Allie, that you got to see Angkor Wat. Not at all. You see, we had your copy to keep us happy. Thanks, girl.

Ben Wilkinson *Visayas and Mindanao*

Ben wrote this book. No really, he did. The editor of *Let's Go: Southeast Asia 1999*, he not only undertook the longest itinerary known to mankind but turned in copy so perfect that we had nothing left to edit. As an Editorial Manager the year before and Publishing Director the year before that, Ben has *Let's Go* in his blood and proved it yet again. Though you made us all feel inadequate in every way, Big B., we must have done something right to get you.

Jason D. Williams *Luzon, Manila, Palawan*

Cute as a button, even Jason had his doubts before setting off. But with one breath of Manila air, he had swarms of Filipino girls blushing (nothing he's not used to, we're sure) with his fluent Tagalog. Undaunted by lost luggage, typhoons, a volcano eruption, a broken *banca*, and Manila humidity that had him begging us for anti-frizz conditioner, Jason took on everything from rice terraces to bars, proving a better guide than his resident cousins. This superstar even overcame personal tragedy and insisted on finishing his itinerary, leaving us all in awe of his strength.

Jonathan Williams *Myanmar, Bangkok*

Blessed with natural North Dakotan charm and rugged good looks, this *Let's Go: Southeast Asia 2001* vet did what no one thought was possible: he came back to the SEAS mothership. Unperturbed by anonymous midnight calls, Jon smiled his way through approximately eleven million pagodas and a few slightly suspicious military officials on his way to "researching" the steamy streets of Patpong in Bangkok (see North Dakotan good looks, above). As if his brilliant copy wasn't enough, he came straight from the airport to help us edit. We feel the love, J.

Michael Wheeler *North and Northeast Thailand*

After hanging from ropes in a Moscow theater production, Michael took off to hang from ropes in the mountains of Northern Thailand. Brushing off ATM fraud and recurrent bouts of what he claimed was the "Russian flu" (we believe you, Mike...promise), he marched through his route with the last of his baht hidden in his socks. His hard work was rewarded when, in his own words, "Mike + beach + Swedish girl + no flu = happy."

ACKNOWLEDGMENTS

The Let's Go 2002 series is dedicated to the memory of Haley Surti

SEAS THANKS. SEASism: Marly=■. ■=Marly. Thanks to I&N for spice markets, kraftwerk, and Gabe. To 4th fl. love. To the prod pod and our legion of typists and proofers. To the goddess of maps, J-dawg. To Olivia for HCMC and Julie Wecsler for Hong Kong. To our RWs: how much do you rock?

GB THANKS. To Marly for being da boss. To my Charlie's Angels/AEs: I knew I was smart to hire you on your sexy looks alone. Y'all rock my world. To Pos: thank you types yaar. To 9 Wyatt skank. To the purple flower and India in December (We're going!!). To home: ma, baba, sheenu, abs. To the Am'erst gang: I miss ya too. To endless nights and rain on the footbridge. To the fire escape and stairwells everywhere. To a year gone by and one to come. To Pride in golden harem pants. To Southeast Asia and learning how to be alone. Alvida.

MD THANKS. GB for skank. KM for Rufus and yummy food. GP for always being so happy! Marly for being so ridiculously on top of things. You rule! Brooke and Jason for being such cute and stupendous researchers. Anna for waking me up every morning and enduring the MBTA with me. Mom and Dad for ESL emails and too many phone calls. Rach for care packages, Montreal, and shopping. The Wrap for Jimmy Carters. Luna bars. 'Nuff said. 17a Belmont for a bed. Chris for all the format quirks. OZ for much-needed distractions. I&N for being so hilarious.

KM THANKS. GB for hiring little old me, it's been great and totally worth it. Megha for early morning looniness and the smoothie times. Gretchen for all the songs and coffee breaks. Marly for showing up in the AM. 318 Beacon roomies Chris, Collin, and J for the IHOP nights and cable days. Nelson for putting up with me and keeping me fan-cooled full-time. Mom, Dad, Dom and Mike for the emails and pep-talks. The fourth floor for being fabulous. My RWs for the presents and pictures. Friends for seeing me through the craziness. And SEAS for the long names and laughs.

GP THANKS. To G-daddy (thinking in NC-17), Kiri (good music and kitchen wonders), and Megha (someday you'll run with middle-aged me!) for taking me back after the affair and allowing me to enjoy the everlasting skankdom that is SEAS love. To Marly for being so kick-ass. To Kate, Chi Trung, and Quang Trung for opening me up to the world of Vietnam. To LKP for reminding me to step back and see the things that really matter. To the fam for DI bonding, early-morning chaul, and helping me find some peace in the middle of the craziness.

HOW TO USE THIS BOOK

Southeast Asia is a land of tradition and flux, so be prepared to experience and enjoy both. *Let's Go* lists thousand-year-old temples that will still be around when you get there and two-year-old guest houses that will have bitten the proverbial dust before these pages go to press. Choose the right guest house during the bumpy bus ride into town; if it's out of business, move down the list and relish in the uncertainty of life on the road. Slide your index finger into the "Sights" section as you wander from pagoda to pagoda. Use the absorbent pages to mop your brow in the sweltering Southeast Asian heat. Swat mosquitoes with the book as you sit on your favorite guest house patio, and utilize its used pages as toilet paper in the ubiquitous squat toilets. Let these pages and your instinct be your guides and trust no other.

ORGANIZATION OF THIS BOOK

INTRODUCTORY MATERIAL. The first chapter, **Discover Southeast Asia,** provides an overview of travel in the region. The **suggested itineraries** give an idea of the places you shouldn't miss and how long it takes to see them. Check out the snazzy maps in this section—we like 'em a lot. The **Essentials** section outlines practical information, like bureaucratic formalities, health and safety concerns, and transport information, that you'll need both before you leave and once you're there .

COVERAGE. Each chapter covers a country, beginning with Brunei and tracing the alphabet to Vietnam. Each chapter's **Life and Times** section outlines country-specific history, culture, and practical information. The **black tabs** in the margins—and knowing that "V" comes after "M"—will help you to navigate between chapters quickly and easily.

APPENDIX. The appendix has useful **conversions,** a **phrasebook** of handy phrases in the gamut of Southeast Asian languages, another **map** to decode Southeast Asia's bizarre time zones, a **climate** chart, and a list of all major **holidays and festivals.**

A FEW NOTES ABOUT LET'S GO FORMAT

RANKING ESTABLISHMENTS. In each section (accommodations, food, etc.), we rank establishments, starting with our favorites. Our absolute favorites are so denoted by *Let's Go's* highest honor, the *Let's Go* thumbs-up (■).

GRAYBOXES AND IKONBOXES. Grayboxes often provide wonderful cultural insights but, once in a while, are simply expressions of our often bizarre sense of humor. In any case, they're usually amusing, so enjoy. **Whiteboxes,** on the other hand, provide important practical information, such as warnings (■), helpful hints and resources (■), and border crossing information (■).

OUR QUIRKS. Southeast Asia has more islands than the Sultan of Brunei has fornicating watches (see p. 59) or Imelda Marcos has shoes (see p. 515). To aid your island hopping ideas, **View from Above** boxes summarize the highlights of major islands. Additionally, refer to p. 464 for a note on our coverage of Myanmar, and note that **HCMC** and **KL** are used in place of Ho Chi Minh City and Kuala Lumpur.

A NOTE TO OUR READERS The information for this book was gathered by *Let's Go* researchers from May through August of 2001. Each listing is based on one researcher's opinion, formed during his or her visit at a particular time. Those traveling at other times may have different experiences since prices, dates, hours, and conditions are always subject to change. You are urged to check the facts presented in this book beforehand to avoid inconvenience and surprises.

DISCOVER SOUTHEAST ASIA

Southeast Asia is the offspring of thousands of years of sea trade, religious conflict, colonial influence, expanding empires, political maneuvering, and continuous ethnic redefinition. Legend, mixed with scientific evidence, says that the story began when the Tai-Kadai people arrived from southern China and formed the Thai and Lao kingdoms. Indonesian Malays intermarried with Indian traders and princes to become the Khmer people, and a Chinese migration enriched the blood lines. Kingdoms mixed, matched and migrated; European powers divided, conquered, and colonized; and in the wake of colonialism, nation-states formed, collapsed, and rebuilt themselves. From these shared origins, the countries of Southeast Asia have formed distinct, proud, and historic national identities that flaunt themselves amidst the stunning geographic and cultural diversity that has come to characterize the region. Shimmering crater lakes await the tranquil traveler, while the steamy streets of the bustling big cities challenge even the hardiest urban adventurer. Every trip to Southeast Asia is an experience that awes, frightens, challenges, educates, and spell-binds. Though little is certain in Southeast Asia, one thing is guaranteed: looking back on one of the world's most incredible regions, you'll have one heck of a story to tell.

FACTS AND FIGURES

POPULATION: 479,500,000.

COUPS SINCE 1950: 42.

WATS, PAGODAS, OR TEMPLES PER CAPITA: We stopped counting at 17,500,000–give or take a few.

AVG. # OF WHEELS PER VEHICLE: 2.79.

COUNTRIES: 11.

SEX CHANGE OPERATIONS: 21,473.

ISLANDS: 25,390.

AVG. LENGTH OF THAI ISLAND PARTIES: 31hr.

AVG. COST OF 31HR. THAI ISLAND PARTIES: 6$.

WHEN TO GO

Southeast Asia has dry and rainy seasons which roughly correspond to high and low tourism seasons. During the low season, sights are less crowded, and fewer services are offered at reduced prices. Some beaches and islands close down and fewer trekking opportunities are available.

The rainy season spans May to September in the north and runs later in the year the farther south you travel. For example, in Bali, the rains last from November to May. Closer to the Equator, the hotter the weather and the less the variations among seasons. The weather in Southeast Asia is hot and humid; temperatures fluctuate around 27°C (80°F) year-round everywhere except the extreme uplands of mainland Southeast Asia, where night-time temperatures can fall to near freezing. For a rough conversion from °C to °F, multiply by two and add 30. (See the conversion chart in the **Appendix,** p. 912.)

WHAT TO DO

With eleven countries and countless destinations to choose from, planning an itinerary in Southeast Asia can be as difficult as getting yaks to mate at low altitudes. Luckily for you—and the yaks—this section details routes, **suggested itineraries,** must-do's, and must-dont's to give you an idea of the country-hopping, beach-bumming, mountain-climbing, budget-living days that lie ahead of you. Rock on.

LA ISLA BONITA

Southeast Asia boasts some of the most inviting strips of sand in the world. Luxury resorts are invading famous destinations such as **Phuket,** Thailand or **Bali,** Indonesia, but budget hideaways—bathed in the same sunlight as the five-star resorts—are still available nearly everywhere. The islands of **Ko Samet, Ko Chang, Ko Phangan,** and **Ko Tao** in Thailand; **Pulau Tioman** and the **Perhentian Islands** in Malaysia; **Pulau Nias** off Sumatra, **Kuta Beach** on Bali, and the **Gilis** off Lombok in Indonesia; and **Boracay** and **Biliran** in the Philippines should be on every self-respecting beach bummer's to-do list. In general, Thailand's beach scene is the most raucous; Ko Phangan's infamous Full Moon Party thrown every month is an all-night rave not to be missed. To challenge the Full Moon Party's dominance of the party scene, head to Bali's legendary Kuta Beach or Philippines' Boracay island, both newcomers that are rising in infamy with faster, longer and deeper trances into partydom. If the partying crowds are exactly what you want to avoid, head to **Lovina** or **Sanur** off Bali in Indonesia, or the quieter beaches on the **Vietnamese coast.**

Bali is the undisputed surfing mecca of Southeast Asia. **Legundi Beach** on **Pulau Nias** is well known for its monstrous surf, and other islands in **Nusa Tenggara,** especially **Sumbawa,** have consistent breaks and minimal crowds. Southeast Asia is also an excellent place to learn to scuba dive; PADI certification courses are cheaper here than anywhere else in the world and only in Southeast Asia can non-certified divers get taken on "try dives." Most divers gravitate to **Ko Tao** or **Phuket** in Thailand, but clearer waters and more marine life are on **Apo** and **Panglao Islands** in the Philippines and **Manado** on Sulawesi, Indonesia.

AIN'T NO MOUNTAIN HIGH ENOUGH

Since the mid-1980s, jungle trekking and its trendy 90s cousin, "eco-tourism," have become premier tourist draws to the region. National parks abound and offer a cool and peaceful respite from the summer heat. For high-quality, affordable treks, head to **Northern Thailand,** where the rage began 20 years ago. (For more coverage of trekking in Thailand, see **Hill Tribes and Trekking,** p. 626, and **Trekking around Chiang Mai,** p. 699.) Backpackers trek, climb and spelunk in the national parks of **Sabah** and **Sarawak. Taman Negara,** a national park in the world's oldest rainforest, offers everything from canopy walking on rickety rope bridges to week long camping stays. **Palawan** in the Philippines has the world's longest underground river. For hikers, Southeast Asia presents peaks of varying difficulty, including **Fansipan** in northern Vietnam, **Gunung Kinabalu** in Sabah, **Gunung Agung** in Bali, **Gunung Rinjani** in Lombok, and the **Mayon** volcano and **Mt. Apo** in the Philippines, though the last has an annoying habit of erupting every once in a while.

GHETTO SUPERSTARS

In every major city, backpackers huddle in their ghettoes, meeting fellow travelers, exchanging tales of travel and diarrhea, and watching locals with interest as the same locals watch them with amusement. During the high season, grungy, scantily clad foreigners seem to outnumber the locals. Some travelers shun contact with fellow *farang;* others relish the opportunity to spend weeks holed up in cheap guest houses jawing with others and avoiding the outside world. Love 'em or hate 'em, these hangouts are places to pick up travel tips, get a new book, or just remember what English sounds like. Among the backpacker haunts of Southeast Asia are: **Bangkok's Khao San Rd., Chiang Mai, Nong Khai,** and the islands in Thailand; **Georgetown,** the **Perhentian Islands,** and **Pulau Tioman** in Malaysia; **Jogjakarta** on Java, **Ubud** and **Kuta** on Bali, the **Gilis** off Lombok, and **Bukit Tinggi** and **Lake Toba** on Sumatra, all in Indonesia; **Sabang** and **Boracay** in the Philippines; **Hồ Chí Minh City** and **Hội An** in Vietnam; and **Singapore.**

Some of the more isolated regions that see less backpacker traffic are: **Northeast Thailand,** the Cambodia's **Mekong River,** the **Mekong Delta** of Vietnam, Malaysia's east coast, **Flores** and **northern Sulawesi** in Indonesia, **Negros,** and **Davao** in the Philippines, **southern Laos,** and all of **Myanmar.** Traveling during the low season is an excellent way to dodge the crowds almost anywhere though fewer services are available and some resorts even close for the entire period.

STAYIN' ALIVE

Many tourists come to the region seeking "traditional" Southeast Asian culture. At its worst, "ethnotourism" leads to human zoos such as the long-neck **Karen villages** of Northern Thailand or the so-called **"Chicken Village"** outside Đà Lạt, Vietnam; in most cases, however, travelers are welcome to observe and participate in local ceremonies and festivals. Chances to respectfully interact with indigenous cultures include: visiting **longhouses** in **Sarawak** and **Sabah;** participating in massive **funerals** in **Tana Toraja** in Sulawesi; traveling down the **Mekong** by barge with a Lao family; staying with a **hill-tribe village** in **Mai Châu,** Vietnam; or living in a **Malay kampung,** a **Thai Muslim fishing community,** or an **Ifugao village** in the **Central Cordillera** of Luzon. Be sensitive, respective, and aware of your surroundings.

PAPA WAS A ROLLING STONE

Southeast Asia has been the site of many great civilizations, most of which seem to have been obsessed either with building things, or with breaking the things that others built. As a result, awe-inspiring temples, palaces, and wats abound, side-by-side with the ruins of those that didn't make it. The three wonders of classical Southeast Asia are **Angkor** in Cambodia, **Bagan** in Myanmar, and **Borobudur** on Java in Indonesia. The imperial city in **Huế,** Vietnam, a microcosm of Beijing's Forbidden City, provides a fascinating counterpoint to the Indic-influenced monuments elsewhere in the region. **Luang Prabang** in Laos may be the best-preserved ancient city in the region. In Thailand, the former capitals of **Sukhothai** and **Ayutthaya** shouldn't be missed.

THINGS THAT MAKE YOU GO HMMM...

Food. Good, cheap food. The unbelievable cuisine alone is worth the trip to Southeast Asia. Among the culinary highlights are the **hawker stalls** of Singapore, the *nyonya* cuisine of Penang and Melaka in Malaysia, the spicy *padang* food of Sumatra, the Vietnamese delicacies found in Huế, the hybridized dishes of European inspiration in **Ubud,** the **dim sum** of Hong Kong, and just about anything in Thailand. Eating at the vibrant **night markets** of Thailand and Malaysia, where the locals dine, is one of the truly great pleasures of traveling here. Menu headings range from pigeon and rat to squid and cobra. Abundant vegetarian options everywhere will keep the less carnivorously inclined well-fed and content.

PARADISE CITY

You've got to see 'em to believe 'em. Southeast Asia's big cities are stories in themselves. Though **Bangkok, Jakarta,** and **Manila** are often portrayed as smoke-infested, choking ovens, these cities bustle with an unmatched energy, diversity, and chaos that captures the essence of modern-day Southeast Asia, gathering its architectural, cultural and culinary attractions all in one place. **Hong Kong** and **Singapore** are respites from the chaos of other Southeast Asian cities, while **Hanoi, Luang Prabang, Yangon, Kuching, Davao,** and **Cebu** deserve a gawk. For nightlife, Bangkok, **Ho Chi Minh City, Kuala Lumpur,** Jakarta, and Manila lead the pack.

LET'S GO PICKS

BEST GENITALIA-SHAPED ROCK: Despite stiff competition, the "grandmother and grandfather" rocks of **Ko Samui** (p. 787) in Thailand, win this hard-fought prize.

BEST NAME GAME: Looking for hostels? Stay at the **Shadow of the Moon at Half past Four**, in Cherating, Malaysia, or at **Nigi Nigi Nu Noos 'e' Nu Nu Noos** (p. 584), in Boracay, Philippines.

BEST SCHLONG-PINS: The Thai, Myanmarese, and Cambodian people are experts in penile insertions. Metal balls (up to 30), pins, needles, metal extensions have all been assimilated into the Southeast Asian men's best friend.

BEST REASON TO GET UP IN THE MORNING: The sunrise over **Angkor Wat** (p. 90) is one of the world's most spectacular sights. In another vein, after a particularly steamy night in **Bangkok** (p. 629), getting out of bed fast might be a good idea as well.

BEST HOT SPRINGS TO MAKE IT IN: **Makin It Hot Springs** (p. 595), El Nido, the Philippines.

BEST WAY TO SWEAT WITH THE LOCALS: Catch an impromptu soccer game in the parks of **Hanoi,** or indulge in the **Philippine's** favorite: basketball. If you fancy yourself a real athlete, try *sepak takraw* in **Kuala Lumpur.**

BEST PLACE TO SEE WILDLIFE: Catch the mini-dinosaurs on **Komodo Island** (p. 248) in Indonesia, on your way to **Gunung Leseur National Park** (p. 295). Malaysia's **Taman Negara National Park** and the *babirusa* (pig-deer) of **Sulawesi** finish off your list.

BEST PLACE TO EAT WILDLIFE: You can choose: Cambodian crickets; Filipino duck embryos, ox balls, or blood soup; Vietnamese snakes and rats; Indonesian squids. What can we get you today?

BEST PLACE TO LOSE YOUR LOINS: **Bangkok's** best hospitals have one special skill: they help Michael find the Michelle within.

BEST TRADITIONAL REMEDY: Sabang Beach, the Philippines, offers the **"Feeling Shitty"** breakfast of coffee, 2 cigarettes, coke and ibuprofen for P70.

SUGGESTED ITINERARIES

THE THREE COUNTRY CIRCUIT

MENAGE A TROIS: THE THREE COUNTRY CIRCUIT (5 WEEKS)

The markets in lazy **Trat** (p. 683) are a short hop from Bangkok and an ideal stop on the way to **Sihanoukville,** Cambodia (p. 79). Journey north to **Phnom Penh** (p. 69) to see the poignant Killing Fields. Next, head to **Siem Reap** (p. 86), the gateway to the spectacular **Angkor Wat** (p. 90). Backtrack through Phnom Penh to **Ho Chi Minh City,** Vietnam (p. 888). Be sure to spend a few easy days in the **Mekong Delta** (p. 899) before heading to the mountains of **Dalat** (p. 884). and the beaches of **Nha Trang** (p. 881). History buffs rejoice in **Hoi An** (p. 877) and in the imperial capital city of **Hue** (p. 859). The trek north finishes at **Hanoi** (p. 826), Vietnam's other metropolis. From here, the mountains of **Sapa** (p. 846) and the spellbindgin **Halong Bay** (p. 842) are both a must. Fly across the border to **Vientiane** (p. 333) and welcome the lazy pace of Laos. **Luang Prabang** (p. 342) and **Luang Nam Tha** (p. 350) are home to some of Southeast Asia's last undisturbed indigenous cultures.

THE BEST OF THAILAND AND MYANMAR

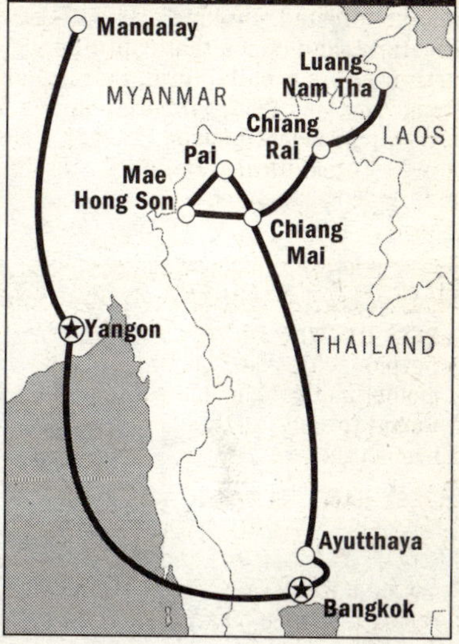

FROM PAGODAS TO PATPONG: THE BEST OF THAILAND AND MYANMAR (4 WEEKS)

Begin where all good trips do, in bustling **Bangkok** (p. 629). Fly to **Yangon** (p. 471) and pay your respects at the Shwegadon Pagoda. Complete your Myanmar odyssey by booking it up to **Mandalay** (p. 488) where cafes stand side by side pagodas. Backtrack through Bangkok towards the north, reaching the hills of **Chiang Mai** (p. 690)where the best trekking in region awaits you. The infamous **Golden Triangle** of Chiang Mai, **Pai** (p. 706) and **Mae Hong Son** (p. 702) bring together the best of indigenous Thai culture, amazing mountain views, and respite from the sizzling Southeast Asian summer. Having conquered the triangle, move onto the gentler **Chiang Rai** (p. 710) for more insights into northern culture. Head back to Bangkok via the ancient capital of **Sukhothai** (p. 729), whose ruins will remind you of the deep history of Thailand. Another former capital, **Ayutthaya** (p. 654), showcases the deep Indic influences on Thai history. Click your ruby heels, and you're back in Bangkok, where it all began.

THE BEST OF INDONESIA

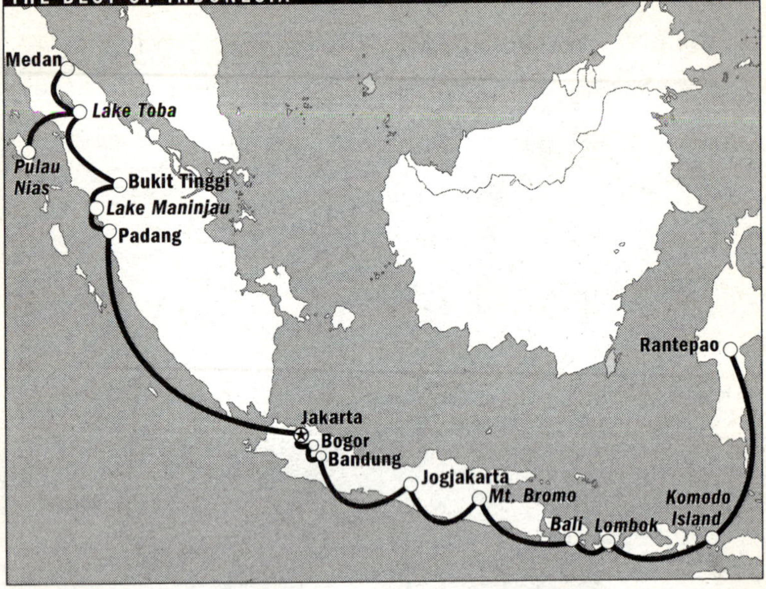

ISLAND-HOPPING: THE BEST OF INDONESIA(6 WEEKS)

Sprint through **Medan** (p. 279) to **Lake Toba** (p. 288), the world's largest crater lake, Next, take an overnight ferry to **Pulau Nias** (p. 296), which boasts great surf and untouched beaches. Continue to **Bukit Tinggi** (p. 302) and immerse yourself in the traditional Minangkubau culture. Then head over to **Lake Maninjau** (p. 306) to catch a fiery sunset over the crater-lake before moving on to **Padang** (p. 306) to sample the region's famous spicy-hot cuisine. **Jakarta** (p. 140) awaits, but stay only as long as your lungs can take it. Continue on to **Bogor's** (p. 154) botanical gardens, and then on to bustling and intellectual **Bandung** (p. 159) via the breathtaking **Puncak Pass** (p. 158), before reaching **Jogjakarta** (p. 169). After indulging in daytrips from here, move to **Gunung Bromo** (p. 192), which is Java at its best. Partying calls in **Bali** (p. 194), especially in **Kuta** (p. 204). Find your own plot of sand in **Sanur** (p. 200) or **Lovina** (p. 216). For more beach and less fanfare, head to the **Gili Islands** (p. 241). Reptile-lovers must stop at **Komodo Island** (p. 248), though those less enthusiastic should continue to **Rantepao** (p. 267).

THE BEST OF THE PHILIPPINES

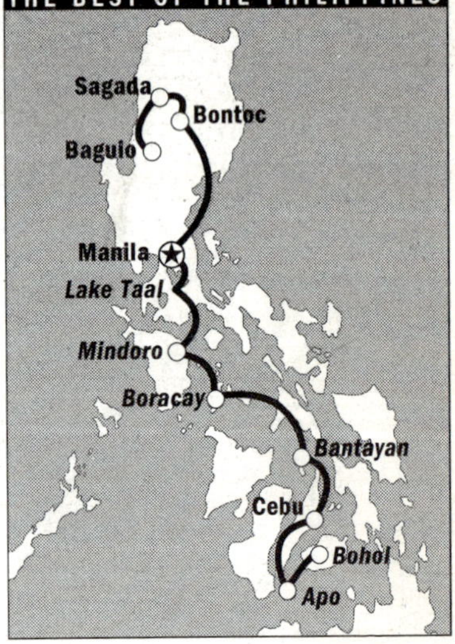

BEACHES, MOUNTAINS AND THE ODD SKYSCRAPER

TALES OF AMPHIBIOUS TOURISTS: THE BEST OF THE PHILIPPINES (4 WEEKS)

Stay in **Manila** (p. 519) long enough to hit the pumping nightlife and check out Intramuros, then catch your breadth amidst the rice paddies in the northern hills of **Banaue** (p. 538). Linger in lazy **Sagada** (p. 536) for a while, then backtrack through Manila south to beautiful **Lake Taal** (p. 547). Next, hop over to **Mindoro Island** (p. 553) for an introduction to Filipino beach culture, then quickly push on to **Boracay's** (p. 582) famous White Beach. After an overnight stay in **Panay** (p. 578), and a brief sun-soaking session on **Bantayan Island** (p. 566) or undiscovered **Malapascua Island** (p. 568), steam into **Cebu City** (p. 558) to appease your Bacchanalian impulses. Catch a ferry to **Bohol** (p. 568), indulge in the Chocolate Hills, and bask on the isolated beaches of **Panglao Island** (p. 571). Continue island-hopping to your finale at **Apo Island** (p. 577), where you'll find the Philippine's best-preserved marine sanctuary.

YOU, ME, AND MAMA NATURE: BEACHES, MOUNTAINS AND THE ODD SKYSCRAPER (5 WEEKS)

Begin in **Bangkok** (p. 629) and just take it all in. Start the journey south at **Hua Hin** (p. 670) for an introduction to Thailand's pristine white sand. Now, island hop from the diver's paradise of **Ko Tao** (p. 799) to the **Full Moon Party** on **Ko Phangnan** (p. 795) to tourist-friendly **Ko Samui** (p. 787). More beaches? Cut across to **Krabi** (p. 810) and **Phuket** (p. 803). On to **Penang,** Malaysia (p. 396) and its scrumptious street food. Then venture inland to the **Cameron Highlands** (p. 407) and recharge on the jungle hikes. **Kuala Lumpur** (p. 374) will serve as a fitting urban trek. As a reward, plunge into Malaysian history in **Melaka** (p. 384). Take a respite in sanitized **Singapore** (p. 598) before flying into wild Borneo. Climb Southeast Asia's highest peak, **Gunung Kinabalu** (p. 455) and then bask in the wealth of tiny **Brunei** (p. 51). Having greeted the Sultan, head on to **Niah National Park** (p. 444), a spelunker's dream. Out of the caves, **Kuching's** (p. 433) waterfront esplanade is an ideal final step.

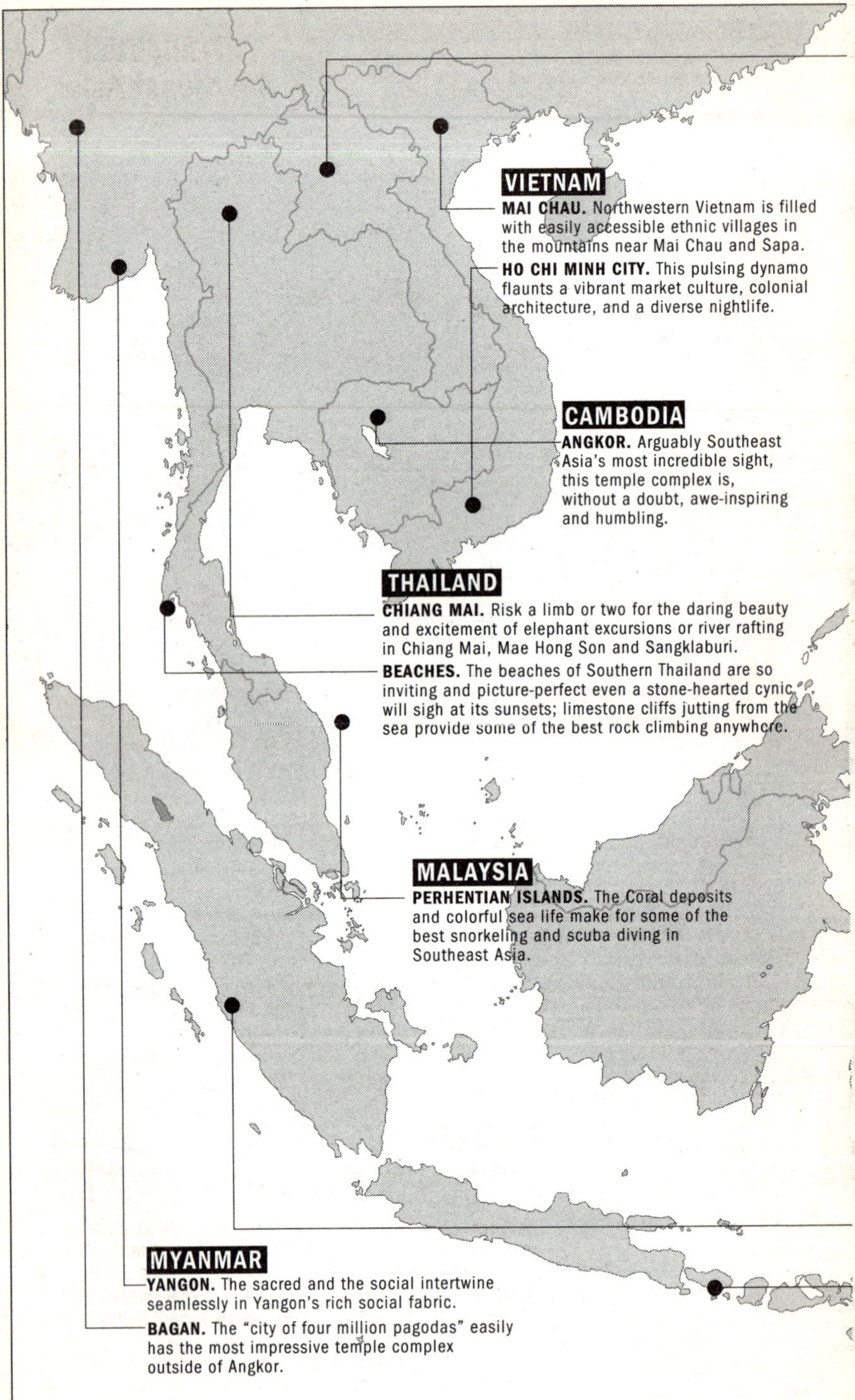
VIETNAM
MAI CHAU. Northwestern Vietnam is filled with easily accessible ethnic villages in the mountains near Mai Chau and Sapa.
HO CHI MINH CITY. This pulsing dynamo flaunts a vibrant market culture, colonial architecture, and a diverse nightlife.
CAMBODIA
ANGKOR. Arguably Southeast Asia's most incredible sight, this temple complex is, without a doubt, awe-inspiring and humbling.
THAILAND
CHIANG MAI. Risk a limb or two for the daring beauty and excitement of elephant excursions or river rafting in Chiang Mai, Mae Hong Son and Sangklaburi.
BEACHES. The beaches of Southern Thailand are so inviting and picture-perfect even a stone-hearted cynic will sigh at its sunsets; limestone cliffs jutting from the sea provide some of the best rock climbing anywhere.
MALAYSIA
PERHENTIAN ISLANDS. The Coral deposits and colorful sea life make for some of the best snorkeling and scuba diving in Southeast Asia.
MYANMAR
YANGON. The sacred and the social intertwine seamlessly in Yangon's rich social fabric.
BAGAN. The "city of four million pagodas" easily has the most impressive temple complex outside of Angkor.

Highlights of Southeast Asia

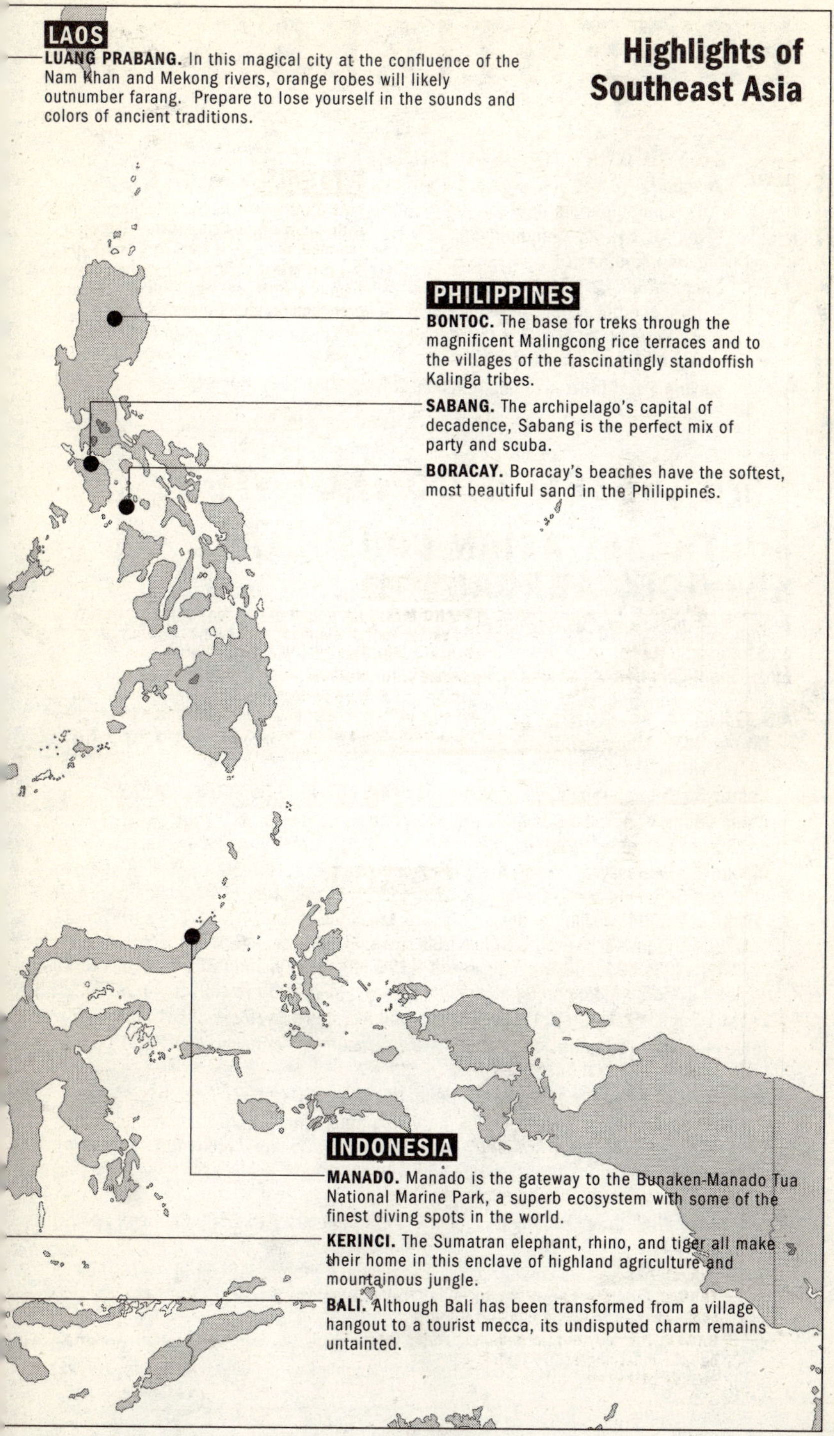

LAOS

LUANG PRABANG. In this magical city at the confluence of the Nam Khan and Mekong rivers, orange robes will likely outnumber farang. Prepare to lose yourself in the sounds and colors of ancient traditions.

PHILIPPINES

BONTOC. The base for treks through the magnificent Malingcong rice terraces and to the villages of the fascinatingly standoffish Kalinga tribes.

SABANG. The archipelago's capital of decadence, Sabang is the perfect mix of party and scuba.

BORACAY. Boracay's beaches have the softest, most beautiful sand in the Philippines.

INDONESIA

MANADO. Manado is the gateway to the Bunaken-Manado Tua National Marine Park, a superb ecosystem with some of the finest diving spots in the world.

KERINCI. The Sumatran elephant, rhino, and tiger all make their home in this enclave of highland agriculture and mountainous jungle.

BALI. Although Bali has been transformed from a village hangout to a tourist mecca, its undisputed charm remains untainted.

ESSENTIALS

SO YOU WANT TO GO TO SOUTHEAST ASIA

Passports (p. 13): Required of all travelers. Must be valid for at 6 months after anticipated departure date.

Visas (p. 14): Visa requirements vary by country. See individual countries for more information.

Inoculations (p. 25): Visitors who have been in Africa or South America must have a certificate of vaccination against yellow fever.

Work Permits (p. 14): Required for all foreigners planning to work in Southeast Asia. Hence the name.

Driving Permits (p. 42): International Driving Permits required for car rental in many countries.

EMBASSIES & CONSULATES

SOUTHEAST ASIAN CONSULAR SERVICES ABROAD

Check out www.embassyworld.com for easy access to many embassy web pages and to download forms. Embassies and consulates within Southeast Asia are listed in the **Practical Information** sections of individual cities.

AUSTRALIA

Brunei: High Commission, 16 Bulwarra Close, O'Malley, Canberra, ACT 2606 (☎(02) 6290 1801/2).

Cambodia: 5 Canterbury Cres., Deakin, Canberra, ACT 2600 (☎(02) 6273 1259).

China (Hong Kong): 15 Coronation Dr., Yarralumla, Canberra, ACT 2600 (☎(02) 6273 4780; www.chinaembassy.org.au).

Indonesia: Embassy, 8 Darwin Ave., Yarralumla, Canberra, ACT 2600; mailing address: P.O. Box 616, Kingston 2604 (☎(02) 6250 8600). **Consulates,** 134 Adelaide Terr., East Perth, WA 6004; mailing address: P.O. Box 6683 East Perth, WA 6892 (☎(08) 9221 5858); 20 Harry Chan Ave., Darwin NT 800; mailing address: P.O. Box 1953 Darwin, NT 0801 (☎(08) 8941 0048); 72 Queens Rd., Melbourne, Victoria 3004 (☎(03) 9525 2755); 236-238 Maroubra Rd., Maroubra, Sydney, NSW 2035 (☎(02) 9344 9933).

Laos: 1 Dalman Cres.Cres., O'Malley, Canberra, ACT 2606 (☎(02) 6286 4595).

Malaysia: High Commission, 7 Perth Ave., Yarralumla, Canberra, ACT 2600 (☎(02) 6273 1543).

Myanmar: 22 Arkana St., Yarralumla, Canberra, ACT 2600 (☎(02) 73 3751/3811).

Philippines: Embassy, 1 Moonah Pl., Yarralumla, Canberra, ACT 2600; mailing address: P.O. Box 3297, Manuka ACT 2603 (☎(02) 6273 2535; www.philembassy.au.com). **Consulate,** Philippine Ctr., Level 1, 27-33 Wenthworth Ave. Sydney NSW 2000 (☎(02) 9262 7377; www.emanila.com/phconsul).

Singapore: High Commission, 17 Forster Cres., Yarralumla, ACT 2600 Canberra (☎(02) 6273 3944).

Thailand: Embassy, 111 Empire Circuit, Yarralumla, Canberra, ACT 2600 (☎(02) 6273 1149; www.geocities.com/CapitolHill/7789). **Consulate General,** 2nd fl., 75-77 Pitt St., Sydney NSW 2000 (☎(02) 9241 2542/3).

Vietnam: Embassy, 6 Timbarra Cres., O'Malley, Canberra, ACT 2606 (☎(02) 6286 6059). **Consulate,** 489 New South Head Rd., Double Bay, NSW 2028, Sydney (☎(02) 9327 2539).

CANADA

Brunei: 395 Laurier Ave. E, Ottawa, ON K1N 6R4 (☎(613) 234 5656).

China (Hong Kong): 515 St. Patrick St., Ottawa, ON KIN 5H3; mailing address: P.O. Box 8935 New Terminal, Alta Vista, Ottawa ON (☎(613) 789 3434).

Indonesia: Embassy, 55 Parkdale Ave., Ottawa, ON K1Y 1E5 (☎(613) 724 1100; www.indonesia-ottawa.org). **Consulates,** 1630 Alberni St. Vancouver, BC V6G 1A6 (☎(604) 682 8855; www.kjrivcr.org); 129 Jarvis St., Toronto, ON M5C 2H6 (☎(416) 360 4020).

Malaysia: High Commission, 60 Boteler St., Ottawa, ON K1N 8Y7 (☎(613) 241 5182; home.istar.ca/~mwottawa). **Consulate,** 1805-1111 W. Georgia St., Vancouver, BC V6C 4M3 (☎(604) 685 9550).

Myanmar: 85 Range Rd. #902-903, Sandringham, Ottawa, ON K1N 8J6 (☎(613) 232 6446 or 232 6434).

Philippines: Embassy, 130 Albert St. #606, Ottawa, ON K1P 5G4 (☎(613) 233 1121; www.philembassyca.org). **Consulate,** 151 Bloor St. W #365, Toronto, ON M5S 1S4 (☎(416) 922 7181; www.philcongen-toronto.com); 700 W Pender #1405, Vancouver, BC V6C 1G5 (☎(604) 685 7645).

Singapore: Consulate, 999 W Hastings St., #1305, Vancouver, BC V6C 2W2 (☎(604) 669 5115).

Thailand: Embassy, 180 Island Park Dr., Ottawa, ON K1Y OA2 (☎(613) 722 4444). **Consulate,** 1040 Burrard St., Vancouver, BC V6Z 2R9 (☎(604) 687 1143; www.thai-congenvancouver.org).

Vietnam: Embassy, 470 Wilbrod St., Ottawa, ON K1N 6M8 (☎(613) 236 0772).

NEW ZEALAND

Indonesia: 70 Glen Rd., Kelburn; P.O. Box 3543, Wellington (☎(04) 475 8697/8/9).

Malaysia: High Commission, 10 Washington Ave., Brooklyn, Wellington (☎(04) 385 2439, 801-0943).

Philippines: 50 Hobson St., Thorndon; P.O. Box 12-042, Wellington (☎(04) 472 9921).

Singapore: High Commission, 17 Kabul St., Khandallah Wellington; Johnsonville, P.O. Box 13-140, Wellington (☎(04) 479 2076, -2077).

Thailand: 2 Cook St., Karori, P.O. Box 17-226, Wellington (☎(04) 476 8618); Level 5, 18 Shortland St. Auckland (☎(09) 302 3378).

SOUTH AFRICA

Indonesia: Embassy, 949 Schoeman St., Arcadia, P.O. Box 13155, Hatfield 0028, Pretoria (☎(012) 342 3352). **Consulate,** 59-61 Loop St., P.O Box 10129, Caledon Sq. 7905, Cape Town 8001 (☎(021) 423 2321).

Malaysia: High Commission, 1007 Schoeman St., Pretoria 0083 (☎(012) 342 5990).

Myanmar: 319 Murray St., Brooklyn, Pretoria 0181; mailing address: P.O. Box 12121 Queenswood 0121 (☎(012) 460 6544).

Philippines: Embassy and Consulate, 54 Nicolson St., Muckleneuk, Pretoria 0181; mailing address: P.O. Box 2560, Brooklyn Square, 0075 (☎(012) 346 0451/2).

Singapore: High Commission, 1980 Schoeman St., Hatfield, Pretoria 0028; mailing address: Box 11809, Hatfield 0028, Pretoria (☎(012) 343 4371).

Thailand: Embassy, 428 Hill St., Arcadia, Pretoria 0083 (☎(012) 342 4600/5470).

Vietnam: Embassy, 955 Arcadia St., Arcadia, Pretoria 0001 (☎(012) 430 3738, 343 7673).

UNITED KINGDOM

Brunei: High Commission, 19/20 Belgrave Sq., London SW1X 8PG (☎(020) 7581 0521).

China (Hong Kong): 31 Portland Pl., London W1B 1QD (☎(020) 7631 1430).

Indonesia: 38 Grosvenor Sq., London W1K 2HW (☎(020) 7499 7661).

Myanmar: 19A Charles St., London W1X 8ER (☎(020) 7629 9531).

Philippines: 9A Palace Green, London W8 4QE (☎(020) 7937 1600; fax 7376 0819).

Singapore: High Commission, 9 Wilton Cres., Belgravia, London SW1X 8ST (☎(020) 7235 8315/9852).
Thailand: 29-30 Queen's Gate, London SW7 5JB (☎(020) 7589 2944).
Vietnam: Victoria 12-14, London W8 (☎(020) 7937 1912).

UNITED STATES

Brunei: Watergate, 2600 Virginia Ave. NW #300, Washington, DC 20037 (☎(202) 342-0159).

Cambodia: Embassy, 4530 16th St. NW, Washington, DC 20011 (☎(202) 726-7742; www.embassy.org/cambodia). **Mission to the UN:** 866 UN Plaza #420, New York, NY 10017 (☎(212) 223-0676; www.un.int/cambodia).

China (Hong Kong): Embassy, 2300 Connecticut Ave. NW, Washington, DC 20008 (☎(202) 328-2500; www.china-embassy.org). **Visa office,** 2201 Wisconsin Ave. NW #110, Washington, DC 20007 (☎(202) 338-6688). **Consulates,** 520 12th Ave., New York, NY 10036 (☎(212) 868-7752); 100 W Erie St., Chicago, IL 60610 (☎(312) 803-0098); 3417 Montrose Blvd., Houston, TX 77006 (☎(713) 524-4311); 1450 Laguna St., San Francisco, CA 94115 (☎(415) 674-2900); 443 Shatto Pl., Los Angeles, CA 90020 (☎(213) 807-8088).

Indonesia: Embassy, 2020 Massachusetts Ave. NW, Washington, DC 20036 (☎(202) 775-5200). **Consulates,** 5 E 68th St., New York, NY 10021 (☎(212) 879-0600); 72 E. Randolph St., Chicago, IL 60601 ☎(312) 595-1777; 3457 Wilshire Blvd., Los Angeles, CA 90010 (☎(213) 383-5126; www.kjri-la.com); 1111 Columbus Ave., San Francisco, CA 94133 (☎(415) 474-9571); 10900 Richmond Ave., Houston, TX 77042 (☎(713) 785-1691). **Mission to the UN,** 325 E 38th St., New York, NY 10016 (☎(212) 972-8333).

Laos: Embassy, 2222 S St. NW, Washington, DC 20008 (☎(202) 332-6416; www.laoembassy.com). **Mission to the UN,** 317 E 51st St., New York, NY 10022 (☎(212) 832-2734; www.un.int/lao).

Malaysia: Embassy, 2401 Massachusetts Ave. NW, Washington, DC 20038 (☎(202) 328-2700). **Consulate,** Two Grand Central Tower, 140 E 45th St. 43rd Fl., New York, NY 10017 (☎(212) 490-2722/2723); 875 N Michigan Ave. #4101, Chicago, IL 60611 (☎(312) 280-9632); 350 S Figuera St. #400, Los Angeles, CA 90071-1203 (☎(213) 621-2991). **Mission to the UN,** 313 E 43rd St., New York, NY 10017 (☎(212) 986-6310).

Myanmar: Embassy, 2300 S St. NW, Washington, DC 20008 (☎(202) 332-9044 or 332-9045). **Consulates,** 10 E 77th St., New York, NY 10021 (☎(212) 535-1310).

Philippines: Embassy, 1600 Massachusetts Ave. NW, Washington, DC 20036 (☎(202) 467-9300). **Consulates,** 556 Fifth Ave., New York, NY 10036 (☎(212) 764-1330; 30 N Michigan Ave. #2100, Chicago, IL 60602 (☎(312) 332-6458); 5th fl., Philippine Center Bldg., 447 Sutter St., San Francisco, CA 94108 (☎(415) 433-6666); 3600 Wilshire Blvd. #500, Los Angeles, CA 90010 (☎(213) 639-3220); 2433 Pall Hwy., Honolulu, HI 96817 (☎(808) 595-6316). **Permanent Mission to the UN:** Philippine Center Bldg., 556 5th Ave., New York, NY 10036 (☎(212) 764-1300; www.undp.org/missions/philippine).

Singapore: Embassy, 3501 International Pl. NW, Washington, DC 20008 (☎(202) 537-3100, www.gov.sg.mfa.washington/). **Consulates,** 231 E 51st St., New York, NY 10022 (☎(212) 223-3331); 609 Deep Valley Dr. #200, Rolling Hills Estate, CA 90274 (☎(310) 373-7622); 595 Market St. #2450, San Francisco, CA 94105. **Mission to the UN,** 231 E 51st St., New York, NY 10022 (☎(212) 826-0840).

Thailand: Embassy, 1024 Wisconsin Ave. NW #401, Washington, DC 20007 (☎(202) 944-3600; www.thaiembdc.org). **Consulates,** 351 E 52nd St., New York, NY 10022 (☎(212) 754-1770, 754-2536); 700 N Rush St., Chicago, IL 60611 (☎(312) 664-3129); 611 N. Larchmont Blvd., 2nd fl., Los Angeles, CA 90004 (☎(323) 962-9574; www.thai-la.net); 1024 Wisconsin Ave. NW #101, Washington, DC 20007 (☎(202) 944-3608).

Vietnam: Embassy, 1233 20th St. NW #400, Washington, DC 20037 (☎(202) 861-0737; www.vietnamembassy-usa.org). **Consulate,** 1700 California St. #430, San Francisco 94109 (☎(415) 922-1577). **Mission to the UN,** 866 UN Plaza #435, New York, NY 10017 (☎(212) 644-0594).

ESSENTIALS

TOURIST AND GOVERNMENT INFORMATION OFFICES

Hong Kong Tourist Association (www.hkta.org). **Australia,** Level 4, Hong Kong House, 80 Druitt St., Sydney NSW 2000 (☎(02) 9283 3083). **Canada,** 9 Temperance St., 3rd fl., Toronto, ON M5H 1Y6 (☎(416) 366-2389). **New Zealand,** P.O.Box 2120, Auckland, 1001 (☎(09) 307 2580). **South Africa,** c/o Development Promotions Ltd. 7th fl., Everite House, 20 De Korte St., Braamfontein 2017; mailing address, Everite House, 30615 Braamfontein 2017 (☎(011) 339 4865). **UK,** 6 Grafton St., London W1X 3LB (☎(020) 7533 7100). **US,** 115 E 54th St., 2nd fl., New York, NY 10022-4512 (☎(212) 421-3382); 401 N Michigan Ave. #1640, Chicago, IL 60611 (☎(312) 329-1828); 10940 Wilshire Blvd. #2050, Los Angeles, CA 90024-3915 (☎(310) 208-4582).

Tourism Malaysia (www.tourismmalaysia.com). **Australia,** 65 York St., Sydney NSW 2000 (☎(02) 9299 4441); 56 William St., Perth, WA 6000 (☎(09) 481 0400). **Canada,** 830 Burrard St., Vancouver, BC V6Z 1X9 (☎(604) 689 8899). **South Africa,** Hutton Ct., 1st fl., CNR Jan Smuts Ave. & Summit Rd., Hyde Park, 2196 Johannesburg (☎(011) 327 0400). **UK,** 57 Trafalgar Sq., London WC2N 5DU (☎(020) 7930 7932). **US,** 595 Madison Ave. #1800, New York, NY 10022 (☎(212) 754-1113); 818 W 7th St. #802, Los Angeles, CA 90017 (☎(213) 689-9702).

Philippines Department of Tourism (www.tourism.gov.ph). **Australia,** Tourism Information Officer, Level 1 Philippine Centre, 27-33 Wentworth Ave., Sydney NSW 2000 (☎(02) 9283 0711). **UK,** Embassy of the Philippines, Dept. of Tourism, 146 Cromwell Rd., London SW7 4EF (☎(020) 7835 1100). **US,** Philippine Center, 556 5th Ave., New York, NY 10036 (☎(212) 575-7915); c/o Consulate General, 447 Sutter St., 5th fl. #507, San Francisco, CA 94108 (☎(415) 956-4060); 3660 Wilshire Blvd. #216, Los Angeles, CA 90010 (☎(213) 487-4527).

Singapore Tourist Promotion Board (www.stb.com.sg). **Australia,** 47 York St., Level 11, AWA Building, Sydney NSW 2000 (☎(02) 9290 2888); Unit 2, 226 James St., Perth WA 6000 (☎(08) 9228 8166). **Canada,** 2 Bloor St. W #404, Toronto, ON M4W 3E2 (☎(416) 363-8898; www.singapore-ca.com). **New Zealand,** c/o Vivaldi World Limited, 85B Hebron Rd. Waiake, Auckland (☎(09) 473 8658). **UK,** Carrington House, 1st fl., 126-130 Regent St., London W1R 5FE (☎(020) 7437 0033). **US,** 590 5th Ave., 12th fl., New York, NY 10036 (☎(212) 302-4861; www.singapore-usa.com); 2 Prudential Plaza, 180 N Stetson Ave. #2615, Chicago, IL 60601 (☎(312) 938-1888); 8484 Wilshire Blvd. #510, Beverly Hills, CA 90211 (☎(323) 852-1901).

Tourism Authority of Thailand (TAT). Australia, 75 Pitt St., 2nd fl., Sydney NSW 2000 (☎(02) 9247 7549). **UK,** 49 Albemarle St., London WIX 3FE (☎(020) 7499 7679). **US,** 1 World Trade Ctr. #3729, New York, NY 10048 (☎(212) 432-0433).

DOCUMENTS & FORMALITIES

PASSPORTS

REQUIREMENTS. You need a valid passport for travel in Southeast Asia. Most countries will require that your passport be valid for six months beyond your anticipated departure date. Visa requirements differ from country to country; see individual country introductions for specifics.

PHOTOCOPIES. Photocopy the page of your passport that contains your photograph, passport number, and other identifying information, along with other important documents such as visas, insurance policies, plane tickets, credit cards (front and back), and traveler's check serial numbers, in case you lose anything. Carry one set of copies in a safe place apart from the originals and leave another at home. Consulates also recommend that you carry an expired passport or an official copy of your birth certificate separate from other documents.

LOST PASSPORTS. If you lose your passport, immediately notify the local police and the nearest embassy or consulate of your home government. To expedite its replacement, you will need to know all information previously recorded and show identification and proof of citizenship. In some cases, a replacement may take weeks to process may be valid only for a limited time. Your passport is a public document belonging to your nation's government. You may have to surrender it to a foreign government official, but if you don't get it back in a reasonable amount of time, inform the nearest mission of your home country.

NEW PASSPORTS. All applications for new passports or renewals should be filed several weeks or months in advance of your planned departure date. Most passport offices offer emergency passport services for an extra charge. Citizens living abroad who need passport or renewal services should contact the nearest consular service in their home country.

VISAS, INVITATIONS, & WORK PERMITS

VISAS. Many countries in Southeast Asia require an entry visa that must be obtained in advance from a consulate abroad. For multiple entries, applying for re-entry permits may be necessary. For specific visa requirements (as of Aug. 2001), see the **Essentials** section in individual countries. Check entrance requirements at the nearest embassy for up-to-date information before departure. US citizens can take advantage of the **Center for International Business and Travel** (☎800 925 2428), which secures visas for travel to almost all countries for a variable service charge.

VISA REQUIREMENTS

	AUS	CAN	IRE	NZ	SA	UK	US
BRUNEI	N3	N3	N1	N1	Y	N1	N2
CAMBODIA	Y	Y	Y	Y	Y	Y	Y
HONG KONG	N2	N2	N4	N2	N1	N4	N2
INDONESIA	N5	N5	N5	N5	Y	N5	N5
LAOS	Y	Y	Y	Y	Y	Y	Y
MALAYSIA	N2	N2	N5	N2	N2	N2	N2
MYANMAR	Y	Y	Y	Y	Y	Y	Y
PHILIPPINES	N6	N6	N6	N6	N6	N6	N6
SINGAPORE	N3	N3	N1	N3	N3	N1	N3
THAILAND	N1	N1	N1	N2	N1	N1	N1
VIETNAM	Y	Y	Y	Y	Y	Y	Y

KEY 1 tourists can stay up to 30 days without visa; **2** tourists can stay up to 90 days without visa; **3** tourists can stay up to 14 days without a visa; **4** tourists can stay for 6 months.; **5** tourists can stay up to 60 days without visa; **6** tourists can stay 21 days without a visa. Extensions issued within country.

INVITATIONS. Letters of sponsorship or invitation from businesses or organizations in Southeast Asia are often required to obtain business visas or work permits. Contact the embassy for specific details.

WORK PERMITS. Entering countries in Southeast Asia to study or work often requires a special visa. Contact the country's embassy for specific details. For more information, see **Alternatives to Tourism,** p. 46.

IDENTIFICATION

When you travel, always carry two or more forms of identification on your person, including one photo ID. A passport and driver's license or birth certificate usually serve as adequate proof of your identity and citizenship. Never carry all your forms of ID together; split them up in case of theft or loss. It is useful to carry extra passport-size photos (2"x2") to affix to the visas and IDs you may acquire.

STUDENT AND TEACHER IDENTIFICATION. The **International Student Identity Card (ISIC)** is accepted in only a few Southeast Asian countries, most notably Myanmar and Myanmar. Flashing this card might get you discounts for sights and other services, like car rentals, cinemas, and restaurants. Check out the ISIC discount database (www.istcnet.org/DiscountDatabase) for more information. Cardholders have access to a 24-hour emergency helpline for medical, legal, and financial emergencies (in North America call ☎(877) 370-ISIC, elsewhere call US collect ☎+1 (715) 345-0505). US cardholders are also eligible for insurance benefits (see **Insurance**, p. 31). Many student travel agencies issue ISICs and will require them for the purchase of student tickets, including **STA Travel** in Australia and New Zealand; **Travel CUTS** in Canada; **Usit** in the Republic of Ireland and Northern Ireland; **SASTS** in South Africa; **Campus Travel** and STA Travel in the UK; **Council Travel** (www.counciltravel.com/idcards/default.asp) and STA Travel in the US (see p. 40).

The card is valid from September of one year to December of the following year and costs AUS$15 or US$20. Applicants must be degree-seeking students of a secondary or post-secondary school and must be at least 12 years old. Because of the proliferation of fake ISICs, some services (particularly airlines) require additional proof of student identity, such as a school ID or a letter attesting to your student status, signed by your registrar and stamped with your school seal. The **International Teacher Identity Card (ITIC)** offers the same insurance coverage and limited discounts. The fee is AUS$13 or US$20. For more info, contact the **International Student Travel Confederation (ISTC),** Herengracht 479, 1017 BS Amsterdam, Netherlands (☎+31 (20) 421 28 00; fax 421 28 10; istcinfo@istc.org; www.istc.org).

YOUTH IDENTIFICATION. The International Student Travel Confederation issues a discount card to travelers who 25 years old or under but not students. This one-year **International Youth Travel Card** (**IYTC;** formerly the **GO 25** Card) offers many of the same benefits as the ISIC and is sold in the same places (US$20).

CUSTOMS

Customs requirements vary from country to country in Southeast Asia. Upon entering you must declare certain items from abroad and pay a duty on the value of those articles if they exceed the allowance established by that country's customs service. Southeast Asian governments have harsh penalties for **drug possession and trafficking.** Some of them will kill you if you are found guilty. Note that goods and gifts purchased at **duty-free** shops abroad are not exempt from duty or sales tax at your point of return and thus must be declared as well; "duty-free" merely means that you need not pay a tax in the country of purchase. Upon returning home, you must similarly declare all articles acquired abroad and pay a duty on the value of articles in excess of your home country's allowance. In order to expedite your return, make a list of any valuables brought from home and register them with customs before traveling abroad, and keep all receipts for goods purchased.

Additionally, several countries in Southeast Asia require official certification before cultural goods or artifacts can be taken out of the country. Such certification often takes 3-5 days to process; make sure you leave enough time to complete the process or your purchases cannot leave the country with you. The import of **firearms, weapons,** and **pornography** is prohibited by all Southeast Asian countries. Additional country specific customs regulations are listed below.

Indonesia: Chinese medicine, and text in Chinese characters are prohibited. Import or export of more than Rp50,000 is prohibited.

Laos: Customs procedures are informal. No antique cultural items or Buddha images may leave the country without government authorization. Silver or copper items subject to custom duty.

Malaysia: No restrictions on import or export of currency, but it is inadvisable to carry more than RM10,000 in cash. Pornography, prejudicial publications, knives, and most broadcast receivers are prohibited. A permit is necessary to import precious stones or gold (except coins issued by the Central Bank of Malaysia and personal jewelry).

Myanmar: Non-residents can bring the equivalent of US$2000 without declaration. Jewelry, electrical goods, and cameras must be declared but are exempt from duty. Antique souvenirs cannot be exported. Gems, jewelry, and silverware accompanied by an export-guarantee voucher from authorized gift shops may be exported.

Philippines: Visitors bringing in over US$3000 must declare the total at the Central Bank counter at customs. Drugs, coral, certain orchid species, mussels, animal parts (e.g. turtle shells), and local currency over P1000 may not leave the country. A certificate from the National Museum must accompany all antiques purchased in the country.

Singapore: Prohibited from importation are chewing gum, chewing or imitation tobacco, obscene material, "seditious and treasonable material," and toy currency. Drug possession is considered trafficking in Singapore.

Thailand: Travelers may bring 1 still camera with 5 rolls of film, or 1 video camera with 3 tapes. Firearms and pornography are prohibited. The total amount of currency taken out should not exceed the amount taken in (max. US$10,000). No Buddha or Bodhisattva images, or fragments thereof, may be exported without permission from the Bangkok National Museum (☎02 224 1333) and the Ministry of Commerce; you must prove you are a practicing Buddhist or are using them for cultural or academic purposes. These rules do not apply to souvenirs bought in department stores. For art purchased in the country, keep receipts for customs. 500฿ airport tax on departure.

Vietnam: Visitors must declare cameras, videos and camcorders, tape recorders, and all other electric equipment. Foreign currency in excess of US$3000 must be declared. Antiques are not allowed out of the country without approval from the Ministry of Culture and Information. No đồng allowed out of the country. You must present your customs and immigration cards when leaving the country, or face a fine.

MONEY

CURRENCY & EXCHANGE

Up-to-date **exchange rates** and information on local currencies in this guide are in each country's **Essentials** section. Check the currency converter on the *Let's Go* homepage (www.letsgo.com/thumb) or a major newspaper for the latest rates. As a general rule, it's cheaper to convert money at your destination. Bring enough currency to last for the first 72 hours of a trip—banks might be closed when you arrive. Travelers from the US can get foreign currency from the comfort of home: **International Currency Express** (☎(888) 278-6628) delivers currency or traveler's checks overnight (US$15) or second-day (US$12) at competitive exchange rates.

Banks generally have the best rates outside the black market. A good rule of thumb is to go only to banks that have at most a 5% margin between their buy and sell prices. Since you lose money with each transaction, convert in large sums (unless the currency is depreciating rapidly).

Smart travelers will carry US dollars even if it isn't their national currency. Especially in Cambodia and Vietnam, exchanging money isn't necessary if you're carrying US dollars and bank tellers favor changing US dollars over other currencies. There are also some companies (e.g., Lao Aviation) and establishments that will only accept dollars. If you use traveler's checks or bills, carry some in small denominations (US$50 or less), especially for times when you are forced to exchange money at disadvantageous rates. However, it is good to carry a range of denominations since charges may be levied per check cashed.

Store your money in a variety of forms; ideally you will at any given time be carrying some cash, some traveler's checks, and an ATM and/or credit card. For small transactions though, put your dollars away and use local currency. Throwing dollars around for preferential treatment is offensive, and it attracts thieves.

Many travelers illegally change currency on the black market from unofficial changers. Freelancers often offer much better rates than the banks, but you run the risk of being swindled or arrested.

TRAVELER'S CHECKS

Traveler's checks (**American Express** and **Visa** are the most recognized) are one of the safest and least troublesome means of carrying funds. Several agencies and banks sell them for a small commission. Each agency provides refunds if your checks are lost or stolen, and many provide additional services, such as toll-free refund hotlines abroad, emergency message services, and stolen credit card assistance.

While traveling, keep check receipts and a record of which checks you've cashed separate from the checks themselves. Also leave a list of check numbers with someone at home. Never countersign checks until you're ready to cash them, and always bring your passport with you to cash them. If your checks are lost or stolen, immediately contact a refund center (of the company that issued your checks) to be reimbursed; they may require a police report verifying the loss or theft. Less-touristed countries may not have refund centers at all, in which case you might have to wait to be reimbursed. Ask about toll-free refund hotlines and the location of refund centers when purchasing checks, and always carry emergency cash.

Most Southeast Asian countries accept traveler's checks in well-travelled areas, especially at banks and hotels. They are less widely-accepted in smaller towns and rural areas. Check individual city listings for more information.

American Express: In Australia, call ☎(800) 251 902; in New Zealand ☎(0800) 441 068; in the UK ☎(0800) 521 313; in the US and Canada ☎(800) 221-7282. Elsewhere US collect ☎+1 (801) 964-6665; www.aexp.com. Traveler's Cheques are available for a small fee (1-4%) at AmEx offices and banks, commission-free at AAA offices. *Cheques for Two* can be signed by either of 2 people traveling together.

Thomas Cook MasterCard: In the US and Canada ☎(800) 223-7373; in the UK ☎(0800) 62 21 01; elsewhere UK collect ☎+44 (1733) 31 89 50. Checks available in 13 currencies at 2% commission. Thomas Cook offices cash checks commission-free.

Visa: In the US call (800) 227-6811; in the UK ☎(0800) 89 50 78; elsewhere UK collect ☎+44 (20) 79 37 80 91. Call for the location of their nearest office.

CREDIT CARDS

Where they are accepted, credit cards often offer superior exchange rates—up to 5% better than the retail rate used by banks and other currency exchange establishments. Credit cards may also offer services such as insurance or emergency help, and are sometimes required to reserve hotel rooms or rental cars. **MasterCard** and **Visa** are the most welcomed; **American Express** cards work at some ATMs and at AmEx offices and major airports. However, budget travelers will find that few of the establishments they frequent will accepts credit cards; you will probably have to reserve your credit card for financial emergenciess.

Credit cards are also useful for **cash advances,** which allow you to withdraw local currency from associated banks and ATMs throughout Southeast Asia instantly. However, transaction fees for all credit card advances (up to US$10 per advance, plus 2-3% extra on foreign transactions after conversion) tend to make credit cards a more costly way of withdrawing cash than ATMs or traveler's checks. In an emergency, however, the transaction fee may prove worth the cost. To be eligible for an advance, you'll need to get a **Personal Identification Number (PIN)** from your credit

A HAGGLE A DAY In Southeast Asia, bargaining is more than a pricing system. Understanding this is step one on your way to becoming a master heckler. Bargaining is an art form, a crucial part of everyday social interactions, the lifeblood of every market, a riveting, exciting and skillful mind game, and, if your attitude is right, SO much fun. The fleeting, yet deep, personal relationship that bargaining fosters between the seller and the tourist bridges many cultural gaps, which are often as wide as the vast disparity between the "tourist price" and the local (read: real) price; not to mention "morning price" in Bali. So how does one become a master Mr. Heckler? Always keep in mind the concept of "face," deeply embedded in many Asian cultures and fundamental to an understanding of bargaining. In short, humiliation in the company of others, or "losing face," is avoided at all costs. Equally problematic is forcing others into this predicament. Put your cut-throatness aside; this game of skill is built on a foundation of mutual respect and cheeky smiles of understanding. The bargaining-fairy says:

1. Bargaining shouldn't be a fierce struggle laced with barbs. Always approach with a smile, it'll start things off on the right foot.

2. Don't leave your poker face at home. As a rule, visible interest is inversely proportional to actual desire; covetous eyes are the cat's meow to sellers and the kiss of death to buyers. But don't confuse a calm manner of carefully calculated semi-disinterest with putting on a look of disdain. The latter will simply lose a friend you might have made a deal with.

3. Know when to bargain. In most cases, it's clear when it's appropriate to pull out your guns. When in doubt, smile (see rule 1, above) and ask tactfully, "Oh! Is that the best we can do?" or whether discounts are given. Never bargain for prepared food.

4. Never underestimate the power of peer pressure. A buyer's market, with hordes of sellers and one buyer, does not prove advantageous. Bargaining with more than one person at a time—particularly taxi, *tuk-tuk*, and cyclo drivers—almost always yields higher prices. Thus, it's always best to pull one person aside and settle in private. If you begin talking to one seller though, **you must finish bargaining with him/her before talking to someone else.** Openly talking to several sellers is unacceptable.

5. To start bargaining without an intention to buy constitutes a major *faux pas* and makes you not very nice. Agreeing on a price and declining it is the lowest of the low. One effective strategy is to turn away slowly, as if to walk away, with a smile and "thank you," upon hearing a ridiculous price. Turn around with the same nonchalance and the price may plummet.

6. Losing sight of the value of money—and the traveler's place in the world economy—can be downright disgraceful. Cut throat bargaining to a rock-bottom price often results in the seller's losing face. It's also worth considering that an hour of work in most Western nations yields enough to feed a family for a week in many parts of Southeast Asia.

card company (see **Cash Cards (ATM)**, below). Be sure to check with your credit card company before you leave home, though; in certain circumstances companies have started to charge a foreign transaction fee.

CASH CARDS (ATMS)

Cash cards are an increasingly popular way to get money in Southeast Asia. ATMs are common in Brunei, Indonesia, Hong Kong, Malaysia, the Philippines, Singapore, and Thailand. They are rare in Cambodia, Laos, Myanmar, and Vietnam, except in large, central cities. ATMs get the same wholesale exchange rate as credit cards, but there is often a limit on the amount you can withdraw per day (around US$500), and computer networks sometimes fail. There is typically also a surcharge of US$1-5 per withdrawal.

Have your home bank issue you a four-digit PIN, the only variety accepted at some Southeast Asian ATMs. Be sure to memorize your PIN code in numeric form, since machines abroad often don't have letters on their keys. Also, check which account your card will withdraw from (checking or savings) and plan accordingly.

The two major international money networks are **Cirrus** (☎(800) 424-7787) and **PLUS** (☎(800) 843-7587). To locate ATMs around the world, call the above numbers, or consult www.visa.com/pd/atm or www.mastercard.com/atm.

Visa TravelMoney is a system that allows you to access money from any Visa ATM. Deposit money before you travel (plus a small administration fee), and you can withdraw up to that sum. The cards give you the same favorable exchange rate for withdrawals as a regular Visa. Check with your local bank to see if it issues Travel-Money cards. (☎(877) 394-2247; www.visa.com/pd/trav/main.html.) **Road Cash** (☎(877) 762-3227; www.roadcash.com) issues cards in the US with a minimum US$300 deposit.

GETTING MONEY FROM HOME

AMERICAN EXPRESS. AmEx has ATMs throughout Southeast Asia, concentrated in major cities. Cardholders can withdraw cash from their checking accounts at any of AmEx's major offices and many representative offices (up to US$1000 every 21 days; no service charge, no interest). AmEx "Express Cash" withdrawals from any AmEx ATM are automatically debited from the cardholder's checking account or line of credit. Green card holders may withdraw up to US$1000 in any seven-day period (2% transaction fee; minimum US$2.50, maximum US$20). To enroll in Express Cash, call 800-227-4669 in the US. The AmEx international travel assistance number is ☎(800) 732-1991; call from Southeast Asia for the nearest AmEx ATM. For other inquiries, in the US, Caribbean, Canada, and the Philippines, call ☎(800) 678-0745; the international direct number is ☎(336) 393-1111.

WESTERN UNION. Travelers from the US, Canada, and the UK can wire money abroad through Western Union's international money transfer services. In the US, call ☎(800) 325-6000; in Canada, ☎(800) 235-0000; in the UK, ☎(0800) 833 833. Money can be wired online from www.westernunion.com. The rates for sending cash are generally US$10-11 cheaper than with a credit card, and the money is usually available at the location you're sending it to within an hour. Western Union agents are emerging everywhere throughout Southeast Asia; you're almost guaranteed to find some at well-known banks in large cities. To locate the nearest Western Union location, consult the website.

FEDERAL EXPRESS. Some people choose to send money abroad in cash via FedEx to avoid transmission fees and taxes. In the US and Canada, ☎(800) 463-3339; in the UK, ☎(0800) 123 800; in Ireland, ☎(800) 535 800; in Australia, ☎13 26 10; in New Zealand, ☎(0800) 733 339; in South Africa, ☎(021) 551 7610. FedEx is reliable, but note that this method is illegal and somewhat risky. Also, it may take anywhere from a few days to several weeks for the package to reach you in Southeast Asia, depending on from where it was sent and where it is going.

US STATE DEPARTMENT (US CITIZENS ONLY). In dire emergencies, the US State Department will forward money to the nearest consular office, which will then disburse it for a US$15 fee. Contact the Overseas Citizens Service, Consular Affairs, Room 4811, US Department of State, Washington, DC 20520 (☎(202) 647-5225; nights, Sundays, and holidays 647-4000; http://travel.state.gov).

COSTS

The cost of your trip will vary considerably, depending on where you go, how you travel, and where you stay. The single biggest cost of your trip will probably be your round-trip (return) **airfare** (see **Getting to Southeast Asia: By Plane,** p. 35). Traveling Southeast Asia can be done on a rather small budget, spending as little as US$5 per day in some parts of the region. However, prices vary considerably from places like

Bangkok to Vientiane. Before you go, spend some time calculating a reasonable per-day **budget** that will meet your needs. See the **Essentials** section for each country for a breakdown of expected daily costs in individual countries.

STAYING ON A BUDGET. To meet your daily needs in Southeast Asia (sleeping in hostels/guest houses, buying food at markets, and seeing sights) is very cheap in Southeast Asia, relative to most Western countries. This is particularly true after the Asian Financial crisis which made travel very cheap for foreigners in the region. The difference between the cheapest option and the mid-range options is often only a few dollars in Southeast Asia, giving the budget traveler the option of an occasional night of luxury. Travelers looking to spend more than one night in comfort also have that option, especially in the more populated areas and beach resorts. At the moment, package tours are on the rise. Tours wary widely in terms of expense and desirability. Often, they offer more efficient ways to travel while still being affordable but, for many travelers, packaged trails can feel limiting. In any case, travel in Southeast Asia will not drain your savings. Your bowels might not, but your wallet will certainly thank you. Always keep emergency reserve funds (at least US$200) when planning how much money you'll need.

TIPPING & BRIBERY

Tipping is not customary in Southeast Asia. Upscale hotels or restaurants might expect a 5-10% tip, but avoid tipping too much, since it can set a precedent for others. Still, most will welcome the extra kip, riel, đồng, or baht, as the average yearly income for some is as low as US$150. If an establishment includes a service charge in the bill, however, tipping is not necessary.

While corruption is rife in many Southeast Asian countries, as a general rule, officials are unwilling to accept bribes from foreigners, and it is unwise to initiate an under-the-table transaction. If an official demands a fine that you feel may be illegal, proceed with caution. Paying the bribe might be preferable to the alternative, but keep in mind that it is also illegal. If you politely ask for a receipt, or to speak with the official's superior, you might be able to defuse the situation. Threatening to contact your embassy may also be effective.

SAFETY & SECURITY

PERSONAL SAFETY

BLENDING IN. Be careful about leaving yourself vulnerable to criminals. Tourists carry a lot of cash and are not as street savvy as locals; criminals know this. You can forget about "blending in" or "passing as a local." Locals are neither blind nor stupid and will spot your ruse quickly, even if your physical appearance doesn't instantly give you away. You can, however, reduce your risk of getting robbed or hurt by **keeping a low profile:** the loudmouthed camera-toting gawker generally looks more witless than a quietly thoughtful—but friendly—traveler. Keep in mind that tie-dyed shirts, multiple piercings, and dreadlocks do not help you keep a low profile in Southeast Asia, though you might succeed in keeping many at a wary distance. Be open-minded; be nice, and smile. Smile all you can. You'll be surprised how far it will get you and how much it will get you out of. If you show genuine interest in locals' language and practices, the locals are more likely to watch your back when a mugger starts trailing you. Know your surroundings before setting out; if you must check a map on the street, duck into a cafe or shop. If you are traveling alone, be sure that someone at home knows your itinerary and **never admit that you're traveling alone.**

When walking at night, stick to busy, well-lit streets, and avoid dark alleyways. Do not attempt to cross through parks, parking lots, or other large, deserted areas.

Look for children playing, women walking in the open, and other signs of an active community. If you feel uncomfortable, leave as quickly and directly as you can, but don't allow fear of the unknown to turn you into a hermit. Careful, persistent exploration will build confidence and make your stay even more rewarding.

GETTING AROUND. Renting a **motorbike** is one of the cheapest and most convenient ways to explore Southeast Asia. Register as an organ donor before you ride, since you stand a good chance of dying in a wreck. Wearing a helmet will help ensure that your head remains intact, even if it is not attached to the rest of your body, after your first collision. It's a good idea to simply watch traffic before you venture out for the first time. Different parts of Southeast Asia drive on different sides of the road, but most drive on both at once. Lanes are "suggested" and often ignored. Remember also that honking a car horn is part of a complicated system of understanding on Southeast Asian roads; do as other drivers do and you'll soon get the hang of it. Though not for the weak-hearted, the roads of Southeast Asia are an adventure in themselves. *Let's Go* does not recommend hitchhiking.

SELF DEFENSE. There aren't any sure-fire precautions that will protect you when you travel, but a good self-defense course will help you react effectively to aggression. **Impact, Prepare, and Model Mugging** can refer you to self-defense courses in the US (☎800 345 5425). Visit the website at www.impactsafety.org/chapters.htm for a list of nearby chapters. (2-3 hr. workshops from US$50; full courses US$350-500). Women and men are welcome. If you end up needing self-defense, remember that the best strategy is usually to run and scream "help" or "fire" in the local language. In Southeast Asia, especially, attracting attention to yourself in public could help deter any immediate threat to your safety.

! **TRAVEL ADVISORIES** The following government offices provide travel information or advisories by telephone, by fax, or via the web:

Australian Department of Foreign Affairs and Trade: ☎2 6261 1111; www.dfat.gov.au.

Canadian Department of Foreign Affairs and International Trade (DFAIT): In Canada ☎800-267-8316, elsewhere ☎+1 613-944-4000; www.dfait-maeci.gc.ca. Call for their free booklet, *Bon Voyage...But.*

New Zealand Ministry of Foreign Affairs: ☎04 494 8500; www.mft.govt.nz/trav.html.

United Kingdom Foreign and Commonwealth Office. ☎020 7008 0232; www.fco.gov.uk.

United States Department of State. ☎202 647-5225, http://travel.state.gov. For *A Safe Trip Abroad,* ☎(202) 512-1800.

POLITICS AND TERRORISM. Travelers to Southeast Asia should always check travel advisories and world news for the countries they will be visiting before departure. Once there, the best way to stay out of trouble is to avoid talking politics altogether. However, it is always helpful to be aware of the political situation in the region, and using current, proper titles for government officials and organizations is a must. Currently, one of the most prominent terrorist groups in Southeast Asia is the Abu Sayyaf Group (ASG), an Islamic separatist organization operating primarily in the Philippines but also in nearby parts of Malaysia and Indonesia. While ASG has taken to kidnapping, other terrorist groups have also been responsible for bombings and violence. The military government of Myanmar is not a threat to foreigners, but talking about politics in any way might endanger both you and your conversation partner. At the time of press, a US State Dept. travel warning was in place for Indonesia in the wake of political instability rising from the impeachment of the President. Travel in rural Cambodia should be avoided, as active landmines from the war are still a major concern.

COUNTRY-SPECIFIC CONCERNS

CAMBODIA. Landmines litter the country. Though de-mining operations have made significant progress, much of Cambodia remains mined, especially in rural areas. **Stay on well-travelled roads at all times.** Additionally, bandits are still at large, and corrupt police forces are always looking for extra cash. Overland travel is the most dangerous mode of transport, because of raids, unofficial police "checkpoints," and road conditions.

INDONESIA. Though violence is rare in Indonesia, there is still reason for caution. As of August 2001, the country was undergoing a process to impeach President Wahid, and though no serious outbreaks of violence have occurred as of yet, tension persists in the political and social climate. Travel is also currently considered unsafe in the **Aceh province, Central Sulawesi, East Timor,** and **Irian Jaya.** Check with your embassy for up-to-date safety information before attempting any travel in these areas.

LAOS. Laos has a low crime rate, but travelers shouldn't let their guard down. The **Vang Vieng-Luang Prabang Rd.** is no longer a major bandit target, but some travelers feel safer avoiding it. Be especially careful in the **Golden Triangle** area near the Thai-Burmese-Lao border, which is known for its opium production. In Xieng Khouang Province, the Bolovens Plateau, and along the Ho Chi Minh Trail, unexploded ordnance is still a threat. Although several non-governmental organizations have taken up demining, some bombs remain, killing or injuring about 10 people per month. Laos has strict rules regarding **public morality.** (Remember, this is the country that outlawed karaoke in its capital city.) Bringing a Laotian into your hotel room could land you in prison.

MALAYSIA. Trafficking in illegal drugs carries the death penalty. This warning, and ones similar to it, are plastered across Malaysian tourist literature for good reason—Malaysia does not take kindly to drugs. On the bright side, very little violent crime threatens travelers; criminals stop at petty theft, and minor cons.

MYANMAR. Do not talk about politics. Stay away from demonstrations, and do not engage in political conversations, no matter how harmless the topic may seem. **Political conversations put locals at risk of interrogation and arrest.** Do not photograph bridges, military installations, or anything else of economic or military importance.

Officials carefully screen books and magazines at the airport. The officials may not understand English, but they are attentive to political articles, books, and pictures related to Aung San Suu Kyi.

THAILAND. Thailand has a good safety record. Nevertheless, scams abound: taxi and *tuk-tuk* drivers, guest house operators, and fellow travelers have all been known to attempt various con-games and thievery. On buses and trains and in the airport, be careful when accepting food or drink from strangers; travelers have been drugged and robbed. Most likely their friendliness is genuine, but exercise common sense. Crime committed against foreigners is usually petty thievery; violence is rare. Most Thai cities have separate tourist police forces. All narcotic drugs in Thailand are illegal, despite what your guest house owner may tell you. Penalties for drug-related crimes can be very stiff—up to life in prison.

SINGAPORE. Singaporean law has no sense of humor. Do not: jaywalk within 50m of a street crossing (S$50 fine); import or possess chewing gum; litter; smoke in enclosed public areas; or eat or drink on the MRT. Most offenses carry fines of S$1000-2000 for first-time offenders. The penalty for importing illegal drugs involves rotting in jail or being executed. Foreign embassies cannot intervene. Don't be scared, though; Singapore is one of the safest places in the world—if you don't break any laws. Women are rarely cat-called, and it's not unusual to see women walking by themselves after dark. Nevertheless, petty crime happens, and travelers shouldn't surrender common street smarts.

THE PHILIPPINES. Personable Filipinos go to great lengths to give directions and point out proper jeepney routes. Be wary of taking drinks from anyone you don't know—unsuspecting travelers have been given drinks spiked with **sedatives.** Manila seems to be the haven for these wayward pharmacists, but exercise caution everywhere. Declining seedy request disguised as amicable gestures usually requires special social skills, especially when assailants are graying grandmas dishing out soup, but a moment's awkwardness far outweighs a ruined trip. Another concern for travelers is the use of firearms by security guards protecting restaurants, banks, and clubs. Hanging out in front of banks and armored vehicles is not wise, as these are often targets.

VIETNAM. Never leave valuables unguarded (especially your passport); thefts are not uncommon within guest houses, sometimes even under the management's orchestration. Keep an eye out for con artists, pickpockets, and purse/backpack snatchers, especially prevalent in Hồ Chí Minh City. Also, remember that Vietnamese police can be unfriendly and should generally be avoided. A new law prohibits the police from collecting fines directly—they can only hand out tickets—so don't be fooled into paying cash. **Avoid photographing bridges, border crossings, power stations, and military and government structures.**

FINANCIAL SECURITY

If you keep all your valuables (money, important documents) in one place, you will lose them all at the same time. Have different stashes of money, passports, as well as **photocopies** of all important documents. Be sure to photocopy both the visa page and the identification page of your passport. Carry one copy separate from the documents and leave another copy at home. Label your luggage both inside and out. **Don't put a wallet with money in your back pocket or your backpack.** Never count your money in public, and carry as little as possible. Secure packs with small combination padlocks which slip through the two zippers; even twist-ties or dental floss will slow down pickpockets. These precautions do not always suffice: moped riders who snatch purses and backpacks sometimes cut straps with knives. If you carry valuables in the handcrafted cloth bags that abound in Southeast Asia, you might as well put a sign around your neck that says "Am rookie tourist. Please steal from me." A **money belt** is the best way to carry cash; you can buy one at camping supply stores. Keep some money separate from the rest to use in an emergency.

Con artists abound in all large cities in Southeast Asia. They often work in groups, and children are among the most effective. They are wily and have a large bag of tricks. In city crowds and especially on public transportation, **pickpockets** are impressively deft. Be aware of your surroundings and look sure of yourself. Confidence is the greatest anti-theft device you can have.

Never leave your belongings unattended; crime occurs in the safest-looking guesthouse or hotel. If you feel unsafe, look for places with a curfew or a night attendant. *Let's Go* lists locker availability in guesthouses, hotels, and train stations, but you'll need your own **padlock.** Lockers are useful if you don't want to lug everything with you, but don't store valuables in them.

Be particularly careful on buses. Carry your backpack in front of you where you can see it, and don't trust anyone to "watch your bag for a second." Thieves thrive on trains; professionals wait for tourists to fall asleep and then carry off their bags.

DRUGS & ALCOHOL

Drugs are often easily accessible in Southeast Asia and, especially in some rural communities, drug use may seem to be common and public. All drug use, however, is illegal. Buying or selling *any* type of drugs may lead to anything from a prison sentence to the death penalty, especially in Malaysia, Singapore, and Cambodia. A meek "I didn't know it was illegal" will not suffice; if you break the law, your home embassies will visit you in jail and bring you candy, but they **cannot and will not do anything else** to help.

HEALTH

Common sense is the simplest prescription for good health while you travel. Travel in Southeast Asia can be dreary, requiring you to be in hot, humid weather. Foreign foods and water may cause diarrhea, so dehydration is a major concern. Drink lots of fluids and bring anti-diarrheal medicines and salt-tablets to prevent dehydration and constipation. Wear sturdy, broken-in shoes and clean socks, and use talcum powder to keep your feet dry.

BEFORE YOU GO

Preparation can help minimize the likelihood of contracting a disease and maximize the chances of receiving effective health care in the event of an emergency. For tips on packing a basic **first-aid kit** and other health essentials, see p. 25.

In your **passport**, write the names of any people you wish to be contacted in case of a medical emergency, and also list any allergies or medical conditions of which you would want doctors to be aware. Matching a prescription to a foreign equivalent is not always easy, safe, or possible. Carry up-to-date, legible prescriptions or a statement from your doctor stating the medication's trade name, manufacturer, chemical name, and dosage. To be extra careful, bring any medication you think you might need with you. Major gateway cities like Bangkok, Manila, Jakarta etc. will have most over the counter medications that you might need; stock up here before you travel out. While traveling, be sure to keep all medication with you in your carry-on luggage.

IMMUNIZATIONS & PRECAUTIONS

See **Inoculations Requirements and Recommendations,** below, for a list of inoculations that are required/recommended. **Malaria** is prevalent in most of Southeast Asia, and strains that are resistant to certain prophylactics are not uncommon. Ask your doctor to recommend the best preventative drug for your region of travel. While yellow fever is only endemic to parts of South America and sub-Saharan Africa, many countries may require travelers arriving from affected regions to have been vaccinated for **yellow fever.** In general, travelers from North America, Europe, Australia, most of Central America, North Africa, India, and the Middle East need not worry about being vaccinated for Yellow Fever. The **Center for Disease Control (CDC),** in the US, does, however, recommend that travellers from South American or South African countries get a yellow fever vaccination and signed certificate. For recommendations on immunizations and prophylactics, consult the CDC (see below) in the US or the equivalent in your home country, and check with a doctor for guidance.

USEFUL ORGANIZATIONS & PUBLICATIONS

The **CDC** (☎(888) 232-3299; www.cdc.gov) provides medical information for travelers. The CDC also publishes the booklet "Health Information for International Travelers" (US$20), a global rundown of disease, immunization, and health advice, including risks in particular countries. Orders can be made by phone (☎(202) 512-1800) with a major credit card.

The **United States State Department** (http://travel.state.gov) compiles consular information sheets on health, entry requirements, and other issues for all countries of the world. For quick information about health and travel warnings, call the **Overseas Citizens' Services** (☎(202) 647-5225; after-hours 647-4000). To receive the same consular information sheets by fax, dial (202) 647-3000 from a fax machine and follow the instructions.

EMERGENCY MEDICAL ASSISTANCE

If you are concerned about having medical support while traveling, contact one of these three services: Global Emergency Medical Services (GEMS) has *Med-Pass* that provides 24-hour international medical assistance and support coordinated through registered nurses who have online access to your medical information, your primary physician, and a worldwide network of screened, cre-

INOCULATION REQUIREMENTS & RECOMMENDATIONS. Travelling to Southeast Asia necessitates some, but not all of the following inoculations. Check with a doctor for guidance through this maze of injections. Be sure to keep your inoculation records with you as you travel-you may be required to show them to border officials.

Diptheria and tetanus, recommended.

Polio, recommended.

Typhoid, recommended.

Hepatitis B, if travelling for 4 weeks or more or if blood transfusions, needle-sharing, or sexual contact is likely.

Hepatitis A, recommended for those traveling for 4 weeks or more.

Cholera, not recommended because of the vaccination's serious side effects; all countries have dropped cholera vaccination as a requirement for entry.

Yellow Fever, if travelling from South America or southern Africa; certificate or vaccination may be required.

Rabies, if travelling for 4 weeks or more, especially if you will be cycling, handling animals, or caving.

Japanese Encephalitis, if you plan to visit rural areas for 4 weeks or more; elevated risk usually from May-Oct.; no risk in Honk Kong and Singapore.

Tuberculosis, for stays of 3 months or more.

dentialed English-speaking doctors. Subscribers also receive a personal medical record that contains vital information in case of emergencies, and GEMS will pay for medical evacuation if necessary. Prices start at about US$35 for a 30-day trip and run up to about $100 for annual services. For more information contact them at 2001 Westside Dr. #120, Alpharetta, GA 30004 (☎(800) 860-1111; www.globalems.com). International Security Overseas (ISOS) (worldwide headquarters: 331 N Bridge Rd., #17-00 Odeon Towers, Singapore 188720; www.internationalsos.com) provides emergency assistance services, medical services, managed health care solutions, and security overseas services (SOS Security). ISOS especially prides itself for its around-the-clock quality care in developing countries and medical clinics worldwide. ISOS offers medical insurance for short-term travels for 1-14 days ($143, $8 each additional day) or on a monthly basis ($190/month, $8 each additional day). Families and couples can purchase cheaper packages. Call US (800) 523-8662 to enroll in a plan. Contact ISOS offices in Singapore (☎(65) 338-7800); Ho Chi Min City, Vietnam (☎(848) 829-8250); Bangkok, Thailand (☎(66 2) 256-7146); and Phnom Penh, Cambodia (☎(855 23) 216 911). The International Association for Medical Assistance to Travelers (IAMAT) has free membership and offers a directory of English-speaking doctors around the world who treat members for a set fee schedule. Chapters include: US, 417 Center St., Lewiston, NY 14092 (☎(716) 754-4883, 8am-4pm; www.sentex.net/~iamat); Canada, 40 Regal Rd., Guelph, ON N1K 1B5 (☎(519) 836-0102) or 1287 St. Clair Ave. W, Toronto, ON M6E 1B8 (☎(416) 652-0137); New Zealand, P.O. Box 5049, Christchurch 5.

If your regular **insurance** policy does not cover travel abroad, you may wish to purchase additional coverage, particularly for traveling in Southeast Asia. For more information, see p. 31.

MEDICAL CONDITIONS

Hospitals in Southeast Asia vary from region to region, but generally larger, centralized cities like Singapore, Bangkok, and Kuala Lumpur have high-quality facilities. Public hospitals tend be more crowded and less expensive than private hospitals, which are more likely to have English-speaking doctors, language interpreters, foreign insurance claim assistance, international emergency medical evacuation access, and embassy liaison services. For the most trusted medical care, go to Thailand or Singapore.

If you are still concerned about being able to access medical support while traveling, there are special support services you may employ. The *MedPass* from **GlobalCare, Inc.,** 2001 Westside Pkwy., #120, Alpharetta, GA 30004, USA (☎800 860 1111; www.globalems.com), provides 24hr. international medical assistance, support, and medical evacuation resources. The **International Association for Medical Assistance to Travelers (IAMAT;** US ☎(716) 754-4883, Canada ☎(416) 652-0137, New Zealand ☎(03) 352 20 53; www.sentex.net/~iamat) has free membership, lists English-speaking doctors worldwide, and offers detailed info on immunization requirements and sanitation.

Those with medical conditions (e.g., diabetes, allergies to antibiotics, epilepsy, heart conditions) may want to obtain a stainless steel Medic Alert identification tag (US$35 the first year, $15 annually thereafter), which identifies the condition and gives a 24-hour collect-call information number. Contact the **Medic Alert Foundation,** 2323 Colorado Ave., Turlock, CA 95382 (☎800 825 3785; www.medicalert.org). Diabetics can contact the American Diabetes Association, 1660 Duke St., Alexandria, VA 22314 (☎800 232 3472), to receive copies of the article "Travel and Diabetes" and a diabetic ID card, which carries messages in 18 languages explaining the carrier's diabetic status.

ESSENTIALS

ONCE IN SOUTHEAST ASIA

ENVIRONMENTAL HAZARDS

Heat exhaustion, characterized by **dehydration** and **salt deficiency,** can lead to fatigue, headaches, and wooziness. Drink water and plenty of other fluids as water doesn't stay in the system for long. Adding salt or some lemon juice to water helps. Eat salty foods, and avoid dehydrating beverages (e.g. alcohol, coffee, tea, and caffeinated soda).

Sunburn: If prone to sunburn or planning to spend time near water or in the desert, bring sunscreen with you. Apply liberally and often to avoid burns and risk of skin cancer. If sunburned, drink more fluids than usual and apply Calamine or an aloe-based lotion.

INSECT-BORNE DISEASES

Many diseases are transmitted by insects—mainly mosquitoes. Be aware of insects in wet or forested areas, especially while hiking and camping. **Mosquitoes** are most active from dusk to dawn. Wear long pants and long sleeves, tuck your pants into your socks, and buy a mosquito net. Use insect repellents, such as DEET, and soak or spray your gear with permethrin (licensed in the US for use on clothing). Consider natural repellents like vitamin B-12 or garlic pills. To stop the itch after being bitten, try Calamine lotion or topical cortisones (like Cortaid), or take a bath with a half-cup of baking soda or oatmeal.

Malaria: Symptoms include fever, chills, aches, and fatigue, followed by high fever and sweating, sometimes with vomiting and diarrhea. See a doctor for any flu-like sickness that occurs after travel in a risk area. Use mosquito repellent, particularly in the evenings and when visiting forested areas, and take oral prophylactics, like **mefloquine** (sold under the name Lariam) or **doxycycline** (ask your doctor for a prescription or visit the CDC website, www.cdc.gov). Be aware that these drugs can have very serious side effects, including slowed heart rate and nightmares.

Dengue fever: A viral infection transmitted by *Aedes* mosquitoes, which bite during the day. Has flu-like symptoms and is often indicated by a rash 3-4 days after the onset of fever. Early symptoms include chills, high fever, headaches, swollen lymph nodes, muscle aches, and in some instances, a pink rash on the face. See a doctor **immediately,** drink plenty of liquids, and take fever-reducing medication such as acetaminophen (Tylenol). *Never take aspirin to treat dengue fever.*

Japanese encephalitis: Symptoms include delirium, chills, headache, fever, vomiting, muscle fatigue. Go to a hospital as soon as any symptoms appear. According to the CDC, there is little chance of being infected if proper precautions are taken, such as using mosquito repellents containing DEET and sleeping under mosquito tents.

!

MALARIA RISK BY COUNTRY

Brunei, Hong Kong, and **Singapore:** Little risk.
Cambodia: Risk in all areas, except Phnom Penh.
Indonesia: Risk in rural areas only, except there is high risk in all areas of Irian Java. Little risk in Java, Sumatra, and the main resort areas of Bali.
Laos: Risk in all areas, except Vientiane.
Malaysia: Risk in remote areas of peninsular Malaysia and Sarawak. Sabah (NE Borneo) has risk throughout. Urban and coastal areas are nearly risk-free.
Myanmar: Risk in rural areas; there is little danger in Yangon or Mandalay.
Philippines: Rural areas only; little risk in the provinces of Bohol, Catanduanes, Cebu, and metropolitan Manila. Subic Bay is a risk area.
Thailand: Risk is largely confined to the borders of Cambodia and Myanmar. Little risk in major cities and tourist resorts (Bangkok, Chiang Mai, and Phuket).
Vietnam: Rural areas, except little risk in the Red River Delta and the coastal plain north of Nha Trang.

Filariasis: A roundworm infestation transmitted by mosquitoes. Infection causes enlargement of extremities and has no vaccine. Use mosquito repellents and sleep under mosquito tents.

Plague: Recent outbreaks in Myanmar, Laos, and Vietnam. Early symptoms include fever, nausea, sore throat, and swollen lymph nodes. Travellers in endemic areas can take antibiotics with malaria medication and should use insect repellents with DEET.

FOOD- & WATER-BORNE DISEASES

The **tap water** in Southeast Asia (with the exception of Singapore) is not safe, even for teeth-brushing. Prevention is the best cure; be sure that your food is properly cooked and the water you drink is clean. Never drink unbottled water that you have not treated yourself. Ice cubes are just as dangerous as impure water in liquid form. Salads and uncooked vegetables are full of untreated water. Other culprits are raw shellfish, unpasteurized milk, and sauces containing raw eggs. Peel fruits and veggies and avoid tap water (including ice cubes and anything washed in tap water, like salad). Buy bottled water or purify your own water by bringing it to a rolling boil or treating it with **iodine tablets;** note however that some parasites such as *giardia* have exteriors that resist iodine treatment, making boiling a more reliable treatment for water. Always wash your hands before eating or bring a quick-drying purifying liquid hand cleaner. Your bowels will thank you.

Traveler's diarrhea: A rite of passage caused by bacteria in untreated drinking water and uncooked foods. Symptoms include nausea, bloating, and urgency. Try quick-energy, non-sugary foods with protein and carbohydrates to keep your strength up. Over-the-counter anti-diarrheals (e.g. Immodium) should be used in moderation for temporary relief. Drink sweetened liquids, uncaffeinated soft drinks, or salted crackers to avoid dehydration. Consult a doctor for treatment of diarrhea in children.

Dysentery: Symptoms include bloody diarrhea, fever, and abdominal pain. Bacillary dysentery generally only lasts a week but is highly contagious. Amoebic dysentery is more serious and may cause long-term damage if left untreated. Dysentery can be treated with the drugs norfloxacin or ciprofloxacin (commonly known as Cipro). Consider obtaining a prescription before you leave home.

Cholera: Symptoms include diarrhea, dehydration, vomiting, and muscle cramps. See a doctor immediately; if left untreated, it may be deadly. Antibiotics are available, but the most important treatment is rehydration.

Hepatitis A: Symptoms include fatigue, fever, nausea, dark urine, jaundice, vomiting, and light stools. Ask your doctor about the vaccine (Havrix or Vaqta) or an injection of immune globulin (IG; formerly called gamma globulin).

Typhoid fever: Caused by the salmonella bacteria; common in villages and rural areas. While mostly transmitted through contaminated food and water, it may also be acquired by direct contact with another person. Early symptoms include fever, headaches, fatigue, loss of appetite, constipation, and sometimes a rash on the abdomen or chest. Antibiotics can treat typhoid, but a vaccination (70-90% effective) is recommended if you will be hiking, camping, or staying in rural areas.

OTHER INFECTIOUS DISEASES

Hepatitis B: A viral infection of the liver transmitted via bodily fluids or needle-sharing. Symptoms may not surface until years after infection. Vaccinations are recommended for health-care workers, sexually-active travelers, and anyone planning to seek medical treatment abroad. The 3-shot vaccination series must begin 6 mo. before traveling.

Hepatitis C: Like Hep B, but the mode of transmission differs. IV drug users, those with occupational exposure to blood, hemodialysis patients, and recipients of blood transfusions are at the highest risk, but the disease can also be spread through sexual contact or sharing items like razors and toothbrushes that may have traces of blood on them.

AIDS, HIV, & STDS

A thriving sex and intravenous drug industry has brought **Acquired Immune Deficiency Syndrome (AIDS)** to epidemic status in parts of Southeast Asia. A full 2.3% of Thailand's adult population now has HIV/AIDS, although the rate of new infections has started to fall. Condom use has increased, but not enough to combat the dramatic spread of this disease within Cambodia, Myanmar, Thailand, and Vietnam. Indonesia, Laos, Malaysia, the Philippines, and Singapore are not as widely affected.

The easiest mode of **HIV** transmission is through direct blood-to-blood contact with an HIV-positive person. *Never* share intravenous drug, tattooing, or other needles. The most common mode of transmission is sexual intercourse. If you're going to have sex, use a condom. Since it isn't always easy to buy condoms when traveling, take a supply with you before you depart for your trip.

Travelers seeking pleasure in the quasi-legal bars, massage parlors, and brothels of Southeast Asia stand a good chance of bringing back unwanted viral souvenirs of their trip. The best advice is to follow all precautions concerning any sexual encounter—use a condom with spermicide, and avoid sex with strangers or with people who engage in high-risk behavior (such as IV drug use or promiscuous or unprotected sex). Many prostitutes do not know that they are infected, and even if they do, they probably won't tell their clients. Some HIV-positive people live symptom-free for ten years or more; others die quickly. There is no cure for AIDS.

Sexually transmitted diseases (STDs) such as gonorrhea, chlamydia, genital warts, syphilis, and herpes are easier to catch than HIV. They can be painful, ghastly, even deadly. **Hepatitis B** and **C** are transmitted sexually (see **Other Infectious Diseases,** above). If you are a traveler with uncommon presence of mind, inspect your partner's genitals for swelling, sores, bumps, or blisters before sex.

WOMEN'S HEALTH

Women traveling in unsanitary conditions are vulnerable to **urinary tract** and **bladder infections,** which are common and severely uncomfortable bacterial diseases that cause a burning sensation and painful, frequent urination. To avoid these infections, drink plenty of vitamin-C-rich juice and clean water, and urinate frequently, especially right after intercourse. Untreated, these infections can lead to kidney infections, sterility, and (rarely) death. If symptoms persist, see a doctor.

The hot and humid climate of Southeast Asia also makes women especially susceptible to **vaginal yeast infections.** Wearing loosely fitting trousers or a skirt and cotton underwear will help, as will over-the-counter remedies like Monistat or Gynelotrimin. Bring supplies from home if you are prone to infection, as they may be difficult to find on the road. In a pinch, some travelers use a natural alternative such as plain yogurt and lemon juice douche.

Tampons and **pads** are sometimes hard to find in Southeast Asia, and your preferred brands may not be available, so take supplies along. **Reliable contraceptive devices** may also be difficult to find. Women using birth control pills should bring

SMART FASHION
would you like to get your own bespoke suit ?(Specialized Chinese Tailors)
TREND 2002
WIR SPRECHEN DEUTSCH (WE CAN SPEAK MANY LANGUAGES)
Exhibition in Europe, Benelux, Scandinavia, United Kingdom, USA & Australia
Contact us to make a personal appointment on our next visit to your city for made-to-measure clothing. You get to choose your suits made from high quality fabrics ranging from Super 100's, Super 120's and wool / cashmere blends.
A visit to your home or office is also possible
To make an appointment on our next visit list kindly fill up your request at www.smartfashion.com/europe.htm
Order our fabric-sample catalogue online at: www.smartfashion.com/catalog.htm
Our staff will get in touch with you and will confirm the appointment to send our sales representative to measure you
CENTRALLLY LOCATED NEXT TO ALL MAJOR HOTELS, EMBASSIES, AND SHOPPING AREAS.-(25 MIN FROM AIRPORT)
PRI: 02-259-9412 (SUNDAY) FAX: +662-255-4518
HIGHLY RECOMMENDED CLOTHIERS FOR BIG & TALL PEOPLE
Special "Let's Go" offer..
from US$ 125
Gents:
1 Cashmere Suit
1 Summer Suit
3 Extra Trousers
3 Shirts
2 Silk Ties
Ladies:
2 Suits
1 Dress
2 Skirts
3 Blouses
1 Silk Kimono
BEST BUY
While in Bangkok, Call for free pick up to our showroom
BOSS, UOMO VALENTINO, VERSACE & ARMANI CUTS ARE OUR SPECIALITY
02-651-0303
02-651-0304
Leave Voice Mail or send faxes at the following numbers:
USA: 1-888-2890861
UK: (020) 76011794
Switzerland: (01) 3553232
Germany: (069) 25577773
Netherlands: (020) 5241550
Belgium: (02) 7062445
France: (01) 53016997
Australia: (02) 9475 0279
To reach us by BTS (Sky Train), 3 minute walk from the Nana Station into Soi 11
Order From us and Enjoy our Special Fringe Benefit Services
1) Free delivery to hotel and anywhere within Thailand
2) Our tailor will personally go to your hotel to do the fitting
3) Free alteration
4) Free transportation to our shop
5) Free after sales services.
6) Clothes can be ready within 3 hours upon request
7) Size are keep for 5 years
TAILOR OF THE YEAR AWARD
MAXIMUM AWARDED TAILOR IN THAILAND
We keep all the sizes in the computer. So in future you can order by E-mail or fax. Tourguides, taxi drivers, tuk-tuk drivers get commission for taking you to different stores, CALL DIRECT, you will PAY LESS
Call: 02-255-4516
For your hotel reservations and airticket inquiries,visit our new venture at www.thailandtravel.net
OPEN 7 DAYS A WEEK
IMPORTANT: SOME OTHER SHOPS VERY NEAR TO OUR FASHION SHOP ARE ALSO USING THE NAME SAM MAKE SURE YOU ARE IN THE RIGHT SHOP BY LOOKING FOR SMART FASHION SIGN BOARD
SMART FASHION.COM
LADIES & GENTS CUSTOM TAILOR
E-mail: info@smartfashion.com
Showroom Address: 1/10-11 Sukhumvit Soi 11, Bangkok, Thailand
Mailing Address: P.O. Box 1424, Nana Post Office, Bangkok 10112, Thailand

enough to allow for possible loss or extended stays. Bring a prescription, since forms of the pill vary considerably. Women who use a diaphragm should bring enough contraceptive jelly. Condoms are easily found in all major Southeast Asian cities and its a good idea to stock up before there before heading out.

INSURANCE

Travel insurance covers four basic areas: medical/health problems, property loss, trip cancellation/interruption, and emergency evacuation. Even if your regular insurance policies extend to travel-related accidents, consider purchasing travel insurance if the cost of potential trip cancellation/interruption or emergency medical evacuation is greater than you could absorb. Prices for travel insurance purchased separately run about US$50 per week for full coverage, while trip cancellation/interruption may be purchased at US$5.50 per US$100 of coverage.

Medical insurance (especially university policies) often covers costs incurred abroad; check with your provider. **US Medicare** does not cover foreign travel. **Canadians** are protected by their home province's health insurance plan for up to 90 days after leaving the country; check with the provincial Ministry of Health or Health Plan Headquarters for details. **Homeowners' insurance** (or your family's coverage) often covers theft during travel and loss of travel documents (passport, plane ticket, railpass, etc.) up to US$500.

ISIC and ITIC (see p. 15) provide basic insurance benefits, including US$100 per day of in-hospital sickness for up to 60 days, US$3000 of accident-related medical reimbursement, and US$25,000 for emergency medical transport. Cardholders have access to a toll-free 24-hour helpline for medical, legal, and financial emergencies overseas (US and Canada ☎(877) 370-4724, elsewhere call US collect +1 (715) 345-0505). American Express (US ☎(800) 528-4800) grants most cardholders automatic car rental insurance (collision and theft, but not liability) and ground travel accident coverage of US$100,000 on flight purchases made with the card.

INSURANCE PROVIDERS. **Council** and **STA** (see p. 39) offer a range of plans that can supplement your basic coverage. Other private insurance providers in the **US and Canada** include: **Access America** (☎(800) 284-8300); **Berkely Group/Carefree Travel Insurance** (☎(800) 323-3149; www.berkely.com); **Globalcare Travel Insurance** (☎(800) 821-2488; www.globalcare-cocco.com); and **Travel Assistance International** (☎(800) 821-2828; www.worldwide-assistance.com). Providers in the **UK** include **Campus Travel** (☎(01865) 258 000) and **Columbus Travel Insurance** (☎(020) 7375 0011). In **Australia,** try **CIC Insurance** (☎9202 8000).

PACKING

PACK LIGHT. To appreciate the virtue of traveling light, pack your bag with what you think are only the bare essentials, strap it on, and imagine walking uphill for three hours on hot asphalt. Now pack again. After trekking a mile in 90-degree heat and humidity to the bus station, and then wedging yourself into a Vietnamese vehicle made for people two feet shorter, you will rue the day that you packed that hair-dryer "just in case," or, for that matter, the unnecessary handle end of your toothbrush. Don't forget that you can purchase all necessary items in Southeast Asia for a fraction of the cost.

LUGGAGE. For traveling in Southeast Asia, a sturdy **frame backpack** is unbeatable. Toting a **suitcase** or **trunk** is all right if you plan to live in one or two cities and explore from there but a very bad idea if you're going to be moving at all. Regardless, a **daypack** (a small backpack or courier bag) is a must. A pack that locks is good for state-of-mind and as a initial deterrent, but shouldn't replace heads-up common sense. Plastic bags will come in handy for keeping things dry and sorted. If you use a brightly-colored fanny pack, you deserve to get robbed.

ESSENTIALS

ESSENTIALS

CLOTHING. The clothes you bring should be sturdy, comfortable, and quick-drying. Try to bring only two outfits, one to wash and one to wear. Clothing is very inexpensive in Southeast Asia, so it's best to pack light and buy what you need on the road. Essentials that you should bring with you might include a good waterproof jacket, underwear, and study boots.

CONVERTERS AND ADAPTERS. Electricity in Southeast Asia is 220 volts AC, enough to fry any 110V appliance. **Americans** and **Canadians** should pick up an **adapter** and a **converter** (US$20) at a hardware store-most appliances need both. **New Zealanders, South Africans**, and **Australians** won't need a converter, but will need adapters for anything electrical.

TOILETRIES. Most toiletries are readily available and cheap in Southeast Asia. To be safe, stock up in larger cities before going to rural areas. Contact lenses may be expensive, so bring enough pairs and solution for your entire trip. Bring your glasses and a copy of your prescription in case you need emergency replacements. If you use heat-disinfection, check if you can switch temporarily to a chemical disinfection system or buy a 220/240V converter.

OTHER USEFUL ITEMS. It's always a good idea to carry a first-aid kit including sunscreen and insect repellent. Other useful items include: an umbrella, alarm clock, moleskin (for blisters), safety pins, sunglasses, pocketknife, compass, padlock, flashlight, duct tape (for patching tears), and a moneybelt.

IMPORTANT DOCUMENTS. Don't forget your passport, traveler's checks, ATM and/or credit cards, and adequate IDs (see p. 14).

ACCOMMODATIONS

Choosing accommodations in Southeast Asia can sometimes be a gamble, as electricity, running water, and air-conditioning have not yet reached many of the rural areas throughout the region. Finding inexpensive accommodations, however, never proves to be a real problem. Hotels and guesthouses line the streets of major cities and towns throughout Southeast Asia, many equipped with Internet facilities and small cafes. For a few dollars facilities can vary from a shared room with several beds, to a single room with an ensuite bathroom and fan. Modern and more expensive hotels can be found in highly touristed areas, allowing for a cooler and more comfortable stay.

While you should make reservations at the more expensive lodgings, finding a hotel on the same day as your stay is not difficult. It is not uncommon, and most often expected, to ask to see rooms before committing to a hotel; this also allows room for bargaining. Some hotels and guesthouses in Southeast Asia, and all places in Vietnam, require by governmental law that you leave your passport with them during your stay. If you feel uncomfortable about doing this, some places will allow for you to leave your customs slip from immigration.

KEEPING IN TOUCH

BY MAIL

SENDING MAIL HOME FROM SOUTHEAST ASIA

Airmail letters under 1 oz. between North America and most Southeast Asian nations cost US$1. Envelopes should be marked "air mail" or "*par avion*" to avoid having letters sent by sea. There are several ways to arrange pick-up of letters sent to you by friends and relatives while you are abroad.

General Delivery: Mail can be sent through **Poste Restante** (the international phrase for General Delivery to almost any town with a post office). Address Poste Restante letters to the recipient, with the last name underlined and in capital letters: "Darren TESSITORE, Poste Restante, Bangkok, Thailand." The mail will go to a desk in the central post office, unless you specify a post office by street address or postal code. As a rule, it is best to use the largest post office in the area, and mail may be sent there regardless of what is written on the envelope. When picking up mail, bring a form of photo ID, preferably a passport. There is generally no surcharge. If the clerks insist that there is nothing for you, have them check under your first name as well. *Let's Go* lists post offices in the **Practical Information** section for each city and most towns.

American Express: AmEx's travel offices throughout the world will act as a mail service for cardholders if you contact them in advance. Under this free **Client Letter Service,** they will hold mail for up to 30 days and forward upon request. Address the letter in the same way shown above. Some offices will offer these services to non-cardholders, but you must call ahead to make sure. Check the **Practical Information** section of the countries you plan to visit; *Let's Go* lists AmEx office locations for most large cities. A complete list is available free from AmEx (US ☎(800) 528-4800).

Surface mail: By far the cheapest and slowest way to mail. It takes 1-3 months to cross the Atlantic and 2-4 to cross the Pacific–appropriate for sending large items you won't need to see for a while. When ordering books and materials from abroad, always include one or two **International Reply Coupons (IRCs)**–a way of providing the postage to cover delivery. IRCs should be available from your local post office (US$1.05).

SENDING MAIL TO SOUTHEAST ASIA

In general, mail in Southeast Asia is unreliable. Mark envelopes "air mail" or *par avion* or your letter or postcard will never arrive. Expect standard mail to take 2-3 weeks to reach major cities and longer to get to rural areas. **Federal Express** (Australia ☎13 26 10; US and Canada ☎800 247 4747; New Zealand ☎0800 73 33 39; UK ☎0800 12 38 00) handles express mail services from most home countries to all countries in Southeast Asian countries; for example, they can get a letter from New York to Vietnam in three days for US$31.98, and from London to Brunei in three days for UK£30.

RECEIVING MAIL IN SOUTHEAST ASIA

There are several ways to arrange pick-up of letters sent to you by friends and relatives while you are abroad. Mail can be sent via **Poste Restante** (General Delivery; to almost any city or town in Southeast Asia) with a post office, but is not very reliable. (see **Sending Mail home from Southeast Asia: General Delivery,** above). **American Express's** travel offices throughout the world offer a free **Client Letter Service** (mail held up to 30 days and forwarded upon request) for cardholders who contact them in advance (see **Sending Mail home from Southeast Asia: American Express,** above).

BY TELEPHONE

CALLING HOME FROM SOUTHEAST ASIA

A calling card is probably your cheapest bet. Calls are billed collect or to your account. You can frequently call collect without even possessing a company's calling card just by calling their access number and following the instructions. To obtain a calling card from your national telecommunications service before leaving home, contact the appropriate company listed below (using the numbers in the first column). To call home with a calling card, contact the operator for your service provider in Southeast Asia by dialing the appropriate toll-free access number (listed below). International calling booths abound in Southeast Asia; for a small fee, some may let you receive a call as well if you ask nicely. Many hostels also have International Direct Dial (IDD) facilities.

Country	Code	Australia Direct (Telstra)	Telecom New Zealand	Bell Canada Direct	BT Direct *Telkom South Africa*	AT&T MCI Sprint
Brunei	673	800 061	800 064	800 010	800 044	800 1111
Cambodia	855	1 800 881 061	N/A	N/A	N/A	1 800 881 001
Hong Kong	852	800 0061	800 96 0064	800 96 1100	800 961044	800 96 1111
Indonesia	62	001 801 61	008 801 64	008 801 16	001 801 44	001 801 10
Malaysia	60	800 0061	1 800 80 0064	1 800 800 0017	1 800 800 044	1 800 80 0011
Philippines	63	105 61 102 661	105 64	105 10	105 44 *105 78*	105 11 105 14
Singapore	65	8000 610 610	8000 640 640	8000 100 100	8000 440 441	8000 111 111 8000 112 112
Thailand	66	001 999 61 1000	001 999 64 1066	001 999 15 1000	001 999 44 1066	001 999 11111 001 999 12001
Vietnam	84	120 061 111	N/A	120 11 010	N/A N/A	120 10 288 120 11 022

CALLING WITHIN SOUTHEAST ASIA

The simplest way to call within the country is to use a coin-operated phone. **Prepaid phone cards** (available at many guest houses, shops, and restaurants) which carry a certain amount of phone time depending on the card's denomination, usually save time and money in the long run. Just insert them into the phone and proceed with your call. Other prepaid phone cards come with a Personal Identification Number (PIN) and a toll-free access number. Call the access number and follow the directions on the phone. They can be used to make both international and domestic calls. Purchase them in advance from major telephone companies in your country, and check to make sure that service from the company will be available in the region you'll be traveling. Phone rates typically tend to be highest in the morning, lower in the evening, and lowest on Sunday and late at night.

BY EMAIL AND BY INTERNET

Internet cafes are everywhere in Southeast Asia, even in some of the smallest towns. Many guest houses have Internet access, or log on for free at a public library. *Let's Go* lists Internet access locations in the Practical Information sections. It's usually difficult to forge a remote link with your home server from Southeast Asia, so take advantage of free web-based email accounts (e.g., www.hotmail.com, www.yahoo.com, www.rocketmail.com).

GETTING TO SOUTHEAST ASIA

BY PLANE

A little effort can save you a bundle. If your plans are flexible enough to deal with the restrictions, courier fares are the cheapest. Tickets bought from consolidators and standby seating are also good deals, but last-minute specials, airfare wars, and charter flights often beat these fares. The key is to hunt around, be patient, be flexible, and ask persistently about discounts. Students, seniors, and those under 26 should never pay full price for a ticket.

Southeast Asia regional package tickets (offered by Cathay Pacific Airlines), and round-the-world (RTW) flights are pricier but reasonable alternatives. Patching one-way flights together is the least economical way to travel.

DETAILS AND TIPS

Timing: Airfare to Southeast Asia peak between May and September; holidays are also expensive. The cheapest times to travel are October and April. Midweek (M-Th morning) round-trip flights run US$40-50 cheaper than weekend flights. They are generally more crowded and less likely to permit frequent-flier upgrades. Traveling with an "open return" ticket can be pricier than fixing a return date when buying the ticket.

Route: Round-trip flights are cheapest; "open-jaw" (arriving in and departing from different cities, e.g. New York-Hanoi, Bangkok-New York) tickets tend to be pricier. A route like this is best tackled by purchasing a round-trip ticket to Bangkok and then buying a one-way flight to Hanoi upon arrival. That way you can purchase another one-way ticket from another city to Bangkok, which is very cheap. In general, flying into regional hubs (especially Singapore, Bangkok, and Kuala Lumpur) is cheaper. Regional transportation is easier to handle while in Southeast Asia, and domestic flights can usually be purchased just hours or days in advance.

Round-the-World (RTW): If Southeast Asia is only one stop on a more extensive globe-hop, consider a RTW ticket. Tickets usually include at least 5 stops and are valid for about a year; prices range US$1200-5000. Try **Northwest Airlines/KLM** (US ☎(800) 447-4747; www.nwa.com) or **Star Alliance,** a consortium of 13 airlines including United Airlines (US ☎(800) 241-6522; www.star-alliance.com).

Boarding: Confirm international flights by phone within 72hr. of departure. Most airlines require that passengers arrive at the airport at least 2hr. before departure. One carry-on item and 2 checked bags is the norm for non-courier flights.

AVERAGE ROUND TRIP FARES (US$)

	Bangkok	HCMC	Jakarta	Manila	Singapore
Auckland	US$600-700	700-900	600-750	700-800	550-650
Brisbane	670-800	700-900	550-800	650-750	650-800
Dublin	500-650	700-900	700-900	700-900	700-900
Johannesburg	550-650	1300-2000	600-900	600-850	550-700
London	500-650	1000-1300	700-850	800-900	650-750
New York City	750-850	900-1050	850-1000	800-900	750-900
Perth	600-750	1050-1150	350-600	1500-2000	450-600
San Francisco	600-700	700-900	750-850	700-800	650-750
Sydney	670-800	700-900	500-750	650-800	650-750
Toronto	1150-1300	1300-1400	1300-1400	1150-1300	1200-1350
Vancouver	950-1100	1200	1150-1250	950-1050	1000-1150

BUDGET AND STUDENT TRAVEL AGENCIES

While knowledgeable agents can make your life easy and help you save, they may not spend the time to find you the lowest possible fare—they get paid on commission. Students and under-26ers holding **ISIC and IYTC cards** (see p. 15) qualify for discounts from student travel agencies. Most flights are on major airlines, but in peak season some may sell seats on less reliable chartered aircraft.

usit world (www.usitworld.com). Over 50 **usit campus** branches in the UK (www.usitcampus.co.uk), including 52 Grosvenor Gardens, **London** SW1W 0AG (☎(0870) 240 1010); **Manchester** (☎(0161) 273 1880; and **Edinburgh** (☎(0131) 668 3303). Nearly 20 **usit now** offices in Ireland, including 19-21 Aston Quay, O'Connell Bridge, **Dublin** 2 (☎(01) 602 1600; www.usitnow.ie), and **Belfast** (☎02 890 327 111; www.usitnow.com). Offices also in Athens, Auckland, Brussels, Frankfurt, Johannesburg, Lisbon, Luxembourg, Madrid, Paris, Sofia, and Warsaw.

Council Travel (www.counciltravel.com). Countless US offices, including branches in Atlanta, Boston, Chicago, LA, New York, San Francisco, Seattle, and Washington D.C. Check the website or call 800-2-COUNCIL (226-8624) for the office nearest you. UK's office is at 28A Poland St. (Oxford Circus), **London** W1V 3DB (☎0207 437 77 67).

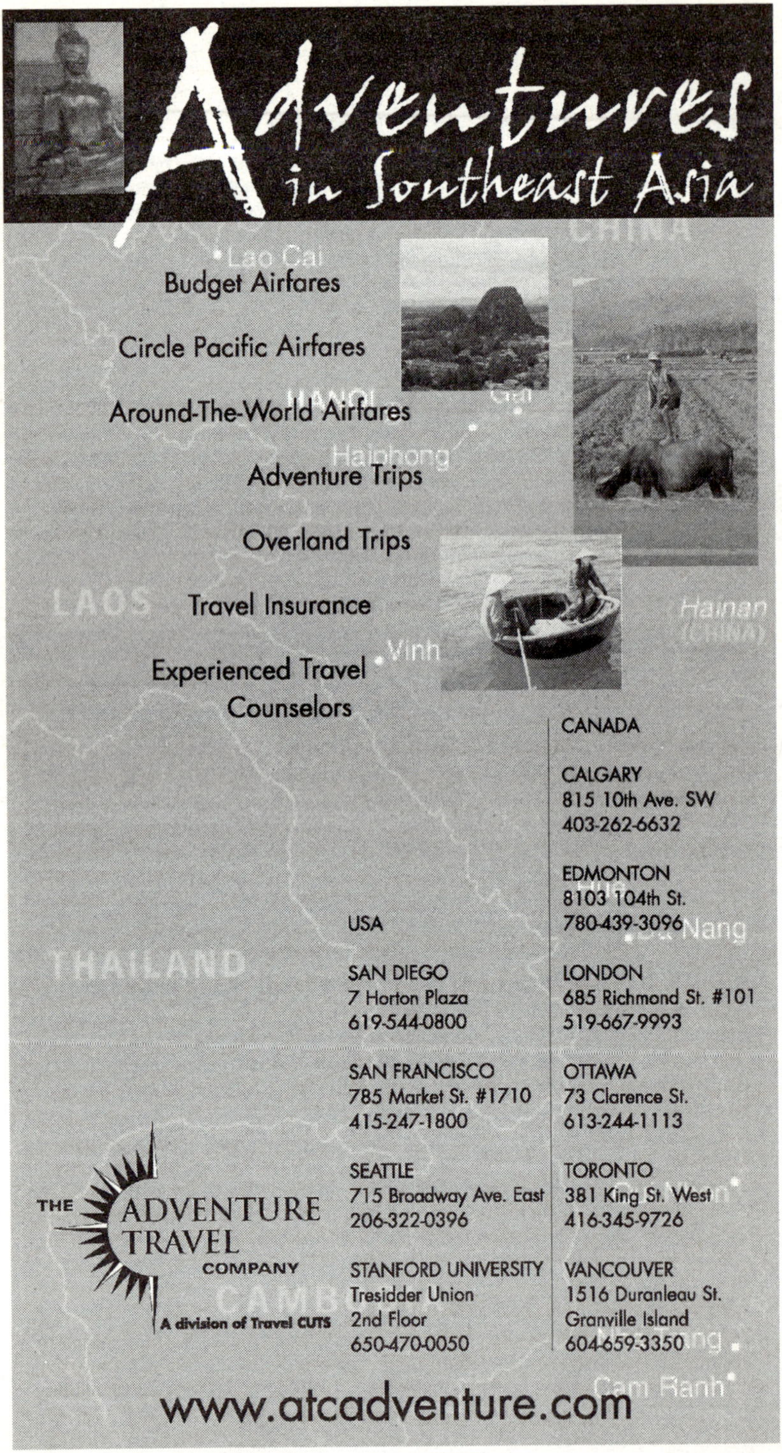
Adventures in Southeast Asia
Budget Airfares
Circle Pacific Airfares
Around-The-World Airfares
Adventure Trips
Overland Trips
Travel Insurance
Experienced Travel Counselors
Lao Cai
CHINA
HANOI
Haiphong
LAOS
Vinh
Hainan (CHINA)
THAILAND
USA
SAN DIEGO
7 Horton Plaza
619-544-0800
SAN FRANCISCO
785 Market St. #1710
415-247-1800
SEATTLE
715 Broadway Ave. East
206-322-0396
STANFORD UNIVERSITY
Tresidder Union
2nd Floor
650-470-0050
CANADA
CALGARY
815 10th Ave. SW
403-262-6632
EDMONTON
8103 104th St.
780-439-3096
LONDON
685 Richmond St. #101
519-667-9993
OTTAWA
73 Clarence St.
613-244-1113
TORONTO
381 King St. West
416-345-9726
VANCOUVER
1516 Duranleau St.
Granville Island
604-659-3350
THE ADVENTURE TRAVEL COMPANY
A division of Travel CUTS
Cam Ranh
www.atcadventure.com

CTS Travel, 44 Goodge St., **London** W1T 2AD (☎0207 636 0031; ctsinfo@ctstravel.com.uk).

STA Travel, 7890 S. Hardy Dr. Ste. 110, Tempe, AZ 85284 (24hr. reservations and info ☎800-777-0112; fax 480-592-0876; www.statravel.com). A student and youth travel organization with over 250 offices worldwide (check website for a listing of all offices), including US offices in Boston, Chicago, LA, New York, San Francisco, Seattle, and Washington, DC Ticket booking, travel insurance, railpasses, and more. In the UK, walk-in office at 11 Goodge St., **London** W1T 2PF (☎0870 160 6070). In New Zealand, 10 High St., **Auckland** (☎09 309 0458). In Australia, 366 Lygon St., **Melbourne** Vic 3053 (☎03 9349 4344).

Travel CUTS (Canadian Universities Travel Services Limited), 187 College St., **Toronto,** ON M5T 1P7 (☎416-979-8167; fax 979-8167; www.travelcuts.com). 60 offices across Canada. Also in the UK, 295-A Regent St., **London** W1R 7YA (☎0207-255-1944).

COMMERCIAL AIRLINES

The commercial airlines' lowest regular offer is the **APEX** (Advance Purchase Excursion) fare, which provides confirmed reservations and allows "open-jaw" tickets. Generally, reservations must be made seven to 21 days ahead of departure, with seven to 14-day minimum-stay and up to 90-day maximum-stay restrictions. These fares carry hefty cancellation and change penalties (fees rise in summer). Book peak season APEX fares early; by May you will have a hard time getting your desired departure date. Use **Microsoft Expedia** (msn.expedia.com) or **Travelocity** (www.travelocity.com) to get an idea of the lowest published fares, then use the resources outlined here to beat those fares. Low-season fares should be appreciably cheaper than high-season (May to Sept.).

AIR COURIER FLIGHTS

Those who travel light should consider courier flights. Couriers help transport cargo on international flights by using their checked luggage space for freight. Generally, couriers must travel with carry-ons only and deal with complex flight restrictions. Most flights are round-trip only with short fixed-length stays (usually one week) and a limit of one ticket per issue. Most of these flights operate only out of major North American gateway cities. Generally, you must be over 21 (in some cases 18). Groups such as the **Air Courier Association** (☎(800) 282-1202; www.aircourier.org) and the **International Association of Air Travel Couriers,** 220 S Dixie Hwy. #3, P.O. Box 1349, Lake Worth, FL 33460 (☎(561) 582-8320; www.courier.org) provide lists of opportunities and courier brokers worldwide for an annual fee. For more information, consult *Air Courier Bargains* by Kelly Monaghan (The Intrepid Traveler, US$15) or the *Courier Air Travel Handbook* by Mark Field (Perpetual Press, US$10).

CHARTER FLIGHTS

Charters are flights a tour operator contracts with an airline to fly extra loads of passengers during peak season. Charter flights fly less frequently than major airlines, make refunds particularly difficult, and are almost always fully booked. Schedules and itineraries may also change or be canceled at the last moment (as late as 48 hours before the trip and without a full refund), and check-in, boarding, and baggage claim are often much slower. But they are usually cheaper than commercial flights.

Discount clubs and **fare brokers** offer members savings on last-minute charter and tour deals. Study contracts closely; you don't want to end up with an unwanted overnight layover. Pay with a credit card if you can and consider traveler's insurance against trip interruption.

TICKET CONSOLIDATORS

Ticket consolidators or **"bucket shops"** buy unsold tickets in bulk from commercial airlines and sell them at discounted rates. Look in the travel section of any major newspaper, where many bucket shops place tiny ads. Call quickly, as availability is typically extremely limited. Not all bucket shops are reliable, so insist on a receipt that gives full details of restrictions, refunds, and tickets. Pay by credit card (in spite of the 2-5% fee) so you can stop payment if you never receive your tickets. For more info, see www.travel-library.com/air-travel/consolidators.html or pick up Kelly Monaghan's *Air Travel's Bargain Basement* (Intrepid Traveler, US$8).

TRAVELING FROM THE US AND CANADA. **Travel Avenue** (☎(800) 333-3335; www.travelavenue.com) rebates commercial fares from the US (5% for over US$550) and will search for cheap flights from anywhere for a fee. Other consolidators worth trying are **Interworld Travel** (☎(800) 468-3796, (305) 443-4929; www.interworldtravel.com); **Cheap Tickets** (☎(800) 377-1000; www.cheaptickets.com); **Travac** (☎(800) 872-8800; www.travac.com), **Internet Travel Network** (www.itn.com); **Travel Information Services** (www.tiss.com); and **TravelHUB** (www.travelhub.com). These are just suggestions to get you started; *Let's Go* does not endorse any of these agencies. Be cautious, and research companies before you hand over your credit card number.

TRAVELING FROM THE UK, AUSTRALIA, AND NEW ZEALAND. In London, the **Air Travel Advisory Bureau** (☎(020) 7636 5000; www.atab.co.uk) can provide names of reliable consolidators and discount flight specialists. From Australia and New Zealand, look for consolidator ads in the travel section of the *Sydney Morning Herald* and other papers.

SPECIALTY CONSOLIDATORS. A limited number of travel agencies deal in unconventional arrangements of flights. Circle Pacific and Circle Asia tickets provide one-way flights to, from, and around Southeast Asia. These tickets are best for extended trips; most have flexible dates, good up to one year from commencement of travel. For itineraries more complicated than a simple round-trip, RTW and other unconventional tickets are often a better deal. Try **Air Treks** (☎(800) 350-0612 or (415) 912-5600; www.airtreks.com) or **Ticket Planet** (☎(800) 799-8888; www.ticketplanet.com) and leave at least a month to book and confirm tickets.

FLIGHT PLANNING ON THE INTERNET

The Web has great travel bargains–it's fast, it's convenient, and you can spend as long as you like exploring options without driving your travel agent insane. The Air Traveler's Handbook provides tips on finding cheap fares (www.cs.cmu.edu/afs/cs.cmu.edu/user/mkant/Public/Travel/airfare.html). Travelhub (www.travelhub.com) is a directory of travel agents that includes a searchable database of fares from over 500 consolidators. Other sites do the legwork and compile the deals for you–try www.bestfares.com, www.onetravel.com, www.lowestfare.com, and www.travelzoo.com. **STA** (www.statravel.com) and **Council** (www.counciltravel.com) provide quotes on student tickets, while **Expedia** (msn.expedia.com) and **Travelocity** (www.travelocity.com) offer full travel services. **Priceline** (www.priceline.com) allows you to specify a price, and obligates you to buy any ticket that meets or beats it; be prepared for odd routes. **Skyauction** (www.skyauction.com) lets you to bid on both last-minute and advance-purchase tickets.

ESSENTIALS

FURTHER READING

The Worldwide Guide to Cheap Airfare, Michael McColl. Insider Publications (US$15).

Discount Airfares: The Insider's Guide, George Hobart. Priceless Publications (US$14).

Air Traveler's Handbook, a detailed, comprehensive guide to consumer travel; (www.cs.cmu.edu/afs/cs/user/mkant/Public/Travel/airfare.html).

GETTING AROUND SOUTHEAST ASIA

BETWEEN COUNTRIES

AIR

Flights between countries in Southeast Asia are inexpensive. Find the best deals on tickets in Bangkok, Singapore, Hong Kong, Kuala Lumpur, and Penang. Popular airlines include Malaysia Airlines, Singapore Airlines, Thai International, Cathay Pacific, and KLM Airlines. Booking tickets should be relatively worry-free, but travel agents can scam you. Be sure to make sure your deal is legitimate before handing over your credit card. *Let's Go* lists reliable tourist offices and travel offices in the **Practical Information** section of large cities. In general, use common sense—don't trust agents vending tickets in coffee bars. To be sure, always reconfirm with the airlines after receiving your ticket.

BUS

Bus travel between countries can be arranged within the regions of Cambodia, Laos, and Vietnam and Myanmar, Thailand, and Malaysia. A/C buses can be very comfortable and reliable, but others offer sparse leg room and bumpy rides. Inquire about purchasing tickets, as some buses require reservations in advance, whereas others sell tickets upon departure and don't leave the station until completely full. Always check visa availability before taking a bus ride; visas may not always be available at the border and must be acquired in advance in other towns. Most tourist cafes can help you with information and reservations.

BORDER CROSSINGS

Overland border crossing points represent legal points of overland transit between Southeast Asian countries. For detailed information on possible crossing points and requirements, refer to the **Getting There** section of individual countries.

WITHIN A COUNTRY

Southeast Asia has every type of vehicle imaginable. From buses to taxis, cyclos to trishaws, *angkot* to jeepney, if it has moves on land and wheels, you'll find detailed information in the **Local Transportation** section of each city. Here's a glimpse of Southeast Asia's mechanical marvels.

MECHANICS FOR DUMMIES			
Bemo **(Indonesia)**	A three-wheeler pick-up truck.	***Honda Om*** **(Vietnam)**	Zooming motorbikes with a rodeo-like feel.
Cyclos **(Vietnam)**	The bastard child of a rickshaw, tricycle, and trishaw.	***Becak*** **(Indonesia)**	Cyclo-trishaws.
Dokar **(Indonesia)**	Two wheels, a little horsey and you.	***Songthaew*** **(Thailand)**	Three wheeler pickup with two rows of seats.
Jeepney **(Philippines)**	Cross a jeep with a school bus, and the outcome with a low rider.	***Trishaw*** **(Vietnam)**	The classic pedal rickshaw still runs on calf power.
Linecars **(Myanmar)**	Like a songthaew; think moving hunks of tin.	***Tuk-tuk*** **(Thailand)**	An opinionated and noisy three wheeler pickup.

An **International Driver's Permit (IDP)** is almost always asked for when renting a car in Southeast Asia, though documentation requirements vary. Some countries allow travelers to drive with a valid American or Canadian license. Apply for an IDP at your home country's Automobile Association. Remember that if you are driving a conventional vehicle on an unpaved road, you are almost never covered by insurance; ask about this at the rental agency.

SPECIFIC CONCERNS

WOMEN TRAVELERS

Women exploring on their own inevitably face some additional safety concerns, but it's easy to be adventurous without taking undue risks. If you are concerned, consider staying in hostels which offer single rooms that lock from the inside or in religious organizations with rooms for women only. Communal showers in some hotels are safer than others; check them before settling in. Stick to centrally located accommodations and avoid solitary late-night treks.

Always carry extra money for a phone call, bus, or taxi. **Hitchiking** is never safe for lone women or even for two women traveling together. Choose train compartments occupied by women or couples; ask the conductor to put together a women-only compartment if there isn't one. Look as if you know where you're going (even when you don't) and consider approaching older women or couples for directions if you're lost or feel uncomfortable.

Generally, the less you look like a tourist, the better off you'll be. Dress conservatively, especially in rural areas. Trying to fit in can be effective, but dressing to the style of an obviously different culture may cause you to be ill at ease and a conspicuous target. Wearing a conspicuous **wedding band** may help prevent unwanted overtures. Some travelers report that carrying pictures of a "husband" or "children" is extremely useful to document marriage status. Even a mention of a husband waiting back at the hotel may be enough in some places to discount your potentially vulnerable, unattached appearance. If someone asks you how long you've been in the country, **always lie** and say three to four weeks.

Your best answer to verbal harassment is no answer at all; feigning deafness, sitting motionless, and staring straight ahead at nothing in particular will do a world of good that reactions usually don't achieve. The extremely persistent can sometimes be dissuaded by a firm, loud and very public "Go away" in the appropriate language. Learn how to say "help" or "fire" in the local language as well. In Southeast Asia, making a public display is the most effective way of getting a heckler off your back. If you feel threatened, **shout** your heart out — help will instantly be on the way.

Don't hesitate to seek out a police officer or a passerby if you are being harassed. Memorize each city's emergency numbers (listed in the **Practical Information** sections). Carry a **whistle** or an airhorn on your keychain, and don't hesitate to use it in an emergency. An **IMPACT Model Mugging** self-defense course will not only prepare you for a potential attack, but will also raise your awareness of your surroundings as well as your confidence (see **Self Defense,** p. 22). Women also face some specific health concerns when traveling (see **Women's Health,** p. 29).

FURTHER READING

A Journey of One's Own: Uncommon Advice for the Independent Woman Traveler, Thalia Zepatos. Eighth Mountain Press (US$17).

Adventures in Good Company: The Complete Guide to Women's Tours and Outdoor Trips, Thalia Zepatos. Eighth Mountain Press (US$7).

Active Women Vacation Guide, Evelyn Kaye. Blue Panda Publications (US$18).

Travelers' Tales: Gutsy Women, Travel Tips and Wisdom for the Road, Marybeth Bond. Traveler's Tales (US$8).

TRAVELING ALONE

There are many benefits to traveling alone, including independence and greater interaction with locals. On the other hand, any solo traveler is a more vulnerable target of harassment and street theft. Lone travelers need to be well-organized and look confident at all times. Try not to stand out as a tourist and be especially careful in deserted or very crowded areas. If questioned, never admit that you are traveling alone and lie about how long you've been in the country — always say you've been there at least for 3-4 weeks. Maintain regular contact with someone at home who knows your itinerary. For more tips, pick up *Traveling Solo* by Eleanor Berman (Globe Pequot Press, US$17) or subscribe to **Connecting: Solo Travel Network,** 689 Park Road, Unit 6, Gibsons, BC V0N 1V7 (☎604 886 9099; www.cstn.org; membership US$28).

Alternatively, several services link solo travelers with companions who have similar travel habits and interests; for a bi-monthly newsletter for single travelers seeking a travel partner (subscription US$48), contact the **Travel Companion Exchange,** P.O. Box 833, Amityville, NY 11701 (☎631 454 0880 or 800 392 1256; www.whytravelalone.com; US$48).

American International Homestays, P.O. Box 1754, Nederland, CO 80466, USA (☎800 876-2048). Lodgings with English-speaking host families in Southeast Asia.

OLDER TRAVELERS

Travel in Southeast Asia has the potential to be particularly taxing for senior citizens. However, there may be some extra benefits to age, including greater respect from the people you encounter. Agencies for senior group travel are growing in enrollment and popularity. These are only a few:

ElderTreks, 597 Markham St., Toronto, ON M6G 2L7 (☎(800)741-7956; eldertreks@eldertreks.com; www.eldertreks.com). Tours offered in Cambodia, Indonesia, Laos, Malaysian Borneo, Myanmar, Thailand, and Vietnam.

Elderhostel, 11 Ave. de Lafayette, Boston, MA 02111 (☎(877) 426-2166; www.elderhostel.org). Programs at colleges, universities, and other learning centers in Cambodia, Indonesia, Laos, Malaysia, Thailand, and Vietnam (and other countries depending on season) on varied subjects lasting 1-4 weeks. Must be 55 or over (spouse can be of any age).

The Mature Traveler, P.O. Box 15791, Sacramento, CA 95852 (☎800 460 6676). Deals, discounts, and travel packages for the 50+ traveler. Subscription$30.

BISEXUAL, GAY, & LESBIAN TRAVELERS

The enormous range of sexualities in Southeast Asia defies easy categorization. From the *waria* communities of Indonesia to the *bakla* of the Philippines and the *kathoey* transgender communities of Thailand, the perceptive gay traveler can find a trip to Southeast Asia an enlightening experience. The most active gay communities exist in **Bangkok, Manila, Jakarta,** and **Hong Kong,** with lower-profile communities in **Kuala Lumpur** and **Singapore.** The stigma of the sex trade is such that many gay travelers find it difficult to integrate themselves into local communities. Lesbian life tends to be inaccessible to outsiders. Wherever possible, *Let's Go* lists resources for gay and lesbian travelers in the **Practical Information** sections of specific cities. Travelers should keep in mind that the people of Southeast Asia often disapprove of public displays of affection, be they among homosexuals or heterosexuals. Listed below are contact organizations, mail-order bookstores and publishers that offer materials addressing some specific concerns. **Out and About** (www.planetout.com) offers a bi-weekly newsletter addressing travel concerns.

International Gay and Lesbian Travel Association, 4331 N Federal Hwy. #304, Fort Lauderdale, FL 33308, USA (☎(954) 776-2626, (800) 448-8550; www.iglta.com). An organization of over 1350 companies serving gay and lesbian travelers worldwide.

Gay's the Word, 66 Marchmont St., London WC1N 1AB (☎44 20 7278 7654; www.gaystheword.co.uk). The largest gay and lesbian bookshop in the UK, with both fiction and non-fiction titles. Mail-order service available.

Giovanni's Room, 1145 Pine St., Philadelphia, PA 19107 (☎215 923 2960; www.queerbooks.com). An international lesbian/feminist and gay bookstore with mail-order service (carries many of the publications listed below).

International Lesbian and Gay Association (ILGA), 81 rue Marché-au-Charbon, B-1000 Brussels, Belgium (☎+32 2 502 2471; www.ilga.org). Provides political information, such as homosexuality laws of individual countries.

FURTHER READING.

Utopia-Asia (www.utopia-asia.com): The best and most comprehensive resource for the gay or lesbian traveler in Southeast Asia.

Spartacus International Gay Guide 2001-2002, by Bruno Gmunder Verlag. US$33.

Ferrari Guides' Gay Travel A to Z, Ferrari Guides' Men's Travel in Your Pocket, and *Ferrari Guides' Inn Places.* Ferrari Publications. Purchase the guides online at www.ferrariguides.com. US$16-20.

The Gay Vacation Guide: The Best Trips and How to Plan Them, by Mark Chesnut. Citadel Press US$15.

TRAVELERS WITH DISABILITIES

Southeast Asia, excluding Hong Kong and Singapore, is ill-equipped to deal with disabled travelers. Those with disabilities should inform airlines and hotels of their disabilities when making arrangements for travel; some time may be needed to prepare special accommodations. Hospitals cannot be relied upon to replace broken braces or prostheses; orthopedic materials, even in Bangkok, Jakarta, and Manila, are faulty at best. Public transportation (trains, buses, *songthaew*, *tuk-tuk*, etc.) is completely inaccessible. Rural areas have no sidewalks, and larger cities are packed with curbs and steps.

Attitudes toward disabled people vary. In Laos and Cambodia, where an uncommonly large part of the population consists of amputees (from landmines and cluster-bombs), disabilities are common. Thai people with disabilities rarely come out in public. Despite this, bold travelers will find many people eager to aid them.

USEFUL ORGANIZATIONS

Mobility International USA (MIUSA), P.O. Box 10767, Eugene, OR 97440, USA (☎541 343-1284 voice and TDD; www.miusa.org). Sells *A World of Options: A Guide to International Educational Exchange, Community Service, and Travel for Persons with Disabilities* (US$35).

Moss Rehab Hospital Travel Information Service (☎215 456-9600 or 800 CALL-MOSS; netstaff@mossresourcenet.org; www.mossresourcenet.org). An information resource center on travel-related concerns for those with disabilities.

Society for the Advancement of Travel for the Handicapped (SATH), 347 5th Ave., #610, New York, NY 10016 (☎212 447 7284; www.sath.org). An advocacy group that publishes free online travel information and the travel magazine *OPEN WORLD* (US$18, free for members). Annual membership US$45, students and seniors US$30.

TOUR AGENCIES

Directions Unlimited, 123 Green Ln., Bedford Hills, NY 10507 (☎800-533-5343). Books individual and group vacations for the physically disabled; not an info service.

MINORITY TRAVELERS

People in Southeast Asia are largely tolerant and accepting of minority travelers. However, travelers of African descent have reported stray incidents of harassment, though there have been no reports of violence. To be safe, travelers of African descent are advised not to travel alone in rural areas. In addition, ethnic Chinese in Indonesia and Malaysia have been a target of discrimination (see **Plight of the Chinese,** p. 135). Though violence is rare, some travelers report inferior service and stray incidents of harassment.

TRAVELERS WITH CHILDREN

Travel in Southeast Asia with young children can prove a hassle. Hygienic environments and proper medical facilities are scarce. The combination of heat, mosquitoes, and dirty water might prove too much for a young child. All this said, it is possible to bring children along as long as you take extra precautions and remain especially alert to potential dangers. Family vacations often require that you slow your pace and always require that you plan ahead. When deciding where to stay, call ahead to inquire about an establishment's ability to meet the special needs of young children. Be sure that your child carries some sort of ID in case of an emergency or he or she gets lost and arrange a reunion spot in case of separation when sight-seeing. International fares are usually discounted 25% for children from two to eleven. Finding a private place for **breast feeding** is often a problem while traveling. For more information, consult one of the following books:

Backpacking with Babies and Small Children, Goldie Silverman. Wilderness Press (US$10).

How to take Great Trips with Your Kids, Sanford and Jane Portnoy. Harvard Common Press (US $10).

Have Kid, Will Travel: 101 Survival Strategies for Vacationing With Babies and Young Children, Claire and Lucille Tristram. Andrews McMeel Publishing (US$9).

DIETARY CONCERNS

Although Southeast Asian food often contains meat or uses meat bases, **vegetarian** dishes abound throughout the region. For more information about vegetarian travel, contact **North American Vegetarian Society,** P.O. Box 72, Dolgeville, NY 13329 (☎(518) 568-7970; www.navs-online.org), which publishes Vegetarian Asia ($10). While **kosher** meals are practically nonexistent, the Muslim presence in Southeast Asia makes **halal** food a large part of the cuisine (especially in the Malay-speaking

THE RAMAYANA Arguably the most culturally influential work of literature in India and Southeast Asia, the *Ramayana* (literally, "the romance of Rama") has inspired thousands of dances, paintings, shadow puppet shows, inter-religious riots and its own TV mini-series in addition from gracing the murals of every wat from Bangkok to Angkor. The Sanskrit poet Valmiki is thought to have composed the *Ramayana* around 400 BC, basing it on events that took place between 1000 and 700 BC. The epic's main characters, Rama and Sita, are revered as archetypes of those who unwaveringly follow their *dharma* (duty, or fate).

Act I, Scene 1: Rama is born to King Dasaratha's wife Kausalya in Ayodhya, capital of Kosala and also the city after which the ancient Thai capital of Ayutthaya is named. Dasaratha's other wives, Kaikeyi and Sumithra, bear him Bharata and the twins Lakshman and Shatrugna, respectively. **Scene 2:** Rama journeys with his guru Viswamitra to the kingdom of Mithila, where he falls in love at first sight with King Janaka's beautiful daughter, Sita. But winning her hand is not an easy task. Being a tad possessive as a father, Janaka declares that only he who is able to break Shiva's divine bow can have her hand in marriage. **Scene 3:** In true hero fashion, Rama breaks the bow, and the two kingdoms delight in the wedding of Rama and Sita. **Scene 4:** the aging Dasaratha names Rama as his successor, but his wife Kaikeyi (read: evil step-mother) refuses to accept Rama as king and forces Dasaratha to banish Rama to the forest for 14 years, so her son, Bharata, can be crowned king instead.

Act II, Scene 1: Rama, Sita, and Rama's faithful brother Lakshman leave Ayodhya for the forest. The sorrowful Dasaratha soon dies, and Bharata rushes to the forest, begging Rama to return to claim the throne. Unwilling to break his promise to his father, Rama stays in the forest for the next 14 years. **Scene 2:** Ravana, chief of the *asuras* (demons), abducts Sita to his island kingdom of Lanka. **Scene 3:** Rama and Lakshman journey in search of Sita, encountering en route the clever monkey Hanuman, son of the wind god. Rama sends Hanuman to Lanka to assess the situation and deliver a token to his beloved wife. Hanuman does so and also manages to set fire to the entire capital of Lanka before he leaves. **Scene 4:** With the help of a Lankan spy, Rama and his army of monkeys advance on Lanka. The valiant monkeys build a bridge to Lanka, and a celestial battle ensues. Rama emerges victorious, vanquishing Ravana and winning back Sita. **Scene 5:** 14 years finally end, and Rama, Lakshman, Sita, and Hanuman return to Kosala. Rama is crowned king, and Ayodhya erupts in celebration upon the revelation that Rama is an avatar of Vishnu. **Scene 6:** Sita's fidelity during Rama's absence is questioned. Subordinating his trust in Sita to his princely duty, Rama subjects her to an ordeal of fire, from which she emerges unscathed, vindicated, and more than a little angry at being doubted. Teaching Rama a lesson in marital trust, she returns to her mother, the Goddess of the Earth and is swallowed up into the ground. **Moral:** When you use a monkey army to defeat the demon who kidnapped your wife, trust her enough not to make her sit through fire.

world). If you are strict in your observance, consider preparing your own food on the road. For more information, visit your local bookstore, health food store, or library, and consult *The Vegetarian Traveler: Where to Stay if You're Vegetarian*, by Jed and Susan Civic (Larson Publications, US$16).

ALTERNATIVES TO TOURISM

For an extensive listing of "off-the-beaten-track" and specialty travel opportunities, try the **Specialty Travel Index,** 305 San Anselmo Ave., #313, San Anselmo, CA 94960, USA (☎888 624 4030 or 415 455 1643; www.specialtytravel.com; US$6). **Transitions Abroad** (www.transabroad.com) publishes a bimonthly on-line newsletter for work, study, and specialized travel abroad.

STUDYING ABROAD

Foreign study programs vary tremendously in expense, academic quality, living conditions, degree of contact with local students, and exposure to culture and language. While not as many programs are available in Southeast Asia as in other regions, they do exist. Check out the organizations below for a start.

UNIVERSITIES

Association of Commonwealth Universities (ACU), John Foster House, 36 Gordon Sq., London WC1H OPF (☎44 020 7380 6700; www.acu.ac.uk). Publishes information about Commonwealth universities including University of Brunei Darussalam, National University of Malaysia, and National University of Singapore.

School for International Training, College Semester Abroad, Admissions, Kipling Rd., P.O. Box 676, Brattleboro, VT 05302, USA (☎800 336 1616 or 802 258 3267; www.sit.edu). Runs semester- and year-long programs in Bali, Indonesia, and Vietnam. Programs cost US$8200-10,300, all expenses included. Financial aid available and US financial aid is transferable. Also runs the **Experiment in International Living** (☎800 345 2929; fax 802 258 3428; eil@worldlearning.org). Founded in 1932, it offers cross-cultural, educational homestays, community service programs in Thailand. Programs are 5 weeks long and run US$1800-5000.

Council on International Educational Exchange (CIEE), 633 3rd Ave. 20th flr., New York, NY 10017-6706 (☎888 268 6245 or 800 407 8839; www.ciee.org/study) sponsors volunteer and study abroad programs in Indonesia, Thailand, and Vietnam.

International Association for the Exchange of Students for Technical Experience (IAESTE), 10400 Little Patuxent Pkwy. #250, Columbia, MD 21044-3510, USA (☎410 997 2200; www.aipt.org). 8- to 12-week programs in Hong Kong, Thailand and Vietnam for college students who have done 2 years of technical study. US$25 application fee.

LANGUAGE SCHOOLS

Study abroad language schools are far rarer in Southeast Asia than in Europe, but if you're dying to learn Thai in Thailand, start your search at the following websites:

LanguagesAbroad.Com: www.languagesabroad.com gives country and language school overviews.

Study Abroad Links: www.studyabroadlinks.com/language.htm offers information by country or category, including language programs.

Language Schools: www.languageschoolsguides.com is searchable by country or language, providing list of schools with Internet links.

WORKING & VOLUNTEERING

There's no better way to submerge yourself in a foreign culture than to become part of its economy. Officially, you need a special visa that will allow you to be employed in the country of your choice. Your employer must obtain this document, usually by demonstrating that you have skills that locals lack—not the easiest of tasks. Inquire at the embassy or consulate for more specific information. Teaching English abroad is a common and practical choice. Students can check with their universities' foreign language departments, which may have connections to job openings abroad, or contact the organizations listed below.

TEACHING ENGLISH

International Schools Services, Educational Staffing Program, P.O. Box 5910, Princeton, NJ 08543, USA (☎(609) 452-0990; www.iss.edu). Recruits teachers and administrators for American and English schools. US$150 program fee.

Office of Overseas Schools, US Department of State, Room H328, SA-1, Washington, DC 20522 (☎(202) 261-8200; www.state.gov/www/about_state/schools/). Keeps a

ESSENTIALS

comprehensive list of schools abroad and agencies that arrange placement for Americans to teach abroad, including schools in Cambodia, Indonesia, Laos, Malaysia, Myanmar, the Philippines, Singapore, Thailand and Vietnam.

ARCHAEOLOGICAL DIGS

Archaeological Institute of America, 656 Beacon St., Boston, MA 02215, USA (☎(617) 353-9361; www.archaeological.org). The *Archeological Fieldwork Opportunities Bulletin* ($20 for non-members) lists field sites in Southeast Asia. Buy the bulletin from Kendall/ Hunt Publishing, 4050 Westmark Dr., Dubuque, Iowa 52002, USA (☎(800) 228-0810).

ESSENTIALS

VOLUNTEERING

Volunteer jobs are readily available, and many provide room and board in exchange for labor. You can sometimes avoid high application fees by contacting the individual workcamps directly.

Earthwatch, 3 Clocktower Pl., P.O. Box 75, Maynard, MA 01754 (☎(800) 776-0188 or (978) 461-0081; www.earthwatch.org). Arranges 1- to 3-week programs in Cambodia, Malaysia and the Philippines to promote conservation of natural resources. Programs average US$1600.

Habitat for Humanity International, 121 Habitat St., Americus, GA 31709, USA (☎(800) 422-4828; www.habitat.org). Offers international opportunities in Indonesia, Malaysia and the Philippines to live with and build houses in a host community. Costs range US$1200-3500.

Peace Corps, Office of Volunteer Recruitment and Selection, 1111 20th St. NW, Washington, DC 20526 (☎(800) 424-8580; www.peacecorps.gov). Opportunities in 78 developing nations including Thailand and the Philippines. Volunteers must be US citizens ages 18+ willing to make a 2-year commitment. A bachelor's degree is usually required.

Service Civil International Voluntary Service (SCI-IVS), 814 NE 40th St., Seattle, WA 98105, USA (☎/fax (206) 545-6585; www.sci-ivs.org). Arranges placement in workcamps in Malaysia, Thailand and Vietnam for those 21+. A special application form and previous workcamp experience is required for those applying to work in Southeast Asia. Registration fee US$65-150.

Volunteers for Peace, 1034 Tiffany Rd., Belmont, VT 05730, USA (☎(802) 259-2759; www.vfp.org). Arranges placement in workcamps in Cambodia, Indonesia, Thailand, and Vietnam. Annual International Work*camp Directory* US$20. Registration fee US$200. Free newsletter.

OTHER RESOURCES

Let's Go's brief historical and cultural sketches of each country at the beginning of each chapter are no substitute for further reading and research. As a rule, the more background knowledge you can acquire before you leave, the better equipped you will be to make sense of the different cultures of Southeast Asia. Moreover, Southeast Asians are always pleased to meet foreigners who have made the effort to learn something about their heritage.

ECOLOGICALLY RESPONSIBLE TOURISM

Traveling through Southeast Asia takes visitors into ecologically sensitive areas. Avoid buying natural souvenirs such as teeth, hides, coral, butterflies, or turtle shells. Products made of animals often come at the expense of endangered species. Women may consider buying feminine hygiene products with minimal packaging. Choose glass soda bottles over marginally recyclable plastic equivalents and reuse plastic bags. Bucket showers and squat toilets are more water-efficient than their Western counterparts. To be even more water-friendly, carry a water bottle or canteen. While tap water is unsafe, purifying tablets or iodine drops save buying countless plastic water bottles.

ESSENTIALS

BOOKS

Southeast Asia: An Introductory History, by Milton Osborne (1997). A basic survey of Southeast Asian history, revised and updated many times.

The Lands of Charm and Cruelty: Travels in Southeast Asia, by Stan Sesser (1993). A collection of essays originally published in the New Yorker.

TRAVEL PUBLISHERS & BOOKSTORES

Hippocrene Books, Inc., 171 Madison Ave., New York, NY 10016 (☎(212) 685-4371; orders (718) 454-2366; www.netcom.com/~hippocre). Free catalog. Publishes foreign language dictionaries and language learning guides.

Hunter Publishing, 130 Campus Dr., Edison, NJ 08818, USA (☎(800) 255-0343; www.hunterpublishing.com). Has an extensive catalog of travel guides and diving and adventure travel books.

Rand McNally, 150 S. Wacker Dr., Chicago, IL 60606, USA (☎(800) 234-0679 or (312) 332-2009; www.randmcnally.com), publishes road atlases (each US$10).

Adventurous Traveler Bookstore, 245 S. Champlain St., Burlington, VT 05401, USA (☎(800) 282-3963 or (802) 860-6776; www.adventuroustraveler.com).

Travel Books & Language Center, Inc., 4437 Wisconsin Ave. NW, Washington, DC 20016 (☎(800) 220-2665 or (202) 237-1322; www.travelbks.com). Over 60,000 titles from around the world.

WORLD WIDE WEB

There is a wealth of information on Southeast Asia available on the World Wide Web. Recently many regional newspapers, including the *Bangkok Post* and the *Straits Times* (Singapore), have launched on-line editions. Listed here are some budget travel sites to start off your surfing; other relevant web sites are listed throughout the book. Because website turnover is high, use search engines (such as www.google.com) to strike out on your own.

THE ART OF BUDGET TRAVEL

How to See the World: www.artoftravel.com. A compendium of great travel tips, from cheap flights to self defense to interacting with local culture.

Rec. Travel Library: www.travel-library.com. A fantastic set of links for general information and personal travelogues.

Lycos: cityguide.lycos.com. General introductions to cities and regions throughout Southeast Asia, accompanied by links to applicable histories, news, and local tourism sites.

INFORMATION ON SOUTHEAST ASIA

CIA World Factbook: www.odci.gov/cia/publications/factbook/index.html. Tons of vital statistics on Southeast Asia's geography, government, economy, and people.

Foreign Language for Travelers: www.travlang.com. Provides free online lists of phrases in Cantonese, Mandarin, Malay, Bahasa Indonesia, Tagalag, Thai, and Vietnamese.

MyTravelGuide: www.mytravelguide.com. Country overviews, with everything from history to transportation to live web cam coverage of Southeast Asia.

Geographia: www.geographia.com. Highlights, culture, and people of Indonesia, Malaysia, Myanmar, Thailand, and Vietnam.

Atevo Travel: www.atevo.com/guides/destinations. Detailed introductions, travel tips, and suggested itineraries for Cambodia, Indonesia, Malaysia, the Philippines, Singapore, Thailand, and Vietnam.

World Travel Guide: www.travel-guides.com/navigate/world.asp. Helpful practical info.

TravelPage: www.travelpage.com. Links to official tourist office sites in Southeast Asia.

PlanetRider: www.planetrider.com. A subjective list of links to the "best" websites covering the culture and tourist attractions of Hong Kong, Indonesia, Thailand and Vietnam.

Time-Asia Now: www.time.com/time/asia/ is the international version of popular Time Magazine, and covers current events, cultural information, and technology news throughout Asia.

Cornell University Southeast Asia Program: www.einaudi.cornell.edu/southeastasia. Has links to hundreds of Southeast Asia-related sites.

Australia National University: http://coombs.anu.edu.au/WWWVL-AsianStudies.html. Maintains a fantastic "virtual library" of Asia-related materials.

AND OUR PERSONAL FAVORITE...

Let's Go: www.letsgo.com. Our constantly expanding website features photos and streaming video, online ordering of all our titles, info about our books, a travel forum buzzing with stories and tips, and links that will help you find everything you ever wanted to know about Southeast Asia.

BRUNEI DARUSSALAM

BRUNEI DOLLAR

US$1 = B$1.75	B$1 = US$0.57
CDN$1 = B$1.13	B$1 = CDN$0.88
EURO€1 = B$1.59	B$1 = EURO€0.63
UK£1 = B$2.54	B$1 = UK£0.39
IR£1 = B$2.02	B$1 = IR£0.49
AUS$1 = B$0.93	B$1 = AUS$1.08
NZ$1 = B$0.77	B$1 = NZ$1.30
ZAR1 = B$0.21	B$1 = ZAR4.77

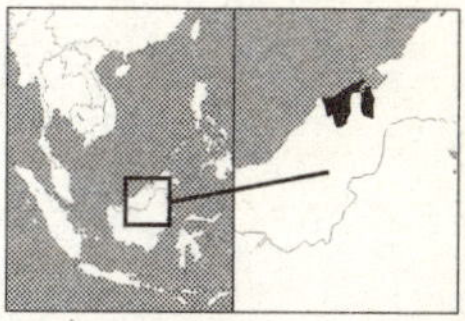

PHONE CODE **Country Code:** 673. **International dialing prefix:** 001.

Though Brunei is geographically tiny, everything here is big and fabulously wealthy. Over the past 20 years, oil has transformed this Islamic sultanate into an impressive "Shellfare state" that offers its citizens free education and health care, no income tax, and subsidized houses, cars, and pilgrimages to Mecca. Benefiting even more from Brunei's opulent offshore wells is Sultan Hassanal Bolkiah, whose estimated worth was over US$25 billion in 1994. Fortunately, the oil industry hasn't spoiled much of Brunei's rainforests and urban areas, which are home to large-scale attractions ranging from luxurious historic mosques and sprawling water villages, to the decadent and free Jerudong Park Playground and architectural orgasm of the royal palace. The nightlife is nonexistent (the sale and public consumption of liquor have been banned since 1991), and the country boasts just one hostel, making Brunei less than ideal for the budget traveler. Still, if traveling through Borneo, you'll want to check out this small-scale country, even if only for a glimpse of the stunning capital.

FACTS AND FIGURES

Official Names: Brunei Darussalam, State of Brunei: Abode of Peace.
Government: Islamic Autocratic Sultanate.
Capital: Bandar Seri Bagawan.
Land Area: 5765 sq. km.
Geography: Sits in Borneo's northwest corner bounded by the South China Sea.
Climate: Tropical and rainy year-round.
Population: 330,700.
Languages: Malay, Chinese, English.
Religion: Islam.
Average Income Per Capita: US$17,400.
Major Exports: Crude oil, natural gas.

LIFE AND TIMES

THE PEOPLE OF BRUNEI

More than two-thirds of Bruneians are Malay; Chinese, Indians, and other indigenous groups make up the remaining third. Most live in Bandar Seri Begawan and the coastal oil areas of the Belait District. About a quarter of the labor force is foreign-born, mostly expats from Europe and Asia. Budget travelers may come in contact primarily with this latter group, as natives inhabit the upper economic reaches of their oil-fed society.

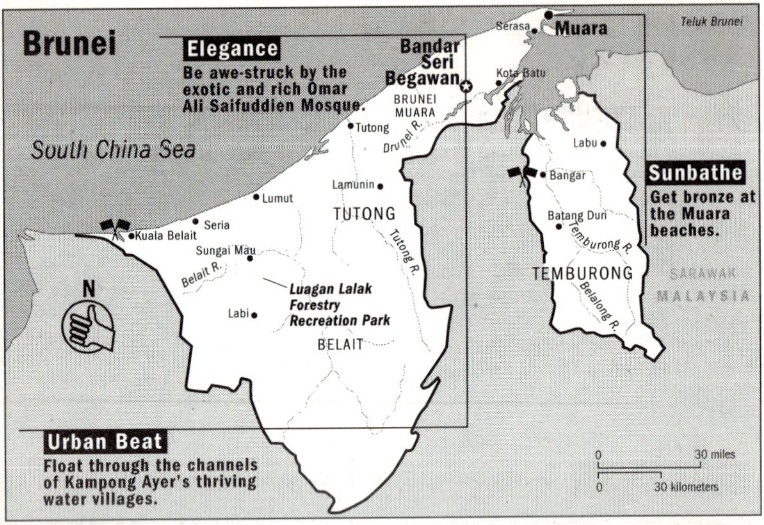

HIGHLIGHTS OF BRUNEI

CULTURAL HERITAGE. **Omar Ali Saifuddien** and **Jame'Asr Hassanal Bolkiah Mosques** (p. 59) are some of the most opulent religious structures in the world.

URBAN BEAT. Don't come for the non-existent bar and club scene; do come for completely free **Jerudong Park Playground,** Borneo's leading amusement park (p. 59), and a sunset boat ride through the channels of **Kampung Ayer** (p. 59).

HISTORY

ORIGINS AND INFLUENCES (1500–1700)

Rule #3 of the Fight Club: Colonizers don't like Islam.

Little is known about Brunei before the early 1500s, but Muslim influence is believed to have been in place from before 1000. Brunei's close relations with China remained until strong until the Europeans arrived. The first European missions were established in 1521, the prime-time to take advantage of Brunei's growing wealth and power. Consequently, many Muslim leaders fled to Borneo, laying a foundation for **Islam,** which Brunei officially adopted in 1521. Catholic European colonists were, as usual, displeased with growing Islamic trends and invaded Brunei to put an end to the silliness, burning mosques as they went. Threatened by further European intrusion, rulers of the Sulu Archipelago took half of Brunei's Bornean holdings. Brunei subsequently lost importance and dissolved into a jumble of chiefdoms, falling into Spanish and then British control.

ENTER THE BRITISH (1847–1906)

I'd like some tea, crumpets, and a little country please. Put it on the Queen's tab.

The 19th century saw the rise of the **"white rajah"** Brooke family, industrial magnates and political minds extraordinaire. Despite a treaty that required any cessions to be approved by the Crown, the greedy Brookes snatched up bits of Brunei for annual cash infusions into the Sultanate. Thus divided, Brunei's power and size dwindled to a tragic degree by late in the century. It became a British protectorate in 1888 and a British Residency in 1906, both of which established British control over foreign policy and guaranteed Brunei's territorial distinctness.

A 20TH-CENTURY SULTANATE (1959–84)

Who said money doesn't buy happiness?

In 1959 Sultan Omar gained power over domestic affairs through a new constitution under the British. Moving toward constitutional monarchy, the **Parti Rakyat Brunei (PRB)** swept the 1962 elections. This left-wing party hoped to unite the Malay states, Indonesia, and the Philippines with Brunei at the center and itself on top. The PRB led the Brunei Revolt, which was crushed by British Gurkha and Highlander troops. Discouraged from pursuing democracy, Brunei's strict Sultan has held no elections since, and his power remains uncontested today.

By 1963 the movement for a **Malay Federation** was in its home stretch. Reluctant to relinquish his oil and power, however, the Sultan declined membership. Oil and natural gas were struck that same year, paving the way to a burst of prosperity for the small nation. Brunei became an independent state in 1984.

1521
Europeans arrive; Islam adopted

1578
Spanish attack Brunei. Tropical diseases attack the Spanish

17c
Not so hot: Brunei loses power, prestige, and property

19c
"White Rajah" follows British tradition by taking Brunei's territory

1929
Jackpot! Oil discovered in Seria

1959
New constitution written

1962
PRB gains power, leads Brunei Revolt

1963
Sultan hordes money, turns down Malay Federation

1967
Sultan Hassanal Bolkiah rises to power

1984
Sultan proclaims Brunei an independent Muslim monarchy

BRUNEI

BRUNEI TODAY

Shell Oil rules the economy in modern-day Brunei and has produced massive wealth since the black gold started flowing in 1929. With only 21 years' worth of oil and natural gas left in reserves, however, the Sultan has begun to take diversification initiatives more seriously. The Asian economic crisis of 1998 and falling oil prices have demonstrated to Brunei that even oil has it limits. The Sultan and his brother nonetheless continue to spend extravagantly (i.e. the purchase of ten watches depicting a couple fornicating every hour for UK£312,000 each), while rumors abound that the royal family can no longer live on the interest accumulated by its stockpiles of money.

CUSTOMS AND CULTURE

HERE COME THE MIB

Islam is not just a religion in Brunei—it's the way of life. In1984, the Sultan officially proclaimed the **Melayu Islam Beraja (MIB)** philosophy, which propagates Islamic values and the monarchy government. It claims to be tolerant of other religions, but Islamic influences abound in every area of life, and the practice of other faiths, particularly Christianity, is routinely prohibited. Government officials roam the streets at night in search of unmarried Muslim couples too close to each other. Everything from magazines to food is checked for non-Islamic references; pictures of the cross or articles about Christianity are blackened out, and foods not prepared in accordance to *halal* requirements are confiscated. Still, Bruneians are very respectful to foreigners and are not nearly as extreme as their government.

MIND YOUR MANNERS

Be careful of your manners, as many will take offense to conduct in breach of Islamic standards. Use your right hand while eating and giving and receiving things; the left hand is considered unclean. Sitting on the floor is common, but don't extend your legs fully; ladies sit with their legs tucked to one side and men with legs folded at the ankles. Public displays of affection are taboo—shaking hands, hugging, and kissing will make Bruneians feel awkward.

HUMAN RIGHTS

Brunei's government hasn't yet welcomed gender equality. Women are regularly denied equal status in divorce and inheritance. Citizenship is also only granted through males, so female citizens can't transmit citizenship to children fathered by foreigners. As a result, a growing population of residents cannot enjoy full privileges of citizenship. Unlike men, women can't hold government positions without university degrees and get fewer benefits than males. Still, a growing number of women are entering the workplace and enrolling in universities.

BISEXUAL, GAY, AND LESBIAN TRAVELERS. As a strict Islamic country, Brunei does not accept homosexuality. There is no open gay life, and the subject is still taboo in modern Brunei. Travelers are advised to be discreet.

ADDITIONAL SOURCES

The Richest Man in the World, by James Bartholomew (1989). An amusingly sensationalistic biography short on facts but long on opinions, most of them negative.

ON THE WEB

The Government of Brunei Official Website (www.brunei.gov.bn/). A comprehensive resource for basic history, current events, culture, and government links.

Asia Travel-Brunei (www.asiatravel.com/brunei/bruinfo.html). Browse through a brief overview of contemporary history and highlight of tourist interests.

ESSENTIALS

VISAS

US citizens may stay in Brunei without a visa for up to 90 days; British Commonwealth and New Zealand citizens may stay for 30 days; Canadian, Dutch, French, Italian, Spanish, Swedish, and Swiss citizens may stay for 14 days. Australian citizens are advised to get visas before their trip, although it's possible to obtain a 14-day visa from the Brunei International Airport upon arrival. Single-entry visas are valid for 3 months. Just about anyone can enter Brunei from Sabah or Sarawak in Malaysia and stay for a week.

MONEY

The **Brunei dollar (B$)** comes in denominations of B$1, $5, $10, $50, $100, $500, $1000, and $10,000, and coins come in 1, 5, 10, 20, and 50 cents. Most banks open M-F 9am-3pm and Sa 9am-11pm. Most places appreciate a 5-10% **tip** for good service.

BANDAR SERI BAGAWAN ☎02

The oil boom hit Brunei during an unfortunately tasteless era for architecture, so downtown Bandar Seri Bagawan (BSB) looks boxy. Most of its appeal is in Kampung Ayer, the water village communities along the Brunei River. Lavish royal monuments such as Omar Ali Saifuddien Mosque and the new Yayasan Sultan Haji Hassanal Bolkiah Mall portray Brunei's true faith—Islam and opulence.

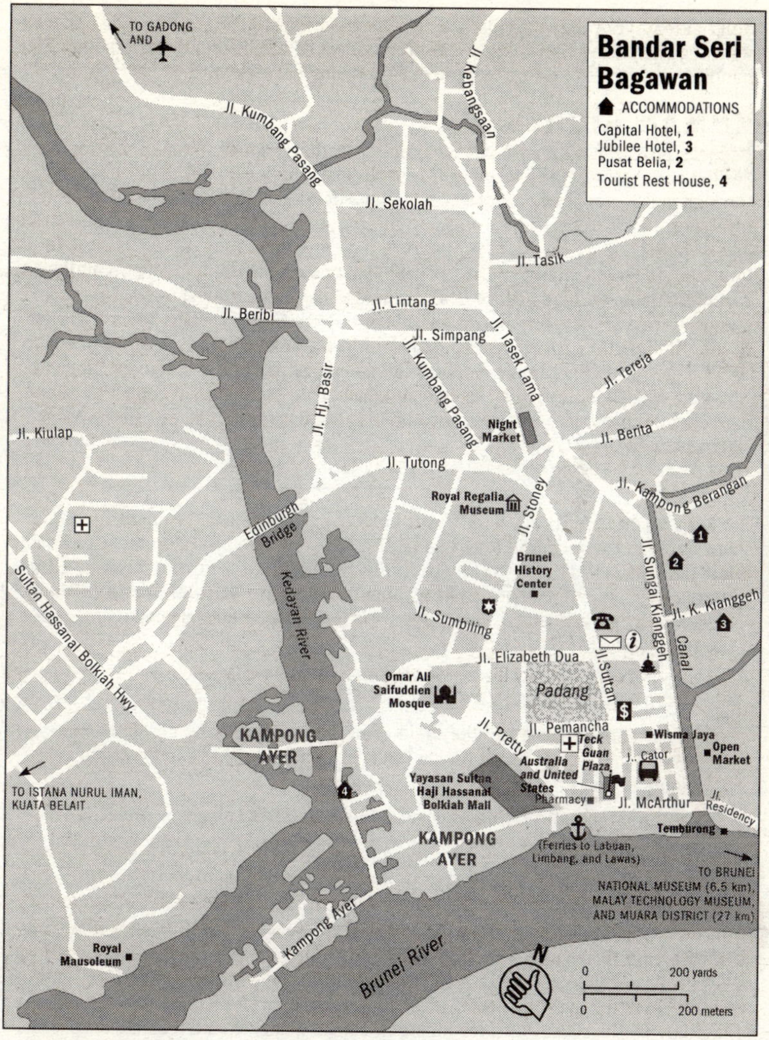

INTERCITY TRANSPORTATION

BY PLANE

The international airport, **Lapangan Terbang Antarabangsa,** is accessible by bus #11, 23, 24, 36, 38, and 57 from downtown BSB (B$1). A PPP taxi costs B$25. Airport tax is B$5 for destinations in Malaysia and Singapore and $12 for other destinations. **Garuda Indonesia** is at 49-50 Jl. Sultan, Wisma Raya Building, 3rd fl. (☎2 235 870. Open M-F 9am-5pm, Sa 9am-1pm.) **MAS** is at 144 Jl. Pemancha (☎2 224 141. **Royal Brunei Airlines,** has an office at RBA Plaza, Jl. Sultan (☎242 222). **Singapore Airlines** is at 49-50 Jl. Sultan, G/F Wisma Raya Bldg. (☎227 253). Travel agents offer cheaper airfare than the airlines.

THE MILE-HIGH CLUB					
DESTINATION	**FREQUENCY**	**PRICE**	**DESTINATION**	**FREQUENCY**	**PRICE**
Bangkok	3 per week	B$350	**Kuala Lumpur**	19 per week	B$350-441
Denpasar	2 per week	B$410	**Kuching**	3 per week	B$150-243
Hong Kong	3 per week	B$430	**Manila**	5 per week	B$455
Jakarta	4 per week	B$410	**Singapore**	1 per week	B$350-389
Kota Kinabalu	7 per week	B$81	**Surabaya**	3 per week	B$340

BY BOAT

Boats to and from **Lawas** in Sarawak and **Pulau Labuan** in Sabah (5 per day, B$15) stop at **Muara Port,** 30km east of BSB, accessible by the express bus to Muara from the bus station (every 20min. 6:50am-4:50pm, B$2). Contact **Halim Tours & Travels,** No. 61, Jl. McArthur for tickets to **Lawas** and **Kota Kinabalu.** (☎226 688. Open M-F 8am-4:30pm, Sa 8am-12pm.) Boats to **Limbang** (12 passengers, leave when full, 7am-4pm, B$10) depart from the **ferry terminal** on Jl. McArthur in BSB. For departures check the *Borneo Bulletin,* available at local newsstands, or call the Marine Department (☎771 347).

BRUNEI

BY BUS

The **bus station** in BSB is on Jl. Cator between Jl. Sultan and Sungai Kianggeh. Buses leave in the morning for **Seria** (1½hr., B$6), where buses connect to **Kuala Belait** (20min., every hr., B$1). At Kuala Belait, take a border crossing bus (30min., free) to the border, where buses depart for **Miri, Malaysia** (45min., RM4.70). Get an early start; buses depart infrequently but post departure times in the front windows.

BORDER CROSSINGS

MALAYSIA–SARAWAK. The main overland crossing is by bus from **Kuala Belait** in Brunei to **Kuala Baram (Miri)** in Sarawak (p. 445). To cross into **Limbang** or **Liwas,** ferries are most convenient.

MALAYSIA–SABAH. Ferries connect Brunei to **Pulau Labuan** in Sabah.

ORIENTATION

Brunei Darussalam is divided into four areas from west to east: **Belait, Tutong, Brunei-Muara,** and **Temburong,** which is separated from the others by Limbang, a sliver of Sarawak in Malaysia. BSB is in Brunei-Muara. Downtown BSB, often called "Bandar," extends over the **Brunei River.** The **bus station** sits on **Jl. Cator** in the heart of Bandar. To the right, Jl. Cator meets **Jl. Sungai Kianggeh** and a canal; across the canal are the **market** and **Pusat Belia.** Both Jl. Sungai Kianggeh and **Jl. Sultan** end at **Jl. McArthur,** which runs west along the waterfront to the **water taxi stand** and enormous **Yayasan Sultan Haji Hassanal Bolkiah Mall.** Behind the mall is the **Omar Ali Saifuddien Mosque.** Across the river is **Kampung Ayer,** the city's water village. The **Gadong** area houses the **Yaohan Shopping Mall, Kiarong Complex,** and the **Jame'Asr Hassanal Bolkiah Mosque.**

LOCAL TRANSPORTATION

Buses: Purple A/C **City Transport Service (CTS)** buses run from the **bus station** on Jl. Cator from 6:30am-6pm or earlier. B$1, express bus to Murara B$2. Bus #1 runs most frequently, making a circular route by the hospital, Center Point shopping district, government buildings, and the immigration office. Bus #55 goes to Jerudong Park, #39 to the museum, #21 to Kiarong Complex, and #22 to Jame'Asr Hassanal Bolkiah Mosque.

Taxis: Purple Pelangi (PPP) taxis (☎394 949) wait outside major hotels and the bus station. Open daily until 4pm. Taxis run from 6am-10pm to: **airport** (B$20); **Gadong** (B$10); **Jeradong Park** (B$20). B$3 within town. It's difficult to hail cabs, so call the office instead. Booking fee B$1.

Water taxis: Hail popular water taxis at the stand behind the Yayasan Sultan Haji Hassanal Bolkiah Mall or along the canal by the market on Jl. Sungai Kianggeh. B$0.50-3, tours B$10 per 30-60min. Fares are negotiable.

Rentals: Budget U-Drive, Unit E17, 1st fl., Bangvnan G. P Satu, Jl. Gadong (☎345 573), rents cars from B$85 per day.

PRACTICAL INFORMATION

TOURIST, FINANCIAL, AND LOCAL SERVICES

Tourist Offices: Information counter at airport (☎330 142, ext. 364). **Tourist Information Center,** Jl. Elizabeth Dua, next door to the post office. Free maps and brochures. Useful *Explore Brunei* booklet at both locations. Both open M-Th and Sa 8am-4:30pm.

Tours: Freme Travel Service Sdn., Unit 403B, Wisma Jaya, Jl. Pemancha (☎234 280). Tours of BSB (B$36 per person, 2-person min.) and Brunei's national park (B$140 per person, 3-person min.). Open M-F 8am-noon and 1:30-5pm, Sa 8am-noon. Local tourism guru **Danny** (danny25174@hotmail.com) hangs out near the bus station and loves giving advice and exciting tours, often for free.

Embassies: Australian High Commission, 4th fl., Teck Guan Plaza, Jl. Sultan (☎229 435). Open M-Th 8am-4:30pm, F 8am-4pm. **British High Commission,** 2nd fl., Block D, Complex Yayasan Sultan Haji Hassanal Bolkiah (☎222 231). Open M-Th 8:30am-5pm, F 8:30am-12:30pm. **Canadian High Commission,** 5th fl., 1 Jl. McArthur (☎220 043). Open M-F 8:30am-5pm. **Indonesia,** Lot No. 4498, Simpang 528, Sungai Hanching Baru, Jl. Muara (☎330 180). Open M-Sa 8:30am-12:30pm. **Malaysia High Commission,** No. 27 and 29, Simpang 396-39, Kampung Sungai Akar, Mukim Berakas B, Jl. Kebangsaan (☎345 652). Open M-Th, Sa 9am-noon and 3-4pm. **New Zealand Consulate,** 36A Seri Lambak Complex, Jl. Berakas (☎331 612). Open M-F 8am-5pm, Sa 8am-noon. **Philippines,** Rooms 1 and 2, 6th fl., Badi'ah Building, Mile 1, Jl. Tutong (☎241 465). Open M-F 8:30am-12:30pm and 1:30-5:30pm, Sa 9am-noon. **Singapore High Commission,** No. 8 Simpang 74, Jl. Subo (☎262 741). Open M-F 8:30am-5pm. **Thailand,** No. 2 Simpang 52-86-16, Kampong Bunut, Jl. Tutong BF 1320 (☎653 108). **US,** 3rd fl., Teck Guan Plaza, Jl. Sultan (☎229 670). Open M-F 8am-4:30pm. **Vietnam,** House 16, Simpang 538-37-2. Jl. Kebangsaan Lama (☎343 167). Open M-Sa 8-10am and 2-4:30pm.

Currency Exchange: Several moneychangers are in shopping complexes near the bus station. **Hong Kong Bank** (☎242 305), at Jl. Sultan and Jl. Pemancha. Open M-F 9am-3pm, Sa 9-11am. **ATM** (Cirrus). **Standard Chartered Bank,** 51-55 Jl. Sultan (☎242 386). Unlimited exchange B$15. Open M-F 9am-3pm, Sa 9-11am.

Markets: Tamu Kianggeh Market, on the opposite side of the canal from Jl. Sungai Kianggeh. Open daily 8am-6pm. **Pasar Malam** (night market), opposite Sheraton Hotel on Jl. Tasek. Savory *satay* and good souvenirs.

EMERGENCY AND COMMUNICATIONS

Emergency ☎993. **Fire** ☎995. **Ambulance** ☎991.

Police: ☎242 334. On Jl. Stoney near the intersection with Jl. Elizabeth Dua.

Pharmacies: Guardian Pharmacy, Yayasan Sultan Haji Hassanal Bolkiah Mall, ground fl. Open daily 10am-9:45pm.

Hospital: RIPAS (Rajah Isteri Pengiran Anak Saheha Hospital; ☎242 424), on Jl. Putera Al-Muhtadee Billah across Edinburgh Bridge. Take CTS bus #1. **Klinik Kuin Mee,** 72 Jl. Roberts (☎243 546). Open daily 7:30am-1pm and 2-5:30pm.

Telephones: Telegraph Office, on Jl. Sultan (☎222 323), behind the post office. International phone/fax. Open daily 8am-10pm. **Directory Assistance:** ☎113.

Internet Access: LA Cybercafé, 2nd fl., Block B, Yayasan Sultan Haji Hassanal Bolkiah Mall (☎225 298). B$1 per 15min. Open M-Sa 9:30am-9:30pm, Su 10am-6pm.

Post Office: ☎228 291. At the corner of Jl. Sultan and Jl. Elizabeth Dua. *Poste Restante.* Open M-Th and Sa 8am-4:30pm, F 8-11am and 2-4pm. **Postal code:** BS8611.

ACCOMMODATIONS

BSB has few budget accommodations, but they're rarely full. The exception is during celebrations of the Sultan's birthday (July 15-31) when budget travelers scramble for cover. At mid-range hotels, always ask for the "promotion" or "discount" rates, which may be 25-30% cheaper than listed prices. Expect a 10% service charge.

Pusat Belia, Jl. Sungai Kianggeh (☎222 900). With the canal on the right, it's to the right of the youth center building. Complete with pool (B$1) and gym. No towels. Bring ISIC or youth hostel ID. Curfew 10:30pm. Closed for 2 weeks following the Sultan's birthday. Clean, single-sex 4-bed A/C dorm rooms with shared baths. Dorm beds B$10.

Tourist Rest House, Ketua Kampong (☎202 139), across the river on the border of the Kampung Ayer. Take a boat across town (B$0.50) and aim for the cream building with a green roof. Clean rooms with A/C, Internet, and common bath B$20 per person.

Capital Hotel, No. 7, Simpang 2, Kampung Berangan (☎223 561), behind Pusat Belia. Go down Jl. Sungai Kianggeh, right on Jl. Berangan, and right onto Simpang 2. Singles B$80-118; doubles B$95-138. AmEx/MC/V.

Jubilee Hotel, Jubilee Plaza, Jl. Kampung Kianggeh (☎228 070). With the canal to your right, turn right past the Chinese temple; it's before Pusat Belia. Cafe on 1st fl. TV, A/C, and full bath in each room. Singles/doubles B$70. AmEx/MC/V.

FOOD

If you've spent all your money on accommodations, don't worry; eating in Brunei is cheap. Near Pusat Belia, the night market behind the Chinese temple on Jl. Elizabeth Dua provides a selection of dishes and iced drinks (most items B$1). A similar night market sets up at the end of Jl. Sungai Kianggeh on the waterfront. (Both open sundown-midnight.) Locals prefer the larger night market in Gadong.

Kedai Makan Dan Minum Hajah Halimah Sulaiman, No. 34 Jl. Sultan, opposite the Shell building near Jl. Pemancha. The best Indian/Malay fare on the block. Generous servings. *Dosai* with chicken B$3.50. Open daily 6:30am-8:45pm.

Padian Food Court, Yayasan Sultan Haji Hassanal Bolkiah Mall. Range of Asian cuisines at budget prices (B$3-5). A/C. Open daily 9am-10pm.

Hualtua Restaurant, No. 48 Jl. Sultan, next to Standard Chartered Bank. One of 4 Chinese restaurants downtown. *Wanton* soup B$3. Open daily 7am-8:45pm.

SIGHTS

For those short on time, the best of Brunei can be seen via water taxi; ask for an hour tour (B$10-20, negotiable).

OMAR ALI SAIFUDDIEN MOSQUE. The 28th Sultan built this eye-poppingly opulent structure in 1958 at a cost of US$500 million. Worshippers wash before entering at the fountain on the far side. Dress conservatively and remove shoes before entering. *(On the west side of downtown BSB; entrance on Jl. Elizabeth Dua. Open Su-W 8am-noon, 1-3:30pm, and 4:30-5:30pm, F 4:30-5:30pm. Closed Th to non-Muslims.)*

FAST TIMES IN NEW BRUNEI In 1967, 21-year-old Hassanal Bolkiah became the Sultan of Brunei. As the country's oil and natural gas reserves were exploited in the 1970s and 80s, the Sultan grew richer than Midas. His palace, the largest on the planet, tops Versailles, with 1788 rooms, 500 chandeliers, 14 acres of marble, and hundreds of polo ponies in air-conditioned stables. For years, the Sultan was the wealthiest person alive, until software magnate Bill Gates stole the honor. The Sultan and his brother, children, wives, lovers, and advisers have blown nearly US$21.8 billion since 1987, making them the biggest spenders in history.

All in all, 1998 and 1999 were unsettling years for Brunei's royalty. Prince Jefri, the Sultan's youngest brother, battled for control of the financially flailing Amedeo Development Corporation and the Brunei Investment Agency, but the Sultan's accountants shut them down. Jefri claims that the Sultan and another brother, Prince Mohamed, were conspiring with Muslim traditionalists to oppose his liberal and modern views, which he expresses by buying hundreds of cars and sailing around on his yacht, the good ship *Tits*, known to have two lifeboats aptly named *Nipple I* and *Nipple II*. He has also been known to fly in prostitutes from around the world for sex parties; a former Miss USA sued both him and the Sultan for US$56 million for bringing her into such a situation, but her case was dismissed because of state immunity. Meanwhile in August 1998, the Sultan, engulfed by scandal, and with 22 years of oil left, named his snooker-loving son Billah heir to the throne.

KAMPUNG AYER AND ENVIRONS. Behind the mosque is a path to the **water villages,** a network of brightly-colored homes built on stilts above the Brunei River. Wooden boardwalks link the neighborhoods of Kampung Ayer, which merit hours of wandering and chatting with friendly residents. A less strenuous option is to explore by water taxi (see **Local Transportation,** p. 56). Make sure the taxi driver goes to the newest development at the far end, where white cookie-cutter homes stand on concrete piles, in contrast to the rickety wooden structures closer to town.

While barreling around the Brunei River, check out the **Istana Nurul Iman,** the world's largest palace and residence of Sultan Haji Hassanal Bolkiah Mu'izzadin Waddaulah. Visitors are allowed inside the palace once a year at the end of Ramadan. The **Persiaran Damuan,** a landscaped park across the river on Jl. Tutong, features sculptures by ASEAN artists and evening food stalls.

BRUNEI MUSEUM. His Majesty's Muslim art and artifacts, rescued from shipwrecks, exhibit the long history of wealth in the Sultanate. *(6½km east of BSB. Take bus #39 or an express bus to Muara. Open Su-Th 9:30am-5pm, F 9:30-11:30am and 2:30-5pm.)*

JAME'ASR HASSANAL BOLKIAH MOSQUE. This fancy mosque beckons worshippers, architecture enthusiasts, and tourists alike. Completed a few years ago in commemoration of His Majesty's 25 years on the throne, Jame'Asr Hassanal Bolkiah Mosque, the largest in Brunei, trumps Omar Ali Saifuddien Mosque in every category, including gaudiness. Upon entry, remove your shoes and register at the security post. The Sultan prays here on Fridays. *(In Gadong. Take bus #21 or 22. Open Su-W 8am-noon, 1-1:30pm, and 4:30-5:30pm; F 4:30-5:30pm. Closed Th to non-Muslims.*

OTHER SIGHTS. For more displays of wealth, check out the **Royal Regalia Building.** *(In a gray domed building on the left side of Jl. Sultan, past the Telekom Office. Open Th 8:30am-5pm, F 9-11:30am and 2:30-5pm. Free.)* Behind the Brunei Museum, **Malay Technology Museum** exhibits traditional fishing and steel-making techniques used in Kampung Ayer. *(Open Sa-M and W-TH 9am-5pm, F 9-11:30am and 2:30-5pm.)*

ENTERTAINMENT

The greatest attraction in BSB and, perhaps, the country, is **Jerudong Park Playground,** a state-of-the-art amusement park in the Brunei-Muara district. Bruneians boast that the park, a gift from the Sultan to his subjects, is better than Disneyworld. Laser lightshows, death-defying speed, botanical beauty, and palatial promenades electrify the senses. A food court is next to the parking lot.

Jerudong is beyond the Bandar city limits. Take bus #55 before 5pm and arrange for a PPP cab to take you back (B$20). Alternatively, the manager of Pusat Belia takes groups of four (B$10). No sleeveless shirts are allowed. On weekdays the park is deserted; it's even hard to muster up the six-person minimum required to get the coasters rolling. (Grounds open daily 2pm-2am. Games and rides open M-W 5pm-midnight; Th, Sa 5pm-2am; F, Su, and holidays 2pm-midnight; Ramadan 8pm-2am. B$3-5 per ride.)

For quiet nights in alcohol-free Brunei, stroll the night markets or the promenade along **Yayasan Sultan Haji Hassanal Bolkiah Mall.** Alternatively, catch a flick at the **Hasanal Bolkiah and Marina Theater,** on Jl. Sungai Kianggeh near the bus station and waterfront. (☎238 074. Movies B$3.50-4.) BSB shuts down by unofficial decree at 10pm, and loiterers may be eyed with suspicion during the wee hours. In Gadong (a 45min. walk), cafes stay open until midnight but are still quiet.

Outside BSB and the amusement park are a few scattered sights, all difficult to reach by public transportation. **Muara and Surasa beaches,** in Muara District, are considered Brunei's finest. Temburong District is home to **Ulu Temburong National Park, Peradayan Forest Recreational Park,** and the **Rainforest Field Studies Center (FSC)** at Kuala Belalong in Batu Apoi Forest Reserve. Travelers must go with a tour. **Freme Travel** (see **Practical Information: Tourist Information,** p. 57) runs tours. (B$140, with rafting B$180; overnight tours from B$220. All require at least 2 people.)

CAMBODIA

RIEL

US$1 = 3835.38R	1000R = US$0.26
CDN$1 = 2482.45R	1000R = CDN$0.40
UK£1 = 5569.70R	1000R = UK£0.18
IR£1 = 4432.53R	1000R = IR£0.23
EUR€1 = 3490.90R	1000R = EUR€0.29
AUS$1 = 2032.36R	1000R = AUS$0.49
NZ$1 = 1690.37R	1000R = NZ$0.59
ZAR1 = 460.02R	1000R = ZAR2.18

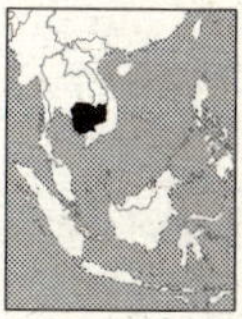

PHONE CODE **Country Code:** 855. **International dialing prefix:** 00.

The story of modern Cambodia is one of the darkest in modern history. Perhaps because of the tragedy of their present, Cambodia's people look to their past for inspiration. It has been a thousand years since the god-kings of Angkor built their vast empire, but the Cambodians still strive to recapture a sliver of their ancestors' glory with Angkor Wat's distinctive five-column silhouette emblazoned on every national flag since independence. Today the image adorns a popular brand of beer (Angkor: My Country, My Beer), and school girls study the ancient art of Khmer dance, inspired by the graceful *apsaras* that adorn Angkor's walls. The veneration of the past, however, cannot hide the reality of the present. North of Phnom Penh, a once graceful temple lies in ruins, its central sanctuary pockmarked with bullet holes. Many travelers come seeking precisely this unsettling mixture of glorious and ghastly legacies—to admire the ancient beauty of Angkor and then reflect on the horrors depicted in Phnom Penh's genocide museum. Others come on a whim and stay longer than they meant to, drawn to the lazy, peaceful beach at Sihanoukville, the cheap, easy livin' in Phnom Penh, and the resilience and hospitality of people everywhere. The relative stability of recent years is a welcome change from the constant civil war since the 1970s, but no one is celebrating just yet. The Khmer Rouge may be defunct, but political corruption, violence, massive unemployment, illiteracy, and land mines are the legacies of today's Cambodia. Perhaps one day Cambodia will leave its past behind, but for now it lingers, a comfort and a curse for its people.

FACTS AND FIGURES

Official Name: Kingdom of Cambodia.
Government: Multi-party democracy under a constitutional monarchy.
Capital: Phnom Penh.
Land Area: 176,520 sq. km.
Geography: Borders Thailand, Laos, and Vietnam. River systems: Mekong, Bassac, Tonle Sap. Mountain ranges: Cardamom, Dangrek, Elephant.
Climate: Dry (high season) Dec.-Apr., rainy (low season) May-Nov.
Major Cities: Battambang, Siem Reap, Sihanoukville (Kompong Som).
Population: 11,60,000.
Languages: Khmer, French.
Religions: Buddhism (95%), Islam (5%).
Average Income Per Capita: US$60.
Major Exports: Timber, rubber, soybeans.

LIFE AND TIMES

THE PEOPLE OF CAMBODIA

Cambodia's pre-1975 population included **Khmer, Khmer Loeu** (upland Khmer hill tribes), and minority ethnic groups, including **Chinese, Vietnamese,** and **Chams.** The Khmer Rouge genocide (see **Civil War and the Rise of the Khmer Rouge,** p. 65), how-

HIGHLIGHTS OF CAMBODIA

CULTURAL HERITAGE. **Angkor** (p. 90) is arguably the most awe-inspiring collection of sights in Southeast Asia and reason enough to visit Cambodia. The **Tuol Sleng Genocide Museum** in Phnom Penh (p. 69) is a must-see.

HANGING OUT. Guest houses and restaurants in **Phnom Penh** (p. 69) and **Siem Reap** (p. 86) attract a fun-loving bunch who almost always stay longer than they expect. Nature lovers will enjoy quiet **Ban Lung** (p. 84).

BEACHES. The beaches of **Sihanoukville** (p. 79), with their fine white sand, affordable guest houses, and delicious seafood, have really only been discovered by the weekending Cambodian crowd and remain largely deserted during the week.

ever, targeted minority populations, and Cambodia's population is now, consequently, almost 90% Khmer. The Chinese minority, which had been a large part of the merchant class of pre-Khmer Rouge Cambodia, is now rebounding. The Vietnamese, many of whom live in the cities and on the Tonle Sap, remain subject to virulent racism and are known by the pejorative term *yuon*. Hill tribes practice subsistence agriculture in the highlands along the Vietnamese border, but the growing logging industry threatens their lifestyle.

AD 100-500 Funan kingdom established.

7c Indian culture gains influence and begins to meld in with Khmer; Sanskrit becomes language of the elite

8c Founding of the Angkor state; Construction of Angkor Wat begins

800 King Jayavarman II ascends throne; declares himself "God-King" because he can

1113 Suryavarman II expands Khmer territory and builds more wats

1177 Too many wats drain resources; Cham invade weakened Kambujadesa

1181 Jayavarman VII reunites Kambujadesa

15c Phnom Penh becomes capital

1557 First European missionaries arrive

HISTORY

EARLY KINGDOMS AND INDIANIZATION (AD 100-800)

—I'll take Indian culture for 200, please.

Scholars base the little they know about pre-Angkorian Cambodia on Chinese travel logs and a handful of cryptic inscriptions. These accounts describe the **Funan Kingdom** (AD 100-500) as the first unified Cambodian polity. Recent scholarship, however, cautions that many accounts in the logs may have exaggerated the descriptions of the empire to enhance the prestige of the Chinese Court.

Contact between Khmer and Indian traders led to an **Indianization** of Khmer society as Indian culture influenced politics, religion, art, and literature. Sanskrit became the language of the elite, and traditional Khmer concepts of power combined with Indic notions of divine kingship in a peaceful process of cultural borrowing and localization that was never considered a loss of real Khmer culture.

THE ANGKOR PERIOD (802–1432)

—I know wat will make me happy...

Cambodia's Khmer civilization (*Kambujadesa* in inscriptions) was the mightiest kingdom in Southeast Asia during this period, drawing tribute from as far away as present-day Thailand, Myanmar, and Malaysia. **Jayavarman II** founded the Angkor state (from the Sanskrit word for "city") and declared himself *devaraja*, or god-king. After uniting many disparate kingdoms, he established his capital northeast of the Tonle Sap and began constructing the mammoth temple complex of **Angkor** (p. 92).

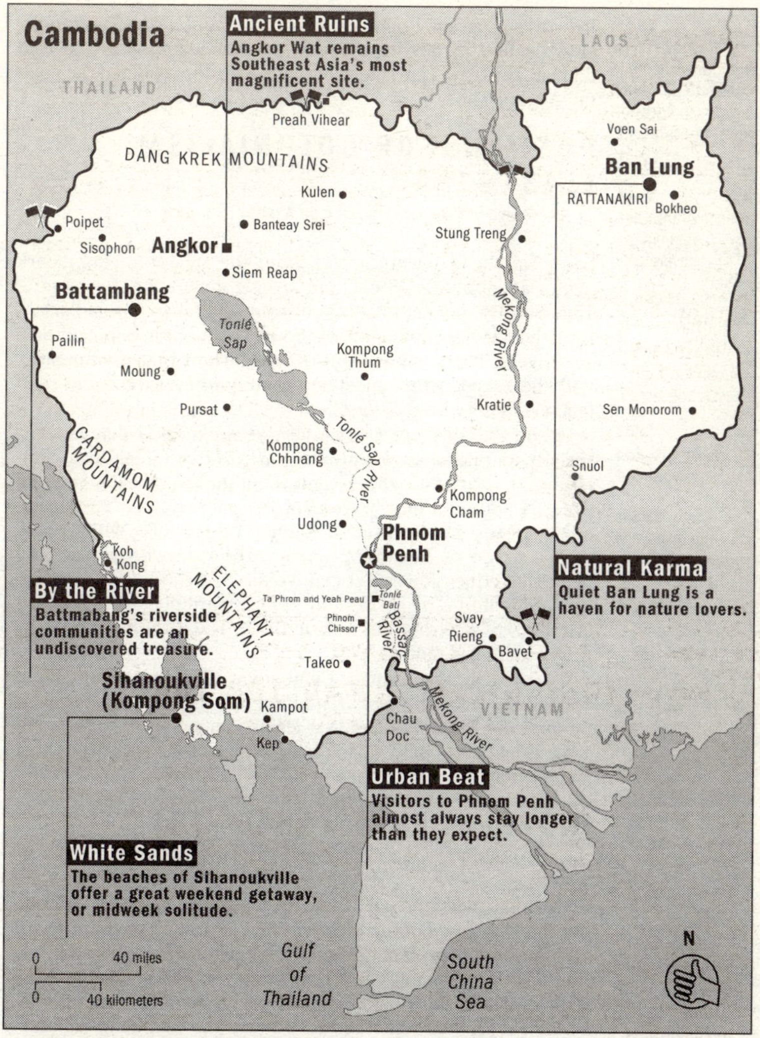

The Angkor state had important cosmological and economic underpinnings. Under the idea of divine kingship, the Khmer king was seen as an embodiment of the Hindu goddess Shiva (see **Angkor's Motley Crew**, p. 95). If the king was indeed a spiritual god, however, he certainly reconciled himself with materialism, as Angkor's wealth grew to astounding proportions. Most scholars attribute Angkor's wealth to booming agriculture and a strong irrigation system, and it didn't hurt that the King single-handedly commanded the country's entire labor force.

Angkor's power waxed and waned under its monarchs. Under **Suryavarman II**, Khmer territory expanded, and construction on Angkor Wat increased, ultimately sapping the country's strength and leaving it vulnerable to Cham invasions in 1177. In 1181 **Jayavarman VII** reunited the kingdom and instituted an ambitious pub-

1800-50
Numerous Vietnamese and Thai invasions

1863
French Rule begins; Cambodian people's welfare neglected

1930s
New educated elite promotes nationalism

1941
Playboy Prince Norodom Sihanouk comes to power as supposed "puppet king" but surprises everyone

1949
French grant Cambodia limited sovereignty

1950s
Pol Pot returns to Cambodia from France and joins KPRP

1953
Cambodia gets independence

1960s
Communist Party renamed Khmer Rouge; gains in power under Pol Pot

1970
Vietnam War leads to US invasion of Cambodia

1970
Khmer Rouge controls most of the country

1975
Pol Pot founds Democratic Kampuchea (DK); Declaration of Year Zero by the Khmer

1975-79
Cambodian genocide engineered by the Khmer Rouge; millions killed

1977
Increased border conflicts with the Vietnamese

1978
Vietnamese invasion finally ends Khmer Rouge power

lic works program. Following his death, Kambujadesa suffered a slow decline, its territory steadily encroached upon by the Thai and Lao. In 1431, The Thai Ayutthaya Kingdom claimed the capital, Angkor Thom.

POST-ANGKOR COLONIALISM (1431–1945)

–Give 'em an inch, they'll take a mile.

Some call the five centuries following the sack of Angkor a dark age of economic, political, and artistic stagnation. In the mid-15th century, the capital shifted from Angkor to **Phnom Penh,** a trade hub at the confluence of the Mekong, Tonle Sap, and Bassac Rivers. The move to Phnom Penh meant increased contact with the outside world, most importantly with Vietnam and Thailand and later with the West.

By the 19th century, Cambodia was caught between its territorially ambitious and mutually antagonistic neighbors, Vietnam and Thailand, which each invaded the country several times. Cambodia may well have been swallowed up permanently were it not for French colonial rule in 1863, which came at the price of heavy taxes, onerous *corvée* labor, and neglected education and social welfare. By the 1930s, an emergent educated elite in Phnom Penh responded with the first stirrings of Cambodian nationalism, recalling the pride of Angkor and Cambodia's past.

Co-opted by the French, Cambodian kings were content to collaborate with colonists. Thinking they had selected a pliant puppet, the French placed **Norodom Sihanouk** on the throne in 1941. Equal parts playboy and patriot, Sihanouk surprised them all by agitating for independence.

INDEPENDENCE (1945–70)

–Would you like land mines with your independence?

Cambodian independence came in stages with neither the drama nor the bloodshed of the Vietnamese war against the French. An attempt to romanize the Khmer language catalyzed the formation of pro-independence groups, like the **Khmer Issarak** (Free Khmer) party which established a government-in-exile in Thailand. In 1949, the French signed a treaty granting Cambodia limited sovereignty, and complete independence peacefully followed in 1953. The next decade belonged to Sihanouk, who consolidated his autocratic domestic rule and plotted a neutral course in international affairs.

Sihanouk's neutrality was thwarted as the war in South Vietnam intensified. He gave the North Vietnamese tacit permission to transport soldiers and supplies through Cambodian territory. **National Liberation Front** (**NLF** or **Viet Cong**) guerrilla forces used Cambodia as a sanctuary and staging ground for operations in South Vietnam. Desperate to eliminate the NLF sanctuaries, US military commanders requested permission from the Nixon White House (and, some say, from Sihanouk) to begin a series of secret, devastating bombing campaigns over Cambodia, eventually invading the country outright in 1970 and planting mines that still haunt Cambodia today.

CIVIL WAR AND THE KHMER ROUGE (1970–75)

—The Pol Pot begins to boil....

The Cambodian revolutionary movement started in the mid-1940s when the Vietnamese-dominated **Indochinese Communist Party (ICP)** began promoting Cambodian membership. The **Khmer People's Revolutionary Party (KPRP)** became Cambodia's revolutionary party in the 1950s, drawing its support from leftist Khmer Issarak members and Khmer students returning from study in France. In this group of students, known as the **"Paris Circle,"** was Saloth Sar, better known as **Pol Pot.** He had studied engineering in Paris but spent most of his time reading Rousseau and attending Stalinist discussion groups. Poor showings on exams led to the rescinding of his scholarship, and he returned to Cambodia in the early 1950s.

The Marxist revolutionary movement renamed itself the **Communist Party of Kampuchea (CPK)** but was known popularly as the **Khmer Rouge.** Led by Pol Pot, the Khmer Rouge steadily expanded its influence until it had almost a quarter of the country's votes by 1970. In March 1970, Cambodia's Prime Minister, the US-backed General **Lon Nol,** deposed Sihanouk in a bloodless coup. In Sihanouk's absence, the Khmer Rouge rapidly expanded its territory until April 1975, when Pol Pot's forces marched into Phnom Penh and declared the founding of **Democratic Kampuchea (DK).**

1979
Pro-Hanoi government installed at center; Hun Sen appointed prime minister

1980
US places embargo and recognizes Khmer Rouge as Cambodian government

1989
Vietnamese forces withdraw from Cambodia

1991
Paris Peace Accords; UNCTAC tries, unsuccessfully, to resolve internal conflict

1993
Elections result in shaky coalition government

1997
Hun Sen seizes control of government in coup

1998
General elections held, Hun Sen gains power

DEMOCRATIC KAMPUCHEA (1975-79)

—... and boils over.

The Khmer Rouge leadership quickly implemented a program to transform Cambodia into a self-sufficient agrarian utopia. Pol Pot, a shadowy figure whose true identity few knew, declared that the present day, **"Year Zero,"** would mark the beginning of a massive restructuring of Cambodian society. The Khmer Rouge ordered the evacuation of all cities, including Phnom Penh, whose two million residents fled US bombing in the countryside and were relocated to slave labor camps. The government systematically eradicated all vestiges of pre-revolutionary society, including schools, hospitals, and religion, and the doctors, teachers, and artists that worked there. Anyone thought to be educated—as evidenced by wearing glasses or speaking a foreign language, for example—was shot or clubbed to death and then buried in the mass graves of the "killing fields" (see **The Killing Fields,** above). Children were indoctrinated to expose their own parents and friends, who were then taken to the camps or killed. No one knows for certain how many people were murdered or perished of malnutrition and disease, but estimates range from one to two million, approximately one-eighth of the 1975 population. The Cambodian genocide was never recognized as such by the world until years later. Arguing that the ideals of sovereignty kept them from acting against another country's government, the rest of the world was silent in the face of the senseless mass killings, an action that many consider tantamount to condoning the Khmer Rouge itself.

The Khmer Rouge loathed the Vietnamese, whom they blamed for the steady decline of the Khmer nation. DK raids on Vietnamese border villages eventually provoked a full-scale Vietnamese invasion of Cambodia in December 1978. Two weeks later, Vietnamese forces seized Phnom Penh. Pol Pot and his followers carried on their struggle from jungle strongholds along the Thai-Cambodian border,

THE KILLING FIELDS Over 25 years of civil war has left Cambodia with many sad legacies, but perhaps the worst are the millions of land mines. If you stray far from Phnom Penh, you're bound to see warning signs; Cambodia's land is sown with 6-10 million anti-personnel mines. Additionally, there are 500,000 tons of unexploded ordnance (UXO), small bombs that failed to explode when the US dropped them during the Vietnam War. Injuries number between 100 and 300 each month, about half of whom survive with amputations; one in 236 Cambodians has lost a limb due to a mine explosion. Children are disproportionately at risk, as they frequently mistake UXOs for toys.

As of 1996, demining groups estimated that at current rates it would take nearly 300 years to clear the fields. Generous international donations have enabled the Cambodia Mine Action Center (CMAC) to carry out demining efforts, but the group is beset with allegations of corruption and misallocation of resources. Improved technology, however, may speed up the project. In December 1997, a Japanese company introduced Mine Eye, a new landmine sensor (field-tested on Cambodian soil) that differentiates between mines and scrap metal. If contributions continue to increase, CMAC may clear the fields within 10 or 20 years. For now, **when traveling outside touristed centers, never, ever, ever stray from paths.**

supporting themselves through timber and gem smuggling. More than two million refugees flooded across the border into Thailand where many languished in refugee camps for years.

FOREIGN INTERVENTION AND HUN SEN'S COUP (1979–97)

–An acronymous peace accord: UNTAC, FUNCINPEC, CPP, PRK.

The Vietnamese installed the **People's Republic of Kampuchea (PRK),** a pro-Hanoi regime. Led by Heng Samrin and a young **Hun Sen** (current Prime Minister), both former DK leaders who had defected to Vietnam, the PRK struggled to rebuild the shattered country, but the guerrilla war in the countryside hampered their efforts. The US, which recognized the Khmer Rouge as the legitimate government of Cambodia, engineered an embargo that further stifled recovery.

In September 1989, the Vietnamese announced a unilateral withdrawal of their forces from Cambodia and cleared the way for the 1991 **Paris Peace Accords.** The UN oversaw the **United Nations Transitional Authority in Cambodia** (UNTAC), an ambitious mission to resolve the civil war and hold elections. Widely-regarded as a fiasco, UNTAC failed to disarm the Khmer Rouge, which, rather than participating in the peace process, marred the elections with intimidation and violence. The May 1993 election resulted in a shaky coalition between **Prince Norodom Ranariddh's United Front for an Independent, Neutral, Peaceful, and Cooperative Cambodia (FUNCINPEC)** and Hun Sen's **Cambodia People's Party (CPP).** But the two factions were never more than uneasy partners, and the Khmer Rouge continued to wage war from its border-area strongholds. Hun Sen seized sole control of the government in a July 1997 coup, for which he was condemned by the international community. Meanwhile, Ranariddh went into exile.

CAMBODIA TODAY

In April 1998, Pol Pot died in a Khmer Rouge camp near the Thai border. The former dictator, held under house arrest by former allies since the summer of 1997, had declared, "my conscience is clear" in an interview with a US journalist. In the intervening months, the remaining Khmer Rouge forces had split into rival factions and began defecting en masse. During the early spring of 1998, a Japanese-brokered peace agreement paved the way for general elections in July by permitting the return of Prince Ranariddh. A wave of political violence swept the country in the weeks leading up to the elections as did violence against the Vietnamese population in Cambodia. Strongman Hun Sen claimed victory, although opponents accused him of fraud and intimidation.

The **Association of Southeast Asian Nations (ASEAN)** admitted Cambodia in April 1999. A lack of basic infrastructure in the countryside continues to hinder economic development. The mammoth task of de-mining the country—which still has approximately 140 mines per square mile—has been taken up mainly by Cambodian women, creating an employment niche.

CULTURE AND CUSTOMS

A CARTOGRAPHER'S NIGHTMARE

"Cambodia" is no longer called Kambujadesa, the original name of the country during the Angkor period, but that may be the only definite thing one can say about its name. "Cambodia" is the English translation of "Kampuche," though many now associate Kampuchea with the Khmer Rouge and freely interchange its use with Cambodia, even in Khmer. The French, of course, do their own thing and call it "Cambodge." Phnom Penh is often Phnom Penh, and where you really are simply depends on whom you ask.

EASY ON THE KARMA

Cambodia is often considered less fervent about Buddhist doctrine than neighboring Indo-China. However, the basics still hold: don't point your feet towards people or images of the Buddha, don't touch people on the head, don't lose your calm publicly. Unlike the rest of Southeast Asia, shorts and T-shirts are accepted at some temples.

HUMAN RIGHTS

Much to the dismay of human rights organizations, human rights violators (past and present) are often granted immunity in Cambodia. In the past, the government failed to prosecute military officials and civilians for killing and torture. In the months leading up to the July 1998 elections, over 50 people were killed in political violence. During elections, opposition parties are subject to intense intimidation. Anti-Vietnamese sentiment (a long-standing theme in Cambodia) continues, with massacres of Vietnamese Cambodians reported as recently as the spring and summer of 1998. However, strides have been made to hold offenders accountable: two senior Khmer Rouge leaders, Ta Mok and Kaing Khek Leu, were arrested in spring of 1999, and the latter was charged with ordering the killing of over 16,000 people during the Khmer regime. Nuon Chea and Khieu Samphan, two top-level Khmer Rouge cadres who surrendered in December 1998, have not yet been charged with war crimes or genocide.

BISEXUAL, GAY, AND LESBIAN TRAVELERS

There is little or no openly gay life in Cambodia. Rumors of underground communities abound, but finding them is entirely a matter of luck. Be careful and discreet; con men are known to run scams involving gay travelers.

PINK INK. For more information on Cambodia's gay life (or lack thereof), check out the Utopia-Asia web site (www.utopia-asia.com/tipscam.htm).

ARTS AND RECREATION

Pol Pot targeted artists for execution. Today, the Cambodians are still struggling to resurrect old art forms, but a lack of resources and the stark fact that few can teach them hinders efforts. Angkor civilization produced a distinct **classical dance** that has influenced Thailand and Laos. Believed to be the earthly embodiment of the *apsaras*, the celestial nymphs of Angkorian cosmology, dancers re-enact great

Indian epics. Cambodia's national dance is the **lamthon,** typified by slow, graceful gestures. **Folk** and **shadow plays** are popular in the countryside.

Angkor civilization also produced an indigenous style of architecture called **roulos,** in which temples are enclosed in concentric moats and walls. **Preah Ko** (sacred cow; see **Most Sacred Cow in the East,** p. 90) is the first example of this style. Cambodia's artistic tradition of hand-weaving has persisted for centuries. The production of the material used for sarong and *krama* scarves remains a vibrant art form. Using crude hand-looms, village weavers produce beautiful silk and cotton cloth in simple linear and plaid patterns and more complicated designs using tie-dyed thread. Vegetable dyes are specially mixed for each *sampot* (traditional women's sarong) so that no two lengths of material are exactly the same.

ADDITIONAL SOURCES

A History of Cambodia, by David Chandler (1983). A classic textbook on Cambodian history by Cambodia's foremost Western historian.

The Killing Fields, directed by Roland Joffé (1984). Based on a true story of a foreign correspondent and his assistant, this Academy Award-winning film captures the stunning landscape of Southeast Asia and the atrocities of the Khmer Rouge.

Sideshow: Kissinger, Nixon, and the Destruction of Cambodia, by William Shawcross (1979). A damning indictment of America's war in Cambodia.

ON THE WEB

Cambodia Genocide Project (www.yale.edu/cgp). Comprehensive story of the genocide.

Cambodia Info (www.cambodia.org). Great site with info, links, resources and photographs. One stop shopping, anyone?

ESSENTIALS

VISAS

All travelers must obtain visas before entering Cambodia overland. One-month visas obtained from international consulates cost US$20, and 2-month extensions cost US$45; allow three business days for processing. Thirty-day tourist visas are available at **Pochentong International Airport** in Phnom Penh (p. 69) or **Siem Reap Airport** in Siem Reap (p. 86) upon arrival. Those traveling overland from Vietnam can apply for same-day visas (US$30) in Ho Chi Minh City at the Cambodian General Consulate. The Cambodian Embassy in Bangkok issues 30-day visas (1000฿, 2-days processing); many travel agencies can secure visas in one day. **Extensions** may be obtained through the Immigration Office at No. 5, St. 200 in Phnom Penh.

MONEY

The Cambodian **riel (r)** comes in denominations of 50, 100, 200, 500, 1000, and 10,000r notes. It's usually not necessary to exchange money if you pay in US dollars—you'll be given change (at a fair rate) in Cambodian riel. **Tipping** is not necessary but appreciated—the average Cambodian makes about US$5 per month. A tip of 2000-2500r is appropriate for moto and cyclo drivers and at cheap restaurants. It's wise to keep small bills handy. Credit cards are not widely accepted.

GETTING THERE

BY PLANE. Cambodia has two **international airports:** Pochentong International Airport in Phnom Penh (p. 69) and Siem Reap Airport in Siem Reap (p. 86). The country doesn't have a national airline, but several major Southeast Asian airlines, like **MAS, Silk Air, Thai Airways,** and **Vietnam Airlines,** fly into these airports.

BY LAND. Refer to the following table for overland border crossings in Cambodia.

BORDER CROSSINGS

LAOS. The border crossing between **Stung Treng** (p. 84) in northern Cambodia and **Don Khong** in southern Laos recently opened.

THAILAND. Boats run regularly from **Sihanoukville** (p. 79) to **Trat** (p. 683). From Siem Reap, trucks take travelers through Sisophon to the border at **Aranyaprathet/Poipet** (p. 673). The 7hr. overland route is uncomfortable and bumpy, and during the rainy season muddy roads sometimes make the route impassable.

VIETNAM. Buses and share-taxis head from Phnom Penh through **Bavet** (Svay Rieng) to **Mộc Bài** (Tây Ninh), Vietnam, from which connections can be made to Saigon. The trip to the Vietnamese border takes 4-5hr.

GETTING AROUND

ON THE BEATEN TRACK. Cambodia has the most landmines per capita of any country in the world. Though de-mining efforts continue, landmines are a serious threat, especially in rural areas. **Stay on well-traveled roads and at all times.** Bandits also threaten travelers in rural areas. Never travel alone or at night.

Inexpensive daily **flights** connect cities within the country. **Boats** provide a fairly safe, enjoyable method of travel between Phnom Penh and Siem Reap and along the Mekong River. Most of the roads in Cambodia, with a few notable exceptions, are an unpaved, pot-holed sin against one's internal organs. **Private bus lines** run between the capital and major cities, but foreigners should avoid public transportation whenever possible. Hiring a **shared taxi** is a smart option for border crossings; it's cheaper than flying and faster and more secure than taking a bus.

KEEPING IN TOUCH

Cambodia's **postal service** is unreliable—**postal codes** are not used, and mail takes over two weeks to get to and from Cambodia. Phnom Penh and Siem Reap offer *Poste Restante* and **telephone** service. **Long distance calls** placed from Cambodia are costly. Incoming calls are accepted at most hotels and some communication centers. **IDD calls** can be placed from Telstra phone booths around Phnom Penh. For **Home Country Direct (HCD)** numbers from Cambodia, refer to the table on the inside back cover of this book. HCD calls can be made from phone booths with orange handsets instead of blue ones.

SOUTHERN CAMBODIA

PHNOM PENH ☎ 23

Phnom Penh's citizens have spent the past 21 years improvising with the leftovers from disaster. Purged of its population in April 1975, Phnom Penh sat empty for the four-year Pol Pot regime, while nearby provinces faced hard labor, famine, fear, and death. Though more stable than in recent years, the past is more than a memory: water damage from its ghost-town years remains unmended; blackouts are common; fading French colonial architecture mixes with modern kitsch; bored policemen loiter on street corners with AK-47s slung over their shoulders, idle and workday icons of Cambodian law and order. As

Phnom Penh gets back on its feet, memories of a devastating past lurk in the minds of a majority of its inhabitants. However, this city of about one million has an admirable sensibility—as rural as it is street-smart, as gentle as it is jaded.

INTERCITY TRANSPORTATION

BY PLANE

Most guest houses and hotels offer bus, boat, taxi, and air services to Siem Reap, Sihanoukville, and Vietnam. Non-guests can also use these services.

I BELIEVE I CAN FLY...

DESTINATION	FREQUENCY	PRICE	DESTINATION	FREQUENCY	PRICE
Bangkok	2 per day	US$125	Siem Reap	1 per day	US$61
Ho Chi Minh City	2 per day	US$75	Singapore	1 per day	US$260
Kuala Lumpur	4 per week	US$191	Vientiane	1 per day	US$130

Flights to Phnom Penh arrive at **Pochentong Airport,** 3km west of the city. Airport tax US$20 on international flights, US$10 on domestic flights. Buses go to the airport from GST Express (see **Buses,** below) for 2000r. Ticketing can be done at the airport or at these offices in and around the city: **Lao Aviation,** 58B R.V. Samdech Preah Sihanouk (☎216 563); **Malaysia Airlines,** 172-184 M.V. Preah Monivong (☎426 688), on the first floor of the Diamond Hotel; **Royal Air Cambodge,** 24 Kramuon Sar Ave. (☎428 830), near the intersection with M.V. Preah Monivong; **Silk Air,** 219BC M.V. Preah Monivong (☎364 443), on the first floor of the Pailin Hotel; **Thai Airways,** Regency Sq., 294 Mao Tsé Toung (☎214 359), in the Hotel Inter-Continental; **Vietnam Airlines,** 41 P. 214 (☎363 396).

CAMBODIA

BY TRAIN

! Train travel for foreigners was recently legalized, and although cheap, remains somewhat dangerous. In the past, when train travel for foreigners was illegal, kidnappers and bandits targeted Westerners on the rails, in extreme cases, resulting in death. While legal, train travel is not yet recommended, especially for those traveling alone. The **train station** is a yellow art-deco building set back from M.V. Preah Monivong, north of M.V. Confederation de la Russie (Pochentong Blvd.).

BY BUS

The two major **bus** companies have stations near the New Market, between M.V. Charles de Gaulle and P. 67. **GST Express,** 13 P. 142, goes to: **HCMC** (7-8hr.; Tu, Th, Sa 6:30am; US$16); **Kampong Cham** (5 per day 6:45am-4pm, 7000r); **Sihanoukville** (5 per day 6:55am-1:30pm, 8000-12,000r); and **Udang** (3000r). **Ho Wah Genting Transport Co. Ltd.** goes to **Sihanoukville** (5 per day, last leaves 1:30pm, 10,000r). Inquire about share-trucks and minibuses to **Siem Reap** (US$5-10). **Capitol Guest House** has a daily bus to **HCMC** at 6:45am. Note: the station lacks English-speakers and service frequently changes. *Let's Go* advises avoiding all night travel.

BY BOAT

With an abundance of bad roads and wide rivers, **boat** travel serves as an expedient travel option. Most guest houses can arrange **express boat** service to **Siem Reap** (4-5hr., US$22-25). The ferries, many of which lack adequate safety equipment, can be overloaded, so it's best to travel on the roof. Boats leave from 6 to 7am.

BY TAXI

Taxis can be hired on M.V. Charles de Gaulle between M.V. Preah Monivong and the New Market. Hire a taxi by the seat or by the car; a car to **Sihanoukville** costs around US$20. If you purchase just a seat (around US$3), expect to be crammed into a Toyota Corolla with six other people; buying two seats is a more comfort-

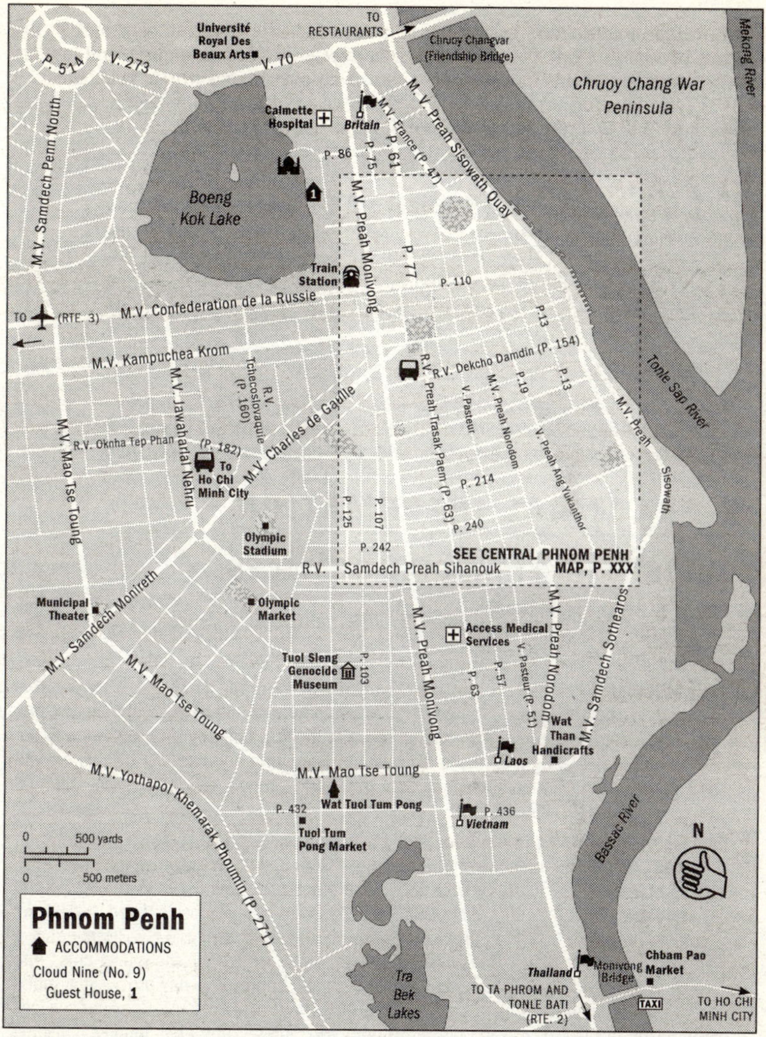

able option. Share-taxis to: Vietnamese border at **Bavet/Mộc Bài** (US$10 per person); and **Siem Reap** (US$80 per person). Most destinations between 2-4hr. from Phnom Penh cost US$15-20 per car. Before hiring a taxi by the New Market, check with guest houses for cheaper options.

ORIENTATION

Three major north-south boulevards divide the central Phnom Penh. In the east, **M.V. Preah Sisowath,** with its cafes and bars, runs alongside the **Tonle Sap** river. **M.V. Preah Norodom,** west of the river, is lined with embassies, government ministries, banks, and NGOs; one block to the east, towards the Tonle Sap, are the **National Museum, Royal Palace,** and **Silver Pagoda.** The main commercial, financial, and residential thoroughfare, **M.V. Preah Monivong,** runs straight down the center of the city. Most accommodations, and restaurants are between the Tonle Sap River and M.V Preah Monivong. The **New Market** (known to most as **Psar Thmei**) sits between M.V. Preah Monivong and Norodom just south of **M.V. Confederation de la Russie** (called **Pochentong Blvd.** everywhere but on maps). The east-west thoroughfares (from north to south) are M.V. Confederation de la Russie (Pochentong Blvd.), **R.V. Samdech Preah Sihanouk,** and **M.V. Mao Tsé Toung.** Most named streets have a number as well; both are printed on street signs.

LOCAL TRANSPORTATION

Motos and pedicabs: Motorcycle taxis (motos) and **pedicabs** go anywhere in the city for low fares (1000-2000r). Some guest houses recommend taxi travel as the best option after dark, but expect to pay more. Moto drivers also take passengers to sites outside of town, such as **Chœng Ek, Tonle Bati,** and **Udong.** Drivers outside expat and backpacker haunts speak some English. Female travelers should note that while sitting side-saddle might be customary, it is also dangerous on longer and less-traveled routes.

Rentals: Lucky Motorcycles, 413 M.V. Preah Monivong (☎212 788), north of the Hong Kong Hotel near Wat Koh. Motos (US$3 per day), dirtbikes (US$6), motorcycles (US$10). A passport or cash **deposit** is required. English spoken. Open daily 7am-6pm.

PRACTICAL INFORMATION

TOURIST AND FINANCIAL SERVICES

Tourist Offices: The understaffed and underbudgeted tourist offices are useless. Speak to a guest house manager for good travel advice and bookings. Information regarding safety outside Phnom Penh should be verified at an embassy.

Tours: Diethelm Travel, 65 P. 240 (☎214 059). West of the American Embassy, it is better than most agencies. Arranges trips to Sihanoukville and Siem Reap. English spoken, credit cards accepted. Also has an office in the FCC building, 363 Sisowath Quay. Both open M-F 11:30am-6pm, Sa 10am-1pm. **Hanuman Tourism,** 233 P. 13 (☎428 883), north of the National Museum, is a trustworthy option. English spoken. Open M-Sa 7:30am-noon and 2-5:30pm.

Embassies: Australia and Canada, Villa 11, P. 254 (☎213 470 or 213 459). Consular services open M-Th 8am-noon and 1:30-5pm, F 8am-noon and 1:30-4:15pm. **Lao PDR,** 15-17 M.V. Mao Tsé Toung (☎982 632). Visa office open M-F 8-11:30am and 2-5pm. 15-day and 1 month tourist visas US$35. 2 passport-size photos required. 1-day processing. **Thailand,** 196 M.V. Preah Norodom (☎363 870). Open M-F 8:30am-noon. 1 month single-entry transit visa US$15. Foreigners are no longer allowed to cross into Thailand through Poipet or Koh Kong without special approval. 1-day processing; emergency same-day processing available. **UK,** 27-29 P. 75 (☎427 124). Consular services open M-Tu and Th-F 8am-noon and 1:30-5pm, W 8:30am-1pm. Also handles concerns of **New Zealand** citizens. **United States,** 16-18 P. 228 (☎216 436). Open M-Th 8am-noon and 1-5pm. Consular services open M-Th 9am-noon and 1-3pm. In an after-hours emergency, speak to the guard. **Vietnam,** 436 M.V. Preah Monivong (☎362 531). Visa office open M-F 8-11am and 2-4pm, Sa 8-11am. **Visa applicant must specify point of entry.** Travelers with visas obtained in Thailand have also been turned back despite having correct point of entry stamped. Single-entry visa US$35; double-entry US$70. 3-day processing.

Immigration Office: Direction des Etrangers, on P. 200, off M.V. Preah Norodom and to the right. Visa extensions: 1-month US$30, 3-month US$60, 6-month US$100. 1-day processing US$45, US$75, and US$155, respectively. Must leave passport. Open M-F 8-10:30am and 2:30-4:30pm. Visa applications accepted 8-10am only.

Currency Exchange: Moneychangers on the street who post their exchange rates may offer good rates, but banks are more trustworthy. **Cambodian Commercial Bank,** 26 M.V. Preah Monivong (☎426 145), on the corner of M.V. Confederation de la Russie on

the right. MC/V cash advances. Open M-F 8am-3pm. **Thai Farmers Bank** (☎426 536), on M.V. Preah Monivong near the Mittapheap Hotel. MC/V cash advances. (US$10 fee; max. US$500 per day). 2% commission on traveler's checks. Open M-F 8am-3pm.

American Express: At **Diethelm Travel,** 65 P. 240, near the intersection with M.V. Preah Monivong. No surcharge on AmEx purchases. Can issue Traveler's Cheques. Also accepts V, MC. Open M-F 7:30-11:30am and 1:30-5:30pm, Sa 7:30-11:30am.

LOCAL SERVICES

English-Language Bookstore: Monument Books, 46 M.V. Preah Norodom (☎723 020). Good selection of English books on Cambodian politics and history. Open M-Sa 8am-7pm, Su 8am-noon and 2-5pm. V accepted. For second hand fiction, head to the **London Book Center,** 65 P. 240 (☎214 258).

English-Language Newspapers: The **Phnom Penh Post** (3500r) publishes long stories on current events bi-monthly. Includes a map of the city. **The Cambodia Daily** (1200r) offers harder-hitting coverage of daily Cambodian, regional, and international news.

EMERGENCY AND COMMUNICATIONS

Emergency: Police ☎117. **Medical** ☎119. Free from any orange phone.

Police: Bureau des Etrangers (Office of Foreign Affairs), P. 154 (☎226 847), off V. Pasteur/P. 151. Some English spoken. Come here with complaints, but in emergencies go immediately to your embassy. Open daily 7-11am and 2-5pm.

Pharmacies: A high percentage of drugs sold in Phnom Penh have expired or are flat-out fakes. **Pharmacie de la Gare,** 81 M.V. Preah Monivong (☎426 855), on the corner of Confederation de la Russie just before the train station, is the best in Phnom Penh. Some English spoken. Open M-Sa 7am-7pm, Su 7-11am.

Hospitals: Health care in Cambodia is well below international standards. **AEA International/SOS Assistance,** 161 P. 51 (24hr. ☎216 911), near P. 228, specializes in emergency care and will provide evacuation to Bangkok. Australian or Khmer-French doctor on-call 24hr. Open M-F 8:30am-5pm, Sa 8am-noon. **Tropical & Travelers Medical Clinic,** 88 P. 108 (☎366 802 or 012 898 981), specializes in travelers' needs. British doctor. Open M-F 8:30am-noon and 2-5pm, Sa 8am-noon.

CAMBODIA

Telephones: IDD calls can be made from Telstra phone booths at the GPO, the Ministry of Tourism, and outside many hotels on M.V. Preah Monivong. Phone cards sold at GPO and many hotels.

Internet Access: Mekong Cyber, 253 M.V. Preah Sisowath (☎012 888 788). **Friend Net,** 273 M.V. Preah Sisowath (☎216 225). US$3 per hr. There are also Internet cafes among the guest houses on Bœng Kak Lake, and some along M.V. Preah Monivong south of the New Market.

Post Office: GPO, on P. 13, at the intersection with P. 102 south of Wat Phnom. A large, yellow colonial building. Overseas calls, fax, telegram service. EMS mail available. Sells phone cards for local phone booths. *Poste Restante.* Open daily 7am-6pm.

Express Mail: DHL, 28 M.V. Preah Monivong (☎426 726), north past the intersection with Confederation de la Russie. Open M-F 8am-6pm, Sa 8am-5pm.

ACCOMMODATIONS

Guest houses (US$3-10) in Phnom Penh provide beds and a backpacker-friendly atmosphere. Hotels (US$10 and up) keep travelers cooler and cleaner, but many of them are nondescript. Prices and amenities are similar, so differing levels of cleanliness or noise can make or break a stay.

Narin Guest House No. 50, 50 P. 125 (☎213 657). Follow M.V. Preah Monivong from the city center, turn right at the Ministry of Tourism (P. 232), then left on P. 125. Good food (US$1-3) and clean rooms. Patio and balcony give guests a place to socialize. Organizes onward travel; taxis to Vietnam US$5 per person. Book rooms in advance. Singles US$3; doubles US$5, with bath US$6, with balcony US$7.

The Walkabout Hotel (☎851 787), on the corner of P. 51 and P. 174. Centrally-located with a security guard at the door, offers clean rooms, with bath and satellite TV. The lobby doubles as a popular bar. Doubles with fan US$8, with A/C US$12.

Cloud Nine (No. 9) Guest House, 9 P. 93. Head toward Bœng Kak Lake on M.V. Preah Monivong, then turn left on V. Moat Chrouk (P. 86). At the end of the street, just before the mosque, turn left and walk 500m; it's on the right. Loll in hammocks on the lakeside porch with fellow packers. TV and billiards. Rooms have mosquito nets. 10-bed dorm US$1; singles US$2, with bath US$3; doubles US$3/$4.

Capital Guest House and Restaurant, 14 P. 182 (☎364 104), on the corner, 1 block off M.V. Preah Monivong. One of the longest-standing backpacker institutions in Phnom Penh. Loud neighborhood. Good English spoken. Arranges visas to Vietnam and Laos. Singles US$3, with bath $4; doubles US$4/$5, with A/C US$10-12.

Royal Guest House, 91 P. 154 (☎854 806). Near the intersection with M.V. Preah Norodom. Location and wide range of room options make the few extra dollars worth it. Good English spoken. Arranges moto driver for US$3 per day. Reservations recommended. Singles with shared bath US$3. All other rooms with bath, fridge, and cable television. Singles US$8, with A/C and hot water US$10; doubles US$12.

The Last Home, 47 P. 108 (☎724 917). 2 blocks west of the Old Market. Cramped rooms have mosquito nets, desks, and small fans. Arranges buses to Sihanoukville (10,000r), boats to Siem Reap (US$22), and transportation to the airport (taxi US$5, moto US$2), from the Internet cafe downstairs. Call ahead. 4-bed dorms US$2; singles US$3, with bath US$4; doubles US$5, with A/C US$8.

Keov Mean Guest House, 1 V. Pasteur St. (☎723 067), near P. 51 between P. 118 and P. 126. Tidy rooms within 2 blocks of the New Market. Wrap-around balconies. Rooms have fan and bath (with decent water pressure!). Rooms US$6, with A/C US$10.

Pailin Hotel, 219 M.V. Preah Monivong (☎426 698), at the intersection with M.V. Charles de Gaulle. Away from the tourist hustle and bustle, but still centrally located. Good but pricey Thai restaurant. All rooms have A/C, cable TV, phones, mini-fridges, and baths. Singles US$20; doubles US$28.

FOOD

Dozens of restaurants worthy of exploration line **M.V. Preah Monivong** and **M.V. Samdech Preah Sihanouk.** Cheap and adventurous eats are at the markets. **Lucky Market Group** has two stores, one at 160 Samdech Preah Sihanouk (open daily 8am-8pm), and a large one in the Parkway Square complex, on M.V. Mao Tsé Toung, near the intersection with M.V. Preah Monivong (open M-F 9am-8:30pm, Sa-Su 9am-9pm). There's a wide selection of imported products. At 5:30pm, food stalls materialize near **Wat Koh** at the Independence Monument. More expensive and touristed restaurants line **M.V. Preah Sisowath,** north of the Royal Palace. Also try the restaurants over the **Chruoy Changvar** (Cambodian-Japanese Friendship bridge), northeast of the city. Of the restaurants in this area, **Boeng Meas** (on the left) has the best food, **Heng Lay** (on the right) has the best comedy act, and **Hang Neak** (farther down the strip on the right) has great decor and entertainment. Restaurants are open from 9am to 10pm. They start filling up on weekends after 8pm.

Phnom Khiev, 138 R.V. Samdech Preah Sihanouk, on the corner of P. 63. The intimate interior (with A/C) lends a gentle ambience. Typical Cambodian dishes and some French fare. Generous, inexpensive portions US$2-6. Cocktails, aperitifs, wine, and imported beer served. Open daily 7am-11pm.

Friends, The Restaurant, P.13, one block north of the National Museum, on the left. Cool and brightly-decorated, the cafe wins applauds, doubling as a program to fund employment for street children. Lemon-garlic fried squid US$1. Frozen margarita US$2.50. Helping a child (free). Open Tu-Sa 11am-9pm.

Globe Cafe and Restaurant, 389 M.V. Preah Sisowath, north of the Royal Palace. Good Western and Asian food US$3-8. Beautiful French building; terrace overlooking the river. Live music. Open daily 10am-3pm and 5-10pm. Bar open later.

Happy Herb's Pizza, 50m north of the FCCC (see **Nightlife,** below) on the river.

Restaurant Ponlok Special Soup, 319-323 Preah Sisowath. Balcony seating overlooks the river and catches the breeze at night. Excellent Chinese and Khmer fare, especially the shrimp dishes and sour soup. French and English menus with pictures. Dishes US$3-8. Open daily 10am-11pm.

La Terasse, on the corner of P. 262 and P. 51, one block west of the Victory Monument. Pricey French food, located in a colonial-style building, also serves food in the secluded garden. Enjoy a *croque monsieur* US$5. Open M-Sa 10am-6pm.

"KT" Khmer-Thai Restaurant, 15 P. 49, north of Wat Phnom. Very tasty, inexpensive Khmer and Thai food. Good *tom kha gai* (spicy Thai chicken and coconut milk soup) and grilled chicken US$3. Open daily 9am-11pm.

Mount Everest, 98 M.V. Samdech Preah Sihanouk, 500m west of the Independence Monument. Indian and Nepalese cuisine (mains around US$5). Open daily 9am-11pm.

SIGHTS

Phnom Penh is better for aimless exploration than scheduled sightseeing. There are few jaw-dropping tourist attractions, but some are more profound, deserving plenty of time and attention. Chief among these are the **Tuol Sleng Genocide Museum** and the **Killing Fields** at **Chœng Ek.** Guest houses arrange motorcycle drivers for the day (US$7, more for a trip to the Killing Fields). Many government tourist attractions close on Mondays, but a gratuity may open the doors.

TUOL SLENG GENOCIDE MUSEUM. At this former high school in a residential neighborhood of Southern Phnom Penh, the Khmer Rouge imprisoned and killed over 14,000 people. Only seven survived; the rest were sent to the Killing Fields of Choeng Ek. When the Vietnamese arrived in 1979, they found at Tuol Sleng a morbidly well-documented hell. The most telling memorial of the Khmer Rouge years, Tuol Sleng has been left as it was found in 1979. There are no velvet museum barricades—visitors walk through closet-sized detention cells and torture chambers freely. Many documents of torture are now displayed on the walls, including hundreds of photographs, taken of each victim upon arrival. *(On P. 103. Open Tu-Sa 7:30-11am and 2-5pm. $2 donation expected. Photography permitted.)*

CAMBODIA

CHŒNG EK "KILLING FIELDS". The killing fields were the final destination for more than 40,000 victims of Pol Pot's reign of terror. A *stupa* was erected in 1988; a glass case inside contains 17 levels of human skulls and bones from exhumed bodies. Bits of bone and cloth still come up from the earth. *(17km south of the city. Open Tu-Su 7am-5pm, though on M a donation might open the gates. Entry US$2.)*

WAT PHNOM. With its beautiful lawn and Buddhist statues, Wat Phnom is the most sacred sight in Phnom Penh. According to legend, an aristocrat named Lady Penh founded a monastery atop this hill to house Buddha statues that she had found inside a log. *Phnom* means hill—hence, Phnom Penh. *(On a hill north of the Old Market on M.V. Preah Norodom. Entry US$1.)*

ROYAL PALACE AND SILVER PAGODA COMPLEX. The Royal Palace is closed when the royal family is at home, but visitors can peek in the huge open windows of the throne hall. English-speaking guides or English programs orient and inform the visitor, as most of the artifacts and buildings are unlabeled. Along the walls of the Silver Pagoda complex, which occupies the southeast corner of the Royal Palace complex, frescoes portray scenes from the *Ramayana* and the palace in ancient times. A large *stupa* holds the ashes of King Ang Duong (reigned 1845-59). The pavilion beyond shelters a mighty statue of King Norodom on horseback and a footprint of the Buddha. At the center of the complex is the **Silver Pagoda,** which derives its name from the 5000 silver blocks covering the floor. An **emerald Buddha** dating from the 1600s surveys the room, fittingly named the Temple of the Emerald Buddha (Wat Phra Kaew). A Buddha statue in the likeness of King Norodom, made of gold and inlaid with thousands of diamonds, is also on display. *(Along M.V. Sothearos, south of Wat Ounalom. Open daily 8-11am and 2-5pm. US$3, camera fee US$2, video camera fee US$5.)*

NATIONAL MUSEUM OF ARTS. Designed by a French architect, the museum actually houses fine pre-Angkorian sculptures, as well as wooden and stone figures from the Angkor period. *(North of the Royal Palace along P. 13. Open Tu-Su 8-11am and 2-5:30pm. US$2.)*

OTHER SIGHTS. In the park at the intersection of Norodom and Sihanouk, the **Cambodia-Laos-Vietnam Monument** (the Liberation Monument) features a giant statue of three figures that commemorates the 1979 Vietnamese liberation of Cambodia.

Phnom Penh also has wats, though many were wrecked by the Khmer Rouge in the late 1970s. The remaining ones serve as schools and shelters for the poor and disabled; they are not designed for tourists. **Wat Ounalom,** on the corner of P. 154 and Preah Sisowath Quay, is the cornerstone of Cambodian Buddhism. **Wat Tuol Tum Pong,** on the corner of M.V. Mao Tsé Toung and P.155, just before the market, has budding linguists who greet visitors with enthusiastic "hellos." **Wat Koh,** on M.V. Preah Monivong, south of the New Market, has an English school.

ENTERTAINMENT

Check the calendar of *The Cambodia Daily's* Friday edition for cultural events.

The **Sovanna Phum Association,** 111 P. 360, near the Tuol Sleng Genocide Museum, performs dance and shadow-puppet shows. (☎012 846 020. Shows every 15 days. Tickets US$3.) The **Mekong Island Park,** intended as an "authentic showcase" of traditional Cambodian culture, hosts Khmer music and theater. Trips leave daily from the **Mekong Island Park Office,** 13 P. 240, at the corner of P. 19, returning at 3pm. Tickets include lunch, a visit to the zoo, an elephant ride, and a dance show. (☎016 851 1361. US$32; 4-person min.)

The easiest and cheapest way to observe Khmer music and dance is to visit the **Université Royale des Beaux-Arts,** on P. 70, off M.V. Preah Monivong, north of the French Embassy. Head north on M.V. Preah Monivong and turn left at the rotary, just beyond the Thai Embassy. The university is on the right. The faculty struggles to preserve Khmer art, which was eradicated during the Pol Pot years. Students learn the *apsara* dance, flute music, and scenes from the *Ramayana*. Unobtrusive foreigners are welcome. (Classes M-F 7-11am and Sa 8-11am.)

At sundown, locals head to the strip of decorated restaurants northeast of the city center, where cool river breezes accompany diverse menus and lively entertainment. Line-dancing Khmer and American pop-singing youngsters keep things upbeat, before local comedians take the stage; even if you don't enjoy dirty, slapstick comedy, the scene alone is truly unique and entertaining.

MARKETS

Phnom Penh supports more than seven markets, all of which are food havens. Most vendors set up at 6:30am and don't leave until 5pm. Markets are best visited during early morning. **Cobblers,** on P. 143, due west of the Tuol Sleng Genocide Museum, sell fine, custom-fit, all-leather shoes or sandals (US$10-40).

New Market (Psar Thmei). The hub of Phnom Penh, this large yellow structure is often referred to as "Central Market." The large art deco structure was built in the 1930s, but today the market has barely a third of the merchants it once housed. Generally has higher prices than the other markets. Purchase up-to-date maps, Angkor guides, and Khmer phrasebooks here.

Russian Market (Tuol Tom Pong Market), between P. 163 and P. 155, south of the wat of the same name. This market wins high marks for its beautiful silk, cotton print *sarongs*, *krama* (the combination scarf, headdress, and bathing suit), and wide selection of cheap pirated CDs.

Old Market (Psar Char), northeast of the New Market along P. 108 and P. 15. If you want to purchase silk by the yard, this is the place. The atmosphere is less touristy and the vendors are less pushy than in the other markets.

O Russei Market, on P. 182, between M.V. Charles de Gaulle and M.V. Preah Monivong. This large market is housed in a new, indoor facility and sells electronics.

Wat Tan Handicrafts, 206a M.V. Preah Norodom, next to the Royal Air Cambodge Office. Wat Tan trains students in tailoring, weaving, and carpentry as part of an effort to aid the thousands of men and women disabled by landmines and polio. The fruits of their labor are sold at the Wat Than showroom. Items include silk pillows, clothing, and pocketbooks. Tailor-made outfits specially-ordered. Open M-Sa 7:30am-5:30pm.

NIGHTLIFE

Popular bars and cafes, such as **The Globe** and **La Croissette,** line **Preah Sisowath**—the Globe has live music. Earthier pubs, such as the **Irish Rover** and the **Ettamogah Pub,** are on **M.V. Samdech Preah Sihanouk,** between the Independence Monument and M.V. Preah Monivong. Be careful at night—tourists have been mugged.

Heart of Darkness Bar, 26 P. 51, near the corner of P. 174. Red-lit bamboo and Angkor-inspired decor, good music and ambience. The expat/backpacker bar *par excellence*. Inexpensive beer and mixed drinks US$1-3. Open daily 8pm-sunrise.

Foreign Correspondents Club of Cambodia (FCCC), 363 Sisowath Quay (☎724 014), on the river north of the Royal Palace. Mission-style furniture on a terrace overlooking the Tonle Sap River. Western menu, pool table. Imported beers, mixed drinks, and restaurant. A bit pricey, but great scenery. Happy hour 5-7pm. Open daily 7am-midnight.

Martini Pub, on M.V. Mao Tsé Toung, next to the giant Hotel Inter-Continental. Not so pub-like, but oddly more like an outdoor dance club out of an episode of *Star Wars*. Dancing gets going around 11pm. Beam me to the beer garden to watch the giant video screen in the late-night heat. Open M-Th 7pm-2am, F-Sa 7pm-sunrise.

Manhattan Club, on P. 84, just east of M.V. Preah Monivong and Calmette Hospital. Part of the Holiday International Hotel. One of the best dance clubs in Phnom Penh with an interesting, high-rolling Asian clientele. Buy beer at the street stalls outside. Otherwise, it's US$6 a drink. Dancing gets going around 11pm, and goes on until dawn.

DAYTRIPS FROM PHNOM PENH

UDONG

The city bus from Phnom Penh has the cheapest rate to Udong. Buses leave from the bus station at the New Market (every 45min. 6:30am-6:30pm, 2500r) for the village of Udong; from there, it is a cycle ride (2000r) to the temples. Capitol Travel at the Capitol Guest House in Phnom Penh offers an A/C bus to Udong daily (US$5, 9am, 4-person min.). Alternatively, a cycle can be chartered round-trip for US$8. Get there early, as the hill tends to simmer even when the surrounding countryside basks in a picnicker-friendly breeze.

Udong, Cambodia's capital from 1618 to 1866, sits 45km northwest of Phnom Penh; a daytrip there makes for a quiet respite from the city's hubbub. The site sees few tourists, though Phnom Penhois pour in for weekend picnics.

The **twin hills of Udong** are visible from miles away; one bristles with temples and *stupas*. From the parking lot/picnic area at the hill's base, the road on the extreme left leads to a mosque and temple, both of which suffered greatly in the civil war. From there, paths lead to countless vistas and *stupas*.

Phnom Tamao is a wildlife center and zoological preserve near Tonle Bati, a small lake south of the city (see **Other Sights,** below). Monkeys, tigers, birds, and bears are caged in the setting of lush jungles, except during the dry season. (US$1.)

PHNOM CHISSOR

Phnom Chissor is 22km from Phnom Tamao. The turn-off is on the left beyond the school. From there, a dusty dirt track winds 6km through a small village and past lush rice fields to the foot of the hill. Inquire at most guest houses for a tour or hire a moto.

Phnom Chissor temple rises high above the flat plains of Takeo Province. The kings had elephants, but visitors must now walk up more than 500 steps to get there. Built in 1150 of laterite and sandstone, the temple was a regular stop on the god-king pilgrimage circuit. The central sanctuary houses the original reclining Buddha statue. To protect it from thieves, the monks have concealed it behind newer images. The original can be viewed only by climbing back into the tiny sanctuary with a candle and a 500r tip.

Facing east, in line with Phnom Chissor, stand two laterite gates, **Sen Thomol** and **Sen Ravang.** On the way to Phnom Chissor, the Brahman priests would bathe in Tonle Oun, the lake in front of the first gate. The original steps leading down to the gates are still visible. Tragically, the temple was nearly destroyed by US bombers in 1973. The modern pagoda next to the ruins houses a valuable statue of the Buddha. Resourceful monks painted the stone statue silver to guard against art thieves—it is the fat one in the center surrounded by other more modern images.

ALONG RTE. 2

There are several worthwhile sights near the capital, each of which can be visited on a half-day excursion. The easiest way to reach them is by motorcycle or car; most drivers charge tourists about US$10-15.

Ta Phrom temple is 32km south of Phnom Penh along Rte. 2. The turn-off is on the right; look for a gate with three large Angkor-inspired towers. The first Phrom temple was constructed in the 7th century. The current one, built of laterite and sandstone in the Bayon style, is believed to have been erected during the rule of Jayavarman VII (1191-1218). Originally constructed as a Brahmanic temple, it was later reconsecrated to Buddhism. Nearby, **Yeah Peau** temple is also worth a peak.

The nearby lake of **Tonle Bati** is a popular weekend retreat for urbanites. For a few thousand riel, small, thatched-roof, waterfront shacks can be rented. Vendors offer beer, fried chicken, cold drinks, fruit, and young coconut juice out of the shell.

SIHANOUKVILLE ☎034

All but destroyed during the Pol Pot years, Sihanoukville was rebuilt with Soviet aid. Now, as the country's only deep-water port, this city of 30,000 may be a key to the kingdom's economic survival. Tourism has been on the rise in recent years, but while the number of hotels in the town has grown, the beaches remain largely deserted. Hang up the rucksack and take it easy for a couple of days—as if you hadn't been doing that already.

TRANSPORTATION

Buses: Guest houses and hotels can arrange bus tickets to **Phnom Penh.** 3 bus companies, all along V. Ekareach, go to Phnom Penh: **D.H. Cambodia,** east of the city center (7:30am, 12:30pm; 12,000r); **GST Express** (☎012 820 559), next to Chaok Sakor Hotel (3½hr., 4 per day 7:15am-1:30pm, 10,000r); **Ho Wah Genting Transport Co. Ltd.** (☎933 888), next to the Cambodian Commercial Bank (4hr., 5 per day 7:10am-2pm, 12,000r). Arrive 15min. early.

Ferries: Look for signs saying "Port of Passenger Ship" at the ferry dock north of Sihanoukville, off of Hun Sen Beach Dr. Take the boat to **Koh Kong** (3½-4hr., daily noon, US$15), where smaller boats run to the **Thai border** (10min., 100฿).

Local Transportation: Motorcycle taxis cost 1000-2500r, depending on distance. Arrange early morning transport in advance. Hire a **taxi** at the **Central Market** (Psar Loer). To **Phnom Penh** US$30. Night travel not recommended.

Rentals: For the bad boy in all of us, uncrowded roads make Sihanoukville an ideal place to rent **motorbikes.** Check your guest house or go to the GST and D.H. bus stations. Most places charge US$5 per day.

ORIENTATION AND PRACTICAL INFORMATION

The town is spread thinly over hills, with long stretches of road between it and the beaches. The town's main thoroughfare is **V. Ekareach,** which runs east-west from **Victory Beach** to the city center (2km) and then elbows south to the **Golden Lion Traffic Circle** (1½km). The main beach road, **2 Thnou St.,** follows the coast past **Independence** and **Sokha Beaches. Ochheuteal Beach** lies to the south of the Golden Lion Traffic Circle. The most popular guest houses and the main **post office** are near Victory Beach. The *Sihanoukville Visitors Guide*, published yearly and available in restaurants and hotels, includes a map. **Mekong Bank,** on V. Ekareach in the center of town, offers Visa cash advances (US$5 min.), and changes traveler's checks. (☎933 867. Open M-F 8:30am-4pm, Sa 8:30am-midday.) The **Central Market (Psar**

Loer) is a raucous night market near the Okinawa Thmey Hotel. (Open daily 5am-6pm.) Other services include the **police,** on V. Ekareach at the top of the hill 1km west of city center and the **Chuen Min Hospital** (☎933 111), on V. Ekareach near the city center. **International calls** can be made at the **Local Center** on V. Ekareach 50m west of the intersection with V. Sophakmongkol. **Open 24hr.** The post office is in building across the street from the market on 7 Makara. (Open M-F 7am-6pm.)

ACCOMMODATIONS

MASH & Melting Pot (☎012 924 205), on Weather Station hill above Victory Beach. From the red scooter above the entrance to the individually decorated rooms in the MASH section, this guest house is characterized by its idiosyncratic charm. Includes the 'Melting Pot,' a restaurant serving Western and Indian food, a bar, and a library of books about Cambodia and Southeast Asia. All rooms with bath. MASH section 1-2 person US$3-4; Melting Pot section US$4-6.

Mealy Chenda Guest House (☎933 472), on a bluff above Victory Beach. A brand-new backpacker friendly haven with open-air balcony and restaurant with a great view. Moto rental $4 per day. 3-bed dorms with shared bath US$2; singles with shared bath US$3; spacious singles/doubles with bath US$5-6, with balcony US$7-8.

Chuck's Other Place (☎012 854 309), on 'Serendipity Beach' west of Ochheutal Beach. Follow the signs from the Golden Lion Traffic Circle. Situated on the edge of the sand, this simple guest house features a 24hr. bar/restaurant complete with pool tables. All rooms with shared bath and squat toilet. Singles US$3; doubles US$5.

FOOD

Sihanoukville has excellent seafood, especially shrimp and crab. Most guest houses sport wide selections of food but the intrepid can feast at the **night market.** Food stalls line **V. Ekareach.** (Open daily 6-11pm.) **Les Feuilles Restaurant,** 400m east of the Golden Lion Traffic Circle on Kanda 1 St., serves excellent French, Western, and Khmer food. Great *Luk-Lak* US$5. (Open daily 7am-9pm.) **Chez Claude Restaurant,** off 2 Thnou St. on a ridge high above Sokha Beach, has a beautiful view and fantastic Asian and French cuisine. It's a perfect place to catch sunset over the Gulf of Thailand. (Entrees US$5-10.)

SIGHTS AND ENTERTAINMENT

Sihanoukville's big draw are the many stretches of sugary sand that surround the town. A few other sights, however, are worth a look. Atop the 132m high Sihanoukville Mountain, the town's wat overlooks a stunning panorama of land and seascape. The best place for a view is several hundred meters past the temple. Head east on National Rte. 4 (towards Phnom Penh), turn right at the Cambrew Brewery (home of Angkor Beer; open M-Th), and follow the dirt road up the ridge. About an hour by moto outside of the town is a waterfall that is a popular bathing spot. Moto drivers will do the round-trip for US$4. Angkor Arms Pub, on V. Ekareach near the city center, is a self-proclaimed traditional British pub and a Sihanoukville institution offering beer, darts, and a restaurant. (Open daily 4pm-midnight or whenever the last person leaves.)

BEACHES

At the southeastern end of the peninsula is **Ochheuteal Beach**—long, uncrowded, and backed by some of Sihanoukville's nicest hotels. Farther west is **Independence Beach,** which has clear water and few hawkers. There is great boulder-hopping on the rocky shorelines between beaches. **Sokha Beach,** back to the east a bit, is the most popular beach. Throngs of vendors sell snacks and fresh coconuts (1000r) here, and inner tubes can be rented. **Victory Beach,** just south of the Port of Sihanoukville, has little to speak of. Get a motorbike there for 2500r.

UP THE MEKONG

KOMPONG CHAM ☎042

Kompong Cham is the first major stop for travelers heading up the Mekong from Phnom Penh and an important transit point to the east of the country. With the Lao border opening north of Stung Treng and the scheduled 2002 completion of the gargantuan bridge now under construction, tourists are sure to follow. For now, though, Kompong Cham feels nothing like the third-largest city in Cambodia. One of the easiest to explore of the country's 22 provincial capitals, Kompong Cham's friendly residents easily merit a drowsy day of strolling the streets.

TRANSPORTATION. The road from Phnom Penh to Kompong Cham is in excellent condition. **Buses** leave from near **Phnom Penh's** New Market twice a day (3hr.; 10am, 1pm; 5000r). The road to **Kratie** is hellish. It's also plagued by bandits. Those willing to brave the northern roads catch a pickup from Kompong Cham's market (7-9hr.; 7am; 25,000r inside, 15,000r outside).

Travel by **boat** north to Kratie is preferable (fast boat 3hr.; 7, 9:30am, 1pm; 20,000r; slow boat 4hr., check at dock for schedule, 10,000r). Boats are also an excellent option between **Phnom Penh** and Kompong Cham (fast boat 2½hr., 7am, 10,000r; slow boat 3hr., 8am, 6000r).

ORIENTATION. Kompong Cham sits on the west bank of the Mekong River, 120km northeast of Phnom Penh. Fast boats from Phnom Penh and Kratie dock opposite the imposing Mekong Hotel, on **Preas Bat Sihanouk,** the riverside road. Just south of the Mekong Hotel, Sihanouk supports a string of guest houses and intersects **Rue Pasteur,** which runs inland past the police station. Heading north from the Mekong Hotel, Sihanouk bends inland to a six-way intersection, abutting the market, also a bus stop. One block north, **Kosamak Neary Roth** runs inland through a major traffic circle to the governor's mansion.

PRACTICAL INFORMATION. The **tourist office,** in front of the governor's mansion on Kosamak Neary Rath, is eager to help but is low on resources. (Open M-F 8-11am and 2-4pm.) **Canadia Bank** will exchange currency and cash traveler's checks, but will not take credit cards. (Open M-F 8:30am-3:30pm.) A **standard pro-**

THE TIDES THEY ARE A CHANGING Every year between July and October, a strange natural phenomenon plays itself out between the banks of the Tonle Sap River. During these months the current of the river is reversed—the waters actually flow away from the ocean into Tonle Sap (The Great Lake). The sheer volume of the melted snows descending from the Himalayas overflows the Mekong River. The backlog turns the waters of the Tonle Sap River upon themselves. This reversal of fortune has had significant consequences in both contemporary and ancient Cambodia. During the months of the reversed current, Tonle Sap more than doubles in size, creating the world's most fertile fishing grounds. A thousand years ago, the alternating current came in handy for transporting raw material to the Angkor monument. The reversal enabled builders to float in sandstone blocks from Phnom Kulen, almost 40km away. The Tonle Sap's reversal explains why the Mekong Delta in south Vietnam rarely floods; the lake serves as a massive overflow pool, absorbing excess water that might otherwise wreak havoc on low-lying towns. Sadly, this hydraulic wonder is threatened by deforestation and damming upriver in Laos and Thailand.

vincial market sits next to the six-way intersection of Preas Bat Sihanouk. Here you can buy fine *kramas* (the traditional checkered scarves found everywhere around Cambodia). The **police,** on Rue Pasteur one block from the river, speak no English. The **Kompong Cham Provincial Hospital** runs a bare-bones operation on Rue Pasteur, one block from the river. The **post office** is on Khemarak Pumin, one block north of Osamak Neary Rath. (Open M-F 7-11am and 2-5pm.) **Long distance calls** can be made from shops around the city, including some on Rue Jayavarman VII, one block north of the police station. Most international calls are US$3 per min. (Open daily 7am-9pm, the "24hr." sign notwithstanding.)

ACCOMMODATIONS. Cheap guest houses line Preas Bat Sihanouk south of the dock. Bridge construction begins to shake the town before 6am; moving upriver or inland may help a bit. The **Sengly Thmei Guest House** (☎ 012 915 122), on Preas Bat Sihanouk, is one block south of the dock. Rooms are small but have high ceilings and clean bathrooms (US$3 ; US$1 extra for use of a TV). The **Bophear Guest House,** just behind the Mekong Hotel on the left of the dock, has a helpful staff and tidy doubles with bathrooms for US$4. A little down the river from the Mekong Hotel, the **Chumnor Tonle Guest House** provides the most room for your riel, but the staff speaks little English. (Singles US$3, with TV US$4; doubles with TV US$5, with A/C US$9.) A glut of rooms in Kompong Cham means classy hotel-style accommodations come cheap; the **Mittapheap Hotel,** across the traffic circle from Canadia Bank, has flush toilets and rooms with fans for US$5 (with A/C US$10).

CAMBODIA

FOOD. Along the river, many vendors sell pots of food for 2000r, including steamed rice. More formal restaurants are scarce. One quality eatery is **Hoa An,** four blocks inland on Rue Pasteur. This local institution serves up Chinese and Khmer food with lots of beer. (Fried rice with pork sausage and egg 6500r. Large Angkor beer 5500r. Open daily 6am-8:30pm.)

SIGHTS AND ENTERTAINMENT. Wat Nokor, an 11th-century sandstone and laterite Buddhist temple, claims top billing in Kompong Cham, which is not saying much. The ruins contain an active temple in raucous neon 2km west of town. From the road to Phnom Penh, take a left at the traffic circle or hire a moto driver (US$1). **Phnom Pros** and **Phnom Sray** (Man Hill and Woman Hill) are 5km farther toward Phnom Penh. The former houses a clan of hungry monkeys, and the latter's vista is worthwhile. A moto-trip costs US$2 round-trip.

Nightlife is not one of Kompong Cham's strong points. Only the **Phnom Prosh Nightclub** in the hotel of the same name even pretends to be a spot for nighttime entertainment. A far more entertaining option is simply to stroll around the city and be a foreigner; you will likely draw stares and excitement. There is a good table tennis set up in Rue Pasteur's first block from the river, on the left; quality play is not hard to find.

KRATIE

Kratie (KRA-cheh) is an unassuming provincial capital along the Mekong. It would deserve little attention, were it not the best place in the world to see the brandishing of blowholes and hear the exclamations from the majestic and rare Irrawaddy dolphin. For this and for the glory of the sunset over the river, Kratie is a worthy breakpoint to any journey, or even a destination in its own right.

TRANSPORTATION. Road travel around Kratie is no fun. Due to bandits, the roads south to **Kompong Cham** and north to **Stung Treng** are some of the most dangerous in the country. Nevertheless, **pickups** travel these roads north to Stung Treng (6-8hr.; 7am; 20,000r inside, 15,000r outside) and south to Kompong Cham (7-9hr.; 7am; 25,000r inside, 15,000r outside). Boats are a much friendlier mode of

TRAVEL ON THE RIVER With the opening to foreigners of the Cambodia-Laos border at Don Khong, travel on the Cambodian Mekong has acquired a purpose other than sunbathing. Indeed, there are few better ways to start the day than atop a ferry watching the Mekong slide by. However, not all Cambodian ferries are created equal. All fast boats are Malaysian-made. **Khemara** runs the tightest ship, complete with luxuriantly existent emergency exits and plenty of leg room, as well as the flattest, most buttock-friendly roof. **Rambo** has the oldest, smallest, and creakiest fast boats. Phnom Penh's other ferry outfits fall in-between these two extremes. Companies alternate days and routes, so ask guest house owners for details. So-called slow boats are Cambodian-made, and have no need for emergency exits, as they have no windowpanes. Security and safety on slow boats is suspect; they should only be taken where fast boats fear to tread. Boats leave all piers at 7am.

transportation. From July to January, **fast boats** speed north to Stung Treng (4hr.; 7am, 12:30pm; 30,000r). Cambodian-made **slow boats** make the journey year-round (6hr.; 7am, 12:30pm; 30,000r).

ORIENTATION AND PRACTICAL INFORMATION. Kratie dozes on the east bank of the Mekong, northeast of Kompong Cham and Phnom Penh. Navigation couldn't be easier. Kratie's two main streets run parallel to the river, **V. Preah Sura Marit** along the bank and **V. Samdech Preah Sihanouk** one block back. Streets numbered from north to south, with the town's center situated between Rue 7 and Rue 10, intersect these two roads. The **market** is on Sihanouk between Rue 8 and Rue 10, and the **post office** (open M-F 7-11am and 2-5pm) sits between the two main streets on Rue 12.

ACCOMMODATIONS AND FOOD. A profusion of cheap rooms graces P. Sihanouk near the market. Most guest house owners speak little English. **Nyta Guest House,** on Preah Sihanouk just south of Rue 10, is Kratie's best value. Its spotless rooms boast private toilets. (All rooms 10,000r.) At **Hy Heng Guest House,** just up Sihanouk from the market behind a beauty parlor, absurdly low hallways lead to bright and airy rooms. (All bathrooms shared. Singles US$2; doubles US$3.) The owners of the **Star Guest House** on Sihanouk and Rue 10 speak excellent English, and the rooms are modern and clean. However, the volume at the karaoke bars next door rises at an early hour. (Rooms with private bath US$4, with TV$5.) The guest house next door, **Vimean Tip Guest House,** has little to offer other than rock-bottom prices. (third floor rooms 5000r; lower rooms 7000r.)

Market food is exceptionally cheap in Kratie. The standard market meal costs 1500r; most of the town shows up to partake. Should you require a more formal setting, the **Mekong Restaurant,** on Rue 9, has attentive service, a host of local patrons, and quality french fries (fried chicken and chips 6000r). Between is **Apsara Restaurant,** on Sihanouk and Rue 7, where the attached guest house actually takes a back seat to the excellent local cuisine downstairs. The "boiled sea alga (moss)" for 4000r is a lot like a heartier *miso* soup.

SIGHTS. The only sight in town isn't even in town, but it's well worth seeing. The best place in Cambodia to see endangered **Irrawaddy dolphins** is 15km north of Kratie. Hundreds more survive in Laos (see p. 365). Confined to a stretch of the Mekong where the water is deep, the animals' size and stateliness invite wonder. Any moto driver in town can take you to the dolphin-viewing pavilion (US$2). Once there, a friendly boatman will pole you out on the river for a closer look (US$1).

STUNG TRENG

Stung Treng is a tiny town on the San River, just off the Mekong, that unfortunately constitutes a near-necessary overnight stop for those heading north to Laos or east to Rattanakiri. Perhaps the opening of the Lao border will spur a growth in Stung Treng's tourist attractions and infrastructure. Right now, though, one night here is plenty for most travelers.

From July to January, **express boats** reach Stung Treng from **Phnom Penh** (10hr., 7am, 60,000r). **Slow boats** run between **Kratie** and Stung Treng year-round (6hr., 7am, 30,000r). Roads around Stung Treng are extremely shoddy, though construction of a decent road to Rattanakiri is rumored to begin in August 2000. For now, **four-wheel-drive** vehicles spend most of their time in the jungle, rather than the roads. They leave and arrive from just in front of the dock (7-9hr, 7am, 30,000r). **Pickups** also traverse the bandit-plagued and pothole-cursed rut from Kratie (6-8hr.; 7am from Kratie; 20,000r inside, 15,000r outside). **Planes** fly into the airport 6km north of the town from **Phnom Penh** (45min.; 4-5 per week, 10am; one-way US$45, round-trip US$85) and **Rattanakiri** (25min.; W 11:30am; one-way US$30, round-trip US$45). **President Airlines** (☎074 973 790, in the Sok Sombat Hotel next to the market), and **Phnom Penh Airlines** (☎074 973 963; open daily 7am-5pm) alternate days of service.

The only budget accommodation in town is the **Amatak Guest House** opposite the docks, where basic rooms with mosquito nets and fans go for 10,000r. The genial owner is in charge of immigration and can help those headed to Laos. The other option is the overpriced **Sok Sombat Hotel** on the north side of the market. The lobby is gloomy, but rooms are standard hotel affairs. (Rooms with flush toilet US$8, with TV US$10, with A/C US$20.) Eating options are confined to the choose-and-chomp at the small but busy **market** one block behind the Amatak Guest House (2000r).

CAMBODIA

BORDER CROSSING: STUNG TRENG/DON KHONG. This crossing opened recently and is currently in a state of flux; check in Phnom Penh or Vientiane for the latest information. As of August 2000, to pass into Laos on the Mekong River from Stung Treng, travelers had to obtain a Lao visa in Phnom Penh and also pay a fee of US$30 at the border. **Slow boats** head north from Stung Treng every morning (4-5hr., 7am, 25,000r), while **speedboats** make the trip as well (2½hr., US$10). Ask the owner of the Amatak Guest House in Stung Treng for details.

BAN LUNG ☎075

Far removed from the bustle of Phnom Penh, Rattanakiri province is defined by its countryside, dusty clay roads, and populations of fiercely independent minorities, who make up over three-quarters of the inhabitants. Isolated in the mountainous northeast border with Laos and Vietnam, the people of the region have resisted lowland hegemony for centuries. Even the Khmer Rouge largely left the ethnic minorities to their own devices. Consequently, Rattanakiri remains perhaps Cambodia's safest region. Since 1986, when Ban Lung was made the provincial capital, increasing numbers of Khmer, Vietnamese, and Chinese have migrated here, but a vibrant mix of Jarai, Krung, and Tumpuon people continue to dwell in small, insular communities and farms.

ORIENTATION AND PRACTICAL INFORMATION. With only one main road, finding one's way around Ban Lung isn't difficult. The dirt strip **airfield** is 400m south of town. Heading north on the airport road brings you to the intersection with **Route 19,** Ban Lung's wide artery, which runs east-west through town and on to the Vietnamese border only 70km away. A right turn leads to town. Another right at the *naga* pillars leads past a **police station** and Ban Lung's utilitarian **market,** where pickups leave for Stung Treng (7-9hr., 7am, 30,000r). The road also passes the **President Airlines office** (open daily 7am-noon and 2-5pm), which offers three flights per week to Phnom Penh (Tu, Th, Sa 11:55am; one-way US$55, round-trip US$105). **Phnom Penh Airlines,** to the left of the market (open daily 7am-noon and 2-5pm) offers slightly cheaper flights the other days (Su, M, W, F in the late morning; one-way US$51, round-trip US$101). All flights must be reconfirmed, and departures can change without formal notice. A few stands at the front of the market sell a meager assortment of hill tribe handicrafts. **Rattanakiri Provincial Hospital** is 2km north of the airport road-Rte. 19 intersection; it's not for the faint of heart. The **post office** (open daily 7:30-11am and 2-5pm) is 1km east of the *naga* pillar, next to the **telecommunications office** (☎974 006; open daily 7:30-11am and 2-5pm), which has no international service.

ACCOMMODATIONS AND FOOD. Some shrewd bargaining can cause prices to plunge from March to June. The **Mountain Guest House** (☎974 047), Ban Lung's best accommodation, is on the airport road 400m north of Rte. 19. The Chinese owners speak several languages. Plates of fruit mysteriously appear as you lounge on the veranda. Large rooms with double beds, fans, and shared baths are US$5. **Ban Lung Guest House I,** left of the road heading from the Naga to the market, has the ideal price and location. (☎974 137. Basic rooms with double beds, fans, and shared baths are just US$3.) Larger and more motel-like, the **Ban Lung Guest House** (☎974 066) is just 100m from the airport toward Rte. 19. (Clean rooms with private flush toilet and shower US$5, with A/C US$10.) Hidden among the vegetation, the **Restaurant Rattanakiri,** west of the airport road-Rte. 19 intersection and known as American Restaurant, is bound to be a highlight of any visit. Locally renowned Cambodian pizza costs 4000r. (Open daily 7am-10pm.)

SIGHTS. There is little to see in Ban Lung proper. About 2km west of the airport road intersection on Rte. 19 is **Wat Phnom Suay.** At the top of Phnom Suay, 1km beyond the temple along the dirt path that runs through the temple grounds, is a large statue of the **Sleeping Buddha.** The Enlightened One's view from the top, with the jagged peaks of the Central Highlands in the distance, is magnificent, especially at sunset. **Yak Lom Lake,** a magical little crater lake, is 4km east on Rte. 19. The water is quite clear and the swimming excellent. To get there, head east on Rte. 19 past several rubber plantations. After 2km, there's a roundabout topped with statues of hill tribesmen. Take a right here, and the lake is 1½km farther, past a hill tribe village. It makes a nice walk, if the weather cooperates.

DAYTRIPS FROM BAN LUNG. Many travelers use Ban Lung merely as a base camp from which to see the province's attractions, both anthropological and ecological. The region is a patchwork of highland minorities, many of whom continue to live as they have for millennia in small, isolated communities. Indeed, during the rainy season, many villages may be largely, if not completely, deserted. At this time families head off into the forest to clear and cultivate mountain rice, their staple crop.

DEATH IN THE JUNGLE In July 1999, goons in Kratie province decided to rob Khmer cigarette importers in Rattanakiri on Rte. 19, a trade artery from Vietnam. The plan hit a snag when the bandits got hopelessly lost in the jungles in Ou Ya Dau district, in southeast Rattanakiri. Unfazed, they kidnapped a large group of Jarai villagers and asked them for directions. The Jarai, who spoke only tribal languages, shrugged in incomprehension. The bandits grew surlier by the hour, and began slicing Jarai throats one-by-one. Police soon gave chase, having been clued in by escaped Jarai. The chase ended in a mining town in the west, where the bandits were apprehended. Hill tribe justice took its course; the lives of the 13 slain Jarai were avenged with 9 bandit executions, including a mob lynching in which villagers, armed with bamboo poles and their bare hands, beat a bandit to a mash.

Since roads are unmarked and the villages are frequently hidden from main roads, the best way to see the countryside is to hire a motorcycle and driver in Ban Lung (US$10 per day; inquire at the Mountain Guest House). Several **Krung villages** lie west of town. A typical settlement consists of a meeting house, a "groom house" where young men sleep, and family dwellings. There are three **waterfalls** off the main road, the most impressive of which is **Seven Waterfalls,** near the village of Jum Rum Bay S'rop, 35km south of Ban Lung.

Thirty kilometers northwest of Ban Lung is **Voeun District.** The tiny town is the gateway to **Virachay National Park,** which is still largely unexplored and may hold tigers, elephants, and kouprey. Ask at the ranger station in Voeun Sai for details. To get to Voeun Sai, hire a motorcycle for the 1½hr. ride in Ban Lung (US$7) or catch the 6am minibus (4000r) or slightly earlier but slower jeep (3000r) from the marketplace on selected days; ask at guest houses (return trips at 8am and 3pm).

East on the road to Vietnam is **Bokeo District,** home to several Lao and hill tribe villages, a waterfall, and several **sapphire mines.** About 30km south of Ban Lung stands the small town of **Lumphat,** famed for its **gold mines.** Unfortunately, the town was bombed heavily by the US in covert operations from 1970-75. It is past its heyday, doesn't have any guest houses, and is not as safe as the rest of the province. Foreigners should exercise caution while visiting mines.

A truck leaves the Ban Lung market for Bokeo every Sunday and Thursday at 6am (8000r). The Bokeo Guest House next to the market offers rooms for US$2.

NORTHERN CAMBODIA

SIEM REAP ☎063

Functioning chiefly as a gateway to the nearby temples of Angkor and spurred by improved safety in the region, the little dusty city of Siem Reap is starting to attract more travelers. Driving through the outskirts of town is like taking a tour through the five-star resorts of tomorrow. Package tours have yet to really hit this town, and from secluded waterfalls decorated with Angkorian carvings to isolated temples, there remain hidden secrets that the traveler can explore in peace.

TRANSPORTATION

The **airport** is 8km northwest of town off Rte. 6. International departure tax is US$20 and domestic is US$4. Visas are available on arrival (US$70, passport photo required). **Bangkok Airways,** 571 Rte. 6 (☎380 191), near Royal Air Cambodge. (Open daily 8am-4:30pm) flies to **Bangkok** (5 per day, reduced service in low season, US$155). **Royal Air Cambodge,** 362 Rte. 6 (☎963 422), next to Diethelm Travel, 1km west of the intersection with V. Sivatha (open daily 7:15-11:30am and 1:30-5:30pm) flies to **Bangkok** (10:15am, no flights July 15-Aug. 15, US$140) and **Phnom Penh** (8:10am, 8pm; US$61). **Vietnam Airlines,** 108 Route 6 (☎063 964 488), flies to **Ho Chi Minh City** (9:30am, 1:15, 6:15pm; US$100). **Motos** (US$2) and **taxis** (US$5) swarm outside the airport entrance to whisk travelers away. Most guest houses organize taxis and buses to **Angkor** (US$2-3), **Phnom Penh** (10hr., US$9), and **Thailand** (7hr., US$56).

ORIENTATION AND PRACTICAL INFORMATION

Siem Reap can be navigated by foot, but the heat and unlabeled streets make traveling by moto preferable. **Rte. 6** cuts through the north part of town, running east to the **New Market** and west to the **airport.** Those arriving by boat will follow a road heading north from Tonle Sap. The road forks into **V. Sivatha** on the left and the **West Bank River Road** on the right. V. Sivatha traces the west edge of town, intersecting Rte. 6 in a flurry of guest house signs. North of its intersection with Rte. 6,

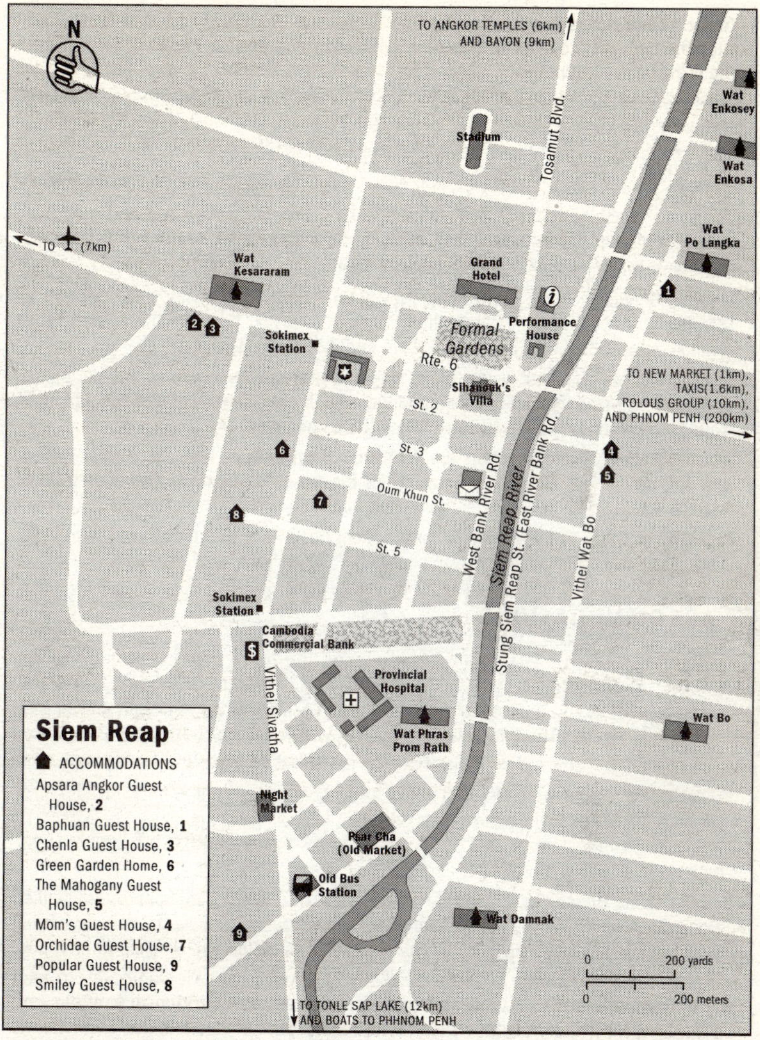

the West Bank River Road runs past the traffic circle and the Grand Hotel, and on to Angkor, 7km away. Running north-south, the **Siem Reap River** traces the east edge of town, with roads lining both banks. The dirt road parallel to the east bank road is **V. Wat Bo,** home to several popular guest houses. The best source of information about Siem Reap is the indispensable and free *Angkor Guide*, available in guest houses, hotels, and restaurants. Inside is a color map of the town and temples complex.

Tourist Office: Opposite the Grand Hotel on the road to Angkor. Not very useful for travelers but is a base for guides leading tours to the temples. Maps of Angkor and Siem Reap. Sells temple passes (1-day US$20, 3-day US$40, 1-week US$60). Motorcycle with driver US$8 per day. A/C car with driver US$20 per day. Licensed guides US$20 per day. Open M-F 7:30-11am and 2-3pm, Sa 7:30-11am, but the office is often closed as the employees double as guides.

Tours: Airline Ticket Services (☎011 630 808), on V. Sivatha just north of Cambodian Commercial Bank. Flights to **Bangkok** (US$140) and **Phnom Penh** (US$60). Open daily 7:30am-10:30pm.

Currency Exchange: US$ and Thai฿ are accepted everywhere. **Cambodian Commercial Bank** (☎964 392), south of Hotel de la Paix on V. Sivatha, exchanges traveler's checks (2% commission). MC/V cash advances. Open M-F 8am-3pm.

Markets: New Market *(Psar Leu)*, 1km east of town on Rte. 6. The touristy **Old Market** *(Psar Cha)* is at the southern end of the west bank river road.

Police: Foreigner Office (☎012 893 297), on the corner of Rte. 6 and V. Sivatha.

Pharmacies: Many located around the town center.

Medical Services: Rustic **Siem Reap Provincial Hospital,** down the side street off V. Sivatha that veers east at Cambodian Commercial Bank; opposite the Apsara Tours branch office. Doctors on call M-F 7-11am and 2-5pm, Sa 6am-noon.

Telephones: The cheapest way to place **international calls** is to use an Internet phone in one of the many Internet cafes around town. For those attached to traditional phones (and their privacy), head to the post office (US$5 per min.).

Internet Access: Internet centers are springing up everywhere. US$2-3 per hr. A pleasant A/C option is **E Cafe Siem Reap,** 147B Sivatha Blvd., opposite Cambodian Commercial Bank. US$2 per hr. Open daily 7am-9pm.

Post Office: GPO, on the west bank of the Siem Reap River 500m north of the market. EMS mail service. *Poste Restante.* Open daily 7:30am-5pm.

ACCOMMODATIONS

Siem Reap is teeming with places to stay, and there are new accommodations open every month, packed by tourists heading to the temples of Angkor. Travelers planning to visit in the high season should make reservations. Guest houses cluster near the **V. Sivatha-Rte. 6 intersection** and on **V. Wat Bo,** south of Rte. 6. Flush toilets are standard. Prices may drop up to 20% in the rainy season.

Smiley Guest House No. 019 (☎012 852 955). Coming from Rte. 6 on V. Sivatha, turn left onto the dirt alley opposite 10 Makara High School. Very popular with backpackers with a pleasant restaurant and porch. Singles with shared bath US$2-3; doubles with bath US$5-6, with A/C $10.

Popular Guest House, 33 Boboos St. (☎012 916 165). Head south from the old market along the river; it's on the right 200m after the bus station. Popular by name, popular by nature. Backpackers hang out in the leafy veranda restaurant. Singles with fan and shared bath US$2-4; doubles US$3-7, with A/C US$14.

Green Garden Home, 051 V. Sivatha (☎012 890 363), about 200m south of the Rte. 6 intersection; look for the blue sign. Lovely rooms with bamboo furniture and relaxing verandas all set in a flower garden. Doubles with bath, hot water, fridge, cable TV, fan US$10-13, with A/C US$15-20. Call ahead in high season.

Mom's Guest House, 99 V. Wat Bo (☎964 037), next to Mahogany Guest House. Very clean. Good English spoken. In the old building, rooms are functional; in the new place they're a treat. Singles with shared bath US$3; doubles with private bath US$10, with A/C US$15, with hot water US$20.

Chenla Guest House No. 260, 260 Rte. 6 (☎012 835 488), 200m west of the V. Sivatha intersection. Best rooms are in the new building. Some rooms have cable TV and fridge. Singles with shared bath and fan US$3; doubles US$4, with private bath US$6, with hot water US$10, with A/C $15-20.

The Mahogany Guest House, 0593 V. Wat Bo (☎012 631 066). About 30m south of the intersection with Rte. 6. Large mahogany house with veranda decorated with a bizarre wooden moosehead. Small rooms with rich wood walls. Singles US$5, with bath US$8, with A/C US$12.

Apsara Angkor Guest House No. 279, 279 Rte. 6 (☎015 630 125). 100m west of Chenla Guest House. Functional rooms. Good English spoken. Singles with shared bath US$3, with bath US$5-6; doubles with TV, hot water, bath, US$15.

Baphuan Guest House, 117 V. Wat Bo (☎834 181), 120m north of Rte. 6. Clean and modern rooms. Singles US$3, with bath US$5; doubles US$6.

Orchidae Guest House (☎012 898 178). From Rte. 6, go 500m south on V. Sivatha and take a right before the Sokimex station; it's 30m ahead on the left. Clean rooms and central location. Singles US$3, with bath $4; doubles US$4/5, with A/C US$12.

FOOD

A small **night market** on V. Sivatha north of Cambodian Commercial Bank serves noodles for under US$1. A **fruit market** is next door. **Food vendors** also line the road to Angkor and the east bank of the river parallel to the guest house strip. Small restaurants offering good value meals are at the north end of the old market.

Arun Restaurant, off the East Bank River Road 50m north of the Rte. 6 intersection on the right. Generous portions of Cambodian and Chinese food. Numerous veggie options. Grilled beef with tofu sauce US$4. Open daily 10am-10pm.

Chivit Thai, 130 V. Wat Bo, string of guest houses. Charming, open air terrace with great Pad Thai (US$2.50). Open daily 7am-10pm.

Restaurant Sampheap, on the east bank of the river just south of the Rte. 6 bridge. Riverfront dining and large Khmer, Thai, Chinese, and Western menu. Specializes in traditional Khmer candy (US$0.50 per pack), available Oct.-Apr.

Blue Pumpkin, across the road from the provincial hospital. Serves teas and snacks. Arguably the best fruit shakes in town (3000r). Open daily 8am-10pm.

SIGHTS

A **memorial** to Khmer Rouge atrocities is on the road to Angkor. Take the dirt road turn-off at the "Welcome" sign, 500m past the Grand Hotel. Follow the road to a small wat, next to the ramshackle wooden pavilion that is filled waist deep with human skulls and bones, serving as a grisly reminder of the Khmer Rouge massacres. For those who can't get enough of Angkor architecture, **Wat Leah,** along the east bank of the river north of Arun Restaurant, has two well-preserved Angkor-period brick sanctuaries behind the modern pagoda. For a chance to watch highly skilled craftsmen create traditional Khmer wood carvings head to the **Khmer Art of Carving Center.** Look for the sign on the left heading out of town on the road to the temples. (Open daily 7:30am-5pm.) Across the road there is also a small **stone carving workshop.** Small pieces sell for US$10-15.

NIGHTLIFE

Nightlife in Siem Reap is picking up. The amusingly named **Angkor What?,** a block north of the Old Market on one of V. Sivatha's side streets, and the **Ivy Bar,** at the south end of the Old Market, are both youthful late night drinking spots. **Lotus Bar,** at the north end of the market, is open 24hr. For an expensive nightcap, try the **Elephant Bar** in the Grand Hotel d'Angkor, at the north end of the West Bank River Road. The **Grand Hotel's Performance House,** just across the west bank river road from the hotel proper, offers a rare (and costly) chance to see traditional **Khmer dance and drama.** (☎963 417. Shows M, W, Sa. US$22 includes 7pm buffet dinner, 8pm performance.) The **Red Piano,** 50m northwest of the old market, is a chic restaurant/bar whose claim to fame is that it was the headquarters of the "Tomb Raider" cast and crew while they filmed at Angkor. Good food beckons everyday travelers to kick back and have a good time after a day of sight-seeing.

MOST DANGEROUS COW IN THE EAST Cambodia's national animal is the critically endangered kouprey *(Bos sauveli)*, a wild forest-dwelling cow. Males have frayed horns and a huge dewlap, stand 2m at the shoulder, and weigh up to 900kg. There are probably no more than 200 kouprey left in north Cambodia, with a few spilling into Northeast Thailand, south Laos, and central Vietnam. Thanks to human warfare, the unlucky cow has always been almost impossible to study. In the late 30s, a captive kouprey calf starved to death in a Paris zoo during German occupation. Since then, a handful of 50s field notes, one grainy 1967 photograph, and a few unverified sightings have comprised the best research in the kouprey's war-torn home turf; the official U.N. Conservation Plan states that kouprey data is "of a very sketchy nature." Beyond its mystery and rarity, the kouprey could be profitably interbred with domestic cattle to produce disease-resistant, tropics-adapted livestock. When hiking through Rattanakiri in search of this elusive bovine, be sure to bring the proper equipment: malaria pills, a flashlight, an armed escort, de-mining equipment, and for God's sake, a decent camera.

ANGKOR

With their unrivalled beauty and majesty, the temples of Angkor deserve their reputation as one of the great man-made wonders of the world. Begun in the 9th century, the building process lasted over 600 years, with the last of the temples being built in the later 15th century. The temples are the remains of the mighty Khmer empire that, at its height, extended its reign over most of the Malay peninsula and modern-day Cambodia, Laos, and Vietnam. The name 'Angkor' is believed to be a mispronunciation of the Khmer word *nakhon* meaning 'city.' In the 15th century the Khmer kings abandoned Angkor and moved their capital to the site of modern-day Phnom Penh. Angkor lay in relative obscurity until the diaries of French Naturalist Henri Mouhot were published in 1864. Mouhot's description of the beautiful temples sparked international interest, drawing the droves of travelers who now come to see the rising sun break over the temple *stupas* in what the Khmer believe is the gateway between the mortal and celestial worlds.

TRANSPORTATION

If not on a package tour, most travelers stay the night in Siem Reap and hire a **motorcycle** (US$6-10 per day) or **bicycle** (US$3 per day) to see the temples. Rentals can be arranged through guest houses or at the Siem Reap Tourist Office (see p. 86) and require a passport as a deposit. **Cars** with drivers can be hired for US$25 per day.

PRACTICAL INFORMATION

Foreigners can buy one-day (US$20), three-day (US$40), or seven-day (US$60) passes from the Siem Reap Tourist Office or the on-site ticket checkpoint (1 passport-sized photo required). Multi-day passes must be used on consecutive days. There is a steep US$80 fine for misusing tickets.

SIGHTS

THE GRAND CIRCUIT

The following descriptions are arranged in the order that most travelers see the monuments. Beginning at Angkor Wat, the route proceeds clockwise on a roughly rectangular track. During the high season, it may be wise to do the circuit in reverse, since almost everyone starts at the same time and goes the same way.

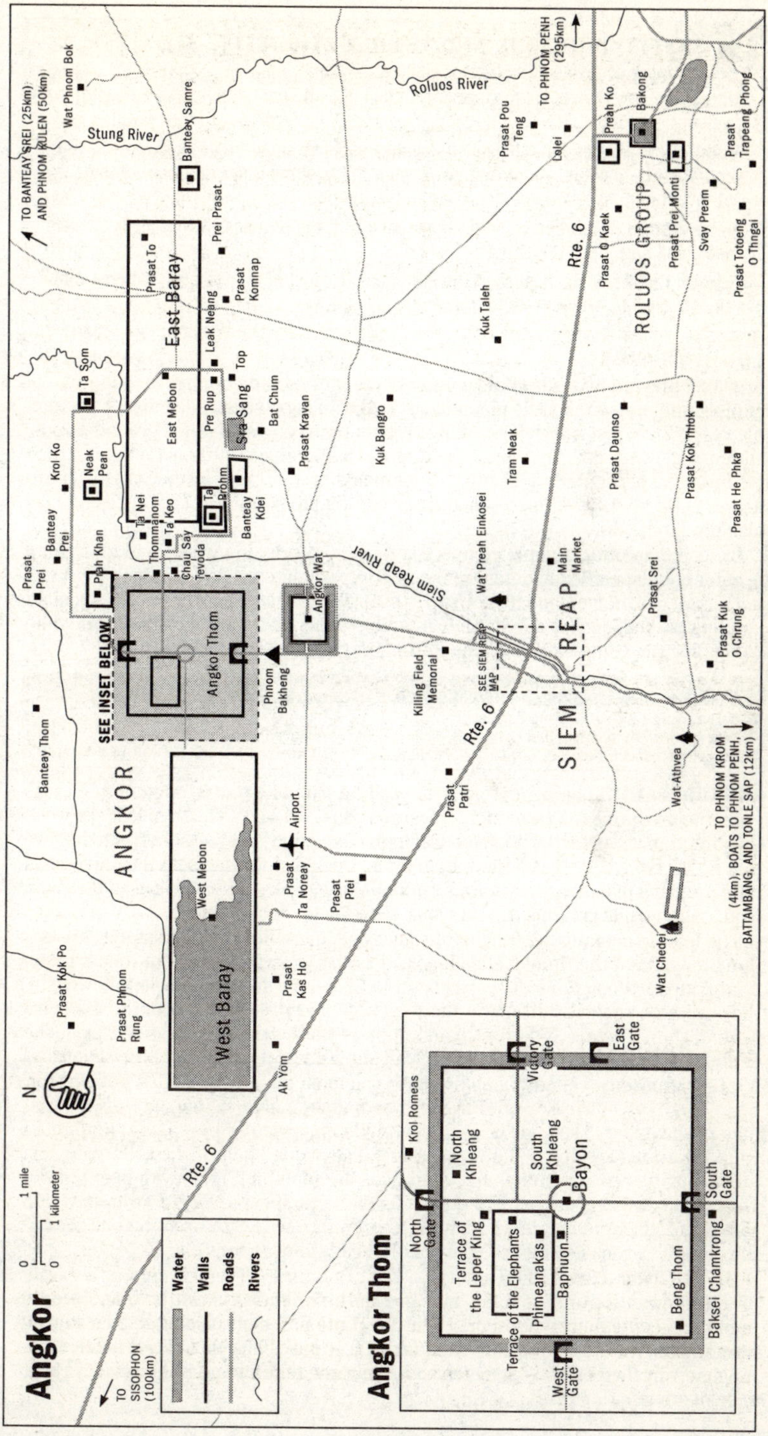
Angkor
0 1 mile
0 1 kilometer
N
Water
Walls
Roads
Rivers
TO SISOPHON (100km)
TO BANTEAY SREI (25km) AND PHNOM KULEN (50km)
TO PHNOM PENH (295km)
TO PHNOM KROM (4km), BOATS TO PHNOM PENH, BATTAMBANG, AND TONLE SAP (12km)
Rte. 6
ANGKOR
SIEM REAP
ROLUOS GROUP
SEE INSET BELOW
SEE SIEM REAP MAP
Wat Phnom Bok
Stung River
Roluos River
Siem Reap River
Banteay Samre
Prei Prasat
Prasat To
East Baray
Prasat Komnap
Leak Neang
Top
East Mebon
Pre Rup
Ta Som
Sra Sang
Bat Chum
Neak Pean
Krol Ko
Banteay Prei
Prasat Prei
Preah Khan
Ta Nei
Thommanom
Ta Keo
Ta Prohm
Banteay Kdei
Chau Say Tevoda
Prasat Kravan
Kuk Bangro
Angkor Wat
Angkor Thom
Phnom Bakheng
Banteay Thom
West Baray
West Mebon
Airport
Prasat Ta Noreay
Prasat Prei
Prasat Kas Ho
Prasat Phnom Rung
Prasat Kok Po
Ak Yom
Killing Field Memorial
Prasat Patri
Wat Preah Einkosei
Main Market
Tram Neak
Kuk Taleh
Prasat Pou Teng
Lolei
Preah Ko
Bakong
Prasat Trapeang Phong
Prasat Prei Monti
Svay Pream
Prasat Totoeng O Thngai
Prasat Ó Kaek
Prasat Daunso
Prasat Kok Thlok
Prasat He Phka
Prasat Srei
Prasat Kuk O Chrung
Wat Athvea
Wat Chedei
Angkor Thom
North Gate
Terrace of the Leper King
Terrace of the Elephants
Phimeanakas
Baphuon
Krol Romeas
North Khleang
South Khleang
Bayon
Victory Gate
East Gate
South Gate
West Gate
Beng Thom
Baksei Chamkrong

> **! SAFETY CONCERNS AND TEMPLE ETIQUETTE.** Keep in mind the following concerns and customs while at Angkor:
>
> **Mines:** The government claims that Angkor has been de-mined, but to be safe, stay on well-trodden paths.
>
> **Wildlife:** The jungles have poisonous snakes such as small bright green *kraits.* King cobras, with enough venom to bring down a bull elephant, are rare but not unheard of–avoid dark, isolated chambers within the temples.
>
> **Preservation:** Don't remove stone fragments from the temples. Government officials search all bags upon departure.
>
> **Tickets:** Guards check passes at the entrances to most of the temples; it's now virtually impossible to slip in without paying.

TOURING TIPS

Angkor's magnificent ruins hold enough secret nooks and crannies for a lifetime of exploration, but with a little planning and prioritizing you can see most of the temple complex in just a few days. Many visitors try to cover as much ground as possible on the first day (including the major sites) and spend their remaining time returning to particularly intriguing monuments or venturing farther afield. Try to get an early start; by 11am temperatures can rise to over 39°C (100°F). Mornings also tend to be drier.

Bring a map of the temple complex, a flashlight, drinking water, and extra film. A guidebook specifically detailing the history, architecture, and myths of individual temples is recommended. *A Guide to Angkor*, by Dawn Rooney, sold by child vendors at Angkor Wat (US$3-6), has temple plans and is especially useful while navigating the complexities of Tha Phrom, Bayon, and Angkor Wat.

THE BOX OF S

Best carvings: Angkor Wat and Banteay Srei.
Best spots to sit in quiet bliss: Banteay Kdei, Prah Khan, East Mebon, and Ta Som.
Best views: Phnom Bakheng, East Mebon, Pre Rup, and Angkor Wat.

ANGKOR WAT. This magnificent 213m tall laterite-and-sandstone complex was constructed during the reign of Suryavarman II (r. 1113-50). The temple faces west, the direction associated with death in Hindu cosmology, leading scholars to believe that it was constructed as a funerary temple. Designed to represent the universe in miniature, it's five-tower *quincunx* symbolize the peaks of Mt. Meru used by Hindu God Vishnu while creating the Universe. (See **Churn, Baby, Churn,** p. 93).

The temple contains 1200 sq. m of sandstone; incredibly detailed stone carvings line the walls of the first-level gallery and form the largest series of reliefs in the world. Mostly depictions of scenes from Indian epics and Angkor period warfare, they are best viewed starting on the west side and proceeding counterclockwise around the structure. The first panel depicts the battle of Kuruksetra from the Hindu epic *Mahabharata*. The south wall shows a mighty military procession and a rather gruesome vision of hell. Perhaps the most famous relief in all of Angkor, *The Churning of the Sea of Milk* (see **Churn, Baby, Churn**, below), adorns the east face of the gallery. The north wall depicts Vishnu's victory over Bana the Demon King, a curious-looking hellion on a rhino. The second half of the gallery depicts more universe-saving battles between gods and demons. The north panel of the west gallery depicts the battle of Lanka from the Hindu epic *Ramayana*, in which Rama and his monkey army sought to free Rama's wife Sita from the clutches of the demon Ravana (recognizable by his 10 heads and 20 arms).

On the second level, the Gallery of 1000 Buddhas (of which only a few fragments remain) is on the right, and the Hall of Echoes is on the left. Temple explorers can stand in one corner of the Hall of Echoes, pound their chests like Tarzan, and feel the room thunder in response. The third level has a stunning view of the perfectly symmetrical Angkor Wat complex. Angkor Wat is best seen at sunrise or sunset.

ANGKOR THOM. The large temple complex of Angkor Thom (literally "great city"), constructed by Jayavarman VII (1181-1219), lies 1½km north of Angkor Wat. Angkor Thom shares Angkor Wat's cosmological layout: a moat symbolizes the oceans, the walls are the land, and the towers represent the peaks of Mt. Meru. The remaining ruins are mainly temples, though it's believed that this vast city once housed many administrative buildings that didn't survive the test of time. The south entrance to Angkor Thom passes through a causeway lined with 54 guardian statues of gods and demons; the Angkor Conservancy, however, has replaced many of the original heads to prevent theft. An all-seeing, four-faced, smiling head tops the tower gates.

THE BAYON. Rising in the exact center of Angkor Thom, the Bayon was erected by Jayavarman VII and is dedicated to Buddhism. Its reliefs depict, in addition to the usual epics, scenes of everyday life in Angkorian Cambodia (fishing, chess-playing, hunting, etc.). The Bayon contains two sets of bas-reliefs meant to be viewed clockwise. The lower gallery adorning the outer wall depicts life in the capital. The south gallery contains perhaps the finest of the Bayon's bas-reliefs depicting a battle between the Khmers and Chams, while the lower tier of reliefs present a more peaceful view of Angkorian life. The north gallery, only some of which was completed, contains a depiction of an Angkor circus. The upper gallery contains stories from Hindu epics dotted with faces believed to represent the Bodhisattva Avalokitesvara, who selflessly delayed attaining enlightenment in order to aid humanity

BAPHUON. A few hundred meters northwest of the Bayon stands the Hindu temple of Baphuon, built by Udayadityavarman II in the late 11th century.

PHIMEANAKAS. Situated just north of Baphuon, this Hindu monument was erected by three successive kings, Rajendravarman, Jayavarman V, and Udayadityavarman I. If open, the steep climb to the top of the central sanctuary is worth the view that waits at the top. The steep laterite "stairs" are best attempted early in the day before the sun or rain set in. The west staircase has a metal rail that makes climbing slightly easier.

TERRACE OF THE ELEPHANTS. First laid out by Suryavarman I, the Terrace of the Elephants (the Royal Terrace) stretches for 300m from Baphuon to the beginning of the Terrace of the Leper King, past Phimeanakas. The bas-reliefs of near life-sized elephants seem to emerge like ghosts from within the stones. Along the wall near the Terrace of the Leper King is a carving of a five-headed horse.

TERRACE OF THE LEPER KING. Another legacy of Jayavarman VII, the monument lies north of the Terrace of the Elephants. Two galleries of bas-reliefs line the terrace, while mythological creatures and *apsaras* (see **Angkor's Motley Crew,** p. 95) decorate the outer wall. The statue of the Leper King himself is a replica; the National Museum in Phnom Penh now houses the original. Some historians believe Jayavarman VII may have suffered from leprosy himself, though others believe that the statue portrays the Hindu god of death, Yama or Kubera, the god of wealth.

CHURN, BABY, CHURN! An ancient Hindu legend, "The Churning of the Sea of Milk" recalls the problem-solving methods of ancient Hindu gods during the turbulent days when they were busy creating the world. Being new at world-creation, they ran into a small glitch—they lost the elixir of immortality while churning the cosmic sea. It took a 1000 years before the gods and demons, in a rare joint effort—aided by Sesha, the sea snake, and Vishnu—recovered the potion. The design of Angkor's temples is based on this ancient legend. The moat represents the ocean, and the gods use Mt. Meru, represented by the tower, as their churning stick. The cosmic serpent, in a rare cameo as the good guy, selflessly offered himself as a rope to enable the gods and demons to twirl the stick and save the Universe.

PRAH KHAN. Located northwest of the Bayon outside Angkor Thom, Prah Khan was built as a Buddhist temples by Jayavarman VII in memory of his father. Literally, Prah Khan means "sacred sword," and some archaeologists believe that the two-story building in the northeast corner of the compound, a location rarely used in Khmer architecture, might once have housed an Asian excalibur left by Jayavarman VII for his descendants.

NEAK PEAN. Neak Pean, a Buddhist temple situated east of Prah Khan along the Grand Circuit access road, was also built by Jayavarman VII. Unlike any other Angkor temple, this small and charming temple is made up of five ponds that are now covered in grass. A temple stands in the exact center of what was the large, central pond. Neak Pean is said to represent Lake Anayatapa, a sacred body of water in the Himalayas. The four symmetrical ponds, one at each cardinal point, represent the earth's four rivers. A stone horse, believed to be the sacred steed *Balaha*, drags several marooned sailors toward the island sanctuary in the middle of Neak Pean.

TA SOM. Lying east of Neak Pean along the access road, Ta Som was also built by Jayavarman VII. A small, quiet temple with one sanctuary, it is unrestored and largely in ruins. A four-faced bayon casts its inscrutable smile over visitors as they enter from the west. Continuing to the east gate, the bayon almost entirely in the clutches of fig tree roots, giving its smile an almost eerie feel.

EAST MEBON. Built in the 10th century by Rajendravarman II in memory of his parents, tranquil East Mebon stands southwest of Ta Som and is accessible only by boat. In the Angkor era, the temple stood in the middle of the large man-made lake *(baray)*. Impressive sculptures of elephants and lions guard each entrance.

PHNOM BAKHENG. Just north and slightly west of Angkor Wat, Phnom Bakheng was built by Yasovarman I in the late 9th century. Travelers struggle up the steep and rocky slope to enjoy a spectacular sunset and view of Angkor Wat. For the tired and style-conscious, an elephant carriage is available to take you to the top (US$15). Originally, 109 towers, corresponding to the animal zodiac cycle, graced the *phnom*. In January and February, a glorious sunrise directly over Angkor rewards early risers.

TA PROHM. Located west of Pre Rup and bordering Banteay Kdei, Ta Prohm was built by as a Buddhist temple Jayavarman VII in memory of his mother. This vast, crumbling temple competes with the Bayon and Angkor Wat as the most awe-inspiring of Angkor's treasures. Ancient trees have grown into and out of the buildings themselves, creating the visage of a "lost city." Inscriptions reveal that during its heyday, 79,365 people were employed in Ta Prohm's upkeep. Early risers can witness the temple's stunning beauty in the morning light.

PRE RUP. Five hundred meters due south of East Mebon lies Pre Rup, a Hindu temple built by Rajendravarman II in the second half of the 10th century to honor Shiva. More impressive than its contemporary, East Mebon, this multi-tiered structure affords views of East Baray to the north. Two halls parallel to the laterite wall as you enter from the east are believed to have housed pilgrims who journeyed here to worship. The temple has traditionally been thought to have funerary associations; the vat near the east staircase is thought to have been used at cremations.

BANTEAY KDEI. Banteay Kdei is a Buddhist temple built by Jayavarman VII, southeast of Pre Rup near the Sra Srang Reservoir. A bayon oversees the entrance to this unrestored temple. Lying largely in ruins, Banteay Kdei is more a spot for calm reflection than active exploration.

BANTEAY SREI. Five kilometers northeast of the main cluster of Angkor temples stands detailed and beautiful Banteay Srei ("Citadel of Women"). Described as the 'precious queen' by French archaeologists, Banteay Srei's construction spanned two kingships in the second half of the 10th century. Though smaller in scale than the temples at Angkor, this temple is home many exquisite carvings that are based

ANGKOR'S MOTLEY CREW Several figures and objects make appearances in Angkor's carvings. *Let's Go*'s guide to who's who in Angkor:

Naga: Sanskrit for snake, these mythical, multi-headed serpents seem to be everywhere at Angkor and often form balustrades. Possibly the most abundant motif in Southeast Asia, *naga* play a marked role in Khmer legends. It is said that the Khmer are descended from the union between a foreigner and a *naga.* According to Hindu myths, the *naga* swallowed the waters of life and were either ruptured by Indra or squeezed by Vishnu's entourage to set the waters free. Either way, the moral of the story is not to be a *naga* while the Universe is being created.

Apsara: These celestial beauties, who sprang forth during the *Churning of the Sea of Milk* (See **Churn, Baby, Churn,** p. 93) have become virtually synonymous with Khmer architecture. Their perfect, sensuous beauty was believed to have highly refined powers of seduction and are typically depicted facing outward with only their feet in profile. Angkor Wat *apsaras,* widely regarded as the most beautiful (and most well endowed) nymphs of all the temples, appear individually—unlike the Bayon *apsaras* who appear in groups of three.

Vishnu: An important Hindu deity, Vishnu was widely worshipped during the height of the Angkor period. Married to Lakshmi, he is frequently portrayed with four arms and an ornamental waist sash *(sampot).* Whenever the earth is threatened by evil, he acts as its savior, assuming an *avatara* (earthly incarnation). He is seen in the bas-reliefs of Angkor Wat both in human form and as a tortoise in the *Churning of the Sea of Milk.*

Ganesha: Parvati created Ganesha, the elephant-headed Hindu god of wisdom, to guard her bath. When her husband, the powerful god Shiva, tried to gain admittance, Ganesha refused to let him pass. Shiva called upon Vishnu for help and together they decapitated him. Rightly furious, Parvati wrought destruction on the world. Since even the mighty Shiva could not handle a women scorned, he resurrected Ganesha and placed upon his body the head of the first being he saw—an elephant.

Garuda: A late addition to Angkor's characters, this half-man, half-bird enemy of the *naga* is Vishnu's preferred means of transport.

Makara: With a face like a Chinese dragon, a body of a crocodile, and a dance costume, this demonic sea monster is often represented on lintels with hideous creatures, such as *naga,* coming from his mouth. Lolei, one of the Roluos temples, has a fine representation of the creature.

on Indian epics. The south library shows Ravana shaking Mt. Kailusa (east pediment). The north library depicts Indra casting down heavenly rain (east pediment) and Krishna killing his murderous uncle King Kamsa (west pediment).

WEST BARAY. West of Angkor Thom, the half-filled lake is best seen from Phnom Bakheng. Believed to date from the 11th century, West Baray was built during the reign of Udayadityavarman II. A small, largely destroyed temple, West Mebon, stands in the center of the *baray* and is accessible by boat.

ROLUOS GROUP. About 30min. by moto on the incredibly dusty Rte. 6, this collection of three temples represents the very earliest of the Angkor period and is interesting only to die-hard Angkor enthusiasts. Jayavarman II made this capital of Hariharalaya in the 9th century. All three temples were originally consecrated to Hinduism. **Lolei** (north of the other two off Rte. 6), the site of a modern Buddhist wat, has not been preserved very well but boasts a few beautiful lintels on the four brick towers of the main sanctuary. **Preah Ko** (south of Rte. 6 and north of Bakong), or "Sacred Ox," consists of a central sanctuary with six brick towers. Bakong, the largest and most impressive of the Roluos Group is a temple mountain representing Mt. Meru and was once the ancient capital of Hariharalaya.

KBAL SPEAN. Situated about 10km down the road form Banteay Srei, Kbal Spean, "the head of the bridge," offers a free and less crowded opportunity to see riverbed *linga.* A *linga* is a symbol of the creative power of nature and is shaped like a male phallus. Water that flows through the channel carved into the side of the *linga* is thought to be blessed. About 15min. up the hill lies the secluded **River of the Thousand Linga.** The stretch of riverbed before the waterfall is carved with *linga* and images of deities. The carvings bless the river's waters as they flow to the temples of Angkor. Its proximity to Banteay Srei make it practical to combine a visit to the two sites. **Stay on the path marked by red tree-trunks, as mines remain a risk.**

PHNOM KULEN. Phnom Kulen looms 50km northeast of Angkor Thom. Due to its distance from Siem Reap, the US$20 entry fee, and the presence of more impressive riverbed carvings at Kbal Spean, the trek to Phnom Kulen is not for those temple-weary. The mountain is one of Cambodia's most sacred sites and on the weekend plays host to hordes of pilgrims. They come to see the **reclining Buddha,** perched on top of a huge boulder on one of the mountain's peaks. The temple sheltering the Buddha has magnificent views over the surrounding mountains, but remember to remove your shoes before climbing the staircase. Ten meters down the hill from the river on the right is a side road leading to a **waterfall,** a popular bathing spot. Vendors set up stalls to cater to picknicking Khmer families on the weekend. The quickest way to get to Phnom Kulen is by **moto** (1½hr. each way, US$20-25 for the whole day). **Be sure you have a reliable guide before venturing off the main road; keep to well trodden paths.**

HONG KONG

HONG KONG DOLLAR

US$1 = 7.999HK$	1HK$ = US$0.130
CDN$1 = 5.049HK$	1HK$ = CDN$0.198
UK£1 = 11.369HK$	1HK$ = UK£0.085
EUR€1 = 7.138HK$	1HK$ = EUR€0.140
AUS$1 = 4.150HK$	1HK$ = AUS$0.240
NZ$1 = 3.449	1HK$ = NZ$0.289
ZAR1 = 0.930HK$	1HK$ = ZAR1.074

PHONE CODE **Country Code:** 852. **International dialing prefix:** 00.

Despite Britain's flight from Victoria Harbour and Hong's status as a Special Administrative Region (SAR) of China, business is as usual in the former colony—lightning-fast and devil-may-care. Capitalism is the name of the game, and everybody's playing; Suzie Wong has become a corporate boss, and the *taipan* of Hong Kong's mythical past are eager, Armani-clad moguls. Beneath all the ultra-modern clothes, chic haircuts, and glossy building exteriors, however, beats the heart of old Hong Kong. CEOs head home to light joss sticks and pay homage to Buddha in front of ancestral shrines. The gliding junks and incense-clouded temples of Hong Kong's past endure, somewhat obscured by Victoria Harbour's neon lights and the all-too-ubiquitous golden arches. Chinese opera and Canto-pop duke it out in the streets with N'Sync and the Beatles. Indeed, Mr. Rolex, Ms. Rolls-Royce, and little Rémy Martin lead a peaceful cheek-by-jowl coexistence with seahorse aphrodisiacs and roast-duck banquets. A city in search of free-trade nirvana, Hong Kong works hard but plays harder, leaving many visitors stunned and slightly out of breath, but invigorated, nonetheless.

HIGHLIGHTS OF HONG KONG

BEACHES. Deepwater Bay (p. 121) has the best of Hong Kong's waters.

URBAN BEAT. See the classic view of the Hong Kong skyline from the Star Ferry across **Victoria Harbour** (p. 105), or just jump into the bustle of Hong Kong's dizzying streets.

HIKING. Try the MacLehose Trail for the lush lowlands, demure beaches, and misty mountains of Hong Kong's **New Territories** (p. 122).

ESSENTIALS

VISAS

British citizens can stay in Hong Kong visa-free for six months; US, Canadian, Australian, New Zealand, Western European, and most Central and South American citizens can stay for three. Eastern European and African citizens usually require a visa. The Hong Kong Immigration Department handles **visa extensions.** This may take 1-5 days, and prices vary (HK$100-200 for single entry, 1-month tourist visa). Photo machines in every subway station (HK$35) and in the CTS office (HK$30) provide fast visa and passport photos.

MONEY

Legal tender in Hong Kong is the **Hong Kong dollar** (HK$), which is divided into 100 **cents.** Bronze-colored, government-issued coins come in 10¢, 20¢, and 50¢ denominations; silver-colored coins come in $1, $2, $5, $10, and $100. Three private banks issue notes in denominations of $10, $20, $50, $100, $500, and $1000. Currency can be exchanged at banks, hotels, money changers, or 24hr. automatic currency exchange machines called **EA$YXCHANGE,** which can be found at a few Wing Lung banks (HK$30 handling fee); banks usually have the best rates.

All major **credit cards** (AmEx, Diner's Club, JCB, MC, and Visa) are generally accepted in Hong Kong, although some shops charge extra for their use. **ATMs** connected to international money networks like Cirrus, Plus, Mondex, and NYCE dispense Hong Kong dollars and can be found around the city and in MTR and KCR stations. All **HongkongBank ETC** machines accept Cirrus, Plus, Visa, and MasterCard. In general, look for machines that are marked "For International Cards."

Tipping is not common, so don't feel obligated to tip waiters, bellhops, or other attendants. Most restaurants automatically levy a 10% service charge, and expect to keep the change. For taxis, round the fare up to the nearest dollar.

LANGUAGE

Chinese and English are the official languages of Hong Kong. Even though the use of Mandarin is on the rise in Hong Kong, **Cantonese** is above and beyond the most widely spoken dialect. English and other foreign words have crept into Cantonese to such an extent that you might take a "teik si" or a "bas si" from the airport or buy a "fon kad" at the 7-Eleven. Most people who work in the tourist industry speak English, but many shopkeepers, vendors, and restaurant owners do not; learning to count and say a few key phrases in Cantonese can prove very useful.

INTERCITY TRANSPORTATION

BY AIR

The frighteningly modern **Hong Kong International Airport** at **Chek Lap Kok** sits just off Lantau Island's northern rim, 30km from central Hong Kong. New arrivals enjoy all the latest airport perks, including 54 moving walkways, a mall, and a high-speed rail link between the airport and Victoria Harbour. There is an adult (12 years and over) departure tax of HK$50. A direct **Mass Transit Railway Airport Express Line (AEL)** jets every 10min. from the airport to Kowloon (20min., single journey or same-day return HK$90, round-trip valid for 1 month HK$110) and to Hong Kong Island (23min., single journey or same-day return HK$100, round-trip HK$180).

Airbuses run from the airport to Hong Kong Island, Kowloon, and the New Territories. **A11** goes to Causeway Bay (every 15min., HK$40); **A12** to Siu Sai Wan (every 15min., HK$45); **A21** to the Hung Hom KCR Station (every 10min., HK$33); **A22** to the Lam Tin MTR Station (every 15min., HK$39); **A31** to Tsuen Wan (every 15-20min., HK$17); **A35** to Mui Wo (every 30-40min., HK$14, Su HK$23); **A41** to Sha Tin (every 20min., HK$20); and **A43** to Fanling (every hr., HK$28). Less-expensive, conventional **bus** routes include **E11** to Causeway Bay (every 10-20min., HK$21); **E22** to Kowloon City (every 6-20min., HK$18); **E33** to Tuen Mun (every 11-20min., HK$13); **E41** to Tai Po (every 12-20min., HK$13); and **E42** to Sha Tin (every 15-20min., HK$13).

DESTINATION	FREQUENCY	PRICE	DESTINATION	FREQUENCY	PRICE
Bangkok	3-5 per day	HK$1500	**Phnom Penh**	2 per day	HK$2750
Jakarta	2-3 per day	HK$7630	**Manila**	3-5 per day	HK$3500
Ho Chi Minh City	2 per day	HK$549	**Singapore**	5-6 per day	HK$2050
Kuala Lumpur	3-5 per day	HK$2850	**Yangon**	1 per day	HK$2750

Taxis wait outside the airport terminal. A ride from the airport to TST costs about HK$270; to Causeway Bay HK$335; to Central Hong Kong HK$330; and to Tsuen Wan HK$235. There is a HK$5 surcharge per piece of luggage.

Hong Kong's official airline is **Cathay Pacific,** New World Shopping Centre, 20 Salisbury Rd., Basement, Shop 53, TST East. It also has offices at Swire House, 9 Connaught Rd., 4th fl., Central (☎2747 1888). Several major international airlines serve Hong Kong, including: **Air Canada,** Wheelock House, 20 Pedder St., Rm. 1002, Central (☎2522 1001); **Air New Zealand,** Lipo Chun Chambers, 189 Des Voeux Rd., 17th fl., Central (☎2524 9041); **American Airlines,** New World Tower, 18 Queen's Rd. Central, Tower 1, 16th fl., Central (☎2826 9269); **Ansett Australia,** Lipo Chun Chambers, 189 Des Voeux Rd., 17th fl., Central (☎2527 7883); **British Airways,** Jardine House, 1 Connaught Pl., 24th fl. (☎2882 9000, ticketing 2822 9090); **Garuda Indonesia,** Henley Bldg., 5 Queen's Rd., 7th fl., Central (☎2840 0000); **MAS,** Central Tower, 28 Queen's Rd., 23rd fl., Central (☎2521 8181); **Myanma Airlines,** Shun Tak Centre, 168-200 Connaught Rd., #2206, Central (☎2526 0100); **Northwest Airlines,** Alexandra House, 20 Chater Rd., 29th fl., Central (☎2810 4288); **PAL,** East Ocean Center, 98 Granville Rd., Ground fl., TST East (☎2301 9300); **Qantas,** Jardine House, 1 Connaught Place, 37th fl., #3701, Central (☎2822 2900, ticketing 2842 1400); **Singapore Airlines,** United Center, 95 Queensway, 17th fl., Admiralty (☎2520 2233); **Thai Airways,** United Center, 95 Queensway, 24th fl., Admiralty (☎2876 6888); **United Airlines,** Gloucester Tower, 11 Pedder St., Landmark, 29th fl., Central (☎2810 4888).

ORIENTATION

Sandwiched between the **Kowloon Peninsula** and **Hong Kong Island, Victoria Harbour** is the heart of Hong Kong.

KOWLOON. North of the harbor, at the tip of the **Kowloon** peninsula, is **Tsim Sha Tsui (TST),** the city's tourist center. Along the eastern banks of the harbor, **Tsim Sha Tsui East (TST East),** with its more upscale shopping malls and hotels, struggles to compete with Tsim Sha Tsui proper for tourism business. Quiet **Hung Hom** sits on the other side of Tsim Sha Tsui East; tourists rarely visit this area except to visit the Whampoa Gardens. **New Kowloon,** north of Tsim Sha Tsui, marks the frontier between the waterfront districts and the New Territories.

HONG KONG ISLAND. Situated across Victoria Harbour from Kowloon, Hong Kong Island is accessible by three harbor tunnels, the MTR's island line, and the Star Ferry. To the west, **Sheung Wan** is a honeycomb of cluttered streets and alleys. Right in the thick of things, **Central** and **Admiralty** sprout vertiginous skyscrapers. **Wan Chai** is one stop east from Admiralty on the MTR; **Causeway Bay** is one stop farther. The predominantly rural southern part of Hong Kong Island is marked by the expat haven of **Stanley** and the beaches at **Repulse Bay.** A short skip to the west is **Aberdeen,** home to the grandiose Jumbo Floating Restaurant.

NEW TERRITORIES. The New Territories sprawl all the way to Shenzhen and the border with mainland China. In the New Territories, **Tsuen Wan, Sha Tin,** and **Tai Po** are fast-developing "new towns"; the **Sai Kung Peninsula** boasts hiking trails and sparkling beaches.

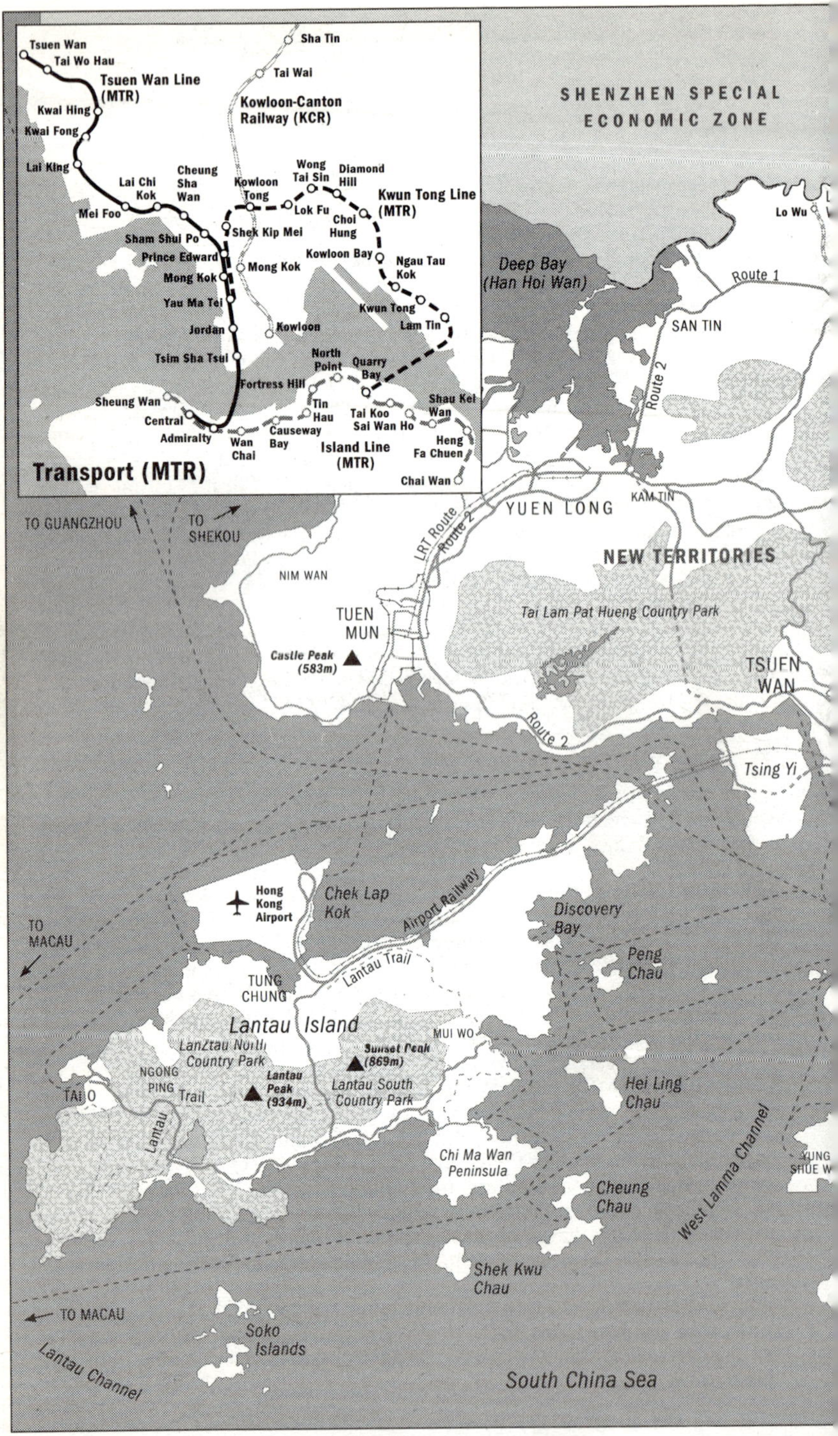
Transport (MTR)
Tsuen Wan Line (MTR)
Kowloon-Canton Railway (KCR)
Kwun Tong Line (MTR)
Island Line (MTR)
Tsuen Wan
Tai Wo Hau
Kwai Hing
Kwai Fong
Lai King
Lai Chi Kok
Cheung Sha Wan
Mei Foo
Sham Shui Po
Prince Edward
Mong Kok
Yau Ma Tei
Jordan
Tsim Sha Tsui
Sha Tin
Tai Wai
Kowloon Tong
Shek Kip Mei
Mong Kok
Kowloon
Wong Tai Sin
Diamond Hill
Lok Fu
Choi Hung
Kowloon Bay
Ngau Tau Kok
Kwun Tong
Lam Tin
North Point
Quarry Bay
Fortress Hill
Sheung Wan
Central
Admiralty
Wan Chai
Causeway Bay
Tin Hau
Tai Koo
Sai Wan Ho
Shau Kei Wan
Heng Fa Chuen
Chai Wan
SHENZHEN SPECIAL ECONOMIC ZONE
Lo Wu
Deep Bay (Han Hoi Wan)
Route 1
SAN TIN
Route 2
KAM TIN
YUEN LONG
LRT Route
NEW TERRITORIES
TO GUANGZHOU
TO SHEKOU
NIM WAN
TUEN MUN
Castle Peak (583m)
Tai Lam Pat Hueng Country Park
TSUEN WAN
Route 2
Tsing Yi
Hong Kong Airport
Chek Lap Kok
Airport Railway
TO MACAU
Discovery Bay
Peng Chau
Lantau Trail
TUNG CHUNG
Lantau Island
MUI WO
Lantau North Country Park
Sunset Peak (869m)
NGONG PING
Trail
Lantau Peak (934m)
Lantau South Country Park
TAI O
Lantau
Hei Ling Chau
Chi Ma Wan Peninsula
Cheung Chau
West Lamma Channel
YUNG SHUE W
Shek Kwu Chau
TO MACAU
Soko Islands
Lantau Channel
South China Sea

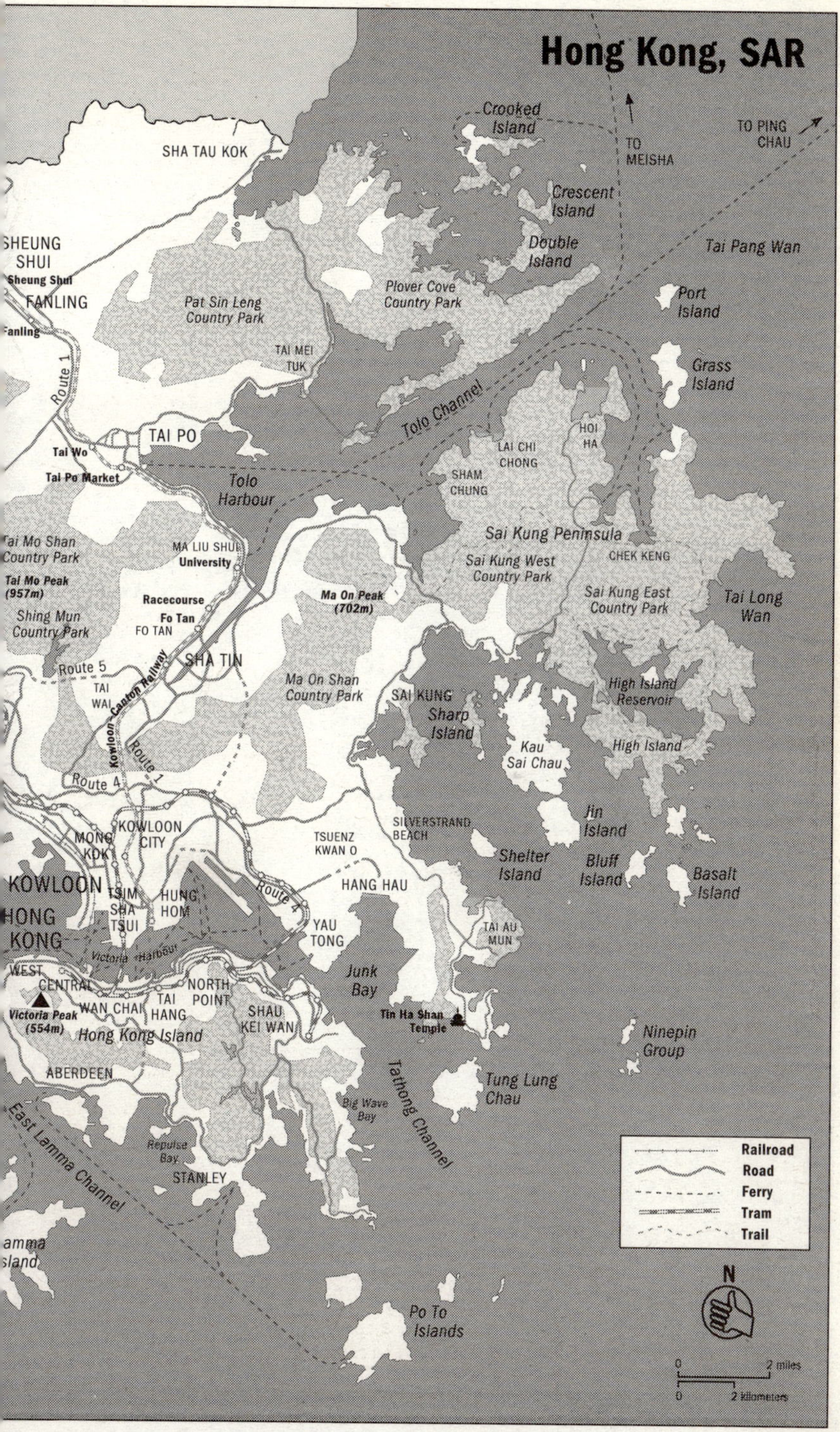
Hong Kong, SAR
Crooked Island
TO MEISHA
TO PING CHAU
SHA TAU KOK
Crescent Island
Double Island
Tai Pang Wan
SHEUNG SHUI
Sheung Shui
FANLING
Fanling
Pat Sin Leng Country Park
Plover Cove Country Park
Port Island
Grass Island
TAI MEI TUK
Route 1
Tolo Channel
TAI PO
Tai Wo
Tai Po Market
Tolo Harbour
LAI CHI CHONG
HOI HA
SHAM CHUNG
Sai Kung Peninsula
CHEK KENG
Tai Mo Shan Country Park
MA LIU SHUI
University
Sai Kung West Country Park
Tai Mo Peak (957m)
Ma On Peak (702m)
Sai Kung East Country Park
Tai Long Wan
Racecourse
Fo Tan
FO TAN
Shing Mun Country Park
SHA TIN
Route 5
Kowloon-Canton Railway
TAI WAI
Ma On Shan Country Park
SAI KUNG
Sharp Island
High Island Reservoir
Kau Sai Chau
High Island
Route 1
Route 4
MONG KOK
KOWLOON CITY
TSUENZ KWAN O
SILVERSTRAND BEACH
Jin Island
Shelter Island
Bluff Island
Basalt Island
KOWLOON
TSIM SHA TSUI
HUNG HOM
HANG HAU
Route 4
HONG KONG
YAU TONG
TAI AU MUN
Victoria Harbour
WEST
CENTRAL
NORTH POINT
Junk Bay
Victoria Peak (554m)
WAN CHAI
TAI HANG
SHAU KEI WAN
Tin Ha Shan Temple
Hong Kong Island
Ninepin Group
ABERDEEN
Tathong Channel
Tung Lung Chau
Big Wave Bay
East Lamma Channel
Repulse Bay
STANLEY
Railroad
Road
Ferry
Tram
Trail
Lamma Island
N
Po To Islands
0
2 miles
0
2 kilometers

Hong Kong City Center and Kowloon Peninsula
ACCOMMODATIONS
Chungking Mansions, 3
Mirador Mansions, 2
Victoria Hostel, 1
YMCA, 4
HUNG HOM
TO WONDERFUL WORLD OF WHAMPOA (100m) AND HUNG HOM FERRYS (150m)
TO NORTH POINT
Cross Harbour Tunnel
Hung Hom (Kowloon) Station
Coliseum
Hong Kong Polytechnic University
Hong Kong Museum of History
Hong Kong Science Museum
TSIM SHA TSUI EAST
Hong Kong Tourist Association
Tsim Sha Tsui West Ferry Pier
New World Centre
Promenade
Queen Elizabeth Hospital
Chi Man St.
Wylie Rd.
Gascoigne Rd.
Chatham Rd. N
Chatham Rd. S
Salisbury Rd.
Science Museum Rd.
Mody Rd.
Nathan Rd.
Austin Rd.
Jordan Rd.
Canton Rd.
Ferry St.
JORDAN
TSIM SHA TSUI
American Express
China Travel Service
Peninsula Hotel
Hong Kong Space Museum
Hong Kong Museum of Art
Hong Kong Cultural Centre
Clock Tower
Star House
Star Ferry Concourse
Kowloon Mosque and Islamic Centre
Harbour City
China Hong Kong City
China Ferry Terminal
Ocean Terminal
Jordan Rd. Ferry Terminal
KOWLOON STATION
KOWLOON
Tin Hau Temple
Western Harbour Crossing
TO MACAU AND CHINA
CENTRAL-TSIM SHA TSUI FERRY
TO TSING YI AND TSUEN WAN
TO CHEUNG CHAU AND PENG CHAU
TO LAMMA ISLAND
TO TUEN MUN, TUNG CHUNG WAN, AND TAI O
TO MACAU
HK Macau Ferry Terminal
Pier 1

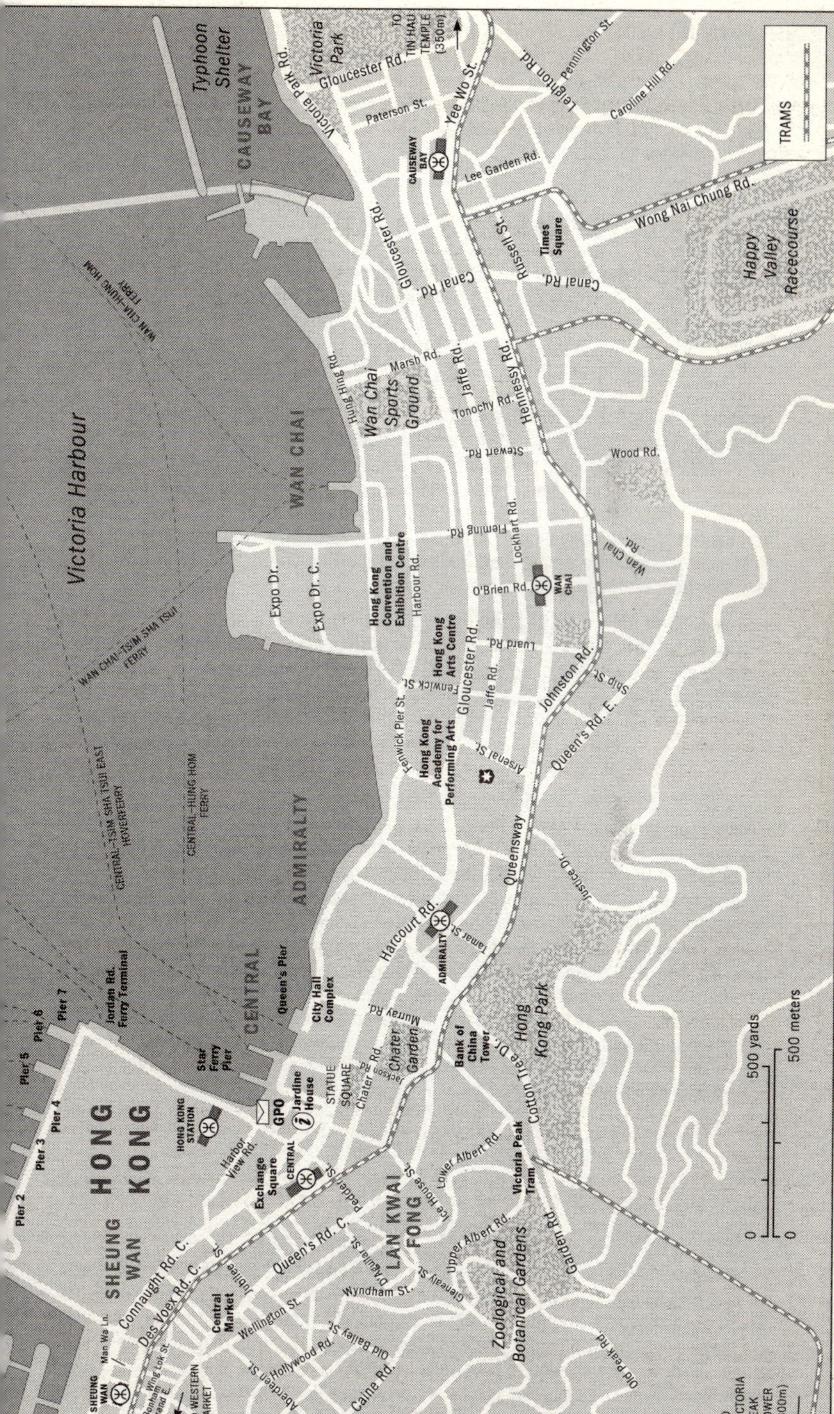
Victoria Harbour
Typhoon Shelter
CAUSEWAY BAY
Victoria Park
Victoria Park Rd.
Gloucester Rd.
TO TIN HAU TEMPLE (350m)
Paterson St.
Yee Wo St.
CAUSEWAY BAY
Lee Garden Rd.
Pennington St.
Leighton Rd.
Caroline Hill Rd.
TRAMS
Wong Nai Chung Rd.
Times Square
Russell St.
Canal Rd.
Happy Valley Racecourse
WAN CHAI–HUNG HOM FERRY
Hung Hing Rd.
Marsh Rd.
Jaffe Rd.
Hennessy Rd.
Wan Chai Sports Ground
Tonochy Rd.
WAN CHAI
Stewart Rd.
Wood Rd.
Fleming Rd.
Lockhart Rd.
Wan Chai Rd.
Expo Dr.
Expo Dr. C.
Hong Kong Convention and Exhibition Centre
Harbour Rd.
O'Brien Rd.
WAN CHAI
WAN CHAI–TSIM SHA TSUI FERRY
Hong Kong Arts Centre
Gloucester Rd.
Luard Rd.
Fenwick St.
Jaffe Rd.
Johnston Rd.
Ship St.
Fenwick Pier St.
Hong Kong Academy for Performing Arts
Arsenal St.
Queen's Rd. E.
CENTRAL–TSIM SHA TSUI EAST HOVERFERRY
CENTRAL–HUNG HOM FERRY
ADMIRALTY
Queensway
Justice Dr.
Harcourt Rd.
ADMIRALTY
Tamar St.
Jordan Rd. Ferry Terminal
Pier 7
Pier 6
Pier 5
Pier 4
Pier 3
Pier 2
CENTRAL
Queen's Pier
City Hall Complex
Murray Rd.
Star Ferry Pier
Chater Garden
Bank of China Tower
Hong Kong Park
Cotton Tree Dr.
HONG KONG STATION
GPO
Jardine House
STATUE SQUARE
Chater Rd.
Jackson Rd.
HONG KONG
Harbor View Rd.
Exchange Square
CENTRAL
Pedder St.
LAN KWAI FONG
Ice House St.
Lower Albert Rd.
Victoria Peak Tram
SHEUNG WAN
Connaught Rd. C.
Des Voeux Rd. C.
Queen's Rd. C.
D'Aguilar St.
Wyndham St.
Glenealy St.
Upper Albert Rd.
Garden Rd.
Zoological and Botanical Gardens
Jubilee St.
Central Market
Wellington St.
Man Wa Ln.
Hollywood Rd.
Old Bailey St.
Aberdeen St.
Caine Rd.
Old Peak Rd.
SHEUNG WAN
Bonham Strand E.
Wing Lok St.
TO WESTERN MARKET
TO VICTORIA PEAK TOWER (300m)
0
500 yards
500 meters

OUTLYING ISLANDS. The Hong Kong archipelago is not limited to Hong Kong Island. Among many smaller islands, scenic **Lamma Island** (see p. 128) off the coast of Aberdeen, has walking trails, caves, and beaches. **Lantau Island** (see p. 125), the site of the international airport, also houses the giant Tian Tan Buddha and the Po Lin and Po Lam Zen Monasteries. **Cheung Chau Island** boasts flamboyant character and great scenery.

LOCAL TRANSPORTATION

Mass Transit Railway (MTR): The MTR (information ☎2881 8888) is Hong Kong in a nutshell: super-efficient, automated, and lightning-fast; unfortunately, it's also the most expensive of Hong Kong's public transport options. Five MTR lines connect Kowloon, Hong Kong Island, the New Territories, Chek Lap Kok Airport, and most points in between. Tickets (HK$4-13; maximum HK$26) are valid for 90min. of travel on the day of issue. You can also purchase a long-term, multiple-use ticket called an **Octopus** (hotline ☎2993 8880) for HK$70 (ages 3-12 and the elderly), HK$100 (for Hong Kong students), or HK$150 (for adults); the card can be used on the MTR, KCR, AEL, most KMB and Citybus cross-harbor buses, Hong Kong & Yaumati Ferry routes to the outlying islands, and even in the photo booths in subway stations. The refundable deposit is HK$50; for short-term visitors, it is probably not worth the hassle. Information centers in MTR stations sell Octopus cards, give change, and answer questions. Most tickets cost more during **rush hour** (7:30-9:30am and 5:30-7:30pm). The system runs from 6am-1am, although a few stations are only open 7am-midnight.

HONG KONG

Kowloon-Canton Railway (KCR) and light rail (LR): The KCR (☎2602 7799), an older version of the MTR, runs from Kowloon Station in TST East, through the New Territories, and to the Chinese border at Lo Wu (HK$3.50-9, children and seniors half-price). Passengers can change from the MTR to the KCR at Kowloon Tong Station. Trains run every three minutes 5:30am-12:20am. The LR (☎2468 7788) joins the towns of Yuen Long and Tuen Mun in the New Territories. Tickets are HK$4-5.80 and can be purchased at vending machines along the route. Trains run daily 5:40am-12:30am.

Buses: Hong Kong's five-star bus system (HK$1.20-$45) ventures into any area worth visiting (and even some places better left alone). Schedules and fares are posted at bus stops and available at any tourist office. Buses with numbers followed by an "M" run to MTR stations; those with numbers followed by a "K" go to KCR stations, and those followed by "X" indicate express routes. On Hong Kong Island, **New World First Bus** (☎2136 8888) runs cream-and-blue buses; **Citybus** (☎2873 0818) operates orange buses. In Kowloon, cream-and-red caravans are run by **Kowloon Motor Bus** (☎2745 4466). Air-conditioned buses cost extra. Red-and-cream **minibuses** stop anywhere along their routes except at busy intersections and city bus stops. Tell the driver your stop; pay as you disembark. Green-and-cream minibuses called **maxicabs** only stop at marked maxicab stops; pay once on board. In both cases, destinations are on the front of the bus, but the English is often small and hard to read. Buses accept only exact fare (HK$1.50-20).

Taxis: Taxis are **red** in Kowloon and Hong Kong Island, **blue** on Lantau Island, and **green** in the New Territories. Base fare for red taxis is HK$15, and each additional 200m or minute of waiting time is HK$1.40. Red taxis will take you to Hong Kong Island and vice versa, but there are surcharges for the Cross-Harbour Tunnel (HK$20), the Eastern Harbour Tunnel (HK$30), and the Western Harbour Tunnel (HK$45) to cover the cab's round-trip tunnel toll. Base fare for blue taxis is HK$12; each additional 200m or minute of waiting time costs HK$1.20. Base fare for green taxis is HK$12.50; each additional 200m or minute of waiting time costs HK$1.20. Green taxis only pick up and drop off passengers within the New Territories. Taxi drivers may also charge HK$5 per piece of luggage. Most major thoroughfares have taxi stands. Taxis are not allowed to pick up or set down passengers in areas marked with yellow lines. To file a complaint against a driver, copy down the taxi number displayed on the dashboard and call the **police hotline** (☎2527 7177).

TRANSPORT INFORMATION. For the most up-to-date information on all types of transportation into, out of, and around Hong Kong, contact one of the following companies. If all else fails, contact the **Hong Kong Tourist Association hotline** (☎2508 1234). For links to up-to-date transport information on the Internet, go to www.igsd.gov.hk.

Hong Kong International Airport (☎2181 0000).

To and From the Airport: Airbus Coach (☎2745 4466) or **Airport Express** (☎2881 8888).

Trains: MTR (☎2881 8888). **KCR:** East Rail (☎2602 7799), Light Rail (☎2468 7788), and West Rail (☎2684 8833).

Buses: New World First Bus (☎2136 8888). **Kowloon Motor Bus** (☎2745 4466). **City Bus** (☎2873 0818). **Lantao Bus Co.** (☎2984 9848).

Taxis: Hong Kong Island (☎2861 1008), Kowloon/New Territories (☎2397 0922). **Taxi Union Loss Report Hotline** (☎2385 8288).

Hong Kong Tramway (☎2548 7102).

Peak Tramway (☎2522 0922).

Star Ferry (☎2367 7065).

Hong Kong Ferry (☎2815 6063).

Trams: Aging trams have lumbered along northern Hong Kong Island since 1904 and are an inexpensive way to see Hong Kong Island. The tram follows a route from Kennedy Town to Shau Kei Wan, past Central, Admiralty, Wan Chai, and Causeway Bay. Fare is HK$2.20 (children and seniors half-price). Board at the rear and pay with exact change as you exit. The tram's last stop is written in English on the front. Contact **Hong Kong Tramways** (☎2118 6338) for more information. Trams run 6am-1am.

Boats: The **Star Ferry** (☎2367 7065) has been in operation for over 100 years. The Star Ferry Terminal in TST is at the end of Salisbury Rd. Ferries glide between TST and **Central** (every 5-10min. 6:30am-11:30pm; lower deck HK$1.70, upper deck HK$2.20) and between TST and **Wan Chai** (every 8-20min. 7:30am-11pm, HK$2.20). There is also service to **Hung Hom** from the Star Ferry pier in Central, in front of Jardine House and the post office in Exchange Square (7am-7pm, HK$5.30). Ferries to the outlying islands leave from the **New Ferry Piers,** off the Exchange Square in Central, to **Lamma** from Pier 5 (30min.; every hr. 6:30am-12:30am; M-Sa HK$10, Su HK$14); **Cheung Chau** from Pier 6 (48min.; every hr. 6:20am-11:15pm; M-Sa HK$10, deluxe class HK$16; Su and public holidays HK$15, deluxe class HK$24); **Lantau** from Pier 7 (48min.; every 1½-2hr. 6:10am-10:30pm; M-Sa HK$10-16; Su HK$15-24); and **Peng Chau** (38min.; every 30min. 7am-11:30pm; M-Sa HK$10-16; Su HK$15-24). For schedules and fares, contact the tourist office or the **Hongkong & Yaumati Ferry Co. Ltd.** (☎2736 1381 or 2516 9581).

HONG KONG

PRACTICAL INFORMATION

TOURIST AND FINANCIAL SERVICES

Hong Kong Tourist Association (HKTA), The Center, 99 Queen's Rd. Ground fl., Central (☎2807 6543; fax 2806 0303; info@hkta.org; www.hkta.org), Hong Kong Island. MTR: Central, D exit. Turn left on Pedder St., and then turn left onto Des Voeux Rd. Central. Walk about 10min. until you reach a set of escalators on your left. Take the escalator one level up and walk through the maze of steel mirrors between the two water pools until you reach another set of escalators. Take the escalator down into the basement, turn left and voilà! An important stop for any visitor to the SAR. Scores of glossy new brochures and information pamphlets on events, festivals, and activities line the shelves, created in accordance to HKTA's two-year campaign for tourism since April 2001. Open daily 8am-6pm. Other HKTA offices at **Star Ferry Concourse,** TST (open daily 8am-6pm) and **Hong Kong International Airport** in Buffer Halls A and B in the transit area (open 24hr.). All HKTA offices have maps, subway, bus, and ferry route maps and schedules, and the official guides to shopping, dining, and sightseeing. Weekly *Hong Kong Diary* lists current festivals and events. Visitors with foreign passports who plan to do some shopping can also ask for a free **Hong Kong VIP card** that offers special discounts at many upscale stores. Self-guided **walking tour** guides with portable CD-ROM player and headphone cost HK$50 (HK$500 refundable deposit). *Exploring Hong Kong's Countryside* by Edwards Stokes (HK$80) serves as an excellent reference for walks, hikes on Hong Kong Island, Lamma, Lantau, and New Territories. You can also request a complimentary copy of any one of the guides to Hong Kong's 18 districts, each of which lists the sights and all relevant tourist information.

Additional help can be found at:

Multilingual HKTA Visitor Hotline (☎2508 1234). Open daily 8am-6pm.

24hr. Infofax Facsimile Information Service (☎(900) 6077 1128). Local calls HK$1 per min.

Sincerity Travel, 835A Star House East Block (☎2730 3269), next to the Star Ferry pier. Offers discounts for ISIC holders (ISIC HK$100). Open M-F 9:30am-7:30pm, Sa 9:30am-6:30pm. Credit cards accepted (2.25% surcharge).

Armaan Travel Service, Alpha House, 27-33 Nathan Rd., 5th fl., Flat C (☎2723 3330; atsl@armaantravel.com). Mostly deals with air travel; arranges visas to India. Open M-F 9:30am-6pm, Sa 9:30am-1pm. Credit cards accepted.

Immigration office: Hong Kong Immigration Department, Immigration Tower, 7 Gloucester Rd., Wan Chai (24hr. ☎2824 6111; www.info.gov.hk/immd). For **visa extensions,** bring your passport, airplane ticket, and HK$135 and fill out form ID91. Work and study visas require an ID card, passport, a completed ID91 application form, and a letter from the appropriate company or school. Open M-F 8:45am-4:30pm, Sa 9-11:30am. **The Visa Office of the Ministry of Foreign Affairs of the People's Republic of China in Hong Kong,** China Resources Bldg., 26 Harbour Rd., Lower Block, 5th fl., Wan Chai (☎2827 1881). The entrance is off Gloucester Rd., in the red/white building. Issues single-entry tourist visas (1-month, HK$100); dual-entry visa (1-month, HK$150); multiple-entry visa (HK$400). Visa processing takes 1 working day. Express 1hr. service (HK$150). Open M-F 9:30am-12:20pm and 2-5:30pm.

Currency Exchange: Banks usually offer the best rates, but there are several avenues for currency exchange. In **Chungking Mansions,** 36-44 Nathan Rd., stalls on the 1st fl. (not the very first booth at the entrance) have competitive rates and are usually open daily 9:30am-6pm. AmEx cardholders can use Jetco **ATMs** for cash advances in Hong Kong currency. MC and Visa holders can use HongkongBank's "Electronic Money" ATMs as well as Citibank ATMs.

Traveler's checks: American Express: Henley Bldg., 5 Queen's Rd., 1st fl., Central (☎2277 1010, 24hr. hotline 2528 3247). MTR: Central Station, Landmark exit. Exchanges currency and AmEx traveler's checks (no fcc). Handles credit card payments. Open M-F 9am-5pm, Sa 9am-12:30pm. China Plaza, 48 Cameron Rd., 1st fl., TST (☎2926 1606). Exchanges traveler's checks. Open M-F 9am-5pm, Sa 9am-12:30pm. Taikoo Place, Somerset House, 979 King's Rd., 18th fl., Quarry Branch (☎2811 6888). Offers client mail services, mail held 30 days at no fee for members and holders of AmEx traveler's checks; does not exchange traveler's checks. Open M-F 9am-5pm, Sa 9am-12:30pm. **Thomas Cook:** ☎2854 4938. **Western Union:** ☎2528 5631.

Lost or Stolen Credit Cards: American Express (☎2811 6122); **Citibank** (☎2823 2323; **JCB** (☎2366 7211); **Mastercard** (☎2511 6387); **Visa** (☎2810 8033).

Weather and Local Information: Weather Conditions in English (☎187 8066). **Special Weather,** such as typhoons, (☎2835 1473). **English Newsline** (☎(900) 0038 7177).

Gay Organizations: HORIZONS, Winning Commercial Bldg., 46-48 Hillwood Rd., TST (☎2815 9268; fax 2542 3714). Information on gay nightlife and events around town as well as support and counseling. Open Tu and Th 7:30-10:30pm.

EMERGENCY AND COMMUNICATIONS

Emergency: ☎999.

Police: Crime Hotline and Taxi Complaints (☎2527 7177). To locate the nearest police station, call 2860 2000.

Medical Services: Hong Kong Island: **Queen Mary Hospital** (☎2855 3111); Kowloon: **Queen Elizabeth Hospital** (☎2958 8888); New Territories: **Prince of Wales Hospital** (☎2632 2211). **Free ambulance service:** Hong Kong Island (☎2576 6555); Kowloon and New Territories (☎2713 5555).

Internet Access: All public libraries have free Internet access, with so many computers that you usually don't have to wait too long, especially not on weekdays. Also, universities such as the Hong Kong Polytechnic University on Yuk Choi Rd., Hung Hom, often have many computers with Internet access.

Cash Online (☎2366 0060), on Nathan Rd. just before Peking Rd., TST (MTR: Tsim Sha Tsui, Hong Kong Museum of Art exit.). HK$20 per 30min.; free hot beverage, juice, or soft drink. HK$10 per additional 30min. Open daily 8:30am-10pm.

Post Offices: GPO, 2 Connaught Pl., **Central** (☎2921 2333). MTR: Central, Jardine House exit. Immediately to the right of Star Ferry and in front of the Jardine House. Poste Restante held for 2 weeks. Open M-Sa 8am-6pm, Su 8am-2pm. Hermes House, 10 Middle Rd., Ground fl., **TST** (☎2366 4111). MTR: TST, Nathan Rd. exit. Walk past Chungking Mansions toward the harbor, and turn left onto Middle Rd.; Hermes House is at the end of the street on the left. *Poste Restante* held for 3 months. Open M-F 8am-6pm, Sa 8am-2pm, Su 8am-6pm.

Telephones: HK$70 or HK$100 IDD phonecards sold at Hong Kong Telecom Service centers, HKTA offices, or 7-Eleven and Circle K stores. Hong Kong Telecom sells cards in denominations of HK$200, HK$300, and HK$500. The office on 10 Middle Rd. is open 24hr. Local calls HK$1 per 5min.

Telephone Information: Directory Assistance (☎1081). **Operator assistance** (☎10010) for IDD inquiries, collect calls, and/or phonecard inquiries.

KOWLOON

Kowloon, the jam-packed 11 sq. km peninsula off the New Territories, is the quintessential picture of Hong Kong. Kowloon (*gau lung* in Cantonese) is named for the nine mythical dragons that are said to inhabit the peninsula—one for each of the peninsula's eight mountain peaks and one more for Ping, an ancient child-emperor. Today, the color and fury of these legendary winged beasts still lingers in the resplendent natural beauty of the area, but apartment blocks, hotels, restaurants, and plazas encroach on their traditional turf. Crowds along Nathan Rd. in TST linger in front of jewelry stores, inhale the subtle hue of saffron in restaurants, or don 3in. dancing shoes at night to paint the town red. All the while, the dragon's fiery breath still blows throughout the land—a pulsing heat that travelers to Hong Kong simply cannot avoid.

ORIENTATION

At the southernmost tip of Victoria Harbour are the roads **Tsim Sha Tsui (TST)** and **Tsim Sha Tsui East (TST East),** separated by **Chatham Rd. South** and bounded in the south by **Salisbury Rd.** Along the waterfront are some of Kowloon's most recognizable landmarks, including the Star Ferry Pier, the Cultural Centre, the Hong Kong Space Museum, and the New World Centre. **Nathan Rd.** begins at Salisbury Rd. and runs north into the smaller districts of **Yau Ma Tei** and **Mong Kok,** both of which are famous for their crowded street markets. The red line of the **MTR** subway system runs along Nathan Rd. and under the harbor to Hong Kong Island. To the east, past the **terminus of the KCR** and the **Hong Kong Coliseum,** lies **Hung Hom.** In the north, **Boundary Rd.** separates Kowloon from the New Territories.

ACCOMMODATIONS

Tsim Sha Tsui offers numerous accommodations in the center of the chaos, dirt, noise, and decadent luxury that is Hong Kong. Budget digs in TST consist mainly of guesthouses that are tucked away inside vast "mansions"—basically cavernous apartment buildings where the flats have been partitioned into smaller rooms. Be wary of individuals along Nathan Rd. and outside Mirador Mansions and Chungking Mansions who aggressively tout their "very clean, very quiet, very cheap" rooms; also, if you have decided where to stay, it's best to keep this information to yourself.

CHUNGKING MANSIONS

Chungking Mansions, located at 36-44 Nathan Rd. (MTR: Tsim Sha Tsui, Hong Kong Museum of Art exit), is far and away the most notorious of the TST mansions. The elegant dark marble and gold lettering outside hide Chungking's chaotic interior; it is legendary for its dim labyrinth of hallways and dank staircases, crowded elevators, and disreputable inhabitants. Chungking Mansions in fact does have very quiet, very clean rooms, but it is unlikely that the touts on the ground floor are affiliated with such establishments.

Chungking Mansions is divided into five blocks, unimaginatively called A, B, C, D, and E block. From the entrance to the arcade, the A, B, and C elevators are on the left, while D and E are on the right. Each block has a pair of elevators: one services even-numbered floors, the other odd-numbered ones. Quality varies more than price, so choose guesthouses carefully; ask to look at a room before agreeing to spend the night. All guesthouses accept cash only.

Women traveling alone should take particular care: they may find themselves the object of unwanted attention from some long-term Chungking residents.

Travelers Hostel, A Block, 16th fl. (☎2368 2505 or 2368 7710; digand@hotmail.com). Spacious, fairly clean dorms popular with backpackers. Cable TV in common room. Free lockers for guests, but no padlocks provided. Luggage storage HK$5-10 per day. **Internet access** HK$10 per 15min. IDD service. 6-bed dorms with A/C HK$65; singles HK$100, with A/C HK$130.

Kyoto Guesthouse, A8, 15th fl. (☎2721 3574 or 9077 8297). Colorful rooms and cheerful staff. Singles HK$80-100, with A/C and bath HK$120; doubles with A/C and bath HK$150-160. HK$10 discount for individual travelers.

Harbour Guesthouse, B8, 4th fl. (☎2721 2207 or 2367 2777). All rooms have A/C and TV. Discounts for longer stays; rates increase by about HK$10 in summer. Singles HK$100, with bath HK$110; doubles HK$160, with bath HK$200.

Mandarin Guesthouse, E5, 13th fl. (☎2366 0073). A location in block E means less crowded elevators. Every room in this average guesthouse has A/C, bath, phone, sandals, towels, and toilet paper. IDD service. Singles HK$130-150; doubles HK$200. Prices very negotiable.

Welcome Guesthouse, A5, 7th fl. (☎2721 7793 or 2721 7436; gloriak@netvigator.com). Run by a father-son team that readily offers travel advice, it rents out clean but aging rooms with A/C, fridge, large windows, towels, and TV. Singles HK$100, with bath HK$130-150; doubles with twin beds and bath HK$200-220. In July prices rise 10-20%. 10-15% student discount available.

MIRADOR MANSIONS

These days, many backpackers seem to be moving from Chungking to Mirador Mansions, a few doors down at 54-64 Nathan Rd.; Mirador's few guesthouses are interspersed with private residences. Unlike Chungking, it is relatively clean, quiet, and uncrowded. Two elevators (one for odd-numbered floors, one for even) are to the right as you enter the arcade.

Cosmic Guesthouse, A1, A2, and F1, 12th fl. (☎2721 3077 or 2369 6669). Open for just over 3 years, and run by a very friendly family, the Cosmic Guesthouse is truly out of this world. Spotless rooms have A/C, phone, and TV. Communal fridge and hot water dispenser in the hallway. IDD service. Check-out 11am. Deposit HK$100. 8-bed dorms HK$60; singles HK$110-130, with bath HK$150; doubles with bath $200-220; triples with bath $240-270. Discounts for anyone with a copy of *Let's Go*.

Man Hing Lung Hotel, F2, 14th fl. (☎2311 8807 or 2722 0678; mhlhotel@hkstar.com). This fairly clean guesthouse even meets government safety standards, unusual for guesthouses in Mirador. A/C, phone, and TV. Singles HK$120, with private bath HK$150; doubles HK$150-220; triples HK$220-270.

Garden Guesthouse, F4, 3rd fl. (☎2311 1183). Very popular with backpackers for its dorm rooms, Garden's best feature is its large outdoor balcony. A/C, phone, and TV in the common room. 6-bed single-sex dorms HK$60; doubles with bath HK$200.

BEYOND THE MANSIONS

YMCA, 41 Salisbury Rd. (☎2268 7000; room@ymcahk.org.hk), next to the Peninsula Hotel and opposite the Hong Kong Cultural Centre. MTR: Tsim Sha Tsui. This posh establishment features a swimming pool, squash courts, and indoor climbing walls. Reservations recommended, especially during summer and holidays. IDD service and Internet access. Wheelchair accessible. Closet-sized lockers with personal safes. Deposit HK$150 room deposit. 7-night max stay; dorm guests must show a visa proving that they've been in Hong Kong 10 days or fewer. 4-bed dorms with A/C and bath HK$190. 10% service charge. 10% discount for YMCA associates. Credit cards accepted.

Victoria Hostel, 33 Hankow Rd., 3rd fl. (☎2376 0621; vhostel@hkstar.com), 2 blocks from Nathan Rd. MTR: Tsim Sha Tsui, Hong Kong Museum of Art exit. Walk onto Middle Rd., turn right, walk ahead until Hankow Rd., turn right and walk until you see the blue and white sign for the hostel. Don't worry—the building's grimy outside is not indicative of its interior. A/C, common baths, phone, and TV. Deposit HK$100. 10-bed dorms HK$60; 4-bed dorms HK$140; singles HK$220; doubles HK$280.

FOOD

Hong Kong is a self-acclaimed culinary heaven, with restaurants and food stalls lining every road. The *Official Dining and Entertainment Guide* (available at HKTA offices), the *HK Magazine*, and *bc Magazine* all list and rank restaurants and are free and widely available at most hotels and restaurants.

Dim sum is the soul of Hong Kong. Meaning "to touch the heart," *dim sum* is positive proof that the fastest way to someone's heart is through their stomach. Enjoyed in the late morning or early afternoon, *dim sum* is a selection of bite-sized morsels shared by three or four people as they drink pot after pot of tea. Most Cantonese restaurants serve *dim sum* from 11am to 2pm, although some establishments devoted solely to *dim sum* continue on through the evening. The usual procedure for ordering *dim sum* involves either checking off a desired dish on a slip of paper or pointing at waiters that wander by with rolling carts.

Some of the best culinary bargains are found in decrepit, no-name shops and stalls. Food vendors come out in the late evening (after 11pm) to refuel eager shoppers along **Nathan, Carnarvon,** and **Mody Rd.** Also, try the small streets west of Nathan Rd. While many Indian restaurants have members-only rules, the first and mezzanine floors of Chungking Mansions host a number of jam-packed but dirt-cheap stalls serving delectable South Asian dishes (often under HK$20).

Small cafes along **Haiphong** and **Canton Rd.** post menus listing Cantonese and Western food items outside their windows (HK$30-40). For those seeking Western food, **Ashley Rd.** features restaurants and pubs that serve up hearty portions of Australian, Italian, and English food at mid-range prices. **Kimberly Rd.,** which branches off Nathan Rd. farther inland, is packed to the brim with restaurants. The area bounded by **Hart Ave.** and **Prat Ave.,** on the opposite side of Nathan Rd. to Kowloon

Park, has an exciting selection of both Western and Asian fare—and nightlife venues to help sated diners work away the extra calories.

Most malls in the city have **food courts,** which usually offer a great selection of cheap Asian and Western fast food. **City's Super,** inside Harbour City Mall on Canton road in TST, has a dizzying selection of international fast food cuisine that's a little more upscale than most food-court fare. Set meals run about HK$26-60. (Open Su-Th 10:30am-9:30pm, F-Sa, and public holidays 10:30am-10pm.)

The Sweet Dynasty, 88 Canton Rd., Ground fl., TST (☎2375 9119), opposite the Harbour City shopping plaza. Famed for its *tong shui,* sweet soups traditionally served after meals. Flour and peanut balls, pudding soups, and more curiously named dishes like *stewed snow frog fat* are also on the menu. You may want to start off with a delicious bowl of almond soup (HK$15) and plunge into a bowl of fresh pork kidney and pig's tripe congee (HK$36). Open Su-Th 7:30am-midnight, F-Sa 7:30am-1am.

Cheerful Ginseng Congee, Fullcorp Centre, 53-55 Chatham Rd. South, TST East (☎2368 9203), near Cameron Rd. True to its name, this restaurant serves up delicious bowls of hot congee for a palatable HK$16-30. Some meat congees are slightly more expensive (HK$38-88). Health-friendly, vegetarian-friendly, and people-friendly. English and Chinese menu. Take out available. Open daily 7:30am-4am.

Han Wo Korean Restaurant, Multifield Plaza, 3-7A Prat Ave., Ground fl., Flat 9, TST (☎2739 7798). Open atmosphere, and open to all budgets, with prices ranging from HK$15 to HK$550. Open daily 11am-1am. Credit cards accepted.

Wing Fat Restaurant, 448 Nathan Rd., Ground fl., Yau Ma Tei (☎2385 8167). The unpretentious fare, cheap prices, long hours, and plastic-vinyl decor are as down-to-earth as you can get. Dishes HK$30-45, french toast HK$15. Open daily 7am-4am.

Jade Court Seafood Restaurant, Pacific Centre, 16-38 Hankow Rd., 2nd fl., TST (☎2723 1823). A festive atmosphere prevails in this local favorite. Light *dim sum* for 3 people (3-4 dishes) costs a reasonable HK$200. Top it off with mango pudding. Open daily 7am-midnight. Credit cards accepted.

Her Thai Restaurant, Shop 1, Promenade Level Tower 1, on Canton Rd. (☎2735 8898), in China Hong Kong City, TST. Outdoor tables and a stunning view of the harbor. Entrees HK$50-70, seafood dishes HK$100-120, and drinks HK$27-30. The *longan* drink is a sweet refreshment. Stick with the less expensive set menus (HK$138-298). Open daily noon-11pm, happy hour 3-7pm. Credit cards accepted.

SHOPPING

There is no need to go looking for good shopping in Hong Kong—it's everywhere and it's hard to resist. Serious shoppers may want to pick up *The Official Shopping Guide* from HKTA offices. It features shipping and insurance advice, bargaining and bargain-hunting hints, and the hours and addresses of almost every store in the city. HKTA also offers a free VIP card, which lists discounts available for tourists at upscale tours.

Bargaining is inappropriate in large boutiques and department stores, where prices are indicated. In many smaller shops and especially in street market stalls, it's expected—don't hesitate to ask for a "special price."

For short shopping sojourns near any of TST's "mansions," head to Nathan Rd.'s **Golden Mile,** the road's final stretch on the way to Victoria Harbour. **Granville Rd.,** off Nathan Rd., is also lined with shops selling clothing at incredible discounts. Street-side vendors emerge with their carts along **Salisbury Rd.** and Nathan Rd. and beside major hotels most evenings. Watches and shirts (from "Rolax" to "Tammy Hillfinger") cost about half what they do in the more crowded street markets. Buying electronics along Nathan Rd. may appear tempting but is extremely risky, as vendors usually don't include the packaging, prices vary wildly, and buyers often lug their purchases home only to discover that a few key internal parts have mysteriously disappeared.

STREET MARKETS. A visit to Kowloon's noisy, chaotic street markets is an incomparable experience. You might find some good deals here, but prices that seem too good to be true probably are. Most designer labels are cheap—albeit convincing—imitations.

You'll find the best deals on clothing at **Fa Yuen St. Market** (MTR: Prince Edward, B2 exit). From Prince Edward Rd. West, walk against traffic (not literally, of course); Fa Yuen St. is two blocks ahead, on the right. Walk one block along Fa Yuen St. away from Prince Edward Rd. and turn right onto the street parallel to Fa Yuen St. to find the **Tung Choi St. Aquarium Market,** on Tungchoi St. Shops have walls lined with water-filled plastic bags housing goldfish, which are said to bring good luck and are always in demand. (Open daily 10am-6pm.)

Off Sai Yee St. is **Flower Market Rd.,** Hong Kong's best-smelling street. (MTR: Prince Edward, B3 exit; turn left on Prince Edward Rd. West, walk past Sai Yee St. on the left; Flower Market Rd. is on the right.) Petals give way to feathers at the end of the road and the entrance to **Yuen Po St. Bird Garden.** Recently built to replace the old Bird Street Market on Hong Lok St., the Bird Garden houses vendors selling birds, cages, and live grasshoppers. Old men also come here daily to "walk" their birds. (Open daily 10am-6pm.)

Mong Kok and **Yau Ma Tei** also bustle with street markets. **Mong Kong Market** is on Tung Choi St. (MTR: Mong Kok, D2 exit). Walk straight ahead for one block. At the traffic light, turn right and cross the street. Otherwise known as **Ladies' Street Market,** this is the place for handbags, shirts, dresses, and even underwear. (Open daily 10am-10:30pm.) To reach **Temple St. Night Market** (MTR: Jordan, Temple St. exit), walk three blocks from the station before turning right on Temple St. Imitation designer shirts, watches, and handbags are all for sale, while palm-readers and fortune-tellers prophesize outside the temple. Shoppers can also sample snacks from stalls or enjoy performances of Chinese opera. (Open daily 7-10pm.) From Temple St., turn left on Kansu St. and walk three blocks to reach the **Jade Market,** where vendors hawk real and fake jade trinkets and souvenirs, as well as sunglasses, nail clippers, and other odds and ends. (Open daily 10am-3:30pm.)

CHINESE MEDICINE. Throughout Hong Kong, **Chinese medicine** emporiums beckon passersby with their bitter odors and jars of antlers, seahorses, and other oddities. Since the staff at most stalls generally speaks little or no English, try visiting **Eu Yan Sang (Hong Kong) Limited,** Eu Yan Sang Tower, 11-15 Chatham Rd. South, Ground fl., for an overview of herbal remedies and other Chinese cures in English. En Yan Sang displays samples of a whole array of Chinese medicinal plants, rocks, and animal parts, all with tags identifying the maladies each one cures. Call the central office hotline (☎2544 3268) to inquire about the location of other branches. (☎2366 8321; www.euyansang.com. Open daily 10am-8:30pm.)

NIGHTLIFE

Bars and pubs pack the odd quadrilateral formed by Carnarvon, Cameron, Chatham, and Mody Rd. and the area bounded by Hart Ave. and Prat Ave. Bars in TMT often have a dance floor, so bring your dancing shoes.

Ned Kelly's Last Stand, 11A Ashley Rd. (☎2376 0562). This Aussie saloon immortalizes a famed outlaw. For jazz lovers, this is the place to be. Live jazz 9pm-2am. Happy hour 11:30am-10pm. Menu items HK$48-130. Fried eggs, bacon, sausages, chips, toast, and tea/coffee/juice HK$64. Open daily 11:30am-2am.

Grammy's Lounge, Supreme House, 2A Hart Ave., Ground fl.(☎2368 3833). A favorite local hangout, Grammy's boasts multi-colored lights, shimmering gold curtains, and Canto-pop performances. Karaoke M-Sa 5-9pm and all day Sunday. Live band M-Th 2-5pm, F-Sa 1-5pm. Happy hour 3-10pm; most drinks HK$18. Cover HK$15, HK$10 during happy hour. Open M-Th 1pm-2am, F-Sa 1pm-1am, all day Su. Credit cards accepted

Rick's Cafe, 53-59 Kimberly Rd. (☎2367 2939). When you visit this popular nightstop, snazz it up; men in shorts and anyone with sandals are not allowed inside. The DJ has a penchant for love songs. Happy hour 5-10pm (mixed drinks and bottled beer HK$22). Open M-Th 5pm-3am, F-Sa 5pm-5am.

K.K. Pub & Cafe, 45-51 Chatham Rd., Shop B, basement (☎2312 2808). The techno beat and popular DJ keep hearts thumping M-Sa 8pm-3am. This large establishment has many, many, many screens to watch soccer–as if watching the dancers weren't entertaining enough. Drinks HK$32-50, HK$18-40 during happy hour (daily 3-9pm). Open M-F 11am-5am, Sa 11am-6am, Su 4:30pm-5am.

SIGHTS

TSIM SHA TSUI

NATHAN ROAD. Nathan Road is as crazy, chaotic, and hectic as Hong Kong gets. TST's most important thoroughfare is also its greatest tourist attraction. The distinguished **Peninsula Hotel** marks one end of the boutique-packed road.; a few minutes away are the legendary **Chungking Mansions.**

Covering the vast area between Nathan and Canton Rd., **Kowloon Park** (MTR: Tsim Sha Tsui, A1 exit) is a verdant oasis amid Hong Kong's endless stretches of concrete. The park features lush foliage and wildlife (flamingos and rare Asian birds share an open-air aviary) and postmodern sculptures. The footbridge to the Royal Pacific Hotel offers great views of the harbor. *(Open daily 6am-midnight.)* Near the park's Nathan Rd. entrance sits the majestic **Kowloon Mosque and Islamic Centre.** *(105 Nathan Rd. ☎2724 0095. Visitors must wear pants or long skirts. Open daily 4:30am-10pm. Free.)*

HONG KONG

ON THE WATERFRONT. Many of TST's ultra-modern museums and landmark attractions cluster along the waterfront near the Star Ferry Pier, far from the neon lights and bargain-bonanza commotion of Nathan Rd. From the Clock Tower, a lonely remnant of the old KCR station, a concrete walkway known as the Promenade stretches along the northern banks of Victoria Harbour and into TST East. The Promenade passes by the Hong Kong Cultural Centre, the city's prime venue for Cantonese opera, Andrew Lloyd Weber musicals, and symphony concerts.

Directly adjacent to the Cultural Centre is the **Hong Kong Space Museum,** a golf-ball shaped building filled with hands-on exhibits. The **planetarium** (the world's largest) and the **Omnimax Theater** each present at least three shows a day. *(10 Salisbury Rd. Shows usually start every hr. 11:30am-8:30pm. HK$32, students and seniors HK$16. ☎2734 2722. Open M, W-F 1-9pm, Sa-Su 10am-9pm. Cantonese, English, Japanese, and Mandarin recorded tours. HK$10, students and seniors HK$5, free W.)* Behind the Space Museum, the **Hong Kong Museum of Art** houses large, well-maintained exhibits of ancient and modern Chinese art. *(☎2721 0116. Open daily 10am-6pm. HK$10, students and seniors HK$5, free W.)*

TSIM SHA TSUI EAST

The waterfront **promenade** begins in TST and ends in TST East. Nearby, fishermen dangle makeshift lines in Victoria Harbour, but they seem to catch more oil cans, boots, and rubbish than fish as couples cuddle in corners of the second-level walkway (open daily 7am-11pm) behind the Cultural Centre. Farther down, the Promenade runs past the **New World Centre,** near an artificial waterfall and a gigantic watch embedded in a rock.

Chatham Rd. South, the boundary between the two TMTs, veers off Salisbury Rd., away from the waterfront, just after the New World Centre. Noodle, rice, and *dim sum* restaurants line one side of the street, while parks and covered rest areas proffer benches for tired sightseers on the other. At the intersection of Chatham Rd. and Austin Rd. is the brand-new **Hong Kong Museum of History.** *(☎2724 9042. Open Tu-Sa 1-6pm. HK$10; students, seniors, and handicapped HK$5.)*

NEW KOWLOON

Squeezed between Mong Kok and the New Territories, New Kowloon has neither the glamour of Kowloon nor the seclusion of the New Territories.

CHI LIN NUNNERY. Reputedly built without a single nail over the course of 10 years, Chi Lin Nunnery is the latest architectural wonder of Hong Kong. This newly opened Tang dynasty-style Buddhist complex is visually very impressive, with 16 halls and a beautiful rock garden. Its elegant grandeur in the midst of such an urban setting is rather bizarre—as is the aura of newness for a building constructed exactly as a monastery would have been a thousand years ago. *(5 Chi Lin Dr. MTR: Diamond Hall, C exit. Follow the yellow signs. ☎2354 1604 or 2354 1882. Open daily 9am-3:30pm except W; Western Lotus Pond Garden open daily 6:30am-7pm.)*

WONG TAI SIN TEMPLE COMPLEX. This complex is named after a legendary healer and dedicated to Daoist and Buddhist deities and Confucius. Old ladies sell incense sticks to temple-goers; while tourists look on, the devout come to bow and pray in this active place of worship, bringing offerings of fruit and cooked chickens. Donations go to support education and temple maintenance. *(2 Chuk Yuen Village. MTR: Wong Tai Sin, B exit. ☎2327 8141. Open daily 7am-5pm. Free.)*

The peaceful **Good Wish Garden** stretches behind the main temple. Artificial rock formations, marred only by lovers' graffiti, offer shade from the sun. As you exit the garden, Kowloon's nine coiled dragons bid you farewell. *(Open Tu-Su 9am-4pm.)*

HONG KONG ISLAND

ORIENTATION

When viewed from across the harbor, Hong Kong Island's impressive skyline looks like an unbroken string of high-rises. From left to right (east to west), Hong Kong Island is divided into the districts of Sheung Wan, Central, Admiralty, Wan Chai, and Causeway Bay; Stanley is farther south. The island's center is dominated by mountains like Victoria Peak, most of which are largely pristine and undeveloped.

SHEUNG WAN. At the end of the MTR Island line, Sheung Wan is also the home of the Macau Ferry Terminal. Connaught Rd. Central, the area's main thoroughfare, follows the edge of the harbor. Moving south away from the coast, Des Voeux Rd. Central and Queen's Rd. Central run parallel to Connaught Rd. Central. Hollywood Rd. marks the edge of SoHo district, roughly three blocks south of Queen's Rd. Central.

CENTRAL AND ADMIRALTY. Most of Central's major landmarks and sights are easily to find if you use the **Star Ferry Pier** as a reference point. **Connaught Rd. Central/Harcourt Rd.** runs parallel to the pier, passing **Jardine House,** a silver rectangle with glass. Queen's Rd. Central and Des Voeux Rd. Central merge to become **Queensway;** the austere black **Cheung Kong Centre,** the gleaming blue **Bank of China Tower,** and the beige pillar-and-dome structure of the **Legislative Council (Legco) building** can be found at this intersection. Three blocks beyond Queen's Road Central is the infamous expat playpen **Lan Kwai Fong.**

WAN CHAI. The Hong Kong Convention and Exhibition Centre juts out into the harbor, dominating the waterfront when viewed from afar. Center Plaza is farther inland, behind the Convention Centre and Harbour Rd. and is home to the Hong Kong Revenue Tower and the Immigration Tower. Gloucester, Hennessy, and Johnston Rds. run east-west, roughly parallel to one another, and are intersected by Fenwick, Luard, O'Brien, and Fleming Rds.

CAUSEWAY BAY. Causeway Bay is roughly divided into northern and southern sections by the broad swath of **Hennessy Rd.,** which becomes **Yee Wo St.** and then **Causeway Rd.** as it runs eastward. **Gloucester Rd.** runs parallel to and north of Hennessy until it hits **Victoria Park** and makes a sharp right-angle turn, eventually crossing Yee Wo St./Causeway Rd. The tightly packed **Jardine's Bazaar** and **Jardine's Crescent** streets are parallel to Yee Wo St.

STANLEY. Most of Stanley's attractions (including its famous market) are on **Stanley Main St.,** an intricate thread of connected lanes. The frenzied clusters of shopping stalls and restaurants that line this street make it nearly impossible to use addresses to navigate.

ACCOMMODATIONS

The accommodations on Hong Kong Island, apart from a few semi-affordable options in Causeway Bay, are usually at least twice as expensive as the guesthouses on the Kowloon peninsula.

Ma Wui Mt. Davis Youth Hostel (HI) (☎2817 5715) is far, far away on top of Mt. Davis Path, off Victoria Rd., in Kennedy Town. A shuttle runs to the hostel from the Macau Ferry Terminal in Sheung Wan (20min.; 9:30am, 7, 9, 10:30pm; HK$10). Call ahead to ensure there are vacancies. The only inexpensive option on Hong Kong Island. Large, clean dorm rooms and an upbeat, communal atmosphere. A/C and linens provided. Common kitchen, bathrooms, and phones. Simple chores required daily. Lights out 11pm, curfew midnight. Dorm beds (single-sex) HK$65, non-members HK$95; 4-person rooms available at HK$75, non-members HK$105.

Jetvan Traveller's House, Fairview Mansion, 51 Paterson St., Flat 4A, Causeway Bay (☎2890 8133 or 2984 8539). A nondescript establishment with a spacious area and a large TV. Rooms come with A/C, phone, towels, sheets, and TV. Singles HK$250, with bath HK$300; doubles with bath HK$350; triples HK$450.

Payless Inn, Fairview Mansion, 51 Paterson St., Flat 5A (☎2808 1030 or 2808 1004; fax 2890 7798). The smell of ginseng greets guests of this clean guest house. IDD service in lobby. Singles with double beds have A/C, bath, phone, and TV HK$250; HK$50 for an additional person. Expect a 20% price increase during peak tourist season.

An Zhang Hang, Fairview Mansion, 51 Paterson St., Flat 2A (☎2895 0626 or 2577 5758; fax 2895 2895). The cleanest and most pleasant atmosphere on the island. Rooms have A/C, phone, and TV. Doubles HK$350; triples HK$450.

HONG KONG

FOOD

SHEUNG WAN

Hankering for a taste of Russian caviar, Argentinian steak, or Japanese *sashimi?* If so, head to **SoHo** ("South of Hollywood Rd."). A couple of flights up the Mid-Level E escalators, SoHo is an uneasy collection of expensive international restaurants on otherwise lackluster streets. Most of SoHo's restaurants are open for dinner (6-11pm); some also serve lunch (noon-3pm). Most of the culinary action happens on **Staunton St.,** parallel to Hollywood Rd., and **Elgin St.,** which begins slightly south of the intersection of Staunton St. and Peel St.

Just off the well-beaten path, **La Piazetta,** 5 Tsun Wing Ln., is a classy Italian restaurant that serves up pizza (HK$38-78), pasta (HK$37-60), and specials like deer *ragout.* (☎2522 9505. Open daily noon-11:30pm.) The **Singapore Restaurant,** Alliance Building, 130-131 Connaught Rd., offers an extensive menu with low-end prices. The menu includes chicken *à la portuguese* (HK$55), shredded beef stroganoff (HK$38), and ice cream sundaes. (☎2815 1566. Open daily 11am-11pm.)

CENTRAL

Midnight Express, 3 Lan Kwai Fong (☎2525 5010 or 2523 4041). Serves generous portions of Greek, Indian, and Italian dishes for under HK$55; the kebabs (HK$35-55) are tasty and filling. On weeknights, the small eating booth is a refreshing escape from the glitz and sparkle of Lan Kwai Fong. On weekends, it is filled with beer-guzzling businesspeople. Beer HK$20-30. Free delivery in Central and Wan Chai. Open M-Sa 10am-3am, Su 11am-3pm.

Dai Pai Dong, 128 Queen's Rd. (☎2851 6389). Choose from more than 10 noodle combination meals. Those with a sweet tooth may want to try the Dai Pai Dong toast (HK$13) or a sweet Chinese pancake (HK$26). Scrambled egg on toast HK$26. 10% service charge. Open M-Sa 8am-10pm, Su 9:30am-7pm.

South East Garden Vietnamese Food, 8 Queen Victoria St. (☎2525 3953). Sit at a small glass table and enjoy the unique ambience created by dark wooden furniture and plastic flowers. Barbecued pork HK$20; sandwiches HK$8-11. No English or Mandarin is spoken in this local hangout. Open daily 7am-5:30pm.

Bravo. Le Cafe, 34-37 Connaught Rd. Central (☎2104 7129). The black roof, varnished wood tile and scattered fruit baskets make think you're in Europe. Chefs deftly serve up buttered French toast (HK$16), Indian *samosa* platters, Chinese-style chicken, and other sumptuous platters from the open kitchen. Open M-Sa 7am-9pm.

WAN CHAI

Banana Leaf Curry House, 440 Jaffe Rd., 1st fl. (☎2573 8187). Other locations in TST, Mong Kok, Whampoa Garden, and Causeway Bay. Waitresses in traditional dress scoop rice from a large wooden bucket onto a banana leaf. A comfortable setting for families. Pork satay appetizer HK$48, curry HK$24-48, and vegetables HK$20. Open M-F 11:30am-3pm and 6pm-midnight, Sa-Su and public holidays 11am-11:30pm. Credit cards accepted.

Healthy Vegetarian Restaurant, 51-53 Hennessy Rd., Ground fl. (☎2527 3918), uses the culinary marvels of bean curd to create uncanny meat imitations (entrees HK$38-138). The strict vegetarian can even try shark's fin (HK$68). Takeout available. Open M-Sa 10:30am-11pm, Su 5pm-11pm. DC/MC/V.

CAUSEWAY BAY

Laurel Noodle, 462 Lockhart Rd. (☎2904 7867). Eat spare ribs in pineapple sauce (HK$28) off porcelain dishes and propose a toast with mineral juice (HK$8) to the gods of cheap food. Open daily noon-11pm.

Fantasy Vegetarian Restaurant, 66 Electric Rd. (☎2887 3886 or 2807 0569). MTR: Tin Hau Electric Rd. exit. One of the few vegetarian options in town features an English menu and a friendly, English-speaking staff. The lineup includes noodles (HK$17-29), congee (HK$48-60), vegetables with mock kidney (HK$52), and a dozen other veggie dishes (HK$48-60). Open daily 11am-10pm; *dim sum* stalls open 9am-11:30pm.

STANLEY

Pepperoni's, 18B Stanley Main St., Ground fl. (☎2813 8605), resembles an Italian bistro with tables that spill out onto the sidewalk. Delicious pizza is available in small (HK$50-65), medium (HK$65-85), and large (HK$80-100) sizes; ask for the special secret sauce. Open daily 10am-10pm.

Al Fresco's, 30A Stanley Main St., Ground fl. (☎2813 2520), a colorful eatery with a varied menu that includes Mexican tacos (HK$65). Open daily 10am-10pm. Under the same management as Pepperoni's; both have branches throughout Hong Kong Island.

The King of Pasta, 928 Stanley Main St. (☎2813 7313). Create your own dish from a choice of 10 pastas, 24 ingredients, and 8 sauces (from HK$60). Breezy Mediterranean atmosphere. Open daily 11am-midnight or 1am. AmEx.

SHOPPING

Unlike Kowloon, Hong Kong Island only has few cheap street markets where budget travelers can haggle for discounts on rip-offs of brand-name goods. Older, upscale tourists flex their financial might in boutiques that sell Yves St. Laurent, sparkling gold jewelry, and other 24-carat emblems of conspicuous consumption.

Li Yuen St. Market, in Central. **Li Yuen St. East** lies between Des Voeux Rd. and Queen's Rd. Excellent bargains for traditional Chinese dresses. Open daily 7am-10pm. **Li Yuen St. West** is parallel to and 1 block left of Li Yuen St. East, if you are standing with Jardine House behind you. More shops than its sister street and a selection of shoes that will make the shoe-lover delirious. Open daily 7am-10pm.

Central Market, at the intersection of Queen Victoria St. and Queen's Rd., Central. 3 floors packed with produce, meat, and customers. Fierce smells and questionable cleanliness, but low prices and undeniably fresh food. Open daily 6am-8pm.

Graham Street Fruit and Vegetable Market, on Graham St., off Queen's Rd., Central, between the Union Bank of Hong Kong and the V. Heun Building. This open-air market is a fruit connoisseur's fantasy, very clean and very well-stocked. Nuts, corn on the cob, and fresh tofu also available. Open daily 6am-8pm.

Jardine's Bazaar and **Jardine's Crescent,** in Causeway Bay. MTR: Causeway Bay, Jardine's Crescent exit. The Crescent is the small tunnel of clothing stalls to the right of the Giordano store. The Bazaar is the next street on the left. Peddlers sell traditional herbal medicines, preserved bean curd, and tea. Open daily noon-10pm.

NIGHTLIFE

Before heading out for a night on the town, stop by a restaurant, hotel, or newsstand and pick up a free copy of *HK Magazine* or *bc magazine*, two English-language weeklies with up-to-date entertainment and event listings.

CENTRAL AND ADMIRALTY

The L-shaped **Lan Kwai Fong** area overflows with trendy restaurants and bars. During the day, the area is packed with mild-mannered eateries that cater to a mellow clientele. As dusk falls, Lan Kwai Fong becomes the happening hot spot for Hong Kong's expats. The city-slicker material girl regulars provide enough entertainment to justify the upwardly mobile cover charges and bar tabs at these posh, upscale places. Credit cards are accepted in most bars and clubs.

Oscar's, 2 Lan Kwai Fong (☎2804 6561). Amid high ceilings and elegant decor, Oscar's caters to a cosmopolitan crowd. Tasteful style, good music, and a great bar manager who might even buy you a drink. Happy Hour daily 4-8pm (Budweiser HK$30). Open M-F 11am-1am, Sa-Su 11am-3:30am. Check out the Australian restaurant (☎2861 1511) in Causeway Bay, run by the same management.

The Fringe Club, 2 Lower Albert Rd. (☎2521 7485). A funky art gallery and bar in one. Lunch buffet daily noon-2:30pm HK$75 (M-F vegetarian). Drinks HK$35-55. Happy Hour daily M-Sa 4-9pm. Open M-Th noon-midnight, F-Sa noon-2am.

Club 64, 12-14 Wing Wah Ln., Ground fl. (☎2523 2801), off D'Aguilar St. Popular with both expats and backpackers, this laid-back bar is normally packed on weekends. Happy Hour daily 2-9pm. Drinks normally HK$40-60; during Happy Hour a Carlsberg goes for HK$15. Open M-Th noon-2am, F-Sa 10am-3am, Su 6pm-1am.

Post 97, 9-11 Lan Kwai Fong (☎2810 9333), part of the elite 97 group that includes the members-only **Club 97** in the same building. Bottled beer HK$47. Happy Hour daily 3-7pm, dinner served until 11pm. Open M-Th 10am-12:30am, F-Sa 10am-3am, Su 10am-midnight.

LA Cafe, Lippo Centre, 89 Queensway, Ground fl., Shops 2-3 (☎2526 6863). Conjures up a stereotypical Hollywood scene from its neon lights to its palm trees. Mexican dishes HK$75-125, burgers HK$90-95, pasta HK$85-105. Happy hour daily 2-8pm. Bottled beer HK$24. Open M-F 11am-midnight, Sa-Su 10am-12:30am.

Sherman's, California Entertainment Bldg., 34-36 D'Aguilar St., Ground fl. (☎2801 4946). Sophisticated patrons blow smoke rings from long, thin cigarettes in this dim bar and restaurant. Great food includes pastas HK$40, soups HK$55-60, sandwiches HK$80-110, and tiramisu HK$55. Open M-Th noon-2am, F-Sa noon-4am, Su 4pm-1am.

Yeltsinn, 42 D'Aguilar St., Ground fl. (☎2524 7790 or 2523 4448). Hammers, sickles, and jocular Russians decorate the walls; real-life expats decorate the bar. Happy hour daily 5-9pm. Drinks normally about HK$45. Open daily 5pm-4am.

Zip, 2 Glenealy St. (☎2523 3595). Around the corner from The Noodle Box and opposite St. Paul's Church, a subtle black door opens into an inferno of pink curves and artsy decor. Drinks HK$40-50. Open daily 7pm-2am.

WAN CHAI

As the setting of Richard Mason's novel *The World of Suzie Wong*, Wan Chai will never quite shake its image of a dissolute area filled with brothels, bars, and furloughed sailors, even though the district today bears little resemblance to its sordid past and caters to a flashy crowd. Pubs and bars cluster on **Jaffe** and **Luard Rds.;** their neon signs lighting the path to drunken revelry.

Joe Bananas, 23 Luard Rd. (☎2529 1811), at Jaffe Rd. Despite the dress code—no furs, t-shirts, or shorts—this swinging spot is a Hong Kong landmark in its own right. The tropical, sunny place features palm trees and tin-foil-covered walls. Asian, European, and New World food served until midnight. Unplugged every F. Happy hour 7-10pm. 21+ after 6pm. Open M-Sa noon-6am, Su 3pm-6am.

The Wanch, 54 Jaffe Rd. (☎2861 1621). MTR: Wan Chai, Lockhart Rd. exit. An ode to Hong Kong pop culture. Set lunches (HK$65-80), pub grub dinner, and Hong Kong souvenirs. Live music nightly beginning at 10pm. Happy Hour daily 11am-6pm, and 7-10pm (drinks HK$24-30); "Crazy hour" M-Sa (drinks HK$19). Open M-Th 11am-2am, F-Sa 11am-3am, Su noon-late.

Carnegie's, 53-55 Lockhart Rd. (☎2866 6289). This popular pub has specials nightly. DJ every night except Th and Su, when local groups show their stuff. Cocktails HK$40-150. Happy Hour M-Sa 11am-10pm. "Crazy hour" daily 6-7pm (drinks HK$19). Open M-Sa 11am-5am, Su 5pm-2am.

Nickleby's, 57-73 Lockhart Rd. (☎2862 1023). In the basement of the Wharney Hotel, amid suspended model airplanes and clouds on the ceiling, a Filipino band plays English and Tagalog pop songs nightly (M-Th 6:15pm-12:15am, F-Sa 6:15pm-1:15am). Very mellow, relaxed atmosphere with a devoted following of regulars. Big screen broadcasts live soccer games. Cocktails HK$60. Happy hour M-Th all day, F-Sa 4:30-9pm. Open M-Th 4:30pm-1am, F-Sa 4:30pm-2am.

Cinta-J, 69 Jaffe Rd., Shop G-4, Malaysia Bldg. (☎2529 6622). A Malaysian-Filipino-Indonesian restaurant and lounge. Lunch sets M-F 11am-3pm HK$43. Happy hour M-F 3-9pm (half-pints HK$15-16, pints HK$25-27). Live music M-Sa 5pm-1am, Su 11am-1am. Major credit cards accepted; HK$200 minimum charge. Open daily 11am-5am.

Beer Castle, 15-19 Luard Rd. (☎2527 7211). Big TV, red vinyl bar stools, and enough beer to keep things afloat. A healthy mix of expats and locals. Imported beers HK$31-40, snacks HK$30. Happy hour M-Th 11am-5pm, F-Sa 11am-9pm, Su 6-9pm. Open daily 11am-6am.

Delaney's, One Capital Pl., 18 Luard Rd., 2nd fl. (☎2804 2880). Supposedly all you need to say to a taxi driver to get to this famous Irish joint is "Jay Faye Doe." The manager greets clients with a genuine brogue. HK$59 for a pint of Guinness. Happy hour daily 5-9pm. Open Su-Th noon-2am, F-Sa noon-3am. Another branch in **Kowloon** (☎2301 3980). To get to this one, just tell the driver "Buck King Doe."

The Devil's Advocate, 48-50 Lockhart Rd. (☎2865 7271). Customers crowd this bar in search of a night of devilish delights, and the Advocate does not disappoint. Western food during Happy hour daily noon-9:30pm and 1-2am. Open daily noon-late.

CAUSEWAY BAY

Most of the bars in Causeway Bay are joined to hotels and close early, but there are a few tucked away with relatively late hours.

Dickens, The Excelsior Hotel, 281 Gloucester Rd., Lower Ground fl. (☎2837 6782). Sports buffs will appreciate the autographed pictures of tennis, soccer, and marathon champions. Very classy—don't underdress. Beer HK$50. Happy Hour 5-8pm, dinner menu 6-10pm. Open Su-Th 11am-1:30am, F-Sa 11am-2:30am.

SIGHTS

SHEUNG WAN

When the Royal Navy arrived to raised the Union Jack in 1841, it was here that they did it. Ironically, this area is rich in local character, and overflows with little shops, streetside markets, and moldy apartments. The **Macau Ferry Terminal** sits on the northern edge of the district. Farther south, on the corner of Ladder St. and Hollywood Rd., looms **Man Mo Temple,** where the lovelorn shake fortune-telling sticks to check on the state of their star-crossed destinies. Dedicated to the ancient gods of *Man* ("Literature") and *Mo* ("Warfare"), the temple also houses shrines to the city god and the 10 divine judges. *Feng shui* advice and palm-reading is available. *(☎2540 0350. Open daily 8am-6pm. Free.)*

Hollywood Rd. curves across the center of Sheung Wan, lined by shops selling antiques and Chinese artwork (daily 10am-6pm). The **Central Mid-Level Escalators,** the longest covered escalator in the world, follow Hollywood Rd. to the eastern edge of Sheung Wan, on Cochrane and Shelley St. Over 800m of moving stairs (and a total of 20 exits) transport residents down the hill (6-10am) and up again (10am-11pm). Bars and restaurants are constantly sprouting up on the hillside along the Escalators, and toward the top is Hong Kong's own **SoHo.**

HONG KONG

CENTRAL

VICTORIA PEAK. The quintessential Hong Kong experience is a trip to Victoria Peak. At 396m above sea level, the Peak provides a spectacular view of Hong Kong; binoculars (HK$2 per 5min.) are available on levels two, four, and five of the Peak Tower. Entertainment options on the Peak (shopping, a motion simulator, a theme gallery, a movie) are expensive and crowded with tourists. Sitting quietly and absorbing the panoramic view from the Level Four terrace is free, as is a walk around the trails at the top. The **peak tram** offers an exhilarating ride up a 45° incline, at a speed leisurely enough for you to take in the view. *(33 Garden Rd., behind the Murray Building. A double-decker bus (HK$3.20) departs from the Central Star Ferry pier to the tram station daily every 15min. 7am-midnight. Alternatively, walk the 600m by following Garden Rd. away from the Harbour. ☎2522 0922. Tram departs every 10-15min. 7am-midnight; HK$20, round-trip HK$30; children 3-11 HK$6/HK$9; seniors over 65 HK$7/HK$14.)*

HONG KONG PARK. For a park, this place boasts an impressive amount of cement, and in spite of its eight hectares, it has a cramped air. Perhaps the park's most worthwhile site is the **Flagstaff Museum of Teaware.** Constructed between 1844 and 1846, the Flagstaff House was both home and office to the Commander of the British forces in Hong Kong. The museum offers a comprehensive and innovative study of British and Chinese tea and tea customs. *(☎2869 0690. Video at 11:30am, 1:30, and 3:30pm; groups of 10 or more can inquire about additional screenings. Open Th-Tu 10am-5pm.)* The **Edward Youde Aviary, Forsgate Conservatory, K.S. Lo Gallery,** and the **Visual Arts Centre** are also on the premises, and a small but lovely *bonsai* and rock garden is hidden behind the aviary. *(Park ☎2521 5041. Open daily 6:30am-*

BANKING ON FENG SHUI Belief in the ancient practice of *feng shui*, or wind-water geomantic principles, still inspires modern-day engineers and architects in Hong Kong. Prime examples are the **Bank of China** and the **Hong Kong & Shanghai Banking Corporation** buildings in Central, both of which rank as internationally recognized architectural marvels. The 70-story Bank of China building earned its acclaim as the tallest building in Hong Kong until Central Plaza snatched the title a few years ago, while the Hong Kong & Shanghai Banking Corporation building, made of titanium, was the most expensive building in the world at the time of its construction.

I. M. Pei designed the Bank of China Tower to resemble a budding bamboo shoot. When it was finally completed in 1990, occupants of the surrounding structures complained of the bad *feng shui* generated by their newest neighbor. Indeed, the Hong Kong & Shanghai Banking Corporation registered a loss in profits that very year. As a defensive measure, the Hong Kong & Shanghai Banking Corporation employed a *feng shui* expert who advised the company to board up the windows of the transparent tower and to erect two arms to jut out from the side of the building closest to the rival bank. With red blinking lights and round barrels, the arms look more like guns trained on the Bank of China than manifestations of an ancient faith. In any case, business for the Hong Kong & Shanghai Banking Corporation did improve the following year. The HKTA offers a free lecture on the principles of *feng shui* every Sunday 10-11am at the HKTA office in Central (☎2564 1234).

11pm. Aviary and Conservatory open daily 9am-5pm. Gallery ☎2869 6690. Open Th-Tu 10am-5pm. Visual Arts Centre ☎2521 3008. Open W-M 10am-9pm. Wheelchair accessible. All free.)

ZOOLOGICAL AND BOTANICAL GARDENS. The Zoological and Botanical Gardens sit just off Garden Rd., a 10min. walk from the Hong Kong Hilton past St. John's Cathedral. The main entrance is at the intersection of Garden Rd. and Upper Albert Rd. Stick to the maze of pedestrian walkways and keep your eyes alert for signs pointing to the Gardens. The Gardens are a pleasure for flora and fauna enthusiasts. Jaguars, reptiles, monkeys, and butterflies also call this home. *(☎2530 0153. Open daily 6am-7pm; greenhouse open 9am-4:30pm.)*

OTHER SIGHTS. Some of the most tranquil gardens found anywhere in Hong Kong are in the midst of Central's gleaming urban landscape. **Statue Square** (a three-minute walk from the Star Ferry through the pedestrian underpass) sprouts a crop of picnic-goers on Sundays and public holidays. In the center of the square, the statue of Sir Thomas Jackson, one of Hong Kong's beloved capitalists, surveys the ever-thriving business district with approval. Farther inland, the **Chater Garden** is a shady vantage point for observing Central's most famous buildings. The concrete pavilion that embraces the garden, well camouflaged in green creepers, is a subdued break from the busy streets around it.

WAN CHAI

In keeping with Wan Chai's fascination for lights, **Central Plaza,** the tallest building in Hong Kong, is easily spotted from most locations on Hong Kong Island. Its color beams serve as a clock: the color of the bottom light indicates the hour (red 6pm, white 7pm, purple 8pm, yellow 9pm, pink 10pm, and green 11pm); if the top light is a different color, it's a quarter past; if the top two and bottom two lights differ, it's a half past; if the top three match, it's 45min. past the hour; and when all four lights match, it is on the hour.

HONG KONG CONVENTION AND EXHIBITION CENTRE (HKCEC). This grand waterfront building stands as an impressive testament to Hong Kong's ability to put on a good show. Opened in 1997 for the handover ceremonies, the Centre is a quiet, sprawling marvel of glass, sunlight, and expansive floor-to-ceiling windows. It was supposedly constructed to look like a bird on the brink of takeoff, but many claim that it slightly resembles the Sydney Opera House. Exhibits, cafes, and restaurants keep the HKCEC active at night. *(☎2582 8888. No slippers or* *shorts. Open 24hr.)* The outdoor garden and waterfront promenade come as a welcome surprise in this otherwise urban desert. The **Hong Kong Arts Centre,** to your right as you leave the HKCEC, sells tickets for shows in its auditoriums. Brochures and posters in front of the box office on the ground floor advertise upcoming performances. *(Program inquiries ☎2582 0202; URBTIX hotline ☎2734 9009. Box office open daily 10am-6pm.)*

CAUSEWAY BAY

VICTORIA PARK. At dawn and dusk, this haven of sprawling green lawns and leafy boulevards is peppered with *tai chi* devotees. Sports facilities include tennis courts, rollerskating rink, bowling green, and swimming pool (all for a fee). Free jogging trails wind through spacious lawns, an aviary, and a topiary garden. The park is home to a large flower fair during the **Chinese New Year,** and during the **Mid-Autumn Festival,** local families come here to eat lotus-seed cakes and gaze at the moon. *(Enter on Gloucester Rd., opposite the Park Lane Hotel. ☎2890 5824. Park open 24hr. Rollerskating rink open daily 9am-11pm; HK$16 per hr. Swimming pool open daily 6:30am-noon and 1-10pm; HK$19, children HK$9.)* A single footbridge in the northwest corner of the park, along the path from the Model Boat Pool, leads to **Causeway Bay Typhoon Shelter,** where floating homes bob next to sleek yachts.

HAPPY VALLEY RACECOURSE AND HONG KONG RACING MUSEUM. Built in the 1840s when horse racing first became popular among wealthy Hong Kong residents, Happy Valley's track was recently widened in 1995 to allow 14 horses to race at once. The racecourse also played host to the Millennium Extravaganza as Hong Kong and Happy Valley welcomed the new century with one enormous party. During night races, lights flood the track to compete with the glitter of the surrounding skyline. The **Hong Kong Racing Museum** on the second floor of the stand tells the story behind one of Hong Kong's greatest passions. *(MTR: Causeway Bay, exit A. From the exit, it's a 20min. walk via Leighton Rd. and Morrison Hill Rd. Racecourse ☎2966 8111. Museum ☎2966 806. Museum open Tu-Su 10am-5pm; 10am-12:30pm on daytime race days.)*

HONG KONG

NOON-DAY GUN. This famous gun, featured in Noel Coward's 1924 satire *Mad Dogs and Englishmen* ("In Hong Kong they strike a gong and fire a noon-day gun"), squats on the waterfront across from the Excelsior Hotel. In 19th century Hong Kong, the famous Jardine Matheson company had their own private artillery as protection against pirates. This unlicensed show of military might finally angered a new naval officer; he demanded the company be punished. Jardine Matheson had to fire the gun every day at noon to signal the time—a tradition that continues to this day. *(Take Jaffe Rd. toward Victoria Park; walk straight toward the alley near the Excelsior Hotel car park. Just after you pass the 7-Eleven on your left, look ahead and follow the red-letter sign to the gun. Open daily 7am-midnight.)*

OTHER SIGHTS. Past Victoria Park, on Tin Hau Rd., is the small **Tin Hau Temple.** Take the tram or MTR to Tin Hau MTR station, and take exit B onto King's Rd. Cross the street, turn right and go around the block onto Tin Hau Temple Rd. An air of hushed stillness extends from the main altar to the courtyard garden. Next to the Tin Hau Temple, on Dragon Rd., the **Raja Yoga Meditation Centre** helps teach the art of blessed repose with free classes in meditation, vegetarian cooking, and positive thinking. *(☎2806 3008; fax 2887 0104. Call ahead; registration required. Open M-F 9am-1pm and 2-9pm, Sa-Su and holidays 9am-1pm and 2-7pm.)*

STANLEY

Stanley's main attraction is **Stanley Market.** Stanley Main St. runs through clean stalls and petite shops full of every garment known to man, from snake-skin boots to the street's specialty, silk pajamas. **Stanley Main Beach,** just east of the market along Stanley Beach Rd., is often packed on weekends. **St. Stephen Beach** is a 10min. walk south along Wong Ma Kok Rd., away from the market and toward the hills. From the bus station terminus on Stanley Village St., turn left and follow the signs in pink print all the way to the beach entrance. In the opposite direction from the bus station, follow the signs for **Stanley Plaza** to reach the new shopping mall. Beside it is Stanley's **Tin Hau Temple,** which provided shelter to villagers during WWII Japanese bombings. *(To get to Stanley, take bus #973 from the Star Ferry Pier in TST (HK$13) or Express Bus #260 from the Star Ferry Pier in Central. Market open daily 9am-6:30pm. Beaches open 24hr. Shower facilities available at Stanley Beach.)*

WALKS ON HONG KONG ISLAND

Perhaps one of the most intriguing aspects of Hong Kong is that its dense urban fabric is nestled between sweeping, unspoiled hills and mountains. Over 40% of the territory has been preserved in public parks, most of which feature an intricate network of extremely well-maintained trails. The *Magic Walks* series (HK$45-85), available in major bookstores and at the HKTA, covers most hiking options. The HKTA also distributes pamphlets about specific trails. Happy trekkers should bring sunscreen, proper shoes, and plenty of water.

The **Wilson Trail,** named after an ex-governor and inveterate hiker, starts in Stanley and ends in the New Territories; the **Shing Mun Jogging Trail,** the **Sai Kung Coddle Stones** path, and the southern valley of **Mount Butler** are some of the trail's highlights. The entire route takes 27hr. The **Wan Chai Green Trail** begins at the Wan Chai Old Post Office on Queen's Rd. East and ends at Stubbs Rd. Eleven educational stations along the trail point out plants of interest. The **Hong Kong Trail** passes through five country parks on Hong Kong Island, offering scenic views of some of the island's most beautiful areas.

SOUTHERN HONG KONG ISLAND

A few kilometers from the hubbub of northern part of Hong Kong Island are the serene shores, clear waters, and good hiking of Southern Hong Kong Island.

KENNEDY TOWN

Although it's a long trek to **Hong Kong University,** which is hidden on the side of a mountain in Kennedy Town on Hong Kong Island's western edge, the **University Museum and Art Gallery** is definitely worth a visit. The museum houses permanent exhibits of bronzes and ceramics that date back to the Shang (1600-1066 BC) and Zhou (1066-221 BC) dynasties. Relics from the Yuan dynasty (AD 1279-1368) also grace the display shelves. *(To get to Hong Kong University, take bus #7 from Pier 7 in Central (every 10-15min., HK$5.30) or bus #5A from along Des Voeux Rd., Queensway, or Queen's Rd. East (every 10-12min., HK$3.40). Ask a student to point out the building upon arrival at the University. ☎2241 5500. Open M-Sa 9:30am-6pm, Su 1:30-5:30pm. Free.)*

SHEK O

On the southeast coast of Hong Kong Island, not far from Stanley, lies the lovely Shek O Beach. Crowded with oiled-up sun-worshipers fanned by breezes that filter down from the mountains, this long, well-maintained stretch of shore is one of the most popular beaches on Hong Kong Island. Stake out a spot and rent an umbrella tent for the day (HK$30). Several shops rent bikes (HK$15-20 per hr., HK$35-40 per day) for exploring the surrounding hillside. Wander around the markets in Shau Kei Wan if you have time on your hands before getting on the bus. Allow at least 2hr. to get to the beach if you're going this way. (Bus #309 goes to Shek O from Central (50min., Su every 30min., HK$11). On weekdays, ride the tram to its last stop and board bus #9 for Shek O at the Shau Kei Wan MTR Station (A1 or A2 exits; every 15-30min. 6am-11pm; HK$4.20, A/C HK$6.20).

DEEPWATER BAY AND REPULSE BAY

Deepwater Bay beach has a long coast, a beautiful view, and powdery soft sand. (Take bus #6 from Central Exchange Square to the Deepwater Bay stop, every 10-

30min., HK$5.30). Repulse Bay, ironically, is the gem of Hong Kong Island. (Take bus #6 to the Shell station stop on Repulse Bay Rd.) Sturdy nets anchored offshore keep out unwanted sea creatures and two large statues of Gwan Tum and Tin Mau, traditional protectors of local fishermen, guard the shores. Bus #73 connects Aberdeen, Repulse Bay, and Stanley (every 15-25min., HK$5.80).

ABERDEEN

Once just a small fishing village with a harbor full of floating *sampan*, Aberdeen and its pricey floating restaurants are now a must-see for many tourists. The **Aberdeen Promenade,** a smaller version of the TST walkway, passes junks, *sampan*, and teenagers fishing in waters clearly marked with pollution warnings. The **Jumbo Floating Restaurant,** the self-proclaimed "most luxurious floating restaurant in the world," offers overpriced seafood. Little old ladies waylay tourists near the bus stop for *sampan* cruises around the harbor (HK$40-50 for 30min.). Bus #70 runs between Central and Aberdeen (every 6-15min. 6am-midnight, HK$4.70).

Ocean Park features nerve-wracking, stomach-dropping rollercoasters, a goldfish pagoda, shark aquarium, dolphin university, and Hong Kong's two giant pandas, An An and Jia Jia. The pandas occupy a 2000m^2 habitat that is within walking distance of **Atoll Reef,** where 400 species of fish can be viewed through a glass gallery. The **Middle Kingdom,** which showcases 17 Chinese dynasties, is near the back. *(A Citybus shuttle runs from the Aberdeen bus terminal to Ocean Park (HK$12). Take bus #70 from Exchange Square in Central (every 6-15min., HK$4.70) or bus #72 from Causeway Bay (every 10-20min., HK$4.70); get off at the stop after the Aberdeen Tunnel and follow the blue signs to Ocean Park. ☎2552 0291. Ocean Park open daily 10am-6pm. HK$140, ages 3-11 HK$70 with purchase of adult ticket, 1 child age 3-11 free.)*

NEW TERRITORIES

The quiet, rural and somewhat reserved New Territores stretch over 794km^2 of rugged mountains and unexplored beaches. Home to almost half of Hong Kong's population, the area is rich in temples, rock carvings, hiking trails, and cultural relics. Because of its wide open spaces, the New Territories are often targeted for development. HKTA has free booklets that outline sights and hiking trails in detail for each of the New Territories' nine districts.

TRANSPORTATION AND ORIENTATION

The best way to get around the New Territories is to use the KCR and MTR. Each stop has buses, minibuses/maxicabs, and green New Territories taxis. The KCR East Rail runs south-north, beginning at Hung Hom and zigzagging through **Mong Kok, Sha Tin, Fotan,** the **Chinese University,** and **Tai Po,** ending at **Lo Wu** on the Chinese border. From Central, the MTR red line runs north, finishing at **Tseun Wan.** Accessible by ferry or bus, **Tuen Mun,** a residential center in the far west, is connected to **Yuen Long** in the northeast by KCR Light Rail (LR). The beaches of **Sai Kung Peninsula** and **Clearwater Bay,** in the southeast corner, are accessible by bus #299 from University KCR Station.

FOOD

After a day exploring **Sai Kung**'s tropical forests and enjoying its spectacular views, a meal in Sai Kung town can be the perfect way to wind down. Sai Kung town overflows with seafood restaurants, many of which boast live specimens in tanks. **Fuk Man Rd.** runs alongside the bus station. Little English is spoken in the local bars, but music proves to be a universal language—karaoke is everywhere.

Pepperoni's, 1592 Po Tung Rd. (☎2792 2083). A warm ambience and an excellent apple crumble topped with vanilla ice cream keep Pepperoni's busy; expect to wait for a table. Famed pizzas (HK$55) include small margheritas (HK$70) and small pepperoni specials. Credit cards accepted. Delivery to New Territories. Open daily 9am-11pm.

Indian Curry Hut, 64 Po Tung Rd. (☎2791 2929 or 2791 2333). Serves tandoori specialties, including tandoori squid (HK$66) and chicken tikka (HK$48). Rice, bread, mutton, and vegetarian plates available. Open daily 11:30am-11:30pm.

Tapas Tree, 10A Po Tung Rd. (☎2792 6608). Features upbeat music, classy decor, flowers on every table, and attentive service. *Souvlakis* (lamb and lemon kebabs with minted tomato sauce) go for HK$40. Open M-Th noon-midnight, F-Su noon-2am.

Susannah's Seafood, 76 Po Tung Rd. (☎2792 2139). The baked lobster with cheese, chili crab, and salt-fried prawns is a local favorite. Chinese dishes (HK$48-60). English menus. Open M-F noon-2:30pm and 6-10:30pm, Sa-Su noon-3:30pm and 6-10:30pm.

SHOPPING

In the past, Hong Kong Island and Kowloon competed fiercely to construct bigger malls. The New Territories used to look on in dazed bewilderment, but now they too have joined the melee, and every major stop on the KRC (East Rail) boasts an impressive mall complex. **Festival Walk,** 80 Tat Chee Ave., Kowloon Tong, is a gleaming complex with glass floors, more than 200 shops, a movie theater, and ice skating rink. (MTR: Kowloon Tong; KCR: Kowloon Tong. ☎2520 8028.) **New Town Plaza and Grand Central Plaza** puts on musical water shows at 12:45pm and 9:30pm on weekdays at the central fountain on the first floor, with additional shows at 10am and 5:30pm on weekends and holidays. (KCR: Sha Tin. ☎2683 9175.)

SIGHTS

TSUEN WAN

At the end of the red Tsuen Wan MTR line is a major cultural and spiritual center, the ever-expanding city of Tsuen Wan. Temples here see more prayer and incense than any others in Hong Kong. Not surprisingly, the town has capitalized on its spiritual popularity and is the most expensive place to deposit the ashes of the departed. **Tai Mo Shan,** the biggest mountain in Hong Kong, is also in Tsuen Wan.

The **Sam Tung Uk Museum** is a restored, walled Hakka village dating back to 1786 and has rooms furnished with tools and other knickknacks. A small exhibition hall also houses a rotating exhibit. *(2 Kwu Uk Lane, near the Tsuen Wan MTR station. ☎2411 2001. Open W-M 9am-5pm. Free.)*

The **Western Monastery** holds religious ceremonies on the second floor that are sometimes open to tourists. Along with its neighbor, the famous **Yuen Yuen Institute,** the temple complex is dedicated to Confucianism, Buddhism, and Daoism. A stroll around the complex reveals a bronze statue of Confucius, a *bonsai* garden, and a temple containing 60 statues of deities, one for each year in the Chinese 60-year cycle. Yuen Yuen also shelters three of Hong Kong's largest "Precious Buddha" statues inside its walls. *(Take green minibus #81 to Lo Wai Village. From B3 exit at Tseun Wan MTR Station, follow the pedestrian overpass until the end. Once on the street below, with your back to the MTR station, take a left. Make a right turn at Chung On St. Walk up the block, turn right at the corner, and minibus #81 will be on your right. Monastery ☎2411 5111. Institute ☎2429 2220. Both open daily 9am-5pm. Free.)*

TAI PO AND PLOVER COVE RESERVOIR

Take the KCR to Tai Po Market, exit at Uptown Plaza, take the pedestrian underpass, and hop on bus #75K at the far back corner of the bus station (50min., HK$3.60). The reservoir is the last stop on the bus line.

Tai Po is a typical New Territories town—a mess of construction, a marvel of tall, identical apartments, and a stone's throw away from stunning panoramic views of land and sea. Plover Cove Reservoir is a favorite for both hikers and picnickers.

Visitors can barbecue by the water's edge or rent boats on the weekends. A family walk begins next to the Bradbury Lodge and tours the surrounding area in under an hour; numerous side trails await exploration by the more adventurous.

Bradbury Lodge (HI), on Tai Mei Tuk Rd. (look for the sign and trail at the back of the bus terminal), puts up guests who wish to stay at the Plover Cove Reservoir for the night. The lodge has a rustic and communal atmosphere with A/C, a large, shared kitchen and dining area, a TV in the common room, and a rooftop balcony with a splendid view of Plover Cove. The drawbacks are the six shared showers, Chinese-style toilets for up to 48 guests, and cleaning duties. Reservations are recommended on weekends. (☎2662 5123. Reception daily 7-10am and 4-11pm; lockout 10am-noon. Lights-out at 11pm. 8- and 12-bed dorms HK$55; doubles HK$150.)

CHINESE UNIVERSITY

A shuttle bus (☎2609 7990) runs from the University KCR station to the center of campus (every 30min. M-F 9am-5:15pm, Sa 9am-1am; HK$1). Art museum ☎2609 7416. Open M-Sa 10am-4:45pm, Su 12:30-5:30pm; closed on public holidays. Free.

The Chinese University's lovely campus, just one stop south of Tai Po Market on the KCR, is built into the side of a mountain in Ma Liu Shui. The beautiful surrounding green parks and peaceful lakes, however, are prime landslide territory during monsoon season. A visit to the art museum (next to the university library and miniature hedge maze) is worth the risk. The museum has an extensive collection of modern and ancient Chinese art (free audio tour available).

HONG KONG

SHA TIN

Sha Tin's **Shing Man River** is a popular venue for dragon boat racing during the **Dragon Boat Festival,** or **Tuen Ng.** The **Bo Fook Ancestral Worship Halls** on Tai Po Rd. also sits among Sha Tin's attractions. Situated in the mountains, these halls have a pristine tranquility that dramatically contrasts the industrial sprawl below. Use the escalator at the base of the building for easy access. For the more athletically-inclined, the **Ten Thousand Buddhas Temple** is a 450 strenuous steps away. The climb is steep and winds its way through heaps of rusting iron and poorer New Territories residences. Turn left at the entrance to the Worship Halls to ask for directions; watch for the little yellow signs. *(Exit through the left entrance of the Sha Tin KCR station and follow the yellow signs. Both Halls and Temple open daily 9am-5pm.)*

The **Shatin Race Course** draws thousands of spectators on race days, which are Wednesday evenings or weekend afternoons from September to June. In the center of the track is the lush **Penfold Park** and a bird sanctuary. *(Take the KCR to Fo Tan Station; from the C exit (Jubilee Garden), cross the street, turn left, and walk until Jubilee Garden is on your right. Soon after, enter the garden; just before the Jubilee Wet Market, go into the tunnel on the left and follow it until you reach the horse racing stadium. Bus #888 also leaves from the Sha Tin KCR to the racecourse. Overseas visitors to Hong Kong who are over 18 and have been in the area for less than 21 days can snag admission badges for entrance into the coveted Member's Enclosure at the track. Call the Hong Kong Jockey Club for details at 1817. Penfold Park open daily Tu-Su; 9am-5pm. Closed on race days.)*

SAI KUNG

On a late Sunday afternoon, **Sai Kung** town feels like an old fishing village. It is relaxed, foreigner-friendly, and filled with hikers, campers, and beach-lovers.

The area is scattered with temples over 300-years-old. The **Tin Hau Temple,** built in honor of the Goddess of the Sea, is a popular place of worship for fishermen whose lives are inextricably bound to her will. *(With the waterfront behind you, walk left from the bus station. ☎2461 5725.)* You can also explore Sai Kung's **Country Park** and the famous **MacLehose Trail,** which begins in Pak Tam Chung, (take bus #94 from Sai Kung station). The HKTA provides a free booklet outlining a walk in Sai Kung that includes a visit to **Sheung Yiu Village Museum,** a restored Hakka village in Pak Tam Chung. *(☎2792 6365. Open W-M 9am-4pm.)*

Sai Kung's **Clearwater Bay Beaches No. 1** and **2** are famed for their water quality. To windsurf, canoe, row a *sampan*, or kayak, contact **Chong Hing Water Sports Centre** (☎2792 6810). Clearwater Bay, a part of Sai Kung and a popular beach, has pristine white sand and turquoise water. Beware the ominous fins that may circle offshore; the shark attack warnings plastered all over the beach are serious. Clearwater Bay comes fully equipped, with showers, changing rooms, first aid station, and lifeguards who will stand between you and Jaws's jagged teeth. *(To reach the beach, take the MTR to Diamond Hill station, and take bus #91 every 12-18min. 6am-10pm; HK$4.7, with A/C HK$6.50.)*

KWAI TSING

The **Kwai Tsing** district, in the southwestern corner of the New Territories, consist of Tsing Yi Island and Kwai Chung. This unpretentious industrial area has some breathtaking sights, including the **Tsing Ma Bridge,** one of the world's largest suspension bridges, and the **Lantau Link View Point,** which overlooks Tsing Ma, Ting Kau Bridge, and the Ma Wan Channel. *(From Maritime Square, take minibus 304M to the Viewpoint. Open M-F 9:30am-6:30pm, Sa-Su and public holidays 10am-8pm.)* Another way to view the surrounding area is to take a hike along the **Kwai Tsing Reunification Health Trail** which winds through Liuto Valley in Tsing Yi. *(To get to the trail, take bus 248M from Maritime Square.)*

LANTAU ISLAND

If God lived in Hong Kong, then Lantau Island, with its breathtaking natural grandeur, would be the Garden of Eden. Lantau's craggy mountains, isolated monasteries, giant Buddha statue, and wide open skies give the island an otherworldly feel. However, even on Lantau it's hard to get away from city life entirely. The new Chek Lap Kok airport on Lantau has made it easier than ever to reach the island, and Lantau greets business travelers and tourists everyday. On weekends, Hong Kong residents descend upon Lantau, to dine on fresh seafood, visit temples, and picnic in the mountains. After daytrippers leave, quiet descends, leaving residents and hikers camping in the wilderness to marvel at the beautiful night sky.

ORIENTATION AND PRACTICAL INFORMATION

Lantau Island is essentially comprised of small towns that span the island's coastal perimeter. On the northeast coast, **Discovery Bay** is a tightly knit community of high-income individuals who can afford to maintain a picture-perfect neighborhood. **Pui O,** along the Southern coast, is a residential area that eventually leads to the famous beaches of **Tong Fuk Village. Tai O** is an old fishing village on the west coast. **Ngong Ping,** in the inner Western region of Lantau, is surveyed by the immense Tian Tan Buddha atop Po Lin Monastery. The quickly developing central town, **Tung Chung,** was previously the remote site of an old fort built to keep out opium traders. **Chek Lap Kok,** the site of the new airport, was once an insignificant appendage on the northwest coast, hanging onto Lantau by a thin thread of land. The newly constructed 2.2km road and rail suspension bridge, **Tsing Ma Bridge,** the longest in the world, links Chek Lap Kok, Lantau Island, and Hong Kong.

Government and financial services are concentrated in **Mui Wo** and **Tung Chung.** In **Mui Wo,** banks, **ATMs,** grocery stores, and 7-Elevens cluster the square surrounding the bus station. Mui Wo police station, clinic, and post office are all in the same government complex. To reach them, walk toward Silvermine Bay beach on **Ngan Kwong Wan Rd.** Just after the bridge to the beach (Mui Wo Chung Hau St.) branches off Ngan Kwong Wan Rd., you will see gray complex on the left labeled "Government Offices." The **police** force (☎2721 2486) is in Rm. 215. The **clinic** (☎2984 2178) and **post office** are on the ground floor. (Open M-F 9am-4:30pm, Sa 9am-12:30pm.) **Tung Chung MTR Station** has a small bank with **ATM** machines; **Citygate Mall,** attached to the station, has a large grocery store.

TRANSPORTATION

Trains: Trains travel along the yellow Tung Chung line, beginning at Hong Kong station and ending in Tung Chung MTR Station (HK$23).

Buses: Mui Wo, Tung Chung, Pui O, Tong Fuk, Tai O, and Ngong Ping each have conspicuous bus stations with fares and schedules. Buses are run by the New Lantau Bus Co. (☎2984 9848). Blue **taxis** are available at all bus stations (☎2984 1328), but since all the major routes spiral up mountains in a leisurely fashion, taking a taxi is not recommended. Base fare HK$12 for the first 2km, HK$1.20 each additional 0.2km or 1min. of waiting time. Luggage HK$5 extra per piece.

Ferries: Ferries depart from Pier 7 at the Central Star Ferry to Mui Wo port (daily, every 30min. 1:30am-11:30pm). Free schedules are available from HKTA offices and the Star Ferry ticket office.

Local Transportation: Bus E31 leaves from Tseun Wan and Discovery Park to Tung Chung MTR; **E32** leaves from Kwai Fong MTR on Red line via Tung Chung MTR to the Chek Lap Kok airport terminus. Both buses run every 10-20min. and cost HK$10.

Bicycles: Friendly Bicycle Shop (☎2984 2278), behind McDonald's in Mui Wo. HK$10 per hr.; weekdays HK$30 per day, weekends HK$40 per day. HK$5 student discount on weekdays. Open daily 10am-8pm. **King of Bicycle** (☎2984 7704), two stores down from Friendly Bicycle. HK$10 per hr., HK$30 per day (overnight included). Discounts available for large groups. Open daily 10:30am-8:30pm.

HONG KONG

ACCOMMODATIONS

S.G. Davis Hostel (HI), Ngong Ping (☎2985 5610). From the Mui Wo bus station at the ferry port, take bus #2 to Po Lin Monastery, Ngong Ping. Follow the sign to the left of the Buddha statue; the hostel is a 7min. walk away. Quiet, serene, and run by an exceptionally friendly couple. Reservations recommended for weekend stays. Simple chores required. Curfew 11pm. Dorms HK$45 for HI members, HK$75 for non-members. Doubles HK$150.

Jockey Club Mong Tung Wan Hostel (HI), Pui O (☎2984 1389). From the Mui Wo bus station, take bus #7 to the Pui O terminus. Signs for the hostel are on Chi Ma Wan Rd., which loops around the bus station. Follow them; it's about a 45min. walk. Alternatively, take the ferry from Pier 6 (Central Hong Kong Island) to Cheung Chau Island. Hire a *sampan* to the jetty at Mong Tung Wan (HK$100). The hostel is a few minutes' walk away and within walking distance (45min.) of Pui O beach. Prices and curfew times same as at the S.G. Davis Hostel.

Mui Wo Inn, 24 Tung Wan Tau Rd., Silvermine Bay/Mui Wo (☎2984 8597). From the Mui Wo bus station, walk toward Silvermine Bay beach; Tung Wan Tau Rd. runs along the beach. A/C, beach views, bath, refrigerator, TV, and VCR. Singles HK$280, waterfront singles HK$400; on weekends singles HK$480, waterfront singles HK$600.

FOOD

MUI WO. The **Mui Wo Square** surrounding the bus station has a few small Chinese restaurants tucked between the stores. McDonald's is by the ferry terminal, and the **China Bear Bar and Restaurant** is just behind it, serving up nachos (HK$45), bangers and mash (HK$55), and an all-day breakfast platter (HK$58). The locals come here to enjoy the great waterfront view and laid-back atmosphere. (☎2984 9720. Open M-F noon-11pm, Sa-Su 11am-11pm.) The **Mui Wo Cooked Food Market,** also by the ferry terminal, consists of small blocks of restaurants that share an outdoor seating area. (Open daily 6am-midnight.)

PUI O AND TAI O. Apart from Mui Wo, **Pui O** is your best bet for a selection of good restaurants in the midst of rural Lantau. From Mui Wo bus station, take bus #7 to Pui O bus terminus. A string of mostly Chinese restaurants lines the street opposite the bus station. If you want to eat as the Chinese do, take bus #1 from Mui Wo bus station and get off at **Tai O.** This small, densely populated fishing village is famous for its seafood restaurants. Unfortunately, the village is hard to navigate and restaurants are hard to find.

OTHER OPTIONS ON LANTAU ISLAND. For vegans, **Po Lin Monastery** in **Ngong Ping** is the place to eat. On arrival at Po Lin (take bus #2 from Mui Wo station at ferry pier), walk straight from the Buddha statue through the stone gateway to the main hall. The cafeteria is on the left, in the Arhat temple. A meal ticket costs HK$60, and light snacks are available. (Noodles or tofu HK$20, desserts HK$10. ☎2985 5248. Open daily 11:30am-5pm.)

The **Tung Chung** MTR station exits into the new Citygate Mall. On the other side of a Delifrance is the **Catstreet Cafe,** with outdoor seating, upscale decor, and reasonable prices. The menu includes Western and Chinese dishes, like sumptuous fried rice noodles with satay beef (HK$40) and grilled steak with black pepper sauce for HK$48. (☎2109 1131. Open daily 11am-10pm. MC/V.)

SIGHTS

NGONG PING. Perhaps Lantau Island's most popular sight is the giant **Tian Tan Buddha statue,** the largest outdoor seated bronze Buddha in the world. Completed in October 1989, the statue is 33.95m tall and covers an area of $3284m^2$. Be prepared to walk up 260 steps to view the Buddha statue up close. High atop his altar, Buddha raises his right hand as if greeting his visitors while peacefully surveying the lives of those below at the **Po Lin Monastery.** Every feature of the statue is symbolic; its broad forehead and elongated ears signify virtue, wisdom, and perfection. *(☎2985 5248. Open daily 10am-6pm. Free, museum admission with food purchase.)*

The beauty of the surrounding mist-covered mountains makes for inspirational hiking. The **Lantau Trail** passes **Sunset Peak,** the second highest mountain on Lantau. Early birds who catch the sunrise from the mountain can take in this unforgettable sight. Although the path can be dangerous when wet, tourists can still manage the climb to **Po Lam Zen Monastery** (45min. from Po Lin Monastery), winding up and down through incredible scenery.

OTHER AREAS. The **Silvermine Waterfall,** a short walk from the ferry terminal in **Mui Wo,** is a hidden treasure, unknown even to many of the residents. To get to the waterfall, take a right out of the ferry terminal; continue down the road and turn right on Ngen Shek St. Follow Ngen Shek St. as it curves to the right, and then turn left onto Wong Tong Rd. Keep to the left at the two forks, and you'll soon hear the falls in the distance. The walk from the ferry to the falls takes about 35min.

Pui O beach, accessible by bus #7, is popular with locals. The **Cheung Sha Upper beach,** accessible by bus #4 (specify to the driver that you are going to Cheung Sha *Upper* beach), has lovely views and high water quality. *(Beach hotline ☎2414 5555. All beaches in Lantau open daily 9am-6pm.)*

HIKING

Lantau is rich in country parks and hiking terrain. A large map pointing out walking trails, campsites, and country parks often greets visitors to each town. For the dedicated hiker, E. Stokes's book *Exploring Hong Kong's Countryside* is highly recommended (HK$80, available at HKTA main office and major bookstores). The

HKTA also publishes a free guide to five walking trails, one of which is on Lantau. **Mui Wo** is a good starting point, with a **Country Parks Information Post** in the ferry station. (Open M-F 8:30am-noon, Sa-Su 8:30am-4pm.)

LAMMA ISLAND

Though Hong Kong and Lamma Islands are separated only by an island, it might as well be an entire planet away. On one island, life never stands still; on the other, life is in a perpetually languorous state. Lamma shuns cars, business suits, and stress, enjoying the beach instead. Needless to say, it is an escapist haven for expats in search of a more bohemian atmosphere.

ORIENTATION AND PRACTICAL INFORMATION

Lamma has a northern and southern half held together by a strip of land. The port of arrival in the north region is **Yung Shue Wan;** in the south, **Sok Kwu Wan.** A ferry shuttles from the Lamma port to Pier 5 in Central. Lamma is so small that a walk from Yung Shue Wan to Sok Kwu Wan takes under an hour.

There are no cars on the island; most people walk or ride bikes. **Bikes** can be rented at Hoi Nam bicycle store in front of the Shai Po New Village street sign. (☎2982 2500. HK$15 per hr. Open daily 7am-11pm.) There are two public **Internet** facilities, both in Yung Shue Wan. **Scorpio,** on Back St., has four terminals with net access for Hong Kong. (☎2982 4121. Open M-Th 9am-8pm, Su noon-6pm. For Hong Kong, $1 per min., 15min. minimum.) The **Bookworm Cafe,** 79 Yung Shue Wan Main St., has one terminal. A small selection of books is also available for loan or purchase. (☎2982 4838 or 2982 2521. Open Sa-M and W 10am-10pm; Tu, Th-F 10am-6pm. HK$1 per min.) The **website** www.lamma.net has invaluable information on Lamma Island happenings and establishments.

HONG KONG

ACCOMMODATIONS

Man Lai Wah Hotel (☎2982 0220 or 2982 0600), right off the ferry terminal at Yung Shue Wan. A/C, bath, phone, and TV. Rooms are clean and many have balconies. Doubles HK$350-400; on weekends HK$500 and up.

Lamma Vacation House, 29 Yung Shue Wan Main St., 1st fl. (☎2982 0427). A/C, bath, fridge, and TV. Doubles HK$200; on weekends HK$500.

FOOD AND ENTERTAINMENT

Lamma's undisputed culinary specialty is seafood. The docks and walkways along the bay in **Sok Kwu Wan** are lined with seafood restaurants that showcase entire aquariums of edible fish. In **Yung Shue Wan,** seafood restaurants cluster around the ferry terminal; plenty of alternatives are also in Yung Shue Wan.

Bookworm Cafe, 79 Yung Shue Wan Main St. (☎2982 4838). Cool your body with a pineapple smoothie or warm your heart by chatting with the friendly proprietor. Pricey but very tantalizing salads. Open M, W, Sa-Su 10am-10pm; Tu, Th-F 10am-6pm.

Deli Lamma, 36 Main St. (☎2982 1583). Serves hefty, high-quality portions of both Western and Indian delights and occasionally hosts typhoon-watching parties. Open daily 9am-11pm.

Lamma Seaview Man Fung Restaurant, 5 Main St. (☎5982 0719). Vegetable dishes and open-air dining tables complete with fresh roses gracing each table top. Plenty of seafood, plenty of sea views. Open daily 11am-10pm. Credit cards accepted.

The Islander (☎2982 1376), on Main St. Unabashedly prides itself on being Lamma's *true* bar (they do not serve snacks) and subsequently draws a mixed crowd. Happy Hour daily 6-8pm. Open M-F 6pm-late, Sa-Su noon-late.

HIKING

The trail from **Yung Shue Wan** to **Sok Kwu Wan** passes breathtaking beaches and caves before emerging near the ferries bound for Central. From Yung Shue Wan, turn onto Yung Shue Wan Back St. and follow the concrete path through tiny villages until you hit the countryside. The trail veers past the fully equipped and staffed **Hung Shing Ye Beach** (a 25min. walk) before continuing over and around **Kamikaze Cave.** In Sok Kwu Wan, you can catch a ferry back to Central or continue on to **Mo Tat Wan** or **Lo So Shing** beaches. From Sok Kwu Wan, the trail follows the curve of the mini-bay. Walking the entire trail takes under an hour. Watch for signs for the trail in both cities.

CHEUNG CHAU

Tiny in landmass but abundant in character, Cheung Chau Island, is perhaps the most buoyant of the outlying islands. It boasts quite a list of flamboyant characters, from Lee Lai-Shan, Hong Kong's first Olympic gold medalist, to Cheung Po Tsai, a legendary pirate who supposedly hid in a cave that now bears his name. Ride the ferry from Pier 6 in Central and cruise through stunning visions of mountain and sea. The Cheung Chau ferry pier has **ATMs, grocery stores,** and the **police** station. Wander down **Pak She St.,** which runs between the waterfront and the procession of restaurants, bars, shopping stalls, and numerous ice cream stalls. The island is a colorful collection of three-tiered buildings that host restaurants and bars on the lower floors and sun-loving islanders on the third.

INDONESIA

RUPIAH

US$1 = RP3835.38	RP1000 = US$0.11
CDN$1 = RP2482.45	RP1000 = CDN$0.17
EURO€1 = RP3490.90	RP1000 = EURO€0.12
UK£1 = RP5568.70	RP1000 = UK£0.08
IR£1 = RP4432.53	RP1000 = IR£0.09
AUS$1 = RP2032.36	RP1000 = AUS$0.21
NZ$1 = RP1690.37	RP1000 = NZ$0.25
ZAR1 = RP460.02	RP1000 = ZAR0.91

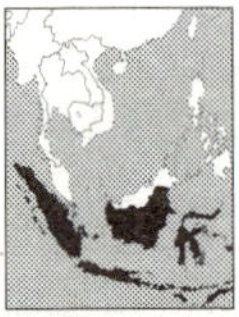

PHONE CODE **Country Code:** 855. **International dialing prefix:** 001,008.

Indonesia's national motto, "*Bhinneka Tunggal Ika*," translates to "Unity In Diversity." This simple idea has recently become the goal of political leaders, who have found that unity isn't as easy as diversity. The country is home to over 350 ethnic groups that add cultural hodgepodge to the geographic mix of volcanoes, islands, and beaches. Achieving political unity has been most challenging; President Suharto's resignation signaled the end of the iron-fisted New Order era and the beginning of *Reformasi*, complete with student protests, strikes, and rioting. The recovering tourist industry and peaceful parliamentary elections of 1999 sparked renewed hope in divided Indonesia, although violence in East Timor, the Malukus, and Aceh Province signifies that unity remains tenuous in the wake of continuing political upheaval. Still, wary travelers can maneuver around points of instability and immerse themselves in the strongholds of Indonesian culture—its stunning landscapes, cultural diversity, historical legacies, and gracious people.

FACTS AND FIGURES

Official Name: Republic of Indonesia.
Government: Constitutional Democracy.
Capital: Jakarta.
Land Area: 1,826,440 sq. km.
Geography: Archipelago of 17,508 islands bordered by the Indian Ocean. Shares Borneo with Malaysia and New Guinea with Papua New Guinea.
Climate: Dry (high season) May-Oct., wet (low season) Nov.-Apr.
Major Cities: Bandung, Medan, Palembang, Semarang, Surabaya.
Population: 224,800,000.
Language: Bahasa Indonesia.
Religions: Islam 87%, Christianity 9%, Hinduism 2%, Mahayana Buddhism 1%, Taoism and other religions 1%.
Average Income Per Capita: US$684.
Major Exports: Petroleum, timber, jewels, textiles.

LIFE AND TIMES

THE PEOPLE OF INDONESIA

With over 200 million people, 350 ethnic groups, and 250 spoken languages, Indonesia is the fourth most populous nation in the world and has the world's largest **Muslim** population. Over 75% of Indonesians live on Java and Sumatra, which together represent only a fraction of the country's total land mass. The sea-based Islamic **Bugis** (from which "boogeyman" is derived) and the **Torajans** inhabit Sulawesi; the **Acehnese, Batak,** and **Minangkabau** people live in Sumatra. The **Balinese,** known for their flourishing arts and dedication to Hinduism, host Indonesia's most popular tourist destination. The **Javanese** and **Sundanese,** Indonesia's largest and most politically influential ethnic groups, live in Java.

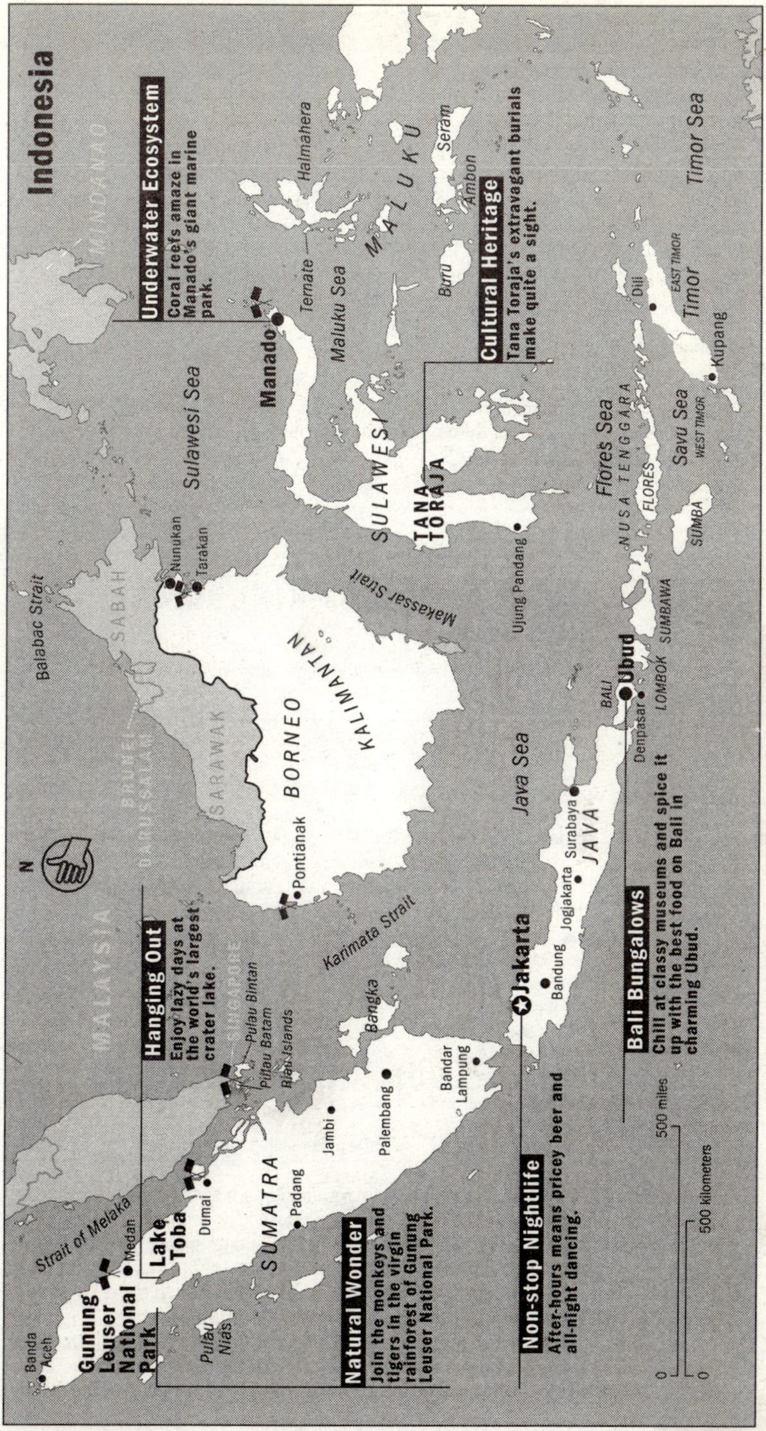
Indonesia
Underwater Ecosystem
Coral reefs amaze in Manado's giant marine park.
Cultural Heritage
Tana Toraja's extravagant burials make quite a sight.
Hanging Out
Enjoy lazy days at the world's largest crater lake.
Natural Wonder
Join the monkeys and tigers in the virgin rainforest of Gunung Leuser National Park.
Non-stop Nightlife
After-hours means pricey beer and all-night dancing.
Bali Bungalows
Chill at classy museums and spice it up with the best food on Bali in charming Ubud.
Gunung Leuser National Park
Lake Toba
Banda Aceh
Medan
Strait of Melaka
Pulau Nias
Dumai
Padang
SUMATRA
Jambi
Palembang
Bandar Lampung
Bangka
Riau Islands
Pulau Batam
Pulau Bintan
SINGAPORE
MALAYSIA
BRUNEI DARUSSALAM
SARAWAK
SABAH
Balabac Strait
Karimata Strait
Pontianak
BORNEO
KALIMANTAN
Nunukan
Tarakan
Makassar Strait
Jakarta
Bandung
Jogjakarta
Surabaya
JAVA
Java Sea
BALI
Ubud
Denpasar
LOMBOK
SUMBAWA
SUMBA
FLORES
NUSA TENGGARA
Flores Sea
Savu Sea
WEST TIMOR
EAST TIMOR
Timor
Dili
Kupang
Timor Sea
Ujung Pandang
SULAWESI
TANA TORAJA
Sulawesi Sea
Manado
Maluku Sea
Ternate
Halmahera
MALUKU
Buru
Seram
Ambon
MINDANAO
N
500 miles
500 kilometers
0

HIGHLIGHTS OF INDONESIA

BEACHES. Bali, especially **Lovina** (p. 216) and **Kuta** (p. 204), needs no introduction. Lombok's **Northwest Gilis** (p. 241) has smooth sands. **Manado** (p. 273), at Sulawesi's north tip, offers first-rate scuba diving. Java's **Pantai Parangtritis** (p. 176) is striking albeit not swimmable. **Pulau Nias** (p. 296) off Sumatra draws a surfer crowd.

CULTURAL HERITAGE. Jogjakarta (p. 169) is easily Java's best city. Colorful **Tana Toraja** (p. 267) in Sulawesi throws killer funerals. **Besakih** (p. 221) is the mother of Balinese temples. **Bukit Tinggi** (p. 302) and **Padang** (p. 306) showcase both the artistic and culinary culture of Sumatra's Minangkabau people.

HANGING OUT. Hip **Ubud** (p. 208) on Bali has the best cafes and meditation workshops. **Malang** (p. 187) dishes out the Javanese delicacies. Lombok's **Tetebatu** (p. 240), Flore's **Ende** (p. 255), and Sulawesi's **Rantepao** (p. 267) all offer cool respite from the lowland heat. **Lake Toba** (p. 288) on Sumatra is an ethereal detour.

NATURAL WONDERS. Gunung Leuser National Park (p. 295) counts **whitewater rafters, trekkers,** and **orangutans** among its denizens. Berestagi's **Karo Highlands** (p. 283) welcome hikers. Climbing **Gunung Rinjani** (p. 239) is an exhilarating challenge.

URBAN BEAT. Jakarta's nightlife (p. 140) pulses with unmatched panache. **Bandung** (p. 159) rocks, but **Kuta** (p. 204) reigns as *the* place to party on Bali.

HISTORY

7c Indian traders introduce Buddhism, Hinduism

7-12c Shrivijaya: first of many rulers and phallic shrines

8-10c Size matters: Saliendra Kingdom expands into Indochina

1292-1478 Majapahit Empire leads Java's Golden Age

13c 1st Sumatran Muslim Kingdom. Islamization begins

14-15c Islam keeps spreading

16c Breaking news: Islam keeps spreading

16-17c Zenith of Achinese sultanate

HINDU-BUDDHIST KINGDOMS (600–1478)

—The golden age: Trade, temples, the Hindu trinity.

Indonesian history begins with the **Shrivijaya Kingdom** (comprised of Sumatra, the Malay peninsula, west Java, and parts of Borneo), which gained power by controlling Indonesian trade routes. Simultaneously, a succession of neighboring kingdoms in central Java prospered through intensive agricultural development. At its height, the Mahayana Buddhist **Sailendra Kingdom** re-conquered parts of Indochina, while the **Sanjaya Kingdom** built phallic monuments, such as the temples of **Prambanan,** to the Hindu god Shiva. Indonesia's last great Hindu-Buddhist kingdom was East Java's **Majapahit Empire,** which is known for unifying the islands before the Dutch arrived. Its greatest rulers, **Hayam Wuruk** and **Gajah Mada,** fostered Java's Golden Age, though the empire's glory withered away due to internal feuds and a languishing economy.

ISLAMIC SULTANATES (1200–1700)

—In other news, Islam kept spreading today.

Arab and Indian traders introduced Islam as early as the 7th century, but Muslim communities weren't prominent in Indonesia until 600 years later when the first sultanates were established in northern Sumatra. These soon became centralized under the state of **Aceh,** with their capital at **Banda Aceh,** known as an important port and learning center in the 17th century.

Islam then spread as far east as Maluku and the southern Philippines; Bali remained staunchly Hindu. During the 15th and 16th centuries, a series of sultanates arose along the northern coast of Java, and Islam finally penetrated inland, mixing with pre-existing Hindu-Buddhist tradition. Under the **Mataram Kingdom,** the last of Java's great sultanates, **Sultan Agung** united nearly all of Java under this hybrid form of Islam.

DUTCH COLONIALISM (1700–1927)

–If by "Indonesia" you mean the Dutch East Indies...

The Portuguese left Indonesia some ruins, a few street names, and about five serious Catholics; the Dutch, monitored by the **Dutch East India Company,** were the colonizers of choice. Military force and exploitative diplomacy gave the Dutch a regional trade monopoly and funneled all profits away from locals. A "divide and subjugate" strategy created power imbalances between increasingly Dutch-dependent local rulers.

The Dutch East India Company went bankrupt in 1799, but the Dutch, intent on trade, stepped in to pursue what came to be known as the **Dutch East Indies.** Colonists set up an administration with compliant local rulers as middlemen. Initial colonial rule was centralized on Java; control over the outer islands took longer to establish, especially in rebellious areas like Aceh.

The early 20th century saw the creation of the **Ethical Policy,** improving education and public health and bringing Indonesians closer to European ideals. Educated Indonesians, particularly the Javanese and Minangkabau, began organizing themselves by religious or ethnic identity and political ideology. Trade cooperatives, Communist parties, and other organizations became vehicles for political action, but internal conflicts prevented the emergence of a united nationalist movement.

REVOLUTION AND INDEPENDENCE (1927–1950)

–"Who's your daddy?" says Sukarno to the Dutch.

The stage was set for the rise of the **Partai Nasional Indonesia (PNI),** a nationalist party founded in 1927 that practiced civil disobedience and was led by charismatic **President Sukarno.** Bahasa Indonesia, the national language, was adopted in 1928 to further an ever-increasing sense of national unity.

During WWII, Japan defeated the Dutch and invaded Indonesia for its rich oil deposits. Indonesians welcomed the Japanese for liberating them but soon discovered that incorporation into the **Greater East Asia Co-Prosperity Sphere** was a fate worse than Dutch rule. Power again changed hands as Japan's 3½-year brutal regime ended with their surrender to the Allies in 1945. Eager to take charge before the Dutch returned, Sukarno declared independence two days later.

The Dutch had hoped to restore their former colonial empire, but, to their dismay, they found a mobilized and chaotic population willing to fight for the newly declared **Republik Indonesia.** Lacking support from the UN and facing US pressure, the Dutch soon realized their efforts were futile. The **Indonesian Revolution** (1945-50) further unified the nation against the Dutch, who for once quietly bowed out. The new government, however, met raging internal disputes, especially among the **Indonesian Communist Party (PKI),** the Nationalists and their ragtag military, and an array of Islamic parties.

1602
Colonizers? Us? Never! Dutch East India Co. formed

1825-30
Locals lose Java to Dutch. Dutch East Indies: 1, Indonesia: 0

1873-80
Achinese War: Aceh province rebels against Dutch armies

1900-30
Cloning 101: Ethical policy tries to spread European values

1924
Indonesian Communist Party (PKI) established

1927
Partai Nasional Indonesia (PNI) founded

1928
Bahasa Indonesia adopted

1942
Brief Japanese rule makes even the Dutch look good

1945
Independence declared; Dutch not happy

1945-50
Indonesians *really* not happy—Dutch get the point

1957
Sukarno's "Guided Democracy"

1963
Konfrontasi with Malaysia

1965
Rise of Suharto's "New Order"

1975
East Timor annexed

1991
Dili Massacre

1997-98
Anti-Suharto student protests

1998
Suharto resigns presidency to VP Habibie

1999
Wahid is first democratically-elected president.

SUKARNO'S RULE (1950–1965)

–You can dress him up, but you can't take him out.

By 1950, the Dutch, embarrassed by international criticism, officially transferred sovereignty to Indonesia. Sukarno wrote the **Pancasila,** the ideological basis of the Indonesian constitution, which consisted of **Five Principles**: belief in one supreme God, humanitarianism, nationalism and national unity, social justice, and democracy. From 1950-57, Sukarno's attempts to form a government based on representative democracy were the most politically free years in Indonesian history but, in a largely poor and illiterate nation, resulted in corruption and stagnation.

By 1957, after economic failure and several regional rebellions, Sukarno announced his **Guided Democracy** concept, which abolished political parties and granted the president dictatorial powers. In the early 60s, matters came to a head when the masses called for "liberation" of western **New Guinea.** With US pressure, the Dutch handed over the territory to the UN, which transferred the territory to Indonesia with the understanding that a vote of self-determination would take place within five years. The vote never came, and the province was officially incorporated with the Indonesia Republic under the name **Irian Jaya.** To this day, conflict over the region's sovereignty persist.

In 1963, Sukarno launched his **konfrontasi** campaign against Malaysia and deployed troops in response to the country's supposedly neo-colonialist arrangements with the British.

THE NEW ORDER (1965–98)

–Danger is my middle name.

INDONESIA

Sukarno's balancing act collapsed tragically in 1965, when he was implicated in a failed coup, supposedly perpetrated by the PKI. The coup involved the murder of six high-ranking generals and resulted in a right-wing military backlash (see **Human Rights,** p. 135). During the following "Year of Living Dangerously," the military slaughtered 500,000 to one million suspected communists. Pragmatic and mild-mannered **Major General Suharto** emerged as supreme commander, dismantling Sukarno's powers and replacing the Guided Democracy with his **New Order** government, which ended the *konfrontasi* campaign. He promptly banned the PKI and encouraged investment from the West.

Under the New Order the next 30 years brought political stability, impressive economic growth, and major improvements in infrastructure, public health, and education, albeit at the expense of free speech and individual human rights under military control. Newly independent **East Timor** was on the verge of forming its own government when civil war broke out. Claiming that the Timorese posed a communist threat to the region, the Indonesian army invaded in 1975.

INDONESIA TODAY

In March 1998, economic crisis brought about by regional currency devaluation and stringent IMF regulations resulted in factory closings, bank liquidations, withdrawal of foreign investment, and spiraling inflation and unemployment rates. Popular opinion turned decisively against Suharto. In 1998, the military killed four student protesters in Jakarta, outraging Indonesians throughout the island. Rioting, fires, and looting quickly swept cities throughout the archipelago. Meanwhile, thousands of students staged a sit-in at the House of Represen-

PLIGHT OF THE CHINESE In the aftermath of the financial crisis that annulled 30 years of growth, Indonesia's 7 million Chinese bear an increasing burden of blame; comprising only 3.5% of the population, they control 70% of the nation's wealth. Tycoons include Liem Sioe Liong, the Suharto family's financier, and Sofjan Wanandi, head of the Gamelan music empire. Their wealth, however, is their only security against institutionalized repression and violence. Even though most Chinese are Indonesian-born rather than first generation immigrants, they're are always reminded of their place as second-class citizens. Until recently, identity cards coded them as Chinese. Chinese-language schools and chambers of commerce, publications bearing Chinese characters, and publicly-spoken Chinese are restricted, and all Chinese must adopt indigenous Indonesian surnames and can't service in the military.

In spring 1998, anti-Chinese riots rocked Indonesia; Pamanukan, Java, Jakarta, Balung, and Ugung Pandang all have stories of blood, shattered glass, and smoky ruins. Many are convinced that the government, through incendiary statements and ambivalence, encourage anti-Chinese sentiment to deflect blame from government policies and provide a scapegoat for those frustrated by economic conditions. The violence has led to an exodus of Chinese and their billions in capital, which threatens to worsen the economy and heighten racial hatred. For more information, check www.huaren.com.

tatives demanding Suharto's resignation. One by one, government ministers and high-ranking political figures handed over their resignations, calling upon Suharto to do the same. Suharto finally resigned the presidency to Vice President **B.J. Habibie** in May 1998.

Protests subsided as Habibie, in a bid to regain confidence in the Indonesian presidency and government, released political prisoners, opened dialogue on the East Timor issue, distanced himself from Suharto, and addressed the concerns of ethnic Chinese, who had been the victims of many attacks during the riots. The most dramatic change during this so-called *reformasi* (reformation) era has been in freedom of the press: political pundits now openly criticize the government. Fifty new political parties formed before the 1999 parliamentary elections, each espousing the aspirations of some portion of Indonesian society. Megawati's **Indonesian Democratic Party (PDI)** received the most votes, followed by Habibie's **GOLKAR** party.

After Suharto stepped down, his enforced unity fell apart as various groups sought to assert their political, religious, and ethnic identities. The most violent and potentially destabilizing separatist movements erupted in East Timor and Aceh. East Timor voted for independence in 1999; UN peacekeeping forces were sent in to control the resulting violence between pro-Indonesia and pro-independence factions. Aceh remains strongly Muslim, rich in natural gas, and very dangerous.

In late 1999, **Abdurrahman Wahid,** former leader of the Nahdlatul Ulama Muslim Organization, was elected President, and Megawati became Vice President. Wahid's erratic leadership over the next months, including accusations of financial scandal, however, led to his impeachment in July 2001, with Megawati gaining control. Amid political turmoil, Indonesia's economy remains unstable.

CUSTOMS AND CULTURE

THE UNWRITTEN RULES

Despite continuing ethnic and religious strife, most Indonesians are relaxed and friendly. Just keep smiling, since Indonesians are known to hide negative feelings and avoid confrontation, rarely raising their voices. Remove your shoes in temples and accept hosts' offers of food and drink. Don't use your left hand for eating, pointing, or receiving objects, and never use your feet to point to objects or people.

Adat, or common law, explains many customs. Present in all parts of everyday life, *adat*, originally rooted in religion and adapted over many years, is one of the few things that diverse Indonesians have in common. Though unwritten and unspoken, *adat* still remains an important code of conduct.

HUMAN RIGHTS

The suppression of independence movements by Suharto's regime resulted in the deaths of 200,000 people in East Timor and 2000 in northern Sumatra; Aceh continues to clamor for freedom and suffers in its efforts. Under global pressure, Indonesia removed troops from East Timor and renounced claims to the territory following the August 1999 referendum; East Timor is currently under UN administration. Continued violence drove one-fourth East Timor into West Timor. Recently, the Indonesian government has been criticized for its treatment of East Timorese refugees and displaced persons from Aceh and the Malukus and for its handling of human rights abuses. Continuing tensions keep these areas dangerous.

BISEXUAL, GAY, AND LESBIAN TRAVELERS

Homosexuality is legal in Indonesia, but public displays of affection are not advisable for *any* couples, straight or gay. All large Indonesian cities have a substantial gay nightlife scene, but it may take some time or the advice of locals to figure out what's currently *en vogue*. Defying categories assigned by the West, Indonesia has an alternate gender, known as *waria*, which is defined as a man *(pria)* with the soul of a woman *(wanita)*. While not wholly accepted by Indonesian society, *waria* participate in a subculture of their own (see **Waria,** p. 198). Although no laws deal specifically with AIDS or HIV, affected persons may be denied entry or even quarantined under other restrictions.

PINK INK. For more information on Indonesia's gay and lesbian scene, *waria* communities, and AIDS activism, pick up a copy of *GAYa Nusantara*, a magazine published in Surabaya. (☎593 4924. Offices at Jl. Mulyosari Timur 46, Surabaya, East Java, 60112.)

INDONESIA

ARTS AND RECREATION

ARCHITECTURE

The ancient **candi** (shrines) of central and eastern Java testify to the architectural grandeur of Indonesia. Among the achievements of the first millennium are the monuments of Borobudur and Prambanan. Bali contains 20,000 **pura** (temples), the largest and most sacred of which is Pura Besakih on Gunung Agung. With the arrival of Islam on Java, mosques replaced temples; the **kraton** (walled palace) complexes in Jogjakarta and Surakarta exemplify the blend of Islamic and Hindu-Buddhist architectural traditions. A common structure used in the *kraton* and Javanese households is the **pendopo,** an open-sided pavilion with a raised floor and wooden pillars supporting a roof of beams. Every region has its own **rumah adat** (traditional house), such as the western Sumatran Minang houses whose roofs slope up like buffalo horns, and Batak longhouses, built with spaces for storing ancestors' bones.

BATIK AND OTHER CRAFTS

Batik, a world-renowned textile art of producing intricate patterns, often with animal motifs, is common throughout Southeast Asia. Originally done by hand, **batik tulis** is now made with a tool that holds a small amount of liquid wax and is used like a pencil to create designs on fabric. Various colored dyes are absorbed by the parts of the fabric not covered by wax. The cheaper **batik cap** is made with pre-patterned metal stamps dipped in wax and then pressed repeatedly onto fabric. *Batik* shirts are common formal dress for men, and women often wear *batik* sarongs. In the past 20 years or so, **batik paintings** have become a popular art form. The best and cheapest *batik* paintings are around Jogjakarta tourist areas; many galleries also give visitors a chance to make their own paintings.

Ikat is a type of weaving in which already-dyed threads are woven into designs, while the rest of the fabric is dyed in a contrasting color. **Traditional wood-carvings,** from masks and life-size puppets to weapons and furniture, are uniquely reflective of Indonesia's many cultures. In places where Hindu culture was strongest, metalworking recreates the ancient artifacts of **moko,** bronze kettle drums, and the legendary **kris,** a ceremonial sword. For those with a hankering for gold, silver, and semi-precious stones, Indonesian artists offer inexpensive and intricate jewelry.

DANCE AND DRAMA

Indonesian dance traditions are highly developed, especially in Java and Bali. Javanese dance is meditative, deliberate, and extremely challenging. It requires limber movements, contemplative pauses, and distant stares. Balinese dancing also requires meticulous maneuvering but is distinct for its fast, jerky movements accompanied by the explosive Balinese *gamelan*. The most popular dances are the **Barong,** which is a battle between good and evil, and **Kecak (Monkey Dance),** which reenacts a scene of the Hindu epic *Ramayana* around flame torches while 100 or more men sit in concentric circles shouting and chanting in rhythm. Most modern drama has developed in Java. **Ludruk** is an all-male performance in which roles of women are humorously, if somewhat derogatorily, depicted on stage. **Kethoprak** adds a contemporary twist on classic epic stories and myths of India and Java.

MUSIC AND WAYANG

The **gamelan** orchestra, a sophisticated ensemble of gongs, metallophones, drums, vocalists, and string and wind instruments, is unique to Java and Bali. Javanese *gamelan* is trance-like, while the Balinese version is fast-paced and dramatic. *Gamelan* accompanies many events, among them dance and *wayang* (shadow puppetry). Indonesia's diverse set of popular music traditions draws upon outside influences and traditions across the islands. Lilting **kroncong** music reflects the influence of the Portuguese, while **dangdut** music shares Indian and Arabic rhythms. The Batak of North Sumatra are famed for their beautiful voices and melancholy tunes, which frequently feature unabashed sobbing by the vocalists.

The ancient Javanese art of **shadow puppetry** probably has its roots in ancestor worship, with the *dalang* (puppeteer) considered a conduit of spirits. Today he's highly respected for his ability to manipulate several puppets at once, to conduct the *gamelan* orchestra behind him, be familiar with an entire pantheon of characters, and keep it going nonstop for nine hours. The stories are drawn from the *Ramayana* and *Mahabharata* Indian epics as well as indigenous stories. **Wayang kulit** is the original shadow puppet art form, but it has been built upon by subsequent traditions on Java and Bali. **Wayang golek** shows, more common in western Java, are similar, but the puppets are wooden, three-dimensional figures.

ARE YOU OUT OF YOUR GOURD? Salon.com reports that in the 1970s, well-clad Indonesian officials attempted to deny Dani tribesmen in Irian Jaya their sole piece of clothing—the "penis gourd." Traditionally, Dani men tote several of these "phallocrypts," adorned with fur, feathers, and embroidery, on a string around the waist to hold money and smokes. Officials describe the Dani fashion as backward and have banned it from government offices. Wearing a penis gourd has thus become a government-defying act. Elder Sopaluma Elosak, grabbing his gourd, exclaimed "Freedom to Papua," when asked how he felt about Indonesia.

OUTDOORS

Pick any island, and some sun or sea adventure awaits. **Wildlife lover?** Explore bat caves in Bukit Lawang, rhinos in Ujung Kulon National Park, dragons on Komodo Island, and the endless flora and fauna of Kerinci Seblat National Park. **Born to swim?** Try surfing at Pura Uluwatu, snorkeling and dolphin-watching in Lovina, and the coral reefs of Bunaken-Manado Tua National Marine Park. **Totally a trekker?** The paradise of Puncak, the trails of Tana Toraja, and hikes and rafting of Gunung Leuser National Park are just the beginning. Indonesia boasts numerous volcanoes, hot springs, and rainforests for the outdoorsy traveler. Activities range from beginner to world-class; any trip to Indonesia should include at least one trek or dive and can easily be organized solely around Indonesia's natural wonders.

ADDITIONAL SOURCES

A History of Modern Indonesia (1993), by MC Ricklefs. A comprehensive but readable history of Indonesia, with a focus on the colonial period.

The Buru Tetralogy: This Earth of Mankind, Child of All Nations, Footsteps, and *House of Glass*, by Pramoedya Ananta Toer. Historical novels about the Indonesian national consciousness by Indonesia's most famous dissident writer. Pramoedya languished in prison and has been under house arrest since 1965.

ON THE WEB

Indonesian Homepage (http://indonesia.elga.net.id/). Info on all things Indonesian.

Inside Indonesia (www.insideindonesia.org). The online version of this quarterly magazine offers information on current events.

ESSENTIALS

INDONESIA

VISAS

For tourist stays of up to 60 days, visas aren't required for citizens of Australia, Canada, Ireland, New Zealand, the UK, and the US, provided that they enter Indonesia through special **gateways:** by air at Balik Papan, Bandung, Batam, Biak, Denpasar, Jakarta, Kupang, Manado, Mataram, Medan, Padang, Pekan Baru, Pontianak, Solo, Surabaya, or Ujung Pandang; by sea at Bali, Batam, Bintan, Jakarta, Maluku, Medan, North Sulawesi, Semarang, or Surabaya; or by land at West Kalimantan. Other nationals and travelers entering from other cities must obtain a 60-day non-extendable tourist visa at an Indonesian embassy or consulate. Single-entry tourist visas are valid for 3 months, and multiple-entry visas are valid for 1 year.

MONEY

The Indonesian **rupiah (Rp)** comes in denominations of Rp100, 500, 1000, 5000, 10,000, 20,000, and 50,000, and coins come in Rp50, 100, and 500. The US dollar is the most readily accepted foreign currency. Traveler's checks can be exchanged at banks, moneychangers, and some hotels. Only major hotels, restaurants, and travel agencies accept credit cards. Most major cities have **ATMs.** Bills at major hotels usually include a 10% service charge. **Gratuity** is not expected, but a 5-10% **tip** is always appreciated. Tips for taxi and hired car drivers are not necessary, but for satisfactory taxi service a Rp1000 tip is appropriate; give a bit more for a hired car. Airport **porters** should be given Rp2000 for small bags and Rp3000 for bags over 20kg.

GETTING THERE

BY PLANE. Indonesia has four **international airports:** Adi Sumarmo Airport in Surakarta (p. 176), Juanda Airport in Surabaya (p. 183), Ngurah Rai International Airport on Bali (p. 194), and Soekarno-Hatta Airport in Jakarta (p. 140). **Garuda** (www.garuda-indonesia.com) runs the most flights to these airports.

BY LAND. Refer to the following table for overland border crossings in Indonesia.

BORDER CROSSINGS. Any entry or exit without a special visa must be made through **specific gateways** (see **Visas,** p. 138).

MALAYSIA–SARAWAK & SABAH. You can cross from **Entikong** in West Kalimantan (near Pontianak) to **Tebedu** in Sarawak (near **Kuching,** p. 433), or from **Tarakan/Nunukan** in East Kalimantan to **Tawau** in Sabah (p. 450).

MALAYSIA–PENINSULAR. Ferries connect Sumatra and Peninsular Malaysia via a number of routes: **Medan** (p. 279) to **Penang** (p. 396); **Dumai** to **Melaka** (p. 384); and **Pulau Batam** to **Johor Bahru** (near Singapore, p. 598).

SINGAPORE. Ferries connect Singapore (p. 598) to **Pulau Bintan** in Sumatra (p. 277).

GETTING AROUND

BY PLANE. Air travel is the easiest and most comfortable way to get around Indonesia, although the economic crisis has forced many airlines to bump up fares. National carriers **Garuda** and **Merpati** run to all provincial district capitals, and **Bouraq** and **Mandala** fly to more domestic destinations.

BY BOAT. Government-owned A/C **Pelayaran Nasional Indonesia (PELNI)** ships serve all domestic main points biweekly with spartan accommodations, basic food, slow journeys, and mediocre prices. Reserve ahead. PELNI operates less comfortable **Pelayran Perintis** to smaller ports. Go early to claim a mattress and floor space.

BY TRAIN OR BUS. Trains run in Java and parts of Sumatra; they're often slow and delayed but generally cheaper and more comfortable than buses for long trips. Most locals take the buses, which are usually slow, overcrowded, unpredictable, and cheap. Combined bus/ferry tickets make island-hopping easy. Overnight buses are usually faster but more nerve-wracking and arrive at inconvenient hours. Beware of pickpockets on any public transportation.

BY CAR OR TAXI. Hired cars with driver cost Rp75,000-200,000 per day in major cities. Taxis are metered in large cities and carry five passengers on major routes. If there's no meter, agree on a price before hopping in. The government advises travelers to stick with registered taxis, marked with yellow license plates.

OTHER LOCAL TRANSPORTATION. Other forms of transport include the **andong** (horse-drawn cart), **bajaj** (ba-JA-ee; orange motorized three-wheeler), **becak** (BAY-chuck; bicycle rickshaw), **bemo** (minibus), **ojek** (motorcycle taxi), and **oplet** (a larger form of *bemo*, a.k.a. **angkutan, angkot, colt, daihatsu, mikrolet,** or **sudako**) Some can be hired for private use. When navigating by foot or **bicycle,** keep in mind that Jl. is an abbreviation of *jalan* (street).

KEEPING IN TOUCH

Kantor pos means "post office." Indonesia's postal service is not terribly reliable—**register important mail.** Check **Practical Information** listings in each town for *Poste Restante* availability. For **telephone calls,** bigger towns have Perumtel or *wartel* offices, which often also send **faxes.** Major cities and several hotels in Bali and Jakarta have IDD. For **Home Country Direct (HCD)** numbers from Indonesia, refer to the table on the inside back cover of this book. Indonesia falls into three separate **time zones:** west (Java and Sumatra) is seven hours ahead of GMT; central (Nusa Tenggara and Sulawesi) is eight hours ahead; and east (Irian Jaya and Maluku) is nine hours ahead.

JAVA

Packing over 60% of Indonesia's population on only 8% of its landmass, Java takes center stage both politically and culturally across the archipelago. Java's fertile volcanic soil has supported the development of sophisticated court cultures from the 7th century through the Republic's modern government. Although alone it presents an incomplete portrait of Indonesia, no trip to the islands would be complete without taking in the wealth of ancient, colonial, and modern sites that Java has to offer. Most make a beeline from Jogjakarta to Gunung Bromo and on to more exciting places, but for those waiting to step off the beaten path, sprawls of labyrinthine cities and mountainous landscapes are ripe for exploration.

JAKARTA ☎021

Plagued by overcrowding and political instability, Jakarta remains a city caught in transition, with one foot among the world's most cosmopolitan cities and the other steeped in the chaos and frenetic energy of the developing world. Underpaid officials and sluggish land developers have slowed the growth of the capital of the world's fourth most populous country. Shiny skyscrapers sidle up next to weathered metal shacks while sleek Mercedes cut off smog-spewing *bajaj* on the streets—all caught in the space between old and new. Recently, many tourists have preferred scattering themselves to other parts of the archipelago, but for those willing to venture out from backpacker ghettos, fascinating sights await—including a thriving harbor and exciting nightlife. As a big city, travelers should be extra sensitive to potential crime. Pickpocketing is the main problem, but walking the streets late at night might be tempting fate.

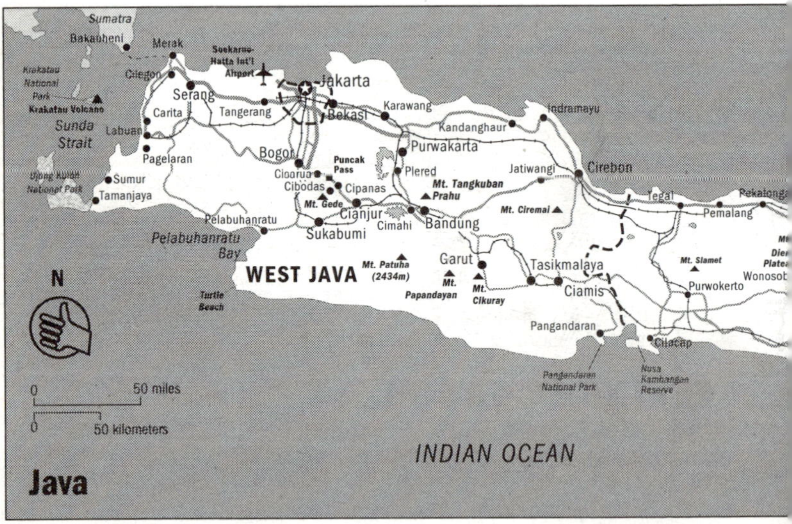

Java

INTERCITY TRANSPORTATION

BY PLANE

International and domestic flights arrive at **Soekarno-Hatta Airport** (departure/arrival info ☎550 5307), 35km northwest of the city. Departure tax is Rp50,000. From the airport, **DAMRI** buses go to **Gambir Station** (every hr., A/C Rp5000), **Bogor** (Rp8000), and other locations. A metered taxi to the city costs roughly Rp52,000 (including toll). Armed with this knowledge, you can now confidently ignore the swarming hordes of taxi drivers trying to rip you off.

LOVE IS FOR THE BIRDS

DESTINATION	FREQUENCY	PRICE	DESTINATION	FREQUENCY	PRICE
Bangkok	1 per day	US$300	**Kuala Lumpur**	1 per day	US$135
Denpasar	10 per day	Rp802,200	**Medan**	5 per day	Rp1,156,400
Hong Kong	1 per day	US$300	**Singapore**	10 per day	Rp594,000

Major airlines that serve Jakarta include: **Bouraq,** Jl. Angkasa 1 (☎628 8827); **Garuda,** Jl. Merdeka Selatan #13 (☎231 1801); **Malaysian Airlines,** World Trade Center, Jl. Sudirman (☎522 9682); **Mandala,** Jl. Veteran near Istiqlal Mosque (☎381 1107); **Merpati,** Jl. Angasa, Kemayoran, in front of the PELNI office (☎654 6789); and **Singapore Airlines/Silk Air,** Jl. Rasuda Said (☎5790 3747). Other international airlines are in the BDN Building, Jl. Thamrin 5, next to the Sari Pan Pacific Hotel, including: **American Airlines** (☎230 0033; open M-F 8am-5pm, Sa 9am-1pm); **British Airways/Quantas** (☎230 0277; open M-F 8:30am-5pm, Sa 8:30am-12:30pm); **Continental** (☎334 417; open M-F 8:30am-4:30pm, Sa 8:30am-1pm); and **Thai Airlines** (☎230 2551; open M-F 8am-5pm, Sa 8am-noon).

BY TRAIN

Trains are more comfortable and reliable than other land transport between cities. **Gambir Station** (☎384 2777), at the center of Jakarta in Merdeka Square, is a 10min. walk from budget-friendly Jl. Jaksa. The information counter at the station helps decode the cryptic schedule. Tickets are sold for three **classes: first-class** provides reclining seats, meals and A/C; **second-class** means smokers galore and non-reclining seats; **economy** trains have wooden benches and broken fans. First-class tickets

INDONESIA

are sold at Jl. Juanda 1, Narinda Building, across the street from Mesjid Istiqlal; buy other tickets at the station or for a Rp15,000 markup at travel agents. Seats can be reserved one to seven days in advance. Weekend tickets often sell out by Friday, and tickets during school holidays sell out days in advance. Many trains from Gambir run through **Kota Station** in North Jakarta, where express trains to Bogor begin. All other trains (listed below) leave from Gambir Station.

DESTINATION	DURATION	FREQUENCY	PRICE
Bandung	3hr.	16 per day	Rp20,000-32,000
Bogor	express 1hr.	6 per day	Rp6000
Jogjakarta	7-9hr.	8 per day	Rp36,000-140,000
Semarang	7hr.	4 per day	Rp31,500-130,000
Solo	10hr.	4 per day	Rp41,500-140,000
Surabaya	9-13hr.	7 per day	Rp48,000-190,000

BY BUS

Travel agencies around Jl. Jaksa hire comfortable private buses (non-stop, usually with A/C, and far less crowded than public buses) that whisk travelers away from guest houses to tourist destinations on Java. Pay for public buses on board. Bus terminals are outside Jakarta and require a complicated 1-2hr. of travel by public transportation; ask your travel agent for help on getting there.

DESTINATION	TIME	FREQUENCY	PRICE
	FROM KALI DERES STASIUN		
Bandar Lampung	6hr.	many daily	Rp40,000; A/C Rp96,500
Bengkulu	36hr.	5 per day	Rp50,000; A/C Rp160,000
Bukit Tinggi	38hr.	3 per day	Rp50,500; A/C Rp130,600
Medan	48hr.	4 per day	Rp100,000; A/C Rp200,000
Padang	36hr.	3 per day	Rp50,500; A/C Rp130,600
Palembang	12hr.	many daily	Rp40,000; A/C Rp96,500
	FROM PULO GADANG TERMINAL		
Denpasar	13hr.	many, 3-5pm	A/C Rp130,000
Jogjakarta	13hr.	many, 3-5pm	A/C Rp70,000
Surabaya	14hr.	many, 2-5pm	A/C Rp90,000
	FROM KP. RAMBUTAN TERMINAL		
Bandung	3-4hr.	every 20min. 6am-10pm	Rp9000; A/C Rp15,000
Banjat	6hr.	hourly	Rp18,000; A/C Rp35,000
Bogor	1hr.	every 20min. 6am-10pm	Rp3000-4000

INDONESIA

BUS SAVVY. The buses *Let's Go* lists are only suggestions; hundreds of buses are sure to go your way. Yelling out your destination or asking someone at the stop is a good way to make sure you're on the right bus. Overcharging foreigners for bus fares is common. Some bus operators will insist on high fares; others will laugh and accept the lower fare when they realize that you know their ploy. Ask another passenger to make sure you don't pay too much.

BY BOAT

The state-run **PELNI Company** on Jl. Angkasa #18, Kemayoran (sales ☎421 1921, info ☎6385 7773) has a small fleet of A/C ships that wind their way between major harbors throughout Indonesia. Those with a supply of dramamine and a tolerance for spartan accommodations and erratic schedules can travel on them between islands at a reasonable cost. For tickets, head to the PELNI office or pay a surcharge and buy from a travel agency around Jl. Jaksa. PELNI ships offers four

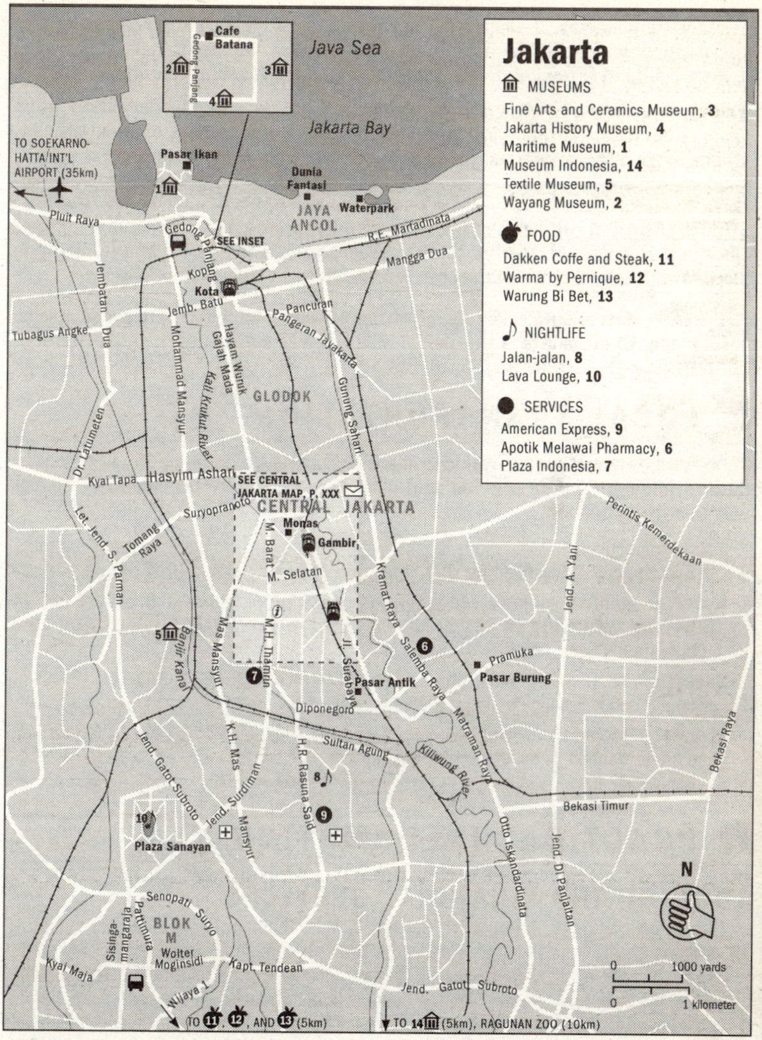

classes with variously crowded cabins (2-8 people): the expensive first and second classes have toilets and TVs, third and fourth don't; *wisata* class provides a bed and a locker; economy is split into seat and non-seat (read: floor) areas.

ORIENTATION

Jakarta is divided into five regions: central Jakarta and four quadrants: north, south, east, and west.

CENTRAL JAKARTA (JAKARTA DUSIT). The area revolves around **Medan Merdeka (Freedom Square),** home to **Monas,** the national monument, and **Gambir Station.** Bordering the square is the **National Museum** to the west, **Istana Merdeka** (the Presidential Palace) to the northwest, and the **Mesjid Istiqlal mosque** to the northeast. A 10min. walk away is **Jl. Jaksa,** home to myriad budget *losmen* and eateries.

Another 10min. away, **Jl. Thamrin** boasts skyscrapers, banks, shopping plazas, and international hotels. Jl. Thamrin runs north-south; at Medan Merdeka it becomes **Jl. Merdeka Barat** (Freedom Road West) and **Jl. Hayum Wuuk** further north.

NORTH JAKARTA (TANJUNG PRIOK). The district includes the harbor (sunda kelapa), the museum-filled old Dutch district (Kota), the electronics-peddling Chinatown (Glodok), and enormous Jaya Ancol leisure park. To go north, hop on any bus bound for Kota Bus Terminal.

SOUTH JAKARTA. Jl. Kemang is expat-friendly, lined with expensive bars, jazz clubs, and restaurants. Further south is **Ragunan Zoo.** The heart of south Jakarta is **Block M** station and much of the area is referred to as "Block M."

THE REST. East Jakarta is largely industrial. Closer to Block M is **Taman Mini Indonesia Indah. West Jakarta** is the site of mass flower cultivation and distribution, offering little else to visitors.

LOCAL TRANSPORTATION

There's no easy way to get around in Jakarta. Patience, a combination of transportation trickery, a *Let's Go* guide, and a sense of adventure provide the quickest way to any destination.

Bajaj: Pronounced "BA-jai." Bone-crunching, smog-spewing orange three wheelers zoom all over the city. Convenient for short trips; fix a price beforehand (Rp3000 per km).

Taxis: A/C comfort and less need for life-insurance. For pick-up, call **Blue Bird** (☎794 1234), the best, **Citra** (☎781 7771), or **Kosti Jaya** (☎780 1333). Rp20,000 for a 20min. ride in light traffic.

Buses: Run on all major roads; look for destination on windshield. Tickets sold on bus or at major stops. Ask locals to find the right route.

Microlet: Minbuses and **vans,** also known as *oplet,* run various routes. Look for destination on windshield or tell driver your destination.

Rentals: Avis, Jl. Diponegoro 25 (☎314 2900). Rp275,000-400,000 per day.

PRACTICAL INFORMATION

TOURIST AND FINANCIAL SERVICES

Tourist Office: Visitor Information Center, Jl. M.H. Thamrin 9 (☎314 2067), opposite Sarinah Plaza. From Jl. Jaksa, walk south (away from Monas) to the end of the street and turn right on Jl. Wahid Hasyim. The entrance is in the Djakarta Theater building. Open M-F 9am-5pm, Sa 9am-1pm. A booth is in the **airport** near baggage claim, before customs. Both have free maps, brochures, shopping guides, and English-speaking help. **Information** ☎108.

Tours: Many Jl. Jaksa establishments book bus tours and transportation. Budget travel offices on Jl. Jaksa and K.H. Wahid Hasyim cover the travel spectrum, booking seats on chartered buses to **Denpasar, Jogjakarta,** and other destinations at a small markup. **STA,** in the BDN building, Jl. Thamrin 5 (☎230 0336), has 3-day package tours to Southeast Asian cities. Open M-F 8:30am-5pm, Sa 8:30am-noon.

Embassies and Consulates: Australia, Jl. Rasuna Said Kav. C15-16 (☎2550 5555). Take bus #P11 or #19 to Kuningan Plaza. Open M-F 8am-4pm. **Brunei,** 19th fl. Wisma GKBI Jl. Sudirman 28 (☎574 1437). Open M-F 8:30am-2:30pm. **Canada,** Wisma Metropolitan I, 5th fl., Jl. Sudirman Kav. 29 (☎525 0709). Take bus for Block M and stop at Karet in front of the Meridian Hotel. Open M-Th 7:30am-4pm, F 7:30am-1pm. Visas 8:30am-noon. **Laos,** Jl. Patra Kuningan 14 #1A. Open M-F 8-11:30am and 2-4pm. **Malaysia,** Jl. H.R. Rasuna Said Kav. X/6 1-3 (☎522 4947). Take bus #P11 or #66 to Jl. Prof. Dr. Satriol. Open M-F 9am-4pm. **New Zealand** (☎570 9460), 23rd fl. BRI building, Jl. Sudirman Kav. 44-46. Open M-Th 7:30am-4pm, F 7:30am-1pm. **Philip-**

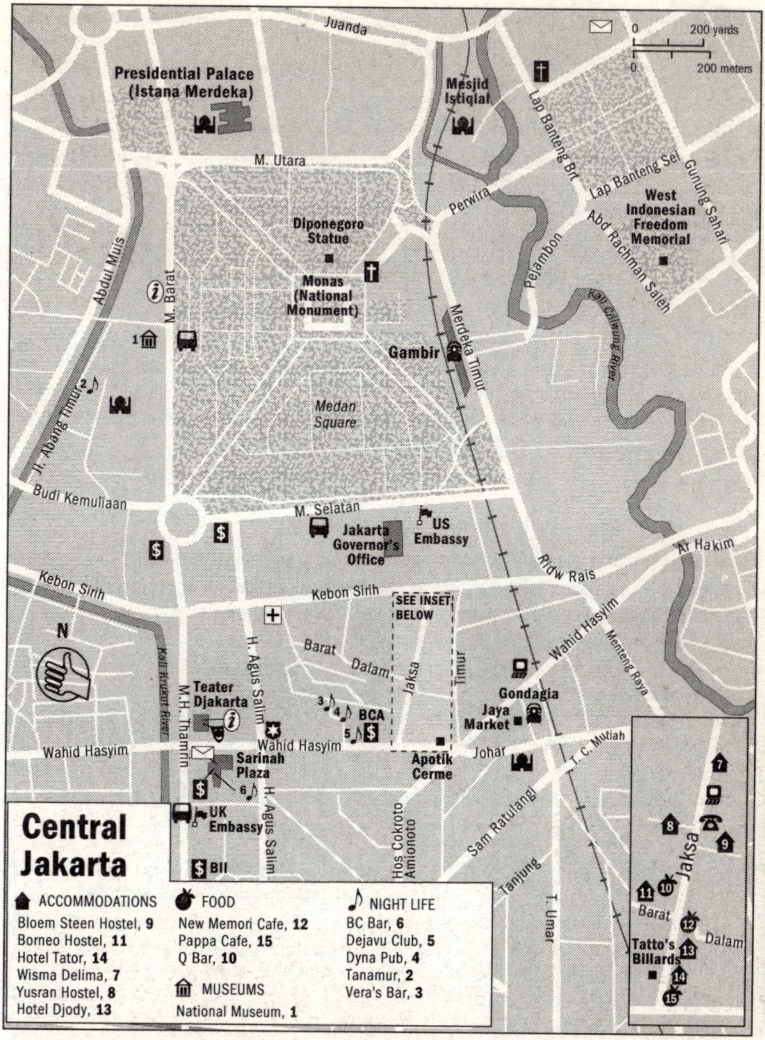

INDONESIA

pines, Jl. Imam Bonjol 6-8, Menteng (☎314 9329). Open M-F 8am-4pm. **Singapore,** Jl. H.R. Rasuna Said Blok X4 Kav. 2 (☎520 1489). Take bus #P11 to Mesjid. Open M-F 8:30am-5pm. Visas 8:30am-noon. **Thailand,** Jl. Imam Bonjol 74 (☎390 4052). Head 500m southwest from the traffic circle on Jl. Imam Bonjol. Open M-F 9am-2:30pm. **UK,** Jl. M.H. Thamrin 75 (☎315 6264), near Jl. Jaksa. Open M-Th 7:45am-4pm, F 7:45am-12:45pm. **US,** Jl. Merdeka Selatan 5 (☎3435 9000). Open M-F 7:30am-4pm. **Vietnam,** Jl. Teuku Umar 25 (☎310 0357), southeast of Jl. Jaksa. Open M-Sa 9-11:30am and 1:30-4pm.

Currency Exchange: Airport banks offer decent rates without commission. In the city, many banks and **ATMs,** which offer slightly better rates, cluster near the Jl. Jaksa area. Traveler's checks not in US$ can be difficult to cash, except at international banks. **BCA Bank,** Jl. Wayid Hasim 82 (☎390 3979). Cashes traveler's checks. Open 6am-10pm. **Citibank,** Landmark Bldg., Jl. Jend Suriman 1 (☎252 9999). Hordes of **24hr. ATMs** can be found at most banks, Sarinah Plaza, and elsewhere.

American Express: Jl. Rasuna Said Blok X/1 (☎521 6111). Traveler's check services. Open M-F 8:30am-3pm.

LOCAL SERVICES

Luggage Storage: ☎550 5581. Airport Terminal D. Rp3300 per day. **Open 24hr.**

English Bookstores and Publications: Times, on the lower level of Plaza Indonesia Shopping Center beneath the Grand Hyatt on Jl. M.H. Thamrin, has British tabloids and English books. Open daily 10am-9pm. Several small book-trading posts and book-peddlers cluster along Jl. Jaksa. **The Jakarta Post** is the daily English language newspaper. The weekly **Djakarta** magazine is half in English, half in Bahasa Indonesia and has nightlife, film, and theater listings.

Pharmacies: Apotik Cerme, Jl. Wahid Hasyim 64 (☎326 207). Walk north on Jl. Jaksa and turn left; it's a 100m down on the left. Open daily 8am-11:30pm.

Medical Services: Best service by doctors between 8am and 8pm. All are open **24hr.** for emergencies. General hospitals **MMC Kuningan,** Jl. Rasuna Said Kav. C21 (☎522 5201), and **RS Jakarta,** Jl. Sudirman Kav. 49 (☎573 22 41). **Ufar Madica Clinic** (☎310 2870), next to Gambir Apotik on Jl. Kebon Sirih.

EMERGENCY AND COMMUNICATIONS

Emergency: Police ☎110. **Fire** ☎113. **Ambulance** ☎118 or 119.

Tourist Police: ☎526 43 47. Some English spoken.

Police: Jl. Sudirman 55 (☎525 0110). Another post at the corner of Jl. Wahid Hasyim and Jl. Agus Salim, near Jl. Jaksa.

Telephones: Coin (blue) and card (gray) phones on almost every street block are for local use only. For better connections, try phones in shopping centers and public buildings. **Indosat** offers **HCD** service from phones at the airport. There are several *wartels* on Jl. Jaksa. The one in the **Graha Building,** Jl. Jaksa 15A, offers HCD for Rp5000. **Click Internet,** Jl. Jaksa 29, has a free HCD phone. Open daily 9am-midnight.

Internet Access: Access can be found in travel agencies along Jl. Jaksa, public buildings like the Central Post Office, and, of all places, McDonald's. **Bloem Steen Hostel,** Jl. K.S. Timur 174. Rp10,000 per hr. Open 24hr. **Click Internet** (see above) charges Rp3000 per 15min. Open daily 9am-midnight.

Post Offices: GPO, Jl. Pos 2, Pasar Baru (☎385 9889), opposite the West Indonesia Freedom Memorial and 3 buildings east of the Cathedral. Take bus #P12. *Poste Restante* at counter 43 (open M-Sa 8am-3pm). Open M-F 8am-8pm, Sa 8am-7pm, Su 8:30am-2pm. Closer to Jl. Jaksa is **Pt. Pos Indonesia,** on the 5th fl. of Sarinah Plaza on Jl. M.H. Thamrin (☎381 4427). Open M-Th 8am-3pm, F 8am-2pm, Sa 8am-noon. **Postal code:** 10000.

Express Mail: DHL (☎314 1708, ext. 2128), in the Djakarta Theater building, opposite the information center. Open M-F 8am-4:30pm.

ACCOMMODATIONS

Jakarta's accommodations, known locally as *losmen*, span a wide range of both prices and comfort. **Jl. Jaksa** (1km south of Gambir Station, a 15min. walk or Rp2000-2500 by *bajaj*) hosts the backpacker district. Hostel doors often close at midnight. Mosquitoes are bad, so pick up some incense coils, buy a net, or get an A/C room. Almost all accommodations in Jakarta have Western toilets, but you'll have to get used to using a *mandi*, which involves bathing with a bucket of water.

Bloem Steen Hostel, Jl. K.S. Timur I 174 (☎323 002), 50m up the path by Le Margot Seafood. Clean and quiet rooms with fans are the best bargain in town. Upstairs balcony, shared bathrooms, 24hr. Internet. Singles Rp15,000; doubles Rp20,000-25,000.

Wisma Delima, Jl. Jaksa 5 (☎392 3850). The closest accommodation to Gambir Station, this popular but weathered guest house offers minimal rooms with fans. Cafe. Midnight lockout. Books A/C buses. Rooms have shared bathroom downstairs. Rp25,000.

Borneo Hostel, Jl. K.S. Barat Dalam 35 (☎314 0095), on a small road off Jl. Jaksa, opposite Hotel Djody. Patrons preferring an active nightlife will appreciate Borneo's no-lockout policy; everyone will appreciate the spacious rooms. Central courtyard floods with light. Doubles with fan and shared *mandi* Rp30,000, with private bath Rp40,000.

Yusran Hostel, Jl. Jaksa 9 (☎314 0373). Removed from the bustle of the street. Earth-tone rooms (with fan) are cheap and quiet. Tiny singles Rp20,000; doubles Rp25,000.

Hotel Djody, Jl. Jaksa 33 (☎315 1404). Large range of rooms with fan or A/C. No lockout. Downstairs small singles Rp24,000; A/C doubles with bath Rp52,000; upstairs doubles/triples with shared bathrooms and Western toilets Rp37,0000/48,000.

Hotel Tator, Jl. Jaksa 37 (☎323 940). A higher-end budget accommodation, the black-and-white tiled Hotel Tator has private baths and provides free toast and coffee. Singles with fan Rp40,000; doubles with fan Rp55,000, with A/C and phone Rp65,000, with hot water, A/C, and phone Rp70,000.

FOOD

In Jakarta, you're never more than a block away from **warung** (food stalls), which specialize in delicious *sate*, fresh seafood, and spicy *padang* food. Ranging from little stalls to bigger areas with chairs and tables, these are your best bet for good, cheap food all over the city. The homesick can rely on international chains at one of the many malls ("plazas") in town.

Cheap backpacker menus cluster on **Jl. Jaksa** and one block over on **Jl. H.A. Salim.** Jl. Salim also yields fancier restaurants, including some with air conditioning. Famous food chains pack **Jl. Wahid Hasyim** and the **Sarinah Plaza** on the corner of Jl. Hasyim and Jl. Thamrin. **Hero** and **Ramayana** supermarkets, at Sarinah and 22A/B Jl. Salim respectively, offer the do-it-yourself option. Popular with expats and Indonesians alike, **Jl. Kemang Raya** hops with fancier Western bars and restaurants that charge higher prices. Take a cab (Rp20,000) or a bus from Block M.

Q Bar, Jl. Jaksa 18 (☎335 508), is the top place on Jl. Jaksa. Pizzas (Rp24,000-35,000), crepes (Rp8500-10,000), or Indonesian grub (Rp10,000-15,000) in a relaxing pastel-colored atmosphere. Pool table and big bar open onto a little pool outside. Cable TV shows major sporting events. Open daily 9am-4am.

Pappa Cafe, Jl. Jaksa 41 (☎323 452), serves up backpacker and Indonesian menus by day and comes alive with music and beer after sundown. A bit more comfortable than other places on Jl. Jaksa.

New Memori Cafe, Jl. Jaksa 17, next to the Army Hostel sign. Jam to contemporary music and rub elbows with locals and backpackers while enjoying Indonesian and Western food. Typical meal Rp6000-8000. **Open 24hr.**

Jimbani Cafe and Gallery, Jl. Kemang Raya 85 (☎719 8938). One of many "resto-galleries" on this trendy street. In reality, this one's more of a food-serving bar frequented by young Indonesians and some expats. Pool table and live music on weekends. Fried scampi Rp17,500, Irish coffee Rp28,500. Open Su-Th 11am-1am, F-Sa 11am-1:30am.

Warung Bi Bet, Jl. Kemang Raya 90A (☎718 0859), across from Jimbani. Serves coffee and local fare in a mellow setting. Dishes Rp3000-10,000. Open daily 10am-10pm.

Warna by Pernique, Jl. Kemang Selatan 101 (☎7179 3536). A real "resto-gallery." You have to walk through a furniture gallery to get to the food. Lovely open-air courtyard with fountain caters to a higher-end crowd. Mellow music plays most of the time; a live band revs it up F-Sa 8-11pm. Expensive drinks. Fish and chips Rp24,500. Open Su-Th 11am-11pm, F-Sa 11am-1am.

Dakken Coffe and Steak, Jl. Kemang Selatan 150 (☎7883 7628), at the bottom of Jl. Kemang Raya. Less character than other places on the street, but serves exciting coffees. Avocado coffee Rp12,000. Omelette Rp10,000. Open daily 11am-11pm.

LET'S GO TO THE MOVIES With the explosion of Video CDs across backpacker districts everywhere, we *Let's Go* editors feel justified in declaring ourselves *bona fide* movie critics. Watch out Ebert, we have thumbs of our own. Let's Go rates 4 Southeast Asian blockbusters:

Bridge Over the River Kwai (1957)

Synopsis: A pre Obi Wan Kenobi Alec Guiness foregoes tea and crumpets to maintain honor in the Burmese jungle, only to have an American private blow it all to hell.

Pluses: Spectacular jungle trekking scenes, British and Japanese working side-by-side, improving poor relations of the time.

Minuses: British officers too proud to get their hands dirty languish for days without food. American private leaves beach paradise in southern India to re-enter the jungle, only to be shot in the back and die in a river.

Score:

Return to Paradise (1997)

Synopsis: An American languishes in a Malaysian prison awaiting execution for trafficking hash unless two fellow travellers return to paradise and claim their share of the responsibility.

Pluses: Backpackers learn what happens if they get busted with a brick of hash.

Minuses: Backpackers learn what happens if they get busted with a brick of hash.

Score:

The Beach (1999)

Synopsis: One American and two French backpackers stumble out of Khaosan Rd. and into a hidden community of travelers in the gulf of Thailand.

Pluses: Impressive cinematics, the stunning scenery of Ko Phi Phi, an accurate depiction of the backpacker scene, Virginie Ledoyen taking off her shirt, and Leonardo DiCaprio taking off his shirt.

Minuses: Leonardo DiCaprio taking his shirt off, the script, the plot, damaging to Ko Phi Phi during filming, and Leonardo DiCaprio.

Score: (We admit we're superficial.)

The Man with the Golden Gun (James Bond) (1974)

Synopsis: Taking time from out dueling the stylish assassin Scaramanga, the British superspy conquers Hong Kong, Bangkok, and the South China Sea (filming occurred near Phuket) before saving the world and winning the affection of his female co-spy.

Pluses: 007 lives out every backpacker's dream: in a time-efficient 109min., Bond steals a longtail boat, throws an elephant-obsessed boy into the river, masters the Bangkok canal system, and snubs and ignorant American tourist—all before escaping to Southern Thailand and getting the girl.

Minuses: Sub-nemesis Knick-Knack, for the senseless waste of vintage champagne as Bond gets the girl. It's hard to find a decent midget *cordon bleu* chef these days.

Score:

SIGHTS

MEDAN MERDEKA (FREEDOM SQUARE)

MONAS. In the center of the square is Monas, Indonesia's national monument. Also known as Sukarno's Last Erection, this 137m intentionally phallic monument represents the strength, freedom, and fertility of the nation (and perhaps of Sukarno himself), and also makes a good reference point. The base of the monument contains a diorama of Indonesia's fight for independence. *(Monument and museum open daily 8:30am-5pm, closed last M of every month. Museum and tower Rp5100, students Rp3600, children Rp2600.)*

NATIONAL MUSEUM. Across the street 300m to the west, the museum is recognizable by a small elephant statue out front. It has a vast stockpile of artifacts from all over the archipelago, ranging from Ming Dynasty pottery to models of traditional houses from the islands. *(Open Tu-Th, Su 8:30am-2:30pm, F 8:30-11:30am, Sa 8:30am-1:30pm. Free tours Tu-Th 9:30am, second Sa and last Su of every month 10:30am. Rp750, students Rp250, children Rp150.)*

TEXTILE MUSEUM. The museum displays over 300 types of fabric, including colorful *batik* sarongs, woven pieces and traditional instruments with some English descriptions. *(Jl. K.S. Tubun 4. Take a* bajaj *from Jl. Jaksa (Rp6000). Open Tu-Sa 9am-3pm, Su 9am-2pm. Rp2000, students Rp1000, children Rp600.)*

ISTANA MERDEKA (PRESIDENTIAL PALACE). Dominating the top of the square, the palace is used only for presidential functions. Northeast of the square is the dome of **Mesjid Istiqlal,** the largest mosque in Southeast Asia, with a capacity of 100,000 and a razor-sharp minaret. Visitors are welcome but should avoid the noon prayer; remember to cover legs and shoulders. The entrance is on the north side, on Jl. Veteran. *(Free.)*

FATAHILLAH SQUARE

One kilometer northeast of Kota Station is Fatahillah Square, surrounded by Dutch period buildings where public executions were held.

JAKARTA HISTORY MUSEUM. This weathered building with teal shutters was formerly known as the Batavia Town Hall. Antique Dutch and traditional Indonesian furniture and a dozen ornate muskets are displayed. Some descriptions are in English. *(☎692 9101. Open Tu-Su 9am-3pm. Rp2000, student Rp1000, children Rp600.)*

WAYANG MUSEUM. The triangle-roofed Dutch museum on the west side of the square houses an extensive collection of *wayang kulit* (leather) and *wayang golek* (wooden) puppets. There are puppets of modern-day bureaucrats and vignettes from revolutionary movements. Descriptions are somewhat lacking, making the displays hard to follow. *(☎629 2560. Open Tu-Su 9am-3pm. Rp2000, student Rp1000, children Rp600.)*

FINE ARTS AND CERAMICS MUSEUM. The museum is located in a big Greek-looking building set back on the east side of the square. Ceramics include modern *kreatif*, foreign pieces, and eerily carved tree-trunk totems. *(☎690 7062. Open Tu-Su 9am-3pm. Rp2000, student Rp1000, children Rp600.)*

CAFE BATAVIA. On the north side of the square Cafe Batavia is a living museum transporting patrons back in time before the 1930s. The Javan teak bar upstairs was added in 1930 and has remained unchanged since. Background swing music, slow-spinning fans, and glamorous drinks draw an expat crowd to Sunday brunch and a thirty-something crowd in the evenings. Food and drink are expensive but it's worth popping in for a look. *(Beer Rp20,000. Cocktail Rp57,000. Open 24hr.)*

OTHER SIGHTS

SUNDA KELAPA (OLD HARBOR). Northwest of Fatahillah Square, the Old Harbor features panoramic **Jl. Pasar Ikan,** which begins under a metal gate and continues past shops of all sorts and to the water (see **Markets,** below). The **Museum Bahari (Maritime Museum),** on the beginning of Jl. Pasar Ilkan, is in the breezy storehouses of the Dutch East India Company, where the feel of old Batavia still lingers. An interesting collection of boats and marine life explains Indonesia's history with the sea. *(☎669 3406.* Bajaj *(Rp3000) or 20min. walk. Open Tu-Th, Su 9am-3pm, F 9am-2pm, Sa 9am-1pm. Rp2000, students 1000, children Rp600.)*

RAGUNAN ZOO. A large and green zoo where animals are kept in their natural habitats, a rarity in Indonesian zoos. All sorts of standard zoo animals roam here, but the most fabulous by far are the Komodo Dragons who bask like mini-dinosaurs. *(Open daily 7am-6pm. Take any bus for Ragunan. Rp3000, children under 12 Rp2000; Rp1500. Extra for snake house.)*

TAMAN MINI INDONESIA INDAH. In this huge complex on the southeast corner of Jakarta, "you can see all of Indonesia in a day." The complex includes a visit to **Museum Indonesia,** which displays traditional artwork, cultural dioramas, and flicks about Indonesia at the Imax Theater. English-speaking guides lead tours of 27 full size provincial houses. Other areas, from the aviary to the Islamic museum, should satisfy specialized interests. On crowded Sunday mornings, there are traditional dance performances in the pavilions. (☎ *840 9210. Take bus #P11 from Sarinah, or bus #P15 from Blok M, and then take a* mikrolet *from the Kampung Rambutan Station. Open T-Su 8am-5pm. Rp4000, children Rp3000, Sa-Su Rp1000 extra. Museum of Indonesia open daily 9am-4pm. Rp3000. Imax every hr. 11am-4pm. Rp6000.)*

MARKETS

Huge malls and open-air markets are scattered throughout Jakarta and frequented by chic families. Other markets cater to the everyday man.

Pasar Ikan, in Sunda Kelapa. The fish market is a tile-roofed building on Jl. Pasar Ikan, 400m up from the Maritime Museum. Activity is almost endless but when the catch comes in after 9pm, everything else shuts down. The fish on sale come in every shape, size, and color imaginable. More interesting, though, is the nearby area, collectively referred to by locals as "Pasar Ikan." Beyond the Maritime Museum, shops sell gear to prepare ships for sea–huge anchors, chains, and cables are carted from place to place. Off the colorful and bustling main drag, smaller alleys are woven together in an unnavigable maze; some flood with light, while others never see the light of day.

Pasar Antik, running along Jl. Surabaya, a Rp5000 *bajaj* ride from Jl. Jaksa, is as full of beautiful handicrafts from around the archipelago as any of Jakarta's museums. Decorative items from ships' wheels to ebony sculpture and ashtrays overflow from innumerous stalls. Shopkeepers do their utmost to get you bargaining–once you've started it's expected you'll buy. Travelers head here to buy the best of Indonesia and hone their haggling skills. Open daily 8am-6pm.

Pasar Burung, on Jl. Pramuka behind the big yellow and blue Pasar Pramuka, a Rp4000 *bajaj* ride from Jl. Jaksa. The twitter of birds slowly grows louder until millions are visible in their cages. Birds, from colorful budgies to magnificent (and outlawed) eagles, are on sale. Pesky peddlers are known to hassle travelers. Open daily 6am-6pm.

Pasar Mangga Dua, on Jl. Mangga Dua, is full of electronics. Shops continue down from the top of Jl. Hayam Wuruk. **Jl. Pancuran** leads off Jl. Hayam Wuruk 300m down and through Glodok, boasting a huge **fruit market** running the length of the street.

SHOPPING

Teenage mall culture is all the rage in Jakarta. Pricey and sterile food stalls cater to hordes of school kids while the chi-chi head straight to the designer stores.

Sarinah Plaza, on the corner of Jl. Wahid Hasyim Romald and Jl. Thamrin, a 10min. walk from Jl. Jaksa. Look for a frighteningly large inflatable McDonald. Less extravagant than some malls in town, Sarinah is the place for lesser designer clothes, Rp70,000 CDs and a big supermarket downstairs. A plethora of **24hr. ATMS** outside.

Plaza Sanayan, on Jl. Sudirman, a few kilometers from Jl. Thamrin. Sanayan has a cinema, bowling alley, and pool as well as American food chains and European couturiers. A daytime hangout for rich kids, it's best used for its recreational facilities. Open M-F 8am-9pm, Sa-Su 8am-midnight.

Plaza Indonesia, Grand Hyatt Hotel, Jl. Thamrin. One kilometer up from Sarinah on the right. Much of the Hyatt's grandeur has leaked down to this 5-floor mall. In the main hall piano music wafts through the air and Italian shoes sell for Rp3,000,000. It's a good place to get away from it all in A/C comfort–if you can afford a Rp12,000 coffee or Rp10,000 crepe. Open daily 10am-10pm.

ENTERTAINMENT

When sights don't take priority, Jakarta has the typical big city offerings. Many worthwhile distractions are in the many malls around town (see **Shopping,** above).

CENTRAL JAKARTA. Teater Djakarta, at the corner of Jl. Wahid Hasyim and Jl. Thamrin, 10min. from Jl. Jaksa, has three screens showing last year's English movies beginning at 3pm. A similar setup runs at **Plaza Sunayan** on Jl. Sudirman. Plaza Sunayan also boasts 30 **bowling lanes** (Rp12,000 before 4pm, Rp15,000 after) and an even larger pool hall. (Rp18,000 per hr. before 4pm, Rp24,000 after. Open daily 10am-10pm.) **Tatto's Billiards,** Jl. Jaksa 38, has tables for Rp1500 per game. (Open daily 11am-2am.)

NORTHERN JAKARTA. Jaya Ancol is a massive entertainment complex of Disney-like proportions. A resort facility on the coast, it's next to the mercury-laden sea, but the nearby **waterpark** is safer and sports decent slides. (M-F Rp12,000, Sa-Su 15,000. Open daily 7am-7pm.) Near the main entrance to Jaya Ancol is **Jaya Ancol Bowl,** where bowling a game will set you back Rp9000 until 4pm, and Rp13,000 thereafter. (Shoes Rp3000. Open daily 10am-1am.) **Dunia Fantasi** has a roller coaster, a ferris wheel, and other rides and games for children. (Open M-Sa 10am-6pm, Su and holidays 10am-8pm. Admission M-F Rp29,000, Sa-Su Rp35,000.)

Sea World aquarium boasts over 6000 aquatic animals and daily ray and shark feedings in the main aquarium. To get there, take bus #P64 from Kota, *mikrolet* #15 from Sunda Kelapa, or bus #60 up Jl. Gunung Sahan. (☎641 0080. Open M-F 9am-6pm, Sa-Su 9am-7:30pm. Feedings M-F 11am, 3:30pm, Sa-Su 11am, 2:30, 5:30pm.)

NIGHTLIFE

Cheap beer flows nightly along Jl. Jaksa as live music softens the murmur of backpacker chit-chat. The dancing queen in everyone is well served by Jakarta's many nightclubs. Some are rather seedy and skin-trade oriented, while others are the height of glamour. Cover charges listed include first drink.

NEAR JL. JAKSA

BC Bar, Sarinah Plaza, at the corner of Jl. Wahid Hasyim and Jl. Thamrin, next to the Hard Rock Cafe. The hippest joint in town for young party-goers hosts Balinese and Javanese emcees spinning techno. Drinking followed by dancing on the bar is the order of play. Beer Rp19,000. Cover varies depending on first drink Rp25,000-50,000. Open W, F, Sa 9pm-4am.

Vera's Pub, Jl. Wahid Hasyim 116 (☎391 3592), 5min. from Jl. Jaksa down a side street after Dyna Pub, caters to the Jl. Jaksa crowd. Stake out your space on the smallish dance floor. Beer Rp16,500. Open daily 9pm-3am.

Dyna Pub, Jl. Wahid Hasyim 116A, down the side street after Bank BCA. Quiet and cosy—somewhere between an Irish pub and old gentlemen's club. Ideal for a drink away from the backpacker droves. Bintang or Guinness Rp15,000. Open daily 11am-2am.

Dejavu Club, Jl. Wahid Hasyim 88, upstairs from Parkit Restaurant. Boasting an "artist" clientele and gentle, jazz-like music nightly. Older Indonesian family crowd. Partner dancing and a lack of heavy drinking. Beer Rp15,000. Open daily 9pm-2am.

ELSEWHERE IN JAKARTA

Jl. Hayam Wuruk in **Glodok** has a reputation for extremely large, overwhelming, and seedier clubs. The most happening places are in luxurious hotels. Cover charges and drinks aren't budget-friendly but to see the top end of Indonesian society in the swankest venues is worth the extra rupiah. Taxis are the only feasible transportation; get them to run their meter if you can.

Lava Lounge, on Jl. Sudirman, in Sanayan Plaza. Taman Ria is *the* place to be seen. Models mix with *asmods* (young executive big spenders), mobile phones ring incessantly, and people watching is the sport of choice. Good dance floor and expensive beer. Beer Rp30,000. Cover Rp50,000. Escape from the Lava crowds at **Manna,** a wine bar in the same complex. Also super chic, of course.

Retro, on Jl. Sudirman, in the Crown Plaza Hotel. Another hangout of the rich and beautiful (and some mere mortals). Patrons stand and talk until the unspoken hour when the dancing starts. Reputedly some of the best music in town, good lights, and space to boot. Torn trousers won't do. Cover W, F, Sa Rp50,000, free other days. Open M, Tu, Th, Su 10pm-1am, W 10pm-3am, F-Sa 10pm-4am.

Jalan-Jalan, Menera Imporium Building 36th fl., Superblok Kau 1, Jl. H.R. Rasuna Said (☎835 3976). Dance to classic disco, sample the pricey winebar, or grab a beer (Rp25,000). Pool table and food. Live music Th-Sa 9pm-2am. Ladies free Th. F-Sa mixed gay/straight. Gay night Su with a live show including lipsynching. Cover Rp30,000, Th Rp25,000. Open Th-Su 9pm-2am.

Tanamur, Jl. Abang Timur 14 (☎380 5233). Jostle with tourists, expats, and Indonesians in this biggish club. Fast music. Beer Rp25,000. Go-go dancers M-Sa at midnight, 1 and 2am. Mixed gay/straight F-Sa. Cover Rp30,000. Open daily 9pm-3am.

CARITA AND LABUAN ☎0253

These neighboring coastal towns are a 3hr. drive or bus ride from Jakarta, give respite from the chaotic metropolis, and make good stops on the way to Ujung Kulon National Park. Carita Beach brims with vacationing Indonesians while Labuan, a neighboring fishing town, offers a glimpse into small city Javanese life.

TRANSPORTATION

The **bus terminal** in Labuan is between the market and police station and has buses to: **Bogor** (5-6hr., 5 per day, Rp12,000) and **Jakarta** (3-4hr., 5am-10pm, Rp10,000). Minibuses also go to **Sumur** (2½hr., hourly, Rp10,000). **Becak** swarm around Labuan and are ideal for short hops. Take an **angkot** minibus (Rp2000) or **ojek** (Rp6000) from the road or at the bus terminal to Carita.

INDONESIA

ORIENTATION AND PRACTICAL INFORMATION

One main road goes through Labuan and Carita (kilometer distances are measured from the Labuan terminal). **Jl. Jenderal Sudirman** begins in Labuan and changes its name frequently as it runs west past the **bus terminal.** At **Pasar Labuan,** it swings right and becomes **Jl. Printis Kemerdekaan.** One kilometer further it bends left, then crosses a bridge. Seven kilometers further, now **Jl. Raya Carita,** it passes **Pantai Carita,** the **beach,** and a strip of densely-packed guest houses. A 1½hr. trek through the hills behind Carita on a well-marked path leads to scenic **Curug Endang** (Drum Falls Waterfall.)

Tourist Office: PHPA Office, Jl. Printis Kemerdekaan 51 (☎801 731), in Labuan. 1½km up the road toward Carita. Insurance Rp2500. One-week permits to Ujung Kulon and Krakatau (Rp2000). Helpful maps and information for solo travelers. Open M-Th 8am-3:30pm, F 8am-11am and 1:30-3:30pm.

Tours: Black Rhino Tourist Information Service, Jl. Raya Carita Km10 (☎802 818), offers 2-4 day group trips to trek, dive, or surf in Ujung Kulon (min. 2-4 people, 4 days/3 nights US$100-150) and day trips to Krakatau (US$30-60). Slashed prices for big groups. **Wanawisata,** Jl. Printis Kemerdekaan 43 (☎803 845), near Hotel Rawayana, organizes tours, 3hr. canoe trips in the park to see monkeys, pythons, and other jungle beasties. US$8.

Currency Exchange: Banks and moneychangers offer poor rates; a handful of ATMs in town give better ones. Labuan's **BRI,** Jl. Jend. Sudirman 156 (☎801 214), has poor rates and a **24hr. ATM.** Head 200m past the bus terminal from the market. To cash traveler's checks, take a 2hr. minibus ride north to bustling **Cilegon.**

Rentals: Pricey **Marina Lippo Carita,** Jl. Raya Carita Km10, rents water sports gear.

Markets: Pasar Labuan, at the bend of Jl. Jend. Sudirman, is small but lively and sells ordinary wares–clothes and grub. Stock up for a market at the **Super Bazaar Supermarket,** run by the ever present Matahari company. Open daily 9am-9pm.

Police: Jl. Jend. Sudirman 176 (☎801 110), 50m from the bus terminal with the market to your back.

Pharmacy: Toko Obat Sumber Sehat, Jl. Jend. Sudirman 190C (☎801 153), next to Super Bazaar. Open daily 8am-8pm.

Medical Services: Clinic, Jl. Jend. Sudirman 164 (☎801 009), beside the green cross sign 100m down from the police.

Telephones: Several *wartels* dot Labuan. Most offer international calls and are open daily 7am-9pm.

Post Office: GPO, Jl. Printis Kemerdekaan 40, 2km from the bus terminal in Labuan, beyond the bridge toward Carita. Open M-Th 7:30am-3pm, F 7:30-11am, Sa 7:30am-1pm. **Postal code:** 42264.

ACCOMMODATIONS

CARITA

Hotels and guest houses line a 4km strip on Jl. Raya Carita, a 15min. minibus ride from Labuan bus terminal. Weekend and holiday rates are sky high.

Restoran Seafood Carita Krakatau, Jl. Raya Carita Km10.3 (☎803 027). The roadside restaurant is but a front for the best value stay in town. Clean rooms with Western toilet, and shower. Su-Th Rp30,000, F-Sa Rp40,000, holidays Rp60,000.

Bandok Lucia, Jl. Raya Carita Km11 (☎801 261), further up the road. Spacious rooms in a relaxed atmosphere. Attached cafe, ping-pong table, and a pool. Clean doubles with fan and private *mandi* Su-Th Rp50,000, F-Sa Rp60,000, holidays Rp80,000.

Yusi Inn, Jl. Raya Carita Km10 (☎801 074), next to Black Rhino Tours. Clean rooms with pleasant balconies and sitting areas offer fan-cooled respite from the beach. Doubles with shared *mandi* Su-Th Rp40,000, F-Sa Rp45,000, holidays Rp80,000.

Pondok Pandawa, Jl. Raya Carita Km9 (☎802 139). Bamboo bungalows in the thick of it on the beach. Doubles with private *mandi,* Western toilet, and fan Su-Th Rp50,000, F-Sa Rp70,000, holidays Rp170,000.

LABUAN

There's not much to do in Labuan though it's less resort-like than Carita.

Hotel Rawayana, Jl. Printis Kemerdekaan 41 (☎801 386), past the bridge toward Carita, 100m before the PHPA office. Outside town and set back from main road. Big, clean bungalows for 2 with fan, Western toilet, and *mandi* Rp30,000.

Hotel Caringin, Jl. Printis Kemerdekaan 9 (☎801 388), on the way to Carita, 300m after the bridge. Friendly management. Clean doubles with *mandi* Rp30,000, with fan Rp40,000; triples with fan Rp50,000.

FOOD

Labuan's *padang* restaurants and *warung* serve delicious, cheap Indonesian food. Carita has fewer *warung* along the road but a greater number of small, inexpensive Indonesian restaurants. Check out **Rumah Makan Diminati,** 50m from Black Rhino Tours for an excellent Western, Chinese, and Indonesian menu in English. (Beef steak Rp17,500. Local fare Rp3000-8000. Open daily 6:30am-9pm.) **Maya Kantin Restaurant** right next door to Black Rhino, has Indonesian eats and an English menu. (Dishes Rp3000-8000. Open daily 6am-9pm.) For excellent, generous portions of grilled crab, squid, and fish (Rp10,000-15,000), try the woven-bamboo restaurants along the road. Particularly notable is **Rumah Makan Lancar,** halfway between Labuan and Carita. Filling and tasty *otak-otak* (fish cakes) sell for Rp1500.

DAYTRIPS FROM CARITA

UJUNG KULON NATIONAL PARK

The park is 4hr. southwest of Labuan. Leave bags at your hostel, but load up on food and water before leaving, as they're cheaper at the supermarket than in the park. Take a minibus to Sumer (3hr., last bus 3pm, Rp10,000) and then an ojek *to Tamanjaya (1hr., Rp20,000). Alternatively, 2 direct buses leave Ujung Kulon at 5:30am and return from Labuan between 11am and 1pm.*

The park is famous for Javan rhinos and its rich assortment of rainforest wildlife. A UNESCO World Heritage Site, it has seen major preservation efforts in the last few years. Permits allow one-week access. Off the coast and on the beaches, evidence of the 1883 **Krakatau explosion** and the ensuing 40m high *tsunami* remain visible (see **The Wrath of Krakatau,** p. 324). The spectacular secluded beaches of the south coast are still totally undeveloped. The best wildlife inhabits the least accessible areas around **Pulau Handeleum** and **Pulau Peucang.** (Rp750,000 by boat from Tamanjaya for 15 people, but fewer people may be able to tear the fishermen away from their work for less.) A five-day hike around Ujung Kulon will give cheaper access to wildlife. A boat to Pulau Peucang can be taken from a guidepost (US$3). Consider packing snacks and lounging on one of several beautiful empty **beaches** you pass between Sumur and Tamanjaya—they're worth the trip from Labuan.

Tickets, information, and advice on the park are available in Labuan from locals and the **PHPA office.** Tourist agencies in Carita sell expensive package tours, but freelance guides are cheaper. There is another PHPA office in Tamanjaya, but employees there speak less English than in Labuan (Rp25,000-30,000 per person per day, including food and cigarettes, Rp20,000 without). Spiritual pilgrims hire *kuncen* who tap into the powers of the forest using special rituals (Rp50,000).

There are two s in Tamanjaya. **Wisma Wisata Alam** has bungalow doubles opening onto a well-manicured lawn and gorgeous sunset view. Shared bathrooms have Western toilets. Mosquito net and/or coils are a must. The owner is well-informed and speaks the best English in town. (Rp35,000 with breakfast.) **Penginapau Sunda Jaya,** down the road, offers mosquito nets and a better value for single travelers. (Rp15,000 per person.)

In the park, camping with a mosquito net and waterproof ground pad is feasible. Leaving Rp20,000 (more for bigger groups) for the watchman is a common courtesy best fulfilled via your guide. **Cimayang** is a favorite campground near the river. Rangers' houses throughout the park also have rooms available (Rp20,000 or less), though many are in poor condition. One exception is on **Pulau Pcucang** (doubles Rp50,000); another favorite spot is with the **lighthouse keeper.** Those stranded in Sumer can stay in the **Penginapan Citra Ayu.** (Rp20,000 for clean quiet rooms.)

BOGOR ☎0251

Dubbed "*Sans-Souci*" or "without worries" by the Dutch, Bogor was originally the site (chosen for its temperate climate) of capitals built by ancient Hindu-Buddhist kings. Centuries later, colonists made the town a site for weekend retreats, and the city retains a similar role today. Virtually a suburb of Jakarta, Bogor is cosmopolitan enough to satisfy a traveler's longing for creature comforts, yet small enough to provide refuge from the madness of the city. Most find it preferable to stay in Bogor and explore Jakarta rather than vice-versa. Bogor's world-renowned botanical gardens, the city's heart and soul, endure 320 tempestuous days a year, nourished by the highest average rainfall in West Java.

TRANSPORTATION

Trains: The **train station** (☎324 529), on Jl. Permas, is west of the Botanical Gardens off Jl. Kapten Muslihat. To **Jakarta** (economy 1hr., every 15min. 4am-9:30pm, Rp1500; business express 30min., Rp4000). Major central and east Javanese city routes go through Jakarta; ask a travel agent for these destinations.

Buses: The **terminal** is 1km southeast of the Botanical Gardens on Jl. Raya Pajajaran. To **Bandung** (3hr., every 30min., Rp7000-13,000) and **Jakarta** (Kali Deres, Tanjung Priok, and Pulo Gadung, 1½ hr., every 15min., Rp3000-5000; Kp. Rambutan, 45 min., every 15min., Rp3000-5000). Buses to **Jogjakarta** and **Surabaya** go through Jakarta.

Local Transportation: Short-distance **angkot** head to the Puncak and surrounding areas from the Sukasari minibus "terminal" in South Bogor–take *angkot* #2. *Angkot* swarm local roads on fixed routes at fixed rates (Rp600), and **becak** are everywhere. Prices vary depending on weight and distance but should generally be around Rp3000 and never exceed Rp5000. Slower ***delman*** (pony carts) linger by gardens, but the ride is not so romantic when stuck in traffic.

ORIENTATION AND PRACTICAL INFORMATION

Bogor is built around the rectangular **Botanical Gardens,** home to many plant species and one of five Indonesian Presidential Palaces, the **Istana Bogor.** The gardens are bounded by **Jl. Ir. H. Juanda** to the west, **Jl. Otista** to the south, and **Jl. Raya Paja-**

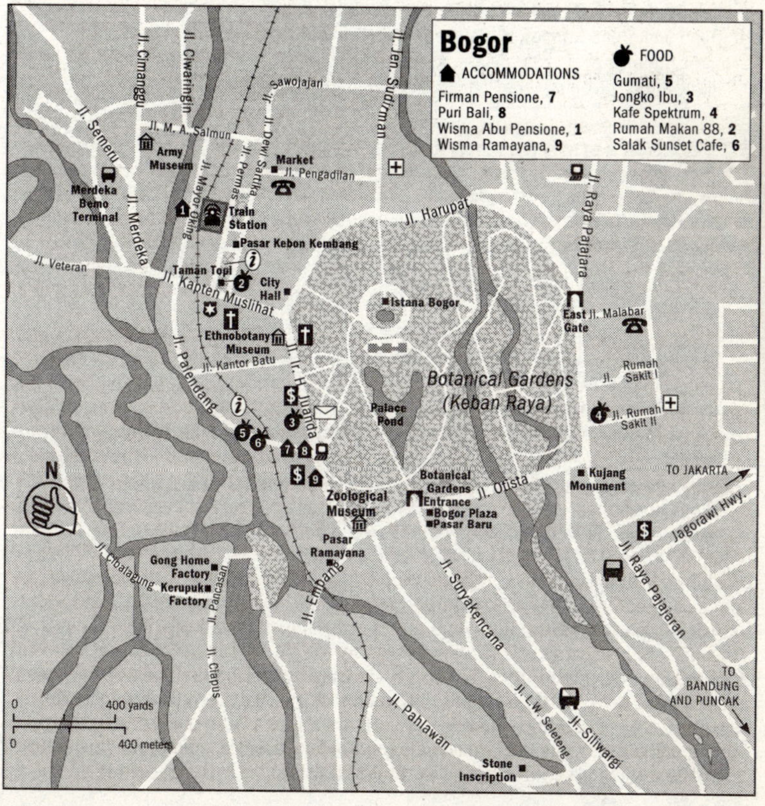

INDONESIA

jaran to the east (which leads to the **bus station**). Extending away from the palace to the west is **Jl. Kapten Muslihat,** toward **Taman Topi (Hat Park)** and the **train station.** Most guest houses lie on **Jl. Raya Pajajaran** and **Jl. Palendang.**

Tourist Offices: Jl. Paledang 35 (☎332 775). Hidden behind two white buildings. Maps and palace tours available. Open M-F 8am-4pm. **Tourist Information Center,** in Taman Topi, on Jl. Permas side. Unreliably open M-F 8am-4pm.

Tours: Travel Bureau Mulia Rahayu, Jl. Mayor Oking 18-20 (☎324 150). Books airplane and PELNI boat tickets. Open daily 8am-6pm. **Larasati Tours and Travel** (☎338 361), on Jl. Kapten Muslihat, in a hat-shaped building at Taman Topi, southeast of the train station. Open M-F 8am-6pm, Sa 8am-4pm, Su 9am-1pm.

Currency Exchange: Bank Bali, Jl. Kapten Muslihat 17A (☎312 990). Near the railway station. **ATM.** Open M-F 8am-3pm; exchange available M-F 10am-2pm. Numerous other banks with ATMs are along Jl. Raya Pajajaran and Jl. Juauda.

Emergency: Police ☎110. **Fire** ☎113. **Ambulance** ☎118.

Police: Jl. Kapten Muslihat 16 (☎381 360). Opposite soldier statue at Taman Topi. Open 24hr.

Medical Services: RS Salak, Jl. Jend. Sudirman 8 (☎344 609), with **pharmacy** (☎320 496) next door. **RSU PMI,** on Jl. Rumah Sakit II. Both open 24hr.

Telephones: Wartel, Jl. Pengadilan 14, to the left of Telkom, offers **international calls** daily 4:30am-midnight. **Wartel Exotica,** Jl. Kapten Muslihat 51. At Taman Topi. Open daily 7am-midnight.

Internet Access: Internet cafes full of schoolchildren on "Lovemail" abound. Around Rp5000 per hr. **B@linet,** Jl. Palendang 50. Attached to Puri Bali Guest House (see below). Open 9am-midnight. **Blue Corner Net,** at Taman Topi, is a college hangout. Open 9am-9pm. **Infonet,** Jl. Pajajaran 34. Next to Pangrango Hotel. Open 24hr.

Post Office: GPO, Jl. Ir. H. Juanda 5. 200m north of where Jl. Palendang intersects with the gardens. *Poste Restante.* Open M-Sa 8am-4pm. **Postal code:** 16124.

INDONESIA

ACCOMMODATIONS AND FOOD

Bogor has numerous guest houses. In addition to those listed, several more are on **Jl. Raya Pajajaran** east of the gardens. All of these listings offer free tea and laundry service, need no reservations, and accept cash only.

Wisma Abu Pensione, Jl. Mayor Oking 15. Walk down Jl. Kapten Muslihat and turn right at the pedestrian footbridge onto Jl. Mayor Oking; it's 300m down on the left. Wonderfully serene guest house. Courtyard and small cafe/kitchen overlooking the stream below. Singles/doubles with shared *mandi* Rp35,000-45,000; with hot water, private bath, and A/C Rp60,000.

Wisma Ramayana, Jl. Ir. H. Juanda 54. Across from the gardens, past the small iron gate left of the bank. *Pajungs* and private patios provide a shaded and relaxed atmosphere. Singles, doubles with shared *mandi* Rp35,000-40,000. Surcharge for private bath.

Firman Pensione, Jl. Palendang. Past Puri Bali on the left. This social *wisma* has several sitting areas that look out over the valley to the peak. Breakfast included; cafe offers other meals as well. Doubles with shared *mandi* Rp25,000, with private *mandi* Rp30,000-40,000. Rp5000 cheaper for solo travelers.

Puri Bali, Jl. Palendang 50. Close to the gardens. Spacious but still a bit stuffy and antique. Cafe and pool table next door has evening entertainment for a younger crowd. Singles/doubles with private *mandi* Rp30,000-40,000; triples Rp50,000.

Warung line Jl. Dewi Sartika. Those by the railway station are seedier but make scrumptious *martabak*. **Bakeries** are in almost every supermarket and on each street corner. The **Salak Sunset Cafe,** Jl. Palendang, across the train tracks, boasts a great view and a relaxed setting. Your wallet will enjoy their refreshing house drink (Sirsak juice Rp4500) and the fantastic local and foreign food.

(Open M-F noon-11pm, Su 4-11pm.) For great Sundanese food, try **Jongko Ibu** across from the post office, and **Mirah Sari,** Jl. Merdeka 48. (Open daily 9am-10:30pm.) Taman Topi has a slew of restaurants including **Rumah Makan 88,** which serves cheap Sundanese and Indonesian food. **Kafe Spektrum,** Jl. Pajajaran 35, before the hospital, has nightly live music, karaoke, and Western-style food at Western prices. (Open daily 11am-midnight.) Come to **Gumati,** Jl. Paledang 26, 150m from the gardens, for the best yet priciest view in town, and stay for a mediocre meal (cowtail Rp21,000) and a decent Top 40 band. (☎313 422. Open M-F 10am-11pm, Sa-Su 10am-midnight. Bands F-Sa 7:30-10:30pm. Reservations recommended Sa-Su. Credit card friendly.)

SIGHTS

At a sprawling 87 hectares in the center of Bogor sits the stately **Istana Bogor** and the surrounding **Kebun Raya (Botanical Gardens).** Established for the Dutch governor of Indonesia Baron Van Imhoff as an escape from the capital, these grounds housed many guests of the state and became a presidential retreat upon the country's independence in 1945. History buffs will notice Sukarno's influence in the inordinate number of statues and paintings of nude women. These women, along with his four wives, surely brightened up Sukarno's house arrest here (1967-70). Gaining admission to the grounds is a bit tricky—a consequence of ever-present Indonesian politics. Groups of 10 can visit if requested one week in advance, but all are welcome on national holidays.

Viewing **Kebun Raya** is simpler. The park's entrance is on the south side on Jl. Otista. Formerly part of Bogor Palace, these gardens were converted to a collection of indigenous, foreign, and exotic botanical species for educational and scientific purpose in the late 18th and early 19th centuries. Those in the mood for a soothing stroll can meander along the four recommended routes (about 1hr. each), and guides give naturalists the scoop on the thousands of unique species. (Open daily 8am-5pm. Rp3000. Guides Rp25,000.)

Across the street from the Pasar Ramayana food market are the inanimate skeletons and stuffed animals of the **Zoological Museum,** 200m west of the entrance to the gardens. (Open daily 8am-4pm. Rp1000.) On Jl. Kantor Batu, opposite a castle-like church, is the **Ethnobotany Museum,** Jl. Ir. H. Juanda 22-24. Enter on the north side of the building to see traditional Indonesian instruments, baskets, and pottery. (Open daily 9am-3pm. Rp2000.)

Tourists can also visit the **Gong Home Factory,** Jl. Pancasan 17. A small donation of a couple thousand rupiahs is expected. Bring a pack of cigarettes to make a whole bunch of friends while enjoying the musical rhythms of metal-hammering. (Take *angkot* #2. Open Sa-Th 8am-noon and 1-4pm.) Head up the hill and turn right at the dentist sign to visit a **kerupuk factory.** The dough is kneaded, spun into cakes, dried, and dropped into hot oil. (Open daily 6am-noon and 1-4pm.) An ancient **stone inscription** batutulis, dating from the mid-14th century and the Pajajaran Kingdom, can be seen on Jl. Batutulis. Take *angkot* #2. 10min. south of the garden.

MARKETS

Pasar Kebon Kembang, on Jl. Dewi Sartika beside Taman Topi, offers everything from *anjaman* (weaving) to *zaitun minyac* (olive oil). **Pasar Baru,** Jl. Suryakencana 3, is near the gate to the Botanical Gardens behind **Bogor Plaza Shopping Center.** Watch your step; this hectic food market also offers odorous puddles. Public execution of chickens may dismay the lighthearted. **Pasar Ramayan** on Jl. Empang is a low-key market with high-key musical accompaniment (canary Rp120,000). Bargaining rule of thumb: always aim for a fifth of the price, reluctantly settle for half.

DAYTRIPS FROM BOGOR

Buses from the main bus terminal or the Sukusari bus terminal (via *angkot* #2) reach countless destinations in the outlying areas near Bogor. Travelers can escape to **Pelabuhanratu,** a hill-bounded coastal town to the southwest. It takes four hours by share-taxi and an indeterminate amount of time by bus (Rp10,000). Unfortunately currents render it unsafe for swimming in all but the bay area. Beaches around **Ujung Genteng** have great surfing and reasonable accommodations. Share the beaches at twilight with night-loving giant turtles. From Pelabuhanratu a bus will take you to Suradi and a bemo will get you to Genteng. For Rp50,000, a stay at **Mama's** will keep you well-fed and happy.

To reach the seven **Air Terjun Cilember** (Cilember Waterfalls), take *angkot* #2 to Terminal Sukasari and then a blue #2 minibus halfway to Cisarva (Rp1500). Look for the blue gates and then catch an *ojek* (Rp2000-4000) to the entrance. The tough hike is deserted on weekdays; solo travelers might consider visiting on weekends. (Entrance fee Rp1500, guides for less traversed routes roughly Rp5000-10,000.)

Taman Safari, in Cisarva, is more a drive-thru zoo than a safari. A swimming pool and other entertainment help make this a fun half-day trip from Puncak. (☎0251 253 222. Take an *angkot* 30 min. from Cilember, Rp1000; tell the driver to stop at the Safari. An *ojek*, Rp1500, will take you to the gate. Open M-F 9am-5pm, Sa-Su 8:30am-5:30pm. Tour Rp30,000, children Rp25,000. Night tours on the Taman Safari bus, Sa 7-9pm.)

THE PUNCAK ☎0263

Meaning "peak" in Bahasa Indonesia, "Puncak" understates the beauty of the mountain pass connecting Jakarta and Bogor to Bandung. Tea plantations stretch for miles on either side of Rte. 2 (Jl. Raya), which winds through the towns of Cisarua and Cipanas. From here the floral Jl. Raya Cobodas branches off and leads to the Gede Pangrango National Park and the Cibodas Botanical Gardens. Terraced rice paddies and the peaks of Gunung Gede and Gunung Pangrango are visible from any patio on the hill. Beyond the park's gates, avid trekkers see exciting wildlife, impressive waterfalls, and seemingly bottomless volcano craters on the way to the top. The view of the mountain path alone is well worth the challenging hike.

TRANSPORTATION. On weekdays, **buses** run almost every 30min. from **Jakarta, Bogor,** and **Bandung.** On the weekend, public buses are forbidden from traveling on Rte. 2 (Jl. Raya) because traffic is so heavy, though white minibuses do still make the trip from Bogor (1hr., Rp3000-5000). From Bandung, reach **Cibodas** by taking a bus to **Cianjur** and then travelling via *angkot* to Cibodas via **Cipanas** (total Rp6000-7000).

PRACTICAL INFORMATION. The **medical clinic, post office, wartel,** and **bank** reside on **Jl. Raya Cipanas,** the stretch of the road connecting Bogor and Bandung. A couple of kilometers from the heart of Cipanas toward Bogor, **Jl. Raya Cibodas** branches off and stretches to the parks and gardens above, where most guest houses are located.

The Cipanas **angkot station** is next to the **post office,** Jl. Raya Cipanas 109. (Open M-Th 8am-3pm, F 8-11am, Sa 8am-1pm.) Painfully slow Internet and a **wartel** are next door. (Open daily 6am-midnight.) A few hundred meters back toward the pass is **Bank BNI Cipanas,** Jl. Raya Cipanas 167, which has a **24hr. ATM.** (☎512 022. Open M-F 8am-3pm.) BCA **ATM** (Cirrus/MC/V) is 100m toward Bandung and across the street. Next door is a general **pharmacy.** There is a **24hr. health clinic** (☎512 465) at the Jl. Raya Cibodas and Jl. Raya Cipanas intersection. **Postal code:** 43253.

ACCOMMODATIONS AND FOOD. A short *angkot* ride up Jl. Raya Cibodas leads to several well-situated accommodations, overlooking the beautiful terraced valley and a mere 10min. walk from the Botanical Gardens and Gunung Gede.

Freddy's, 500m from the Cibodas gate, is the lodging of choice. This relaxed, friendly home has the only knowledgeable English-speaking guides in the area. Shared *mandi*, breakfast and tea are complimentary. (☎515 473. Doubles Rp50,000.) Past the Cibodas Gate to the right is the **Wisma Jamur,** a good option for groups of three to six, offering bright and clean rooms with great views of the Puncak from its veranda. (Around Rp50,000 with private *mandi*, depending on size and degree of privacy.) Next door, the **Pondok Pemuda Hostel,** intended for groups of four to 24, evokes memories of summer camp with its dorm-style rooms. (☎512 807. Quads Rp40,000.) Expect these hostels to be packed on weekends and holidays.

The best option for delicious satiating eats are the guest houses above, all of which offer hot, home-cooked meals. Dozens of fruit stands and countless *warung* offering fried noodles and rice line the road leading to the garden gates, providing a quick post-trek snack for a few thousand rupiah. Several cafes inside the gardens offer somewhat more extensive menus. **Jl. Raya Cipanas** supplies fancy hotel-restaurants, sleepless *warung*, and cheap *padang* joints for spice fanatics.

SIGHTS. The walk or ride up **Jl. Raya Cibodas** is breathtaking (*angkot* Rp1000). Thanks to residents who participate in the nursery business, flowering plants and bonsai line the whole 4km stretch. The **Kebun Raya Cibodas,** an extension of the Bogor Botanical Gardens 1km beyond the Cibodas gates, is a hiking and bird-watching paradise. **Avoid crowded weekend and holiday explorations.** (Open daily 7am-6pm; last ticket sold at 4pm. Rp3000.) The gardens spread out on the lower fringe of **Gede Pangrango National Park,** a volcanic range that extends from Sumatra through Java. For Rp2500, visitors can hike roughly one hour to a mystical bat cave (guide required) and three waterfalls. Another 90min. finds a hot spring. A round-trip day-hike to the summit of Gunung Gede (14km) is another option for those who start early enough. Those with a tent and sleeping bag can spend the night near the summit of **Gunung Pangrango,** a neighboring mountain. Quality maps with suggested trails and required visitor's permits are available at the visitors center. Though costly, guides are strongly recommended for night hiking.

While not exactly the bower of flowers the name suggests, the **Taman Bunga Nusantara** (National Flower Garden) provides more landscaped wonder filled with colorful greenhouses (around Rp10,000). An *angkot* headed toward Mariwati from Cipanas will drop you at the gate. The tea-picking process can be seen at the fascinating **Gunung Mas Pabrik Teh** (Gunung Mas Tea Factory) between Bogor and Cipanas. From the gates, walk past a teahouse, gift shop, and women passionately picking away 10min. to get to the factory. (Grounds open daily 8am-6pm; Rp1500. Factory open Sa-Th 8am-2pm; Rp2000, plus Rp5000 for required guide.)

BANDUNG

☎022

From the late 19th century until WWII, the Dutch knew Bandung as a favorite vacation spot. As the capital of West Have province and home to 50 schools and universities, Bandung is a center for brains and power. Known as "The Paris of the East Indies" because of its residual European sophistication, Bandung still offers a backdrop of cool mountain nights against which a melange of tropical Deco architecture from the 1920s, modern nightclubs, and traditional Indonesian arts are set.

TRANSPORTATION

Flights: Husen Sastra Negara Airport, 5km west of the city. Take a taxi from the town center (10min., Rp15,000-20,000). Contact **Merpati,** a travel agency located at the airport (☎603 4744) and in Hotel Papandayan on Jl. Gabot Sobroto (☎730 27 37) for flight times and arrangements (open M-F 8am-4:30pm, Sa 9am-2pm, Su 9am-1pm). Flights Tu, Th, and Sa to: **Denpasar** (Rp772,000); **Lombok** (Rp 912,000); **Surabaya** (Rp530,500); **Ujung Pandang** (Rp1,199,000).

Trains: Terminal Stasiun (☎420 69 17), behind the *angkot* station on Jl. Stasiun Barat, off Jl. Kebonjati. To: **Jakarta** (3hr.; every hr. on the hr. 5am-6pm; Express/Special M-F 6:30 and 9pm, F-Sa 4pm, Su and holidays 7, 8pm; Rp20,000-50,000); **Surabaya** (11hr.; 7am, 5, 7pm; Rp60,000-150,000); **Jogjakarta** (around 7hr., 4 per day, Rp40,000-72,000). Prices depend on class (1st, 2nd) and type (standard, executive) of train.

Buses: Intercity buses leave Leuwi Panjang Terminal going west and Terminal Cicaheum going east. **Leuwi Panjang Terminal** (☎522 07 68), is on Jl. Sukarno-Hatta a few kilometers south of the train station. Take bus Ledeng-Leuwi Panjang or an *angkot* from *alun-alun.* To **Bogor** (3hr., every hr. 24hr., Rp5000-10,000) and **Jakarta** (4hr., every hr. 24hr., Rp10,000-15,000). **Terminal Cicaheum** (☎727 95 49) is on Jl. A. Yani northeast of the town center. Take bus Cicaheum-Kebon Kelapa or bus #9 Cicaheum-Leuwi Panjang from *alun-alun.* To: **Cirebon** (4hr., every hr. 6am-6pm, Rp15,000-20,000); **Denpasar** (24hr., 2pm, Rp132,000); **Surabaya** (12hr., 2pm, Rp82,000); **Jogjakarta** (10hr., 6:30pm, Rp52,000).

Local Transportation: City buses (Rp500-700) have north-south and east-west routes. A complex network of **angkot** ply city streets (Rp500-700) and surrounding regions but locals are always willing to help. Terminals are at the railway station at **Station Hall** and at **Kebon Kelapa** (old bus terminal). **Becak** are convenient for downtown jaunts. **Taxis** rarely use meters, so bargain. Share-taxi to **Pangandaran** (6hr.) Rp25,000.

ORIENTATION AND PRACTICAL INFORMATION

Busy **Jl. Asia-Afrika** runs east-west passing *alun-alun*, the center of town. **Jl. Otto Iskandardinata** runs north-south and ends at the Governor's Mansion, where **Jl. Merdeka** takes over as the major north-south route two blocks east. **Jl. Kebonjati** becomes **Jl. Suniaraja** in front of the train station and then runs parallel to and north of Jl. Asia-Afrika. **Jl. Braga** runs north-south by the **Museum Asia-Afrika.** Keep in mind that street signs are placed perpendicular to the streets they name.

Tourist Office: Tourist Information Center (☎420 66 44), at the northeast corner of *alun-alun.* Books tours in and around Bandung. Open M-Sa 8am-5pm. **Information counter** (☎421 66 48), at the railway station. Has locked luggage storage (Rp1500 per day). Open daily 8am-5:30pm.

Tours: Sari Holiday, Jl. Naicpan 45 (☎422 07 16), 1 block northeast of the Museum Asia-Afrika. Open M-Sa 8am-4pm. **Pacto Tours and Travel,** Jl. Karapitan 87 (☎733 39 42). Provides AmEx services. Open M-F 8:30am-4:30pm, Sa 8:30am-1pm.

Currency Exchange: Golden Moneychanger, Jl. Otto Iskandardinata 180 (☎423 84 38). Open M-F 9am-4:30pm, Sa 9am-1pm. Banks and ATMs are all over the city, including a **BCA ATM** at the corner of Jl. Suniaraya and Jl. Banceuy, and a full-service **Bank Bali,** Jl. Merdeka 66 (☎423 43 66). Open M-F 8am-3pm.

Emergency: Police ☎110. **Ambulance** ☎118. **Fire** ☎113.

Police: Main Station (☎420 35 00), on Jl. Merdeka.

Pharmacy: Kimia Farma 12, Jl. Ir. H. Juanda 1 (☎420 54 21) at the intersection with Jl. Hasannudin. Open 24hr. Pharmacies in town are open 8am-8pm.

Medical Services: Hospital RS Kebonjati, Jl. Kebonjati 152 (☎601 40 58). **24hr.** emergency clinic.

Telephones: International phones at **GPO** and **Wartels** are abundant in town.

Internet Access: Ega Kineta, Jl. Braga 111 (☎420 62 91). Rp5000 per hr. Open M-Sa 8am-7pm. **Cybernet,** Jl. Gardu Jati 33. Rp5000 per hr. Open daily 10am-10pm. **Warposnet,** in the far back of the GPO. Rp6000 per hr.

Express Mail: DHL, Jl. Asia-Afrika 81 (☎423 16 31), in the Grand Hotel Preanger. Open M-F 8am-5pm, Sa 8am-1pm.

Post Office: GPO, Jl. Asia-Afrika 49 (☎420 70 81). Enter on the side past the stands. International phones. *Poste Restante.* Open daily 8am-8pm. **Postal code:** 40111.

Bandung
ACCOMMODATIONS
By "Moritz," 16
Hotel Patrudissa II, 11
Hotel Surabaya, 13
Le Yossie Homestay, 15
Le Yossie Homestay II, 14
Losmen Sakardana, 12
FOOD
Braga Permai Bakery, 18
Dago Tea House, 1
Kampung Daun, 2
Rumah Makan Sari Sunda, 26
Sindang Reret, 4
SIGHTS
Army Museum, 19
Bandung Institute of Technology (ITB), 3
Bandung Society for Heritage Conservation, 10
Gedung Merdeka, 23
Gedung Sate, 7
Geology Museum, 6
Museum Asia-Afrika, 24
Pakuan Building (Governor's Residence), 9
Pasar Baru, 20
Plaza Bandung Indah, 8
Wayang Golek Factory, 27
NIGHTLIFE
Fame Station, 25
L.A. Dream Palace, 22
North Sea, 17
Planet 2001, 21
Sapulidi, 5
0 500 yards
0 500 meters
N
TO JL. SETIA BUDI AND 2
TO 1 (2km)
Advent Hospital
Borromaeus Hospital
Hassan Sadikin Hospital
Hospital RS Kebonjati
Zoo
Ganesha Park
Merdeka Park
Alun Alun
Kebon Kelapa Bus Terminal
Taman Ria Tegellega Sport Center
TO (5km)
TO CICAHEUM BUS STATION (1km)
TO 25 (300m)
TO LEUWI PANJANG BUS STATION (500m)
BCA
Bank Bali
Jl. Teku Umar
Jl. Ganeca
Jl. Dago
Jl. Hasannudin
Jl. Dipati Ukur
Jl. Surapati (Jl. Suci)
Jl. Diponegoro
Jl. Sulanjan
Jl. Jipang
Jl. Cipaganti
Jl. Jurang
Jl. Eyckman
Jl. Sukajadi
Jl. Rumahsakit
Jl. Pasteur
Jl. Cihampelas (Jeans St.)
Cikapundung
Jl. Taman Sari
Jl. Juanda
Jl. R. Gading
Jl. Trunojoyo
Jl. Cilamaya
Jl. Citarum
Jl. Cilliwung
Jl. Otten
Jl. Cipto
Jl. Wastu Kencana
Jl. Pajajaran
Jl. Martadinata (Jl. Riau)
Jl. Maratadinata
Jl. Ambon
Jl. Banda
Jl. Sulawesi
Jl. Aceh
Jl. Cicendo
Jl. Kebon Kawung
Jl. Merdeka
Jl. Sumatra
Jl. Kalimantan
Jl. Sumbawa
Jl. Lombok
Jl. Patra Komala
Jl. Belitung
Jl. Jawa
Jl. Pasir Kaliki
Jl. Kebonjati
Jl. Suniaraja
Jl. Tera
Jl. Belakang Pasar
Jl. Banceuy
Jl. Lembong
Jl. Braga
Jl. Veteran
Jl. Gardu Jati
Jl. ABC
Jl. Naripan
Jl. Jend. Sudirman
Jl. Asia-Afrika
Jl. Cibadak
Jl. Dalem Kaum
Jl. Karang Anyar
Jl. Pagarsih
Jl. Kalipahapo
Jl. Tamblong
Jl. Lengkong Kecil
Jl. Pangarang
Jl. Pacedang
Jl. Astana Anyar
Jl. Dewi Sartika
Jl. Pasir Koja
Jl. Pungkur
Jl. Lengkong Besar
Jl. Ciateul
Jl. Otto Iskandardinata
Jl. Mohamad Toha
Jl. Kopo
Jl. Bojongloa
Jl. Mohamad Ramadan
Jl. BKR

ACCOMMODATIONS

Cheap accommodations line both streets near the railway station and Jl. Pangarang, two blocks south of the Museum Asia-Afrika.

By "Moritz," Luxor Permai 35 (☎420 57 88), at intersection with Jl. Belakang Pasar. A sign on the south side of Jl. Kebonjati leads the way. Named after the owner's oldest son, this comfortable, colorful and backpacker-filled home has clean rooms. Arranges mountain tours. Breakfast and virtuoso guitarists included. Extendable midnight curfew. Dorms Rp15,500; singles Rp19,500; doubles Rp28,000; triples Rp39,500.

Hotel Patrudissa II, Jl. Pasirkaliki 12 (☎420 26 45). Follow the "Hotel" sign down a short, well-lit alley. Private *mandi,* hot water, maps, and info about Bandung. Colored light bulbs give the squeaky clean and rather bland rooms some character. Blue, green, or red singles/doubles Rp40,000.

Hotel Surabaya, Jl. Kebonjati 71-75 (☎423 36 79). Echoey, spacious rooms that share the building's colonial feel, all the way down to the stained glass. Free tea. Singles Rp20,000; doubles Rp30,000; triples Rp42,500; quads Rp47,500; deluxe Rp52,500.

Le Yossie II, Jl. Belakang Pasar 112 (☎426 60 36). Bar and pool table may compromise an early trekker's shut-eye. Arranges mountain tours. Singles Rp20,000; doubles Rp25,000.

Le Yossie , Jl. Kebonjati 53 (☎420 54 53). Look for the pastel-green shutters of the less popular older brother of Le Yossie II. One bathroom per floor. Singles Rp20,000; doubles Rp25,000.

Losmen Sakardana, Jl. Kebonjati 50-7/B (☎423 98 97). Follow signs down a short alley to "Sakadarna International." Has upstairs terrace, but small rooms. Knock after midnight. Avoid less sanitary "Sakarda" housing further down the narrow, sketchy alley. Singles Rp15,000; doubles Rp25,000; triples Rp35,000.

FOOD

Warung set up nightly on **Jl. Gardu Jati.** Try *bakso,* a noodle soup with meat and *tahu* (tofu). Sweet drinks like ginger *bandrek* and *bajigur,* made of creamy cool coconut milk, shouldn't be missed. Scrumptious *ikan gurame,* a freshwater fish grilled *(bakar)* or fried *(goreng)* is a signature of local cuisine. Enjoy a delish dish of fish on Chinese-themed Jl. Gardu Jati and **Jl. Sudirman** (**Siang Siang** open nightly 10pm-4am) or just unwind at one of **Jl. Braga's** many fine cafes and aromatic bakeries (**Braga Permai** serves a killer banana split Rp9500).

Kampung Daun (☎278 79 15), in the Trinity Villas Complex on Jl. Cihideung. *Angkot* up Jl. Setia Budi toward Lembang (15min). Transit in Parongpong onto Jl. Cihideung on the left (10min). Taxi Rp25-30,000. Plan a trip to this hideaway in the beautiful hills of Dago, Bandung's superb suburb. Fine Sundanese and Mediterranean cuisine and romantic private huts by a stream make a memorable experience. *Jaipong* upon request. Traditional music Sa. Reserve during the week. Open Tu-F 11am-midnight.

Rumah Makan Sari Sunda, Jl. Jend. Sudirman 103-107. Let the calming sounds of *gamelan* music and falling water wash away stress in a spectacular open-air garden. The mouth-watering Sudanese menu (especially the *ikan gurame,* smaller portion Rp23,000, or *kelapa muda,* a coconut and syrup sipper, Rp5500) does not fall short of the atmosphere. Open daily 10am-11pm.

Dago Tea House, Jl. Bukit Dago Utara. Take an *angkot* toward Dago and ask to be let out at the Dago Tea House, then ask the locals for directions. Buried in the hills north of the city; the exquisite food, thatched huts, and spectacular view of the city, mountains, and setting sun, is worth the hike. Admission Rp500, entrees Rp7000-18,000.

Sindang Reret, Jl. Surapati 53 (☎250 14 74), past the running track. Performance hall restaurant provides not only a great Sudanese feast (fish dishes Rp9000-18,000, rice entrees Rp3000-8000) but also the only *wayang golek* show in town (Sa 7:30-10pm). Delicious *sarikaya* pudding Rp1750. (Open daily 10am-11pm.)

INDONESIA

SIGHTS

Though Bandung has a handful of interesting cultural attractions, its best sights are outside the city in the volcanoes (see **Daytrips from Bandung,** p. 164). An Art Deco movement swept through here in the 1930s (courtesy of architects Wolf Shoemacher, A.F. Aalbers, and F.W. Brinkman). Curious visitors can take free one-hour tours through the **Bandung Society for Heritage Conservation** in the Hotel Panghegar, on the fifth floor of Jl. Merdeka 2. (☎423 22 86, ext.8554. Open M-F 10am-4pm.) Two blocks southwest is the **Gedung Merdeka,** marked by its several dozen flagpoles, which houses the **Museum Asia-Afrika** at Jl. Asia-Afrika 81. The museum has memorabilia from the 1955 Non-Aligned Movement Conference in Bandung, at which 29 African and Asian nations collectively agreed to pursue non-alignment policies during the Cold War between the US and erstwhile USSR. (Open M-F 8am-3pm. Free.) At the **Army Museum,** Jl. Lembong 38, military buffs can compare older weapons and tanks to modern devices on display. Enter from the interior courtyard of the military building. (☎420 33 93. Open M-Sa 8am-1pm. Donation requested.)

A. Ruchiyat's **wayang golek factory,** in a twisting alley two blocks south of the Savoy Homan Hotel off Jl. Pangarang, produces and sells *wayang golek* puppets (miniature marionette Rp6000). The care and precision that goes into carving the special albasia wood may leave you dazed. Enter beyond Hotel Mawar; ask around for directions. (☎420 13 35. Open M-Sa 8am-9pm.)

North of the city, the **Bandung Institute of Technology (ITB)** stands in an impressive Art Deco building. Take an *angkot* toward Dago and get off at ITB. Also in the north suburbs is the stately **Gedung Sate,** a colonial-era building that is now the regional capital. It faces the **Geology Museum,** Jl. Diponegoro 57(☎720 32 05), which houses fantastic fossils, including those of an enormous elephant, a Tyrannosaurus Rex, and prehistoric **Java Man's skull** (see **History,** p. 130).

ENTERTAINMENT AND NIGHTLIFE

The nexi of Bandung's nightlife are **Jl. Braga** and **Jl. Cihapelas (Jeans Street).** *Wayang golek* puppet performances are free with dinner at **Sindang Reret** on Jl. Surapati (Sa 7:30-10pm), Jl. Tegalega offers traditional *jaipong* dance, and weekend *dangdut* (live) music is featured at most clubs. Saturday is the best night to go clubbing.

Planet 2001, on Jl. Sudirman 29 in the paramount building. Glow-in-the-dark planets and big, clumsy rockets coat the semi-galactic dance hall. Best techno in Bandung gets twenty-somethings and professional dancers bumping. Open nightly 9pm-4am.

North Sea, Jl. Braga 82. Nautically-themed bar with international crowd. Drown your sorrows and have a maritime. Bir Bintang Rp12,000. Live music F and Sa. Free pool table. Open M-F 5pm-1am, Sa-Su noon-3am.

Fame Station, on the 11th floor of the Wisma Lippo tower on Jl. Asia-Afrika. Hesitant dancers share the dance floor and pool hall with the occasional foreigners and graceless teenagers looking for a good time. Live house music. Cover Rp30,000. Birthday cupcake Rp15,000. Tyson, an 18 liquor compound, Rp165,000. Open M-Sa 9pm-2am.

Sapulidi, Jl. Cihampelas 107. Self-proclaimed "Fancy Bar" packed with local hipsters and serious cover bands. Cover Rp25,000, one drink included. Open M-Sa 11pm-2am.

L.A. Dream Palace, 2nd fl., Jl. Asia-Afrika 21-27, in Plaza Asia-Afrika. This is what people in the '70s imagined the future to be like. Cheesy flashing lights and a thumping sound system give a pulse to the awkward dancing of local teenagers. *Dangdut* music M, gay night W. Cover Rp10,000. Open M-Sa 10pm-3am, Su 2:30pm-2am.

MARKETS

Most of Bandung's wares are straight from the production line. Food markets, such as Pasar Malam by *alun-alun*, seem to appear in excessive abundance. Claustrophobic **Pasar Baru,** along Jl. Otto Iskandardinata in Chinatown, is Bandung's oldest market, dating back to 1812. An adventurous maze of vendors sell textiles, shoes, dried foods, fish, meat, and fruit. (Open daily 7am-4pm.) West of town is the even larger **Pasar Ciroyom,** selling a mix of second-hand goods, food, and household products (catch a westward *angkot* from the train station). Cheap **night markets** along Jl. Sudirman and Jl. Belakang Pasar provide a tasty cure for midnight munchies. A flashy shopping strip two blocks north of the train station, on **Jeans Street** (Jl. Cihampelas), sells cheap denim products. **Plaza Bandung Indah,** Jl. Merdeka 56, called "Bay-Ee-Pay" or "Beef" by locals, is swank with its big-name foreign stores and a seven-screen cinema featuring movies in their original language. (Open daily 8am-6pm.) For *warung*, try **Pasar Malam,** off *alun-alun*'s northeast corner. **Pasar Baru** offers textiles, clothing, and fruit on Jl. Otto Iskandardinata, near Jl. ABC.

DAYTRIPS FROM BANDUNG

Bandung hides a wealth of sights in its mountain ridges, best seen through tours led by guides (about Rp75,000 per day trip). You can brave the *angkot*/minibus system for a cheaper viewing (take *angkot* from the train station toward Lembong and get out before Subang). Travelers can trek to **Tangkuban Prahu,** the "capsized boat" crater, from the town of **Lembang,** a 90min. *angkot* ride from the railway station. Those with time should get off at Jl. Jayagiri after one hour and hike the remaining 10km straight up through pine and tropical forests. The forest trail emerges at the lower parking lot and gate. (Open daily 6am-5pm.) The big gray **Ratu** spits sulfur and steam, at 1830m. A path leads to the smaller **Domas Caldera** from the lower lot; get a guide for this route, available at the tourist office. Those who have had their fill of vistas can take an *angkot* toward Subang. After winding through tea plantations, get off at the top of the road at the "Air Panas Crater," the **hot springs** at **Sari Ater Resort,** Jl. Taman Sari 72. To catch some stars, it's best to settle in the therapeutic hot baths among natural waterfalls around 9pm. (☎250 31 88. Open 24hr.)

Check out a **silk factory** in Garut at the **Candi Cangkuang Temple,** the oldest Hindu temple on West Java, dating from the 8th century. Take an *angkot* from Terminal Cicaheum, direction Garut, and after one hour get out in Kadungora. It's a 4km walk or *delman* ride from there. Continue on to Garut, switch *angkots* and head to Cisurupan, a 9km hike from the crystal studded **Papandayan Volcano.** After the hike, a soak in the **Tarogong Hot Springs** at the base will help you relax (take *angkot* from Garut directly to Tarogong).

If you're headed to Dago Tea House, check out the historic cave in **Maribaya Park** (Rp2600). Take a 15min. ride from Lembang to the park and then walk to Dago (Rp2100). During WWII, the Japanese used this cave to store their weapons (Rp2000 for guide and flashlight).

CIREBON ☎0231

At the Sudanese-Javanese crossroads on the north coast lies Cirebon, a former seat for ancient Muslim kingdoms. Today the city produces *kerupuk* (shrimp crackers) and cigarettes, two of the most important consumer items in Indonesia and is also a major stop on the railway from Jakarta to all points east. Travelers willing to detrain and face the sweltering coastal heat find lesser-known sites, such as the three *kratons* (palaces) and the sacred tomb of Sultan Gunung Jati, that make Cirebon an afternoon of discovery and adventure.

TRANSPORTATION

Trains: Stasiun Cirebon (☎208 888), on Jl. Stasiun off Jl. Siliwangi. Express trains to: **Jakarta** (3½hr.; 3:55, 5:55am, 1:30, 3:30, 10:25pm; Rp18,000-32,000); **Jogjakarta** (5-8hr., 10 per day, Rp36,000-100,000); **Surabaya** (9hr.; 8am, noon, 6pm;

Rp42,000-155,000). Cirebon is also a stopping point for most non-express trains, including those headed to **Jogjakarta, Solo,** and **Surabaya.**

Buses: Terminal Harjamukti Kodya Cirebon (☎248 902), 5km from town. Take *angkot* D5, D7, or D8 (Rp1000). Service to: **Denpasar** (20hr., Rp80,000-200,000); **Jakarta-Pulo Gadung** (4hr., every 30min., Rp12,000-20,000); **Jogjakarta** (5hr., Rp25,000-50,000); **Surabaya** (12hr., Rp40,000-100,000).

Local Transportation: *Angkot* have set rates of R700 around town. G5 and G6 run up and down Jl. Siliwangi. Over-eager *becak* drivers lounge on every street corner. Be sure to bargain, as usual, and expect to pay about Rp1000-2000 per km. Don't bother asking for directions; this will only result in deriding remarks. To most *becak* drivers, you deserve no help.

ORIENTATION AND PRACTICAL INFORMATION

Cirebon is on the coast, and its center is bound by train tracks and the shoreline, which run parallel from the northwest to the southeast. The **tomb of Sultan Gunung Jati** stands a few kilometers north of town on the major thoroughfare **Jl. Siliwangi/ Jl. Karanggetas.** Heading southeast from the tomb, Jl. Siliwangi leads to the **train station** and the **hotel area** of town. It is intersected by **Jl. Karitini/Jl. Veteran** (host of Grage Mall, Cirebon's largest shopping complex), and again by the **Kali Sukalila,** a narrow waterway. Jl. Siliwangi becomes **Jl. Karanggetas** at the channel heading through **commercial and shopping districts**, and passing the **New Jogja** and **Asia malls** before reaching the **three kratons.** The **post office, banks,** and **harbor** are east of this area; the **hospital** (RS Gunung Jati) is a few kilometers south.

Tourist Office: Jl. Brig. Gen. Darsono 5 (☎486 856). Near Stadium Bima. Dispenses brochures and pamphlets. Open M-Th 7am-2pm, F 7-11am, Sa 7am-1pm.

Currency Exchange: Banks line Jl. Siliwangi and Jl. Yos Sudarso. **Bank Niaga,** Jl. Siliwangi 110 (☎201 833), cashes checks from US banks. Open M-F 8:15am-2:30pm.

Markets: Fully-equipped **Pasar Pagi** sprawls under and behind the colossal Matahari on Jl. Karaggetas; **Pasar Kanoman,** specializing in fresh edibles, lies in front of Keraton Kanoman on Jl. Winawon and disperses into narrow alleyways.

Emergency: Ambulance ☎118. **Police** ☎110. **Fire** ☎113.

Pharmacies: Kimia Farma Apotek, Jl. Parujakan 12 (☎208 954). Turn right onto Jl. Surya Negra from Jl. Karanggetas, then walk 400m and turn left. **Open 24hr.**

Medical Services: RS Gunung Jati, Jl. Kesambi 56 (☎206 330), several km south of the town center. Take *angkot* G6 south from the train station down Jl. Siliwangi.

Telephones: Wartel Citra, Jl. Inspeks 53, next to the train station. **Open 24hr.**

Internet Access: At the **GPO,** Rp1500 per 15min. Open M-Sa 8am-5pm, Su 8am-2pm. **Warnet Catur,** Jl. Karanggetas, opposite Marina Seafood on the 4th fl. of the New Jogja department store. Rp5000 per hr. Open daily 8am-9pm. A microscopic Internet station hides timidly among bullying big-names on the top floor of **Grage Mall,** on Jl. Kartini.

Post Offices: GPO, Jl. Yos Sudarso 9 (☎200 511). Take *angkot* D1. Coin and card phone. *Poste Restante* (☎204 411). Open M-Sa 7:30am-8pm, letter service Su 8am-1pm. **Branch** (☎200 731) in the town center next to the Jogja mall on Jl. Karanggeta. **Postal code:** 45111.

ACCOMMODATIONS

Middle and upper range hotels are near the train station. Because Cirebon-bound packers are such a rarity, budget spots are few and far between and must be hunted down. If you're desperate and feeling lucky, try **Jl. Siliwangi.** Reserve in advance from October through November.

Hotel Slamet, Jl. Siliwangi 95 (☎203 296). Opposite the train station. Considering the options, definitely worth the extra rupiahs. Breakfast included. Each well-kept room has 2 beds, TV, and private bath. Doubles with fan Rp57,000, with A/C Rp70,000; extra bed Rp20,000.

Hotel Baru, Jl. Kali Baru Selatan 3 (☎201 728). From the train station, turn right onto Jl. Siliwangi; after 1km cross the bridge, then turn left and walk 400m. Breakfast included. Restaurant and karaoke available and intriguing. Quality doubles with fan and bath Rp35,000, with TV Rp45,000, with A/C and hot water Rp102,000; extra bed Rp20,000.

Hotel Asia, Jl. Kali Baru Selatan 11A (☎202 183). Next to the Hotel Baru. Courtyard. Simple doubles Rp20,400, with *mandi* and fan Rp35,100.

Losmen Famili, Jl. Siliwangi 66 (☎207 935). 100m straight ahead from the train station. Shared *mandi.* Best bargain around; 6-legged roommates pick up their share of the bill. Basic singles Rp14,000, doubles Rp20,000-30,000.

FOOD

Cirebon specialties such as *nasi lengko* (rice with bean sprouts, onion, cucumber, and *tempe*) and *nasi jamblang* (rice in dried teak leaves) taste best right off the food carts on Jl. Siliwangi. Countless restaurants, *warung,* and markets in the area serve fresh fish and shellfish.

Kang Kabayan, Jl. Dr. Wahidin 68, across the street 100m from the Grage Mall on Jl. Kartini. Neon lights adorn the best bamboo house known to Cirebon. Dishes Rp5000-35,000. Open daily 10am-11pm.

Marina Seafood Restaurant, 4th fl., Jl. Karanggetas 64, over the New Jogja Department Store. Fantastic views of the harbor inspire marine and terrestrial dishes for Rp12,000-55,000. The killer Aruana is not on the menu. Live music Sa. Open M-Sa 11am-10pm, Su *dim sum* 8-11am.

SIGHTS

Cirebon's **Tomb of Sultan Gunung Jati** is one of Java's holiest sites. One of the first Muslim missionaries to Java, the Sultan is revered for pushing out the Hindu kingdom of Pajajaran and conquering the Cirebon empire. In November, Muslim devotees pour in to celebrate his birthday. To reach the tomb, take *angkot* CG or GG from Jl. Siliwangi north to Makam Gunung Jati, walk to the lane's end, and turn right. A small donation (Rp500-1000) buys a tour of the grounds.

At the east end of Jl. Gudang/Pasuketan overlooking the harbor is **Klenteng Thiaw Kak Sie,** a temple that serves the Chinese residents of Cirebon (15% of the city's population). Built in 1658, Thiaw Kak Sie is Indonesia's oldest Chinese temple and one of its most beautiful.

Angkots D6 and G5 lead to the south end of town, where three separate **kratons** (palaces) lie two or three blocks past the end of Jl. Karanggetas. Farthest south is **Kraton Kasepuhan,** built in 1527. Here, visitors can view one of the main halls still furnished; a museum of 16th-century weapons, armor, and *gamelan* pieces; and a stable containing cannons and the **Singa Barong Carriage**, the sultan's personal ride. The buffalo-powered Oldsmobile celebrates harmony among Chinese Buddhists, Indian Hindus, and Egyptian Muslims, respectively symbolized by its dragon head, elephant tusks, and bird wings that function as car doors and flap when underway. (☎204 001. Museum open M-Sa 8am-4pm, Su 8am-5pm. Rp2000.) **Kraton Kanoman,** on Jl. beyond Pasar Kanoman, holds **the Paksi Naga Liman** (elephant-serpent-bird), another magnificent coach. (Open daily 8am-4pm. Rp2000.)

East of Kraton Kanoman is **Mesjid Agung** (long pants required). **Kraton Kacirebonan,** to the north, is still inhabited by the sultanate and is thus closed to the public.

Four and a half kilometers southwest of town is **Taman Sunyaragi,** which houses Cirebon's botanical gardens in an odd red-brick structure. Built in the 15th century as a rest house for the royal family, Sunyaragi has been a country palace, an armory, and a rebel base during the colonial wars. Take *angkot* G2 to the Jl. Bypass and walk right.

PANGANDARAN ☎0265

Pangandaran is a peninsula on the untamed south coast of Java. Its usually vacant stretches of beachfront and quiet streets are a welcome change from Indonesia's commercial beach resorts. However, tourist shops are sprouting along the beach, so travelers may prefer exploring the lush forests and waterfalls and visiting less developed nearby villages while they can. Beachgoers beware: dangerous currents render much of Pangandaran's shore unsafe for swimming.

TRANSPORTATION

Trains: No direct trains to Pangandaran. **Banjar's** station serves all major cities.

Buses: The **bus terminal** is 50m from main gates. To: **Bandung** (6hr.; every hour 4-9am, and noon, 3, 6, 9pm; Rp12,500); **Banjar** (1½hr., every 10min. 4am-4pm, Rp5000); **Bogor** (8hr.; 7am, 7pm; Rp23,000); **Jakarta** (9hr.; 5, 7, 9am, and every hour 5-9pm; Rp30,000).

Local Transportation: *Becak,* **motorcycles,** and **bicycles** rule the roads.

Rentals: Rent bicycles (Rp 20,000 per day) and mopeds (Rp 35,000 per day) from the *ojek* stand opposite the market, or from most hotels. Charter minibuses available at Lotus Tours (see **Practical Information,** below).

ORIENTATION AND PRACTICAL INFORMATION

From the bus terminal, turn left and enter the first red gates. Sign the guest book and pay a one-time cover charge of Rp2000 to get into the city and onto a well-lit boulevard that leads directly into the waves of the **west beach.** Perpendicular at the boulevard's end, mainstream **Jl. Pamugaran/Pantai Barat** stretches north-south along the shore. One kilometer southward, busy **Jl. Bulak Laut** connects Jl. Pantai Barat with **Jl. Kidang Pananjung,** the town's former main road that is furnished with cheap *losmen* and restaurants extending all the way back to the bus station.

Tours: Countless tourist information services, hotels, and restaurants sell the same package tours. One of the more popular is **Lotus Tours,** Jl. Bulak Laut 7. (☎639 635. Open daily 6am-10pm.) Buses head to: **Bandung** (Rp25,000, with A/C Rp35,000); **Jakarta** (Rp35,000); **Wonosobo** (Rp50,000). A wonderful **river boat/bus trip** offers a stress-free trip to **Jogjakarta** (10hr., Rp50,000 through an agent). Don't want to spend RP50,000? Take an early Banjar-bound bus to **Calipucang** (Rp3000), a *becak* to the harbor (Rp5000), a boat to **Cilacap** (6am, though known to launch late; 4hr; Rp5000), a *becak* to the bus station (Rp4000), and a bus to **Jogjakarta** (6hr., Rp15,000).

Currency Exchange: The town's greatest tourist attraction is its only **ATM (24hr.),** behind the market by **Bank Negara Indonesia,** Jl. Merdeka 312 (☎639 700). **Bank Rakyat Indonesia,** Jl. Kidang Pananjung 212 (☎639 288), by the intersection with Jl. E. Jaga Lautan. An additional branch is on Jl. Merdeka behind the market. Cashes traveler's checks at reasonable rates. All banks are open M-F 8am-2pm.

Markets: A narrow **main market** is outside the entrance gates by the bus terminal. Supplier of all goods known to man. Open daily 6am-4pm; crowded on Monday and Thursday. The **fish market** and a mass of tourist shops are in the south, by the east beach and west beach respectively. Open daily 5am-4pm.

Emergency: Police ☎110.

Police: Jl. Merdeka 177 (☎639 110), behind the main market and 400m to the left. Open M-Sa 7am-2pm. Police officers stationed at main gate **24hr.**

Pharmacy: Apotik Pangandaran Farma (☎639 524), in back of the main market. A second resides on Jl. Kidang Pananjung (☎639 983), 100m west of the hospital.

Medical Services: Hospital, Jl. Parapat 1 (☎639 118). Small hospital with ambulance service. **24hr. emergency care.**

Telephones: Telkom office, Jl. Kidang Pananjung 65 (☎639 333). **Open 24hr. HCD** and fax. **Adam's ,** Jl. Pantai Barat 164, has international phone service 8am-10pm.

Post Office: Jl. Kidang Pananjung 129 (☎639 284). *Poste Restante.* Open M-Th 7:30am-3pm, F 7:30-11:30am, Sa 7:30am-1pm. **Postal code:** 49396.

ACCOMMODATIONS

The town has a surplus of exceptional budget accommodations. Sundry accommodations are cluttered on the west beach road. The more inland you go, the cheaper they get. Most places have a two-night minimum and prices decrease with length of stay. Indonesia's tourism slump has hit Pangandaran hard, driving prices down and forcing some establishments to close.

Laguna Beach Bungalows (☎639 761), off of Jl. Pengadilan Kebon, 2km outside the city. Hopeless to find on your own, serene Laguna offers 24hr. free pick-up service (call reception or ☎081 223 68806). A raft-ride from the beach and a 30min. walk from the city, the most popular stay in Pangandaran entertains with traditional dance performances Sa, a lip-smacking welcome drink from the full-fledged restaurant, and rooms with porches. Standard singles Rp35,000; doubles and triples Rp40,000-70,000.

Pondok Cocobana (☎630 510), 200m north from the street to the west beach. Beautiful, spacious rooms with fan, shower, and porch. Singles Rp25,000; doubles Rp45,000; triples Rp60,000.

Bamboo House (☎639 419), on Jl. Baru. This popular stay offers quality bungalows far from traffic. Breakfast Rp5000. Private bath. Singles Rp20,000; doubles Rp25,000-30,000; triples Rp35,000.

Holiday Beach, Jl. Bulak Laut 50 (☎639 285). A block off the beach. Popular restaurant and tourist service. Bare rooms with fan and private *mandi*. Singles Rp20,000; doubles Rp30,000.

FOOD

Pangandaran's food scene ranges from the usual *warung* to busy cafes and seafood spots. Eateries in the old center, the southern end of Jl. Kidang Pananjung, are cheap (Rp5000-10,000 per meal) and open daily 8am to 11pm. Further north on the east beach road, the **fish market** offers the freshest grub in town.

Green Garden Cafe, Jl. Kidang Pananjung 116. Next to Pondok Ibu . Seafood with a Western twist and tasty Indonesian dinner served *al fresco* (Rp6000-10,000). Very relaxed atmosphere. Open daily 5-10pm.

Bunga Laut Restaurant, Jl. Bulak Laut 8-11. Off Jl. Pantai Barat opposite Lotus Tours. Savory soups (Rp5000), delightful desserts (Rp2000-4000), and delicious chicken and seafood entrees (Rp7000-15,000). The fried banana alone is worth the trip.

Bamboo Cafe, on Jl. Pantai Barat beside Adam's , is a popular roadside grotto known to grill a mean fish (around Rp25,000) and chicken (around Rp10,000). Essential fried rice Rp5000.

SIGHTS

Pangandaran has two major sights: **Penanjung National Park** and **Green Canyon.** Travelers can enter Penanjung National Park (Rp2000, open daily 7am-4pm) and check out white- and black-sand beaches that promise great snorkeling (Rp60,000) and hungry monkeys. Although much of the park is technically closed, hikers can see some areas on their own or hire a guide for eco-friendly tours (Rp30,000). Expect to see limestone caves, bats with 2m wingspans, lizards, monkeys, deer, porcupines, and enormous rafflesia flowers that bloom for only four days and reek from 30m away. The Green Canyon follows a jade-colored river through cliffs and waterfalls. Majestic rock formations surround clear pools separated from the main river. Bring a swimsuit, but ask hotels about safe bathing areas. Tours include stops at **Batu Keras Beach,** ideal for beginners looking to ride the wave (plastic boards Rp20,000).

JOGJAKARTA ☎0274

In 1755, Prince Mangkubumi built Jogjakarta's royal kraton and named himself Sultan Hamengku Buwono, meaning "the universe on the lap of the king." His lineage survives today, ten sultans later, illustrating the respect for tradition and the tradition of respect encapsulated in the heart of Jogja, the sultan's palace. The famed Kraton pumps history, culture, and art through the city's pulsating arteries, animating international curiosity and enlivening its locals with an energy uniquely Jogjan.

TRANSPORTATION

Flights: The **airport** (☎566 666) is on Jl. Adisucipto, 5km from the city center. Take a taxi—by public transportation, the trip is excessively complicated, requiring 2-3 bus transfers. **Garuda** (☎522 148) in Amparukmu Hotel on Jl. Laksta Adisucipto. Open daily 5:30am-8pm. Daily flights to: **Denpasar, Jakarta,** and **Mataram. Merpati** (airport office ☎512 727) open daily 8am-4:30pm. Daily flights to **Surabaya.** Purchase tickets through a travel agent.

Trains: Tugu Train Station, Jl. Mangkubumi 1 (☎589 685), on Jl. Pasar Kembang. To: **Bandung** (7hr., 4per day, Rp40,000-70,000); **Jakarta** (7-8hr., 10 per day, Rp36,000-100,000); **Solo** (1hr., 5 per day, Rp3000); **Surabaya** (5hr., 7 per day, Rp36,000-150,000). Tourist info staff at the station can help demystify the schedule. Arrive 30min. in advance to purchase tickets. **Lempuyangan Train Station** on Jl. Lempuyangan serves economy trains only.

Buses: Umbulharjo Terminal, Jl. Veteran (☎376 013), southeast of the city. Take buses #4 and 2 from Malioboro and Prawirotaman areas, respectively. Buses (usually with evening departures) zoom all over Java, Sumatra, and Bali. Schedules, fares, express buses, and peace of mind available at ticket agencies on Jl. Mangkubumi, Sosrowijayan, and Prawirotaman. To: **Denpasar** (17hr., 1:30pm, Rp80,000); **Jakarta** (9-14hr., 3pm, Rp30,000-65,000); **Semarang** (4hr., every hr., Rp10,500).

Local Transportation: City buses (Rp1000) run north-south between Umbulharjo Terminal and Gajah Mada University along Jogja's main streets. Buses are less frequent after 5pm, when unmetered **taxis** become best for long-distance transport. *Becak* is the best way to tour the city; agree on a price before boarding (Rp5000 per 5km is standard). *Andong,* horse-drawn carriages, are available for hire (Rp15,000 per hr.).

Rentals: Places all along Jl. Prawirotaman rent motorbikes for Rp30,000-40,000 per day. **Fortuna Rental,** Jl. Jlagran 20-21 (☎564 680), 50m to the right of Tugu Station. Bikes Rp5000 per day, motorbikes Rp50,000-75,000 per day. Tackle mountains in a jeep (Rp150,000) or sedan (Rp350,000 with driver). Bring a passport and a credit card. Open daily 9am-6pm.

ORIENTATION AND PRACTICAL INFORMATION

Jogjakarta rests at the base of **Gunung Merapi** (2911m), 603km southeast of Jakarta. The city is built around the 10-hectare fortress of the **kraton complex** and the two square fields to the south **(Alun-alun Kidul or Selatan)** and north **(Alun-alun Lor or Utara),** from which **Jl. Yani** runs northward. As Yani runs through the city, it turns into **Jl. Malioboro** and becomes the main boulevard, passing the major living and dining areas. Beyond Tugu Train Station, Malioboro becomes Jl. Mangkubumi, terminating at the **Tugu Monument.** The monument stands in the middle of a major four-street intersection: **Jl. Kangkubumi, Diponegoro, Sangaji,** and **Sudirman,** which leads east to the **airport** and eventually to Prambanan and Solo.

THE PEOPLE'S SULTAN Jogjakarta's reigning Sultan, Hamengkubuwono X, has a tough act to follow. His father, Hamengkubuwono IX, was instrumental during Indonesia's war of independence from Dutch rule, offering the fledgling republic his city as a capital. The move earned Jogjakarta a semi-autonomous status, and himself the positions of Jogja's governor-for-life and vice president to Suharto. It's no wonder that Hamengkubuwono X found himself living in a long shadow when the elder passed away in 1988. But if there were any doubts, the Sultan silenced them in the demonstrations and rioting that led to Suharto's resignation in May 1998. With Jogja's sister city, Solo, in flames, and students planning a march without official consent, he called for *reformasi damai* (peaceful reform) and led the march with his family, from Gadjah Mada University to the *alun-alun* in front of his *kraton*, where he asked students to disperse peacefully. Suharto resigned the next day. Typically Javanese, Hamengkubuwono X brings together contradictions as both a reformist and the head of Jogja's GOLKAR party. He seems to have no intention of running for political office, though GOLKAR probably wishes he would.

Tourist Office: Jl. Malioboro 16 (☎566 000), south on Malioboro past the modern Mutiara Hotel on the left. Brochures, maps, tickets, and tours. International phone service. Open M-Sa 7:30am-7pm.

Tourist Police: Jl. Malioboro 16 (☎566 165), at the tourist office.

Immigration Offices: Jl. Solo Km10 (☎586 130), near the airport. Open M-Th 8am-noon, F 8-11:30am, Sa 8am-noon.

Currency Exchange: Many banks and ATMs in Sosrowijayan and Prawirotaman areas. Bring passport. **BNI Bank,** across from the post office. Open M-F 8am-4pm.

American Express: In Natour Garuda Hotel on Jl. Malioboro. Open M-F 8:30am-4pm, Sa 8:30am-1pm. Also at **Pacto Tours and Travel,** Jl. Laksda Adisucipto Km8.7, in the Sheraton Hotel.

Luggage Storage: At Tugu Train Station. Rp2000-6000 per 6hr., Rp4000-12000 for 24hr. Counter open daily 5:30am-9:30pm.

Emergency: Ambulance ☎118. **Fire** ☎113. **Police** ☎110.

Police: Kapolresta (☎512 511), on Jl. Reksobayan. Posts throughout the city.

Pharmacy: Kimia Farma 21, Jl. Malioboro 123 (☎514 980). **Open 24hr. Apotek Ratna,** Jl. Parangtritis, near intersection with Jl. Prawirotaman (☎371 028). Open M-Sa 8am-9pm.

Medical Services: Ludira Husada Tama Hospital, Jl. Wiratama 4 (☎620 333). English-speaking doctors. **Open 24hr.**

Telephones: *Wartel* all over town place international calls (no credit cards). The **IDD** phones at the **Telkom** office, next to Komodor Yos Sudarso Rotary, and at the **Natour Garuda Hotel,** Jl. Malioboro 89, are unreliable. Those on Jl. Sosrowijayan are overpriced.

Internet Access: Küpi Net, on Jl. Mataram, is cheap and fast, much like many other 24 hr. cyber cafes along Prawirotaman and Jl. Jend. Sudirman (Rp3500 per hr.). Cyber cafes in the back packer community are slower and overpriced.

Post Offices: GPO, Jl. Senopati 2 (☎384 237), on the corner with Jl. A. Yani. *Poste Restante.* Open M-Sa 8am-8:30pm. Get stamps at a small office on Jl. Sosrowijaya 53. Open M-Th, Sa 8am-2pm, F 8am-noon. **Postal code:** 55000.

Express Mail: DHL, Jl. Dr. Wahidin 58 (☎511 950).

ACCOMMODATIONS

Budget accommodations cluster south of the train station in the *gang* (alleys) that connect **Jl. Pasar Kembang** to **Jl. Sosrowijayan.** Near the train and bus stations, commission-earning "friends" claim to know the cheapest and most popular places in

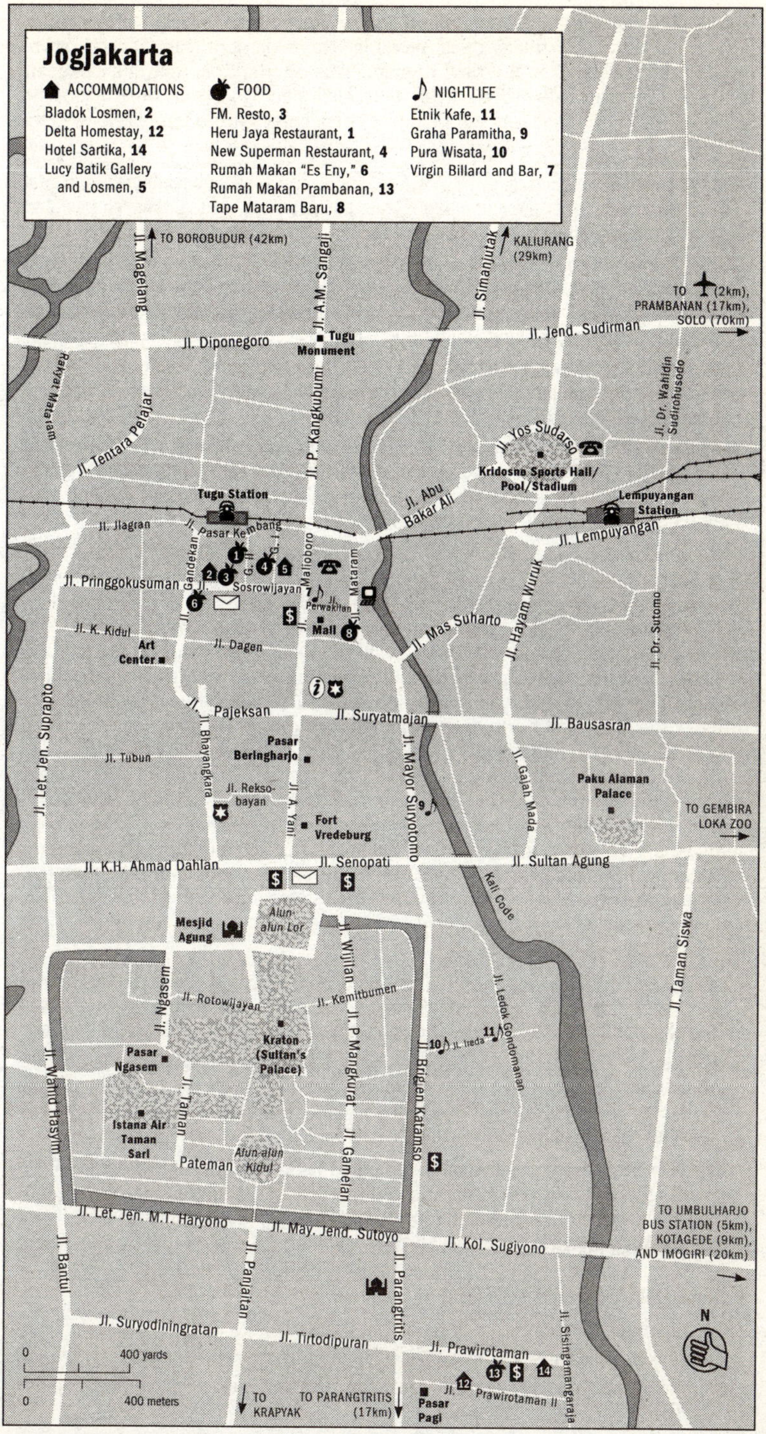
Jogjakarta
ACCOMMODATIONS
Bladok Losmen, 2
Delta Homestay, 12
Hotel Sartika, 14
Lucy Batik Gallery and Losmen, 5
FOOD
FM. Resto, 3
Heru Jaya Restaurant, 1
New Superman Restaurant, 4
Rumah Makan "Es Eny," 6
Rumah Makan Prambanan, 13
Tape Mataram Baru, 8
NIGHTLIFE
Etnik Kafe, 11
Graha Paramitha, 9
Pura Wisata, 10
Virgin Billard and Bar, 7
TO BOROBUDUR (42km)
KALIURANG (29km)
TO (2km), PRAMBANAN (17km), SOLO (70km)
Jl. Magelang
Jl. A.M. Sangaji
Jl. Simanjutak
Jl. Diponegoro
Tugu Monument
Jl. Jend. Sudirman
Rakyat Mataram
Jl. Tentara Pelajar
Jl. P. Kangkubumi
Jl. Dr. Wahidin Sudirohusodo
Jl. Yos Sudarso
Kridosno Sports Hall/ Pool/Stadium
Tugu Station
Jl. Abu Bakar Ali
Lempuyangan Station
Jl. Jlagran
Jl. Pasar Kembang
Jl. Lempuyangan
Malioboro
Mataram
Jl. Pringgokusuman
Jl. Gandekan
Sosrowijayan
Jl. Perwakilan
Jl. Hayam Wuruk
Jl. Dr. Sutomo
Jl. K. Kidul
Mall
Jl. Mas Suharto
Art Center
Jl. Dagen
Jl. Pajeksan
Jl. Suryatmajan
Jl. Bausasran
Jl. Let. Jen. Suprapto
Pasar Beringharjo
Jl. Tubun
Jl. Bhayangkara
Jl. Reksobayan
Jl. A. Yani
Jl. Mayor Suryotomo
Jl. Gajah Mada
Paku Alaman Palace
Fort Vredeburg
TO GEMBIRA LOKA ZOO
Jl. K.H. Ahmad Dahlan
Jl. Senopati
Jl. Sultan Agung
Kali Code
Alun-alun Lor
Mesjid Agung
Jl. Taman Siswa
Jl. Ngasem
Jl. Rotowijayan
Jl. Kemitbumen
Jl. Ledok Gondomanan
Jl. Wijilan
Kraton (Sultan's Palace)
Jl. Ireda
Pasar Ngasem
Jl. Wahid Hasyim
Jl. P Mangkurat
Jl. Brigjen Katamso
Jl. Taman
Istana Air Taman Sari
Pateman
Alun-alun Kidul
Jl. Gamelan
Jl. Let. Jen. M.T. Haryono
Jl. May. Jend. Sutoyo
Jl. Kol. Sugiyono
TO UMBULHARJO BUS STATION (5km), KOTAGEDE (9km), AND IMOGIRI (20km)
Jl. Bantul
Jl. Panjaitan
Jl. Parangtritis
Jl. Suryodiningratan
Jl. Tirtodipuran
Jl. Prawirotaman
Jl. Sisingamangaraja
Jl. Prawirotaman II
N
0 400 yards
0 400 meters
TO KRAPYAK
TO PARANGTRITIS (17km)
Pasar Pagi

INDONESIA

Jogja; close your ears to them. A 15min. expedition will lead you to the best stays in the area. Worth considering are the budget *losmen*, southeast of the kraton, found in the oasis that is Jl. Prawirotoman. This discount district, in a desert of destitution, is commonly referred to as "that other place" by trendy Sosrowijanese, and its uncommercial charm and financial convenience are often overlooked by outsiders.

Bladok Losmen, Jl. Sosrowijayan 76 (☎/fax 523 832). Casual atmosphere plus colorful and classy rooms with fan and *mandi* attract packers of all ages. Swimming pool and great restaurant. Check-out 2pm. Singles and doubles begin around Rp50,000.

Delta, Jl. Prawirotaman II MG 111 597A (☎082 274 3177). Less popular, but a great deal. Relaxed, a well-kept courtyard with swimming pool and free safebox. Breakfast included. Singles Rp25,000, with private *mandi* Rp45,000-70,000; doubles Rp32,500, with private *mandi* Rp50,000-75,000.

Hotel Sartika, Jl. Prawirotaman 44A (☎372 669). Need a bath? This quiet refuge has spacious rooms with fans and bathtubs! Free breakfast. Singles and doubles beginning at Rp35,000. Tubs with rooms Rp40,000 and up.

Lucy Batik Gallery and Losmen (☎513 429), on Sosrowijayan Wetan GT I/87 *(losmen)* and GT I/94 (gallery). Off Sosrowijayan, walk 25m down *gang* 1, the heart of cheap housing, and turn right. *Batik* courses start at 9am (Rp30,000-75,000). Basic singles Rp20,000; doubles Rp30,000; triples Rp55,000.

FOOD

Pricier restaurants on **Jl. Sosrowijayan** and **Jl. Prawirotaman** serve Western, Chinese, and Indonesian food (Rp10,000-20,000). Locals prefer the *warung* in the upper levels of the **Pasar Beringharjo.** In the evening many eat *lesehan*-style and play cards on woven mats along the sidewalks of **Jl. Malioboro** at the northeast corner of the Mall. Just down Jl. Perwakilan and around the bend, booths along Jl. Mataram sell Jogja's specialty sweets, but only **Tape Mataram Baru** at 191 sells *wajik*, sticky rice soaked in palm sugar and coconut milk (Rp9000). Other treats here include *bakpia*, a sweet green or red bean pastry (Rp9,000 per box); *yangko*, flavored bite-sized rice flour chewables (Rp5000 per box); and *geplak* candy, colored coconut-sugar bombs, Rp9000 per kg. (Open daily 7:30am-10pm.) Jogja's specialties are *gudeg*, a sweet jackfruit-and-coconut dish with chicken, boiled egg, *tempe*, and *kercek* (cow hide); and sweet-and-spicy *sambal*, both found at the markets.

Rumah Makan "Es Eny," Jl. Gandekan Lor 42A. From Malioboro, head down Jl. Sosrowijayan past Bladok Losmen, and turn left onto Jl. Gandekan Lor. For anyone who's ever had trouble understanding Indonesian menus. Excellent native food, cafeteria-style. Full plate Rp5000-7000. Sweet icy drinks Rp2000-3500. Open daily 10am-9pm.

FM. Resto, Jl. Sosrowijayan 54. Colonized by exhausted travelers who enjoy the mellow yellow atmosphere, decked with casual decor and a handful of local teens. Killer combo: Spaghetti *a la* FM (Rp12,500), lemon honey pancake (Rp4000), mix fruit juice (Rp6000). Open and occupied 24 hr.

Heru Jaya Restaurant, come on down *gang* II off Jl. Sosrowijayan. Simple, hidden cafe on the left serves delectable dishes (Rp4500), a gargantuan breakfast menu (Rp1000-5000), and French cuisine (Rp12,500). The price is right. Open daily 8am-10pm.

Rumah Makan Prambanan, Jl. Prawirotaman 14. Great cosmopolitan cuisine (Rp5000-12,000). Fantastic beef stroganoff (Rp11,000) and spicy grilled cobra meat (Rp18,000) are a treat. Open daily 11am-11pm.

New Superman Restaurant, Jl. Sosrowijayan Wetan GT I/71. Follow the sign on Pasar Kembang. A backpacker haunt in an Indonesian pavilion. Entrees Rp5000-15,000 but the service is supermalas. Open daily 7:30am-11pm.

SIGHTS

Many of Jogja's historical and cultural sights are within the kraton walls. The **Sultan's Palace** and its pavilions sit at the center of the enclosure. Time-spanning buildings display the development of Javanese architecture since 1755 and highlight Jogja's regional prominence. Multilingual guides lead visitors through the home of Jogja's past 10 sultans. Hamengku Buwono X, the beloved current Sultan, resides in the kraton with his family. (Open M-Th 8:30am-2pm, F 8:30am-1pm. Rp7500. Camera Rp500 extra, video Rp1000. Respectable dress required—tank tops and short-shorts are a no-no.)

The ruins of **Istana Air Taman Sari** (water castle and fragrant garden) can be seen a few blocks west behind **Pasar Ngasem** (a bird market) and are worth the trip. A mixture of Javanese and Portuguese architecture built shortly after the kraton, Taman Sari (meaning beautiful park) was used briefly as the royal family's pleasure garden (Rp2000 at the pool complex). Past the initially unimpressive view awaits a network of tunnels, a deteriorated underground mosque, and ruins (best climbed early in the morning, when Gunung Merapi is still visible). According to legend, the tunnels extend 27km all the way to Parangtritis (see p. 176). Parts of Taman Sari have been restored, including the now goopy green bathing pools of the 20 royal wives in which boys sit on the stone lily pads and fish the day away. When nobody's watching, they sneak up the restored tower and stare at the imaginary 20 royal wives bathing, the Sultan's second favorite pastime.

Mesjid Agung, the grand mosque of the kraton, stands at the southwest corner of the *alun-alun* Utara. For over two centuries, the yearly **sekaten** festival has honored the Prophet Muhammed's birth. *Sekaten* is celebrated annually from June 7-July 7, during which the *alun-alun* is filled with amusement-park-style games.

MARKETS

Ironically, the cheapest way to spend an afternoon in Jogja is to go shopping. Just a walk through the narrow passageways of **Pasar Beringharjo** can be very enriching. Hard bargaining is rewarded with excellent deals on *batik* bedsheets and *sarung;* the early bird catches the discount (open until 4pm). For the barter-worn, **Mirota Batik** opposite Pasar Beringharjo, sells quality *batik* clothes and other crafts at fixed prices. Any of many *penjahit* (tailors) will convert *batik* cloth into an outfit of your liking. **Pasar Ngasem** sell the masters' and their students' works, which are reliable but a bit more pricey. For a good deal, try the turquoise **Art Center,** 20m down an alley off Jl. Pajeksan. An informal bazaar on the west side of **Jl. Malioboro** sells Jogja's signature handcrafts: *batik*, leather *wayang kulit*, bags, and silver. **Kotagede,** to the southeast of Jogja, is renowned for its silver. Take bus #8 south to Basen. Jl. Kemasan is lined with shops that take orders for brass, copper, and silver pieces. A stop at buyer-friendly "Borobudur Silver" is included in most packages.

ENTERTAINMENT AND NIGHTLIFE

Once a religious ceremony, **Wayang Kulit** is now a Javanese art form that depicts the heroism of mythological ancestors. The leather shadow puppet theater is performed at the **Sonobudoyo Archaeological Museum** on Jl. Trikora (daily 8-10pm) and in Alun-alun Selatan (every second Saturday of the month 9pm-5:30am). Tickets for world renowned *Ramayana* **ballets** are available at the tourist office and every street corner. The stories of Prince Rama can be enjoyed in the open air with a spectacular view of the lit Prambanan temples (May-Oct. nightly 7-9pm). Nearby, the complete and condensed version is danced indoors at the Trimurti Theater (Tu and Th 7:30-9:30pm). **Purawisata Open Air Theater** on Jl. Brigjen Katamso has nightly performances for those who can't make the trip (8-10pm). Free cultural performances, such as classical Jogjanese dance (at the Sultan's Palace, Jl. KHA Dahlan

71, Su 10:30am-noon), and *wayang golek* puppet shows (with traditional gamelan music, M-Sa 11am-1pm), exemplify the city's aesthetic interests. At night, **fire-eaters** perform at the south end of the Jl. Malioboro/A. Yani or participate in a **blindfold walk** between the banyan trees at **Alun-alun Kidul,** south of the *kraton.* For nocturnal affairs, **Etnik Kafe** on Jl. Ireda is a pleasant outdoor bar with live music and an underpopulated dance floor. (Open M-F and Su 6pm-1am, Sa 6pm-2am.)

Closer to Jl. Brigjen Katamso, Taman Ria at the **Pura Wisata** entertainment complex has live *dangdut (*Hindu-influenced rock) performances. (W and Sa 9pm-midnight. Rp5000.) If you love **dancing** alone, head over to **Graha Paramitha,** Jl. Mayor Suryotomo 26. Once Jogja's hottest nightclub (formerly called Papillion), this place has seen better nights. (☎564 343. Cover Rp15,000. Ladies' night Th, Su, M, and Tu; gay night F. Open M, T, Th, Su 10pm-2am; W, F, Sa 10pm-3am.) **Virgin Billiard and Bar** off Jl. Malioboro on Jl. Perwakilan, caters Bintang at Rp16,000 and pool for Rp700.

DAYTRIPS FROM JOGJAKARTA

BOROBUDUR

Forty kilometers northwest of Jogja, Borobudur can be reached by local buses from ***Umbulharjo*** *(Jl. Veteran), which take pilgrims straight to Borobudur (6am-6pm, Rp2-6000) or Muntilan, a transfer point. Tourist offices along Jl. Sosrowijayan and Jl. Prawirotaman and most hotels offer package tours.*

Few sights on the planet can compare to the misty sunrise over Borobudur, the world's largest Buddhist temple. Built around AD 800 during the Sailendra dynasty, Borobudur is one of the three wonders of classical Southeast Asia (along with Myanmar's Bagan and Cambodia's Angkor Wat). The temple, topped by a 40m *stupa,* consists of ten levels, symbolic of the ten stages of the Buddhist cosmic system. Along the walls, carvings depict scenes from the life of Buddha, the thousands of reincarnations and manifestations, and the final quest for truth. The three highest levels of Arupadhatu stand for the freedom from earthly bonds and represent "Karma," the highest stage of Buddhahood. Here, an exposed stone Buddha figure meditates among encapsulated neighbors. His expression of suffering preaches that life is pain because of desire, which can only be controlled by meditation. (Road to salvation open daily 6am-5:30pm. US $5; guides Rp30,000.)

Before facing the breathtaking climb and view, visitors often go to the **Audio Visual Center** to watch an enlightening 35min. video. (First showing 8am. Rp4000.) Many visitors try to improve their luck by reaching into any of the 432 *stupas* to touch the stone Buddhas' hands and navels. Use your right hand, as the left hand is considered unclean. Make the pilgrimage early, preferably during the week, to avoid the crowds. For an awesome view, visit the hills behind the monument.

Mendut and **Pawon,** two nearby historic temples, are sites of the actual religious ceremonies (included in tours). Devotees from as far away as China have walked across Java to attain enlightenment from Borobudur via Mendut and Pawon.

PRAMBANAN TEMPLES

The Prambanan temples are 17km northeast of Jogja toward Solo; a direct bus from Umbulharjo Terminal (45min., Rp2000). Upon arrival, the peaks of Gunung Merapi and the main Prambanan temple should be visible. Maps are complimentary at the tourist office inside the entrance gate ($5). Those planning to avoid the tourist scene and see more than the main Prambanan temple can do so by bike (Rp5000 per day).

Built in the 9th century during the Hindu Sanjaya dynasty, the complex consists of temples dedicated to Shiva, Vishnu, and Brahma. The rubble littering the area is the remains of temples destroyed by Gunung Merapi's eruption in 1006. Within the park, smaller temples, including **Candi Lumbung, Bubrah, Sewu,** and **Sojiwan,** are worth checking out. Monuments to the north (**Candi Plaosan, Banyunibo, Sari, Kalasan,** and **Sambisari**) are best seen by bike or *becak,* but beware the gods of inflation. Two kilometers south of Prambanam, **Kraton Ratu Boko** offers a splendid view. Ride a bike south along the road west of the market and follow signs to the palace gate (Rp750). Available maps two-dimensionalize the mountainous view and assist visitors through the mysterious palace of stone foundations built on plateaus.

The Prambanan park holds Ramayana ballets in an outdoor theater almost every night May through October; it's indoors on occasion for the rest of the year (see **Entertainment,** above). Grab a free story line (in several languages) inside the inner gate. (Open daily 7:30-9:30pm. Camera pass Rp2500, video pass Rp25,000.)

Ny Muharti Guest House (☎496 103), Jl. Tampumas Ngankruk 2-3, opposite the entrance to the Prambanan temple, is worth considering for temple-goers wanting to rise with the sun.

GUNUNG MERAPI AND KALIURANG

Gunung Merapi killed dozens when it erupted in November 1994. In July 1998, Merapi erupted for days in a row, spewing ash over the countryside. It's now closed, although guides offer to take visitors up with assurances that it is safe. Hiking up to see live lava can be exciting, but it is extremely risky. Let's Go does not recommend live lava.

Gunung Merapi, 30km north of Jogja, rises triumphantly high above sea level and can be seen from all surrounding areas. From the Umbulharjo Terminal, take a bus to Kartosuro, then to Boyolali, then to Selo. Start at 1am to reach the summit in time for sunrise, as the hike will take around 4hr. **Vogel's** , Jl. Astamulya 76, offers recommended and reasonably priced tours. Wear layers, as temperatures increases dramatically as daybreak hits. Consider spending the night at the hostel, thus avoiding risky bussing in the dark. (☎895 208. Rp25,000-30,000.)

For a tamer adventure, stick around **Kaliurang,** 28km north of Jogja on the slopes of Merapi. From Jogja, take a 1hr. bus ride from Umbulharjo or an *angkot* from the Terban Terminal on Jl. Simanjuntak (both Rp2000). Kaliurang offers several cheap hotels, a campground, and a youth hostel, **Vogel's .** (Dorms Rp6000, 10% discount for HI members. Singles Rp12,500; doubles Rp17,500-25,000.) While in the **market,** look out for Kaliurang's specialties: sweet, brown-red *tempe* or *tahu bacem* and the mild *jadah,* made from glutinous rice.

To explore the town's hiking paths and nature park, head to **Hutan Wisata Kaliurang,** a 1km walk from the youth hostel. Cool off by clambering up the observatory for a stunning view of the valley and Mt. Merapi.

IMOGIRI ROYAL CEMETERY

Buses to Imogiri leave from Umbulharjo bus terminal (45min., Rp2000). Open M 10am-noon, F 1-4pm. Rp1500 for outfit.

Imogiri Royal Cemetery, 17km south of Jogja, houses the deceased members of the Royal Houses of Jogjakarta and Surakarta (Solo), including Jogjakarta's first sultan, Hamengku Buwono I. Imogiri is less touristed than other famous sights, but the pleasant walk affords a rare glimpse of the ancestor worship and the regard most Jogjakartans retain for members of royalty. Built in 1645 by Sultan Agung, three distinct courtyards constitute the cemetery. To the left rests the royalty of Solo; to the right, the sultans of Jogja; and at the center, the ancient Mat-

IT'S NOT EASY BEING GREEN At Parangkusumo, 1km west of Parangtritis, there's a shrine commemorating the mythical romance between Sultan Senopati of the Mataram kingdom and the goddess Nyai Loro Kidul, Queen of the South Seas. Forever heartbroken over the Sultan's decision to return to Mataram, Nyai Loro Kidul has been known to kidnap and drown anyone who wears her favorite color, green, along her beaches. Locals at Parangtritis offer prayers and gifts to the angry goddess each week–and to this day the old clothes, hair, fingernail clippings, and assorted other offerings from the Sultan himself are sent out on a raft to appease her. Visitors are warned to leave something for her at the shrine and to leave their green clothing at home.

aram kings. All visitors are expected to wear formal Javanese clothing in the tombs; after climbing the 345 steps, discard your sweaty garments and rent appropriate attire (Rp500). Men should wear a sarong, a long-sleeved shirt, and a hat. Women can be less modestly dressed in a sarong and *batik* halter top. The tombs are best visited with a guide, but maps are available at the dressing station. In each room, enter quietly, make a donation (Rp100 will do), and kneel by the cool marble. After paying your respects, visit the sacred burial chambers of Sultan Agung and Hamengkubuwono I.

PARANGTRITIS

27km south of Jogja. Take a public bus (Rp3000) from Umbulharjo Terminal, or a minibus from Jl. Parangtritis (Rp3000) at the southeast corner of the kraton. The last bus back leaves Parangtritis at 5pm. For those left stranded, dozens of guest houses line the beachfront (Rp15,000-50,000 per night).

Stark and beautiful **Parangtritis Beach** is revered by day trippers who drink *es kelapa muda* (young coconut milk) and cross the black sand in horse-drawn carriages. Dramatic cliffs to the east shelter meditation caves. The strong undertow of the Indian Ocean renders the beach dangerous for swimmers and surfers.

SURAKARTA (SOLO) ☎0271

As any Solonese will tell you, Solo is Java's cultural heart. Residents seem to be indoctrinated with city pride even before they're weaned onto *nasi liwet*, the local specialty. Solo's two large *kraton* (palaces), topped with Indonesia's second-oldest museum, and a side order of classical art and *batik*, all served with a uniquely Javanese old-world charm, make for one budget-happy meal. Add a refreshingly small portion of tourist traffic, compliments of the chef, for the perfect visit.

TRANSPORTATION

Flights: Adi Sumarmo Airport (☎780 400), 10km northwest of Solo. To get to town, take a blue minibus to Kartosuro Terminal (Rp700-1000) and a bus to Jl. Slamet Riyadi or a taxi (Rp20,000). **Garuda,** Jl. Slamet Riyadi 201, in Hotel Cakra (☎630 082). Open M-F 7:30am-5pm, Sa-Su 9am-noon. To **Jakarta** (3 per day; 8:20am, 1:30, 5:45pm; Rp455,900). **Silk Air,** at Hotel Novotel, Jl. Slamet Riyadi 272 (☎724 606), flies to **Singapore** (M, Sa, Su 10:20am, Tu 3pm; US$220). Domestic airport tax Rp8000; international tax Rp30,000.

Trains: Balapan Railway Station (☎644 122), Jl. Monginsidi 112. Trains to: **Bandung** (7hr., 8pm, Rp30,000-120,000); **Jakarta** (8-12hr., 8pm, Rp35,000-185,000); **Jogjakarta** (1hr., 7 per day 6am-7pm, Rp3000); **Surabaya** (3hr.; 2:45, 4:30pm; Rp40,000-130,000). Bandung and Jakarta trains stop in Jogjakarta.

Buses: The **main intercity bus terminal** is **Tirtonadi,** Jl. A. Yani 262 (☎717 297), on the north side of town. Buses to: **Bandung** (11hr., 4pm, Rp25,000-60,000); **Jakarta** (12hr.; 5, 7pm; Rp32,500-87,500); **Jogjakarta** (1½hr., every 30min., Rp3000); **Semarang** (3½hr., every 30min., Rp5000-8000); **Surabaya** (6hr., every hr., Rp15,000-25,000). **Gilingan Minibus Terminal,** connected to Tirtonadi, serves all major destinations. Seats on special overnight buses must be booked in advance. Contact **Raya,** Jl. Sultan Syahir 13 (☎635 838), for buses to **Bogor** and **Jakarta; Bandung Cepat,** Jl. Kapten Mulyadi 27 (☎653 836), for buses to **Bandung;** and **Cakrawala,** Jl. Setia Budi (☎711 710) for buses to **Denpasar**.

Local Transportation: Becak are plentiful, friendly, and the best way to get around. Metered **taxis** congregate at all major hotels. **Double-decker** and **regular buses** are the cheapest option and travel along Jl. Slamet Riyadi and Jl. Veteran (every 10min. 5am-9pm, Rp750). Orange **minibuses** (Rp1000) run most other routes.

ORIENTATION AND PRACTICAL INFORMATION

The city's main boulevard and bus artery, **Jl. Slamet Riyadi,** runs east-west through town. The **tourist office** is on its west side, and many restaurants and food stalls cluster on streets off its center. The **Puro Mangkunegaran Kraton** is at the northern edge. The **post** and **telephone offices** are off **Jl. Sudirman** on Jl. Slamet Riyadi's east side. Home stays are off Jl. Slamet Riyadi: to the north by **Jl. A. Dahlan,** and in the alleys between **Jl. Gatot Subroto** and **Jl. Yos Sudarso** to the south. The **Kraton Surakarta** and the bustling **batik market** are southwest, while **Tirtonadi/Gilingan Terminal** and **Balapan Train Station** are north of the city center.

Tourist Offices: Dinas Pariwisata, Jl. Slamet Riyadi 275 (☎711 435), behind the Museum Radya Pustaka on the far west end of Solo's main boulevard. Brochures, calendar of events, and a super useful booklet. Free city maps. Open M-Sa 12am-4pm.

Tours: High-priced tours at agencies along Jl. Slamet Riyadi and many *losmen.* Try **Warung Baru Restaurant** on Jl. A. Dahlan.

Currency Exchange: BNI, Jl. Arifin 2 (☎645 909). Open M-F 7am-noon and 1-3pm. Numerous others are on Jl. Slamet Riyadi and the south end of Jl. Sudirman.

Emergency: Police ☎110. Fire ☎113. Ambulance ☎118.

Police: Adisucipto Manahan (☎712 600), and other posts all over town.

Pharmacy: Pasar Pon, Jl. Slamet Riyadi 124 (☎645 802) and **Rapi,** Jl. Ranggowarsito 161 (☎713 067) are convenient and extensive. The apotik at **Rumah Sakit Kasih Ibu Hospital** is **open 24hr.**

Medical Services: Rumah Sakit PKU Muhammadiyah, Jl. Ronggowarsito 130 (☎719 743). **Open 24hr. Klinik Prodia Laboratorium,** Jl. Ronggowarsito 143 (☎463 78), is a modern diagnostic clinic. Open M-F 7am-8pm, Sa 7am-5pm. MC/V.

Telephones: Telkom Office, Jl. Mayor Kusmanto 1 (☎644 606), opposite the GPO. Open 24hr.

Internet Access: Aloha Internet Cafe, at the Hotel Sahid Kusuma. Rp3600 per hr. Delightfully speedy. Open daily 8am-10:30pm. **NETPluzz,** Jl. Yos Sudarso 174, 500m off Jl. Slamet Riyadi. Rp4000 per hr. Open 9am-11pm.

Post Office: GPO, Jl. Sudirman 8, off the east end of Jl. Slamet Riyadi. *Poste Restante.* Open M-Sa 7am-8pm. **Postal code:** 57111.

ACCOMMODATIONS

Quality *losmen* abound near **Jl. A. Dahlan** and **Kemlayan Kidul,** the street that connects Jl. Gatot Subroto and Jl. Yos Sudarso. Cafe owners in the area point the way.

Lucie Pension, Jl. Ambon 12 (☎653 375), east of Mangkunegaran Palace. Owner Topik keeps his library interesting, sitting area comfy, and prices low. Mattresses on the floor attest to the down-to-earth atmosphere. Singles Rp20,000; doubles Rp30,000.

Dagdan's Home Stay, Baluwerti 02/7 42 (☎669 324), within the *kraton* 400m past the museum entrance. Lush courtyard, meditation garden, and airy rooms. Special long-term rates. Singles Rp15,000; doubles Rp20,000.

Paradiso Home Stay, Kem Layan Kidul 1/3 (☎652 960). Gorgeous open-air Dutch building furnished with plants, pottery, and a cafe. Ring bell after 10pm. Singles Rp11,000-17,000, with *mandi* Rp25,000; doubles Rp25,000-50,000.

The Westerner's Home Stay, Kemlayan Kidul 11 (☎633 106), past a white garage door in an alley between Jl. Yos Sudarso and Jl. Gatot Subroto. Basic rooms and pleasant sitting areas. Ring bell after 10pm. Free hot tea. Singles Rp18,000, doubles Rp20,000.

Joyokusuman (Hendra Guest House and Painting Studio), Jl. Gajahan 7 Rt. 2/3. From Jl. Yos Sudarso, head through the elephant gate by the Irma Jaya store, turn left, and continue through the columned gate. Tranquil *kraton* courtyard and nice rooms. Singles Rp40,000; doubles Rp50,000; single private bungalows Rp60,000; double Rp70,000.

Wisma Bahagia (Happy Home Stay), Jl. Honggowongso Gg. Karagan 12 (☎712 449). Laundry service Rp5000 per 20 pieces. Breakfast included. Discounts for long-term guests. Rooms Rp15,000-25,000.

Cendana Home Stay, Gang Empu Panuluh III 4 (☎652 821), on a street between Jl. Yos Sudarso and Jl. Gatot Subroto. Turn at the ADA textile sign and follow the arrows. Typically filled with families. Clean, well-lit. Ring bell after 11pm. Singles Rp13,000-15,000; doubles Rp15,000-20,000.

FOOD

Nasi liwet, a sweet coconut cream and spice-based rice dish, is a Solonese specialty. Genuine *nasi liwet,* carried on the backs of village women, is sold on street corners early in the morning and late at night. For a traditional *srabi* (a part-crispy, part-soft concoction of sweet coconut milk and rice flour Rp500), check out the carts that line Jl. Slamet Riyadi. *Warung* gather along Jl. Gatot Subroto and Jl. Teuku Umar at night. Tourist restaurants line Jl. A. Dahlan.

O-Solo-Mio, Jl. Slamet Riyadi 253, beyond the intersection with Jl. Honggowongso (☎727 264). Small, yellow Italian *restoran* opens into courtyard decorated with Javanese art. *Bellisimo* cappuccinos Rp8000. Prima oven-baked pizza Rp22,000-28,500. Open daily 10am-midnight.

Monggo Dinarak, Jl. A. Dahlar 22. Not as popular as Warung Baru across the street, but outstanding Indian curry and *masala* dishes (Rp6000-7000) washed down with tasty *chai* (Rp2500) plus the elegant furniture puts this cafe in a league of its own. Ask to see the travelers' note/joke book. Open daily 7am-10pm.

Warung Baru, Jl. A. Dahlan 23, off Jl. Slamet Riyadi. Rightfully famous for a titanic menu of good, cheap food. Homemade bread Rp4500-6000. Pizzas Rp6000-7500. Tours and travel info. Open daily 7am-10pm.

Bakmi Surabaya Sraten, Jl. Gatot Subroto 265. Great lunch stop. Fantastic *bakmi* noodles compensate for the cafeteria ambience. *Komplit* order (Rp9000) includes *siomay, bakso,* and *pangsit*. Open daily 9am-9pm.

American Bakery, Jl. Slamet Riyadi 90. Sweet alternatives for sugar-lovers who've had too many banana pancakes. Snacks Rp1000-3000. Open M-Sa 8:30am-5pm.

SIGHTS

Solo's real beauty lies in its people. Most locals are extremely friendly, and a walk through town is sure to reveal numerous **home industries.** Most hotels organize bike tours to nearby weaving, *gamelan* instrument, tofu and rice cracker, and *batik* processing and stamping industries.

Though not visually stunning, Solo's two **kratons** embody important historical and architectural features of Solonese culture. The smaller **Kraton Mangkunegaran,** built in the 18th century, houses the current prince and his family. Visitors can see the ornate *pendapa* where the first-rate *gamelan* orchestra rehearses (W 10:30am-noon), peek into the Prince's private gardens, and wonder at the regal holdings of the palace museum. English-speaking guides are available for a small donation. (Open M-Sa 8:30am-2pm, Su 8:30am-1pm. Rp5000.)

The **Kraton Surakarta,** in the southeast section of town, was built in 1745 by Pakubuwono II. It currently houses the present Sultan, 74-year-old Pakubuwono XII, and his six wives and 35 children. Partially restored after a devastating fire in 1985, the *kraton* limits respectfully-dressed visitors (no shorts) to the unimpressive main receiving hall and the palace museum. (*Kraton* open daily 8:30am-2pm. Free dance performances Su noon-2pm. Rp5000.)

The **Radya Pustaka Museum,** beside the tourist office on Jl. Slamet Riyadi, exhibits Mataram artifacts, including *wayang* puppets, *keris* daggers, and ancient Javanese philosophical texts. (Open M-Th 8am-1pm, F-Sa 8-11am. Rp1000.)

MARKETS

Pasar Triwindu, the antique market near Mang Kunegaran Palace, has as many ancient car parts as antiques. **Pasar Klewer,** near *Kraton* Surakarta, is an endless indoor maze of *batiks*. **Pasar Gede,** on Jl. Slamet Riyadi near Alun-alun, sells fruits, vegetables, and spices. **Pasar Burung** is an outdoor aviary on the outskirts of town near Tirtonadi/Gilingan Terminal. All are open daily 8am-4pm.

ENTERTAINMENT AND NIGHTLIFE

Traditional *wayang orang* dancers perform at **Sriwedari Park** beside the tourist office on Jl. Slamet Riyadi. (M-Sa 8-11pm. Rp3000.) Nightlife is surprisingly vibrant, with five major discos and many billiard halls. Get down to house techno with a handful of locals at intimate **Nirwana** on Jl. Suryo Prawato. (☎648 845. Bintang Rp17,000. Cover Rp10,000, Sa Rp15,000; includes 1 soft drink. Open daily 9pm-3am, Sa until 4am.) A few beats to the left, bouncing **New Legenda** hosts an older crowd in a larger, darker environment. (☎664 715. Bintang Rp20,000. Cover Rp10,000, Sa15,000. Open M-Su 10pm-3am, Sa until 4am.)

DAYTRIPS FROM SURAKARTA

SANGIRAN MUSEUM

Take a minibus from Jl. Slamet Riyadi or Gilingan Terminal toward Purwodadi or Kalijambe and ask to get off near Sangiran (1hr.), where ojek *haul visitors up the hill to the museum. To return to Solo from the* ojek *stand, hop on a large bus with "Berseri" printed on the front. Open M-Sa 8am-5pm. Rp1500.*

In 1936, a Dutch paleontologist found the fossil skull of *Pithecanthropus erectus* **(Java Man)** in Sangiran, 15km north of Solo. The site's numerous fossils and pictures are interesting, but the trip may not be worth it unless you're an archaeology buff.

SUKUH TEMPLE

Catch a double-decker bus from Jl. Slamet Riyadi to Palur and then a big bus to Karang Pandan (30min.). From here, take a minibus to Sukuh (20min.). Unless you travel on a market day, the minibus will drop you off at the bottom of a hill. Take an ojek *to the temple (Rp3500) or walk up the steep hill (45min.).*

On the slopes of Gunung Lawu 34km northeast of Solo, the Sukuh Temple is difficult to reach, but its views make the journey worthwhile. Built in the 15th century, it was one of the last Hindu temples constructed before the rise of Islam. On the basis of some very suggestive and descriptive reliefs, many believe a fertility cult built the temple as a "sex education" exhibit, but the resemblance the temple bears to those of the Maya in Mexico and Guatemala is far more interesting and mysterious than ancient erotica.

Even more difficult to reach (*ojek* is the only reliable way, and therefore a bit more expensive), **Candi Cetho,** 8km away, offers more stunning views of the tobacco and tea plantations below in addition to a larger temple complex now used exclusively for meditation.

SEMARANG ☎024

A former Dutch delight fallen from favor with tourists, the coastal capital of Semarang has few notable cultural sights and even fewer budget accommodations. Architecture buffs will appreciate the Dutch colonial buildings, but most backpackers will only visit Semarang en route to more picturesque destinations nearby.

TRANSPORTATION

Flights: A. Yani Airport (☎760 8735), on Jl. Siliwangi, 5km west of town. **Garuda** (☎844 9331) flies to **Jakarta** (7, 8:40am, noon, 3:20, 6:40pm; Rp386,400). **Merpati** (☎351 7137) flies to **Surabaya** (daily 6:30am, and Su 1:45pm; Rp267,600).

Trains: Tawang Railway Station (☎354 4544), off Jl. Merak. Trains to **Jakarta** (6hr.; 5, 8am, 12:25, 8, 9, 11pm, midnight; Rp40,000-210,000) and **Surabaya** (3½hr.; 1:30, 3am, 3, 11:40pm; Rp14,000-130,000). **Lockers** Rp2000 per hr.

Buses: Terboyo (☎658 1924), on Jl. Terboyo. Buses to: **Jakarta** (12hr.; every hr. 4-8pm; Rp27,500, with A/C Rp45,000); **Jogjakarta** (3½hr., every 10min. 9am-5pm; Rp15,000); **Solo** (2½hr.; every 10 min.; Rp10,000, with A/C Rp16,000); **Surabaya** (6hr.; every 10 min.; Rp25,000, with A/C Rp40,000).

Local Transportation: Semarang's orange **angkot** and large **bis kota** (city buses) have overlapping, inefficient routes. **Minibuses** head out of town and are scarce after 9pm (Rp1000). Ask a local (*not* the driver) for the *harga biasa* (usual price). Prohibited from busy streets, **becak, ojek,** and **andong** improvise through alleyways.

ORIENTATION AND PRACTICAL INFORMATION

The major transportation centers—the **airport, train station,** and **bus terminal**—form the northern edge of the city from west to east, each a few kilometers apart. The **harbor** lies to the north of the train station. The heart of the city is contained by three rotaries linked by streets with exhaustive shopping and eating opportunities. The **Johar** complex, from which the ever-equipped market **Pasar Johar** stretches east, is a few blocks from the train station, southwest of the **Old Dutch District.** From Johar, **Jl. Pemuda** (which has many tourist services) runs 2km southwest to the **Tugu Muda Monument. Jl. Pandanaran** heads 1-2km eastward from Tugu Muda until **Simpang Lima** (the main square and shopping complex), from which **Jl. Gajah Mada** goes north and connects back to Jl. Pemuda. Architecture buffs should explore the Old Dutch District, **Chinatown,** the area south of the market, and the ritzy colonial-style hills of the **Candi-Kintelan district,** southwest of downtown.

Tourist Offices: Kota Semarang Tourist Office, on Jl. Sriwijaya 29 (☎831 12 20). Useful maps and info. Open M-Th 7am-3pm, F 7-11am.

Currency Exchange: Banks line major streets and are usually open M-F 8am-2pm. **P.T. Supit,** Jl. Pemuda 39C (☎354 24 61), exchanges cash and checks. Open M-F 8am-4pm, Sa 8am-1pm. **BCA,** Jl. Permuda 90-92, has a **24hr. ATM.**

Emergency: Police ☎110. **Ambulance** ☎118. **Fire** ☎113.

Police: Central station, Jl. Dr. Sutomo 19 (☎844 4444). Open 24hr.

Pharmacies: Kimia Farma, Jl. Pemuda 135 (☎354 3646). Open 24hr.

Medical Services: Telogorejo Hospital (☎844 6444) on Jl. A. Dahlan, 1 block from Simpang Lima. Some English spoken.

Telephones: International **wartel** all over. No credit card calls. **Kopegtel,** Jl. Alun-alun Timur 2, behind GPO. Fax. **Telkom Office,** Jl. Lt. Gen. Suprapto 7. Both open 24hr.

Internet Access: Zone, 5th fl. Plaza Simpang Lima (☎831 8831). Rp6000 per hr. Open daily 10am-10pm. **Wasantara Net,** at the GPO. Rp5000 per hr. Open daily 8am-10pm.

Post Office: GPO, Jl. Pemuda 4 (☎554 563). *Poste Restante.* Open daily 8am-8pm. **Postal code:** 50000. Downtown **branch,** Jl. Imam Bardjo 3 (☎841 2135). *Poste Restante.* Open M-Th 8am-4pm, F-Sa 8am-3:30pm. **Postal code:** 50243.

ACCOMMODATIONS AND FOOD

Noteworthy budget accommodations and restaurants are few and far between in this businessman's city, and the lack of demand will probably keep it that way.

Hotel Blambangan, Jl. Pemuda 23 (☎541 649). A safe, immaculate, and conveniently-located oasis. Often fully booked. All rooms include private bath and morning snack. Doubles Rp27,500, with A/C Rp50,000; triples Rp36,000.

Hotel Oewas Asia, Jl. Kol Sugiono 12 (☎354 2547), 1 block northeast of the Metro Grand Park Hotel on Jl. Pemuda. Cement floors, piercing bright lights, and not exactly cozy, but one of the cheapest in town and close to the train station. Singles/doubles Rp25,000, with A/C 35,000, with TV and A/C Rp40,000.

Natour/Dibya Puri, Jl. Pemuda 11 (☎354 7821), at the intersection with Jl. Imam Bonjol near the post office. Old colonial building looks a bit abused but is well kept with huge doubles, comfortable beds, and private verandas. Breakfast buffet included. Rooms with TV Rp35,000-70,000.

Hotel Bojong, Jl. Pemuda 8 (☎354 6240), at the end of the short alley across Hotel Dibya Puri (south of the intersection of Jl. Permuda and Jl. Agus Salim). Clean, basic *mandis*. Standard doubles Rp15,000 with fan Rp20,000; doubles with *mandi* Rp50,000, with TV and A/C Rp75,000; Rp10,000 for extra bed.

REFORMASI Before and during the Indonesian War of Independence of the 1940s, the phrase *"Merdeka, Bung!"* ("independence, brother!") was first a secret greeting among resistance fighters and then, once the movement gained momentum, a rallying cry for freedom throughout all of Indonesian society. Similarly, the term *"reformasi"* ("reform") in the late 1990s was at first subversive, uttered by only the most radical intellectuals and students opposed to Suharto's New Order government. What has happened since the May 1998 riots, and Suharto's subsequent resignation, is nothing less than a linguistic revolution surrounding this potent buzzword. Friends now greet each other and sign letters with the phrase *"salam reformasi"*; countless businesses and public institutions have emblazoned their buildings with broad banners proclaiming *"pro-reformasi!"* and "we support *reformasi* 100%," as if the term were a charm to ward off mob attacks such as those that destroyed Java in May 1998. Bank IFI is offering a *Tabungan Reformasi* (Reform Savings Account) that allows clients "freedom" from various administrative fees and the "freedom" to withdraw large amounts from their ATMs. The popular fast-food restaurant California Fried Chicken now markets their own *Paket "Refo"* equivalent to a fast-food combination value-pack in less "politically zealous" nations. The dizzying array of *reformasi* supporters, movements, and advertisements obscures the intentions of the campus radicals who first dared to put a name to their vision of a post-Suharto era. If they could have foreseen that their success meant that well-intentioned, *reformasi*-minded Indonesians could now channel their political aspirations by saving a couple hundred rupiah at the downtown CFC, would they have even bothered?

Semarang teems with stalls and fast food chains along Jl. Permuda and Jl. Gajah Mada's south end. Citraland Mall has Western and Indonesian fare at good prices. Vegetarians, however, often have to resort to *gado-gado* and *nasi goreng*. **Nusantara,** Jl. Pandanaran 6 Ruko 11 & 12, near Tugu Muda, is popular for its spicy, meaty options over hot rice. (Dishes Rp1000-6000. Open 24hr.)

INDONESIA

NEAR SEMARANG

GEDONG SONGO PARK

An ambitious hike reveals the five (of the original nine) remaining Gedong Songo Temples. Hidden on the hillside, their beauty and pleasant shade attract hikers of every level. Voyaging on weekdays avoids tent-toting teens at the base and crowded trails. Experienced hikers can head toward the peak on a trail that begins 200m before the hospitable hot spring. A stone creature stands watch among the trees and marks the path, which becomes heavily overgrown higher up. A guide is recommended for those climbing to the summit. Freelance and official guides are available in and outside the tourist office (Rp15,000). Guides inside the gates can also show you a spectacular view of the surrounding mountains and lowlands by horseback. (Open daily 7am-5pm. Admission Rp2500.)

Since the temples are a two-day trip from Jogjakarta and an exhausting day trip from Semarang, nearby Bandungan offers cheap *losmen*. **Sari Marin Indah,** on Jl. Kauma Sari, offers doubles with hot water. (☎711 485. Rooms Rp30,000.) On the same street, **Losmen Lestari** has small, damp doubles with private *mandi* (Rp7500).

Gedong Songo Park is in the town of **Sumowomo.** To get there, take a bus from Semarang's Terboyo Terminal for Bandungan (1½hr., Rp2000, extra for large bags), from which a 20min. *angkot* ride leads to Sumowono. From the bottom of the hill below Gedong Songo, take an *ojek* to the gates (Rp2000-3000). To reach Gedong Songo from Jogjakarta, take a bus toward Semarang (Rp5000-10,000) and ask to get off at Ambarawa (2hr.). Take a minibus to Bandungan (Rp1000), where you may have to spend the night. Many buses head from town to the gates. (Rp1000.)

DIENG PLATEAU

Between tourist-packed Jogjakarta and sweltering Semarang, the quiet mountain village of Dieng offers cool, clean air and a wealth of unspoiled natural and man-made sights. A 2-3hr. walk reveals the multi-colored **Telaga Warna Lake** (fed from a sulfur hot spring), mushroom and potato terraces, smoldering craters, and ancient Hindu temples. The eerie plateau of **Kawahsi Kidang** is one of many hidden intricacies that merit endless exploration.

Dieng Plateau is best accessed and explored from the town of **Wonosobo,** from which buses scurry to the highland (45min., 7am-3pm, Rp2500). Jogjakarta has direct buses to Wonosobo, but the trip from Semarang and Suryakarta requires transfers at Bawen Magelang. From the Wonosobo **bus terminal** (open daily 7am-3pm), connect to **Magelang** (1½hr.; every 15min., last bus 5pm; Rp2500). Head left from where the bus drops you off and walk 1km or ride an *ojek* to the gate, where maps are available (Rp2000).

The **tourist office** next to the bus terminal **stores luggage.** Minibuses go from the terminal into town. Travelers who wish to enjoy the mountain air for a little longer can stay at **Dieng Plateau,** opposite the *ojek* stand. (☎92 823. Singles Rp15,000; doubles Rp20,000.) It serves food (Rp3000-7000), as do numerous *warung* on the street. **Losmen Jawa Tengah,** toward the department store on Jl. A. Yani, 150m north of the intersection with Jl. Pasman, has minimal but satisfactory rooms (Rp20,000).

SURABAYA ☎031

As the second-largest city in Indonesia, Surabaya has six-lane streets, a formidable skyline, and five indoor shopping complexes the size of small towns. Travelers seeking an "authentic Java" may be put off by the city's glitz and restless pace, but with connections to every island in the archipelago by ferry, plane, or bus, it's an important transit city with luxuries not found in other parts of east Java.

TRANSPORTATION

Flights: Juanda Airport (☎866 7513, ext. 9), 18km south of Surabaya. Taxis (Rp20,000-30,000) and Damri buses (Rp2500) shuttle visitors into town, leaving when full. To: **Bandar Seri Bagawan** (M, W, F; US$237, $351 round-trip); **Denpasar** (6am, 7:20pm; Rp295,000-310,000); **Jakarta** (every 2hr. 6am-8pm, Rp457,000-625,000); **Jogjakarta** (4:20pm, Rp230,000). **Garuda** (☎534 5886; open M and Sa 9am-1pm, Tu-Th 7:30am-4:30pm, F 7:30am-5pm) and **Royal Brunei Airlines** (☎532 6407, open M-F 9am-5pm, Sa 9am-noon), are both on Jl. Jend. Basuki Rahmat 106-128, next door to the Hyatt Regency. **Merpati,** Jl. Raya Darmo 111 (☎568 8111).

Trains: Surabaya's train stations are **Gubeng,** on Jl. Gubeng Masjid (☎503 3115); **Kota/Semut,** on Jl. Stasiun Kota; and **Pasar Turi** (☎534 5014), on Jl. Semarang. Trains traveling through Gubeng stop at Kota/Semut. From Gubeng trains go to: **Bandung** (10½hr., 7am, Rp158,800) via **Solo** (4½hr.) and **Jogjakarta** (5hr., Rp48,500-138,500); **Banyuwangi** (5hr.; 8am, 10pm; Rp27,000-40,000); **Jakarta** (12hr., 6pm, Rp148,500); **Malang** (1hr., every hr., Rp10,000). From Pasar Turi, executive trains go to **Jakarta** (12-13hr., 6 per day 9am-9pm, Rp56,000-227,000) via **Semarang** (8hr., Rp44,500-217,000) and **Cirebon** (10hr., Rp44,500-217,000). Ticket offices open daily 8am-5pm.

Buses: Bungurasih/Purabaya Terminal (☎853 1701), 10km south of town. All south-bound **Damri** and **Patas buses** finish their routes at Bungurasih/Purabaya. Executive/deluxe buses with A/C, video, reclining seat, toilet, and food go to: **Bandung** (10hr.; 3, 3:30, 4, 4:30pm; Rp87,500); **Banyuwangi** (6hr., every 15min., Rp30,000); **Denpasar** (7hr., every hr. 4-9pm, Rp55,000); **Jakarta** (11hr., every 30min. 2-4:30pm, Rp87,500); **Malang** (1¼hr., every 10min., Rp8500); **Probolingo** (1½hr., every 10min., Rp10,000); **Solo/Jogjakarta** (4½-5½hr.; every hr. 10am-midnight, 12:30am;

INDONESIA

Rp24,000-28,500). Pay on the bus. Economy buses are slower, more crowded, leave when full, and charge half the price.

Ferries: The **port** is 100m from Tanjung Perak Terminal (see **Local Transportation,** below). **PELNI office,** Jl. Pahlawan 112 (☎355 9950). Open M-Th 8am-4pm, F 8-11am and 1-4pm. Purchase tickets at least 3 days in advance; cash only. To: **Bali** (Rp90,000-127,000); **Jakarta** (Rp105,000-327,000); **Ujung Padang** (Rp119,000-374,000). Ask at the PELNI office for departure times and other destinations.

Local Transportation: Joyoboyo Terminal, on Jl. Joyoboyo by Surabaya Zoo, is the main local bus terminal. From Bungurasih Terminal, Damri (Rp1000) and P-1 Patas (Rp2000) **buses** run by the zoo, Tunjungan Plaza, Pasar Turi Station, the PELNI office, the GPO, and the Madura Ferry Terminal, ending at **Tanjung Perak Terminal.** Buses run 6am-9pm. There are 30 **bemo** routes, labeled alphabetically; almost half use Joyoboyo Terminal as a base. Yellow **angguna** (un-metered taxis) can be flagged down; agree on a price first. **Becak** are useful for short distances (Rp2000-3000).

Taxis: The best way to get around. If they don't turn on the meter, hop out and catch another. Rp2800 for 1st km, about Rp800 each additional km. **Taxi Citra,** Jl. Arif Rahmuin 147 (☎592 5555). **Zebra Taxi** (☎841 1111).

Rentals: Toyota Rent-A-Car, Jl. Raya Waru Km15 (☎853 0909), 2km from the airport, and Jl. Basuki Rakhamad 116 (☎546 2500). Rp275,000 per day. IDP (see p. 42) or driver (Rp99,000 per day) required. Open daily 8am-4pm.

ORIENTATION AND PRACTICAL INFORMATION

Surabaya is a sprawling harbor city with a branching river that snakes around its more popular spots, making navigation difficult. The huge **Tunjungan Plaza** marks the intersection of **Jl. Tunjungan** and **Jl. Pemuda,** two main commercial streets. **Jl. Yos Sudarso** and Jl. Pemuda meet four blocks east around the center of town. **Gubeng Train Station** is a few blocks down at the end of Jl. Pemuda across the river, after the Surabaya Plaza. Following the river north brings you to **Jl. Peneleh,** which has some reasonably priced accommodations. Farther upriver is the **GPO, Kota Station,** the **Arab Quarter,** and **Chinatown. Jl. Tanjung Perak** and the river eventually head to the **Madura Ferry Terminal** and to Surabaya's harbor.

Tourist Offices: Regional Office (☎853 1815), 7km south of the city toward the airport on Jl. Wisata Menanggal. More convenient **branch** at Jl. Basuki Rakhmat 121 (☎534 4710), opposite the Hyatt Regency. Both open M-F 7am-1pm.

Tours: Dozens of agencies around Tunjungan Plaza and the Hyatt Regency on Jl. Basuki Rakhmat. **P.T. Haryono Tours and Travel,** Jl. Sulawesi 27-29 (☎503 4000), books transport as well as tours. **Branch,** Jl. Sudirman 93 (☎532 5800).

Embassies and Consulates: UK, Jl. Basuki Rakhmad 106-128 3rd fl., Hyatt Regency (☎550 5500). Open M-F 9am-5pm. **US,** Jl. Dr. Sutomo 33 (☎567 6880). Open M-F 8am-4pm.

Currency Exchange: Banks with ATMs line Jl. Pemuda and Jl. Urip Sumoharjo. **Danamon** (☎534 8700), on Jl. Pemuda. AmEx Traveler's Cheques. MC/V cash advances. Open M-F 8:30am-3pm. **Bank Bali,** Jl. Tunjungan 52. **24hr. ATM** (AmEx/Cirrus/V).

American Express: Pacto, Jl. Basuki Rakhmad (☎531 1234), in the Hyatt Regency. Open M-F 9am-5pm, Sa 9am-1pm.

Luggage Storage: At Gubeng Train Station. Rp2000 per day.

Markets: Pasar Kayun, on Jl. Kayun, is a flower market lined with eateries. **Pasar Genteng,** on Jl. Genteng Kali, is an all-purpose market by day and a food market by night. **Pasar Blawuran,** on Jl. Blawuran at the end of Jl. Embong Malang, is a gold market.

Emergency: Police ☎110. **Fire** ☎113. **Ambulance** ☎118.

Police: At Jl. Raden Saleh 2 (☎532 8535).

Pharmacy: Kimia Farma, Jl. Raya Darmo 2-4 (☎567 7777). **Open 24hr.**

Medical Services: Dr. Soetomo General Hospital, Jl. Dharmahusada 6 (☎502 0079). **William Booth General Hospital,** Jl. Diponegoro 34 (☎567 8917).

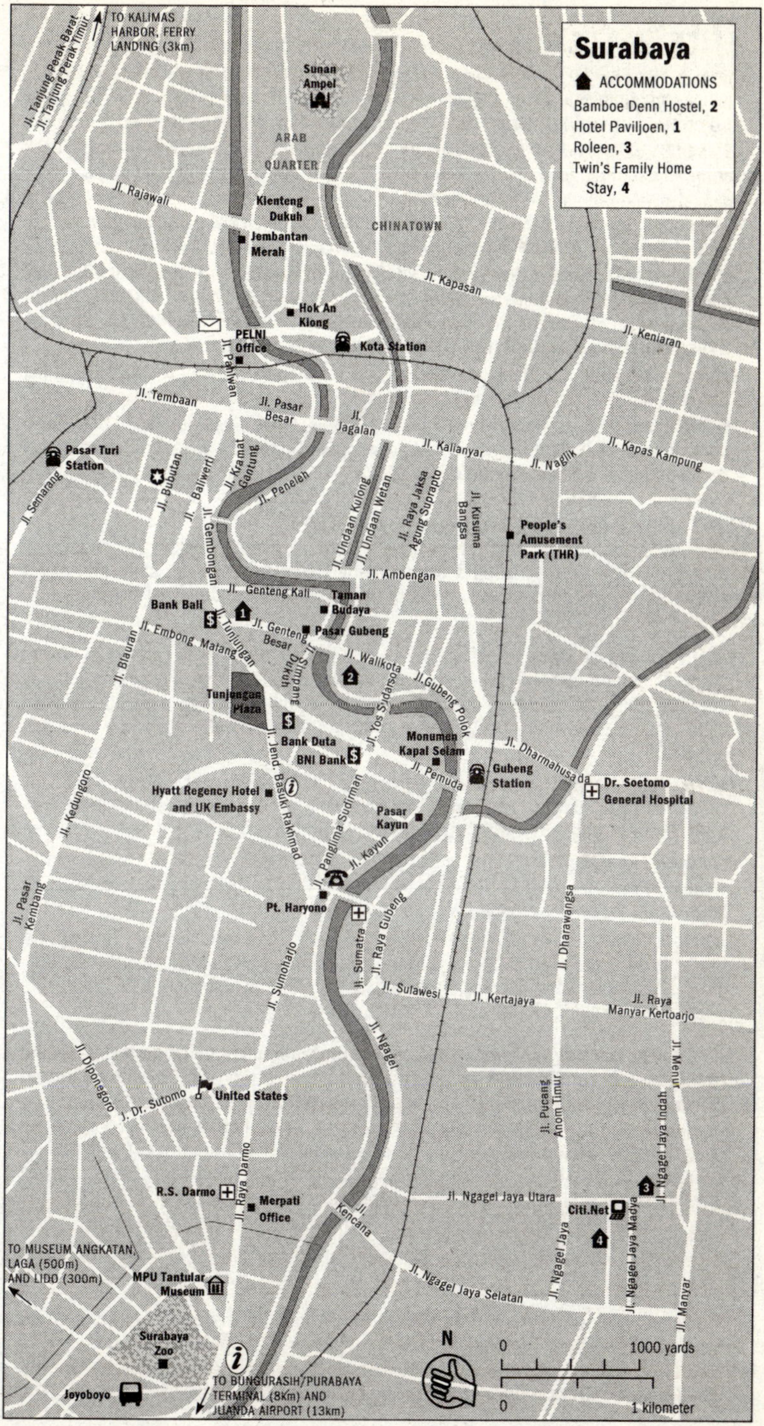
Surabaya
ACCOMMODATIONS
Bamboe Denn Hostel, 2
Hotel Paviljoen, 1
Roleen, 3
Twin's Family Home Stay, 4
TO KALIMAS HARBOR, FERRY LANDING (3km)
Jl. Tanjung Perak Barat
Jl. Tanjung Perak Timur
Sunan Ampel
ARAB QUARTER
Jl. Rajawali
Kienteng Dukuh
Jembantan Merah
CHINATOWN
Jl. Kapasan
Jl. Kenjaran
Hok An Kiong
PELNI Office
Kota Station
Jl. Pahlawan
Jl. Tembaan
Jl. Pasar Besar
Jl. Jagalan
Jl. Kalianyar
Jl. Naglik
Jl. Kapas Kampung
Pasar Turi Station
Jl. Semarang
Jl. Bubutan
Jl. Baliwerti
Jl. Kramat Gantung
Jl. Peneleh
Jl. Undaan Kulon
Jl. Undaan Wetan
Jl. Raya Jaksa Agung Suprapto
Jl. Kusuma Bangsa
People's Amusement Park (THR)
Jl. Gembongan
Jl. Ambengan
Jl. Genteng Kali
Taman Budaya
Bank Bali
Jl. Genteng Besar
Pasar Gubeng
Jl. Embong Malang
Jl. Tunjungan
Jl. Simpang Dukuh
Jl. Blauran
Jl. Walikota
Jl. Gubeng Polok
Tunjungan Plaza
Jl. Yos Sudarso
Monumen Kapal Selam
Jl. Dharmahusada
Bank Duta
BNI Bank
Jl. Pemuda
Gubeng Station
Dr. Soetomo General Hospital
Hyatt Regency Hotel and UK Embassy
Jl. Jend. Basuki Rakhmad
Jl. Panglima Sudirman
Pasar Kayun
Jl. Kayun
Jl. Kedungdoro
Pt. Haryono
Jl. Pasar Kembang
Jl. Sumatra
Jl. Raya Gubeng
Jl. Dharawangsa
Jl. Sumoharjo
Jl. Sulawesi
Jl. Kertajaya
Jl. Raya Manyar Kertoarjo
Jl. Ngagel
Jl. Menur
Jl. Diponegoro
Jl. Dr. Sutomo
United States
Jl. Pucang Anom Timur
Jl. Ngagel Jaya Indah
Jl. Raya Darmo
R.S. Darmo
Merpati Office
Jl. Ngagel Jaya Utara
Citi.Net
Jl. Kencana
Jl. Ngagel Jaya
Jl. Ngagel Jaya Madya
TO MUSEUM ANGKATAN LAGA (500m) AND LIDO (300m)
MPU Tantular Museum
Jl. Ngagel Jaya Selatan
Jl. Manyar
Surabaya Zoo
N
0
1000 yards
1 kilometer
Joyoboyo
TO BUNGURASIH/PURABAYA TERMINAL (8km) AND JUANDA AIRPORT (13km)

FIRE WATER At well over 120 proof (i.e. over 60% alcohol), and likely closer to the ethanol content of your aftershave, Indonesian *arak* packs a punch to unsuspecting foreigners. A rice wine akin to *tuak* (fermented palm sap), *arak* is illegal to produce in mass quantities, but moonshine manufacturers brew the liquid poison behind closed doors. Your guest house owner is your best bet in locating some, but be sure it's fresh (*arak* goes bad fast) and that someone's around to take you home.

Telephones: Indosat, Jl. Kayun 72. **HCD** phones. Most malls have international **wartel. Wartel Surabaya Yudha Pratama,** Jl. Tunjungan 53k. Open 24hr.

Internet Access: Kokuyo Net (☎547 5848), 1st fl., Tunjungan Plaza, by the ice rink. Fastest connection around. Rp15,000 per hr. Open daily 8am-10pm. **Citi.Net,** Jl. Ngagel Jaya Utara 80 (☎502 5249), between Roleen and Twin's s. Rp4000 per hr. Open 24hr. Also at the main **GPO.** Rp1500 per 15min. Open daily 8am-5pm.

Express Mail: DHL, Jl. H.R. Muhammad 111 (☎734 3435). **Branch,** Jl. Basuki Rakhmat 57 (☎534 0852), by Tunjungan Plaza. Open M-F 8am-5pm, Sa 8-11am.

Post Offices: GPO, Jl. Kebonrojo 10 (☎352 2099). *Poste Restante.* Open daily 8am-9pm. **Branch** at Jl. Pemuda, past the General Soerjo statue on the left. Open M-Th and Sa 8am-2pm, F 8-11am. **Postal code:** 60175.

ACCOMMODATIONS AND FOOD

Surabaya has few quality budget hotels aside from those listed. The only other inexpensive option is a group of dingy hotels north of the center around Jl. Peneleh.

Hotel Paviljoen, Jl. Genteng Besar 94-98 (☎534 3449), near Jl. Tunjungan. In a posh Dutch colonial structure. If they say their cheap rooms are full, say you're going to nearby Bamboe Denn Hostel and start walking out; they'll start to bargain. Breakfast included. Doubles Rp40,000; triples Rp60,000-65,000, with A/C and hot water Rp85,000.

Twin's Family Home Stay, Jl. Ngagel Tama A-12 (☎504 1026), on the side street connecting Jl. Jaya Utara and Selatan. Large hotel with wooden interior and winding stairwells. Doubles with A/C Rp65,000, extra bed Rp30,000.

Bamboe Denn Hostel, Jl. Ketabang Kali 6A (☎534 0333), west of Jl. Yos Sudarso intersection toward the river. Cheapest beds in town. Only some rooms have locks. Bunk beds Rp5,000; singles/doubles with shared *mandi* Rp27,500.

Roleen , Jl. Ngagel Jaya Indah I/18 (☎502 2619), on the corner with Jl. Ngagel Jaya Utara, south of the town center. A converted family home owned by super-friendly Robert and Kathleen. Worth the taxi ride for refuge from the city. Rooms with A/C, bath, hot water, and TV from Rp90,000.

INDONESIA

Most of Surabaya's restaurants are many rupiah beyond most budget travelers' budgets. Shopping malls offer an overwhelming collection of food options at better prices, but the food at the riverside restaurants along **Jl. Kayun** and at *warung* and night stalls along **Jl. Genteng Besar** is superior. **Kayun Park** is bordered by cheap eateries that serve excellent seafood. Local specialties include *ular* (fried snake). Clean, cheap **Duta Cafe,** Jl. Genteng Kali, opposite Siola Department Store, serves Indonesian standards. (Open daily 7am-10pm.) **San Thauw,** Jl. Raya Gubeng 64, specializes in Chinese cuisine and seafood. (Open daily 10am-4pm and 6-9pm).

SIGHTS

Surabaya's malls are worth a visit, if only to gawk at their size and enjoy soft ice cream in A/C comfort. **Tunjungan Plaza** is allegedly the archipelago's largest and flatters itself with an ice rink, movie theater, and enough stores to challenge even professional shoppers. (Open daily 10am-11pm; most shops close by 9pm). The

People's Amusement Park (THR), behind the THR Mall, has traditional dance and music performances. Schedules are available at the tourist office. (☎534 0956. Open Th and Sa 7pm-midnight. Rp350.) The real thrills, however, are at nearby **Taman Remaja's** ferris wheel and mini roller-coasters (Rp2000).

The **Surabaya Zoo** is Southeast Asia's largest, but unnatural and cramped living spaces as well as crude spectators can make it a nightmare for animal lovers. From the Tunjungan area, catch a bus (15min.) south on Jl. Sudirman; tell the attendant you're heading to "Kebun Binatang." (Open daily 7am-6pm. Komodo dragon feedings the 5th and 20th of every month. Rp3000. Elephant and camel rides Rp2000.)

The **Arab Quarter** and the monumental **Sunan Ampel Mosque,** the oldest mosque in East Java, can be visited in a few hours and are worth the trip for architecture buffs. The mosque was built by Sunan Ampel, one of the *wali songo*, nine Muslim holy men who initiated the spread of Islam in Java. To get there, take any *bemo* (#10 is ideal) to Jembatan Merah Terminal and then hop on a *becak* (Rp2000) or walk 15min. northeast to Sunan Ampel. Be warned that tensions are high in this area as a result of recent religious fighting—exercise caution.

NIGHTLIFE

Plenty of *diskoteks* and karaoke bars scattered around **Tunjungan Plaza** are crowded with friendly young adults on weekends. With arguably the best nightlife options in Java, all major hotels have bars with nightly live music, Bintang beer at around Rp20,000, and decent vibes for a Rp40,000 cover charge. Low-key **Tavern Pub** in the Hyatt Regency, Chinese-filled **Desperado** in Sanggrila Hotel, tropical **Bongos** in the Sheraton, and strikingly similar **Java Jimmies** in the Westin complete the inter-hotel pub crawl. All close around 3am. You'll need to get a cab to get around, so make sure it's metered.

Colors, Jl. Sumatra 81. Cozy bar/cafe crowded with hungry hip cats and kittens on the prowl. Excellent live pop bands after 9pm. Reasonably priced drinks. Bintang Rp11,000, pitchers Rp36,000. Happy hour 7-9pm daily. Open daily 5pm-2am.

Laga, Jl. May Jen Sungkono 107 (☎568 1826). Cheap and popular on weekends. One of a few "bars" that neither costs more than a hotel room nor blasts deafening dance music. Live music starting at 10:30pm. Cover F Rp3000, Sa Rp5000. Open M-F 6pm-1:30am, Sa until 2:30am.

INDONESIA

MALANG ☎0341

Travelers to East Java instinctively choose Malang over sweaty Surabaya as a base from which to explore the province. Tourists come for the eye-catching scenery, stay for the cool temperatures, and never leave thanks to the succulent cuisine. With untouristed beaches to the south, the lunar-landscape of Gunung Bromo to the east, and the finest *nasi pecel*, Malang satisfies every traveler's need.

TRANSPORTATION

Trains: Stasiun Kereta Api Kota Baru, Jl. Trunojoyo 10 (☎362 208), is visible from Tugu Monument. Trains to: **Blitar** (2hr., 5 per day 7am-6:50pm, Rp2400); **Jakarta** (express 10hr., 3:20pm, Rp100,000-150,000; economy 16hr., 2:30pm, Rp35,000) via **Jogjakarta** (express 6hr., Rp90,000-140,000; economy 8hr., Rp24,000); **Solo** (6hr., 2:30pm, Rp24,000); **Surabaya** (2½hr., 7per day 4:30am-5:20pm, Rp3000). Ask the helpful information desk about destinations not listed above, as departure from Surabaya may be advisable.

Buses: Buses leave from **Arjosari, Gadang and Landungsari terminals. Arjosari,** Jl. Terusan Raden Intan 1 (☎397 058), 6km north of the city by *angkot* A-G or G-A. Buses to: **Denpasar** (11hr., many daily 4-7pm, Rp75,000-90,000); **Jakarta** (18hr., 12 per day 12:30-2:30pm, Rp97,500-125,000); **Surabaya** (2hr., every 15min., Rp3500-7500).

Many express tickets are on night buses. For **Gunung Bromo,** take a bus to **Probolinggo** (2hr., Rp3500-8000) and catch a *bemo* for the final leg of the trip (1-2hr.). **Gadang Terminal,** 5km south by angkot A-G or G-A from Tugu Monument or *Alun-alun,* has **mini-buses** that head toward **Bale Kambang** and other beaches to the south (1-1½hr., Rp3500). **Landungsari,** 6km northwest by *angkot* ADL from Tugu Monument, sends buses to **Selecta** (1½hr., Rp3500) via **Batu** (1hr., Rp2500).

Local Transportation: Ubiquitous **becak** can only use smaller roads. **Angkot** (Rp850), labeled as follows, run between terminals: **A-L** and **A-D-L,** Arjosari to Landungsari; **A-G, G-A** (**A-B-G, A-J-G,** and **A-M-G**), Arjosari past Tugu Monument and *Alun-alun* to Gadang; **L-G, G-L** and **L-D-G,** Landungsari past *Alun-alun* to Gadang. **M-M** runs past the train to Tugu Monument, down Jl. Majapahit to the *Alun-alun,* up Jl. Kawi, and back. *Angkot* run daily 4am-10pm.

Taxis: Can be hailed from hotels around Tugu Monument or called for pickup. Rp2000 plus Rp1200 per km. Try **Argo** (☎490 444), **Bima** (☎717 171), or **Citra** (☎490 555).

ORIENTATION AND PRACTICAL INFORMATION

Malang, 90km south of Surabaya, is bordered by volcanos—**Gunung Butak** (2868m) to the west, **Gunung Arjuna** (3339m) to the north, and **Gunung Semeru** (3676m) and **Bromo** (2329m) to the east—and is rightly the region's most active hot spot. The city centers on two public spaces: the **Tugu Monument,** a traffic rotary with government buildings, hotels, and a view of the **train station** to the east; and the *Alun-alun* (the town center), 500m south of Tugu Monument, near the GPO and the center of the busiest shopping areas. Three bus terminals lie on the outer rim of the city; Arjosari, the main station to the northeast, Landungsari to the northwest, and Gadang to the south.

Tourist Offices: Bunga Wisata, Jl. Basuki Rakhmat 6H (☎323 966). Hut on the side of the road with limited info and overpriced tours. Open daily 9am-4pm. **Tourist Information Center,** Jl. Basuki Rakhmat 5 (☎364 052), inside Toko Oen (see **Food,** below) may be more helpful. Maps, brochures, travel advice, and tickets. Open daily 9am-9pm. **Branch** at the train station (☎362 208). Fewer brochures, but great travel info.

Tours: Pt. Mujur Surya, Jl. Bromo 33A (☎279 55). Books PELNI and air tickets. **N and N Traveler's Shop,** Jl. Suropati 19 (☎345 612), 50m from Helio's Hotel. Organizes tours and travel arrangements. Open daily 7am-9:30pm. All tourist offices, most hotels, and a dozen counters in Arjosari Terminal arrange tours and express bus bookings to major cities.

Currency Exchange: Banks are open M-F 8am-2:30pm. **Bank BCA** has a **24hr. ATM** (Cirrus/MC/V) on Jl. Basuki Rakhmat in the alley between McDonald's and Sarinah Plaza. A **moneychanger** and more ATMs are in the same building.

Luggage Storage: At the train station. Rp1000 per item. No overnight storage.

Markets: Malang is crowded with shopping. The **Alun-alun** never stops bustling with *warung* and merchants. Over the river and through Jl. Brawijaya lies the ever chirping **Pasar Burung** with its congested cages, and the **Pasar Bunga** (flower market), a fragrant relief from the concrete jungle. Open daily 8am-5pm.

Emergency: Police ☎110. **Fire** ☎113. **Ambulance** ☎116.

Police: Polresta, Jl. Slamet Riyadi 1 (☎366 444). **Open 24hr.**

24hr. Pharmacies: In all shopping plazas along Jl. Salim. **Kimia Farma 53,** Jl. Kawi 22A (☎362 301), at the intersection with Jl. Bromo 1km past Hotel Riche.

Medical Services: R.S. Saiful Anwar, Jl. J.A. Suprapto 2 (☎362 101), on the north side of town. **24hr. emergency care.** Cash only. **Prodia Labortorium Klinik,** Jl. Achmad Dahlan 17 (☎366 042). With your back to Hotel Toseri, walk right 25m. Open M-F 6am-8pm, Sa 7am-2pm. AmEx/MC/V.

Telephones: 24hr. wartel at the Telkom Office next to Toko Oen Restaurant on Jl. Basuki Rakhmat. Free **HCD phone** at Toko Oen.

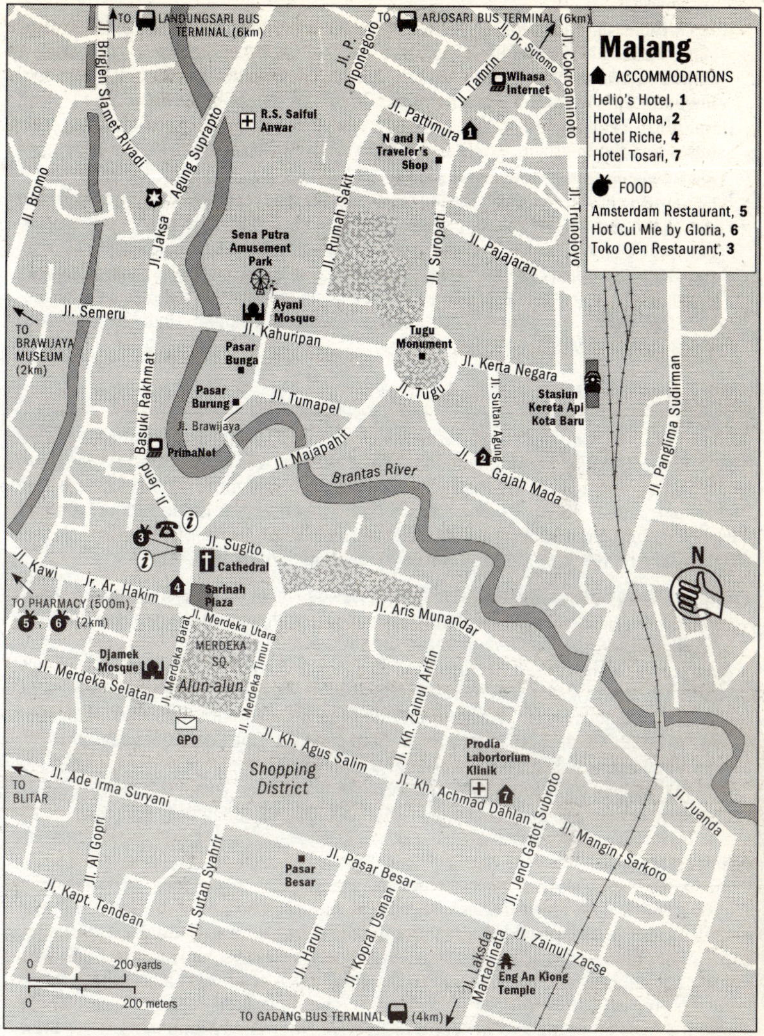

Internet Access: PrimaNet, Jl. Bakusi Rachmat 24 (☎340 043). Rp4000 per hr. MTV for the homesick. Open 24hr. **Wihasa Internet,** behind Helio's Hotel at Jl. Thamrin 6. Rp6000 per hr. Open daily 8am-10pm. **Warnet Kantor Pos,** at the GPO. Rp1500 per 15min. Open 24hr.

Express Mail: DHL, Jl. Jaksa Agung Suprapto 60 (☎365 060). Open M-F 8am-5pm, Sa 8am-1pm.

Post Offices: GPO, Jl. Merdeka Selatan 5 (☎736 2254). Open M-F 8am-8pm, Sa 8am-7pm, Su 9am-2pm. *Poste Restante.* Open M-Th 8am-4pm, F 8-11am, Sa 8am-2pm. **Postal code:** 65119.

ACCOMMODATIONS

Truly budget accommodations are scarce in Malang. Hotels, mostly mid-range to upscale, cluster around the Tugu Monument and the *Alun-alun.*

Helio's Hotel, Jl. Pattimura 37 (☎362 741). From the train station, walk to the Tugu rotary and head 2 blocks up Jl. Suropati. Humble rooms with porches overlooking a tranquil courtyard. Tours to Bali (Rp375,000) and Bromo (Rp90,000-120,000). Doubles Rp22,000, with private *mandi* Rp38,500; triples Rp30,500/55,000.

Hotel Aloha, Jl. Gajah Mada 7 (☎326 950). Walk toward Tugu Monument from the train station and turn left onto Jl. Sultan Agung; it's down and on the right. Full body massages Rp15,000 per hr. Clean doubles with *mandi* Rp40,000; triples Rp50,000.

Hotel Tosari, Jl. K.H. Achmad Dahlan 31 (☎326 945), a 10min. walk from *Alun-alun* down Jl. Kh. Agus Salim. Cheap, clean, spartan rooms worth considering for their location. Doubles Rp27,500, with private *mandi* Rp50,000; triples Rp75,000.

Hotel Riche, Jl. Basuki Rahmat 1 (☎325 460), next to Toko Oen Restaurant opposite Sarinah Plaza. A fresh coat of paint breathes some life into this old colonial building. Expensive rooms are worth the extra rupiah. Breakfast included. Doubles Rp30,000, with private *mandi* Rp35,000-60,000.

FOOD

While in Malang, be sure to try *nasi pecel*, an east Javanese specialty of boiled vegetables with spicy peanut sauce and fried *tempe* over rice. Countless *warung* encircling the *Alun-alun* are loaded with *nasi pecel* and more. Quieter stands line Jl. Suropati and Jl. Kawi. Pricier cafes attached to hotels provide Indonesian and Western dishes. **Hero** supermarket inside Sarinah Plaza north of the *Alun-alun* is a good place to stock up on food for daytrips. (Open daily 9am-9pm.)

Hot Cui Mie by Gloria, Ruko Kawi Atas 43B, beside Planet Surf 2-3km west on Jl. Kawi. *Angkot* M-M. Packed with locals. Noodle, meat, and soup masterpieces (Rp4500-7000). Full juice bar cools your tongue (Rp3500-5000). Open daily 9am-9pm.

Amsterdam Restaurant, Jl. Terusan Kawi 2, opposite the entrance to Taman Buah-Buahan on Jl. Kawi. *Angkot* M-M. Indoor-outdoor seating and a dessert menu of ice cream concoctions. Indonesian, Western, and Chinese dishes Rp3000-20,000. Numerous steaks Rp19,000-42,500. Nightly music 8pm-midnight. Open daily 9am-midnight.

Toko Oen Restaurant, Jl. Basuki Rakhmat 5, opposite McDonald's. A colonial relic serving fresh juices (Rp5000-7500) and locally produced ice cream (Rp3500-12,500). Excellent homemade pastries. Entrees Rp10,000-30,000. Open daily 8am-9pm.

SIGHTS

The colorful **Eng An Kiong Chinese Pagoda,** at the intersection of Jl. Gatot Subroto and Jl. Zainul Zakse, provides a fascinating view of Chinese Buddhist, Confucian, and Taoist cultures. Intricate carvings, enormous archways, and shrines filled with homemade candles and incense add to the quiet mystery of this place, where locals come to give offerings to their ancestors. (Open daily 6am-8:30pm. Free.) Those searching for something less peaceful head west from Tugu Monument to the **Brawijaya Museum,** behind the welcoming tanks at Jl. Besar Ljen 25A. The two halls are draped in war photographs and battle plans, and filled with Javanese military memorabilia such as stained flags, intimidating guns, and a street car named "Desoto," all to the pleasant tunes of marching music. (Open daily 7am-5pm. Donations, about Rp1000 per person, expected.) The **Sena Putra Amusement Park** has dancing. Check with the Tourist Information Center for exact times. After lunch at Toko Oen Restaurant many stroll, bike, or take a *becak* ride down lovely tree-lined boulevards, especially Jl. Kawi and Jl. Semeru, past Malang's many colonial buildings.

DAYTRIPS FROM MALANG

CANDI SINGOSARI

Open daily 8am-5pm. Donations accepted, usually Rp1000. From Arjosari bus terminal, nab a public bus 12km north to Singosari town (20min., Rp1000). Ask to get off at the candi *(temple).*

Singosari Temple was built between 1268 and 1292 in honor of King Kertanagara, the last ruler of the Singosari Dynasty. The small *candi* has been well-restored and retains its mystique, although only one of the six interior statues remains at this location; the Dutch claimed the other *patung* for themselves.

BALE KAMBANG BEACH

From Malang, take any G-A angkot *to Gadang Terminal. From here,* bemo *go south toward Bantur (2hr., Rp3500), where* ojek *scurry to the beach (30min., Rp7500). Rare minibuses make a less enjoyable trip (Rp3000).*

Bale Kambang, 75km south of Malang, is a stretch of sea backed by dense forest. The *ojek* ride from Bantur to the beach is a highlight—12km of terraced fields, villages, and woods laced with scenic trails. Three offshore islands, accessible by bridges, provide spectacular views of the ocean and mainland. *Candi* Bale Kambang rests on the largest of the three, which lets visitors spend the night. Those seeking solitude should come on weekdays. Although the sands are packed on weekends, loitering young men might harass women traveling alone. Other beaches in the area include: **Ngliyep,** with white sands enveloped by dense jungle (bus from Gadang Bus Terminal; nearby **Tamban,** a less spectacular waterfront that offers peace and quiet; and **Sendang Biru,** nice sands with a view of Pulau Sempu, a dramatic island offering an exciting 2hr. hike through the nature reserve to Segara Anak, a crystal-clear laguna fed by the teeming ocean.

BLITAR ☎0342

Blitar is the birthplace and final resting place of former President Sukarno (known as "Bung Karno"). Residents use only the most superlative and respectful terms when speaking of the charismatic leader of the Indonesian revolution. Not surprisingly, Blitar has thrown its support behind the reformist President Megawati Sukarnoputri, Sukarno's daughter. As a regional hub in the heart of East Java, Blitar exudes a relaxed atmosphere and is an ideal stopover between Solo and Malang.

TRANSPORTATION. Blitar's **train station** (☎801 940) is on Jl. Mastrip, which runs east-west on the south side of town. Trains run daily to: **Jakarta** (11-14hr.; 4, 4:30pm; economy Rp31,000) via **Cirebon**; **Jogjakarta** (6-7hr., 4:30pm, economy Rp24,000) via **Solo** (5-6hr.; 4, 4:30, 9pm; Rp24,000); and **Surabaya** (5hr., 6 per day 5am-3:10pm, Rp4000) via **Malang** (2hr., Rp2400). *Angkot* headed south down Jl. Anggrek go to the **bus terminal** on the southern outskirts of town. Buses run to: **Denpasar** (15hr., 2:30pm, Rp90,000); **Jakarta** (12hr., 11:30am, Rp90,000); **Malang** (2hr., dozens per day, Rp4500); and **Solo** (7hr., every hr. 6am-1pm, Rp12,000). If arriving in Blitar from Malang, ask to be let off on the main road near the Herlingga Jaya Hotel, where *becak* (around Rp4000) greet passengers heading to the hotels near Bung Karno's grave. Otherwise it's a long wait for an *angkot* or an expensive *becak* ride from the terminal into town and north to **Jl. Slamet Riyadi** and the tomb.

ORIENTATION AND PRACTICAL INFORMATION. One block north and parallel to **Jl. Mastrip** (home to the train station), **Jl. Merdeka** runs east-west past the *Alun-alun.* Two blocks to the west of this town center, the main boulevard intersects with Jl. Anggrek, which heads south to the **bus station.** Three blocks to the east, Jl. Merdeka turns into **Jl. A. Yani** as it crosses **Jl. Sudirman,** which leads to **Sukarno's tomb** in the north.

The **Kantor Pos Blitar (post office),** Jl. Mastrip 87 (☎801 544; open M-Th 8am-2pm, F 8-11:30am, Sa 8am-1pm), offers **Internet** (Rp3000 per 30min.). With your back to the post office, **BNI,** Jl. Kenonogo 7, is two blocks on your right. It has a **24hr. ATM** (Cirrus/MC/V) and exchanges currency. (☎801 946; open M-F 8am-3pm.) Further east, the **Apotek Nirmala** pharmacy is at Jl. Seruni 45. (☎800 666. Open M-Sa 6am-10:30pm.) Continuing north and two blocks right on Jl. Merdeka are a **24hr. Telkom Office** and **Internet** access (Rp5000 per hr.) at Jl. A.Yani 10. Heading north, the **police station** is at Jl. Sudirman 32 (☎802 790).

ACCOMMODATIONS AND FOOD. Finding a room around June 21 (the anniversary of Bung Karno's death) and June 6 (his birthday) is virtually impossible, but the sight of thousands of Javanese descending on Blitar might be worth the hassle. To escape the Sukarnoist hordes, consider staying at **Herlingga Jaya Hotel II,** Jl. Jaksa Agung Suprapto 49 (behind the main hotel), to the northeast on the outskirts of town. A pool and karaoke bar are nestled in the back. (☎806 325. Check-out 2pm. Rooms Rp30,000, with A/C Rp50,000.) **Hotel Saptra Mandala,** Jl. Slamet Riyadi 31, 150m south of Bung Karno's grave, is the city's best value. (☎801 810. Rooms Rp20,000, with TV and hot water Rp55,000. Extra bed Rp8000.)

Restaurant Mandala, in the same complex, offers *nasi pecel* for Rp3000. About 150m north of the tomb at Jl. Slamet Riyadi 66, **Depot Pojok** serves point-and-eat dishes such as fried chicken or fish over rice. (Rp3000 per plate. Open daily 7am-9pm.) Dozens of hotels and eateries are scattered north of the train station and the alleyways off Jl. Anggrek (left of the train station) house several dirt-cheap *losmen.*

SIGHTS. Sukarno wished to be buried near his family residence in Bogor, but the New Order had him interred in an unmarked grave next to his mother in his hometown of Blitar. Eight years after his death, the Suharto regime rehabilitated Sukarno, *proklamator* of Indonesian independence, and constructed a US$1 million shrine around his grave. **Makam Bung Karno,** the mausoleum complex, borrows from Balinese and Javanese styles to reflect the liberator's mixed ethnicity. Beyond the massive stone entrance and within the Javanese *pendopo* pavilion, reverent visitors gather below the elaborate wooden ceiling and surround the grave in silence and meditation. Follow their example and point your bare feet away from the tomb. Sukarno's children are rumored to be working on fulfilling their father's wish by moving his grave to Bogor. (Open daily 8am-5pm.)

Dating back to the Majapahit period (15th-century), **Candi Penataran,** 8km north of Makam Bung Karno, East Java's largest Hindu-Buddhist temple, shouldn't be missed. Take a Penataran-bound minibus from Jl. W.R. Supratman (Rp1500), 400m below Bung Karno's grave, and ask to be let off at *Candi* Penataran. (Open daily 7am-5pm. Donation Rp1000.)

GUNUNG BROMO ☎0335

At 2923m, dramatic Gunung Bromo is one of the most magnificent sights in Indonesia. "Bromo" refers not only to the ash-gray, semi-active crater named after the Hindu god Brahma but also to an entire cluster of active and dormant volcanos set in an enormous 40km wide crater, the Bromo-Semera Massif, known as Tengger. An overnight stay and breathtaking sunrise followed by a 5hr. hike is enough time to take in the vistas, but the mountain air merits an extra night or two for those who don't mind the hordes of tourists.

TRANSPORTATION. Gunung Bromo is 50km east of Malang. It's most commonly reached by tourist bus via the unfriendly town of **Probolinggo.** From there, take a crowded public *bemo* to **Cemorolawang** (2½hr. last bus 5pm, Rp6000), the stop for the Gunung Bromo area. Most locals will get out at the market halfway to Gunung Bromo; refuse any offers for express buses and wait for the *bemo* to refill (around 10min.). For late arrivals, direct **minibuses** can be chartered at one of the travel agents in the Probolinggo bus terminal (1hr., Rp50,000-60,000). Alternatively, Gunung Bromo can also be approached from its northern edge via the coastal town of **Pasuruan.** From Pasuruan, minibuses run to **Tosari,** where visitors can hire a jeep to the crater or take a minibus to **Penanjakan,** the premier sunrise viewpoint.

To leave, purchase bus tickets at the **Probolinggo bus terminal** or a travel agency in Cemorolawang. Minibuses constantly run downhill to Probolinggo, from where buses continue to **Denpasar** (8hr.; 10:30am, 12:15, 7, 8, 9pm; Rp60,000) and **Solo/Jogjakarta** (economy 11-12hr.; 7, 8, 9pm; Rp45,000; executive 9-10hr.; 10:30am,

THE GODFODDER *Kadasa*, a Hindu celebration of life, attracts droves of visitors annually, filling the *laut pasir* (a desert-like sea of sand in Bromo's 40km long "Tengger" crater). Around 1000 religious participants and two million interested onlookers cram under October's full moon to witness spiritual festivities of volcanic proportions: horses dance to the accompaniment of bongo-like *ketipung*, and flowers come down like rain from the main road all the way up to the lip of the crater. After the ceremonial prayer in the *Pure*, a temple in the middle of *laut pasir*, the holy *pak jai* (priest) leads up participants through the night to the top of Gunung Bromo. Loaded with sacrificial ammunition, the holy men take aim and erupt in a flame of flying fare, flinging a full menu of fresh produce into the fiery furnace. Bouquets, boxes of rice, and chickens with their legs bound descend in a leap of faith, with high hopes of appeasing the gods. But the gods will have to be appeased another day, for here's the catch: the destitute and homeless crouch inside the sulfuric crater, awaiting their projectile provisions as the religious providers dish up an airborne carte du jour. Every good *filche noir*, however, ends in a final twist of victory. Aware of the theives' weakness, the priests cunningly pitch cigarettes into the pit. With no choice but to give in, the would-be thieves irresistibly indulge in their vulnerability, their lit cravings revealing their location and aiding their capture by the poultry police. And so it goes: the classic tale of an ongoing struggle between good and evil...and chickens.

8pm; Rp60,000). Alternatively, take a bus to **Panuangi** (4hr., every 30min., Rp8000), a bemo to **Ketapong** (45min., Rp1750), and a final bus to **Denpasar** (3½hr., Rp7500). **Public buses** travel to **Malang** and **Surabaya** (both 2hr., every 30min., Rp8000).

ACCOMMODATIONS AND FOOD. The best deal in the Gunung Bromo area is **Yoschi,** Jl. Wonokerto Km2, Ngadisari, 7km before Cemorolawang. Though it's a *bemo* ride or a steep 45min. walk from the crater, classy facilities, including a restaurant and morning jacket rentals, trump the competition. (☎541 018. Doubles with shared hot-water *mandi* Rp25,000.) In Cemorolawang, on the lip of the crater, *losmen* are close together and travelers should shop around; note that *bemo* drivers often take commissions from *losmen* operators. **Hotel Lava's,** beyond the entrance gate 50m up the left road, has a friendly and comfortable cafe (try the pancakes) and attracts the most tourists. (☎541 020. Doubles Rp30,000, with *mandi* and breakfast Rp85,000.) **Cemara Indah** is 100m up the road to the right, where you're most likely to get dropped off. It's not the best stay around, but it's worth a look-see. (☎541 019. Singles Rp20,000; doubles Rp25,000-30,000.) Since the town shuts down after 8pm and restaurants are limited to those attached to hotels, backpackers tend not to dine out. *Warung* are easy to come by on village roads (Rp1000-4000). Hotel restaurants bustle with backpackers (Rp5000-15,000).

If you're stranded in Probolinggo, **Hotel Ratna,** Jl. Sudirman 16, has pricey rooms. (☎421 597. Breakfast included. Rooms Rp35,000-75,000.) **Rumah Makan Sumber Hidup,** next to Hotel Ratna at the corner at Jl. Moch Saleh 2, serves ice cream and Indonesian fare. (Dishes Rp8000-15,000. Open daily 7am-9pm).

CLIMBING GUNUNG BROMO. Gunung Bromo and its surrounding peaks can be climbed at any point in the day, but to hike to the magnificent sunrise, set your alarm clock for 1:30am. Alternatively, a convoy of jeeps leaving at 4am hauls a mass of people making the pre-dawn pilgrimage to nearby **Gunung Penanjaka,** which provides a premium postcard panorama at daybreak. Purchase tickets for Rp25,000 through any Cemorolawang accommodation. After the crack of dawn, jeeps scurry back down the mountain across *Laut Pasir*, the "sea of sand," and to Gunung Bromo, where a short 15min. jaunt up the trail will take you to the caldera's edge. Expect to be surrounded by desperate men trying to rent wheezing horses for Rp20,000 to the top and back. Practice your bargaining skills and remember that the ride downhill may be more strenuous than walking. By foot, Gunung Bromo is a short 2½km hike from Cemorolawang and makes for a daytrip, but the hike to **Pen-**

anjakan viewpoint is up a long, winding, and potentially-dangerous path (6km). Early trekkers should bring warm clothes, water, explicit directions, and a flashlight. After sunrise, the crowds melt away, but promising and creative hiking possibilities remain (10km to Gunung Bromo; 2km around its crater).

BALI

One million tourists flock to this little island (5700 sq. km) every year, seeking everything from enlightenment to drunken debauchery. For many, this exotic paradise could be Eden; foolish travelers, however, dismiss it as Eden after the Fall. The truth lies somewhere in between: though McDonalds is allowed in Kuta, escapists can still find virgin expanse and a paradise not yet lost. Though no part of Bali's main attractions remains untouched by tourism, the island is undeniably beautiful. You may have to share the beaches and volcanoes with droves of fellow voyagers, but the white coral, black lava beaches, world-class watersports, and gorgeous vistas make it all worthwhile. Bali has transformed from a village to a tourist mecca for a reason—that reason was its charm, which if you look closely, still prevails.

THE VIEW FROM ABOVE

Main cities: Denpasar, Sanur, Singaraja, and Ubud.
Highlights: Enjoying secluded beaches in Lovina, partying at Kuta, recovering in Ubud.
Something fun: Climb Gunung Agung and Gunung Batur, bungee jump in Kuta, visit the Monkey Forest.

DENPASAR ☎0361

Chock full of art, markets, malls, karaoke, museums, and international cuisine, Denpasar is Bali's urban center of schmooze. Typically not visited by many travelers, this city reveals the ritual daily idiosyncrasies of its Indonesian denizens. Though the streets can be filthy, they offer a mosaic of treasures, from the literal to the metaphoric. With puppies and birds for sale and paintings and Dutch cannons to admire, the eclectic nature of Denpasar's streets should not be missed.

INTERCITY TRANSPORTATION

BY PLANE

Ngurah Rai International Airport (☎751 011, 24hr. info ext. 164) lies 30min. south of Kuta by taxi or direct shuttle. A moneychanger, baggage storage (Rp5500 per day), and **ATM** (Cirrus/MC/Plus/V) are available. The Rp75,000 international departure tax must be paid in cash; the domestic departure tax is Rp30,000. From the airport, fixed-rate taxis go to: **Denpasar** (Rp27,000-37,500); **Nusa Dua** (Rp30,000); **Sanur** (Rp30,000); **Ubud** (Rp90,000). Cheaper public *bemo* and chartered transport vehicles linger outside the airport on the main road. Beware of porters who carry your luggage without being asked and then demand large sums for their effort.

SUPA DUPA FLY...

DESTINATION	FREQUENCY	PRICE	DESTINATION	FREQUENCY	PRICE
Bima	1 per day	Rp478,800	**Mataram**	5 per day	Rp233,500
Jakarta	8 per day	Rp802,200	**Singapore**	1 per day	US$255
Jogjakarta	3 per day	Rp426,000	**Sumbawa Besar**	M, W	Rp303,900
Kupang	1 per day	Rp803,300	**Ujung Pandang**	1 per day	Rp555,800

Singapore Airlines, Garuda, and **Merpati** have information desks at the airport between the domestic and international terminals, and head offices in Denpasar: **Garuda,** Jl. Melati 61 (☎225 245, open M-Th 7:30am-4:30pm, F 7:30am-5pm, Sa 9am-

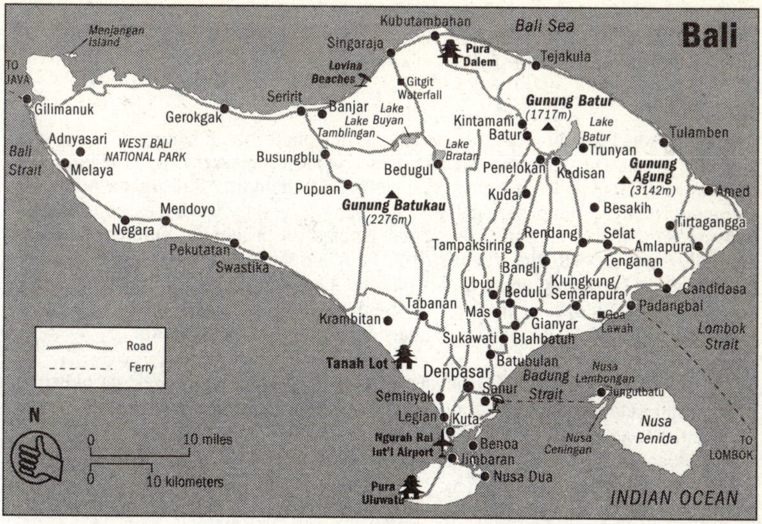
Bali
Bali Sea
Menjangan Island
TO JAVA
Gilimanuk
Bali Strait
Adnyasari
Melaya
WEST BALI NATIONAL PARK
Gerokgak
Seririt
Singaraja
Lovina Beaches
Kubutambahan
Pura Dalem
Tejakula
Gitgit Waterfall
Banjar
Lake Buyan
Lake Tamblingan
Busungblu
Pupuan
Bedugul
Lake Bratan
Gunung Batukau (2276m)
Kintamani
Batur
Gunung Batur (1717m)
Lake Batur
Trunyan
Tulamben
Penelokan
Kedisan
Gunung Agung (3142m)
Amed
Kuda
Besakih
Mendoyo
Negara
Pekutatan
Swastika
Rendang
Selat
Tirtagangga
Tampaksiring
Amlapura
Tenganan
Bangli
Ubud
Bedulu
Klungkung/ Semarapura
Candidasa
Tabanan
Mas
Goa Lawah
Padangbai
Krambitan
Gianyar
Lombok Strait
Sukawati
Blahbatuh
Road
Ferry
Tanah Lot
Batubulan
Denpasar
Badung Strait
Nusa Lembongan
Jungutbatu
Seminyak
Sanur
Legian
Kuta
Nusa Penida
Ngurah Rai Int'l Airport
Benoa
Nusa Ceningan
TO LOMBOK
Jimbaran
Nusa Dua
Pura Uluwatu
N
0 10 miles
0 10 kilometers
INDIAN OCEAN

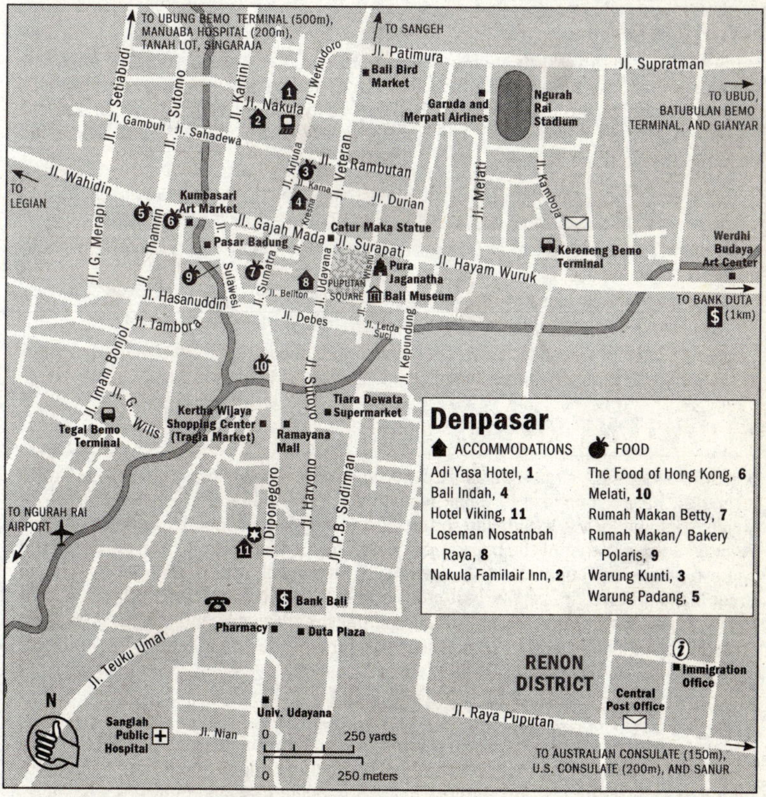
TO UBUNG BEMO TERMINAL (500m), MANUABA HOSPITAL (200m), TANAH LOT, SINGARAJA
TO SANGEH
Jl. Patimura
Jl. Supratman
Bali Bird Market
Garuda and Merpati Airlines
Ngurah Rai Stadium
TO UBUD, BATUBULAN BEMO TERMINAL, AND GIANYAR
Jl. Setiabudi
Jl. Sutomo
Jl. Kartini
Jl. Werkudoro
Jl. Nakula
Jl. Gambuh
Jl. Sahadewa
Jl. Arjuna
Jl. Veteran
Jl. Rambutan
Jl. Wahidin
TO LEGIAN
Jl. Kama
Jl. Kresna
Jl. Durian
Jl. Melati
Jl. Kamboja
Kumbasari Art Market
Jl. Gajah Mada
Catur Maka Statue
Jl. Surapati
Jl. G. Merapi
Jl. Thamrin
Pasar Badung
Pura Jaganatha
Jl. Hayam Wuruk
Kereneng Bemo Terminal
Werdhi Budaya Art Center
Jl. Sulawesi
Jl. Sumatra
Jl. Udayana
Jl. Wisnu
PUPUTAN SQUARE
Bali Museum
Jl. Beliton
Jl. Hasanuddin
Jl. Debes
TO BANK DUTA (1km)
Jl. Tambora
Jl. Letda Suci
Jl. Kepundung
Jl. Imam Bonjol
Jl. Sutoyo
Jl. G. Wilis
Tiara Dewata Supermarket
Kertha Wijaya Shopping Center (Tragia Market)
Tegal Bemo Terminal
Ramayana Mall
Jl. Haryono
Jl. P.B. Sudirman
Jl. Diponegoro
TO NGURAH RAI AIRPORT
Denpasar
ACCOMMODATIONS
Adi Yasa Hotel, 1
Bali Indah, 4
Hotel Viking, 11
Loseman Nosatnbah Raya, 8
Nakula Familair Inn, 2
FOOD
The Food of Hong Kong, 6
Melati, 10
Rumah Makan Betty, 7
Rumah Makan/ Bakery Polaris, 9
Warung Kunti, 3
Warung Padang, 5
Bank Bali
Pharmacy
Duta Plaza
Jl. Teuku Umar
RENON DISTRICT
Immigration Office
Univ. Udayana
Central Post Office
Jl. Raya Puputan
N
Sanglah Public Hospital
Jl. Nian
0 250 yards
0 250 meters
TO AUSTRALIAN CONSULATE (150m), U.S. CONSULATE (200m), AND SANUR

1pm); **Merpati,** Jl. Melati 51 (☎235 556; open M-F 8am-5pm, Sa-Su 9am-5pm); **Singapore Airlines,** 3rd fl., Bank Bali on Jl. Dewi Sartika (☎261 666, weekend ☎261 669; open M-F 8am-5pm, Sa 8am-1pm).

BY BUS

Overnight buses leave in mid-afternoon for Java from terminal Ubung in Denpasar, and vice versa. Buy tickets to **Jakarta** (Rp170,500), **Jogjakarta** (Rp110,000), and **Surabaya** (Rp50,000) from tour agencies in Bali, including **Bali Buana Artha,** Jl. Diponegoro 131A, Denpasar (☎227 370), or the terminal. A/C buses go to **Bima/Sape** on Sumbawa. Fares include ferries. **Perama,** Jl. Legian 39, Kuta (☎751 551), has daily departures to **Bima/Sape** (Rp130,000) and **Mataram** (Rp50,000). Other bus lines include **Langsung Indah, Safari Dharma Raya,** and **Simpatik,** but due to the accessibility of its offices and English-speaking staff, Perama is the most accommodating for tourists. Be vigilant onboard buses, as theft is common.

ISLAND-HOPPING Ferries run between **Gilimanuk** on the west tip of Bali and **Ketapang** on east Java (20min., every 30min. 5am-9pm, Rp10,000). Ferries to **Lombok** leave from **Padangbai** (see p. 228) on Bali's east coast (4-5hr., every 1½hr., Rp9500). **Mabua Express** leaves for **Lembar** (2½hr., 8am, US$25-30) from **Benoa Harbor** (☎721 272) in south Bali. **PELNI** ships also serve Benoa Harbor. For schedules and tickets, contact their ticket office in Benoa (☎721 377). To get to Benoa, take a taxi from Denpasar (15min.)

BY BEMO

Public *bemo*, identified by yellow license plates (government vehicles have red plates; private ones have black), are best caught in the early morning and generally stop running after 9pm in southern Bali and 6pm in the north. They can also be chartered privately. **Denpasar** is the hub of *bemo* activity for southern Bali. Four terminals serve the island.

Batubulan, 6km northeast of Denpasar, runs *bemo* east to Bangli, Padangbai, Candidasa, Amlapura, and Tirtagangga and north to Ubud via Kediri and Penelokan.

Kereneng, on the east end of Denpasar off Jl. Hayam Wuruk, has connecting *bemo* to the other terminals.

Tegal, on the west end near the intersection of Jl. G. Willis and Jl. Imam Bonjol, runs *bemo* south to Kuta, Legian, Ngurah Rai Airport, Sanur, Nusa Dua, and Uluwatu.

Ubung, north of Denpasar on Jl. Cokroaminoto, handles trips to the north and west, including Singaraja, Bedugul, Tanah Lot, Gilimanuk, and points in Java.

ORIENTATION

North of Denpasar, dense Pasar Badung lies between the two parallel east-west streets **Jl. Hasanuddin** and **Jl. Gajah Mada,** which are connected by **Jl. Sulawesi.** Jl. Gajah Mada becomes **Jl. Surapati** to the east, which later becomes **Jl. Hayam Wuruk. Puputan Square** is east of the market, between the same streets. At one corner of the square, where Jl. Gajah Mada, **Jl. Veteran, Jl. Surapadial,** and **Jl. Udayana** meet, sits **Catur Maka statue.** The **central post office** and **Bali Government Tourist Office** are both in the **Renon District** near **Jl. Raya Puputan. Udayan University** and the massive **Duta Plaza Shopping Center** border **Jl. Diponegoro,** which heads northward to the market.

LOCAL TRANSPORTATION

Metered taxis start at Rp3000; bargaining is usually more expensive. Taxis don't stop where *bemo* or local drivers are parked, so catch one elsewhere. The light-blue **Bali Taxi** (☎701 111) offers professional service. **Ojek** can be hired anywhere. **Dokar** (horse-drawn carts) are used in Denpasar.

TOURIST PRICE. Tourists are usually charged more than locals for transportation. If you're up to the challenge, ask locals how much they pay to determine a fair price and then bargain away. *Let's Go* wishes you luck.

PRACTICAL INFORMATION

Tourist Offices: Dinas Pariwisata, Jl. Surapati 7 (☎234 569), near the Bali Museum. Friendly and informative. Free maps, brochures, and schedule of events. Staff helps decipher *bemo* routes. Open M-Th 7am-2pm, F 7-11am, Sa 7am-12:30pm.

Tours: Miraz Tours, Jl. Diponegoro 81 (☎246 007), books tours around Bali. Open M-Sa 8am-8pm, Su 8am-4pm.

Embassies and Consulates: Australia, Jl. Prof. Yamin 4, Renon District (☎235 092). Open M-F 8am-4pm. **US,** Jl. Hayam Wuruk 188 (☎233 605), next to Hotel Sanno. Open M-F 8am-4:30pm.

Immigration Office: Jl. Niti Mandala, Renon District (☎227 828). With your back to the GPO, turn left and then left again. Visa extensions. Open M-Th 7am-2pm, F-Sa 7-11am.

Currency Exchange: Big **banks** cluster on **Jl. Gajah Mada** between Badung Market and Puputan Square. There are dozens of **ATMs;** one is at **Bank Bali,** on Jl. Diponegoro at Jl. Teuku Umar near the telephone office. **Bank Duta,** Jl. Hayam Wuruk 165 (☎226 578), has MC/V cash advances. Open M-F 8am-3pm.

Gay and Lesbian Organizations: Gaya Dewata/Citra Usadua Foundation, at Jl. Sari Gading 1, off Jl. Ratna (☎246 757). Focuses on AIDS education.

PELNI Office: Jl. Diponegoro 165 (☎234 680). Helps with transportation and other tourist-related questions. Open daily 8am-7pm.

Emergency: Police ☎110. **Ambulance** ☎118.

Police: ☎424 346. On Jl. Gunung Sangiong. **Branch** (☎234 928), on Jl. Diponegoro near the Tragia Shopping center.

Pharmacies: Kimia Farma 34, Jl. Diponegoro 125 (☎227 811), at the intersection with Jl. Teuku Umar. Doctors available **24hr. Bulan Farma,** Jl. Diponegoro 126 (☎227 605), specializes in pediatric care. House calls. Open daily 5am-9pm.

Medical Services: Sanglah Public Hospital, Jl. Kesehatan Selatan 1 (☎227 911). **Manuaba Hospital,** Jl. Cokroaminoto 28 (☎426 393). Both open 24hr.

Telephones: The **phone office,** Jl. Teuku Umar 6, near the intersection with Jl. Diponegoro, offers reliable international, collect, and calling-card calls. **Wartel,** also offering international calls, are scattered about town.

Internet Access: Several Internet cafes are scattered around Jl. Diponegoro. **Methel Internet Cafe,** across from Adi Yasa, Jl. Nakula 23B. Rp4000 per hr. 6:30am-3pm, Rp5000 3-10pm. Open daily 6:30am-10pm.

Post Offices: GPO (☎223 565), south on Jl. Raya Puputan in Renon District. *Poste Restante.* **Branch,** Jl. Kamboja 6 (☎222 004), outside Kereneng Terminal. Both open daily 8am-8pm. **Postal code:** 80235.

Express Mail: DHL, Jl. Hayam Wuruk 146 (☎262 713). Open M-F 8am-5pm, Sa 8am-1pm.

ACCOMMODATIONS

Nakula Familiar Inn, Jl. Nakula 4 (☎226 446), on the same street as Adi Yasa Hotel. Run by a friendly local family, it's easily the top pick in the city. Guest rooms in separate buildings in a traditional Balinese compound. Breakfast Rp15000. Laundry service with ironing Rp2500 per article. Huge, clean singles or doubles with porch, ceiling fan, private bath (combination *mandi* style). Singles Rp40,000; doubles Rp60,000.

Adi Yasa Hotel, Jl. Nakula 23B (☎222 679), 50m from Nakula Familiar Inn. *Losmen*-style accommodation. Inexpensive, worn rooms with private combination *mandi* and fan. Neighbor's pet monkey can be hellishly noisy. Breakfast included. Singles Rp25,000; doubles Rp35,000.

WARIA Fitra is anatomically male, but insists that she and her boyfriend, a Javanese policeman who visits her on his lunch breaks, are not gay. "He doesn't like men," Fitra insists as she brushes her long, black hair. As a teenager, she began to wear dresses and makeup. Though no one has ever explained it to her, she, like most *waria*, members of Indonesia's alternate gender, believes that God gave her a female soul inside a male body. When Fitra was 13, she dressed in a female's tunic and veil, went to the mosque with her family, and confronted this belief. She sat for a few moments on the female side of the room, since she couldn't in the male section dressed as she was. The women nearby began to shift away uneasily, making it clear they were uncomfortable in Fitra's presence. As Fitra explains it, they felt she was polluting the purity of their prayer.

Fitra doesn't go to the mosque anymore. She prays alone on the red prayer mat that hangs over the door to her room, a concrete cell in a compound filled with other Javanese immigrants hoping to strike it rich in Denpasar. The intricacies of Fitra's belief distinguish her from the transvestites, hermaphrodites, homosexuals, and transsexuals. According to Fitra, she is neither "cross-dressing" nor wearing the clothes of another gender. She has a masculine body, but she believes that her female soul distinguishes her from homosexual men attracted to other men. She has not had nor wishes to have genital surgery. Fitra has recently updated her National Identity Card, an identification card carried by all Indonesians. The card describes her status—once printed as male beneath her long-haired photograph—as *waria*.

Bali Indah, Jl. Kresna 11 (☎225 226). From the Catur Maka statue, the first right off Jl. Gajah Mada. A quiet hotel in noisy Denpasar, Bali Indah is near all the sights. Fewer tourists make it ideal for mingling with locals. Doubles with private combination *mandi* and fan Rp50,000; with A/C, TV, bath and hot water Rp120,000. Open 24hr.

Hotel Viking, Jl. Diponegoro 120 (☎223 992). With your back to Bank Bali, turn right onto Jl. Diponegoro; it's 100m down on the left. Noisy. Free tea. Singles Rp60,000; cottages set back from road Rp70,000, with A/C Rp80,000.

Losmen Nusatnbah Raya, Jl Beliton 10 (☎226 951), 2 blocks from Bali Museum on a quiet side street. Neighborly, clean outfit. Singles Rp25,000; doubles Rp35,000.

FOOD

Denpasar's diverse ethnic population makes for exciting dining. You'll find *warung* and cheap eateries everywhere in town, especially along **Jl. Sumatra-Diponegoro** and at the Kereneng *bemo* terminal. A **night market** behind Pasar Badung offers *warung* dishes. (Open daily 6pm-midnight.) Another night market comes to life on Jl. Diponegoro near the **Kertha Wijaya Shopping Center. Tiara Dewata Supermarket** is at the north end of Jl. Sudirman. **Tragia Market,** Jl. Diponegoro 98, part of the Kertha Wijaya Shopping Center, sells a large selection of fruits and vegetables. (Open until 10pm.) If you're not adventurous, Western cuisine is easy to find.

Rumah Makan Betty, Jl. Sumatra 56. 1 block east of Jl. Sulawesi. A small, low-budget cafeteria on Jl. Sumatra. Clean, roomy, friendly. East Javanese food and some vegetarian options. Open M-Sa 8am-9pm, Su 8am-2pm.

Warung Kunti, Jl. Arjuna 37. Take 2nd right down Jl. Gajah Mada from the Catur Maka statue. A tiny mom-and-pop operation, Kunti is far from traffic and serves spicy Balinese food. The owner likes to practice his English and show off his 100-year-old Dutch mirror. Meal with rice Rp5000. Open daily 7am-2pm.

Melati, Jl. Diponegoro 48. *Sate* house with English menu. Impressive array of dishes and juices. Meals and juice drinks from Rp5000.

Rumah Makan/Bakery Polaris, Jl. Sulawesi 40, next to Pasar Badung. Local bakery and restaurant. Try *onde-onde* (fried dough balls in sesame seeds). Refreshing *es kolak* (ice, banana, pineapple in bright pink coconut milk) Rp2500. Open daily 6am-8pm.

Warung Padang, Jl. Dr. Wahidin 1. From Pasur Kumbasari, go down Jl. Gajah Mada with your back to the river; it's at the big intersection. A good place to chow down on *otak* or brains Rp3000. Open 24hr.

The Food of Hong Kong, J1 Gajah Mada 99 (434 926), next door to Pasar Badung, serves up delectable and diverse Southeast Asian meals. Dishes Rp10,000-50,000.

SIGHTS

BALI MUSEUM. Rebuilt in 1932 after the original collapsed in a 1917 earthquake, the museum is Denpasar's primary attraction. The building itself, with its blend of Balinese temple and palace architecture, is the finest exhibit. It also houses artifacts that provide an introduction to Balinese society and culture from the prehistoric age up until today. While the museum lacks English-speaking guides and detailed labels, wandering through the well-maintained courtyards and rooms is nonetheless informative, especially for those interested in traditional Balinese woodcarving, weaving, and painting. *(On Jl. Mayor Wisnu east of Puputan Sq. Open Tu-Th, F 8am-2:45pm, Sa 8am-3:15pm, Su 8am-3:45pm. Rp750, children Rp250.)*

PURA JAGANATHA. This temple, dedicated to the supreme god Sanghyang Widi, is a symbolic representation of the cosmos. Sanghyang Widi, symbolized by a gold statue, sits atop a tall spire. The eight gods, each clad in a symbolic color, are beneath, and under them are two dragons that balance the earth. The spire, built of white coral, is surrounded by a moat with goldfish and sacred lilies. Guides, often religion or history students, will give you a crash course on Balinese Hinduism for a few dollars. At 7pm during *purnama* (full moon) and *tilem* (dark moon), the temple becomes crowded, as Balinese bring offerings and prayers, and Hindu intellectuals meet for religious readings. *Wayang kulit* (shadow puppet performances) begin on *purnama* around 10pm. *(Next to the Bali Museum. Open daily 7am-6pm.)*

WERDHI BUDAYA ART CENTER. Every June and July, the **Bali Arts Festival** kicks off in Denpasar at Werdhi Budaya Art Center. The large, Balinese-inspired outdoor amphitheater and display wings make it the perfect home for Balinese arts, especially painting. The tourist office (see **Practical Information**, p. 197) provides a schedule of events. Call ahead to find out what's on display. English-speaking guides are available—haggle well. *(On the corner of Jl. Hayam Wuruk and Jl. Nusa Indah. ☎227 176. Open daily 8am-2pm. Rp1000.)*

PUPUTAN SQUARE. This large park, with a fountain and monument depicting a family preparing for battle, commemorates the solemn, suicidal *puputan* (final flight) of 1906, when Badung's last king, followed by family and court, refused to surrender and marched into the bullets of Dutch soldiers. Locals eat lunch and lounge around the square throughout the week. *(Opposite the Bali Museum.)*

MARKETS

Denpasar offers a panoply of shopping, but its markets, some of the oldest in Bali, offer a rich display of Balinese culture. **Pasar Badung,** located at Jl. Gajah Mada and Jl. Sulawesi, the oldest and largest market in Bali, masks itself as a produce market, with spices and fruit galore. It also carries daily appliances and ritual accoutrements such as *pajong* (Bali umbrellas). Across the river is the **Kumbasari Art Market,** which sells everything from house appliances to elaborate works of art. Other markets include one on **Jl. Abimanyu** (connected to Jl. Nokula) and Jl. Veteran; farther down Jl. Veteran is the **Bali Bird Market,** selling birds and fabric of varying qualities and colors.

DAYTRIP FROM DENPASAR

PURA ULUWATU

Reaching Uluwatu can be challenging. Renting your own transport is the best option (motorcycle Rp30,000, taxi Rp60,000, jeep Rp70,000 per day). If you can't sport a rental, it's musical bemos for you. From Denpasar's Tegal Station, catch a bemo to Jimbaran, where you must catch another one to Uluwatu. (Rp10,000 is a bargain, as there are no direct bemo routes to the temples.) If leaving from Kuta, pick up a bemo from Tegal by waiting on the road heading away from the Duty Free Shop, near the gas pump on Jl. Raya Kuta. Private transport can also be hired from Kuta. The distance from Uluwatu to Kuta is bikeable (20km), but the roads near the temple are steep; a bemo will once again be best. Returning from Uluwatu is even harder than getting there. Have an ojek drop you at Jimbaran, where you can catch bemos that run sporadically until 10pm to Kuta and Denpasar. Stow your caps and sunglasses, or monkeys around the temple may snatch them and flee. (Open daily 7am-6pm.)

One of the *Sad Kahyangan*—the six most important temples in Bali—Pura Uluwatu overlooks cliffs on the southwest tip of Bukit Peninsula, the mushroom-shaped area south of Denpasar and Kuta. Thought to date back to the 11th century, Uluwatu honors the Hindu saint **Danhyang Nirartha,** who explored Bali in 1500 BC and reputedly achieved *moksa* (liberation from worldly life) at the site of this temple. Only visitors with appropriate temple clothes (sarong and sash rental included in the Rp3000 admission) and offerings may enter the temple. There is no official tour, but unofficial English-speaking guides work at the entrance. They can be helpful and informative, but agree on a price beforehand, or they can be pricey too.

Surrounding Pura Uluwatu are some of the most challenging **surfing sites** in the world. The nearby breaks of Uluwatu, Padang Padang, and Bingin, north of Pura Uluwatu, host world-class local and international surfing contests. Take an *ojek* (Rp10,000) down the sharp descent to the beaches outside the entrance for Pura Uluwatu. Facilities range from simple *warungs* to board waxing and repair. The Badung Tourist Information (in Kuta) and surf shops have details about other beaches ideal for surfing.

If passing through Jimbaran on the way back from Pura Uluwatu at dusk, be sure to cut down to the bay where candlelit *warung* prepare fish, lobster, and king prawns at "tourist" prices (fish Rp50,000 per kg; crab, lobster and prawns Rp100,000 per kg). A taxi to Jimbaran Bay costs approximately Rp10,000 from Kuta, although most cafes will provide free transportation.

SANUR ☎0361

Sanur's beach is particularly good, but the surf is only decent in the wet season, and the shallow reef makes swimming inconvenient. But the typical Sanur tourist doesn't care—he's too busy floating potbelly-up, sipping piña coladas from poolside bars. Sanur is Bali's first attempt at corporate development: sterile, predictable, and unexciting. Although Sanur is essentially a mid-range resort town (most tourists here are families who couldn't afford a place in Nusa Dua), it's not a hopeless cause for the budgeteer—there are a few reasonably priced s of better quality than the budget accommodations in Kuta. The rupiah-conscious can entertain themselves by getting to the beach and hotel pools through A/C lobbies. Sanur is a good place to crash en route to Nusa Lembongan.

TRANSPORTATION

Flights: Bali's **Ngurah Rai Airport,** 40min. by taxi or blue *bemo* (to Tegal Station). The Bali Beach Hotel has an entire wing with international airline offices. Open M-F 8:30am-4:30pm, Sa 8am-1:30pm.

Bemo: For **Denpasar,** take a green *bemo* to Kereneng Station (10min., Rp1000). Blue *bemo* go south to Tegal Station (20min., Rp1500), where connections are available to **Kuta** and the airport. Private shuttles to destinations in Bali are available from tour offices.

Boats: Perama (Kuta office ☎751 551), has daily **boat** service to **Nusa Lembongan** (10:30am, Rp27,500), but tickets have to be bought through the Kuta office and not the kiosk in Sanur (☎287 594), at Warung Pojok on Jl. Hang Tuah opposite the Radisson).

Rentals: Wirasana, Jl. Danau Tamblingan 126 (☎288 706), and Jl. Ngurah Rai Bypass 545x (☎286 066), opposite police station. Cheap **cars** (Rp100,000) and **motorcycles** (Rp60,000) rented by the day. Cars only at Bypass store. MC/V.

ORIENTATION AND PRACTICAL INFORMATION

Sanur divides into three parallel strips. Along the beach is an almost continuous boardwalk, lined with large hotels, restaurants, and watersports centers. Parallel to the boardwalk 50m inland, **Jl. Danau Tamblingan** (**Jl. Tanjung Sari** at its south end), is studded with resorts, restaurants, boutiques, postal agents, craft shops, and tour agencies. Parallel to Jl. Danau Tamblingan 150m inland is busy **Jl. Ngurah Rai Bypass** (also known as **Bypass Rd.**), a highway whose shops and services are geared toward locals. The Bali Hyatt dominates Sanur's south end, and the even bigger Bali Beach Hotel dominates the north. At the beach end of the northernmost cross-street is the boat service to Nusa Lembongan. **Jl. Hang Tuah** becomes **Jl. Raya Sanur** on its way to Denpasar. Jl. Segara Ayu becomes Jl. Danau Buyan as it crosses Jl. Ngurah Rai; the same happens to Jl. Pantai Sindhu which becomes Jl. Danau Tondano. **Bemo** congregate at Jl. Matasari/Suadamala at the southern end of Jl. Danau Tamblingan.

Tourist Offices: Nearest office in Kuta, but hotels and tour operators provide info and guided tours to anywhere. Private travel offices abound on Jl. Danau Tamblingan. In Bali Beach Hotel, **Barata Tours** arranges trips to Lembongam and vicinity. Open daily 8am-9pm.

Currency Exchange: Moneychangers on Jl. Danau Tamblingan and beach boardwalk have better rates than hotels (except for bank offices in Bali Beach Hotel). **Bank BNI** (☎282 590), on Jl. Danau Tamblingan next to Bali Moon, offers cash advances. Open M-F 8am-noon and 1-3pm. **Bali Bank ATM** at the supermarket (Cirrus/MC/V). Beware of hidden commissions and shortchanging at moneychangers.

American Express: Representative office in the Bali Beach Hotel (☎288 449). Cardholders can buy traveler's checks. The office does not hold packages, but holds letters if addressed c/o PACTO (AmEx), Hotel Bali Beach, Sanur, Denpasar. Open M-F 8:30am-4:30pm, Sa 8:30am-12:30pm.

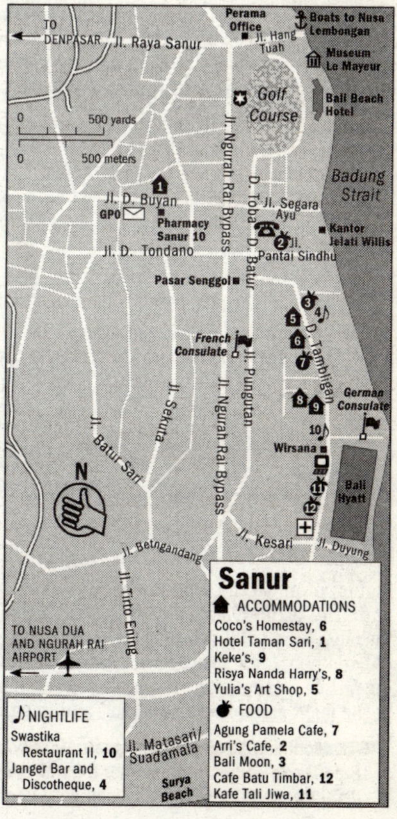

Markets: Pasar Senggol, at the northern end of Jl. Danau Tamblingan, starts at 5pm and winds down at 10pm. **Alas Arum Agung Sanur,** Jl. Danau Tamblingan, near Swastika II restaurant, stocks imported food at high prices. Open daily 8am-10pm.

Emergency: Police ☎ 110. **Ambulance** ☎ 118.

Police: ☎ 288 597, on Bypass Rd. at the edge of the golf course.

Pharmacy: Pharmacy Sanur 10 (☎ 288 744), on Jl. Danau Buyan opposite Hotel Tamon Sari.

Medical Services: Bali Beach Hotel has an **emergency clinic** (☎ 288 511; ask for the clinic). Open M-F 7am-9pm, Sa 7am-8pm, Su and holidays 10am-6pm. Doctor on duty M-Sa 8am-noon, otherwise on-call only. **Legian Medical Clinic II** (☎ 287 446), Jl. Danau Tamblingan, offers 24hr. medical service.

Telephones: Make local, collect, and cash international calls at the **Wartel** near where Jl. Segara crosses Bypass Rd. Wartel also on Jl. Hang Tuah. **Bali Beach Hotel** has **24hr. HCD** phone accepting credit card calls behind the main lobby.

Internet Access: Hotel Santai, Jl. Danau Tamblingan 148. Rp7500 per 15min.

Express Mail: Bali Prima Cargo, Jl. Danau Tamblingan 160 (☎ 287 360), offers DHL, FedEx, and worldwide delivery service. Open M-Sa 8am-8pm, Su 8am-5pm.

Post Offices: GPO, Jl. Danau Buyan. Send *Poste Restante* to GPO, Banjar Taman. Open M-Th 8am-2pm, F 8am-noon, Sa 8am-1pm. **Postal code:** 80228.

ACCOMMODATIONS

Most of the accommodations in Sanur are mid-range or upscale and charge prices in US dollars far from budget range. The few places that do cater to backpackers are pricier than those in Kuta and Denpasar, but the difference in price generally translates to cleaner bathrooms and better rooms.

Coco's, Jl. Danau Tamblingan 42 (☎ 287 391). Family-run with rooms facing a lovely tropical garden. Best value in Sanur. Clean rooms with private bath, ceiling fan, and breakfast Rp50,000 for up to 2 people.

Risya Nanda Harry's, 19 Jl. Bumi Ayu (☎ 288 390). Walk south from Besakih Hotel to Jl. Bumi Ayu, walk to the end of the street and turn left. Walk 50m more and turn left again and it's at the end of the alley between two enclosed lots. Run by Harry (who speaks English) and Risyal (who speaks German and English), the rooms are gorgeously furnished and mosquito-netted. Call ahead for reservations. Doubles US$10.

Hotel Taman Sari, Jl. Danau Buyan 37 (☎ 288 578). With your back to post office, turn right; it's 100m on the left. The cheapest option. Doubles with fan Rp40,000.

Keke's (☎ 287 282), on Jl. Tamblingan 100m south of Coco's and Yulia's. With the same amenities as Coco's, but pricier. Singles Rp60,000; doubles Rp75,000.

Yulia Art Shop, Jl. Danau Tamblingan 38 (☎ 288 089). Don't let the attached souvenir shop put you off; Yulia's offers fully furnished rooms in a garden setting. Private bath, fan, and breakfast included, all for Rp60,000 (2 people).

FOOD

Sanur caters to the mild tastes of package tourists, so deep-fried squid and steak with fries is often as exotic as the cuisine gets. Eating well is possible, as many restaurants blend Balinese fare with Western, and the result is often hit-or-miss. For cheap, tasty local grub, try a *padang* restaurant on Bypass Rd. **Warung** carts serving *bakso* and roast corn scatter along the north end of the beach and are plentiful at the **night market** on Jl. Danau Tamblingan's north end.

Bali Moon, Jl. Danau Tamblinghan 19. Airy, tropical restaurant with salads, Italian and Indonesian dishes. Happy hour 6-8pm; one free drink. Bali Moon offers free drop-off. Pizza Capriciosa Rp23,900. Open daily 9am-11pm.

WHOSE SYMBOL? Upon coming to Bali for the first time, a number of tourists are shocked by the use of a familiar, threatening symbol: the swastika. Now reviled in the west, the symbol actually dates back over three millennia. Swastika is a Sanskrit sun symbol common to Hindu statues and architecture and has been adopted by Buddhism. The four "legs" represent dynamic cyclical change. In Bali and other areas influenced by Hinduism, the swastika is an ubiquitous blessing that imbues statues and buildings with religious significance. Hitler and the Nazis appropriated and corrupted this symbol, among their other evil deeds. Though it takes some time to get used to the swastika's presence, rest assured that you'll have achieved a new liberation of the mind once you can look at the symbol without the revulsion that accompanies memories of the Third Reich.

Arri's Cafe, Jl. Pantai Sindhu 7, in the north near the night market. English-trained Arrie serves cottage pie (Rp12,000) and local meals like *rendang daging* (beef with cream, *kemiri*, ginger, *galangal*, palm sugar, and lime leaves; Rp20,000). Open daily 8am-11pm.

Cafe Batu Timbar, Jl. Danau Tamblingan 152. What being a vegetarian is all about: delicious salads, fresh fruit juices. Open M-Sa 7:30am-10:30pm, Su 7:30am-3:30pm.

Kafé Tali Jiwa, Jl. Danau Tamblingan 148. Part of the environmentally-conscious Hotel Santai, this place offers healthy vegetarian dishes at affordable prices. Popular hummus, guacamole, and homemade ice cream. Water bottle refill and **Internet access.**

Agung Pamela Cafe, Jl. Danau Tamblingan 52. Sanur's Little Vienna. Dine with the gnome in the corner–share an apple strudel (Rp6800). If you *Oktoberfest* a little too hard, there's a free drop-off service. Open noon-10pm.

SIGHTS

The north part of Sanur's coast is rocky and dark and is dominated by local wildlife; crabs, seabirds, and children flying kites dominate the scene. Farther south, on the sandy beach part of the coast, the fauna are exotic foreign species (German and Japanese sunbathers) and their parasites (countless hawkers, peddlers, massage women, and boat captains). The wise traveler out on safari knows that this is an ecosystem best observed from afar.

MUSEUM LE MAYEUR. Sanur's only non-beach related sight has seen better days. The former home of Belgian artist Le Mayeur (who lived in Bali from 1932 to 1958) is crumbling, unswept, and filled with mostly faded paintings. Le Mayeur's work is mostly Impressionist portraits of Balinese women. The collection here shows little range. The cheap ticket price makes it worth a quick walk-through while you wait for the boat to Nusa Lembongan, but don't go out of your way. *(The museum is north of Bali Beach Hotel grounds, on the beach boardwalk. ☎ 286 201. Open Tu-Th and Su 8am-2pm, F 8-11am, Sa 8am-12:30pm. Rp750; children Rp250.)*

ENTERTAINMENT AND ACTIVITIES

Sanur caters to the Elton John and John Tesh crowd, the same crowd that finds Kuta too loud and wild. **Janger Bar and Discotheque,** Jl. Danau Tamblingan 21, is a local interpretation of Western hipness. It's the largest club on the island and features four bars and a mix of Balinese (younger than in Kuta) and foreign (older than in Kuta) clientele. (☎ 288 88. Cover M-Th Rp25,000, W-Su Rp30,000, no cover 9-10:30pm Su-Th. Open daily 9pm-dawn.)

Check restaurants for schedules of Balinese dance and *gamelan* performances. The **Bali Beach Hotel** (☎ 288 511), at the north end of the beach, has dinner performances of *Ramayana* dance on Wednesdays at 7:30pm. **Swastika Restaurant II,** Jl. Danau Tamblingan 124 (☎ 288 573), has frog dance performances on Thursday and

Legong dance on Sunday (both at 8:30pm). These are not full traditional shows, however, but rather half-hour excerpts.

Sanur is livelier during the day, when watersports are available. The **Kantor Jelati Willis** booth on Sanur Beach, where Jl. Segara runs into the sand, offers the most options, including traditional sailing (US$20 per hr.), windsurfing, snorkeling, waterskiing (US$20 per 15min.), parasailing (US$10 per time around, approximately 4-5min.), and scuba diving. For similar activities and trips to neighboring islands, visit the booth on the boardwalk's end, where the boats are docked. Windsurfing and snorkeling require caution, as passing motorboats have killed tourists.

NEAR SANUR

NUSA LEMBONGAN

The local proverb recounts a familiar story: "I came here for a day, and went back to Kuta, but I quickly returned. I've been here now for two weeks." Welcome home. With white sand, blue waters, and barreling waves, Nusa Lembongan is the domain of surfers who brave the three large breaks over its reef. Looking from the beach to the off-shore reefs, the major breaks (from right to left) are: Shipwreck, Lacerations, and Playground. The most reliable surf is at Shipwreck, a clean right-hand break. Almost as good as the surf is the snorkeling at Mangrove Bay.

The cheapest way to get to Nusa Lembongan is by boat from the end of Jl. Hang Tuah. The boat leaves at 8am but requires a minimum number of people to set sail (Rp30,000). Perama boats leave at 10:30am. Tickets cost Rp30,000 and must be ordered 2hr. ahead from the Kuta office (☎751 551); they'll be waiting at the Warung Pojok depot at 10:15am. Returning boats from Nusa Lembongan leave around 8am. Coming back in the evening by public transportation is not possible. The strait between the islands is rough and the only way to navigate it is by chartering a boat. On the island, boats are readily available for rent and guides will take you around the island for some of the best snorkeling on Bali. (Rp100,000; Rp20,000 when boat is full.)

The best places for food and accommodations are on the northwest corner of the island at Jungubatu Village, 500m from the boat drop-off (with the water to your back, walk left). There is little difference among the many bungalows along the shore. **Ketut's Losmen** has new, modern bungalows. (Singles Rp50,000; doubles Rp60,000.) **Agung's Lodge** offers a carnival atmosphere and full amenities. (Singles Rp40,000; doubles Rp50,000.) The best place to eat is beachside at the **Main Ski Inn and Restaurant,** which offers fresh seafood and shows American movies. The 2½hr. walk around the whole island is pleasant, especially at dusk.

KUTA ☎0361

People seeking Balinese surf, sun, and good times may find fulfillment in Kuta. For the rest of Bali's sake, this may be a good thing. Opinions about Kuta range from disgust to bemusement to love. Crowds, commercialization, and chaos aside, Kuta supports a vibrant international scene of shopping, cheap restaurants, accommodations, markets, and crowded nightspots—all along what was once the most stunning, and is still the most surfable, beach on Bali. If you have the right sense of humor and take nothing too seriously, Kuta is your kind of place.

TRANSPORTATION

Flights: Ngurah Rai International Airport, 15min. by taxi (Rp20,000); convince the driver to turn on the meter, or agree on fares before getting in. A bus also runs from Jl. Legian 39 (hourly, Rp6000). **Garuda,** Natour Kuta Beach Hotel, Jl. Pantai Kuta 1 (☎270 535). Open M-Th 7:30am-4:30pm, F 7:30am-5pm, Sa-Su 9am-1pm. Several airlines have offices at the airport. Private tourist offices offer reservation services.

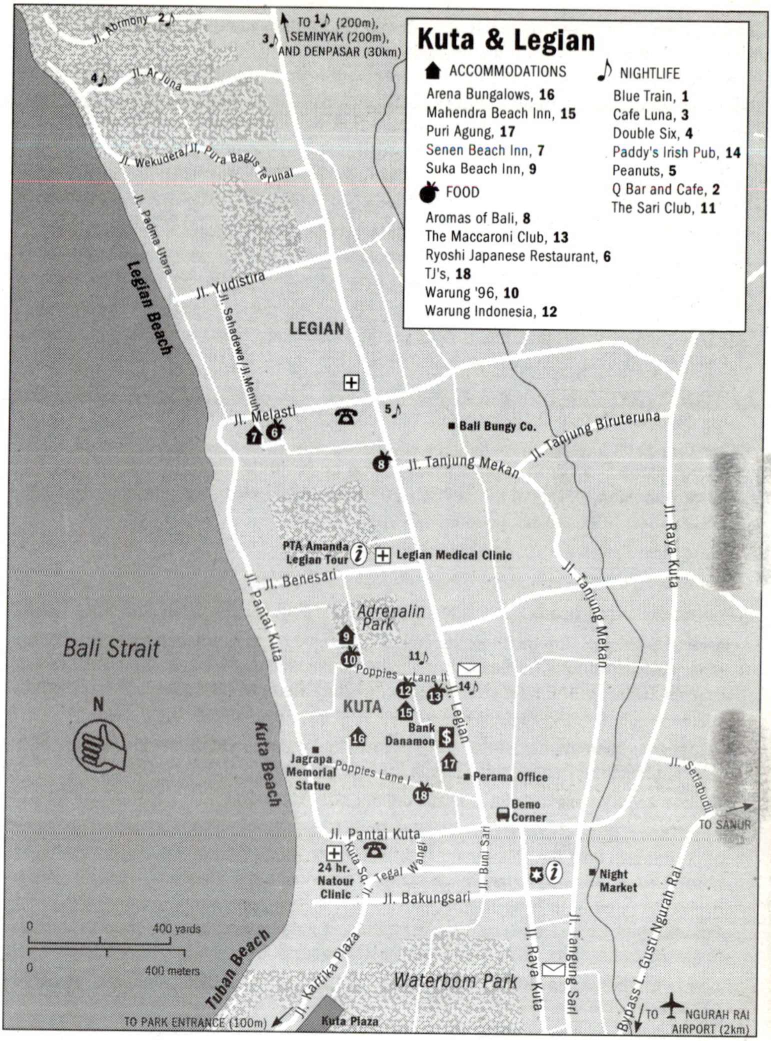

Local Transportation: Bemo run from the *bemo* corner along Jl. Pantai Kuta to the beach and **Legian.** Catch *bemo* to Denpasar's **Tegal Station** (30min.) on Jl. Tanjung Sari or from the corner of Jl. Raya Kuta/Imam Bonjol (Rp1000). **Perama,** Jl. Legian 39, has **buses** to destinations on **Bali, Lombok,** and **Java.**

Rentals: Cars can be rented by the day at most tour and travel agencies and hotels. You don't need an international driver's license to rent the car, but chances are you'll be asked to present one at one of the many check-points in the area.

ORIENTATION AND PRACTICAL INFORMATION

Kilometers long but only a couple of blocks wide, Kuta sprawls along the beach from **Tuban** in the south to **Legian** in the north. Most of the action is between **Jl. Pantai Kuta** and **Jl. Legian,** the main north-south streets. They're connected by one major street, **Jl. Melasti,** and by several small *gang*, only wide enough for *bemo* to

INDONESIA

pass through. The more traveled of these *gang*, **Poppies Lane I** and **Poppies Lane II,** have cheap hotels and restaurants along their cluttered streets. The *bemo* corner is at the intersection of Jl. Legian and Pantai Kuta. In Legian there's an added complication to navigating the already labyrinthine streets. **Jl. Pura Bagus Teruna** is also called **Jl. Werkudera,** and **Jl. Sahadewa** is also **Jl. Menuh**. There's no clear point when one becomes the other; in fact you can walk by five buildings with a Werkudera address, five more with Pura Bagus Teruna on the door and then a couple of Werkudera pop up.

Tourist Offices: Badung Regency Tourism Information Center. Helpful staff gives advice about the best surfing. Free maps and copies of *Bali Plus* guide and entertaining *Hello Bali* and *Bali Travel News*. Open M-Th 7am-2pm, F 7-11am, Sa 7am-12:30pm.

Tours: Agencies spill out every street and alleyway. The large **PT. Amanda Legian Tour,** Jl. Bini Sari (☎754 090), has a helpful office staff and offers tours and trips around Bali, Lombok, and Java. Open daily 8am-8pm.

Immigration Offices: Jl. Airport Ngurah Rai (☎751 038), Tuban. Arrive 1hr. in advance to ensure service. Open M-Th 7am-2pm, F 7-11am, Sa 7am-12:30pm.

Currency Exchange: Moneychangers and banks line **Jl. Legian** and **Jl. Pantai Kuta.** Banks generally close by 2pm weekdays and noon on Sa, and are not open on Su. **Bank Danamon,** Jl. Legian 87 (☎761 620), offers credit card cash advances. Open M-F 8am-3pm. **ATMs** are scattered along Poppies Lane I.

Emergency: Police ☎110. **Ambulance** ☎118.

Police: ☎751 598. On Jl. Raya Tuban, opposite Bank Duta.

Pharmacy: Krisna Usada, next to the Legian Clinic, Jl. Benesari. Open daily 8am-10pm.

Medical Services: Natour Clinic (☎751 361, ext. 110), at the beach end of Jl. Pantai Kuta, next to Natour Kuta Beach Hotel. English-speaking staff. Open 24hr. **Kuta Clinic** (☎753 268), on Jl. Raya Kuta. In Legian, **Legian Medical Clinic** (☎758 503), off Jl. Legian on Gang Benesari, next to Century Plaza. Medi-evacuation. Open 24hr.

Telephones: International **wartel** all over, including Kuta Square Shopping Center. **HCD** booth in Matahari Department Store in Kuta Sq. Open daily 9:30am-10pm.

Internet Access: One Internet cafe per square inch. Get wired.

Post Offices: GPO (☎754 012), set off Jl. Raya Tuban south of central Kuta. Head south on Jl. Bunisari from the *bemo* corner, turn left on Jl. Kartika Plaza/Bakungsari, and right onto Jl. Raya Tuban. Follow orange signs; it's opposite the elementary school. *Poste Restante*. Open M-Th 8am-2pm, F 8am-noon, Sa 8am-1pm. More convenient is **Ida's Postal Agent** (☎751 574), on Jl. Legian Kuta at the intersection with Poppies Lane II. *Poste Restante*. Open M-Sa 8am-8pm. **Postal code:** 80361.

Express Mail: Perama Office, Jl. Legian 39 (☎751 551), is a **DHL**-authorized representative and will forward **FedEx** letters.

INDONESIA

ACCOMMODATIONS

Poppies Lane II is just meters from the surf shops and nightlife, and attracts the younger crowd. **Poppies Lane I** is quieter, and north of Jl. Melasti is quieter still. Cheap accommodation is hard to come by in Legian; however, what does exist exudes the general air of sophistication found in the area.

Senen Beach Inn, Camplung Mas Lane 25 (☎755 470), in an alley off Jl. Melasti. One of the cheapest options in Legian. Unusually friendly and laid-back staff mingles with an older and more European clientele. Quiet garden. Good restaurant. Tea fairy leaves you a fresh thermos every night. Fan, private outside bath. Singles Rp25,000; doubles Rp30,000.

Puri Agung (☎750 054), on Gang Bedugul. Turn onto Poppies Lane I from Jl. Legian, and turn right at T.J.'s; it's a short way down on the right. Central location and gated entrance. Singles with fan and private bath Rp30,000; doubles Rp40,000.

Suka Beach Inn (☎752 793). Turn onto Poppies Lane II from Jl. Legian and then turn right at Adrenalin Park and walk 100m. Extremely popular among surfers. Free storage for boards and bags. Breakfast included. Singles Rp30,000; doubles Rp40,000.

Arena Bungalows (☎752 974), on Poppies Lane I. Walking toward the beach, take the 2nd right past T.J.'s. These once-luxurious bungalows are aging, but the isolated location, pool, and veranda make up for the cracks. Breakfast included. Singles Rp40,000, with A/C Rp60,000; doubles Rp60,000/80,000.

Mahendra Beach Inn (☎752 371). From Jl. Legian take the first left off Poppies Lane II. Secluded *losmen,* with oh-so-classy blue-tile decor. Fan and private bath (extra fans available for Rp1000). Breakfast included. Singles from Rp40,000; doubles Rp50,000. The more expensive rooms are worth it.

FOOD

Kuta's tourist hordes eschew local food and instead eat at a variety of Western-style restaurants (anything from McDonald's fast food to fine European cuisine). The locals, however, will share their own cooking at the night market. (From Jl. Pantai Kuta, walk away from the beach and take the third right; it's 100m down on the left.) For cheaper eats, a few *warung* dot the beach boardwalk.

The Maccaroni Club, Jl. Legian 52. Pretentious. Expensive. To die for. Delicious Balinese-flavored Italian food. Divine desserts Rp18,000. First-rate *gnocchi* Rp33,500. 15min. free Internet with food or drink purchase. MC/V.

Aromas of Bali, on Jl. Legian, 300m south of the intersection with Jl. Melasti. More Bombay than Bali, this venue for "exotic vegetarian cuisine" will tempt even the most carnivorous. Black Goddess (iced coffee and ice cream drink) Rp9700. MC/V.

T.J.'s, on Poppies Lane I, on the side street nearest Jl. Pantai Kuta. Romantic, classy, tropical atmosphere with indoor reflecting pool. The food isn't authentic Mexican but still is fresh and tasty. Enchiladas with crab meat and green chili Rp35,000. MC/V.

Ryoshi Japanese Restaurant, on Jl. Melasti Teron, 300m from the water. Fresh sushi. Spicy tuna roll with fresh *sambal* Rp9500. MC/V.

Warung '96, off Poppies Lane II. Serves burgers and way too much Backstreet Boys. Join the surfers for a King Sized Burger (with beef, bacon, ham, pineapple, egg, and cheese) Rp7500. Open daily 7am-midnight.

Warung Indonesia, on Poppies Lane II, the first left from J. Legion. Fresh Indonesian food. Entrees Rp8000.

ACTIVITIES

If you're a surfer, welcome home. If you aren't, now is the time to become one. While the surf is relatively safe, the quality and size selection of boards for rent is rather poor. **Motor boats** regularly go from **Kuta Beach** to the airport reefs (Rp10,000, but don't pay full price in advance to ensure a quick pickup). Swing by **Tubes Surf Bar and Restaurant** and pick up a free tide chart or drop in on a conversation on where the best waves are crashing. (☎753 510. Open daily 10am-midnight.)

If "getting crazy barrel" is not your thing, Kuta will still get your adrenalin pumping. With four **bungee-jumping** towers, a **waterslide park,** several **billiard halls,** and a few **arcades,** all's fun and games in this little paradise. **Waterbom Park,** on Jl. Kartika Plaza in Tuban, a 5min. walk south from the *bemo* corner, has waterslides, a wave pool, and masseurs. (☎755 676. US$15; massage extra. Open daily 9am-6pm.) Bungee-jumping packages are available at **A.J. Hackett** (☎730 666), next to Double Six Nightclub; **Bali Bungy Co.,** on Jl. Pura Puseh (☎752 658; open 9am-7pm); and **Bungee in Bali** (☎941 102), 30min. away in Gianyar. Bungee in Bali drops jumpers over a waterfall; the others do it over a pool. **Adrenalin Park,** on Jl. Bina Sari 69 in Legian, also offers jumps. (☎757 841. Open noon-7pm.)

NIGHTLIFE

Kuta's nightlife is legendary. The bars are packed every night from midnight to dawn, when the revelers take a break to surf and sleep before starting again the next night. The Legian and Seminyak scenes are slightly older, trendier, and gay-friendly, while Kuta's bars and clubs tend to be popular with hormonal Aussie college kids. Join the rambunctious few for the Kuta-Legian happy hour (6-8pm) for substantially cheaper booze.

Double Six (☎251 266), in north Legian, at the beach end of Jl. Arjuna. Trendy place with hefty cover (Rp40,000; includes 1 drink) attracts disco sophisticates. Mixed crowd boogies to Euro-house/trance music. Open midnight-dawn.

Q Bar and Cafe, on Jl. Abimony off Jl. Rayo Seminyak in Seminyak. Gay-friendly establishment with nightly dancing, a clothing boutique, and occasional fashion shows.

Cafe Luna (☎730 805), in north Legian on Jl. Raya Seminyak, 100m north of Jl. Padman Bagus Teruna. Salsa with live bands (T and Th 10pm-midnight) or go-go dancers (Sa midnight). Mixed crowd. Drinks Rp20,000-30,000.

Blue Train, on Jl. Raya Basangkasa No. 28, in Seminyak. Best jazz on Bali. Bands vary throughout the week. Open Tu-Su 11am-2am.

The Sari Club (☎754 903), near the corner of Poppies Lane II and Legian. Aussie surfers and beach-bunnies love this place; it's always packed by midnight, and single males line up outside. Tiki bar atmosphere and top 40 playlist.

Paddy's Irish Pub (☎752 363), opposite the Sari Club on Jl. Legian. Standard dance club plays standard house tunes for a standard crowd. Of course, that doesn't mean it isn't hopping every night. Cheap drinks. Open daily 11am-3am.

Peanuts (☎754 149) attracts a fast crowd looking to hook up. In high season it hosts a pub crawl (Tu, Sa); cover includes transport, entrance fees, and drop-off at the end. Otherwise, Peanuts is just Sari Club overflow.

INDONESIA

DAYTRIP FROM KUTA

TANAH LOT

From Kuta Beach, with the water on your left, hike 4½hr. along the coast. Sharp rocks necessitate short detours from the beach, but paths are easy to find and quickly lead back to the beach. Bring plenty of water and sunscreen and try to leave early (6am) to avoid the hot midday sun. From Tanah Lot, it's a circuitous bemo *trip back to Kuta: take one to Kediri (20min.) to catch another to Denpasar's Ubung Terminal. From there, take another to Tegal Station, where large minibuses leave constantly for Kuta. Be sure to get to Tanah Lot before 4pm, as* bemo *run unpredictably after that. To do the trip in reverse,* bemo *it to Tanah Lot and walk along the water back to Kuta with the sun on your back.*

In the 16th-century, the Brahman priest Danghyang Nirartha was so impressed by Tanah Lot's beauty that he convinced locals to build a temple. If he saw today what became of it, he would probably regret his decision. The temple, whose name means "Temple of the Earth in the Sea," is dwarfed by the tourist infrastructure around it. Cafes, food stalls, and souvenir shops compete for tourists' attention and photo-snapping tour groups swarm. To avoid the hordes of tourists, make the trip a morning pilgrimage.

UBUD ☎0361

A deluge of foreigners coming to landlocked Ubud to experience "authentic" Balinese culture has gentrified the city, spawning tasteful boutiques and cafes, cozy bungalows, world-class art museums, and Bali's finest restaurants. This also means that villages and rice paddies have been inaccurately preserved for the tourists. Despite all its pandering to outsiders, however, Ubud remains a lovely, charming city and, with a keen eye, still a Balinese one.

TRANSPORTATION

Local Transportation: Bemo congregate in front of markets and on major streets. In theory, *bemo* colors designate destinations, but this system doesn't always work. Brown *bemo* go south to **Batubulan** (40min.), where connections can be made to other cities. Orange *bemo* go to **Gianyar** (15min.), where connections can be made to: **Amlapura** (1½hr.); **Besakih** (1½hr.); **Candidasa** (1½hr.); **Klungkung** (1hr.); each ride is Rp2000. Shops and tourist centers offer **shuttle bus** services; departure times and fares are listed on storefronts. Fares vary from company to company. Destinations include: **airport/Kuta** (1½hr.); **Candidasa/Padangbai; Lovina** (2½hr.); **Sanur** (1hr.). Tourist offices also rent **bicycles** (Rp20,000) and **motorcycles** (Rp30,000).

ORIENTATION AND PRACTICAL INFORMATION

Ubud's main drag, **Jl. Raya Ubud**, runs east-west through the town's tourist center. Most major roads are perpendicular to Jl. Raya Ubud. On the west side of town, **Jl. Monkey Forest (Jl. Warana Wana)** runs alongside the **market** to Ubud's **monkey forest.** There it makes a U-turn and becomes **Jl. Hanoman,** which leads back to Jl. Raya Ubud east of the market. North of Jl. Raya Ubud, **Jl. Raya Peliatan** becomes **Jl. Raya Andong/Tegalalang,** which runs past the **police station** toward Kintamani. The market also serves as a **bemo terminal.**

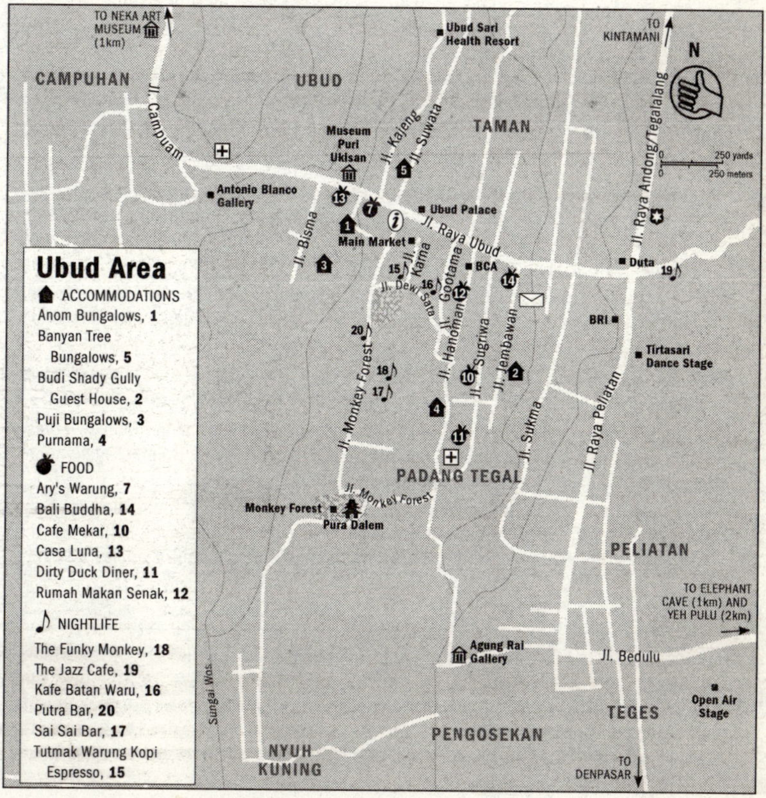

Tourist Offices: Ubud Tourist Information (☎973 285), on Jl. Raya Ubud. Provides performance schedules and workshop info. Books Perama buses 1 day in advance. Open daily 8am-7:30pm. Many **private tourist information centers** offer transport, car and bicycle rentals, guides, and other services.

Currency Exchange: Bank BNI, Jl. Monkey Forest 2 (☎875 986). Open M-F 8am-2:30pm. Many **ATMs** along Jl. Raya Ubud. Moneychangers abound.

English-language bookstores: Along **Jl. Raya Ubud. Ary's Book Shop** sells maps, novels and books on Bali. Open daily 8am-10pm.

Markets: At the corner of Jl. Raya Ubud and Jl. Monkey Forest. Fruit and vegetable sales from dawn to dusk.

Emergency: Police ☎110. **Ambulance** ☎118.

Police: ☎975 316. On Jl. Raya Andong.

Pharmacies: Ubud Farma (☎974 214), on Jl. Raya Ubud opposite the post office. **Branch** (☎976 149), on Jl. Monkey Forest. Both open daily 8am-9:30pm.

Medical Services: Ubud Clinic, Jl. Raya Campuhan 36 (☎974 911), toward Campuhan. **Legian Clinic 5 Ubud** (☎976 457), on a small alley off the south end of Jl. Monkey Forest. Housecalls. English-spoken. Both **open 24hr.**

Telephones: 24hr. HCD booths at the post office and main Ubud market. **Telkom Offices** opposite Duta Bank on Jl. Raya Ubud and at Ary's Warung on Jl. Raya Ubud. **Wartel** on Jl. Raya Ubud and on Jl. Monkey Forest. **Information** ☎108.

Internet Access: Internet cafes line every street and alley-way (Rp250 per min.).

Post Office: Kantor Pos (☎975 764), on Jl. Jembawan off Jl. Raya. *Poste Restante.* Open M-Th 8am-2pm, F 8-11am, Sa 8am-12:30pm. **Postal code:** 80571.

ACCOMMODATIONS

Thanks to a large number of bungalows and cheap, clean lodgings in central Ubud, it's hard to go wrong. Signs on the main road and Jl. Monkey Forest direct travelers to several dozen establishments. Breakfast is usually included.

Puji Bungalows (☎977 493), on Jl. Bisma. Facing the tourist office, turn right and take the first left; it's 200m down. Spacious bungalows with individual porches overlooking rice paddies. Removed from the street. Screened rooms with overhead fan and private bath. Singles Rp35,000; doubles Rp45,000.

Banyan Tree Bungalows, on Jl. Suwata, across from the palace. Roomy bungalows clad in some of Ubud's finest art. Screened rooms with porch, writing desk, tea, and coffee. Singles Rp35,000; doubles Rp45,000.

Anom Bungalows (☎978 491), on a small lane off Jl. Raya Ubud. Large bungalows with ceiling fans and torn mosquito screens. Singles Rp20,000; doubles Rp30,000.

Purnama (☎978 371), at the end of Jl. Hanoman heading toward the Monkey Forest. Rooms open onto a lush garden. Clean rooms with verandas in a Balinese-style home. Tea included. Singles Rp50,000; doubles Rp60,000.

Budi Shady Gully Guest House (☎976 027), on Jl. Jembawan. A 5min. walk from the intersection with Jl. Raya Ubud. Serene jungle views overlooking a river. Family-run and impeccably well-maintained. Pricey but old rooms with outside bath. Doubles US$10.

FOOD

Ubud lives up to its reputation for having Bali's best food. Unlike in other Balinese destinations, Ubud's international cuisine may beat out local fare for ingenuity and flavor. Trendy cafes, health food, and vegetarian restaurants are popular among expats—their quality and selection leave no doubt as to why. Tino Drug Store, on Jl. Raya Ubud near the Tourist Information Center, has a supermarket. (☎975 020. Open daily 8am-10pm.)

Casa Luna, on Jl. Raya. Not only the best bread in Bali, but also incredible entrees and desserts. Outdoor patio overlooks dense tropical forest. English-language movies shown most nights at 7pm. "Killer brownie" concoction Rp9000. MC/V.

Bali Buddha, on Jl. Jembawan, opposite the post office. Garish, bright hippie-esque colors and tasty, trendy drinks. 3-level sitting area and a sandbox for the kids. Banana-date soy milkshake Rp6500. Open daily 7am-10pm.

Dirty Duck Diner, on Jl. Hanoman opposite Purnama Accommodation. Artsy types eat black Russian pie (Rp18,500) and sirloin steak (Rp49,500) on platforms above a tropical garden, complete with pools and streams. Romantic dinners by candlelight with chamber music playing in the background. Open daily 10am-11pm. MC/V.

Ary's Warung, on Jl. Raya Ubud by the Tourist Information Office. Classy atmosphere and walls covered with black and white photos from Ary's backpacker days. Expensive, though *paella* sets you back only Rp35,000. Open daily 7:30am-1am. MC/V.

Cafe Mekar, Jl. Sugriwa 33. Minimal atmosphere, but cheap and hearty Indonesian food. Entrees under Rp15,000. Open daily 10am-11pm.

Rumah Makan Senak, Jl. Hanoman No. 7. Cheap, clean, and basic, with *padang* (Sumatran) style sauces. Rice with tofu Rp1500, with beef Rp3500.

SIGHTS

Ubud, with its classy cafes, up-market souvenir shops, scenic boulevards, and nearby villages, is one giant sight in itself. Once you're done with the city, however, more treats await.

MONKEY FOREST. Ubud's most popular site is a well-preserved miniature jungle in the middle of the city. Giant trees loom on either side of the trail, providing cool shade for humans and a habitat for the 200 monkeys that live here. The monkeys aren't shy, so the problem isn't spotting them but keeping them from stealing your hat, sunglasses, and wallet. Inside the Monkey Forest is Ubud's Pura Dalem ("Temple of the Dead"), flanked by statues of ogres devouring children. Paths lead from the forest to southern villages, including Nyuhkuning, which houses a woodcarving museum. *(On the south bend of Jl. Monkey Forest. Open daily 8am-5:30pm. Rp3000.)*

NEKA ART MUSEUM. Set in idyllic grounds overlooking a river valley, this museum displays an extensive collection of Balinese and Bali-inspired art. One of the museum's annexes, the Arie Smit Pavilion, houses work by the Dutch expat and examples of the "Young Artist" style he established. The photography archive collection preserved photographs of Balinese ceremonies from colonial times, while its back room houses a megalomaniacal tribute to the museum's founder, Suteja Neka. All paintings are labeled in English. *(Follow Jl. Raya Ubud east until it crosses the river and becomes Jl. Raya Campuhan. Walk 1km along Jl. Raya Campuhan until it turns right. ☎975 074. Open daily 9am-5pm. Rp10,000.)*

ANTONIO BLANCO GALLERY. The former home of the "Dali of Bali" now showcases his art. Antonio Blanco's style was above all eccentric, expressive, exotic, and highly erotic. The house itself is a great exhibit; the architecture is Balinese done with over-the-top pastel colors and a giant archway. *(Facing the Tourist Information Office, turn right down Jl. Raya Ubud and take the first left before the suspension bridge. ☎975 502. Open daily 8am-5pm. Rp10,000.)*

AGUNG RAI MUSEUM OF ART. Opened in 1996, ARMA holds examples of every traditional style of Balinese painting as well as Bali's only works of the Russian-German artist Walter Spies. An open-air stage hosts traditional dances every night at 6pm. *(500m south of the intersection of Jl. Monkey Forest and Jl. Hanoman. ☎976 659. Open daily 9am-6pm. Rp10,000.)*

MUSEUM PURI LUKISAN. Built to preserve Balinese art heritage, the museum focuses on traditional painting styles and woodcarvings. At the center of the museum compound is a lotus pool set in a garden complete with elegant shrine islands. *(Opposite the Tourist Information Office. ☎975 136. Open daily 8am-4pm. Rp10,000.)*

ENTERTAINMENT

PERFORMANCES. Dance, *gamelan*, and other types of performances are held nightly at temples and stages. Ubud's shows are well-rehearsed and elaborately staged. The more natural and traditional performances, however, are performed in the surrounding area. Ubud Tourist Information Center has a list of performances. (Shows 7pm. Tickets sold at the Tourist Information Center, tour agencies, or on the street. For shows in neighboring villages, the Tourist Information Center provides free transport). Particularly worthwhile are the *wayang kulit* (shadow puppet show) and the powerful *kecak* (monkey) dance, in which men beat out rhythms on their bare chests.

WORKSHOPS AND CLASSES. Ganesha Bookstore, on Jl. Raya Ubud, offers **gamelan lessons;** no previous musical knowledge is required. (☎963 59. Rp45,000.) **Balinese dance courses** are available at **Dewi Sekar Ayu,** Jl. Hanoman 26. With your back to Jl. Dewi Sita, turn right at the intersection with Jl. Hanoman and walk 100m; it's on the left. Take away a lasting memento from the **batik course** offered at the **Crackpot Gallery** on Jl. Monkey Forest. With the football field on the left, the Crackpot is 100m down on the left. Design your own T-shirt or cushion cover. (☎973 411. Open daily 9am-8pm.) The **Meditation Shop,** on Jl. Monkey Forest 400m from the Monkey Forest, allows visitors to observe **meditation workshops** for free. Stop by for details or join the daily 6-7pm meditation. (☎976 206. Open 5-9:30pm.) **Casa Luna Restaurant** offers **Balinese cooking classes.** Sign up early for the Tuesday **market tour,** as spots are limited to eight. (M, W 10am-2pm, Tu 8am-noon. Rp100,000, includes 1 meal.) **Massages** and **skin treatments** are available at competitive prices. De-stress and rejuvenate at **Ubud Sari Health Resort,** Jl. Kajeng 35, at the end of the road. (Massages US$12 per hr.) A health-food restaurant and juice bar serves high-quality food. (☎974 393. Open daily 8am-8pm.)

SPORTS. Although most of Ubud's draws are cultural or artistic, rafting and other adventure sport options exist for thrill seekers. Contact **Sobek** (☎287 059), **Unda Adventures** (Jl. Raya Ubud No. 33; ☎977 169), or **Bali Adventure Tours** (☎751 292). You can also arrange whitewater rafting tours in the area. Day trips includes transportation and a meal (about US$60).

MAY THE BIGGEST COCK WIN On the day of the fight, the cock-master prepares a concoction of meat and purified jackfruit–a sure mix to thicken the blood and make the cock stand strong, tall, and ready. Cockfights in Ubud are common, but they take on additional meaning on the day of *tabah rah*–literally "pouring of the blood"–a sacred event in which sacrifices feed the demons. After the *Demangku* (lay priest) gives the initial offering of rice wine, it's down to business. The masters pass their cocks around to be prodded, pulled, and plucked, so spectators can evaluate the cock's strength and ferocity. The owner then attaches the 10-15cm long *taji* (blade) to the cock's leg. From there, it's a winner-take-all pool between the two owners. Bets are placed in codes: the cry of "cok, cok, cok" in quick succession means 4:3 odds that the underdog will win. As the gong is struck, the cocks fly at each other in a frenzy of feathers and feet until the fatal blow is struck. The *pemsang taji* (master of the winning cock) wins the leg of the losing cock with the *taji* still attached. Hoisted up high, the winning cock lives to fight another day; the loser becomes dinner. Though gruesome, the relationship between cock and man is not viewed as inhumane. All cocks are eventually sacrificed, they reason; the process by which the sacrifice occurs is irrelevant.

NIGHTLIFE

An artsy town inhabited by bohemian tourists, Ubud's nightlife isn't as intense or wild as Kuta's and tends to be more cafe- than bar-oriented. The coffee shops on Jl. Dewi Sata are popular; both **Tutmak Warung Kopi Espresso** (☎975 754; open daily 9am-11pm) and **Kafe Batan Waru** (☎977 528; open daily 8am-midnight) fill up after dance performances end. A few places on Jl. Monkey Forest pit American movies against the Balinese dancing. For the bar-goer, the **Sai Sai Bar** plays reggae and rock-and-roll for a slightly older crowd. The **Funky Monkey** is known for its mysterious trance atmosphere, where patrons sit under a black-lit, star-studded ceiling. (☎390 3729. Open daily 11am-1am.) The **Jazz Cafe** is packed nightly and plays pop, jazz, and blues. (Open daily 11am-midnight.) As the evening winds down and the night starts, crowds head to **Putra Bar.** (Open daily from 11am until the last person leaves.)

DAYTRIPS FROM UBUD

Villages and rice paddies are within 1km of Ubud, and any road leading away from the main drag will reward the explorer with breathtaking scenery.

ON FOOT. In 2½-3½ hr., you can take a decent walking tour of Ubud's surroundings. Start from the west end of Jl. Raya Ubud, circle through the picturesque landscape, and eventually get back onto Jl. Kajeng near the Ubud Sari Health Resort. With your back to Museum Puri Lukisan, walk down Jl. Raya Ubud until you come to Abangan Bungalows. Walk up the steep driveway and to the left side of the main building along a small trail that runs parallel to a stream. The trail will bear left; follow it for 30-45min. and take the first right. Take a left on the trail that leads down a small hill for a few steps and then cross the bridge on the right. Turn right and follow this trail the rest of the way. If you get lost, ask someone, *"Bagimana ke Jalan Kajeng?"* ("How do I get to Jl. Kajeng?") or *"Ke Ubud?"* ("To Ubud?").

ORGANIZED WALKS. It's also possible to join an organized walking tour. A guided **Herb Walk** (☎975 051), led by husband-and-wife team Lilir and Westi, explores native plants and medicinal herbs (US$18 includes herbal teas, drinks, and snacks). Another possibility is the **Bali Bird Walk** (☎975 609) offered by an Englishman, Victor Mason (US$3, including walk, lunch, and bird guide).

The road that connects Ubud to Denpasar via Batubulan links a string of **craft villages**: **Mas** (wood carving), **Sukawati** (wind chimes and baskets), **Celuk** (silver work), and **Batubulan** (stone carving). Sukawati is also the site of an early morning produce market. Brown *bemo* pass through these villages, offering views of artists working on open verandas. Alternatively, it's an easy downhill ride by bike (bring string to tie the bike to the *bemo* back).

GOA GAJAH (ELEPHANT CAVE). There never were elephants on Bali; Goa Gajah gets its name from the floppy-eared demon carved around its entrance. One section contains idols of Ganesha, the other *hingham* (phallic representation) and the Hindu trinity: Brahma, Vishnu, and Shiva. A thousand years of existence have taken their toll on Goa Gajah's carvings—many appear worn. Whether it's worth the hassle of pushy souvenir hawkers is up to you. *(1km outside of Ubud on the bemo-plied road to Gianyar. Take a red or green* bemo *Rp2000.)*

YEH PULU. For the time being, the bas-relief of Yeh Pulu is vendor-free. The walk there passes an ungentrified Balinese neighborhood and terraced rice fields. *(1km from Gao Gajah. From the entrance to Goa Gajah, walk away from Ubud; the way is clearly marked by signs on the road.)*

GUNUNG KAWI. **Tampaksiring village's** Gunung Kawi is a mysterious complex of tombs amid a central temple. The river divides the two cliff faces, hewn from rock in the 11th century. The area left of the stone archway is thought to be the burial site of King Anak Wungsu's four concubines. Across the river are the tombs of the king and his four wives. Beside the royal tombs lie a courtyard and a series of caves and rock passages. Gunung Kawi is best seen in the early morning or late afternoon, when visitors will share the grounds with only local villagers who bathe in the river instead of the hordes of tourists that flock to the area during the day. **Titra Empul,** at the north end of Tampaksiring village, is a temple around natural spring pools. The holy water is said to have therapeutic power. *(Take an orange or blue* bemo *for Gianyar and get off in the town of Bedulu. From there, take a* bemo *or* ojek *north to Tampaksiring. If you bike, be prepared for an arduous 15km ride uphill that lasts about 1hr. Each sight Rp3100. Where necessary, sarong and sash are provided free of charge.)*

ANIMAL PARKS. Two animal parks were recently built in **Singapadu.** The **Bali Reptile Park** (Rimba Reptil) features reptiles from around the world, including cobras and komodo dragons, as well as a petting zoo with huge pythons and iguanas. *(☎299 344. Open daily 8:30am-6pm. Rp57,000.)* Next door is the **Bali Bird Park** (Taman Burung), which has exquisite landscaping and fantastic birds, including the endangered Bali starling. *(Catch a* bemo *toward Batubulan from Jl. Raya Ubud and tell the driver you want to go to the "tempat burung, di Singapadu" (the bird place in Singapadu). The trip takes 30min., and the* bemo *will probably let you off at the turn-off to Celuk. From here it's a 20min. walk to the parks. Private vans may be easier to get there or back, but bargain hard; don't pay more than 5 times what the* bemo *ride would cost. ☎299 352. Open daily 8am-7pm. Rp57,000. Combination ticket for both parks Rp103,000.)*

SINGARAJA ☎0362

Singaraja is Bali's second city—sleepier and more traditional than Denpasar. Originally designed to be the capital of Bali and neighboring Nusa Tenggara, the once-important colonial port must settle for being capital of the Buleleng (north) region. With few tourist sights and little tourist infrastructure, most tourists value Singaraja for its big-city services and for its function as the transport hub of the region.

INDONESIA

TRANSPORTATION

Buses leave from **Banyuasri Terminal,** on the west end of Jl. A. Yani, for **Lovina** (10min., Rp1000). **Minibuses** leave for **Gilimanuk** (2hr.) and **Denpasar** (2½hr.). **Sukasada Terminal** at south end of Singaraja has buses to: **Denpasar, Bedugul/Danau Bratan** (1hr.), and **Gitgit Waterfall** (15min.). **Penarukan Terminal,** on Jl. Surapati on east side of town, has buses to: **Amlapura** (2½hr.), **Kintamani** (2hr.), **Klungkung** (3hr.), and **Yeh Sanih** (1¼hr.). *Bemo* shuttle between bus terminals until 6pm.

ORIENTATION AND PRACTICAL INFORMATION

Singaraja is bordered to the north by the harbor and to the south by the mountains. The main street, **Jl. A. Yani,** runs parallel to the harbor. The Banuasri **bus terminal,** where *bemo* from Lovina stop, is on the west end of Jl. A. Yani. *Bemo* from Den-

DEMON MANICURE Once upon a time, a great demon assembled his finest warriors and assaulted the gates of heaven. A fierce battle raged, and the gods triumphed over the demons. Instead of destroying them, however, the gods forced them to swear an oath of service. As a sign of submission, the demons had all but one of the claws on each of their hands shorn. Demon statues guarding temples and bridges thus have one long claw on each arm. The practice exists among Balinese people as well as Balinese demons; people both young and old have one long fingernail to signify that they are practitioners of white magic. In theory, as a person grows in evil, all of their fingernails lengthen and turn black.

pasar stop at the Sukasada terminal on the south end of town. Most commercial activity is centered on the east side of town at the intersections of Jl. A. Yani with **Jl. Diponegoro** and **Jl. Imam Bonjol.** Other points of interest are on the south side of town on **Jl. Veteran.**

Tourist Office: Dinas Pariwisata, Jl. Veteran 23 (☎251 41), near the corner of Jl. Gajah Mada, on the southeast side. Ask for Pak Putu Tastra Wijaya and get free maps, brochures, and plenty of advice. Open M-F 7am-2pm, Sa 7am-noon.

Currency Exchange: BCA Bank (☎237 66), on Jl. A. Yani, east of Jl. Diponegoro. MC/V cash advance. **24hr. ATM** (Cirrus/PLUS/V). Open M-F 8am-2pm.

Markets: Buleleng Market, at the corner of Jl. Veteran/Semeru and Jl. Gajah Mada/ Mayor Metra, sells fruit. **Pasar Anyar,** off Jl. Dr. Sutomo on north side, sells fruit and other foods. **Tirta Dewata** supermarket, intersection of Jl. A. Yani and Jl. Pramuka.

Emergency: Police ☎110. **Ambulance** ☎118.

Police: ☎225 10. On Jl. Pramuka, south of Jl. A. Yani, opposite Jagat Nata temple.

Pharmacies: Wijaya Kusuma Apotik, Jl. Ngurah Rai 23 (☎228 90). Open 24hr.

Medical Services: Singaraja Private Hospital, Jl. Cendrawasih 5 (☎262 77), 50m off Jl. A Yani on the left. English-speaking staff. **Open 24hr.**

Telephones: Wartel Kopegtel, Jl. Gajah Mada 154. Collect or cash international calls. **HCD** phone outside. Open 24hr. **Wartel,** Jl. A Yani 124.

Post Offices: Jl. Gajah Mada 156 (☎217 88), intersection with Jl. A. Yani. **Internet access.** Poste Restante. Open M-Sa 8am-3pm, Su 9am-1pm. **Postal code:** 81113.

ACCOMMODATIONS AND FOOD

While Lovina is better promoted and more traveler-friendly, Singaraja has a some options for a good night's sleep. At the east end of the main strip, several *losmen* have fans, cold showers, and laundry services. **Wijaya Hotel,** Jl. Sudirman 74 (☎219 15), has the most options—from basic rooms with fan and shared bath (singles Rp20,000; doubles Rp 25,000) to nicer ones with private *mandi* and fan (Rp30,000; Rp35,000) to plush suites with A/C, TV, and a phone (Rp70,000; Rp75,000). **Hotel Sentral,** Jl. A. Yani 48, offers clean basic rooms without flush toilets. (☎218 96. Singles Rp25,000; double Rp30,000. With A/C and flush toilets Rp60,000; Rp70,000.) With your back to the post office, turn right and walk 15min. Slightly better rooms with firmer beds can be found across the road at **Losmen Duta Karya,** Jl. A. Yani 59. (☎214 67. Doubles with fan Rp35,000; rooms with A/C start at Rp60,000.)

Jet-Z (say "Jet-Zet") **Cafe** on Jl. Seruni, 100m in from Jl. Achmed Yani, is Bali's only punk-rock cafe. Run by the drummer of the Singaraja garage-band Jet-Z, it's a great place to listen to NoFX and reminisce about Kurt Cobain while snacking on cheap and tasty Indonesian food (most items under Rp7000).

For Singaraja seafood, head to **Ikan Laut Warung,** Jl. Gajah Mada 65, to enjoy a sampler plate with spicy fish at super-cheap prices. Hindu and Muslim *warung* congregate by the harbor, to form a mini-food-market offering a wide selection of seafood dishes and fresh fruit dishes. (Open daily 9am-9pm.) With the mountains behind you, follow Jl. Diponegroro to its north edge, then turn right and cross the bridge. Grab a cheap plate of *nasur lampur* and take it to a local vantage point, where you can watch the setting sun over the harbor.

SIGHTS

Singaraja is off the well-beaten tourist track, and its sights get few outside visitors. While this means you'll often have the place all to yourself, it also means the temples of Singaraja aren't expecting you. They are poorly maintained and few among the staff (if there is anyone around at all) speak English.

GEDONG KIRTYA. Gedong Kirtya holds Indonesia's largest collection of palm-leaf manuscripts. The palm-leaves are etched, then covered in charcoal to make the

ART COLONY Bali attracts loads of Westerners—not all of whom leave. Expat artists are a fixture here. A tour around the Ubud galleries will acquaint you with Antonio Blanco, Walter Spies, and Arie Smit, all first-rate European artists who came into their own on Bali, then never left. Smit was taken by local artists, Blanco married a local, but it's undeniable that the culture and beauty of Bali were conducive to great art. Even now the island teems with artists: Perry Farrel (lead singer of Porno for Pyros) devoted an album to his Bali experience, and the spiritual depth of the island and its lush natural beauty has made permanent visitors out of the French Buddhist photographer Jacques Guyot and the American Yogic Furniture designer Nathan Winsor.

writing legible. More a depository than a museum, there's little here. A better place to see *lontor* produced is the Tengaran village near Candidasa. *(Right next to the tourist center, on Jl. Veteran next to the tourist office. ☎226 45. Open M-F 7am-noon.)*

PURA DALEM. sits Singaraja's Pura Dalem (Temple of the Dead). The *pura* displays a wall of fantastic reliefs depicting the Balinese *sorga* (heaven) and *neraka* (hell), and the earthly behavior associated with both. The intricate carvings of demons on the walls of the temple proper more than make up for the weeds in the courtyard. It can be viewed at anytime. Next to Pura Dalem, the **Balinese Hindu Cemetery** is open to visitors. It is essential to the Balinese that the body be cremated, as it is the soul's way to reincarnation. Because of the high cost of cremation ceremonies in Bali, many Hindus are buried in temporary graves until their families can afford to have their corpses retrieved and cremated. Perhaps because these graves are not final resting places, the graveyard has an overgrown, wild-garden character to it. Wild flowers, birds, animals and insects surround the headstones. *(With your back to Gedong Kirtya, turn right down Jl. Veteran and, 60m later, left down Jl. Gajah Mada. Pura Dalem is 200m ahead on the right.)*

TEMPLE SUCI SU SAN YEE. The fascinating *tridarma* temple **Tempat Suci Su San Yee** contains three altars, one for Taoism, Buddhism, and Confucianism, hence the *tridarma* ("3 truths"). Since 1985 the Chinese-style temple has served as a center for traditional healing for people of all faiths. *(From the cemetery, 10min. farther up Jl. Gajah Mada, around house #97 on the left. ☎213 22.)*

OTHER SIGHTS. Balinese Hindus believe that the divine is everywhere and that certain places and images are supercharged with spirit. **Pura Agung Jagat Natha,** the largest temple of its kind on Bali, is one such place. *(Follow Jl. Gajah Mada for 120m more and take a left. Open daily 6am-8pm. Sarongs available to borrow.)* According to legend, the 200-year-old **Chinese temple** was impervious to shells fired by the Japanese during WWII. In April 1998, when an angry mob set fire to it, only the meeting room was destroyed; the temple stands unscathed. *(From the tourist information office, walk to the left on Jl. Gajah Mada for 10min.; it's on the right.)* **Pura Dalem Jagaraga** has comic carvings in its soft rock walls. *(12km southeast of Singaraja. The temple can be reached by* bemo.*)*

INDONESIA

LOVINA ☎0362

Get it all in Lovina: multicolor sunsets, great snorkeling, superb dolphin-watching, a black lava beach, exquisite Balinese seafood, and cheap accommodations. It's a refuge for ocean-goers who want to trade in the crowded beach scene for calmer waters and relaxed Balinese hospitality. Locals try to maintain the quiet village atmosphere, but as tourist dollars roll in, loud nightlife and beach-swelling hecklers are an ever-rising threat to Lovina's serenity.

TRANSPORTATION

Buses: *Bemo* run west to **Gilimanuk,** where a ferry goes to **East Java** and **Singaraja;** from here connections are available to anywhere in Bali. **Perama** (☎411 04), on the main road next to B.U. Warung, goes to: **Denpasar/Kuta** (2hr., Rp40,000); **Candidasa**

(3hr., Rp50,000); **Gunung Batur** (2hr., Rp20,000); **Ubud** (2½hr., Rp40,000). For the cheapest rates but rougher, longer travel, take a *bemo* to Singaraja's **Banyuasri Terminal** and catch public bus connections there.

Rentals: Motorcycle and **bicycle** rentals available with uniform prices. **Su-kha Rentals** (☎411 56), on Jl. Bhina Ria, rents bikes for Rp10,000 per day. Open daily 8am-10pm.

ORIENTATION AND PRACTICAL INFORMATION

"Lovina" describes an 8km stretch of beach along the Bali Sea. The main road, **Jl. Singaraja,** runs parallel to the beach and is lined with restaurants and hotels. The strip includes several villages. From east to west, they are **Pemaron, Tukadmungga Anturan** (Happy Beach), **Kalibukbuk,** and **Kaliasem** (Lovina). Tourist activity centers on Kalibukbuk and Kaliasem. Marked by a dolphin statue, **Jl. Bhina Ria** is the main road to the beach. A smaller beach road, **Jl. Pantai Mawar,** branches from Jl. Singaraja 300m farther east. In addition, there are many smaller, unnamed beach roads lined with bungalows and restaurants. As Jl. Singaraja leaves town, it heads east to **Singaraja** (10min.) and west to the ferry point of **Gilimanuk** (2hr.) and the **Bali Barat National Park** (1¼hr.).

Tourist Office: ☎419 10. On Jl. Singaraja in Kalibukbuk between B.U. Warung and Malibu Restaurant. Diving information and directions to local sights. Open M-Sa 8am-8pm.

Currency Exchange: Several moneychangers along the main road offer slightly better rates than at Singaraja's banks. Most are open until 5pm. Bank BCA **ATM** on Jl. Singaraja in Kalibukuk (Cirrus/MC/Plus/V).

Emergency: Police ☎110. **Ambulance** ☎118.

Police: ☎419 10. On the main road between Jl. Singaraja and Seririt.

Medical Services: Darma Bakti (☎412 11), on Jl. Singaraja, 1km to the right (with your back to the tourist office). English-speaking doctor. Open M-Sa 9am-noon and 5-7pm. Lovina has no pharmacy, but **Angosaka Mini-Market** (☎411 30), in front of Pasar Kalibukbuk on the main road, sells some medicine. Open daily 8am-10pm.

Telephones: Several **wartel** along the Lovina stretch charge a small fee for international calling cards. **Telkom Wartel Mitsuya** (☎417 25), next to Surya Restaurant, has similar fees. Open daily 8am-midnight.

Internet Access: Internet cafes line Jl. Bhina Ria and they charge Rp300 per min.

Post Office: GPO (☎413 92), on Jl. Singaraja. With your back to tourist office, turn right and walk 20min.; it's on the left. Open M-Sa 8am-2pm.

INDONESIA

ACCOMMODATIONS

Despite the inflationary pressures of the Indonesian economic crisis, tight competition has kept prices down. Rates are uniform, so the hardest choice is whether to stay in Lovina's rowdy late-night bar scene or it's quieter but slightly more expensive resort-style fringes. The region is known for its mosquitoes and for gigolos. Pick up a mosquito coil from a corner store; you're on your own with the gigolos. Expect to pay more during peak season.

Susila 2 Backpackers Hostel (☎410 80), on Jl. Bhina Ria. Best value in town. Clean with mosquito nets, fan, and private bath. Singles Rp30,000; doubles Rp40,000.

Pulesti Beach Hotel (☎410 35), 25m from the beach on the main beach road. Hard to miss; the bright facade opens to a landscaped pool with man-made waterfalls. Singles with fan and mosquito net Rp70,000; doubles with open-air bathroom Rp80,000.

Billibo Beach Cottages (☎413 55), opposite the post office on Lovina's west edge. Owner helps plan fun-filled days. Slightly-more-than-cheap rooms scant meters from the beach with fans and screened windows from Rp75,000.

Hotel Dupa (☎413 84), on the main road opposite the beach, is cheap, clean, and close to the action. The view of rice fields from upper rooms is worth the extra rupiah. Laundry service. Low rooms from Rp20,000; extra Rp15,000 for higher floors.

Mas Bungalows (☎417 73). Facing the tourist information office, walk 1km to the right or catch a *bemo*. Take a left on Jl. Lasiana; it's on the right. Sheltered from downtown but close enough to the hub. Singles Rp35,000; doubles Rp40,000.

FOOD

Although Western dishes are available, Lovina's premier tastebud sensation is Balinese seafood and roasted duck. Establishments offering these local specialties have signs posted on their windows; be sure to order a few hours in advance for dinner. **Kakatu Bar & Restaurant,** on Jl. Bhina Ria right before the beach, has the most international menu in Lovina. Mexican and Thai dishes go for Rp15,000-30,000. (Open daily 8am-11pm.) **Bali Bintang,** on Jl. Bhina Ria, has great people-watching potential with a typical Western/Indonesian menu. (Open daily 8am-11pm.) **Seabreeze Cafe & Restaurant,** also on Bhina Ria, is an unmatched location for sunsets and late-night drinks. (☎411 38. Open daily 8am-midnight.) **Waru Bali,** at the end of Jl. Mawar, is the place for breakfast after chasing dolphins. (☎415 53. Open daily 7am-10pm.) **B.U. Warung,** next door to the Perama office, is cheap and unpretentious, with scrumptious *pepes*, tuna, and lemon papaya juice. (Open noon-9pm.)

SIGHTS AND ENTERTAINMENT

Lovina's main attractions are pre-dawn boat rides to see **dolphins** and midday **snorkeling** excursions. Local fishermen offer early morning rides past the reef for roughly Rp15,000 with hard bargaining. If the dolphins don't show (80% chance they will), the sunrise is a glorious consolation. Lovina's snorkeling is some of Bali's best, and shallow waters make it safe for beginners and children. **Scuba diving** possibilities abound. **Spice Dive** (☎415 09), is a professional, PADI-certified outfit. Facing the tourist information office, head left 500m; it's on the left, opposite Joni's Restaurant. Spice offers full certification courses (4 days US$250), night dives, and dives for beginners (US$45-60). Fishing enthusiasts can rent boats, motorboats, traditional *sanpan* (bamboo-stabilized canoes), and other equipment on the beach. (Fishing with guide Rp20,000.)

Tiga Wasa village, a pleasant 1½hr. walk from the west edge of Lovina, makes ornate bamboo handicrafts. Follow the main road to the west past the post office; the turn-off is clearly marked on the left—it is then a 5km climb uphill. There are no stores, but bamboo items are visible from the road. Once reaching the first house, a pathway to the right leads you to the **Sing Sing Waterfalls** for a swim. There are no signs, but ask and someone will help you. Although no problems have been documented, the village and waterfall are remote, so it is best to visit with a group.

Starting earlier in the night, the best place to catch a film is on top of **Mailaku Bar and Restaurant.** Seats fill up, so get there early. (Shows 6 and 8pm.) Following dinner, the hot, friendly bar in town is **Zigiz,** on Jl. Bhina Ria, with a full bar and live music every night. (Open daily 11am-midnight.) If you're still going strong, it's on to the **Malibu Cafe,** on the main road, for more live music, dancing, and partying until dawn. Malibu offers free pickup from all hotels until midnight.

DAYTRIPS FROM LOVINA

Though bemo transport is both easy and cheap to Lovina's three main excursions, many tourists still charter a car and driver. A full six-person bemo should cost Rp30,000.

GITGIT WATERFALL. The only thing more spectacular than the 40m high waterfall is the kilometer-long line of souvenir stalls. Local legend says that couples who swim together in the pools beneath the falls will soon separate. If you've been looking for a way out, here's your chance. *(Take a bemo from Sukasada Terminal in Singaraja toward Ubung Station (15min., Rp2000). At the sign to Gitgit, walk 1km along the path to the falls. Open daily 8:30am-5pm. Rp3100.)*

BANJAR BUDDHIST MONASTERY. On a forested hilltop with stunning ocean views, the monastery was damaged in the 1976 earthquake that flattened Seririt, but the monks have since repaired it and it now houses Buddha sculptures and a lotus pool. Proper dress is required and can be borrowed from the shop next door. Talking is frowned upon in monastery grounds, and a donation (albeit a small one) is expected. *(Open daily 8am-6pm. Rp3000.)*

BANJAR HOT SPRINGS. The **Banjar Hot Springs** are among manicured gardens and palm trees. *(Catch a* bemo *from Lovina toward Seririt and get off at Dencarik Village (15min.). Grab an* ojek *or* bemo *3km to the monastery; ask the driver to go to "tempat buddha.")*

GUNUNG AGUNG

For the Balinese, Gunung Agung is the religious focus of the universe—the vantage point from which the gods observe human life in Bali and beyond. Some 3142m high and thought to be the son of the larger Mt. Semuru on Java, Gunung Agung dominates east Bali. An active volcano, Gunung Agung erupted most recently in 1963, killing thousands. Many believed the eruption to be a punishment for neglecting religious duty, so high priests were sent to appease the gods at Mt. Semuru. The most sacred temple complex on Bali lies on the southern slope of Gunung Agung, 6km from the village Besakih. Once a year, representatives from every town in Bali come to Besakih, the "mother temple," for the Betara Turun Kabeh ceremony.

TRANSPORTATION. Public **bemo** run from **Klungkung** to **Besakih** (50min., Rp3500). While the official schedule is every half-hour until the last *bemo* at 3pm, it may be necessary to flag down local *ojeks* or trucks. A common place to change *bemo* is at **Redang** between Besakih and Klungkung. Here, *bemo* can be caught to **Selat** (30min., Rp2000).

PRACTICAL INFORMATION. Though most foreign visitors to the area come on package tours from Candidasa and Ubud, tourist facilities do exist. Below the main parking lot, beyond the ticket booth, is a *dinas pariwisata*, or **tourist information bureau.** Arrive by 1pm to ensure that it's open, or make do with maps at the end of the road leading to the temples.

ACCOMMODATIONS AND FOOD. If you're climbing from Besakih, it is more convenient to stay at one of the many unmarked **losmen** that line the street from the car park to the hotel. Ask any local; they will show you where they are. Usually the *mandi* is shared and rooms are noisy, so bargain for a cheap price. Rp15,000 is fair. At the temple, be wary of guides who demand outrageous sums after a 5min. "tour" of the complex, or a 1min. *ojek* ride up to the temple—they will tell you it is 1km.

For those staying the night, food may be found at the base of the mountain, after the parking lot. Hit the *sate ayam* cart before dark for a cheap, filling meal. Fruit and souvenir vendors line the path up to the temple.

SIGHTS. Pura Besakih (The Mother Temple) is the most sacred Balinese sanctuary. The largest temple complex in Bali, consisting of nearly 30 temples, it sits 900m above sea level on the southwest slope of Gunung Agung, affording fantastic views of southern Bali. A pantheon of Hindu gods and goddesses is worshipped at Besakih; Shiva, Brahma, and Vishnu are most important. The Shiva temple is the first and largest. A phalanx of statues protect Shiva; those on the left represent *fandwa* (good spirits), the ones on the right *krawa* (bad spirits). The three gods sit inside the temple, with Shiva in the center, Brahma on the right, and Vishnu on the left. The temple at the far right belongs to Brahma and the one at the far left belongs to Vishnu.

The temple complex is extensive, and the lack of brochures or other English-language tourist information makes hiring a local guide tempting. The same organization that supervises the Gunung Agung guides also manages those at Pura Besakih. The set price is Rp25,000, the only required fee, although the guide may want more than this as a tip or commission or as an extra *ojek* charge if you took the ride up. It is important to note that the organization has a monopoly on tours of Besakih; if you bring an outside guide, you are still expected to pay the organization Rp25,000. Additionally, the central temple at Besakih is off-limits to all save for worshippers. The path around the temple's rather low outer walls gives good views of the inside, however. Another option is to pay one of the temple "caretakers" that mass at its front gates Rp20,000 to be led in to "worship" (and take pictures). While Rp20,000 may seem like a bargain, during the requisite prayer at one of Besakih's shrines, tourists are pressured to make "offerings" of Rp50,000 or more. *(The complex is open daily 6am-6pm. Admission is Rp1500, but parking costs extra and there is a Rp1000 charge for cameras and a Rp2500 charge for video.)* Besakih's great annual festival, **Bhatara Turun Kabeh** (Gods Descend Together), occurs on the full moon of the 10th lunar month *(purnama kadasa)*, in March or April. This month-long festival, during which the gods of all temples in Bali take up residence in Besakih's main shrine, attracts thousands of worshippers from all over Bali.

CLIMBING GUNUNG AGUNG. Gunung Agung is a rigorous climb, dangerous in its steeper portions, but it's an exhilarating experience for the physically fit who want a perch from which to view Bali—provided they arrive at the summit before the clouds do. Climbers should aim to reach the summit near daybreak, and definitely no later than 8am, when the mist begins to roll in. The two most popular climbs from Besakih and Selat require climbers to spend a night in the region. The popular route from the Besakih temple is a four- to six-hour, 6km ascent to the highest point on Gunung Agung. Another route starting in **Selat** enables hikers to take transportation up to within 2km of the summit, although the climb is a steeper ascent. From Selat, one should leave around 4am; from Besakih, 2am. A guide is necessary as parts of the trail are hard to find; arrangements should be made at least a day in advance. The police tourist stations in Besakih (☎230 82) and Selat (☎241 87) have lists of **guides** in the area. In Selat it's possible to shop around among different guides. Gung Bawa Trekking (☎243 79) is one reputable outfit. (1 person Rp100,000; decreases to Rp50,000 per person with 4 people, guide and breakfast included. A night in Selat is required; the affiliated is Rp50,000 per person.) The guides from Besakih have recently been cartelized, and the standard price from there is US$50 for one person, US$75 for 2, and US$100 for three people. You cannot choose your guide, however; the cartel's members take turns on a strict system. Wear sturdy shoes and warm clothing, and bring a flashlight and something to eat. Beware of loose topsoil and falling rocks.

INDONESIA

PLACATING THE DEMONS On Bali, belief in demons is widespread. You'll see offerings on the ground wherever you go; these are gifts to the evil spirits, to placate them and keep the gift-givers from harm. In a woven leaf basket, supplicants place flowers, colored rice, chicken entrails, *arak* and spices. Three times a day, but more often in the evening, armed with a woven leaf basket filled with flowers, bouquets, rice, chicken entrails and incense, Balinese set out to battle with the local wild ghosts, or what we might call demons. Here in Bali, misfortune is thought to be caused by demons. As a means to curb potential mishaps, these baskets are given as gifts on the streets, on porches, in temples, around the home, on motorcycles, and even under the hoods of cars. Once the gift is given, it is the demon's to dispose of; humans don't protect it, so it often gets eaten by dogs—perhaps demons in dog form?—or crushed by passersby. Demons dwell at the sites of accidents and deaths. Shrines flank the roads at the sites of fatal accidents. To avoid curses, drivers slow down and honk twice to ask permission to pass. If a Balinese is asked about this belief they will go on about its irrationality, how weird it must seem, but "it's good luck!"

GUNUNG BATUR

The serene beauty of Lake Batur, which rests inside an enormous volcanic crater, and the mountain villages that cling to the crater's edge veils volatility. Gunung Batur's 1917 eruption engulfed the village of Batur, killing 1400 and destroying 65,000 homes, curiously sparing only the town's temple. Believing this to be a sign of good fortune, the villagers remained in Batur until the eruption of 1926, which destroyed the village again and convinced Batur residents to relocate to the outer rim. The most recent eruption occurred in 1994. The Batur region offers lavish physical beauty, but be warned: aggressive merchants, pricey accommodations, and mediocre food have marred many a traveler's time here.

TRANSPORTATION. Orange **bemo** travel between **Bangli** and **Penulisan** (30min., Rp2000). To see Gunung Batur from the rim, get off at **Penelokan.** *Bemo* arriving in the Gunung Batur area stop in **Kintamani,** where connections run to other villages. **Taxis** and **ojek** also pick up passengers at the *bemo* stop. **Public bus** connections depart from Penelokan to other island destinations. Morning departures (7-9am) are most frequent. Alternatively, travelers can arrange for a shuttle connection through transport agents along the main road in **Toya Bungkah** (also known as **Tirta**). **Perama's** prices are: **Kuta** (3hr., Rp30,000); **Lovina** (2½hr., Rp20,000); **Ubud** (1½hr., Rp20,000).

ORIENTATION AND PRACTICAL INFORMATION. The Batur area is on Bali's northeast corner. The villages of **Penulisan, Batur, Kintamani,** and **Penelokan,** on the crater's west edge, are at the highest elevations and offer spectacular views. Of the two most frequented, **Kedisan** (on the west corner) runs boat trips across the lake, while **Toya Bungkah** (at the southern base of Batur) provides easy access to the mountains. The village of **Trunyan,** famed for its aboriginal Balinese residents, the **Bali Aga,** lies across the lake.

The near-useless **tourist office** is opposite the fork in the road at Penelokan. (Open daily 9am-3pm.) By far the best resource for tourists serious about exploring the area is the freelance guide **Made "Dizzy" Darsana** (☎517 54). Climbing Gunung Batur since he was twelve, his knowledge of the area is unsurpassed; in addition, his English is excellent. He is at Hotel Putra Mulya. Visitors should change money elsewhere, as rates here are poor. The **post office** is on Jl. Bayung Gede in Kintamani. (Open M-Th 8am-2pm, F 8am-11pm, Sa 8am-12:30pm.)

ACCOMMODATIONS AND FOOD. Toya Bungkah is the place to stay if you are climbing Batur or soaking up the view from the lakeside. If circumstances require a night on the rim, **Miranda** (☎520 22), 5km from Penelokan in Kintamani, has basic singles with *mandi* (Rp20,000) and doubles (Rp40,000). Be sure to get a room off the main road. In Toya Bungkah, **Arlinas Bungalows** (☎511 65) have attractive singles (from Rp30,000) and doubles (Rp40,000) and its helpful staff arranges treks up Gunung Batur. **Under the Volcano I** is nestled in a peaceful garden setting. (☎511 66. Bungalows with *mandi* Rp30,000, with toilets Rp45,000.) Lakeside rooms at **Under the Volcano II,** farther down the road, all have toilets (Rp65,000). **Wisma Tirtha Yatra,** on the lake's edge, is the cheapest in town. Follow the main road from Penelokan and take the first right after the hot springs. (Singles Rp20,000.)

Segara Cafe, opposite the boat harbor in Kedisan, prepares small but delicious fish for Rp10,000. (☎511 35. Open daily 7am-10pm.) If you are only visiting the rim, a simple bite with an unforgettable view and reasonable prices can be found at **Ramana.** Facing the Penelokan police station at the fork in the road, turn left and walk 5min. around the corner. (Open daily 10am-5pm.) Don't leave the area without visiting a neighborhood *warung* to taste *bantal* (pillow cake): coconut, rice, and banana or peanuts wrapped in a coconut leaf.

SIGHTS. Close to Kintamani in the village of **Penulisan,** at an altitude of 1745m, stands **Pura Tegeh Kuripan,** Bali's highest temple. Built in the 9th century, the temple offers exquisite views of both Gunung Batur and Bali's north coast. The temple houses little *linga* statues, symbols of the god Shiva. (Open during daylight. Rp3000.) Tours of **Lake Batur** can be arranged form the harbor in **Kedisan.** Guides are assigned and prices are fixed. (Rp196,500 for 1 person, includes admission and donation at Trunyan and the cemetery; prices go down with more people.)

From Kedison the boat goes to the **Bali Aga** village of Trunyan, **Trunyan cemetery** (both the village and cemetery are accessible only by boat), and the hot springs at **Toya Bungkah** (US$5 to swim). The boat waits as long as you like at each stop. Standard tours last 1½-2hr. Beware of locals aggressively asking you for "donations."

The base of Gunung Batur is encircled by a road; the walk around the base takes a scenic 4-5hr. Among the highlights is **Lucky Temple** in the northwest corner, which has miraculously survived all lava flows. After an exhausting trek up, down, and around the mountain, relax in the **Hot Springs** in Toya Bungkah. The price is steep at US$5, but worth it. (Open daily 8am-8pm.)

CLIMBING GUNUNG BATUR. A steep climb in some places and a bit of a challenge in the dark, the hike rewards the stamina-laden with a sensational view of the sunrise and the entire Gunung Batur area; even Lombok's Gunung Rinjani is visible from the peak. During the day, a guide is unnecessary; however, locals claim it is "illegal" to climb in the dark (to catch the sunrise) without a guide. This "law" is enforced by the Komesariat Gunung Bator, the union of local guides, which harasses and threatens would-be independent climbers to preserve its monopoly. All guides must be hired through the Komesariat. (☎523 62. Rp150,000 for up to four people, an additional Rp20,000 for breakfast and ground transportation.) Many *losmen* charge commissions that can double or triple this price. Wear warm clothes.

To climb on your own, first find the yellow "Welcome to Toya Bungkah" sign at the Kedisan side of town. A dirt road next to the sign heads toward the mountain. Take this road and, once it bears right after the houses, continue following it 70m. It will then bear left; follow it. When the road reaches a temple on the right, take the narrow foot path that branches from the road (it's just before the temple wall) and follow it around the temple and into the woods. Stick with the path for 45min. until the trees stop and the terrain turns to volcanic rock, sand, and ash. From here, there are no real "paths;" the only way to go is up. Most day-trekkers leave between 8 and 9am. Departing much later could result in being shrouded in mist before reaching the summit (2hr.).

AMLAPURA ☎0363

Side stepping from the eventful tourist locals surrounding it, Amlapura is simple in its manner, but royal in its history. With just a few main streets and one lively night market, this city has little to offer the "intending to hang for a few days traveler." However for the historically minded, the police and nearby royal retreats offer a unique look into the regal lifestyle of a bygone era.

TRANSPORTATION AND PRACTICAL INFORMATION. *Bemo* from the **main terminal** in the market area leave for **Denpasar** (2½hr.) via **Candidasa** (20min.); **Padangbai** (40min.); **Klungkung** (1hr.); **Gianyar** (1½hr.); and to **Singaraja** (1½hr.) via **Tirtagangga** (15min.), **Culik** (½hr.), **Tulamben** (40min.), and **Yeh Sanih** (1hr.). Amlapura's main road runs north-south at the town's very east end, disguising itself with many names. From north to south: **Jl. Sultan Agung** becomes **Jl. Teuku Umar,** then **Jl. Gajah Mada,** and finally, near the Ujung Water Palace, **Jl. Bayangkara.** Jl. Gajah Mada and **Jl. Kesatrian,** which run parallel to each other, border the town center. At the south end, Jl. Kesatrian turns sharply and intersects Jl. Gajah Mada. The *bemo* and bus stop is at the south end of Jl. Kesatrian as it bends back to Jl. Gajah Mada. **Bank BNI,** next to the *bemo* terminal on Jl. Kesatrian, changes currency and traveler's checks. (☎220 57. Open M-F 8am-4pm.) The **hospital,** Jl. Ngurah Rai 40 (☎21 470), is near the Telkom office. The **police station,** Jl. Bayangkara 1 (☎212 20), is near the center of town at the transition of Jl. Gajah Mada to Jl. Bayangkara. The **post office,** Jl. Gatot Subroto 29, is at the entrance to Amlapura. (☎210 10. Open M-Th 8am-2pm, F 8-11am, Sa 8am-noon.) A **wartel** sits on Jl. Gajah Mada for cash calls. (Open daily 7am-11pm.) **Postal code:** 80800.

ACCOMMODATIONS AND FOOD. Options for accommodation in Amlapura are slim—most travelers prefer to stay in resort-style Candidasa or in the hillside s of Tirtagangga. **Villa Amlapura,** 100m downhill from the palace on Jl. Sultan Agung has excellent rooms at Rp50,000, including Western bath & breakfast, surrounded by late 70s, yet retro modern, designer furniture & fixtures. (☎232 46). The extremely bare **Losmen Lahar Mas** is at the entrance of town, before the post office on Jl. Gatot Subroto; it has basic rooms with baths. (☎213 45. Singles Rp20,000; doubles Rp30,000.) Food is largely limited to the *pasar*'s **warung.** A **night market** sets up next to the turn-off to Singaraja at 5pm, but usually winds down by 8pm. **Sumber Rasa,** on Jl. Gajah Mada, is one of the few sit-down joints in Amlapura that serves Indonesian-style Chinese food. Most dishes run under Rp10,000. (Open daily 8am-8pm.)

SIGHTS. Visitors to Amlapura can stroll through what remains of the once-prosperous Karangasem kingdom. **Puri Agung,** also known as Puri Kanginan, the former residence of the last Karangasem king and his family, is open to the public. There are no tours of the palace and little labeling, but visitors can pick up a useful information sheet from the ticket window. On weekends, one of the king's sons is on hand to show off cheerfully his childhood home. Note the evidence of Dutch artwork and furniture—the Karangasem retained power long into the 20th century because of their collaboration with the Dutch. The *puri* is north of the *pasar* along Jl. Sultan Agung. (Open daily 8am-6pm. Rp2000.) The **Ujung Water Palace,** a more modest version of what the Karangasem king built in Tirtagangga (see below), is south of town. Built in 1919, it was used as a private retreat for the royal family. The 1963 eruption of Gunung Agung and the earthquake of 1979 destroyed much of the palace, and all that remains now are ruins jutting up through the rice paddies and water lilies with the main palace in the center left for exploration and imagination. Few tourists come here; there is no formal admission. Some local farmers have converted a few of the lily pools into rice paddies, and they have the area to themselves most of the time. Take a blue *bemo*, from the corner of Jl. Gajah Mada and Jl. Kesatrian (10min., frequent departures, Rp500), or enjoy the passing scenery to Ujung on a *dokar*. Clamber up the surrounding hills to get a better look at the garden's pools and fountains and a view of the Indian ocean.

TIRTAGANGGA

Bali's *rajah* built Tirtagangga in 1947 as a holiday retreat and named it after Hinduism's holiest river, the Ganges. Lying 6km northwest of Amlapura, Tirtagangga houses multi-leveled, ornate pools fed by a spring on the slopes of Gunung Agung. The idyllic pools offer the perfect setting in which to swim, rest, and rejuvenate. (Open daily 6am-6pm. Admission to the springs Rp1000 for adults, Rp600 for children; still cameras Rp1500; video cameras Rp2500; Rp4000 to swim, Rp2000 for children.) *Bemo* run between Amlapura (15min.) and Tirtagangga (every 20min. until 6pm); Tirtagangga is also served by Perama shuttles. Buy tickets to destinations all over the island at the Good Karma Restaurant and (☎224 45), at the entrance to the carpark. The main road from Tirtagangga, leading away from Amlapura to Culik (30min.), passes some of the most picture-perfect scenery in Bali, from dense tropical forests to rugged arid mountains.

For those staying here overnight, the best value is at **Pondok Lembeh-Dukuh**, three secluded bungalows on a hill. Getting there is an adventure. From the parking lot, head toward Singaraja on the main road until you come across an irrigation canal.

Follow the canal through rice paddies and past houses until you reach the forest. A path there leads to a long stairway to Pondok Lembeh-Dukuh. Gorgeous views of the area more than compensate for the trek. (Breakfast included. Singles Rp25,000; doubles Rp40,000.)

The ritzier **Tirta Ayu Hotel/Restaurant** (☎216 97) is the beautifully kept former residence of the *rajah*. The lavish rooms start at Rp100,000; price includes breakfast and unlimited use of the pools. Cheaper accommodations can be found at **Kusuma Taya Inn** (☎212 50). On the main road, with your back to the pools, turn left and climb up the stairs 300m. Standard rooms start at Rp40,000, but fluctuate depending on availability (breakfast included).

AMED (LIPAH)

The sleepy fishing village of Amed conjures up the Bali of 30 years ago. Bargain hunters can find great deals in the low season. The village's quiet seaside air is conducive to relaxing on the warm lava-black beaches or snorkeling in the clear calm waters. Along the main road north of Amlapura/Tirtagangga, *bemo* pass the village of Culik, from which *bemo* run from Culik to Amed up until 11am (after that, hire an *ojek*). The nearby wreck of the **USAT Liberty** makes Amed a mecca for divers. All accommodations rent diving and snorkeling equipment and normally offer dive packages. No longer inexpensive, many budget places in Amed have renovated up-market or closed down. It is hard to find accommodation for under Rp60,000. The best option is the newly merged **Amed Beach Cottages/Amed Cafe.** On the main drag at the center of town, its cheaper rooms are clean and well-maintained, with fan, private bath and mosquito nets. (Doubles Rp80,000.) The cheaper option with equal quality is 50m further away from Amed, **Bamboo Bali Bungalows.** (Singles Rp70,000; doubles Rp90,000.) **Amed Dive Shop** offers 1-day, 2-dive package US$85, and introductory courses US$55. V, MC.) **Warung Congkang Three Brothers** will cook your catch and serve it with good humor. Cost of grilling outside fish varies; most menu entrees are under Rp15,000. (Open daily 8am-9pm.) Change money before arriving—in case you end up staying awhile.

CANDIDASA ☎0363

Once upon a time, there was a beach at Candidasa. The beach attracted tourists. The tourists needed bungalows. To build the bungalows, the locals needed cement. To make cement, the coral along the coast was ripped out and ground up. Without the coral to break the tides, the beach washed away. There is no beach in Candidasa anymore, but there are still bungalows. Despite the lack of a beach, watersports still attract tourists to the area. Candidasa is also the only designated resort area in east Bali; budget accommodation and decent restaurants are numerous here and scant in the rest of the area. The sights in Bangli, Klungkung, and Amlapura, along with the two Tenganan villages, make a few nights in Candidasa worthwhile.

TRANSPORTATION

Local Transportation: Bemo run regularly on the main road until 6pm. With your back to the water, *bemo* going right are headed to Amlapura (20min., with connections to Tirtagangga and Singaraja). Those going left are headed to **Padangbai** (20min.) and **Klungkung** (40min., with connections to Gianyar, Besakih, Penelokan, Batubulan). **Perama,** next to the police office at the west end of town, has daily morning departures to: **Denpasar/Kuta/Sanur/Airport** (Rp20,000); **Ubud** (1½hr., Rp15,000); **Lovina/Singaraja** (3hr., Rp50,000); and **Penelokan/Kintamani** (2½hr., Rp30,000).

Rentals and Diving: Many accommodations and tour agents rent **bicycles** (Rp10,000), **motor bikes** (Rp30,000), and **snorkeling equipment** (Rp15,000) by the day. **Baruna Dive** (☎411 85), at the center of Candidasa's main road, offers diving and snorkeling expeditions to surrounding areas.

ORIENTATION AND PRACTICAL INFORMATION

Candidasa is a 1km strip on Bali's east coast along the Klungkung-Amlapura Rd. With your back to the water, Klungkung is to the left (west) and Amlapura is to the right (east). Murky **Candidasa Lagoon** is on the sea-side of the main road at its east end; the local temple is directly across the lagoon. The waters of **Amuk Bay** border Candidasa on the south and hilly rice terraces to the north. From the sand, the island straight ahead is Nusa Penida.

Tourist Offices: Besides the plethora of private tourist information centers offering tours, rentals and shuttle services, there is the official (but not very useful) **Candidasa Tourist Information Office** (☎412 04). As you're walking on the main road with the lagoon on the right, the office is one house past the end of the lagoon. Open daily 8am-noon.

Currency Exchange: Moneychangers all along the main road offer reasonable rates and take traveler's checks. Most close by 9pm.

Emergency: Police ☎110. **Ambulance** ☎118.

Police: ☎416 77. At the west end of the main road, where the road runs along the bay.

Hospital: Candidasa Clinic Laboratory & Apotik (☎413 21). Traveling on the road to Padangbai, it's 100m past the turn-off to Tenganan on the left. Open M-Sa. On Sunday, the area is serviced by a doctor from Denpasar (☎0361 463 093). Another general practice is next to Bali Kebu hotel.

Telephones: Wartel at the center of town on the main road. International cash calls only. Open daily 8am-11pm. **HCD** booth at Tourist Information.

Post Offices: There are several **postal agents** on the main street, including **Asri's Convenience Store.** These may take mail and sell stamps, but no more. Open until 10pm. The nearest **post office** is 20min. away in Amlapura. **Postal code:** 80851.

ACCOMMODATIONS

Budget beachside bungalows run the length of Candidasa, but the quieter ones cluster at either end. In the low season, it's possible to negotiate a bargain price.

Barong Beach Inn (☎411 27). When the road bends sharply to Amplapura at the east end, go straight ahead and take the 1st right. Best price in Candidasa. Breakfast included. Singles Rp20,000; doubles Rp25,000; beachfront rooms but nothing special Rp40,000.

Ida Home Stay (☎410 96), on the west side of the lagoon. 6 private bungalows with large rooms, modern bathrooms, and deck chairs on private verandas. Rooms available for 4 or more. Breakfast included. Singles Rp66,000; doubles Rp75,000.

Rama Bungalows (☎419 07). With the lagoon on the right, walk down the path to the beach; it's on the left. Set among gardens. Quiet and well-screened rooms with fan and full bath. Singles Rp50,000; doubles Rp60,000, with hot water Rp70,000.

FOOD

For a small strip along the beach, Candidasa offers a surprisingly large selection of culinary delights. Cheap tourist-oriented restaurants face the street. *Warung*, only slightly cheaper, cluster at the west end of town. More expensive restaurants have superior service and atmosphere, and are worth the extra cost. Some restaurants have a double role, also serving as the source of nighttime entertainment with dance floors and live bands on Saturdays.

TJ's, on the non-lagoon side of Candidasa, is on the exquisite side of food consumption with fantastically and creatively prepared daily catches (Rp30,000)

Raja's Bar and Restaurant, opposite the Tourist Information Office on the main road, offers a large Western menu with burgers, pasta, and barbecue. American movies shown from 7:30pm. V, MC. Open daily 10am-11pm.

Ciao, set back off the main road near Candidasa Beach Bungalows, features great Italian spaghetti, pizzas, and gelato. Entrees Rp14,500-21,000. On Saturdays, a band plays and a dance floor opens up below the dining area. Open daily 9am-10pm.

Warung Astawa, on the main road at the east edge of Candidasa. Seafood sampler with shrimp cocktail, fish in banana leaves, and dessert Rp15,000. Tropical atmosphere, bamboo furniture. *Legong* dancing at 7:45pm. Open daily 7am-10pm.

Warung Srijati, opposite the Gandhi Reading Room by the mucky lagoon. Nicer than a real *warung*, cheaper than a real restaurant. Tasty Balinese food for under Rp10,000. Fresh fruit juice. Vegetarian-friendly. Open daily 7am-10pm.

Warung Agung, 200m west of the lagoon. Tiki decor, good place to try roast suckling pig (Rp19,500). Entrees Rp12,500. Free pickup service. Open daily 7am-10pm.

DAYTRIP FROM CANDIDASA

TENGANAN

One km west of Candidasa. An ojek from Candidasa should cost no more than Rp5000. Walking takes two hours, and is best to do in the early hours to avoid traffic. Small donation (Rp5000 is acceptable) to enter the village.

Tenganan consists of not one, but two villages. One, clearly marked as Tenganan (Bali Aga), is an enclave of the Bali Aga, the aboriginal Balinese. Unlike those in Trunyan, the Bali Aga here do not aggressively pursue donations other than the entrance donation; in fact, while they do depend on souvenir sales for their livelihood, even the shopping here is surprisingly low-pressure. Tourists can observe the weaving of double-ikat (*geringsing*) cloth as well as the inscribing on *lontar* scrolls. The other Trunyan hosts a month-long festival (Usaba Sambah) in May/June; tourists may view it for a donation. A very bright and lively affair, it features traditional *pandanus* fighting, in which combatants try to draw blood with spiky leaves.

KLUNGKUNG (SEMERAPURA) ☎0366

INDONESIA

Klungkung's fame as the seat of the powerful precolonial Gelgel Kingdom makes it an important historical landmark on east Bali. The kingdom fell long ago in the bloody Battle of Klungkung, but its legacy lives on in the old palace grounds and monuments commemorating the 1908 battle. With ordinary accommodations and maniacal traffic, Klungkung's intriguing sights are best seen as a daytrip on the way to Candidasa, Besakih, or Ubud.

TRANSPORTATION AND PRACTICAL INFORMATION. **Bemo** run 6am to 6pm to: **Amlapura** (1¼hr.) via **Padangbai** (25min.) and **Candidasa** (50min.); **Batubulan** (1hr.) via **Gianyar** (25min.); and **Besakih** (45min.). The yellow *bemo* at the main terminal go 1km to the city center. Officially named Semarapura, Klungkung sits 40km east of Denpasar. Klungkung's city center is small, consisting of an intersection and four streets heading in four directions. The central landmark is a **traffic rotary,** where the main east-west thoroughfare, **Jl. Diponegoro/Untung Surapati,** runs into north-south **Jl. Gajah Mada/Puputan.** From the rotary, the **Puputan Monument** and the old palace grounds (Island Gardens or Taman Gili) are visible. South from the rotary 1km along Jl. Puputan, the *bemo* terminal is on the right. Next to the terminal is an enormous **market.** East on Jl. Diponegoro are the main commercial area and the few accommodations.

Several **banks** along Jl. Diponegoro change money and transfer cash from V and MC. **Bank BCA** (☎213 21), on Jl. Diponegoro between Jl. Puputan and Jl. Nakula, has an **ATM** that accepts V, MC, Cirrus, and PLUS. The Klungkung government **tourism office,** Jl. Untung Surapati 3 (☎214 48), lies within the Faman Gili complex. A **hospital** (☎211 72) is on Jl. Flamboyan on the outskirts of town. For English, head to Ubud or Kuta's 24-hour clinics. Next to the hospital is an **apotik** (pharmacy), and a more central apotik is at Jl. Diponegoro (open 24hr). (Open M-Th 7:30am-

1:30pm, F 7:30-10:30am, Sa 7:30-noon.) The **police** (☎211 72) are on Jl. Untung Surapati to the far west, past the post office. A 24-hour **wartel** is at the corner of Jl. Diponegoro and Jl. Puputan. **HCD** booths allow collect and credit-card calls. The **GPO,** on the west side of Jl. Untung Surapati holds Poste Restante. (☎210 10. Open M-Th 8am-2pm, F 8-11am, Sa 8am-2pm.) **Postal code**: 80700.

ACCOMMODATIONS AND FOOD. It's better to stay in Candidasa and Padangbai, where options are more plentiful, and the trip to Klungkung can be made easily as a daytrip. To get to **Loji Ramayana Hotel,** Jl. Diponegoro 152, stand at the rotary with the palace at your back and walk straight ahead on Jl. Diponegoro. (☎210 44. Doubles with *mandi* Rp30,000, with flush toilets Rp50,000.) For lower prices, cross the street to **Cahaya Pusaka Losmen** (look for the "Losmen 20m" sign), where bare rooms face a small garden. (☎221 18. Singles Rp25,000; doubles Rp30,000.) The usual *warung* fare is widely available, but is best at the lively *pasar senggol.* (Open daily 4pm-midnight.) Two Chinese restaurants, **Sumber Rasa** (☎250 97) and **Restoran Bali Indah** (☎210 56), are both on Jl. Nakula. Take Jl. Diponegoro east from the rotary; Jl. Nakula is the first road on the right. Prices range from Rp6500 for chicken fried rice to Rp12,5000 for stir-fried chicken with mushrooms and vegetables. (Sumber Rasa open daily 7am-11pm. Restoran Indah open daily 7am-9pm.)

SIGHTS. Klungkung's historical and religious significance provides visitors with an opportunity to understand the various influences that have shaped Bali. **Kerta Gosa,** the Court of Justice, is a pavilion in the northwest corner of the Taman Gili compound. One ticket includes admission to all sights. (Rp2000, children Rp1000.) The ceiling is lined with 267 painted panels that depict the story of **Bhima Swarga,** Indonesia's Dante. In his journeys, Bhima Swarga traveled through the various levels of *paradiso* and *inferno* in order to save his parents' souls. For the accused, these paintings illustrate the punishment for the guilty (bottom rows) or the rewards for the innocent (culminating with the birds at the top) that lay ahead in the after life. (Open daily 7am-6pm.) Also in the complex is the **Bale Kambang** (Floating Pavilion). In dynastic times, the *bale* was the receiving area for important guests. The paintings on the inside of the roof depict the story of **King Sutasoma,** a Buddhist king. Many paintings show the Hindu demon **Kala** hurling weapons at Sutasoma, which transform into flowers right before hitting him. The painting is a chronicle of the union of Buddhism and Hinduism in Bali—the final painting shows Buddha emerging from the mouth of **Naga,** a symbol of Hinduism. The paintings are all a bit faded. They do not, in content or style, break from traditional Balinese themes. If the museums in Ubud were too much for you, don't come here. The **museum** is at the west edge of the Taman Gili complex. Built by the Dutch, the museum houses fascinating photographs of the *rajah* and royal residence as well as artifacts from Bali's history. Everything is labeled in English and provides great insight into Bali's past. Across the street is the **Puputan Monument,** whose base contains labelled dioramas providing a visual crash course in Balinese history. (Open daily 7am-6pm.)

The fabled **Goa Lawah** (bat caves), 9km east of Klungkung on the way to Padangbai, are home to thousands of bats, and at least 1000 are visible, hanging over a make-shift temple, to the visitor's eye. Snakes prey on bats in the area, giving rise to the story about a mythical serpent who dwells inside the caves. The caves can only be seen from the outside, not entered. Doing so would be both sacrilegious and stupid—not only would you anger the locals, you'd be covered in bat guano in an instant. According to the Balinese, these caves extend all the way to Gunung Agung. *Bemo* heading to Padangbai pass Goa Lawah frequently (10min., Rp1500).

BANGLI ☎0366

Of the three former eastern kingdoms—Amlapura, Klungkung, and Bangli—Bangli has the most trees and the fewest modern buildings. Superb night market fare, clean and uncrowded streets, one of the most important temples on Bali, and a magnificent waterfall more than compensate for the lack of tourist facilities.

TRANSPORTATION AND PRACTICAL INFORMATION. Bangli is 40km north of Denpasar. The **bemo terminal**, south of the **Jl. Kusumayuda/Jl. Merdeka** junction, offers connections to: **Gianyar** (45 min., Rp3000); **Kintamani** (30min., Rp2500); **Batubulan** (1hr. Rp3000); and **Klungkung** (30min. Rp1500). The **night market** is one block south of the *bemo* terminal along Jl. Merdeka, while the **day market** is directly opposite. Along Kusuma Yuda away from the day market are **banks;** the **post office;** and the **hospital,** at Jl. Kusuma Yuda 27 (☎910 02). The *wartel*, Jl. Merdeka 62, offers cash **international calls**. (☎911 50; open 24hr.) The **Telkom office,** Brigen Ngurah Rai 60, offers calling-card and collect calls as well as HCD phones outside.

ACCOMMODATIONS AND FOOD. Great food and centralized accommodations make Bangli a pleasant place to spend the night. The best place in town is the **Bangli Inn,** in a modern two-story building. With your back to the *bemo* terminal, turn left and then right at the roundabout; it's 200m on the right. (☎/fax 914 19. Rooms Rp50,000.) **Artha Sastra Inn,** directly opposite the *bemo* terminal, was the palace of the last king of Bangli. The grandson of the last king, Agung Artha Sastra, will happily talk with guests. (☎911 79. Singles Rp25,000; doubles Rp45,000.) The cheapest option is the **Catur Adnyana,** Jl. Lettu Lila 2. Take the first right after the police station, 1km from the bemo terminal, as you walk south on Jl. Merdeka. (☎912 44. Rooms Rp25,000.) The night market, starting approximately 5pm, off Jl. Merdeka boasts a festive atmosphere and good cheap eats. Try *martabak mesir* (egg and onion pancake) for dinner, and *martabak manis* (chocolate and butter concoction) for dessert.

SIGHTS. Bangli's not-to-miss sight is the 11th-century **Pura Kehen** temple, with an enormous sacred banyan tree in the courtyard. The *kulkul* is precariously high up in the banyan to call the villagers to worship. With your back turned to the *bemo* station, turn left onto Jl. Merdeka, and walk 1km. When the road forks, take the right and the temple will be 200m on the left. (Rp2500. Sarong available to borrow.)

The countryside around Bangli reveals hidden wonders. The small village of **Taman Bali,** out the south end of Jl. Meraka, offers to the faithful the spectacular **Dusin Kuing waterfall.** Find an *ojek* driver who has heard of Dusin Kuing; be patient, as this place still remains a mystery to most locals. **Desmulih** is another tiny village that offers great walks and magnificent views. Behind the town lies **Bukit Demulih.** When in Demulih ask *"Dimama tangga manugu ke puncak?"* ("where are the stairs to the top?") to find the flight of 200 steps cut into the hill. To get to Demulih village, follow Jl. Kusuma Yada out of Bangli to the west for 3km until the turn-off to Giangar appears on the left. Demulih will be the first town you pass. *Bemo* don't access this area; organize an *ojek* guide.

PADANGBAI ☎0363

For a modest port village, Padangbai has much to offer. Set along a crescent of narrow beach, the village is a quiet pocket of colorful outriggers and cheap seafood. For many, Padangbai is no more than a busy transit point on the way to Lombok. But the ocean-view bungalows, grilled prawn dinners, and small sandy beaches make Padangbai a travel destination in its own right.

TRANSPORTATION. Buses whisk travelers to destinations on Bali, Lombok, and Java. Prices include ferry fees. Tickets can be purchased along the water. **Perama** (☎414 19), situated at Dona cafe opposite the *bemo* on the entrance road, runs several shuttles to: **Ubud** (1hr., Rp15,000); **Sanur** (2hr., Rp25,000); **Kuta** (2½hr., Rp25,000); **Kintamani** (2hr., Rp30,000); **Mataram** (5hr., Rp30,000); **Senggigi** (5½hr.,

Rp30,000); **Bangsal** (5½hr., Rp30,000); **Gili Air** (7hr.); **Gili Meno** (7hr.); and **Gili Trawangan** (7hr. Rp60,000). Buses run to **Jakarta, Jogjakarta/Surakarta, Probolinggo/Surabaya,** and **Malang. Ferries** run continuously to **Lombok** (4hr., every 1½hr., Rp9500, 1st-class with A/C Rp17,000).

> **WARNING.** When waiting for a boat, keep your luggage with you at all times and do not let the porters take it. Some have known to threaten to throw it overboard unless you pay a ridiculous amount (avg. Rp100,000 per bag).

ORIENTATION AND PRACTICAL INFORMATION. Tiny Padangbai is 50km northeast of Denpasar, off the main road between Klungkung and Candidasa. At the end of the road entering Padangbai are the harbor gates and the overbearing ferry terminal. Facing the terminal, in the left corner closest to the water, is **Jl. Segaran.** This runs into **Jl. Siliyuti,** which heads away from the bay. Most of the accommodations lie off Jl. Segaran and Jl. Siliyuti, with s closer to the ferry port. *Bemo* wait at the ferry terminal end of the entrance road. A helpful **tourist office** at the front of the ferry terminal can direct you toward the best snorkeling and beaches in the area, but has no printed information.

Snorkeling equipment is available everywhere. **Motorcycle** and **car rentals** are available through Hotel Puri Rai and Kerti Beach Inn. To get to the **post office,** walk to the harbor gates next to the ferry, walk straight ahead, and take the first left at the police station; it's 50m ahead on the right. (Open M-Th 8am-2pm, F 8-11am, Sa 8am-12:30pm. Poste Restante.) A **wartel** on the street leading from the harbor gates toward the main road to Candidasa offers cash-only international calls and faxes. (Open daily 6am-12:30pm.) **Moneychangers** abound on the beach boardwalk and market; most take traveler's checks. **Postal code:** 80872.

ACCOMMODATIONS AND FOOD. Several cheap accommodation options lie to the left of Jl. Siliyuti at the point where it meets Jl. Segara. **Parta** is the best maintained. Rooms are worth the extra rupiah for the space, privacy, fan, and private bath. (Singles Rp25-35,000; doubles Rp35-50,000.) The **Bagus Inn** has basic rooms with ceiling fans and *mandi*-style bathrooms. (Singles Rp25,000; doubles Rp30,000.) For a bed closer to the water, continue away from the port along the beach. At **Topi Inn,** try for one of the three rooms that have private *mandi.* (Singles Rp30,000; doubles Rp40,000; bungalows Rp50,000.) **Kerti Beach Inn,** next to Hotel Puri Rai, has clean rooms and well-designed bungalows with an open-air lounge room and mosquito nets. (Breakfast included. Singles Rp40,000; doubles Rp50,000; bungalows Rp60,000.)

Padangbai's seafood is exceptional—prawns, shark, and barracuda are local specialties, served with generous amounts of garlic. The cheapest prices are found away from the water and at hotel-attached restaurants. **Kendedes Restaurant** on Jl. Silayuti, has a sizeable menu of cheap, tasty Indonesian food. The second-floor seating has a good view of the ocean or, if you prefer, a better one of the graveyard. **Ozone Cafe** before Parta has a laid-back, backpacker-friendly atmosphere and an owner who will beat you at Scrabble. (Scrumptious pizzas from Rp15,000). **Puri Rai Restaurant,** attached to the similarly-named hotel, is a classy tiki bar where you can catch all your favorite soccer tournaments (usually 2am). On the water, **Warung Pantai Ayu** is cheap. (Garlic prawns Rp15,000.)

BEACHES AND SIGHTS. Padangbai offers a surprisingly large range of water recreation options. **Equator,** the local PADI- and CAMS-certified dive shop, offers dives in nearby waters (full dayUS$50, cash only). PADI-certified **Geko Dive** in Pandan Restaurant offers similar packages. All-inclusive diving packages to Nusa Penida cost US$70. If you can find a group of four or more divers, tagging along to snorkel is only US$10, including lunch. The best swimming option is the popular **Bias Tugel.** With your back to the water at the ferry port, turn left at the police station; the turn-off to Bias Tugel is 50m ahead on the left before the road rises steeply. Another popular recreation area is **Blue Lagoon,** at the opposite end of the ferry port bay. Walk along the beachfront roads; the turn-off to the Blue Lagoon is immediately after Topi Inn. The best place to explore the surrounding rocky coastline is from **Pura Silayukti,** the temple commemorating the man who introduced the caste system to Bali. It's a 5min. walk along the sealed road from Topi Inn. When the road forks, head to the left, and Pura Silayukti is the temple to the left. From high on the ridge, dirt paths lead to the shoreline, where several *pantai kecil* (little beaches) can be found. Immaculate and deserted, these beaches provide shelter from the hecklers and access to interesting rock pools.

NUSA TENGGARA

LOMBOK

Since the riots of January 2000 (see **Riot2k,**p. 233), tourists have been wary of embarking upon this island and as a consequence, prices are cheap, tourists are few, and some extraordinary sights are missed. With increased security and with an improved safety rating, however, the unhurried strolls through rice and tobacco paddies in Tetebatu are slowly drawing tourists back. The trek through Gunung Rinjani is more than just a touristy sleep-over, and there are more types of beaches than can be categorized.

THE VIEW FROM ABOVE

The lowdown: Bali's quieter, gentler sibling.
Major towns: Greater Mataram, Senggigi, Tetebatu
Highlights: Climbing Gunung Rinjani, walking through the rice paddies of Tetebatu, partying in the discos of Senggigi.

GETTING TO LOMBOK

BY PLANE

Lombok's **Selaparang Airport** (☎622 987, ext. 108) marks the northern edge of Mataram, the official capital. **Taxis** have set rates and are in front of the airport (Mataram Rp9500, Senggigi Rp15,000). **Bemo** go to Ampenan (Rp1000). **Merpati** flies to: **Bima** (1¼hr., Th and Sa, Rp475,500); **Denpasar** (30min., 3 per day, Rp233,500);

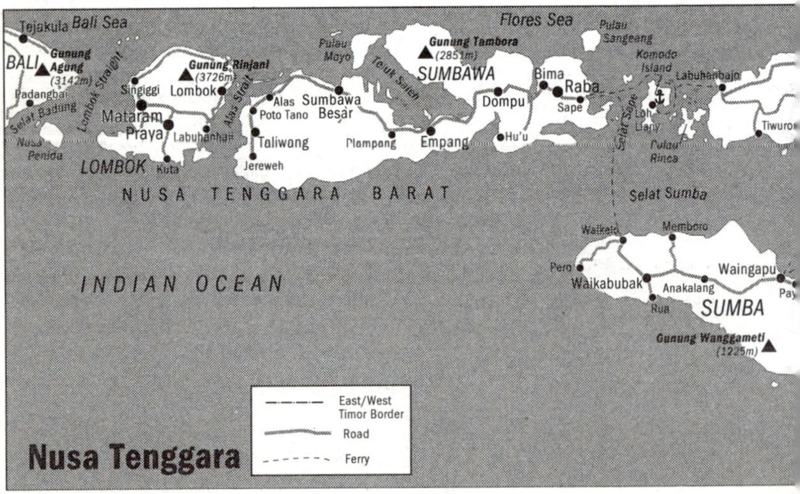

Jakarta (1 per day, Rp.888,000) via **Jogjakarta** (1 per day, Rp527,200); **Sumbawa Besar** (45min.; M, W, Sa; Rp248,900); **Surabaya** (M, W, Sa; Rp380,900). **Silk Air** flies to **Singapore** (Tu, F, Sa, Su; one-way US$220, round-trip US$350). International departure tax is Rp60,000; domestic departure tax is Rp8000.

BY BOAT

Ferries cross from **Labuhan,** Lombok and **Poto Tano,** Sumbawa (1½hr., every hr., Rp10,000) and a similar ferry system runs between **Lembar,** Lombok to **Padangbai,** Bali (4-5hr., every 1½hr., Rp10,000). The **Mabua Express** (☎811 95) operates daily between Lembar and **Benoa,** Bali (2½hr., returns 5:30pm, US$25-30). Two **PELNI** ships dock at Lembar. The KM *Awu* departs once every two weeks to: **Berau; Denpasar** (Rp21,500); **Dili; Ende; Kaladahi; Kupang; Makasar; Maumere; Nunukan; Tarakan;** and **Waingapu.** The KM *Tilongkabilu* leaves every two weeks and travels to: **Bima** (Rp53,000); **Denpasar; Kumai; Labuanbajo** (Rp79,300); **Makasar; Sampit;** and **Surabaya.** Buy tickets and confirm ship arrival dates at the harbor in Lembar or at the PELNI office on Jl. Industri (☎637 212), opposite Hotel Nitour in Ampenan.

BY BUS

Buses to destinations on other islands depart Sweta Terminal, on the east side of Greater Mataram (see p. 232) around noon to: **Denpasar** (7hr., Rp50,000); **Jakarta** (Rp175,000); **Jogjakarta** (Rp135,000); and **Surabaya** (19hr., Rp85,000). **Langsung Indah** has the most comfortable buses, departing daily at noon and 2:30pm to: **Bima** (13hr., Rp44,400); **Dompu** (11hr., Rp40,500); **Sape** (15hr., Rp47,500); and **Sumbawa Besar** (7hr., Rp27,000). There are also buses to: **Jereveh** (Rp20,000); **Lonyuk** (Rp28,000); **Plompang** (Rp30,000); **Taliwerg** (Rp15,000-20,000). Confirm times a day in advance. Buy tickets for night buses 24hr. before departure. Long rides often include dinner.

GETTING AROUND LOMBOK

Buses departing from Sweta Terminal cost less than **bemo** and run to the same places. **Taxis** run in greater Mataram, but aren't common outside the city. **Ojeks** save time but not money. **Bemo** will run almost anywhere. Beware of empty *bemo*—drivers will assume that you are chartering the vehicle. *Cidomo*—horse-drawn carts with car tires and axles—ferry people around small locales. They're ubiquitous on Lombok, even in cosmopolitan Mataram. The following terminals serve Lombok:

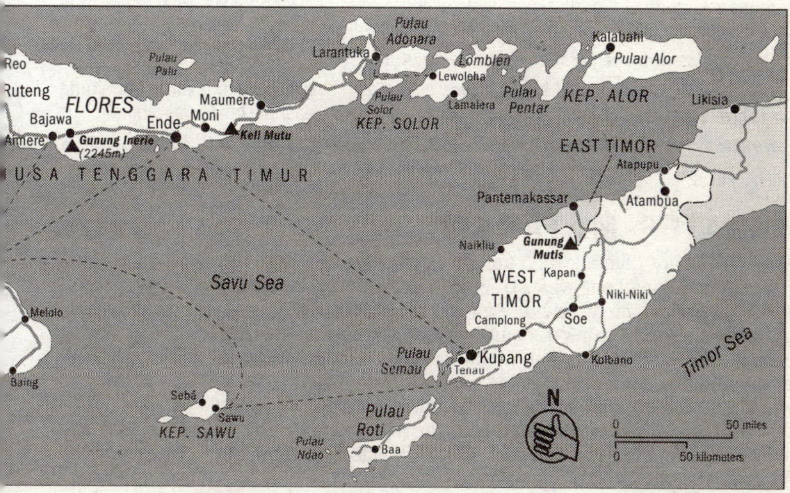

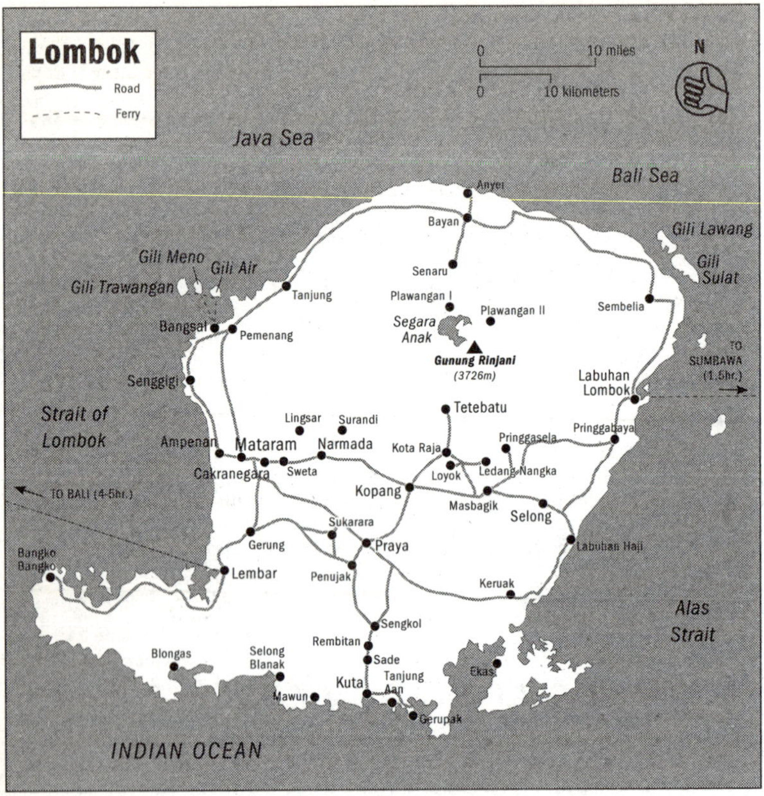

Sweta, on the east side of greater Mataram. Lombok's transportation hub. Serves: **Bangsal** (1½hr.); **Bayan** (20min.); **Labuhan** (2hr.); **Lembar** (1hr.); **Greater Mataram** (10min.); **Narmada** (20min.); **Praya** (1hr.).

Ampenan, north of the city's main intersection. Serves as a stop for Mataram routes from Sweta Terminal, with *bemo* running north to **Senggigi** (15min.).

Praya, in the town center. Serves the south: **Kuta** (30min.); **Sengkol** (30min.).

Narmada, in the center of town. Serves central Lombok: **Masbagik** (2hr.); **Pomotong** (1hr.); **Suranadi** (15min.); **Tetebatu** (2hr.); and points east of Greater Mataram.

Rentals: Rinjani Rent Car (☎632 259), Jl. Panca Usaha. Rents Suzuki Jimmys Rp75,000. Motorcycle rentals are everywhere.

GREATER MATARAM ☎0370

Home to 10% of Lombok's 2.5 million people, greater Mataram consists of three cities along 10km of one wide street. The worst rioting in January 2000 ravaged hot and dusty Ampenan. As you browse the art and jewelry stores, you won't be able to ignore the burnt ruins of churches that serve as a sobering backdrop. As the capital of Nusa Tenggora Barat, Mataram has seen development and investment. In the mid 90s, Mataram was busy transforming itself from a sleepy provincial headquarters into a modern city. The currency crisis and January's riots halted that process, and now Mataram is in the process of reintroducing tourism and enlivening shopping and nightlife—although outside night markets, nightlife is, so far, nonexistent.

RIOT2K These days, if you ask locals what happened in January 200, some might say "politics" or "religion," but most will simply look confused and say "I don't know." It seems that the riots that swept through Lombok two years ago are largely unexplained. Some believe that Western tourists were the target, while others are adamant that foreigners had nothing to do with the riots. Here's what we do know:

On January 17th, 2000, during a Muslim Solidarity holiday, a group of Muslims in Ampenon began a public rally. Over the next three days, churches and two discos were burned, and a few Muslim activists were shot and killed by the police. No tourists or non-Muslims were harmed. Tourists in Senggigi were evacuated and taken to Bali.

Locals say that the two discos that were burnt down were well-known for drug trafficking and prostitution, leading some to conclude that the Muslim group wasn't after tourists, but rather was trying to rid their community of its problems—drugs and prostitution. This explanation, however, doesn't explain the burning of the churches.

The riots left many unanswered questions, including that of the safety of the tourists. Today, the Office of Tourism, as well as Lombok at large, realizes Lombok cannot survive without tourism. Amidst the finger pointing for the jobs lost and sore economy, one thing's for certain: Lombok, with enforced police and security, is working hard to insure peace on the island and welcome tourists back.

ORIENTATION AND PRACTICAL INFORMATION

Traffic courses through Greater Mataram on two parallel roads. *Bemo* circle between terminals at both ends. **Jl. Yos Sudarso** goes from Ampenan to Cakra, then turns into **Jl. Langko, Jl. Pejanggik,** and finally **Jl. Selaparang. Jl. Tumpang Sari** runs east-west from Cakra to Ampernan, one block south, and becomes **Jl. Panca Usaha, Jl. Pancawarga,** and finally **Jl. Pendidikan.** Giant, official-looking buildings flank the tree-lined streets of **Mataram,** the administrative center. Outside Cakra are the transportation hubs of **Sweta** and **Bertais.**

Tourist Offices: Provincial Tourist Service, Jl. Singosari 2 (☎634 800), off Jl. Majapahit near central post office. Friendly staff dispenses maps and pamphlets. Open M-Th 7am-2pm, F 7-11am, Sa 7am-12:30pm.

Tours: Perama, Jl. Pejanggik 66 (☎635 928), east of the hospital. Runs buses and cruises to Flores, Java, and Sumbawa.

Immigration Offices: ☎635 220. On Jl. Udayana, 300m north of Jl. Pejanggik on the way to the airport. Open M-Th 8am-2pm, F 8-11am, Sa 8am-1pm.

Currency Exchange: Moneychangers and **ATMs** abound at the main intersection in Ampenan, on Jl. Pejanggik in Cakra, and opposite Sweta Terminal on Jl. Sandubaya. **BCA** (☎632 588), on Jl. Pejanggik, has a **24hr. ATM** (Cirrus/MC/PLUS/V). Open M-F 8am-2:30pm.

Emergency: Police ☎110. **Ambulance** ☎118.

Police: Ampenan, Jl. Langko 17 (☎633 733). **Sweta** (☎632 682), on Jl. Selaparang.

Medical Services: Rumah Sakit Umum Mataram (☎213 45), on Jl. Pejanggik, east of the Governor's office. English-speaking female doctor available in the morning. Attached **Apotik** (☎637 326). MC/V. **Both open 24hr.**

Telephones: The big **Telkom office,** Jl. Langko 23 (☎634 466), has an **HCD** telephone.

Internet Access: *Warposnet* room of the central post office. Rp250 per 15min. More convenient is **Global Internet**, in the strip mall opposite the Lombok Raya Hotel. Rp750 per hr. Open daily 8am-8pm.

Express Mail: DHL, Jl. Pejanggik 20, west of the Governor's Office. Open M-F 8am-4:30pm, Sa 8am-1pm.

Post Offices: GPO, on Jl. Majapahit. *Poste Restante.* Open M-Th 8am-3pm, F-Sa 8-11am. **Postal code:** 83114.

ACCOMMODATIONS

Accommodations pander equally to tourists and locals. Generally comfortable and cheap, they are far from the beach and nightlife. If being close to the action is important, **Senggigi** (see p. 237) is the better bet. The cheapest lodgings, in Ampanen along **Jl. Koperasi,** are noisier and dustier than in Cakra.

Shanti Puri Hotel and Restaurant, Jl. Maktal 15 (☎632 649), 100m south off Jl. Pejanggik in east Cakra. Comfort exceeds price. Friendly staff, cozy restaurant. Clean rooms with fan. Doubles with toilets Rp35,000, with *mandi* Rp25,000-30,000.

Inap Keluagra Oka (Oka), Jl. Repatmaja 5 (☎622 406), 200m south of Jl. Pejanggik at Bank Pembanguan Indonesia in Cakra, on a side street. Shady courtyard and *losmen*-quality rooms. Friendly staff. Breakfast included. Singles Rp20,000; doubles Rp25,000.

Losmen Ayu (☎621 761), on Jl. Nursiwan, 100m south of the BCA ATM in Cakra, has clean rooms. Doubles with *mandi* Rp25,000, with Western toilets Rp35,000.

Hotel Wisata, Jl. Koperasi 19 (☎269 71), in Ampenon. A variety of rooms just secluded enough to get away from street noise. Close to antique and art shops. Singles with bath Rp35,000; doubles Rp40,000.

Losmen Horas, Jl. Koperasi 62 (☎631 695). Basic and cheap. Singles Rp17,500; doubles Rp20,000.

Chandra Hotel, Jl. Caturwarga 55 (☎623 979), south of the hospital. Cut down Jl. Prisaian to Jl. Caturwarga and turn right. In the heart (and heat) of Mataram. Simple, windowless rooms. Doubles Rp35,000, with A/C Rp60,000.

FOOD

Closed due to the 2000 riots in Ampenon, Restaurant Betawi, famous amongst expats, has since re-opened and is the top choice for food in Ampenon. In Cakra, there is a variety of restaurants and numerous scrumptious night stalls. The region specialty is spicy *sasak taliwang*, food smothered in hot chili peppers. If you can't handle the heat, ask for it *"kurang pedes"* (less spicy) and ignore the snickers.

Restaurant Betawi, at the intersection of Jl. Koperasai, Jl. SalehSongkar and Jl. Yos Sudarso, in a "Colonial Grand Style." On a balcony overlooking the heart of Ampenon, Betawi offers up some lip-smacking dishes. Red snapper with Rico Rico (sweet tomato with chili) sauce Rp22,000, including rice and bread with cheese.

Suharti Sate House, Jl. Maktal 9 (☎ 6379 58), next to the Shanti Puri. Run by Romy Rahiem, a Mataram-renowned Indonesian master chef. Best *nasi goreng* on Lombok (Rp5000). Open daily 9am-10pm.

Kania Satu-Rumah Makan Taliwang, on Jl. Pejanggik, opposite Bank BCA in Cakra. Spicy Lombok-style food. *Ayam goreng taliwang* Rp15,000. Open daily 7am-11pm.

Aroma, Jl. Palapa I 2, in west Cakra, south of Jl. Pejanggik at Bank BTN. Clean, quiet, and cool. Large portions of Chinese seafood. Young pigeon Rp18,000.

SHOPPING

If it's modernity—escalators, bright lights, A/C, and fixed prices—you seek, then the **Mataram Mall** (formerly Glinoya Shopping Center) on Jl. Pejonggik is your place. Here you'll find clothes and electronics, and a bookstore with English texts to boot. If you prefer a noisy rush and bargaining, then the **market** in Cakra, at the Mataram Complex further up Jl. Pejanggik and condenses at the intersection of Jl. Pejanggik and Jl. Gede Ngurah, is for you; it offers similar items, minus the English books, for cheaper prices. For art and antiques, go to **Jl. Saleh Sungklar,** in Ampenon center. One certainly worth the trip is the Yufi Artshop, Jl. Saleh Sungklar 22, which has brilliant and affordable pottery in all shapes and sizes.

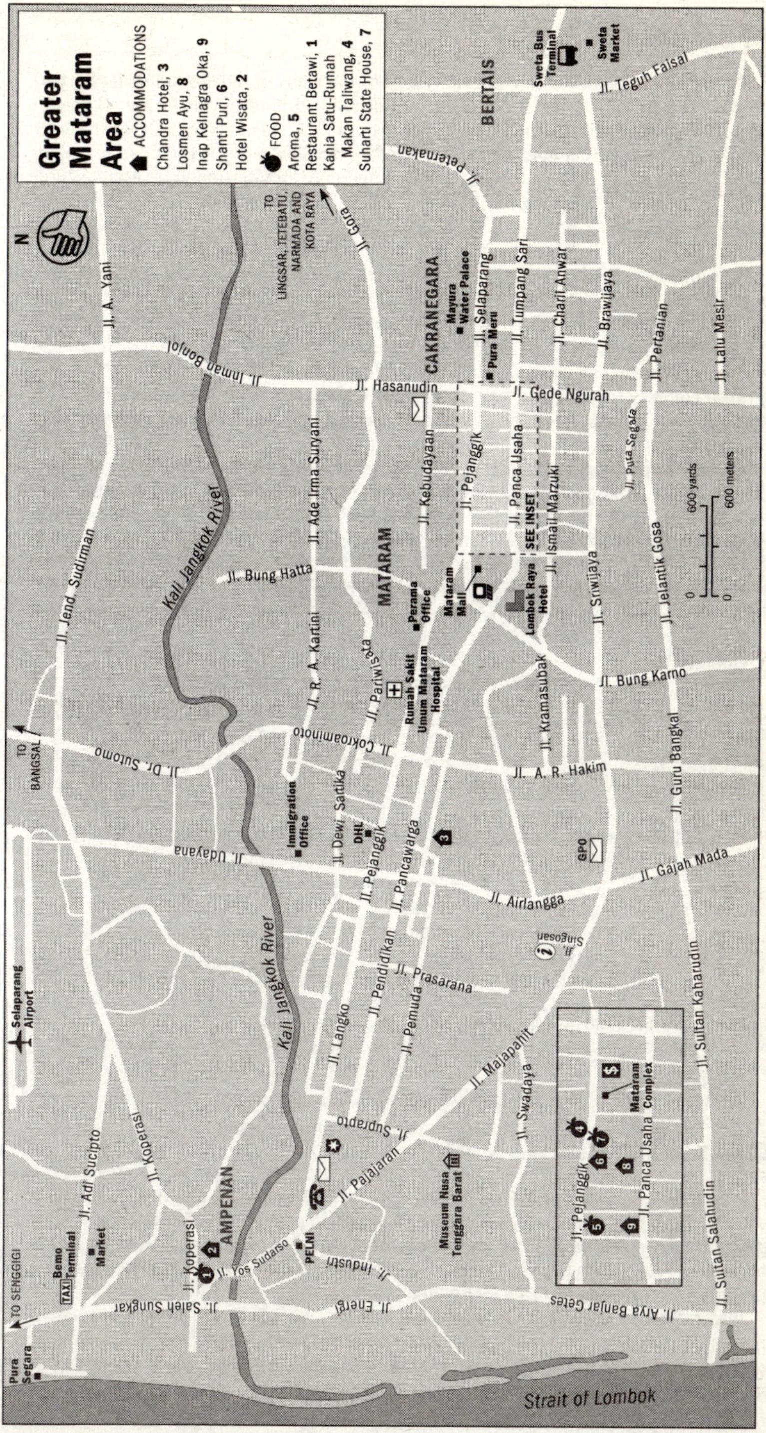
Greater Mataram Area
ACCOMMODATIONS
Chandra Hotel, 3
Losmen Ayu, 8
Inap Kelnagra Oka, 9
Shanti Puri, 6
Hotel Wisata, 2
FOOD
Aroma, 5
Restaurant Betawi, 1
Kania Satu-Rumah
Makan Taliwang, 4
Suharti State House, 7
N
TO LINGSAR, TETEBATU, NARMADA AND KOTA RAYA
BERTAIS
Sweta Bus Terminal
Sweta Market
Jl. Teguh Faisal
Jl. Peternakan
Jl. Gora
CAKRANEGARA
Mayura Water Palace
Pura Meru
Jl. Selaparang
Jl. Tumpang Sari
Jl. Chairil Anwar
Jl. Brawijaya
Jl. Pertanian
Jl. Lalu Mesir
Jl. A. Yani
Jl. Imam Bonjol
Jl. Hasanudin
Jl. Gede Ngurah
Jl. Kebudayaan
Jl. Pejanggik
Jl. Panca Usaha
SEE INSET
Jl. Ismail Marzuki
Jl. Pura Segara
600 yards
600 meters
Jl. Jend. Sudirman
Kali Jangkok River
Jl. Ade Irma Suryani
Jl. Bung Hatta
MATARAM
Perama Office
Mataram Mall
Lombok Raya Hotel
Jl. Sriwijaya
Jl. Jelantik Gosa
Jl. R. A. Kartini
Jl. Pariwisata
Rumah Sakit Umum Mataram Hospital
Jl. Kramasubak
Jl. Bung Karno
TO BANGSAL
Jl. Dr. Sutomo
Jl. Cokroaminoto
Jl. A. R. Hakim
Jl. Guru Bangkal
Immigration Office
Jl. Dewi Sartika
DHL
Jl. Udayana
Jl. Pejanggik
Jl. Pancawarga
GPO
Jl. Gajah Mada
Jl. Airlangga
Jl. Singosari
Selaparang Airport
Kali Jangkok River
Jl. Langko
Jl. Pendidikan
Jl. Pemuda
Jl. Prasarana
Jl. Sultan Kaharudin
Jl. Majapahit
Jl. Swadaya
Mataram Complex
Jl. Suprapto
Jl. Adi Sucipto
Jl. Koperasi
AMPENAN
Jl. Pajajaran
Museum Nusa Tenggara Barat
Jl. Pejanggik
Jl. Panca Usaha
Bemo Terminal
TAXI
Market
Jl. Koperasi
Jl. Yos Sudarso
PELNI
Jl. Industri
TO SENGGIGI
Jl. Saleh Sungkar
Jl. Energi
Jl. Arya Banjar Getas
Jl. Sultan Salahudin
Pura Segara
Strait of Lombok

INDONESIA

SIGHTS

In 1894, Balinese and Western *Sasaks* crept to the walls of the **Mayura Water Palace,** fired on Dutch soldiers camped there, and drove them out of this former Balinese court. Fountains, statues, and cannons are all that remain (Rp2000 entrance). Across Jl. Pejanggik is **Pura Meru,** Lombok's *grande dame* of Balinese temples, with 33 shrines and three big, plain, empty pagodas. Commissioned by Anak Agung Made Karang of the Singosari Kingdom in 1772, the three pagodas honor the Hindu trinity of Brahma, Vishnu, and Shiva, and the three volcanos, Agung, Bromo, and Rinjani. Sashes are lent out for free, but the entrance fee is Rp10,000.

More interesting is **Pura Segara,** on the north side of Ampenan in a shaded neighborhood off of Jl. Yos Sudars. Still used for Hindu burial ceremonies, the gates are locked, although a peek around the surrounding fishing village warrants the trip. Pura Segara is best visited early, when the rugged foothills of Gunung Rinjani are visible. A **Chinese cemetery,** on the way to Pura Segara, is an exhibition of above-ground tombs enshrined in ornate tiles of Chinese characters and colors. The grounds have gone to seed, however, and it is not unusual for locals to graze their cattle inside.

Museum Nusa Tenggara Barat, on Jl. Panji Tilar Negara in southeast Ampenan, displays 1239 palm-leaf Indonesian manuscripts and exhibits in English on the history, geology, and cultures of Lombok and Sumbawa. One of the curators speaks English and leads tours. (Open Tu-Su 8am-4pm. Rp750.)

DAYTRIPS FROM GREATER MATARAM

NARMADA

Bemo *run from the Sweta Terminal eastward to Narmada (15min., Rp1000).*

On the south side of the main road in Narmada, is the **Pura Kalasa Water Palace,** a temple built into a hill and encircled by three pools. The surroundings are a reproduction of Gunung Rinjani: the central pool replicates Lake Segara Anak, the small pools represent the cascading hot springs near the lake, and the temple itself, built at the top of the hill, symbolizes Gununj Rinjani's peak. A popular story states that the water palace sated the King's lust; the Balinese monarch would peep at the village virgins in the pool. Guides (fairly useless) will approach you near the entrance. The water palace is more popular with the locals than with tourists—it's packed on weekends. During the summer, youth groups often camp out here. Locals use the lower pools for swimming and laundry, while it is believed that the higher pool's water gives eternal life if drunk. Tourists can join in the splashing for a small fee (Rp1000, Rp1000 extra to bathe). During the full moon of the 5th Balinese lunar month in December, townspeople give live ducks and other offerings to the lake in a ritual called *pujawali.*

LINGSAR

Bemo *run to Lingsar from Narmada (10min., Rp1000).*

The **Pura Lingsar** temples, consisting of the Muslim **Kemaliq** and the Hindu **Pura Gaduh,** built in 1714, sits 7km northwest of Narmada (15min. from Sindu), near the village Lingsar. Both temples are simple and sparse. The complex celebrates the peaceful coexistence of Balinese and Sasaks; annual week-long ceremonies at the start of the wet season known as **Perang Topat** (Topat War) mark these events. Hindus and Muslims pelt each other with *ketupat* (rice wrapped in coconut leaves) after giving thanks for last year's rain and asking for it to return again as a symbol of tolerance between the two religions.

A spring water eel pool lays within the Kemaliq section of Pura Lingsar. Eggs to feed the eels are sold at the gate. It is said that if an eel rises to eat your egg, you will have good luck. There is no fee to enter the complex, but a donation is expected for the two temples (sash provided).

SENGGIGI

☎0370

With one main drag and paradise-like bungalow resorts, Senggigi is the small but hip height of nightlife and leisure on Lombok, offering everything from fine food and dancing to drag shows, but not before the early evening ritual of watching the sunset over the Gilis.

ORIENTATION AND PRACTICAL INFORMATION. Only 15min. from Ampenan by *bemo* (Rp1000), it's possible to make Senggigi a base for exploration into north and west Lombok. Most hotels and restaurants are spread out along a 2km strip that incorporates two sandy bays.

Services, which cluster near **Pacific Supermarket** (☎693 005), on Jl. Raya Senggigi (open daily 8:30am-9:30pm), include: the **Perama Office** (☎693 007), opposite Lina's Cottages, which provides information on trips to the Gilis and Gunung Rinjani; **Bank BNI,** next to the supermarket (☎693 546; **24hr. ATM** accepts MC/PLUS/V); the **police** (☎693 267), at the north end of Jl. Raya Senggigi; a **24hr. medical clinic** (☎693 210, ext. 1730), at the Senggigi Beach Hotel; a **Telekom Office,** opposite the Sheraton Hotel; a **wartel,** in Pacific Supermarket (offers cash international calls; open daily 8am-10pm); an **HCD** booth outside the supermarket; several Internet cafes along the main strip (all open around 8am-11pm; Rp200 per min.); and the **post office,** opposite the supermarket (*Poste Restante;* open M-Sa 8am-8pm, Su 8am-noon). **Postal code:** 83355.

ACCOMMODATIONS AND FOOD. Although Senggigi is resort-oriented, the lack of tourists has depressed prices considerably. With some bargaining, you can have plush accommodations at budget prices. **Batu Bolong Hotel** offers daily cleaning services, towels, and free tea all day long. Opposite the beach, it's a 10min walk below the main strip (on the same street), or a 3min. *bemo* ride. (☎693 065. Doubles Rp55,000.) **Lombok Coconut,** at the far north end of Jl. Raya Senggigi past the Sheraton, has ocean views from the swimming pool and free transport into town. (☎693 195. Singles Rp35,000; doubles Rp60,000.) **Sonya** , on the main road behind Kastika Restaurant, is the cheapest place in town with warm hospitality and a delicious breakfast. (☎693 447. Singles Rp15,000; doubles Rp20,000.)

Fine international cuisine is on **Jl. Raya Senggigi** (Rp20,000-30,000 per dish), but cheaper eats are scarce. Some establishments offer transportation to and from restaurants; call ahead. **Restoran Taman Senggigi** (☎693 842) features a fountain with goldfish, multi-level seating, and Cajun Tuna Steak (Rp26,000). **Bambo** has the best curry dishes (Rp15,000-25,000) in Senggigi. The art market in the north end is cluttered with beachside dining. **Cafe Coco Loco,** next to the Sheraton Hotel end of the market, prepares an excellent *olah olah,* an extremely spicy Sasak dish with vegetables in coconut milk. For basic dining, four *warung,* located before the bridge leading to the center of town serve scrumptious *ikan laut* (ocean fish). **Senang Restaurant,** in the supermarket complex, is cheap and acceptable, and offers spicy *nasi pecal* for Rp6000. (Open daily 9am-9pm.)

SIGHTS AND ENTERTAINMENT. **Pura Batu Bolong** (Hole-in-Rock Temple), one of Lombok's most stunning Balinese temples, is within walking distance of the main strip to the south, on a rocky promontory with a gorgeous view of the ocean. It is thought that the Balinese once hurled virgins from Batu Bolong into the sea. A donation is expected, and sashes can be borrowed for free at the gate.

Despite the increasingly grand views, the tourism wanes as you go further north. Much of the desolate beach between cities is accessible from the road. *Bemo* run sporadically along the long road as far as Mangsit (15min., Rp1000), and most rented motorbikes can manage the hills. On the way to Mangit, buy some coconut milk from a roadside vendor, sit atop a lookout hill on the coastal road, and watch the sun drop behind the Gilis and Gunung Agung. At 10pm the to-and-fro migration between two dance clubs begins: **Club Tropicana** and **The Blue Coral,** about a half-kilometer apart on the main drag. Both offer contemporary dance music with the occasional 70s or 80s song. At some point in the evening, a band comes on; if you don't like it, just move on to the other club. (☎693 173. Cover Rp20,000-25,000.) **Pondok Senggigi** hosts an all-male cabaret (Sa 11pm) and **Warung Pojok,** next to Millenium Internet, titillates with an evening drag show (9pm).

KUTA ☎0370

Kuta, not to be confused with Kuta on Bali, is a rock-bottom-cheap stop for surfers, beachcombers, and budget travelers in the center of Lombok's south coast, where pristine white sand clashes with a jagged shoreline of unusual rock formations. A fishing town once slated for massive tourist development, Kuta has recently been hit hard by the economic crisis. While the villagers are friendly, the struggling populace has become desperate, and robberies are on the rise; check on safety in Mataram before making the trip.

TRANSPORTATION AND PRACTICAL INFORMATION. A Perama **bus** to Kuta costs five times more than a *bemo* but saves hours of travel (2hr., Rp45,000). Explore Sasak villages on the way to Kuta (Rp1500) by taking a bus from **Mataram** via **Praya** (Rp2000) and **Sengkol** (Rp1500). *Bemo* from Sengkol continue on to Tanjung Aan Beach.

The bulk of tourist services, including a **police station, Perama Office,** money-changer/*warung* hybrids, and the Ocean Blue Surf Shop, are on the beachfront road, **Jl. Raya Pantai Kuta.** The closest **hospital** is in Praya, but Kuta has a **public health clinic** 500m from Kuta on the road to Sengkol (doctor available M-Sa 4-6pm; attached **apotik open 24hr.**). There is a **wartel** (open M-Sa 7:30am-10:30pm) and another Perama office across the intersection from Matahari Inn. International and collect calls can be made from Wisma Segara Anak and Kuta Indah.

ACCOMMODATIONS AND FOOD. The bungalows along the beachfront are of similar quality and price. **Ketapang Cafe and Bungalow,** on the corner of the beachfront and road leading inland, is immaculate, with a leisurely restaurant. (Singles Rp15,000; doubles Rp25,000). **Anda Bungalows and Restaurant** provides service and care worthy of a resort, although it's best to eat elsewhere. (Singles Rp25,000; doubles Rp35,000). Farther toward Mandalika Tourist Resort, **Rinjani Agung** has a range of rooms with safes and night security. (☎654 852. Rp30,000.) Landscaped gardens and the luxury of a pool at **Matahari Inn** win it the non-beach prize. (Rp50,000. MC/V.)

Most accommodations in Kuta have their own restaurants, but the half-dozen waterfront *warung* are cheaper and closer to main street's activity. **Rinjani Agung** features international dishes like Thai chicken salad (Rp10,500) and spinach and feta crêpes (Rp14,000).

INDONESIA

BEACHES. Kuta's beach, **Putri Nyale,** is too rocky for swimming but great for exploring. It hosts the **Bau Nyale,** a celebration of the mating of *nyale* seaworms, four to eight days after the second full moon of the year (in February or March). The origin of the festival stems from the story of the beautiful princess Mandalika, who, instead of choosing one man, threw herself into the ocean where she was transformed into a *nyale* and could be shared by everyone. The celebration marks the anniversary of her transformation. Thousands of people camp on the beach before the *nyale* make their appearance. Young people eat the worms, which are supposedly powerful aphrodisiacs.

The region also boasts great **surf,** and boats can be chartered to choice spots. Check the **Blue Ocean Surf Shop** for local excursions as well as trips to the breaks on Sumbawa. (☎653 911. Board rentals Rp25,000 per day.) A local favorite for surfing is **Maun Beach,** 30min. outside Kuta. (*Ojeks* Rp25,000.) **Tanjungon Beach,** good for swimming and snorkeling, is 5km east of Kuta. (*Bemo* from Kuta Rp1500.) **Sartinng Beach,** completely isolated although still visited by locals, is another swimmable white sand beach with bizarre surrounding rock formations.

NIGHTLIFE. Jungle Bay, across from the Matahari Inn, sometimes has live music, but the eclectic selection of jazz and more tickles just fine. The bar serves a parade of cocktails and Bintang draught beer (Rp10,000). Their pool is free of charge. (☎655 410. Open 11am until the last person leave_s.)

> **SOUTH COAST BEACHES** Due to threats against foreigners since 1998, coverage of the South Coast Beaches is not included in *Let's Go: Southeast Asia 2002.* Check embassies for current safety information.

GUNUNG RINJANI

Magnificent Gunung Rinjani, which last erupted in 1994, rises 3726m in the center of the north coast and is Lombok's holiest site. Many local Balinese Hindus make an annual pilgrimage to the summit to chuck goldfish and jewelry into Segara Anak, the crater lake, much to the delight of local fisherman. The Sasak Muslims believe that on the ninth day after death, spirits travel to Gununj Rinjani. By journeying to the volcano, Sasaks draw power from their ancestors.

TRANSPORTATION. Due to the popularity of treks, private tourist information centers in Senggigi and on the Gili Islands arrange transportation from **Senaru**—the gateway town—as part of a package tour. Cars (Rp100,000) and *ojeks* (Rp35,000) can be hired from Senggigi or Senaru. Self-fashioned expeditions cost less but require finding a guide and transportion. *Bemo* to **Bayan** start in Mataram (3hr., Rp5000) or can be picked up on the northwest coastal road in Pemenang or Tanjung. Past Bayan, *bemo* run from Bayan to Senaru (30min., Rp1500). Transportation is possible to Bayan from **Labuhan Lombok** or **Pringgabaya.**

ACCOMMODATIONS AND FOOD. All accommodations in Senaru rent out trekking equipment and arrange guides and porters. Staying in a *pondok* (guest house) doesn't bind a guest to use that *pondok's* guides and sleeping bags; trekkers should choose a room they like, then shop around. **Pondok Indah,** on the south end of Senaru, has new rooms and a great view of the coastline and valley below. The professional staff offers an excellent trekking service and organizes transport for travelers starting or completing the climb in Sembalan Lawang. (Singles Rp25,000; doubles Rp30,000.) **Segara Anak Restaurant and ,** across the road from Pondok Indah and not as helpful with trekking information, offers an equally stunning view of Senaru's river valley but is plainer than Pondok Indah. (Singles Rp20,000; doubles Rp25,000.) The most convenient option is the **Bale Bayan,** on the trailhead opposite the village. (Singles Rp25,000; doubles Rp50,000.)

INDONESIA

CLIMBING GUNUNG RINJANI. Climbing Gununj Rinjani, one of the most exhilarating experiences on Lombok, should only be tried by those prepared for a long trek. Climbers can reach the summit from nearly all sides—Tetebatu, Saesot, or Torean. The most popular route is by way of Batu Koq/Senaru and Sembalun Lawangon on Gununj Rinjani's northern foothills. The two most popular climbing options are available from almost every *pondok* in Senaru: a two-day/one-night package (Rp150,000-200,000), or a three-day/two-night package (Rp250,000-300,000). If you want more time to climb the summit, guides are available for longer programs. All packages include guide, tent, sleeping bag, mat, and water. Prices drop for groups. Inexperienced hikers may also hire porters to carry everything but personal items. Porters usually carry 40kg and cost Rp40,000-70,000 per day, depending on time of year, demand, and your bargaining skills. Both porters and guides prepare meals and carry gear. Be friendly and generous with your guide; hard bargaining and mistreatment make them cranky and possibly less disposed to warn you about those loose rocks and hidden plunges. Bring a flashlight and warm clothing; the temperature drops at night.

The most popular route to the summit is the three-day/two-night trek from **Sembalun Lawang.** The first night ends at **Plawagan II** on the crater rim, a 6-8hr. climb from Sembalun Lawang. From there, it is a 3hr. climb to the summit in the wee hours of the second day to watch the sunrise. Trekkers descend from the rim to the crater lake (2hr.), take a dip in the lake and hot springs, then climb back out of the crater to **Plawagan I** on the rim above **Senaru** (2hr.). When going down into the caldera, watch your step; past hikers have slipped to their deaths. The final descent to Senaru is a 3-4hr. hike on the third day.

Senaru, in Gunung Rinjani's picturesque foothills, contains the spectacular **Sindang Gile Waterfall.** The path leading to the falls appears off the main road in Senaru when the falls first come into view. A second waterfall upstream from Sindang Gile is equally powerful and has a pool ideal for swimming. Although locals will tell you that a guide is needed to reach the second falls, trekkers can follow the path at the bottom of the steps as they descend to Sindang Gile. The path crosses an aqueduct and fades out 500m before the waterfall at the bend in the river. From there, follow the noise and the riverbed to reach the base of the falls.

TETEBATU ☎0370

Tetebatu sits on the cusp between foothills and farmland. *Pondok* and *losmen* stand between fields of rice and tobacco in picturesque contrast to Lombok's beach attractions. Wander through the fields toward the Monkey Forest to the north, the jungle waterfalls to the east, or the natural springs to the west. If placid Tetebatu loses its charm, visit the nearby local craft villages by motorbike.

TRANSPORTATION AND PRACTICAL INFORMATION. To get to Tetebatu, catch a *bemo* to Promotong. From there, *bemo* go as far as **Kotaraja** (Rp1000), where *ojek* and *cidomo* go the extra distance to Tetebatu (Rp2000). Tetebatu's northern and southern central areas are 1km apart. *Losmen* are in two clusters, one between Tetebatu's two centers, the other on the eastbound side road, **Jl. Waterfall.** The Monkey Forest is to the north. A **Perama office** is in the **Green Orry Inn** on the south side of Jl. Waterfall from lower Tetebatu. Soedjones Hotel offers **currency exchange.** Warung Salabusa rents motorbikes (Rp30,000) and cars (Rp100,000), and the **wartel,** next door, offers cash international and collect calls. The nearest **post office** and **police station** are in Masbagik.

ACCOMMODATIONS AND FOOD. Tetebatu has high-quality accommodations south of the town center and along the eastbound road. The lack of tourists means that all prices are negotiable. **Centrawasih Cottages,** along Jl. Waterfall, has colorful *Sasak*-style Lumbung bungalows. Only one of the four has a Western bathroom, but all are spotless and cheap. (Doubles Rp30,000.) **Pondok Tetebatu,** along the main road, has bright bungalows with private *mandi* facing a charming garden (only Rp20,000-25,000). Directly behind, **Onong Garden** has similar rooms farther from the road (Rp20,000). **Soedjones Hotel,** at the north end of the main road, has slightly over-priced rooms and a swimming pool. (☎62 376 22522. Bungalows with *mandi* Rp35,000; cottages with Western bath Rp45,000.)

Every hotel comes with a good-quality restaurant or cafe. **Green Orry Inn's cafe** serves delicious *lassis* (Rp3000-3500) and chicken curry (Rp15,000). **Harmony Cafe,** on the main road, is vegetarian-friendly (vegetables with coconut milk Rp7500). **Tetebatu Cafe** has pool tables and an occasional band on Fridays and Saturdays and serves a small menu of cheap food (fried chicken Rp12,500). **Warung Salabusa,** the other nightspot, is down the main road from Harmony Cafe and is also open for lunch. Nightly movies, Saturday night bands, and karaoke round out this lively cafe.

SIGHTS. Local hospitality makes Tetebatu a peaceful retreat. The paths around the glorious tobacco fields and terraced rice paddies merit days of exploring. To get to the **Monkey Forest,** follow the main road north until it veers right; a dirt road marked by a park sign continues north for 4km before reaching the *hutan.* Local boys gather here to offer their services as guides. **Otak Kokok Gading** (Joben Waterfall), west of Tetebatu, is frequented by locals who believe the natural springs have healing powers. Far more impressive are the **Jeruk Manis Waterfalls,** 7km to the east of Tetebatu. To reach these falls, follow the signs along the eastbound road out of Tetebatu's southern hub to a carpark. From there it's a 30min. walk to the falls. There's a new police station at the entrance. Guides are recommended. (Guides Rp20,000 for the falls, Rp50,000 to walk to all sights. Admission to Jeruk Manis Waterfalls Rp1500.)

DAYTRIPS FROM TETEBATU. Rural Lombok towns are full of textiles and craftwork. *Ojek* drivers and bungalow owners offer tourists various packages around the handicraft loop. *Bemo* and *cidomo* cover all destinations and, if you travel early, shouldn't be hard to catch. The frugal can walk to nearby villages.

The market town of **Kotaraja** is 3km south of Tetebatu. Its daily market, which carries mainly produce, is dwarfed by the massive turnouts on Wednesday and Friday. The next village, **Loyok,** is known for bamboo and rattan weaving. On its main street is a "handicraft center," but residential shops are more interesting. Visitors who ask to see weaving can get a lesson in bamboo ring-making. Locals sell burnt-sienna pots that resemble overbaked Grecian urns 500m east in **Rungkang. Masbagik,** however, is the commercial center for terracotta pieces. East of Pomotong on the main drag, Masbagik has a market on Mondays. **Pringgasela** lies farther from Masbagik (go east toward Rempung and then veer north off the main road), but it's worth the trip to see *Sasak* ikat weaving at its finest.

The **Radiah** in **Lendang Nangka** is an unorthodox way to experience central Lombok. Radiah is a teacher who leads walks through rice fields and teaches guests how to plant and harvest rice. Meals consist of Sasok food: *urap-urap* (veggies with young coconut and garlic); *olah olah* (veggies with coconut milk); *sayurbening* (plain boiled veggies); and *pelecing kangkung* (very spicy boiled veggies). There are two walks a day—one (from sunrise until 7:30am) to witness how Sasak farmers start their day, and another (from 4pm to sunset) to see how their day ends. Walks are free for guests, but non-guests can also tag along for Rp25,000. Buses stop at Masbagik from Labuhan Lombok and Sweta. Take a *cidomo* (Rp1500) to Lendang Nangka and ask for Radiah. (Rooms include meals. Singles Rp25,000; doubles Rp35,000; plantation room Rp45,000. If business is slow, the plantation rooms close and guests are boarded with the family.)

NORTHWEST GILI

Gili Trawangan, Gili Air, and Gili Meno are tourist magnets, popular for their glorious blue-green reefs, white sand, and fun-loving crowds. Each island has a niche of its own: Gili Trawangan hops with an eternal party, Gili Air is the perfect romantic getaway, and Gili Meno is the best place to hide from the first two. Look elsewhere for lush tropical vegetation and jungle wildlife though—the islands are all flat and, without hills to break the clouds, there is little rainfall. Environmental changes and rising water temperatures have endangered the coral reefs along the shore and sparked wide conservation efforts.

THE VIEW FROM ABOVE

The lowdown: Three islands–Gili Air, Gili Meno, and Gili Trawangan–between Bali and Sumbawa.
Highlights: Partying the bar shacks of Gili Trawangan, scuba diving in Gili Air's coral reefs, and finding quiet on Gili Meno.

GETTING AROUND NORTHWEST GILI

From **Mataram** (see p. 232), take a *bemo* to **Pemenang** (1½hr., Rp4000), where **cidomo** go 1km to the port of **Bangsal.** Once at Bangsal, you can reach the Gilis by public, shuttle, or chartered boats. **Public boats,** the cheapest option, leave when full (at least 15 passengers and up to 2hr. wait) for Gili Air (Rp1500), Gili Meno (Rp1900), and Gili Trawangan (Rp2000). **Shuttle boats** run at 10am and 4:30pm to

Gili Air (Rp3500), Gili Meno (Rp4000), and Gili Trawangan (Rp4500) and leave at 8:15am from Gili Air and Gili Meno and 8:30am from Gili Trawangan on the return journey. **Perama** is a reputable boat operator that runs boats to the Gilis from virtually anywhere on Bali and Lombok. Direct boats leave from **Senggigi** (Rp30,000). The **ticket office,** by the landing as you get off the boat, also runs expensive **charter boats;** after 4:30pm the prices are no longer fixed, so bargain hard. **Island-hopping shuttles** (Rp7000 one-way) make it possible to daytrip to other islands and leave twice daily from Gili Air at 8:30am and 3pm; other information is available at the ticket office.

GILI TRAWANGAN

Gili Trawangan, the party center of the Gilis, bustles with backpackers who come for several bars and a hip beach resort with low prices. In 1992, President Suharto marked the northwest corner of the island for massive tourist development and ordered all establishments to shut down. In July 1998, following Suharto's resignation, the people of Trawangan demanded their land back. As they returned to their beachside plots, most set up stores and simple *warungs* that contrast with the more upscale resorts near the landing. The island is a great place for snorkeling and scuba diving, and stretches of undeveloped beach await exploration.

TRANSPORTATION AND PRACTICAL INFORMATION. The **boat landing** is at the midpoint of the eastern coast. The **Perama Office** is south of the landing, 100m inland. A **medical clinic** is next door to Villa-Ombok on the south side of the main strip. The **wartel,** south of the boat landing, offers collect and calling-card calls for Rp10,000. (Open daily 8am-midnight.) **Wiggis Internet,** next to the Perama Office, suffers the fewest chance disconnections. (Open daily 8:30am-11pm). *Cidomo*, bicycles, and walking suffice for local transportation. There is **no post office.** Trawangan has the best diving infrastructure in the Gilis. **Blue Marlin Dive Center,** with a PADI 5-star IDC rating, is one of the island's three professional dive centers. (2 dives US$45). Compare prices with **Reef Seekers** and **Dream Divers.** Bargain for **snorkeling** prices around US$10 (☎/fax 0370 632 424).

ACCOMMODATIONS AND FOOD. Most accommodations line a narrow strip along the eastern coast; the northern and southern ends are more secluded. Lodging comes with electricity, fan, mosquito nets, and breakfast. In the high season, the better hotels may be booked, forcing travelers to put down a deposit while staying elsewhere for the first night, or possibly finding a bench on the beach.

Creatif Bungalows II, a 15min. walk from the boat landing and just a short stroll to the best swimming area, has private hammocks in a beautiful garden. (Singles Rp25,000; doubles Rp35,000.) The cheapest option is **Mawar I Bungalows,** at the southern end of the strip, with bamboo bungalows and slightly worn outdoor *mandi*. (Singles Rp7500; doubles Rp10,000). For peace and quiet, head to **Pondok Santi,** south of Mawar I (singles Rp25,000; doubles Rp30,000) or **Pondok Jessica,** 100m inland, which has new cottages and fresh-water showers. (Rp40,000-60,000.)

In addition to the *warung* that line the beach north of the landing, many fine restaurants line the southern end of the beach strip. **Dream Divers** grills fresh fish every night. **Blue-Marlin Dive Center** serves tasty meals on beachside tables. (Sweet and sour prawns Rp25,000.) **Villa-Ombok** has delicious food that's almost worth the price tag. (entrees Rp30,000). Try the crêpes *partisia* (apple or mango and custard in a crepe and drizzled with orange sauce Rp15,500). Most of the backpacker cafes and *warungs* serve the local specialty—Indonesian magic mushrooms.

GILI AIR

Gili Air is just busy enough. It buzzes with the bustle of a tourist town yet retains a small town air. Less arid than the other Gilis, the island supports coconut groves. Gili Air also has the largest permanent population of the Gilis and the local pres-

INDONESIA

ence is felt beyond the hawkers and massage-ladies. Swimming is best in the southeast corner of the island, but snorkeling sites have deteriorated due to seaweed farming and dynamite fishing.

TRANSPORTATION AND PRACTICAL INFORMATION. A road traces the perimeter of the island, and a few unnamed roads cut through the village center. Most tourist services are on the beachfront. **Boats** land on the south side of the island. **Bicycles** are the sole and most efficient local transport.

The **Perama Office** (☎637 816), 100m inland from the jetty, arranges **glass-bottom boat trips** and **tours** all over Lombok. Most hotels offer tickets to destinations in Bali, Lombok, and Sumbawa at similar prices. Gili Air has **no hospital, police, post office,** or **banks** but there's a **health clinic** (*Puskesmas*) on the south side in the village, and **moneychangers** are everywhere. Hotel Gili Indah has a **wartel.** (☎636 341. Open daily 7am-10pm.) **Internet cafes** are popping up all over. (Rp500 per min.)

Several dive shops and guest houses offer **scuba-diving** trips and courses, and most bungalows rent **snorkeling** equipment. Even if you don't dive with **Reefseekers** (☎641 008), stop by to ask the staff for tour of the **Turtle Farm.** After endangered turtle eggs are bought from markets and hatched, the turtles are returned to the sea.

ACCOMMODATIONS AND FOOD. Night owls will be grateful for the island's 24hr. electricity. Most bungalows offer standards including mosquito nets, *mandi*, and breakfast, with the variables being showers, hammocks, and location. Prices increase during high season, and rooms fill up early in the day. **Safari Cottages,** along the south coast, has respectable bungalows on a stretch of secluded, if scruffy, beach. (Singles Rp30,000; doubles Rp45,000.) **Gili Air Santay,** halfway along the east shoreline, is more expensive than others, but the cleanliness and tiled bathrooms make it worth the extra rupiah. (Singles Rp35,000; doubles Rp50,000.) Next door, **Coconut Cottages** has a range of accommodations in a torch-lit, tropical garden. (Bamboo bungalows with veranda Rp30,000-50,000.)

The restaurant in **Hotel Gili Air,** with beachside seating along the northern coast, is a great place to watch the sunset and chow down on grilled tuna (Rp20,000). Next door, the **Pondok Wisata Santi** features pavilions and delicious sweet-and-sour chicken (Rp15,000). **Il Pirata,** in a pirate ship 100m west and inland from the landing (follow the signs), serves Italian cuisine (most entrees Rp20,000-25,000).

GILI MENO

Gili Meno is the least visited of the Gilis, making it the preferred island for a romantic retreat. The northern part of the island is empty but the livelier southeast shore is entrancing, considerably better-groomed, and has the island's only decent beach. An inland **salt-water lake** can be reached by cutting through the island on the road next to Royal Reef Hotel. During the low season, Gili Meno operates at half-speed; bungalows remain open, but restaurants usually close down.

Boats arrive at the southeast shore. Most tourist facilities, including a **Perama** outpost and **moneychangers**, are near the landing. The **wartel,** south of the landing at the Gazebo Meno Hotel, has unreliable connections. **Royal Reef Hotel,** north of the landing, offers **phone service.** There is **no post office** on Meno.

Generators produce the only electricity on Gili Meno; lights are switched off from 10pm-midnight. **Kontiki Cottages,** south of the landing, has elegant, clean bungalows with Western bathrooms. (Singles Rp60,000; doubles Rp80,000.) **Mallia's Child Bungalows,** next door to Kontiki, tempts travelers with its beachfront location. (Bungalows with *mandi* Rp50,000-60,000.) The remote **Blue Coral,** 1km north of the boat landing, boasts views of both the sunrise and sunset from new, classy huts. (Singles Rp50,000; doubles Rp70,000.)

Saleswomen hawk *gado-gado* and *nasi campur* on the beach. Most of the accommodations have restaurants attached.The restaurant at Kontiki Cottages has great views of the beach and cheap, tasty meals (entrees Rp10,000-15,000). A trip to the cheap **Good Heart Restaurant,** on the northwest side of the island, is a good excuse for walking the island perimeter (entrees Rp10,000). Time your visit with the setting sun—but bring a flashlight for the walk back.

SUMBAWA

Hot and dry Sumbawa is off the beaten path. Rarely visited by tourists and neglected by Jakarta, Western culture and modernization haven't really touched this island. Though an excellent transport system exists, Sumbawa is still primarily a residential island—not a tourist one. The friendly residents are eager to practise their English with visitors, but otherwise keep their culture to themselves. Surfers will appreciate Hu'u's waves—for others, however, Sumbawa is probably still best known as the island between Lombok and Flores.

THE VIEW FROM ABOVE

The lowdown: The island that Indonesia forgot lies between Lombok and Flores.
Gateway Cities: Poto Tano, Sape.
Major Towns: Bima, Hu'u, Sape, Sumbawa Besar, Taliwang.
Highlights: Climbing Gunung Tambora, surfing Lakey's Beach in Hu'u and the waters of Taliwang, dropping in on the Sultan's Palace in Sumbawa Besar, taking off for Komodo Island.

GETTING TO SUMBAWA

BY PLANE

Bima's airport lies 19km from town along the main road to Bima. As a major regional hub for **Merpati,** Bima offers island-hopping flights to: **Denpasar** (Tu, Th, Sa, Su; Rp478,800); **Kupang** (Th, Su; Rp699,900) via **Ruteng** (Rp284,100); **Labuhanbajo,** Flores (M, Sa; Rp164,200); **Mataram** (Th, Sa; Rp352,300). **Sumbawa Besar's airport,** on Jl. Garuda at the western edge of town, is easily reached by yellow *bemo* (Rp1000). Merpati has flights to **Jogjakarta, Semarang,** and **Surabaya.**

BY FERRY

Ferries run between **Labuhan Lombok** on Lombok's east coast to **Poto Tano** on Sumbawa's west coast (1½hr., every hr., Rp8000). Purchase tickets at the pier. Alterna-

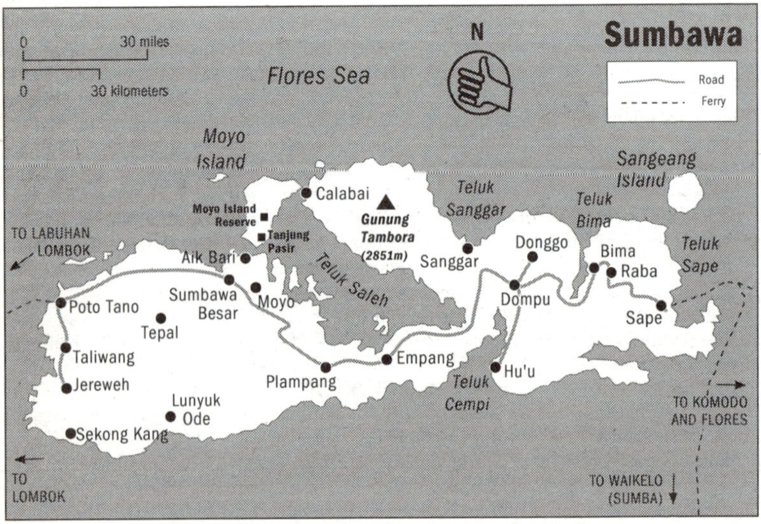

INDONESIA

tively, buy a combined ferry and A/C bus ticket (Rp27,000) at Tiora Mas on Jl. Yos Sudarso (☎214 28), which will take you directly to **Mataram** (p. 232) on Lombok. Ferries also leave **Sape** for: **Labuhanbajo,** Flores (8-12hr., 8am, Rp16,000); **Komodo Island** (7hr.; W, Sa 8am; Rp9700); and **Waikelo,** Sumba (F 9pm, Rp15,500).

BY BOAT

PELNI ships dock at **Bima** and **Badas,** both 5km from Sumbawa Besar. The KM *Tata Mailau* departs from both harbors every two weeks for **Denpasar, Dobo, Labuhanbajo, Larantuka, Saumlaki,** and **Tual.** The KM *Tilongkabila* sporadically leaves from Bima for **Denpasar, Kumai, Lembar, Sampit,** and **Surabaya.** The KM *Pangrango* leaves from Badas about once a week to **Ende, Labuhanbajo, Surabaya, Waingapu,** and beyond. The Bima **PELNI Office,** Jl. Pelabuhan 103, is beside the harbor. **Barito,** Jl. Hasanudin (☎437 37), runs express boats from Bima to **Denpasar** (6hr.; business Rp146,000, executive Rp176,000).

SUMBAWA BESAR ☎0371

Aside from the comfort of that its relative wealth affords, Sumbawa Besar has little to offer visitors. The famous *beraban kebo* (buffalo race) is held every Sunday for tourist edification, provided there are enough tourists to warrant one. For those with the luxury of private transport, the countryside offers some fascinating sites.

ORIENTATION AND PRACTICAL INFORMATION. All of Sumbawa Besar lies north of a river except for **Jl. Garuda,** which crosses southward toward Hotel Tambora. **Brangbiji Airport,** the tourist office, and the main **post office** are all on Jl. Garuda. The rest of the city is enclosed by **Jl. Diponegoro** (which becomes Jl. Yos Sudarso, then Jl. Setia Budi) to the north, **Jl. Hasanuddin** (which becomes Jl. Dr. Wahidin) to the south, their juncture in the west, and **Jl. Merdeka/Jl. Urip Sumoharjo** to the east. **Jl. Kartini** is lined with shops selling everything you could want. Yellow and blue *bemo* ply these streets and congregate at the *bemo* corner behind **Seketeng Market** in the northeast part of the town.

Services in Sumbawa Besar include: **Dinas Pariwisata Tourist Information,** on Jl. Garuda between the airport and the bus terminal (☎237 14; open M-Th 7am-2pm, F 7am-11:30pm, Sa 7am-1:30pm); **Perama Office,** Jl. Hasanuddin 48 (☎225 41); **BNI** (☎217 86), on Jl. Kartini, which changes traveler's checks and has a **24hr. ATM** (Cirrus/MC); **police,** Jl. Hasanuddin 105 (**emergency** ☎110), at Jl. Diponegoro; **Apotik Dynasty,** Jl. Garuda 4 (☎220 33), opposite the **hospital,** Jl. Garuda 5 (☎210 78; **ambulance** ☎118); and **GPO,** Jl. Garuda 99, close to the airport and town center (*Poste Restante*, open M-Th 7:30am-5pm, F 7:30-11:30am, Sa 7:30am-1pm). The **Telkom office,** Jl. Yos Sudarso 6 (☎210 00), opposite the **branch post office,** has **Internet** access (Rp10,000 per hr.).

ACCOMMODATIONS AND FOOD. Losmen Mekersari, on the first side street after Jl. Kamboja as you head into town along Jl. Hasanuddin, has basic but clean accommodations with private *mandi*. (☎213 51. Breakfast included. Singles Rp20,000; doubles Rp30,000.) **Losmen Suci,** across the street, has similar budget rooms. (☎215 89. Singles Rp20,000; doubles Rp25,000.) **Hotel Tambora,** on the western edge of town, is overpriced for its filthy condition. (☎215 55. Rooms with shared *mandi* Rp17,500; with private *mandi* Rp30,000.)

Although it's possible to find English menus, dining in the city often involves the "pick and pray" method of choosing dinner. Restaurants cluster along **Jl. Diponegoro,** and **food carts** line the perimeter. **Cirebon 2,** Jl. Kebayan 4, up the street from Hotel Tambora, has a gigantic non-English menu. (Dishes Rp5000-6500. Open daily 7am-10pm.) **Aneka Rasa Jaya,** at the east end of Jl. Hasanuddin, is a Chinese *rumah makan* with delicious seafood and panoramic views (entrees Rp7500-10,000). **Cirebon 1,** Cirebon 2's older sibling, is further up Jl. Kebayan and serves inexpensive Indonesian food (Rp5000-7000).

SIGHTS AND ENTERTAINMENT. The old Sultan's palace, **Dalam Loka,** off Jl. Sudirman, is the city's prime attraction. Built at the end of the 19th century and recently restored, it's one of the largest all-wood buildings in the world. The 99 wooden pillars that adorn the palace symbolize the different representations of Allah. Extensive information labels explain everything—in Indonesian. Apart from the bare rooms of the palace itself, a small number of traditional artifacts are also on display. (Open Sa-Th 7am-2pm, F 7-11am; visits outside these hours can be arranged with the resident caretaker. Small donation expected.) The **Pura Agung Giri Natha** temple, next to the post office, serves a now-scant Hindu population.

Bull racing is traditionally organized before rice planting in August, but due to the flow of tourists through the area, races are now held whenever there are enough tourists to warrant one. The Perama Office can help arrange transportation to and from these events.

NEAR SUMBAWA BESAR

Bemo and fishing boats are the best way to see sights outside Sumbawa Besar.

AI' BELING. Surrounded by dense forest and swimmable pools, this 50m high terrace-like waterfall is 36km outside Sumbawa Besar and once was the Sultan's hunting ground. On a good day you'll see monkeys, butterflies, and the occasional wild pig (*ojek* from Sumbawa Besar Rp30,000).

POTO VILLAGE. Poto Village, 12km east of Sumbawa Besar (Rp500 by *bemo*), is known for *songket* cloth, used to make sarongs laced with silver and gold. Ask around to find local weavers.

MOYO ISLAND. A short hop from Sumbawa Besar, Moyo Island is home to a nature reserve inhabited by wild pigs, deer, and other creatures. If the $900 per night resort on the west side of the island isn't ritzy enough, shelter is available at **Tanjung Pasir** (rooms Rp35,000). Snorkeling equipment is available, though food isn't. Fishing **boats** can be hired (Rp50,000) from the nearby town of Air Bari (*ojek* from Sumbawa Besar Rp40,000). For more information and maps, call the National Forestry Office (PHPA; ☎239 41), located on Jl. Desa Nijong.

INDONESIA

TALIWANG. Some of the finest, least crowded waves in the Indonesian archipelago are off the west coast of Sumbawa in Taliwang, accessible by bus (3hr.; Rp15,000) from Sumbawa Besar. Moving south along the coast line, **Jelenga (Scar Reef)** is a challenging left hand break. The surf breaks over sharp coral reefs that can mangle the careless. Beautiful Tanjung Malok has **Malok**—known as **Super Suck**—and a long sandy beach great for swimming when the water is calm. Luxurious surfing tours from Bali dock farther south at **Sekongkang (Yo-Yo's).** Most accommodations are nestled in Taliwang, but many travelers stay in Jelenga. From Taliwang, *ojek* and *bemo* can be chartered to Jelenga, Malok (Super Suck), and Sekongkang (Yo-Yo's).

HU'U ☎0373

Surf-lovers and professionals come to roast, play, and be photographed in Hu'u's aquamarine Cempi Bay before rainy season winds dampen surfing conditions. The surrounding reefs make for great snorkeling opportunities for non-surfers.

To get to Hu'u, take a bus from **Bima** (2hr., Rp5000) or **Sumbawa Besar** (4-5hr., Rp15,000) to **Dompu,** a transit point for buses to Hu'u. In Dompu, take a *bemo* from the Northern Terminal to the city center (Rp500) and then a *cidomo*(Rp500) to the Southern Terminal before continuing to Hu'u.

Surfers will appreciate the easy offshore access to the successive breaks from Lakey's Beach: **Lakey's Peak, Lakey's Pipe,** and **Nanges.** For intrepid surfers, two right-hand breaks of Lakey's Beach lie to the north (**Cobblestone,** a 15min. walk) and south (**Periscope,** a 30min. walk). If you're not a professional surfer and can't tell the difference, ask anyone with a board and they'll help.

Exchange **currency** in Bima or Sumbawa—rates in Hu'u are terrible. Intan Lestari rents **bicycles** (Rp 15,000) and **snorkeling gear** (Rp10,000). Most hotels and bungalows offer **international calls.** Fatma's Hand Restaurant provides **fax** service, transportation **bookings,** and **surfboard rental** (Rp25,000 per day).

Accommodations on **Lakey's Beach** are kilometers away from the nearest villages, so most lodgings have restaurants and general stores. **Mona Lisa Bungalows,** about the fourth hotel from the northern edge of Lakey's Beach, has straw and bamboo huts with private *mandi*. (Singles Rp20,000; doubles Rp30,000.) **Puma Cottages** are larger with Western-style bathrooms. (Singles Rp35,000; doubles Rp60,000.) The rooms and the service at **Hotel Aman Gadi** are exquisite. (☎623 031. Rooms US$14-18, with A/C and hot water US$22-28.) Once the low tide kills the surf, the happening **Fatma's Hand Restaurant** gets lively. Come for the quiche (from Rp22,000), a movie, or just to hear the word "gnarly" spoken without irony.

GUNUNG TAMBORA

Gunung Tambora, the rocky giant on the northern peninsula of central Sulawesi, last blew its top in 1815, a blast that resulted in a summerless 1816. Some say it was more destructive than even the eruption of Gunung Krakatau. The two-colored crater lake and far-reaching vistas are amazing rewards for those who reach the summit. The town of **Calabai** is the launching pad for the three-day ascent, but there are few trekking and transportation packages available. Transportation is easiest from from Dompu (8hr.). From here, buses leave to Calabai (3 per day; 8am, noon and 4pm; Rp10,000). From Calabai, *bemo* go to **Prancasila,** the base point for the trek.

BIMA ☎0374

If Sumbawa Besar is mild-mannered, then Bima is its hot-blooded sibling with spice, charisma, and even a touch of bawdiness. Whether in the vendors of the night market or in the *dokar* that careen down its streets, Bima's energy envelopes every visitor as hundreds of bright, colored lights light up every awning, store front, and mosque, while teenagers blast music that turns downtown into a virtual discotheque. The main attraction is the Sultan's Palace (now a museum), with its impressive display of ceremonial *kris* (swords).

Buses go from **Kumbe Terminal** on Jl. Sukarno-Hatta and the **Town Bus Terminal** to: **Dompu** (2hr., Rp3500); **Sape** (1½hr., every 30min. 7am-4pm, Rp3000); and **Sumbawa Besar** (Rp12,000). Bima sits between two rivers. **Jl. Terminal Baru** stretches north from the airport (south of the southern river) and becomes **Jl. Kaharnuddin,** the main street. It first intersects **Jl. Karantina/Sukarno-Hatta,** the main eastbound road that leads to **Raba**, Bima's administrative center. **Jl. Sumbawa,** which collides with the Sultan's Palace complex, runs two blocks up and parallel to Jl. Sukarno-Hatta. Along Jl. Sukarno-Hatta, Raba has a **24hr. Telkom Office** with collect calls and **Internet;** the **police** (☎430 26; **emergency** ☎110); and the **hospital,** Jl. Langsat 1 (**24hr. emergency** ☎431 42; **ambulance** ☎118). **Bank BNI,** on Jl. Sultan Hasanuddin, has a **24hr. ATM.** (Open M-F 8am-3pm. Cirrus/MC.) The **GPO** is on the eastern extension of Jl. Hasanuddin/Diponegoro at Jl. Gajah Mada. (*Poste Restante.* Open M-Sa 8am-2:30pm, Su 9am-noon.) **Postal code:** 84100.

La'mbitu Hotel (☎422 22) is easily the best value on Sumbawa. (Classy rooms with private bath Rp40,000, with A/C and TV Rp60,000). Next door, **Hotel Liligraha,** older and more worn, gives you less for the money. (Rooms with shared bath Rp15,000-20,000; doubles with bath Rp50,000, with bath and fan Rp60,000.)

The numerous food carts that line Bima's back streets and the **night market** (just south of Jl. Hasanuddin) compensate for a paucity of restaurants. Both hotels listed above have cheap, tasty eateries inside. In town, **Rumah Makan Anda,** on Jl. Kaharuddin before the bridge on the way to the terminal, delights with freshly baked goods and a large Chinese menu. (Limited vegetarian dishes. Open daily 8am-10pm.) **Ayam Goreng Pemuda,** Jl. Sulawesi 12, by the night market, weighs a bit heavier on the vegetarian side. Try the vegetables in chili sauce for Rp4000. Large fish with tomato Rp20,000. (Open daily 9am-3pm and 5pm-10pm.)

SAPE

Sape is the port for ferries to: **Labuhanbajo,** Flores (9-12hr.; 8am; economy A with soft chairs and American movies Rp16,000, economy B with hard chairs and Indonesian TV Rp11,000); **Komodo Island** (see below); **Waikelo Somba** (14hr.; F 9pm; economy A Rp15,500, economy B Rp11,5000; bicycles Rp5150, motorbikes Rp16,000, cars Rp170,000). Apart from the ferry, there isn't much in Sape. *Dokar*—chariot like vehicles jokingly called "Ben Hur"—race along the lone road from Sape to the port village of **Pelabuhan Sape,** 4km east. The **bus terminal** and the local **produce market** bustle on the east side, at the fringe of the farm fields 3km west of Sape. One *losmen* and the **ferry** are in Pelabuhan Sape, but most services line the Sape stretch of the main road. There are a handful of restaurants, a few *losmen,* a **police office,** a **post office,** and the **medical services** of Dr. H. Maknum, near the police station (open daily 4pm-8pm). One **wartel** (cash-only; open daily 6am-midnight) stands 200m before the harbor in Pelabuhan Sape and another is by the bus station (cash only; open daily 6am-midnight). **Balai Taman Nasional Komodo,** 1km from Pelabuhan Sape, provides advice and dioramas of Komodo Island.

If you don't want take the 1hr. ride to/from Bima (Rp4000), then staying at the pier is your best bet. **Losmen Mutiara** is close to the ferry and more immediate than the 20min. buggy ride through rice fields to the other end of Sape. (Doubles with shared *mandi* Rp22,000.) If you choose to make the trip, **Losmen Friendship** compensates for its considerable distance from the ferry landing with complimentary hot beverages. (☎710 06. Rooms with shared *mandi* Rp15,000, with private *mandi* Rp20,000, with private *mandi* and fan Rp30,000.)

Sape's small market is not a great place to scrounge for a meal and certainly not for alcohol (there is none in this Muslim port), and the smattering of *rumah makan* don't offer many alternatives. At **Rumah Makan Arema,** by the ferry landing, a hopping crowd enjoys cheap dishes. (Grilled prawns Rp10,500. Open daily till 10pm.) **Novita's** (across from Losmen Friendship) limited menu includes Western favorites like spaghetti (Rp4500) and pizza (Rp7500), but the food isn't stellar.

INDONESIA

DAYTRIP FROM SAPE: KOMODO ISLAND. Beautiful blue water and multiple islands line the route to Flores. The island is known for its reptilian inhabitants and their ravenous appetites. The **Komodo dragon,** over 3m long and a hefty 150kg heavy, is the largest of the monitor lizard family. The dragons have long claws, sharp teeth, and powerful tails. Although they're sedentary in the heat of day, they can sprint short distances and hunt with considerable prowess. Much like a snake, a Komodo can expand its chest cavity enough to swallow a goat whole.

Wandering the island alone has been forbidden since 1974, when an elderly Swiss gentleman took a walk and never came back. The national park office leads tours in the early morning and late afternoon (Rp2000 each for 3 or more people, Rp6000 each for 1-2 people). Most guides lead the 30min. walk to **Banu Ngulung,** a dry riverbed where the lazy dragons sunbathe. For the motivated, a hike up **Gunung Gara** (7-8km) affords magnificent views of the rugged landscape. The neighboring island of **Rinca** has accommodations at **Loh Buaya,** more dragons, and other wild animals such as pigs, deer and cobras.

SAFETY WATCH. Before accepting a 4-day cruise around Komodo and Rinca, check the boat. Typically, boats do not have life vests or a radio, making stormy nights uncomfortable. There have been reports of women being molested in the middle of the night. **Women should not go alone.**

Getting to Komodo can be difficult. Two **ferries** shuttle passengers to the island from **Sape** (8am; W, Sa; economy A Rp9700, economy B Rp7200) and **Labuhanbajo** (8am; W, Sa; Rp8000). A small boat meets both ferries and whisks passengers to **Loh Liang** (Rp2000), where most accommodations are situated. Alternatively, fishing boats can be chartered from Labuhanbajo (around Rp100,000; discounts for groups). Tours make one-day trips from Labuhanbajo to Rinca (Rp150,000), or one to four day trips to Rinca and Komodo ($5 a day), which include meals, snorkeling, and a bed on the deck of the boat. Shop around for the best price.

SUMBA

A dry, dusty island where most people live in traditional, walled *kampungs*, Sumba is as rugged and ancient a place as you'll find. Waingapu and Waikabubak are sleepy little towns where nothing seems to happen, but don't be deceived. The tranquil appearance of this tropical island masks deep-seated tensions, especially between the Loli and Wewewa tribes in western Sumba, where tribal warfare has raged sporadically since 1960. The violent streak is perpetuated every year by the island's famous ritual, the *pasola*, in which mounted horsemen with blunted spears engage in "mock" battles (often lethal) for a crowd. But despite the tension, visitors are greeted warmly by locals—whether they are searching for an the exquisite *ikat* cloth or wandering the coastline for a perfect beach.

THE VIEW FROM ABOVE

The lowdown: A rugged island still clinging to its tribal roots.
Gateway cities: Denpasar
Major towns: Waikabubak, Waingapu.
Highlights: The fantastic surf in Rua and the weaving villages near Waingapu.

GETTING TO SUMBA

Sumba has two **airports**: **Tambolaka Airport,** in the west, 2km from Waikabubak; and **Mau Hau Airport,** in the east, 10min. outside Waingapu. **Merpati** runs flights from Mau Hau to **Denpasar** (M, W; Rp691,900) and **Kupang** (M, W; Rp434,500) and also from Tambolaka to **Denpasar** (W, F; Rp618,300) and **Kupang** (W, F; Rp542,300).

Waingapu has regular **ferry** service to **Aimere, Ende, Kupang,** and **Sabu.** Check the city listings for details. A ferry also runs from Waikelo in west Sumba to **Sape** or **Sumbawa** (Tu, F; Rp15,5000). Waingapu also is the port for **PELNI** boats; the office is 100m from the harbor entrance. With the help of the KM *Awu* and KM *Pangrango*, Sumba is connected to many ports, including **Benoa, Ende, Kupang,** and **Surabaya.** Check the PELNI office or your hotel for schedules.

GETTING AROUND SUMBA

Sumba is an island where **bus travel** is popular but often unreliable. Buses run between **Waikabubak** and **Waingapu** (5½hr.; 8-9am, noon-1pm, 3-4pm, 10pm; Rp10,000) and to surrounding destinations (about Rp2000). The surface of the main road between Waingapu and Waikabubak is good, but side routes are in bad shape.

WAIKUBUBAK ☎0387

Nestled in the plateaus of western Sumba, Waikabubak is cooler and wetter than the coast. It's a small town with around 25,000 people, split evenly between traditional grass and bamboo houses and paved streets lined with plywood and sheet metal stores and shacks. Beyond the city, the countryside is isolated and traditional, and head hunting and ritual warfare are the local traditions. The *kampung* clashed in 1992 and again in 1998, resulting in the destruction of several villages and more than 40 deaths. Even in hotels that pander to tourists, English is barely spoken, so a local guide is near essential for those not fluent in Bahasa Indonesia.

TRANSPORTATION. **Tambaloka Airport** is 42km north of town. Rare public buses (Rp5000) and chartered bemos (Rp60,000) make the trip into town. **Merpati,** Jl. A. Yani, runs flights to **Denpasar** (W, F; Rp618,500) and **Kupang** (W,F; Rp542,300). (Open M-F 8am-4pm.) The **bus** and **bemo terminals** are on Jl. Pisang, off Jl. A. Yani.

INDONESIA

Buses leave frequently to **Waingapu** (Rp10,000) and **Waitabula** (Rp5000), and bemo go as far as **Anakalang** to the east and **Lamboya** and **Wanokaka** to the south (all Rp1000). **Waikelo,** north of Waikabubak and the airport, runs **ferries** to **Sape** twice per week (inquire at the harbor for details).

ORIENTATION AND PRACTICAL INFORMATION. The city's main north-south street, **Jl. A. Yani,** has most shops and services. **Jl. Gajah Mada** runs parallel, and both cross the short east-west **Jl. Pattimura** at their southernmost points. **Jl. Pemuda** and **Jl. Adiaksa,** which becomes **Jl. Sudirman,** cut through the center of Jl. A. Yani and Jl. Gajah Mada. The northern end of Jl. A. Yani terminates at **Jl. Bhayangkara.** To the east is the road to Waingapu; to the west is **Tambaloka Airport.**

Services in Waikabubak include: **Bank BNI,** Jl. A. Yani 46, which changes currency and traveler's checks (☎215 40; open M-Th 8am-2pm, F 8-11am); **Rumah Sakit Lende Moripa**, on Jl. Jend. Sudirman (☎210 86; **24hr. emergency care;** ambulance ☎118); **Apotik Ezri Farma,** Jl. Pattimura 12 (open M-Sa 8am-1pm and 5-9pm, Su 6-8:30pm); the **police** (☎211 10; **emergency** ☎110), on Jl. Bhayangkara; **GPO,** Jl. Bhayangkara 1, across the street (*Poste Restante;* open M-Th 8am-3pm, F 8am-noon, Sa 8am-1pm). The 24hr. **Telkom Office,** Jl. Pattimura 7, has no HCD phone but allows collect calls. A 24hr. **wartel** is on Jl. A. Yani. **Postal code:** 87211.

ACCOMMODATIONS AND FOOD. Breakfast is included at all listed accommodations. Most hotels organize guides (Rp30,000 per day) and transportation. **Hotel Manandang,** Jl. Pemuda 4, has a restaurant and clean rooms with sinks and a phone. (☎211 97. Singles with shared *mandi* Rp20,000; doubles Rp27,500; deluxe singles with hot water, TV, and fan Rp65,000; deluxe doubles Rp75,000.) **Hotel Tarung Wisata,** Jl. Pisang 26, near the bus and *bemo* terminals, also has clean rooms and a restaurant. (☎213 32. Small singles with shared *mandi* Rp6000-Rp15,000, with private bath Rp20,000; doubles Rp10,000-20,000/25,000.)

Culinary experiences outside hotel restaurants are limited to streetside *warung* like the ones along **Jl. A. Yani. Manandang Restaurant** in Hotel Manandang is the most tourist-friendly. *Tempe goreng* (Rp6000) and *sayur asam* (sour vegetable soup; Rp6500) satisfies vegetarians. (Open daily 6am-11pm.) **Rumah Makan Sumba Indah,** on the outskirts of town leading toward the airport, specializes in Balinese cuisine and **rents motorcycles.** (Motorcycles Rp30,000 per day. Open M-Sa 6am-10pm.) **Rumah Makan Bali Indah,** opposite the Telkom Office, serves cheap *padang* food.

INDONESIA

DAYTRIPS FROM WAIKABUBAK. *Bemos* (45min., Rp1000) ride east to the town of **Anakalang's** numerous *kampung* and stately tombs. **Kampung Pasunga,** along the main road, is noteworthy for its large **stone tombs**, some of which took six months to carve. Over 100 buffalo were sacrificed during the construction of the five-person tomb. Ask for directions to **Lai Tarung,** the hilltop ancestral village of the area clans. The deserted village has old tombs and a ceremonial building.

In the opposite direction, a trip to **Pero** in the **Kodi District** delights with its beautiful scenery and sea breezes. On the west coast, the villages around Pero (**Pronbaroro** and **Wainyapu**) have impressive tombs and *kampung*. People flock to Pero for the **surf** at **Pantai Radukapal,** across the river, but legend has it that the best place to surf in western Sumba is **Rua** in the **Lamboya District.**

To reach **Kodi District** from the bus terminal in Waikabubak, take a bus to Waitabula (Rp1500) toward the airport and then catch a bus to Kodi (3 harrowing hours, Rp1500). You'll be dropped off in the middle of a field near a market that comes to life on Saturdays and Wednesdays. Visit **Wainyapu** by *ojek* via the inland road connecting Wainyapu and Pronbaroro.

WAINGAPU ☎0387

Waingapu offers more restaurants and accommodations than its western neighbor Waikabubak, but the dry, dusty streets that line Waingapu's coast are no match for Waikabubak's temperate highlands. *Ikat* vendors wait outside hotels, and art shops peddle collections of expensive cloth and traditional blades. The market near the *bemo* terminal offers the best selection of eclectic goods. Even if you're not into cloth, Waingapu is a good place to wait for infrequent flights and boats; just put down your luggage and rest your arms in the east Sumba sunshine.

TRANSPORTATION. Frequent **buses** go to **Melolo** (2hr., Rp2000) and **Waikabubak** (5½hr., Rp10,000) and **Mangili** and **Baing** in southeast Sumba. **PELNI,** Jl. Pelabuhan 2, is near the harbor. Check postings for the boat schedule to: **Benoa** (Rp71,000); **Ende** (Rp23,000); **Kupang** (Rp41,500); **Labuhanbajo** (Rp28,000); **Lembar** (Rp69,500); **Surabaya** (Rp109,500); **Ujung Pandang** (Rp148,000). A regular **ferry** service operates between Flores, Sabu, and West Timor; ferries go to: **Airmere** (M 7pm, Rp19,500); **Ende** (W 7pm, Rp19,500); **Kupang** (F 2pm, Rp37,000); **Sabu** (F 4pm, Rp21,500). Check at the harbor to be sure that ferries still operate.

ORIENTATION AND PRACTICAL INFORMATION. Waingapu's two centers are the **port** in the north and the **bus terminal** in the south, along **Jl. Eltari,** which also hosts the **market. Jl. Yos Sudarso** loops about the north area, turning into **Jl. Hasanuddin** and **Jl. Wanggameti. Jl. A. Yani** connects the two centers.

Services in Waingapu include: **BNI,** on Jl. Ampere, which exchanges major traveler's checks and currencies (☎621 46; open M-F 8am-2pm); **police** (☎629 55), on Jl. R. Suprapto toward the airport; **Apotik Waingapu Farma,** Jl. Wanggameti 33 (☎215 33; open daily 8am-1pm and 5-10pm); **Rumah Sakit Kristen Lindimara,** Jl. Prof. Dr. WZ Johanes 6 (☎610 19; 24hr. emergency ☎110; ambulance ☎118); 24hr. **Telkom Office,** Jl. Cut Nya Dien 19; **wartel,** on Jl. Panjaitan in Surabaya Hotel (open daily 5am-1am); **GPO,** Jl. Sutomo 21 (*Poste Restante;* open M-Th 8am-2pm, F 8-11am, Sa 8am-noon); **Postal code:** 87100.

ACCOMMODATIONS AND FOOD. Hotel Sandal Wood, Jl. D.T. Panjaitan 23, practically in the bus station, has a wide selection of clean, comfortable rooms. (☎211 99. Breakfast included. Singles with shared *mandi* Rp20,000, with private bath Rp30-55,000; doubles Rp25,000/35,000-65,000.) **Hotel Merlin,** around the corner from Hotel Sandal Wood, on Jl. D. I. Panjaitan, is the most luxurious accommodation in town. All rooms have private baths with showers and Western toilets. (☎613 00. Singles Rp27,500, with A/C and TV Rp44,000; doubles Rp33,000/55,000.)

Cheap, excellent *rumah makan* are on almost every corner in Waingapu. **Mini Indah,** on then northern end of Jl. A. Yani, has cheap, tasty *padang* entrees (Rp5500 per plate).

DAYTRIPS FROM WAINGAPU: MELOLO, PAU, AND RENDE. Engulf yourself in tribal culture in the **weaving villages** of southeastern Sumba. Guides are available at local hotels (Rp50,000 per day plus transportation), or you can make the 62km trip by bus from Waingapu yourself (2hr., Rp2000).

The **Pau** village, a 1½hr. walk from Melolo, is popular with cloth aficionados and features four impressive tombs of past *rajahs.* Here you can see all the hard labor that goes into weaving *ikat* (dyed cloth) and *hikung* (cloth with woven patterns). *Bemo* don't go as far as Pau, but if you're coming from Waingapu, ask to be dropped off at the turn-off for Pau. Otherwise, walk toward Waingapu on the road from Melolo. Cross the bridge with the mouth of the river to your right, take the paved road to the left, and then veer right at the fork with the horse statue. The walk has scenery that rivals Bali's best.

Rende, 7km south of Melolo and accessible by foot or bemo, is best known for its tombs carved intricately with animal features and the *ikat* made for village royalty. Because of its royal presence, Rende is more touristy and expensive than Pau.

FLORES

For its magnificent landscape, Flores ranks as one of Indonesia's most spectacular islands. Volcanic mountains and ridges that break the passing clouds have nurtured and protected the growth of the lush rainforests that set Flores apart from barren Sumba and Sumbawa. Flores was virgin ground for the arrival of the Europeans and bears the legacy of their stay to this day. Personal and place names are

I'M TOTALLY DEAD Unlike the other islands of Nusa Tenggara—which are all, in their own way, modernizing—Sumba stubbornly holds on to tradition. Unapologetically animist, Sumba adheres to an ancient ancestor worship called Marapu. In accordance with the roles assigned to the sexes by the "original ancestors," only men can plant rice or feed beasts, while only females can make the famous Sumba *ikat*. Marapu also dictates burial tradition; dead ancestors are supposed to influence earthly life, so at the funerals of chiefs and aristocrats, animals are sacrificed, and monumental stone slabs are erected. Sumbans believe that the spirits require the spilling of human blood, so rituals such as the Pesola (a "mock" cavalry battle between interior and coastal villages, which claims at least a few casualties annually) and head hunting is still considered cool. So no you know: the long machetes worn by Sumban men are not decorations.

often in Portuguese, and Roman Catholicism is the faith of choice. Old habits die hard, however, and European influences have not supplanted traditional culture; in most remote areas "Catholic" villages still practice traditional animistic rites and rituals in their own compromise between the past and the present.

THE VIEW FROM ABOVE

The lowdown: Bali's quieter neighbor rocks to nature's wondrous beat.
Main cities: Labuhanjo, Ruteng, Bajawa, Ende, Maumere
Highlights: Tricolored crater lakes; Sunrises over Golo Curu; *caci* demonstrations.

GETTING TO FLORES

BY PLANE

The **airport** is 2km southeast of Labuhanbaho; take the road heading inland at the south end of town and turn left at the sign. **Merpati** (☎411 77) has an office on the way, as well as in Ende (see Ende: Transportation, p. 256) and flies a few times per week to **Denpasar** (once a week via Bima), **Jakarta,** and **Kupang.** Be warned that flights are often cancelled and, in the high season, often booked well in advance (especially the Maumere-Denpasar route). **Bajawa Airport,** 25km north of Bajawa, has three flights per week to **Denpasar** (Rp6500) and **Kupang** (Rp6500).

BY BOAT

A main **ferry landing** is at the north end of the city. Ferries go to **Sape** (8-12hr.; W, Sa; Rp16,000) via **Komodo** (3-4hr., Rp8000). Check at the harbor to confirm the erratic ferry schedule. To get to the **PELNI office** (☎411 06), walk away from the water at the harbor, take the main road to the right, and then take the first left. Go through the intersection up the dirt road; it's 50m up on the left, cleverly disguised as a house. Check on boats to **Bali, Lombok, Sumba, Surabaya,** and **Timor** here.

LABUHANBAJO ☎0385

While Labuhanbajo's excellent accommodations and relaxing sea-side atmosphere should make it a destination in its own right, it is still mostly a point of departure to Rinca, Komodo, and Sumbawa. Accommodations boast views of spectacular sunsets over the bay, best enjoyed while indulging in the freshly caught seafood. A 15min. walk yields a fine stretch of sand and beach hotels; isolated resorts lie on islands or the mainland beaches north of town.

TRANSPORTATION. While Labuhanbajo has no bus terminal, it's a major stop for **buses** bound for **Ruteng** (6hr., Rp15,000) and through buses to **Bajawa** (10hr., Rp20,000); they can be caught along the main road. Check with hotels for times or to arrange a pickup.

ORIENTATION AND PRACTICAL INFORMATION. Labuhanbajo is a simple coastal crescent 1½km long. The **national parks office,** on the inland road before the turn-off to the airport, has brochures, maps, and information about **Rinca** and

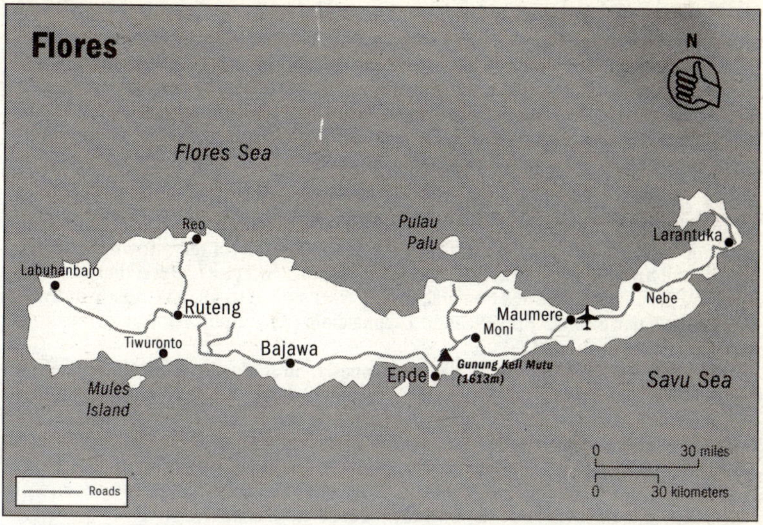

Komodo, as well as a komodo dragon skeleton that's worth a gawk. (☎410 04. Open M-Sa 7am-2pm.) Most hotels on **Jl. Sukarno/Yos Sudarso/Pelabuhan** arrange snorkeling trips and island treks. The national parks office and local rental shops take visitors diving (about US$75 per day). Hotels also rent out snorkeling equipment.

Bank Negara Indonesia, in the market across from Hotel Witasa, has good rates. (Open M-F 7:30am-2:30pm, Sa 7:30-11:30am.) The main **police station** (☎411 10) is inconveniently south of the town center on the road to the *pasar baru* ("new market"). A 24hr. **Telkom office,** with **HCD** phone, is 1km south of the ferry landing. Take the first left after the bridge, and then a right after the national parks office. The **GPO** is 400m south of the ferry landing. (Open M-Th 7:30am-3pm, F 7:30-11am, Sa 7:30am-1pm.)

INDONESIA

ACCOMMODATIONS AND FOOD. Labuhanbajo has a good range of budget and mid-range establishments that include complimentary breakfast. For those who desire seclusion, beach hotels offer free transport to bungalows (Rp20,000-40,000, including 3 meals) and on to nearby beaches. The best value in town is the **Hotel Wisata,** about 1.2km south of the ferry dock. Walking south from the ferry dock, turn left at the sign (about 800m) and walk uphill another 200m. All rooms come with private bath, Western toilet, and fan. (☎410 20. 2nd-class singles Rp15,000-20,000; doubles Rp20,000-30,000.) **Gardena Bungalows,** 150m south of the ferry landing, has the best view of the sunset. (☎412 58. Singles with fan, private *mandi* and mosquito net Rp20,000; doubles Rp25,000.) Gardena also provides free transport to its sister bungalow, **Seraya,** located on an isolated island 1hr. away (singles Rp20,000; doubles Rp25,000). **Chez Felix,** Jl. Prof. Dr. Johanes, 1km south of the ferry landing, is a wonderful place to watch the street bustle without the noise. (☎410 32. Singles with shared *mandi* Rp15,000, with private *mandi* Rp20,000, with mosquito nets and flush toilets Rp40,000; doubles Rp20,000-50,000.)

The restaurants at Gardena Bungalows, Hotel Wisata, and Chez Felix have lively atmospheres and the prices are the cheapest in town. **Borobudur Restaurant,** a couple of doors south of Gardena Bungalows, has a spectacular view and food to match. The chocolate milkshakes are an incredible treat (Rp6000), especially after a plate of sweet and sour prawns (Rp15,000). **Dewata Ayu Restaurant,** also next door to Gardena, has steak, chicken, and prawn dishes that are all worth the wait (Rp20,000). Both restaurants are open until 10pm.

RUTENG ☎0385

Although traversing Flores's circuitous interior can be arduous, persistent travelers will be rewarded with cool days in highland market towns such as Ruteng. The town is a logical stopover for the traveler who prefers 5hr. of jarring bus travel to ten. The surrounding scenery is worth exploring, as are the nearby caves and Manggarai villages. Hotels and locals can offer guidance and even arrange for a *caci* (traditional whip fighting) demonstration.

TRANSPORTATION AND PRACTICAL INFORMATION. Most of Ruteng is conveniently laid out in rectangles, and distances are short. The town center is up the hill, while most accommodations are on the far side of downtown. **Merpati** is on a side street between the town and the airport. (☎211 47. Open daily 7:30am-1pm; W, Sa 4-5pm.) The **bus terminal,** on the west side of town, has mostly morning buses to: **Bajawa** (5hr., Rp6500) and **Labuhanbajo** (5hr., Rp6500). Have your hotel arrange to have you picked up.

For currency exchange, **Bank Negara Indonesia,** on Jl. Kartini (next to the Telkom office), has the best rates. (Open M-F 7:30am-12:30pm and 1:30-4:45pm, Sa 7:30-11:30am and 1:30-4:45pm.) In case of **emergency,** call ☎110; for an **ambulance,** call ☎118. The **police station** (☎211 10) is on Jl. Bhayangkara, opposite the soccer field, near the bus terminal. The **post office,** Jl. Dewi Sartika 6, near the former king's house, and the **Telkom office,** Jl. Kartini 8-10, near the government offices, are on the south side of town (Both open 24hr.). **Postal code:** 86511.

ACCOMMODATIONS AND FOOD. As the least visited of the major towns on the Trans-Flores Hwy., Ruteng offers few budget options, but it's still possible to find an affordable place to stay. **Hotel Sinda,** Jl. Sudarso 26, has spacious rooms that open up to a lush garden. An English speaking crowd swaps travel stories at night. **Hotel Rima,** though a fair trek up to the Bajawa end of Jl. Ahmed Yani, is an attractive building with a fine restaurant and immaculate rooms. (☎221 96. Singles Rp15,000, with bath Rp25,000; doubles Rp25,000/35,000; triples Rp35,000-45,000.) **Losmen Agong I** is a few hundred meters north of town on Jl. Motang Rua. Economy rooms with shared *mandi* are tidy and bathrooms are clean, but the concrete construction is vintage Sing-Sing. (☎210 80. Singles Rp20,000, with private bath Rp20,000-25,000.) **Wismat Agong II,** on a side street northeast of the main soccer field, is more central but simple. (☎218 35. Singles Rp15,000; doubles Rp20,000.)

Dining options are rather skimpy, but the food is hearty. Smaller, independent eateries are most affordable. **Bambooden Restaurant,** Jl. Motang Rua 30, serves an array of entrees starting around Rp8000. **Dunia Baru,** Jl. Yos Sudarso 10, carries usual Chinese and Indonesian dishes (Rp6,000-12,000).

SIGHTS. **Golo Curu** is a godsend for the wannabe hiker in all of us—it's enough of a climb to give a good view, but doesn't take a great deal of time or preparation. Follow Jl. Motang Rua 1km north of the town center until the road crosses a bridge and immediately veers left. Follow the smaller road to the right. Travelers should stay on the paved pathway. The entire climb is a fascinating glimpse into Indonesian Catholicism; as the hill steepens, a series of Christian reliefs begin to appear on the mountain's sides. As you ascend the hill, so does Jesus, bearing a cross, shrugging off Roman guards, and eventually rising to Heaven. That's not all—Golo Curu is crowned by a shrine to the Virgin Mary. On a clear day, one can see the local volcano, Gunung Ranaka. Mornings and late afternoons, when the sun is reflecting off the spider web rice fields are the best times to climb. For local caci (traditional whip fighting) demonstrations, ask your hotel owner.

BAJAWA ☎0384

This market town of the Ngada people has weathered its transition into the modern world with grace. Although Bajawa's hotels are seldom empty, life goes on undisturbed, and the town's clean streets have avoided the tension prevalent in other Indonesian tourist towns.

TRANSPORTATION AND PRACTICAL INFORMATION. The road branching off the **Trans-Flores Hwy.** enters from the south, running into **Jl. Ahmet Yani,** which marks the town's southern boundary. **Watujaji Bus Terminal,** 3km south of town, is a Rp500 bemo ride away. Hotel Sunflower arranges pickup in the morning. Buses go to **Ende** (4hr., Rp5000) and **Ruteng** (4hr., Rp5000). **Bajawa Airport,** 25km north, is accessible by a Merpati shuttle (Rp5000) or chartered *bemo* (Rp20,000). **Merpati** (☎210 50) has an office near the market (open daily 8am-1pm).

The tiny town isn't a tough to navigate. **Bank Rakyat Indonesia** (☎210 24; open M-F 7:30am-3:45pm, Sa 7:30-11:30am), the **Telkom office** (☎210 00; open 24hr.), and the **post office** (open M-Th 7:30am-3pm, F 7:30-11:30am, Sa 7:30am-1pm; **postal code:** 86415) are all on **Jl. Sukarno-Hatta,** which marks the east side of town. Perpendicular to it, **Jl. Gajah Mada** runs through the center of town, past the **bemo stand.** The **market** is in the middle of town. For medical services, **Rumah Sakit Umum** (☎210 30) is on Jl. Diponegoro in the north of town. For an **ambulance,** call ☎118, and for the **police,** call ☎110.

ACCOMMODATIONS AND FOOD. Bajawa has many hotels but few good values. Bargaining is possible and profitable, especially in the low season. Breakfast is always included, blankets often aren't; highland nights can get quite cold. **Hotel Elizabeth** is the nicest place around, with bright, airy rooms and private baths. (☎212 23. Singles Rp35,000; doubles Rp40,000.) To get there, take the first left from Jl. Soekarno Hatta after tourist information, and then take the next left. **Hotel Karina,** on Jl. Ahmed Yani at the southern end of town, has decent rooms with bath. (Singles Rp20,000; doubles Rp25,000.) One of the few budget places that still charges budget rates, **Hotel Dam,** on a side street with the church, south of the market, has cozy rooms. (Rp7500 per person with shared bath.)

The local specialty is **dog,** but few tourists are interested in trying it, so it's left off the menu at any of the more touristy spots. Ask a local to bring you to his favorite *warung* for a taste. Otherwise, several *padang* joints cluster near the market. For more ambience, try the restaurant at **Hotel Anggrek. Restaurant Carmellia,** Jl. A. Yani 82, east of Hotel Dagalos, is acclaimed for its spring rolls and guacamole. **Restaurant Kasih Bahagia,** on Jl. Gajah Mada east of the town center, serves typical Chinese favorites. Entrees at all listed establishments cost around Rp10,000.

DAYTRIP FROM BAJAWA

NGADA HIGHLANDS

Occasional bemo *run from Bajawa to Bena in the Ngada Highlands. Hotel and independent guides run tours (Rp50,000 for groups of five or more, including transport, admission, a guide, lunch, and a soak at the hot springs in Soa).*

Traditional **Ngada villages** dot the mountainous region around Bajawa. They are characterized by thatched-roof houses, intricate carvings, clusters of monoliths, and two unique local structures related to the ancestor worship still practiced in the area: the *bhaga*, a small carved thatched-roof house commemorating female ancestors, and the *ngadhu*, a wooden pole topped by a conical thatched roof, often surmounted by arms holding a spear and axe, for male predecessors.

Bena, 13km south of Bajawa, is the most interesting village (Rp2500). Although it's possible to visit Bena and other villages on your own, you'll get the most for your money on a guided tour, even if the guide doesn't know that much about Ngada history. Don't miss a relaxing soak at the **superb hot springs** near **Soa,** north of Bajawa.

ENDE ☎038

One of Flores's more developed cities, Ende stretches along a coastline of black sand beaches, and is surrounded by rolling hills and islands. As a port city to Sumba and Kelimutu, Ende is a haven for the services-starved with speedy Internet, bustling markets, and all the comforts you thought you could do without.

TRANSPORTATION

Flights: Merpati (☎213 55), on Jl. Nangka. Open M-Tu and Th-Sa 8am-1pm and 4-5pm, Su and holidays 10am-noon.

Buses: Ende has the best bus connections anywhere on Flores—at least 2 buses per day go to both extremes of the Trans-Flores Hwy. **Ndao Bus Terminal** is on Jl. Mesjid, north of the city proper. Several buses per day go to: **Bajawa** (5hr., Rp8000); **Labuhanbajo** (10hr., Rp27,000); **Ruteng** (8hr., Rp20,000). **Wolowana Terminal,** on Jl. A. Yani, east of town has buses to: **Larantuka** (10hr., Rp17,000); **Maumere** (6hr., Rp10,000); **Moni** (2hr., Rp5,000).

Ferries: PELNI, Jl. Katedral 2 (☎210 43), has information for the two PELNI ships that dock here, and for smaller, more frequent ferries to Timor (Rp31,000) and Waigapu (Rp22,000).

Local Transportation: *Bemo* buzz along the main streets (Rp500). *Ojek*, or motorcycle taxis, are quicker. Prices vary according to distance and bargaining skill.

Rentals: Hotel Ikhlas (See **Accommodations,** below) has **car** and **motorcycle** rentals.

ORIENTATION AND PRACTICAL INFORMATION

Ende stretches across the neck of a peninsula, with **Ende Harbor** to the west and **Ipi Harbor** to the southeast. **Jl. Mesjid, Hatta,** and **Mahon/Sukarno** run north-south from Ende Harbor. **Jl. Kartini/Pahjawan Wirajaya,** the northernmost thoroughfare, runs northeast past the Protestant and Catholic churches and the hospital. The narrowest area between Jl. Pahjawan and **Jl. Katedral** forms downtown Ende. Jl. Katedral/A. Yani bounds the city on the south, forking near a cluster of *losmen;* one prong goes east; the other, **Jl. Adisucipto,** goes southeast toward the ferry office and Ipi Harbor. On the east side of town, **Jl. El Tari** runs northwest-southeast through Jl. Pahjawan past Jl. A. Yani and ends at the **airport.** From the Jl. El Tari and Jl. A. Yani intersection, **Jl. Kelimutu** extends northwest past the **pasar malam** to the **telephone office.** Running north and parallel to Jl. Kelimutu is **Jl. Nangka.**

Tourist Office: PT Kelimutu Permai Tour and Travel (☎213 55), on Jl. Nangka.

Currency Exchange: Bank Rakyat Indonesia, Jl. Yos Sudarso 27 (☎216 15), in the Dwi Putra Hotel. Open M-F 8am-3pm.

Medical Services: Rumah Sakit Umum (☎210 31), far from the town center on Jl. Prof. Johanes.

Pharmacy: Sumber Sehat, Jl. Sudirman 6 (☎216 15). Open daily 8am-1am.

Emergency: Police ☎110. **Ambulance** ☎118.

Police: ☎210 95. On Jl. Polisi, a few blocks up Jl. Pahlawan, on the right.

Telephones: 24hr. Telkom office, Jl. Kelimutu 5.

Post Offices: GPO, Jl. Basuki Rahmat 15 (☎212 03), northeast of town, near the Pahjawan-El Tari intersection. (Jl. Basuki Rahmat is the continuation of Jl. El Tari.) *Poste Restante*. Has one of the only Internet connections on Flores (Rp10,000). Open **24 hr.** Another branch is at Jl. Yos Sudarso 4, opposite Dwi Putri Hotel. Open M-Th 7:30am-3pm, F 7:30-11am, Sa 7:30am-1pm. **Postal code:** 86318.

ACCOMMODATIONS AND FOOD

Ende's accommodations are cheaper and more tourist-friendly than most other places in Flores. The nicest digs are east of the town center. Breakfast is usually included in the price of the room (Hotel Ikhlas is an exception).

Dwi Putri, Jl. Yos Sudarso, next door to Bank Rakyat Indonesia. Lounge with cable TV and spacious rooms. The main attraction is the not-to-be-missed aerobics class. Singles Rp25,000; doubles Rp30,000.

Hotel Ikhlas (☎216 95), on Jl. A. Yani, 200m from the traffic rotary to the airport. Cheap rooms, lounge (with CNN), restaurant, and HCD phone. Basic singles Rp10,000, with bath Rp15-20,000; doubles Rp15,000/Rp20,000-25,000.

Nurjaya Hotel, Jl. A. Yani 20 (☎212 52), closer to town center. Clean, simply furnished rooms with shared bath. Singles Rp10,000; doubles Rp20,000.

The capital's proximity to the ocean translates into a lot of seafood. Downtown abounds with local Indonesian restaurants sporting delicious window displays that can prove torture for the indecisive. **Istana Bambu,** Jl. Pasar 39, in the heart of downtown, offers Chinese and Indonesian food. A rival restaurant, the other **Istana Bambu,** Jl. Kemakmuran 30, one block east, tempts with fresh sweet-and-sour squid (Rp10,000) and baked goods.

DAYTRIP FROM ENDE

WEAVING VILLAGES

Buses run directly from Ende to Nggela, usually once per day in the morning. Alternatively, take a bus from Ende to Wolowaru (or get off a Maumere-bound bus there; Rp4000) and walk south to Nggela. A bemo *usually heads to Wolowaru in the afternoon (Rp1000). From Wolowaru, catch a bus to Moni or Ende.*

Central Flores is renowned for its gorgeous *ikat* weaving. Sarongs, shawls, and blankets can be found in rich rust and orange tones with elaborate patterns featuring mountains, spiders, gongs, flowers, and other motifs. The entire process, from the dying of the cotton to the stitching of the cloth, is done by hand. Although it's easy to find affordable, decent cloth in Moni and Ende, the villages south of **Wolowaru,** 12km east of Moni on the Maumere road, display the best work. **Jopu** is the first village, 5km south of Wolowaru, followed by **Wolonjita** 6km farther south. At the end of the road, a full 17km from Wolowaru, is **Nggela,** on a promontory overlooking the Savu Sea. Nggela's weaving is the best in the area, and the finest examples can sells for millions of rupiah. At any of the villages, simply ask in any house and usually a few sarongs will be brought out for display. The asking price for a sarong of good quality is usually Rp100,000, but it's often possible to end up paying half that or less. Keep in mind though that the aim of haggling is to reach an acceptable price for both parties, and one that recognizes the work that goes into the making of *ikat* cloth. For a place to stay, ask around for the **Ngglet Sare.**

MONI

Moni is a small village swollen with home stays. Its fabulous views, cool weather, hot springs, waterfalls, and close proximity to the base of Keli Mutu's tricolored crater lakes make this town a convenient respite en route to the nearby peaks.

Moni is 50km from Ende and 100km from Maumere. Buses run regularly from both ends (Ende 2hr., Rp5000; Maumere 4hr., Rp6500). The queasy traveler should note that the road from Ende winds along the narrow sides of a jagged ravine and over antiquated bridges. The road to **Keli Mutu** is farther uphill on the Ende side of town. There's a **wartel** at **Restaurant Kelimutu,** 100m from the **police office** near the turn-off to Keli Mutu. **Arwanti Bungalows,** 20min. up the hill from the market in the town center, is the best bet for groups who can fill up the bungalow suites (Rp60,000) which have two separate rooms and a sitting area with chairs and couches. Homestays that were once notably cheap now lean toward being overpriced and dirty. Be sure to bargain and don't pay more than Rp10,000 per person and Rp20,000 for private *mandi*, including breakfast. The villages are near identical with basic rooms. The staff at **Wisma Kelimutu Moni** is often praised for its helpfulness and honesty. **Nusa Bunga** (first as you enter on the Ende road), and **Daniel** (in the center of the village) are both adequate for a nights sleep. Some establishments that are farther away can be even better, considering their isolation, wondrous vistas, and bungalow-style housing. One of the most pleasant is **Watugana Bungalows,** not far uphill from the market. (Singles Rp25,000; doubles Rp40,000.)

The **Arwanti** restaurant, located in the bungalows (see above), serves real vermicelli that the owners swear is not out of a box. **Restaurant Kelimutu** attracts more view-mongers than food connoisseurs, but is worth a simple meal. Mary, of **Mary's,** can cook up a traditional dinner banquet for Rp10,000 per person if you ask her by

2pm. Since people often do, her house is packed with nightly diners. Lovers of green have to check out the "vegetarian feast" at **John** (also known as **Sao Wisata Lelegana,** next to **Amina Moe I**). Let John know that you're coming, and you can choose from several wonderful vegetable dishes served by candlelight for Rp11,000. Bring your own drinks to both banquets, since quantities can be limited and pricey (Rp15,000) at the s.

While you're here, enjoy the nightly **traditional dance performance** at the *rumah adat*, 20m off the main road, opposite the market. The bamboo dance alone—traditionally performed only every few years to bless children—is worth the Rp10,000 admission. (Show daily at 8pm.)

NEAR MONI: KELI MUTU

Moni's tourist trappings are due to its proximity to Flores' grandest natural wonder—the tricolored crater lakes. The water changes color over time, owing to a geological process not fully understood. As of July 2001, the three lakes were green, black, and mocha. Previously, the middle lake was milky white; for a long time before that the lakes were maroon, blue, and white. Locals consider the pools to be the resting place of spirits, where color indicates morality; the three pools are akin to Heaven, Hell, and Purgatory.

A daily truck up Keli Mutu (Rp15,000) begins early in the morning and stops once at the park office, where visitors are asked to pay another Rp1000 to enter. The ride down (Rp15,000) leaves at 7am . Those who prefer to avoid the hordes on the truck can charter a *bemo* (Rp30,000) or walk the 13km. A shortcut *(jalan potong)* begins opposite Rumah Makan Sarty on the road to Ende, 500m from the market, and ends near the park office but it's only feasible for the descent, as the way up can be steep and slippery. It's possible to ascend Keli Mutu at times other than sunrise, but those who wait to climb not only miss a gorgeous sunrise but also risk a cloud cover that almost invariably descends on the lakes by mid-morning, obscuring the view. By road, the ascent takes 3-4hr., while the shortcut-aided descent is 2hr.

MAUMERE ☎0382

Hit hard by the 1992 earthquake and a resulting *tsunami* that rocked east Flores, Maumere is slowly rebuilding itself. Upon close inspection on the waterfront, one can see hints of what was once a pier. Still, there's not much to occupy tourists—most stay only to catch a flight out, to head west to Moni and Keli Mutu, or to venture east to Larantuka, gateway to the islands off the east coast. Those who linger stay at one of several beachside resorts east of the city, or wander through the markets and surrounding villages, many of which are known for their *ikat* weavings.

TRANSPORTATION. The **airport** is 3km east of the town center. *Bemo* and taxis ask Rp10,000 for the trip, but ignore them and walk an easy 500m to the highway, where passing *bemo* can be hailed (Rp500). **Merpati,** Jl. Don Tomas da Silva 19, is in the center of town. (☎213 42. Open daily 8am-8pm.) Frequent **buses** heading east to **Larantuka** (4hr., Rp7000) leave from **Terminal Waioti,** several kilometers east of town, but you can catch them as they swing through downtown on their way out of the city. **Terminal Madawat,** a couple of kilometers southwest of town, is the departure point for transport headed west to **Ende** (6hr., Rp10,000), **Moni** (it's usually convenient to use an Ende-bound bus, as direct *bemo* are infrequent; 4hr., Rp7500), and cities farther west. The **PELNI office** (☎210 13), on Jl. Slamet Riyadi, across the west bridge at the end of town, handles ship reservations for the *KM Awu.*

ORIENTATION AND PRACTICAL INFORMATION. Most of the town is concentrated in a wedge between the main east-west road (the Trans-Flores Hwy.) and the water. The downtown area is centered at the **old market** on **Jl. A. Yani** in the west part of town. The market's west edge is formed by **Jl. Raja Centris,** which houses most of the restaurants in Maumere. The **New Market,** on Jl. Anylik, is on the the western border of the city.

The **Sikka Regency tourist information office,** in the west reaches of town, has a helpful, wacky staff and maps of Maumere to boot. Turn left on Jl. Gajah Mada, follow Jl. A. Yani as it turns left across the river and take the second right onto Jl. Wairklau at the sign; it's 250m up. (☎216 52. Open M-Th 7am-2pm, F 7-11am, Sa 7am-12:30pm.) The best place to change money is **Bank BNI,** Jl. Sukarno-Hatta 4, about a block south of the highway. (Open M-F 8am-3pm.) The new **hospital,** Rumah Sakit Umum Daerah (☎216 17), is on Jl. Wairklau, past the tourist information office. On Jl. Moa Toda are a **pharmacy** and the **Harapan Jaya Artshop,** the latter of which has a collection of high-quality weavings and various art objects from across Indonesia. (Open M-Sa 7:15am-8pm, Su 8am-noon and 4-8pm.) The **police** (☎211 10) are at the west end of Jl. A. Yani. Opposite is the **24hr. Telkom office** with **HCD** phone inside. The **post office** is one block east of Jl. Sukarno-Hatta on the corner of the main road. *Poste Restante.* (Open M-F 8am-5pm, Sa 8am-4pm.) **Postal code:** 86100.

ACCOMMODATIONS AND FOOD. Despite a relative lack of tourists, Maumere has several decent budget spots that serve complimentary breakfasts. **Gardena Hotel,** one block north of the soccer field on Jl. Patirangga, has very clean and inexpensive rooms. (Single with private bath and fan Rp15,000, with A/C Rp25,000; doubles Rp22,500-30,000.) The hotel can arrange an English-speaking guide. Call ahead for reservations. **Wini Rai Hotel,** Jl. Gagahmada 50, down the street from terminal Madawat and 2km walk into the town center, has a clean and welcoming with a garden and a great location. (☎213 88. Singles with fan Rp25,000, with A/C Rp40,000; doubles Rp50,000-66,000.) Long popular **Senja Wair Bubuk,** Jl. Komodor Yos Sudarso 81, on the waterfront street in the east part of the town center, is a friendly place. (☎214 98. Singles Rp12,000-22,000, with A/C Rp27,500; doubles Rp17,800-30,500/35,200.) Dining options are limited. **Jl. Raja Centris** has a couple of decent places, the Chinese **Restaurant Sarinah** being the best. The tourist favorite is the **Golden Fish Restaurant,** on Jl. Hasanuddin as you walk toward the pier. It has fresh seafood, but also the highest prices in town (lobster Rp100,000).

Only 27km east of Maumere in **Wairterang** lie some of the best values in beach resorts in Indonesia. **Ankermi Bungalows** and **Flores Froggies** sit 50m apart in a secluded bay shared only with local fishermen. They offer activities ranging from climbing the island volcano to diving and snorkeling. Jump in one of the canoes (free at either resort) at night and observe the mesmerizing phosphorescent glow in the water. The bungalows at Ankermi are immaculate and have spotless outdoor *mandi.* They also offer dive trips (US$30 per dive) and are PADI-certified. (Singles Rp16,500; doubles Rp22,500; quad bungalows Rp27,500.) The bamboo huts at Flores Froggies are romantic on the beach. (Dorm bungalow Rp5000 per person; single bungalows with *mandi* Rp10,000; doubles Rp12,500.) Flores Froggies gives out snorkeling equipment to guests for free. Since there is no electricity in the area, gas lanterns are provided at night. The food is exceptional at both establishments. Try a freshly caught fish for under Rp5000. To get to Wairterang, take any *bemo* or bus east toward Lurantuka and ask for Ankermi or Flores Froggies (Rp1000).

NEAR MAUMERE: LARANTUKA AND BEYOND

Larantuka is a seaport 4hr. east of Maumere, the last stop on the Trans-Flores Hwy. (almost 700km from its beginning in Labuhanbajo). The town's setting is its most attractive feature—it runs along the coast and up the slopes of volcanic **Mount Ile Mandiri.** Although the surrounding area has a few good beaches and interesting villages, there's little of note in the town itself. Most people visit here on their way to the islands off Flores' east coast. The **Solor** and **Alor Archipelagos** offer scenic seclusion and the chance to join a whale-hunting expedition in Lamalera (on the island of **Lembata**); hunters still use hand-thrown harpoons. Daily **boats** head from Larantuka to **Lewoleba,** the largest city on Lembata (from where infrequent boats go to Lamalera). Less frequent ones head to other islands in the archipelagos and to Timor. Several **buses** per day voyage west to Maumere (4hr., Rp7000), and a few continue to further west. The bus terminal is several kilometers southwest of town.

BAHASA INDONESIA 101 On buses on rugged, rural islands like Timor, knowledge of Bahasa Indonesia is essential. Destination signs are not always accurate—ask the driver before hopping on. Useful phrases include *Apakah masih ada bis dari sini ke ____ hari ini?* ("Is there still a bus from here to ____ today?"), *Di mana bisa saya naik bis ke ____?* ("Where can I catch a bus to ____?"), and *Berapa ongkos dari sini ke ____?* ("How much is the fare from here to ____?"). If you hear responses like *Tidak ada lagi* or *Besok pagi* ("there are no more" or "tomorrow morning"), then ask about spending the night (*Di mana bisa saya menginap malam ini?* means "Where can I spend the night this evening?") or chartering private transport to the highway junction (*Apakah ada orang di sini yang bisa mengantar saya ke jalan raya?* means "Is there someone here who can take me to the highway?"). Be prepared to shell out rupiah for an *ojek* or private *bemo* ride. Distant journeys are not recommended if you need to fly out of Kupang the next morning.

Everything you need is laid out on the waterfront boulevard or the parallel street a block uphill. Money can be changed (at horrible rates) at the **Bank BNI** (open M-F 7:30am-1:30pm) or at the main **Bank Rakyat Indonesia** (open M-F 7:30am-2:30pm, Sa 7:30-11:30am), around the corner from its branch on the main road. The **PELNI office** is on the main road in the west part of town. (Open daily 7:30am-5pm.)

There aren't too many places to stay in the area. **Hotel Rulies,** on the main street a bit west of what might be called downtown Lewoleba, is the most popular spot with backpackers. (☎0383 211 98. Singles with shared *mandi* Rp10,000; doubles Rp15,000.) **Hotel Tresna,** next door, caters more to townspeople. (☎0383 210 72. Singles Rp10,000, with *mandi* Rp13,000; doubles Rp15,000-18,000.) Dining options are similarly limited. A few *rumah makan* cluster in the center of town by the monument, but **Restaurant Nirwana's** Chinese food, east on the waterfront, is a better bet.

SULAWESI

Indonesia's third largest island, Sulawesi, has a population of 11 million. The fiery Muslim Makarese and Bugis inhabit the south, the gentile and affluent Minahasans live in the north, and the animist-Christian Torajans dwell in the central-south region. While major tourist spots are accessible by plane and are Western-traveler friendly, many of the twisty roads are damaged, and the rickety smoke-filled vehicles overcrowded. Nonetheless, travelers tend to stay longer than intended, and see more than any guidebook could cover. For those who are up to the challenge of traveling in Sulawesi, the rewards of exquisite natural beauty and unforgettable cultural exchanges are plentiful.

SOUTHERN SULAWESI (SULAWESI SELATAN)

Convoluted Sulawesi seems to have as much coastline as land. Nowhere is its wealth of beachfront life as rich or textured as in the ports of Southern Sulawesi. The peninsula becomes increasingly lush as travelers move north from the arid land below Ujung Pandang, unearthing rice over maize as the crop of choice. Flat fields stretch to the base of mountains, accentuating the contrast between coastal plain and mountain. Further north, Tana Toraja gives way to the labyrinthine topography of winding mountain valleys, offering even more natural beauty.

UJUNG PANDANG (MAKASSAR) ☎0411

Centuries after the Gowa Kingdom established Ujung Padang as a trading *entrepot*, the site retains all the characteristics of a lively port city. Cluttered markets clatter with consumer opportunities, and waterfront bars help sailors drown their sorrows

and dip their tip. Equally fascinating is the ethnic diversity resulting from ages of fighting over the largest city in the spice islands. Violent anti-Chinese riots in 1998 and continued racism reveal that the racial mix is not necessarily a stable one.

TRANSPORTATION

Flights: Hasanuddin Airport, 23km from downtown. Walk 500m to the "Halte bus" hut or to the main road and flag down a *bemo* (Rp2000) to Makassar Mall or take a taxi (Rp30,000-35,000). **Merpati,** Jl. Bawakaraeng 109 (☎442 471). **Garuda,** Jl. A.P. Pettarani 18B-C (☎423 737). **Bouraq,** Jl. Veteran 1 (☎453 139). **Mandala,** Latanet Plaza and on Jl. Cokroaminoto (info ☎323 592, reservations ☎314 880). Ask offices for exact departure times. Flights to: **Denpasar** (1hr., Rp555,000); **Jakarta** (2½hr., Rp985,000-1,196,000); **Kuala Lumpur** (4hr., US$165); **Manado** (Rp649,800-853,900); **Surabaya** (1hr., Rp625,000-727,000); **Singapore** (3hr., round-trip US$365).

Buses: Panaikan Station, a few kilometers out of town on the airport road, serves points north and east. Take a *bemo* from Makassar Mall. Be flexible—the buses get packed. The **Trans-Sulawesi Highway (Transul)** connects **Ujung Pandang** in the south to **Manado** at the northernmost tip of the island. **Public buses** to: **Mamasa** (10hr., Rp30,000); **Parepare** (3hr., Rp8000), **Rantepao** (6hr., Rp35,000-52,000); **Sengkang** (5hr., Rp12,000).

> **TRANS-SULAWESI TRAVEL WARNING.** Recent trouble in Central Sulawesi makes the Trans-Sulawesi Hwy. unsafe to travel. Check with your embassy for updated information.

Boats: PELNI office, Jl. Sudirman 38 (☎331 401). Buy tickets there or at a travel agent. Fares are cheaper than air tickets (Rp70,000-450,000), but travel time is in the scale of days. Most are on 2-week loops. 1st, 2nd, 3rd, 4th, and economy classes available. Ferries to: **Bima; Denpasar; Jakarta; Kupang; Labuhanbajo; Surabaya.** Non-PELNI **ferries** (although some of them may be less safe) also make inter-island trips. **Travelers running out of days on their visas** can leave and re-enter by 3-day PELNI trips (2 per week). Check PELNI office for times and prices of all boats.

ORIENTATION AND PRACTICAL INFORMATION

Although the clamor of Ujung Pandang seems to reach as far as the **airport** some 23km to the east, the heart of the city is compact. **Jl. A. Yani,** the main thoroughfare, springs from the Western shore with **Jl. Martadinata** to its north and **Jl. Ujung Pandang** (which passes **Fort Rotterdam** and morphs into **Jl. Pasar Ikan, Penghibur,** and **Rajawali)** to its south. One block inland, Jl. A. Yani becomes **Jl. Slamet Riyadi, Jl. Hasanuddin** and **Jl. Cendrawasih** as it heads south out of town. Two blocks further east, Jl. A. Yani passes **Lapangan Karebosi,** the city center, changes to Jl. Bulusarung, and then intersects **Jl. Cokroaminoto,** a major boulevard and home to **Makassar Mall** and the central **Bemo Station.** Jl. Bulusarung continues eastward to meet northbound **Jl. Andalas,** which heads to **Paotere Harbor** via **Jl. Yos Sudarso.**

Tourist Office: Government Tourist Office (☎443 355), off Jl. Sudirman by the Mandala Monument. Open M-Th 8am-3pm, F 8am-noon, Sa 8am-1pm. Staff at Legends Hostel and other hotels are more helpful.

Tours: Sena Tours, Jl. Jampea 1A (☎323 906).

Immigration Office: Jl. Tantura Pelajar 2 (☎315 731), in the northern part of town between Jl. Nusantara and Jl. Sulawesi near the harbor. Open M-Th 7am-2pm, F 7am-11pm, Sa 7am-1pm.

Currency Exchange: Jl. A. Yani is lined with over a dozen **banks,** several of which have **24hr. ATMs.** Most open M-F 8am-2pm. For the best rates, try **Bank Central Asia** (☎319 208). Check exchange until noon. Open M-F 8am-5pm.

American Express: Pacto Travel, Jl. Sudirman 56 (☎873 208). Accepts client mail but doesn't change checks. Open M-F 8am-12:30pm and 1:30-4pm, Sa 8am-1pm.

Markets: Renowned primarily for its jewelry, **Jl. Somba Opu,** runs parallel to the waterfront a bit south of the fort. Watch for fakes. **Sutera Alam,** Jl. Onta Lama 47, is a silk-weaving center on a side street running east off Jl. Dr. Ratulangi. Sneak a peak at the weavers in action.

Emergency: Police ☎110. **Fire** ☎113. **Ambulance** ☎118.

Police: Jl. A. Yani 9, opposite Jl. Balaikota. **Branch,** Jl. Hasanuddin 3 (☎325 850), next to Hotel Marannu.

Tourist Police: ☎319 377.

Pharmacy: Apotik Kimia Farma are abundant, including **24hr. branches** at Jl. Hasanuddin 36 (☎324 442), south of Galael supermarket, and Jl. A. Yani 17-19 (☎316 722).

Medical Services: Rumah Sakit Akademis Jaury (☎317 343), on Jl. Akademis off Jl. Bulusarung. **24hr. emergency care.**

Telephones: Telkom offices on Jl. Balaikota are of little help. **Wartel** are at Jl. Bali 71, Jl. Kajaolaliddo 2G-4, Jl. Balaikota 2, Jl. Veteran 28, and on Jl. Sulawesi and Jl. Nusantara. **HCD** phones can be found in big hotels; try the Makassar Golden Hotel. **Directory Assistance** ☎108.

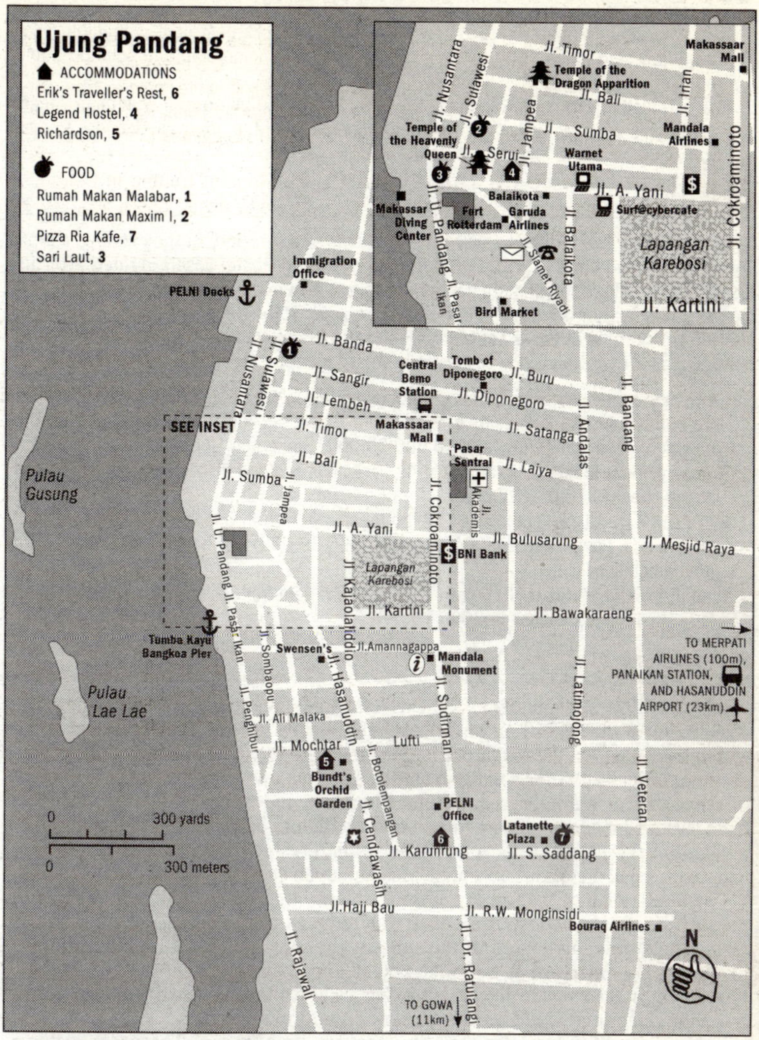

Internet Access: Warnet Utama, Jl. A. Yani 17. Best price in town. Rp3000 per hr. **Surf@cybercafe,** Jl. A. Yani 2, 3rd fl., above Pizza Ria Kafe. Booths with a view and a little surf island with cute baby turtles. Rp4000 per hr. Open daily 9am-midnight.

Post Office: Jl. Slamet Riyadi 10 (☎323 180), 1 block south of Jl. A. Yani. *Poste Restante*. Open M-Sa 8am-8pm, Su 9am-4pm. **Postal code:** 90111.

ACCOMMODATIONS

Budget haunts are remarkably hard to find, except those frequented by fluttering Surabayan "night-butterflies" (read: prostitutes). This scarcity has resulted in the virtual monopolization of the backpacker trade by the renowned "Legend."

Legend Hostel, Jl. Jampea 5G (☎328 203), next to Yasmin Hotel north of Jl. A. Yani. Backpacker's heaven: an in-house travel agency, cafe, sitting room, bottomless teacups, dozens of travelers and cheap rooms. Dorms Rp12,500; singles Rp25,000-28,000; doubles Rp28,000-32,000; triples Rp39,000.

Richardson, Jl. Mochtar Lufti 21 (☎320 348), 2 blocks east of Jl. Penghibur near Bundt's Orchid. Fireda and her dog Burner keep this home safe and sound. Simple rooms Rp35,000, with A/C Rp50,000.

Erik's Traveller's Rest, Jl. Karunrung 9A (☎321 998), 600m down Jl. Sudirman. Makeshift rooms will eventually make you shift hotels. Clean, but not overly friendly. Rooms Rp35,000, with A/C and shower Rp45,000.

FOOD

Ujung Pandang has a diverse assortment of eats and seafood. In the evening, a motley crew of **food carts** line Jl. Penghibur to make up **Pantai Losari,** named after its beachside locale. Typical dishes like *mie ayam* and *bakso* are served, but the *ikan bakar* stalls farther down yield delicious denizens of the deep sea. Savor other non-restaurant options at **Pasar Sentral** opposite the *bemo* station. **Toko Hawa Baru,** Jl. A. Yani 2, is a convenient place to stock up for roadtrips. (Open daily 8am-11pm.)

Sari Laut, on the corner of Jl. Ujung Pandang and Jl. A. Yani. Something smells fishy! Get the *cumi-cumi* and *kakap* for a full-fledged feast. Cooked right in front of you, the *esjeruk* hits the spot. Entrees Rp10,000-30,000. Open daily 3pm-4am.

Rumah Makan Maxim I, Jl. Sulawesi 42. Delicious seafood dishes in large, larger, and insane sizes (Rp10,000-27,500).

Pizza Ria Kafe, Jl. G. Latimojong 152, on the corner with Jl. Saddang. As close as you'll get to a deli. Pizza (slice Rp5000; pie Rp11,000-39,000) and bakery goods make for a great lunch snack.

Rumah Makan Malabar, Jl. Sulawesi 264. Indian fare from chicken curry to goat-head soup (Rp17,500). Dishes Rp8000-15,000.

SIGHTS

Once called Fort Jumpandang (from which Ujung Pandang derives its name), the structure near the waterfront on Jl. Penghibur was renamed **Fort Rotterdam** after the Dutch overpowered the Makarese and claimed the fort. The site now houses government offices and the **La Galigo Museum,** in which one wing displays a collection of ethnographic exhibits from around Indonesia and a second features artifacts from various kingdoms of southern Sulawesi. History buffs will get the most out of a visit, but the pleasant courtyard keeps uninterested amused. (Fort open daily 8am-6pm; small donations accepted. Museum open Sa-Th 8am-6pm, F 8am-2pm.)

Clustered north of the fort are several Chinese temples, including the **Temple of the Heavenly Queen,** whose front altar was reduced to rubble during anti-Chinese riots. The shrine, dedicated to the sailor-protecting goddess Tian Hou Gong, is located at the corner of Jl. Sulawesi and Jl. Serui, one block north of Jl. A. Yani. Farther up Jl. Sulawesi at Jl. Bali is the **Temple of the Dragon Apparition,** whose central altar celebrates Xian Mu, the mother of immortals.

Venturing further north leads to the Javanese-style **Tomb of Diponegoro,** inside a rustic cemetery near the intersection of Jl. Diponegoro and Jl. Akademis. Diponegoro was a beloved prince of Jogjakarta who led Indonesians against the Dutch in the Java War of 1825-30, only to be imprisoned in Makassar until his death in 1855.

South of the fort off Jl. Penghibur is **Bundt's Orchid Garden,** Jl. Mochtar Lufti 15, a pleasantly shaded yard with a stunning seashell shop. After repeating that three times, ask multi-lingual Clara to show you the "Golden Cowrie" and "Glory of the Sea." (☎322 572. Open daily from dawn to dusk.)

DAYTRIPS FROM UJUNG PANDANG

MAKASSAR BAY

Charter boats (up to 6 people; Rp100,000 each) jet from Tumba Kayu Bangkoa Pier, south of the intersection of Jl. Pattimura and Jl. Penghibur, to the islands of Barang Caddi (1hr.), Barang Lompo (1hr.), and Samalona (30min.). Boats to Kodingareng Keke (1hr.) and Bone Tambung (1½hr.) cost Rp200,000.

Home to some of the finest coral reefs in the region and a collection of white-sand islands, Makassar Bay is ideal for aquatic exploration. Unfortunately, careless snorkelling and explosives used in dynamite fishing have nearly destroyed reefs close to shore; decent dives sites are at least 10km out. **Samalona** is the jewel of the bay, with budget bamboo huts on the beach. **Kodingareng Keke** is a secluded oasis, while in **Kapoposang,** the ocean floor drops dramatically and teems with sea life.

In Ujung Padang, sporting goods stores on Jl. Somba Opu sell and rent snorkeling gear. **Makassar Diving Center,** Jl. Ujung Pandang 4, 50m north of the fort, rents masks, snorkels, and fins to those with or without experience and offers 4hr. snorkeling and island sightseeing trips (US$25), 1-day diving trips (US$50-100), or multi-day all-inclusive package tours (US$25-200).

MAROS CAVES

Take a bemo *(Rp2000) or DAMRI bus (Rp3500) directly to Maros. Once there, take a* bemo *(Rp1500) into the Bantimurung grounds, get off 3km before the waterfall (look for an arch labeled "Leang-Leang") and walk 5km to the site. Bring a flashlight. Open daily 7am-5pm. Rp5000.*

With over 55 caverns, the Maros Caves are a wonderland of bizarre rock formations, running streams, and painted walls. The most visited site is **Leang-Leang,** whose two caves contain paintings of *babirusa* (Indonesian wild pig) and Lascaux-like handprints believed to be 5000 years old.

BANTIMURUNG WATERFALL

Take a bemo *(Rp2000) or DAMRI bus (Rp3500) from Ujung Pandang's Makassar Mall to Maros, and then jump on a* bemo *to Bantimurung (Rp1500).*

An hour northeast of Ujung Pandang is **Bantimurung Falls,** a park reserve surrounded by massive cliffs that are worth the trip in themselves. The waterfalls aren't breathtaking, but the butterfly-filled walk up the stairs to the left is delightful (keep your eyes open for the occasional monkey). A 15min. promenade up the riverbed leads to **Store Cave,** harboring a waterfall, secluded pool, and smaller caves within. Before the main waterfall, there's a quieter walk up to **Gua Mimpi,** a pitch-dark cave filled with pushy flashlight-donning guides (Rp20,000)—bring your own light and maybe they'll leave you alone. The whole valley was once home to clouds of gorgeous butterflies, but "collectors" (Rp1000-10,000 per souvenir) have decimated the population despite the efforts of the on-site **Center for Butterfly Breeding,** which runs the free **Butterfly Museum.**

GOWA

Take a bemo *from Makassar Mall and get off at Tangul Patompo (Rp1000). From there, boats cross the river (Rp1000).*

Along the Jeneberang River, the remains of the once great kingdom of Gowa lies scattered 11km south of Ujung Pandang. Ruins of the fortress **Somba Opu,** the strongest of the forts that once protected Makassarat lie scattered around the area.

Old Gowa, where ancient mosques, royal tombs, and legendary coronation stones remain standing, is further east. The sacred **Tomb of Syech Yusuf** stands in the northwest section. A religious scholar turned resistance fighter, Syech Yusuf (1626-94) purportedly brought Islam to Sri Lanka and South Africa during his Dutch-imposed exile. A road south of the tomb runs southeast to **Katangka Mosque,** the oldest mosque on Sulawesi. It was allegedly built in 1605, shortly after Islam became Gowa's official religion. Walk 300m down the road from the mosque, make a right and then right again to get to **Batu Pelantikan** (Coronation Stone), on which the kings of Gowa were crowned. Next to it is the **Tomb of Hasanuddin,** the celebrated 12th king of Gowa, who waged a long war against the Dutch before his final defeat in 1660. *Bis kota* run from the bus terminal to Old Gowa (Rp1000); alternatively, walk 3km along the Jeneberang River from Somba Opu.

PAREPARE ☎0421

Situated between Ujung Pandang and Tana Toraja, Parepare lacks the cosmopolitan panache and natural beauty of most Sulawesian villages. As a commercial port and administrative center there is little to see, but connections to Tana Toraja, Sengkang, Kalimantan, and Ujung Pandang mean that most travelers pass through at some point in their travels.

TRANSPORTATION. **Buses** run from the station, Jl. A. Yani 4 (☎242 34), 1km south of town, to: **Rantepao** (4-5hr.; 9am, 5pm; Rp15,000); **Sengkang** (2hr.; 1, 2, 4pm; Rp7000); **Ujung Pandang** (3hr.; 7am, 5pm; Rp10,000). Get to the terminal early to ensure a seat. Another small station, 4km north of town, has buses for **Polewali** (2hr., Rp10,000), which connect onward to **Mamasa** (5-6hr., Rp15,000). For **ferries,** contact the **PELNI Office,** Jl. Andi Cammi 96. (☎210 17. Open daily 3-11am and 1-2pm.) **Bemo** run from the terminal in the town center along Jl. Pinggir Laut to points north and down Jl. A. Yani to the bus station (Rp800).

PRACTICAL INFORMATION. Parepare's streets run north-south and parallel to the western waterfront. In the north, **Jl. Pinggir Laut** runs parallel to the water, with **Jl. Baso Dg. Patompo/Jl. Hasanuddin** one block inland. **Jl. Bau Massepe,** one block further inland, accommodates most hotels and **banks, the post office,** and the **Telkom office.**

Bank BNI, Jl. Veteran 41, north of the football field, has the best exchange rates and the only **ATM** in town. (Both open M-Sa 8am-3pm.) The **hospital,** Jl. Ilham 3 (☎218 47), is one block up from the northeast corner of the football field between Jl. Bau Massepe and Jl. Veteran. The **post office,** Jl. Karang Burane 1, at the intersection with Jl. Bau Massepe, has *Poste Restante.* (☎219 44. Open M 8am-noon, Tu-Sa 8am-6pm.) A **Telkom office,** Jl. Bau Massepe 262, is opposite Hotel Gemini and has **Internet** for Rp10,000 per hr. (☎223 21. Open 8am-5pm.) **Wartel** are at Jl. Dg. Parani 25 and Jl. Bau Massepe 306. (Open 24hr.) **Postal code:** 91111.

ACCOMMODATIONS AND FOOD. Parepare's budget hotels are dives; unless you're stuck overnight or taking an early ferry or bus, you'll do better to continue to your final destination or make the journey to Sengkang. **Hotel Gandaria,** Jl. Bau Massepe 395, would be an exception, if not for its punctured ceiling and noisy location. (☎210 93. Rooms Rp30,000-42,500, with A/C Rp42,500-60,000.) **Hotel Gemini,** Jl. Bau Massepe 451 (☎217 54), is split by a dirt driveway that is reminiscent of its rooms.

Parepare's best food is at *warung* along the waterfront that have fresh seafood for lunch and dinner. **Sejathera,** on Jl. Bau Massepe near Hotel Gemini, is a supermarket with cheap water and snacks for the road. (Open daily 8am-10pm.) **Rumah Makan Padang Raya,** Jl. Bau Massepe 389, just south of Hotel Gandaria, has flavorful *padang* fare (entrees Rp1000-6000).

DAYTRIP FROM PAREPARE: SENGKANG. A daytrip from Parepare or an overnight journey from Ujung Pandang, this attractive town is a wonderful side trip before or after visiting Tana Toraja further north.

Buses link Sengkang to **Parepare** (2hr., Rp5000) and **Ujung Pandang** (5hr., Rp10,000). Central Sengkang is easy to navigate: the street with the bus station, **Jl. Kartini,** merges into **Jl. Sudirman** south of the terminal, and forks at the **Bank BNI.** A **24hr. Telkom** is at Jl. Pahlawan 6; from Jl. Sudirman, turn left at the Bank BNI and take the first left. The **post office** is north of the center on Jl. Veteran. **Pondok Eka,** Jl. Maluku 12, offers clean and quiet rooms with bathrooms and breakfast. The English-speaking staff also arranges boat tours. (☎0485 212 96. Rooms Rp30,000; with A/C Rp50,000.) **Hotel Al'Salam,** on Jl. Emmi Saelan off Jl. Sudirman, buzzes with backpackers. (☎0485 212 78. Singles Rp15,000, with private *mandi* Rp20,000; doubles Rp20,000-30,000.) Several restaurants and seafood *warung,* including a decent *padang* joint, are on Jl. Kartini and Jl. Sudirman (Rp5000-10,000).

From the shores of **Danau Tempe,** a lake formed millions of years ago when the two middle spurs of Sulawesi rammed into the landmass that now forms the island's two outer branches; a boat trip to the floating village of **Tempe** is not to be missed. Villagers are friendly and may let you visit their home, so bring small gifts such as sweets or cigarettes. Longboats can be hired at the river (2-3hr., Rp20,000-

30,000). A late trip ensures good lighting for photography, waterfowl, and a spectacular sunset. Sengkang's other main attraction is its position at the heart of Southern Sulawesi's **silk** industry. Off-the-rack clothes are easy to find, but beware of cotton blends. To see garment production, walk 10min. from the bus station on Jl. Kartini (which becomes Jl. Magga Amirullah) to **Toko Sumber Sutera,** Jl. Magga Amirullah 140, where you can also buy material. Hotels lead tours from the village where silk worms are raised (an incredible sight) to the village where silk is dyed and woven, and finally to a "soft-selling" silk clothing store (Rp50,000 per person).

TANA TORAJA

Untarnished Tana Toraja (or "Tator") is the heart of Sulawesi's tourist trade, welcoming travelers to partake in lavishly ceremonial Torajan funerals, marvel over cliff-graves, and trek through paddies and mountains. The only way to really be one with Sulawesi's magnificence, however, is to hike west from Rantepao to Mamasa, an unforgettable three-day affair through the true nature of Indonesia.

RANTEPAO ☎0423

Rantepao is geared toward the affluent outsider. Tour buses buzz past bewildered rice farmers, and "traditional houses" are touched up annually with fresh paint. Restaurants cater to Westerners, and guides think they know exactly what you want to see but just beyond the town limits, stretching in all directions, lies a paradise that even the most aggressive tout can't spoil. Creative exploring options lead to unique and unforgettable experiences for those who make the effort to leave the tourist-ridden city.

TRANSPORTATION

Buses: Bus companies line Jl. Mappanyuki. **Limon Express** and **Litha & Co.** run frequently. Daily service to **Palu** (26hr., Rp30,000) and **Ujung Pandang** (9hr., Rp25,000-42,000). Some continue to nearby local locations and **Manado** (3 days). Regional instability has made routes unpredictable; keep your ears open and ask agencies and hotels for up-to-date information.

Local Transportation: Bemo ply the streets. Most run between Terminal Bolu, 2km northeast of Rantepao, and points south. **Becak** are also hard to miss.

Rentals: Motorcycles (Rp50,000 per day) and **bicycles** (Rp25,000 per day) available at several establishments around town, including Holiday Tourist Service, Jl. Mangoldil 25 (☎254 68), close to Wisma Maria I.

ORIENTATION AND PRACTICAL INFORMATION

Rantepao, 18km north of Makale, is defined by its mercantile north-south thoroughfare, which enters from the south as **Jl. Pongtiku,** becomes **Jl. A. Yani** in the center of town, switches to **Jl. Mappanyuki** past the large intersection with Jl. Diponegoro, and continues north as **Jl. Pahlawan.** Jl. Pahlawan crosses the north curve of the **Sa'dan River** and leads to some of the better accommodations on **Jl. Suloara** to the left beyond the bridge. A general **market** is in the center of town, but real market life is 1km up Jl. Diponegoro.

Tourist Office: Pusat Informasi Wisata, Jl. A. Yani 62A (☎212 77). Free maps and a listing of ceremonies. Open M-Sa 8am-2pm.

Tours: Several agencies and guide services are on Jl. A. Yani/Mappanyuki. Maps of Tana Toraja, rentals, and whitewater rafting trips. **Holiday Tourist Service** (see **Rentals,** above), can arrange Torajan natives who are excellent funeral guides.

Currency Exchange: Bank BNI, Jl. A. Yani 84 (☎243 16). MC/V cash advances (Rp50,000 commission). Bring passport. Open M-F 8am-2pm.

Emergency: Police: ☎110. **Ambulance:** ☎118.

Police: A few **posts** in town, including at the corner of Jl. A. Yani and Jl. Diponegoro.

INDONESIA

Pharmacy: Rayndi Farma, Jl. A. Yani 99 (☎210 13). Open M-Sa 8am-8:30pm.

Medical Services: Rumah Sakit Elim, Jl. A. Yani 68 (☎212 58). **Open 24hr.**

Telephones: Telkom office (☎211 08), next to the post office. Allows collect and credit card calls from a card phone. **Open 24hr.**

Post Office: Jl. A. Yani 111, opposite the bigger of the two Bank Rakyats. Open M-Th 8am-2pm, F 8-11am, Sa 8am-1pm. *Poste Restante.* **Postal code:** 91831.

ACCOMMODATIONS AND FOOD

Rantepao's supply of rooms exceeds demand most of the year. Because visitors come for exhausting treks and daytrips, most prefer quieter locales on the outskirts of town to regain their energy for further ventures. All guest houses offer free breakfasts.

Wisma Malita, Jl. Suloara 110 (☎210 11). Go north on the main road through town until you cross the Sa'dan river, then take a left on Jl. Suloara; it's on the right. A quiet refuge from tourist chaos with newly renovated rooms and gardens. Rooms Rp25,000-35,000, with bath and hot water Rp35,000-50,000.

Wisma Surya, Jl. Monginsidi 36 (☎213 12), right by the river. Friendly. Singles/doubles Rp25,000.

Wisma Maria I, Jl. Ratulangi 23 (☎211 65). Backpacker favorite. Communal balcony. Singles Rp20,000-40,000; doubles Rp25,000-50,000.

Wisma Monika, Jl. Ratulangi 36 (☎212 16), a few doors down from Maria I. Simple, family-run rooms. Doubles Rp30,000.

Wisma Wisata, Jl. Monginsidi 40 (☎217 46). Central location and low prices make a great combination. Singles Rp15,000; doubles Rp25,000; triples Rp30,000.

Wisma Sarla, Jl. A. Mappanyuki 83 (☎211 67). Noisy but convenient. Rooms vary, so be sure to look first. Singles Rp20,000; doubles Rp25,000.

The tourist restaurants in Rantepao reduce the local specialties of bamboo-tube-cooked meats *(pa' piong)*, black rice, and palm wine to bland fare. Small restaurants and *warung*, however, serve *pa' piong* the old-fashioned way. To eat with locals, ask around for directions to **Warung Ni'Buri.'** *Tuak* (palm wine) is cheapest in markets, but taste before you buy (it quickly goes bad). **Riman,** Jl. Mappanyuki 115, and **Restaurant Mambo,** opposite the Wisma Maria, are places to satiate pancake cravings and meet trekking guides. **Sallebayu,** which translates into "many shirts," is 50m beyond Kete Kesu and hosts a spectacular view of a rice paddied valley. The food is less spectacular and a bit overpriced at that, but the surrounding area makes for great meal overall.

TORAJAN FUNERALS The Torajan people have embraced Christianity, but their funerals still echo animist beliefs. Even Dutch missionaries, finding the death rites too entrenched, gave up on trying to make the Torajans change their practices. Today, the extravagant burials last up to a week and cost millions of rupiah. To raise necessary funds and to carve *tau-tau* effigies, most Torajans get two funerals. Immediately after death, the body is injected with a preservative to make the body last until the ceremonial burial, which takes place six months to a year later. Nobles sacrifice 24 buffalo and pigs; slave descendants might kill one or two. The soul is meant to ride the buffalo over a huge mountain range to reach Puka, the afterworld. After the slaughter, guests divide the meat; portion sizes reflect status and generosity. Tourists who want to see a ceremony should hire a guide and buy a gift (like a carton of *kretek* cigarettes) for the family of the deceased.

SIGHTS

A short walk out of the city takes travelers through the countryside and its secluded villages. The best time to trek is March through October, when clouds at the end of the dry season protect trekkers from the harsh sun. Avoid the wet season, when roads turn into leech-infested mudslides. Guides are recommended for longer trips.

Tana Toraja is a pedestrian's paradise. Travelers can hike for hours in any direction and take in the endless supply of Torajan culture and life among the rice paddies. Tourist attractions all have Rp6000 entrance fees, with an optional, and often necessary, guide (Rp10,000) with lamp for cave explorations. The villages south of Rantepao have some of the area's most interesting sites. **Londa,** 6km from Rantepao off the road to Makale, hosts a small collection of *tau-tau* (effigies created for Torajan burial ceremonies) and two caves filled with decaying coffins and skeletons. The two caverns are connected by a wee passageway to be taken on only by headstrong spelunkers. Guides can help explore bat caves and the 1km crawl to villages on the other hillside. **Lemo,** 6km further south, has one of the most spectacular cliff-graves in all of Tana Toraja and features dozens of *tau-tau* that stare straight ahead with their right hand extended to symbolically accepting offerings, and their left protecting the graves from evil spirits. Unfortunately, most are replicas financed by the government after a heist in the late 1980s. Arrive before 9am to see the figures' faces in the sun. For a relaxing daytrip, catch a Makale-bound *bemo* in Rantepao and get off at the road to Lemo. After enjoying the *tau-tau*, walk north along small paths and through paddies to **Tilanga** and its refreshing swimming hole, then continue to Londa and catch a *bemo* to Rantepao.

Ke'te Kesu', whose well-preserved *tongkonan* houses and rice barns (see **Tongkonan Houses,** p. 271) and "bon-bon" begging kids have become amongst the most-visited in Tana Toraja, is 4km southeast from Rantepao. Follow the path back from the row of houses to a cliff gravesite, overflowing coffins, and a set of *tau-tau*. *Bemo* from Rantepao to Labo or Buntao can drop you off; or you can take any *bemo* toward Makale, 2km south of Rantepao.

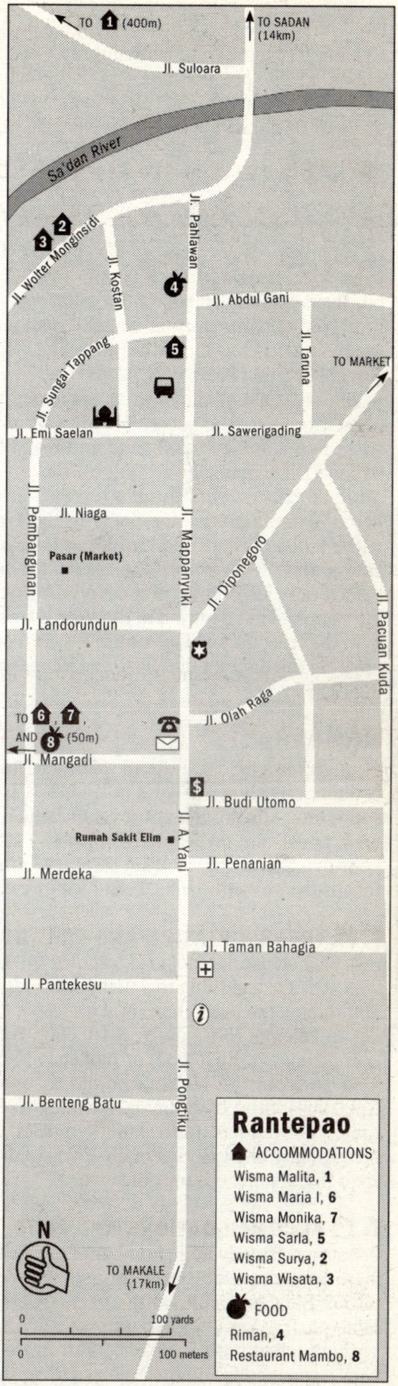

Walks north of Rantepao yield fewer *tau-tau* but more spectacular scenery. One of the popular routes is to take a *bemo* from **Terminal Bolu** north of Rantepao to Lempo (45min.) and walk uphill to **Batutumonga,** an almost spiritual view of the region. From here, continue uphill to the turn-off for **Pana.** Pana has a modest cliff-grave with some nearby tree-graves used for infants. An enjoyable downhill walk leads to **Tikala,** which has *bemo* back to Rantepao.

MAKALE

Makale's poor accommodations, less-than-stellar food, and less impressive scenery conspire to keep tourists away, but its location between nearby Rantepao (20min. by *bemo*) and more spectacular sites further north make it a hub for day-trips. **Jl. Nusantara,** the road south from Rantepao, passes guest houses, the **hospital, Rumah Sakit Fahima,** and a **24hr. wartel** before reaching Jl. Tritura, an uphill road to the *bemo* station near the man-made lotus pond. Transport heads to villages and towns, including **Bittuang** (Rp7000), **Mamasa** (Rp25,000), **Parepare** (Rp20,000), and **Polewali** (Rp25,000).

The sites east of Makale at **Suaya** and nearby **Tampangallo** can be seen in an afternoon. Both sites are accessible by *bemo* from Makale before 3pm (30min.). Otherwise, hop a *bemo* to Sangalla and backtrack to Suaya (3km by road or through paddies). Tampangallo is 1km off the road from Suaya to Sangalla. Suaya has 20 original *tau-tau* and though the cliff-grave is less spectacular than the one at Lemo, the miniatures are closer to the ground. The cave at Tampangallo is filled with skulls, coffins, and half-sized *tau-tau*. Be sure to see the treetop **Sarapung baby graves,** 400m before the main site. Babies who die before growing teeth are placed in holes in trees and covered by woven doors, since babies are considered pure enough to be buried in the sacred trees. It is also believed that by being joined with the tree, the babies continue to live on. Bark eventually grows over the body, creating the distinct dimples. The **Hot springs** at **Makula** are a few kilometers south of Sangalla.

MAMASA

Though outside Torajaland, Mamasa has loads of natural beauty without the ostentatious show of Torajan tradition. Isolated by ruined roads, the town offers something almost shameful to advertise: unspoiled rural calmness and friendliness. Locals are on the delightfully shy side of hospitable, and the place feels like your own when—as is often the case—tourism is slow. In the morning, Christian hymns drift over the hills, countering vestiges of former animalist religions.

TRANSPORTATION AND PRACTICAL INFORMATION. Cut off from the rest of the island, Mamasa straddles the **Mamasa River,** a bumpy 93km from Polewali. The closest thing to a main drag is **Jl. A. Yani,** which houses *Losmen* Mini and Marampan, the market, several *warung*, and the *wartel*. **Buses** head from the market to **Polewali** (5hr., daily, Rp10,000), from which you can continue to **Parepare** (2hr., frequent, Rp10,000) or **Rantepao** (5-6hr., at least 3 per day, Rp17,000). Buses also go from the Matana Lodge to **Ujung Pandang** (10-12hr., 1 or 2 per day, Rp20,000). Stop by a day in advance to reserve a seat and confirm a departure time. Polewali has a **BNJ** bank with **ATM,** but **Mamasa's banks don't change money;** bring plenty of cash, especially if you plan to hire a guide. A **hospital** lies across the river in the northern part of town.

ACCOMMODATIONS AND FOOD. Given its size and isolation, Mamasa boasts a relatively large number of places to stay. **Matana Lodge,** on a side street off Jl. A. Yani, draws the most tourists with some of the nicest rooms around. (☎0423 23 558. Singles/doubles with attached bath and hot water Rp25,000-65,000.) **Losmen Mini,** on Jl A Yani in the center of town, is the best budget option. (Clean rooms with attached bath Rp20,000.) For more peace and quiet, **Toraja Mamasa Church** runs a guest house on the Mamasa River on the road north to Rante Buda. (Singles/

TONGKONAN HOUSES Rantepaoean residents have exploited *tongkonan*-style houses for tourism, but functional ones still exist in countryside villages. Identifiable by their saddle-shaped roofs and ornamentation, these homes symbolize traditional beliefs about the afterlife. Shaped as a pair of buffalo horns, the house is always entered from the east. The soul is believed to ride the back of the buffalo to Puka, the afterworld, after death. Each structure has three floors, but daily life centers on the middle floor–the open lower level houses buffalo and goats at night, and the top floor in the ceiling is primarily structural. Three multifunctional rooms on the middle floor house mom, dad, and the kids; the northernmost is a prayer space and a guest room, the central room is a reception and living room, as well as the children's bedroom, and the parents sleep in the southern room. New houses are built upon marriage.

doubles Rp20,000.) **Losmen Marampan,** on Jl. A. Yani, has small rooms, some of which have bath. (Rp15-20,000.)

Don't get your hopes up for really good food here, as *mie* noodles and *nasiputih* (white rice) dominate the menus. All accommodations listed except Toraja Mamasa Church have restaurants, but *warung* sell cheaper food.

DAYTRIPS FROM MAMASA. As long as you don't mind asking directions from villagers, guides are not necessary for day hikes in **Mamasa Valley.** For multi-day treks, you might want a guide; your hotel's staff can help you find one. (Guides about Rp40,000 per day. Local kids may follow you at points and later demand payment for their "guide" services; if you didn't ask for their services, it's fine not to pay, but try to shake them off early.

Day hikes abound in the hills and nearby villages. The best way to figure out the possibilities is to check out **Matana Lodge** or the other *losmen*—most have maps and suggestions for travelers. Martinos, at **Losmen Marampan,** has an amazing hand-drawn map that he may let you photocopy.

A relaxing half-day trip to the northern villages of **Kole** and **Rante Buda** leads to a pool fed by a hot springs and the oldest *banua layuk* (High House). *Bemos* head south to **Pena,** the resting grounds for 18 traditional, buffalo-shaped coffins (sometimes called **Teron-Terong**). From here, head through the traditional villages of **Pidara** and **Balla Peu** for a view of the valley from Mussa. The 2hr. side trip to a 100m waterfall at **Allodio** is worthwhile if you want to swim, but the roads are a bit rough, and the trip isn't especially pretty. Those in the mood for more culture should head west to the villages of **Tanete** and **Tai Bassi** for a look into **traditional weaving.**

More ambitious trekkers can undertake **multi-day hikes** around Mamasa or head toward Tana Toraja on a three-day, 67km trek east to **Bittuang,** from which *bemos* run to Makale. Finding accommodations and food isn't a problem, especially at the usual stopping points each night (Rp30,000-40,000 per night), but pack plenty of water each day. The first day's hike is generally from Mamasa to Timbaan. (Head north past the hospital to the village of Mama, where the road ends, and the trail begins.) Stop in Paku on the second day, and land in Bittuang on the third.

NORTHERN SULAWESI (SULAWESI UTARA)

The smallest of the island's four provinces, northern Sulawesi is the most prosperous; its education and health are the envy of much of Indonesia. Blessed with fertile soil fed by volcanic ash and seasonally heavy rains, the region has cashed in on coconuts and cloves, although rice is what first drew the Dutch here in the 1600s. Looking to feed their factories on the nearby Moluccas (Spice Islands), the Dutch

SULAWESI'S WILD SIDE In the 19th century, British naturalist Alfred Russel Wallace asserted that wildlife in Borneo is Asian, while Sulawesi's animal friends are Austronesian. Indeed, Sulawesi's bizarre fauna often has more in common with Australia's creatures than with those of much closer Indonesian islands. The island's isolation from larger landmasses has resulted in a proliferation of unique species; over 60% of Sulawesi's mammals and a third of its birds are endemic. Three species are particularly celebrated on the island. Lucky travelers might catch a glimpse the famous *babirusa* (pig deer), which has monstrous tusks that curve through the roof of its mouth. Another fearsome beast is the *anoa* (miniature buffalo), whose size belies its ferocity. Rounding out the trio is the *maleo* bird, a megapode. Development and poaching, however, threaten these species with extinction.

established a fort near present-day Manado. The most visible result of their colonial presence is the overwhelming Christian sector of the Minahasa people, who constitute the province's largest ethnic group. Today most tourists come to northern Sulawesi for the exquisite diving near Manado.

PALU ☎0451

Even though Palu is surrounded by lush rainforest, this coastal town is one of Indonesia's driest spots. With its eerie silence and sickly warm winds, being in Palu can feel like being stuck in a concrete purgatory. Yup, that's Palu—an oasis of boredom in an otherwise enthralling island. Travelers use the town as a transportation hub, coming to get trekking permits and catch a movie before catching the earliest flight, bus, or boat out. Palu's redeeming feature, however, is its proximity to Donggala's Elysian sands.

INDONESIA

TRANSPORTATION AND PRACTICAL INFORMATION. Bandara Multiara Palu Airport (☎234 99) is 7km southeast of town, accessible by *bemo* (30min.). **Merpati** (☎211 72), on Jl. Has Anuddin, flies to **Manado** (Tu, Th; Rp413,900) and **Ujung Pandang** (11:15am, Rp360,000). **Bouraq** (☎278 95) is on Jl. Mawar, while **Garuda** (☎211 72) is on Jl. Said Idus Aldjufrie. Call hotels or government tourist offices for bus departure locations. **Buses** go to **Gorontalo** (1½ days); **Manado** (2 days), **Poso** (8hr.); **Rantepao** (1½ days). **Bemos** go just about everywhere from **Mosomba terminal.**

Kantor Parawisata, Jl. Rajamoili 103, the tourist office, is on the beach. (☎268 10. Open M-Sa 7am-2pm.) **PHPA,** on Jl. Moh-Yahim, sells **trekking permits.** (☎211 06. Open M-Th 7am-noon, F 7-11am, Sa 7am-1pm.) Other services in Palu include: **BNI,** Jl. Sudirman 21 (☎212 80), which has the best rates for **currency change; police** (☎213 15) on Jl. Pemuda; **Rumah Sakit Umum Undata** (the **hospital**), on Jl. Soeharto, which has a **pharmacy** (☎212 70; **open 24hr.**); **wartels** around town that offer collect and international calls; **post office**, on Jl. Moh-Yamin (☎211 02; open M-Th 8am-6pm, F 8-11am and 2-6pm, Sa 8am-6pm).

ACCOMMODATIONS AND FOOD. Many Palu hotels are dodgy, so you'll have to search a little for acceptable lodgings. **Alam Raya Hotel,** Jl. Sis Aljufri 65, making it your best bet in Palu. **Wisata Hotel,** Jl. S Parman 39 (☎211 75), has a cool lobby and clean rooms but too few windows. **Losmen Pasifik,** Jl. Gajah Mada 42 (☎233 54), is mediocre.

Palu's proximity to the ocean unfortunately doesn't mean it has tasty seafood. Food stalls set up on **Jl. Gadjah Mada** every night. **Masomba Market** sells fruits and vegetables. The **supermarket,** at the corner of Jl. Hasan Uddin and Jl. Dr. Wahidin, sells an array of food and other goods. **Salero Minang,** Jl. S. Parman 61, has good *padang* food.

EXCURSION FROM PALU: DONGGALA. Once a bustling seaport, Donggala now is rundown and crowded. The secluded village **Tanjung Karang,** however, teems with white beaches, excellent snorkeling and diving, and good food only 1½km from Donggala. The scarcity of fresh water has put a limit on the number of *losmen,* creating a high-priced market and dearth of rooms during peak season (July-Aug.). Beachside **Harmoni** and **Mariyna** are the most desirable budget lodgings. **Natural Cottages** (☎253 34) is more expensive. If all the *losmen* are booked, travelers can sleep on the beach or inquire about renting a room with local families. Dining options are pretty limited, but at **Prince John Dive Resort** (☎457 717 10), all guests are served at the same time, buffet-style. Prince John also offers diving instruction and excursions. Bring plenty of cash—there are no banks, and the diving isn't cheap.

MANADO ☎0431

The prosperity of Manado, the capital of northern Sulawesi, is evident in its lively markets and Chinese and Minahasa traditions and cuisine. Thus far, the city has avoided direct ethnic tension; during the 1998 riots, Chinese from across the archipelago flocked here as a haven from racial violence. For most tourists, Manado is the gateway to the Bunaken-Manado Tua National Marine Park, a superb ecosystem with some of the finest diving spots in the world.

TRANSPORTATION

Flights: Sam Ratulangi Airport, 15km out of town. Walk left downhill to catch a *mikrolet* to Paal 2 or take a cab (Rp20,000). **Bouraq,** Jl. Sarapung 28 (☎841 470), flies to **Davao, Philippines** (M, F; US$150) and **Surabaya** (1pm, Rp1,040,000). **Garuda,** Jl. Diponegoro 15 (☎852 154), flies daily to: **Denpasar** (Rp1,320,000); **Jakarta** (Rp1,365,000); **Ujung Pandang** (1:20pm, Rp845,000). **Merpati,** Jl. Martadinata 43 (☎853 213), near the Paal 2 terminal, flies daily to **Ujung Pandang** (1pm, Rp1,040,000). **Silk Air,** Jl. Sarapung 5 (☎863 744), flies to **Singapore** (Tu, Sa 2:10pm; US$220). Open M-F 8am-5pm.

Ferries: PELNI boats departs from **Bitung** (see **Near Manado,** p. 276). **PELNI office,** Jl. Sam Ratulangi 7 (☎855 114). Open M-F 8am-3pm. Infrequent ferries go to: **Denpasar** (2 per month Rp210,5000, 1st-class Rp467,500); **General Santos** (3days, leaves M, US$25); **Surabaya** (2 per month; economy Rp200,000, 1st-class Rp658,000); **Ujung Pandang** (2 per month Rp145,000, 1st-class Rp457,500).

Buses: Bus leave from the **Paal 2** terminal, east of the city, to: **Airmadidi** (30min. by *mikrolet* Rp750); **Bitung** (1hr., every 30min. 7am-9pm, Rp1500); **Tondano** (1hr., Rp2000). From **Karombasan Station,** south of town in Wanea, buses leave for **Tomohon** (30min., Rp1500) and destinations farther into the Minahasan heartland. From the **Malalayang Terminal,** southwest of Manado, buses leave for: **Kotamobagu** (4hr., Rp6000); **Palu** (24-30hr., Rp50,000); **Ujung Pandang** (3 days, 9am, Rp115,000).

ORIENTATION AND PRACTICAL INFORMATION

North-south **Jl. Sam Ratulangi,** parallel to **Jl. Piere Tendean (Waterfront Blvd.),** has all the goods and services a traveler needs. Another road, called **Jl. Lasut** at the top and **Jl. Sarapung** at the bottom, runs one block inland from the northern part of Jl. Sam Ratulangi. **Jl. Walanda Maramis** (sometimes called **Jl. Tendean),** is a shopping street that runs farther inland from Jl. Sam Ratulangi and Jl. Lasut. At the far northern end of **Pasar 45,** *mikrolets* head anywhere in the city for Rp400 but are often full and sometimes unwilling to stop for travelers with large bags.

Tourist Office: Government tourist office, Jl. Diponegoro 111 (☎851 723). Unhelpful. Open M-Th 8am-2pm, F 8-11am, Sa 8am-1pm. Better maps at **Smiling Hostel** and **Manado Bersehati Hotel.**

Currency Exchange: BNI, at the north end of Jl. Lasut. open M-F 8am-4pm. Also an airport branch. **BCA,** on Jl. Sam Ratulangi near the post office. **24hr. ATM.** (AmEx/MC/V).

Markets: Pasar Bersehati is north of the harbor, past the end of Jl. Sam Ratulangi. Smaller market between the upper ends of Jl. Sam Ratulangi and Jl. Sarapung.

Police: Central station, on southern Jl. Diponegoro and at the telecommunications office on Jl. Sam Ratulangi.

Emergency: ☎110. **Ambulance:** ☎118.

Medical Services: Rumah Sakit Gmim, Jl. Raya Talete 1 (☎352 712), in Tomohon, 30min. from Manado, at the end of the *mikrolet* line. The region's best hospital.

Pharmacies: On lower Jl. Sam Ratulangi and around the square at the top of Jl. Lasut.

Telephones: Telkom office, on Jl. Sam Ratulangi. **Open 24hr.**

Internet Access: Cybernet, Jl. Sam Ratulangi 23. Rp8000 per hr. Open 8am-10pm.

Post Offices: GPO, Jl. Sam Ratulangi 19 (☎852 301). *Poste Restante.* Open M-Th 8am-8pm, F 8-11am and 2-8pm, Sa 8am-6pm, Su 2-6pm. **Express Mail: DHL** (☎852 778), on Jl. Sam Ratulangi between Jl. Sudirman and Jl. Walanda Maramis. Open M-F 8am-6pm. **Postal code:** 95111.

ACCOMMODATIONS

Manado Bersehati Hotel, Jl. Jend. Sudirman 20 (☎855 022), on a side street 1 block inland from the Jl. Sudirman and Jl. Sarapung intersection. Singles Rp17,500, with bath Rp30,000; doubles Rp30,000/35,000; rooms with A/C Rp50,000.

Smiling Hostel, Jl. Rumambi 7 (☎868 463), on a short extension of a street at the northern end of Jl. Sam Ratulangi. Head toward the port; it's next door to Hotel Celebes. Cheap rooms are popular with young travelers. Plenty of tourist info. Restaurant upstairs. Dorms Rp8000; singles Rp12,000; doubles Rp18,500; deluxe doubles Rp24,000.

Hotel Minahasa, Jl. Sam Ratulangi 199 (☎862 559), on the far southern end of Jl. Sam Ratulangi. Rooms have private *mandi* and fine views. Breakfast included. Singles Rp48,000, with A/C Rp100,000; doubles Rp64,000, Rp116,000. MC/V.

Rex Hotel, Jl. Sugiono 3 (☎851 136). Head inland on Jl. Watanda Maramis from Jl. Sam Ratulang and make the 4th left. Clean and affordable. Laundry. Singles with common *mandi* Rp15,000, with A/C Rp40,000; doubles Rp25,000/50,000.

FOOD

Minahasan cuisine features famously spicy and risqué specialties, including forest rat, bat, dog, and *tinutuan* (vegetable breakfast porridge). The best place to sample these delicacies is the string of restaurants overlooking Manado near the town of Tinoor on the road to Tomohon. More conventional fare is accessible from cheap *warung* lining the upper part of Jl. Sam Ratulangi. **Supermarkets** line Jl. Sam Ratulangi and Jl. Sudirman, and seafood restaurants are appropriately by the water.

Surabaya, Jl. Sarapung 33, near the intersection of Jl. Sarapung and Jl. Sam Ratulangi. Javanese-style restaurant. Long English menu. Good for vegetarians. *Gado-gado* Rp7000. *Ikan mas* Rp17,000. Open daily 10am-10pm.

Tinoor Jaya, Jl. Sam Ratulangi 167, close to Hotel Minahasa. Yummy Minahasan cuisine. Man's best friend–fried Rp5000. *Ayam kam* (hairy bat) Rp2000.

Kawan Baru, on Jl. Walanda Maramis, near the Jl. Sam Ratulangi intersection. Great home cooking. *Nasi goreng* Rp5000. *Cumi* (squid) *goreng tepung* Rp15,000. Open daily 9am-9pm.

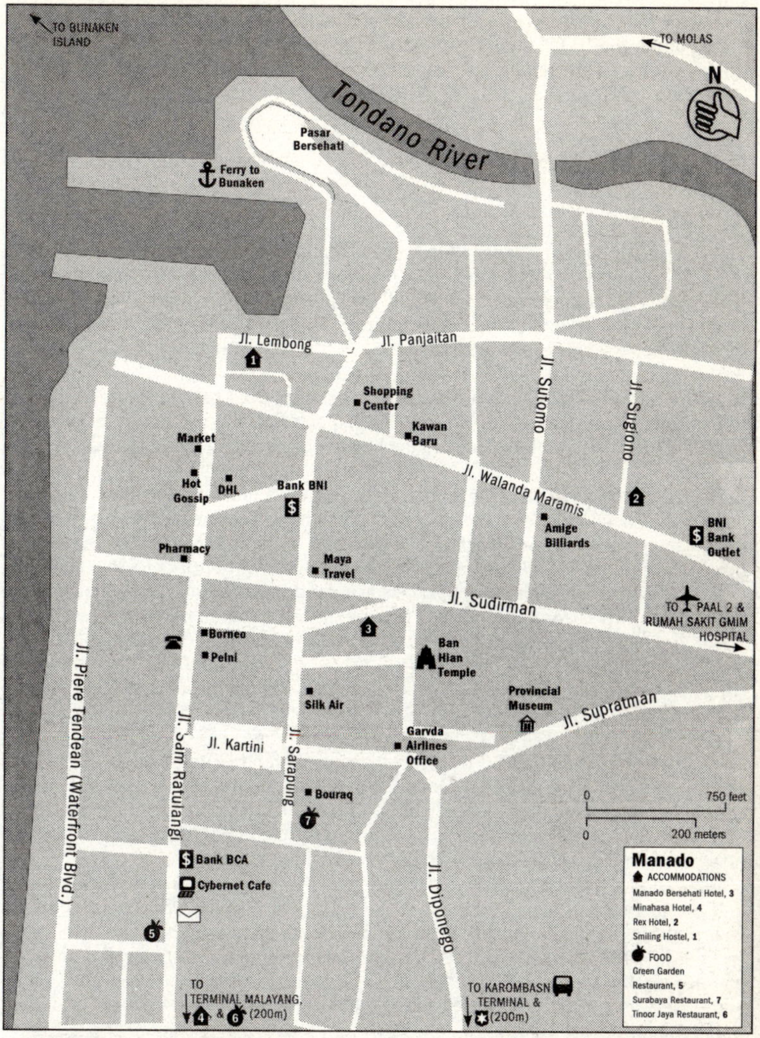

INDONESIA

Green Garden, on Jl. Sam Ratulangi, near the KFC. Generous portions of Chinese food. 22 different juice flavors Rp3500-6000. Open daily 9am-2am.

SIGHTS AND ENTERTAINMENT

The **Provincial Museum of North Sulawesi,** on Jl. Supratman 72, has impressive greenery and architecture, traditional clothing, weaving, and pottery from around northern Sulawesi. (Open M-F 8am-2pm.) The **Ban Hian Kiong Buddhist-Confucian Temple,** on Jl. Panjaitan in the city center, serves Manado's large Chinese population. In February, two weeks after the Chinese New Year, it's home to one of Southeast Asia's largest Toa Pa Kong Festival celebrations.

Amigo Billiards Hall, on Jl. Walanda Maramis, is as friendly as the name suggests. (Pool Rp8000 per hr. Open daily 9am-1am.) **Borneo,** a tropically-themed disco, is on Jl. Sam Ratulangi, opposite the Telkom Office. (No cover. Open daily

9pm-4am.) Word travels quickly about **Hot Gossip,** a bit farther down Jl. Sam Ratulangi under the "H.G." sign. Despite the high cover, it's packed by midnight with folks grinding to house music. (Cover Rp15,000; includes 1 drink. Beer Rp10,000. Open 7am-4am.)

NEAR MANADO

BUNAKEN

The 753 sq. km **Bunaken-Manado Tua National Marine Park** has turned Manado into a major stop on the backpacker circuit. Coral walls with drop-offs to 200m teem with marine life. Experienced divers will find plenty of water action, while rookies can test-dive the several introductory courses. Underwater visibility is superb, and the rich ecosystem is easily accessible.

TRANSPORTATION. From Manado, take a **boat** from behind Pasar Bersehati to **Bunaken** (1½hr.; leaves 1:30pm, returns 6:45pm; Rp5000) or charter an **outrigger** (Rp50,000-100,000). Smiling Hostel may be able to arrange a free charter.

ACCOMMODATIONS. The best way to explore Bunaken is to stay on one of its islands. Each has its own character, so if you have the time and energy, it might pay to shop around. **Liang Beach,** 100m from the drop-off, hosts two of Bunaken's three dive centers. (Meals included. Simple cottages with *mandi* Rp30-60,000 per person.) **Santika** and **Panorama Cottages** are good budget options. **Bastiaano's,** in the center of the beach, has larger, more expensive rooms that are all near the water and enjoy spectacular sunsets. (Rooms Rp60,000.) On the other side of the island, **Pangalingan Beach** has similarly priced accommodations, including **MC** (Rp30,000), **Daniel's** (Rooms Rp35,000), **Lerenzo's Cottage** (Rooms Rp30,000), and **Seabreeze** (Rooms Rp40,000-60,000).

DIVING AND BEACHES. Bunaken's beaches aren't quite paradise, but its 18 world-class dive sites make up for it. Turtles, tuna, and whitetip sharks frequent **Lekuan,** a superb wall dive. Schools of barracuda are often spotted in **Pangalingan,** and **Sachiko's** spectacular density of fish and strong currents attract schools of pelagics. **Cela Cela** is an ideal site to observe reef life at night.

Sulawesi Dive Quest is the island's best dive center. The gear is in mint condition, and the instructors are knowledgeable. (☎812 816. 2 dives US$50; PADI open-water course US$300.) **Froggies** is an impressive all-inclusive hotel and dive shop. (☎82 431 34 78. 2 dives US$75, PADI open-water course US$410.) On Jl. Pangalingan, **Indopacific Divers** (☎82 431 35 41), at Seabreeze, offers two dives for US$75 and open-water courses for US$400. Fins and mask rental runs Rp10,000 per day. Snorkeling tours are US$15.

The pricier dive centers on Manado offer better accommodations, more amenities, and easier access to shops and banks. The only downside is a 1hr. commute to the dive sites. **Nisantara Diving Center** (**NDC;** ☎863 988) is in Molas, north of Manado. (Take a *mikrolet* to **Tuminting** and then an *oplet* to **Molas,** or call NDC for pickup from Manado. Glass-bottom boat tours US$20-40.) **Murex,** small and intimate, has bungalows south of the city. (☎662 80. 2 dives US$80-90; dive course US$395-500.)

MINAHASA

The Minahasan highlands around Manado offer many pleasant daytrips. To get there, catch a bus from Manado's Karombasan Terminal south to **Tomohon** (30min., frequent departures). A 30min. drive east of Tomohon brings you to **Tondan,** the cultural heart of Minahasa. A few kilometers out of town toward **Airmadidi** are caves built by slave labor under the Japanese occupation during WWII.

INDONESIA

Farther north along the road to Airmadidi rests the small town of **Sawangan** (30min.) and its *waruga*, traditional stone houses for the deceased. Concerns about the hygiene of this kind of burial led to the abandonment of the practice in the 19th century, and *waruga* (144 in total) from across the region were collected here. Another set, including a 3m high tomb that held a king, was brought to Airmadidi proper. Airmadidi is on the main Manado-Bitung road (30min. from Manado); the *waruga* lot is off the road to Tondano, 500m from the Manado-Bitung road.

BITUNG AND TANGKOKO

By the 1960s, Manado's port was too silted for cargo boats, so most commercial traffic moved to **Bitung** on the other side of the peninsula. The only reason to come here is to catch the PELNI **ferry** leaving Manado. From the Paal 2 terminal in Manado, take a bus to Bitung (Rp250, 1hr., frequent departures). **Tangkoko's** main is the **Tangkoko-Batuangus Dua Saudara National Park,** named after the reserve's three mountains. Home to the endemic *maleo* bird, *aroa*, and the Tarsius monkey (see **Sulawesi's Wild Side,** p. 272), Tangkoko supports a wealth of species in a small area. To get to Tangkoko, take the Bitung bus to **Girian** (45min., Rp2000) and catch a jeep north to **Batuputih** (30min., Rp2500).

BOLAANG MONGONDOU DISTRICT

Although **Kotamobagu** is the capital of Bolaang Mongondou, the central district of North Sulawesi, most tourists find little reason to linger there. The bus from **Manado** (5hr., 5 per day, Rp12,500) stops at a station not far from town; take a *mikrolet* into the main square, past the roundabout. A few buses also head west to **Gorontalo** (5hr., Rp7000). Buy tickets, change money, and place phone calls from the **bus agency,** left of the supermarket. From Gorontalo, an overnight ferry leaves daily for the desolate paradise of the **Togian Islands**.

DUMOGA-BONE NATIONAL PARK. With 3000 sq. km of protected land, **Dumoga-Bone National Park** (☎225 47 in Kotamobagu), is Sulawesi's largest wildlife preserve and the finest place to see the island's fauna (see **Sulawesi's Wild Side,** p. 272). Bring long pants and a long-sleeve shirt, as the bugs and the spines of rattan plants can hurt. A tent is key for treks, and binoculars are useful to spot the *maleo* birds. Transportation to the park requires patience and skillful bargaining. From Kotamobagu's *mikrolet* terminal (a block from the supermarket), take a *mikrolet* to **Doloduo** (1hr., Rp2500). Use the word "public" and avoid paying drivers Rp30,000 for a "charter" trip. Once in Doloduo, catch another *mikrolet* (15min., Rp2500) to **Toraut,** where you'll find the park entrance complex, next to Wallacea Cottage. Ask Mr. Suroji for a tour (Rp35,000 per 5hr.). **Wallacea Cottage** is the park's only option for overnight stays, at Rp45,000 per person. (Park entrance fee Rp1500 per day.)

SUMATRA

As the westernmost—and one of the largest—of Indonesia's islands, Sumatra plays second fiddle only to Java in politics and economics. Notorious for its poor roads and fickle climate, Sumatra is no jetsetter's paradise. Many regions prove inaccessible for even the most determined, and women traveling alone may experience harassment. Still, the Medan-Padang route via Lake Toba, Nias, and Bukit Tinggi is well traveled and insures intrepid visitors a memorable experience. Laced with hikable jungle terrain, crystalline crater lakes, and cultural character, Sumatra should not be overlooked by those with the desire—and stomach—for adventure.

Pulau Weh
Banda Aceh
0 100 miles
0 100 kilometers
Phuket
THAILAND
N
Meulaboh
Takengon
ACEH
Simeulue
Blangkejeren
Tapaktuan
Ketambe
Bukit Lawang
Kutacane
Belawan
Gunung Leuser National Park
Straits of Melaka
Penang
Georgetown
Kabanjahe
Medan
Berastagi
Pulau Banyak
Lake Toba
Pangururan
Parapat
MALAYSIA
Gunung Sitoli
Pulau Samosir
Sibolga
Tarutung
Lagundi Bay
Nias
NORTH SUMATRA
Kuala Lumpur
Tanahmasa
Pini
Tanahbala
Dumai
Rupat
Siberut
Bengkalis
Pekanbaru
Melaka
Danau Maninjau
Bukit Tinggi
Rangsang
Padang
RIAU
SINGAPORE
Kundur
Sipura
WEST SUMATRA
Pulau Batam
Rengat
Pagai Utara
Riau Islands
Pulau Bintan
Tanjung Pinang
Kayu Aro
Sungai Penuh
Danau Kerinci
Pagai Selatan
Kerinci Sablat National Park
JAMBI
Singkep
Lingga
Jambi
Road
Ferry
Province Border
BENGKULU
Bengkulu
SOUTH SUMATRA
Baturaya
Palembang
Pankalpinang
Bangka
Enggano
Danau Ranau
INDIAN OCEAN
LAMPUNG
Tanjungpadan
Belitung
Bandar Lampung
Java Sea
Krakatau
TO JAVA AND ANAK KRAKATAU VOLCANO

Sumatra

NORTH SUMATRA

MEDAN

☎061

City slickers will take comfort in Medan's bustling urban chaos as this home of nearly two million people marches to its own hectic beat. Beyond the smoke and grime of the city streets that makes travellers hurry to Penang or Lake Toba, however, lie neighborhoods full of character, with a richness of food and architecture that reflects the city's diverse population. Mosques dot the city, from the handsome Masjid Raya to small, decrepit constructions weathered by the past. Colorful Hindu temples and Buddhist monasteries find their place east and west of the town's center in Chinatown and Little India, neighborhoods bursting with the their own tales, tongues, and tastes. Travellers to Medan will be rewarded with friendliness, curiosity and urban comforts absent in the rest of Sumatra.

TRANSPORTATION

Flights: Polonia International Airport (☎456 7084), 3km south of town at the end of Jl. Imam Bonjol. The international terminal lies directly behind the main gate; the domestic terminal is 300m to the right. From town, take a *becak* (Rp5000) or taxi (Rp15,000). Pick up a map (Rp39,000) at the **Airport Tourist Information Office.**

Garuda, Jl. Mongsidi 34A (☎455 6777), across from the post office on Jl. Balai Kota 2 (☎451 6400). Open M-F 8am-5pm, Sa 9am-5pm, Su 9am-1pm. To: **Banda Aceh** (1hr., Rp396,300); **Denpasar** (3hr., Rp1,677,000); **Jakarta** (2hr., Rp1,156,400).

Malaysian Airlines (MAS), Jl. Imam Bonjol 17 (☎451 9333), ground fl., in the Danau Toba Hotel. Open M-F 8am-5pm, Sa 8am-3pm. AmEx/MC/V. To: **Kuala Lumpur** (US$92) and **Penang** (US$92).

Merpati, Jl. Brigjen Katamso 219 (☎455 1888). Open M-F 8am-4:30 pm, Sa 9am-2pm, Su 9am-1pm. To: **Palembang** (Rp 1,094,000); **Pekan Baru** (Rp 492,000); **Pontiana** (Rp.1,548,300).

Silk Air/Singapore Airlines (☎453 7744), on the lower back side of the Tiara Convention Center off Jl. Imam Bonjol and Jl. Cut Meutiah. Open M-F 8am-5pm, Sa 8am-3pm. To: **Singapore** (US$144).

Buses: The cheapest are rattle-trap **public buses** with no A/C and no price guarantees (pay on the bus). Ideal for short trips, even if the only space you can find is on the roof. Locals can point to the correct bus, but ask several people to be sure. For longer trips, purchase tickets in advance for faster, less crowded **private buses.** Most locals purchase tickets directly from individual bus companies along **Jl. Sisingamangaraja.** Shuttle buses pick up passengers at company office before heading to main terminals.

Amplas Terminal, 12km south of the town center, goes to: **Bukititinggi** (18hr.; 3 per day; Rp50,000, with A/C Rp70,000); **Jakarta** (48hr.; 5 per day; Rp135,000, with A/C Rp260,000); **Padang** (20hr.; Rp55,000, with A/C Rp75,000); **Parapat** (4hr.; every hr. 8am-8pm; Rp20,000, with A/C Rp30,000).

Pinang Baris Terminal, 10km west of town center, services points north and west of Medan. Entrance fee Rp100. To: **Banda Aceh** (12hr.; 5 per day 8am-9pm; Rp50,000, with A/C Rp60,000); **Berastagi** (2hr., every 30min. 7am-5pm, Rp3000); **Bukit Lawang** (2½hr., every 30min. 7am-5pm, Rp4000).

Ferries: Leave from **Belawan,** 26km north of Medan. Companies run ferries to **Penang,** Malaysia (90 Malaysian Ringgitt (RM), round trip 120RM; 4hr., 10am.) Buy tickets at **Penang Express Bahagia,** Jl. SiSingaMangaRaja 92A (☎732 0421). Open M-F 7:30am-4:30pm, Sa 7:30am-3:30pm, Su 7:30am-1:30pm. Cash only. **Perdana Ekspress,** Jl. Brigjen Katamso 35D (☎456 6222), offers the same service. Open M-F 7:30am-5:30pm, Sa 7:30am-4pm, Su 7:30-11:30am. Tickets purchased from hotels or travel agents cost about Rp15,000 extra, and include a tourist bus to Belawan. **PELNI,** Jl. Kol. Sugiono 5 (☎453 8772), connects to domestic ports. To: **Jakarta** (42hr., every 4 days, Rp172,000) via **Batan** (Rp89,900).

Local Transportation: *Sudako* (or *bemo* as they're known in larger cities) are rickety, yellow, and door-free mini-vans that careen along set routes; major stops are usually written on windshields. They leave from **Sambu** near the **Pasar Sentral** (Central Market) for **Amplas** (30min., Rp1000). To get to **Belawan,** take a *sudako* marked "Morina" from Jl. A. Yani or Jl. Sisingamangaraja (30min., Rp1000-1500). To get to **Pinang Baris,** take *bis damris* or *sudako* marked "P. Baris" running along Jl. A. Yani/Balai Kota (30min., Rp1000-1500). *Sudako* #64 travels between bus terminals via Jl. Juanda and Jl. Palang Merah (Rp1000). *Becak* and *becak mesin* (motorized) prowl downtown (Rp2000-5000). If you're not staying long and don't mind a few moments of life-flashing panic, they're probably your most efficient way of getting around town. Metered **taxis** no longer have or use their meters, so bargain for a rate. Airport to downtown Rp13,500.

ORIENTATION AND PRACTICAL INFORMATION

Medan rambles with little rhyme or reason. The heart of the city is comprised of major one-way avenues which change names throughout their length. The main north-south road starts as **Jl. Putri Hijau** and changes to **Jl. Balai Kota** at the **Deli Plaza Shopping Center.** After passing **Merdeka Square,** it becomes **Jl. A. Yani.** South of the intersection with **Jl. Palang Merah,** it becomes **Jl. Pemuda** before changing to **Jl. Brigjen Katamso,** passing the **Istana Maimun** and several travel agencies. **Jl. Palang Merah,** which leads west from Jl. A. Yani (and quickly becomes **Jl. H. Z. Arifin**), passes through the **Chinese** and **Indian areas** of the city. The other important road is **Jl. Sisingamangaraja,** which roughly parallels Jl. Pemuda/Brigjen Katamso, past the **Mesjid Raya,** where hotels catering to every budget abound. Medan's two **bus terminals, Stasiun Pinang Baris** and **Stasiun Amplas,** are on the city's west and south edges.

Tourist Office: Provincial Tourism Office of North Sumatra, Jl. A. Yani 107 (☎453 8101). Friendly, English-speaking staff. Maps, information booklets, and directions readily available. Open M-F 7:30am-4pm.

Tours: Most agents line Jl. Brigjen Katamso south of Jl. Letjen Suprapto. **Trophy Travel and Tour,** Jl. Brigjen Katamso 33DE (☎415 5666), is Medan's largest travel agency. Open M-Sa 8am-5pm, Su 8am-noon. AmEx/MC/V.

Consulates: Australia, Jl. Kartini 32 (☎415 7810). Open M-F 9am-1pm. **Malaysia,** Jl. Diponegoro 43 (☎453 1342). Open M-F 8am-1pm and 2-4pm. **Singapore,** Jl. Tengku Daud 3 (☎451 3366). Open M-F 8am-12:30pm and 1:30-4:30pm. **UK,** Jl. Kaptan Pattimura 459 (☎821 0559). Open M-F 8am-noon.

Immigration Offices: Jl. Binjei 268A (☎852 2112). Several km north of town; take a *Damri* bus from Jl. A. Yani and ask to get out at "Kantor Imigrasi." Use for visa questions and service. Open M-Th 7:30am-2:30pm, F 7:30-11:30am, Sa 7:30am-1:30pm.

Currency Exchange: Change money here–rates outside Medan are poor. Most banks are along Jl. Palang Merah and Jl. Pemuda/A. Yani. Best rates at **Bank Buana Indonesia,** Jl. Palang Merah 30 (☎415 6574), just east of Jl. A. Yani. Traveler's checks accepted only M-F 8-11am. Open M-F 8am-2pm. On the weekends, use the moneychangers, or **ATMs** (Cirrus/MC/V) at shopping centers, banks, and hotels.

English-Language Bookstore: Firma Rimbow Bookstore, Jl. SiSingaMangaRaja 14 (☎736 8538). Carries guidebooks and maps. Open daily 9am-8:30 pm.

Shopping Centers: Seven American-style behemoth malls dot the Medan landscape. Cheap Internet, 6 screen cinemas, abundant toiletries, and if nothing else, blissful A/C shops await. **Deli Plaza,** on Jl. Balai Kota north of the post office, has upscale Chinese and Thai food (Rp. 20,000-35,000) and is the size of a small country. **Perisai Plaza,** on Jl. Pemuda opposite the Lippo Bank, has a disco, a bowling alley, and a café.

Public Swimming Pool: Jl. Sisingamangaraja 6. A welcome break from the grime of Medan. Rp 2500 per person. Open 6am-6pm.

Emergency: Police ☎255 110. **Ambulance** ☎118.

Police: Jl. H.Z. Arifin 7 (☎515 513).

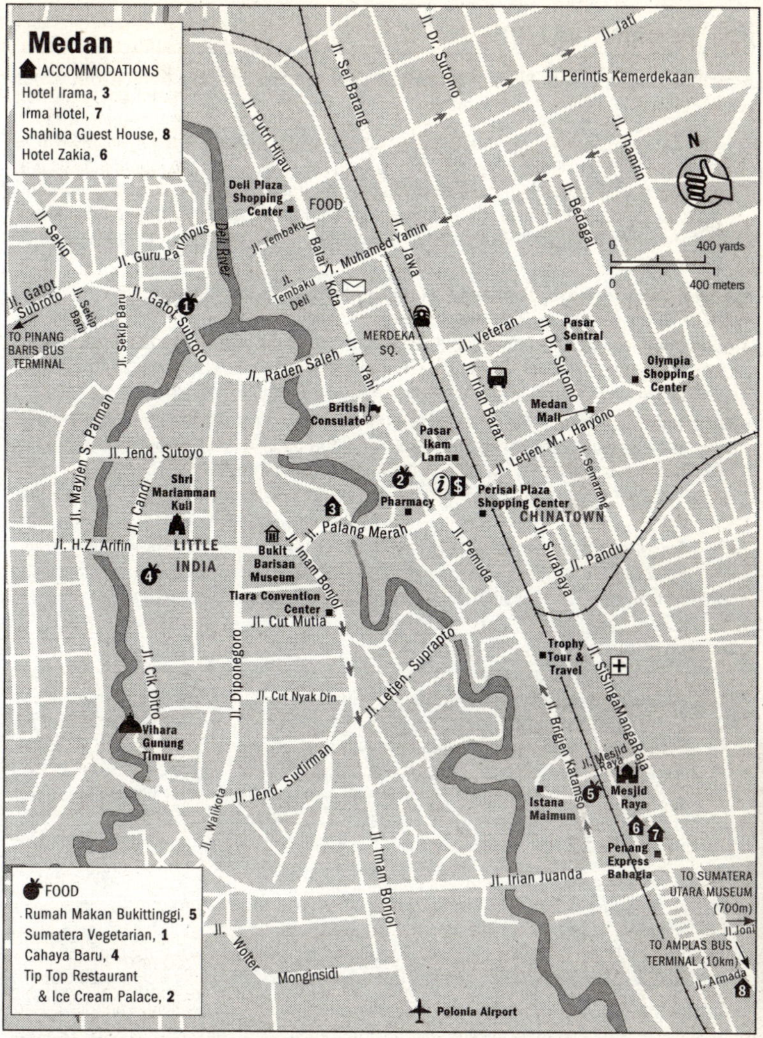

Pharmacies: Apotik Kimia Farmia, Jl. Palang Merah 32. Toiletries and over-the-counter medicine are most easily purchased in shopping malls. **Open 24hr.**

Medical Services: Klinic Specialis Bunda, Jl. SiSingaMangaRaja 17 (☎736 5772). Considered the best facility in Medan. English-speaking "specialist" (daily 6-8pm). Open 24hr.

Telephones: Indosat Phones permit calling cards; **HCDB** at **Hotel Zakia** (collect calls Rp3000); and **Hotel Irama** allows free collect calls.

Internet: Mita Internet, Jl. SiSingaMangaRaja 53, near Mesjid Raya (Rp5000 per hr.) Get even better rates at **Perisai Plaza** or **Deli Plaza,** Rp2500-4000 per hr.

Post Offices: GPO, Jl. Pos 1 (☎456 8940), at the intersection with Jl. Balai Kota, opposite Merdeka Sq. Poste Restante. Open M-Sa 8am-4pm, Su 10am-2pm. **Postal code:** 20111.

ACCOMMODATIONS

Accommodations on **Jl. SiSingaMangaRaja** near the Mesjid Raya range from backpacker hotels to classy establishments.

Hotel Zakia (☎732 2413), on Jl. Sipiso Piso, off Jl. SiSingaMangaRaja 1 block south of the mosque. A backpacker favorite. Free coffee, tea, and rolls in the morning. Greenery downstairs and a rooftop patio overlooking Mesjid Raya puts your ears in close proximity to the 5am call to prayer. HCD phone (collect calls Rp3000). Western toilets. Dorms with fan Rp8000; singles Rp15,000; doubles Rp. 20,000, with private *mandi* Rp25,000.

Shahiba Guest House, Jl. Armada 1A (☎736 8528). Head south on Jl. SiSingaMangaRaja; at the far end of Bukit Barisan Hero's Cemetery, turn right onto Jl. Armada. It's 20m down on left. Quiet and friendly on a charming street with good size rooms, all with private *mandi* or shower. Dorms Rp7000; doubles Rp12,000, with *mandi* Rp20,000, with shower Rp25,000; deluxe room with A/C and TV Rp50,000.

Irma Hotel, Jl. Tengah 1B. Just south of Mesjid Raya, around the corner from Hotel Zakia. Clean with comfy beds and a small rooftop patio, it shares Zakia's proximity to the morning call to prayer. Doubles with *mandi* outside Rp20,000.

Hotel Irama, Jl. Palang Merah 112S (☎457 9118). In the center of town, opposite Hotel Danau Toba. From the Jl. Pemuda intersection, head west and cross the river to the traffic triangle with a tall, white violinist sculpture. It's on the next street to the right. Small shared *mandi*. HCD phone with collect calls. Drinking or returning drunk not permitted. Midnight curfew. Fan Rp2500. Dorms Rp11,000; doubles/triples Rp25,000.

FOOD

Medan's chief culinary specialty is spicy *padang* food, the ethnic specialty of West Sumatra's *Minang* people. Stalls freckle the city and crowd across from Mesjid Raya. In the evenings, delicious and cheap Chinese *warung* fill the genial **Jl. Semarang,** in Chinatown between Jl. Pandu and Jl. Letjen M.T. Haryono. (Crab claw RP 3000. Open daily 6pm-midnight.) Bakeries and Indian food stalls cluster near the intersection of Jl. H.Z. Arifin and Jl. Cik Ditro in **Little India.** *Sate* and juice stands on Jl. SiSingaMangaRaja toward the Bukit Barisan Heros graveyard are open until late.

Tip Top Restaurant and Ice Cream Palace, Jl. A. Yani 92. North of the Jl. Sukamulia-Palang intersection, on the left before Merdeka Sq. Exotic Western, Chinese, and Indonesian menu and ice cream to cool the soul. Shark's fin soup Rp15,000; *otak* (ox brain curry) Rp4000; ice cream concoctions Rp4000-10,000. Open daily 8:30am-10:30pm.

Cahaya Baru, Jl. Cik Ditro 8L. In the southern part of Kampung Keling. Friendly Indian staff serve genuine Indian cuisine. Curries Rp8,000-10,000; biryanis Rp7,000-12,000. Open M-Sa 9am-10pm.

Rumah Makan Bukittinggi, Jl. Brigjen Katamso 456. Opposite Maimoon Palace. Great *padang* food. Pick from the display. Spicy fish with rice and cabbage Rp 5000. Fish Rp3000. Spicy eggplant Rp3000. Open daily 10am-10pm.

Sumatera Vegetarian, Jl. Gatot Subroto 36. Across from the roundabout where Jl. L. S. Parman intersects Jl. Subroto. Rice with a platter of 6 vegetable dishes (menu changes daily) Rp4000. Open daily 6am-8pm.

SIGHTS

In addition to the real life charm of Medan's residential neighborhoods, the city's chief crowd-pleaser is its architecture. The black domes, turquoise tiles, and minarets of the **Mesjid Raya** (Grand Mosque), at Jl. SiSingaMangaRaja and Jl. Mesjid Raya, were built by a Dutch architect in 1908. Once the midday sun descends, young boys play football in the lawns behind the Masjid, while the elderly pray beside the graveyard where the Sultan and his favorites now rest.

Not far from Mesjid Raya, where Jl. Brigjen Katamso meets Jl. Mesjid Raya, is the **Istana Maimun** (Maimun Palace). Built with tobacco money, the palace has been the home of the Deli Sultans since its construction in 1888. The 12th Sultan and his family still live here. Only the throne room is open to the public. (Open daily 8am-5pm. Donation Rp2000.)

Vihara Gunung Timur, a Buddhist temple sacred to Medan's influential yet low-profile Chinese community, stands on Jl. Hang Tuah off Jl. Cik Ditiro and makes you forget that you aren't a thousand miles north. Incense smoke rises to a roof emblazoned with colorful dragons as a gentle quiet descends upon the temple in the cool evenings. (Open daily 6am-5pm.) The Hindu temple, **Shri Mariamman Kuil,** is on Jl. Tenku Umar, just off Jl. H. Z. Arifin. Built in 1991, it turns heads with its brightly colored and ornate depictions of gods, heroes, and mythical creatures. Inside, small shrines and marble walls are well-kept at the behest of the local Indian community.

The **Museum Sumatera Utara,** Jl. H.M. Joni 51, whose collection documents the geological and cultural history of the province, is the more interesting of Medan's two museums. An informative tour takes about an hour. (Take *sudako* #01 or 04, or walk 1½km from Mesjid Raya. From the south end of the Bukit Barisan Hero's Cemetery, Jl. H.M. Joni is on the left and the museum is 700m down on the right. Open Tu-Su 8am-4pm. Tip discretionary, about Rp5,000.) The **Museum Bukit Barisan,** Jl. H.Z. Arifin 8, near the police station, documents North Sumatra's role in the struggle against Dutch colonial forces. It has one room crammed with weapons. (Open M-Th 9am-2pm.)

MARKETS

Pasar Sentral (Central Market), off Jl. Sutomo, east of the Sambu *sudako* station. You've reached it when you find the crowd by the roadside amidst shops covered in blue tarpaulin. Fresh clothes, *batik's* by the pound, and "Disco India" cds abound. **Pasar Ikam Lama,** on Jl. Pernigaan parallel to Jl. A. Yani is a quieter experience with rolls and rolls of fabric. (Both open daily 8am-5pm.)

BERASTAGI ☎0628

Set against the ethereal beauty of North Sumatra's mountainous hinterland, Berastagi brims with natural and cultural attractions. Its fertile volcanic soil yields a cornucopia of succulent fruits, including the *marquisa* passion fruit. The surrounding Karo Highlands shelter traditional Batak Karo villages. Using Berastagi as a base, climbers can tackle steaming Gunung Sibayak or jungle-covered Gunung Sinabung. Those less sweat-inclined can take a stroll in one of the town's parks or pass the time in a local coffeehouse with some of the friendliest people in Sumatra.

TRANSPORTATION

Most buses from Berastagi are **minibuses,** though larger buses from Medan sometimes stop in Berastagi, too. The **station** is in front of the central market on Jl. Veteran. Buses go to: **Kutacane** (5-6hr.; every 20min. 9am-6pm; Rp15,000, RP5000 for backpacks); **Medan** (1½hr., every 10min. 5am-9pm, Rp2500); and **Pangururan** (4hr., every 20 min., Rp5000). **Minibuses** to **Tapaktuan** (13hr., 4-5 per day, Rp20,000) and **Kutacane** (4hr., every hr. 8am-8pm, Rp15,000) leave from **Cv. Karsima,** Jl. Veteran 51 (☎919 66). Large nightbuses go to **Tapaktuan** (10hr.; every hr. 6-10pm; Rp40,000, with A/C Rp70,000). **Tourist buses** provide the only direct service to **Bukit Lawang** (4hr., Rp30,000) and **Parapat** (4hr., Rp30,000-35,000), leaving at around 10am and 2pm. Purchase tickets at any *losmen* at least 1 day in advance.

ORIENTATION AND PRACTICAL INFORMATION

Downtown Berastagi consists of a single, divided thoroughfare, **Jl. Veteran,** which forks at a 25m high **war memorial** near the north end. The left branch becomes **Jl. Gundaling,** which leads up the hill past the **fruit market** toward **Mt. Sibayak;** the right branch leads downhill out of town and becomes the **Berastagi-Medan Hwy.** The **tourist information center, post office,** and **wartel** cluster near the memorial. Heading south, Jl. Veteran passes the **bus terminal** and **central market** on the left before forking again. The left branch continues 11km to **Kabanjahe,** and the right branch, **Jl. Udara,** leads to **Gunung Sinabung** and the well-touristed Karo village of **Lingga.**

Tourist Offices: Tourist Information Center, Jl. Gundaling 1 (☎910 84). Left of the war memorial. Excellent transportation info. Check for upcoming Karo ceremonies, guides and maps for Gunung Sinabung and Gunung Sibayak, and rafting and trekking trips in Gunung Leuser National Park. Blackboards in *losmen* advertise travelers assembling groups for climbing, trekking, and rafting. Open daily 8am-6pm.

Tours: Mr. Telah Bangun, an excellent **guide** who speaks English and organizes expeditions (US$20 per person per day) in Gunung Leuser National Park, is at **Tobali Tour and Travel,** Jl. Veteran 49 (☎921 60). Above Raymond's Steak House. Available M-Sa 8am-8pm, varies Sunday.

Currency Exchange: The best rates are at **P.T. Bank Sumut,** Jl. Veteran 135 (☎926 61). There is an **ATM** 100m down from the war memorial on the right. Open M-Sa 8am-4pm, Su 8am-1pm.

Pharmacy: Dharma Bakti (☎913 21), Jl. Veteran 49A, is past the central market on the same side of the road as Wisma Sibayak. Open daily 8am-8pm.

Medical Services: Public Health Center, Jl. Veteran 34. (☎910 28). English-speaking doctors on call M-Sa 8am-noon. **Open 24hr.**

Telephones: Telkom office, Jl. Perwira 1 (☎911 98), next to the post office. **HCD** phones outside. Open daily 7am-midnight.

Internet Access: Sporadic service at **Michie Holiday Hotel,** 3km south on Berastagi-Medan Hwy. (*sudako* Rp500). Rp5000 per hr. Open daily 10am-7pm.

Post Office: Jl. Veteran 4, next to the tourist office. Poste Restante. Open M-Th 8am-2pm, F-Sa 8am-noon. **Postal code:** 22156.

ACCOMMODATIONS AND FOOD

Berastagi boasts some of the finest guest houses in North Sumatra, with good facilities (i.e. Western toilets), friendly atmospheres, excellent information, and extensive, cheap Western and Indonesian menus. Many double as trek and rafting organizers and travel agents.

Wisma Ikut Guest House, Jl. Gundaling 24 (☎911 71). Up past the fruit market on a hill, on the right. Stunning views of Gunung Sibayak from a beautiful Dutch house. Menu includes a packed lunch option (chicken, tomato and cheese sandwich; Rp7000). Shared *mandi* with hot shower Rp2000. Dorms Rp7000; doubles Rp12,000; room with a porch leading into the garden Rp15,000.

Elshaddai Hotel and Restaurant, Jl. Veteran 65-66 (☎910 23). Just north of the monument on the right. Shared *mandi* with hot shower and a rooftop patio with a view of the mountain. Front side gets noise from Jl. Veteran. Exciting menu (fried rice with veggies and cuttlefish Rp7500). Singles Rp7500; doubles Rp10,000.

Losmen Sibayak Guest House, Jl. Veteran 119 (☎911 22). Head south from the war memorial; it's 200m down on the left. Information on sights and *Karo* culture and rituals. Lounge sports a cable TV and a cafe with Western food at decent prices. Hot showers Rp2000. 3 person dorms Rp6000; larger rooms for 1 or 2 Rp10,000.

Wisma Sibayak Guest House, Jl. Udara 1 (☎911 04). Head south on Jl. Veteran from the bus terminal; it's set back from the road where Jl. Udara branches left. Outside bathrooms with Asian-style toilets. Hot shower Rp2000. Dorms Rp5000; singles Rp7000; doubles Rp10,000; triples Rp15,000. Big rooms with private *mandi* and patio opening onto grass. Singles Rp25,000; doubles Rp35,000.

Berastagi is a food lover's paradise. All of the *losmen* offer extensive menus including hearty breakfasts. In town, options range from fried banana stands to shiny *Batak* restaurants with mouth watering window displays. Every night, **Jl. Veteran,** between the monument and **Losmen Sibayak,** comes alive with cheap *warung* (chicken *sate* with rice cakes Rp5000). **Muslimin,** Jl. Veteran 128, next to the bus terminal, boasts delicious *padang* food in a slightly grubby but very local atmosphere. *Ikan gulai* (fish with vegetables) runs Rp6000. (Open daily 7am-10pm.) **Sehat Restaurant,** Jl. Veteran 315, just south of Losmen Sibayak, is one of the town's Chinese joints and dishes out generous portions. (Fried veggies, egg and crab Rp12,000; sweet and sour pig stomach Rp16,000. Open daily 7am-8pm.) **Noodle Soup Shop,** Jl. Perniagaan 39, at the *sudako* station by Pasar Sentral, serves delicious noodle soup with chicken, veggies and eggs. (Open daily 6am-7pm.) **Bundok Andung,** Jl. Veteran 20, up near the post office is one of several shiny *batak* restaurants in the small area. It's a bit pricier, but spotless and delicious. (Fried shrimp with rice Rp17,000. Open daily 7am-11pm.)

SIGHTS

At **Tahura National Park,** 10min. from the town center by *sudako* (Rp500), you might encounter gibbons, hornbills, and other wildlife on a day hike (Rp1100). Trails are marked. Small **Tahura Park** (Rp3000), is a popular hangout for local kids and has a museum. Live monkeys and orangutans survive on food from visitors and park employees. On Sunday, the main plaza features traditional Karo music and dancing (noon-5pm).

The **highland region** constitutes the heart of Karo Batak country; several **Karo villages** can be visited in a day. Entrance fees (Rp500) and hawkers are the norm. **Peceren,** 2km past the war memorial on the road to Medan, is the closest. Karo dwellings, complete with buffalo horns and thatched roofs, stand alongside modern, concrete houses with satellite dishes. Although guest house operators decry Perceren as "impure," it provides a more realistic look at Karo life than other artificially "traditional" settlements. It's best to visit in the evening, when souvenir vendors have packed up. Other Karo villages, including **Serdang** and **Dokan,** lie farther away. Minibuses run direct from Berastagi to Serdang (Rp1500). For Dokan, go via Kabanjahe (Rp700-1000). Tobali Tour and Travel (See **Practical Information,** above) offers an overnight tour of Serdang during which you sleep and eat in a Batak longhouse. (Rp60,000. 3-person min.) The Losmen Sibayak Guest House offers a three-hour walking tour from Berastagi through several smaller villages and the larger, tourist-oriented village of **Lingga.** Check its office for details. **Arihta,** Jl. Veteran 36, near the *Apotik* is the town pool hall. An inventive way of killing some time with the locals. (Rp500. Open daily 7am-10pm.)

COMMODE, COMMODE... WHEREVER YOU ARE! If you've been in Indonesia more than a day, or rather if a few hours have passed since your first meal here, you've discovered the Southeast Asian, and indeed Indonesian, version of the toilet. Known for its simplicity and minimalist design, many might call it just a "hole in the ground," but it is so much more. Scientists have confirmed that squatting over a "hole in the ground" toilet is far easier on your bowels and leads to much improved bowel movement. If that wasn't enough, it also reduces your risk of hemorrhoids. So, put a smile on your face as you sit back on your haunches, and remember, your bowels are now your friends.

MARKETS

The spice of Berastagi's market life is to be found in the **Pasar Buah** (fruit market) which is on the left of Jl. Gundaling just north of the memorial. Small mountains of fruit, including delicious miniature oranges and Berastagi's trademark *marquisa* passion fruit, are at every turn and delightfully tacky wool "*Berastagi!*" hats are also on sale. (Open M-Sa 7am-8pm, Su 7am-9pm.) **Pasar Sentral** is the place to go to buy shoes, clothes, music, and day-packs. Fish and rubber boots are available among the narrow passages that seem to be lit blue from the tarps that cover them. (Open daily 6am-9pm.)

HIKING

Berastagi has been a tourist town since its founding in the early 1900s, when colonial officials from British Malaysia came to play golf, ride horses, and attend dinner parties. Today, most visitors come to hike on the spectacular volcanos. Most popular is the 2100m **Gunung Sibayak,** whose summit smokes from the active sulfur steam jets that shoot from its apex. A well-maintained trail with concrete steps, winds up the west slope to the crater. The route to the higher summit is dangerous and only should be attempted with a **guide** (Rp60,000 for 3 climbers). A second route runs on the east slope of Sibayak from Semangat Gunung Hot Springs to the lip of the crater. The trail is steep and treacherous, especially when wet. A further "jungle" route winds up from the Berastagi-Medan Hwy. *Sudako* run between Pasar Sentral and Semangat Gunung (Rp1000).

To reach the west route, walk 30min. or take a *sudako*. Go north on Jl. Veteran, bearing left at the war memorial onto Jl. Gundaling. Turn right at the end of the football field before the Sibayak Multinational Hotel, follow the road uphill (past the Karo Hill Bungalows) and turn left onto a dirt road where the paved road turns right (entrance Rp1000). Climbing Gunung Sibayak takes two and a half hours. Start early to avoid early afternoon clouds, which ruin the lovely vista. A guide is not necessary to climb Gunung Sibayak via the west route. But don't climb alone—find a group to hook onto.

There are two hot springs near the foot of Sibayak: the **Lau Debuk-debuk Hot Springs,** 12km from Berastagi, and the **Semangat Gunung Hot Springs,** 2km farther down the road toward the volcano. Lau Debuk-debuk is larger, with several bathing pools for comfortable, sulfurous soaks, though the sulphur smell can be a bit much. Be modest—local women bathe fully clothed. You can get here from town on the Semangat Gunung *sudako* or hike down from Sibayak; the walk affords beautiful views of lush countryside. (Open during daylight hours. Rp500-1000.)

The more pristine and challenging **Gunung Sinabung** (2417m), 27km west of Berastagi, is higher and should be attempted only by experienced climbers. The trails are crude and completely devoid of markings. Several people have died on Sinabung recently. Climbers should **hire a guide** licensed by the HPL (around Rp100,000 per day, transportation included). Most hikers begin at the village of **Sigaranggarang** and end at **Lake Kawar** for a post-climb swim. Much of the hike is unspoiled jungle. The final few hundred meters cover loose rock. The ascent takes three hours; the earlier you begin, the better the view. On a clear day, it is possible to see the northern tip of shimmering Lake Toba, 30km to the south. Leave by 9am for the safest, most well-lit climb, as well as the most comfortable (cool on the way up, warm on top).

INDONESIA

BUKIT LAWANG ☎061

"Welcome to the jungle" is a common greeting in Bukit Lawang. But the "jungle" in this town, beautifully set on the Bohorok River, is as often a description of the tourist colony that it is rapidly becoming, as it is of the nature that cradles it. Carved out of the rubber and cocoa plantations northwest of Medan it consists of a string of guest houses lining the riverbank. Many come to see the Bohorok Orangutan Station where perhaps the world's gentlest primates are reintroduced to their natural habitat. Some get caught up in the beauty of the place and while away time trekking, rafting, or tubing down the lazy river. On the weekends, however, the party bus drives in from Medan as droves of Medanites come to party, often leaving devastation in their wake.

TRANSPORTATION

The **bus terminal** is near the Visitors Center. Buses go to **Medan** (2½hr., every 30min. 5am-5pm, Rp3500). Tourist buses leave daily for **Berastagi** (5hr., 8:30am, Rp30,000) and **Parapat** (10hr., Rp42,000). Book at least 1 day in advance. Purchase tickets pretty much anywhere in town.

ORIENTATION AND PRACTICAL INFORMATION

The **visitors center, PHPA office,** and **tourist office** cluster near a dirt lot known as the **bus terminal.** The path leading upriver from the bus stop is **Jl. Orang-utan.** About 500m upriver is an elaborate gate marking the entrance to a **public campground;** many of the most popular guest houses are beyond the campground along the river. The **Bohorok Orangutan Center** is 1km upriver from the **Visitors Center** on the opposite bank.

Tourist Offices: PHPA Ranger Station (☎414 2571), on Jl. Orangutan opposite the bus "terminal." Organizes treks and nature walks and answers questions about safety and permits. Purchase permits to see orangutan feedings. Rp4500 per person, good for 2feedings in a day. Open daily 7am-3pm. **Bukit Lawang Visitors Center** is next door and has interesting exhibits about the local wildlife plus an impressive 3D map. Open daily 8am-3pm. **Tourist Information Center** is down a path, left of the visitors center. Organizes treks, rafting, and tube-trips downriver to Bohorok. Usually open daily 8am-2pm.

Currency Exchange: Cash traveler's checks at the *wartel* kiosk. Some travel agents and some guest houses offer decent rates.

Tourist Police: Opposite the bus terminal. Open 24hr.

Medical Services: A tiny **polyclinic** sits next to the PHPA office. Open daily 8am-5pm.

Telephones: Wartel kiosk off path to Bukit Lawang Cottages; turn left off Jl. Orangutan before Goa Restaurant. International collect calls Rp2000. Open daily 6am-midnight.

Internet: Dita Internet, opposite the Ranger Station. 30min. Rp10,000; 30min. minimum. Open daily 8:30am-10pm.

Post Offices: No post office; use letter-collection boxes (and a prayer!) near Dita Internet. Good luck! **Postal code:** 20774.

ACCOMMODATIONS AND FOOD

In Bukit Lawang, you pay by the room rather than by the person, and most rooms consist of one double bed so get cozy and save money. After dark, use a flashlight when walking up to guest houses on the right bank. A small **campground** rests 500m upriver from the PHPA office but offers bamboo tent frameworks and little else. No reservations needed. A flat Rp500 covers clean-up costs.

Bukit Lawang Cottages, across the river in the direction of the bat cave. Offers a range of slightly pricier bungalows. Close to "town" but away from the crowds on gorgeous grounds. Be warned—it's known to be a place that's hard to leave. Slightly pricey menu. Decent size bungalows with bathroom and second floor patio Rp15,000; big bungalow with verandah Rp40,000; super-deluxe bungalow with greenery inside Rp50,000.

Ariko Inn, 800m through the jungle beyond the Orangutan Center, a 30min. walk from the bus station. Set in a bamboo grove with an excellent splash pool. The main lodge, on stilts over a tributary, is shaped like a boat. Charming bungalows with *mandi* Rp10,000 (negotiable).

Jungle Inn, 400m beyond the campground entrance gate, near the Orangutan Center. A 2-story jungle-style restaurant. Large, immaculate doubles with bathrooms Rp40,000; enormous honeymoon suite Rp60,000.

Queen Resort, 300m beyond the campground, sign says "Tourist Information." Main area advertises "bloody cold beer" (Rp11,000). Simple rooms with comfy bed and *mandi* Rp10,000.

Cheap *warung* and *padang* joints are all along the river near the bus terminal. The **Jungle Inn Restaurant,** part of the main inn (see above), offers a large Western/Indonesian menu (chicken, rice and veggies Rp10,000, "jungle food" with fish Rp20,000) and boasts fresh brown bread. For Italian food, try the **Queen Resort.** (Freshly baked banana bread Rp3000.)

GOING APE? Rumors are the latest beast to jump from tree to tree in Bukit Lawang and neighboring areas. Talk of a possible **relocation** of the Orangutan Station at Bukit Lawang is on everyone's lips. Newspapers report that the number of orangutans in Gunung Leuser National Park fell from 13,000 in 1993 to just 6000 in 1999 and speculate that too much tourist contact has hurt population size. Unconfirmed monkey-mouths are also chattering about corruption linked to the station's finances, and the World Wildlife Fund (WWF) has withdrawn support. A possible relocation site? Maybe Sibolangit between Medan and Berastagi, or maybe somewhere top secret. Whatever the case, some primates are having trouble digesting this fruit from the gossip tree.

SIGHTS AND ENTERTAINMENT

Bukit Lawang's most famous guests are not backpackers but *Pongo pygmaeus abelli*, otherwise known as orangutans. The station was founded in 1973 with grants from the World Wildlife Fund and the Frankfurt Zoological Society to reintroduce illegally captured orangutans to their natural habitat. Since then, the rehabilitation project has returned 124 animals to the rainforest. Cross the river in a canoe only during the half hour prior to the feeding. Visitors may observe the two daily feedings (8am and 3pm). **Day-long permits** (Rp4500) can be purchased at the PHPA office.

Caves abound near the south of town, including the superb **Bat Cave.** Take the trail beyond the Bukit Lawang Cottages; it winds through a rubber plantation before turning right to the cave. To reaclh the vine-covered entrance, clamber up rickety wooden ladders. The cavern is filled with bats (a flashlight is essential—bring one or rent one for Rp3000). A narrow corridor leads from the back of the cavern some 600m into the hillside (Rp1000). About 1km beyond is the **Swallow Cave,** named for its chief inhabitants. For human-oriented entertainment, check out the **Acoustic Cave,** where beer is accompanied by a remarkable band with songs in Spanish, English, Indonesian, and Padang. (Su, W, F 9pm.) During the daytime the garden in this cave is gorgeous. Also open for revelry are **Tony's Restaurant** where it's happy hour every night from 6-9pm (beer Rp9000) and English videos are screened at 7:30 and 9:30pm, and **Lina's Coffeeshop** (beer Rp10,000), which advertises a dance party every Saturday at 9pm (beer Rp15,000).

DANAU TOBA (LAKE TOBA)

Lake Toba sits majestically not only as Southeast Asia's largest freshwater lake, but as the world's largest crater lake. The steep slopes that ring Toba form the rim of an ancient volcano, whose cataclysmic eruption some 75,000 years ago created the lake, and may have even triggered the last ice age. Unseen by Western eyes until the 1850s, *Tano Batak* is the homeland for the *Batak Toba*, the largest of five principal peoples of North Sumatra's interior. Today, many travelers see Lake Toba as a vacation from a vacation, and the best place to enjoy a hot shower and a pizza between jungle treks.

TONGGING

Unspoiled and resplendent at the head of Lake Toba, Tongging's location is so marvellous that it's pictured on the Rp1000 note. An isolated Christian stronghold within a Muslim country, Christian tombs dot lush hills that roll into the lake where fishermen venture out in wooden canoes or remain ashore repairing their nets.

Heaven isn't easy to get to and, in this case, is accessible only by a small road. Buses run to and from **Situngaling** (30 min., every hr. 7:30am-3pm, Rp1500) which is in turn accessible from **Kabanjahe** (30min., Rp2500). The ride on the roof is worthwhile for the brave. One bus a day runs direct to **Kabanjahe** (1½hr., 5pm, Rp4000). Buses run from nearby **Merek** down the western shore of the lake to **Pangururan** on Samosir (3hr., every hr. 7:30am-5pm, Rp10,000). A ferry takes market-goers to **Haranggaol** (1½hr., M 7:30am, Rp5000) where another ferry goes on to **Samosir Island** (2 hr.; M, Th 3pm; Rp6000).

Phone, post and **police** services are all to be found up the road at **Merek,** though there are two **nurses** in town—ask for Berukaro or Berusimbolon. Any useful travel and **tourist information** can be found at the **Wisma Sibayak** (See **Accommodations,** below). Tongging is a tiny village with no street names or telephone numbers. The road to town descends from the Sipisopiso Waterfall and

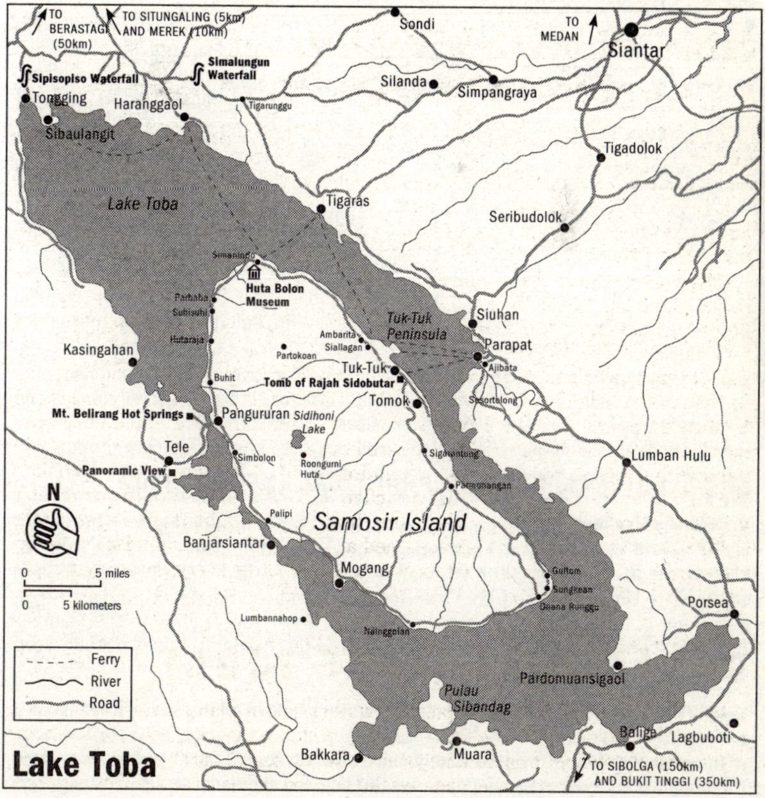

Lake Toba

arrives at the main drag at the top of the lake. Here you can find a few good-looking fish and *padang* joints. The only guest house in town is the lovely **Wisma Sibayak,** on the other side of the lake and 1.5km down the road. They offer large, immaculate rooms with private *mandi* and Western toilets (Rp25,000), or slightly smaller rooms with porch and *mandi* outside (Rp10,000-12,000). Activities and a pricey menu are also available (BBQ fish for 2 Rp30,000).

There is plenty to do around Tongging for the free-spirited. Picturesque Sipisopiso and Sidompah waterfalls are both within a two-hour hike and the view of Lake Toba from atop Gunung Sipisopiso is breathtaking. Several nearby villages afford spectacular views (Sibaulangit), longhouses (Bage) and a monument to the Batak ancestors (Silalahi). For the more stomach-minded, the Wisma rents canoes (Rp20,000) and fishing rods (Rp5000) by the day and supplies you with all the equipment to cook your catch.

PARAPAT ☎0625

The rolling hills on Lake Toba's east shore make Parapat a perfect vantage point for overlooking the lake and Samosir Island. Pricey hotels have sprung up at warp speed, and are filled on weekends and holidays by urban Medanites. Most backpackers leap onto the first ferry for Samosir for lack of any appreciable local sights, but grabbing some fresh fish or a drink, and admiring the view of the island make a restful day.

TRANSPORTATION

Buses: Public buses and private coaches depart from the terminal on Jl. SiSingaMangaRaja, 1km east of the police station. All buses originate in Medan and get to Parapat around midday; talk to travel agents about times. To: **Bukit Tinggi** (15hr.; 1, 4, 7pm; Rp65,000; A/C 4pm, Rp75,000-90,000); **Jakarta** (45hr., noon, Rp150,000; A/C 12:30 and 1pm, Rp250,000); **Medan** via **Siantar** (4hr.; 8, 11am, 1, 4pm; Rp20,000, irregular minibuses); **Padang** (17hr., 2pm, Rp65,000; A/C 2, 4pm, Rp90,000); **Sibolga** (5hr.; 11:30am, noon, 12:30pm; Rp30,000; minibus 11:30am, 1pm; Rp35,000-50,000). Tourist buses head to **Bukit Lawang** (7hr., 10:30am, Rp42,000) via **Berestagi** (4hr., Rp30,000). Book at any travel agency.

Ferries: Passenger ferries to **Pulau Samosir** leave from Tiga Raja Pier, stopping at your accommodation in **Tuk-Tuk** (every hr. 8:30am-7:30pm, Rp2000). Ferries from Tiga Raja also run to **Ambarita** on market days (Tu, Th, and Sa; Rp2000). A **car ferry** shuttles between Ajibata Pier (south of Tiga Raja) and Tomok.

Local Transportation: *Sudako* follow streets counter-clockwise (with your back to Samosir Island), usually from Tiga Raja Pier to the bus terminal, down Jl. SiSingaMangaRaja and then down Jl. Sinagara/Haranggaol back to Tiga Raja (Rp500).

ORIENTATION AND PRACTICAL INFORMATION

Jl. SiSingaMangaRaja, the main road, swings west-east through town, passing the **police, wartel, post office,** and **bus terminal** before heading toward Bukit Tinggi. **Jl. Kol. TPR Sinaga** (formerly Jl. Pulau Samosir) branches off Jl. SiSingaMangaRaja at a Welcome Gate along the lake and follows the shore before crossing a ridge, becoming **Jl. Haranggaol** at the Natour Parapat Hotel, and leading to the Samosir **Tiga Raja Pier.** Cafes line **Jl. Haranggaol** near the ferry launch. Buses usually drop backpackers off at the ferry.

Tourist Information: Use travel agents. Try helpful **PT Dolok Silau,** Jl. SiSingaMangaRaja 56 (☎414 67).

Tours: Andilo Nancy Travel Service, Parapat's largest agency, has 2 offices: one at the bus terminal (☎415 48, open daily 6am-10pm), and another at Jl. SiSingaMangaRaja

76 (☎414 33, open daily 8am-7pm). Alternately, try PT Dolok Silau at their main office (see **Tourist Information,** above) or at Jl. Haranggaol 118 (☎415 49) near the ferry. Also reliable is **Tobali Tours,** with a main office opposite the Tuk-Tuk ferry landing at Jl. Pelabuhan 1 (☎417 47) and a branch at Jl. Haranggaol 3 (☎411 56).

Currency Exchange: Moneychangers line Jl. Haranggaol. The best rates are at **Bank BNI,** Jl. SiSingaMangaRaja (☎417 41), 200m past Singgalang Hotel. **ATM** and AmEx Traveler's Cheques after 10am. Open M-F 8:30am-3:30pm. **Restoran Singgalang,** Jl. SiSingaMangaRaja 52, in Hotel Singgalang (☎412 60), offers MC/V advances for a 10% rate.

Police: ☎415 71. On Jl. SiSingaMangaRaja next to the large Welcome Gate.

Medical Services: Parapat Public Hospital (☎413 32), on Jl. Rumah Sakit, 800m past the bus terminal, left off Jl. SiSingaMangaRaja at the sign, and set back 300m on a hill.

Telephones: Telkom office, Jl. Josep Sinaga 28 (☎411 08), next to communications towers. **HCD** phone. Open daily 8am-midnight.

Post Office: Jl. SiSingaMangaRaja 75 (☎414 88). Open M-Th 7:30am-3pm, F 7:30-11:30am, Sa 7:30am-1pm. **Postal code:** 21174.

ACCOMMODATIONS

While resorts line the water on Jl. TPR Sinagara, cheaper hotels are on **Jl. Haranggaol** and lower **Jl. SiSingaMangaRaja.**

Baringin Tua Inn, Jl. Kapten Karmel Napitupulu 2 (☎413 94), opposite the ferry landing. A good spot if you miss the last ferry or want to catch the first. Rooms overlook the pier. Rooms with 2-3 beds and cold shower Rp15,000.

Singgalang Hotel, Jl. SiSingaMangaRaja 52 (☎412 60), 50m up from the police station. Large rooms with 3-4 beds. Squeaky-clean shared *mandi*. Chinese restaurant downstairs showing TV reruns of "Friends" (Rp20-30,000 per dish). MC/V cash advances. Rp20,000 per person.

Riris Inn, Jl. Haranggaol 43 (☎413 92), 250m up the road from the ferry on the right. Beautiful views form flowery porch. Clean doubles or triples with *mandi* outside Rp22,000, with cold shower and Western toilet Rp25,000; big room Rp35,000.

FOOD

Expensive but good *batak* and *padang* restaurants abound on **Jl. SiSingaMangaRaja** and **Jl. Haranggaol,** specializing in fresh fish from the lake. A small **fruit market** sets up near Tiga Raja Pier every day, and sometimes a larger **Batak Market** will sell all sorts of food and second-hand T-shirts. Come early for the best deals, especially on Saturday. Open Tu and Th 6am-2pm, Sa 6am-6pm.

Mitudo Cafe, Jl. Kol TPR Sinaga, 200m beyond the Welcome Gate. A wonderful deck on the shore has the best view in town. Limited menu. Guinness Rp15,000. Fried rice Rp5000. Open **24hr.**

Rumah Makan Marina, Jl. Haranggaol 48, adjacent to Pago Pago Inn. A cozy *padang* place specializing in luscious seafood dishes and a fabulous *cap cai*. Stir-fried veggies Rp10,000. Open daily 8am-10pm.

Hong Kong Restaurant, Jl. Haranggaol 9/11, near the crest of the hill opposite the souvenir and sarong stalls. *Gado-gado* (veggies with spinach sauce) Rp12,000. Spicy prawns Rp25,000. Open daily 8am-9pm.

Hidangan Khas Minang, Jl. SiSingaMangaRaja 108, 100m up from Singgalang Hotel on the right. Clean, and has an English menu. *Padang* favorites. *Rendang* (beef curry with coconut milk) Rp4000. Octopus chili Rp8000. Open daily 6am-midnight.

Saroha, Jl. SiSingaMangaRaja 145, 100m up from Singgalang. Hotel across the street. A good veggie option, they serve fried noodles or noodle soup with egg and a ton of vegetables (Rp3000). Open daily 6am-1am.

PULAU SAMOSIR

Samosir Island, larger in area than Singapore, is attached to the western shore of Lake Toba by a bridge. Many travelers never make it further than Tuk-Tuk, staying to worship the sun, lake and company. Those that do will find ancient relics of Batak culture, unspoiled hinterland and spectacular scenery.

TRANSPORTATION

Buses: Nearly all travelers to Samosir use the ferry to and from **Parapat,** but those who take the bus from Pangururan are rewarded with stunning views from the mountains on Lake Toba's Western shore. Buses to **Medan** (3½hr., 3 per day, Rp15,000) via **Berastagi** (4hr., Rp12,000) and **Tarutung** (3hr., 8am, Rp6,000-10,000) for connections to **Bukit Tinggi** (15hr.) and **Sibolga** (2hr.).

Ferries: Ferries leave every hr. from shoreline and past guest houses. From **Tuk-Tuk** to **Parapat** (7am-6pm, Rp2000). Wave from your pier to flag one down. Also from **Tomok** (8am-7pm, Rp2000), and on market days from **Ambarita** (Tu, Th, and Sa; Rp2000).

Local Transportation: Buses shuttle between **Pangururan** and **Tomok** (every hr. 6am-5pm, Rp4000) tracing the north shore via **Simanindo** (Rp3000). From Tuk-Tuk, catch a bus by walking to the main road.

Rentals: Guest houses and cafes in Tuk-Tuk rent snazzy mountain bikes (Rp20,000) and motorcycles (Rp45,000); must be returned by sundown. Bargain for a reduced price later in the day and be sure to get a helmet.

ORIENTATION AND PRACTICAL INFORMATION

Pulau Samosir is 40km long and 20km wide. The largest town is **Pangururan,** the seat of local government, on the west shore. A single **perimeter road** circles the north half of the island, connecting Pangururan with **Tomok** on the east. At the north tip is the village of **Simanindo.** Most visitors stay on the mushroom-shaped **Tuk-Tuk Peninsula,** 4km north of Tomok. The **Tuk-Tuk Ring Rd.** branches off the main road to the right, 3km north of Tomok. After 2km, at the south neck of the peninsula, the shortcut to the small village of **Ambarita** branches left, and guest houses appear on the right. The narrow pavement follows Tuk-Tuk's gold coast of guest houses and *warung* for 2km, joining the shortcut at the north neck and continuing to Ambarita, 3km up the coast. About 8km inland from Ambarita is the hamlet of **Partokoan,** a popular stopover point on the Ambarita-Pangururan traverse.

INDONESIA

Tours: Agencies in Tuk-Tuk sell tourist-bus tickets, ferry tickets from Medan to Penang, and airline tickets. Guest houses also book tourist bus tickets, at slightly higher rates than you'll get in Parapat. Buses leave from Parapat to: **Berastagi** (Rp30,000); **Bukit Lawang** (Rp45,000); **Bukit Tinggi** (Rp80,000); **Medan** (Rp35,000).

Currency Exchanges: At guest houses, but Medan and Berestagi have better rates.

Police: The **main station** (☎451 091), opposite the football field on the road to Tuk-Tuk. **Police post** in Tuk-Tuk near Carolina Cottages. Open M-Sa 8am-2pm.

Medical Services: Health center (☎451 075) in Tuk-Tuk, near Mafir Guest House. Doctor speaks some English. **Open 24hr.** In an **emergency,** return to Parapat or Medan.

Telephones: Overseas calls at guest houses in Tuk-Tuk and Ambarita (Rp5000). You can also try the Wartel just after Pog's Pub. Rp5000 for 10min. Open daily 8am-10pm.

Internet access: Tabo Cottages and **Samosir Cottages** offer rates ranging from Rp55,000-150,000 per hr., depending on time of day.

Post Offices: Ambarita, Jl. Raya 39. Open M-Th 7:30am-3pm, F 7:30-11:30am, Sa 7:30am-1pm. **Postal code:** 22395.

ACCOMMODATIONS

As North Sumatra's premier tourist destination, the area around Tuk-Tuk and Ambarita has cheap guest houses and optimal services. Almost all accommodations have cafes that will show movies upon request. Except for the best-known guest houses, rates depend on the proprietor's whim and your bargaining skills.

Tony's Guest House (☎451 209), on the north end of the peninsula. Beautiful rooms with patios facing the lake, Western toilets, and hot showers, catering to a slightly cleaner-cut crowd. Cafe and TV/living room overlook the water (pizza Rp10,500). Sunbathing platform. Good value. Doubles Rp15,000; triples Rp25,000.

Bagus Bay Stayhouse (☎414 81), just south of Tabo cottages. Tuk-Tuk's most popular establishment, with a cafe that's never empty (pizza Rp12,000). Movies every night, Batak music W and Sa night. Ping-pong, pool, and mini-golf. Hot showers. Singles Rp7500; doubles Rp15,000; bungalows with *mandi* Rp20,000.

Timbul Bungalows (☎413 74), off the road between Tuk-Tuk and Ambarita. An almost surreal peacefulness for those seeking to escape Tuk-Tuk. Views of Tuk-Tuk and Parapat. Bungalows with *mandi* Rp8000, with Western toilet and cold shower Rp15,000, with hot shower R25,000.

Tabo Cottages (☎416 14), on the south neck, past the Ambarita shortcut road, hosts a very chill crowd. Offers incense sticks, a "wellness program," and table tennis. A luxurious cafe playing mellow tunes serves fresh-baked German bread and cakes (Rp3000). Single with *mandi* Rp10,000; double Rp15,000, with Western toilet and hot shower Rp25,000; huge Batak Villa Rp80,000-100,000.

FOOD

Most travelers eat at guest houses, which supply fairly comprehensive Western and Indonesian menus (the staple being pizza), but there are also cafes and small restaurants in Tomok and Tuk-Tuk—many offering "magic mushroom omelettes." Visitors have reported getting "sick" from these illegal hallucinogens.

Tabo Vegetarian Restaurant and Bakery, in Tuk-Tuk, on the south neck of the peninsula, 70m east of Bagus Bay. Excellent fish and vegetarian food in a beautiful wooden veranda. Best are the homemade German bread (Rp2500), cake (Rp3000), and ice cream (Rp3500).

Pizzeria Rumba, with branches on the north and south ends of Tuk-Tuk Peninsula, is run by a mother and her daughter. Rumba was the first of Tuk-Tuk's countless pizzerias, and some say that it's still the best. Pizza Rp15,000, toppings Rp1000-3000 apiece. Open daily 8am-10pm (north), **24hr.** (south).

Matir, 50 meters behind Rog's Pub, offers a delicious menu in cozy, clean surroundings. Steak a la Mafir Rp20,000. Long drinks Rp12,000. Open daily 7am-10pm.

Juanita Cafe, next door to Mafir, offers good veggie options and curries in an easy to reach location. Eggplant curry with rice Rp8500. Sweet and sour tofu with rice Rp8500. Open daily 7am-10pm.

Rumah Makan Islam Murne, just after the police post on the left. One of the few places in Tuk-Tuk where you can find *padang* (spicy chicken with rice Rp7500). Catchy music playing. Open daily 7am-10pm.

SIGHTS

Most travelers come to spend a few lazy days splashing in the lake, but there are also cultural attractions along the east shore, within 20km of Tomok. Motorcycles and bicycles are the most convenient transport, but be careful: the only roads safely navigable by motorcycle are the north coast roads from Tomok to Pangururan (passing through Ambarita and Simanindo) and the Tuk-Tuk Ring Rd. The whole island can be circled in about seven hours, but the southern end is treacherous and must be done in good light.

TOMOK AND AMBARITA. Several megalithic **tomb complexes** reside in Tomok. Featuring moss-covered stone statues of humans and animals, they were built to hold the remains of local Batak kings, the Sidobutars, whose descendants reside in Tomok. The path past the first tombs leads to the **Museum of King Sidobutar,** situated in a traditional Batak house with Batak artifacts. The **tomb of Rajah Ompu Soribuntu Sidobutar** is further uphill, under a *hariam* tree. More interesting and slightly less commercialized, **Siallagan village** lies 8km up the road near Ambarita, behind the post office near the town harbor. Hidden behind a row of houses are stone chairs and table. Here, village honchos arbitrated quarrels; if the accused committed a serious offense, the loser would be marinated, cooked, and then eaten. *Let's Go* does not recommend such cannibalistic rituals.

SIMANINDO AND PANGURURAN. North of Ambarita, the island perimeter road passes through peaceful farmland, as the cliffs behind Tomok and Tuk-Tuk gradually recede into rolling hills dotted with Batak shrines. Some 20km later the road reaches the village of **Simanindo,** on the north tip of the island. Simanindo is home to the **Huta Bolon Museum,** famed for the traditional Toba Batak dances in its Huta Bolon Village, a small, well-preserved Batak village surrounded by a high stone wall. The large *jabu raja* (king's house) is worth a peek. (Museum open daily 9am-4pm. Rp5000. Dance performances M-Sa 10:30am and 12:30pm, Su 12:30pm depending on demand. Rp4500.) Uninspiring **Pangururan** provides a base for forays into the hills on the mainland. The **Mt. Belirang Hot Springs** (Rp1000) offer sulfurous comfort 4km west of town. Motorcycle enthusiasts can take a trip up **Mount Tele,** the steep ridge on the mainland. Beware of buses careening downhill. Visitors stranded in Pangururan can stay at **Hotel Wisata Samosir,** 42 Dr. T.B. Simatupang, next to the Telkom office on Sisinga Mangarata. (☎200 50. Dorms with shared *mandi* Rp12,000.) A tour of all these villages can be organized at Bagus Bay Stayhouse (1 day for Rp50,000).

ENTERTAINMENT

Many guest houses have showings of English movies nightly, in a cosy atmosphere with drinks. If you're looking for something a bit more upbeat, then lace up your dancing shoes.

Roy's Pub, atop the hill on the south side of the peninsula. Describes itself as a "Bob Marley Bar," but plays tunes with a considerably stronger beat. Bar, lounge area, and dance floor with DJ. Large beer Rp12,000. Open 7pm-late.

Tumba Discotique, follow signs south of Roy's or the southern Pizzeria Rumba. A big dance hall with bar. Large beer Rp15,000. Small bottles of stronger stuff Rp20,000-40,000. Open 8pm-late.

HIKING ACROSS PULAU SAMOSIR

An invigorating hike across the island uncovers less tarnished Batak life. The nicest route runs from Ambarita west to Pangururan. It's possible to finish in one day if you start early. Well-marked trails wind around coffee and tapioca plantations.

Alternatively, you can stay overnight in one of several villages with s. Hikers setting out from Ambarita pass tiny **Partokoan,** which has two guest houses, **John's** and **Jennie's.** From Partokoan, a rocky cart path heads 9km up to the larger village of **Roongurni Huta,** where it meets the road left to Tomok (24km) and right to Pangururan (16km). The latter arrives after 6km at **Sidihoni Lake,** where **Weny Guest House** puts up hikers for Rp5000 per night on the shore of the lake. The last 10km down to Pangururan offers stunning views of the steep crater walls and **Gunung Pusuk Buhit** on the western mainland.

From Ambarita, the path begins opposite the Batak Restaurant. From Pangururan, the dirt road to Roongurni Huta branches left off Jl. Dr. Tobing, opposite a Catholic church. Another trail leads from Tuk-Tuk to the narrow waterfall opposite the tiny peninsula, beginning on the right of the "gas station" near the intersection of the main road and the Tuk-Tuk perimeter road (2km); follow this path as far as you can (800m), then turn left. A scenic path from Tuk-Tuk to Ambarita also begins here. Follow the path to the waterfall and then turn right. The narrow dirt road winds through several small villages, past churches and across rice fields, before rejoining the main road near Ambarita.

ACEH PROVINCE

! Due to clashes between government forces and Acehnese nationalists, *Let's Go* last updated coverage of the Aceh outside Kutacane and Ketambe in the summer of 1998 and has hence removed coverage of the province from *Let's Go: Southeast Asia 2002.* Travel is dangerous. Check with your embassy before visiting.

GUNUNG LEUSER NATIONAL PARK

The virgin rainforest enveloping the fault lines of the Alas and Kluet River Valleys constitutes the largest national park in Southeast Asia. The Alas and Kluet River Valleys comprise lowland forest (1000m) with vines, spiny palms, and the malodorous rafflesia, while meadows of alpine flowers grace the higher altitudes (up to 2500m). Trekkers can see and hear hundreds of species of birds and watch acrobatic gibbons soar through trees. Macaques and orangutans abound, while Sumatran tigers, elephants, clouded leopards, and the rare Sumatran rhinos are more scattered. The Gayo, who live in the hilly highlands, raise water buffalo and grow tobacco, rice, and coffee; the Alas, who have moved up the Alas River Valley, cultivate the fertile rice *sawah* of the ancient Danau Alas. While the park lies largely in Aceh Province, parts extend into North Sumatra, where hikers head in from Bukit Lawang. The more adventurous head to Ketambe and Blangkejeren for less traveled treks and rafting.

TREKKING

Trekking is the most popular activity in the park. With a smaller group and a more obscure area, wildlife sightings become more likely. Prices vary substantially: in general, the closer you are to the starting point, the cheaper the hike. Nearly every tourist office and guest house in nearby towns organizes treks; the most exorbitant treks originate in Medan. Prices include food, drink, camping equipment, necessary permits, a guide, and transport to the starting point. Most guide services can arrange transportation from the finish point to the next destination. Prices are listed in US$ and translated to rupiah according to the daily quote.

Employ guides licensed with the **HPI** (the Indonesian Guide Association) whenever possible for legal, environmental, and safety reasons. However, some guides may have other local licenses which work just as well—check a prospective guide's license. Browsing through comment books of guest houses may also indicate the outstanding guides. Beware that prepackaged multiple day treks often involve only a few hours of hiking each day, with the rest of the time for "relaxing." Trekkers should make sure they get the level of intensity that they want.

Many trekkers start their trips in **Bukit Lawang.** Standard HPI prices are US$15 for one-day treks, US$35 for two-day, and US$55 for three-day; group size is usually a minimum of three people. Prices may be reduced for large groups.

Those wishing to escape tourist traffic can start from **Ketambe,** where prices tend to be lower ($10 for a 1 day trek, no min. group size). Most treks organized in

Berastagi actually begin in Ketambe, but you may want to compare the trekking companies in Kutacane if you are planning a longer expedition. As jaunts become expeditions prices per day rise to pay for extra porters and more experienced guides. For a six-day hike from Ketambe, prices get lowered to the US$30 a day per person. Such treks include the route between Bukit Lawang and Ketambe and climbs up **Gunung Kemiri** and **Gunung Bendahara. Gunung Leuser** (3119m) and **Loser** (3404m) are best attempted from **Blangkegeren** and will take up to 10 days.

RAFTING

Rafting expeditions range from the boisterous water-park feel of the **Bohorok River** in Bukit Lawang to multiple-day adventures down the **Wampu River** near Ketambe. Rafting prices, which include all expenses, tend to be higher than trekking prices to cover multiple guides and expensive equipment. From Bukit Lawang, trips down the Wampu River average US$75 per person per day for one- to four-day jaunts. In the Kutacane area, rafting trips down the Alas River start in Ketambe and head toward Gelombang. The most competitive rates are available from tour services in Kutacane. One-day floats from Ketambe to Kutacane cost as little as Rp200,000 per person. Three- or four-day adventures cost US$80-100 per person. **Combined rafting/trekking trips** are becoming more popular. Arrange these in the Bukit Lawang or Kutacane/Ketambe areas. Trips (3 days rafting and 2 days trekking) can be organized out of Kutacane. A two-day combination trip out of Bukit Lawang runs US$130-145.

Most guest houses at Bukit Lawang have **inner tubes** for use on the Bohorok River (Rp3000 per day). While loads of fun, tubing can also be dangerous—injuries caused by unseen rocks or submerged logs are common. During the dry season (Feb.-June), the water level may be too low to float safely. Check with the Visitors Center first. It is possible, although perhaps a bit chilly, to float 6km to Bohorok village (2-3hr.). Local buses ferry the drenched back to Bukit Lawang (Rp500).

PULAU NIAS

Pulau Nias is a tropical island paradise. Lush green palm forests give way to white beaches and rolling surf from a clean sea. The island is inhabited by the Niha, whose ancestors are believed to have been proto-Malays, even though they display physical characteristics of north Asians, speak a unique language, and produce art forms with Indian and Vietnamese influences. Today, an eclectic mix of people come to Pulau Nias not for the depth of its history but to ride the waves at one of Indonesia's premier surfing spots.

> **WARNING.** Pulau Nias was hit by a tropical storm in July 2001. Severe flooding caused serious damage to the island. Listings below may have since been affected.

SIBOLGA ☎0631

> **FERRY TICKETS.** Buying ferry tickets in Sibolga is tricky. Insist on a written receipt. Otherwise don't pay until you are on the boat in your chosen class. Many tourists face the added trouble of being falsely accused of having drugs in their bags, or of having been seen dumping drugs into the water. "Police," either off-duty cops or just pretenders, then extract exorbitant bribes. Causing a big scene and refusing to budge may or may not get you out of paying.

You gotta go to hell to get to heaven. **Sibolga** is the transit point to Pulau Nias, and has unbearably aggressive hustlers at the ferry and bus terminals. A recent increase in legitimate tourist business, however, has helped push hustlers back. **Scuba diving** and the **Internet** are two things that you'll find in Sibolga and not on Pulau Nias.

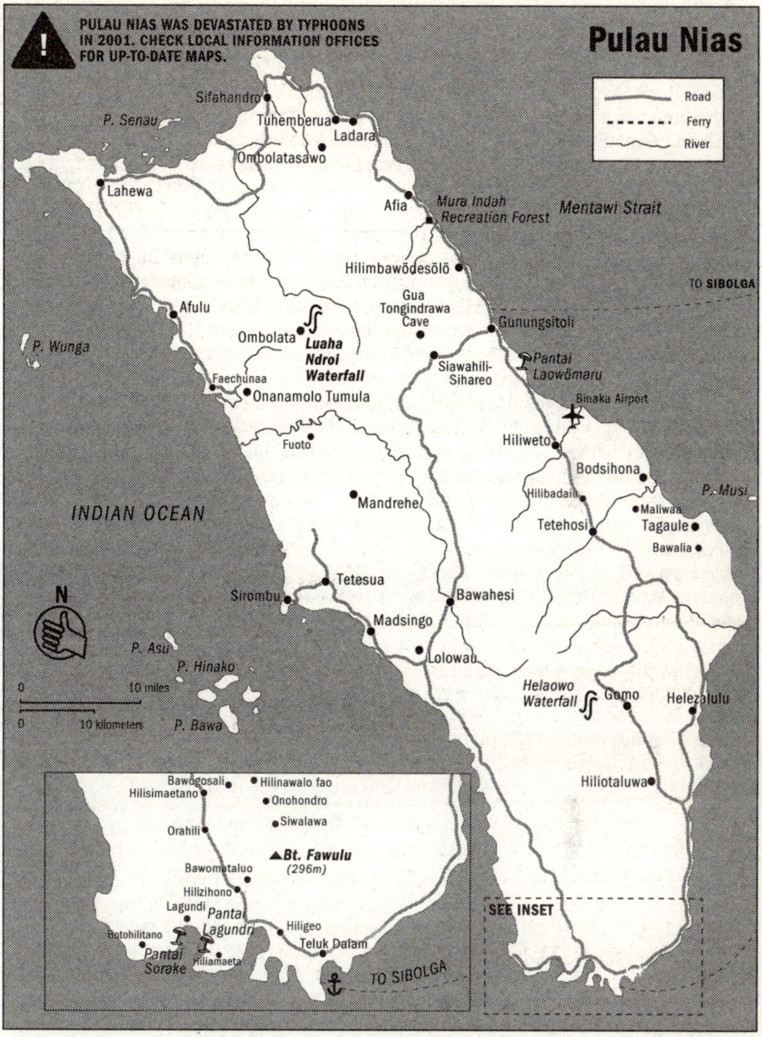

Away from the main bus terminals, there are bus and shipping companies that will help you out. If you're willing to pay, **Helen's Tourist Information Service,** Jl. Diponegoro 33 (☎250 71), a shack across from Masjid Agung Mosque offers a good service—ferry tickets at a small markup and bus tickets for a bit more (let them know you know the real price and negotiate), as well as safe transport and temporary bag storage (Rp10,000, including transport). As always, rates are better for groups.

Buses go from the **terminal** on Jl. SiSingaMangaRaja in Sibolga (Rp1000 by *becak* from the pier) to: **Jakarta** (3 days per week, 4pm, Rp180,000); **Medan** (8hr., 8am, Rp30,000; Minibus 7, 8, 9am, Rp50,000); **Padang** (16hr.) via **Bukit Tinggi** (14hr., 2, 4pm; Rp30,000; Minibuses 8hr., several daily, Rp50,000); **Parapat** (6hr., 7, 8, 9am; Rp30,000; Minibuses 8hr., Rp40,000). If you miss the bus that goes to Parapat and Medan, you can charter a car (Rp250,000); a minivan (Rp350,000 after hard bargaining), or you can take a public bus to Taratung (2hr., every 30min., Rp10,000), where more buses run north.

Overnight **ferries** shuttle from Sibolga to Gunung Sitoli and Teluk Dalam. **PT Simeulue,** Jl. Pelabuhan 59 (☎214 97), operates small wooden boats from Sibolga to **Teluk Dalam** (10-12hr.; Tu, Th, Sa 8pm, return M, W, F 8pm; deck Rp25,000, cabin Rp45,000). Boats also go to **Gunung Sitoli** (9-10hr.; Tu, Th, F 8pm; deck Rp15,000, cabin Rp25,000). Cabins can also be purchased on board from the captain for Rp20,000 per person. **PT ASDP,** Jl. SiSingaMangaRaja 161, regularly runs large boats from Sibolga to Gunung Sitoli and back. (☎217 52. Open M-Sa 8am-5pm. 10hr.; M Sa 8pm; economy Rp19,500, A/C lounge Rp26,000, non-A/C cabin Rp30,000-35,000.)

Alternating **PELNI** ships arrive Saturday from **Padang.** The *Lambelu* arrives in Sibolga at 2pm and leaves at 4pm for **Padang** (arrives Su 4am, Rp49,500) and departs at 10am for **Jakarta** (arrives M 4pm, Rp120,000). On alternating Saturdays, the *Kambona* arrives in Sibolga at 7am and leaves at 10am for **Gunung Sitoli** (arrives at 2pm), at 3pm for **Padang** (arrives Su 4am, Rp63,500), and at 10am for **Jakarta** (arrives M 4pm, Rp116,500). For **local transportation,** use *becak* (about Rp2000).

Hotel Melati, Jl. Horas 100, opposite Citra Nasional Bus office, has the best rates in town. (☎228 57. Double with fan, *mandi* outside Rp20,000, with Western toilet and shower Rp30,000.) **Scuba diving** can be organized through **Hotel Wisara Indah,** Jl. B. Katamso 51. A day includes two dives, lunch, and boat. (US$75 per person for 1-2 people, US $65 for 3-4 people, and US $50 for 5 people. ☎236 88. Book ahead.)

Sibolga has a 24-hr. **police station,** Jl. Tobing 35 (☎251 10). There are decent exchange rates and an **ATM** at **Bank BNI,** Jl. S. Parman 34. (☎227 24. Open M-Th 8am-4pm, Sa 8am-noon.) **RSU Dr. F.L. Tobing Hospital** is nearby at Jl. Tobing 35A, at the corner of Jl. Yos Sudarso. (☎213 99. Open 24hr.) There is an **Internet cafe** next to the post office. (Open daily 9am-10pm. Rp10,000 per hr.) A **post office,** across the street at Jl. Sutomo 40 (☎221 62; open M-Sa 8am-5pm), offers *Poste Restante.* **Postal code:** 22500.

GUNUNG SITOLI ☎0639

As the capital of the island, Gunung Sitoli is a convenient base for exploring the stunning architecture and isolated beaches of seldom-touristed north Nias. The antidote to the hostile *becak* drivers who swarm here are the friendly locals who will happily assist the daring souls who don't hop on the first bus south.

TRANSPORTATION

Binaka Airport lies 20km south of Gunung Sitoli. Confirm flights the day before departure. Regular buses run from the bus station to Binaka (30min., Rp2000). **SMAC,** Jl. Lagundi 46 (☎210 10, open M-Sa 8am-4pm), has flights to: **Medan** (1 hr.; W 1pm, Sa noon; Rp552,500); **Padang** (1½hr., W 8am, Rp190,600); **Pulau Batu** (30min., W 8am, Rp83,900).

Several buses and *oplet* leave the **bus station** going south to **Teluk Dalam** (5hr., 7am-2pm, Rp15,000). To avoid paying exorbitant "tourist prices," don't pay until other passengers do. A private car to Teluk Dalam can be chartered for Rp300,000 at the bus terminal. Buses and *oplet* to the north regularly depart from here. **Ferries** depart from the harbor, 3km north of town, off the main road (Rp1000 by *oplet,* Rp5000 by *becak*). **PT ASDP,** Jl. Yos Sudarso 201 (☎224 10, open M-Sa 8am-4pm), runs large ships to **Sibolga** (10-12hr.; M-Sa 8pm; economy Rp19,5000, A/C lounge Rp26,000, cabin with fan Rp30,000-35,000). Buy at the dock if the office has closed. **PT Simeulue,** on Jl. Sirao opposite Hotel Gomo, runs smaller wooden boats. (Open M-Sa 8am-6pm. 10hr.; W, F 8pm; economy R15,000, cabin 25,000.) **PELNI,** Jl. Ceugeh 38, off Jl. Lagundi has Padang-bound ships on Saturday. (Open daily 8am-4pm.)

ORIENTATION AND PRACTICAL INFORMATION

The main thoroughfare, **Jl. Sirao,** starts from the grassy main square by the Hotel Wisata and runs west-east until it kinks south (right) and then crosses a bridge after 100m. Hotels cluster along Jl. Sirao and most of the action is north of the bridge. South of the bridge (where Jl. Sirao becomes **Jl. Diponegoro**), the **bus station** is 200m down on the right. **Jl. Lagundi** branches off Jl. Sirao to the east (toward the water), and **Jl. Gomo/Yos Sudarso** runs parallel to Jl. Sirao to the west. The **ferry port** is 3km north of town.

The **tourist office,** Jl. Sukarno 6, across the main square from the Hotel Wisata, has brochures and maps. (☎215 45. Open M-Sa 7:30am-4pm.) **Bank BNI,** Jl. Imam Bonjol 40, 150m south of the telephone office, offers poor exchange rates for cash and traveler's checks, but it does have an **ATM.** (☎219 46. Open M-F 8am-4pm.) **Apotik Mira Lina,** Jl. Sirao 179, on the left heading south, is well stocked. (☎217 79. Open daily 9am-7pm.) **RSU Gunung Sitoli Hospital,** Jl. Dr. Ciptomangunkusomo 15 (☎214 74), the best on the island, is 100m uphill on the right from the phone office. To find the regional **police office,** Jl. Melati 5 (☎215 58), take one of the side streets off Jl. Diponegoro on the same side as the bus station and 100m south; Jl. Melati runs parallel with Jl. Diponegoro. The **post office,** Jl. Hatta 1, on the southeast corner of the main square, offers *Poste Restante.* (☎214 40. Open M-Th 8am-3pm, F 8am-noon, Sa 8am-1pm.) **Postal code:** 22813.

ACCOMMODATIONS

Most establishments in Gunung Sitoli are overpriced. Millions of mosquitoes and the risk of malaria make protection a must. If you don't have a net or A/C, mozzie coils are readily available (Rp1700 for a box).

Hotel Gomo, Jl. Gomo 148 (☎219 26), with another entrance off Jl. Sirao. Offers simple rooms with fan and *mandi* and karaoke videos of all your favorite hits of the late 60s and 70s. Doubles Rp25,000, with A/C and Western toilet Rp40,000; big room with A/C, TV, and Western toilet Rp55,000.

Hawaii Hotel, Jl. Sirao 20 (☎210 21). Friendly staff manages clean rooms. Doubles with *mandi* outside Rp20,000, inside Rp30,000, with A/C Rp45,000; AC, TV, and Western toilet Rp55,000.

Losmen Serasi, Jl. Sirao 6. Cheapest beds; you get what you pay for, but there's a lively little cafe downstairs. Dorm bed with communal *mandi* downstairs Rp5000.

FOOD

High food prices reflect the fact that chicken and beef has to be imported from the mainland; your best bet is to order fish.

Rumah Makan Nasional, Jl. Sirao 87. Sample the wide variety of *padang* dishes; try the *pergadel* (potatoes prepared in an almost Swiss fashion). Expect to pay Rp10,000 for a good meal. Open daily 9am-6pm.

Restoran Bintang Terang, Jl. Sirao 10. In a family's comfy front room. Serves a large selection of BBQ seafood and Chinese dishes. Fried rice and shrimp Rp6000, fried prawn with flour Rp18,000.

Warung Damai, at the corner of Jl. Gomo and Jl. Sudirman. Delightful little tea place with yummy tidbits. Cupcake Rp250, tea Rp1500. Open daily 6am-6pm.

Rumah Makan Saiyo, Jl. Sirao 57. Serves *padang* in a room filled with chirping birds and exotic fish. Buffalo meat Rp5000. Open daily 8am-10pm.

SIGHTS

The cost of seclusion is frustrating transportation. Buses and minivans connect northern sights to Gunung Sitoli bus station, but at unpredictable times. Being stranded at a beach after the tide comes in is risky. You can hire a motorcycle guide/driver to navigate the unmarked roads by asking at your hotel or just about anywhere you hear English. (After bargaining, Rp150,000 per day is the best you can hope for.)

Nearby, traditional north **Niha villages** have houses characterized by large oval shapes with thatched roofs of up to 10m in height. It's possible to stay several nights in some villages, where you can see traditional dancing and music. Be respectful of local customs, and ask permission before taking photos. **Siawahili-Sihare'ö,** 5km west of town, with magnificent *rumah adat* lining the streets, is the most authentic (Rp2500 by *ojek*). The **Gua Tögindrawa Cave,** perfect for the daring and flashlight-armed spelunker, lies 1km away. Walking from Gua Tögindrawa Cave to Siawahili-Sihare'ö and back is an enjoyable daytrip. **Hilimbawödesölö,** 8km north of Gunung Sitoli, is another remarkable village. **Muara Indah Recreation Forest,** 14km north, boasts a lake, a beach, and a meandering estuary to the ocean. (Public bus every 1½hr., 7am-6:30pm, Rp1000-1500.) White **Pantai Laowömaru,** 7km on the road to the airport is a beach popular with locals (*becak* Rp5000).

Museum Pusaka Nias, Jl. Yos Sudarso 134A, halfway between Gunung Sitoli and the ferry port, has carved figurines, war costumes, and models of traditional Nias houses, as well as a mini-zoo hosting crocs. The friendly staff gives tours. The free film on Niha culture (see "Neee Haaa!" below) is undoubtedly the cheapest way to see the stone-jumping ceremony. (☎219 20. Open Tu-Su 8am-5pm. Rp500; extra Rp2000 to take pictures.)

There is a **clothes market** on Jl. Mongsidi, between Jl. Sirao (before the bend) and Jl. Gomo. Pick up paradise's essentials: boardshorts, t-shirts, and sunglasses.

LAGUNDI BAY ☎0630

Only 12km west of Teluk Dalam, this horseshoe-shaped bay's perpetual surf and razor-sharp coral reefs have made it a hot spot on the international surfing circuit. Non-surfers enjoy fresh fish, spectacular views, and trips to traditional villages. Since many surfers stay for months at a time, there is a sense of community at Sorake Beach, which ages nicely the longer you stay.

TRANSPORTATION. Motorcycle (*ojek*) drivers take you to and from **Teluk Dalam** (Rp3000) and minibuses are usually handy at the ferry if you've got boards (Rp5000). The inspired can rent **motorbikes** (post-haggling Rp15,000 per hr.), but roads are in patchy condition. Buses leave the bus station for **Gunung Sitoli** at about 7am and 1pm. The eastern route follows an awful road along the coast and into the hills (6-7hr.). The inland route is better paved (4hr.), but only fate determines bus size and route chosen (Rp20,000-25,000). Buses taking the inland route will pass **Lagundi Village** on the way and you can flag one down. For **Binaka Airport** change bus in Gunung Sitoli. The **ferry** leaves for **Sibolga** on M, W, F at 8pm (12hr.; deck Rp25,500, cabin Rp45,500). Occasionally, smaller ferries replace the larger one (deck Rp25,500, cabin 55,500). **Cargo ships** head to **Padang** twice a week. You can organize a ride at PT Martika on Jl. Panigoro across from the school in Teluk Dalam (12hr., cabin Rp90,000).

PRACTICAL INFORMATION. In town are the **police,** 100m north of the bus station on Jl. Mohamata, and the **post office** at Jl. Imam Bonjol2 (open M-Th 8am-2pm, F 8-11am, Sa 8am-noon). **Postal code:** 22865.

For medical services in English, the **Puskesman Lagundri** is on the main road in Lagundi village. (☎212 02. Open daily 8:30am-2pm. **24hr.** emergency care.) A road junction lies across a trestle bridge 150m west of Pukesman Lagundri. The road to Gunung Sitoli heads north, the road to **Botohilitanö Village** heads west, and the **Sorake Beach Rd.** heads south. South down Sorake Beach Rd. with the bay on the left, the string of *losmen* stretches for 1km. A three-story judging tower (for surfing competitions) dominates the beach 50m south of the wartel office. The latter has an **HCD** phone (open 24hr., collect calls Rp20,000).

ACCOMMODATIONS AND FOOD. Lodgings stretch around from the **lighthouse** on Lagundi Beach to **Sorake Beach** on the west end, where *losmen* cluster. Rooms range from Rp5000 to Rp10,000 per night and better deals can be struck on

NEEE HAAA! Traditionally, the ultimate organization of Niha culture was the village and its most important resident the king. In times of war, every village's primary defense was a 2m tall fence surrounding the village. In the heat of battle, warriors would leap over these fences and chop off their enemies' heads before returning home to present their liege with the bloody trophies. Such gory presents excited any self-respecting king, and the bearer of such good gifts was rewarded with a life in the lap of luxury. To be recognized as a warrior, a man had to demonstrate his aptitude by leaping over a 2m stone monument, thus indicating that he was ready for battle. Extra spice was added to the equation by the stipulation that only once a man could hurdle the hump could he marry...thus the stone-jumping ceremony recalls two integral aspects of Niha survival: defense in the present and reproduction in the future.

long stays. The real money is made off food. Prices are highish, and many *losmen* expect you to eat on premises. The most peaceful option, a 30min. walk away from surf and surfers, is **Aman Inn** on Lagundi beach just past the "lighthouse." (Rooms Rp5000 with porch, mosquito net, *mandi* and Western toilet; bungalow Rp10,000.) For a place near the surf, try **Marlynto's,** 150m south of the patio. Rp10,000 gets you a well-kept room with all the perks: a fan, Western toilet, and spacious patio with a great view of the surf. Another 200m south, **New Raya** offers quiet bungalows with private *mandi* and Western toilet for Rp5000 and a proprietor who doesn't mind where you eat. Canoeing and boogie boarding is free and there's a bonfire and dinner on the beach every night. The owner is very talkative, friendly and helpful. For utter seclusion, try his brother's similar place next door at **Risky Guest House.**

Check out different *losmen* when you arrive; it is considered unacceptable to change accommodations. Although backpackers usually want to be left alone, here it is very easy to become dependent on your mama and papa (*losmen* proprietors), especially for meals. It's crucial to choose a place with the dynamic that you are looking for. Theft is a common problem, so choose a place with locks, don't leave clothing outside, and beware of "safe deposit boxes."

Sorake Beach has three cafes with similar offerings; most of the *losmen* have basic menus as well. The real prize is the local fish, shark, and octopus, which can be bought on the beach and cooked in your *losmen.* Expect to pay about Rp5000-10,000 per person for the fish, and Rp5000-10,000 for the preparation.

SIGHTS AND ENTERTAINMENT. Competition-class **surf** draws wave riders from around the world to **Sorake Beach.** The waves off Sorake (3-4m high June-Sept.) should be treated with respect—a wrong turn can crash you into the reef. When the waves shrink they're perfect for beginners, but seasoned experts head west to the Hinako Islands, especially Asu, where the break is better in small surf. A chartered boat out can hold 12 people (Rp600,000) or there's a ferry from Sirombu to Hinako and Bawa (1½hr., 11am M-Sa, Rp5000). Accommodation runs about Rp30,000 for a double on Asu, less elsewhere. Surfboards are sold, fixed, and rented along Sorake Beach (Rp15,000 per day). **Lagundi Beach's** smaller waves offer pleasant swimming. Surfer hangouts include **Toho Bar and Cafe** on Sorake Beach Rd., for beer, table tennis, Western food, and movies, and **Dolin Cafe** at the judging tower (fried octopus with chili sauce Rp16,000).

DAYTRIP FROM LAGUNDI BAY: THE NIHA VILLAGES. The hills of south Nias have **Niha villages** that can be visited as a daytrip from Lagundi Bay or Teluk Dalam. *Rumah adat* (traditional houses) line cobbled streets. Locals once laid their deceased on the carved stone benches lining the streets. At the center of each village is a large square in front of the chief's house, where village meetings convene and traditional dancing, including stone-jumping, is performed. Upon arriving at any village, head first for the chief's house to pay your respects. Usually he will ask for a small donation. After visiting the chief, visitors are free to roam about the village.

Considered the Joshua Tree of Niha culture, **Gomo Village,** 40km north of Teluk Dalam, boasts numerous megalithic stone chairs that are over 2000 years old. The 2½hr. trip to Gomo is most easily accomplished via motorbike by guides in Teluk Dalam and Lagundi (round-trip Rp100,000). **Bawömataluo,** standing 300m above the ocean 12km from Lagundi, has a massive ceremonial drum and is the most touristed. Take a motorcycle (Rp10,000) or a *sudako* (Rp1500) from Teluk Dalam.

Hiliameta is a smaller village, a 45min. walk from Lagundi Bay. The village is 500m up a walkway that turns into stone steps, starting off the main road 1km east of Lagundi village. The turn-off is a 45min. walk from Sorake Beach (less than Rp5000). Another village, **Botohilitanö,** rests on the hill 1km west of Sorake Beach.

Niha war dances, featured on the back of the Rp1000 note, are a spectacular sight. Most performances include **stone-jumping,** the ancient rite wherein young men launch themselves from a small stone onto a 2m high platform (see **Neee Haaa!** p. 301). Locals can arrange traditional Niha dancing in Botohilitanö or (cheaper) Hilimaeta Village (Rp300,000 for dancing only, Rp50,000 extra for stone-jumping).

It's possible to make **day hikes** through villages, which are linked by well-marked stone paths. A pleasant route from Orahili to Hilisimaetano passes through seven villages, including Bawömataluo. Hikers can arrange for a motorbike to pick them up at the terminus. Alternatively, stay in Hiliwanalo or one of the many villages that lodge visitors for around Rp10,000 per night (including meals). Consider leaving your valuables at home; there have been reports of theft in the villages.

CENTRAL SUMATRA

BUKIT TINGGI ☎0752

A thriving market town, Bukit Tinggi is among the most urban of Sumatra's backpacker haunts and well-populated with travelers. The city's pleasant residents and well-developed infrastructure make it easy to explore the unique food, architecture, and performing arts of the Minangkabau culture. Have fun and climb volcanoes, visit remote Minangkabau villages, or strike out for the Mentawi Islands.

TRANSPORTATION

Buses: Purchase long-distance tickets from bus companies at **Aur Kuning bus terminal,** 3km southeast of Jam Gadang. Buses to: **Danau Maninjau** (1½hr., every hr. 7am-5pm, Rp2500); **Medan** (18hr.; noon, 4, 5pm; with A/C Rp85,000); **Padang** (2-3hr., every 30min. 5am-7pm, Rp5000); and **Solok** (1½hr., every 15min. 6am-6pm, Rp3000). For more options, go to Pekan Baru and change buses there (6hr., every 2hr. 7am-4pm, Rp15,000). **Tourist buses** to **Parapat** stop at the equator and a hot spring and include a ferry to **Pulau Samosir,** though a night in Parapat is required. (13hr., 8am, Rp72,500). Book at hotels and travel agents.

Ferries: Take a bus (12hr.; 7, 9am, 4pm; Rp30,000) or minibus (10hr., 8pm, Rp50,000) to **Dumai.** From there, ferries run to **Melaka** (1¾hr., every hr. 11am-3pm, Rp110,000). A bus to **Sibolga** (10hr, 10am and 7pm, Rp50,000) will get you to the Nias ferries.

Local Transportation: Mikrolet minivans follow a roughly clockwise route up Jl. Sudirman, Jl. A. Yani, Pasar Bawah (lower market), and Aur Kuning bus terminal (Rp500). **Dokar** (horse-drawn carriages) clop around (Rp5000 in town).

ORIENTATION AND PRACTICAL INFORMATION

Jam Gadang—the Dutch clock tower—and the surrounding square dominate the town center. **Pasar Atas** (upper market) is next to the square on the northeast. **Jl. A. Yani** heads roughly northwest from the square until it bends right at a four-way

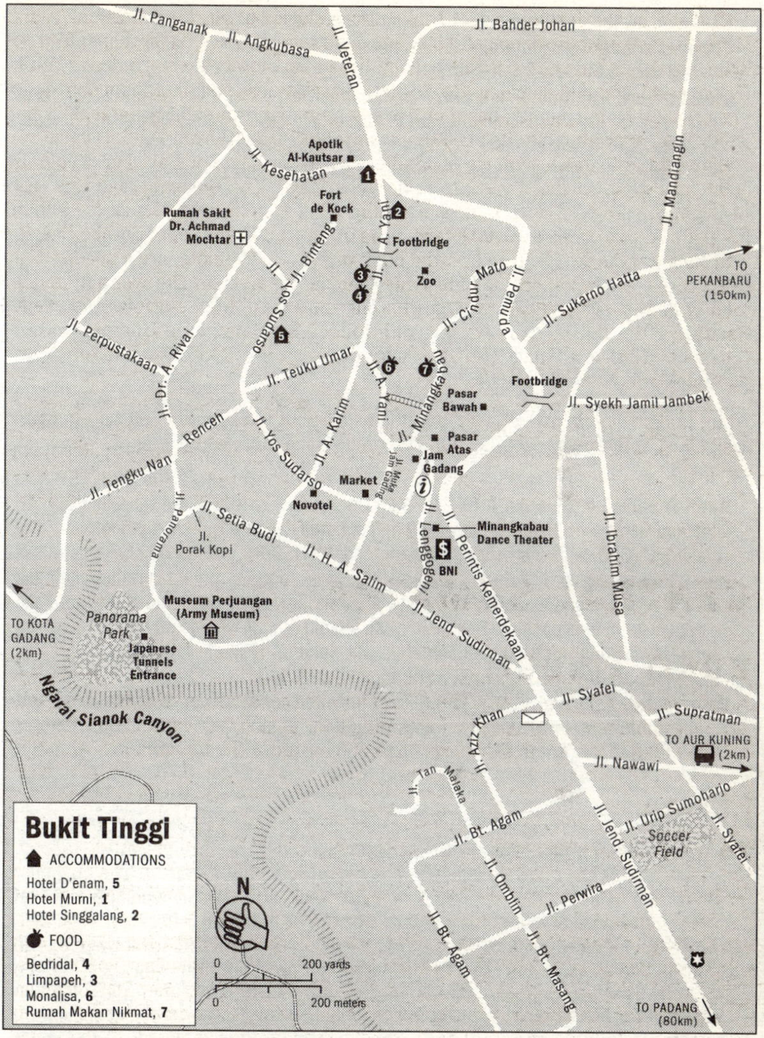

intersection and continues downhill where it passes beneath the towering footbridge with a great view, and passes the **zoo** and the old Dutch **Fort de Kock,** into **Kampung Cina (Chinatown).** Budget *losmen,* cafes, and travel companies abound here. Back from the four-way intersection, **Jl. A. Karim** climbs to the southwest (with **Novotel** at its summit), and **Jl. Teuku Umar** (which becomes **Jl. Tengku Nan Renceh**) climbs uphill to the west, intersecting Jl. Yos Sudarso.

Tours: Outfits on Jl. A. Yani arrange flights, buses, and taxis, rent motorbikes, and offer tours. **PT Maju Indosari,** Jl. Jam Gadang 17, 20m from the clock tower is right next to the old tourist information office and has inherited its karma.

Currency Exchange: Bank BNI, Perintis Kemerdekaan #15 (☎225 78), cashes traveler's checks. **ATM.** Open M-F 7:30am-3:15pm.

English-Language Bookstores: 3 on Jl. A. Yani and one on Jl. Teuku Umar; all of which buy, sell, and trade.

Police: Jl. Sudirman 23 (☎311 10), 500m south of the post office. Open 24hr.

Pharmacies: Apotik Al-Kautsar, Jl. Kesehatan 17 (☎312 34), is past the bottom of Jl. A. Yani and to the left. **Open 24hr.**

Medical Services: Rumah Sakit Dr. Achmad Mochtar, Jl. Dr. Rivai 1 (☎213 22). From the bottom of Jl. A. Yani, bear left onto Jl. Kesehatan. Take a left at the fork in the road; the **24hr.** emergency entrance is 100m ahead on the right.

Telephones: The **HCD** phones in the public phone bank next to Jam Gadang are generally out of order; try the free one in the lobby of Novotel, 300m southwest of Jam Gadang.

Internet cafes: Abound on Jl. A Yani. All charge Rp20,000 per hr. Connections are slow. Your best bet is in the morning or late at night.

Post Offices: GPO, Jl. Sudirman, up the road from BNI. *Poste Restante.* Open M-Sa 8am-4:30pm. **Postal code:** 26116.

ACCOMMODATIONS

While budget hotels are all over Bukit Tinggi, most backpackers end up in **Kampung Cina** (Chinatown). Hotels on **Jl. Yani** are in the action, while quieter s are on **Jl. Sudirman.**

Hotel D'enam, Jl. Sudarso 4 (☎213 33). One of several hotels on the quiet hill. An upstairs porch with beautiful view and friendly staff, all in a quiet neighborhood. Doubles Rp13,000, with shower and Western toilet Rp15,000; triples Rp22,500.

Hotel Singgalang, Jl. A. Yani 130 (☎215 76), at the bottom of the hill on the right just after the footbridge. An extremely friendly staff and a welcoming center courtyard make it popular with backpackers. Tidy rooms with shared *mandi.* Rooms off the courtyard are quietest. Lockout midnight, but someone will wake up if you're arriving in town early. Singles Rp15,000; doubles Rp17,000; triples Rp25,000.

Hotel Murni, Jl. A. Yani 115 (☎355 69). At the intersection with Jl. Pemuda on the left. Clean rooms, mellow balcony, and sitting area upstairs. Cheap option. Doubles Rp11,000; triples Rp16,500; quads Rp30,000—all with shared *mandi.*

INDONESIA

FOOD

Tasty, atomic-hot Minangkabau cuisine (known across the archipelago as *padang* food) dominates the culinary spectrum of restaurants and *warung.* The cheapest meals can be had in the maze of stalls in **Pasar Atas** or at one or two stalls right on Jl. A. Yani. **Backpacker cafes** cluster at the bottom of **Jl. A. Yani,** offering a wide variety of Western dishes. **Bedridal,** Jl. A. Yani 95-105, just before the footbridge on the left, offers incensed air and chilled tunes to go with padded floor seating. (Chicken salad with avocado, tomato, lettuce, and sprouts Rp12,500. Open daily 8:30am-midnight.) Good, inexpensive *padang* food can be found next door at **Limpapeh,** Jl. Yani 111 (open daily 10am-10pm), or **Rumah Makan Nikmat,** Jl. Minankabau 77 (open daily 6am-9pm). **Monalisa,** on Jl. A. Yani, serves quality Chinese food at reasonable prices (open daily 7am-11pm).

WHERE WOMEN RULE West Sumatra, land of the Minangkabau people, has one of the world's only enduring matrilineal societies. In this world where women rule, property is passed from mother to daughter, rather than from father to son, and children take the mother's family name. Evidence of the perseverance of this system in Minangkabau culture is their great reverence for the role of the mother—she is child-rearer, educator, and protector. Since she is seen as responsible for the family, she is honored with the responsibility of passing on her name and prosperity. The mother's eldest brother acts as the *tungganai* (manager of the clan's affairs), but Minangkabau women are quick to point out that although the men may run a business, the women own it! *Let's Go* believes that women should rule the world everywhere.

SIGHTS

Towering above Bukit Tinggi's skyline, the Minangkabau-Dutch hybrid **Jam Gadang** clock tower oversees the frenetic market. Almost nothing remains of the Dutch **Fort de Kock** at the end of Jl. Bintang; young folks bring guitars to its hilltop benches to while away the hours in song. The footbridge over Jl. Yani boasts a juxtaposed view over the busy city to the powerful Mt. Merapi. It connects Fort de Kock to the **city zoo,** where a decent collection of jungle wildlife is kept in depressingly small quarters. (Fort and zoo open daily 7am-6pm. Rp1600 for both.)

Panorama Park sits on top of **Ngarai Sianok Canyon,** and its clusters of *warung* afford spectacular views. The park houses **Japanese Tunnels,** built with forced labor during WWII; they're nothing to write home about. (Open daily 8am-6pm. Rp1100.) Opposite Panorama Park is the **Museum Perjuangan** (Army Museum) with an old fighter plane outside, displaying military relics and photos from the independence struggle. (Open daily 8am-5pm, donation optional.) An invigorating 2½km hike across the canyon will bring you to **Kota Gadang,** a silver-smithing town filled with small jewelry shops.

Two volcanoes, **Gunung Singgalang** (2878m) and **Gunung Merapi** (2891m), dominate Bukit Tinggi's horizon. A **guide** is recommended for either nine-hour roundtrip ascent; the trail may be hard to find alone. Travel companies in Bukit Tinggi leave at 11pm in order to catch the sunrise and charge US$15. Most adventurers climb Merapi for its spectacular view. Having erupted in 1974, it is still active and the police will close it down if it starts smoking.

Slightly further afield, there are a number of traditional Minangkabau villages, native reserves, and a swimming lake. Public transportation can be unpredictable; either rent a motorbike or go with a tour. Lake Singkarak and surrounding villages can be comfortably visited in six hours on a motorbike (Rp65,000 per day). **Harau Canyon** is a pristine reserve northeast of Bukit Tinggi. Rental places can give you good directions.

Pandai Sikat, a handicraft town specializing in carvings and *songket* weavings, is a popular stop on most Minangkabau area tours before returning to Bukit Tinggi; it's also accessible by *mikrolet* from the bus station (Rp1000). **Pariangan** is a traditional village with *rumah gadang* homes; take a bus from **Aur Kuning** (1hr., every hr. 7am-6pm, Rp2000). Buses also run to **Batang Palupuh** (15min., Rp1000), a nature reserve for the rafflesia flower. Worthwhile day tours of the whole region can be arranged in any hotel or cafe for Rp65,000 per person.

MARKETS

One of the most happening markets around, **Pasar Atas (upper market),** begins in the southwest corner of the Jam Gadang square. Food ranging from pancakes to *padang*, glossy magazines, clothes, and masses of women's underwear are just the tip of the iceberg in this maze of stalls under refreshingly different orange tarpaulins. On a lower level **Pasar Bawah (lower market),** offers up smells of fresh produce mixed with the smell of horses and minibuses which throng here on their way around town. Across the square there is a **smaller market** with food stalls.

ENTERTAINMENT

Bukit Tinggi hosts nightly **Minangkabau dance performances** at a theater on Jl. Lenggogeni 1 (behind the tourist office, next to Hotel Jogja). Different local dance groups give a colorful musical performance nearly every night (8:30-10pm). The show includes local martial arts, wedding celebrations with beautiful costumes, and culminates with the harvest celebration dance, involving several dancers jumping and trashing around in a heap of shattered china. Purchase tickets at hotels, travel agencies or at the door (Rp20,000). **Buffalo fighting** is also popular. Tuesday and Wednesday evening duels don't always occur in the same place; con-

HOOK 'EM HORNS The people of West Sumatra, now known as the Minangkabau, earned the moniker from their cunning victory over their enemies in battle. Realizing that they had no chance in combat, they suggested that the battle be settled by bullfight. The invaders agreed, returning with an enormous, champion bull. The clever locals, on the other hand, brought only a tiny buffalo calf, just separated from its mother, then tied knives to its horns. The enemies sneered, sure that victory was in their future. To their surprise, the calf rushed to the bull to suckle, thereby slicing the bull open and winning the battle. In tribute to their ingenuity and to the calf, the West Sumatrans called themselves the "Minang" (Winning) "Kabau" (Buffalo), and thereafter designed their roofs and ceremonial headdresses in the shape of buffalo horns.

sult the tourist office for locations. Saturday matches take place at **Batagak,** 9km away (take a bus to Padang Panjang and ask the driver to drop you off). The hour-long events begin at 5pm (Rp2000). Area daytrips on fight days finish with the matchup.

NEAR BUKIT TINGGI

DANAU MANINJAU

A smaller, less touristed version of Lake Toba, Lake Maninjau is a crater lake 36km west of Bukit Tinggi. Extreme weather patterns created by the crater's micro-climate cause eerie mists, freak downpours, and dazzling sunsets. For daytrips around the lake, **bicycles** can be rented in Maninjau Village (Rp10,000 per day). The **Internet** has also found its way to Maninjau Village and two cafes offer different speed connections for different prices.

A number of waterfront s have sprouted north of Maninjau Village and past **Bayur,** 3km north of Maninjau. Those in Maninjau Village are surrounded by backpacker cafes, many of which show American movies every night at 8pm. The cheapest food in Maninjau Village can be found at the market in the center of town. Homestays in Bayur are more peaceful, separated from the road by rice paddies. **Lili's** offers Western toilets as well as doubles for Rp15,000, or lakeside bungalows for Rp25,000. A dip in the clean lake is a nice alternative to the shared *mandi*. Buses and *oplets* between Maninjau Village and Bayur run all day for Rp500.

Travel to Maninjau is an ordeal: the last descent from Bukit Tinggi involves 44 hairpin bends. Although all the **buses** from Bukit Tinggi to **Maninjau** (1½hr., every hr. 7am-5pm) willingly drop guests in front of any of the lakeside s, hikers can alight at **Lawang,** climb two hours uphill to **Puncak Lawang** ("top of Lawang," the highest point around the lake), and then hike four hours down to Bayur village. As always, if venturing into the jungle, a guide is a good idea.

INDONESIA

PADANG ☎0751

The offshore islands near Padang, the southernmost stop on northern Sumatra's backpacker ant-trail, offer excellent opportunities for beach frolicking. Aside from roaming the Pasar Raya, there's not much to do in this sprawling city. Padang's catch-22 weather complicates any travels: the scorching sun makes lengthy wandering unbearable, and frequent rains wash out the vistas. Logically enough, the city is the place for *padang* food—if that's too spicy, try a bowl of bananas.

TRANSPORTATION

Flights: Bandara Tabing Airport, 9km north of town. Catch *bis kota* #14A up Jl. Sudirman (Rp800) or an *oplet* (Rp1000) up Jl. Pemuda. Taxis Rp9000. Departure tax Rp9000. **Merpati,** Jl. Juanda 79 (☎444 832), flies to: **Batam** (M, W, F, and Su noon;

Rp464,500) and **Palembang** (M, W, F, and Su 2pm; Rp926,000). Open M-F 8am-4:30pm, Sa and Su 9am-1pm. **Garuda,** Jl. Sudirman 2 (☎301 73), in front of Bank Bumi Daya, flies to **Jakarta** (daily 9am, 3:25pm; Rp870,000). Open M-F 8am-4pm. **Mandala,** Jl. Sooteran 19C (☎327 73). Open M-F 8am-5pm, Sa-Su 9am-2pm. **Pelangi,** Jl. Veteran 18 (☎381 03), flies to **Johor Baru** (Tu, Th, F, Su, 11am; US$107) and **Kuala Lumpur** (Tu, Th, F, Su, 11am; US$127). Open M-F 9am-4pm, Sa 9am-2pm.

Buses: The **terminal** is on Jl. Pemuda, west of Pasar Raya. Buy tickets from the many companies at the bus station. Each company handles one or two routes; ask around. To: **Bengkulu** (16hr.; 2pm; Rp30,000, with A/C Rp50,000); **Bukit Tinggi** (2½hr., every hr. 6am-6pm, Rp5000); **Jakarta** (30hr.; economy 1pm, Rp85,000; A/C 1pm Rp150,000; A/C toilet, 10am, Rp250,000); **Jambi** (13hr.; 4pm; Rp30,000, with A/C Rp55000); **Medan** (17hr.; economy 11am Rp52,000, A/C 1pm, A/C toilet 2pm, Rp120,000); **Pekanbaru** (10hr., 8am and 7pm, Rp20,000); **Sungai Penuh** (10hr., 5pm, Rp25,000; minibuses 5hr.; 9, 9:30am, 6, 6:30pm, Rp25,000; 1pm Rp35,000). Access **Palembang** through Jambi and Bandar Lampung en route to Jakarta.

Ferries: Private companies line **Muara Harbor,** along Jl. Batang Arau, in the southwest corner of town. *Bemo* shuttle from Pasar Raya to the harbor regularly, or catch *bis kota* #14A heading south on Jl. Sudirman (Rp800). **PELNI,** Jl. Teluk Bayur 32 (☎616 24), in Teluk Bayur, has ships from Teluk Bayur Harbor to: **Gunung Sitoli** (15hr.; F 8pm; *Lambelu* Rp57,500-189,500, *Kambana* Rp62,500-206,500); **Jakarta** (36hr., Su 9am, Rp117,000-391,000); **Sibolga** (10hr.; F 8pm; *Lambelu* Rp62,500-250,000, *Kambana* Rp35,000-180,500); and **Surabaya** (2 days, Su 9am, Rp204,000-697,000). **Bungus** and **Teluk Bayur** harbors run ferries to similar destinations.

Local Transportation: Bis Kota (big city bus) Rp800, **oplet** Rp700-1200, depending on distance. Pasar Raya is a hub for buses and *oplets*.

ORIENTATION AND PRACTICAL INFORMATION

The coast runs north-south along Padang's west edge. The **bus terminal** is on the main north-south road, **Jl. Pemuda** (called **Jl. Diponegoro** south of the terminal and **Jl. Damar** in the north), one block inland. The main street is **Jl. M. Yamin,** which runs east-west past the **Pasar Raya Market** and the unmistakable Matahari Department Store. The tall Minangkabau-roofed **post office** stands 300m farther, at the intersection of **Jl. Aziz Chan/Sudirman,** where Jl. M. Yamin continues east as **Jl. Proklamasi.**

Tourist Offices: Dinas Pariwisata, Jl. Sudirman 43 (☎342 32), 1km north of the post office on the left. Maps and brochures. Open M-Th 8am-2:30pm, F 8-11am, Sa 8am-12:30pm. **Cab Dinas Pariwisata,** Jl. Hayam Wuruk 51 (☎341 86), at the intersection with Jl. Samudera. Open M-Th 8am-3pm, F-Sa 7:30am-11:30pm. Beware of staff walking you places and asking for money. Travel agencies are on Jl. Permuda, but agencies in Bukit Tinggi are more helpful.

Immigration Offices: Kantor Imigrasi Padang (☎551 13), Jl. Khatib Sulaiman, 1km north of the Telkom. Visa questions and not much else. Open M-Th 7:30am-2:30pm, F 7:30-11:30am, Sa 7:30am-1pm.

Currency Exchange: BII, Jl. Sudirman 14 (☎308 11). **ATM** here and all over town. Open daily 8am-3pm. **Moneychangers** on Jl. Pemuda offer inferior rates.

Markets: Pasar Raya, east of the bus terminal and the minibus hub is an action hotspot, selling many familiar objects in its maze. Tasty *warung* set up nearby every evening. Open daily 4am-7pm. The **night market** on Jl. Permindo at the west edge of the pasar is open until 9pm.

Police: Jl. M. Yamin 1 (☎337 24), next to the post office. Open **24hr.**

Pharmacies: Apotik Al Azhar, Jl. Proklamasi 54 (☎326 14), 100m east of the post office, next to several other pharmacies. **Open 24hr.**

Medical Services: Rumah Sakit Dr. M. Jamil (☎225 35), on Jl. Kemerdekaan. From 400m past the post office, take a right on Jl. Dr. H. Abdullah Ahmad; it's 300m up.

Telephones: There is a free **HCD** phone in the **Dipo International Hotel,** Jl. Diponegoro 13. **Open 24hr.**

Internet access: At the post office (see below). Rp5000 per hr. **Terminal Oleh-Oleh,** Jl. Pemuda 29 (☎274 81). Open 8:30am-midnight, Rp5000 per hr. **Bl@ntoeng,** Jl. Sudirman 5, opposite the bus station. Rp4000 per hr. Open 10am-11pm.

Post Office: Pos Besar Padang, Jl. Aziz Chan 7 (☎343 58). *Poste Restante.* Open daily 8am-6pm. **Postal code:** 25000.

ACCOMMODATIONS

Budget hotels are along **Jl. Pemuda** near the bus terminal; quieter places lie scattered about town. Most offer several "classes" of accommodation. A fan will combat the stifling heat and bloodthirsty mosquitoes.

Hotel Tiga Tiga, Jl. Pemuda 31 (☎226 33), opposite the bus terminal. Good location for a short stay. Popular with backpackers. Cafe and TV room. Singles Rp16,000; doubles Rp25,000; triples Rp32,000; quads Rp39,000; with fan, *mandi* and Western toilet Rp32,000-44,000.

Hotel Sriwijaya, Jl. Alang Lawas I 15 (☎235 77). Head right 100m east of the post office on Jl. M. Yamin/Proklamasi, down Jl. Alang Lawas I; it's 70m up on the right. Quiet street inhabited by several tasty breakfast stalls. TV room, comfy lounge. Singles Rp20,000, with *mandi* Rp25,000, with A/C Rp35,000; Rp5000 per extra person.

Hotel Cendrawasih, Jl. Pemuda 27 (☎228 94), next to Tiga Tiga offers slightly cheaper standards for a bit less. Singles Rp12,500; doubles Rp20,000; triples Rp25,000; with fan and *mandi* Rp10,000 extra.

FOOD

For the daring, restaurants prepare spicier-than-average (a.k.a. *en fuego*) *padang* fare. Lunch *warung* cluster at the bus terminal and east toward Pasar Raya. At night, Jl. M. Yamin and Jl. Permindo on the west edge of the *pasar* come to life with activity; *warung* with a view set up along **Pantai Padang,** where Jl. M. Yamin ends on the west edge of town, until the evening. *Teh telur* (tea with egg) is local fare.

Restaurant Tanpa Nama, Jl. Rohana Kudus 87. Head 300m north on Jl. Permido from Pasar Raya to Jl. Rohana Kudus. A shiny joint with neon lights, advertising A/C and music. Serves cheap *padang* and has a small bar. *Nasi Rendang* (special beef with rice) Rp5500. Open M-Th and Sa-Su 10am-9pm.

Restoran Kubang, Jl. M. Yamin 138, east of the bus terminal, sets up a street stall out front. Indonesian dishes served to locals and tourists alike. Masterfully created *martabak mesir* (pancakes with meat and veggies inside) can be found streetside Rp5500. English menu available. Open daily 2pm-12:30am.

Safari Bakery, Jl. Damar 50C, 500m north of the bus station on the right. Serves regular fare, but go out of your way for the flakiest, most buttery pastries in West Sumatra (Rp1200-2000). Also has a phenomenal juice bar (Rp3000). Open daily 9am-10pm.

Bofet Baru Sianok, Jl. P. S. Raya II Blok A 5B, off Jl. Pasar Raya. Local hangout for cheap good noodle soup with rice, meat, and veggies (Rp3000). Open daily 8am-6pm.

SIGHTS

The graceful **Adhytiawarman Museum,** Jl. Diponegoro 10, presides over a fenced park with a playground, garden, and pleasant benches. Inside the museum, cultural exhibits are accompanied by English descriptions. (Open Tu-Su 8am-6pm. Rp800, children Rp300.) Traditional musical events are staged on Sundays. Across the street at Jl. Diponegoro 19 is the **Taman Budaya (Cultural Center),** which sometimes stages outdoor dance and martial arts shows. A schedule is usually posted.

Pantai Padang extends along the west edge of town and hosts numerous vendors and *warung* until evening. The beach and water are dirty, but the sunset views are spectacular. A short hike away is calm **Air Manis,** Padang's most famous beach, with stunning views of **Pulau Pisang Ketek** (Small Banana Island), to which you can wade during low tide. Other nearby islands tempt onlookers with clean sandy beaches. To get to Air Manis, walk south along Pantai Padang to the Arau River, where rickety canoes ferry you across for Rp1000. On the other side, the scenic path leads past Japanese fortifications, through a Chinese cemetery, and eventually to the beach 4km down. (M-Sa free, Su Rp500.) Alternatively, *oplets* run from Pasar Raya for Rp1000 or pick one up on Jl. Thamrin. You'll have to change *oplet* at the turnoff to the beach (another Rp1000). In Air Manis, feast on fresh crab (Rp4000) or a coconut (Rp2000) at **Papa Chili Chili's .** (Rooms Rp6000 per person after bargaining.) In the opposite direction, Pasir Jambak (15km north of the city) is Padang's best beach for swimming. (M-Sa free, Su Rp500.)

Straight out of an Indiana Jones flick, the **Jembatan Akar** (Root Bridge) in **Pulut-Pulut** spans 40m over raging rapids. The bridge is formed entirely from the interwoven roots of two giant Beringin trees on either side of the river. Usually three buses travel daily to the village of Pulut-Pulut (2hr., Rp6000).

KERINCI SEBLAT NATIONAL PARK

Animal lovers come to Kerinci National Park in search of the rare Sumatran tiger, rhino, and elephant, as well as many species of primates. Botanists come to see the world's largest (rafflesia) and the tallest (amorphophallus) flowers. Bird-

APEMAN While trekking in Kerinci National Park, look for *orang pendek* (short man), a legendary creature less than one meter tall with the head of a man and the body of an immensely strong ape. Although *orang pendek* officially does not exist, there have been many sightings by both locals and Westerners, all with nearly identical descriptions of this hairy, dark gray creature. Early attempts to trap or kill an *orang pendek* kept producing Malay sunbears, which are known to walk on two legs. Scientists closed the book on this legend in 1992, when a supposed *orang pendek* body that had made international headlines turned out to be a common monkey, altered by locals hoping to claim a reward. Still, park officials will tell you of the *orang pendek* sightings in recent years, and many will tell you that they themselves have seen one.

watchers marvel at such exotic species as the bronze-tailed peacock pheasant. Spanning four provinces, Kerinci Seblat National Park—sometimes called "the wildest place on earth"—is Sumatra's hotspot for ecotourism. The World Wildlife Fund (WWF) has worked closely with local farmers to curtail illegal cultivation and poaching. Designated as a national park in 1982 and now an ASEAN heritage site, the 15,000 sq. km park is dominated by 3805m Gunung Kerinci, Indonesia's second-highest volcano. The valley around Sungai Penuh and Danau Kerinci rests at 800m, allowing for pleasantly cool nights, while the villages in the Kayu Aro region, at the 1500m base of Gunung Kerinci, have brisk morning showers.

SUNGAI PENUH ☎0748

The people of Sungai Penuh consider themselves more closely related to the Minangkabau of West Sumatra than to the provincial administration in Jambi. Not surprisingly, Sungai Penuh is much more touristed than other parts of the province. Though most foreigners whisk through the capital of Kerinci en route to the nearby countryside and mountains, this laid-back hillside town, as the center of a cluster of villages with rich musical and dance traditions, has much to offer.

ORIENTATION, TRANSPORTATION AND PRACTICAL INFORMATION.

As a small town with a defined center, it's not hard to find your bearings in Sungai Penuh. With occasional roadsigns, shop addresses and residents all disagreeing on street names, however, it's hard to find an address! The town rests on a hillside with a large grass square at its center, corners at the four points of the compass. In the south corner of the square, an obelisk rests at the tops of Jl. Marthadinata. 100m down on the left **Jl. Agus Salini** leads past the main market, **Pasar Sayur** to the **bus terminal**. The square is flanked on the northwest by Jl. Sudirman and on the southeast and northeast by Jl. Diponegoro which becomes Jl. Mudari. Buses depart from **Terminal Sungai Penuh** to: **Padang** (9hr., 7pm, Rp20,000); minibuses (7hr., 9am, Rp30,000); **Jambi** (11hr., 4pm, Rp20,000); **Bengkulu** (17hr., noon, Rp21,000); **Bedeng Dua, Kersik Tua,** and **Pelompek** (1½hr., every 15min., Rp2500).

To get to **Kerinci National Park Headquarters,** at Jl. Basuki Rahmat 11, follow Jl. Muradi 300m from the square. At the intersection with small islands in the middle of the road, turn left onto Jl. Basuki Ramhat; the office is 100m uphill. The office issues permits to climb Kerinci or visit Danau Gunung Tujuh, has guides for trekking, and gives information about the region. (☎222 50. Open M-Th 7:30am-2:30pm, F 7:30-11am, Sa 7:30am-1pm).) **Bank BNI,** Jl. Yani opposite Hotel Matahari, has an **ATM. Apotik Usaha Baru,** Jl. Diponegoro 4-12, is on the southeast side of the square (open daily 9am-9pm.) The **police,** Jl. Diponegoro 2, (☎211 70) are on the east corner of the square. The **Telkom office,** on Jl. Imam Bonjol, is at the west corner of the square. Collect calls advertised but questionable validity. (☎211 08. Open 24hr.).The **post office,** at Jl. Sudirman 1A, on the north corner of the square, has Poste Restante. (☎210 10. Open M-Sa 8am-5pm, Su 9am-1pm.) **Postal code:** 37114. The **hospital**, **Rumah Sahit Umum Daerah,** (☎210 18) is on Jl. Basuki Rahmat before the National Parks office on the left. (Intensive Care Unit open 24hr.)

ACCOMMODATIONS AND FOOD. A block beyond of the post office and 150m uphill on the left is the **Hotel Matahari,** Jl A. Yani 25, which offers a nice mountain breeze and comfortable beds. (☎210 61. Doubles Rp18,000 with *mandi* Rp35,000, with bath and Western toilet Rp45,000. Triples Rp27,000.) Just off the square on the right, the **Yani Hotel,** Jl. Muradi 1 (☎214 09), has doubles for Rp20,000, Rp10,000 extra per person. With *mandi* inside add Rp13,000 again. **Hotel Kayu Manis,** Jl. Martadinata 34, offers decent rooms with a cozy upstairs. Best value. (Singles Rp7500; doubles Rp15,000, triples Rp20,000. With private *mandi* Rp15,000-single to Rp50,000-quint.)To get to **Losmen Anak Gunung,** Jl. Agus Salim 43, take the first major left on Jl. Martadinata coming from the square; the hotel is 30m ahead on the right. Go through back and upstairs. Cheapest in town. (☎230 18. Singles Rp6000; doubles Rp10,000.)

Warung and hole-in-the-wall establishments flourish around the square's north-east edge and continue down along Jl. Muradi, but the happening place is **Jl. Martadinata,** which brims with *nasi goreng* joints, *sate* and *martabak* vendors, and syrupy-sweet *es* (iced) goodies. **Sari Manggis,** (☎231 50) on Jl. Depati Parbo, is a popular *padang* joint offering a cozy and clean restaurant atmosphere. 300m down Jl. Marthadinata forks right; it's 100m more on the left. (Open daily 8am-9pm.) **Bofet Sate Kambing,** Jl. Marthadinata 45, offers meat or vegetarian *Martabak* pancakes for Rp4000 and iced fruit drinks for Rp2500.

SIGHTS AND ENTERTAINMENT. Mesjid Agung Pondok Tinggi is 200m from the post office on Jl. Deputi Payung. Rumored to be over 500 years old, the mosque was built in 1874 without a single nail. Tourists may enter. (Rp10,000.)

The unimpressive **Semurup Hot Springs,** 9km north of town, soothe travelers with mildly sulfurous waters. (Open M-Sa 8am-6pm, Su 6am-6pm. Rp1500)daily 6am-6pm. Rp10,000.) Communal *mandi* disperse hot water in the long building directly before the springs. Catch a minivan from the bus terminal; ask for "Air Panas Semurup." Most buses will drop you off at the intersection of the main road (Rp1000). From the intersection, it's a 2km walk or Rp1000 *ojek* ride; bear right at the fork after 1km and then left after another 700m.

Traditional Kerinci dances include *Asyiek,* which contacts the spirits of dead ancestors, and **Pencak Silat,** a swordfighting martial art. Also unique to the area are *Basikie* music, a complex mix of various drum beats, and *Seruling Bambu* music, involving bamboo flutes and singing. To see or hear these traditional performances, ask about festivals in local villages.

KAYU ARO REGION

As the bus putters uphill from Sungai Penuh to the foot of Gunung Kerinci, tea plantations roll out to cinnamon groves, and magnificent Gunung Kerinci dominates the scenery. The region, collectively called Kayu Aro, embodies a slow, rural lifestyle and friendly people, and divides into three towns: Bedeng Dua, home of a tea factory; Kersik Tua, 7km north and the base for mountain treks; and Pelompek, another 10km up, the start for hikes to Danau Gunung Tujuh. A few visitors may be treated to *Kuda Kepang,* a frenetic fruit-throwing, bamboo-pounding ceremony that blends Kerinci and Javanese culture.

TRANSPORTATION AND PRACTICAL INFORMATION. Bedeng Dua, Kersik Tua, and **Pelompek** are easily negotiated, one-street towns. Buses and minivans shuttle between **Kayu Aro** and **Sungai Penuh** (1-1½hr., every 15min. 6am-4pm, Rp2500-3000), but can be flagged down for transit among the three Kayu Aro towns (Rp1000). Buses to **Padang** pass through around 9pm (7hr. Rp20,000), and minibuses at 10am (5hr., Rp25,000, reservation recommended). To climb Gunung Kerinci or visit Danau Gunung Tujuh, buy permits (Rp1500 per site) at **park headquarters** in Sungai Penuh or at one of two **PHPA** huts. The first (usually open daily 7am-5pm) lies 2km west of Kersik Tuo (follow road next to tiger statue); the second (open daily 24hr) is in **Sungai Jernih** village 2km east of Pelompek. Each town has a **police post** and **health clinic.** and a local **wartel. Postal code:** 37163.

ACCOMMODATIONS AND FOOD. Kayu Aro has five s along the road in Kersik Tua, all of which offer clean rooms, a cozy atmosphere, complimentary tea or coffee, shared Western toilets, and ice-cold *mandi*. The most popular is **Subandi,** as Mr. Subandi is an excellent source of information. (Doubles with or without private *mandi* and Western toilet Rp20,000 per person. Breakfast Rp5000, dinner Rp10,000). Down the road, **Darmin and Wandi s** offer rooms with shared *mandi* and Western toilet for Rp15,000 per person. If you want to eat out, **Ojo Lall** across from the tiger statue, makes great *bakso* noodle soup with meatballs and all the fixins for Rp3000. (open daily 7am-9pm).

Several *losmen* and restaurants dot Pelompek, but the real getaways are up the hill at the park border, near Sungai Jernih village. 150m from the PHPA hut, **Losmen Mt. Solok,** with bundles of sweet cinnamon downstairs, is a prime spot for hikers who want to get an early start to Danau Gunung Tujuh. (Rooms Rp10,000 negotiable per person; meals Rp4000.)

SIGHTS. The sprawling 5000 hectares of the **PTP Nusantara-VI tea plantation** yield 18 tons of black tea daily, most of which is exported to Europe. (Complimentary tours 7am-5pm. Rp2000 tip recommended.) A force of 3200 workers collects leaves in the fields.

Ensconced in dense virgin jungle, **Danau Gunung Tujuh,** at 1996m, is the highest freshwater lake in Southeast Asia. Travelers can hike from Pelompek to marvel at the seven mountains from which the lake takes its name, or to take a dip in its icy waters. A guide is helpful but not needed for the 7km hike from Sungai Jernih village. From the end of the asphalt road at Sungai Jernih (2km east of Pelompek), a gate marks the park's entrance. Buy your permit at the PHPA hut (Rp1500) and follow the path, making sure not to take the turn-off to the left at the bridge 1km up. Grab a walking stick, and remember to take snacks, water, rain gear, insect repellent, and a sweater. **Telun Berasap Waterfall** cascades off the mountain into a pool 50m below. (Rp500.) From Pelompek, catch a northbound bus 4km to **Letter** village (Rp500); the waterfall is 300m away. Guides (preferably HPI-licensed) are available for all activities and charge Rp70,000 per day.

CLIMBING KERINCI. Take a guide for the two-day climb up Gunung Kerinci. As recently as 1999, an experienced Swiss climber disappeared on the mountain. The first day of hiking is not strenuous—about six hours through the tea plantation to the park boundary (Permits Rp1500 at the PPA hut here), climbing up through the jungle to Camp 2, a shelter at 3000m. The final steep ascent to the summit can be accomplished in the morning, when there's the greatest chance of clear skies. Sleeping bags can be rented in Kersik Tua for Rp10,000 per night, and guides run Rp70,000 per day. The weather at high altitudes can be freezing and fickle (snow or hail is possible), so climbers should take warm clothes, a sleeping bag, and a large supply of water, as there may be no sources for replenishment on the trail.

PULAU BINTAN

Three times the size of Singapore, but with only a fraction of its population, the majority of Pulau Bintan remains largely undeveloped, replacing skyscrapers with rain forests and quiet white sand beaches lined with palm trees. The locals seem to know one another and coexist peacefully despite the evenly proportioned practice of Islam, Hinduism, Christianity, Buddhism, and Kong Hochu. Many stay in Tanjung Pinang to access the Buddhist temples in Senggarang or Pulau Penyengat, a popular pilgrimage site for Malays. Others head to Trikora Beach to pretend they're on a deserted island, many with success. Hotel prices are steep in the posh Bintan resorts, but most Singaporeans come anyway, bringing their families to Trikora Beach for the weekend to fish and break some of the rules of their hometown.

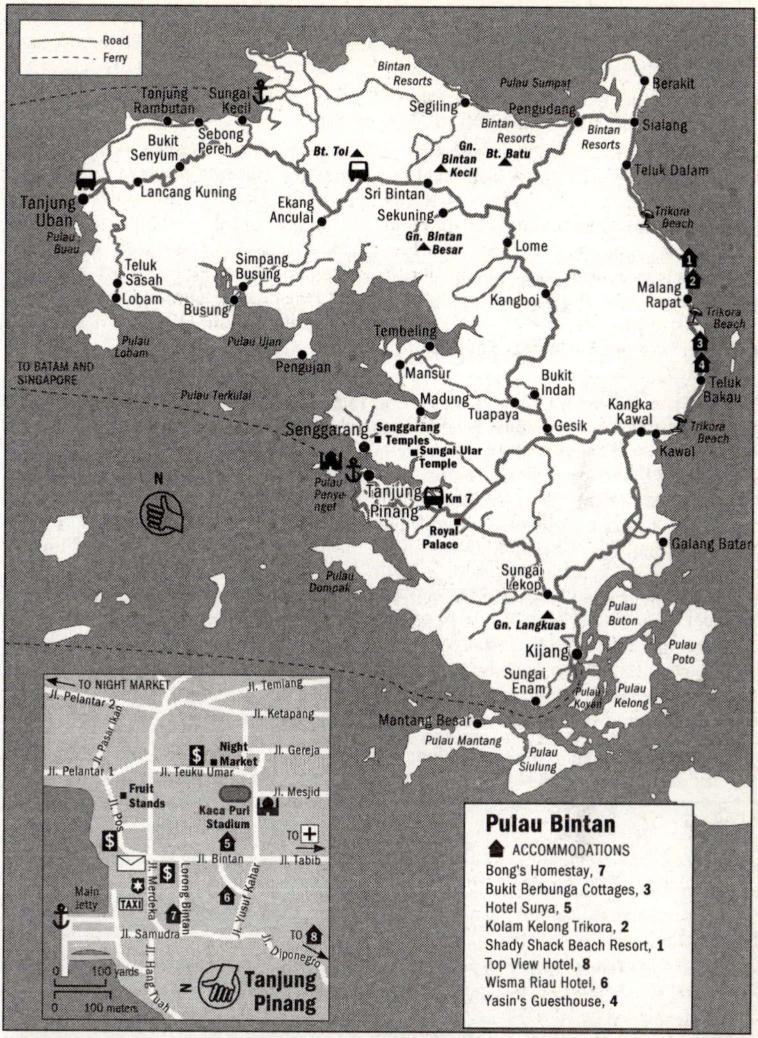

THE VIEW FROM ABOVE

Main cities: Tanjung Pinang, Senggarang, Kijang, Tanjung Uban.
Highlights: Pulau Penyenget, Trikora Beach.
Something Fun: Snorkeling at Pulau Bralas, Tanjung Pinang's water village.

TANJUNG PINANG ☎0771

Home to many services on Pulau Bintan, Tanjung Pinang is primarily a gateway city, but also boasts an intriguing water village and nearby temples.

TRANSPORTATION

Ferries: Ferry schedule and prices vary with season. Check with travel agents around the port exit on Jl. Merdeka. To: **Singapore** (1½hr.; 10 per day 7am-6:40pm; Rp120,000-200,000, round-trip Rp150,000-260,000). Exit tax to Singapore is Rp15,000.

Buses: The **bus terminal** is best reached by taxi (20min., Rp30,000). From here, buses circle travel northwest towards **Tanjung Uban** (every 30min. until 3am, Rp12,000) via **Bt. Toi** (Rp10,000).

Taxis: Bargain upon getting off the jetty for fares to **Kijang** (Rp30,000-50,000 per car/bus) or **Trikora Beach** (Rp70,000-80,000 per car).

Boat Rental: To get to **Pulau Penyenget,** face away from the docks and go to the jetty on the very left. Pick up a **motorboat** to **Senggarang** from Jl. Pelantar I by the water (Rp150,000 per 2-3hr. trip). **Pulau Batam speedboats** leave from the main pier (every 30min. until 4:30pm, Rp90,000-100,000) and **Tanjung Uban** (Rp60,000-80,000).

Local Transportation: Honking **minibuses** abound. Within the city Rp500, past Km5 mark Rp2000. **Motorcycle rental** Rp70,000-80,000 per day, includes helmet, which is required by law. Motorcycle "taxis" may also be hitched for Rp5000 per ½ kilometer.

ORIENTATION AND PRACTICAL INFORMATION

Ferries from Singapore dock at the port in **Tanjung Pinang** or north of the island at **Bintan Resort. Pulau Penyenget** is offshore to the west. **Trikora Beach** hugs the east coast, but is cut off from ferry ports by lack of transportation. Development will soon bring resorts to the entire northern coast of Pulau Bintan. Upon arrival at **Bandar Bintan Telani** (BBT) in Bintan Resort, take a **taxi** to the resort area (US$3). Getting to Tanjung Pinang is more difficult. From the drop-off point, take a bus to the **bus terminal** (2hr., Rp40,000), and a minibus onward to Tanjung Pinang (Rp10,000).

In Tanjung Pinang, most travelers arrive at the main pier on the east end. Down the pier past the dock offices is **Jl. Merdeka,** which runs east-west from the arch near the pier to the fruit market. Walking through the Merdeka intersection leads to **Jl. Bintan.** Parallel to the east is **Jl. Teuku Umar,** home to the night market. **Jl. Pos** begins opposite Jl. Bintan, close to the post office, and curls by the wharves. The **police station** and **bus terminal** outside of town are accessible by minibus (Rp1000).

Currency Exchange: Bank Negara Indonesia, Jl. Teuku Umar 630 (☎214 32). Cashes traveler's checks. Open M-F 8am-6:15pm, Sa 8:30-11:30am. **Moneychangers** are near the Jl. Pos and Jl. Merdeka intersection. Open daily 8am-8pm. Many s will also accept Singaporean dollars.

Police: ☎311 10. At Km5 Jl. Ahmad Yani. There is a **police box** at the corner of Jl. Merdeka and Jl. Ketapang.

Medical Services: Along Jl. Sudirman, in the south of the city or in the General or Navy Hospitals near the Top View Hotel.

Telephones: Telkom office (☎281 83), on Jl. Hang Tuah. Follow the road to your right from the main pier near the large waterfront seashell statue. Long distance 24hr.

Post Offices: GPO on Jl. Katamso, 3km out of town. *Poste Restante.* Open M-Th and Sa 8am-2pm, F 8am-11pm. Another office is at the corner of Jl. Pos and Jl. Merdeka, 100m through the west arch on the left. Open M-Sa 8am-8pm, Su 8am-1pm. **Postal code:** 29111.

ACCOMMODATIONS AND FOOD

Hotel Laut Jaya, Jl. Plantar II No. 98, has a view of the beautiful **water village** and is next to the best night market in town. All rooms have A/C and include breakfast. (☎62 771. Standard S$20; deluxe S$25.) **Top View Hotel,** Jl. Ciptadi No. 3, is a hilltop hotel with a restaurant, karaoke lounge, laundry service and swimming pool. All rooms have A/C and include breakfast. (☎24 221. Standard S$32; deluxe S$42; S$3 more on weekends.) The **Wisma Riau Hotel,** Jl. Yusuf Kahar No. 8, is a bit dark but the rooms are spacious and have A/C and TV. (☎21 023. Standard Rp95,000; double Rp130,000. Breakfast included.) Cheap dorms abound in Tanjung Pinang. **Hotel Surya,** Jl. Bintan 49, combines a hotel atmosphere with hostel prices. It gets packed on weekends, so its best to make a reservation before walking over. (☎21 811. Rp30,000, with A/C Rp50,000.) **Bong's**, Lorong Bintan II 20, at the end of the alley, is a family-run place with a comfortable kitchen. Rooms have dipper baths and no sinks. (☎22 605. Dorms Rp15,000; doubles Rp28,000.)

If you don't find the local chicken heart and beef lung curry appetizing, it's best to head to the **night markets,** open from 7pm to 2am. Try the one on Jl Delantar 2, easily the most serene. Opposite Bank Degong Negara on Jl. Teuka Umar, and on Jl. Ganbir, three blocks up Jl. Merdeka, plenty of options exist to appease taste-buds, such as Malay satay, *mie goreng* (Rp5000), and *gado gado* (Rp4000).

SIGHTS

One of the truly amazing sights of Tanjung Pinang is the **water village** found at the north end of the town, down Jl. Pasar Ikan or Jl. Pasar. The rickety boardwalk is unsafe and best avoided at night. The water village is only visible in the daytime, anyway. **Senggarang,** home of impressive 200-year-old Buddhist temples and colorful modern statues, can be reached by motorboat (2hr., Rp150,000) from the fishing village on stilts at Jl Pelantar I.

DAYTRIP FROM TANJUNG PINANG

PULAU PENYENGET

Catch a motorboat (10min., Rp10,000-15,000) from the pier to the left of the middle pier when you are facing Tanjung Pinang. On Pulau Penyenget, the pier is off Jl. Pos, hidden opposite the bank. The boats drop anchor at Penyenget jetty.

Pulau Penyenget, the seat of the Riau *rajah*'s far-flung kingdom for hundreds of years, is Bintan's greatest treasure. Just beyond the jetty shines **Mesjid Raya Sultan Riau,** a 178-year-old mosque. Jl. Ahmadi, to the left of this mosque, leads to the **Raja Ali Grave.** Directly past this grave, is the **Tengku Bilik Building** and the **Raja Jakfar Grave,** the oldest building on the island. The **tomb of Rajah Abdurrachman** is 100m to the right, and the **island fort,** the highest point on the island, is directly behind the tomb. The path then winds through the quiet **Rajah Ali's palace,** abandoned this century. Go farther down the track to the road's end and take a right to get to the modern **Riau palace.** Pilgrims travel here to venerate the royal internments of **Rajah Ali Jajai,** writer of the first Malay grammar, who received the isle as her dowry.

INDONESIA

NEAR TANJUNG PINANG

TRIKORA

About 45km from Tanjung Pinang, Trikora is a smooth white sand beach that's always breezy. Travelers often come here in twos—especially when the rainy season hits the beaches of Southern Thailand. To the east of Trikora Beach, sand and snorkeling is the name of the game at **Pulau Bralas** (25-30min. by boat). Resort owners have friends with boats who make the rounds (S$5 per person). To get to Trikora Beach, rent a taxi from Tanjung Pinang (2hr., Rp70,000-100,000).

For those who've ever found the term "oceanfront property" appealing, **Shady Shack Beach Resort's** water-practically-under-your-feet bungalows will be a dream come true. The water is particularly clean and optimal for swimming. The owner is friendly and speaks fluent English. (Breakfast included. Rp60,000. S$ accepted.) Although the entire facility is on the water, **Kolam Kelong Trikora** is set up with a television, telephone, plumbing, and a view of distant floating fishermen's houses. They also are famous for their Chinese-style seafood dishes. (☎312 645. Single S$15; double S$20.) **Yasin's Guest House** (☎267 70) has sturdy beds. Try to stay in bungalow #7, which is built on stilts over the water. The **Bukit Berbunga Cottages** are right next door. Bungalows with sleeping lofts and mosquito nets are complete with bathrooms and bucket shower are Rp60,000 a night. The pool table and open air bar promise good times at night. **BBC Restaurant** serves breakfast and offers huts with inside dipper bath and toilet for S$10. (Open daily 8am-midnight.)

SOUTHERN SUMATRA

BENGKULU ☎0736

Though Bengkulu's June 2000 earthquake claimed over a hundred lives, this resilient city is slowly coming back to life. Fortunately, most of the damage occurred on the outskirts of the town, leaving the city itself as a relaxing respite for the frenzied traveler. Whether hunting for rafflesia (discovered in Bengkulu in 1818) or enjoying the uncrowded beaches and crushed-ice drinks, travelers will appreciate the atmosphere in southern Sumatra's mellowest city.

TRANSPORTATION

Flights: Padang Kemiling airport, 14km east of city, is accessible via yellow *angkot* minibus or taxi (Rp10,000). To: **Jakarta** (daily 12:40pm; Rp584,400). **Merpati,** Jl. Sudirman 246 (☎271 11), at the Hotel Samudera Dwinka. Open M-F 8am-4:30pm, Sa-Su 9am-1pm. Travel agents such as **C.S.H.'88** (See **Orientation,** below) also book flights at the same prices.

Buses: Inter-provincial buses stop at **Terminal Panorama,** 7km from town. Private companies, mostly on Jl. Haryono, have A/C buses to **Bukit Tinggi** (18hr.; 10am, 1pm, Rp30,000; 2pm, Rp50,000) via **Padang** (16hr.); **Jakarta** (24hr., 10am, Rp115,000); **Jogjakarta** (28hr., 1pm, Rp72,000); **Medan** (48hr., 10am, Rp161,000); **Palembang** (14hr.; 3pm, 4pm; Rp50-60,000).

ORIENTATION AND PRACTICAL INFORMATION

The town's main road runs southeast to northwest, changing names from **Jl. S. Parman** to **Jl. Suprapto** at the gray BNI Bank boat sculpture. At the **Mesjid Jamik** it changes again to **Jl. Sudirman,** then weaves west as **Jl. Yani** past a square (with a tall obelisk), Fort Malboboro, and Kampung Cine. **Jl. Haryono** heads northeast at the intersection with Mesjid Jamik. The **beach** is on the southwest coast—just follow the signs for the Hotel Horison.

Tourist Office: Dinas Pariwisata ("Bengkulu Government Tourist Office"), Jl. Tendean (☎212 72). Not really worth the trek. Open M-Th 7:30am-2pm, F 7:30am-noon, Sa 7:30am-1pm.

Tours: G.T. Sanindo Wisata, Jl. Haryono 73 (☎275 22), next to Hotel Vista and **CSH '88,** Jl. Suprapto 88 (☎223 85) can help you with bus and flight details. Both open M-Sa 8am-4pm, Su 8am-2pm.

Currency Exchange: Bank BII, Jl. Suprapto 205 (☎344 100), changes money and accepts AmEx Traveler's Cheques. Open M-F 8am-3pm. **ATMs** abound on Jl. Suprato.

Markets: Pasar Minggu, extends off Jl. Suprapto onto Jl. Abidin. Cruising mobile food carts feature fresh produce and cheap *martabak*. **Baru Koto,** near Fort Marlboro on Jl. A. Yani, sports a number of cheap *sate* and juice stands.

Police: ☎221 10. Opposite the obelisk on Jl. A. Yani 1.

Pharmacies: Apotik Purnama, Jl. Suprapto 4 (☎262 86). Open daily 8am-9pm.

Medical Services: Rafflesia Hospital, Jl. Mahoni 10 (☎217 10). From Mesjid Jamik, turn left 150m after the BNI boat. It's another 150m on the right. Very friendly staff and sterile facilities.

Telephones: Telkom office, Jl. Suprapto 132 (☎211 08). International calls. **No HCD.** Open 24hr.

Internet: There are a number of places up Jl. S. Parman charging about Rp5000 per hr. **Warnet,** Jl. S. Parman 21, next to BNI 100m up from the boat statue is one. Open daily 8am-10pm. Rp5400 per hour gets a "bonus" soda.

Post Offices: GPO, Jl. A. Yani 38, near Ft. Marlboro. Open M-F 8am-3pm, Sa 8am-noon. **Postal code:** 38000.

ACCOMMODATIONS AND FOOD

Bengkulu offers the full spectrum of accommodations, from dirt-cheap *losmen* to friendly, family-run hotels to swank beach resorts. Hot, muggy weather makes it worthwhile to invest in some mosquito coils or A/C.

Hotel Vista, Jl. Haryono 67 (☎208 20). Spotless rooms. All rooms open onto balconies that get glorious morning light. Doubles with fan and *mandi* Rp22,000; with A/C, TV, and breakfast Rp55,000.

Wisma Balai Buntan, Jl. Khadijah 122 (☎212 54). Run by a friendly lady with good English and better advice. Enormous rooms and plenty of natural light. All rooms include A/C, private *mandi* with Western toilet, and breakfast. Singles Rp35,000; doubles with hot shower Rp45,000; extra bed Rp12,500.

Losmen Surya, Jl. Abidin 26 (☎213 41), near Pasar Minggu. A host of *warung* set up outside every evening. All rooms with clean, shared *mandi* Rp15,000. Treat yourself to a rented electric fan (Rp1000).

Losmen Hyani, Jl. Parman 5 (☎207 18). A colorful building when lit, a 10min. *microlet* ride from the action of Fort Marlborough. All rooms have fans with smallish shared *mandi*. Doubles Rp10,000, with big clean *mandi* Rp30,000; triples Rp15,000.

Permata Gading Resort, Jl. Pantai Nala 133 (☎218 55). Each cottage's deck faces an empty beach 50m away. Breakfast and tax included. Restaurant features typical *padang* fare. Doubles with *mandi*, Western toilet, A/C Rp80,000.

In Bengkulu, you are never far from a refreshing *es pokat*, a smooth and creamy blend of avocado and ice. Other local specialties are *bakso*, a meatball and noodle soup; and *martabak*, a gooey sort of pancake that comes in two varieties: sweet (cheese and sugar) or meat (beef and onions). The best *martabak* are on **Jl. Sudirman** near Mesjid Jamik and on **Jl. Abidin** after 6pm (Rp5000-8000).

Many restaurants and bakeries can be found on **Jl. Suprapto** in the center of town. **Sri Solo,** Jl. Suprapto 117, offers a wide selection of Indonesian food (Rp3000-5000), in addition to *es pokat* and fresh fruit drinks. (Open daily 7:30am-9:30pm.) Another source of cheap sustenance is **Pasar Barn Koto,** where Rp4000 will buy you a plate of chicken *sates* and *kaching* (rice cakes) doused in peanut sauce. **Roti Holland**, Jl. Suprapto 124, has deliciously sticky pastries. (Open daily 8am-9pm.) **Sari Rasa**, Jl. A. Yani 329B, near Wisma Balai Buntan, has an exciting Chinese menu. Try the fried frogs legs or the crab omelette. (Rp20,000. Open daily 8am-9pm.)

SIGHTS

Bengkulu's claim to fame is the **rafflesia,** the world's largest flower. Depictions of the flower are found all over, but those hoping for the real thing should head to the **PHPA office** (Dept. of Forestry), Jl. Mahoni 11 (☎216 97), opposite the Rafflesia hospital, which can tell you where to look. Rafflesia typically bloom briefly during July and August and can be up to a meter or more across. The **Mesjid Jamik,** an unspectacular red-roofed mosque considered spectacular because it was designed by the engineer-turned-president Sukarno, is in downtown Bengkulu, where Jl. Sudirman and Jl. Suprapto meet. To the southeast is **Negeri (Bengkulu Museum),** on Jl. Pembangunan, which houses a bizarre collection of hatchets, coral, and doll houses. (☎220 98. Open Su and Tu-Th 8am-1pm, F 8-10:30am, Sa 8am-noon.) North of Mesjid Jamik, at the intersection of Jl. Berlian and Jl. A. Yani, intact **Fort Marlborough** has a commanding view of the sea. (Open daily 8am-5pm. Rp1000.) Completed in 1719, it's the second-oldest British fort in the East after Fort George in India. Abutting the fort to the west, **Kampung Cina** (Chinatown), the oldest section of the city, was demolished during the February 1998 riots. Now almost completely reconstructed by its ethnic Chinese inhabitants, Kampung Cina spreads out behind Pasar Baru Koto by the sea (look for the remains of red-roofed buildings). The hill behind Fort Marlborough is a great place to go to watch the sunset. Heading south from Mesjid Jamik on Jl. Suprapto, then west on Jl. Soekaino-Hatta, leads to **Rumah Bung Karno** (Brother Karno's Home), where Sukarno served in Dutch-imposed exile from 1938 to 1941. (Open 8am-5pm. Rp1000.) 100m farther up on the left is the massive, pristinely white **Mesjid Agung.** Continuing west from the Jl. Hasan and Sentoso intersection leads to the **Hamilton Monument,** a memorial to a Mr. Hamilton, who died for the British cause. From here, Bengkulu's prime beaches are within walking distance.

BEACHES

The 1.8km **Pantai Panjang** is empty except for fishermen. Large surf and sharp coral can make swimming dangerous. To swim, try 1km south of the Horison Hotel, or just fake it and dip in the **Horison Hotel's pool** (Rp4500 for the whole day.) Farther south of the hotel is **Pasir Putih Beach,** near Pulau Baai Harbor, 19km away. The harbor is the departure point for bi-weekly ship service to the villages of **Enggano Island.** To stay on the island, contact the *kepala desa* (village head) upon arrival, as is the only option. The **Samudera Dwinka Hotel,** Jl. Sudirman 246 (☎216 04), opposite Mesjid Jamik, arranges boats to **Pulau Tikus** (Rat Island) for up to ten people (Rp300,000 per person), with diving and snorkeling.

MARKETS

Pasar Minggu is a delicious, dirt-floored den of life. All sorts of animal products—each at various stages of life and death—are sold here and the smell is kind of hard not to notice. The Jl. Abidin end of the market comes alive at sunset. (Open daily 8am-5pm.) **Pasar Baru Koto,** at the edge of Chinatown off J.L. Yani, has an outdoor department store feel to it by day and sells many ordinary wares. If you're looking for Wellington boots or toddler-sized British football outfits, you're going to be a happy shopper. At night, the entrance fills with *martabah*, *sate*, and *paday* vendors, all offering *es pokat* drinks on the side.

BANDAR LAMPUNG ☎0721

The capital of Lampung Province and a bustling transportation hub, Bandar Lampung provides an easy rest stop between the rest of Sumatra and Jakarta. Comprised of the port city, Teluk Betung, and its hillside neighbor, Tanjung Karang, this urban region is known for its distinctive "ship cloth" tapestries and *tapis* sarongs, embroidered with gold and silver thread. Its proximity to many nearby natural attractions, including Way Kambas Elephant Training Center, and the infamous Krakatau, the island-volcano that demolished Telukbetung in 1883, make it an ideal exploration point. Every July, the people of Lampung attempt to appease the volcano gods with traditional Lampung dances and music, along with parades, races, car rallies, and a running/boating biathlon.

TRANSPORTATION

Flights: Radin Inten II Airport, 24km north of town. Take a public DAMRI bus near Rajabasa bus station (Rp900-1000) or spend 5min. in a purple *angkot* bound for Teluk Betung. **Herodiza Taksi** offers door-to-door service to Radin Inten (Rp50,000). **Mer-**

THAT WAS MY FOOD DOWN BELOW, COMING UP TO SAY HELLO! The international sport of hurling is widely practiced in Indonesia. Played since prehistoric times, the game tests mankind's oldest reflex by vomiting out his latest meal and sharing with others around him. Nowhere in the world is the sport more popular than on buses in the mountains of Sumatra where youngsters do their nation proud as they "go internal for Indonesia." Power is the name of the game so be careful not to get in the way. The sport's only (optional) accessory is the black plastic bag. Often distributed free on buses, its use contributes to hurling's finesse by adding a tangible accuracy factor (T.A.F.) to the more basic force factor (F.F.) Travelers anxious that they not "barf for Britain" are advised to request a window seat–*"boleh saya duduk dekat jendela"*–as watching the outside would help prevent dizziness, thus decreasing the F.F. to below ignition levels. If this doesn't work, and "spewing for Spain" seems likely, *"saya sukah muntah"* to let your neighbor know that it's your turn.

pati, Jl. Diponegoro 189 (☎268 466), at Jl. A. Yani, sells tickets to **Jakarta** (40min., 3pm, Rp428,200). Open M-F 8am-4:30pm, Sa-Su 8am-1pm.

Trains: Stasium Tanjung Karang, Jl. Kotaraja 1. Ticket office (☎262 854). Open daily 7am-9pm. Trains to **Palembang** (8hr., 3 per day, Rp10,000-60,000) via **Baturaja.**

Buses: Rajabasa, 25min. north via light blue *mikrolet.* Buses to and from anywhere in Sumatra and Java pass through Bandar Lampung. To: **Bahanheri** (2hr., every 30min., Rp5600); **Baturaja** (6hr., many per day, Rp135,000); **Bengkulu** (18hr., 7pm, Rp55,000); **Jakarta** (7hr.; many per day; Rp30,000, A/C Rp50,000); **Jambi** (16hr., 5 per day, Rp35,000); **Medan** (48hr.; many per day; Rp120,000, A/C Rp210,000); **Padang** (20hr.; 4pm, Rp80,000; A/C 7pm, Rp150,000); **Palembang,** (8-12hr., 5 per day, Rp20,000; A/C 3pm, Rp115,000).

Ferries: Run to and from **Jakarta** and other points on Java to **Bahanheri,** 90km southeast of Bandar Lampung. Ask tour operators in Bandar Lampung for details. Smaller faster boats also run passengers (45min., every hr., Rp15,000).

Local Transportation: *Angkot* or "mobiles" ably zip around the city: **purple** (Tanjungkarang to Teluk Betung); **green** (Tanjung Karang to Garuntang); **red** (Kemiling to Bambukuning); and **blue** (Tanjung Karang to Rajabasa Bus Terminal). Rp750-1250 depending on the length of your trip. If you know where you are going, public DAMRI buses (Rp500-650) are more comfortable. The main station is next to the train station at the corner of Jl. Kotaraja and Jl. Raden Intan.

Taxis: All over town. For door-to-door service, try **Herodiza Taksi** (☎270 139).

ORIENTATION AND PRACTICAL INFORMATION

The bus terminal and airport are north of the city. The **train station** is down the road from cheap accommodations on **Jl. Kotaraja,** which intersects **Jl. Kartini,** the main drag, in the center of **Tanjung Karang.** Jl. Kartini runs north-south and changes into **Jl. Teuku Umar** farther north and to **Jl. Monginsidi** in the south. **Jl. Diponegoro** runs from Tanjung Karang towards Teluk Betung.

Tourist Office: Kantor BKPMD, Jl. J. Sudirman 29 (☎261 430), can be reached via green *angkot.* Maps, brochures, and English speaking staff. Open M-Sa 7am-3:30pm.

Tours: Many tour agencies offer expensive trips to Way Kambus, Way Kanan, Krakatau, and more. **Elendra Tours and Travel,** Jl. Sultan Agung 32 (☎704 737), is open M-F 8am-9pm.

Currency Exchange: Banks with **ATMs** are everywhere. For currency exchange, try **Bank BNI,** Jl. Teuku Umar 17 (☎252 145). Open M-F 8:30am-2:30pm.

Markets: Bambu Kuning Plaza, on Jl. Imam Bonjol, offers fresh mangoes, American films, and everything in between. **Tanjung Karang Plaza,** a slightly glitzier version, 1km down Jl. Kartini, offers McD's, cinemas, and tackola. **Pasar Seni,** Jl. Majapahit, features local artwork and *batik.* Not really much of a *market* but live music and a grassy softball diamond make it a nice place to chill. At night, **Teluk Betung's Pasar Mambo** at Jl. Malahayti and Jl. Hasanudin is renowned for its seafood and porridge. Well worthwhile. Open daily 6pm-1am. To return to Jl. Kartini, take a DAMRI bus on Jl. Malahayti.

Pharmacy: Apotik Tanjung Karang, Jl. Buhttinggi 12. Opposite the telephone office, walk 1 block up from the **police** on the right. Open daily 8am-11pm.

Police: ☎253 283. At Jl. Kartini and Jl. Imam Bonjol, by the overpass.

Medical Services: RS Dr. H. Abdul Moeloek, Jl. Dr. Rivai (☎703 312), 2km down Jl. Tenku Umar in a blue *angkot.*

Telephones: Wartel, in the Telkom building on Jl. Bukit Tinggi, past the police station. Open daily 7am-11pm. **Information** ☎255 108.

Internet Access: Internet cafe's are dotted around town within a 10min. walk of hotels. They tend to close early if empty. **Fajar Net,** Jl. Raden Intan 61. Rp100 per min. Free soft drink. Open daily 8am-midnight. **Indo Internet,** Jl. Kartini 134, 600m up from Hotel Miri on the left. Rp4000 per hr. Open daily 8am-9pm. **Warnet @ 4000,** Jl. Kartini 20, opposite Tanjung Karang Plaza. Rp4000 per hr. Open daily 8am-8pm. Also available at the main **post office** (see below).

Post Office: GPO, Jl. A. Dahlan 21. Take a green *mikrolet.* Open M-Sa 8am-6pm. Also at Jl. Kotaraja, off Jl. Kartini, open M-Sa 9am-5pm. **Postal code:** 35111.

ACCOMMODATIONS AND FOOD

Affordable accommodations cluster in the center of Tanjung Karang. From the bus terminal, take a light-blue *mikrolet* into town, and get dropped off at the intersection of Jl. Kartini and Jl. Kotaraja (by the rotary with the gray marble obelisk) or at a hotel. The cheapest accommodations lie along **Jl. Kotaraja.** Those on **Jl. Kartini** and **Jl. Raden Intan** cater to local businessmen and excel in cleanliness and comfort. Arrive early or call ahead as cheaper rooms fill up first.

Lampung Inn, Jl. W. Monginsidi 178 (☎471 674), 3km south of Bambu Kuning after Jl. Mongsidi goes down a hill. It's near the bottom on the left. Rickety-looking but has tidy rooms with *mandi* and fan. Garden sitting area. Doubles Rp35,000.

Hotel Mini, Jl. Dwi Warna 71 (☎255 928), off Jl. Kartini. Walk 1 block north of Bambu Kuning. Free tea/coffee. Clean rooms with private *mandi* Rp27,500.

Hotel Ria, Jl. Kartini 79, near Hotel Mini. Comfy beds. Clean shared *mandi.* Small breakfast. Rooms with A/C and *mandi* Rp68,000.

Losmen Gunung Sari, Jl. Kotaraja 21 (☎252 072), near the mosque. Rooms a little shabby, *mandi* a bit dark. Decent overall feel. It's a cheapie. Singles Rp15,000.

Bakeries with names like "Roti French, London, and European" abound on Jl. Kartini and Jl. Pamuda. For later-day fare, head to the side streets and curbs off of Jl. Kartini, where many *warung* and *padang* restaurants cluster, including the local favorite, **Kamang,** on Jl. Dwi Warma, past Hotel Mini. Fruit and *martabak* (warm, peanut butter-filled pancake) stands are plentiful around Bambu Kuning Plaza. The marvelously tacky **Garuda Restaurant,** Jl. Kartini 31, just before Tanjung Karang Plaza offers *padang* plates (Rp3000-8000) and a juice bar. (Open daily 7am-10pm.) Down Jl. Mongsidi 44B, **Rumah Mahari Shinta** supplies *padang,* softdrinks and a clean, quiet atmosphere.

DAYTRIPS FROM BANDAR LAMPUNG

Reaching sights and beaches by public transportation can be frustrating. A more comfortable but pricier way to see the area is through a tour operator.

The tour to Krakatau, through the Hotel Beringin in **Kalianda,** visits **Pulau Sebesi, Sebuku,** and **Harimau,** a few of the islands dotting Lampung Bay. Those averse to group travel can try the traditional boats, which leave from **Canti,** a small town 10km from the Bakauheni port, and travel to Sebesi. Accommodations are available in Canti. **Pasir Putih,** a small, delightful beach with pricey hotels looking out to **Pulau Condong,** sits idle just southeast of Bandar Lampung. All these sights are accessible on the Rajabasa-Bakauheni bus.

The **Way Kambas National Park and Elephant Training Center,** a 2hr. drive northeast of the city, is where wild elephants are tamed. It also harbors Sumatran tigers and rhinos. To the dismay of the tigers, camping is prohibited. It is possible to stay in bungalows (doubles Rp30,000-40,000) and play Hannibal for a day with an elephant-powered jaunt through the jungle. The nearby **Way Kanan River** shelters 258 documented species of Sumatra's most exotic feathered friends. To the west, **Bukit Barisan** (Marching Hills) sprawls spine-like on the coast. To get there, take a bus to Metro, and then onward to **Way Jepara.** Get dropped off on the way and finish by *mobile* or *ojek*. **Bukit Barisan National Park** begins at the southernmost tip at Tampang, and climbs up the west coast. Travelers can explore the **Danau Menjukut** area by boat from Kota Agung to Tampang, or use the camping area near **Wonsobo. Krui,** near the border with Bengkulu Province, neighbors surfing beaches. Take a bus through **Liwa** (6hr.) to reach the beautiful and secluded **Danau Ranau. Pugang Raharjo Archaeological Site** houses megaliths from a Buddhist period in the 12th to 17th centuries. It can be reached from Talang Padian.

PALEMBANG ☎0711

Sumatra's second largest city, Palembang is caught in the endless struggle to hold onto its rich cultural heritage while establishing itself as a modern urban center. A historical capital of Hindu, Buddhist, and Muslim kingdoms, every Sunday traditional wedding ceremonies all over town showcase the music, dance, and costumes of the Sriwijaya kingdom; in the same neighborhoods plagued by big-city problems of crime and danger. Nowhere is Palembang's identity better exemplified than at the traditional market Pasar 16, where merchants from throughout the region come to peddle their wares amid gangsters, pickpockets, and middle-class shoppers.

TRANSPORTATION

Flights: Sultan Mahmud Badaruddin II Airport, known as "Talang Betutu," can be reached by taking a yellow bus up Jl. Sudirman to Km 12, and then switching to a grey airport *angkot*. If you're decent at bargaining, a taxi runs about Rp20,000. **Garuda,** Jl. Kapten A. Rivai 35 (☎315 333), flies to **Jakarta** (1hr., 5 per day, Rp456,800). **Merpati,** Jl. Kapten A. Rivai 6193 (☎37 23 66), also flies to Jakarta (2 per day, Rp405,000) and other domestic destinations. **Pelangi,** Jl. Let. Kol. Iskandar 201 (☎355 669), 100m up from the Internasional Plaza on the left, plies the same route (M, W, Sa 4pm; US$142).

Trains: The **Kertapadi train station** sits across the river from downtown Palembang, at the end of the yellow bus line. Take the "Tanjong Karang" train to **Bandar Lampung** (7hr., 3 per day, Rp26,000-62,000).

Buses: Private bus companies line Jl. Kol Atmo. To: **Bandau Lampung** (2pm; Rp40,000, A/C Rp80,000); **Baturaja** (4hr., 10am, Rp12,500); **Bukit Tinggi** (14hr., Rp110,000); **Dumai** (2pm; Rp70,000, A/C Rp85,000); **Medan** (32hr., 2pm, Rp130,000) via **Padang** (13hr., Rp110,000); **Jakarta** (19hr.; several per day; Rp55,000, A/C Rp95,000-110,000); **Jambi** (2pm; Rp25,000, A/C Rp45,000).

Ferries: Take a red Pusri-bound bus to Bombaru to catch a ferry to **Bantam** (10hr.; Tu, Th, Sa; Rp250,000) or **Mentok** (3hr., daily 7am, Rp40,000).

Local Transportation: Color-coded *angkot* minibuses and larger buses run all over the city (Rp700). The yellow bus runs from Kertapati to Ampera Bridge to Km12 on Jl. Sudirman. To call a taxi, try **Sriwijaya** (☎815 555).

ORIENTATION AND PRACTICAL INFORMATION

Palembang's main drag is **Jl. Sudirman,** which runs northwest from the **Ampera Bridge** where it passes over **Pasar Enamblas** and the **Mesjid Agung** in the center of town. Sights and neighborhoods along Jl. Sudirman are indexed by their distance from the bridge in kilometers. The neighborhood near **Kamboja,** at Km3.5, is a safe, large student community centered around the nearby university. Just before Kamboja, Jl. Sudirman intersects **Jl. Letkol Iskandar,** which is home to several decently priced hotels. Completing a "V" with Jl. Sudirman and Jl. Ishandar, **Jl. Kolonel Atmo** is home to travel agents and bus companies. Further up Jl. Sudirman, **Jl. Kaplen A. Rivai** is a relatively safe and quiet street, with pricey hotels that offer an alternative to the madness of downtown Palembang. Across Jl. Sudirman, it becomes **Jl. Veteran.** Be careful in Palembang at night, especially near Pasar 16 or the Musi River.

Tourist Offices: Jl. Sultan M. Badarrudin 1 (☎358 450). At the **Museum Sultan Mahmud Badaruddin,** 150m before the Mesjid Agung, behind the huge concrete monument with an eagle on it. Some English-speaking help, maps, and a great free publication about the area. Open M-F 8am-4pm. If closed, ask around for Mr. Abi Sofyan.

Tours: PT Nikita, Jl. Kol Atmo 576D (☎368 417). Books plane and ferry tickets and is near bus companies. Open M-F 8am-5pm, Sa 8am-4pm, Su 9am-noon.

Currency Exchange: Bank BCA, Jl. Kapten A. Rivai 22 (☎31 22 44). Open M-F 7:30am-2:30pm.

Markets: Pasar 16 *(Enambelas),* along the river near Ampera Bridge. **Pasar Cinde,** on Jl. Sudirman at the intersection with Jl. Kol. Atmo. **International Plaza,** Jl. Sudirman 147, with 6 stories of shops and an American cinema.

Police: POLDA statran (☎350 404), up at Km5.5 on Jl. Sudirman.

Pharmacies: Apotik Aldo, Jl. Sudirman 1269 (☎374 933).

Medical Services: Hospital Charitas, Jl. Sudirman 1054 at intersection with Jl. Kapten A. Rivai (☎353 374).

Telephones: Telkom office at Jl. Kapten A. Rivai 7. **Open 24hr.**

Internet: Various places around town charge about Rp50,000 per hr. **Wartel**, Jl. Veteran 761, is on the left coming from Jl. Sudirman. Open daily 7am-midnight. **Warnet**, Jl. Sudirman 3007, is at Km3.5 on the left side when coming from town. Open daily 9am-9pm. Access is also available at the **Post Office.**

Post Office: GPO at Jl. Merdeka 3. Open M-Sa 8am-7pm, Su 9am-4pm. Branch at Jl. Kapten Rivai 63. Open M-Th 8am-2pm, F 8-11am, Sa 8am-12:30pm. **Postal code:** 30000.

ACCOMMODATIONS

The cheapest accommodations are near **Pasar 16,** but they are unsafe for tourists. Hotels on **Jl. Sudirman** are centrally located, but noisy. Travelers and local businessmen prefer the quieter places on **Jl. Kapten A. Rivai,** a 15min. walk or *angkot* from Jl. Sudirman, and Jl. Kol. Iskandar. All hotels have private *mandi* and include a small breakfast. As many hotels are very busy, calling ahead is a good idea.

Hotel Sriwidjaja, Jl. Kol. Iskandar 39 (☎355 555). 100m from the Internasional Plaza. Clean wide halls, white tiled floors, and Western toilets. Singles with fan Rp33,000; double Rp36,500, with A/C Rp60,500.

Hotel Indayuh, Jl. Natunah 24 (☎359 453), off Jl. Kapten A. Rival, 10m after the post office. Well worth the rupiah. Western toilets. Doubles Rp40,000-60,000.

Hotel Nusantara, Jl. Let. Kol. Iskandar 563/17 (☎353 306). Offers slightly cheaper rooms in a grim-looking corner. Doubles with fan Rp30,000, with A/C and TV Rp40,000, with Western toilet Rp60,000. 10% tax extra.

Hotel Mahasar, Jl. Let. Kol. Iskandar 715 (☎359 565). Doubles with fan and less-than-perfect *mandi* for Rp30,000.

FOOD

The culinary specialty of Palembang is *pempek*, a boiled or fried concoction of seafood, egg, and flour. You can buy *pempek* just about anywhere in Palembang, whether in a restaurant, on the street, or on a train. *Martabak* and *bakso* stalls cram Jl. Let. Kol. Iskandar.

Pempek Nony 168, Jl. Sudirman 168. Km3.5 near Pokda. A good place for *pempek* (small Rp700, large Rp3500). Popular with locals. A few good *warung* outside make for a choice selection. Open daily 7am-7pm.

Roh Holland, Jl. Sudirman 828. Shelves and shelves of amazing cakes are the dessert to the *pempek* you had next door at Pempek Nony 168. Open daily 7am-9pm.

Rumah Makan Eko Enak, Jl. Sudirman 98B, opposite the Sari Hotel. Serves Indonesian favorites in clean and tasty-smelling premises. Open daily 9am-9pm.

Moriska Bakery, Jl. Kapten A. Rivai 55. Beyond Hotel Arjuna and Jl. Sudirman at Km3.5 #953. Tasty pastries Rp1000-4000. Open daily 8am-9pm.

Lezat, Jl. Kapten A. Rivai 1372, serves an assortment of Indonesian, Chinese, and Western dishes, from *pempek* to noodles and sirloin steak. Try one of the exotic fruit juices, made fresh for Rp2000-3000. Open daily 8:30am-9pm.

SIGHTS

Crossing the Musi River on the Ampera Bridge, you will see the towering **Masjid Agung mosque,** completed in 1748, on your left and the infamous **Pasar 16** on your right. The river itself can be explored by rented speedboats (Rp50,000 per hr.) During the **Sriwijaya Festival** (June 16-20), it is filled with *bidars*—traditional Indonesian racing boats. Off to the left 100m before the mosque is the **Museum Sultan Mahmud Badaruddin,** which relays the history of the Muslim sultanate Palembang Dar es Salaam (Palembang Place of Peace), which lasted from 1659 until the Dutch came in 1821. (Open M-F 8am-4pm. Small donation required.) Behind the aging Masjid Agung, **Jl. Pakih Jalalludin** is packed with stores that sell ornate traditional Palembang wood carvings and cabinets. At Jl. Sudirman Km6 is the **Museum Balaputra Dewa,** with exhibits on the history and culture of the Sriwijaya Kingdom, of which Palembang was once the capital. (Open T-Su 8:30am-2pm. Rp500.) Outside the urban jungle, the **Punti Kayu** (at Km 7), is a small park and zoo, featuring crocodiles, a bear, an orangutan, and an elephant. (Open daily 8am-5pm.)

MARKETS

In addition to **Matahan Internasional Plaza** at Jl. Sudirman and Jl. L.K. Iskandar, which has a five story movie theater, and the self-contained **Pasar Cinde** at the intersection with the Jl. Kol. Atmo, there are several self-proclaimed "Pasars," or markets, in town. However, none comes close to the real deal, **Pasar Enemblas (16),** which, sprawling from under the bridge, is an embodiment of the bustle of Southeast Asia. Mind bogglingly enormous, the market is an intricate maze of seemingly foundation-less stalls leading to more permanent fixtures. Seeds sit, chicks chirp, and fish fester in their own filth; in some corners, the smell is overwhelming while in others fragrances abound. Strap on something sturdier than flimsy flip-flops if you decide to head to the most lively and eye-opening market in Sumatra. Keep your wallet secure, but more importantly, keep your mind open.

KALIANDA

Small, charming, and unspoiled, Kalianda overlooks a south Sumatran inlet, half an hour from the ferry port of Bakauheni and 1½ hours from Bandar Lampung. In addition to offering the cheapest trips to Krakatau, Kalianda provides strenuous climbs, relaxing beaches, and seldom touristed hot springs. Tours depart from the **Penginapan Beringin,** Jl. Kesuma Bangsa 55, a hotel on the town's major thorough-

THE WRATH OF KRAKATAU On August 27, 1883, Krakatau exploded violently and left marks of destruction around the world. As the explosion weakened the island's foundations, water rushed into its lava interior, producing an even more terrible explosion that pitched tons of debris 20km high. The explosion was heard in Australia, volcanic rocks scattered as far as Madagascar, and ash encircled the earth for three years. Giant, 40m tsunamis devastated hundreds of villages along the Sumatran and Javanese coasts, and their effects were felt as far as Europe. An enormous ship buoy tossed onto shore by the tidal waves can still be seen on the south end of Jl. Monginsidi. Krakatau's peak was destroyed, and, in its place, the explosions left a crater 400m below sea level. For nearly half a century, Krakatau seemed at peace. Then in 1927, from the depths of the crater, a plume of steam unexpectedly flared up. Continued activity has already piled enough rocks and ashes together to create **Anak Krakatau** (Son of Krakatau), which now rises 150m above sea level. Seismic activity was again detected in 1979 and it began to appear as though the volcano had merely been resting this past century. Tension mounts as geologists ponder whether Sumatra and Java—and, indeed, the world—can take another eruption.

fare. This hotel's huge rooms open onto a lush atrium. (☎2008. Rooms Rp15,000, with private *mandi* Rp22,000; fan and breakfast included.)

The Sukarno-Hatta Highway passes Kalianda between Bandar Lampung and Bakaukuri. Ask to be let off there (from Bandar Lampung 1½hr., Rp5500; from Jakarta 6hr., Rp30,000). A Rp1500 motorcycle ride will take you to the Penginapan Beringin. Kalianda has a host of food stalls and small restaurants specializing in seafood and tasty *neshmeh* all along **Jl. Kasuma Bangsa,** though it's most hopping down at the bottom of **Jl. Veteran.** There is a **wartel** (☎0727) 100m down from the Beringin on the left (open 24hr.); **Apotik Rajabasa** is 200m uphill on the right. There's no currency exchange, and the ATM only speaks Bahasa Indonesia; bring all the rupiah you'll need. The main **police** office is on the way to Pantai Laguna (☎2110) and the **hospital (Rumah Sakit Umum Kalianda)** is half way to the highway (☎2159).

INDONESIA

One and a half kilometers up the road, **PantaiWay Urang** is a decent beach with a gorgeous view, overlooked by scenic **Gunung Rajabasa.** Two kilometers in the other direction, **Way Belerang Hot Springs** offer a pleasant soak. Either can be reached by foot, but an *ojek* uphill to Way Belerang might be preferable (Rp2000). A bit farther afield is luxurious and small **Pantai Laguna Beach,** 3km up from Way Urang. Motorbikes can be rented everywhere (Rp30,000 per day).

The islands of Krakatau mark the edge of a huge underwater crater. In ancient times Krakatau was over 2000m high, later blown away and replaced by a set of smaller islands. After 1883 **Rakata** was the tallest island remaining and seen today. **Anak Krakatau** (Son of Krakatau) is the site of volcanic activity today. Constantly growing and erupting since it appeared in 1930, this island of ash and rock entices adventurous souls to stroll around its base and peek (see **The Wrath of Krakatau,** p. 324). Keep in mind that this is dangerous, despite guides' assurances to the contrary. As recently as 1993, Krakatau performed unexpectedly and killed two.

Boats for **Gunung Krakatau** leave from nearby fishing villages. An overnight tour leaving at 8am from Penginapan Beringin costs Rp150,000 per person in a group (Rp200,000 for a single person) with meals included. The three- to five-hour boat ride stops at the jungle-covered "coral garden" islands of Sebuku and Sebesi for snorkeling and spends a night on the beach at Sertung, less than 1km away from Krakatau.

DANAU RANAU

Danau Ranau (Lake Ranau), flanked by hills and **Gunung Seminung** (1900m) to the south, is a popular retreat for Indonesians, but has remained hidden from foreign interest. Paying the price for this untainted splendor involves enduring the arduous six- to eight-hour northbound transport via **Liwa** from Bandar Lampung, or a *transit* minibus-hopping adventure from Baturaja (Rp8000 direct, otherwise more). The transport hub for the area is **Simpang Sender.** Buses to and from Bandur Lampung and Jakarta begin on the lake. The place to hit is **Pusri.** Get dropped off there if you can, otherwise get a minibus from Simpang Sender (20min Rp3000.) From the dropoff point, walk 1km steep downhill to hotels. **Pusri** has a number of hotels and bungalows, all offering scenic views of the lake. For Rp75,000, **Danau Ranau Cottages** offers enormous and beautiful bungalows with patios overlooking the water. Rp40,000 gets a room with *mandi.* 200 meters down the road, the friendly staff of the more secluded **Putri Gunung** offers clean rooms. (Rp30,000; with private *mandi.*) The cottages monopolize access to food.

Danau Ranau offers a retreat, not only from the noisy cities but from activity in general. There's not much to do around the lake but row a canoe, enjoy the blissful scenery, take a dip in the refreshing water, and lounge around with the Indonesian vacationers. Cool off from the heat below **Air Terjun,** a a gorgeous 30m waterfall with a damned-good dammed-off swimming area that is a 10min. walk from the cottages past Putri Gunung (Rp1000.) A noisy Rp50,000 chartered motorboat can take travelers 20min. across the lake to **Gemuhak Springs** (1½hr.), a pool of hot springs abutting the lake at the base of Seminung.

Buses leave from Banding Agung, via Simpang Sender and Pusri, for Bandar Lampung (7hr., 7am, noon, Rp20,000) and Baturaja (3hr., Rp8000) twice daily.

LAOS

KIP

US$1 = 8000.80KIP	1000KIP = US$0.13
CDN$1 = 5178.51KIP	1000KIP = CDN$0.19
EURO€1 = 7282.19KIP	1000KIP = EURO€0.14
UK£1 = 4572.15KIP	1000KIP = UK£0.22
IR£1 = 9246.48KIP	1000KIP = IR£0.11
AUS$1 = 4239.60KIP	1000KIP = AUS$0.24
NZ$1 = 3526.20KIP	1000KIP = NZ$0.28
ZAR1 = 959.63KIP	1000KIP = ZAR1.04

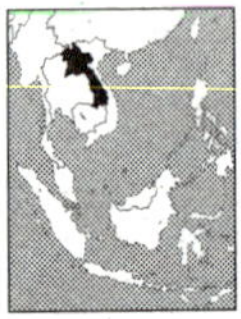

PHONE CODE **Country Code:** 855. **International dialing prefix:** 00.

There's a saying in Indochina: the Vietnamese plant the rice, the Khmer watch the rice, and the Lao listen to the rice grow. Visitors entering Laos from Vietnam, Thailand, or China are often shocked by the dramatic change in the pace of life. An undeveloped land dominated by mountains and forests, the "Land of a Million Elephants" is home to more than 60 ethnic groups, and "tourist" has yet to become prominent among them. After two decades of isolation, Laos has only recently opened its gates to foreigners, giving rise to a rather frail tourism infrastructure that is part of its allure. Whether traveling the mountainous, exploring the jeweled temples of Luang Prabang, venturing into the thick jungles of the Bolovens Plateau, or kicking back in the 4000 Islands Region, visitors are often content to just sit back and listen to the rice grow.

FACTS AND FIGURES

Official Name: Lao People's Democratic Republic.

Government: Communist State.

Capital: Vientiane.

Land Area: 237,000 sq. km.

Geography: Borders Thailand, China, Myanmar, Vietnam, and Cambodia. 85% of the country is mountainous. River systems: Mekong River.

Climate: Dry (high season) Nov.-Apr. Rainy (low season) May-Oct.

Major Cities: Luang Prabang, Pakse, Savannakhet.

Population: 5,827,500.

Language: Lao, French, English, hill tribe languages.

Religion: Theravada Buddhism (60%), Animist and other (40%).

Average Income per Capita: US$385.

Major Exports: Timber, coffee, tin.

LIFE AND TIMES

THE PEOPLE OF LAOS

Laos' 68 ethnic groups are conventionally divided into three categories. The **Lao Loum,** or ethnic Lao, live in lowland areas along the Mekong River, comprise over two-thirds of the population, enjoy high literacy rates and incomes, and wield the most political influence. The semi-nomadic **Lao Theung** live in the mountains along the Lao-Vietnamese border and on the Bolovens Plateau. The **Lao Soung** include the Hmong and Yao peoples, who emigrated from China in the 19th century and are often politically and economically marginalized.

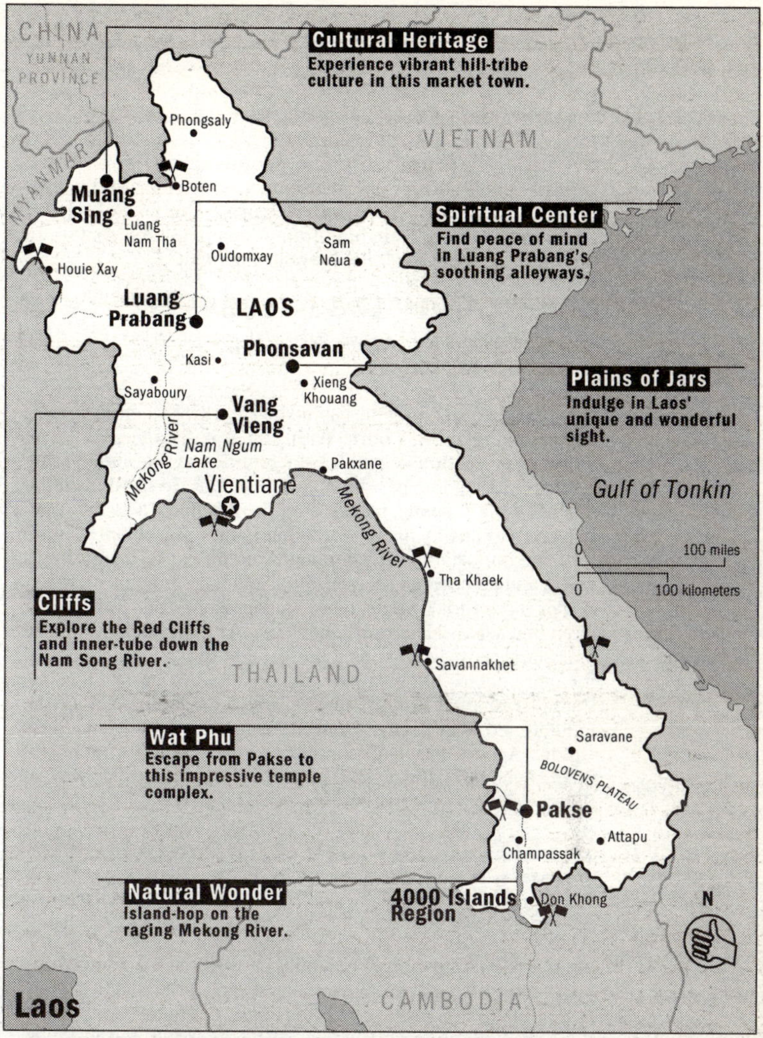

HIGHLIGHTS OF LAOS

CULTURAL HERITAGE. Serene **Luang Prabang** (p. 342) is Laos' spiritual center. The **Plain of Jars** (p. 347) is anything but ordinary. For vibrant hill tribe culture, **Muang Sing** (p. 352) and the far north is unparalleled. Pakse's **Wat Phu** (p. 363) is the largest Angkorian temple complex outside of Cambodia.

NATURAL WONDERS. Surreal **Nam Ngum Lake** (p. 339) and **Vang Vieng's jagged cliffs** (p. 341) are within striking distance from Vientiane. The **Bolovens Plateau** (p. 364) and **4000 Islands Region** (p. 365) are tops for rugged beauty and pure mystique.

HANGING OUT. From lazy Mekong voyages to peaceful mountain walks, Laos's laid-back atmosphere is its number one attraction.

8c
Tai Kadai emigrate from China

14c
Fa Ngum establishes Lane Xang Kingdom

16c
Capital moved to Vientiane; Emerald Buddha moved from Thailand

1637-94
Lane Xang's Golden Age

1694
Soulinga Vongsa's death; Vietnamese warlords enter

18c
Fight Club 2: Burmese and Thai forces want to play

1791
Then there was one: Bangkok gains control

1805
Chou Anou attempts to restore Lang Xang

1827
Bangkok's armies sack Vientiene

1880s
French enter Laos, give Khorat Plateau to Bangkok

1941
Japan invades, triggers Lao nationalism

1945
King Sisavangvong declares independence under pressure from Japan and internal groups

1954-62
Efforts for a neutral Lao government

HISTORY

EARLY HISTORY

–Even gourds have class distinctions.

According to legend, the Lao people sprung from three gourds—nobility from one, peasants from another, and indigenous hill tribes from the third. The proto-Laotians of the Tai Kadai ethnic group emigrated from China in the 8th century to take shelter from the Mongols in the mountains.

LANE XANG (1353–1694)

–Buddha image: elephant ratio in "Kingdom of Million Elephants" 23:1

The first recorded date in Lao history is 1316, when Prince Fa Ngum of Angkor was born. With Khmer assistance, Fa Ngum united a collection of small principalities and founded Lane Xang, the "Kingdom of a Million Elephants." He ruled from the city of Luang Prabang, named after the **Pha Bang,** a golden Buddha given to him by his Khmer father-in-law. The statue symbolized the importance of Theravada Buddhism to Lane Xang's rulers and manifested their spiritual and temporal power.

For the next 300 years, Lane Xang prospered; at its zenith, it stretched across all of north Indochina. Threatened by Burmese and Siamese invasions, **King Setthathirat** moved the capital to the more defensible Vientiane and brought the **Emerald Buddha,** the most revered Buddha in Thailand, from Lanna. Under the enlightened **King Souligna Vongsa**, Lane Xang experienced its Golden Age as its borders expanded to Yunnan to the north, Shan Myanmar to the west, Cambodia to the south, and Vietnam to the east.

INTERNAL DIVISION AND SIAMESE CONTROL (1694–1885)

–Sold to the Thai army in the corner!

Many crises following King Vongsa's death in 1694 led to the fragmentation of Lane Xang into three weak principalities: Vientiane, Luang Prabang, and Champassak. Vietnamese warlords threatened all borders, and chaos was the result. In the 1700s, the Burmese and Thai attacked the divided kingdoms, beginning Bangkok's control over much of Laos. In 1805, **Chou Anou,** a Vientiane prince, tried to end Thai rule. In turn, Bangkok sacked Vientiane in 1827 and depopulated the area—an event that still haunts Thai-Lao relations today. By the mid-19th century, only Luang Prabang maintained a modicum of independence.

COLONIAL RULE (1885–1954)

–Unity: a common hatred of the French.

As the French consolidated their rule over Vietnam, they also assumed traditional Vietnamese interests in Laos. After establishing a protectorate over Luang Prabang, the French expanded territory in Laos through many treaties with the Thai.

Blithely ignoring traditional boundaries, the French divided Laos at the Mekong, ceding all of the Khorat Plateau to Bangkok.

French rule in Laos was laissez-faire; they used the area primarily as a buffer between British interests to the west and their colonial claims in Vietnam. Health care and education were for the most part ignored. Nationalism came slowly, but the 1941 invasion of Indochina by Japan catalyzed independence movements. Several anti-French movements, including the **Lao Issara** (Free Lao) and the communist **Pathet Lao** (Lao Nation), arose to counter French imperialism. **King Sisavangvong,** initially reluctant to break with France, was pressured to declare independence for his country in 1945 backed by Japanese support.

1965-75
Second Indochina War. Lao gets bombed from all sides

1975
Pathet Lao found LPDR and LPRP; Kaysone Phomvihane leads LPRP

1970s
Fear of communists drives out the educated Lao

1980s
Laos becomes Vietnam's puppet state

1986
"New Thinking" copies Vietnamese communism

1992
Nouhak Phoumsavan gains power

1998
Pre-reform General Khamtai Siphandon to power

THE WAR YEARS (1954–80)

–History's most bombed country fights to stay alive.

The first attempt to establish a neutral Lao, conceived at the Geneva Conference in 1954, lasted only eight months. Another attempt in 1962 failed after the small kingdom was dragged into the Vietnam War. The North Vietnamese would accept a neutral Laos only if they could transport supplies through Laos along the Ho Chi Minh Trail, while the US remained intent on shutting the trail and preventing the Pathet Lao from seizing power.

The US waged a secret war in Laos, pouring aid to the right-wing government, recruiting highland minorities like the Hmong and Yao, and waging a destructive air campaign. From 1964-72, US bombers dropped more than two billion kilograms of bombs on Laos, making it the most heavily bombed country in history.

In 1975 after 30 years of division and war, the Pathet Lao marched into Vientiane and established the **Lao People's Democratic Republic (LPDR),** with the **Lao People's Revolutionary Party (LPRP)** as the sole political party. Abolishing Laos' 600-year-old monarchy, they gave leadership to **Kaysone Phomvihane.** Fear of communists sparked a mass exodus of educated lowland Lao in the 70s and left the LPDR with very few educated bureaucrats and technicians. Hmong rebels continued to wage guerrilla wars against the LPDR. In the 1980s, Laos was a puppet state of Vietnam, with upward of 60,000 Vietnamese troops still on Lao soil.

LAOS TODAY

Corruption and economic mismanagement contributed to Laos' status as one of the world's poorest countries. The LPRP followed Hanoi's lead in 1986 by approving an economic liberalization program dubbed "New Thinking." In November 1992 after Phomvihane's death, **Nouhak Phoumsavan** came to power. At the Sixth Party Congress, held in 1996, the LPRP upheld "New Thinking" but reaffirmed the state's role in the economy and its monopoly of power. Laos joined the **Association of Southeast Asian Nations (ASEAN)** in July 1997. In February 1998, the pro-reform **General Khamtai Siphandon** replaced President Nouhak.

Today, the Lao government remains committed to shielding the country from foreign influence. Since 1986, however, the government has made strides in decentralizing economic control and encouraging private enterprise; consequently, the average economic growth rate grew 7% from 1988 to 1996. The Asian economic crisis dealt the Lao economy a strong blow due to its close ties to Thailand, and in many ways Laos still reels from this blow. Vientiane has earned US praise for its cooperation in the "war on drugs" and search for American MIAs. Laos receives aid as one of the world's 20 least developed nations, but the government has trouble distributing and implementing programs to help its people. Up to 90% of the Lao people are subsistence farmers who benefit little from the country's fledgling capitalist economy.

CUSTOMS AND CULTURE

HUMAN RIGHTS

The LPRP remains the country's only legal political party. In January 1998, 43 Christians were arrested in Vientiane, provoking international criticism of Lao government. The position of the Hmong hill tribesmen (formerly funded by the American CIA) remains a thorny political issue; a dwindling band of Hmong insurgents continues to wage a low-level guerrilla war by occasionally raiding government convoys on the highway from the capital to Luang Prabang, but many analysts agree that their days are numbered.

BISEXUAL, GAY, AND LESBIAN TRAVELERS

The Laotian gay scene does exist—but without the flamboyance of the scene in neighboring Thailand. Attitudes towards gays may be improving, but for all travelers—straight or gay—public displays of affections are frowned upon.

PINK INK. For information on gay tours to Lao, check out Utopia Tours web site (www.utopia-tours.com/laos.htm.).

ARTS AND RECREATION

Influenced by Thai, Burmese, and Khmer styles, Lao art is unique and expressive, frequently inspired by Buddhist themes. Sadly, however, much of the country's artistic heritage has been lost or destroyed.

ARCHITECTURE

Buddhist temples, Laos' architectural genius, come in three chief styles. High, pointed, and layered roofs distinguish the **Vientiane style** of architecture found in the capital city. The **Luang Prabang style,** with multi-layered roofs and graceful, sweeping eaves that nearly touch the ground, is similar to that of Northern Thailand. A third temple style, **Xieng Khouang,** was irrevocably lost when American bombers razed Laos during the war. A few temples built in stone or brick with wide and sloping but layerless roofs in the Xieng style remain in Luang Prabang.

DANCE AND DRAMA

Classical dance and drama came to Laos from India via Cambodia in the 14th century, but it wasn't until the 16th and 17th centuries that **classical theater** fully developed. The Royal Court organized dance and drama, which were accompanied by a grand orchestra of xylophones, gongs, trumpets, tambourines, violins, mandolins, and, later, chanting. **Mimic dancers** wore rich and vibrant costumes with masks and diadems. Today, the Royal Lao Ballet, who also perform a number of Lao folk dances, is the only remaining court troupe in Southeast Asia.

MUSIC

Songs and music are indispensable accompaniments to all celebrations and prominent features of everyday life. Live **mor lam** performances, involving singing jousts of Lao epic poems, occasionally take place at markets and temple fairs. The haunting, hollow sound of the **khene,** a complex bamboo reed organ that Lao musicians play at celebrations and funerals, is the center of Lao traditional music. The Hmong are renowned for their *khene* players who often perform at New Year festivals. A Lao orchestra consists of the *khene*, the **so** (a two-stringed cello), the **khouy** (a bamboo flute), and the **nang-hat** (a wooden xylophone).

WEAVING AND HILL TRIBE ART

Young girls learn the traditional art of weaving cotton and silk with shimmering gold and silver threads (called **tdinjok**); a woman's ability to weave is considered an asset during courtship. The **pha sin** (Lao sarong), **pha baeng** (Lao shawl), and **sin** (bridal skirt with an elaborately embroidered hem), are made from these cloths.

The Yao and Hmong are renowned for their excellent **silversmiths.** Both groups traditionally assessed their wealth in terms of family silver. The Hmong are the only people in Laos who make **batik,** created by dyeing fabric with resistant wax designs (see p. 136). **Appliqué** is a craft form in which cloth is layered and stitched to create a rich collage of contrasting colors, textures, and geometric shapes. Most hill tribes, other as the Akha, make beautiful appliqué.

OUTDOORS

In Laos, "outdoors" will likely mean getting wet; Laos offers more waterfalls and watersports than trekking. **Swim** in Nam Ngum Lake and **raft** down the Nam Ngum River. For some mystery and excitement, the cliffs near Vang Vieng offer **spelunking, underground swimming, waterfalls,** and **inner-tubing** down the Nam Song River. For a more laid-back experience, go **boating** in the 4000 Islands Region and spot a rare Irrawaddy dolphin.

ADDITIONAL SOURCES

A History of Laos, by Martin Stuart Fox (1997). One of the few general histories of Laos. The author covers all of Lao history, emphasizing on the colonial and modern periods.

The Politics of Heroin in Southeast Asia, by Alfred McCoy (1972). A fascinating account of the opium trade in Southeast Asia, focusing on America's role in opium smuggling during the Vietnam War. Since republished as *The Politics of Heroin.*

ON THE WEB

Laos News.net (www.laosnews.net). Links to Lao history and updates on daily news and current events.

Visit Laos (www.visit-laos.com). Practical tips and hotel, tour and travel info.

ESSENTIALS

VISAS

All travelers must obtain visas before entering Laos overland. One-month family visas and 15-day tourist visas are issued at **Wattay International Airport** (p. 333) in Vientiane, **Friendship Bridge** (p. 756) at Nong Khai, **Luang Prabang Airport** (p. 342) in Luang Prabang, and **Ban Muang Kao/Chong Mek** (p. 752); bring a passport-sized photo and US$30. If entering the country from another international checkpoint, obtain a visa in advance. Lao consulates abroad issue non-extendable 15-day tourist visas that are valid for two months. Travel agencies and Lao consulates in **Bangkok** issue visas for 300฿ (2-day processing); in **Hanoi,** US$60 (1- to 3-day processing); in **Saigon,** US$65 (2-month; same-day processing).

MONEY

The Lao **kip** comes in denominations of 100, 500, 1000, 2000, and 5000 and is divided into 100 cents. Thai baht and US dollars are the most widely exchanged currencies, especially since the government devalued the kip in early 1998. Vendors in markets are eager to change US dollar and baht into kip, often at better rates than in the banks. Travelers checks and credit cards are only accepted at major banks and businesses. It's customary to **tip** guides, but tipping in restaurants and hotels is uncommon. Feel free to **bargain** whenever a price isn't indicated.

GETTING THERE

BY PLANE. Laos has two **international airports:** Wattay International Airport in Vientiane (p. 333) and Luang Prabang Airport in Luang Prabang (p. 342). **Lao Aviation** (www.laoaviation.com) runs the most international flights between major Southeast Asia gateways, but the US State Department has issued a warning regarding Lao Aviation's safety record, advising visitors to limit their use of the carrier to essential travel only. Consult your embassy for the latest safety reports. Alternatively, use **Thai Airways** or **Vietnam Airlines** for flights to Bangkok, Hanoi, and Ho Chi Minh City.

BY LAND. Refer to the following table for overland border crossings in Laos.

BORDER CROSSINGS

CAMBODIA. The border crossing between **Don Khong** in southern Laos and **Stung Treng** (p. 83) in northern Cambodia recently opened. Cambodian visas are not available at the border.

CHINA. The only legal crossing is from the small town of **Boten** in northern Laos to **Mohan/Mengla** (p. 352) in southwest China.

THAILAND. There are 5 border crossings from Laos to Thailand: **Houie Xay** (p. 355) to **Chiang Khong** (p. 719); **Vientiane** (p. 333) to **Nong Khai** (p. 756); **Thakhek** to **Nakhon Phanom** (p. 757); **Savannakhet** (p. 357) to **Mukdahan** (p. 752); and **Pakse** (p. 360) to **Chong Mek** (p. 752).

VIETNAM. Travelers pass between **Savannakhet** (p. 357) in Laos and **Đà Nẵng/Huế** (p. 859) in Vietnam via **Lao Bảo** (6-7hr. from Savannakhet, 7-8hr. from Huế; p. 360). It's rumored that the crossing at **Điện Biên Phủ** will open soon; check with an embassy for up-to-date info. You may be denied passage if your visa doesn't specify the correct points of entry and exit.

MYANMAR. It isn't currently possible to travel overland to Myanmar from Laos.

GETTING AROUND

Travel in Laos can make travel in other parts of Southeast Asia feel luxurious. Most roads are old, pot-holed, and bumpy or are just dirt tracks that become rivers of mud during the rainy season. Boat and air travel are infinitely more popular than buses and cars.

BY PLANE. During the rainy season, air travel may be the only way to reach remote areas like Phonsavanh. **Lao Aviation** has domestic flights that link the capital with every region of the country. Buy your ticket several days in advance and confirm your flight one day in advance, as some routes only run occasionally, and other forms of transportation aren't always available. Some travelers report showing up at the airport terminal only to find their seat unceremoniously sold to someone else. The only accepted method of payment for foreigners is US dollars.

BY BUS. Buses, trucks, and pickups run regularly in most provinces. Buses are cheap but take and inordinate amount of time. Overcrowded buses often stop at the driver's whim. In the north, the best way to ensure a seat is to show up around 7am; in the south, departure times vary more. The fully paved road between Savannakhet and Luang Prabang along with less bandit activity in the north, has made bus trips to most major towns bearable, but the dirt roads south of Savannakhet and the partially paved road through the Lao Bảo border crossing to Vietnam make travel in these areas a painful experience. Due to banditry along Rte. 7, travelers headed to Phonsavanh should inquire at their embassy about road status and safety.

BY BOAT. For centuries, boat travel was the chief means of transportation within Laos (besides elephants, of course). A jaunt down the Mekong, Nam Ou, or Nam Tha rivers remains an intriguing option, and many travelers find **slow boat travel** so relaxing that they spend a good portion of their time in Laos on the water. In some areas, passenger boats have fixed prices, while in other areas, travelers need to organize a group and charter an entire vessel or bargain for a place on cargo vessels. Whatever the case, bring a sleeping bag if traveling overnight, and stock up on food and water. During the dry season, water levels drop, and boats may get stuck. Exact travel times depend on several variables, including the river current, amount of cargo, number of passengers, and number of stops made along the way.

Speedboats are a different matter. These ear-splitting, leg-cramping, light-speed contraptions will (somehow) get you to your destination more quickly than slow boats but for more money and discomfort. Insist on a helmet and life vest, especially during the rainy season, and make sure your bag is securely tied to the boat, as choppy waters pitch luggage overboard. Bring earplugs, hang on tight, and pray.

KEEPING IN TOUCH

Mail from Laos is unreliable and slow. Postage is cheap, but many prefer to send overseas packages from Thailand. Receiving mail in Laos is possible through *Poste Restante* in Vientiane. Postal officers will inspect anything that's not a letter.

The brand-new **Lao Telecom** phone service has made international calls from Laos possible for the first time. Post offices in medium-sized towns sell US$3, US$6, and US$9 phone cards, stock English-language white pages, and invariably have a card phone outside. Cities like Luang Prabang and Vientiane have telecommunication bureaus that place calls but charge more for fewer services (no collect, credit card, or incoming calls allowed). For **Home Country Direct (HCD)** numbers from Laos, refer to the table on the inside back cover of this book.

NORTHERN LAOS

VIENTIANE ☎21

To adventurers from a bygone era, Vientiane conjures up sepia-tinged images of an exotic colonial backwater, where days melted into years and life remained as sluggish as the current of the Mekong. Today, save for some French expats, restaurants, and a few wine shops, the "City of Sandalwood" has shed its colonial legacy for the impersonality of a larger metropolis. For most travelers, this capital's chief appeal is its provincial feel; most linger here a day or two before heading into rural Laos.

TRANSPORTATION

Flights: Wattay International Airport (☎513 200), on Luang Prabang Rd. 4km from the center of town. Taxi to downtown US$5. **Lao Air Booking Co.,** 43/1 Setthathirat Rd. (☎216 761). Open M-F 8am-noon and 1-4pm, Sa 8am-noon. AmEx/V. **Lao Aviation,** 2 Pang Kham Rd. (domestic ☎212 057, international ☎212 051). To: **Bangkok** (1 per day, US$70); **Chiang Mai** (2 per week, US$85); **Hanoi** (2per day, US$100); **Ho Chi Minh City** (2½hr., US$150); **Houie Xay** (1 per day, US$88); **Luang Nam Tha** (5 per week, US$80); **Luang Prabang** (2-3 per day, US$55); **Pakse** (1 per day,$95); **Phonsavanh** (1 per day, US$44); **Phnom Penh** (1 per day, US$130); **Savannakhet** (1 per day, US$61); **Udom Xai** (5 per week; US$71). **Thai Airways,** 27/1 Pang Kham Rd. (☎222 527). Open M-F 8:30am-noon and 1-5pm, Sa 8:30am-noon. AmEx/V. To **Bangkok** (1 per day, US$115). **Vietnam Airlines,** 63 Samsenthai Rd. (☎217 562), in Lao Plaza Hotel. Open M-Sa 8am-noon and 1:30-4:30pm. To **Hanoi** (US$108) and **Ho Chi Minh City** (US$170).

Buses: The **Northern Bus Terminal** (☎216 507), on the corner of Mahosot and Khou Vieng Rd. Buses go to: **Friendship Bridge** (#14, 30min., every 30 min. 7am-5pm, 1000kip); **Paksan** (3hr.; 7, 11am, 2pm; 6000kip); **Pakse** (#35; 13hr.; 11am, 1, 3pm; 35,000kip); **Savannakhet** (#36; 8hr.; 7:30, 10am; 25,000kip); **Tha Dua** (#14,

45min., every 20min. 7am-5pm); **Vang Vieng** (#1; 4hr.; 7, 10:30am, 1:30pm; 6000kip). Other buses leave from **Thalat Laeng** (☎413 297), accessible by *tuk-tuk* (3000kip). To: **Luang Prabang** (8hr.; 7, 8:30, 10:30am, 1, 5pm; 50,000kip); **Oudomxay** (15hr., 6am, 60,000kip); **Phonsavanh** (10hr., 7:30am, 60,000kip); **Xamnena** (30hr., 7am, 80,000kip).

Boats: Boat travel to northern towns is possible, but erratic schedules make buses the preferred means of transport. **Speedboats** go from **Kao Liao Pier,** 3km from the city center, to **Luang Prabang** and **Pak Lay. Private boats** can also be chartered to **Luang Prabang** (10hr., 5000kip).

Local Transportation: Taxis congregate at the morning market on Lane Xang Ave. and in front of the Novotel on Luang Prabang Rd. 10,000-15,000kip per hr. or 200,000kip per day. To **Tha Dua** (Buddha Park) 50,000kip. **Tuk-tuk** 6000-8000kip. **Saysouly Guest House** (☎218 383), on Manthatulath Rd. 1 block west of Pang Kham Rd., rents **bicycles** ($2 per day) and **motorbikes** ($10 per day).

ORIENTATION AND PRACTICAL INFORMATION

The **Nam Phou Fountain,** obscured by trees on **Setthathirat Rd.** serves as a convenient landmark while exploring the city. Vientiane's three main thoroughfares are **Samsenthai Rd.** one block north of the fountain; Setthathirat Rd., one block south of the fountain; and **Lane Xang Ave.,** which runs perpendicular to the **Mekong River** till the **Anousavari Monument** and is home to **Talat Sao** (the morning market), **GPO,** and most **embassies.** Most restaurants are on **Quay Fa Ngum Rd.,** parallel to the Mekong River. **Mahosot Rd.,** parallel to and one block east of Lane Xang Ave., passes the **Northern Bus Terminal. Khoun Boulom Rd.** runs inland from Quay Fa Ngum Rd. and loops toward Talat Sao and Lane Xang Ave.

TOURIST AND FINANCIAL SERVICES

Tourist Offices: National Tourism Authority (☎212 248), on Lane Xang Ave. 300m before Anousavari Monument. Friendly English-speaking staff. Flight and bus schedules and travel info. Open M-F 8am-noon and 1-4pm. **Inter-Lao Tourism** (☎214 232), on Luang Prabang Rd. near the Novotel. Open M-F 8am-5pm and Sa 8am-noon.

Tours: Diethelm Travel (☎213 833), on Setthathirat Rd. beside the Nam Phou Fountain. Arranges transport. Open M-F 8am-noon and 1:30-5pm, Sa 8am-noon. **Sadetour** (☎216 314), on Quay Fa Ngum Rd. near the residential palace, is Laos' oldest tour company. Open M-F 8am-6pm, Sa 8am-noon.

Immigration Offices: Immigration Department (☎212 520), on Khoun Boulom Rd. before the Lane Xang Ave. intersection. 15- or 30-day visas can be extended for up to 4 days (US$1 per day). Open M-F 8am-noon and 1-4pm. Other immigration offices are at the airport and next to Mithaphrap bridge (☎812 040).

Embassies: Australia (☎413 600), on the corner of Nehru and Phone Xay Rd., near Anousavari Monument. Open M-Th 9am-noon and 1:30-5pm, F 9am-noon. Serves **UK, Canada,** and **NZ** citizens. **Cambodia** (☎315 251), on Tha Dua Rd., 2km outside the city center. Same-day visa US$20. Open M-F 7:30-11:30am and 2-5pm. **China** (☎315 103), on War Nak Rd. past Myanmar Embassy. 30-day visa US$50. Open M-F 9-11:30am. **Myanmar** (☎314 910), on Sokpaluang Rd. 500m past Wat Sokpaluang on the left. Tourist visas US$18; 2-3 days processing. Bring a passport and 4 photos. Open M-F 8:30am-noon and 1-4:30pm. **Thailand** (☎214 582), on Phone Keng Rd.; Consular office (☎217 154), on Lane Xang Rd., 300m before the Anousavari Monument. 60-day tourist visa 300฿, transit visa 200฿; 2-day processing. Open M-F 8:30am-noon. **US** (☎212 581), on Bartholomie Rd. Open M-F 8am-noon and 1-5pm. **Vietnam,** 60 That Luang Rd. (☎413 400). Tourist visas US$55; 3-day processing. Bring passport and 1 photo. Open M-F 8-11:30am and 2-4pm, Sa 8-11:30am.

Currency Exchange: Banque Pour le Commerce Exterieur Lao, 1 Pang Kham Rd. (☎213 200). V cash advances. Traveler's checks cashed. Open M-F 8:30am-3:30pm. **Lao May Bank** (☎213 300), 39 Pang Kham Rd., and **Lane Xang Bank** (☎213 400), on Setthathirat Rd., provide similar services. Both open M-F 8am-4pm.

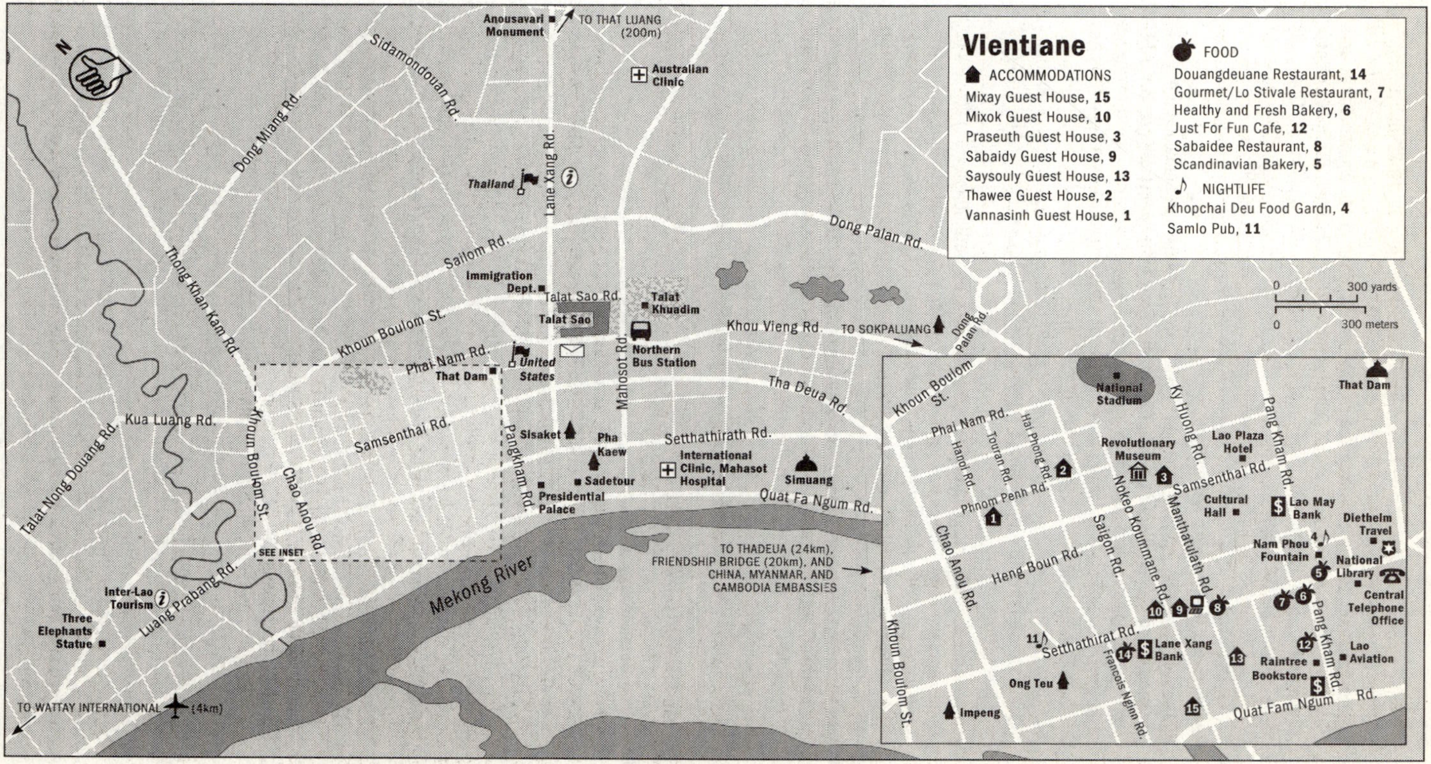
Vientiane
ACCOMMODATIONS
Mixay Guest House, 15
Mixok Guest House, 10
Praseuth Guest House, 3
Sabaidy Guest House, 9
Saysouly Guest House, 13
Thawee Guest House, 2
Vannasinh Guest House, 1
FOOD
Douangdeuane Restaurant, 14
Gourmet/Lo Stivale Restaurant, 7
Healthy and Fresh Bakery, 6
Just For Fun Cafe, 12
Sabaidee Restaurant, 8
Scandinavian Bakery, 5
NIGHTLIFE
Khopchai Deu Food Gardn, 4
Samlo Pub, 11
Anousavari Monument
TO THAT LUANG (200m)
Australian Clinic
Sidamondouan Rd.
Dong Miang Rd.
Thailand
Lane Xang Rd.
Dong Palan Rd.
Sailom Rd.
Immigration Dept.
Talat Sao Rd.
Talat Khuadim
Talat Sao
Khoun Boulom St.
Khou Vieng Rd.
TO SOKPALUANG
Dong Palan Rd.
Northern Bus Station
Mahosot Rd.
Phai Nam Rd.
That Dam
United States
Tha Deua Rd.
Thong Khan Kam Rd.
Kua Luang Rd.
Samsenthai Rd.
Pangkham Rd.
Sisaket
Pha Kaew
Setthathirath Rd.
International Clinic, Mahasot Hospital
Simuang
Sadetour
Presidential Palace
Quat Fa Ngum Rd.
Talat Nong Douang Rd.
Chao Anou Rd.
SEE INSET
Mekong River
TO THADEUA (24km), FRIENDSHIP BRIDGE (20km), AND CHINA, MYANMAR, AND CAMBODIA EMBASSIES
Inter-Lao Tourism
Luang Prabang Rd.
Three Elephants Statue
TO WATTAY INTERNATIONAL (4km)
0 300 yards
0 300 meters
National Stadium
That Dam
Ky Huong Rd.
Pang Kham Rd.
Revolutionary Museum
Lao Plaza Hotel
Hai Phong Rd.
Touran Rd.
Hanoi Rd.
Phnom Penh Rd.
Samsenthai Rd.
Cultural Hall
Lao May Bank
Diethelm Travel
Nokeo Koummane Rd.
Manthatulath Rd.
Nam Phou Fountain
National Library
Central Telephone Office
Heng Boun Rd.
Saigon Rd.
Setthathirat Rd.
Lane Xang Bank
Raintree Bookstore
Lao Aviation
Ong Teu
Francois Nginn Rd.
Quat Fam Ngum Rd.
Impeng

LAOS

American Express: Diethelm Travel (see **Tours,** above) is the Lao representative. Traveler's checks (2% commission) for AmEx cardholders.

English-Language Bookstore: Raintree Bookstore, 25 Pang Kham Rd. *Newsweek* and English books on Laos. Open M-F 8:30am-5:30pm, Sa 8:30am-4:30pm. **Vientiane Bookcenter,** on Pang Kham Rd., sells maps, used guidebooks, and novels. Open M-F 9am-5:30pm, Sa 9am-4pm.

EMERGENCY AND COMMUNICATIONS

Police: ☎191. **Fire:** ☎190. **Ambulance:** ☎195.

Pharmacy: Seng Thong Osoth Pharmacy (☎213 732), on the road between the morning market and the Northern Bus Terminal. Moving away from the river, it's on the right. Friendly, English-speaking staff. Open 8am-5pm.

Medical Services: Australian Embassy Clinic (☎413 603), on Nehru Rd. near the Australian Embassy. Serves Australian, British, Canadian, and NZ citizens. Initial consultation US$50. By appointment only. Open M-Th 8:30am-noon and 2-5pm, F 8:30am-noon. **International Clinic, Mahosot Hospital** (☎214 022), on Mahosot Rd past Wat Pha Kaew. **Open 24hr.**

Telephones: Central Telephone Office (☎214 977), on Setthathirat Rd. Facing Nam Phou Fountain, head 1 block right on Setthathirat Rd.; it's a yellow building on the left. Cash calls only. Fax 500kip per page. Phone cards. Open daily 7am-10pm. International phones also at GPO (card calls only). The **Lao Plaza Hotel** on Samsenthai Rd. offers international credit card calls.

Internet Access: Planet Online, 205 Setthathirat Rd. (☎218 972), at the corner of Manthatulath Rd., has many terminals, free tea and coffee, and a giant TV usually tuned to MTVAsia (150kip per min).

Post Office: GPO (☎/fax 217 327), on Khou Vieng Rd. Head away from the river on Lane Xang Rd. and take a right before the morning market. *Poste Restante.*

ACCOMMODATIONS

Thawee Guest House, 64 Ban Ann (☎217 903), two blocks northwest of the Cultural Hall. Great guest house with energizing orange walls and wonderfully comfortable rooms. Singles with satellite TV and outside bath with hot water US$7; doubles US$14.

Saysouly Guest House, 23 Manthatulath Rd. (☎218 383), near the Setthathirat Rd. intersection. Large clean rooms and plenty of tourist info. Laundry 1000-2000kip per piece. Singles with shared bath US$6-10; doubles with A/C US$8, with shared bath US$10-12; triples US$15.

Praseuth Guest House, 312 Samsenthai Rd. (☎217 932), next to the Cultural Hall. Amicable, family-run business with small but spotless rooms in the heart of the city. Laundry. Rooms US$6-7, with A/C US$7, with bath US$8.

Mixay Guest House, 39 Nokeo Koummane Rd. (☎217 023). From the Nam Phou Fountain, walk 3 blocks down Setthathirat Rd. with the river on your left and turn left onto Nokeo Koummane Rd.; it's on the right near the end. Apart from the giant snakeskin on the lobby wall, Mixay is similar to most guest houses–clean and comfortable. Internet. Singles US$4; doubles US$6.

Vannasinh Guest House, 051 Phnom Penh Rd. (☎222 020). Walk down on Samsenthai Rd., and look for the sign 2 blocks before Khoun Boulom Rd. Pretty and in a quiet yet central location. French-and English-speaking staff manage clean, pleasant rooms. Rooms with shared bath US$8; doubles with private bath US$10, with A/C and hot water US$16.

Mixok Guest House, on Setthathirat Rd. 2 blocks west of the Nam Phou Fountain. Small but good value rooms with dorm bunk beds. Motorbikes US$8-10 per day. All rooms have shared bath. Dorms 15,000kip; singles 30,000kip, with larger bed 36,000kip; doubles 36,000kip; triples 51,000kip.

Sabaidy Guest House, 203 Setthathirat Rd. (☎/fax 213 929). Basic but clean dorms. Communal TV complete with karaoke. Hot water. Dorms US$2; rooms 40,000kip.

FOOD

For cheap and delicious Lao food, head to one of the many eateries along the river. Most are open from dawn until late evening and serve a mix of Lao, Thai, and Western style dishes (7000-15,000kip). French bakeries and restaurants cluster near the Nam Phou Fountain.

Scandinavian Bakery, 74/1 Pang Kham Rd. beside Nam Phou Fountain. Expensive but popular. Excellent pastries (5000kip) and lunch options (10,000-18,000kip), CNN, and foreign magazines. Open daily 7am-7pm.

Healthy and Fresh Bakery, on Setthathirat Rd. near the Nam Phou Fountain. Popular eatery with big breakfasts, pack lunches (30,000kip), and a variety of snacks. Great coffee 8,000kip. Open daily 7am-7pm.

Gourmet/Lo Stivale Restaurant, 44 Setthathirat Rd. Gourmet is a cafe, while Lo Stivale is a full restaurant. Pricey but authentic and utterly delicious food. Comprehensive Western menu (US$1-3 per dish). Panini US$2.50. Gourmet open daily 7am-8pm; Lo Stivale open daily 10am-10pm. MC/V.

Douangdeuane Restaurant, on François Nginn Rd. off of Setthathirat Rd. Delicious vegetarian Lao, Thai, and Vietnamese menus (entrees 7000-20,000kip) and English- and French-speaking staff. Open daily 8am-10pm.

Just for Fun, 15/2 Pang Kham Rd. between the Nam Phou Fountain and Quay Fa Ngum Rd. This quirky eatery specializes in vegetarian food and sells ethnic products, clothing etc. Most dishes US$1-2. Open M-Sa 9am-9pm.

Sabaidee Restaurant, on the corner of Setthathirat Rd. and Manthathlat St. A pretty courtyard restaurant offering Lao and Western dishes. Breakfast menu. Chicken *laap* 10,000kip. Open daily 7am-11pm.

SIGHTS

Several temples and some of the best-preserved colonial architecture in the city grace tree-lined **Setthathirat Rd.** and **Quay Fa Ngum Rd.** Away from the city center are That Luang, the Anousavari Monument, and the steam baths of Wat Sokpaluang.

THAT LUANG. This 45m gold *stupa* is the Lao national symbol and also one of the most important religious sites in Laos. Four wats once surrounded the lotus-bud-shaped *stupa*, but only the north and south wats remain. Originally built in 1566, it was restored in 1935 by the French colonial regime. Each November, That Luang hosts the **That Luang Festival,** when hundreds of monks gather to accept alms and floral gifts from the faithful. *(On That Luang Rd. Open Tu-Su 8am-noon and 1-4pm. 1000kip donation expected).*

HO PHRA KEO (HALL OF THE EMERALD BUDDHA). Vientiane's oldest temple has housed Buddhist sculpture and artifacts since 1970. The original temple was built in the mid-16th century by King Setthathirat to house the Emerald Buddha he brought from Chiang Mai. Razed by Thais in 1827, the wat was restored in the 1940s. *(From the Nam Phou Fountain, follow Setthathirat Rd. 100m past the Lane Xang Ave. intersection; the entrance is on the right. Open daily 8am-noon and 1-4pm. 1000kip.)*

WAT SISAKET. Built by King Anou in 1818, the temple houses 7000 Buddha statues and a sanctuary with elaborate murals. *(On the corner of Setthathirat Rd. and Lane Xang Ave. Open daily 8am-noon and 1-4pm. 1000kip.)*

WAT ONG TEU. The largest temple in the capital, Wat Ong Teu has one of the country's most prestigious Buddhist schools and a massive meditating Buddha. *(At the north end of Setthathirat Rd. at the Chao Anou Rd. intersection.)*

THAT DAM (BLACK STUPA). According to legend, a seven-headed dragon lies under the *stupa* to protect the people of Vientiane from Siamese invaders in 1828. Ever since, the *stupa* is seen as the city's protector. *(In a square left off Samsenthai Rd.when heading east.)*

WAT SOKPALUANG. This wat offers wonderfully refreshing herbal saunas (5000kip) and rigorous 40min. massages for 15,000kip. *(1½km southeast of the city center. Take a tuk-tuk (4000kip) or walk away from Lane Xang Ave. on Khou Vieng Rd., which runs between the morning market and the post office. The turn-off for the wat is unmarked; it is visible through the trees from the main road. Open daily late morning-8pm.)*

WAT SIMUANG. Built by King Setthathirat in 1566, this wat houses the foundation pillar of Vientiane, which, according to legend, crushed a pregnant woman, Nang Si, as it was lowered. Nang Si is revered as the guardian spirit of the city. *(On Quay Fa Ngum Rd. at the eastern end of town. Open Tu-Sa 8am-8pm.)*

ANOUSAVARI MONUMENT (VICTORY GATE). This bizarre looking monument, at the end of Lane Xang Ave., is akin to a concrete mix between Paris's Arc de Triomphe (the creator's inspiration) and a wedding cake. It was built by the government in memory of those who died during Loas' struggle for independence. When builders ran out of concrete, they completed the memorial in 1969 with US cement earmarked for use in construction of Wattay International Airport. Known to some as the "vertical runway," it has a wonderful panoramic view of town. *(At the north end of town on Lane Xang Ave. Open daily 8am-5pm. 1000kip.)*

ENTERTAINMENT

There is little raucous nightlife in Vientiane—bars and clubs must close by midnight. **Khopchai Deu Food Garden,** next to the Nam Phou Fountain on Setthathirat Rd., has beautiful courtyard surrounding an aging French colonial building. It's nightly barbecues are one of Vientiane's most popular nighttime hangouts. Sit at the outside bar, enjoy a Lao wine cocktail (7500kip), and listen to the live band every Friday and Saturday. (Open M-Sa 9am-11:30pm, Su 5:30-11:30pm.) British **Samlo Pub,** 101 Setthathirat Rd., caters to a tourist/expat crowd. Hang out, shoot pool, or play foosball. (☎222 308. Open daily 11:30am-2pm and 5pm-midnight.)

MARKETS

Talat Sao (the morning market) and **Talat Khuadim** (the evening market) are two of Vientiane's main attractions. Talat Sao is in two green-roofed buildings off Lane Xang Ave., the first selling cheap electric and silver goods, and the second selling clothes and wall-hangings. (Open daily 6am-6pm.) Talat Khuadim is the large open-air market behind the Northern Bus Terminal. **Magninom Market,** on Khounboulom Rd., is piled high with everything a traveler may need. (Open daily 8am-9:30pm.)

LAOS

DAYTRIP FROM VIENTIANE

THA DEUA

Tha Deua, 24km from Vientiane, can be reached by bus from the Northern Bus Terminal (#14, 50min., every 20min. 6am-5pm, 1000kip) or tuk-tuk (45min.; 40,000kip, 1000kip for parking.) Open daily 8am-5pm. 2000kip.

Buddha sculptures are everywhere in this sculpture park built by the same self-described "half-man, half-animal" Lao monk/mystic who designed Sala Kaew Ku following the communist victory 23 years ago. Both temples have a mix of Hindu and Buddhist themes brought to life in cement sculptures. Fat Buddhas, thin Buddhas, big Buddhas, little Buddhas, Buddha family scenes, and reclining Buddhas all make an appearance.

NEAR VIENTIANE

NAM NGUM LAKE

Nam Ngum Lake, 90km northeast of Vientiane, is a vast reservoir formed by the damming of Nam Ngum River in the late 1970s. Today, the hydroelectric power plant supplies electricity to much of Laos and parts of Thailand. Nam Ngum's natural setting is spectacular; emerald islets, many of which were prisons and political re-education camps during the 1980s, dot the lake. In the hurry to complete the dam, however, no one thought to harvest the surrounding forest, which was soon submerged. Ingenious Lao loggers have now developed underwater chain saws, as lumberjacks trade in boots for flippers to keep the show going on.

Travelers seeking peace and quiet head to **Santipap Island,** the site of a dilapidated but charming guest house. An ethereal setting, great swimming, and gorgeous sunsets compensate for the simple lodgings (rooms 6000kip). The **Nam Ngum Restaurant** (☎20 513 521), surrounded by plants to the left of the pier, serves fresh fish (10,000-18,000kip). Long-tail boats make the trip to Santipap Island (30min., 10,000kip per person). The guest house runs a boat that returns to the lake at 10am.

To reach the lake, take a bus from Vientiane's Northern Bus Terminal (see **Transportation,** p. 333) to Ban Thalat. From there, *songthaew* and *tuk-tuk* run to the lake (3500kip), passing the dam complex. Photography is prohibited. To continue farther north of Nam Ngum Lake, head back to Ban Thalat and hop on a *songthaew* to **Phon Hong** (30min., 2000kip). If you get to Phon Hong early enough, you may be able to flag down a bus to Luang Prabang or at least Kasi. Otherwise, *songthaew* also leave when full to **Vang Vieng** (1½hr., 5000kip).

LAO PAKO

A small eco-tourist lodge, **Lao Pako** is popular with Vientiane's expats and lies south of Nam Ngum Lake on the Nam Ngum River, 50km from Vientiane. Austrian owner Mr. Pfabigan organizes treks, river-rafting expeditions, and village visits. The bar/restaurant is popular but expensive; bring your own food and drink if you're staying a few days. (☎212 981. Dorms 20,000kip; doubles 60,000kip; 2- to 3-person bungalows 150,000kip.)

To get to Lao Pako, take a Pakxap bus from the Northern Bus Terminal to Som Sa Mai (#19; 1½hr.; 6:30, 11am, 3pm; 1500kip) and then a motorboat to Lao Pako resort (25min., 25,000kip per boat). The resort runs boats back to Som Sa Mai (25,000kip per boat), where buses leave for Vientiane (every 2hr. 7:30am-4pm, 1500kip).

VANG VIENG ☎23

The small town of Vang Vieng has held various roles throughout its diverse history. During the Vietnam War, the area was a stronghold of Vang Pao's Hmong guerillas, recruited by the US Central Intelligence Agency to fight the Pathet Lao and Vietnamese communists. More recently, the area has been home to Hmong and Yao minority communities. The town's latest claim to fame is as a mecca for Laos's backpackers, drawn by the dramatic limestone cliffs dotted with spectacular caves.

> **TRAVEL WARNING.** Incidents of bandit and insurgent attacks have been reported along Route 13 in northeastern Vientiane Province and southeastern Luang Prabang Province. Those who decide to travel on Route 13 from Vang Vieng to Luang Prabang should travel in daylight, avoid unnecessary stops, and travel in convoy if possible.

TRANSPORTATION

All **buses** leave from the **bus station** next to old airstrip on Rte. 13. Arrive at least 30min. in advance to ensure a seat on crowded south-bound buses. Buses run to

Luang Prabang (6-8hr., 9am, 40,000kip) and **Vientiane** (4-5hr.; 5:30, 5:50, 6:10am, 1, 2:30pm; 8000kip). To visit **Nam Ngum Reservoir,** take a *songthaew* to **Ban Thalat** (3hr., 8am, 6000kip), and then a *tuk-tuk* to the reservoir (3500kip per person).

ORIENTATION AND PRACTICAL INFORMATION

Vang Vieng lies along **Rte. 13,** which runs between Vientiane and Luang Prabang. The town spans two unnamed roads that are parallel to Rte. 13 and west of the airstrip. The first one originates at the **bus station** east of town. One block west, the 2nd road runs along the **Nam Song River.** At the north end of the road is the **market,** where *tuk-tuk* gather. Two kilometers south on the river road is the **Vang Vieng Resort** and **Tham Chang Cave.** Maps are available from shops all over town (3000kip).

The **post office,** which sells phone cards for international calls, is on the river road next to the market. (☎511 009. Open M-F 8-11am and 1:30-4:30pm.) A **card phone** is outside. Heading away from the market is the **district hospital** (☎211 109). The **Keo** and **Aikham Pharmacies** sit opposite the hospital. (Open daily 8am-8pm.) The large, well-stocked **Kheamphone Pharmacy** (open daily 6am-10pm) is on the right on the same road heading north from **Lane Xang Bank,** which **exchanges currency** and traveler's checks. (☎511 458. Open M-F 8:30am-6pm.) International calls can be made from **Lao Telecom,** opposite the police station. (☎511 000. Open daily 8am-5pm.) **Bicycle rental** is available from most guest houses and shops on the side road leading to the market (5000-7000kip per day). **Internet** access is available at **Xayoh Internet Restaurant,** at the north end of the first road parallel to Rte. 13. (250kip per min; open daily 9am-11:30pm) and **Planet Online,** further down toward the post office. (350kip per min. Open daily 8am-11pm.)

ACCOMMODATIONS AND FOOD

The rapid growth of tourism in Vang Vieng has led to a frenzy of hotel and guest house construction, most with similar prices and uniformly bland architecture. The north end of town has most of the restaurants and nightlife activity, while the south is quieter. The centrally-located **Doukkhoun 1 Guest House,** 50m east of the market, has clean rooms. (☎511 032. Doubles with bath and hot water 20,000kip, with A/C 70,000kip; 2-3 person rooms 30,000kip.) Around the corner, **Nglun Phanith Guest House** has friendly owners and views of the street life below. (☎511 150. Doubles with bath 20,000kip.) At the south end of town on the road that runs parallel to and east of the airstrip, the **Nana Guest House** has a restaurant and clean, quiet rooms. (Doubles with bath 20,000-25,000kip.) South of the hospital on the riverbank is **Les Jardins de Vang Vieng,** a guest house with simple, traditional bungalows set in tranquil surroundings. (☎511 192. Doubles 40,000kip; triples 50,000kip.)

For a chance to see traditional silk worm breeding and the production of green tea and starfruit wine, head 3km north of Vang Vieng to **Mr. T's Phondindaeng Organic Farm.** Spending a night in Mr. T's guest house is the ideal way to experience farm life first hand. Guests are welcome to help with the farm work. (☎511 220. Singles 25,000kip; doubles 30,000kip. If you plan to stay, write to Mr. Thanongassi Salangkoun, GPO Box 7893, Vientiane, LAO PDR. The owner prefers guests who plan to help out to stay at least two weeks.)

The **Sunset Restaurant,** an old favorite, is 300m south of the hospital down a lane to the left off the river road and offers gorgeous views over the Nam Song River. Further north, opposite the hospital, is **Ban Sabai Riverside Restaurant,** serving good but pricey French food. (Spaghetti 18,500kip. Open daily 10am-10pm.) **Khamla Restaurant,** 20m north of Nana Guest House, has many tasty dishes, including organic and vegetarian options. (Fried rice 6000kip. Open daily 6am-11:30pm.) A recent addition to Vang Vieng's selection of eateries is the **Organic Farm Cafe,** just north of Lao Telekom, which serves produce from the Phoudindaeng Organic Farm. (Starfruit wine 5000kip per glass. Open daily 8am-10:30pm.)

SIGHTS

By far the most popular activity around Vang Vieng is **inner-tubing** down Nam Song River. Shops along the road linking Luang Prabang Rd. and the river road arrange excursions 7km north of town (5,000kip including *tuk-tuk* and tube rental). The numerous **limestone caves** in the cliffs surrounding Vang Vieng are a spelunker's dream. Apart from **Tham Chang,** which is well-lit, the caves are unspoiled, beautiful, and easy to get lost in. **Mr. Keo,** a veteran guide at Nang Bot Restaurant, leads tours that include spelunking, hikes to waterfalls, subterranean swimming, and inner-tubing (1-day 30,000kip; 2-day/1-night 150,000kip). Flashlights and sturdy footwear are a must for spelunking. Many shops near the market sell maps of Vang Vieng and environs (2,000kip) for those wishing to venture alone.

> **!** Many travelers explore the caves on their own and do not die. Still, unaccompanied foreign explorers make tempting targets for rogues and bandits in more remote areas around Vang Vieng. Consider hiring a guide; doing so reduces your chances of getting lost, hurt, or robbed.

North of town lie the largest, most spectacular caves. **Tham Xang** (Elephant Caves) are 15km north of town and accessible by *tuk-tuk* (10,000kip), bicycle, or foot. Take Rte. 13 north to Ban Tham Xang Village where a dirt road to the left leads to the cave. A few paddies down, villagers run an informal ferry service across the river (1000kip), though in the dry season you may have to wade or cross a bamboo bridge. The first elephant cave rises out of the rice fields like a shark fin. Buddha images, a single footprint, and a stalactite bearing an uncanny resemblance to an elephant's head all await inside.

Vang Vieng's largest cave, **Tham Nang Phomhorm** (Cave of the Fragrant-haired Woman), is 4km past Ban Tham Xang. Take the turn-off right at the village of **Ban Patthana.** The two-level cave is 15km down this road, which passes **Ban Nam Yen,** a Yao hill tribe village 3km before the cave entrance (*tuk-tuk* 2500kip). It's a good idea to pay extra to get the *tuk-tuk* driver to wait while you explore. The most popular way to visit the caves is on one of the numerous tours (1-day tour of caves and local villages US$5) offered by guides around Vang Vieng. Some companies also offer white water rafting and rock-climbing trips (about US$15 per day).

South of town and across the Nam Song River lie **Tham Pourke** and **Tham Phou Kham** (Cave of the Golden Crabs). Tham Pourke is closer but less impressive. To reach the caves, head south of town toward the river and turn right down the path next to the Sunset Restaurant. In the dry season it's possible to cross the bridge to get to the caves, but in rainy season you'll need to cross by boat (2000kip). Over the bridge to the right is **Tham Chang.** (Open daily 7:30-11:30am and 1-4:30pm. 4000kip.) Bring a flashlight.

Other highlights around Vang Vieng include ethnic villages that are best visited by bicycle. Across the river west of town are the Hmong villages of **Naxom** and **Namouang.** South of town off Rte. 13 toward Vientiane are the Yao villages of **Namone** and **Vangheua,** which offer splendid views of the surrounding mountains across paddy fields. A Hmong village of some 300 households, comprised mainly of repatriated refugees from Thailand, is 13km north of Vang Vieng and south of Tham Xang village still west of Nam Song River. The United Nations High Commissioner for Refugees (UNHCR) oversees their reassimilation. Ask before taking photos.

NIGHTLIFE

Vang Vieng's popularity has led to the birth of a small nightlife scene. Currently there are only a few options, and many locals would like to keep it that way. **Hope's Oasis,** 50m east of the market, is a lively bar/restaurant with dancing in an attractive garden. The **Monkey Bar,** across from the market, also has dancing. (Open M-W

11am-11pm, Th 11am-11:30pm, F-Sa 11am-midnight, Su 11am-11:30pm.) The **Xayoh Cyber Pub,** next to Hope's Oasis, has a pool table. (Open daily 9:30am-11:30pm.)

LUANG PRABANG ☎71

Luang Prabang's name is synonymous with Lane Xang, the magnificent "Kingdom of a Million Elephants" that stretched across Indochina from the 14th-17th centuries. Substitute palanquins and pachyderms for bicycles and *tuk-tuk*, and it really seems like the city hasn't changed much since. From Mt. Phousi in the center of town, the gold peaks of Luang Prabang's many wats shine through the palm-tree canopy, as monks in saffron robes add color to the streets below. King Setthathirat shifted the capital to Vientiane in 1556, leaving Luang Prabang in a peaceful isolation that has helped it resist the urbanization that has swept other Laotian cities and stands as an ideal springboard for trips north and lazy rides down the Mekong.

TRANSPORTATION

Flights: Luang Prabang Airport (☎212 173), on Airport Rd., 5km from the town center. *Tuk-tuks* to Central Station on Chao Xomphou Rd. 10,000kip. Flights to: **Chiang Mai** (Th and Su, US$60); **Houie Xay** (1 per day, US$46); **Luang Nam Tha** (4-5 per week, US$37); **Phonsavanh** (1 per day, US$35); **Vientiane** (2-3 per day, US$55). Departure times vary, so ask at **Lao Aviation** (☎212 172), on Wisunalat Rd., near the Kitsalat Setthathirat Rd. intersection (open daily 7:30am-4:30pm) or at **Kian Min Lao Office,** 3/064 Ban Viengxay Rd. Better English spoken. Open daily 8am-5pm. MC/V. Domestic tax 1000kip; international tax US$10.

Buses: Northern Bus Terminal (☎252 729), 5km north of city in Ban Don. *Tuk-tuk* 4000kip. Buses leave when full after 7:30am for: **Muang Ngoi** (3-4hr., 15,000kip); **Nambak** (2½-3hr., 14,000kip); **Oudomxay** (5hr., 3 per day, 22,000kip); **Pakmong** (2½hr., 11,000kip). **Southern Bus Terminal** (☎252 066), south of the city off Phothisane Rd. next to the city stadium. *Tuk-tuk* from town center 4000kip. Buses to: **Vang Vieng** (6-7 hr., daily 9:30am, 40,000kip) and **Vientiane** (10-11hr.; daily 6:30, 7:30, 9, 10, 11:30am; 50,000kip). Arrive before 8am to ensure a seat.

Boats: Book tickets for **slow boats** at the Navigation Office (☎212 237) on Souvanabalang Rd. behind the Royal Palace. Service to: **Chiang Khong,** Thailand (2-3 days, 150฿); **Pakbeng** (1-2 days, 250฿); **Pak Ou Caves** (5hr. round-trip, 90,000kip per boat); **Tha Shang** (1 day, 200฿). **Charter boats** for up to 20 people go to: **Muong Ngoi** (1 day, 4500฿); **Paklay** (2 days, 5600฿); **Tha Deua** (1 day, 2500฿); **Vientiane** (3 days, 11,500฿ per boat). **Speedboats** leave when full from **Ban Don** (*tuk-tuk* 4000kip), 5km north of Luang Prabang; tell the driver "speedboat." Boats go to: **Houie Xay** (6hr., 1000฿); **Pakbeng** (3hr., 500฿); **Pak Ou Caves** (20min., 30,000kip). Speedboats can also be chartered. Prices listed are per boat for up to 8 passengers. To: **Muang Ngoi** (2hr., 2600฿); **Paklay** (4hr., 4000฿); **Tha Deua** (1½hr, 1750฿); **Vientiane** (9hr., 8300฿). For long journeys (to Houie Xay or Vientiane), arrive before 10am or you'll have to stop overnight.

Local Transportation: Fishing **boats** run across the river to and from **Ban Chiang Man** (5min., 1000kip), the gateway to **Wat Long Khoune** and **Wat Tham,** and to **Ban Chan Pottery Village** (40min., 20,000kip round-trip). **Songthaew** run to: **Ban Hat Hien** (10min., 4000kip); **Ban Phanom Pottery Village** (15min., 10,000kip); **Khouang Si Waterfalls** (2hr., 80,000kip); **Pak on Caves** (80,000kip).

Rentals: Many guest houses and rental shops across the city rent **motorbikes** (US$10 per day) and **bicycles** (US$2 per day).

LAOS

ORIENTATION AND PRACTICAL INFORMATION

Luang Prabang is small enough to easily navigate. The main road, running southwest to northeast from the **football stadium** to the **Nam Khan River,** is **Sisavong Rd.,** called **Phothisarath Rd.** between the football stadium and the post office. After the post office, Sisavong/Phothisarath Rd. briefly becomes **Chao Fa Ngum Rd.** and finally **Sakavongsa Rd.;** the **post office, tourist office, national museum, Wat Xieng Thong,** and the entrance to Mt. Phousi all lie along this road. Parallel to Phothisarath Rd., **Souvanabalang Rd.** runs along the Mekong River, becoming **Ounkham Rd.** to the northeast and then **Souvanna Khamphong Rd.** at the tip of the peninsula between the Nam Khan and Mekong Rivers. The main cross-street, **Kitsalat Setthathirat Rd.,** runs away from the waterfront, eventually intersecting **Naneng Kham Rd.** Lao Aviation, the **police,** the Rama Hotel, and numerous restaurants sit on **Wisunalat Rd.,** which runs parallel to Naneng Kham Rd.

Tourist Office: Luang Prabang Tourism Office (☎212 487), on Wisunalat Rd. near the intersection with Chao Xan Phon Rd. Friendly if slightly clueless staff. Arranges tours to sights and ethnic villages, but guest houses do the same for less. Open M-F 8am-noon and 1-4pm.

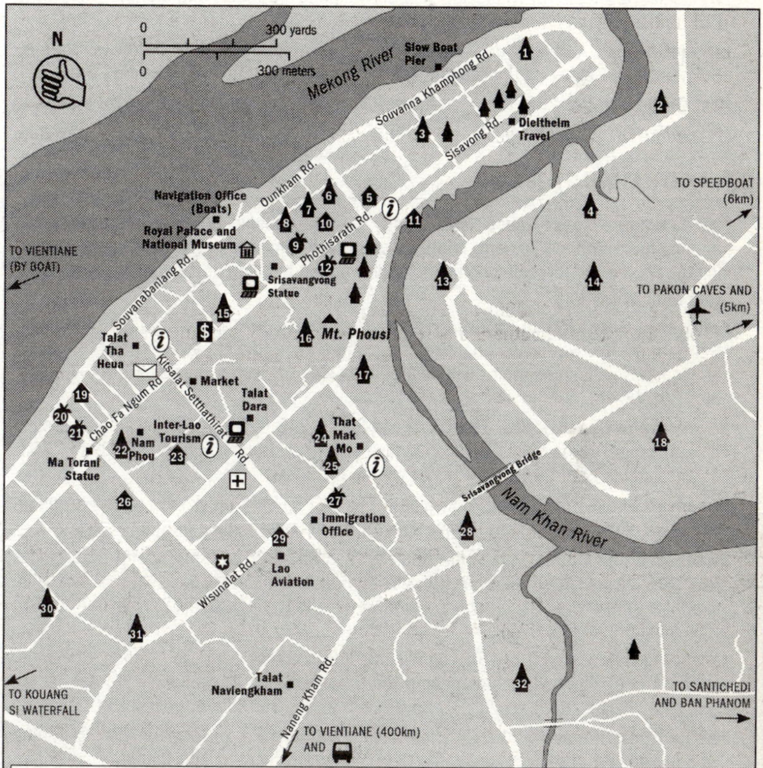

Luang Prabang

ACCOMMODATIONS
Kounsavan Guest House, **23**
Jaliya Guest House, **29**
Pathoumphone Guest House, **11**
Phounsab Guest House, **10**
Souansavahn Guest House, **26**
Paphai Guest House, **5**
Viradesa & Viradesa II Guest House, **19**

FOOD
Indochina Spirit Restaurant, **21**
Domchan Restaurant, **20**
Luang Prabang Bakery, **12**
Nazim Restaurant, **27**
Scandinavian Bakery, **9**

WATS
Aham, **24**
Aphai, **17**
Chom Phousi, **16**
Choum Kong, **8**
Mai, **15**
Munna, **28**
Nong, **3**
Pa Kha, **4**
Pa Nha Thiop, **32**
Phan Luang, **13**
Phon Sang, **14**
Phonsaat, **2**
Sene, **6**
Sieng Mouane, **7**
Tao Mai, **18**
Tham Phousi, **25**
That Luang, **30**
That, **22**
Wanorom, **31**
Xieng Thong, **1**

Tours: Lane Xang Travel, 46 Phothisarath Rd. (☎212 725). Tours of craft villages US$5-20 per day depending on size of group. Open M-Sa 8am-noon and 2-5pm.

Immigration Office: ☎212 453. On Wisunalat Rd. near the Kitsalat Setthathirat Rd. intersection. **No visa extensions.**

Currency Exchange: Lane Xang Bank, 90/8 Phothisarath Rd. (☎212 107). Exchanges currency (min. exchange US$100; commission 3.5%) and cashes traveler's checks. V cash advances. Open 8:30am-3pm.

Police: Provincial Headquarters (☎212 151). On Wisunalat Rd. past the Lao Aviation office. Some French spoken.

Pharmacies: Many on Kitsalat Setthathirat Rd. next to the hospital, on the Mekong side of Phothisarath Rd. Open daily 7am-7pm.

Medical Services: Luang Prabang Provincial Hospital (☎212 054), on Kitsalat Setthathirat Rd. 75m from the Wisunalat Rd. intersection. **Red Cross** (☎212 259). On Winusalat Rd. near Wat Winusalat. Herbal saunas (10,000kip) and aromatic massages (25,000kip). Open daily 8am-9pm, 5-9pm for massages.

Internet Access: All over town. About 250kip per min. **Planet Online,** 1 block east of the Scandinavian Bakery on Photisalat Rd. offers free coffee and tea and shows CNN.

Post Offices: ☎212 288. At the corner of Photisalat and Kitsalat Setthathirat Rd. *Poste Restante.* International calls 60,000kip per 3min. Cash only. Open M-F 8am-5pm.

ACCOMMODATIONS

Pathoumphone Guest House (☎212 946), on Soukhaseum Rd. From the base of Mt. Phousi, head up the riverbank 75m; it's on the left. Small, quiet guest house overlooking the Nam Khan River. Reception is in the wooden building next door. Doubles US$5, with bath US$6-10

Kounsavan Guest House (☎212 297), on Chaotonkham Rd., the 1st right off Kitsalat Setthathirat Rd. when heading away from the Mekong River. Swiss chalet-like guest house has small, clean rooms with shared bath with hot water. Singles 25,000kip; doubles 30,000kip.

Souansavahn Guest House, 132 Boukhong Rd. (☎213 020). Spacious, clean rooms in an impersonal guest house. All rooms have hot water. Double with outside bath US$3-4, with private bath US$6; "VIP" room with A/C US$15.

Phounsab Guest House, 6/7 Photisalat Rd. (☎212 975). 1 block right of the Royal Palace. Airy, clean, and friendly. Convenient location. English spoken. Rooms US$7.

Viradesa Guest House, 13/2 Hoa Khoie Rd. (☎252 026). From Kitsalat Setthathirat Rd., turn left on Chao Fa Ngum Rd. and right down a lane marked by a "silversmith" sign; it's at the end. Basic rooms. Dorm beds US$1; singles US$2, with bath US$5; rooms for 3-4 people US$8.

Jaliya Guest House (☎252 154), on Wisunalat Rd., across from Lao Aviation. Spacious, spotless bungalow-style rooms behind the main building. Convenience store in reception area. Singes/doubles 20,000-25,000kip; triples 35,000kip; quads 45,000kip.

Paphai Guest House (☎212 752), on Savang Vathana Rd. off Sisavong Rd. Charming wooden guest house with traditional decor. Centrally located with friendly English-and French-speaking staff. All rooms have shared bath. Singles US$4, doubles US$8.

FOOD

Luang Prabang brims with good restaurants that offer traditional Lao dishes, like watercress salad, *laap kai* (spicy chicken salad), and brown sticky rice. Restaurants are located along **Sisavong** and **Wisuhalat Rd.** For the best food at rock-bottom prices, head to **Talat Tha Heua.** (Open daily 6am-8pm.) In the evenings, vendors here set up on Kitsalat Setthathirat Rd. near the river. Noodle vendors and *khao jii pâté* sellers gather at **Talat Dara.** Fresh fruits and vegetables are sold at **Talat Naviengkham** on Phothisane Rd. (Open daily 6am-6pm.)

Indochina Spirit Restaurant, on Chao Fa Ngum Rd. before the Ma Torani statue. In a traditional wooden stilt house. Floor seating on cushions. Wide selection of Lao, Thai and Western dishes. Delicious selection of *tam yam* (Lao soup), curries, and grilled dishes 10,000-20,000kip. Traditional Lao music every night. Open daily 10am-11pm.

The Scandinavian Bakery, 52/6 Photisalat Rd., 1 block east of the Royal Palace. Mix of Lao and Western foods. Great breakfasts (13,000-18,000kip). Open daily 7am-7pm.

Luang Prabang Bakery, on Photisalat Rd. 50m east of the Royal Palace. Superb home-baked goodies. Lao/Western menu. "Big" baguette sandwiches 12,000-15,000kip. Open daily 7am-10pm.

Nazim Restaurant, 78/4 Ban Visoun, between the Immigration Office and Red Cross. Great Indian food and friendly service. Vegetarian options. Open daily 11am-11pm.

Domchan Restaurant, on Souvanabanlang Rd. by the Mekong River. Wooden house with gorgeous sunsets. Tasty hot papaya salad. Traditional Lao dishes 10,000-15,000kip. Open daily 7am-10pm.

SIGHTS

The former capital of a great Buddhist kingdom, Luang Prabang has many vestiges of its glorious past. Most notable are its many wats, which show off the Luang Prabang-style five-tier roofs that dot the city. Many of the most interesting sights line **Phothisarath Rd.,** which culminates with the magnificent Wat Xieng Thong. If you have time for only a few sights, start there and work your way up to the Royal Palace and Museum, Wat Mai, and Mt. Phousi. End the day relaxing by the Khouang Sy Waterfall or with a Lao massage at the Red Cross. Wats are locked to prevent theft, but a polite request can open them.

WAT XIENG THONG (TEMPLE OF THE GOLDEN CITY). Built by King Setthathirat in 1559, the temple is widely regarded as the *magnum opus* of Lao religious architecture, boasting elaborate golden reliefs and a mosaic of the Buddhist Tree of Life. The pagoda on the right if you enter from the Sisavong Rd. entrance, houses King Sisavangvong's funeral chariot, used to transport the funerary urn to the cremation site after his death in 1959. *(On Souvanna Khampong Rd. near the Mekong River. Open daily 6am-5pm. 5000kip.)*

ROYAL PALACE AND NATIONAL MUSEUM. The Royal Palace and its contents are a highlight of many a traveler's visit to Luang Prabang. Built by King Sisavangvong in 1904, it remained the home of the royal family until the monarchy was abolished in 1975. It houses a copy of the **Pha Bang,** a golden Buddha that is Lao Buddhism's most revered image. A gift to Lane Xang's first king from the Khmer court in the 1300s, the original figure is made of 50kg of pure gold and sealed in a Vientiane bank vault. The elephant motif seen in much of the palace symbolizes the kingdoms of Luang Prabang, Champassak, and Vientiane, which were unified under Lane Xang in the 15th century. Inside the Royal Palace is the National Museum, home to a fine collection of Lao art. *(Next to Wat Mai. Museum open M-F 8-11am and 1:30-4pm. No bare thighs, upper arms, or midriffs. 10,000kip.)*

MT. PHOUSI (MARVELOUS MOUNTAIN). Despite its name, "Mt." Phousi is not very high. A leisurely climb up 329 steps takes visitors to small **Wat Chom Phousi,** whose glittering *stupa* is visible from miles away. There is no better spot to take in Luang Prabang's sunsets than from the summit. Past the wat and up a staircase on the left, a rotund Buddha sits at the entrance of a cave. Bring a flashlight. Beyond the pavilion is a deep footprint of the Buddha. Continuing along the path down the mountain leads to an exit onto Sisavong Rd. *(Open daily 8am-9pm. 8000kip.)*

WAT MAI. It took 70 years to construct this impressive wat. It was completed in 1797 and housed the Pha Bang Buddha from 1894-1947. The north side of the wat is adorned with gold bas-reliefs depicting the story of *Veisantara*, Buddha's ultimate mortal reincarnation. *(Opposite Mt. Phousi. Open daily 6am-late.)*

WAT WISOUNNNARATH. Built in 1523, this wat was razed by Chinese mercenaries and then rebuilt at the turn of the 19th century. The towering *sim* houses Buddhist art, overseen by the largest Buddha in the city. Stacked haphazardly along the walls are hundreds of Buddha images. Also located on the temple grounds, **That Mak Mo Stupa** (aptly named the "**Melon Stupa**") was constructed in 1504 and held many Buddha statues that are now on display in the national museum. *(Open M-Sa 5am-7:30pm, Su 9-11am and 5-7:30pm.)*

STATUE OF MA TORANI. This small statue depicts Ma Torani (Mother of the Earth) as a young maiden washing her hair. According to legend, this cleansing act protected the Buddha from a demon who was washed away in a flood of suds. Images of Ma Tarani in the same contorted pose adorn wats all over town. *(Opposite the Provincial Hall on Phalongxay Rd.)*

OTHER SIGHTS. **Wat That Luang,** the final resting place of many royals, including King Sisavangvong, is another sunset-viewing spot. *(On Phalongxay Rd. south of the sMa Torani statue.)* Wacky **Wat Prabouthabat** was built in the 1950s with money from local Chinese and Vietnamese communities. *(Farther down Phalongxay Rd., opposite a Shell station. Open daily 8am-6pm. 500kip.)*

MARKETS

Luang Prabang's **markets,** although not large by Southeast Asian standards, are some of the city's most engrossing sights. **Talat Dara,** at the intersection of Kitsalat Setthathirat and Samsenthai Rd., sells everything imaginable. (Open daily 6am-6pm.) **Talat Tha Heua** is on Kitsalat Setthathirat Rd. near the waterfront. **Talat Navi-engkham,** on Phothisane Rd., near the Kitsalat Setthathirat Rd. intersection, is the morning market. (Open daily 5-6am.) **Handicraft and textile shops** along **Photisalat Rd.** display a wide range of products crafted from traditional woven fabrics including silks and cottons. Inspired by diverse ethnic styles and once patronized by the royal family, the industry accounts for much of Luang Prabang's trade. Embroidered fabric and off-the-rack garments, such as blue-and-black Hmong vests, are available. Bargaining is acceptable.

DAYTRIPS FROM LUANG PRABANG

KHOUANG SY WATERFALL

30km south of the city. Tuk-tuk (1½hr.; 80,000kip). Entrance fee 8500kip.

Numerous pools of cool, crystal water are dotted up the slope of the hill making the waterfall a popular swimming spot for travelers. Many travellers aren't deterred by the "Do Not Swim" signs next to the pools at the base of the falls. Climb the steps cut into the clay slope to the pool at the first tier. From here you can cross the river and climb natural, water-eroded steps to the top. Careful— the steps are steep and slippery.

PAK OU CAVES

At the confluence of the Mekong and Nam Ou Rivers, 25km upriver from Luang Prabang. Charter a boat on Souvanna Khamphong Rd., at the bank of the Mekong River (1hr., US$10 per boat, up to 6 people) or tuk-tuk (1hr., 80,000kip, up to 6 people) to Pak On Village and then hire a boat to the caves (3000kip per person). Entrance 8000kip.

The two caves, **Tham Ting** (lower) and **Tham Phum** (upper), are home to hundreds of Buddha statues. The boat journey has fantastic scenery and is worth the trip in itself. Every April during Phimai (Lao New Year), thousands flock to the caves to pray, a tradition dating back to King Setthathirat's discovery of the caves in the 1500s. Bring a flashlight.

Close to the caves is **Xang Hai Village,** famed for its *lao khao* (rice whiskey) distillation industry. Locals brew the firewater from sticky rice in oil drums along the riverbank. Many of the handicraft stalls offer visitors free samples and bottles are sold for US$1. Traditionally, women drink the less abrasive colored whisky, but locals are happy to provide the stonger variety to anyone who dares.

ACROSS THE RIVER

To get to the other bank, hire boats all along the Mekong River.

Few temples match **Wat Long Khoune's** location, a tranquil tropical garden above the Mekong. **Wat Tham** (Temple Cave) is 20m up the path from Wat Long Khoune. A labyrinthine passageway twists 50m underground, ending at a quartz stalactite as thick as a tree trunk. Monks guide spelunkers and point out Buddha statues and rock formations along the way. Bring a flashlight.

CRAFT VILLAGES

To get to Ban Phanom by bicycle, head away from Mt. Phousi on Vatmuenna Rd. and turn left at a large paved intersection 100m past Wat Pa Nha Thiup. After 1km take a dirt road marked by a "Luang Prabang Pre-Stress Concrete Plant" at the base of a hill with a pagoda on top. Follow the dirt road into Ban Phanom (tuk-tuk 8500kip). To get to Ban Chan, hire a boat from Luang Prabang or Ban Chiang Man (20min.).

Each of the craft villages near Luang Prabang specializes in a specific item, and workshops let visitors see the manufacturing process. **Ban Phanom,** a weaving village 4km east of the city on the banks of the Nam Khan River, is a 300-year-old Lu village which has enjoyed considerable royal patronage, and many villagers served as royal weavers and tailors. Come early before tour groups arrive.

Ban Chan, a pottery village 45km south of Luang Prabang, is on the opposite side of the Mekong River. The entire village participates in making large *thong* (water jugs) and clay roofing tiles. Visitors can watch the entire process, from grinding clumps of clay into fine sand to throwing pots on hand-turned pottery wheels to baking the pots and tiles in large underground kilns.

Ban Xang Chang, 7km east of Luang Prabang, is home to a paper producing workshop on the village's main road. Artisans use traditional techniques to produce the distinctive paper. A small shop sells paper products (notebooks 8000-20,000kip).

> **!** The US government has advised its citizens to avoid to Xieng Khouang Province (except for Phonsavanh town and the districts of Muang Kham and Muang Nong Haet) due to ongoing insurgent and bandit activity. Ask your embassy for up-to-date conditions before traveling. Also note that Rte. 7, the main road to Phonsavanh from Vientiane, is periodically closed due to bad conditions. It is always closed during rainy season.

PHONSAVANH

The terrain of Xieng Khouang Province, northeast of Vientiane along the Vietnamese border, is composed of rugged mountains and beautiful rolling hills, more reminiscent of Ireland than Indochina. Its elevation ensures cool, at times chilly, temperatures. During November and December the mountains near the border are ablaze with poppy blossoms; opium, grown by the hill tribes, is the province's chief cash crop. Xieng Khouang is best known for Thong Hay Hin (Plain of Jars), an area scattered with mysterious 3000-year-old stone vessels. Xieng Khouang was one of two Lao provinces heavily bombed during the Vietnam War. Xieng Khouang City, the former provincial capital, was so severely damaged by B-52s that after the war the provincial seat was moved to Phonsavanh, 36km north. The landscape is pocked with craters, and cluster bombs litter the countryside, exacting a gruesome toll in limbs and lives from the local population.

> **!** **WARNING.** Reports indicate that Phonsavanh, including Plain of Jars, Xieng Khouang Province, and Muang Kham District, may be unsafe for lone female travelers. Check with your embassy before planning a trip.

TRANSPORTATION

Flights: Xieng Khouang airport, 5km from town down Rte. 4 (5000kip by *tuk-tuk*). To **Luang Prabang** (3 per week, US$35) and **Vientiane** (1 per day, US$44). **Lao Aviation** office (☎312 177) is at the airport by the exit, a small booth on the left. Book a day before departure. Cash only (US$) for foreigners. Open 7am-noon and 1-4pm.

Helicopters: The chopper that flew to Vientiane (US$44) is suspended due to an accident in May 2000. Inquire at the Lao Aviation booth to see if service has been restored.

Buses: Ramshackle buses and trucks leave from an empty lot on Rte. 7 adjacent to the market. Buses go to: **Ban Thatcho** (1hr.; noon, 3pm; 500kip); **Muang Kham** (22k; noon, 4pm; 600kip); **Xieng Khouang** (36km, 600kip). Bus travel to **Vientiane** was impossible as of July 2000. Buses run daily to **Luang Prabang** (2 days, 8am, 30,000kip–much more if the 2nd bus is empty; the 1st bus stops in the middle of nowhere). Buses to **Vietnam** run daily (6-7 hr.; 8, 9am; 25,000-30,000kip).

Local Transportation: Tuk-tuk are plentiful and go anywhere except the Plain of Jars for 4000-5000kip (15,000kip for 30min.). To **Ban Thatcho** 120,000kip round-trip.

Rentals: Cars and 4WD vehicles can be rented from tour companies. US$50 per day; to caves US$70; minibus seating 8 US$80. No self-drive. Check at hotels or guest houses.

ORIENTATION AND PRACTICAL INFORMATION

Phonsavanh consists of three main streets—**Rte. 4, Rte. 1** (also called **Phonsavanh Rd.**), and **Rte. 7**—forming three sides of a rectangle. Rte. 4 runs from the **airport** past the orphan school, **government buildings,** the **hospital,** and the construction site of a forthcoming museum to the **bank** (left) and the Phudoi Hotel (right). From there, it becomes Rte. 1, which passes the town's hotels and shops and ends with the **post office** (right) and a small unkempt park. Rte. 7 runs perpendicular to Rte. 1, left toward Vientiane, and right past more hotels and restaurants. Rte. 7 runs east-west and makes a "T" at the **market** when it crosses Phonsavanh. Budget hotels and guest houses line its east arm. South of the Phudoi Hotel, Phonsavanh Rd. veers west, passing the hospital on its way to the airport. **Electricity (and therefore hot water) is only available 6-11pm.** Bring a flashlight.

Tours: Manophet, at the **Kong Keo Hotel,** is a well-regarded guide. Tours to all three Plains of Jars or trips to the villages and hot springs US$50 for 5-6 people. **Plain of Jars Agency Travel** (also called **Sodetour:** ☎312 403), is well-run and cheap and has offices in Vientiane (☎21 216314) and Luang Prabang (☎71 212092). English and French spoken. Day trips to Plain of Jars US$30-50 depending on size of group. Open daily 8-11:30am and 1-5pm. **Lane Xang Travel** (☎312 171) opposite the Phudoi Hotel, near the bank, provides similar services. Prices according to size of group and season. Connected to Dao Phouane Hotel (☎312 092).

Currency Exchange: Lane Xang Bank (☎312 041), on Phonsavon Rd. opposite Phudoi Hotel. Exchanges traveler's checks. No credit cards. Open M-Sa 8am-3:30pm.

Markets: Central market, on Rte. 7 next to bus station and opposite post office. Well stocked with clothes, food, produce, and supplies. Open daily 6am-6pm. **Dry market,** next to bank, sells tinned food and hardware. Open daily 6am-5pm.

Police: Xieng Khouang Provincial Police (☎212 141), on Phonsavanh Rd., in a 2-story concrete building in the field opposite the hospital. No English spoken.

Medical Services: Xieng Khouang Provincial Hospital (☎212 240), on Phonsavanh Rd., southwest of town past the provincial hall on the right. Some English spoken.

Post Office/Telephones: Post and Telegram Office (☎212 166), on the corner of Rte. 7 and Phonsavanh Rd. opposite the market. International phone cards. Direct card phone and dial using ordinary magnetic and credit cards. Up to 61,000kip can be used in the 2 booths outside post office (expect a wait).

ACCOMMODATIONS AND FOOD

Phimmahaxay Guest House (☎312 208), near the bus station on Rte. 7. New, airy, and has satellite TV. All rooms US$12 including breakfast and bath (Japanese-style).

Phudoi Hotel (☎312 048), opposite the bank. Midnight curfew. Tours in English. Doubles with hot water Apr.-Sept. US$10, Oct.-Mar. US$15.

Dao Phouan Hotel (☎312 092), in a green marble building opposite the post office. Provides tours via Lane Xang Travel. Doubles Apr.-Sept. US$8, Oct.-Mar. US$10.

Dok Khoune Guest House (☎312 189), on Rte. 7 near the market. A bit of color: the lobby is decorated with (fake) defused bombs and expended cartridges as keychains. Medium-sized rooms with bath and toilet 40,000-60,000kip.

Phonesavanh Hotel (☎312 206). Basic and has a restaurant (entrees 10,000-20,000kip). Ask for larger 1st floor rooms. Shower and toilet. Singles US$7; doubles US$8.

The **food market** behind the post office sells fruit, vegetables, French bread, and some prepared snack foods. (Open 6am-7pm.) There are a few **noodle stands** here and across the street in the **main market. Sanha Restaurant,** on Rte. 7 opposite the post office, is the largest and most popular in town. (Huge portions, large menu. Delicious steak with fries 12,000kip; most entrees 10,000-20,000kip. Open 6:30-9pm.) **Tuoy Restaurant,** across the street by the Photo Express, serves delicious sweet-and-sour pork (12,000kip) and fruit shakes. (Most entrees 10,000kip. Open 11am-11pm.)

> **!** Areas immediately surrounding the jars are clear of mines and cluster bombs, but the rest of the countryside is not safe. Permission from the local Department of Commerce and Tourism (on Rte. 4 near the governor's office) is required to get to the official sights. Though *tuk-tuk* drivers will offer to take you to the Plain for cheaper prices than most package tours, it is recommended to stick to well-trodden paths and to go with an authorized guide.

DAYTRIPS FROM PHONSAVANH

THONG HAY HIN (PLAIN OF JARS)

The best way to see the plains is to take a day-tour of the three main jar sights. Tours cost US$10-30 per person depending on group size. Seen individually, sights cost 2000kip each.

The Plain of Jars consists of 3000 jars scattered in clusters on hill-tops, ranging from 200 plus urns down to one measly jar. The largest jars are up to 3.5m high and weigh as much as three cars. They are believed to be between 2500 and 3000 years old. A theory, strengthened by the discovery of human remains in one of the jars in 1963, holds that the jars are funerary urns hewn from solid stone by ancestors of the Khamu people, who continued to place the remains of their dead in jars well into this century. Others guess that an ancient civilization use the jars to store rice or wine. Many locals claim the jars were Stone Age kegs, made to brew vats of *lao khao* for the troops of a Chinese king after their victory on the Bolovens Plateau. No one really knows yet, but they are a wonderful and somewhat odd sight.

Hay Hin 1, 12km from town down Rte. 4 near the military airport, is the most impressive. Over 200 large urns cover three hill-tops in a small area marked by bomb-craters. This sight includes the heaviest urn (3.7 tons) as well as a cave where locals took shelter from bombs during the Second Indochina War (Vietnam War) and which is said to be one of the possible sights in which the urns were originally made (it looks like a furnace). **Hay Hin 2** (24km) and **Hay Hin 3** (32km) are accessible only by a car ride, and, during the rainy season, by Russian jeeps. The jars are smaller than those of Hay Hin 1, but Hay Hin 2—also spread over two hilltops—boasts the longest jar (3.5m) and a sweeping view of the landscape. Hay Hin 3, accessible by foot through paddy fields and villages, is the quaintest, and known for its Buddha statues in the jars, which are themselves unimpressive.

XIENG KHOUANG PROVINCE

To get to Ban Thatcho, take a tuk-tuk (6000-7000kip), taxi (10,000-15,000kip), or local bus (noon, 3pm; 1000kip).

Other highlights of the area include the ancient capital, **Xieng Khouang City,** 36km from Phonsavanh and difficult to access during rainy season, which despite bombing boasts two temples and a few Buddhas. Xieng Khouang is accessible by local bus. Beyond are hot springs and waterfalls, best reached by foot (with a guide to avoid bombs), and Hmong villages. **Ban Dong Dan,** near Hay Hin 2, and the larger **Ban Thatcho,** 24km from Phonsavanh, are the most visited. Xieng Khouang province, bordering Vietnam, is rife with ethnic minorities, consisting of 61% lowland Lao including Black Tai, 7% Khmu people, and 32% Hmong.

MUANG KHAM DISTRICT

*The Phonsavanh branch of **Sodetour Travel** is Hmong-run and recommended by travelers. A one-day trip to Tham Phyu and Hmong villages costs 30,000kip for car, driver, and guide. Sodetour organizes three-day treks into the mountains near the Lao-Vietnamese border, where trekkers sleep in remote villages (40,000-80,000kip per person). More independent travelers can take a bus to Nong Haet from Phonsavanh and request to stop at the turn-off for Tham Pin (around 1500kip). The trek to the cave is difficult.*

Muang Kham District uses war scraps—bomb casings, shells, and scrap metal—cleverly, in everything from farmyard troughs to fences. **Tham Phyu,** a cave 56km from Phonsavanh, was a civilian bomb shelter until 1968, when an aircraft fired a rocket into the cave and killed 400. Bone fragments are scattered around the cave.

Near the caves are **Hmong villages** worth exploring. Relatively far from the control of the Lao government, these villages are interspersed with poppy fields, despite the government's war on drugs. Go with a guide who can translate for you.

LUANG NAM THA ☎86

Relaxed and friendly Luang Nam Tha is the principal city of Laos's most ethnically diverse region. Surrounded by luscious landscapes and home to Nam Tha National Biodiversity Conservation area, it's a picturesque gateway to surrounding villages and also to the Chinese border crossing at Boten.

TRANSPORTATION. The **airport** is 7km south of town. **Lao Aviation's** offices are on the main road just north of Darasavath Guest House and at the airport (☎312 180; airport ☎312 053. Open daily 8-11:30am and 1:30-4pm.) Flights go to: **Houie Xay** (Tu, Sa; US$41); **Luang Prabang** (M, Th; US$37); **Vientiane** (Th, Sa, Su; US$80). Due to low demand, low season flights may be cancelled; check for current schedules.

The Tourist Information boards at the **bus station** (☎312 164) and guest houses list up-to-date travel information. Most **buses** depart by 8:30am but fill up quickly, so show up around 7 or 7:30am. Buses and **songthaew** depart daily from the bus station for: **Bokeo** (8hr., 8:30am, 60,000kip); **Boten** (2hr., hourly 8-11am, 10,000kip); **Muang Long** (4hr., 8:30am, 20,000kip); **Muang Sing** (2-2½hr., hourly 8-11am, 10,000kip); **Nalae** (3hr., 9:30am, 30,000kip); **Oudomxay** (4-5½hr.; dry season 8:30, 9:30, 10:30, 11:30am; rainy season 8:30, 11am; 18,000kip); **Xiengkok** (4½hr., 8:30am, 25,000kip). During the rainy season, the road to **Houie Xay** is impassable, but *songthaew* may ply the route during the dry season (8-11hr.).

Boats vary in size and carry 4-10 people. Go to the bus landing, 7km south of Luang Nam Tha (*tuk-tuk* 10,000kip) the night before you wish to leave to arrange the boat. Travelers may also save money, though not time, by agreeing to let the boatman do business along the route. Boats go to **Houie Xay** (dry season 3 days; rainy season 1 day, US$75-100/boat) via **Nalè** (2 days); and **Luang Prabang** (3 days);

SHAKY GROUND Laos is still fighting a war that ended 27 years ago for its primary combatants. Officially neutral, Laos allowed North Vietnamese troops on its land to start the Ho Chi Minh Trail, a conduit for supplies that eventually spelled ruin for South Vietnam and, ultimately, US troops.

Neutrality came with a price: nearly 3 million tons of explosive dropped in a never-ending series of raids, one every eight minutes every day for nine years. Around 30% of that ordnance–only 4% of it actual mines–never exploded and is still there, experts reckon. International NGOs have tried to help, but the Lao government thinks it can do the job with locally-trained staff. Time will tell, but it's not on the Lao side. In Phonsavanh, one of the main target areas during "The War," the largest building is an orphanage with 500 residents, their parents the victims of ordnance in supposedly clear paddies. The school authorities plan to accept another 300 students soon.

bring supplies. It may be quicker to hire a boat to **Pak Tha** on the Mekong (US$65-95), and then a faster boat to Houie Xay or Luang Prabang. Boats also go to **Nalè** (4hr., 40,000-50,000kip per person).

PRACTICAL INFORMATION. Luang Nam Tha lies along the main north-south road, Rte. 3, 217km northeast of Houie Xay and 117km northwest of Oudomxay via Rte. 2. The town center is marked by the large Kaysone Monument on Rte. 3. The **airport** and **boat landing** on the Nam Tha River both lie off this road, 7km south of town; heading north on the same road leads to **Muang Sing. Luang Nam Tha Tourism**, next to the Kaysone Monument, provides maps of the area and rents bicycles for US$2 per day. (☎312 047. Open M-F 8am-noon and 1:30-5pm.) A few doors right is **Lane Xang Bank,** which changes US dollars, baht, Chinese yuan, and traveler's checks into kip. (☎312 073. Open M-F 8:30am-3:30pm and Sa 8:30-10:30am.) **Bank for Exterior Commerce,** across the road from the Manichan Guest House, exchanges US dollars and yuan and offers Visa cash advances. (☎211 141. Open daily 8:30am-3:30pm). **Lao Aviation** and the **old market** are north of the guest house on the main road. At the south edge of town, a dirt road leads uphill to the **hospital, bus lot,** and **main market.** The **Telecom Office** (☎312 004), 100m past Lane Xang Bank, provides **international phone/fax.** (Open M-F 8am-noon and 1-4:30pm.) You can also make international calls from the two payphones outside the Telecom Office or from the phone booth 100m south on the same side of the road. Phone cards are available from the Telecom Office and various shops. The yellow **post office** (☎312 007) is opposite the Telecom Office. **Luang Nam Tha has electricity from about 7:30-10:30pm.**

ACCOMMODATIONS AND FOOD. Luang Nam Tha has many budget accommodations of varying quality. The best value is **Manichang Guest House,** on the main road across the post office. The friendly staff speaks good English and offers comfortable rooms with clean, shared bathrooms. (☎312 209. Bike rental 8000kip per day. Curfew 10pm. Doubles with hot water when available high season 20,000kip, low season 15,000kip.) About 200m up the road on the left is pricier **Darasavath Guest House,** which features charming bungalow-style rooms and a bar/restaurant. (Rooms with shared bath 20,000kip, with private bath 40,180kip.) At the north end of the main road is **Sing Savananh Guest House,** set apart by its clean rooms and family feel. (☎211 141. Doubles 15,000kip, with bath 20,500kip.) Seven kilometers from town following the main road south is **Boat Landing Guest House,** offering delightful, secluded bungalows and a restaurant. (☎312 398. Doubles with bath, hot water, and solar-powered light high season US$12, low season US$6.25; larger double US$15/7.50.)

Many guest houses have good restaurants serving Lao and Western dishes. Manichang Guest House's restaurant is especially popular. (Entrees 6500-10,000kip.) **Saikhonglongsak Restaurant,** to the right of the post office, has an excellent selection of Lao dishes. (10,000-25,000kip. Open daily 6:30am-10pm.)

SIGHTS. There is more to Luang Nam Tha than meets the eye. The town itself offers little, but superb excursions and scenery are a few minutes away by bicycle. Keep to roads and well-trodden paths. Luang Nam Tha Tourism (see **Practical Information,** above), in conjunction with local guides, organizes **treks to local villages.** Consult the visitor's boards or your guest house for up-to-date information. The **Nam Tha Guides Association** (☎211 131), around the corner from the Saikhonglongsak Guest House, organizes treks for up to eight people to villages along the Nam Tha River in the **Nam Tha National Biodiversity Conservation Area** and plans to start white water rafting trips soon. Travelers visiting villages should do so only with an accredited guide who can ensure that the cultural sensitivities of the villagers are respected. One popular excursion is to **Hmong Had Yao village,** 3km down the road to Muang Sing. Head north out of town and continue past the turn-off with the bridge. The **waterfall** at Ban Nam Dee (10,000kip by bike or *tuk-tuk*), 6km north of Luang Nam Tha off Rte. 3, is worth a detour. From December to March, the waterfall is the site of local papermaking. A visit to **Ban Thong Tai,** past the bridge north of town, affords views of **weaving and silk production.** Behind the Kaysone Monument, the local **museum** displays local textiles, clothing, and religious artifacts.

BORDER CROSSING: BOTEN/MOHAN. Wooden buildings, 60km northeast of Luang Nam Tha and northwest of Oudomxay, constitute Boten village, the only legal border crossing between Laos and China, open daily from 8am to 4:30pm. Boten has two roads: a paved road leading to the border checkpoint and a parallel dirt road with most of the town's buildings. Before the checkpoint, on the left, sits an **exchange booth** that trades Chinese yuan, US dollars, Thai baht, and kip, but no traveler's checks. (Open daily 8am-noon and 1-4pm.) Noodle shops on the dirt road have dorm-style **rooms** with mattresses on the floor or a raised platform (3000-4000kip per person).

For those coming from China, **songthaew** leave from near the exchange booth into the early afternoon for **Luang Nam Tha** (2½hr., 5000kip) and **Oudomxay** (3hr., 7000kip). If the only *songthaew* available is going to the destination you don't want, it may be possible to take it as far as Na Toei and change there.

Those crossing into China must have a Chinese **visa,** available from the Chinese embassy in Vientiane, on hand. After the border checkpoint, you can board a *tuk-tuk* to **Mohan,** China (1-2km, 1500kip), and proceed to Mengla, the closest sizeable town in southwest China's Xishuangbanna region.

MUANG SING

No one knows how the tourist industry got started in this one-road hamlet on Laos's north frontier (perhaps the cloud of opium smoke obscuring Muang Sing's past had something to do with it), but few can question that tourists are, indeed, here. Nestled among small villages and rice paddies, Muang Sing is just a short walk to rural northern Laos's world of minority ethnic groups and age-old traditions.

TRANSPORTATION. Muang Sing is 58km northwest of Luang Nam Tha on a bad road (prone to mudslides in the rainy season) that continues 10km to the Chinese border. Arriving from Luang Nam Tha, the **bus** drops off passengers at Muang Sing's large **market,** on the main road. From here, **songthaew** return daily to Luang Nam Tha (2½-3½hr., 8am-3pm, 101,500kip). *Songthaew* departure times vary; inquire at the ticket office. **Bicycle rentals** are available from guest houses (8000kip per day).

PRACTICAL INFORMATION. Opposite the market, a branch of **Lane Xang Bank** exchanges currency. (Open M-Sa 8am-4:30pm.) Left of the bank sits a tiny **post office;** look for the "La Poste" sign. (Open M-F 7:30-11:30am and 1-4:30pm, Sa 7:30-11:30am.) With the market on your right, head up the main road through the center of town. After 200m or so the road crosses a small bridge; 200m farther down on the left is the **hospital,** a cluster of wooden buildings with blue shutters. (Open 8am-4:30pm). There is **no international phone service** in Muang Sing. **Muang Sing has electricity from 7-10pm.**

ACCOMMODATIONS AND FOOD. Many cheap accommodations line Muang Sing's main road. The **Viengxay Guest House,** 20m to the left of the market, has friendly management and a restaurant. (Hot water when available. Singles 15,000kip; doubles 20,000kip; triples 25,000kip.) The **Taïlu** next door gets positive reports from travelers. (Doubles 35,000kip.) A little farther up the road on the left is the **Muang Sing Guest House,** which offers small but charming rooms for 20,000kip.

Some guest houses have restaurants. Apart from these, a few nameless food stalls, especially around the market, offer cheap meals.

SIGHTS. For many travelers, Muang Sing's main draws are its remoteness and proximity to ethnic villages. Booths along the main road organize guided trips (up to 3 people, up to US$40 per day per group). Stop by the **morning market** for another chance to experience the local cultures. Every morning the market bustles with buyers from surrounding villages. Market activity dies down by 6:30-7am, so come early. During the rainy season, market activity may drop as travel becomes difficult.

OUDOMXAY ☎81

Nestled amidst gentle hills and small farming villages, Oudomxay's beautiful surroundings and its lively market make up for the town's unattractiveness and lack of interesting sights. The journey from Luang Prabang is especially spectacular. Sixty kilometers from the Chinese border, Oudomxay—also known as Moung Xai—straddles both cultures: the language is peppered with Chinese and the televisions are tuned into Chinese stations.

TRANSPORTATION. The **airport** sits 1km outside town off the road to Pakbeng. **Lao Aviation** (☎312 047) flies to: **Houie Xay** (T, Sa); **Luang Prabang; Vientiane** (M, T, Th, F, Su; US$71). Buy tickets at least a day in advance from the Lao Aviation desk at the airport. Scheduled flights may be cancelled if demand is low. **Buses, trucks,** and **songthaew** leave from a lot on Rte. 2. Departures start between 8 and 9am and continue into the afternoon, going to: **Boten** (5hr., up to 3 per day, 14,000kip); **Luang Nam Tha** (4-5hr.; 8, 11am, 2pm; 18,000kip); **Luang Prabang** (5-6hr., 3-4 per day, 20,000kip); **Pakbeng** (7hr.; 8-9am or later; 21,500kip). To get to **Nong Khiew** take a Luang Prabang-bound bus to **Nambak** and continue from there, or catch a direct *songthaew* to Nambak (3-4hr., several per day, 12,500kip). You can also reach Luang Prabang via **Pak Mong** (3hr., 3-4 per day, 12,000kip), from which buses run to Luang Prabang (2-3hr., afternoon, 17,000kip).

PRACTICAL INFORMATION. Oudomxay lies on the intersection of **Rte. 1,** which leads east to Nambak and Nong Khiew, and **Rte. 2,** which heads north to Boten and Luang Nam Tha and south to Pakbeng. **Lang Xang Bank,** on the left about 400m up Rte. 1 from the intersection, **exchanges currency** and traveler's checks. (☎312 059. Open M-F 8:30am-5:30pm, Sa 8-10am.) The **Bank for Exterior Commerce,** next to the bus station, also exchanges currency and gives Visa cash advances. (3.5% commission, no commission on traveler's checks. ☎211 260. Open M-F 8:30am-3:30pm, Sa 8:30-10:30am.) Other services in Oudomxay include: a string of **pharmacies** opposite the market on the small road off of Rte. 2; the **hospital,** 3km south on Rte. 1., 400m down the first road on the right after Rte. 1 becomes a dirt road (☎312 043; open M-F 8am-noon and 1-4pm); the **Telecom Office,** on Rte. 2, 100m from the main intersection away from the pagoda hill on the right, with **international phone/fax** (☎312 001; open M-F 8am-noon and 1-4pm); a box for international calls, opposite the Bank for Exterior Commerce; **Friendly Internet,** next door to the Linda Guest House (500kip per min.; open daily 7am-10:30pm); and the **post office,** next to the Telecom Office (☎312 007; open M-F 8am-noon and 1-5pm, Sa 8am-noon). **Postal code:** 0400.

ACCOMMODATIONS AND FOOD. A family feel and very friendly owners sets **Sivankham Guest House,** across the bridge after the main intersection and past the gas station, apart from others. (☎312 253. Shared baths, squat toilet. Singles 15,000kip, doubles 20,000kip.) **Pholay Guest House,** on Rte. 2 100m past the bridge on the right before the gas station, has clean rooms with private bathrooms and a restaurant downstairs (☎312 324. Doubles 30,000kip). Across the road, pricier **Linda Guest House** has comfortable rooms, but traffic noise from Rte. 2. spills into the front room. (☎312 147. Doubles 30,000kip, with bath 40,000kip; "VIP" room with fridge and A/C US$10.) Up the hill from the bus station, behind the Kaysone Monument, is plain **Linda 2 Guest House,** conveniently near the bus station. (☎211 242. Triples 30,000kip).

There are few dining options in Oudomxay. The **market** offers fresh fruit and vegetables, and every morning stalls all over town serve baguettes with condensed milk filling (1,000kip). Of Oudomxay's few restaurants, **Noisavat Restaurant,** on Rte. 2 next to the post office, stands out with locals for its extensive menu and family feel. (Entrees 15,000-20,000kip. Open daily 7am-10pm.) Next door, **Supailin Restaurant** serves hearty breakfasts, filled baguettes, and Lao and Chinese entrees. (Breakfast 5000-10,000kip. Entrees 10,000-15,000kip. Open daily 8am-10pm.) **Sainamkor Restaurant,** at the bridge on Rte. 2, takes its name from the river it overlooks and serves substantial dinners, from eel to duck. (Dinners 10,000-20,000kip. Open daily 7am-10pm.)

SIGHTS AND ENTERTAINMENT. To ease the pain inflicted by bumpy roads to town, the Red Cross operates a **herbal sauna and massage** center, behind the Phon Xay Hotel down the road from the Sivankham Guest House. (Sauna 10,000kip. 1hr. massage 20,000kip. ☎312 391. Open daily 4-7pm.) A **snooker hall** next to Sainamkor Restaurant has four tables—locals will challenge you to a game. (Open daily 10am until you lose.) Apart from the large **market** (open daily 7am-7pm), which occupies a large block off Rte. 2 and sells colorful wall-hangings and clothes, only the eye-catching **pagoda,** which offers a panoramic view of the town and countryside, is worth a detour. As with all the northern towns, beautiful landscapes await those walk along the roads leading away from town.

PAKBENG

On the threshold of dense primary forest at the confluence of the Nam Beng and Mekong Rivers, tiny Pakbeng is a colorful though calm escape, relatively untouched by the tourist industry. Most travelers stay one night on their way to the Thai border or Luang Prabang and find this enough to soak in Pakbeng's ambience; others find its remoteness enticing enough to extend their visit.

TRANSPORTATION AND PRACTICAL INFORMATION. Overlooking the Mekong between Luang Prabang to the east and Houie Xay to the northwest, one-road Pakbeng winds along Rte. 2 for 2km. **Buses, trucks,** and **songthaew** depart when full from a lot out of town (*tuk-tuks* leave from the pier; 4000kip to get there) for **Oudomxay** (7hr., 8am until passengers stop showing up, 20,000kip). **Slow boats** leave for Luang Prabang (6-8hr., 50,000kip) and Houie Xay (9-11hr., 50,000kip). **Speedboats** depart to Luang Prabang (3hr., leave 8am-4pm when full, 100,000kip) and Houie Xay (3hr., leave 8am-4pm when full, 80,000kip). There is **no official currency** exchange in Pakbeng, although you can try the market 1km from the pier to the left. A **pharmacy** is on the main road to the right 500m from the pier opposite an improvised cinema. (Open daily 7am-9pm.) The **local hospital,** 1km

BETELMANIA From Mandalay to Mindanao, few things link the disparate cultures of Southeast Asia like the chewing of betel (pronounced "beetle"). Betelnut is chewed in China and South Asia but is believed to have originated in Southeast Asia. Leaves from the betel vine *(Piper betle)* are wrapped around slices of areca nut *(Areca catechu)* and powdered lime (chalk, not fruit) to form a quid. When chewed, this venerable wad produces a mouthful of blood-colored juice and a mind full of mellow vibes. Betel juice reddens the lips and stains the teeth black, a feature once considered oddly sexy throughout Southeast Asia. Since time immemorial, rulers retained betel-bearing slaves, and the betel trade made a great city out of Penang (named from the Malay word for areca nut). Beyond its role in traditional healing, betel is used in all manner of social functions, from offerings in the Thai Water Festival and exorcisms in Sarawak to Vietnamese courtships and Burmese divorces. In many languages, betel and marriage are linked concepts; in many cultures, the exchange of betel is the proper starting point for a romantic relationship and a necessity for mind-melting sex. Nobody is sure whether betel is addictive or carcinogenic, but many believe it's outmoded. The Thai government tried to outlaw betel in 1945, and in the 50s the Vietnamese communists launched an aggressive campaign against this supposed *hủ tục* ("backward custom"). As Southeast Asia continues to Westernize, betel-chewing has declined, and fewer people sport the telltale ring around the mouth.

WARNING. Reports indicate that Pakbeng may be unsafe for lone female travelers. Check with your embassy before planning a trip.

from the pier on the right, sits opposite the **post office.** (Open M-F 8am-noon and 1-4:30pm.) Pakbeng has **no telephone office,** and has **electricity from 6 to 10pm.**

ACCOMMODATIONS AND FOOD. Of the dozens of guest houses near the pier (and of the dozens more to come), a few stand out for cleanliness and good service. **Mon Savan Guest House,** 300m from the pier to the left, has clean doubles in bamboo houses (15,000kip with net and fan). A little farther and to the right, **Dockhoune Guest House** offers similar rooms and boasts a restaurant overlooking the Mekong. (Doubles 10,000-15,000kip.) **Sarika Guest House,** the large white building next to the ticket office, is more expensive but larger. Its restaurant overlooks the Mekong. (Doubles with private bath 20,000kip. Entrees 10,000-20,000kip.) A dozen restaurants cluster around the guest houses in and around town. All offer standard, though greasy, Lao rice and noodle dishes. (Open 6:30am-10pm.) **Pine Kham Restaurant,** 200m from the pier on the left, and **Bounmy Restaurant,** 100m farther, serve large and tasty fried rice dishes and soup (10,000-15,000kip). The **main market,** 300m from the pier on the left, is an excellent place to pick up fruits and other munchies.

HOUIE XAY ☎084

Houie Xay, Laos's little link to the infamous Golden Triangle—now little more than a tourist attraction—serves utilitarian purposes, but defies classification as just another border town. A 10min. walk in any direction finds hills of red clay or thatch huts on stilts, and if you walk for several hours, you'll surely come across hill tribe villages. As underappreciated (and overpriced) as it may be, Houie Xay still provides a taste of "unsullied" Laos: children play in the street after dark, the power goes out during storms, and if you do take a walk, you may go kilometers without seeing a car.

WARNING. Reports indicate that Houie Xay may be unsafe for lone female travelers. Check with your embassy before planning a trip.

TRANSPORTATION. **Ferries** to and from **Chiang Khong** (20฿) dock right by the center of town, down behind the Manirath Hotel. They leave when full, between 8:30am and 5pm, which are the official hours of the **border passport control** by the landing. It is possible to pass customs after hours for (an unofficial) 2500kip. **Speedboats** to **Luang Prabang** (6-7hr., 8-9am, 180,000kip) via **Pakbeng** (3-4hr., 80,000kip) depart from a small pier 5km south of town (2000kip per person by *tuk-tuk*). **Slow boats** heading north and south share a landing 1½km north of the town center. Boats don't depart on weekends. During the week, show up in the morning and hope for the best. You'll probably have to barter with the captain, but most will agree to set fares to **Luang Prabang** (48hr., 500฿ or 100,000kip) and to **Pakbeng** (5½hr.; 9, 11am; 86,000kip). Speedboats heading upriver dock north of the slow boats. During the dry season, you can explore northern provinces, including Muang Sing and Luang Nam Tha (up to 7hr., leaves early, 30,000kip) via **passenger trucks** that leave from a station by the market. **Lao Aviation** has flights (subject to weather conditions and frequently postponed during rainy season) to: **Luang Nam Tha** (1-2 per week, US$41); **Luang Prabang** (1hr., Tu, US$46); **Oudomxay** (2 per week, US$51); **Vientiane** (2-3 per week, US$88). The airstrip is 7km south of town; pay 4000kip per person for *tuk-tuk*. With your back to the Manirath Hotel, head right, then take the first left; the Lao Aviation office is 30m down on the left. (☎312 022. Open daily 8am-4pm.) **Bokeo Travel** (☎661 980 6242), off the main road by the post office, rents **jeeps** with drivers (US$100 per day).

ORIENTATION AND PRACTICAL INFORMATION. North of Luang Prabang and a few hundred meters east of Chiang Khong, Thailand, tiny Houie Xay hugs the Mekong. The main road runs north-south parallel to the river, and a small road passes shops and the customs to the pier on the Mekong. Perpendicular to the main road and opposite the pier, steps lead up the hill to a **Buddhist Temple.** Heading south, the main road also passes a **market** to the left and forks west (away from the river) toward the once French-occupied **Fort Carno,** now occupied by Lao officials. A dirt track on the way (to the left) leads uptown to the **post office.** The main road runs north-south, parallel to the river; the other road of note forks east from the main road at the north end of town, moving east (away from the river).

Lane Xang Bank (☎312 020), opposite Arimid Guest House's back entrance, cashes traveler's checks and exchanges US dollars and Thai baht. An exchange counter by the customs office on the Mekong provides similar services. (Open M-F 8am-3pm.) The **Bokeo Tourism Authority Office** has free maps. (Open M-F 9am-4pm.) To get to the **market,** head south (with your back to the river, turn right) on the main road, and then turn left at the big field with the pavilion 1½km down; it's another 1km. A smaller market sits at the center of town opposite the post office. **Bokeo Hospital** is on the back road, 1km south of the bank; **pharmacies** dot the main road. On the hill above the slow boat landing, **police** hang out in a stucco house. The **post office** is on a dirt track left when you are heading south on the main road. (☎312 026. Open M-F 8am-4:30pm.) An international **card phone** is outside.

ACCOMMODATIONS AND FOOD. As a border town, Houie Xay has a captive audience; its prices reflect that fact. The place that most deserves to be charging Vientiane-style prices is **Aramid Guest House,** on the main road, 1km north of the border ferry. Aramid rents bicycles for 4000kip per hour and has a friendly ambience and decent restaurant. (Doubles US$5, with A/C US$10; triples US$9, with A/C and mini-fridge US$12.) **Manirant Hotel** (☎312 040), on the main road, has doubles with private baths for 175฿ or 45,000kip. **Hotel Houei Sai,** 200m south, has the cheapest rooms in town. (Doubles 170฿ or 35,000kip.) A more comfy option is **Keochampa Guest House,** left from the border pier, with decent doubles. (☎312 035. Doubles with A/C and bath 200฿.) Cheap **restaurants** cluster along the main road. There are two good food stalls at the pier (soup 5000kip) and a Lao-Chinese restaurant north of the pier (entrees 8000-15,000kip). The market has lunchtime **food stalls.**

SPIES IN THE SKIES The Vietnam War made it to the living room TV of every US family, but the military missions in Laos remained covert and hushed. One of the most colorful and storied of these missions was Air America, an airline owned by the CIA and used exclusively to accomplish military objectives in Laos. The airline began in China in the early 1950s but was quickly and quietly taken over by US intelligence, which used it to ferry people discreetly around points in Asia. During the Vietnam War, Air America employed hundreds of pilots and mechanics to fly and maintain a fleet of 70 aircraft. Missions involved photo reconnaissance, airdrops, and searches-and-rescues for downed airmen. Some have alleged (notably in the 1990 film *Air America*) that the agency was also involved deeply in the Lao opium trade.

SOUTHERN LAOS

WARNING. Reports indicate that Savannakhet, Pakse, and the 4000 Islands Region may be unsafe for lone female travelers. Check with your embassy before planning a trip.

SAVANNAKHET ☎41

Nearly 500km south of Vientiane and on the west bank of the Mekong, Savannakhet—"Savan" to locals—is the center of Laos's most populated province. The town's charm lies in its buildings, its odd mixture of colonial French and modern, and its riverside walk. Most travelers don't stop long en route to the Vietnamese cities of Huế and Đà Nẵng or to Wat Phu and 4000 Islands region farther south.

TRANSPORTATION

Flights: The **Lao Aviation office** (☎212 140), at the south end of Sisavangvong Rd. Flights to **Pakse** (3-4 per week, US$44) and **Vientiane** (9-10am, US$61). Schedule is erratic. Buy tickets at least 1 day ahead and confirm. Cash only. Open M-F 8am-noon and 1-4pm, Sa 8am-noon.

Buses: The **bus station** (☎212 143) is at the intersection of Sisavangvong and Visouthat Rd., 1½km north of town center. Buses to **Pakse** (9-10hr., 6am, 17,000kip) and **Vientiane** (7-8hr., several per day 6am-1:30pm, 20,000kip) via **Thakhek** (3hr., 10,000kip). Through-buses from Vientiane to Pakse pass through at 4pm, but can arrive a few hours early or late. Times for buses from Pakse passing through en route to Vientiane are equally ambiguous. Buses along the unpaved road to **Đà Nẵng, Vietnam** (21hr.; Tu-W, F-Sa 10pm; 105,000kip) via the **Lao Bảo** border crossing (6-7hr., 65,000kip) and **Huế** (13-15hr., 83,000kip). Arrive 1hr. early. Buses also leave daily to **Lao Bảo** (6-7hr.; 6, 9am; 65,000kip), where transportation is possible to Vietnam.

Ferries: Pier is at the immigration office, near Simuang-Tha Heua Rd. intersection. Buy tickets at the desk downstairs to: **Mukdahan, Thailand** (15min.; M-F 9:10, 10, 11:10am, 1:30, 4:15pm, Sa 10:30am,2:45pm, Su 10:30am; 10,000kip).

Local Transportation: Tuk-tuk roam streets in large numbers, 4am-10pm. Around town, don't pay more than 3000kip during daylight hours. To **That Inheng** (40min., round-trip 30,000kip) and **That Phon** (2hr., 70,000-80,000kip).

Rentals: Sensabay restaurant on Thanon Simuang Rd. rents **bicycles** for 7000kip per day with passport deposit. DAFI tours (see above) rents **cars** for US$70 per day.

ORIENTATION AND PRACTICAL INFORMATION

The town's main road is **Phtisalath Rd.,** north-south parallel to the river and several blocks away. **Tha Heua Rd.,** along the bank, **Khantabouli Rd.** one block east and **Sisavangvong Rd.** farther east are also important and are linked by streets running east-west, the main one being **Oudomsinh Rd.** at the north end of town, which passes the deserted old market (a good landmark). **Simuang Rd.** (also known as **Chaleunmuang Rd.**), five blocks south of Oudomsinh Rd., is home to the immigration pier, Hotel Santyphab, and cheap restaurants. The **bus station** and the **new market** are at the north end of Sisavangvong Rd., and the **airport** is at the south end.

Tours: Savan Travel and Tour, 644 Senna Rd. (☎/fax 212 944), in Savan Banhao Hotel. Tours are the best way to visit the Ho Chi Minh Trail near Xepon, 160km east of Savan. Open M-Sa 8am-noon and 1-4pm. **DAFI Travel and Tour,** 127 Ratsavongseuk Rd. (☎212 341). Organizes tours down the Ho Chi Minh Trail and to the dinosaur remains at Ban Tangwai (car with driver US$80-100 a day) as well as minibuses to Lao Bảo (US$10 per person). Open M-Sa 8am-4pm.

Consulates: Vietnam (☎212 418), on Sisavangvong Rd. From the south end of the old market, head away from the river on Oudomsinh Rd., take the 1st right onto Sisavangvong Rd.; it's half a block down. **Visas** for crossing at Lao Bảo US$50; bring 2 photos. 3- to 5-day processing (best to obtain visa from Vientiane, Thailand, or Cambodia). Open M-F 7:30-11am and 1:30-4:30pm, Sa 7:30am-noon.

Currency Exchange: Banque Pour le Commerce Exterieur Lao (☎212 261), opposite old market. AmEx/V Traveler's Cheques, V cash advances (4% commission; min. US$100). Open M-F 8:30am-3:30pm. The cash exchange booth is in the post office. Exchange is possible at the **Lao May Bank** (☎212 362) inside the immigration office.

Markets: Savanxay market, 200m toward the river from the bus station, near the north end of Sisavangvong Rd. A sight to behold.

Police: ☎212 212. On Khanthabouli Rd., opposite the post office.

Pharmacies: Many near the old market. **Pharmesco,** 236/1 Ratsavongseuk Rd. (☎212 313), south of the old market. Anti-malarials and other Western drugs. Open 8am-5pm.

Medical Services: Savannakhet Provincial Hospital (☎212 131), on Khanthabouli Rd. 5 blocks south of Simuang Rd. on the right. English spoken.

Internet: Hotmail Cafe, Photisalath Rd. at Simuang Rd. near the Catholic Church. 1000kip per min.; 900kip per min. for over 30min. use. Open daily 8am-9pm.

Post Offices/Telephones: ☎212 295. On Khanthabouli Rd. From the intersection with Simuang Rd., the **post office** is 1 block south beside the radio tower. Cash exchange booth. Cash **overseas telephone** and **fax** service. *Poste Restante.* Open M-F 8am-5pm, Sa-Su 8am-noon. **Postal code:** 1300.

ACCOMMODATIONS

Sayamungkun Hotel, 85 Ratsavongseuk Rd. (☎212 426), 1 block south of the Simuang Rd. intersection; look for the sign. Towering ceilings, tiled floors, large terrace, and lovely 2nd-floor patio. Doubles with bath and fan 30,000kip, with A/C 52,000kip.

Soulinsouk Guest House (☎213 436,) opposite the bus station on Makhasavan Rd. This modern and comfortable guest house is ideally located for catching an early bus. Large doubles with bathroom 25,000kip.

Savan Banhao Hotel, 644 Senna Rd. (☎212 202). From the side of the old market nearest the Mekong, walk 1½ blocks south; it's on the right. Sometimes called the Silan Hotel. Quality varies markedly with price. 4 "classes" of rooms, from dingy (23,500kip) to decent with bathroom (41,000kip).

Savanphattana Guest House (☎313 955), the large gray concrete building next to Savan Banhao Hotel on Senna Rd. Clean doubles with individual bathrooms and fan 30,000kip, with A/C 40,000kip, VIP 60,000kip.

FOOD

The market boasts a large food section with *phở* (3000kip), spring rolls (1000kip each), and other Lao and Vietnamese snacks. Stalls along **Tha Heua Rd.** are an excellent place to sit back with a drink and watch sunsets over the Mekong.

Mekong Riverside Restaurant, at the north end of Tha Heua Rd. behind a hedge. Lao, Vietnamese, and Thai dishes 10,000-15,000kip. Grilled fish in chili sauce (12,000kip) and priceless views. Open daily 9am-10pm.

Lao and French Food Restaurant, 30 Chaleunmuang Rd., in a Chinese-style house at the corner with Tha Heua Rd., near the immigration office. European and Asian dishes, including omelettes (entrees 8000-15,000kip). Open daily 8am-11pm.

Sensabay Restaurant, 15 Chaleunmuang Rd., left before the Lao-Paris restaurant. Rice and noodle dishes; steaks and French fries (10,000-17,000kip). Open daily 8am-10pm.

SIGHTS

Wat Sayaphum, on Tha Heua Rd. north of the pier, is the only historically significant wat in Savan. The complex dates to 1896 and contains two main *sim;* the largest is a secondary school for monks decorated with murals depicting scenes from the *Ramakien.* Savan's French colonial buildings along Phagnapui Rd. and Simuang Rd. near the Mekong are also of interest.

That Inheng, the city's most revered religious shrine, is 15km north of Savan. The 25m *stupa*—built to hold the Buddha's spine—is all that remains of the ancient city of Sikhottabong. The road is poor; biking isn't advisable. Buses leave from the central station on Makhasavan Rd. every hour on the hour (5000kip).

That Phon stands 60km south of Savannakhet on Rte. 13. with a tall, white *stupa.* It isn't awe-inspiring, but it is sacred. Dating from the Angkor period, the story behind its construction is one of the most unusual Buddhist anecdotes. According to legend, Buddha was in the middle of a sermon when nature's call came on strong. Exercising the prerogative of the "World-Honored One," he had a *naga* build a toilet for him on the spot. That Phon's white spire now commemorates the site. **The Museum of Dinosaurs,** on Kanthabouli Rd. near some tennis courts (head north from Santyphals Hotel), is a surprising sight. The local archaeologist gives an interesting tour of the remains found northwest of Savan in the early 1990's. (☎212 597. Open daily 8am-noon and 4-10pm. 1000kip.)

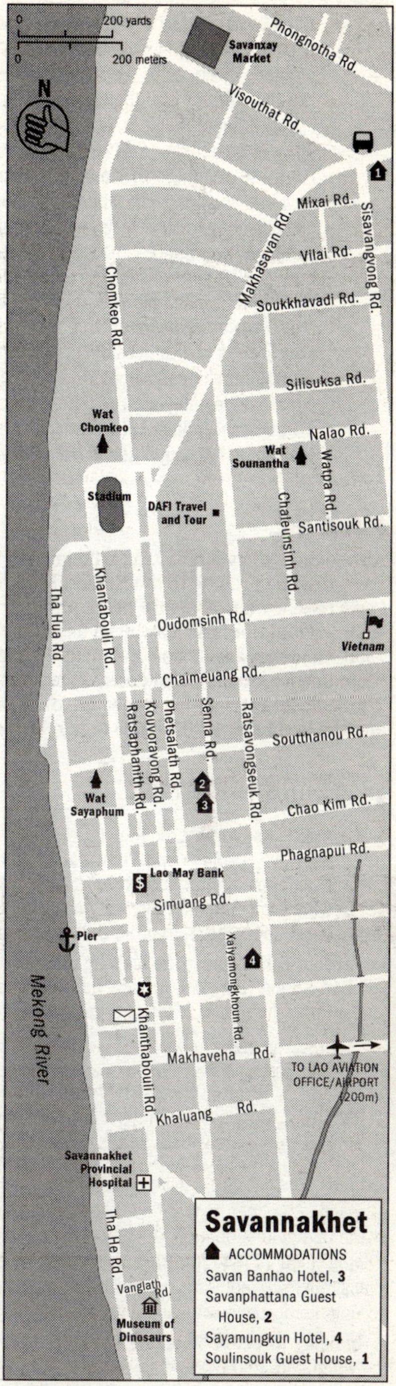

BORDER CROSSING: LAO BẢO The border town of Lao Bảo lies 200 buttock-bruising kilometers east of Savannakhet along Rte. 9, which winds around the slopes of the Annamite Mountains, on the Lao-Vietnamese border. The bus ride isn't for the faint of heart. If you opt to stay the night in Lao Bảo, Friendly Guest House is the only accommodation. The English-speaking owner offers basic meals (5000kip) and plain rooms (10,000kip).

For those heading into Vietnam, Lao customs at Lao Bảo is a formality, though travelers must show passports and pay a fine of US$5 for each day they have overstayed their visa. Vietnamese immigration requires a **visa** stamped with the correct entry point (get the stamp in Vientiane, Savannakhet, or Pakse). Passing through Vietnamese customs takes 3-5 hours, as the bus is combed for contraband and every bag is searched. You might take the bus only to the border and pass through customs on foot to avoid the wait; catch a motorcycle taxi to the next town. It is also possible to hop back on the bus and continue on to **Huế** for a US$2 surcharge (7-8hr.). There are currency exchanges at both checkpoints.

For those heading into Laos, the only bus to **Savannakhet** leaves at 8am (7hr., 13,000kip). Though *Let's Go* doesn't recommend it, travelers who miss the bus report that hitching a ride is easy, as trucks pass through at all hours.

PAKSE ☎031

Although its dirty streets and wild growth may be forbidding at first, Pakse offers a worthwhile prelude to the Emerald Triangle region, where the natural beauty of Laos reaches a crescendo of mountains, gorges, and islands. Its lively market stands out of doors as it awaits a new home—the previous market burned down in 1998—and spreads its colorful stalls in all directions. Pakse also boasts the largest Vietnamese population in Laos, a presence felt in the brisk pace on in its streets. The atmosphere stands in contrast to the far-flung Saravane and Attapu provinces, and the laid back 4000 Islands region farther south.

TRANSPORTATION

Flights: Pakse Airport, on Rte. 13 1km west of Xedone River Bridge. To **Savannakhet** (2-3 per week, US$44) and **Vientiane** (1 per day, US$95). **Lao Aviation office** (☎212 252), before the airfield on left or in town (☎212 252), on Xedone Quay (Rd. 11) between the Bangue Pour le Commerce Exte'neur Lao and the pier. Both open M-F 8:30am-noon and 1-4pm, Sa 8:30am-noon.

Ferries: Ferries cross the Mekong to Ban Muang Kao (7am-6pm, 20,000kip). **Boats** to **Don Khong** (8hr., 15,000kip) via **Champassak** (1½hr., 5000kip) leave when full from the waterfront right of the ferry pier (daily 7am-noon).

LAOS

CURIOSITY KILLED THE KING In the 11th century, King Khamatha of Champassak accepted a wager from a rival to prove that he could build a temple more rapidly. Khamatha set about the task of constructing Wat Phu, and his challenger ordered a group of women to erect Wat That Phanom (in present-day Thailand). The female engineers removed their shirts to work in the heat. When word reached the men at Wat Phu that That Phanom employed a topless construction crew, the contractors abandoned their own site to observe the effort upstream. Wat Phu lay unfinished as That Phanom's triumphant spire was raised aloft. Khamatha, ashamed of his failure, killed himself. The voyeuristic builders returned to Champassak to find their king dead. Heavy with guilt, they constructed a *stupa* for their ruined leader, which still stands a few hundred meters from Wat Phu. The temple remained unfinished until the Khmer King Suryavarman II completed it a century later.

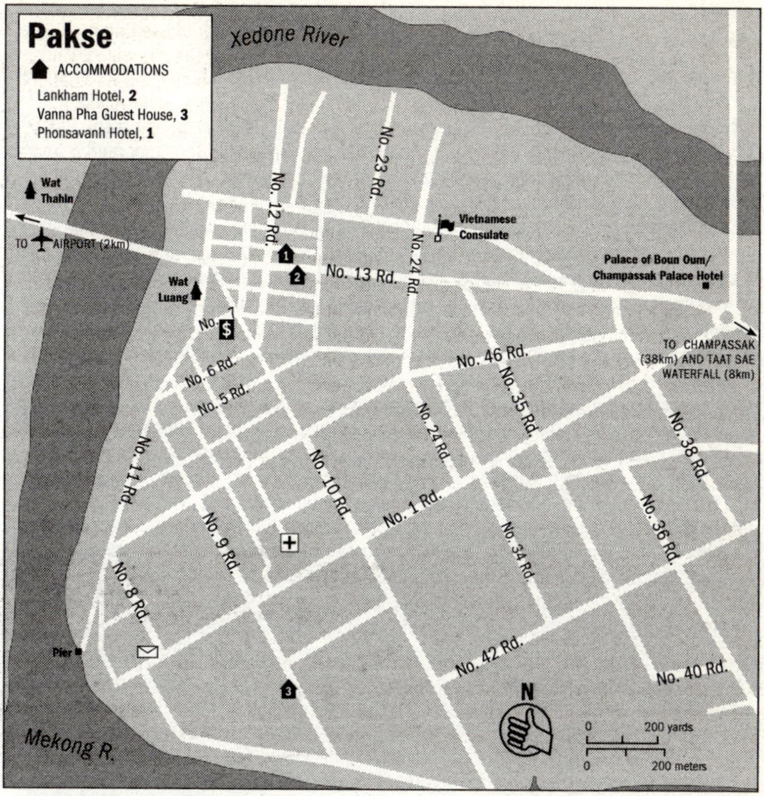

Buses: The **southbound** bus station is 8km east off Rte. 13; **northbound** buses depart from a station 10km west of town on Rte. 13. *Tuk-tuk* run to either for 3000kip.

Southbound station: Buses leave daily for: **Attapeu** (4-7hr.; 7:30, 9am, 1pm; 17,000kip); **Champassak** (1-2hr.; 9, 11am; 4000kip); **Muang Khong** (on the island of Don Khong; 2-3hr.; 7:30, 9am; 10,000kip); **Pakxong** (1½hr., every hr. 6am-4pm, 4000kip); **Saravane** via **Thad Lo** (3hr.; 7, 9, 11am, 1, 2pm; 8000kip).

Northbound station: Buses leave daily for **Vientiane** (15-17hr., up to 6 per day roughly 6am-3:30pm, 24,000kip) via **Savannakhet** (9-12hr., 17,000kip). Catch the ferry across the river, where *songthaew* go to **Vang Tao border crossing** (45min., 4000kip). *Tuk-tuk* can be chartered for 15,000kip. The ferry will be obsolete when the bridge (completed in July 2000) is open.

Local Transportation: The **tuk-tuk** hang-out is the parking area on Xedone Quay from the pier to Lao Aviation Office. *Tuk-tuk* will take you anywhere in town for 2000-3000kip.

ORIENTATION AND PRACTICAL INFORMATION

Pakse is confusing to navigate; maps are available. The **Xedone River** borders the town to the north and west; the **Mekong River** borders to the south. **Rte. 13,** the main road, goes past the **airport** and over the Xedone at the western end of town, passes by Lankham and Phonesavan hotels, **Lao May Bank** and the impressive Champaisak Palace Hotel before leaving town at the eastern end. Most budget hotels, restaurants, and shops are along Rte. 13, around the central market, and on the Xedone River. All streets are numbered: **Rd. 6, 5,** and **1** run parallel to Rte. 13, with Rd. 1 closest to the Mekong. **Rd. 8, 9, 10,** and **12** are perpendicular to Rte. 13. **Xedone Quay** (also known as **Rd. 11**) runs along the Xedone River from Rte. 13 to the **ferry pier** at the river. **Unhila market** is between Rd. 9 and 10; the **outdoors market** spreads its tentacles all over the center of town, making passage difficult.

Tourist Office: Lao National Tourism Authority (☎/fax 212 021), on Rd. 11 near the ferry pier. Map of Pakse 3000kip. Open M-F 8am-noon and 1-4pm.

Tours: Inter-Lao Tourism, #121 on Rd. 13 (☎/fax 212 226), at Champassak Palace Hotel. 4WD pickups with driver US$90-100 per day. Open M-F 8am-noon and 1-4pm, Sa 8am-noon. **Sodetour** (☎/fax 212 122), at the intersection of Rd. 13 and 24. Information desk. French and English spoken. Open M-F 8am-noon and 1-4pm. **DAFI Travel and Tours** (☎212 329), on Rd. 13 near Lankham Hotel. Rents cars and organizes minibus tours of the 4000 Islands region ($100 for 3 days).

Consulates: Vietnam (☎212 058), on Rd. 24 past Ketmany Restaurant on the right as you head toward Xedone River from Champassak Palace Hotel. Visas US$50. Passport and 2 photos required. 5-day processing. Open M-F 8-11am and 2-4:30pm.

Immigration Office: At the police station. Open M-F 8am-4pm. English spoken. No visa extensions–go to Vientiane.

Currency Exchange: Banque Pour Le Commerce Exterieur Lao (☎212 779), in the white concrete and glass building on the Xedone Quay (Rd. 11), 150m from the Xedone bridge. Exchanges currency. V, AmEx, traveler's checks, and cash advances (4% commission; US$-to-kip only, US$100 min.). Open M-F 8:30am-3:30pm. **Lao May Bank** (☎213 550), on Rd. 13 just before the large Honda sign (left as you head away from Xedone bridge), provides the same services. Open M-F 8:30am-3:30pm. **Lane Xang Bank,** farther down Rd. 13 on the right, and **Lao Agricultural Bank,** off a right 150m down Rd. 13, exchange currency. Both open Sa 8-11am.

Markets: Pakse's morning market burned in January of 1998. Two new ones are currently being built–near the airport (dry goods only) and near Dedone Restaurant on Rd. 1–until they are completed, the market sprawls between Thanon 10 and the Xedone River (and beyond on weekends)

Pharmacies: Seng Souk Osoth, 5 Rd. 9 (☎212 272), next to the old market lot. Anti-malarial drugs. Some English spoken. Open daily 7am-5pm. **Yingchokchay Pharmacy** (☎218 139), on Rd. 12 just off Rd. 13 near Suksamlan Hotel. Open daily 7am-10pm.

Medical Services: ☎212 018, **emergency** ☎212 041. Sandwiched between Rd. 46 and Rd. 1, behind old market lot. Doctor on duty M-F 7:30-11:30am and 1:30-4:30pm.

Police: ☎212 145. On Rd. 12, on the right, away from the market past Pakse Hotel.

Telephones: Telephone office (☎/fax 212 056), at the corner of Rd. 38 and Rd. 1. Take a right before the Champassak Palace Hotel on Rte. 13, then a right on Rd. 1; it's on the right. Cash **overseas telephone** and **fax** service (open daily 7am-9pm) and Lao Telkom **phone cards.** Card phones outside post office and Champassak Palace Hotel.

Internet Access: T and K E-mail and Internet Service (☎212 232), next to Lankham Hotel on Rd. 13. 1000kip per min. Open daily 7am-7pm. **Pakse Internet Cafe,** at the corner of Rd. 1 and Rd. 35, near the old market. Same price but faster connection. Also provides maps of Pakse and useful information. Open daily 8am-10pm.

Post Offices: ☎212 199, on Rd. 8 at Rd. 1. Head down Rd. 8 to the left of the gas station next to pier; it's near the end on right. Open 7:30am-9pm. **Postal code:** 1600.

ACCOMMODATIONS

Lankham Hotel (☎212 125), on Rd. 13 opposite Lao May Bank. A white-and-green concrete building with yellow sign. Modern and clean with friendly service. Internet access 1000kip per min. Doubles with bath and fan 40,000kip, with A/C 50,000kip.

Vanna Pha Guest House (☎212 502), on Rd. 9. From the market, head south on Rd. 9 toward the Mekong; it's 120m past the Rd. 1 intersection. Large shaded courtyard and decent rooms. Doubles with fan 30,000kip, with A/C 50,000kip.

Phonsavanh Hotel, 294 Rte. 13 (☎212 842), opposite the Lankham Hotel. Long dark corridors. Cheap but slightly dingy rooms with fan. Dorm 10,000kip per bed; singles 10,000-15,000kip; doubles 20,000kip; triples 30,000kip.

FOOD

Pakse has the largest Vietnamese population in Laos; *phở* shops are abundant. The **evening market** features a pavilion that is home to very cheap *kai ping*, *khao niaw*, and noodle soups. For top-notch spring rolls (5000kip), head to **Xuan Mai** at the intersection of Rd. 5 and Rd. 10. (Open daily 7:30am-midnight.)

Dorn Sokdee Restaurant, 94/95 Rd. 6, near Rd. 10, behind the Pakse Hotel. *Sukiyaki* 20,000-30,000kip, feeds 3-5. Lao and Thai dishes 3000-6000kip. Open daily 9am-11pm.

Sedone Restaurant, 110 Rd. 5, 2 shops to the left of Pakse Hotel, opposite the empty market lot. Doubles as a supermarket. Great Vietnamese food (*neuns* 4000kip) and decent Lao and Thai. Most dishes 6000-10,000kip. Open daily 7am-10pm.

Lien Huong Restaurant, on Rd. 13 next to Phonsavanh Hotel and opposite DAFI Tours. Serves basic Vietnamese food for 5000-8000kip.

Okeo Restaurant, on Rte. 13 past the Honda sign. The sign's in Lao; look for Ketmany Restaurant, which is next door. Cook-it-yourself meat and fish in vegetable soup. Delicious and healthy, though pricey (40,000kip for 2 servings).

SIGHTS

The **Palace of Boun Oum,** between the Xedone River and the bus station on Rte. 13, is one of the more bizarre landmarks in Laos. Construction of the six-story former residence of the Prince of Champassak began in 1969 and had not been completed when the communists deposed the prince in 1975. The impressive huge white structure presiding over the Xedone River now houses the **Champassak Palace Hotel.** Visitors can take the elevator to the top floor for the view of the Bolovens Plateau; sunsets are gorgeous. **Taat Sae Waterfall,** 8km east of town on Rte. 13, makes for a pleasant half-day trip. Large artificial pools lead to three waterfalls, two of which fall 40m. Locals bring their children to swim here. (*Tuk-tuk* 3000kip per person.)

Ban Saphay, a weaving village 13km west of town off Rte. 13, is renowned for *ikat* silk and *mutmee* cotton. Two shops along the main road sell fabric by the meter and a few ready-made garments. The **Lao Women's Union** operates one, but the privately owned **Lao Homemade Silk Skirt Shop** carries a better selection. *Mutmee* cotton costs 10,000kip per meter, *ikat* silk 8000kip per meter. Materials are cheaper and often better from the producers in nearby homes. Take a *songthaew* from the ferry pier (30min., leaves when full, 2000kip) or a *tuk-tuk* (3000kip per person).

CHAMPASSAK

The small town of Champassak lies 38km down river from Pakse, sandwiched between the Mekong and steep, craggy limestone hills. A quiet town, it offers an alternative to Pakse as a place to stay for travelers on their way south.

Wat Phu is open daily from 8am to 4:30pm (2000kip). Boats from Pakse to Don Khong stop at Champassak (3-4hr., several 8am-noon, 5000kip), as do occasional buses. Wat Phu is easily visited on a daytrip from Pakse via Champassak, accessible by bus and boat from Pakse. The latter is the more relaxing and scenic of the two options. Buses leave the southern bus station in Pakse 8km east of town on Rte. 13 (1hr.; 9am, 2pm; 5000kip). Buses leave Champassak for Pakse (1-2hr.; 6, 7, 9am; 5000kip). Boats heading upriver to Pakse stop at the landing near the center of town (3hr., last boat between 1-2pm, 5000kip). Boats continuing downriver to Don Khong stop at the landing at the center of town (6-8hr., leaves around 9:30am, 20,000kip). Those desperate to return to Pakse can take a ferry across the river and hire a *tuk-tuk* for the 40km ride (50,000kip) or charter a fast boat from Champassak for 60,000kip (1½hr.)

Boats and buses drop off passengers outside **Sala Wat Phou Hotel and Restaurant,** by the traffic circle that marks the small town's center. (☎213 280. Singles US$20; doubles US$25; triples US$35; US$5 more per room in high season.) For cheaper digs, head past the traffic circle with the small fountain and straight ahead until you reach a large wooden house on your left marked **Say Thong Restaurant;** this is also **Mr. Seng's Guest House,** an agreeable stop overlooking the Mekong. (Singles 15,000kip; large doubles with private bathroom 20,000kip.) The restaurant serves a mix of Lao and Viet food (entrees 7000-12,000kip). **Dok Champa Guest House,** on the left 50m after a right turn at the traffic circle, offers basic rooms with fan in little bamboo houses. (Singles 10,000kip; doubles 15,000kip.) The attached **Dok Champa Restaurant** serves Lao, Viet, and French food with many breakfast options and has great curries and fruit salad (entrees 8000-15,000kip). A bank on the left by the pier before the traffic circle changes US dollars and baht. (Open M-F 8:30am-4pm.)

Wat Phu (Hill Temple), or rather its ruins, lie 11km south of Champassak. An ancient Khmer temple known as **Muang Kao** (Old City) constitutes one of the finest examples of Khmer art outside Cambodia. Archaeologists believe the site dates to the 500s, although construction was completed in the 12th century by King Suryavarman II (1113-50) of Angkor. The temple bears stylistic similarities to Angkor Wat, and may have served as its prototype. UNESCO is planning renovations. Some of the walls are not stable; exercise caution while exploring.

Tuk-tuk to Wat Phu run 10,000kip per person roundtrip; bicycle rental from a guest house or hotel costs around 5000kip. The temple's main gate is 8km south (downriver), along Champassak's main road.

The temple's access road skirts a large *baray*, which symbolizes the waters of the earth and helped irrigate the surrounding rice fields. Originally, visitors entered the complex by a causeway lined with *naga* balustrades, as at Angkor Wat. The causeway is now fenced off; two large rectangular galleries flank the entrance.

Crowning a series of moss-covered laterite tiers is a small central sanctuary. Lithe celestial nymphs guard the entrance, above which Shiva rides a three-headed elephant. A rather incongruous Buddha sits where the *linga* once did, reflecting the empire's overlapping Hindu-Buddhist influences.

THAD LO

Against the backdrop of the Bolovens Plateau, 80km northeast of Pakse and 30km from Saravane, idyllic Thad Lo sits on a bend in the Xedone River. Travelers soak their road-weary bodies in natural pools, visit out-of-the-way villages, or kick back in bungalows, lulled to sleep by the sound of waterfalls.

Thad Lo can be visited as a daytrip from Saravane or Pakse, or as a lunch stop en route between the two. Buses run from Saravane to Pakse and stop at Thad Lo (every hr. 5am-1pm; return 1-2hr., 6am-1pm; 5000kip each way). Buses from Pakse to Saravane (2-3hr., every hr. 7am to 1pm, 3000kip) run from the station 8km east of town via Thad Lo. Be at the junction by noon to guarantee a ride.

Bamboo huts cluster along the main road between Pakse and Saravane, where the bus drops off passengers. **Thad Lo village** is some 2km down a dirt road (follow the signs). Continuing through the village and bearing right leads to a small bridge below Thad Heng Falls. The government-run **Thad Lo Resort,** up the path to the bridge, consists of a collection of bungalows around a main lodge (the White House). The open-sided lodge with a bamboo bar is an inviting hangout. (☎212 725. Bungalows US$5-10.) Less-comfortable **Saise Guest House,** across the bridge, offers cramped rooms with common baths for 20,000kip. **The Green House,** near Thad Heng Falls, has clean wooden rooms with gorgeous views for 28,000-40,000kip; the more expensive ones have a balcony. Two restaurants serve unexciting Thai and Lao and charge a fortune (breakfast 35,000kip). Attractions, include hikes, leaving from the waterfall (guides 10,000-15,000kip from the White House), explorations of the Bolovens Plateau ($10 per day), or the more exotic option of a ride on a elephant's back.

BOLOVENS PLATEAU

Northeast of Pakse looms the Bolovens Plateau, one of Southeast Asia's last frontiers. Laced with white water rivers, gorges, and valleys, the plateau is home to

FLIPPER, INDOCHINA-STYLE Once numbering nearly a thousand, the freshwater Irrawaddy dolphin population is now estimated at under 50. Increased fishing in the Mekong, as well as in rivers in Bangladesh and Myanmar, is threatening the dolphin's survival. Beyond the risk of being caught in fishing nets, the greatest menace to these mammals is the explosives used by unsporting Cambodian fishermen. Though banned in Laos, this practice is not uncommon across the river; unless it is stopped, the Irrawaddy dolphins may disappear.

ethnic minorities, many of whom were forced to flee their homelands in Vietnam's Central Highlands during the war. Among the larger groups are the Ngai, Suk, Katou, and Alak. Tea, coffee, fruit, and cardamom are grown on plantations, which were founded by the French to make Laos a more productive colony.

On the vast plateau, 113km northeast of Pakse, lies the sleepy provincial capital **Saravane.** Along its unnamed dirt roads, turkeys and cattle outnumber bicycles; cars are rare. Travel requires patience, flexibility, and cash, as many towns with accommodations cater to tour groups and charge high rates for rooms.

Saravane, northeast of Pakse, lies on the bank of the **Xedone River.** The road from Pakse passes the **bus station** and **airport** on the southwest edge of town, then rings the town center. Daily **buses** and trucks go to Kongsedone (1hr.; 10am, noon, 2pm; 9000kip), Pakse (3hr.; 6, 8:15, 10am, noon, 1pm; 9000kip), and Sekong (2-3hr.; 7:30am, 1:30pm; 8500kip). The **market** is the center of town and the main attraction, with the **post office** and **bank** to the west and the **hospital** and football field to the north. The post office sells phone cards, and has a card phone out front.

Saise Guest House, at the northeast corner of town near the river, has a helpful, hand-drawn map of the town and also offers not-so-clean rooms with fan and shared bathroom (18,000kip). **Susai Guest House,** 5min. out of town, is a little friendlier and has nice views. (Doubles with fan 20,000kip, with balcony 30,000kip.) *Tuk-tuk* from the bus station cost 2000kip to Saise Guest House, 1000kip to the market, and 3000kip to Susai Guest House. The restaurant opposite Susai Guest House serves unoriginal though tasty Lao food. (Entrees 8000-15,000kip.) *Phở* shops around the market and vendors selling fresh fruit abound. Inquire at Saise about exploring the Bolovens Plateau by car (US$25-40 per day) or hire a *tuk-tuk* from the lot near the market (50,000-60,000kip for 5hr.). Visits to animist villages, waterfalls, archaeological sites, and the plateau towns of **Attapu, Tataeng,** and **Pakxong** are options, though not always possible during rainy season. Other opportunities include visiting villages and waterfalls, or imbibing *lao hai* in traditional drinking circles.

4000 ISLANDS REGION ☎31

There are no long sandy beaches, but there are chances to lounge by the waterside. The area from Ban Munla Pamok to the Cambodian border is a tropical paradise at a point where the lazy waters of the Mekong become a raging torrent 10km wide. Thousands of islets dot the branches and tributaries, earning the region its nickname. The larger, inhabited islands maintain a distance from mainland affairs, and have a pace dictated by the cycles of the river. Welcome to the edge of the world.

TRANSPORTATION AND PRACTICAL INFORMATION. The largest island, and a good starting point for explorations, is **Don Khong,** with several guest houses in **Muang Khong,** the main village.

To get to Don Khong from Pakse, take a **boat** (8hr., several 7am-noon, 20,000kip) or **bus** (3½hr.; 7:30, 9am; 10,000kip). The boat stops at Muang Sen, on the west side of the island. The 20min. *tuk-tuk* ride to Muang Khong costs up to 6000kip per person. Buses stop in **Hat Xai Khun;** take a skiff to Muang Khong (2000kip per person). Buses return to **Pakse** from Hat Xai Khun daily (3hr., every hr. 7am-noon). An 8am bus leaves Muang Khong (at the intersection of the main road and Kang Khong villa) but takes longer, as it has to cross the Mekong (4hr., 15,000kip). Boats back to Pakse leave from Muang Sen near 5am, but they do not leave daily; the trip upriver is long and arduous. Ask at the pier in Muang Sen one day in advance.

A **post/telephone office** is a few meters upriver from Don Khong's pier and can place cash-only international calls. (☎212 073. Open M-F 8am-noon and 1-4:30pm, Sa 8am-noon.) A **morning market** is upriver from Muang Khong pier but ends between 6 and 7am.

ACCOMMODATIONS AND FOOD. Muang Khong has pleasant budget guest houses and many more under construction. The first, in front of the pier, is **Done Khong Guest House.** The French-speaking proprietor offers basic, tidy singles and doubles with shared bath and doubles with private bath. Her English-speaking son runs the **Done Khong Guest House No. 2,** 200m up the road past the post office, which has a beautiful veranda overlooking rice fields. (Singles 10,000kip; doubles 20,000kip.) **Kang Khong Villa,** a large wood and concrete building with balcony and front garden, is 30m past the original Done Khong. (☎213 529. Huge doubles with private bath 25,000kip; smaller doubles 20,000kip.) Every guest house rents **bicycles** for 8000kip per day.

Mr. Pon was a chef in Vientiane and now operates **Pon's Restaurant,** 50m upstream from Muang Khong pier. Delicious steamed fish (15,000kip) must be ordered two hours in advance. (Open daily 6am-10pm.) Mr. Pon also organizes boat tours of the islands (10,000kip per person). Done Khong Guest House also has a good restaurant that serves quality Viet and Lao food (8000-15,000kip).

Don Det and **Don Khone**—two relatively large islands, 20km south (downriver) of Don Khong and connected by a bridge constructed by the French, are becoming popular as a destination to avoid crowds on Don Khong. With palm trees, tropical flowers and tiny bungalows on the Mekong (10,000kip per person), Don Det is a paradise. Travelers rush there to swim in the Mekong and relax in hammocks. Don Det and Don Khone are accessible by boats from Muang Khong pier (most leave at 9am, 10,000kip). It's also possible to stay overnight in Muang Sen if the boat is late. **Muang Sen Guest House** and **Saykhong Guest House,** near the pier, offer rooms and meals. (Doubles 15,000kip.)

SIGHTS. The main attractions of the 4000 Islands are the waterfalls downstream from Don Khong. **Li Phi Falls,** on the southwestern tip of the island of Don Khone, are accessible by boat (10,000kip). They are rapids and are not so impressive. Don Khone shelters a 5km railroad line (now inoperative). Both sights are part of a government-owned resort. (Open daily 8am-6pm. 2000kip.) **Khone Pha Pheng (Voice of the Mekong),** the largest cascade in Southeast Asia, is farther south on the left bank, off Rte. 13. This so-called "Niagara of the Mekong" is (once again) nothing more than large rapids. Both waterfalls can be visited in a day with an early start. Guest houses and Pon's Restaurant organize trips (group of 4-10 people and boats with skipper 10,000kip per person). As the final stretch of river is not navigable, travelers stop on the mainland 12km away and take a *tuk-tuk* to Khone Pha Pheng (whole *tuk-tuk* 60,000kip). This region is home to the Lao population of the endangered freshwater **Irrawaddy dolphins,** who come upriver to spawn between January and March. They can't pass the rapids, but nevertheless try on a yearly basis. You might see them jumping out of the water in attempts to get to the other side (see p. 82).

MALAYSIA

RINGGIT

US$1 = RM3.80 (RINGGIT)	RM1 = US$0.26
CDN$1 = RM2.46	RM1 = CDN$0.41
EURO€1 = RM3.46	RM1 = EURO€0.29
UK£1 = RM5.52	RM1 = UK£0.18
IR£1 = RM4.39	RM1 = IR£0.23
AUS$1 = RM2.01	RM1 = AUS$0.50
NZ$1 = RM1.68	RM1 = NZ$0.60
ZAR1 = RM0.46	RM1 = ZAR2.19

PHONE CODE **Country Code:** 60. **International dialing prefix:** 007.

Malaysians have much to be proud of—Southeast Asia's most sophisticated transportation infrastructure; clean, diverse cities; and a reasonably well-protected natural environment. For the traveler, Malaysia offers the comforts of rapid Westernization as well as the grandeur of carefully preserved traditional cultures. Although the interaction between the country's Malay majority and sizable Chinese population isn't without tension, it's a credit to the Malaysians that in the wake of regional depression their society has stuck together, while Indonesia to the south has erupted in a bonfire of racial hatred. Malaysia's ethnic mix mingles most in the cities of the cosmopolitan west coast, while the sparsely populated east coast remains a bastion of seafaring Malay culture, but fantastic island beaches beckon eager travelers to both coasts. The eastern states of Sabah and Sarawak offer a chance to explore the wilds of Borneo, Malaysian-style, with accessible national parks, efficient tourist services, and buses that never run late.

FACTS AND FIGURES

Official Name: Federation of Malaysia.
Government: Constitutional Monarchy.
Capital: Kuala Lumpur.
Land Area: 329,758 sq. km.
Geography: Separated from the mainland by the South China Sea; borders Thailand to the north and Singapore to the south.
Climate: Dry (high season) Apr.-Oct. in the east, Oct.-Mar. in the west; Rainy (low season) Nov.-Mar./May-Sept.
Major Cities: Ipoh, Georgetown, Kuala Terengganu.
Population: 22,083,000.
Languages: Malay, Chinese, English, Tamil, Itan Dusan, Bajau.
Religions: Islam, Christianity, Buddhism, Hinduism, Confucianism.
Average Income Per Capita: US$4,458.
Major Exports: Petroleum, timber, natural gas, electronic components, textiles.

LIFE AND TIMES

THE PEOPLE OF MALAYSIA

Malaysia's true natives are the *Orang Asli* (original people), who most probably migrated to the peninsula from China some 10,000 years ago. Now, most of Malaysia's 22 million residents live on the peninsula, and the rest inhabit Sabah and Sarawak to the east. The terms "Malaysian," "Malayan," and "Malay" are distinct. **"Malaysian"** is a reference to a citizen of the country, **"Malayan"** denotes anyone from the peninsula, while **"Malay"** is a term for the ethnic Malay who constitute 50% of the population. Almost all Malays are **Muslim.** Sarawak is home to the Dayak, Malaysia's small Christian population. Indians constitute the third-largest race in Malaysia, while Chinese-Malaysians comprise a third of the total population.

HIGHLIGHTS OF MALAYSIA

BEACHES. **Pulau Langkawi** (p. 404) harbors budget haunts, but **Pulau Tioman** (p. 430) and the **Perhentian Islands** (p. 413) take the prize. **Similajau National Park** (p. 443) proves there's more to Borneo than jungle.

NATURAL WONDERS. **Taman Negara National Park** (p. 411) provides cool respite. Spelunk in **Niah National Park** (p. 444) or scale **Gunung Kinabalu** (p. 455), Southeast Asia's highest peak.

URBAN BEAT. Slick and never dull, **Kuala Lumpur** (p. 374) boasts capital sights, services, and after-hours elan. **Melaka** (p. 384) blends east and west both in the kitchen and on the street. **Georgetown** (p. 398) exudes the feel of a Chinese city. **Kota Bharu** (p. 418) is the heart of Malay culture. **Kuching's** (p. 433) vibrant waterfront scene and sights on the edge of the jungle are the cat's meow.

7-12c Trade increases Indic influences until Javanese and Chinese stop by

1400-1511 Melaka converts to Islam

1511 Portuguese invasion. Muslim loyalists flee to Johor

16c Dutch give Portuguese the boot

1699 Sultan Mahmud assassinated; Sulawesi groups jump into the fray

1786 More loot for the Queen: British acquire Pulau Penang

1795 British rule begins

18-19c British consolidate rule; anti-colonial sentiments grow

1819 British claim uninhabited Singapore

1824 Anglo-Dutch Treaty gives Malaya to Britain

HISTORY

EARLY KINGDOMS (100–1400)

–The Malay melting pot: gold, trade, and fleeing Chinese.

As early as the 1st century AD, the Straits of Melaka linked China and India through trade as traders from both countries came seeking gold. Indic influence spread throughout Malaya. Malaysia was temporarily seized by the Javanese Empire around 1080 until the Chinese, fleeing from the threatening Siamese, founded Melaka in the early 15th century. Melaka then grew quickly as a naval port and trading center for merchants from Arabia, China, Java, India, and Myanmar.

RISE OF ISLAM AND WESTERN EXPLORATION (1400–1800)

–A ruler a day...

The 15th century also saw the spread of Islam under Muslim **Muzaffar Shah,** who helped Melaka get rid of Thai vassals. By the late 15th-century reign of **Mahmud Shah,** Melaka included Peninsular Malaysia, Singapore, and parts of Thailand and northern Sumatra. The **Portuguese invasion** in 1511 marked the beginning of Malaysia's "age of exploration." Unruffled by the Portuguese presence, locals remained loyal to the Shah Dynasty and fled south to establish the state of **Johor.** The chaos following the assassination of Melaka's **Sultan Mahmud** attracted the **Bugis** and other groups from southern Sulawesi. They competed with the Sultan of Johor and the **Dutch,** who had replaced the Portuguese.

COLONIAL RULE (1795–1945)

–Once upon a time, the British colonized everyone.

The chaos continued until the oppressive but stabilizing English presence in Malaya began in 1795, when the Dutch gave up the island of Penang to Britain. Malaya fell under British influence, and the Dutch, in turn, took the islands south of Singapore. The **Treaty of Pangkor of 1879** saw the import of ill-prepared English "residents" to Malaysia, who influenced all aspects of life except religion and customs. By WWI, all of Peninsular Malaysia had submitted to some sort of British control, though not without resistance. Throughout the 1920s-40s, anti-colonial sentiment grew, evidenced in the popular uprisings and suppressions that characterized the colonial period.

FORGING A NATION (1945–70)

–1960s Malaysia: If everything bad happened at once, what would it be like?

During WWII, the Japanese moved into Malaya and returned the northern states to Thailand, hoping to exploit Malaya's resources and strategic location. The British, who had fled and left the country defenseless, returned to Malaya after the war but were unable to return the country to its former calm. In 1946, Britain's plan for refederation—which proposed that all Malayan territories except for Singapore be included in a single union—was opposed by the newly formed **United Malay National Organization (UMNO)** and the **Malay Communist Party.** But communist hopes were soon dashed, in part due to the deportation of half a million Chinese. The government plan then shifted to unifying Malaya and guaranteeing Malay rights. In 1957, the independent **Federation of Malaya** was established.

The 1960s were tumultuous. Supporting insurgency in Malaysia's eastern states and border skirmishes between Sabah/Sarawak and Kalimantan, Indonesian President **Sukarno** declared **Konfrontasi** ("confrontation") against Malaya in January 1963. With England's support, Malaya became Malaysia on September 16, 1963. This infuriated the Philippines, which held an ancient claim to Sabah; Indonesia, meanwhile, regarded Malaya's action as covert British neo-colonialism.

Within Malaysia, ethnic tensions rose. The diverse nation was home to a proud Malayan majority that dominated politics but lagged in economics. The official attitude toward Singapore's predominantly Chinese population created more problems for the Malay-oriented government, which had established Islam and Bahasa Malay as its official religion and language. In 1965, Malaysia passed an amendment allowing Singapore to secede. In May 1969, ethnic riots erupted in Kuala Lumpur after the Malay majority party, **Alliance** (which consisted of the UMNO and the conservative Malayan Chinese Association), lost a number of seats to non-Malay-supported parties.

Feeling their own culture should be adopted, at least in part, by other nationalities, the Malay forced the use of Malay language in Parliament and the courts. Malay political leaders called mass meetings but quickly lost control of the armed mobs that gathered. Ensuing riots lasted four days, leaving over 200 Chinese dead and more than 5000 homeless. Some Malays blamed the prime minister for the riots, but most blamed them on concessions to non-Malay groups rather than their own racial attitudes. **Deputy Prime Minister Tun Abdul Razak** replaced former Prime Minister Tunku Abdul when he retired in 1970.

1841
Sarawak given to James Brooke

1879
Treaty of Pangkor brings English residents to Malaysia

1942-45
Japanese occupation, British desertion, and Malay nationalism

1946
UMNO established

1957
Independence: Federation of Malaysia formed

1960s
Government tries to enforce Islam and Malay language

1963
Indonesian President Sukarno declares *Konfrontasi*

1965
Singapore secedes

1969
Ethnic riots in Kuala Lumpur

1971
Islamic National Culture Policy established

1981
Mahatir elected Prime Minister, slowly consolidates power

1996
First satellites launched; financial restrictions on Australia lifted

1997
Mahathir's policies called off

1999
Ibrahim receives six-year prison sentence

2000
Ibrahim convicted of sodomy

MALAY DOMINATION (1970-94)

—Mirror, mirror on the wall, aren't Malays fairest of all?

Under Razak's rule, UMNO's power increased, and the country continued to promote Malay interests. Additional political alliances increased the status and political clout of Malay citizens, and economic policies were implemented to support Malay business ownership. The **Islamic National Culture Policy,** established in 1971, defined "national culture" as encompassing the indigenous traditions of the Malay people, which disregarded not only pre-Islamic Chinese and Indian influences but also those of the Orang Asli, who had populated the region thousands of years before the proto-Malay. Policy makers insisted on education in Bahasa Malay alone and provided federal support only for ethnic Malay art and literature. The 1980s saw rapid growth and industrialization. Though he faced allegations of human rights violations and a court's declaration that the UMNO was unconstitutional, then-in-power **Mahathir Mohammed** prevailed and organized the **UMNO Baru** (New UMNO).

MALAYSIA TODAY

Mahathir intertwined Western economic models with a **"Look East"** policy when seeking foreign investment and trade to pull Malaysia out of the financial crisis. Malaysia remains an active member of the **Association of Southeast Asian Nations (ASEAN).** Under Mahathir's administration, the country has become less dependent on tin and rubber resources and toward industrialization. As a step toward the **Vision 2020** plan, which aims to attain developed-nation status by 2020 by improving technology, Malaysia launched its first two space satellites in August 1996.

The Asian financial crisis has since slowed Malaysia's development. Although Mahathir stopped blaming various segments of the population (from the Jewish population to currency traders) for the financial crisis, only recently has he accepted the gravity of the situation and the responsibility to address it. To avoid the imposing IMF regulations, Deputy Prime Minister **Anwar Ibrahim** called off Mahathir's high-growth policies in December 1997 to help stabilize the ringgit and the plummeting stock market. While stagflation may continue, it seems that Ibrahim's policy changes have at least stabilized the situation.

The downside of development has been severe **environmental degradation.** Once-beautiful bus rides are now marked by hills scarred by mining, single-crop plantations, and wastelands of factories and construction sites. Environmental awareness has gained popularity, but much of it's little more than rhetoric. The **Environmental Quality Act,** however, imposes stiff penalties for mishandling hazardous wastes.

Recent years have seen corruption in Malaysia's government. In April 1999, Ibrahim was condemned to a six-year prison sentence for allegedly interfering with police investigations into accusations of sexual misconduct, and in a year later, the court convicted Ibrahim of sodomy, ending a controversial year-long trial. Ibrahim viewed the ordeal as a staged maneuver to halt their struggle for more liberal politics. To many human rights watchdogs worldwide, however, the trials illustrated the government's backlash against peaceful political demonstrations.

CUSTOMS AND CULTURE

BUMIPUTRA

Though improving, Malaysia's Chinese-dominated economy suffers from serious income inequality, most notably between the Malay and Chinese. The Malay government hopes to balance the situation through the **New Economic Policy (NEP)**, a state-run program dedicated to streamline society and redistribute wealth to the native Malay, known as the *bumiputra* (literally "sons of the soil"). The NEP extends the *bumiputra* certain privileges to promote their economic advancement. Malaysian companies are encouraged to hire Malays over Chinese for top positions and must have at least 51% Malay shareholders, though recent economic development has loosened some of these requirements. Malays also get discounts on housing and loans. Consequently, Malays have risen economically, though critics denounce the NEP for discriminating towards Chinese, an giving unfair preference to the well-off *bumiputra*, and helping few poor still working in rice fields.

FROM THE HEART

As with most dominantly Muslim countries in Southeast Asia, the standard conservative codes of conduct apply. Remove shoes before entering a home or mosque, dress modestly, and use your right hand when handling food and greeting someone. Handshakes are usually suitable for both men and women, though Malays traditionally use the *salam*, a handshake in which the hands are touched to the chest to mean, "I greet you from the heart."

HUMAN RIGHTS

In its quest for unity, the Malaysian government has used a heavy hand regarding freedom of expression, particularly in the media. Amnesty International has criticized Malaysia for its dealings with the media, use of capital punishment, and restrictions on religion. Though the constitution provides for religious freedom, the practice of Islamic beliefs other than Sunni Islam is severely restricted, and religious minorities like Buddhists, Hindus, and Christians frequently face restrictions. In addition, some accuse Malaysian police of being trigger-happy; according to Mahathir, police use force appropriately to limit crime. However, this doesn't change the fact that suspected criminals under arrest face a very high death rate.

BISEXUAL, GAY, AND LESBIAN TRAVELERS

As a predominantly Muslim country, Malaysia is quite intolerant of homosexuality. Both Malay and visiting Muslims face flogging or imprisonment for gay or lesbian activity. Though non-Muslims are exempt from Muslim religious law, police may arrest any publicly gay person. Discretion is advised.

PINK INK. For more information, try **Pink Triangle,** 1st fl., 7C-2 Jl. Ipoh Kecil, Kuala Lampur, an organization devoted to HIV/AIDS and sexuality issues. The staff has information on GLBT venues in Kuala Lumpur and holds socials. (☎4044 4611; hotline ☎4044 9622. Open M-F 10am-7pm, hotline open M-F 7:30-9:30pm.)

ARTS AND RECREATION

DRAMA AND DANCE

Malaysian dance and drama are closely related, as exemplified by the **Ma'Yong,** a Malay dance-drama that gained prominence as a court tradition over 400 years ago. All roles are traditionally reserved for young women, except for the role of the buffoon. The stories are romantic dramas with nearly identical plots in which a heroic boy saves a princess from an ogre. **Malay shadow play** is an ancient and elaborate form of puppetry found across Southeast Asia. The central story is the **Ramayana,** Valmiki's epic Hindu poem, in which Rama leads an army of monkeys from India to Ceylon to rescue his wife Sita. **Malay dance** comes in many popular forms. The most famous of the court dances is the **Ashek,** a three-part dance in which the lead dancer weaves her way among stationary partners. Open-air **Malay folk dances,** performed during crop production or the fish harvest, are thought to appease spirits.

MUSIC

Cambodia, India, and the Middle East all influence Malay music. Among the most well-known instrument is the **rebab** (spike fiddle). Its nasal sound leads the orchestra in the Ma'Yong. The large Arabic **gendang** drums, provide the tempo for Malay drama and dance events. Popular singing styles include: **pantun,** Islamic devotionals of improvisational duets; **ghazals,** mournful Islamic love songs; and the vocal accompaniment to the powerful, percussion-heavy **dondang.**

OUTDOORS

Though more than 60% of Malaysia's rainforests have been destroyed to logging, the nation still offers magnificent activities for the adventurous traveler. Scale **2376m-Gunung Mulu** in Sarawak's Gunung Mulu National Park or try a **jungle hike** through **Taman Negara National Park,** one of the world's oldest tropical rainforests. For daring cave expeditions, **explore** the extensive underground limestone caves of Gunung Mulu or **spelunk** through the bat- and swiftlet-inhabited caves at **Niah National Park.** Malaysia's unspoiled coastal areas and islands offer some of Southeast Asia's best **snorkeling** and **diving**. Check out Shark Point and D' Lagoon on the Perhentian Islands to explore a sunken Vietnamese ship. For the less hard-core outdoors-lovers, Taman Negara, Gunung Mulu, and Kinabalu boast exotic **bird-watching**.

ADDITIONAL SOURCES

The Malay Dilemma, by Mahathir Mohammed (1970). A controversial treatise on Malaysia's racial issues. Banned in Malaysia until Mahathir's election.

The Lands of Charm and Cruelty: Travels in Southeast Asia, by Stan Sesser (1993). Includes an essay on logging in Sarawak originally published in *The New Yorker.*

ON THE WEB

Malaysia Tourism Board (www.interknowledge.com/malaysia/). Where to go, what to see, and how to do it.

NewMalaysia (www.newmalaysia.com/). Current events and a Malaysia search engine.

ESSENTIALS

VISAS

American, Australian, Canadian, New Zealand, South African, and most European citizens don't need visas for stays of up to 3 months. Irish citizens can stay for 2 months without a visa, and Greek and Portuguese citizens can stay for 1 month. Immigration offices in Johor, Kuala Lumpur, and Penang give **visa extensions.** Travelers who leave Malaysia and come back must apply for a US$10 **re-entry permit.**

MONEY

Malaysia's **ringgit (RM)** is issued in denominations of RM1, 2, 5, 10, 20, 50, 100, 500, and 1000. Each ringgit is divided into 100 **sen,** which come in coins of 1, 5, 10, 20, and 50. British pounds and US dollars are the most widely accepted foreign currencies. Travelers checks are accepted at all banks, hotels, and major department stores. A 5% government tax and 10% service charge is added to most bills, making **tipping** unnecessary but appropriate for exceptional service.

GETTING THERE

BY PLANE. Malaysia has four **international airports:** Bayan Lepas International Airport in Georgetown (p. 398), Kuala Lumpur International Airport (KLIA) in Kuala Lumpur (p. 374), Kuching International Airport in Kuching (p. 433), and Malaysia Airport Berhad in Kota Kinabalu (p. 450). **Malaysia Airlines** (**MAS,** www.malaysiaairlines.com.my/) flies from KLIA to over 100 domestic and international locations. Kuala Lumpur, Penang, and Singapore are the major international gateways.

BY LAND. Refer to the following table for overland border crossings in Malaysia.

BORDER CROSSINGS

BRUNEI. From Kuala Baram in **Sarawak** (near Miri, p. 445) take the bus that stops at the border in Kuala Belait and have your passport stamped before going on into Seria and **Bandar Seri Begawan** (p. 54). Alternatively, from Lawas or Limbang (also in Sarawak), cross over to Temburong or Bangar, stopping by the immigration post near Bangar. From **Sabah,** take a ferry to **Pulau Labuan.**

INDONESIA. Buses connect Tebedu in Sarawak (near Kuching, p. 433) with **Entikong** (near Pontianak) in West Kalimantan. The border crossing is open daily 6am-5pm; Indonesian visas are available in Kuching. Ferries run from Tarakan/Nunukan in East Kalimantan to **Tawau** in Sabah. To reach Sumatra from Peninsular Malaysia, take a ferry from **Penang** (p. 396) to **Medan** (p. 279).

SINGAPORE. A 1056m causeway connects Singapore (p. 604) to **Johor Bahru**. Buses and trains from Malaysia run over this causeway into Woodlands town.

THAILAND. Most Western tourists can travel to Thailand from Malaysia without buying a visa before crossing borders. Obtain transit visas at the border stops instead. By ferry, you can travel from **Kuala Perlis** and **Pulau Langkawi** (p. 404) to **Satun** (p. 777); remember to stop by the immigration office at Thammalang pier to have your passport stamped. Other common crossings are (listed from Malaysia to Thailand): **Rantau Ranjang/Kota Bharu** (p. 418) to **Sungai Kolok** (p. 778) in the east and **Kangar** to **Padang Besar, Alor Setar** to **Sadao,** and **Keroh** to **Betong** in the west.

GETTING AROUND

BY PLANE. Malaysia's abundance of domestic airports makes plane travel between cities easy and safe. **MAS** monopolizes the domestic market.

BY BUS OR TRAIN. Both A/C and non-A/C **buses** run between major towns at reasonable prices. **Malayan Railways (Keretapi Tanah Melayu Berhad, KTM)** runs up and down the west coast from Kangar to Singapore. KTM railpasses allow unlimited travel on passenger trains in Malaysia and Singapore for 10 days (US$28, children US$28) or 30 days (US$120, children US$60). The slow but scenic **Jungle Train** connects Wakat Baru (near Kota Bharu) to Singapore via Jerantut. Bus travel is quick and efficient along **Hwy. 3,** a well-maintained road connecting Johor Bahru in the south to Kota Bharu in the north.

BY CAR. Fixed-rate inter-city **taxis** connect many towns and cities; split the ride with up to three others. Local taxis are often unmetered, so agree on a price beforehand. Surchages apply to taxis booked by phone, trips from midnight-7am, and rides for more than two passengers. To **rent a car,** you should have an **International Driver's Permit (IDP)** or a government-issued license (see **Within a Country,** p. 42). Some hotels rent cars for RM160-350. Malaysian drivers travel on the left side of the road and wear seatbelts when riding in the front seat.

KEEPING IN TOUCH

Malaysia's **postal system** does quality work. Airmail across the globe should take one to two weeks. **Long-distance calls** are easiest from card phones, most of which offer IDD, but you'll have to pay local charges in addition to long distance fees. Telephone offices and convenience stores sell **phone cards.** The most convenient is the Telekom Malaysia card, except in Kuala Lumpur, where the Uniphone card is most useful. For **Home Country Direct (HCD)** numbers from Malaysia, refer to the table on the inside back cover of this book.

PENINSULAR MALAYSIA

WEST COAST

Rich with colonial history and natural beauty yet polished with a cosmopolitan veneer, peninsular Malaysia's west coast offers plenty of sights and modern amenities. With user-friendly transportation, tourist facilities, and many English speakers, the west coast may well be the best introduction to Southeast Asia. The west coast also represents Malaysia's ethnic mix well: sizeable Chinese and Indian communities coexist with ethnic Malay. Although many tourists complain that industrialization has hindered local culture, it has also created many jobs and comforts.

KUALA LUMPUR ☎03

Approaching Kuala Lumpur, two breathtaking towers appear, beckoning visitors from afar. Once in the city center, however, the bustling activity of this efficient city overtakes the towers' quiet grandeur. Kuala Lumpur asserts itself through elegant Muslim architecture and exerts patriotism through "Proud to be Malaysian" songs, ubiquitous Malay flags, and the highest flagpole in Asia. A country that has been in the hands of everyone from India to Portugal, and the Netherlands to Britain, Malaysia's multi-ethnic history is still visible: up to 7% of the population is of mixed European and Asian blood. With the opening of the KL Sentral Railway Station and a monorail, Kuala Lumpur looks to be on its way. As Malaysians chant "Malaysia Boleh!" ("Malaysia Can!") at sports events, the rumblings of numerous construction projects throughout the city reiterate the same sentiment.

INTERCITY TRANSPORTATION

BY PLANE

Ultra-modern **Kuala Lumpur International Airport** (**KLIA;** ☎8776 2000) lies 90km southwest of the city. Take a commuter train from the KL Sentral Railway Station to Nilai station (1hr., every 15-30min. 5:45am-10:45pm, RM4.5) and connect to a KLIA-bound bus (40min., every 10min. 6:15am-10:15pm, RM2.5) from Chansowlin Station or Jl. Duta Station. Alternatively, take Intrakota bus #19 from Klang bus station to the Duta Hockey Stadium at Hentian Duta (30min., RM1.20 or 1.60) and an airport shuttle from Hentian Duta to KLIA (1hr., every 20-30min. 5:45am-10:15pm, RM20). Airport taxis (☎8787 3030) between Kuala Lumpur and KLIA charge exorbitant rates (1-1½hr., RM70-90). Don't ride in a taxi without a meter.

FLY ME TO THE MOON

DESTINATION	FREQUENCY	PRICE	DESTINATION	FREQUENCY	PRICE
Bangkok	2 per day	RM620	**Penang**	12 per day	RM109
Hong Kong	1 per day	RM880	**Phnom Penh**	4 per week	RM790
Jakarta	2 per day	RM650	**Saigon**	4 per week	RM739
Manila	2 per day	RM1025	**Singapore**	10 per day	RM262

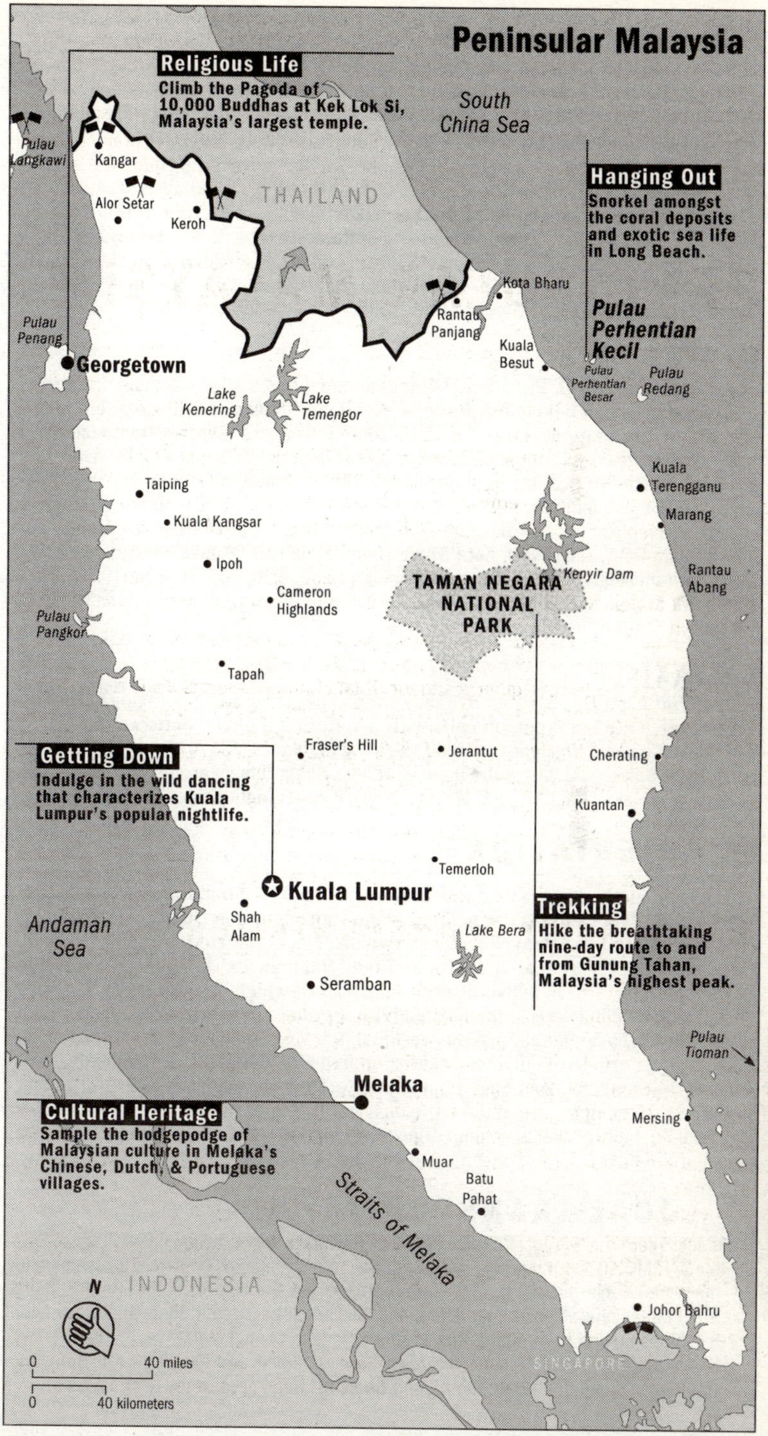
Peninsular Malaysia
Religious Life
Climb the Pagoda of 10,000 Buddhas at Kek Lok Si, Malaysia's largest temple.
South China Sea
Pulau Langkawi
Kangar
Alor Setar
Keroh
THAILAND
Hanging Out
Snorkel amongst the coral deposits and exotic sea life in Long Beach.
Kota Bharu
Rantau Panjang
Pulau Perhentian Kecil
Pulau Penang
Georgetown
Kuala Besut
Pulau Perhentian Besar
Pulau Redang
Lake Kenering
Lake Temengor
Kuala Terengganu
Taiping
Kuala Kangsar
Marang
Ipoh
Kenyir Dam
Rantau Abang
Cameron Highlands
TAMAN NEGARA NATIONAL PARK
Pulau Pangkor
Tapah
Getting Down
Indulge in the wild dancing that characterizes Kuala Lumpur's popular nightlife.
Fraser's Hill
Jerantut
Cherating
Kuantan
Temerloh
Kuala Lumpur
Trekking
Hike the breathtaking nine-day route to and from Gunung Tahan, Malaysia's highest peak.
Andaman Sea
Shah Alam
Lake Bera
Seramban
Pulau Tioman
Melaka
Cultural Heritage
Sample the hodgepodge of Malaysian culture in Melaka's Chinese, Dutch, & Portuguese villages.
Mersing
Muar
Batu Pahat
Straits of Melaka
INDONESIA
N
Johor Bahru
SINGAPORE
0 40 miles
0 40 kilometers

MALAYSIA

Airlines which fly out of Kuala Lumpur include: **Garuda Indonesia,** 19th fl., Citybank Bldg., Jl. Ampang (☎2162 2811); **Malaysian Airlines (MAS),** MAS Bldg., Jl. Sultan Ismail (☎746 3000); **Royal Brunei Airlines,** 2nd fl., UBN Tower, 10 Jl. P. Ramlee (☎230 7166); **Singapore Airlines (SIA),** Wisma Singapore Airlines, 2/4 Jl. Dang Wangi (☎2692 3122); **Thai Airways,** Ste. 3001, 30th fl., Wisma Gold Hill, 67 Jl. Rajah Chulian (☎2031 2900); and **Vietnam Airlines,** Wisma Cosway 2nd fl., Bukit Bintang (☎2141 2416).

BY TRAIN

The **railway station,** known as **KL Sentral** (☎2273 8000), is in front of the National Museum, off Jl. Travers. Express trains to **Butterworth** (8hr.; 2:50pm daily; 3rd-class RM17, 2nd-class RM30) and **Singapore** (7hr.; 7:30am, 3, 10:30pm; 3rd-class RM19, 2nd-class RM34). Regular trains to **Hat Yai** (12hr., 8:30pm, 2nd-class sleeper RM46) via **Butterworth** (8hr.) and **Tumpat** (12hr.; 7am, 8pm) via **Jerantut** (6hr.).

BY BUS

Puduraya Station on Jl. Pudu is KL's long-distance bus station. Dozens of express bus companies sell tickets for destinations all over Malaysia. The counters inside the station are more accurate for last-minute purchases. **Ekspres Transnasional** is one of the largest bus companies. (☎230 3300. Open daily 6am-midnight.) Buses go to: **Butterworth** (10 per day 9am-midnight, RM20); **Kuantan** (10 per day 9am-midnight, RM14.30); **Singapore** (2 per day 9:30am-11pm, RM31.10). Most bus companies run to **Melaka** (12 per day 8am-7pm, RM8). Other companies go to: **Ipoh** (3 per day 8:30am-9pm, RM11.30); **Kota Bharu** (9pm, RM26.10); **Kuala Terengganu** (5 per day 10am-midnight, RM25.10); and **Mersing** (12:30, 5:30, 10:30pm; RM19.50). **Hantian Putra Station** serves Malaysia's east coast and has the same prices as those at Puduraya Station.

BY TAXI

Above Puduraya Bus Station, five taxi companies serve various regions. The following rates are per 4-person cabs with A/C during the day: **Butterworth** (RM260 plus toll); **Cameron Highlands** (RM260); **Genting Highlands** (RM70); **Ipoh** (RM120 plus toll); **Johor Bahru** (RM200); **Kota Bharu** (RM200); **Kuala Terengganu** (RM240); **Kuantan** (RM120); **Melaka** (RM100); and **Muar** (RM60). Expect higher rates at night.

ORIENTATION

There is no method to the madness of Kuala Lumpur's layout. **Jl. Tuanku Abdul Rahman** and **Jl. Raja Laut** are the main six-lane thoroughfares running north-south. Most Intrakota buses travel on these two streets, connected in the north by **Jl. Chow Kit,** a busy market area. Jl. Tunku Abdul Rahman and Jl. Raja Laut converge in the south to form **Jl. Sultan Hishamuddin,** east of which lies **Chinatown. Jl. Cheng Lock** borders Chinatown to the north, and **Jl. Petaling** runs through its heart to the south. Parallel to Jl. Petaling to the west is **Jl. Tun H.S. Lee,** which runs through Chinatown and north to the financial center, ending at **Jl. Gereja.** Jl. Gereja starts westbound, becomes **Jl. Ampang** (sometimes called Embassy Row), and heads northeast. Most sights are in the city's western half near the old railway station or **Merdeka Sq.** Luxury hotels, malls, offices, and nightclubs fill the east and northeast areas of the city.

LOCAL TRANSPORTATION

Buses: There are two local bus companies, **Intrakota** and **Cityliner.** Fares vary by distance (RM0.70-1.60). Match your destination with route maps posted at bus stops and the signs visible through the front windows and ask the bus driver for the fare. Bring exact fare; change won't be refunded, and bills are not accepted. There are three major bus stops around town: **Klang Bus Station** (close to Central Market on Jl. Cheng Lock) heads south of Kuala Lumpur, including Subang airport and Petaling Jaya; **Bangkok Bank** goes to the north Batu Caves; and **Chow Kit Road** goes to the Keramat area.

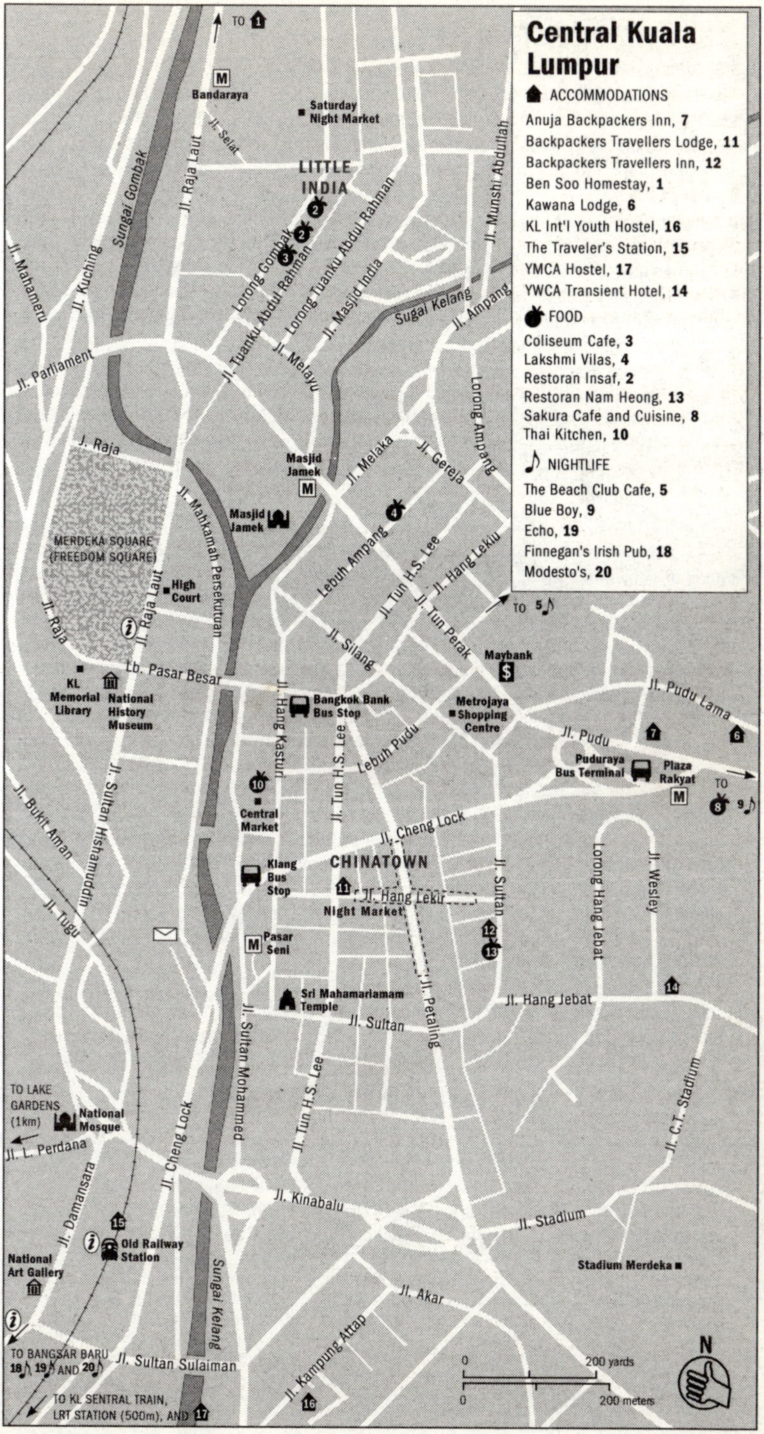
Central Kuala Lumpur
ACCOMMODATIONS
Anuja Backpackers Inn, 7
Backpackers Travellers Lodge, 11
Backpackers Travellers Inn, 12
Ben Soo Homestay, 1
Kawana Lodge, 6
KL Int'l Youth Hostel, 16
The Traveler's Station, 15
YMCA Hostel, 17
YWCA Transient Hotel, 14
FOOD
Coliseum Cafe, 3
Lakshmi Vilas, 4
Restoran Insaf, 2
Restoran Nam Heong, 13
Sakura Cafe and Cuisine, 8
Thai Kitchen, 10
NIGHTLIFE
The Beach Club Cafe, 5
Blue Boy, 9
Echo, 19
Finnegan's Irish Pub, 18
Modesto's, 20
Bandaraya
Saturday Night Market
LITTLE INDIA
Jl. Selat
Jl. Raja Laut
Sungai Gombak
Jl. Mahameru
Jl. Kuching
Lorong Gombak
Jl. Tuanku Abdul Rahman
Lorong Tuanku Abdul Rahman
Jl. Masjid India
Jl. Munshi Abdullah
Sugai Kelang
Jl. Ampang
Jl. Parliament
Jl. Melayu
Lorong Ampang
J. Raja
Masjid Jamek
Jl. Melaka
Jl. Gereja
Jl. Mahkamah Persekutuan
MERDEKA SQUARE (FREEDOM SQUARE)
High Court
Lebuh Ampang
Jl. Tun H.S. Lee
Jl. Hang Lekiu
Jl. Tun Perak
Jl. Raja
Jl. Silang
Maybank
Lb. Pasar Besar
KL Memorial Library
National History Museum
Jl. Hang Kasturi
Bangkok Bank Bus Stop
Metrojaya Shopping Centre
Jl. Pudu Lama
Jl. Pudu
Lebuh Pudu
Puduraya Bus Terminal
Plaza Rakyat
Jl. Sultan Hishamuddin
Jl. Bukit Aman
Central Market
Jl. Cheng Lock
CHINATOWN
Klang Bus Stop
Jl. Hang Lekir
Night Market
Jl. Sultan
Lorong Hang Jebat
Jl. Wesley
Jl. Tugu
Pasar Seni
Sri Mahamariamam Temple
Jl. Hang Jebat
Jl. Petaling
Jl. Sultan Mohammed
TO LAKE GARDENS (1km)
National Mosque
Jl. L. Perdana
Jl. C.T. Stadium
Jl. Kinabalu
Jl. Stadium
Jl. Damansara
Old Railway Station
National Art Gallery
Stadium Merdeka
Sungai Kelang
Jl. Akar
Jl. Kampung Attap
TO BANGSAR BARU 18 19 AND 20
Jl. Sultan Sulaiman
TO KL SENTRAL TRAIN, LRT STATION (500m), AND 17
0 200 yards
0 200 meters
N

MALAYSIA

SHIVER ME TIMBERS! Very few of them wear eye patches, walk on peg legs, or have parrots named Polly, but pirates aren't relics of dusty fantasy novels and history books. In Southeast Asia, maritime piracy is alive and kicking. In the late 1980s, when Vietnamese refugees were being repatriated, the Gulf of Thailand was particularly dangerous. Pirates, mostly Thai fishermen, attacked refugee boats and sometimes raped and murdered the passengers and kidnapped young children to sell into prostitution. Piracy dissipated as the refugee flow slowed, and since the 1990s, the major trouble spot has been the Straits of Melaka and Singapore. Pirates here are more sophisticated than those in Thailand. Often, they are seasoned professionals with links to organized crime and drug smuggling. They tend to target international shipping boats, including oil tankers, which they approach with speedboats and board via grappling hooks. Some steal the ships (called "phantom ship" operations). Most tie up or kill the crew, take the money on board, then depart.

Piracy is, of course, nothing new to these parts. Pirates based in the Sulu Islands and Sulawesi struck fear in the hearts of European sailors until well into the 19th century. (The phrase "boogie man" comes from the Bugis, among the most dreaded sea raiders.) In 1992, the International Maritime Bureau established the Regional Piracy Center (RPC) in Kuala Lumpur, which coordinates the maritime law enforcement efforts of Singapore, Malaysia, and Indonesia, tracks boats in the area, and warns shippers of possible attacks. The RPC documented 229 pirate attacks in 1997, and while its efforts have successfully decreased the number of attacks in target areas like the Straits of Singapore, piracy may merely have moved offshore to the South China Sea or other channels along the vast Indonesian coast. "Yo ho ho and a bottle of rum" is a catchy jingle, but for Southeast Asia, it's no laughing matter.

Taxis: Most taxis are metered; if not, agree on a price beforehand. Metered cabs start at RM2 and increase by RM0.10 per 200m. Surcharges apply for trips between midnight and 6am (50%), for luggage in the trunk (RM1), and for booking by phone (RM1). To call a cab, try **Telecab** (☎9221 1011), **Kuala Lumpur Taxi Driver's Association** (☎9221 9241), **Comfort Radio Taxi** (☎5633 0507), or **Supercab** (☎7875 7333). All are open 24hr.

Trains: Light Rail Transit System STAR is Kuala Lumpur's new intra-city elevated train. **Phase 1** is an above ground train with two lines, running from Ampang Station to Sentul Timur. **Phase 2,** known as **PUTRA,** stops at the Petronas Twin Towers (KLCC), Chinatown (Pasar Seni), and Bangsar Bar (Bangsar) and is most commonly used by tourists. Trains operate M-Sa 6am to 11:30pm, and Su and public holidays 8am-11pm at 5-15min. intervals (fares RM0.75-3.60). Obtain a free transit system map from a nearby STAR or PUTRA station or the tourist office.

Rentals: The nightly traffic jams and convoluted layout of Kuala Lumpur are a good reasons to take public transport, but if you need your own wheels, try **Avis** (☎2141 7144), **Budget** (☎1 800 88 3191), **Hertz** (☎2148 6433), or **Mayflower Car Rental** (☎6252 1888, at the airport 746 3223). A local or international driving license is required.

MALAYSIA

PRACTICAL INFORMATION

TOURIST AND FINANCIAL SERVICES

Tourist Offices: Kuala Lumpur Visitor's Center, 3 Jl. Hishamuddin (☎2274 0831), near the old railway station. Open M-F 8:30am-5pm, Sa 8:30am-12:30pm. **Tourist Information Center,** at the airport, Satellite Bldg. Open daily 9am-9pm. **Malaysian Tourism Center (MTC),** 109 Jl. Ampang (☎2164 3929), after the intersection with Jl. Sultan Ismail opposite the Renaissance Hotel. Walk through the parking lot and into the white building with the red roof. Open daily 9am-6pm.

Tours and Travel: MSL Travel, 66 Jl. Putra (☎4042 4722), off Jl. Chow Kit, next to the Grand Central Hotel. Offers Eurotrain Explorer Pass for unlimited travel on KTM-Malayan Railway (1 week US$38, 21 days US$60) or SRT Railway of Thailand (1 week US$32, 21 days US$48). Open M-F 9am-5pm, Sa 9am-1pm.

Immigration Offices: Pusat Bandar Daman Sara (☎255 5077), on Jl. Damai Selatan, near the Road Transport Dept. Block I. Same-day visa extensions RM50 per month. Open M-Th 8am-12:45pm and 2-3:30pm, F 8-11:30am and 2:45-3:30pm.

Embassies: Australia, 6 Jl. Yap Kwan Seng (☎2142 3122, after hours 2140 6642). Open M-Tu, Th-F 9-11:30am and 1:30-3pm, W 9-11:30am. **Brunei,** MBF Plaza, 172 Jalan Ampang (☎2161 2800). **Canada,** 7th fl., Plaza MBF, 172 Jl. Ampang (☎2161 2000, after hours 2161 2031). Open M-F 8am-noon and 1-4pm. **Indonesia,** 233 Jl. Tun Razak (☎2945 2011). Open M-Th 8:30am-1pm and 2-4:30pm, F 8:30am-1:30pm and 2:30-4:30pm. **Laos,** 108 Jl. Damai (☎2148 3895). Open M-F 8:30am-noon and 2-5pm. **Myanmar,** 15 Taman U Thant Satu (☎2142 3863). Visas RM70; 3-day processing. Open M-F 9am-1pm. **New Zealand,** Menara IMC (☎238 2533). Open M-F 8am-12:30pm and 1:30-4:30pm. **Singapore,** 209 Jl. Tun Razak (☎2161 6277). Open M-F 8:30am-1pm and 2-5pm. **South Africa,** Empire Tower Jl. Tun Razak (☎2164 2653). Open M-F 8:30-11:30am and 1:30-4pm. **Thailand,** 206 Jl. Ampang (☎2148 8333). Open M-F 9am-12:30pm and 2-5pm; consul open M-F 9am-12:30pm. **UK,** 185 Jl. Ampang (☎2148 2122). Open M-F 8am-12:30pm and 1:30-4:30pm. **US,** 376 Jl. Tun Razak (☎2148 9011). Open M-F 7:45am-12:30pm and 1:15-4:30pm. **Vietnam,** 4 Persiaran Stonor (☎2148 4036). Open M-F 9am-noon and 2-4:30pm, Sa 9am-noon.

Currency Exchange: Moneychangers concentrate on Jl. Hang Lekir and banks are ubiquitous. **MayBank,** 100 Jl. Tun Perak (☎230 8833), close to Puduraya Station, opposite Metrojaya. Traveler's check fee RM5 plus RM0.20 per check. Open M-F 9:30am-4pm, Sa 9:30-11:30am. Most **ATMs** accept Cirrus/MC/PLUS/V (RM5 charge).

American Express: 18th fl. of Weld Building on corner of Raja Chulan and Jl. P. Ramlee (☎2161 0000). Mail-holding services offered. Open M-F 8:30am-5pm.

LOCAL SERVICES

Luggage Storage: Akijaya Enterprise (☎230 5334), in Puduraya Bus Station, near Ekspres Nasional counter. RM1.50 per bag per day. Open daily 8am-10pm. **Matang Luggage Service** (☎2274 5561), at the old railway station on platform 4. Open daily 7am-10:30pm.

English-Language Resources: MPH Bookstores has branches at No. 2 Jl. Telawi, Bangsar Baru and Metrojaya Sinar Kota Level 3, Jl. Tun Perak. Open daily 11am-9pm. **Kuala Lumpur Memorial Library,** 92 Jl. Raja (☎2693 2908), next to the National History Museum. Foreigners prohibited from note-taking. Open Tu-F 9:30am-4:30pm, Sa 1-4:45pm, Su 9:30am-1:30pm.

Lesbian, Gay, Bisexual Organizations: Pink Triangle, 1st fl., 7C-2 Jl. Ipoh Kecil (☎4044 4611), off Jl. Raja Laut. Counseling hotline (☎4044 9622), open M-F 7:30-9:30pm. Devoted to issues related to HIV/AIDS and sexuality; engages participants with movies, socials, and discussions. Su sessions for gay men. Staff provides info about LGBT venues in Kuala Lumpur. Call for directions. Open M-F 10am-7pm.

EMERGENCY AND COMMUNICATIONS

Emergency: ☎999. **Fire** ☎994.

Tourist Police: ☎2149 6593. Main office at corner of Jl. Pudu and Jl. Hang Tuah. Another office at Puduraya Bus Terminal. **Open 24hr.**

Police: ☎2146 0522. Kuala Lumpur Police HQ, 13th fl. Jl. Hang Tuah.

Pharmacies: All around Jl. Sultan/Cheng Lock. **Georgetown Pharmacy,** 41 Jl. Silang (☎201 6924), in the heart of Chinatown. AmEx/MC/V. Open daily 8am-10pm.

Medical Services: Kuala Lumpur General Hospital (☎2692 1044), in city's north end on Jl. Pahang near Grand Season Hotel. **City Medical Center,** 415-427 Jl. Pudu (☎9221 1255), is privately run. Most doctors speak English.

Telephones: Pusat Telekom (☎239 6025), Jl. Raja Chulan. **Perkhidmantan Biro,** at the corner of Jl. Rajah Chulan and Jl. Bukit Mahkamah. Open daily 8:30am-9pm. **HCD** phones, fax. **Assisted International Calls** ☎108. **Directory Assistance** ☎103.

Internet Access: Traveler's Station, Platform A in the Old Railway Station (☎2272 2237). RM6 per hr. Open daily 9am-10pm. **Starsurf Cyber Cafe,** 1st fl., 105 Jl. Sultan (☎206 0200). Four stores down from corner of Jl. Cheng Lock, on the left. MTV in the background. RM6 per hr. Open Su-Th 10am-11pm, F-Sa 10am-1am.

Post Offices: GPO, Jl. Sultan Hishamuddin 9 (☎2274 1122). *Poste Restante.* Open M-Sa 8am-6pm. **Pos 2020** on the ground floor is usually sufficient. **Postal code:** 50670.

ACCOMMODATIONS

Chinatown has many cheap hotels and hostels that cater to backpackers, but the convenient location comes with a great deal of noise. Travelers looking for a quiet location should go elsewhere, but if you can sleep heavily, being just steps from Chinatown's famous chicken rice can't be beat.

CHINATOWN AREA

Anuja Backpackers Inn, 28 Jl. Pudu (☎2026 6479). Best accommodation in Chinatown and right opposite Puduraya Bus Station. Great location, exceptionally clean, but a little noisy. Hangout on the rooftop. Cafe next door. Internet. Laundry. Dorms with A/C RM10; singles/doubles RM18-22, with A/C RM30-40; triples RM38/RM50.

Backpackers Travelers Inn, 60 Jl. Sultan (☎2078 2473), off Jl. Cheng Lock, on the right; look for a red sign. Rooftop bar encourages partiers. Tour reservations. Bakery downstairs. Lockers. Laundry RM9. Dorms with A/C RM10; singles/doubles RM22-30, with A/C RM28-60.

Backpacker's Traveler's Lodge, 158A Jl. Tun H.S. Lee (☎2031 0889), at Jl. Hang Lekir. Convenient but cramped. Rooms with or without showers RM25-40.

Kawana Lodge, 68 Jl. Pudu Lama (☎2078 6714). Exit Puduraya Bus Terminal, cross Jl. Pudu and walk away from the white Maybank building. Climb the stairs to the top; it's on the right. A bit run-down. Laundry RM1 per piece. Dorms RM15; doubles RM40, with A/C RM50.

YWCA Transient Hostel, 12 Jl. Hang Jebat (☎230 1623), up the hill on the left past Jl. Wesley. Most take a taxi. Squeaky clean. Large, quiet rooms with hardwood floors. Library. Building behind (YWCA VTOC) offers A/C hotel-like doubles. Reservations recommended, especially if arriving before 9am or after 5pm. Women and married couples only. Singles RM30; doubles RM50; triples RM70; quads RM80.

OLD RAILWAY STATION

The Traveler's Station (☎2272 2237), on Platform 1 of the old railway station, above the Kentucky Fried Chicken. Taxi from KL Sentral RM3. Owned by 2 former backpackers who know how to have fun. Free movie everyday after 3pm. Internet access. Laundry RM12. 24hr. reception. Dorms with A/C RM10; singles and doubles with fan RM20-30, with A/C RM35-45.

Kuala Lumpur International Youth Hostel (HI), 21 Jl. Kampung Attap (☎2273 6870; myha@pd.jaring.my). Turn off Jl. Attaponto Jin Manau. Clean bathrooms and comfortable beds live up to the HI reputation. Separate bathrooms and accommodations for men and women. Lockout midnight. Bookings advisable in May, Nov., and Dec. HI cards for foreigners RM30 (one year membership). Dorms RM25, members RM20. MC/V.

FURTHER AFIELD

Ben Soo Homestay & Travel Services, 61B Jl. Tiong Nam, 2nd fl. (☎2691 8096). Exudes a family feel, complete with light breakfast and travel tips by Ben Soo, ex-travel agent and taxi driver extraordinaire. Laundry RM8. Singles RM27; doubles RM40.

YMCA Hostel, 95 Jl. Radang Belia (☎2274 1439), a 5min. walk from KL Sentral/LRT. Great facilities, comfortable rooms. Unmarried couples may not share a room; they say they can "tell" after they've grilled you with questions. Tennis court. Singles RM38, with A/C and bath RM68; doubles RM50/RM78; triples RM65/RM90; quads RM75. MC/V.

FOOD

Head to **Chinatown** for 24hr. service and delectable delights. **Jl. Sultan** and **Jl. Hang Lekir** host an open-air carnival of steamboat restaurants, *satay* sellers, and exotic fruit-juice vendors, while the **Chinatown night market** rages along Jl. Petaling. Those with a sweet-tooth should sample the coconut pancakes (RM40). Beware of pick-

A DRINKING CLUB WITH A RUNNING PROBLEM In 1938, a small group of British expats founded the Hash House Harriers in Kuala Lumpur. These first inspired "Hashers," named for the uninspiring grub at the Selangor Club, married the traditional game of Paper Chase with ample alcohol. The group leader, or "hare," would blaze a tangled trail across challenging terrain, leaving behind scraps of paper and the occasional case of beer for his friends, the "hounds," to pick up. The sport was interrupted by the Japanese invasion of Malaysia during WWII, though afterward one of the Hashers was able to finagle reparation payments for some damaged mugs. During the Emergency of 1948, some hashers followed a paper path straight past a group of dangerous bandits, rushed to inform the police, and received enough bounty to buy two new cars.

In the 60s, Hash House chapters sprouted up throughout Malaysia, spread to Singapore and Brunei, engulfed the rest of Southeast Asia, and subsequently exploded to over 1300 confirmed Hashes worldwide, sending their co-ed constituents over 6-8km courses with a tipsy cry of "On-on!" Though generally a safer English-style sport than, say, ferret-legging, at least one death has occurred in the history of Southeast Asian Hashing: in Myanmar, one hapless hound toppled from a waterfall. A mega-Hash celebrating the 60th anniversary of the first Hash was held in KL in October 1998. For a more trenchant and nuanced perspective on the original HHH, see www.mtiz.com/kl_hhh/home/index.html; for chapter contacts throughout the globe, see www.gthhh.com. Tally-ho and bottoms up!

pockets. **Little India,** north of Chinatown around **Jl. Mesjid India,** tantalizes travelers with a blend of South Indian and Malay flavors. The **Kampung Bahru Sunday Market,** near the Muslim cemetery on Jl. Sungai Baharu, is also tasty. For more info, see **Markets,** below.

Restoran Nam Heong, 56 Jl. Sultan, off Jl. Cheng Lock, next to the Backpackers Traveler's Inn. Has a near-historic stronghold on having the most authentic chicken rice in town. Some think it's gotten too commercial, but the laughing grannies who bring their friends and families can't lie–this place is for keeps. Chicken rice with vegetables RM9.

Sakura Cafe and Cuisine, 163-169 Jl. Imbi, off Jl. Sultan Ismail. Where Malays come when they long for authentic *nyonya* food. Order the house special, *nasi lemak* (RM14.50) which comes with beef *rendang,* coconut rice, and *achar.* Top off your feast with a soothing *chendol* (shaved ice topped with coconut syrup, RM4.50). Open daily noon-2:30pm and 6:30-11:45pm.

Coliseum Cafe, 98-100 Jl. Tuanku Abdul Rahman, 3 blocks from the intersection with Jl. Perak. A legendary restaurant/bar serving hearty Western food. Old leathers chairs and teak interior give it a colonial ambience. Roast chicken, veggies, and chips RM8.50. Steak RM26. Open daily 10am-10pm. AmEx/MC/V.

Lakshmi Vilas, 57 Lh. Ampang, near Masjid Jamek LRT Station. *Crème de la crème* for vegetarians. Best South Indian cuisine in town. *Dosai* RM1. *Lassi* RM2.50. Veggie set meals RM4-4.5. *Biryani* RM6. Open daily 7:30am-8:30pm.

Restoran Insaf, 116 Jl. Tuanku Abdul Rahman, near Coliseum Cafe. Another branch 50m down same street (open daily 8am-8pm). Lively, informal atmosphere. Enjoy beef *rendang* (RM4) and *biryani* (RM7). Open daily 10:30am-9pm.

Thai Kitchen, Lot M13-16 in the Central Market. Set meals include coffee and Thai dessert for RM9 from 2:30-6:30pm. The *tom yum* soup is delicious and spicy, with a price (RM18) that's harder to swallow. Open daily 11am-9:30pm.

SIGHTS

MERDEKA SQUARE (FREEDOM SQUARE)

As Kuala Lumpur's most architecturally rich area, this expansive square was once a colonial cricket field, the site of Malaysia's independence ceremonies in 1957, and is now home to the tallest flagpole in Asia. On one side of the square, opposite the Natural History Museum, is Kuala Lumpur's Justice Hall (High Court) in the Sultan Abdul Samad Building. With its clock tower and Muslim influences, the High Court blends well with neighboring buildings.

NATIONAL HISTORY MUSEUM. Originally Kuala Lumpur's first bank, the museum now exhibits artifacts dating from prehistoric to present. *(29 Jl. Raja. North of the old railway station, where Jl. Sultan Hishamuddin becomes Jl. Raja. Open daily 9am-6pm.)*

MASJID JAMEK. This stunning mosque stands where the first settlers landed in Kuala Lumpur. It was built in 1909 by the same architect who designed the railway station. *(Follow Jl. Hang Kasturi north. Open Sa-Th 9am-12:45pm and 2:30-4:15pm, F 8-10:30am and 2:45-4:15pm.)*

NATIONAL MUSEUM. This museum houses the usual weapons, royal ceremonies, and *Orang Asli* crafts and artifacts. The best exhibits are the shadow puppet display and the natural history section, which features stuffed wildlife, including the largest crocodile ever caught. The cultural showcases of Malaysia's different ethnic groups are also worth seeing. *(On Jl. Sultan Hishamuddin, 500m past the Kuala Lumpur Visitors Center. Open daily 9am-6pm. RM1, under 12 free.)*

LAKE GARDENS. Next to the National Museum is the pedestrian overpass leading to the Lake Gardens—91.6 hectares of spectacular greenery. The complex features a **planetarium, dinosaur museum,** and **war memorials.** The most popular draw is **Taman Burung,** an outdoor aviary housing tropical birds, including the blue-tailed bee-eater and striking Malaysian hornbill (RM5).

In the north section of the garden, the **National Monument** is dedicated to Malaysians who died during the two World Wars and the Emergency of 1948-1960. Other attractions in the garden include Taman Orkid dan Bunga Raya (Orchid and Hibiscus Gardens). Two-person boats can be rented to cruise the lake. Musicians usually perform at the band shell on Sundays around 5:30pm. On a hill, the parks are a great place to see Kuala Lumpur's impressive skyline. *(☎2698 3253. Open daily 9am-5pm.)*

SOUTH OF MERDEKA

NATIONAL MOSQUE. This modern white-marble mosque is a stark contrast to the Masjid Jamek across the river. The upper deck houses the main prayer hall and a reflecting pool. Visitors may borrow a robe (*jubah*) or a head scarf (*tudong*, for women) and explore. *(At the intersection of Jl. Sultan Hishamuddin and Jl. Perdana. Open Sa-Th 9am-12:45pm and 2:30-4:15pm, F 8-10:30am and 2:45-4:15pm.)*

KUALA LUMPUR OLD RAILWAY STATION. Built by a British architect in 1900, this magnificent station is a contrast of domes, minarets, and archways that house everything from a tourist office to a hostel. Commuter trains stop here. *(On Jl. Sultan Hishamuddin. Open 24hr.)*

THE NATIONAL ART GALLERY (BALAI SENI LUKIS NEGARA). The art museum houses a diverse collection of Malaysian artwork, a sculpture garden, and a photography studio. *(On Jl. Temerloh, off Jl. Tun Razak. A hike from Chinatown. ☎4025 4980. Open daily 10am-6pm.)*

NEAR CHINATOWN

SRI MAHAMARIAMAN TEMPLE. In the heart of Chinatown, this Hindu temple is often unfairly overlooked. The deity Mahamariman is thought to protect his devotees against illness. The focus of the 124-year-old temple is a silver chariot, prominent in the Thaipusam Festival's procession to the Batu Caves. *(From the Central Market, turn left on Jl. Cheng Lock and then right on Jl. Tun H.S. Lee. Open daily 6am-9pm.)*

OTHER SIGHTS

Along with Asia's tallest flagpole, Kuala Lumpur boasts the fourth-tallest building in the world. The 88-story **Petronas Twin Towers,** in the northeast part of the city, are the loftiest twin towers in the world. The lowest floors have the largest mall in the country and show off Malay arts and crafts in an immaculate setting, along with fancy boutiques like Escada and DKNY. Tourists are permitted to go as far as the Sky Bridge. *(Mall open daily 10am-10pm. Sky Bridge open 10am-12:45pm and 2:30-4:45pm. Free entry.)* The **Menara Tower,** or **KL Tower** as it is commonly called, offers a spectacular view of the city. *(Open M-F 10am-9:30pm, Sa-Su 10am-10pm. RM8.)*

MARKETS

Chinatown, south of Jl. Cheng Lock and east of the Klang River, is the liveliest place in Kuala Lumpur. At dusk, central Jl. Petaling becomes a *pasar malam* **(night market).** Food stalls and open-air restaurants roll their tables onto Jl. Hang Lekir and Jl. Sultan, as do traders selling pirated movies and CDs.

Central Market, on the corner of Jl. Cheng Lock and Jl. Hang Kasturi, is an arts and crafts center with 150 shops selling batik dresses, Muslim pajamas, intricate silver jewelry, and Malay kites and masks.

Saturday Night Markets, on Jl. Tuanku Abdul Rahman between Jl. Tun Perak and Jl. Dang Wangi, have food hawkers galore. The locations and times of the largest night markets are: M, section 1 in **Wangsa Maju,** northeast of town toward the zoo; T, **Seri Petaling,** south toward Serembau; Th, Jl. Kaskas in **Taman Cheras;** and F, **Taman Melati Gombak.** The markets are difficult to reach. Ask your guest house for directions.

NIGHTLIFE

The mix of yuppies, expats, and rich teens means that Kuala Lumpur has many nightlife options. The life span of clubs here is typically six to 12 months, so new clubs and hot nightspots emerge often. For a guaranteed wild night, head to **Bangsar Baru,** a haven for popular pubs and great food. Prices are as out of control as the dancing, though, so don't be surprised at a RM20 beer on weekends. There is also a growing interest in theater and dance, and major hotels host performances. For information, call **MTC** (☎2164 3929) or **Istana Budaya** (☎4025 2525).

The Beach Club Cafe, 97 Jl. P. Ramlee (☎2166 9919) off Jl. Sultan Ismail. Buzzing even on Monday nights, the all-ages crowd loosens their collars to kick back under a large grassy-eared "hut," enjoying brick oven pizza outside or bopping around the bar's shark tank. Try the beach party margaritas on Th. Happy hour noon-9pm. Beers RM14.50. Open daily noon-3am.

Finnegan's Irish Pub, 6 Jl. Telawi Lima (☎2284 0187), in Bangsar Baru. The friendliest authentic Irish pub in Kuala Lumpur. Pumps the best retro tunes and serves exclusive beers like Kilkenny and Cream Ale. Have the Shepard's Pie (RM24) upstairs before the dancing on tables begins downstairs. Happy Hour 5-8pm. Open daily noon-3am.

Echo, 21 Jl. Telawi Tiga (☎2284 3022), in Bangsar Baru. Both retro and modern by design, Echo makes you feel like you're in a Stanley Kubrick movie. Each night of the week has a different sound scene: Tuesdays beers are RM10 with trancey, progressive tunes, Th ladies get a free alcoholic slushy and swing to French house and Latin disco tunes. Beer jugs RM51. Open M-Th 6pm-2am, F-Sa 6pm-3am.

Modesto's (☎2284 2446), Telawi Tiga, in Bangsar Baru. A jeans-and-T-shirt pub with billiards, foosball, and good pizzas and pasta (RM18-25). Happy hour 5-9pm. Ladies' night Tu and Th. Open daily noon-3am.

Blue Boy, 54 Jl. Sultan Ismail (☎2142 1067), in a small alley off Jl. Sultan Ismail across from the 7-11, behind the Regent Hotel. Mixed crowd. Cocktails RM15. Cover RM16 on weekends, includes one drink. Open daily 8:30pm-3am.

DAYTRIPS FROM KUALA LUMPUR

BATU CAVES. The most famous attractions outside KL are the Batu Caves. In January and February, hundreds of Hindu devotees from around the world descend here for the annual **Thaipusam Festival,** armed with hooks and needles with which to pierce their skin in a ritual of penance. For the rest of the year, the immense caves are home to wild monkeys who prostitute themselves by performing tricks for peanuts, bananas, bags, and the odd passport. Visitors can climb the 272 steps to the main cave for free. *(Take #11 Intrakota 45min. from Bangkok Bank or Central Market. ☎238 3467. Open daily 7:30am-6:30pm.)*

KUALA SELANGOR. Fireflies are attracted to the berembang trees that flank both sides of the river. Watch thousands of them flash in unison on a boat ride on the Selangor River. The tiny creatures are not as precious as the Batu Cave monkeys and have not yet learned to spell names in the air. *(From Puduraya Bus Station, take Selangor Omni Bus #141 from Platform 23 (leaves every hr.). Returning to Kuala Lumpur requires chartering a taxi for RM60. Ferry Ride RM2. Seafood restaurant on the premises.)*

ROYAL SELANGOR PEWTER FACTORY. As befits the makers of the world's most famous pewter goods, this factory has the world's largest pewter tankard. *(4 Jl. Usahawan Enam, Setapak Jaya. Take bus W12 or #10 from the Lebuh Ampang bus stand or Intrakota #49D, 326, or 326D (30-45min., RM0.70, with A/C RM0.90) from Central Market. ☎422 1000. Open M-F 8:30am-4:45pm, Sa-Su 9am-4pm.)*

ORANG ASLI MUSEUM. This fascinating museum features exhibits relating to Malaysia's indigenous people. *(Take bus #174 from Lebuh Ampang (RM1.70). ☎6189 2122. Open Sa-Th 9am-5:30pm. Free.)*

NATIONAL ZOO AND AQUARIUM. Start counting—this complex is home to 500 species of animals and fish. *(Intrakota #20 from Central Market or bus #17 from Lh. Ampang (45min., RM1.60). ☎408 3422. Open daily 9am-5pm. RM8, children RM4.)*

MELAKA ☎06

Founded around 1400 by the exiled Sumatran prince Paremaswara, Melaka succumbed to Portuguese conquest in 1511. The Dutch and British soon took over and dominated it for the next four centuries. The imperial era ended when Malaysia's first Prime Minister, Tunku Abdul Rahman, proclaimed independence at Padang Pahlawan in the heart of Melaka. This historical city maintains Malaysia's oldest Buddhist temple and mosque and is famous for antiques over 400 years old. Melaka's many cultural layers are best experienced by strolling through Chinatown, past the crimson hues of the Dutch square, and around the waterfront abodes of the Portuguese Settlement. Soak in Melaka's easygoing charm and let your taste buds sample *nyonya* food, an often spicy blend of Chinese and Malay cooking—full flavors that capture Melaka's rich heritage.

TRANSPORTATION

Trains: The nearest station is at **Tampin,** 38km to the north. Take a taxi to the station (45min., shared RM6, charter RM40). Trains to: **Butterworth** (10hr., 12:45pm, 2nd-class RM17); **KL** (12:40, 7:20pm; 2nd-class RM27); **Singapore** (9:35am, 1:40, 4:55, 12:55pm; 2nd-class RM27).

Buses: Express bus station, on Jl. Tun Ali. Long-distance buses run by private companies. **Kuala Lumpur-Melaka Express,** 324 Jl. Kilang (☎282 2503) goes to **KL** (2hr., 7 per day 9am-5:45pm, RM7.90). **Malacca-Singapore Express** (☎282 4470) goes to **Singapore** (every hr. 8am-8pm, RM11.50). Several bus companies go to: **Alor Setar** (8hr., 9am and 9pm, RM30-33); **Butterworth** (9hr., 4 per day, RM27); **Ipoh** (5hr., 5 per day, RM20); **Johor Bahru** (3hr., 8 per day, RM12.30); **Kanga** (10hr., 9am, RM38); **Kota Bharu** (11hr., 8pm, RM28.10); **Penang** (8hr., 4 per day, RM28-30); **Perlis** (10hr., 9am, RM38); **Sungei Petani** (7hr., 9am and 9pm, RM30-33); **Taiping** (6hr., 3 per day, RM20-28).

Taxis: Jl. Tun Ali (☎284 7163), down the street from the bus station. Shared cabs to: **Batu Pahet** (RM20); **KL** (RM120); **Muar** (RM30-40); **Port Dickson** (RM80).

Local Transportation: The town is compact enough to cover by foot, but to rest your feet, take a **trishaw** from Jl. Kota (RM5-10 per trip, RM25-30 per hr.). All local buses meet at the traffic circle in front of Hotel Equatorial. Bus #17 goes to the Portuguese Settlement (every 10min.). Bus #19 heads for the zoo at Ayer Keroh (every 30min., RM1.70).

Bicycle Rentals: Muhibbah Enterprise (☎283 0631), on Jl. Munshi Abdullah in Intan Plaza Shopping Arcade. RM10 per day. Open daily 10am-6pm.

ORIENTATION AND PRACTICAL INFORMATION

The city sprawls on both sides of **Melaka River,** which winds its way southwest as it empties into the **Straits of Melaka.** The streets extending from Lorong Hang Jebat lead to the heart of **Chinatown.** Buddhist temples, antique shops, and the *Baba-Nyonya* homes of **Old Melaka** run along **Jl. Tun Tan Cheng Lock** and **Jl. Hang Jebat (Jonkers Walk),** both of which are parallel to the southern coast. Melaka Raya, the hostel area, is in the southeast of town. The bridge that extends from Jl. Hang Jebat leads to a cluster of many historical museums and sights, easily recognizable by the bright red **Christ Church** and the **Stadthuys.** South of the numerous sights and east of the Mahkota Parade Mall lies the gateway to backpacker heaven: **Jl. Merdeka. Taman Melaka Raya,** a series of side streets off Jl. Merdeka, offers some of the best values for budget accommodations in Malaysia. Further east is the **Portuguese Settlement.**

Tourist Office: Melaka Tourist Information Center (☎281 4803), on Jl. Kota near bridge connecting Jl. Laksamana and Lorong Hang Jebat. Free maps. Open M-Sa 8:45am-5pm, Su 9am-4:30pm. Sometimes closes for lunch.

Tours and Travel: The Tourist Center runs 45min. boat tours on Melaka River (RM8). Frequency depends on tide and demand. **Stadthuys Tours and Travel,** 151 Jl. Beadahara (☎284 6373), offers night tours, plantation tours, and trips to Ayer Keroh.

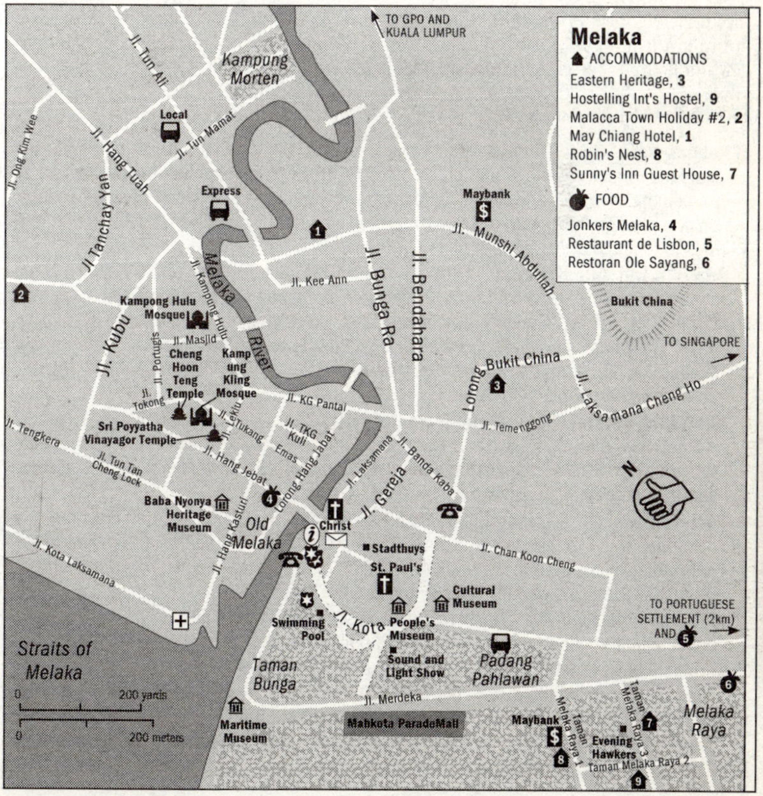

MALAYSIA

Currency Exchange: MayBank, 6 Jl. Hang Tuah (☎282 2477), near the bus and taxi stations. Closed 1st and 3rd Sa of the month. Open M-F 9:30am-4pm, Sa 9:30-11am. **Branch Office** on Jl. Melaka Raya 1 off traffic circle. Open M-F 9am-4:30pm, Sa 9am-12:30pm. Stops currency exchange service 1hr. before closing. Both have **ATMs** (Cirrus/MC/V). The **bank** in the Mahkota Parade Mall is open daily 10am-9pm.

Emergency: ☎999. **Fire** ☎994.

Tourist Police: ☎285 4222. On the pedestrian mall section of Jl. Kota, opposite the tourist center. Open daily 8am-11pm.

Pharmacies: Guardian Pharmacy (☎282 9499), on the ground floor of Mahkota Parade Mall. Open daily 10:15am-10:15pm.

Medical Services: Mahkota Medical Center, 3 Mahkota Melaka (☎281 4071), next to Mahkota Parade Mall. Private hospital with **24hr. emergency care.** Open M-Sa 8:30am-5:30pm.

Telephones: Compaka Technology (☎283 5955), on Jl. Merdeka opposite the Perwira Habib Bank. Offers fax, long-distance calls, and **Internet** (RM5 per hr.). Open M-F 10am-10:30pm, Sa-Su 8:30am-1pm. **HCD** available from "KADFON" card phones.

Internet Access: CMS Computer Shop, 1st fl. of the Makhota Parade Mall. RM5 per hr.

Post Offices: GPO (☎283 3860), on Jl. Bukit Baru, 6km north of town center. Take bus #19 20min. from the local bus station. *Poste Restante.* Open M-Sa 8am-6pm, Su 10am-1pm. **Pos 2020,** in the Youth Museum on Jl. Laksamana next to Christ Church and off south Jl. Merdaka. *Poste Restante.* Open M-Sa 8am-5pm. **Postal codes:** Old Melaka 75200; business district 75100.

ACCOMMODATIONS

Inexpensive options cluster in the area known as **Taman Melaka Raya,** beyond Mahkota Parade Mall off Jl. Merdeka. Closer to the express bus terminal, several budget hotels are located on **Jl. Munshi Abdullah.**

TAMAN MELAKA RAYA

Robin's Nest, 205B Taman Melaka Raya 1 (☎282 9142). Take the first right after the Mahkota Parade Mall; it's 50m up on the right. Highly recommended by travelers for its welcoming, friendly, and clean atmosphere. Owner speaks English. Laundry service, book exchange, free movies. Dorms RM9; singles RM16; doubles RM18-21, with A/C RM40; triples with A/C RM50.

Sunny's Inn Guest House, 270A/B Taman Melaka Raya 3 (☎277 5446; sunnysinn@hotmail.com). Take the 2nd right from Jl. Merdeka behind the traffic circle; it's 20m up on the left. Friendly staff and well-stocked kitchen. Lounge, laundry service, travel info board, and 2 movies every night. Bicycle rental RM5 per day. Dorms RM9; singles RM15, with A/C RM25; doubles RM18-25/RM30-35; triples RM30/RM40, attached shower RM10-20 extra.

Hostelling International Melaka Hostel (HI), 341 Taman Melaka Raya 3 (☎282 9715). Take the 2nd right off Jl. Merdeka; it's a 2min. walk down on the right. Clean, spacious dorms and large common room. Dorms reserved for women and families have an attached bathroom. Dorms with fan RM10, with A/C RM14.

Eastern Heritage, 8 Lorong Bukit China (☎283 30 26). Old Chinese architecture and paintings in the rooms give a distinct Eastern flavor. Guests can try their hand in the *batik* studio (RM30). Bar at entrance. Small dipping pool downstairs. Lockout midnight. Dorms RM8; singles with fan RM18; doubles RM20-30.

May Chiang Hotel, 52 Jl. Munshi Abdullah (☎283 9535). A 5min. walk from the express bus terminal. A good place to unpack and begin exploring. All A/C doubles RM40.

Malacca Town Holiday Lodge #2, 52 A,B,C Jl. Kampong Empat (☎284 6905), in the Wine and Spirits building, near the express bus terminal. From Jl. Kubu, turn right on Jl. Kampung Empat/Jl. Tanchay Yan and stay left as the road forks. They'll buzz you in. Western breakfast, kitchen facilities, laundry service (RM5), bike rentals (RM5). Singles RM25-35; doubles RM25-40.

FOOD

Melaka's concoctions offer a palate of excellent food, including *sate celup*, a hotpot of spicy broth into which *sate* sticks are dipped. For a cheap meal, try the few **food stalls** in the alley between Jl. Melaka Raya 1 and 3. Plenty of Chinese and Indian coffee shops line **Lorong Bukit China** and **Jl. Temenggong.**

Restoran Ole Sayang, 198-199 Taman Melaka Raya, on the right corner where the shops end on Jl. Merdeka. The best *nyonya* food in Melaka. Try *ayam pong teh,* a spicy chicken dish (RM7.50). Open Th-Tu 11:30am-2:30pm and 6-9:30pm.

Jonkers Melaka, 17 Jl. Hang Jebat. From the Tourist Information Center, cross the bridge and go down the road; it's 10 doors down on the left. Proceed through the artsy gift shop into the breezy courtyard. Expensive, delicious *nyonya* and Western cuisine. Soup and sandwich RM15. Set special RM20. Open daily 10am-5pm.

Restaurant de Lisbon, Portuguese Square. Eat home-cooked Portuguese fare at this 17-year-old restaurant, made all the more special because Prime Minister Mahatir ate here. Owner George suggests the baked fish with seven spices (RM20). Watch Portuguese dancers prance about the square on Sa nights. Open daily noon-midnight.

SIGHTS

HISTORICAL DISTRICT

STADTHUYS AND MELAKA ETHNOGRAPHICAL AND HISTORICAL MUSEUMS. The Stadthuys, a dark pink residence built by the Dutch in the mid-1600s for the Governor of Melaka, now displays Melakan porcelain, weaponry, and coins, as well as the boxing gloves of Muhammad Ali. Upstairs detailed paintings narrate Melaka's historical development. If the paintings don't cut it, the nightly **sound and light show** features an informative history of Melaka. *(Opposite the Tourist Information Center. ☎284 1934. Open Sa-Th 9am-6pm, F 9am-12:15pm and 2:45-6pm. RM2, children RM1. English light show 9:30pm; tickets sold at Cultural Museum booth; RM10.)*

CHRIST CHURCH. One of the most famous landmarks in Melaka, this church was built by the Dutch in 1741 to commemorate a century of colonial rule in Melaka. Check out the Dutch, Armenian, and Portuguese inscriptions, dating back to 1776, in the stone floor near the entrance. *(Between Jl. Kota and Jl. Laksamana. ☎284 8804.)*

ST. PAUL'S CHURCH AND A FAMOSA FORTRESS. Built by a Portuguese captain grateful for his safe arrival, this church was originally dedicated to Mary and called Our Lady of the Hill; the name changed to St. Paul's under Portuguese rule in 1641. Before falling into ruin due to British neglect, the building served as a fortress, lighthouse, Dutch burial ground, Catholic chapel, and Protestant church. Near the altar is an open crypt that housed the body of St. Francis Xavier, missionary extraordinaire, for nine months before he was sent to Goa, India. The hill has a beautiful panorama of the colonial district. *(Climb steps from Jl. Kota.)* Down the steps from St. Paul's Church and through an English cemetery, the last remnants of the **Porta de Santiago** act as a gateway to the Portuguese fortress of **A Famosa.** The Dutch used the fort, but the British demolished it in the early 1800s to ensure that Melaka could not compete with Penang for controlling trade in the Strait of Melaka.

MUZIUM RAKYAT (PEOPLE'S MUSEUM). The "Enduring Beauty" exhibit displays the lengths that humans will go to embody beauty ideals, from male corsets and lip plates to cranium manipulations and Padaung neck coils. Also check out the Governors of Malacca Gallery and the spartan Kites of the World exhibit on the top floor. *(Down Jl. Kota away from the clock tower. ☎282 6526. Open Tu-Su 9am-12:15pm and 2:45pm-5:30pm. RM2.)*

OTHER SIGHTS. Inside a Portuguese ship, the **Maritime Museum** has three floors of ship models and exhibits on Melakan sea trade and piracy. *(On Jl. Laksamana toward the river's mouth. ☎284 1934. Open daily 9am-6pm.)* The **Cultural Museum** is housed in a replica of the old Sultan's Palace. *(On Jl. Parameswara, near Jl. Kota. ☎282 74 64. Open*

Su-Th and Sa 9am-6pm, F 9am-12:15pm and 2:45-6pm. RM1.50.) Across the river from the historic European buildings is **Old Melaka,** a district of narrow, winding streets and architecturally interesting Chinese homes.

CHINATOWN

BUKIT CHINA. This site housed Princess Hang Li Poh's hundreds of attendants when she came from China to marry the sultan. Now it's the largest Chinese cemetery outside of China. Many of its 12,000 tombs date back to the 12th century. At the foot of the hill is Hang Li Poh's well. Legend has long held that anyone who drinks from the well will someday return to Melaka; spoilsport Dutchmen and the forces of the Johor Sultanate disproved this by poisoning the well during the wars of the 1500s and 1600s. *(At the end of Jl. Temenggong, northeast from of the city center.)*

CHENG HOON TENG TEMPLE. The oldest functioning temple in the country (founded in 1673), it was converted into a city hall, a courthouse, and a prison for the Melakan Chinese when the Portuguese arrived. The temple is still an active place of worship for Confucians, Taoists, and Buddhists. *(On Jl. Tokong, below the intersection with Jl. Lekiu.)*

MASJID KAMPUNG HULU. Built in 1748, Kampung Hulu is Malaysia's oldest mosque. Along with Kampang Kling, Hulu has a pagoda-like minaret and a three-tiered roof, a combination of Sumatran and Chinese architectural styles. *(On the corner of Jl. Kampung Hulu and Jl. Masjid. Open Sa-Th 9am-7pm.)*

BABA NYONYA HERITAGE MUSEUM. Constructed in the 1890s as a private residence and converted into a museum in 1985, this home tells the tale of Chinese Malays. *(48-50 Jl. Tun Tan Cheng Lock. From the Tourist Information Center, cross the river and turn left on Jl. Kasturi; take the next right and it's on the right. ☎ 283 1273. Open daily 10am-12:30pm and 2-4:30pm. Admission and tour RM8.)*

KAMPUNG KLING MOSQUE. Melaka's second-oldest mosque demonstrates the city's historical diversity. Built in 1784, its construction was influenced by Sumatran, English, Greek, Portuguese, Chinese, Indian, and Moorish architecture. Intricately sculpted cast iron-lamps surround the outdoor pools for "ablution," or cleansing before prayer. In addition to being one of Melaka's most beautiful architectural sites, it is still a center of Malay life. *(1 block down from Cheng Hoon Teng on the opposite side of Jl. Lekiu.)*

SRI POYYATHA VINAYAGOR TEMPLE. The third holy building on the "Street of Harmony," this Hindu temple contains the shrine of Vinayagor, the remover of obstacles and the god of filial piety. *(Next door to Kampung Kling. Open daily 8am-7pm.)*

PORTUGUESE SETTLEMENT. Three kilometers east of the historic area, the Portuguese Settlement's main attractions are the seafood restaurants around the Medan Portugis (Portuguese Square) and a glimpse of a couple Portuguese houses that are adorned with representations of both Jesus and Buddha. The Festa San Pedro, an extravagant festival with Portuguese dancers, singers, and beauty pageants, takes place during the weekend closest to June 29; ask the tourist office for details. *(Take bus #17 from the front of Pos 2020 next to Christ Church.)*

IPOH ☎ 05

Ipoh's reputation as one of the richest mines in the world at the end of the 19th-century drew an influx of English, Chinese, Indian, and French fortune hunters to the region. Within ten years, Ipoh's size and population had grown tenfold. Now, the driving forces of this mini-metropolis include light industries, mega-malls, and fast food. Chinese-Malaysian tourists don't leave without having had a bowl of *koay teow* (which purportedly tastes different because of the limestone deposits in the water) and several cups of the local favorite, white coffee. As the capital of the state of Perak, Ipoh offers excursions to Buddhist cave temples and has nearly 25 heritage buildings in the old town.

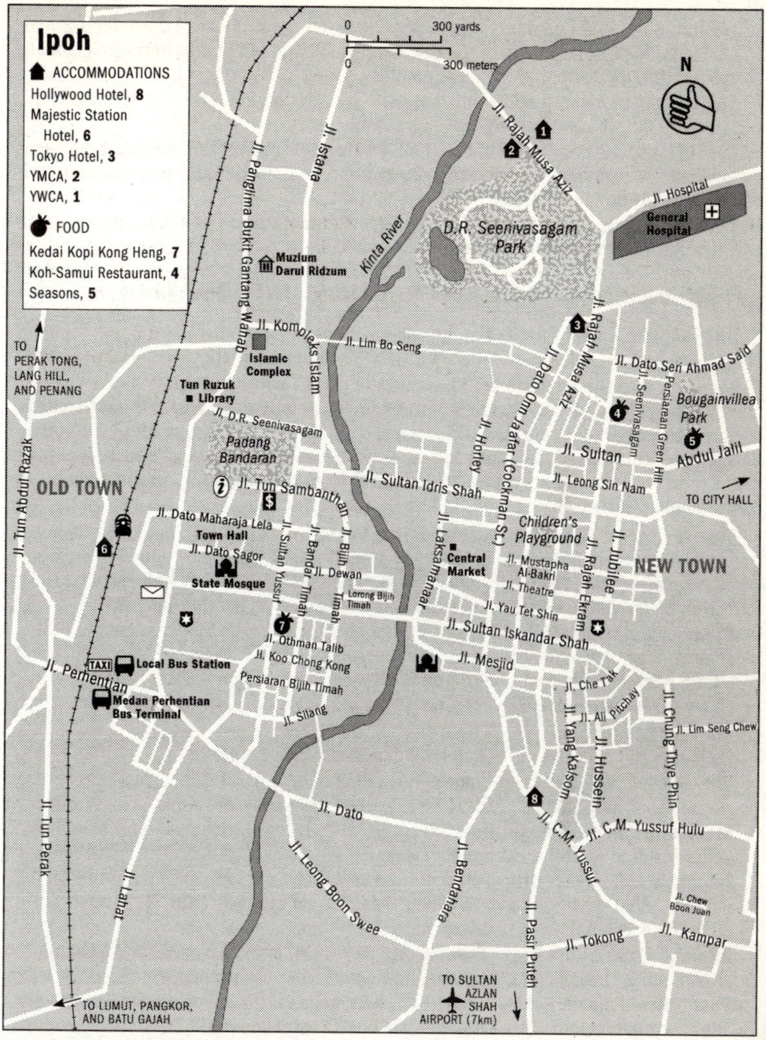

TRANSPORTATION

Flights: Sultan Azlan Shah Airport, on Jl. Lapangan Terbang, 7km outside town. Taxi to town RM10. Airport tax RM5. **MAS,** Lot 108, Bangunan Seri Kinta, Jl. Sultan Idris Shah (airport ☎2414 4155; reservations ☎312 2459). Open M-Sa 8:30am-5:30pm. Flights to **KL** (35min., 3 per day 6:45am-7pm, RM66).

Trains: KTMB Ipoh (☎254 7987), Majestic Ipoh Station Hotel on Jl. Panglima Bukit Gantang Wahab. To: **Butterworth** (express 4½hr.; 1:45am, 6:45pm; RM21); **KL** (express 3hr.; 1:55am, 11:10pm; RM22; mail trains 4hr., RM18); **Singapore** (express 8hr.; 1:55am, 11:10pm; 2nd class RM48).

Buses: Medan Perhentian Bus Terminal, on Jl. Perhentian in the southwest corner of town. Buses to: **Alor Setar** (9am, 1, 4:30pm; RM14.20); **Butterworth** (2½hr., 8:30am, RM9); **Cameron Highlands** (11am, 6:30pm; RM15); **Hat Yai** (6-7hr.; midnight, 1am; RM35); **Kota Baru** (9:30am, 9:30pm; RM21.50); **Kuala Kangsar** (every hr. 6:45am-6pm, RM2.90); **KL** (3hr., frequently 8:30am-6:15pm, RM11.30); **Kuala Terengannu**

(12hr., 8pm, RM37); **Kuantan** (8hr., 8pm, RM22); **Lumut** (1½hr., 12 per day 1:30pm-1:30am, RM4.60); **Melaka** (5 per day, RM20); **Penang** (4 per day, RM12); **Singapore** (5 per day, RM43).

Taxis: Long-distance **taxi stand,** opposite the Medan Perhentian Terminal. To **KL** (RM100 per car) and **Penang** (RM96 per car).

Local Transportation: 12 **local bus** (RM0.70) lines ply main roads, ending at the terminal on Jl. Perhentian. **Local taxis** around town are RM5 (RM20 per hr.). **Radio Cab** (☎253 4188).

Rentals: Pacific Budget (☎1 800 883 191) and **Maju Jaya** (☎255 5510) are at the airport. Open M-Su 8am-5pm.

ORIENTATION AND PRACTICAL INFORMATION

Ipoh is 205km north of Kuala Lumpur along Rte. 1 between the capital and Penang. The main thoroughfares form a grid of six north-south streets. The **Kinta River** splits Ipoh into the western **old town** and the proud white buildings of the eastern **new town.** The new town scurries with business activity; the **bus** and **train stations** and the **tourist office** are in the old town. To get to the **old town,** walk to the traffic circle from the bus station, turn left on **Jl. Panglima Bukit Gantang Wahab,** and turn right onto **Jl. Dato Maharaja Lela.** The **Central Market** is bounded on the west by **Jl. Laksamanaar** and on the east by **Jl. Dato Onn Jaafar.**

Tourist Offices: Perak Tourist Information Center (☎241 2959), on Jl. Tun Sambanthan near the northwest corner of Padang Ipoh (the soccer field). Info on Perak and great map of Ipoh. Open M-F 8am-4:30pm, Sa 8am-12:50pm. **City Hall** (☎241 3733), on Jl. Sultan Abdul Jalil toward the far northeast side of town, also has maps.

Currency Exchange: Moneychangers cluster on Jl. Sultan Idris Shah around the central market area, and in the basement of the Yik Foong Complex. Open M-F 9am-5pm. **Hong Kong Bank** and **Standard Chartered Bank,** near Town Hall on Jl. Dato Maharajah Lela, have **ATMs** (Cirrus/MC/V).

Emergency: ☎999.

Police: ☎253 5522. On Jl. Sultan Iskandar Shah. English spoken.

Pharmacies: *Farmasi* are everywhere. **Apex Pharmacy,** Lots 11-12, ground fl., Yik Foong Complex, Jl. Laksamanaar (☎254 5833). Open daily 10am-9:30pm.

Medical Services: General Hospital (☎253 3333), on Jl. Hospital, on the northeast outskirts of town. **24hr. emergency room.** English-speaking doctors. No credit cards.

Telephones: Telekom Office, Jl. Dato Onn Jaafar (☎249 9292), south of the central market. Also on Jl. Sultan Idris Shah, near the Kinta River. **HCD.** Both open Sa-Th 8:30am-4:15pm, F 8am-12:15pm and 2:45-4:45pm.

Internet Access: City Comp Training (☎241 7612), in Ipoh Parade, 2nd level, on Jl. Sultan Abdul Jalil. Email RM2.50 per hr. Open daily 10am-10pm.

Post Office: Pejabat Pos Besar (☎254 6555), opposite the police, next to the train station. *Poste Restante.* Open M-Sa 8:30am-6pm. **Postal code:** 30670.

ACCOMMODATIONS

Inexpensive accommodations congregate in the eastern half of the new town. **Jl. Raja Musa Aziz** (Anderson Rd.) has the best options. Cheaper places line **Jl. Yang Kalsom** in the south, but numerous massage parlors lend it a seedy air.

The Majestic Station Hotel, Bangunan Stesen Keretapi, Jl. Panglima Bukit Gantang Wahab (☎255 4217), on the upper levels of the historic railway station. Breezy veranda with restaurant, bar, and old photos provides easy-going ambiance. "Superior" standards with shower RM63; "deluxe" with long bath RM78.

YMCA, 211 Jl. Rajah Musa Aziz (☎254 0809), surrounded by green parks. Take a taxi from bus or train station. Slightly far from town, but spotless rooms. Dorms for 1-5 people RM12; singles with phone, A/C, and bath RM30; doubles from RM40.

Toyko Hotel, 159-161 Jl. Raja Musa Aziz (☎254 2005), at the corner of Jl. Dato Onn Jaafar. Near the heart of the new town. Spacious, furnished rooms and free filtered water. Singles/doubles with fan and bath RM30, with A/C and bath RM40-45.

YWCA, opposite the YMCA. Advisable to check-in before 5pm. Offers singles and doubles for women travelers. Single with fan, desk, and shared toilet RM35.

Hollywood Hotel, 72-76 Jl. C.M. Yussuf (☎241 5405), at the corner of Jl. Yang Kolsom. Singles RM35; doubles/triples RM55.

FOOD

Ipoh serves everything from Western breakfast to Hainan chicken rice. Find the best and biggest options at **The Food Center (Pusat Makaran Majestic),** on Jl. Dato Tahwil Azar, which serves Ipoh's signature dish (*koey teow* RM2.20; open daily 9am-11pm) and at **Pusat Penjaja Podeng Kamak** (The Children's Playground), on Jl. Raja Musa Aziz, south of Jl. Sultan Idris Shah. For Malay cuisine, look for shop names preceded by *kedai kopi*, meaning "coffee shop." While coffee is served, the name refers to a space where hawkers set up stalls.

Koh-Samui Restaurant, 83-85 Jl. Rajah Ekram, is in the northern part of new town, 1 block from Practical Internet. Upscale Thai restaurant. Prices average RM8. Beef in lime juice and garlic RM9.80. Open daily 11:30am-2:45pm and 6-10:30pm.

Kedai Kopi Kong Heng, 65 Jl. Bandar Timah, 2 blocks below Jl. Sultan Iskandar Shah. One of many excellent coffee shops along this street. Chinese from around Malaysia come here to try the white coffee, only available in Ipoh. Try the takeaway freshly squeezed orange juice (in a plastic bag!) for RM1.70. Open daily 7:30am-4pm.

Seasons, 88 Jl. Sultan at the Syuen Hotel. Specializes in Italian food in an elegant setting. Spaghetti Carbonara RM17. Open 24hr.

SIGHTS

Ipoh's significant sights are mostly architectural, but the cave temples on the outskirts of the city are also worth a visit. **Jl. Panglima Bukit Gantang Wahab** has many impressive colonial buildings, including the train station and town hall. **D. R. Seenivasagam Park** spans the broad strip between the YMCA and the traffic circle on Jl. Rajah Musa Aziz and has soccer fields, gazebos, trees, fish ponds, and a Japanese garden. Smaller but more stylish are **Bougainvillea Park** and **Tugu Park,** which flank Ipoh City Hall southeast of D.R. Seenivasagam Park.

Limestone caves, used as Buddhist temples by Chinese immigrants, surround the city. North of Ipoh on the road to Kuala Kangsar is **Perak Tong,** a temple known for its paintings and endless stairwell. Though the climb to the top of the mountain is good exercise and the breeze a true blessing, the industrial view is uninspiring. (Accessible by bus #141. Open daily 9am-5pm.) Other cave temples are **Sam Poh Tong,** 6 km south of Ipoh on the main road (RM1; open daily 8am-5pm), and **Kek Lok Tong,** before Gunung Rapat (open daily 7:30am-7pm). Sam Poh Tong is the oldest in the region, built 128 years ago; it shelters ponds brimming with fish and turtles. (Both cave temples are accessible by buses #66 or 73.)

The road to **Lumut,** southwest of Ipoh, passes through countryside dotted with elaborate Chinese cemeteries, open-cast mines, and small mining towns gone bust. One such town is **Papan.** Built in the 1890s, it has become a near-ghost town since the demise of the tin industry. **Kellie's Castle,** 30min. outside town, is the beautifully landscaped abode of William Kellie Smith, a wealthy Scottish planter who died during the building's construction in 1926. Take a peek at the castle's empty rooms and rubble walls. (Accessible by taxi or a short ride from Batu Gajah on the Gopeng Bus. RM0.50.) In the **Clearwater Century Golf Resort,** you can tour the set for *Anna and the King.* The fee (RM15) includes high tea at 4pm.

LUMUT

As the gateway to **Pulau Pangkor,** buses drop off visitors opposite the ferry terminal. Two types of ferries run from **Lumut** to Pangkor: the **express** (20min.; M-F every 2hr., Sa-Su every hr.; 8:45am-6:45pm; RM5) and the **local** (45min., M-F every 30min. every 6:30am-8pm RM3), via Sungai Pinang Cecil. The **Pangkor Tourist Information Center** is in Lumut, across the street from the jetty. If you miss a ferry, don't despair—there are two decent hotels near the Lumut-Pangkor jetty. **Indah Hotel,**

208 Jl. Iskandar Shah, a couple blocks from the bus station, offers singles with A/C, attached bath, and TV. (☎683 5064. RM60.) **Hotel Era,** 7 and 9 Jln. Raja Muda Musa, slightly closer to the bus station, has a tasty Indian restaurant downstairs. (☎683 8525. Singles with fan RM30, with A/C RM50.) Malay food stalls between the two hotels serve *nasi goreng* well into the night. The **tourist information center** on the other side of the gas station, opposite the jetty, can answer any questions. (Open M-F 9am-5pm, Sa 9am-1:45pm.)

PULAU PANGKOR

Despite the island's commercial success, much of Pulau Pangkor's coastline and jungle interior remain untouched. The island's 25,000 inhabitants reside mostly on the east coast, while travelers flock to the west coast beaches to view the vibrant sunsets, sit on white beaches, and watch black hornbills fly from one palm tree to the next. Rustling breezes, deserted sands, and shops brimming with sacks of dried fish create the laid-back Pangkor atmosphere. Pulau Pangkor's waters reveal the diversity of its travelers; Muslim women swim fully-clothed next to bikini-clad Westerners, but the groups unite in efforts to relax and enjoy.

TRANSPORTATION AND PRACTICAL INFORMATION

The **Pangkor jetty** is on the island's southeast side. Ferries arrive frequently from Lumut, (see p. 391) the island's mainland gateway. Coming from the jetty, Pangkor's main road, which generally follows the coastline, is to the left. Heading south, the road goes past the fishing village of **Teluk Gedung** and the **Fota Belanda** (Dutch Fort). Off the main road is **Jl. Pasir Bogak,** which leads to the **post office, police station,** and the beaches of **Coral Beach, Pasir Bogak,** and **Teluk Nipah.**

Pink taxivans at the Teluk Nipah jetty and by the south end of Pantai Pasir Bogak go anywhere for RM10. Several shops and hotels on the main road rent **motorcycles** (RM30 per 24hr.) and **bicycles** (RM15 per 12hr.). Wear a helmet and make sure rented bikes have brakes that can handle steep hills and hairpin turns. Opposite the jetty, **Maybank** changes currency and has an **ATM.** (☎685 1494. Open M-F 9:30am-3:30pm, Sa 9:30-11:30am.) Prescriptions can be filled at the **24hr. clinic** opposite the post office, near the Pangkor jetty. Downstairs from the Chuan Full Hotel, the Fisherman Cafe provides **Internet access** (RM6 per hr.). The staff at the **post office** are very helpful. (☎685 1281. Open M-Sa 8:30am-5pm.)

ACCOMMODATIONS

Most of Pulau Pangkor's budget accommodations cluster on two side roads at Teluk Nipah. Travelers gather here for the beautiful sunsets and proximity to the whiter sands and bluer waters of **Coral Beach,** as well as kayaking, fishing, and island-hopping. Prepare to bargain, as many mediocre hotels ask ridiculous prices (rooms RM50). Prices fluctuate dramatically between high and low seasons, as well as on school holidays.

Takana Juo, 4458 Teluk Nipah, has delicious food and comfortable rooms 50m from the beach. (☎685 4733. Singles/doubles with toilet and shower RM25.) **Joe's Fisherman Village,** also at Teluk Nipah, down the lane from Restoran Horizon, pro-

SLIMY, SCALY, SPIKY Koperal Rashid Noordin, leader of an anti-smuggling police unit in Changlun, Malaysia, knelt to get a better look at the 22 black shriveled objects being hawked road-side by an unlicensed vendor. Eight inches long with three prongs and numerous tiny spikes, the objects were—you guessed it—dried crocodile genitalia. The 30-year-old vendor claimed the croc willies were akin to a natural Viagra, the *New Straits-Times* reported in December 1999. Police alleged that he smuggled the objects from Indonesia. It is not uncommon in Malaysia and elsewhere in Southeast Asia for "traditional" vendors to sell bizarre concoctions—sometimes of herbs, sometimes of animal parts—as aphrodisiacs. Koperal Rashid Noordin confiscated the wrinkled penises.

vides cheap beds, A-frames, and a small library. A super-friendly staff and family-style meals with vegetarian options round out this guest house. (☎685 2389. Doubles RM20, triples/quads RM10 per person.) **Pangkor Paradise Village Holiday Resort,** at Pasir Bogak on a great secluded beach, attracts couples. Turn left off the main road and right toward the school. Take a left and it's 50m straight ahead. (☎685 1496. Doubles with A/C and bath RM125 in high season; RM35 in low season.) Near the jetty, the **Chuan Full Hotel,** 60 Main Rd., offers immaculate rooms farther from the beach. (☎685 1123. Doubles with bathroom and fan RM20, with A/C RM35.)

FOOD

A few stalls sell burgers and snacks at Teluk Nipah. The south end of Pasir Bogak, 5min. from Pangkor Paradise Village Holiday Resort, has your ordinary night hawkers. Also, most accommodations have attached restaurants. **TJ's Restoran,** at Teluk Nipah (connected to Takana Juo), is known for its Malay and Indonesian dishes. (Banana milkshake RM1.50. Open daily 8:30am-11pm.) One of Pankor's culinary specialties is fish, which restaurants purchase fresh from the piers each morning. **Restoran Horizon,** 4438 Teluk Nipah, next to the Rumah Rehat on the main road, has excellent squid dishes (RM9). Across the street from Chuan Full Hotel, **Sin Nam Huan Restaurant** serves tantalizing garlic butter prawns (RM16).

SIGHTS

Pulau Pangkor's best sights are its beaches and green hills. A leisurely island tour takes 30min. by motorcycle or 1½hr. by bicycle. Taxivans charge RM40 to circle the island, so share the ride to offset costs.

On the west side of the island between Teluk Nipah and Pasar Bogak, is the trail-head to the top of **Tortoise Hill,** as well as the **Jungle Information Center,** which provides tips on trekking through the island interior. Trips with a guide and water are RM25 per person. Those who go on their own can expect a 4-5hr. hike to get to the other side. Farther north is **Turtle Beach,** a delightfully deserted stretch of golden sand separated from the main road by waves of wild grass. Off Teluk Nipah's coast lies **Giam Island,** which has another small beach. Boats from Teluk Nipah motor here for a hefty RM30, so it's best to share with others. You can also hire a boat to island-hop and snorkel for several hours (RM50). Arrange boats with **Sam'Ong and Zukies' Watersport Center.** Other attractions include night fishing, canoeing, and an old man with an unusual affinity for king cobras. Kayaks are RM6 per hour. Sunsets are best from the beach at Teluk Nipah. North of Teluk Nipah is beautiful **Coral Beach,** with a small seaside Chinese temple at its northernmost end.

Pangkor Hill is 2km farther southeast on the right; a wooden sign reading "Hutan Simpan Sg. Pinang" marks the trailhead. The 1.8km hike reaches 371m above sea level. Some 2km south, a paved road to the right marked by a Coca-Cola sign leads to the **Fu Lin Kung Chinese Temple,** which should not be missed. Nestled at the base of a hill surrounded by dense jungle, the temple contains pools of turtles and orange *koi* fish, a garden, and a replica of the Great Wall.

KUALA KANGSAR ☎05

Dwarfed by its neighbors Ipoh and Taiping, Kuala Kangsar remains a quiet little town with grace and dignity worthy of the Sultan of Perak himself. For decades, Muslim heads of state inhabited the palace of Istana Iskandariah overlooking the serene Perak River. Although Kuala Kangsar can easily be explored in a few hours, its scenic riverside walk beside manicured playgrounds and parks offers relaxation that may make you want to put your feet up and stick around for a bit.

TRANSPORTATION AND PRACTICAL INFORMATION

Kuala Kangsar's commercial center sprawls near the **clock tower** roundabout which intersects **Jl. Taiping, Jl. Kangsar, Jl. Daeng Selili,** and **Jl. Istana.** Jl. Istana crosses the river and leads to Kangsar's major sights. The main street is Jl. Kangsar, whose back side is part of the square near the bus station.

The **bus station** on Jl. Raja Bendahara lies between Jl. Taiping and Jl. Kangsar, a 5min. walk from the clock tower toward Jl. Taiping. Buses go to **Ipoh** (1hr., every 15min. 6:15am-9:30pm, RM3.05) and **Taiping** (1hr.; every 15min. 6:15am-9:30pm; local RM2.50, express 2.70). **Transnasional Ekspres** (☎776 1033) runs buses to: **Butterworth** (11:45am, 3:45, 7:45pm; RM6.30); **Ipoh** (1hr., every 10min. 6:15am-9:30pm, RM3.95); **KL** (4½hr., 8 per day 9am-9pm, RM14.10). Next to the bus station is a **taxi stand** with service to: **Ipoh** (RM22); **KL** (RM100); **Taiping** (RM16). Refer to the rate board on the side of the taxi building if they try to scam you. (1hr. taxi service RM20.) The **train station** (☎776 1094) is on Jl. Stesyen, 2km from the central clock tower; walk 20min. down Jl. Taiping and make a right onto the street with the general hospital. Trains leave for **Butterworth** (2:30am, RM9) and **KL** (1:20am, RM22).

In town, **Maybank** is in the square behind the bus station (**ATM** accepts V; open M-F 9:30am-4pm, Sa 9:30-11:30am). The **Vitro Farmasi,** 88Jl. Kangsar, on the far side of the strip mall near Maybank, has a greater selection. (Open M-Sa 9am-9pm, Su 9:30am-7pm.) The **general hospital** (☎776 3333; **emergency** ☎999), is on Jl. Taiping. A **Telekom Office,** which sells international calling cards, is on Jl. Rajah Chulan. **HCD** is available here and from card phones. (☎776 9191. Open M-F 8:30am-4:30pm, Sa 8:30am-12:30pm.) **Pusat Komputer,** 86.2 Bandar Baru, Jl. Kangsar, provides **Internet access** (☎777 6320; open daily 9:30am-midnight), and the **post office** is on Jl. Daeng Selili by the clock tower (☎776 4555; open M-Sa 8:30am-5pm). **Postal code:** 33000.

ACCOMMODATIONS AND FOOD

Kuala Kangsar is a favorite weekend destination for Malaysians, not backpackers, and budget accommodations are scarce. The **Double Lion Inn,** 74 Jl. Kangsar, on the traffic circle where Jl. Kangsar meets Jl. Raja Bendahara, has cheaper, rundown singles, renovated doubles with soft sheets, TV, phone, and a bakery. From the bus station, the inn is visible on the left. (☎776 1010. Bicycle rental RM5. Singles/doubles RM25, with A/C RM40; triples with A/C and bath RM50; renovated doubles with A/C RM70.) **Rumah Rehat Kerajaan-Government Rest House,** 300m on the right from the bridge on Jl. Istana, is on the hill overlooking the river. Cheaper rooms are small but tidy and comfortable. All have A/C, bath, and double beds. (☎776 3872. Rooms in basement RM70; old wing RM80; new wing RM100.)

Chinese, Indian, and Malay restaurants abound on **Jl. Kangsar** and in the **square** between Jl. Kangsar and the bus station. Stalls at the **Sunday market** between Jl. Daeng Salili and the river sell peanut pancakes and corn. Restaurants on the other side of the river, away from Jl. Kangsar, serve *laksa* (fish and vegetable soup). **Restoran Rahmaniah,** 33 Jl. Kangsar, serves traditional Malay food with a kick. (*Mee goreng* RM2.30. *Nasi lemak* RM0.60. Open M-Sa 8am-9pm.) **Rumah Rehat Rest House's restaurant** overlooks the river and has a Western and Malaysian menu. (*Sambal* beef RM9. Mixed vegetable soup RM4. Open daily 8am-11pm.)

SIGHTS

Most of the town's attractions are across the river from town along Jl. Istana. The gold-domed **Masjid Ubudiah,** one of Malaysia's grandest, was commissioned in 1917 by Sultan Idris Murshidul'adzam Shah I, the 28th Sultan of Perak, as thanksgiving for his recovery from a chronic illness. (Open daily 9am-noon, 3-4pm, and 5:30-6pm.) The abandoned but impressive **Istana Kota** was formerly the palace of Sultan Idris Shah. It's beyond the bridge, 700m up the hill on the right. Ask the guard to show you the doors to the veranda above. (Open daily 9am-5pm.)

Down the road 250m stands **Istana Iskandariah,** the barricaded Sultan's Palace, providing another glimpse of Moorish architecture. Built in 1931 to house the royal family, it is now an empty monument, sometimes used for official ceremonies. Unfortunately, it's not open to the public. Built in the shape of a sword, the **Royal Museum** is right of the palace, 5min. down the road where it forks; look for yellow curtains. Once known as Istana Kenangan ("memory palace"), this structure served as the home of the 30th Sultan, Iskandar Shah, as he awaited the completion of the present Istana Iskandariah in 1931. Visitors can trace the history of Perak's royal families, admire the royal regalia, and learn about the heyday of the Perak state. (Open Sa-Th 9:30am-5pm.)

On the river's other side stands **Kolej Melayu** (Malay College). Opened in 1905 by the British government, this secondary school/junior college has turned out many statesmen and business leaders. The school was the first to give Malays an English education and still admits only Malays. Malaysia's **oldest rubber tree** is down from the police department, fenced in on Jl. Rajah Chulan.

TAIPING ☎05

Once the state of Perak's capital, proud Taiping is a city of firsts: the country's first museum, hill station, radio station, and public garden. Downtown Taiping reveals a predominantly Chinese city, evident in the local *dim sum's* popularity. For those who like long strolls among lake gardens and cool hills, Taiping is an ideal break.

TRANSPORTATION

Trains: Stesyen Keretapi Taiping (☎807 2591), on Jl. Stesyen, 700m west from the downtown area on the left. Office open 24hr. 2nd-class to **Butterworth** (3:20am, RM11) and **KL** (8hr., 12:30am, RM24).

Buses: Stesyen Bus, at the west end of Jl. Panggong Wayang. To **Kuala Kangsar** (every 15min. 6am-9:30pm, RM2.50). **Express bus terminal** is in **Kamunting,** a 20min. bus/taxi ride from Taiping. To: **Butterworth** (every 30min. 6:30am-8:30pm, RM5) via **Alor Setar; Ipoh** (1hr., every 30min. 6:30am-8:30pm, RM3.80); **Johor Bahru** (8hr.; 9:30am, 9, 10:30pm; RM35); **KL** (4½hr., 26 per day 7:30am-11pm, RM13.30); **Penang** (1½hr.; 9, 11:30am, 4, 6:30pm; RM7.35).

Taxis: ☎808 1691. In Kamunting at the express bus terminal and Taiping on Jl. Iskandar between West Jl. Kota and Jl. Panggong Wayang. To: **Ipoh** (RM48); **Kamunting** (RM5); **Kuala Kangsar** (RM28).

ORIENTATION AND PRACTICAL INFORMATION

Taiping's center is set up in a grid. The main drags (running east-west) are, from north to south, **Jl. Panggong Wayang, Jl. Kota, Jl. Pasar, Jl. Taming Sari, Jl. Barrack,** and **Jl. Stesyen.** To the east are the government offices, lake garden, zoo, museum, and library. **Jl. Iskandar** is off the west end of Jl. Panggong Wayang.

Tourist Information: Taiping Visitor & Information Center (☎805 3245), on Jl. Kota, under the pink clock tower. Very helpful. Provides transportation info. Open M-F 8:30am-5:30pm, Sa 8:30am-3pm.

Currency Exchange: Bank Bumiputra Malaysia Berhad (☎807 2422), on Jl. Kota, next to the pink clock tower. Open M-F 9:30am-4pm, Sa 9:30am-noon. **Maybank,** on east Jl. Taming Sari, has an **ATM** (Cirrus/MC/V).

Emergency: ☎999.

Police: ☎808 2222. On Jl. Taming Sari, in front of the white and stately land office. Attentive and helpful.

Pharmacy: Farmasi Kota, 182 Jl. Kota (☎805 6750), 2 blocks behind the store. Open daily 9am-10pm.

Medical Service: Hospital Taiping (☎808 3333), at the west end of Jl. Taming Sari. **24hr. emergency care.** English spoken. No credit cards.

Telephones: Telekom office (☎809 9841), next to the post office. IDD/fax. Open M-F 8:45am-5pm, Sa 8:45am-1pm.

Internet Access: Net Surfer, 36-38 Jl. Tupai, off Jl. Kota, visible from the pink clock tower. Busy. Open daily 11am-2am.

Post Office: (☎807 7555), uptown on the far east side of Jl. Barrack. *Poste Restante.* Open M-Sa 8:30am-5pm. **Postal code:** 34000.

ACCOMMODATIONS

Hotel Malaya, 52 Market Sq. (☎807 3733), in the heart of Taiping. From the bus station, walk towards the Gardens and Zoo and turn left before the film developing shop; it's 50m down on the left. Clean rooms have A/C, phones, and new bathrooms. Laundry. Free filtered water. Rooms with 2 twin beds RM30; 2 full-size beds RM40.

Swiss Hotel, 37 Theater Rd. (☎807 4899), opposite Jl. Ketab Cina and Jl. Panggong Wayang, behind the Kedai Kopi Dan Swiss restaurant. Noisy. All rooms have showers, toilets, blankets, and towels. Singles RM20; doubles RM30, with A/C RM40.

FOOD

This Chinese-dominated city is a great place to fill up on Cantonese and Hokkien treats. Taiping's **day market** is in the town center between Jl. Taming Sari and Jl. Panggong Wayang, and the **night market** is south of Jl. Panggong Wayang. (Open daily 6am-midnight.) Taiping's best food is at the huge center at **Market Square** near the local bus station. Look for the large *Fajar* sign. (Open daily 6am-midnight.)

Kum Loong, 45-47 Jl. Kota, east of the pink clock tower. *The* choice for *dim sum.* Rice and vegetables with Chinese tea RM6. Endless tea and tidbits. Open daily 5am-11pm.

Bismillah Restaurant, 138 Jl. Taming Sari, at the intersection with Jl. China. Malay/Indian restaurant. Enjoy *roti canai* for breakfast (RM.60) or *nasi biryani,* before it runs out (M, Sa; RM3.50). Intimate, friendly atmosphere. Open daily 6am-9pm.

SIGHTS

The **Taiping Lake Gardens and Zoo,** Malaysia's first recreational garden, is one of the country's biggest and most beautiful. Wander the road encircling the park, sheltered by ancient, Tolkien-esque *samanea saman* trees. (Paddle boat RM10 per 30min. Zoo open daily 8am-7pm. Feeding time 10am-noon. RM4, children RM2.)

Malaysia's oldest hill station, **Bukit Larut,** formerly known as Maxwell's Hill, lies 1250m above sea level in the mountains that form Taiping's scenic background. It's popular for its cool temperatures, mountain greenery, and seclusion. Government-operated Land Rovers ply the only route to the hill station from the base in Taiping on Jl. Air Terjun, past the northeast end of the Lake Gardens (35min., every hr. 8am-5pm, roundtrip RM4). Taxi drivers will tell you that the station base is within walking distance, but it's a 45min. walk. Bukit Larut guest houses and bungalows run about RM80-200, while run-down rooms cost RM15. Accommodations offer simple Malaysian meals. To make reservations, call the officer in charge at the Bukit Larut Hill Resort (☎807 7243).

Muzium Perak, built in 1883, is Malaysia's first museum. One kilometer east of the town center on the left of Jl. Taming Sari, it maintains a compact and eclectic permanent exhibit, including a Vietnam War-era CAC Avon Saber, photos of old Taiping, exhibits of royal garb and accoutrements, a large collection of Orang Asli tools, and a collection of animal skeletons and taxidermy. (☎807 2057. Open Sa-Th 9am-5pm, F 9am-12:15pm and 2:45-5pm.)

PENANG (PULAU PINANG)

Those with illusions of a sweet little island are in for a shock. With the second largest economy in Malaysia, Penang is more powerhouse than paradise as it struggles to balance conscientious productivity with down-to-earth congeniality. The island is home to a number of multinational corporations by the airport, two universities, and Malaysia's largest Buddhist temple, as well as numerous Malaysian *kampongs* and *kongsi* (clans) scattered in the rural areas. The dense jungles contain durian, jackfruit, and nutmeg plantations, and visitors can choose from the prestigious Butterfly Farm, new aquarium, botanical garden, and Forestry Museum and Arboretum. Other delights include relaxing by Batu Ferringhi's beaches, temple hopping in Georgetown, and devouring one of Penang's culinary contributions to the world—the minty yet spicy *assam laksa.*

THE VIEW FROM ABOVE

The lowdown: A bustling island off the west coast with a life of its own.
Major towns: Batu Ferringhi, Georgetown, Teluk Bahang.
Highlights: Penang cuisine, lush jungles, unspoiled beaches, and Malaysia's largest Buddhist temple.

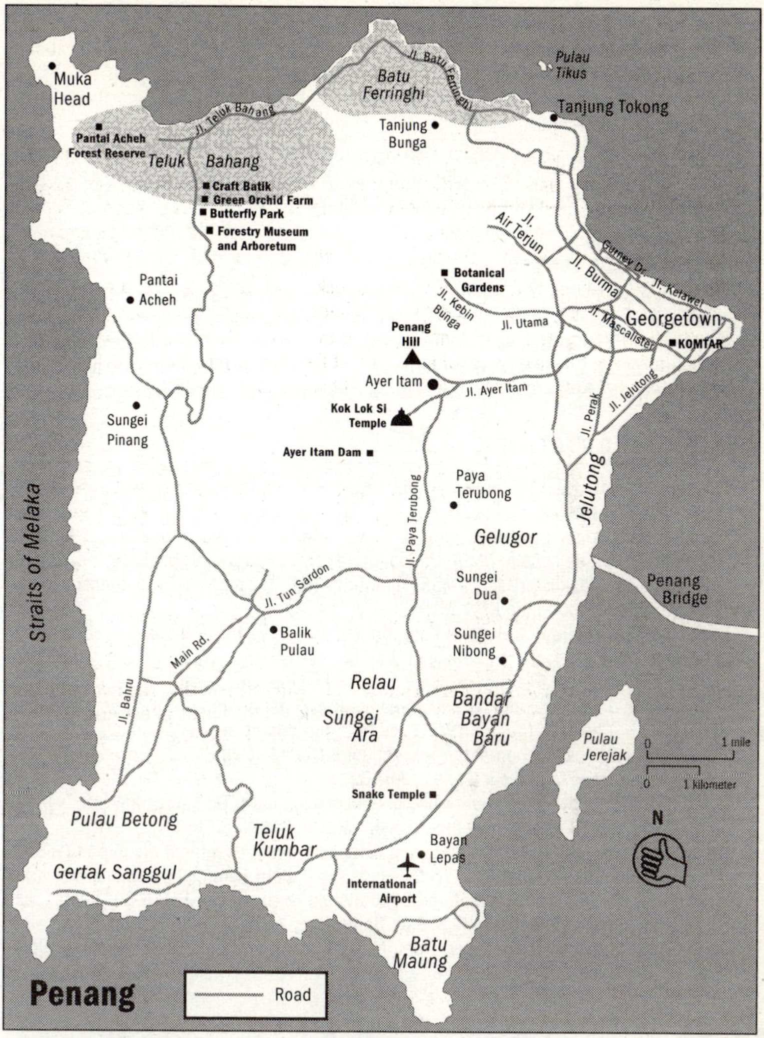

GETTING TO PENANG

Flights: Bayan Lepas International Airport (☎643 0811), 20km south of Georgetown. Yellow bus #83 (every hr. 6am-10pm) and minibus #32 run between the airport and Pengkalan Weld in Georgetown. **MAS** (☎262 0011) flies to **KL** (45min., every hr., RM109) and **Medan, Indonesia** (45min., 12:55pm, RM253). **Singapore Airlines** (☎226 3201) flies to **Singapore** (1hr., 3 per day, RM295). **Thai Airlines** flies to **Bangkok** (1¾hr., 8am, RM499).

Trains: The **train station** (☎331 2796) is below the ferry landing in Butterworth. To: **Bangkok** (20hr., 2:10pm, RM94.20) via **Hat Yai**; **KL** (6½hr.; 7:50am, 9:30pm, F-Su also 3:20pm; RM30); **Johor Bahru** (12hr., 8am, RM58); **Singapore** (13hr., 8am, RM60). Prices are for 2nd-class.

Buses: There are two **bus stations:** one at KOMTAR in Penang and the other below the Butterworth ferry landing. Buses run to **Johor Bahru** (10hr., 10:30pm, RM40.60) and **KL** (5hr., every hr., RM21). **Kurnia Bistari** buses go to **Cameron Highlands** (5hr.;

8:30am, 2:30pm; RM20). **Gunung Raya** buses go to **Alor Setar** (1½hr., every 30min., RM6.30); **Kota Bharu** (7hr.; 10am,10pm; Rm19); **Lumut** (RM13); **Melaka** (10:30am; 3, 11pm; RM28).

Ferries: A 24hr. ferry runs between Georgetown and **Butterworth** on the mainland (every 20min., and after midnight every hr.; RM0.60 to Penang, free to Butterworth).

Taxis: Taxis can be hired in Butterworth. To: **Alor Setar** (RM180); **Cameron Highlands** (RM250); **Hat Yai** (RM180); **Ipoh** (RM120); **KL** (RM260); **Kuala Kedar** (RM180); **Lumut** (RM140); **Padang Besar** (RM120); **Taiping** (RM120).

GEORGETOWN ☎04

Georgetown is a cultural and culinary mecca, where each street has a blend of ethnic influences. Chulia St. is the main backpacker hangout, but the entire city begs to be explored. On Jl. Masjid Kapitan Keling alone, there are five different religious establishments. Narrow streets and markets pulse with life late into the night, and wandering walks reveal one of Asia's most diverse architectural collections.

TRANSPORTATION

Ferries: To **Butterworth** (every 20min., RM0.60, cars RM7). Express services to **Langkawi** and **Medan, Indonesia** run from the tourist office building. **KPLFS Company** (☎262 56 30) goes to Langkawi (2hr.; 8am; RM35, round-trip RM60) and Medan, Indonesia (5hr.; daily 8am; RM96, round-trip RM166). **Ekspres Bahagia** (☎263 1943) also goes to Langkawi (8am; RM35, round-trip RM60) and Medan, Indonesia (daily 8:30am; RM96, round-trip RM166).

Local Transportation: Bas Mini (minibuses) run from the *jeti* (ferry station) and KOMTAR. **Taxis** are faster and cheaper than *beca* (trishaws), which will charge RM5 no matter how short the trip and are more likely to swindle you. In either case, confirm the price before departing. Both taxi and *beca* are RM20 per hr. and taxis charge 20% more at night. Lh. Chulia to the *jeti* RM5. Taxis from the airport are hired through a coupon system. Purchase a coupon at the Teksi counter (Georgetown RM23). Buses to the rest of the island leave from the *jeti* and KOMTAR ground fl. (6am-11pm). Colorful lines refer to routes. Yellow buses go south while blue buses go north. Take red-and-white bus #1 or 101 to Central Penang, blue bus #93 and transit line #202 to the north shore.

Rentals: IDL required for all car rentals. **Hawk** has a rental counter in the airport (☎881 3886). **Ruhanmas Rent-A-Car,** 76-C-1 and 157-B Batu Ferringgi (☎881 1760), has 4WD from RM105 per day. Motorbike rentals along Lh. Chulia RM18-30. Rental services also provide car delivery. **H.S. Sam Bookstore,** 144 Chulia St. in Georgetown also rents cars, from RM125 per day. Open M-Sa 9:30am-8:30pm, Su 10:30am-1:30pm and 6:30-8:30pm.

ORIENTATION AND PRACTICAL INFORMATION

Georgetown sits on a peninsula on Penang's east coast. The **ferry terminal** *(jeti)* and **bus station** are on **Pengkalan Weld Quay,** along Georgetown's southeast coast. Opposite the southern end of the ferry terminal, **Lh. Chulia** has many budget hotels and delicious food stalls. Guarding the city at the peninsula's northeast tip is **Fort Cornwallis,** which is bordered by Lh. Light. **Jl. Macalister** leads to the **KOMTAR,** the tall cylindrical building that dominates Penang's skyline, and becomes **Jl. Magazine** east of the traffic circle. From this traffic circle, **Jl. Penang** runs north toward the coast.

Tourist Offices: Penang Tourist Center (☎261 6663), on Pesara King Edward by the rotary. Maps and info. Open M-Th 8:30am-1pm and 2-4:30pm, F 12:30-2:30pm, Sa 8:30am-1pm. **Tourist Guides Association** (☎261 4461), 3rd fl. of KOMTAR, has more detailed info. Open M-Sa 10am-6pm; closed for irregular lunch breaks. Sells *Penang Tourist Newspaper* that has essential phone numbers and a calendar of events. **Tourism Malaysia** (Northern Region), 10 Jl. Tun Syed Sheh Barakbah (☎262 0066). Open M-F 8am-5pm, Sa 8am-1pm. Very informative.

Tours and Travel: MSL Travel Sd. Bhd., Agora Hotel, Jl. Macalister (☎227 2655). Malay and Thai rail-passes available with ISIC. Smaller companies along Lh. Pantai and Lh. Chulia offer tours. **Eva Ting Enterprise,** 487 Lh. Chulia (☎262 9996), is very helpful. Open daily 9am-3pm and 6-10:30pm.

Consulates: Indonesia, 467 Jl. Burma (☎227 4686). **Thailand,** 1 Jl. Tuanku Abdul Rahman (☎226 8029).

Currency Exchange: Several moneychangers on Lh. Chulia and major banks along Lh. Pantai have good rates. Open 8:30am-6pm. **Maybank,** on Lh. Campbell near Lh. Chulia, has an **ATM** (Cirrus/MC). Banks at KOMTAR and **Hong Kong Bank** (☎262 3000) and **Standard Chartered** (☎650 3667), both on Lh. Pantai, have **ATMs** (Cirrus/Nexus/Plus/V).

Emergency: Police ☎999. **Fire** ☎994.

Tourist Police: ☎261 5522, ext. 409.

Pharmacies: A few large pharmacies are on Lh. Pantai. **Boon Chemist Pharmacy,** ground fl., KOMTAR Lh. Tek Soon (☎263 1119). Open daily 10am-9:30pm.

Medical Service: General Hospital (☎229 3333), on Jl. Hospital. English spoken. **24hr. emergency room.** Consultation fee RM2. Minor surgery. No credit cards.

Telephones: Telekom office (☎220 9321), on Jl. Downing next to the post office. Open M-F 8:30am-4:30pm. **HCD/fax. IDD** from any card phone.

Internet Access: Many on J.H. Chulia. RM2 per hr.

Post Office: GPO Penang (☎261 9222), on the corner of Lh. Downing and Pengkalan Weld. Open M-F 8:30am-6pm, Sa 8am-4pm. *Poste Restante.* **Postal code:** 10670 (for post office only).

ACCOMMODATIONS

Budget hotels are on or near Lh. Chulia. Love Lane, named for the Chinese matchmakers who once lived there, intersects the center of Lh. Chulia.

Olive Spring Hotel, 302 Lh. Chulia (☎261 4641), above Rainforest Restaurant. Lovely welcome crew and walls awash with Caribbean purples and blues. No skimping on cleanliness here. Singles with fan RM15; doubles RM22-25

Hang Chow Hotel, 511 Lh. Chulia (☎261 0810). From Penang Rd., it's on the 1st block on the right. Clean and spacious rooms with hardwood floors and a sink. Fan doubles RM22; with 2 double beds RM30; doubles with A/C RM33.

SD Motel, 24 Lh. Muntri (☎264 3743). From Lh. Chulia, take a left off Love Ln. Off the main drag and very quiet. Immaculate rooms and sheets you want to sleep on. Hot and cold showers. Friendly management, but lacks a space to socialize. A/C dorms RM13; doubles with fan RM20, with A/C RM28; triples with fan RM24/38.

Oasis Hotel, 23 Love Ln. (☎261 67 78). Coming from Lh. Chulia, it's on the right. Cross-breezes, cushy chairs in the lobby, and the best hot showers in Malaysia. Laundry service and motorcycle rental. All rooms have fans. Single-sex dorms RM8; singles/doubles RM20-25, with shower RM30/35.

Wan Hai Hotel, 35 Love Ln. (☎261 6853), on the right. Faded, clean rooms with fans and sinks in an old Chinese shop house. Nice balcony, but the bathrooms are a bit far. Laundry, motorcycle (RM20 per day), bike (RM10 per day), and travel booking services. Dorms RM17; singles/doubles RM18; triples RM25.

Blue Diamond Hotel, 422 Ln. Chulia (☎261 1089), 1 block before the intersection with Jl. Penang. Beautiful old building with soaring (and echoey) ceilings. Beer garden outside. Movies every night. Email, motorbike rental, and travel booking services. Dorms RM8; singles/doubles RM20-30, with A/C and bath RM45.

Cathay Hotel, 15 Leith St. (☎262 6271). Traveling buddies and couples enjoy this antique colonial with lofty ceilings and white sheets. Check out the antique telephone switchboard and feel like you're walking through a sepia photograph. Doubles with fan RM57.50; standards with A/C RM69; deluxe with A/C RM92.

FOOD

The hybrid *nyonya* cuisine reigns supreme in Penang. The best food is found streetside: Chinese hawkers ladle out sugarcane juice, *ais kacang* (shaved ice, sweet corn, sweet red beans, *saso*, and syrup), *chendol* (shaved ice with green pea noodles in coconut milk and *pandan* syrup), and *bubur cha cha* (sweet coconut milk over ice with chunks of fruit and colorful rice gummies). General rule of thumb: if it's steaming when you get it, it's sanitary. Ask locals for their favorite stalls or head to the west end of **Gurney Dr.** overlooking the water (on the outskirts of town on the way to Batu Ferringhi), which is well known for its good *rojak*. Point to the fruits and veggies you want inside, and they'll mix it up for you. The best *popia* (a fresh spring roll), can be found at the **Popia Lazat Enak** stall with the tweetie bird decoration (on Gurney Dr., RM1.10 each). The same stall also sells scrumptious *top hats* (crispy bite-size pastries filled with cooked turnips, RM0.50 each). Hokkien Chinese food dominates **Kg. Malabar,** while Malaysian food stalls line **Lh. Tamil.** Join locals for dinner at the **Pasar Malam (night market).** (Call ☎263 8818 for current location.) Lh. Carnavan, between Lh. Chulia and Lh. Campbell, hosts a bustling **morning market.**

Oriental Seafood Cafe, 62 Jl. MacAlister, near KOMTAR Building. Some of the best Chinese seafood in town, cooked any way you want. Open daily 5:30pm-midnight.

Hameediyah, 164A Lebuh Campbell. Reputable Indian Muslim restaurant with a selection of *Murtabak* curries. Signature Curry Kapitan dish RM7. Open daily noon-10pm.

The Tandoori House, 34-36 Jl. Hutton, 2 blocks north of the intersection with Penang Rd. Georgetown's finest Mughal restaurant. A whopping 19 varieties of *naan* and 11 types of rice. Try *gulab jamun* (fried milk balls soaked in syrup, RM4) for dessert. Tandoori chicken and kebabs RM12. Refreshing freshly squeezed lime juice RM5. Tax 15%. Open daily 11:30am-3pm and 6:30-10:30pm.

Green Planet, 63 Lh. Cintra. Hang out in a welcoming makeshift hut with framed photographs of animals and the Orang Asli people while flipping through books of traveling advice. The scrumptious curry *devil* (RM12) made with lemongrass and tumeric stands out among Western alternatives. Vegetarian burger RM7. Open M-Sa 10am-3pm and 7pm-midnight, Su 7pm-midnight.

Rainforest Restaurant, 300 Lh. Chulia. Enveloped by the orange glow from the walls, customers always look happy. Western staples like milkshakes and sandwiches. Internet access RM2 per hr. Open M-Sa 8am-midnight.

Hard Life Cafe, 363 Lh. Chulia, 400m from the intersection with Lh. Penang, on the right. Pool table and reggae all the time. Cool beer RM5. Mostly vegetarian dishes RM6-10. Rooms upstairs RM10, for 2 people RM12. Open daily 5pm-3am.

Kean Lai Seng, 55 Kg. Malabar, off Jl. Penang under the Coca-Cola signs. *Laska* RM2. A Chinese "economy rice" buffet (until 2pm) that features amazing fried prawn fritters and other delectable selections for RM3.40. Authentic seafood *char koay teow* RM3. Open daily 8:30am-10pm.

SIGHTS

All sights listed except for Wat Chayamang Kalaram, Fort Cornwallis, and the State Art Gallery are near Jl. Masjid Kapitan Keling (formerly Lh. Pitt).

WAT CHAYAMANG KALARAM. The 36m reclining Buddha at this Thai temple is Malaysia's largest, and reputedly the third largest in the world. Photography is not allowed. *(Accessible by blue bus #93 and transit link bus #202. Off the main road to Batu Ferringhi on Ln. Burma.)* Opposite the temple is **Wat Dhammikarama,** the only Burmese temple in Malaysia, with intricately carved decorations and a 9m tall standing Buddha. *(Open daily 9am-5pm.)*

FORT CORNWALLIS. A hankering for the imperial past might take you to Fort Cornwallis's cannons and old brickwork at the northeast tip of town. Built by Captain Francis Light as a defense against the French, Kedah, pirates, and Siam in 1786, the fort was the point from which Penang's settlement began. Walk along the old cannons and prisons; plaques will guide you along. *(On Lh. Pantai beyond the clocktower and tourist information. Open daily 8:30am-7pm. RM1.)*

PENANG STATE MUSEUM. Fantastic displays give a flavor of Penang's history and culture without the dusty aftertaste of many museum exhibits. *(On Lh. Farquar, between St. George's Church and the Cathedral of the Assumption. Open Su-Th 9am-5pm. RM1.)*

KUAN YIN/TENG TEMPLE. Built in 1800, the temple is devoted to the Buddhist Goddess of Mercy. Devotees at Penang's oldest Chinese temple burn joss paper money for prosperity in the afterlife, with prayers for health, wealth, and longevity in a fog of sandalwood incense. *(1 block from St. George's. Open daily 9am-6pm.)*

KHOO KONGSI TEMPLE. Signs for various *kongsi*, meaning "dan house," are visible throughout the island. This one stands out for its lavish decoration and innumerable ancestral pillars. *(On Jl. Masjid Kapitan Kling, near Lh. Acheh. Go through the temple entrance; the meeting hall is on the right and the temple is down the drive.)*

SRI MARIAMMAN TEMPLE. Lord Shiva and his consort Parvati preside over this active Hindu temple, which also shelters the Shrine of the Nine Planets. *(The back of the Temple is down Jl. Masjid Kapitan Keling on the left before the intersection with Lh. Chulia. The front is one block over on Lh. Queen. Open daily 8am-noon and 4-9pm.)*

ST. GEORGE'S CHURCH. The church has English services on Sundays and offers interesting contrast with the Hindu and Buddhist temples in Penang. *(On Lh. Farquar, next to the Penang Museum.)*

MASJID KAPITAN KELING. A stark contrast to the frenzied activity of the Kuan Yin Temple, the mosque's marbled floors are cool on your feet (you must take off your shoes) and its silence a relief to the senses. It may still be undergoing renovations. *(From Sri Mariamman Temple, cross Lh. Chulia and walk one block down Jl. Masjid Kapitan Keling. Open daily 9am-5:30pm.)*

DAYTRIPS FROM GEORGETOWN

KEK LOK SI TEMPLE

Accessible via bus #1, 85, or 101 (25min.). Open daily 9am-6pm.

The largest Buddhist temple in Malaysia, its intricate blend of Chinese, Thai, and Burmese architecture makes it a must-see. Buddhist laity from all over Malaysia and Thailand flood the temple on Buddhist holidays. A vegetarian restaurant and turtle pond are on the lower level. Remember to take off your shoes in all six sanctuaries; taking pictures of nuns and monks is forbidden. The seven-tiered **Pagoda of 10,000 Buddhas** has eight flights of stairs leading to a narrow balcony, which offers a raven's-eye view of Ayer Itam and the countryside as well as a close look at the giant statue of Buddha at the top of the hill.

BOTANICAL GARDENS

Take bus #7 from the jeti, *Lh. Chulia, or KOMTAR. Open daily 5am-8pm.*

Northwest of Georgetown, the 30-hectare Botanical Gardens are great for a stroll, jog, or picnic, and on the weekend you're likely to have the rest of Georgetown to keep you company. Admire the rhesus monkeys roaming amid the greenery, but don't feed them. Stray from the main paths to avoid crowds.

PENANG HILL

Take bus #1 from Georgetown to Ayer Itam's Roundabout Junction. Locals will direct you to the cable train (10min. walk), which creeps up 740m Penang Hill (45min.; every 30min., every 15min. in late afternoon, M-W and F 6:30am-6:15pm, Th and Sa 6:30am-11:30pm; RM3, round-trip RM4). From the top, you can walk back by jungle path (once again, ask for directions and watch weather conditions, as rain may thwart your descent).

Penang Hill offers wonderful views of Georgetown. You can stop halfway up the cable train to view the rubber plantations of old. A small bird park houses sad but gloriously feathered birds (RM3). Before going home, stop by the Ayer Itam market to try one of the best *laksa* (RM2) in front of the red sign that says "LAKSA."

NEAR PENANG

BATU FERRINGHI

Graced with the natural beauty that earned Penang the nickname "Pearl of the Orient," Batu Ferringhi ("Portuguese Rock") is a seafood dining mecca and local hangout. The stretches of beach welcome honeymooners from abroad, even if the water is not crystal clear. You can roll out of bed and onto the sand from any of these guest houses. From the main road toward Teluk Bahang, look for the Coca-Cola sign with "Bayu Senja Kompleks 50m." Keep in mind that taxi drivers may badmouth certain guest houses and send you elsewhere for a commission. To get to **Baba Guest House,** 52 Batu Ferringhi, turn right down this road and left at the end. Baba is the first guest house on this lane. Laundry service and motorbike rental are available. (☎881 1686. Singles RM25; doubles RM30, with A/C RM50-60.) **Shalini's,** 56 Batu Ferringhi, cooks up breakfast and dinner from an extensive menu of Malay, Indian, and Chinese food. Guests hang out on the balcony to watch the sunset. (☎881 1859. Doubles with fan RM30, with A/C RM40.) **Ali's Guest House,** 53 and 54-B Batu Ferringhi, is the oldest in Batu Ferringhi. Laundry service and bike rental are available. (☎881 1316. Bar/lounge open daily 8-10pm. Singles/doubles RM30-35, with A/C and bath RM60-70; doubles on 2nd floor RM60; triples with A/C and bath RM75; quads with toilet and shower RM75.)

Hawker stalls and waterfront cafes are scattered amid high-class restaurants; nearly everywhere, a plate of *mee* or a bowl of *laksa* goes for RM3. The best bargain is the *nasi* packaged in newspaper. (Get it plain or with curry sauce RM0.50.) For the cheapest food in town, try **Bayu Senja Corner Cafe,** on the corner of Jl. Teluk Bahang and Bayu Senja, which serves Malaysian, Chinese, and Thai food. (Fried noodles RM3. Open daily 4pm-5am.) **Blue Bayou Seafood,** to the right of the guest houses, is a popular beachfront seafood cafe. Confirm prices before ordering. (Open daily noon-11pm.)

TELUK BAHANG

Known as "the end of the world" to local Malays because the road out of Georgetown once ended here, Teluk Bahang counterbalances the pressure-cooker atmosphere of Georgetown. Along the tree-lined streets, free-range roosters dodge school children, and laid-back vendors arrange piles of durian and rambutan. At the far end of town lies a *kampung nelayan* (fishing village). Rickety piers, a few weather-beaten boats, and a handful of equally weather-worn folks panning for *goleng* (tiny clams) are all that keep the *nelayan* in this *kampung.* Many travelers stay to enjoy the seafood and explore the nearby monkey beach, **Pantai Acheh Forest Preserve,** and the **Butterfly Park.** To reach Teluk Bahang from Georgetown, take blue bus #93 from the jetty.

The **Fisherman's Village Guest House,** in a turquoise house in the fishing *kampung* off the main road to the right, has clean rooms in a longhouse. The owners make you feel at home. (☎885 29 36. Standards with fan RM18, with A/C RM30.) **Hotbay Motel,** 48 Jl. Teluk Bahang, has attentive staff and brand new rooms; the sheets are white and clean. All rooms have two twin beds. (☎885 1323. Doubles with fan RM40, with A/C RM60; family rooms RM80.) To get to **Miss Loh's Guest House,** coming from Georgetown, turn left at the traffic circle, continue 300m, and take the first right past the Telekom station; it's the first unlabeled gate on the left after the bridge. Miss Loh's sits on a picturesque patch of land with an orchard of jackfruit trees and dogs and cats underfoot. Cook your own food. The rooms are clean and bright, but bring your mosquito net. (Dorms RM8-10; singles RM15-20.)

As you enter town, the main center for food is before the traffic circle on Teluk Bahang. Fare is simple but tasty (RM5). The **night market** by the traffic circle vends *sate, nasi kandar,* chili burgers, and local desserts. (Open daily 7:30-10:30pm.) The **morning market** on the left, beyond the public park on Jl. Teluk Bahang, sells fruits and veggies. (Open daily 6:30am-noon.) **Sun Stall,** on the right side of the main road before the traffic circle, is a Malay and Indian Muslim restaurant serving *char koay teow* (fried flat rice noodles RM2) and banana *roti* with ice cream (RM3). Sun also offers plenty of curries; just point and eat. **(Open 24hr.)** For Chinese fare, try the **Yellow Point Restaurant,** 486 Mk2, directly on the traffic circle. The menu includes claypot bean curd (RM6) and Taiwanese shark's fin soup (RM12). Seafood sells at market prices. (Open M and W-Su 11am-3pm and 6-11:30pm.) **Fisherman's Village Restaurant,** off the road from Rama's Guest House and before Fisherman's Village Guest House, serves fresh seafood (RM16-45).

DAYTRIPS FROM TELUK BAHANG. Hard-core nature enthusiasts hike at the **Pantai Acheh Forest Reserve,** between Teluk Bahang and Balik Pulau. There, the **Forestry Museum and Arboretum** display the local variety of rainforest trees and plants. (Open Tu-Su 9am-noon and 2:45-5pm.) The trail begins where Jl. Teluk Bahang ends, near the beach at the fishing village. From the trailhead, walk 30min. to a campsite with a wooden shelter near a swaying footbridge where the trail forks.

To the right, it leads to a **lighthouse** at the northwest tip of the island; the left branch goes to **Keracut Beach,** where there are crowded camping facilities. Those who take the adventurous 2hr. hike to the lighthouse should bring plenty of water. Beware of broken walkways and incredibly deep crevices. The dangerous parts of the trail have been marked with white squares of paper pointing out the best path. The trail leads to an empty beach, beyond which stands an out-of-date "Do Not Enter" sign. Hikers are now permitted to climb the crumbling trail to the lighthouse. (Forest Reserve open daily 7am-7pm.)

Erected in memory of the Buddhist priest and healer Chor Soo Kong, the **nake Temple** boasts snakes that are free to wind around the mantelpiece. They're more pit viper than cobra, but check it out, if only because every traveler in Malaysia will ask whether you went. (Take yellow bus #66 or minibus #32. Open daily 7am-7pm. Donations voluntary.)

The **Craft Batik,** 651 Teluk Bahang Rd., offers free tours of their factory. (☎885 10 44. Open M-Sa 8:30am-5:30pm, Su 8:30am-noon.) Lim Song at the **Green Orchid Farm,** 500m down the road, gives tours of his exquisite flora. The **Penang Butterfly Farm,** 830 Mk2, is 500m farther down the road. It's won numerous tourism awards and breeds 120 species of butterflies. The farm also has an insect museum and garden. (☎885 12 53. Open M-F 9am-5pm, Sa-Su 9am-5:30pm. RM10.) The **Pinang Cultural Center,** 288 Teluk Bahang Rd., though a bit touristy, has dinner shows with award-winning performances. (☎885 1175. Shows 8pm-10:30pm, RM110 including dinner.)

PULAU LANGKAWI

Slated to become the Phuket of Malaysia, sparsely populated Langkawi transformed from a fisherman's outpost into an efficient island resort in the early 1990s. After declaring itself duty-free, it has drawn tourists to shop in Kuah and drink cheap beer. The main attractions are eagle-feeding and cave viewing, with hours and hours of relaxation to spare. Snorkelers and divers head south for day trips to Pulau Payar to swim with blacktip sharks and schools of tropical fish.

THE VIEW FROM ABOVE

The lowdown: A well-developed island with everything from parties to sandy beaches.
Major city: Kuah.
Beaches: Pantai Cenang, Pantai Tengah.

KUAH ☎04

Kuah lays claim to *chendol* hawkers, duty-free shops, blocks of souvenir shops, and five out of Pulau Langkawi's six traffic lights. For the most part, however, it serves as base to explore nearby beaches and the island's lush landscape.

MALAYSIA

TRANSPORTATION

Flights: Langkawi airport, at Padang Matsirat, 20km from Kuah. **MAS** (☎966 6622) flies to: **Johor Bahru** via **Penang** (2½hr., 2:30pm, RM295); **Kuala Lumpur** (1hr., 7 per day 6:35am-9:40pm, RM205); **Penang** (30min.; daily 11:35am, 7:45pm, Su-M 1:50pm); and **Singapore** (1½hr.; Tu, F 3:55pm, Su 5:10pm; RM345).

Boats: Ferry companies have counters at the **jetty.** Ferries go to: **Kuala Perlis** (1hr., every 30min. 7am-6pm, RM12); **Kuala Kedah** (1½hr., every 30min. 7am-6pm, RM15); **Penang** (2½hr., 5:30pm, RM35); and **Satun,** Thailand (1hr.; 9, 10am, 3pm; RM18).

Taxis: Fixed fare taxis abound. From the jetty to Kuah town (RM4) and **Pantai Cenang** (RM15), or circumnavigate the island (RM 80-100).

Rentals: Major hotels rent **cars** (RM60-150 per day). **Motorcycle** (RM35-40 per day) and **bicycle** (RM10-15 per day) rentals are everywhere.

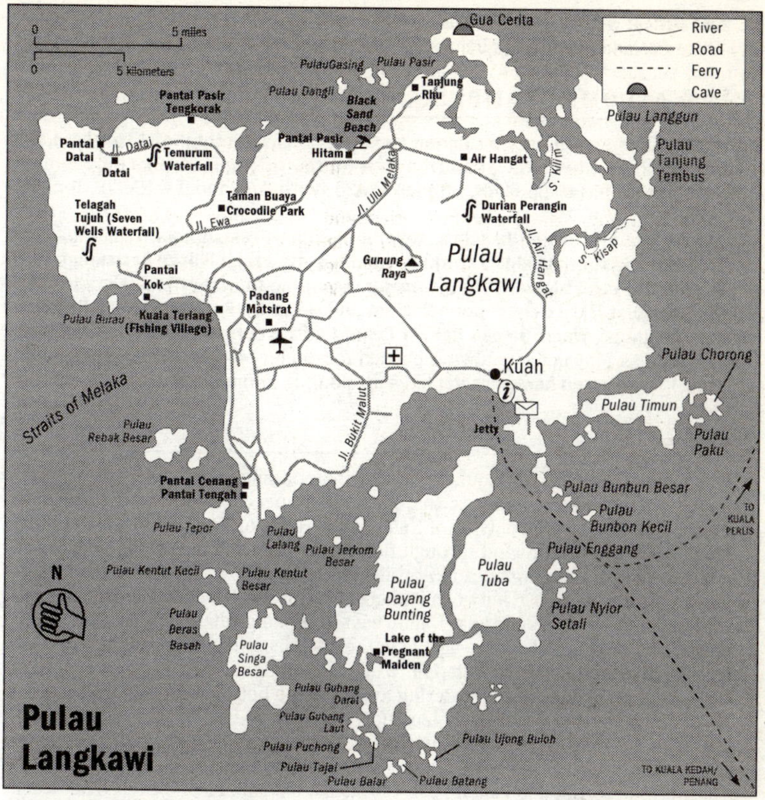

PRACTICAL INFORMATION

Tourist Office: Tourism Malaysia (☎966 7789), on Persiaran Putra. Coming from the jetty into Kuah, it's on the left. Open Sa-W 9am-5pm, Th 9am-1pm.

Tours and Travel: Zarminda Holidays (☎019 479 4123). Competitive prices, excursions around Langkawi, and snorkeling or island-hopping tours. Ask for Shawn.

Currency Exchange: Moneychangers abound. **Bumiputra Commerce Berhat,** 1 and 3 Jl. Pandak Mayah 1 (☎966 6725), opposite the hawker stalls. **24hr. ATM** (Cirrus/MC). Open Sa-W 9:30am-4:30pm.

Markets: Langkawi's big **Pasar Malam** changes location nightly. It rotates among Ulu Melaka (M), Kedawang (Tu), Kuah (W), Temoyong (Th), Air Hangat (F), Kuah (Sa), and Padang Matsirat (Su).

Emergency: ☎999.

Police: ☎966 6222. On Jl. Leboh Kisap opposite the old hospital.

Pharmacy: MNY Multi-Pharmacy, 102 Persiaran Mutiara (☎966 0066). Open daily 9am-10:45pm.

Medical Service: The **hospital** (☎966 3333) is on Bukit Tekoh, 10km toward Pantai Cenang. English-speaking doctors. **24hr. emergency care.** No credit cards.

Telephones: Telekom Office, Jl. Pandak Mayah 6 (☎966 7202), a few blocks off the main road. Open Sa-W 8:30am-4:30pm, Th 8:30am-1pm. **IDD** from public phones.

Internet Access: Along Pantai Cenang. RM6 per hr. Most open daily noon-midnight.

Post Office: ☎966 8690. Coming from the jetty, it's 500m before the tourist office. *Poste Restante.* Open Sa-Th 9am-5pm. **Postal code:** 07000.

ACCOMMODATIONS AND FOOD

Most travelers stay in nearby Pantai Cenang. Consequently, **Hotel Langkawi,** 6-8 Persiaran Putra, down the road from the tourist office, is Kuah's only budget accommodation. (☎966 6248. Singles RM25, with A/C and TV RM30; doubles RM35/40).

Despite the lure of the beaches, several of Kuah's restaurants remain packed with locals and tourists alike. For tastebud bliss, try **Prawn Village Restaurant,** 7-10 Jl. Persiaran Putra, between Hotel Langkawi and the tourist office. (Noodle soup RM3. Fish fillet RM10. Open noon-2:30pm and 6-11pm). **Rootian Seafood Restoran** and its neighbor, **Water Garden Hawker Center,** at the corner of Jl. Pandak Mayah and Jl. Pandak Mayah 6, are always packed for dinner on weekends. (Open Sa-Th 5-11pm.) The **open-air hawker center** lines up along Jl. Persiaran Putra with seafood.

SIGHTS

Pulau Langkawi is full of exquisite beaches, mountains, stone cliffs, and waterfalls. Driving around is painless, thanks to the impeccable infrastructure, clear signs, and minimal traffic outside of Kuah. Small roads off Rte. 115 between Pantai Cenang and Pantai Kok wind through fields, the **Kuala Teriang fishing village,** and Padang Matsirat. If you're on a motorbike, you can follow the many small paths that lead off the main road between Padang Matsirat and Ulu Melaka to a quiet and traditional *kampung*. **Pantai Kok,** 15min. past the fishing village, is slated for development, and wave breakers are visible in the distance. Northwest of Pantai Kok is **Telaga Tujuh,** the **Seven Wells Waterfall.** While the 20min. hike is steep (it descends 300m), a splendid view of the waterfall awaits at the bottom. For the more adventurous, in the wet season the full hike affords spectacular views, refreshing swims in the fall's six wells (the seventh, according to locals, is only found by those who get lost in the village), and close contact with monkeys.

On the road to Datai is **Pantai Pasir Tengkorak,** a small, clean beach. The beach gets crowded on Fridays, when families take advantage of the rest day to picnic by the water. The beach is good for swimming, but beware of sharp stones farther from the shore. Down the road is the **Temurum waterfall.** A 15min. walk will lead to the pool at the base of the falls. During the rainy season (June), the overflowing pool makes this a beautiful picnic spot. During the dry months, the waterfall is reduced to a trickle, but the beauty of the sheer cliff and surrounding trees still make the walk worthwhile. T-shirt vendors can be hired as guides for those who want to see the spectacular views from the top of Temurum (45min., about RM20).

Pantai Pasir Hitam, a black sand beach, is west on Rte. 113. After the rotary coming from Pantai Cenang, Rte. K33 leads to **Tanjung Rhu,** Langkawi's most secluded beach. At low tide, walk to the neighboring beach and watch fishermen cast their nets. Tours of nearby caves in the Killem River—**Gua Cerita** and **Gua Kelawar** (the bat cave)—are available. You can also see eagle feedings at a nearby mangrove swamp. (Cave tours: ☎955 2745. RM35. Eagle feedings: RM250-350 per boat or RM110 per person.)

In the center of the island, a road leads off Rte. 112 to the top of **Gunung Raya,** the tallest mountain on Langkawi. The reward at the end of the 13km stretch is a breathtaking view of the surrounding rice fields, Kuah, and the ocean. Off Rte. 113 east of the traffic circle, a road leads to **Durian Perangin Waterfall,** whose large pool and thick foliage distinguish it from its higher brethren. Farther south, Rte. 113 leads past a **rubber plantation.**

The clearest water and best **snorkeling** are at **Pulau Payar Marine Park** south of Langkawi, which has the best coral reefs off Malaysia's west coast. Full day excursions can be arranged with several train agencies at the Kuah jetty for RM130 (includes snorkeling gear and ferry transport). Many hotels along Lh. Pantai Cenang arrange island-hopping tours (4hr.; 9:30am, 2pm; RM25-45 not including snorkeling gear) which include snorkeling around Pulau Beras Basah, tours of the wildlife park on Pulau Singa Besar, and a visit to the gorgeous **Lake of the Pregnant Maiden** on Pulau Dayang Bunting. Many of the hotels also offer watersports such as water-skiing and jet-skiing. Fishing boats travel between the Kuah jetty and **Pulau Tuba** (30min., every 30min., RM3). Tuba's beach, fishing village, and bungalows are popular among backpackers and are worth a day trip.

PANTAI CENANG

Pantai Cenang is an up-and-coming backpacker center, with cheap beer and friendly regulars. Travelers spend they days on the beach looking for shells before catching a Langkawi sunset to begin the night. The easiest way to get here is by taxi from the airport (RM15) or Kuah.

Pantai Cenang offers numerous beachfront chalets with similar prices. **AB Motel,** 1km from the intersection of Lh. Pantai Cenang and the road from Kuah, has huts right on the beach. (☎955 1300. Huts with bath RM40; triples with A/C RM70.) **Delta Motel,** the first on the left as you're coming from Kuah, boasts real mattresses. (☎955 1307. Singles/doubles with shower RM40; triples with A/C and hot water RM85; longhouse quads with Western toilet and shower RM95.) **Yahok Homestay** is homey, but a couple of minutes from the beach. From Kuah, continue past **Breakfast Bar** (a local favorite) and take the paved road to the right. The porch is nice at sunset. (☎955 8120. Dorms RM10; singles/doubles with private bath RM15-20.)

Beach Garden Bistro and Beer Garden, on the beach 500m past AB Motel toward Pantai Kok, serves excellent but expensive international cuisine. (Happy hour 4-6pm. Open daily 8am-11pm.) **Hot Wok Cafe,** past the AB Motel on the right has tasty, inexpensive shrimp fried rice. (Open daily 10:30am-3pm and 6-11pm.) Nightlife consists of canned beer and other bubblies. The hottest spot on Langkawi is the **Coco Jam,** at the Langkawi Village Resort on Jl. Teluk Baru, where music blasts until the wee hours. (☎955 1511. RM15 cover includes first drink. Open daily 10pm-3am.) At **Bananas Fun Pub,** in the Awana Hotel, beers cost RM10 and beer jugs are only RM34. There are also pool tables on the second level and a Karaoke bar tucked behind the main bar room. (Open daily 6pm-2am.)

Check out marine life at **Underwater World,** left at the beginning of town coming from Kuah. (☎955 6100. Open daily 10am-6pm. RM18, children RM10.) The **Taman Buaya Crocodile Park,** on the road to Datai, has croc shows and a 25-foot python. (☎955 2559. Shows 11:45am, 2:15pm. Open Th-Tu 9am-6pm. RM8.)

CAMERON HIGHLANDS

Cool breezes, lush giant ferns, and fuscia orchids await travelers at this historic retreat. Since 1885, when government surveyor William Cameron hacked away wild jungles to a "fine plateau," the Cameron Highlands have provided a sweet escape for overheated, homesick Brits and, more recently, ornithologists documenting the variety of bird species. Outside the cool jungle are vegetable and strawberry farms and vast tea plantations that supply the pekoe tea consumed by lowlanders. There are three towns: Ringlet, Tanah Rata, and Brinchang. Ringlet, the lowest, is primarily a farmers' hub; Brinchang, the highest, attracts locals for its night market; and Tanah Rata is the main town where most jungle treks commence and offers the most conveniences, though it is also the most expensive.

TANAH RATA ☎05

In the clouds 14km north of Ringlet and 8km before Brinchang, Tanah Rata emerges with tall, mock-Tudor apartments and hotels interspersed around the main drag, which is lined with restaurants, bus and taxi stands, and entrances to jungle treks. Travelers from around the world come here for laid-back and late-night sidewalk dining and access to hostels and hotels.

TRANSPORTATION

Buses: From the **bus station** halfway down the main road, **Regal Transport Co.** (☎491 1311) operates local routes to **Brinchang** (10min., 21 per day 6:30am-5:40pm, RM0.50) and **Tapah,** a common stopover en route to the Cameron Highlands (1½hr., 8 per day 8am-5:30pm, RM3.70). **Express buses** (☎491 2978) go to: **Ipoh** (3hr., 8:30am and 2:30pm, RM15); **KL** (4½hr.; 8:30, 10:30am, 1:30, 4pm; RM13.95); **Penang/Butterworth** (7hr., 8:30am and 2:30pm, RM18).

Taxis: Next to the bus station. RM18 per hr. is the lowest price. To **Brinchang** or anywhere between Tanah Rata and Brinchang RM4. Taxis usually pick up at the taxi stand.

ORIENTATION AND PRACTICAL INFORMATION

The town of Tanah Rata begins with a row of restaurants, hotels, and shops on both sides of the street. Two hundred meters down the road, the **bus station** and **Malay food stalls** constitute the end of central Tanah Rata. Past the heart of town, the road leads to Bala's Holiday Chalets 1km away, and then to Brinchang.

Tourist Information: Souvenir shops sell maps. Guest houses provide detailed tourist information and jungle trail maps (RM5).

Currency Exchange: Hong Kong Bank, 31-32 Main Rd. (☎491 1217). Open M-F 9:30am-3:30pm, Sa 9:30-11:30am. **ATM** (Cirrus/MC/PLUS/V). **Maybank,** 20-21 Main Rd. (☎491 2873), exchanges currency. Open M-F 9:30am-4pm, Sa 9:30-11:30am.

Emergency: ☎999.

Police: ☎491 1222. Past the hospital beyond the main part of town.

Medical Service: Hospital (☎491 1966), on the left of the main road at the end of town. During office hours (8am-4:15pm), check in at registration room on left. **24hr. emergency care.** English spoken. No credit cards.

Telephones: No available Telekom office, but Telekom card phones all over town.

Internet Access: Most guest houses offer Internet access.

Post Office (☎491 10 51), on the left of the main road near Orient Hotel. Open M-Sa 8:30am-5pm. **Postal code:** 39000.

ACCOMMODATIONS

Nearly all guest houses provide attractive services, including bus reservations, international phone service, hot water (you'll need it), kitchen facilities, book exchange, movies, food, Internet service, and tourist information.

Father's Guest House, P.O. Box 15 (☎491 2484). Runs like clockwork. They pick you up the moment you step off the bus, provide a quick tour of the town and guest house, answer all your questions, and set you off exploring. Fall asleep to the laughter of jovial backpackers and get dropped off at the bus station when you leave. Laundry service nearby. Excellent Internet services. Lower rates for stays over one week. Dorms RM7; doubles RM18, with bath and shower RM30.

Daniel's Travelers Lodge, 9 Lorong Perdah (☎491 5823). From the bus station, take the 2nd right off the main road. Large patio with pool table provides a social atmosphere. 4 movies a day. Trekking guide accompanies patrons into the jungle. Dorms with backpack lockers RM6-8; singles/doubles RM16-24, with bath RM25-45.

Cameronian Holiday Inn, Jl. Mentigi 16 (☎491 1327), in a quiet area off the main road. Great location, comfortable beds, and a restaurant. Helpful trail maps, currency exchange, Internet, and motorbike rentals. Dorms RM6; singles/doubles RM15-25, with shower RM30-50.

Bala's Holiday Chalets, Lot 55 (☎491 1660), 2km up the road from town (sign indicates the turn-off), about a 20min. walk. Serene surroundings and elegant architecture:

perfect for those seeking solitude. Free pickup from the bus station. Make reservations on weekends. Doubles RM66, RM120 on weekends; family rooms from RM120.

FOOD

Delicious, inexpensive food is everywhere. Don't miss the **steam boat hot pot** offered by most restaurants. As you enter town, head for the right side of the road before the bus station for food stalls serving cheap, standard Malay and Chinese fare. The best are **Excellent Food Stall** (open daily 7am-5pm) and **Zainab San,** which serves Malay food. Several good Indian and Chinese restaurants are on the left side of the road. Guest houses have menus as well.

Mayflower Restaurant, on Main Rd. opposite the bus station. Locals agree that it's the best restaurant in town. *Tom yam* (RM10) and steamboat hot pots.

Restoran Bunga Suria, 66A Persiaran Camellia 3, beyond the electric palm trees on the left when facing Ringlet. Runner up on the "local favorites" list. Set meals satisfy trekking hunger (from RM4-5.50). Vegetarian meals available. Open daily 7am-10pm.

Warung Kek Rich Bake and Coffee House, 54-A Persiaran Camellia 3, 100m from the bus station toward Ringlet, on the left. Learn about Chinese tea ceremonies or enjoy thick pancakes with fruit (RM4). Open daily 10am-5pm and 6-11pm.

SIGHTS

Second to its natural beauty, the Highlands' best sights are agricultural. Picturesque tea plantations and terraced vegetable, strawberry, and dairy farms make a surreal "food pyramid." Check out the tiles with minuscule Buddhas at **Sam Poh Buddhist Temple,** near Brinchang, and the camouflaged leaf frogs and foot-long stick insects at the **Butterfly Park.** (Open daily 8am-6pm, RM3.)

Hiking is the preferred Highlands activity. Most guest houses offer trail maps. Count on each hike being more difficult than its description and be careful after it rains, when trails are treacherous. Highland forests are covered with slippery moss.

The hikes' levels of difficulty vary widely: Path #1 is very steep and reaches almost 2000m with a lookout at the top on Gunung Brinchang. You can also climb up and arrange a car back. Path #2, to Gunung Berembun, is not well marked and very challenging; paths #3, 5, and 8 are steep and don't offer the best views. It's always best to take someone along and take several breaks, as wildlife tends to appear when you're still. Head down the Tanah Rata-Brinchang road directly opposite the hospital to reach the beginning of Walk #9A, which passes **Robinson Waterfall** and descends easily to the **Mini Dairy Farm.** Budget 4-5hr. round-trip for all paths except for #1, which may take a strenuous full day.

The **Boh Tea Estates,** the oldest tea plantation in the Highlands, are accessible by bus or taxi. Smaller **Sungei Palas Tea Estate** is more picturesque. Visitors can have a cup of tea and some homemade shortbread in the open cafe and take a free tour of the factory. (Open Tu-Su 9am-4:30pm.) **Daily countryside tours** are available at all accommodations and include a visit to the tea plantation and factory, Buddhist temple, strawberry garden, vegetable farms, butterfly garden, and market center. (4hr., 9am-2pm, RM15. Tea estates closed on M.)

BRINCHANG ☎05

Brinchang is a short **taxi** (RM5) or **bus** ride (RM0.50), some 5km from Tanah Rata. It's less sophisticated than Tanah Rata, but still attracts tourists for its markets. **Jl. Bandar,** also known as the Main Road, loops around the central square. The market occupies most of the square, which consists of restaurants, hotels, clinics, and shops. West of the square behind the Hong Kong Hotel is **Bandar Baru,** with laundry, bank, and a drugstore. The local **bus stop** is on the main road next to the Hong Kong Hotel. **Public Bank Berhad** is at 41-43 Bandar Baru. (☎491 1590. Open M-F

9:30am-4pm, Sa 9:30am-noon.) The **GPO** is on the Main Rd. past the square on the left. (☎491 1016. Open M-Sa 8:30am-12:30pm and 2:30-5pm.) The **day market** is in the central square. **Postal code:** 39100.

Brinchang's budget accommodations are frequently booked on weekends. For backpacker camaraderie, stay in Tanah Rata. The **Chua Gin Hotel,** 11 Main Rd., has a friendly staff and honors guests' privacy. (☎491 1801. Doubles with bathroom RM35.) **Highlands Hotel,** 29-32 Jl. Bandar, offers spacious rooms but lacks character. (☎491 1588. Doubles RM42; triples RM55; quads RM65.)

Brinchang's Chinese food is good. **Malay food stalls** cluster in the central square. **Shal's Curry House,** 25 Main Rd., with a fish-head logo, is one of the finest South Indian restaurants in Malaysia. Try the *mulligatawny* soup (RM5.50), *murtabak,* (a savory stuffed roti RM5.90), or Shal's famous apple strudel (RM5.90) and be bowled over by the warm hospitality. (Open daily 8am-10pm.)

INTERIOR PENINSULAR MALAYSIA

Malaysia's development has wrought enormous environmental harm throughout the peninsula. The protected parklands of Taman Negara, the interior's premiere attraction, sometimes seem to be the lone pristine oasis. Eco-conscious travelers still sneer at the unabashed marketing and development of this "virgin jungle paradise," but these trappings are only in the main resort—the rest remains relatively untouched and the efforts to maintain Malaysia's natural heritage deserve applause.

JERANTUT ☎09

Jerantut is mainly a gateway to Taman Negara and the best place to stock up on supplies and information about treks and other adventures. However, a night spent here before plunging into the jungle is not wasted. If you have time to explore, wander down a few of Jerantut's back streets, teeming with bougainvillea and the shy smiles of little kids.

TRANSPORTATION AND PRACTICAL INFORMATION. **Boats** leave for Taman Negara from **Kuala Tembeling,** 20min. outside Jerantut. To get there, take a shuttle from any of the hotels (RM5), or use a **taxi** (RM18, with A/C RM26). The **bus station** is on Jl. Diwangsa. **Local buses** go to **Kuala Tembeling** (30min., 4 per day 8:15am-5:15pm, RM2). **Express buses** run to **Kuantan** (8:30, 11am, RM8.50). Express Perwira buses depart at 8:30, 10:30am, 2:30, and 4pm for **Klang** (4hr., RM11.40); **KL** (3hr., RM9.40); **Temerloh** (1hr., RM3.50). If the Jerantut station doesn't go to your destination, try the station in Temerloh. The **train station** (☎266 2219) is on Jl. Stesen Keretapi. Jungle trains with great views crawl to **Singapore** (8½hr., 8:45am, RM15; express 7hr., 1:20am, RM19) and to **Wakaf Bharu,** near Kota Bharu (11:30am, RM12.60; express 6hr., 1:50, 3:30pm, RM19). Taxis zoom to **Kota Bharu** (RM240); **KL** (RM88); **Kuantan** (RM80).

The two main roads are **Jl. Besar** and **Jl. Diwangsa. MBF Finance Berhad,** with **ATM** and **currency exchange,** is opposite the bus station. The **hospital** (☎266 3333) is located outside the town off Jl. Besar. Stock up on supplies at **Aktif** on Jl. Diwangsa. (open 10am-10pm.) Turn left from the bus station onto Jl. Bomba and the **post office** is at the end of the street. (☎266 2201. Open M-Sa 8:30am-5pm.) **Postal code:** 27000.

ACCOMMODATIONS AND FOOD. **Green Park Guest House,** Lot. 34 Jl. Besar, is the friendliest guest house in town. The amiable proprietor, Azam, holds a forestry degree and has 15 years experience as a tour guide. He holds nightly talks on park trails in addition to leading two tours (3 days 350RM, 2 days 250RM) which are geared towards the more adventurous tourist. (☎266 3884. Dorms RM8;

singles RM10; doubles RM20; triples RM27.) In the center of town, **Sri Emas** (☎266 4499), on Jl.Besar, offers clean rooms at great prices. Staff provide information on transport and activities and make bookings for tours. A large sign marks **Hotel Chet Fatt,** Lot 1755 Jl. Diwangsa, second floor, opposite the bus station. The friendly owner manages immaculate rooms. For weekend stays, reserve in advance. There is a pool table and Internet downstairs. (☎266 58 05. Doubles with fan RM15, with A/C RM18, with A/C and private bath RM23-28.) **Jerantut Guest House** has clean rooms with grungy bathrooms but no perks except for the cheapest rates in town. (☎266 99 77. Doubles with fan RM10, with A/C RM25; triples with fan RM15.) Pusat Dobi Pelanggi on Jl.Besar has same-day laundry (RM4 per kilo).

Dine outside at one of the many restaurants across from the market on Jl. Pasar Besar. The **night market** offers the standard *kavay teow*/fried rice/*satay* standards for around RM4-5. (Open Sa dusk-10:30pm.) Look for *roti canai* stands hawking late-night snacks.

TAMAN NEGARA NATIONAL PARK ☎09

The shrieking cicadas and tall trees of Taman Negara have an awesome and uneasy beauty. As powerful as this rainforest seems, it is all that is left of its kind on the peninsula due to heavy deforestation. As Malaysia's first and largest national park, Taman Negara is one of the world's best-kept rainforests, yet it still teeters on the brink of ecological disaster. Increased river traffic, land development, and noise pollution ensure that the wildlife stays far from resort areas. Fortunately, few visitors venture more than 2km from park headquarters and the Taman Negara Resort, making it easy to dodge crowds.

AT A GLANCE

AREA: 4300 sq. km.

CLIMATE: Rainy season Nov.-Jan. Moderate temperatures near 25°C.

HIGHLIGHTS: Hiking, canopy walking, river rafting, tubing.

GATEWAYS: Jerantut and Kuala Tembeling.

FEES AND RESERVATIONS: Entry permit RM1. Photography permit RM5. Fishing permit RM10.

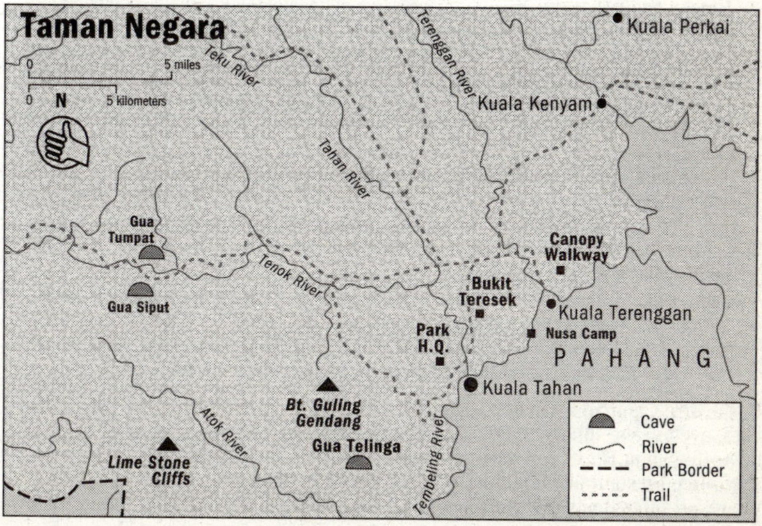

TRANSPORTATION

Taman Negara and its gateways, **Jerantut** and **Kuala Tembeling,** are accessible by **bus** from **KL** or **Kuantan,** and by **train** from **Wakaf Bharu** or **Singapore.** The park can be reached by privately arranged **bus** or **taxi,** or by **boat** on the Tembeling River. Boats to the park (3-3½hr.; 9am, 2pm; RM19; return 2-2½hr., same times) leave from the village of **Kuala Tembeling,** accessible by bus (RM1.20) or share-taxi (RM4 per person) from Jerantut. Look for monkeys, lizards, and colorful birds on the shores. **Boats** shuttle across the river for RM0.50. Nusa Camp runs **river buses** (RM30-290 per day) within the park that are cheaper than private charters. **Nusa Riverbus** routes go from Nusa Camp to **Blau and Yong observation hides** (RM7), **Kuala Tahan** (RM7), **Kuala Terengganu** (RM8), and the **cave** (RM5) several times per day, stopping at 6pm. In Kuala Tembeling, fixed-price **share-taxis** (4-passenger max.) go to: **Jerantut** (RM16, with A/C RM18); **Kuala Lumpur** (RM120); **Kuantan** (RM120).

ORIENTATION AND PRACTICAL INFORMATION

Book your boat ride and accommodations at least one night in advance (either with the resort or with Nusa Camp), especially during weekends and holidays. Hold on to your permits (see **At A Glance,** above), as you'll be asked to produce them when you leave. Bring lots of water, fruit, and snacks; the mini-markets are expensive.

The **park headquarters,** next door to a mini-market, is on the left of the Tembeling River, near the park's south entrance. Across the river is the village of **Kuala Tahan** with cheaper hostels and restaurants. The reception area at the resort offers **telephone service** at rip-off prices. Good **maps** (RM2) with trails and points of interest are available at the Wildlife Office at the park headquarters. The resort office next to reception rents hiking and camping gear (RM14 for 2-person tent). If you're undertaking a lengthy hike or are inexperienced, consider hiring one of the expensive but knowledgeable guides (around RM120 per day). For the Taman Negara environs (including Kuala Tahan, Kuala Tembeling, and Jerantut) the **postal code** is 27000. Drop off mail at the resort reception desk.

ACCOMMODATIONS AND FOOD

For cheaper accommodations, cross the river to Kuala Tahan.

Nusa Camp, 16 Jl. Diwangsa, 27000 Jerantut, Pahang Darul Makmur (☎266 2369). At Jerantut bus station. **KL Office:** Express National Counter, Malaysia Tourist Information Center, 109 Jl. Ampang, 50450 (☎03 230 5401). **Kuala Tembeling Office:** No. 5, Taman Negara Jetty, Kuala Tembeling, Jerantut, 27000, Kuala Tembeling (☎266 1832). Reservations recommended for boats and accommodations. Upriver from the Taman Negara Resort and quieter than jetty area lodging. Campsite RM2 with tent RM8; dorms RM15; A-frame chalet RM55; Malay cottages RM90; Malay house RM100.

Teresek View Village (☎266 9744). Although it is a bit of a hike to get up the hill, RM10 hostel beds can't be beat. Ask for Ahmad, the receptionist/resident nature guide, for information on trails. The A-frames RM40. Clean and cozy Malay houses RM 60-100.

Agoh's Chalets (☎266 9570), on the embankment 50m to the right with your back to the river. 4-bed dorm rooms RM15, with A/C 20; fan chalet for 2 RM35; family room with TV, A/C and beds for 4 RM100.

Taman Negara Resort, Kuala Tahan, 27000 Jerantut, Pahang Darul Makmur (☎266 2500). Call ahead to book rooms and boats to Kuala Tahan. Expensive and luxurious. Camping arranged with Wildlife Dept. (RM2). Make reservations a week in advance from Apr.-Nov. Dorms are a rip off at RM45; doubles RM185, extra bed RM55. MC/V.

Both Nusa Camp and Taman Negara Resort have restaurants, but the prices are high, even in the "budget cafeteria." The resort is the only place in town to get a beer, though at RM18 you have to question whether it's worth it. Several reasonably priced restaurants line the river. The **Family Restaurant** on the shore opposite the resort offers tasty Malay dishes as well as standard Western fare. Burgers run

RM2.50. (Open daily 8am-11pm.) Up the hill, the **Off Road Cafe** serves up hearty breakfasts for the early riser and hosts a crowd of locals and guests who gather to watch football on TV in the evenings.

OUTDOOR ACTIVITIES

Taman Negara never experienced an ice age and, as a result, is the oldest rainforest in the world. Trails are clearly marked, so it's easy to slip away in the early morning and surround yourself in the virgin jungle. The larger mammals—elephants, tigers, rhinos, leopards, and cattle—are rarer sights these days but amazing insects, birds, and lush forest makes this a forest a must-see. Start your trip with the nightly showing of an informational video about Taman Negara, next door to an exhibit on the plants and animals in the park (8:45pm at the Interpretive Center).

HIKING. The **nine-day trek** to and from **Gunung Tahan,** Peninsular Malaysia's highest peak, and the nearby four-tiered waterfall is the best way to take in the ecological riches. The trip requires massive planning. Food and camping materials must be purchased in Kuala Tahan. Travelers must consult with park authorities beforehand and hire a **guide** (RM500 for 1 week, RM50 for each subsequent day. The information desk at the resort has postings from people willing to split costs. The mostly uphill climb to **Bukit Teresek** (1.7km, 1hr.) offers breathtaking panoramas of the forest as far as Gunung Tahan. Bring plenty of water.

CANOPY WALKWAY. Suspended by a web of ropes, wires, cables, and wooden planks along the treetops, the canopy walk is the longest crossing of its kind. This can be its selling point, although for those afraid of heights, it is 470m of sheer torture. The view 40m above the forest floor is tremendous; bring, buy, or steal a camera. Authorities regularly test the safety of the walkway. (Open Sa-Th 11am-3pm, F 8am-noon. RM5.)

GUA TELINGA. This limestone cave is a tourist favorite. Look for bats and non-poisonous snakes. The cave is slippery and dirty, so bring old clothes, sturdy shoes, and a flashlight. (2.6km, 1½ hr. each way).

RIVER RAFTING AND TUBING. Ride the rapids in a "boat" or float down the river in a rubber tube for a new vantage point from which to see the forest—on your back. Book trips at the Family Restaurant at least an hour in advance. (10am, 11am, and at varying times in the afternoon; RM25 per person).

NIGHT ADVENTURES. The rainforest really comes to life at night. Explore it on a guided night hike (RM15), 4WD safari tour (RM25), or river cruise (RM35). Hikes focus more on insects and phosphorescent fungi, while safaris attempt to track the more elusive wildlife. Check for times and book through the Family Restaurant.

PERHENTIAN ISLANDS ☎09

One of the world's most beautiful beaches, the sands of Long Beach have brought widespread fame to the Perhentian Islands. Tourists come in search of great coral deposits, snorkeling, and scuba diving and settle for the evening barbecues and starry nights that make up the islands' nightlife, which is limited by meager alcohol reserves. Those hoping for a taste of indigenous culture will be disappointed, as vacationers from around the world flock to the islands during tourist season. In rainy months, however, visitors find cheap hostels, fewer tourists, and great surf.

THE VIEW FROM ABOVE

The lowdown: Western Malaysia's northernmost island group.
Islands: Pulau Perhentian Kecil ("Little Island") and Pulau Perhentian Besar ("Big Island"). Neither island is more than 4km across.
Gateway city: Kuala Besut.
Beaches: On Kecil: Coral Bay, Long Beach, Mira Beach, Petani Beach. On Besar: Blue Lagoon, Flora Beach, Main Beach.

GETTING TO PERHENTIAN ISLANDS

The easiest way to get to the Perhentians is via Kuala Besut from Kota Bharu or Kuala Terengganu. From Kuala Besut, take a boat to the islands.

TO KUALA BESUT: From **Kota Bharu,** take a taxi to Kuala Besut (1½hr., RM24 per 4 people). If you can't find other passengers to split the cost, take a bus to **Pasir Putih** (1hr., every 30min. 6:30am-7:30pm, RM2.8) and catch another bus to Kuala Besut (30min., every 30min. 6:30am-6:30pm, RM1.6). From **Kuala Terengganu,** take a taxi (2hr., RM40 per 4 people) or a bus to **Jertih** (1½hr., every 30min. 6:30am-7pm, RM5.5) and then a bus to Kuala Besut (20min., every 20min. 6:30am-6pm, RM1).

TO THE PERHENTIANS: Boats leave for the islands from **Kuala Besut** and **Tok Bali** (taxi from Kota Bharu 70min., RM24 per 4 people). Boats drop passengers off at their beach of choice on either Besar or Kecil. Return boats leave around 8:30am and noon. Well-known boat companies are **Perhentian Ferry Travel and Tours** (☎ 691 9679) and **Tanjung Enterprise** (☎691 0189). The Tourist Information Center and many guest houses in Kota Bharu and Kuala Besut sell boat tickets.

WHAT TO EXPECT. Accommodations can be difficult to find during the high season (June-Aug. and public holidays). **Arrive in Kuala Besut for the 10am boat departure, as accommodations on the islands fill up quickly.** Most accommodations close from Nov.-Feb. Reservations usually aren't accepted, and scant telephone lines make connecting to local numbers unreliable.

PULAU PERHENTIAN KECIL ☎09

With the constant criss-crossing of motorboats, the monotone hum of generators, and cheap bungalows on every available plot of land, Kecil isn't a mecca of serenity. But past the crowds, Long Beach is arguably Malaysia's most beautiful locale.

ORIENTATION AND PRACTICAL INFORMATION

Long Beach is on the island's east coast. Accommodations span the entire length of the beach, while restaurants, dive shops, and convenience stores take up the center. On the west coast, a 15min. walk from **Mohsin Chalets,** is quieter **Coral Bay.** A 45min. walk south is **Mira Beach.** Another 20min. takes you to the southern coast and larger **Petani Beach. Perhentian Village,** home to the **police station** and **medical services** is on the island's southeast tip, 20min. from Petani Beach.

Motorboat taxis line up along **Long Beach** and go to: **Coral Bay** (RM14); **D'Lagoon** (RM4); **Mira Beach** (RM12); **Perhentian Village** (RM8); **Petani Beach** (RM10); **Pulau Perhentian Besar** (RM7-15). Don't buy round-trip tickets, since they are honored only if you have the same driver going both ways.

Tourist Offices: No official tourist office, although **Turtle Shop** (☎010 983 3538), at the center of Long Beach, offers info on entertainment, transportation, and the turtle hatchery. Snorkeling trips run RM30 including equipment rental. Open daily 9am-7pm.

Currency Exchange: Both Turtle Shop and **Mama's Place** in Coral Bay change traveler's checks. **Bring cash from the mainland.**

Medical Services: ☎697 7680, behind the police, across a small bridge to right. Basic care only. Some English spoken. Open M-W, Sa 8am-4:50pm, closed Th, F, Su. Go to the mainland for emergency care.

Police: ☎697 7722, in a blue building along the village beach behind a rusting fence. Little English spoken. Open daily 8am-4pm.

Telephones: International calls available at high rates at some accommodations. Usually RM10 per min. A **Telekom Malaysia** booth is next to the police station.

Post Offices: Turtle Shop has stamps and more frequent mail service than the village **post office. Postal code:** 22200.

ACCOMMODATIONS

Most accommodations on Long Beach are full throughout the tourist season (June-Aug.). Some travelers head to less-frenzied Coral Bay or hire a boat to one of Besar's smaller beaches.

LONG BEACH

Chempaka (☎010 985 7329) has a variety of standard, clean options. Tents RM12; A-frames with shared, Western toilets and mosquito nets RM25; longhouses for 2 with bath RM40; bungalows RM60.

Mohsin (☎010 333 8897) has large bungalows on the hillside above the beach. Linens and towels provided. Restaurant attached. Bungalows with bath RM50. MC/V.

Panorama (☎010 912 2518), set back from the beach. TV in restaurant shows movies. 2 pool tables. Chalets RM30, with bath RM50-60.

Mateheri (☎019 956 5756), in the center of the beach. Bungalows set back in the woods RM30, with bath RM45-75.

Rock Garden has simple A-frames on the hillside. Squat toilets in rooms farther from the beach. All rooms with common bath and mosquito nets RM20-30.

Simfony (☎019 910 4236) offers cheap but shabby thatch-roofed A-frames with bathrooms crowded close to the beach. Rooms with common bath RM25.

CORAL BAY

A 15min. stroll across the island from Long Beach is Coral Bay, Kecil's second most popular beach.

Rajaweli Corel Beach Resort (☎011 344 5688), at Coral Bay's north end. Balcony cafe and friendly staff make for a pleasant stay. Clean, spacious dorms RM15; A-frames RM35-80; great family rooms with A/C, carpet, and TV RM80.

Maya Beach Resort. New chalets with Western toilets RM50, beachfront RM80.

DJ Chalet (☎010 985 2546) has basic chalets in a wooded area. The cheapest lodging on the beach. Indulge in the sinful "DJ special" (chocolate banana shake RM3.5) at the restaurant. Internet access RM0.40 per min. Chalets with mosquito nets and squat toilets RM25, with bath RM30.

Butterfly, at the south end of Coral Bay. Vaulted bungalows with private baths, Western toilets, and breathtaking sunset views RM45-60.

Aur Beach Chalets (☎010 985 8584), where the trail to Long Beach starts. Clean A-frames with mosquito nets and bath RM30-40. Prices expected to rise in Aug. 2001.

OTHER BEACHES

From the south end of Coral Bay, a trail (follow the splotches of white paint on rocks and trees) heads for quiet **Mira Beach** (45min.) and **Petani Beach** (1-1½hr.).

Mira Beach, accessible by boat or hike from Coral Bay. Hillside rooms surround the small beach. Restaurant open daily 7am-midnight. Set dinners RM5-10. Snorkel gear rental RM4-5 per hr., RM12 per day. Malay longhouses RM25-40.

Petani Beach Resort (☎019 957 1624), between Mira Beach and the village. Restaurant fish special RM15. Reservations recommended. Bungalows with bath RM50-60.

D'Lagoon (☎010 985 7089), in a cove on the island's northeast tip, accessible only by boat or water taxi. 10min. hike to west coast beaches. Restaurant open daily 7am-10pm. Group dinners (usually fish) RM10 per person. Snorkeling equipment and turtle trips RM21. Camping RM5; dorms RM10; treehouse RM20; rooms with bath RM25-50.

FOOD

Most accommodations have attached cafes that serve breakfast and lunch. By night, restaurants in the center of Long Beach set up barbecues with fresh seafood, chicken, and veggie options (meat, sauce, and fruit RM8). **Shake Shack** mixes up gigantic shakes for RM4. On Coral Bay, try the homemade cakes (RM2.50) from the **Cake Lady** in front of DJ Chalets.

ACTIVITIES

Gorgeous coral reef and clear waters make Kecil ideal for **diving.** Several dive shops near the beach offer PADI courses. **Turtle Bay Divers** (☎010 333 6647) has shops in Long Beach, and **Perhentian Dive Center** (☎018 836 1442) operates on Coral Bay. Almost all dive shops on the islands arrange four-day open-water courses (RM750), two-day advanced courses (RM550), one-day discover scuba courses (RM150), and fun dives for certified divers (2 dives RM140, with own equipment RM110). MC/V is accepted. All certified divers receive a discount on breakfast and lunch at the **Safety Stop Cafe** at Chempaka Chalets on Long Beach.

Snorkeling trips can be arranged at **Turtle Shop** (see **Practical Information,** p. 414) and most accommodations (4hr., RM30; rentals RM6-8). The **turtle hatchery** in front of Turtle Shop lets travelers watch baby turtles as they make their moonlit trek to the waves. Starting in June, drop by at 11pm to see if they are being released (no noise, flashlights, or flash photography). **Nightlife** is limited to barbecues, card-playing, and expensive booze on Long Beach (Beer RM8). Bring alcohol from the mainland or seek out Western expats for hidden stashes.

PULAU PERHENTIAN BESAR ☎09

Known as "The Big Island," Besar languidly awaits travelers looking for more space, calm, and waves. Dive shops along the west coast attract younger travelers, while peaceful beaches lull backpackers, newlyweds, and families alike. All visitors, however, sample the local way of life, which remains far less disturbed than on Kecil, the budding Waikiki next door.

TRANSPORTATION AND PRACTICAL INFORMATION

Most services and accommodations cluster on two chief beaches, **Main Beach** and **Flora Bay.** There is no official **tourist office,** but most guest houses and shops provide basic information. **Mama's Place** (see **Accommodations,** below) exchanges **traveler's checks** at poor rates and runs **boats** to: **Abdul's Chalets** (RM4); **Coral Bay** (RM10); **D'Lagoon** (RM10); **Flora Bay** (RM10); **Long Beach** (RM7); **Perhentian Village** (RM4).

ACCOMMODATIONS

Budget accommodations are concentrated along the south and west coasts on Main Beach and Flora Bay. Upscale resorts cluster farther north.

MAIN BEACH

Facing Kecil along Besar's southwest coast, the endless Main Beach is packed with budget accommodations.

Mama's Place. Isolated by a tumble of rocks. A favorite with couples and families. Nightly feast RM13-25; make reservations before 5pm. Daytrips to Turtle Beach RM12. Sea canoe rental RM30 per day. Sunset boat rides RM12. Snorkeling trips RM20. Bungalows RM25, often filled; doubles with bath RM60-80; triples RM90.

Abdul's Chalet (☎010 983 7303), on the south end of the beach. Popular with families. Bungalows, some right on the water, have Western bath RM40-50.

Seahorse Chalet. Cheapest bungalows on the beach. No electricity. Basic A-frames with mosquito nets and common bath with squat toilet RM20.

Cozy Chalet Villas (☎019 959 5465), high on the rocks. Longhouses with bath and squat toilet RM50; bungalows RM60; family rooms with bath RM100.

ABC Chalet Rooms (☎967 7568), overlooking the ocean. Rooms with bath RM30-40.

FLORA BAY

Farther east along the island's forested southern coast (accessible by ferry, water taxi, or a 30min. hike on the jungle trail) is spacious and quieter Flora Bay, boasting cheaper accommodations, personal attention, and the best dining in the Perhentians.

Wanderer's Inn. Popular for its cheap rates, clean bathrooms and delicious barbecue. Camping RM15 with tent rental; bungalows with common bath RM25.

Flora Bay (☎697 7266) offers a variety of well-kept rooms, large cafe, and friendly staff. Internet access RM0.35 per min. Moneychanger. Reservations accepted. Longhouse doubles RM42; bungalows RM60-120; family rooms for 5 RM90. MC/V.

Ocean Blue (☎010 281 9689). Bungalows with an attached Western bath RM50.

Fauna Beach Chalet (☎697 7607), in the center of the beach. Pricier rooms have ocean views. Spacious doubles with bath RM35-65; family rooms RM80.

Samudra Beach Chalet (☎697 7608). Clean, standard A-frames and chalets. Doubles with bath (RM30-50).

FOOD

Nearly all accommodations have attached cafes. **Mama's Place** and **Abdul's** are big hits for breakfast and lunch. At night, try **Wanderer's Cafe** at Flora Bay for a delicious barbecue with daily catches of squid, kingfish, and tuna, and grab a few beers at **Sea Horse Cafe.** The best Malay food is on Flora Bay. **Samudra Cafe** serves especially tasty *sotong* (squid cooked in chili sauce RM5), while **Fauna Bay Cafe's** monstrous menus are sure to please even the most finicky eaters.

ACTIVITIES

Like Kecil, Besar boasts fabulous **snorkeling** and **scuba diving**. Most guest houses rent snorkeling equipment (RM15). **D'Lagoon, Shark Point,** and the water in front of **Mama's Place** are the best snorkeling sites. At Shark Point, popular with adventurous divers, you'll have the best chance to see sharks. **Bay Watch** arranges snorkeling trips (RM20) and excursions to **Rawa Island** (RM45) and **Redang** (RM60). For a touch of romance, pack your snorkeling gear and head to **Blue Lagoon,** a deserted beach on the north shore. If snorkeling doesn't fill your marine needs, head 30m from Mama's Place to watch the giant sea turtles that haunt Malaysia's east coast.

For the water babies, Besar's diving opportunities are not to be missed. **Trumba Toga** offers a breathtaking swim around a tumble of rocks. Wreck dives center on a Vietnamese ship that sunk in the Vietnam War. Dive shops have standard scuba prices (4-day PADI open-water certification course RM750; 2-day advanced course RM550; 1-day discover scuba course RM150; 2 fun dives for certified divers RM140, with own equipment RM110). On the main beach next to Check Point and Coco Hut, respectively, **Sea Horse Dive Center** (☎010 983 4079) and **Bujang Senang Dive Center** (☎010 985 8171) are small shops with easy-going staffs. On the beach near Mama's Place are a branch of **Turtle Bay Divers** (☎010 280 8791) and **Watercolours Dive Center** (☎019 9811852). **Flora Bay Divers** (☎697 7266) is the best choice in Flora Bay.

EAST COAST

The fishing villages of Peninsular Malaysia's east coast offer a remarkable contrast to west-coast city life. In a decidedly laid-back atmosphere, visitors relax on endless stretches of white beaches, observe with awe the arrival of leatherback turtles on shore, and get to know traditional Malay life. The predominantly Malay communities adhere strongly to Muslim values; keep this in mind before stripping down to your skivvies on the beach.

KOTA BHARU ☎09

Among a handful of cities in Malaysia with a majority Malay population, Kota Bharu, the capital of Kelantan State, has recently seen a revival of traditional Muslim values in its laws—such as different check out-lines for men and women in supermarkets, gender-segregated seating at movies, and enforcement of *purdah* for women—most of which have failed to last. The daily performance of local cultural pastimes (top spinning, kite flying, *silat*, drum beating, dancing, and puppeteering) are certainly worth a some time.

> **WARNING.** This region is unstable and may not be safe to visit. Check with your embassy before planning a trip. This section was last updated in 2000.

TRANSPORTATION

Flights: Airport (☎737 000), 9km northeast of town. Take bus #4 (RM0.90) into town. **MAS** (☎744 7000), at traffic circle on Jl. Gajah Mati flies to **KL** (8 flights daily 7am-9:30pm, RM109; 11:10pm, RM78).

Trains: Station (☎719 6986), 7km west of town in **Wakaf Bharu.** Take a taxi (RM2.50) or local bus #19 from town. **Jungle trains** go to **Gemas** (13hr., 6am, RM28) via **Jerantut** (8½hr., RM17). Daily **express trains** go to **KL** (12hr., 6:40pm, 3rd-class RM28) and **Singapore** (12½hr., 8:20pm, 3rd-class RM32).

Buses: Local bus terminal (☎744 0114), on Jl. Padang Garong in town center. To **Kuala Terengganu** (3hr.; 7 per day 8:30am-7:30pm; one-way RM3.70, round-trip RM7.40). The **Express Bus Terminal/Langgar Station** (☎748 3807) is on Jl. Pasir Puteh outside town. To: **KL** (9-10hr.; 9am, 8pm, 9pm; RM22); **Kuantan** (5 per day 8:30am-5:30pm, RM1720); **Penang** (8hr., 9am 9:30pm; RM19.40); **Singapore** (12hr., 8am, RM45). Reserve at either bus station, regardless of destination, 1 day in advance. **Regional buses** also leave from or near the central station to the **Thai border crossing** at **Rantau Panjang** (opposite Sungai Kolok), catch local bus #29 (1hr., every 30min. 6:45am-6:30pm, RM2.70).

Taxis: Long distance taxi stand, next to the bus station in town center. Drivers depart when full (4 people) for: **Butterworth** (RM40); **KL** (RM45); **Kuala Besut** (RM6); **Kuala Terengganu** (RM16); **Kuantan** (RM35); **Rantau Panjang** (RM5); **Wakaf Bharu** (RM2.50). Chartered taxis cost 4 times as much as the prices listed.

Local Transportation: Trishaw rides within town average RM3-5.

Rentals: Avis Rent-A-Car (☎748 4457) operated from Perdana Hotel on Jl. Mahmud. From RM143 per day. Credit cards only.

ORIENTATION AND PRACTICAL INFORMATION

Kota Bharu lies along the east bank of the north-south **Kelantan River.** Running roughly parallel to the river are six major thoroughfares. **Jl. Post Office Lama** (called **Jl. Atas Banggol** on many maps) traces the river and runs into **Padang Merdeka (Independence Square)** in the northern part of the city. The next street east is **Jl. Sultanah Zainab,** with a traffic rotary at its south end. **Jl. Temenggong** parallels Jl. Sultanah Zainab before hitting a busy clock-tower rotary and becoming **Jl. Sultan Ibrahim. Jl. Doktor** and **Jl. Kebun Sultan/Jl. Mahmud** are next, the latter converging with Jl. Sultan Ibrahim. The primary east-west avenues are **Jl. Tok Hakim/Jl. Padang Garong/Jl. Pengkalan Chepa,** which runs through the city center and **Jl. Gajah Mati/Jl. Hospital,** which wraps around the clock tower.

Tourist Offices: Tourist Information Center (☎748 5534), on Jl. Sultan Ibrahim, near traffic the circle with the clock tower. Maps. Organizes tours and home stays. Open Su-Th 8am-4:45pm.

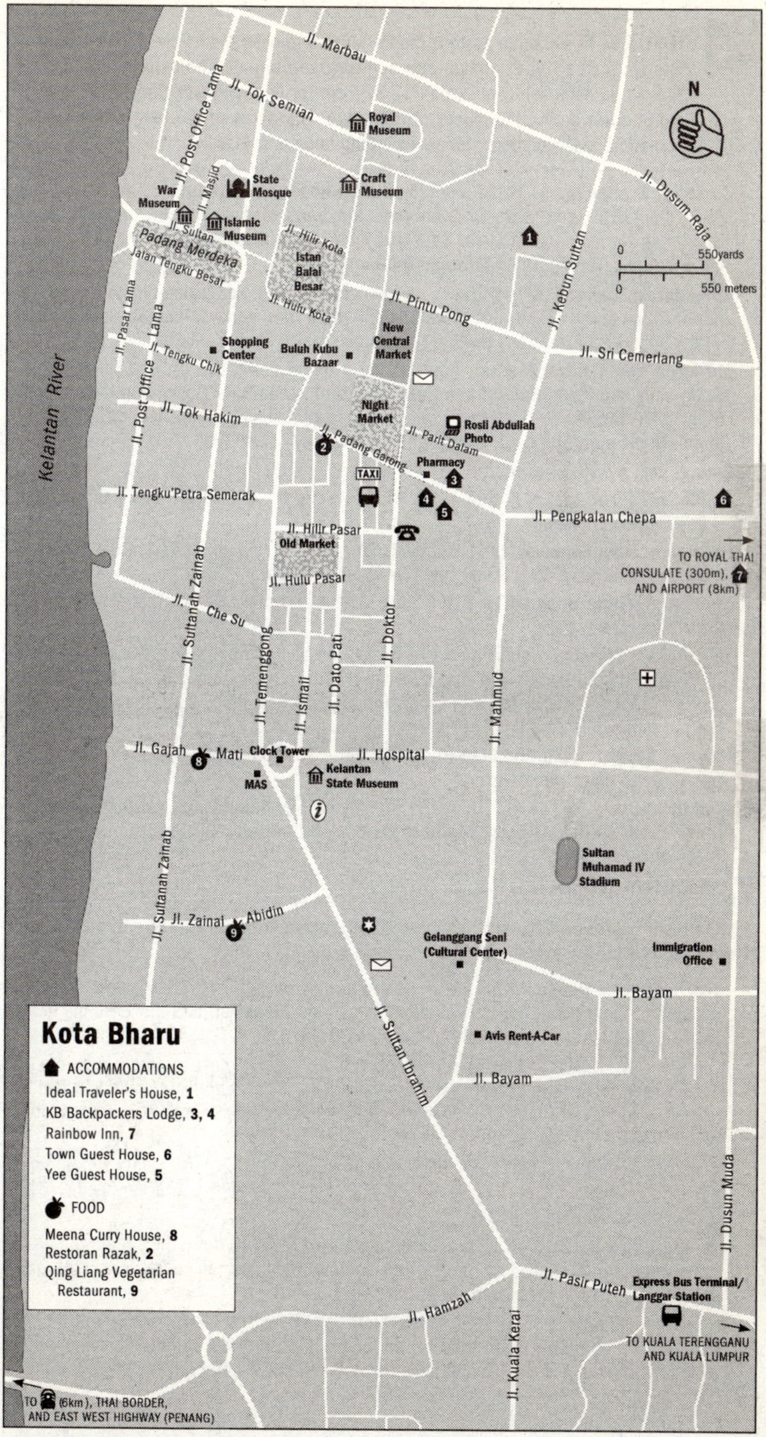
Kota Bharu
ACCOMMODATIONS
Ideal Traveler's House, 1
KB Backpackers Lodge, 3, 4
Rainbow Inn, 7
Town Guest House, 6
Yee Guest House, 5
FOOD
Meena Curry House, 8
Restoran Razak, 2
Qing Liang Vegetarian Restaurant, 9
N
Jl. Merbau
Jl. Tok Semian
Royal Museum
Jl. Post Office Lama
Jl. Masjid
State Mosque
Craft Museum
War Museum
Islamic Museum
Jl. Sultan
Padang Merdeka
Jalan Tengku Besar
Jl. Hilir Kota
Istan Balai Besar
Jl. Hulu Kota
Jl. Dusum Raja
Jl. Kebun Sultan
0 550yards
0 550 meters
Jl. Pintu Pong
New Central Market
Jl. Sri Cemerlang
Jl. Pasar Lama
Jl. Tengku Chik
Shopping Center
Buluh Kubu Bazaar
Kelantan River
Jl. Post Office Lama
Jl. Tok Hakim
Night Market
Rosli Abdullah Photo
Jl. Parit Dalam
Jl. Padang Garong
Pharmacy
TAXI
Jl. Tengku Petra Semerak
Jl. Pengkalan Chepa
Jl. Hilir Pasar
Old Market
TO ROYAL THAI CONSULATE (300m), AND AIRPORT (8km)
Jl. Hulu Pasar
Jl. Che Su
Jl. Sultanah Zainab
Jl. Temenggong
Jl. Ismail
Jl. Dato Pati
Jl. Doktor
Jl. Mahmud
Jl. Gajah Mati
Clock Tower
Jl. Hospital
MAS
Kelantan State Museum
Sultan Muhamad IV Stadium
Jl. Sultanah Zainab
Jl. Zainal Abidin
Gelanggang Seni (Cultural Center)
Immigration Office
Jl. Bayam
Avis Rent-A-Car
Jl. Sultan Ibrahim
Jl. Bayam
Jl. Dusun Muda
Jl. Pasir Puteh
Express Bus Terminal/ Langgar Station
Jl. Hamzah
Jl. Kuala Keral
TO KUALA TERENGGANU AND KUALA LUMPUR
TO (6km), THAI BORDER, AND EAST WEST HIGHWAY (PENANG)

MALAYSIA

HOURS. As Kelantan State is mostly Muslim, most establishments are closed Fridays instead of Sundays, and some close early on Thursday afternoons. Almost all establishments close 12:30-2pm for Friday Prayer. The whole town shuts down during the month of Ramadan. The dates of the fast, which falls sometime in December, change according to lunar cycles.

Currency Exchange: No banks open F. **Bank Simpanan National,** 61 Jl. Pintu Pong (☎744 9433). Open M-Th, Sa 9am-4pm. **Maybank Moneychanger,** opposite Bank Simpanan National. Open M-Th, Sa 11am-7pm. **Azam Moneychanger** (☎744 1786), on Jl. Padong Garong. Open M-Th, Sa 9:30am-9:30pm.

Consulates: Thailand (☎748 2545), on the right side of Jl. Pengkalan Chepa toward the airport. Take bus #4 (RM0.50) or walk 15min. from town center. Open Su-Th 9am-noon and 2-3pm. Visa extensions RM33 (1-day processing); bring 2 photos.

Markets: New Central Market, bounded by Jl. Pintu Pong, Doktor, and Tengku Chik. Open daily 8am-6pm. **Buluh Kubu Bazaar,** next to Istana Balai Besar, and the top floor of the **Old Market,** bounded by Jl. Dato Pati and Temenggong, have fabrics and handicrafts. **Night market,** near the bus station. Open daily 6am-3pm.

Emergency: ☎999. **Fire:** ☎994.

Police: ☎748 5522. On Jl. Sultan Ibrahim, between the post office and tourist office. Some English spoken.

Pharmacy: Kian Farmasi, 2981 B-C Jl. Padang Garong (☎744 1267), in the center of town opposite Hong Kong Bank. Open Sa-Th 9am-10pm.

Medical Service: Hospital (☎748 5533), at the end of Jl. Hospital. English spoken. **24hr. emergency care.**

Telephones: Telekom Malaysia (☎744 6609), on Jl. Doktor in the center of town near Jl. Padang Garong. Open M-W and 8:30am-4:30pm, Th 8:30am-1:15pm. **HCD calling cards** cannot be used at Telekom Office or public phones. Place calls at hotels or guest houses to reach international operators.

Internet Access: Rosli Abdullah Photo, 165 Jl. Parit Dalam (☎744-2770). RM1.50-3 per hr. Open daily 9am-noon.

Post Office: GPO (☎748 4073), on the left side of Jl. Sultan Ibrahim, south of the clocktower. Open Sa-Th 8am-5pm. **Postal code:** 15670 (for post office only).

ACCOMMODATIONS

Kotu Bharu has over 40 guest houses within walking distance of the town center. Most help book onward travel.

Ideal Traveler's House, 3954 F-G Jl. Kebun Sultan (☎/fax 744 2246), down a small road off Jl. Pintu Pong. Popular. All rooms have fan. Breakfast RM3-3.50. Dorms RM6; doubles RM12-25, with bath and balcony RM30-35.

Rainbow Inn, 423-A Jl. Pengkalan Chepa (☎743 4936), next to Thai consulate. A 15min. walk from town center, but very friendly, family-style lodging make you feel at home. All rooms with fans and shared bath. Internet access. Dorms RM6; singles/doubles RM10-20.

KB Backpackers Lodge, 2981-F Jl. Padang Garong (☎743 2125). Breakfast and Internet access included. Singles/doubles RM18-25. Its affiliate, KB Backpackers Lodge Two, across the street, has dorms with A/C for RM10.

Yee Guest House, 1872 A-B Jl. Padang Garong (☎744 1944), down the street from A&W opposite a small alley. Free drinks and cooking facilities. All rooms with fans and shared bath. Dorms RM6; singles/doubles RM12-14.

Town Guest House, 286 S/12 Jl. Pengkalan Chepa (☎981-1416), 500m on the left past the Jl. Kebun Sultan intersection and 1 block past Caltex station. Many services, including Internet access, included. Dorms RM7; doubles with bath RM25; rooms with A/C RM30.

FOOD

Local specialties include *ayam percik* (chicken grilled on sticks) and *nasi dagang* (coconut-based rice topped with tuna). Several Chinese joints line **Jl. Kebun Sultan,** near Ideal Traveler's House. **Jl. Gajah Mati,** the road heading toward the river from the clock-tower rotary, has a handful of Indian eateries.

Meena Curry House, 3377-G Jl. Gajah Mati, east of Jl. Sultanah Zainab. Some of the best fish-head curry in town. Ladles deposit rice and toppings onto clean banana leaves. Vegetarian curry RM3. Chicken curry RM4.5-6. Open daily 11am-9:30pm.

Qing Liang Vegetarian Restaurant, 3400-H Jl. Zainal Abidin, on a side street connecting Jl. Sultan Ibrahim and Jl. Sultanah Zainab. Good value for great food. 3 toppings plus rice RM4. Open daily 11am-9pm.

Restoran Razak, on the corner of Dato Pati and Jl. Pudang Garong. Blissful vegetables and *beriani ayam* (Indian chicken rice) RM4.50. Open daily 6am-8pm.

SIGHTS

Kota Bharu's sights are within walking distance of each other but require a good day or two to explore. The **Gelanggang Seni (Cultural Center),** on Jl. Mahmud opposite the Perdana Hotel, sponsors free top-spinning, kite-flying, drum-beating, and *silat* demonstrations (Sa, M, W 3:30-5:30pm). On the same days from 9-11pm, there are performances of *wayang kulit* (shadow-puppet shows), dance, and drama. Check with the tourist office for a schedule of these free events.

Padang Merdeka (Independence Square) commemorates the Malay struggle against British rule. At the east end of the rectangle away from the river is the **Istana Balai Besar,** a large wooden hall built in 1844. Closer to the river to the right of the square are the **War Museum, Islamic Museum, Royal Custom Museum, Royal Museum,** and **Craft Museum.** (All open M-Th and Sa 8:30am-4:45pm. RM2.) **Kelantan State Museum,** next to the tourist office on Jl. Sultan Ibrahim, is worth a gawk for its cultural exhibits.

The **Pantai Cahaya Bulan (PCB) Beach** makes a pleasant excursion with cheap accommodations (look for homes with signs that say *tempat penginapan, asrama,* or "budget accommodations"). Buses leaves from the Royal Museum for PCB (#10, every 20min, last returning bus 7:30pm, RM0.70).

If relaxing on the beach wasn't enough, take a **river cruise** through the surrounding jungle. Roselan "Fabulous" Hanafiah, an award-winning guide, leads a half-day tour for 3-10 people through the canals and rivers of Kelantan. Check the tourist office to find Roselan. (roselan71@hotmail.com. Runs 10am-1pm; RM75 per person with lunch.) Travelers on a smaller budget can cruise on a public boat and return by bus. Boats depart from **Kuala Krai,** accessible by bus from the central terminal.

Roselan can also help make reservations to stay with a family in the village, through a program called **The Kampung Experience.** Visitors choose the families with whom they stay (kite and *batik* makers, fishermen, potters, etc.). (Meals and transportation included. 3-day packages RM225 per person. 1-day workshops RM75. Or, for a taste of Malaysia, try Roselan's authentic Malay cooking class (RM55) taught in the comfort of his home.

KUALA TERENGGANU ☎09

Capital of the conservative Muslim state of Terengganu, Kuala Terengganu lies beside the inlet of the Terengganu River. Until recently a large fishing village, KT, as it's commonly called, now thrives on oil and seems upstaged by the sunny beach destinations nearby. Though attractions and nightlife here are minimal, KT isn't just a gateway city to nearby Marang and Merang; its Malay-dominated population and low-key seaside warrant exploration.

TRANSPORTATION

Flights: Airport (☎666 4204), 18km from town. **MAS,** 13 Jl. Sultan Omar (☎622 2266), flies to **KL** (4 per day, RM109). Open M-W and Sa-Su 8:30am-4:30pm, Th 8:30am-12:30pm. AmEx/MC/V. **Taxi** from the airport RM18.

Ferries: Pulau Duyong (Duyong Island), off the west coast, is accessible by ferry or bridge from the west shores.

Buses: Local buses leave from the **large bus station** (☎623 6239) at the intersection of Jl. Masjid Abidin and Jl. Syed Hussain. To: **Dungun** (every 30min. 7:30am-6pm, RM4); **Duyong** (#16 or 20, every hr. 7:40am-5:40pm, RM0.60); **Marang** (every 30min. 7:30am-6pm, RM1.50); **Rantau Abang** (every 30min. 7:30am-6pm, RM3). **Express buses** stop at the large bus station and at the **express bus station** (☎622 5335) on Jl. Sultan Zainal Abidin near the Jl. Tok Lam intersection. To: **Kota Bharu** (3hr., 6-7 per day 8:30am-7:30pm, RM7.50); **KL** (8hr.; 4-5 per day 9:30am-10pm; RM25.10, with A/C RM34.70); **Kuantan** (3½hr., 6-7 per day 8:30am-7:30pm, RM11.60); **Mersing** (6hr., 12:30 and 10pm, RM16.10); **Singapore** (9-10hr.; 9am and 8:30pm; RM30.20, with A/C RM39).

Taxis: From the **taxi stand** (☎626 5150) on Jl. Masjid Abidin, near the large bus station, taxis go to: **Kota Bharu** (RM56, A/C RM70); **Kuala Besut** (RM40, A/C RM60); **Kuantan** (RM70, A/C RM90); **Marang** (RM15, A/C RM20); **Mersing** (RM150, A/C RM160). Passengers can split fares 4 ways. No bargaining.

Local Transportation: Trishaw rides cost RM3-5. **Taxis** run RM5-10 in town.

ORIENTATION AND PRACTICAL INFORMATION

Jl. Sultan Zainal Abidin runs east-west along the city's shore, along which sit the **post office, Tourist Information Center,** and **express bus terminal.** Further south along the shoreline is **Chinatown.** Major sights, including **Bukit Putein (Princess Hill), Maziah Palace,** and the **Central Market,** also line the shore. The city's commercial spine, **Jl. Sultan Ismail,** runs parallel to Jl. Sultan Zainal Abidin. Its west edge begins with Hotel Terengganu, while the **police station** and **immigration office** flank its east edge. These two streets sandwich **Jl. Dato' Isaacs.** From the city's center north to its shores, **Jl. Tok Lam** connects all three boulevards. Parallel and to the west is **Jl. Masjid Abidin;** walking from Jl. Sultan Ismail will lead to the **taxi stand** and **local bus station.** Accommodations flank the north and east sides of the mosque in the center of the city.

Tourist Office: Tourist Information Center (☎622 1553), on Jl. Sultan Zainal Abidin. Free maps. Open M-W and Sa-Su 8am-5pm, Th 8am-12:45pm.

Immigration Offices: (☎622 1424), on the 1st fl. of Wisma Persekutuan Bldg., at the intersection of Jl. Pejabat and Jl. Sultan Ismail. Same-day visa extensions RM50 per month. Open M-W and Su 8am-12:45pm and 2-4pm, Th 8am-1pm.

Currency Exchange: Bank Bumiputra (☎622 2611), on Jl. Sultan Ismail. AmEx/MC/V/traveler's checks. Currency exchange upstairs next to **ATM.** Open Sa-W 9:30am-4pm, Th 9:30am-12pm. All banks closed every other Sa.

Police: ☎622 2222. On the corner of Jl. Sultan Omar and Jl. Sultan Ismail.

Pharmacy: Dew Ma, 10-D Jl. Tok Lam (☎622 0200), near the northern tip, with a large English sign. Open M-W and Sa 9am-10pm, Th 9am-6pm.

Medical Service: Kuala Terengganu General Hospital (☎623 3333), on Jl. Sultan Mahmud, south of the rotary. English-speaking doctors. **24hr. emergency care.**

Telephones: Telekom Malaysia (☎622 1554), on the corner of Jl. Sultan Ismail and Jl. Banggol. Free access to international operators. Direct international calls. Open M-Th and Su 8:30am-4:30pm. IDD calls can also be made from the Telekom booth on Jl. Tok Lam near Dew Ma pharmacy using phone cards.

Internet Access: Golden Wood Internet Cafe, 59 Jl. Tok Lam (☎624 6171), near Jl. Dato Isaac. RM3 per hr. Open Sa-Th 10am-12:30am. **Creative Computer Communication,** No. 1-I Jalen Syed Hussin (☎956 7211), opposite bus station. RM2.50 per hr. Open daily 9am-7pm.

Post Office: (☎622 8555). On Jl. Sultan Zainal Abidin. Facing the river, it's 100m left of Jl. Masjid Abidin. *Poste Restante*. Open Su-Th 8am-5pm. **Postal code:** 20000.

ACCOMMODATIONS

Ping Anchorage Traveler's Homestay, 77A Jl. Dato' Isaacs (☎622 0851), near the Jl. Tok Lam intersection. From the mosque, it's on the left. Accepts backpackers only. Travel service available. Bright dorms RM6; singles/doubles with common bath RM12-18, with A/C and private bath RM30.

Seaview Hotel (☎622 1911), across from the palace. Clean, roomy singles with bath RM40; doubles RM50.

Awi's House. The only accommodation along the shores of Pulau Duyong. Accessible by infrequent boats from the jetty opposite the tourist office. Basic wooden rooms on stilts over the water. Surrounded by wildlife; peaceful and homey. Cooking facilities and refrigerator. River plumbing but clean tap water drawn from KT. Dorms RM5; private doubles with common or private bath RM15.

Check Point Homestay (☎626 1400), Lot 3, 2nd fl. Jalan Pejabat, near the stadium off Jl. Sultan Ismail. Dorms RM10.

FOOD

Many cheap **food stalls** crowd the first floor of the bus station on Jl. Syed Hussain, and Chinese food spots line the shores of **Pantai Batu Buruk** on the east coast. Try *keropok*, a Terengannu specialty of fried ground fish with chili sauce. The food court above the **central market** offers a great selection of fruits and Malay dishes.

M.D. Curry House, 19-C Jl. Tok Lam, opposite Dew Ma pharmacy. A popular banana-leaf restaurant. All meals come with rice, veggies, and *papadam* (an Indian lentil wafer). Chicken curry RM4.80. Vegetarian curry RM3.80. Open daily 7:30am-10pm.

City Cake House, 59G Jl. Tok Lam. Large selection of breads, mini pizzas, and pastries. Delicious banana bread RM6.

Golden Dragon, Jl. Bandar, in Chinatown near the Dragon Gate. Chinese buffet with vegetarian selections RM2-3. Open daily 11am-3pm and 6:30-9:30pm.

SIGHTS AND ENTERTAINMENT

Kuala Terengganu's main tourist attractions cluster near the Tourist Information Center. The **central market,** on Jl. Sultan Zaimal Abidin, sells handicrafts and produce. Nearby, next to the GPO, are **Istana Maziah,** the Sultan's stately palace, and **Bukit Puteri,** the "hill of the princess." Climb the stairs next to the Tourist Information Center for great views over the waterfront and the remains of a fort and a lighthouse. (Open Sa-Th 9am-5pm. RM1.)

Outside town, the **Muzium Negeri,** Malaysia's largest museum, features a set of Terengganu-style buildings on stilts. The main museum showcases the *batu bersurat*, an inscribed stone dated 702 which proclaims Islam as Terengganu's religion. The complex also includes botanical gardens, traditional houses, and a zoo. Bus #10 (RM0.60) runs between the local bus terminal and the museum. (☎622 1444. Open Sa-Th 9am-5pm. RM5.)

Off the mainland, **Pulau Duyong's** locals still construct boats of all sizes with traditional techniques—without plans or diagrams. Boats to Pulau Duyong depart from behind the **Seri Malaysia Hotel** at the southern tip of Jl. Bandar and from the jetty opposite the tourist office on Jl. Sultan Zainal Abidin (15min., 5am-6pm, RM0.60). On the road south to Marang, 4½km from KT (take local bus #13), sits

Masjid Tengku Zaharah (Floating Mosque), a striking white building that seems to float on the water. (Open 24hr., but only Muslims can enter the mosque. Free.)

MARANG ☎09

Government bulldozers have ended Marang's (not to be confused with Merang) peaceful days as a picturesque Malay fishing village. Construction projects have devastated half the town. Breakwaters line the beach, and good food and budget accommodations are scarce. The park near the main jetty is a pleasant place to have lunch and watch the boats pass, but for most, Marang is a transit town en route to the deserted beaches of Kapas Island.

TRANSPORTATION AND PRACTICAL INFORMATION. Marang is 20km south of Kuala Terengganu. From KT, get to Marang via Dungun **buses** (30min., every 30min. 7:30am-6pm, RM1.50) or **share-taxi** from the Terengganu-Kuantan Hwy. The **bus stop** is on the highway. Most people get dropped off at the four-way intersection next to the squid-and-prawn statue. The main part of town is on **Kampung Paya,** the street parallel to and east of the highway, running close to the river and beaches. In the opposite direction, Kampung Paya passes shop houses and two footbridges before reaching the budget accommodations. The footbridges cross the river to a sandy stretch lined with palm trees and homes on stilts. Opposite the post office (☎618 2215; open Su-Th 8:30am-5pm) is the **Klinik Kesinatan Clinic** (☎618 2216; open Su-W 8am-1pm and 2-4:15pm). Ask for English-speaking Dr. Mohd. Reze bin Rashid. The **police station** (☎618 2222) is on the highway before the bridge. A **laundromat** is on the road leading to the shore from the four-way intersection (RM2 per kg). **Postal code:** 21600.

ACCOMMODATIONS AND FOOD. Green Mango Inn, A-71 Bandar Marang, up a small hill opposite the largest tourist-boat jetty, offers homey rooms in a wooden house. (☎618 2040. Singles RM15; doubles RM20.) **Kamal Guest House,** B283 Kg. Paya, between the two footbridges north of the jetty and market area, has friendly staff and cheap, clean rooms. (☎03 618 2181. Singles/doubles RM13, with bath RM18.) **Marang Guest House and Restaurant,** Lot 1367 and 1368 Kampung Paya, up the hill next to Kamal Guest House, has rooms in a garden setting and offers laundry service (RM5), massages (RM30), Internet (RM3/hr) and travel information. (☎/fax 618 1976. Doubles with baths RM20-25, with A/C and bath RM50.)

Devour the cheapest and best meals at the **food stalls** opposite the market near the tourist boat agencies and at the Sunday night market. Choose from Malay-style fish or *murtabak*, fried dough with assorted fillings.

SIGHTS. Although fewer travelers have visited beautiful **Kapas Island** since Marang's storm of development, many still spend time here walking through the jungle or snorkeling. **Tourist boats** to the island cost RM16-26 round-trip, including RM1 insurance. Buy tickets from agents along the shore or guest houses. Boats leave from 9am to 3pm and return from 10am to 4pm, though schedules change with the tides. **Bukit Api Beach** and **Pasir Cina Beach** are the best on the island, and the north coast is best for **snorkeling.** Rent snorkel gear from almost anywhere for RM15. Friendly Zakaria at the **Marang Tourist Jetty** (☎010 983 9454) can help to arrange **diving** courses, sea sport rentals, and room reservations. **Mak Cik Gemuk Resort** (☎09 624 5120) offers three-day, two-night packages including accommodation, boat transfers, and meals for RM100-RM167; nightly rates for doubles with mosquito nets and common bath are RM25. Two campsites on the island rent tents (campsite use RM5, with tent rental RM15).

CHERATING ☎09

On Rte. 3 lies Cherating, the town Malaysia forgot. Cherating's more attractive aspects include a windsurfing beach, an occasional leatherback turtle, beachfront fun, cultural diversions, and a few bars. Less titillating are the omnipresent tourists.

TRANSPORTATION. Cherating is 50km north of Kuantan, accessible by local bus (40min., RM3). From **Kuala Terengganu,** take a bus from the **main bus station** (RM11.50). The beach road meets the highway at the two bus stops on the way. The west stop, closer to **Juantan,** is near the Cherating River and marked by a "Culture Center" billboard. This stop is closer to Masnah and Mataheri Chalets. The east stop is marked by a "Residence Inn" billboard; get off here for the Moon Guest House.

ORIENTATION AND PRACTICAL INFORMATION. The town has two main roads: the **Kuantan-Terengganu Hwy.,** which bends east-west through town, and the Y-shaped **beach road** that runs along the river and the sea. On the highway between the bus stops is the **police office** (☎581 9322). There are **no medical services** available in Cherating. Call hospitals in **Kemaman** (☎859 3333) or **Juantan** (☎513 3333) for **24hr. emergency care;** both have English-speaking doctors. The closest **clinic** is in **Kampung Balok,** 10km south of Cherating. The beach road is lined with restaurants, accommodations and bars. Towards the center of the road is **Travel Post,** which provides tours, **Internet** (RM8 per hr.), laundry (RM4 per kg), **mail service,** international phone service (RM7 per min.), and **currency exchange. Badgerlines,** further down the road, provides similar services. (Open daily 9:30am-12:30pm, 2:30-4pm, 8-10pm.)

ACCOMMODATIONS. A variety of guest houses pack the beach road, offering standard A-frame or small chalet-style huts. **Matahari Chalet,** 100m down the road from the west bus stop, maintains solid, well-kept huts. Friendly management and a range of amenities, including an attached do-it-yourself *batik* studio, make Matahari one of the best abodes in the village. (☎581 9835. Twin chalets RM15; doubles with fridge RM20.) **Maznah Guest House,** also near the west bus stop, has a cozy common area with TV and movies. (Breakfast and kitchen facilities included. Internet RM4 per hr. for guests, RM5 for non-guests. Dorms RM12; twin chalets with fans and common bath RM15; family rooms RM50.) **The Shadow of Moon at Half Past 4,** on the hillside 100m down the beach road from the east bus stop, offers a haunting atmosphere and superb bungalows, accentuated by knobby handmade furniture, glowing red lanterns, and monkeys in the trees. (☎581 9186. Double chalets with bath RM35.) **Ranting Resort** (☎581 9068), in the center of the beach road across from Rhana Pippins (see **Sights and Entertainment,** below), provides clean, well-built bungalows with bath for RM45, with A/C RM60.

FOOD. Can't Forget Seafood, on the beach road, serves superb Chinese fare. Try the sweet-and-sour chicken or squid for RM6. (Open daily 11am-10pm.) **Payong Cafe,** run by a kind Swiss woman, makes huge pans of pizza for RM8.50-12. (Open daily 10:30am-2:30pm and 7-10:30pm.) The **Ranting Resort** has a pleasant veranda cafe which has great breakfast options. Homemade bread runs RM3.50. For romantic dining in private gazebos, try the Indian clay pot dishes (RM5) at the **Cherating Ria Garden** on the beach road near Badgerlines.

SIGHTS AND ENTERTAINMENT. At surfside in front of Rhana Pippins, **Kelaut Sports** rents watersports equipment. (Kayaks RM15 per hr., RM60 per day. Windsurfing RM25 per hr., RM30 with instructor. Surfboards RM15 per hr., RM50 per day.) Surfing is best from January to March, but windsurfing is great anytime.

If you're in Cherating between June and September, don't miss the opportunity to see the **giant leatherback turtles** lay their eggs. The Fisheries Department has set up a hatchery near the Club Med Beach. Upon request, most accommodations will wake you if there is a sighting and take you to the beach (RM15). Leatherback sightings are rare due to declining numbers.

Two kilometers east of Cherating is breathtaking **Club Med Beach.** You may have to do some detective work to find an incognito approach to the beach (Club Med officials may not let you in). Alternatively, ask guest house managers about trails through the hills that will take you from the village beach to the promised shore.

The best nightspots are Pop Inn Pub (live cover band F and Sa) and Rhana Pippins (2-for-1 drink specials until midnight). Both are on the same side of beach road..

KUANTAN ☎09

Kuantan offers little in the way of cultural attractions or remarkable cuisine, but for those coming from the east coast, the capital of the state of Pahang will seem either rejuvenating or overwhelmingly modern and cosmopolitan. Surrounded by waterfalls, caves, and beaches, the town itself is home to the beautiful State Mosque, and the beaches of Teluk Chempedak are only 4km away.

TRANSPORTATION

Flights: Airport (☎538 1291), 16km west of town. Take a bus from the local terminal (every hr. 7am-5pm) or a taxi (RM15-20). **MAS** (☎515 7055, weekends and holidays ☎03 746 3000), on the ground floor of Wisma Bolasepak Bldg. on Jl. Gambut, has flights to **KL** (45min., 4 per day 6:20am-9:30pm, RM79) and **Singapore** (1hr., F 11:45am and Su 1:20pm, RM244). Open M-F 8:30am-5:30pm. AmEx/DC/MC/V.

Buses: The **express bus terminal** is on Jl. Stadium. To: **Butterworth** (10hr., 9am-9pm, RM32); **Jerantut** (3½hr., 4 per day 8am-5pm, RM10.50); **Johor Bahru** (6hr., 6 per day 8:30am-1:30am, RM20); **Kota Bharu** (7hr., 7 per day 8am-midnight, RM19); **KL** (5hr., 17 per day 8am-1am, RM14.20); **Kuala Terengganu** (3½hr., 8 per day, RM11.50); **Melaka** (5hr., 9am and 2:30pm, RM16); **Mersing** (3hr, 9am and 5pm, RM10.60); **Singapore** (7hr., 8 per day 9am-11pm, RM19.40). **Luggage storage** on 2nd fl. (RM1 per day; open daily 7am-12:30am). The **local bus terminal** on Jl. Besar, 1 block south of Jl. Mahkota, runs buses to **Cherating** and **Kemaman** (every hr., RM3 and RM3.70). Buses to the **airport** leave from both terminals (every hr. 7am-5pm). **City buses** ply the streets at RM0.60-0.80.

Taxis: Taxis leave from the express bus terminal or **city taxi stand** on Jl. Mahkota, close to the pedestrian overpass. Taxis go anywhere in town for RM4. **Shared taxis** also leave from the stand. Fare per car (4-people max.) to: **Jerantut** (RM100); **Johor Bahru** (RM180); **Kota Bharu** (RM180); **KL** (RM120); **Mersing** (RM120).

Rentals: Orix Rent-A-Car (☎515 7488), at Hotel Grand Continental on Jl. Gambut. From RM148 per day. Open M-F 9am-5pm, Sa 9am-1pm.

ORIENTATION AND PRACTICAL INFORMATION

Kuantan lies at the crossroads of **Rte. 2 and 3,** some 260km from KL. The city sprawls in an ambitious flurry of high-rises, but the main points of interest to the visitor are the southwest parts of town (the commercial district) along the **Kuantan River.** The two main streets, **Jl. Besar** and **Jl. Mahkota,** run parallel along the river. The town's central landmark is the large blue and white mosque, **Masjid Negeri. Jl. Bukit Ubi.** Nearby are many guest houses and restaurants.

Tourist Office: (☎516 1007). On Jl. Mahkota, near the taxi station opposite Kompleks Terantum. Free maps, tips, and tour info offered by a friendly staff. Open daily 9am-1pm and 2-5pm.

Immigration Offices: (☎514 373). On Wisma Persekutuan. Same-day visa extensions RM100 per month. Open M-F 8am-12:45pm and 2-3:45pm.

Currency Exchange: HSBC, Jl. Mahkota (☎552 4666). Open M-F 9:30am-3:30pm, Sa 9:30-11:30am. **Maybank ATMs,** opposite the bus station on Jl. Tun Ismail and on Jl. Makhota, a block past the mosque on the left. Cirrus/MC/V. **Hamid Bros.,** 23 Jl. Mahkota (☎521 119), opposite the mosque. Open daily 9am-7pm.

Markets: The Sunday **day market** is off Jl. Mahkota opposite the post office. The Saturday **night market** is on Jl. Gambut.

MISS MANNERS' BANANA LEAF ETIQUETTE Those who find cutlery restrictive will enjoy banana leaf dining, common throughout Malaysia and Southeast Asia. Eating with your hands, however, doesn't mean you get to throw your manners out with the fork and knife–it's just a different set of rules.

1. Use only your right hand. The left hand is traditionally used for cleaning one's nether regions. Ever wonder why toilet paper is sometimes hard to find in Malaysia?
2. Mash toppings into your rice so that you get a little bit of everything in each bite.
3. If necessary, use your *papadam* (a crispy, round salty cracker) as a rice shovel. Too much reliance on this will bring trouble when you run out of *papadam*.
4. If you eat something with bones, just spit 'em out.
5. Burping is acceptable only by the older generation.
6. When you're through, fold your banana leaf in half.
7. *Bon apetit!*

Emergency: ☎999.

Police: ☎513 2222, on Jl. Mahkota.

Medical Service: Hospital Besar Kuantan (☎513 3333), on Jl. Tanah Putih, opposite Kompleks Terantun. Head southwest on Jl. Besar, away from Teluk Chempedak; the road becomes Jl. Tanah Putih. English-speaking doctors available. **Open 24hr.**

Telephones: Telekom Office (☎513 9292), next to the post office. Sells phone cards. Open M-F 8:45am-4:15pm, Sa 8:30am-12:30pm. **Cyberpoint** on Jl. Besar, 3rd fl. RM2.50 per hr. Open 9am-9pm.

Internet Access: Blue Lane Computer (☎513 6424), on the ground fl. of Kompleks Makmur next to the express bus terminal. RM2 per hr. Open 10am-10pm.

Post Office: Pejabat Pos Besar (☎552 1032), on Jl. Mahkota at Jl. Merdeka intersection. Turn left coming from Jl. Bukit Ubi. *Poste Restante,* at side of building, open Sa-Th 8:30am-5pm. Post office open M-Sa 8am-4:30pm. **Postal code:** 25670.

ACCOMMODATIONS

New Capital Hotel, 55-59 Jl. Bukit Ubi (☎524 222), 350m from the corner of Jl. Makhota. Friendly owner. Incoming international calls free of charge. Worth the extra ringgit. Clean, spacious rooms RM16, with bath RM17.90.

Hotel Kristal, 2/F, 59-61A Jl. Mahkota (☎552 6577). Next to Standard Chartered Bank near the mosque. Spartan but soothing, with warm proprietors. For the A/C-lovers. Doubles RM30, with TV and bath RM35; triples with shower and TV but no toilet RM45.

Kuantan Planet Hotel, 77 Jl. Bukit Ubi, 2nd and 3rd fl. (☎513 9852). On the last side street on the left before the Jl. Tun Ismail intersection. Barebones accommodations, all with common bath. Closets with bed RM12; double/triples RM16, with A/C RM25.

FOOD

Food stalls on **Jl. Mahkota** near the State Mosque behind Ocean Shopping Center on Jl. Tun Ismail are great for cheap, convenient meals. For scenic late-night eats, head to the river behind the local bus terminal. Try the steamed shredded coconut with *gula melaka* placed inside a short bamboo cylinder (RM0.50). For breakfast, sample the classic *nasi lemak* (rice cooked in coconut milk served with peanuts, dried anchovies, sliced cucumber, and chili sauce) from one of the bakeries along Jl. Bukit Ubi and Jl. Mahkota.

Restoran Chan Poh, 52 Jl. Bukit Ubi, opposite the Snooker Bistro and a few stores down. A great place for late-night *dim sum*. Shrimp dumplings RM1.80. Fried *mie* RM3. Open daily 6pm-midnight.

Mikee Bakery and Cakeshop, on Jl. Mahkota past the mosque opposite Maybank. Feast on *nasi lemak* and assorted pastries. Open daily 8am-10pm.

Restoren Parvathy, 75 Jl. Bukit Ubi. Heading away from Jl. Mahkota, it's 7 stores past the Snooker Bistro on the left. Veggie dishes and the old standbys: *dosa, roti, chapati,* and a host of curry selections RM2.50-4. Open daily 7am-10pm.

SIGHTS

The only noteworthy attraction is the **Masjid Negeri** (State Mosque), whose enormous blue domes are the most colorful on the peninsula. Visitors are allowed inside if they are dressed appropriately (long pants or skirt, no bare shoulders) and do not walk on the elevated areas. Admission is free, but you must ask to enter at the front desk. Early morning and late afternoon are the best times to visit.

The most popular attraction around Kuantan is **Teluk Chempedak,** 4km from town on the east-coast shore. Teluk Chempedak's sandy 2km beach is bound by rocky headlands. At the north end, a promenade passes restaurants, souvenir shops, and cheap food stalls. Expect crowds on public holidays. Walk over the bridge to do the **Denai Tebling Pelindung** (cliff walk), which leads to a secluded beach inhabited by monkeys. Although the only budget accommodation recently closed, the **Kuantan Hotel** (opposite the Hyatt) offers rooms for RM44. Get to Teluk Chempedak by taking bus #39 from the bus stop by Masjid Negeri on Jl. Mahkota (7am-10pm, RM1).

DAYTRIPS FROM KUANTAN

For even more scenic, relaxing activities, check out several worthwhile daytrips from Kuantan. **Sungai Pandan Waterfall** is a 50m cascade with eight tiers and a large pool at the bottom. Take a bus (every 2hr., RM3) from the local bus station to **Felda Panching** (30km), from which it's a 3½km hike to the falls. Nearby is **Paching Cave,** a four-million-year-old limestone cavern enclosing a statue of the "Natural Buddha" carved by water drops (RM1). Take bus #48 (toward Sungai Lembing) from the local bus station to Panching (RM3). From town, it's a 4km hike. **Tasik Chini,** Malaysia's second-largest lake, is well worth a sidetrip of one or two days. The lake and its environs are a natural playground where you can fish, jog, trek, take a boat ride through seven interconnected lakes, or absorb the serene landscape. To get there, take a taxi (RM50) or a bus to Chini Town (RM5.20), which will bring you 12km from the lake. From here you can walk, take an unlicensed taxi at exorbitant rates (RM30), or try to catch a ride with locals; *Let's Go* does not recommend hitchhiking. "Uncle" Rajan Jones runs a home stay in an Orang Asli village (RM18). There is no phone but locals should be able to direct you or give you a lift.

MERSING ☎07

The bustling town of Mersing is cluttered with signs of tourists in transit—backpackers roam the sidewalks in search of food stalls, moneychangers, and short-term distractions. For visitors who want to rest before taking the ferry to Tioman, Mersing is ideal to take advantage of services designed for tourist comfort.

TRANSPORTATION

Buses: Express Bus Terminal in **Plaza R&R** next to the jetty. To: **KL** (5½hr.; 11:30am, noon, 10pm; RM16.60); **Kuala Terengganu** (6-7hr., noon, RM18.80); **Kuantan** (3hr., 1pm, RM10.40); **Penang** (9hr., 5pm, RM26); **Singapore** via **Johor Baru** (3hr.,12:30pm, RM11).

Ferries: Buy ferry tickets in **Plaza R&R.** To **Pulau Tioman** (1½-2hr.; 5 per day 7:30am-4:30pm; RM25, children RM15-20; speedboat 1hr., RM30). Don't buy round-trip tickets–they may not be honored on the return journey.

Taxis: ☎ 799 1393. On Jl. Sulaiman. From the roundabout, walk down Jl. Abu Bakar, turn left at 1st intersection and right at end of the road. Open daily 7:30am-6pm.

ORIENTATION AND PRACTICAL INFORMATION

Next to the jetty is the blue-and-white tiled **Plaza R&R,** housing a **tourist center** and **express bus terminal.** To the left of the plaza, travel agencies and restaurants line the street. Jl. Abu Bakar runs in front of the jetty and through the main part of town. Many **guest houses** and the **post office** lie along Jl. Abu Bakar within a 5min. walk of the jetty.

Tourist Offices: Mersing Tourist Information Center (☎ 799 5212), on Jl. Abu Bakar. Friendly and knowledgeable staff. Open M-Th 2-4:30pm, F 2:45-4:30pm. **Sun and Sand Holiday** (☎ 799 4995), in Embassy Hotel.

Tours: Omar's Backpacker's Hostel offers 1-day tours to nearby islands (RM60; includes guide, transport, lunch, and snorkeling gear; 4-12 people) and day-trips to Mersing (RM60; includes transport, lunch, and drink; 2-6 people).

Currency Exchange: Bank Bumiputra Malaysia Berhad, 4-5 Jl. Ismail (☎ 799 1600), next to Embassy Hotel. Cashes traveler's checks RM2.15. MC/V cash advances RM4. Open M-F 9am-4:30pm, Sa 9:30am-noon. **MBF,** on Jl. Abu Bakar, 50m past 1st rotary on left. **ATM** (Cirrus/MC). Open daily 7am-midnight. **Moneychangers** line Jl. Abu Bakar. Generally open daily 9am-6pm.

Emergency: ☎ 999.

Police: ☎ 799 2222. From jetty, walk down Jl. Abu Bakar and turn left on Jl. Sultan.

Pharmacies/Medical Services: Hospital Daerah (☎ 799 3333), at end of Jl. Ismail. English spoken. **24hr.** emergency care. Open daily 8am-4:15pm.

Telephones: Card phones everywhere, especially around jetty and inside Plaza R&R. Many shops along Jl. Abu Bakar sell phonecards.

Internet: Mersing IT Center, 30 Jl. Aku Bakar (☎ 799 6072), to the right of the jetty. RM5 per hr. Open daily 9am-6pm.

Post Office: ☎ 799 1031. On Jl. Abu Bakar. Open M-Sa 8:30am-5pm.

ACCOMMODATIONS

Comfort Guest House, 60-2 Jl. Abu Bakar (☎ 012 762 4983), near rotary on Jl. Dato Muhammed Ali. Fans and lockers with locks. Breakfast included. Large dorm rooms with Japanese-style private partitions RM10.

Backpacker's Guest House, 66-3 Jl. Abu Bakar (☎ 019 371 1792). Clean 2-bed dorms. Breakfast included. RM10 per person.

Embassy Hotel, 2 Jl. Ismail (☎ 799 3545), near rotary by Bank Bumiputra. Firm mattresses. Doubles with shared bath RM16, with private bath RM28, with A/C RM40; triples with private bath RM30, with A/C RM45, with TV RM55.

Omar's Backpacker's Hostel, 1D1 Jl. Abu Bakar (☎ 799 5096), opposite the post office. 5min. from the jetty. Shared bath. Dorms RM8; doubles RM20.

FOOD

Food stalls at **Plaza R&R** sell cheap Malay food. (Open daily 5am-10pm.) For late night hunger pangs, stalls stay open late on the **Jl. Muhammed Ali.** Open-air seafood restaurants abound on **Jl. Abu Bakar,** while the **market** opposite the taxi and bus station on Jl. Sulaiman specializes in fruit. **Restoran Sea View,** at the roundabout where Jl. Abu Bakar and Jl. Dato Muhammed Ali meet, serves good seafood and chicken rice specialties. (Most dishes RM4. Open daily 8am-9pm.) For breakfast, **Restoran**

Al-Arif, 44 Jl. Ismail, opposite Parkson Supermarket, has good coffee and excellent *roti telur* (RM1). **Rio del Mar,** 53 Jl. Abu Bakar, makes pizzas (RM6.50-20), chicken wings (RM4-7.50), and sandwiches. (Open Tu-Su 10am-1am.)

PULAU TIOMAN

The locals say that, with a little bit of imagination, Pulau Tioman looks like a fuzzy green dragon when viewed from overhead. According to legend, a magical dragon princess inhabits the island to maintain its peaceful beauty. The princess is certainly doing her job, given the island's superb beaches and clear waters that are transparent to depths of over 20m. Though the ugly jetties and the sometimes mobbed beaches may not be everyone's image of paradise, pockets of seclusion are never too far for the determined traveler.

THE VIEW FROM ABOVE

The lowdown: One of the most spectacular islands off the Malaysia's east coast.
Towns: Kamung Air Batang (ABC), Kampung Juara, Kampung Saland, Kampung Tetek.
Highlights: Unspoiled beaches, crowded beaches, big beaches, small beaches... you get the idea. Snorkelling, daytrips to Coral Island, diving, and jungle trekking.

GETTING AROUND PULAU TIOMAN

The **airport** is in Kampung Tekek. **Berjaya Air** (☎419 1309) has daily flights to **KL** (1hr.; 11:30am, 1:50pm; RM141, children RM71) and **Singapore** (40min., 11am, RM280). Make reservations one day in advance (AmEx/MC/V).

Most travelers catch a **boat** from **Mersing** to get to Pularu Tioman. Buy tickets at a travel agency for a **ferry** (4hr.; 11am, 4:30pm; RM25, children RM15) or a **speedboat** (2hr., RM30). Ferries to Mersing leave from: **Kampung Air Batang** (7am); **Kampung Salang** (6:30am); **Kampung Tekek** (daily 7-8:30am). Speedboats to Mersing also leave from all three piers (10am-noon). Ferries leave for **Singapore** from the **Berjaya Resort.** (4-4½hr.; 2:30pm; RM199.50, cash only). Schedules vary with the tides; check with ticket sellers and locals. Don't buy-round trip tickets as they may not be honored on the return journey.

An expensive local **sea taxi,** booked at any hostel, travels between beaches (RM15-20 for 4min. ride). A daily ferry leaves from **Juara** at 3pm to: **Berjaya Resorts** (RM25); **Kampung Salang** (1hr., RM17); **Kampung Tekek** (2hr., RM20). Chartering a boat runs upward of RM200.

KAMPUNG TEKEK ☎09

Kampung Tekek, Pulau Tioman's largest village, has a few cheap accommodations and food stalls. A **police station** is located 500m to the right of the jetty. (☎419 1167. Open 24hr.) The **clinic** is next door in a pale yellow building. (☎419 1880. Open M-F 8am-4:30pm, Sa 8am-12:50pm.) For emergencies, an on-site doctor is available 24hr, ask locals to wake him. A **moneychanger** is on the second floor of **Kompleks Terminal Kampung** (known simply as **"Kompleks"**) across from the jetty. It also cashes traveler's checks at poor rates—**bring cash from the mainland. Telekom card phones** are clustered at the jetty and in the Kompleks. Purchase phone cards at the Kompleks, which also has an **Internet cafe** (RM7 per hr.). The **post office** is to the right of the jetty, beyond the police station. (Open M-F 8am-noon and 2:30-5pm, Sa 8-11am.) **Sri Tiomen,** next to the police station, has mid-range bungalows with an excellent beach. (☎419 1189. Doubles with bath RM40, with A/C RM70.) Next door is **Scuba Point,** which offers PADI courses. **Food stalls** at the Kompleks serve Malay dishes at cheap prices.

KAMPUNG SALANG ☎010

Kampung Salang is at the north tip of Tioman Island. The small, dreamy beach is delightful, but the town is crammed with travelers on their way to Coral Island and nearby dive sites. Beach and budget accommodations stretch out on both sides of the pier. Most restaurants, cafes, and shops are to the right of the jetty. Exchange **currency** at most budget hotels or at **Salang Indah mini-mart,** to the left of the jetty, which cashes traveler's checks, sells phone cards, and will let you make **international telephone calls** (RM12-13 per min.).

B&J Diving Center, left of the jetty, is a five-step PADI center. (☎419 1218. 2-dive daytrip RM160, equipment included; 2-day advanced courses RM525; 4-day open water courses RM750. AmEx/MC/V. Traveler's checks accepted. Next to B&J's, **Fishermen Dive Center,** is also well equipped. (☎419 5014. Same prices. Open daily 9am-6pm. MC/V.)

Half a dozen inexpensive hotels line Salang's beach and most have restaurants with Malay, Chinese, and Western dishes. **Salang Huts** offers quiet chalets at the north end of the village. (☎419 5027. Doubles with fan and bath RM25.) **Salang Sayang (Zaid's Place),** at the beachy end of the village, has clean rooms with a great view and beach. Reserve in advance for August. (☎419 5019; doubles with fan and bath RM60-80; triples RM90; triples with A/C and hot shower RM150; quads with A/C and hot shower RM200.) Right of the jetty, **Salang Dreams Restaurant** serves chili or curry fish, prawns, and omelettes. (☎419 5003. Dishes from RM12. Open daily 8am-11pm.) Nightlife stumbles on at **Four-S Cafe** with RM7 beers. (Open daily 6pm-1am. MC/V.)

KAMPUNG AIR BATANG (ABC) ☎10

ABC is a backpacker haven buzzing with accommodations, food, and souvenir shops. The beach is rocky but the snazzier nightlife makes up for it. The **tourist information hut** is immediately opposite the ferry landing spot, but is rarely open. Diving and snorkeling can be led by **B&J Diving** (See **Kampung Salang,** above).

Bamboo Hill Chalets, left of the jetty, offer picturesque accommodations with sea views, Internet access (RM10 per hour), purified Tioman water (RM1 per bottle), and international calls. Susan, the hospitable owner, is an unofficial information center herself. (☎419 1339. 2-person bungalows with bath RM70; family chalets with bath and fridge RM100-120. MC/V.) **Nazri's Place** is at the south end of the village with a small beach. (☎419 1329. Campground RM3; A-frame huts with common bath RM10; doubles with fan RM20, with A/C and hot shower RM80; quads with fan RM50, with A/C and hot shower RM 60.) Nazri's also has a **restaurant.** (Open daily 8am-midnight or later.) Closer to the jetty, **Tioman Guest House** offers sturdy chalets with mosquito nets, fan, and bath. (Doubles RM20, with A/C RM50.) To the right of the jetty, **My Friend's Place** offers spacious chalets with private baths and cheap eats. (☎09 419 1150. Doubles RM30; triples with A/C RM60; quads with A/C RM80.) **Mokhtar's Place** has the cheapest rooms of its kind. (☎419 1148. Doubles with fan and bath RM15.) For dinner, **Mawars** has an astounding array of Malay dishes (vegetable curry RM3; BBQ fish with chips and salad, RM12).

KAMPUNG JUARA ☎10

Kampung Juara is the hardest place to reach on the island but trekkers will be rewarded with some of Pulau Tioman's best beaches all to themselves. The most scenic route to Juara is a cross-island walk from **Kampung Tekek** (2½hr., 6km). The trek is cool and insect-free. From the jetty, turn left on the cement path and walk 500m, turning right at the sign on the paved path before the mini-mart. Past the mosque, the trail narrows to a thin dirt path. The halfway point is marked by the **Jungle Cafe,** after which the path becomes a downhill cement walkway. From Juara, take a **sea bus** (3pm, RM20) back to Kampung Tekek.

The road set back from the beach meets the **jungle trail** to Tekek south of the jetty. **Happy Cafe Mini-Mart,** next to the jetty, exchanges traveler's checks and major currencies, but rates are unpredictable. (Open daily 7:30am-9pm.) Ferry and sea bus tickets are sold at the **Happy Cafe** and **Hamden Beach Cafe** next door. Rent snorkeling equipment at the hut next to **Mini Cafe,** left of the jungle trail as you come out. (RM10. Open daily 8:30am-5pm.)

Paradise Point, to the right of the jetty, has basic two-person chalets with private bath (RM15). The restaurant serves an extensive menu and has outdoor seating. (Open daily 7am-10:30pm.) Next door is the **Riverview.** (Doubles with bath, fan, and mosquito net RM20.) **Juara Mutiara Resort** is left of the jetty with newly built chalets and a mini-mart. (Singles with fan and bath RM25; doubles RM40.) **Rainbow Chalet** is the cheapest on the block, with sea view chalets. (Doubles with fan and bath RM15; triples RM25; quads RM30.) The banana milkshakes (RM2) at **Bushman Cafe** are divine. The cafe also serves pizza and beer. **Beruntan Dive Shop,** at the cafe, offers two dives for RM120.

NEAR KAMPUNG JUARA

Coral Island, more beautiful than Pulau Tioman itself, has reefs with abundant marine life that are perfect for snorkeling. **Scuba Point,** on the beach next to **Sri Tioman Chalets** in Kampung Tetek, offers a 5hr., 2-dive trip to Coral Island (☎419 1228. RM180, including equipment. Open daily 9am-late. MC/V.) **Kampung Salang Indah** organizes snorkeling trips. (☎419 5015. Departs 10am; RM35, children RM15.) **Monkey Beach** is a secluded bay halfway between Kampung Salang and ABC. Follow the well-marked jungle trails going in each direction (2hr. return). The hike is steep; bring water and look out for monkeys.

If you're exhausted from the effort of laying around on the beach all day, try **Tioman Marine Park,** near the border of Kampung Tekek and ABC, which has a museum and video screenings from 11am to 3pm. (Open daily 8am-4:15pm. Free.) Look skyward at night—the islands offer excellent star-gazing opportunities.

SARAWAK

Sarawak earned its name when the Sultan of Brunei handed it over to James Brooke, the first White Rajah (See **Dynasty of the White Rajah,** p. 395), with the words "*Serah kapada awak*" ("I give this to you"). Though he really doesn't need the money, the Sultan is probably kicking himself now—Sarawak is Malaysia's richest state and boasts nine national parks, lush jungles, secluded beaches, and giant limestone caves. The state is also home to 26 distinct ethnic groups, including the famed Iban who live in longhouses along the Rajang River. Environmental degradation is threatening Sarawak's natural beauty and its indigenous cultures, though major conservation efforts are now underway.

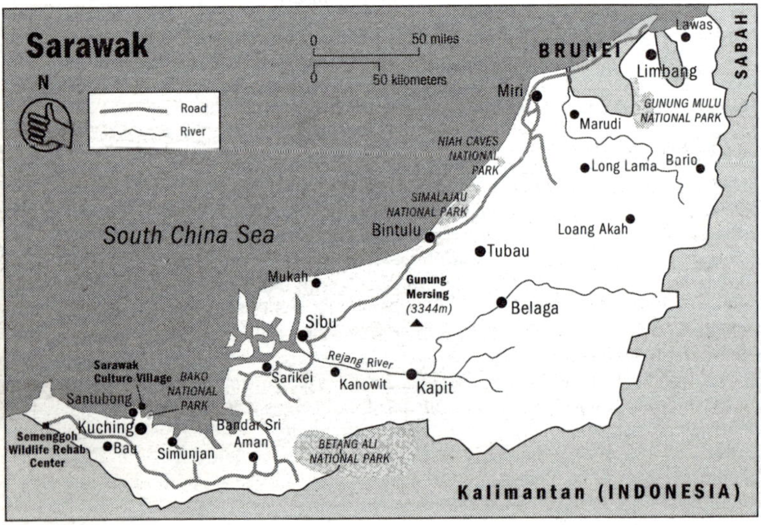

KUCHING

☎082

Kuching means "cat" in Malay, and residents celebrate that appellation with gleaming feline statues. Thoroughly modern, Kuching's waterfront esplanade is the place to unwind as you look back on a day spent at world-renowned museums and historical buildings. Kuching is also an ideal base from which to explore Bako National Park, the Sarawak Cultural Village, and Iban and Bidayuh longhouses.

TRANSPORTATION

Flights: Kuching International Airport (☎457 373), 10km south of the city. Take Sarawak Transport Company bus #12A from town (30min., every hr. 6am-7:20pm, RM1) or buy coupons for taxis (RM16.50) outside customs and use themon your return trip. **Storage lockers** RM3 per day. **Singapore Airlines** (☎240 266), in Wisma Bukit Mata, next to Crown Plaza Hotel on Jl. Tunku Abdul Rahman. Open M-F 8:30am-noon and 1:30-4:30pm, Sa 8:30am-12:30pm. To: **Singapore** (W, Sa 6pm; RM326). **MAS** (☎246 622), on Jl. Song Thian Cheok. To: **Bintulu** (RM117); **Hong Kong** (RM1167); **Kota Kinabalu** (RM228); **KL** (am RM197; pm RM272); **Miri** (RM164); **Sandakan** (RM289); **Sibu** (RM72); **Singapore** (RM286). **Royal Brunei Airlines,** 1st fl., Rugayah Building, Jl. Song Thian Cheok (☎243 344). Open M-F 8:30am-5pm, Sa 8:30am-12:30pm, Su 9am-1pm. To: **Bandar Seri Begawan** (Tu, Th, Sa; RM309).

Buses: Three main local bus companies run local and intercity routes. Green-and-cream **Sarawak Transport Company (STC)** buses run from the bus stop at **Ban Hock Wharf.** Blue-and-white **Chin Lian Long (CLL)** buses depart in front of the mosque on Jl. Masjid. **Petra Jaya's (PJs)** red, yellow, and black buses run from Jl. Khoo Hun Yeang near the night market. All serve: **Bintulu** (12hr., 5 per day, RM60); **Miri** (14hr., 4 per day, RM70) via **Sibu** (7hr., 5 per day, RM40); and **Pontianak, Indonesia** (8hr., 3 per day, RM34.50).

Boats: Express boats depart from **Bintawa Express Wharf,** accessible by CLL buses #17 and 19 (30min., RM0.80). **Express Bahagia,** 50 Padungan Rd. (☎421 948), runs boats to **Sibu** (4hr.; 12:30pm; RM35, 1st-class RM40).

Rentals: Pronto Car Rental, 1st fl., 98 Jl. Padungan (☎237 889). Sedans RM180 per day. 4WD RM350 including insurance. International Driving Permit required (see p. 42.) Open M-F 8:30am-5pm, Sa 8:30am-1pm. AmEx/MC/V.

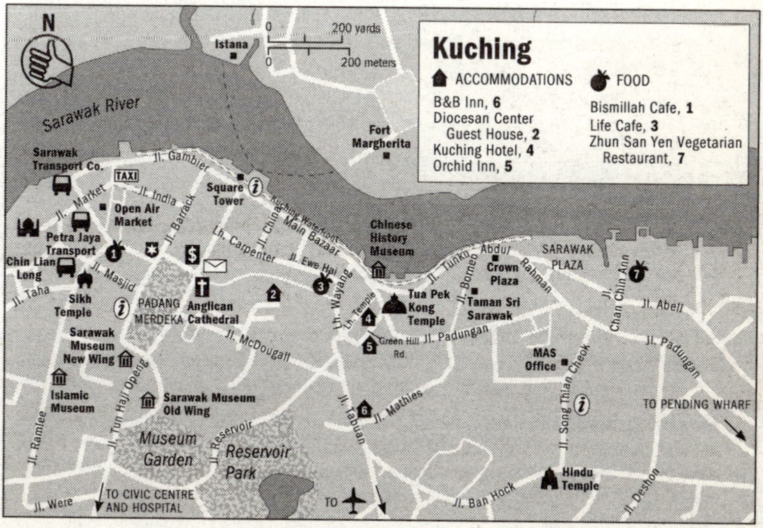

ORIENTATION AND PRACTICAL INFORMATION

Kuching unfolds along the southern banks of the **Sarawak River.** Its western border is **Jl. Gambier,** which becomes **Jl. Main Bazaar. Local bus terminals,** the **mosque,** and the **waterfront promenade** are in this vicinity. **Fort Margherita** stands across the river. The **central district** begins past the souvenir shops on Jl. Main Bazaar near **Tua Pek Kong Temple.** Turning right leads to **Lh. Temple** and most budget accommodations.

Tourist Offices: Visitors Information Center, Lot 31, Jl. Masjid (☎410 942). Entrance faces Padang Merdeka on Jl. Barrack, before new wing of Sarawak Museum. Helpful staff and free maps. **National Parks Office** (☎/fax 248 088), in the same building. Make reservations for Bako National Park and get permits for Semanggoh Rehabilitation Center. Open M-F 8am-6pm; 1st and 3rd Sa 9am-3pm; 2nd and 4th Sa 8am-4pm.

Consulates: Canada, Wisma Ting Pek Khiing, 1 Jl. Padungan (☎237 000). **Indonesia,** 111 Jl. Tun Haji Openg (☎241 734), opposite the hospital. **British Council** (☎256 044), on corner of Jl. Abell and Jl. Pandugen Utara.

Immigration Offices: 2nd fl., Bangunan Sultan Iskandar, Jl. Simpang Tiga (☎245 661). CLL bus #14A/14B to Petra Jaya (20min., RM0.50). 1-month visa extensions; RM1 filing fee. Open M-Th 8am-noon and 2-3:30pm, F 8-11am and 2-3:30pm, Sa 8am-noon.

Currency Exchange: Public Bank, 28-30 Jl. Tun Haji Openg (☎417 922), opposite the post office. RM3 for cashing 1st traveler's check; RM0.15 per additional check. Open M-F 9:30am-4pm, Sa 9:30-12:30am. Standard Chartered Bank on Jl. Padungan near Holiday Inn. **24hr. ATM.**

American Express: At **CPH Travel Agency,** 70 Jl. Padungan (☎243 708), off the intersection with Jl. Chan Chin Ann. Open M-F 8:30am-5pm, Sa 8:30am-noon.

English-Language Bookstore: Times Bookshop, 1st fl., 103 Crown Plaza Complex, Jl. Tunku Abdul Rahman (☎234 009). Open daily 10am-9:30pm.

Emergency: ☎999.

Police: ☎241 222. At the corner of Jl. Khoo Hun Yeang and Jl. Barrack.

Hospital: Sarawak General Hospital (☎257 555) on Jl. Ong Keattwi. Taxi RM10.

Pharmacies: PharmaCARE Medicine Shoppe (☎239 091), in the Crown Plaza Complex basement. Open daily 10am-9:30pm. AmEx/MC/V.

Telephones: Credit card phones at the GPO and airport. Most hotels send faxes.

Internet Access: Cyber Borneo & Cafe (☎239 425), Medan Pelita. RM4 per hr. Open daily 9am-10:30pm.

Post Office: GPO (☎241 311), on Jl. Tun Haji Openg. *Poste Restante.* Closed 1st Sa of the month. Open M-Sa 8am-4:30pm. **Postal code:** 93100.

ACCOMMODATIONS

B&B Inn (☎237 366), Tabuen Rd. Walk up Jl. Temple to rotary and veer left. Clean rooms and storage space. Light breakfast included. Dorms RM16; singles RM24, with A/C RM30; doubles RM32/38.

Orchid Inn, 2 Jl. Green Hill (☎411 417), past Furama Lodging House. Quiet. A/C, hot water, and private bath. Singles RM28; doubles RM35; triples RM45.

Kuching Hotel, 6 Lh. Temple (☎413 985), across from CyberBorneo. Large singles with fan, common baths, and friendly management. SIngles RM22; doubles RM26.

Diocesan Center Guest House (☎240 188), on Jl. McDougall. Enter driveway right of the cathedral parking lot and veer right at the end. Commonly known as Anglican Cathedral Lodging. Basic rooms with fan. Singles RM18-20; doubles RM23-25; 2 small apartments RM30, double occupancy RM35.

FOOD

Sarawak's signature dish, *laksa mee* (a spicy noodle dish), makes for a breakfast. **Vendors** cluster in the west end of town, south of the **Jl. Gambier** terminals and opposite the Chinese temple on **Jl. Carpenter.** The **Siang Siang Food Center** is in the basement of Medan Pelita car park between Lh. Temple and Lh. Wayang.

Zhun San Yen Vegetarian, Lot 165, Jl. Chan Chin Ann. Follow Jl. Tunku Abdul Rahman past Sarawak Plaza and turn left at Pizza Hut. Vegetarian heaven with over 30 dishes (RM1.30 per 100g). Open M-Sa 8am-2:30pm and 5-9pm.

Bismillah Cafe, 19 Jl. Khoo Hun Yeang. North Indian Muslim restaurant. Buffet style. *Lassi* RM2. Open M-Sa 8am-5pm.

Life Cafe, 108 Jl. Ewe Hai. Close to the intersection with Lh. Wayang; look for red lanterns. The best coffee in Sarawak (RM3), light food, and Chinese and Western teas. Clay pot noodles RM3.50. Open M, W-Sa 11am-10pm.

Khatulistiwa Cafe, Jl. Tunku Abdul Rahman. Great views of the river and large portions of Malay food. Breakfast served 24hr.

SIGHTS

Kuching's colonial architecture was spared from WWII bombing that leveled other cities on Malaysia's east coast. All the sights lie along the **Kuching Heritage Trail.** Maps are available at any tourist information office.

Along the esplanade and Jl. Main Bazaar, the **courthouse** faces the **Square Tower,** built in 1879 as a fortress and prison. Across the river are the pavilions of the **Istana,** built by Charles Brooke as a gift to his wife, and now used as the residence of Sarawak's head of state. On Jl. Tun Haji Openg is the **Round Tower,** built in the 1880s as a hospital and fortress. Sarawak's oldest Taoist temple, **Tua Pek Kong,** stands on Jl. Temple opposite the esplanade.

The region's best **museums** are within Kuching center. Follow Jl. Tun Haji Openg away from the river and past the town green to get to **Sarawak Museum.** The pedestrian overpass to the new wing is visible from the road; turn left and walk to the main entrance in the old wing. The exhibits upstairs focus on Sarawak's 27 ethnic groups. (Open daily 9am-6pm.) The **Sarawak Islamic Museum** showcases seven galleries of Muslim art. (Open Sa-Th 9am-6pm.)

The real treat, however, is Kuching's **Cat Museum,** in the City North Council office complex in the Petra Jaya district. Take Petra Jaya Transport bus #2B (RM0.60). The cat-crazy converge each November and December for **Pesta Meoww,** seven weekends of cat bazaars, cartoons, and other festivities. The nearby **Timber Museum** was established by timber companies to respond to foreign environmentalists. (Open M-Th 8:30am-4pm, F 8:30am-4:30pm, Sa 8:30am-12:30pm.)

Across the river, **Fort Margherita,** named after Charles Brooke's wife, houses a **Police Museum.** (Open Tu-Su 10am-6pm.) Take local *sampans* (RM0.30) from the esplanade across the river and walk past the park to the road beyond. Turn right and head up the hill. At the gate, surrender your passport and pick up a pass. The **Chinese Museum,** along the esplanade opposite Tua Pek Kong Temple, traces the history of Sarawak's Chinese community. (Open M-Th, Sa-Su 9am-6pm.)

MARKETS

The **Sunday Market,** which actually starts on Saturday afternoon, is held weekly on **Jl. Satok** on the outskirts of town. Get lost in aisles of handicrafts, local foods, and forest products including fresh wild honey. The best times to go are Saturday night and Sunday morning (open all night). Sarawak is also a great place to buy local handicrafts such as wood carvings and woven mats. Most shops are on **Jl. Bazaar.** Bargain hard.

ENTERTAINMENT AND NIGHTLIFE

Many residents head to the **esplanade** along Sarawak River to people-watch or take a moon-lit cruise (*sampan* boats RM15-20 per hr.) For nightlife, amble to mellow **De Tavern,** Lot G21, Taman Sri Sarawak, Jl. Borneo. Unbeatable happy hour 4:30-9:30pm. Barflies can add *tuak* (rice wine, RM3 per glass) to more traditional malts like Carlsberg. (☎419 723. Open daily 4:30pm-1:30am.) Afterward, crawl to **Cat City** down the street for live music and a game of pool. **Pepper's Two** at the Hilton holds Kuching's premiere discotheque on the lower level; a karaoke lounge is on the upper level. (Cover RM30 includes 1 drink. Ladies' night W, F. Open daily 6pm-2:30am.) The **Victoria Arms** at Merdeka Palace Hotel on Jl. Tun Abang Haji Openg is an English-style pub.

DAYTRIPS FROM KUCHING

SARAWAK CULTURAL VILLAGE

PJ bus #2B departs from Jl. Khoo Hun Yeang for Damai and the Sarawak Cultural Village (45min., 6 per day 7:20am-6pm, RM2.80). For the return trip, PJ buses depart from the rotary in front of the village entrance (6 per day 8:20am-7pm). When the buses stop running, catch a shuttle from the Holiday Inn at Damai to Kuching (5 per day 10:00am-9:30pm, RM10). Village open daily 9am-5pm, dances 11:30am and 4:30pm. RM45, under 12 RM22.50.

The Sarawak Cultural Village claims you can "visit all of Sarawak in half a day." In the shadow of Gunung Santubong, the village highlights seven reconstructions of Bidayuh, Iban, Penan, Orang Ulu, Melanau, Malay, and Chinese dwellings, each inhabited by a cast of English-speaking actors who engage in typical domestic activities and answer visitors' queries. Each day ends with tribal dancing and singing in the village theater.

SEMENGGOH WILDLIFE REHABILITATION CENTER

STC bus #6 departs from the bus stop at the west end of the esplanade on Jl. Gambier (45min.; 7:15, 8:10, 10:20, 10:50, 11:20am, 1:20pm; RM1.50) and drops passengers off at the Forest Department nursery. From here it's a 30min. stroll to the feeding stations. Buses return from Semenggoh nursery at 7:55, 8:50, 11am, noon, 12:30, 2, 4pm. Obtain permits at the Visitor's Information Center, on Jl. Barrack in Kuching. Center open daily 8am-4:15pm.

The Semenggoh Wildlife Rehabilitation Center lets you see the region's peculiar forest inhabitants up close. Semenggoh takes custody of injured or ill animals and birds and gradually rehabilitates them to the point where they can survive on their own. Residents of the center include orangutans, proboscis monkeys, honey bears, eagles, and hornbills. Feeding times are 8:30am and 3pm; arrive 30min. early. Gifts of fruit are appreciated. Morning feedings tend to be more populated.

BAKO NATIONAL PARK

PJ bus #6 departs from Jl. Khoo Hun Yeang (45min., every hr. 6:40am-6pm, RM2.10). Buses returning from the pier follow a similar schedule (6:30am-5:40pm). Or take a taxi (RM30). Buses and taxis go to Kampung Bako, where you can charter a boat (30min., RM30, 7 person max.) to park headquarters. Note that low tides interfere with transport.

Within Bako's 2700 hectares, trails squirm to cliff-lined beaches through almost every type of vegetation in Sarawak. The rare proboscis monkey is active during early mornings and late evenings. Pick up permits while arranging advance accommodations from the Kuching's Visitors Information Center. (See **Practical Information,** p. 399.) Daytrippers can obtain a permit directly at the Bako jetty.

The **park office** is over the bridge, left of the compound as you disembark; arrange a ride back with the driver. Drop by the park office to check in (RM3, cameras RM5). Hostel beds (with cooking facilities) cost RM10.50; camping spaces are

RM4. A **canteen** serves up fried rice and noodles for RM3. (Open daily 8am-10pm. Rooms RM42; entire lodge RM84.) There's a limited selection of snacks and drinks, so **bring your own rations.** Wildlife is abundant even around the park headquarters; monitor lizards, wild boar, and silvered leaf-monkeys are common. Macaques will raid dustbins in rest houses as well as steal food and unguarded bags at the canteen. The **Lintang Trail** (5¼km, 3½hr.) is great for a day-hike. **Telok Pandan Kecil** (2.5km each way, 1½hr.) takes you to a breathtaking beach.

Several tour companies in downtown Kuching can arrange day and overnight trips to **local longhouses. Borneo Inbound Tours and Travel** (☎082 237 287), No. 98, 1st fl. Main Bazaar, offers a variety of trips including daytrips on the Lemanak River with a visit to an Iban longhouse (RM280), half-day trips to Land Dayak longhouses (RM100), and overnight trips (RM350-500). Home stays in Malay fishing villages can also be arranged.

SIBU ☎084

In the early 20th century, Foochow immigrants from southern China settled in Sibu, gradually transforming this river town into Sarawak's second-largest city and an economic dynamo. A collection of recent public works projects entices visitors en route to Kuching, Similajau, or Niah to spend a night in Sibu for a taste of the conveniences they thought they could do without.

TRANSPORTATION

Flights: Airport (☎307 770), 23km outside town. Take Bus #3A from Lanang Rd. (every 30min. 6:30am-6pm, RM2). Taxi RM21. **MAS,** 61 Jl. Tuanku Osman (☎326 166). Open M-F 8:30am-4:30pm, Sa 8:30am-12:30pm. Daily to: **Bintulu** (RM64); **Kota Kinabalu** (RM180); **KL** (RM320); **Kuching** (RM72); **Miri** (RM112); **Sandakan** (RM218). Buy tickets at the terminal.

Buses: Sungei Antu Express Bus Terminal, on the outskirts of town. Take bus #2, 7, or 9 (all RM0.60) from the local bus station on **Lanang Rd.** Taxi (RM8). To: **Bintulu** (3½hr., every hr. 6am-6pm, RM20); **Kuching** (6hr., 12 per day 6:30am-10pm, RM40); **Miri** (6½hr., every 2hr. 6am-12:30am, RM40).

Boats: Express Bahagia boats to **Kuching** depart from the wharf near the Chinese temple (4½hr., 11:30am, RM35-38). Boats to **Kapit** depart upriver, near the Sungei Antu Express Bus Terminal (3hr., 6am-2:30pm, RM15). Buy tickets on board.

ORIENTATION AND PRACTICAL INFORMATION

Sibu is 60km upriver of Kuching on the banks of the **Rejang River.** Most hotels, restaurants, sights, and services are south of **Jl. Kampong Nyabor.** More hotels cluster around **Jl. Lintong** and **Jl. Wong Nai Siang.** A row of markets begins at the **wet market** on the **waterfront** and move north to end at the **night market** in the center of the city. **Taxi** and **bus stations** are on the waterfront near Jl. Khoo Peng Loong.

Tourist Offices: Sarawak Visitors' Information Center, ground floor, 32 Jl. Lintang (☎340 980). Helpful. Free maps and info on Belaga, Kapit, and Sibu. Open M-Th 8am-4pm, F 8am-5pm, Sa 8am-12:45pm.

Tours and Travel: Sazhong Travel, 4 Jl. Central (☎336 017). Air tickets, longhouse tours (2-day RM250 per person for 2-4 people, 3-day from RM450). Open M-F 8am-noon and 1:30-4:45pm, Sa 8am-noon and 1:30-4:15pm, Su 8:30am-noon. AmEx/MC/V.

Currency Exchange: Public Bank, on Jl. Pulau in a tall white building close to the Chinese temple. Cashes traveler's checks (RM3.15 for the 1st, RM0.15 per additional check). Open M-F 9:30am-4pm, Sa 9:30am-12:30pm. **Standard Chartered Bank** near the Visitor's Information Center has a **24hr. ATM.**

Police: ☎322 222. On Jl. Kampung Nyabor near the post office.

Pharmacies: Zhunian Pharmacy, 1st fl. of Wisma Sanyon (☎328 392). English spoken. Open M-Sa 8am-10pm, Su 8am-noon.

Medical Services: ☎343 333. Take a taxi (RM10), or Sungei Merah bus #9.

Telephones: Telekom Office (☎329 292), on Persiaran Brooke near the communications tower 200m from Jl. Kampung Nyabor. Open M-F 8:30am-12:45pm and 2-4:45pm, Sa 8:30am-1pm. **IDD phones** along Jl. Tuanku Osman.

Internet Access: Several Internet cafes on the 4th fl. of Wisma Sanyon, a tall white building at the west end of town. All cost 3RM per hr. and close at 10pm. The **Civic Center** offers 30min. free Internet. Open M-F 8am-5pm, Sa 8am-12:30pm.

Post Office: ☎337 700. On Jl. Kampung Nyabor. *Poste Restante.* Open M-Sa 8am-5pm. **Postal code:** 96000.

ACCOMMODATIONS

Hoover House, 22 Jl. Pulau (☎332 491), to the left of the church near the Chinese temple. Faded white structure with a blue trim. A/C, hot water, and private bath. Dorms RM15; singles RM20; doubles RM30.

Sentosa Inn (☎349 875), on Jl. Pulau. Newly renovated with A/C, TV, hot water, and private bath. Singles RM30; doubles RM35.

Sarawak Hotel, 34 Ramin Way (☎333 455), at Jl. Wong Nai Siong, before the Sugar Bun Outlet. Smiling staff eager for patronage. A/C, TV, phones, and private baths. Singles RM35; doubles RM50.

River View Hotel, No. 65 Jl. Mission (☎325 241), near Lanang Rd. bus station and close to wharf. A/C, private bath, and hot water. Singles RM30; doubles RM36.

FOOD

Chinese *kedai kopi* (food stalls) line Ramin Way, Jl. Wong Nai Siang, and Jl. Morshidi Sidek. Don't leave Sibu without sampling *foochow* noodles, served in a broth of soy and oyster sauce with onions and shrimp. All *kedai kopi* serve them—ask for *kampua mee.* **Sin Yung Kiaw Cafe 98,** No. 5 Ramin Way, opposite Kee Supermarket, serves *kampua mee* for RM1.60. (Open daily 6am-10pm.) Specify *daging* (beef), *ayam* (chicken), or *udong* (shrimp). *Kong bian,* Sibu's version of a sesame bagel, is another *foochow* specialty. Pick up a freshly baked dozen at **Seng Kee Agencies** on Jl. Tinggi. **Hawker stalls** line the first floor of the **SMC Market** on Jl. Channel. At the end of Jl. Market is the circular **SEDC Food Center,** commonly known as "Bulatan Tanahmas," which serves *halal* Malay food. The *Pasar Malam* market serves a smorgasbord of *satay,* steamed dumplings, and cakes (about RM4). **All The Best Vegetarian Restaurant,** No. 39 Jl. Tuanku Osman, is on the left if you're coming from Jl. Kampong Nyabor walking toward the MAS Office. (Sweet and Sour tofu RM2.50. Open M-Sa 6am-4pm, Su 6am-2pm.)

SIGHTS

Tua Pek Kong Temple (Great Uncle's Temple), built in 1870, survived the fire that swallowed Sibu in 1928, only to be destroyed during WWII bombing. The altar, however, somehow survived even this. Ask caretaker Tan Teck Chiang for the keys to climb the seven-story tower. Sibu's **cultural center** is a copy of Kuching's Sarawak Museum. Be prepared for a lesson on temple structure and philosophy, complete with props. (☎331 315. Open Tu-Su 10:30am-5:30pm.) Take a taxi (RM5) or Sungei Merah bus #4; get off at "Dewan Suarah" (RM0.40).

DAYTRIPS FROM SIBU

REJANG RIVER LONGHOUSES. Sibu is the starting point for all longhouse tours along the Rejang River. Most people arrange tours either in Sibu or Kapit, choosing from simple daytrips to strenuous week-long expeditions. Sazhong Travel (see **Practical Information,** p. 437) offers a large variety of trips and will custom design itineraries; contact Frankie Ting two weeks in advance. For those attempting a visit on their own, Kapit is a good starting point. Hang out in the coffee shops and chat with locals for advice. Never approach a longhouse without an invitation. Permits, available for free at the Resident's Office in Kapit, are required for travel beyond Kapit.

KAPIT ☎084

As the last outpost of civilization along the heavily deforested Rejang River, Kapit is used by international travelers as a jumping-off point into the surrounding jungles and for visits to Orang Ulu longhouses. The city itself offers little cultural enrichment; most of the longhouses have become modernized, and traditional dances are saved for special holidays. Thus, Kapit has less tourist traffic than Kuching. Still, travelers with plenty of time, money, and tolerance for leeches can venture upriver to the most remote reaches of Borneo.

> **WARNING.** This region is unstable and may not be safe to visit. Check with your embassy before planning a trip. This section was last updated in 2000.

TRANSPORTATION

From the jetty to the right (facing the river), boats depart downriver to **Sibu** (3hr., frequent until 3pm, RM16 and up). Sit on the boat rooftop to see longhouses and logging sites along the way. Boats upriver depart from the jetty to the left. During the rainy season, **express boats** leave from Kapit and Sibu to **Pelagus Rapids** and **Belaga** (5-6hr., RM25); when the river is low, take a **speedboat** (2 daily before 11am, RM50-80). Longboat rental runs RM200 per day and up.

ORIENTATION AND PRACTICAL INFORMATION

Kapit stretches south of the **Rejang River. Jl. Wharf** leads from the main jetty. The new Rejang Inn is a block down on the right. Another block up at the **Hock Hua Bank,** Jl. Wharf intersects the main road, **Jl. Teo Chow Beng.** The **town square** is on the right, bounded to the east by **Jl. Tan Sit Leong** and to the west by **Jl. Kapitan Chua Leong Kee. Jl. Tiong Ung Hong** past the square to the west. Farther along where Jl. Teo Chow Beng intersects **Jl. Temenggong Jugah** is the **post office** and the Meligai Hotel.

Currency Exchange: Hock Hua Bank; 63-64 Jl. Wharf (☎797 677), at the east end of Jl. Teo Chow Beng. Open M-F 9:30am-3:30pm, Sa 9:30-11:30am. Cashes traveler's checks RM2.15 for the 1st check, RM0.15 per additional (up to 5). **Maybank**, near Hotel Meligai. **ATM** (Cirrus/PLUS/MC/V).

Resident's Office (☎796 963). From Jl. Wharf, go past Hock Hua Bank, continue straight through a small playground and onto a road besides the Telekom. Up ahead behind a fence, the office is on the 1st floor of a blue-trimmed building. Permits for upriver travel to Balleh and Belaga available. Open M-Th 8am-12:45pm and 2-4:15pm, F 8-11:30am and 2:30-4:45pm, Sa 8am-12:45pm.

Markets: Day Market, on Jl. Teo Chow Beng, past the town square on the right. Stalls set up between Rejang Hotel and the river on Jl. Temenggong Jugah.

Police: ☎796 222. On east end of town, past the lake and the turn-off onto Jl. Hospital.

Pharmacy: James Pharmacy, 17 Jl. Tan Sit Leon (☎013 820 70 15). Open M-Sa 7:30am-6:30pm, Su 7:30am-noon.

Medical: Hospital (☎796 333), at the east end on Jl. Hospital. English spoken.

Telephones: Kedei Telekom Kapit (☎796 991), on a hill opposite resident's office. Open M-F 8:30am-4:45pm, Sa 8:30am-1pm.

Internet Access: Lee Cyber Center (☎013 820 0891), Lot 65 1st fl., No 14 Jalan Tang Sit Leong (RM4 per hr., minimum15min.).

Post Office: ☎ 796 332. On Jl. Teo Chow Beng, west of the square. Open M-F 8am-noon and 2-5pm, Sa 8am-noon. **Postal code:** 96800.

ACCOMMODATIONS AND FOOD

Many budget hotels have degenerated into brothels, but fortunately you'll still be able to find some less not-so-seedy, affordable options.

Rejang Hotel, No. 28 Jl. Temenggong Jugah (☎ 796 709). Spotless rooms with A/C and private bath RM20.

New Rejang Inn, No. 104 Jl. Teo Chow Beng (☎ 796 600), facing Jl. Wharf. A bit ritzier. Singles RM40; doubles RM45.

Hotel Meligai, (☎ 798 103) at the far west end of Jl. Teo Chow Beng, past the post office. Kapit's swank option. All rooms have A/C, TV, and phones. Singles RM50; doubles RM60; deluxe rooms with carpeting and fridge RM70-80.

Greenland Inn, lot 463-464 Jl. Teo Chow Bang (☎ 796 388), above the Sugarbun Restaurant. Rooms similar to Meligai's. Singles RM65; doubles with hot water, A/C, TV, and fridge RM75.

For the cheapest eats in town, head to the **food court** at the end of Jl. Tiong Ung Hong, one block uphill from the **hawker stalls** fronting the day market on Jl. Teo Chow Beng—look for the "Gelanggang Kenyalang" sign. (Open until 9pm.) A **night market** serving *halal* Malay staples sets up by the post office. Local cuisine includes *babi hutan* (wild boar) and *rusa* (venison). Yummy. (Open 7pm-midnight).

Ung Tong Bakery, opposite the day market. A popular morning stop for a cup of Milo and a plateful of fragrant rolls. Red bean buns RM0.50 each. Open daily 6:15am-5pm.

99 Seafood Cafe (☎ 797 321), up on a hill behind Hotel Meligai and the post office. One of the few restaurants open all afternoon and evening. Open daily 1pm-midnight.

SIGHTS AND ENTERTAINMENT

Named after the third Rajah's wife, **Fort Sylvia** was built in 1880 as a demonstration of the government's intent to end intertribal hostilities and head-hunting. The **museum,** within the Civic Center on the east edge of town, is worth a visit. (Open M-F 9am-12:45pm and 2-4:15pm, Sa 9am-12:45pm.) Evening entertainment varies from karaoke clubs and snooker halls to the more insidious brothels staffed by Indonesian immigrants. If you hear loud drumming near Rejang Inn, children may be practicing Lion Dancing at the Chinese Temple.

DAYTRIPS FROM KAPIT: LONGHOUSES

An entire Malay community resides in the sturdy walls of a longhouse. Structures are built from ironwood and bamboo and held together with rattan cord. The size of a longhouse is reckoned by the number of doors; some have hundreds and are well over 1km in length. The building is raised to take advantage of cooling drafts and for safety. A *tuai* (headman), who enforces strict rules to maintain harmony, traditionally presides over the longhouse community.

In the past, a visit to east Malaysia was not considered complete without a trip to a longhouse. Guests brought news to the isolated communities and were welcomed as an excuse to throw raucous parties. As these communities became more affluent, they sought to improve their standard of living by building sturdier tin-roofed cement structures—much to the dismay of tourists. Longhouse dwellers started to resent the well-to-do foreign travelers who showed up on their doorstep expecting to be feted like a Rajah in exchange for a box of cigarettes. Needless to say, more remote areas have more traditional longhouses and less cynical residents. However, no longhouse visit is a mere tourist attraction. A cultural home stay, even for a few hours, proves far superior to any museum.

PASS THE POTATOES, PLEASE Don't throw your manners out the window at a longhouse. The *Orang Ulu*, like any other people, will warm up to visitors once they are comfortable. *Let's Go* offers some basic dos and don'ts:

1. Wait for an invitation to enter a longhouse.
2. Take off your shoes before entering.
3. Dress modestly. When bathing, men should wear their underwear and women should use a sarong.
4. At meals, be sure to sample any offered food. Evenings sometimes culminate in a small celebration with *tuak* (traditional rice wine–take at least a small sip if offered) and plenty of dancing and music. Visitors are expected to contribute, and your hosts will love you if you participate wholeheartedly, even if it means making a bit of a fool of yourself.
5. Gifts are appreciated. Bring pencils and crayons for the children, and practical clothing, such as shirts and hats, and luxuries, like foreign cigarettes, for adults. Avoid giving sweets and alcohol. It's also nice to bring some pictures of your family, postcards, coins, stamps, or a book about your home country. For instant and enduring fame, bring a Polaroid camera and lots of spare film.
6. Otherwise, basic courtesy is the rule: don't touch anything or take pictures of anyone unless properly introduced. Remember to quietly ask permission as well.

Those looking for a traditional longhouse stay should try **Bareo** in eastern Sarawak or **Belaga** further upriver from Kapit. For those short on time, pricey longhouse stays can be arranged through tour guides in Kuching and Kapit. Before signing with any guide, check with the hotel staff and other travelers; not all of Kapit's tour guides are genuine. Also confirm the price, mode of transportation, and name and location of the longhouse to assure safety. **Mr. Tan Teck Chuan** at Kapit Adventure Tours, 11 Jl. Tan Sit Leong, on the western edge of the town square, is one of the area's most reputable guides. (☎796 352. 11 Jl. Tan Sit Leong, P.O. Box 16, 96807 Kapit, Sarawak, Malaysia. Daytrips to Iban longhouse RM380 per person, RM650 per person for two-day trips.) Chuan also coordinates trips farther upriver to more remote settlements. For extensive treks into the extreme hinterlands, he requests one to two months' advance notice. **Mr. Joshua M. G.,** at Regang Travel & Tours, is another experienced guide who offers daytrips (RM75) as well as a four- to five-day jungle treks. (☎796 600. New Regang Inn, 104 Teo Chow Beng Road, 96807 Kapit, Sarawak, Malaysia.)

The best time to visit longhouses is in early June during the **Dayak Gawai** (harvest festival) celebrations, but the best weather is from July to September. Bring a plastic bag for cameras, raingear, toilet paper, flashlight, sunscreen, mosquito repellent, aspirin, and basic toiletries. **Permits** from the resident's office are required for journeys upriver from Kapit. Most guides can help you through this harmless formality.

BINTULU ☎086

According to the Guinness Book of World Records, Bintulu is closer to an airport than any other city in the world; the runway cuts through the middle of town. Since Bintulu offers poor values for accommodations and food, visitors are better off arriving early to take advantage of banks, supermarkets, and other services while there's still time to catch connections to the polished sands of Similajau National Park and other alluring destinations.

TRANSPORTATION

Flights: Airport (☎331 073), in the middle of town, a few minutes north of most hotels. **MAS** (☎331 554), on Jl. Masjid, next to Chef Fried Chicken. Airport tax RM5. Open M-F 8:30am-4:30pm, Sa 8:30am-1pm. AmEx/MC/V. Flies daily to: **Kota Kinabalu** (RM132); **Kuching** (RM122); **Miri** (RM69); **Sibu** (RM69).

Buses: Medan Jaya Bus Terminal, on the outskirts of town. Accessible by local bus (RM0.60) or taxi (RM8) from downtown. To: **Batu Niah** (2½hr., 8 per day 6am-4:30pm, RM15); **Kuching** (5 per day 6am-5:30pm, RM60); **Miri** (3½hr., 12 per day 6am-8:30pm, RM20); **Sibu** (3½hr., 8 per day 6am-6pm, RM20).

Boats: Express boats leave from the waterfront daily at 8am and 1pm to **Binyo** (RM18) and at 7, 9, 10:30am, noon, and 1:30pm to: **Labang** (RM12); **Pandan** (RM9); **Sebauh** (RM8); **Tubau** (RM18).

Local Transportation: Local bus terminal is next to the markets on Jl. Main Bazaar/Masjid. Buses shuttle to **Medan Jaya Bus Terminal** (20min., every 15min. 6:15am-10:15pm, RM0.50). **Taxis** congregate opposite the station and charge high fares. To **Medan Jaya** (RM8); **Similajau National Park** (RM40).

ORIENTATION AND PRACTICAL INFORMATION

Bintulu has two parallel main streets: **Jl. Abang Galau,** which becomes **Jl. Keppel,** and **Jl. Masjid,** which becomes **Jl. Main Bazaar. Hotels, restaurants,** and **banks** line these two streets. The **markets, taxi station,** and **local bus terminal** are clustered around the center of Jl. Masjid.

Tourist Offices: Bintulu Development Authority, 1 Jl. Tanjung Kidurong (☎332 011). Welcome center in the basement of the white, cone-shaped building. Staff members fall over themselves to assist you. Open M-Th 8am-12:30pm and 2-5pm, F 8-11:45am and 2:30-5pm, Sa 8am-12:45pm.

Currency Exchange: Public Bank (☎331 433), on Jl. Somerville. Cashes traveler's checks (RM1.15 for the 1st, RM0.15 per additional check). Open M-F 9am-3:30pm, Sa 9:30-11:30am. **Standard Chartered Bank,** on Jl. Keppel down the street from the Capital Hotel, has a **24hr. ATM** (Cirrus).

Markets: The **day market's** twin cones reach skyward along Jl. Main Bazaar. The **night market** lights up near the airport at the end of Jl. Pedada.

Emergency: ☎994.

Police: ☎312 531. On Jl. Tun Razak.

Pharmacies: L.T. Ling Pharmacy, 61 Medang Sebadoh (☎335 996). Near Plaza Hotel. Open M-Sa 8:30am-9pm, Su 8:30am-1pm.

Medical Services: Hospital (☎331 455). Traveling west on Lh. Raya Abang Galau, it's on the left, opposite Bank Bumiputra. English-speaking staff. **24hr.** emergency care.

Telephones: Telekom office (☎319 292), on Jl. Law Gek Soon, north of the intersection with Jl. Keppel. International phone/fax. Open M-Th 8:30am-12:30pm and 2-4:15pm, F 8:30-11:30am and 2:15-4:15pm, Sa 8:30am-noon.

Post Offices: GPO (☎332 375), on Jl. Tun Razak, opposite the airport. *Poste Restante.* Open M-F 8am-4pm, Sa 8am-3pm. A reliable **courier service** (☎339 164), on Jl. Somerville opposite Hock Hua Bank, offers good rates. Open M-F 8am-5pm, Sa 8am-1pm. **Mini post office,** in the Medan Jaya Bus Terminal. **Postal code:** 97000.

MALAYSIA

ACCOMMODATIONS AND FOOD

AA Inn, 107 Taman Sri Dagang, Jl. Pedada (☎335 733). On the corner of Jl. Masjid and Jl. Pedada. Rooms with carpet, TV, and A/C RM32; "family-sized" RM36.

Kemena Inn, 78 Jl. Keppel (☎331 533), facing the Chinese temple on Jl. Keppel. Worth the extra ringgit. Bath with hot water. Singles RM50; doubles RM55.

City Inn, 150 Jl. Aban Galau (☎337 711), near Plaza Hotel. Clean A/C rooms with TV. Singles/doubles RM36.

Night markets, offering an excellent selection of *sate*, grilled fish, and fruit, set up at the local bus terminal and at the former long distance bus terminal east of Jl. Somerville, beside the airport runway. (Open daily 7-10pm.) An alley near Plaza Hotel at the east end of town hosts a variety of open-air restaurants. There, **Famous**

Mama Cafe serves up a delicious array of meat and veggie selections, *bacadile* (veggie potato puff; RM2), and freshly made *roti canai* (RM1). **Sea View Restaurant,** next to the Riverfront Inn on the east edge of the waterfront, serves fried rice or noodles for RM2.50. (Open daily 6am-10pm.) **Honey Bakery,** No. 63 Medan Sepadu, on Jl. Abang Galau, serves a dazzling array of pastries; its coffee shop also serves breakfast. (Pastries RM0.50-2. Open daily 7:30am-10pm.)

SIMILAJAU NATIONAL PARK

Some of Sarawak's finest beaches are 30min. northeast of Bintulu, nestled in Similajau National Park. Only 1½km wide, the park boasts 30km of sand and coastal cliffs, inlaid with orchids and pitcher plants. The 9km of trails that snake through coastal forest lead to the fine sands of Turtle and Golden Beaches. Along the way are the Sentunsur Rapids and the Batu Anchau rock formation, and boats are available to Kolam Sebubong pool. If you arrive during the week, you may have the entire park to yourself.

TRANSPORTATION. To reach park headquarters, contact **Mr. Syaidi,** who runs the park's canteen (☎010 884 18 88) and picks up guests in Bintulu for RM20. If you can't reach him, take a **taxi** from Bintulu (30min., RM40), and arrange a ride back with Mr. Syaidi. Bus #1322 leaves from the local bus station for Similajou (RM180); from here, it's a 1hr. (4km) walk to the park. Also negotiable is a chartered **minivan** from the park canteen to **Niah Caves** (around RM150).

PRACTICAL INFORMATION. The **park office** (☎391 284) is down a path from the parking lot and to the right. Drop by to pick up brochures, maps, and **permits** for park entrance (RM3), cameras (RM5), and video recorders (RM10). The office assigns rooms and arranges transport to the mouth of Sungai Sebubong for trekking to Koam Sebubong Pool. Next door to the park office is a **visitors center** with a fine collection of photographs of the area's wildlife. A ranger is usually on duty, but it's best to arrive during office hours. (Open Sa-Th 8am-12:45pm and 2-4:15pm, F 8-11:30am and 2:30-4:45pm).

ACCOMMODATIONS AND FOOD. Call Mr. Rahman at the **park office** (☎391 284) to reserve accommodations. The park has two **hostels,** each with cooking facilities, communal toilets, showers, and a large veranda. Each room sleeps four in bunk beds with sheets, blankets, fan, and storage cubbies (RM10.50). Closer to park headquarters are three **chalets,** each with two four-person rooms (RM63 per room; RM126 for the entire 8-bed chalet). All accommodations face a stretch of white sand and are set back in vegetation. Shaded **camping** areas are nearby (RM4).

A simple open-air **canteen** offers staples like snacks, bottled water, fried rice (RM3), and welcome extravagances like chocolate-dipped ice-cream bars (RM1-4). Dinner usually consists of a set menu of fresh fish and vegetable stir-fries (RM10-15). For an extended stay, it's wise to bring your own supplies. (Opens at 8am; closing time varies.) For a late afternoon trek, notify the canteen of your destination to ensure an evening meal.

SIGHTS. Many visitors are content to romp in the surf and loll on the sand near the park's accommodations. Further afield are more secluded beaches accessible only by marked forest paths. Treks range in length and difficulty. A good full-day hike goes from the park office to Setensur Rapids (15km/8hr. return). The trail passes through beaches and dipterocarp forests. **Turtle Beach** is an 8km hike from headquarters (permit required). **Kolam Sebubong** is an isolated pool on the upper reaches of the Sebubong River. Arrange with the park office to hire a boat for the day (RM150). Similajau has **saltwater crocodiles.** These ferocious beasts are hard to spot and attack with lightning speed. **Do not wade across larger streams. Use boat transfers wherever possible.**

NIAH NATIONAL PARK

Niah National Park's fame relies on its birds' nests and human skulls. In 1958, excavators discovered a 40,000-year-old intact skull at the mouth of the Great Cave. In nearby Painted Cave, Iron Age coffins were unearthed. Today, swiftlet nests, gathered by shimmying up rickety, 30m bamboo poles, fetch up to RM1200 per kilogram in markets. Although its size is not as grand and its rock formations not as glamorous as the caves at Mulu National Park, Niah is both a spectacle and great bargain for budget travelers.

TRANSPORTATION. **Batu Niah** is the gateway to Niah Park. Buses from Miri and Bintulu deposit passengers near the town jetty on the Niah River. The park is a **longboat** ride downriver (10min., RM10 for 1-5 people, RM2 per person for more than 5), or a 2km **taxi** ride (RM10). Returning to Batu Niah is possible by boat or taxi or via a shaded concrete path along the river. **Buses** depart from Batu Niah square for **Bintulu** (2hr., 6 per day 6am-4pm, RM10) and **Miri** (2hr., every hr. 6:30am-3:30pm, RM8.50). Buy tickets on board.

PRACTICAL INFORMATION. The **Park Reception Area** is a few hundred feet from the river's edge. If you don't have a reservation, pay the park entrance fee and arrange accommodations here. (☎085 737 450. Entrance fee RM3, cameras RM5, video RM10. Open Su-Th 8am-12:30pm and 2-4:30pm, F 8-11am and 2:30-4:45pm, Sa 8am-12:45pm.)

ACCOMMODATIONS AND FOOD. The park hostel's wood-paneled rooms and modern baths are a bonus for those visiting Niah. Each fan-cooled dorm has four beds and a bathroom with hot water. If visitors are scarce, ask for a room to yourself. (Beds RM10.50; eight-person chalets RM94.50.) A cheap open-air **restaurant** on the park grounds has fried rice or noodles for RM4. (Open daily 8am-9pm.) The park has no minimart so purchase snacks in Batu Niah.

SIGHTS. A boat ride across the river ends at the start of the trail to **Niah Caves** (RM0.50, after 6pm RM1). Be sure to bring a flashlight, as the caves are unlit. Rent flashlights from the **museum** immediately on your right, which houses artifacts excavated from the caves. (Open daily 10am-5pm.) It's a pleasant 3km (45min.) walk from the museum through cool forest air to the caves. The sometimes slippery plank walk doesn't require a guide (RM35). The trail leads through the **Traders Cave** before arriving at the 60m by 250m mouth of the **Great Cave.** Here, in 1958, Tom Harrison and his staff from the Sarawak Museum unearthed the 40,000-year-old human skull. Excavations along the cave's left flank uncovered stone tools and other human relics. Next, the trail crosses the **Cave of Bones** and **Beunt Cave,** where bamboo poles are positioned by bird's nest collectors, and eventually leads to **Moon Cave.** It's impossible to proceed beyond this point without a flashlight, but fear not—a brief walk through the caverns

HOLY BUCKETS OF BAT SHIT The few who care to examine the Niah Caves' floor will find a bizarre feast of bat dung, attracting not only cockroaches and worms but humans as well. Guano collectors have gathered bat and swiftlet feces as fertilizer for local *Iban* farmers since 1929. Despite the increasing availability of chemical fertilizer, guano remains the standby in *Iban* societies—not only for its low price but also for its ability to prevent foot-rotting disease in pepper vines. Today's harvests are nowhere near the 1950s recorded average of 476 tons per year, but 20 to 30 professional collectors still work the cave floor. In case you were wondering, quality guano tastes salty.

leads visitors back to sunlight. The fern-covered plank walk continues to the **Painted Cave,** which originally contained coffins. The relics have since been removed for conservation, but faded paintings are faintly visible behind a locked gate. At dusk, bats swoop and circle before finally pouring from the cave, as swiftlets make their way back to their shelters. **Iban longhouses** are a 30min. walk from the main plank walk; turn left at the marked sign. Though the longhouses are not traditional, the *Iban* villagers, especially the English-speaking schoolchildren, are welcoming.

MIRI

☎085

Profits from Mother Nature assure that Miri is well-poised for the 21st century. Bustling streets display new signs of wealth—the Mega Hotel prominent among them—soon to be eclipsed by even glitzier projects. This conspicuous consumption comes courtesy of oil and timber. The oil was followed by expats, resulting in the curious array of cowboy saloons and Southwest cuisine.

TRANSPORTATION

Flights: Airport (☎615 433) west of the city limits. Taxis (RM14) and infrequent public buses run into town. **MAS office** (☎414 144), on the corner of Jl. Yu Seng. Open M-F 8:30am-4:30pm, Sa 8:30am-12:30pm. To: **Gunung Mulu National Park** (3-4 per day, RM74); **Kota Kinabalu** (5 per day 9:25am-9:10pm, RM109); **Kuching** (5 per day 8:40am-9:30pm, RM169). **Royal Brunei Airlines,** ground fl., Lot 263, Jl. South Yu Seng (☎426 322). Open M-F 8:30am-noon and 1-5pm, Sa 8:30am-12:30pm.

Buses: Pujut Padang Kerbau Long Distance Bus Station, several kilometers outside downtown Miri. The A1 Shuttle Bus (every 20min., RM.50) take you to the **local bus terminal** in town. Several private bus companies go to major destinations in Sarawak: **SYKT Express** (☎439 325) and **Rejang Express** (☎435 336) are neighbors on Jl. Malay; **P.B. Express** and **Biara Mas Express** are at the bus terminal. All go to **Bintulu** (3½hr., every hr. 6am-6pm, RM20). SYKT Express also runs buses to Bintulu from the local bus station (every 2hr., 6am-4:30pm, RM20). Frequent buses run to **Kuching** (RM70) and **Sibu** (RM40). **Miri-Belait Transport Co.** (☎419 129) sends buses to **Kuala Belait,** over the Brunei border (daily 7, 9, 10:30am, 1, 3:30pm; RM12.20). Bus changes at the border, so take all belongings off when getting your passport stamped and hold onto your ticket. From Kuala Belait, continue onward to **Seria** and switch to a **Bandar Seri Begawan-bound** bus there. Leave Miri before 10:30am to avoid getting stuck in Seria for the night.

Local Transportation: Local bus station, behind Wisma Pelita on Jl. Padang. Bus #28 goes to the **airport** (every hr. 6:10am-7pm, RM1). **Taxis** (☎432 277) meet at the bus station and in front of the Fairland Inn. Buses to **Batu Niah** (2hr., every hr. 6:45am-4pm, RM8.50) and **Taman Selera** (#11; 1hr., every 20min. 6:30am-9pm, RM0.50) depart from the other long distance bus terminal on Jl. Padang.

ORIENTATION AND PRACTICAL INFORMATION

The heart of the old town is near the towering **Wisma Pelita Tunku** complex. On the south side of the complex are the **bus station** and **Visitor's Information Center.** Miri's tangle of streets are between **Jl. Kingsway,** running north west of the Wisma Pelita running north, and **Jl. Bendahara,** several blocks west along the edge of the **Miri River** and leading to the bulky blue-and-white Mega Hotel. Opposite the hotel, which is now the center of the city, **Jl. Yu Seng** heads north past the **Imperial Mall Shopping Center** and the gold-domed **mosque,** where Yu Seng morphs into **Jl. Datuk Merpati.**

Tourist Offices: Visitor's Information Center, Lot 452, Jl. Melayu (☎434 181). From Wisma Pelita, walk through the bus terminal; it's a white building in a park to the right. Staff provides maps and brochures. Reserve accommodations in Lambir, Niah, and Gunung Mulu Parks here. Open M-F 8am-5pm, Sa 8am-12:50pm; closed holidays.

Tours and Travels: Tropical Adventure (☎419 337), in the lobby of the Mega Hotel. 4-day packages to the Pinnacles in Gunung Mulu National Park (RM870 for 2), and 4-day treks back via Head-Hunters Trail to Limbang (RM1260 for 2). Cash preferred. Open M-F 8:30am-5pm, Sa 8:30-12:30pm. **Transworld Travel Services,** 2nd fl., Wisma Pelita Tunku Complex (☎422 277), offers similar packages. 5hr. trip to Lambir Falls and Iban longhouse for 4 people RM65 per person. Open M-F 8:30am-5pm, Sa 8:30am-4:30pm. AmEx/MC/V.

Immigration Offices: ☎442 105. Follow Jl. Brooke east until it becomes Jl. Sylvia and then Jl. Gartak; turn left at Jl. Persekutuan. In the pink building on the ground floor behind door 3. Free visa extensions up to 2 months. Open M-Th 8am-12:30pm and 2-4pm, F 8-11:30am and 2:30-4:15pm, Sa 8am-12:30pm.

Currency Exchange: Bank Bumiputra (☎420 371), beyond the Mega Hotel on Jl. Indica, off Jl. Bendahara. RM2.15 per check. **24hr. ATM** (Cirrus/MC/V). Open M-F 9:30am-4pm, Sa 9:30am-noon. **Bank Utama** (☎411 882) is the futuristic building on Jl. Nahoda Gampar. Open M-F 9:30am-3:30pm, Sa 9:30-11:30am.

Police: ☎433 222. In 2 buildings on the corner of Jl. Kingsway and Jl. Chia Tze Chi.

Pharmacies: Guardian Farmasi, ground floor Bintang Plaza, on the corner of Jl. Merbau and Jl. Min Pujut. Well-stocked prescription counter. Open daily 10am-10pm.

Medical Services: Hospital Umum Miri (☎420 033), on Jl. Cahaya-Lopeng, south of the city on the road to Bintulu. **Open 24hr.**

Telephones: Telekom Office next to the post office on Jl. Post, near the rear of the Imperial Mall. Open M-Th 8:30am-12:45pm and 2-4:15pm, F 8:30-11:45am and 2:30-4:15pm, Sa 8:30am-12:30pm. **IDD phones** opposite Wisma Pelita, on Jl. Padang.

Internet Access: Cyber Corner, 1st fl. Wisma Pelita. RM4 per hr. **Public library** at Dewan Suarah also has access. Take Jl. Yu Seng-Datuk Merpati north and turn right on Jl. Persekutuan before the gold domed mosque. Follow the street until it ends; the library is a glass and whitewashed-concrete creation. 10 terminals; free usage for 30min. Open Tu-F 9am-8pm, Sa 8am-8pm, Su 9am-3pm; closed holidays.

Post Office: ☎432 887. On Jl. Sylvia on the east fringe of town. *Poste Restante.* Open M-F 8am-4pm, Sa 8am-3pm. **Postal code:** 98000.

ACCOMMODATIONS

Muhibba Inn, Lot 548, South Yu Seng Rd. (☎412 003), above Sin Mui Pin Restaurant near Mega Hotel. Gate locks at 2am, but someone is always on duty. Singles and doubles with bath, A/C, and TV RM33.

Tai Tong Lodging House, 1st fl., 26 Jl. China (☎411 498), opposite the Chinese temple. Men only dorm. Lockout midnight. Dorms RM10; singles with shared bath RM28; doubles with A/C RM36, with private bath RM42.

Brooke Inn, 14 Brooke Road (☎412 881). Hot water, A/C, TV, and free storage. Singles RM40; doubles RM45; family rooms RM50.

Fairland Inn, 1st fl., 21 Jl. Kingsway (☎413 981). From Wisma Pelita, it's across Jl. Kingsway, down Jl. Anatto, above Sunmay Refreshment Center on the left corner. Gate locks at 11pm. Singles with bath and hot water RM20, with A/C RM25; doubles RM28.

Silverwood Inn, 20A Jl. Bendahara (☎420 577), a few shops from KFC. Phones, TVs, and bathrooms with hot water. Lockout midnight. Singles RM50; doubles with bathtub RM60. AmEx/D.

FOOD

North Indian eateries line the covered promenades of the beautiful **Jade Center** on either side of **Jl. Nahkoda Gampar.**

Bilal Restaurant, near Mega Hotel on Persiaran Kabor. Savory Indian cuisine. English-language menu. Dig into generous plates of *tandoori* chicken (RM7). Tender *rogani naan* RM2. *Lassi* RM2.50. Open daily 6am-9pm.

Hengyap Noodle Factory, Jl. N. Yu Seng, near Standard Chartered Bank. Look for the yellow "vegetarian" sign. Vegetarian buffet with Chinese specialties.

Yi-Hah-Hai Seafood, on Miri Waterfront off Jl Bendahara. Turn left after Bank Bumiputra; look for red tablecloths and orange chairs. Worth the extra ringgit. Exquisite *makan laut* (seafood) RM10-15. Open daily 4:15am-1:30am.

Sin Mui Pin, 5-7 Jl. South Yu Seng, opposite MAS office. A popular, open-air restaurant. Batter-fried cuttlefish RM8. Deer meat with ginger RM10. Light meals only after 9pm. Open daily 7am-2am.

NIGHTLIFE

Before partaking in Miri's vibrant nightlife, visitors can walk along Jl. Melayu to a roundabout, where a right turn leads to the free ferry across the Miri River. Follow the road 100m to **Long Jetty**—a perfect spot to catch Miri's stunning sunsets. Across the river, catch bus #11 to **Taman Selera** (last bus 9pm), 2km south of town, for a cheap dinner from the food stalls, then savor a stroll along the beach.

The **Ranch,** Lot 585-586, Jl. North Yu Seng, a few blocks north of the Mega Hotel, blasts live English music nightly. (Ladies night Th; Happy hour daily 5-9pm. Cover RM10. Open M-Th 10pm-2am, F-Sa 10pm-3am.) The Rihga Royal Hotel's **Rigs Fun Pub,** before Taman Selera on the right, hosts more dancing fun. (No shorts or slippers. Cover RM15. Beer RM14.50, RM7.25 M-Th. Open M-Sa 9pm-1:30am.)

Several bars also dot **Jl. Mebau.** For karaoke fun with locals, a **bowling alley** (RM4.60 per game; open 9am-1am) and **movie theater** (RM7; shows every 2hr. 12:30-11pm) entertain for hours on the fourth floor of Bintang Plaza.

GUNUNG MULU NATIONAL PARK

The largest park in Sarawak, Gunung Mulu National Park encompasses 544 sq. km of peat swamp, heath, dipterocarp forest, moss thickets, and mountain vegetation. Over 3500 plant species and 20,000 animal species, including eight of the reclusive hornbill, have been documented in the park's wildlands. Geology, however, not biology, is the main draw for tourists. Above-ground adventures include a two-day hike to the razor-sharp Pinnacles on the slopes of Gunung Api and a three-day ascent of Gunung Mulu. Some 500km of mostly undiscovered caves lurk underground, including the world's largest cave passage, in Deer Cave. With careful planning, savvy travelers can get the most out of Mulu without sacrificing their backpacker budgets.

TRANSPORTATION

Flights: The **airport** (☎011 205 285) is a 20min. walk from park headquarters. **MAS** runs flights from Miri to **Gunung Mulu** (2-3 daily, RM69). Reserve early or try to fly standby. Vans drive visitors to park headquarters (3min., RM3). Arrange return transport at park headquarters on the day before leaving.

Ferries: Returning to **Miri** by boat involves an entire day (and possibly night) of travel via **longboat,** starting with the trip to **Long Terawan.** Charter a boat (1-4 people, RM150). To make the next connection, some travelers leave by 4pm the day before and arrange accommodation at longhouses in Long Terawan. Residents may let you sleep on their floor in return for a small gift or gratuity; ask at the park office. Alternatively, leave from park headquarters by 4am and try to catch the boat to **Marudi** (express 3-4hr., 6am, RM20; speedboat 2½hr., 6am, RM22). From the Marudi jetty, take an express boat to **Kuala Baram** (3hr., 4-5 per day 7am-3pm, RM18). **Buses** from Kuala Baram go to Miri (45min., every 30min. 5:30am-9:30pm, RM2.50).

On Foot: After conquering the Pinnacles, you can hike from Camp 5 to the settlement of **Lubang Cina** on the Terikan River. The next leg involves taking a boat, with an overnight stop at Bala Losong, to **Medamit.** It's possible to catch a taxi here into **Limbang,** with cheap sea and air connections to **Kota Kinabalu** and **Miri.** Trekking the Head-Hunters' trail requires prodigious logistical coordination; package tours are easiest.

PRACTICAL INFORMATION

Obtain all **permits** for Gunung Mulu at the park headquarters upon arrival, rendering pricey **tour operators** unnecessary unless you fancy **adventure caving.** Gunung Mulu's airport harbors the park's only **minimart,** which sells noodles, nuts, candy, and water. Trekkers to Camp 5 can avoid a trip back by stocking up here upon arrival, or better yet in Miri before arrival. Head to the **park office,** left of the boat dock, to pay park fees and for accommodations, camera and video permits and to arrange guides and transportation for adventures within the park. (☎434 561. Open daily 8am-5pm.) There are no equipment rentals (try **Mulu Resort** downriver), but lockers (RM3) are available.

ACCOMMODATIONS AND FOOD

Lodgings cluster near the parks office. (Dorm beds RM10.50; 4-bed chalet RM63; double bed VIP suite RM157.50.) Call the park's office or drop by the Visitor's Center (☎085 434 181) in Miri. Electricity is available until midnight. A **hostel** across the river offers dorm rooms of significantly lower quality, and a chance to mix with locals. Take a left 30m past the canteen onto a dirt path, cross a stream, and the hostel is the first building in sight. (RM10 per room.) The sole **restaurant** on the park grounds offers staples such as fried rice and noodles (RM4), set breakfasts (RM7), bottled water (RM6), and beer (RM6). Across the park entrance bridge another restaurant serves large set dinners (3 courses RM15) on an open deck with loud music.

SIGHTS

Gunung Mulu's numerous fees may seem high for the budget traveler, but permit fees are charged per group; cut costs significantly by joining other travelers. Permit fees for the Pinnacles and Gunung Mulu include a knowledgeable guide.

SHOW CAVES. The Show Caves are Gunung Mulu's most accessible and least strenuous attraction. All have been fitted with boardwalks, and some have dramatic lights highlighting the fluid rock forms and passages.

Bring a flashlight, a raincoat, and a plastic bag for cameras and video recorders. **Permits** are mandatory for all visits. Standard fees for permits are (for groups of 1-5/6-10 people; all prices per group): Deer Cave and Lang's Cave RM18/20; Garden of Eden RM18/20; Wind Cave and Clear Water Cave RM18/20; Langang's Caves RM66/72; and Simon's Caves RM66/72.

The **Clear Water Cave** and **Wind Cave** systems (lit 9:30am-12:30pm) were first explored 16 years ago by a Sarawak Royal Geographic Society expedition which mapped 25km of passages. Over the past decade, exploration has brought the mapped terrain to over 107km, making Clear Water Cave Asia's longest. To get there, walk 4km on wooden planks, through Mook Milk Cave (flashlight required). Alternatively, charter a boat (15min., 1-4 persons, RM85) up the Melanau River. The first stop is Wind Cave, up a wooden plank walk to the right of the boat dock. Clear Water Cave is a 5min. walk along the river. The path first passes through **Young Lady's Cave** and ends at a 50m chasm littered with bones of boars who got lost in the caverns. Beware of guano-coated handrails (see **Holy Bat Shit,** p. 444). Outside Clear Water Cave, travelers can swim in clear water.

The path into **Deer Cave** hugs the base of the mountain. Deer Cave has the world's largest cave passage; at over 2km, even the shrill screeches of the two million horseshoe bats living in the cave are lost in the vast opening passage. The trail snakes relentlessly onward to a lone rocky outcrop, where visitors can take in the **Garden of Eden** a few hundred feet beyond. The entrance to **Lang's Cave** is a few minutes walk from Deer Cave; the formations are easiest to observe here. A 3km boardwalk has been built from the park's office to these two caves, and makes for excellent hornbill spotting around dawn. The lush, scenic trip takes 30-45min. (Officially open daily 2:30-4:30pm, when the lights are on.) Just outside the two caves, a hot observatory is a good vantage point for the continuous stream of bats emerging from Deer Cave at 6pm (lasts 20min.).

ADVENTURE CAVING. Guides lead the daring into Gunung Mulu's lesser-known passages to scramble over boulders, wade through subterranean rivers, and rappel into pits. **Sarawak Chambers,** the world's largest natural chamber, is the size of 16 football fields. Eight hours of round-trip romp-and-stomp through its midnight landscapes cost approximately RM88 per guide for groups of up to five people. Other destinations include the **Drunken Forest** and the **Stone Horse Cave** systems. Arranging expeditions through tour operators in Miri only if you need equipment. (Some caves require technical rope work.) Park Headquarters does not supply extensive caving equipment but will lend the mandatory head lamp, helmet, and Carbide (for lamps) for RM40 per day.

THE PINNACLES. Over five million years old, the Pinnacles knife their way skyward from the upper reaches of Gunung Api. The trek begins with a scenic 2hr. longboat ride from park headquarters to Long Berar. In times of low water you may spend more time pushing the boat than riding in it. From Long Berar, it's another 2-3hr. (8km) to **Camp 5,** the Pinnacles base camp, with basic lodging (claim your piece of wood floor) and cooking facilities (scrounge for firewood). Bring your own food, dishes, utensils, and water bottles. River water can be boiled for drinking. The next morning trekkers tackle the steep, slick, stone-mired hillside of Gunung Api. Although the path is only 2.4km long, you need to be fit and focused to conquer the 3-5hr. hike. With 400m to go, climbers are greeted with ropes and ladders, some nearly vertical and others horizontally bridging 20m chasms. Hikers find this part of the climb the easiest (albeit the most unnerving). For determined trekkers, the hike concludes at a narrow vantage point overlooking the surreal spires of the stone forest. The trail downhill is tricky and slippery after rain; it takes 3-5hr. to reach Camp 5. Most visitors spend another night here before returning to headquarters.

A boat to Long Berar, the first leg of the journey to the Pinnacles, costs RM350 for up to four people or RM85 per person; the permit fee is RM110 per group, which includes a guide for the three-day/two-night trek. Almost as impressive as the Pinnacles is **Larry,** Camp 5's park ranger, who makes the journey to the top three to four times per week. Bring your lunch, raingear, and at least 3L of water.

GUNUNG MULU. Rhinos were the first to enjoy Mulu's craggy summit, and the trail used by most trekkers today follows their footsteps. The journey takes four days for moderately fit travelers, although the experienced climber can conquer Gunung Mulu in three. Visitors to Camp 1 deal with muddy trails populated with leeches. The second day is a tough uphill battle. It takes nine leech-infested hours to reach Camp 4, at an elevation of 1800m. The next day, the most zealous of climbers are up before sunrise. The journey up to the wind-scarred peak involves 2hr. of climbing, some of it using thick lengths of rope to steady wobbly legs. After capturing the sunrise and a spectacular panorama all the way to Brunei Bay, most visitors return to camp for a night before trudging back to park headquarters on day four.

SABAH

Known as the "land below the winds," Sabah was once rumored to be a storehouse of gems. At lower altitudes, a jungle teeming with wildlife and vegetation entices the adventurous to Sabah's more remote locations. Shop-a-holics feast on handicrafts at the Filipino market, while divers enjoy the underwater paradise of Sabah's reefs. The stark granite of Gunung Kinabalu, however, is the primary attraction.

KOTA KINABALU ☎088

Kota Kinabalu (KK) is a raw, big-boned city where, despite the locals' best efforts, few visitors linger. But though they might not stay long, they come in hordes seeking the austere grandeur of the granite summit of Gunung Kinabalu. KK is an excellent base for sorting through travel logistics and planning daytrips. The overlooked beaches of nearby Tunku Abdul Rahman Park Islands are an off-beat surf-and-turf combo, and visits to the House of Skulls and Sabah's State Museum are intriguing.

TRANSPORTATION

Flights: Malaysia Airport Berhad (☎238 555), 6km from the city. From the highway outside the terminal, minibuses, Putatan Buses (RM1), and taxis (RM13.50) go to the city center. **MAS offices** are in the departure hall (☎240 632; open daily 5:30am-7pm), and in the Kompleks Karamunsing (☎239 310). MAS flies daily to: **Bandar Sen Bagawan, Brunei** (RM103); **Hong Kong** (RM825); **Jakarta** (RM825); **Johor Bahru** (RM347); **Kuching** (RM228); **Manila** (RM700); **Miri** (RM104); **Sandakan** (RM83); **Singapore** (RM584). **Singapore Airlines,** Lot 12-13, ground fl., Block C, Kompleks Kuwasa

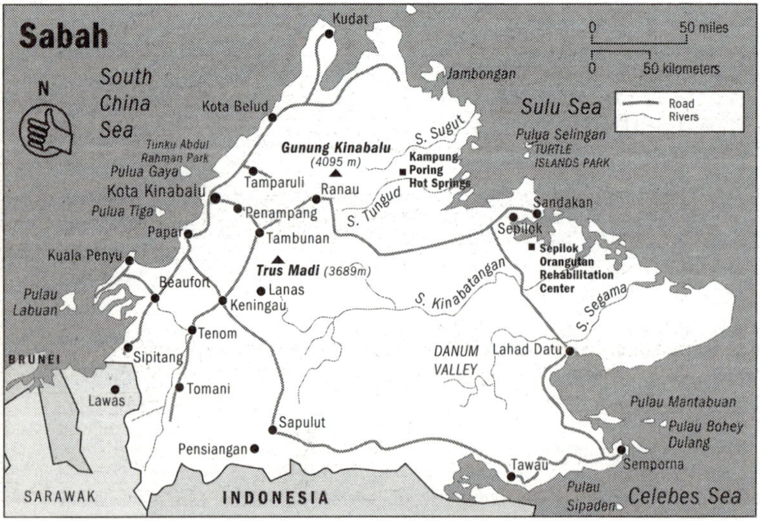

(☎255 444), flies to **Singapore** (Tu, Th; RM315). **Dragon Air,** Lot CG01-CG04, ground fl., Block C Kompleks Kuwasa (☎254 733), flies to **Hong Kong** (RM825).

Buses: Long-distance bus terminal, next to a field on Jl. Tunku Abdul Rahman opposite the library. Buses to **Kota Belud** (1hr., RM5) depart when full until 4pm. Buses to **Gunung Kinabalu Park** (2hr., RM6-7) and **Ranau** (2½hr., RM7-10) depart until noon. Buses to **Sandakan** (6½hr., RM29.75) leave most frequently in the morning.

Ferries: Park boats leave from the **Sabah Parks Jetty** behind the Hyatt Hotel to islands in **Tunku Abdul Rahman Park** (4 per day 8:30am-4:30pm, RM10 per person for groups of 4 or more). Beware of locals who offer to take visitors on speedboats; there are frequent tales of tourists being cheated and stranded. To get to **Bandar Seri Bagawan, Brunei,** catch the Labuan Express ferry to **Pulau Labuan** (2½hr., 8am, RM28) and another from Labuan to BSB (1hr., 12:15pm, RM24). Purchase tickets at the jetty office (☎236 834). Open daily 7am-3pm.

Local Transportation: Local minibus terminals are opposite the post office on Jl. Tun Razak and next to the Centrepoint building. **Putatan Buses** go to the **airport** (RM1), and buses marked "Beach" go to **Tanjung Aru Beach** (RM1). **Taxis** congregate near large hotels and charge RM6-7 for intra-city hops.

Rentals: Inno Travel and Tours Sdn. Bhd., Lot 31, ground fl., Wisma Sabah (☎222 708). 4-door sedan without insurance from RM160 per day (additional RM100 for a driver). IDP required (see **Essentials: Within a Country,** p. 42). AmEx/MC/V. Open daily M-Sa 8am-5pm.

ORIENTATION AND PRACTICAL INFORMATION

Completely destroyed in WWII, KK's center was rebuilt in a grid system dominated by three north-south roads. **Jl. Tun Fuad Stephens** curves along the waterfront west of the city center and houses the **jetty, city market,** and **Sabah Parks Office.** The **GPO** and **minibus terminal** are on **Jl. Tun Razak,** the city's central boulevard. The Backpacker Lodge, **police station, long-distance bus terminal,** and **immigration office** all line **Jl. Tunku Abdul Rahman** along the city's east edge. Other major landmarks are the Wisma Sabah, Wisma Merdeka, and Centrepoint complexes. Wisma Sabah is the L-shaped building by the Hyatt Hotel, Merdeka is down the street on Jl. Tun Razak, and Centrepoint is next to the Sinsuran neighborhood in the town's west end.

Tourist Offices: Sabah Tourism Promotion Corp., 51 Jl. Gaya (☎212 121), in the old post office. Multilingual pamphlets. Free comprehensive map. Open M-F 8am-5pm, Sa 8am-2pm. **Sabah Parks Office** (☎211 881), opposite the Filipino Market. Advice on Sabah's national parks. Open M-F 8am-1pm and 2-4:30pm, Sa 8am-12:50pm. **Tourism Malaysia** (☎211 732), opposite Sabah Tourism, ground fl., EON CMG Bldg. Open M-F 8am-4:30pm, Sa 8am-12:50pm.

Tours: Kinabalu Nature Resorts Sdn. Bhd. G15, ground fl., Wismah Sabah (☎243 629). Handles all accommodations in Gunung Kinabalu Park, Poring Hot Springs and Tunku Abdul Rahman Park. Book at least 3 days in advance. **Borneo Divers** (☎222 226), 9th fl. Stanford College near Sabah Tourism. 5-star PADI dive center. 4-day open water course RM900, min. 2 people. Day tours to Tunku Abdul Rahman Park RM180 (includes 2 dives, transportation, and park entrance fee). Wreck dives off Pulau Labuan RM185-250 (2 dives).

Consulates: Indonesia (☎219 110), on Jl. Kemajuan opposite Karamunsing Hotel, north of Jl. Tunku Abdul Rahman. Open M-F 8am-noon and 2-4pm.

Immigration Offices: 4th fl., Wisma Dang Bandang, Jl. H. J. Yaakob (☎280 700; visa inquiries 224 349). 1-month visa extensions RM6. Open M-Th 8am-12:45pm and 2-4:15pm, F 8-11:30am, Sa 8am-12:45pm.

Currency Exchange: Banks cluster by Wisma Merdeka on Jl. Tugu. **Standard Chartered Bank** and **Bank Bumiputra** have **24hr. ATMs. Maybank** (☎254 295), at the corner of Jl. Pantai and Jl. 3. Open M-F 9:30-11:30am. **Airport branch** (☎268 906) cashes traveler's checks. RM5 per transaction, RM0.15 per check. Open daily 8am-10:30pm.

English-Language Bookstores: Iwase Bookshop, ground fl., Wisma Merdeka (☎233 757). Borneo field guides and maps of Sabah and KK RM14.90. Open M-Sa 10am-8:30pm, Su 10am-2pm.

Emergency: ☎999.

Police: ☎242 111, on Jl. Balai, east of town.

Pharmacies: Pharmex, ground fl., Lot 6, Block F, Kompleks Segama on Jl. Tun Razak (☎231 457). Open M-Sa 8:30am-7:30pm, Su 9:30am-1:30pm. **Syarikat Kaca Mata** (☎258 589), next door, has contact lens supplies. Open daily 8:30am-7:30pm.

Medical Services: Perdana Polyklinik (☎235 100), on Jl. Pantai. **Queen Elizabeth Hospital** (☎218 166), near State Museum. English spoken. Both **open 24hr.**

Telephones: Public phones place collect calls, and some accept Foncards. **Telekom Office,** ground fl., Block I, Jl. Ikan Juara 1, Karamunsing (☎257 676). Open M-F 8:30am-4:45pm, Sa 8:30am-1pm. **Airport branch** (☎261 261). Open daily 8am-5pm.

Internet Access: Vision De Net Cafe, Lot 91, 1st fl. Jl. Gaya (☎019 873 3475), near RHB Bank and Sabah Tourism. RM3 per hr., students RM2.50 per hr. Open daily 9am-2am. **PlayNet,** ground fl. Wismah Sabah. RM2 per hr. 7pm-2am, RM3 per hr. 9am-7pm. Open daily 9am-2am.

Post Office: GPO, on Jl. Tun Razak (☎210 855), near pedestrian overpass and Kompleks Segama. *Poste Restante.* Open M-Sa 8am-5pm. **Postal code:** 88806.

ACCOMMODATIONS

Backpacker Lodge, 1st fl., Lot 25, Lorong Dewan, Australia Place on Jl. Tun Razak. (☎261 495). Travel info, TV, VCR, stereo, and library. Breakfast included. Curfew 11pm. Laundry. Single-sex 12-bed dorms with shared bath RM18; doubles RM40.

Trekkers Lodge, 46 Jl. Pantai (☎213 888), opposite Pizza Hut. Clean rooms and outgoing staff. Great deals for daytrips. Breakfast included. 4-bed dorms RM17, with A/C RM20; doubles RM37/43. Additional rooms available in **Sinsuran Complex,** 2nd fl. (☎252 263); turn right from the Filipino Market and look for large red-lettered sign.

City Park Inn, Jl. Pasar Baru 2 (☎260 607), across from the Sinsuran Complex. Popular owner Jimmy Wong has been known to treat his guests to dinner and has helpful travel advice and insight into local culture. Clean rooms with lockers, A/C, and attached bath. Dorm RM15; singles RM45; doubles RM50.

FOOD

Affordable Malay, Indian, and Chinese restaurants dot the city. The **Kompleks Sedco,** off Jl. Laiman Diki, is an open-air food court with the feel of a family reunion gone nuts. The A/C food court in the basement of the **Centrepoint Complex** offers similar bargains and a vegetarian stall.

Ang's, on Jl. Haji Saman, opposite Wisma Merdeka. Packed with locals. Hefty portions of Chinese seafood and meat. Sizzling Japanese bean curd RM6 each.

Restoran Sri Melaka, No. 9, Jl. Laiman Diki, Kampung Air, opposite the restaurants of Kompleks Sedco. English menu. A/C. Patrons rave about *assam* fish head (RM10). Vegetarian options. Chicken RM6. Open daily 9:30am-9:30pm.

Restoran Bilal, ground fl., Block B, Kompleks Segama. The best cheap North Indian food in KK. Buffet. *Roti canai* RM0.80. Curries RM2.50. Open daily 7am-7:30pm.

Port View Seafood Restaurant, on Jl. Haji Sama opposite the old customs wharf. Follow Jl. Tun Razak east out of town, 200m past Wisma Sabah; look for the blazing blue and red neon sign. Scrumptious Chinese seafood. Menu priced seasonally—never a cheap season. Fried cuttlefish with chilies RM10. Lobster RM80. Open daily 6pm-midnight.

SIGHTS AND ENTERTAINMENT

STATE MUSEUM AND ENVIRONS. KK's main cultural destination, the State Museum is a modern interpretation of traditional Rugus longhouses. Its cavernous interior has exhibits on ethnography, natural history, ceramics, and archaeology. Ironically, the **Science and Technology Center,** just beyond the museum, houses a small art gallery with a few noteworthy modern paintings depicting everyday life in Sabah. **Kampung Warisan (Heritage Village)** is at the compound's opposite end, past the waterfall. Visitors can pose with a traditional Bajau or Chinese farm house or a Murut longhouse before continuing to the nearby **Ethno-botanic Gardens,** where plants used for ornamentation, commerce, and medicine vie for space and sunlight. *(30min. walk southwest from the city center along Jl. Tunku Abdul Rahman. Walk*

400m past the intersection with Jl. Kemajuan and turn left on Jl Penampang. A small gate on the left leads uphill to the museum. Alternatively, catch a minibus from a bus stop along Jl. Tunku Abdul Rahman (RM0.50). Museum open M-Th 10am-6pm, Sa-Su and holidays 9am-6pm. RM5. Science and Technology Center open M-Th 10am-4:30pm, Sa-Su and holidays 9:30am-5pm. Heritage Village and Ethno-botanic Gardens open Sa-Th 10am-5pm, except F.)

TANJUNG ARU BEACH. While the warm water and soft sand make this beach ideal for relaxation, Tanjung Aru comes to life at sunset and on weekends. Hawkers sell steamed corn (RM1 per cob), peanuts, fried noodles, and chicken *sate* (RM0.40 per stick). Kampung Nalayan Restaurant in Tun Feud Stephens Park, several kilometers east of town center, has daily Malay and Kandazan dance performances around 7:30pm. Take a minibus bound for Luyang. *(2½km from the museum. Take one of the buses labeled "Beach" or "Shangri-La Resort" opposite the post office.)*

The **Poring** and **Kilan Cinemas,** at the intersection of Jl. Tunku Abdul Rahman and Jl. Laiman Diki, often show English movies. (Most seats RM6-8. Open daily noon-midnight.) **Asia City,** off Lh. Raya Pantai Baru, across from Centrepoint, and **Lintas Plaza** are home to many karaoke bars, clubs, and discos. **Shenanigan's,** ground fl. Hyatt Hotel, next to Wisma Sabah, is a popular backpacker hangout with live music. (No shorts or slippers. Beer from RM7.50. Cover RM15. Happy hour daily 5-9pm. Open M-Th 5pm-1am, F-Sa 5pm-2am, Su 5pm-midnight.)

MARKETS

KK's market area is along the waterfront. The **Pesar Besar (big market)** lays out fresh fruit and veggies. Look for cheap clothing and cloth upstairs. (Open daily 8am-6pm.) Next door, the **Filipino Market** sells souvenirs and T-shirts. At night, hawkers barbecue fresh fish (RM8-15). On Sunday mornings, **street stalls** on Jl. Gaya Browse sell everything from Chinese medicines to puppies. Beware of pick-pockets.

DAYTRIPS FROM KOTA KINABALU

MONSOPIAD CULTURAL VILLAGE

Several kilometers south of KK in Donggonggon. Take a taxi (RM20) or Penampang Bus from the local bus terminal in KK to the last stop in Donggonggon (RM0.80), connect to a minibus to Terawi (RM0.80), and ask to be let off at Monsopiad. ☎ 761 336. Open M-F 10am-5pm. Cultural shows Sa 11am, 1pm. Guided tours 9:30, 11am, 12:30, 2, 3:30pm. RM25, but most backpacker hostels arrange discounts.

Famed Kadazan warrior Monsopiad is still revered at Monsopiad Cultural Village where he lived over 300 years ago. His 42 trophy-heads remain in the House of Skulls. Monsopiad's direct descendants run the village and vividly detail the warrior's adventures.

KOTA BELUD

Arrive in Kota Belud early. Buses from the long-distance terminal in KK drop off passengers on the highway in the city center. Head for the pink spires and gilt dome of the city mosque and bear right down Jl. Hasbollah. The tamu *grounds are a 5-10min. walk from town past the post office. Minibuses back to KK depart when full from the Esso gas station near the bookstore (1½hr., last bus 4pm, RM5).*

Coastal Kota Belud, 75km north of KK, makes a welcome diversion from KK's urban rhythms. Surrounded by rubber plantations and shaggy dipterocarp forests, Kota Belud is famous for its lively *tamu* (market and trade fair), one of the largest in Sabah. (Open Su 6am-noon.) Historically, *tamu* allowed the upland Rugus and Kadazan/Dusun people to meet and trade goods with the coastal

Bajau. The Bajau, Sabah's famed "cowboys of the east," wear brilliantly stitched garb on special occasions, like the **Tamu Besar** in late November. The real attractions are not so much the standard market wares but, rather, the raucous, friendly atmosphere and bustling trade in the shaded fairgrounds.

NEAR KOTA KINABALU

TUNKU ABDUL RAHMAN PARK

Idyllic Tunku Abdul Rahman Park is made up of five placid islands 3-8km from KK. Inexpensive park boats leave from the wooden Sabah Parks Jetty behind the Hyatt Hotel to the park (4 per day 8:30am-4:30pm, RM10 per person for groups of 4 or more). Beware of locals who offer their speedboats; some tourists report being cheated or stranded. Admission for any island is RM3.

Palau Gaya, the largest island, is home to Filipino immigrants who have settled in the stilt village off the east coast. Over 20km of trails criss-cross the island through an intact **dipterocarp forest;** the trail from **Park Headquarters** leads through a dense mangrove thicket in which you'll hear the cat-like call of the shy megapode bird. Although crowded and dirty, tiny **Pulau Sapi** (Cow Island), off Pulau Gaya's southwest coast, is also popular. **Police Beach,** once used by police recruits as a shooting range, is the most secluded, while **Manukan** and **Manutik Beaches** get crowded with large tour groups' barbecues. **Pulau Sulug** is the least developed of the park's islands and popular with divers and snorkelers.

Camping is permitted on Pulau Sapi and Pulau Sulug. (RM5 per person, under 18 RM2.) Campers must obtain written permission from the park headquarters and bring their own food and equipment. **Chalets** are available on Manukan. (4-person rooms M-Th RM161, Sa-Su and holidays RM230.) Make reservations with Kinabalu Nature Resorts Sdn. Bhd. (see **Practical Information: Tours,** p. 452). Accommodation on Mamutik is a training base under Borneo Divers. For more information, consult Sabah Parks Office in Komplex Sinsuran.

GUNUNG KINABALU

Gunung Kinabalu is the world's youngest non-volcanic mountain, Southeast Asia's highest peak, and Sabah's premier tourist draw. The mountain has a solid granite core that began pushing through the surrounding sandstone and shale a million years ago. Already 4101m above sea level, it inches skyward at 5mm per year. Sir Hugh Low attempted to climb the seductive mountain in 1851 and 1856—and though the summit was named in his honor, he never quite made it that far. "Inaccessible to any but winged animals" was his appraisal of the peak, surveyed from the brink of the terrifying Lows Gully, a 1.6km-deep chasm. In 1888, John Whitehead, a bird specialist, became the first human to prove him wrong. Scaling Gunung Kinabalu is not to be attempted by the unprepared, but thousands ascend yearly and are rewarded with more than just an experience to write home about.

TRANSPORTATION AND PRACTICAL INFORMATION. Regular **buses** run from the long-distance terminal in KK to the park (1½hr., RM10) and also from the smaller town of **Ranau** (RM4-5). **Minibuses** make the journey until noon. Flag down buses back to KK on the highway in front of the park entrance (2hr., last bus 4pm, RM10). Daily **shuttles** also make the trip (1hr., every 1½hr., RM10). Admission to **Kinabalu Park** is RM3. Travelers usually arrive at **park headquarters** the day before ascending the mountain and spend their afternoon exploring forest trails. The **Visitor Center** is past the hostels before the access road loops back to the park reception. Upstairs is a small but intriguing exhibit on park history and wildlife. (Slide show daily 2pm, F-Su also at 7:30pm. RM2.) Learn about ecology at the **Sabah Parks Office** near the park entrance. Behind the Visitor Center is the **Mountain Garden.** Flora endemic to the park have red labels, plants used medicinally are tagged blue, and more common species bear black tags. The garden has a beautiful selection of Kinabalu's 1200 orchid species, including the world's smallest flowering orchid, with a blossom the size of a pin head. (Required tours 9am, noon, 3pm. RM5.)

ACCOMMODATIONS. Kinabalu Nature Resorts Sdn. Bhd. (www.kinabalunatureresorts.com; see **Practical Information: Tours,** p. 452), runs most park accommodations. Make reservations one week in advance. To the right of the park entrance, the **reception office** will give you a room assignment and a map of the park with directions to accommodations. (☎088 889 077. Open daily 7am-10pm.) Many trekkers stay at **Medang Hostel** or **Menggilan Hostel.** (Dorms RM12, under 18 RM6; doubles RM92; quads RM184; 5- and 6-person cabins RM230.) **Camping is not allowed.**

Halfway up the mountain, the most popular dig is the **Laban Rata Rest House.** Dorm rooms (54 beds) have heaters, hot water, and electricity. (Doubles with attached bath RM115; quads RM230.) Rooms at **Gunting Lagadan Hut, Panar Laban Hut,** and **Waras Hut** are unheated but provide cooking facilities and sleeping bags. (Dorms RM12, under 18 RM6.) The most basic accommodations (cooking facilities only) are at **Sayat Sayat Hut,** a 2hr. climb up the Panar Laban rock face. Many visitors rave about the Sayat's camaraderie-fostering seclusion, where groups gather in sleeping bags under the stars and chat late into the bitter cold night. Lock up food to avoid rats. (RM12, under 18 RM6.)

Outside the park, **Traveler's Adventure Lodge Kinabalu** (TALK; ☎088 266 124) offers dorm-style (RM18) and A-frame (RM40) huts with free breakfast. By bus, ask to be let off at Bundu Tukan junction; it's 2km from park headquarters.

FOOD. The **Kinabalu Balsam Canteen,** below the park office, offers excellent sunset views of the mountain from its veranda. (Dishes from RM5. Open daily 6:30am-9:30pm.) Meals at **Mt. Kinabalu Restaurant,** part of the Visitor Center complex, are comparable to those at canteens. (Entrees RM8. Open M-F 6:30am-10pm, Sa and holidays 6:30am-11pm.) A canteen at **Laban Rata** sells a modest supply of provisions and meals. (Scrambled egg RM5. Noodle soup RM6. Open daily 7:30am-7:30pm, 2-3:30am). Outside the park, **Restoran Tenompok** serves the cheapest fare around. (Open daily 9am-11pm).

CLIMBING GUNUNG KINABALU

Arrive at Park Headquarters by 7am, wallet in hand. You'll need a **permit** (RM50, under 18 RM20), **accident insurance** (RM3.50), and possibly a **porter** (RM50 for the first10kg, RM5 per additional kg). **Guides** are mandatory for climbing past Laban Rata. Groups with special interests can make requests for specific guides (fluent English-speakers, plant and bird specialists, etc.) when they arrive. (Guides for 1-3 people RM60 per day, 4-6 people RM64 per day, 7-8 people RM70 per day.) Park officers place independent travelers in groups. Bring a change of warm clothes (temperatures can drop to below freezing), gloves, hat, raingear, sunscreen, a small flashlight, comfortable shoes with traction, toilet paper, aspirin, bandages, hard candy or chocolate for quick energy, and a water bottle. Store baggage at the park office; free lockers are provided for valuables.

DAY 1. The first day takes you halfway up the mountain in 3-6hr. The trail starts at the power station, a brief bus ride (RM25 per bus) or 1hr. trek away. After a brief walk to picturesque **Carson Falls,** it's all uphill along narrow but well-maintained trails. Travelers soon arrive at the first of six rest shelters built along the trail. Pop-eyed tree shrews cautiously emerge from the shrubs to frolic for handouts. Over half the plants above 912m, such as the unusual **Kinabalu Balsam** with iridescent purple flowers, are unique to the park. Farther on, you'll see **pitcher plants,** whose large, liquid-filled leaves attract insects that fall and drown in the plants' digestive juices. The largest of the species holds up to two liters of fluid. Gradually, the trail gets steeper, rockier, and increasingly barren. The rare **Kinabalu Warbler** and **Mountain Blackbird** live in these landscapes. In late August and early September, the **rafflesia,** the world's largest flower, blossoms to a striking 1m in diameter. Most climbers spend the night at Laban Rata or one of the nearby huts; a hardy few trek 1½km farther to Sayat (see **Accommodations,** p. 456). The afternoon is spent recharging for the next day's push to the top.

DAY 2. By 3am the next day, bundled-up climbers set out with flashlights to reach the summit by sunrise. Above Laban Rata is the Panar Laban rock face, where wooden staircases become steep ladders that soon give way to shelves of bare gray granite. Ropes aid climbers up the sheerest bits. The Kadazan guides of early explorers offered sacrifices to appease the spirits of the dead at **Panar Laban** (Place of Sacrifice). The treeline stops here, and the thinner air renders the rest of the climb tougher. Take it slow and steady to avoid altitude sickness and exhaustion. **Low's Peak,** at 4101m, rises in a gentle curve from this austere landscape of windswept granite. Tourists vie for the ideal vantage point to capture the sunrise over Borneo. The descent takes 4-8hr. Every climber receives a handsome certificate of achievement from the park office that makes all the effort worthwhile (RM2).

DAYTRIP FROM GUNUNG KINABALU: PORING HOT SPRINGS. Poring's steaming, sulphurous waters are advertised as a miraculous cure for Kinabalu-weary legs. The springs (glorified bathtubs filled with hot, yellowish water) may disappoint, but nowhere else in the region are there free baths. Poring's isolated setting makes for a soothing visit. The 50-60°C (120-140°F) waters are piped into open-air tiled tubs. Jacuzzis, small swimming pools, and a new seven-tiered swimming pool and waterslide are at your service for an additional fee. A brief walk past the baths leads to the **canopy walkway,** a series of suspended boardwalks 60m above the ground. The view of the lowland dipterocarp forest is enthralling but a bit nerve-wracking. Those intent on seeing wildlife eye-to-eye in the forest area can negotiate nocturnal visits for higher fees. Many trails meander through bamboo thickets and formerly bat-infested caves. A 10min. stroll to the right of the baths is **Kepungit Falls** and a small, chilly pool. Another 2hr. through difficult trails, **Langanan Waterfall** drops 150m. Lepidoptera flitter at the **Butterfly Farm.**

Reserve **accommodations** at Kinabalu Nature Resorts in KK. (ground fl., Wisma Sabah. ☎243 629. Dorms RM12, under 18 RM6.) The park **restaurant** serves excellent meals. (Banana milkshake RM3. Claypot bean curd RM9.) Several local restaurants are outside the park and cooking facilities are available in the dorms. *(43km east of Kinabalu Park Headquarters. Baths RM2. Canopy walkway open daily 10am-4pm; RM5, cameras RM5, video RM30. Butterfly Farm open Tu-Su 10am-3pm; RM4.)*

SANDAKAN ☎089

Grim and artless, Sandakan's grid of numbered streets and concrete blocks of shops have the charm of army barracks. Most travelers go to nearby Sepilok, by the Kinabatangan River, which is home to the Orangutan Rehabilitation Center.

MALAYSIA

TRANSPORTATION

Flights: Airport (☎669 969), 11km outside town. **MAS office,** on Jl. Pelabuhan at Jl. Lebuh Dua, Sabah Bldg., 1st fl. (☎273 966). Open M-F 8:30am-5pm, Sa 8:30am-1pm. Flights to: **Kota Kinabalu** (RM83); **Kuching** (RM284); **Miri** (RM152).

Buses: Long-distance bus terminal, on Jl. Pryer on the west edge of town. Follow Jl. Tiga out of town and turn left before the pedestrian overpass. To **Kota Kinabalu** (A/C 7½hr., 4 per day, RM15-25; regular 3 per day 6:30am-noon, RM20-25; minibuses depart until 2pm, RM25) and **Ranau/Park Headquarters** (A/C 4hr., RM15-18; minibuses depart until 2pm, RM20).

Local Transportation: The **local bus terminal** sends green- and red- striped buses down **Jl. Leila** (RM0.40 to Bandar Ramai-Ramai). Blue *labuk* buses head north on Jl. Utara toward the **airport** (RM1.50); some buses cut the route short, so specify your destination before hopping on. Buses show how far—in kilometers (*batu*)—they go from town. *Batu* 14 runs to the **Sepilok Orangutan Rehabilitation Center** (RM 1.80). **Taxis** cost RM3-5 within a few kilometers of the city center.

ORIENTATION AND PRACTICAL INFORMATION

Many of Sandakan's streets have similar names, and street signs are scarce. **Lh. Tiga** (not to be confused with **Jl. Tiga,** a cross-street at the east end of town) is the town's main thoroughfare and changes to **Jl. Leila** near the post office. South of Lh. Tiga along the waterfront is **Jl. Pryer.** At Lh. Tiga's extreme east end is the **Wisma Koo Siak Chew Bdg.,** which houses the **Sabah Park Office** and **Telekom Office.** West of town are the **long-distance bus terminal, night market,** and **post office.**

Tourist Offices: Tourist Information Office (☎229 751), across the town square from the police station on Jalan Empat, has a helpful staff. Open daily 8am-4:30pm. **Sabah Park Office,** Wisma Khoo Siak Chew, 9th fl. (☎273 453). Open M-Th 8am-1pm and 2-4:30pm, F 8-11:30am and 2-4:30pm, Sa 8am-12:30pm.

Currency Exchange: Banks cluster at the Bulatan Merdeka traffic circle at the intersection of Jl. Tiga and Jl. Pelabuhan. **Hong Kong Bank** (☎213 122). Cashes traveler's checks. 1st check RM2.15, each additional RM0.15. **24hr. ATM.** Open M-F 9:30am-3pm, Sa 9:30-11:30am.

Police: ☎211 222. On Lh. Empat, north of town.

Pharmacies: Borneo Dispensary, 65 Lh. Tiga (☎213 981), 2 doors from KFC. English spoken. Open M-Sa 8am-5:30pm, Su 8am-12:30pm.

Hospital: ☎212 111. On Jl. Utara towards the airport. English spoken.

Telephones: Near the long-distance bus terminal. No credit card phones. **Telekom Office,** 6th fl., Wisma Khoo Siak Chew (☎219 292), at east end of Lh. Tiga. International phone/fax. Open M-F 8:30am-4:45pm, Sa 8:30am-1pm.

Internet Access: Sandakan Cybercafe, Lot 305, Wisma Sandakan (☎216 158), near Hotel Sandalacan. Fast connections. RM5 per hr. Open M-Sa 9am-10pm, Su 9am-8pm.

Post Office: ☎201 501. On Jl. Leila next to the supermarket on the outskirts of town. *Poste Restante*. Open M-Sa 8am-5pm. **Postal code:** 90000.

MALAYSIA

ACCOMMODATIONS

Travelers Rest Hostel, Apt. 2, Block E, 2nd fl., Bandar Ramai-Ramai. 10-15min. walk down and 1 block from Jl. Leila, near MayBank Finance. Organizes trips to Turtle Island and Kinabatangan River. Spacious rooms with common bath. Light breakfast included. Dorms RM12, with A/C RM15; rooms RM25.

Rose B8B, opposite Travelers Rest House. Immaculate rooms with common bath. Communal TV. Arranges trekking trips to Sukau. Internet RM4.50 per hr. Breakfast included. Dorms RM15; doubles with A/C RM38.

May Fair Hotel, No. 24, Block 26, 1st fl., Jl. Pryer (☎219 855), in front of the market. Rustic but clean. Friendly owner speaks many languages. All rooms have A/C and private bath with hot shower. Singles RM36; doubles RM45.

FOOD

Stingray-steak vendors compete with used-clothing stalls at Sandakan's **night market** on Jl. Tiga. (Open daily 7pm-late.) Several Indian restaurants and more market stalls line **Jl. Pryer.**

Habeeb III, on Jl. Tiga between Lh. Tiga and Lh. Empat, opposite the Wisma Sandakan. Small, friendly, and A/C. English menu. Indonesian, Malaysian, and Chinese dishes RM3-5. Western dishes RM5-9. Open daily 8am-11pm.

Kedai Makanan King Cheong, Block 19, Lot 5A, 2 blocks from MAS office. Cheap Chinese meals and an excellent veggie selection. Owner speaks English. Dishes RM3-4.

Supreme Garden Vegetarian Restaurant, Block 30, Lots 2-3, Bandar Ramai-Ramai, off Jl. Leila; look for a red and gold sign. English menu and A/C. *Faux*-pork lunch specials (served M-Sa 11am-1:30pm) RM3.50. Seaweed soup RM4. Bean curd RM6. Open daily 9:30am-1:45pm and 5:30-8:45pm; closed Tu evening.

Restaurant Shamrock, Lot 9, Block 20, on Jl. Tiga near Wisma Sandakan. Excellent beer selection and an up-to-date jukebox. Large Heineken RM10. Open daily 8am-2am.

NEAR SANDAKAN

TURTLE ISLANDS PARK

Forty kilometers from Sandakan's coast, government-built Turtle Islands Park is made up of three islands—**Selingaan, Gulisan,** and **Bakkungan Kecil.** It protects **Green** and **Hawksbill Turtles,** whose eggs and flesh are considered delicacies and have been harvested for centuries by the local Cagayan people. Egg counts dropped from 700,000 in the late 1960s to less than 250,000 in 1987. The Green Turtles (which constitute 83% of those sighted) prefer to lay their eggs on Selingaan from July to September, while the more elusive Hawksbills favor Gulisan from February to April. All eggs laid in Selingaan are collected and resettled at the park's turtle hatcheries. After 50-60 days, the turtles emerge and are released into the sea. It's estimated that a mere 3% survive into adulthood. Especially during the full moon, turtles can be seen crawling to the high-water mark to dig nests. Green turtles are seen year round, and it's extremely rare for a night to pass without at least one sighting.

Pricey accommodations are run by **Crystal Quest Sdn. Bhd.** Make reservations one month in advance at Wisman Khoo Siak Chiew, 12th fl., Room 1204 in Sandakan. (☎212 711; mailing address: PO Box 848, 90709, Sandakan, Sabah, Malaysia. Doubles RM125 with shared bath, A/C, and 2 meals RM150 per person.) Crystal Quest is often booked way in advance because it sells its rooms to local tour agencies that jack up the prices. Many guest houses offer package tours. Roundtrip transport from Sandakan to the park costs RM100.

KINABATANGAN RIVER

Sabah's largest river, the Kinabatangan supports one of the densest wildlife concentrations in the world. Proboscis monkeys frolic in the thick canopies at the river's lower reaches every morning and evening. Other treetop denizens include gibbons, macaques, and the occasional orangutan. On the ground, aardvarks, porcupines, deer, and boar meander through the trees. Civet cats are frequent night visitors to the jungle camp kitchens.

The most distinctive way to see the Kinabatangan River is on an excursion to a local jungle camp. **Uncle Tan's** is the traditional choice, but a management slump has led to food shortages and cramped conditions. (Transport RM130. Meals included. Rooms RM15.) A better alternative is the **Jungle Sanctuary,** run by Sandakan's **Travelers' Rest Hostel.** The friendly staff leads free excursions for guests and prepare delicious meals. Manager Nelson takes visitors fishing on the lake, but beware of crocodiles! (Transport RM150. Meals included. Rooms RM15.)

SEPILOK ORANGUTAN REHABILITATION CENTER

One of Sandakan's prime (and cheapest) attractions, the Center reintroduces infant orangutans taken from their mothers into the reserve. Visitors can watch orangutans scoop handfuls of milk into their mouths.

Keep in mind these rules when you visit: don't leave trash anywhere; don't smoke or carry insect repellent; don't get closer than 2m to the animals at all times; and never attempt to feed any of the animals on the trail. Orangutans are strong, and their idea of play could put you in traction. They'll jump on your head, steal your camera, strip you naked (as they did to a visitor in 1992), and drop it (the camera) from the tree-tops. Forest trails allow visitors to witness orangutans and other primates in a more natural setting. Watch your head.

There are two daily feedings on platform A (10am and 3pm); arrive 30min. before feeding time. The **reception office** (☎215 189) is to the right of the entrance; documentaries on the Center's activities can be viewed on request. There are free video showings at 8:40am, 10:40am, and 3:30pm. To reach the center from Sandakan, catch a blue-and-white Sepilok "Batu 14" bus (45min., 8 per day, RM1.50) from the long-distance bus station. Buses will drop you at the turnoff to the center; from there it's a 3km walk. (Open daily 9-11am and 2-3pm. RM10, video cameras RM10.)

Most visitors to the center stay at the **Sepilok Jungle Resort** on Labuk Rd., 500m from the park entrance, which boasts an ideal location, resort-style settings, and management that falls over itself to help with trips and travel. (☎533 031. Breakfast included. Dorms RM18; doubles RM40, with A/C RM60; family rooms RM100.) Call for pickup from the main road. **Uncle Tan's,** on Labuk Rd., Lot 8 Block B, SEDCO Complex/Mile 16, Gum Gum, is another great value option. From Sandakan, take any bus going beyond Batu 16 and ask to be dropped off at Gum Gum. Uncle Tan is a local legend as a former newspaperman, an environmental activist, and a geography teacher. He regales visitors with anecdotes and draws an eclectic mix of travelers. (☎531 917. Meals included. Rooms with mosquito nets and shared bathroom RM20. Reservations recommended.)

MYANMAR

KYAT

US$1 =6KYAT*, 600KYAT*	10KYAT = US$1.51, $0.016
EUR€1 = 6KYAT, 600KYAT	10KYAT = EUR€1.51, €0.016
UK£1 = 9KYAT, 800KYAT	10KYAT = UK£1.01, £0.012
IR£1 = 7KYAT, 700KYAT	10KYAT = IR£1.31, £0.014
AUS$1 = 3KYAT, 300KYAT	10KYAT = AUS$2.85, $0.033

*Dual exchange rates reflect disparity between pegged government rate and the market rate. The official rate is listed first, followed by the black market rate. Rates change as much as 20% daily (see **Money,** P. 468). Only hard currencies such as those listed above are accepted for FEC conversion. Travelers should carry some amount of the above currencies when traveling to Myanmar.

PHONE CODE **Country Code:** 95. **International dialing prefix:** 00.

There are two visions of Myanmar. One is a country with glittering pagodas and a glorious past, where village life thrives undisturbed and the serenity of the country's Buddhist faith steeps into a culture of gentleness and respect. The other describes one of the poorest countries in Southeast Asia, where real incomes are lower than they were at independence, a government represses and tortures its own people, the will of a people for democratic freedom is ruthlessly suppressed, and slave labor is a norm for public works. Both these visions grasp at some aspect of the reality of Myanmar today. Known until recently as Burma, it has been a hermit state since the 1960s and opened up to foreign investment and tourism only in 1989—a change that many hope will be the primary agent of some movement of reform in the country. Travelers who step down at Yangon Airport will find golden stupas, picturesque lakes, and unspoiled mountain scenery. Myanmar's arid central plains gave rise to some of Southeast Asia's greatest civilizations. The country's jewel, the ancient city of Bagan, is rivaled only by Angkor Wat as the most breathtaking sight in Southeast Asia. Perhaps the greatest treasure in Myanmar, however, is the grace of the Burmese people amidst the fierceness of their repression. The paradoxes of Myanmar are truly still alive.

FACTS AND FIGURES

Official Name: Union of Myanmar.
Government: Military rule.
Capital: Yangon.
Land Area: 676,522 sq. km.
Geography: Borders Bangladesh, India, China, Thailand, and Laos. River Systems: Ayeyarwady, Chindwin, Mekong, Sittang, Salween. Mountain Ranges: Himalayas in northern Myanmar.
Climate: Dry (high season) Oct.-May, rainy (low season) June-Sept.
Major Cities: Mandalay, Yangon.
Population: 47,300,000.
Languages: Burmese, English.
Religion: Buddhism, Islam, Christianity, Hinduism, other.
Average Income Per Capita: US$150.
Major Exports: Teak, rice, rubber, wood.

LIFE AND TIMES

THE PEOPLE OF MYANMAR

As of the last official census taken in 1931, Myanmar's population consisted of **Burmans** (60%), **Karen** and **Shan** (10%), **Arakanese, Chin, Chinese, Kachin, Mon,** and **Wa.**

HIGHLIGHTS OF MYANMAR

CULTURAL HERITAGE. The Golden Age shines on the **Bagan** Archaeological Zone (p. 501). Yangon's **Shwedagon Pagoda** (p. 479), the temples of **Mandalay** (p. 488), and Mon State's **Golden Mount** (p. 486) stand as reminders of Myanmar's past.

NATURAL WONDERS. Self-sufficient waterborne communities thrive on **Inle Lake** (p. 505). Shan, Danu, Pa-O, and Palaung villages beckon trekkers into the splendid mountain scenery around **Kalaw** (p. 509).

URBAN BEAT. The temples, parks, and tea houses of **Yangon** (p. 471) and the arts scene of **Mandalay** (p. 488) all give insight into traditional Burmese rhythms of life.

HISTORY

PREHISTORY

—A: Ayeyarwady, Austro-Asiatic, and Ancient.

Five thousand years ago, the first humans settled in the **Ayeyarwady Valley,** which divided Myanmar culturally and geographically into upper and lower regions. The **Pyu** (Tibeto-Burmese people) joined the upper valley around 200 BC and grew wealthy by controlling the lucrative trade route from China to India. Two centuries later, the **Mon,** an Austro-Asiatic people related to the Khmer, arrived farther south at the Sittang River Valley and established a capital at Thaton. As their last major city fell to the Chinese in 832, the Burmese took over the Pyu River area and established the city of **Bagan** in 849.

BAGAN AND TOUNGOO DYNASTIES(1044-1752)

—B: Baganites, Buddhists, and Border warriors.

Myanmar's first unified kingdom rose under the **Bagan Dynasty**, founded in 1044 by powerful **King Anawrahta**, who decreed Theravada Buddhism as the state religion. The kingdom expanded under the powerful king, reclaiming the Mon capital of Thaton in 1057. Under **King Alaungsithu**, Theravada Buddhism became increasingly dominant, allowing for the establishment of a unified and stable social system based at Bagan's peak during the early 13th century. Now seen as the **"classical age"** of Bagan, the dynasty saw the building of an estimated 3000 temples, 100 of which still stand today. The beginning of the end of the empire was marked by the Mongol invasion of 1287 by **Kublai Khan**.

1044
Bagan Dynasty established under King Anawratha

10-12c
Classical Age; 3000 temples built

1287
Mongol Invasion of lower Myanmar

1546
Tabinshweti reunifies Myanmar

1752
Toungnoo dynasty falls

18c
Border wars with Siam

In the 16th century, Burmese forces rose again. Declaring himself king, **Tabinshwehti** reunified Myanmar under the **Toungoo Dynasty** and established its capital at Pegu in 1546. But frequent wars with the Thai kings and the Arakanese minorities led to the fall of the Toungoo rulers in 1752. **Alaungpaya** emerged as a powerful leader against the Toungoo and regained control of Myanmar, establishing the new city of Yangon. Following Alaungpaya's death in 1760, however, border conflicts escalated to war with Siam. **King Hsinbyushin** conquered Ayutthaya in 1776 and killed the king of Siam, creating an enmity that still festers today. Ayutthaya, however, was soon lost again to Thai forces.

King Bodawpaya's tyrannical reign saw several failed attempts to re-invade Siam. His frustration with the failed invasions turned into religious persecution against anyone breaching strict Buddhist doctrine, and he declared the death penalty for smoking opium. The second Burmese invasion of the Arakan region, bordering British territory in India, instilled fear in the British that Myanmar would continue to expand.

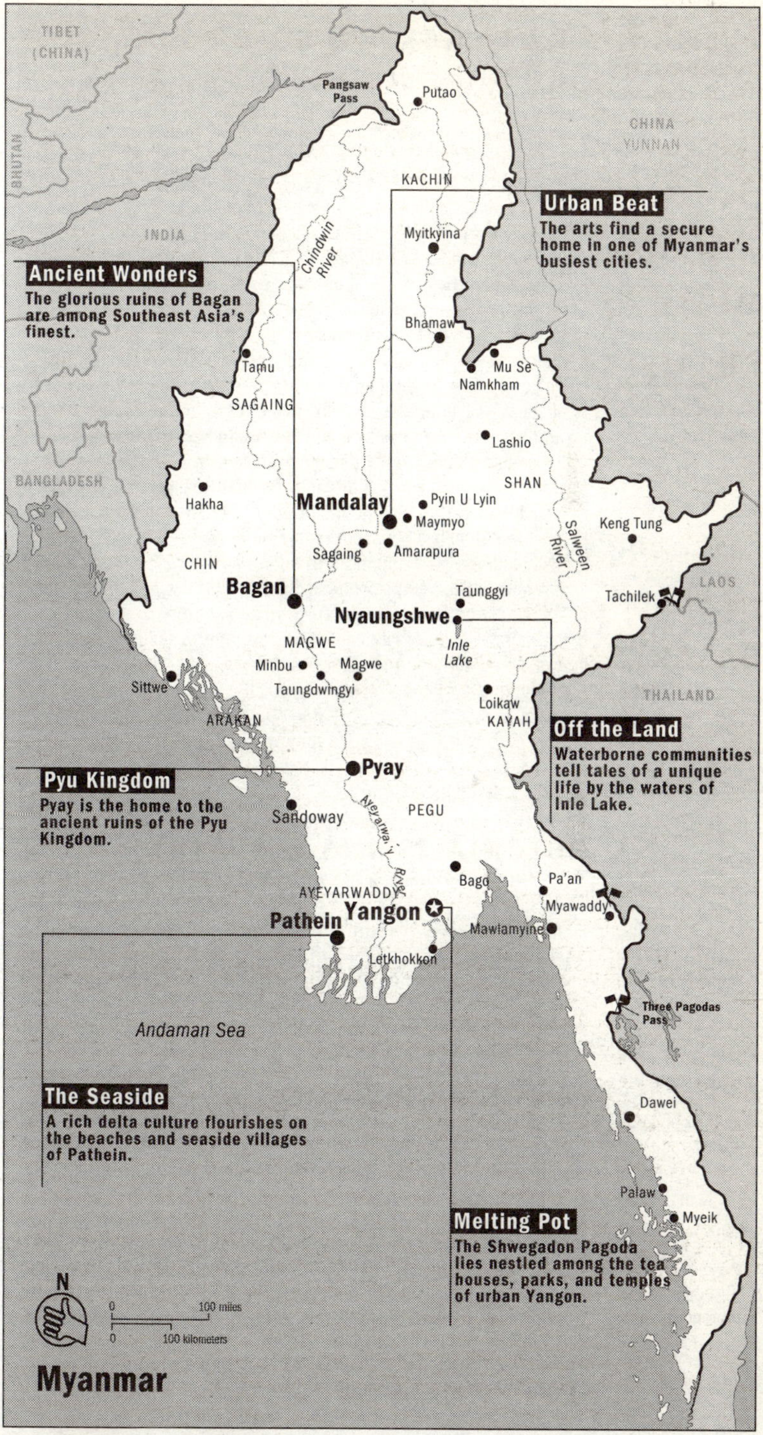
TIBET (CHINA)
Pangsaw Pass
Putao
CHINA YUNNAN
BHUTAN
KACHIN
INDIA
Urban Beat
The arts find a secure home in one of Myanmar's busiest cities.
Myitkyina
Chindwin River
Ancient Wonders
The glorious ruins of Bagan are among Southeast Asia's finest.
Bhamaw
Mu Se
Namkham
Tamu
SAGAING
Lashio
BANGLADESH
SHAN
Hakha
Mandalay
Pyin U Lyin
Maymyo
Keng Tung
Salween River
Sagaing
Amarapura
CHIN
Bagan
Taunggyi
Tachilek
LAOS
Nyaungshwe
MAGWE
Inle Lake
Minbu
Magwe
Sittwe
Taungdwingyi
Loikaw
THAILAND
ARAKAN
KAYAH
Off the Land
Waterborne communities tell tales of a unique life by the waters of Inle Lake.
Pyay
Pyu Kingdom
Pyay is the home to the ancient ruins of the Pyu Kingdom.
Sandoway
Ayeyarwady River
PEGU
Bago
Pa'an
AYEYARWADDY
Myawaddy
Yangon
Pathein
Mawlamyine
Letkhokkon
Three Pagodas Pass
Andaman Sea
The Seaside
A rich delta culture flourishes on the beaches and seaside villages of Pathein.
Dawei
Palaw
Myeik
Melting Pot
The Shwegadon Pagoda lies nestled among the tea houses, parks, and temples of urban Yangon.
N
0 100 miles
0 100 kilometers
Myanmar

1782
King Bodawpaya establishes strict Buddhist doctrine

1824
First Anglo-Burmese war

1886
Third Anglo-Burmese war gives British control over Myanmar

1900-30
British Rule

1930
Burmese Liberation movement

1937
New Constitution adopted

1942
Rangoon seized in WWII

1943
Aung San founds AFPFL

1948
Burma gains independence

1950
Civil war breaks out with minority rebel armies

1962
First Military Government; BSPP established

1962
Citizens protest crushed by military

1960s
"Home Guard" police force established

MYANMAR: TO GO OR NOT TO GO? The question of whether or not to go to Myanmar echoes a similar debate that once plagued tourists visiting South Africa under apartheid. Tourism in Myanmar undoubtedly financially supports one of the world's worst military regimes, but the reality for the people of Myanmar is not nearly so simple. In one of Southeast Asia's poorest countries, the fledging tourist industry is, for many, the only alternative to state-sponsored slave labor to eke out a living. Increasingly relaxed tourist regulations mean that an informed tourists can direct their money to Myanmar's people, not to its repressive government (See **Keeping the Bucks Where They Belong,** p. 469). Many Burmese hope that more tourists will visit their impoverished nation and bring money with them; some also want travelers to witness the political situation and tell others about it. The Burmese government's abuses are not a new story, yet they have only recently come to the attention of the world after the country opened up to foreign investment and tourism in 1989. Many argue that responsible and informed tourism is a far more effective means to change rather than isolating a military government that then has no incentive to stop its abuse of power.

Nonetheless, it is important to note that Burmese citizens have disappeared or been beaten severely for discussing politics with foreigners, no doubt due to an insidious network of government informants. Military intelligence interrogated a family-restaurant owner for 24hr. after he spoke with tourists who tried to visit one of Myanmar's "no-go" areas. For locals' sake, if you decide to travel to Myanmar, **avoid discussion of politics** and educate yourself about how to avoid empowering the military junta. The choice to travel to Myanmar is yours. *Let's Go* only asks that you make it an informed one.

COLONIALISM (1824–1945)

—C: Colonialism, Conflict, and Constitution

Tension between Britain and Myanmar climaxed during the **Anglo-Burmese Wars** of 1824 and 1852. Britain won both wars and subsequently annexed the Pegu Province, renaming it **Lower Burma.** The third Anglo-Burmese War gave Britain control over Myanmar in 1886; they renamed it "Burma" and made it a province of India with a capital at Yangon, renamed "Rangoon."

During colonial occupation, Britain began fledgling industries in the country, building railways in 1918, mainly seeking to exploit the country's oil and mineral deposits. Education levels increased, especially in monastic studies. Despite these economic boosts, the people of Burma didn't receive many benefits. The British eliminated the monarchy and separated church and state, thereby precipitating the demise of the two primary pillars of Burmese society. An increase in the number of Indian immigrants (already over 7% of the population) began to displace local labor and caused increasing economic duress. Resentment toward the Indians culminated in the violent anti-Indian riots of the Burmese national liberation movement in 1930 as well as in the expulsion of over half a million Indians by the Burmese army during WWII.

1937 saw the adoption of a new constitution that gave Burma control of its own affairs. **Dr. Ba Maw** was elected Prime Minister in 1936 in the first and only election under British control. Burma's abundant natural resources and access road to China made it attractive to the **Japanese** during WWII. Aiming to claim the road and oil resources, the Japanese seized Rangoon in March 1942. As the Japanese began to lose in WWII, they withdrew from Burma in 1943 and installed a puppet government. Meanwhile, Minister of Defense **Aung San** began a movement of organized resistance against the Japanese and planned to achieve complete independence for Burma with his **Anti-Fascist People's Freedom League (AFPFL).**

1980s
Government seeks foreign aid to aid economic recovery

1987
Anti-government riots in Rangoon

1988
SLORC takes over,

1989
"Burma" becomes "Myanmar"

1990
NLD wins elections; SLORC ignores results

1991
Aung San Suu Kyi wins Nobel Peace Prize

1995
Aung San Suu Kyi is released from house arrest

1997
SLORC dissolves; leaves SPDC in power

INDEPENDENCE (1945–1960)

–D: Democracy, Declaration and Division

After WWII, the British took over, suspended the 1937 constitution, and implemented a governor system. As the new leader of the Council of Ministers, Aung San expelled the communists from the AFPFL in 1946 and began to pressure the British to free Burma completely. Slain by right-wing politician **U Saw** in July 1947, Aung San didn't live to see the Union Jack lowered. Under Thakin Nu, the **Burma Constituent Assembly** earned complete independence in September 1947, and the Republic of the Union of Burma was recognized by the British in January 1948.

In opposition to the declaration, communists and other minority factions revolted within Burma, causing the government to lose control of most of the country. In 1948, minority Karen groups rebelled and cut off Rangoon's river, rail, and road communication systems. At the height of the **civil war** in 1950, many nations, including Britain and India, supplied the Burmese government with weaponry and money.

MILITARY RULE (1962–1990)

–E: Ethnicities, Economics, and Elections

In March 1962, **General Ne Win,** tired of threats of secession from ethnic groups, responded by arresting prominent leaders, revoking the 1947 constitution, and establishing a military government. Citizens raged at restrictions on their freedom, and students demonstrated against the military regime at Rangoon University. Under the indirect order of General Ne Win, soldiers fired into the crowds and bombed the Students' Union building, a Burmese nationalist symbol since 1930. Eyewitnesses reported hundreds of bodies strewn across the campus, but the official report cited only 15 deaths and 27 wounded.

To protect Burma from insurgent groups, the government established **Ka Kwe Ye (KKY)**, or "Home Guard," a local militia group supported with help from the area's druglords. Government drug enforcement officials were frequently bribed into dispensing with laws prohibiting opium trade. After General Ne Win retired in 1972, the country sought foreign aid to battle serious economic stagnation caused by the government's economic mismanagement and rampant corruption. By the late 1980s, resource-rich Burma had become one of the poorest nations in the world.

Widespread anti-government riots erupted in Rangoon in October 1987, again accompanied by demonstrations and violent suppression by the military. By March 1988, **Aung San Suu Kyi,** daughter of Aung San, had become the driving force for such movements for democracy in Burma. One of General Ne Win's military groups, the **State Law and Order Restoration Council (SLORC),** took power and sus-

THE ARMY OF SPIRITS In early 1999, two 12-year-old twins named Luther and Johnny, cigars hanging from their mouths and machine guns casually slung over their shoulders, gained international infamy for leading a fundamentalist Christian group of 200 Karen rebels known as "God's Army" near the Myanmar-Thailand border. Their followers swear that the adolescent twins can't be killed by bullets or mine fields. In a Burmese army attack on their village, the twins emerged unscathed from a cavalcade of bullets and defeated the Burmese with what many believe is an "army of spirits" that fights for the messiahs. But this rebel group bit off more than it could chew in February 2000, when it tried to take mare than 100 hostages in a Thai hospital across the border. Not amused, the Thai army launched a secret attack and executed 10 members of the God's Army and brought their bodies out wrapped in white sheets, letting the world know that Thailand doesn't succumb to blackmail. Last heard, the twins entered Thailand asking for refuge and were taken to a Thai refugee camp where their mother awaited their return.

pended the 1974 constitution, revoking the limited autonomy that had been granted to ethnic minority groups. Under the guise of change, a free market "open door" economic policy took effect in late 1988. The dictatorship, under the rule of **General Saw Maung,** changed the name of the nation from "Union of Burma" to "Union of Myanmar" in June 1989. Aung San Suu Kyi was placed under house arrest in July 1989, for speaking openly against the government. Under her leadership, the **National League for Democracy (NLD)** won the majority in the national elections of May 1990, but SLORC refused to honor the election results, jailing most of the party leaders. Aung San Suu Kyi won the Nobel Peace Prize in 1991, and the government released her from house arrest in 1995. SLORC continues to exclude her from negotiations, and she remains under close guard, though her stature in Myanmar is as great as ever.

MYANMAR TODAY

Myanmar has started to broaden its international ties. The government joined the **Association of Southeast Asian Nations (ASEAN)** in July 1997 and established diplomatic ties with China, Indonesia, and the Philippines. Relations with the US and the European Union, however, remain strained due to human rights abuses. SLORC dissolved in November 1997 in order to "speed up economic development," leaving the **State Peace and Development Council (SPDC)** in power. Tensions with minority groups continue to heighten, especially near the Thai border.

Myanmar and Afghanistan together control 90% of the world's opium and are responsible for 60% of heroin in the US. Some 1400kg of heroin (only a small proportion of total production) were seized in Myanmar in 2000 alone. Despite government denial, Myanmar is also thought to be suffering from an AIDS epidemic; in 1995, the World Health Organization estimated that half a million people in the country were infected with HIV.

CUSTOMS AND CULTURE

BAMAHASIN CHIN

Bamahasin Chin describes an idea of an essential "Burmese-ness" that encapsulates Burmese ideals of good behavior. It prizes the subtle and quiet over the loud and direct, knowledge of Buddhist scriptures, respect for elders, discretion in dress and attitudes towards the opposite sex, and the ability to speak idiomatic Burmese. It is unseemly to show too much emotion, especially in public, and loss of temper is seen as a loss of face. The head is considered the most spiritual part of the body, and images of the Buddha, however old, ruined or broken, are sacred above all. The more your *bamahasin chin*, the more respect you'll get, regardless of your station or wealth.

NAT FOR NOW, BUDDHA FOR LATER

Though Buddhism is the state religion, the practice of *nat* worship still remains popular among the people of Myanmar. A *nat* is a traditional animistic spirit and considered the embodiment of a god. The Burmese *nat* has evolved over time into a spirit that can hold power over a place, person, field, or experience; most are still animistic in form, and all possess the power to wreak havoc on life. The Burmese reconcile *nat* worship with Buddhism with an easy maxim: *nat* worship tackles problems in this life, while Buddhism takes care of karma in the life to come. For many, *nat* worship is a way to repent a misdeed in this life and have it not affect one's karma negatively in the next one.

HUMAN RIGHTS

The military government ignored the landslide pro-democracy verdict in the 1990 election and has abandoned human rights ever since. The SLORC has a galling record of human rights atrocities. A full 385 **National League of Democracy** (NLD) members won election to Parliament in 1990, but almost half continue to face exile, imprisonment, or banishment from Parliament. The government stopped **Aung San Suu Kyi's** car in July 1998, as she traveled to visit party supporters. After a six-day standoff during which she received neither food nor water, authorities took the car and drove her back to Yangon. When the top US envoy in Myanmar visited her home, state-controlled newspapers wrote that Aung San Suu Kyi was trying to instigate unrest. Another standoff in August 2000 lasted nine days.

The military junta has banned gatherings of more than five people, established 4pm curfews, sentenced citizens to seven years in prison for hosting unregistered guests, forcibly relocated thousands of citizens to desolate locales, and established forced labor projects. The US Department of Labor cites documented evidence of more than 5 million Burmese forced laborers between 1992 and 1998, many of whom work on tourism projects, including a runway extension at Yangon Airport that inaugurated tourist jet landings in Myanmar. Documented acts of torture include electrocuting a pregnant woman during interrogation, hanging people from electric fans, and tying naked people to blocks of ice.

BISEXUAL, GAY, AND LESBIAN TRAVELERS. There is virtually no acknowledgement of homosexuality in Myanmar. Travelers should be discreet.

ARTS AND RECREATION

ARMT AND ARCHITECTURE

Much of Burmese art is associated with *nats*, deities ranging from ghosts of people to spirits of trees who wreak vengeance on those who frustrate them. The Buddha is the most important *nat*, and thus Buddhist monasteries and temples are lavishly adorned like divine palaces. *Stupas* and brick structures with bell-like apexes characterize architecture from the Mon period. Modern structures show an Indian influence, with thicker apexes that taper to the top. Burmese iconography deals with Buddha's life. Other artwork, including various **sculptures** made of wood, gold, and stone, portrays *nats* and sacred objects.

DANCE AND DRAMA

All-female **dance shows** feature solo performers who sing a shrill-sounding song and dance using their feet, head, and arms to create thousands of movements reminiscent of the Chinese style. Dramatic streetside performances are often ceremonies portraying various *nat* stories. Men dressed as women (and vice-versa) are the dominant performers at these shows. **Marionette theater,** or *yok-thei pwe*, which flourished in the late 18th century, has almost ceased to exist but occasionally appears at temple fairs or local festivals with a lighthearted dance and a more dramatic play.

MUSIC

The Burmese orchestra is dominated by its drummer, who sits within a railing enclosing 21 drums. Other instruments include a gong ensemble, bass and tenor drums, cymbals, and bamboo clappers. In larger orchestras, melody instruments such as oboes or flutes are added. Burmese music characteristically has full sounds and repetitive rhythms and melodies that intertwine in complex patterns.

ADDITIONAL SOURCES

Burma in Revolt: Opium and Insurgency Since 1948, by Bertil Lintner (1994). Unravels the complex relationship between drug trade and the country's ethnic insurgencies.

Freedom From Fear and Other Writings, by Aung San Suu Kyi (1991). A must-read for anyone wishing to familiarize himself with the struggle to bring democracy to Myanmar.

Burmese Days, by George Orwell (1962). A classic. An insightful treatment of colonial Burma, drawing on Orwell's experience as a colonial official in the early 20th century.

ON THE WEB

Myanmar.com (www.myanmar.com). Official government web site has information steeped in propaganda, including a link to the Ministry of Defense that publishes an online ten volume book called "The Truth."

Free Burma (www.freeburma.org). The other side of the story, with links to pro-democracy and activists groups.

Culture and History (www.soros.org/burma/CRISIS/index.htm). The Burma Briefing Book is an excellent overview of recent Burmese history, ethnic tensions, and tales of Burmese culture.

ESSENTIALS

VISAS

Single-entry 28-day tourist visas are required of all visitors. They are issued at Myanmar's diplomatic missions abroad, the most convenient locations being Bangkok, KL, and Hong Kong. Allow 1-3 days for processing times. Once in Myanmar, you can usually get a **visa extension** for up to 30 days.

> **ISIC.** The **International Student Identity Card** (**ISIC;** see p. 14) is useful in Myanmar. Although no consistent policy prevails, presentation of the ISIC often entitles holders to reduced admission prices.

MONEY

The Myanmar **kyat** (pronounced "chat") comes in denominations of 5, 10, 20, 50, 100, 200, 500, and 1000. Particularly in tourism industries and international trade, US dollars and their one-to-one equivalent, **Foreign Exchange Certificates (FECs),** operate as legal tender. FECs are printed in denominations of 1, 5, 10, and 20.

As of July 2001, 1 FEC equals 500-550kyat at the free market rate, while US$1 yielded 570-600kyat. Individual travelers (called "Foreign Independent Travelers" in bureaucratic jargon) are supposedly required to exchange US$300 (£, DM, and traveler's checks also accepted) for 300FEC upon arrival at Yangon International Airport. Doing so puts cold, hard cash straight into government coffers (see **Keeping the Bucks where they Belong,** p. 469). A small "gift" to the desk attendant, however, has been known to allow the traveler to exchange only US$100. Only FEC bought in excess of the US$300 requirement, accompanied by an official receipt, are eligible for reconversion into dollars. Since travelers cannot use kyat to cover accommodation expenses, train, boat, or plane tickets, or admission fees—and US dollars and FEC prove impractical for smaller purchases—a supply of both forms

KEEP THE BUCKS WHERE THEY BELONG

Stupendous sights, vibrant cultures, and the friendliest people in the world aren't enough to draw more than a trickle of tourists to Myanmar each year. "Do not let your tourist dollars pay for SLORC's bullets," urge flyers in Bangkok guest houses, and socially conscious backpackers seem to listen. Many argue that visiting Myanmar may end up helping the vicious regime that controls it, but others counter that educated and responsible tourism may be an agent of change and, more importantly, may transfer valuable and scarce tourist dollars to Myanmar's impoverished citizens who otherwise have no source of income. (See **Myanmar: To go or not to go?**, p. 464) There are simple ways to minimize one's contribution to SLORC and to maximize the portion that goes to citizens who make their livelihood from the tourist industry.

Foreign Exchange Certificates (FECs): The government insists that tourists change US$300 for 300 FECs, the flimsy notes that serve as a second currency in Myanmar. Doing so means trading cold, hard cash to the government. Weaseling out of the requirement was once common but is becoming more difficult. The best way is to arrive on a business visa, which can be obtained at Burmese embassies fairly easily with a letter of sponsorship. Not only will you be entitled to stay for several months, but you also won't have to convert your currency. Visas that indicate that you are on a package tour also exempt you. A small unofficial donation at the FEC counter has been known to help reduce the requirement to $100.

Government-owned agencies: Government run agencies listed in *Let's Go* are marked with a **M**. Using agencies thus marked implies giving money directly to the military government. Private alternatives providing the same services are always listed.

Transportation: Use only privately-run transport. Don't take trains, Myanmar Tours & Travels boats, or Myanma Airways, all of which are state-owned. Look for the **M**.

Accommodation: Stay in private guest houses. **All accommodations listed in this guide are privately owned.**

Sights: Many of Myanmar's sights carry hefty entrance fees, and it's unclear where the cash ends up. If you have an ISIC or student ID card, wave it in front of every attendant you see; some will give discounts. Ticket sellers also tend to neglect their duties very early and late in the day; if you go then, you might not have to pay at all.

of currency is essential; a 50/50 split between US$/FEC and kyat, totaling about US$15 per day, is a good rule of thumb for budget travelers.

The government has fixed the exchange rate at 6kyat to the US$1, but the free market rate hovers around 550kyat, with each US dollar reaping 50kyat more than an FEC. The best places to change money at the free market rate are at officially licensed booths, guest houses, and private travel agencies. Many people will solicit you to change money on the street; not only do you stand a good chance of being cheated, but also police may attempt to interfere. Foreigners aren't much at risk, but local changers in markets have been arrested to prevent black market rates from soaring. Rates in larger cities like Yangon and Mandalay tend to be 10-20kyat better than in smaller towns like Kalow or Nyaungshwe, so it pays to convert before heading into the countryside. Apart from government banks and some luxury hotels and restaurants, credit cards (besides AmEx/V) and traveler's checks aren't readily accepted in Myanmar, so it's necessary to carry hard cash. Credit cards also usually incur an additional fee.

GETTING THERE

BY PLANE. Mingaladon Airport in Yangon is the international gateway to Myanmar for the majority of travelers. **Air Mandalay** (www.air-mandalay.com/), **M Myanma Airlines,** and **Yangon Airlines** (www.myanmars.net/ygnair/) are the major international and domestic carriers.

BY LAND. Refer to the following table for overland border crossings in Myanmar. .

BORDER CROSSINGS. Due to periodic fighting and fickle government regulations, the status of these border crossings changes frequently. Get an update from the nearest Burmese embassy before attempting an overland crossing.

THAILAND. As of July 2001, foreigners could officially enter Myanmar by land from 3 points from Thailand: from **Thachilek** to **Mae Sai** (p. 715) from **Mae Sot** (p. 733) to **Myawaddy,** and from **Sangkhlaburi** to **Phayathonzu** via the **Three Pagodas Pass.** In the past it has also been possible to take a ferry between **Ranong** in southern Thailand and **Kawthaung.** All 3 crossings include customs and immigration checkpoints, and foreigners may be required to exchange US$200 into FECs. Depending on the level of insurgent activity, you may be confined to the immediate area near your point of entry.

GETTING AROUND

The notion of "fixed price" finds few moorings here. It's perfectly legal for bus or linecar operators to charge widely different prices for the same service—don't take it personally. As of July 2001, travelers could travel by land as far northeast as Lashio, as far east as Taunggyi in the Shan State, and as far south as Mawlamyaing. By air, these borders stretch to Myitkyna in the north, Kengtung in the east, Sittwe in the west, and Kawthaung in the south. For more remote regions, such as the otherwise completely off-limits Chin and Kayah States, the MTT may require that you book an expensive tour.

BY PLANE. Air travel is the fastest, safest, most comfortable, and most expensive means of getting around the country. Frequent connections and increasing competition on routes between the major tourist destinations make flying very convenient.The British Foreign and Commonwealth Office bans its staff from the domestic airline **Myanma Airways** and warns others that it is best avoided citing its four accidents since 1998. Preferable are **Yangon Airways** and **Air Mandalay.** Air Mandalay's fares are higher than its competitors, but many travelers will pay extra for its safety and in-flight service standards. Private travel agencies charge 10-15% less than the airline offices.

BY BUS. Bus travel is the cheapest mode of transport. The recent proliferation of private bus lines has led to improvements in comfort and convenience, though no luxury can compensate for the road conditions, some of the worst in Southeast Asia. Book at least a day in advance to reserve a good seat; avoid rows in the back or over wheels. During long journeys (up to 20 hours), the bus will (thankfully) stop several times for food and bathroom breaks.

WHAT'S IN A NAME? In 1988, the State Law and Order Restoration Council (SLORC) changed the name "Union of Burma" to "Union of Myanmar," claiming that "Burma" was a British colonial construction. Indeed, "Burma" is a derivative of "*bamar,*" which refers to the Burman ethnic group, just 60% of Myanmar's population. "Myanmar," the government argues, has a longer history, dating back to the 11th century. This shift was repeated for toponyms throughout the country; thus "Rangoon" became "Yangon," "Pegu" "Bago," and the "Irrawaddy" River the "Ayeyarwady" River. Generally speaking, the international community has accepted the new names. More problematic is the use of "Burmese" as a term for the people of Myanmar, when, in fact, the term refers to one ethnic group. Pro-democracy activists, taking their cue from Aung San Suu Kyi, refuse to acknowledge the change, believing that doing so would implicitly recognize the regime they oppose.

BY TRAIN. All train travel in Myanmar is state-owned and operated. **Myanmar Railways** offers three classes: sleeper, upper, and normal; most travelers find the last intolerable. Fares for beds in sleeper class and reclining seats in upper-class rise considerably but remain fairly competitive internationally. The most trafficked route is the **Yangon-Bago-Thazi-Mandalay** line. An extension from Thazi to **Shwenaung (Inle Lake)** is excruciatingly slow but scenic, and there is also service between Mandalay and **Bagan.**

BY BOAT. Powerful river currents render boat travel impractical for visitors on a limited tourist visa. The journey from Yangon to Pyay takes three days. The only exception is the **Inland Water Transport** boat service from Mandalay to Bagan, which takes 9-14hr. During the dry season, exposed sandbars have snagged boats—inquire about current conditions.

KEEPING IN TOUCH

Myanmar's **postal system** is difficult and unreliable. Sending letters is straightforward and inexpensive (35kyat or less for letters, 25kyat or less for postcards), but mailing parcels is a convoluted, time-consuming process—set aside at least 1½hr. Customers are required to buy regulation boxes and tape at the post office and complete a host of customs and address forms. Packages for specific destinations are only accepted on certain days of the week (Tu, Th to Australia, Europe, and the US; no service to Canada). Fees amount to 900-1100kyat for a 10kg maximum limit to most parts of the world. Many locals hire private agents to handle this process. **DHL** services are available in Yangon and Mandalay.

The **telephone system** further reveals the inadequacies of Myanmar's communications infrastructure. Placing international calls can be accomplished using the expensive IDD services at government telephone offices and private telephone offices, hotels, and guest houses. (Calls to North America about US$6 per min.) Savvy planners who manage to forward itineraries and guest house numbers to acquaintances can receive calls along the way. For **Home Country Direct (HCD)** numbers from Myanmar, refer to the table on the inside back cover of this book.

LOWER MYANMAR

YANGON ရန်ကုန် ☎ 1

Even amid the cacophony of a packed city bus, all heads turn, all conversations stop, and all hands move gracefully to bowed foreheads at the sight of Shwedagon Pagoda. The reverence surrounding Yangon's main landmark captures the extent to which the sacred and social intertwine in the city's social fabric. As the administrative, commercial, and transport hub of central Myanmar, Yangon cradles 6.4 million people. But while other capitals have developed into modernized metropolises, Myanmar's closed-door policies have given way to Yangon's deterioration from its colonial glory days. Dirt paths through backdrops masquerading as jungle villages abruptly give way to a sensory overload of avenues surging with *longgyi*-clad locals forced to pound the shackled pavement to eke out a living. Visitors find themselves immersed in a culture whose rigors can exhaust and whose intersections can befuddle. Just 33km from the ocean via the mighty Yangon River, Yangon is less well-known as one of the great port cities of Southeast Asia.

GOVERNMENT LISTINGS. All government listings are marked with a symbol. Money spent at such establishments goes directly into the government's hands. For more information, see **Keeping the Bucks Where They Belong,** p. 469.

MYANMAR

INTERCITY TRANSPORTATION

BY PLANE

International and domestic flights arrive at **Mingaladon Airport,** 19km northwest of Yangon. There is a US$10 departure tax payable in US$ or FEC. Touts from hotels and transport services mob foreigners exiting the customs and immigration area. **Taxis** monopolize transport into the city. Several companies charge flat rates to most points. **M Myanmar Travel and Tours (MTT)** is high quality but pricey (US$5). They often provide maps. To avoid giving money to the government, walk past the MTT booth to the throng of taxis outside (US$2-4). Beware of drivers offering the lowest fares or anyone who mentions currency exchange. Many are cons looking for naive tourists. Many guest houses, including Motherlands II and White House Hotel, offer free transport for patrons.

I'M LIKE A BIRD...

DESTINATION	FREQUENCY	PRICE	DESTINATION	FREQUENCY	PRICE
Bagan	3 per day	US$90-128	**Kuala Lumpur**	4 per week	US$185-198
Bangkok	4-9 per day	US$75-95	**Lashio**	2 per week	US$110
Heho	2-3 per day	US$75-128	**Mandalay**	6 per day	US$90-138
Hong Kong	2 per week	US$212	**Singapore**	1 per day	US$285

CURRENCY EXCHANGE. After inching through immigration, all passengers (except those on group tours and with business visas) are required to exchange "hard" foreign currency (US$, £, DM) equivalent to 300 Foreign Exchange Certificates (FEC) at the Myanmar Foreign Trade Bank counter. (See **Money,** p. 466.) Money thus exchanged goes directly to the coffers of the state. The recent introduction of AmEx and Visa cash advances and traveler's check acceptance has made it difficult to circumvent this requirement. "Donating" a small sum to the desk attendant, however, has been known to allow passage with the exchange of only US$100. Officials spot-check about half of all travelers' luggage, paying special attention to foreign magazines and periodicals, which could be confiscated.

Several flights and carriers serve each destination. Contact the airlines for exact fares and schedules: **Biman Bangladesh,** 106 Pansodan Rd. (☎27 58 82; open M-F 9:30am-4pm, Sa 9:30am-1pm); **MAS,** Central Hotel, Bogyoke Aung San Rd. (☎24 10 07; open M-F 8:30am-12:30pm and 1:30-5:30pm, Sa 8:30am-1:30pm); **M Myanmar Airways International,** 123 Sule Pagoda Rd. (☎28 97 72); **Silk Air,** Sakura Tower, 2nd fl., 339 Bogyoke Aung San Rd., opposite Traders Hotel (☎25 52 87; open M-F 9am-5pm, Sa 9am-noon); **Thai,** Sakura Tower, ground fl., 339 Bogyoke Aung San Rd. (☎25 54 99; open M-F 9:30am-4:30pm, Sa-Su 9:30am-12:30pm). Most travel agents sell tickets for US$5-10 cheaper than airlines.

Three major airlines serve domestic routes in Myanmar: **Air Mandalay,** 146 Dhammazedi Rd. (☎28 25 61; open M-F 9am-5:30pm, Sa-Su 9am-noon); **M Myanma Airways,** 104 Strand Rd. (☎27 48 74; open M-F 8:30am-3pm, Sa-Su 8:30am-1:30pm); **Yangon Airways,** 22/24 Pansodan St. Contact them for exact schedules.

M BY TRAIN

Yangon Central Railway Station monopolizes Kun Chan St., north of Bogyoke Aung San Rd., between Sule Pagoda Rd. and Pansodan St. Book tickets for **M Myanma Railways** at the station or at the **advance booking office** on Bogyoke Aung San Rd. (☎27 75 03. Open daily 6am-4pm.)

Ordinary-class tickets provide wooden seats. Shelling out a bit more money will buy you a seat in an **A/C upper-class** cabin with video programming. Sleeper trains have two options: the sleeper cars or upper-class sleeper. **Sleeper cars** have A/C and audio, but the **upper-class sleeper,** a four-person cabin, has attached bath, fridge, A/C, audio, *and* video. The **foreigner ticket office** handles same-day bookings; be wary of touts whose prices reflect hefty commissions. (Open daily 9am-

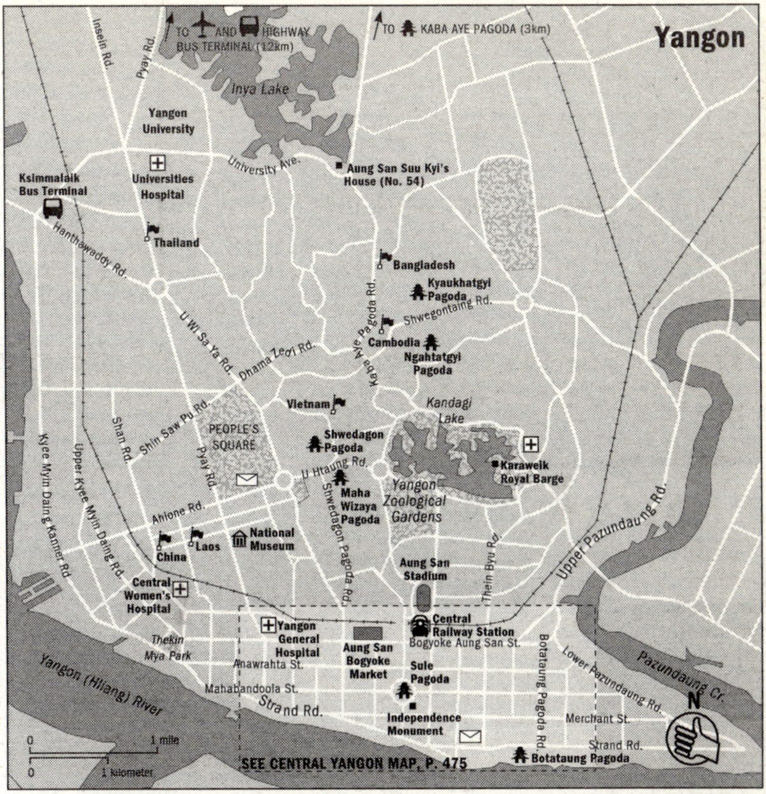

4pm.) The advance booking office takes upper-class and sleeper reservations three days in advance and ordinary-class reservations one day in advance. Making reservations through a guest house or travel agent incurs an additional fee. Trains go to: **Mandalay** (14-15hr.; 7 per day 6am-9pm; upper-class US$30-45, sleeper US$50) via **Bago** (2hr.; US$2, upper-class US$5) and **Thazi** (11-12hr.; US$12, upper-class US$32-35).

BY BUS AND LINECAR

Myanmar's buses are not nearly as comfortable as trains. Expect long, crowded rides. Companies with major long-distance routes operate from the **Highway Bus Terminal,** 18km north of Yangon, past the airport. Tickets, however, should be purchased at branch offices at the south end of Aung San Stadium, north of the railway station. At least seven companies ply the **Mandalay** route (14-15hr., 4-5pm). **Leo Express,** 23-25 Aung San Stadium, on the east side (☎25 20 01; open daily 8am-8pm), and **No. 4,** Room 7D, Highway Bus Terminal (☎24 74 42), have a reputation for the roomiest buses as well as free breakfast, lunch, and dinner (5pm, 2500kyat). Next door to **Rubyland Tourism Services** (See **Practical Information,** p. 438), **Hnin Thu Wai** (☎24 62 83; 19hr.; noon; 2500kyat) and **Ye Thu Aung** (☎64 21 22, ext. 96; 18hr.; 1pm; 2500kyat) both serve **Taunggyi** (Inle Lake). **New Bagan Express** books tickets to **Bagan** (17hr., 3pm, 2500kyat). Both Ye Thu Aung and New Bagan Express book through Rubyland Tourism Services.

Buses and linecars to **Kyaiktiyo** (Golden Mount; 4hr.; 7, 9, 11:30am, 1:30, 3pm; 500kyat) via **Bago** (3hr., 300kyat) and buses to **Pathein** (5hr.; 8:30, 10:30am; 400-500kyat) leave from the **Ksimmalaik Bus Terminal** in northwest Yangon at the intersection of Hanthawady Rd. and Hledan St. Taxis from downtown to the bus terminal cost 700-1000kyat. Buses to **Thanlyin** (1½hr., every 15min. 5:30am-6pm, 30kyat) leave from **Mahabandoola Rd.** near the corner of 37th St., in front of Nilar Win's Cold Drink and Yogurt Shop.

ORIENTATION

Flanked to the south and west by the Yangon River, the capital sprawls over 350 sq. km. In the southern part of town near the Yangon River, the **downtown** area has most accommodations, cafes, services, and markets. The area enjoys a compact grid layout, making navigation by foot feasible. In downtown, the four east-west thoroughfares are, from north to south: **Bogyoke Aung San St.,** the site of the Bogyoke Aung San Market; **Anawrahta St.,** on which City Hall rests; **Mahabandoola St.,** bisected by the **Sule Pagoda Rotary;** and **Merchant St.** The area circumscribed by Bogyoke Aung San and Anawrahta St. is the **top block,** by Anawrahta and Mahabandoola St. is the **middle block,** and by Mahabandoola and Merchant St. is the **lower block. Sule Pagoda Rd.** bisects the downtown area. The short north-south streets in downtown are numbered one to sixty; streets bearing proper names comprise every third to sixth street. **Shwedagon Pagoda** is 4km north of Yangon, while **Yangon International Airport** and the **Highway Bus Terminal** are about 19km northwest.

LOCAL TRANSPORTATION

Buses: Dilapidated and dirty 1970s Korean and Japanese buses provide the cheapest but most uncomfortable transportation. **As most bus numbers are labeled in Burmese numbers, finding the right one can be challenging.** Just for you, there's a Burmese numeral chart below. Open-air **linecars** resembling military vehicles with canvas-covered truck beds (front seat 30kyat, back seat 15kyat), **regular buses** brimming with passengers (5-15kyat), and **A/C buses** (20-30kyat), which mysteriously lack A/C, ply overlapping routes. Fares vary according to distance; after 6pm expect higher linecar fares. Routes include:

#3: Latha Rd. (in the upper block of Chinatown, 20min. west of Sule Pagoda)-Shwedagon Pagoda
#37: Sule Pagoda (leaves from the east side of Mahaboolanda Gardens)-Shwedagon Pagoda
#43, #44 (A/C): Downtown-east side of Kabe Aye Pagoda-Maelamu Pagoda
#46: Shwedagon Pagoda-Kyaukhatgyi Pagoda
#47: Sule Pagoda-Shwedagon Pagoda Rd.-Shwedagon Pagoda-Inya Lake (east side)
#51 (A/C): Mahabandoola Park (Mahabandoola Garden Rd.)-Inya Lake (west side)

BURMESE NUMERALS

1	2	3	4	5	6	7	8	9	0
၁	၂	၃	၄	၅	၆	၇	၈	၉	၀
Cheat Sheet for major routes: #37=၃၇ #43=၄၃ #44=၄၄ #46=၄၆ #47=၄၇ #51=၅၁									

Taxis: Four-door 1980s-style Japanese taxis provide the most convenient albeit expensive transport around Yangon. None have meters; settle on a price before departing. 200kyat or less within downtown. Typical fares from Sule Pagoda to: **airport** (500-600kyat); **Highway Bus Terminal** (500kyat); **Ksimmalaik Bus Terminal** (500kyat); **Shwedagon Pagoda** (300-400kyat). Longer excursions US$30-40 per day.

Trains: A circular train line—cheap and scenic, but neither comfortable nor useful—follows a route from **Yangon Central Railway Station** to **Mingaladon** (near the airport) via **Insein** on the west and **Okklapa** on the east. Five or six trains make the entire loop in each direction daily (2½hr., 6am-5pm, 50kyat), and numerous additional trains make shorter runs throughout the day.

Pedicabs (Sica): In Myanmar's version of the pedicab, the passenger sits next to the pedicab driver. Though exiled from the downtown area, *sica* are easy to track down and convenient for trips around the outskirts of the city, including many of the pagodas. Short distances 50-100kyat. Shwedagon Pagoda to Yangon River 200-300kyat.

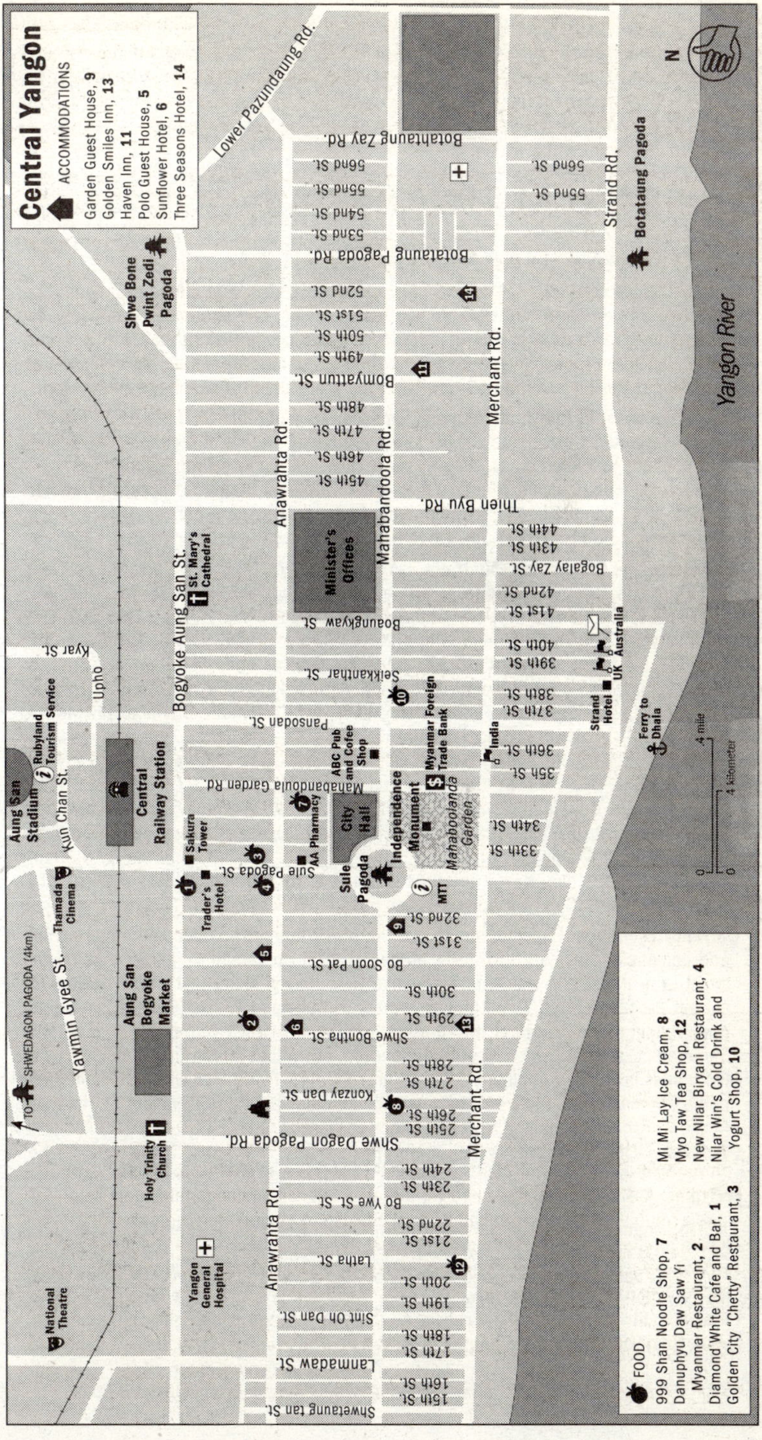
Central Yangon
ACCOMMODATIONS
Garden Guest House, 9
Golden Smiles Inn, 13
Haven Inn, 11
Polo Guest House, 5
Sunflower Hotel, 6
Three Seasons Hotel, 14
FOOD
999 Shan Noodle Shop, 7
Danuphyu Daw Saw Yi Myanmar Restaurant, 2
Diamond White Cafe and Bar, 1
Golden City "Chetty" Restaurant, 3
Mi Mi Lay Ice Cream, 8
Myo Taw Tea Shop, 12
New Nilar Biryani Restaurant, 4
Nilar Win's Cold Drink and Yogurt Shop, 10
TO SHWEDAGON PAGODA (4km)
National Theatre
Yawmin Gyee St.
Thamada Cinema
Kun Chan St.
Aung San Stadium
Rubyland Tourism Service
Upho
Kyar St.
Central Railway Station
Aung San Bogyoke Market
Holy Trinity Church
Yangon General Hospital
Trader's Hotel
Sakura Tower
Bogyoke Aung San St.
St. Mary's Cathedral
Shwe Bone Pwint Zedi Pagoda
Lower Pazundaung Rd.
Anawrahta Rd.
Shwetaung tan St.
Lanmadaw St.
Sint Oh Dan St.
Latha St.
Bo Ywe St. St.
Shwe Dagon Pagoda Rd.
Konzay Dan St.
Shwe Bontha St.
Bo Soon Pat St.
Sule Pagoda St.
Mahabandoula Garden Rd.
Pansodan St.
Seikkanthar St.
Boangkyaw St.
Minister's Offices
Mahabandoola Rd.
Bomyattun St.
Botataung Pagoda Rd.
Botahtaung Zay Rd.
15th St.
16th St.
17th St.
18th St.
19th St.
20th St.
21st St.
22nd St.
23th St.
24th St.
25th St.
26th St.
27th St.
28th St.
29th St.
30th St.
31st St.
32nd St.
33th St.
34th St.
35th St.
36th St.
37th St.
38th St.
39th St.
40th St.
41st St.
42nd St.
Bogalay Zay St.
43th St.
44th St.
45th St.
46th St.
47th St.
48th St.
49th St.
50th St.
51st St.
52nd St.
53nd St.
54nd St.
55nd St.
56nd St.
Merchant Rd.
Thien Byu Rd.
Strand Rd.
Sule Pagoda
MTT
City Hall
AA Pharmacy
ABC Pub and Cofee Shop
Independence Monument
Mahabandoola Garden
Myanmar Foreign Trade Bank
India
Strand Hotel
UK
Australia
Ferry to Dhala
Botataung Pagoda
Yangon River
0 .4 mile
0 .4 kilometer
N

MYANMAR

Ferries: To go to **Letkhokkon Beach** or **Twante** or cross the **Yangon River** to the small town of **Dhala,** known for its furniture, rice, fishing, and excellent views of the port and Yangon skyline, take a M steamer. Once a cheap thrill at 3kyat, the government has now raised the price for foreigners to US$1 each way. Ferries leave from the jetty opposite Strand Rd. from the Port Commissioner building near Pansodan St. (every 10-15min. daily 5am-9pm).

PRACTICAL INORMATION

TOURIST AND FINANCIAL SERVICES

Tourist Offices: M **MTT,** 77-91 Sule Pagoda Rd. (☎28 39 97). State-run organization that arranges tours and travel services (planes, trains, and ferries). Not as useful for general information. Maps 50kyat. Tourist **visa extensions** US$39 for up to 2 weeks. (However, the airport charges US$3 per day for overstaying a visa, so don't get an extension if staying less than 13 days after the expiry date.) Open daily 8am-5:30pm.

Travel Agencies: **Rubyland Tourism Services,** 16 Aung San Stadium (☎24 50 51). One of Myanmar's most established travel companies. Adept at organizing excursions into normally restricted areas. Also arranges buses for many private companies. A reliable source for currency exchange. Open M-Sa 9:30am-4:30pm. **Adventure Myanmar,** 89/91 32nd St. (☎70 47 83), near Sule Pagoda. Long-term car rental with driver. Guide service US$15-25 per day. Open daily 9:30am-6:30pm.

Embassies and Consulates: Australia, 88 Strand Rd. (☎25 18 10). Open M-F 8:30am-12:30pm and 1-4pm. **Bangladesh,** 56 Kaba Aye Pagoda Rd. (☎54 95 56). Open M-F 8:30am-12:30pm and 2-4:30pm. **China,** 1 Pyidaungzu Yeiktha Rd. (☎22 19 26). Consular services open M-F 9am-noon and 2:30-4:30pm. 30-day visa US$25-30. **India,** 545-547 Merchant St. (☎24 06 33). Consular services open M-F 9am-12:30pm. 6-month visa US$55-75. **Indonesia,** 100 Pyidaungzu Yeiktha Rd. (☎25 44 65). Open M-Th 8am-noon and 1:30-4pm, F 9am-noon. **Laos,** A-1 Diplomatic Quarters, Tawwin Rd. (☎22 24 82). Visas US$33, for US citizens US$43. Open M-F 8am-3pm. **Malaysia,** 82 Pyidaungzu Yeiktha Rd. (☎22 18 40). Open M-F 8am-3pm. **Singapore,** 326 Pyay Rd. (☎52 56 88). Open M-F 8:30am-1pm and 2-5pm. **Thailand,** 437 Pyay Rd., 8 Ward (☎53 30 82). Consular services open M-F 9-11:30am. **Vietnam,** 36 Wingaba Rd., Bahan (☎54 89 05). Visas US$50. Open M-F 8-11:30am and 1-4pm. **UK,** 80 Strand Rd. (☎28 17 00). Open M, Tu, Th, F 8:30am-12:30pm and 2:30-4:30pm, W 8:30am-12:30pm. Also serves **New Zealand** citizens. **US,** 581 Merchant St. (☎28 20 55). Open M-F 8am-4:30pm. Consular services open M, W 8-11am.

Currency Exchange: Changing money on the **black market** has become more difficult and complicated since 2000. (See **Money,** p.432) Be careful to ignore cons on the street or at the airport who want to change your money. **Ask guest house owners** for current exchange rates. Guest house owners or **Rubyland Tourist Service,** an authorized changer (see **Practical Information,** p.438), will assist you in finding a reliable free market rate. Discretion is advised, and be aware that locals face a much greater risk under law than foreigners. M **Myanmar Foreign Trade Bank,** 80/86 Mahabandoola Garden St. (☎28 49 11), between Mahabandoola St. and Merchant St., handles AmEx/V cash advances and traveler's check conversion to FEC. US$2 fee for each traveler's check changed. Open M-F 9:30am-3pm.

LOCAL SERVICES

English Language Bookstores: Pagan Book House, 100 37th St., lower block (☎27 72 27). Carries old novels and books on Myanmar. English spoken. Open daily 9am-5:30pm. Numerous **book stalls** line the upper block of 29th St., but non-Burmese language books are rare. The best is **Theingi Maw Bookstall,** 185 29th St. (☎24 63 62), which carries a collection of pulp novels and old magazines. Books 350-1000kyat. Open M-Sa 9:30am-5pm. **Open Eyes Bookstore,** 365 Bogyoke Aung San St., (☎70 05 79), at the corner of Bo Soon Pat Rd, carries 1- to 2-day old issues of the *Bangkok Post* and *Straits Times* and recent issues of *Newsweek* and *The Economist*. Open daily 9am-6:30pm.

Libraries: British Council, 78 Strand Rd. (☎25 62 90), in the same building as the embassy. Operates a small library with current newspapers, magazines, and BBC broadcasts. Open M-F 8:30am-5:30pm, Sa 8:30am-4:30pm. **American Center,** 14 Tawwin St., Dagon (☎22 31 40), has comparable facilities. Open M-F 9am-4pm, Sa 9am-1pm.

EMERGENCY AND COMMUNICATIONS

Emergency: Fire ☎191. **Ambulance** ☎192. **Police** ☎199.

Pharmacies: Super One Pharmacy, 394 Shwebontha St. (☎25 02 68), at the corner of Bogyoke Aung San St. Some English spoken. Pharmacies cluster around here. **AA Pharmacy,** 146 Sule Pagoda Rd. (☎25 32 31), opposite Traders Hotel. **Open 24hr.**

Medical Services: Bahosi Medical Center, 31/36 Bahosi Housing Complex (☎21 16 97), off Bogyoke Aung San St., Lan Madaw. Quality outpatient/inpatient services. Fine English spoken. **Open 24hr.**

Telephones: Calling from Myanmar is difficult; there are nearly no lines of communication into or out of the country. **Telephone/Telegraph Office,** 393 Mahabandoola Rd. (See **Keeping in Touch,** p. 471). Calls booked in 3min. increments; sometimes hour-long delays before connection. It is often easier to make calls and send faxes from **private phone shops** that line every street. Service US$5-8 per min. to most parts of North America and Western Europe. **Telegrams** (4kyat per word) are the quickest and cheapest way to send messages. Take 1-5 days to arrive. Open daily 7am-8pm.

Internet Access: The Business Center at the Traders Hotel, 3rd fl., 223 Sule Pagoda Rd. (☎24 28 28). Allows people to send emails from the hotel's address for US$1 per 5KB and to receive emails sent to that address for US$1 per page. By far the best (and almost the only) deal in town, as the government has only recently introduced Internet access to the country and strongly regulates its use. Open daily 7am-10pm.

Post Office: GPO, 80 Bo Aung Kyaw St., at Strand Rd. Open M-F 9:30am-3pm; closing time isn't set in stone. International airmail available but unreliable. *Poste Restante* on 2nd floor. Do not have valuables sent to you in Myanmar. **DHL** service is available on the 1st fl. of the Trader's Hotel. **Postal code:** 11181.4

ACCOMMODATIONS

Recent privatization of hotel and guest houses has sparked an orgy of construction and the competition has made owners very amenable to bargaining. Budget hotels are scattered downtown, to the west of Sule Pagoda Rd. Prices drop by a few dollars in the low season (June-Sept.) and owners lower prices for longer stays. Prices usually include breakfast.

Golden Smiles Inn, 644 Merchant Rd. (☎27 35 89), between Shwebontha St. and 29th St., on the 2nd fl. behind the door marked "Full Gospel Assembly." Friendly hosts, large breakfasts, and a streetside balcony promise a sociable stay. Large, cozy (though not soundproof) rooms with bath and A/C. Singles US$4-5; doubles US$8-10.

Garden Guest House, 441-5 Mahabandoola St. (☎25 37 79), facing the southwest side of Sule Pagoda. *Primo* location and a gracious staff make up for the 5-story climb. Incredible view of Sule Pagoda from the lobby. Clean, brand-new singles with fans and shared baths US$4, with A/C and bath US$6; doubles US$12.

Polo Guest House, 240 Anawrahta Rd. (☎24 12 52). Entrance on 30th St. Clean, standard rooms with bath and fan. Singles US$5, with A/C US$8; doubles US$10, US$15.

Haven Inn, 216 Bo Myat Tun St. (☎29 55 00), between Anawrahta Rd. and Mahabandoola Rd. Cozy and homey with Western- and Burmese-style breakfasts. Away from the hubbub of downtown. Free transport to and from airport with advance notice. Large, immaculate wood-floored rooms have A/C, fridge, and hot water bath. Singles US$10; doubles US$15.

Three Seasons Hotel, 83/85 52nd St. (☎29 33 04), between Anawrahta Rd. and Mahabandoola St. Personable staff and quality rooms make it worth the extra kyat. Large, spacious rooms with TV, fridge, and A/C. Free airport pickup with advance notice. Singles US$15; doubles US$20; triples US$25.

Sunflower Hotel, 259/263 Anawrahta Rd. (☎24 00 14), of Shwebontha St. Sitting areas offer good views of bustling city streets, but the noise is hard to escape. International phone/fax. Basic singles with shared bath US$5, with A/C US$10; spacious singles with A/C, TV, fridge, and private bath US$15; doubles with shared bath US$15, with private bath, A/C and extras US$20.

FOOD

Yangon's Shan, Burmese, Chinese, and Indian cuisines deliciously reflect the city's ethnic diversity. The quintessential meal includes a savory curry of fish, meat, or vegetables; a soup dominated by gourd or bitter greens; and a plate of steamed rice and boiled vegetables. In the evenings, downtown Yangon overflows with vendors offering snacks. Teahouses, which spill out into the streets, are also great place for cheap eats; most offer pastries and dumplings for 50kyat or less.

RESTAURANTS

New Nilar Biryani Restaurant, 203 Anawrahta Rd., between Sule Pagoda Rd. and 32nd St. Mountainous portions of superb chicken, mutton, and vegetable *biryani* (210-230kyat) served by a restless staff. Just watching the serving mayhem is nearly as satisfying as the fantastic food. Breakfast *chapatis* (60-70kyat) are a great way to start the day. Open daily 4:30am-10pm.

Golden City "Chetty" Restaurant, 170 Sule Pagoda Rd., 1 block north of Sule Pagoda. At meals, a true eating frenzy erupts at this fantastic Indian restaurant. Sizable staff ensures that *biryani* dishes (170-400kyat) are never empty. Open daily 8am-10pm.

999 Shan Noodle Shop, 130B 34th St., between City Hall and Anawrahta St. Best Shan noodles in town. Great for breakfast or a light meal. Savory Shan rice salad 100kyat. Rice or wheat noodles with soup or salad dressing 150kyat. Open daily 6am-7pm.

Danuphyu Daw Saw Yi Myanmar Restaurant, 175/177 29th St., upper block. Great introduction to Burmese cuisine. Steamed butter beans or bamboo shoots 200kyat. Steamed catfish, chicken, and mutton 300kyat. Meals include soup and sides. Open daily 9am-9pm.

TEAHOUSES AND CAFES

Mi Mi Lay Ice Cream, Konzayolan St., lower block, near Mahaboolanda St. Relive your pre-teen years and melt your worries away with two icy scoops. Several flavors 150kyat per bowl. Open daily 11am-8pm.

Diamond White Cafe and Bar, on Bogyoke Aung San St., between 31st and 32nd St., next to the Central Hotel. Hip teahouse by day, popular bar by night, and, simply, *the* place to hang out. Pastries and tea 50kyat. *Dim sum* 100kyat. Open daily 7am-10pm.

Myo Taw Tea Shop, 434 Strand Rd., at the corner of 18th St. next to the Chinese temple. They don't come any more local than this. Tea 30kyat. Savory *shu mai* (dumplings) 30kyat. Scrumptious pork buns 45kyat. Open daily 4am-10pm.

Nilar Win's Cold Drink and Yogurt Shop, 377 Mahabandoola St. (☎27 83 64), between 37th and 38th St. Founded by a famous kickboxer. Excellent way to beat the heat. Avocado salad 150kyat. Refreshing *lassi* 200kyat. Open daily 8am-11pm.

MARKETS

Downtown Yangon is constantly abuzz with **hawkers** pandering their wares to the masses. Each afternoon, vendors meticulously line up their selection of durable goods, from pens to padlocks and pants to parasols before they sit to watch the world go by. Few passersby pay much attention, but those who do are likely to strike a good deal with some bargaining. Most of the action occurs on the main east-west streets off **Sule Pagoda Rd. Streetside shops** provide an alternative to the ever present vendors. North-south streets tend to specialize in a certain merchandise. 31st St., between Mahaboolanda St. and Anawrahta St., sports at least a dozen paper shops, while **Konzaydau St.,** has nearly 20 wall paint stores.

Markets are relatively few and far between in Yangon. **Bogyoke Aung San Market,** clearly the granddaddy of them all, is on the street bearing its name west of the Central Railway Station. This massive space (indoors and out) houses a wealth of clothing and textile stores, carvings and handicrafts sellers, and **government-registered** gem and jewelry shops. A few food stalls in the market satiate hungry shoppers' appetites. Though more popular on weekends, the market remains fairly empty midweek. The result is a buyer's market; bargaining is favorable and recommended, as shopkeepers gear prices toward tourist crowds. (Open daily 9am-5pm.)

> **BUYERS BEWARE!** Buying jewelry from Myanmar essentially requires a purchase from a government shop, since exporting jewelry from the country requires an accompanying government-issued certificate. See **Keeping the Bucks Where They Belong,** p. 469.

SIGHTS

A day in the life of a sightseer: Wake up early and make a trip to **Shwedagon Pagoda** for a glimpse of praying Buddhists before crossing the street to see the Maha **Wizaya Pagoda** commissioned by General Ne Win. After a morning strolling through the gardens around **Kandawgyi Lake,** stop to see the royal **Karaweik Boat.** After lunch, head downtown to the **Sule and Botataung Pagodas,** and catch a glimpse of the sparkling **Strand Hotel.** Cap off the day people-watching on the consumer-filled streets or relax with a cup of tea at one of Myanmar's many teahouses.

SHWEDAGON PAGODA AND ENVIRONS

SHWEDAGON PAGODA ရွှေတိဂုံဘုရား**.** Its colossal spine visible from many points in the city, Shwedagon Pagoda is Myanmar's most sacred structure and Yangon's marquee attraction. As legend has it, two traders from Okkala (as Yangon was known 2500 years ago) traveled to India, where they met the recently enlightened Siddartha Gautama under a *bodhi* tree. When the travelers presented the Buddha rice cakes and honey, he conveyed his wisdom in a sermon and gave them eight of his hairs. Upon the traders' return, King Okkalapa ordered the enshrinement of the hairs in a pagoda on Singutlara Hill. Builders constructed a sequence of superimposed pagodas of iron, marble, lead, copper, tin, silver, and gold, before encrusting the temple in jewels. While the original structure measured only 22m, Shwedagon now reaches 109m.

Leading to the top of the hill are four stairways full of vendors selling overpriced Buddhist paraphernalia, woodcarvings, and palm readings (200-2000kyat). Exquisite **woodwork** and **paintings** depicting scenes from the Buddha's life adorn the stairs. Sixty-four **miniature pagodas,** four larger ones, and several lions and *manokthihas* (twin-bodied, sphinx-like creatures) surround the pagoda. Pilgrims make offerings and pour cups of water on the heads of Buddha statues at eight equally spaced planetary post shrines. In the southeast quadrant stands a *bodhi* tree, supposedly descended from the one sheltering the Buddha's enlightenment in India.

Midday trips yield the fewest crowds, but the best time to see the pagoda is early in the morning or dusk: views are best, temperature is most tolerable, and atmosphere is liveliest. Though a quick tour of the temple grounds takes just 15min., many visitors spend at least an hour absorbing the Buddhist community.

As the heart and soul of religion in Myanmar, Shwedagon also serves as a sort of political icon. In 1988, the honorable **Aung San Suu Kyi** made her first public speech against the government here. (See **History,** p. 462) As a result, the military keeps a watchful eye on the pagoda and government informers pay close attention to contact between locals and foreigners and gatherings of local citizens. (*3km northwest of Sule Pagoda. Accessible via bus #37. Private guides near the entrance to the south staircase give good tours for US$5. No sleeveless shirts or shorts. Remove shoes. Open daily 4am-9pm. US$5 from about 7am-7pm.*)

THANK GOODNESS ITS VENUS-PIG DAY!

The Burmese astrological system is the base principle of the architecture of many pagodas. Eight planetary posts, each corresponding to a point of the compass and a day of the week, line the structure's circumference, while shrines at each post pay homage to a host of galactic and mythical entities.

DIRECTION	DAY	PLANET	GUARDIAN SPIRIT
Northeast	Sunday	Sun	Garuda
East	Monday	Moon	Tiger
Southeast	Tuesday	Mars	Lion
South	Wednesday am	Mercury	Elephant with tusks
Southwest	Saturday	Saturn	Dragon
West	Thursday	Jupiter	Rat
Northwest	Wednesday pm	Rahu	Elephant without tusks
North	Friday	Venus	Pig

A Buddhist's visit to a pagoda usually has a dual purpose: to gain brownie points by doing good deeds and to get insurance against bad luck in the future. A worshipper visits the planetary shrine linked to his birthdate to propitiate its guardian spirit—kind of like giving it a "come hither" look. The ritual consists of pouring cups of water on the image of the guardian spirit (the number of cups depends on the person's age) and reciting prayers. Those especially eager to ward off impending misfortune offer eugenia sprigs, a plant associated with victory, for added protection. The planetary posts of Saturn and Rahu—notorious as evil planets, the latter believed to swallow the moon during eclipses—inspire anxiety and fear.

MAHA WIZAYA PAGODA. In 1980, General Ne Win commissioned the construction of Maha Wizaya Pagoda with public funds. Although it's impressive, with an 11-tier *hti* (the bell-covered cap on the *stupa*) and a hollow interior containing commemorations of Burmese constellations, many locals boycott this pagoda, skeptical of Ne Win's motivations. Believing it to be more a monument to the General than to Buddhism, some jokingly call it—though never too loudly—the "Ne Win Pagoda." *(Near the base of the south entrance to Shwedagon Pagoda.)*

DOWNTOWN YANGON

SULE PAGODA ဆူးလေဘုရား. The center of downtown Yangon, 2000 year-old Sule Pagoda provides a natural starting point for exploring the city's sights. Its Mon name, *Kyaik Athok*, means "the pagoda enshrining the sacred hair" and, sure enough, the pagoda enshrines a hair relic of the Buddha brought by two missionaries from India and presented to Dagon minister Maha Sura. The octagonal shape, unusually tapered to the bell and inverted bowl, architecturally delineates the eight planetary posts of the Burmese zodiac. *(On Sule Pagoda Rd. in the middle of a rotary.)*

MAHABANDOOLA GARDENS. Southeast from the Sule Pagoda rotary, the gardens provide a visual refuge from the surrounding city. A hotbed of student activism during the late 80s, the park now hosts sedate morning *tai chi* and lively afternoon chats. The **Independence Monument** rests at its center. The colonial architecture of **City Hall,** the **Supreme Court,** and the **High Court** surrounds the park. *(20kyat.)*

BOTATAUNG PAGODA ဗိုလ်တထောင်ဘုရား. Over 2000 years old, Botataung Pagoda rivals Shwedagon Pagoda in its antiquity and, like most pagodas in the country, enshrines relics of the Buddha transported from India. Its name, meaning "1000 officers," refers to the military escort these relics received upon their presentation by the king of Syriam. Allied bombing in 1943 almost completely destroyed the temple, but its restored state has a hollow, walk-in center. Mirror-enhanced views of some relics are available, but the most sacred ones are locked below away from view. *(Along the Yangon River on Strand Rd. in the southeast part of town.)*

NORTH TO INYA LAKE

KYAUKHATGYI PAGODA ကျောက်တော်ကြီးဘုရား. The selling point of Kyaukhatgyi "six-story" Pagoda is its enormous, 70m long reclining Buddha. Kyaukhatgyi also lends its name to a famous attached **monastery,** where 600 monks study ancient Buddhist scriptures and Pali language and literature. Opposite Kyaukhatgyi, the shorter **Ngahtatgyi Pagoda** holds a Buddha resting on the grounds of **Ashay Tawya Monastery.** Don't miss the ornate footprint highlighting the distinguishing marks of the Buddha. *(2km northeast of Shwedagon Pagoda on Shwe Gone Thing Rd. Accessible via bus #47. Kyaukhatgyi free, Ngadatkyi US$2.)*

KANDAWGYI LAKE. This breezy lake and its sculpted parks are a godsend amidst Yangon's urban landscape. At the east end is the picture-perfect **Karaweik Boat,** constructed in the 1970s as a replica of a royal barge from the old monarchy days. This 2000-ton, 90m behemoth understandably doesn't float but rests firmly embedded in the lake bed. The main objective in its construction was the revival and preservation of traditional Burmese art; today, it has a restaurant featuring a titanic buffet and traditional dance performances. *(The lake can be reached from Shwedagon Pagoda via U Htaung Bo Rd. 10kyat. Dance performances US$5. Open 6am to 5pm.)*

INYA LAKE. Not to be confused with Inle Lake in Northern Myanmar, Inya's surrounding parks and footpaths are well worth an afternoon's exploration, despite their considerable distance from downtown. Bordering **Yangon University,** it is often closed, but twenty-something couples still sneak around here after sunset. Though off-limits, **Aung San Suu Kyi's house,** which doubled as her prison for years, is at 54 University Ave., on the southeast tip of the lake. *(4km northwest of Kandawgyi Lake.)*

OUTLYING TOWNSHIPS

NATIONAL MUSEUM အမျိုးသားပြတိုက်. A disappointing representation of a nation wealthy in culture and history, the National Museum's five stories teem with lackluster exhibits. Topics include royal regalia, neolithic stone artifacts, clay votive tablets, and other objects from the Bagan period, as well as diverse Buddha images, cave paintings, and information on the cultures of national minorities. The big deal on the ground floor is the 180-year-old Great Lion Throne, originally used in the Mandalay Palace by the last Burmese king. *(66/74 Pyay Rd. in Dagon Township. ☎28 25 63. Open daily 10am-4pm. US$5.)*

KABA AYE PAGODA ကမ္ဘာအေးဘုရား. The first Prime Minister of postcolonial Burma commissioned the building of Kaba Aye Pagoda, nicknamed the "world peace" pagoda. Its five entrances correspond to the four historical Buddhas and the Buddha of the future and lead to an inner chamber sheltering a 500kg silver Buddha image. *(11km north of downtown, past Inya Lake on Kabe Aye Rd. Accessible via bus #43.)*

OTHER SIGHTS. Maha Pasan Guha, adjacent to Kaba Aye Pagoda, is an enormous cave built to hold 10,000 people for the Synod, which commemorated the 2500th anniversary of the Buddha's enlightenment. Adjacent to the cave is a Buddhist university. **Ah Lain Nga Sint Pagoda,** farther northwest in Insein, has a five-story tower on Pyay Rd., opposite the turn-off to the airport.

ENTERTAINMENT

Backpackers seeking a deeper spiritual experience should try **meditation.** Most meditation courses require a 10-day minimum stay for the first retreat. Those with previous experience find it more worthwhile. Travelers recommend **International Meditation Center,** 31A Inya Myaing Rd. (☎53 15 49) and **Chan Mye Yeiktha Meditation Center** (☎66 14 79), north of Inya Lake Hotel on Kaba Aye Rd.

THE LADY AND YOU Any talk of the honorable Aung San Suu Kyi, charismatic leader of the National League for Democracy and the most internationally prominent thorn in the government's side, is taboo. Rather than facing her *mano y mano*, the government seeks a hear no evil, see no evil, speak not-at-all policy in public. The mere whisper of her name suggests anti-government sentiments. Locals who complain about the government hush their voices and hesitate to mention her, even in the privacy of their homes, and the media avoid even negative references to her. If only for the sake of locals, **travelers should tread lightly around this subject.** Mentioning her name may spell trouble for anyone around you. Aung San Suu Kyi's house is off-limits; attempting to visit it might be fun, but **you'll risk deportation and place your guest house proprietor and taxi driver at great risk,** should a driver be crazy enough to take you there. If locals discuss her, they will do so on their own and only when sure of their safety. Follow their cues; when they don't wish to talk further, let it go.

Thamada Cinema, 5 Signal Pagoda Rd. (☎24 69 62), 1 block northwest of the train station, opposite Aung San Stadium. Very popular with locals. Burmese and foreign films (usually in their original language, some in English) play frequently during the day and night. 100-500kyat, depending on seat.

ABC Pub and Coffee Shop, on Mahabandoola Rd. at the intersection with 36th St. Join expats and upscale Burmese at this restaurant/bar and jam to a live band on weekends. Things get cooking around 9pm. Tiger or Myanma Beer 300kyat per glass, 550kyat per bottle. Open daily 11:30am-11pm.

DAYTRIPS FROM YANGON

THANLYIN သံလျင် AND KYAUKTAN ကျောက်တန်း

Thanlyin and Kyauktan, across the Bago River southeast of the capital, are best visited via a loop from Yangon (Yangon-Thanlyin-Kyuaktan-Yangon). Buses and linecars to Thanlyin (1½hr., every 15min. 5:30am-6pm, 30kyat) leave from Mahabandoola Rd., near the corner of 37th St. in front of Nilar Win's Cold Drink and Yogurt Shop. Buses back to Yangon leave from the marketplace (2hr., every 20min. until early evening, 40-50kyat).

For those in need of a breath of country air and rural life after a few days amid Yangon's bustle, the tiny towns of Thanlyin and Kyauktan provide a daytrip's worth of sweet refuge. **Thanlyin** was the base for Portuguese explorer Philip De Brito, who tried to establish a kingdom here in the 1600s before meeting a violent death at the hands of the Burmese. Today, Thanlyin has little more to offer than a bustling marketplace and rustic charm, easily absorbed on a walk through its streets.

From Thanlyin's marketplace, horsecarts make the 3km journey south to **Kyaikkhauk Pagoda,** Thanlyin's primary attraction (600kyat). Get off when you see the large pagoda staircase up the hill at the right of the road. The pagoda's Shwedagon-esque golden spire is a worthwhile sight, but even better are the stunning views yielded by a short walk to the top. On clear days, you can see over the surrounding peanut groves and across the delta to Shwedagon Pagoda.

The road in front of the pagoda continues 10km or so to **Kyauktan.** This quaint collection of wooden houses has a lively marketplace and tasty restaurants along the breezy riverbank. On an island in the middle of the river, **Yele Pagoda,** the highlight of the greater Yangon area, dominates the view from the village. The pagoda is a collection of shrines, some of which feature pictures of Myanmar's famous pagodas—if nothing else, nice teasers for up-country forays. To get to the pagoda, buy a round-trip boat ticket (30kyat) at the pavilion on the shore opposite the pagoda. Boats leave when full. Remove shoes before stepping ashore. (US$1 if someone happens to be manning the admission booth, free otherwise.) Opposite Yele Pagoda on a small hill overlooking town, **Kyauktauk Pagoda's** pavilion is a nirvana for the heat-sensitive as it receives steady waves of cool, blustery wind.

TWANTE တွံတေး

To get to Twante, cross the Yangon River to Dalah from the jetty on the intersection of Pansodan and Strand Rd. (every 20min. 5:20am-8:40pm, US$1) and take a linecar to Twnate (1hr., every 30min. 6am-5pm, 50-70kyat). Taxis go for 4000-5000kyat round-trip.

Pottery aficionados will enjoy the village of Twante and its fascinating craft industry. Artisans operate from thatch-roof sheds throughout the Oh Bo District, eager to sell their inexpensive wares. **Shwesandaw Pagoda** (ရွှေဆံတော်ဘုရား) features a 76m golden *stupa* that rivals Shwedagon in antiquity, plus a small display of antique pottery and royal artifacts from the Mon and Burman kingdoms. A "wish-fulfilling" station marks a corner of the pagoda and commemorates the defeat of King Bayinnaung's uprising. *Sicas* cluster around the marketplace and peddle to the Oh Bo District or Shwesandaw Pagoda for around 100kyat.

LETKHOKKON BEACH

To get to Letkhokkon, cross the Yangon River to Dalah at the jetty on the intersection of Pansodan and Strand Rd. (every 20min. 5:20am-8:40pm, US$1) and then take a linecar to the beach (3hr., every 1-2hr., 300kyat). Poor road conditions prevent linecars from running as regularly in the rainy season (June-Oct.). In such cases, the only option is to hire an expensive taxi (5000kyat each way).

Given that most travelers confine themselves to Yangon, Mandalay, Bagan, and Inle Lake, it's likely that Letkhokkon Beach will remain off the beaten path for some time. While the rainy season (June-Oct.) brings mud and fewer sunbathing opportunities, the dry season reveals the town's appeal: fresh air, powdery sand, fine views, and invigorating breezes. The water, while certainly clean enough for swimming, often looks murky because of silt discharged by the mighty delta. **Letkhokkon Beach Hotel,** the only place to stay as of summer 2001, maintains well-kept bungalows. (☎247 538. Singles US$24; doubles US$36.)

BAGO (PEGU) ပဲခူး ☎052

There are two Bagos. The Bago at eye-level is a hot but endearing little country town with a nondescript main street and exceptionally polite residents—a place for napping through the midday heat and sipping drinks with locals at the riverside teahouse in the evenings. The Bago seen from above—from the upper reaches of the Mahazedi Pagoda or a guest house rooftop—floats in a sea of rice paddies and wilderness that stretches out of sight, peppered in every direction with gleaming pagoda spires and dominated by the Shwemawdaw Pagoda, Myanmar's tallest *stupa*. Come to see both—the Bago of today, provincial in scope and influence, and the Bago that exists only in legends and glittering ruins.

TRANSPORTATION

The **train station,** 250m west of the river and 100m north of the Main Rd., runs connections to **Mandalay** (14hr.; 4 per day 7:45am-10:45pm; standard US$11, upper-class US$30) and **Yangon** (2hr.; 8 per day 1:45am-7:20pm; standard US$2, upper-class US$5). The bustling **Main Rd.,** has **linecar** and **bus service** to Ksimmalaik Bus Terminal in **Yangon** (2hr.; every 15min. 6am-6pm; 150kyat, front seat 300kyat). Many travelers choose to stop in Bago to break up the long journey between Yangon and up-country destinations. Those wishing to continue by bus to Mandalay can arrange tickets at Myananda or San Francisco Guest Houses, or the first floor of Emperor Motel for 2000-2500kyat. Book one day in advance.

ORIENTATION AND PRACTICAL INFORMATION

As Main Rd., a section of the **Yangon-Mandalay Hwy.** slicing through the heart of town from southeast to northwest, enters Bago from Yangon, it passes sights and the railway before reaching many accommodations. The shop- and restaurant-lined thoroughfare continues for 200m to the river, just before the center of the town. Continuing northward on Main Rd. leads to a small **clock tower** near a fork in the road. To the left, Main Rd. continues towards Mandalay and the **Shwemawdaw Pagoda.** The right fork leads to: **Myanmar Economic Bank,** which exchanges travelers checks to FEC at a 5% commission rate (☎212 97; open M-F 9:30am-3pm); the **post office** (open M-F 9:30am-4pm); and **Myananda Pharmacy,** marked by a blue-and-white Burmese sign below Myananda Guest House (open daily 5am-9pm).

ACCOMMODATIONS

Three guest houses and a motel vie for the patronage of budget travelers. All are near the train station. The best choice is **Myananda Guest House,** 10 Main Rd., which has clean rooms, provides information on Bago and Kyaiktiyo, and arranges cheap car transport. (☎222 75. Singles with fan US$3, with A/C US$4, with private bath US$5; doubles US$6-8, with private bath US$10.) For an extra dollar or two, the comfortable **Emperor Motel,** opposite Myananda Guest House, has spic'n' span rooms, a friendly staff, excellent views, and a helpful travel agency in the lobby. The only drawback is the crew of pushy *sica* drivers who congregate near the entrance. (☎230 24. Singles US$5-10; doubles US$10-20.) **San Francisco Guest House,** 14 Main Rd., a half-block south of the other two, has cheaper, dimmer, and older rooms and extensive travel information. Rooftop rooms afford stupendous views. (☎222 65. US$2-5.) Popular with Burmese vacationers, **Silver Snow Guest House,** 527 Main Rd., before the clock tower on the other side of the bridge, offers basic rooms and fewer tourist services. (☎221 13. Rooms with shared bath US$5, with private bath US$8, with A/C US$15.)

FOOD AND NIGHTLIFE

A number of decent tourist-oriented restaurants line Main Rd. between the railroad tracks and the clock tower. **Panda Restaurant,** next to the bridge, and **Three Fire Restaurant,** next to the Emperor Motel, serve up a massive array of chicken, beef, prawn, and noodle dishes (250-600kyat). For Burmese food at its best, try **Cho Pyone Family Restaurant,** on Main Rd. before the clock tower; look for the orange "Crusher" sign. A full spread of curry, soup, and vegetable sides costs 250-300kyat. (Open daily 8:30am-8pm.) For a lively after-dark atmosphere, open-air **Ngwe Pon Gyi Cafe,** next to the bridge on the east bank of the river, serves mouth-watering pastries with coconut, peanut, pork, or lotus paste (25-50kyat) and tea. (Open daily 6am-6pm.) A number of **"Beer Stations"** and cafes fuel all-male socializing for young and old alike. Taps flow freely near the bridge and around Shwemawdaw Pagoda.

SIGHTS

Though the town's atmosphere merits a few days' stay, Bago's sights can be covered in a day or less. Energetic travelers do a walking tour of the sights (about 8km total), but the best way to soak in the town's atmosphere is by bicycle or trishaw. Rent the former at San Francisco Guest House (200kyat per day); hire the latter for 500-1000kyat per day. **Manni** is an exceptionally popular driver—guest house owners will help locate him, though he will likely find you first. Attractions stay open daily 5am to 9pm. Most cost US$2, but paying US$6 at any sight buys a ticket to all of them. On the other hand, by visiting early (before 7am) or late (after 7pm) it may be possible to avoid paying altogether.

A morning journey to the **Shwethalyang Buddha** sheds light on Buddhist prayer rituals, and the nearby pagodas, monasteries, and **ordination hall** illustrate Buddhist history and architecture. This part of the village is a fascinating area to see the Myanmarese way of life and enjoy the countryside, which can easily take half a day. Stop in the **market** for lunch on the way to **Shwemawdaw Pagoda** and **Hinthagone Hill,** which are best-visited under the late afternoon sun, when locals come to pray.

CARE FOR SOME MOUTHWASH? The sight of Myanmar's men and women spewing crimson liquid from their mouths or a bloody-red grin is not indicative of a gum disease epidemic. It is however, an epidemic of tradition. *Betel nuts*–the nut of the areca palm stuffed into betel vine leaves–comprise a social activity similar to chewing tobacco. A leafy green wad, characterized by a pungent, unmistakable odor, is removed from a small storage box or can and crammed between the gums and cheek, where it steeps for up to an hour. Instead of swallowing their now-caustic saliva, users project the mess onto streets and sidewalks (watch your step!), creating sanguine scars for the streets.

SHWEMAWDAW PAGODA. Contrary to popular belief, Shwedagon Pagoda is not Myanmar's tallest. Monopolizing Bago's skyline at 114m, impressive Shwemawdaw Pagoda wins the title by 5m. Over 1000 years old, it was constructed to enshrine two hairs of the Buddha bequeathed to two merchant brothers. After an earthquake leveled the structure in 1930, successive reconstructions propelled it to its present height in 1953. The pagoda is a fascinating mecca of modernization and tradition, well worth the trip. The grounds contain electric contraptions including revolving boats and bobbing serpents set amid glittery waves designed to collect projectile coin and paper money donations. *(US$2. Free after sunset. Camera fee 50kyat; video fee 200kyat. Walk 2km from Bago up Main Rd. and turn right past the clock tower.)*

SHWETHALYANG BUDDHA. Debate rages over which of Bago's sights is more awe-inspiring—the massive Shwemawdaw Pagoda, or the colossal 55m by 16m Swethalyang Buddha (reclining Buddha). Built in 994, it languished in decay until King Dhammaceti ordered its restoration in the 15th century. By 1900, it again stood in disrepair and underwent a sweeping face-lift. Colorful murals along the entrance recount the events inspiring its original construction. *(From the center of town, cross the train tracks and turn onto the right-hand turn-off; it's 2km down. US$2; camera fee 50kyat; video fee 200kyat.)*

HINTHAGONE HILL. East of Shwemawdaw Pagoda is a smaller pagoda on Hinthagone Hill. According to legend, two *hamsa* birds perched over the water here, fulfilling a prophecy of the Buddha. Over the years, the river and surrounding delta shifted course, and that fated spot emerged as the summit of the huge hillock and the center of the ancient Mon kingdom.

KALYANI SIMA (SACRED ORDINATION HALL). A tranquil, wooded respite from linecars and teashops awaits at these temple grounds on the way to Swethalyang Buddha. While its present incarnation is only 48 years old, the hall stands on the site of one of the oldest structures of its kind in Myanmar. King Dhammaceti, an ardent supporter of Buddhism, sent monks to Ceylon in 1475 for re-ordination by the famed Mahavihara sect. Upon their return, he commissioned the building of Kalyani Sima, and monks consecrated the site with sand from the sacred Kalyani River. West of the ordination hall stand 10 huge stone pillars covered with inscriptions in Pali and Mon. Scholars prize the pillars for their insights into the early history of Buddhism in Myanmar and the role of Buddhism in 15th century Bago and Ceylon. *(On the road to Shwethalyang Buddha, roughly halfway on the left.)*

MAHAZEDI PAGODA. In 1560 this pagoda enshrined a tooth of the Buddha obtained from Ceylon. Fifty years later, the relic was captured and taken north to Sagaing. Male visitors are allowed to climb to the *stupa's* upper echelons to see Bago's finest views. In the vicinity, a handful of interesting pagodas warrant a visit for those with time. *(Continue past the front of the Shwethalyang Buddha and turn left at the "T"-intersection; it's a few hundred meters down at the end of the road. US$2.)*

KYAIKPUN PAGODA. Also built by the ever-building King Dhammaceti, Kyaikpun Pagoda features an unusual design of four 30m Buddhas sitting back-to-back against a pillar. *(3km southwest of Bago, off the Yangon-Mandalay Hwy. US$2.)*

MARKETS

Two blocks off Main Rd. behind Emperor Motel, Bago's day and night markets don't offer much besides raw vegetables and hygienic supplies, but the area starts moving after sunset and is worthwhile if one doesn't mind the constant attention from locals. Escape to the nearby teahouses if it gets to be too much.

DAYTRIP FROM BAGO

KYAIKTIYO PAGODA (GOLDEN MOUNT)

The trek begins at a base camp in Kyaiktiyo, 65km east of Bago. Taxi, available at Myananda or San Francisco Guest Houses (4hr., US$20). Buses or linecars are trickier and less comfortable though cheaper. Go from Bago to Kyaiktiyo by bus or linecar (3-4hr., 400-600kyat), then from Kyaiktiyo to the base camp by linecar (40min., 70kyat), and finally from the base camp to the pagoda area by truck (45min.; last truck to the top 4pm, last truck back 6pm; 150-400kyat). Buses run from the base camp to Yangon via Bago (3 per day in dry season, 1 per day in wet season). Buses leave Kyaiktiyo for Yangon (6, 6:30, 8am, noon; 500kyat). Trains also go from Bago to Kyaiktiyo (#81, 3hr., 6am).

At 7.3m, Kyaiktiyo Pagoda soars above other Burmese pilgrimage sights in terms of popularity, altitude, and significance. Perched on a colossal golden boulder balanced on the edge of a cliff, the pagoda, like most Myanmarese pagodas, claims to enshrine a hair of the Buddha passed on to a hermit monk. After tucking away the relic in his own hair knot for safekeeping, the monk set out to fulfill the Buddha's final request: to erect a pagoda housing the sacred hair on top of a rock resembling the Buddha's head. It's often said that the power of the hair alone prevents the boulder from toppling off its base. A careful look reveals a deceptively small area of contact upon which, as the caretakers readily demonstrate, the mount rocks back and forth on the pivot point. Adding to the sight's appeal, the journey to Kyaiktiyo Pagoda is breathtaking.

Reaching the Golden Rock from the base camp is an adventure. Trucks rumble out of the base camp around 7 or 8am, earlier in the high season. There are no seats in the back; passengers simply bunch together on the floor of the open air cargo bay. The trucks are not allowed to take foreigners all the way to the summit, who must make a steep 45min. trek up the road, either on foot or aloft a chair carried by bearers (US$5). Reliable footwear is essential. The US$6 fee is payable at a checkpoint at the top. It is also possible to join the pilgrims who trek from the base camp to the pagoda. The scenic but steep 13km climb takes 4-8hr. Locals at the base camp will point you towards the path. Kyaiktiyo is best visited, though overrun with pilgrims, in the cool season. Visitors taper off considerably in the rainy season, but the journey to the top is more arduous and the views less expansive. Trucks to the pagoda rarely fill up in the afternoons (either way), leaving visitors no choice but to walk or wait for the last trucks up (4pm) and back (6pm). It is not recommended that travelers begin hiking up after 1pm or down after 2pm.

Those who wish to spend more time visiting Kyaiktiyo can stay overnight at the base camp. This is necessary during the rainy season since fewer options remain to get to Bago, but the quiet village is a refreshing change from busier towns and cities. This option also allows for the possibility of witnessing the sunrise or sunset or for reaching the top by foot. **Sea Sar Guest House,** in the middle of the main road of the base camp, has basic rooms for 500kyat and more furnished bungalows with private bath and A/C in the dry season for US$3-10. There are plenty of English-speaking restaurants and teahouses in the area.

PATHEIN ☎42

Known as the jewel of the Ayeyarwady Delta, Pathein was once a Mon stronghold but lost its prominence under the Burmese Empire. Today, Myanmar's fourth largest city is known for its parasol workshops, rice production, and friendly Karen, Rahkine, and Burmese population. There aren't many sights, but with at a relaxed pace, fascinating home industries, and some of the most hospitable people in Myanmar, Pathein is a welcome respite.

DON'T LEAVE HOME WITHOUT IT. Unlike other towns listed in this book, entering Pathein requires passing an immigration checkpoint. Buses stop upon entering town, and valid **visas** are required for entry. If you've overstayed your visa, you'll be sent back to Yangon.

TRANSPORTATION. The **highway bus terminal** is several kilometers south of the town center. **Jeeps** run between the terminal and town (20kyat). **Buses** to **Chaungtha Beach** (2-3hr.; 7, 11am, 1pm; 400kyat) leave from Shwezedi Rd., between Merchant St. and Mingyi Rd. Buses to **Yangon** (6hr., 1 per hr. 5am-2pm, 600-1000kyat) leave from the corner of Mingyi Rd. and Two Pagodas St., north of Mahabandoola Rd. Buy tickets one day in advance. The **train station,** on **Station Rd.** three blocks south of Mahabandoola Rd., offers connections to **Hinthada** (4hr., 4:30pm, 105kyat). **Trishaws** charge 50-100kyat anywhere in the city and provide the only other reliable method of transport, besides your feet.

ORIENTATION AND PRACTICAL INFORMATION. Pathein Hwy. enters Pathein from the east and becomes **Mahabandoola Rd.** as it approaches the heart of the city. A **clock tower** stands at its intersection with **Merchant Rd.,** two blocks before Mahabandoola Rd. ends at **Pathein River** (north-south). **Strand Rd.** runs alongside the river, perpendicular to Mahabandoola Rd. **Shwemokhtaw Pagoda** sits in the middle of Merchant, Strand, Mahabandoola, and Shwezedi Rd. **Myanmar Commercial Bank,** on Shwezedi Rd. opposite the pagoda, converts cash and checks to FEC at the fixed rate. (☎210 81. Open M-F 10am-2pm.) Several **pharmacies** (open daily 8am-9pm) cluster opposite the **hospital,** on the corner of Mahabandoola and Mingyi Rd. (parallel to and one block east of Merchant Rd.). The **telephone** and **post office** are on Mahabandoola Rd., one block west of the clock tower. **Postal Code:** 10011.

ACCOMMODATIONS AND FOOD. Of the four facilities authorized to house foreigners in Pathein, **Taan Taan Ta Hotel,** 7 Merchant St., near the corner of Shwezedi Rd., is the best buy. (☎222 90. Well-kept singles with fan US$3; doubles US$4; special doubles with bath, A/C, and TV US$6.) **Pamawady Inn,** 14A Mingyi Rd., is polished but slightly overpriced in the dry season, though quite reasonable in the rainy season. (☎211 65. Singles with fan US$4-7; doubles US$5-10, with A/C US$6-15, with attached bath and TV US$10-20; quads US$30.) **Delta Guest House,** 44 Mingyi Rd., though not quite as nice as Taan Taan Ta, is another good bargain, boasting clean rooms and a warm staff. (☎221 31. Singles with fan US$3, with A/C and bath US$5; doubles US$6/8.) The most expensive and well-groomed place in town is the motel-style **Pathein Hotel,** on Mahabandoola Rd. several kilometers from the town center, next to a golf course. (☎225 99. Doubles with large bathrooms, A/C, and TV US$25; 2 people US$40.) **Electricity is sporadic everywhere.**

Pathein's restaurants are not accustomed to catering to tourists, so don't be surprised when restaurant owners stare at you, shocked. Good eats, however, are plentiful. **Amayar Restaurant,** 44 Mingyi Rd., near the corner of Myenu Rd., and **Khe Kha Gyi,** 68 Mingalar St., opposite the east entrance to Shwemokhtaw Pagoda, both serve excellent, full spreads of Burmese food for around 250kyat. (Open daily 9am-9pm.) For regional Asian cuisine, try the **Morning Star Restaurant,** on Myenu Rd., where curry and thin wheat noodle soup cost 150-200kyat each.

SIGHTS. Shwemokhtaw Pagoda, at the intersection of Shwezedi and Merchant Rd., and the smaller Buddha figures along its perimeter create a serene spiritual scene. Though smaller than its cousins in Yangon and Bago, Shwemokhtaw's sequined designs prove that size doesn't matter when it comes to beauty. **Settayaw Pagoda,** off Pathein Hwy. as you enter the city, which pays homage to the footprint of the enlightened one, and **Twenty-Eight Pagodas,** featuring 28 images of the Buddha, both deserve a look by travelers craving for more splendid Buddhist abodes. Countless other small pagodas sit amidst the twisting back roads of Pathein; locals can help point the way.

Pathein is known to make Myanmar's most decorative parasols, and two **parasol workshops** along Shwezedi Rd. near Mingyi Rd. detail the fascinating production process. (Open daily 9am-7pm.) Guides near Shwemokhtaw help tourists find the string of family-run shops that sell the colorful umbrellas. On Strand Rd. near Mahabandoola Rd., Pathein's massive **night market** sells everything from vegetables to bicycle tires. (Open daily 5-9pm, closed during rainy season.)

DAYTRIP FROM PATHEIN: CHAUNG THA BEACH. Ranked by most visitors as one of Myanmar's best beaches (after hard-to-reach Ngapali Beach in Rakhaine State), Chaung Tha's sand and surf attract visitors—Burmese and foreign alike, but mainly Burmese—seeking idyllic respite from Yangon's city bustle. When the monsoon hits, however, poor weather dampens spirits as well as the beach's appeal. Nestled in the Bay of Bengal, Chaung Tha can be reached by **bus** from Pathein (2-3hr., 500kyat).

UPPER MYANMAR

GOVERNMENT LISTINGS. All government listings are marked with a **M** symbol. Money spent at such establishments goes directly into the government's hands. See **Keeping the Bucks Where They Belong,** p. 469.

MANDALAY မန္တလေး ☎02

Sprawling, dusty Mandalay may not exactly be eye candy, but the joy of Myanmar's second-largest city lies not in its appearance but in the cultural fabric woven into its patchwork grid of streets. The last capital of Myanmar before British rule, Mandalay retains the artistic traditions that were once the object of royal patronage, and quarters of the city still brim with performers and artisans. Daytime affords opportunities to observe wood carvers, weavers, and gold leaf workers, and the night brings out performers who stage marionette and traditional variety shows. Four nearby towns provide escape from the bustle and invite travelers to linger for a few days before slipping off to a more sedate respite on Inle Lake or Bagan.

INTERCITY TRANSPORTATION

BY PLANE

Mandalay International Airport (☎347 07) is a distant 35km south of the city center. (Taxi into town US$10-15.) **Air Mandalay** (☎315 48; open M-F 8:30am-5pm, Sa-Su 8:30am-1pm), on 82nd St. between 26th and 27th St., flies to: **Bagan** (6:20pm, US$48); **Heho/Inle Lake** (9am, US$48); **Yangon** (1½hr.; 9am, 5pm; US$138). **M Myanma Airways** (☎362 21; open M-F 9:30am-4:30pm, Sa-Su 9:30am-4:30pm), on 81st St. between 25th and 26th St., flies to: **Bagan** (25min., 9am, US$40); **Heho/Inle Lake** (M 3:10pm, W 9:40am; US$35); **Yangon** (M, Tu, Th-Sa 8am; W, Su 6:30am; US$100). Tickets bought one day in advance are only sold between 9:30-10:30am. **Yangon Airways** (☎360 12; open daily 9am-5pm), on 78th St. between 29th and 30th, opposite the train station, flies to **Heho/Inle Lake** (9:15am) and **Yangon** (9:15am, US$110). **Credit card** payments (AmEx/V) incur added fees of up to US$20.

BY BOAT

Boats sail to **Bagan** (regular: 14hr.; W and Su 5:30am; deck US$11, cabin US$33; express: 9hr.; M, Tu, Th-Sa 6am; US$18). The **M Inland Water Transport** jetty (also known as **Gaw Wein** jetty) on the west end of 35th St., a 200kyat *sica* ride from the palace area, and **M Myanmar Tours & Travel** sell tickets to foreigners. Tickets pur-

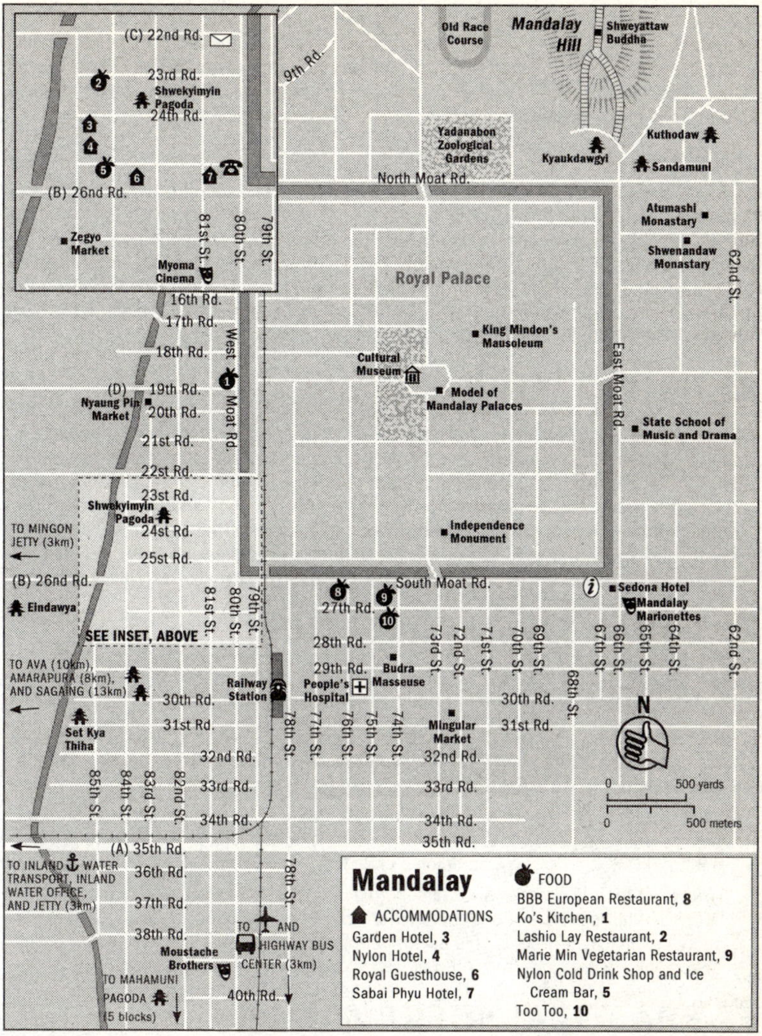

chased from the jetty cost US$2-4 less but can only be bought one day before departure. The **Mingun** jetty, at the west end of 26th St., organizes a tourist boat to **Mingun** (1hr.; 9am, return 1pm; 200kyat). Private charters to Mingun cost 3000kyat.

BY BUS

Private bus companies at the **Kywe Ser Kan Highway Bus Station,** 10km south of Mandalay Palace, serve major destinations like Bagan, Inle Lake, and Yangon. A trishaw to the bus station costs 300-400kyat from most guest houses, which can also arrange tickets for 60-150kyat extra. **Nyaung U Man Express** (☎212 80) runs buses to **Bagan** (7-8hr.; 9am, 2, 9pm; 1200kyat). **Honey Express,** 203 82nd St. (☎229 35), between 22nd and 23rd St. and at the bus station, goes to **Shwenyaung** (Inle Lake; 7-8hr., 5:30am, 1500kyat). Seven companies serve **Yangon** (14-15hr., depart 4-6pm). The best is **Leo Express** (☎885 12), on 84rd St. & 33rd St. (5, 6pm; 2500kyat).

From the corner of 29th and 84th St., **linecars** depart to **Sagaing** (#8, 1¼hr., every 15min. 6am-6pm, 50kyat) via **Amarapura** (30min., 30kyat) and **Ava** (1hr., 30-50kyat). From the corner of 82nd and 26th St., linecars depart to **Pyin Oo Lwin** (3hr., every 30min. 6am-4pm, 200-500kyat). Direct buses to **Lashio** are off-limits to foreigners, but you can go to **Hsipaw,** and transfer.

BY TRAIN

Standard tickets are available one day in advance on the second floor of the new **Railway Station,** on the corner of 78th and 30th St. (☎213 85. Open daily 6-11am and noon-4pm.) Buy **upper-class tickets** three days in advance from the office right of the main counter. Trains go to: **Bagan** (7½hr.; 10pm; standard US$4, upper-class US$9); **Lashio** (19hr.; 4:45am; standard US$5, upper-class US$12); **Myitkyina** (27hr.; 1:15pm; standard US$10, upper-class US$27); **Pyin Oo Lwin** (3-4hr., 4:30am, US$4); **Yangon** (14-15hr., 8 per day 6am-8:30pm, sleeper US$33-36).

ORIENTATION

Mandalay Palace and **Mandalay Hill** (behind it) dominate northeastern Mandalay. A 3.2km square moat surrounds the palace. Most accommodations, restaurants, services, travel services, and the **train station** cluster a few blocks southwest of the palace; the **airport** and **bus station** are further south. The city's western edge, 3km from the palace, meets the **Ayeyarwady River** and its several ferry jetties. The city's streets follow a simple grid structure: north-south streets count up from 50 to 90 (moving west) while east-west streets are labelled from 1 to 45 (moving south).

LOCAL TRANSPORTATION

Rent a bicycle or hire one of Mandalay's 17,000 pedicabs instead of walking to the attractions around the hot, spread-out city—you'll thank us later.

Bicycles: A great way to get around. Several guest houses near 25th and 82nd St. rent bicycles. **Nylon Hotel** and **Royal Guest House** charge 300-500kyat per day; **O Khin Maung,** opposite the Royal Guest House, charges 200kyat per day.

Taxis: Two types of taxis are available: small **blue** taxis resemble mini linecars (500kyat per hr., US$6-10 per day); larger **white** taxis are typically Japanese sedans (1000kyat per hr., US$20-25 per day). Settle on a price first.

Trishaws (Sica): In downtown, drivers' hard sell borders on harassment. Expect to pay 200kyat from downtown to Mandalay Hill (500kyat round-trip) and a little less for shorter distances. Drivers charge 8000-10,000kyat for a day of sightseeing, but prices depend on commissions from souvenir shops. Make your destination clear.

PRACTICAL INFORMATION

Tourist Office: **Myanmar Tours & Travels** (☎271 93), on 68th St. between 26th and 27th St. Myanma Airways and boat bookings. Maps 50kyat. English spoken. Open daily 8am-6pm. Guides at travel agencies and MTT US$15 per day.

Currency Exchange: Central Money Changer (☎285 92), on 27th St. between 80th and 81st St. Fair rates for kyat and traveler's check conversion and AmEx cash advances. Open daily 9am-8pm.

Emergency: Fire ☎191. **Ambulance** ☎192. **Police** ☎199.

Pharmacy: AA Pharmacy (☎312 91), at 82nd and 26th St. Open daily 8am-6:30pm.

Medical Services: **Mandalar Hospital** (☎357 99), on 68th St., between 32nd and 33rd St. Private clinics are better. **Myat Thu Kha,** 392 80th St. (☎350 66), between 24th and 25th St. English spoken. **Open 24hr.** A smaller **clinic** (☎278 59) at 81st St., between 28th and 29th St.

Telephones: **Telephone/Telegraph Office** (☎214 44), on 26th St. between 80th and 81st St. International calls, but expect delays. Open daily 7am-8pm. **IDD** at numerous hotels and the Central Money Changer (see **Currency Exchange,** above) US$6 per min. Calling cards don't work. **Telegraphs** (4kyat per word) arrive in one-day.

Internet Access: Sedona Hotel (☎364 88), at the corner of 26th and 66th St. US$2 per KB to send, US$1 per page to receive. Open M-F 8am-5pm.

Post Office: GPO, on 81st St. between 21st and 22nd St. *Poste Restante*. Open daily 9:30am-3:30pm. **Postal code:** 05071.

ACCOMMODATIONS

Mandalay's budget accommodations are west of Mandalay Palace. Cheaper than counterparts in Yangon, standards are high and breakfast is often included.

Nylon Hotel (☎334 60), at the corner of 25th and 83rd St. Pleasant staff manage well-furnished, cheap, and clean rooms with TV, refrigerator, phone, bath, and A/C. Higher prices buy larger rooms with bathtubs. Basic rooftop rooms with breezy deck and nice views US$3 per person; singles US$4-6; doubles US$8-12.

Royal Guest House, 41 25th St. (☎314 00), between 82nd and 83rd St. Personable staff and less crowded than Nylon Hotel. Travel info and international phone. Singles with shared bath US$3, with A/C and private bath US$4-5; doubles US$6/$8-10.

Sabai Phyu Hotel, 58 81st St. (☎253 77), between 25th and 26th St. Basic rooms but useful travel info and fantastic views of the city from the rooftop dining room. Rooms with hot shower US$4; singles with A/C US$5; doubles US$8-10; cavernous family room with TV and bathtub US$10 per person.

Garden Hotel, 174 83rd St. (☎276 57), between 24th and 25th St., next to Nylon Hotel. Spacious rooms with A/C, hot shower, TV, fridge, and pink curtains aren't significantly nicer than elsewhere, despite the higher prices. Car rental and international phone. Discounts for longer stays. Singles US$6; doubles US$12; fancier rooms with bathtubs and tile floors US$10-18.

FOOD

Most of Mandalay's restaurants are on 23rd St., between 83rd and 84th St., near Mandalay Palace. *Kyomok* (glutinous rice cooked with coconut milk, raisins, sugar, and oil) prevails as the Mandalay delicacy; look for it in Zegyo Market.

Marie Min Vegetarian Restaurant, on 27th St., between 74th and 75th St. With refreshing drinks, veggie food, and travel info, it's a herbivore's dream come true. Shakes 130-200kyat. Guacamole with *chapati* 275kyat. Open daily 8am-10pm.

Nylon Cold Drink Shop and Ice Cream Bar, on 83rd St., between 25th and 26th St. As close to a soda shop as you'll find in Southeast Asia, complete with high school groupies and outdoor seating. Divine ice cream, shakes, custards, and *lassis* 80-120kyat. Durian ice cream 80kyat. Open daily 7am-10pm.

Lashio Lay Restaurant, on 23rd St. between 83rd and 84th St. Talkative staff shells out mouth-watering Shan dishes with all the fixings. Shan and Chinese dishes 100-250kyat. Shan noodles with chicken 200kyat. Open daily 8am-10pm.

BBB European Restaurant, 242 76th St. between 26th and 27th St. Don't let the name or ritzy appearance scare you away. Great, reasonably-priced Western food and wine make it popular amongst the local clientele, but tourists dine here too. Burgers 450kyat. Set breakfast 700kyat; steak 900kyat. Open daily 8am-11pm.

Too Too, on 27th St. between 74th and 75th St., opposite Marie Min Vegetarian Restaurant. Locals say its the best Burmese food in the area. Succulent meat and fish curries and superb sides with lentil and broadbean curries. Meals 300-350kyat, veggie-only 100kyat. Open daily 11am-8pm.

Ko's Kitchen, on the corner of 80th St. and 19th St., along the palace's western moat. Friendly staff offers delicious Thai delights from an exhaustive list of curries, seafood, vegetables, and drinks (700-1700kyat). Expensive but worth it. Open daily 11am-9pm.

SIGHTS

Mandalay's historical sights are in the northwest, with the exception of Mahamuni Pagoda and the artisan quarters in the southern reaches. Due to the considerable distance between the downtown area and the sights, bicycles and trishaws are preferred modes of transport. Visitors on a tight schedule should be sure not to miss Mahamuni Pagoda or Mandalay Hill.

MANDALAY HILL မန္တလေးတောင်**.** Covered stairways climb the south and west faces of the sacred hill, rising 236m above the northeast corner of town; ascending the 700-odd stairs takes at least 30min. The less ambitious can use linecar service to the top (30-100kyat). The temples leading to the summit seem newfangled and lacking in distinction, but the Shweyattaw image, close to the top, is an exception. The towering Buddha image points toward the city, a representation of a famous legend in which the Buddha predicted that a great Buddhist city would arise at the base of the hill. The sweeping views at the summit provide relief from the surrounding plain. At sunset on the weekends, local teens come to practice their foreign languages with tourists. *(Open daily 6am-8pm. US$3.)*

SHWE NANDAW KYAUNG (GOLDEN PALACE MONASTERY) AND ATUMASHI (INCOMPARABLE MONASTERY). One of the few teak monasteries to survive WWII, the architecture and ornamentation of **Shwe Nandaw Kyaung** yield one of Mandalay's more impressive sights. Originally built by King Mindon in 1878, it highlights a royal medication couch and a replica of the great Lion Throne. **Atumashi,** behind Shwe Nandaw Kyaung, is much less stunning. Before burning down in 1892, it was considered Mandalay's most beautiful monument, with elaborate stucco carvings, glass mosaics, fine masonry work, and a revered, diamond-encrusted Buddha image (which the British stole in 1885). The fruit of intense prison labor, the reconstructed building looks so modern that it's difficult to fathom its prior splendor. *(South of Kuthodaw Pagoda. Open 8:30am-5:30pm. US$5.)*

MAHAMUNI PAGODA. The "Pagoda of the Great Buddha Image" remains the holiest object in Upper Myanmar. According to legend, the Buddha brought this 3.8m bronze temple to life, after embracing it seven times during a visit to the Rakhine (Arakan) State. Mahamuni was presented to Mandalay in 1784 by the Crown Prince of Amarapura, who claimed it upon his victory over the Arakan King.

Devout Buddhists consider the statue a replica of Gautama Buddha, alive and endowed with supernatural powers. Every morning around 4am, the head monk gives the image a ceremonial facial, right down to brushing its teeth. Women grind sandalwood for the ceremony in one of the side courtyards during the day but are prohibited from entering the inner sanctuary. Male pilgrims flock daily to the podium to affix gold leaves to the Buddha. Over the years, the golden buildup has accumulated to a layer over 16cm thick. The face has reputedly expanded proportionally with this growth, stirring evidence, some say, that Mahamuni is a living entity. *Longgyi*-clad male visitors are welcome to place gold leaves on the image (*longgyi* rental 50kyat, 5 gold leaves 200kyat).

Behind the image and to the right stand **six bronze statues.** The interest here lies not so much in artistic merit but in the statues' travels. Originating in Cambodia's Angkor Wat, the statues were moved to Ayutthaya, the Burmese Kingdom of Bago, the Arakan Kingdom, and finally to Mandalay along with the Mahamuni Pagoda. Many believe that rubbing the figures in a particular place cures ailments in the corresponding part of the body.

The temple's atmosphere is lively. Artisans selling wood-carvings, miniature gongs, and other handicrafts crowd the walkways to the temple. *(In southern Mandalay. The main entrance is at the intersection of 82nd and 45th St. Open daily 4am-4pm. No sleeveless shirts or shorts. US$4.)*

THE ROYAL PALACE မန္တလေးနန်းတော်**.** Surrounded by stately walls and a formidable moat, the Royal Palace, built in the 1860s, monopolizes northern Mandalay on a 3.2 sq. km plot of land. These walls of King Mindon's teak palace and their associated guard towers are all that remain of the original structure. East of the current palace, a scale model of the original grounds hints at its former grandeur. While the structure once consisted of a main audience hall and 100 chambers to house the king's 53 wives and countless concubines, the site today serves as a military encampment. A few concrete reconstructions (including the palace itself and a watchtower) make up the main tourist attractions.

The palace may not be worth the steep admission; the best-preserved elements of the fort, the moat and walls, are visible from the outside; nearby Mandalay Hill affords fine views of the palace and surrounding area. Many travelers boycott the palace to protest the forced labor involved in its reconstruction. The enormous moat, for example, is the result of the mass mobilization of Mandalay's citizens, who had to bring their own tools to the work site. *(Open daily 8:30am-5pm. US$5.)*

KYAUKDAWGYI PAGODA. Built by King Mindon from 1853-78, this pagoda rests at Mandalay Hill's base opposite the main southern walkway. The Buddha statue was cut from an 3.5 million kg block of green marble; moving it from the quarry required a herculean effort of 10,000 laborers, who dug a canal to transport it. The image is impressive, but if the cash-strapped want a rest from Mandalay's expensive sights, this is one that can be missed. *(Open daily 7:30am-6pm. US$2.)*

KUTHODAW PAGODA AND SANDAMUNI PAGODA. Crafted in 1857 on the model of Bagan's Shwezigon Pagoda, **Kuthodaw,** a 5min. walk east of Mandalay Hill, holds the distinction of housing the world's biggest book, a tome with all Buddhist scriptures in Pali. The text is inscribed on 729 stone slabs, each sheltered in masonry shrines surrounding the pagoda. One hundred meters southwest of Kuthodaw, **Sandamuni Pagoda** marks where King Mindon's younger brother, hand-picked to succeed him, was murdered in 1866 by two of the King's miffed sons. Much more interesting than the pagoda's iron Buddha are the surrounding miniature *stupas*, which shelter 1774 marble slabs containing commentaries on the Tripitaka called *Sutta Vinaya Abidhamma.* *(Open 6:30am-6pm. US$5; includes admission to both pagodas.)*

ARTISAN WORKSHOPS. The arts thrive in Mandalay, thanks to **artisan guilds** in the south of the city. **Marble** and **wood workshops** craft Buddha statues of every size. Mahamuni Pagoda is a good place to catch artisans at work; wood-carvers and gong-makers display their craft on the temple's covered walkways. *(South of Mahamuni Pagoda on 84th St., between 45th and 46th St. Open daily 9am-5pm.)*

In the **Myit Pa Yup Quarter,** 200 families dedicate their energy to the production of **gold leaf,** which is used to gild *stupas* and sacred images. The labor-intensive hammering and delicate packaging processes are an eye-opening look at the effort required to make the 0.02cm thick leaves. It is well worth a stop on a bicycle or trishaw tour. *(On 37th St. between 76th and 78th St. Open daily 8am-6pm. Gold leaf 30kyat.)*

MARKETS

Equidistant from India, Bangladesh, China, and Thailand, Mandalay serves as a major shopping hub and arts center. **Handicrafts**—teak, marble, and jade carvings, lacquer ware, and metalworking—abound, particularly in the south of the city around Mahamuni Pagoda. **Zegyo Market,** a three-block shopping and socializing extravaganza, provides just about everything else, including hours of people-watching entertainment. Fruit and vegetable merchants set up around midnight, and locals crowd side streets to buy produce each morning. Around midday, the inventory shifts gears: plastic and stainless steel kitchenware, *longgyi*, and bamboo weavings replace foodstuffs. The **night market** continues the selling frenzy with less practical goods like military knives, brass knuckles, and fake designer watches. *(Southwest off the corner of 84th and 26th St. Open daily 5am-10pm.)*

ENTERTAINMENT

No trip to Mandalay is complete without a performance of the **Mandalay Marionettes,** an entertaining traditional art form in Myanmar. Dating to 11th century Bagan, Burmese puppetry adapts themes from stories of the Buddha and colorful

CAN'T TAKE A JOKE? *A-nyeint* theater has a long history. People flock to this synthesis of cabaret, burlesque, and vaudeville, sometimes at all-night festivals called *pwe*. For the past 30 years, the Moustache Brothers in Mandalay have been the art's most popular practitioners and have played to packed houses nightly. Recognizing the potentially subversive nature of the performances, the government imposed strict curbs on *a-nyeint* artists, banning all-night performances, censoring advertising, and requiring comedians to submit written copies of jokes for approval. Comedians have to be subtle and clever; they refer to aspects of daily life to offer masked critiques of government policies. In January 1996, Moustache Brother Par Par Lay and cousin U Lu Zaw were invited to the NLD's celebration of the 48th anniversary of Burmese independence, at Aung San Suu Kyi's compound, before government officials and dignitaries. Par Par Lay prefaced his routine by declaring he would speak his mind, despite the threat of reprisal. In one skit, he played an imprisoned activist who refuses to die after being shot multiple times by a general. The pun hinges on the homonymy of "hit" and "right" in Burmese. In response to the general's insistence that he die after being hit, the prisoner responds, "Why should I die if I am right?" Three days after their return to Mandalay, security forces arrested dancers, musicians, comedians, and NLD attendees. The two comedians were imprisoned after a short trial and remain incarcerated, despite Par Par Lay's failing health. Lu Maw, the remaining Moustache Brother, hosts shows in his home. Between acts and jokes, Lu Maw explains that he and his brother flipped a coin to determine who would attend the NLD celebration. The wife of Par Par Lay is also a part of the show. Her exceptional dancing is occasionally upstaged by the despair that colors her face. Her husband has become an international symbol as part of the movement for human rights in Myanmar. In 1997, 10 Hollywood comedians wrote to the government to urge that Par Par Lay and Lu Zaw be released. In 1998, anti-government demonstrators in front of Myanmar's London embassy created a 6m-by-4m portrait of the comedians by applying 1.6 million thumbprints to a canvas. The portrait hangs in London's National Gallery. Meanwhile, the family counts down the days, months, and years until the two men's release.

events in Burmese mythology. Starring characters include alchemists, giant birds, ogres, and serpents. Seasoned puppeteers deliver quality shows at the **Garden Villa Theater** on 66th St. between 26th and 27th St. (1hr., daily 8:30pm, 1000kyat.)

Mandalay also boasts its own **"Little Broadway."** Covering 39th to 43rd St. between 80th and 81st St., the **theater district** has 75 performance troupes fronted by colorful, often campy, signs. The best interface with this scene is the **Moustache Brothers,** on 39th St. between 80th and 81st St. Backed by 30 years experience, this troupe performs *a-nyeint*, starring enthusiastic comedian Lu Maw (see **Can't Take a Joke?,** p. 494). The performances interweave commentary, conjugal infidelity jokes, and dances with elaborate costumes, culminating in a spin-off of the Demi Moore movie *Striptease*. (Shows 8pm. Audiences of four or fewer 3000kyat per group; audiences over four 600kyat per person.)

For a quieter evening, head to **Myoma Cinema**, at the corner of 81st and 28th St., which shows foreign films in their original language (often with Myanmar-language subtitles) and local films without subtitles. Many patient travelers still find the melodramatic Myanmarese low-budget films entertaining (or rather, amusing) even without understanding the dialogue. (☎387 19. Showtimes 12:30am, 3:30, 6:30, 9:30pm. 125-200kyat.)

DAYTRIPS FROM MANDALAY

A few kilometers from Mandalay, four small villages flaunt momentous pasts that belie their presence as tiny blips along the Ayeyarwady River: **Amarapura, Ava,** and **Sagaing** downriver from the city, and **Mingun** upriver. All not only dwarf their larger sibling in antiquity but also provide a peaceful counterpoint to the city's mayhem and are worth visiting for their historical and religious sites and splendid scenery.

Mingun is accessible only by boat, while the others can be reached by linecar or taxi. By hiring a blue taxi (US$6-10 per day) or a guide (**U Aye Pe** at Eindawya Pagoda is knowledgeable and fun; US$6-15 per day) or starting early enough on your own, you can see the three down-river towns leisurely in one day. The natural progression of sights makes it best to work your way further away from Mandalay over the course of the day: from Amarapura to Ava to Sagaing. Though many finish at U Bein's bridge in Amarapura, try to finish in Sagaing for views of the sunset, cities, and surrounding plains from atop the pagoda-covered splendor of Sagaing Hill. Alternately, it's possible to see Mingun by boat in the morning, return to Mandalay, catch a linecar or taxi to Sagaing in the afternoon, and visit Amarapura and Ava by linecar another day. Linecar #8 leaves from the corner of 29th and 84th St. and heads to Sagaing (1¼hr., every 15min. 6am-6pm, 50kyat) via Ava (1hr., 30-50kyat) and Amarapura (30min., 30kyat).

MINGUN မင်းကွန်း

Foreign tourists are limited to 3hr. visits and required to use the daily **M** *MTT "tourist boat" that departs from the 26th St. jetty in Mandalay (1½hr., 1hr. return; 9am, returns 1pm; 300kyat). If you want to stay longer, charter a private boat (3000kyat), but 3hr. is ample time to enjoy the town. US$3.*

Mingun's three main sights are often accompanied by hordes of children who greet tourists at the dock and hound visitors at every turn, scrapping their way through explanations of the sights in hopes of earning a few kyat. All it takes is one step off this well-beaten track, however, and the traveler is alone, free to wander Mingun's fields and hills and enjoy splendid views all the way to Mandalay and a worthwhile glimpse into Myanmar's rural life.

MINGUN PAGODA. Size mattered to King Bodawpaya, who in 1790 began construction of a 150m pagoda to dwarf the Minwun mountain range behind. In true autocratic fashion, he mobilized 20,000 Arakanese slaves for 39 years, but the pagoda only made it to 50m before suffering damage from the 1838 earthquake. Today, the remains of the King's arrogance bear the dubious title of "largest stack of bricks in the world," and the temple carries an alternative tag, Patodawgyi Pagoda, or "Unfinished Pagoda." Brisk breezes and views extending to Mandalay make the strenuous, 174-step climb to the top more than worthwhile.

MINGUN BELL. This massive appendage to the pagoda was completed in 1790 and continues to hang as King Bodawpaya's crowning achievement. The impressive 82,000kg bell, 4m high and 5m in diameter, is the largest un-cracked bell in the world. Thrill-seekers crawl underneath to hear its resonance from within.

HSINBYUME PAGODA. North of Mingun Pagoda, Hsinbyume humbles in comparison. Built in 1816, it finds its architectural inspiration in the cosmological vision of Sulamani Pagoda atop the heavens of Mount Meru. Its seven concentric terraces symbolize the mountain ranges surrounding Meru.

COUNTRY LIFE. A good place to escape Mingun's beaten path is the horse cart track behind Hsinbyume Pagoda. After passing peanut fields and a crumbling pagoda, the trail reaches the hills that paint Mingun's backdrop. Most of the souvenir-hawking crowd disappears by the time you reach Hsinbyume Pagoda, thus allowing visitors to hike the foothills unpestered, take in excellent views of Mingun Pagoda and the river, listen to farmers singing in the fields, and make it back to Mingun in time for a quick lunch before the boat leaves.

AMARAPURA အမရပူရ

Linecars to Amarapura leave from the intersection of 29th and 84th St. From the market in Amarapura, it's easy to pick up linecar #8 onward to Ava and Sagaing or back to Mandalay (25min., every 15min. 8am-5pm, 30kyat).

From the late 18th century until the mid-1800s, Amarapura swapped roles with Ava several times as the Burmese capital before losing the title to Mandalay. In its heyday, one writer has contended, Amarapura stood as a "microcosm of Burmese civilization"—a center not only of wealth, fashion, and beauty but also erudition and scholarship. Apart from a few structures and four pagodas marking the original corners of the city, Amarapura ("The City of Immortals") has nothing to show for this regal legacy. Nonetheless, the lively market, provincial atmosphere, and opportunities for leisurely people-watching on the town's famous bridge will please those seeking respite from Mandalay clamor.

U BEIN'S BRIDGE. At the west end of town, rickety U Bein's Bridge spans much of scenic **Lake Taungthaman.** Over 1km in length, it's the longest teak bridge in the world, all the more impressive given that it's nearly 250 years old. The lake itself is a local source of food. Townspeople flock to the bridge during the rainy season to fish the shallow lake, while the dry season sees farmers tilling and harvesting paddy fields where the lake once was. Regardless of the season, however, the relationship between the people and their land is worth a look. *(Ponycarts run from the market to the bridge for 100kyat each way. During the rainy season rowboats provide an alternative route across the lake 300kyat.)*

SILK WEAVING. With nearly every house in town weaving silk, Amarapura has emerged as one of Myanmar's premier weaving centers. Family-run silk businesses have functioned for generations here. Weaving households line the street from the market to the bridge, and many are amenable to visitors and will demonstrate the entire painstaking process. *(Cotton-and-silk* longgyi *US$3. Intricate silk skirts US$5.)*

OTHER SIGHTS. South of the bridge entrance lies **Mahagandayon Monastery.** The 1000 monks uphold rigorous standards in the study of Pali and meditation techniques. On the other side of the footbridge is the dusty village of **Taungthaman.** There you'll find **Kyauktawgyi Pagoda,** which was constructed in 1847 using Bagan's Ananda Temple as its blueprint. It features an impressive Buddha image and evidence of British influence (frescoes portray tailcoated figures). During the rainy season, reaching the temple may require a stroll through knee-deep muddy water.

Neither of these sights merits value over wandering the **market**. Fresh fruits, vegetables, and bamboo weavings dominate the menu, but the locals manning the stalls are welcoming and excited to have foreigners attempt conversation.

AVA (INWA) အင်းဝ

Linecars from Amarapura drop off passengers at the base of a long wooden road (trishaw 50kyat). At its opposite end is a ferry landing where boats shuttle to Ava (5min., every 30min., 10kyat; US$4 fee payable at tourist booth before crossing).

Ava (commonly referred to as Inwa) lies 20km southwest of Mandalay and 7km beyond Amarapura at the junction of the Ayeyarwady and the Myitnge Rivers. Thado Minbya established Ava as the capital of Burma in 1364, a position it retained until 1823—the longest streak in Burmese history. Today, disembarking on the triangular island—which has a handful of motorized vehicles, a legion of horse carts, and one backwater village in the northeast—is like stepping back in time. The old walls of the city remain intact guarding cultivated land, hamlets, monasteries, and pagoda ruins. Pony carts provide the best means of navigation; flurries of them await arrivals at the two flock landings. The circuit around the "hit parade" of sights— the "leaning" watchtower, King Bagyidaw's Palace, Ava Fort, Okkyaung Monastery, and a host of pagodas—takes an hour or two and costs 600-1000kyat. Guides are best hired through Mandalay guest houses (US$6-10).

A lone 30m watchtower marks **King Bagyidaw's Palace,** inhabited from 1819-37. Though an 1838 earthquake left the palace slanting, people are allowed to climb the reinforced stairways for a breezy panorama of the area. The nearby **Maha Aungmye Bonzan Monastery** (Okkyaung Monastery), was built in 1818 by Bagyidaw's notorious queen, Nanmadaw Me, to house her religious preceptor, Nyaunggan Sayadaw. The upper chambers are desolate and not particularly interesting, but carvings of Buddhist imagery fill the lower levels and the dark, grotto-like series of walkways used for meditating. Crumbling **Bagaya Monas-**

tery, constructed in 1834, represents Myanmar's famous teakwood monasteries and maintains many of its original carvings despite its dilapidated present condition. Many **ruined pagodas** visible from Bagaya may prove more interesting than the monasteries.

SAGAING စစ်ကိုင်း

Linecar #8 departs for Mandalay via Ava and Amarapura until 8pm (1hr., 50kyat).

Sagaing is 21km southwest of Mandalay, across the Ayeyarwady River from Ava. The religious center of Myanmar, Sagaing teems with *stupas* and monasteries, mostly scattered near Sagaing Hill to the northeast. Sagaing is best visited late, when Sagaing Hill affords sunset panoramas to the chanting of the town's 5000 monks and nuns.

SAGAING HILL. With 300 temples and pagodas, Sagaing Hill rises majestically with tremendous views of Mandalay, Ava, Amarapura, and Sagaing. The walk up the front of the hill is good exercise but offers far fewer lookouts along the way than the back staircase, which passes several pagodas. Due to the difficulty (for non-Burmese speakers) in finding the back stairs, the best route may be to head up the front and down the back before flagging down a horse cart back to the linecar drop off point. Some of Sagaing Hill's attractions include: **Padamya Zedi,** built by a monk in 1300 (perched atop one of the less-accessible peaks, Padamya Zedi requires a full day to visit); **Ohnmin Thonze** ("30 Caves"), which shelters Buddha images in a crescent-like chamber; **Ponnyashin Pagoda,** housing the Buddha's hair relics; and **Tilawkaguru,** at the bast of the hill, built in 1672 and displaying murals depicting the Buddha's past lives. *(The hill is 4km north of the town center; take a horse cart or trishaw (300kyat one-way) or linecar (15min.; every 20min. 7:30-11am, return until 2pm; 30-40kyat) from the bus compound outside town to the base of the mountain. Covered walkways shelter the 30min. climb. US$4.)*

KAUNGHMUDAW PAGODA. Sagaing's most renowned temple, Kaunghmudaw rests 10km outside town. In 1536, with Ceylon's Mahaceti Pagoda as his ambitious model, King Thalun of Ava built the Kaunghmudaw Pagoda, also known as **Rajamanicula,** which reputedly houses the Buddha's sacred tooth and hair relics transferred from Bagan's Mahazedi Pagoda. Some believe that its architectural signature, a 46m high white Indian-style dome, was made in the likeness of the voluptuous breast of King Thalun's queen. *(Linecars from the Sagaing bus compound outside town leave for the temple (10min., every 30min. 7:30am-4pm, 30kyat). US$3.)*

MYITTAKAN. This sacred pond is surrounded by a parapet wall. Legend has it that no autumn leaves from the tangle of nearby trees have ever dared to break its surface. *(Behind Kaunghmudaw Pagoda.)*

BAGAN (PAGAN) ပုဂံ

☎062

Sunsets in Bagan illuminate pagoda spires that look like rosebuds rising from a caramel sea. Little is known about Bagan's founding, but scholars agree that its splendor prevailed for 250 years following King Anawrahta's ascension to the throne in 1044. Dissatisfied with the religious practices predominant among his people, Anawrahta launched a rejuvenation of Theravada Buddhism that was accompanied by a flurry of temple building. The results of this religious revival are still evident today, as the 42 sq. km Bagan Archaeological Zone's "city of four million."

> **GOVERNMENT LISTINGS.** All government listings are marked with a M symbol. Money spent at such establishments goes directly into the government's hands. For more information, see **Keeping the Bucks Where They Belong,** p. 469.

TRANSPORTATION

Flights: Nyaung U Airport (☎702 06), 4km southeast of Nyaung U, off the road to Mandalay. Taxis from airport to most destinations in Bagan 500-700kyat. **Air Mandalay** (☎701 16; open daily 9:30am-5pm), next to the pagoda rotary on the Main Rd. in New Bagan, serves **Heho/Inle Lake** (US$68) and **Yangon** (8:15am, US$128) via **Mandalay** (US$48). **Yangon Airways** (☎704 51; open daily 10am-6pm), in Nyaung U on Anawrahta Rd., on the right about 200m past the post office heading away from the market, flies to **Heho** (US$90) and **Yangon** (8:10am, US$105) via **Mandalay** (US$45). **Myanma Airways** (☎701 99; open daily 9:30am-4:30pm), 150m inside Tharaba Gate in Old Bagan, flies to **Mandalay** (7:50am, US$40) and **Yangon** (M-Tu, Th-Sa 11:20am; W, Su 9:20am; US$90). Air tickets are cheaper from ticket agents who cluster on Bagan-Nyaung U Rd. 75m south of the market area. Most daily open 8am-6pm. Discounts are frequent, seasonal, and require cash payment.

Buses: Highway Bus Center, in front of Shwezigon Pagoda on Bagan-Nyaung U Rd. in Nyaung U. Book tickets at guest houses or in person. **Nyaung U Man Express** (☎704 00) goes to **Mandalay** (7hr.; 7, 9am; 1200kyat) and **Taunggyi** (Inle Lake, 9-12hr., 5am, 1700kyat). **New Bagan Express** (☎704 79), and **Popa Dagon Express** go to **Yangon** (15-16hr., 3:30pm, 2000-2300kyat).

Trains: The **train station** is 6km south of Nyaung U and 10km west of New Bagan off the road to Mandalay. Taxis 800-1000kyat. Buy tickets a day in advance at the station ticket office or the branch 200m west of the market in Nyaung U on Bagan-Nyaung U Rd. (☎704 17; open daily 8am-8pm) or arrange through guest houses. Trains to **Mandalay** (7-8hr., 7am, up to US$9) and **Yangon** (12hr., times vary, up to US$33).

Boats: Popular express boats to **Mandalay** depart from the Nyaung U jetty, where Bagan-Nyaung U Rd. meets the river beyond the Nyaung U market (at least 12hr., Tu-W and F-Su 5am, US$16). Most scenic and comfortable, but the schedule is unreliable. Check at least a day in advance. Buy tickets at the jetty or through guest houses.

Local Transportation: Linecars depart from the market in Nyaung U to **New Bagan** via **Old Bagan** (6am-5pm, less frequent in the afternoon, 100kyat). **Pony carts** provide a comfortable way to skim the sights in one day (3-person max., 1500kyat per day). **Trishaws** in Nyaung U or New Bagan make intra-town trips (up to 150kyat). **Private taxis** can be hired through most guest houses to **Inle Lake** (7-9hr., US$50-60), usually via **Mount Poppa** (1hr., US$12-15).

Rentals: Car US$15-20 per day. **Bicycles** available at guest houses (200-300kyat, depending on quality). Nicer models are worth the extra kyat.

ORIENTATION AND PRACTICAL INFORMATION

The **Bagan Archaeological Zone** is along the banks of the **Ayeyarwady** At the river's bend, **Old Bagan** is a historic and geographic focus. Two parallel highways, **Bagan-Nyaung U Rd.** and **Anawrahta Rd.,** extend 5km northeast from Old Bagan and through most of the temple complexes before meeting at **Nyaung U market,** home to **Shwezigon Pagoda.** The adjacent **highway bus center** handles regional long-distance buses. **New Bagan,** 3km south of Old Bagan, is organized around **Main Rd.** that begins at the intersection with Bagan-Nyaung U Rd. and runs east all the way to the **airport** 4km south of Nyaung U. A pagoda in the middle of a rotary rests on Main Rd. at the center of town. The historic village of **Myinkaba** lies between New Bagan and Old Bagan, 1km south of the latter. Throughout the region, street names and addresses are rarely used.

Tourist Offices: MTT (☎702 17), on Bagan-Nyaung U Rd. near Ananda Temple. Maps of Bagan 200kyat. Open 8am-5pm. If *Glimpses of Glorious Bagan* isn't enough (see **Sights,** p. 501), guides (about US$10 per day) can help you understand Bagan's temples; it seems like every local is licensed to provide this service. U Zaw Weik is among the most learned guides. Inquire at **Thiri Sandar Guest House** (☎700 45) near the pagoda rotary in New Bagan.

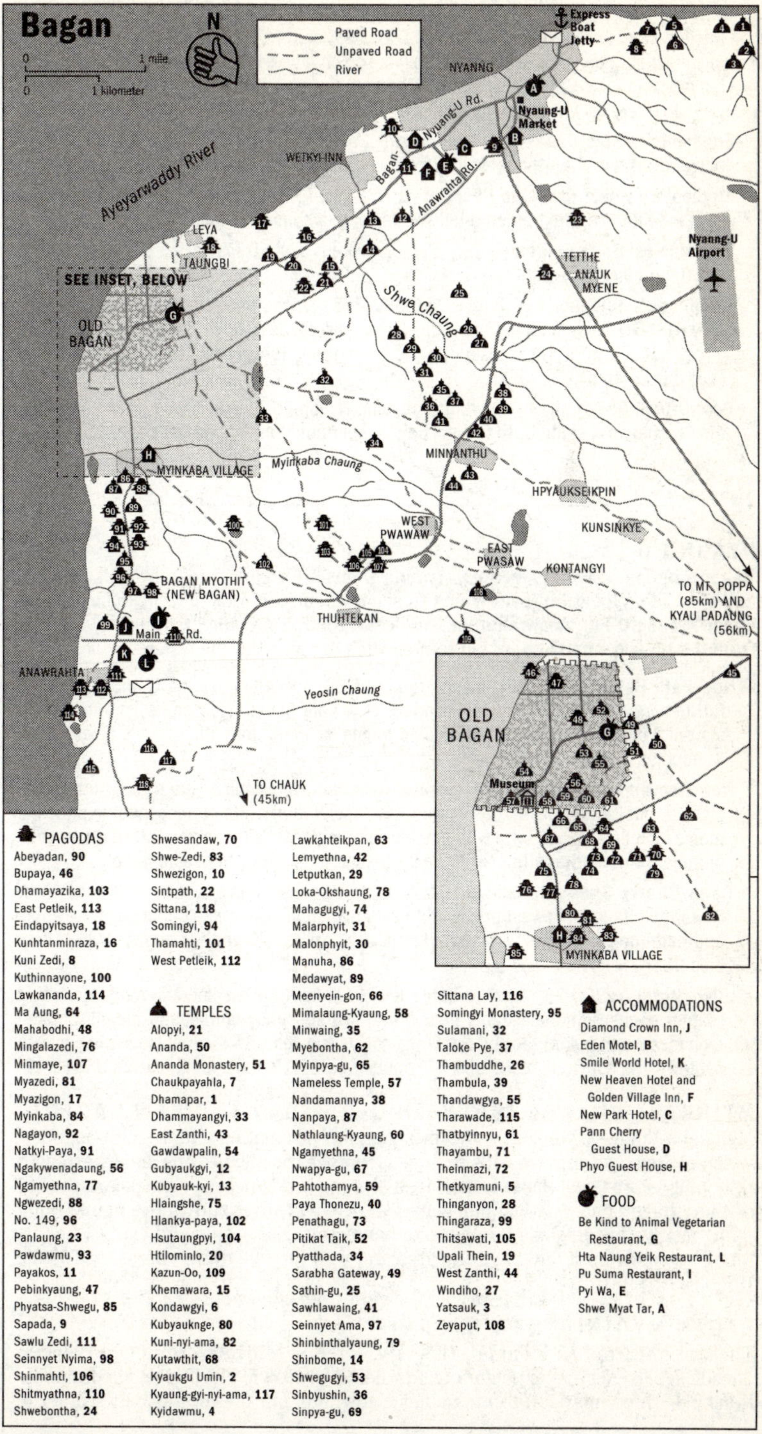

PAGODAS

Abeyadan, **90**
Bupaya, **46**
Dhamayazika, **103**
East Petleik, **113**
Eindapyitsaya, **18**
Kunhtanminraza, **16**
Kuni Zedi, **8**
Kuthinnayone, **100**
Lawkananda, **114**
Ma Aung, **64**
Mahabodhi, **48**
Mingalazedi, **76**
Minmaye, **107**
Myazedi, **81**
Myazigon, **17**
Myinkaba, **84**
Nagayon, **92**
Natkyi-Paya, **91**
Ngakywenadaung, **56**
Ngamyethna, **77**
Ngwezedi, **88**
No. 149, **96**
Panlaung, **23**
Pawdawmu, **93**
Payakos, **11**
Pebinkyaung, **47**
Phyatsa-Shwegu, **85**
Sapada, **9**
Sawlu Zedi, **111**
Seinnyet Nyima, **98**
Shinmahti, **106**
Shitmyathna, **110**
Shwebontha, **24**
Shwesandaw, **70**
Shwe-Zedi, **83**
Shwezigon, **10**
Sintpath, **22**
Sittana, **118**
Somingyi, **94**
Thamahti, **101**
West Petleik, **112**

TEMPLES

Alopyi, **21**
Ananda, **50**
Ananda Monastery, **51**
Chaukpayahla, **7**
Dhamapar, **1**
Dhammayangyi, **33**
East Zanthi, **43**
Gawdawpalin, **54**
Gubyaukgyi, **12**
Kubyauk-kyi, **13**
Hlaingshe, **75**
Hlankya-paya, **102**
Hsutaungpyi, **104**
Htilominlo, **20**
Kazun-Oo, **109**
Khemawara, **15**
Kondawgyi, **6**
Kubyaukngе, **80**
Kuni-nyi-ama, **82**
Kutawthit, **68**
Kyaukgu Umin, **2**
Kyaung-gyi-nyi-ama, **117**
Kyidawmu, **4**
Lawkahteikpan, **63**
Lemyethna, **42**
Letputkan, **29**
Loka-Okshaung, **78**
Mahagugyi, **74**
Malarphyit, **31**
Malonphyit, **30**
Manuha, **86**
Medawyat, **89**
Meenyein-gon, **66**
Mimalaung-Kyaung, **58**
Minwaing, **35**
Myebontha, **62**
Myinpya-gu, **65**
Nameless Temple, **57**
Nandamannya, **38**
Nanpaya, **87**
Nathlaung-Kyaung, **60**
Ngamyethna, **45**
Nwapya-gu, **67**
Pahtothamya, **59**
Paya Thonezu, **40**
Penathagu, **73**
Pitikat Taik, **52**
Pyatthada, **34**
Sarabha Gateway, **49**
Sathin-gu, **25**
Sawhlawaing, **41**
Seinnyet Ama, **97**
Shinbinthalyaung, **79**
Shinbome, **14**
Shwegugyi, **53**
Sinbyushin, **36**
Sinpya-gu, **69**
Sittana Lay, **116**
Somingyi Monastery, **95**
Sulamani, **32**
Taloke Pye, **37**
Thambuddhe, **26**
Thambula, **39**
Thandawgya, **55**
Tharawade, **115**
Thatbyinnyu, **61**
Thayambu, **71**
Theinmazi, **72**
Thetkyamuni, **5**
Thinganyon, **28**
Thingaraza, **99**
Thitsawati, **105**
Upali Thein, **19**
West Zanthi, **44**
Windiho, **27**
Yatsauk, **3**
Zeyaput, **108**

ACCOMMODATIONS

Diamond Crown Inn, **J**
Eden Motel, **B**
Smile World Hotel, **K**
New Heaven Hotel and Golden Village Inn, **F**
New Park Hotel, **C**
Pann Cherry Guest House, **D**
Phyo Guest House, **H**

FOOD

Be Kind to Animal Vegetarian Restaurant, **G**
Hta Naung Yeik Restaurant, **L**
Pu Suma Restaurant, **I**
Pyi Wa, **E**
Shwe Myat Tar, **A**

Currency Exchange: Aungzeyar, a travel agent on Bagan-Nyaung U Rd., 75m towards the jetty from the Nyaung U Market. US$ and FEC conversion at 50-100kyat less than in bigger cities. Open daily 8am-6pm. Unlicensed changers in the market offer slightly better rates. In New Bagan, try **Money Changer Counter,** on Main Rd. 15m before the pagoda rotary as you come from the river. Open daily 7am-8pm.

English-Language Bookstore: Several small shops and stalls in Nyaung U sell paperback novels. For the best selection, try the New Park Hotel and Pyiula Restaurant.

Medical Services: Township Hospital (☎702 19), 1½km outside Nyaung U on the road to Mandalay. Western-trained, English-speaking doctors available **24hr.**

Pharmacies: Sadana Mon (☎703 51), opposite Nyaung U Market on Bagan-Nyaung U Rd. Open daily 7am-5pm.

Telephones: Telephone Office (☎951 580 255), at the post office in Nyaung U. IDD only (US$6-9 to Western nations). Call-back service US$2. Open daily 8am-8pm. Some guest houses offer similar service. Send cheaper **telegrams** from the post office (15kyat per word).

Post Office: 750m down Anawrahta Rd. from Nyaung U market. Open daily 9am-4pm. Also on Bagan-Nyaung U Rd in New Bagan, south of Main Rd. **Postal code:** 05191.

ACCOMMODATIONS

NYAUNG U

Bagan's budget travelers' center, Nyaung U has affordable, pleasant guest houses and is an ideal location from which to see the temples. Most guest houses are on **Bagan-Nyaung U Rd., Anawrahta Rd.,** and off a road that connects the two, running from the bus terminal at one end to near the post office at the other.

New Park Hotel (☎701 22), off the road connecting Bagan-Nyaung U and Anawrahta Rd. Recently renovated and landscaped, New Park prides itself on its knowledgeable staff and comfortable rooms. Affordable rooms have A/C and hot water. Singles US$3-4; doubles US$6-8.

New Heaven Hotel (☎700 61), close to New Park Hotel; follow the signs north of the highway bus center. Clean, basic rooms and useful tourist info at a reasonable price. All rooms include A/C and bath with hot shower. Singles US$3; doubles US$6. If full, comparable **Golden Village Inn** (☎700 88), behind it, is run by the same people.

Pann Cherry Guest House (☎701 47), on Bagan-Nyaung U Rd., 300m north of Shwezigon Pagoda. Lowest prices and best location in town make up for concrete floors and bare rooms. Singles with shared bath US$2, with A/C and hot shower US$3; doubles US$4/6.

Eden Motel (☎700 78), on Anawrahta Rd., 15m from the market. Mid-range quality at budget prices. Fantastic deals possible in low season. High season means booked rooms and a popular balcony. Small, basic A/C singles US$4, super-clean singles with cable TV and spacious baths US$4-6; doubles US$8-12; huge family rooms US$12-18.

MYINKABA VILLAGE (BETWEEN OLD BAGAN AND NEW BAGAN)

Myinkaba Village, 1km south of Old Bagan, has fascinating temples and pagodas. With only two guest houses, it's removed from the travelers' scene and awash with tranquility. **Phyo Guest House** is on Bagan-Nyaung U Rd., near a white pagoda, north of the village center. A lacquer ware factory next door shows the painstaking effort involved in Bagan's number-one handicraft. Enjoy splendid views of cloistered *stupas* from its main sitting area and well-furnished A/C rooms. (☎700 86. Doubles US$10-15.)

BAGAN MYOTHIT (NEW BAGAN)

The warmhearted residents of this city, forcibly relocated from Old Bagan a decade ago, have great expectations for their dusty town. The budget accommodations pale in comparison to the values elsewhere, but the food is better and the atmosphere less touristy than Nyaung U, particularly in the low season, when the town's numerous guest houses all stand empty.

Smile World Hotel (☎701 12), 25m up Main Rd. from Bagan-Nyaung U Rd., on the right. Spotless bungalow-style rooms with front porch, A/C, and hot water showers are bound to make travelers smile, too. Singles US$6; doubles US$10.

Diamond Crown Inn, on Bagan-Nyuang U Rd. 50m before Main Rd. Simple singles as cheap as they come in this area, with A/C and hot water bath US$5.

FOOD

Bagan cuisine narrows the gap between the delicious and the mediocre, such that the same restaurant may serve you a mouth watering lunch and an uninspired dinner. In Nyaung U, it pays to avoid the countless tourist eateries; in New Bagan, consistently delectable delights are easier to find.

Pyi Wa, on the road that connects Bagan-Nyaung U and Anawrahta Rd. near New Park and New Heaven Hotels. Typical Bagan food is served in an unbeatable atmosphere: candlelit open air tables in a ruined temple's shadow. Chinese, Burmese, and Italian food with complimentary fruit salad 200-1000kyat. Open daily 7:30am-10pm.

Shwe Myat Tar, 50m north of the rotary where Bagan-Nyaung U Rd. and Anawrahta Rd. intersect by the market. Look for the sign at the entrance to an alley. Burmese food in a family atmosphere provides sweet culinary refuge, but vegetarians need look elsewhere. Curries with side dishes 350kyat. Open daily 10am-9pm.

Be Kind to Animal Vegetarian Restaurant and Cold Drinks, 30m inside Tharaba Gate on Bagan-Nyaung U Rd. An oasis in the culinary (and vegetarian) desert of Old Bagan, serving mango *lassi* (100kyat), yogurt with fruit (200kyat), and meatless Burmese set meals (375kyat). Open daily 7am-11pm.

Hta Naung Yeik (Acacia Shade Restaurant), at the turn-off to the right before the pagoda rotary on the Main Rd. Heaping portions of Burmese dishes served in the shade of an acacia tree by a friendly family. Vegetarian meal 300kyat. Meat curries 400-500kyat. Open daily 6am-10pm.

Pu Suma Restaurant, on the left adjacent to the pagoda rotary with your back to Bagan-Nyaung U Rd. An unassuming green shack with a yellow Burmese sign. Join locals in their well-earned adoration of Pu Suma's scrumptious, affordable Burmese food. Tasty noodles with pork 150kyat. Curries 250kyat. Open daily 7am-8pm.

SIGHTS

Three days is enough to explore the 4000-plus ancient temples and pagodas adorning the **Bagan Plain.** The US$10 admission is collected at checkpoints in the region and at the airport; presentation of the receipt is mandatory upon check-in at guest houses and hotels. This one-time fee allows access to all of the temples from around sunrise to after sunset (the larger temples close between 7 and 9pm).

The helpful *Glimpses of Glorious Bagan*, available at souvenir shops and temple entrances (600-1000kyat), is an ideal consort for deeper knowledge of these sights. It's also essential to talk to guest house owners, pony cart drivers, and tour guides for insight into off-the-beaten-path destinations—valuable gems abound. A quintessential Bagan experience involves viewing the sunset from a temple roof; Mingalazedi and Shwesandaw Pagodas are rightfully the most popular viewpoints, although numerous other temples provide fabulous (and quieter) views. Get around by **bicycle** (200-300kyat per day) or **horse cart** (all-day itinerary around 1500kyat). Many travelers take a one-day horse cart ride first, then strike out on their own by bicycle. A guide is useful (most US$5-10 per day).

If you're pressed for time, be sure to see Ananda Temple and Mahabodhi Pagoda in Old Bagan, Shwezigon Pagoda near Nyaung U, and Sulamani and Dhammayangyi Temples between Old Bagan and New Bagan, before soaking in a red and purple sunset from atop Shwesandaw.

OLD BAGAN

Old Bagan contains many of the archaeological zone's marquee temples. The area is navigable on foot and warrants a full day of exploration.

ANANDA TEMPLE (အာနန္ဒာ). The showcase of Old Bagan, Ananda represents the pinnacle of Bagan's Early Period design, with its sweeping terraces and symmetrical square Greek cross design. The 12th-century temple is commanding and awe-inspiring in size and grandeur, with 17 *stupas* rising from its walls and exterior structure. The interior walkways feature hundreds of Buddhas staring down from their alcoves, as well as four 10m standing Buddhas (one for each reincarnation of the Buddha) in each entrance. *(East of the city walls. Camera fee 30kyat, video 50kyat.)*

THATBYINNYU TEMPLE (သဗ္ဗညု). This 61m two-tiered temple was built in 1144 by King Alaungsithu and is the tallest structure in Bagan. Unfortunately, tourists are no longer allowed to go to the upper terraces. Its most interesting features are its exemplary brickwork and the intricate multilevel architectural design, characteristic of the transition to the late Bagan style. *(West of Ananda.)*

BAGAN MUSEUM. The Bagan Museum complex tells the story of the cataclysmic earthquake of 1975 and features Buddha images from the 10th and 11th centuries. It's worth it only for the dedicated museum hounds. *(West of Thatbyinnyu. US$5.)*

NAMELESS TEMPLE. This tiny temple without a name is worthy of mention. Attempting to find treasure in a plaster Buddha statue, a thief performed open-heart surgery on the image. He discovered a smaller plaster Buddha whose face emerged from the chest cavity. The owners, craving the merit granted to grand figures, had simply built a larger statue over the old one. *(Opposite Bagan Museum.)*

PITAKATTAIK (LIBRARY). According to legend, King Anawrahta built this structure in 1057 to house 30 sets of the Buddhist canon, carried by a caravan of 32 elephants from Thaton. At 16m square, its design carries many similarities to a temple, with a central room surrounded by a processional hallway. The distinctive five-tiered roof emerged as a later renovation at the hands of King Bodawpaya in 1783. *(North of Thatbyinnyu.)*

MAHABODHI PAGODA. This pagoda maintains spiritual ties with Bodh Gaya in India, where the Buddha attained Enlightenment under the *bodhi* tree. In the early 13th century, King Htilominlo modeled its design after the original Mahabodhi Pagoda in Bodh Gaya, accounting for its pyramidal spire and many seated Buddhas occupying niches in horizontal shelves. *(Northwest of the Pitakattaik.)*

BUPAYA PAGODA. Bupaya rests on a bank overlooking a bend of the Ayeyarwaddy River. It was destroyed in the 1975 earthquake, but reconstruction has restored it. The real reason to visit isn't for the temple but rather the amazing views of the river and mountain scenery beyond. *(At the northwest corner of Bagan.)*

BETWEEN B5AGAN AND NYAUNG U

SHWEZIGON PAGODA (ရွှေစည်းခုံဘုရား). According to legend, Buddha's tooth, collar bone, and frontlet relics are enshrined in this "Ground of Victory" Pagoda. It's said that King Anawrahta placed the frontlet relic atop a white elephant and declared that wherever the elephant knelt would be the relic's resting place; it was here that Shwezigon was built. The temple is the most revered and visited by locals, and current pagoda architecture bears its influence. *(5km northeast of Old Bagan, 500m before Nyaung U.)*

UPALI THEIN (ဥပါလိသိမ်). Allegedly dating back to the 13th century, Upali Thein is the only ordination hall for monks *(sima)* in the Bagan area. *(Halfway between Nyaung U and Bagan on the north side of Bagan-Nyaung U Rd.)*

NYUANG U MARKET. Built in the latest Bagan architectural style (wood and corrugated tin), this temple enshrines nothing Buddhist whatsoever and, instead, honors the US dollar. Alcoves contain lacquer ware plates and opium weights as well as dried fish and bamboo ware. While the market is overpriced for tourists and not particularly awe-inspiring, a walk through the wares provides simple entertainment. *(Open daily 6am-5pm.)*

SOUTH OF THE OLD CITY: BETWEEN BAGAN AND NEW BAGAN

SHWESANDAW PAGODA (ရွှေဆံတော်ဘုရား). King Anawrahta built Shwesandaw in the late 11th century to shelter a single Buddha hair. Archaeologists consider its design, featuring a bell-shaped dome atop five terraces, a forerunner to Shwezigon. A steep climb to the top affords a spectacular (and popular) sunset view. Also interesting is the original top (with *hti*) felled by the 1975 earthquake, left on the pagoda's south side. *(5km west of Nyaung U on Bagan-Nyaung U Rd.)*

MANUHA TEMPLE. Manuha was named after the King of Thaton, who suffered exile and imprisonment in Bagan after King Anawrahta sacked his kingdom in 1057. King Manuha sold his last possessions, even his crown jewels, to build the temple. Of interest is the claustrophobic nature of the Buddha images and temple—it's believed that the king chose to show his displeasure in imprisonment through the temple's design. *(South along the Bagan-Nyaung U Rd. in Myinkaba Village.)*

MINGALAZEDI PAGODA (မင်္ဂလာစေတီဘုရား). King Narathithapate inaugurated the construction of the "Auspicious Pagoda" in 1268 but held off completion for six years upon hearing a prophecy that it would bring his kingdom's destruction. Lo and behold, the Mongols sacked Bagan 10 years later. Its smooth, precise design cause archaeologists to consider it the last great pagoda of Bagan, and it offers prime views of the sunset from its scalable upper platform. *(South of Old Bagan.)*

SOUTHEAST OF THE OLD CITY

SULAMANI TEMPLE (စူဠာမဏိ). King Narapatisithu built Sulamani, dubbed "Crowning Jewel" in Pali, around the turn of the 13th century. This massive, two-story structure contains a vaulted corridor encircling brickwork, each side sporting a Buddha image seated on a pedestal. Interesting wall paintings adorn many walls and ceilings, but many are believed to have been added in the 18th century.

IF YOU WANN, I SHOW YOU While most Myanmar locals are shy and wary of foreigners, Bagan "wall painters" (from "wall painting copy makers") are notorious tourist hunters. Touring the desert on bicycle with their own copies of temple murals, these 20-year-old artistic nomads hone in on fresh travelers in attempts to turn their creations into hard-earned dollars. Many new arrivals to Bagan are overwhelmed by the throngs of aggressive sellers, but proper preparation will leave you ready for battle. Careful analysis reveals at least four types of selling techniques.

1. The Helpful Friend. The most common of wall-painters, the helpful friend usually rides solo along Bagan's paths and roads looking for tourists on rental bikes. He commonly initiates conversation with "Hello, where you go?" or "Where are you from?" and may even offer advice on the temple sights. Quickly, however, he shifts the topic with "You want to see my paintings? No problem, no money." The helpful friend is easily dispelled, but can also be of benefit with useful advice.

2. Squatters. At each of the large temples await the less energetic wall-painters. These young men claim their stake near the entrance and lounge with fellow squatters as they wait for inbound tourists. Like most souvenir sellers, squatters are easily ignored or shrugged off.

3. Pack Hunters. These are less frequently seen in the wild, as they only make their appearance known when a potential buyer shows interest. If one should respond favorably to the helpful friend's "Have a look? No problem..." pack hunters appear from nowhere and the foreigner is surrounded by painters and their wares. Pack hunters are more difficult to escape; only the determined will survive.

4. Freeloaders. The least successful of wall painters are often friends of the helpful friend or squatters. Freeloaders may function as translators or assist in a transaction but inevitably end up pushing their own wares, citing different styles and colors in replica-making.

DHAMMAYANGYI TEMPLE (ဓမ္မရံကြီး). This is one of Bagan's largest temples. Although its design, with porticos projecting from all sides of a square to form a Greek cross, follows Ananda's model, Dhammayangyi is loftier. Its unsurpassed brickwork, considered a crowning achievement of the Later Period, is airtight. Like its rough contemporary Sulamani, only the four porches and the outer corridors are accessible, while the interior is blocked.

MINNANTHU VILLAGE

Several temples in Minnanthu are worth a visit, and many other small temple complexes lie nearby. Few tourists come here. *(4-5km northeast of New Bagan.)*

NANDAMANNYA TEMPLE. Built by King Kyazawa in 1248, Nandamannya houses the best preserved wall paintings around, depicting scenes from the life of the most recent Buddha, Gautama. A racy picture on the west wall depicts women modeling see-through clothing in provocative postures; some postulate that this picture shows the temptation of Buddha by Mara.

PAYATHONEZU TEMPLE (THREE TEMPLES). The unique structural design, involving a uniform trio of temples joined at the hip via narrow vaulted passages, invokes its share of curiosity. These temples also contain 11th-century wall paintings depicting Gautama Buddha's life and showing mysterious deities from outside Theravada Buddhism.

DAYTRIPS FROM BAGAN

MOUNT POPPA ပုပ္ပားတောင်

Mount Poppa, 85km southeast of Bagan, is best reached by car. Guest houses and hotels in Nyaung U and New Bagan arrange transport (2hr., US$15). Find other travelers to split costs. Alternatively, a pickup leaves daily from the Nyaung U Bus Terminal (3hr.; 8:30am, returns 1pm; 400kyat).

Volcanic Mount Poppa rose to 1518m above sea level after a colossal earthquake in 442 BC, its volcanic ash transforming the barren Myingan plains below into fertile soil. Today, the mesa serves as the seat of all magical power and *nat* worship in Myanmar; adorned with *nat* shrines, monasteries, bells, and *stupas*, Mount Poppa is an important pilgrimage site. Stunning views and cool air await those who navigate the 20min. staircase to the top. Watch your step—the staircase houses mischievous monkeys. Visitors should do as the pilgrims do to avoid offending the *nat:* be careful not to wear red or black, speak ill of others, or carry meat on the climb.

FLOWER POWER "Mountain of Flowers" is rooted in ancient legend: Bagan's King Anawrahta loved Mount Poppa's flowers so much that he sent the Indian runner Byatta to fetch bundles of them every day—from over 50km away. Between runs, Byatta fell in love with a flower-eating ogress from Poppa named Mai Wunna. Together they bore two sons, named **Shwe Phyin Gyi** and **ShwePhyin Ngai**, or "Big Gold Pot" and "Small Gold Pot," who were wild, irreverent young men; they met their deaths for neglecting duties during the construction of the pagoda atop the mountain. After their executions, their spirits begged the king for forgiveness, and he graciously bestowed to them rights and territories to rule. By some twist of fate, the slacker sons have since become objects of worship, with Mount Poppa as the site of their veneration. Lavish festivals enlivened by transvestite *nat pwe* dancers honor them in July or August. Pilgrims follow their spirits around an ambitious circuit that includes Mount Poppa, Taungbyong (near Mandalay), and China.

INLE LAKE REGION

NYAUNGSHWE ညောင်ရွှေ ☎081

Idyllic Nyaungshwe rests in a fertile plain between twin corridors of rolling mountains. Visitors frazzled from the bustle of the cities or enervated from the swelter of Bagan will find relief here. Intha, Pa-O, Shan, and Burmese traditions combine to create a congenial and multifaceted culture unlike any other in Myanmar. Nyaungshwe is not merely the springboard to Inle Lake, Myanmar's most celebrated natural attraction, but constitutes a destination in itself. With scenic treks leading to hill-tribe villages, motorboat forays on the lake, canoe paddling around the canals, and invigorating bike rides, plenty exists to delight visitors, though for many the greatest appeal is the tiny town's relaxed atmosphere.

> **GOVERNMENT LISTINGS.** All government listings are marked with a **M** symbol. Money spent at such establishments goes directly into the government's hands. For more information, see **Keeping the Bucks Where They Belong,** p. 469.

TRANSPORTATION

Flights: Heho Airport lies 25km northwest (by taxi 1hr., 4500kyat). Airline offices are in **Taunggyi,** but guest houses and travel agencies arrange tickets at the same price. **Air Mandalay** flies daily to: **Kengtung** (US$80); **Mandalay** (US$45); **Yangon** (1¼hr., US$95) via **Bagan** (US$65-70). **Yangon Airways** flies daily to **Mandalay** (US$45) and **Yangon** (1¼hr., US$90). **M Myanma Airways** goes to **Mandalay** and **Yangon** (2 per week).

Buses: Company offices are in **Taunggyi,** but guest houses and travel agencies sell tickets. Buses leave from **Shwenyaung Junction,** 11km north. **Nyaung U Man Express** runs minibuses to **Bagan** (11hr., 5:30am, 2300kyat). **Honey Express** runs **minibuses** and **Shwe La Min** runs buses to **Mandalay** (9hr., 5:30am, 1900kyat). **Ye Thu Aung** and **Taung Paw Thar** run parallel routes to **Yangon** via **Bago,** the former getting the nod for comfort (17-20hr., 12:30pm, 2600kyat).

Local Transportation: Linecars leave from the street one block west of the market for **Shwenyaung Junction** (every 30min., 50kyat) and **Taunggyi** (1hr., every 30-60min., 70kyat). From Shwenyaung Junction, connections run to **Kalaw** (3hr., every 30-60min. 7am-evening, 400-500kyat) via **Heho** (1hr., 200kyat) and **Aungban** (2hr.); and **Thazi** (4-5hr., every hr. 7am-noon, 500-600kyat). All services run daily 7am-4:30pm during the cold season, and 7am-5pm during summer months.

M Trains: The closest station is 11km away in **Shwenyaung,** from which a daily train winds its way to **Thazi** (8hr.; 8:30am; ordinary US$3, upper US$7) via **Kalaw** (3hr.; 8am; ordinary US$1, upper US$3). From Thazi, connections run to **Mandalay** (3hr.; 8 per day; ordinary US$3, upper US$8) and **Yangon** (9 per day; ordinary US$9, upper US$25, sleeper US$33) abound. Trains are increasingly delayed in the rainy season.

Taxis: Can be hired at most guest houses and travel agencies. To: **Bagan** (US$70); **Heho** airport (4500kyat); **Kalaw** (5000kyat); **Meiktila** (US$40); **Pindaya Cave** (8500kyat); **Shwenyaung Junction** (1500kyat); **Taunggyi** (3500kyat); **Thazi** (US$40).

Rental: Guest houses and travel agencies rent **bicycles** (400kyat per day), **canoes** (300kyat per person per hr.) and teak **motorboats** (driver included, 300kyat per day).

ORIENTATION AND PRACTICAL INFORMATION

Nyaungshwe is set in a rectangular grid and easily navigable on foot. Landmarks, rather than addresses, provide the fulcrums for navigation. Linecars from Swenyaung stop at the northwest corner of the **market,** in the north of town. Along the southern edge of the market is **Yonegyi Rd.,** home to countless **travel agencies, shops,** and **local cafes.** Yonegyi and **Phaungdawsaik Rd.** (two blocks south and recognizable by its numerous pagodas) run parallel and west to the **canal.** Most **guest houses** and **restaurants** are found here, east of the canal and southwest of the market. The canal (with **Canal Rd.**) forms the west edge of town and runs north-south along its length.

Tourist Office: **MTT,** off the canal at the end of Phaungdawsaik Rd. Its sole purpose is to collect the US$3 Inle Lake admission fee. Open daily 9am-4pm.

Tours and Travel: Comet Travel Agency, 27 Yonegyi Rd., near the southeast corner of the market. Run by friendly Nwe Ni Soe. Arranges bus, train, and air tickets and rents boats, canoes, bikes, and taxis. **Treks** US$3-5 per day, including lunch. Open daily 8am-8pm. Many others in this area provide similar services.

Currency Exchange: Guest houses offer the most reliable rates, but at 50-80kyat less than in Yangon or Mandalay. Offers on the street are generally worse.

Markets: Mingala Market, on Yonegyi Rd., sells handicrafts (including Shan handbags, cannibals, and wood carvings), clothes, and vegetables. Relatively tame, except when the rotating market comes (see **Round and Round,** below), but foreigners can expect a hard sell. Open daily 6am-6pm except on full moons and holidays.

Emergency: ☎0 for the operator.

Medical Services: A small **hospital** is 3 blocks south of the post office. The nearest decent hospital is **Mandalar Hospital** in Taunggyi (see p. 508).

Pharmacies: Win Tin and **Zizoa,** on Yonegyi Rd., south side of market. Both open daily 6am-8pm.

Telephones: IDD available at **King Rabbit Tours** (☎229 42), 15m east of the market on Yonegyi Rd. US$7 per min. Call back service 500kyat per 8min. (plus the 1min. to call and give your number).

Post Office: On Phaungdawpyan Rd., by the Golden Express Hotel. Open M-F 9am-4:30pm.

ACCOMMODATIONS

Splendid budget guest houses and hotels offer clean, cozy rooms and reliable information on Inle Lake. Lodgings often provide free breakfast, laundry service, boat and canoe rentals, bus bookings, and taxi service.

Remember Inn, down the road that runs along the northern edge of the market; it's a 3-5min. walk east from the canal. Bountiful breakfasts, backpackers, and big bamboo bungalows with bath and hot water. Singles US$3; doubles US$6.

Four Sisters Inn, at the south end of Canal Rd. Four Sisters has home-spun hospitality, not to mention the tastiest home-cooked food in Myanmar and a garden. Big, clean bungalows with bamboo walls and hot showers. Singles US$6; doubles US$10-12.

Teakwood Guest House, 3 blocks from the canal, above Phaungdawsaik Rd. Run by a Mon-Shan couple, this popular guest house offers spacious rooms and tasty Shan cooking. Western breakfast and Shan dinner included. Singles US$3, with bath US$4; doubles US$6/8.

Joy Guest House, down Yonegyi Rd. from the market toward the canal; follow the signs. The extra dollar means fewer people, a great location, traditional furniture, and clean bathrooms. Breakfast served on balcony with view of sunrise. Singles with bath US$4-5; doubles US$8-10; family rooms with bathtub US$15.

FOOD AND ENTERTAINMENT

Four Sisters Restaurant, 105 Nan Pan Quarter, at the southern end of Canal Rd. One of the finest dining experiences. Enhanced by fresh ingredients and traditional music, din-

ROUND AND ROUND Throughout the state the Shan princes established a rotating market to provide villagers regular opportunities to sell their crops and buy their near-weekly needs. Every fifth day, villagers trek through the Shan hills with kilos of tea leaves, jack fruits, strawberries, and cheroot (cigar) leaves on their backs or heads to market. Though there is little tourists would want to purchase, the markets are an insightful look into the agricultural life of the area. The bustling morning market moves according to the following schedule: Kalaw Shwenyaung Kaungtaung to Pindaya Nyaungshwe Nanpan to Heho Kyone to Ywama (floating market) Aungban Taunggyi to Pin Loung Nan Taing Mine Thout and back.

ner takes the form of a home-cooked Myanmar meal; there is no menu. Pay what you feel is appropriate. Open daily 6:30-9pm, but stop in early and make a reservation.

Pancake Kingdom, towards the canal on Yonegyi Rd., follow the signs, and **Golden Kite,** 3 blocks away from the canal on Yonegyi Rd., duke it out for the best Western food in Backpackerland. It's a photo finish, but fresh homemade pasta dishes (500-600kyat) gives the title to GK by a nose despite PK's cool name. Both serve excellent banana, chocolate, or strawberry pancakes 100-250kyat. Both open daily 7:30am-9:30pm.

Big Drum Restaurant, across the canal bridge at the end of Yonegyi Rd. and 50m to the left. Shan specialties in A-frame bungalows on the canal. Set meals with curry, soup, and fried potato or tomato 650kyat. Vegetable curries 250kyat. Open daily 9am-9pm.

Shwe Pyi Soe Tea House. Head 3 blocks south from the market on the road that runs along its west side; it's just past the pagoda on the left. Rock to the latest in Myanmar pop music. Samosas 10kyat. Best tea in town 40kyat. Open daily 6am-6pm.

Nyaungshwe also hosts numerous makeshift **"pubs"** (cafes) after dark. Tourists stick to guest houses while locals take their pick of pubs along Yonegyi Rd. Check out **Kaung Kaung Restaurant,** on the west side of the market, for 120kyat taps of Myanmar beer. (Open daily 9am to 10pm.)

Those who missed the Mandalay Marionettes might take in a show at the **Aung Traditional Puppet Show** on Yonegyi Rd., 100m east of the market. The master puppeteer puts on excellent half-hour shows throughout the day. (500kyat per person. Open daily 9am-9pm.)

DAYTRIPS FROM NYAUNGSHWE

INLE LAKE အင်းလေးကန်

US$3, payable at the MTT office at the canal entrance.

Inle Lake, 2km down the canal from Nyaungshwe, is the showpiece of the Shan Plateau. From the lake's center, power lines, bamboo stakes, wooden homes on stilts, and the occasional palm tree punctuate the mountainous horizon. The Intha, as the lake area's residents are known, build homes on stilts over the water and succeed admirably in "living off the lake." There's little space on this 10km by 40km lake that isn't harvested, fished, or lived on. Intha farmers tend to floating gardens that yield flowers, vegetables, and fruit (especially tomatoes) and fish from their narrow teak canoes. The Intha are also gifted weavers, carpenters, canoe builders, and metalworkers. Boatmen seek hefty commissions to escort visitors to the factories and workshops that dot the lake. Though the home industries are interesting and informative, those who feel that this tends to reduce a trip to a tour of souvenir shops should establish a desired itinerary before setting off for the lake.

YWAMA. The village of Ywama was once an essential stop on any Inle Lake foray. Its **floating market** (see **Round and Round,** p. 507) appears in full vigor every fifth day. Recently, however, the market has been redubbed the "Souvenir Market." On official market days, it's an interesting lesson in nautical trade (although why they don't step ashore to facilitate the process remains a mystery), but check with your guest house owner first, lest you end up being ambushed by ambitious venders with souvenir-laden canoes. The most sacred religious site in north Shan State, **Phaung Daw U Kyaung,** can be reached via the main boat landing in town. Though the (reconstructed) exterior architecture is impressive, the structure's contents are not. Owing to generous gold-leaf donations over the years, the Buddha images have ballooned considerably in size, rendering their original dimensions a mystery and leaving five lumps of gold in their place. Every September or October, the 20-day **Phaung Daw U Kyaung Festival** features their procession in highly decorated barges, along with hundreds of accompanying vessels, around the lake's villages. At the northern outskirts of Ywama stands the stilted **Nga Phe Kyaung,** the oldest monastery among the 268 that dot the lake's shores. The beautiful teak structure houses Bagan, Intha, Shan, and Tibetan Buddha images. For generations, the monks have trained cats to jump through hoops. Exactly how this "cat and pony" contributes to enlightenment is open to debate.

NUN TE. For a substantially more down-to-earth and personal encounter with Inle Lake monastic life, wander to the village of Nun Te, 5min. south of Four Sisters Inn as Canal Rd. becomes a dirt path. The village contains four monasteries, **Le Bien, Pien Tha, Pai Ah Gyi,** and **Moke Thoke,** the last of which serves as home base for 17 studious monks. All welcome visitors. The ethereally gracious U Aw Bar Tha at Moke Thoke speaks excellent English and is happy to show visitors around.

OTHER TOWNS. The farther out you head on the lake, the better your chances are of escaping the souvenir scene. One good bet is **Intain,** known for its market and *stupas.* To get there, cross the lake by boat and continue on foot. At the lake's far southern end, the villages of **Taung Doe** and **Kyauk Taing,** which have recently become accessible to foreign travelers, offer opportunities to explore stone carvings and ancient *stupas.* Because of their distance from Nyaungshwe, visiting them adds 500-1000kyat to the normal price of boat hire.

Dozens of villages to the east and west afford other exploring options. Day-hike guides are available for US$3-5 (lunch included), with higher prices for longer treks up to 20 miles. Closer forays can be done without a guide, so long as you aren't afraid to ask for directions on occasion. Hire guides from your guest house or a travel agent to avoid scams.

TAUNGGYI

Take a pickup or taxi from Nyaungshwe (see Nyaungshwe's Practical Information, above). Pickups back to Nyaungshwe leave from just north of the market (1hr., leaves when full 7am-4:30pm, 100kyat).

The capital of Shan State, Taunggyi would feel like just another big town were it not for the frontier atmosphere of its location, nestled among the peaks of picturesque highlands 28km northeast of Inle Lake. Its Shan, Burmese, Chinese, Indian, and Nepali populations as well as its fine market make it a stimulating daytrip from Nyangshwe, but few travelers find reason to spend the night. Opium and insurgency intrigue in the area beyond make Taunggyi the easternmost point accessible by land in Shan State.

Bogyoke Aung San Rd., the main drag in Taunggyi, bisects the city as it goes uphill from north to south. Pickups from Nyaungshwe may drop passengers in a lot on the northwest outskirts of town; from here, bus #9 heads toward the town center (10min., 20kyat). The town's main draw is the **central market,** on Bogyoke Aung San Rd., which sells everything from handicrafts to traditional Shan dress. Taunggyi's market is less touristed and busier than Nyaungshwe's, resulting in a larger selection of goods and better bartering opportunities. The other reason travelers might visit Taunggyi is for treatment at the private **Mandalar Hospital,** 222 Bogyoke Aung San Rd. (☎227 33), near the north end of town, which has an English-speaking staff and 24hr. service. At the opposite end of town, also on Bogyoke Aung San Rd., Taunggyi's **post office** offers the most services of any in the region, while the **telephone office** next door provides the usual exorbitantly expensive IDD (US$4-8 per min.) and reasonable but unpredictable telegraph (4-15kyat per word) services. (Both open M-F 9am-4pm.)

For those with time to spare, the **Shan State Museum,** south of the post office, manages to pack religious, cultural, and artistic artifacts into relatively few exhibits. (Open M-F 9:30am-3:30pm. US$2.) Affordable accommodations are at **Khemarat Hotel,** 403 Bogyoke Aung San Rd. opposite Mandalar Hospital. (☎224 64. Clean and comfortable rooms are well-kept. Singles US$6; doubles US$12.)

KALAW ကလော ☎081

The sedate alpine charm of Kalaw is nothing short of paradise to travelers coming from the dusty swelter of Bagan or the frenzied sprawl of Mandalay or Yangon. The British must have thought similarly when they founded a hill station here; a colonial legacy lingers in the wide, uncluttered streets and missionary-built schools, even though most tourists do not. With jungle trekking trails and traditional villages in the surrounding hills, Kalaw serves as a base camp for hikes or the perfect place to sit back, relish the air, and take in the scenery.

TRANSPORTATION. The **train station** (booking office open daily 9am-5pm) at the southeast corner of town only serves **Thazi** (5hr.; 11:30am, 1:20, 3pm; US$3). Trains are often hours late in the rainy season. **Buses** originating in Taunggyi pass through on their way to points west and south. Book tickets at numerous travel and trekking agencies near the market. Buses go to: **Bagan** (8hr., 7am, around 2000kyat); **Mandalay** (7-8hr., 7am, 1500kyat); **Yangon** (15-18hr., 2pm, 2500kyat). Two buses depart from Parami Hotel, one block west of the market, for **Taunggyi** (3hr.; 6:30, 7am; 400kyat) via **Shwenyaung Junction** (the turn-off to Inle Lake; 2hr., 400kyat). Buy tickets one day in advance through guest houses or travel agencies. If these buses are full, **pickups** rattle eastbound on Union Rd. (6am-4 or 5pm, 300-400kyat).

PRACTICAL INFORMATION. Kalaw's layout is simple. **Pye Daung Su (Union) Rd.,** which runs west to Thazi and east to Taunggyi, forms the northern boundary of town. Ten parallel streets extend southward. Just before the **market, Main Rd.** bisects Union Rd. and has a large **banyan tree,** the town landmark. Travel agencies and guest houses **exchange** US dollars and FEC at free-market rates 50-70kyat less than what you'll get in the bigger cities. On Main Rd. about halfway between Union Rd. and the banyan tree, on the market side, sits a well-stocked **pharmacy.** (☎500 08. Open daily 7am-7pm.) A private **clinic** sits on the road that runs along the southern side of the market. From Union Rd., walk down Main Rd. to the banyan tree and turn right; look for the red cross 2½ blocks down on the left. (☎501 86. Open daily 8-11am and 3-7pm.) IDD overseas calls can be made from the **post office,** at the west end of Union Rd opposite Natsin Rd. (☎500 57. Open daily 9am-4pm.)

Trekking agencies line Union Rd. around the market. The hillside outside Kalaw hosts several different 1-3 day treks. Routes focus on visits to the villages of four regional tribes. Guide fees (US$5-7 per person per day) cover food and accommodations in the villages. It pays to shop around for a guide in Kalaw; ask locals for their recommendations and try to find someone who speaks the languages of the peoples on the itinerary. Guides range from highly experienced and knowledgeable to utterly ignorant. **Sam's Trekking** (☎502 37), on Union Rd. on the north side of the market, receives raves, as does **Eddie,** owner of the Golden Kalaw Hotel. Treks to the north visit tribes that live more traditionally than the south, but all routes have spectacular scenery. Hiking in the rainy season, however, brings slippery conditions; hiking boots and an optimistic attitude are necessary.

ACCOMMODATIONS AND FOOD. Hotel and guest house rooms outnumber visitors, so quality is high and prices are low. **Winner Hotel,** in the town center on Union Rd., has excellent rooms and satellite TV in the sitting area. (☎502 79. Singles US$3, with bath US$5-7; doubles US$6/10; rooms with tub, fridge, satellite

TV, and teak decor US$20-25.) **Golden Lily Guest House,** at the town's west end on Nat Sin Rd., is a quiet, simpler, but clean place run by a helpful family. (☎501 08. Rooms with shared bath US$2 per person, with private bath US$3.) It doesn't get any cheaper—or more basic—than **Pine Land Inn,** next to Winner Hotel. (☎500 20. Small, bare rooms US$1 per person, with bath US$2-3 per person.)

Thirigayhar (Seven Sisters) Restaurant, 7 Union St., 100m west of the post office, serves delicious Burmese, Chinese, Indian, and European food ranging from sour mustard soup to vegetable spaghetti. (Dishes 200-600kyat. Open daily 7am-10pm.) **Everest Nepali Food Center,** on Aung Chan Tha St. (look for the sign near the banyan tree) is the best NFC in town, with all-you-can-eat *dhaal bhat* for 450kyat and curries for 250-300kyat. (Open daily 6am-9pm.) **Ye Baw Gyi,** on Union Rd. at the north side of the market, is popular for its traditional Myanmar curries and fried noodles. (Dishes 250-350kyat. Open daily 6am-9pm.)

DAYTRIPS FROM KALAW: PINDAYA AND SHWE U MIN. The "Switzerland of Myanmar," **Pindaya,** 1180m above sea level and 39km north of the town of **Aungban,** has crisp air, excellent scenery, and fertile farmland. The town's reputation is built on **Shwe U Min Pagoda,** or "Golden Cave Pagoda." The strenuous climb up 200 steps to the cave entrance is worth it. Stalagmites, stalactites, and 8000 Buddha images crafted in every conceivable style adorn the limestone caves. Over the years, pilgrims and adherents have donated these images to the caves, but the monument is now saturated, and trustees have put a cap on further offerings. The smaller caves serve as meditation chambers for monks and laypeople. Bring a flashlight and US$3 for admission. During the full moon in February or March, the cave hosts a lively festival attracting devotees from all over the country. The **rotating market** comes through town every five days (see **Round and Round,** p. 507). Pindaya is best reached from Kalaw, but public transportation is difficult, especially in the rainy season. When Pindaya hosts the market, a linecar makes the journey from Kalaw to Pindaya, leaving when full (1½hr.; around 6am, return around noon; 200kyat). If it's not a market day, traveling to Pindaya by public transportation is nearly impossible; it involves an overnight stay and the possibility of having to return to Kalaw via an expensive taxi ride. This situation changes frequently, so ask in Kalaw. The more stable option is to go by **taxi** (4500-5000kyat round-trip), which allows you to stop around Pindaya to view **handicraft centers** specializing in bamboo hats, tree bark paper, umbrellas, clay pots, and the local version of potato chips.

PHILIPPINES

PESO

US$1 = P51.30 (PESO)	P100 = US$1.96
CDN$1 = P33.20	P100 = CDN$3.01
EURO€1 = P46.69	P100 = EURO€2.14
UK£1 = P74.48	P100 = UK£1.34
IR£1 = P59.29	P100 = IR£1.69
AUS$1 = P27.18	P100 = AUS$3.68
NZ$1 = P22.61	P100 = NZ$4.42
ZAR1 = P6.15	P100 = ZAR16.25

PHONE CODE **Country Code:** 63. **International dialing prefix:** 00.

Possessing a history laden with Spanish and American influences, the Philippines has been perhaps permanently thrown out of sync with the rest of Southeast Asia. Described as a hodgepodge of "Malay, Madrid, and Madison Avenue," Filipino culture fosters a range of ethnicities, languages, and lifestyles among which natives have somehow found unity and an unparalleled love for life. Their willingness to drop everything for a basketball game or cockfighting match reflects the national philosophy of *bahala na*, roughly translated as "whatever will be, will be." At the heart of Filipino tradition is a strong sense of community; Filipinos can't bear doing things by themselves and value family, friendliness, and personal loyalty above all. This cheerful attitude, along with safe streets, convenient transportation, numerous English speakers, and abundant inexpensive locales, make the Philippines a budget traveler's paradise.

FACTS AND FIGURES

Official Name: Republic of the Philippines.
Government: Republic.
Capital: Manila.
Land Area: 300,176 sq. km.
Geography: A 7100-island archipelago stretching 1851km north-south and 1107km east-west. Divides into four zones: Luzon, the Visayas, Palawan, and Mindanao. Mountain ranges: Central Cordillera and Sierra Madre in Luzon. Mindanao's Mt. Apo(2954m) is the highest peak.
Climate: Two seasons in western Luzon and the Visayas: Dry (high season) Nov.-Mar., and rainy (low season) Apr.-Oct. Rest of country has a balance of wet and dry weather.
Major Cities: Bacolod, Cagayan de Oro, Cebu, Davao, Iloilo, Zamboanga.
Population: 81,159,644.
Languages: Tagalog, English.
Religions: Roman Catholic (83%), Protestant (9%), Muslim (5%), Buddhist (3%).
Average Income Per Capita: US$1050.
Major Exports: Electronics, textiles, agricultural products.

LIFE AND TIMES

THE PEOPLE OF THE PHILIPPINES

Though they inhabit over 1000 islands, Filipinos are relatively homogenous. Thanks to Spanish colonialism and its Christian legacy, Christian Malays account for 92% of Filipinos. Still, a growing number of ethnic and religious minorities, such as tribal groups and Muslims, diversify the islands. The Chinese and *mestizo* populations, mostly Filipino-Spanish and Filipino-American, are also becoming more prominent. The dwindling *Negrito* population, the Philippines' most exploited minority and oldest surviving race, lives mostly in upland forests as nomadic hunters and fishermen.

HIGHLIGHTS OF THE PHILIPPINES

BEACHES. The sugar-fine sand of Boracay's **White Beach** (p. 582) lures jet setters and backpackers alike, while **Palawan** (p. 590) draws an adventurous crowd. **Bantayan** (p. 566) and **Malapascua** (p. 568) are restful island detours en route to Cebu.

DIVING. Visayan dive sites are Southeast Asia's best; **Moalboal** (p. 565), **Panglao Island** (p. 571), and **Apo Island** (p. 577) are the diver's pilgrimage trail.

CULTURAL HERITAGE. Manila's walled city of **Intramuros** (p. 527), **museums** (p. 527), and **Fort San Pedro** (p. 564) simulate the drama between *conquistadors* and natives, while **Vigan's** (p. 545) churches attest to the lasting Christian influence. Indigenous Cordilleran cultures around **Banaue** (p. 538) delight ethnographers.

NATURAL WONDERS. Mountain air cleanses Manila-marred lungs around **Bontoc's rice terraces** (p. 535). The **Mayon Volcano** (p. 552) in Legazpi and **Mt. Kanla-on** (p. 574) near Bacolod challenge with their height and fiery tempers. Palawan's **Cabayugan River** (p. 594) offers a surreal float through the bowels of Earth. Hikers meander through Bohol's **Chocolate Hills** (p. 570) to peek at the precious primate, the *tarsier*.

1380 Islam slowly begins to spread

1521 Magellan arrives; Spanish rule begins

1565 Spanish unify and colonize the Philippines; Manila becomes capital

16c Catholicism takes over

17-18c Revolution begins as tensions rise

1762 British seize Manila but promptly relinquish it to Spain

1896 *ilustrados* grow in power; Rizal's execution spurs nationalism

19c Radical Katipunan society wages war with Spanish

HISTORY

EARLY HISTORY

The first immigrants probably came to the Philippines 30,000 years ago from southern China, Vietnam, and Malaysia. Malays soon became dominant in the Visayas and southern Luzon, but the Chinese still managed to establish strong trading communities that aided the spread of Islam in the 14th and 15th centuries.

SPANISH YEARS (1521–1888)

–The colonial maxim: Ask not what you can do for your country, ask what your country can do for us.

Like any greedy observer, the Spanish recognized the Philippines' precious metals, foothold along the spice route, and easily Catholicized population and moved in for the kill. In 1521, **Ferdinand Magellan** led an expedition to the Visayas, signaling the beginning of almost 400 years of Spanish rule. Relying on the Philippines' lack of unity, **Miguel López de Legazpi** quickly consolidated Spanish rule and unified the nation for the first time. The Spanish claimed the Philippines as a colony in 1565, moved the capital to Manila, and Catholicized the majority of the Philippine people except the Muslims in the south. Friars controlled religious life, government, and education, while Spanish colonists only cared about trade and consequently were concentrated in urban areas. This feudal system bred tension between the friars and an educated Filipino elite. Known as the *ilustrados*, they were the first driving force in the revolution to come.

REFORM MOVEMENT AND EARLY NATIONALISM (1888–96)

–Sore losers and sour independence: what happens when you don't share.

Few challenged the strong-minded Spanish for the first 200 years of rule. But during the Seven Years' War, the Filipinos grew disenchanted with Spanish rule, and the omnipresent

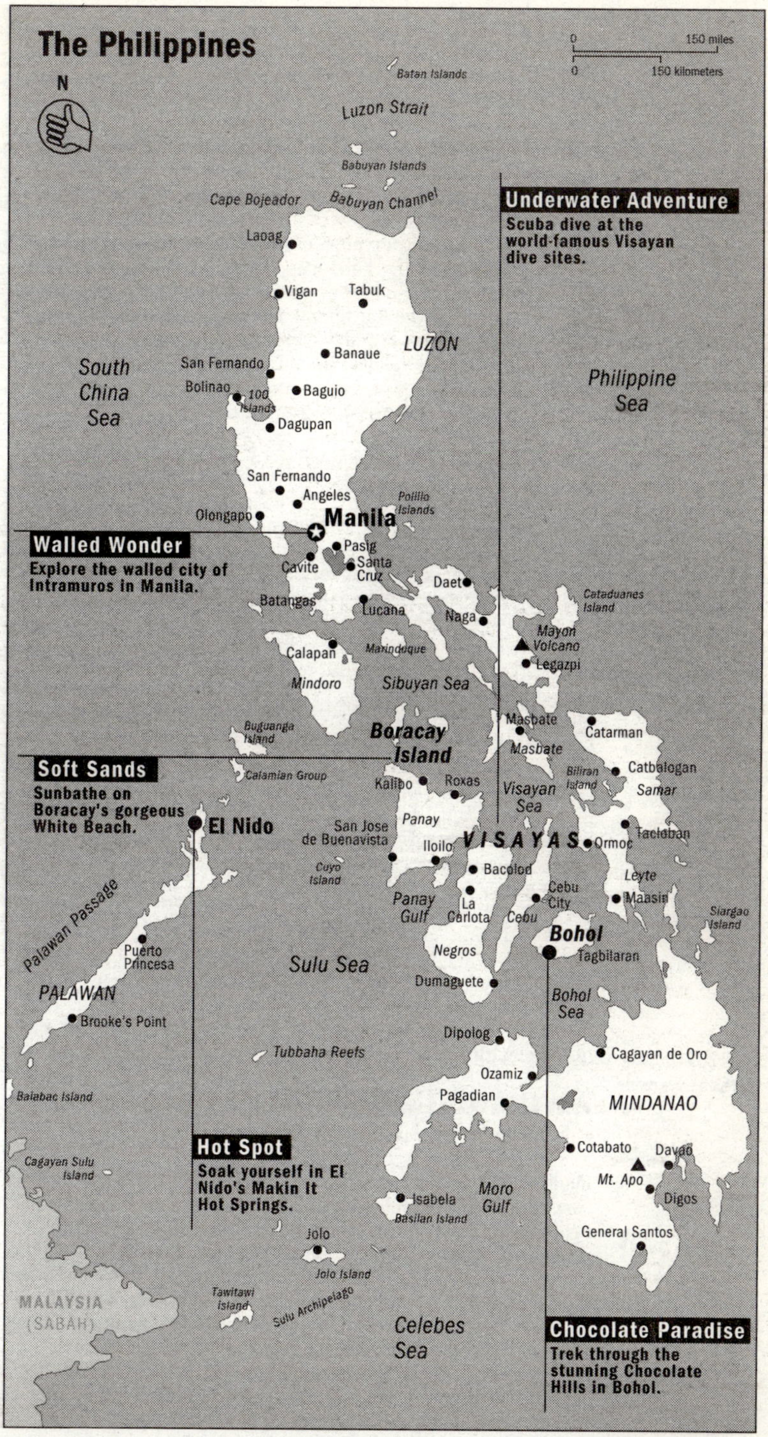
The Philippines
N
0 150 miles
0 150 kilometers
Batan Islands
Luzon Strait
Babuyan Islands
Cape Bojeador
Babuyan Channel
Underwater Adventure
Scuba dive at the world-famous Visayan dive sites.
Laoag
Vigan
Tabuk
LUZON
Banaue
San Fernando
Bolinao
100 Islands
Baguio
Dagupan
South China Sea
Philippine Sea
San Fernando
Angeles
Polillo Islands
Olongapo
Manila
Walled Wonder
Explore the walled city of Intramuros in Manila.
Pasig
Cavite
Santa Cruz
Daet
Batangas
Lucena
Catanduanes Island
Naga
Mayon Volcano
Calapan
Marinduque
Legazpi
Mindoro
Sibuyan Sea
Busuanga Island
Boracay Island
Masbate
Catarman
Masbate
Soft Sands
Sunbathe on Boracay's gorgeous White Beach.
Calamian Group
Kalibo
Roxas
Biliran Island
Catbalogan
Samar
Visayan Sea
El Nido
San Jose de Buenavista
Panay
Iloilo
VISAYAS
Ormoc
Tacloban
Cuyo Island
Bacolod
Leyte
Cebu City
Maasin
Siargao Island
Palawan Passage
Panay Gulf
La Carlota
Cebu
Bohol
Puerto Princesa
Negros
Tagbilaran
Sulu Sea
PALAWAN
Dumaguete
Bohol Sea
Brooke's Point
Dipolog
Cagayan de Oro
Tubbataha Reefs
Ozamiz
Balabac Island
Pagadian
MINDANAO
Hot Spot
Soak yourself in El Nido's Makin It Hot Springs.
Cotabato
Davao
Cagayan Sulu Island
Mt. Apo
Moro Gulf
Digos
Isabela
Basilan Island
General Santos
Jolo
Jolo Island
MALAYSIA (SABAH)
Tawitawi Island
Sulu Archipelago
Celebes Sea
Chocolate Paradise
Trek through the stunning Chocolate Hills in Bohol.

1898 Spanish-American War; US defeats Spain and buys the Philippines in giant 3-for-1 bargain

1900s Philippine-American War; Aguinaldo leads the revolt

1910 US crushes insurrection, changes tactics, and begins cultural invasion

1942-45 Japanese invade Luzon, defeating MacArthur

1945 Angry MacArthur gets revenge; Philippines gets independence under Roxas

1953 Magsaysay suppresses Huk Rebellion and is elected president

1953-63 The bad and the ugly: a decade of inept rule

1963 Popular Marcos elected president, and wife buys more shoes

1968 NPA established; Marcos brands them communist, calls coup, and declares martial law

British snuck in and occupied Manila in 1762 only to give it back to Spain in 1763. Continued economic development in the 1800s led to the growth of the educated elite—the *ilustrados*—who, initially encouraged by reforms promised by the Spanish, strove for cultural assimilation with Spain rather than independence. **Jose Rizal,** from Luzon, anchored the *ilustrados'* fight for independence, choosing literature as his weapon. His famous novel *Noli Me Tángere (Touch Me Not)* galvanized the Filipino elite. Distrustful colonial authorities executed Rizal in 1896, spurring a wave of nationalism that fueled the development of the **Katipunan,** a radical secret society for independence through revolution. When the *ilustrados* refused to support the Katipunan, its founder, **Andres Bonifacio,** forged their signatures on the Katipunan's membership list and showed it to Spanish authorities. Bonifacio waged war on the Spanish and was executed soon after. The Filipinos and Spanish signed a truce, but tensions remained high.

AMERICA IN THE PHILIPPINES (1896–1945)

–Problem+America=Bigger problem

The **Spanish American War** erupted in 1898 when the US Navy under Gen. Dewey attacked the Spanish fleet in Manila Bay. In the peace treaty that ended the war, the US bought the Philippines, Guam, and Puerto Rico for a bargain US$20 million. Opposed to American intentions to "civilize and Christianize" the Filipinos—especially since Dewey didn't notice that most Filipinos were already Catholic—President Emilio Aguinaldo initiated the **Philippine Insurrection** or **Philippine-American War.** The US crushed the insurrection and, instead of being acrimonious, adopted a policy of "benevolent assimilation" toward their "little brown brothers" (so dubbed by William Taft, the first American governor of the Philippines). Education became the method of Americanization, and the Filipinos embraced assimilation into American culture. Though the US increased literacy, developed a public health system, and improved roads and communications, its involvement in the Philippines came at a heavy price. Promotion of English devalued indigenous culture, and little was done to bridge the gap between the burgeoning middle class and the rural *barrios*. To this day, inequality persists, as one-fifth of the population controls 50% of the wealth.

WWII AND INDEPENDENCE (1942–69)

–Never break a promise: MacArthur strikes back.

Feeling lucky after a successful invasion of Pearl Harbor just two days earlier, the Japanese pushed on and invaded Luzon, proceeding to occupy the islands for four years. Like all pissed-off, dispossessed generals, MacArthur vowed "I shall return," and did in 1945, defeating the Japanese and liberating the Philippines. Independence began with the election of **Manuel Roxas** as the first president of the post-war Commonwealth. Defense Secretary **Ramon Magsaysay** quelled the **Hukbalahap** (or **Huk,** People's Anti-Japanese Army), an anti-Roxas peasant organization which was denounced as communist by pro-

Americans, and became President in 1953. Following victory, the government passed from one inept regime to another until **Ferdinand Marcos** came to power in 1963. His aggression in tackling the problems of education, poverty, transportation, and land reform won him widespread approval. In 1969 he became the first president to win a second term. He was accompanied into office by his wife, the former beauty queen and shoe aficionado **Imelda Marcos.**

1979
Holy plummeting pesos! Economic recession

1983
B. Aquino killed in Manila; shoe queen Imelda suspected

1986
"Cory" Aquino romps all over Marcos in election

1986-92
Cory curbs government abuse of power, releases political prisoners, and shuts up greedy Imelda Marcos

THE MARCOS DYNASTY (1963–86)

—"It wasn't me! Blame the communists!"

After years of success, Marcos' liberal spending led to a currency devaluation that weakened his power and sparked skepticism from the press. Claiming to protect his country from internal communist threats from the **New People's Army (NPA),** Marcos staged a coup in 1972 and declared martial law. Many Filipinos supported him initially but soon became aware of the corruption within the state and their disenchantment with Marcos grew. In 1977, Marcos' arch rival, Senator **Benigno "Ninoy" Aquino,** was arrested on trumped-up charges of treason and murder. Upon arrival in Manila after years of exile, he was assassinated at the airport. Many suspect either First Lady Imelda Marcos or military chief Fabian Ver as his killer.

PEOPLE POWER (1986–1992)

—The First Wives Club: Cory and Imelda show who wears the pants in this archipelago

Aquino's assassination marked the end of Marcos' rule. **Corazon Aquino,** Benigno's widow, ran against Marcos and received overwhelming support. The **EDSA Revolution,** named for the street on which local masses faced marines and tanks in support of "Cory," gained international attention as one of the first successful pro-democracy revolutions in the developing world. Aquino released all political prisoners and drafted a new constitution that would reduce executive power. She also dealt with the continuing demands of Imelda Marcos, who was found guilty of stealing millions from the treasury. Succeeding Aquino in 1992, **Fidel Ramos** faced an economic crisis caused by several volcanic eruptions and the US termination of its lease on the Subic Bay naval base, a move that cost the Philippines thousands of jobs.

THE PHILIPPINES TODAY

When Ramos' supporters failed to amend the constitution to allow him to run for a second term, **Joseph Estrada,** a college-drop out and movie star, took his place as president. The Supreme Court removed Estrada from office in January of 2001, following massive resignations from his government, and installed Vice President **Gloria Arroyo.** Estrada now faces a corruption trial. The biggest challenges facing Arroyo's new administration are the swelling government budget deficit (estimated at 74.2 billion pesos), corruption, poverty, and the high crime rates. He must also deal with increasing domestic terrorism from left-wing groups and Muslim separatists. The **Abu Sayyaf Group (ASG)** is responsible for a rash of bombings in Manila and kidnappings as well as killings of tourists and locals in Mindanao and Palawan in 2000 and 2001. The **Moro Islamic Liberation Front (MILF)**, another Muslim insurgent group demanding the formation of an autonomous Islamic state in the southern Philippines, has racked up impressive military forces and threatens the stability of the Republic with bombings, bus hijackings, and sniper shootings. **Tourists to the southern Philippines, especially Minandao, should check travel warnings and contact the Philippines embassy in their home country before traveling.**

CUSTOMS AND CULTURE

LET IT BE

Though scattered among thousands of islands and speaking nearly 70 languages, the Filipino people unite through unique, sanguine values. *Bahala na*, the principle of leaving things be, breeds the worry-free attitudes found in village squares on warm afternoons when locals drop whatever they're doing to play basketball. Good sportsmanship is a must, though, as Filipinos will make every effort to avoid causing others *hiya*, or shame. Frankness is traded for subtlety to preserve rapport. Give-and-take is also valued; Filipinos honor *utang na loob*, a debt of gratitude expected to be repaid by the recipient of a favor. Relationships depends on *tiwala*, or trust; betraying personal loyalty is uncouth. If nothing else, be polite—negativity is especially disrespectful in the Philippines. Extend your most kind words even to beggars with the phrase, "*Patawarin po,*" which means "Forgive me, sir."

HUMAN RIGHTS

The Philippine government has publicly denounced human rights abuses and the number of violations continues to drop year after year. The **Armed Forces of the Philippines (AFP), Philippine National Police (PNP),** and military officials are notorious for arbitrary arrests and killings of individuals associated with revolutionary political groups. In the wake of the Marcos government's human rights abuses, the country has failed to impress the international community with its recent efforts to deal with perpetrators. Groups such as the **Communist Party of the Philippines (CPP)** continue to engage in illegal activities. Of greatest concern, however, are the civilian militia units, otherwise known as **CAFGUs (Citizens Armed Forces Geographical Units),** which have been reported to torture and abuse prisoners. Muslim extremists, most notably the MILF, have been implicated in terrorist bombings since 1993.

Though Filipinas enjoy greater equality than women in other parts of Southeast Asia, prostitution, rape, and domestic problems still run rampant. Until the government cracks down, other nations will continue to place pressure on the Philippines; in 1996, a US court upheld a $2 billion fine against the estate of Ferdinand Marcos for human rights abuses.

BISEXUAL, GAY, AND LESBIAN TRAVELERS

Homosexuality, far more readily accepted for both men and women in the Philippines than in other parts of Southeast Asia, takes a unique form in Filipino communities. Gay men, known as *bakla*, consider themselves men with the souls of women and are attracted more to heterosexual men than other gay men. Often invited to beauty pageants and asked to work at salons, the *bakla* occupy a well-accepted niche within Philippine society, though many fear being trivialized as superficial and appearance-obsessed. Travelers to the Philippines will have no trouble finding bars, clubs, and beaches that cater to a mixed crowd.

PINK INK. Utopia Asia (www.utopia-asia.com/tipsphil.htm) has great resources and event listings for major cities as well as updated links.

ARTS AND RECREATION

LITERATURE

Though artistically hindered under Spanish rule in the 1800s, the upwardly mobile class of educated, native-born Filipino *ilustrados* wrote about their discontent with revolutionary results. Jose Rizal, leader of the *ilustrados* and considered the grandfather of modern Filipino literature, criticized the oppressive power of the Spanish in his spanish novel, *Noli Me Tángere (Touch Me Not)*. Other writers wrote in Tagalog to encourage the Filipino tradition. American occupation in the early to mid-1900s left a deep imprint on Philippine literature. Many writers, such as Bienvenido Santos *(The Scent of Green Apples)*, wrote in English to imitate Anglophone greats like Hemingway. In recent years, Philippine literature seems to have begun a second renaissance. Some acclaimed members of the burgeoning corps of Filipino writers include Nick Joaquin *(The Woman Who Had Two Navels)*, R. Zamora Linmark *(Rolling the R's)*, Jessica Hagedorn *(Dogeaters)*, and F. Sionil Jose *(Sins)*.

DANCE

The internationally acclaimed **Bayanihan Dance Company** has been performing to standing ovations from Brussels to Broadway since the 1950s. Dancers balance oil lamps or candles in small glasses on the head and the palms of the hands while they turn, sway, and even roll on the floor. Other well-known dances are **barrio** dances, which originated in rural lowland areas of the country and are known for their spirited music, playful characters, and colorful costumes. The quintessential *barrio* dance is the ever-popular **tinikling.** Dancers beat pairs of long bamboo sticks rhythmically against the ground and each other, as couples skip, twirl, and hop in and out of the sticks. Another dance tradition comes from the Muslim areas of the Philippines (like Mindanao), where dances are characterized by their theatricality. In the **Langka-batuang,** men act like angry monkeys, scuttling about in chimp fashion and nimbly climbing poles propped up by other dancers.

OUTDOORS

The Philippines' collection of some 7000 islands make it a sure-spot for slip-'n'-sliding fun. The best **diving** and **snorkeling** trips depart from Mindoro, particularly Sabang Beach and Big Lalaguna. **Boracay's** immaculate **windsurfing** beaches and caves offer opportunities to **surf, dive,** and **sleep with sharks.** Scuba dive off Tabbataha Reef in Puerto Princessa, or take a PADI course if you're a diving virgin. For the water-timid, the Philippines is becoming increasingly popular for **mountain biking.**

ADDITIONAL SOURCES

The Philippines: A Singular and Plural Place, David Joel Steinburg (1990). A textbook-style introduction to contemporary Philippine society

Noli Me Tángere (Touch Me Not), Jose Rizal (1886). Rizal's diagnosis of the injustices of Philippine society under Spanish rule.

ON THE WEB

Philippines.com (www.phillipines.com). Quirky and practical tidbits on Philippines travel, culture, and news.

Philippines Department of Tourism (www.tourism.gov.ph). General information, guides to 25 popular destinations, events calendar, and details of package tours.

ESSENTIALS

VISAS

American, Australian, British, Canadian, European, and South African citizens may enter without visas and stay for 21 days. For longer stays, obtain a 59-day visa beforehand (single-entry visas US$25; multiple-entry US$50) or get an **extension** from the immigration office (P510). Extensions for longer stays require approval from the government, which can take three weeks or more.

MONEY

The Philippine **peso (P)** is divided into 100 **centavos.** Bills come in denominations of P5, 10, 20, 50, 100, 500, and 1000. Coins come in 1, 5, 10, and 25 centavos and P1, P2, and P5. Carry small bills, as a 5-10% **tip** is expected for many services, including restaurants, even if a service charge is included. Fares for taxis should be rounded up for a tip of P5-10. **ATMs** abound in most cities.

GETTING THERE

BY PLANE. The Philippines has two **international airports:** Mactan Cebu International Airport in Cebu (p. 558) and Nino Aquino International Airport in Manila (p. 519). **Philippine Airlines** (**PAL;** www.philippineair.com) operates international flights from dozens of countries

GETTING AROUND

BY PLANE. Air travel is a godsend for island-hoppers in the Philippines. Multiple-day journeys by bus or ferry are shrunk to 1-2hr. plane rides. PAL is the national airline, but competitors include **Air Philippines** (which has some of the best student rates), **Asian Spirit,** and **Cebu Pacific.**

BY BUS AND JEEPNEY. A competitive market of bus companies runs across Luzon, with a few epic 45hr. journeys. "Ordinary" buses are hot and stuffy, while first-class and "premier" buses have A/C and more spacious seats. Jeepney (see **Jeepers Creepers,** p. 522) offer cheap, convenient transportation (approximately P2.50 per km) for shorter journeys. Drivers keep crucifixes on their dashboards; their reckless driving might make you appreciate the divine protection.

BY BOAT. Ferry travel provides a cheap but dangerous means of traversing the seas; many fatal ferry wrecks occur every year, and pirates have been a recent threat. Regulation is improving steadily, and fast, safer catamarans with radars and night-vision equipment ply many popular routes. On overnight voyages, women should sleep in cots next to other women and should not travel alone. Inter-island shipping schedules are published in daily newspapers. Journey times to the same destination vary significantly between ships—inquire about the fastest option.

KEEPING IN TOUCH

Even in some larger cities, the Philippine *Poste Restante* system is unreliable at best; use AmEx mail holding service instead. Mail usually reaches Manila from the west in 5-10 days, but it takes a few more days to snake its way through the islands. For **telephone calls,** a number of public calling offices handle domestic and international communication. The **Philippines Long Distance Telephone Company (PLDT)** is most prevalent, but **RCPI/Bayantel, Islacom,** and a few smaller companies pick up the slack in more remote areas. Unfortunately, not all public calling offices allow phone card calls. PLDT has phone cards which can be used for international or domestic calls, but coin-operated payphones are still commonplace. A few resort areas still lack phone service, but cell phones keep the lines of communication open for reservations and emergency calls. For **Home Country Direct (HCD)** numbers from the Philippines, refer to the table on the inside back cover of this book. The Philippines is **8 hours ahead of GMT.**

LUZON

The largest of the Philippines' 7107 islands, Luzon accounts for a third of the country's landmass and half its population. Anchored by sprawling Metro Manila to the south, Luzon extends northward along teeth-shattering rural roads. On the ride through the countryside, the Central Cordillera mountains overlook the Banaue rice terraces, which lay claim to the world's 8th natural wonder. Thanks to millennia of back-breaking labor by the *Ifugao* people, gigantic stone staircases climb skyward, carpeted with emerald puffs of rice seedlings. If these steps recount lives of labor, then the coffins hanging from Sagada's limestone cliffs are haunting reminders of the afterlife. Leisurely treks through mountain tribe homelands grant glimpses of indigenous traditions, Pangasinan's Hundred Islands Park and Subic

Bay provide a taste of Philippine beaches, and nearby Baguio entertains a thriving student and artist community. While Legazpi's Mayon Volcano is the most fiery of Luzon's hotspots, the scene in Manila is doubtlessly the feistiest. Luzon is worth every minute of the rickety journey, which in itself is breathtaking.

MANILA

☎2

In 1571, Spanish conquistador Miguel López de Legazpi swept into Manila Bay and wrested control of Rajah Sulayman's settlement easily. That was the last time, however, that Manila was a pushover for any visitor. Now residents battle for space to move and air to breathe; traffic and trade deluge the city mercilessly. The struggle can be wearisome, and much of Manila's upper-crust population has retreated to developments in the suburbs leaving the city center for poorer newcomers from the provinces. Though it's easy to seal yourself off from the city's heat and noise in the many A/C malls, it's well worth the sweat and dust to let loose and enjoy the lively bar and cafe scene and restaurants that celebrate Filipino cuisine.

INTERCITY TRANSPORTATION

BY PLANE

Manila has separate international and domestic airports. International flights arrive at **Ninoy Aquino International Airport (NAIA;** ☎877 1109 for Department of Tourism, ☎877 1200 for international flight info), off Ninoy Aquino Ave. in Parañaque, 9km south of Rizal Park. The tourist reception kiosk provides **maps.** Banks in the arrivals hall **change currency** at poor rates, but **ATMs** near the car rental booths offer better rates (Cirrus/MC/NYCE/V). Domestic flights arrive at **Manila Domestic Airport** (☎871 0000), off Domestic Rd. in Parañaque, 1km closer to town than the international airport. The international departure tax is P550; domestic is P100.

Taxis run between NAIA and Manila Domestic Airport(P85) and into **Metro Manila** (P255). To avoid the mass of pushy taxi drivers, head to the "coupon" taxi counter in the arrivals hall. You'll pay a little more but won't get driven in circles. **PAL passengers** can take the **free shuttle** between terminals. Brave travelers can venture out to Ninoy Aquino Ave., where **jeepney, buses,** and **taxis** are available. Jeepney head along Domestic Rd. to **Baclaran Market** (P4) and **Manila Domestic Airport** ("Baclaran-MIA" route, P4). To get to Manila from the market, take the **Light Rail Transit (LRT;** P12) or a "Sucat-Hwy." or "New MIA" jeepney. Jeepneys may charge extra for large baggage. Buses bound for **Fairview, Monumento,** or **Santa Cruz** pass by Ermita and Malate Districts along Taft Ave. (P17).

LEAVING ON A JET PLANE...

DESTINATION	FREQUENCY	PRICE	DESTINATION	FREQUENCY	PRICE
Bangkok	5 per week	US$638	**Jakarta**	4 per week	US$867
Bacolod	2 per day	P2343	**Kuala Lampur**	3 per week	US$801
Cebu	13-14 per day	P1736-2183	**Legazpi**	1 per day	P1611
Ho Chi Minh City	3 per week	US$528	**Puerto Princesa**	2 per day	P2071
Hong Kong	4 per day	US$421	**Singapore**	1 per day	US$801
Iloilo	3 per day	P2342	**Tacloban**	3 per day	P2298

Most airlines have offices in the Makati Business District, though many have branches closer to Ermita and Malate. Major **international airlines** that serve Manila are: **Cathay Pacific,** second fl., Tetra Global Bldg., 1616 Dr. Vasquez St., Pedro Gil, Ermita (☎525 9367); **Malaysia Airlines,** G/F Legazpi Towers, 300, Roxas Blvd. (☎525 9404); **Philippine Airlines (PAL),** 540 P. Faura St., Cov. Adriatico St., Ermita (☎521 4512); **Royal Brunei,** 7 Saville Bldg., at the corner of Gil Puyat Ave. and Paseo de Roxas St., Makati City (☎897 3309); **Singapore Airlines,** 138 H.V. de la Costa St., Salcedo Village, Makati City (☎810 4960); **Thai Airways,** Escolta Twin Towers, 288

Escolta St., Paco (☎243 2645). Major **domestic airlines** that serve Manila are: **Air Philippines,** 15th fl., Multinational Bank Corporation Center, 6805 Ayala Ave., Makati (☎843 7770); **Asian Spirit,** ground floor, LPL Towers, 112 Legazpi St., Legazpi Village, Makati (☎840 3811); **Cebu Pacific,** Manila Midtown Hotel, on the corner of Adriatico St. and Pedro Gil, Ermita (☎636 4938); **PAL,** S&L Bldg., Roxas Blvd., Ermita (☎521 8821, 24hr. info ☎816 6691).

BY BUS

Buses heading north leave from terminals clustered around **Epifanio de los Santos Ave. (EDSA)** in the Cubao District, accessible by a Cubao-bound jeepney or bus. Buses headed south leave from terminals along EDSA in Pasay City, best reached by LRT: EDSA Station. Call for schedules and specific prices. Major transit companies include: **Autobus,** at the corner of Dimasalang and Laong-Laan St., Sampaloc (☎743 2227); **BLTB,** 3 EDSA, Pasay City (☎833 5501); **Jam Transit,** at the corner of Taft Ave. and Gil Puyat, Pasay City (☎831 4390); **Dagupan Bus,** at the corner of EDSA and New York St., Cubao, Quezon City (☎928 5639); **Dangwa Tranco,** at the corner of Aurora Blvd., and Driod St., Cubao, Quezon City (☎410 1991); **Partas,** at the corner of Aurora Blvd. and Arayat, Cubao, Quezon City (☎724 9820); **Philippine Rabbit:** Santa Cruz Terminal, at the corner of 819 Oroquieta St. and C.M. Recto (☎734 9836); Quezon Terminal, 1240 EDSA (☎456 7659); **Philtranco,** at the corner of EDSA and Apelo Cruz St., Pasay City (☎833 5061); **Victory Liner,** Caloocan Terminal, Grays Park Ave. (☎361 1506); Cubao Terminal, 853 Immaculate Conception Rd., along EDSA (☎833 0293); Pasay City Terminal, 561 EDSA (☎727 4268). Bring a blanket on overnight A/C bus rides.

DESTINATION	DURATION/ FREQUENCY	PRICE	DESTINATION	DURATION/ FREQUENCY	PRICE
Baguio	6½hr., 21 per day	P187	Santa Cruz	2hr., 25 per day	P58
Banaue	9hr., 2 per day	P150	San Fernando	8hr., 24 per day	P200
Batangas City	30min., 20 per day	P70	Tagaytay	1½hr., 15 per day	P47
Legazpi	12hr., 15per day	P270	Vigan	9hr., 20 per day	P321

BY TRAIN

The **Philippine National Railway** (☎234 9772) runs between Manila and **Ragay City** (from Tayuman Station: 8hr., daily 4pm, P179-234; from Blumentritt Station: daily 7:40pm, with A/C P234). Antiquated cars and slow speed make this government-backed operation a last resort for travelers.

BY BOAT

Boats leave from two terminals: the **North Harbor** and **PTA Bay Terminal.**

North Port District: In the North Port District along Marcos Rd., north of the Pasig River, accessible by taxi from Ermita (P65) or "North Harbor" jeepney from Divisoria Market. **WG&A Lines,** Pier 4 and 14, North Harbor (☎894 3211) sends boats to: **Catbalogan, Samar** (25hr., M 9am, P611); **Cebu** (19-20hr.; M 7pm, Tu 3pm, Th 7pm, Su 9am; P1185); **Coron** (7-8hr., F 4pm, P800); **Davao** (2 days; M 9am, W, Sa noon; P1600); **Dumaguete** (15hr., P1185); **Iloilo** (21hr.; W, Sa 9, 10am; P1245); **Puerto Princesa** (28hr., F 4pm, P1120); **Tagbilaran** (28hr., F, Su midnight, P1007). **Negros Navigation** (☎243 5359), offers fewer destinations at similar prices.

PTA Bay Terminal: On Roxas Blvd. in the CCP Complex in Pasay City, accessible by orange jeepney from LRT: Vito Cruz. **Bullet Express** (☎551 0476) sends boats to **Lamao, Bataan** (55min.; 5 per day 6:20am-4:30pm; P130, students P110).

ORIENTATION

"Metro Manila" comprises 12 cities and five municipalities. The clogged main artery, **Epifanio de los Santos Ave. (EDSA),** traces a wide loop (24km) around the metropolis, running through **Caloocan City** and **Quezon City** in the northeast, **Makati**

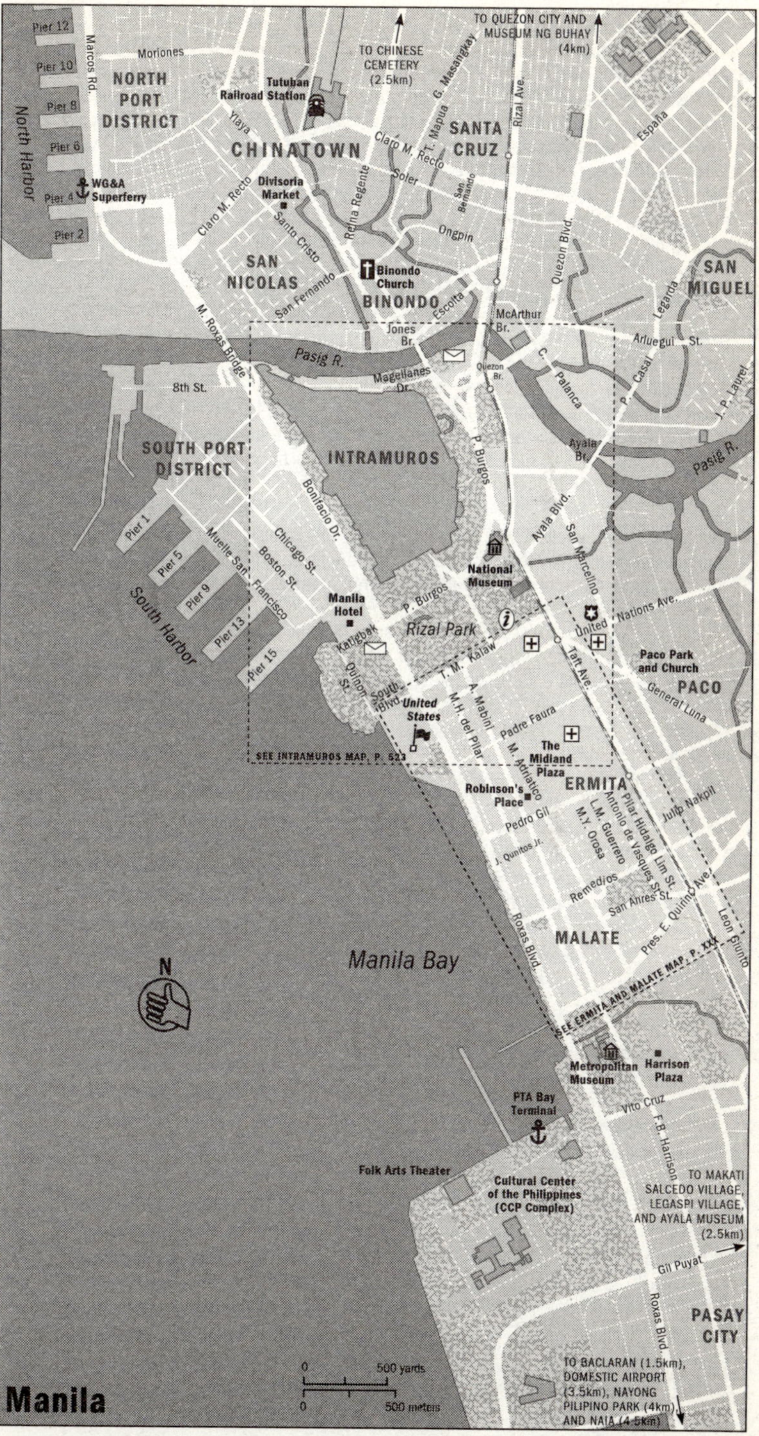
Manila
Manila Bay
North Harbor
South Harbor
NORTH PORT DISTRICT
SOUTH PORT DISTRICT
CHINATOWN
SANTA CRUZ
SAN NICOLAS
BINONDO
SAN MIGUEL
INTRAMUROS
ERMITA
PACO
MALATE
PASAY CITY
Pier 12
Pier 10
Pier 8
Pier 6
Pier 4
Pier 2
Pier 1
Pier 5
Pier 9
Pier 13
Pier 15
WG&A Superferry
Tutuban Railroad Station
Divisoria Market
Binondo Church
TO CHINESE CEMETERY (2.5km)
TO QUEZON CITY AND MUSEUM NG BUHAY (4km)
Pasig R.
Rizal Park
Manila Hotel
National Museum
United States
The Midland Plaza
Robinson's Place
Paco Park and Church
Metropolitan Museum
Harrison Plaza
PTA Bay Terminal
Folk Arts Theater
Cultural Center of the Philippines (CCP Complex)
TO MAKATI SALCEDO VILLAGE, LEGASPI VILLAGE, AND AYALA MUSEUM (2.5km)
TO BACLARAN (1.5km), DOMESTIC AIRPORT (3.5km), NAYONG PILIPINO PARK (4km), AND NAIA (4.5km)
SEE INTRAMUROS MAP, P. 523
SEE ERMITA AND MALATE MAP, P. XXX
0 500 yards
0 500 meters
N
PHILIPPINES

in the southeast, and **Pasay City** in the south. **Manila proper** sprawls along the bay, straddling the **Pasig River. Rizal Park,** also known as **Luneta,** is a widely-used landmark in the heart of the city. The tourist ghettos of **Ermita** and **Malate** lie south of Rizal Park, bounded by **Taft Ave.** to the east and Malate Church to the south. The **Cultural Center of the Philippines (CCP)** sits south of Malate towards Pasay City. The walled city of **Intramuros** sits north of Rizal Park, extending to the Pasig River. The **Chinatown** districts of **Binondo** and **Santa Cruz** form the other bank of the Pasig River. The LRT above Taft Ave. connects north and south. Affluent **Makati City** is 7km southeast. **Note:** Manila maps often use the abbreviation "cor." for "at the corner of," particularly when street numbers are absent.

LOCAL TRANSPORTATION

Taxis: An affordable and comfortable way to get around and an ideal stepping stone for new travelers before braving the chaotic jeepney circuits. Metered A/C taxis may be reluctant to go short distances or into congested areas unless you agree to a high fixed price. Beware of taxis that charge exorbitant rates as set down in a fare-book with the deceptive title "Meters." Always look for an electronic meter above the gear stick. Taxis charge a base fare of P25 plus P2 for every 200m (1½min. wait in traffic). If drivers refuse to turn on their meters, they can be fined and, in some cases, lose their licenses. So let 'em know who's boss.

Jeepneys: Jeepney follow set routes all over the city (first 4km P4, P0.50 per additional km). A signboard declares destinations, and the route is detailed below the windscreen or to the side. A useful route connects the Ermita and Malate Districts to **Baclaran Market** in Pasay City to the south. Other jeepney run from Baclaran or LRT: Buendia (Gil Puyat Ave.) along Taft Ave. to **Quiapo, Santa Cruz,** and **Monumento** north of the Pasig River. Jeepney marked **Project 2** and **3** head for the **Quirino District, Project 4** go to **Cubao,** and **Project 6** and **8** head to the center of **Quezon City.** The Cubao jeepney are useful for reaching several **EDSA bus terminals,** while Baclaran jeepney cross EDSA to a cluster of **Pasay City bus terminals.** Jeepney with the same destinations can take entirely different routes with different stops, depending on where you catch them from. Don't be afraid to ask the driver or other passengers for directions to your destination, and, as always, be aware of your surroundings and property inside a jeep. Often overcrowded, they are prime pickpocketing locations and can be unsafe at night.

LRT and MRT (Elevated Railways): Manila's LRT is the only way to avoid hectic traffic. Trains run frequently 5am-9pm between 15 stations at 800m intervals, along a 15km route from **Monumento Station** in Caloocan City in the north to **Baclaran** in the south (30min. end to end, flat rate P12). Completed in 2001, the MRT, another elevated railway, has two lines: MRT 1 (6am-11pm, P12) and MRT 3 (6am-11:30pm, P9.50-16). MRT 1 has 18 stops along Rizal and Taft Ave. North, Central, and South Terminal stops are transfer stations to buses and jeepney. MRT 3, commonly called Metrostar, has 13 stops along EDSA Ave.

Other Moving Objects: Pedi-cabs, small BMX bikes with sidecars, roam Ermita and Malate's back streets (P15-30). In Binondo, Divisoria, Intramuros, and Rizal Park, **calesas** *(horse-drawn carriages)* cruise the city (P40 per 1km). Eight-seater Toyota Tamaraw FX **"mega-taxis"** threaten to surpass jeepney as the city's most rampant vehicles (from P10). These large vehicles run routes similar to jeepney and have A/C—a life-saver dur-

JEEPERS CREEPERS Cross a jeep with a school bus, and cross that with a low-rider and... Voila! You'll have what Filipinos call a jeepney. The chosen form of mid-distance travel in the Philippines, jeepney are built for 18 passengers but usually pack in about 25. Puffing diesel smoke, jeepney don't have many set stops—flag one down, jump in the open back door, and be ready to bang on the roof or yell "Ooooo!" to get off. Two-man teams staff some popular jeepney; one drives, while the other recruits passengers and takes money. Pay the driver through the open divider while in motion, hang on, and enjoy the ride.

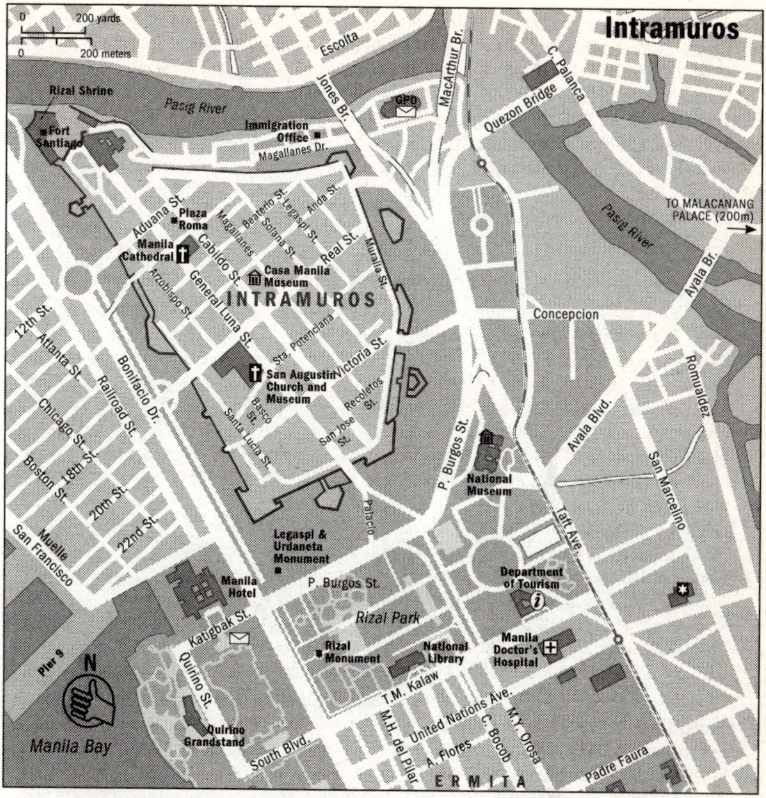

ing Manila's severe traffic jams. **Local buses** grind along major thoroughfares, particularly Taft Ave. and EDSA (about P10 per 4km). Destinations are posted in the front windows. "Ayala" buses run along Taft Ave. to Ayala Ave. in Makati City (P14). **Tricycles** run in Caloocan City (P5 per 2min.).

PRACTICAL INFORMATION

TOURIST AND FINANCIAL SERVICES

Tourist Offices: Head Office, #106, Dept. of Tourism Bldg., Teodoro Valencia Circle, T.M. Kalaw St., Ermita (☎524 1703), at the corner of Rizal Park near the Taft Ave. and T.M. Kalaw St. intersection. LRT: UN Ave. Station. Free *Tourist Map of the Philippines plus Street Map of Manila.* Open M-Sa 7am-6pm. To reach **Airport Tourist Information,** take the elevator to the 4th floor and look for a door with a Filipino flag draped over it.

Travel and Tours: The Ermita and Malate areas have many travel agencies. **Swagman Travel,** 411 A. Flores St., Ermita (☎524 5816), a well-established Aussie outfit with 15 outposts all over the Philippines. Organizes tours to Mt. Pinatubo and Corregidor Island. **Southeast Travel Corp.,** at the corner of Pedro Gil and Mtt. del Pilar St., Ermita (☎524 5676), handles international and domestic air ticketing and local tours. Open M-F 8am-6pm, Sa 8am-noon. **Aqua Travel & Tours,** Ste. #201, Manila Midtown Hotel, Pedro Gil St., Ermita (☎523 1989), specializes in scuba holidays. Open daily 9am-6pm.

Embassies: Embassies are normally open M-F 9am-3pm. **Australia,** 1st and 5th fl., Doña Salustiana Bldg., 104 Paseo de Roxas, Makati (☎750 2850). **Brunei,** 11th fl., Ayala Wing, BPI Bldg., at the corner of Ayala Ave. and Paseo de Roxas St. (☎816

2836). **Canada,** 9-11th fl., Allied Bank Center, 6754 Ayala Ave., Makati (☎867 0001). **France,** 16/F Pacific Star Bldg, Makati Ave., Makati (☎810 1981). **Indonesia,** 185 Salcedo St., Legazpi Village, Makati (☎892 5061). **Ireland,** 3rd fl., Port Royal Palace, 118 Rada St., Legazpi Village, Makati (☎819 1581). **Malaysia,** 107 Tordesillas St., Salcedo Village, Makati (☎817 4581). **Myanmar,** 8/F, Xanland Center, 152 Amorsolo St., Legazpi Village, Makati (☎817 2373). **New Zealand,** 23rd fl., Far East Bank Center, Sen. Gil Puyat Ave. near Makati Ave., Makati (☎891 5358). **Singapore,** 6th fl., ODC International Plaza, 219 Salcedo St., Legazpi Village, Makati (☎816 1764). **Thailand,** Royal Thai Embassy Bldg., 107 Rada St., Legazpi Village, Makati (☎815 4219). **UK,** 15-17th fl., L.V. Locsin Bldg., at the corner of Ayala and Makati Ave., Makati (☎816 7116). **US,** Chancery Bldg., 1201 Roxas Blvd. (☎523 1001). **Vietnam,** 554 Pablo Ocampo St., Malate (☎524 0364).

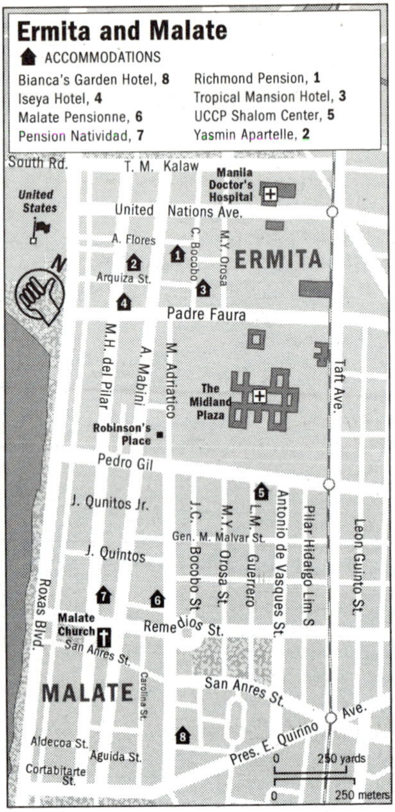

Immigration Office: Bureau of Immigration and Deportation, Magallanes Dr., Intramuros (☎527 3263), near Jones Bridge. Extends tourist visas to 59 days for P1570. No shorts or sandals. Open M-F 8am-noon and 1-5pm. Many travel agencies extend visas just as quickly for similar prices and shorter lines.

Currency Exchange: Ermita and Malate are rife with late-night moneychangers and **24hr. ATMs. Equitable PCI Bank,** EBC Bldg., at the corner of J. Bocobo St. and UN Ave., Ermita (☎524 9661). **Branches** throughout the city. MC/V cash advances. **24hr. ATM.** Open M-F 9am-4pm. "Traveler's check" is almost nonexistent in the Filipino moneychanger's vocabulary; bring plenty of cash.

American Express: 1810 Mabini St., at the corner with Remedios St., Malate (☎524 8681). Mail held for free. Open M-F 8:30am-4pm, Sa 9am-noon.

LOCAL SERVICES

Luggage Storage: Most pension houses look after guests' luggage free for a few hours or P5-10 per day for longer periods.

Bookstores: National Book Store, Robinson's Mall, Pedro Gil. St., Ermita (☎733 8265). English books, Filipiniana section, maps, and travel guides. *Metro Manila Street Map* P80. Open daily 10am-9pm. **Solidaridad Bookshop,** 531 Padre Faura St., Ermita (☎523 0870). Owned by F. Sionil "Frankie" Jose, one of the Philippines' foremost contemporary novelists. *International Herald Tribune* and *Financial Times* delivered by 5:30pm. Open M-Sa 9am-6pm.

Women's Resources: Women in Travel Club, c/o Philippine Airlines, S&L Bldg., 1500 Roxas Blvd., Manila (☎525 5420).

Lesbian and Gay Resources: Library Foundation, 1066 Remedios St., coordinates gay activities in the capital. Ask at The Library Bar, 1779 Adriatico St. **Womyn Supporting Womyn Center (WSWC),** 43-44 University of the Philippines Shopping Center, U.P. Diliman, Quezon City. Lesbian info service.

EMERGENCY AND COMMUNICATIONS

Emergency: ☎166.

Police: Western District Police, ☎523 8391. Smaller police branch on the corner of U.N. Ave. and San Marcelino St., east of Taft Ave.

Tourist Police: Dept. of Tourism Bldg., #112, Teodoro Valencia Circle, T.M. Kalaw St., Ermita. **24hr. Tourist Assistance Hotlines,** ☎524 1728 or 524 1660.

Pharmacies: Well-stocked **Mercury Drug** branches in every major shopping mall. Most branches open daily 7am-10pm. **Manila Doctors Hospital Pharmacy** (☎524 3090, see **Medical Services,** below). **Open 24hr.**

Medical Services: Manila Doctors Hospital, 667 U.N. Ave., Ermita (☎524 3011), opposite the Philam Bldg., is close to most accommodations. **Open 24hr.**

Telephones: Most shops and guest houses provide local phone service (P5 per 3min.). Prepaid PLDT "Fonkards" (P100-1000), available in stores throughout the city, connect local or long-distance calls from PLDT card phones. Green Eastern card phones line the streets of Ermita and Malate as an alternative for international calls.

Internet Access: Several Internet cafes line Pedro Gil St. in front of Robinson's Mall. P30 per hr. **Shuttle.com** on Pedro Gil St. and Adriatico St. has 20 stations for Internet and network gaming.

Post Offices: GPO, Liwasang Bonifacio, Intramuros (☎527 8561). LRT: Central Station and walk past Manila City Library and through the Quezon Blvd. underpass. It's near MacArthur Bridge on Pasig River. *Poste Restante* at Counter 218. Open M-F 7am-5pm, Sa 8am-noon. **Postal code:** 1000.

ACCOMMODATIONS

Manila can be a carbon-monoxide sauna—A/C rooms might be worth the extra pesos. Most accommodations enforce noon checkout. Ermita and Malate, in the heart of Metro Manila, have the best accommodations choice amidst restaurants, sights, services, and entertainment.

Malate Pensionne, 1771 Adriatico St., Malate (☎523 8304). Solid accommodations with a beautiful, shady courtyard and a waterfall. Fax and Internet access. Dorms with A/C P275, with common room P300; super economy singles P450; doubles P550, with common room P825, with A/C, TV, and bath P1050.

Yasmin Apartelle, 453 Arquiza St., Ermita (☎523 5107). Very friendly staff. Live large, pay little. Doubles with TV, refrigerator, A/C, and private common room P700.

Pension Natividad, 1690 M.H. del Pilar St., near J. Quintos St., Malate (☎521 0524) The best-kept secret of backpackers and Peace Corps volunteers visiting Manila, and for good reason: Natividad has clean, no-frills rooms at dirt-cheap prices. Same-sex dorms P200; doubles P550, with common room P650; doubles with A/C and bath P900.

UCCP Shalom Center, 1660 L.M. Guerrero St. (☎524 8430), calls itself your "Christian home in Manila," but all are welcome. Average rooms, but heavenly service redeems. Dorms P325; doubles with A/C and common room P1000.

Tropical Mansion Hotel, 1242 J.C. Bocobo St., Ermita (☎521 2639). Neither tropical nor a mansion, but A/C in all rooms makes this urban hotel a temporary oasis from the city heat. Singles P605; larger singles P715, with cable TV P935; rooms with 2 twin beds, couch, and TV P1430. AmEx/V.

Bianca's Garden Hotel, 2139 Adriatico St., Malate (☎525 2846), at the south end of Adriatico St. near Quirino Ave. Beautiful house in an enclave with pool. Rooms with shared bath P700, with A/C, TV, and phone P1300.

Iseya Hotel, 1241 M.H. del Pilar St., Ermita (☎523 8166), near the corner of Padre Faura St. Centrally located, but the rooms are dim and dusty. Rooms with A/C, cable TV, phone, fridge, and private common room P1100.

Richmond Pension, 1165 Grey St. (Jaycee Way), Ermita (☎525 3864), behind Barrio Fiesta Restaurant. Some of the cheapest, most spartan dorm rooms around—only for the extremely frugal. Dorm beds P160; doubles P390, with A/C P560, P50 per additional head.

Hotels in **Chinatown** (Binondo and Santa Cruz Districts) cater mainly to Asian guests and offer little personality. **Hotel Merchants,** at the corner of San Fernando and Soler St., has large rooms with A/C and private common rooms. (☎733 8111. Singles P590, with TV P770.) **Premier Hotel,** on T. Mapua St. off Soler St., is more expensive but has finer furnishings. (☎733 8301. Doubles P800; triples P990.) Guest houses around **Makati Ave.** enjoy a pristine neighborhood as well as sky-high prices. No true budget traveler would admit to staying here. **Inn Suites,** 5012 P. Burgood St., off Makati Ave., has all the creature comforts—TV, A/C, and phone. (☎897 2053. Doubles in high season P1900, in low season P1100.) In **Quezon City,** several pension houses operate along E. Rodriquez Sr. Blvd. **Quezon City Apartelle,** on the corner of E. Rodriguez Blvd. and J.D. Jimenez St., provides clean and comfortable rooms. (☎922 1460. Singles with A/C and private bath P700; suites with kitchen P1200.)

FOOD

Manila overflows with fast-food joints and high-quality, expensive sit-down restaurants, offering little selection in between. The **Food Plaza,** on the corner of Padre Faura and Bocobo St., Ermita, lacks the charm of street stalls but offers a wide selection of Filipino dishes such as *chicken adobo* (P35). Street stalls and canteens line **Santa Monica St.,** particularly between Adriatico and M.H. del Pilar St.

Cabalen, in Robinson's Place, 2nd fl., Ermita and Ayala Center, Quad 3, 2nd fl. Makati City, Ermita. All-you-can-eat cornucopia enables you to quickly sort through the good, the bad, and the ugly of Filipino cuisine (P220). Novices dig the *lechon* (roasted whole pig), while the truly brave go for *dinuguan* (pig blood stew). Open daily 11am-midnight.

Hap Chang Tea House, 563 Gen. Malvar St., at the intersection with Adriatico St., Malate. Hordes of hungry patrons spill into the streets at all hours to delight in the dirt-cheap grub. Beef brisket noodles are greasy but oh, so good (P65). Hong Kong soy duck P150. Open daily 10am-3am.

Harbor View, South Gate A, New Luneta Park (☎524 1532), across from Quirino Grandstand. Expensive, but fine oceanfront views and exquisite seafood make it easier to fork over the dough. Crab in chili sauce P120 per 100g (most crabs weigh at least 500g). Reservations recommended. Open daily 11am-midnight.

Penguin Cafe and Gallery, 604 Remedios St., off Remedios Circle. Artsy atmosphere. Breakfast staples (*bangus, atsara,* papayas, garlic rice) served anytime but in the morning P65. Open Tu-Th noon-2pm and 6pm-1am, F-Sa 6pm-2am, Su 7pm-1am.

Kamayan, 532 Padre Faura, Ermita. Eat with your hands, but watch out for the sizzling buffalo steak (P355). Cool your digits with the rather pricey *halo-halo* for dessert. Open daily 11am-10:30pm.

L'Eau Vive, 1499 Paz. M. Gauzon Ave., Paco. UN Ave. turns into Paz M. Gauzon Ave. 15min. east of Rizal Park after the traffic circle. Run by nuns, "the living water" spreads the gospel through French cuisine. Prayers at noon and 9pm; meals in between. Fixed menu P150. Open M-Sa 11am-3pm and 7-11pm.

Three Amigos, 613 J. Nakpil St., Malate. Quality Mexican food and quick service. Enchilada combo plates P110-180. Open M-Th 6pm-2am, F-Sa 6pm-3am, Su 6pm-1am.

Kashmir, 523 Padre Faura St., Ermita, opposite Adriatico St. Indian, Malaysian, and Middle Eastern cuisine. Vegetarian friendly. Samosas P110. Open 11am-11pm.

LEAN, MEAN, PHILIPPINE CUISINE Experimenting with Philippine cuisine is hit-or-miss. The seafood tends to be better than meat-based dishes, which are usually prepared with fatty cuts of meat. The most common types of fish are the thin *bangus*, *tilapia* (fleshier and more expensive), and *lapu-lapu* (more expensive still). Many dishes combine two major ingredients such as pork and chicken. Common sauces, such as those used on *adobo* dishes, tend to be garlic-, vinegar-, and soy-based; Filipino dishes typically aren't as spicy as other Southeast Asian dishes. *Sinigang* soups, including pork *(sinigang na baboy)* or shrimp *(sinigang na hipon)*, noodle dishes such as *pancit canton* (thick baked noodles with pork and vegetable), and *lumpia* (spring rolls) are good standbys. Unsweetened *calamansi* juice, a citrus fruit juice, is a godsend. Filipinos often eat *merienda*, a mid-morning snack, and many restaurants offer cheap *merienda* options. Widely acknowledged as one of the highlights of Filipino cuisine, *halo-halo* is a dessert made from crushed ice, condensed milk, sweets, and fruit. Most regions have a specialty worth trying, though sometimes there's a good reason why a dish has remained local. Vegetarians will find vegetable chop suey in most Filipino restaurants but should beware of "vegetarian dishes" that may contain fish or meats other than beef.

SIGHTS

LUNETA AND INTRAMUROS

MANILA BAY. In May 1898, Spanish colonial rule ended suddenly when US Commodore Dewey wiped out the Spanish fleet in 3hr. in Manila Bay. **International Golden Horizon Cruise,** Gate A, South Rd., Rizal Park next to Golden Horizon Restaurant, arranges **Manila Bay cruises** (1hr.), which give mildly interesting lectures on the bay's history. The first-hand view of villagers living along the waters against the background of Makati's skyscrapers, however, is a sobering reminder of the gap between Manila's rich and poor. *(Boats depart from the PTA Bay Terminal at the CCP Complex in Pasay City. ☎525 5698. Call for reservations.)*

RIZAL PARK. Once known as "Luneta," or Little Moon, Rizal Park is the heart of Manila. The Spanish executed Filipino rebels here, including national hero **Dr. Jose Rizal,** whose remains are entombed in the **Rizal Monument.** The souls of other Filipino greats rest on canvas and in clay in the **National Museum,** P. Burgos St., on the northeast corner of the park. The collection includes painter Juan Roma's awe-inspiring *Spolarium*. *(Museum ☎527 1214. Open Tu-Su 9am-5pm.)*

INTRAMUROS. Hundreds of years ago, the Spaniards surrounded the colonial city of Intramuros with 4½km of protective walls as a first line of defense; today the area serves as the best reflection of life in 16th century Manila. **Fort Santiago,** wedged between Bonifacio Dr. and the Pasig River on the northwest promontory of Intramuros, also houses the **Rizal Shrine.** An exquisite and informative tribute to the martyr, the shrine also marks the beginning of Manila's "Freedom Trail." Follow the yellow footsteps showing Rizal's final walk on the day of his execution; the **Intramuros Visitors Center (IVC)** provides maps. *(IVC ☎527 2961. Fort open daily 8am-6pm. P40, students/children P15. Rizal Shrine open Tu-Su 8am-5pm.).*

OTHER SIGHTS. Strolling down Gen. Luna St. from Fort Santiago, sights pop up in every direction. **Manila Cathedral,** in Plaza Roma on Postigo St., was rebuilt in 1958 by Fernando Ocampo after being razed in WWII. With imposing high arches and heavenly blue lighting, the cathedral now hosts the weddings of Manila's rich and famous. The **Casa Manila Museum,** on the corner of Real and Gen. Luna St., is a replica of an 1850 *illustrado* home. *(Museum ☎527 4084. Open Tu-Su 9am-6pm. Guided tours 2hr.; depart every 2hr. from 9am.)*

San Augustin Church and Museum, on the corner of Gen. Luna and Real St., didn't need to be resurrected after WWII; this baroque church and its *trompe l'oeil* ceiling have staggered through repeated natural disasters and foreign invasions since their incarnation in 1571. The museum houses 17th to 19th century sanctuary art. *(☎527 4060. Open daily 9am-noon and 1-5pm. Church and museum P45, college students P20, high school students P15, children P10.)*

CCP AND ENVIRONS

CULTURAL CENTER OF THE PHILIPPINES (CCP) COMPLEX. The CCP is built on land reclaimed from Manila Bay. The main building has **three theaters,** an **ethnographic museum,** and a changing contemporary **Filipino art exhibit.** The ethnographic **Museo ng Kalinangang Pilipino** concentrates on local cultural traditions. **Museo ng Sinig,** in GSIS Bldg., exhibits experimental art, including mixed media, sculptures, and tapestries by Frederico Alcuaz. *(On Roxas Blvd. in Malate. Take an orange jeepney with yellow stripes from the LRT: Vito Cruz. ☎832 1125. Art exhibit open Tu-Su 10am-5pm. Free. Museo ng Kalinangang Pilipino open Tu-Su 10am-5pm and 8pm for evening performances. P20. Museo ng Sinig ☎891 6161. Open Tu-Sa 10am-5pm. Free.)*

METROPOLITAN MUSEUM OF MANILA. Changing exhibitions feature a mix of contemporary and early 20th century art. Save for a stunning exhibition of pre-Hispanic gold ornaments, there are few notable items in the collections. *(In the Bangko Sentral ng Pilipinas Complex, on the corner of Roxas Blvd. and Vito Cruz, left of the CCP. ☎/fax 523 7855. Open M-Sa 10am-6pm. Basement open daily 10am-4:30pm. P50, students P30.)*

ON THE PERIPHERY

MALACAÑANG PALACE. A slurred conglomerate of the Tagalog expression "a rich man lives there," Malacañang stays true to its name as the official residence of the Philippine President and a museum with rooms dedicated to past presidents. Hear the tour guide's spin on the recent overthrow of former president Joseph Estrada. *(In San Miguel, across the Pasig River from Intramuros. ☎733 3721. No shorts, slippers, singlet tops, bags, cameras, or kids under 7. Open daily 9am-3pm. Guided tours M-W every 15min., Th-Su every 30-40min. P200.)*

CHINESE CEMETERY. The Spanish, who evidently were quite territorial about their burial grounds, forced the Chinese to establish their own cemetery. Huge 3m marble mausoleums testify to the wealth and status of the Chinese businessmen buried here. On most Sundays (especially All Saints Day, Nov. 1), families come to make offerings. *(Off P. Huertas St. in Tondo District. Catch the LRT to Blumentritt Station, walk a few yards up Blumentritt St., and turn left on P. Huertas St; follow it to Aurora Blvd. to reach the cemetery. ☎/fax 253 4204. Open daily 7am-7pm. Mausoleum keepers arrange guided tours; bargain around P50-P100.)*

PACO PARK AND CHURCH. The park originally held the remains of Dr. Jose Rizal, buried here to keep him from becoming a cult figure. The plan backfired spectacularly—his body has been exhumed twice. The park remains a peaceful, shady, out-of-the-way spot. Live Filipino folk groups perform every Friday at 6pm. *(On Padre Faura St. at the San Marcelino St. intersection. Catch a Taft jeepney to the Taft-Padre Faura intersection. ☎526 8163. Open daily 8am-5pm. P5.)*

NAYONG PILIPINO PARK. Six miniature replicas of Philippine regions display a range of flora and fauna. Included on the grounds of the park are the **Philippine Museum of Ethnology,** where you can learn how to play an *Ifugao* nose flute, and the **Museum ng Buhay Filipino** antiques museum. Replicas of natural wonders such as the Mayon Volcano verge on being childish, but the architecture in each mini-region offers an informative crash course on the Philippines. A dance troupe performs at the Mindanao Pavilion on weekends at 2:30 and 4:30pm. *(Off MIA Rd. adjacent to the airport. Park open Tu-Su 7am-6pm. P40, under 12 P25. Museum ng Buhay Filipino ☎832 3766. Both museums open Tu-Su 9am-5pm. Free.)*

AYALA MUSEUM. Ayala Museum has superb sea vessels, art exhibits, and dioramas depicting Philippine history. *(On Makati Ave., Ayala Center, opposite Shangri-La Hotel. ☎812 1191. Open Tu-Su 8am-6pm. P50, children P25. Tours P30, students P25.)*

ENTERTAINMENT

CULTURE AND COCKS

Manila supports several venues for cultural performances. The **Cultural Center of the Philippines,** CCP Complex, Roxas Blvd., Malate, presents concerts, ballet, drama, and films. (☎832 3704; box office ☎832 1125, ext. 240. Open M-F 9am-5pm, Sa-Su 1-5pm. Tickets from P200.) Various plays grace the stages of the **William J. Shaw Theater,** Shangri-La Shopping Mall, 5th fl., EDSA, Mandaluyong. (☎633 4821. Box office open daily 10am-7pm.) **Intramuros Evenings** (formerly Puerto Real Evenings) feature music, dance, and madrigal singing. (☎527 3138. Shows about 6:30pm around Intramuros). The **Araneta Coliseum** (☎911 3101), on the corner of Gen. Roxas and Gen. Araneta Ave., stages **cockfights** in September (P120-450) and hosts **Philippine Basketball Association (PBA)** games the rest of the year. Cheer on your favorite corporate product and their sponsored players. (Game tickets from P100.)

Dragon Acupressure Center, 2nd fl., 1811 LM Guerrero St., Malate, on the road that connects J.M. Nakpil St. and Remedios Cir., offers herbal steam baths with massage for P500. (☎526 7342. Open noon-1am.) Beware of "massage" offers outside massage parlors; your "masseuse" will rub down more than just sore muscles.

Movie theaters are a great place to kick back and cool off. **Robinson's Place** in Ermita and **Glorieta** in Makati boast two particularly impressive theaters. (P50, balcony seats P80. Movies run 10am-10pm.)

PHILIPPINES

BARS AND CAFES

A vibrant bar and cafe scene thrives in Manila, especially on **J. Nakpil St.** and **Remedios Circle** in Malate and on **P. Burgos St.** in Makati.

Hobbit House, 1801 A. Mabini St., Malate (☎521 7604). Great live rock, blues, and country. "The smallest waiters in the world"–all midgets and dwarves–are ready to serve you and even pose for cheesy pictures. Gimmick aside, one of the best bars in Manila. Food served. Beers P55. Cover P95. Open daily 6pm-2am.

The Library, 1779 A.M. Adriatico St., Malate (☎522 2484), near Remedios Circle. The country's funniest *baklas* (see **Bakla,** p. 530) become balladeers for the night. Gay patrons especially welcome, while foreigners are prime targets for (relatively painless) jokes. Bookish cocktails for bibliophilic imbibers. The "Reader's Digest" P90-P125. No slippers or vests. Cover P50. Open 7pm-4am.

The Verve Bar, 607 J. Nakpil St. off Adriatico St. Musically one step above the rest. Bar and DJ compete for the most innovative mixes: trip-hop, progressive house, and acid jazz. The "Adios Motherfucker," an 8-alcohol blend, will knock your socks off (P145). Open Tu-Sa 8:30pm-5am.

Cafe Havana, 1903 M. Adriatico St., Malate (☎521 8097). Manila's only Cuban restaurant/dance club. "Limoncito" cocktail P140. Che T-shirts P250. Afro-Cuban music F-Sa 11pm. No cover. Open daily 10am-2pm.

Gotham, 2nd fl., 610 J. Nakpil, Malate (☎450 1645). One of the most popular bars in town; the average patron is 22, impeccably stylish, and holds a cigarette in one hand and a cell phone in the other. Show up in your Batmobile and order the "Gotham Mist" cocktail (P135). Live music F-Sa. Open M-Th 6pm-1am, F-Sa 7pm-3am.

DISCOS

Many discos are actually bars with go-go dancers, gyrating sadly. **Solution,** 369 Libertad St., in Pasay City, is cheap, cheerful, refreshingly innocent and tourist-free, with bop to pop and club classics. (☎833 1641. San Miguel P35. Happy hour M-F and Su 7-10pm. Cover M-Th and Su P30, F P50, Sa P70. Open daily 8pm-5am.) **Mars,** 2 San Lorenzo Dr., on Pasay Rd. in Makati, is glitzy and crowded with spotlights, steam, and attitude. (☎841 0088. San Miguel P100. Cover M-Th and Su P200, F-Sa P300 includes 1 drink. Open daily 9:30pm-4am.)

PHILIPPINES

BAKLA! Homosexuality is far more open and readily accepted in the Philippines than in other parts of Southeast Asia. The day after the Philippines celebrated the centennial anniversary of its 1898 declaration of independence, a well-attended gay-pride march paraded through Manila. While this march and the gay scene in Manila are not so far removed from their counterparts in the West, homosexuality takes a distinct form. The *bakla,* as gay men are known, consider themselves men with the souls of women. Rather than being sexually oriented toward other gay men, their sexual preferences are for men who like heterosexual women, whom they affectionately nickname "Papa." The *bakla* occupy a well-accepted niche within Philippine society and are considered arbiters of fashion, glamour, and even humor. It is common for *bakla* to work in hair and beauty salons even in the smallest Filipino towns, and they often take roles as comedians in the country's most popular television shows and movies. To some, this role may seem narrow or even frivolous; *bakla,* too, are constantly wary of being perceived as masters of appearances and slaves of the superficial.

SHOPPING

Malls are omnipresent. **SM Megamall** in Mandaluyong offers two behemoth six-floor buildings to challenge the most ardent shopper. If shopping wears you out, take a spin on its ice-skating rink or catch a flick at the theaters. **Robinson's Place,** conveniently located in the tourist district, has two levels of restaurants and a large bowling alley. Ooh-la-la your way through upscale boutiques like DKNY and Louis Vuitton at **Shangri-La Plaza,** next door to SM Megamall. **Harrison Plaza,** on the corner of FB Harrison and Vito Cruz, mainly caters to families.

Divisoria Market, outside Binondo, is the mecca of marketplaces. Everything under the sun is sold at bargain prices. **Baclaran Market** in Paranaque is similar. The **Ilalim ng Tulay Market** in Quiapo hawks cheap tokens of Filipino culture, while Cubao's **Farmer's Plaza** is a collision of department stores and flea markets. In **Chinatown,** shops along Ongpin St. near Santa Cruz Church sell Chinese desserts, textiles, and herbal medicines. The heavyweight among antiques and handicraft stores is the Silahis Center, 744 Gen. Luna St., Inramuros (☎527 2111), near P. Burgos St.

DAYTRIPS FROM MANILA

LAS PIÑAS BAMBOO ORGAN AND SARAO JEEPNEY FACTORY

Buses on Taft Ave. bound for Zapote or Cavite pass through Las Piñas. Alternatively, from LRT: Baclaran Station, catch a "Las Piñas" jeepney (20min., P4). Bamboo Organ Factory ☎826 7718. Open M-F 9pm-midnight and 2-6pm. P20, children/students P5. The jeepney factory is on Padre Diego Cerra Ave., Pulanglupa, Las Piñas, 3km south. ☎874 7885. Open M-Sa 8am-4pm.

In 1819, Friar Diego Cera became a legend among budget-organ enthusiasts by building a working instrument entirely of bamboo. The **bamboo organ** of St. Joseph (San Jose) Church, in Las Piñas parish, produces a unique sound and is the centerpiece of an international bamboo organ festival for a week each February. Kitsch-lovers will want to see the **Sarao Jeepney Factory,** where WWII jeeps have been converted into fume-spewing *objets d'art.*

PAGSANJAN FALLS

Pagsanjan is 5km from Santa Cruz, accessible by BLTB buses from 3 EDSA, Pasay City (every hr. 4am-7pm, P61.50) and JAM Transit buses leaving from Taft Ave. at Gil Puyat St., Pasay City (2hr., every 30min. 4am-10:30pm, with A/C P72).

The final scenes of Francis Ford Coppola's *Apocalypse Now* were filmed along this tropical gorge. Though more likely to see a crazed man bathing his bald head back at the guest house, tourists still pay high prices to have *banqueros* canoe them 7km upstream to the **Magdapio Falls** and shoot the rapids back down (2hr.; last trip 2hr. before sundown; standard fares for 2-3 passengers P580 per person, single passenger P1080, plus P100-200 tip). The rapids are most active in the rainy

season. At the top of the river you can float on a bamboo raft (P50 per person) to **Devil's Cavern** behind the falls. Because boatmen have been known to harass tourists, it's advisable to arrange a boat through the PTA-operated **Pagsanjan Garden Resort,** Pagsanjan (☎049 808 4451), a short tricycle ride from town. Accommodations line Garcia St., which runs along the northern bank of the river.

CORREGIDOR ISLAND

The Corregidor Visitors' Information Center, Dept. of Tourism Bldg., #212, Agrifina Circle, T.M. Kalaw St., Manila (☎525 3420, ext. 329) gives advice about tours. Most visitors take a package tour (P1698); book with Sun Cruises, PTA Bay Cruise Terminal, CCP Complex, Roxas Blvd. (☎831 8140). Tours depart at 8am from PTA Bay Cruise Terminal.

Leafy, tadpole-shaped Corregidor Island, christened the "cork in the bottle" of Manila Bay by General MacArthur, was the scene of military humiliation and defeat for first the US and then the Japanese during WWII. One of the last places to fall to the Japanese, it earned the terrible distinction of being the most bombed island of the war. Today knowledgeable guides and a light-and-sound show (P150) retell the story to visitors from both sides of the conflict. The island is a can't miss for WWII buffs, but for everybody else, the hollowed out shells of bombed buildings can become monotonous. Lodging (P400) is offered by **Corregidor Youth Hostel** offers lodging. (☎0912 304 0692. Rooms 400.) Camping at the South Dock Beach or Middleside Camping Grounds costs P10 per day.

PHILIPPINES

BAGUIO ☎74

Sprawled amid a rugged, pine-bedecked landscape, Baguio rests 1400m above sea level. Its cooler temperatures make it the "summer capital" of the Philippines. Both tourists and Filipinos, many on their way to Sagada or Banaue, others vacationing or honeymooning, flee Manila's scorching heat to pack Baguio from March to May. Although popularity has put pressure on the mountain milieu, highland mountain tribes subsist on the thriving produce market, which draws avid tourists looking for a taste of the Filipino way of life, as well as legions of artists and students attempting to preserve the pre-colonial Cordilleran culture.

TRANSPORTATION

Flights: Take a taxi from Session Rd. to the **Loakan Airport** (P60). **Asian Spirit** (☎447 3914) flies daily to **Manila** (1hr., P1583).

Buses: Several bus companies send buses from different terminals in Baguio City. From the terminals on Gov. Pack Rd. near the corner of Session Rd.: **Autobus** (☎444 9056), **Byron Express** (☎442 5708), **Philippine Rabbit** (☎442 5945), **Partas** (☎444 8431), **Victory Liner** (☎442 5708). From the terminal on Rajah Soliman St. behind Baguio Central Mall: **Dangwa Tranco** and **Lizardo.** From the terminal on Otek St., **Eso-Nice Liner** (☎443 3076). Travelers report Victory Liner buses are the safest and most comfortable and Partas the fastest. Buses to:

Alaminos: Byron Express (4hr., every hr. 6am-6pm, P75).

Banaue: Autobus (8-9hr., 7:30pm, P233); Dangwa (7am, 7pm; P185); Lizardo (8-9 hr.; 2:30pm, 7:30pm; P230).

Bontoc: Dangwa (7hr., every hr. 5-10am, P145).

Dagupan: Byron Express (2½hr.; every hr. 6am-6pm; P47, with A/C P57).

Manila: Partas (midnight, 5, 6, 10am, 2pm; with A/C to Cubao District P235); Philippine Rabbit (every hr. 24hr.; P225); Victory Liner (5-6hr.; every hr. 24hr.; with A/C to Cubao District P236, with A/C to Pasay City P250).

Sagada: Lizardo (6½hr.; every 30min. 7-9:30am, 11am; P139, students P115).

San Fernando (La Union): Eso-Nice Liner (2hr., every 30min. 5:30am-6pm, P40).

Vigan: Partas (5hr.; 6:30, 10am, noon, 3:15, 6, 8:45pm; P154, with A/C P215); Philippine Rabbit (5hr.; every hr. until 7pm; P150, with A/C P170).

Local Transportation: Taxis start at P20 for the first 250m, P1 for each 100m thereafter. **Jeepneys** cost about P4 per trip but are slower than taxis.

DON'T MESS WITH FENG SHUI. Before building a home, Filipinos often hire a consultant to make sure nothing structurally violates *feng shui*—a set of spiritual rules that bring ill luck when broken. More than a few bank closings have been blamed on choices that made these spirits angry. Rules include: not allowing the front door to face the back, not pointing the foot of the bed toward the door, and having a specific number of stairs leading to the front door. The stipulations are so numerous and so difficult to avoid that "consulting" can be quite a lucrative job.

ORIENTATION AND PRACTICAL INFORMATION

Rose-colored **Baguio Cathedral** overlooks the main commercial thoroughfare, **Session Rd.,** which climbs from its intersection with **Magsaysay Ave.** to the top of a hill. Session Rd. then splits into **Leonard Wood Rd.,** which leads to the **Botanical Gardens, Wright Park,** and **Mines View Park,** and the **Session Rd. extension.** Northbound highways leading into Baguio go to **Governor (Gov.) Pack Rd.,** which borders **Burnham Park.** Half a kilometer down the road is the **Department of Tourism Complex** in front of Baguio City High School. Another kilometer down is the main **bus terminal** and a roundabout into Session Rd. Near the **City Hall, Rizal Pack,** and **Malcom Sq., Otek St.** forms an arc around the northwest end of Burnham Park. Ease your navigation dilemmas by purchasing the *E-Z Map to Baguio 2001*, which plots all major buildings in the city (P80) or the *Map of Baguio* by Island Viewing Publishing. A free but quite useless map is available at the **Department of Transportation (DOT).**

Tourist Office: DOT Complex (☎442 6708). 10min. down Gov. Pack Rd. from bus terminals, opposite Baguio City High School. Open M-F 7:30am-noon and 1-6:30pm.

Travel and Tours: Swagman Travel, Swagman Attic Inn, 90 Abanao St. (☎442 5139). 3hr. city tour P850. 4-day tours to Banaue, Sagada, and Bontoc depart from Swagman Attic Inn at 6am daily. Visa extensions P2050. Open M-Sa 8am-5pm.

Currency Exchange: Philippine National Bank (PNB) (☎442 7795), on Session Rd. Open M-F 9am-3pm. **24hr. ATM** (AmEx/Cirrus/MC/V). Better exchange rates might be found in the city market.

Bookstores: Bookmark (☎442 4912), on Session Rd. at the foot of the steps to Baguio Cathedral. Glossy coffee-table books in Tagalog and English. Useful maps. Open daily 9am-7pm.

Emergency: Medical Services ☎169.

Police: ☎166. Station on Abanao St.

Pharmacy: Store Plus (☎442 8156), in YMCA bldg. on Session Rd. at the top of the hill, opposite Banco de Oro. Open 24hr.

Medical Services: Baguio Medical Center, 9 Military Cut Off Rd. (☎442 4216). Past the DOT complex near St. Francis Convent.

Telephones: Piltel Office (☎422 4567), on Session Rd., corner of Gov. Pack Rd. Accepts all Filipino and major international calling cards. Collect calls (deposit P46). Open daily 7am-8pm.

Internet Access: PhilCi.Com, Juniper Bldg., Bonifacio Ave. opposite Baguio City University. Fast access. P40 per hr. Telnet and web cam available. Open 24hr.

Post Office: Post Office at corner of Gov. Pack and Session Rd. Poste Restante at counter in adjoining lockbox section (closed Sa). Open M-F 8am-noon and 1-5pm, Sa 8am-noon. **Postal code:** 2600.

ACCOMMODATIONS

Walking down **Abanao St.** and onto Session Rd. will take you past many accommodations. Prices are more expensive than other mountain locations and sensitive to seasonal demand. Ask for a discount in the low season. Prepare to pay 50% more than the prices listed below during peak season.

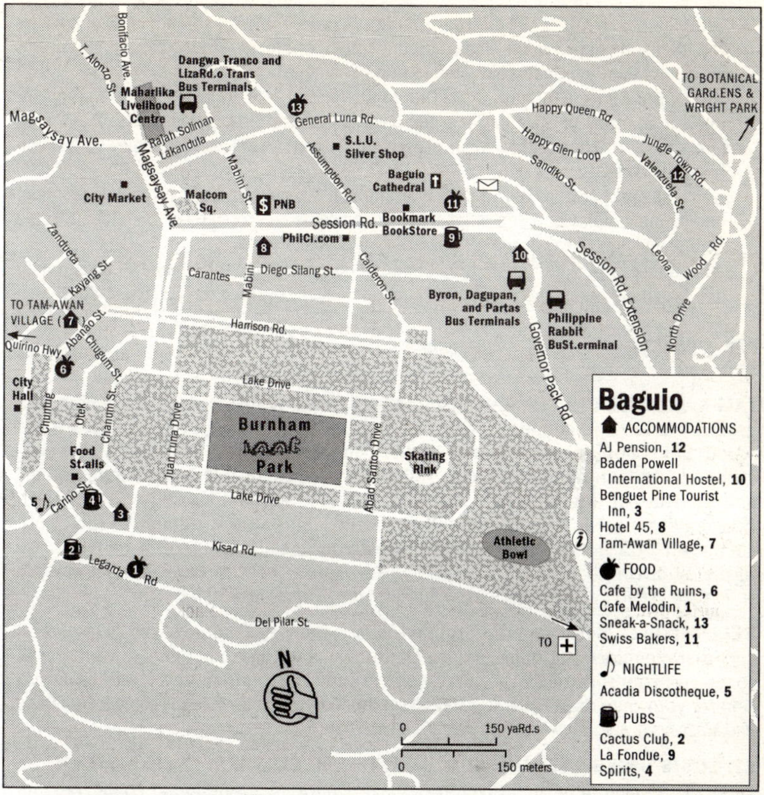

Benguet Pine Tourist Inn, 82 Chanum St. (☎442 7325). Doesn't offer the cheapest rates, but the amazing service, clean and spacious rooms, and great views of Burnham Park compensate adequately. Breakfast included. Singles P795, with common room P995; doubles P800, with common room P1200.

Hotel 45, 58 Session Rd. (☎442 6634). This multi-story hotel offers cheap rooms in a central location, but common floor toilets may not bode comfort. Singles P250; doubles P380, with private common room P650.

Baden Powell International Hostel, 26 Gov. Pack Rd. (☎442 5836). At the intersection with Session Rd. Proximity to bus stations guarantees early morning honk-imposed wake-up calls. Breakfast included. Laundry services available. Dorms P300; rooms for 1-2 P900; quads P1350. 10% surcharge on credit cards.

Tam-awan Village (see **Sights,** below), Purok 1, Tam-awan, Pinsao Proper (☎446 2949). Off Tacay Rd. on the way to La Trinidad (P35 taxi ride from Session Rd.). A slightly more expensive form of camping, the traditional *ifugao* huts rise 1½m off the ground. Toilets steps away. Singles P500; doubles P900, each extra person P200.

AJ Pension (☎442 2206), on Jungle Town Rd. Offers great rooms with hot water, TV, and telephone. Far from city center. Singles P600; doubles P800.

FOOD

Fruits you won't find anywhere else in the Philippines thrive in Baguio's cool climate. Street stalls on **Shanum St.** around Burnham Park sell spit-roasted chicken, while those around **Otek St.** play the juiciest karaoke hits. Other cheap eateries cluster around the bus terminals and the city markets. A quick walk down Session Rd. gives you an idea of options.

Cafe Melodin (☎442 7734), on Legarda Rd. Renews one's appetite for Filipino cuisine. The all-day breakfast menu, including the cured pork *tocino* (P69), can fill you up for the rest of the day. Open daily 10am-10pm. Cash only.

Cafe by the Ruins, 25 Chuntug St. One of the best vegetarian selections in the region. Choose from any of 20 meat and non-meat selections. Delicious noodles. Fixed-price lunch P200. Dinner slightly more expensive. Orgasmic shakes P55. Open daily 7am-9pm. AmEx/MC/V.

Sneak-a-Snack, at Gen. Luna St. and Assumption Rd. near St. Louis School. Lunch-time budget meal of rice and one other selection available on school days to entice St. Louis School children (P35). It works. Open daily 6:30am-6:30pm.

Swiss Bakers, on Session Rd. Uphill from the steps to Baguio Cathedral. Cakes, buns, and bread are quick and delicious. Cinnamon rolls P20. Open daily 7:15am-8pm.

SIGHTS

TAM-AWAN VILLAGE. Tam-Awan, literally "vantage point" in the local dialect, is a gateway to the indigenous Cordilleran culture. The cluster of authentic *ifugao* wood and *cogon* grass huts, dismantled from their original location and reconstructed less than an hour outside Baguio City, serves as a living museum and art gallery. Huts of this kind face extinction as mountain tribes switch to modern housing structures. Walk up the hill to "Batad" hut to get a glimpse of the South China Sea. Stay in the huts overnight (see **Accommodations,** above) for a true taste of the culture. *(☎446 2949. Purok 1, Tam-awan, Pinsao Proper, off Tacay Rd., on the way to La Trinidad. A P40 taxi ride from Session Rd. Open daily 9am-6pm. P20.)*

BELL TEMPLE. Bordering the Trinidad Valley, the Bell Temple serves a syncretic sect that combines Buddhist, Taoist, Confucian, and Christian beliefs. Ask a priest to tell you your fortune (P4) or take a trip around the fountain of waterlilies as you ponder your own existence. *(Off Magsaysay Ave. Take a jeepney from the corner of Bonifacio and Magsaysay Ave. Cameras prohibited. Open M-F 6am-5pm. Free.)*

ST. LOUIS UNIVERSITY MUSEUM OF ARTS AND CULTURE. Established in 1969, this museum, in the university's Msgr. Charles Vath building, conserves cultural artifacts of the Cordilleras. On display is a carabao-powered grinding machine called a *dadapilan*, normally used to squeeze juice from sugar cane but allegedly used during WWII to squeeze confessions out of prisoners. *(☎442 3043, ext. 260. Open M-Sa 7:30am-noon and 1:30-5pm. Free.)*

PARKS. Take a horse for a spin in the **Botanical Gardens, Wright Park,** and **Mines View Park**. Set routes (up to 5hr.) take you to **Mt. Santo Tomas,** the limestone peak 8km away. Behind a blockade of tourist shops, a small promontory gives a wide-angled view of Amburayan Valley and Benguet's gold and copper mines. *(The Botanical Gardens and Wright Park are on the route to Mines View Park, 4km from the city. Open daily 6am-sunset. Horses P100 per 30min. plus P100 for guide.)*

OTHER SIGHTS. On top of a hill with a view of Session Rd., the lavender **Baguio Cathedral** is a funky church with multi-colored daisies in the stained glass. Less authentic than the Tam-Awan Village, the **Ifugao Woodcarvers Village** churns out figurines and animals, including Buddhas, *ifugao* warriors, and potency symbols for P35-150. *(Along Asin Rd. off Naguilian Rd. Take a San Luis jeepney or a taxi to Km 5 for P40.)*

MARKETS

The **City Market** on Magsaysay Ave. showcases gruesome livestock parts as well as vegetables, fruit, *ube*-flavored jam, peanut and cashew brittle, and strawberry wine. For the skilled bargainer, all will be wondrously cheap. (Open daily 5:30am-8pm.) Across the street is the multi-story **Maharlika Livelihood Center.** Tourists' anti-modern predilections have made the traditional garb, personal adornments, and handicrafts of the mountain tribes people highly marketable.

The **Easter Weaving Room,** on Easter Rd., on the northwest outskirts of Guisad, is the commercial counterpart to the Easter Weaving School. Watch weavers stitch clothes and tablecloths. (☎442 4972. Open M-F 8am-5pm. Tablecloths P800-1000)

ENTERTAINMENT AND NIGHTLIFE

City Center Burnham Park, named after urban planner Daniel Burnham, boasts an orchidarium, lake, boats, playground, and roller-skating rink. (Roller-skating P50 per hr., roller blades P50 per hr., available 8am-midnight; boating P60 per boat, P25 per additional person, max. 5 per boat, available 8am-10pm.) The **Baguio Arts Festival,** held each November, features visual, performing, and folk arts, many of which are staged in the park. The **Modern Age Spa,** in the YMCA building on Session Rd. opposite Banco de Oro, offers shiatsu and Swedish massage. (P350; with aromatherapy P450.)

Spirits, 34 Otek St. (☎442 6406). Climb the steps from Burnham Park's northwest corner and turn left onto Otek St. before Rizal Park. Multi-level club. Slouch in comfy chairs, strut on the dance floor, or retire to the bar. San Miguel beer P90. Tu ladies night. No collarless shirts. Cover charge P120; Su-Th includes free drink. Open daily 9pm-2am.

Le Fondue (☎414 3920), on Session Rd. A lounge bar with a live band covering classic hits (James Taylor, anyone?). Cozy atmosphere and happy denial of the "No Smoking" sign. Beer P40; Long island iced tea P95. Open daily 6pm-1am.

Cactus Club, on Legarda Rd., serves its twenty-something patrons with a live band and a pulsating rock and blues mix from 10pm onwards, turning the small bar into a mini club. Great whiskey sours P45. Live band 7-10pm. Open daily 7pm-2:30am.

Acadia Discotheque (☎300 1227), on Cariño St. Baguio's new disco geared toward the hipper-than-thou college crowd. San Miguel P70. Cover P60; M-Th from 7-10pm P25. Open daily 6pm-3am.

BONTOC ☎74

At a mere 1000m, Bontoc lies low within the Chico River Valley. The capital of Mountain Province, it is primarily a commercial town and exhibits the rusticity of other mountain settlements but without the charm or cool climate. However, its friendly people, inexpensive quality accommodations, and proximity to the unparalleled Maligcong rice terraces make it worth a visit. In addition, Bontoc is an excellent place to experience *Igorot* culture, including the standoffish Kalinga tribes whose tattooed members walk the streets alongside Levi-legged locals.

TRANSPORTATION. Several companies run **buses** to nearby towns. Dangwas buses leaving from the **bus terminal** behind the Mountain Hotel go to **Baguio** (7hr., every hr. 6-10am, P145) and **Banaue** (signs read "Tabuk," 2hr., 8am, P80). Rising Sun buses leave from outside City Hall to **Baguio** (every hr. 7am-1pm, P130). Von-Von buses leave from opposite the culture station going to **Banaue** (sign reads "Tabuk" or "Paracelis;" 7:30, 8:30am; P80). **Jeepney** leave from beside Municipal Hall to go to **Banaue** (8:30, 9:30, 11:30am, noon, and sometimes 1pm; P80); those leaving from behind the Kodac building near Old Saints Mission Elementary School go to **Sagada** (1hr., every hr. or when full, 8:30am-4:30pm, P40).

ORIENTATION AND PRACTICAL INFORMATION. Bontoc streets are unmarked and, as far as the residents know, unnamed. "Main St." runs parallel to Chico River through the town's center. Most transportation arrives at the town circle (marked by a large tree) on Main St. Adjacent to the circle and up the hill are **Rizal Plaza** and **Pines Kitchenette and Inn.** The latter gives helpful travel information, arranges guides, and sells the Bontoc-Kalinga trekking map (P10; also available at the Bontoc Museum). Main St. is intersected by five major streets. Between the circle and the first street lies **Xijen,** where you'll find the town's only Internet access. (P2 per min. Open M-Sa 8am-7:30pm, occasionally Su 9am-2pm.) Opposite the second street, a road curves back up the hill past the **post office** (*Poste Res-*

tante; open M-F 8am-noon and 1-5pm). The **Philippine National Bank** exchanges currency and AmEx Traveler's Cheques at no charge. (☎602 1078. Open M-F 8:30am-2:30pm.) **Bontoc General Hospital** (open M-F 8am-noon and 1-4pm, Sa 8am-noon for consultation) has a **24hr. pharmacy** and emergency care. The **Bayantel** office on Main St. places **international calls.** (Collect calls P45. Open M-Sa 8am-noon and 2-7pm.) **Postal code:** 2616.

ACCOMMODATIONS AND FOOD. During the dry season, accommodations suffer from intermittent water supply. **Pines Kitchenette and Inn,** opposite Rizal Plaza, has large rooms and exquisite service. (☎602 1509. Breakfast included. P100 per person; doubles with common room P500.) The road to Samoki, which runs across the river from the town circle, passes the newly furnished **Ridgebrooke Hotel, Cafe & Restaurant,** offering one of the few laundry services in town. It's only disadvantage is its considerable distance from the town center. (Laundry P25 per piece for guests only. Rooms with shared common room P150 per person; private room P600.) The **Eastern Star Hotel & Restaurant** has friendly management, but the rooms are dark, and the bathrooms need a good scrub. (Singles P70; doubles P140.)

Julia-A Restaurant on Main St. offers sumptuous food in a cool, clean diner. (*Bistek* P60. Red Horse beer P30. Open daily 9am-9:30pm.) **Bluebirds Restaurant,** between the third and fourth streets intersecting Main St., flies high with large, tasty portions. ("Budget meal" P45. Open daily 9am-9pm.)

SIGHTS AND ENTERTAINMENT. Before heading into the villages, you can get background information from the **Bontoc Museum,** opposite the post office. (Open daily 8am-noon and 1-5pm. Minimum donation P25.) Artifacts demonstrate the distinct cultures of the four tribes in the area. The highlight is a collection of photographs from 1908-09 that record earnest Americans trying to introduce games of tug-of-war to the males of rival villages to divert them from head-hunting. At the end of the day, there's always the **Massage Clinic,** located on the road to Samoki near the Department of Social Welfare building, where blind masseurs will rub your aches away. (Whole body P140, half-body P70, foot or back P35. Open daily 7am-7pm.) After the massage, visit **Koykie Lite Bar,** Bontoc's PG-rated version of nightlife.

TREKKING AROUND BONTOC. You're asking for trouble if you don't hire a guide to smooth out cultural and linguistic barriers. Ask Arlene at Pines Kitchenette to contact private guide Francis Pa-in, a Kalinga, highly recommended by several publications. (☎462 4225. Around P500 per day for groups of 1-5.)

Treks last anywhere from one morning to three days. A typical day-hike could involve a three-hour walk from Bontoc to the **Maligcong rice terraces,** a 2hr. trek from Maligcong to **Guina-ang,** and then a 45min. hike to the **Mainit Hot Springs,** where optimistic miners pan for gold. The return to Bontoc is a 3hr. downhill walk. Jeepney leave for Maligcong from the town circle (8am, noon, 2:30, 4:30pm; P30). From the drop-off point, it's a 2km trek to the village. It is customary for trekkers to bring gifts. Adults want matches, and children delight at candy. It's also possible to take two- or three-day treks into Kalinga province. You'll have to rely on the hospitality of the villages for food and accommodation. One such expedition includes a trip to the village of **Butbut.** From Bontoc, it's a long jeepney ride to Basao (P40), then a 2hr. hike up the mountain to reach the Butbut. The views of Tinglayen village from along the ridge are unbeatable.

SAGADA ☎74

The long and bumpy ride to Sagada is punishment worth enduring to reach this quiet and spiritual town. Sacred burial grounds, caves, statuesque limestone formations, and heavy waterfalls offer an alternative to yet more rice terraces. Despite a scarcity of nightlife, visitors tend to linger in Sagada, partaking in the bohemian cafes and restaurants.

DON'T MESS WITH THE KALINGA The Kalinga only recently began tolerating outsiders. A troubled relationship with the Marcos administration led to a frigid attitude toward strangers. President Marcos proposed to build a giant dam in the Chico Valley that would flood Kalinga villages and force them to relocate. The Kalinga refused offers of compensation and banded together with local communists (the NPA) to sabotage construction. They succeeded in delaying the dam until Marcos was ousted in 1986, when the project was scaled down. The Kalinga have continued their subversive stance since then by producing high-quality marijuana, mostly exported to Boracay. They are friendlier to travelers now, but a guide is essential to help orient you to the villages.

TRANSPORTATION AND PRACTICAL INFORMATION. The road that ascends into Sagada also serves as the town's main street. It passes **St. Theodore's Hospital,** then reaches the **town center** and **Municipal Hall** about ½km down the road. Also in the town center are: the **tourist information center** (open daily 7am-5pm); **Sagada Rural Bank** (open Tu-Sa 8-11:45am and 1:15-4:30pm); **police station** (open 24hr.); **post office** (Poste Restante, open M-F 8am-noon and 1-4:30pm; **postal code:** 2619). Lizardo **buses** go to **Baguio** (7hr.; every hr. 5-10am, 6:30pm; P149). **Jeepney** to **Bontoc** leave from the market (1hr.; every 20min. 6-7am, every hr. 7:45-8:45am and 10am-noon; P25). To reach **Banaue** from Sagada, you must go through Bontoc.

ACCOMMODATIONS AND FOOD. **Masferré Inn and Restaurant** offers spacious, clean rooms in the center of town. (P100 per person, shared bath.) The dining area serves decent sandwiches (ham P45, tuna P50) and lukewarm beer (P30). **St. Joseph's Lodge,** opposite St. Theodore's Hospital, has cheaper rooms but lacks the comfort of Masferré. (Singles P85; doubles P180, with private common room P500.) The **Sagada Guest House** (P75 per person), **Greenhouse Inn** (P85 per person) and the **Ganduyan Inn** (doubles P180), all in the town center, offer basic accommodations. Along with a particularly pious curfew (9pm), these three accommodations impose a merciless 9am check-out.

Down the hill from Masferré's is the **Yoghurt House,** highly recommended for delicious veggie fried rice (P90). Listen to great 80s music or rent a book while you wait. (Open daily 6am-9pm.) Near the town hall is the **Shamrock,** whipping up fabulous flapjacks (P25).

SIGHTS. The **Masferré Gallery,** about 1km down the road from St. Theodore's, displays the work of the late Eduardo Masferré, the son of a Spanish soldier who settled in the mountains at the turn of the century. His photographs of friends and neighbors have enjoyed international success. (Open daily 6am-9pm. Free.) **RJ's Souvenirs and Gift Shops,** across from the Yoghurt House, offers plenty of cheap souvenirs to take home. (P15-100. Open daily 7am-6:30pm.)

TREKKING AROUND SAGADA. The **Sagada Environmental Guides Association (SEGA)** has fixed rates; only SEGA guides can be hired at the tourist information center. Typical tours include the **Sugong Hanging Coffins, Lumiang Burial Cave,** and **Sumaging Cave,** popularly known as "Big Cave." (4-5hr. 1-4 people P300; group of 5 P350; group of 6-9 P600. Prices double after 5hr.) Another alternative is a one-day trek encompassing the 1800m **Mt. Ampacao** (1½hr.), **Lake Danom,** and the **Bokong Falls,** including a climb up the **Kiltepan Tower** to survey the rice terraces. (1-4 people P400; group of 5 P500; 6-9 P600. Guides strongly recommended for novice hikers.)

If you'd prefer not to take a tour, try exploring some of the sights on your own. Fifteen minutes past the Prime Hotel, the road forks. The left fork, leading to Suyo Rd., passes the Sugong Hanging Coffins, tethered to a cliff face. Thirty minutes farther along Suyo Rd., a path leads to the Lumiang Burial Cave. Walk 10min. past the burial cave to Sumaging Cave, which offers unmatched adventure as you wade in waist-deep water, cling to ropes, and crawl through crevices. Either get a guide or become bat feed.

From Bontoc Rd. a path to the right leads past St. Mary's Episcopal Church to a **cemetery** and **Calvary Hill.** To the right, the path takes you to a boulder, and another path takes you to the floor of **Echo Valley.** The path is slippery; be prepared to come back drenched in mud. These trails are unmarked, and it's easy to get lost without a guide. Wear hiking boots and pack light. Hanging coffins are visible in the limestone cliff faces, accompanied by a smattering of "death chairs." In certain rituals, the deceased sits in the chair while funeral-goers perform sacrifices and songs.

Fifteen minutes along the road to Bontoc, the **Matangkib Burial Cave** is at the foot of a path opposite the Rocky Valley Inn. Passing by the left of the cave leads you to the **Latang Underground River.** With a strong flashlight, the river can be followed to the Bokong waterfall. If you don't want to follow the underground river, you can take the concrete steps leading up from Bontoc Rd. past Sagada Weaving to a path down to the river, then cross the river and head upstream to the falls.

To visit the 40m high **Bomod-ok (Big) Waterfalls,** register with the tourist information center and obtain a guide. Jeepney go to the Banga-an Elementary School from the basketball court (30min.; on school days only 8am departure, 1pm return; P25). A trail leads from Banga-an to the Bomod-ok waterfalls (1½hr. trek). On weekends and holidays hire a jeepney for a "Special Ride" to Banga-an (P200 plus P150 for waiting), or walk (2-3hr.). Follow the road to Banga-an for about an hour, turn down the cement steps beyond the Banga-an Elementary School, then take the path through Fidelsian village to the waterfalls.

BANAUE ☎74

Generations of *Ifugao* farmers have grown vast rice terraces on every mountain face in and around Banaue. The rugged terrain is now a spectacular gallery of geological sculptures. As the *Ifugao* have shaped their habitat, it has shaped them, leaving its mark in the deeply stooped backs of the older tribeswomen, a calendar of rituals that punctuate the rice-growing cycle, and indigenous artistic tradition which has produced an outpouring of jewelry, carvings, bronze works, and textiles. Unfortunately, swarming tourists and tricycles slightly spoil the terrace panoramas. A short trek to Batad affords spectacular terraces views.

TRANSPORTATION. Most buses and jeepney leave from the Sanafe Lodge. **Dangwa buses** run to **Manila** (9hr., 5pm, P250). The dispatch office in Niclyn's Store at the marketplace makes reservations one day in advance from 3 to 7pm. **Autobuses** leave from near the Banaue Hotel and go to **Manila** (5pm, A/C P250). Make reservations at the craftshop opposite Cool Winds. To get to **Baguio,** take a **KMS** bus from the top of the stairs near Cool Winds (9hr., 3pm, P180), a Dangwa bus (7am, and 4pm, P210), or an Autobus, which departs from the Banaue Hotel (5:30pm, P230). Jeepney run to **Bontoc** (2½hr., 7am, P80). A second jeepney may leave when full (P1800). A jeepney to **Sagada** costs P2500.

OF RICE AND MEN Countless hours passing through countless acres of nearly identical terraces will begin to dampen your awe of the Cordillera landscape. Once you've seen one piece of rice-growing genius, you've seen it all, right? Wrong. A true rice-terrace connoisseur knows that each terrace is different: they can be convex or concave, equiaxial or isomorphic, stone-walled or clay-packed. Though the Banaue terraces are credited by some as being 2000 years old, it is misleading to think of them as completed sculptures that have stood immutable over the centuries. The terraces are an ongoing project, requiring constant upkeep. Terraces change over the year. In January, they are segmented pools of water, muddy plots plowed and harrowed by farmers and their carabao-sparring partners. Weeks later they are transformed into lush green lawns of seedlings. By July the terraces have started to turn yellow and brown, becoming ripe for harvest. In addition to producing high-grade rice, the terraces provide a constant source of work, worry, celebration, status, and territorial dispute for the village people who depend on them.

ORIENTATION AND PRACTICAL INFORMATION. The unnamed main street starts at a parking area for **buses** and **jeepney,** surrounded by market stalls, shops, and the town hall, which houses a branch of the **post office** (☎386 4104; *Poste restante;* open M-F 8am-noon and 1-5pm) and a desk where jeepney and **tricycles** can be chartered. The **tourist information center** is on the second floor of the Town Hall. (Open daily 8am-5pm.) Area maps are available at **People's Inn** (see below, P10). **RSR Merchandising** at the market **exchanges US dollars** and **traveler's checks** at poor rates; bring enough pesos with you. From the **market,** the main street runs beside the river to its right before it veers, crosses the river, and becomes a national road that heads back on the other side of the gully past the **Guihob Natural Pool** (4km) to the **Batad Junction** (12km). A left at the fork by the market leads uphill past the **Good News Clinic** to the Banaue Hotel overlooking **Tam-An village** (15min. walk). At the top of the drive are the main post office and the **Digitel telephone office** (☎386 9850; open M-F 8am-6pm.) **Postal code:** 3601.

ACCOMMODATIONS AND FOOD. Hostels generally observe a 9pm curfew and a 10am check-out. **People's Inn and Restaurant** offers solid accommodations in addition to Banaue's hottest lounge. Mingle with tourists and locals of all ages while enjoying a serene view of the terraces. (☎386 4014. Singles P100-150, with common room P300; doubles P200, with common room P500; quads with common room P500.) **Green View Lodge** boasts spacious rooms with balconies but unfortunately lacks People's views. (☎386 4021. Rooms with shared common room P100 per person; twins with balcony, hot shower, and private common room P400-600; quads with common room P600; family room with common room P700.) **Stairway Lodge** rooms are clean and pleasant. (Singles P100; doubles P200, with common room and hot shower P230.) For something a little more private, try **Cozy Nook,** opposite the Stairway Lodge, a homey inn run by an affectionate old woman and her family. (Doubles P200; triples P350; P100 extra for high season.) Both the **Banaue Hotel and Youth Hostel** and **Sanafe Lodge** are pristine, but rooms other than dorms will cost you an arm and a leg. (Banaue: ☎386 4088. Dorms P200; singles with common room P2300; doubles with common room P2800; includes hot shower and pool access. Sanafe: ☎386 4085. Dorms US$3.65; doubles with common room US$18; family room with common room US$25.) Around the corner from the Stairway Lodge, the **Cool Winds Restaurant** delivers hot meals in a breeze. (Pork, fish, and chicken dishes P50-70. Veggie fried rice P65. Open daily 6am-9pm.)

SIGHTS AND ENTERTAINMENT. The established viewpoint of the famous **Banaue rice terraces** is 4km along the road to Bontoc (round-trip tricycle to Banaue Viewpoint P100, jeepney P350). The terraces are visually spectacular, but, literally, lack true grit. Producing much less grain than the Batad terraces, only subsidies from the United Nations keep the land plowed and the villagers working (guide P300). Before the viewpoint, turn left onto the Hapao-Hungduan Rd. to see the **mummified couple of Hiwang,** smoked and embalmed by their children in the early 70s. (Round-trip tricycle 15-20min., P150; jeepney P350.) The **Banaue Museum** at the Banaue View Inn (on main street) holds the collection of anthropologist H. Ottley Beyer, one of the first outsiders to treasure *Ifugao* culture. (☎386 4078. Open M-Sa 8am-noon and 1-5pm. P25.) On a sunny day, visitors cool off in the **Guihob Natural Pool** along the road to Batad. (Round-trip tricycle P120, jeepney P350.)

An established two-day trek from Banaue includes the villages of Batad, Cambulo, and Pula. Cambulo, a village circumscribed by a river, has two guest houses, the **Riverside Inn** and the **Friends Inn** (P75 per person). The treks can be difficult during the rainy season. Arrange your trip at the Banaue Viewpoint or Banaue Hotel. (1-2 people P1200 per day; 3-4 people P500 per person per day.)

DAYTRIP FROM BANAUE: BATAD. Rightfully so, travelers rave about the abundant cheap rooms and phenomenal rice terraces in Batad. Jeepney (50min., 10am-noon, P40) leave from the market area outside the Sanafe Lodge for the **Batad Junction** (special round-trip by tricycle P400; jeepney P1000). A stone path leads from the junction around the "saddle" to Batad (2hr.). About 15min. into the walk, the "mountaineer's shortcut" veers left over the saddle, cutting the walk in half. Signs blocking the first view of the valley entreat hikers to stay in their lodgings. Try a room in either **Simon's Inn and Restaurant** (singles P50 per person) or **Hillside Inn** (rooms P50 per person). Batad's cuisine is good, even though the lack of electricity (bring a flashlight for the outhouse) makes refrigeration impossible. Simon's serves pita-bread dishes, pancakes (P45), *chapati* bread, and pizza, a fresh break from everyday Filipino cuisine.

OLONGAPO CITY ☎47

Olongapo prides itself for prohibiting laziness; it's a city that has learned to work hard. Life here was once idyllic: the mountains and beaches that border Subic Bay were once home to one of the largest American naval bases outside the US. However, the sudden and violent eruption of Mount Pinatubo in 1991 followed by the pullout of the US forces a year later left a city that was physically destroyed and economically debilitated. Under the charismatic leadership of Mayor Richard Gordon, thousands of unpaid volunteers cleaned the base of its former ashes, paving the way for the creation of the **Subic Bay Metropolitan Area (SBMA).** As a new free-port region, Olongapo hopes to reclaim some of its former economic glory and continue its path toward revitalization.

TRANSPORTATION

Buses: Victory Liner has a virtual monopoly on the region with a terminal on the **Ulong Apo Rotunda** (Rizal Ave. and National Hwy.). Buses to: **Baguio** (5hr., every hr. 8am-10:30pm, with A/C P225); **Caloocan** (3½ hr., every hr. 4am-midnight, with A/C P128); **Pasay** and **Cubao** (4hr., every hr. 5:30am-11:30pm, with A/C P140).

Local Transportation: Jeepney routes are easily distinguishable by the color of the vehicles. Yellow jeepney take the busy Rizal Ave. route to Magsaysay Dr., while blue ones start from the Ulong Apo Rotunda and pass through the city beaches (P4). **Tricycles** are color coded as well, but are able to take passengers to different areas as well (about P5 for first 2km).

ORIENTATION AND PRACTICAL INFORMATION

Entering from Manila, the northbound **National Highway** turns into **Rizal Ave.,** the city's main commercial thoroughfare. The **Ulong Apo Rotunda** connects Rizal Ave.to the National Hwy., the road to **Barrio Baretto** (also known as **Beach Blvd.**), Olongapo's beach area. Continuing down Rizal Ave. takes you to a second major rotunda, this time intersecting **Magsaysay Dr.,** the entrance to SBMA and home to most of Olongapo's clubs and restaurants.

Tours: Swagman Travel, 30 National Hwy. (☎223 4356). Open M-Sa 8am-5pm. Free maps.

Currency Exchange: Bank of the Philippine Islands (BPI), 1925 Rizal Ave. (☎223 7376), near City Hall. **24hr. ATM** (AmEx/Cirrus/MC/V). Open M-F 9am-4pm.

Bookstores: National Bookstore, 1885 Bennet Rd., SBMA (☎223 7341). English and Tagalog titles. Open daily 9am-8pm.

Emergency: Medical Services ☎169. **Police** ☎166.

Police Station: ☎222 4554.

Pharmacy: Mercury Drug (☎222 2520), on Rizal Ave., 250m south of City Hall. Opposite the **public market.**

Medical Services: James Gordon Memorial Hospital (☎222 4120, emergency ☎169), on Rizal Ave. near Magsaysay Dr.

Telephones: Piltel Office (☎222 5050), on De la Cruz Dr., next to Marikit Park facing Rizal Ave. Open M-F 8am-4pm.

Internet Access: AMA Internet Center, 1040 Rizal Ave. (☎222 8531). Telnet, printing, and fax machines available. Internet P60 per hr. **Telesubic Internet Center,** 960 Rizal Ave. (☎224 8846). Internet P40 per hr.

Post Office: On Rizal Ave. in front of City Hall. *Poste Restante.* Open M-F 8am-noon and 1-5pm. **Postal Code:** 2200.

ACCOMMODATIONS

The lodgings in SBMA are over-touristed and overpriced, and resort inns along Beach Blvd. put a premium on the view. Magsaysay Dr. hotels give the best value and location.

Arlene's Inn I, Magsaysay Dr. and 5th St. (☎222 5320). Great location and a knowledgeable staff makes Arlene's a prime choice in the city. Singles with A/C P700; doubles with A/C P800.

Arlene's Inn II (☎222 2629), right in front of the Victory Liner bus terminal. Same perks and prices as above.

Subic Bayside Hotel, 85 Beach Blvd., (☎222 4580). Beachfront rooms without having to sell your first-born. *Nipa hut* cottage P385; doubles P550, with A/C P900.

SBMA Hotels (☎252 4463). If you're into large Navy barracks remodeled and turned into an international lodge, then this is your spot. The cheapest option in SBMA. Single Su-Th P900, F-Sa P1000, extra bed P200.

Ridgecrest Gardens Hotel, 15 Magsaysay Dr. (☎222 2006). Barest amenities means cheap rates. Treat yourself to a drink with the money you've saved. Singles P600, with A/C P800; extra bed P200.

FOOD

The numerous ethnic restaurants in Olongapo reflects the diversity in taste and growing tourist influence. Several restaurants line Rizal Ave. and Magsaysay Dr., and **Times Square,** a 2min. walk from the SBMA entrance, offers a myriad of choices ranging in price from expensive to "are you kidding?" **Wimpy's,** on Magsaysay Dr. and also in front of the Ulong Apo Rotunda, is named after Popeye's rotund friend and specializes in amazingly good hamburgers (P55). Try the tropical ice cream flavors as well (mango P20). **Subic Garden,** 99 Beach Blvd. (☎222 2888), offers relaxing meals before you head out to the beach. Try the seafood in spicy sauce (P160) or the *pancit* (P60).

SIGHTS AND ENTERTAINMENT

The natural beauty of Subic Bay's beaches is the highlight of the area. SBMA delivers the finest ones in the area, especially the **Officer's Club** and **All Hands** beaches.

Subic Bay houses Luzon island's remaining untouched patch of rain forest. The **Jungle Environment Survival Course (JEST)** teaches you how to live off bamboo in the wilderness, just like the Marines. (Call JEST at ☎252 9072 for specific courses, prices, and times.) With more than seven shipwrecks sprinkled along the harbor, Subic Bay also attracts divers. **Johan's Adventure Dive Center** in Baloy Long Beach offers two dives for US$41.50. (☎224 8915; www.subicdive.com.) **Baloy's Long Beach** on Beach Blvd. is a small city in and of itself. Housing a myriad of restaurants, bars, cottages, and more bars, many visitors have found themselves becoming permanent residents of the neighborhood. (Entrance fee P30, but mention that you're staying in one of the hotels to get in free.)

Finally, instead of throwing away your hard-earned cash, why not slowly lose it via **Casino Filipino's** one-armed bandits on Magsaysay Dr. Roulette, blackjack, poker, and bingo are also available. (☎222 4565. Open 24hr.)

MARKETS

The **public market** on Rizal Ave. is one of the cleanest in the country, but don't be afraid to get dirty with the bargaining. Everything from clothing to souvenirs to meat is available. (Open daily 8am-dusk.) At the end of Magsaysay Dr. next to the SBMA entrance is the **night market** where vendors hawk the latest retail fashions and pirated electronics.

For a more formal shopping experience, try **Ocampo's,** on Rizal Ave., a mini-department store that attracts a primarily after-school teen crowd. There's no haggling here. (Open daily 9am-8pm.)

NIGHTLIFE

The absence of free spending American sailors has defanged Olongapo's nefarious reputation as a meat market, but the city is still far from tame. Magsaysay's Dr. offers a multitude of exciting discos and great live bands, while the bars along Beach Blvd. attract retired expats with colorful stories. All the clubs are welcoming, but don't be surprised to discover that the hot girl winking at you actually works for the club.

Gigolo Club, on Magsaysay Dr. off Rizal Ave. Don't let the name fool you. Gigolo is one of the hottest spots in the city, playing the latest dance hits all night long. Very crowded on weekends. Cover F-Sa P50. Beer P45. Open 9pm-4am.

Blue Note Cafe, 24 Magsaysay Dr., has the city's best live music and the most comfortable booths. San Miguel Beer P45.

THE WEST COAST

The west coast of Luzon, from the Hundred Islands National Park in Pangasinan to Vigan in Ilocos Sur, may seem like a sideshow compared to the more traveled route north through the Cordillera. The beaches around San Fernando are popular with domestic tourists from Manila, but if beaches are your final goal, you would be better off heading south to Mindoro or the Visayas. But for the traveler who wants to decipher the old patterns of colonialism, the well-preserved Spanish city of Vigan, established by Legazpi's protégé Juan de Salcedo, is a Rosetta Stone. And if Vigan is the mecca for such a pilgrimage, messing about on boats around the Hundred Islands National Park and unwinding on the beaches around San Fernando can be frivolous diversions along the way.

SAN FERNANDO (LA UNION) ☎72

The capital of La Union province, San Fernando is a city with great civic pride. Bearing slogans declaring love for the city, tricycles buzz through the streets painted a uniform blue and white, uncannily color-coordinated with the pastel shades of the town plaza. The streets are crowded and the air reeks of pollution, yet peace can be found at the spectacular Ma-cho temple. A stretch of beach between San Fernando and Bauang to the south attracts swarms of townies on weekends, but won't impress those familiar with Visayan beaches. Rougher waters to the north, at San Juan beach, support a loyal surfers between November and February.

TRANSPORTATION

Partas (☎242 0465), on Quezon Ave. 100m north of P. Burgos St. intersection, runs buses to **Baguio** (2hr., sporadic departures 9am-7:15pm, with A/C P56) and **Manila** (6hrs., 6am-12:30am, with A/C P235). **Philippine Rabbit** (☎888 2035) buses depart from the terminal off Quezon Ave. on the southernmost border of town for **Vigan** (2¾hr., every hr. 7:30am-4pm, with A/C P108) and **Laoag** (4½hr., P169). **Minibuses,** including Eso-Nice, depart from Gov. Luna St. to **Baguio** (2hr., every 15min. 5:30am-6pm, P40). For **Dagupan,** catch minibuses departing from Rizal Ave. (2hr., every 5min. 4:30am-6pm, P50). For **Alaminos,** change minibuses at Dagupan.

ORIENTATION AND PRACTICAL INFORMATION

San Fernando is 270km north of Manila, stretched between the seven hills and the South China Sea and bracketed between the beaches of **Buang** (6km) to the south and **San Juan** (10km) to the north. The town is arranged linearly, and the South China Sea makes a north-south orientation easy. **Quezon Ave.** (which becomes **National Highway**) connects the beaches and the city's main road. Most budget accommodations lie north of the **town plaza** along Quezon Ave. The major streets running east-west include **Gen. Luna St.** (not to be confused with adjacent Gov. Luna St.), **Rizal Ave.,** and **P. Burgos St.,** where jeepney are available for the beaches of San Juan. The sights sit on polar ends of town, with the **Ma-Cho Temple** at the north extreme, and other sights (**Freedom Park, Fil-Chinese Pagoda,** and the **Museo de La Union**) to the south. Taking Rizal Ave. west away from the hill leads to the coast.

Tourist Office: on Gen. Luna St. (☎888 2411). In Mabanag Justice Hall on one side of the town plaza. Better maps available at the **Office of the City Planner** in the Marcos Bldg. Open M-F 7am-6pm.

Currency Exchange: Philippine National Bank, on Quezon Ave., at Gov. Luna St. (☎242 0908). **24hr. ATM** (Cirrus/MC/PLUS/V). Open M-F 9am-3pm.

Bookstore: Triva, Quezon Ave. (☎888 2996). Open M-Sa 7:30am-8pm.

Pharmacy: Mercury Drug, on Quezon Ave. opposite Far East Bank. Open 6:30am-9pm.

Emergency: ☎166.

Police: ☎242 4702. North of town plaza on Quezon Ave.

Medical Services: Bethany Hospital, Widdoes St. (☎888 2355). Past Union Christian College, off Gen. Luna St. toward the hill. **Open 24hr.**

Internet Access: The NET Cafe, Quezon Ave. (☎242 2222), 30m from P. Burgos St. intersection. P25 per hr. during peak times. P38 per hr. during non-peak times. Open M-Sa 8am-9pm, Su 1pm-7pm. **Union City Cafe,** Juanita Commercial Building on Quezon Ave. next to Mikka Hotel (☎888 0407). P42 per hr. Telnet and AOL Instant Messenger available. Open M-Sa 10am-10pm, Su 2am-10pm.

Post Office: Marcos Bldg., Rizal Ave., at the corner of P. Tavera St. (☎888 2933). *Poste Restante.* **Branch** on Mabini St., Catbangen. Open M-F 8am-6pm. **Postal code:** 2600.

ACCOMMODATIONS AND FOOD

You get what you pay for in San Fernando: you'll be charged only for the roof at the Mandarin House Hotel, but for newer fittings and cable TV at Hotel Mikka. Even the view will cost you at the Sea & Sky Hotel and Restaurant. Ambience is only sold north of town at **Las Villas** (see **Beaches around San Fernando,** p. 544) where good lodging and great food are available at reasonable prices.

Mandarin House Hotel (☎888 5309), on Quezon Ave., 100m south of town plaza. Decent budget option. Doubles P165, with A/C and common room P435.

Hotel Mikka (☎242 5737), on Quezon Ave., next to Partas bus terminal 150m north of P. Burgos St. intersection toward Ma-cho Temple. Knowledgeable, professional staff. All rooms equipped with phones, A/C, cable TV. Singles P625; doubles P750; family room P1250.

Sea & Sky Hotel & Restaurant, Pagdaraoan (☎888 5579). Affordable basement rooms forego views of the South China Sea. All rooms have phones, A/C, and cable TV. Singles/doubles P675; sea-view singles/doubles P875; quads with fridge P1275.

The Chinese influence in San Fernando gives restaurants added flavor. The **Danish Baker,** on Quezon Ave. past the plaza on the left, offers delicious tuna turnovers (P18.50) and *pandisuelo* bread, a local favorite (P2). The fresh seafood at well-run **Las Villas,** 2514 San Juan., 400m toward the sea from the National Highway (Quezon Ave.) in San Juan., provides fresh seafood that will melt in your mouth as you cool in the shade of the palms by the sea. The "Fisherman's Basket" feeds two for P375. It's well worth the trek out of town.

SIGHTS AND ENTERTAINMENT

A joint group of Filipinos and Taiwanese fisherman built the **Ma-cho Temple,** in the lush green hillside off Quezon Ave., 400m to the north of the town plaza, in gratitude for local hospitality. Ma-cho, the Taoist goddess of the sea, looks out upon the South China Sea from atop her hill—visitors can borrow her vista from the balcony, or step inside to ask her questions. A Chinese deity of the Sung dynasty, Macho is known in the Philippines as the Virgin of Caysasay. On the second week of September, the original statue of the Virgin is brought to the temple from Taal for the **Feast of Our Lady of Caysasay.** (Open daily 6am-6pm.)

The hills behind San Fernando afford views of the South China Sea to the west and the Cordillera to the east. Down Quezon Ave., beside the Caltex station, a flight of steps leads up to the hauntingly decrepit **Heroes Hill,** surrounded by white, gypsum-like statues of the usual suspects (Rizal, Bonifacio, et al.). The steps end abruptly, and around a communications outpost is the **Museo de la Union,** which exhibits archaeological finds in La Union predating the Spanish arrival. (Open M-F 8am-5pm.) The view from the balcony is better than anything you will see inside. A path leads to the north along a ridge to the **Fil-Chinese Pagoda,** a gesture of friendship by the Filipino-Chinese toward their adopted county.

Like most of San Fernando's attractions, its preeminent disco is atop a hill. The **High Altitude Disco,** on Gapuz Zig-Zag Rd., features pop/dance on Friday nights (☎888 2025. Cover P100 includes one beer. Open W-Sa 9pm-2am.)

BEACHES

SAN JUAN. The best local beach is 8km north of San Fernando near San Juan. The rough waves make it less suitable for swimming and instead attract a cadre of surfers from November to February. Catch a jeepney (P5) bearing the signboard "Bacnotan" from the corner of Quezon and Burgos St. in San Fernando. Get off prior to arriving in San Juan when you see your resort's advertisement. **Las Villas,** St. Jude Village, Ili Norte, is 400m from the National Highway toward the sea. Management invests fastidious pride in the food and rooms of this peaceful outpost; set in a cactus garden. An eclectic group of adventurers and expatriates mingle at the bar nightly. (☎242 3770. Doubles P850-950; family room for 5P1800.) **San Juan Surf Resort (Surf Camp),** 238 Urbiztondo, on the path past the Billabong Guest House rents rooms and surfboards, and is San Juan's surfer mecca. The amiable Aussie owner rents surfboards and rooms. (☎242 4544. No hot water. Dorm rooms with common cooking facility P150; singles P300; bungalow P650. Surfboards P100 per hr., P300 per half-day, P500 per whole day.) The occupancy rate of **Mona Liza,** in Urbiztondo, rises and falls with the height of the waves. (☎888 4892. "Budget" rooms with common room P300; doubles P400; triples P600. P50 for refrigerator.)

BAUANG. A stretch of beach runs from Baccuit to Pagdalagan 6km south of San Fernando and 1km north of Bauang proper. Take a jeepney bound for Naguilian or Agoo (P3). The beaches are not visible from the road, but advertisements for beach resorts certainly are. Prices increase up to 25% in summer months (Nov.-May). For travelers staying elsewhere, resorts charge a fee for use of their facilities.

Farther north, the **China Sea Beach Resort,** in Paringao, offers a swimming pool. (☎242 6101. Standard doubles with A/C, private common room, and breakfast P1050; "deluxe" with cable TV P1700.) Other options along the beach include the boisterous **Southern Palms Beach Resort,** Arturo Balagot St., Pagdalagan. (☎242 0854. Doubles with A/C P595.) Their nightclub, **Stiletto's,** is open daily 4pm-midnight.

VIGAN ☎77

In the late 16th century, conquistador Miguel de Legazpi awarded the rule of Ilocos Province to his grandson Juan de Salcedo, who set about emulating his grandfather by styling Vigan, the provincial capital, after Legazpi's Intramuros in Manila. Spared the wartime devastation that gutted Intramuros, Vigan remains the best-preserved of the old Spanish colonial cities.

TRANSPORTATION. The **Philippine Rabbit** terminal, on Gov. Reyes St., is the launching pad for buses to: **Baguio** (4½hr.; every hr. 3am-midnight; P138, A/C P158); **Laoag** (1hr., every 30min., A/C P64); **Manila** (8hr.; every 1-2hr. 4am-5pm; P284, A/C P324). **Dominion Bus Lines** (☎722 2053), near the south end of Quezon Ave., sends buses to **Manila** (8-10 per day 4:30am-10pm, with A/C P340). The **Partas** terminal (☎722 2933) is behind the cemetery, with buses to **Cubao** and **Manila** (every 30-60min. 4:45am-10:30pm, P340).

ORIENTATION AND PRACTICAL INFORMATION. Vigan lies on the west side of the Mestizo River. Its grid-patterned streets are easily covered on foot or by horse-drawn *calesa.* **Quezon Ave.,** which runs parallel to the river, intersects P. Burgos St. on the east side of the city's main plaza area. The main plaza area is beside Municipal Hall, which houses the **police** station (☎166) and the **Office of the Mayor** (☎722 2466). The newly restored **Mena Crisologo St.,** distinguished by its cobblestones and antique shops, runs south of the Plaza Brugos near the provincial **tourist office** (open M-F 8am-5pm). One block south of Burgos St., Florentino St. runs east-west and passes a branch of **Philippine National Bank,** with a **24hr. ATM.** (Cirrus/MC/PLUS/V. Open M-F 9am-3pm.) The **post office** is one block farther down on Bonifacio St. near the corner of Gov. A. Reyes St. **Postal code**: 2700. The next major east-west street is Gen. Luna St., home to the **PT&T Telephone Office.** (☎722 2273. Open M-W 7am-8pm, Th-F 8am-8pm, Sa-Su 8am-5pm.)

The **Gabriela Silang General Hospital** is on Quirino Blvd., which runs north-south on the east side of town along the river. (☎169, office ☎722-2782. Open M-F 8am-5pm.) Local pharmacies include **Farmacia Fernandina,** on Quezon Ave., between Bonifacio and Gen. Luna St. (☎722 2470. Open daily 7am-10pm.) **Internet access** is available at **Powernet,** 32 Gov. A. Reyes St. (☎722 1830), two blocks west of Mena Crisologo St. (First hr. P60, P0.83 each additional min. Open daily 8am-7:30pm.)

ACCOMMODATIONS AND FOOD. Grandpa's Inn, 1 Bonifacio St., on the corner of Quirino Blvd. not far from the river, is an affordable way to experience old-world chic. Famous for its knick-knacks, it's worth a visit if not an overnight stay. (☎722 2118. Doubles P250, with private common room P350, with A/C P550.) **El Juliana Hotel,** Quirino Blvd., on the corner of Liberation Blvd. in the southeast corner of town, attempts to recreate the Spanish villa experience while staying cool in the Vigan heat. (☎722 2994. Singles/doubles with private common room, A/C, and TV P500.) The swimming pool is open to the public 7am-6pm (P35) and 6-11pm (P50). The **Vigan Hotel,** at the corner of P. Burgos St. and V. Pelos Reyes, features spacious rooms at decent rates. (☎722 1906. Singles with A/C and cable TV P695; doubles P850.)

THE PBA It seems ironic that some of the world's shortest people would play one of the world's tallest sports, let alone with the skill and intensity of the basketball players of the Philippines. The Philippines Basketball Association (PBA), the focus of a national sports obsession, is celebrating its 25th year. Each of its ten teams, rather than representing a region, is sponsored by a corporation, so names like "San Miguel" are plastered across jerseys in boldface letters. The early years of the league were dominated by Toyota and Crispa, whose rivalry resembled the Celtics-Lakers battles of the NBA in the 1980s. Despite the league's many great successes, it has had its share of controversy. During the Marcos years, league officials (including the commissioner) were given jobs allegedly based less on their knowledge of the sport than their familial connections. Game-fixing and blue-chipping have plagued the league since its inception. Nonetheless, the talents of the players have inspired youngsters to don replica jerseys and take up the sport themselves. Basketball is truly the sport of the Philippines, and one of the pleasures of traveling here is watching the PBA-hopefuls hoop it up just about anywhere, with just about anything resembling a ball and hoop.

The local cuisine is blessed with glorious Spanish *empanadas* (deep-fried rice tortillas filled with local vegetables for P3 or meat and eggs for P15) and *okoy* (crispy shrimp and onion pancakes for P15) prepared along Plaza Burgos from late afternoon until early morning. Vigan also claims pork specialties, such as sour and spicy *longganiza* sausage and crispy pork belly *bagnet*, available in cafes surrounding the plaza. **Cafe Floresita,** set within attractive arches by the Ancieto Mansion, has fabulous *longganiza*. (Most dishes P40-180. Open 6am-9pm.) **Cafe Leona's Courtyard,** on Mena Crisologo St., is Vigan's sole outlet for Thai and Japanese entrees. (Sushi P90-190. ☎722 3089. Open 8am-10pm.) Branching out from the plaza, the **8.88 Restaurant and Pool Hall,** on Rizal Ave., draws the local crowd with pool tables and a variety of entrees for P40-60, from squid balls (P50) to *longsilog* (P46), a combination of egg, fried garlic rice, and *longganiza*. (☎722 2208. Open 8am-2am.) **Quality Cool Spot Restaurant,** behind the Vigan Hotel on Quirino Blvd., is a local favorite renowned for its homemade *bagnet* (P200) and *longganiza* (P70).

SIGHTS. The legacy of the Spanish conquistadores is well preserved in the town's architectural template, but Vigan has also been deeply influenced by its participation in the lucrative galleon trade with Europe, Asia, and Mexico. The city's antique stores, many of which line Mena Crisologo St., reflect these influences. **Rowilda's Hand Loom,** on Crisologo St. near Cordillera Inn, reprises the hand-weaving craft that once contributed to the international textile trade of colonial times. (Woven handbags P150-180. Open daily 8am-6pm.)

Pagburnayan Potteries, on the corner of Liberation Blvd. and Rizal St., an almost-hidden jewel, produces the stoneware *burnay* jar used by the Ilocanos to store everything from vinegar to wine. A water buffalo squashes the clay under hoof while mammoth wood-fired kilns bake the sculptured clay.

Padre Burgos House National Museum, 6 Burgos St., adjacent to St. Paul's cathedral, commemorates the death of Padre Burgos, one of the most famous Chinese mestizo residents of Vigan, whose martyrdom in 1872 galvanized the revolutionary movement. On display, among other things, are ancient *itneg* (ovens) of the Tinggian Tribe, which were recently discovered inside a rat cave in Ilocos Sur. (Open M-F 8:30-11am and 1:30-4:30pm, Sa-Su by appointment. P10.)

Crisologo Museum, 23 Liberation Blvd., is another ancestral home that has evolved into a museum. This one-time residence of Congressman, Governor, and war hero Floro Crisologo contains *santos* (icons), natural history exhibits, and ancestral furnishings. (Open daily 8:30-11:30am and 1:30-4:30pm.)

SOUTHERN LUZON

South of Manila, the sights come thick and fast, starting with the Taal Volcano and its own beautiful lake and moving across the straits to Mindoro's decadent beaches and world-class dive sites. Southeast down the Bicol Peninsula, many fly to Legazpi to see the imposing and frequently erupting 2000m Mayon Volcano.

LAKE TAAL REGION ☎43

The Taal Volcano is actually a volcano within a volcano: Lake Taal, which surrounds it, is itself the caldera of a massive ancient volcano. A smaller lake has formed in the main crater, enabling visitors to swim in a crater lake of a volcano in the crater lake of a larger volcano. The great views and cool climate on Tagaytay Ridge have made it a sought-after site for developers. The volcano itself is magnificent, but the town surrounding Lake Taal is dreary and uncomfortable; no more than a daytrip is necessary to see the volcano and neighboring Tagaytay.

TRANSPORTATION. Resorts line the lakefront between **Talisay** and **Leynes. Buses** from **Batangas** and **Manila** pass through **Tanauan. Jeepney** travel from the public market in Tanauan to **Talisay** (20min., 5am-7pm, P9), from which a **tricycle** (P20) can be taken toward Leynes to reach the resorts. On an alternate route, buses from Manila en route to **Nasugbu** or **Calatagan** pass **Tagaytay Ridge,** which has the best views of the volcano. To get to the lakefront from the ridge, get off the bus at **Olivares Plaza,** catch a jeepney (P3.50) to the top of **Ligaya Dr.,** and transfer to another jeepney down Ligaya Dr., which ends at the water (last trip 6pm, P15). Jeepney turn left to Talisay, but you can catch a tricycle to the right if you're heading toward Leynes. Jeepney to Tanauan depart from the corner of Laurel and Wencislao St. (3am-5pm, P9). Buses to **Batangas** and **Batangas Pier** pass along J.P. Laurel St. in Tanauan (1½hr.; P35, A/C P45). Buses also go the other way to **Manila** (1½hr.; P40, A/C P50).

PRACTICAL INFORMATION. The **Tanauan Shoppers Market (TSM)** on A. Mabini St. changes **currency** and traveler's checks. (Open daily 7am-6pm.) The **PLDT telephone office** on the lakefront road near the Ligaya Dr. intersection, provides international phone service, and pay phones provide collect and calling card calls. In Talisay proper, the **Municipal Hall** on Wencislao St. houses the **police** (☎773 0241; **emergency** ☎166) and **post office** (open M-F 8am-5pm). Farther along the street (with the lake to your right), **St. Andrew's Hospital** (☎773 0196) has a **24hr. pharmacy. Postal code:** 4220.

ACCOMMODATIONS AND FOOD. Tourists flock to the lake during summer months (Mar.-May); book well in advance. **San Roque Beach Resort,** 5min. from Ligaya Dr. off Tagaytay Rd., is a labor of love for owners Lita and Leo. (☎733 0271. *Nipa* huts with common room P850; 3-bedroom guest house with living room and kitchen P4000.) **Vista Hazel's Beach Resort,** down the road from San Roque and right on the beach, has a swimming pool. (☎773 0257. Cottages P350; gigantic doubles with A/C P1500.) **Buco Resort,** next to the Taal Volcano Science House (see **Sights,** below), is a 5min. walk toward Leynes from San Roque. (☎773 0306. Doubles P600, with A/C P700; family room P1500.)

SIGHTS. Pick up some background knowledge on Taal and other Philippine volcanoes at the **Taal Volcano Science House,** next to the Buco Resort, halfway between Talisay and Leynes. (Open 24hr. Free.) The locals call it "Vulcanology," so if you're lost and need directions, address it as such. **Taal Volcano** actually has two craters, the younger of which erupted in 1965. There are two popular ways to tackle the old crater. A boat can take you to the front of the island (30min., about P500), where a trail (by foot or horseback) leads to the lip of the old crater. From here, you can gaze into the crater, but there's no route to the lake. Alternatively, you can pay extra for a boat to take you around the back of the island (45min., P750-1000), where islanders guide visitors into the crater to the water's edge (P300). **Resort International,** opposite Ligaya Dr. junction, and many other hotels arrange boats for daytrippers. You're free to bathe in the sulfurous waters, which are said to have medicinal value, but don't swim to the rocky outcrop in the center of the lake and avoid areas with rising steam—the water can scald. It takes 2-4hr. to visit Taal Volcano—go early and bring water.

DAET ☎54

Daet (pronounce dah-et), the capital of Camarines Norte Province, was a trendsetter in Rizal-mania. Two years after Rizal's death, the city erected the first monument to the national hero in 1898, an understated white obelisk. Aside from this seminal act, Daet remains an unassuming town in the corner of the Bicol peninsula, near the western cusp of San Miguel Bay. The tiny coastal village of Mercedes, 7km east, probably attracts more attention, drawing in a flotilla of fishing boats for its morning fish market. The mainland beaches near Daet run the gamut from Bagasbas Beach—with its pizza parlors and videoke bars—to San Jose Beach, patronized only by the occasional picnicker or fisherman.

TRANSPORTATION

The **Philtranco** bus terminal is on F. Martinez St. off Gov. Panotes Ave. (☎571 2718), a short jeepney ride from the town center. Buses depart for Pasay and Cubao in **Manila** (8-9hr.; 9-12 per day 6:30am-9:40pm; P191, premiere P207, A/C P244). Buses also leave from **Superlines** bus terminal (☎721 2961), a short tricycle ride from Vinzons Ave. (P10), for Cubao in **Manila** (8-9hr.; every hr. 5:30am-9:30pm; P171, A/C P205). **AMDG** buses leave from the Caltex Station opposite the hospital for **Legazpi** (4½hr., every 30-45min. 5am-3:30pm, A/C P170.50).

ORIENTATION AND PRACTICAL INFORMATION

Vinzons Ave., Daet's main street, parallel to the north side of the river, is home to a congregation of hotels and restaurants. At the easternmost end of Vinzons Ave., an elevated **town plaza,** housing the town market, rises near the cross streets of **J. Cereses** and **Moreno St.** Vinzons Ave. narrows to become **Gov. Panotes Ave.,** which continues to **Mercedes.**

Camarines Norte Doctors' Hospital (☎571 2302), is on Vinzons Ave. opposite the Wiltan Hotel (open 24hr.; front door open 5am-11pm). Taking J. Lukban St. across the river leads past the Rizal monument and Freedom Park to Magana St., where the **Philippine National Bank** (☎571 2815) exchanges traveler's checks (open M-F 9am-3pm). The **post office** is in Camambugan, a P2.50 tricycle ride from the town center (*Poste Restante;* open M-F 8am-noon and 1-5pm). A **Bayantel** telephone office (☎440 0568; open daily 7am-7:30pm) can be found on Vinzons Ave. not far from the J. Lukban St. intersection. For the **police,** dial ☎166 or 571 2815. **Postal code:** 4600.

ACCOMMODATIONS AND FOOD

Sampaguita Lodging House (☎571 2221), Vinzons Ave., past town plaza near intersection with Pimentel Ave. Some showers. Cable TV P50. 24hr. coffeeshop. Singles P75, with private common room P175, with A/C P300; doubles P150/P250/P395.

Hotel Dolor (☎721 2167), Vinzons Ave., opposite elevated town plaza. Nightclub upstairs. 24hr. room service. Cable TV P50. Economy singles P220, deluxe with A/C, TV, hot water, and refrigerator P450; doubles P400-450/650-850.

Wiltan Hotel & Restaurant, Vinzons Ave. (☎511 2907), adjacent to Caltex Station, opposite Camarines Norte Doctors' Hospital. Restaurant. Singles with clean, private common room P200, with A/C P450; doubles P300, with A/C P550, with TV P600.

Nautiloux Resort (☎440 036), at the end of the Bagasbas Beach beside the defunct Daet airstrip. Swedish or shiatsu massage P500. Food upon request. A/C rooms with mirrors. Ordinary rooms lack showers. Doubles P250, with A/C P500.

During June, Daet raves it up in honor of the pineapple. But not just any pineapple—the sweet Formosa pineapple. Apart from a food festival and agricultural exhibit, the Daet Pineapple Festival features beauty contests and sports events.

Golden House, Zabala St., by Metrobank off Vinzons Ave. in a distinctive red and yellow building. Chinese food. Sea cucumber P200, set meals P70-85. Open daily 7am-10pm.

Sandok at Palayok, 2nd fl., F. Pimentel Ave., opposite the elevated town plaza. Cozy, low-ceilinged room. Portions almost big enough for 2. Special vegetable meal P150. Bicol express P50. Open daily 8am-10pm.

SIGHTS AND ENTERTAINMENT

Bagasbas Beach is an unbroken stretch of sand, with surfing on particularly rough days. Pizza joints, videoke bars, and darts houses line the road behind the beach, and a light smattering of litter collects beyond the reach of the tide. Bagasbas Beach is 4km from Daet town center along J. Lukban St. (10min. tricycle ride P10).

A relaxing beach experience can be had at the **San Jose Beach,** near the Talisay district (15min. tricycle ride north of Daet center). A vast sweep of sand matched by a deep blue horizon, the beach can almost claim to make featurelessness a feature. Crickets chirp on low sand dunes with benches that provide the perfect picnic spot, but an almost total absence of shade will probably keep any stay short.

Stroll Jazz Bar, in Daet on the fourth floor of the Hotel Dolor Bldg. on Vinzons Ave., is better than other bars on Bagasbas Beach. (Happy hour 7-9pm. "Hard drinks" ½-price Sa. Billiards, darts. No sandals or shorts. Open daily 6pm-2am.)

As much as it is a quaint, old-fashioned fishing village, **Mercedes,** 7km from Daet up Gov. Panotes Rd., is also a successful industrial outlet. Hundreds of fishing vessels congregate here for its seafood market. The Mercedes "Fishtival" is held August 4-8th to give thanks for the abundance of fish and the natural harbor. Jeepney to Mercedes depart from the fork in Vinzons Ave. (P3). A boat can be hired from Mercedes to **Apuao Grande Island** (45min., up to 6 persons P300) or you can wait for the barrio *banca*, the local village boat (6-8am, P50, returns to Mercedes 9-10am), which departs from a spot on the Mercedes coast marked by a Caltex gas pump off Eco Ave.

The island has some fine beaches and trails, but is dominated by the **Apuao Grande Island Resort,** run by Swagman Travel, which offers a nine-hole golf course, scuba diving, sports, and fishing trips for guests. Bookings can be made in Daet at T.S. Resorts booking office, 1085 Vicente Basit St., off Pimentel Ave. near the town plaza. (☎721 1545. Open daily 8am-6pm. Singles/doubles with private common room P600. Quads with 2 double beds and private common room P800. Brutal 7am check-out.)

LEGAZPI ☎52

In 1565, Esteban Rodriguez, captain of a galleon returning from Acapulco, sighted a land veiled in smoke. Four hundred fifty years later, the Mayon Volcano is still belching smoke skyward, a constant reminder that what is beautiful— "Mayon" is derived from *magayan* or "beautiful"—can also be dangerous. As this book went to press, Mt. Mayon had erupted again, spewing ash 15km

> **!** On June 25th, 2001, Mt.Mayon erupted, spewing ash and lava and leading to the evacuation of over 23,000 people. At time of press, a warning is in place for all living near or traveling to the volcano. Check with the local tourist office or your embassy for updated news on safety.

high, as rivers of lava flowed down its sides. The government had begun evacuating local villagers from the area. Mayon had most recently erupted in February, 2000. Before that, in 1993, a series of eruptions claimed 30 lives. Most travelers come here to climb the volcano, but this seldom-frequented region shelters several other noteworthy attractions, including Donsol's mighty *butanding* (whale sharks). Legazpi itself is quite pleasant, and the friendly populace is eager to share their region's many delights, including the fiery local cuisine. Legazpi also makes an ideal springboard for excursions south into the eastern Visayas, via Matnog in neighboring Sorsogon province.

TRANSPORTATION

Flights: As of Spring 2001, only **Philippine Airlines** (☎245 5024) served Legazpi, with 10 flights per week to **Manila** (daily 9am and M, W, Sa 3:45pm; P2463). An agent is at **Hotel Victoria** (☎214 3476) on Rizal St. Open daily 8am-noon and 1:30-5pm.

Buses: There are two **bus terminals.** Local buses and **jeepney** leave from the **Old Market terminal** on Circumferential Rd. To: **Donsol** (2½hr; 15 per day, last bus 4:30pm; P47) and **Sorsogon** (1hr., every 15 min. until 6pm, P25). Buses to Manila leave from the **Satellite Bus Terminal. Philtranco** (☎820 2794), goes to **Manila** (11hr.; 9 per day, last bus 7pm; P485). **BLTB** (☎480 8907), on Peñaranda St. past Casablanca Hotel, goes to **Ormoc** (15hr., 11pm, P412) and **Tacloban** (12hr., midnight, P338).

ORIENTATION AND PRACTICAL INFORMATION

Legazpi has three districts. The main commercial district, also home to most of Legazpi's budget accommodations, lies between **Albay** to the south and **Rawis** to the north. **Rizcl St.** links central Legazpi with Albay and is plied by hordes of **jeepney** (most rides P4). The **Battle of Legazpi Monument's** concrete obelisk stands in the middle of central Legazpi. To the west, **Circumferential Rd.** leads to the local bus and jeepney terminal and the **Satellite Bus Terminal.** One block east (towards the bay) is **Peñaranda St.,** Legazpi's principle commercial artery. The **airport** is 2km northwest of town at the end of **Aquende St.**, which then becomes **Washington Dr.** The fishing quarter, known as **Victory Village,** lies along the black sand beach south of central Legazpi at the foot of **Kapuntaken Hill.**

The very helpful **tourist office** is in Rawis, just across the bridge on the right. (☎408 3105. Open M-F 8am-5pm.) There are a number of **banks** on Rizcl St. in central Legazpi (most open M-F 9am-3pm). Many have **24hr. ATMs. Ago General Hospital** is in Albay, past the provincial capitol on the left. (☎481 5807. Open 24hr.) Next door, **Mercury Drug** is on Rizcl St. opposite the Bayantel office. (Open daily 6am-9pm.) The **Bayantel** office on Rizcl St. at the corner of Imperial St. charges P33 for collect calls and provides email access. (☎480 6187. Open daily 8am-5pm.) The **PLDT office** on Rizcl St. in Albay has an **IDD phone.** (☎214 3896. Open daily 7am-9pm.) Internet access is available at **Joycom** on Rizcl St. (☎480 4777. Open daily 9am-10pm. P30 per hr.) The **post office** is on Lapu-Lapu St. near the Legazpi Tourist Inn. (Open M-F 8am-noon and 1-5pm.) **Postal code:** 4500.

ACCOMMODATIONS

Most of Legazpi's budget accommodations are clustered within a few blocks of the monument. The friendly **Legazpi Tourist Inn,** on the third floor of the U&O Building on Lapu-Lapu St., is the best combination of price and value. (☎480 6147. Singles

WHOSE SYMBOL? PART II Seeing Southeast Asian swastikas? Ran across an advertisement for KKK in the Philippines? You aren't alone. Visitors to the Philippines may be taken aback by the blood-red flags emblazoned with "KKK" above government buildings. Don't worry, the flag has no connection to the Ku Klux Klan in the US; on the contrary, it is a symbol of Philippine nationalism. Here, "KKK" stands for "Kataastaasan Kagalanggalangang Katipunan ng mga Anak ng Bayan" ("Highest and Respected Society of the Sons of the People"). "Katipunan," for those challenged in the art of tongue acrobatics, was founded in 1892. Like any respectable secret society, the Katipunan had passwords, blood oaths of loyalty, and color-coded masks denoting rank. Unfortunately, founder Andres Bonifacio proved a better schemer than leader. When the revolt against the Spanish rulers erupted, Bonifacio's troops were defeated repeatedly. Co-founder General Emilio Aguinaldo proved himself far more capable and became president of the Katipunan. Indignant, Bonifacio, naturally, crowned himself King, appointed a vice-King, and was later executed for treason by President Aguinaldo.

P450, with A/C P700; doubles P510/800.) The **Rex Hotel,** at the corner of Peñaranda and Aguinaldo next to the church, offers cheap, reasonably clean lodgings. (☎480 7101. Singles P240, with A/C P540; doubles P275/580.) The **Xandra Hotel,** on Peñaranda, one block north of the Rizal intersection on the left, is the cheapest bed in town but isn't for the squeamish. (☎22 688. Singles P170-270, with A/C P450; doubles P230-410, with A/C P600.)

FOOD

Legazpi is a great place to sample the area's signature dish, **Bicol Express,** a mildly vile concoction whose principle ingredient is fiery chili peppers. **Doña Alice,** in Rawis 1km north of the bridge on the left, is a pleasant, airy establishment specializing in seafood, serving scrumptious garlic prawns (P160) and Bikolano delicacies. (Open daily 10am-10pm.) Closer to town, on Peñaranda just beyond the BLTB bus terminal, the **Paayahayan Beer Garden** serves delicious seafood in *nipa* huts. (Open daily 10am-1am. Crabs in chili sauce P150.) There are also a number of fast food joints and several nondescript Chinese restaurants in central Legazpi. For after hours entertainment, locals hit the **Bicharra Entertainment Center** in central Legazpi, opposite the statue of Jose Rizcl. Inside you'll find a movie theater, cafes, ice cream shops, and a bar with live music.

SIGHTS AND ACTIVITIES

CAGSAWA RUINS. The ruins are the remains of a church destroyed by Mt. Mayon during the cataclysmic 1814 eruption. Early in the day, there is an eeriness that encapsulates the church. Its forlorn belfry, encroached upon by the foliage, frames views of the beautiful mountain that covered it in ash. At other times, clouds obscure the volcano as hawkers and ice cream salesmen noisily break any enchantment you might find. **Cagsawa National Museum** features an exhibit covering the major volcanoes in the Philippines. *(Take a jeepney bound to Guinobatan or Camalig and ask the driver to stop at the Cagsawa turn-off (20min., P5), which is marked by advertising for the Cagsawa 1814 restaurant. It is 500m from the turn-off to the ruins. Open M-Sa 8-11am and 1-4pm. P5, students P2.)*

CAVES. The three-tiered **Hoyop-Hoyopan Caves** have crystal formations that guides insist resemble everything from the Banaue rice terraces to the Philippine eagle. Hoyop-Hoyopan literally means "blow-blow," supposedly the sound of the whispering wind at the caves' exit. Only guided tours are permitted. The **Calabidongan Caves** (Cave of the Bats), 3km from Hoyop-Hoyopan cave, are much more extensive. It takes 3hr. and a chest-deep dip in the underground river to get here. Bring a flashlight—and be prepared to get wet. *(For Hoyop-Hoyopan, take a Guinobatan-bound or Camalig jeepney to Camalig town proper (20-30min., last trip 8pm, P8), and find a jeepney bound for Barangay Cotmon (6am-6pm, P8), 12km away. Tell the driver to stop at the junction for the Hoyop-Hoyopan cave. It's an additional 100m to the entrance. Guided tours P45-60min.; P100. For Calabidongan, P500 for 1-2 people, each additional person P250.)*

BUSAY WATERFALLS. These seven-tiered falls in Malilipot are a godsend in the heat of the rainy season, when the water falls thick and fast. Kids play in the larger pools at each tier and dare you to stand under the pummeling waters of the highest waterfall. If you're up to it, you'll earn their deepest respect and a flash of whooping smiles. *(Take a jeepney or bus to Malilipot (35min., P15), and get off when you see the large "Busay Falls" sign. It is a 35min. walk to the falls. P5.)*

! Mt. Mayon is regarded as one of the world's most volatile volcanoes. Since 1616 it is known to have erupted at least 40 times, most recently in June, 2001. The Philippine Institute of Vulcanology and Seismology (PHILVOLCS) monitors the volcano closely; at the time of this research a ban on climbing had been in effect since spring 2000. Check with the Department of Transportation in Legazpi for the latest update.

MAYON VOLCANO. In northeast Albay, Mt. Mayon peaks at 2457m. A challenging but popular climb, it's normally scaled over two days. Expeditions set out at 7am. Base camps punctuate the climb at 750m and 1500m, where climbers pitch tents for the night. The second day's trek begins at 6am and reaches the "knife edge," 2250m high, around 9:30am. Loose rocks make it risky for inexperienced mountaineers to cover the remaining 500m to the rim. Expeditions return to Legazpi by 6pm the second day. The climb is possible year-round, though March and April are ideal times. Wear long sleeves and trousers to avoid grass cuts. Temperatures can fall to 10-15°F on upper parts of the mountain.

Guides charge P4500 for one or two climbers (each additional person P1500). The fee includes transportation, a five-person tent, rope, and food. The tourist office organizes guides (book before 5pm one day in advance). You might be able to hire a guide directly. True penny-pinchers and the stamina-filled can consider attempting the peak in one day for P2500. In the third week of May, the DOT conducts the "Mayon Conquest"—a free, organized climb of the volcano. For travelers wishing to get close, but not *that* close, to the volcano, the ramshackle **Mayon Rest House** sits at 840m. To get there, take a jeepney to Tabaco, 26km north of Legazpi, and then transfer to a **Ligao-bound** jeepney; ask to be let off at the junction leading to the guest house—it's an 8km hike from there, unless you charter transportation.

DARAGA HILLTOP CHURCH. Established in 1773 by Franciscan missionaries as "Our Lady of the Gate," Daraga is a monumental reinterpretation of a traditional Basilican Church. Built of volcanic rock, it appears to be formed as much by geology as by human hand. Enjoy a meal at the **Terraza Cafe.** *(Jeepney (30min., P3) head west into Daraga (Locsin). Get off at the Shell station on Gen. Luna St.; walk up St. Maria St.; or take the Daraga Water District stairs next to Sarko Cafe & Bookstore. Open daily 7am-midnight.)*

OTHER SIGHTS. Visitors can take a pre-dusk stroll through **Victory Village,** an old fishing enclave incongruously appended to the characterless city. From the end of Elizondo St., pass through the entrance to the covered fish market. On the other side, the village huddles on the black-sand beach. At the far end, steps take you up **Kapuntukan Hill** for a stunning view of the volcano, the sunset and the city.

Twenty kilometers north of Legazpi is the little village of **Santa Domingo.** The town itself has little to offer but there are several decent black sand beaches popular with locals. The beaches are fairly unimpressive by Philippine standards but are clean and the water is refreshing after a hard morning climbing or caving. The **Mayon Spring Resort** has two swimming pools, water slides, a nice strip of beach as well as a restaurant/bar and well-appointed bungalows (P600 per night). They'll let you use the facilities for P50 per day. To get there, take a "Santa Domingo" bound jeepney (25min., P8) and ask to be let off at the Mayon Spring Resort turnoff. The last jeepney back to Legazpi leaves at 6pm.

Every October, the province-wide **Ibalong Festival** reenacts early ancestral legends interwoven with subsequent Catholic influences. The **Karangahan Albay Festival** in May is a celebration of abundance in thanks for a good harvest. During Holy Week every April **banca races** are held in Bacacay, a village north of Santo Domingo. (Accessible via jeepney from Legazpi.)

NEAR LEGAZPI

DONSOL

Some 30km southeast of Legazpi in neighboring Sorsogon province, lies this sleepy fishing village. With a single phoneline shared by the entire village, it's the kind of place where older residents still fondly recall the day former president Magsasay passed through on the campaign trail some 50 years ago. Donsol remained an anonymous speck on the map until, in the words of provincial tourist literature, "by twist of fate, an amazing discovery of grandest scale surfaced" in the form of mighty whale sharks **(Rhicodon typus).** Actually, schools of *butanding*, as the whale sharks are known locally, have been gathering in the waters off Donsol for generations, keeping the local fishermen company. In the late 1990s, word of the *butanding* spread, attracting divers and poachers from far and wide. Recognizing the potential value of the *butanding* as a tourist attraction, local authorities promptly passed legislation banning the hunting of the sharks and, with the assistance of the WWF and the United Nations Development Program, established what has become a model for eco-tourism and sustainable development projects. The opportunity to swim alongside the *butanding* is a truly once-in-a-lifetime experience.

Donsol is accessible by local bus from Legazpi (See **Practical Information,** p. 550). Excursions leave at 8am and return at 5pm. It's wise to show up at the visitors' center by about 7am to secure a spot (each boat holds six people). Solo travelers can usually find groups to join; ask around the night before. A "Butanding Interaction Officer" oversees each boat and advises you on safety. (P2500 per boat, plus a P300 fee per person. Snorkeling gear P220. Scuba diving is banned.)

Prime *butanding* watching season is December to May, though they have been known to gather earlier and stay longer. For more information, call the Bayantel phone in Donsol (☎56 411 1109) and ask for Nita Pedragoza at the visitors' center. The regional DOT office in Legazpi can also help (see **Practical Information,** p. 550).

You will probably have to spend at least one night in Donsol. Check in at the **visitor's center,** where officials will help you find a place to stay. There are several homestays in the village, including **Hernandez Lodging House** and **Santiago Homestay** (both P300 for a 3-person room). Pricier "beach resorts," **Amor Farm Beach Resort** and **Woodland Beach Resort** (both P500 per room), are accessible from Donsol by boat.

MINDORO

Four hours by bus from Manila, the steamy smog gives way to the salty air of the island of Mindoro, 26km off the coast of Luzon. Teeming marine life replaces the crowds, and the island's interior wilderness is as impenetrable as Manila's urban jungle. While the local Mangyan people are eager to avoid tourists, the Manileño hawkers are eager to scam them. That said, if visitors pitch ashore after dusk on Sabang Beach outside the coastal town of Puerto Galera, they might be forgiven for thinking that they had been brought to nothing more than a seaside meatmarket. The imported international cuisine is even more expensive, but the hollow ennui of the bored hooker and her slovenly customers is all too familiar. However, reefs and wrecks near shore, excellent underwater visibility, and dazzling aquatic life make Mindoro an exquisite dive site. Stick to the diving and steer clear of the dives.

THE VIEW FROM ABOVE

Main towns: Batangas, Puerto Galera.
Beaches: Big Lalaguna Beach, Sabang, Small Lalaguna Beach, and White Beach, all near Puerto Galera.
Something fun: Hash House Harrier runs and treks to Mt. Calavite and Mt. Halcon.

PUERTO GALERA ☎43

The beaches surrounding Puerto Galera are the destinations of choice for island-hoppers from Luzon. Sabang Beach, the most popular in the area, lays the amenities and services on thick, while other beaches exist in tranquility. The harbor at Puerto Galera proper is beautiful, and accommodations await those who don't want to be on the front line of tourism development. Dive sites lie near the coast, and the interior provides numerous trekking opportunities amongst largely unspoiled wilderness.

TRANSPORTATION

Buses: The Si-Kat office on Muelle Pier sells combined ferry/bus tickets to **Manila.** Open daily 7:30am-4pm. **Si-Kat II** ferry departs from Muelle Pier and arrives at Centerpoint Hotel in **Ermita** (5½hr., 9:30am, P350).

Ferries: Boats go to **Batangas** from Muelle Pier, Balatero Pier, and Sabang Beach. From **Muelle Pier: Blue Eagle** (1hr.; 7am, 1:30pm; P125) and **Si-Kat** (2hr., 9:30am, P150). From **Balatero Pier: Viva Lines'** M/V *St. Lawrence* (2hr.; 5, 10:30am, 2:30pm; P100). From **Sabang Beach: DSL Big Bancas** outriggers (☎0912 306 5332, c/o Angelyn's Beach Resort; 1½hr.; 6, 7, 8, 11:30am; P80). "Special Ride" to Batangas in a *banca* P1500. To get to **Boracay,** take jeepney from the R.J. Store in Puerto Galera market to **Calapan** (2hr., 5am-2:30pm, P50), then catch a bus from the wharf in Calapan to **Roxas** (3-4hr., P82). Spend the night in Roxas (a hotel is nearby the stone beach). In the morning take the M/V *Flor B* to **Boracay** (5hr.; M-Tu, Th-F 10:30am; P250). Alternatively, several **outrigger boats** leave Roxas for **Romblon Island** and **Tablas Island** north of Boracay. From Romblon Island, regular ferries cross to Tablas Island. A jeepney to **Santa Fe** on Tablas Island and a ferry across to Boracay completes the journey. An alternate route to Boracay is to travel via Batangas.

Local Transportation: *Banca*s go to common coastal destinations from Muelle Pier (P100-500). Tricycles are abundant but expensive (P80-150). Jeepney to **Puerto Galera's** town proper congregate around **Sabang Fast Food** (depart when full; 15min., 6am-5pm, P10; return approx. every hr. 6am-5pm, P25). Tricycle to Sabang Beach runs P80.

ORIENTATION AND PRACTICAL INFORMATION

Puerto Galera (or Población) is in **Muelle Bay** on the north coast of Mindoro, at the neck of a Y-shaped peninsula surrounded by coves and beaches. A lighthouse at Escarcero Point makes the easternmost tip of the peninsula. **Sabang Beach** stretches out 1-2km west along the coast. A road connects Sabang beach to Población, 5km away. A short walk west from Sabang Beach, with the sea to your right, leads around a rocky point to **Small** and **Big Lalaguna Beach.** Small Lalaguna Beach is actually bigger than Big Lalaguna Beach—the names refer to inland lagoons, not the beaches. The west tip of the "Y" shelters ritzy and exclusive **Coco Beach.** From Población, a 7km ride west goes to **San Isidro. White Beach,** a more placid tract of sand than the eastern beaches, lines the San Isidro coast.

Tourist Office: On Muelle Pier in Población. Open M-F 8am-noon and 1pm-5pm. *Puerto Galera Tourist Map,* available in guest houses, the tourist office, and from travel agents, features resort listings, transport, and diving information (P70).

Travel and Tours: Swagman Travel (☎0912 319 9587), on Muelle Pier in Población. Open daily 8am-5pm. A branch on **Sabang Beach** (☎0912 347 6993) doubles as a tourist office. Cash advances available (MC/V; 8% surcharge). **Island Trekking Tours,** at Havanna Moon Cottage (☎0973 497 503), offers treks and kayaking.

Currency Exchange: Moneychangers abound on Muelle Pier in Población. Sabang Beach offers better rates than Población and Manila.

Police: ☎442 0051. Municipal Hall, H. Axalan St. opposite Puerto Galera Academy. **Open 24hr.**

Medical Services: The Puerto Galera Lying-In Clinic (☎0912 352 9531), next to the Municipal Hall, takes care of prescriptions. **Dr. Carmelita Atienza** works in Sabang down the road that turns off near Tropicana Restaurant. Open M-Sa 9am-5pm.

Telephone: IDD available at outlet next to a mini-mart and *barangay* security office in Sabang (☎0912 318 2840; open daily 6am-10pm). **Bayantel,** in Muelle, Población, has lowest fees for international collect calls. Open M-F 7am-8:30pm, Sa-Su 7am-6pm.

Post Office: In Municipal Hall. Open M-F 8am-5pm. **Postal code:** 5203 (Sabang).

ACCOMMODATIONS

Only the pricier beach resorts have hot water and A/C. Peak season is November-May and prices on some beaches reach for the heavens during Christmas and Holy Week. In the low season, most accommodations have cheaper rates for longer stays. Seasonal room rates are listed as high/low.

POBLACIÓN (PUERTO GALERA PROPER)

Melxa's Greenhills Nipa Hut, E. Cobarrubias Sr. St. (☎0912 270 6248). Turn right at the crossroads 50m past Municipal Hall. Wonderfully rustic *nipa* huts have balconies hedged with hanging baskets of flowers. Singles/doubles with shared kitchen and common room P200; triples P250; family room with refrigerator, common room, and kitchen P1000.

Coco Point Hotel & Restaurant (☎442 0191). Proximity to busy Muelle Pier can be a visual blessing or a noisy annoyance. Upstairs rooms arrayed along balcony. Solid bamboo furnishings. Restaurant open daily 6am-9pm. Doubles with common room P400; family double with common room P500.

SABANG BEACH

JAA Lodge (☎0973 864 616), west of Ed's Bar and Pool Hall, is a tropical mansion that won't burn a hole in your pocket. Well-equipped, comfortable rooms with balcony/porch and couch. Doubles with TV, refrigerator, stove, and private common room downstairs P400, upstairs with amazing views of the sea P500.

Villa Sabang (☎/fax 0912 313 4486), on the east edge of the beach. Currency exchange, international telephone. Spacious doubles with balcony hammocks P600/450; 2-person cottages with refrigerator and TV P800/700; A/C room with patio, refrigerator, and TV P1200/990; triples with A/C P1500.

VIP Lodge, behind Action Divers. No-nonsense rooms with the beach's lowest rates. Laundry. Check-out 11am. Upstairs rooms have a balcony with sea views. Singles with common room P200; doubles with TV and refrigerator P600/400.

Sabang Inn (☎0973 490 101), beside Villa Sabang. Doubles with A/C, TV, and complete kitchen P450-680/P650-850.

Capt'n Gregg's Dive Resort (☎/fax 0973 496 691). For the hardcore divers or the wannabes. Front and center on the beach, west of Puerto Galera Rd. Rooms 10% off with 6 dives or dive course. Singles/doubles with private common room P500/400, with A/C and hot water P900/800, with TV P1200/1000.

SMALL LALAGUNA BEACH

Small Lalaguna Beach provides one of the most strategic locations for a relaxed stay. All modern amenities and foodstuffs are within walking distance.

Nick & Sonia's Cottages (☎0917 562 0032), in the center of the beach, offers discounts for 10-day stays. (Pair of *nipa* huts P600/500, with kitchen and fridge P900/600; "1st-class" hut with TV, fridge, and cooking facilities P1200/1000.)

BIG LALAGUNA BEACH

Big Lalaguna Beach is a 10min. walk from Sabang Beach. As you round the point between Small and Big Lalaguna Beaches, you'll traverse "Penman's Mountain Pass." A stone notes the dizzying altitude—6.7m above sea level. The near-spotless beach has crystal-clear teal waters interspersed with coral, ideal for snorkeling.

Miller's Corner is as far away from Sabang as possible, with doubles on the rocks. (With common room P950/750, with A/C P1100/950; *nipa* huts P450.)

WHITE BEACH

This grainy-sand beach is a 5min. walk from San Isidoro Rd. Jeepney run from Puerto Galera to San Isidro and vice versa (depart when full, 6am-5pm, P10). A "special" jeepney from Puerto Galera to White Beach costs P100-200; a "special" *banca* trip from Sabang costs P400-500. The resorts have become very territorial, with fences running all the way to the road. Iraya villagers nearby have nicknamed tourists "Papaya" because of their overzealous passion for the fruit.

Summer Connection, at the farthest, most secluded end of the beach. Lattice-work cottages with grass roofs and hammocks. Arranges treks into Mindoro's wilderness interior. Reservations advised in peak season. Restaurant open daily 6am-10pm. Singles with private common room P550/400; doubles with common room and porch P800/500; suites P1500/700.

White Beach Resort (☎0912 367 0657). Green walls and pink cupboards make an attempt to move the plain wood *nipa* style into the Art Deco era. Peak season disco and bar. International phone/fax. Collection of books. Doubles with private common room P900/600; cottages with TV, refrigerator, and kitchen P1500/800.

OTHER BEACHES

New Encenada Beach Resort, Palangan, in Varadero Bay (☎450 8259), is a 15min. walk from Puerto Galera town proper (3km by jeepney P10, tricycle P20). It's a large 40-room resort with a restaurant, dive shop, and billiard hall. For real seclusion, explore **Talipanan Beach** (35min. by jeepney from Muelle Pier, P20).

FOOD

SABANG BEACH

Relax Thai Restaurant, west of the center. Bulwark against Sabang's tendency toward "anything-but-Asian" cuisine. Relaxed atmosphere offers a break from Sabang's bustle. Unusual but tasty *pad thai* P120. Open 10:30am-10pm.

McRom's, on the southeast corner of the main street. Good enough that you may not want to eat elsewhere. Any of the "sizzling platters," especially "chicken with special McRom's peanut sauce" (P120), will enrapture your taste buds. Open daily 9am-10pm.

Sunshine Coast Restaurant & Bar. Tu night Indian banquet P235. "Feeling shitty" breakfast of coffee, 2 cigarettes, coke, and ibuprofen P70. A sign prohibits "riff raff"—you know who you are. Open daily 7am-10pm.

Janelle's Fastfood, near Deco Stop. Good, round-the-clock dining. Sandwiches P25-95. Vegetable curry P60. Open 24hr.

Sabang Fast Food, where jeepney leave for Puerto Galera. Serves a first-rate chocolate shake (P50) and a mean chicken *cordon bleu* P130. Open 9am-3am.

ELSEWHERE

Pier Pub & Pizza Restaurant, on Muelle pier, at end of the bay-side boardwalk. Sandwiches P48-95. Small pizza P135-195. Buttered shrimp P220. Open daily 7am-9pm.

The Point, where Small Lalaguna and Sabang Beaches meet. Catches the breeze nicely on its rocky promontory. Try the African Passage three shooter set (P400) and get your name on a plaque. Superb steak sandwich P145. Open daily 10am-midnight.

ACTIVITIES

Thirty well-established dive sites are within a 20min. boat ride from Sabang Beach. Abundant reef fish, including triggerfish, lionfish, frogfish, and scorpionfish, populate the coral. Rays, giant turtles, and whitetip sharks are seen less frequently. Visibility averages 24-30m, and can be up to 45m February-July.

A score of dive shops line the shore from Sabang to Big Lalaguna Beaches; prices are uniform. **South Sea Divers** (☎918 865 0264), on Sabang beach, stands out. Owners Sky and Paul define the word "laid-back," and divemasters Carlos and Rob will show you Sabang's nightlife.

Most dive shops offer dives with equipment, boat, and guide (US$25, night dives US$32) and PADI dive courses (Discover courses US$50; open-water course US$300; advanced open-water course US$200; assistant instructor course US$750). Beachside stands rent snorkels and masks (P50 per day).

ENTERTAINMENT AND NIGHTLIFE

If the sun's shining, most of Sabang is on the beach or in the reefs. Only a few meters from the shore, the dive sites are tops in Luzon and among the finest in the world. Go-go bars shimmy with sleazy expats and sex tourists, but are easily avoidable, as numerous bars, pool halls, and a disco offer enjoyable alternatives. When the moon comes out, however, so do the ladies of the night, and Sabang transforms into the Sin City of the Philippines.

Stretch your lungs and join the **Hash House Harriers,** a beer-drinking and running club founded in 1938 in Kuala Lampur that now has branches all over the world. Runs start from Cap'n Gregg's. (☎0912 305 0652. Su 4:30pm; P200 for first-time runners, including beer and t-shirt; P100 for repeat runners. See **A Drinking Club with a Running Problem,** p. 381.) **The Lounge** on Sabang Beach, surprisingly stylish and laid-back, sports a bar with soccer shirts on the walls and sports on the TV. (Happy hour 5-6pm. Open daily 9am-midnight.)

There is no shortage of **pool halls** on the beaches (P10 per game). Try **Ed's Pool and Restaurant** for excellent competition, but be wary of hustlers when betting on a game. If you need to supplement your budget, enter the peak season **pool tournament** at Le Bistrot restaurant (☎0973 861 425), on Sabang Beach, where winner takes all (Sa 5pm, P50). If you really want to be a shark (or at least look like one), you can purchase a beautiful handmade cue (1500P).

DAYTRIPS FROM PUERTO GALERA

A jeepney from the R.J. Store in Puerto Galera market goes to **Calapan** (2hr., 5am-3pm, P30). **Cockfights** in Calapan city center start at 10am on Sundays. If you're lucky, you might see one during the day in the area behind Janelle's Fastfood.

The **Tamaraw Falls** are only 30min. from Sabang Beach via the jeepney bound for Calapan (jeepney P25; entrance P15). Also within easy striking distance is the **Light House** on Escarcero Point, where cliffs fall away on three sides (jeepney to Sinandigan near Escarcero Point P15, "special" jeepney to the Light House P150). It's also a pleasant trek by foot.

You can take longer treks into Mindoro's unspoiled interior wilderness. Past White Beach, where the road thins and disintegrates, large tracts of rainforest have yet to be penetrated by roads. With the exception of the village 1km behind White Beach, the Mangyan tribes in the interior are unaccustomed to tourists.

A trek from White Beach to **Mt. Malisimbo** (1230m) near Ponderosa, south of White Beach, takes 3hr. Guides should be arranged from the Tourist Information Center, at Muelle pier, or via the **Summer Connection** on White Beach.

Island Trekking Tours (☎/fax 0973 497 503; ask for Ralf) organizes treks into the interior. The **Bogdong Beach trek** leaves from Sabang beach's Sunshine Coast Restaurant. A native outrigger takes trekkers to Bogdong Beach, followed by a

2hr. trek through Mangyan valleys that ends at a lagoon with waterfalls. (Sa, W 7:30am, returns to Sabang 6pm. US$35 per person including food, additional US$17 for overnight stay. 8-person min.) If there are enough people, Island Trekking Tours or Summer Connection can arrange more extensive treks. Longer treks might include **Mt. Calavite,** where communities live on bamboo rafts at the confluence of two rivers. One-week hikes head to **Mt. Halcon,** the highest mountain in Mindoro at 2587m.

THE VISAYAS

After endless bus rides in the mountains of north Luzon, island-hopping brings a welcome reminder that the Philippines is, in fact, an archipelago. The ancient coral beds and volcano tips that compose the Visayas include six major islands: Samar and Leyte in the Eastern Visayas, Negros and Panay in the Western Visayas, and Cebu and Bohol at the heart of the chain. There are four main dialects: Cebuano (spoken in Cebu and Bohol), Waray Waray (spoken in Samar and Eastern Leyte), Ilonggo (spoken in Panay and Negros Occidental), and Aklan (spoken in Northern Panay). Amid this confusing tropical Tower of Babel, the Visayas bore witness to two unifying events in Filipino history: the spread of Catholicism in the 16th century and the wrestling of the islands from Japanese oppression in the 20th. Although travelers are not often drawn away from the beaches of Bantayan, Panglao, and Boracay, among the loveliest in Southeast Asia, Visayan cities try their best with a generous dash of frenzied charm. From Bohol's Chocolate Hills to Mt. Kanla on Negros, inland adventures also await. Whether bounding up a hill, frolicking on a beach, or jumping into a jeepney, friendly Visayans won't hesitate to greet you with a shriek of "Hey Joe!"

CEBU

Once upon a time, Ming vases and Spanish doubloons were the currencies of choice on Cebu. Nowadays, tourist cash runs the island, and mammoth resorts on Mactan Island serve as a testament to the new industry. The northern islands of Bantayan and Malapascua run at a slower pace, their calm broken only by the dynamite fishing that has driven divers to Pescador Island near Moalboal. For the nocturnal traveler, the nightlife in Cebu City provides evenings of endless excitement.

THE VIEW FROM ABOVE

Main cities: Cebu City, Maolboal.
Island fever: Diving off Mactan and Malapascua Islands, vegging out at deserted Bantayan Island.
Blast from the past: Discover the lingering history from Cebu City's colonial era.

CEBU CITY ☎32

Miguel Lopez de Legazpi anchored off the shores of Cebu in 1565, took one look at the droves of hostile natives, and aimed his galleons in the direction of friendlier shores. Two months later, the *conquistadores* returned, set Cebu ablaze, and erected the first fortified settlement in the archipelago. Modern travelers follow Legazpi's footsteps, taking off for excursions around the other islands before returning to raze Cebu in their own way. Little can prepare travelers for the energy of this "Queen City of the South," where historical and religious relics are entangled with the contemporary trappings of a major port city and transport hub. Today's visitors can expect a much warmer welcome than Legazpi received, losing themselves in Cebu's first-class restaurants, vibrant nightlife, and cultural attractions.

TRANSPORTATION

BY AIR

Mactan Cebu International Airport (☎340 2468) serves all of Cebu Island. From Cebu City, **Metro Ferry** runs from Pier 3 to Mactan Island (45min., every 15min. 6am-7:30pm, P6). From the pier on Mactan, take a tricycle (25min., P30) or a taxi (15min., about P40 from downtown Cebu). Another option is to take the 23D Jeepney from S.M. City Mall to Lapu-Lapu city (P4.5) and then a tricycle (P30) to the airport. Aircon "U-hires" minibuses leave from the terminal opposite the S.M. City Mall for Lapu Lapu City (20 min, P12). The **tourist info counter** in the arrival area can help. (☎340 8229. Open M-F 8am-5pm.) Tickets are subject to a P3 airport fee.

INTERNATIONAL CARRIERS. To: **Hong Kong:** Cathay Pacific (☎254 0740) flies four times per week (Tu, Th, F, Su US$400). To: **Kuala Lumpur**: MAS flies to KL (Tu, Th; US$303), via **Kota Kinabalu** (US$241). Offices are at the airport (☎340 2978) and Unit 312 in Ayala Shopping Center (☎231 3887). To: **Singapore:** Silk Air flies daily (US$450). Offices are at the airport (☎232 6211) and Suite 302, Cebu Holding Center in Cebu Business Park (☎254 0740).

DOMESTIC CARRIERS. Cebu is the principle transportation hub for the Visayas, making it impossible to throw a stone in the city and not hit a travel agent. Airline and ferry booking agencies abound downtown and uptown, around **Fuente Osmeña. PAL,** at the airport (☎340 0191, open daily 8am-5pm), **S.M. City Mall** (☎232

8412), and on Plaridel St. in downtown Cebu (☎254 4136, open M-F 8:30am-6pm, Sa 8:30am-noon), flies to: **Davao** (daily, P1598-1804); **Iloilo** (Th, Sa; P1598-1804); **Manila** (6 per day, P2398-3308); **Puerto Princessa** (M,F; P2798-2308). **Cebu Pacific**, at the airport (☎255 4040) and in the Capitol Commercial Complex on N. Escario St. (☎255 0201), flies to: **Bacolod** (M, Tu, Th, Sa; P1414); **Davao** (2 per day, P2054); **Kalibo** (Tu, F, Su; P2054); **Manila** (8 per day, P2064-2324); **Zamboanga** (M, W, Th, Sa; P2104). **Air Philippines** (☎340 0752) has an office in the Century Hotel lobby on Pelaez St. near the intersection with Colon St. (☎255 1341, open daily 8:30am-noon, 2-8:30pm) and flies to: **General Santos** (daily, P2078-2378); **Manila** (3 per day, P2308-2608); **Zamboanga** (M, W, F, Su; P2088-2388). **Asian Spirit** (☎256 3478) flies to **Cagayan de O'ro** (daily except Tu, P1499); **Caticlan** (Tu, W, F, Su; P1950); **Naga** (daily except Tu, P1499). **Seair** flies to: **Camiguin** (M, Th; P1390); **Caticlan** (daily except W, P1990); and **Siargao** (Tu, F, Su; P1990).

PHILIPPINES

BY BOAT

Ferries clutter the harbor. For schedules, go to the S.M. City Mall complex, which houses the **S.M. Traveler's Lounge** (☎232 0291, open daily 6am-8pm) as well as independent ferry offices. Take a jeepney from Colon St. headed toward "Colon, S.M., N. Terminal" (30min., every 20min., P4). **Alboitz Express** operates a similar service on the third floor of the **Robinson Mall** at Fuente Osmeña. The catamaran **Supercats** (☎232 3455) leaves from Pier 4 to: **Dumaguete** (2hr., 3 per day, P430, 15% student discount); **Ormac** (2hr., 3 per day, P410); **Tagbilaran** on Bohol (1½hr., 3 per day, P320). **WG&A Superferry** (☎232 0490) pulls out of Pier 6 for **Manila** (20 hr.; M, W, F, Su; P1185) and **Surigao** (Tu, P365). **Trans-Asia** (☎254 6491), located on M. J. Cuenco Ave. by Osmeña Blvd (open daily 8am-noon, M-Sa 1:30-5pm), goes to: **Iloilo** on Panay (12hr., daily, P394); **Masbate** (14hr.; M, W, F; P320); **Tagbilaran** (4hr.; W, Sa, Su; P100). **Cebu Ferries** (call S.M. Traveller's Lounge) goes to: **Cagayan** (12hr., M-Sa, P425); **Ormoc** (5hr.; W, F, Su; P295); **Tacloban** (12hr.; M, W, F; P300).

BY BUS

Northbound buses leave from **Cebu North Bus Terminal,** outside the city center along the north coast, for **Hagnaya** (3hr., every hr. 4am-6am and every 20min. 6am-10pm, P70) via **Liloan** (45min., every 20min. 4am-10:30pm, P25). Schedules for other destinations are available at the station. For southbound and westbound buses, walk west down P. Del Rosario St. away from Osmeña Blvd. to **Cebu South Bus Terminal.** Buses to **Moalboal** (2½hr., every 30min. 5am-6pm, P30, A/C P50) and other nearby destinations.

LOCAL TRANSPORTATION

Jeepney: Link uptown and downtown (P4). To venture downtown, look for jeepney headed toward "Colon St.," any of the piers, "Carbon Market," or "Sto. Niño." To head back uptown, look for "Capitol Bldg.," "Escario," or "Fuente Osmeña." These routes run along Osmeña Blvd. The "Colon St.-SM-H. Terminal" covers S.M. City Mall complex (P4), North Bus Terminal, and Colon St. The "Colon St.-Ayala" jeepney will take you to the Ayala Mall and the Waterfront Hotel/Casino.
Taxis: Meters start at P25 and click upward in P2 increments.

ORIENTATION AND PRACTICAL INFORMATION

Halfway down the east coast, Cebu City is about 600km south of Manila. **Mactan Island,** home of Mactan Cebu International Airport, is accessible by ferry and bridge. Cebu City has two sections: downtown and uptown. **Downtown** sprawls along the piers to **P. del Rosario.** On the seafront, **Quezon Blvd.** passes all piers, **Fort San Pedro,** and **Carbon Market. Jakosalem St.** starts at City Hall (and Magellan's Cross) and runs uptown to **Gen. Maxilom (Mango) Ave. Osmeña Blvd.** runs from **Plaza Independencia** (downtown) though **Fuente Osmeña** (uptown) to **Escarin St. Gen. Maxilom (Mango) Ave.** radiates east from Fuente Osmeña and intersects **F. Ramos St.,** Jakosalem St., and **San Jose St.** on its way back to the sea and Quezon Blvd.

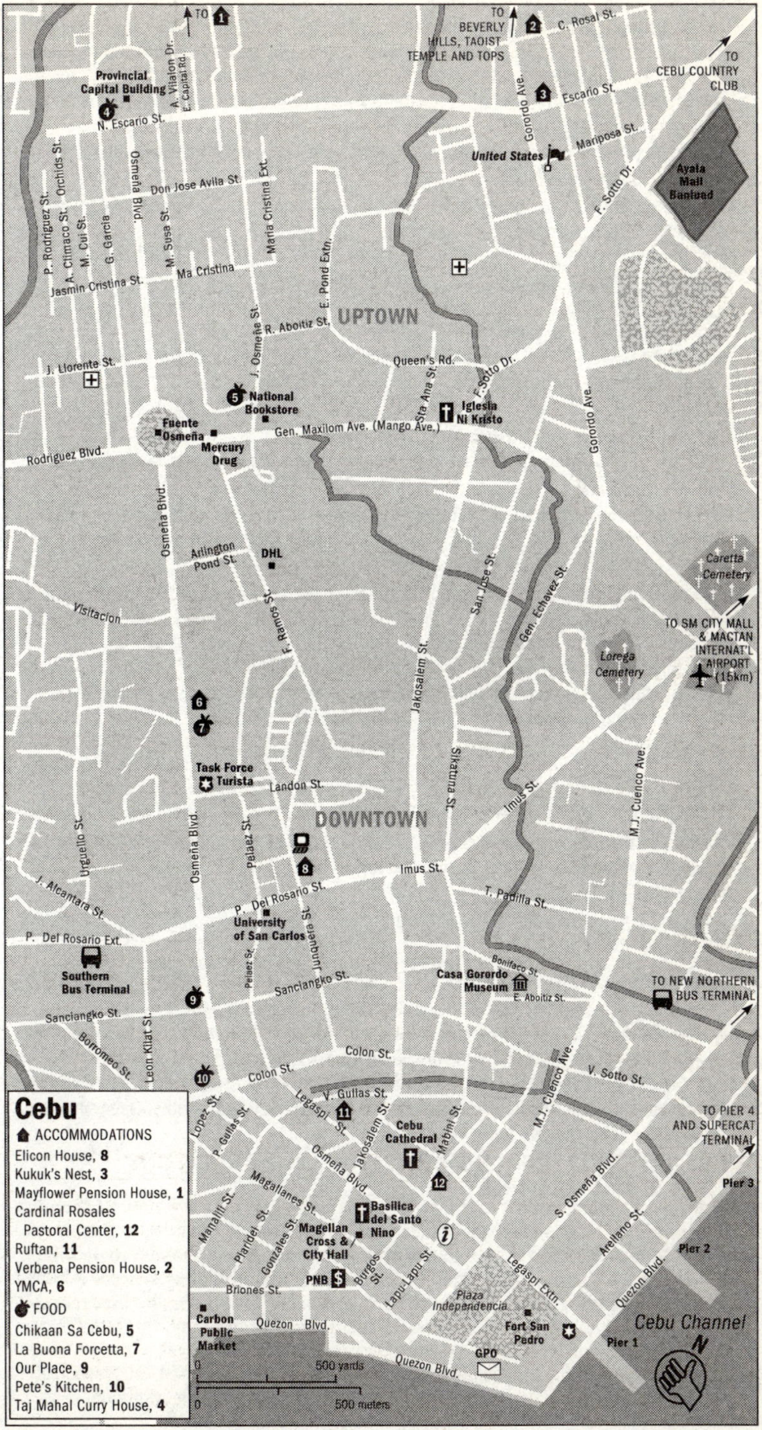
TO 1
TO BEVERLY HILLS, TAOIST TEMPLE AND TOPS
C. Rosal St.
TO CEBU COUNTRY CLUB
Provincial Capital Building
A. Villalon Dr.
E. Capital Rd.
N. Escario St.
Escario St.
Gorordo Ave.
United States
Mariposa St.
Ayala Mall Banilad
F. Sotto Dr.
Orchids St.
Osmeña Blvd.
Don Jose Avila St.
Maria Cristina Ext.
P. Rodriguez St.
A. Climaco St.
M. Cui St.
G. Garcia
M. Susa St.
Ma Cristina
Jasmin Cristina St.
E. Pond Extn.
R. Aboitiz St.
UPTOWN
J. Osmeña St.
J. Llorente St.
Queen's Rd.
Sta Ana St.
National Bookstore
Iglesia Ni Kristo
Fuente Osmeña
Mercury Drug
Gen. Maxilom Ave. (Mango Ave.)
Rodriguez Blvd.
Arlington Pond St.
DHL
Visitacion
F. Ramos St.
San Jose St.
Gen. Echavez St.
Caretta Cemetery
TO SM CITY MALL & MACTAN INTERNAT'L AIRPORT (15km)
Lorega Cemetery
Jakosalem St.
Sikatuna St.
Task Force Turista
Landon St.
Imus St.
DOWNTOWN
M.J. Cuenco Ave.
Urguello St.
Pelaez St.
J. Alcantara St.
P. Del Rosario St.
University of San Carlos
Junquera St.
T. Padilla St.
P. Del Rosario Ext.
Southern Bus Terminal
Sanciangko St.
Casa Gorordo Museum
Bonifaco St.
E. Aboitiz St.
TO NEW NORTHERN BUS TERMINAL
Borromeo St.
Leon Kilat St.
Colon St.
V. Sotto St.
V. Gullas St.
Legaspi St.
Lopez St.
P. Gullas St.
Cebu Cathedral
Mabini St.
TO PIER 4 AND SUPERCAT TERMINAL
Osmeña Blvd.
Magallanes St.
S. Osmeña Blvd.
Pier 3
Manalili St.
Plaridel St.
Gonzales St.
Basilica del Santo Nino
Magellan Cross & City Hall
Arellano St.
Pier 2
PNB
Burgos St.
Lapu-Lapu St.
Legaspi Extn.
Quezon Blvd.
Briones St.
Plaza Independencia
Carbon Public Market
Fort San Pedro
Cebu Channel
Pier 1
GPO
N
0
500 yards
500 meters
Cebu
ACCOMMODATIONS
Elicon House, 8
Kukuk's Nest, 3
Mayflower Pension House, 1
Cardinal Rosales Pastoral Center, 12
Ruftan, 11
Verbena Pension House, 2
YMCA, 6
FOOD
Chikaan Sa Cebu, 5
La Buona Forcetta, 7
Our Place, 9
Pete's Kitchen, 10
Taj Mahal Curry House, 4

Tourist Office: The **main tourist office** (☎254 2811), is at the corner of Lapu-Lapu St. and Legaspi St. near Fort San Pedro. Head for glass doors midway down the block in the LDM Building. Free maps and brochures. Open M-F 8am-noon and 1-5pm. The **Airport tourist counter** (☎340 8229) is in the arrival area of Mactan International Airport. Open M-F 6am-5pm.

Travel Agencies: Swagman Travel, 301 F. Ramos St. (☎254 1365). Very helpful branch of Australian-owned agency.

Consulates: US (☎231 1261). 3rd fl. PCI Equitable Bldg. on Gorordo Ave. Open M-F 8-11am. The **UK** has an "honorary" consulate on 44 Pasee Eulalia, but it is of little use to British travelers.

Immigration Office: Cebu Bureau of Immigration (☎/fax 253 4339), in Mandaue City, 10km north of Cebu City. Take the 21B or 22B jeepney from S.M. City Mall to Mandaue City (20min., P4). From the Jollibee, walk past City Hall and turn right on P. Burgos St.; the office is 800m down on the right. Passport, airline ticket, visa, and patience required. Be sure to **dress neatly** – long pants and a collared shirt are appropriate. 38-day visa P2100; 59-day visa P2800. Open M-F 8am-noon and 1-5pm.

Currency Exchange: Banks, many with 24hr. **ATMs,** are all over town, particularly around Fuente Osmeña uptown. **HSBC** is on the corner of Gen. Maxilom and Juana Osmeña St. Open M-F 9am-4pm.

English-Language Bookstore: National Bookstore (☎255 4644), down Gen. Maxilom St. from Fuente Osmeña; it's on the corner with Juana Osmeña St. Open daily 9:30am-8pm.

Outdoor Equipment: Hagabat (☎256 3896), on Juana Osmeña St., 3 blocks north of the Gen. Maxilom intersection, in the Baseline Recreation Center. Carries top-quality outdoor equipment including packs, stoves, and climbing gear. Also a branch in the S.M. City Mall. Open M-Sa 10am-8pm.

Market: Carbon Market, on Briones and Calderon St., south of the downtown area. Catch a "Carbon" jeepney (P4). Sells everything from fruit to tires.

Emergency: ☎166.

Police: Central Police Station (☎253 5636), on F. Ramos St.

Tourist Police: Task Force Turista (☎254 4023), aids tourists 24hr.

Pharmacy: Mercury Drug (☎255 4187), uptown on Fuente Osmeña, at the intersection of Gen. Maxilom and Osmeña Blvd. **Open 24hr.**

Hospital: Cebu Doctors Hospital (☎253 7511), on Osmeña Blvd. Travel up Osmeña and pass Fuente Osmeña; it's on the right after the intersection with Maria Cristina and before the Provincial Capitol.

Telephones: Bayantel (☎255 0057) operates around Fuente Osmeña in the uptown area. Open M-F 8am-10pm, Sa-Su 8am-5pm.

Internet Access: Internet cafes have sprouted up all over town, especially on Del Rosario St., near the University of San Carlos and Fuente Osmeña. Expect to pay P20-30 per hr.

Post Office: Cebu Central Post Office (☎256 1696), on Quezon Blvd., south of the downtown area and opposite Fort San Pedro. *Poste Restante* available. Open M-F 8am-noon and 1-5pm. **Postal code:** 6000.

ACCOMMODATIONS

There are plenty of good budget choices downtown and uptown. Note that downtown is grimier and more chaotic, and that after dark touts pushing their "bikini bars" can get a bit oppressive; most travelers will find uptown more agreeable. To avoid the skin trade, look for hotel rooms that don't allow visitors in their rooms.

DOWNTOWN

Elicon House (☎256 1435), on Junquera St. near its P. Del Rosario St. intersection and the University of San Carlos. Posh service and vibrant artwork. Cafe with room service.

Laundry service. TV P50. Singles P175, with A/C P350-450; doubles with A/C P450-550. MC/V.

Cardinal Rosales Pastoral Center (☎255 1269), Opposite Cebu Cathedral on Burgos St. Look for "Patria de Cebu, Inc." sign. Share a dimly lit hallway with the Archbishop's office. Singles P150-200; doubles P250, with A/C P600; extra person P100.

Ruftan Cafe and Pension, 61 Legaspi St. (☎256 2613), near Basilica del Santo Niño. Backpacker haven in the heart of Cebu. Good food and travel stories. Internet P15 per hr. Doubles P165-350.

UPTOWN

Mayflower Pension House (☎255 2800; mayflower@cebu.webling.com), on Villalon Dr., off Escario St. east of the Capitol Building. Cafe, tickets, a library, IDD, and TV in A/C rooms. Laundry service. Check-out 1pm. Singles P210-435; doubles P275-540; triples P340-675. MC/V.

Verbena Pension House 584 Don Gil Garcia St. (☎/fax 253 3430), off Osmeña Blvd. Walk a block down Jasmin St. and turn left onto Don Gil Garcia St. Tall eucalyptus trees grow in the courtyard of this pleasant establishment. Free local calls. Canteen open 6am-7:30pm. Booking service. All rooms A/C. Singles P390; doubles P440; triples P500; quads P560.

Kukuk's Nest 157 Gorordo Ave. (☎231 5180; kukus@nexus.com.ph), at Escario St. Spacious, clean rooms with a Bohemian atmosphere. Excellent base to explore Cebu. Beer garden/restaurant open 24hr. Roast chicken P130. Diving and transportation arrangements available. Singles P200; doubles P500-560, with A/C P450.

YMCA 51 Osmeña Blvd. (☎253 4057), opposite the Shell gas station. Conveniently located midway between Colon St. and Fuente Osmeña. Cafeteria, pool, bowling, billiards. Free local calls. TV P50. Refrigerator P70. Singles P200, with A/C 250, extra bed P100; doubles P250-500; triples P360-750; quads with fan and private common room P600.

FOOD

Both swanky uptown and gritty downtown provide fine food, local and foreign. Some of the tastiest and cheapest food can be found in the food courts of Cebu's many shopping malls, including the **Robinson** complex at Fuente Osmeña and the **Ayala Center.** The mother of all food courts can be found at the **S.M. City Mall.**

DOWNTOWN

Pete's Kitchen, on Paelaez St. From Colon St. walk north; it's on the right. Local grub served up cafeteria style. *Lumpia* P6-40; grilled squid P65; fried rice P15. Takeout counter open daily 6am-8:30pm. Restaurant open daily 5:30am-10:30pm.

Our Place, upstairs at the corner of Pelaez St. and Sanciangko. Haunt of the (mostly male) expat community. Steak P100; spaghetti P80. Open M-Sa 9am-11pm.

UPTOWN

Taj Mahal Curry House (☎253 6745), on Escario St. at the Osmeña St intersection. Facing the capitol, it's to the left. Tasty and cheap Indian food and lots of vegetarian entrees. Try the spinach *kofta* (P55) or the mushroom curry (P65). Also has a branch in the Ayala Center. Open M-Sa 11am-11pm.

Chikaan Sa Cebu, on Juana Osmeña St. From Fuente Osmeña, go down Gen. Maxilom Ave., turn left up Juana Osmeña, then left again into the shopping plaza. A worthwhile splurge, seafood menus with *adobong kangkong* (sauteed vegetables) P135. Sizzling blue marlin P135. Open daily 11am-2pm and 6-10pm. AmEx/MC/V.

SIGHTS

One day is more than enough for Cebu's limited array of sights.

BASILICA DEL SANTO NINO. Planted on April 14, 1521, by Ferdinand Magellan, the **Cross of Magellan** on Magallanes St. marks the location where missionaries baptized the first Christian Filipinos. Two weeks later, after Chief Lapu-Lapu killed Magellan, the expedition fled and the Spanish influence waned until Legazpi returned to raze Cebu in April 1565. Next door, in the **Bascilla del Santo Niño** on Osmeña Blvd., Queen Juana's baptismal gift is prominently displayed. A conquistador discovered the unmarred Santa Niño figure given to the Queen by Magellan, the oldest religious relic in the Philippines. The Bascilla was originally built as a *nipa* hut in 1565, the church suffered numerous fires until the current structure was built from 1735-37. One of the oldest churches in the Philippines, it exemplifies the imported architecture of the conquering Spaniards. *(Open M-Th and Sa-Su 5am-7:30pm, F 6am-6pm. Free.)*

FORT SAN PEDRO. When Legazpi began construction of **Fort San Pedro** on May 8, 1565, the days of friendly blood compacts with native chieftains were over. Swords, then crosses, became the order of the day. The triangular bastion has been reincarnated as a schoolhouse, barracks, and zoo. The shaded interior garden is one of the most peaceful spots in Cebu, a perk not missed by young lovers. The eight-foot thick walls also guard the **Fort San Pedro National Museum.** The museum displays the artifacts of the Spanish galleon *San Diego*. *(In the pier area in southern Cebu on Quezon Blvd. opposite the post office. ☎255 7748. Fort open daily 9am-11pm; P10. Museum open W-Su 9am-5pm; free. San Pedro Museum open daily 9am-noon and 1-5pm; P5.)*

UNIVERSITY OF SAN CARLOS. The oldest school in the Philippines, the **University of San Carlos** on P. Del Rosario began as a seminary in 1595. Get a glimpse of gender inequalities of a bygone era and cranial deformation, a purely aesthetic pursuit to flatten the front of the skull by using boards and straps, inside the ethnographic gallery of the **University Museum.** *(☎253 1000. Open M-F 8:30am-noon and 1:30-5:30pm, Sa 8:30am-noon. P10, students P1.)*

OTHER SIGHTS. A jaunt north to **Beverly Hills** (taxi P70-80) shows you the world of the wealthy Chinese Cebuanos. Lavish mansions surround the **Taoist Temple** high above the city. With Bohol and Mactan in the distance, this is a great place to see the sunset. The **Casa Gorordo Museum** provides an unparalleled glimpse into Cebu's late colonial past. Built in the 1860s, this beautiful Spanish colonial house was constructed without a single nail. *(35 Lopez Jaena St. ☎255 5630. Open M-Sa 9am-noon and 1-5pm. P15, students P5.)*

OUTDOORS. Outdoor enthusiasts usually strike out for other islands in search of adventure. Nevertheless, there are some activities in and around Cebu to catch the traveler's attention. **Swagman Travel** (see **Practical Information** above) organizes eco- and adventure day trips, including **kayak tours** and **trekking** through Cebu's mountainous interior. The **Hagabat Outdoor Gear Shop** (see **Practical Information** above) is a meeting spot for the local hiking, climbing (there's a climbing gym next door) and diving scene; get all your updated information on diving here. The shop frequently organizes weekend day-trips—contact Warlito "Monski" Momongan.

ENTERTAINMENT

Don't miss Cebu's fantastic live music venues, typically featuring local bands that cover pop hits from James Taylor to Jennifer Lopez with frightening accuracy.

Cities (☎255 4562), on the left side of Gen. Maxilom Ave. heading away from Fuente Osmeña. Fantastic cover bands as well as zany stage acts, like dancing nuns. Beer P40-60; pitchers P200. Ladies' night Tu and Th. Cover P100. Open M-Th 7pm-1am, F-Sa 7pm-2am. MC/V.

Jerby's Cafe and Music Lounge (☎253 5401), on the north corner of Fuente Osmeña, along Osmeña Blvd, next to Dunkin' Donuts. Live bands and karaoke. San Miguel P30. Happy Hour 6-9pm. F-Sa cover P50. Open M-Sa 10pm-2am.

Waterfront Hotel (☎232 6888). It's nowhere near the water, but The Waterfront does offer some intriguing after hours entertainment including the **Casino Filipino** with card tables, roulette, and slots (P100 cover), and **H_2O,** a hip bar-cum-nightclub that attracts a glamorous late 20s yuppie crowd. Cover P150.

MACTAN ISLAND ☎32

If Magellan were a tourist, the behemoth resorts on Mactan Island would surely have crushed his spirits as quickly as Chief Lapu-Lapu crushed his cranium. Most of Mactan's resorts are far beyond a budget traveler's price range, and the more affordable ones are generally dark, dingy affairs. Unless you are desperate for the beach or absolutely pressed for time, Mactan is best avoided. That said, the island's saving grace is its offshore diving, though the underwater ecosystem has been hit hard by "dynamite fishing," where fishermen simply use dynamite to blow up all the fish and then grab them as they float up to the surface.

TRANSPORTATION AND PRACTICAL INFORMATION. Just off the east coast of Cebu Island, Mactan Island is linked to Cebu City by ferry and land. A bridge connects Mactan to mainland Cebu in **Mandaue,** a small area of the metro sprawl 8km north of Cebu City. The island's capital city, **Lapu-Lapu City,** is on the northwest coast, facing Cebu. **Beaches** dot the east coast. The **airport** spreads through much of the island and provides service to Cebu City. **Metro Ferries** leave from Cebu City's Pier 3. (45 min., 6am-7:30pm, P7.) **Jeepney's** leave from the S.M.City Mall in Cebu City and drop passengers at the **jeepney terminal** north of Lapu-Lapu City. (30-45 min., every 20 min. 4am-11pm, P5.) From Cebu City, A/C **minibuses** head to Lapu-Lapu City from the lot opposite the S.M.City Mall. (25 min., P11.) Trips to beaches on **tricycle** require skillful negotiation (around P60). Other airport services include a **tourist office** (☎340 8229; open M-F 8am-5pm) and a **post office** (open M-F 8am). **Postal Code**: 6015.

ACCOMMODATIONS AND FOOD. The **Buyong Hotel and Restaurant** on Maribago Beach offers adequate but unpretentious abodes by Mactan standards. (☎492 0118. Doubles P500-1200.) Next door, the posh facilities of the man-made desert island of the **Bluewater Beach Resort** are available for P350. Check out the shark pond. Rooms at **Club Kontiki** (☎495 2471) start at US$30. The nearby **Triancolori Pensionne** (☎495 2375) has decent A/C rooms for P500. Next to the Kontiki Divers, the **Lapu-Lapu Monument** has seafood eateries (squid P100 per kg).

SIGHTS AND DIVING. On the northeast tip of the island in Punta Engano, the **Magellan Marker,** built in 1866, honors the explorer's death on April 27, 1521. The nearby Lapu-Lapu Monument commemorates the local hero (tricycle P50). Mactan's waters offer several dive sites. **Marigondon Cave** is the Philippines' largest underwater cave, recommended for advanced divers only; **Kontiki Reef** is suitable for all levels. The waters off Mactan are home to jet-skiing Japanese businessmen as well as snapper, tuna, and occasionally, shark. **Kontiki Divers,** next to the Kon Tiki Club, is a top-flight outfit. (☎495 2471; 7seas@mozcom.com. Dives US$22, nitrox dives US$30. Open-water courses US$360, advanced courses US$300. Ask Maki about diving safaris.)

The public beach at **Marigondon** offers everyone a taste of Mactan, on the rocks. The **Tambuli Beach Club and Villa** charges a P200 admission fee and you're likely to spend another P150 at the restaurant and bar. (Open 7am-5pm.)

MOALBOAL ☎32

Sleepy Moalboal has attracted attention for its natural beauty and fine diving. *Nipa* huts balance on rock outcroppings over calm waters, illuminated by sunsets over the mountains of Negros. Back on land after a day at sea, divers sip beers and swap stories of their underwater adventures. Ten years ago a typhoon devastated nearby reefs but spared alluring Pescador Island Marine Park. Reasonably priced diving, nearby outdoor adventures, and a relaxed atmosphere keep the huts full though non-divers should note that there is no sand to be found here, and underwater exploration is the name of the game; beach bums might find Bantayan and Malapascua islands more to their liking.

TRANSPORTATION AND PRACTICAL INFORMATION. The town of Moalboal shares a peninsula with Panagsama and White Beach, 89km southwest of Cebu City on the opposite shore. Tricycle drivers make the 4km hop to Panagsama Beach (30-45min., P40). **Buses** to Cebu (2½hr., every 30min. 3am-6pm, P40) must be flagged down on the main drag. From Moalboal, ABC Liner buses continue south down the coast to **Bato** (2hr., P30), where rickety **ferries** make the short hop to **Tampi,** a port just a few km north of **Dumaguete. Eve's Kiosk** has **currency exchange.** (Open daily 6:30am-9pm.) A **market** lines the left side of the road where the bus stops. The **post office** is in the municipal building at the end of the road. (Open M-F 7:30am-noon and 1-5:30pm.) There's a **telephone office** in back. (Open M-F 8am-noon and 1-10pm, Sa-Su 8am-noon and 1-5pm.) **Postal code:** 6032.

ACCOMMODATIONS AND FOOD. All accommodations are within walking distance of each other and have restaurants serving fresh seafood. Ask about discounts if you dive with their shop. **Mollie's Place** is an immaculate backpacker's haven. (☎918 770 9855. Singles P100-150; doubles P395-400. AmEx/MC/V.) **Pacitas Beach Resort** bungalow offers private *nipa* huts. (☎918 770 9982. Call ahead Oct.-Mar. Doubles P250, with A/C P600.) **Marcoses Cottages** (☎474 0024) has gorgeous bungalows for P550. The exquisite bungalows of the **Quo Vadis Beach Resort** are down the coast to the south. (☎474 0018; quovadisb.r@skyinet.net; www.moalboal.com. Bungalows with fan P350-550; with A/C US$40.) Restaurants along the shore await hungry divers from Pescador. The **Last Filling Station** flanks the main path along the shore. Feast on the Asian table barbecue (P135) while sipping a refreshingly bitter *Kalamansi* juice (P20). **BB's Seaside Restaurant,** over the water in the north part of town, serves up fresh *lapu-lapu* (P120).

SIGHTS AND DIVING. Sun worshippers looking for a sandy beach will be disappointed, but bliss awaits divers. Several dive sites are accessible by a short *banca* trip. For the experienced diver, **Sunken Island** is the spot to see schools of tuna and large pelagics. **Pescador,** suitable for all divers, has vibrant coral life. **White Beach** has a coral wall that leads to a sunken airplane now piloted by turtles.

Diving in Moalboal has an international feel: **Neptune Diving Stop** (www.neptunediving.com) has French and Swiss instructors; **Visaya Divers** is run by a Californian expat; **Ocean Safari** is usually preferred by Japanese divers. **Savedra Dive Center's** (www.savandra.com) professional staff offer quality service. **Planet Action's** Jochen takes pride in finding adventure for his clients. He offers river climbing trips to **Kawasan Falls** (P900), mountain biking, canyoning, and caving expeditions in the jungles of Negros and Cebu (1-3 days US$25-120).

Prices vary little among the well-established dive centers. One dive goes for around US$23 (nitrox US$31). Open-water courses and advanced courses cost US$220-250.

BANTAYAN ISLAND ☎32

Despite local mystic belief in *aswang* (witches), the real magic of Bantayan Island, just northwest of Hagnaya, Cebu, is in the soft white beaches stretching along the southwest coast—a true respite for those making the long trek from Cebu to Boracay. Although dynamite fishing has blasted the hopes of would-be divers, it has left the beaches relatively *banca* free, a godsend for sunbathing purists. Aquanauts should head for nearby Malapascua, whose graceful thresher sharks have made it one of the Visaya's best-known dive sites. With few resorts and such potential, the lack of tourists is surprising, though not unwelcome for the travelers who do make it to the island's two main towns, Santa Fe and Bantayan.

TRANSPORTATION

Bantayan is connected to Cebu by **Island Shipping Corp. ferries,** which depart from **Hagnaya** (1hr.; 4 per day 7:30am-6:30pm; P63, A/C P70-75) and land in **Santa Fe.** Buses run from Cebu City to Hagnaya (3hr., 6 per day, P60). When traveling from Santa Fe to Hagnaya, buy tickets on board (1hr., 4 per day 5:30am-2pm, P5-7). **Jeepney** depart from the ferry pier to the **Bantayan** (30min., every 20-30min. 6am-10pm, P10). The Bantayan ferry pier serves Island Shipping Corp., which offers trips to **Cadiz** on Negros (2¼hr.; 9am; P130-135 upper deck, tickets bought on board). The Island Shipping Corp. office in Bantayan town is at the end of the road after City Hall. (☎352 5103. Open daily 8am-5pm.) **Note:** a hop from Bantayan to Boracay requires an overnight in Iloilo or Kalibo on Panay. By late 2001 Seair may begin offering air service between Bantayan and other points in the archipelago.

PHILIPPINES

ORIENTATION AND PRACTICAL INFORMATION

Off Cebu's northwest coast, **Bantayan** is a stepping stone to Negros and Panay. The main road connects southwest Bantayan with southeast **Santa Fe,** which is surrounded by beaches. For those who want to blaze through northern fields to coastal fishing communities, the northbound road begins as **Pres. Osmeña St.** in central Bantayan. A trip by **dirtbike** to the northernmost community, **Madridejos,** takes 30-45min. **Budyong Beach Resort** rents out dirtbikes (P700 for 8hr.).

Santa Fe is where the fun is. This resource-laden Bantayan town exhibits the best of local life. In Bantayan, **tricycles** cluster where Rizal Ave. meets the plaza. From Santa Fe, jeepney leave from the pier shortly after ferries arrive (30min., P10).

Allied Bank, on the corner of Osmeña and Escario St. in Bantayan, cashes AmEx Traveler's Cheques. (☎352 5144. Open M-F 9am-4pm.) There are **no ATMs** on the island. The **police station** in Bantayan is in the town hall near the ferry pier. **Bantayan District Hospital** (☎352 5231) is 500m down the road to Santa Fe. The town hall hosts the **post office** (open M-F 8-11:30am and 1-4pm) and the **PLDT office** (☎198 5231. Open M-Sa 8am-noon and 1-5pm.) **Postal code:** Santa Fe 6047.

ACCOMMODATIONS AND FOOD

Santa Fe's resorts are far better than those in boring Bantayan, and there's no reason to stay in the latter. All resorts are a P5-10 tricycle ride from the pier. **Budyong Beach Resort** has beautiful bungalows on the nicest resort beach in Santa Fe. (☎438 9040. Doubles P400/600, with A/C P1000/1200.) Across the street, **Kota Beach Resort** (☎438 9042) offers a vast range of rooms from P350 huts to gorgeous P1200 suites. North of the pier, Danish-managed **St. Bernard's** features seven well-appointed bungalows, a true bargain at P300-450. **Moby Dick's,** on the road to Madridejos from Bantayan, is a secluded retreat boasting the island's best sunsets (☎352 5269. Bungalows P500/700.) To arrange transportation, inquire at the eponymous restaurant **Little Moby Dick's,** a fixture in its own right in Bantayan's so-called "nightlife." (Excellent seafood P60-120.) **D'Jungle Bar** in Santa Fe specializes in German food (P120-170) and features a dizzying assortment of alcoholic treats (P55-100).

SIGHTS AND ENTERTAINMENT

Beyond the sand and surf in Santa Fe, Bantayan sights are slim. The nearby community often holds afternoon **cockfights** behind Little Moby Dick's. Follow the men with the chickens. Farther down the beach toward Bantayan town is the cesspool that is **Ogtong Cave,** where snorkelling awaits. (Open daily 7am-6pm, P50.) **"Jungle discos"** happen spontaneously in the forest, where all ages groove to 70s classics. Ask a tricycle driver or the guest house staff for directions.

MALAPASCUA ISLAND ☎32

Off the northeast tip of Cebu, this tiny speck captures travelers' attention as they cross from Cebu City on their way to Boracay. Time seems to stand still on Malapascua's white beach; one might spend days reading in the shade of coconut trees, swimming in crystal-clear waters, or counting passing ships. Malapascua has become one of the Visaya's most popular dive destinations, its popularity fed by the regular appearance of thresher sharks in the channel between Cebu and Leyte.

The starting point from Cebu is Maya. **Pump boats** cover the distance from Maya to Malapascua (10am and whenever full during the day, P25) and also ply the return journey (8am and whenever full during the day, P25). Chartered pumpboats go anytime for P350; from Santa Fe, hire one at a resort or at the pier (2hr., P1000-1500 per boat). Otherwise, take the **ferry** to **Hagnaya** (1hr., P60), a **tricycle** to **Bogo** (30min., P10), and then hop on a bus to Maya (1hr., P15). From there you can catch the scheduled trips or charter a *banca*.

During low season, activity slows down, prices drop, and some establishments close. **Cocobana Beach Resort** has spacious waterfront and garden cottages. (☎0918 775 2942. Waterfront P960/860; garden P760/660.) Next door, the **Malapascua Blue Water Resort** has rooms near the water, large rooms, and "garden rooms." (☎0918 773 4124. Cottages P800/600, P1000/800; small rooms P500.) Farther down the beach, the **Sunset Beach Resort** offers passable beachfront bungalows at good prices (P400-600). A number of dive shops have cropped up along the beach, capitalizing on thresher-mania. Dutch-owned **Exotic Divers,** at the far end of the beach, is a well-established operation which runs daily shark-watching excursions to Monod Point.

Next to the Cocobana, **Sunsplash** (☎091 858 84 666) has great Euro/Filipino food and a floating bar. Specialties include crepes (P60), pasta (P120), and pizza (P110).

BOHOL

In the heart of the Boholano forest, the tarsier swivels its head and leaps from tree to tree, clinging with elongated suction-cup fingers. Just north of its home, the majestic Chocolate Hills pop out of the flat landscape and offer unparalleled sunrises and sunsets. Off southwest Panglao Island, porpoises and whales slip through world-class diving reefs in the Mindanao Sea. Luckily for Bohol, tourists who come to enjoy this island have not much impacted the Boholano lifestyle, which, along with its many beaches, remains undisturbed.

THE VIEW FROM ABOVE

Main towns: Carmen, Tagbilaran.
Highlights: Diving off the coast, swimming with dolphins, or just lounging on the Panglao Island beaches.
Something sweet: North of Tagbilaran, the Chocolate Hills might be your true soul food.

TAGBILARAN ☎38

The rulers of the Bohol Kingdom once used Panglao Island, off the southeastern coast of Bohol, to hide from Muslim raiders, the *Bilaan*, who swept north from Mindanao. Modern-day marauders find little in Tagbilaran but telephones, Internet terminals, and ATMs. Once these are plundered, you can explore the island's inspiring interior without getting entangled in the city.

TRANSPORTATION

Flights: Tagbilaran airport, 1½km north of the city. **Asian Spirit** (☎411 5701; www.asianspirit.com) flies to **Manila** (Tu, W, F, Sa, Su; P2499). **Tarsier Tours and Travel Services,** 25 Maria Clara St. (☎411 3615), near the University of Bohol, handles reservations. Tricycle into town P5.

Boats: The ferry pier extends from the northwest part of the city. Walking along the pier, turn right onto Gallares St. to head into town (1km). Take a tricycle to Tagbilaran center (5-10min., P4) or directly to **Alona Beach** on Panglao Island (1¼hr., P100). Ferries are operated by 3 companies with offices in the terminal (open 5am-9pm); all grant a 15% student discount. Tickets for all lines at **Alboitz Express office,** Carlos Garcia Ave., opposite the tourist office. **Supercat** (☎232 4511) to: **Cebu** (1½hr.; 3 per day; P320) and **Dumaguete** (1½hr., 2:15pm, P430). **WG&A** to: **Cagayan** (4hr., Sa, P269); **Diplong** (3hr., Su 9am, P270); **Manila** (29hr.; M, W 10am; P1185). Ferries to **Siguijor** (M,W,F 7pm; P150); purchase tickets on the pier.

Buses: Dao Integrated Bus Terminal serves all of Bohol's major sights. Take a jeepney from Grupo St. or any marked "Dao" or "Int. Bus Terminal" (15-20min., P4). Buses to: **Baclayon** (15-20min., P5); **Bilar** (1½hr., P18); **Carmen** (2hr., every hr. 4am-5:30pm, P52), passing the **Chocolate Hills Complex** (6km before Carmen proper); **Loboc** (30-40min., P14); **Loon** (45min., P10). Buses marked "Talibon; Tubigon" follow the north-coast road to **Maribojoc** (25min., every 30min. 4am-6:30pm, P5).

Jeepney: Leave from Grupo St. near **Jacinto St.** and from the **Cogon Public Market.** They go north to Punta Cruz in **Maribojoc** (40min., every 45min. 7am-5pm, P10) and south from **Dao Integrated Bus Terminal** to the Blood Compact site in **Bool** (5-10min., 7am-5pm, P4) on their way to **Baclayon** (20min., P4). Flag down jeepney leaving from Boholand near the cathedral in Tagbiliran. Those marked "Panglao" head to **Doljo Beach** (45min., every hr. 7am-5pm, P11). Those marked with the number 80 or "Panglao-Tawala" pass **Alona Beach** but stop running by 4pm.

Tricycles: P3-5 per trip in town. To: Panglao P100-150.

Rentals: Chocolate Hills Travels and Tours (☎411 5907), at the Slim Pension House (see **Accommodations,** below). Car with driver P1500. Open 8am-4pm. **Dirtbikes** can be rented at resorts along Alona Beach (P100 per hr., P600 per day).

ORIENTATION AND PRACTICAL INFORMATION

Tagbilaran, on the southwest tip of Bohol, guards the narrow strait separating **Bohol** and **Panglao.** From the pier, **Gallares St.** follows the shore and terminates at **St. Joseph's Cathedral** and **City Hall.** In front of the cathedral, **Plaza Rizal** is bounded on the other side by **Carlos P. Garcia (CPG) Ave.,** Taghilaran's main commercial street, on which you can find the very helpful **tourist office** opposite the **Bohol Quality** department store (☎411 3666. Open M-F 8am-8pm.) Come here to book whale watching excursions or arrange for a tour of the Chocolate Hills (guided full-day tour P1500). **PCI Equity Bank** is just down the street. (Open M-F 9am-4pm.) Further down is the **Mercury Drug pharmacy.** (Open daily 7am-9pm.) Private **Ramiro Hospital** is on Gallares St., on the way to the pier. There are **Internet cafes** all over town, especially along Lesage St., near Divine World College. The **post office** is behind the Cathedral. (Open M-F 8am-noon and 1-5pm.) **Postal Code**: 6300.

ACCOMMODATIONS AND FOOD

Taghilaran has a number of cheap, forgettable budget accommodations. **Slim Pension house** on F.R. Ingles St. behind the Agora market, is the best value in town. (☎411 4858. A/C singles P480, doubles P620.)On CPG Ave. opposite the PCI Equitable Bank, the optimistically named **Charisma Lodge** has clean if noisy rooms. (☎411 3094. Singles P115-280, doubles P490.) The **Everglory Hotel** on C. Galleres St. overlooking the pier, has decent views of the harbor (☎411 3200. Singles P350, with view P400, with A/C P500.) There are several very dirt-cheap lodging houses on Lesage St. opposite the Divine World College with singles for P70.

Seafood is the passion here, and if it's removed from the pier, it's not considered fresh. Try **M-R Seafood** set on a triangle of mango trunks in front of the pier. (P50-150. Open daily 6am-10pm.) The usual fastfood joints and eateries crowd the center of town.

DAYTRIPS FROM TAGBILARAN

THE CHOCOLATE HILLS

The Chocolate Hills are Bohol's signature attraction. The terrain is certainly unique, though whether or not the Hills live up to the tourist hype is questionable. All 1268 of the 40m mounds dollop the relatively flat paddy land. Geologists believe that eons of erosion sculpted coral and limestone into this bizarre topography.

The hills are best viewed from **Carmen,** 59km northeast of Tagbilaran. The only truly acceptable place to stay for the full dawn spectacle is on top of one of the hills themselves. The **Chocolate Hills Complex** perches atop the tallest hill 6km before Carmen; make sure the driver knows your destination. (Dorms P75; doubles P250-800; triples P350-800; extra person P200.) The **observation patio,** 214 steps up from the complex, is the highest point in the hills. (☎912 856 1559. Admission P10. Open daily 6am-9pm.) Motorcyclists congregate at the turn-off to the complex and take you on a meandering tour back to Tagbilaran, stopping to see the sights along the way. (Half-day P600 for two.)

Visit **Nuts Huts,** which has beautiful *nipa* huts on the Loboc River surrounded by lush forest. It's a relaxed backpacker hangout and a base for adventure activities. Nuts is 3km after Loboc on the road to Carmen. A sign on the left indicates a dirt road turn-off; it's 750m down the road. Enjoy breathtaking views and imaginative Euro-Asian cuisine at the hilltop restaurant. Ask Walter about mountain biking, hiking, and river swimming. (Dorms P150; cottages P350; large cottages P550.)

BOOL, BACLAYON, AND MARIBOJOC

A handful of dull but historically significant sights collect dust near Tagbilaran. The sights in Bool and Bacloyan are accessible by any eastbound jeepney leaving Taglibiran City (P7). **Bool,** 3km away, boasts a small roadside memorial to the **Blood Compact Site,** where Miguel Lopez de Legazpi swore a blood oath with Chieftain Datu Sikatuna in 1565. Farther down the coastal road is the Philippines' first church **Baclayon Church.** Next door, the convent houses a centuries-long accumulation of religious relics. (Open M-Sa 8:15am-noon and 1:30-5pm, Su 9am-noon and 1:30-5pm; P15.) In **Maribojoc** is the watchtower **Punta Cruz,** built by the Spanish in 1796. Jeepney leave Tagbilaran for Maribojoc daily, passing the tower (40min., 7am-5pm, P7).

FOWL PLAY Take a feisty cock, a 10cm blade, and a fierce bet, and you have the Pinoy national obsession. Begun during the Spanish colonial era, cockfighting permeated the culture of every province, city, and remote *barangay* in the archipelago's 7107 islands. Although large arenas have been built in bigger towns solely for cockfighting, it is best to witness them at a rustic bamboo-pen crowded with captivated local children. On Sundays and holidays, the day-long event commences with an intense discussion about the pairing of combatants. Size, speed, and spirit are all important criteria to be weighed before placing a bet. The number of fingers held aloft signifies the numerical value of the wager. Pointing upward places a conservative bet in the tens of pesos, pointing sideways connotes a bet in the hundreds, and a gesture downward signals a bet of heroic or insane proportions. Farmers lose (or win) the equivalent of a week's wages over the two-minute explosion of blood and feathers. Before doing battle, two cocks are fitted with 10cm curved blades protruding backward from their left foot. Held firmly by their owners, each cock is allowed to peck at its opponent's neck to incite rage and make sure the combatants come out fighting. The unlucky cluckers peck and pounce their way to freedom, attempting to escape the grill for one more night. The fight ends with one cock, fatally impaled, flopping on the ground. When the referee hoists the two into the air and the injured no longer has the life to peck at the victor, the match ends and money changes hands.

NEAR TAGBILARAN

PANGLAO ISLAND

With exquisite sand beaches and first-class diving, Panglao Island has much to offer travelers of every stripe; it is arguably the Visaya's best beach destination. Underwater fanatics dominate Alona Beach, the most developed of the island's beaches. For more seclusion, escape to Doljo Beach. Either way, arrange to watch the magnificent whales cavorting off Panglao's south coast.

The well-paved central road connects Panglao in the west with Bool and the new bridge. Most amenities can only be found in Tagbilaran. Few roads are paved, so allow for extra travel time. International calls can be made from hotels or from the **PLDT** in Panglao town. (☎198 8109. Open daily 7am-10pm.) **Jeepney** passing Alona Beach go to Panglao town (15min., P4), but don't go back; return by **tricycle** (15min., P20-30).

All of the following are near each other on Alona Beach, except for the Palm Island Beach Resort on Doljo beach. Most lodgings have an attached restaurant, but exploring waterfront eateries is a tasty option. Prices rise during the high season (Dec.-Mar.). **Alonaville Beach Resort** has touristy **Sam & Jerry's Bar** downstairs. (Doubles without fan P300, Apr.-Nov. P200; cottages for 2 with fan P600, Apr.-Nov. P500.) No shoes are allowed upstairs at **Peter's House,** which has tasty pizza (P90-125) and exotic rooms in a beautiful three-story *nipa* house. (Cell ☎0918 770 8434. Singles with fan P400; doubles P550; discounts for divers.) Down the beach, the **Tierra Azul Beach House** is a good value with well-appointed A/C rooms for P500. **Palm Island Beach Resort** is a secluded resort on Doljo Beach. (☎500 0777. *Nipa* dorms P200; doubles with fan P500.)

For the best diving, head to **Balicasag Island,** southwest of Doljo Point. **Black Forest** is an excellent site for drift-diving, where black coral can be found. **Pamalican Island** is known as the "nesting place of manta rays." **Doljo Beach,** on the other side of Panglao, has rich coral walls. Dive shops along **Alona Beach** go to every hot spot and offer the entire range of PADI courses. (US$34 per dive; open-water courses US$300; advanced open-water US$195-220.) Friendly **Bohol Divers** (☎411 4983) is a notch above the rest.

Whales save their best performances for early-birds, but hyperactive dolphins perform at the drop of a hat. Ask your guest house about chartering a boat. The shoreline also yields numerous locals with idle pumpboats. Organized tours leave **Bacloyan Pier** east of Tagbiliran City and cruise to Pamilican Island. (☎540 9279. 7-person boat P500 per person; 3-person boat P600 per person.)

BETWEEN TAGBILARAN AND CARMEN

Rajah Sikatuna National Park, south of the Chocolate Hills, covers 9000 hectares of molave forest and grasslands honeycombed with caves (P20). Among the animals inhabiting the park is the petite **tarsier,** the world's smallest primate. To get there, take a Carmen-bound bus from the Integrated Bus Terminal; get out at the market in **Bilar** (1hr., P18). From there, ask for directions or try to swindle some transportation to cover the few kilometers to **Camp Magsaysay.** The park is best visited with plenty of time and your own transportation — unless you've got an obsessive interest in tarsier habitats, the park is best skipped. Before going, groups should contact the National Park (☎032 411 2357). *Nipa* cottages are available for rent (P50), and camping is possible (P50). The Logarita Spring-fed **swimming pool,** 2½km from the Bilar market, is available for use (P5).

The best and most humane place to view the tarsier is at the **Philippine Tarsier Breeding Center** in Carella. It is 11km west of Loboc; take a jeepney bound for Sikatua. The Center is 2km past Sikatua on the right. At **Supercarp's,** you can commandeer a small pumpboat (local crew included) to head upriver to a waterfall that is ideal for swimming (15min., P400). In Loboc, **St. Peter's Church,** the second oldest stone church in the Philippines, stands as a monument to Filipino piety. The unfinished bridge across the river is a monument to American presumptuousness. US engineers began the bridge on the assumption that the locals wouldn't mind dismantling their church. They minded, and construction halted.

NEGROS

When Spanish missionaries deemed Negros' island mountains too formidable to traverse, even for the glory of God, they split the island diagonally into Negros Occidental and Negros Oriental. Spotless Bacolod became the capital of Negros Occidental, and vibrant Dumaguete became Negros Oriental's capital. The island's main sights are the lush jungle around Mt. Kanla-on and the white beaches of Apo Island. The plains of Negros Occidental are known for their sugar crop, but the worldwide sugar market crash has devastated that industry. The jarring economic results have contributed to the rise of the communist New People's Army (NPA), an active force in the area.

THE VIEW FROM ABOVE

Gateway city: Bacolod.
Major towns: Dumaguete in the south, Silay and Victorias in the north.
Nearby islands: Apo Island, Siquitor Islands.
Beaches: Head south to Apo Island for, yup, you guessed it, another great dive.
Something big: Mt. Kanla-on is the tallest peak in central Philippines.

BACOLOD ☎34

Most travelers will find little reason to linger in Bacolod. It's dusty, chaotic streets lack the charm of Iloilo City across the Guimaras Straights. Bacolod sits in the heartland of Negros' once-thriving sugar industry. The island's historic wealth is preserved in the excellent Negros Museum and in the fading grandeur of the sugar baron's *haciendas* in Silay and Victorias. South of the city, Mt. Kanla-on rises dramatically from the cane fields, a challenge to be taken by only the hardiest trekkers.

TRANSPORTATION

Flights: The **airport** is south of the city, on Araneta St. Taxis to/from airport P35-40. To go downtown, flag down a jeepney marked "Pta. Taytay–Central Market" (P3). **PAL** (☎835 29), in the main terminal, flies to **Cebu** (M, W, F, and Su 7:05am; P1263) and **Manila** (4 per day, P2563). **Air Philippines** ticketing is opposite the main terminal (☎434 2520; open M-Sa 8:30am-4:30pm); the domestic terminal (☎433 9210) is on the same side as the main terminal; the downtown office (☎433 9570; open M-Sa 8:30am-6pm) is in Victorina Arcade on Rizal St. near the plaza. Flies to **Cebu** (daily, P1599) and **Manila** (daily, P2498). **Cebu Pacific's** terminal (☎433 1969) is near Air Philippines; the downtown office (☎434 2020) is on Rizal St. near the plaza. Open daily 9am-5:30pm. To: **Cebu** (1 per day, 7:10am, P1039) and **Manila** (3 per day, P1549).

Buses: Ceres North Terminal, on Lopez Jaena St. near corner of B.S. Aquino Dr. (15min. by taxi from city center, P30). Buses to: **Cadiz** (1½hr., P30); **Cebu City** via **Toledo** (7-8hr.; 1, 5:45, 9:30, and 9:45am; P115-140); **Dumaguete** (8hr., 8 per day 3am-midnight, P122) via San Carlos; **San Carlos** (4hr., every 30min. 4am-7:30pm, P67) via **Silay** (20min., P6); **Victorias** (30-40min., P10). **Public North Bus Terminal,** a few meters down Lopez Jaena St., has buses and jeepney to: **Cadiz** (1½hr., every 30min. 6:30am-7:30pm, P25); **San Carlos** (3½hr., every 30min. 4am-4pm, P60); **Victorias** (30-40min.; every 15min. 6am-8pm, last return 6pm; P10). Down Lopez Jaena St., between the Luzuriaga and San Sebastian St. intersection, **Public South Bus Terminal** has buses to: **Canalaon** (3½hr., every hr. 4am-4pm, P46); **Candoni** (3hr., 8 per day 4am-3pm, P56); **Dumaguete** via **Mabinay** (5hr., 6 per day 5:30am-4pm, P164);

Hinoba-an (5½hr., 12 per day 3am-10pm, P90); **Kabankalan** (2hr., 8 per day 6am-8:45pm, P58). Jeepneys leave from opposite the Robinson's Mall for **Cadiz** (P30), **Silay** (P10), and **Victorias** (P12).

Ferries: All shipping lines grant 15% student discount and half fare for ages 4-11. Two port areas serve Bacolod. The one closest to town is at the end of the reclamation area. Banago Port is several miles north of the center of town. **Bullet Express** (☎838 31; open daily 6am-5pm) goes to **Iloilo** (1hr., 4-5 per day last trip 5pm, P140). **Negros Navigation** (☎434 4291) runs to **Cagayan d' Oro** on **Mindanao** (14hr., Tu 7:10am, P930) and to **Manila** (18-24hr.; W 10am, Th 11am, F noon; P930). The **branch office** (☎297 95; open M-F 8:30am-5pm, Sa 8:30am-4pm), at the corner of Rizal and Gatuslao St., sells Negros Navigation and **SeaAngels** tickets. A **shuttle** to Banago leaves 30min. before ferry's scheduled departure (10min., P25) from the reclamation area (a P5 tricycle ride from the plaza). SeaAngels (main office ☎434 2350, terminal ☎441 0659) runs fast ferries to **Iloilo** (1hr., 4 per day 6am-5pm, P230). Office next to Negros Navigation at 6th St. off Lacson St. Open M-F 8am-5pm, Sa 8am-noon. **WG&A** Lines sends ferries to: **Batangas** (14hr., W 2pm, P1245); **Cagayan d'Oro** (12hr., Sa, P1230); and **Manila** (24hr.; W 2pm, Su 2pm; P1245).

Jeepney: Intra-city jeepney routes: "Pta. Taytay-Central Market" to airport; "Bata" and "Mandalagan" pass Negros Museum to Robinson's Mall (15min., P3); "Shopping" to Ceres bus terminals; "Libertad" to Libertad Market. For **Mambukal,** take a jeepney from Libertad Market (1hr., every 15min. 7am-9pm, P12).

Taxis: Fares start at P25, to the airport P50, to Banago ferry pier P50.

PHILIPPINES

ORIENTATION AND PRACTICAL INFORMATION

Bacolod is on the northwest tip of Negros Occidental. The **ferry pier** sits west of the **plaza. Lacson St.** bisects the city. Three blocks closer to the coast, **Araneta St.** begins at the plaza and continues south to the airport. Between the two, **Gatuslao St.** passes the **post office** and **Negros Museum. Burgos St.** intersects Lacson and Araneta St. and ends at the ferry pier. In the east, Burgos St. cuts across **Lopez Jaena St.,** which hosts the **bus terminals.**

Tourist Offices: City Tourism Office (☎434 7472), in Bacolod Plaza. Open M-F 8am-noon and 1-5pm, Sa 10am-3pm. **Provincial Tourism Office** (☎433 2515), in the provincial government complex, north of the lagoon near the Negros Museum. Tina will help facilitate your travels. Open M-F 8am-5pm.

Budget Travel: Manna Travel Agency (☎920 405; mannatrvl@yahoo.com), on San Juan St. near the Plaza. Open M-Sa 9am-6pm.

Immigration Office: Luzuriaga St. (☎438 8581). Near San Juan. Bring your passport and stamp of entry to the Philippines. No shorts or sandals. Open M-F 8am-5pm.

Banks: PCI Bank (☎277 28), on the corner of Araneta and Gonzaga St. near the plaza. No commission on AmEx checks. **24hr. ATM** (Cirrus/MC). Open M-F 8:30am-5pm.

Luggage Storage: Daytime storage at the tourist office in Bacolod Plaza.

Markets: Fruit vendors line Ballesteros, barbecue grills clutter Gatuslao on the corner of Hernadez and Mabini St. and the **Libertad** market has fresh fish and produce.

Emergency: Police ☎166. **Fire** ☎161. **Ambulance** ☎166.

Police: There is a **PNP** office next to the City Tourism Bldg. in the plaza.

Pharmacy: Mercury Drug (☎433 6604), on the corner of Araneta and Luzuriaga St. Open daily 7am-10pm.

Hospitals: Riverside Medical Center (☎433 7331), is on B.S. Aquino Dr. in the north of the city.

Telephones: PLDT (☎433 6700), on Galo St. off Lacson St. Booths close at 4:30pm. Open M-F 8am-noon and 1-5pm.

Internet Access: Cyberworld, on Araneta St. near the Plaza. P30 per hr. Open daily 9am-midnight.

Post Office: (☎433 0436), on Gatuslao St. near intersection with Burgos St. *Poste Restante.* Open M-F 8am-noon and 1-5pm, Sa 8:30-11:30am. **Postal code:** 6100.

ACCOMMODATIONS AND FOOD

Pension Bacolod (☎433 3377). 11th St. on corner of Hilado St. The cheapest A/C and hot water in town. Singles P110-170, with A/C P289; doubles P145-208, with A/C P355; triples P205-260, P420. MC/V with 10% surcharge.

Halili Inn, (☎433 3342). On Locsin St. north of the San Sebastian intersection. Price and location compensate for passable cleanliness. Doubles with fan P120, with common room P200, with A/C P350.

King's Hotel (☎433 0572). On Gatuslao St., at the corner of San Sebastian. Gleaming rooms. A/C, telephone, private common room. Doubles P600. MC/V with 8% surcharge.

Hotel Las Rocas (☎434 1578). On Gatuslao St. between Galo and Rizal St. near the public plaza. Shabby, but with a TV in every room. Singles with fan and private common room P190; doubles with fan and private bath P300, with A/C P500.

Bacolod's fast-food gives a tired traveler an easy way out. For better quality and ambience, head to the **Goldenfield Commercial Complex,** which has bistros and cafes, or hit the area of **Lascon St.** between 20th and 24th St. **Cyberazia,** on the corner of 22 and Lacson St., is an Internet cafe and trendy neon bar. (Wings P70. Internet P25 per hr. Open M-Sa 9am-2am.) Nearby **Chicken House,** on Lacson St. at the corner of 24th St., proves that not all chicken is created equal. (*Pecho* (breast), or *paa* (thigh) P45. Open daily 10am-2pm and 4-11pm.) Bacolod also offers sweet delicacies, including *piyaya* (hardened crêpe with melted sugar) and *bay ibayi* (sugar and coconut in a coconut half shell), all in the central market downtown. For excellent Japanese nosh at bargain prices (by Western standards), try **Inaka** on Lacson St., near the 22nd St. intersection. (☎434 4045. Sushi P30-90, tempura P70. Open daily 10:30am-2pm and 6-10:30pm.)

SIGHTS AND ENTERTAINMENT

Nearly everything in the **Negros Museum,** in the Old Capitol Building, has something to do with the colonial sugar industry. (☎233 95. Open M-Sa 9am-6pm. P30, students P20.) The **Old Capitol Building,** built in 1921, sprawls beautifully from Gatuslao to Lacson St. Across the street from the Negros Museum is the Negros Forest and Ecological Foundation's **Biodiversity Center.** The center is devoted to preserving what remains of Negros' indigenous flora and fauna. Endangered species such as the Visayan pig and the striking bleeding heart pigeon are held in remarkably clean and humane enclosures, in hopes that they will procreate. (Open M-Sa 10am-5pm.) The third week of October sees the celebration of **Masskara,** a melange of Mardi Gras and Rio party styles.

In the Goldenfield Commercial Complex, **bars** and **karaoke joints** galore stay open daily from 9pm to 2am. **Quorum,** near the back of the complex at the Kundutel, is an enormous arena with space-tech flair. (Cover P100. Beer P25. Open 9pm-2am.)

DAYTRIPS FROM BACOLOD

MT. KANLA-ON NATURAL PARK

Take a jeepney from Bacolod (1hr., every 15min. 7:20am-9pm, P15). The last jeepney to Bacolod leaves Mambukal at 5pm. Guides cost around P500 per day with package deals running P4000 for two climbers, including equipment, food, and transport. To secure a permit and find accredited guides, tourists should consult the tourist office in Bacolod or check out the Mt. Kanla-on Natural Park Bacolod Liaison Office in the Department of Environmental and Natural Resources office in the Penro Compound on Gatuslao St. near the Hall of Justice. (☎434 7769. Open M-F 8am-5pm.) Permits to explore the park and climb the volcano cost P300.

The tallest peak in the central Philippines (2465m), Mt. Kanla-on offers a challenge, an impressive landscape, and danger. Two expeditions got caught at the edge of a 1996 eruption; one British trekker and two Filipino guides died. Its unique structure consists of a small active opening on the southwest edge of the larger collapsed caldera of the original volcano, also called the Margaja Valley. The rainy season creates a small lake inside this caldera. The surrounding rainforest has pythons, monitor lizards, tube-nose bats, *dahoy palay* (poisonous green tree snakes), and monkeys. The trails within 4km of the summit are treacherous during the rainy season, January to March and July to September. During those months, the mountain is closed for safety and to allow for the peaceful mating of the non-human animals.

The best entrance point into the park is from the **Mambukal Mountain Resort,** near many hot springs and waterfalls. (☎433 8887. 2-person cottages P400; 4-person cottages P600.)

SILAY AND VICTORIAS

To either town, take a bus connecting Bacolod with Cadiz (Bacolod to Silay 20min., every 30min. 4am-7pm, P10; to Victorias 30-40min., P10) or a jeepney from opposite Robinson's Mall (P10).

Silay and Victorias are the centers of Negros' sugar industry. Silay, the "Paris of Negros," is known for arts and culture. Enthusiasts come for the sugar trains and most find the Angry Christ rewarding, too.

Hop a jeepney at the corner of Rizal and Severino St. (10min., P4) to get to Silay's **Hawaiian Philippines Sugar Corp.** (☎495 3200) and see the sugar trains. A letter of introduction from the Silay tourist office is recommended. The best time to visit the Sugar Corp. is in the tourist season from October to May. Sandals and shorts are not allowed. *Bagasse*, a by-product of sugar production, fuels the "iron dinosaurs." The **Balay Negrenses Museum** is on Cinco de Noviembre St. near the corner of McKinley St. Attendants claim French sugar baron Yves Leopold Gaston built the house in 1898 from a single tree trunk. (☎495 4855. Open Tu-Su 10am-6pm. P15, students P5.) On the National Rd. two blocks beyond the plaza on the right is the **Bernardino-Ysabel Jalandoni Ancestral House,** Silay's other museum, which documents the lifestyle of a leading sugar baron and his family. (Open Tu-Su 8am-noon, 1-5pm.) The **Tourism and Cultural Arts Office,** in the City Hall opposite the plaza, can point out ancestral homes and sights and give you the low-down on the **Kansilay Festival** held November 5-13. (☎495 5145. Open M-F 8am-noon and 1-5pm.) Don't miss the **El Ideal Bakery** on the corner of National Rd. and Zulueta St. near the plaza. El Ideal satiates Silay's sweet tooth with local treats like *lumpia ubod* (fresh spring rolls) and *piaya* (sesame cakes).

The **Victorias Milling Company, Inc. (Vicmico)** is the largest sugar mill in Asia. It is accessible from the main road in Victorias by jeepney. Grab the one marked "VMC" at the corner of Osmeña and Jover St. (10min., every 30min. 5:30am-8:30pm, P3). Ask to be let off at the **Vicmico Public Relations Office** on Ossorio Rd. below the Personnel Building. Tours can be arranged at the factory and the Church of St. Joseph the Worker, but call ahead. (☎0912 503 1510. Open Tu-F 9-11:30am and 2-4pm. Tours 30-40min.; M-F 9am and 2pm; P15, students P10.) Vicmico's real attraction is the **Church of St. Joseph the Worker** and its mural, known as the "Angry Christ," where Jesus sits in front of the hands of God, straddling a serpent-spewing skull. No mini-skirts, shorts, or sleeveless shirts are allowed.

DUMAGUETE ☎35

The City of Gentle People guards its peace carefully. Dumaguete doubles as the capital of Negros Oriental and as a haven from turbulent Mindanao to the south and the alleged witchcraft of nearby Siquijor Island. It is a convenient springboard for exploring Siquijor or lovely Apo Island, which shelters some of the finest diving in the country while also being one of the most pleasant cities of the archipelago. The energy of its student population combat the relaxed atmosphere of its beautiful waterfront in a city that has a little bit of it all.

TRANSPORTATION

Flights: To get to the **airport,** take Dumaguete North Rd. off Silliman Ave. **Air Philippines** is at the airport (☎225 4266) and the ticket outlet is on Katada St. (☎255 034). Open

M-F 9am-noon and 1-3pm. Flies daily to **Manila** (7:50am and 4:30pm, P2353). **Cebu Pacific** (☎225 6850) flies daily to **Manila** (3:20pm, P2354); purchase tickets at the airport or at a travel agent in town.

Buses: Dumaguete Ceres Terminal is in the south of the city across the river on Calindagan South Rd. Follow Perdices St. (tricycle P2.50). Buses to: **Bacolod** via **Cadiz** (6hr., P110); **Kaban Kalan** (5hr., every hr. 4am-10pm, P112); **San Carlos** (7hr., every hr. 3am-11pm, P130). Buses going north stop at **Ceres Sub Terminal Northbound** near the ferry pier. Walking away from the pier, take a right up Flores St. Terminal; it is 5min. up on the right. Locals call the area **"Looc." Royal Express Bus Terminal** (☎225 2234) sends buses to **Bacolod** (5hr., 6am and 2pm, P164) via **Mabinay** (2hr., P70).

Ferries: The **pier** is at the north end of Rizal Ave. Shipping companies send representatives to pier area 1hr. before departure. There is a P10 terminal fee for all ferries. 15% student discount. **Supercat** sends ferries to **Cebu** (2¼hr., 4:15pm, P415) via **Tagbilaran** (P350). Purchase tickets at the **Aboitiz Express** office on Ma. Cristina St. behind the Metrobank branch. Open M-Sa 8am-noon and 1-5pm. The branch office (☎225 5799) is near the pier opposite Ceres Sub Terminal in Looc. **Delta Fast Ferries** (☎225 6358, ticket outlet ☎225 3881) whisks passengers to: **Cebu City** via **Oslob** (2½hr.; 7:45am, 11:30am; P240) and **Larena** on **Siquijar** (45min.; 6, 9:15am, 1:30, 4:30pm; P110). Ticket outlet is in the **Gold Label Bakeshoppe** on Perdices St. Open M-Sa 9am-noon and 1-7pm. Ferries leave from Tampi, several kilometers north of Dumaguete, for the quick hop to **Bato** on Cebu, a short bus ride from **Moalboal** (45min., leaves when full, P27). **WG&A** sends ferries to **Cagayan de Oro** on **Mindanao** (6hr., F 6am, P430) and **Manila** (25hr.; W 4pm, Sa 9am; P1185). WG&A tickets can be purchased at Supercat offices. **Negros Navigation** cruises to **Manila** (24hr., Tu 1pm, P1110).

Local Transportation: Tricycles P5.

Rentals: Boni Rent-a-Car (☎225 2261), on corner of San Jose and Real St., rents cars with drivers. Open daily 7:30am-8pm. P200 per hr. **Manna Motorbike Rentals,** 36 San Juan St. (☎225 4505). Open 24hr. Scooters P500 per day.

ORIENTATION AND PRACTICAL INFORMATION

Downtown is easily navigable by foot. **Rizal Ave.** borders the coast connecting the ferry pier in the north with roads heading inland. Silliman University sprawls north of nearby **Silliman Ave.,** which runs west from the shore. Originating at Silliman Ave., **Perdices St.** bisects the city, heads south, crosses the **Banica River,** and ends at the main bus terminals. **Dr. V. Locsin St.** intersects Perdices midway through downtown; the market, park, and post office are a few blocks south.

Tourist Office: ☎225 0549. In the city hall complex near the corner of Colon and Santa Catalina St. Open M-F 8am-noon and 1-5pm.

Budget Travel: Maganda Travel and Tours (☎225 8256). On the corner of Dr. V. Locsin and Santa Catalina St. Visa extension service, airline ticketing, and tour packages. P200 service charge over standard fares. Open M-Sa 9am-6pm.

Immigration Office: 38 Dr. V. Locsin St., door 9, Lu Pega Bldg. (☎225 4401). Passport and visa extensions, and airline tickets. Open M-F 8am-noon and 1-5pm.

Currency Exchange: PCI Bank (☎225 4787). On the corner of Perdices and Legaspi St. Cashes traveler's checks. **24hr. ATM** (Cirrus/MC). Open M-F 9am-3pm.

English-Language Bookstore: The Old San Francisco Bookstore (☎225 8230), on Real St. opposite the provincial capital. Used books, paperbacks P50-60. Open M-Sa 9:30am-7:30pm.

Emergency: ☎111 or 166. **Fire:** ☎113.

Police: Philippine National Police (☎225 1766). At corner of Cervantes and Locsin St.

Pharmacy: Mercury Drug (☎225 0425). On Colon St. opposite the fish market. The largest of many. Open daily 6am-10pm. MC/V.

Hospitals: Holy Child Hospital (☎225 0247). On Legaspi St.

Telephones: RCPI (☎225 1733). At the corner of San Jose and Santa Catalina St. Open M-F 8am-8pm, Sa 9am-6pm.

Internet Access: Scooby's (☎425 4452). On the corner of Perdices and Silliman Ave., upstairs from the fast-food joint. 1hr. P15. Open daily 8am-midnight.

Post Offices: GPO (☎255 5877). At the corner of Santa Catalina and Pedro Teves St. *Poste Restante*. Open M-F 8am-noon and 1-5pm. **Postal code:** 6200.

ACCOMMODATIONS AND FOOD

Budget accommodations are within walking distance of the market and town plaza. Tricycle drivers make the trip with baggage from the ferry pier (P10-20).

Home Quest Lodge (☎225 3327). On Silliman Ave. near the Perdices St. intersection, on the 2nd fl. Complimentary coffee 6-8am. Cable TV in lobby. Singles P177, with A/C P262; doubles with shared common room P283, with A/C P395-437.

Theresa's Lodge (☎225 4827). On San Juan St. between the intersections with Perdices and Maria Cristina St. Minimalist rooms with shared common room, fan, and ripped screens. Singles P140; doubles P200; triples P270.

Vintage Inn (☎225 1076). On Legaspi St. opposite the public market, near the Real St. intersection. Clean rooms in a large airy building. Restaurant open daily 7am-10pm. Singles P220, with A/C P330; doubles P330/495.

Silliman University Alumni Hall Dormitory (☎/fax 225 4323). Walk north along Perdices St. which becomes campus drive; turn right at the first gate. Spacious A/C rooms in the university. Dine at the University cafeteria next door. Doubles P400; quads P500.

Barbecue chicken reigns supreme in Dumaguete. There are several BBQ hotspots on Silliman Ave., and smaller evening operations set up along Rizal Ave. The **Silliman Avenue Cafe** opposite the university is a student hangout and serves tasty *panini* and coffee concoctions (P30-70). Along Rizal, **Chin Loong,** at the corner of San Jose St., serves heaping portions of Chinese and Filipino favorites (P40-125).

SIGHTS AND ENTERTAINMENT

Dumaguete's cleanliness makes strolls through town and seaside **Rizal Blvd.** a genuine pleasure. A block inland, **Quezon Park** is the favorite of younger Negrenses; the more mature venture to the spotless market. In the distance rises Mt. Talinas, romantically known as the Horns of Negros. **Silliman University** was the first Protestant university in the Philippines. The university's museums of ethnology and anthropology are on the corner of Silliman Ave. and Perdices St.

All nightlife inquirers will be pointed to the **Why Not Complex** (☎225 4488) on Rizal Ave., which has an Internet cafe (24hr., 1hr. P35), a disco with live music (open daily 9pm-2:30am; P50 cover), and a karaoke lounge with billiards (open daily 8pm-2am). The **Sandurot Festival,** in the third week of November, celebrates multiculturalism. After ceremonial gift giving, various costumed Negrenses parade and celebrate their *sandurot* (friendship).

NEAR DUMAGUETE

APO ISLAND

Together with Moalboal (Cebu) and Panglao Island (Bohol), Apo Island completes the trinity of world-class diving spots in the Visayas. With its ultra-relaxed environment, seclusion, and fine accommodations it may be the finest dive destination in the Philippines. A marine sanctuary has been established around the island to preserve this underwater world. Secluded beaches dot the island coast, and cliffs poke through the green jungle. Fishermen inhabit a small village and tend a lighthouse with over 300 steps leading down to the water. The reefs around Coconut Point are suitable for all levels, while the crystal-clear waters of the sanctuary give snorkelers a view of this underwater community. Barracuda swim at **Coconut Point,** a site perfect for drift diving.

To get to Apo take a **jeepney** from the market in Dumaguete bound for Danin or Zamboangita; ask to be let off in **Malatapay** (1¼hr., P12). From Malatapay pumpboats make the 20min. run to Apo (P100). The two accommodations on Apo can pick you up in Malatapay by prior arrangement. From Apo, you can charter a **pumpboat** to take you to **Siquijor** (P2500-3000).

Apo is finding its way onto backpacker radar and is well within a budget traveller's grasp (P20 landing fee on the island). At **Liberty's,** bamboo rooms let in onshore breezes, and Paul, the English owner, guides divers to the Marine Sanctuary. (☎424 0888; reservations apo@filnet.com. Dive with equipment US$23; PADI open-water certification US$295; advanced open-water US$245; Discover Scuba US$45. Restaurant open daily 6am-9pm. 5-bed dorms P200 per person; doubles P550-800.) Next door, **Apo Island Beach Resort** is in a secluded cove on a great beach. (☎369 949 01626. Dorms P250; hillside huts P700, beachside P800, extra person P200. Restaurant open daily 6am-10pm. 1 dive US$25 with equipment, 2 dives US$48.) Several local families rent cottages for P100-200 per night; make inquiries in the village.

BAIS AND SIQUIJOR

Bais, 40km north of Dumaguete, is named for a species of eel, though most people slither to Bais to see whales and dolphins in the Tanon Strait between Cebu and Negros. The smallest province in the Philippines, Siquijor sits 20km off of the southeast tip of Negros Oriental, casting its own spell with its beaches, mountains, and rice fields. A fire road encircles the island, making it an excellent place to explore by motorbike, which can be rented at most accommodations. Dubbed "Isla del Fuego" ("Island of Fire") by Spaniards who saw strange lights in the mountains, Siquijor's name is synonymous with the black-magic shenanigans of *aswang,* witches who transform into pigs. Although mysticism is not immediately visible, healers dwell in the interior mountains. Juan Bance, a famous witch-healer, sells amulets and massage oil in San Antonio, south of Siquijor City.

Contact travel agencies in Dumaguete for information on Bais and Siquijor. Buses from the Ceres Terminal headed for **Cadiz** go via Bais (1½hr., every hr. 4am-10pm, P19). A handful of pricey accommodations are on the island. **Casa de la Playa,** 7km from Larena on Sandugan Beach, is a quiet retreat to calm the body and soul. The restaurant specializes in exotic vegetarian fare. (☎035 397 2291. Beachside houses with kitchen and fridge P600; hill top cottages P500.) **Charisma,** run by an Aussie expat, is a small resort with personalized service. (Motorbike rental P350-500 per day. Snorkeling P50 per day. Rooms with fan P400-500, with A/C P600-700.) Next to Casa de la Playa, **Kiwi Dive Resort** is the only permanent dive shop. (1 dive US$20; PADI open-water courses US$300; advanced open water US$250. Cottages P350-490.) Siquijor's diving is unspectacular; most expeditions head to nearby Apo.

PANAY

A Goliath of an island, Panay has never matched the quick-footed and savvy tourist tendencies of its David—little Boracay off its northwest tip. The four provinces of Capiz, Iloilo, Antique, and Aklan carve up the mainland, but for pilgrims eager to reach Boracay, there are simply four provinces too many. Tourism officials are developing Panay's potential attractions, such as trekking in the mountains of Antique and diving off the southern coast. For now, though, the main attraction remains Kalibo's Atiatihan festival.

THE VIEW FROM ABOVE

Main cities: Iloilo in the south and Kalibo in the north.
Nearby islands: North of Panay, Boracay Island rivals some of the world's most beautiful tropical havens.
Tasty mangoes: Guimaras Island, an easy daytrip from Ioloilo, is famous for its nice mangoes and beaches.

ILOILO ☎33

A century ago, Iloilo (pronounced "Eelo-Eelo") was the world's gateway to the sugar of Negros; today it is the most lively of the stopovers on Panay for travelers on their way to Boracay. The Iloilo and Batiano rivers carve a distinct facial feature resulting in the name "Ilong-ilong," meaning "noselike," but travelers en route to Boracay would be hard-pressed to sniff out much of interest. More patient folks should consider making the short hop to Guimaras, a rather undeveloped island which rewards visitors with idyllic beaches and the world's sweetest mangos.

TRANSPORTATION

Flights: Iloilo's **airport** is northwest of the city in Mandurriao. Take a "Mandurriao Iloilo" jeepney heading west on Gen. Luna (20-25min., P3); a pedicab goes the rest of the way (3min., P3). **PAL** (☎320 3030) has flights to: **Cebu** (5 per week, P1995); **Manila** (4 per day, P2785); **Puerta Princesa** (M, F; P2328). **Air Philippines** (☎320 8048) has flights to **Manila** (3 per day, P2243). **Cebu Pacific** (airport ☎320 6889) has flights to: **Cebu** (daily, P1799); **Davao** (daily, P3295); **Manila** (3 per day, P2498). All have branch offices open daily 9:30am-6pm in Atrium Mall at the Gen. Luna-Bonifacio intersection. Terminal fee P45.

Buses: Buses from 2 stations connect Iloilo with towns in the rest of Panay. **Ceres Bus Terminal** (☎337 0456) on Tanza St. near Ledesma St. intersection. 15% student discount. To: **Caticlan,** the gateway to **Boracay** (6hr., 6 per day, P130); **Kalibo** (3¾hr., every 30min. 3am-3:15pm, P112); **Roxas** (3hr., every 30min. 4:15am-5:30pm, P63). Buses to **Antique** leave from the **R. M. Panay Transport** office (☎336 8341) on Gen. Luna opposite the John B. Lacson Colleges Foundation.

Ferries: Fast ferries dock on the river after the 1st bend, near City Hall. **SeaAngels** (☎336 1316) motors speedily to **Bacolod** (1hr.; 8 per day 6am-5pm; P210, 15% student discount). From Arrastre Pier by Fort San Pedro, **Negros Navigation** (☎336 2396) serves: **Cagayan d'Oro** (13hr., Sa, P1190); **Manila** (20hr., 5 per week, P1245); **Puerta Princesa** on Palawan (18hr., W 3pm, P980); **Zamboanga** (14hr., Tu, P695.) Some times vary, so call ahead. Negros Navigation (☎336 8910) also has an outlet on 2nd fl., Atrium Mall. Open daily 8am-6pm. **WG&A** (☎336 2776), in Atrium Mall, has similar routes. Outriggers to **Buenavista** and **Jordan** on Guimaras island (15min., departs when full 6am-6pm, P7.50) leave from the pier to the right of the large ferries.

Local Transportation: Jeepney cost P4 to most destinations. Southbound jeepney gather at the corner of de Leon and Fuentes St. **A/C taxis** P25 plus P2 increments. **Tricycles** P5-10.

ORIENTATION AND PRACTICAL INFORMATION

The largest city on Panay, Iloilo (pop. 350,000) sits on the southeastern coast across the straits from Bacolod on Negros. Iloilo covers five subdivisions and is trisected by the Iloilo and Batiano river system. The **provincial capitol** sits on the northern edge at the intersection of **Gen. Luna St.** and **Bonifacio Dr.,** which leads north across the river into **La Paz** and **Jaro.** Separated by a tributary, **Mandurriao** lies west of Jaro and is home to the **airport.** The main river separates **Molo,** west of the city and south of Mandurriao. Downtown revolves around the Gen. Luna St.-Bonifacio St. intersection, site of the **Atrium Mall.** From here, **jeepney** head to the five subdivisions.

Tourist Office: ☎337 5411; on Bonifacio Dr., 2min. north of the capitol by the pedestrian bridge. Helpful staff. Maps. Open M-F 8am-5:30pm.

Budget Travel: Panay Island Holidays, (☎336 8069). At the Casa Plaza Building. Offers city and Guimaras Island tours and Boracay packages. Open M-Sa 8:30am-5pm.

Immigration Office: Iloilo's Bureau of Immigration (☎509 9665). 2nd fl., old Customs House on Aduana St. Near intersection of J.M. Basa St. and Plaza Libertad. Extensions on visas arranged through Manila. Open M-F 8am-4:30pm.

Bank: Philippine National Bank, (☎337 2476), on the corner of Gen. Luna and Valeria St. **24hr. ATM** (MC/V). Open M-F 9am-4pm.

Emergency: ☎166.

Police: ☎337 9022. On Gen. Luna St. west of the Provincial Capitol building.

Hospital: St. Paul's Hospital, (☎337 2741). A 5min. walk from the Provincial Capitol building down Gen. Luna St. on the right.

Pharmacy: Mercury Drug (☎335 0037), on Iznart St. near J.M. Basa St. **Open 24 hr.**

Telephones: RCPI (☎336 2225), at the corner of Iznart and Yulo St. Open M-F 7am-7pm, Sa 8am-5pm, Su 9am-2pm.

Internet Access: Cyberworld, on Gen. Luna opposite the Provincial Capitol. P25 per hr. Open daily 9am-11pm.

Post Office: ☎337 3880. In the old Customs House on Aduana St. *Poste Restante.* Open M-F 8am-noon and 1-5pm, Sa 9-11am. **Postal code:** 5000.

ACCOMMODATIONS

Family Pension House (☎335 0070). On Gen. Luna St. at the Mabini intersection. The best budget option in an otherwise grim town. Treehouse restaurant and pool table (P10). Singles P250; doubles P325, with A/C P525.

Eros Travellers Pensione (☎337 1359). On Gen. Luna St. opposite St. Paul's Hospital. Set back from the street. Sterile and the cheapest A/C in town. Singles P240-335; doubles P305-405; extra person P80.

River Queen (☎335 0176). On Bonifacio Dr. 50m past the Provincial Capitol on the left. Iloilo's oldest hotel; recently renovated, it's quite a good deal (grotty common rooms aside). Singles P295, with A/C P510; doubles P320/580.

Castle Hotel (☎338 1022). On Bonifacio Dr., just beyond the museum. Friendly place housed in a rambling 19th-century mansion. All rooms with A/C and TV. Singles P503, doubles P592.

FOOD

Iloilo prepares specialty dishes disguised with innocuous names. *Lapaz batchoy* mixes liver, beef, and pork with noodles. *Mud soup* contains hearty amounts of pigs' intestines soaked in blood. "Soup #5" is made from a bull's penis and testicles. Food stalls along Valeria and Gen. Luna St. offer cheap, late-night eats. For finer dining, try the **Marina,** on Iloilo Diversion Rd. in Mandurriao, in an airy *nipa* pavilion on the river. (Delicious *kinican* P85; *adobo* P140; *lechon* P165. Open daily 9am-1am.) **Nena's Manokan,** on Gen. Luna St. before the Diversion Rd. intersection, serves first-rate grilled chicken (with rice P45) on balconies perched over the river. (Open daily 11am-11pm.) **Sisa's Bar and Cafe,** adjacent to the Family Home Pensione, serves excellent American-style bar food. (Open daily 4pm-1:30am.)

SIGHTS AND ENTERTAINMENT

The **Museo Iloilo,** behind the capitol on Bonifacio Dr., records the history and traditions of the Western Visayas (Panay and Negros) with local art and life-size dioramas. (☎729 86. Open M-Sa 9am-5pm. P15, students P3.)

The **Dinagyang Festival,** held on the fourth weekend of January, pays tribute in the form of colorful street dancing to the Santo Niño (Christ Child) and the heritage of tribes. The southwest coast of Panay offers Spanish churches, including **Molo** and **San Joaquin. Miag-ao,** a church built of coral with a facade ornamented by palm trees and bananas, is a rare vernacular baroque. (Jeepney to Miag-ao leave from the intersection of Gen. Luna St. and Bonifacio Drive; P15).

Iloilo's student population ensures that there are plenty of nightlife options around town. For good live music, a friendly, raucous crowd, and San Miguel's (P30), try the military-themed **Barracks,** on Iloilo Diversion Rd. past the S. M. City mall. (Open M-Sa 6pm-1am. No cover. Taxi P40.) **Vega,** off Gen. Luna St., is a chic restaurant/disco, which attracts a hipper-than-thou scene. (Open M-Sa 11am-4am. Cover P100, includes one drink.) There are several bars and a disco in the **Serabia Hotel Complex** on Gen. Luna St. **Sisa's Cafe and Bar** (see **Food,** above) is a great place to chill out and shoot some pool over a few beers.

DAYTRIP FROM ILOILO

GUIMARAS ISLAND

15min. by pumpboat from Iloilo harbor (every hr. 5am-5:30pm, P5).

Guimaras is famous throughout the archipelago for its mangoes, said to be the country's tastiest. The island is home to a Trappist monastery whose monks produce candies and preserves from local produce. Other attractions include the **Macopo Falls** and, of course, the **Oro Verde Mango Plantation.** There are several beach resorts on **Alubihod Beach** in Nueva Valencia offering picnicking facilities as well as lodging (P300-800). Local boat owners can be hired to take you to the many outlying islands. On an idyllic islet off Lawi, the **Baras Beach Resort** offers its guests an array of aquatic activities, including sailing, snorkeling, and windsurfing. (☎0917 9387159. Cottages P750-900, ask for Mike or Baby to arrange transportation to the island.) There is a very helpful **tourist information kiosk** on the pier in Jordan, the provincial capital. (Open daily 9am-6pm.) All of Guimaras' sights can be seen in a daytrip from Iloilo (tricycles can be hired for P200-400) or by using one of Nueva Valencia's resorts as a base. Ask at the tourist kiosk about the International Mountain Biking Tournament, held every year in March.

KALIBO ☎36

During the third week in January, the capital city of Aklan explodes in merriment that even Boracay can't rival. Celebrating the original inhabitants of Panay island, the *Atis*, revelers smear their faces with black soot and dance about the streets in the *Ati-atihan* (meaning "to make like the Atis") Festival. When the last native headdress is laid to rest, Kalibo and its airport resume their appointed duty as a way station on the well-beaten path to Caticlan and Boracay.

TRANSPORTATION

Flights: Kalibo's **airport** is the main transportation hub for traffic to Boracay. **PAL** (☎262 3263) and **Air Philippines** (☎262 4444) both fly to **Manila** (P2700). **Cebu Pacific** (☎262 5409) serves: **Cebu** (T, F, Su; P1799); **Davao** (T, F, Su; P3295); **Manila** (P2700). PAL's office is in the terminal; the other 2 are across the street. From the airport parking lot, **Southwest Tours** (☎268 5100) runs buses to **Caticlan** via **Boracay** (round-trip 3hr., P250). The cheapest option from the airport to Boracay includes a tricycle to town (P20), a jeepney to Caticlan jetty (P45), and then a pumpboat to Boracay itself (P17.50).

Buses: Ceres Bus Terminal has buses to **Iloilo** (4hr., every 30-60min. 2:30am-3:30pm, P112). **Paradise Tours** offers A/C vans to **Caticlan** (1hr., P100) and **Iloilo** (3hr., 7am-5pm, P100). **Delmabel** heads to **Roxas** (2hr., every hr. 4:30am-2:30pm, P50). Buses and jeepney to Caticlan also depart from the corner of Roxas Ave. and Barrios St., and from the corner of Roxas and Pastrana Ave. when full (1½hr., P45).

Ferries: Ferry service is inconvenient. First take a jeepney from Gonzales St. market to **Dumaguit** (30-45min., roughly every 30min., P12). From Dumaguit, take an outrigger to **Batan** (5min., every 30min. 6am-5:30pm, P7). Last jeepney from Dumaguit to Kalibo 4pm. **Negros Navigation** (☎262 4943) has service to **Manila** (16hr.; Th, Sa; economy P700). Call the office for exact times. Open M-F 8am-noon and 1-4pm, Sa 8am-noon. **WG&A's office** (☎268 4391) is on C. Laserna St. near the market. A more convenient option if you're going to be on Boracay is to take an **MBRS Lines** ferry from Caticlan to Manila (W, F, Su; P750). Book tickets at a travel agency on the island.

ORIENTATION AND PRACTICAL INFORMATION

Kalibo lies along Panay's north highway a few kilometers from the sea at the confluence of the Sooc and Aklan Rivers. **Roxas Ave.** links the city center with the Aklan Bridge. In a skewed grid south of Roxas, **Burgos St., Archbishop Reyes St.,** and **XIX Martyrs St.** link the main city center with Pastrana Park. Each street terminates at **Mabini St.,** which leads from Roxas Ave. to **Maagma Ave.** Maagma Ave. eventually becomes **Quezon Ave.** heading southeast to Kalibo Airport.

Travel Agencies: Southwest Tours (☎268 5100) offers connecting bus and boat transfers to and from **Caticlan** and from Kalibo airport to **Boracay** (1½hr., P175). Open M-F 8am-noon and 1:30-5pm, Sa 8am-noon.

Banks: BPI (☎262 3504). On Martelino St. at the corner of XIX Martyrs St. Cashes AmEx Traveler's Cheques. **24hr. ATM.** Open M-F 9am-3pm.

English-Language Bookstore: Thumbelina (☎262 4017). Next to the police station on XIX Martyrs St. New and used books. Open M-Sa 8am-5:30pm.

Emergency: ☎166. **Hospital:** ☎141 or 16900.

Police: On XIX Martyrs St. in city center.

Hospital: Kalibo Provincial Hospital (☎268 4565). On Mabini St.

Telephone: Bayantel (☎268-4006). At the corner of Barrios and Burgos St. Fax and calling cards. Open M-F 7am-7pm, Sa-Su 7am-5pm.

Internet: Aero Comm (☎262 1232). In the Royal Supermart on Roxas Ave. P50 per hr.

Post Office: GPO (☎262 3215). In the capitol (P5-10 tricycle ride). *Poste Restante.* Open M-F 8am-noon and 1-5pm. **Postal code:** 5600.

ACCOMMODATIONS AND FOOD

Rooms are easy to find, except during the Ati-atihan Festival in January, when you should make reservations weeks ahead. Prices launch into the stratosphere.

Garcia Legaspi Mansion, 159 Roxas Ave. 4th fl. (☎262 5800). Near the corner with Barrios St. Rooms vary from comfortable to luxurious. Helpful owner runs Kalibo Tourist Association. Singles P300, with common room P450; doubles with A/C and bath P500-800.

Gervy's (☎262 4190). On Pastrad St. near XIX Martyrs. Dirt cheap. Doubles P125.

Casa Felicidad, on Archbishop Reyes St. near plaza. On the 3rd fl. of the Aklan Academy High School. Singles with fan P300; doubles P400, with A/C P600.

Glowmoon Hotel (☎262 3073). On Martelino St. near the plaza. Simple fan rooms with common room P250, ritzier A/C rooms P650.

Cheap eats abound in Kalibo. Basic eateries and Filipino fast food joints encircle the plaza. **Kalibo Peking House,** on the corner of XIX Martyrs and Barrio St., serves cheap "Chinoy" meals (P70). **Kusina sa Kalibo** (☎262 3466) on D. Maagma St. is a pleasant beer garden serving favorites like ox tongue soup for P100 (tricycle P4).

BORACAY ISLAND ☎36

Filipinos all over the archipelago will ask if you've been to Boracay; if you haven't, they'll emphatically encourage a visit. Tempting postcards display the 4km White Beach, arguably the softest, most beautiful sand in the country. Boracay has fast become a flagship for the tourism industry as resorts, restaurants, and shops line up in dense rows. For tropical seclusion, look elsewhere; Boracay's raucous nightlife now approximates the hedonistic scene found on Ko Samui or Ko Phangan in Thailand. But with its *nipa* cottage rentals, the island remains as budget-friendly as it was in the 70s, when dinner meant bartering with fishermen.

TRANSPORTATION

Flights: Most tourists fly to **Kalibo,** the capital of Aklan, and then take a van bus to the small town of **Caticlan,** where outriggers run to Boracay. Vans to Kalibo's airport vary by season (1½hr., 3-4 per day in low season, P100). **Southwest** (☎288 3010), south of the boat station on Boracay, runs a bus to the airport (1½hr., departs 4hr. before flight departure, P200). Several airlines link Manila with Caticlan's small airport, a 15min walk from the ferry pier (P20-30 by tricycle). The tourist center books plane tickets. **Asian Spirit** (☎288 3465) flies from Caticlan to **Manila** (6-7 flights per day, P2250). **Seair** (☎288 7163) flies from Caticlan to **Busuanga** on Palawan (F, Su; P2500); **Cebu** (daily except W, P1990); and **Manila** (daily, P2200). **Air Philippines** (☎288 3999) flies to **Manila** (10:30am and 3:15pm, P1798). **PAL** (☎288 3502) flies to **Manila** (3 per day, P1899).

Ferries: Outriggers link Caticlan with three boat stations on White Beach and stop at the south station first (30min., every 15min. 6am-5pm, P19.50). In wavy conditions, the ferries land on the southeast tip of the island; from there, it's a P20 tricycle to White Beach. Boats also run to: **Carabao,** north of Boracay (1hr., 3 per day, P20); **Roxas,** on Mindoro (6hr.; M, Th 10am; P150); **Santa Fe,** on Romblon (2hr., 9am, P100); **Tablas** (2hr., P100). Check at the tourist office on the Caticlan pier for the latest schedules and prices. **MBRS Lines** operates a convenient ferry service to Manila (W, F, Su; P750).

Buses: Bus and van connections between Kalibo and Caticlan are frequent. **GM Liner** sends buses to **Iloilo** (6hr., 7:30 and 9:30am, P160). **Jeepney** (P45) and buses (P45) run to **Kalibo,** but most don't go to the airport (1½hr., 6am-4:30pm, P30).

Tricycles and Pedicabs: Tricycles sputter up and down the jeepney-free main road. Daytime rides P7 per person, at night P12. **Pedicabs** along White Beach P20-30.

Rentals: Mopeds can be rented everywhere. Bargain hard (half-day P600). **Mountain bike** rentals run about P50 per hr.

ORIENTATION AND PRACTICAL INFORMATION

Boracay is north of Panay between the Sulu and Sibuyan Seas. The 4km **White Beach** stretches along its west coast. Boracay's main road bisects the island vertically. **Barangay Yapak,** topped by Puka Beach, occupies the north. White Beach, in **Barangay Balabag,** has three boat stations. Accommodations are everywhere, but the southernmost **Boat Station 3** has the most shops and services. **Boat Station 2** has many restaurants and bars. **Boat Station 1** is bigger and quieter. Shady forests and rocky coves cover **Barangay Manok-Manok** in the south.

Tourist Office: DOT office (☎/fax 288 3689), is a *nipa* cottage in the Mall d' Boracay near Boat Station 2. Helpful staff. Immigration officer extends visas W 9am-3pm. Open M-F 8am-noon and 1-5pm. **Tourist Center** centralizes many helpful resources: **telecommunications services** (open daily 9am-9pm, no calling card access); **foreign exchange;** safety deposit (P100 per month); Activities desk (open daily 9:30am-7pm). Helpful staff. (☎288 3704. Center open 9am-6pm.)

Budget Travel: Tourist Center. Ticketing, visa extension services, and package tours. MC/V. Open M-F 9am-6pm, Sa 9am-noon. **Tribal Adventures** (☎288 3207; www.tribal-adventures.com). At Sand Castle Resort south of Boat Station 1. Mountain biking, kayaking, and windsurfing. Open daily 7:30am-10pm.

Currency Exchange/Banks: Allied Bank (☎288 3048), on the main road between Boat Station 2 and 3. Open M-F 9am-4pm. Branches lie beside Boat Stations 1 and 3.

Luggage Storage: DOT office (see above) will guard valuables while you select a room.

Market: Talipapa Market, north of Boat Station 3.

Emergency: Police ☎166. **Medical** ☎141.

Police: Philippine National Police (☎288 3066). Between Boat Stations 2 and 3.

Medical Services: Boracay Island Emergency Hospital (☎141). On the main road; take the road next to Boracay Regency Hotel near Boat Station 2, then turn left at the

PHILIPPINES

main road. **Boracay Medical Clinic** (☎288 3147), is on the main road in Balabag. **Open 24hr.**

Telephones: Cruztelco phone booth near Lapu-Lapu Divers, north of Boat Station 2. **Pantelco,** north of Boat Station 2 opposite Mango Ray's. **RCPI-Bayantel,** (☎/fax 288 3012). At Oro Beach Resort, Boat Station 3. Open M-Th 8am-8pm, F-Su 8am-noon and 1-5pm. P33 charge for calling cards.

Internet Access: Tourist Center, blazing connections P60 per hr.

Post Office: In Balahag north of Boat Station 1 on the main road. Open M-F 8am-noon and 1-4:30pm. *Poste Restante.* **Tourist Center** (see above) has a postal center (letters only) with *Poste Restante,* which they deliver from Manila every 2 days. P5 service charge per letter. Address: "PO Box 552, Manila 1099, Philippines." Open daily in high season 9am-8pm; in low season 9am-6pm.

ACCOMMODATIONS

Heading north toward Boat Station 1, the sand gets finer, and (in general) prices rise. The coast guard banned cottages on the beach, so all are set beyond the trees. Prices here reflect those in high/low season. Always bargain and ask for discounts for extended stays.

Michelle's Bungalows (☎288 3086). A short walk north of Boat Station 3. Between Beach Life Diving and La Isla Resort; take a right and head 35m from beach. Location yields lower prices and a safe, comfy feel. Doubles P500-600.

Trafalgar Garden Lodge (☎288 3711). From Boat Station 3, head north, turning right into the market at Beach Life. Trafalgar is 200m down on the left. Operated by a friendly British-Filipino couple, Trafalgar is one of the last truly budget accommodations on the island. Singles P200-600, doubles P250-700.

Nigi Nigi Nu Noos 'e' Nu Nu Noos (☎288 3101). Between Tourist Center and Boat Station 2. Polynesian pagodas in a tropical garden. Free 20min. email per day. Cashes travelers' checks. Huts with fan P2000-3000, with A/C P2500-3500. MC/V.

Bans Beach Resort (☎288 3837). Near Boat Station 1. Has airy, comfortable *nipas* in a quiet garden. Doubles P800/P500.

Fiesta Cottages (☎288 3818). South of Boat Station 1 near Fisheye Divers. Friendly Filipina owner oversees *nipas* with hammocks. 3 huts face the beach. Small library. Motorboat and bike rentals P150. Cottages with fan and common room P600/400, with A/C P2000/1500.

Saigon Beach Resort (☎/fax 288 3203). Near the path leading to Talipapa Market, north of Boat Station 3. Newer *nipas* with linoleum floors only a short stroll to the beach. Safety deposit free for guests. Doubles P1000/P700.

Welcome Inn (☎367 9603). In the market north of Boat Station 3, near Trafalgar Garden. Airy bungalows in a tropical oasis setting P500.

Villa de Oro (☎288 5466). Simple *nipas* south of Boat Station 2. Good value in low season. Restaurant with bar. Open daily 6am-noon. Huts P1000/P400; 10% discount for Hostelling International members.

FOOD

Boracay's restaurants offer travelers a break from blandness. International cuisine dots White Beach and a few months' stay would barely exhaust the options.

Shennan Restaurant, next to Lapu-Lapu Divers. Superb inexpensive 3-course dinner combo P115. Excellent pineapple shake P45. Open daily 7am-10pm.

Nigi Nigi Nu Noos 'e' Nu Nu Noos (see **Accommodations,** above). Pry the name's hidden meaning out of the owners. Unforgettable seafood cuisine P190-195. Delectable set meal P210. Happy Hour 5-7pm. Jazz and blues Th and F. Open daily 6:30am-11pm. AmEx/V.

Mango Ray, north of Boat Station 2. Savory BBQ and international grub. 4-course meal P230. "Mango Ray Baby" mixes *kalamansi,* mango, and rum P55. Open 8am-11pm.

Gorios, south of Boat Station 1, makes tasty crepes (P40-95). Open 6:30am-11pm.

Sea Lovers, north of Boat Station 2. Reasonable prices and snappy service. Open 24hr.

SIGHTS AND ACTIVITIES

Sunset on White Beach is Boracay's premier sight. The beach is uniform, except for **Willy's Rock,** north of Boat Station 1. The north is often marvelously neglected. **Puka Beach** is isolated on the northern shore (tricycle from White Beach 30min., P30). Snorkeling tubes crisscross the water off **Ilig-Iligan Beach** to the northeast. From the beach, the **Bat Cave** is easily reached (P50). The **windsurfing beach** sits a short walk across the narrowest point of the island from White Beach. Between White Beach and the south tip, the **Dead Forest Preserve,** really just a mosquito preserve, hardly merits attention (P20). More worthy are trails through the **southern rainforest** in *barangay* Manok-Manok.

Watersports equipment can be rented at **Scuba World,** south of Boat Station 1. (☎288 3310. Windsurfing gear P300 per hr., with instruction P500. Kayaks are P150-300 for the first hr., each additional hr. P75-150. Wakeboarding P650 per 30min. Open daily 8am-6pm.) The **Tourist Center** (see **Practical Information,** above) rents water-skiing equipment (P650 per 15min.), wakeboarding (P1100 per 30min.), and speedboating (P2800 per hr.). Local boat owners hawk snorkeling tours (P500).

Boracay is surrounded by wall dives, channel drift dives, plunges into bat-and-snake-infested caves, and deep dives. One site ranks among the Philippines' best: **Yapak,** on the coast of Panay. At 35m, the strong currents attract pelagic fish, tuna, and whitetip sharks. On **Maniguin Island,** 48km southwest of Boracay, whitetip sharks sleep in caves. An overnight stay is recommended on Maniguin, although it can be reached in a day by boat (2hr., around US$90). To explore shallower reefs, divers head for the coral of **Crocodile Island** and the fish frenzy at **Friday's Rock.**

Dive shops litter the sands of White Beach. Shop around, keeping in mind that diving in the Philippines is already cheap, and that experienced divemasters and quality gear is a must. Typically, dives cost US$20-25, PADI open-water courses are US$285-310, and advanced courses cost US$185-200. **Lapu-Lapu Diving Center,** next to Mango Ray north of Boat Station 2, was the first on the beach. (☎288 3302; www.lapulapu.com. Open daily 7am-8pm.) **Calypso Divers** is north of the Tourist Center and has great instructional facilities. (☎288 3206. Open daily 8am-10pm.) **Victory Divers,** next to Nigi's and south of Boat Station 2, changes equipment annually. (☎288 3209; www.pny-web.i-next.net/~victory/. Open daily 7am-midnight.)

Arrange **horseback riding** through the Tourist Center (P400 per hr.) or go straight to **Boracay Horse Riding Stables** (☎288 3311), north of Boat Station 1.

NIGHTLIFE

At times, Boracay seems like an island that floats not only on water, but on a seas of free-flowing alcohol. White Beach is dotted by a seemingly endless parade of bars, most of which offer budget-friendly happy hour deals, ensuring that by the time the specials end, you'll be too sloshed to care. To the delight of some and the horror of others, several Boracay clubs have begun staging "full moon parties" a la Thailand's Ko Phangnan. Dare to drink two or more "coconut killers" (P130) and Barracuda, south of Boat Station 2, will enshrine you in their Hall of Fame. (Open daily 5pm-1am.) Beachcomber, north of Boat Station 1, is Boracay's premier open air disco. (Beer P40. Open daily 5pm-3am.)

LEYTE

Sipping a blood cocktail with a local chieftain and planting the first of many crosses, Ferdinand Magellan staked his claim for the glory of Spain on the tiny Leyteno island of Limasawa in 1521. Four centuries later in 1944, General Douglas MacArthur made his triumphant return to the archipelago here. Historical significance aside, there is little of interest in Leyte to most travelers, who (unlike MacArthur) often have no desire to return.

THE VIEW FROM ABOVE

Major towns: Tacloban at the edge of Samar, Ormoc on the western coast.
Something different: Escape the beach on Bilican Island, host to one of the Philippines' only hinterlands.
Natural wonders: From Tacloban, head to Sohoton Natural Bridge National Park to see nature at its best.

TACLOBAN ☎53

Tacloban is the geographical and historical heart of the Eastern Visayas. Choking smog, *kamikaze* jeepney, and a lack of sights won't give travelers much cause to linger. Indeed, today's Tacloban provides the same strategic significance to travelers that it provided MacArthur—namely, a base from which to reach other islands.

TRANSPORTATION

Flights: Daniel Z. Romualdez Airport (☎325 5893), 11km east of Tacloban in San Jose. Cross the airport parking lot for the cheapest jeepney into town (P5). Flights from Tacloban go only to **Manila. Cebu Pacific** (airport office ☎325 8484, downtown office on Sen. Enage St. ☎325 7740) has 3 flights per day (P1999). Both offices open M-F 8am-4:30pm. **Philippine Airlines** (☎321 2212) has 2 flights per day (P2343). Open daily 5:30-11:30am and 1-4:30pm. **Air Philippines** (airport office ☎323 6800, downtown office on Sen Enage St. ☎321 7771) flies to Manila at 5:25pm daily (P1998). Both offices open daily 8am-4pm.

Buses: To find the bus terminal, walk away from the city on Quezon Blvd. To: **Manila** (24hr.; 11 per day; P569, with A/C P650) via several destinations in **Samar** including **Catbologan** (2-3hr., 15 per day, P60-70), **Calbayog** (5hr., 11 per day, P126), **San Isidro** (4hr.; 3 per day; P149, with A/C P163), and **Allen** (6hr., 6 per day, P140). San Isidro and Allen ferries run to **Matnog,** on Luzon (1½hr., P52). Other destinations include: **Davao** (12hr., 2 per day, P355); **Naval** on Biliran (3½-4hr., 4 per day, P70-100); and **Ormoc** (2hr., every 20min. 6:30am-6:30pm, P63-70). **Jeepney** strike out for **Basey** on Samar (45min., depart when full, last return 3pm, P10). Jeepney also head south every 20min. until 7pm to **Palo** (20min., P5) and **Tolosa** (30min., P10).

Ferries: William Lines (☎321 2536) goes to **Cebu** (14hr., M-F 4pm, P200). **Sulpicio Lines** (☎321 2303) goes to **Manila** (21hr.; Tu 5am, F noon; P547).

Local Transportation: Jeepney cruise Magsaysay Blvd., Real St., and Veteranos St. Cross-town fare P2.50, from jeepney stop along Quezon Blvd. **Taxis,** ☎321 4713.

ORIENTATION AND PRACTICAL INFORMATION

On Leyte's east coast 108km from Ormoc, Tacloban is a portal to and from Samar, across the San Juanico Straits to the northeast. The city is sandwiched between **Panalaron Bay** to the north and **Cancabato Bay** to the south. The pier, market, and bus/jeepney terminal overlook Panalaron Bay. **Magsaysay Blvd.** wraps around the northern and eastern boundaries of the peninsula, originating in the north by **Children's Park,** the **tourist office,** and Leyte's **Provincial Capitol** building, and terminating in the south at **Real St.** Jeepney blaze down southwest **Veteranos St.** and southeastern Real St., converging to funnel passengers southward to **Palo** or the **airport** across Cancabato Bay.

Tourist Offices: The **main office** (☎321 2048) is at Children's Park, on Sen. Enage St. Open M-F 8am-6pm. **Airport branch,** ☎325 5893.

Tours: MacArthur Landing Tours and Travel, 122 Lopez Jaena St. (☎321 5685). Off St. Niño St. which is off Magsaysay Blvd. Very helpful. Open M-F 8am-noon and 1-5pm.

Currency Exchange: ATMs are available at most banks. **Philippine National Bank** (☎321 2053), at the corner of St. Niño St. and J. Romualdez St. Passport photocopy required to cash traveler's checks. **24hr. ATM** (Cirrus/MC/PLUS/V). Open M-F 9am-3pm. **PDCP Bank** (☎321 2881), on Salazar St. near intersection with Zamora St. Open M-F 9am-3pm.

Markets: Quezon Blvd., Torres St., and Tarcela St., sell fruit, straw goods, and clothes.

Emergency: Police (☎166), on the Paterno Ext. **Fire** ☎911. **Ambulance** ☎321 2427. **Medical emergency** ☎321 2816.

Pharmacy: Mercury Drug (☎321 2852), on Salazar St. at the intersection with P. Zamora. Open daily 7am-10pm.

Medical Services: The **Eastern Visayas Regional Medical Center** (☎325 5471), near the gate of Children's Park on Sen. Enage St.

Telephones: Bayantel, 109 Romualdez St. (☎321 2207). Open M-F 7am-7pm.

Internet Access: Continental Internet Cafe, 170 Veteranos St. (☎321 3427). P0.80 per min.

Post Office: ☎321 3509. On Trece Martirez St. along the harbor. Open M-F 7am-noon and 1-5:30pm, Sa 8am-noon. **Postal code:** 6500.

ACCOMMODATIONS

Manabo Lodge, 191 P. Zamora St. (☎321 3727), in the heart of Tacloban, north of the intersection with del Pilar St., past the neon blue Metrobank sign, on the left. Rooms are basic with shared bathrooms. Showers P30. Singles P250; twins with private bath P400; extra person P50, folding bed P30.

LNU House (☎321 3175), at the corner of Paterno and Santa Cruz St., next to the pedestrian bridge, is a barrack for students at Leyte Normal University. Balcony and TV room. Laundry service. A/C in every room. TV P50. Refrigerator P50. Singles P400; twins P500; extra bed P120.

Cecilia's Lodge, 178 Paterno St. (☎321 2815), near Veteranos St. Simple but adequate rooms and an amicable owner. Singles with fan P150, with private bath P220, with A/C and private bath P250; doubles with private bath and fan P350.

Rosvenil Pensionne, 302 P. Burgos St. (☎321 2676), at the corner of Real St. and P. Burgos. Turn left on P. Burgos; it's on the left before the computer college. Singles P210-230, with A/C P290-340; doubles P250-280/320-420.

FOOD

Visitors can slurp a San Miguel while watching a Filipino soap opera at a **roadside barbecue** along Real St. The **fish and vegetable market** along the streets outside the bus terminal provide a great medium for the culinary artist.

Join Us Cuisine, on Veteranos St. near the intersection with Rizal Ave. A spotless venue good for sampling local cuisine like *giniling* (spicy chopped pork; P20). *Halo-halo* P10. *Lichee flan* P12. Open M-Sa 8am-9pm.

Guiseppe's Restaurant, on Veteranos St. at the corner of MH del Pilar St. This unlikely blend of Italian and Filipino cuisine is the best food in town. Steak P250. Mango shake P50. Open daily 10:30am-10:30pm. AmEx/MC/V.

Sheu-Zheu Mami House, on Samora St. in the Dynasty Square Shopping Center near the MH del Pilar St. intersection. Local Chinese dishes. All entrees P35. Open daily 7:30am-7:30pm. Free delivery.

SIGHTS AND ENTERTAINMENT

The white Neoclassical façade of the **Leyte Provincial Capitol,** built in 1902, on the corner of Sen. Enage St. and Magsaysay Blvd., is architectural evidence of colonial influences. **Santo Niño Church,** at the corner of Real and Zamora St., houses the city's patron saint. In 1889, en route to a makeover in Manila, a venerated image of the Christ child was tossed overboard. Months later, natives on north Mindoro recovered the crate, which was then stolen back by impassioned residents of Tacloban. The **Santo Niño Shrine and Heritage Museum,** on Real St., founded by Imelda Marcos, displays local artists' paintings of the stations of the cross. (☎321 9775. Open M-Sa 8-11:30am and 1-4:30pm. P200. Video permit P200, camera permit P30.)

South of Tacloban, the **General Douglas MacArthur Landing Memorial** commemorates the charismatic commander's return on October 20, 1944. Take a jeepney from Veteranos St. to Palo via Baras (20min., last return 4:30pm, P5). Ask the driver to drop you off in front of the memorial. Hide in foxholes on nearby **Hill 522.** The **Battle of Baluarte Marker,** 52km away in Barugo, commemorates a battle between guerrillas and Japanese troops. North of the city, the **San Juanico Bridge**—the longest span of its kind in Southeast Asia—links Leyte to Samar.

DAYTRIP FROM TACLOBAN: SOHOTON

Sohoton Natural Bridge National Park is across the straits in Samar. A subterranean river snakes underneath two mountain ridges, creating the natural stone bridge for which the park is named. From Tacloban's bus terminal, take a jeepney to **Basey** (30min., P90). Get off at Basey's City Hall, and find the **Department of the Environment and Natural Resources (DENR)** across the street. (☎276 1151. Open M-F 9am-5pm.) Admission to the park is US$2. Francisco Corales Jr. arranges the necessary boat trip (1½hr., P500 per person) and provides kerosene lamps (P50). The guide expects a tip (around P200). Boats do not go out in the rain.

In Basey, the only accommodations are at **St. Michael's Lodging House** next to the jeepney stop, to the left of Elsie's Bakery. (☎276 1003. Dorms P100.) While in Basey, navigate the picturesque streets to **St. Michael's Church,** built in 1636.

There are a few attractions in **Western Samar.** The area around **Calbayog** is replete with caves and waterfalls. The **Samar Archaeological Museum and Research Center,** at Christ the King College in Calbayog, documents the island's history.

ORMOC ☎53

Ormoc became a poster-city for the dangers of environmental degradation when Typhoon Uring pummeled Leyte in November 1991. Deforestation of the surrounding hills proved deadly when torrential rains swept massive amounts of topsoil into town, claiming 8000 lives. Ormoc has since been rebuilt and remains a busy gateway to the Eastern Visayas. Travelers may first look at Ormoc as a transportation hub, but a second look reveals a surprisingly clean city with vibrant and festive nightlife along the water.

TRANSPORTATION. At the bus terminal, **Philtranco** takes off for **Manila** at 5am (24hr., with A/C P810) and also at 9am and 5pm (26hr., P608). These buses stop at **Tacloban** (2hr.; P70, with A/C P77) and the cities of Samar: **Catbologan** (4hr.; P136, with A/C P149), **Calbayog** (P181, with A/C P198), **San Isidro** (P216, with A/C P236), and **Allen** (P228, with A/C P249). Ferries connect San Isidro and Allen to **Matnog** on Luzon (1½hr., P52). **JD Bus Line** (☎255 2890) rolls to **Tacloban** (2hr., 5-7 per day 6am-8:30pm, P100) and **Naval** on Biliran (1½hr., 6 per day 6:30am-9pm, P100). **Eagle Star**

(☎255 5166) and **Velmar** alternate service to **Tacloban** (2½hr., every 20min. 3:30am-5pm, P62.75) and **Catbologan** (4hr.; 3, 5a, 8, 9am; P124). **MC Bus Lines** heads south to **Baybay** (1hr., 9am, P20). **Bachelor Express** runs to **Davao** (11:30am, 11pm; P375).

SuperCat ferries (☎255 3511; open 5am-7pm), at the end of the pier, chug to **Cebu** (2hr.; 6, 8:30am, 1:30, 6:30pm; P370). Student discount (15%) with ID. **Sulpicio Lines** (☎255 2041) heads for **Cebu** (5hr., Su midnight, P97) and **Manila** (52hr., Tu 5pm, P549).

ORIENTATION AND PRACTICAL INFORMATION. Ormoc is in northwest Leyte, 109km across the central range from Tacloban. Tucked into the north coast of **Ormoc Bay,** the **city pier** juts directly southward. Walking out of the pier area, the bus terminal and jeepney pick-up are on the left. The first road perpendicular to the pier is **Larrazabal Blvd.,** which has street barbecues and fresh pineapple. **Bonifacio St.** heads north, crossing Larrazabal Blvd. and **Aviles St.** Farther east, **Navarro** and **San Pedro St.** run north to south from the memorial park along the water.

Services include: the **Philippine National Bank** (☎255 4538), on Bonifacio St. with an **ATM** (open M-F 9am-3pm); the **post office** (☎255 3181; open M-F 7am-noon and 1-5:30pm, Sa 8am-noon; **postal code** 6541), in Cogon district; **Internet access** at **OrmocNet** (☎561 7912; P30 per hr.), on San Pedro St. in the Ormoc Days Hotel; **telephones** in the PLDT office (☎/fax 255 4737; open daily 7am-10pm) on the corner of Bonifacio and Catag St.; a **hospital** (☎255 2475); and the **police** (☎166).

ACCOMMODATIONS AND FOOD. Opposite the bus terminal is the **Hotel Don Felipe.** (☎255 2460. Singles P360; doubles P420.) A bit farther down Bonifacio St., the **Pongos Hotel** has clean, spacious rooms. (☎255 2540. Singles P216, with A/C P420; doubles P336/600; extra bed P120.) The **Ormoc Bay Lodging House** is on Real St. near the intersection with Aviles St. (☎255 5745. Singles P120; doubles P310-450.)

Barbecues line the waterfront. For a more formal affair, cruise along Larrazabal Blvd. away from the bus terminal. **Chitos Chow** serves up Filipino dishes for P45-150. (Open daily 9am-11:30pm.)

SIGHTS AND ENTERTAINMENT. Magellan left behind a bridge by Larrazabal Blvd. The **Leyte Mountain Trail** snakes east 40km to Mahagnao National Park, terminating in Burauen, 66km from Tacloban. A national park since 1992, **Lake Danao** is an oasis in the heart of a wild forest. From the Ormoc bus terminal take a jeepney (1½hr., leaves when full, P20) to the Lake Danao stop. Next walk (15min.) or take a *bangka* (5min., P5) to the Department of Environment and Natural Resources (DENR), where park ranger Quinciano Abiertas Jr. arranges *bangka* trips around the lake (P40 per hr.) and treks in the forest (park entrance fee US$2; tip expected for forest treks). Camping is allowed for free. The station has showers, and for a day stay, huts cost P50 per person per day.

Fred's Bar, on Jaena Lopez St. near the corner of J. Navarro St., shows the local flavor of entertainment: karaoke. The regulars sing quite well. (☎255 2953. San Miguel P20. Open daily 7pm-1am.) Within the Don Felipe complex, the **Swing Disco** is mainly ballroom (Tu-F 8:30pm-2am) and disco (F 11:30pm-3am, Sa 9pm-3am, Su 11:30pm-2am). Cover costs P100.

BILIRAN ISLAND

Welcome to the virtually untouched Filipino hinterland. On Biliran, water buffalo trudge through rice paddies with farmers in tow; the police chief bemoans his lack of a patrol car; and local Visayans chase *tuba* (a homemade wine concoction derived from coconut tree sap) with a quick gulp of soda. The island has managed to stay off the beaten track, but new infrastructure and a growing European-dominated tourist force may soon put Biliran on the mainstream map.

Tacloban and Ormoc are the easiest gateways to Biliran. **Eagle Star, PP Bus Lines,** and **JD Bus Lines** alternate departures to **Tacloban** (3hr., every 30min. 10:30am-4:30pm, P70; A/C buses 10:30am, 4:30pm; P100). The same companies cover **Ormoc**

(2hr., every 2-3hr. 3:30am-4:30pm, with A/C P100). The arrival times of the buses to Ormoc coincide with the departure times of the **SuperCat ferries** to **Cebu** (4½hr., 4 per day, P370). There are slower ferries from Naval to Cebu: **Michael's** (8hr.; Su, Th, F 8pm; P185) and **John Carrier** (8hr.; Su, Tu, Th 9pm; P185).

Roughly 110km northwest of Tacloban, the province of Biliran crowns the north coast of Leyte. **Biliran,** the southernmost town, is the island's chief entry point. The capital, **Naval,** lies midway up the west coast, followed by **Almeria** and **Kawayan.** A dirt road circles the island, linking **Culaba** on the northeast coast, **Caibiran** on the east coast, and **Cabucgayan** on the southeast coast. A trans-island road skirts Caibiran volcano, connecting Naval with Caibiran and Culaba. **Maripipi Island,** a snorkeler's dream, sits off Biliran's northwest coast. **Higatagan Island** lies west of Naval.

NAVAL

Cebuano-speaking Naval stole the title of the provincial capital from its eastern Waray-waray-speaking sister city Caibiran when Biliran became a province in 1992. The hectic activity of the **pier/bus terminal,** with its eateries and large market, emanates eastward by way of two parallel roads, north **Vicentillo St.** and south **P. Inocentes St.** A 15min. hike down P. Inocentes or a 5min. pedicab ride will bring you to the **Naval Institute of Technology** on the right. Enroll in night school or stay at their hostel for a modest P70 (with A/C P200). For more privacy, strike out down Vicentillo St. The **Brigida Inn** adjoins LM's Auto Supply. (Singles with fan P70; doubles with fan P160-300.) Suffer the financial consequences of A/C in the dimly lit rooms of the **Rosevic Lodging House,** farther up Vicentillo St. on the left. (Singles with A/C P350; doubles P400-P500.)

The **PLDT,** on P. Inocentes St., offers free calling card calls. (☎198 2029. Open daily 7am-10pm.) The **Philippine National Bank** is at the left end of Ballesteros St. looking toward the ocean. (No ATM. Open M-F 9am-noon and 1-3pm.) At the other end of Ballesteros St., a right on Caneja St. leads to the **police station.** From another path leading down P. Inocentes, a right on Ballesteros St. will lead to a **hospital,** 2km outside Naval. **Chapeland Pharmacy** on Casfin St. is open 24hr. Naval's pier and jeepney/bus terminal has daily departures for coastal cities and nearby islands (jeepney service ceases around 4:30pm). From the pier, walk 10-15m along P. Inocentes St. and take a right through the market to reach the **post office.** (Open M-F 7:30am-noon and 1-5:30pm. **Postal code:** 6543.) **Gee Bee VI's Place,** on P. Inocentes St., a 5min. walk from the bus terminal, serves Filipino and Italian food for P40. (Open daily 8am-5pm; beer served 5pm-midnight.) **Upperdeck,** across the road and above the Bayan Telephone Office, has live music everyday, 5pm-2am.

DAYTRIPS FROM NAVAL. Naval's pier bus terminal has daily departures for coastal cities and nearby islands. The rugged highway unlocks rewards for those willing to swap sweat for seclusion. Outriggers run west to **Higatagan Island** (1hr., 11am, P20-25). A home stay is the only option on the island (lodging should cost around P200-300). Higatagan's attractions include the beach and snake-infested **Ka Ventong Cave.** The snorkeling heaven of **Maripipi Island** can be reached by boat (3hr., noon, P30). **Caibiran** is convenient for launching an expedition to Mt. Biliran. Surrounding villages shelter sulfur hot springs, **Caibiran Falls,** and the spring-fed **San Bernardo** pool. Jeepney cross the island every hour (P30). Daytrippers may hire a motorcycle with driver (P300 per day). Sunsets are wonderful at secluded Agta Beach. Take the jeepney bound for Koiwayan and tell the driver you want to get off at Asta (30min. P6.) **Agta's** beach faces **Dalutan Island.** Outriggers make daytrips to Dalutan (P25). Inhabited by a hospitable family, **Agta Beach Resort** has thatched huts. (Singles P100; doubles with A/C P400.) Pump boats make the trip to **Tingkasan Bat Cave** (10-15min., P200-300) on Tingkasan Island.

PALAWAN

Once connected to Borneo, the large, finger-shaped island of Palawan is understandably different from the rest of the Philippines. Most of the country is virtually wildlife-free, but Palawan teems with bizarre beasts, ranging from the scaly anteater and Palawan bearcat to the stink badger. Instead of volcanoes, Palawan has limestone cliffs resembling those of China and Vietnam. Palawan takes pride in its cultural preservation as well; while most of the Philippines hurtles toward modernity, Palawan remains frozen in time. Outside Puerto Princesa, electricity and running water are rare. More than 80 tribes, untouched rainforest, and incomparably beautiful beaches earn Palawan its title: "The Last Frontier."

THE VIEW FROM ABOVE

Main city: Puerto Princesa.
Other towns: Coron, El Nido, Port Barton.
Highlights: Scuba diving at Tabbataha Reef, Honda Bay, or Coron's Japanese wrecks; St. Paul Subterranean River National Park; island-hopping and snorkeling in Bacuit Bay; and a visit to Makin It Hot Springs.

PUERTO PRINCESA ☎48

The lone urban outpost in Palawan, Puerto Princesa has become a environmentalist, ferociously fending off loggers from the wilderness, and protecting its several indigenous cultures. The cleanest city in the Philippines, "Puerto" levies heavy fines on litterers. At least one night here is needed to stock up on supplies and funds, which are lacking elsewhere, but cafes, restaurants, and hopping bars often lull travelers to linger longer on the island.

TRANSPORTATION

Flights: The **airport** is 1km from the National Hwy. intersection with Rizal Ave. **PAL** (☎433 4565; open daily 8-11:30am and 1-3:30pm), is in the building to the right of the airport and flies to: **Cebu** (M, F 2:50pm; P3000); **Iloilo** (M, F 2:50pm; P2200); **Manila** (daily 11am, P3096). **Air Philippines,** 420 Rizal Ave. (☎433 7003; open daily 8am-5pm), flies to **Manila** (noon, P2553). **Seair** (☎891 8708; open daily 8am-5pm), flies to **Coron** (Tu, F, Su 11:20am; P2200) and **El Nido** (Tu, F, Su 11:20am; P1700).

Ferries: The **wharf** is on the western tip of the city. Walking up the hill and to the right connects you to Rizal Ave. Tickets are sold at the wharf, but reserve a spot beforehand at the ferry offices downtown. **Negros Navigation** has an office on Roxas St. near the corner with Rizal Ave. (☎/fax 433 7204). Open M-Sa 8am-noon and 1-5pm. Ferries sail to **Manila** (22hr., F 7pm, from P1205). **WG&A** is on the right side of Rizal Ave. in the ARL building, a 5-10min. walk from the airport. (☎433 4875). Open M-F 8am-5pm. **Super ferries** sail to **Manila** (24hr.; Su 9am; P895, with meal P1120) via **Coron** (6-7hr., P800).

Local Transportation: Since public transportation is spotty when demand is low, hiring a **private vehicle** is often necessary. A jeepney-derivative costs P2500 per day. An A/C 4WD runs P4500 (P3000 in low season) per day to **Sabang** and the **Underground River.** A/C vehicles to **El Nido** cost P15,000. Some agencies slap a P500-1000 overnight fee on top of a 2nd day's charge. All rentals come with a driver. **Go Palawan** (see **Travel Agencies,** below) rents dirtbikes for P800 per day.

ORIENTATION AND PRACTICAL INFORMATION

Puerto Princesa is huge, spanning the width of the island from Sabang in the north to Long Point in the south. The city is on a peninsula jutting into the Sulu Sea, south of Honda Bay on the east coast. Ferries dock on the western tip, where **Rizal Ave.,** the main drag, ends. **Roxas, Burgos,** and **Valencia St.** intersect Rizal Ave. The **National Hwy.** intersects Rizal Ave. on the east tip of the commercial area near the **Provincial Capital.** The only paved road outside the city center leads south to **Quezon.**

Tourist Offices: City Tourism (☎434 4211). Offices at air and sea ports. Open daily 8am-noon and 1-6pm. More helpful is the **Provincial Tourism Office** (☎433 2968), at the corner of Rizal Ave. and the National Hwy. Excellent "Palawan Tourism Map" P50. Open M-F 8am-noon and 1-5pm. The unofficial tourist office at **Backpackers' Cafe** has a humorous and helpful "comments book." Open daily 7am-11pm. **Pat Murray,** one of Palawan's original settlers, is a walking Palawan encyclopedia. He frequents Trattoria Inn and happily offers advice.

Travel Agencies: **Go Palawan,** 353 Rizal Ave. at Trattoria Inn (☎433 4570). Phenomenal staff and countless brochures. Open M-Sa 9am-6pm. **Coron Tours and Travel,** 38-B R. San Juan St. at Unit 6 Bundal Business Center (☎/fax 434 2638), between the airport and the city in nearby Barangay San Miguel. Offers hints on getting to and exploring the northern islands. Open M-F 8am-5pm, Sa 8am-noon. The new branch of **Swagman Travel** (☎434 2595) is open M-Sa 8am-5pm.

Banks: Many on Rizal Ave. near Valencia St. All banks open M-F 9am-3pm. **Bank of the Philippine Islands** has an **ATM** (Cirrus/Maestro/MC).

Bookstore: Leonar's Merrimart Bookstore carries English and Tagalog titles. Open M-Sa 8am-7pm, Su 9am-7pm.

Markets: The central market is on Malvar St. between Burgos and Valencia St.

Emergency: ☎166.

Police: Police Assistance Center (☎433 9826), on Rizal Ave. near the Palawan Museum.

Pharmacies: Mercury Drug (☎433 2498), on Rizal Ave. Another branch on Valencia St. opposite the Renzel Hotel. Open daily 7am-10pm.

Medical Services: Adventist Hospital (☎433 2156), on San Pedro National Hwy. near the Santa Monica Rd. intersection. **Open 24hr.**

Telephones: Bayantel, 293 Rizal Ave. (☎433 4892), past the Provincial Capital. Open M-F 8am-10pm, Sa 8am-5pm. International and domestic calls. **Piltel,** 42 Roxas St. (☎433 2346). AT&T calling cards with no service charge. Open daily 6am-10pm.

Internet Access: Big Bad Wolf, on Valencia St. next to the market. P60 per hr. Open M-Sa 10am-10pm, Su 2-10pm. **Trattoria Inn** is the fastest. P100 per hr.

Post Office: ☎433 2556. On Burgos St. near the corner of Rizal Ave. *Poste Restante.* Open daily 8am-noon and 1-5pm. **Postal code:** 5300.

ACCOMMODATIONS

Puerto Pension, 35 Malvar St. (☎433 2969). Gorgeous, polished, bamboo rooms. Restaurant with panoramic bay view. Singles P250; doubles P380, with A/C and common room P750.

Abelardo's Pension, 63 D. Manga St. (☎433 2049), off Burgos St. Immaculate, well-run guest house. "Clean is our best asset," boasts the convivial owner. Singles P150; twins P250, with A/C and private bath P600; add P50 for TV.

Trattoria Inn & Swiss Bistro, 353 Rizal Ave. (☎433 2719). Superb service. Spotless singles P270-320, with A/C, common room, hot water, phone, and cable TV P650. AmEx/MC/V/traveler's checks.

Backpackers' Cafe, Bookshop, and Inn, 112 Valencia St., 5min. past the Palawan Museum. A fusion of cafe, bookstore, travel agency, guest house, and island-guru hangout. People stay for the company and travel advice, not the rooms. Common room. Office open daily 7:30am-11pm. Singles P150; doubles P220.

FOOD

Kalui Restaurant, on Rizal Ave., toward the airport from Trattoria Inn. Easily the best restaurant in Palawan and possibly the Philippines' best seafood. Set menu changes with catch and includes soup and heavenly dessert fruit plate (regular P100, special for 2 P275). Open M-Sa 11am-2pm and 6-11pm.

Vegetarian House, 79 Burgos St., at the corner of Manalo St. Wise sayings adorn the walls of this Buddhist eatery. I can't believe it's not cow! "Beef steak" and other "meat" dishes that'll fool any carnivore P50-120. Open M-Sa 9am-2pm and 4-10pm.

Pho Vietnamese Restaurant, a 5min. tricycle ride past the airport. Fondues P106-200. Filling noodle soups P52-88. Vermicelli P44-52. Open daily 8am-9pm.

Trattoria Inn, on Rizal Ave., toward the airport. Large international selection. Superb "Filipino breakfast" (fried rice, eggs, and cured pork) P85. Yummy coffee shakes P55.

Phoenix, on Abrea Rd., 200m from the airport. Considered the best Chinese food around. Delivery service. Lobster P140 per 100g. Open daily 11am-10pm.

SIGHTS

The **Kamarikutan Kape & Art Galeri,** on Rizal Ave. near the airport, provides an interesting glimpse at local art. The airy complex, constructed in Palawan and *Ifugao* styles, exhibits area artists. *Ifugao* huts are available for rent (high season P400; low season P280). Every April or May, locals hold an arts festival and teach native crafts. (☎433 5182. Open daily 7:30am-11pm.)

The **Palawan Museum,** at the corner of Rizal Ave. and Valencia St. behind Mendoza Park, places the island in historical and cultural context. Its collection includes artifacts from the Tabon Caves, the "Cradle of Philippine Civilization." Their library contains books on Palawan. (☎433 2963. Open M-Sa 8am-noon and 1:30-5pm, Su 9-11am. P10, students P5, children P2.)

At the west end of Rizal Ave. by the cathedral, a **memorial** marks where 143 US POWs were herded into a tunnel, doused with gasoline, and set on fire by Japanese captors on December 15, 1944. Eleven men survived by jumping off the cliff and swimming across Puerto Princesa Bay.

Supporting the local ethno-environmental craze, many shops hawk native goods. **Culture Shack,** on Rizal Ave. opposite Bayantel, sells cashew wine (P65), basketry, and clothing. (Open M-Sa 8:40am-7:40pm.)

ACTIVITIES

Tabbataha Reef, 150km southeast of Puerto Princesa, is the archipelago's most sought-after dive site. It's remoteness and limited availability (Mar.-June) make the trip to the reef difficult, but the certainty of spotting large marine life draws divers nonetheless. **Queen Anne Divers,** 353 Rizal Ave. (☎433 2719), at the Trattoria Inn, operates two dive ships to Tabbataha Reef (5-7 days; US$660-900, must be booked six months in advance). Non-divers pay lower rates to snorkel and bird watch. Queen Anne also runs trips to **Busuanga** and **Coron** (which are famous for their Japanese wrecks), daytrips to reefs off the southern coast near Puerto Princesa (2-dive packages with lunch and boat US$55, with rentals US$60), and PADI courses (open-water US$300, advanced open-water US$230). **Island Divers,** 371 Rizal Ave., frequents southern Puerto Princesa Bay around Pete's Reef, Light House, and Table Head (2-dive daytrip US$50, with rentals US$60) and offers PADI courses for US$200-280. (☎433 5103. Open M-F 8am-5pm.)

NIGHTLIFE

Most Filipinos won't let foreigners sneak out of Puerto Princesa's numerous **karaoke joints** without wailing a song, but for a night free from the spotlight, the cozy **Tom-Tom Club** leaves the music to the professionals. **Nick's Venue,** in the Admiral Hotel on Rizal Junction, is the main hotspot for Palawan's 20-something partiers. (Cover P100-150. Open daily 8pm-2am.) **Spice Bar & Disco,** on Rizal Ave., also keeps the crowd hopping until after midnight. (San Miguel P35. No cover, but P100 minimum tab. No shorts or slippers. Open M-Th 8pm-2am, F-Su 8pm-3am.)

DAYTRIPS FROM PUERTO PRINCESA

HONDA BAY

Bancas (P250-1200) leave for Honda Bay from St. Lourdes Wharf, a 30min. tricycle ride from town (P250). A tourist shack organizes bancas and gear (P100 per day).

North of the city, these waters are peppered with islands ideal for **snorkeling. Snake Island** (P600) makes a pleasant daytrip. For a longer stay, use **Starfish Island** (P500) or **Meara Marina Island** (P400) as a base to explore the bay. **Starfish Sandbar Resort** (☎433 2740) has pumpboat trips (daytrip P200, overnight P400), quads on stilts (P500-800), and facilities for serving canned food. **Meara Marina Island Resort** (contact Trattoria Inn in Puerto Princesa, see p. 592) offers bigger bungalows with a *nipa* bar and restaurant and scuba diving in the high season. (Tent P150; huts P590, extra bed P100. Snorkeling gear P190 per day.)

CROCODILE FARM

To get to Irawan, hop on a "Manginisda" jeepney (15min., 6:30am-7pm, P16) from the corner of Malvar and Burgos St. in Puerto Princesa.

At the **Crocodile Farming Institute,** the freshwater Mindoro crocodile and the Indo-Pacific saltwater crocodile have multiplied from an initial population of seven to 5000. An exhibition hall enlightens visitors about the reptiles' life and a mini-zoo displays the crocs in depressingly small cages. (Open M-Sa 9am-4pm. Tours every hr. Feedings M and Th afternoons.) At the **Butterfly Garden,** on the road to Crocodile Farm, you can view Palawan's gorgeous butterflies. (Open daily 8:30am-4:30pm. Live pupae are P20 at the giftshop.)

IWAHIG PRISON AND PENAL FARM

Tricycle to the Penal Colony P350. Jeepney marked "Iwahig" run from Valencia St. on the way to the Backpackers Cafe (30min., 2-3 per day 10am-3pm, P16).

Across the bay from the city proper, brown-shirt-clad prisoners work the Iwahig rice paddies, shackle-free. Iwahig is a community with basketball courts, a town center, and residential sections for the prisoners' families. One small jail houses maximum-security prisoners. When the "minimums" aren't farming, the 2000 prisoners fashion handicrafts. Lucky travelers might convince a prisoner to sell an "Inmate—Minimum" T-shirt (P200). The gift shop is at the turn-off from the main highway running around the bay. (Open daily 6am-6pm.)

TABON CAVE

South of Puerto Princesa in Quezon. Charing Bus Lines runs trips to Quezon leaving from the market on Malvar St. (daily, 2 buses leave when full, P132) or take a shuttle van from the airport (P140 per person). From Quezon, hire a pumpboat to the caves (P500 round-trip). Bring a flashlight and hiking shoes.

Named after the bird that lays it eggs in holes found in the caves' floor, this system of 200 caves is known as the oldest habitated site in Southeast Asia. Excavations in the 1970s led to the discovery of the 22,000-year-old Tabon man. Stone tools found here, however, show use of the cave by even earlier humans.

ST. PAUL SUBTERRANEAN RIVER NATIONAL PARK

On the west coast of Palawan between Port Barton and Puerto Princesa, the giant St. Paul Subterranean River National Park lies with its gaping mouth pointed toward the South China Sea. The **Cabayugan River,** the longest underground river in the world, weaves 8.2km through a natural growth forest, home to macaques and monitor lizards, and carves out a habitat for 40,000 bats, thousands of birds, and a natural stone statue of the Virgin Mary. Absolutely fabulous, this is a must-see for anyone on Palawan.

The National Park is best reached from **Sabang. Jeepney** to Sabang leave from Malvar St. near the Shell station in Puerto Princesa (3hr. private, 7am-2am, P95 plus P15 for baggage). From Sabang, **motorboats** (one way P400, round-trip P500) leave from the pier where jeepney from Puerto Princesa stop, or you can hike the **Monkey Trail** along the beach that ends at the park entrance. Jeepney to Puerto Princesa leave from the ferry pier (3hr., 3 per day 6:30am-1:30pm, P75), but aren't very reliable. **A/C vans** offer a more comfortable ride, but are just as infrequent (P400). The desperate can hire a jeep (P2000) or A/C van (P2500) from the park office.

It's best to stop by the **St. Paul's Subterranean River National Park Office** on Manalo St. near the corner with Fernandez St. in Puerto Princesa, to get **permits.** (Cave entrance P200, children P100. General entrance P30. ☎433 2409. Open M-F 8am-noon and 1-5pm.) You can, however, also grab a permit at the **Visitor's Assistance Center.** (Open daily 8am-noon and 1-5pm.) Snorkelers should rent equipment in Puerto Princesa. Post offices, banks, and telephones are nonexistent.

From the pier, beaches stretch north toward the subterranean cave, with a few resorts within walking distance. Walking up the beach from the pier with the ocean to your left, you'll first encounter **Tom's Cottages,** offering charmingly cozy and rustic private huts. (Hut for 2 P200, beachfront P300.) A 10min. walk down the first beach ends at **Mary's Cottages,** in a quiet cove with hammocks and similar amenities. (Huts with common room P300, beachfront P400.) Mary's also rents outriggers to navigate the Puyo-puyo River (P50). Pricey **Panaguman Beach Resort** (☎433 2719), is the sole occupant of the coastline on the other side of the underground cave. Although the isolation is nice, the resort has a monopoly on comings, goings, and recreation. Bookings can be made in Puerto Princesa.

PORT BARTON

Lack of phone service, roads, and reliable electricity has not stopped Port Barton from becoming a backpacker hotspot. Perhaps it's the very absence of modern features which pulls travelers to explore, snorkel, and swim at these pristine islands.

Jeepney go to **Puerto Princesa** (5-6hr.; 8-9am; P140, private P4500). In high season **boats** go to **El Nido** (5hr.; M, W 9:30am, Th, Su 10:30am; P1000, private P5000) and **Sabang** (3hr.; Tu, Th noon, W, Sa 12:30pm; P650, private P2500).

Rizal Ave. hugs the coast, cradling the port's cottages. Fellow statesmen **Quezon, Mabini,** and **Ballesleros** cross Rizal Ave. toward the ocean. **The Adventist Health Care Clinic** on Bonafacio Ave., a block from Rizal Ave. between Quezon and Ballesleros Ave., gives malaria tests and provides basic care. The nearest **post office** and **phones** are in Roxas (2hr. by jeepney).

Port Barton rides the tide of tourism. During high season, the tourist swell requires tents, while in low season, restaurants and cottages often shut down. **Ausan's Cottages** stands out for quality, cheap rooms. (☎433 4825. Singles P150.) **Swissippini Lodge and Resort** (Puerto Princesa ☎433 4757; cottages P500, with common room P700) and **El Dorado Sunset Cottages** (☎433 2110; cottages P300-400) offer similar lodging and a beautiful seafood buffet (P225). The **Bamboo House** is a terrific dining choice. (Entrees P35-95. Open 7am-10pm.)

Port Barton's **beach** is mediocre and crowded by *bancas* (pumpboats), but white sandy shores beckon nearby. Another beach is around the rocky point to the south, a 30min. walk from town, and more options hide in island coves. *Bancas* island-hop for P800-1000. Cacnipa, Exolica, and Albaguin islands all have snorkeling sites, and scuba diving can be arranged through the **El Busero Inn** ($50 for 2 dives). For a freshwater experience, walk 1½ hr. inland to cascading waterfalls. Pick up a map from behind the bar at El Dorado Sunset Cottages (see **Accommodations,** above).

EL NIDO ☎48

El Nido is the frontier of travel on this "last frontier" island. The limestone cliffs surrounding the gorgeous beach add to the atmosphere, shielding the tourist from tourism. If this seems like paradise to you, get here while you can.

TRANSPORTATION. Flights to: **Busuanga** (30min.; M, F, Su 9am; P2100); **Manila** (1½hr.; Tu, F, Su 9am; P4400); **Puerto Princesa** (40min.; Tu, F, Su 11:20am; P1700). In high season, jeepney go directly to **Puerto Princesa** (12-14hr., 8am, P400). Alternate routes to Puerto Princesa include taking a **jeepney** to **Sibaltan** (2-2½hr., 7am, P60) where a **boat** leaves for **Taytay** (3-4hr., 9:30am, P160); from Taytay, jeepneys head to **Puerto Princesa** (8-10hr.; 2, 4pm; P190). Boats also leave for **Sabang** (7-8hr.; W, Sa 7am; P850). All boats leave from the pier at the end of the beach, but they are often out of commission in the low season.

PRACTICAL INFORMATION. Calle Hama, which turns into **Palmera St.,** runs along the coast; **Calle Real** runs parallel. **Rizal St.** cuts through the two and heads to the ocean. All other roads are unmarked, unnamed, and unpaved. Buy a **map** at El Nido Boutique. The **Department of Tourism** doubles as the **post office** on Calle Real.

(Open M-F 8am-5pm.) There are no banks, but **Palawan Pawnshop** and **Lim's Store** exchange cash. The **police station** is in the Municipal Building on the corner of Calle Real. **Farmacia Comprendio** has most non-prescription drugs. (Open daily 7am-9pm.) There is also a **clinic** next to El Nido High School. (Open M-F 8am-noon and 1-5pm.) **Bayantel** offers **collect call** service for P45. (Open M-F 7:30am-10pm, Su 9am-10pm.)

ACCOMMODATIONS AND FOOD. Like most of Palawan, El Nido is deserted in the off season but receives large crowds of backpackers and adventurers during peak months. In the off season, prices of cottages are halved and many restaurants shut down; prices listed reflect high/low season rates. **Lally and Abet Cottages,** at the far end of the beach, is popular and quiet. (Cottages P350/250, beachfront P900/600, with A/C P1200/800). Nearby, **Gloria's Beach Cottages** is run by motherly Ms. Fernandez, who gives advice on El Nido and arranges island-hopping. (Cottages P400/250.) **New Bayview Inn** is another possible alternative (P250 per person, common room).

El Nido's food options are surprisingly diverse. **Ric Son's,** on the beachfront, has gorgeous views of Bacuit Bay and a large seafood menu. (Fish with black bean sauce P65. Open daily 6am-10pm.) **Mac-Mac Restaurant,** on Calle Hama, has a large selection of German dishes and pizza. (Whopping cheeseburger on French bread P70. Open daily 8am-10pm.) **Elm St. Cafe and Restaurant,** off Rizal St., has a seafood buffet (P200) but is closed to tourists in the off season unless reserved in advance. (Open daily 7am-9pm.)

SIGHTS AND ENTERTAINMENT. El Nido's prime attractions are **Bacuit Bay's islands,** featuring white sand **beaches** at the foot of towering limestone cliffs. Asia's Galapagos, these isles boast coral, three species of endangered giant turtles, and brilliant fish. Among the best are **Miniloc Island,** with a small lagoon; **Pinsail Island,** where a marble cave lies complete with a skeleton of a WWII Japanese soldier; and **Inabuyatan,** which has a spotless white beach. Arrange **island-hopping tours** through cottages (P1000 per day) and **snorkeling** through **Bacuit Divers** on Calle Hama (P50 per day).

El Nido's vast rainforests offer unparalleled adventure. Jungle trekking to **Bulalacau** and **Nagkalit Kalit Falls,** **Makin It Hot Springs, Marble Cliff,** and **Cudugnon Cave,** an ancient burial site, can be arranged with a guide at the Department of Tourism (P150-350). Arrange **spear-fishing trips** with local fishermen (P800). Bacuit Divers offers dive trips around the archipelago, but Coron Island has better diving.

On most Sundays, especially holidays, **cockfights** erupt at the cockpit on Rizal Ave. **Shipwreck Bar,** on Palmera St., is a popular tourist hangout. (San Miguel P25. Open daily 4pm-midnight.) Locals get down at **Bom Disco,** opposite Mac-Mac Restaurant. (Cover P10. Open daily 8pm-midnight.)

CORON

While Port Barton calms the most critical beachcombers, and El Nido caters to island-hoppers, Northern Palawan is a wreck diver's Shangri-La. The waters off Coron Island and the separate town of Coron earn the curious distinction of housing the second-highest number of sunken Japanese WWII vessels, next to the Mar-

DEATH, PHILIPPINES STYLE In 1997, the Supreme Court affirmed the death penalty for three criminals, ending a 20-year no-killing streak. The Department of Corrections, however, lacked funds to build the gas chamber required by law. Instead, they assembled a lethal injection device, which they have been using zealously ever since. Before the 1998 executions, the last man to die was Emiliano San Jose, a 1976 victim of the electric chair. The new lethal injection system, operated by technicians trained in Texas, replaces the chair, which was destroyed by lightning in 1977.

ianas Islands. Diving aside, the azure waters, countless islets, and a gorgeous inland lake are enough reasons to visit for one day or four.

TRANSPORTATION AND PRACTICAL INFORMATION. Seair flies to **Manila** (1½hr.; Tu, F, Su; P2300), while flights from neighboring **Busuanga** fly to **Manila** (daily, 1½hr., P2300) and **Puerto Princesa** (P2200). **Jeepneys** depart from the public market regularly for **Busuanga** (2hr., 7am-4pm, P50). **WG&A Superferry** (☎12 31 48) sails to **Manila** (12hr., Su, P400) and **Puerto Princesa** (12hr., Sa, P400). **San Nicolas Lines** also goes to **Manila** (M, F, Su; P350). As with many small towns, roads are few and unnamed. The **National Hi-Way** connects Coron only to the western side of Busuanga Island, and the town's two main streets run parallel to the Hi-Way. The "first" street is anchored by **City Hall,** which also houses the **police station** and **post office** (M-F 8am-noon and 1-5pm). On the opposite end is the town **market** and **pier** for small boats. **Swagman Travel** (with a **Western Union** branch) lies at the intersection of the "second" street and the National Hi-Way. The **hospital** lies 3km north along the Hi-Way, next to the KokusNuss Resort.

ACCOMMODATIONS AND FOOD. Most of Coron's accommodations are concentrated between its two ports. **KokusNuss Resort,** 5316 Coron, is about 1½km towards Busuanga, but its amazing service and amenities make well worth the distance. (☎02 804 0331. Small cottage P300; large cottage P500,with private common room P700.) **Darayonan Lodge** (☎02 521 0637) and **Village Lodge** offer similar accommodations within the same price range but are more conveniently located next to City Hall. **Sea Dive Resort** offers scrumptious seafood with changing menus depending on the day's catch (dishes P80-250).

SIGHTS. There are over 10 Japanese wrecks within **diving** depths around Coron. The islands' countless dive shops have uniform prices ($25-35 per dive for all experience levels). PADI courses are also widely available ($200-450). **SeaDive** offers a diving special which includes two dives, divemaster, boat, lunch, and drinks. (P1200. ☎048 550 9207) **Scubaworld** offers a "Dive Safari" of three dives per day at Black Island. (2-3 days; $70 per day, including meals and kayaks.)

Island-hopping is the best way to enjoy Coron's unspoiled beauty. Coron Island's lakes are among the cleanest and greenest in the world. (Pumpboat with driver P800-1000 per day). El Nido's **Makin It Hot Springs** can be reached by a 3½km trail or a 15min. boat ride (P500 round-trip).

MINDANAO

TRAVEL WARNING. Due to dangerous travel conditions, this section was last updated in 1999. Security has improved since the 1980s, but crime and insurgent activity remain a concern outside Davao, particularly in Tawi-Tawi, Maguindanao, Lanao del Sur, Lanao del Norte, Sulu, Basilan, Zamboanga del Sur, Zamboanga del Norte, North and South Cotabato, and Sultan Kudarat. In 2000 and 2001, Muslim rebels took hostages in Jolo and Sanal Island. Travelers considering visiting Mindanao should contact their embassy for the latest information.

SINGAPORE

SINGAPORE DOLLAR

US$1 = S$1.75	S$1 = US$0.57
CDN$1 = S$1.13	S$1 = CDN$0.88
EURO€1 = S$1.59	S$1 = EURO€0.63
UK£1 = S$2.54	S$1 = UK£0.39
IR£1 = S$2.02	S$1 = IR£0.50
AUS$1 = S$0.93	S$1 = AUS$1.08
NZ$1 = S$0.77	S$1 = NZ$1.30
ZAR1 = S$0.21	S$1 = ZAR4.77

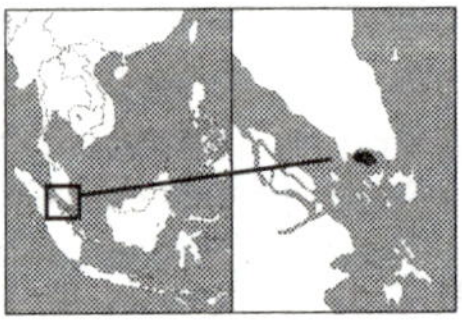

PHONE CODE **Country Code:** 65. **International dialing prefix:** 011.

Singapore can be shocking after traveling in other Southeast Asian countries. High-tech skyscrapers, clean streets, cutting-edge communication, and even potable tap water distinguish the "Lion City" from its neighbors. But there's more to Singapore than an affinity for hygiene; visitors are amazed by the contrast between its stringent laws and extreme wealth and the busy, multicultural metropolis burgeoning from the street markets and shops that seem to march to a different urban beat. Nodding bougainvillea at the Botanical Gardens give way to cash registers ringing in downtown department stores, while sidewalks bustle with the controversy surrounding the city-state's human rights violations or interplay of the its four ethnicities. Yes, Singapore is known for its harsh penalties for chewing gum, but the crab at East Coast Seafood and treks up Bukit Timah tell their own stories. Exploring Singapore means choosing between the financially and culturally rich and between designer shopping and a plate of chicken rice—the decision is yours to make.

FACTS AND FIGURES

Official Name: Republic of Singapore.
Government: Parliamentary Democracy.
Capital: Singapore.
Land Area: 647½ sq. km.
Geography: On the southern tip of the Malay peninsula.
Climate: Dry (high season) Mar.-Oct., rainy (low season) Nov.-Jan.
Population: 4,300,500.
Languages: English, Chinese, Malay, Tamil.
Religions: Islam, Hinduism, Taoism, Mahayana Buddhism.
Average Income Per Capita: US$30,900.
Major Exports: Petroleum, ships, electronics.

LIFE AND TIMES

THE PEOPLE OF SINGAPORE

Singapore's ethnic makeup is 77% **Chinese,** 14% **Malays,** and 8% **Indian,** the majority of whom are **Tamil** and were brought by the British as laborers. Singapore has welcomed immigrants since the 1300s; combine the many foreign-born residents with increasing Westernization, and it's understandable why there's concern about whether Singapore can forge a strong sense of national unity. Recognizing this, the government strives to promote a multicultural Singapore free of Western influence.

HIGHLIGHTS OF SINGAPORE

CULTURAL HERITAGE. Singapore's colorful past lingers at the **Raffles Hotel** (p. 613), in **Chinatown** (p. 614), and in **Little India** (p. 614). Hawker stalls make dining a truly cultural experience.

URBAN BEAT. Bars and clubs (p. 616) crowd the **Raffles Hotel Area,** the **Quays,** and **Mohamed Sultan Rd.** Shopping is expensive, but Chinatown is full of hidden bargains.

NATURAL WONDERS. Yup, even in a city-state. The **Zoological Gardens** (p. 615), **Botanical Gardens** (p. 615), and **offshore islands** (p. 615) are lush and orderly.

HISTORY

EARLY YEARS AND ISLAND COLONY (1300-1965)

—From lions to Lee Kuan Yew

The island state of Singapore, or **Tumasek** ("sea town") as it was once known, was established in the 14th century. One legend says it was founded by a Shrivijayan prince claiming relation to Alexander the Great, while another claims the island was named by an Indian prince, who saw a lion on the horizon and, in turn, named it **Singhapura** ("lion town").

In the 15th and 16th centuries, raids by the Portuguese and mighty Southeast Asian empires took their toll; the small island city sank into obscurity for two centuries. Prized only for its position along important trade routes, the island remained little more than a pirate's pit stop, free of Europeans until **Sir Stamford Raffles** of the **British East India Company** docked in Singapore's harbor in January 1819. Raffles transformed Singapore into a thriving port city, which became a British colony in 1867.

Piracy, intrigue, trade, exploitation, and prosperity all shook up the area during the 19th century as waves of immigration created a cultural mix. British expats strolled about the *kampung*, Chinese traders grew rich off Malayan exports, and indentured Indian convicts built St. Andrew's Cathedral. By 1915, the government began to address opium abuse, fund public works, and improve social services.

Despite its large British naval base, Singapore quickly surrendered to an unexpected **Japanese invasion** on the Chinese New Year in February 1941. The Japanese proceeded to terrorize the little colony, carting Europeans off to Changi Prison en masse and raping, pillaging, and slaughtering local Chinese.

After the war, a battered Singapore fell into political disarray, welcoming back Britain even as its residents began yearning for independence; strikes and student demonstrations crescendoed in the 1950s. For three years, **Lee Kuan Yew** negotiated for Singapore's independence, and a new constitution was written in 1959. After Lee and the left-leaning **People's Action Party (PAP)** won the 1959 elections, Singapore embarked on a steep path to stability and modernization, dissolving all ties to Britain and pursuing an alliance with the strongly nationalist **Federated States of Malaya.** This partnership, however, ended in bitter divorce, and Singapore assumed its present status in August 1965, independent from Malaysia.

14c
Singapore established

17-18c
Dutch and British struggle to control Singapore

1867
Singapore becomes British colony

1915
Singapore Sling invented by Ngiam Tong Boon at the Raffles Hotel

1915
Singapore takes control of the opium market, cracks down on Chinese secret societies

1941
Japanese invade

1959
New constitution written

1965
Independence

1990
Lee Kuan Yew steps down, succeeded by Goh Chok Tong

1996
Singapore achieves developed nation status

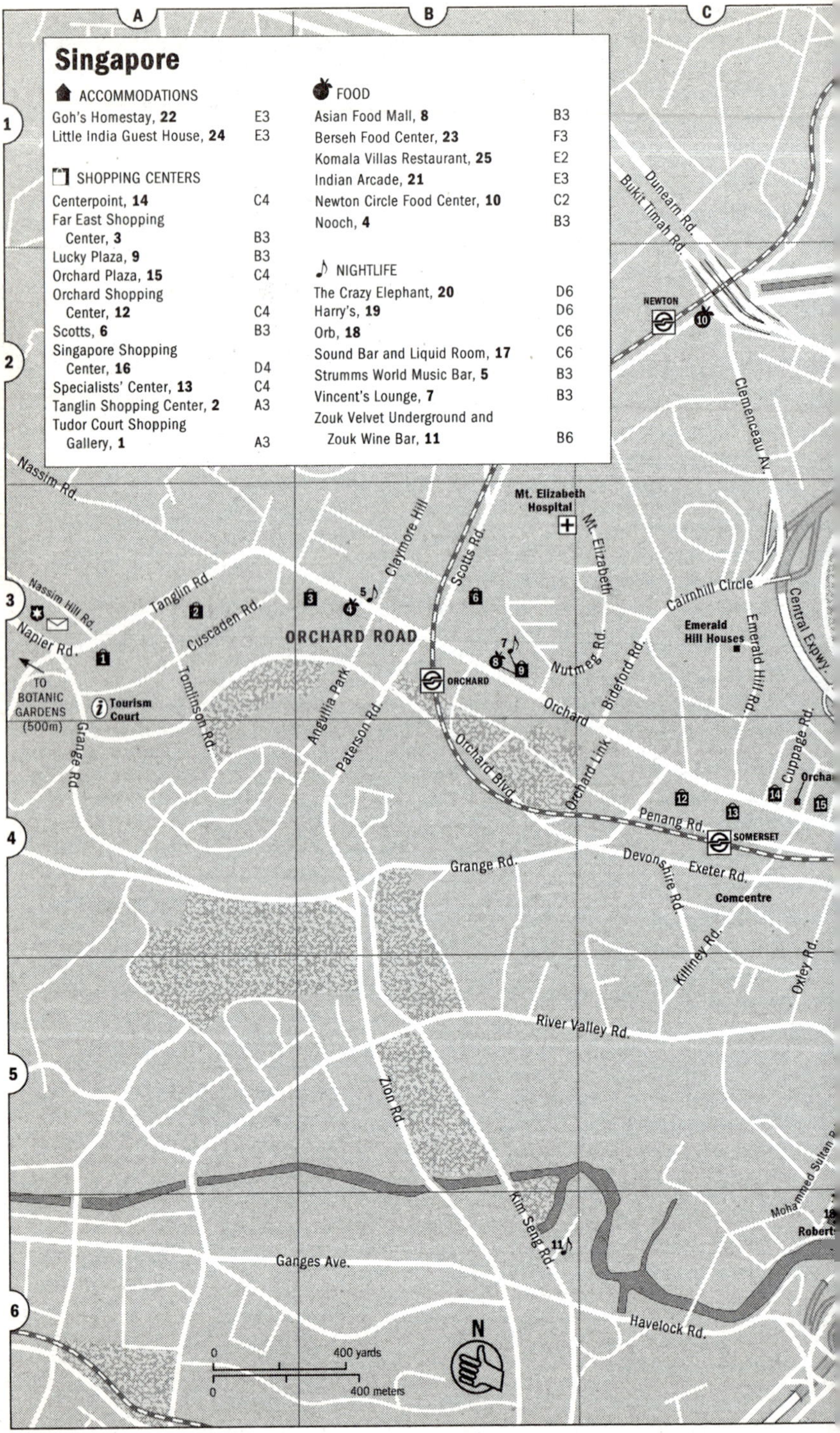
Singapore
ACCOMMODATIONS
Goh's Homestay, 22 E3
Little India Guest House, 24 E3
SHOPPING CENTERS
Centerpoint, 14 C4
Far East Shopping Center, 3 B3
Lucky Plaza, 9 B3
Orchard Plaza, 15 C4
Orchard Shopping Center, 12 C4
Scotts, 6 B3
Singapore Shopping Center, 16 D4
Specialists' Center, 13 C4
Tanglin Shopping Center, 2 A3
Tudor Court Shopping Gallery, 1 A3
FOOD
Asian Food Mall, 8 B3
Berseh Food Center, 23 F3
Komala Villas Restaurant, 25 E2
Indian Arcade, 21 E3
Newton Circle Food Center, 10 C2
Nooch, 4 B3
NIGHTLIFE
The Crazy Elephant, 20 D6
Harry's, 19 D6
Orb, 18 C6
Sound Bar and Liquid Room, 17 C6
Strumms World Music Bar, 5 B3
Vincent's Lounge, 7 B3
Zouk Velvet Underground and Zouk Wine Bar, 11 B6
A
B
C
1
2
3
4
5
6
Dunearn Rd.
Bukit Timah Rd.
NEWTON
Clemenceau Av.
Nassim Rd.
Mt. Elizabeth Hospital
Mt. Elizabeth
Claymore Hill
Scotts Rd.
Cairnhill Circle
Central Expwy.
Nassim Hill Rd.
Tanglin Rd.
Napier Rd.
Cuscaden Rd.
ORCHARD ROAD
Emerald Hill Houses
Emerald Hill Rd.
Nutmeg Rd.
Bideford Rd.
ORCHARD
TO BOTANIC GARDENS (500m)
Tourism Court
Tomlinson Rd.
Anguilla Park
Paterson Rd.
Orchard
Grange Rd.
Orchard Blvd.
Orchard Link
Cuppage Rd.
Penang Rd.
SOMERSET
Grange Rd.
Devonshire Rd.
Exeter Rd.
Comcentre
Killiney Rd.
Oxley Rd.
River Valley Rd.
Zion Rd.
Kim Seng Rd.
Ganges Ave.
Havelock Rd.
N
0
400 yards
0
400 meters

D
E
F
Central Expressway
Balestier Rd.
Serangoon Rd.
Leong San Ci
Shakya Muni Buddha Gaya Temple
Race Course Rd.
Lavender St.
Cambridge Rd.
Owen Rd.
Rangoon Rd.
LITTLE INDIA
Sri Srinivasa Temple
Perumal Rd.
Jl. Besar
Kampong Java Rd.
Keng Lee Rd.
Kampong Java Rd.
Farrar Park
Anguilla Mosque
Kitchener Rd.
Horne Rd.
Bukit Timah Rd.
Cavenagh Rd.
Race Course Rd.
Roberts Ln.
Kinta Rd.
Race Course Ln.
Syed Alwi Rd.
Sam Leong Rd.
Desker Rd.
Rowell Rd.
King George's Ave.
Belilios Ln.
Baboo Ln.
Hindoo Rd.
Sri Veerama Kali Amman Temple
Norris Rd.
Kg. Kapor Rd.
Veerasamy Rd.
Berseh Food Center
Serangoon Rd.
Buffalo Rd.
Cuff Rd.
Istana
Bukit Timah Rd.
Bukit Timah Rd.
Little India Arcade
Chitty Rd.
Upper Weld Rd.
Jl. Berseh
MacKenzie Rd.
Tekka Center
Hastings Rd.
Clive St.
Dunlop St.
Dickson Rd.
Weld Rd.
Malabar Muslim Jam-Ath
Jl. Kubor
SEE COLONIAL DISTRICT MAP, P. 607
Perak Rd.
Sungei Rd.
Rochor Canal
Arab St.
Wilkie Rd.
Edinburgh
Sophia Rd.
Short St.
Selegie Rd.
Prinsep St.
Albert St.
Rochor Rd.
Queen St.
Ophir Rd.
N. Bridge Rd.
Jl. Sultan
Sultan Mosque
Bussorah St.
Mt. Sophia
Kwan Im
Bugis Village
Sri Krishnan
Middle Rd.
BUGIS
Kramat Ln.
Handy Rd.
Princep Link
Bencoolen St.
Liang Seah St.
Tan Quee Lan St.
TO GOLDEN MILE COMPLEX (500m)
Penang Rd.
DHOBY GHAUNT
Waterloo St.
Queen St.
Victoria St.
Oxley Rise
Penang Ln.
Orchard
Fort Canning Rd.
Bras Basah Rd.
Singapore Art Museum
Bain St.
Purvis St.
Seah St.
Beach Rd.
National Museum
COLONIAL DISTRICT
N. Bridge Rd.
Raffles Hotel
Nicholl Hwy.
Fort Canning Park
Canning Rise
National Library
Stamford Rd.
Chijmes
Raffles Arcade
Suntec City
Temasek Blvd.
Temasek Ave.
Clemenceau Av.
Armenian St.
United States
War Memorial Park
Central Expwy. Tunnel
CITY HALL
Raffles Blvd.
TO CHANGI AIRPORT (10km)
River Valley Rd.
Hill St.
Coleman St.
St. Andrew's Cathedral
St. Andrews Rd.
Marina Square
Clarke Quay
Padang
Connaught Dr.
Raffles Av.
Singapore R.
High St.
Nicholl Hwy.
Boat Quay
Guardian Pharmacy
Upper Circular
Boat Quay
Tew Chew
Raffle's Landing Site
Explanade Bridge
Hongkong St.
Fullerton Rd.
Merlion
Marina Bay
Havelock Rd.
Laundry
TO CHINATOWN (SEE MAP, P. XXX)
Anderson Bridge

SINCE INDEPENDENCE (1965-2001)

—The price of dictatorship: prosperity.

When Lee Kuan Yew became a de facto and de jure dictator, he masterminded Singapore's miraculous transformation into a full-fledged city-state and economic powerhouse, complete with social welfare trimmings. Lee maintained that democracy and free speech, though important, meant little to individuals with nothing to eat and nowhere to live. These freedoms have therefore been sacrificed for the privileges of progress. Lee stepped down in 1990 to be succeeded by **Goh Chok Tong,** whose administration readmitted political exiles. Lee remains active in the Cabinet, however, and his popularity has waned little since his resignation. Many eye his son Deputy Prime Minister **Lee Hsien Loong** a shoo-in heir to the dynasty.

SINGAPORE TODAY

Technologically-advanced Singapore offers social and material benefits to its citizens. Unlike other Asian bureaucracies, efficiency defines Singaporean government; its overarching administration has the power to establish and fund programs that seek to improve education, cultural pursuits, and economic growth as well as fill potholes promptly. Because of their meteoric rise to progress and success over the past few decades, Singaporeans are justifiably proud of their country and bristle at criticisms from Western governments. In a speech to the Asia Society in 1989, Lee Hsien Loong asked, "Can the Singapore government really be so benighted and wrongheaded as not to see what is so patently in Singapore's interests? ...Speaking English does not make us an Anglo-Saxon people, much less Americans... We are not a Western society and have never sought to become one."

Opposition parties have grown, but since they boycotted elections in 1971, PAP has dominated politics. In a major victory for Prime Minister Goh Chok Tong, PAP won the parliamentary elections of January 1997. While Singapore has not been immune to the Asian economic crisis, its robust economy, low inflation, strong commercial banks, and lack of foreign debts have shielded it from the serious economic turmoil that has plagued its neighbors.

HUMAN RIGHTS

Singapore's harsh stance on drugs and crime has been internationally publicized and has come under fire from human rights groups such as Amnesty International. Criticism heightened in May 1994 when 18-year-old American **Michael Fay** was flogged for spray-painting cars and throwing eggs. US President Clinton claimed the punishment was extreme and cruel, but Singapore refused to buckle. The Singapore government also strictly control press by regularly filing (and wining) libel suits against its opponents. Though not technically censored, newspapers critical of the government are rarely allowed into the country. In 1997, the Singaporean government even began censoring the Internet, denying access to "unsuitable" web sites with references to sex, politics, or religion. Still, everyday Singaporean life remains at least superficially free. Small but pervasive reminders that Big Brother is watching include restricting those under 21 from watching movies with homosexual content and government posters gently encouraging procreation.

BISEXUAL, GAY, AND LESBIAN TRAVELERS

Homosexuality is illegal, but law prohibiting it are rarely enforced. Numerous clubs and hangouts, as well as a large online community, make up Singapore's thriving gay scene (see **Adam and Steve, Darling!**, p. 617). Every local knows this, but officials would like to believe that none of it exists; Singaporean media and government have been known to treat gays harshly.

PINK INK. For a complete listing of gay venues in Singapore, check out the Dragoncastle Gay Asia web site (www.dragoncastle.net/singapore/html).

SEMI-AUTOCRATIC WEAPONS Singapore's zeal for fining gum-chewers, litterbugs, vandals, and spitters is well-known, but the government also sponsors other "harmony-imposing" initiatives.

Freedom from smut: The recently passed Undesirable Publications Act staves off the Western cultural agenda by forbidding 170 magazines, books, and computer media on sexual, political, and religious grounds.

Freedom from smog: High car prices, automotive taxes, and a fantastic public transportation system are disincentives to drive in Singapore. Beginning in 1998, a debit card on every windshield is automatically zapped of funds depending on the road and the time of day. Those driving without a card have their license plates automatically photographed; a fine arrives by mail soon afterward.

Freedom to schmooze: The state-sponsored Social Development Unit serves as both a matchmaking and mildly eugenic family planning service, offering over 800 matrimony-making mixers each year for single university graduates. Recent events include a Beverage Knowledge Class, Go-Karting, and Self-Defense for Executives.

Freedom from stench: In an effort "to drive home the message that clean toilets are achievable," the Environment Ministry has sponsored both a People's Choice contest for particularly spankin' johns and a Toilets of Shame hotline for citizens to snitch on those who shirk their legal obligation to flush. Many elevators in Singapore contain **automated urine-sniffers,** which trap incontinent occupants inside until law enforcement agents arrive to levy fines.

Freedom from stings: Once a month, every home in Singapore is inspected for puddles of standing water, which breed malaria-carrying mosquitoes and other pests. If a stray puddle is found in a flower pot or trash bin, a stiff fine follows.

SINGAPORE

ARTS AND RECREATION

Singapore's **architecture** integrates Western, Indian, Arabic, and Chinese styles, old and new. While urban renewal has destroyed many older fishing villages and bungalow-style *kampung*, conservation has maintained some classic structures and neighborhoods. The Emerald Hill area, off Orchard Rd., boasts beautiful shophouses. Colonial architecture is predominantly found in "black and white" style houses, such as Adam Park, off Adams Rd. near the Bukit Timah intersection. Modern skyscrapers serve as constant reminders of the city's dramatic transformation. Architect **I.M. Pei's** wizardry, including the **Gateway Building** on Beach Rd. and the **OCBC Center** on Church St., dots the landscape.

Other visual arts are mostly modern, although certain genres, like traditional **pen and ink drawing,** are influenced by older Chinese styles. Local cultural shows present other traditional forms, such as **Malay shadow plays** and **kite-flying** or **Chinese lion dances.** Western and Chinese drama are popular, but Hollywood and Hong Kong blockbusters along with popular Malay and Indian hits take center stage. **Chinese opera** combines high (melo)drama with elaborate costumes.

ADDITIONAL SOURCES

The Lands of Charm and Cruelty: Travels in Southeast Asia, by Stan Sesser (1993). Includes an essay on contemporary Singapore originally published in *The New Yorker.*

Fistful of Colours, by Suchen Christine Lim (1993). Celebrates the destinies of three women shaped by the uniqueness of Singapore's early multi-ethnic society.

ON THE WEB

New Asia-Singapore (www.newasia-singapore.com). Choose a language and learn everything it takes to "Live it up in Singapore."

Singapore Infomap (www.sg/). Endless links and information grace this page.

ESSENTIALS

VISAS

All travelers to Singapore must obtain a **Social Visit Pass,** issued at arrival and valid for 3 months. British and Irish citizens can stay for up to 30 days, while citizens of all other countries can stay for a maximum of 14 days. The immigration office provides **visa extensions** for up to 90 days. For stays over 3 months, travelers must apply for a Long Term Social Visit Pass backed by a Singapore organization.

MONEY

The **Singapore dollar (S$)** comes in denominations of S$2, 5, 10, 20, 50, 100, 500, 1000, and 10,000, and coins come in 1, 5, 10, 20, and 50 cents and S$1. **Credit cards** are widely accepted, and **ATMs** are abundant. **Tipping** is discouraged and illegal at the airport. Clubs, bars, and classy restaurants and hotels label themselves either "plus," indicating a 10% service charge, or "plus plus," indicating a 10% charge plus a 4% tax. The 3% Goods and Services Tax (GST) can be partially refunded by shopping at stores with "Tax Refund" signs. Ask for a Global Refund Cheque and present it at airport customs before departure. Unless you see a "fixed price" sign, feel free to **bargain** in outdoor markets, at most shops in Chinatown and Little India, and on trishaw rides. For information on **currency exchange,** see p. 608.

KEEPING IN TOUCH

Singapore's postal service is probably the most reliable in all of Southeast Asia. Many *Poste Restante* packages actually make it (gasp!) to the post office counter. High-tech communications equipment make phone connections clear and consistent. **International operator** number is ☎104; **directory assistance** is ☎100. For **Home Country Direct (HCD)** numbers from Singapore, refer to the table on the inside back cover of this book.

THE CITY ☎65

INTERCITY TRANSPORTATION

BY PLANE

Changi Airport (☎1 800 542 1122, flight info 542 4422) is 25min. east of the city center. A S$15 **airport tax** is usually included in the price of your ticket. To get downtown, take **bus** #36 (6am-midnight, S$1.50) to the **Raffles City** and **Orchard Rd.** areas. **Taxis** run S$15-20, plus a S$3 (S$5 on weekends) airport charge. The **Maxicab,** an A/C six-seat coach, takes you to within blocks of any budget accommodation. (☎552 2222. Every 30min. 9am-11pm from airport to city, S$7; 8:20am-10:30pm from city to airport; S$8 in advance.)

ONE DAY I'LL FLY AWAY...

DESTINATION	FREQUENCY	PRICE	DESTINATION	FREQUENCY	PRICE
Bangkok	6 per day	S$806	**Jakarta**	5 per day	S$330
Brunei	6 per day	S$466	**Kuala Lumpur**	9 per day	S$338
Cebu	1 per day	S$750	**Manila**	3 per day	S$895
Hanoi	3 per week	S$900	**Phuket**	2 per day	S$360
Hong Kong	2-4 per day	S$700	**Yangon**	1 per day	S$764

Singapore International Airlines (SIA) is in airport terminal 2, DBS tower, 290 Orchard Rd., and SIA building on 77 Robinson Rd. #01-01. (24hr. ☎223 8888, ticketing 223 6030; www.singaporeair.com.) **Silk Air,** 8 Shenton Way #08-01 Temasek Tower, is a subsidiary of Singapore International Airlines. (☎225 4488, ticketing 332 6891; 24hr.

reservations available through SIA. Ticketing open M-F 8:30am-5:30pm.). Other air services are provided by: **Bangkok Airways,** airport terminal 1, #041-04F (☎545 8481); **Cathay Pacific Airways,** 10 Collyer Quay, #16-01 Ocean Building (reservations ☎533 1333); **Garuda Indonesia,** 101 Thomson Rd., #13-03 (reservations ☎250 5666); **Malaysia Airlines,** 190 Clemenceau Ave., #02-09/11 (reservations ☎336 6777; open M-F 9am-6pm); **Myanma Airways,** Singapore Station 50 HPL House Cuscaden Rd. #07-00 (☎235 5005); **Philippine Airlines (PAL),** 35 Selegie Rd., #10-02 Parklane Shopping Mall (reservations ☎336 1611); **Royal Brunei Airlines,** 25 Scotts Rd., #04-08 Scottswalk (☎235 4672); **Thai Airways,** 100 Cecil St. (reservations ☎224 9977, ticketing 224 2024); and **Vietnam Airlines,** 260 Orchard Rd., #08-08 (reservations ☎339 3552).

BY TRAIN

The **railway station,** 30 Keppel Rd., is on the south tip of the main island, 20min. from downtown by bus. (☎222 5165 for 24hr. automated schedules and fares. Open daily 6am-11pm.) Buses run every 5-15min. to the station from the **Raffles Hotel** (#84, 97, 100, and 131), **Selegie Rd.** (#97 and 131), and **Little India** (#97 and 131). Buy tickets before travel during booking hours (8:30am-7pm). The **Malayan Railway** (☎222 5165) has two train routes: one runs along the west coast up to **Hat Yai** (Haadyai) in Thailand while another cuts through the middle of Malaysia and **Taman Negara National Park,** ending in **Tumpat,** the northeastern corner of Peninsular Malaysia. The Hat Yai (via Butterworth) line leaves from Kuala Lumpur. **Express trains** with A/C go to **Kuala Lumpur** (7hr.; 8:10am, 3, 10:10pm, plus F-Su 10:25am; S$19) via **Tampin** (5hr., S$15). To go to Taman Negara National Park, take the **Gua Musang** train to **Jerantut** (8½hr., 9:30am), or the **Tumpat** (14hr., 8:06pm, 2nd-class lower bunk S$51) train that travels via **Jerantut** (8hr., 2nd-class lower bunk S$38).

BY BUS

In addition to the stations below, buses also leave from the Golden Mile Complex, near Lavender St. Bus Station.

Lavender St. Bus Station: On the corner of Lavender St. and Kallang Bahru in Little India. **Hasry Express** (☎294 9306; open M-Sa 7:45am-8pm, Su 7:45am-4pm) to **Kuala Lumpur** (9:30, 10:30am, noon, 2:30, 10pm, midnight) and **Melaka** (4½hr.; 8:30, 10:30am, 2:30, 4:30pm; S$11). **Transnasional Express** (☎294 7034; open daily 8am-8pm) to **Kuala Lumpur** (daily 9, 11am, 4:30, 10pm, plus Th-Sa 6pm; S$25-30) and other Malaysian destinations.

Lucking Station: At Queen and Arab Rd. **Singapore-Johor Bahru Express** (☎292 8149) to **Johor Bahru** (1hr., every 15min. 6:30am-midnight, S$2.40). **Kuala Lumpur-Singapore Express** (☎292 8254) to **Kuala Lumpur** (6hr.; 9am, 1, 5, 10pm; S$25).

Hotel Royal: On Newton Rd. **Nice/Plusliner** to **Ipoh** (9:30am, 10pm; S$45, children S$35) and **Kuala Lumpur** (24 per day 7am-10pm; S$37, children S$27).

BY BOAT

Changi Ferry Terminal: In the northeast part of the city. **Ferrylink** (☎545 3600) boats to **Tanjong Belungkor,** gateway to the Peninsula's east coast (45min.; 4 per day 9:45am-6:45pm; S$19, round-trip S$26); check in 1hr. in advance.

Tanah Merah Ferry Terminal: On the southeast corner of the island. Take MRT to Tanah Merah station and then bus #36 to the Ferry Terminal. Gates close 20min. before departure. **Dino Shipping** (☎276 9722) ferries to **Batam** (30min.; every 2hr. 8am-6pm; S$15, round-trip S$25).**Auto Batam Ferries** (☎542 7105) boats to **Pulau Bintan** (1½hr.; 9:10am, 1:10, 5:25pm; S$39, round-trip S$49) and **Pulau Tioman** (4½hr.; 8:30am; S$90, round-trip S$148).

ATTENTION ISLAND-HOPPERS If you're off to Pulau Penyenget, take the ferries to Tanjong Pinang, the main city, and not to Bintan Resort. Transport from Bintan Resort to Tanjong Pinang involves a taxi and a 2hr. local bus ride.

World Trade Center Ferry Terminal: At the southern tip of the island, accessible by bus #97 or 131 from Bencoolen St. or Bras Basah Rd., #61, 84, or 145 from North Bridge Rd., or #143 from Orchard Rd. **Auto Batam** (☎271 4866) ferries to **Batam** (40min.; every 30min. 8:40am-9:45pm; S$15, round-trip S$20). From Batam, travelers to **Sumatra, Indonesia** can take a high-speed boat to **Pekanbaru** (7hr., 9:45am).

ORIENTATION

The city divides into four areas. **Orchard Rd.** stretches from west to east of the city center, where it turns into Stamford Rd. Stamford Rd. and its parallel street to the north, **Bras Basah Rd.,** are at the heart of the **Colonial District.** When Selengie Rd., which protrudes from the eastern end of Orchard Rd. becomes Serangoon Rd. to the north, you've reached **Little India.** South of the Singapore River, below Upper Cross and Cross Streets, **Chinatown's** many shops and restaurants extend as far as Cantonment Rd. The **airport** is at the east fringe of the city. The **railway station** is south of Chinatown. Free maps and the useful "Official Guide to Singapore" are available at the airport and major hotels.

BENCOOLEN STREET. Backpackers gather here to avoid the frenzied shoppers of nearby Orchard Rd. Rumor has it that Bencoolen has been slated for development into a high-wattage strip of shops and hotels. For now, it remains a land of small discount stores, vacant lots, and unremarkable coffee houses between the National Museum on Bras Basah Rd. and Rochor Canal. To reach Bencoolen St. from the airport, take the Maxicab, or take bus #36 to the YMCA on Orchard Rd.

COLONIAL DISTRICT. The extensively renovated Raffles Hotel captures the grandiose splendor of colonial Singapore, as do all of the three neighborhood museums. Many visitors stop by for a drink by the fountain at Chijmes, the convent-turned shopping gallery. Backpackers flock to accommodations on North Bridge Rd., near Rocher Rd., to soak in the outer rays of the Colonial District, which is gradually expanding northward.

ORCHARD ROAD. Shopaholics are free to roam about the street's numerous department stores and underground food courts. While designer boutiques are normally empty, department stores are always packed with cosmopolitan consumers who stay at 5-star hotels nearby. Bars and pubs are hard to find, as they are located underground or at the top of shopping centers.

CHINATOWN. To get to Chinatown from the airport, take public bus #36 to the Stamford and North Bridge Rd. intersection, then catch #81 to Sri Mariamman Temple. Chinatown stands as a testament to Singapore's pride in its newfound national heritage—Chinese-colonial shophouses have been gutted, refurbished, and repainted in lively pastels. The MRT extension has sent property values through the roof, and old coffee shops have given way to new offices and boutiques. Don't worry, you can still find a competitively-priced stuffed frog. These streets host many Buddhist and Hindu temples, as well as culinary centers like Lau Pa Sat Festival market and the Maxwell Market food center.

LITTLE INDIA. Indian immigrants used to raise cattle on the fertile land around the Rochor River. As more immigrants flocked to Singapore in the late 19th century, Little India grew into a thriving trade center and an Indian cultural haven. Scrubbed and purified in Singaporean fashion, Little India provides the best compromise for budget travelers—accommodations are reasonable, worthwhile sights are within easy reach, and cheap food is everywhere.

LOCAL TRANSPORTATION

Buses: Local buses run 6am-midnight. Yellow-and-orange-roofed stops have information boards listing buses by street and destination. **Night Rider buses** run from 11:30pm to as late as 3:56am; bus stops have yellow NR signs and the time of the last bus. Bus fares are S$0.60-1.50. Ask the driver for the fare to your destination and pay the exact fare or insert your **Farecard** (available at any MRT stop, vail on buses and trains). **Transit Link Travel Map** (S$5) at any bookstore.

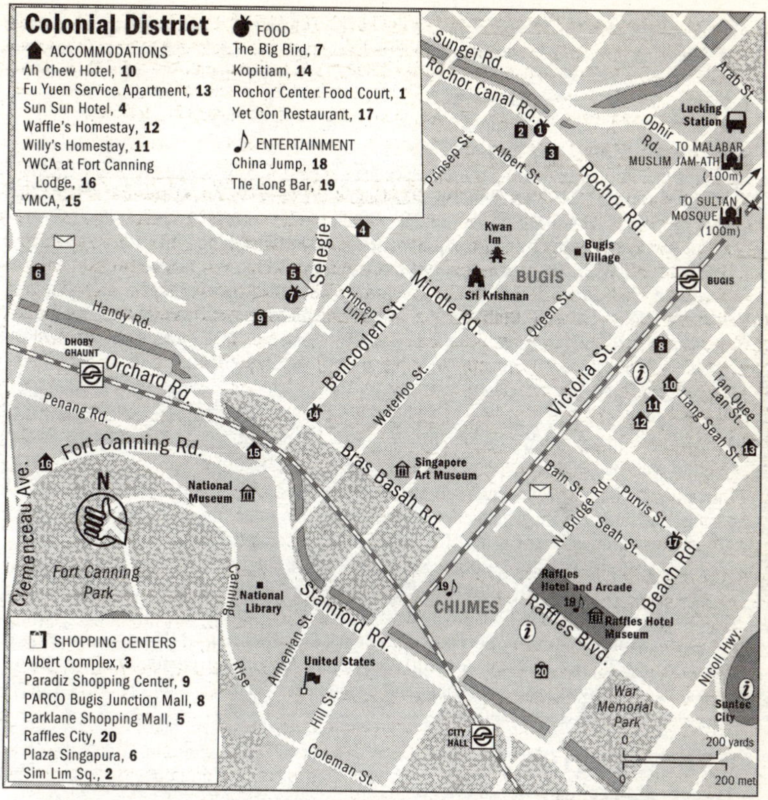

Mass Rapid Transit (MRT): ☎1 800 336 8900; www.smrt.com.sg. Two main A/C lines run 6am-midnight. Single-use card S$0.80 for the three stops closest to where you board, S$0.90-1.60 for more. **Farecards** save 5-10¢ per ride (S$12 plus S$2 deposit, returned when card is returned; unused portion is refunded). Most MRT counters (open M-F 8am-9pm, Sa 8am-6pm) sell Transit Link Guides (S$1.50) and MRT maps (S$5).

Taxis and Trishaws: With an efficient bus and train system, there is little reason to use taxis. Taxis are government-owned, which means fares are standardized but surprisingly low. The meter starts at S$2.40; each additional 240m is S$0.10; most city fares cost S$3-7. 50% surcharge midnight-6am. Try **Comfort Cab** (☎552 1111), but expect a S$2.80 surcharge. Expensive **trishaws,** at Bras Basah Park on Orchard Rd. and outside of Bugis St. food market, are unnecessary for most sightseers.

PRACTICAL INFORMATION

TOURIST AND FINANCIAL SERVICES

Tourist Offices: Tourism Court, 1 Orchard Spring Ln. (☎1 800 738 3778). Open M-F 8:30am-5pm, Sa 8:30am-1pm. **Singapore Visitors Center at Suntec City,** 3 Temasek Blvd. (☎332 5066). Open daily 8am-6:30pm.

Tours and Travel: Airpower Travel, 131A Bencoolen St. (☎334 6571). Most competitive prices for regional flights. **STA Travel,** 1 Tanglin Rd., #02-17 Orchard Parade Hotel (☎737 7188). Student/youth-rate tickets, ISIC cards, and train packages to Thailand and Malaysia. MC/V (3% surcharge). Open M-F 9am-5pm, Sa 9am-noon. For international bus tickets, try **Singapore Travel Service,** 6001 Beach Rd. #01-11 Golden Mile Complex. Open daily 8am-8pm. Other popular bus operators include **707 Travel Services** (☎292 3633) and **T&L Tours** (☎293 9118).

Embassies: Australia, 25 Napier Rd. (☎836 4100). Open M-F 9am-12:30pm and 1:30-4:45pm. **Brunei Darussalam,** 325 Tanglin Rd. (☎733 9055). Open M-F 8:30am-4:30pm. **Canada,** 80 Anson Rd., 14th-15th fl., IBM Towers (☎325 3200). Open M-F 8am-noon and 2-4pm. **Indonesia,** 7 Chatsworth Rd. (☎737 7422). Open M-F 9am-4pm. **Ireland,** 298 Tieng Bahru Rd., #08-06 Tieng Bahru Plaza (☎276 8935). Open M-F 9:30am-12:30pm and 2:30-4pm. **Malaysia,** 301 Jervois Rd. (☎235 0111). Open M-F 8am-5:15pm. **Myanmar,** 15 St. Martin's Dr. (☎735 6576). Open M-F 9:30am-12:30pm and 2-5pm. **New Zealand,** 391A Orchard Rd., Ngee Ann City Tower A, 15th fl. (☎235 9966). Open M-F 8:30am-5pm. **Philippines,** 20 Nassim Rd. (☎737 3977). Open M-F 9am-noon and 1-4pm. **South Africa,** 331 North Bridge Rd., #15-12 Odeon Towers (☎339 3319). Open M-F 8:30am-1pm and 2-5:30pm. Visas M-F 9am-noon. **Thailand,** 370 Orchard Rd. (☎737 2158). Open M-F 9:30am-12:30pm and 2-5pm. Visas 9:15am-noon. **UK,** 100 Tanglin Rd. (☎473 9333). Open M-F 8:45am-5pm. Visas 8:30am-noon. **US,** 27 Napier Rd. (☎476 9100). Open M-F 8:30am-5:15pm. Visas M-F 9-11am. **Vietnam,** 10 Leedon Park (☎462 5938). Open M-Sa 9am-noon.

Immigration Offices: 10 Kallang Rd. (☎391 6100). MRT: Lavender. **Visa extensions** require a local sponsor, confirmed departing air ticket, and passport. Usually no fee, and 1-day processing. To avoid the hassle of visa extensions, some travelers go to Johor Bahru, Malaysia and re-enter. Open M-F 8am-5pm, Sa 8am-1pm.

Currency Exchange: Moneychangers are often the best deal. Most open daily 9am-9pm. Arab Street moneychangers provide competitive rates but close at 5pm. Try **Saj Drug Store Money Change,** #01-09 Raffles City Shopping Center (☎339 1723). Open M-F 8am-10pm, Sa 8am-9:30pm, Su 10am-9pm. **Banks** mostly open M-F 9:30am-3pm, Sa 9:30-11:30am. **American Express Bank,** 16 Collyer Quay (☎538 4833), opposite Clifford Pier. No card member services. Open M-F 10am-3:30pm.

American Express: Member Services, 300 Beach Rd., 18th fl. #18-01 Concourse Bldg. 199 555 (☎299 8133, 24hr. ☎1 800 733 0833). Mail held 1 month for card or traveler's check holders. Replaces cards and cashes personal checks for members. Open M-F 9am-5pm, Sa 9am-12:30pm.

LOCAL SERVICES

Luggage Storage: Train Station (☎222 5165). S$3 per piece per day. Open daily 7am-9pm. **Changi Airport** (☎546 2738), in the basement and in both terminals; S$4-5 per day including S$500 insurance. Follow the signs. **Open 24hr.**

Library: National Library, 91 Stamford Rd. (☎332 3255). English and Chinese books. Open M 11am-9pm, Tu-F 10am-9pm, Sa 10am-5pm, Su 1-5pm.

Bookstores: MPH, 63 Robinson Rd. (☎222 6423). Office supplies, English-language best-sellers, maps, magazines, and international newspapers. Open M-F 10am-7pm, Sa 10am-3pm. There's a branch on Stamford Rd. next to the National Library. Open daily 10am-9:30pm. **Sunny's Bookshop,** 14 Scotts Rd. #03-58 (☎733 1583), is small but has reasonable prices. Open M-Sa 10am-8pm.

EMERGENCY AND COMMUNICATIONS

Emergency: Police ☎999. **Ambulance** ☎995. **Fire** ☎995. Toll-free from pay phones.

Pharmacies: Guardian Raffles City Pharmacy, 252 North Bridge Rd., Raffles City Shopping Center basement #11 (☎339 2137). MRT: City Hall. Knowledgeable staff. Call ahead for prescriptions. Open daily 10:30am-9:30pm.

Medical Services: Raffles Medical Group Clinic (☎543 1118), in the basement of Changi Airport Terminal 2. Doctors available 8am-midnight S$30; after midnight S$180. **Open 24hr.** for consultations. **Singapore General Hospital** (☎222 3322). MRT: Outram Park. Walk-in clinic open daily 8am-11pm. All major hospitals have **24hr.** on-call doctors.

Telephones: See **Keeping in Touch,** p. 604.

Internet Access: Youth Resource Center, 113 Somerset Rd. (☎734 4233). S$5 per hr. Open M-F 9am-6pm, Sa 9am-8pm. **Cybernet Cafe** in Changi Airport, passenger terminal 2. Open daily 8am-10pm. **Internet City,** #02-066 Suntee City Mall (☎357 1155).

S$3 per 30 min., S$5 per hr. Open daily 10am-10pm. Another branch is at 11 Stamford Rd. #01-19 (☎338 9100). **One Stop Cafe,** 44 Smith St. Students S$3 per hr. Open daily 10am-8pm.

Post Office: GPO, 10 Eunos Road 8, Level 1 West Entrance 408600 (☎741 8857). MRT: Paya Lebar. *Poste Restante.* Open M-F 8am-9pm, Sa 8am-6pm, Su 10am-4pm.

ACCOMMODATIONS

Tiny Singapore has enough hotel beds to house its 7 million annual visitors—which is no small feat, considering Singapore's permanent population is under 3.5 million. Accommodations may not be as budget-friendly as those in the rest of Southeast Asia, but aside from ritzy Orchard Rd., most hotels are an excellent value.

COLONIAL DISTRICT

Sun Sun Hotel, 260A and B-262A Middle Rd. (☎338 4911), in the classy old David Elias Bldg. Convenient location. Chinese bakery downstairs. Clean common baths and tidy beds. High ceilings make the rooms seem large. Highly recommended by regulars. Singles with fan S$35; doubles with fan S$45, with A/C S$50; extra person S$10.

YWCA at the Fort Canning Lodge, 6 Fort Canning Rd. (☎338 4222; ywcasin@singnet.com.sg). Conveniently close to Orchard Rd. and the Colonial District, but without the five-star prices. Immaculate brand-new facilities, with fantastic views of the adjoining country club and the city. Take a dip in the pool, play tennis, sing karaoke, or get your hair done on the premises. Notify to cancel reservations. Singles S$95-120, doubles S$105-140; women-only dorms S$45 (groups preferred, reserve in advance). S$3.09 surcharge first night for YWCA membership. Prices don't include taxes.

Fu Yuen Service Apartment, 75 Beach Rd. 6th fl. #06-02 Fu Yuen Bldg. (☎339 5490), 2½ blocks past the Raffles Hotel; look for a brown elevator. Comfortable common room. Laundry S$10. Dorms S$8-10; with A/C S$35-45.

YMCA, 1 Orchard Rd. (☎336 6000; hostel@ymca.org.sg). Despite 70s motif bedsheets, the Y is well-kept and runs like clockwork. All rooms have A/C, TV, telephone, and attached bathroom. Has a fitness center, billiards room, and rooftop swimming pool. "Student room" dorms S$28.33; singles S$107.64; doubles S$124.63; extra bed S$17. Surcharge of S$5 per room on first night to get temporary YMCA membership.

Willy's Homestay, 494 North Bridge Rd. (☎337 0916). Go through the restaurant and upstairs. Breezy, fun atmosphere. Free lockers. 9-person dorms with fan S$8, with A/C S$10; double with fan S$26, with A/C S$30. Use the back entrance 10pm-8am.

Ah Chew Hotel, 496 North Bridge Rd. (☎837 0356), above Tongseng Kopitiam. For those who just want to lay down their weary heads. Cubby-sized dorms with bunk beds. Laundry starts at S$5. Storage S$5. 24hr. reception. No reservations. Dorms with fan S$10 or A/C S$12; singles and doubles with fan S$26/30.

Waffle's Homestay, 490 North Bridge Rd. (☎338 88 26), through loud Naj Indian Cafe. Nice balcony with breezes and flowers. A/C 8am-8pm only. Check-out 11am. Big dorms S$8; 4-bed dorms S$9; singles and doubles S$26-30; triples S$35. 10% off for 7-day advance payment.

CHINATOWN

Majestic Hotel, 31-37 Bukit Pasoh Rd. (☎222 3377; majestichotel@pacific.net.sg). A short walk to Outram Park MRT, popular among Malays and foreign couples for neat and recently restored rooms with A/C. Contact to reserve room and confirm promotional room rates for A/C singles and doubles S$60-90.

Chinatown Guest House, 325D New Bridge Rd., 5th fl. (☎/fax 220 0671). MRT: Outram Park. Opposite Pearl's Center Mall on the southwest edge of Chinatown. Go to Eu Tong Sen St., cross the street, and proceed right (New Bridge Rd.). Helpful attendant, rooftop view of streets below and nearby office buildings. Kitchen available. 2 common baths. Dorms S$10; singles S$25; doubles S$30, with A/C and bath S$45.

LITTLE INDIA

Goh's Homestay, 40-43 Upper Weld Rd. (☎339 6561; minggoh@pacific.net.sg). Part hostel owner, part universal mother, Goh's owner will stay up at night awaiting your safe return. Located between Serangoon and Jalan Besar, Grace and Snowy (the outdoor cat) are part of the welcoming committee. This tightly-run ship abounds with amenities: local fax S$1 per page, storage S$6 per week, laundry S$12, breakfast S$4. Email S$5 per hour. Bicycle rental S$10 per day. Reservations recommended. High season A/C dorms S$25; singles S$44; doubles S$55; triples S$69.

Little India Guest House, 3 Veerasamy Rd. (☎294 2866), off Serangoon Rd. The beds are a bit springy and the towels could be a bit fresher, but all rooms have TV and phones. Squeaky clean common bathrooms. 24hr. reception. Check-in anytime. Locker service. Singles S$35, with A/C S$40; doubles S$40, with A/C S$50; triples S$60, with A/C S$70.

MURDER OF CROWS The Singapore Gun Club, a venerable institution of heat-packing private citizens, has been tapped by the city for a public duty: the massacre of crows. The crows, a non-native species, bring disease and contagion and leave droppings all over the otherwise sparkling clean city-state. To combat the pesky birds, the government provides free ammo to the Gun Club, whose members are mostly wealthy Singaporeans with a love of weapons and/or killing things. The club totes its shotguns to parks and shipyards and blows away anything that's black and has wings. They bag a few hundred per night.

FOOD

Food prices in Singapore range from S$3 *laksa* (a spicy coconut-based soup) to S$150 steak dinners downtown. Luckily, there's a happy medium at Singapore's **hawker centers.** These food markets hold countless stalls serving everything from fruit juice and iced desserts to seafood, rice, and vegetarian curry, all for about S$2-3 each. The bustle of centers is worth exploring for its own sake. Hawker centers in the city centers are often open 24 hr.

Rojak is a salad of fruit and vegetables, including cucumber, turnip, pineapple, and mango. Fish balls *(ta mee)* combine fried noodles and fish paté. Chicken rice is a specialty of the Hainan region of China. To make *char kuay teow*, cooks sauté wide rice noodles with sea cockles, vegetables, soy sauce, and vinegar. Desserts of shaved ice and fruit or jelly, such as *ice kachang*, mitigate the effects of Singapore's jungle climate. Diners rush to slurp it up as they melt in the tropical heat.

Just about every shopping center or department store has a food court on the lower level, so no one can accuse Singapore of starving them. "Good Food in Singapore" signs mark kiosks that were rated high by local food critics.

So, hungry yet?

BEST OF SINGAPORE FOOD FINDS

Best Hawker Centers:
The Rochor Center, Newton Circle Food Center, Lau Pa Sat Center, Maxwell Market Food Center and The Indian Arcade

Best Chicken Rice:
The Big Bird

Best Viagra Alternative:
The Soup Restaurant's culinary cures

COLONIAL DISTRICT

Yet Con, 25 Purvis St. Two blocks north of the Raffles Hotel, this wellspring of authentic Hainanese cuisine has dished up chicken and *charsiu* roast pork (S$3) to a fanatical following for 60 years. The specialty is the "steamboat," (around S$14 for 2 people) a silver hotpot with a chimney to release the steam emitted from the charcoal burning below. Open daily 11am-8pm.

The Big Bird (The Chicken Rice restaurant), 35 Selegie Rd. #01-07, Parklane Shopping Mall. Chicken rice is a Singapore delicacy that is sumptuous, thrilling, titillating, and so chock full of chicken fat it hurts your arteries just to think about it. The Big Bird offers a recipe that satisfies, judging by the crowded tables. Plate for one is S$4.50.

Kopitiam, 51 Bras Basah Plaza, at the corner of Bras Basah Rd. and Bencoolen St. Opposite the Singapore Art Museum. It's predecessor is under the Le Meridien Hotel at Orchard Rd. With shiny multi-colored seating, this food court is bustling even late on weekday nights. Marvelous selection of fruit juices (S$2), fish and chips, beer, wonton soup, and Indian biryani. Full meals S$3-5. Open 24hr.

The Rochor Center, at the corner of Bencoolen St. and Rochor Canal Rd. has food stalls open daily 6:30am-10:30pm and a supermarket open daily 9am-10pm.

ORCHARD ROAD

Nooch, 501 Orchard Rd., #02-16 Wheelock Place. Above Border's Books and near the Orchard MRT station, this "Noodle Bar" promises to be MSG-free and eco-friendly (note the bamboo chopsticks). Nooch scores points for its street view, prompt service, and heaps of Thai and Japanese noodles. Try the chicken curry noodles (S$8.50) or the crispy *thung negen yueng* (minced chicken wrapped in deep fried bean curd, S$6). Open M-Th noon-3pm and 6-10:30pm; F 6-11pm; Sa-Su noon-3pm and 6-11pm.

Newton Circle Food Center, right next to Newton MRT stop, using the Newton Food Circus exit. One of the best examples of how open-air eating in Singapore can be more fun than a controlled climate, Newton shows off the true spirit of hawker centers. A generous helping of fried rice, frog legs, or whatever fare you choose costs S$3-5. Beers S$3.50; sodas S$2; fresh fruit juice S$1.50-2. Open 24 hours.

Asian Food Mall, Lucky Plaza #B1-31-38/135-143/148, 304 Orchard Rd. An alternative to the fancy restaurants and Western food chains that crowd Orchard Rd. Much like indoor hawker centers, these food courts provide such local delicacies as *Nasi goreng* (S$3.80), Malay curry rice, 2 vegetables and a meat (S$4) or an "east meets west" special offer of fried rice and a grilled drumstick for S$4.50. Drinks range from S$1.20 sodas to S$2.90 for freshly squeezed juice. It won't be the best Asian food you'll find, but it's quick and convenient.

CHINATOWN

Markets and Hawker Centers: Lau Pa Sat Center, the oldest hawker center in Singapore, a carnival of cuisine on the corner of Cross St. and Shenton Way, is a 5min. walk south of the Raffles Place MRT stop. Banana leaf meal S$3. After midnight, the side street is blocked off for stalls that offer your choice of prawn, beef, mutton, chicken, or duck satay for S$0.40 a stick. Open 24hr. **Maxwell Market Food Center,** at the intersection of Maxwell and South Bridge Rd., is perhaps Singapore's most modern hawker center. Vendors hawk traditional Chinese and Middle Eastern fare, including *char kuay teow* (S$2-3) and turtle soup (S$6-12). Open daily 6am-11pm; some stalls open 24hr. Behind **People's Park Center,** on Eu Tong St., is a large variety of food stalls. Take bus #81 from Bencoolen St. or take the MRT to Outram Park and look for Eu Tong Sen St.; it's beyond the Pearl's Center Mall. Rice cakes are recommended (S$6). Full meals S$3-5. Open daily 10am-10:30pm.

Ci Yan Vegetarian Health Food, 2 Smith St. Off the corner where Smith and S. Bridge Rd. intersect. This small cafe has MSG-free brown rice meal sets for vegetarians and the health conscious (S$4.50) and a bookcase of Buddhist literature to read during your meal. If you were put off by the antlers for sale next door, Ci Yan's may be the perfect creature-friendly alternative. Open daily 8am-8pm.

The Soup Restaurant, 25 Smith St. MRT: Outram Park. Walk north up New Bridge Rd., turn right on Smith St. after New Bridge Center; it's on the right. A healing culinary experience with family recipes; it seeks to improve anything from eyesight to sexual potency. Samsui ginger chicken S$12-22. Soak in old-Singapore atmosphere with your Chinese tea. Open daily noon-2:30pm and 5:30-9:30pm.

Muang Myint Restaurant, 65 Temple St., features popular Burmese dishes such as tea-leaves salad (S$3) and prawns (S$7). Curry catfish is a steal at S$5. Tiger beer S$6. Open daily noon-10pm.

Murray Food Terrace, opposite the Maxwell Market Food Center off Maxwell Rd. Walk from the Tanjong Pagar MRT stop down Peck Seah St. toward Maxwell St., turn left, then left again before the Bank of China. Renowned for pricier restaurants, such as **Moti Mahal,** 18 Murray St., serving tandoori chicken (½bird S$13.80), and **Moi Kong,** 22 Murray St., a Hakka restaurant that serves the popular salt baked chicken (S$8).

LITTLE INDIA

Komala Villas, 76-78 Serangoon Rd., around the corner from Upper Dickson Rd. Branch down the street at 12-14 Buffalo Rd. Indian vegetarian food. *Masala dosa,* a sassy mix of sauces and spices, scooped up with a huge pancake around a potato base is S$2.50. Affiliated bakery next door sells Indian sweets (S$0.80), fruit, and cold drinks. A souped-up version of Komala Villa's is around the corner on Upper Dickson. Komala's Restaurant, more expensive with its glass doors and fast-food interior, sells the same vegetarian delights (South Indian meal S$6.60) as well as crispy spice-dusted fries. Open daily 8:30am-10pm.

Indian Arcade, the corner of Campbell Ln. and Serangoon Rd. Find the hawker center of Indian food below the Indian Arcade. Mutton *biryani* S$3, vegetarian *biryani* set S$4. Open daily 9am-9:30pm.

Berseh Food Center, on Jl. Besar at the corner of Jl. Berseh and close to the International Hotel, serves *kuay teow,* Hokkien Prawn Mee soup, and *roti.* Dishes S$2-5. Open daily 5am-1am

SINGAPORE

SIGHTS

COLONIAL DISTRICT

RAFFLES HOTEL. This pristine white behemoth, built in the early 20th century by the Armenian Sarkies brothers, is a testament to Singapore's colonial past. Legend has it that a tiger once escaped from a street circus nearby and wandered into the hotel's billiard room, where a guest shot it dead. Tigers haven't run amok for some time, but the prices at shops in **Raffles Arcade** are just as scary. The only thing free is the ambience and the peanuts at the **Long Bar** inside. The **Raffles Hotel Museum,** on the third floor, traces the hotel's history from its founding in 1887 through New Year's Eve 1993. *(The entire block between North Bridge and Beach Rd. along Raffles Blvd. ☎237 1886. Open daily 10am-9pm.)*

CHIJMES. This area was the home of the Convent of the Holy Infant Jesus, an orphanage run by French nuns. After five years of restoration, this four-acre city jewel has been transformed into an esplanade of outdoor shops and cafes. Raffles City Shopping Center, across the park from Chijmes, is an intriguing contemporary structure housing many designer boutiques. *(30 Victoria St. between Stamford Rd. and Bras Basah Rd.)*

NATIONAL MUSEUM. Also known as the Singapore History Museum, found at the beginning of Bencoolen St., focuses on Singaporean history and boasts exhibits of Chinese porcelain and Aw Boon Haw's jade collection. *(93 Stamford Rd. ☎837 9940. Open Tu-Su 9am-6pm, F until 9pm. S$3, students S$1.50. Free tours Tu-F 11am and 2pm; Sa-Su 11am, 2, 3pm.)*

SINGAPORE ART MUSEUM. Opposite the National Museum, the Singapore Art Museum houses an array of multimedia works by regional artists and hosts traveling exhibits by artists ranging from Monet to Leonardo. *(☎332 3222. Open Tu-Su 9am-6pm, F 9am-9pm. S$3, children and students S$1.50. Free guided tours Tu-Su 11am and 2pm; Sa-Su 11am, 2, 3:30pm.)*

BUGIS VILLAGE AND FOOD CENTER. Always bustling with activity, the Bugis area, stretching over Waterloo and Qreen St., used to serve as a stage where transvestites and transsexuals paraded openly. After a government crackdown, residents complained of decreased business and the demise of Bugis life, but government efforts to reintroduce Bugis culture failed. At the fruit market, vendors advertise their wares while potential buyers sniff, shake, and pat the selections. The adjoining market has restaurants and flea market stalls. Performances by Chinese singers or Thai dancers may be hidden on adjacent side streets, so go peek. *(Open daily 9am-10pm.)*

OTHER SIGHTS. The **Sultan Mosque,** off Arab St. on North Bridge Rd. and a 3min. walk from the Bugis MRT stop, should be entered from Brussorah or Muscat St. Inspired by Indian traditions, it was originally built with a S$3000 grant from Sir Stamford Raffles. *(Visiting hours 9am-1pm and 2-4pm; no visits F 11:30am-2:30pm.)* **Malabar Muslim Jam-Ath** is a smaller mosque that sits north of the Sultan Mosque. *(471 Victoria St., on corner of Victoria St. and Jl. Sultan. ☎294 3862. Open daily 5:30am-9:30pm.)*

Near the Bugis area, the section of Waterloo St. between Middle and Rocher Rd. is closed to traffic. People wander among the flower vendors and fortune tellers on the street opposite the **Chinese Goddess of Mercy** and **Sri Krishnan Temples.** *Puja* ceremonies (ceremonies of worship), happen at 7am, noon, 5:30pm, and 9pm. The **Kwan Im Temple** (Goddess of Mercy) next door shines in gold splendor. Take a canister of fortune-sticks from the monks' desk, kneel in the middle of floor and shake the canister until a stick falls out. Tell the monks the number on your stick and they'll give you a sheet of paper with your fortune on it. Or, for the latest in fortune-telling technology, try the **palm-reading** computer opposite the temple—one of the two is sure to get your fortune right. *(Open daily 10am-5:30pm; 1st and 15th days of lunar month 6am-6:15pm and 5am-6:45pm; festive days 4am-6:45pm.)*

In **Sim Lim Square,** six floors of every imaginable form of electronics are ready to be sold to the best bargainer. From heart rate monitors to cameras, fax machines, cell phones, satellite dishes, computers and their accessories, this place has it all. *(1 Rochor Canal Rd. Open 11:30am-8:30pm.)*

CHINATOWN

The **Chinatown Historic District,** on Telok Ayer St., parallel to Amoy St., used to be home to Chinese and Malay immigrants in the 19th-century, later becoming the Chinese commercial district and serving as a slave-trade hub on shore.

TIAN HOCK KENG TEMPLE. Of the three temples along Telok Ayer St., only the Escher-like "Temple of Heavenly Happiness" merits more than a cursory pause. The **statue of Ma Cho Po,** goddess of the sea, was installed in 1840. Sailors donated tile and ironwork, as well as a spate of stone dragons slinking on the roof, pillars, and walls. *(On Telok Ayer St. between Boon Tat and McCallum St. Open daily 6am-5:30pm.)*

SRI MARIAMMAN TEMPLE. Locals say they know they're in Chinatown when they see this colorful temple. It stokes up a pit 4m wide for **Thimithi,** the **Firewalking Festival.** Hindu stalwarts wrap their feet with faith alone for the yearly October stroll over fire. *(At 244 South Bridge Rd. at the southeast end of Temple St. MRT: Outram Park; follow Eu Tong Sen St. past Pearl's Center and the People's Park complex, turn right onto Temple St., and walk to the end of the street. ☎223 4064. Open daily 7am-noon and 6pm-9pm. Inner part closed noon-6pm. Camera use S$3, video camera S$6.)*

OTHER SIGHTS. Evening visitors to the **Sri Vinayager Hindu Temple,** at the intersection of Kreta Ayer and New Bridge Rd., may be privileged to witness Hindus praying and cracking coconuts on the ground. Shops nearby, along Trengganu, Smith, and Temple St., sell clothes, fabric, medicine, and countless souvenirs. The **Chinese Theater Circle,** features Cantonese opera with English and Chinese subtitles. *(5 Smith St. ☎323 4862. Open noon-3pm and 7:30-9:30pm. Tickets S$10-50.)* **Rainbow Reflexology and Massage,** one block over from the Chinese Theater Circle, performs reflexology, Thai, Chinese, Swedish and injury massage, and pulls the limbs into relaxing positions. *(59 Temple St. Massage S$35 for 45min.; reflexology S$20 for 40min.)*

LITTLE INDIA

Shops near Serangoon Rd. emit clouds of incense and freshly ground spices. Proprietors fuss with displays of jewelry, gold, *saris*, and Hindu gods—take your pick.

SRI SRINIVASA TEMPLE. The broken coconuts in the inner courtyard are for the elephant-headed Vinayagar, revered for his filial piety. The temple is the launching pad for the **Thaipusam Festival.** On a decreed religious day in January or February, Hindus honor Lord Subramaniam with a pilgrimage from this temple to the Chettiar Hindu Temple. They carry a *kavadi* (metal cage) decorated with offerings, hooks, and spikes, with which worshippers pierce their skin so the *kavadi* can hang from their flesh. The zealots never bleed, a phenomenon attributed to their trance-like state. *(397 Serangoon Rd., past Perumal Rd. ☎298 5771. Open Su-Th 6:30am-noon and 6-9pm, F-Sa 6:30am-noon and 5-9:30pm.)*

SRI VEERAMA KALI AMMAN TEMPLE. The temple draws devotees of the fearsome Kali. Friday evenings see a steady mass of visitors. *(141 Serangoon Rd. on the corner of Belilios Rd. ☎293 4634. Open daily 5:30am-12:30pm and 4-9pm.)*

OTHER SIGHTS. Sakya Muni Buddha Gaya Temple (Temple of 1000 Lights), boasts a 50-foot Buddha adorned in yellow and orange robes. The Thai temple was placed in Little India to recognize the Buddha's Indian background and to encourage Buddhist and Hindu dialogue. *(366 Race Course Rd. Open daily 8am-4:45pm.)*

Across the street, the large **Leong San Temple** (Dragon Mountain Temple) has impressive fountains and a back room full of ancestral tablets of patrons. The main hall replicates a Chinese palace and was built in 1917. Reverend Zhuan Wu established the temple with a statue of Kwan Yin that he brought from Fujian Province. *(Open 6am-6pm.)*

The neighborhood around **Desker St.** holds Singapore's **red-light district.** House after house shines red fluorescent lights on bored women reading or chatting. Transsexuals and transvestites pose and approach men in the streets; con artists play card and ball tricks for bets. **Angullia Mosque,** on Serangoon Rd., is a unique specimen of religious architecture that mixes traditional and contemporary styles. On Serangoon Rd. across the from Angullia Mosque, **Mustafa's** shopping complex, said to have the best prices in town, hums with the activity of busy shoppers.

NEAR SINGAPORE

SINGAPORE ZOOLOGICAL GARDENS AND NIGHT SAFARI. The zoo is well kept and renowned for its no-cage policy. Some animals wander at their leisure; others are separated by moats or trees. The zoo has a rare collection of four **Komodo dragons,** which are publicly fed at 2pm on the second and last Sundays of the month. Visitors also come for breakfast or high tea with the **orangutans.** Catch nocturnal creatures at their loveliest on the **Night Safari,** next door to the zoo. Tour a recreated landscape of rainforests and river valleys from the Himalayas to the Americas, communing with "pig bears," tigers, and rhinos by tram. *(Travel there in luxury on the Zoo Express in the evenings from Orchard Rd. hotels, or take the MRT to Ang Mo Kio and transfer to bus #138. 80 Mandai Lake Rd. ☎269 3411. Zoo express ☎481 01 66. Open daily 8:30am-6pm. S$12, ages 3-12 S$5. Breakfast 9am S$16, tea 4pm S$13; no tea on Su and public holidays. Night safari open daily 7:30pm-midnight; last entry 11pm. S$15-15, children S$10.30.)*

SINGAPORE

SENTOSA ISLAND. The Singaporean mother-of-all-tourist-traps has an Asian Village, Central Beach, water park, Underwater World, and insect museum. Don't be tempted by a guided tour. Avoid volcano land like it's a real disaster—$12 gets you the kind of experience that dominates grade-school field trips. Saturday nights, **Siloso Beach** hops with expats and Singaporean *yuppies* at the weekly beach party. For island **camping,** reserve three days in advance. *(Take Sentosa Bus E from Orchard Rd. or C from Tiong Bahru MRT, or take the cable car from the World Trade Center. ☎275 0388. Admission to the island before 6:30pm S$5, children S$3; after 6:30pm S$3, children S$1.80. Camping ☎472 5130. 4-person tents S$14; 8-person tents S$19.)*

JURONG BIRD PARK. This park contains over 600 bird species, including Antarctic penguins and the cassowary from Papua New Guinea, known for its ability to charge humans and rip their hearts out with its bare claws. For a cheerful start to your day, have "breakfast with the birds" in the park, on Jl. Ahmad Ibrahim. *(Take the MRT to Boon Lay Station and transfer to bus #194 or #251. ☎265 0022. Open daily 8am-6pm. S$12, children S$5.)*

THE BOTANIC GARDENS. This 52 sq. km haven shelters the world's largest orchid display and houses a virgin rainforest that has been preserved through decades of industrial development. *(Take the MRT to Orchard, then take bus #7, 105, or 106. ☎471 7361. Open daily 5am-midnight. Free, except S$2 for Orchid Garden.)*

JURONG REPTILE PARK. The park is next door to the Bird Park on Jl. Ahmad Ibrahim. You can gape at over 2500 crocodiles and see crocodile wrestling at 11:45am and 2pm. *(☎261 8866. Open daily 9am-10pm. S$8, children S$7.50.)*

CHINESE AND JAPANESE GARDENS. Built on a pair of islands in Jurong Lake connected by a carved stone footbridge, the gardens are at Jurong Park on Yuan Ching Rd. *(Take the MRT to the Chinese Garden station and follow the signs. ☎264 3455. Open daily 9am-6m. S$4.50, children S$2.)*

EAST COAST PARKWAY. Offers good seafood and ocean views. Excellent choices are always pepper prawns and chilli crab. The UDMC Seafood Center to the right and East Coast Lagoon Food Center to the left are recommended eateries. *(Take bus #36 (S$1.20) from Bras Basah Rd. to Marine Crescent, block 34. Walk across the street toward the main road or take a taxi from Bedok MRT. Open 5pm-10pm.)*

OTHER SIGHTS. Changi Prison Chapel and Museum is a chilling reminder of the Allied POWs during WWII. *(Take the MRT to Tanah Merah, then the SBS bus #2. ☎214*

2451. Open M-Sa 9:30am-4:30pm.) From the Changi Point Ferry Terminal, boats leave for **Pulau Ubin**, a quiet island of fishing *kelong*, ideal for hiking or biking (S$2 per trip). More island getaways lie south of Singapore. **Kusu Island** is home to a hill sacred to Muslims and Taoists that offers panoramic views of the mainland. *(S$9, children S$6; includes ferry ticket.)* **St. John's Island** offers beaches and walking paths. *(Ferries leave from the World Trade Center to both destinations. ☎270 7881. M-Sa 10am and 1:30pm, Su 6 per day 8:45am-5:15pm; S$6.20, children S$3.10.)* Equipped with lots of water, sunscreen, and comfortable clothing, a day or afternoon spent exploring Singapore's parks can bring a true appreciation for local flora and fauna, and you may even spy a monkey or two. **Macritchie Reservoir,** accessible by many buses is off Thompson Rd. after the TCS building. The large reservoir is an ideal place to jog, read a book, or watch one of Singapore's famous thunderstorms. The **Bukit Timah Nature Reserve** is home to the only real hike in Singapore; Bukit Timah "hill" rises 164m above sea level and is host to such strange birds as the "striped tit-babbler." *(177 Hindhede Dr. Take bus #171. From Newton MRT take bus #171. Open daily 7am-7pm.)*

NIGHTLIFE

There's no dancing on bar-stools (or chewing gum on bar-stools, for that matter), but Singapore's classy club and bar scene offers a great opportunity to splurge.

COLONIAL DISTRICT

The Long Bar (☎337 1886, ext. 1230), in the Raffles Arcade, is the birthplace of the Singapore Sling (S$16). The atmosphere is reminiscent of colonial times. Get fanned by palm leaves and engage in pleasant conversation while brushing peanut shells onto the floor. Cover bands perform on the 3rd fl. Beers S$10-12; spirits S$13. Open Su-Th 11am-1am, F-Sa 11am-2am.

Harry's, 28 Boat Quay (☎538 3029), near Tew Chew St. on Boat Quay. Features live jazz and rhythm-and-blues Tu-Su 9:30pm and F 10pm. Expat hangout, like the rest of Boat Quay. Happy Hour (until 9pm) beer S$6, spirits S$7. Bar and restaurant open Su-Th 5pm-1am, F-Sa 5pm-2am.

The Crazy Elephant, #01-07 Clarke Quay (☎337 1990), has live bands from 10pm-1am, and an open jam every Su. Great blues and jazz and laid back atmosphere. Happy Hour daily 5-9pm. Open Su-Th 5pm-1am, F-Sa 5pm-2am.

China Jump, #B1-07/08 Fountain Court (☎338 9388), in Chijmes, has 1930s Shanghai-style furniture and bartenders who do fancy tricks. Get your "teeth cleaned" in the dentist's chair with tequila and lime juice, or try the FBI (Bailey's, vanilla ice cream, vodka, and Kahlua). Beer and spirits S$11.50. Cover W and F-Sa: women S$20, men S$25. Open M, Tu, Su 5pm-1am, W, Th-Sa 5pm-3am.

MOHAMED SULTAN RD.

Club-hopping is the local ritual on Mohamed Sultan Rd., but everyone's content to stay at the end of the road at Robertson Quay.

Sound Bar and Liquid Room, 76 Robertson Quay, #01-05 Gallery Evason Hotel (☎333 8117). On the ground level, Sound Bar plays chill-out music at the al fresco bar. Prime seating is by the glowing fish tank or on the couches outside. Have the house special, a lychee martini (S$15), while the fans blow mist in your direction. Lava lamps sparkle; everyone is beautiful here. Open Su-Tu 7pm-2am, W-Sa 7pm-3am. A propeller-sized fan cools off the crowd upstairs at **Liquid Room,** which pumps trance and techno music mixed by local DJs and guest DJs from Japan and the UK. Packed on the weekends. No cover. W-Th 11:30pm-3am, F 10:30pm-3am, Sa 11pm-3am.

Orb, 76 Robertson Quay, The Gallery Evason Hotel #01-08 (☎333 8506). A circular lounge with frosted glass panes. Shoot pool downstairs while jiving to hip-hop or chat under the ambient tunes on cushy cubes in an intimate setting. Premium beers S$14, house wine S$12. Open M-Sa 6pm-3am.

ADAM AND STEVE, DARLING! "You! In the tight T-shirt...gyrating in leather pants and blowing kisses! Hands in the air! You're under arrest!" If this is your view of homosexuality being illegal in Singapore, the answer is: Not quite. Yes, that episode where Ally McBeal and Lucy Liu kiss was taken off the television airwaves, and Janet Jackson's recent album was not released here for its racy lyrics, but the gay scene is burgeoning behind the turned head of the Singapore government. Many straight folks go to the **Boom Boom Room** to see the cabaret show of lovely drag comedian Kumar, who is loved for his signature Singaporean humor. Gays and lesbians alike congregate to drink and outshine one another on the dance floor at **Taboo Cafe & Bar,** and **Vincent's Lounge,** which just celebrated its twelfth anniversary, and is regarded as somewhat of a gay institution or headquarters for its tenacity throughout the years. Lesbian bars **Cow and Coolies Pub** and **Loosen Up** are packed despite the stiff beer prices (S$25) after 9pm. There's even been a "Butch Hunt" competition at **Zouk,** which hosts a Girls' Party on the first Tuesday of every month. Everyone is having a ball at "KTV" Karaoke Pubs like **Babylon** for yuppie gay Singaporeans along Tanjong Pagar Rd., despite the crooning of melodramatic love songs from the 80s. With limited access to gay and lesbian literature, many Singaporeans still view homosexuality as being "unnatural," leaving communities to find venues on the internet (like www.sgboy.com and www.utopia-asia.com/tipssing.htm). So while the gay pride parade is more than just around the corner, venues are slowly being publicized, guaranteeing visitors a very gay stay in spite of their supposed invisibility.

Boom Boom Room, 132 Amoy St., Far East Square (☎435 0030).

Taboo Cafe & Bar, 21 Tanjong Pagar (☎225 6256).

Vincent's Lounge, 6th fl., Lucky Plaza, 304 Orchard Rd. unit #05. Open Su-Th 7pm-1am, F-Sa 7pm-2am.

Cow and Coolies Pub, 30 Mosque St. (☎221 1239).

Loosen Up, 15 Neil Rd. Open M-Th 6pm-1am, F-Sa 6pm-3am.

Zouk Velvet Underground, 17 Jiak Kim St. (☎738 2988).

Babylon, 52 Tanjong Pagar Rd. (☎227 7466).

Zouk Velvet Underground, 17 Jiak Kim St. (☎738 2988). The premiere nightclub in Singapore. World-renowned DJs, but steep covers. Psychedelic TVs, strobe lights and pulsating beats. W is Retro Night, when you can get lost in the crowd and pretend you're a local. Happy Hour daily 11pm-midnight. Cover S$20-35. Open Tu-Su 8pm-3am.

Zouk Wine Bar (☎738 2988). Has older crowd and self-described down tempo music. No cover. Open Tu and Th 9pm-3am, W and F-Sa 6pm-3am, Tu and Su 1pm-1am.

ELSEWHERE

Many pubs and clubs flash in Chinatown along **Tanjong Pagar and Duxton Rd.,** accessible by the MRT stop of the same name. Exit the station, turn left, pass Peck Seah on Wallich, and turn right on to Tanjong Pagar. **Strumms World Music Bar,** 400 Orchard Rd., #02-43 Orchard Towers, has a live band in tight leather, funky Southwestern decor, and a generous dance space, all make it one of Singapore's hottest nightspots. (☎738 3483. First-drink charge on weekdays, S$15 cover charge F-Sa. Free cover and 5 drinks for ladies on Tu. Happy Hour 6-8pm. Women 18+, men 23+. Open daily 6pm-3am.)

SINGAPORE

THAILAND

BAHT

US$1 = 44.25฿	10฿ = US$0.23
CDN$1 = 23.45฿	10฿ = CDN$0.43
EUR€1 = 40.28฿	10฿ = EUR€0.25
UK£1 = 64.25฿	10฿ = UK£0.16
IR£1 = 51.14	10฿ = IR£0.20
AUS$1 = 28.64฿	10฿ = AUS$0.35
NZ$1 = 19.50฿	10฿ = NZ$0.51
ZAR1 = 5.31฿	10฿ = ZAR1.88

PHONE CODE **Country Code:** 66. **International dialing prefix:** 001.

The only people of Southeast Asia not to have been colonized, the Thai have a proud and independent history that infuses the spirit of Thai society even today, in spite of the hordes of tourists who trample the country's beaches, temples, and jungles. A period of economic depression has made living very cheap for foreigners, even as the Thai economy slowly begins the road to recovery. Fifteen years ago, a million people descended on the "Land of Smiles" every year—today, that number has risen to 8½ million, and catering to tourists has become Thailand's lifeblood. There are sights for everyone: beachgoers head to the islands off the eastern and southern coasts, while the more adventurous trek through hill tribe homelands in the mountainous north. Others explore the ancient cities of central Thailand, where the ruins of once-great kingdoms now lie in silent majesty, testament to a glorious past. Throughout Thailand, mouth-watering cuisine and gracious people will be your companions, and a smile will be your currency. For travelers new to Southeast Asia, there is no better place to start than *Amazing Thailand.*

FACTS AND FIGURES

Official Name: Kingdom of Thailand.
Government: Constitutional Monarchy.
Capital: Bangkok.
Land Area: 514,000 sq. km.
Geography: Borders Malaysia, Myanmar, Laos, and Cambodia. Chao Praya River flows through the fertile central plain. Northern Thailand and the Burmese border to the west are mountainous.

Climate: Dry (high season) Nov.-Mar., rainy (low season) Apr.-Oct.
Major Cities: Chiang Mai, Khon Khaen, Nakhon Ratchasima, Ubon Ratchathani.
Population: 61,000,000.
Languages: Thai, English.
Religions: Theravada Buddhism (95%), Muslim, Christian, Hindu (5%).
Average Income Per Capita: US$3100.

LIFE AND TIMES

THE PEOPLE OF THAILAND

Use of the word "Thai" began in the 20th century as a political/geographical designation referring to all citizens of Thailand. "Tai," however, refers to the ethnic Tai-Kadai people, who speak Tai-based languages, live mostly in China, Laos, and Myanmar (where they are known as the Shan), and account for 75% of Thai people. At 12% of the population, the **Chinese** are Thailand's largest minority. Hill tribe groups, including the **Karen, Hmong, Yao, Lahu, Akha,** and **Lisu,** concentrate in the north, while the country's one million Muslims are concentrated in the south.

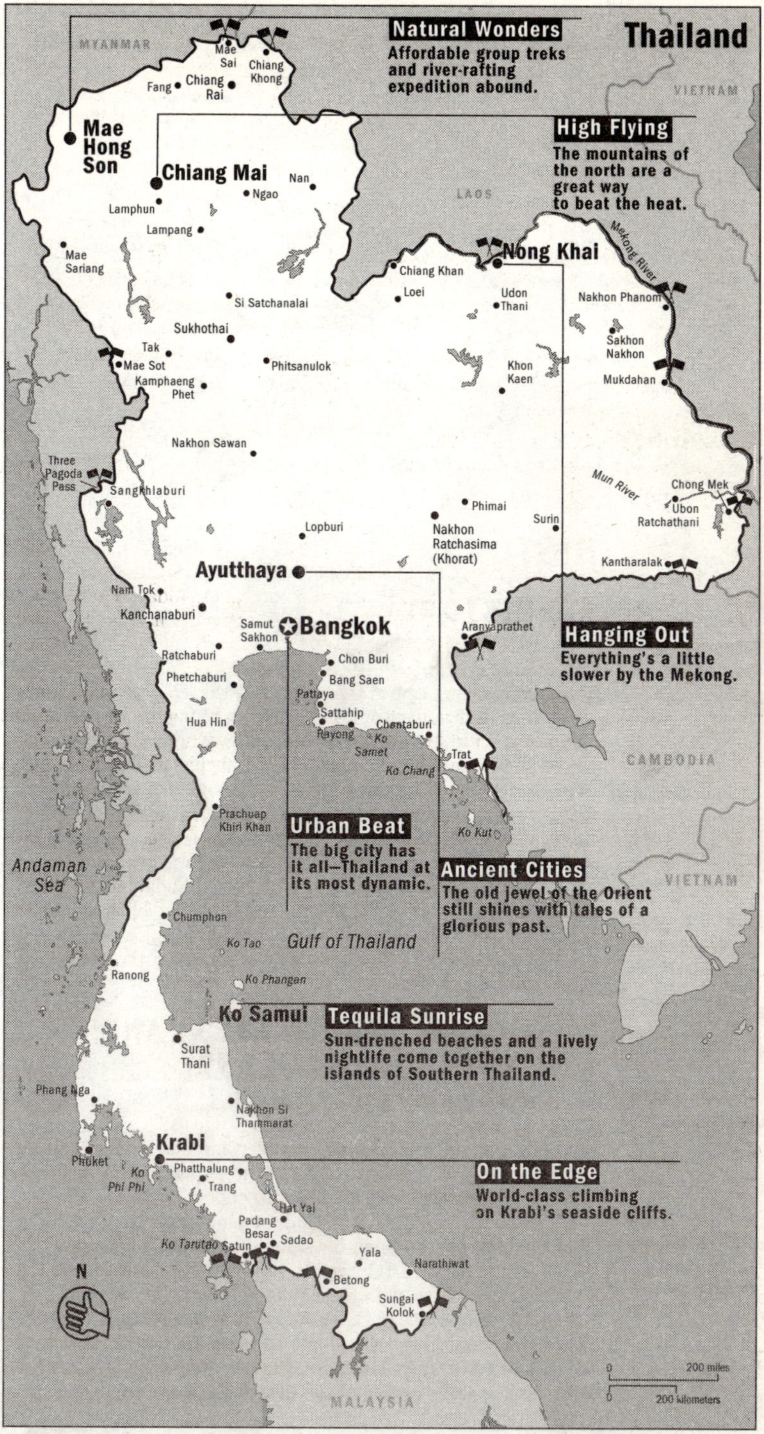
Thailand
Natural Wonders
Affordable group treks and river-rafting expedition abound.
High Flying
The mountains of the north are a great way to beat the heat.
Hanging Out
Everything's a little slower by the Mekong.
Urban Beat
The big city has it all—Thailand at its most dynamic.
Ancient Cities
The old jewel of the Orient still shines with tales of a glorious past.
Tequila Sunrise
Sun-drenched beaches and a lively nightlife come together on the islands of Southern Thailand.
On the Edge
World-class climbing on Krabi's seaside cliffs.
MYANMAR
LAOS
VIETNAM
CAMBODIA
MALAYSIA
Mae Sai
Chiang Khong
Fang
Chiang Rai
Mae Hong Son
Chiang Mai
Nan
Ngao
Lamphun
Lampang
Mae Sariang
Nong Khai
Mekong River
Chiang Khan
Loei
Udon Thani
Nakhon Phanom
Sakhon Nakhon
Mukdahan
Si Satchanalai
Sukhothai
Tak
Mae Sot
Phitsanulok
Kamphaeng Phet
Khon Kaen
Nakhon Sawan
Three Pagoda Pass
Sangkhlaburi
Mun River
Chong Mek
Ubon Ratchathani
Phimai
Surin
Lopburi
Nakhon Ratchasima (Khorat)
Ayutthaya
Kantharalak
Nam Tok
Kanchanaburi
Samut Sakhon
Bangkok
Aranyaprathet
Ratchaburi
Chon Buri
Phetchaburi
Bang Saen
Pattaya
Sattahip
Hua Hin
Rayong
Chantaburi
Ko Samet
Trat
Ko Chang
Prachuap Khiri Khan
Ko Kut
Andaman Sea
Chumphon
Ko Tao
Gulf of Thailand
Ranong
Ko Phangan
Ko Samui
Surat Thani
Phang Nga
Nakhon Si Thammarat
Krabi
Phuket
Ko Phi Phi
Phatthalung
Trang
Hat Yai
Padang Besar
Sadao
Ko Tarutao
Satun
Yala
Narathiwat
Betong
Sungai Kolok
N
0
200 miles
0
200 kilometers

THAILAND

HIGHLIGHTS OF THAILAND

BEACHES. Idyllic **Ko Samet** (p. 677) and **Ko Chang** (p. 685) off the east coast are cheap and mellow. Down south, **Ko Samui** (p. 787), **Ko Phangan** (p. 795), and **Ko Tao** (p. 799) offer a more raucous brand of sun-and-fun with a broader slate of aquatic activities. **Krabi's** (p. 810) seaside cliffs offer world-class climbing.

HIKING AND TREKKING. **Northern Thailand** (p. 690) offers the greatest range of affordable treks. Less-touristed **Mae Hong Son** (p. 702) and **Sangkhlaburi** (p. 665) are less touristed have activities ranging from elephant excursions to river rafting.

HANGING OUT. Towns along the Mekong, including **That Phnom** (p. 754) and **Nong Khai** (p. 756), are unparalleled spots to unwind and take in stunning natural settings. Nothing tops **Kanchanaburi** (p. 658) for top-notch accommodations and tasty victuals. Itsy-bitsy **Pai** (p. 706), nestled in the northern highlands, has much to explore.

CULTURAL HERITAGE. The temples and palaces of **Bangkok** (p. 629), the ancient capitals of **Sukhothai** (p. 729) and **Ayutthaya** (p. 628), and the Angkorian ruins of the **Phimai** (p. 743) are engrossing and accessible.

NIGHTLIFE. **Bangkok** (p. 629), **Chiang Mai** (p. 690), **Ko Phangan** (p. 795), **Ko Samui** (p. 787), and **Khon Kaen** (p. 768) rock on when the rest of the kingdom has gone to bed.

4000BC Farmers settle in Khorat Plateau

651AD First kingdom of Thai tribes formed

7-12c Tai-Kadai tribes establish kingdoms and city states

1238 Sukothai Kingdom established

1275 Thai alphabet established

1350 Ayutthaya established

13-16c Ayutthaya grows in stature and number of temples per capita

1688 Foreigners plot, lie, and steal; get expelled from the kingdom

HISTORY

PREHISTORY

–The little tribes that did.

Scholars disagree about the origins of the Thai people. Some argue that their ancestors originated in Mongolia or northern China and were driven south to Yunnan, where the tribes coalesced and established the kingdom of Nanchao in 651. Other theorists trace the origins to what is now northeast Thailand. Recently discovered **human remains** in Ban Chiang (see p. 767) in the Khorat Plateau suggest that farmers settled there around 4000BC before leaving for Nanchao two centuries later. In the next four centuries, various tribes of the Tai-Kadai moved south into northern Myanmar, Thailand, and Laos, establishing minor kingdoms and city states. In 1238, southern Thai tribes moved north and founded the kingdom of Sukothai under the tutelage of the neighboring **Angkor.**

SUKHOTHAI (1200–1351) AND AYUTTHAYA (1351–1767)

–The bigger your wat...

Sukhothai reached its zenith in power and size (incorporating present-day Laos, Thailand, Singapore, and Malaysia) in 1275, when **King Ramkhamhaeng the Great** ascended the throne. His rule marked the first unification of Thais under a single monarch as he abolished slavery, codified laws, and instituted Theravada Buddhism as the national religion. In 1283, the King introduced the Thai alphabet which, with few changes, remains in use today.

In 1350, **King U Thong** (later called **King Ramathibodi I**) established the magnificent island-city of **Ayutthaya,** which served as the capital for the next 416 years. The rise of Ayutthaya coincided with the inevitable arrival of the first of the Europeans, as a dispute over the territory of Melaka brought the Portuguese into the picture. Under **King Narai,** Ayutthaya reached its peak, boasting a population larger than that of London. But in 1688 while the king was seriously ill, his chief minister was accused of conspiring to replace the king with a puppet-king loyal to France. Relations with the French were cut off, and virtually all foreigners were expelled from Ayutthaya for 150 years.

AYUTTHAYA'S FALL (1767–82)

—... the harder it falls.

After a nine-year siege, Burmese forces stormed Ayutthaya in 1767. Keeping with the to-do list when invading another country, they burned it to the ground, killed the king, and slaughtered thousands along the way. Only 10,000 of over a million people survived, some of them being **General Phraya Taksin** and a few hundred of his followers. Regrouping on the east coast, Taksin led an army of several thousand men to expel the Burmese and gain sweet revenge. Within 15 years, the Thais had recaptured Chiang Mai, Cambodia, and parts of Laos and established the kingdom's capital at Thonburi. Soon after he won the war, however, King Taksin declared himself the reincarnation of Buddha. Bad idea—in their counter-declaration, the other royals and generals decided that not only was Taksin not the Buddha but also that he was insane to think he was. In turn, he was executed in royal fashion: he was placed in a sack (so as not to spill any royal blood) and beaten to death. Commander-in-chief **Chao Phraya Chakri** became king and took the title **Rama I.**

THE EARLY BANGKOK PERIOD (1782–1910)

—"I am English and always right. Get over it, " said Anna to her king.

When Thonburi became too vulnerable, Rama I moved the capital across the Chao Phraya River to Bangkok. There he built the Grand Palace and Royal Chapel (Temple of the Emerald Buddha) and unified the kingdom's many fiefdoms. Ordering an overhaul of the Buddhist priesthood, he created the "Law of the Three Seals," which set economic, political, and military rules.

The reign of King Mongkut, or **King Rama IV,** was one of the most significant transition periods in modern Thailand. Unfairly portrayed as a flippant and frivolous monarch in Margaret Landon's *Anna and the King of Siam*, Mongkut was actually a serious man. Seeking to strengthen the nation and silence Western critics, Siam negotiated a foreign trade treaty with the British in 1885—reversing 150 years of virtual isolation—and imported Western technologies. Malaria cut short Mongkut's rule, however, and the government fell into the able hands of his fifteen-year-old son, Prince Chulalongkorn, who was crowned **King Rama V.** His 42 years of rule were marked by reforms in Thai justice, education, and public welfare and a courageous foreign policy in an era of aggressive European colonialism.

In 1893, after prolonged tension between France and Siam in the northeast, two French gunboats shelled Siamese defenses at the mouth of the Chao Phraya River and sailed into Bangkok. Thanks to the swift diplomatic action of Foreign Minister Prince

1767
Burmese annex Ayutthaya

1767-83
General Taksin reclaims Thai kingdom, think's he's the Buddha, but everyone else thinks he's crazy.

1782
King Rama I comes to power

1785
Bangkok becomes capital; King builds Grand Palace

1851
King Rama IV ascends the throne

1855
King signs treaty with British. imports Western technology

1868-1910
King Rama V attains god-like status

1893
French ships enter Bangkok

1932
People's Party to power

1932-52
Phibun and Dr. Banomyong dominate Thai politics

1940-50s
Economy prospers as interactions with the West increase

1957
Military regains power

1963
US builds bases against Vietnam

1971
King intervenes in October Massacre

1974
New constitution adopted

1975
Second student demonstration; military regains control; New Prime Minister promises freedom

1992
Pro-democracy movement rises

1992-96
Economic prosperity slows down

1996
Stock market crashes

1997
ASian financial crisis

1999
Thai economy begins recovery

2000
"Amazing Thailand" launched by TAT

Devawongse, however, war between the two countries was narrowly averted. A treaty with the French established Siam as a buffer state in the region, guaranteeing its independence. By his death in 1910, Rama V had become the most revered Thai monarch in modern history and the last Thai royal revered as a god.

THE RISE OF THE MILITARY (1932–1975)

–Years: 40. Coups:16. Coups per year: 0.4.

During the Great Depression, the Thai treasury nearly went bankrupt due to public works projects. Prominent academics and intellectuals demanded a civil constitution. In June 1932, government workers and the military launched a bloodless coup. Proclaiming themselves the **People's Party,** the revolutionaries, led by Major Luang Phibunsongkhram (commonly known as **Phibun**) and Dr. Pridi Banomyong, moved quickly to occupy high government posts. For the next three decades, they remained the dominant forces in Thai politics as the monarchy's influence waned in the face of military control.

In 1946, after his brother was found shot dead in his bed, the current monarch, King Rama IX, began his reign. Thailand continued to develop economically through the late 1940s and early 50s and adopted increasingly democratic practices, although corruption persisted in the government.

In 1957, the military staged a *coup d'état* during the general elections, and Field Marshal **Sarit Thanarat** took over. The new government re-established full military control while purging the police force of corruption, executing drug dealers, and suppressing communist propaganda. By the time Thanarat died in 1963, Thailand had become a staunch US ally in Southeast Asia. Under his successor, US forces were permitted to build air bases in Thailand to support the war in Vietnam.

By late 1971, Thailand had reverted to full military rule. In June 1973, university students led demonstrations in the streets, calling for a democratic government. Radicals left the cities to join communist guerrilla forces. In October, the government responded, sending troops into Thammasat University to quell demonstrations; more than 100 people were killed in what was called the **October Massacre**.

TOWARD DEMOCRACY (1975–92)

–Wham, bam, thank you ma'am.

The October Massacre was curtailed only due to the intervention of the king. Although he had no legal authority, he commanded great respect and loyalty among the people, and his intervention shamed the Prime Minister and other high-ranking officials into voluntary exile. The new interim government drafted a new, democratic constitution that provided universal suffrage for all Thai citizens over 20 and greater freedom of speech and religion. But democracy was short-lived, as the military reclaimed power by claiming that an increasing number of demonstrations (which many believed were staged) pointed to a resurgence of socialist and communist tendencies nurtured by democratic lassitude. A stand-off between students and police at Thammasat University, Thailand's hotbed of political activism, exploded into another bloody assault. Scores of people were killed, and the military once again took control of the government.

In 1988, after 16 coups in 40 years, public dissatisfaction and shrinking military support culminated in general elections and the end of military rule. But in February 1991, the army launched a successful bloodless coup under General **Suchinda Kraprayoon.** Citing corruption, he abolished the 1978 constitution, dissolved the legislature, and curtailed freedoms.

Thousands took to the streets in May 1992 to protest against military rule amidst accusations that the army influenced the framing of the new constitution to institutionalize its rule. Under Suchinda's orders, the military killed between 100 and 1000 people, many in front of Bangkok's Democracy Monument and Western TV cameras. Horrified, King Bhumibol pushed Suchinda out of office and appointed **Panyarachun** as a transitional prime minister.

END OF MILITARY RULE 1992-97

—Baht seriously....

Panyarachun fired the top four military officers in August 1992, kicking off a new era in Thai politics that promised to distance the military from politics. The following governments, however, faced charges of corruption and mismanagement; the resultant political instability caused Thailand's economy to suffer after years of spectacular 8-10% growth rates. In 1996, Thailand had a 7.4% inflation rate (its highest in five years), 0% export growth, and a drop of 30% in stock market prices. Then Prime Minister Silpa-archa was harshly criticized for meddling in economic affairs and was held responsible for the nation's dire economic situation.

Tougher times were still to come. In July 1997, years of heavy external debts, financial deregulation, and an unrealistic and unsustainable fixed exchange rate culminated in the collapse of the Thai baht under what eventually became known as the **Asian Financial Crisis,** which shook the entire region. Shock waves of currency devaluations, accompanied by economic and political havoc, spread across Southeast Asia. In response, the IMF initiated a US$17.2 billion emergency international rescue package in August of that year. Nevertheless, the baht's value fell 40%, over 350 factories shut down, and Thailand's stock market hit a nine-year low.

THAILAND TODAY

With positive growth rates since 1999, Thailand seems to be well on its way to recovery, aided by the unprecedented popularity enjoyed by the government of Prime Minister Chuan Leekpai. The Tourism Authority of Thailand (TAT) inaugurated the ambitious **Amazing Thailand** campaign to boost the economy, and by February 2000, officials declared the worst of the economic crisis to be over.

CUSTOMS AND CULTURE

THE THREE SPIRITS

The Thai attitude towards life rests on three main concepts. The first, *jai yen*, explains the Thai aversion to any sort of confrontation. Most Thais avoid raising their voices or displaying any visible irritation, instead embracing the idea of *mai pen rai*, literally translated as "it can't be helped, so why bother?" This verbal equivalent of a shrug is ideally complemented by the last of the three Thai spirits, *sanuk*, which literally means "fun." Thais believe that everything in life should have a little bit of *sanuk*, or else everything degenerates to mere drudgery. See the national water fight in April for a healthy helping of *sanuk* in action.

HEADS UP

According to an ancient Hindu belief (now incorporated into Buddhism as well), the head is the most sacred part of the body, and, by extension, the feet are the most unclean. A pat on the head in Thailand is neither playful nor cute—it's simply disrespectful. Similarly, don't stretch your feet out towards an image of the Buddha in a temple or towards another person sitting across from you, especially if they are older. Shoes, even more unclean than feet, are thus unwelcome in temples and most private homes.

MONKS AND MONARCHS

King Bhumibol Adulyadej is the longest-reigning monarch in the world. Born in December 1927 in Cambridge, Massachusetts, he's revered for his dedication to the underprivileged, his role in resolving government conflicts, and his commitment to the peace and unity of his country. He may have no direct legal power but his word commands tremendous loyalty and respect. A musician and composer (particularly of jazz), the king has written 73 songs, including the Royal Anthem, *"Falling Rain,"* which you will hear far more frequently than you expect.

The Thai speak in a special language of higher respect when referring to the Monarchy. Don't ever speak disparagingly of the monarchy and avoid defacing or even stepping on currency or stamps, which carry the king's portrait. In short, don't mess with the man whose name means "Strength of the Land, Incomparable Power."

Theravada Buddhism is the religion of 95% of the Thai people, and informs both their faith and lifestyle. Monks are a common sight in Thailand; their saffron robes, shaved heads, and gentle manner serve as a reminder of a search for inner peace that is the mainstay of Theravada Buddhism. Monks are below only the monarchy in social hierarchy and are also discussed in a special language of greater respect.

BISEXUAL, GAY, AND LESBIAN TRAVELERS

The spirit of Buddhist tolerance and non-confrontation make Thailand largely tolerant, if not actively supportive, of same-sex relationships. Most Thais believe that sexuality is a private matter and should be treated with discretion, regardless of one's sexuality. Public displays of affection are thus frowned upon for both homosexual or heterosexual couples. However, most Thai's are horrified at the idea of gay-bashing and would regard it unthinkable to spurn a child simply because he was gay. Due largely to familial structures that stress carrying on the family lineage, however, most lesbians and gays feel pressured to stay closeted. The absence of blatant discrimination based on sexual orientation in Thai society takes away any impetus for the community to mobilize itself. It comes as no surprise, then, that informal social networks predominate over political organizations.

Many Thais feel that the preponderance of male *farang* who frequent the "no money, no honey" scenes centered in Pattaya and Bangkok misrepresents the gay lifestyle. However, a booming gay nightlife—much of it divorced from the sex industry—remains quite accessible to foreigners. Lesbian communities remain largely underground, their nightlife comparatively subdued.

PINK INK. Utopia, 116/1 Soi 23, Sukhumvit Road, is Bangkok's best resource for gay and lesbian listings and support groups, with a cafe and gallery to boot. Their web site includes detailed information on clubs, events, and accommodations. (☎02 259 9619; www.utopia-asia.com). **Dreaded Ned's** (www.dreadedned.com) has detailed info on gay venues throughout Thailand.

ARTS AND RECREATION

ARCHITECTURE

During the early part of the Sukhothai period, Thai architecture was greatly influenced by the Khmer of central and eastern Thailand. Structures built during that period often have ornate gold leaf, mother-of-pearl inlay, and porcelain tiles. They consist principally of carved stone and are bound by vegetable glue.

Buddhist monasteries are the finest examples of Thai architecture. The **bot,** or main chapel, is a tall, oblong building with a three-level, highly sloped, layered roof that houses the principal Buddha image and serves as the site of most ceremonies.

STAND AND DELIVER Remember your national anthem? The Thais certainly remember their's. Visitors to Thailand are struck by how Thais respond so patriotically to their national anthem and the national flag. Whether they're in the bus or train station, on the street or in the market, all Thai people stop what they're doing when they hear the anthem (and they do, indeed, hear it often). In some smaller cities, traffic comes to a screeching halt. Thailand's national flag is raised each morning at 8am and lowered at 6pm. If you don't stand still, old ladies stares with disapproval, children laugh and point, and your karma value will take a serious nosedive, greatly increasing your chances of being reborn as, say, a termite. So, to be termite-free in the after life, respect Thailand's national custom—be still and stand up when the anthem is played before movies and public events.

The highest corners of the *bot* end in sharp points called **chofa,** which represent swans, the carriers of Brahma. Similar to the *bot*, the **wiharn** holds fewer Buddha images and functions primarily as a place for meetings, meditation, and sermons. The **sala** is an open, gazebo-like structure for meditation and preaching.

Above some monastic compounds looms a tapering, spire-like tower, a **phra chedi**. Derived from the Indian **stupa**, the *chedi* houses the possessions and cremated remains of high priests, members of royalty, and the Buddha.

THAILAND

DRAMA AND DANCE

Thai classical drama and dance are closely related. The three main types of dramatic media in Thai culture are the **khon, lakhon,** and **likay.** The first two forms are generally patronized by the elite, while the *likay* is popular in the countryside among poorer Thais, making it the most popular of the three.

The *khon*, or masked dance drama, is based on Indian dancing and ritual; its various stories come exclusively from the epic Indian tale known as the *Ramayana*. During the Ayutthaya period, only men performed; women didn't appear on stage until the mid-19th century. With the exception of the leading male and female characters, all actors wear elaborate masks. As in Greek drama, verses are recited by a chorus that sits next to a small band. The *khon* is performed with a great deal of stylized action; the movements are suggested by motifs in the music.

The *lakhon* form of drama is less structured. Masks are reserved for monkeys, demons, and other non-human, non-celestial creatures. Like the *khon*, the *lakhon* is derived from the *Ramayana* but also adds stories from Thai folk tales and Buddhist JaHat Katas. **Lakhon chatri** is a simple play performed at shrines for the benefit of gods. **Lakhon nai,** with a traditionally all-female cast, dramatizes romantic stories and focuses on graceful movements. *Lakhon nok*, once performed only by men, is characterized by quick movements, fast-paced music, and humor.

In contrast to the *khon* and *lakhon*, the *likay* is bawdy and humorous with loud, sharp music, lyrics sprinkled with sexual innuendos, and improvisation. It's often performed at festivals, combining local and court stories to create a workable plot.

MUSIC

Unique Thai musical instruments have been given onomatopoeic names such as **krong, chap, ching, krap,** and **pia.** Simpler instruments were combined to create more complex sounds. Still more instruments were developed as Thai music assimilated elements of Indian, Mon, and Khmer styles.

The oldest surviving Thai songs are from the Sukhothai period. In the Ayutthaya period, music was an official part of court life. Territorial expansion brought instruments and musical styles from neighboring regions such as Myanmar, Malaya, and Java. During this period, rules defining musical forms were introduced. Songs were composed in a form called **phleng ruang,** a suite of melodies. Three orchestral types of music, appropriate to different occasions, further order Thai musical form: **pi phat** is used at ceremonies and in the theatre; **kruang sai** is used in performance at village festivals; and **mahori** often accompanies vocalists.

Contemporary Thai music takes many forms. Regional folk music, less studied than classical music, is common. One of the most popular styles is **luk thung,** country music, which has developed into upbeat electronic versions. The northeastern **mo lam** is a well-known folk style; it is fast-paced and features a male and a female vocalist who sing as if courting one another, accompanied by a **khaen.**

MUAY THAI (THAI BOXING)

Muay Thai was developed to keep Thai soldiers battle-ready in the 15th and 16th centuries. The first boxer to win historic recognition was **Nai Khanom Tom.** Captured by the Burmese, he won his freedom after dispatching a dozen Burmese soldiers in a boxing challenge. When word of his amazing feat reached Thailand, King Naresuan and his generals made Muay Thai a mandatory part of military training. Today these fights, full of ritual, music, and blood, are put on display. Every blow imaginable is legal, with the exception of head-butting. Fighters exchange blows for five three-minute rounds; the winner either knocks out his victim or takes the bout by points (most bouts are decided in the latter manner). Fights are packed with screaming fans, most of whom have money riding on the outcome. While many provinces have venues, most of the best fighting occurs in **Bangkok's Ratchadamnoen** and **Lumpini Boxing Stadiums** (see **Muay Thai (Thai Boxing)** p. 649).

TRADITIONAL PASTIMES

Every year during the hot season, a strong southerly wind lifts handmade **kites** high over Bangkok. Kites are often shaped to represent animals and are sometimes flown in games of aerial tag. Kite fighting is even patronized by the King.

Crowds watch and bet on the ill-tempered **Siamese fighting fish.** When let loose in a tank with another, these fish battle to the death in a flurry of fins and scales. The fish are so aggressive that they will often kill themselves trying to attack fish in neighboring jars or tanks. **Cockfighting** is also popular in the countryside.

HILL TRIBES AND TREKKING

The safest bet when searching for tour guides is to use companies that meet **Tourism Authority of Thailand (TAT)** and **Northern Thailand Jungle Club** regulations (see **Trekking in Chiang Mai,** p. 699). Ask around when picking a company and talk to fellow travelers; reputable operations make reports from former customers available. Treks affiliated with guest houses are generally safer than the packages arranged by independent organizations.

TAT publishes a list of trekking agencies, indicating those that use licensed guides (who have studied at the Tribal Research Institute in Chiang Mai). Trekking companies, guides, and customers are required by TAT regulations to be registered with the tourist police. Most companies provide insurance, food, accommodations, transportation, and extra supplies like small backpacks. Bring water with you. Go in a group of eight or fewer people, as smaller groups are less disruptive to village culture. The best way to learn about hill tribe culture is to hire a personal guide (500฿ per day). Make sure your guide speaks both English and the languages of the villages on your itinerary.

HEALTH AND SECURITY. Bring a first-aid kit, sunscreen, a hat, mosquito repellent, a water bottle, and long clothing. Baby wipes and anti-bacterial cream are also a good idea. Some regions contain malarial mosquitoes; be sure to get the proper medications before you go (see **Insect-Borne Diseases,** p. 27). Before embarking on a trek, try to find a safe place to leave valuables in your absence. TAT recommends that trekkers utilize a bank safety deposit box; there have been numerous reports of credit cards being lifted from guest house "security" boxes. **Bandits** have been known to raid trekking groups. Should this occur, hand over your belongings to the bandits to avoid physical harm. **TAT discourages independent trekking.**

TREKKING ETIQUETTE. Hill tribe societies are being rapidly integrated into Thai society. Their unique, centuries-old cultures are ever changing, and there's no question that tourism speeds the process. **Always ask before taking photographs.** Some individuals or even whole villages may object even if your guide says it's okay. Ask permission from the specific people you want to photograph. Smile and give a "thumbs-up" sign. Respect people, space, and things, particularly hill tribe beliefs, and be careful about what you touch. For example, the gate at the entrance to Akha villages marks the point past which spirits may not enter; don't touch this. Use the old hiking maxim: see as it is, leave as it was.

WHEN TO GO. Of Northern Thailand's three distinct seasons, the cool season (Oct.-Feb.) is the best time for trekking. The vegetation is most lush, and temperatures are usually in the mid-20s (°C) by day, falling to near freezing at night. In the rainy season (July-Sept.), paths are muddy, and raging rivers make rafting fun but dangerous. In the hot season (Mar.-May), the land is parched and the air is dry.

ADDITIONAL SOURCES

Thailand: A Short History, by David Wyatt (1982). The best one-volume history of Thailand. Available in Thailand.

ON THE WEB

Tourism Authority of Thailand (www.tat.or.th). Official website of TAT is possibly the best launching pad for information on visiting Thailand.

Thailand Youth Hostel Association (www.tyha.org). The name says it all: solid budget accommodations.

Thailand.com (www.thailand.com/travel/). Great resources on everything from nightlife to accommodations.

ESSENTIALS

VISAS

American, Australia, British, Canadian, European, and South African citizen can stay for 30 days without a visa, while New Zealand citizens may stay up to three months without a visa. For longer stays, Thai consulates abroad issue 60-day tourist visas, or travelers can apply for **extensions** in Thailand. If you wish to sojourn to nearby countries, obtain a **re-entry permit** at an immigration office before departure.

MONEY

The Thai **baht (฿)** comes in denominations of 20, 50, 100, 500, 1000, and coins come in 1, 5, 10฿ and 25 and 50 satang. Thailand has a **10% VAT** (value-added tax) on most items, including hotel rooms and food; it's usually already included in stated prices. Menus, tariff sheets, etc. specify if VAT is not included in the listed price. **Tipping** is not customary but much appreciated; in restaurants that don't levy service charges, a 15% gratuity is appropriate. Foreigners should expect to pay higher entrance fees at some places, including beaches, museums, and monuments.

> One of the most common cons is the selling of gems. Con-men will tell you that there is a one-week special on gems, and you will not be charged tax "if you buy today." There is no such special, and there are no government export agencies.

GETTING THERE

BY PLANE. Thailand has four major **international airports:** Bangkok (p. 629), Chiang Mai International Airport in Chiang Mai (p. 691), Phuket International Airport in Phuket (p. 803), and Hat Yai International Airport in Hat Yai (p. 775). Numerous international airlines, including **Thai Airways** (www.thaiair.com), fly to each of these destinations.

BY LAND. Refer to the following table for overland border crossings in Thailand.

BORDER CROSSINGS

CAMBODIA. Travelers can access Cambodia from **Aranyaprathet** (p. 673) to **Poipet,** or via a **Trat-Sihanoukville** boat (p. 685).

LAOS. Numerous land crossings exist across the Mekong River: **Chiang Khong** to **Houie Xay** (p. 721); **Nong Khai** (p. 756) to **Vientiane** (p. 333); **Nakhon Phanom** to **Thakkek** (p. 757); **Mukdahan** (p. 752) to **Savannakhet** (); **Chong Mek** to **Pakse** (p. 752).

MALAYSIA. The border is traversed from **Satun** (p. 777) to **Kuala Perlis**; **Padang Besar** to **Kangar**; **Sadao** to **Alor Setar; Betong** to **Keroh;** or **Sungai Kolok** to **Kota Bharu** (p. 779).

MYANMAR. Foreigners may enter Myanmar by land at: **Mae Sai** (p. 718), **Mae Sot** (p. 733), and the **Three Pagodas Pass** (p. 667).

GETTING AROUND

BY PLANE. Thai Airways has a near-monopoly within Thailand, with extensive domestic connections. An alternative is **Bangkok Airways** (☎2 229 34 56), whose major routes go from Bangkok to Ko Samui and Phuket.

BY TRAIN. The **State Railway of Thailand** (☎2 225 03 00) operates an efficient and cheap rail system; call for schedules and fares. The four main train routes in Thailand start in Bangkok and run north to Chiang Mai, south to Malaysia and Singapore, and northeast to Nong Khai and Ubon Ratchathani. Minor routes connect Bangkok to Kanchanaburi and cities north of the eastern seaboard. For long rides (over 3hr.), **third-class** travel can be uncomfortable. **Second-class** sleeping berths carry an additional charge of 100-320฿ (depending on the type of train, fan or A/C, and upper or lower bunk) and often sell out; reserve a few days early. **Rapid** (40฿ extra), **Express** (60฿ extra), and **Special Express** (80฿) trains come next in price and are speedier than ordinary trains.

BY BUS. Public buses are the cheapest and easiest way to travel short distances but blue **A/C buses** are recommended for longer transits. These buses cost twice as much, make fewer stops, and are mostly used by tourists.

KEEPING IN TOUCH

The Thai **postal system** is reliable and efficient. Airmail across the globe from Bangkok takes from 7-10 days. Overseas mail from rural areas takes two weeks but almost always gets to its destination. For 3-day overseas mail, **Express Mail Service (EMS)** is often available. Guest houses and TAT offices usually offer international phone service. For **Home Country Direct (HCD)** numbers from Thailand, refer to the table on the inside back cover of this book.

CENTRAL THAILAND

Fertile central Thailand, also known as the Chao Phraya River Basin, stretches from Hua Hin in the south to Nakhon Sawan in the north. The region's attractions include the awe-inspiring ruins and monuments of Ayutthaya and the lush landscapes fanning west of Bangkok around Kanchanaburi, which attract travelers to the banks of the River Kwai and the province's national parks. Southbound buses

and trains wind through the beginnings of peninsular Thailand, a teaser for the sandy playgrounds farther south.

BANGKOK

☎ 02

After a day or two in the city, most travelers marvel that Bangkok still remains standing at each sunset. Armadas of BMW's and Mercedes meet at each intersections littered with heart-wrenching traffic as seething legions battle for territory on the city sidewalks and ooze from every bus. The incessant, predatory heat and humidity reduce crisp clothing to saline sludge in seconds and when the umpteenth tout insists that your life won't ever be complete without his ride, Thai massage, or his sister, an old expat joke—"the good thing about Bangkok is that it's near Thailand"—seems to make sense.

Bangkok wasn't fashioned by city planners; it was hewn from unsuspecting paddies by the double-edged sword of Thailand's growing economy. To the western eye, the city today resembles home more than ever: Nintendo has taken children permanently away from their mothers, 7-11's abound on every corner, and modern medication, education, and technology are taken for granted. Yet, in rare but precious moments, the heart of Bangkok peeks over the shoulder of the city bustle when a well-heeled businessmen sets aside his cellular phone to pray at a wayside shrine and walkman-toting college students give up their seats to a parade of smiling Buddhist monks.

INTERCITY TRANSPORTATION

TOUT-FREE LIVIN'. Be wary of touts offering free advice outside airports or bus and train stations; experienced con artists wait to prey on unsuspecting tourists. Trust your handy *Let's Go* guide instead—we would never rip you off.

THE WIND BENEATH MY WINGS

Most flights to Thailand arrive at **Don Muang International Airport,** 171 Vibhavadi-Ransot Rd. (the main northern highway), 25km from the city center. The airport includes the **International Terminal 1** (departure info ☎535 12 54, arrival info ☎535 13 10), **International Terminal 2** (departure info ☎535 13 86, arrival info ☎535 13 01), and **Domestic Passenger Travel** (info ☎535 12 53). The **24hr. post office,** in the departure hall of International Terminal 1, has **international phones, EMS,** and **stamps.** Each terminal has **left baggage service** (70฿ per bag per day, each additional day over 3 months 140฿). Departure tax is 500฿ international, 30฿ domestic.

TAKE ME TO THE CITY! Take one of the **metered taxis** (250-400฿ depending on traffic) waiting as you exit customs or the useful and comfortable A/C **airport buses (AB)** which run four routes into the city center (every 30min. 4:30am-12:30am, 100฿). To get to the infamous Khaosan Rd., take AB2.

ROUTE #	STOPS
AB1: DON MUANG-SILOM	Don Muang Tollway, Dindaeng Rd., Pratunam, Ratchadamri Rd., Lumpini Park, Silom Rd., Charoen Krung Rd., Silom Rd.
AB2: DON MUANG-SANAM LUANG	Don Muang Tollway, Dindaeng Rd., Rachavithi Rd., Victory Monument, Phyathai Rd., Petchaburi Rd., Larn Luang Rd., Tanao Rd., Phrasumen Rd., Chakrapong Rd., Banglamphu (Khaosan Rd.), Democracy Monument, Ratchadamnoen Klang Rd., Sanam Luang.
AB3: DON MUANG-THONGLOR	Don Muang Tollway, Dindaeng Expressway, Sukhumvit Rd., Asok, Eastern Bus Terminal (Ekamai), New Petchaburi Rd., Thonglor Rd.
AB4: DON MUANG-HUALAMPHONG	Don Muang Tollway, Dindaeng Expressway, Ploenchit Rd., Siam Square, Phayathai Rd., Mahboonkrong, Rama IV Rd., Wongwien 2, Hualamphong Railway Station.

The Cheap Way: from the airport, cross the bridge to the Don Muang Train Station and catch one of the many **trains** heading inbound to Hualamphong Railway Station (5-10฿) and then take a **city bus.** Night service is infrequent.

Suffocating **public buses** are available on the highway just outside the exit for 3.5-16฿ (A/C #4, 10, 29, regular #3, 24, 52), and other modes of transport are more reliable. A list of fares and schedules can be found at the **Tourist Authority of Thailand (TAT)** in the arrivals area of Terminal 1. (**Open 24hr.**)

DESTINATION	FREQUENCY	PRICE	DESTINATION	FREQUENCY	PRICE
Chiang Mai		1650฿	Phnom Penh		3050฿
Hanoi		4700฿	Phuket		2000฿
Ho Chi Minh City		4400฿	Singapore		2050฿
Hong Kong		3600฿	Udon Thani		1310฿
Jakarta		6950฿	Ubon Ratchatani		1405฿
Kuala Lumpur		4480฿	Vientiane		2350฿
Manila		5500฿	Yangon		2450฿

RIDE THE LOVE TRAIN

Second only to elephant-transport in style and peanut holding capacity, train travel is cheap, efficient, and safe. Five train lines, traveling the north, northeast (two lines), east, and south, start and end at **Hualamphong Railway Station** (☎220 43 34,

24hr. info ☎1690), on Rama IV Rd. in the dead center of the metropolis. *Klong* (canal) and river ferries, coupled with public buses (see **Local Transportation,** p. 633) are the easiest ways to reach the station from the city. Metered taxis or *tuk-tuk* at the side entrance of the station are the best ways into town from the station. Otherwise, walk down Rama IV Rd. to a bus stop from which A/C bus #1 and regular buses #25 and 40 go to Siam Square and down Sukhumvit Rd. and regular bus #53 goes to Banglamphu (Khaosan Rd. area) and continues to Thewet.

Daily ticket booking is left of the main entrance; advanced booking is to the right. The lower information counter has train schedules. **Upper class** seats have A/C and bathrooms; **lower-class** seats put you right in the middle of many friendly Thai people. **Sleeper berths** are popular, so buy tickets eight to 10 days before departure. In order of increasing speed, price, and service, the trains are: normal (*rot thamada*); fast (*rot reaw*); express (*rot duan*); and special (*rot pheeset*).

Left of the main entrance is a **police booth** (☎225 03 00, ext. 5295). A **luggage storage center** is at Platform 12. (10฿ per day. Open daily 4am-10pm.) An **information booth** sits near the right hand ticket counter. **24hr. ATMs** cluster near the main entrance. A **post office** is outside the entrance. (Open M-F 7am-7pm, Sa 8am-4pm.)

DESTINATION	DURATION	FREQUENCY/TIME	PRICE (฿)
CHIANG MAI LINE			
Ayutthaya	2hr.	21 per day 5:45am-11:25pm	no sleeper: 15; 35
Chiang Mai	10-14hr.	7 per day 6:40am-10pm	121; 281; 381; 593
Don Muang Intl. Airport	1hr.	25 per day 5:45am-11:25pm	5
Lampang	9hr.	8 per day 6:40am-10pm	118; 273; 373; 575
Lopburi	3hr.	8 per day 7:45am-10pm	no sleeper: 28; 64
Phitsanulok	7hr.	11 per day 6:40am-11:10pm	69; 159; 324
NONG KHAI LINE			
Nong Khai	13hr.	daily 6:15am, 7, 8:30pm	103; 238; 338; 497
PADANG BESAR LINE			
Hua Hin	4hr.	12 per day 12:25pm-10:50pm	no sleeper: 44; 102
Hat Yai	17hr.	5 per day 12:25pm-10:50pm	149; 345; 445; 734
Surat Thani	10hr.	10 per day 12:25pm-10:50pm	107; 248; 348; 519
UBON RATCHATANI LINE			
Surin	11hr.	10 per day 5:45am-11:25pm	73; 169; 269; 346
Ubon Ratchatani	13hr.	7 per day 5:45am-11:25pm	95; 221; 321; 460

THAILAND

! THE PRICE IS RIGHT! Prices listed are base fares for specific classes (3rd; 2nd; 2nd A/C; 1st). Add 40฿ for fast trains, 60฿ for express trains, and 80฿ for specials. Sleeper cars cost 100-500฿, depending on class. Duration listed is for fast trains; add 2-3hr. per 10 hours for normal trains.

WHEELS ON THE BUS

Government buses depart from four terminals. The **Eastern Bus Terminal** (**E;** ☎391 25 04) is on Sukhumvit Rd., accessible via the Skytrain's Ekamai Station or by local A/C bus #1, 8, 11, or 13, or regular bus #2, 25, 38, 40, 48, or 98. The **Northern** (**N;** ☎537 80 55), **Central** (**C;** ☎936 19 72), and **Northeastern** (**N;** ☎936 36 60) **Bus Terminals** are in a new building west of Chatachak Park. Take the Skytrain's Sukhumvit Line to Mo Chit and a motorcycle taxi (5 min., 30฿) from there to the terminals. The **Southern Bus Terminal** (**S;** ☎435 11 99) is on Boromat Chonnani (Pinklao-Nakhonchaisi) Rd. across the river in Thonburi. Tickets for government and **private buses** can be bought at the Southern Bus Terminal. To get here, take A/C bus#11 from the Democracy Monument, or regular bus #30 from Sanam Luang. Although private companies can be cheaper and convenient, and sometimes offer more modern accommodations, they have higher scam and accident rates.

DESTINATION	DURATION	TERMINAL, FREQUENCY	PRICE (฿)
Ayutthaya	1½hr.	C, every 20min. 5:40am-7:20pm	41; 52
Banpae for Ko Samet	3½hr.	E, every hr. 7am-5pm	A/C only: 124
Chanthaburi	4hr.	E, every 30min. 4:30am-midnight	82-103; 115-148
Chiang Mai	10hr.	N, 32 per day	205; 290; 369; 570
Chiang Rai	11-13hr.	N, 32 per day	229; 241; 321; 337; 412; 640
Hat Yai	14hr.	S, 14 per day	535; 830
Khon Kaen	7½hr.	NE, 27 per day	202; 259; 400
Krabi	12hr.	S, 6 per day	459-486; 710
Mae Hong Son	14hr.	N, 3 per day	292; 509
Nong Khai	7½-10hr.	NE, 5per day	454; 705
Pattaya	2½hr.	E, every 30min. 6am-10:30pm	50; 70; 90
Phang-Nga	13hr.	S, 5 per day	326; 403; 419; 625
Phuket	14hr.	S, 12 per day	441; 685
Si Racha	2hr.	E, every 20-40min. 5:45am-7pm	39; 55; 70
Sukothai	7hr.	N, 16 per day	128; 230
Surat Thani	10hr.	S, 8 per day	142
Surin	6-8hr.	NE, approx. every hr. 6am-midnight	131; 225; 355
Trat	5hr.	E, every 1½hr. 7am-11:30pm	120; 147-176; 190
Ubon Ratchathani	5hr.	NE, 27 per day	297; 382

THAILAND

ORIENTATION

Beyond the cliff top shelters of **Khaosan Rd.** and other backpacker districts lies a bastion of ripe and unclaimed sights and experiences. The north-south **Chao Praya River** is a worthy landmark and launch site. To the river's east rests the heart of the city: **Banglamphu** (home to Khaosan Rd.) is immediately north of **Ratchadamnoen/Ko Rattanakosin,** home of Sanam Luang Park, Wat Phra Kaew, and the Royal Palace. Further north is **Thewet/Dusit,** a backpacker area and the location of the Dusit Zoo and the former royal mansions. Heading southeast along the river leads to **Chinatown,** the Indian district **Pahurat,** and the **Hualamphong Railway Station.** Further south is the wealthy **Silom** financial district and its less upstanding bedfellow, the **Patpong** red-light district. East of the Hualamphong Railway Station are **Siam Square's** shopping mall and the World Trade Center. Rama I. Rd. slices through, connecting Wat Phra Kaew (on its western end) with the Bangkok's eastern edge and the **Sukhumvit Rd.** area, where Thais and foreigners party until the wee hours. The *Bangkok Tourist Map* (40฿) or Nancy Chandler's Map of Bangkok (150฿) will make all of this clearer than we ever could. Our own guide to the neighborhoods, however, might offer a different kind of help:

KNOW THY NEIGHBOR BEFORE LOVING HIM...	
Wat center: Ratchadamoen	**Expat zoo:** Sukhumvit
No wat in sight: Patpong	**Real zoo:** Dusit
Backpacker's ghetto: Banglamphu	**Curry heaven:** Pahurat
Chinatown: Chinatown	**Shopaholics anonymous:** Siam Square

ADDRESSES. Buildings are often numbered twice in Bangkok—the first number represents the building's lot, and the second number signifies where on the lot it is. For example, 127/8-10 Sukhumvit Rd. signifies that the building is on lot 127 and occupies numbers 8-10. Minor roads that split off a main thoroughfare are called soi (alleys), although they can often be sizeable roads.

LOCAL TRANSPORTATION

Maneuvering Bangkok traffic is enough to bring out the Hyde in any Jekyll. Traffic has decreased recently, but getting from north to south is still frustrating. The traffic monster sleeps from10am-4pm; taking canal boats and river taxis means less time sweating on buses and breathing exhaust. Travelers hoping to maneuver Bangkok by public transportation will love the **Bangkok Tourist Map** (40฿), which has bus, water taxi, and Skytrain routes as well as information on sights.

BY BUS

The shiny, happy bus system, run by the Bangkok Metropolitan Transit Authority (BMTA), is extensive and cheap. Red-and-cream buses have no A/C (3½฿); blue-and-white and yellow-and-white buses both have A/C (8-16฿). Pea-green **minibuses** (3½฿) supposedly run the same routes as the buses but tend to stray easily. **Microbuses** cover long distances and stop only at designated places (5am-10pm, 30฿). Paying a higher price guarantees a seat and fewer stops. Buses run 5am-midnight or later. Make sure you get on the right type of bus, not just the right route number. Pick up a free **bus map** at any TAT office.

REGULAR BUSES WITH NO A/C (RED-AND-CREAM)

#1: Wat Pho–Yaowarat Rd. (Chinatown)–General Post Office–Oriental Hotel

15: Banglamphu (Phra Athit Rd., Phrasumen Rd.)–Sanam Luang–Democracy Monument–Wat Saket–Siam Sq.–Ratchadamri Rd.–Lumpini Park–Silom Rd.

18 and **28:** Vimarnmek Teak Museum–Dusit Zoo–Chitralada Palace–Victory Monument

25: Wat Phra Kaew–Wat Po–Charoen Krung Rd.–Rama IV Rd. (near Hualamphong Railway Station)–Phayathai Rd.–Mahboonkrong Center–Siam Sq.–World Trade Center–Ploenchit Rd.–Sukhumvit Rd. to outer Bangkok

48: Sanam Chai Rd.–Bamrung Muang Rd.–Siam Sq.–along Sukhumvit Rd.

59: Don Muang International Airport–Victory Monument–Phahonyothin Rd.–Phetburi Rd.–Larnluang Rd.–Democracy Monument–Sanam Luang

70: Democracy Monument–TAT–Boxing Stadium–Dusit Zoo

72: Ratchaprarop Rd.–Si Ayutthaya Rd.–Marble Temple–Samsen Rd.–Thewet

74: Rama IV Rd. (outside Soi Ngam Duphli)–Lumpini Park–Ratchadamri Rd.–World Trade Center–Pratunam-Ratchaprarop Rd.–Victory Monument

115: Silom Rd.–Rama IV Rd.–along Rama IV Rd. until Sukhumvit Rd.

116: Sathon Nua Rd.–along Rama IV Rd. (passes Soi Ngam Duphli)–Sathon Tai Rd.

204: Victory Monument–Ratchaprarop Rd.–World Trade Center–Siam Sq.–Bamrung Muang Rd.

A/C BUSES (BLUE-AND-WHITE, YELLOW-AND-WHITE)

#1: Wat Pho–Charoen Krung Rd.–Rama IV Rd. (near Hualamphong Railway Station)–Phayathai Rd. (Mahboonkrong Center)–Siam Sq.–along Sukhumvit Rd.

8: Sanam Luang–Bamrung Muang Rd.–Rama I Rd.–Ploenchit Rd.–Sukhumvit Rd. to outer Bangkok

10: National Assembly (Ratchawithi Rd.)–Dusit Zoo–Chitralada Palace–Victory Monument–Phahonyothin Rd.–Don Muang International Airport

11: Khaosan Rd.–Phra Sumen Rd.–Democracy Monument (Ratchadamnoen Klang Rd.)–Phetchaburi Rd.–World Trade Center–Sukhumvit Rd.

BY TAXI

Your lungs will thank you for using Bangkok's extensive taxi system. Simple and cost-efficient, taxis are under-utilized by most travelers. Single women find taxis much safer than *tuk-tuks* or motorcycles.

A
B
C
1
2
3
4
5
6
TO DON M
Samsen Rd.
Nakhon Chai Si Rd.
Rama V Rd.
Charan Sanitwong Rd.
Krung Thon Bridge
Sukhothai Rd.
Chao Phraya River
THEWET
Tha Thewet
Ratchsima Rd.
Ratchawithi Rd.
TO SOUTHERN BUS TERMINAL (1km)
New Arun Amarin Rd.
Samsen Rd.
Luk Kuang Rd.
Krung Kasem Rd.
Prachathipatai Rd.
Si Ayutthaya Rd.
Rama V Rd.
Sawankhalok Rd.
SEE KHAOSAN ROAD AREA MAP, P. 639
Tha Phra Athit
Tha Banglamphu
Phra Athit Rd.
Chakrapong Rd.
Phra Sumen Rd.
Ratchadamnoen Nok Rd.
Royal Turf Club
Phra Pinklao Bridge
BANGLAMPHU
TAT
Phitsanulok Rd.
Rama VI Rd. (Below Expre
Khaosan Rd.
Nakhon Sawan Rd.
Thonburi Railway Station
Klong Taxi Pier
Larn Luang Rd.
RATCHADAMNOEN
Mahachai Rd.
Bamrung Muang Rd.
Tha Chang
Na Phra Lan Rd.
Na Phra That Rd.
Saman Luang
Ratchadamnoen Nai Rd.
Ratchini Rd.
Atsadang Rd.
Tanao Rd.
Dinso Rd.
Boriphat Rd.
Worachak Rd.
Sua Pa Rd.
Luang Rd.
Rama I Rd.
Tha Tien
Maharat Rd.
Sanam Chai Rd.
Charoen Krung Rd.
Ti Thong Rd.
Maitri Chit Rd.
Krung Kasem Rd.
Luk Luang Rd.
Rong Muang Rd.
Banthat Thong Rd.
Pahurat Rd.
Yaowarat Rd.
Tri Phet Rd.
Chakraphet Rd.
Ratchawong Rd.
Song Sawan Rd.
Itsaraphap Rd.
Memorial Bridge
Hualumphong Railway Station
CHINATOWN
Tha Ratchanong
Song Wat Rd.
Khao Lam Rd.
Rama IV Rd.
Phayathai Rd.
Mahanakhon Rd.
Pratchadipok Rd.
Somdet Chao Phraya Rd.
Si Phraya Rd.
Sap Rd.
Naret Rd.
Patpong
Tha Si Phraya
GPO
Chao Phraya River
Lat Ya Rd.
Surawong Rd.
Indraphitak Rd.
SILOM & PATPONG
Decho Rd.
Canada
Mahesak Rd.
Silom Rd.
Tha Oriental
CHONG NONSI
Surasak Rd.
Pramuan Rd.
Pan Rd.
Myanmar
Taksin Bridge
Charoen Krung (New) Rd.
Taksin Rd.
SURASAK
SAPHAM TAKSIN
2
3
4
5
6
8
9
10
11
12
13
14
15
16
17
18
19
20
21
23
24
25
26
27
28
29
30
35
36
40

D
E
F
(20km)
TO NORTH/NORTHEASTERN BUS TERMINAL (5km) AND CHATUCHAK MARKET (5km)
Bangkok
SITES
Chitralada Palace, 6 C2
Chulalongkorn University, 37 D5
Democracy Monument, 18 B3
Dusit Zoo, 5 C2
Grand Palace, 24 A4
Jim Thompson's House, 29 C4
King Rama VI Monument, 39 D5
King Taskin Monument, 35 A5
La Muang (City Shrine), 15 A3
Lumpini Boxing Stadium, 41 D6
Mahboonkrong Center, 31 C4
National Assembly, 4 B2
National Gallery, 10 A3
National Library, 3 B2
National Museum, 12 A3
National Stadium, 30 C4
Oriental Hotel, 40 B6
Ratchadamnoen Boxing Stadium, 17 B3
Royal Barge Museum, 9 A3
Royal Theater, 11 A3
Saovabha Institute (Snake Farm), 38 D5
Siam Center, 32 D4
Student Christian Center, 1 C1
Suan Pakkerd Palace, 22 D3
Thammasat University, 13 A3
Thieves Market, 21 B3
Victory Monument, 7 D2
Vimanmek Palace, 2 B2
World Trade Center, 34 D4
WATS
Arun (Temple of Dawn), 25 A4
Benchamabophit (Marble Temple), 8 B2
Bowonniwet, 16 B3
Mahathat, 14 A3
Patum Wanaram, 33 D4
Phra Kaew, 23 A4
Pho, 26 A4
Ratchabophit, 28 B4
Ratchanada, 20 B3
Saket, 19 B3
Suthat, 27 B4
Traimit, 36 B5
Guest house areas
ARI
Rama VI Rd.
Phahonyothin Rd.
Vibhavadi Rangsit Rd.
SANAM PAO
Expressway
VICTORY MONUMENT
Din Daeng Rd.
PRATUNAM
Ratchaprarop Rd.
Makkasan Rd.
Indonesia
Phetchaburi Rd.
RATCHATHEWI
New Phetchaburi Rd.
PHLOENCHIT
Chit Lom Rd.
CHIT LOM
United Kingdom
PHLOEN CHIT
Ploenchit Rd.
New Zealand
NANA
Soi Nana Nua (Soi 3)
Soi 5
Soi 7
Soi 11
Soi 13
Soi 15
Soi 19
Soi 21 (Soi Asoke)
Soi 23
Soi 29
Soi 31
Soi 33
Sukhumvit Rd.
ASOK
Soi 6
Soi Nana Tai (Soi 4)
SUKHUMVIT
Soi Lang Suan
Witthayu Rd. (Wireless Rd.)
Soi Ruam Rudi
RATCHADAMRI
Royal Bangkok Sports Club
Henri Dunant Rd.
Malaysia
Cambodia
United States
Sarasin Rd.
Lumpini Park
Queen Sirikit Park
Ratchadaphisok Rd.
Soi 16
SILOM RD. MAP p. 637
SALA DAENG
Saladaeng Rd.
SATHON
Soi Ngam Duphli
Expressway
Rama IV Rd.
Australia
Soi Suan Phlu
Immigration Office
Kasem Rat Rd.
N
EASTERN BUS TERMINAL
0 yards 550
0 meters 500

BY TUK-TUK

Tuk-tuk scour the city and slither through the traffic that brings taxis to a halt. Negotiation is key: drivers may charge you twice they would a local. Skillful negotiators can get prices 30% cheaper than taxi fares.

> **!** **SCAM ME A TOURIST** *Tuk-tuk* drivers are often con artists and have been known to harass women travelers. Drivers have also been known to drive off with passenger luggage, tell travelers that sights are closed, and take them to jewelry and tailor shops instead, push the skin industry, and deliver passengers to expensive restaurants. To entice *farangs,* they offer tours of the city for low rates (10-20฿ per hr.), but all you'll get is a sales pitch and inflated prices. Beware of these words: *free, sexy, massage, jewelry, tailor shop, Go-Go* (unless of course you really want to go to a tailor, masseur, or a prostitute). *Tuk-tuk's* aren't all bad—just be firm and make it clear that you want to go to your intended destination and nowhere else.

BY MOTORCYCLE TAXI

Motorcycle taxi drivers loiter on street corners in brightly colored vests. Though faster in traffic and 10-25% cheaper than *tuk-tuk's*, motorcycle taxis can only a carry a single passenger, can be dangerous for long journeys, and require calm nerves. Travelers should insist on a helmet, as police will fine non-wearers.

BY BOAT

Chao Phraya River Express ferries (6am-6pm; 6-15฿) are the best way to travel along the river and provide easy access to the Skytrain. Buy tickets at the booth at the pier or from the ticket collector on board. Specify your stop, as boats will stop only if passengers are waiting at the pier. Disembark quickly.

The main stops, from north to south, are **Thewet** (for the National Library and Dusit guest houses), **Phra Athit** (for Khaosan Rd./Banglamphu), **Bangkok Noi** (for Thonburi Railway Station and Royal Barges), **Chang** (for Wat Phra Kaew and Royal Palace), **Tien** (for Wat Pho), **Ratchawong** (for Chinatown and Hualumphong Railway Station), **Si Phraya** (for GPO), **Oriental** (for the Oriental Hotel and Silom), and **Sathon** (for the Skytrain to Silom). Small brown, box-like ferries with bench seats, easily confused with river taxis, shuttle across the river to every major stop. A small sign identifies each *tha* (pier).

Klongs are small canals that zig-zag through the city's interior. Thonburi, west of Chao Praya, has an extensive network, and Bangkok Proper has two useful lines. **Klong Saen Saep** links Democracy Monument near Banglamphu with the area around Siam Sq. and the World Trade Center (10min., 6-15฿).

Another route links **Klong Banglamphu** and **Klong Phadung Krung Kasem.** From Tha Banglamphu, at the Chakraphong and Phrasumen Rd. intersection, you can reach Hualumphong Railway Station (15min., 6am-6pm, 6฿). Boats run every 45min. during off-peak hours and weekends and every 30min. during rush hour.

Longtail boat rentals are available at almost every pier for tourist destinations on the river and *klangs*—agree on a price before setting off. Usual rates are 400฿ for the first hour, 300฿ each additional hour.

BY SKYTRAIN

The Skytrain (**Bangkok Mass Transit System, BTS**) is an A/C orgasm. Incredibly useful for navigating Siam Sq., Silom, and Sukhumvit, the train has two lines that meet at Siam Sq. The **Sukhumvit Line** runs from Mo Chit next to Chatuchak Market, past the Victory Monument to Siam Sq., through Sukhumvit Rd. and terminates at On Nut, beyond the Eastern Bus Terminal. The **Silom Line** runs from the National Stadium, past Siam Sq. and Lumpini Park, and along part of Silom Rd. before terminating at Taksin Bridge. All stations have useful **maps. Fares** are based on distance (10-40฿), and ticket purchase is automated. 10-, 15-, and 30- trip passes are the most cost-effective for students; flaunt that ISIC card. (160-360฿, adults 500-540฿). Insert the card at the turnstile to enter the station; **hold onto it and insert it at the turnstile at your destination to leave the station.** The Skytrain operates daily from 6am-midnight.

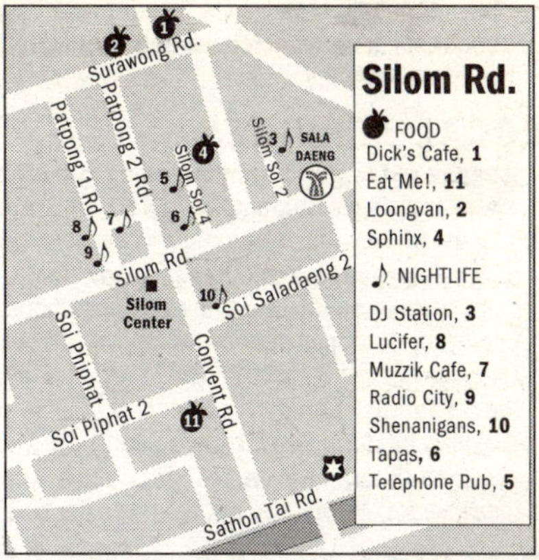

BY CAR

Travelers should avoid cars, as driving in Bangkok can be dangerous. An International Driver's Permit (see p. 42) and major credit card are required. Rental agencies include **Avis,** 2/12 Witthayu Rd. (☎255 53 00), **Dollar,** 272 Si Phraya Rd. (☎233 08 48), and **Hertz,** 420 Sukhumvit Rd. (☎390 0341). Renting a small sedan costs 1000-1500฿ per day and insurance costs 250฿.

PRACTICAL INFORMATION

TOURIST AND FINANCIAL SERVICES

Tourist Offices: TAT, 4 Ratchadamnoen Nok Rd. (☎282 97 73). 500m down on the right from the 8-way intersection east of the Democracy Monument. Very helpful staff doles out free maps and advice in English, French, Japanese, bad Italian, and worse German. Open daily 8:30am-4:30pm.

Immigration Office: 507 Soi Suan Phlu (☎287 31 01), off Sathon Tai Rd. 30-day transit visas extended for 10 days; 60-day tourist visas extended for 30 days (500฿). Open M-F 8:30am-4:30pm.

Embassies and Consulates: Australia, 37 Sathon Tai Rd. (☎287 26 80). Open M-F 8am-5pm. **Cambodia,** 185 Ratchadamri Rd. (☎254 66 30). Consular services around the corner off Sarasin Rd. on first soi on left. 30-day visa; 2-day processing (1000฿). Open M-F 9-11am and 1:30-4pm. **Canada,** Abdulrahim Bldg., 15th fl., 990 Rama IV Rd. (☎636 05 41). Open M-F 8am-noon. **China,** 57 Ratchadaphisek Rd. (☎245 70 32). Open M-F 9-11:30am and 2:30-5pm. **Indonesia,** 600 New Phetchaburi Rd. (☎252 31 35). Take regular bus #2 or 11; or A/C bus #5, 11, or 12. Open M-F 8am-noon and 1-4pm. **Ireland,** 205 United Flour Mill Bldg., 11th fl., Ratchawong Rd. (☎223 08 76). Open M-F 9am-noon and 1:30-4pm. **Laos,** 502/1-3 Soi Ramkhamhaeng 39 (☎539 66 67). Visa 300฿; 2-day processing. Open M-F 8am-noon and 1-4pm. **Malaysia,** 33-35 Sathorn Tai Rd. (☎679 21 90). Open M-F 8:30-noon and 1-4pm. **Myanmar,** 132 Sathon Nua Rd. (☎233 22 37). Consular services on Pan Rd., off Sathorn Nua Rd., 1½ blocks from the Skytrain Surasak Station. 30-day visa 800฿ (inquire at embassy for up-to-date status of land crossings); 24hr. processing. Open M-F 8:30am-noon and 2-4:30pm. **New Zealand,** 93 Witthayu Rd. (☎254 25 30). Open M-F 7:30am-noon and 1-4pm. **Singapore,** 129 Sathon Tai Rd. (☎286 14 34). Open M-F 8:30am-noon and 1-4:30pm. **South Africa,** Park Palace, 6th fl., 231 Soi Sarasin, Ratchadamri Rd. (☎253 84 73). Open M-Th 7:45am-4:30pm, F 7:45am-3:15pm. **UK,** 1031 Ploenchit Rd. (☎253 01 91). Open M-Th 7:45am-noon and 12:45-4:30pm, F 7:45am-1:15pm. **US,** 120-122 Witthayu Rd. (☎205 40 00). Consular services M-F 7-10am. **Vietnam,** 83/1 Witthayu Rd. (☎251 58 36). Visa 2050฿; 2- to 3-day processing. Open M-F 8:30-11:30am and 1:30-4:30pm.

Currency Exchange: 24hr. ATMs abound. Those with "ATM" spelled in blue dots or with a purple hand holding an ATM card accept AmEx/Cirrus/MC/V. You can't throw a stone in Bangkok without hitting a bank, particularly in **Silom.**

American Express: IBM Building, 388 Phahonyothin Rd. (☎273 00 33). Open M-F 8:30am-5pm. **Branch** at Sea Tours Co. Ltd, 8th fl., 128 Phayathai Plaza Bldg. (☎216 5783), on Phayathai Rd. between Phetchaburi and Si Ayutthaya Rd., next to Phayathai

Skytrain station. Mail held for up to 60 days; no packages. Passport and AmEx card, check, or travel receipt needed for pickup. Open M-F 8:30am-noon and 1-5pm, Sa 8:30am-noon.

LOCAL SERVICES

Luggage Storage: The **airport** is the most reliable but a bit pricey (open 24hr., 70฿ per day). Also available at **Hualamphong Railway Station** for 10฿ per day. Open daily 4am-10pm. Guest houses may also offer this service, but proceed at your own risk.

English-language Bookstores: Aporia Books, 131 Tanao Rd. (☎629 2129), opposite the end of Khaosan Rd. One of the best bookshops in Bangkok with new and used books for sale, trade, or rent. Open daily 9am-8:30pm. **D.K. Books** offers similar merchandise. Branch on Sukhumvit Soi 8 (☎252 62 61). Open daily 9am-8pm.

Local Publications: *The Bangkok Post* is an English daily, sold everywhere (20฿). Weekly *Metro* (www.bkmetro.com) divulges secrets on the trendiest nightlife (100฿).

Gay and Lesbian Resources: Anjaree (☎477 17 76). Lesbian organization with monthly newsletter. *Metro* (see above) has extensive listings of Bangkok's gay nightlife.

EMERGENCY AND COMMUNICATIONS

THAILAND

Emergency: Police ☎191. **Tourist Police** ☎1155. **Ambulance** ☎252 21 71.

Tourist Police: Tourist-specific grievances and complaints handled. Most useful office next to TAT, 4 Ratchadamnoen Nok Rd. (☎282 8129). All other stations will refer you here. **Branches** at 2911 Unico House Bldg., Soi Lang Suan (☎652 17 21), off Ploenchit Rd. in Siam Sq., and at the corner of Khaosan Rd. and Chakraphonh Rd. English spoken. **24hr. booths** (☎221 62 06) opposite Dusit Thani Hotel in Lumpini Park and at Don Muang International Airport (☎535 16 41).

Pharmacies: Fortune Pharmacy (Banglamphu), in front of Khaosan Palace Hotel on Khaosan Rd. Open daily 8am-midnight. **Siam Drug** (Silom/Financial), at the cul-de-sac of Patpong 2 Rd. Open M-Sa 10am-3am, Su 3pm-3am. A large number of pharmacies cluster on **Sukhumvit Rd.** between Soi Nana and Soi II. Most open daily 8am-late.

Medical Services: Bamrungrad Hospital, 33 Sukhumvit Rd. Soi 3 (☎253 02 50). **Open 24hr. Chulalongkorn Hospital,** 1873 Rama IV Rd. (☎252 81 81). Ambulance service. The best and largest public hospital is **Siriraj Hospital** (Thonburi), 2 Pran Nok Rd. (☎411 02 41). Take regular bus #19 from Sanam Luang. 24hr. ambulance. Cheapest vaccinations at **Red Cross Society's Queen Saovabha Institute** on Rama IV Rd.

Telephones: Make domestic calls at "cardphone" booths (5฿ per 3min.) and international calls at yellow "international cardphone" booths. Upper right metal button connects directly to an AT&T operator. Most post offices have international phone services (see below). The **Public Telecommunication Service Center** next to GPO offers fax and telex. **Open 24hr.**

Internet Access: Try **Khaosan Rd.** and other backpacker areas. Average 40-60฿ per hr.

Post Offices: GPO (☎233 10 50), in Communications Authority of Thailand building on Charoen Krung Rd. near Soi 32. *Poste Restante*. Mail held for 2 months. Pick-up fee (1฿ per item, 2฿ for parcels). Open M-F 8am-8pm, Sa-Su 8am-1pm. **Banglamphu Office** on Khaosan Rd.; turn left onto Bowon Niwet Rd. and walk to small square at bend in road. Open M-F 8:30am-5:30pm, Sa 9am-noon. **Overseas Telephone Office** on 2nd fl. of **Silom/Financial Office,** 113/6-7 Suriwongse Center Rd. From Silom Rd., head up Patpong Rd. to Surawong Rd. and turn left; it's a few lanes down to the left. Open M-F 8:30am-4:30pm, Sa 9am-noon. **Sukhumvit Rd. Office,** 118-122 Sukhumvit Rd. (☎251 79 72), between Soi 4 (Nana Tai) and Landmark Plaza. International calls 8am-10pm. Another at Soi 23, Sukhumvit Rd. (☎258 41 97), on right. EMS and international calls. Open M-F 8:30am-5:30pm, Sa 9am-noon. **Postal code:** 10500; 10501 for *Poste Restante*.

ACCOMMODATIONS

The tourism explosion witnessed under the *Amazing Thailand* campaign in past years has led to the formation of cookie-cutter guest houses by the soi-ful. Always check prices and rooms first to discern differences in quality between lodgings.

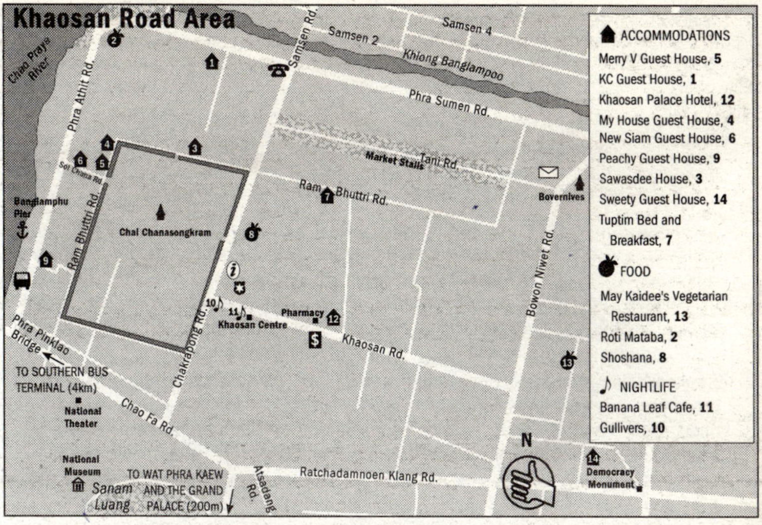

BANGLAMPHU AND KO RATTANAKOSIN

Within walking distance of Wat Phra Keow, Wat Pho, the Grand Palace, and the National Museum, this hub of royal Buddhism and ancient architecture functions as a kind of depressurization chamber for international travelers and budget backpackers as they enter Thailand. The heart of the fanfare is just to the north along **Khaosan Rd.**, a dubious mecca of cheap accommodations, free-flowing *chang* beer, and fake designer clothing. Tourist services abound, but rooms are often cramped, noisy, and full—reserve ahead by phone. About as un-Thai an experience as is imaginable, "Khaosan" is laden with drunken *farang*, who haggle with Thais for overpriced goods and swap travel stories over banana pancakes.

GETTING TO BANGLAMPHU. Chao Phraya River Express stop: Phra Athit. Buses: Airport Bus AB2, regular bus#15, A/C bus#11.

My House Guest House, 37 Soi Chanasongkram (☎282 92 63). From Khaosan Rd., go toward the river and across the temple grounds; it's 50m to the right. A socialite's dream, My House features a popular sitting area and proximity to cafes and bars but still maintains a relatively quiet atmosphere and clean rooms. Singles 120฿, with bath 160฿; doubles 200/300฿, with A/C 500฿.

KC Guest House, 58 Trok Kai Chae, Phra Sumen Rd. (☎282 06 18), 2 blocks north and 1 block west of Khaosan Rd. Set back from the chaos with refreshing garden, this homey guest house shines. Singles 120฿; doubles 150฿.

New Siam Guest House, 21 Soi Chanasongkram (☎282 45 54). On the small soi that connects the wat to the river. Though a few banana pancakes pricier than the competition, this recently renovated guest house has a comfortable feel that's worth the extra baht. Singles 200฿; doubles 245-320฿, with bath 395-450฿, with bath and A/C 550฿.

Peachy Guest House, 10 Phra Athit Rd. (☎281 64 71). Serene garden, Internet cafe, and bar are bonuses to a clean and well-run guest house. 4-bed dorms 80฿; singles with shared bath 100฿; doubles 160฿, with A/C 200฿, with A/C and shower 250฿, with A/C, shower, and toilet 350฿.

Merry V. Guest House, 33-35 Soi Chanasongkram (☎282 92 67). Typical of most accommodations in the area. Rooms and baths are cramped but cheap, and the cafe out front is popular. That it's not on Khaosan Rd. makes it worthwhile. Singles with fan and shared bath 120฿; doubles 180฿.

Sweety Guest House, 49 Ratchadamnoen Rd. (☎280 21 91). Walk away from the river to the end of Khaosan Rd., cross Bowon Nivet Rd., and go 100m down the soi to the right. The cheapest stay in town. Singles 80-100฿; doubles 140-160฿, with bath 200฿, with A/C 350฿.

Tuptim Bed and Breakfast, 82 Rambhuttri Rd. (☎629 15 35). From Khaosan Rd. walk to Chakrapong Rd., turn right, and right again onto Rambhuttri Rd.; it's about halfway down on the right. Well-kept wood-floored rooms and filling breakfasts (included) make this a fantastic bargain. Singles 250฿, with A/C 399฿; doubles with A/C 550฿.

Sawasdee House, 147 Soi Rambhuttri (☎281 81 38). From Khaosan Rd., cross Chakrapong Rd. and walk down the soi along the right side of the temple wall; it's halfway down on the right. If looks were everything, this would be it: a beautiful restaurant and loads of traditional decor. Rooms are well-kept but often full–plan ahead. Singles with fan 180฿, with balcony 250฿; twins 350฿, with A/C and bath 500฿; doubles 350฿, with balcony 400฿, with bath 420฿, with A/C and bath 500฿.

Khaosan Palace Hotel, 139 Khaosan Rd. (☎282 05 78), walk down the alley beneath the large green neon sign. For party animals willing to pay for comfort, the Palace is an oasis in the heart of the action. Rooms include private bath and towels. Singles with bath 280฿, with A/C, hot shower, and TV 400฿; doubles 350-580฿; triples 730฿.

THAILAND

DUSIT AND THEWET

Just a quiet bus ride, boat jaunt, or walk from the sights of Ko Rattanakosin and Banglamphu, the guest houses behind the National Library on Thewet are some of Bangkok's best-kept secrets. Catering to those who wish to escape Khaosan Rd.'s frenetic atmosphere while retaining its affordability and accessibility, the area is quiet and has little nightlife. Some taxi and *tuk-tuk* drivers don't even know it exists; be sure to tell them to go to Thewet, behind the National Library.

GETTING TO DUSIT. Chao Praya River Express stop: Thewet. Skytrain: Si Ayutthaya Rd. Regular Buses #30, 31, 32, 33, and 53. A/C bus #1.

Shanti Lodge, 37 Si Ayutthaya, Soi 16 (☎281 24 97). Billed as "The Oasis of Bangkok," Shanti has some of the best accommodations in city. Artsy explorer decor hangs from the walls, and with smoking and shoes prohibited inside, the place feels like paradise. Sparkling shared baths and the vegetarian restaurant only enhance this spectacular guest house. Dorms 100฿; doubles 250-280฿, with shower 400-500฿, with A/C and shower bathroom 600฿.

Tavee Guest House, 83 Si Ayutthaya Rd., Soi 14 (☎280 14 47). Large common spaces with fish tanks, well decorated rooms, and a family atmosphere. All rooms with clean shared bathrooms. Dorms 80฿; singles 140-220฿; doubles 250฿.

Original Sawutdee Guest House, 71 Si Ayutthaya (☎281 07 57). Similar lodgings to Shanti and Tavee but not quite as carefully decorated. All rooms with fans and clean, shared baths. Dorms 60฿; singles 200฿; doubles 250฿; family room 300฿.

Bangkok International Youth Hostel (HI), 25/2 Phitsanulok Rd. (☎281 03 61), 300m from the Samsen Rd. intersection. Head south a short block from Si Ayutthaya Rd. and turn left on Phitsanulok Rd.; it's 500m on the left. Great, spacious dorm rooms. Sex-segregated. Good restaurant. Lockout. No smoking or alcohol. No reservations. HI members only; non-members can buy a year-long membership on the spot for 300฿ or 50฿ per night. Dorm-style rooms 70฿, with A/C 120฿; singles with A/C and shared bath 280฿; doubles with fan 250฿, with A/C and shared bath 350฿.

CHINATOWN, PAHURAT, AND HUALAMPHONG

Accommodations line **Yaowarat Rd., Pahurat Rd., Chakraphet Rd.,** and **Rong Muang Rd.** Travelers staying here are either evading *farang* hordes or jumping on and off early morning trains. Chinatown offers few budget rooms that are clean and safe. Some are rip-offs, others welcome only Asians, and many are brothels.

GETTING TO CHINATOWN, PAHURAT, AND HULAMPHONG. Chao Praya River Express stop: Ratchawong. Regular bus #1. A/C bus #1.

T.T. Guest House, 516-518 Soi Sawang, Si Phraya Rd. (☎236 29 46). Exit Hualamphong Railway Station, take a left on enormous Rama IV Rd., turn right on Mahanakhon Rd. and take the 1st left; it's at the end of the soi. Popular in high season (reserve ahead), this family-run home has clean rooms and a friendly atmosphere. Strict midnight lockout. Dorms 100฿; singles 160-200฿; doubles 250฿.

New Empire Hotel, 572 Yaowarat Rd. (☎234 69 90), opposite the Bank of Ayudhya near the intersection with Charoen Krung Rd. and Wat Traimit. Higher prices pay for security, A/C, and phone in this impersonal hotel. Singles 400-480฿, with TV 580฿; doubles 593฿; triples 750฿; deluxe rooms 650฿.

Station Hotel (☎214 27 94), opposite the Hualamphong Railway Station. Good location for those with a train to catch, but there's not much special here. Decent doubles 250฿, with A/C 400฿.

SILOM ROAD

Although towering skyscrapers dominate **Silom Rd.,** the surrounding area houses diverse neighborhoods. On **Pan Rd.,** a Burmese community lives between the Burmese Embassy and the Hindu temple. The world-famous **Patpong** red-light district explores the raunchier side of Bangkok, while the wealthy trot in and out of the Oriental Hotel. Most budget establishments are 2km from Silom Rd. along **Soi Ngam Duphli** and **Soi Si Bamphen,** off Rama IV Rd., a bus or *tuk-tuk* ride away.

GETTING TO SILOM RD. Chao Praya River Express stop: Oriental. Skytrain: Silom Rd. Regular buses #15, 74, 115, 116.

Sala Thai Daily Mansion, 15 Soi Sapankoo (☎287 14 36). From Rama IV Rd., walk up Soi Ngam Duphli and turn left onto Soi Si Bamphen; take the 1st soi to the left and then turn right. Quiet during low season and happenin' during high season, Sala Thai features sizable rooms with shared bath, a sitting area with cable TV, and a rooftop garden. Singles 200-300฿; doubles 300-400฿.

J.M. Kennedy, 93 Pan Rd., Silom (☎635 23 85), opposite the Myanma Airlines office. Walk down Silom Rd. toward the river, and turn left at the Indian temple or take Skytrain to Surasak Station and walk 1½ blocks away from the river and turn left onto Pan Rd. Owner Michael dishes out Burmese and Indian food (curries with rice 30-60฿) and advice on Myanmar. Breakfast included. Basic but clean rooms with TV. Dorms 100฿; doubles with shared bath 200-250฿.

Lee Guest House 3, 13 Soi Sapankoo (☎679 70 45) and **Lee Mansion 4,** 9 Soi Sapankoo (☎286 78 74), next to Sala Thai, offer clean, fan-cooled rooms at reasonable prices. Small rooms 120฿; large 160฿, with bath 200฿, with A/C 350฿.

SIAM SQUARE

In the shadow of Bangkok's ritziest malls, **Soi Kasem San 1** lies off Rama I Rd., opposite the National Stadium. Quieter than Khaosan Rd. and almost tout-free, Siam Sq. claims a loyal following of travelers. Prices tend to run high, but the accommodations are a good deal for those willing to splurge a little. Proximity to the Skytrain makes much of Bangkok's nightlife and the Eastern Bus Terminal easily accessible.

GETTING TO SIAM SQUARE. Skytrain: Siam Sq. Regular buses #15, 25, 48, 204. A/C bus #1.

The Bed and Breakfast, 36/42-43 Soi Kasem San 1 (☎215 30 04). This brightly painted oasis is a heavenly respite from the city. A/C, phone, hot shower, and breakfast included. Reserve ahead Nov.-Feb. Singles 380฿; doubles 480-550฿; triples 650฿.

Pranee Building, 931/12 Soi Kasem San 1 (☎216 31 81). The fan-cooled rooms make this the place if you're willing to pay extra for location but not luxury. Windowless singles with bath 300฿; nicer doubles with A/C and hot water bath 400-450฿; triples 500฿.

SUKHUMVIT ROAD

The concrete, pavement, and skyscrapers of Sukhumvit Rd. have few affordable guest houses, but the side soi off Sukhumvit Rd. have Bangkok's trendiest (and most infamous) nightspots.

GETTING TO SUKHUMVIT RD. Skytrain: Nana or Asok. Regular buses #25, 48, 115. A/C buses #1, 8, 11.

S.V. Guest House, 19/35-36 Soi 19, Sukhumvit Rd. (☎253 35 56), near Asok Station. Good prices, great location (close, but not too close, to the action), and quiet, furnished rooms. Reserve in high season. Singles 250฿, with A/C 300฿; doubles with A/C 350฿, with bath 400฿.

Uncle Rey's Guest House, 7/10 Soi 4 (Nana Tai), Sukhumvit Rd. (☎252 55 65), on left opposite Nana Hotel. Follow signs through alley, then walk to the back left corner of parking lot. Close to bars on Soi Nana. Those seeking a quiet neighborhood should look elsewhere. Rooms have dressers, well-kept baths, and A/C. Reserve 2 days ahead. Singles and doubles 400-450฿.

FOOD

While most guest houses connect to overpriced Thai and Western cafes, the most authentic, best tasting, and cheapest Thai victuals are served from carts and no-name restaurants lining back-alleys. Lose your fears and find your senses.

BANGLAMPHU AND KO RATTANAKOSIN

For good food stalls, stroll down **Soi Rambuttri, Krai Si Rd.** (in the evening), or **Phra Chan Rd.** (during the day) opposite **Thammasat University.** The University's **Cafeteria** has good street grub at cheap prices. On weekends, hawkers hang out the area around **Sanam Luang. Khaosan Rd**. bursts with overpriced Thai and Western cuisine.

WHAT'S LOVE GOT TO DO WITH IT? The wholesome Thailand of temples, beaches, and smiles hides a shadowy country of sex servants and whorehouses. Some work freelance as elite call-girls, some split earnings 50-50 with their go-go bars, and an unfortunate few indentured prostitutes pay off their "debt" in brothels. Most work 1-2 years before leaving the industry; many work until they get AIDS and die.

Prostitution has existed in Thailand since Chinese sailors arrived and started taking "minor wives" centuries ago; today, scholars estimate that 150,000-200,000 women staff brothels and streets all over the country servicing primarily Thai locals. Bangkok, Pattaya, Phuket, Hat Yai, and Chiang Mai are the premiere skin carnivals for foreigners. Most travelers' first experience with the sex trade is in Bangkok, in the Patpong and Nana districts (See **Red Light, Green Light,** p. 652).

The Asian economic crisis has forced more women into prostitution to feed their families. More and more of the prostitutes hail from Thailand's poorer neighbors, where desperation among the neediest has reached unthinkable proportions. Child prostitutes are in especially high demand: clients–mostly Thai men–fear AIDS and believe that children are less likely to pass on AIDS than older prostitutes.

Under a 1960 law, the sex trade is illegal, but the law is unenforced, full of loopholes, and punishes prostitutes more than pimps and clients. The skin trade is lucrative and not a matter of much debate among Thais. Reforms have been proposed, but for now, Patpong and Pattaya attract overweight, aging Western sex tourists by the busload.

One or two blocks north on **Tani Rd.** and at **Wat Chai Chanasongkram,** food stalls fry noodles and rice dishes all day and into the night.

May Kaidee's Vegetarian Restaurant (☎282 57 02). Walk to Bowon Niwet Rd. at the end of Khaosan Rd. Take a right, a quick left, and left again down the first soi; it's 50m down. An expat favorite. Lounge on a street side stool and suck on sweet Thai specialties like black sticky rice with coconut milk and fruit (20฿) or noodles with coconut soup (35฿). Open daily roughly 9am-9pm.

Shoshana, on Chakrapong Rd. Facing the temple at the end of Khaosan Rd., turn right and right again at the first alley. This guest house restaurant specializes in delicious Israeli and Middle Eastern cuisine such as *falafel* (50฿), *schwarma* (60฿), and salads. Plenty of vegetarian options. Open daily 11am-11pm.

Roti Mataba, at the bend in Phra Athit Rd. where it becomes Phra Sumen Rd. This roadside corner is home to some of the best Muslim Thai food in the area; curry stuffed *roti* (35฿) or beef *mataba* (25฿) are sure to satisfy. Abundant breakfast *roti* options (8-20฿). Open T-Su 7am-8pm.

DUSIT AND THEWET

The pavement opposite the guest houses on **Si Ayutthaya Rd.** bustles with food stalls, as does the market a little ways down the road. With just about every Thai rice, noodle, and curry dish available at rock-bottom prices (20-30฿), these stalls are the best dining for guests in this area.

Si Amnouai, on Si Ayutthaya Rd., at the corner with Samsen Rd., opposite the National Library. No English sign. Si Amnouai serves the same rice and noodle dishes as the stalls outside at the same prices—only indoors. Open daily 5am-late.

Bangkok Youth Hostel Cafe, 25/2 Phitsanulok Rd. Mostly Thai clientele despite international flags. Menu features noodles, curries, and a few Western treats (60-130฿). Live music some nights 8-11pm. Open M-F 9am-1am, Sa-Su 10am-1am.

CHINATOWN, PAHURAT, AND HUALAMPHONG

The center of **Yaowarat Rd.** is a treasure of outdoors dining; the soi that branch off from it overflow with culinary delights prepared on the street. Excellent Indian restaurants abound near **Chakraphet Rd.** where it meets **Pahurat Rd.** In general, however, eating in this area requires more adventurous tastes.

Royal India Restaurant, 392/1 Chakraphet Rd., near the river; look for the sign on the left as you come from Yaowarat Rd. Delicious food makes up for a sparse decor. Menu features Indian dishes of all flavors and tastes (vegetarian included) at 50-100฿. The *thali,* curry, masala, and *naan* sampler (125-165฿), saves you from making a difficult choice. Open daily 10am-10pm.

White Orchid Restaurant and Coffee Shop, 409-421 Yaowarat Rd., in White Orchid Hotel. Famed *dim sum* (30฿ per dish) and the F night all-you-can-eat dinner buffet (160฿) is worth the trip for reliably delicious Chinese food. Open 24hr.

SILOM ROAD

Silom Rd. brims with delicious, expensive restaurants, particularly near Silom Center. Small tourist cafes set up at night on **Surawong Rd.** opposite Patpong. Look for local fare along **Convent Rd.** and inside **Soi Ngam Duphli.**

Eat Me!, 1/6 Piphat Soi 2 (☎238 0931), off Convent Rd. to the right. Creativity and food collide in this stylish, modern restaurant. Photography and sculpture downstairs, roasted capsicum stuffed with red chicken curry upstairs (170฿). Live jazz Su 8-11pm. Open 3pm-1am. MC/V.

Sphinx, 98-104 Soi 4 Silom Rd. (☎234 7249). This trendy, gay-friendly (though not exclusive) restaurant and bar serves set Thai meals (275-295฿) and Thai/Western dishes (80-150฿) over candle light. The bar picks up around 11pm and doesn't let up until closing (cocktails 125฿). Open 6pm-2am. AmEx/MC/V.

Loongvan, 37/3 Surawong Rd., off Patpong II Rd. Heaps of Thai curry dishes all night long. Curries, soups, and salads, with or without meat (20-30฿). Open until 3am.

Dick's Cafe, 894/7-8 Soi Pratoochai (☎637 0078). From Patpong cross Surawong Rd. and head two sois to the right. This classy gay cafe and bar draws a *farang* male clientele of all ages. Well-lit with wicker chairs, sofas, and gay art decor, it's perfect for lunch (Thai/Western food 60-130฿) or late-night socializing (beer from 70฿, cocktails 140฿).

Sun Far Myanmar Food Center, 107/1 Pan Rd.; look for the Hindu temple; it's on the left halfway down. Myanmar curries and sides (30-50฿). Open daily 9am-8pm.

SIAM SQUARE

Siam Sq. houses hundreds of restaurants, from independent cafes to well-known Western chains. In the afternoon and evening, vendors hawk in front of the **National Stadium** on Rama I Rd., at the mouth of **Soi Kasem 1,** and along the soi weaving through Siam Sq. Sidewalk restaurants dot **Ratchaprarop Rd.** and **Soi Wattanasin** opposite the Indra Regent Hotel.

Yum Zap, 430/11-12 Siam Sq. Soi 10. Look for the yellow smiley face and the "Spicy Salad" sign. Numerous scrumptious northeastern-style salads. Papaya salad with seafood (35฿). Open daily 10am-8pm.

Witthyakit Building Food Court. Walk through Soi 10 in Siam Sq., cross the street, and enter the basement of the tall building resembling a parking structure. Students and faculty from nearby Chulalongkorn University pack this food court for dozens of Thai dishes at 15฿ per plate. Open daily 6-11:15am and 12:45-6pm.

Daidomon, 266/11-13 Siam Sq. Soi 3. Do away with "atmosphere," get down to business, and eat at this fast-food-esque all-you-can-eat Japanese buffet. Lunch 79฿. Dinner 99฿. Weekends 109฿ all day. Open daily 10:30am-10pm.

THAILAND

SUKHUMVIT ROAD

Sukhumvit Rd. brims with expensive quality restaurants and tourist cafes for wealthier travelers. If you want to burn baht for a fancy meal and get your money's worth, this is where to do it. **Soi 3/1** specializes in Middle Eastern cuisine. The usual food stalls set up on many soi during lunchtime to sell Thai dishes for 20-40฿.

Cabbages and Condoms, 10 Sukhumvit Rd., Soi 12 (☎229 46 11). The brainchild of Dr. Vichit, a family planning advocate, this restaurant, bar, and handicraft shop was established in 1986 to help support the PDA. Exceptional Thai food served in a beautiful garden. Try the basil and chili chicken 90฿. Most dishes 80-200฿. Reserve on weekends. Open daily 11am-10pm. AmEx/V.

Crêpes and Co., 18/1 Soi 12, Sukhumvit Rd.(☎653 39 90), past Cabbages and Condoms. Every type of crêpe imaginable: sweet, rich, Western, Thai—or design your own (80-250฿, most around 150฿). *Tapas* (80-120฿). Open daily 9am-midnight. AmEx/V.

Moghul Room, 1/16 Soi 11, Sukhumvit Rd. (☎253 44 65), down the short alley opposite "Sea Food Center." One of Bangkok's best Indian restaurants. Muslim and Indian curries. Vegetarian dishes 80-90฿. Excellent *dosas* 110-150฿. Open daily 11am-11pm. AmEx/MC/V.

SIGHTS

BANGLAMPHU AND KO RATTANAKOSIN

Ko Rattanakosin requires at least a full day to explore fully. Because this area is compact, a walking tour is the perfect way to see the sights. Although extremely touristed, **Wat Phra Kaew** and the **Grand Palace** remain two of the most impressive sights in Bangkok. Chao Phraya River Express (Tha Chang) and buses (#1, 25, 47, 82; A/C #43, 44) stop near the compound. History and art buffs will drool over the treasures in the nearby **National Museum.** A circuit of **monasteries** is also nearby.

WAT PHRA KAEW (TEMPLE OF THE EMERALD BUDDHA) AND THE GRAND PALACE. The Temple of the Emerald Buddha was initially the Royal Chapel of the Chakri Dynasty. Inside the main chapel building *(bot)* is the actual **Emerald Buddha,** Thailand's most sacred Buddha figure. The Emerald Buddha was discovered in 1434, when lightning shattered a *chedi* in Chiang Rai and an abbot found a stucco

Buddha inside. He sloughed off all the stucco and found the glorious Emerald Buddha hidden underneath. The image stayed in Lampang until 1468 before being carted off to Vientiane, Laos. General Chao Phraya Chakri captured Vientiane 214 years later and reclaimed the statue. In 1782, then King Rama I ascended the throne, moved the capital to Bangkok, and built the Royal Chapel—Wat Phra Kaew— for the Buddha. Take a look at the frescoes that encircle the compound; the scenes are taken from the ancient Indian epic, *Ramayana.*

Next door to the Temple of the Emerald Buddha is the **Grand Palace,** accessible through a gate connecting the two compounds. Inside the gate, turn right and stroll down the path past important buildings on the left. The first is **Amarinda Vinichai Hall,** which once held court ceremonies. Next, **Chakri Mahaprasad Hall,** the residence of King Chulalongkorn, is a hybrid of European and Thai design. Today, the reception areas and central throne hall are used for royal ceremonies and are off-limits to mere mortal backpackers. Farther on, **Dusit Hall** is a symmetrical Thai building with a mother-of-pearl throne.

The **Wat Phra Kaew Museum** is inside the Grand Palace (take a right after the gift shop). The first floor displays relics and parts from original buildings that have been replaced. The second floor contains hundreds of Buddhas and enamel and crystal wares. *(☎222 00 94, ext. 40. Free English tours at 10, 10:30, 11am, 1:30, 2pm. Headphone audio tours 100฿ for 2hr., with guidebook and map 200฿. Admission to Wat Phra Kaew and the Grand Palace includes admission to Vimanmek Palace in Dusit and the Royal Thai Decorations and Coins Pavilion. Polite dress–full shoes, pants, and sleeves–required. Long pants, shirts, and shoes are available at the entrance. Complex open daily 8:30am-3:30pm. Museum open daily 9am-3:30pm. Entrance 500฿.)*

THAILAND

WAT PHO (THE TEMPLE OF THE RECLINING BUDDHA). Wat Pho is the oldest, largest, and most architecturally spectacular temple in Bangkok. Its grounds are divided by Soi Chetuphon: one side is home to the monastery, while the other contains temple buildings. Wat Pho was built in the 16th century during the Ayutthaya period and expanded by King Rama I; his grandson, King Rama III, built the *wiharn* that houses the Reclining Buddha, 46m in length and 15m in height. Wat Pho is also home to Thailand's first university, a monastery that taught Thai medicine a century before Bangkok was founded. A world-famous Thai massage school (see **Traditional Thai Massage,** p. 649) is its latest achievement. *(From Wat Phra Kaew, walk around the block and take three left turns from the entrance. ☎222 09 33. Open daily 9am-5pm. 20฿.)*

WAT MAHATHAT. Also known as the Temple of the Great Relic, Wat Mahathat houses a large sitting Buddha, and was home to King Rama I, who was an abbot before he took up military campaigning. Today the temple is a famous center of Buddhist teaching and home to one of Thailand's two Buddhist colleges. The southern part of the complex offers English instruction in Buddhist meditation. *(Between Silpakorn University and Thammasat University on Na Phra That Rd., opposite Sanam Luang. Open daily 9am-5pm.)*

SANAM LUANG. Sanam Luang is the "national common" of Thailand. In its old days, criminals were lined up and shot here. Although public executions have been discontinued, summer soccer matches and kite-fighting contests—in which the large "male" kites *(chula)* pursue the fleeing smaller "female" kites *(pukpao)*—have not. *(On Na Phra That Rd.)*

NATIONAL MUSEUM. Southeast Asia's largest museum, this branch is the crown jewel of Thailand's national museum system. King Chulalongkorn (Rama V) founded the museum in 1874 with the opening of a public showroom inside the Grand Palace to exhibit collections from the reign of his father, King Rama IV. *(On Na Phra That Rd. past Thammasat University. ☎224 13 33. Open W-Su 9am-4pm; tickets sold until 3:30pm. Free English tours W, Th 9:30am. 40฿.)*

NATIONAL GALLERY. The gallery contains classical and contemporary Thai artwork and the National Film Archives. Rooms upstairs display paintings of scenes from epics such as *Ramayana* and classical plays. *(On Chao Fa Rd. opposite the Phra Pinklao Bridge from the National Theater. ☎282 26 39. Open W-Su 9am-4pm. 30฿.)*

DEMOCRACY MONUMENT. Commemorating Thailand's transition from an absolute monarchy to a constitutional one in the Revolution of 1932, the monument is built on the site of bloody demonstrations held in May 1992, when students and citizens protested the dictatorial rule of General Suchinda Kraprayoon.

WAT SAKET. Notable for its Golden Mount (an artificial hill topped with a gilded pagoda) soaring 80m high, this popular mount was formerly the highest point in the city. Today, its spectacular 360° panoramic view and golden *chedi* reward those fit enough to make the trek to the top. *(On Worachak Rd. Open daily 7:30am-5:30pm. 10฿.)*

WAT SUTHAT. The wat is famous for housing the Sao Ching Cha (Giant Swing) and Thailand's largest cast-bronze Buddha. In the past, Sao Ching Cha was the scene of several of the more curious Brahmin rituals, including one in which a priest would swing on a rope to try to use his teeth to catch money suspended 25m high. Many priests lost their lives attempting this until a law passed during the reign of King Rama VII prohibited the ritual. The best part of the complex is the main *wiharn* compound, with marble floors, ornate statues, and impressive murals. *(On the right as you follow Worachak Rd. from Wat Saket to Bamrung Muang Rd. Open daily 9am-5pm.)*

WAT BOWONNIWET. This less-touristed temple is where King Rama IV spent 27 years as chief abbot and King Bhumibol Adulyadej spent his time as a monk. The wat is home to Thailand's second Buddhist college, Mahamakut University. Drop by and admire the chapel's gorgeous ornamental borders and Chinese-style statues or observe the Western monks who live here. Be polite and cautious. *(On the corner of Phra Sawn and Bowon Nivet Rd. in Banglamphu, near Khaosan Rd. Open daily 9am-5pm.)*

THAILAND

DUSIT AND THEWET

The sights of Dusit and Thewet are quieter then those in the heart of the city and make for a relaxing morning or afternoon of sightseeing.

VIMANMEK PALACE. Built of golden teak during the reign of King Chulalongkorn (Rama V), the palace is the largest teak mansion in the world. Held together with wooden pegs, the 72-room structure served as the king's favorite palace from 1902-06. The palace displays many items from his reign. The museum in Aphisek Dusit Hall houses an impressive collection of silver jewelry, silk, and soapstone carvings. *(Entrance is on the left on U Thong Nai Rd. Bus #70 stops nearby. Open daily 9:30am-4pm, last admission 3pm. Thai dancing daily 10:30am, 2pm. 50฿, 5-15yrs. 20฿, under 5 free; free with a Wat Phra Kaew and Grand Palace admission ticket. The palace can only be viewed on a tour. 45min. tours are given in English every 30min. Shorts and sleeveless shirts are not allowed. Admission to the palace includes a visit to the museum. Open daily 10am-4pm.)*

DUSIT ZOO. Thailand's largest zoo was once part of the gardens of the Chitralada Palace. It now hosts a large collection of regional animals as well as some rare species, including white-handed gibbons and Komodo dragons. *(On the right on U Thong Nai Rd. Entrances also on Rama V and Ratchawithi Rd. Open daily 9am-6pm. 30฿, under 10 5฿.)*

WAT BENCHAMABOPHIT (MARBLE TEMPLE). The wat's symmetrical architecture and white Carrara marble walls were built in 1899 by King Chulalongkorn. The courtyard is lined with 52 bronze Buddhas that represent styles from different periods, while the garden contains sacred turtles given to the temple by worshippers. Early in the morning (6-7:30am), the monks line the streets to accept donations of food and incense. In February and May, the wat hosts Buddhist festivals and candlelight processions around the *bot*. *(On the right after the Ratchadamnoen Nok Rd. intersection. Bus #72. Open daily 8am-5:30pm. 20฿.)*

OTHER SIGHTS. Past the Si Ayutthaya Rd. light, Ratchadamnoen Nok Rd. opens into Suan Amphon, site of the revered **statue of King Chulalongkorn (Rama V).** This beloved king, who ruled from 1868 to 1910, is remembered for abolishing slavery, modernizing Thai society (including the introduction of the first indoor bathroom), and fending off power-hungry British and French colonialists.

Behind the statue, guarded by an iron fence and a well-kept garden, stands the former **National Assembly** (Parliament Building). The domed building was commis-

ANTIDISESTABLISHMENTARIANISM, TAKE THAT! "Bangkok," the capital city's Western name, is rarely heard in Thailand. Instead, Thais prefer "Krung Thep," or "City of Angels." But Krung Thep is an abbreviation: with over 100 letters, the city's name is an orthographer's nightmare; in fact, it is so long that a song was written to make it easier for schoolchildren to memorize. Try saying *this* five times fast:

กรุงเทพมหานครอมรรัตนโกสินทร์มหินทรายุธยามหาดิลกภพนพพระรัตนราชธานีบุรีรมย์อุดมราชนิเวศน์มหาสถานอมรพิมานอวตารสถิตย์สักกะขันติยะวิษณุกรรมประสิทธิ

Krungthep Maha Nakhon Amon Ratanakosin Mahinthra Ayutthaya Maha Dilok Phopnop Praratana Ratchathani Burirom Udom Ratchaniwet Maha Sathan Amon Phiman Awatan Sathit Sakkakhantiya Wisanukam Prasit.

sioned by King Chulalongkorn in 1908 to replace his old residence. The new Royal Palace, called **Anantasamakhom,** was patterned after St. Peter's Basilica in Rome. Following the 1932 coup, the palace became the National Assembly building; but the Assembly has since been moved to Dusit. Past Wat Benchamabophit and Rama V Rd. on the left is **Chitralada Palace,** a walled compound protected by a moat and specially trained soldiers and the official home of the Royal Family. The palace is closed to the public.

THAILAND

CHINATOWN, PAHURAT, AND HUALAMPHONG

Chinese immigrants first settled southeast of the royal center along the Chao Phraya River in the 18th century, just after construction of the Grand Palace evicted them from Bangkok's first Chinatown. Today, this area is called **Yaowarat** (after the road that runs through Chinatown) or **Sampeng.** The neighborhood's narrow streets and vibrant street life make it worth exploring on foot, especially at night, when the area really comes alive.

Near Yaowarat, in an area marked by Pahurat Rd., Chakraphet Rd., and countless alleys in between, is **Pahurat District,** home of Bangkok's Indian population. Pahurat's markets are a great place to buy cheap clothing sold by Sikhs and Hindus.

WAT TRAIMIT. The only major temple in this area is home to the Giant Golden Buddha—a 3m, five-ton, gold Sukhothai-style statue. When the Burmese sacked Ayutthaya, residents saved the statue by covering it with stucco. Its identity remained secret until 1955, when the statue slipped from a moving crane as it was being transported to Wat Traimit. Cracks developed in the plaster, the stucco was removed, and the Golden Buddha was rediscovered. *(Main entrance on Yaowarat Rd. near the Charoen Krung Rd. intersection; a smaller entrance on Traimit Rd., accessible by bus #73. ☎225 97 75. Open daily 9am-5pm. 20฿.)*

SILOM ROAD

LUMPINI PARK. Lumpini Park, the largest park in Bangkok, is an oasis in Bangkok's glass and steel. In the mornings, the Chinese practice *tai chi* while others rent paddleboats and cruise the park's lakes. During the day, locals and expats relax at nearby cafes along Ratchadamri Rd. *(The park is bordered by Ratchadamri, Rama IV, Sarasin, and Witthayu Rd. and is accessible from Silom by regular bus #15, 77, 115 or from Siam Sq. and Banglamphu by regular bus #15. Skytrain: Ratchadamri. Open daily 5:30am-7pm.)*

ORIENTAL HOTEL. Founded by two Danish sea captains, the Oriental is one of the world's most famous hotels. H.N. Andersen built the grand Italianate building in 1887, which still stands as the "Authors' Residence" wing of the hotel, and shelters some of its finest and most expensive rooms. *(48 Oriental Ave. along the Chao Phraya River. Chao Praya River Express: Tha Oriental.)*

SIAM SQUARE

Famed for its shopping malls, Siam Sq. also has some sights worth a look and is easily reached on the Skytrain.

JIM THOMPSON'S HOUSE. This elegant house was home to American Jim Thompson, who revitalized the Thai silk industry after WWII and later disappeared in 1967 during a trip to Malaysia. Actually a combination of six teak buildings, the house is home to one of Thailand's best collections of Ayutthaya- and Rattanakosin-period art. Admission includes an English tour, during which guides discuss ingenious architectural oddities in Thai houses. *(Soi Kasem San 2, opposite the National Stadium. All Rama I Rd. buses access this site. Skytrain: National Stadium. ☎612 37 44. Open daily 9am-4:30pm. Tours required; every 10min. 100฿, under 25 50฿.)*

CHULALONGKORN UNIVERSITY. Thailand's most prestigious academic institution is worth a visit. The buildings are an architectural representation of Thai classicism, and the bookstore contains a fine selection of English books. *(On the east and west sides of Phayathai Rd., south of Siam Sq. From MBK, cross Phayathai Rd. on the footbridge or take any bus heading south on Phayathai Rd. until you see the campus on the left.)*

SUAN PAKKAD PALACE. The palace has five traditional houses in an immaculate garden with plants from all over the world. In the back of the garden is the Lacquer Pavilion, filled with porcelain, Buddhas, and Ban Chiang pottery. *(352 Si Ayutthaya Rd. Take regular bus #54, 73, or 204 from Siam Sq. past the Indra Regent on Ratchaprarop Rd. Get off near the corner of Ratchaprarop and Si Ayutthaya Rd. and turn down Si Ayutthaya Rd.; it's on the left. Skytrain: Phayathai. ☎245 49 34. Open M-Sa 9am-4pm. 150฿, students 30฿.)*

THAILAND

GODDESS TUPTIM SHRINE. One of Bangkok's more arousing sights, the shrine is famous for the large numbers of phallic objects around its spirit house, brought there by couples seeking help for infertility. *(Near the Hilton International Hotel on Wireless Rd. at Phetchaburi Rd.)*

OTHER SIGHTS. Opposite Jim Thompson's House is the **National Stadium,** the most noticeable landmark on Rama I Rd. aside from the Mahboonkrong Shopping Complex and the Siam Sq. Shopping Center. The famous **Erawan Shrine,** built after workers died in mysterious accidents during the construction of the Erawan Hotel, is farther along Rama I Rd. where it becomes Ploenchit Rd. Dancers hired by grateful worshippers often perform around the shrine.

SUKHUMVIT ROAD AREA

When Rama I/Ploenchit Blvd. crosses Witthaya Rd., it becomes Sukhumvit Rd., stretching southeast out of the city. The Sukhumvit Rd. area houses trendy nightlife, upper-crust travelers, red-light districts, and great restaurants.

KAMTHIENG HOUSE. This ethnological museum is home to the Siam Society, a cultural society supported by the royals. The museum reconstructs daily life in 19th-century Thailand with exhibits on tools, utensils, and other objects. *(131 Soi 21 Asoke, on the left as you walk from Sukhumvit Rd. Near the Asok Skytrain station. ☎661 64 70.)*

THONBURI: WEST OF THE RIVER

WAT ARUN (TEMPLE OF DAWN). Named for Aruna, the Hindu god of dawn, this wat was built in the Ayutthaya period and embellished during the reigns of Kings Rama II and III into its present Khmer-style form. The distinctive 79m *prang* is inlaid with ceramic tiles and porcelain. For the best view of the wat, go to the Chao Praya River's Bangkok side in the early morning or in the evening; the top of the *prang* affords beautiful views as well. *(From Wat Pho, take a right from Chetupon Rd. onto Maharat Rd. and a left at Tani Wang Rd. This path goes to Tha Tien pier. From an adjacent pier, ferries make crossings to the wat for 1฿. ☎465 56 40. Open daily 8:30am-5:30pm. 10฿.)*

ROYAL BARGE MUSEUM. The most impressive barge in the museum is the Suphannahongsa, a 46m vessel reserved for the king when he makes his annual offering of robes to the monks during the Kathin Ceremony. *(On Arun Amarin Rd., under the bridge over Klong Bangkok Noi. Take a river taxi to Bangkok Noi pier and walk upriver, over the canal, to the museum. ☎424 00 04. Open daily 8:30am-4:30pm. 80฿.)*

ENTERTAINMENT

NATIONAL THEATER

Dedicated in 1965, the National Theater, on Na Phra That Rd. past the national museum, has regular drama and dance shows. The performance program changes monthly but usually includes at least one *Khon* or *Lakhon* dance-drama performance and a performance by the Thai National Orchestra. Contact the theater for the month's schedule. (☎224 13 42. Open M-F 9am-3:30pm and 1hr. prior to performances. Tickets 30-80฿ for the government-sponsored shows.)

THAI CLASSICAL DANCE DINNERS

Missed the National Theater show? Don't worry, many restaurants offer Thai classical dance-dinners with half a dozen traditional dances in an hour-long show. Shows usually include *khon* dances from the *Ramakien*. No shorts, sandals, or tank tops are allowed. Reserve at least a day in advance. At **Ruen Thep,** Silom Village, 286 Silom Rd., in the Narai Hotel, enjoy a dance-dinner in a garden of turtle pools. Performances begin at 8pm and include seven dance styles that change monthly. (☎234 45 81. Opens at 7pm; set Thai dinner at 7:30pm. Tickets 450฿. AmEx/MC/V.)

TRADITIONAL THAI MASSAGE

Quality among massage parlors varies tremendously, and many are fronts for prostitution. Pictures of women in the window, for example, are giveaways for the latter. Ask other backpackers about their favorite masseurs and safe places in addition to using the listings below.

At Wat Pho, **The Traditional Massage School** (see **Wat Pho,** p. 644) offers massages for 200฿ per hr. as well as a 10-day, 30hr. course for 6000฿. (☎221 29 74. Open daily 8am-5pm.) **Winwan,** 45 Sukhumvit Rd., between Soi 1 and 3, offers excellent massages. (☎251 74 67. 300฿ plus tip per 2hr. Open daily 10am-midnight.) **Marble House,** 37/18-19 Soi Surawong Plaza, one soi up Surawong Rd. from Patpong 2, has a capable, mostly Wat Pho-trained staff, including a cadre of blind masseurs reputed to be the best in the business. **Mr. Noi** is possibly the world's best masseuse. (☎235 21 48. 2hr. 330฿. Open daily 9am-midnight.) A popular standby in the Banglamphu area is **Pian Massage Center and Beauty Salon,** 108/15 Soi Rambuttri, Khaosan Rd., down the tiny soi next to Nat Guest House on Khaosan Rd. (Massage 80฿ per 30min., 140฿ per hr.; 30hr. certification course 4000฿. Open daily 8am-midnight.)

MUAY THAI (THAI BOXING)

One of the world's more brutal sports, Thai kickboxing is generally fought with both opponents close together, protecting against a kick to the head, which would entail not only a concussion but a sure knockout. For those who don't mind the actual fighting, the rituals and fervor that surround these fights are fascinating aspects of Thai culture. Muay Thai occurs daily at one of two venues. On Mondays, Wednesdays, Thursdays, and Sundays, the action's at **Ratchadamnoen Boxing Stadium** (☎281 42 05), on Ratchadamnoen Nok Rd. near the TAT office. Take regular bus #70 from Sanam Luang. On Tuesdays, Fridays, or Saturdays, head for **Lumpini Boxing Stadium** (☎251 43 03), on Rama IV Rd. near Lumpini Park, which stages better fights—the top card's on Friday. Fights start around 6pm; the main fight starts around 7:30pm. Take regular bus #115 from Silom Rd. Prices vary depending on the venue and are cheaper at Ratchadamnoen (about 220-240฿, ringside from 880฿).

SHOPPING

After a while in the Bangkok sun, the **Siam Sq.** and **Silom Rd.** areas begin to look like one big A/C shopping mall. Siam Sq. houses five immense shopping centers, four movie complexes, 200 restaurants, and a few discos. (Most open daily 10am-10pm.) The area is a hangout for many Bangkok teenagers and college students trickling in from Thailand's prestigious Chulalongkorn University.

The undisputed heavyweight of Bangkok's shopping centers is **Mahboonkrong Center (MBK),** on the corner of Rama I and Phayathai Rd. in the Siam Sq. area. With seven floors of department stores, arcades, electronics, music stores, fast food joints, and a cinema, MBK puts most Western shopping malls to sham. Connected to it by a skyway across Phayathai Rd. is the equally impressive **Siam Square.** Spread over several soi are outdoor clothing and music stores, restaurants, two movie theaters, and a hotel. **Amarin Plaza,** at the intersection of Rama I and Ratchadamri Rd., and MBK's main competitor, the **Zen World Trade Center,** up Patchadamri Rd. toward Phetchaburi Rd., have the same shops as MBK, but are a little less busy.

MARKETS

Street markets *(talat)* all over the city are sources for knock-off designer watches, clothing (from Ralph Lauren to "Ralph Levis"), and pirated CDs and videos.

WEEKEND MARKET. Located in **Chatuchak Park,** the weekend market is a bargain-hunter's dream and a great example of market culture in Southeast Asia. The bustle is unmistakable and addictive as thousands of vendors sell everything from dalmations to toucans, though the main focus is clothing and plants. Bring plenty of free time and patience to navigate the crowds, hone your wallet preservation skills, and bargain with relentless vendors—even the stingiest will be hard-pressed to go home empty-handed. (Skytrain: Mo Chit. Open Sa and Su 7am-6pm.)

THAILAND

BANGLAMPHU MARKET. This frenzied market branches onto Chakrapong, Krai Si, and Tani Rd., but the tourist-oriented section is along Khaosan Rd. A late-afternoon/early-evening affair, the market's offerings include food, souvenirs, leather products, and fake designer clothing. Everything is overpriced, but the feel of the market itself is priceless.

OTHER MARKETS. Thewet Market is on Krung Kasem Rd. along the Chao Phraya River. The selection is not as diverse, but it's the one-stop shopping center for food or garden landscaping. (Chao Praya River Express: Thewet.) A sweet and brilliant sight is **Pakklong Market,** southwest of Pahurat District over Triphet Ave. Take a river taxi to Tha Rachini. A relaxing stroll through this wholesale flower market is worth the trip.

Opposite Chakraphet Rd., and east of the Pahurat Cloth Market is the **Sampaeng Lane Market.** This small alley continues for a few kilometers through the heart of Chinatown. If you need cutlery, jewelry, socks, monk's supplies, hats, or fishing equipment, this outstretched alley is the place to go. Extending northwest from the corner of Yaowarat and Chakrawat Rd. is the **Nakhon Kasea,** or **Thieves Market,** best known for its machinery, ice cream makers, and ninja weaponry.

The **Pratunam Market** operates during the day along Ratchaprarop Rd., opposite the Indra Hotel. Clothes are the main event here, although there is also a wide selection of knick-knacks. In the **Silom** area, vendors set up along **Patpong Soi 1** after nightfall. This is *the* place to buy overpriced fake designer watches, clothing, or soap carvings or to take in the scene as Thais tout live "shows" to elderly couples and housewives.

NIGHTLIFE

Bangkok's entertainment and nightlife need little introduction. The city's reputation as the epicenter of Southeast Asia's internationalism is well-rooted in its effortless mix of traditional art and culture with the hip, connected youth who want to get down and party until dawn. Like other global metropolises, Bangkok has a wealth of activities from sophisticated bars to shady massage parlors, and dance shows to kick boxing to entertain and enlighten every type of traveler.

Silom is the center of after-dark amusement, although Sukhumvit, Siam Sq., and Khaosan Rd. are nothing to scoff at. Silom Sois 2 and 4 are centers for gay nightlife.

Check out the free *Guide to Bangkok* (available at many bars and restaurants) or the *Metro* (100฿ at newsstands) for the latest in "cool." Establishments listed here are not associated with the skin trade (see **Red Light Green Light**, p. 606).

BARS AND PUBS

Tapas, 114/7 Silom Soi 4 (☎632 7982). Resident DJs spin chill house nightly in this "room club" bar. Sink into a couch to soak up the sounds or get up and groove wherever there's space. Outdoor seating for fresh air and people-watching. No cover downstairs. 200฿ cover upstairs. Beers 120฿. Open daily 10pm-2am.

Banana Leaf Cafe, 34/1 Khaosan Rd., 50m from Gullivers. Psst—one of Bangkok's best new bars is on Khaosan Rd., and tourists haven't found it yet. Packed with Thais and just a few *farang*, this wood-furnished cafe is quiet and refreshing. Comprehensive Thai/Western menu 60-120฿. Drinks 40-140฿. Open daily 9am-2am. A dozen similar cafe/bars have recently opened along **Phra Athit Rd.** near the river. Many have live music. Most open 6pm-2am.

Saxophone Pub and Restaurant, 3/8 Phayathai Rd., away from Siam Sq., at the southeast corner of the Victory Monument. The city's best jazz club buzzes. Thai and Western food is delicious and expensive at 100฿ min. per person. Beer from 110฿. Live jazz bands M-W, blues bands Th-Su.

Boh, Tha Tien pier, near Wat Pho. Enjoy the river view of the nearby temples at night, and get tipsy with Thammasat University students. Singha 70฿. Open daily 7pm-12am.

Shenanigans, Sivadon Bldg., 1 Convent Rd. Just off Silom Rd. near Patpong. A classy Irish pub with a 100% *farang* clientele. A bit expensive but well worth it, especially during happy hour (4-7:30pm) when a Jameson and Coke cost 85฿ and a large Carlsberg 90฿. Guinness on tap 285฿ per pint. Open daily 11am-2am.

Telephone Pub and Restaurant, 86-88 Silom Soi 4 (☎234 32 79). All orientations welcome, but frequented by a gay crowd, both Thai and foreign. Signature fixture of numbered telephones at tables provides fiber-optic flirting options. Serves beer and food indoors and out. Drinks 55-125฿. Western and Thai dishes 100-190฿. Open daily 6pm-2am.

Gullivers, 3 Khaosan Rd., at the corner of Chakrapong Rd. Look for the life-size *tuk-tuk* hanging over the door. One of the most popular bars on Khaosan Rd., its specialties are Western food and beer in a dark tavern atmosphere. Pool tables and a bar that won't quit until sun-up. Expect to see hordes of drunk *farangs* flocking here on the prowl for the opposite sex. Beers 60-65฿ per bottle. Open daily 11am-2am.

Radio City and **Muzzik Café,** on the south end of Patpong on opposite sides of the street. After 9pm these colorful and popular bars fill with *farang* seeking either refuge from the madness outside or the nightly live music. Radio City features Elvis Presley (11pm) and Tom Jones (12pm) shows. Open daily 6pm-2am. Muzzik Café stays open until the wee hours and collects much of the drunken, post-go-go bar chaos. Open daily 6pm-5am.

The Toby Jug Pub, 185 Silom Rd. A hole-in-the-wall of a place next to Silom Complex. From the Dusit Thani, walk toward the river; it'll be on your left before Soi 1. Time passes a little slower in this cool, sedate hangout, which somehow mixes British appearance with Thai ambience. Kidney meat pie 160฿. Amstel and Carlsberg on tap 50฿. Open M-F 11am-11pm, Sa 3-11pm.

LIVE MUSIC

Bangkok's most rewarding nightlife centers on jazz establishments with live music and a classy Thai and foreign clientele. Off Ratchadamri Rd., **Soi Sarasin,** just north of Lumpini Rd., has restaurant/bars that play live music nightly. Bands generally start around 8pm, but things get cooking after 11pm. **Brown Sugar Jazz Pub and Restaurant,** 231/20 Sarasin Rd., opposite Lumpini Park, is regarded (along with Saxophone Pub) as one of the best in the city with jazz bands every night that draw well-dressed patrons. Food (90-360฿), beer (120฿), and cocktails (150฿) are served. (☎250 18 26. Happy hour 4-9pm. Open 11am-1am, live music 9:45pm-1am.)

RED LIGHT, GREEN LIGHT. Love it or loathe it, Bangkok's Red Light District will not be denied. Thailand supports a massive sex industry, primarily for locals (**What's love got to do with it?**, p. 642), but entrepreneurial Thais and expats have filled the niche for lonely male foreigners. Three locales—**Patpong** in Silom, and **Nana** and **Soi Cowboy** in Sukhumvit—are home to the densest concentration of these self-proclaimed "entertainment centers." The Sukhumvit area, in general, more prominently displays the skin industry in the higher number of go-go bars and white male-Thai female "couples" visible on the streets.

One can dabble to different degrees in the sex trade. Most innocent are regular bars staffed by Thai women, whose job is to provide company and suck on drinks purchased by male customers. On the next rung up (down?) the ladder are hostess bars, which are almost exclusively for Japanese tourists. Lines of well-dressed Japanese women wait street side to be selected and escorted by the client into their karaoke bars for food, drinks, and singing. Third are go-go bars, which feature stages for topless and/or bottomless dancing, in addition to topless and bottomless girls for "company." Many of these go all the way, with back rooms where live trick shows or sex shows are put on throughout the night. Needless to say, additional "services" are purchased from these women (many or all of whom are heavily intoxicated from various substances) at any and all of these locations.

At first sight, Patpong appears to be yet another of Bangkok's numerous market/tourist attractions, with families and couples roaming between street stalls. But as the laminated "show lists" that street vendors hawk indicate, the goings-on are not as innocent as the crowds. Go-go bars—front rooms and back—host plenty of older single white men and groups of curious younger tourists (including a few women). "Boy go-gos" provide the gay equivalent on nearby sois (women are welcome in some, though all cater towards men). Lesbian go-gos are elusive. Women are generally accepted at most go-gos on Patpong 1 and 2.

The Nana Entertainment Complex (Sukhumvit Soi 4) and Soi Cowboy (between Sukhumvit Sois 21 and 23) do not cater to tourist families (as Patpong does) but set about their missions a little more seriously. Both have the same types of bars, but less wide-eyed *farang* and more business proceedings. There are far fewer women or couples here.

Let's Go does not encourage the support of these industries. Nevertheless, these activities will continue with or without curious budget travelers. Those who wish to enter go-go bars for dancing or shows should be cautious. In Nana and Soi Cowboy, most of these establishments do not charge cover, and your bar tab (the only required charge, beers run 70-100฿) will be set in front of you at all times. If a woman sits with you, you will be expected to buy her drinks to consume at whatever rate she chooses. Be resolute or go to the manager if this is something you do not want. It is possible to sit and drink one beer by yourself for an hour if you so choose, although few people do here. Patpong is a different situation, and stories abound amongst travelers about those who enter these sex shows under the auspices of "no cover charge" only to be prohibited from exiting before paying thousands of baht. A few of the larger clubs really have free shows, but most don't, charging 200-300฿ for a ticket to a night's worth of shows. Lower priced (80-100฿) tickets are rumored to have similar consequences as the "no cover charge except 3000฿" bars. Regardless of where you go, the only way you can really be certain is, immediately upon entry, seek out the manager and tell him what you expect of his club. He (which it always is) is the only one who can guarantee a "free show" and will tell you if that is not the case. If there is any uncertainty, leave immediately, as you are expected to pay for any watching. Exercise caution, do not take pictures, and be discreet.

DISCOS

Given that Thailand is home to some of Southeast Asia's best DJs, it's no surprise that Bangkok has the largest selection of clubs in the region. Not all discotheques charge cover, but all feature pricey drinks. **Concept CM²**, as in "Siam Squared," in the basement of the Novotel Hotel on Soi 6, is as classy as it gets. The city's most recognized club, "Concept" features postmodern decor and talented bartenders. Dance to the beat of Thai and English techno or dine in the restaurant area where the silk menu comes in a bamboo tub. (☎255 68 88. Cover 100฿. Beer 140฿. Dishes 150-300฿. Officially open daily 7pm-2am, but the doors sometimes don't open until after 10pm. No shorts or sandals. 18+.) **DJ Station** was awarded the title of Best Gay Disco 2001 by *Metro*. With the no-nonsense metal decor, great house/techno, and the full range of openness, it's no wonder. It also features a nightly cabaret and hang-out room on the third floor. (Cover F-Sa 200฿, includes 2 drinks; Su-Th 100฿, includes 1 drink. Open daily 11pm-2:30am. No shorts or sandals. 18+.) **Lucifer,** on Patpong Soi I next to Radio City, is delightfully and elaborately designed to look like hell; the club surely takes in its share of devils from the street and bars below. Regardless, this venue still gets kicking around midnight with dance remixes and happy house. (No cover. Drinks 120฿. Open 10pm-2am).

DAYTRIPS FROM BANGKOK

Travel agencies offer pricey daytrips to attractions outside Bangkok, but these sights can be seen more cheaply independently.

SAMUT PRAKAN

Take A/C bus #11 from the World Trade Center; the Crocodile Farm is the last stop. To reach Muang Boran from the bus stop, backtrack to the corner at the Bank of Ayudhya. Along the side street, a row of songthaew 36 go to Muang Boran for 3฿. Muang Boran ☎323 92 53. Open daily 8am-5pm. 50฿, children 25฿. Crocodile Farm ☎703 84 91. Crocodile shows every hr. 9-11am and 1-4pm; additional shows on weekends and holidays at noon and 5pm. Open daily 8am-6pm. 300฿, students with ID 200฿.

The center of Thailand's leather industry, Samut Prakan is 30km south of Bangkok toward the Gulf of Thailand. The main reason to come to Samut Prakan, however, is to see two main attractions: Muang Boran and the Crocodile Farm. Muang Boran, the "Ancient City," is an open-air museum in the shape of Thailand that contains replicas of monuments and sights from around the kingdom. Highlights include the Ayutthaya-style **Saphet Prasat Palace,** the **Dusit Maha Prasat Palace,** and **Khao Phra Wihan,** which sits atop a hill affording a spectacular view. The Crocodile Farm houses the largest crocodile in captivity. At the "Crocodile Wrestling" show, trainers taunt the toothy behemoths. Other attractions include an aviary, snake pits, a dinosaur museum, and go-carts.

NONTHABURI

The best way to get to Wat Chalerm is by the Chao Phraya River Express ferry, which ends at the Nonthaburi Pier. From here, take another ferry to the west bank (1฿) and hire a motorcycle to Wat Chalerm (10฿). Open daily 9am-5pm.

Nonthaburi province straddles the Chao Phraya River 20km north of Bangkok. The town of Nonthaburi, on the east bank, is known for its fruit and earthenware. On the west bank of the river, in Amphoe Bangkluai stands **Wat Chalerm Phra Kliad Wora Wihaan,** known to locals simply as Wat Chalerm. Chinese styles influence the statues around the grounds as well as the ceramics and flowering decorations. Set in a grove, the monastery grounds are as pleasant as the breezy boat ride.

DAMNOEN SADUAK

Buses leave from Bangkok's southern bus terminal for Damnoen Saduak and drop off passengers in the thick of the action (every 30min. 6am-9pm; regular 30฿, with A/C 49฿). Upon arrival, visitors are approached by locals offering hr. long boat tours for up to 600฿; bargaining should bring the cost closer to 300฿. The best time to visit is 8-10am. To return to Bangkok, take a yellow songthaew *(5฿) into the center of Damnoen Saduak and wave down one of the buses as they turn around.*

Traveling 109km southeast of Bangkok takes you to **Damnoen Saduak** and its **floating market.** From 6 to 11am, vendors sitting in their boats amid fresh produce converge to create a temporary commercial center. Depicted in paintings, postcards, and picture books, the bustling scene has become the poster child of traditional Thai life. Some visitors may find the not-so-picture-perfect reality—murky waters, swarming flies, and spitting vendors—disappointing.

AYUTTHAYA ☎035

Entering the city of Ayutthaya is like walking into a weird time warp. For four centuries the city was the capital of Siam, raising 33 kings, withstanding 23 invasions by Burmese troops, and extending its rule west to Bago in Myanmar and east to Angkor in Cambodia. In 1767, however, good times turned bad when the city was sacked by the Burmese (successfully, this time), and the capital was moved to Bangkok, leaving the city a mere echo of its royal past. *Tuk-tuks* and motorcycles weave around the massive ruins that dot the city, and pedestrians walk by former royal palaces without so much as batting an eye. Perhaps most impressively, traffic routinely comes to a standstill as elephants bearing camera-touting tourists head from ruin to ruin. Modern Ayutthaya is loud, busy, and impersonal but comfortable with its royal past and ruins, which blend anachronistically into the cityscape.

TRANSPORTATION

Trains: Ayutthaya Railway Station (☎241 54), on the mainland east of the island. Take the ferry from U Thong Rd. and walk up the street. Otherwise, it's a long walk across **Pridi Damrong Bridge** or a 20฿ *tuk-tuk* ride. Trains to: **Bangkok** (1½-2hr.; 24 per day; 15฿, rapid or express 20฿); **Chiang Mai** via **Phitsanulok** (12hr.; 4 per day; 3rd-class 296฿, 2nd-class sleeper 586฿, 1st-class 1138฿); **Lopburi** (1½hr., 5 per day, 13฿); **Saraburi** (1hr., 10 per day, 9฿); **Udon Thani** (9hr.; 3 per day; 3rd-class 145฿, 2nd-class 306฿).

Buses: Ayutthaya has 2 bus stations.

Naresuan Rd. has a chaotic mess of buses that go to: **Bangkok** (#901; 1½hr.; every 30min. 6am-7pm; 20฿, with A/C 30฿); **Saraburi,** connecting to destinations in the northeast (#358, 2¼hr., every 30min. 6am-5pm, 27฿); **Suphanburi,** connecting with #411 to **Kanchanaburi** (#703, 1¾hr., every 30min. 6am-5pm, 17฿).

Mainland bus terminal, 5km east of the island (50฿ by *tuk-tuk*) serves destinations farther away. Buses to: **Chiang Mai** (9½hr.; 9 per day; 2nd-class with A/C 255฿, VIP 570฿); **Phitsanulok** (5hr.; 9 per day; 85฿, 2nd-class with A/C 120฿, 1st-class with A/C 194฿, VIP 300฿); **Sukhoyhai** (6½hr.; 6 per day; 2nd-class with A/C 146฿, 1st-class with A/C 230฿).

Ferries: Continuous ferries to the mainland (and the train station) leave from an alley off U Thong Rd. near the intersection with Horattanachai Rd. (2฿). **Long-tailed boats** and **cruisers** can be hired at the Chantharkasem Palace pier at the island's northeast tip for a 1hr. trip around the island (600฿, more with stops).

Local Transportation: Tuk-tuk/songthaew hybrids wheel around the island for 30฿ and venture to the mainland for slightly more. Rent by the hour (200฿) or for a full day (700-900฿). Most guest houses rent **bicycles** (30-50฿ per day).

ORIENTATION AND PRACTICAL INFORMATION

The Ayutthaya **city center** is an oval-shaped island at the intersection the **Chao Phraya, Pa Sak,** and **Lopburi Rivers. U Thong Rd.** encircles the island. **Buses** from nearby cities stop next to the **Chao Phrom Market** at the corner of **Naresuan** and **Khlong Makham Rieng Rd.** in the island's northeast corner. Buses from northern Thailand arrive east of the island, 5km beyond the **Pridi Damrong Bridge.** Most tourist attractions cluster near the **TAT** on **Si Sanphet Rd.**

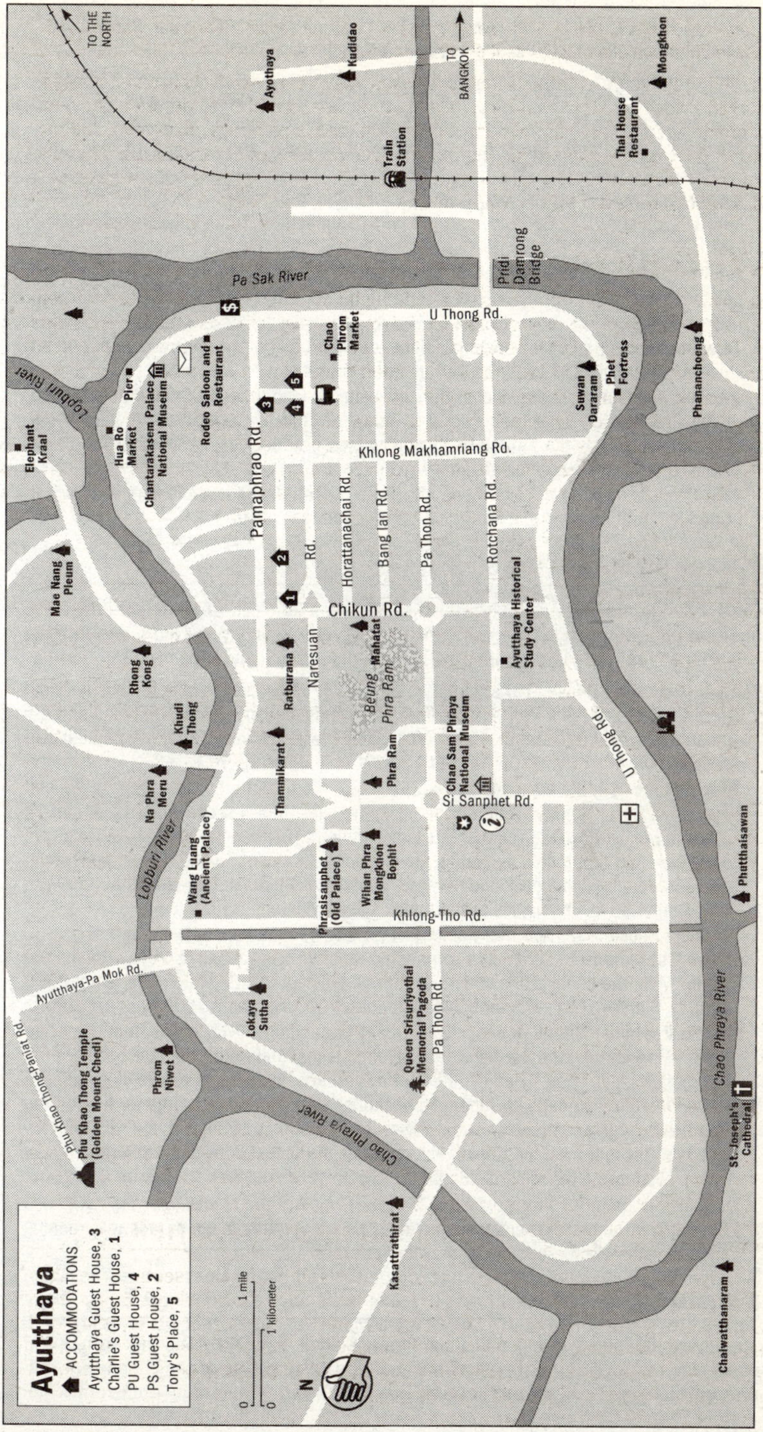
Ayutthaya
ACCOMMODATIONS
Ayutthaya Guest House, 3
Charlie's Guest House, 1
PU Guest House, 4
PS Guest House, 2
Tony's Place, 5
0 1 mile
0 1 kilometer
N
TO THE NORTH
TO BANGKOK
Ayothaya
Kudidao
Train Station
Mongkhon
Thai House Restaurant
Pa Sak River
Pridi Damrong Bridge
U Thong Rd.
Chao Phrom Market
Lopburi River
Elephant Kraal
Hua Ro Market
Pier
Chantarakasem Palace National Museum
Rodeo Saloon and Restaurant
Pamaphrao Rd.
Khlong Makhamriang Rd.
Suwan Dararam
Phet Fortress
Phananchoeng
Mae Nang Pleum
Horattanachai Rd.
Bang Ian Rd.
Pa Thon Rd.
Rotchana Rd.
Naresuan Rd.
Chikun Rd.
Rhong Kong
Ratburana
Mahatat
Beung Phra Ram
Ayutthaya Historical Study Center
Khudi Thong
Thammikarat
Phra Ram
Chao Sam Phraya National Museum
Na Phra Meru
Si Sanphet Rd.
U Thong Rd.
Wang Luang (Ancient Palace)
Phrasisanphet (Old Palace)
Wihan Phra Mongkhon Bophit
Khlong-Tho Rd.
Phutthaisawan
Ayutthaya-Pa Mok Rd.
Lokaya Sutha
Queen Srisuriyothai Memorial Pagoda
Pa Thon Rd.
Chao Phraya River
Phu Khao Thong-Panat Rd.
Phu Khao Thong Temple (Golden Mount Chedi)
Phrom Niwet
St. Joseph's Cathedral
Kasattrathirat
Chaiwatthanaram

Tourist Offices: TAT (☎246 076), Si Senphet Rd., a 5min. walk south of Wat Phra Si Sanphet. Carries timetables and large, handy maps. Open daily 8:30am-4:30pm.

Currency Exchange: Banks abound along the eastern stretch of Naresuan Rd. and the northeastern curve of U Thong Rd.; many have **24hr. ATMs. Bangkok Bank,** 20 U Thong Rd. (☎245 346/7), opposite the school near the GPO. Open M-F 8:30am-3:30pm.

Markets: Chao Phrom Market, at the corner of Naresuan and U Thong Rd. Open daily 7am-7pm.

Emergency: ☎191. **Tourist Police:** ☎1155. **Police:** ☎241 174.

Tourist Police: (☎242 352), next to TAT on Si Sanphet Rd. Some English spoken. Open 24hr.

Medical Services: Phra Nakhon Si Ayutthaya Hospital, 46 U Thong Rd. (☎241 728), at the intersection of Si Sanphet and U Thong Rd. English spoken. No credit cards. Open 24hr.

Telephones: International Telephone Office, on the 2nd fl. of the GPO. Also a booth outside. Collect calls 33฿. Open daily 8am-8pm.

Internet Access: Available all over the city, especially north of the Chao Phrom Market. **9 To Nine Net,** on Bang Lean Rd. off U Thong Rd. 30฿ per hr. Open daily 9am-10pm. More convenient is the **nameless Internet place** next door to The Moon Cafe. 1฿ per 2min. Open daily 9am-midnight.

Post Offices: GPO, 123/11 U Thong Rd. (☎251 233), on the island's northeast corner. Open M-F 8:30am-4:30pm, Sa 9am-noon. **Postal code:** 13000.

THAILAND

ACCOMMODATIONS

Budget accommodations cluster north of **Naresuan Rd.**, a short walk from the local bus terminal. Room rates increase during festival season (Nov.-Dec.), and lodging is harder to find. All lodgings listed offer laundry service and bike rental.

Ayutthaya Guest House, 16/2 Naresuan Rd. (☎232 658), across from the bus terminal at Chao Phrom Market. Worth the extra baht. Rooms are large, clean, and tiled and the modern, shared baths are blessed with flushing Western toilets. Extremely popular and occasionally full. Dorms 70฿; singles 100-120฿; doubles 180฿.

Tony's Place, 12/8 Naresuan Rd. (☎252 578), north of the bus stop across PU and Ayutthaya Guest Houses. A new addition to the guest house scene, Tony's features 12 clean rooms with wooden floors and large windows. Bathrooms, both shared and private, have Western toilets, but some are cleaner than others. The TV lounge, pool table, and outdoor drinking area round out the social atmosphere. Motorcycle rental 250฿ per day. Dorms 80-100฿; singles and doubles 150฿, with bath 250฿.

PU Guest House, 20/1 Soi Thor Korsor (☎251 213). In the lane between TMT and Ayutthaya Guest Houses. Scheduled to undergo massive renovations in 2001. Rooms are clean, while the courtyard is cheerfully messy. Western toilets. Motorcycle rental 200฿ per day. Singles 150฿, with bath 200฿; doubles 200฿, with bath 250฿, with A/C 450฿.

PS (Phatsaporu) Guest House, 23/1 Tanon Pratuchai (☎242 394). From the Chao Phrom Market, take the 1st right after Khlong Makhamriang Rd., then take the 1st left at the light green shop. Friendly, efficient owner. Rooms are large and fairly clean with wooden floors. Popular with Japanese backpackers. If full, ask to camp for free on the front lawn. Vegetarian food served. Singles 100฿; doubles 150฿, with A/C 250฿.

Charlie's Guest House, on Chikun Rd. opposite the entrance to Wat Rotburano. Large rooms overlooking the ruins. Seldom full. Singles 125฿; doubles 150฿, with A/C 250฿.

BJ Guest House, Soi Thor Korsor (☎244 582). Around the corner from the Ayutthaya Guest House. A place to crash if everything else in the area is full or money is running short. Singles 125฿; doubles 150฿, with A/C 250฿.

FOOD

Munch on inexpensive meals at **Chao Phrom Market**, near the local bus stop. Food stalls also line U Thong Rd., particularly on the eastern side of the island. For dinner options, try the night market, the **Hua Ro Market.** (Open daily 4pm-2am.) **Thai**

House Restaurant (Ruenthai Maisuay Restaurant), 8/2 Mu 3 Klongsuanplu District, is down the road from Wat Yai Chai Mongkhon and around the bend on the left. On Friday and Saturday nights, live traditional music (6-9pm) and tasty curry (80-120฿) spice up this sober steak house. (Open daily 11am-10pm.)

SIGHTS

Ayutthaya's crumbling ruins span several dozen kilometers. Exploring all the ruins would take several days. TAT has free maps that locate and explain nearly every sight. Make the best of your time by renting a bicycle or motorcycle, available for rent at most guest houses. Otherwise, *tuk-tuk* drivers will take you to the sights and wait while you visit (200฿ per hr., around 700-900฿ per day).

ANCIENT PALACE AND WAT PHRA SI SANPHET. If you visit only one ruin in Ayutthaya, this should be it. The area was the home of the ancient Royal Palace until 1448, when a monastery was built on the grounds. As a royal monastery, Wat Phra Si Sanphet housed not monks but only important rituals and ceremonies. The site's three charred *chedis* that once held the remains of the king, his father, and his brother are now empty. *(Open daily 8am-6:30pm. 30฿.)*

WIHAN PHRA MONGKHON BROPHIT. At 12.45m high and 9½m wide, the 15th-century Buddha snuggled inside this wat is the largest bronze Buddha in Thailand. On display are photographs and blurbs explaining this restored Buddha's many "incarnations." *(Just south of the Ancient Palace complex. Free.)*

WAT PHRA RAM. Overshadowed by its more glamorous neighbors, the wat of Phra Ram was built in 1369 by King Ramesnan to commemorate the spot where his father and founder of the city, King U Thong, was cremated. Dozens of broken Buddha representations sit silently around the wat's landmark *prang* (corncob-shaped *chedi*), quite likely the town's largest phallic symbol. *(Across the street from the Wihan Phra Mongkhon Brophit. Open daily 8am-6:30pm. 30฿.)*

WAT MAHATHAT. This impressive royal monastery was begun by King Borommarachathirat in 1374 and restored several times, most recently in the 18th century. Excavations done in the 1950s uncovered relics of the Buddha hidden deep in a seven-layered reliquary in the *stupa*. With those finds safely stored at the Chao Sam Phraya National Museum, the wat's most precious part is a representation of the Buddha's face enshrouded in the roots of a tree. *(At the corner of Chikun Rd. and Naresuan Rd., north of Phraram Park. Open daily 8am-6:30pm. 30฿.)*

WAT RATCHABURA. Wat Mahathat's most impressive neighbor was built by King Chao Sam Phraya in 1424. Legend has it that the king's two oldest brothers coveted the throne and killed each other in a heated duel, allowing Chao Sam Phraya to ascend to the throne. To commemorate (or perhaps celebrate) his brothers' deaths, the king ordered the construction of Wat Ratchabura over the site of their cremations. This wat is known for its wealth of gold artifacts and the mural paintings found in its crypt. *(North of Wat Mahathat. Open daily 8am-6:30pm. 30฿.)*

WAT CHAI-MONGKOL. This fabulous wat was founded in 1357 by U Thong who had mastered meditation techniques. The sect grew tremendously, granting its head monk the title of the "Supreme Patriarch." The giant *chedi* was built by King Naresuan the Great to commemorate the 1592 victory over the Burmese. The wat's name, Chai-Mongkol ("Auspicious Victory"), refers to this event. *(On the southeast side of the city. 20min. by bicycle from the island. Open daily 8am-4:30pm. 20฿.)*

WAT PHANANCHOENG. The massive brick-and-mortar Buddha dates back to 1324, 26 years before Ayutthaya was founded. Legend has it that tears formed in its eyes when the city was sacked by the Burmese in 1767. *(West of Chai Mongkol, about 2km farther down the road. Open daily 8am-4:30pm. 20฿.)*

AYUTTHAYA HISTORICAL STUDY CENTER. The modern building houses a US$8 million research institute funded by the Japanese government, featuring displays on the ancient city's political, economic, and social life. Touring the surprisingly small upstairs exhibition hall shouldn't take more than 45min. *(On Rotchana Rd., opposite the Chao Sam Phraya National Museum. Open M-F 9am-4:30pm, Sa-Su 9am-5pm. 100฿, with student ID 50฿.)*

CHAO SAM PHRAYA NATIONAL MUSEUM. An old-school presentation complete with wood-and-glass display cases, dusty artifacts, and missing labels, the Chao Sam Phraya Museum has little to offer besides the splendid jewels taken from Wat Ratchabura. *(On Rotchana Rd., near the intersection with Si Samphet Rd. A 5min. walk from the TAT. Open W-Su. 30฿.)*

OTHER SIGHTS. A short bike ride north of the train station brings you to the impressive **Wats Maheyong** and **Kuidado** and the smaller **Wat Ayothaya**. All three are devoid of tourists. (Free.) North of the island, the **Elephant Kraal Pavilion** was where the king would watch his elephant army train. Ayutthaya is also the site of one of the country's largest **Loi Krathong** festivals, which usually takes place in November on the day of the full moon. Thais gather around **Beung Phra Ram,** the large lake in the center of the island, to see fireworks, watch *likay* (Thai folk dance), and groove to live pop music. The *loi* (floating) of *krathong* (small, lotus-shaped paper boats with candles and incense) takes place at the **Chantorakasem Pier** opposite the Chantorakasem Palace Museum and post office. Legend has it that two people who launch their *krathong* together are destined to become lovers.

THAILAND

ENTERTAINMENT AND NIGHTLIFE

From 7:30 to 9:30pm nightly, **Wat Phra Si Sanphet, Wat Mahatat, Wat Ratburana, Wat Phra Ram** (next to Wat Phra Si Sanphet, toward the TAT), and **Wat Chiawatthanaram** (southwest of the island) are illuminated by floodlights. Although *Let's Go* doesn't recommend it, locals suggest sneaking into the ruins around that time to drink.

Moon Cafe, 10/30 Chao Phrom Rd. (☎232 501). Opposite Ayutthaya Guest House. Look for the English sign. A collection of over 400 jazz, blues, and classic rock CDs makes this small *farang* bar a site for sore ears. Lead sing-alongs from the upright piano in the corner. Open daily 5pm-midnight or whenever the jammin' stops.

Rodeo Saloon and Restaurant, 79/81 U Thong Rd. (☎251 616). Coming from the Chao Phrom Market, it's on the left side of the street 200m before the GPO; look for the Jack Daniels sign. A Thai take on the Old American West (yippee-thai-yai-yay). Large Heineken 95฿. The band doesn't get jumping until 9 or 10pm. Open daily 6pm-1am.

Thai Massage (☎244 582), at the Chao Phrom Market bus station. From Naresuan Rd., it's the 2nd building on the right. Treat yourself to the "good taste" massage. 2hr. of traditional Thai bodywork 240฿. Open daily 10am-midnight.

KANCHANABURI ☎034

The Japanese invasion during WWII immortalized the otherwise unnoteworthy town of Kanchanaburi and its humble River Kwai. Swarms of tourists pack into A/C buses to see the graves of thousands of Allied soldiers and the Death Railway Bridge rather than the several Thai wats that scatter the town. Backpackers, for the most part, use the city as a base for exploring the surrounding waterfalls, caves, and jungles, returning in the evenings to the lively backstreet guest houses to swap travel stories.

TRANSPORTATION

Trains: Kanchanaburi Train Station (☎511 285), on Saeng Chuto Rd. To **Nam Tok** via the **River Kwai Bridge** (2½hr.; 6:10, 11am, 4:30 pm; 15฿) and **Thonburi** (3hr.; 7:25am, 2:50, 5:45pm; 15฿). Call 561 052 for info on weekend trains to **Bangkok** and other destinations (2hr.; Sa-Su 5pm; 28฿). Trains are convenient only for those wanting to ride across the River Kwai Bridge; head to the bus station for other destinations.

Buses: The **Kanchanaburi Bus Station** (☎511 182) is in Ban Noue Village. To: **Bangkok** (#81, 3½hr., every 15min. 4am-6:30pm, 48฿; 1st-class with A/C, 2hr., every 15min. 4am-7pm, 71฿; 2nd-class with A/C, 2hr., every 20min. 3:50am-6:50pm, 62฿); **Erawan National Park** (#8170, 1½hr., every 50min. 8am-5:20pm, 26฿); **Ratchaburi** with connections to **Cha Am, Hua Hin,** and **Phetchaburi** (#461, 2hr., every 15min. 5:10am-6:20pm, 36฿); **Sangkhlaburi** (#8203; 5hr.; 6, 8:40, 10:20am, noon; 84฿); **Suphanburi** (#411, 1½hr., every 20min. 5am-5:45pm, 34฿) with connections to **Ayutthaya** and **Nakhon Sawan.** A/C vans to Sangkhlaburi depart from the corner of Lak Muang Rd. and Saeng Chuto Rd. (3hr.; 7:30, 11:30am, 4:30pm; 118฿).

Local Transportation: Songthaew run up and down Saeng Chuto Rd. (3-5฿). **Samlor** cost 10-20฿ from the railway station to TAT. A **ferry** crosses the river (3฿) at the end of Chai Chumphol Rd.

Rentals: Bicycles available for 20฿ per day near the guest houses on Mae Nam Kwai Rd. Other guest houses and the Punee Cafe rent bicycles for 20-50฿ per day with a deposit of an ID and **motorbikes** for 200฿ with a deposit of a passport.

ORIENTATION AND PRACTICAL INFORMATION

Kanchanaburi is 129km from Bangkok and stretches roughly 4km from northwest to southeast along the banks of the **Kwai River,** which flows parallel to **Saeng Chuto Rd.**, the city's main drag. North of town is the famous **River Kwai Bridge;** 2km south is the **train station** and the river-side **guest house area,** where *farang* congregate. Two kilometers farther south is **Ban Noue Village,** the city's main commercial area and home to the all-important **bus station**. Because Kanchanaburi is quite spread out, consider renting a bicycle to avoid the long, dusty walks between one part of town and the other.

Tourist Office: TAT (☎/fax 511 200), on Saeng Chuto Rd., a 5min. walk south of the bus station. Friendly and helpful English-speaking staff. Maps and bus/train schedules. Open daily 8:30am-4:30pm.

Immigration Office: (☎513 325), on Mae Nam Maeklong Rd., 4km from TAT. Follow Saeng Chuto Rd. south away from Ban Noue Village and turn right at City Hall, 1km past the GPO. A 30min. bicycle ride from the city center. 1-month visa extension 500฿, 1-day turnaround. Open M-F 8:30am-noon and 1-4:30pm.

Currency Exchange: Banks are common on the roads fanning out from the Kanchanaburi Bus Station. Several have **24hr. ATMs.**

Markets: The **Dalat Kao Market,** bounded by Chao Khunnen and Burakamkosol Rd., offers fresh produce and meat. **Phasuk Market,** across from the bus station near Lak Mueng Rd. in Ban Noue Village, sells clothing and accessories. Both open dawn-dusk.

Emergency: ☎191.

Provincial Police Headquarters: ☎512 100. Opposite TAT. Some English spoken. Open 24hr.

PIG HEADED SPIRITS When entering a Thai house, you are likely to see the *san phr pum* ("spirit house"), the dwelling of the household's guardian spirit. An ancient monument, standard *san phr pum* are comprised of a house-shaped shrine, a figurine or tablet representing the guardian spirit, and figurines of followers, household servants, and pets. Raised to eye level and set on a pillar, the location and construction of the shrine are carefully facilitated by a specialist. Allowing the shrine to be overshadowed by the house at any time or facing it toward the house entrance would dishonor the guardian spirit and force it to withdraw its protection. The spirit must be appeased with offerings made during the annual April water festival. Offerings are placed in a banana leaf container called a *bat phlee* and on a tray made of banana trunk. The spirits, it seems, are particularly fond of chicken and pig's head.

Tourist Police: ☎512 795. **Emergency:** ☎1699. 1½km north of the train station on Saeng Chuto Rd. on the right. Free **luggage storage.** English spoken. Open 24hr. Also 2 helpful **booths** at the foot of the Kwai River Bridge and on Song Kwai Rd. Booths open daily 8:30am-6pm.

Medical Services: Saeng Chuto Hospital (☎621 129), 500m north of TAT on Saeng Chuto Rd. English spoken. Open 24hr. MC/V.

Telephones: Data Communications Office (CAT), on Saeng Chuto Rd. Walk past the post office and turn at the 1st left. The office is 200m down the road on the right. International calls, phone cards, and **Internet access.** 1st min. 3฿, each subsequent min. .50฿. Open daily 8:30am-10pm.

Internet: Available all over the city, especially on Saeng Chuto Rd. north of the bus station. The most convenient place is the **Internet & Email Center,** on Mae Nam Kwai Rd. 2 doors down from Jolly Frog Backpacker's. 1฿ per min. (15min. minimum) with the exception of the CAT, above. Open daily 9am-11pm.

Post Office: GPO (☎511 131), on Saeng Chuto Rd., 1km south of TAT on the left. Has *Poste Restante*, but it's a 40min. trek from the guest houses. More convenient is the post office at the corner of Phak Phrak Rd. and Lak Muang Rd. Open M-F 8:30am-4:30pm, Sa-Su 9am-noon. **Postal code:** 71000.

THAILAND

ACCOMMODATIONS

Most of Kanchanaburi's best budget accommodations sit along (or in) the River Kwai in the northern part of the city, a 10min. walk from the train station or a 25min. walk from the bus station. Guest houses on Rong Heep Oil Rd. are quieter, while the ones on Mae Nam Kwai Rd. are always flooded with *farang*. All establishments listed serve Thai and Western food and help arrange tours.

VN Guest House, 44 Rong Heep Oil Rd. (☎514 082). The friendly staff welcomes a crew of easy-going backpackers who congregate on the hotel's river-side veranda late into the night. The small but comfortable rooms are some of the best bargains in town. Singles 50-60฿, with bath 100฿; doubles 180฿, with A/C 250฿.

Jolly Frog Backpacker's, 28 Soi China, Mae Nam Kwai Rd. (☎514 579). Clean, pretty rooms overlook a resort-like courtyard. Large and extremely popular, but if you've had enough of toe rings, tank tops, and tie-dye, keep moving. Nightly movies and free pickup from bus and train stations. Singles 60฿; doubles 110฿, on raft portion 120฿, with bath 150฿; triples 150฿.

Apple's Guest House and Restaurant (Krathom Thai), 52 Rong Heep Oil Rd. (☎512 017). At the juncture with Mae Nam Kwai Rd. Quiet but very popular. The 15 rooms are clean and surround a peaceful courtyard. Hospitable co-owner Apple leads an excellent full-day cooking course (700฿). Free pickup from the bus and train station. Singles 150฿; doubles 200฿.

Rick's Lodge, 45/3 Rong Heep Oil Rd. (☎514 831). Rick's out-luxuries its cheaper neighbors with satellite TVs, a newly expanded restaurant, and recently refurbished rooms. Single bungalows 150฿; double bungalows 200-250฿.

Sam's River Raft House, 48/1 Rong Heep Oil Rd. (☎624 321). Clean, standard raft rooms and more exciting rustic bungalows across the street. Large TV room and good views of the river. Singles 80฿; doubles 150-250฿, with A/C and hot shower 350฿.

Nita Raft House, 27/1 Pakpraek (☎514 521). An easy 10min. walk from the bus station (100m up from the JEATH museum). Proximity to Song Kwai Road's touristy din means floating discos rock right outside until 10pm. Clean but simple rooms. Singles 60฿; doubles 100฿, with shower 150฿.

J's Guest House, 32/4 Rong Heep Oil Rd. (☎620 307). For those traveling on the cheap. Friendly staff, but rooms are bare and made of flimsy plywood. The same family owns the similar **River Guest House** next door. Singles 50฿, with bath 100฿; doubles 80฿/120฿.

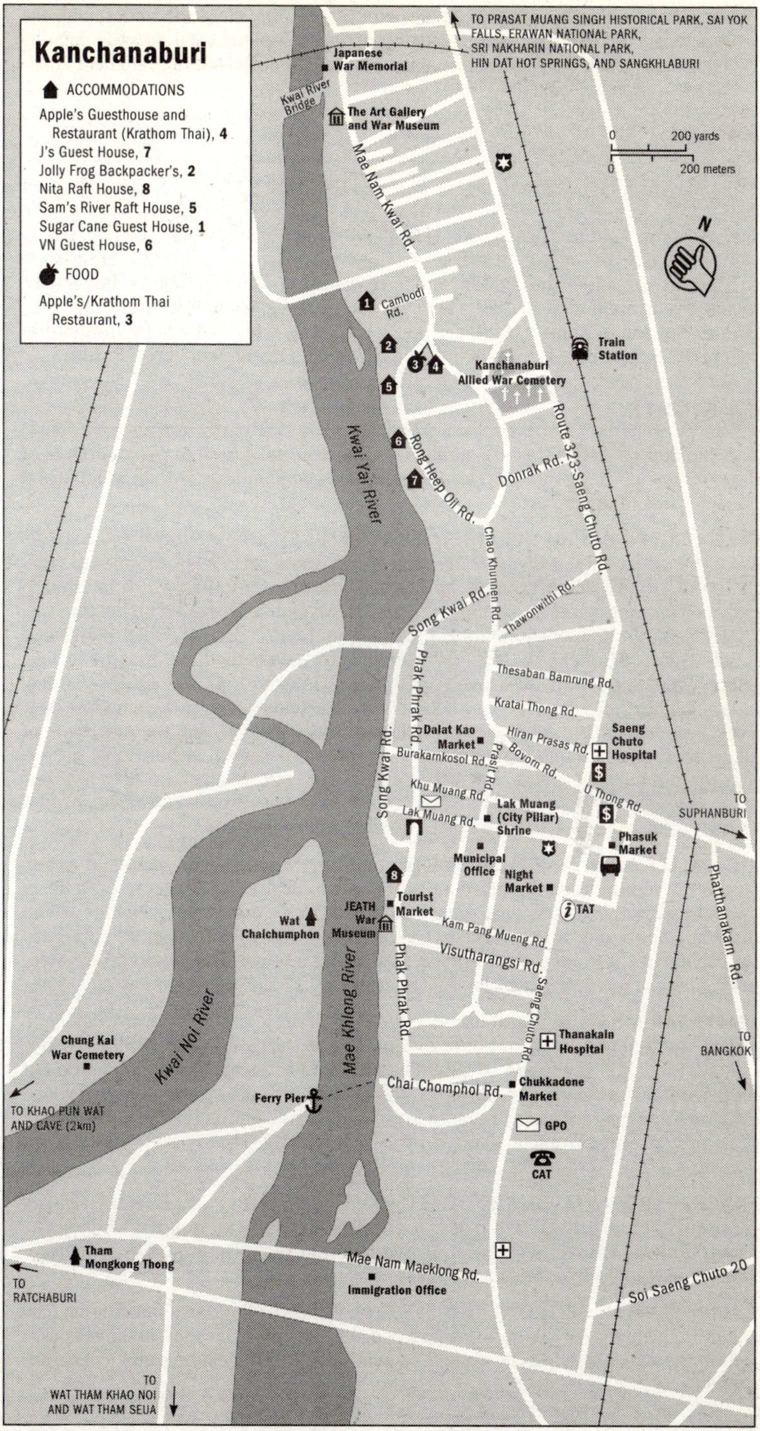
Kanchanaburi
ACCOMMODATIONS
Apple's Guesthouse and Restaurant (Krathom Thai), 4
J's Guest House, 7
Jolly Frog Backpacker's, 2
Nita Raft House, 8
Sam's River Raft House, 5
Sugar Cane Guest House, 1
VN Guest House, 6
FOOD
Apple's/Krathom Thai Restaurant, 3
TO PRASAT MUANG SINGH HISTORICAL PARK, SAI YOK FALLS, ERAWAN NATIONAL PARK, SRI NAKHARIN NATIONAL PARK, HIN DAT HOT SPRINGS, AND SANGKHLABURI
Japanese War Memorial
Kwai River Bridge
The Art Gallery and War Museum
Mae Nam Kwai Rd.
0 200 yards
0 200 meters
N
Cambodi Rd.
Train Station
Kanchanaburi Allied War Cemetery
Kwai Yai River
Rong Heep Oil Rd.
Donrak Rd.
Route 323-Saeng Chuto Rd.
Chao Khunnen Rd.
Song Kwai Rd.
Thawonwithi Rd.
Thesaban Bamrung Rd.
Kratai Thong Rd.
Phak Phrak Rd.
Dalat Kao Market
Hiran Prasas Rd.
Saeng Chuto Hospital
Burakarnkosol Rd.
Bovorn Rd.
Prasit Rd.
Song Kwai Rd.
Khu Muang Rd.
U Thong Rd.
Lak Muang Rd.
Lak Muang (City Pillar) Shrine
TO SUPHANBURI
Phasuk Market
Municipal Office
Night Market
JEATH War Museum
Tourist Market
TAT
Wat Chaichumphon
Kam Pang Mueng Rd.
Visutharangsi Rd.
Phatthanakam Rd.
Kwai Noi River
Mae Khlong River
Phak Phrak Rd.
Saeng Chuto Rd.
Chung Kai War Cemetery
Thanakain Hospital
TO BANGKOK
TO KHAO PUN WAT AND CAVE (2km)
Ferry Pier
Chai Chomphol Rd.
Chukkadone Market
GPO
CAT
Tham Mongkong Thong
TO RATCHABURI
Mae Nam Maeklong Rd.
Immigration Office
Soi Saeng Chuto 20
TO WAT THAM KHAO NOI AND WAT THAM SEUA

Sugar Cane Guest House (☎624 836), on Cambodia Rd. off Mae Nam Kwai Rd. The new location is quite far from the other guest houses and about 7km away from the bridge. The small bungalows are spartan but clean. Doubles with private bath 200฿, with A/C and private bath 400฿.

FOOD

From May to July, be sure to try the *khanun* (jackfruit), a Thai delicacy. This and other tasty victuals can be found in cheap food stalls and open-air eateries that line the streets around the bus station. The **night market,** just north of TAT on Saeng Chuto Rd., is worth a stop. If market eating is not your style, head for Song Kwai Rd., where dozens of indistinguishable restaurants cater almost exclusively to locals. Unfortunately, restaurants near the bridge and guest houses are overpriced. One exception is **Apple's/Krathom Thai Restaurant,** which offers fabulous food (dishes 30-60฿). For a Thai-style Indian dish, try tofu massaman curry (65฿).

SIGHTS

Kanchanaburi's attractions are spread over 6km. To take it all in over a couple of days, rent a bicycle or motorcycle—it's infinitely faster and easier than walking and cheaper than taking taxis.

KWAI RIVER BRIDGE (DEATH RAILWAY BRIDGE). Constructed from 1941-1942, the original Kwai River Bridge was the Japanese army's last attempt to complete the 415km Thai-Myanmar railway line (the "Death Railway") to be used in transporting war materials to military camps in Myanmar. To speed up the process, Japan used all the labor it could get, tapping its rich reserve of Allied POWs and Asian workers. Roughly 16,000 POWs and 96,000 Asians died building the bridge, which was subsequently destroyed by British air raids in 1947. The bridge you see, although impressive, is a reconstruction built as a memorial to those who lost their lives. Kanchanaburi celebrates the **Kwai River Bridge Week** during the first week of December. Activities include archaeological and historical exhibitions, performances and musical events, and a spectacular light and sound show. *(3km northwest of the train station. Orange minibus #2 runs from the Focus Optic shop, 2 traffic lights from TAT (10min., 6am-7pm, 6฿). A 40min. walk from the bus station. Free.)*

ART GALLERY AND WAR MUSEUM. Luring bridge visitors with claims of extensive WWII exhibitions, the museum is actually a bizarre collection of odd, dusty exhibits; everything from Thai stamps to dresses of former Miss Thailands are on display. Follow the "toilet" signs to the basement, where cobwebs hide life-sized portrayals of the bridge construction. It's mildly interesting, but skip it if you're pressed for time. *(50m toward town from the bridge. ☎512 596. Open daily 8am-6pm. 30฿.)*

JEATH WAR MUSEUM. Established in 1977 by the chief abbot of Wat Chaichumphon (Wat Dai to locals) to honor victims of the Death Railway Bridge, JEATH (Japan, England, America/Australia, Thailand, and Holland) sits in a bamboo hut modeled after those used to house POWs. The collection of pictures, articles, and drawings is modest but nevertheless intriguing. Bonus points for the collection of drawings depicting tropical ulcers. *(1km from the town gate down Phak Phraek Rd. ☎515 203. Open daily 8:30am-4:30pm. 30฿.)*

KANCHANABURI ALLIED WAR CEMETERY. The cemetery is the final resting place of 7000 mostly British and Dutch Allied POWs who died working on the Death Railway Bridge. Western tour groups often seem to outnumber the headstones. *(3km north of the bus station on Saeng Chuto Rd., 5min. from the train station. Free.)*

CHUNG KAI WAR CEMETERY. Farther afield, Chung Kai holds the remains of 1700 Death Railway POWs in a setting more peaceful and pleasant than its larger counterpart in town. The trip makes a nice escape from the congestion of Kanchanaburi City. *(4km across the bridge at Song Kwai Road's northern end. Free.)*

WATS. Wat Chaichumphon, opposite JEATH, is the most frequented by townspeople. **Wat Tham Khao Pun,** 1km beyond Chung Kai War Cemetery, has a cave full of Buddhist shrines (5-20฿ donation suggested). Five kilometers across the river, Chinese-influenced Wat Tham Mongkon Thong, Cave Temple of the Golden Dragon, is renowned for its "floating nun," a young woman who can lie on water without sinking. (See **Floating Nun, Golden Dragon,** p. 615). Early weekend mornings are the best time to catch her in action, or you can ask for her. Unless you are with a tour group, she may ask for 200฿ to see her 10 to 15min. performance, which is not all that impressive if you know how to swim. Behind the *bot,* dragon-shaped steps lead up the mountain and into a limestone cave that affords views of the surrounding mountains and valleys. The temple also features a small museum of Kanchanaburi's history. Motorcycle taxis make the trip for 20฿, or you make the bike there.

OTHER SIGHTS. Lak Muang Rd. is home to the **town gate** and the **city pillar shrine.** Drivers honk at the pillar to show respect to the spirit inside.

ENTERTAINMENT

At night, most *farang* stick to bars and restaurants in the well-trodden area around the guest houses. The small but popular **Sports Corner Pub** at the corner of China Rd. and Mae Nam Kwai Rd., entertains Commonwealth folk with nightly showings of football, rugby, and cricket. (Open daily 9am-late.) Though some report the atmosphere is inhospitable to *farang,* head to the **karaoke** and **live music bars** that line the east side of Song Kwai Rd. to experience a more authentic Thai night out. For dives that float, check out the tacky and charmingly mobile floating discos that launch from the west side of Song Kwai Rd. and merrily cruise down the river toward the bridge. A *farang*-friendly option that's both terrestrial and away from the guest houses is the **Punnee Cafe,** 2/15 Ban Nuer Rd., just off Saeng Chuto Rd. The English establishment features a used bookstore and full bar, along with the requisite fish and chips. Danny, the friendly proprietor, organizes treks and gives useful advice. (☎513 503. Open daily 8am-midnight. Treks 150฿.)

THAILAND

DAYTRIPS FROM KANCHANABURI

Kanchanaburi makes an ideal base for exploring the dozens of waterfalls, caves, and parks that stretch all the way to Sangkhlaburi and the Thai-Myanmar border. Most guest houses guide or arrange tours for 400-1000฿, and most have a 3-5 person minimum. More independent travelers can take public transportation but may be limited to visiting only one or two attractions per day. Some report that renting motorcycles is a more time-efficient way of getting around.

Routes 3199 and 323 bisect the province and make good points of reference. The first is a well-paved passage to the Erawan waterfalls. The second heads west to Sangkhlaburi and the Thai-Myanmar border, passing the hot springs, Hellfire Pass, and several more waterfalls.

ALONG ROUTE 3199

ERAWAN NATIONAL PARK. The foremost tourist destination near Kanchanaburi, the spectacular seven-tiered waterfalls may not be the biggest cascades, but they're certainly the most accessible. It's best to arrive early to beat the maddening crowd of locals and *farang.* The first three levels are a five to 10min. walk from the trailhead. The more challenging trails going up the falls lead to clearer water, 50cm long fish, and more seclusion, but watch out—the trails can be slippery. Maps, photos, and a slide show are at the **Visitors Center,** next to where the bus from Kanchanaburi stops. **Accommodations** range from camping (30฿ with own tent) to dorms (mattresses 10฿) and bungalows (4 beds and bath, 250฿ per person). The **National Park Headquarters,** opposite the visitors center, handles emergencies. *(From Kanchanaburi, take public bus #8170 (1½ hr.; every 50min. 8am-5:20pm, last bus back at 4pm; 26฿). Open daily 8am-4:30pm. 20฿; motorcycle 10฿; cars 30฿.)*

GO FISH On your walk toward the River Kwai Bridge, you may have noticed something rather fishy: the street signs. All streets in Kanchanaburi are marked not by typical, boring rectangles but by fish-shaped signs that colorfully point traffic to and fro. The fish guiding those near the Bridge is the *pla yi sok* or Julien's golden-prized carp, a rapidly-disappearing fish native only to Kanchanaburi Province. The names on the fish signs are significant too; all streets linking Mae Nam Kwai Rd. to Saeng Chunto Rd. from the Bridge to the Allied War Cemetery, bear the names of the over 20 countries whose citizens were impressed as POWs by the Japanese.

SRI NAKHARIN NATIONAL PARK. Sri Nakharin has more animals and fewer tourists than Erawan, but getting there demands considerable time, money, and effort. About 105km from Kanchanaburi, **Huay Mae Khamin Waterfalls'** nine tiers are best reached from **Erawan.** Only motorcycles and four-wheel-drive vehicles can travel the 45km dry-weather road parallel to the reservoir, after which you must charter a ferry from Sisawat (150฿). You can also charter a longtail boat (1-2hr., up to 10 people 1000-1500฿) at the **Tha Kradan Pier,** 24km northeast of the Sri Nakharin Dam, 5km past Mongatet Village. **Accommodations** are limited to camping (5฿) and raft houses (1500-2000฿).

THAILAND

ALONG ROUTE 323

HELLFIRE PASS. In their quest to complete the Thai-Myanmar railway (the notorious "Death Railway"), the Japanese Imperial Army would not let a mere mountain stand in their way. Thousands of Allied POWs and impressed Asian laborers worked for months, manually chipping away rock under grueling conditions to create the Hellfire Pass, so named for the ghostly campfire shadows that would dance on the mountain walls at night. Today, the pass is a trail leading down the former railway on a stunning 3km-circuit around the area. The new adjoining Hellfire Pass Memorial Museum showcases pictures, articles, and personal stories of the POWs whose lives were sacrificed in the construction of the pass. When not busy shepherding tourist groups, the knowledgeable Aussie curators are eager to answer questions. *(Between Sai Yok Noi and Sai Yok Yai. Take bus #8203 from Kanchanaburi and tell the attendant where you want to get off. (1½hr.; every 30min. 6am-6:30pm, last bus returns at about 4:45pm; 30฿). Open daily 9am-4pm. Suggested donation 40฿.)*

PRASAT MUANG SINGH HISTORICAL PARK. This walled "City of Lions" rests along the Kwai Noi River and contains 2000 year old artifacts and skeletal remains. Prasat Muang Singh (Tower of the City of Lions) is believed to have constituted the westernmost outpost of the Khmer empire. The Visitors Center, to the right of the main ruins, has a large park map. *(Trains (1hr.; 7:30am, noon, 5:40pm; return 6:20am, 1:50pm, and 4:30pm; 10฿) come closer to the park than buses. Get off at Thakilen; from the train station, walk 1km to the main road and then 1km to the right. Bus #8203 stops 7km from the park; transportation for the final leg may be hard to find. Return buses are best caught before 4pm. ☎591 122. Open daily 8:30am-4:30pm. 40฿.)*

SAI YOK NOI WATERFALL. Although the "little" (*noi*) Sai Yok Falls are fairly large, they offer only food stalls and concrete paths instead of scenery or hiking trails. Tours stop here for five-minute photo ops, and that's probably about enough. *(60 km from Kanchanaburi. Bus #8203 to Sai Yok Noi runs every 30 min. 6am-6:30pm, last return 5pm; the hour-long ride costs25฿. The waterfall is free.)*

WANG BADANG CAVE. This is for spelunkers only, not casual tourists. There are no guided tours, so those who choose to come should bring their own flashlights. *(Turn from Rte. 323, 100m south of Sai Yok Noi, then continue 2½km on the dirt road. Free.)*

HIN DAT HOT SPRINGS. The two springs are rather dingy and small but nevertheless extremely popular with Thai tourists. One stays a constant 40°C, while the other fluctuates between 35 and 38°C. *(1km off Rte. 323. The pools have no English road signs, but their turn-off is 127km from Kanchanaburi and 15km before Thong Pha Phum. Bus #8203 goes from Kanchanaburi every 30min. 6am-6:30pm, last return bus 4pm; 2¾hr. trip, 54฿. Hot Springs 5฿.)*

FLOATING NUN, GOLDEN DRAGON For over 25 years, Wat Thum Mongkong Thong, Cave Temple of the Golden Dragon, was famous for its **"floating nun"**–a young woman who can lie on water without sinking. She was so famous that when she passed away in 1997, another woman (not actually a nun, but apparently pure enough) stepped into fill her floating duties. The 15min. performance takes place in a miniature version of a greek amphitheater surrounding a green pool of water. The "nun," dressed in white, but without the requisite short hair, then floats in various meditation positions. Opinions on the performance vary from "Not impressive if you know how to... you know... swim" to "You try to float in the lotus position!" Best viewed with a tour in the mornings (20฿); otherwise it's 200฿ for a solo float.

SAI YOK YAI WATERFALL AND NATIONAL PARK. Celebrated in poetry and song, the Sai Yok Yai Waterfall dribbles unimpressively, except between July and September, when it gushes unimpressively. One of the world's smallest mammal species, the Kitti hog-nosed bats, lives in the park's Bat Cave, 2km from the visitors center and accessible by trails. You can pick up maps and leave gear at the visitors center. Accommodations include camping (30฿) and rooms for one or two over the river (200-250฿).

Farther away, **Lawa Cave** is the park's largest. Hire a longtail boat (4hr. round-trip, up to 10 people 1000-1500฿) to pass the waterfall and the **Dao Wadung Caves** at the Pak Saeng Pier in Tambon Tha Sao, southwest of Sai Yok Noi. *(45min. by bus from Sai Yok Noi; take any bus or* songthaew *heading north (15฿). Bus #8203 goes from Kanchanaburi every 30min. 6am-6:30pm, last return bus 4:30pm; 2hr. trip, 38฿. You'll still need to walk 3km or take a motorcycle lift (10-15฿) to the Visitors Center. Open daily 6am-7:30pm. 20฿; children 10฿; car with driver 30฿.)*

THAILAND

SANGKHLABURI ☎034

Unlike its neighbor Kanchanaburi, Sangkhlaburi relies mostly on its natural beauty. The few man-made attractions in the town pale in comparison to the fresh air, rugged mountains, and dense jungle that envelop the town. Travelers come for a day and end up staying a week, entranced by the relaxing views of Khao Laem Lake, the numerous jungle-trekking adventures, and the opportunity to mingle with the Karen and Mon migrants who now call this border town home. While the tiny city center offers little to visitors, the natural beauty make it a desirable destination.

TRANSPORTATION AND PRACTICAL INFORMATION. Public transportation from Sangkhlaburi only runs to **Kanchanaburi** (Bus #8203: 4½hr; 6:45, 8:15, 10:15am, 1:15pm; 90฿; with A/C: 3½hr.; 8:45, 10:45am, 2:30pm; 150฿; A/C van: 3hr.; 6:30, 7:30, 9:30, 11:30am, 3:30pm; 118฿) and to the **Three Pagodas Pass** by *songthaew* (30min., every 40min. 6am-6pm, 30-35฿). A/C buses and minibuses from Kanchanaburi drop passengers at the **market** in the middle of town; regular buses and *songthaew* arrive at the end of the street at the **bus station**. The Sangkhlaburi **city center** is laid out in a simple grid. To get to the **wooden bridge** from the bus station, walk right past the post office and turn right at the first paved intersection.

Currency exchange can be handled at **Siam Commercial Bank** opposite the marketplace. (**No ATM.** ☎595 263. Open M-F 8:30am-3:30pm.) In case of emergency, contact the **police** (☎595 300) or the **hospital** (☎595 058). To get to either, walk left two blocks to the end of the street; the hospital staff is 25m to the right, and the police office is right next door. (Limited English. Both open 24hr.) To get to the **immigration office** (☎595 335), walk two blocks left of the bus station and turn left at the post office; it is ¾ of the way down the street on the left. **No visa extensions**, but the office will give you the necessary permit to cross the Three Pagodas Pass into Myanmar. (☎595 335. 2 passport-sized photos and photocopies of the front page of your passport and Thai visa are required for permit. Open daily 8:30am-5pm.) **Internet access** has made its splashy debut down the street from the bank on the right side, around the corner from the Phornpaillin Hotel. (☎595 054. 1฿ per min. Open daily 8am-9pm.) The **post office** is 25m to the right of the regular bus stop and has an **international telephone booth.** (☎595 115. Open M-F 8:30am-4:30pm, Sa 9am-noon.) **Postal code:** 71240.

ACCOMMODATIONS. The **Burmese Inn,** 52/3 Tambon Nong Loo, is 1km to the right from the bus station. Armin, Meo, and their young daughter Alissa make the clean but simple guest house feel like home. Amateur astronomer Armin is a veritable walking tourist office and can arrange individually tailored two- and three-day jungle treks (750-1250฿). The open-air veranda offers stunning views of the bridge. (☎/fax 595 146. Motorbike rentals 200฿ per day. Singles with fan and mosquito net 70฿, with bath 100฿; doubles with fan, net, and bath 180฿; bungalow with bath 300฿; family bungalow with satellite TV 500฿.) **P. Guest House,** 81/2 Tumbon Nong Loo, 300m beyond the Burmese Inn, is worth the extra bhat. The large ranch-style rooms are immaculate and the bathrooms boast some of the cleanest (and most aesthetically pleasing) squat toilets in Thailand. The restaurant offers a lovely view of the lake and a foosball table. (☎595 061. Canoe 100฿ per day. Motorcycle 200฿ per day. Bicycle 100฿ per day. Singles and doubles with shared bath 200฿. Elephant riding, rating, and 1 night accommodation 800฿.)

SIGHTS. Most attractions in Sangkhlaburi are located a ways from the town center. Arrange **trekking trips** through P. Guest House or the Burmese Inn (see **Accommodations,** above). You can also arrange trekking trips in Kanchanaburi where more options exist. Inquire at the Kanchanaburi TAT. Those looking to take it easy might consider a **boat trip** on beautiful Lake Khao Laem, which features a partially submerged wat from pre-dam Sangkhlaburi.

DAYTRIPS FROM SANGKHLABURI. The **longest wooden bridge in Thailand,** the 400m bridge of the Reverend Auttamo, crosses the massive Lake Khao Laem and connects the city of Sangkhlaburi to **The Mon Village.** Although they don't possess Thai citizenship, the Mon people are not quite refugees as they live under the protection of the elderly Luang Phaw Utama, who watches over the temples and households in the area. Utama has oodles of money, thanks to many Chinese who believe he has healing powers and flock to him bearing offerings. To get to his main temple, walk uphill straight from the bridge to the stop sign. Turn left, follow the winding road, and take a left at the next stop sign. The red-and-gold **Wat Wang Wiwekaram** sits at the end of the road, 4km from Sangkhlaburi opposite the **handicraft market** and *chedi*. To get to the bridge and the Mon Village, walk down the road from the Sangkhlaburi GPO toward the guest houses. The first paved right leads to the bridge, 1km away. From here, it's a 30min. walk to the main temple.

Due to poaching, the elephants, tigers, tapirs, bears, gibbons, and peacocks that inhabit **Thung Yai Sanctuary Park,** Thailand's largest conservation area have moved deep into the forest. Most visitors make the trip to see Karen villages. Only four-wheel-drive vehicles can traverse the terrain, even during the dry season. Talk to Armin at the Burmese Inn about accessibility, road conditions, and possible jeep rental (dry season 100฿, more in the wet season).

PHETCHABURI ☎032

Tiny "Phetburi" is something of an oddity. Halfway between Bangkok and the beach getaway of Hua Hin, the town offers neither the beaches nor the overwhelming hustle and bustle of its neighbors. What Phetchaburi does provide, though, is a cultural welcome to Southern Thailand. Numerous wats dot the city's neighborhoods, and a former royal palace overlooks the city from Khao Wang Hill. Despite the city's numerous attractions, most *farang* don't stop here on their way to the southern beaches, leaving the few who do as targets of curious stares.

BORDER CROSSING: THREE PAGODAS PASS. About 24km from Sangkhlaburi, the **Three Pagodas Pass** is an anticlimax for those with visions of border intrigue. The border crossing from Three Pagodas Pass to **Phayathonzu, Myanmar,** recently opened to foreigners with several caveats: prior authorization from the Immigration Office in Sangkhlaburi is required; US$10 (450฿) will get you up to 2km into Myanmar, but only from 6am-6pm; the Burmese military requires one passport picture; and, just as the sign says, "Every foreigner welcome to Myanmar. No videocams are allowed." *Songthaew* leaving from Sangkhlaburi's bus station make the trip (30 min., every 40min. 6am-6pm, 30-35฿). If you're making the trip for a rich, historical experience, you'll be disappointed. The diminutive Three Pagodas communicates little of the place's turbulent past. According to one story, as the Burma Wars came to an end in the mid-1700s, the King of Thailand laid down three stones (representing Siam, Burma, and peaceful unity) to mark the border between the two countries. Villages constructed three pagodas *(Chedi Sam Ong)* over the stones, and monks have used the middle shrine to pray for peace. To make the trip more worthwhile, consider backtracking to the **Sawan Bundarn Cave,** located on the way to the Three Pagodas Pass. From Three Pagodas, walk 2km back toward Sangkhlaburi and turn left. Follow the wide dirt road for 700m and turn right onto a smaller track for 500m. There a monk will lead you on a flashlight tour of the cave—for a donation, of course.

THAILAND

TRANSPORTATION

Trains: The **Phetchaburi Railway Station** (☎425 211) is on the northern edge of town. To get to the city center, head left from the station and take a right 1km later on Damnernkasem Rd. Service to **Bangkok** (6:30, 7:20am, noon, 3pm; 3rd-class 74฿). Buses are more convenient.

Buses: The **A/C bus station** is to the right of Damnernkasem Rd., past the Ratchavidhi Rd. intersection. Buses to **Bangkok** (2½hr., every 30min. 4am-8:30pm, 90฿). The **regular bus station** is on Phetkasem Hwy. on the eastern edge of town, about 300m before the entrance to the Khao Wang cable car. Taxis charge about 20-30฿ for the ride. To **Bangkok** (2½hr., every 20min. 5am-5pm, 70฿). Orange buses to **Cha-am** (1hr., 20฿) and **Hua-Hin** (1½hr., 30฿) depart frequently from Matayawong Rd., around the corner from Wat Kamphaeng Laeng.

Local Transportation: Downtown can be traversed on foot. For longer distances, look for **motorcycle taxis** (up to 20฿ within town, 30฿ outside) and bargain hard.

ORIENTATION AND PRACTICAL INFORMATION

Phetchaburi is 135km south of Bangkok. The town's grid layout is easy to navigate. **Damnernkasem Rd.** is the city's main drag and runs parallel to the **Phetchaburi River** north to south. To the north, the road curves to the left, leading to the **hospital** and **train station.** To the south it intersects **Ratchavidhi Rd.,** leading westward to Khao Wang Hill, and **Phongsuriya Rd.,** leading eastward to several hotels and wats and the **Saphan Chomrut** (the Chomrut Bridge) across the Phetchaburi River.

Tourist Office: Phetchaburi is poorly served by the regional **Tourism Authority of Thailand (TAT) office** in Cha-am (☎ 471 005).

Currency Exchange: Siam Commercial Bank, 2 Damnernkasem Rd. (☎425 303). Halfway between the bridge and the Ratchavidhi Rd. intersection. **ATM.** Open M-F 8:30am-3:30pm.

Emergency: ☎191.

Police: Phetchaburi Police Station (☎425 500), on Ratchavidhi Rd. close to the mountain and opposite the GPO.

Medical Services: Phrachomklao Hospital (☎401 125), 50m from the train station on the left. Some English spoken. No credit cards. Open 24hr. Farther away is the **Petcharat Hospital** (☎417 029), on Phetkasem Hwy. north of town, close to the Khao Wong cable car stop. 24hr. emergency care. No credit cards.

Telephones: 2nd fl. of GPO. **Long-distance** and **international** calls. **Fax**. Open M-F 8:30am-6pm, Sa-Su 9am-5pm.

Internet Access: Internet Cafe, on Chisa-in Rd., just a few blocks west of the Chomrut Bridge. 40฿ per hr. Open daily 9am-midnight.

Post Office: GPO (☎425 146), at the intersection of Ratchavidhi and Damnernkasem Rd. *Poste Restante*. Open M-F 8:30am-4:30pm, Sa-Su 9am-noon. **Postal code:** 76000.

ACCOMMODATIONS AND FOOD

Phetchaburi's few accommodations cluster around **Chomrut Bridge,** a few minutes from the A/C bus station or a 15-20min. walk from the railway station.

Rabieng Guest House (☎425 707), snuggled at the foot of the Chomrut Bridge on the west bank, on a diagonal from the Chom Klao Hotel. The young, friendly staff keeps this small guest house in tip-top shape. The green rooms, although comfortable, are small, but you'll probably spend most of your time in the adjoining restaurant, which offers good food, good views, and good music. Clean shared baths. Request room 104 or 205 for the least street racket. Singles 120฿; doubles 240฿.

Chom Klao Hotel (☎425 398), the 1st building on the river after crossing Chomrut Bridge to the east bank. The large rooms are clean though showing their age with peeling paint and 70s furniture. Some come with balcony, private bath, and Western toilet. Shared baths have squat toilets. Singles 120฿, with bath 160฿; doubles 200฿/240฿.

A feisty **outdoor market** along the curve of Damnernkasem Rd. by the A/C bus station offers a cornucopia of goodies. (Open daily 10am-11pm.) At **Rabieng Restaurant,** next to the guest house, enjoy a long menu of Thai dishes and soups (25-150฿) while overlooking the idle river. (Open daily 8:30am-1am.)

RITES OF PASSAGE In Thailand, Laos, and Cambodia, over half the male Buddhist adolescent population spends a few months as monks. The monastery stay is voluntary, but for many Buddhist boys, it is expected that for a few months before they marry, they will don the orange robes and leave their families, schools, and childhoods. Monks shave their heads, renounce sex and money, spend their days in study and meditation, emerging to resume their old lives with renewed spiritual vigor.

SIGHTS

With the exception of Khao Wang and the Khao Luang Cave, all sights are an easy walk from the town center.

PHRA NAKHON KHIRI HISTORICAL PARK AND NATIONAL MUSEUM (KHAO WANG). In the 1850s, King Rama IV had tired of the heat and exhaustion of Central Thailand and looked south to build a new royal retreat. His search ended in Phra Nakhon Khiri (or Khao Wang), an original mixture of Chinese and Western architecture which scans the hill's three peaks. The westernmost peak houses the **royal residence,** a collection of halls and pavilions where Rama IV and his son relaxed and entertained guests. The palace's original furnishings are still on display. **Phra That Chom Phet,** a 49m tall *chedi*, sits on the middle peak. On the eastern peak is **Wat Phra Kaew,** which Rama IV ordered to be constructed in the same style as the Temple of the Emerald Buddha of the Grand Palace in Bangkok. The park is accessible by a **cable car** running up to the royal residence. Your other option is the long, windy footpath. Every early February, the town celebrates the **Phra Nakhon Khiri Fair,** which features local art shows, cultural performances, and ox-cart races. *(Cable car runs 8:30am-5:15pm; round-trip 30฿, children 10฿. Park open M-F 8:15am-5pm, Sa-Su 8:15am-5:15pm. Museum open daily 9am-4pm. 40฿.)*

WAT YAI SUWANNARAM. This 17th-century religious compound features outstanding examples of Ayutthaya art and architecture. Many of the buildings are currently under renovation but try asking one of the monks to open the two wooden buildings that contain well-preserved 18th-century murals. *(On Phongsuriya Rd., about a 10min. walk east from Chomrut Bridge.)*

WAT KAMPHAENG LAENG. The five impressive laterite-block structures house Buddha images that were originally part of a 12th-century Khmer Hindu shrine, and each of the five *prangs* is thought to be dedicated to one of the five major Hindu deities. In the Ayutthaya period, the temple reconsecrated to Buddhism, and images of the Buddha replaced Hindu sculptures. Currently, the temple is the residence of **Phra Khruu Yanwitmon,** Phetchaburi's most revered monk. *(Follow Phongsuriya Rd. past Wat Yai Suwannaram and turn right on Phogarong Rd., about 500m down. The wat will be on the right after about 500m. If the front gate is locked, turn right on the road just after the wat and enter at the gate on the right.)*

WAT MAHATHAT WORARIHARA. With its giant white *prang* dominating the Phetchaburi skyline, Wat Mahathat Worarihara is understandably one of the most popular religious sites in the city. The dozens of Buddha images surrounding the main *prang* and the stuccos on the *prang* pedestals draw many visitors. *(On Damnernkasem Rd., about a 10min. walk south of its intersection with the bridge.)*

WAT KHAO BANDAI IT. A set of steps between two elephant statues lead to several caves, which, in terms of sheer Buddha quantity, are pretty impressive. A flashlight will help illuminate the "thousand Buddhas" tucked into crevices. *(Take the road leading west from the highway opposite the hospital past Khao Wang. The entrance is on the right side of the road at the series of 3 ornate shelters. Go through the right archway and up the short road guarded by monkeys. Motorcycle taxis from town run 40฿.)*

KHAO LUANG CAVE. This underground religious cave, about 4km north of town, is a bizarre and mildly interesting mix of Buddhist imagery, ill-tempered monkeys, and tourist gimmickry. The cave is best seen between 11am and 2pm, when sunlight illuminates the golden Buddhas and the red-tiled floor. Local entrepreneurs offer flashlight tours of the darker recesses, but the good stuff's out in the open. *(The best way to get there is by taxi. Motorcycle taxis charge 40-50฿ from the town center, 100-150฿ round-trip.)*

DAYTRIPS FROM PHETCHABURI

KAENG KRACHAN NATIONAL PARK. Thailand's largest national park envelops 3000 sq. km of rain forest in the western half of Phetchaburi Province. Since the park's opening in 1981, four white elephants, long considered symbols of royal prestige and good fortune, have been captured here and presented to the king. The Phetchaburi and Phanburi Rivers entice **rafters,** and rangers lead three-day **hikes** in the high season for four people (200฿ per day, with food 352฿). Inquire at the **visitor station** near the park entrance. To reach the park's center and the waterfalls there, get to the park by 9:30am, as the 68km road becomes a one-way road in the wrong direction at 10am. Car rental is 1000฿, and though *Let's Go* doesn't recommend it, hitchhiking is the preferred method of transportation among many park visitors. The alternative, hanging out at **Kaeng Krachan Lake** near park headquarters, gets old quickly. Four-person **bungalows** are 100฿; **tents** can be pitched for 10-30฿. To get to the park, take a dark blue *songthaew* to Tha Yong (20฿). There, switch to a Koeng Krachan *songthaew* to park headquarters (20฿).

CHAO SAMRAN BEACH. Quieter than some beaches to the south, Chao Samran gets crowded on weekends much like it did when the royal family used to bask here. Minibuses leave from the station on Matayawong Rd., and *songthaew* run to the beach until 5pm (10฿).

HUA HIN ☎032

Long before Phuket and Pattaya were catapulted into jet-set stardom, Hua Hin ("Head Rock") catered to the Thai upper crust. Following the example of King Rama VII, who built his summer palace here in the 1920s, wealthy Thai families vacationed on this long stretch of clean sand, mingling with local fishermen and squid vendors. Today, affluent Europeans have replaced the Thais, and towering resorts have stolen the beachfront away from fishermen. Still, there's something about this great dame of beach resorts that remains unchanged; the night market still bustles with activity, the seafood still tantalizes the palate, and the beach still satisfies even the most critical beachcomber. Hua Hin may look different, but the new faces and facades only complement its aging grace.

TRANSPORTATION

Flights: The recently reopened **Hua Hin Airport** (☎520 181), on the north side of the city, is served by Bangkok Airways. One flight per day to **Bangkok** (1hr., 7:30pm) and **Ko Samui** (45min., 9:20am).

Trains: Railway Station, (☎511 073), at the end of Damnernkasem Rd. A 10min. walk from the town center. Fares listed are for 2nd and 3rd class, respectively. **Luggage storage** 10฿ per item per day. To: **Bangkok** (4hr.; 12 per day 12:30am-4:00pm; 102฿, 44฿); **Chumphon** (4hr.; 10 per day 10:40pm-5:10am; 87฿, 38฿); **Phetchaburi** (1hr.; 12 per day; 24฿, 10฿); **Surat Thani** (7hr.; 10 per day; 146฿, 63฿).

Buses: VIP bus station (☎511 654), 1st fl. of the Siripetchkasem Hotel on Srasong Rd. near Decharnuchit Rd. To **Bangkok** (3½hr., 30 per day 3am-9pm, 110฿) and **Cha-am** (20min., 30฿). Buses heading south depart from the **regular bus station** (☎511 230), a dirt path roundabout at the end of Liab Tang Rodfai Rd., about 500m north of the railway station. To: **Bangkok** (4hr., 85฿); **Cha-am** (30min., 15฿); **Chumphon** (5hr., 4 buses per day 8am-midnight, 108฿-250฿); **Phuket** (12hr., 6 per day 10am-11pm, 277฿-457฿); **Surat Thani** (8hr.; 1:30pm, 190฿; 11pm, 340฿).

Local Transportation: Motorcycle taxis and **samlor** go round-trip to **Khao Krilas** and **Khao Takieb** (every 15min. 6am-7pm, 7฿). Green **songthaew** leave from the motorcycle shop at Decharnuchit Rd. and Srasong Rd. (every 15min. 6am-7pm, 7฿).

ORIENTATION AND PRACTICAL INFORMATION

Hua Hin, 232km from Bangkok, is a stop for most southbound buses and trains. **Phetkasem Hwy.** and the train tracks run parallel to the beach. Three major streets cross the highway and head to the sand (from north to south): **Chomsinthu Rd., Decharnuchit Rd.,** and **Damnernkasem Rd.** Parallel to the shore are (from the beach) **Naresdumri Rd., Poolsuk Rd.,** Phetkasem Hwy., and **Srasong Rd.** Free maps are available at the tourist office and several restaurants and bars.

Tourist Offices: Tourist Information Service Center, 114 Phetkasem Hwy. (☎532 433). On the 1st fl. of the municipal building, at the Damnernkasem Rd. intersection. Helpful maps. The free *Hua Hin Observer,* a monthly English journal available at the tourist office and select establishments, provides tourist information, listings, and mildly amusing news articles. Open daily 8:30am-4:30pm.

Tours: Travel agents line **Phetkasem Hwy.** and **Naresdumri Rd.** Half-day excursions 800฿, full-day 1300฿. Includes lunch. 2-day trip prices vary.

Currency Exchange: Banks and exchange booths line **Naresdumri Rd.** by the Hilton Hotel. **Siam Commercial Bank** (☎532 420 5), next to the post office. Open M-F 8am-3:30pm; window open Sa-Su 11am-8pm.

Emergency: ☎191.

Police: (☎511 027). On Damnernkasem Rd., 400m from the beach opposite the post office. No English spoken; go to the tourist police first. Open 24hr.

Tourist Police: (☎515 995). In the little white building on the left side of Damnernkasem Rd. just before the beach. English spoken. Open 24hr.

Medical Services: All services listed provide 24hr. care. **San Pau Lo Hospital** (☎532 576), on Phetkasem Hwy., 400m south of the Tourist Center. Credit cards accepted. **Hua Hin Hospital** (☎520 371) is 4km north of town on Phetkasem Hwy. A **Red Cross station** next door to the municipal building provides basic services.

Telephones: Next to the GPO. International phone/fax. Open daily 8am-midnight.

Internet Access: Rapidly popping up across the city. The **Internet Cafe** on the north side of Phetkasem Hwy. between Decharnuchit Rd., and Amnohayasin Rd., is the cheapest. 1฿ per min. Open daily 10:30am-10:30pm.

Post Offices: GPO (☎511 063), opposite the police station on Damnernkasem Rd. as soon as you turn off Phetkasem Hwy. toward the beach. *Poste Restante.* Open M-F 8:30am-4:30pm, Sa-Su and holidays 9am-noon. **Postal code:** 77110.

THAILAND

ACCOMMODATIONS AND FOOD

For its relatively small size, Hua Hin has an unusually large number of guest houses, which fight for attention in the winding alleyways between Poolsuk Rd. and Naresdamri Rd. Despite this fierce competition, prices in Hua Hin are generally higher than elsewhere. During peak tourist season (Nov.-May), rooms fill up quickly, and prices rise even more.

All Nations Guest House, 10-10/1 Decharnuchit Rd. (☎512 747), on the left about 100m from the beach. Chat with the amiable Canadian manager, chill with other guests in the pub/TV lounge downstairs, or simply unwind in your comfortable room. Shared baths are exceptionally clean and come with hot water. Internet access available. Singles 150-250฿; doubles 300-450฿, with A/C and TV 600฿.

Pattana Guest House, 52 Naresdumri Rd. (☎513 393). Look for the sign pointing down an alley off Naresdumri Rd. 10m to the left of the pier. Traditional 200 year old Thai home with clean rooms and teak furniture and floors. Good staff and relaxed clientele. Singles/doubles 350-400฿, with bath 550฿.

Fulay Guest House (☎513 145), on the ocean, about 25m to the right of the pier on Naresdumri Rd. The boardwalk-like set up lends it character, as do the porches of each of the rooms. Rooms are clean and smartly decorated. All have private baths. Rooms 250-350฿, with A/C and TV 750-1500฿, depending on size of room.

Viking Guest House 23 Selakam Rd. (☎524 021), off Poolsuk Rd. near the Hilton Hotel. With girlie bars galore, the area's a bit seedy at night, but the Viking Guest House's rooms are bright and cheery, complete with large windows, wooden floors, and cartoon-covered bedspreads. Shared baths have hot water. Rooms 250฿.

Banpak Hua-Hin Hotel, 5/1 Poolsuk Rd. (☎511 653), near the intersection with Soi Bintaban opposite the temple. Large and slightly impersonal, but the 70s-style rooms are comfortable and have private baths. Watch Western men hit on Thai women from the seating area. Singles/doubles 250฿, with A/C 350฿; with A/C and TV 450฿.

Though Italian places are moving in, seafood reigns supreme here, and for good reason. Every morning, Hua Hin's fishing fleet returns to the pier with a fresh catch. The lively **night market,** on Donamuchit Rd. between Srasong Rd and Phetkasem Hwy., is the best place to sample authentic Thai seafood. (Dishes 10-50฿. Open daily 5pm-midnight.) **Chatchai Market** sets up during the day between Phetkasem

Hwy. and Srasong Rd. Otherwise, head to Damnernkasem Rd. opposite the Hilton Hotel, where pricier restaurants prepare dishes before your eyes. **Lom Huan,** 250m from the beach, serves bowls of *khao tom* (boiled rice soup) with fresh shrimp for 30-35฿. **Chao Lay Seafood,** 104 Naresdumri Rd., gives large helpings (80-350฿).

SIGHTS AND ENTERTAINMENT

Hua Hin's major attraction is the **Hua Hin Beach,** which rolls along for kilometers in either direction from town. The smelly fishing pier at the base of Chomsintthu Rd. dominates one area of the beach; the entrance to the prettier (and less smelly) part of the beach is just past the entrance to the Sofitel. Farther south, folks wander the sand offering massages, food, and pony rides (100-400฿ for 30min.). If you stroll north (past Hilton Hotel and the pier), you can see the **Klai Kang Won (Far From Worries) Palace.** A royal summer residence in the 1920s, the palace now nurses the ailing King, and the grounds have become closed to visitors.

The **Sofitel Central Hotel,** 1½km south of the pier, recreates a bygone era. Originally the Railway Hotel, it was built by Prince Purachatra, the former Director General of State Railways, and played Phnon Penh's leading hotel in the film *The Killing Fields.* One of Southeast Asia's leading five-star hotels, the Sofitel is outrageously expensive (rooms start at 6000฿). Tourists on a budget can come for high tea (130฿) and meander through the topiary gardens.

The twin hills of **Khao Takieb** (Monkey Mountain) and **Khao Kai Las,** 6km south of Hua Hin on Phetkasem Hwy., are accessible by motorbike or *songthaew* (7฿). Khao Takieb features a temple, hundreds of friendly monkeys (monkey grub sold on the spot for 120฿), and an excellent view of Hua Hin. Khao Kai Las features a small lighthouse and a decent view of Hua Hin. Pine tree-lined **Suan San Beach** is farther south and has unbeatable swimming. Charter a *songthaew* or *tuk-tuk* (150฿). Still farther south is **Khao Tao** (Turtle Hill).

Hua Hin's **nightlife** centers on pubs and beer gardens on **Soi Bintabaht,** which connects Poolsuk and Naresdumri Rd., and the girlie bars liberally sprinkled around the city. If you've had enough of the fat-Western-man-beautiful-Thai-woman combination, head to the **Jamaica Pub,** 70m past All Nations Guest House away from the beach. The local hangout has a band that plays everything from Thai pop to Guns 'n' Roses. Hua Hin's dance halls have a reputation for rowdiness, but **The Rickshaw Club** next to Hilton Hotel is mellow. (Open daily 10am-2am.) For a night away from the booze, hit up the **Thai Boxing Garden,** on Poolsuk Rd. between Damnernkasem and Decharnuchit Rd., to watch amateur and professional boxing matches nearly every weekend (9pm, 250฿).

DAYTRIPS FROM HUA HIN

TANAO SRI AND PA LA-U. The region between Hua Hin and the Burmese border has spectacular natural sights. The **Tanao Sri Range** forms the border and backdrop for the **Pa La-u Forest** in Kaeng Krachan National Park (see p. 669). Deep in the jungle, the twin waterfalls La-u Yai and La-u Noi merge to become **Pa La-u Falls,** an 11-tier cascade. While three days are required to reach the source, trekkers can explore the first few levels in a day's hike. Longer stays require a guide and camping equipment. During high season the park rents **tents** and **bungalows.** It's best to come between November and April.

For a daytrip, taxis are outside Chatchai Market in Hua Hin (up to 1000฿). A more affordable but dangerous option is to rent a motorbike (200฿) in Hua Hin and travel the 60km independently. Follow local Hwy. 3218 from Hua Hin until it meets Hwy. 3219, then follow signs. The route is well paved up to the park entrance and the scenery is inspiring. Past the checkpoint, the road turns to dirt and can be treacherous. Walk the last few kilometers to the waterfall and trailhead. It's a short hike (30min.) to the first cascade and swimming hole. A small eatery on the left-hand side of the road (look for a "Food & Beverages" sign) sells Thai staples (fried rice 20฿). Overnight trekkers should contact the **Sub-Forestry Office** one week in advance by writing to Kaeng Krachan National Park, Pa La Hua Hin, Prachuap Khiri Khan 77110. The office is past the checkpoint at the entrance.

Try spelunking in the three **caves** on the way to Pa La-u on Rte. 3219, 30km from Hua Hin near Nongphlab Village. At the main intersection in town, make a right onto Rte. 3301 and look for signs advertising the **Daow Lap Lae** and **Kailon** caves, which are simultaneously spectacular caves and standard Buddha brigade.

KHAO SAM ROI YOD NATIONAL PARK. Stunning limestone hills (the "Three Hundred Peaks" to which the name refers) rise from the surrounding sea and marshland. The park is 63km south of Hua Hin off Hwy. 4. (Open M-F 8:30am-4:30pm.) Take a southbound bus from Hua Hin, get off at Pranburi Market, and hire a taxi or *songthaew* to park headquarters. Park bungalows accommodate up to 20; reserve in advance (☎02 579 05 29).

ARANYAPRATHET

Aranyaprathet is the border town for the Cambodia-bound. A savvy traveler will arrive early enough to push straight on through without staying the night. The first train from Bangkok arrives early enough for those heading to Siem Reap to arrive the same day. Wide streets and impersonal hotels make friendly locals all Aranyaprathet has to offer.

TRANSPORTATION AND PRACTICAL INFORMATION. In the center of town, **Mahadthai-Suwannasorn Rd.** and **Chaoprayabodin Rd.** intersect at a wee purple clock tower. The **railway station** sits nearby at the north end of **Suwannasorn Rd. Trains** arrive from **Bangkok** at 11:40am and 7:05pm; trains depart for Bangkok at 6:30am and 1:35pm (48฿). The bus station is on the west side of town: walk three blocks straight out and one block to the right to reach the clock tower. **Buses** run to **Bangkok** (every hr., A/C 144฿) and **Sa Gaeo** (every hr., 6am-6pm, 29฿). **Tuk-tuks** and **sambis** putter to hotels from the bus and train stations (20฿).

At the clock tower, the **general post office** has a **Lenso** phone card machine. (Phone cards 300฿ and 500฿. Open M-F 8:30am-4:30pm). For international calls, head to the **Telecommunications Office,** near the corner of Mahadthai and Raduthid Rd., 500m south of the clock tower. (Open M-F 8:30am-4:30pm.) The **pharmacy** is one block north of the Aran Garden I Hotel. (Open M-Sa 6:30am-7:30pm.)

ACCOMMODATIONS AND FOOD. Aranyaprathet has no guest houses and few accommodations of any sort. Many travelers stay at the **Aran Garden I Hotel.** Walk 500m south from the clock tower to Raduthid Rd. and then 600m east to Chitsuwarn Rd.; it's on the corner. (Bicycles 40฿ per day. Singles 150฿; doubles 200฿.) Down Raduthid Rd. one block, **Aran Garden II** has much nicer, quieter rooms. (Bicycles 10฿ per hr. Singles 230฿; doubles 300฿.) Another option, similar in value to the Aran Garden II but removed from the town's hubbub and equipped with a large pool table, is the **Great Hill Hotel,** 1km north of the train station. (Singles with fan 250฿, with A/C 500฿; doubles 300฿/600฿.) In the low season, many travelers crash for free on the office floor of their Siem Reap-bound tour company, which might even provide breakfast. Restaurants are dismal; it's best to enjoy noodles or rice at a street stall near the Aran Garden Hotels.

SHOPPING. The border **market,** on Weruwan Rd., is colossal but caters mostly to Thais trying to look Western, sporting a dull mix of jeans, sunglasses, dresses, and other faux-Western items. (Open daily 6am-7pm.) Motorcycle rides to the market should cost 25-30฿; *tuk-tuks* run 40-50฿.

BORDER CROSSING: ARANYAPRATHET/POIPET. Travelers must obtain visas at the Cambodian embassy in Bangkok. In Aranyaprathet, touts materialize at the train and bus stations to offer trips to Siem Reap. They are helpful in navigating the chaotic bridge and boarding a public pick-up for the painful 7-8hr. ride ahead (in cab 350฿, in the back 200฿). Trucks leave from a station 500m on the Cambodian side on the left. Be sure to obtain an exit stamp from Thai immigration (open daily 7:30am-5:30pm) at the bridge. A *tuk-tuk* from anywhere in town to the bridge costs 60฿.

EAST COAST THAILAND

From Bangkok to Trat, the coastal highway travels the timeline of economic development. Shiny new refineries, power stations, and petrochemical plants dominate the coast from Si Racha to Rayong. East of Rayong up to the Cambodian border, Thailand's coast changes as construction sites and highway traffic thin. Slowly, the groves of durian and mangosteen creep to the edge of the road. Off the coast of Trat, undeveloped Ko Chang and the southern archipelago await exploration by rain forest trekkers and beach-hunters. Farther west, Ko Samet offers convenience and beauty, while charming Ko Si Chang is overlooked by tourists. Perhaps most unfairly neglected, however, is mainland East Coast; Chanthaburi and Trat teem with mountains, jungle, waterfalls, and national parks, most of them completely untouched by backpackers.

SI RACHA ☎038

Thailand may be a culinary heaven, but few towns celebrate the tastebuds like Si Racha does. The maritime heritage of this fishing-village-turned-bustling-town lives on in its restaurants and foodstalls whose blinking lights beckon visitors to sample Thailand's finest and most traditional seafood. Besides its culinary appeal, the town is home to one of Thailand's best zoos. If neither seafood nor caged animals strike your fancy, make sure to arrive with enough time to catch the ferry to Ko Si Chang; there is little other reason to dawdle in Si Racha.

TRANSPORTATION AND PRACTICAL INFORMATION. All transport operates from the de facto **bus stop,** the **Laemthong Department Store,** 2km outside the **city center. Buses** to **Bangkok** (every 20-40min. 5am-6pm; 40฿, with A/C 61฿) and **Rayong** (every 20min. 5am-10pm; 40฿, with A/C 60฿) depart from **Sukhumvit Rd.** next to the department store. Infrequent buses to other eastern destinations stop across from the department store's main entrance. To reach the **city center** and **ferry** to **Ko Si Chang,** either take a *tuk-tuk* or motorcycle-taxi (20฿) from the department store or walk a few blocks north on Sukhumvit Rd. and down service-laden **Surasak I Rd.** Si Racha's main street, **Jermjompol Rd.,** intersects Surasak I Rd. at Soi 10 and runs parallel to the coast, the town's western border. It is bounded to the north by a small, white clock tower and the causeway to the small island Ko Loi, and to the south by a larger clock tower and the **market.**

The **Bank of Ayudhya,** 50m from Jermjompol Rd. on Si Racha Nakom 3rd Rd., exchanges currency and has an **ATM. Siam Commercial Bank,** 98/9 Surasak I Rd., halfway between Sukhumvit Rd. and Jermjompol Rd., exchanges traveler's checks. (☎311 313. Open daily 8:30am-3:30pm.) An infrequently staffed **police booth** stands at the corner of Jermjompol Rd. and Soi 10. (☎311 111; **emergency** ☎191. Open daily 6am-9pm.) **Phyathai General Hospital** is at 90 Si Racha Nakon Rd. 3. (☎770 200/208. Open 24hr.) The **Internet East Co.,** 140 Si Racha Nakon Rd. 1, near Sri Racha Seafood Restaurant, has fast connections. (1฿ per min. Open daily 9am-9pm.) Cheaper access is available on the second floor of the Laemthong Department Store. (25-30฿ per hr. Open M-F 11am-9pm, Sa-Su 9am-9pm.) All services (pharmacies, banks, Internet) are more plentiful and less expensive at the department store. The **post**

office, past the park near the road to Ko Loi at the north end of Jermjompol Rd., a 10min. walk from the city center, has **international phones.** (☎311 202. Open M-F 8:30am-4:30pm, Sa-Su 9am-noon.) **Postal code:** 20110.

ACCOMMODATIONS AND FOOD. All hotels listed are in the city center near the ferry, a 20min. walk or a 20฿ *tuk-tuk* ride from the bus stop. The **Siri Watana,** one block north of Soi 10 opposite Si Racha Nakon Rd., is the best of the bunch. Its nearly 75 year old rooms are plain and clean with wooden floors and private baths. The staff is exceptionally friendly. (☎311 037. Singles 180-200฿; doubles 200-300฿, depending on proximity to the sea.) **Samchai Hotel** (the English sign only says "Hotel"), Soi 10 Phulphiphat 1, at the end of the soi across Jermjompol Rd. near Surasak I Rd., has large rooms with baths and porches overlooking the sea. The bathrooms, though, are grimy, and the staff doesn't speak English. (☎311 800. Doubles with fan 100฿, with A/C and TV 380฿.)

Si Racha is famous for its **seafood,** often prepared with Si Racha Sauce, a spicy red dressing. It appears as **ซอสศรีราชา** on Thai menus. The prime location for gorging on local cuisine is **Si Racha Nakon Rd. 3** not long after it branches off Jermjompol Rd. one block north of Soi 10. This sizable section of road overflows with foodstalls, small restaurants, and larger open-air eateries, allowing diners to stroll through and take their pick. Prices range from 25฿ for staple Thai rice dishes to hundreds of baht for seafood. Sample fresh seafood in the market by the clock tower at the south end of Jermjopol Rd. Those in search of a calmer, fancier dining experience can try **Sri Racha Seafood Restaurant,** 160-164 Si Racha Nakorn Rd. Turn onto Si Racha Nakon Rd. 3 from Jermjompol Rd., veer left at the first fork and right at the next. (Dishes 80-200฿. Open daily 9am-9pm.)

SIGHTS. Si Racha's main attraction is unquestionably the **Si Racha Tiger Zoo,** a rather gimmicky, amusement-park-style zoo 9km east of town. Take a *tuk-tuk* from anywhere in the city (25min., 100฿). The zoo's shows (in Thai only) are quite entertaining; take your pick from elephant, crocodile, and tiger shows or the pig-racing extravaganza. The zoo displays, on the other hand, are disappointing, featuring mostly unhappy-looking caged animals. It's an unusual zoo and an interesting way to kill time waiting for the ferry. (☎296 556. Open daily 8am-6pm. Several shows every hr. 250฿, children 150฿.)

Those with less time can head to the two temples that sit on the mainland. From Jermjompol Rd., **Wat Radniyomtum** is several blocks down Surasak I Rd. on the right. Near the market, Surasak Suguan leads to **Wat Mahasiracha,** on the corner with Tesaban Rd. The town's most touristed temple is **Wat Ko Loi** (Floating Island Temple), reached via a pleasant walk to the causeway at the northern end of Jermjompol Rd. Release a pair of finches at the top (20฿), see enormous **sea turtles** from the nearby moat, or wander around the base, where foodstalls and trinket shops create a lively atmosphere for the picnicking Thais who flock here on weekends. A shady park stretches along the waterfront on Jermjompol Rd.

KO SI CHANG ☎038

Poor Ko Si Chang is all dressed up with no place to go. A tourist boom years back encouraged the residents of this 5000-person fishing village to spruce up their island with new bungalows and English signs and maps. But as the rest of Southeast Asia opened up, more and more visitors cut Ko Si Chang from their itineraries, heading to more spectacular Ko Samet and Ko Chang farther east. Accordingly, Ko Si Chang remains a pretty island with good tourist services, friendly locals, and hardly a trace of the commercialism that seems to have swallowed its larger siblings whole. Those seeking postcard-perfect scenes should keep heading east, but for a sandy respite from hot, dusty Bangkok, Ko Si Chang fits the bill.

ORIENTATION AND PRACTICAL INFORMATION. **Ferries** to Ko Si Chang depart from Si Racha's main pier at the end of Jermjompol Rd., Soi 14 (40min., every hr. 8am-6pm, 20฿). Boats back to Si Racha leave from **Ta Lang Pier** or **Ta Bon Pier** depending on the tide; ask your guest house owner to verify which to head to (every hr. 6am-6pm, 20฿). **Assadang Rd.** runs north along the water past the two piers, curves past the Chinese temple on the hill, and finally doubles back onto itself 4km later next to Tiew Pai Guest House. The road then runs south to **Hat Ta Wang** and **Hat Sai Kaew** beaches, and branches off to **Hat Tampang**, the island's number one beach. *Samlor (tuk-tuk* four-wheel-drive hybrids) go anywhere on the island for 20-50฿, but you can walk most places as well.

Thai Farmers Bank, 9-9½ Assadang Rd., between the piers, exchanges traveler's checks and has an **ATM.** (☎216 132. Open M-F 8:30am-3:30pm.) **The Tiew Pai Guest House** rents **motorcycles** (170฿ for 12hr., 200฿ for 24hr.) and **pickup trucks.** A man named Oo rents **mountain bikes**; look for the sign at the entrance of a small soi 75m before Tiew Pai Guest House on the right as you come from the pier. (☎216 265. Mountain bikes 120฿.) In an **emergency,** dial 191 or call the **police** 216 218. The **post office,** in a white building at the north end of Assadang Rd., offers **Internet access** (3฿ for first minute, 1฿ for every two minutes thereafter) and has **international** and **collect calls** for 30฿. (☎216 227. Open M-F 8:30am-4:30pm.) **Postal code:** 20120.

ACCOMMODATIONS AND FOOD. Ko Si Chang's only budget-minded guest house is **Tiew Pai Guest House,** south of Ta Lang Pier on Assadang Rd. Fortunately, it's cheap, well-kept, and friendly. At night, a karaoke bar thumps to the latest Thai pop. (☎216 084. Breakfast included. Singles with shared bath 100-500฿; doubles 250฿, with A/C and fridge 400; triples and family rooms 500-1000฿.) Pricier bungalows line the beach. The best of these is the **Sichang View Resort,** opposite the Khao Khat Cliffs in the northwest corner of the island, 2km from town, which offers comfortable rooms with TVs in one of the island's most beautiful settings. It's worth the extra baht. (☎216 210. Doubles with fan 500฿, with A/C 800฿, with hot water 900฿; add 200฿ to turn any room into a triple.) **Camping** is free on the beach; bring your own supplies.

Food vendors sell noodle and rice dishes along **Assadang Rd.** Try the tasty breakfast (60฿, included for guests) and entrees from typical rice dishes (25-30฿) to fish 'n' fixin's (180-200฿) at Tiew Pai Guest House. (Open daily 7:30am-1am.) Munch on more rice dishes (35฿) and fresh fish (35฿) at the **Sichang View Resort.** (Open daily 7am-9:30pm.)

SIGHTS. Although a quick tour of Ko Si Chang takes just a few hours by motorcycle or *samlor* (150-200฿), the island rewards more leisurely walks or bike rides extended over a couple days. The town's main street, Assadang Rd., ends in a 163-step climb to a colorful **Chinese temple.** Four hundred steps farther up is an enshrined **Buddha footprint,** whose size makes it a good match for the **Yellow Buddha** on the island's west side. Beneath this 10m-high statue are several caves accessible from the lower platform in front of the Buddha.

Toward the south end of Assadang Rd. near the two eastern beaches are the ruins of **King Rama V's summer palace.** An economic crisis halted the restoration of this royal residence, but you can still see pagodas, reservoirs, and European-influenced buildings. To get there, continue south on Assadang Rd. through the gate of the Marine Research Institute. Find **Hat Tampang,** Ko Si Chang's most swimmable beach, by taking the right branch of the road next to the gate and climbing over a steep hill. North of Hat Tampang, don't miss the **Khao Khat Cliffs,** where Rama V built a pavilion to enjoy the western horizon and compose poetry. The view from the king's seat is stunning. At the bottom, a path by the Sichang View Resort leads down to the cliffs, which are best visited at sunset.

KO SAMET ☎01

Just four hours from Bangkok, Ko Samet is a popular vacation spot for Thais and foreigners alike. Over the last 20 years, beachside bungalows have slowly encroached on much of the shoreline, and loud *farang* pubs and Thai karaoke bars dominate the once still nights. Still, development aside, Ko Samet delivers, and a dip in its tranquil waters or a nap on its clean, white sand beaches will satisfy the relaxation-seeking traveler. Many visitors prefer Samet's low-key atmosphere and friendly locals to that of its rowdier and more developed island neighbors. Commercialism has not yet taken a stronghold on Samet's visitors or residents, so enjoy it while it lasts.

THE VIEW FROM ABOVE

The lowdown: Step 1 in your island hopping trip.
Beaches: At last count, 10. (See **Orientation,** below.)
Highlights: Snorkeling in Ao Kiu's coral reefs, hanging out at Ao Phai, and camping under the starts on Ao Thian (Candlelight Beach).

TRANSPORTATION

Ferries: Nuan Tip Pier and **Tarua Phe Pier** in the town of Ban Phe serve Ko Samet. Buses from Bangkok stop in front of Nuan Tip Pier, which offers service to Na Dan Pier in northern Ko Samet (40min.; June-Oct. 4 per day, Nov.-May 10-20 per day; 20-person minimum; round-trip 100฿). Additional boats with a seven-passenger minimum are available during peak months to: **Ao Kiu/Ao Pakarang** (200฿); **Ao Phrao** (45min., 100฿); **Ao Wai** (50min., 200฿); **Ao Wong Duan** (45min., 125฿). If you arrive via *songthaew* from Rayong, you will be let off at Tarua Phe Pier, opposite the 7-11, about 200m west of Nuan Tip Pier. Ferries here leave more regularly and go to Ao Wong Duan (9:30am, 1:30, 5pm; one-way 60฿) and **Na Dan Pier** (every hr. 8am-5:30pm, one-way 40฿) regardless of the number of passengers.

Buses: Ban Phe Bus Station, (☎651 528), opposite Nuan Tip Pier on the mainland. The A/C buses go to **Bangkok** (3hr., 13 per day 4am-6:30pm, 124฿). If you're heading elsewhere, grab a *songthaew* to **Rayong** (every 15min. 6am-6pm, 15฿) and transfer to **Chanthaburi** (2½hr., every 50min. 5:50am-5:30pm, 55฿); **Khorat** (6hr.; every hr. 4:20am-9pm; 125฿, with A/C 225฿); **Nong Khai** (13hr.; 11 per day 7am-8:30pm; 241฿, with A/C 434฿); **Si Racha** (2hr., every 40min. 5:10am-6:30pm, 40฿); and other destinations. Many Ko Samet bungalows offer expensive but convenient service direct to Bangkok's **Khao San Rd.** (around 220฿).

Local Transportation: Songthaew from Na Dan Pier to: **Ao Kiu** (50฿); **Ao Phai** (20฿); **Ao Phrao** (30฿); **Ao Thian** (40฿); **Ao Tup Tim** (20฿); **Ao Wai** (40฿); **Ao Wong Duan** (30฿); **Hat Sai Kaew** (10฿). For fewer than 8-10 people, *songthaew* must be chartered (100-500฿). *Songthaew* returning to Na Dan Pier or offering taxi service wait at Ao Phai in front of Silver Sands Resort. The island is easily walkable once your pack is off. It's only a 500m stroll from Na Dan Pier to Hat Sai Kaew, and the walk from Ao Wong Duan to Ao Phai takes just 30min.

Rentals: Shops renting **motorbikes** cluster near Na Dan Pier and along the road to Hat Sai Kaew. 120฿ per hr., 500฿ per day with passport or 500฿ deposit. Open daily 7am-8pm.

ORIENTATION AND PRACTICAL INFORMATION

With only two roads strecthing through its 16km, Ko Samet is easily navigable. Boats disembark at **Na Dan Pier** on the island's northeast corner. A paved road runs south to the Park Service entrance booth, where you must pay a hefty **admission fee** to enter the island, a Thai national park (200฿, children under 10 100฿). Here, the path forks. Directly ahead is **Hat Sai Kaew;** the right-hand fork continues south, behind the bungalows of the eastern beaches: **Ao Cho, Ao Hin Klong, Ao Kiu, Ao Phai, Ao Nuan, Ao Thian, Ao Tup Tim, Ao Wai, Ao Wong Duan,** and **Hat Lung Dum.** To get to these beaches, bear left at the fork after Ao Phai. Head straight to go instead to Ko Samet's only west coast beach, **Ao Phrao.** Beach-side paths and jungle trails link all the beaches except Ao Phrao and Ao Kiu, making the island fairly walkable.

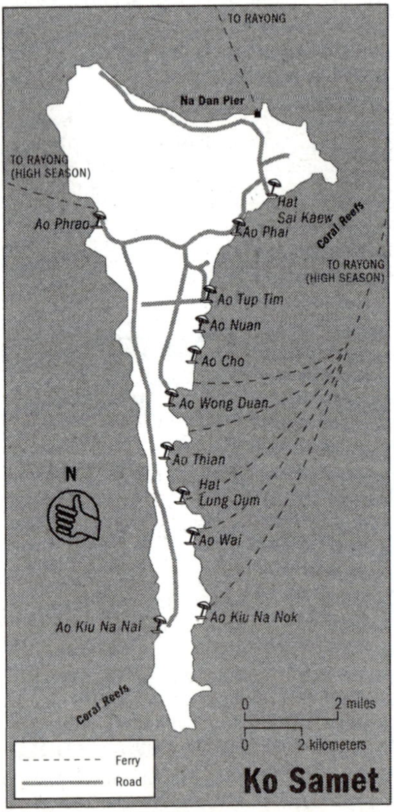

Tourist Office: A **Visitors Center** next to the park entrance by Hat Sai Kaew assists tourists and provides info on local wildlife. An English-speaking man named Thawil staffs the office and can be reached 24hr. in case of emergency (☎ 663 5055). Open daily 8am-4pm.

Tours: Many of Ko Samet's larger establishments offer air ticketing, domestic minibus service, and snorkeling tours.

Currency Exchange: Change as much as you think you'll need at the banks in **Ban Phe,** west of the pier. Otherwise the **post office** at Naga Bungalows offers the most comparable rates for currency, traveler's checks, or cash advances.

English-Language Resources: Several accommodations, including Naga Bungalows and Sea-Breeze Bungalows at Ao Phai and Samet Ville Resort at Ao Wai, operate small libraries.

Markets: Tasty food stalls surround the Nuan Tip Pier area. 25฿ per plate. Open daily 6am-8pm.

Police: (☎651 803), on the paved road between Na Dan and Hat Sai Kaew, next to the health center. No English spoken. Mainland **police** at Ban Phe (☎038 651 111).

Tourist Police: (☎038 651 669), on mainland, a block east of the market at Nuan Tip Pier. English spoken. Open 24hr.

Medical Services: Health Center, halfway between Na Dan Pier and the park entry checkpoint. No telephone. Some English spoken. Open M-Sa 8:30am-4:30pm. In emergencies, phone the **hospital** in Rayong (☎611 104 or 614 708). Ko Samet's emergency services are inadequate.

Telephones: Pay phones are near the Visitors Center and the pier but only make domestic calls. Most establishments offer **international telephone service** run through cellular phones, so service is expensive and faulty. From 100฿ per min.

Internet Access: Access from Samet is like phone service–run on cellular phones and obnoxiously expensive. The **Naga Bungalows Post Office** has the cheapest rates (about 100฿ per 15min.).

Post Offices: Naga Bungalows (☎353 25 75), operates a licensed makeshift post office next door to the hotel. Open M-F 8:30am-noon and 1-4:30pm, Sa 8:30am-noon. **Postal code:** 21160-101.

THAILAND

ACCOMMODATIONS, FOOD, AND BEACHES

All of Ko Samet's beaches offer some bungalow-type accommodation. In general, **Ao Phai** and **Ao Cho** offer the cheapest accommodations, while **Hat Sai Kaew** and **Ao Phrao** cater to the older and more moneyed travelers. Hat Sai Kaew, Ao Phai, and **Ao Wong Duan** are the most heavily touristed beaches, **Ao Nuan** and **Ao Kiu** the most secluded. Establishments without generators have electricity from 6pm-6am. Be prepared for major crowds on weekends and holidays; expect prices to jump then too. **Camping** is available at all beaches, although your best bets are on secluded Ao Kiu, the rocks between Ao Phai and Ao Tup Tim, and the grassy knoll behind the Visitors Center near Hat Sai Kaew.

AO KIU. With good swimming in addition to possibilities for coral reef snorkeling nearby, secluded Ao Kiu is Ko Samet at its best. The security and seclusion come at a price, though; Ao Kiu is relatively hard to reach. A taxi from the pier will cost you a hefty 300-400฿, and from neighboring Ao Wai it's a 20 to 30min. walk along the back road. Once there you can set up at the **Ao Kiu Coral Beach** which rules this remote roost. Bungalows are tiled, screened, and clean. Snorkeling gear rental runs 30฿ per hour. (☎812 20 46. 600-800฿.)

AO PHAI. A five-minute walk from Hat Sai Kaew, Ao Phai is a backpacker haven—a more friendly and welcoming version of Bangkok's Khaosan Rd. Come here for quality, cheap lodging accompanied by a social atmosphere and great screenings of English flicks; don't come for romantic seclusion or quiet nights. Thankfully, free of the litter and bobbing boats that sometimes plague Hat Sai Kaew and Ao Wong Duan, Ao Phai's waters are good for swimming, despite the crowds. Accommodations, while plentiful, fill up quickly; try your best to arrive before 3 or 4pm. At the north end is the cheapest of the hotels, **Naga Bungalows,** an old Ko Samet institution that still remains the most popular spot on the island. The plain bamboo bungalows sit on stilts. The restaurant serves fresh bread, sundaes, tofu-veggie options, and more (20-300฿). Table tennis, a "Tosser's Hour" (10pm-midnight), and all-night food make Naga a lively nightspot. (☎353 25 75. 150฿, with fan 200฿.) **Tok's Little Hut,** south of Naga, is just as popular but slightly more upscale with wood paneled bungalows with fans and bathrooms. (☎218 12 64. 200-350฿, depending on distance from the beach.) The newer, more luxurious **Jep's** features clean, bright rooms and bungalows with added luxuries like extra large beds and sheets. Their restaurant is one of the best on the beach. (Singles 300-350฿; doubles 450-600฿.) The hill-side bungalows at **Ao Phai Hut** are relatively clean but dim and in need of repair. All have private baths. (☎353 26 44. Singles 300฿; doubles 500฿, with A/C 800-1000฿.) **Sea-Breeze Bungalows,** at the south end of Ao Phai where the road branches off to Ao Phrao, has quiet bungalows with private baths. (☎239 47 80. Fan bungalows 100-400฿; A/C rooms and bungalows 600-650฿.)

AO THIAN (CANDLELIGHT BEACH) AND HAT LUNG DUM. These beaches are separated by a a short stretch of rocks and are easily accessible from both Ao Wai and Ao Wong Duan. With cheap bungalows close to some of the island's best swimming and sunbathing, the Ao Thian area is a good choice for the slow-paced beach-lover. Stretching out across both beaches, **Lung Dum Hut** is both remote and mellow though quite busy. The well-priced bungalows have private baths. Ask about their special treehouse option (150฿). In a pinch, they may let you borrow or rent a tent. (☎452 94 72. 300-400฿.)

THAILAND

AO WONG DUAN. "Half Moon Bay" is a spacious beach filled with restaurants, bars, and tour operators. Traffic and congestion make for a lively place to stay, but constant roaring of jet skis and continuous ferry departures make a less than ideal atmosphere for swimming or sunbathing. To get the most bang for your buck, try the red bungalows of **Samet Cabana,** at the north end of the beach, which has rooms with two small beds and shared baths. (☎838 48 53. 300฿, with private bath 500฿.) **Sea Horse Bungalows** (like most other tour operators on the beach) offers snorkeling tours on the island (250฿ per person) and to other islands (500฿ per person).

AO WAI. Clear water and clean, white sand make every second of the 15min. coastal hike from Ao Wong Duan to Ao Wai worth it. Targeting package tourists, **Samet Ville Resort** dominates the beach with pricey rooms. The restaurant serves Thai dishes. (40-300฿. Open daily 7:30am-9pm.) Snorkeling gear rental runs 100฿ per day. (☎949 53 94. 700-1500฿.)

AO PHRAO. A hilly 30min. walk on Ko Samet's back road will drop you onto Ao Phrao, a tidy crescent of sand flanked by jungle. Head straight at the fork just beyond Ao Phai's Silver Sands Resort. The island's only beach with western exposure, Ao Phrao affords beautiful, sky-searing sunsets. Pricey and posh **Dome Bungalows** is the only option that might fit your budget, with large, well-furnished bungalows and wide porches. (☎218 76 93. Singles 600฿, with A/C 1000฿; doubles 800฿/1000฿.)

AO TUP TIM. This small, crescent-shaped beach is an easy five-minute walk along the coast from Ao Phai. Although it's usually less crowded than Ao Phai, it's fairly congested compared to beaches farther south. **Tubtim Resort,** on the southern end of the beach, offers the best deal for accommodations. The comfortable thatch bungalows all have private baths. (☎ 218 77 59. 400฿, with A/C 1200฿.)

AO NUAN. From the south side of Ao Tup Tim, a trail marked "Nuan Bay" leads to this tiny, pretty beach, perhaps overlooked by most tourists because its rocky coastline renders it unsuitable for swimming. The beachfront is monopolized by the rustic **Nuan Bungalows,** which has simple rooms with fans and baths. (Singles 250฿; doubles 300-400฿. No telephone or reservations.)

AO CHO. Small Ao Cho is a quiet break from popular Ao Wong next door, although it's far from being the most secluded or most beautiful beach on the island. Budget accommodations are unfortunately limited to **Wonderland Resort's** bungalows, which are small, grimy, and in need of repair. In this paradise, you get what you pay for. (☎438 84 09. 150฿, with bath 200฿.)

HAT SAI KAEW. A 10min. walk from Na Dan Pier, Hat Sai Kaew caters mostly to package-tour travelers from Europe and Asia and is usually packed with *sarong* vendors, ferries, and overweight seniors bobbing in the water. Consequently, the beach, though good for swimming, is usually too crowded to enjoy. Budget accomodations are scarce. Your best bet is the rather glum **Ploy Thalay Resort** halfway up the beach. The exterior is worn-down, but the tiled rooms are tidy and come with private baths. (☎ 451 13 87. Doubles 500฿, with A/C and TV 800฿.) Farther south on the beach is the large **White Sands Resort,** the only other hotel on Hat Sai Kaew approximating "budget." The dimly lit bungalows are clean but spartan. All come with TV and private bath. (☎353 25 66. 500฿, with A/C 1000฿.)

SIGHTS AND ENTERTAINMENT

With coral reef and clear waters galore, it's no wonder that Ko Samet is popular for **snorkeling** At Ao Phrao and Ao Kiu, reef communities are a five-minute swim from shore. Less-disturbed coral live in more remote reaches of the archipelago. Ko Thalu boasts excellent **skin-diving** and a colony of fruit bats. Many establishments offer snorkeling tours of Ko Samet and the surrounding islets.

There are now several **scuba diving** operations on the island, so it pays to shop around. **Ao Prao Divers,** based in the lobby of the Ao Prao Resort on Ao Phrao, runs a PADI-certified scuba diving school year-round. The school makes daytrips around Ko Samet and to Ko Thalu from November-May. (☎038 616 883. 2 dives 2300฿; 4- to 5-day certification courses 10,000฿; specialty and more extensive dives 10-13,000฿; 3-4hr. introductory courses 1000฿. Open daily 8am-4pm.)

A thirst for sightseeing can be satisfied at the 14m high **sitting Buddha** and the smaller Buddha images at his knees. A gate next to the **golden Buddha** abuts the road between Na Dan Pier and Hat Sai Kaew; follow the path to the statue.

Ko Samet remains free of Ko Phangan's drunken beachside debauchery, but it boasts a lively **nightlife** scene on Ao Phai. The bar at **Naga Bungalows,** which occasionally features a free dancing show, stays open until people go home, which is often as late as sunrise. Nearby **Silver Sands Resort** offers a beachside bar that occasionally becomes an impromptu disco when the crowds are large enough. The other beaches tend to quiet down when their restaurants close.

CHANTHABURI ☎031

Chanthaburi may be the "City of the Moon," but its attraction is grounded in the fertile earth. Between May and July, the city's fruit market bulges with mouth-watering produce, and the precious stones from nearby mines are traded in the famous gem district before being distributed around the world. These, in addition to the neighboring national parks, make Chanthaburi a worthwhile visit.

TRANSPORTATION. The **bus station** on **Saritidet Rd.** (☎311 299) sends buses to: **Aranyaprathet** (8hr.; 15 per day 3am-10pm; 128฿, with A/C 230฿); **Bangkok** (4hr., 27 per day, 101฿-148฿); **Khorat** (6hr.; every hr. 6am-10pm; 104฿, with A/C 146฿); **Mae Sot** (9am, with A/C 401฿); **Rayong** (2hr.; every 30min. 4:20am-6pm; 55฿, with A/C 45฿); **Trat** (1½hr., every hr. 6am-11:30pm, 30฿). **Taxis** go anywhere in town for 30฿.

ORIENTATION AND PRACTICAL INFORMATION. To get downtown from the bus station, head left onto **Saritidet Rd.** After a 10min. walk, Saritidet Rd. ends at **Benchamarachuthis Rd.** at the **Kasemsarn 1 Hotel.** Take the alley to the left of the hotel to reach **Sukhaphibal Rd.,** which runs parallel to Benchamarachuthis Rd. along the river where a few hotels find home. Otherwise head right at the Kasemsarn 1 Hotel to reach the commercial heart of the town. Take a right on **Si Rong Muan Rd.** for the **market.** For the **gem district,** keep straight for one more block and then turn right onto **Kwang Rd.,** which eventually hits **Si Chan Rd.;** take a left. Si Chan Rd. eventually doubles back on itself.

Thai Farmers Bank, 103 Si Rong Muang Rd., is just before the market fountain and has an **ATM.** (☎311 567. Open M-F 8:30am-3:30pm.) The 24hr. **police booth** is at the bus station (**emergency** ☎ 191). The **hospital** is a short 20m walk left of the bus station on Saritidet Rd. (English spoken. Credit cards accepted. Open 24hr.) The **Chanthaburi Telecommunication Center** is next to the **GPO** on Thung Dondang Rd. near the Eastern Hotel, a 3km walk or a 30฿ taxi ride from town. (☎ 325 916. Open daily 7am-11pm.) **Internet access** is available all over, especially on **Tesaban 2 Rd.** which intersects Saritidet Rd. at a traffic light halfway between the bus station and Kasemsarn 1 Hotel. The **Chantani Post Office** (more convenient than the large Chanthaburi GPO) is on Benchamarachuthis Rd. across from the Kasermsarn 1 Hotel. (Open M-F 8:30am-4:30pm, Sa-Su 9am-noon). **Postal code:** 22000.

ACCOMMODATIONS AND FOOD. Accommodations of any sort are scarce in tourist-free Chanthaburi. One of the few choices is the cheap and friendly **Chantra Hotel,** 248 Sukhaphibal Rd. Head down the alley to the left of the Kasemsarn 1 Hotel. The tiled rooms are clean and plain, but the enthusiastic staff and the riverside views more than compensate. (☎ 312 310. Doubles 100฿, with bath 150฿.) The landmark **Kasemsarn 1 Hotel,** 98 Benchamarachuthis Rd. at the intersection with Saritidet Rd., has large, comfortable rooms with private baths but come with traffic clamor and an impersonal atmosphere and staff. (☎ 311 100. 200฿, with A/C 300฿.)

Take your grumbling stomach to Chanthaburi's immense **market,** centered on the low-lying fountain one block west of Benchamarachuthis Rd. down Si Rong Muang Rd. After sundown hordes of food vendors dole out curries and noodle dishes. By day, feast in one of the inexpensive surrounding restaurants. For a classier dining experience, head to the **seafood restaurant** around the corner from the Chantra Hotel on the river. The views are almost as impressive as the extensive menu. (Dishes 50-90฿. Open daily 10am-midnight.)

SIGHTS. Chanthaburi's more spectacular sights are located outside city limits, but a few gems within the town keep travelers entertained for a day or two. Shoppers head to **Si Chan Rd.,** the heart of Chanthaburi's **gem district** on weekends. Some 50-60% of the world's rubies and sapphires pass through Chanthaburi, most through this very street, on their way west from Cambodia, Laos, and even Africa.

The 19th-century **Cathedral of the Immaculate Conception,** across the footbridge near the south end of Sukhaphibal Rd., was built without an architect by French soldiers, who occupied Chanthaburi from 1893-1905. The doors to the magnificent cathedral, however, are closed. On the southwest side of town, **Taksin Park** occupies many well-pruned acres. Chanthaburians come here to relax for an evening or survey the sculpture of the Burmese-bashing King Taksin in the middle of the park. (Open daily 5am-9pm.)

NIGHTLIFE. Chanthaburi boasts a surprisingly dynamic nightlife scene. The enormous **Diamond Pub** on the southwest side of town has taken the place of currently closed **Ritchie Pub.** Live bands belt out Thai pop while a beautiful young crowd schmoozes and looks on. It rocks all week, but it's packed Fridays and Saturdays. Bottles of soda go for 30฿, Singha 80฿. Grab a taxi from the city center for 30฿. (Open daily 8pm to anytime between 11pm and 2:30am.)

DAYTRIPS FROM CHANTHABURI

NAM TOK PHLIU NATIONAL PARK

From Chanthaburi, yellow songthaew *leave from the north side of the market's roundabout and stop at the park gate (30min., 30฿). When leaving, take a taxi to the highway intersection and wait for a passing* songthaew *(Taxis 100-160฿). Open daily 6am-6pm. 200฿.*

Welcoming over 80,000 visitors a year, Nam Tok Phliu is one of Chanthaburi's best-known parks, although it's hardly the most spectacular. A trail cuts through the park linking the entrance to the park's namesake waterfalls, the **Phliu Falls,** where Thai schoolchildren gather to swim and catch the fish in the nearby ponds. A 1km nature trail circles the falls and offers scenic views. The other falls, **Nam Tok Makok, Nam Tok Klong Nalai,** and **Nam Tok Nong,** offer more seclusion. The rest of the park's

184km^2 of rain forest are bereft of trails. The **Park Headquarters and Visitors Center,** on the road leading to the Phliu Falls, has maps in English with directions to the falls as well as information on renting a bungalow (800฿).

KHAO KHITCHAKUT NATIONAL PARK

Songthaew *depart from the corner of Prachaniyon Rd. and Benchamarachuthis Rd., opposite Bangkok Bank south of the post office. The* songthaew *will drop you off at the 1½km access road marked by the number 2511 and a white* fleur-de-lis *(20฿). The 24hr. park headquarters (☎452 074), is beyond the entrance booth. Open daily 6am-6pm. 200฿.*

Thirty kilometers north of town on Hwy. 3249, Khao Khitchakut National Park commences the **Chanthaburi River**, churning down the 13 tiers of **Nam Tok Krathing** (Krathing Falls), the park's most popular attraction. A steep, rocky trail leads up from a Buddha at the mountain's base to the highest fall. Once you've bathed in cascades beneath enormous vines and golden butterflies, you'll understand why 2000 Thai tourists flock to the falls every weekend. Falls #7-13 are great for swimming; the butterflies swarm around #13. The climb is exhilarating and treacherous; come prepared with a swimsuit, good shoes, and lots of water.

A small **canteen** stocks a few basic items and prepares simple rice dishes. (20-25฿. Open daily 6am-6pm.) Food stalls set up on weekends and holidays. The **Visitors Center** has information in English. **Camp** on your own (free), or rent a two-person tent (80฿). Lodging options are limited to **bungalows** for five (200฿), eight (600฿), 12 (1000฿), or 14 (1200฿). They're usually empty on weekdays, but for weekend stays, call the ranger station at least one week in advance.

THAILAND

WAT KHAO SUKIM

Take a taxi (400฿ round-trip) or try to catch a songthaew *for Na Ya-am at Chanthaburi's market, get off at Sathorn, and catch a* songthaew *to the temple.* Songthaew *rarely make the trip to the temple, so a taxi may be your only hope. Open daily 6:30am-5pm.*

On a mountainside 20km outside Chanthaburi, Wat Khao Sukim is the pride of the local Buddhists. Built as a center for meditation, the temple has drawn much attention from Thai and Chinese Buddhists, who have donated Buddhist statues and artwork to the temple. Though the temple is not spectacular, the display halls, crammed with everything from peach trees made of colored glass to furniture inlaid with mother-of-pearl, are overwhelming. Amid all these riches, life-like wax replicas of monks sit in meditation, oblivious to the ornate jade vases around them. The roof offers panoramas of mountains, a waterfall, and fruit groves, providing a glimpse of Chanthaburi's natural beauty for those who don't have time for its parks.

TRAT ☎039

Trat is the least developed of the eastern provinces. Most of its population grows fruit or fish. Travelers who treat this frontier town as a transit point en route to Ko Chang and the southern archipelago are now joined by travelers en route to Cambodia via Klong Yai. For the adventurous backpacker, oft-overlooked Trat Province teems with jungle, waterfalls, temples, and beaches, few of them visited by *farang*. Its guest houses, market, and transportation make Trat a worthy base.

TRANSPORTATION. Trat is a frontier town. **A/C buses** from anywhere north or west of town stop on the east side of **Sukhumvit Rd.,** next to a cinema. Private bus companies offer A/C bus service to **Bangkok** (5hr., 150-200฿); their offices cluster around the market. Buses depart every hour for **Chanthaburi,** where you can transfer to all other major destinations. **Non-A/C buses** to Chanthaburi pull in every two hours from 8:30am to 4:30pm (30฿). Near the pharmacy and market, **minibuses** depart when full for Chanthaburi (1hr., 6am-6pm, 60฿). Blue **songthaew** heading to **Laem Ngop** pull up one block south of the market, next to the pharmacy on Sukhumvit Rd. and leave when full (6am-6pm, 20฿). Blue *songthaew* going to **Klong Yai** wait behind the market on Tat Mai Rd. (1½hr., every hr. 6am-6pm, 35฿). Minibuses to **Klong Yai** wait on Sukhumvit Rd. two blocks north of the market (1½hr., every hr. 6am-6pm, 60-100฿).

ORIENTATION AND PRACTICAL INFORMATION. Trat is easy to navigate. The main road is **Sukhumvit Rd.,** which runs north toward Bangkok and south toward Laem Ngop. Sukhumvit Rd. has two traffic signals; one each at its northern and southern ends, and most services, including the hospital, banks, pharmacy, *songthaew*, minibuses, A/C buses, and the Municipal Market lie between or near them. At the northern traffic light, Sukhumvit intersects **Wiwattana Rd.,** which runs east to the **post office** (☎511 175; *Poste Restante;* open M-F 8:30am-4:30pm, Sa-Su 9am-noon); the **Telecommunications Office,** 315 Chaimongkol Rd., marked by its radio tower and home to overseas phones and fax (☎/fax 512 167; open daily 7am-10pm); and the **police station** (☎520 219). The Foremost Guest House has an attractive wall map.

Krung Thai Bank, 59 Sukhumvit Rd., opposite the pharmacy and next to the Trat Department Store, changes traveler's checks and has a **24hr. ATM.** (☎520 542. 13฿ per check. Open M-F 8:30am-3:30pm.) An outside exchange booth is open only during high season. **Trat Hospital** is on Sukhumvit Rd. just past the traffic light at the northern end. (☎511 040 or 520 216/217, ext. 605. **Emergency**☎191.) A large **pharmacy** sits south of the market, next to the *songthaew* bound for Laem Ngop. (☎512 312. Open daily 7am-10pm.) The lobby of the Trat Inn Hotel, at the corner of Sukhumvit Rd. at the southern traffic light offers **Internet access** (☎532 119; 20฿ for the first 10min., 1฿ per additional minute) and **overseas telephones** (open daily 8am-midnight). **Postal code:** 23000.

THAILAND

ACCOMMODATIONS AND FOOD. To reach the guest houses, walk south on Sukhumvit Rd. one block past the southern traffic light and turn left onto Thana Charoen Rd.; it's a 5min. walk from the buses and *songthaew.* **Windy Guest House,** 64 Thana Charoen Rd., has well-kept wooden rooms with mosquito nets and shared baths in a traditional Thai house overlooking the river and plenty of travel info. (☎523 664. Singles 70฿; doubles 100฿.) They let guests take their rowboat out on the river for free. **Residang Guest House,** near the end of Thana Charoen Rd., is a real bargain, featuring brand new, enormous rooms with large windows that afford views of the river area. Some rooms have balconies; all have shared baths. (☎530 103. Singles 100฿; doubles 150฿.) They also rent **motorcycles** (50฿ per hr.) and **bicycles** (25฿ per hr.). **Foremost Guest House,** 49 Thana Charoen Rd., offers comprehensive travel advice. Slightly worn but clean rooms share toilets and hot showers. (☎511 923. Singles 70฿; doubles 100฿; family room 200฿.) Another worthy option is **N.P. Guest House,** up the soi opposite Windy Guest House. The lobby is adorned with tourist info. The rooms in back are quieter. (☎512 270. Singles 60-70฿; doubles 100฿; family room 200฿.)

There's no excuse for not eating in the **market.** During the day, foodstalls set up on the first floor of the municipal market (elaborate soups with meat or fish 10-20฿). The **night market** moves to the square two blocks north of the municipal market building behind the A/C bus terminal. (Open daily 7pm-midnight.)

SIGHTS AND ENTERTAINMENT. Most attractions lie in the province, not in the town. The travel-weary can relax with a **traditional Thai massage;** look for the sign outside a house on Thana Charoen Rd. just a few meters from the intersection with Sukhumvit Rd. (2hr. massage 200฿. Open daily 8am-8pm.) This may be just enough to loosen your limbs for the 2.3km walk to **Wat Buppharam.** Walking south on Sukhumvit Rd., turn right down the little road before Trat Department Store and follow it out of town to reach this mildly interesting wat on a little hill. The grounds contain buildings constructed in the traditional Thai wooden house style, including monks' picturesque wooden dwellings built on stilts in a little garden. During the day you may catch the wat's monk school in session. The walk to the temple is level; another option is to rent a bicycle from Residang Guest House.

Trat has numerous cafes. A good choice is the new **Sea House,** at the southern traffic light on Sukhumvit Rd., which serves up a variety of drinks and Thai rice dishes to the beat of hip Thai pop music. (Open daily noon-midnight.)

NIGHTLIFE. For a bit of nightlife head to **Jean's Cafe,** next door to the Foremost Guest House, which serves light food and all sorts of drinks. It also sports a great collection of music. (Beer 60-120฿; ginger tea 20฿. Open daily 8am-late.)

DAYTRIP FROM TRAT: LAEM NGOP. A sleepy village with a chaotic pier, Laem Ngop is the place to board ferries to Ko Chang. With Trat a short *songthaew* ride away (20min., 20฿), there is no reason to dawdle here, and certainly no reason to stay the night.

For **visa extensions** (10-30 days, 500฿) and official information on visiting **Cambodia,** head for the **Immigration Office** (☎597 261). The office is on the ground floor of a white building about a 15min. stroll up the road from Laem Ngop to Trat, about 300m beyond Thai Farmers Bank. (Open M-F 8:30am-noon and 1-4:30pm.)

Thai Farmers Bank is 500m from the pier on the Trat-Laem Ngop Rd. (☎597 04 56. 13฿ per check. Open M-F 8:30am-3:30pm.) Laem Ngop's **hospital** (☎597 047), on Trat-Laem Ngop Rd., 2km from Laem Ngop toward Trat, sells **malaria** medication (150mg doxycycline pills 2฿), which is recommended for travelers en route to Ko Chang. A **TAT** office next door has a friendly staff. (☎597 255. Open daily 8:30am-4:30pm.) For information on the National Park, head to the **National Park office.** From the pier, it's a 10min. walk down the first road on the left. (☎538 100. Open 24hr.) The last *songthaew* to Trat leaves after the last boat arrives, usually around 6pm. The only other option is to take a taxi (150฿).

BORDER CROSSING: KLONG YAI/SIHANOUKVILLE. To enter Cambodia, you must have a Cambodian visa. These have recently become available at the border on **Hat Lek** for 1000฿, but to be on the safe side, it is best to obtain your visa at the Cambodian embassy in **Bangkok** before leaving for Trat. The whole process takes 9-13 hours; depending on the departure time of the boat to **Sihanoukville,** an overnight may be necessary. Either way, it pays to get an early start. To get from Trat to Klong Yai, take a blue *songthaew* behind the market (1½hr., every hr. 6am-6pm, 35฿) or a minivan from 2 blocks north of the market (1½hr., every hr. 6am-6pm, 80-100฿). At Klong Yai, take a taxi to the border town **Ban Hat Lek** (30min., 20฿ per person). The border closes at 5pm and there are no guest houses in Ban Hat Lek. When you exit Thailand at the border, remember to obtain an exit stamp. After crossing the border, take a small boat to the town of **Koh Kong** (10min., 100฿), where overnight accommodations can be found. A daily boat departs at 8am (sometimes earlier) for Sihanoukville (3½-4hr., 500-600฿). Stay the night in Sihanoukville (see p. 79) or catch a bus to Phnom Penh (3½hr., 10,000r).

KO CHANG ☎01

Ko Chang used to be a paradise island. To some degree, it has gone the way of Thailand's southern beaches: mounds of garbage, resort commercialism, and late-night parties. However, Ko Chang still has a rugged rainforest interior, towering waterfalls, isolated beaches, and unexplored territory on its east side. In high season, the popularity of Ko Chang opens the gateway to the southern archipelago, making it easy to access the little-touristed, one-bungalow islands. However, malaria and infrequent ferry service makes the islands less appealing in the low season.

THE VIEW FROM ABOVE

Gateway: Dan Mai Pier.
Beaches: Hat Kai Bae, Hat Khlong Phrao, Hat Sai Kaow.
Something fun: Snorkeling and chartering boats to the southern archipelago.

TRANSPORTATION

To reach Ko Chang, take a bus to **Trat,** then a *songthaew* (every 30min. or when full 6am-6pm, 15฿) from the front of the municipal market on Sukhumvit Rd. to **Laem Ngop Pier,** and a ferry to the island. Basic one-way tourist tickets cost 50฿. The ferry lumbers to **Dan Mai Pier** on Ko Chang's north end (1hr). From Ko Chang, an overland ride to the west-coast beach of your choice is 30฿: **Hat Sai Kaow** (15min.); **Hat Khlong Phrao** (30min.); **Hat Kai Bae** (50min.).

Ferries: Ferries returning from **Dan Mai Pier** leave daily (in high season every hr. 7am-5pm; in low season 3-4 per day). Ferries leave **Laem Ngop Pier** daily (in high season every hr.; in low season 3-4 per day). To leave the island outside scheduled departure times, fishermen charter boats (1000-1500฿). **Speedboats** to the mainland cost 1500฿ from Ban Rung Rang Bungalows (☎329 04 64) on Hat Sai Kaow, or 3500฿ from Sea View Resort (☎218 50 55) on Hat Kai Bae.

Local Transportation: Songthaew rule. A ride between beaches is 30฿. In theory, *songthaew* leave from Hat Kai Bae 1hr. before ferry departure, hit the other two beaches on the way up, and reach the pier just in time for departure.

Rentals: Resorts and petrol stalls across the road from Hat Sai Kaow rent **motorbikes,** ideal for exploring the east coast. 60฿ per hr., 400-500฿ per day. Most guest houses rent as well. Contracts and insurance are uncommon.

THAILAND

ORIENTATION AND PRACTICAL INFORMATION

Ko Chang's interior is a trackless rainforest. There is a rudimentary road around part of the perimeter. From **Na Dan Pier** at the island's northeast end, the road goes south to the east coast, passes some waterfall trails, and ends at the village of **Sa Lak Pet.** A right turn at the pier leads down past the west coast's three beaches: **Hat Sai Kaow, Hat Khlong Phrao,** and **Hat Kai Bae.**

Tourist Office: Ko Chang National Park Headquarters (☎039 521 122) in Than Mayom, at the midpoint of the east coast, 20km from Hat Sai Kaow. Open daily 8am-6pm. There is also a national park office in Laem Ngop.

Currency Exchange: Most bungalow operations on Hat Sai Kaow, as well as Thor's Palace Restaurant, exchange traveler's checks for a 3% commission.

Medical Services: Hospitals in Trat handle emergencies. The island's 6 clinics are in Dan Mai, Khlong Son, Sa Lak Pet, Bang Bao, Jek Bae, and Hat Khlong Phrao. All are open 24hr. and have radios but no phones. **Malaria testing** is available at Hat Khlong Phrao and Dan Mai 8:30am-4:30pm. A hospital is planned for Dan Mai.

Telephones: International rates 100-150฿ per min.; 50-100฿ service charge for collect calls (some have a 10-20min. time limit). Calls can be made at most bungalows on Hat Sai Kaow; at Magic Bungalows, K.P. Bungalows, and Chokdee Bungalows on Hat Khlong Phrao; and at Seaview Resort on Hat Kai Bae.

Post Offices: Most bungalows mail letters and postcards. **Postal code:** 26002.

ACCOMMODATIONS, FOOD, AND BEACHES

The north end of the west coast is spiked with soaring cliffs, which soon level off to Ko Chang's celebrated beaches. Of the coast's three principal beaches, **Hat Sai Khaow** (White Sand Beach) is the closest to the pier and the most developed. More privacy can be had at **Hat Khlong Phrao** and **Hat Kai Bae,** 6km and 10km from Hat Sai Khaow, respectively. The ultimate stretch of silica is a 15min. walk through the jungle from Hat Kai Bae's southernmost cove. During the low season, guest houses slash prices and are willing to negotiate.

HAT SAI KHAOW. This white-sand beach has a bad rap. True, the beach is thin and bungalows topple on top of one another, but it is a pleasant brand of commer-

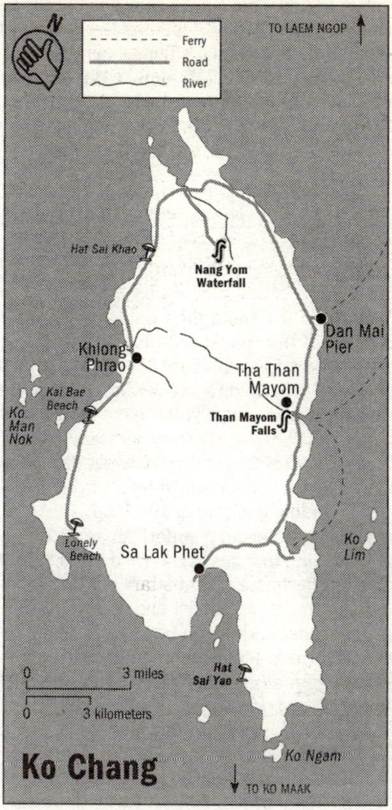

cialism. Extremes of the strip are more sparsely settled. The **White Sand Beach Resort** and its neighbor aren't the only accommodations. Affordable rooms are at **K.C. Sand Beach Resort,** at the north end. (☎211 56 07. Bungalows in high season 170-200฿; in low season 100-150฿.) **Cookie Bungalows,** 300m south, has similar bungalows (150-300฿, depending on the view). At the southernmost point, **Phlamola Cliff Resort** has bamboo huts overlooking the rocky point south of Hat Sai Khaow. (☎323 01 64. Huts in high season 600฿, in low season 300-400฿; concrete rooms with electricity in the evening and private bath in high season 1000฿, in low season 650฿.) The **White Elephant Restaurant** serves the cheapest beer on the island. Walk 10min. south from Hat Sai Khaow, and it's on the right. (Large Chang 40฿; large Singha 50฿. Open daily 6am-2am.)

THAILAND

HAT KHLONG PHRAO. Although not the most remote, Hat Khlong Phrao is the most serene and sparsely settled of Ko Chang's three main beaches. Bungalows are widely spaced on wide expanses of sand, punctuated by creeks from the interior and rock outcroppings. Each establishment has its own entrance, and only a few connect to each other by beach walks. **K.P. Bungalows,** toward the center of the beach, is a travelers' favorite. (☎219 12 25. In high season boxes with one or two beds and shared baths 100-150฿, with fan 300-1000฿ depending on number of people; low season 60-600฿.) Food, laundry service, and motorcycle rentals (60-100฿ per hr., 400-500฿ per day) are available. **Magic Bungalows** (☎329 04 08) offers clean rooms (100฿, with shower and fan 250-400฿), motorbike rentals (80฿ per hr., 400฿ per day), and snorkeling trips to Ko Yauk (3hr., 200฿ per person). **Chokdee Bungalow,** at the south end of the beach, has copious and well-priced accommodations. (☎219 38 14. Huts with shared toilet 100฿, with fan, tidy toilets, and ocean view 500฿. Breakfast combo 40-45฿; *tom yum* 50฿. 3hr. snorkeling outing to Ko Yuak 150฿.)

HAT KAI BAE. The most remote of the beaches, Hat Kai Bae nonetheless has a fun and lively backpacker environment. It also makes a good jumping-off point for exploring the island's south side. **Kai Bae/Comfortable Bungalows** are south past graceful coconut groves. Bungalows with fans and baths (in high season 200฿, in low season 150฿) are maintained by Wee Wat, the young and hospitable owner. Motorcycles cost 60฿ for an hour (around 400฿ per day), but feel free to bargain. Don't miss the chance to kick back at the **Super-Comfortable Kai Bae Bar,** a surreal spot that's open around the clock during the high season, and upon request during the low. **Kaibae Hut,** is where the island taxi will finally disgorge you. (☎219 34 52. Bungalows have attached bathrooms and mosquito nets 100฿; with fan in high season 400฿, in low season 200฿.) Snorkeling tours to Ko Yuak (150฿) last half a day.

The sand-floored restaurant serves plenty of fried Thai food, from pineapples to squid, plus a wide array of cashew dishes. (Dishes 30-80฿. Open daily 7am-9pm.) Swankier **Kai Bae Beach Bungalows** and its popular attached restaurant sprawl north of Kaibae Hut. (☎219 38 61. One bed with no bathroom 100฿; deluxe double with fans and showers 1000฿.) **Siam Bay Resort** has a monopoly on the nice beaches of the far south, offering bungalows with fan and shower (250฿) and nicer rooms (400-600฿).

LONELY BEACH. Find the narrow trail just past Siam Bay Resort at the southern end of Hat Kai Bae and follow it through a shady rainforest. Suddenly, you're on a beach where an old man harvests coconuts and lovers skinny-dip in complete isolation. Complete, except possibly for you. (Treehouse bungalows 100-200฿.)

THE WEST COAST. Consult beach listings for **snorkeling** options. Popular **Mama's Very Famous Snorkel Trips** is just north of the road's end on Hat Kai Bae. A trip to Ko Yuak costs 150฿; special three-island trips run every Thursday (200฿). Fishing boats can be rented for 100฿ per hour. Ko Chang's snorkeling outings are designed for high season crowds. During the low season, you'll have to wait for smooth seas and rustle up a group.

If you do come to Ko Chang in high season, check out the **Seahorse Dive Shop** (☎29 38 44) behind Kaibae Hut. The friendly Swiss instructor offers four-day PADI courses (10,500฿). Dives cost 1200-1500฿, including equipment and food.

If you still hunger for physical and spiritual self-mastery, American Jerry Boxer has developed a unique and personal art, which he teaches at the **Wind Eagle School of Taiji,** a platform beyond Kai Bae Beach Bungalows (lessons 60-75฿ per hr.).

THE EAST COAST. The picturesque east coast is short on beaches but long on scenic beauty. Colonnades of rubber trees alternate with rambutan orchards; several waterfalls are accessible by trails that begin along the shore. While the falls themselves are nothing to write home about, the opportunity to catch a glimpse of the island's rugged interior shouldn't be missed. The town of **Dan Mai** hides a path to **Khlong Nonsi Falls,** a 30min. walk inland. **Than Mayom,** 4km to the south, is home to the **National Park Headquarters** (☎039 521 122), with little to offer save a visitors center, free public toilets, and showers. Nearby **Than Mayom Falls,** a favorite of King Rama V, still bears his initials. Clear mountain water gushes over a 7m high rock into a jungle pool (in rainy season only, July-Dec.). Rent a motorbike or take a *songthaew* to the pier and another down the east coast. Trails to the interior rise up just behind Hat Klong Phrao; ask locals for details. On the west side of the peninsula, jutting out from the southeast corner of the island, Hat Sai Yao awaits those who will settle only for the extremely remote. A **ferry** leaves Laem Ngop at 3pm, stopping at the beach on its way to Ko Wai (100฿); it leaves at 8am from Ko Wai to come back (in low season 3 per week). On the other side of the bay, **Sa Lak Phet** is Ko Chang's most lively fishing village, accessible by ferry (departs for Laem Ngop 6am, returns 1pm; 70฿). You can also charter boats to the southern archipelago.

NEAR KO CHANG: SOUTHERN ARCHIPELAGO

Fifty-one other islands besides Ko Chang make up the national park. Thirteen have accommodations, some of which cater only to package tourists; camping is free and legal anywhere. In the high season, many of these islands are easy to get to and have cheap lodgings. In the low season, most close up shop and head elsewhere. As the area becomes increasingly touristed, new operations pop up monthly. Food is available in island guest houses and is overpriced but tasty.

KO MAAK

A ferry leaves Ko Maak from Ao Nid pier at 8am and Laem Ngop at 3pm (in high season daily, in low season F, Su, Tu; 2½hr.; 170฿). Boats ferry to Ko Kham twice in the morning and return around 4pm (15min., 50฿).

The most accessible of the outer islands, Ko Maak offers the same travel amenities as Ko Chang, but with more solitude and better beaches. The island itself is flat, with volcanic formations on the western tip that frame beaches on either side. In the low season, it is technically closed, but most guest houses will offer lodging and food to anyone who shows up. There is a **clinic** and a **police box** on the road heading into the island from the pier. Expensive bottled water, whiskey, and toilet paper are available at the store at the base of the pier. Just north, a casual **post office** can periodically patch through international phone calls at high rates. (Open daily 7am-8pm.) The complex also has a minimart and bicycle and motorcycle rental. Guest houses are easily accessible by trucks waiting by the pier. There are no official taxi services, so on arrival, pick a truck—each hotel and guest house usually sends one to meet every boat, free of charge. The west beach is very slender and parts have become very trashy, but it basks in the soft glow of splendid sunsets. The farthest south is **Lazy Days,** with accommodations in a relaxed party atmosphere (bungalows and teepees with shared bath 100฿). Just up the beach, **Aukao Resort** has bungalows (with shared bath 100฿, with fan and bath 250฿).

On the north side, the beach is in a long bay with unobtrusive bungalows and calm, coral-strewn waters. At the west end, **Fantasia** (open Oct.-May) has great (though fan-less) A-frame bungalows tucked back on the hill in the coconut grove, with mosquito nets, floor mattresses, and shared baths (100฿). Beachfront bungalows with private baths, beach chairs, and fans run 250฿. Fantasia boasts the best collection of recorded music on the east coast. Up the beach, **Koh Mak Resort** offers high-quality, spacious bungalows (300-600฿).

THAILAND

THE OUTER ISLANDS

To get to Ko Rang, charter a boat in Sa Lak Phet or check at Ko Chang bungalows for scuba or snorkeling tours. Sunsai Bungalows on Hat Sai Kaow runs daytrips to the islands of Ko Loi, Ko Ngam, Ko Gia, and Ko Rang during the high season. Trips leave at 8:30am and return at sunset (350฿). In the high season, a ferry leaves for Ko Wai daily at 3pm from Laem Ngop, returning from Ko Wai at 8am the following morning (2hr., 120฿). A banana boat leaves year-round from the river in Trat (W, Sa 11am) for Ko Kud, returning the next morning (4½hr., 150฿). In addition, a speedboat island-hopper service has started. Tickets cost 250฿. Check with guest houses on the islands in Trat.

The islands off Ko Chang's south coast are famous for fishing, coral, rock formations, bird nests, and bat guano. You can scuba dive at **Ko Rang,** home to an abundance of coral, fish, and toothy sharks.

Ko Wai, a less-remote version of Ko Rang, is surrounded by coral. The fishing is legendary. From Ko Maak, there is a ferry to **Ko Kham,** which features a cheap guest house (open Oct.-June) and more sun and solitude. There are also accommodations on far-flung **Ko Kud** (open Nov.-May). Bungalows on the islands range from 100-300฿ and package tours run 2000฿ per night. Ask at guest houses in Trat.

NORTHERN THAILAND

Northern Thailand's mountains constitute the lowest crags of the Himalayan foothills; its Salawin River flirts with Myanmar before flooding into the Bay of Bengal; and its eastern border is none other than the mighty Mekong. Central **Chiang Mai,** formerly the prosperous Lanna Kingdom, serves as the first stop for many visitors.

The hill tribe haven of **Mae Hong Son** is to the west. **Chiang Rai,** in the north, harbors poppy fields and the Golden Triangle. To the east, **Nan** borders Laos. Throughout the region, Chinese immigrants display pictures of the Thai Royal Family in shop windows, tribal minorities inhabit misty mountainsides, and refugee camps swell with Burmese escaping their military government—the dialect, cuisine, dance, and wat architecture of Northern Thailand owe much to this fusion of cultures.

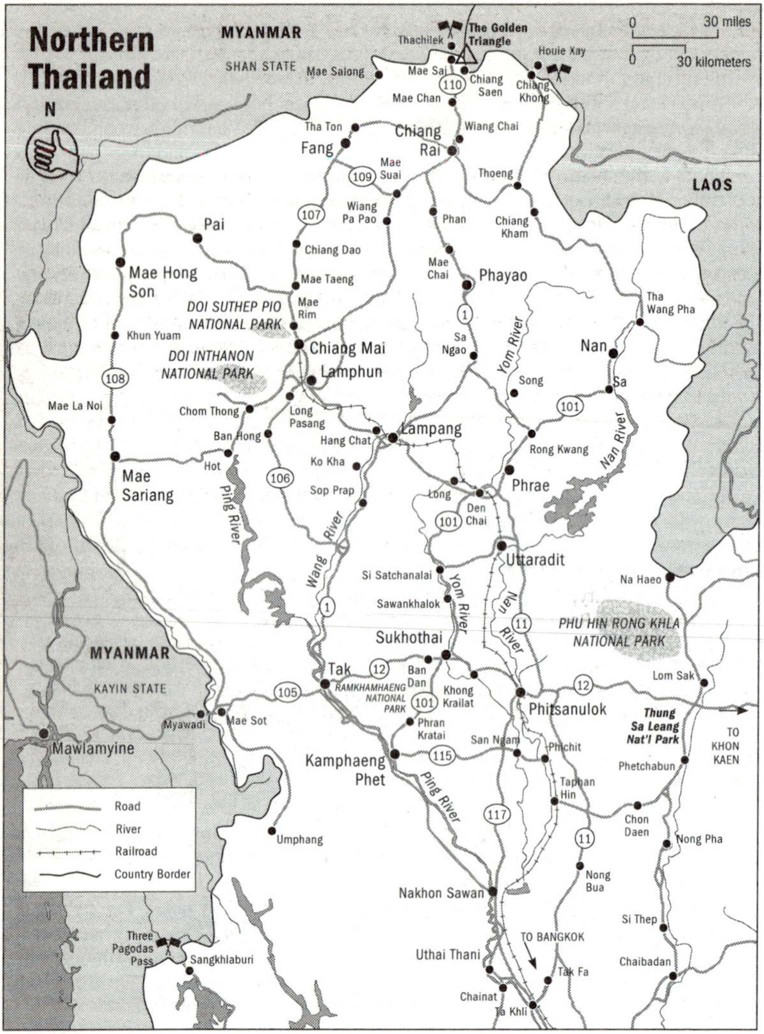

CHIANG MAI

☎053

Nothing more than mice scurrying down a hole convinced King Mengrai to establish the seat of his Lanna Kingdom in Chiang Mai in 1296—an inauspicious beginning for a city that has become Thailand's second-largest in both native population and tourist crowds. Thousands of *farang*, drawn by the promise of adventure and a cool climate, clog the narrow streets of this ancient city. The beautiful "Rose of the North" hustles with a big-city gait, and the increased stampede of tourists heightens concerns that both hill tribe culture and the natural environment are quickly eroding. Lacking a center where local living can strut its stuff, Chiang Mai sinks beneath the waves of Westerners yet somehow seems to retain its cultural autonomy. The distinctive dialect, Burmese-influenced art and architecture, and an abundance of sticky rice (a Northern specialty) prove that Chiang Mai residents are not about to surrender their heritage. This, along with a mountainous backdrop, makes Chiang Mai a necessary stop. The mice were onto something.

INTERCITY TRANSPORTATION

The monthly *What's on Chiang Mai*, available at TAT and travel agencies throughout the city, has comprehensive transportation schedules.

BY PLANE

Chiang Mai International Airport (☎270 222) sits on Sanambin (Airport) Rd., 3km southwest of the city center. From the airport, **taxis** (90฿), *tuk-tuk* (50-60฿), *songthaew* (15-20฿) run to downtown Chiang Mai. **Thai Airways,** 240 Phra Pokklao Rd., has branches around the city (☎211 044; open daily 8am-5pm) and flies to **Bangkok** (13 per day in high season, 9-12 per day in low season; 1900฿) and **Phuket** (11:15am, 3485฿). **Bangkok Airways,** at the airport (☎281 519), flies daily to **Bangkok** (11:50am, 1530฿) via **Sukhothai** (650฿). **Lao Aviation** flies to **Vientiane** (Th, Su 1:10pm; 3400฿). Their contact in Chiang Mai is **Chiang Mai BIS Travel,** 12/1 Loi Krap Rd. (☎206 738. Open daily 8:30am-6pm.) **Air Mandalay** flies to **Yangon** (Th 4:50pm, Su 2:35pm; 3065฿); contact **Charal Business,** 123 Chiang Mai-Lamphun Rd. (☎252 054. Open M-F 8:30am-6pm, Sa 8am-5pm.) **Silk Air,** at the Imperial Maeping Hotel, 153 Sri Donchai Rd. (☎276 459; open M-F 8:30am-5pm, Sa-Su 8:30am-1pm), flies to **Singapore** (Tu, Su 5pm, F 11:25am; 6400฿). **Trans World Travel Service Co. Ltd.,** 259/61 Tha Phae Rd., may offer cheaper student tickets than carriers do.

BY TRAIN

The **Chiang Mai Railway Station,** 27 Charoen Muang Rd. (☎245 363), on the eastern outskirts of the city, is accessible by *songthaew* (10-20฿) and *tuk-tuk* (40-50฿). Trains run daily to **Bangkok** (11-14hr.; 7 per day 6:25am-9:30pm; 3rd-class 161฿, 2nd-class sleeper 421-561฿, 2nd-class with A/C 611-681฿). Most Bangkok-bound trains also stop in **Lampang** (2hr.; 3rd-class 23฿, 2nd-class 53฿) and **Phitsanulok** (6-7hr.; 3rd-class 105฿, 2nd-class 190฿). Many options (including food service) are available for an extra charge. Reserve sleeper tickets well in advance; lower berths are pricier.

BY BUS

Tuk-tuk (30-50฿) and *songthaew* (10-20฿) shuttle between the old city and **Arcade Bus Station,** 3km to the northeast. **Chang Phuak Bus Station** (☎211 586), on Chang Phuak Rd. 1km north of the old city, runs buses within Chiang Mai Province.

DESTINATION, BUS#	DUR.	FREQUENCY/TIME	PRICE
ARCADE BUS STATION			
Bangkok, 18	10hr.	19 per day 6:30am-9pm	A/C only 314-403฿
Chiang Rai, 166	3hr.	17 per day 6am-5:30pm	77฿, A/C 98-139฿
Chiang Khong, 671	6hr.	6:30, 8am, 12:30pm	121฿, A/C 169-218฿
Khon Kaen, 633 or 175	12hr.	11 per day 5am-9pm	219-243฿, A/C 307-437฿
Korat, 635	12hr.	10 per day 3:30am-8:30pm	243฿, A/C 340-510฿
Lampang, 152	2hr.	every 30min. 6am-4pm	29฿
Mae Hong Son, 170	8hr.	6:30, 8, 11am, 8, 9pm	143฿, A/C 257฿
via Mae Sariang	5hr.		78฿, A/C 140฿
Mae Hong Son, 612	8hr.	7, 10:30am, 12:30pm	100฿
via Pai	4hr.		55฿
Mae Sai, 619	4hr.	8 per day 6am-5pm	95฿, A/C 108-171฿
Mae Sot, 672	6hr.	11am, 1:10pm	134฿, A/C 188-241฿
Nan, 169 or 113	6hr.	15 per day 6:15am-10:30pm	117-128฿, A/C 164-230฿
Phitsanulok, 155, 132, or 623	6hr.	11 per day 6:30am-8pm	120-140฿, A/C 184-196฿
Sukhothai, 155	5hr.	12 per day 5am-8pm	122฿, A/C 171฿
Ubon Ratchathani, 587	17	6 per day 12:15-6pm	325฿, A/C 590-685฿
CHANG PHUAK BUS STATION			

DESTINATION, BUS#	DUR.	FREQUENCY/TIME	PRICE
Chom Thong	1¼hr.	every 20min. 5:30am-6:30pm	15฿
Tha Ton	4hr.	6 per day 6am-3:30pm	50฿
via Fang	3½hr.	every 30min. 5:30am-5:30pm	43฿

ORIENTATION

Chiang Mai is 700km north of Bangkok. The primary area of interest is within the old city and the area to its east which stretches 1½km to the **Ping River.** A square moat delineates the old city; within it, the east-west soi numbers increase as you go north. North-south **Phra Pokklao Rd.** and east-west **Ratchadamnoen Rd.** divide the square. **Moon Muang Rd.** follows the inside of the moat and intersects Ratchadamnoen Rd. at **Tha Phae Gate,** the center of backpacker activity. If Tha Phae Gate weren't closed to traffic, Ratchadamnoen Rd. would flow into **Tha Phae Rd.,** which runs east to the Ping River and **Nawarat Bridge.** Along the way, it intersects **Chang Klan Rd.,** home to the night bazaar, and **Charoen Prathet Rd.,** which flanks the Ping's west bank. TAT is on **Chiang Mai-Lamphun Rd.,** which hugs the Ping River's east bank. Guest houses, TAT, and other tourist-geared establishments stock free copies of *Guidelines* and *Welcome to Chiang Mai*, that offer occasionally useful and often amusing practical information.

LOCAL TRANSPORTATION

Thick traffic and numerous one-way streets make exploration on foot appealing.

Songthaew, Tuk-tuk, and Samlor: *Songthaew* 10฿ anywhere in the city, except for along special routes, to the airport or bus station, or at night. Don't pay more than 40฿. Already occupied *songthaew* are cheaper than empty ones. *Tuk-tuk* and *samlor* 20-30฿ within the old city, 40-60฿ for trips across the city, 400-500฿ per day.

Rentals: Bicycles 30-50฿ per day. Often require a passport photocopy and/or 500฿ deposit. **Mr. Mechanic,** 4 Moo Muang Rd. Soi 5 (☎214 708), rents cheap mountain bikes (40฿). **Moped** rental 150฿ per day; **motorcycles** from 200฿. Insurance should be included in the price, but cough up the extra 10฿ for a helmet. Rental shops litter the Tha Phae Gate area; all require a passport photocopy and/or deposit. Mr. Mechanic offers motorbikes for 170฿ with insurance. Need more wheels? **Avis,** Royal Princess Hotel, 112 Chang Klan Rd. (☎281 033), and at the airport. Toyota Corollas 1700฿ per day. Open daily 8am-5pm.

PRACTICAL INFORMATION

TOURIST AND FINANCIAL SERVICES

Tourist Offices: TAT, 105/1 Chiang Mai-Lamphun Rd. (☎248 604), 500m south of Narawat Bridge. Chock full of maps and brochures. Open daily 8:30am-4:30pm.

Consulates: Australia, 165 Sirimungkrajaru Rd. (☎225 975). Open M-F 9am-5pm. **Canada,** (☎850 147). **UK,** Unit 201, Airport Business Park, 90 Mahidol Rd. (☎203 408). Open M-Th 8am-noon and 1-4:30pm, F 8am-1pm. **US,** 387 Vitchayanon Rd. (☎252 629). American citizen services open M and W 1-3:30pm.

Immigration Offices: 97 Sanambin (Airport) Rd. (☎277 510). **Visa extensions** 500฿; 1-day processing. Bring 2 passport photos, 2 copies of passport photo page, visa, and arrival/departure card. Open M-F 8:30am-4pm.

Currency Exchange: Banks line Tha Phae Rd. **Thai Farmers Bank,** 169-171 Tha Phae Rd. (☎270 151). Open M-F 8:30am-3:30pm. Currency exchange daily 8:30am-8pm. **24hr. ATM** (Cirrus/MC/PLUS/V).

American Express: Sea Tours Company, 2/3 Prachasamphan Rd. (☎271 441). The only AmEx affiliate in northern Thailand. Mail held for 3 months, free for check- or card-holders. Open M-F 8:30am-4:30pm, Sa 8:30-11:30am.

HOLD THE STUFFING Thailand is a world leader in penis-reattachment surgery, but if you're considering penile surgical augmentation, make sure your doctor is reputable and has good taste. In October 1999, the Bangkok Post reported that unlicensed physicians had performed 100 penis-enlargement operations by injecting mixtures of olive oil, chalk, and other substances to provide bulk and springiness. According to the always reliable *News of the Weird*, one hospital official in Chiang Mai reported having seen bits of the Bangkok telephone directory stuffed in one unsuspecting penis.

LOCAL SERVICES

Luggage Storage: At the **train station** (☎245 363). 10฿ per day per piece for the1st 5 days, 15฿ per additional day (20-day max.). Open daily 4:50am-8:45pm. Most guest houses store luggage for free, although security can be dubious.

English Language Bookstores: The Lost Bookshop, 34/3 Ratchamanka Rd. Wonderful selection of used novels for sale/trade. Popular titles for rent (80฿). Open M-Sa 9am-2pm and 5-8pm.

Markets: A **night bazaar** with hill tribe goods, expensive furniture, and T-shirts dominates Chang Klan Rd. from 6pm-midnight. Southern end has cheap food stalls.

EMERGENCY AND COMMUNICATIONS

Emergency: ☎191.

Tourist Police: ☎248 974. 50m north of the TAT building. **Open 24hr.**

Pharmacy: Pharma Choice 2 (☎280 136), in Suriwong Plaza at Tha Phae Gate.

Medical Services: McCormick Hospital, 133 Kaew Nawarat Rd. (☎241 311), has ambulance service and a **24hr. pharmacy.** English-speaking doctors.

Telephones: At post offices. **AT&T Direct booths** outside GPO, TAT, and the train station.

Internet Access: Chiang Mai University Library (☎944 531), 10km northwest of old city. Free access. Sign up at reference desk; slots fill up quickly. Open M-F 8am-9pm, Sa-Su 8:30am-4:30pm. Several Internet cafes line the northern half of **Ratchaphakhiani Rd.** 15-20฿ per hr.

Post Offices: GPO (☎245 376), on Charoen Muang Rd., 150m toward the old city from the train station. *Poste Restante.* Open M-F 8:30am-4:30pm, Sa-Su 9am-noon. **Mae Ping Post Office** (☎252 037), on Charoen Prathet Rd., just north of Narawat Bridge. Open M-F 8:30am-4:30pm, Sa 9am-noon. Both provide **international phone/fax. Postal code:** 50000.

ACCOMMODATIONS

Guest house signs sprout from almost every soi entrance within a 1km radius of **Tha Phae Gate.** Prices may inflate during festival periods. Beware of touts who tell you that the guest house you're interested in is closed or full—all they want is a shady competitor's commission.

THA PHAE GATE AREA

Libra Guest House, 28 Moon Muang Rd. Soi 9 (☎/fax 210 687), in the northeast corner of the old city. Popular, family-run establishment offers consistently praised treks (3-day, 1600฿). New cooking school 500฿ per day (3 person min.). Laundry service 25฿ per kg. Free pickup from bus or train station or airport. Check-out 10am. Reservations recommended. Dorms 50฿; doubles 100฿, with hot water 150฿.

Rendezvous Guest House, 3/1 Ratchadamnoen Rd., (☎213 763) near Soi 5. Superb value. Rooms with bath, TV, and fan 280฿, with A/C 380฿.

Rose Guest House, 87 Ratchamanka Rd. (☎273 869), at corner of Ratchaphakinai Rd. It's cheap—who needs windows? Friendly management and rooftop patio, but noisy. Check-out 9am. Dorms 50฿; singles 60฿; doubles 80฿.

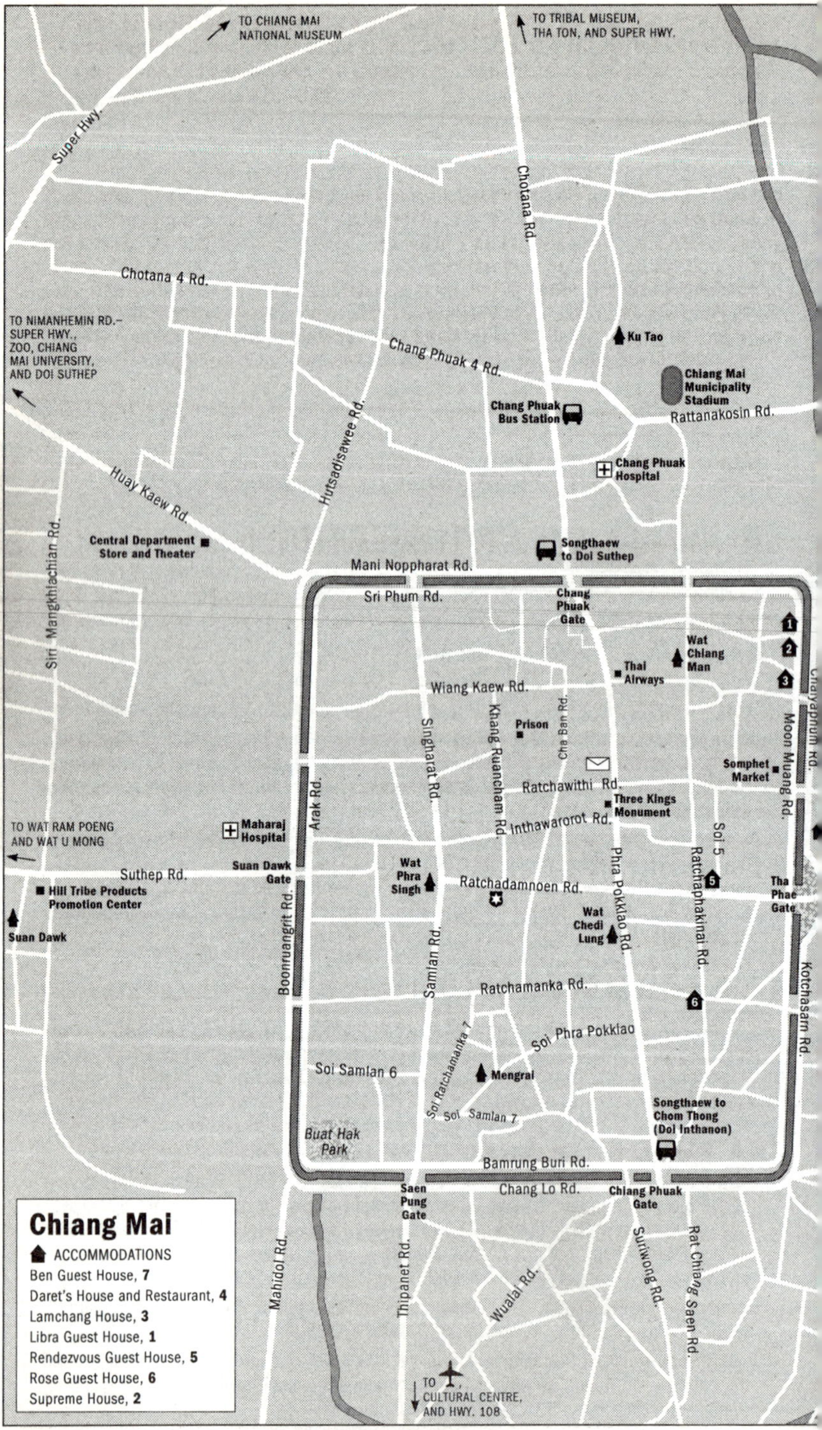
TO CHIANG MAI NATIONAL MUSEUM
TO TRIBAL MUSEUM, THA TON, AND SUPER HWY.
Super Hwy.
Chotana Rd.
Chotana 4 Rd.
TO NIMANHEMIN RD.– SUPER HWY., ZOO, CHIANG MAI UNIVERSITY, AND DOI SUTHEP
Chang Phuak 4 Rd.
Ku Tao
Chiang Mai Municipality Stadium
Rattanakosin Rd.
Chang Phuak Bus Station
Chang Phuak Hospital
Hutsadisawee Rd.
Huay Kaew Rd.
Central Department Store and Theater
Songthaew to Doi Suthep
Siri Mangkhlachian Rd.
Mani Noppharat Rd.
Sri Phum Rd.
Chang Phuak Gate
Wat Chiang Man
Thai Airways
Chaiyaphum Rd.
Wiang Kaew Rd.
Singharat Rd.
Khang Ruancham Rd.
Prison
Cha Ban Rd.
Moon Muang Rd.
Somphet Market
Ratchawithi Rd.
Three Kings Monument
Arak Rd.
Maharaj Hospital
TO WAT RAM POENG AND WAT U MONG
Inthawarorot Rd.
Soi 5
Suthep Rd.
Suan Dawk Gate
Wat Phra Singh
Ratchadamnoen Rd.
Phra Pokklao Rd.
Ratchaphakinai Rd.
Tha Phae Gate
Hill Tribe Products Promotion Center
Suan Dawk
Wat Chedi Lung
Boonruangrit Rd.
Samlan Rd.
Ratchamanka Rd.
Kotchasarn Rd.
Soi Phra Pokklao
Soi Ratchamanka 7
Soi Samlan 6
Mengrai
Songthaew to Chom Thong (Doi Inthanon)
Soi Samlan 7
Buat Hak Park
Bamrung Buri Rd.
Saen Pung Gate
Chang Lo Rd.
Chiang Phuak Gate
Mahidol Rd.
Thipanet Rd.
Wualai Rd.
Suriwong Rd.
Rat Chiang Saen Rd.
TO CULTURAL CENTRE, AND HWY. 108
Chiang Mai
ACCOMMODATIONS
Ben Guest House, 7
Daret's House and Restaurant, 4
Lamchang House, 3
Libra Guest House, 1
Rendezvous Guest House, 5
Rose Guest House, 6
Supreme House, 2

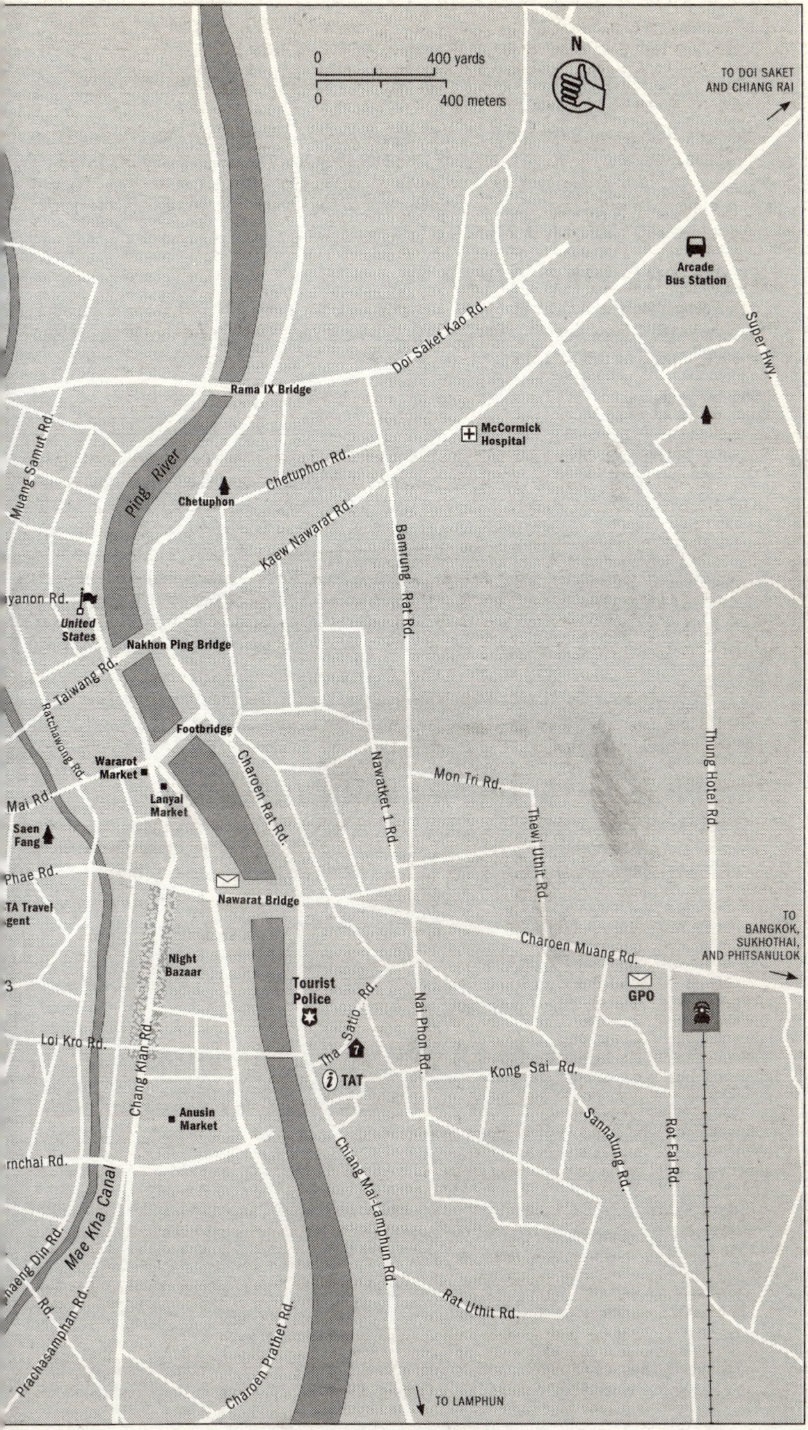
0
400 yards
0
400 meters
N
TO DOI SAKET AND CHIANG RAI
Arcade Bus Station
Super Hwy.
Doi Saket Kao Rd.
Rama IX Bridge
McCormick Hospital
Muang Samut Rd.
Ping River
Chetuphon Rd.
Chetuphon
Kaew Nawarat Rd.
Bamrung Rat Rd.
yanon Rd.
United States
Nakhon Ping Bridge
Taiwang Rd.
Ratchawong Rd.
Footbridge
Wararot Market
Lanyai Market
Charoen Rat Rd.
Nawatket 1 Rd.
Mon Tri Rd.
Thewi Uthit Rd.
Thung Hotel Rd.
Mai Rd.
Saen Fang
Phae Rd.
Nawarat Bridge
TA Travel Agent
Night Bazaar
Charoen Muang Rd.
TO BANGKOK, SUKHOTHAI, AND PHITSANULOK
GPO
Tourist Police
Tha Satio Rd.
Nai Phon Rd.
Loi Kro Rd.
TAT
Kong Sai Rd.
Chang Klan Rd.
Anusin Market
Sannalung Rd.
Rot Fai Rd.
rnchai Rd.
Mae Kha Canal
Chiang Mai-Lamphun Rd.
Rat Uthit Rd.
Prachasamphan Rd.
Charoen Prathet Rd.
TO LAMPHUN

Supreme House, 44/1 Moon Muang Rd. Soi 9 (☎222 480). Helpful owner. Singles/doubles with bath 80฿; triples 150฿; quads 200฿; A/C extra 100฿.

Lamchang House, 24 Moon Muang Rd. Soi 7 (☎210 586). Comfy bamboo rooms. Central. Doubles with shared bath 150฿.

Daret's House and Restaurant, 4/5 Chaiyaphum Rd. (☎235 440), opposite Tha Phae Gate's north end. A *farang* magnet. Perfect location and top-notch restaurant make up for a taciturn owner and unimpressive rooms. Small English bookstore. Weight machines. International phone. Internet 30฿ per hr. Check-out 10am. Singles 120฿; doubles 140-160฿; triples 210฿.

NEAR THE PING RIVER

Ben Guest House, 4/11 Chiang Mai-Lamphun Rd. Soi 2 (☎244 103). Down a soi adjacent to the Tourist Police. Large beds, hot showers, and fans. Check-out 10am. Motorcycle rental. All rooms 150฿.

FOOD

Somphet Market, on Moon Muang Rd. between Soi 6 and 7, serves banana pancakes (10-15฿) and fried noodles (20-40฿). It's open all day, but food stalls don't get going until after 7pm. **Anusin Market,** between Chang Klan and Charoen Prathet Rd., north of Sri Dornchai Rd., is another nocturnal snack zone. **Wahorat Market,** along the Ping River's west bank around Chiang Mai-Lamphun Rd., is Chiang Mai's oldest and largest market and has a wide variety of fresh fruit. For a serious culinary experience, try a *khantoke* dinner. At this formal meal, diners sit on the floor and use their hands to eat rice, two meat dishes, and two vegetable dishes from bowls placed on a *khantoke*, a low tray table. The well-visited **Old Chiang Mai Cultural Center,** 185/3 Wualai Rd., 1½km south of the old city, offers vegetarian and Islamic versions. State your preferences when calling ahead for the necessary reservation. The 2½hr. affair, accompanied by traditional dancing, begins nightly at 7:30pm (270฿, transportation included).

THA PHAE GATE AREA—WITHIN THE MOAT

The Wok, 44 Ratchamanka Rd., east of Ratchaphakinai Rd. Owners run the Chiang Mai Thai Cookery School. Impeccable "special Northern style food" includes yellow curry chicken (60฿) and spicy Chiang Mai sausage (60฿). Open daily 11am-11pm.

Il Forno, 142 Phra Pokklao Rd., south of Ratchamanka Rd. intersection. Fresh bread and pasta. Vegetable panini 45฿. Divine tiramisù 50฿. Open daily 8:30am-10:30pm.

Shuffle Vegetarian Restaurant, 129/3 Moon Muang Rd. Soi 5. Ambiance akin to an French bistro, if it were owned by surfers. Veggie burger 35฿. Mushroom cake spicy salad 35฿. *Tsatsiki* 45฿. Open daily 9am-10pm.

THA PHAE GATE AREA—OUTSIDE THE MOAT

Aroon Rai, 45 Kotchasarn Rd., south of Tha Phae Rd. and before Loi Kroa Rd. Schmooze with Thais and *farang* alike under the portraits of His Ubiquitous Majesty. Curries 40฿. Spicy mushroom soup 40฿. Open daily 8:30am-10pm.

NEAR THE PING RIVER

Shere Shiraz, 23-25 Charoen Prathet Rd. Soi 6, off Chang Klan Rd. down the alley south of Porn Ping Tower Hotel. One of the best South Asian restaurants in town, with Middle Eastern and Thai food too. Chicken *tikka* 100฿. Open daily 9:30am-11:30pm.

Riverside, 9-11 Charoen Rat Rd. From Narawat Bridge, take a left on Charoen Rat Rd; it's the 1st building on left. Phenomenal view from the "*farangda*" (veranda filled with *farang*). Fried bean curd in sauce 55฿. Open daily 10am-1am.

Antique House, 71 Charoen Prathet Rd., across the Ping River from the TAT. Serene feel occasionally spiced up by live music. Dishes 40-180฿. Open daily 10am-10pm.

SIGHTS

DOI SUTHEP AND ENVIRONS

Songthaew leave when full for Wat Phra That Doi Suthep from Chiang Phuak Gate (6am-5pm, 30฿) and the Chiang Mai Zoo (6am-5pm, 30฿). Continuing to the Hmong village costs another 60฿ round-trip; continuing to Doi Phi's summit is 30-50฿ round-trip. Motorbikes are an option, but Huay Kaew Rd. is twisty, and the 4½km dirt road to the Hmong village is rough. Consider renting a bike and storing it atop the songthaew for the ride up.

WAT PHRA THAT DOI SUTHEP. If you only have time to visit one of Chiang Mai's 300 wats, Wat Phra That Doi Suthep, one of Thailand's most sacred pilgrimage sights, should be it. *Phra that* refers to the Buddha's relics enshrined here, namely his *incus* (a teeny anvil-shaped bone in the middle ear); *doi* is a Northern Thai word for mountain; and *suthep* is derived from the Pali *Sudevoy*, the name of the hermit who inhabited the area before the shrine was constructed. While the glint of the brilliant gold *chedi* can be admired from the city's limits, the sweeping survey of the city from the temple's observation deck is sublime.

DOI SUTHEP PIO NATIONAL PARK. A project started in 1987 by a Chiang Mai University professor has thus far collected 2062 species of vascular plants in the park—more than in all of the UK. While the park's flora and fauna are regrettably being forced up the mountain as Chiang Mai expands, the park still offers much for wide-eyed wanderers. **Waterfalls** line Huay Kaew Rd. (Hwy. 1004), which leads up the mountain; keep an eye out for their turn-offs. Doi Phi's summit (1685m), 4½km up the road from Phuphing Palace, makes for a nice hike. Watch for the **Kruba Srivichai Shrine,** the monument on the left just before the road goes up the mountain. Kruba Srivichai was a monk who inspired thousands of volunteers to build the road to Wat Phra That in 1934. Pausing to pay respects is supposed to ensure a safe journey up and down. The **park headquarters** provides trail maps and accommodations. If you want to stay longer, camping costs 10฿ per night and cabins are available for

THAILAND

THE BALLED AND THE BEAUTIFUL

What: A panoply of surgically-inserted, topology-altering penile implants, including bells (jangled by an inner pebble or dried adder's tongue), balls (as many as 30 "up to the size of a small chicken egg"), studs (hewn of gold and jewels), pins (inserted widthwise, sometimes more than once, with rounded terminal pegs), and rings (up to "a full palm in circumference").

When and where: Employed in Myanmar, Thailand, and peninsular Malaysia until the mid-17th century, when newly arrived Muslim and Christian missionaries frowned upon the practice. Recorded in Sumatra, Sulawesi, the Maluku Islands, and the Philippines well into this century. Alive and well in some parts of Borneo.

How: Pins were traditionally inserted by way of a clamp-'n'-lance device far too graphic to describe in any more detail. Some pins included long strings at either end, the better to guide the flaccid johnson into position, from which it could not be removed until pliant once again.

Why: Aye, there's the rub. One Bornean tale explains that these schlong-pins were invented by a resourceful man after being told by several women that he gave them no more pleasure than a rolled-up leaf. Most accounts bespeak the exponentially intensified pleasure derived by women from the cock-inserts ("they are to sex as salt is to food"), while leading modern scholars use them as evidence of the high prestige and power traditionally held by Southeast Asian women. One 17th century Jesuit priest, however, writing about the Visayan Islands of the Philippines, claimed that some men would punish women by affixing sharp pegs to their willy-pins, inflicting great pain or even death during sex.

rent (1000฿ for a 12-person cabin). Reserve at least a week in advance. *(The park headquarters lies 500m up Huay Kaew Rd. from Wat Phra That Doi Suthep. ☎ 248 405. The journey up and down the mountain costs 10฿.)*

SIGHTS NEAR DOI SUTHEP. Doi Pui, a Hmong village 8km past the wat, suffers from tourist overcrowding. The lush garden of the **Hill Tribes Village Museum,** 150m uphill from the parking lot for the wat, contrasts sharply with the squalid village. The museum's main attraction is its collection of tiny pink opium flowers. *(Open whenever there are visitors. 30฿.)* **Phuphing Palace,** 4km up the mountain from the wat at the turn-off to the Hmong village, is the Royal Family's residence from January to February. *(Open F-Su and holidays 8:30-11:30am, 1-4pm.)* The **Chiang Mai Zoo** is by the base of Doi Suthep. No need to wait for feeding time—plates of hippo grub run 5-10฿. *(☎ 221 179. Open daily 8am-6pm. 30฿, children 5฿, bicycles 1฿, motorbikes 10฿, cars 30฿.)* Next door, the **Huay Kaew Arboretum's** rare trees provide a shady respite.

WITHIN THE MOAT

WAT CHIANG MAN. The oldest wat in the city, Chiang Man was built in 1296 by King Mengrai. With its low-sloping roofs and intricate facade, the temple is a classic example of Northern Thai design. The *wiharn* on the right contains two Buddha images: **Phra Setangamani (Crystal Buddha),** thought to have come from Lopburi 1800 years ago, and **Phra Sila (Stone Buddha),** imported from India some 2500 years ago. *(At the north end of Ratchaphakinai Rd. Open daily 9am-5pm.)*

WAT CHEDI LUANG. Built by King Saen Suang Ma in 1401, the temple walls hold the spectacular remains of Chiang Mai's largest *chedi,* which once spiraled 86m toward the sky. A *naga* staircase adorns the *wiharn,* which houses a **standing gold Buddha** and 32 *Jataka* story panels depicting scenes from the Buddha's life. Legend holds that Wat Chedi Luang was home to the Emerald Buddha during its stay in Chiang Mai. *(Head east on Phra Singh Rd. and turn right (south) onto Phra Pokklao Rd.; it's opposite the Yamaha music store.)*

WAT PHRA SINGH. The wat's chief attraction is the bronze **Phra Singh** in **Phra Wihan Lai Kam,** left of and somewhat behind the main *wiharn.* Experts aren't sure if this is the genuine Phra Singh Buddha, as there are identical statues in Bangkok and Nakhon Si Thammarat. The image is the focus of mid-April Songkran festivities. *(On the western side of the old city at Phra Singh Rd.'s end.)*

OUTSIDE THE MOAT

WAT CHED YOT. Inspired by the Mahabodhi Temple in Bodhgaya, India, King Tilokaraja built this shrine in 1455. In 1477, the Eighth World Buddhist Council met here to revise the *Tripitaka* scriptures of Theravada Buddhism. The two Bodhi trees are said to be descendants of the one Gautama sat under during his enlightenment. *(On the highway, 1km from the Huag Kaew Rd. intersection.)*

CHIANG MAI NATIONAL MUSEUM. The museum features art and artifacts collected from Northern Thai royalty, commoners, and hill tribes. *(To the east along the highway. ☎ 221 308. Open W-Su 9am-4pm.)*

TRIBAL MUSEUM. If you're heading out on a trek and can't make it to the National Museum, consider going to the Tribal Museum. The polished exhibits explore daily life, language derivation, gender roles, and costumes of various hill tribes in northern Thailand. *(On Chotana Rd. in Ratchamangkhla Park, 4km north of Chang Phuak Gate. Follow the stadium turn-off to the left and turn right at the 1st sign for the park; the museum is in the middle of a lake. Tuk-tuk from Chang Phuak Gate 30-50฿. ☎ 210 872. Open M-F 9am-4:30pm. English video presentations upstairs 10am, 2pm.)*

CHIANG MAI UNIVERSITY. Though architecturally uninspiring, its 725 park-like acres provide a pleasant break from the city's urban sprawl. *(6km northeast of the old city off Huag Kaew Rd.)*

ENTERTAINMENT

The **Galare Food Center,** 89/2 Chang Klan Rd., features traditional dancing exhibitions, cross-dressing cabaret shows, and Thai boxing on a rotating schedule. (☎272 067. Nightly 7:30-10pm.) The Central Department Store has a **movie theater** on the fourth floor which shows first-run movies (70-90฿).

Baan Nit, 1 Chaiyaphum Rd., has shoulder and back massages to relax sore muscles. Turn onto the soi from Chaiyaphum Rd.; Baan Nit will be on the left. (Massages 30min., 80฿. Open roughly 7:30am-10pm.) South of the old city, the **Old Medicine Hospital,** 78/1 Soi Moh Shivaya Komarapaj, also garners praise for its relaxing massages. (☎275 085. Herbal sauna 50฿; 1½hr. massage 150฿, with A/C 200฿. Open daily 8:30am-4:30pm.)

MARKETS

Chiang Mai is handicraft central. **Tha Phae Rd.** is one of the best daytime hunting grounds, but avid consumerism takes off only after dark. The famed **night bazaar** on **Chang Klan Rd.** showcases a variety of antiques, silver jewelry, hill tribe embroidery, Thai textiles, pottery, and pirated American music, though you'll have to haggle away bloated tourist prices.

The **Hill Tribe Handicraft Project,** 1 Moon Muang Rd., in a brick building at the southeastern corner of the old city, sells audiotapes of Karen, Lisu, Akha, Lahu, Yao, and Hmong village music (90฿), as well as quilts, bags, pullovers, and sculptures. (☎274 877. Open M-F 8:30am-4:30pm.) The better known **Hill Tribe Promotion Center,** 21/17 Suthep Rd., next to Wat Suan Dawk, has a greater selection of traditional and innovative crafts. (☎277 743. Embroidered bag 280฿. Karen dress 650฿. Open daily 9am-5pm.) Both government-run stores seek to shift tribal economies away from opium cultivation by providing alternative means of income.

NIGHTLIFE

Several wildly popular **restaurant/clubs** lie on the Ping's east bank, just north of Narawat Bridge. *Farang* pubs line **Moon Muang Rd.** Those north of Tha Phae Gate attract backpackers; those to the south are seedier.

Riverside, 9-11 Charoen Rat Rd. (☎243 239), has long been the most popular club. Dual stages (one Western, one Thai) start rocking each night around 8pm. Screwdriver 80฿. Large Singha 90฿. Corona 180฿. Open daily 10am-1:30am.

Brasserie, 37 Charoen Rat Rd. (☎241 665), begins jammin' at 10:30pm when owner Took blazes tunes. Whiskey and soda 45฿. Large Singha 130฿. Open daily 6pm-2am.

The Good View, 13 Charoen Rat Rd. (☎302 764), between Riverside and Brasserie. Music is like Riverside's–only louder. Large Singha 100฿. Corona 120฿. Kamikaze 140฿. Open daily 6pm-1:45am.

Bubbles, 46-48 Charoen Prathet Rd. (☎270 099), in the Porn Ping Tower Hotel. Chiang Mai's premiere disco. Mixed crowd. Open daily 9pm-2am.

TREKKING

Chiang Mai has over 200 companies itching to fulfill trekking prospects. Three-day/two-night treks (4 person min.) run 1300฿ per person to the **Maeteang, Poao,** or **Sameong** areas, and 1500฿ per person to **Doi Iuthanon** or **Chiang Dao;** each extra day costs 200฿. These five are the only legal trekking areas around Chiang Mai. With 200 companies tromping through them, there is no such thing as a non-touristed area. This doesn't mean you'll have to elbow your way through mobs of tourists, but some villages see more tourists than they might care to. Maeteang hosts the most trekkers; Chiang Dao gets the fewest because it runs along the sometimes dangerous Myanmar border. Chiang Mai's five areas encompass Akha, Lisu, Karen,

Meo, Yao, and Badong villages; Pai has primarily Lisu and Karen villages and Mae Hong Son has almost exclusively Karen ones. During the low season, it's easier for solo travelers to join a trek in Chiang Mai; in Pai or Mae Hong Son, you might need to assemble your own group or you may end up paying more.

Some Chiang Mai-based companies also run treks to **Mae Hong Son** and **Pai.** (3-day/2-night 2800฿ and 1800฿ per person, respectively; 4-person min.) If either of these locales tickles your fancy, it's better to hop on a bus and book from there, where a three-day trek will cost around 1500฿. Mae Hong Son and Pai see fewer trekkers because Pai's rivers are too low to raft in the hot season and the rivers around Mae Hong Son may become too fast to navigate in the rainy season. Mae Hong Son abuts the troubled border with Myanmar.

WELCOME TO THE JUNGLE. As of summer 1999, only 41 out of 200 trekking companies met TAT and Northern Thailand Jungle Club regulations, which include: stipulations that guides have at least 10 years experience and speak both English and some hill-tribe dialects; that all costs (e.g. food, transportation, insurance, and elephants or bamboo rafts, if offered) be included in the stated price; that treks have no more than nine participants; that the company employ men from the villages they visit as porters and charge the prices set by the Northern Thailand Jungle Club. Not every company with a Jungle Club Plaque is actually a member; many have been expelled for having three or more lawsuits brought against them. For updated information on legitimate outfits, contact the tourist police or Sangduen Chailert, the president of the Northern Thailand Jungle Club and manager of Gem Travel, 29 Charoen Prathet Rd. Soi 6 (☎272 855), which also runs treks.

In terms of specific outfits, treks run by **Libra Guest House** and **Eagle House,** 26 Ratchawithi Rd. Soi 2 (☎210 620), near Somphet market, consistently receive rave reviews. **Chiang Mai Green Tour and Trekking,** 29/31 Chiang Mai-Lampun Rd. (☎247 374), donates a portion of its proceeds to a conservation program and offers nature and bird-watching tours, as well as the more conventional "ethno-tourism" variety. All are genuine Jungle Club Plaque members.

DAYTRIPS FROM CHIANG MAI

LAMPHUN

Buses to Lamphun leave from the Chang Phuak Station in Chiang Mai and from just south of the footbridge near Wararot Market (45min.; every 15min. 6am-6pm; 7฿, with A/C 12฿). Get off as the bus passes through the walled city; the Lamphun bus station is 1km outside of town. Blue songthaew *leave from Chiang Mai-Lamphun Rd., south of TAT (every 20min. 5am-6pm, 15฿). Buses back to Chiang Mai depart from the front of the museum (every 30min. 6am-6pm).*

Tiny Lamphun, 26km southeast of Chiang Mai, offers a handful of worthwhile sights. The town's most exciting event of the year is the **Lum-Yai Festival** in July or August, celebrating the *lum-yai* (longan) season. **Wat Phra That Haribhunchai,** Lamphun's chief landmark, sits on Inthayongyot Rd. in the town center; it's the first temple on the left after you enter the walled city from Chiang Mai. Grassy grounds and little *wiharn* surround the *chedi*, crowned with a nine-tier gold umbrella. A block away is the **Haribhunchai National Museum,** with a small collection of Buddhas, bells, and other bric-a-brac. (☎511 186. Open W-Su 9am-4pm. 30฿.) Take a right (with your back to Chiang Mai) directly after the museum and continue 2km down Chamma Devi Rd. to reach **Wat Chamma Davi.** The stepped-pyramid *chedi* once had a gold coating, but thieves broke it off, giving the temple its other name, Wat Ku Kat ("pagoda without top").

Wat Phra Phut Ta Bat Tak Pah, 20km south of Lamphun, has views that rival Doi Suthep's. Except for oodles of discreet monks, you'll probably be the only one there. Before you reach the 472-step stairway, you'll pass some of the Buddha's footprints. There's an imprint of the Buddha's robe on a cliff somewhere in the vicinity. Ask a monk for guidance—like enlightenment, this print is hard to find. To get to the wat, board a *songthaew* two blocks south of the museum just off Inthayongyot Rd. to the left to Pasang (5฿). After everyone else gets off, the driver can take you the 9km to the wat for 15฿ more.

DOI INTHANON NATIONAL PARK

The 188km route from Chiang Mai to Mae Sariang along Hwy. 108 is ruggedly scenic. The drama picks up 58km away near **Chom Thong,** a convenient place to stop for access to Doi Inthanon National Park, home to **Thailand's highest peak. Buses** from Chiang Mai leave from the Chang Phuak Station (1¼hr., every 20min. 5:30am-6:30pm, 15฿). Yellow *songthaew* leave from Chiang Mai Gate when full (20฿).

From Chom Thong, *songthaew* head to the national park and glorious **Mae Klang Waterfall,** an 8km ride up to the Hwy. 1009 turn-off (10-20฿; leaves when full—which may take a while—6am-5pm). A trip to the **summit** of Doi Inthanon costs 70฿, but that wait is bound to be even longer, unless you want to charter the whole truck (100-500฿). A summit-bound *songthaew* may leave the Mae Klang Waterfall area every 2hr.; a motorbike hired in Chiang Mai can make the trip infinitely easier. The 1km path above the falls to the visitors center can also be reached by driving through the vehicle entrance, a few hundred meters past the Mae Klang turn-off.

Just above the eating spots, cross the bridge and take a left. After 1km, there's a driveway entrance into the grounds of a branch of the **Monk's College of Kamphaeng San** (Wittayalai Sung Kamphaeng San), based near Bangkok. Its hill commands a view of the surrounding mountains amid lush gardens. Just before the visitor center, a 1km path leads to **Borichinda Cave.** Guided tours can be arranged at the visitor center, which also has information and exhibits on local animal life, notably the nocturnal pangolin.

Wachiratan Waterfall is the next stop at the 20.8km mark. At the 31km mark is the elegant **Siriphum Waterfall.** The lane leading to it winds through the park's **Royal Project,** where hill tribes are encouraged to supplant opium production with strawberry and flower cultivation. The road bids farewell at Doi Inthanon's summit, 48km from Chom Thong, usually obscured by mist.

Park admission is 10฿. Motorbikes cost an extra 20฿, and cars cost 50฿. The cool season is the best time to visit. The average park temperature then is 12°C (50°F)—bring raingear, especially if you intend to climb. The park has guest houses (500-2000฿), tents (80฿), and a restaurant at park headquarters just past Siriphum Falls.

MAE SARIANG ☎053

Mae Sariang, a quiet retreat from the cities, is a base for adventurers. Cross-border teak, rice, and heroin trade with Myanmar has fueled a building boom, but it has yet to disrupt the town's drowsiness.

TRANSPORTATION. The **bus terminal** (☎681 347) is on Mae Sariang Rd., 100m north of the traffic light, opposite the gas station. Buses run to **Chiang Mai** (4hr., 4 per day 7am-1am, 69฿; A/C 1:30, 10:30am, 3pm; 124฿) and **Mae Hong Son** (4hr., 4 per day, 69฿; A/C 4 per day 10:30am-1:30am, 124฿). **Yan Yont Tours** (☎681 532) offers VIP buses from the gas station across the street to **Bangkok** (12hr.; 4, 7pm; 420฿). **Songthaew** head to **Mae Sot** (6hr., every hr. 6:30am-12:30pm, 150฿).

ORIENTATION AND PRACTICAL INFORMATION. Mae Sariang is bordered by the **Youm River** to the west and **Hwy. 108** to the east. The main roads form an "H." **Langpanit Rd.** parallels the river. **Mae Sariang Rd.** is one block east, parallel to Langpanit Rd. **Viangmai Rd.** is perpendicular, stretching from the river to the highway and intersecting Mae Sariang Rd. at the traffic light in the town center. **Sridpon Rd.,** site of the miniature morning **market,** connects Mae Sariang and Laeng Phanit Rd. one block south of the traffic light.

Services in Mae Sariang include: **Thai Military Bank,** on Wiang Mai Rd. east of Mae Sariang Rd., which has an **ATM** (Cirrus/PLUS/MC/V) and **exchanges currency** (open M-F 8:30am-3:30pm); **pharmacy,** on the corner of Sridpon Rd. and Langpanit Rd. (open daily 8am-9pm); **government hospital** (☎681 027; **emergency** ☎191) at Viangmai Rd., 200m off Hwy. 108; **police** (☎681 308), on Mae Sariang Rd. 150m south of the traffic light; and **post office,** 31 Viangmai Rd., which has an **international phone/fax** but no IDD (☎681 356; open M-F 8:30am-noon and 1-4:30pm, Sa-Su 9am-noon). **Postal code:** 58110.

ACCOMMODATIONS AND FOOD. For a resplendent setting, try the **Riverside Guest House,** 85 Langpanit Rd., 300m north of Wiang Mai Rd. From the bus station, turn right onto Mae Sariang Rd., left at the first intersection, and left again on Langpanit Rd.; it's 100m down on the right. (☎681 188. Check-out 11:30am. Bicycles 30฿. Basic singles with common baths 70-100฿; doubles 120-200฿.) **Mae Sariang Guest House,** 11 Langpanit Rd., at Viangmai Rd., has dingy ground-floor rooms. (☎621 172. Singles 50฿; doubles 80฿, with bath 100฿.)

Of all the open-air eateries along Wiang Mai Rd., the popular **Renu Restaurant,** 174/2 Wiang Mai Rd., 50m toward the highway from the traffic light, probably has the best eats. (Most entrees 40-70฿. Open daily 6am-midnight.)

THAILAND

DAYTRIPS FROM MAE SARIANG. The country around town, dotted with hill tribe villages, is perfect for walks or bike rides. Riverside Guest House posts a map of a suggested trail posted on the wall. The 6km to **Pha Ma Lo** is particularly scenic and isolated. This affluent White Karen village has a charming setting and a fine temple. Other hamlets speckle the route to Mae Hong Son, which also encounters the **Mae Surin Waterfall,** Thailand's tallest cascade. **Nam Tok Mae Surin National Park** lies 37km from **Khum Yuan,** halfway between Mae Sariang and Mae Hong Son. To get to the park, hop off when the Mae Sariang/Mae Hong Son bus stops in Khum Yuan. Catch a *songthaew* for the remaining distance in front of The Center of Local Culture, 200m toward Mae Sariang from the bus stop, across the main street. This less-traveled route might set you back 500-700฿ for a private *songthaew* ride or leave you waiting for days. **Mae Sam Laep,** 46km west of Mae Sariang, is across the river from Myanmar. (River boats depart 10am, return 3pm, 50฿. Chartered vessels 700฿.) Boats usually won't take foreign passengers aboard due to the dangers of guerrilla warfare and abduction. If you still want to explore Mae Sam Laep, *songthaew* leave Mae Sariang from just east of the bridge. From the center of town, walk south on Langpanit Rd. until it ends, turn right, and the bridge is 100m down. The first *songthaew* (1½hr., 50฿) leaves around 7am; others depart when full. The last comes back in the afternoon—ask your driver for a return time.

MAE HONG SON ☎053

The *songthaew* driver with the "Keep Mae Hong Son Small" sticker across his windshield is fighting a losing battle. While earlier this century the city was converted into a place of exile for criminals and corrupt officials, residence is now voluntary. However, more recent reports of opium smuggling and other sinister border activities can't keep tourists away from this provincial capital. Both Westerners and Thais flood the town year-round, especially during the Bua Tong Blossom Festival in November, when the local wild sunflower turns the hillsides gold.

TRANSPORTATION

Flights: Mae Hong Son Airport (☎611 367), on Nivit Pisan Rd. Turn left at the hospital at the east end of Singhanat Bumrung Rd. To **Chiang Mai** (35min.; 11:10am, 2:05, 5:05pm, with more flights in high season; 420฿). **Thai Airways,** 71 Singhanat Bumrung Rd. (☎612 220). Open M-F 8:30am-5:30pm.

Buses: 33/3 Khunlum Praphat Rd. (☎611 318). To: **Chiang Mai** (7½-8½hr.; 12 per day 7am-9pm; 94-133฿, A/C 132-240฿) via **Mae Sariang** (4hr.; 2pm; 69฿, with A/C

124฿) or **Pai** (3½hr., 4pm, 48฿; A/C 2½hr., 100฿). **Yan Yont Tour,** south of town next to the Shell station, has an A/C bus to **Bangkok** (17hr., 2:30pm, 500฿).

Rentals: Tourists may borrow free **bicycles** from the airport in the high season (M-Sa 8am-4pm); otherwise, it's impossible to find them. Numerous places around the traffic light rent **motorcycles** (150฿ per day). **Highway,** 67/2 Khunlum Praphat Rd. (☎611 620), opposite Thai Farmers Bank, rents a **Jeep 4WD** (1000฿ per day, with driver 1400฿). Open daily 8am-7pm.

ORIENTATION AND PRACTICAL INFORMATION

Mae Hong Son is 348km from Chiang Mai via Mae Sariang (Hwy. 108, the southern route), and 274km via Pai (Hwy. 107 and 1095, the northern route). Buses stop on **Khunlum Praphat Rd.,** which is home to restaurants, trekking outfitters, and motorbike shops and runs north-south through the center of town. As you turn left out of the bus station and head south, the second intersection (with the traffic light) is **Singhanat Bumrung Rd.** Another block south, guest houses dot **Udom Chao Nithet Rd.,** which borders the lake glistening with wat and *chedi* reflections.

Immigration Office: 11 Khunlum Praphet Rd. (☎612 106), 1km north of the bus station. 30-day visa extensions (1-day processing). 2 photos and 2 copies of passport required. 500฿.

Currency Exchange: Bangkok Bank, 68 Khunlum Praphat Rd. (☎611 275). Open M-F 8:30am-3:30pm. **24hr. ATM** (AmEx/MC/PLUS/V).

Markets: The **day market** is on Panit Watana Rd. next to Wat Hua Viang. Roadside stalls sell fruits and vegetables; the covered market is mainly meat. Cookies mix with hill tribe bags and Jem (of the Holograms) umbrellas in the nearby sois. The **night market** (Chang Kham Bazaar) is over-priced and lacks selection.

Emergency: Tourist Police ☎1155. **Ambulance** ☎1669. **Police** ☎191.

Police: ☎611 239. 1km south of the post office on the road to Mae Sariang.

Tourist Police: ☎611 812. At the corner of Rachatampituck and Singhanat Bumrung Rd. Helpful. Maps. **Open 24hr.**

Pharmacy: 37 Singhanat Bumrung Rd. (☎611 380). Open daily 7am-8:30pm.

Medical Services: Srisangval Hospital (☎611 378), at the end of Singhanat Bamrung Rd. English-speaking doctors. No credit cards. **24hr. emergency care.**

Telephones: Mae Hong Son Telecommunication Office, 26 Udom Chao Nithet Rd. (☎611 711), just west of Khunlum Praphat Rd. Overseas calls and fax (cash, collect, or HCD). **Lenso** phone at post office. Open M-F 8:30am-4:30pm.

Internet Access: Kai Comp, just north of the post office. 1฿ per min.

Post Offices: Mae Hong Son Post Office, 79 Khunlum Praphat Rd. (☎611 223). Open M-F 8:30am-4:30pm, Sa-Su 9am-noon. **Postal code:** 58000.

ACCOMMODATIONS

Lakeside guest houses are central, but live and loud renditions of the Beer Chang jingle make for poor lullabies.

Mae Hong Son Guest House, 295 Mucksanti Rd. (☎612 510). Turn right out of the bus station, and left on the 1st street; it's 500m away. Verdant garden and sleepy vibe. Doubles 150฿, with bath 250฿; private bungalows with bath 500฿.

Friend House, 20 Paditchangkam Rd. (☎620 119). Turn right out of the bus station, left at Bangkok Bank, and then the first right; it's 200m down on your right. Cleanest of the lakeside joints, but you might want to kill that rooster. Rooms 100฿, with shower 250฿.

Jong Kam Guest House, 7 Udom Chao Nithet Rd. (☎613 818), north of the lake. Turn left from the bus station, and take the 1st left after the traffic light; it's 250m down on the right. Breakfast. Laundry service. Walking treks to Karen village 1400฿. Rooms 100฿; bungalows of varying quality 80-150฿.

THAILAND

FOOD

Aladdin Home, on Khunlum Praphat Rd., opposite and south of the bus station, has an English menu. Try their specialty, *khao* soy, a northern Thai coconut curry noodle dish for 20฿. (Pineapple chicken 25฿. Lots of tofu dishes 20-40฿. Open daily 7am-11pm.) Stop by the **Sunflower Cafe,** Soi 3 Khunlum Praphat Rd. near the lake, at 8am for oven-fresh bread. To get there, face the post office, and follow the road's left fork 100m; it's on the left. The cafe also offers treks, a tiny book exchange, and information. (Cheesecake 25฿. Open daily 7:30am-11:30pm.)

SIGHTS

Wat Phra That Doi Kongmu, 474m above town, has a panoramic view of the city. Built in 1874, this Shan-influenced temple is Mae Hong Son's most important wat. To get there, head west on Udom Chao Nithet Rd. and turn right at the end. Look for the green pavilion on the left with a stairway to the temple entrance. Nearby **Wat Phra Non** houses a 12m Burmese-style reclining Buddha and the ashes of Mae Hong Son's kings. Get there by turning left at the end of Udom Chao Nithet Rd.

A jogging track circles **Jong Kham Lake.** Feed the fish (fish food 5฿) or visit the lake's south side to see the two famed wat. **Wat Chong Klang** is on the right, with Buddhist glass paintings and wooden dolls brought from Myanmar over 100 years ago. (Open daily 8am-6pm.) Next door, **Wat Chong Khum,** built in 1827, shines with gold-leafed pillars.

TREKKING

Mae Hong Son has some of the best trekking in Thailand—several Chiang Mai-based treks descend here. The surrounding hills support villages of Lisu, Lahu, Hmong, and Karen tribes, as well as Shan and Kuo Min Tang (KMT) zones. During low season, putting your own crew together can lower prices, since Mae Hong Son hosts fewer travelers than Chiang Mai and there aren't always organized groups. Motorbike rental and maps are available from the tourist police. **Sunflower Tours,** in Sunflower Cafe (see **Food,** above), offers butterfly- and bird-watching tours as well as treks featuring elephants, bamboo rafts, and visits to hill tribes. Owner La leads most outings (1- to 5-day trips 500฿ per person per day; 4-person min.). Treks with **Mae Hong Son Guest House,** 20 Singhanat Bamrung Rd., east of the traffic light, also receive favorable reports. (☎620 105. 3-day trek 1800฿ per person; 4-person min.)

DAYTRIPS FROM MAE HONG SON

Border politics dominate Mae Hong Son Province. The Burmese Red Karen state is across the border and further north lie various rebel camps. Trips to Myanmar are illegal and dangerous. No other city in Thailand makes it so easy to experience such an array of ethnic cultures and political backgrounds. A 150฿ motorbike ride provides access to Karen, Lisu, Hmong, and Lahu hill tribe villages, Shan towns, and KMT camps.

NAI SOI (LONG-NECKED KAREN VILLAGE)

Take a songthaew *from Mae Hong Son's day market to the Shan town (leaves when full, 30฿); then walk or hail another for the 3km to Nai Soi. Returning can be tricky; a motorbike is your best bet. 250฿.*

Travelers in Thailand can't make it as far as Mae Hong Son Province without hearing of these Burmese refugees. The women wear metal rings that crush their rib cages and collar bones down; they don't stretch their necks (see **The Plight of the Padong,** below).

THAM PLAA AND HIGHWAY 1095 TO PAI

Hop a Pai-bound bus and signal the driver to stop at the cave. 10฿.

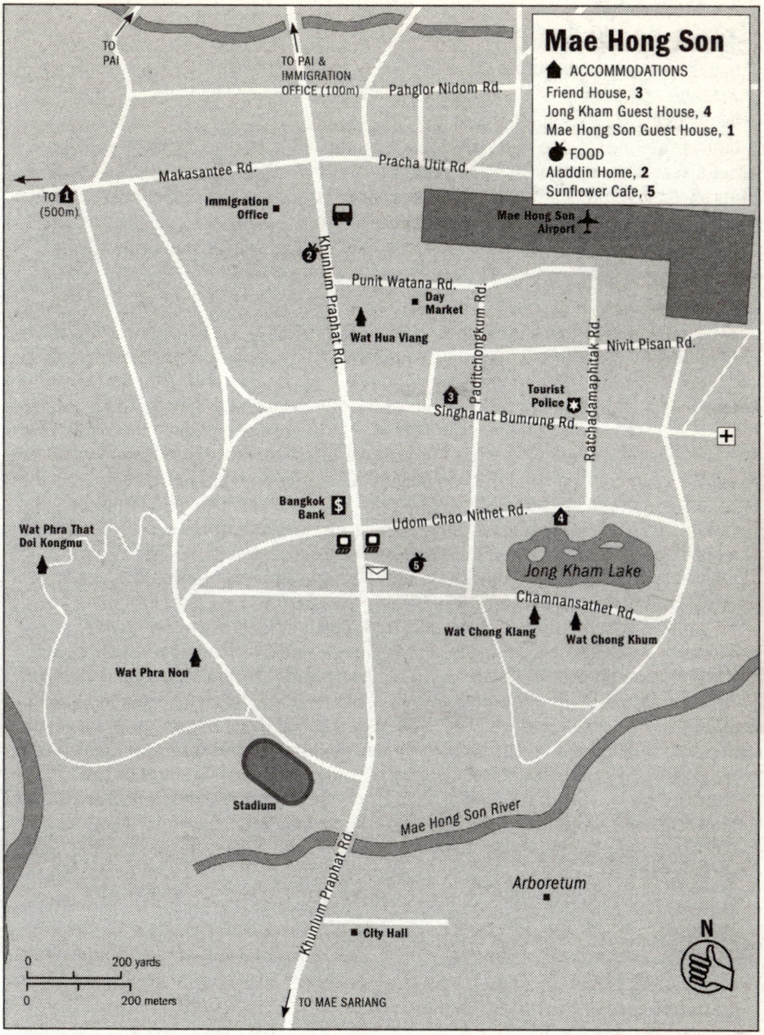

Some of Thailand's most stunning, jagged scenery adorns Hwy. 1095 between Mae Hong Son and Pai (111km). About 35km from Mae Hong Son and 20km before the turn-off to **Mae La Na** are two lone peaks. The **Sunnyata Forest Monastery** is nearby. Shan and Hmong villages, a waterfall, mountain panoramas and the KMT village of **Mae Aw** are situated on a mountaintop right on the Burmese border. You need a motorbike to make it; during the muddy rainy season it's better to have a four-wheel-drive. The Fish Cave—**Tham Plaa**—waits next to the road, 16km north of Mae Hong Son. The Shan villagers who look after the fish never catch them, believing that the spirit of the mountain guards the fish from harm. As a result of their protected status, the fish grow quite large (many more than 80cm long). Recently, a scuba-outfitted Australian camera crew penetrated the pool's depths and discovered a waterfall and an open air cavern within. Local lore has it that Japanese soldiers retreating from Myanmar buried treasure in such caverns.

THE PLIGHT OF THE PADONG A favorite subject of Thailand's postcard photographers is the Padong tribe's "long-neck woman" or "giraffe woman." At the age of five, girls in this subset of the Karen hill tribe are fitted for their first heavy brass neck ring. By adulthood, the rings have compressed the woman's collarbone and ribcage so much that her neck appears stretched. Until recently, the bizarre custom had begun dying out, but when the Karen began to flee Myanmar, enterprising Thais seized the Padong as a potential gold mine. The Padong "villages" in Mae Hong Son Province (Nai Soi primary among them) are creations of these entrepreneurs. There is no "authentic" village life in Nai Soi—just a refugee-camp-turned-tourist-trap.

SOPPONG

Buses stop in Soppong on their way between Mae Hong Son (2hr., 4 per day 10am-5:30pm, 30฿) and Pai (1½hr., 4 per day 8:30am-5:30pm, 25฿); all but the last bus continue to Chiang Mai (5½hr., 76฿).

If you've ever wanted to jump off a bus and frolic through the countryside (to, perhaps, a huge cave and underground river), Soppong's the place to live out your dreams. New Soppong skirts the highway where buses stop; old Soppong dozes along the road curving from the bus station 500m toward Pai. This road follows the 9km route to the **Tham Lod** (Lod Cave). Prehistoric remains have been found among its stalagmites and stalactites. Visitors must hire a guide at the entrance (100฿). During the rainy season, a boatman will take you across the cave's river for another 100฿ per four-person raft. During the dry season, the water's often only at knee-level and many choose to wade. (Open daily 8am-5pm.)

To get to the cave, catch a motorbike taxi (60฿) or acquire your own transportation. The posh **Little Eden,** formerly T-Rex Guest House, on the main road between the bus station and the turn-off to old Soppong and the cave, has two **motorbikes** (200฿ per day) and comfy bungalows in a riverside garden with swimming pool. (☎617 054. 250฿ low season, 350฿ high season.) **Jungle Guest House** offers a **jeep** service (seats 5, 300฿ round-trip) along with a fabulous restaurant. (☎617 099. 3-day treks 1150฿. Dorms 70฿; rooms 100฿; bungalows 200-250฿.) **Cave Lodge,** 500m before Lod Cave, features a roomy restaurant/reading room along with hiking and caving trips (350-500฿ per day) and fanless but bug-netted dorms (60฿), singles (120฿), and bungalows (150฿). Laundry service is available. The less popular **Lang River Guest House,** to the left before Tham Lod's parking lot, boasts a beautiful setting. (Dorms 70฿; singles 100฿; bungalows with bath 100฿ for 1, 150฿ for 2.)

PAI ☎053

Halfway between Chiang Mai and Mae Hong Son, Pai attracts trendy pilgrims, with good reason—the town and surrounding area are astoundingly picturesque. Pai's population is a harmonious melange of cultures and ethnicities and the town has a welcoming and gentle pace. Behind the scenes, however, a clandestine heroin and opium culture has come to the attention of local authorities, who've begun to clamp down on nefarious activities.

TRANSPORTATION

Buses: The **station** is on Chaisongkhram Rd. To **Chiang Mai** (4hr.; 8:30, 10:30am, 1, 4pm; 51฿, with A/C 71฿) and **Mae Hong Son** (4hr.; 8:30, 10:30am, 1, 4pm; 48฿, with A/C 67฿) via **Soppong** (1½hr., 25฿). To go to **Tha Ton,** take a Chiang Mai-bound bus to **Mae Malai** (3hr.; 42฿, with A/C 58฿), then take a bus to **Fang** (2½hr., every 30min. 6:30am-6pm, 35฿). Some buses continue to Tha Ton (8฿); otherwise, *songthaew* make the trip from Fang's bus station.

Rentals: Many shops along Chaisongkhram Rd. and elsewhere rent **motorcycles.** 150฿ per day. Insurance 30฿ extra.

THAILAND

ORIENTATION AND PRACTICAL INFORMATION

Pai is 136km northwest of Chiang Mai and 111km northeast of Mae Hong Son. **Hwy. 1095** cuts through town, but most traffic is channeled away from the town center, skirting the western border formed by **Ketkerang Rd.** The bus station is located in the middle of the town's northern border, **Chaisongkhram Rd.,** also home to numerous Internet cafes and motorbike rental shops. As you leave the bus station, the town's main street, **Rungsiyanon Rd.,** full of restaurants and trekking outfitters, is to your right. The **Pai River,** 400m to the left, forms the town's eastern border.

Currency Exchange: Krung Thai Bank, 90 Moo 3 Rungsiyanon Rd. (☎699 028). Open M-F 8:30am-3:30pm.

Markets: The **night market,** which sets up on Rungsiyanon Rd. between Chaisongkhram and Ratchadamrong Rd., is an eclectic assortment of transient food carts smattered with the occasional hill tribe entrepreneur. The **day market** on Ketkerang Rd., south of Ratchadamrong Rd., is nothing to email home about; it's just a bunch of plastic toys and vegetables.

Emergency: ☎191. **Ambulance** ☎699 031.

Tourist Police: On the road to Chiang Mai, after Ketkerang and Rungsiyanon Rd. merge.

Police: 72 Rungsiyanon Rd. (☎699 217), 500m south of the bus station.

Medical Services: Pai Hospital (☎699 031), on Chaisongkhram Rd. 500m west of the bus station. English spoken. **Open 24hr.**

Pharmacy: 90 Chaisongkhram Rd. (☎699 158), between Ketkerang and Rungsiyanon Rd. Open daily 6am-8pm.

Internet Access: Several around town. **Avu Internet Cafe,** at the corner of Rungsiyanon Rd. and Ratchadamrong Rd. 1฿ per min., 40฿ per hr.

Post/Telephone Office: On Ketkerang Rd. (☎699 208), south of the day market. Overseas phone. *Poste Restante.* Open M-F 8:30am-4:30pm, Sa 9am-noon. **Postal code:** 58130.

ACCOMMODATIONS AND FOOD

The number of guest houses in Pai has risen from 15 in 1944 to over 60 today. Prices are similar but qualities varies widely; check rooms before you check-in.

Blue Mountain Guest Cottages, 174 Chaisongkhram Rd. (☎699 282), is 1km to the right of the bus station past the hospital. Stellar high season restaurant. With two cats named Ham and Bacon, a dog named Mr. Falang, and an adorable white gibbon monkey who exchanges hugs for fruit, you're sure to make at least one new friend. Live music 10pm-2am. Rustic bungalows with mosquito nets 50-80฿; VIP singles with bath and fan 100-150฿.

Wee Huts, off Chaisongkhram Rd. Turn left from the bus station, then left again onto a dirt road before the second wat; it's on the left. The budget traveler's choice. Restaurant with hammocks plays an array of 1960s classics. Particularly well-kept bungalows and chatty staff. Flexible check-out. 1 person 50฿; 2 people 80฿.

Duang Guest House (☎699 101), across the road when you get off the bus. Well kept place with a tasty restaurant. Shows videos at night. Mountain bikes 80฿ per day. Singles 70฿; doubles 130฿, with bath 200฿; V.I.P. rooms with TV and fridge 400฿.

The Golden Hut (☎699 024), just after Wee Huts. Complex of bungalows and bamboo huts. Dorms 40฿; rooms/bungalows 100฿, with bath 150฿.

Hip cafes are in the center of town. For simple open-air joints, try **Ketkerang Rd.** In the evenings, head to the **night market** on Rungsiyanon Rd. Locals also recommend the noodle shop at the back left of the day market. A trendy trattoria, **Mit Thai,** 101 Chaisongkhram Rd. between Rungsiyanon and Ketkerang Rd., has an extensive vegetarian-friendly menu. (*Tom kha hed* soup of coconut milk, mushrooms, and lime leaves 30฿. Open daily 4-10pm.) **Chez Swan,** 13 Rungsiyanon Rd., just south of the Ratchadamrong Rd. intersection, is an authentic French transplant. (Quiche Lorraine 60฿. Open daily 8am-10pm.) The tastiest of the Ketkerang Rd. joints is the oddly named **Nong Beer,** 39/1 Chaisongkhram Rd. (Chicken with cashew nuts 60฿.)

SIGHTS AND ENTERTAINMENT

Wat Phra That Mae Yen has sublime views. To get there, head east on Ratchadamrong Rd. and cross the Pai River; the 360 stairs to the wat are 1km up. Continuing past the Mae Yen River leads to **hot springs,** 7km from town. In the other direction, 9km past Blue Mountain Guest Cottages, is a **waterfall** and Shan and Lisu villages. Beware of locals offering you gifts; quite a few foreigners have been ripped off and/or arrested for illegal drugs. For a less sketchy activity, **Vandee's Cooking Courses,** at Peter and Vandee's Guest House, are widely reported to be some of the best in the country. Head east out of town; it's 500m past the bridge on the way to the hot springs. **Ban Klung Pai,** 200m east of the bus station, shows English movies daily at 2:30 and 7:30pm.

The town boogies nightly to blues at **BeBop,** on Chaisongkhram Rd. between Ketkerang and Rungsiyanon Rd. Show up by 9:30pm to get a seat. (Open daily 6:30pm-12:30am. Music 9-10:30pm.) **Golden Triangle Bar and Restaurant,** on Chaisongkhram Rd. across from the first wat, is a more chill option.

THAILAND

TREKKING AND RAFTING

Trekking outfitters in Pai are diversifying. Everything from hiking to rafting to elephant rides is available, so shop around to see what suits you. **Back Trax,** 67/1 Rungsiyanon Rd., leads groups around the Pai and Soppong areas, giving 15-20% of their proceeds to the villages. Owner Chao, a member of the Lahu tribe, speaks excellent English. (3-days 1500฿. Open daily 8:30am-8:30pm.) **Duang Trekking,** at Duang Guest House, offers hiking-oriented treks that visit Karen, Lisu, and Shan villages along with several waterfalls. (2-day treks 1000฿, with rafting and elephants 1450฿; 3-day treks 1500฿, with rafting 1750฿.)

Bamboo rafting is usually only possible from November to January because Pai's rivers get rather wild in the rainy season. **Thai Adventure Rafting** (☎ 699 111), in Chez Swan Restaurant (see **Food,** above), fills the void from July to December as the only outfit permitted by the Forestry Department to camp in the National Park. By the time you've finished paddling, you're in Mae Hong Son. (Contact Guy Gorias. 2-day whitewater rafting trips along the Pai River daily July-Dec., 1800฿; 4-person min.)

THA TON ☎ 053

The scenic boat trip down the Kok River to Chiang Rai is reason enough to visit idyllic and sleepy Tha Ton. Although few visitors stay long enough to explore the ethnic villages nearby, they come in droves to stay the night. Arriving from Chiang Mai before noon allows travelers to soak up the scenery over lunch, ascend the surrounding hills, and stroll among life-size Chinese, Hindu, and Buddhist figures at Wat Tha Ton—all before hopping back onto a longtailed boat.

TRANSPORTATION. **Rte. 1089,** which continues across the river to Mae Chan 62km away, is Tha Ton's main road. Mae Salong is 43km away, Chang Rai 92km away, and Chiang Mai 175km away. Most **buses** leave from the north side of the bridge; those to **Chiang Mai** (4hr., 7 per day 6:25am-3pm, 55฿) depart from a lot 200m north of the river. Buses to **Mai Sai** (2½hr.; 9, 11am, 2pm; 27฿) stop near the police box just beyond the bus lot. For **Chiang Rai,** take a Mai Sai-bound bus to **Mae Chan** (1hr., 20฿) and wait for a connecting bus (8-15฿). *Songthaew* head to **Fang** (45min., every 10min. 5:30am-3pm, 12฿) from the morning market and to **Mae Salong** (1½hr., every 30min. 7:30am-4pm, 45฿) from a lot north of the bus station and around the bend.

Longtailed boats leave from the pier on the river's south bank for **Chiang Rai** (3-5hr., 12:30pm, 250฿). If you're coming from Chiang Mai, it's necessary to take the 6:25 or 8am bus (3-5hr., 200฿) in order to reach Tha Ton in time to catch the long-tailed boats to Chiang Rai. Reserve a seat at the **Tha Ton Boat Office** by the pier. (☎459 427. Open daily 9am-3pm.) Chartered private craft (seats 6, 1600฿ including guide) won't leave after 3pm, as the ride is dangerous in the dark.

PRACTICAL INFORMATION. While there are no banks or exchange booths, **Tha Ton Tour** at Chankasem Guest House near the pier might exchange small sums. A **morning market** sets up 200m south of the bridge and leaves a fruit stand behind for the rest of the day. (Open daily 5:30-7:30am.) The closest **hospital** (☎459 036) is in Mae Ai, 7km south. In an emergency, call your guest house or the **tourist police** (☎1155) for transportation; ambulances are slower. A **tourist police box** is just before the pier (open 24hr.). There are **no overseas telephones. Tha Ton Internet** (1฿ per min.) is across the street from the pier on the south side on the bridge. A **post office** sits on the main road opposite the entrance to Wat Tha Ton. (Basic postcard and letter service only. Open M-F 8am-4:30pm, Sa 8am-noon.) **Postal code:** 50280.

ACCOMMODATIONS AND FOOD. Most budget digs rest on the Kok's south side while resorts clog the north bank. Affordable **Thip's Travelers House,** just south of the bridge, is run by the lovable English-speaking Mrs. Thip. (☎617 054. Restaurant open daily 7am-9pm. Laundry. Singles with private cold showers 80-100฿; doubles 100-150฿.) **Apple Guest House** has bungalows in two locations. To reach the affordable ones, head south from the bridge and take the first left; it's on the right several hundred meters down. (☎459 315. Mountain bikes with helmet 80฿. Singles 100฿; bungalows 150฿, with hot shower 250฿.) **Tha Ton Garden Riverside** has fabulous bungalows with Western toilets and hot showers in a manicured garden along the river. To get there, walk straight through the lobby of Tha Ton Chalet, between the river and where the Chaing Mai buses drop you off. While you're there, try the *tom yam* soup with shrimp for 50฿. (☎459 286. Restaurant open daily 7am-10pm. English menu. Bungalows 200-300฿.) The best food in Tha Ton is in the open-air joints by the river.

SIGHTS AND ACTIVITIES. Wat Tha Ton dominates the hillside above Thip's Travelers House. The temple features life-size representations of figures from Hindu, Buddhist, and Chinese mythology hidden away in man-made caves, as well as fantastic views of the town and countryside. A visit to the two huge Buddhas is 20฿, but exploring the complex's other scenic areas costs nothing but a climb. The easiest route up the hill begins at the arch across the road from the post office. When you reach the fork in the path marked by the full-fed figure, turn left for the massive golden dragon-headed Buddha, or right for the 12m tall white Buddha.

The Mae Kok River originates in the mountains of Myanmar's Shan states, enters Thailand above Tha Ton, and flows 200km to meet the Mekong River in Chiang Saen. **Bamboo rafting** to Chiang Rai (a 3-day excursion) is a quiet, leisurely method of exploring villages along its banks. The Akha town of **Mae Salak** is the biggest you'll pass; it serves as a starting point for journeys south into the Wawi area, home to numerous Lahu, Lisu, Hmong, Akha, Karen, and Yao hamlets. **Phatai** is a Black Lahu village on the north bank. **Jakue** has numerous Lahu products for sale and a Catholic missionary school. **Pha Khang** has picturesque mountains, and **Pha Keau** has steep cliffs. The stop everyone makes is **Ruammit,** 45min. from Chiang Rai, a large Karen village that offers elephant rides (300฿ per hr.). From there, it's another 20min. to the **Temple Cave. Tha Ton Tour** (☎373 143), at Chankasem Guest House, offers floats (3-days, 1800฿ per person) and treks to Chiang Rai (2-day raft and boat trek, 1500฿ per person; 3-day Akha and Lalu village trek and boating 2000฿ per person; elephant rides 300฿ per hr.). **Thip's Travelers House** (☎459 312) leads bamboo raft trips down the Mae Kok (3-days, 2200฿ with an elephant ride) and is conscious of eco-tourism issues. All prices assume at least four participants.

CHIANG RAI ☎053

Chiang Rai has always played second fiddle to its southern neighbor, Chiang Mai. The rivalry began when King Mengrai built Chiang Rai in 1262 and used it as command central for three decades before switching allegiance to Chiang Mai. Besides offering a stunning landscape and quality guest houses, Chiang Rai also features a night market (that stocks a wider array of tribal handicrafts than the infamous larger Chiang Mai market) and a hill tribe museum. Basking in the poppy glow of the Golden Triangle, the city also serves as an ideal base for treks to villages in the mountains near the Myanmar border.

TRANSPORTATION

Flights: Chiang Rai International Airport (☎798 000), 9km out of town on Hwy. 110. To **Bangkok** (1¼hr.; 9:40am, 12:45, 3:30, 8:50pm; 1970฿) and **Chiang Mai** (40min.; 8:40am, 7:45pm; 450฿). **Thai Airways,** 870 Phahonyothin Rd. (☎711 179), 1 block south of Teepee Bar. Open M-F 8am-noon and 1-5pm.

Buses: Chiang Rai Bus Station (☎711 224), Phahonyothin Rd., opposite the night market. To: **Bangkok** (12hr., 5 per day 7:30am-8pm, 241฿; 2nd-class A/C 7 per day 4am-7:15pm, 337฿); **Chiang Mai** (3½hr., 11 per day 6:45am-5:30pm, 66฿; A/C 13 per day 7am-5pm, 119฿); **Chiang Saen** (2¼-3hr., every 45-60min. 5am-5:45pm, 39-46฿); **Khon Kaen** (13hr.; 5, 9am, 4pm; 226฿; 2nd-class A/C 2pm, 316฿) via **Phitsanulok** (6hr.; 125฿, A/C 175฿); **Lampang** (5hr., every 20min. 5:20am-3pm, 95฿); **Mae Sai** (1½hr., every 15min. 6am-6pm, 20฿); **Mae Sot** (10hr., 7:20am, 176฿; A/C 9:20am, 246฿) via **Lampang** (6hr.; 95฿, A/C 176฿); **Nakhon Ratchasima** (12hr., 3:30pm, 240฿; 1st-class A/C 6:20am, 1, 5:30pm; 432฿; VIP 7pm, 504฿) via **Phitsanulok** (6hr., 125฿); **Nan** (6hr., 9:30am, 90฿); **Pattaya** (16hr., 4 per day, 280฿; A/C 510฿); **Phitsanulok** (8hr.; 7:30, 9:30am; 139฿; A/C 8:30, 10:30am; 195฿) via **Sukhothai** (6hr.; 122฿, A/C 171฿).

Boats: Leave from pier near Dusit Island. To **Tha Ton** (4hr., 10:30am, 200฿) via **Ruammit** (45min., 45฿).

Local Transportation: Songthaew, tuk-tuk, and **samlor** cluster on Uttarakit Rd. around the market. Fares in city 10-20฿. Within 10-15km radius, *songthaew* and *tuk-tuk* should cost under 50฿; trips to airport up to 100฿.

Rentals: Practically every guest house rents motorcycles at similar prices (150-200฿). **Soon Motorcycle,** 197/2 Trirath Rd. (☎714 068), also rents cars. Reduced rates for longer rentals. Open daily 8am-6pm.

ORIENTATION AND PRACTICAL INFORMATION

The **Kok River** flows west to east, forming Chiang Rai's northern border. **Singhaklai Rd.,** site of the TAT office and guest houses, skirts the river. The northern part of town lies between Singhaklai and **Banphraprakan Rd.,** 500m south and parallel to it. The most helpful landmark, the **Haw Nariga** (clock tower), stands in the middle of Banphraprakan Rd. **Jet Yod Rd.,** steaming with food, leads south from there. **Phahonyothin Rd.,** with the bus station and night market, runs parallel one block east.

Tourist Offices: TAT, 448/16 Singhaklai Rd. (☎744 674). Receptive and organized office. Offers free maps (with bus schedules), brochures, trekking and regional info. English spoken. International calling card phone available. Open daily 8:30am-4:30pm.

Currency Exchange: Thai Military Bank, 870/12 Phahonyothin Rd. (☎715 657). Open daily 8:30am-9pm. **ATM** (Cirrus/MC/PLUS/V). Open M-F 6am-10pm.

English-language bookstores: Siam Used Books, 169/157 Pamavipat Rd. Large selection of new and used books. Open daily 9am-9pm.

Emergency: ☎1155 or 191. **Ambulance** ☎711 366.

Police: Chiang Rai Provincial Police Station (☎711 444), on Rattanakhet Rd. near Singhaklai Rd. 1 block east of the TAT.

Tourist Police: ☎717 779. Downstairs from the TAT. **Open 24hr.**

Medical Services: Overbrooke Hospital, 444/3 Singhaklai Rd. (☎711 366), 250m west of TAT. **24hr. pharmacy.** AmEx/MC/V.

Telephones: Telecommunications Office (☎776 738), on Ngam Muang Rd. at the west end of town. Telex, fax, overseas calls. Open daily 7am-10pm. AmEx/MC/V.

Internet Access: Chiang Rai Cyber Net, 869/147 Pamavipat Rd. (☎752 090), between Jet Yod and Phahonyothin Rd. 30฿ per hr., 10min. minimum. A couple of 15฿ per min. places can be found on Sanambin Rd., south of Banphraprakan Rd.

Post Offices: 486/1 Mu 15 Uttarakit Rd. (☎711 421), 150m south of the TAT and 250m north of clock tower. HCD phone booth. *Poste Restante.* Open M-F 8:30am-4:30pm, Sa-Su and holidays 9am-noon. **Postal code:** 57000.

ACCOMMODATIONS

Over 30 guest houses and hotels have opened since a tourist boom hit Chiang Rai, and many boast excellent values. The best ones are located outside the city center, allowing them to be quiet and spacious and worth the 20min. walk or 20฿ *tuk-tuk* to reach them. Check out is usually between 11-11:30am and all have hot water.

Ben Guest House, 351/10 Sankhongnoi Rd., Soi 4 (☎716 775). Call ahead for a free pickup, or head west on Banphraprakan Rd. from the clock tower, turn left at the first traffic signal onto Sanambin Rd., right on Sankhongnoi Rd., right again on Soi 4, and walk to the end. Rooms in tip-top shape. Laundry facilities and periodic massage courses. Singles with shared hot water bath 80฿, with private bath 120฿; doubles 160฿, new wing (with carpet) 200฿, with A/C 450฿.

Chat House, 3/2 Sangkaew Rd. (☎711 481), down the soi directly across from Overbrooke Hospital. Cheap and quiet. Laundry facilities. Offers treks. Comfortable patio. Low season bargaining. Doms 50฿; singles 70฿; doubles 120฿, with A/C 250฿.

Chian House, 172 Koh Loh Rd. (☎/fax 713 388). From the TAT, head east past Rattanakhet Rd. intersection; take next left (onto Koh Loh Rd.), cross bridge and then follow signs. Owner speaks excellent English. Bonuses include restaurant and swimming pool. Laundry 25฿ per kg. Internet 1.50฿ per min. Motorbike rental 150-500฿. Singles 100฿; doubles 120-220฿; bungalows 250฿, with A/C 350฿.

Pintamorn Guest House, 509/1 Rattanaket Rd. (☎714 161). A 5min. walk on Phaonyothin Rd. from the bus station. Backpacker central. 24hr. kitchen big on Western food (cheeseburger 50฿). Cable TV and pool table on the patio. Free luggage storage. Book ahead. Singles 75฿, with private bath 135฿; doubles 90/165฿.

Mae Hong Son Guest House, 126 Singhaklai Rd. (☎715 367), 100m east of TAT. Perks include a bar, laundry service (35฿ per kg), and motorbike rental 150-500฿. Experiment with cooking classes (650฿ per day). Singles/doubles 100฿, with bath 175฿; triples 150฿.

FOOD

Chiang Rai's culinary scene is concentrated in the neighborhood bounded by Jet Yod, Banphraprakan, and Phahonyothin Rd. Guest house kitchens are another alternative; **Chian House** has particularly tasty food (try the baguette sandwiches).

Cabbages and Condoms, 620/25 Thanalai Rd., downstairs from the Hill Tribe Museum. C&C Chiang Rai raises money and awareness for the AIDS campaign. *Tom-yam* 60-70฿. Condoms are free and work better than cabbages. Open daily 11am-midnight.

Golden Triangle Restaurant, 590 Phahonyothin Rd., at Golden Triangle Inn. Thai dining with an English menu. Various curries, rice dishes, and noodles. Delicious *gaeng kiaw wan* (green sweet curry) 45-60฿. Open daily 7am-10pm.

Red Pepper Food Center, 868 Phahonyothin Rd. Thai and Yunnanese food. English menu with pictures. Sizzler chicken with pineapple 100฿. Open daily noon-9pm.

THAILAND

Napoli Pizza, 595/1 Phahonyothin Rd. Pastas, pizza, steak, ice cream 60-80฿ per person. Open daily 3:30-10:30pm.

La Cantina, 1025/40 Jet Yod Rd. High quality Italian food in a relaxing atmosphere. 150-200฿ per person. Open daily 9am-11pm.

SIGHTS

According to local lore, the *stupa* of **Wat Phra Kaew,** originally known as Wat Pa Yier, was struck by lightning in 1434 and revealed an Emerald Buddha; the temple's name changed to "Wat of the Emerald Buddha" as a result. Today, the original sits in Bangkok's Wat Phra Kaew, at the west end of town on Trirat Rd. opposite Overbrooke Hospital, and a new image, commissioned in China and carved from Canadian jade in 1991, sits in its place.

At the west end of town, walking from Trirat Rd. past Chat House, rests **Wat Ngam Muang** on top of the hill of the same name. Its *stupa* contains King Mengrai's ashes and relics.

The **PDA Hill Tribe Museum,** 620/25 Thanlai Rd., 150m east of Phahonyothin Rd., isn't nearly as informative as the one in Chiang Mai. The 25min. slide show on the region's different tribes will give you the basics if you can keep from cracking up when you realize the background music is "Don't Cry For Me Argentina." (☎740 088. Open M-F 8:30am-8pm, Sa-Su 10am-8pm. 50฿.)

THAILAND

ENTERTAINMENT

Take shelter from rented love at **Teepee Hippie Happy Bar,** 542/4 Phahonyothin Rd., just south of Banphaprakan Rd. It's an American West decor shop, hosts an occasional acoustic blues band (after 10pm in high season), and offers a vegetarian menu. (Open daily 11am-5pm and 6:30pm-1am.) Head to expat bar **New Moon Cafe,** 1014/2 Jet Yod Rd. and drain a few Carlsbergs (35฿); the fourth one's free. Chang Beer is an unprecedented 30฿ per glass. (☎714 637. Open daily 8am-10pm or midnight.) Across the street on Jet Yod Rd., an endless row of bars sit next to each other, with comparable music and atmosphere. The disco/bar/karaoke complex at the **Par Club** in the Inn Come Hotel, 172/6 Rajbamrung Rd., is accessible by *songthaew* or *tuk-tuk*. (☎717 850. No cover for foreigners. Open daily 9pm-1am.)

MARKETS

The **day market** is a massive affair encompassing an entire square block, the northeast corner of which nips at the post office on Uttarakit Rd. Lots of vegetables and fresh fruit (pineapple 10฿) roadside are on the north end along Uttarakit Rd. Food vendors hawk everything from soup to noodle dishes to french fries. Inside is a winding maze of, well, everything. Bakeries sit next to tailors next to pharmacies, next to wide selections of plastic combs. The only consistency can be found at the south end, which is full of dead cows, pigs, and fish. The **night market** has a massive amount of hill tribe products on the soi leading to the bus station off Phahonyothin Rd. Following it leads to a wider variety of tapestries, intricately carved boxes, hand bags, instruments, head dresses, and Hello Kitty lights. A great selection of food (fruit shakes 15฿, papaya salad with seafood 30฿) surrounds a courtyard on your left at the end of the soi, and there's a stage where traditional hill tribe music is played 8-10pm daily.

TREKKING

Chiang Rai's bucolic province—full of ethnic hill tribes—offers trekking routes less traveled than those around Chiang Mai. As always, trek prices should include food, transportation, and an informed guide. Typical treks run 3 days/2 nights (2-4 people around 3000฿ per person; 5-7 people around 2500฿ per person; see TAT's pam-

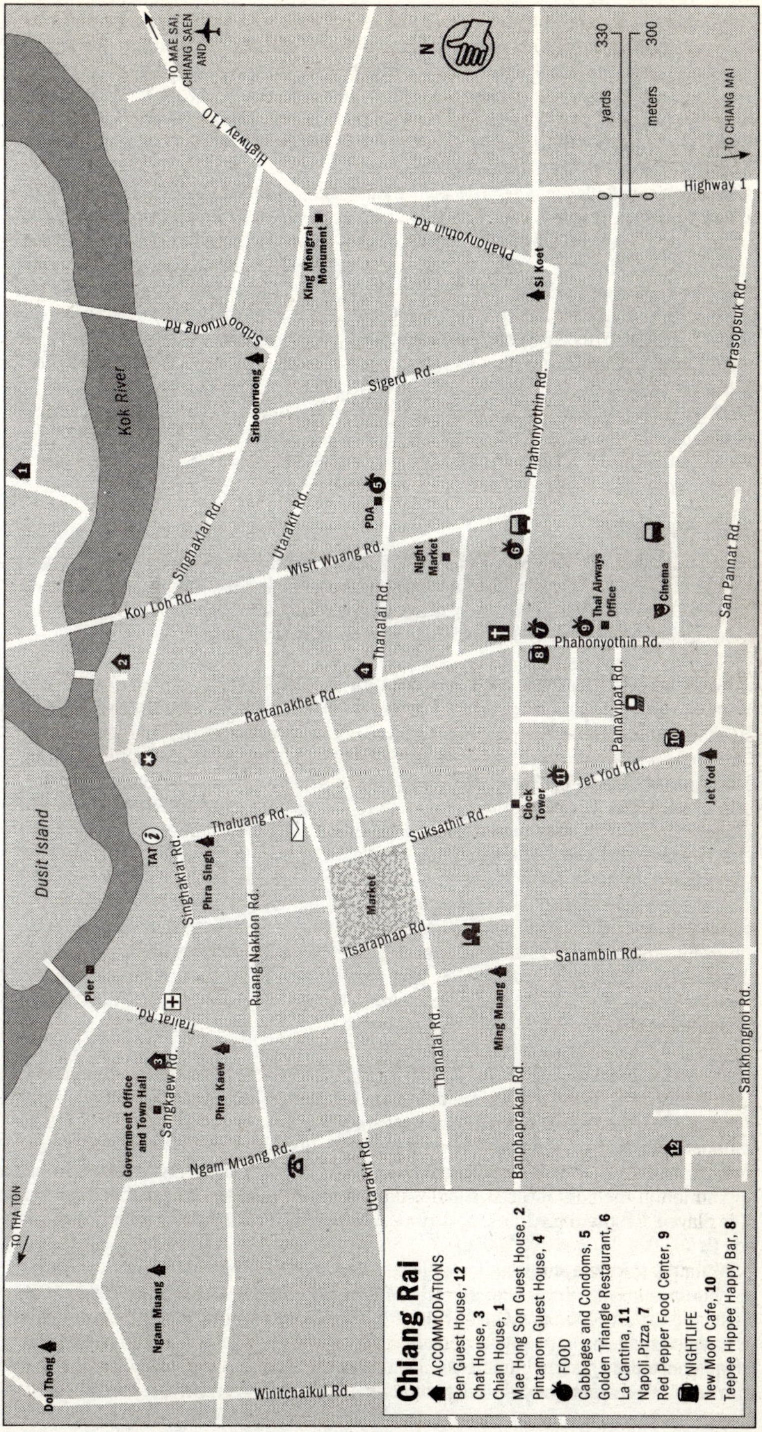
Chiang Rai
ACCOMMODATIONS
Ben Guest House, 12
Chat House, 3
Chian House, 1
Mae Hong Son Guest House, 2
Pintamorn Guest House, 4
FOOD
Cabbages and Condoms, 5
Golden Triangle Restaurant, 6
La Cantina, 11
Napoli Pizza, 7
Red Pepper Food Center, 9
NIGHTLIFE
New Moon Cafe, 10
Teepee Hippee Happy Bar, 8
N
330
yards
0
300
meters
0
TO MAE SAI, CHIANG SAEN AND
TO CHIANG MAI
TO THA TON
Highway 110
Highway 1
Kok River
Dusit Island
King Mengrai Monument
Phahonyothin Rd.
Si Koet
Sriboonruang Rd.
Sriboonruang
Sigerd Rd.
Prasopsuk Rd.
Singhaklai Rd.
Utarakit Rd.
PDA
Wisit Wuang Rd.
Koy Loh Rd.
Night Market
Thai Airways Office
Cinema
San Pannat Rd.
Thanalai Rd.
Rattanakhet Rd.
Pamavipat Rd.
Jet Yod Rd.
Jet Yod
Clock Tower
Suksathit Rd.
Thaluang Rd.
TAT
Phra Singh
Market
Itsaraphap Rd.
Ruang Nakhon Rd.
Sanambin Rd.
Pier
Trairat Rd.
Ming Muang
Phra Kaew
Sankhongnoi Rd.
Banphaprakan Rd.
Government Office and Town Hall
Sangkaew Rd.
Ngam Muang Rd.
Ngam Muang
Doi Thong
Winitchaikul Rd.

THAILAND

phlet), but you can do as short as a day or as long as a week. Many companies have access to horses, elephants, rafts, mountain bikes, and plain old hiking boots; mix and match your itinerary and then consider which hill tribes you'd like to visit, as they're vast and varied in the area. Finally, make sure you like your guide, because your life, fun, and money are in his hands. If you're considering a service that's not listed below, check their status with the TAT. Tours to Laos or Myanmar may be illegal, so check that with the TAT, too.

Population and Community Development Association (PDA), 620/26 Thanalai Rd., which funds rural development, family planning, and AIDS education/treatment/prevention programs among hill tribes, offers treks and one-day tours. If all you crave is to see the world from atop an elephant, the PDA has daytrips to Ruammit (the Karen elephant camp), which stop at a waterfall and some Yao and Akha villages. Company treks are pricier than those run out of many guest houses (see below). PDA also accepts volunteers for many of its health-related projects. If interested, bring a resume and plan to wait a week. In addition, **Ben's Guest House, Chat House,** and **Chian House** all run flexible treks with guides who are registered with the TAT. (PDA: ☎/fax 740 088. 3-day/2-night trek to Lahu and Akha villages, including elephant and longtail boat rides, 2200฿ per person, minimum 4 people or 3000฿ per person, minimum 2 people. Daytrips to the Golden Triangle 1000฿ per person, minimum 4 people or 1900฿ per person, minimum 2 people.)

MAE SALONG ☎053

Fifty years after the Kuo Min Tang (KMT) 93rd Division fled China after the Communist victory and settled in this mountaintop village, Mae Salong maintains its Chinese identity. Chinese characters adorn doorframes, tea houses feature red-lanterns, and the Yunnanese language is more common than Thai.

TRANSPORTATION AND PRACTICAL INFORMATION. *Songthaew* are frequent early in the morning and leave when full; you can pay the full fare (300฿) if the wait is unbearable. To get to Chiang Rai, take a *songthaew* to Ban Pasang (1hr., 7am-2pm, 50฿), and then flag down a passing bus (1hr., every 30min. 6am-6pm, 20฿). *Songthaew* to **Tha Ton** (1½hr., 7am-2pm, 60฿) leave from the small **day market,** 1km toward Tha Ton from the town center. The market features Akha wares and Chinese herbs. The **main road** through Mae Salong is a continuation of roads from Tha Ton and Mae Chan; the Khumnaiphol Resort marks the Tha Ton end, the Mae Salong Villa marks the Mae Chan end. The town center is near the guest houses and has daytime **food vendors** and a **mosque.** Starting before dawn, locals mingle at the **morning market** off the road to the Mae Salong Resort, on the road that leads directly under Shin Sane Guest House. The market also has a **Thai Military Bank.** (☎765 159. Open M-F 8:30am-3:30pm. **ATM** open daily 6am-10pm.) A few part-time **police** have a booth near the Mae Salong Villa. The nearest **hospital** is in Mae Chan. There are **no international phones.**

ACCOMMODATIONS AND FOOD. **Shin Sane Guest House,** off the main road near the mosque, is the most popular among travelers. The owner distributes useful maps (10฿), arranges one-day horse treks (400฿), and speaks English. (☎765 026. Laundry 100฿ per kg. Singles 50฿; doubles 100฿; bungalows with bath 300฿.) Next door, family-style **Akha Mae Salong Guest House** has huge rooms with wood floors and common bath. (☎765 103. Singles/doubles 100฿.) **Golden Dragon,** between the Mae Salong Resort and Akha Guest House, has peaceful bungalows with hot showers. (☎765 009. Rooms 200-300฿.)

Yunnanese noodle shops and noodle vendors abound (5฿ per serving). Tea shops provide a relaxing ambience; a kettle of Mae Salong tea soothes for 100฿. **Mini,** 300m west from Shin Sane Guest House, serves *khanom jun naam ngiaw* (Yunnanese noodle soup), the town specialty. (Beer 65฿. Open daily 7am-10pm.) **Chinese Islam Noodle Shop,** on the main road 250m past the supermarket, has a small selection of Chinese dishes and an English menu. (Open daily 8am-9pm.)

SIGHTS. For an awesome view, follow the road to the Mae Salong Resort and walk up the steps to the **pagoda.** From here, a road continues 4km through mountain scenery and finally curves back into town through the day market. Area hill tribes include **Akha, Lahu,** and **Lisu,** and in smaller numbers, **Hmong** and **Yao.** There aren't many organized trekking groups, although the intrepid can set off alone. Pick up a map at Shin Sane Guest House (10฿), but don't wander too far; in addition to hill tribe villages, pockets of Shan and KMT groups line the Burmese border. Drug trade and clashes have erupted between Khun Sa's Shan United Army and the Wa National Army. Ask in town about the current situation. The walk-weary can inquire about 4hr. **horseback riding treks** at Shin Sane or Akha Mae Salong Guest Houses (400฿ per person).

BORDER INTRIGUE The Golden Triangle, opium capital of the world, produces 70% of the world's heroin. In addition, the Golden Triangle's *yaba*—a methamphetamine often coated in chocolate—has caught on with teenage users as a cheap alternative to opium and heroin. Drug money is the lifeblood of impoverished hill tribes and nearby paramilitary organizations. The drug mystique has resulted in flourishing tour companies, which fill buses with tourists eager to get a whiff of the intrigue. Trekkers with addicted guides are often convinced that opium is an integral part of tribal culture. Although opium was used in tribal medicines as a pain killer, opium use today is considered shameful in most villages.

MAE SAI ☎053

One of Thailand's main links with Myanmar, Mae Sai is a bustling border town during the day, but turns into a ghost town after 5pm when the border shuts down. With a burgeoning gem trade stemming from a recently discovered sapphire mine in the Shan State and an established opium trade, Mae Sai's future as a trade center looked bright—until a full scale three-way battle broke out in February 2001 among the Shan, Thai, and Burmese troops, causing the border to close for four months. Aside from the border intrigue, spelunkers can find impressive caves and national parks near Mae Sai's center.

TRANSPORTATION

Buses and Songthaew: Mae Sai Bus Terminal, 5km south of bridge along Phahonyothin Rd. Green *songthaew* head there every 10min. To: **Bangkok** (14hr.; 7am, 4:30, 5:30pm; 441฿); **Chiang Mai** (5hr.; 4 from 6-9:30am, 1:45, 3:30pm; 83฿, with A/C 149฿); **Chiang Rai** (1½hr., every 15min. 6am-6pm, 20฿) via **Ban Pasang** (30min., 15฿), where *songthaew* go to **Mae Salong** (1hr., leave when full 7am-2pm, 50฿); **Nakhon Ratchasima** (13¾hr., 5 per day 5:15am-6pm, 464฿); **Pattaya** (14hr., 5 per day 5:15am-6pm, 530฿). South of Thai Farmers Bank, blue *songthaew* go to **Chiang Saen** (1hr., every hr. 7am-2pm, 30฿) via **Sop Ruak** (40min., 20฿).

Local Transportation: Motorcycle taxis and **samlor** smother Mae Sai. Rides within the city 10-30฿. Green *songthaew* go up and down Phahonyothin Rd. (5฿).

Rentals: Thong (☎732 815), on Silamjoi Rd. near Porm Charern Minimart, rents **motorcycles.** 150฿ per day. Open daily 8am-5pm.

ORIENTATION AND PRACTICAL INFORMATION

Mae Sai is 61km from Chiang Rai, 68km from Mae Salong, and 35km from the Golden Triangle. Hwy. 110 ends at the **border crossing. Phahonyothin Rd.** hosts a dusty carnival of *farang*, Thais, and Burmese who browse, bargain, and beg at the street stalls. **Silamjoi Rd.** jogs along the river, heading west from the Friendship Bridge toward guest houses.

Tours: King Kobra Guest House, 135/3 Silamjoi Rd. (☎733 055). Regional treks and excursions to Laos and Myanmar.

Immigration Office (☎733 261), on Phahonyothin Rd., 2km south of bridge. 10-day visa extension 500฿; 1-month visa extension for 60-day tourist visas. Open daily 8:30am-4:30pm. For a cheaper option, see **Border Crossing: Mae Sai/Thachilek,** p. 718.

Currency Exchange: All along Phahonyothin Rd. **Thai Farmers Bank,** 122/1 Phahonyothin Rd. (☎640 786). Open M-F 8:30am-3:30pm. **24hr. ATM** (AmEx/MC/V).

Markets: During the day, stalls line Phahonyothin Rd.–check out the base of the bridge for herbs, gems, teak, and flowers; move 400m south for a good fruit selection. Food stalls set up at night near the bridge. Large market on the right of the bridge (as you cross to Thachilek) with stereos, dresses, and gems.

Emergency: ☎191.

Police: ☎731 444. On Phahonyothin Rd. 200m south of bridge. Call Tourist Police first.

Tourist Police: ☎733 850. In a booth next to the bridge. Open daily 8am-5pm.

Medical Services: Mae Sai Hospital, 101 Mu 10 Pomaharat Rd. (☎642 510), off Phahonyothin Rd. With your back to Myanmar, head 2km south; turn right into the soi just after the overpass; hospital is 400m down.

Telephones: Mae Sai Telecommunications Center, next to the post office. **Fax.** No HCD. Open M-F 8:30am-4:30pm. **LENSO** phone at the 7/11 200m south of the bridge.

Internet Access: Take the last right before the bridge, look for the sign leading to the 2nd fl. 20฿ per 30min.; 30฿ per hr.; free coffee after 2hr. Open daily 9am-9pm.

Post Offices: Mae Sai Post and Telegraph Office, 230/40-41 Phahonyothin Rd. (☎731 402), 4km south of the bridge and despite the address, not on the main road. Open M-F 8:30am-4:30pm, Sa-Su 9am-noon. **Postal code:** 57130.

ACCOMMODATIONS AND FOOD

Mae Sai Guest House, 688 Wiengpangkam Rd. (☎732 021), 30ft. from Myanmar at the end of Silamjoi Rd. Idyllic escape with thatch-decorated bungalows, hot water, restaurant, and laundry service. Singles 100฿; doubles 200฿, with bath 300-400฿.

King Kobra Guest House, 135/5 Silamjoi Rd. (☎733 055). Owner Joe gives border and travel info and offers motorcycle treks to Northern Thailand, Myanmar, and Laos. Restaurant, laundry service, and Internet. Singles 80฿, with bath 150฿; doubles 120/200฿; "VIP" room 350฿.

Chad Guest House, 52/1 Soi Wiengpan (☎732 054), off Phahonyothin Rd., 1km south of bridge. Quiet, cheap rooms with shared toilet and shower. Dorms 50฿; singles 100฿; doubles 150฿.

The **night market** along Phahonyothin Rd. has dishes on display, so a quick "point and shoot" will get you what you want. (Open daily 7-10pm.) Pamper your palate at **Jo Jo Coffee House,** 233/1 Phahonyothin Rd., opposite the Thai Farmer's Bank. Bitter melon soup with white gourd on rice is 35฿; curries and "Jelly Boys" are 30฿ each. (Open daily 7am-5pm). Going down the soi directly opposite Thai Farmer's Bank leads to a series of stands with tables that specialize in pad thai (20฿).

DAYTRIPS FROM MAE SAI

Tham Luang National Park (Great Cave) lurks 5km south of Mai Sai 2½km off Hwy. 110. Its caverns burrow 200m into the mountain. Other caverns in the National Park include the **Buddha Cave** and the 7km-deep **Royal Luang Cave.** (Open daily 6am-6pm.) At the other end of the National Park is **Khun Nam Nang Non** (Sleeping Lady Lagoon). Its undulating rock formations are said to resemble a reclining woman. Bring a flashlight.

Two more caves are inside **Wat Tham Pla,** 12km south and 3km west of Mae Sai along Hwy. 110. *Samlor* along the highway will take you for 20฿. Fresh water

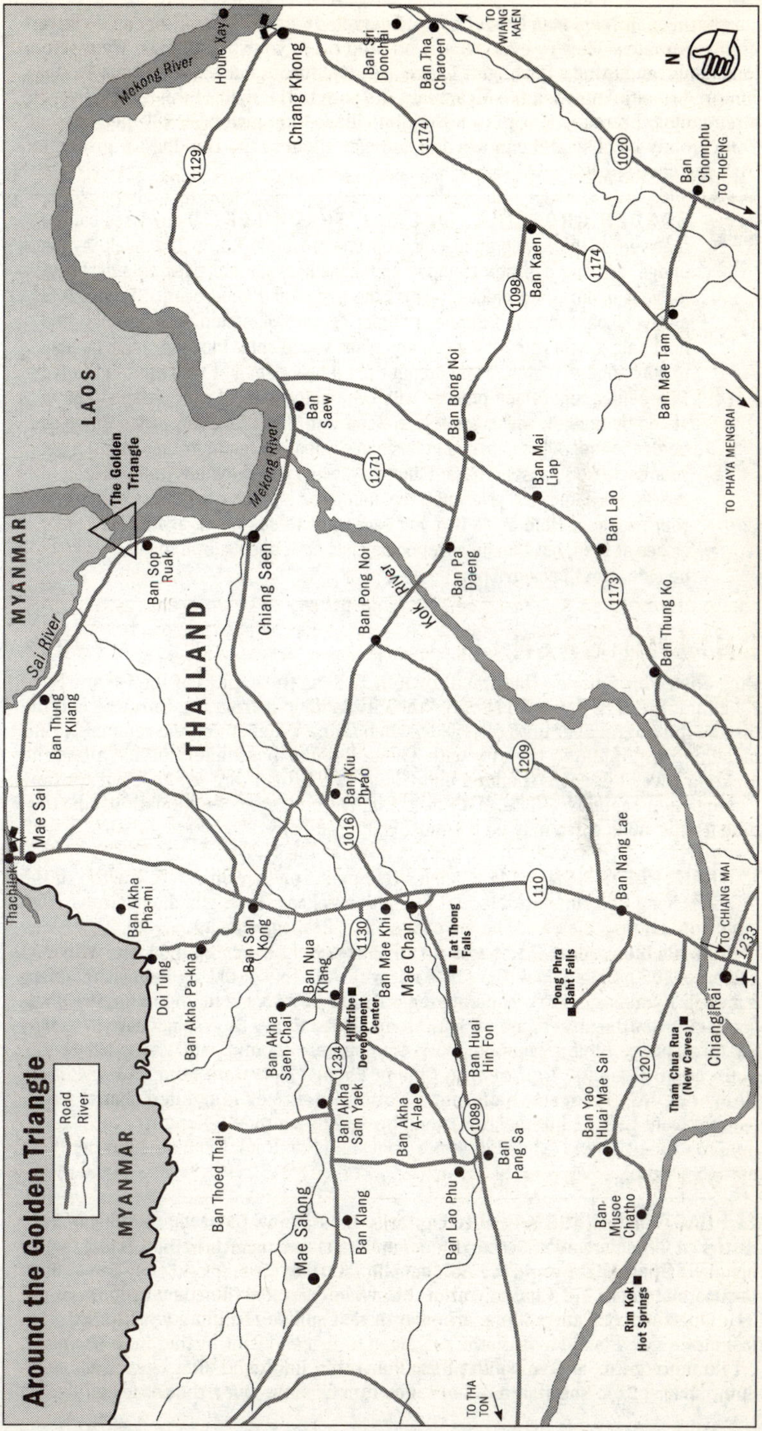
Around the Golden Triangle
Road
River
MYANMAR
LAOS
THAILAND
The Golden Triangle
Mekong River
Sai River
Kok River
Mae Sai
Thachilek
Ban Thung Kliang
Ban Sop Ruak
Chiang Saen
Ban Saew
Chiang Khong
Houie Xay
Ban Sri Donchai
Ban Tha Charoen
TO WIANG KAEN
N
Ban Chomphu
TO THOENG
Ban Kaen
Ban Mae Tam
TO PHAYA MENGRAI
Ban Bong Noi
Ban Mai Liap
Ban Lao
Ban Pa Daeng
Ban Pong Noi
Ban Thung Ko
Ban Kiu Phrao
Ban Nang Lae
TO CHIANG MAI
Chiang Rai
Ban Akha Pha-mi
Doi Tung
Ban Akha Pa-kha
Ban San Kong
Ban Nua Klang
Ban Mae Khi
Mae Chan
Tat Thong Falls
Pong Phra Baht Falls
Hilltribe Development Center
Ban Akha Saen Chai
Ban Akha Sam Yaek
Ban Akha A-lae
Ban Huai Hin Fon
Tham Chua Rua (New Caves)
Ban Yao Huai Mae Sai
Ban Thoed Thai
Ban Pang Sa
Ban Lao Phu
Ban Musoe Chatho
Mae Salong
Ban Klang
Rim Kok Hot Springs
TO THA TON
1129
1174
1020
1098
1271
1173
1209
1016
110
1130
1234
1089
1207
1233

surges through **Tham Plaa** (Fish Cave), also called "Monkey Cave" because of gamboling primates. They're everywhere, so hold on to your belongings. Wear boots, long pants, and bring a flashlight. The more adventurous can explore **Tham Gu Gaeo,** rumored to ultimately lead to Myanmar. The path to the right of the temple leads to attendants who take visitors to a Buddha village 2km away (50-70฿ per person). You can buy incense and candles and dedicate them to the Buddha for protection from the cave spirits.

BORDER CROSSING: MAE SAI/THACHILEK. 30-day visas can be renewed at the immigration office on Phahonyothin Rd. in Thachilek. At the bridge, get your passport stamped and make sure you are given an arrival card for your return. Then proceed across the bridge and hand over US$5 or 250฿ and your passport. The Burmese border control will stamp your passport and hold onto it until you exit the country. When you re-enter Thailand, you'll be able to stay another month. If you do not want a new visa, give your passport to the Thai border control and proceed with two photocopies of your passport (3฿ at stores by bridge), which you'll give along with US$5 or 250฿ to the Burmese border control. All stamps are in this copy; when you return to Thailand, you get your unmarked passport back. Either way, when you surrender your passport to the Burmese, they will give you a very thin piece of paper—that piece of paper is your passport. **Hold on to it if you ever want to see home again.** The border closes at 6pm, but Thai immigration officials have been known to leave early; to be safe, cross back by 5pm.

CHIANG SAEN ☎053

King Saen Phu founded this small town in 1328 as the capital of the Chiang Saen Kingdom. In 1803, Rama I destroyed the city to keep it from the Burmese and the district did not recover until the 1880s, when Rama V kicked out the remaining Burmese and repopulated the city with Thais. Regular passenger service along the Mekong River between Thailand and China may bring more *farang*, but for now Chiang Saen remains sedate. With no attractive budget accommodations, daytripping to this small town may be the most cost efficient.

TRANSPORTATION. Chiang Saen's two main roads form a "T." The top of the "T", **Rimkhong Rd.,** runs north-south along the **Mekong River,** which separates Thailand from Laos to the east. The tail of the "T" is **Phahonyothin Rd.**

From Phahonyothin Rd., **buses** go to: **Bangkok** (12½hr.; 3pm, 261฿; with A/C 4:20pm, 470฿); **Chiang Mai** (6hr., 8:40am, with A/C 150฿); **Chiang Rai** (1½hr., every 30min. 5:15am-5pm, 20฿). The booking office (☎650 822) is in an unmarked house set back from the street east of Siam Commercial Bank. Blue **songthaew** go to **Mae Sai** (1hr., every 40min. 7am-5pm, 30฿) via **Sop Ruak** (20min., 10฿) from across the main road. Green *songthaew* to **Chiang Khong** (2hr., 9am-3pm, 50฿) wait on Rimkhong Rd., 150m south of Phahonyothin Rd. Pricey longtailed **charter boats,** leaving from the "T" intersection, head up and down the Mekong from 8:30am to 6pm to Chiang Khong (2hr., 1200฿ per boat) and Sop Ruak (40min., 400฿ per boat, up to 6 people).

PRACTICAL INFORMATION. Opposite the **National Museum,** the **Chiang Saen Historical City Information Center** offers free maps and an exhibit on Chiang Saen's history. (Open M-F 8am-4pm.) A **24hr. ATM** (AmEx/Cirrus/MC/PLUS/V) is at **Siam Commercial Bank,** 773 Phahonyothin Rd., which also exchanges currency. (☎777 041. Open M-F 8:30am-3:30pm.) The **day market** spills onto Phahonyothin Rd. 75m from the river. Plastic toys on the road lead to fish and fruit further in. A **pharmacy,** on Rimkhong Rd., is 50m south of Phahonyothin Rd. (☎777 019. Open daily 8am-8pm.) **Chiang Saen Hospital** (☎777 017) lies 1km from the river; the **police** (☎793 783) are at the "T" intersection. Gin Guest House has overseas **phones** (20฿ charge). **Fun Fun Internet,** 500m on your left before the museum approaching from the river, has access for 1฿ per min. Along the same road, several places offer motorbike (180฿) and bicycle (70฿) **rentals.** The **post office** is 600m from the river. (☎777 116. Open M-F 8:30am-4:30pm, Sa-Su 9am-noon.) **Postal code:** 57150.

ACCOMMODATIONS AND FOOD. With the river to your back, walk west on Phahonyothin Rd. and turn right before the post office. Just past a bank 100m down on the right, is **J.S. Guest House,** with cozy and quiet rooms with fans and common bath—Chiang Saen's best deal. (☎777 060. Dorms 60฿; singles 100฿.) **Gin Guest House,** on Rimkhong Rd., has collect or credit card international calls (20฿ service charge), but is far. Day hikes are pricey (2400฿ for 1-4 people) and include car and driver but not food, rafting, or elephant riding. (☎650 847. Rooms with fan, bug nets, and hot showers 200฿). **Chiang Saen Guest House,** 45 Rimkhong Rd., just before the wat, papers the walls of its restaurant with "green" editorials. (Concrete singles 70฿; doubles 100฿; twins with bath 150฿).

In the evenings, **food stalls** appear on the **boardwalk** by the Mekong, north of Phahonyothin Rd. (pad thai 25฿). Stalls congregate on **Rim Khong Rd.** 300m south of the "T." *Paw pia thawt* (spring rolls) are great. Those without tongues of steel may want to order dishes *mai champ phèt* (not spicy).

SIGHTS. **Chiang Saen National Museum** is on Phahonyothin Rd., 500m from the river, at the entrance to the city closer to Chiang Rai . Along with a life-size model of a *plaa beuk* (giant Mekong catfish), the museum has a well-done exposé on the nuances of hill tribe cultures and costumes. (☎777 102. Open W-Su 9am-5pm. 30฿.) Next door, a 13th-century brick *chedi* dominates **Wat Chedi Luang,** the tallest Lannathai monument at 58m. **Wat Pasale** is outside the ancient city wall, 200m west of the river. The ornate *chedi* isn't as impressive, but its bucolic location ("Pasale" means "of the teak forest") makes it a pleasant stop. (Open daily 8am-6pm. 30฿ entrance fee.) **Wat Chom Kitti's** hilltop, several kilometers southeast of the city, offers a compelling view of Laos and the Mekong. **Chiang Saen Lake,** a bird-watching site, is a 7km ride southwest.

DAYTRIP FROM CHIANG SAEN: SOP RUAK (GOLDEN TRIANGLE). Sop Ruak may be its official name, but most refer to the confluence of the Sai River and the wider Mekong where Myanmar, Laos, and Thailand meet as **Sam Liam Tongkham (Golden Triangle).**

Songthaew bound for **Mae Sai** (45min., 20฿) and **Chiang Saen** (15min., 10฿) pass through the center of town between 7am and 2pm. Longtail **charter boats** seat up to 6 people and leave from various spots along the river to **Chiang Khong** (2hr., 1500฿) and Chiang Saen (50min., 400฿). Golden Triangle boat rides tour the area (300฿ for 40min.; boats accommodate 1-6 people). The few guest houses that existed have been bulldozed in anticipation of the boom expected to hit the region, now named the **Golden Quadrangle** after the addition of China, resulting in a lack of budget hotels.

In the middle of town, the **House of Opium** features exhibits on the history of opium with pipe and scale displays, and a diorama of a drugged-out old man. (☎784 062. Open daily 7am-7pm. 20฿.) Next door, **Siam Commercial Bank** runs a **currency exchange** booth which accepts all traveler's checks and has MC/V cash advances. (☎784 191. Open daily 9am-5pm.) For a view capturing the three countries, head up the five-dragon-headed staircase to the right of the bank, then follow the road behind the wat up the hill to the viewpoint.

CHIANG KHONG ☎053

Chiang Khong is the archetypal border town. There are no museums, parks, or interesting shops, but a dozen banks line Chiang Khong's dusty main street and wait for tourists en route between countries and currencies. The premiere attrac-

> **THE FRUIT OF HER LOINS** A unique Thai legend provides insight into why the Thai believe that people should smoke tobacco rather than opium. The story goes that an old woman died for no apparent reason. To symbolize the confusion that surrounded her death, she was buried under a busy intersection in her home town. Passersby noticed that three flowers grew from her grave. Tobacco leaves grew from her breasts and opium grew from her genitalia. People, in their natural curiosity, tried both and most liked tobacco better. Wise elders explained that this was no surprise since the tobacco smokers were simply looking for a substitute for their mother's breasts. They declined to comment on what this implies for opium smokers.

tions of Chiang Khong are rest and relaxation. Many guest houses overlook the majestic Mekong and afford alluring views of greener Laos. The engaging surroundings may leave delayed travelers content during the wait.

THAILAND

TRANSPORTATION. **Buses** leave the **station** (☎655 732) and nearby areas beyond the bridge heading away from town. To: **Chiang Mai** (6hr.; 6:30am, 108฿; with A/C 11am, 151฿); **Chiang Rai** (3hr., every hr. 4:30am-5pm, 46฿); **Chiang Saen** (2hr., 7am, 40฿). Buses also leave from Soi 13. **Songthaew** to and from Chiang Saen (2½hr., 8am-noon, 40฿) gather near Soi 3. A few companies run private buses to **Bangkok** from the stops near the bridge, including **999** (7am and 4pm, 450฿); **Karuhart** (4pm, 450฿); **Sombat Tours** (4:30pm, 450฿). The nicest buses are run by **Siamfirst** (4pm; 450฿, VIP 525฿), opposite Thai Farmers Bank. Tickets go quickly; buy a seat in the morning to guarantee an afternoon bus.

PRACTICAL INFORMATION. Chiang Khong is 144km northeast of Chiang Rai and 55km southeast of Chiang Saen. The main drag, **Saiklang Rd.,** runs northwest to southeast, parallel to the Mekong River. Numbered soi run perpendicular to the main road. **Soi 1,** home to the guest houses, is at the northwest end of town; **Soi 13** is at the southeast end near the immigration office. For info, books, and a place to meet fellow backpackers, visit the new **Traveler Corner,** 17/3 Ban Wat Kaew T. Wiang, run by friendly "Apple." It's opposite Ann Travel near Soi 2. (☎655 374. Open daily 9am-5pm.) The **Immigration Office,** next to Soi 13, issues visa extensions for 500฿. (☎791 332. Open M-F 8:30am-noon and 1-4:30pm.) You'll need to go to a tour agency for Laos visas. The **police station** (☎791 426) is next door to the Immigration Office. The **Thai Military Bank** is near Soi 7. (☎655 738. Open M-F 8:30am-3:30pm, **ATM** open daily 7am-10pm.) **Boonchai Pharmacy** is across the street. (☎791 013. Open daily 7am-8pm.) A few hundred meters northwest (toward Soi 1), the **post office** has an international **phone.** (☎791 555. Open M-F 8:30am-4:30pm, Sa-Su 9am-noon.) **Chiang Khong Hospital,** 354 Moo 10, is 3km outside of town. Go straight south on Hwy. 1020 toward Chiang Rai. (☎791 206. Some English spoken. No credit cards. **Open 24hr.**) **Postal code:** 57140.

ACCOMMODATIONS AND FOOD. The best place in town is the new **Bamboo Riverside Guest House,** 71 Huaviang Rd., 75m northwest of Soi 1. In a peaceful spot along the Mekong River, it has a great restaurant with Mexican food, fresh baked bread, and a guitar-playing proprietor. (☎791 621. Dorms 70฿; singles 100฿; bungalows 150฿; doubles with bath 200-250฿.) **Ban Tammila,** by Soi 2, has bungalows with private showers and sells some of the craziest hammock/tent devices you've ever seen for 1200฿. (☎/fax 791 234. Laundry. Bicycle rental 150฿. Bungalows 200-400฿.) **Hua Wiang Country Guest House,** 150m past Bamboo, has cheaper, less romantic rooms. (☎791 134. Dorms 50฿; singles 120฿; doubles 150฿.)

Noodle-and-rice shops line Saiklang Rd. You can find tasty food at Bamboo Riverside Guest House, or head to Ban Tammila's restaurant for an amazing view, vegetarian menu, and small prices for large portions. (Mostly 35-40฿. Open daily 7am-8:30pm.) At **Rimkhong,** by the river between Soi 7 and 9, the freedom from *farang* comes at a price. (Partially translated menu. Green curry 50฿. Open daily 8am-midnight.) **Teepee,** by Soi 2 on Sarklang Rd., plays Bob Marley by day, holds jam sessions by night, and serves fabulous tofu dishes (fried tofu with cashews 60฿).

BORDER CROSSING: CHIANG KHONG/HOUIE XAY. The ferry (20฿) across the Mekong takes less than 15min.; all you need is a visa, available at most guest houses. Alternatively, try **Traveler's Corner** (☎655 374; open daily 8am-4pm) or **Ann Tour** (☎655 198; open daily 7:30am-7:30pm), which both have offices on Saiklang Rd. near Soi 2. Unfortunately, 1-day visas are no longer available. 15-day visas are 1100฿ with a 2-day wait and 800฿ with a 4-day wait. 30-day visas are 1800฿ with a 2-day wait and 1500฿ with a 4-day wait. Going through a guest house instead of a travel agency may raise the price 100฿. To avoid probable delays (up to four-day processing), arrive with a visa obtained in **Bangkok.** Once in Houie Xay, catch a speed boat (6-9hr., 8am-2pm, 950฿), or a slowboat (2 days, 10:30am, 450฿) to **Luang Prabang.** If you do the latter, pack food and water for a whole day. As Laos currency fluctuates constantly, check current exchange rates next to immigration as you enter Laos. Special boats may be organized out of Chaing Khong that make stops along the Mekong for those who want to see more—ask at Travelers' Corner.

SIGHTS. **KMT Cemetery** is 1km out of town on Hwy. 1129 at the top of the big hill on the left. Although the gate is often locked, the caretaker lets visitors explore during daylight; the barking dogs will alert the caretaker of your presence. Ask at guest houses about bike rides to **Hmong villages,** though they may prove inaccessible in the rainy season. In April and May, **Haadkhrai** hosts the annual giant catfish competition. Laos and Thai boats alternate turns trawling the river in search of the 200kg beasts. Only a few are caught every year. To get here, head south out of town, take a left at the Esso service station with the police box in front. Walk 1km to Soi 31 and on to the river. **See Don Chai** is a Lu handweaving village 14km south of the city. Showrooms are scarce and their hours fickle, but poke your head into any house and ask if you can watch for a while. Take a motorcycle south out of town; when you see the 60km stone marker, you're in the town. Alternately, take a Chiang Mai/Chiang Rai-bound bus and tell the driver where you want to get off.

NAN ☎054

Hidden amidst the mountains on the outskirts of the Lanna Kingdom, Nan developed a unique culture and history and remained a semi-autonomous principality until 1931. During the 1960s and 70s, the region's isolation made it a haven for smugglers and the communist rebels of the People's Liberation Army of Thailand (PLAT). Today Nan's seclusion provokes nothing more threatening than frequent shouts of "I love you" from children unfamiliar with *farang.* Doi Phukha National Park beckons explorers, while the superb museum and mural-bedecked wat provide relaxation, and the isolation itself lends a romance to this renegade town.

TRANSPORTATION

Flights: Nan Airport (☎771 729) is on Worawichai Rd., 4km from town center. **Thai Airways,** 34 Mahaphrom Rd. (☎710 377). Open M-F 8am-5pm. Flies to: **Bangkok** (W, F, Su 12:50pm; 1560฿); **Chiang Mai** (M, Tu, Th, Sa 3:05pm; 550฿); **Phrae** (M, T, Th, Sa 11:25am; W, F, Su 12:50pm; 330฿).

Buses: The **bus station** (☎710 737) is on Ananthaworarittidet Rd. To: **Chiang Mai** (6-7hr., 8 per day 7:15am-10:30pm) via **Lampang** (4hr.; 71฿, 2nd-class with A/C 120฿); **Chiang Rai** (blue bus; 5hr., 9am, 90฿); **Pua** (orange bus; 1½hr., every hr. 5am-6pm, 20฿). Other buses arrive and depart from **Khao Luang,** two blocks north of Ananthaworarittidet Rd. To: **Bangkok** (10-13hr., 10 per day, 351-545฿); **Phitsanulok** (5hr.; 7:45, 9:45, 11:45am, 1:45pm 127฿; 6:30pm 165฿); **Sukhothai** (4½hr., 2nd-class with A/C 8:30am, 300฿).

Rentals: Oversea, 488 Sumonthewarat Rd. (☎710 258), at Mahawong Rd. **Mountain bikes** 30฿ per day; **motorcycles** 150฿ per day. Open daily 8am-5:30pm.

ORIENTATION AND PRACTICAL INFORMATION

Buses from the north arrive at the station on **Ananthaworarittidet Rd.,** which runs roughly east-west (perpendicular to the Nan River) through the center of town. **Mahawong Rd.,** a block south, passes the **post office** and goes over the town's bridge. **Suriyaphong Rd.,** flanked by the **police station, City Hall,** and many sights, is two blocks south. The **Nan River** acts as the town's east border and flows four blocks east of the northern bus station. **Sumonthewarat Rd.,** running north-south through the town center, is the primary thoroughfare. Parallel to and one block east is **Khao Luang Rd. Pha Kong Rd.,** which hosts the **night market,** is parallel and two blocks west of Sumonthewarat Rd. The **Dhevaraj Hotel,** a useful point of reference, rests on Sumonthewarat Rd. halfway between the intersections with Ananthaworarittidet and Mahawong Rd.

Tourist Information: In City Hall on Suriyaphong Rd. (☎751 029). Little English spoken. Free maps and pamphlets.

Currency Exchange: Thai Farmers Bank, 434 Sumonthewarat Rd. (☎710 162), has a **24hr. ATM.** Open M-F 8:30am-3:30pm.

Emergency: ☎191.

Police: 52 Suriyaphong Rd. (☎751 033), opposite City Hall.

Pharmacy: 347/5 Sumonthewarat Rd. (☎710 452), opposite Thai Farmers Bank. Open daily 8am-9pm.

Medical Services: Nan Provincial Hospital (☎710 138), on Sumonthewarat Rd., near the bend 3km north of downtown. *Songthaew* leave from the Nara department store, one block north of Dhevaraj Hotel (5฿). **24hr. emergency care.**

Telephone: Telecommunications Office (☎773 214), Mahayod Rd., 2km outside town has phones, Internet, and fax. Open M-F 8am-6pm, Sa-Su 9am-4pm.

Internet access: At the intersection of Mahawong Rd. and Mayahot Rd. **Cybernet,** 328-330 Mahayot Rd., is the best bet. 20฿ per hr. Open daily 8am-midnight.

Post Office: GPO, 70 Mahawong Rd. (☎710 176), west of Sumonthewarat Rd. *Poste Restante.* Open M-F 8am-noon and 1-5pm, Sa-Su 9am-noon.

THAILAND

ACCOMMODATIONS AND FOOD

PK Guest House, 33/12 Premphachraj Rd. (☎751 416). Walk north on Sumontherarat Rd. 1km and make a left after the school; it's down the 2nd soi on the right. Brand new rooms and a charming fountain with fish. Laundry. Shared Western toilets and bath. Wacky singles in oxcarts 100฿; doubles 150฿; triples 200฿; VIP 250฿.

Nan Guest House, 57/16 Mahaphrom Rd. (☎771 849), a 10min. walk from the bus station. Turn left onto Ananthaworarittidet Rd., walk past the market to the intersection with Pha Kong Rd., turn right, and walk 2 blocks. Turn right at Wat Hua Khuang and follow the road until the gravel soi. Centrally located. Great coffee. Laundry 5-10฿ per piece. Rooms 70-120฿.

Amazing Guest House, 25/7 Soi Snow White (☎710 893), 150m past the PK Guest House on the left. Spacious rooms and an intimate environment in the family's teak house. Singles 100฿; doubles 160฿; triples 210฿. Prices drop with longer stays.

Tanaya Kitchen, 75/23-24 Anathaworarittidet Rd., is one block beyond Pha Kong Rd. from the bus station on the right. The friendly owner has maps, a bilingual menu, and bakes great potato bread for 10฿. (Open daily 7:30am-8:30pm.) **Ristorante Da Dario** (☎710 636), next to Amazing Guest House is a little piece of Italy. (Spaghetti pesto Genovese 100฿. Open daily 10am-2pm and 5-10pm. Closed August.)

SIGHTS

The **Nan National Museum,** at the Suriyaphong and Pha Kong Rd. intersection, features informative exhibits on Nan's history and Thailand's hill tribes and has a revered black elephant tusk. (☎710 561. Open daily 9am-4pm. 30฿.)

Across the street is **Wat Phra That Chang Kham,** which houses a walking Buddha made of gold. The 400-year-old **Wat Phumin,** on Pha Kong Rd. south of the museum, contains murals depicting the culture of the Lanna people.

Wat Phra That Chae Haeng, the oldest temple in the region at nearly 700 years old, projects its distinctive golden *chedi* 2km beyond the Nan River bridge. The zoo to the left of the temple has a **statue** of Sa Jao Wang Tao Kha Khaong, the first king of Nan. Southwest of town, **Wat Phra That Khao Noi** offers sweeping views of the valley. Go west on Suriyaphong Rd. to Hwy. 101 and turn right after the bridge. The wat is on top of a hill 2km down the road.

Back in town, the **Thai Payap Project** sells hill tribe **handicrafts** from 15 villages in its showroom on Jettabut Rd. Follow the road directly opposite the Dhevaraj Hotel through the market; it's 400m down on the right. The project also has a new "home stay" project in which travelers may live and work with a family in one of two villages. All proceeds go to community development projects in the surrounding areas. (☎772 520. Open daily 8:30am-5pm.)

MARKETS

A spacious **produce market** sets up in the soi directly opposite the Dhevaraj Hotel with several counters with over 20 dishes which you can point at and buy by the bag (10-15฿). Along Anathaworarittidet Rd. next to the northern bus station is the **day market,** which is big on pineapples and really, really small turtles. The small **night market** on Anathaworarittidet Rd. outside the 7/11 starts around 6pm. Cheap noodle and rice standards are 20฿. Food gets sketchier around the corner on Pha Kong Rd., but there's a fabulous fruit stand at the end of the stalls.

DAYTRIPS FROM NAN

Few travelers get a glimpse of Nan's mountainous back country. Nan is now safe; a few mines remain buried in the most remote areas, but the risks are negligible, especially on roads or trails. Of greater danger is the chance of getting lost due to the lack of English signs—try to bring the names of your destination in writing. **Fhu Travel Service,** 453/4 Sumonthewarat Rd., south of the intersection with Mahawong Rd., leads expeditions around the province. A trek with Mr. Fhu is the only way to visit the **Mrabi** (Phi Tong Lueng, "Spirit of the Yellow Leaves"), a tribe found only in Nan and Phrae provinces. (☎710 636. 1-day trek 700฿ with 4 or more people, 1200฿ with 2 people. 3-day trip 2700฿.)

DOI PHUKHA NATIONAL PARK AND SAPAN WATERFALL

Take Hwy. 1080 from Nan (past an Esso station on the left) for 60km to Pua. Here, turn right just before the market, then left 100m up the road at the English sign for the park. The road stretches 47km over a mountain peak through the park to Ban Bor Kleua. Songthaew, which leave from Pua's market for Ban Bor Kleua, can drop you at the park office (8am, 30฿); others leave infrequently throughout the day. Once you're at the park, there's not much to do without private transportation. To loop back from Ban Bor Kleua, head south to Ban Phak Heuak, then west on Hwy. 1081. Swerve south after Ban Huai Lek Lai (the hilly route) or just before Ban Nam Yao (the flat route), then right onto Rte. 1257 from either, then left onto 1169, which heads south to Nan. Orange buses speed to Pua from the bus station in Nan (1½hr., every hr. 5am-6pm, 20฿).

Doi Phukha National Park, home to Hmong and Mien tribes, has dozens of waterfalls and caves. The **park office** (☎01 602 9844), 25km up the road, can sometimes provide accommodations; call the National Park Division of the Forestry Service in Bangkok first (☎02 579 0529). **Camping** in the park is free and tents are available, but temperatures freeze in the cool season.

A few kilometers past the park office is the prized **Chomphu Phukha tree** *(Bretschneidera sinensis)*. Though not the world's only specimen (as locals tend to claim), it is still extremely rare. The tree blooms in February, and hordes of Thais come to see it. Turn left off the highway and north from Ban Bor Kleua and a road leads to **Ban Sapan,** 10km away. After crossing the bridge just before the village, turn right onto a dirt road to reach the **Sapan Waterfall,** off the road to the right, marked by a red Thai sign and a smaller English one.

LAMPANG ☎054

Lampang's history dates back to the 7th-century Dvaravati period, when it played an integral role in the Lanna Kingdom of the "Million Rice Fields." Like other northern cities, it clings to its heritage; unlike other northern cities, it has little to which to cling. Domestic and foreign tourists alike pass up Lampang's overpriced flower-decked horsecarts and unimpressive Wang River on their way north.

TRANSPORTATION

Flights: The **airport** is on Sanambin Rd. **Thai Airways,** 236 Sanambin Rd. (☎217 078). Open daily 8am-6pm. To **Bangkok** (10:05am, 3:25, 5:30pm; 1980฿).

Trains: Lampang Railroad Station (☎318 648), on Prasanmaitri Rd. To reach the station, flag down a westbound *songthaew* (10-20฿). Trains to: **Bangkok** (10-12hr.; 6 per day; 2nd-class 284฿, 3rd-class 146฿) via **Phitsanulok** (5hr.; 2nd-class 151฿, 3rd-class 88฿) and **Ayutthaya** (9hr.; 2nd-class 261฿, 3rd-class 135฿); and **Chiang Mai** (2hr.; 9 per day; 2nd-class 53฿, 3rd-class 23฿).

Buses: The **bus station** (☎227 410) is off Asia 1 Hwy., several kilometers out of town. All prices listed are with A/C. To: **Bangkok** (8hr., 2nd-class 7 per day, 246฿); **Chiang Mai** (2hr.; every 30min. 2am-9pm; 34฿, 2nd-class 61฿); **Chiang Rai** (5hr., every 45min. 5am-4pm, 71/99฿); **Khorat** (10hr.; 9:30, 11:30am, 8pm; 190/342฿); **Nan** (4hr., 6 per day, 71/99฿); **Sukhothai** (4-5hr., every hr. 8am-9pm, 81/113฿) via **Phitsanulok** (4hr., every hr., 75/135฿); **Udon Thani** (7:20, 9:30am, 2pm) via **Loei** (8½hr., 176/246฿).

Local Transportation: Blue **songthaew** go anywhere in town (10฿)–flag one down on any major street. Trips to the bus and train stations 5-10฿ more. **Samlor** usually cost around 50฿.

THAILAND

ORIENTATION AND PRACTICAL INFORMATION

Most roads radiate from the **clock-tower rotary** near the town center. **Boonyawat Rd.** heads east, passing hotels, banks, and shops. In the opposite direction, **Tah Krao Rd.** runs past the **Aswin Market. Suren Rd.,** off Thakhraonoi Rd., runs to the **train station. Chatchai Rd.** branches out from the station toward the **Wang River** and intersects **Thipchang Rd.,** a commercial avenue parallel to Boonyawat Rd. The **bus station,** off **Asia 1 Hwy.,** is on **Jantsurin Rd.** 2km from the traffic circle.

Tourist Office: ☎218 823. On Boonyawat Rd., just past Praisanee Rd. Go in the gate where the horse carriages line up. It's not either of the "tourist info" places by the clock tower. Free maps and little else. Open daily 8:30am-4:30pm.

Currency Exchange: Banks line Boonyawat Rd. **Bangkok Bank,** 36-44 Thipchang Rd. (☎228 135). **24hr. ATM** (AmEx/Cirrus/MC/PLUS/V). Open M-F 8:30am-3:30pm.

Markets: Large and lively. **Tesaban Market 1** sets up opposite city hall along Praisanee Rd. Dresses, fruit, and underwear in abundance. Watch out for passing motorcycles as you browse. **Aswin Market** is off the traffic circle on Tah Krao Noi Rd. Both are open daily 6am-7pm. **Night food stalls** move in at 7pm and have cheap food until midnight.

Police: ☎221 589. On Boonyawat Rd. opposite City Hall.

Medical Services: Khelang Nakorn-Ram Hospital, 79/12 Thanon Phaholyotin Rd. (☎352 422). **Open 24hr.** AmEx/MC/V.

Telephones: At the GPO. Overseas calls/fax. Open daily 8:30am-4:30pm.

Internet Access: Several places are scattered around the city. **Cyberland,** 258/13-14 Thipchang Rd., is cheap (20฿ per hr.). Open daily 10am-1am.

Post Office: GPO (☎323 497), on Thipchang Rd. Follow Boonyawat Rd. to City Hall and then turn left on Praisanee Rd. *Poste Restante.* Open M-F 8:30am-4:30pm, Sa-Su 9am-noon. **Postal code:** 52000.

ACCOMMODATIONS AND FOOD

Riverside Guest House, 286 Talad Gao Rd. (☎227 005). From the clock tower, walk along Boonyawat Rd. with the river on your left, turn left onto the soi with the sign to the guest house. It's 2 blocks down, where the soi curves. Relaxing veranda over the river. Laundry. Tours of surrounding sights 350฿. Singles 200฿; doubles 250-350฿.

TT&T Guest House, 55 Pahmai Rd. (☎225 361). From the town center, go east on Boonyawat Rd. across the Khelang bridge on the left, take an immediate left; it's 150m on the left. Basic rooms. Bicycles (40฿) and motorbikes (300฿) for rent. Internet. Dorms 80฿; singles 120฿; doubles 200฿.

9 Mituna (Gao Mituna), 285 Boonyawat Rd. (☎217 438), on the 1st block from the clock tower. Clean rooms with hot water and fan. A/C rooms have bathtubs and western toilets. Singles 143฿, with A/C 286฿; doubles 204฿, with A/C 300฿.

Terrace Riverview Restaurant, 4/1 Wank Kua Rd., along the river by the Wang Koa Bridge offers a menu of Thai and Western food that matches the size of its massive patio. (Club sandwich 50฿. Thai entrees 30฿.) **Chom Wang Restaurant,** 276 Talad Gao, serves Thai standards on a peaceful teak patio. (Open daily 5-11:30pm.)

THAILAND

SIGHTS

Wat Phra Kaew Don Tao, in the northeast corner of town, housed the Emerald Buddha during the reign of King Anantayot (r. 1436-68). A building to its left has a golden Buddha. The *wiharn* is open to visitors on Buddhist holidays only. (Wat open daily 6am-6:30pm.)

Despite the dry name, **Lampang Medical Plants Conservation Center** (☎350 787) is the coolest place in Lampang. It's best approached on bicycle. To get there, ride west on Jamatawee Rd. over the big hill, hang a right on the street across from the 7/11, and turn left on the dirt road just before the bridge; it's 100m down on your left. Set in a luscious garden, this spa/research center has the remedy for whatever ails you (herbal vapor bath 80฿, herbal bath 150฿, body scrub with herbs 200฿, massage 100฿ per hr.). There are over 150 herbal products and remedies for sale. Burm-Roong-Rarng-Kye should strengthen health and promote appetite while Ti-Gla Formula 1 may improve your sexual potency. Fancy organic shampoo, is available for earthy types and should be enjoyed after the free barefoot health walk around the gardens.

DAYTRIPS FROM LAMPANG

THAI ELEPHANT CONSERVATION CENTER

Take a Chiang Mai-bound bus; ask to be let off at the Center (35min., 20฿). ☎229 042. Shows 10, 11am, and weekends 1:30pm. 80฿.

HER LEFT FOOT Landmine victims—a common sight in Southeast Asia due to the heavy mining of Cambodia, Laos, and Myanmar—now have the sympathy of the elephant population. In August 1999, on a coffee break from her job as a log-lugger at a Lampang timber camp, a three-ton elephant named Motola stepped on a landmine and blew off her left front foot. The mine was laid in the ongoing guerrilla war between Karen rebels and the Burmese military. After an agonizing three-day trek to safety, Motola arrived at the Hang Chat Elephant Hospital, where doctors immediately pumped her full of elephant-strength painkillers. Thai and international donors contributed over US$125,000 for the three-hour operation to amputate the shredded, infected limb; within a day she was awake and playful, hand-fed bananas and sugar cane by hospital staff. Vets later fitted Motola with a metal prosthesis.

The Thai Elephant Conservation Center, 28km west of Lampang, is on the highway between Chiang Mai and Lampang, outside the Thung Kwian Forest. Elephants begin training here at age three and continue training with one master until they are 61 years old, when they retire from their elephant obligations. Shows feature them walking in procession, carrying teak logs, and *wai*-ing the crowd. Bundles of sugar cane or bananas for the pachyderms are up for sale (10฿), while an extra 100฿ buys a 10min. elephant ride. 400฿ buys a 30min. ride inside the forest.

KEW LOM DAM AND JAE SORN NATIONAL PARK

Songthaew *to Kew Lom line up on Rob Wiang Rd., behind city hall. On weekdays, you may have to charter one. To get a* songthaew *to Jae Sorn Falls, look for the dirt parking lot 100m down the soi off Thip Chang Rd., one block toward the GPO from Bangkok Bank (1½hr., 50฿). Admission to falls 200฿. Camping permitted.*

The Kew Lom Dam is a relaxation spot open from 6am to 6pm. Packed during the holidays, the island can be reached by boat (50฿). Make bungalow reservations with the Royal Irrigation Department (☎02 241 48 06) or Kew Lom Resort (☎223 772). North of the dam, Jae Sorn Waterfalls crash amid tropical forests and hot springs in Jae Sorn National Park.

THAILAND

WAT PHRA THAT LAMPANG LUANG

Songthaew *to Ko Kha leave from Boonyawat Rd., one block west of Praisanee Rd. (20฿). It's a few kilometers farther to the temple—negotiate with a driver.*

About 18km southwest of Lampang in the town of **Ko Kha** sits Wat Phra That Lampang Luang, one of North Thailand's finest displays of religious architecture. Its giant *chedi* and low wooden buildings also hold Lampang's most sacred Buddha.

Through the main gate, the central *wiharn* is an open-air Lanna-style structure, supported by 46 laterite columns. Constructed in 1486, the chapel houses two important Buddha images. **Phra Jao Lan Tang,** cast in 1563, is enclosed in a golden *mondop* near the rear of the temple; **Phra Jao Tan Jai** sits behind the *mondop*. Directly behind the *wiharn*, the *chedi* houses relics of the Buddha. **Wiharn Naamtaen,** to the right of the *chedi*, displays murals dating from 1501, while a 700-year-old Buddha image rests inside **Phra Phuttha Wiharn** (to the left of the *chedi*). A **Buddha footprint** is behind it, in the white building named **Haw Phra Phutthabat** (built in 1149). Beyond the back wall of the compound, a shrine showcases the temple's most valuable Buddha image, a jade Buddha from the Chiang Saen period (1057-1757). In April, during the Thai New Year, the image takes the limelight in a procession through the streets of Lampang.

PHITSANULOK ☎055

A staging ground for Ayutthaya's campaigns against the Burmese and the station of the Third Army during communist uprisings in the Nan hills, Phitsanulok ("Phitlok" or "Philok") still retains its military tradition and hosts the annual Cobra Gold exercises between Thai and American forces. Despite its past martial prowess, however, Phitsanulok is an unthreatening gateway to northern Thailand and home to Phra Buddha Chinnarat, one of the world's most famous Buddha images.

TRANSPORTATION

Flights: Phitsanulok Domestic Airport (☎258 029), on Sanambin Rd. **Thai Airways,** 209/26-28 Srithammatripidok Rd. (☎242 206), in the same building as Able Travel. Open M-F 8am-noon and 1-5pm. Flights to **Bangkok** (daily 6:35am, 12:15, 1:30, 6:40pm; 1110฿) and **Chiang Mai** (every other day 1:20pm, 765฿).

Trains: Phitsanulok Train Station (☎258 005), on Akatossaroth Rd. To **Bangkok** (6-7hr.; 14 per day; 3rd-class 109฿, 2nd-class 159฿) via **Ayuttaya** (5-6hr.; 9 per day; 3rd-class 98฿, 2nd-class 175฿), and **Chiang Mai** (6-8hr.; 7 per day; 3rd-class 105฿, 2nd-class 190฿).

Buses: Bo Ko So Bus Station (☎242 430), on Phitsanulok-Lomsak Rd. north of town. City bus #1 shuttles between the train and bus stations. Buses to: **Bangkok** (6hr.; 26 per day, 115฿; A/C 4pm, 194฿); **Chiang Mai** (5hr., 16 per day, 114฿; A/C 12 per day, 160฿); **Chiang Rai** (6-7hr.; 19 per day, 139฿; A/C 5 per day, 195฿); **Khon Kaen** (5hr.; 9 per day, 110฿; A/C 2, 9:30pm, 12:30, 1:30am; 153฿); **Mae Sot** (A/C van 5hr., 8 per day 7am-4pm, 104฿); **Nakhon Ratchasima** (6-7hr.; 20 per day, 133฿; A/C 10 per day, 221฿); **Phrae** (3hr.; every hr. 8-10am; 57฿, with A/C 103฿) via **Nan; Sukhothai** (1hr.; every 30min. 4:45am-6pm; 19฿, with A/C 34฿); **Udon Thani** (7hr.; 7 per day, 110฿; A/C 11:30pm, 1:30am; 175฿) via **Loei** (4hr.; 69฿, with A/C 110฿).

Local Transportation: City bus station, on Akatossaroth Rd., 1 block left of the train station. Buses run daily 5am-9pm. Bus #1 goes to Bo Ko So Bus Station, Wat Yai, and Naresuan University. Bus #4 goes to the airport. Regular buses 4฿, A/C 6฿.

Rentals: Lady Motor, 7/15 Ramasuan Rd. Motorcycles 200฿ per day. Deposit of passport and 300฿. Open daily 8:30am-5:30pm.

ORIENTATION AND PRACTICAL INFORMATION

Phitsanulok lies along the east bank of the **Nan River,** 377km north of Bangkok. **Akatossaroth Rd.** runs north-south through the center of town. **Putta Boocha** and **Boromtrailokkanart Rd.** run parallel to the train tracks on Akatossaroth Rd. **Narasuan Rd.** connects Putta Boocha and Boromtrailokkanart Rd. through the busiest part of town, shooting out in front of **Phitsanulok Train Station,** in the town center and then crossing the river. The famous **Phra Buddha Chinnarat** is located at **Wat Yai** at the north end of Putta Boocha Rd. The **Bo Ko So Bus Station** is three blocks east of the wat on the other side of the train tracks.

Tourist Offices: TAT, 209/7-8 Surasi Trade Center, Srithammatripidok Rd. (☎/fax 252 742). Info and maps of Sukhothai and Phitsanulok. Open daily 8:30am-4:30pm.

Tours: Able Tours and Travel, 209/26-28 Boromtrailokkanart Rd. (☎/fax 242 206). With your back to TAT, it's 25m to the left. Open M-Sa 8am-5pm.

Currency Exchange: Thai Farmers Bank, 144/1 Boromtrailokkanart Rd. (☎241 497). **24hr. ATM.** Open M-F 8:30am-3:30pm. Several banks are also on **Naresuan Rd.**

Luggage Storage: At the train station. 10฿ per piece per day. Open 24hr.

Markets: Day market, north of the train station behind Akatossaroth Rd. The right-hand side has the standard collection of inane consumer goods, while the left is devoted to tasty and quick meals. Eventually, the two sides converge to 500m of fruits, vegetables, and meats. The **night bazaar** is on Putta Bucha Rd., just south of the bridge where overpriced stone carvings are compensated for by a plethora of great food stalls.

Tourist Police: 31/15 Akatossaroth Rd. (☎245 357), 500m past Wat Yai toward the city stadium. Some English spoken. Open daily 8:30am-midnight.

Medical Services: Buddha Chinnarat Hospital (☎241 608), on Akatossaroth Rd. **24hr. emergency room.** Two more hospitals are nearby.

Telephones: Phitsanulok Telecommunication Center (☎243 116), next to GPO. International phone/fax.

Internet access: Speedy Net, 50m past the bridge on Naresuan Rd. Open daily 8am-midnight. **Skynet,** 141/4 Sanambin Rd. Open daily 8am-midnight. Both 20฿ per hr.

Post Office: GPO (☎258 313), on Putta Boocha Rd. 500m north of the Naresuan Rd. bridge. Open M-F 8:30am-4:30pm, Sa-Su 9am-noon. **Postal code:** 65000.

ACCOMMODATIONS

Phitsanulok Youth Hostel (HI), 38 Sanambin Rd. (☎262 060). From the train station, take bus #4 toward the airport. Cross the train tracks, turn right on Sanambin Rd. and look for the hostel on the left. Clean rooms furnished with Thai antiques and beautiful grounds. Lush garden and small waterfall. Laundry service. International phone. Dorms 120฿; elegant singles with bath 200฿; doubles 300฿; triples 450฿.

London Hotel, 21-22 Putta Boocha Rd. (☎225 145). From the train station, walk left to Sairuthai Rd., take a right and it's 1½ blocks down, just past the Firestone tire store. Retro yellow and green rooms with shared toilets. Singles 100฿; doubles 160฿.

Asia Hotel, 176/1 Akatossaroth Rd. (☎258 378). Take a left from the train station and walk 500m; it's on the left or take bus #1 from the city bus station. Noisy street. Laundry 8฿ per piece. Immaculate singles 200฿; doubles 250฿, with A/C 300-400฿.

FOOD

Phitsanulok is known for its open-air restaurants; **Payalithai Rd.** has the best and cheapest during the day. At night, the food-quake's epicenter is the night market's northern end (see **Practical Information: Markets,** p. 727); nearly a kilometer of solid eateries begins at the Naresuan Rd. bridge. All over the city, flying-vegetable restaurants hurl *pak boong fai deng* (flaming glory vine) from *wok* to distant plates.

Fah-Ke-Rah, 52/2 Pra Ong Dam Rd., near the mosque 35m past the train tracks away from town. Muslim restaurant with arguably the best food in Phitsanulok. *Lassi* (Indian yogurt drink) 20฿. Chicken curry 25฿. Open daily 6am-4pm.

Vegetarian Food Shop, 55/4 Srithammatripidok Rd., 15m north of the TAT. Veggie dish of the day with brown or white rice 10฿. Open daily 6am-2pm.

Payao Bakery, 168 Akatossaroth Rd., opposite train station. Look for brownies in the window. A subdued student hangout. Baked goods, sundaes, and real food too! Open daily 7am-11pm.

SIGHTS AND ENTERTAINMENT

Wat Phra Si Ratana Mahathat (Wat Yai), at the northern end of Putta Boocha Rd., shelters Phitsanulok's jewel. Cast in 1557, the spectacular **Phra Buddha Chinnarat** (Victorious King) is one of the world's most reproduced Buddha images and can be seen glimmering from afar with an ambiguous smile of contemplation. Part of the temple has been turned into a museum. (Museum open W-Su 9am-4pm. Wat open daily 7am-6pm. Sporadically enforced 10฿ admission. Sarongs provided free of charge to the bare-legged.)

The **Sgt. Maj. Thawee Folk Museum,** 26/43 Wisut Kusot Rd., is doing an incredible job of trying to protect folk culture from being swept away in the sea of globalization and only displays items that are no longer in use to preserve local traditions. Detailed English captions explain everything. (☎212 749. Open Tu-Su 8:30am-4:30pm. Free, but donations accepted and deserved.) Across the street, Dr. Thawee runs the **Buranathai Buddha Image Factory** where you can see handcrafted bronze Buddhas, from figurines to goliaths, in different stages of creation. (☎258 715. Open daily 8am-5pm.) **Wat Chulamanee,** built in 1464, is 6km outside the city, best reached by moto-taxi (300฿).

Pubs cluster at the far northern end of **Boromtrailokkanart Rd.** near the Pailyu Hotel and at **Phitsonulok Bazaar** across the Narasuan Rd. bridge.

DAYTRIP FROM PHITSANULOK

PHU HIN RONG KHLA NATIONAL PARK

The park is best visited during the less-crowded weekends. To reach the park, take a bus to Nakhoun Thai (2hr., every hr. 6:30am-6pm, 28฿) and then grab a songthaew to Phu Hin Rong Khla (1½hr., 15-30฿). Private transportation is needed to see much of the park. Contact the Forestry Department in Bangkok (☎02 579 7223) or Phu Hin Rong Khla Park (☎055 233 527) for more information. Park admission 200฿.

The Thai army and People's Liberation Army of Thailand (PLAT) clashed around Phitsanulok. From 1967-1982, PLAT survived in the Phu Hin Rong Khla forests 123km from town near the Lao border; recruits poured in after the clampdown on student demonstrators in Bangkok in 1976. The government then struck a decisive blow by offering amnesty to all students who joined the movement after 1976. In 1982, the area was made into a national park.

SUKHOTHAI ☎055

In 1238, the Thais established the new capital of the Lanna Kingdom near the Yom River, and drove the Khmer to the east. Named "Sukhothai," or "Dawn of Happiness," the city marked the birth of the first Thai nation. Sukhothai's period of glory is preserved in its spectacular ruins. It has recently joined Ayutthaya and Kanchanaburi as a sightseeing hot spot—and while Old Sukhothai is fast becoming a laterite theme park, nearby Si Satchanalai, with some of Thailand's most awe-inspiring ruins, remains untrafficked.

TRANSPORTATION

Flights: The **airport** is 26km out of town. **Bangkok Airways** (☎613 075) at the Pailyn Hotel is nestled on the road to the old city, flies daily to **Bangkok** (12:50pm, 1275฿); **Chiang Mai** (10:45am, 658฿); **Luang Prabang,** Laos. Shuttle bus to the airport is 80฿.

Buses: There is a brand new **bus station** 2km out of town on Bypass Rd. White, pink, and blue *songthaew* run along Bypass Rd. into town (4฿ before 4pm). *Tuk-tuks* to town are a regulated 30฿. Buses go to: **Bangkok** (7hr.; every hr. 7:50am-11:20pm; 106฿, A/C 191฿) via **Ayutthaya** (5hr.); **Chiang Mai** (5hr.; 12 per day 1:20am-5pm; 109฿, A/C 153฿) via **Tak** (1hr., 19 per day 6:50am-6pm, 26฿); **Nan** (6hr.; A/C 2:30, 11pm; 127฿). **Minibuses** to **Mae Sot** (2½hr., 7 per day 8am-4pm, 80฿) leave from a traffic triangle off Charot Withi Thong Rd., 2 blocks north of the main traffic light.

Local Transportation: Tuk-tuks 20-30฿. **Samlor** 10-20฿. At the terminal across the bridge, **songthaew** run to the old city (every 20min. 6am-6pm, 6฿). A bus to **Si Satchanalai** runs from the bus station (every 20min. 7am-4:30pm, 29฿).

Rentals: Lotus Village and Ban Thai Guest House rent **bikes** for 20-50฿ per day. Bikes at the Historical Park cost 20฿ per day and 30฿ at Si Satchanalai. **Motorcycles** are for rent at a bike repair shop (200฿ a day). Crossing the bridge toward the Old City, take the 1st left, which heads back to the river; it's 15m on the right.

ORIENTATION AND PRACTICAL INFORMATION

New Sukhothai city, 12km east of the old city *(muang gao)* and 427km north of Bangkok, appears at an L-shaped bend in the Yom River. **Charot Withi Thong Rd.** and **Sirlintharatid Rd.** run a few blocks in from the Yom's east bank to converge at Sukhothai's largest intersection near the bend in the "L." From there, Charot Withi Thong Rd. crosses **Praruang Bridge** and continues into the old city, intersecting **Nikorn Kasaem Rd.** and **Pravet Nakhon Rd.** along the way.

Currency Exchange: Most banks change currency and traveler's checks. **Thai Farmers Bank,** 134 Charot Withi Thong Rd. (☎611 932), at the base of the bridge, has a **24hr. ATM.** Open M-F 8:30am-3:30pm. Other banks are on **Singhawat Rd.**

Police: 263 Nikorn Kasaem Rd. (☎613 110), 150m beyond the post office.

Medical Services: Patanavej Hospital, 89/9 Singhawat Rd. (☎621 502), 200m from the intersection of Singhawat and Charo Withi Thong Rd., on the right. Some English spoken. **Open 24hr.** MC/V.

Telephones: At the **GPO. Overseas telephone** and **fax** upstairs 8am-6pm.

Internet Access: Cafes are all around town. **CyberMilk,** 51 Treeshod Rd., is on the 2nd right off Singhawat Rd, away from the market. 1฿ per min. Open daily 10am-10pm.

Post Office: GPO, 241 Nikhon Kasem Rd. (☎611 645), 1km south from the bridge. Open M-F 8:30am-4:30pm, Sa-Su 9am-noon. *Poste Restante.* **Postal code:** 64000.

ACCOMMODATIONS

Many guest houses fill up during Sukhothai's long tourist season (Jun.-Feb.)—call a few days in advance to guarantee a room. Many guest house owners complain of *tuk-tuk* drivers who, after being paid by rival guest house owners, lie to tourists at the bus station about certain guest houses being full or dirty. Be firm and check out your intended destination first hand.

Ban Thai Guest House, 38 Pravet Nakhon Rd. (☎610 163), across the Yom River. Take a left after the bridge at Thai Farmers Bank and walk 300m. Friendly owners. Airy restaurant. Twins 120฿, with bath 200฿; bungalows 200฿.

Lotus Village, 170 Ratchathanee Rd. (☎621 484). From Praruang Bridge, walk away from the old city and take the 1st left; it's on the right after the 5th cross-street. Teak rooms over a lotus-bedecked pond. Enjoy real coffee and sumptuous homemade jam. Singles 120฿; doubles with bath 400-500฿; bungalows 400฿, with A/C 800฿.

No. 4 Guest House, 140/4 Soi Klong Maelampan, Charot Withi Thong Rd. (☎610 165). From the bus station take the 2nd right after crossing the bridge and follow the signs (take a *tuk-tuk* after dark). Intimate bamboo bungalow village. Thai cooking lessons 1500฿. Singles 150฿; doubles 180฿.

Yupa House, 44/10 Pravet Nakhon Rd., Soi Mekapat (☎612 578), 100m beyond Ban Thai Guest House. Top floor rooms open onto balconies. There's no patio area, but it's cheap. Dorms 50฿; singles 80฿; doubles 100฿, with bath 150฿.

FOOD

Daytime food stalls congregate on the side streets west of **Charod Withi Thong Rd.;** at night, the best bet is **Ramkhamhaeng Rd.,** the first cross street on the city side of the river. Try the pad thai here; it's a point of pride for the people of Sukhothai.

Thai Noodles Sukhothai 2, 139 Charod Withi Thong Rd. Walk out of the city 700m; it's 100m past the school on the right. Look for a restaurant with small ivy-covered fountains. Phenomenal noodles. Pad thai 30฿. Open daily 10am-3pm.

Ban Thai Restaurant, 38 Pravet Nakhon Rd., next to Ban Thai Guest House. Serves great food on a nice patio. Rice noodles with chicken, vegetables, and egg 25฿. Milk shakes 15฿. Open daily 7am-9pm.

Chopper Bar, 101 Charod Withi Thong Rd., on your left walking from the river to the old city bus stop. Transsexuality is not the theme; it's incidental but adds flavor. Nightspot for *farang* and Thais alike. Large Singha 65฿. Open daily 6pm-midnight.

SIGHTS

WAT THAWET. Not your typical wat, Thawet's grounds are a 3D maze of brightly colored statues which furnish more than a few morbid illustrations of the punishments awaiting those who disobey Buddhist precepts. Inspired entirely by a single dream of the wat's now-deceased monk, highlights include a woman with a rooster head (the head of the animal she killed) and a man being forced to eat his own intestines. *(A beautiful 7km bicycle ride out of town. Ride away from town northeast on Charod Withi Thong Rd. Turn left and go over the bridge and take the 1st paved right; it's 6km down the highway on your right, after the major intersection with another highway. Great fried bananas sold along the highway for lunch.)*

OLD SUKHOTHAI HISTORICAL PARK. Old Sukhothai Historical Park lies within the triple-layered walls of the ancient city. Outside, fragments of an old wat and *chedi* can be explored, ideally by bicycle, along any of the paths branching out from the park's four main gates. **Ramkhamhaeng National Museum,** left of the park's east entrance, houses an eclectic collection testifying to the city's historical and cultural legacy, including a copy of the stone on which King Ramkhamhaeng the Great inscribed the first Thai script, considered by some to be his own invention.

The town centerpiece is **Wat Mahathat.** The main *chedi* is famed for its lotus shape, an architectural feature particular to the Sukhothai period. Also unusual are its several standing Buddha images in the Ceylonese style. Many of the ornate carvings around the wat remain in fantastic condition. Nearby **Wat Sri Sawai,** a south-facing Hindu shrine converted into a Buddhist temple, is the only Sukhothai ruin that doesn't face east. Its centerpiece is a set of three huge *prangs* which shoot out of the temple.

Farther north, 500m outside **San Luang Gate,** is **Wat Phra Phai Luang.** Lying on an island encircled by a moat, the wat has a magnificent Lopburi-style *stupa* and plaster reliefs of the Buddha. There is more room to explore and fewer tourists. The wat is treasured by archeologists for its traces of pre-Sukhothai period art. **Wat Sri Chum** sits just to the west. Its *mondop* houses the 15m tall "talking" Buddha (see **Legends of King Ramkhamhaeng,** p. 731). The tunnels on your right and left as you enter the temple were escape passages for the King. *(Catch a* songthaew *on the west side of the river 300m down the road on the right (20min., 6am-6pm, 6฿). Be firm on the price. Arriving at the park early will help avoid the heat and tour-group mobs. Park open daily 6am-9pm. 40฿; bike 20฿, motorbike 20฿, car 50฿. Museum open daily 9am-4pm; 40฿ entrance fee. Wat Sri Chum additional 40฿.)*

LEGENDS OF KING RAMKHAMHAENG

Sukhothai's King Ramkhamhaeng the Great looms large in Thai legend. The Great Father once sucked clean the fishbones of his dinner, tossed them into the river, and watched them turn into the first *pla paruang*—a fish so transparent that its bones are visible through the skin. (The king, who evidently was quite fond of this sort of trick, also lobbed a tamarind seed into a river and created Thailand's first turtle.) To mobilize Sukhothai for war, he gathered the soldiers in front of Wat Sri Chum's massive Buddha image and, in a terrifying supernatural display, compelled the giant image to speak and urge the soldiers to fight bravely. Since those days of yore, a hidden staircase has been discovered that leads to an opening behind the Buddha's mouth.

SANGKHALOK MUSEUM. The museum displays hundreds of artifacts detailing the daily lives of people who inhabited the nearby ruins. Ceramic masterpieces, around 700 years old, from the Kingdom of Lanna are also on display. *(1.5km outside of town. Follow Singhawat Rd. out of the city as it turns into Hwy. 12 (toward Phitsanulok). Turn left at the first major intersection (Hwy. 101); it's 100m on the left. ☎614 333. Open daily 8am-5pm. 100฿, kids under 17 50฿.)*

MARKETS

The **day market** is defined by the river, Praponbamrung Rd. and Charod Withi Thong Rd. Food stalls on Charot Withi Thong Rd. leading up to the bridge have fantastic meals at great prices (20฿). Off the road to the north in front of the wat are a variety of fruit stalls (watermelon 10฿). Poking your head in and around the area's sois will reveal the usual market produce, meat, and plastic sandals. A **night market** is open Wednesday and Thursday nights on Nikorn Kasaem Rd.

DAYTRIP FROM SUKHOTHAI

SI SATCHANALAI

Park open daily 8:30am-4:30pm. 10฿. Kilns open daily 8am-4:30pm. 40฿.

During the 13th century, Si Satchanalai rivaled Ayutthaya in wealth and sophistication. When Ayutthaya rose to preeminence, Si Satchanalai sunk into anonymity. With Sukhothai's success as a tourist attraction, the competition continues. Si

Satchanalai has excellent tourist facilities, including the **Visitors Information Center,** marked by signs from the roads entering the park. Headquarters contain a model of the area and a museum detailing the history and architectural significance of the ruins. An English brochure, photos, and a cryptic map cost 5฿.

Ruins line the southwestern bank of a bend in the Yom River. After a left at the entrance, ahead on the right is **Wat Chang Lom,** the city's central wat. According to ancient inscriptions, King Ramkhamhaeng ordered the temple's construction in 1287. Across the road, **Wat Chedi Chet Thaew** combines northern, southern, and local styles. Further on, **Wat Nang Phaya** is notable for its magnificent stucco reliefs on one wall of the *wiharn*.

The unearthing of 200 kilns at **Ban Ko Noi,** 5km beyond the park, challenged the conceptions of ancient Siam's isolation and technological simplicity. The city's kilns produced advanced celadons for export to countries as far away as the Philippines. Kiln #61 has an adjacent museum.

TAK ☎055

All roads lead to Tak. Whether your route is Bangkok-Chiang Mai, Sukhothai-Ayutthaya, or Khorat-Mae Sot, you'll pass through this provincial capital—but chances are you won't bother to get off the bus. Despite all of the TAT's attempts to talk it up as a destination in its own right, there's not much in town to do. As direct transportation to trekking destinations further west becomes more common, more travellers will bypass Tak's smiling people and majestic mountain surroundings, perhaps at their own loss.

TRANSPORTATION. The **bus station** (☎511 057), near the intersection of Hwy. 1 and 12, serves: **Bangkok** (7hr.; 15 per day 9am-10pm; 123฿, A/C 221฿, VIP 345฿); **Chiang Mai** (4hr.; 12:30, 1:30, 3, 5, 7pm; 122฿); **Sukhothai** (1½hr., every hr. 8:30am-5:30pm, 40฿). Orange-and-white **minibuses** venture to **Mae Sot** (1½hr., every 30min. 5:30am-7pm, 33฿).

ORIENTATION AND PRACTICAL INFORMATION. Tak's four main roads run parallel on the east side of the **Mae Ping River.** Closest to the river is **Kitticarjon Rd.,** followed by **Chomphon Rd.** and its night market food stalls. Next over are **Taksin Rd.** and **Mahattai Bamruang Rd.,** lined with hotels. On the town's east edge runs **Hwy. 1,** which crosses **Hwy. 12** before going to Chiang Mai.

The **TAT** office, 500m south of the bus station, is a boon to the rare visitor. (☎514 341. Open daily 8:30am-4:30pm.) Other services in Tak include: **Bangkok Bank,** 683 Taksin Rd., near the Sa Nguan Thai Hotel, with a **24hr. ATM** (open M-F 8:30am-3:30pm); the **GPO,** across an athletic field from the TAT (☎511 140; open M-F 8:30am-4:30pm, Sa-Su 9am-noon), with **overseas calls** on the second floor (open M-F 8:30am-4:30pm) and a **Lenso** phone outside; **Taksin Hospital** (☎511 025), on Hwy. 1 in the south part of town; and the **police station** (☎511 354; **emergency** ☎191), on Mahatthai Banruang Rd., east of the footbridge over the river. **Postal code:** 63000.

ACCOMMODATIONS AND FOOD. Sa Nguan Thai Hotel, 6/9 Taksin Rd., one block inland from the night market, is Tak's best value. (☎511 153. All-wood rooms with baths in the old wing 150฿; doubles in the new wing 220฿, with A/C 300฿.) Cheap, with Asian toilets, the **Mae Ping Hotel,** 231/4-5 Mahatthai Bamruang Rd., is another block inland from Sa Nguan Thai and 150m to the right, on the left side. (☎511 807. Singles 110฿; doubles 140฿, with A/C 200฿.)

Tak doesn't have restaurants. Instead, seek out **noodle shops** near the police station, the **night market** on Chompon Rd., or, best of all, **food stalls** dishing out Tak tasties near the footbridge in the park between Kitticarjon Rd. and Chompon Rd.

SIGHTS. The paved riverside path and popular adjoining footbridge offer views of the mountains to the west and, near sunset, billows of beautiful clouds.

Bhumibol Dam is the seventh largest in the world. The resulting reservoir is 100 miles long. A 1½hr. minibus (14฿) from Chompon Rd., near the night market, leads to its base; it's another 3.3km walk up to the dam's crest. There's more than meets the eye—try to finagle a tour of the dam's innards.

Lan Sang National Park is 17km west of Tak on the road to Mae Sot. From the highway it's 3km to headquarters and 5km to the **visitor's center.** Although *Let's Go* does not recommend it, it's possible to hitch a ride with towel-toting Thais. At **Lang Sang Waterfall,** 150m from the visitor's center, clear water cascades down gneiss ledges. Linger on the shady observation deck, or take a plunge. Thai tourists flood the lower falls on weekends but leave the upper falls, **Pha Phung** and **Pha Te,** deserted. (Bungalows 200-800฿; camping 10฿ with your own tent, 100฿ with a rented one. Park open daily 8am-6pm. 200฿.)

MAE SOT

☎055

At Mae Sot's vibrant day market, "Union of Myanmar" currency notes and hill tribe headdresses mingle with the usual fare of pig heads and mangos. This little city's proximity to Myanmar (7km away) and Karen refugee camps lend a sinister side to its multiculturalism: all of the winding routes to the town pass through police border checkpoints. Fair trade coffeehouses and friendly locals abound, however, in this city where travelers crash before trekking adventures or down to Um Phang.

TRANSPORTATION

Flights: Mae Sot Airport (☎535 321) is 3km west of town. Take *songthaew* from the Moei River Market (10฿). **Thai Airways,** 110 Prasatwithi Rd. (☎531 440). Open 8am-5pm. Flies to **Bangkok** (5:30pm, 1625฿) and **Chiang Mai** (M, Tu, Th, Sa 9am; 765฿).

Buses: 6 **bus stations** in town. The station for trips to and from **Bangkok** (10hr.; 9 per day 8-8:30am and 7-10pm; 211฿, VIP 420฿) is 50m from Asia Rd. *Songthaew* to **Mae Sarlang** (5hr., every hr. 6am-noon, 150฿) leave from the market area at the end of a paved path running along the west side of the police station. Orange-and-white minivans to **Tak** (1½hr., every 30min. 6am-6pm, 33฿) gather on the 1st major street north of Intarakepree Rd., west of the police station. The station for buses to and from **Chiang Mai** (6½hr., 6am 115฿, 8am with A/C 207฿) is 1 block east of the police station. To find *songthaew* to **Um Phang** (5hr., every hr. 7:30am-3:30pm, 100฿), head left with your back to the police station. Take the 1st left, and follow the street past Prasatwithi Rd. and the mosque, then take the 2nd left–you'll see a cluster of blue trucks. White vans to **Sukhothai** (3hr., 7 per day 7am-4pm, 80฿) leave from the station south of the market. Maps available at guest houses make this information much clearer.

Local Transportation: To go to the **Moei River Market** and the **border,** catch a blue **songthaew** (10฿) opposite Thai Airways on Prasatwithi Rd. Last one returns at 6pm.

Rentals: A bike shop between No. 4 and Bai Fern Guest Houses, next to the police box, rents **bikes** (50฿) and **motorbikes** (300฿). Open daily 8am-5pm.

ORIENTATION AND PRACTICAL INFORMATION

Mae Sot is 165km west of Sukhothai. **Intirakiri Rd.,** with one-way traffic heading east, runs parallel to **Prasatwithi Rd.,** with one-way traffic heading west toward **Moei Market** and the Burmese border. The **police station** is on Intirakiri Rd. in the center of town. The **market** sprawls south of Prasatwithi Rd. near the Siam Hotel. Prasong, a friendly fellow at the River Restaurant near Bai Fern Guest House (see **Accommodations,** below), has local savvy and provides visitors with town maps.

Tours: For your wallet's sake, go to Um Phang yourself to book a trek. To book in Mae Sot, try TAT-approved **Mae Sot Conservation Tours,** 415/17 Tang Kim Chiang Rd. (☎544 726), 2 doors toward Prasatwithi Rd. from Pim Hut. 5-day trek 7000฿. To avoid scams, make sure your guide is TAT-approved.

Currency Exchange: Banks line Prasatwithi Rd. **Thai Farmers Bank,** 84/9 Prasatwithi Rd. (☎531 938), has a **24hr. ATM** (V, MC, Cirrus, PLUS). Open M-F 8:30am-3:30pm.

English Books: DK Hotel, small bookstore in the back right corner of the department store on the 1st floor. Has a collection of English-language Penguin Classics with a bias towards Dickens—or maybe those are just the ones nobody buys.

Markets: The **day market** is south of Prasatwithi Rd. on either side of the Siam Hotel. Remarkably large for small Mae Sot. Crowded *sois* full of frogs and vegetables bottleneck before opening into large covered areas selling every kind of shirt, from collared to tie dye. The **night market** at the east end of Prasartwithee Rd. is a unimpressive affair where one local entrepreneur offers pad thai in English for 20฿ while blatantly advertising the same in Thai for 15฿. **Moel River market,** at the border 7km west of town, sells Burmese fabrics, foodstuffs, and gems, as well as French skincare products and Sony televisions. Check out the "PolyStation" stand; its graphics make Atari look like DeepBlue. Take a blue *songthaew* from Prasatwithi Rd. opposite Thai Airways (10฿, last return 6pm), or bike past the rice fields for a scenic trip. (Open daily 8am-6pm).

Emergency: ☎ 191.

Police: ☎ 531 112. At the intersection of Tang Kim Chiang and Intirakiri Rd.

Tourist Police: ☎ 533 523. Near Asia Rd. With your back to the police station, head left, take the first left and follow it to the end; it's on the left. No English. **Open 24hr.**

Medical Services: Pawo Hospital (☎ 533 912), south of town past the market, near the vans to Sukhothai. Private. Some English spoken. **Open 24hr.** MC/V.

Telephones: Maesot Telecommunications Office, 784 Intirakiri Rd. (☎ 531 317). Open M-F 8:30am-4:30pm.

Internet Access: SpeciesNet Café, 112/9 Prasatwithi Rd. (☎ 531 909), near Thai Airways. 25฿ per hr. Open daily 9am-9pm.

Post Office: GPO (☎ 531 277), on Intirakiri Rd. Facing the police station, head right; it's 150m down the road on the right. *Poste Restante.* Open M-F 8:30am-4:30pm, Sa-Su 9am-noon. **Postal code:** 63110.

BORDER CROSSING: MOI-MYAWADDY

A 7km *songthaew* ride away from Mae Sot, this Thai/Myanmar border crossing is a relatively hassle-free way to extend your Thai visa. Show up at the bridge, present your passport to the Thai authorities, walk over the bridge, present your passport to be stamped and **US$10,** walk back over the bridge and receive your brand new visa. Bring US$10 with you to Mae Sot, as banks there don't have small bills and authorities are frequently out of change. If you want to see an unrealistic view of Burmese life, daytrips (return by 5pm), usually with a "guide," are permitted; keep in mind that your money will go a government with an atrocious human rights record (see **Myanmar: To Go or Not to Go,** p. 464).

ACCOMMODATIONS AND FOOD

Bai Fern Guest House, 660/2 Intirakiri Rd. (☎ 533 343). Facing the police station, it's 400m to the left. English sign proclaims "Cold Beer," but it's the food that keeps them coming back. Dorm with raised futon 50฿; spic 'n' span twins 100฿; doubles 150฿.

Guest House No. 4, 736 Intirakiri Rd. (☎/fax 544 976), 200m past Bai Fern, on the right. Bicycle rental 30฿. 11pm curfew. No food service. Futons with nets in dorm 50฿; singles 80฿; doubles 100฿.

Bai Fern Restaurant serves fresh bread, great pizzas, and steaming Fair Trade espresso along with traditional Thai food. The **Crocodile Tear** on Intirakiri Rd. before the guest houses has live music daily from 9pm to 1am. The fabulous 2-man band will let you join their heart-wrenching Dylan covers if you feel inspired (Singha 60฿). **Pim Hut,** on Tang Kim Chiang Rd. (near the police station), serves fried serpent (65฿), among other Thai and *farang* entrees. (Open daily 7:30am-10:30pm.) Ask about Mae Sot Conservation Tours.

UM PHANG ☎055

If Um Phang's vistas from the 1500m high peaks don't take your breath away, the speed of your *songthaew* on the hellish trip from Mae Sot will. Sitting on top is illegal and dangerous, but many travellers do so to get a glimpse of the unbelievable view. Tiny Um Phang's 3000 Mon and Thai residents welcomed fewer than 2000 *farang* trekkers last year, compared with the tens of thousands stomping around Chiang Mai.

TRANSPORTATION AND PRACTICAL INFORMATION. Pravesphywan Rd., a continuation of the road from Mae Sot, leads into town. **Sukhomwattana Rd.,** the only other street of note, parallels Pravesphywan Rd. to the west (downhill). For *songthaew*, wait near the end of Pravesphywan Rd. before 3pm.

Services in town include: the **post office** (☎561 127), on the left as you drive into town, which also has **overseas telephone** service (cash and collect calls only; open M-F 8:30am-4:30pm, Sa 9am-noon); the **police station** (☎/fax 561 129), on Sukhumwattana Rd.; and the **hospital** (☎561 121; **open 24hr.;** some English spoken). To get to the hospital, turn left off Pravesphywan Rd. after the road to Trekker's Hill and head onto a road leading uphill. There are **no banks. Postal code:** 63170.

ACCOMMODATIONS AND FOOD. There's been an explosion of guest houses here over the past few years. Beware of high pressure tactics when you arrive, and make it clear that you only want accommodation and will decide on a trek later. More important than where you stay is who your guide will be. Meet him and ensure you like him as your safety and enjoyment will be in his hands. The most reputable (amongst international travelers) are Coco and Johnny (best friends) who have 17 years experience between them. Both speak English, Thai, Burmese, and Karen, and are expert guides and have personal relationships with the hill tribes in the area. Typical treks last 3 days/2 nights with visits to **Tee Lo Su Waterfalls** and a **hill tribe village** by foot, raft, and elephant. **Jungle Huts** offers the nicest and most expensive accommodation with bungalows by the river (200-500฿). **Um Phang House** is directly across the street with cheaper, more basic digs (doubles 120฿). The **Trekker Hill** company is the biggest operation in town and employs many of its own guides. Run by Mr. Jantawong (Mr. T), it has a teak shelter with futons, mosquito nets, and toilet paper. (☎561 090. Dorm 60฿; private mini-bungalow 80฿ per person. Laundry 5฿ per piece. Small food service available.) **Phudoi Guest House and Campsite** is further into town from Trekker Hill, 100m down a dirt road to the left. (☎561 049. Rooms with fan, screens, and hot water bath 100฿ per person.)

Restaurants dot the main street beyond these two accommodations. Only **Phudoi Restaurant,** on the left of Pravesphywan Rd. 200m beyond the turn-off to the associated guest house, gets enough customers to keep the chef interested. (Chicken fried with ginger 60฿. Open daily 7am-10pm.) Um Phang's best **noodle shop** is on Pravesphywan Rd., opposite the wat entrance (10฿ per plate). Beware: during the low season restaurants close.

NORTHEAST THAILAND

This plateau encompasses about one-third of Thailand's total landmass, and supports an equal proportion of the nation's population. Thais call it "Isaan," suggesting prosperity and vastness. Ironically, largely agrarian Isaan is one of the country's poorest regions. The United States set up air force bases in the region's four largest cities during the Vietnam War, and these cities remain centers of transportation, commerce, and education. So close is the relationship with the Lao and Khmers across the Mekong River that the Isaan dialect carries striking similarities to Lao, and in some areas, Thai remains spoken as a second language. For skeptics who hold that any statement containing both "Thailand" and "off the beaten path" is oxymoronic, Isaan emerges as a buried treasure.

KHAO YAI NATIONAL PARK

For travelers wishing to rescue their lungs from the suffocating fumes of Bangkok, Khao Yai National Park offers salvation. Only 160km from Bangkok, this dense jungle teems with wild elephants, tigers, bears, and monkeys. Khao Yai was consecrated as Thailand's first (and perhaps best) national park in 1962, a humbling 2100 sq. km of tropical rainforest. Khao Yai can only be reached via Pak Chong, a dull urban strip featuring little more than basic lodging and supplies.

PAK CHONG ☎044

Approximately 1km long, Pak Chong extends on either side of the **Mitraphap (Friendship) Highway;** all its side streets are designated **Tesaban Rd.** followed by a number. The four major landmarks, starting from the side closest to Bangkok and heading toward Khorat, are the stoplight, the 7-Eleven store, the pedestrian overpass, and the Shell gas station.

Giant light-blue **songthaew** leave for **Khao Yai National Park** from the highway in front of the 7-Eleven (every 30min. 6am-5pm, 12฿). The **train station** (☎311 534) lies at the end of Tesaban 15 (from the overpass, it's the first right after the traffic signals), 400m down the road. Trains go to **Bangkok** via **Ayutthaya** (4½hr., 7 per day, from 76฿) and **Khorat** (1hr., 6 per day, from 18฿). At the **non-A/C bus station,** beside the Thai Farmers Bank near Tesaban 19, you can catch buses en route from Bangkok to **Khorat** (1hr., every 30min. 5am-midnight, 20฿) and make connections to northern and northeastern destinations. An **A/C bus station** is between Tesaban 18 and the overpass, with service to **Bangkok** (3hr.; newer orange and red bus 74฿, blue bus 95฿) and **Khorat** (1hr., every 30min., 39฿). A second A/C bus terminal beneath the overpass has service to **Nakhon Sawan** via **Lopburi** (#121; 6:30, 8:20, 11:20am, 1:20pm) and **Sukhothai** via **Phitsanulok** and **Chang** (#572; 7:10, 9:20, 10:20, 11:20am). A third A/C bus station next to the Shell station serves **Roi Et** and **Chayaphurn.**

The **day market** starts near Tesaban 21 and extends one block uphill from the main road. It is stocked with flashlights, camping gear, and other items useful for Khao Yai treks. (Open dawn-4:30pm.) A **supermarket,** at the corner of Tesaban 16, sells similar wares. (Open daily 9am-10pm.) The **night market** (beneath the overpass) is the place for dinner. **Bank of Ayudhya** (☎311 411), centrally located between Tesaban 18 and the overpass, has an **ATM** (MC/PLUS/V; open daily 6am-11pm), gives cash advances, and cashes traveler's checks (open M-F 8:30am-3:30pm). The **post office** (☎311 736), on the corner of Tesaban 25, handles telegrams, money and postal orders, and faxes (open M-F 8:30am-4:30pm). Directly across the strip, the **Communications Authority of Thailand** (☎311 787) places **domestic and international phone calls** (collect calls 30฿; open M-F 8:30am-4:30pm). Surf yourself silly at the brand-spankin'-new **Internet Zone** between Tesaban 17 and 19 (25฿ per hr.; open daily 9am-midnight). **Postal code:** 30130.

Jungle Guest House, 63 Tesaban 16 (☎313 836), Kongwaksin Rd., Soi 3, is run by Tom and Maew, an amiable Swedish-Thai couple. They provide a wealth of information about Khao Yai and organize expeditions into the park. From the pedestrian overpass, head to the stoplight at Tesaban 17; take a left and, when the road forks, veer left onto Thanon Kong Vaccine Soi 1. A green and white sign announces the guest house, hiding 50m in on the right. Dorms with fans, Western toilets, and small breakfast are 70฿; free upgrades to unoccupied singles, with personal showers (normally 150฿) have been known to occur.

THAILAND

THE PARK

Park open daily 6am-midnight. 20฿. Park Headquarters and Visitor Center open daily 8am-6pm. Trail map 2฿; guide 300-500฿.

Home to one of the last wild elephant herds and some of the world's few remaining wild tigers, the park has over 40km of hiking trails through rainforest and grasslands. Reptiles of all sorts and insects both creepy and crawly scuttle through the vine-entangled jungle while hornbills, gibbons, and rhesus monkeys screech above in the canopy. The waterfalls alone are worth the trek. The **Nong Pak Chi Watch Tower** is where the majority of the park's tigers are sighted. Visitors officially need "approval" for tower access, but the regulation is rarely enforced. Don't trek in sandals and steer clear of salty water to avoid leeches. Leech-guards (70฿) are available at the souvenir shop near Park Headquarters. After stepping off the *songthaew* at the park entrance, it's another 12km to Park Headquarters and the Visitor Center. Though *Let's Go* does not recommend it, most travelers find that they have to hitchhike to headquarters.

When night descends on the forest, there are two accommodation options. **Yao Wa Chon,** 1km from headquarters, has outdoor hammocks (hard floor-space 20฿; blanket rental at headquarters 15฿; 12-person lodges 1200฿). Alternatively, **Orchard Campsite,** 10km from headquarters, offers tent-space for 5฿ (tent rental 80฿). To ensure weekend lodging, call ahead to the **Royal Forest Department** in Bangkok (☎02 579 7221).

For a more convenient tour of the park, try the **Jungle Adventure**—a 1½-day tour operated by the Jungle Guest House in Pak Chong. The tour, which incorporates Buddhist meditation caves, waterfall swims, elephant-trail treks, and a night safari, moves at a blistering pace and costs 950฿. Trips leave at 3pm and end the next evening.

NAKHON RATCHASIMA (KHORAT) ☎044

Known locally as Khorat, the name of the plateau on which it rests, Nakhon Ratchasima straddles the main corridor to all other destinations in Isaan. Although it's Thailand's second largest city, the texture of urban life found here is worlds away from the manic snarls of Bangkok. Built during the Ayutthayan period and surrounded by a moat (the remains of which are still visible), Khorat enjoys close proximity to silk-weaving splendor in Pak Thong Chai, to the pottery manufacturers of Dan Kwian, and to the ruins of Phimai and Phanom Rung.

TRANSPORTATION

Flights: Airport (☎255 899), 28km west of town. Catch a **Buriram** bus at **Bus Terminal 2** (10฿), or a **shuttle bus,** with pickups at hotels (70฿). **Thai Airways** (☎257 211), at the corner of Suranaree and Buarong Rd. Open M-F 8:30am-4:30pm. Flies to **Bangkok** daily (8:40, 10:40am, 8:20pm; 555฿). Airport tax 30฿.

Trains: Nakhon Ratchasima Railway Station (☎242 044), on Mukkhamontri Rd. From the center of town, the station is 500m west on Mukkhamontri Rd., with an old boxcar out front. For a complete list of fares and departures, ask for an English timetable at the ticket booth. To: **Bangkok** (5hr.; 8:40am-11:30am; 3rd-class 58฿, 2nd-class 98฿, 1st-class 173฿) via **Pak Chong** and **Ayutthaya** and **Ubon Ratchathani** (5hr.; 10 per day; 3rd-class 50฿, 2nd-class 110฿, 1st-class 245฿).

Buses: Terminal 1 (☎262 899, for A/C 245 443), on Burin Lane. To: **Bangkok** (#21, 4hr., every 20min. 24hr., A/C with toilet 139฿); **Nakhon Sawan** (#572; 6hr.; every hr. 5am-11pm; A/C 95฿, A/C with toilet 113฿); **Pak Thong Chai** (#1303, 1½hr., every 30min. 5:30am-8:30pm, 12฿); and numerous stops within the province. **Terminal 2** (☎256 007), on Rte. 2 north of town beyond Takhong River. Take a motorcycle or *tuk-tuk* (40-50฿). To: **Bangkok** (#21, 4hr., every 20min. 24hr., A/C 140฿); **Chiang Mai** (#635; 12hr.; 6 per day; 218฿, A/C 392฿); **Chiang Rai** (#651, 13hr., 4 per day, 432฿); **Nong Khai** (#22, 3½hr., every hr. 9am-3pm, 180฿) via **Khon Kaen** (2hr., 104฿) and **Udon Thani** (3hr., 104฿); **Phimai** (#1305, 1½hr., every 30min. 5am-10pm, 21฿); **Surin** (#274, 4hr., every 30min. 11:30am-4pm, 100฿); **Ubon Ratchathani** (#25, 4½hr., 6 per day 12:30-3pm, 185฿).

Local Transportation: **Samlor** and **tuk-tuk** are omnipresent. From the TAT to Thao Suranaree memorial should cost no more than 60฿. City buses are just as convenient (run 5am-4pm; 4฿, A/C 6฿). Buses #1, #2, and #3 start on Mukkhamontri Rd. near the TAT and all go into the center of town. They split where Mukkhamontri forks into Phoklang Rd. (#1), Suranaree Rd. (#2), and Jomsurangyard Rd. (#3). TAT city map has bus routes. Songthaew (4฿) run routes more frequently.

ORIENTATION AND PRACTICAL INFORMATION

Khorat stretches east-west between **Mittraphap Rd.** to the north and the Northeastern Railroad Line to the south. It is bisected by **Ratchadamnoen Rd.** and **Chumphon Rd.,** two parallel streets separated by a park. In the middle of this divider, marking the center of the city, is the dramatic **Thao Suranaree memorial.** The western half of Khorat is bounded to the south by **Mukkhamontri Rd.,** which forks into **Suranaree Rd., Phoklang Rd.,** and **Jomsurangyard Rd.** as it heads toward the town center. These roads intersect Ratchadamnoen Rd. close to the memorial. A rectangular moat, a remnant of the city's old fortifications, circumscribes the city's east half. **Chomphon Rd.,** not to be confused with Chumphon Rd., begins behind Thao Suranaree memorial and cuts east-west through the center of the old city.

Tourist Offices: TAT, 2102-2104 Mittraphap Rd. (☎213 666), on the western edge of town. Take bus #1, #2, or #3 heading west from the memorial and get off just before Mittraphap Rd. and cross the footbridge; it's beside Sima Thani Hotel. English spoken. Brochures, and a useful map (all free). Staff has info on cultural events in Khorat and the status of the Cambodian border. Open daily 8:30am-4:30pm.

Tours: Supatha Tour, 138 Chainarong Rd. (☎242 758).

Currency Exchange: Bank of Ayudhya, 168 Chomphon Rd. (☎242 388). MC/V cash advances and traveler's check exchange 8:30am-3:30pm. **24hr. ATM** (Cirrus/MC/PLUS/V). Other ATMs line Chomphon Rd.

Markets: Mae Kim Heng Market, between Suranaree and Phoklang Rd. about a block beyond the city gate, bustles 24hr. The **night bazaar** fills 2 blocks of Marat Rd. between Chompon and Mahatthai Rd. Open daily 6-10pm. Both offer bargains on Pak Thong Chai's renowned silks and Dan Kwian's famous pottery.

Emergency: ☎191. **Tourist police**: ☎1155.

Tourist Police: ☎341 777. Beside the Thao Suranaree memorial.

Pharmacies: Amarin, 122 Chumphon Rd. (☎242 741), behind the memorial to the left. "Rx" on the glass doors. Adequate English. Open daily 8:30am-8:30pm. Also on the lower level of Klang Plaza II, on Jomsurangyard just off Ratchadamnoen Rd.

Medical Services: St. Mary's Hospital, 307 Mittraphap Rd./Rte. 2 (☎242 385), 50m south of Bus Terminal 2. Private hospital with excellent English-speaking staff. **Khorat Memorial Hospital,** 348 Suranaree Rd. (☎230 215). From the Thao Suranaree memorial, it's past the Sri Pattana Hotel on the right. Look for the new white building proclaiming "KMH." English spoken. Accepts V. **Open 24hr.**

Telephones: Communications Authority of Thailand (☎259 707), next to the post office. Overseas calls, fax, and telex. Open daily 10am-8pm.

Internet Access: Internet World (☎267 854), on the south side of Mittraphap Rd. near the corner of Ratchadanoen Rd., halfway up the footbridge stairwell. 20฿ per hr. Open daily 10am-midnight. **CyNet Cafe,** 154/1 Manat Rd. (☎230 823). Following Chomphon Rd. from the statue's back, take the 2nd left. 40฿ per hr. Espresso 30฿. Open M-F 10am-9pm, Sa-Su 9am-9pm.

Post Office: 48 Jomsurangyard Rd. (☎256 670). Facing the memorial, go right on Ratchadamnoen Rd. until Jomsurangyard Rd. Turn right and pass Klang Plaza II; it's on the right. Open M-F 8:30am-4:30pm, Sa 9am-noon. **Postal code:** 30000.

THAILAND

ACCOMMODATIONS

Siri Hotel, 688-690 Phoklang Rd. (☎241 556), 350m down Phoklang Rd. after Mukkhamontri Rd. forks. Friendly staff, glistening rooms. Singles with fan 130-150฿; doubles 200฿, with A/C 250฿; "special room" for two with TV, A/C, and fridge 400฿.

Potong Hotel, 658 Ratchadamnoen Rd. (☎251 962), at the corner of Phoklang Rd. Popular, with a central (albeit raucous) location. Western toilets. Singles with fan 170฿, with TV and A/C 300฿; doubles with fan 220฿.

Sri Chompon Hotel, 133 Chompon Rd. (☎252 829), a short walk down Chompon Rd. from the memorial, on the left opposite the Buddhist paraphernalia shop. Singles with toilet and fan 160฿, with A/C 240฿; doubles 240/350฿.

Muang Thong Hotel, 46 Chumphon Rd. (☎242 090), next to the AM/PM minimart. Despite its claim to be the "cheapest place in town" and a prime location, it fails to mask the cacophony of the street. Rooms 120฿, with A/C 350฿.

FOOD

Mouth-watering cuisine is plentiful. The markets are fine places to sample regional specialties, such as *sai klog* (pork sausages; 5฿) and small taco-shaped coconut-stuffed pancakes (1฿). **Ran Ahaan Jay Con Im,** 191/2 Suranaree Rd., offers vegetarian entrees running 10-20฿. (Open daily 8am-midnight.) An alternative is the food court in the basement of the Klang Plaza II shopping center on Jomsurangyard Rd.

Suan Sin, 163 Washara Srit Rd. Follow Chomphon Rd. behind Thao Suranaree shrine and take the first right. It's halfway down the 3rd block to the left. Open-air storefront. Isaan specialties like cow-tail soup, pig's neck noodles, and (drumroll please) bull penis salad. Dishes around 60฿. Open daily 9am-8pm.

Dok Som, 130 Chumphon Rd., behind the monument and on the left. Long bar. Bilingual menu of Thai, Chinese, and European dishes. For the adventuresome, a page of Isaan cuisine. Spicy Isaan chicken salad 60฿. Open daily 11am-11pm.

Suan Pak (SPK), 154-158 Chumphon Rd., behind the shrine and to the left, past Dok Som. Soundtrack of repetitive Thai pop contrasts with the more captivating cuisine. 13 pages of Thai, Chinese, and Western entrees 25-120฿. Fried sea bass with chili sauce 45฿. Serpent-head spicy soup 60฿. Ice cream bar. Open daily 10am-midnight.

Cabbages and Condoms (C&C Restaurant), 86/1 Sueb Siri Rd., just past Soi 4 and before the train tracks near Khorat Doctor's House. Look for a tiny bridge on the right below a neon Pepsi sign. C&C is the brainchild of "The Condom King" himself, Meechai Vivaraidya, founder of PDA—an NGO that supports family planning and AIDS education. "Chicken in herb leaf bikinis" 65฿. Open daily 10:30am-10pm.

The VFW Cafeteria, adjacent to Siri Hotel on Phoklang Rd. A slice of displaced Americana straight from the silver screen, exemplifying the "bar-and-grill" G.I. hangout in every Vietnam War flick. Cheeseburger 35฿. Fries 10฿. Open daily 8am-9:30pm.

SIGHTS

Khorat's handful of sights can be visited in a single afternoon. A good starting point is the **Thao Suranaree memorial.** Constructed in 1934, the memorial is a source of identity and inspiration for generations of Khorat citizens.

WAY TO GO, MRS. MO! Embodying the spirit of Khorat like no other symbol, the **Thao Suranaree Memorial** in the town center depicts the heroic Khun Ying Mo, wife of Khorat's deputy governor who, in 1826, rallied 300 women to defend the city from Lao invaders. A 19th century-equivalent to Judith of biblical lore, Thao Suranaree persuaded the women to seduce and then murder the Laotian soldiers, thus playing the key role in the defeat of Prince Anuwong of Vientiane. Locals reverently refer to her as "Yah Mo" (Grandmother Mo), wrap the shrine in ribbons, give offerings of bananas and coconuts, and burn incense. When prayers are answered, they sing thanks in the local Khorat dialect or hire young women to dance in her honor on a raised platform adjacent to the memorial marked "Khorat Song." An annual Thao Suranaree Fair (March 23-April 3) draws thousands to the bronze statue over the city moat between Ratchadamnoen and Chumphon Rd., and entails a parade, folk songs and dances, and a beauty contest.

Wat Sala Loi offers a chance to set sail for new spiritual horizons. Look for its sign on Mittraphap Rd., at the old moat's northeast corner. Sala Loi's architecturally acclaimed inner sanctuary is shaped like a Chinese ship, which symbolizes the passage of the devoted to nirvana.

Every Thai city has a sacred pillar from which distances are measured. Khorat's is enshrined at **Wat Phra Narai Maharat** on Prajak Rd., between Assadang and Chompon Rd. inside the city moat. This wat contains a sandstone image of the Hindu god Narayana, and a *shiva linga* (phallus-shaped pillar).

The **Mahawirawong Museum,** Khorat's branch of the National Museum, is on Ratchadamnoen Rd., two blocks toward the clock tower from the shrine. Its small collection contains artifacts from the Angkor and Ayutthaya periods. (☎242 958. Open daily 9am-noon and 1-4pm. 10฿.)

ENTERTAINMENT

The karaoke plague has reached epidemic proportions here. For temporary relief, the **Sima Thani Hotel,** next to the TAT, holds outdoor performances of Isaan music and dance. (☎213 100. M-Sa 7-8pm. Free with *a la carte* dinner—around 250฿.) **Muay Thai** (Thai boxing) kicks off sporadically at Khorat's stadium; inquire at the TAT. Khorat also has an array of movie theaters and discotheques.

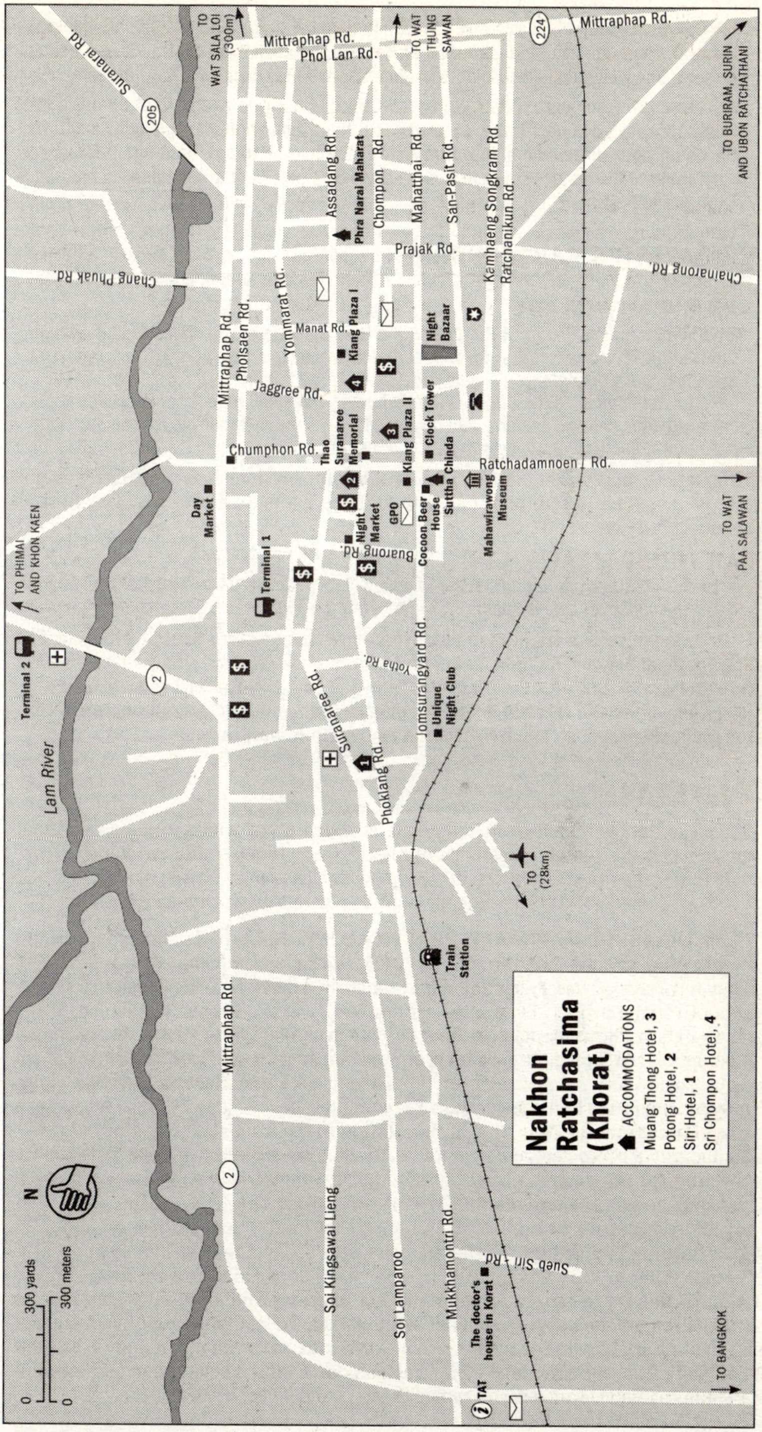
Nakhon Ratchasima (Khorat)
ACCOMMODATIONS
Muang Thong Hotel, 3
Potong Hotel, 2
Siri Hotel, 1
Sri Chompon Hotel, 4
Mittraphap Rd.
Phol Lan Rd.
Suranarai Rd.
TO WAT SALA LOI (300m)
TO WAT THUNG SAWAN
TO BURIRAM, SURIN AND UBON RATCHATHANI
Assadang Rd.
Phra Narai Maharat
Chompon Rd.
Mahatthai Rd.
San-Pasit Rd.
Kamhaeng Songkram Rd.
Ratchanikun Rd.
Prajak Rd.
Chang Phuak Rd.
Chainarong Rd.
Yommarat Rd.
Manat Rd.
Klang Plaza I
Night Bazaar
Pholsaen Rd.
Jaggree Rd.
Chumphon Rd.
Thao Suranaree Memorial
Klang Plaza II
Clock Tower
Ratchadamnoen Rd.
Suttha Chinda
Cocoon Beer House
Mahawirawong Museum
TO WAT PAA SALAWAN
Day Market
Night Market
GPO
Buarong Rd.
Terminal 1
TO PHIMAI AND KHON KAEN
Terminal 2
Yotha Rd.
Jomsurangyard Rd.
Unique Night Club
Suranaree Rd.
Phoklang Rd.
Lam River
TO (28km)
Train Station
N
300 yards
300 meters
Soi Kingsawai Lieng
Soi Lamparoo
Mukkhamontri Rd.
Sueb Siri Rd.
The doctor's house in Korat
TAT
TO BANGKOK
205
224
2

THAILAND

Scorpions' Disco, 191 Assadang Rd. (☎243 184), next to K Stars Hotel. A pillar of the dance scene for Khorat youth. Laser lights and pounding hip-hop. Dance and comedy shows on weekend nights. Cover 60฿, includes 1 beer. Open daily 8:30pm-3am.

Unique, 1372 Jomsurangyard Rd. (☎258 540), 800m down the road from the post office, a half-block past Yotha Rd. on the left. Neon lights brag "Unique: It's Party Time." With an open-air terrace and a 10m waterfall, would-be dancers are often awe-struck, immobile water-watchers. When the novelty wears off, Unique will still be a hip dance destination. Cover 200฿, includes 1 drink. Open daily 9pm-3am.

DAYTRIPS FROM KHORAT

DAN KWIAN VILLAGE

From Khorat, follow Chompon Rd. behind the Thao Suranaree memorial and turn right on Chainarong Rd. At the south gate, turn left onto Kamhaeng Songkhram Rd. and walk past the vendors. On the right, you should see a small blue-striped bus (#1307, 30min., 10฿). Indicate destination to the driver. Disembark when the small road forks into three lanes lined with little shops. To return, wait on the left side of the road back to Khorat. When the bus comes, gesticulate wildly; with luck, it will stop.

Tiny Dan Kwian Village, 15km southeast of Khorat, has long been famous for its distinctive rust-colored pottery, cut with detailed geometric patterns. The work is beautiful but heavy and fragile.

THAILAND

PAK THONG CHAI

Take bus #1303 from Khorat's Bus Terminal 1 (every 30min. 8am-4pm, 12฿); show the driver the center's name in Thai.

Pak Thong Chai is a traditional silk-producing village 32km south of Khorat. The **Pak Tongchai Silk and Cultural Center** gives tours of the factories and allows visitors to observe the silk production cycle, from the raising of silkworms (fed on mulberry leaves) to the threading and weaving of garments. It closes sporadically during the low season, so inquire at the TAT office in Khorat first.

PHIMAI

Since the fall of Angkor in 1432, Phimai has been transformed from an important cultural center to an idyllic satellite of Khorat, 60km to the southeast. Roosters provide free wake-up calls at dawn in the shadow of Thailand's largest stone ruins, and the town's peaceful day lethargically unfolds where a great city once bustled.

TRANSPORTATION AND PRACTICAL INFORMATION. Buses to Phimai depart from Khorat's Bus Terminal 2 (#1305, 1½-2hr., every 30min. 5am-10pm, 21฿). They terminate at **New Primai Town Bus Station,** in a tacky housing development outside of Phimai proper. Be sure to get out earlier at the **Phimai Bus Station,** at the south end of **Chomsudasapet Rd.** Bus #1305 leaves Phimai for **Khorat** (every 30min. 4am-6pm, 21฿). For those headed north to **Khon Kaen, Udon Thani,** or **Nong Khai,** get off at Talad Khae, 10km away from Phimai, and ask someone where to wait. Those moving onward to **Surin** may bypass Khorat and save considerable time by taking a *songthaew* from the New Phimai Bus Station to the train station at Hin Dat (8am, 30min., 20฿). From here, connect to a Surin-bound train (2hr., 3rd-class 22฿).

At the opposite end of **Chomsudasapet Rd.,** the temple is visible. Here, Chomsudasapet meets **Anantajinda Rd.,** which runs along the front of the park. Just around the corner to the left of this intersection is the **Thai Military Bank,** 222 Anantajinda Rd., which exchanges traveler's checks (☎471 334; open M-F 8:30am-3:30pm) and has an **ATM** (Cirrus/MC/V; open daily 6am-10pm). To the right of this intersection, Anantajinda Rd. passes a clock tower, which houses the **police pavilion** and the compact **night market.** To reach the **post and telegraph office,** 123 Srikeaw Rd., go left on Anantajinda Rd. at the gate to the park. **Srikaew Rd.** is the first right; the post office is 150m down on the left. (Open M-F 8:30am-4:30pm, Sa-Su 9-11am.) **Postal code:** 30110.

ACCOMMODATIONS AND FOOD. Phimai boasts two first-rate guest houses and an excellent restaurant, making overnight stays quite rewarding. **Old Phimai Guest House,** 214 Mu 1 Chomsudasapet Rd., 2½ blocks down Chomsudasapet from the bus terminal down a small soi to the left (look for the sign), has palatial rooms in an airy wooden house overseen by an English-speaking family. (☎471 918. Dorms 90฿; singles 150฿, with A/C 200฿; doubles 350฿. HI members receive a 10% discount.) Right across the alley sits the **S&P New Phimai Guest House,** 213 Mu 1 Chomsudasapet Rd. Their cosmopolitan graffiti and a crotchety iguana keep boredom at bay. (☎287 275. Huge singles 80฿; doubles 130฿; triples 210฿.)

Baitely Restaurant, 246/1 Chomsudasapet Rd. (☎471 725), is a block before the soi leading to the guest houses and doubles as an informal tourist info center, distributing free maps of Phimai. The menu features a variety of Thai dishes (30-150฿) but the specialty is *pad mee*, Phimai-style fried noodles (30฿). An English menu is available. (Open daily 7am-midnight.)

SIGHTS. Phimai's *raison d'être* are the stately Khmer ruins smack in the middle of town within the **Prasat Hin Phimai Historical Park.** At its zenith, the Angkor empire covered much of mainland Southeast Asia. Evidence of its power and wealth remain in the hundreds of temples that still dot the region. At one time, a laterite highway linked Phimai, along with nearby Muang Tham and Phanom Rung, with the empire's magnificent capital, Angkor Thom, 225km to the south. This white sandstone temple was built in a style similar to Angkor Wat in the late 11th century, probably during the reign of Suriyavarman I. The encircling walls of red sandstone and laterite were built over the next 150 years. Archaeologists went a bit overboard with their "restoration"—hence the abundance of cement and the incongruous plaster ceiling in the central sanctuary. On the right of the stone causeway with *naga* balustrades is a collection of faded sandstone lintels. Although the temple is dedicated to Buddhism, many of the lintels depict Hindu gods and myths or scenes from the epic *Ramayana*, evidence of the Hindu tradition that preceded the spread of Buddhism. (Open daily 7:30am-6pm. 40฿.)

Phimai National Museum is north of the park, 500m down the road that runs past the eastern perimeter of the temple complex in a large white building with a red tiled roof. The museum includes an extensive collection of Khmer and Dvaravati art, as well as interesting anthropological exhibits documenting the social, political, and economic history of the Isaan region. Those who miss the museum's opening hours can freely explore the pond in front and the outdoor displays of numerous lintels depicting Hindu gods. (☎471 167. Open daily 9am-4pm. 40฿.)

For a less cerebral diversion, **Sai Ngam,** the largest banyan tree in Thailand, stands on the banks of the Moon River 2km east of town. It's about a 10min. bike ride or 40฿ motorcycle jaunt from town. Facing the park, head to the right on Anantajinda Rd. past the clock tower: stick to the main road and follow the signs. Descending under Sai Ngam's thick green canopy is like entering a J.R.R. Tolkien-inspired netherworld. Wizened old men will read your palm for a few baht. At the center, a small pagoda houses the spirit of this 360-year-old miracle. Other attractions include a traditional Isaan house built on stilts, a flower garden, and a statue of **Sook Prasat Hin Phimai,** a famous boxer from Phimai.

PHANOM RUNG AND MUANG THAM

The ancient Khmer temples of Phanom Rung and Muang Tham are the tourist magnets of lower Isaan. Visit Muang Tham first, then explore Phanom Rung. While transportation is not too difficult, set out early to avoid getting stranded. From **Khorat** (Bus Terminal 2) or **Surin,** catch bus #274 or #98 and get off at **Ban Ta-Ko** (2hr., 37฿), which is clearly marked as the turn-off for Phanom Rung (16km) and Muang Tham. If you're just going to Phanom Rung, you can catch a *songthaew* (around 30฿). Another option is to catch the Buriram-bound bus from **Aranyaprathet** (which actually starts in Chanthaburi) as early as possible. The bus passes through Ban Don Nang Nae, only 10km from Phanom Rung, before continuing to Ban Ta-Ko. If you're seeing both Phanom Rung and Muang Tham, **motorcycle** or **pickup** drivers will take you to the temples and wait while you tour the grounds (150-200฿). This latter option is recommended during the low season and on weekdays, when transportation is unpredictable. To return to Surin or Khorat, get back to Ban Ta-Ko before 5pm, as buses run less frequently after that.

Alternatively, book a full-day tour (380฿, 4-person minimum) to both temples at the **Old Phimai Guest House** in Phimai. Tours also visit **Prasat Hin Khau Praviharn,** a magnificent temple just across the Cambodian border (625฿; 4 person minimum).

MUANG THAM. Muang Tham, dating from the 10th century, is situated in a low valley 6km from Phanom Rung. Though fresh from an overhaul at the hands of the Thai Fine Arts Department, Muang Tham cannot match the splendor of Phanom Rung. Still, it provides a detailed picture of a Khmer temple in its present incarnation. *(Open daily 6am-6pm. 30฿.)*

PRASAT HIN KHAO PHANOM RUNG HISTORICAL PARK. This majestic temple, one of the largest surviving Khmer monuments, was built between the 10th and 13th centuries. Standing atop an extinct volcano 383m above sea level, the temple commands dramatic vistas of the surrounding plain, broken in the southeast by the Dongrek Mountains of Cambodia. Inside the complex, three terraced platforms lead up to the "white elephant hall," a partially reconstructed stone structure on the right. The 160m promenade lined with lotus-bud-shaped pillars leads to the main complex and its stairway. The stairs that follow lead to the main temple; at the top is a second bridge and the main gallery. Once you're through the hallway of the gallery, you'll be standing in daylight on the third bridge, facing a portico of the chamber leading to the main sanctuary. The lintel above this entrance, the **Phrai Narai Lintel,** depicts a Hindu creation myth featuring Lord Narayana, an *avatar* (incarnation) of Vishnu. It was stolen, resurfaced in the Art Institute of Chicago, and was returned in 1988. *(Open daily 6am-6pm. 40฿.)*

SURIN ☎044

For one week each November, hordes of Thai and *farang* flood Surin to watch dancing, bejeweled, soccer-playing pachyderms on parade in the Surin Elephant roundup. The other 51 weeks of the year, Surin remains a rare stop on itineraries, as most travelers press on to the Mekong River. Their loss is your gain; this peaceful town, boasting one of the niftiest night markets around, is a jumping-off point for the many small Khmer ruins and traditional villages dotting the surrounding countryside. Only 50km from the Cambodian border, Surin reflects the province's unique mixture of Lao, Khmer, Thai, and indigenous Suay cultures.

TRANSPORTATION

Trains: Surin Railway Station (☎511 295), beside the elephant statue on Thornsarn Rd. Trains to **Khorat** (3hr., 11-13 per day) and **Ubon Ratchathani** (3hr., 11 per day). Many of these trains continue to **Bangkok.** Prices vary according to the type of train and seat (Bangkok 73-229฿; Khorat or Ubon 32-114฿).

Buses: Surin Bus Terminal (☎511 756), on Chit Bam Rung Rd. From the traffic circle, go 1 block east past Mr. Donut, and then 2 blocks to the left; it's on the right. Buses to: **Bangkok** (10 per day 7:30am-9pm; fan 131฿, A/C 183฿, VIP 225฿); **Chiang Mai** (15hr.; 5 per day 2:45-6:50pm; fan 255฿, A/C 455฿, VIP 525฿); **Khorat** (3½hr.; every 15-20min. 3:30am-6pm; fan 60฿, A/C 80฿); **Pattaya** (9hr.; 9 per day 5:30am-9:30pm; fan 150฿, A/C 270฿); **Ubon Ratchathani** (4hr.; 9 per day 7:30am-9:30pm; fan 80฿, A/C 107฿).

Local Transportation: Samlor around town 20-25฿; **tuk-tuk** 30฿.

ORIENTATION AND PRACTICAL INFORMATION

The provincial capital Surin is 452km from Bangkok and easily reached by bus or train from Bangkok, Khorat, or Ubon Ratchathani. Surin has no English street signs. The main street, **Thornsarn Rd.,** runs north-south. At its north end is the **train station,** which faces an elephant statue. Several blocks down Thornsarn Rd. from the train station is a **traffic circle.** To reach the traffic circle from the bus station, exit to the left, pass the soi with the sign for the Petchkason Hotel, and take the next right. Thornsarn Rd. is the first intersection. One block past the traffic circle on Thornsarn is the intersection with **Krung Sri Nai Rd.,** with **day** and **night markets,** the **post office** (on the right past the traffic circle), **banks,** and a **hotel.**

Tourist Offices: Brochure on Surin (but no maps) from the **TAT** in Khorat or at **Surin City Hall** (☎521 361), on Lakmuang Rd. Open M-F 8:30am-3:30pm. Mr. Pirom at Mr. Pirom's House (see **Accommodations,** below) can also provide info.

Currency Exchange: Bangkok Bank, 252 Thornsarn Rd. (☎511 443), just past the traffic circle on the right. **24hr. ATM** (AmEx/MC/PLUS/V). Open M-F 8:30am-3:30pm. Several other banks and ATMs also lie along Thornsarn Rd.

Markets: Day and **night markets** are in the same location along Krung Sri Nai Rd. From the train station walk 1 block past the traffic circle. The permanent market is on the right; the left side of the street comes to life at dusk.

Emergency: ☎191.

Police: Surin Police Station (☎511 007), on Lakmuang Rd.

Pharmacy: Kayang Chelan Pesat, 294 Thornsarn Rd. (☎513 055). Near Krung Sri Nai Rd. Open daily 8:30am-9pm.

Medical Services: Ruam Paet, Tesaban 1 Rd. (☎511 523). In a tall building with a blue and white sign. Facing the train station at the traffic circle, turn right; it's after the 2nd stoplight on the right. English-speaking doctor.

Post Office/Telephones: Surin Post Office (☎511 009), on the corner of Thornsarn and Tesaban 1 Rd. at the traffic circle. Phone and fax available 7am-10pm. International pay phones (one on Thornsarn Rd., 1 block from train station) require phone cards—but phone cards aren't sold in Surin. Open M-F 8:30am-4:30pm, Sa-Su 9am-noon. **Postal code:** 32000.

ACCOMMODATIONS

Except for one superb guest house, accommodations are uninspiring. During the elephant roundup, rates can soar 50% and finding a room is nearly impossible.

Pirom's House, 242 Krung Sri Nai Rd. (☎515 140). From the train station, take a right onto Krung Sri Nai Rd. and walk 600m until it curves sharply left; it's the teak-wood house at the bend. The pond is part of the old city moat. Gates lock at 10:30pm. Mr. Pirom's tours (from 690฿ per day) are famed for their spontaneity. All rooms have shared baths. Dorms 70฿; singles 100฿; doubles 150฿.

Santhong Hotel (Nid Diew Hotel), 279-281 Thornsarn Rd. (☎512 009). From the train station, it's on the left just after the traffic circle, opposite Bangkok Bank. Singles 220฿, with A/C 360฿; doubles 290/390฿.

New Hotel, 6-8 Thornsarn Rd. (☎511 322), outside the train station beside the mini-mart. Convenient. Squat toilets. Singles 160฿; doubles 280฿; A/C rooms 330-500฿.

FOOD

Surin has some of the best Isaan food around, especially at the market. On opposite sides of Krung Sri Nai Rd., at the intersection of Tesaban 3, the day and night markets stay open 24 hours.

THAILAND

Wai Wan Restaurant, 44-46 Sanitnikhomrat Rd. From the train station, take the second left onto Sanitnikhomrat Rd.; it's on the right. Four restaurants in one: Western, Thai, ice cream parlor, and bakery. Tricolored rice (sausage, olive, and crab) 40฿; steak 100-300฿; rice dishes 40฿. English menu. Open daily 7am-11pm.

SIGHTS AND ENTERTAINMENT

Surin is a pleasant place to relax and enjoy Isaan life, but there's not much in the way of "official" sights unless you're there for the annual **Elephant Roundup** at the end of November (check with the TAT in Khorat or with Mr. Pirom for exact dates). The stars of this two-day festival honoring the national animal are the 200 pachyderms who awe audiences with feats of strength and skill. Highlights include a battle reenactment and a staged "elephant hunt" exhibiting traditional Suay techniques. The finale features a soccer match played by the agile beasts.

For those whose idea of fun involves a good beat and a dance floor, **The Sparks Music Complex** is the place. From the traffic circle, head down Tesaban Rd. toward the Mr. Donut sign. Take a left at Sirirat Rd. (the 2nd stoplight) and proceed 300m—look up high for the red sign. Sparks is packed on weekends when locals gather to gyre and gimble. *(☎514 088. Open daily 9am-3am. Cover 70฿.)*

THAILAND

DAYTRIPS FROM SURIN

Anyone can visit the local **silk-weaving villages,** but the communication barrier and sometimes wary villagers make learning the entire silk-making process difficult for the average traveler. Luckily, Mr. Pirom can act as a go-between for travelers and locals (see **Pirom's House,** above); he knows the process and the people well. His tours go to places like **Ban Ta Klang,** a Suay village featuring elephants that are trained and kept as pets, **Ban Khaosinarin,** a group of traditional silk-weaving villages, and numerous Khmer ruins and temples including **Prasat Srikhoraphum.**

To visit the villages solo, walk toward the train station on Thornsarn Rd. After the traffic circle, enter the second alley on the left. From here trucks ferry visitors the 20km or so (approximately every hour 7-9am). Return early to avoid a wait or an overnight stay in the village.

UBON RATCHATHANI ☎045

Ubon Ratchathani (simply "Ubon" to Thais), the trading and communications hub for the northeast corner of Thailand, attracts few travelers, except during the Candle Festival in July. The festival features processions of beeswax-covered serpents, saints, and Buddhas—some candles are larger than the monks that carry them. Not far downstream, the Moon River flows into the "emerald triangle" where Laos, Cambodia, and Thailand converge in the lush jungle. The "Lotus City," with a fine museum and famed silk and cotton cloth, proves a worthy base from which to explore the many fine archaeological sites, national parks, and villages sprinkled along the Mekong River region to the east. Also, those interested in monastic Buddhism can visit many of the region's secluded forest monasteries.

TRANSPORTATION

Flights: Ubon Ratchathani International Airport (☎243 039), on Thepyotee Rd. **Thai Airways,** 364 Chayangkun Rd. (☎313 340), 2km north of the river on the right. Open M-F 8am-4pm. Flights to **Bangkok** (8:30am, 7:40pm; 1435฿).

Trains: Railway Station (☎321 878, advance ticketing ☎321 004), on Sathani Rd., Warin Chamrap District. Buses #2 and #6 run to the station from Uparat Rd. (5฿). Trains go to **Bangkok** (13-14hr.; 6:35, 6:55am, 1:25, 4:15, 4:50, 6:15, 7:40pm; seat with fan 95฿, seat with A/C 120-200฿, sleeper with fan 320-470฿, sleeper with A/C 450-700฿) via **Surin** (31-100฿) and **Khorat** (58-200฿).

Buses: Ubon has 6 privately-run bus stations. At the far north end of town is the **Sahamit bus station,** 327-331 Jangsarit Rd. (☎255 043); take bus #1 or #2. To: **Mukdahan** (2hr.; 6:30, 7:30am, 2, 3pm; fan 51฿, A/C 92฿) via **That Phanom** (45min.); 1st and 3rd buses continue to **Nakhon Phanom** (4hr.; fan 81฿, A/C 146฿); 2nd bus terminates in **Udon Thani** (6½hr.; fan 128฿, A/C 210฿). Buses leave from **Warin Chamrap station** south of the Moon River (take bus #1, #3, #6, or #7; 5฿) to **Phibun** (every 15min. 6:20am-5:30pm, 20฿) and **Surin** (every 30min. 7am-5pm, fan 43฿). From Phibun, *songthaew* run to **Chong Mek** and **Khong Chiam.**

Local Transportation: City buses run 6am-6pm (5฿). From Uparat Rd., buses #2 and #6 run to the train station; buses #1, #3, #6, and #7 go to Warin Chamrap bus station; buses #1 and #2 head to Sahamit bus station. **Tuk-tuk** and **samlor** roam the streets (up to 30฿ from the Moon River to Sahamit bus station).

ORIENTATION AND PRACTICAL INFORMATION

THAILAND

Readily accessible by air, bus, or train, Ubon is the last stop on the northeastern branch of the national railway network. To go farther east or north, travelers must rely on the sometimes-daunting bus system. Ubon's main thoroughfare, **Uparat Rd.,** stretches north-south for 12km. At its north end it is called **Chayangkun Rd.** To the south, it crosses the **Moon River** into the **Warin Chamrap District,** where the train station is. Buses #1, #2, and #6 go there from Ubon proper. North of the river, Uparat Rd. passes the riverside **market** and, two blocks up, intersects **Khuanthani Rd.** The **hospital** and **museum** are here, and the **tourist office** is several blocks to the right. One block farther from the river, Uparat Rd. meets **Sinarong Rd.,** where the **tourist police** and **post office** lie.

Tourist Offices: TAT, 264/1 Khuanthani Rd. (☎243 770), away from the river on Uparat Rd. Turn right onto Khuanthani Rd. at the National Museum; it's on the left 2 blocks down. Free, useful maps and fluent English spoken. Open daily 8am-4pm.

Tours: Siri Ratana Tours (☎245 847), on Palorangit Rd. With your back to the river, turn right onto Palorangit Rd.; it's 1½ blocks down on the left. To: **Bangkok** (10hr.; 7:30am, 8pm; A/C 310฿) via **Surin** (2½hr., 100฿); **Buriram** (4hr., 120฿); **Nakhon Ratchasima** (6hr., 180฿); **Saraburi** (7hr., 310฿). **Sayan Tour,** opposite TAT. To: **Khon Kaen** (4hr., 116฿); **Roi Et** (2½hr., 74฿); **Udon Thani** (#268; 6hr.; 6:40, 8, 11am, 1pm; 162฿) via **Ban Pa Ao** (30min., 15฿). **Nakornchai Air Tour** (☎269 385), on Uparat Rd. 1km south of the Moon River. To: **Bangkok** (#98; 9hr.; 8:15, 9:30am and 5 between 7:30-9:30pm; A/C 393฿) via **Khorat** (6hr.; fan 110฿, A/C 200฿, VIP 300฿); **Chiang Mai** (#587; 13hr.; 6 per day 12:15-6pm; fan 300฿, A/C 540฿, VIP 600฿) via **Surin** (3hr.; fan 50฿, A/C 90฿, VIP 140฿); **Rayong** (#588; 10hr.; 6:30am and 5 between 3:30-7:30pm; fan 215฿, A/C 390฿, VIP 455฿) via **Pattaya** (9hr.; fan 200฿, A/C 355฿, VIP 415฿) and **Surin.**

Currency Exchange: Bangkok Bank, 13 Ratchabut Rd. (☎262 453). **24hr. ATM** (AmEx/MC/PLUS/V). Open M-F 8:30am-3:30pm. Banks line Uparat Rd.

Rentals: Thai Yont has its main office at 302-14 Khuanthani Rd. (☎241 242). Rentals should be returned on Uparat Rd. near Suriyat Rd. Reliable, well-maintained and serviced. **Motorcycles** 200-300฿ per day. Open M-Sa 8am-5pm.

Markets: The **Riverside market** is an around-the-clock affair. As you cross the bridge into Ubon, market is immediately to the right of Uparat Rd.

Emergency: Police ☎191. **Tourist Police** ☎245 505.

Tourist Police: ☎245 505. At the corner of Suriyat and Thebyotee Rd., near the airport. English spoken. Call here before dialing the police.

Pharmacy: Chai Wit, 87 Promtap Rd. (☎254 077). From the TAT, walk 2 blocks toward the river. Chai Wit is 1 block to the left–look for the yellow and green sign across the street. Open M-F 7am-7:30pm, Sa 7am-noon.

Medical Services: Rom Klao, 123 Uparat Rd. (☎244 658), 2 blocks down Uparat Rd. From the bridge, it's on the left before Khuanthani Rd. English spoken. **Open 24hr.**

Internet Access: The cheapest spot on Nakornban Rd. 100m north of Palorangsit (☎01 447 8612). Sign reads: "Internet." 20฿ per hr. Open daily 9am-midnight.

Post Offices/Telephones: GPO (☎260 465), on Sinarong Rd. Walk past the TAT on Khuanthani Rd. and turn left at the 2nd intersection; Sinarong Rd. is 1 block north. The Post office is on the right-hand corner. *Poste Restante* behind the office. AmEx/MC/V. Open M-F 8:30am-4:30pm, Sa-Su 9am-noon. **Telephone** service available M-F 8:30am-4:30pm at a second post office at 159-163 Padaeng Rd. **Lenso** phone. Phone cards sold here. The Warin Chamrap branch office, on Tahaan Rd., has same hours and also offers **Internet** access (Internet cash cards 60฿ per hr.). **Postal code:** 34000.

ACCOMMODATIONS

River Moon House, 21 Si Saket 2 Rd., Warin Chamrap (☎286 093). From the train station, take the second left after the iron horse display out front. Walk 200m until the road merges into Si Saket 2 Rd.; it's across the street, 10m to the right. Four teak houses sit back from the road. Pan, the owner, gives excellent travel advice. Monstrous breakfast 50฿. All rooms have shared baths. Dorms 80฿; singles 100฿; doubles 120฿; room with two double beds 150฿.

Sri Isaan Hotel (☎254 204), end of Ratchabut Rd. near Moon River. Basic rooms 150฿.

New Nakornhuang Hotel, 84-88 Yutthaphan Rd. (☎254 768), a block south of the TAT office. Spartan rooms. Doubles with fan and bath 240฿, with TV 270฿.

Suriyat Hotel, 302 Suriyat Rd. (☎241 144), on the north end of town. Singles with bath and fan 180฿.

FOOD

The **market** off Promathep Rd. east of Uparat Rd. serves up duck salad and *kuay chap*, among other Isaan and Vietnamese dishes, around the clock. At night, **vendors** also gather on Ratchabut Rd. off Khuanthani Rd. near the Ratchathani Hotel. Several Chinese restaurants on nearby Khuanthani Rd. stay open past midnight. With a large population of devout Buddhists, Ubon is a vegetarian's heaven.

Rain Khow Klong. Sit in the rock garden on bamboo furniture and listen to the sounds of an indoor waterfall. Full Thai menu with impressively deceptive imitation meat. Vegetarian only. Meals 40-80฿ per person. Open daily 11am-2pm and 4-10pm.

Vegetarian Restaurant, 79/1 Nakomban Rd. Six-table joint with homemade creations. Soya milk 3฿. Meals 15-25฿. Open M-F 7am-2pm.

Bua Boo Cha Mangsawirat, 11 Si Saket Rd., Warin Chamrap. Specializes in vegetarian food. From Warin Chamrap train station, walk straight and turn right onto Uparat Rd, then left at the next street; it's on the right. Glutinous rice balls stuffed with peanuts 5฿. Open M-Sa 6:30am-3pm.

SIGHTS

The **Ubon Ratchathani National Museum,** on the left side of Khuanthani Rd. immediately after turning right off Uparat Rd., documents the region's history and culture. Considered one of the country's best, this museum features a 1500-year-old bronze kettle drum from Khong Chiam, a 9th-century Dvaravati boundary stone, Khmer lintels, and local crafts. (☎255 071. Open W-Su 8am-4pm. 30฿.)

Wat Thon Sri Muang towers above Luang Rd. opposite the kindergarten. The wat, with interior wall paintings depicting life in ancient Ubon, is over 200 years old. The

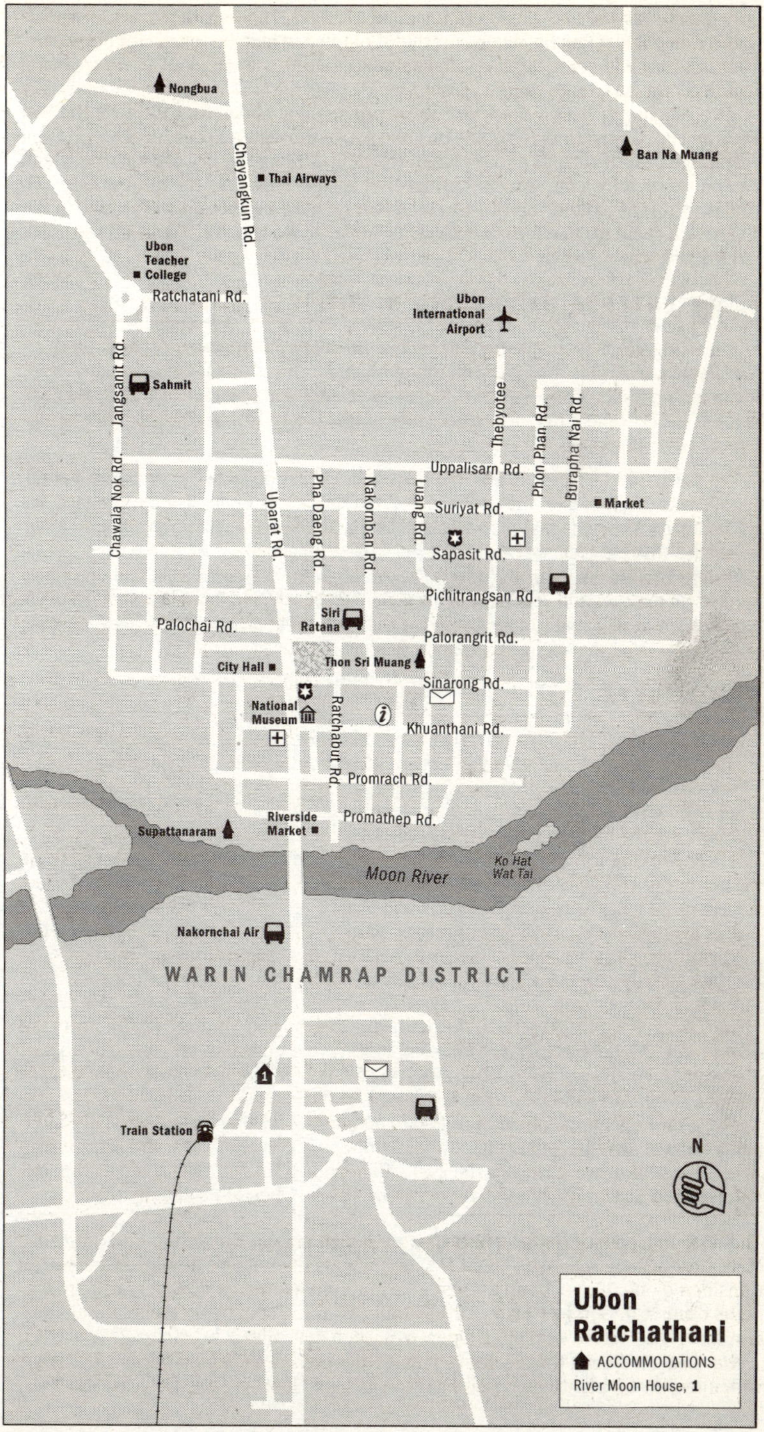
Nongbua
Ban Na Muang
Thai Airways
Chayangkun Rd.
Ubon Teacher College
Ratchatani Rd.
Ubon International Airport
Jangsanit Rd.
Sahmit
Thebyotee
Phon Phan Rd.
Burapha Nai Rd.
Uppalisarn Rd.
Chawala Nok Rd.
Uparat Rd.
Pha Daeng Rd.
Nakornban Rd.
Luang Rd.
Suriyat Rd.
Market
Sapasit Rd.
Pichitrangsan Rd.
Siri Ratana
Palochai Rd.
Palorangrit Rd.
City Hall
Thon Sri Muang
Sinarong Rd.
National Museum
Ratchabut Rd.
Khuanthani Rd.
Promrach Rd.
Supattanaram
Riverside Market
Promathep Rd.
Ko Hat Wat Tai
Moon River
Nakornchai Air
WARIN CHAMRAP DISTRICT
1
Train Station
N
Ubon Ratchathani
ACCOMMODATIONS
River Moon House, 1

THAILAND

July **Candle Festival** takes place in the adjacent field. Those with access to wheels can check out **Wat Ban No Muang,** northeast of town, which features a modern-style, 50m tall, three-headed elephant. Pass underneath to view a giant *wihaan* being paddled away in a large sailing vessel.

Two relaxing spots on the Moon River provide diversions for locals. **Ko Hat Wat Tai** is an island surrounded by huts on stilts above the water. Locals order food from restaurants on the island and picnic in the huts. During the dry season, the island can be reached by a bamboo footbridge, but is inaccessible in the rainy season. To find it, walk east to the end of Promrach Rd., then turn right and walk down to the river bank (no entrance fee). **Hat Khudua,** similar to Ko Hat Wat Tai, is on the north bank 12km west of town.

ENTERTAINMENT AND NIGHTLIFE

Ubon's nightlife is concentrated on Uparat Rd. a few kilometers north of the river. The **Nevada** multiplex, just past the Ratchathani intersection on the right, shows the latest action flicks (60฿). Receive Isaan-style traditional massage at **Traditional Pharmacy,** 359-371 Sapasit Rd., near the corner of Pha Daeng Rd. (☎254 741. 100฿ per hr. Open daily 8am-6pm.)

The Cave, 341 Chayangkun Rd., two blocks out of town past the Uppalisarn-Uparat Rd. intersection on the left. The place to see and be seen in Ubon. Usually has good live bands on weekends that play covers of Thai and English tunes. Cover 80฿, on weekends 140฿, includes two free drinks. Open daily 10pm-3am.

Swing Party House, 140/1-2 Uparat Rd. (☎265 145), between Suriyat and Uppalisarn Rd., on the right with your back to the river. The hottest bar in town. With refined, halogen light fixtures and stuffed leather booths, it's a great place to kick back for a quiet evening. Live soft rock music nightly at 8:30pm. Open daily 5pm-1am.

THAILAND

MARKETS

Ubon is famous for its silk and *khit*-patterned cotton cloth. Two stores sell clothing made from the area's handwoven cotton. **Maybe Cotton Hut,** 124 Sinarong Rd., is a block east of the post office. (☎254 932. Open daily 7:30am-9pm.) **Peaceland,** 189 Thepyothee Rd., is 2½ blocks north of Maybe. Turn left on Thepyothee Rd. and look left beneath the bougainvillea. (☎244 028. Open daily 10am-8pm.)

Those looking for world-famous Isaan silk should try the **Women's Weaving Cooperative** in the village of **Ban Pa Ao,** 17km north of Ubon on Rte. 23. Ban Pa Ao is a 200-year-old village famous for its silk and bronze wares. Their traditional *mutmee* silk is available in an array of colors and patterns. Prices begin at 650฿ per meter, and run into the thousands. Weavers perform demonstrations on request. The clothes, mostly women's blouses and skirts, sold in the showroom, start at 450฿. Any bus heading north from the Sayan Tour bus station passes Ban Pa Ao. (Open daily 8:30am-6:30pm.) Tell the ticket collector to drop you off there (20฿). From the main road, the cooperative is 3km east; motorcycle taxis can take you the rest of the way (20฿). To return to Ubon, flag down any bus heading south to the city, or catch a *songthaew* directly from the village (20฿).

For a more general selection of local handicrafts, try **Ban Phan Chat,** 158 Ratchabut Rd., which sells local silk, cotton, fish traps, rice containers, and bronze trinkets. Exit and turn right from the TAT office and then turn right again at the first intersection; it's on the immediate right. (☎243 433. Open M-Sa 9am-8pm.)

DAYTRIPS FROM UBON RATCHATHANI

FOREST MONASTERIES

Wat Pa Nanachat Beung Wai is behind a rice field off the highway to Si Saket, near Beung Wai village. Catch a Si Saket-bound bus or songthaew from Warin Chamrap bus terminal, and ask to get off at Wat Nanachat. Wat Nong Pa Pong temple is 10km south of Ubon and off the road to Katharalak (ask for directions at Pa Nanachat).

Northeast Thailand is known for its masters of meditation. Forest wat became the home of *dudtong* (serious and ascetic) monks who keep strict vows—limiting food to one meal a day, walking as their only means of transportation, and going barefoot. Ubon province has accessible monasteries. Visitors should wear proper dress and enter quietly, as silent meditation retreats are often in session.

Wat Pa Nanachat Beung Wai, a forest monastery with predominantly Western monks, is 12km west of Ubon on the way to Surin. Those studying meditation and Buddhism may want to visit; serious students can stay the night. It's a branch of the nearby **Wat Nong Pa Pong** temple, known principally for meditation teacher **Ajaan Chaa,** renowned for his clarity, insight, and discipline. Both wat have more than 20 acres of dense forest, providing a pleasant and cool place to spend a morning or afternoon. A major branch of the controversial **Santi Asok** sect resides 6km to the east of town; ask in town for details.

KHAO PHRA WIHAAN

Park open daily 8am-5pm. 100฿. During the week, the grounds are empty, and transportation requires some creativity. Whenever you go, start the 98km haul south early to facilitate a smooth trip. Catch one of the buses to Katharalak, which leave from a lot in Warin Chamrap on Uparat Rd. near the minimart (2hr., every hr. 6am-7pm, 25฿). From Katharalak, tell locals where you want to go. On weekends they will put you on a bus directly to the site, but on weekdays they will direct you to another songthaew that goes to the Poomsalon turn-off 10km north of the site (1hr., leave when full, 15฿). From there, some travelers ignore the greedy motorcycle taxis (200฿ round-trip) and try to hitch a ride from a few hundred meters south on the highway. Drivers and foreigners must cede their passports to police 3km from the park to guarantee return to Thailand.

One kilometer over Thailand's contested southern border, one of Thailand's best monuments is actually in Cambodia. Basking in its own gravity-defying splendor, Khao Phra Wihaan is a temple/monument complex built by the Angkor kings. The complex rises 800m up a steep grade overlooking the Cambodian plains to the south; its principal chapel is on the peak of a great cliff 600m high.

A contemporary of Angkor Wat, the structure was built from the 10th to the 12th century by King Rajendravarman. Large steps lead past four pavilions and many tourist markets. Although officially opened to the public in 1991, it was closed two years later because of violent hill skirmishes between the Khmer Rouge and the Cambodian government. In August 1998, it was reopened. Today, a helicopter with its belly ripped open pays homage to the last government siege in 1998 that captured the mount. It lies near the first pavilion. As of April 2000, the area appears to have stabilized; however, don't stray from the well-trodden path. The area may still contain live landmines.

KHONG CHIAM

The tranquil hamlet of Khong Chiam is 60km east of Ubon, at the confluence of the Moon and Mekong Rivers. To local youths it's "Sticksville," but to the metropolis-weary traveler, it's a paradise where the pace of life echoes the somnolent flow of the river, and where children squeal and hide from *farang*.

TRANSPORTATION. Take a bus from Warin Chamrap bus station in **Ubon** to Phibun Mangsahan (1hr., every 30min. 5am-6pm, 20฿). From the Phibun market, take a *samlor* to the *songthaew* station on the Moon River (10฿ at most). *Songthaew* go to Khong Chiam at least once per hour (45min., 20฿). If you get stuck in Phibun, **Hotel Phibun** has immaculate singles and doubles (with fan 200-250฿, with A/C 300-350฿). To get there, walk from the *songthaew* stop (with the market on the left) to the intersection, and take a right; it's ahead on the right.

ORIENTATION AND PRACTICAL INFORMATION. Khong Chiam is shaped like a triangle: its two main roads come together in a point as they jut out into the two rivers. **Klaewpradit Rd.** runs from the market and bus stop straight through the center of town, ending at a wat. Walking across the temple grounds leads to a pavilion with an excellent view of the Moon and Mekong Rivers, joining to become the "Two-Color" river, an effect created by the different levels of silt suspension in the water. In the dry season, this effect is not as stunning, but the low water level creates a dry mud moonscape from which travelers can almost touch Laos. The **post office** has an **overseas phone.** (☎351 123. Open M-F 8:30am-4:30pm, Sa 9am-noon.) Khong Chiam's lone **bank** doesn't change currency. **Rimkheng Rd.** runs along the Mekong River parallel to Klaewpradit Rd. Here, a stone tablet opposite the **police station** identifies Khong Chiam as the easternmost point in Thailand. **Postal code:** 34220.

ACCOMMODATIONS AND FOOD. Khong Chiam supports several fine guest houses; the **Apple Guest House,** on 267 Klaewpradit Rd., is tops. From the market, head right on Klaewpradit Rd. for 300m; it's on the right, past the bank and opposite the post office. The small restaurant in front has a helpful information board. Motorcycles are rented for 150฿ per day. (☎351 160. Singles and doubles 120฿, with A/C 300฿.) The **Khong Chiam Hotel,** 355 Pakumchai Rd., is off Klaewpradit Rd. From the market, take a right onto Klaewpradit Rd., then another right onto Ratsadonutit Rd. From there, a quick left gets you on Pakumchai Rd.; it's 25m ahead on the left. (☎351 074. Rooms with bath 120฿, with A/C 300฿.) Good **restaurants** line Rimkheng Rd.

THAILAND

SIGHTS. About 30km north of Khong Chiam is **Pha Taem National Park,** housing a 200m stretch of prehistoric rock paintings. There is little public transport, but you can get there easily with a map and rented wheels. Road signs along the way make the trip easier. During the high season, two or three *songthaew* may depart; inquire at Apple Guest House. Once at Pha Taem, it's a 500m walk to the paintings. **Tana Rapids National Park** is 3km south of Khong Chiam on the Moon River.

BORDER CROSSING: CHONG MEK/VANG TAO. Travelers can enter the Laos at the village of Chong Mek, 44km from Phibun. From the village of Vang Tao on the Lao side, it is a short ride to Pakse (see p. 360), an excellent springboard for exploring southern Laos. Other than the border crossing itself, there is little of interest for travelers here except on Saturday and Sunday, when a lively market springs up on both sides of the border. From Ubon, take a bus from the Warin Chamrap station to Phibun (1hr., 5am-6pm, 20฿). At the Phibun market, locals can direct you to *songthaew* heading to Chong Mek (1¼hr., 7am-5pm, 20฿).

Travelers intending to enter Laos must first have a visa stamped with the name of the appropriate entry point (i.e. Vang Tao) from the Lao embassy in Bangkok, or from the Lao consulate in Khon Kaen. Visas obtained in Nong Khai are not valid here. Before crossing the border you must officially register your departure from Thailand at the **immigration office,** 30m before the fence on the right. Once in Laos, present visas to immigration, just beyond the border on the right (entry tax 50฿). From Vang Tao, *songthaew* can drive you to Pakse (10฿).

MUKDAHAN ☎042

Mukdahan Province was carved out of Ubon Ratchathani and Nakhon Phanom Provinces in 1982. Its capital city lies midway along the east border of Isaan with the Mekong River to the east, directly opposite Savannakhet, Laos. Not surprisingly, there is a strong Lao flavor to this town of 30,000. Mukdahan offers unspoiled countryside and beautiful vistas along the river at twilight. Few *farang* make it here, and those who do can expect many attempts at conversation.

TRANSPORTATION

Buses: Main **bus station,** 33 Chayang Koolurd Rd. (☎630 486), 3km away on the side of the highway opposite the town. To walk into town, take a left out of the terminal and a right at Wiwitsurakan Rd., the first major intersection, 500m ahead. Follow this street as it merges and winds to the right. Make a left at Phitak Phanomket Rd. and walk 1km into the heart of town. *Tuk-tuk* to the river 20-40฿. Buses to: **Bangkok** (12hr.; 8, 8:40am, 4:30pm, and 4 between 6:30-7:30pm; fan 184-193฿, A/C 331-347฿, VIP 545฿,) via **Khorat** (6hr.; fan 120฿, A/C 128-202฿). Prices depend on routing. Regular service to: **Nakhon Phanom** (2½hr.; 7 per day 8:30am-5pm; fan 34฿, A/C 61฿); **That Phanom** (45min.; every 30min. 6am-6pm; fan 17฿, A/C 31฿); **Ubon Ratchatani** (2½hr.; every 30min. 6:30am-4:30pm; fan 51฿, A/C 92฿); **Udon Thani** (4½hr.; 6 per day 9:30am-2pm; fan 82฿, A/C 148฿).

Ferries: With a Lao visa, you can take a ferry to **Savannakhet** (see p. 357). Boats depart M-F 9am-3:30pm, Sa 9am-12:30pm; 50฿.

ORIENTATION AND PRACTICAL INFORMATION

The town is laid out on a grid, with streets running roughly parallel (north-south) and perpendicular (east-west) to the Mekong, the town's east border. Along the river bank is **Samron Chaikhong Rd.,** site of the **Indochina Market,** the wat, and the pier. Parallel to Samron Chaikhong, heading from the river, are **Samut Sakdarak (Mukdahan-Domton) Rd.** and **Phitak Santirad Rd.** Perpendicular to these are **Song Nang Sathit Rd.,** which runs from the pier past the Huanum Hotel to the night market, and, one road south, **Phitak Phanomket Rd.,** where the **post office** is. The **bus terminal** is on the main highway (Rte. 212), **Chayang Koolurd Rd.,** 3km northwest.

THAILAND

Currency Exchange: Thai Farmers Bank, 222 Song Nang Sathit Rd. (☎611 056), 2 blocks up the road from the pier and 1 block past Huanum Hotel. Open M-F 8:30am-3:30pm except holidays. **24hr. ATM** (MC/V).

Markets: The **Indochina market** sets up every day at the waterfront. The **day market** is off Phitak Phanomket Rd., 500m west of the traffic circle. The **night market** is 4 blocks from the river on Song Nang Sathit Rd.

Emergency: ☎191.

Police: Mukdahan Police Station (☎611 333), on Phitak Phanomket Rd., between the traffic circle and Song Nang Sathit Rd. Some English spoken.

Pharmacy: Huan Hong Osoth Pharmacy, 38 Samut Sakdarak Rd. (☎612 002), opposite Huanum Hotel. English spoken. Open daily 6am-8pm.

Medical Services: Mukdahan International Hospital (☎611 450), 1km south of downtown on Samut Sakdarak Rd., just past Mukdahan Hotel.

Post Office/Telephones: Mukdahan Post Office, 18 Phitak/Phanomket Rd. (☎611 065), at the traffic circle. Open M-F 8:30am-4:30pm, Sa-Su 9am-noon. The **Telekom office** (☎611 697) is downstairs. Yellow **Lenso** phones accept DC/MC/V and Access AT&T. Open M-F 8:30am-4:30pm. **Postal code:** 49000.

ACCOMMODATIONS AND FOOD

Huanum Hotel, 36 Samut Sakdarak Rd. (☎611 197), on the corner of Samut Sakdarak and Song Nang Sathit Rd., 1 block from the pier. All A/C rooms have hot water and TV. Singles 120฿, with private bath 220฿, with A/C 270฿; doubles 200/270/350฿.

Hong Kong Hotel, 161/1 Phitak Phanomket Rd. (☎611 143), opposite the police station. From the traffic circle facing the river, go left; it's on the left, next to Pith Bakery. Fairly clean rooms with firm beds and Western toilets 160฿, with A/C and TV 250฿.

Riverside restaurants dish out Thai and Chinese entrees (30-120฿). The **night market** along Song Nong Sathit Rd. has Isaan specialties like *som tam* (papaya salad), *larb* *sod* (minced pork), and *kai yang* (roast chicken). *Pa piya* (Vietnamese spring rolls) come *sot* (fresh) or *thawt* (fried). Also, many French-Lao bakeries vend breads, eclairs, and more. To get to **Foremost Restaurant,** 74/1 Samut Sakdarak Rd., from Huanum Hotel, walk 1 block past Huan Hong Osoth Pharmacy. It's at the next intersection. (Thai and Western food 20-80฿. Open daily 7am-11pm.)

SIGHTS

A larger-than-life golden Buddha contemplates the Mekong from **Wat Si Mongkan Tai,** on Samron Chaikhong Rd. **Chao Fa Mung Shrine,** far up Song Nang Sathit Rd., houses the city pillar. If you happen to arrive at the end of Buddhist Lent (in late fall), you'll catch boat races on the Mekong.

DAYTRIPS FROM MUKDAHAN

PHU PHA THEOP NATIONAL PARK

Phu Pha Theop National Park (pronounced poo-PAH-tayp) can be reached from Mukdahan by the orange buses and songthaew leaving town on the Mukdahan-Dontan Rd. (Rte. 2034) past Mukdahan Hotel on the right (2 per hr. 6am-6pm, leave when full, 10-15฿). Exit at Phu Pha Theop. You'll be dropped off on the main road next to a large "Mukdahan National Park" sign on the left. The entrance is a 15min. walk down a small paved road on the right. Open daily 8am-6pm.

Known for its rock formations and caves, **Phu Pha Theop National Park** also boasts prehistoric rock art, stunning landscapes, wildlife, and hiking trails. The collection of huge, oddly shaped rocks at the main entrance are the chief crowd-pleasers. The undersides of many overhanging rocks are decorated with now-faded prehistoric paintings. The rangers know the area well; one speaks English. Trail maps are available from the park office at the entrance.

The main 2km hike to the **Buddha Cave Waterfall** passes the rocks. Other short hikes pass through mountains and cliffs. The trails aren't always easy to follow; explore carefully. Signs in Thai direct trekkers; arrows pointing straight ahead lead to the waterfall. During the dry season, the falls shrink to a trickle. Rickety wooden stairs lead to the **Buddha Cave,** lined with thousands of Buddha images.

THAILAND

THAT PHANOM ☎042

That Phanom is a sleepy town overlooking the Mekong in south Nakhon Phanom Province. Wat That Phanom, the town's signature attraction, rises nearly 60m above ground, its Lao-style *chedi* glinting in the sun. The seamless syncretism of the architecture is mirrored by the food, with the ready availability of Lao and Vietnamese cuisine and the famed biweekly Lao waterfront market. Given That Phanom's pleasing aesthetics, backwater pace of life, and great guest houses, it is not surprising that many enchanted travelers linger here.

TRANSPORTATION AND PRACTICAL INFORMATION. That Phanom, midway between Nakhon Phanom and Mukdahan, is easily reached from either town by bus or *songthaew* (20฿), which stop along **Chayangkun Rd.** (Hwy. 212) and at a small bus station (☎541 087), south of town. Buses leave for **Ubon Ratchathani** (3½hr.; 15 per day 7:10am-3:30pm; fan 66฿, A/C 119฿) via **Mukdahan** (1½hr.; fan 17฿, A/C 31฿) and **Udon Thani** (5hr.; 9 per day 10am-2:45pm; fan 71฿, A/C 119฿) via **Sakhon Nakhon** (1½hr.; fan 24฿, A/C 40฿). Several companies run to **Bangkok,** including **CTP Transport** (☎541 247), opposite the station (11hr.; 8am and frequently between 4:30-6pm; fan 200฿, A/C 284฿). **Thaisgoon Tour,** 158 Chayangkun Rd. (☎541 288), a block from the GPO toward the wat, has daily departures to **Bangkok** (11hr.; 8am and frequently between 5-7:30pm; fan 200฿, A/C 280฿, VIP 358฿) via **Khorat** (7hr.; fan 130฿, A/C 188฿, VIP 230฿). *Songthaew* to **Nakhon Phanom** (1½hr., every 10min., 20฿) leave from a stop 150m north of Thai Military Bank.

Wat That Phanom is on Chayangkun Rd. Facing the wat, the **Thai Military Bank,** 99/13 Chayangkun Rd., is 1½ blocks to the right. (☎541 008. Open M-F 8:30am-3:30pm;

STUPA-STITIOUS That Phanom is a holy town, a *sathanee saksit*, blessed with a temple that radiates tremendous power. Just as the temple can grant everlasting happiness to those who worship there, so too can it bring tragedy to those who defile it. Residents here often point to 1975 as a remarkable year of misfortune. That year, the magnificent *chedi* collapsed following torrential rains. Some locals rushed to pillage "lucky" chunks from the fallen *stupa;* not long afterward, mysterious accidents and inexplicable illnesses befell the culprits and their families. Their abandoned houses stand forlornly to this day.

One late June night a few years ago, the townspeople witnessed another show of divine power. A young *songthaew* driver, unable to pay his rent, clambered up the scaffolding around Wat That Phanom, intending to swipe the three large diamonds embedded in the *chedi*. Unable to get back down, he was spotted in the floodlight's glare. Word spread through the sleeping town, and a crowd soon gathered on the street below, including the police. One officer, convinced that the thief was an illegal Lao immigrant, drew his pistol, and pulled the trigger–it didn't fire. He tried again–to no avail. Exasperated, he grabbed another gun, but it wouldn't shoot. Perhaps the divine one had taken pity on the would-be burglar and protected him. The hapless bandit was finally dragged down, and officers had to forcefully restrain irate townspeople intent on lynching him. Nothing, not even the most innocuous-looking pebble, can be taken beyond the wat's gates. If you inadvertently do so, return it immediately. If not, sleep light–and don't say we didn't warn you.

THAILAND

ATM 6am-10pm.) Past the bank and the *songthaew* stop is the **GPO,** 322 Chayangkun Rd., which has **international phone** service. (☎541 169. Open M-F 8:30am-4:30pm, Sa-Su 9am-noon.) **That Phanom Hospital** (☎541 255) is 2km west on the highway. The **police station** (☎541 266), is also in the north end of town on Phanom Phanarak Rd. **Emergency:** ☎191. **Postal code:** 48110.

ACCOMMODATIONS AND FOOD. Travelers hail **Niyana Guest House,** on 288 Mu 2, Rimkhong Rd., as the best in That Phanom. From the victory arch, head to the pier and turn left onto Rimkhong. Follow the river 800m; it's on a small soi to the left. Niyana serves food, offers tours, exchanges money, gives Thai lessons, and rents out bicycles. (☎540 588. Dorms 50฿; singles 70฿; doubles 100฿.) Another good option is **Pom Guest House,** at 110 Soi Anurakjaydee five soi down Rimkhong Rd. toward the town center from Niyana's. Travelers can cook for themselves and rent bicycles for 25฿ per day. (☎541 450. Dorms 60฿; singles 80฿; doubles 120฿.) **Rimkhong Bungalow,** 103 Soi Prempoochanee, one soi north of Pom Guest House, is clean but pricey. (☎541 634. Singles 200฿, with A/C 400฿; doubles 300/500฿.) Accommodations fill up during the February festival.

At **food stalls** on Chayangkun Rd., 20฿ can buy savory roast chicken, sticky rice, or a bowl of Vietnamese *phở* soup. A **floating restaurant** bobs beside the pier and several terrestrial restaurants are on Phanom Phanarak Rd. A good **night market** sits near the 7-Eleven and dishes up tantalizing cuisine. (Open until around 9pm.)

SIGHTS. **Wat That Phanom** is the most sacred religious structure in Isaan. Legend has it that it was built to house one of the Buddha's clavicle bones, transported from India. Topped by a 110kg gold spire, the shrine has been restored seven times. Depending on who you ask, it's between 12 and 26 centuries old. The most recent reconstruction occurred in 1978, after heavy rains in 1975 collapsed the 57m *chedi*. The temple is circumscribed by a cloister housing dozens of golden Buddha images. At the beginning of February, thousands come to pay their respects during the annual seven-day **Phra That Phanom Homage Fair.**

About 15km northwest of That Phanom is the silk-weaving village of **Renu Nakhon.** Travelers can listen to and see Isaan music and dance at the **Renu Nakhon Wat** on Saturdays during the winter; Niyana knows the performance times. To get there, take any Nakhon Phanom-bound *songthaew* to the Renu Nakhon junction 8km north of town; from there, hire a *tuk-tuk*. Check out the **Lao Market** near Niyana's Guest House on the far end of Rimkhong Rd. (M and Th, 6am-7pm).

NONG KHAI ☎042

Nong Khai's streets are full of tourists passing through, and many that never left. Drawn at first by the popular border crossing with Laos, travelers end up sticking around for a while to experience Nong Khai's polished guest house scene and see one of Southeast Asia's best Buddhist temples—Sala Kaew Ku. The large influx of foreigners mixes with charming Nong Khai's overt Lao-French influence and ornate Buddhist temples to create one of Thailand's authentic tourist towns.

TRANSPORTATION

Trains: Nong Khai Railway Station (☎411 592), on Hwy. 212, 1½km west of town. *Tuk-tuk* ride from Rimkhong Rd. (50฿). Trains to **Bangkok** via **Khon Kaen** and **Udon Thani** (rapid: 10-13hr.; 8:15am, 7:30pm; 3rd-class 163฿, 2nd-class 680฿; express: 11hr.; 6:40pm; 3rd-class 163฿, 2nd-class 298฿) and **Khorat** (6hr., 1pm, 3rd-class 64฿). Booking office open daily 6:30-10:30am and noon-6pm.

Buses: Nong Khai Bus Terminal, on Prajak Rd. at the east end of town. To: **Bangkok** via **Khon Kaen, Khorat,** and **Udon Thani** (#23; 12hr.; every hr. 5:30am-8pm; 200฿, A/C 300฿, VIP 450฿); **Beung Kan** (#507, 3hr., every hr. 6-10:40am, 70฿); **Nakhon Phanom** (#224, 7hr., 5 per day 6:30-9:40am, 160฿); **Udon Thani** (#221, 1hr., every 30min. 5:30am-5:20pm, 17฿). Green buses go to **Loei** and **Pak Chom** (#507, 5hr., 10 per day 6am-3:10pm, 61฿) via **Sangkhom** (2hr., 50฿) and **Si Chiang Mai** (1hr., 30฿), and **Rayong** (12hr.; 13 per day 6am-7:30pm; 211฿, with A/C 328฿). To get to **Chiang Khan,** switch buses at **Pak Chom.**

Local Transportation: For those who just want to walk, **Tuk-tuk** are abundant to the point of distraction as drivers assume all *farang* are desperately in need of their services. 20฿ for short distances, never more than 60฿.

Rentals: Bicycle rental at Mekhong Guest House (30฿ per day) and Mut Mee Guest House (39-52฿ per day). **Motorcycle rental** (200฿ per day) at Nana Motor, 1160 Meechai Rd. (☎411 998), opposite Chayaporn Market. Open daily 6am-6pm.

ORIENTATION AND PRACTICAL INFORMATION

Nong Khai is a major border crossing to **Vientiane, Laos**—the **Friendship Bridge** joins the two countries. In the north, Nong Khai borders the **Mekong River,** while **Hwy. 212** marks the town's southern boundary. Parallel to Hwy. 212, from south to north, are **Prajak Rd., Meechai Rd.,** and **Rimkhong Rd.** The **train station,** on Hwy. 212, 2½km west of the town center, is a bit of a hike. Taking a right out of the **bus station** and stopping at the first intersection will have you facing north on Prajak Rd. Guest houses are scattered to the northeast. Street numbers are haphazard; luckily, maps are available at all guest houses.

Currency Exchange: Bangkok Bank, 372 Soi Srisaket (☎412 675). Open M-F 8:30am-3:30pm. There are **ATMs** and currency exchangers everywhere.

Markets: The **market,** along Rimkhong Rd. near the Mekong river, features a cornucopia of scented soaps, electronics, binoculars, disco balls, and, of course, massive grilled fish from China, Laos, Russia, Thailand, and Vietnam. Open daily 9am-5:30pm.

English Bookstore: Wasambe Bookshop, 1121 Kaeworawat Rd. (☎460 272), off the soi leading to Mut Mee Guest House. 200 of your favorite titles. Open daily 10am-8pm.

Emergency: ☎191.

Police: ☎411 020. On Meechai Rd., facing the hospital.

Pharmacies: Tong Tong Pharmacy, 382/2 Meechai Rd. (☎411 690). Exit left from the post office; it's on the corner. Open daily 7:30am-9pm.

Medical Services: Nong Khai Hospital, 1158 Meechai Rd. (☎411 088), near Mut Mee Guest House and opposite the police station.

THAILAND

BORDER CROSSING: NAKHON PHANOM/THA KHAEK. A pleasant daytrip from That Phanom, Nakhon Phanom has recently become a border crossing to the Lao village of Tha Khaek.

Apibanbuncha Rd. is home to a score of banks and the provincial hospital (☎511 424), at the Tespradit Rd. intersection. **Buses** arrive at the terminal (☎515 780), on Piya Rd. in the southwest corner of town. Buses run to: Mukdahan (2½hr.; 7 per day 6-9:30am and 2pm; fan 35฿, A/C 48฿); Khon Kaen (4hr.; 7 per day 7:30am-4pm; fan 86฿, A/C 155฿); Udon Thani (9hr.; every hr. 6-11am; fan 70฿, A/C 100฿) via Beung Khan (4hr.; fan 62฿, A/C 87฿); Nong Khai (7hr.; fan 100฿, A/C 153฿); and Bangkok (12hr.; 6:45am, 8am, 8:30am, and 9 per day 3:45-9pm; fan 395฿, A/C 421฿, VIP 585฿) via Khorat (8hr., fan 192฿). **Songthaew** leave south of the Thai Farmer's Bank on Apibanbuncha Rd. for That Phanom (1½hr., every 10min., 20฿).

The street adjacent to the river is Sunthon Wichit Rd. The **TAT office,** 184/1 Sunthon Wichit Rd. (☎513 490; open M-F 8:30am-4:30pm), **post office** (☎512 945; open M-F 8:30am-4:30pm; postal code: 48000) and **police station** (☎511 266) cluster here at the north end. Continuing south along the Mekong brings you to the clock tower, where Sunthon Wichit Rd. continues along the river and Si Thep Rd. branches diagonally to the right. **Grand Hotel,** at 2210 Si Thep Rd., sits a couple of blocks after the fork in the road on the right. Although it's a bit pricey, the Grand Hotel is one of the very few decent accommodations in town. (☎511 526. Singles 180฿, with A/C 470฿; doubles 230฿, with A/C 940฿.) Farther down Si Thep Rd. on the right is **Wat Si Thep.** Behind the clock tower, an Indochina **market** sets up during the day next to the river. Tuk-tuk will take you anywhere for 5-10฿.

Nakhon Phanom's restaurants specialize in serving giant golden **catfish** caught in the Mekong River. These denizen of the deep (often weighing 350kg or more) are rare in the Mekong–no more than 35 are caught each year. **New Suan Mai** (☎511 202; open daily 10am-10pm) and **Golden Giant Catfish Restaurant** (open daily 7am-10pm), neighbors south of the clock tower on Sunthon Wichit Rd., serve similarly scrumptious food. If *plaa beuk* isn't listed, ask and you shall receive (180-260฿).

Travelers holding a Lao visa obtained in **Bangkok** or **Khon Kaen** (Nong Khai visas are invalid here) should seek an exit stamp from the **Immigration Office** just opposite the Indochina market on Sunthon Wichit Rd. (☎511 235. Open M-F 8:30am-4:30pm.) A **boat** behind the office shuttles passengers to Tha Khaek (8am-4pm, 50฿). The Lao entry tax vacillates, but currently stands at 70฿.

Internet Access: Cyberkids, 422 Prajak Rd., near the intersection with Haisok Rd. Best prices in town. 20฿ per hr. Open daily 8:30am-9pm. **Wasambe Bookshop** (See **English Bookstores,** above) charges the standard 1฿ per min. The cafe attached to the **Mae Kong Guest House** costs a reasonable 30฿ per hr. Open daily 9am-10pm.

Telephones: Lenso phones in **GPO** and along Meechai Rd.

Post Office: GPO (☎411 521), on Meechai Rd. Open M-F 8:30am-4:30pm. **Postal code:** 43000.

ACCOMMODATIONS

Mut Mee Guest House, 1111/4 Kaeworawat Rd., on the river; look for the sign. Riverside patio, scrumptious food, loads of information, and a steady stream of talkative travelers. Drawing, tai chi, and yoga classes in high season. Dorms 80฿; singles 110฿; doubles 130฿, with private bath and hot water 360฿; triples 240-300฿.

Mekhong Guest House, 519 Rimkhong Rd. (☎460 689), a few stores west of the immigration pier. Well-organized with lots of rooms in classic youth hostel style. Rooms by the river cost more. Internet 30฿ per hr. Dorms 80฿; singles 100-150฿; doubles 250฿.

THAILAND

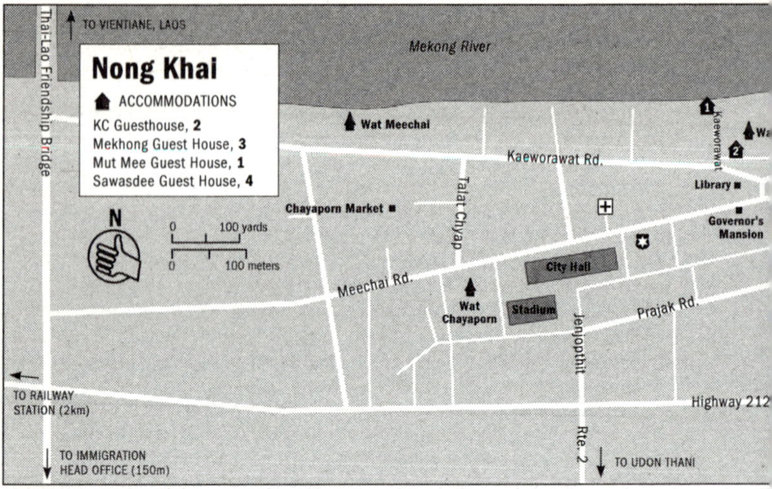

Sawasdee Guest House, 402 Meechai Rd. (☎412 502), 5 blocks east of post office. From the bus station, turn left on Prajak Rd. and then right at Srikuanmuang Rd. Courtyard. Check-in until 10pm. Singles 100฿; doubles 140฿, with A/C and hot water 300฿.

KC Guest House, 1018 Kaeworawat Rd., on the same soi that leads to Mut Mee. Basic rooms almost in view of the river. Singles 100฿; doubles 150฿.

FOOD

Although the anticipated tourism explosion is yet to hit with full force, eateries have already become bland and overpriced to accommodate the just-passing-through traveler. Good, inexpensive Thai food, however, can still be found. **Chayaporn Market** on the west side of town has loads of prepared eats available in clouds of chaos. More food stalls, some offering fresh seafood, crowd the intersection of **Rimkhong** and **Haisok Rd.** Two blocks south where **Prajak Rd.** meets Haisok Rd., skewered meats turn round and round.

Sala Boat, 527 Rimkhong Rd. Look for the telltale Wall's Ice Cream sign, one block from Mekhong Guest House. Enjoy Thai food riverside or set back in A/C comfort. Dishes 30-60฿. Open daily 10am-11pm.

Mut Mee Restaurant, 1111/4 Kaeworawat Rd. Delicious Thai and Western dishes served on the riverside. Great food at unusually low prices. Open daily 8am-10pm.

Udomrod, 423 Rimkhong Rd., next to the immigration pier. A standard restaurant with deluxe views. Budget-decimating but flavorful Mekong River fish dishes. Most dishes 45-100฿; fresh fish 80-160฿. Open daily 8am-8pm.

SIGHTS

SALA KAEW KU (WAT KHAEK). A few kilometers east of Nong Khai on Hwy. 212, Sala Kaew Ku, also known as Wat Khaek, is one of Thailand's most bizarre temples. Towering concrete statues of Hindu and Buddhist figures represent various levels of Buddhist cosmology: the good and the evil, the mundane and the fantastic, the innocent and the freaky—all the brainchild of a Lao mystic, Luang Poo Boun Leya Sourirat. After building a park in Vientiane (see p. 338), Souritat fled to Thailand when the Communists came to power in 1975. Most of the temple's gravity-defying figures are gods, goddesses, demons, and Buddhas found in the Indian pantheon of mythical deities. Enter the giant mouth in back to learn about *samsara*, the Buddhist belief in the endless cycle of rebirth and suffering. A circle shows the

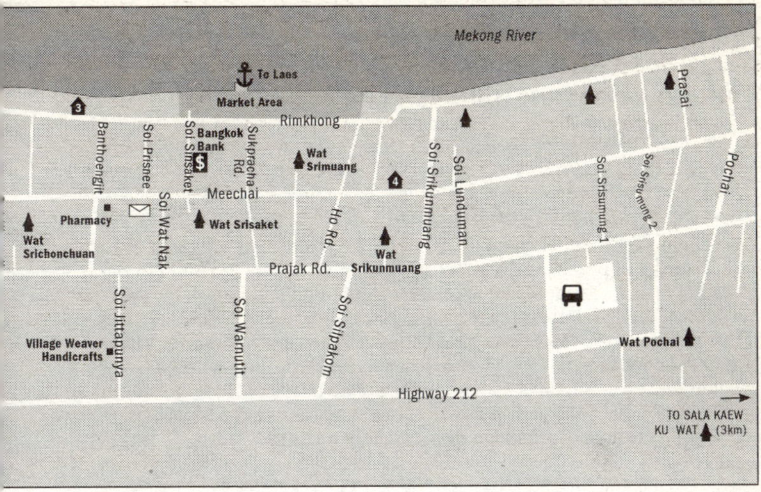

events of one life-cycle. *(By bike (15min.), head east on Rte. 212, past "St. Paul Nong Khai School" on the right; Sala Kaew Ku is 2 turn-offs later. Grab a map for a more scenic river route. Open daily 8am-5pm. 10฿.)*

VILLAGE WEAVER HANDICRAFTS. Seekers of handwoven *mut-mee* fabrics can visit Village Weaver Handicrafts, off Prajak Rd. near the Honda dealership. This 17-year-old project promotes local industry and offers lucrative work to Isaan women who are at risk of turning to brothels for their livelihood. Seamstresses tailor outfits at warp speed and ship them anywhere in the world. *(1151 Soi Jittapunya. ☎411 236. Open daily 8am-5pm, weaving demos closed Su.)*

THE THINGS WE DO FOR LOVE Although Phu Phra Bat Historical Park has attracted international attention for its 3500-year-old cave paintings, it's more renowned among locals for its connection to the legend of Nang Usa and Tao Baros.

Nang Usa was the only child of King Phaya Kong Phan of Phan. A slightly over-protective father, the King decided to have Nang Usa raised by a hermit in the seclusion of Phu Phra Bat where she remained without any social life whatsoever until the age of sixteen. One day, Prince Tao Baros stumbled upon her during a hunting excursion from his neighboring kingdom and they fell madly in love at first sight—perhaps because he was pretty much her only option at that point. When the King arrived the next day, Tao Baros asked him for Nang Usa's hand in marriage. The furious King realized he would lose his daughter's love if he killed Tao Baros and instead proposed a challenge: whoever could build the most beautiful temple from sundown to the rising of the Venus would decide Nang Usa's fate; the loser would be beheaded.

The King requisitioned an entire village to help him, while Tao Baros was left with just one of his men. Tao Baros worked madly on his temple until he had an idea. He climbed a tree on a cliff and lit a fire above the King's temple site. The villagers believed this to be the morning star and left the temple unfinished, leaving Tao Baros free to complete his modest temple. The next morning the King was beheaded, and Tao Baros and Nang Usa were free to be together. But rumors that Nang Usa was untrustworthy and secretly overjoyed at the death of her father devastated her, and she made an irrevocable decision to return to her seclusion in Phu Phra Bat. Tao Baros died of a broken heart from the cruel irony of it all, while Nang Usa lived her life out as it began: without a social life.

DAYTRIPS FROM NONG KHAI

PHU PHRA BAT HISTORICAL PARK

To have enough time to see the park and get back, catch a bus to **Ban Phu** *(#294, 1½ hr., 7:15am, 30฿) from the Nong Khai Bus Terminal. Take a left from the Ban Phu station and walk 100m over the bridge to where* songthaew *(15min., every 15min., 5฿) take you to the park. From here, hike 4km to park headquarters or grab a motorcycle taxi (50฿). Leave the park by 2pm, as the last bus back to Nong Khai leaves Ban Phu at 3pm.*

Some 85km southwest of Nong Khai, not far from the dusty village of Ban Phu, the eerie wizardry of prehistoric hunters and gatherers lingers at Phu Phra Bat Historical Park. On 5.5km^2 of forested mountains in the Phu Pan Range, the park boasts a fine collection of prehistoric cave paintings and rock shelters that date back to 1500 BC. Local lore intertwines these sites with the remains of various locations (see **The Things We Do for Love,** p. 759). Over a dozen excavations lie scattered along a shady well-marked path. Buddhas abound in **Tham Phra** (Cave of Buddha Images). At the top of the mountain, the path yields an astounding vista of **Pha Sadet Cliff,** which has a perfect picnic area overlooking the Laotian mountains.

BORDER CROSSING: NONG KHAI/VIENTIANE. 15-day Lao tourist visas are issued on the Friendship Bridge for US$30 (one passport photo required). 30-day visas are available from the Lao embassy in Bangkok for 1100฿ (3-day processing). Ask Julian at Mut Mee Guest House for the latest wrinkles. A *tuk-tuk* from Nong Khai to the bridge should cost 30-50฿. A bus shuttles people across the bridge for 10฿; once there, expect to pay a 2000kip (10฿) entry tax. On the other side, public buses run the 25km to Vientiane (30฿), or you can take a taxi (150฿).

THAILAND

NEAR NONG KHAI

SANGKHOM

Drowsy Sangkhom is quiet and forlorn, but its geography has stunning vistas, waterfalls, and cliffs. The surrounding jungle is dotted with caves marked on maps available at Bouy Guest House. The impressive **Than Thip Falls** are a 30min. motorbike ride west of town. Bring your bathing suit—the second tier has a swimming hole. **Than Thong Falls** are east of Sangkhom. **Wat Hin Maak Peng** is a monastery set among boulders and bamboo groves.

Sangkhom sits in hills 95km west of Nong Khai. Buses go to Sangkhom from Loei (3½hr., every hr. 5:40-11:40am, 50฿) and Nong Khai (#507, 2hr., every hr. 6am-3pm, 30฿). The **police station** is 700m to the right of the guest houses facing the river. (☎441 080. **Open 24hr.**) The **post office,** 800m to the left, provides international phone service. (☎441 069. Open M-F 8:30am-4:30pm, Sa-Su 9am-noon.) **Postal code:** 43160. The **Bouy Guest House,** 60 M.4 Sangkhom, offers romantic bungalows along the river. Mr. Toy, owner and chef, prepares Thai and Lao specialties (jungle curry 40฿), and has a wealth of tourist information—ask about boat trips. (☎441 065. Singles 80฿; doubles 100฿.) Just west is **TXK Guest House** (formerly Mama's Guest House), famous for 100฿ Thai and Lao feasts. (Free papayas and bananas. Bungalows 100฿.) **River Huts Guest House,** 80m to the right facing the river, has slow Internet access for 2฿ per min and standard bungalows. (Singles 80฿; doubles 100฿; deluxe with private bath, hot water, and 2 fans 280฿.)

WAT PHU THAWK AND BEUNG KHAN

Although it's one of the northeast Thailand's most spectacular sights, Wat Phu Thawk remains un-touristed. In the Isaan dialect, *phu thawk* means "single mountain." The shrine stands on a red sandstone outcropping rising from the Nong Khai plain with each of the wat's seven levels representing a stage of enlightenment.

Level five has a sanctuary built into the cliff and a skeleton encased in glass awaits your company at level six. On the opposite side of the mountain is a hermitage built on a pinnacle nestled under a boulder. Along the walkways are platforms and huts for meditation. Reaching the top involves climbing stairs into a maze of wooden platforms and staircases—don't look down. The view from the Isaan plains makes the sweaty ascent more than worth it, though climbing the stairs isn't recommended in windy weather.

The sheer isolation of Wat Phu Thawk makes tackling it on a daytrip difficult. From the Nong Khai Bus Terminal, take a bus to Bueng Khan (#224, 2hr., every hr. 6am-3pm, 45฿). From the Bueng Khan bus stop (across from the ATMs), catch a bus to Ban Similai (#225, 40min., 17฿). From here, get to Phu Thawk on a motorcycle (30min., 40-50฿) or jump on a *tuk-tuk* (100฿). Beung Khan, the largest town between Nakhon Phanom and Nong Khai along Hwy. 212, is the most sensible place for an overnight stay. Hwy. 222 becomes Thaisamok Rd., home to a small bus stop, clock tower, and rotary near the center of town. To reach the guest houses, turn right onto Maesongnang Rd. (facing the rotary) and left onto Prasatchai Rd. Two hotels are 100m down at the first intersection. **Santisuk Hotel,** 21/2 Prasatchai Rd., is on the right. (☎491 114. Singles with TV and Thai-style bath 150฿; doubles 300฿). **Samanmit Hotel,** 34/3 Prasatchai Rd., is directly across. (☎491 078. Doubles 300฿.)

CHIANG KHAN ☎042

The last decade has seen Chiang Khan develop from a tiny hamlet to a full-blown frontier town. Its charm, punctuated by the meandering Mekong River, has attracted investors, increasing land values tenfold with property near the Kaeng Khut Khu Rapids fetching over two million bhat per $3400m^2$. Life here, however, still remains relatively slow and isolated.

THAILAND

TRANSPORTATION. From Pak Chom, **buses** run to **Nong Khai** and **Sangkhom** (#507; 2hr., 4½hr.; last bus noon). Buses to **Bangkok** leave from Soi 9 south of the market (6pm, 176฿; A/C 8am, 6:30pm; VIP 6:30pm, 490฿). **Songthaew** leave from Chiang Khan Rd. to **Loei** (1hr., every 30min. 5:30am-5pm, 22฿) and **Pak Chom** (1hr., every 30-60min. 6am-4pm, 20฿). Friendship Guest House rents **motorbikes** (150฿ per day), and Zen Guest House rents **mountain bikes** (60฿ per day).

ORIENTATION AND PRACTICAL INFORMATION. Resting on the muddy Mekong River, Chiang Khan is in northern **Loei Province,** 50km from the provincial capital. The two main roads, parallel to each other and the river, are **Chai Khong Rd.,** closer to the water, and **Chiang Khan Rd.,** the highway through town. **Sois 1-24** connect the two roads.

Services in Chiang Khan include: **Immigration Office** past the hospital on the left (☎821 911; visa extensions 500฿; open M-F 8am-8pm); **police** (☎821 181; **emergency** ☎191) on a soi off Chiang Khan Rd. past the hospital; **Ruammith Osoth** pharmacy on Chiang Khan Rd. at Soi 9 (☎821 168; open daily 6am-9pm); **Chiang Khan Hospital** (☎821 101), on Chiang Khan Rd. past Soi 21; **Internet access** at Friendship Guest House (1฿ per min. plus 5฿ connection fee); and **Chiang Khan Post and Telegraph Office,** near the Immigration Office. (☎821 011. International phone. *Poste Restante.* Open M-F 8:30am-4:30pm, Sa-Su 9am-noon.) **Postal code:** 42110.

ACCOMMODATIONS AND FOOD. Zen Guest House, 126/1 Soi 12, maintains simple rooms with bed frames, and mosquito nets. (☎821 825. Singles 100฿; doubles 170฿.) Rooms at the **Ton Khong Guest House,** 299/3 Chai Khong Rd. at Soi 10, are snug and spotless with shared Western baths. (☎821 547. Singles 100฿; doubles 150฿, with bath 200฿, with A/C 300฿.) The balcony restaurant serves delectable Thai and Lao dishes (most entrees 25-50฿). Rooms at **Friendship Guest House,** 300 Chai Khong Rd., are huge teak affairs. (☎822 052. Singles 150฿; doubles 200฿.) **Chiang Khan Guest House 2,** at the intersection of Soi 20 and Chiang Khan Rd., has the cheapest rooms in town with a grubby bathroom. (☎821 023. Rooms 50฿.)

Rabieng, left of Ton Khong Guest House, churns out tasty Chinese food. (Open daily 3pm-midnight). **The Look Kosana,** on Soi 9 near Chai Khong Rd. opposite Phoonsavad Hotel, serves *pad thai* (20฿) and morning glory vine in garlic bean sauce (50฿) to satisfy even the pickiest taste buds. (Open daily 6pm-midnight.)

SIGHTS. About 3km east of town, a turn-off leads left to **Kaeng Khut Khu Rapids,** where picturesque rock piles interrupt the Mekong's seaward schlep. Follow the sign to **Wat Thakhaek** and continue for 1km. A row of covered picnic areas are great for watching rapids from February to May. Some guest houses and hotels provide boat transport to the rapids. *Songthaew* (10฿) and *tuk-tuk* (50฿ round-trip) make the trip from Chiang Khan Rd. The traditional **herbal steam bath** at Zen Guest House uses 40 local plants and herbs to create a relaxing sauna (190฿ per person per hr.). The yellow stain doesn't last long. Traditional Thai massage is also available; remember, *"jèp"* means "that hurts" (150฿ per hr.). Ton Khong and Friendship Guest Houses organize trips ranging from short sunset cruises on the Mekong (800-1200฿) to car tours (Friendship 500฿, min. 3 people). These can be next to impossible to organize in the low season, as there may not be three travelers in town to go with you.

THAILAND

LOEI ☎042

A big billboard on Hwy. 201 greets visitors to Loei with, "Welcome to Loei, Land of the Sea of Mountains and Coldest in All Siam." Grammar aside, the sign captures the essence of this seldom-visited but appealing province. At the end of June, the Phi Ta Khon Festival in Dan Sai in the province's west end features young costumed men and recitations of Buddhist tales. Those who make the trip to Loei find a perfect place to unwind after a day exploring the countryside and national parks.

TRANSPORTATION

Buses: All buses leave from the **main bus terminal** on Maliwan Rd. Green buses go to **Nong Khai** via **Pak Chom, Sangkhom,** and **Tha Bo** (#507, every hr. 5:40-10:40am, 73฿). If you're going straight to Nong Khai, take a bus to **Udon Thani** (every 20min. 10am-5:30pm, 45฿) and then catch a bus to Nong Khai; it's at least 3hr. faster. Buses also run to: **Bangkok** (10-11hr.; 22 per day 7am-8:30pm; 162฿, A/C 227฿); **Chiang Mai** (9hr.; 11:15am, 8:30, 9:30pm; 165฿, A/C 231฿); **Chiang Rai** (11hr.; 6:30am, 10, 10:30pm; 260฿, 1st-class 335฿). Chiang Mai and Chiang Rai buses travel via **Phitsanulok** (4hr.) and **Lampang** (7hr.). Many **long distance buses** may be full upon arrival; guarantee a seat by buying a ticket from the bus terminal counter. *Songthaew* go to **Chiang Khan** (1hr., every 30min. 5:30am-5:30pm, 18฿).

Local Transportation: Samlor and **tuk-tuk** 15-20฿.

Rentals: Bike shop, 20m north of the traffic circle at the intersection of Chum Saai and Sathon Chiang Khan Rd. Look for a row of motorbikes. **Motorbikes** 200฿ per day.

ORIENTATION AND PRACTICAL INFORMATION

Loei town is a tangled mess of streets on Loei River's western bank. **Charoen Rat Rd.** runs the length of the river, beginning in the south at the **night market.** Moving north into town on Charoen Rat Rd., you'll see the **post office** and a white suspension footbridge, followed by **Chum Saai Rd.,** which becomes **Nokkaew Rd.** three blocks down at a busy traffic circle. Continuing up Charoen Rat Rd., **Thai Udom Hotel** is at the intersection with **Ova Aree Rd.** Walk a block more to reach **Ruamjai Rd.,** a major east-west thoroughfare. The **police station** is on **Phipattanamongkhon Rd.,** the city's northern border. The **hospital** and the **main bus terminal** (south of hospital) lie on **Maliwan Rd. (Hwy. 201),** the town's western boundary.

Currency Exchange: Siam Commercial Bank, 3/8 Ruamjai Rd. (☎813 020). Open M-F 8:30am-3:30pm. **ATM** (Cirrus/MC/V) open daily 6am-11pm. **Bangkok Bank,** at the intersection of Ova Aree and Charoen Rat Rd. **24hr. ATM** (AmEx/MC/PLUS/V).

Emergency: ☎191.

Police: Loei Police Station (☎811 254), on Phipattanamongkhon Rd.

Pharmacies: Bun Jung Pesat Pharmacy, 83 Charoen Rat Rd. (☎830 634), on the corner of Ruamjai Rd. Open daily 3am-9pm.

Medical Services: Loei Provincial Hospital (☎811 679), at the intersection of Maliwan and Nok Kaew Rd., opposite provincial offices. Some English spoken. Cash only.

Telephones: International calls may be placed from the GPO, 2nd fl.

Internet Access: PA Computers (☎814 761), on Charoen Rat Rd. between Chum Saai and Ova Aree Rd. 20฿ per hr. Open daily 9am-midnight.

Post Offices: GPO (☎811 713), on Charoen Rat Rd. between the footbridge and night market. Open M-F 8:30am-4:30pm, Sa-Su 9am-noon. **Postal code:** 42000.

ACCOMMODATIONS

Thai Udom Hotel, 122/1 Charoen Rat Rd. (☎811 763), at Ova Aree Rd. Funky, slightly run-down but clean rooms with phones and TV. Hot water during high season. Singles 240฿, with A/C 350฿; doubles 320/500฿; VIP room 600฿.

Friendship Guest House 2, 257/41 Charoen Rat Rd. (☎832 408), at the southern end of the road across from the market. No English sign. Largish, tiled rooms in a concrete complex 150฿.

King Hotel, 11/9-12 Chum Saai Rd. (☎811 701). Lobby fit for a king, and rooms are pretty nice too. Well furnished with TV, phones, and hot water. Slightly impersonal. Singles 240฿, with A/C 380฿; doubles 310/399฿; VIP room with fridge 500฿.

FOOD

Some of the best places to eat are the **open-air restaurants** in front of the movie theater just off Ova Aree Rd., opposite Thai Farmers Bank, and at the main bus terminal. Pyromaniacs can order *pak boong fai daeng* (flaming morning glory vine).

Yang Kin Aeng, at the traffic circle at the intersection of Nok Kaew and Muang Loei Rd. Two-story patio with heaps of Thai classics. Open daily 5-11pm.

Sor Ahan Thai, 32/106 Nok Kaew Rd. (☎813 436). Walking away from the river, it's on the right. Garden restaurant has Thai/English menu. Noodles with shrimp 35฿. Open daily 6am-11pm.

Koouh Tawng, 192/4 Maliwon Rd. (☎832 727). 1km from the main bus terminal. Tasty Thai standards 30-100฿. Open daily 10am-10pm.

ENTERTAINMENT

Discos and Western-style pubs line Rhuamphattana Rd. Walking west on Nokkaew Rd., toward the highway, it's the first right after the traffic circle. Halfway down on the left is **Ban Muang Loei Pub,** which has live country music in Thai (small beer 50฿). Directly across the street is the **Dallas Cowboy,** which is Ban Muang's twin. Continuing down the street, you'll see two Robocop statues on your right; a large, glowing millennium falcon past the gate marks the entrance to **Robot 2029.** Thai rock bands play nightly at 10:30pm in a neon-themed hall. Its rival, **Pegasus Music Hall,** is next door where house music thumps amid strobe lights until a band plays at 10:30pm.

MARKETS

Loei has two day/night markets. One is at the northern end of Charoen Rat Rd., opposite the 7-11. The market has lots of silly things like plastic combs and space guns as well as grilled meats (flies no extra charge). The night market gets going around 6pm but closes between 9-10pm. The second market sets up at the southern end of Charoen Rat Rd. Six long rows under tin roofs deal almost exclusively with all the food under the Thai sky. (Open daily 10am-9pm.)

NEAR LOEI

PHU RUA NATIONAL PARK

The majestic centerpiece of this park is a **1375m mountain.** Personal vehicles can travel to the top, where a large Buddha surveys the scene below. More low-key routes include a 2km trek to a **waterfall,** from which it's a 5½km to the peak. Pick up a map and consult park rangers before your trip. It's possible to complete the circuit in a day, but an overnight stay is recommended. (Tents 50฿; lodging for 5-8 people 250-500฿.) Food is available daily during high season and until 6pm on weekends during low season. Large groups should contact the **National Parks Division** in Bangkok (☎02 579 05 29).

To get to the park, catch a bus to Lom Sak via Phu Rua (#14, 1hr., every hr. 5am-5pm, 25฿); watch for the large English sign on the right. Snacks are available at the market opposite the bus drop-off. Although *Let's Go* doesn't recommend hitchhiking, the easiest way to get to the park headquarters, 3½km away, is to hike up the road and try to snag a lift (remember, the thumb points down). Otherwise, *songthaew* charge an outrageous 300฿. To return to Loei, wait for a bus in front of the market (last bus 6pm). The admission is 200฿.

PHU KRADUNG NATIONAL PARK

The park's bell-shaped mountain inspired the name of this popular sanctuary (*kradung* means bell). Trails criss-cross the 60 sq. km plateau at the summit. The 9km hike from the mountain base to park headquarters is facilitated by bamboo stairways; porters can tote your gear (10฿ per kg). Eager spirits can bid the Khon Kaen bus adieu at Nong Hin, the turn-off for **Ban Pha Ngarm,** a stone forest where limestone outcroppings form a natural labyrinth. Guides promise not to lose you for 100฿ per group. The 18km to Ban Pha Ngarm from the park entrance are traversed only by chartered *songthaew* (500฿). **Mountaintop lodging** starts at 200฿ per bungalow. The park is packed on weekends and holidays and in high season but closes during the rainy season. For more information, contact the **National Park Division** of the Forestry Department in Bangkok (☎02 579 72 23).

Buses to Khon Kaen (25฿) drop you off at the Amphoe Phu Kradung Administrative Office. From here, catch a minibus (15฿) to the National Park Office where trail #9 begins. The admission is 200฿.

UDON THANI ☎042

Sheltering an almost six-digit population, Udon Thani is one the most prosperous cities in the northeast and the Isaan's chief agricultural, commercial, and transportation center. Site of a US Air Force base during the Vietnam War, Udon Thani still evidences an American presence in its Western restaurants and expat community. The province also offers several worthwhile daytrips, most notably Ban Chiang's UNESCO World Heritage archaeological sites.

TRANSPORTATION

Flights: Udon Thani Airport (☎246 567), on Udon Thani-Loei Hwy. 5km southwest of town. Limousine bus to Nong Khai (1hr., 100฿) after all flights from Bangkok. **Thai Airways,** 60 Makkhaeng Rd. (☎243 222). Open M-F 8-11:30am and 1-4:30pm. To **Bangkok** (8:40am, 1, 7:35pm; 1515฿).

Trains: Train station (☎222 061), at the east end of Prajaksilapakom Rd. Booking office open daily 6am-10pm. To **Bangkok** (11hr.; 9:20am, 7:30, 8:30pm; 3rd-class 95฿, 2nd-class 219฿, 1st-class 457฿) via **Khon Kaen** (3hr.); and **Nong Khai** (1hr.; 6:15, 7:45am, 5pm; 12฿).

Buses: Bus terminal #1, at the corner of Sai Uthit and Prajaksilapakom Rd. To: **Ban Chiang/Sakhon Nakhon** (#230, 3hr., every 30min. 4am-7pm, 20฿); **Bangkok** (#407,

11hr., every 15min. 8:30am-11pm, 292฿) via **Khorat** (4½hr., 162฿); **Khon Kaen** (2½hr., every 30min. 4am-6pm, 38฿); **Mukdahan** (5hr., 6 per day 5:45-11:30am, A/C 148฿); **Ubon Ratchathani** (#268, 6hr., 6 per day 7am-2pm, A/C 210฿). Northbound buses leave **bus terminal #2,** 2km northwest of town. To: **Ban Phu** (every 30min. 6am-5pm, 50฿); **Chiang Mai** (11hr.; 7:30am, 6pm, and 8:30pm; 205฿, A/C 369฿); **Loei** (#220, 3½hr., every 20min. 4:20am-6:10pm, 45฿); **Nong Khai** (#221, 1hr., every 1½hr. 6am-7pm, 17฿).

Local Transportation: Songthaew #23 runs between bus terminals #1 and #2 (4฿). Plenty of **samlor** (20-30฿) and **tuk-tuk** (20-50฿) run around town.

ORIENTATION AND PRACTICAL INFORMATION

Udon Thani, 562km northeast of Bangkok, lies between Khon Kaen and Nong Khai along the railroad line and **Friendship Hwy.** Navigating the city requires a decent map, extreme flexibility in interpreting street signs, and an eternal awareness of the landmark **Nong Prajak Reservoir,** a large park on the town's west side. **Prajaksilapakom, Phosri,** and **Srisuk Rd.** run east-west through town toward the reservoir. Each road sports a traffic circle where it intersects **Udon-Dutsadee Rd.,** the major north-south thoroughfare. Away from the reservoir, Prajaksilapakom Rd. ends at the **train station** near **bus terminal #2.** The **airport** and **bus terminal #1** are across the reservoir, west of the town center.

Tourist Office: TAT, 16/5 Mukkhamontri Rd (☎325 406), at the edge of the reservoir. Look for the back door on Tesa Rd. Not too helpful. Open daily 8:30am-4:30pm.

Currency Exchange: Bangkok Bank, 154 Prajaksilapakom Rd. (☎221 505). Open M-F 8:30am-3:30pm; currency exchange open daily 8:30am-5pm. **24hr. ATM.**

Emergency: ☎191.

Police: ☎328 515. At Srisuk and Naresuan Rd.

Pharmacies: Many throughout the city. Try **Aek Udon International Hospital's** pharmacy (see below). **Open 24hr.**

Medical Services: Aek Udon International Hospital, 555/5 Phosri Rd. (☎341 555). One of the best hospitals in the northeast. English-speaking doctors. Ask Peter Davison, Manager of International Services, for health advice. AmEx/MC/V.

Telephones: Communications Authority of Thailand, 108/2 Udon-Dutsadee Rd. (☎222 805). North of the clocktower traffic circle before Wattananuvong Rd. Lenso international phone. Open daily 8am-10pm.

Internet Access: On virtually any street but Phosri Rd. 15-60฿ per hr. **New Com and Good Service,** 1391 Makhaeng Rd., at Prajaksilapakom Rd. Internet and Virtual Cop II 15฿ per hr.

Post Office: GPO (☎222 304), on Wattananuvong Rd. toward the reservoir. Open M-F 8:30am-4:30pm, Sa-Su 9am-noon. **Postal code:** 41000.

ACCOMMODATIONS

If you're looking for a nice room at a good price, you've come to the wrong town.

Chai Porn Hotel, 209-211 Makkhaeng Rd. (☎222 144), next to Mandarin Restaurant. Despite its name and outward appearance, Porn is not a house of ill repute. If you're into that stuff though, congratulations, you're in the right country. Communal TV room. Tidy singles 150฿, with A/C 200฿; doubles 200/250฿.

Thailand Hotel, 4/1-6 Surakan Rd. (☎341 670). From bus terminal #1 or the train station, head down Prajaksilapakom Rd. Turn left on Surakan Rd., cross Phosri Rd., pass "Top World," and it's on the left. Singles 200฿, with A/C 250฿; doubles with A/C 350฿.

Tang Porn Dhi Raksa Hotel, 289 Makhaeng Rd. (☎221 032). If Chai Porn Hotel were a glitzy, pay-per-view flick, this is a grainy home video. Private bath, shared toilets. Singles 140฿; doubles 200฿.

THAILAND

FOOD

Mae Yha, 81 Ratcha Phat Sadur Rd. Walking toward the reservoir from the fountain, take the 2nd left; it's on the 2nd block on the left. Colossal local superstar. An excellent people-watching location and yummy desserts. 9-scoop sundae 95฿. Thai, Chinese, and Western food 25-90฿. Open daily 9:59am-10:59pm, sharp.

Rabieng Pattani Restaurant, 53/1 Rim Nong Prachak. Walk toward the reservoir on Wattananuvong Rd. and make a right on Tesa Rd.; Rim Nong Prachak is 400m down on the left. Slightly out of the way, but well worth it. A local favorite with fabulous seafood (85-150฿). Open daily 8am-11pm.

Mr. T Restaurant, 254 Phosri Rd. at Si Satha Rd. This restaurant/bar/coffeeshop has a mellow atmosphere and acoustic guitar in the evenings. Breakfast (lots of fruit) 80฿. Steaks 100฿. Open 24hr.

Ban Isaan, 177 Adunyadet Rd. Sample all the regional specialties. Thai curries 30-40฿.

Ngee Sun Superstore, 119-123 Phosri Rd., between Makhaeng and Pamphrao Rd. Offers supermarket selection and prices. Open daily 9am-9pm.

PLANTS THAT BOOGIE About 2km northwest of town, the **Udon Sunshine Fragrant Orchid Farm** (☎242 475), 127 Nongsamrong Rd, is a botanical talent show. Mr. Pradit Kampermpoon devoted a decade of his life to develop the first scented orchid, aptly named "Miss Udon Sunshine." The next enclosure over, where Desmodium gyrant makes its home, is even more mind-boggling. These unremarkable-looking herbs perk up and shimmy to the vibes of music or human voice. Thanks to Mr. Kampermpoon's years spent cross-breeding the jinrant plant, the plants respond almost instantaneously as opposed to their more lethargic wild counterparts. "Their performance can be helpful to unhappy people," claims Mr. Kampermpoon, crooning in a falsetto to the plants. Some AIDS patients swear by the plants' healing powers, and sufferers of mental illness show marked improvement through exposure. As if this miracle plant didn't do enough, its tea clears up skin and cures stomach ailments. Next on Mr. Pradit's wish list is a plant that will sing background vocals for his upcoming album. Keep your ears peeled. The orchids thrive from September to April, while the dancing plants strut their stuff year-round. To find these living legends, take Phosri Rd. past the reservoir and bear right on Phoniyom Rd. After the first stoplight, the farm is 100m ahead on the left. If you get lost, say the magic words "Udon Sunshine" to any passer-by. (Open daily 6:30am-6pm. Admission 30฿, goes toward AIDS research.)

SIGHTS AND ENTERTAINMENT

Nong Prajak Reservoir, in the northwest section of town, is sprinkled with benches, pavilions, and footbridges. Join mothers, children, and sweethearts to feed the catfish (bag of fish chow 10฿). For a full 360° view of Udon Thani Province from the northeast's only certified **heliport,** sidle into Aek Udon Hospital and ask for Peter Davison. Bring a beach umbrella and a book to make a day of it.

Udon's nightlife is packed into a thumping section of **Sai Uthit Rd.** between Prajaksilapakom and Wattananuvong Rd. If you like loud techno and wandering elephants, this is the place to be. Starting at Wattananuvong Rd. facing the strip, **Take a Seat** is on the left, and unlike others, it's quiet enough to hold a conversation over the music. Farther down is **Zuzy,** which pumps out Euro-house with Thai lyrics. Next is **Shaken,** almost identical but with a slightly hipper crowd. **Nasa's** larger dance floor rocks with hard-core techno. **Morgan** follows, playing Thai pop to the delight of its screaming patrons. About 200m past the discos, **Mr. Tong's** outdoor bar is a great place to finish the evening. The town's expats and the locals that love them swear by **Harry's Bar,** 19/4 Banliam Bypass. Heading past the reservoir on Srisuk Rd., take a left on Pracha Ruksa Rd. and a right on Suk Rd. *Tuk-tuk* from the town center of town cost 50฿. At all listed establishments, beers cost 60-70฿, mixed drinks 100-110฿. No cover charges apply.

MARKETS

Thai Isaan, on Sai Uthit Rd. west of bus terminal #1, and **Rangsima Market,** across from bus terminal #2, are both uninspiring. The real deal is **Ban Huay Market** at the north end of Udon-Dutsadee Rd. A network of vendor-lined sois surrounds a huge, covered area with tons of delicious goodies. A number of Thai dishes are cooked on the spot and put into a bag for take-away. Not so delicious are the live turtles, eels, and mountain bikes.

DAYTRIPS FROM UDON THANI

BAN CHIANG

Orange and blue songthaew *from beyond the gas station on the left side of Phosri Rd. go to Ban Chiang (#1371, 1½hr., every 30min., 20฿). After crossing the tracks, the road becomes Hwy. 22, the Udon Thani-Sakhon Nakhon Hwy. If the bus drops you off here, take a* tuk-tuk *for the remaining 6km (40-50฿). If you miss the last bus from Ban Chiang to Udon Thani (leaves at noon), hire a* tuk-tuk *back to the highway and catch any of the buses heading to Udon Thani.*

Ban Chiang, 54km east of Udon Thani, is one of Southeast Asia's most significant archaeological discoveries and was recognized as a UNESCO World Heritage Site in 1992. The story of it's discovery begins in 1966, when Stephen Young, a Harvard University archaeology student, tripped over a large root. Catching himself, he found the rim of a partially unearthed pot staring him in the face. Upon closer scru-

tiny, he found that the entire 5m by 15m area was littered with half-buried pots. By the time excavation began in the mid-1970s, many valuable artifacts had been sold to collectors in trading centers worldwide. Since then, archeologists have learned about the people who lived here from 3600-1000 BC. The Ban Chiang people crafted cord-marked vessels and buried their deceased infants in jars. Over 100 skeletons and numerous bronze artifacts indicate that the civilization possessed knowledge of metallurgy much earlier than estimated, casting doubt on the theory that metallurgy came to Thailand from China.

A **village museum** documents the unearthing of Ban Chiang. The 2nd-floor exhibits have comprehensive English captions. *(Open daily 8am-5pm. 30฿.)* At the other end of the village, **Wat Phosi Nai** displays a well-preserved burial site with intact artifacts. Exit left from the museum; the **excavation site** is 500m down on the left.

ERAWAN CAVE

Erawan Cave is just off the Udon Thani-Loei Hwy. (Hwy. 210). Take a tuk-tuk *along the highway until the caves becomes visible. From there, another* tuk-tuk *will transport you the additional 2km from the entrance to the cave.*

The gaping crevice in the cliffs that shelter the large Buddha is clearly visible from the highway. A wat at the base of the cliff marks the end of the road. To the right, a huge flight of stairs ascends the mountain. Eventually the steps branch; take the flight to the left. You can start **spelunking** at the top. A path with a panoramic view of the nearby peaks runs through the mountain to the other side.

KHON KAEN ☎043

Similar to other Isaan cities, Khon Kaen lacks the "big" tourist attraction. Nonetheless, with festive nightlife, open air markets, and an efficient transportation system, Khon Kaen gives visitors the means to enjoy themselves. Khon Kaen University, northeastern Thailand's largest university with 7200 students, brings a vibrant young crowd to the evening scene. Khon Kaen also serves as a base for rewarding daytrips to the rest of the province.

TRANSPORTATION

Flights: Khon Kaen Airport (☎227 701), 5km west of town off Maliwan Rd. **Thai Airways,** 9/9 Prachasamran Rd. (☎227 701), inside Kasa Hotel, flies daily to **Bangkok** (8:30am, 3:20, 8:20pm; 1200฿).

Trains: Khon Kaen Railway Station (☎221 112), Ruenrom Rd. To: **Bangkok** (8hr.; 8:30, 11:20am, 9:00, 9:20, 10:40pm; 3rd-class 117฿, 2nd-class 300฿); **Khorat** (5hr., 5 per day, 38฿); **Udon Thani** (2hr., 7 per day, 25฿); **Nong Khai** (3hr.; 4, 5:30, 9:40am, 3:10pm; 35฿).

Buses: Ordinary bus terminal (☎237 472), on Prachasamosorn Rd. by the pedestrian overpass. Buses to: **Bangkok** (#20, 7hr., every 25min. 6:30am-9:30pm, 129฿); **Khorat** (3hr., every 30min. 5am-10am, 58฿); **Mukdahan** (4hr., every 30min. 8:10am-4:30pm, 72฿); **Ubon Ratchathani** (#282, every hr. 5:40-11:40am, 83฿); **Udon Thani** (#211 or #262; 2hr.; every 20min. 7am-1pm; 3rd-class 38฿, 2nd-class 75฿). **A/C bus terminal** (☎239 910), on Glang Muang Rd. A/C buses to: **Bangkok** (#20, 6hr., 25 per day, 271฿) via **Khorat** (3hr., 140฿); **Loei** (#319; 4hr.; 6:30, 11:30am, 4:30pm; 115฿); **Nong Khai** (#23; 3hr.; 4, 5:30am, 1, 3, 5pm; 95฿); **Ubon Ratchathani** (#268, 5hr., every 2hr. 9am-3pm, 149฿).

Local Transportation: Samlor 20-30฿. **Tuk-tuk** 20-50฿. **Songthaew** 4฿. TAT has a list of stops for all 20 *songthaew* routes. White *songthaew* #11 goes from Khon Kaen Railway Station to TAT. Blue *songthaew* #17 goes from TAT to the National Museum.

ORIENTATION AND PRACTICAL INFORMATION

Khon Kaen, 450km from Bangkok, is easily reached by plane, bus, or train. The main north-south thoroughfares are **Na Muang Rd.** and **Glang Muang Rd.,** lined with

hotels, restaurants, and the **A/C bus terminal.** Farther south, the parallel Muangs cross **Srichant Rd.,** home to the best nightspots. Past Srichant Rd. on Glang Muang Rd. are the **post office, police station,** and **day market,** which ends at **Ruenrom Rd.** A right turn onto Ruenrom Rd. from Na Muang Rd. or Glang Muang Rd. leads to the **train station.** The **regular bus terminal** and **TAT office** are on **Prachasamosorn Rd.**

Tourist Offices: TAT, 15/5 Prachasamosorn Rd. (☎244 498). A brown and white building several blocks left from the regular bus terminal. Essential comprehensive maps and intracity transportation info. Open daily 8:30am-4:30pm.

Consulates: Laos, 171 Prachasamosorn Rd. (☎224 857). 30-day visas US$30-35 available same day if you come early. Open M-F 9am-4pm. **Vietnam,** 65/6 Chatapadung Rd. (☎241 586). 15-day visas about US$40, 2-3 working days to process. Open M-F 8-11:30am and 1:30-4:30pm. Light-blue *songthaew* #10 runs to both consulates.

Currency Exchange: Banks and ATMs on Srichant Rd. **Bangkok Bank,** 254 Srichant Rd. (☎225 142), opposite Parrot Restaurant. After-hours exchange during high season. Open M-F 8:30am-7pm, Sa-Su 9am-5pm. **24hr. ATM.**

Markets: Sizeable **day market** hides behind storefronts along Na Muang and Glang Muang Rd., stretching south to Ruenrom Rd. Fruits, vegetables, and pig heads on sale. Popular items include *mut-mee* silks and triangular pillows. Open daily 5am-6pm. When other shops shut down, the **night market** gets going along Ruenrom Rd. at the south end of the day market. Road side eateries stretch into the horizon.

Emergency: ☎191.

Tourist Police: 15/5 Prachasamosorn Rd. (☎236 937), left of TAT. **Open 24hr.**

THAILAND

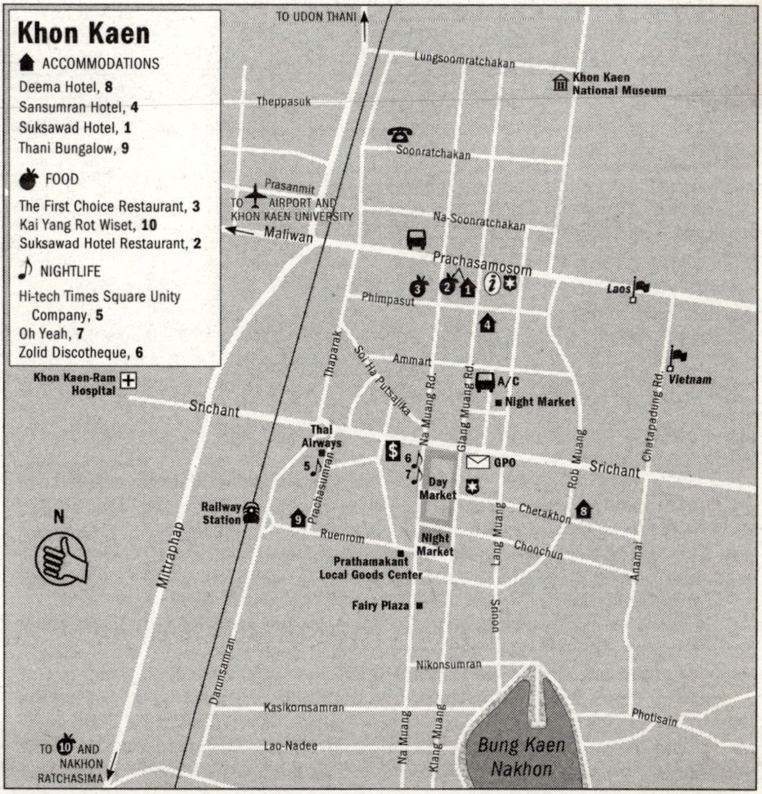

Police: Khon Kaen Police Station (☎221 162), on Glang Muang Rd., between Chetakhon and Srichant Rd.

Pharmacies: On Glang Muang Rd. between Ammart and Phimpasut Rd.

Medical Services: Khon Kaen-Ram Hospital, 193 Srichant Rd. (☎336 789), on the side of the tracks away from town. English-speaking doctors. **Open 24hr.**

Telephones: Khon Kaen Telecommunications Center, 294/1 Soonratchakan Rd. (☎241 569). The real building is behind the one that faces the street.

Internet Access: Several places on Glang Muang Rd. north of Ammart Rd. 15฿ per hour. It's impossible to beat schoolchildren to the computers on Su from 4-7pm.

Post Office: GPO, on Glang Muang Rd., just beyond Srichant Rd. Open M-F 8:30am-4:30pm, Sa-Su 9am-noon. **Postal code:** 40000.

ACCOMMODATIONS

Sansumran Hotel, 55-59 Glang Muang Rd. (☎239 611), between the giant plastic tusks. Spacious rooms with baths and lots of those carved lions so popular in Isaan hotels. Khon Kaen's best value. Singles/doubles 150-250฿.

Suksawad Hotel, 2/2 Glang Muang Rd. (☎236 472), near Prachasamosorn Rd. English-speaking staff. The miser's choice in Khon Kaen. Small rooms 80฿, with toilet 100฿; doubles with toilet 160฿.

Deema Hotel, 113 Chetakhon Rd. (☎321 562). Actually a hotel frequented mainly by domestic tourists. Good value. Singles/doubles 200฿, with A/C 300฿.

Thani Bungalow (☎221 428), at the intersection of Ruenrom and Prachasamran Rd. Small rooms aren't the best deal in Khon Kaen, but colorful bungalows have A/C, TV, and hot water. Singles/doubles 250฿; A/C bungalows 500฿.

THAILAND

FOOD

Sidewalk eateries cluster on Phimpasut and Ammart Rd. Cheap Isaan meals like *sup nau mai* (shredded bamboo shoot salad) tempt hungry passerbyers at **night markets** on Lang Muang and Ruenrom Rd.

The First Choice Restaurant, 18/8 Phimpasut Rd., at the corner of Na Muang Rd. Powerful A/C. Numerous vegetarian choices. Set breakfast 70฿. Thai dishes 50-100฿. Steaks 150-300฿. Open daily 7:30am-11pm.

Suksawad Hotel Restaurant, 2/2 Glang Muang Rd. If you don't like the rooms, you might like the food on this small, outdoor patio. Affordable English/Thai menu. *Thao tom kung* (rice soup with shrimp) 20฿.

Kai Yang Rot Wiset, 177 Mittraphap Rd. Take blue *songthaew* #10 toward Lotus Shopping Center (5฿); it's just beyond PTT gas station on the left. Buffet is easy on the linguistically-challenged as well as the taste buds. Dishes 20฿. Open daily 7am-10pm.

SIGHTS

The only noteworthy sight is the well-run **Khon Kaen National Museum,** at the Lungsoomratchakan and Kasikonthungsang Rd. intersection. Blue *songthaew* stop at the side entrance (3฿). The museum documents the history of the central Northeast. The second floor has articles from the olden days (Lop Buri period) while the first floor is devoted to the really olden days (Ban Chang period, etc.). Check with TAT for the temporary exhibit schedule. (☎246 170. Open daily 9am-4pm. 30฿.)

In the southeast corner of Khon Kaen is **Bung Kaen Nakhon,** a lakeside recreation center circumscribed by four wats and numerous food stalls. Every April it hosts the **Dok Khoon Siang Khaen Flower Festival,** featuring Isaan music, floral processions, and dances. Check with TAT for specific dates. About 4km northwest of town, **Khon Kaen University** is the largest in northeastern Thailand. *Songthaew* #8 and #10 make the trip from town. If you're lucky, friendly students may give you a tour and show you their art work.

Prathamakant Local Goods Center, 79/2-3 Ruenrom Rd., is 30m from the Na Muang Rd. intersection.Those unable to visit Chonabot (See **Daytrips,** below) can enjoy silk handicrafts at Prathamakant Local Goods Center. Lots of *mut-mee* silks, classy and funky shirts and skirts, wooden carvings, and instruments are for sale in A/C comfort. Check out the small museum and huge wooden carving of village life in the back. (☎224 080. Open daily 8am-8:30pm.)

NIGHTLIFE

The arcade near The First Choice Restaurant (see **Food,** above) is packed with karaoke bars, beer gardens, and pubs. Beware: many "karaoke bars" are laden with prostitutes, and travelers report being offered more than a just a beer.

Oh Yeah, 205 Sirichuam Rd. Listen for pumping bass from a soi past Charoen Thani Princess Hotel. Pseudo-underground student dance club. Beers 80-120฿, but everyone seems to bring their own whisky and pay for the mix. Open daily 10pm-2am.

Zolid Discotheque, Chaoren Thani Princess Hotel, bottom floor. Patrons dance on small tables on 3 levels. Huge screen shows music videos. Small Singha 60฿. Cover 60฿. Open daily 9pm-2am.

Hi-tech Times Square Unity Company, where Prachasamran and Darunsamran Rd. converge south of the Srichant Rd. rotary. Student-loved venue with Thai rock bands. Also inside is **Heaven,** a techno club that pulsates 'til dawn. Open daily 6pm-5am.

DAYTRIPS FROM KHON KAEN

Although Khon Kaen Province has plenty of sights, the scant tourist facilities makes exploring the area a healthy challenge.

CHONABOT

Catch a bus to Nakhon Sawan from Khon Kaen's regular bus terminal (1hr., every hr. until 1:30pm, 30฿) and ask to be let off at Chonabot. When you disembark on the highway, face the wagon-wheel fence and police station, walk right to the first intersection and turn left. The first silk factory is on the right before the post office. To return to Khon Kaen, walk down Phosi Sahat Rd. until it meets the highway. Wait in front of the police station for the last bus back to Khon Kaen at 5pm. Most factories open M-Sa 8am-5pm.

The town of Chonabot stocks hand-woven silk. Tour companies offer expensive trips, but it's better to go on your own. There are no formal showrooms, but owners gladly display wares that interest you. Prices vary depending on the thickness and weight of the material. *Mut-mee* silk runs 500฿, and *sipuen* is 220฿.

PHUWIANG

Buses to Phuwiang leave daily from the regular bus terminal.

Those interested in more ancient reptiles should swing by Phuwiang, home to the largest dinosaur fossils in the country. Fossils dug up from the nine quarries located here have added weight to the theory that Tyrannosaurus Rex existed first in Asia Minor before crossing the Bering Channel to North America. Don't try to take any souvenirs from the sites, though, as tourist literature warns, "We must not backstop wrong doings such as taking away a dinosaur fossil to be developed into an amulet of portable Buddha image." Ask TAT to photocopy its single brochure for you.

BAN KOK SA-NGA

50km from Khon Kaen. From the regular bus station, take a bus to Krachuan (#501; every 30min., last return 6pm; 15฿) and ride a tuk-tuk to the village (20฿). Snake breeding center open to the public; 20฿.

Villagers in "King Cobra Village" have been taming deadly king cobras since 1951, using them as attention-getters for their herbal medicine businesses. Villagers stage "boxing" exhibitions: after tempting the snakes to strike, the masters skillfully sidestep death. Wear a cobra like a boa, if you dare.

SOUTHERN THAILAND

South of Surat Thani, mosques slowly replace wats, and women don veils as the ethnic mix changes slowly from Thai to Malay. The people of southern Thailand have traditionally been the country's most prosperous, the sea the source of their livelihood. The steady stream of tourist dollars that started flowing nearly a decade ago is only growing today; nearly every cove and shore is hospitable to tourists, and daytrips can be arranged for diving and snorkeling in the bluest of waters. The sky alone, from sunset to sundown, is enough to make travelers happy to wade many miles in the water simply awaiting another explosive sunset.

ON THE MAINLAND

TRANG ☎075

Trang has been riding the highway (Hwy. 4, that is) of prosperity for 30 years. Though the provincial capital itself is hardly worth writing home about, the surrounding areas stockpile 119km worth of national-park beaches and a formidable collection of small islands, both of which remain undisturbed by the brazen bandits of large-scale development. Off the usual circuit, Trang is nice for travelers seeking relief from *farang*-heavy traffic and a chance to explore undeveloped areas.

TRANSPORTATION

Flights: Trang Airport (☎210 804), on Trang-Palian Rd., 7km south of the city. Take Trang Travel's airport vans (30฿) or a *tuk-tuk* (50฿) into town. **Thai Airways,** 199/2 Visetkul Rd. (☎218 066). Turn right at the clock tower onto Visetkul Rd.; it's several blocks down on the left, just past Soi 5. Open daily 8am-noon and 1-4:30pm. Daily flights to **Bangkok** (9:15pm, additional flights F-Su 6pm; 2575฿).

Trains: Railway station (☎218 012), at the west end of Phraram 6 Rd. Fares listed are express 2nd-class express. Trains to **Bangkok** (16hr.; sleeper 1:55, 5:10pm; 970฿) via **Chumphon** (7hr., 576฿) and **Surat Thani** (5hr., 201฿).

Buses: Bus station (☎210 455), on Huay Yod Rd., north of downtown. Check with TAT for buses that leave from other parts of city. Buses to: **Bangkok** (13hr., 4:30pm, 565฿); **Hat Yai** (every 30min. 6am-6pm, 83฿); **Krabi** (2hr., every hr. 7am-6pm, 90฿); **Phang-Nga** (4½hr., every hr. 7am-6pm, 139฿); **Phuket** (4hr., every hr. 7am-6pm, 189฿); **Satun** (3hr., every hr. 6am-5pm, 86฿; take a *tuk-tuk* to the stop on Ratsada Rd.); **Surat Thani** (3hr., every hr. 9:30am-5pm, 125฿; leaves from train station).

Local Transportation: Tuk-tuk within the city run 10฿. **Taxis** (15฿) and **minivans** (10฿) leave when full and leave from different parts of town (every 20min. 5am-7pm). For vans to **Kantang Pier,** go down Pharam 6 Rd. by the train station, and turn right on Kantang Rd.; vans line up on the right. Vans to **Hat Tao Mai, Hat Yong Ling,** and **Hat Pakmeng** leave from Tha Klang Rd., also by the train station (every hr. 7am-5pm, 50฿).

ORIENTATION AND PRACTICAL INFORMATION

Buses arrive at the **bus station** near the intersection of **Ploenpitak Rd.** and **Huay Yod Rd.,** a 20min. walk north of town or five minutes by motorcycle taxi or *tuk-tuk* (both 20฿). The **railway station** sits at the west end of **Pharam 6 Rd.,** a large hotel-lined avenue with the **TAT office,** landmark **clock tower,** and most other tourist services, including banks, Internet cafes, and travel agencies. North of Pharam 6 Rd., **Ratchadamnoen Rd.** (which becomes **Pattalung Rd.**) winds roughly parallel to the main **day market** and connects to Pharam 6 Rd. by Kantang Rd. to the west and Wisekul Rd. to the east by the clock tower.

Southern Thailand
0 50 miles
0 50 kilometers
Nakhon Pathom
Bangkok
Phetchaburi
Ko Si Chang
Si Racha
Pattaya
Hua Hin
Pran Buri
KHAO SAM ROI YAT NATIONAL PARK
Ko Samet
Kui Buri
Ko Chang
MYANMAR
Prachuap Khiri Khan
Thap Sakae
Andaman Sea
Bang Saphan
Gulf of Thailand
Pathiu
Kra Buri
Chumphon
Tham Prakayang
Punya Ban
Sawi
Ko Tao
Ranong
Lang Sua
Hat Supin
Ko Ta Luang
Ko Phangan
Kapoe
LAEM SON NATIONAL PARK
Chaiya
Don Sak
Ko Samui
Khanom
Khura Buri
Tha Chang
Surat Thani
Sichon
Tham Waram
Takua Pa
Similan Islands
Bang Sak
Phanom
Na San
KHAO SOK NATIONAL PARK
Khao Luk
Phrasaeng
Wiang Sa
Tha Sala
Lam Pi
Than Put
Nakhon Si Thammarat
Phang-Nga
Ao Luk
KHAO PHANOM BENCHA NATIONAL PARK
Khok Kloi
Thung Yai
Thung Sopng
Susarn Hoi
Hua Sai
HAT NAI YANG NATIONAL PARK
Ko Yao Noi
Krabi
Khlong Thom
Huai Yot
Khuan Khanun
Ranot
Phuket
Phuket Town
Phatthalung
Ban Lampam
Ko Phi Phi
Thale Luang
Ko Lanta Yai
Sikao
Trang
Kachong
Thale Sap
Sathing Phra
Pak Mong
Rak Phayun
Yan Ta Khao
Ko Li Bong
Songkhla
N
HAT CHAO MAI NATIONAL PARK
THALE BAN NATIONAL PARK
Thung Wa
Hat Yai
Pattani
Ban Pakbara
Na Thawi
Sai Buri
KO TARUTAO NATIONAL PARK
Ko Tarutao
Sadao
Saba Yoi
Yala
TO KOTA BHARU
Satun
Kangar
Ko Rawi
Betong
Narathiwat
Pulau Langkawi
Kuah
Ban Nang Sata
Alor Setar
MALAYSIA
Sungai Kolok
Road
Railroad
Country Border
TO PENANG
Sungai Petani

Tourist Office: TAT (☎/fax 215 580), next to the Trang Hotel on Phraram 6 Rd. International phone and Internet. Very helpful staff and free maps. Open daily 8:30am-5pm. Private travel agencies offering organized tours and transport line Phraram 6 Rd.

Currency Exchange: Bangkok Bank, 2 Phraram 6 Rd. (☎218 203), one block from the train station on the right. **24hr. ATM.** Open M-F 8:30am-3:30pm.

Emergency: ☎191.

Police: 6 Pattalung Rd. (☎218 019). Some English spoken. **Open 24hr.**

Medical Services: Wattanapat Hospital (☎210 585), on Pattalung Rd. at the intersection with Ploenpitak Rd., north of the clock tower. Some English spoken. **Open 24hr.**

Internet Access: All over Phraram 6 Rd. 30฿ per hr.

Post Offices: GPO (☎218 521), at the bend on Jermpanya Rd., which branches north from Phraram 6 Rd. 20min. walk from train station. *Poste Restante.* Open M-F 8:30am-3:30pm. **Branch office** on Phraram 6 Rd., 1 block from train station. Open M-F 8:30am-4:30pm, Sa-Su 9am-noon. **Postal code:** 92000.

ACCOMMODATIONS AND FOOD

Trang lacks good budget accommodations, but the best selection clusters by the train station. A surprisingly decent abode, fairly popular **Station Inn,** 100m to the left of the train station when exiting, has large doubles that are old but clean. (☎223 393. Singles 200฿; doubles 240฿.) Though it's the most popular backpacker joint in town, almost everything about **Koh Teng Hotel,** 77-79 Phraram 6 Rd., five blocks from the train station on the left, is old. An old notebook documents *farang* travel experiences, and the old staff serves tasty snacks in the old restaurant. The large, old rooms have phones, fans, mirrors, and Western toilets. (☎218 148. Singles/doubles 180฿.)

Trang's cuisine has a distinct Chinese taste. Crispy roasted, honey-dipped pork with *paa tong ko* (Chinese doughnuts) and *dim sum* make delicious breakfasts. The town has several food-serving **night markets,** one next to Diamond Department Store by the train station, and another down Visetkul Rd. from the Phraram 6 Rd. intersection. (Both open daily 6-10pm.) The **Trang Hotel Restaurant,** on Phraram 6 Rd. near the clock tower, serves more upscale cuisine at surprisingly reasonable prices. Sleepy-eyed lounge singers entertain Thai businessmen while friendly teen waiters stare curiously at foreigners. (Thai dishes 80-100฿. Open daily 8am-11pm.)

ENTERTAINMENT

Trang's nightlife doesn't rival that of Phuket or Ko Phi Phi but offers a different kind of fun—the type you'll still remember the next morning. Fierce creatures, not fierce parties, dominate Trang's entertainment. In the morning on Phraram 6 Rd., traders sell colorful **fighting fish.** Makeshift **cock-fighting** arenas set up below stilt houses, and **bullfights** are staged once or twice a year (tickets from 100฿). Direct *tuk-tuk* drivers to Sanam Wuah Chon (10฿) near the bullfight field. The Trang Chamber of Commerce organizes commercial events, like the **Cake Festival** (Aug.) and **Barbecue Festival** (Sept.), which promote Trang's famed dessert and pork.

NEAR TRANG

Trang's surrounding areas offer a bevy of natural oceanside Edens, most of them overlooked by travelers making a beeline from Surat Thani to Ko Phi Phi, Phuket, or Malaysia. Expect few travelers in even busy places like **Ko Mook** and **Pakmeng** and only a smattering of locals on isolated **Hat Yong Ling.** Most towns are accessible from Trang by minivans, which depart from various points around town. **Boats** to islands near Pakmeng, such as **Ko Hai** and Ko Mook, leave from **Pakmeng Pier** (100-300฿). Boats to **Ko Lao Lieng, Ko Petra,** or **Ko Sukorn** (the first two have no accommodations) leave from the pier at **Tasae Cape** in southern Trang Province.

HAT YONG LING. Hat Yong Ling National Park has two coves sheltered by rocky mountains covered in wild orchids. Trek through a lush patch of tropical forest and a bat cave to reach one of the best sand-and-sea combos around. Spelunkers should bring flashlights. Along the mountain base, the waves have carved out coves where locals often camp and grill seafood. Minibuses (50฿) leave every hour or when full from the station by the beach. Hat Yong Ling's **National Park Office** also serves its distant neighbor **Hat Jao Mai.** (☎210 099. Open M-F 9am-5pm.)

HAT PAKMENG. Busier Hat Pakmeng is the only mainland beach with significant commercial presence, as evidenced by the numerous seafood stalls and restaurants that serve customers in their beach chairs. The pretty beach is long and shallow, and several picturesque limestone formations dot the horizon. Minivans (45min., every hr., 50฿) from Trang will take you to the center of the beach or the popular **Pakmeng Resort,** farther south, which has tidy bungalows and private baths. (☎210 321. Singles/doubles 400฿, with A/C 750-800฿.) To return to Trang, flag down a white van from the main road (roughly every hr.).

KO MOOK. Ko Mook is most popular with European budgeteers and, with four resorts, its the most developed of the Trang Province islands. The prettier and cheaper western side of the island boasts a nice white sand beach. Of the island's four resorts, **Had Farung Bungalows** is the cheapest (bungalows 200฿, with bath 300฿), and **Sawatdee Resort** follows close behind (bungalows 300฿). On the west side, similarly-priced **Muk Resort** (☎214 441; bungalows 300฿) and **Muk Garden Resort** (☎211 372; bungalows 300฿) can arrange transportation to the island from their offices in Trang. To get to Ko Mook on your own, take a minivan to **Pakmeng Pier** (1hr., 50฿) and hop on a boat to the island (1hr., 11am, 400฿).

THAILAND

KO HAI (KO NGAI). With white-sand beaches and three pricey resorts, teardrop-shaped Ko Hai (sometimes spelled "Ko Ngai") is not only a true tropical paradise but also an excellent dive spot. **Koh Ngai Villa** has the cheapest rooms and arranges transport to and from the island. (☎210 496. Bungalows with fan 500-800฿.) More upscale **Koh Ngai Resort** has a diving center. (☎210 317. Bungalows 600-780฿.)

KO KRADAN. Under the protection of the Hat Jao Mai National Park, beautiful Ko Kradan is one of the least developed islands in the Andaman Sea. Budget lodging is essentially limited to the **Ko Kradan Paradise Beach.** (☎216 580. Bungalows from 600฿.) Food is as expensive as the rooms, so bring your own from the mainland.

HAT YAI ☎074

Crowded and noisy Hat Yai is southern Thailand's transportation, commerce, and prostitution center. Shopping conquers all in this metropolitan arena, since almost everything—pirated Robbie Williams CDs, pet fish, women—is cheaper here than in Singapore or Malaysia. For the most part, travelers drink away their time while trying to fend off aggressive street hawkers valiantly trying to convince them that buying a fluffy purple ostrich on a string is necessary.

TRANSPORTATION

Flights: Airport (☎251 007), 13km west of Hat Yai. **Thai Airways,** 166/4 Niphat Uthit 2 Rd. (☎233 433). Open M-Sa 8am-5pm, Su 9am-4pm. Flights to: **Bangkok** (1½hr., 9 per day, 2885฿); **KL** (2hr.; F, Su 2:25pm; 9890฿); **Phuket** (45min., 2:25pm, 1180฿); **Singapore** (2½hr., 1:10pm, 5760฿).

Trains: Railway station (☎243 705), at the west end of Thamnoon Vithi Rd. Trains to: **Bangkok** (13-17hr., 5 per day 2:45-6:10pm, 1005฿); **Butterworth, Malaysia** (5½hr., 7am, 233฿); **Sungai Kolok** (3½-4½hr., 4 per day 6:30am-12:15pm, 159฿); **Surat Thani** (4-5hr., 5 per day, 215฿).

Buses: Bus station (☎232 404), on Ranchanawanit Rd. in the southeast corner of town. Buses also stop at the market on Phetkasem Rd. 10-15min. after scheduled departure time. *Tuk-tuk* from town to terminal 10฿. Buses to: **Bangkok** (14hr., 13 per day 7am-7:30pm, 381-760฿); **Chumphon** (7:15, 8:15, 9:30, 10:30am, noon; 147-265฿); **Krabi** (4hr., 11am, 143฿); **Padang Besar, Malaysia** (1½hr., every 10min. 5:45am-7:20pm, 21฿); **Phuket** (7hr., 11 per day 5:30am-9:30pm, 135-243฿); **Satun** (1½hr., every 15min. 5:20am-5:40pm, 32-45฿); **Sungai Kolok** (4hr., 5 per day 6am-3pm, 148฿); **Surat Thani** (5½hr., 10 per day 5:20am-3pm, 103-160฿).

Local Transportation: Tuk-tuks (7฿) and **motorcycle taxis** (20฿) crisscross downtown.

ORIENTATION AND PRACTICAL INFORMATION

Hat Yai is large, confusing, and difficult to navigate without a map; pick one up from TAT or area hotels. Most travelers arrive at the town's train station on the west side of town at the intersection of **Rathakarn Rd.** and **Thamnoon Vithi Rd.,** one of the main commercial thoroughfares. Cheap guest houses and tourist services cluster near the train station. Buses enter the city on **Phetkasem Rd.** and drop off passengers in the rather confusing market area north of downtown. Central Hat Yai is organized by a grid system, marked by **Suphasarnrangsan, Prachathipat,** and Thamnoon Vithi Rd., running eastward from the train station; **Niphat Uthit 1, 2,** and **3 Rd.** intersect them from north to south.

THAILAND

Tourist Office: TAT, 1/1 Soi 2, Niphat Uthit 3 Rd. (☎243 747). Head south on Niphat Uthit 3 Rd. for 15-20min; it's on the left behind the police station. Enthusiastic staff, timetables, and free maps. Open daily 8:30am-4:30pm.

Tours: Ubiquitous on the Niphat Uthit roads. **Pakdee Tour,** 93/1 Niphat Uthit 2 Rd. (☎234 535), in same building as the Cathay Guest House. Specializes in transportation to major Thai and Malaysian tourist destinations. Open daily 7am-8pm.

Immigration Office: ☎243 019. On Phetkasem Rd., west of the train tracks, next to the police station. Open M-F 8:30am-4:30pm.

Currency Exchange: Bangkok Bank, 39 Niphat Uthit 2 Rd. (☎235 330), near Suphasarnrangsan Rd. Open daily 8:30am-3:30pm.

Markets: Morning market on Niphat Uthit 3 Rd. **Day** and **night markets** between Montri 1 and 2 Rd., off Rathakarn Rd., north of the station. Find your special aquatic friend at the **pet fish market** on Niphat Uthit 1 Rd., south of the fountain.

Emergency: ☎191.

Tourist Police: ☎246 733. On Sripoovanart Rd. near its intersection with Niphat Uthit 1 Rd. English spoken. **Open 24hr.**

Pharmacies: Santi Bheasaj, 129/12 Niphat Uthit 3 Rd. (☎246 537).

Medical Services: Hat Yai Public Hospital (☎230 8004), on Rattakarm Rd. The back of the hospital faces the GPO. English spoken. **Open 24hr.**

Telephones: Telecommunication Center, 490/1 Phetkasem Rd. (☎231 080), east of the rotary. Open daily 8am-midnight.

Internet Access: Plentiful and cheap in the area near the train station. 20฿ per hr.

Post Offices: GPO (☎243 013), at the corner of Niphatsongkraw 1 Rd. and Soi 4, 500m north of the rotary. *Poste Restante.* International phone upstairs. Open M-F 8:30am-4:30pm, Sa-Su 9am-noon. **Postal code:** 90110.

ACCOMMODATIONS AND FOOD

Many of the cheapest hotels in Hat Yai offer sleazy services, often under the moniker "ancient Thai massage." To avoid such unpleasantries, opt for one of the slightly more expensive but reputable guest houses suggested by TAT or stick to the tried and trusted train station area.

Cathay Guest House, 93/1 Niphat Uthit 2 Rd. (☎243 815), at the corner with Thamnoon Vithi Rd., a few blocks from the train station. Reminiscent of a university hostel, with backpackers lounging in various ranges of undress and filth. Not the prettiest rooms, but the staff is friendly and offers good tourist services. 4-bed dorms 90฿; singles 160฿; doubles 200฿; triples 250฿.

Ladda Guest House, 13-15 Thamnoon Vithi Rd. (☎220 233). 5min. from train station. Clean bathrooms and a friendly staff make up for the peeling paint. Singles 200฿.

Sorrasilp Guest House, 251/7-8 Phetkasem Rd. (☎232 635), 20m from bus stop. Far from train station and central Hat Yai but convenient if arriving on a late bus. Proximity to Montri Rd. market guarantees noisy afternoons and evenings. Private baths have Western toilets. Singles 160฿; doubles 200฿; 2 double beds 280฿.

Food vendors set up all day and night in the **Niphat Uthit Rd. area** and near the plaza market and cinema on **Phetkasem Rd.** For local flavor, try *khanom bueng* (crêpes with shredded coconut). **T.S. Vegetarian,** 16 Prachathipat Rd., across from Central Department Store, lets you pick three ready-made veggies for your rice. (Platters 20฿. Open daily 7am-8pm.)

ENTERTAINMENT

Your trusty credit card may collapse from shopping on **Phetkasem Rd.** For cheaper, more structured entertainment, check out **Post Laser Disc,** 82-83 Thamnoon Vithi Rd., about two blocks past Niphat Uthit 3 Rd. opposite Indra Hotel. Travelers gather upstairs to watch American movies. (☎232 027. 30฿ cover charge for a table upstairs. Schedule on sandwich board outside. Open daily noon-midnight.)

The **Thai Boxing Stadium** hosts matches one or two weekends a month (around 180฿; *tuk-tuk* to stadium 20-30฿). **Bullfights** are staged on most weekend days. TAT has schedules and prices. A 35m by 15m reclining Buddha rests in **Wat Hat Yai Nai,** 7km west of Hat Yai. (Open daily 8am-5pm; *tuk-tuk* to wat 15-20฿.)

SATUN ☎074

Satun is best known to travelers entering Thailand from Malaysia or passing through Ko Tarutao, the national park off the coast. Since Ko Tarutao is only open from October to May, Satun has little for tourists during the other half of the year. Backpackers sometimes stick around to enjoy Satun's friendly small-town atmosphere, but the town itself has little more than a few open-air bars.

TRANSPORTATION. Non-A/C orange buses go to **Hat Yai** (from the school on Satunthanee Rd., 2hr., every hr., 50฿) and **Trang** (from Sulakanukul, Burivanich, or Satunthanee Rd.; 3hr.; every 30min. 6:30am-5pm; 70฿). For A/C comfort to **Hat Yai,** take a **minivan** from the 7-11 on Satunthanee Rd. Also stops across the street from the Wangmai Hotel, in front of the open-air market (2hr., every 30min. or when full 6am-5pm, 150฿). A daily **ferry** service runs from Tamalang Pier to **Pulau Langkawi** (45min.; 9:30, 1:30, 4pm; 180฿). In high season, **boats** run from Pak Bara Pier, north of Satun, to **Ko Lipe** (departs 10:30am, returns 3pm; round-trip 440฿) and **Ko Tarutao** (10am, 3pm; round-trip 300฿).

ORIENTATION AND PRACTICAL INFORMATION. At its south end, **Satunthanee Rd.** forms a "T" intersection with **Samanthapradit Rd.** South on Satunthanee Rd. just before the mosque, **Burivanich Rd.** splits to the right to the **immigration office.** (☎711 080. Open M-F 8:30am-4:30pm.) Across the road, the **Thai Military Bank** and **Bangkok Bank** both have **24hr. ATMs** (AmEx/Cirrus/MC/V). The **police** are on the corner of Yarttrasawaddee and Satunthanee Rd. (☎711 025. **Emergency** ☎191. **Open 24hr.**) **Pon Phasaj pharmacy,** 62 Burivanish Rd., is near the police box. (Open M-Sa 7am-9pm.) **Satun Hospital,** 55/1 Hatthakumsuksa Rd., is on the corner of Yarttrasawaddee Rd. (☎732 460. English spoken. **Open 24hr.**) Overseas calls can be made from the **Telecom Office,** 7 Satun Thanee Rd., at the base of the red tower. (Open M-F 8:30am4:30pm.) Just east of the intersection of Satunthanee and Samanthapradit Rd. is the **post office.** (*Poste Restante.* Open M-F 8:30am-4:30pm. **Postal code:** 91000.) **Satun Travel and Ferry Service,** 45/8-9 Satunthanee Rd., sells tickets and arranges tours. (☎711 453. Open daily 8am-5pm.)

ACCOMMODATIONS AND FOOD. For the most central location, the **Satultanee Hotel,** 90 Satunthanee Rd., has spacious, bright rooms with attached bathrooms. (Singles with fan 210฿, with A/C 370฿.) Satun's budget accommodation is limited to the **Rain Tong Hotel,** 4 Samanthapradit Rd. From the Satunthanee Rd. intersection, turn onto Samanthapradit Rd. and walk towards the river; it's on the left. The old rooms are plain and clean with attached baths and squat toilets. (☎711 036. Singles/doubles 140฿.) **Satultanee Hotel,** 90 Sathunthanee Rd., has spacious, bright rooms with attached bathrooms. (Singles with fan 210฿, with A/C 370฿.)

Satun's Muslim majority sets the tone for local cuisine. Several breakfast *roti* places serve patrons throughout the day. Both the extensive **day market** on Satunthanee Rd. and **night market** on Tammango Uthit Rd. whip up cheap meals. (Duck noodle soup 20฿. Both open daily 5pm-midnight.) For a spicy nirvana, ask locals to point you to **Sri Trang,** 127 Satunthanee Rd., which has served curry and rice dishes for as long as anyone can remember. (Open daily 4pm-9pm.)

KO TARUTAO NATIONAL MARINE PARK

THAILAND

Once a pirate outpost and then an island prison, Ko Tarutao National Marine Park is an archipelago of 51 spectacular islands in the Andaman Sea. Home to a variety of wildlife, including deer, macaques, and four types of sea turtles, the park is an amazing and delicate ecosystem of coral and tropical jungle that is only now becoming a tourist destination. The park's main island is **Ko Tarutao,** 5_6km from Langkawi Island, a major point of entry into Malaysia. The largest of the park islands, covering 151 sq. km, Ko Tarutao was a labor camp for political prisoners during the 1940s. Today, Ko Tarutao's beaches sprawl on its coral-filled west coast, while further inland, waterfalls, mountains, caves, and wildlife attract adventurous travelers. From October to January, **sea turtles** paddle ashore to deposit eggs on **Ko Khai** (Egg Island), 15km southwest of Ko Tarutao. A popular way to explore the island is the 2hr. **hiking trail** from Ao Phante Melaka to Ao Talo Wao; it extends south for another 3hr. to Ao Talo U-Dang.

Ko Tarutao is open from November to May. The **park office** (☎ 729 002) is at the northern tip of Tarutao on Ao Phante Melaka, near the pier and is only open during peak season. The pier in Pak Bara (☎074 783 485) provides tourist information only during peak season. The beaches along the west coast provide the best campsites (about 10฿ per night). Bring your own tent. Otherwise, Tarutao provides park housing. (4-bed rooms 280฿; bungalows with two bedrooms and two baths 400฿; larger cottages with two bedrooms and one bath 600฿.) Make reservations in advance with the National Park Division of the **Royal Forest Department** in Bangkok (☎02 579 0529) or Pak Bara (☎781 285). For more information on Ko Tarutao, contact **Adang Sea Tour** (☎781 268) in Pak Bara.

To get to Ko Tarutao from **Satun** (see above), take a **songthaew** to **La-Ngu,** 60km from Satun (30฿). Here, *songthaew* and **taxis** go to **Pak Bara Pier** (12฿), from which **boats** leave daily for Ko Tarutao (10:30am, 3pm, return 9:30am; round-trip 300฿). Otherwise, charter a **longtail boat** from the Tarutao pier (from 500฿). From **Hat Yai** (see p. 775), catch a **bus** to La-Ngu or go straight to Pak Bara by minivan (2½hr., every 30min. 7am-5pm, 34฿).

SUNGAI KOLOK

Sungai Kolok is a raucous border town through which Malaysians smuggle booze. Most travelers go straight to the train station without staying at the hotels. Ban Taba, a small town 5km south of Tak Bai, is the preferred border-crossing point. Ferries from Ban Taba (where border hours are the same) to Malaysia cost 15฿.

TRANSPORTATION. From the **railway station** (☎614 060), on Asia 18 Rd. on the right, trains leave for: **Bangkok** (23hr., 11:55am and 2:40pm, 220-260฿) via **Chumphon** (12hr., 150฿); **Surat Thani** (9hr.; 6:30; 126฿); and **Hat Yai** (4-5hr., 5 per day 6:30am-3pm, 82฿). **Thai Airways,** at 53 Soi 1, Charoenkhet Rd. (☎612 132), arranges transport to **Narathiwat Airport** (8am, 140฿), with daily flights to **Bangkok** (10:40am, 2950฿) via **Phuket** (45min., 1155฿). The **bus office,** 95 Vorakamin Rd. (☎612 045), is six blocks from the intersection with Charoenkhet Rd. **Buses** run to **Bangkok** (19hr.; with A/C 8, 11:30am, and 12:30pm; 546-1090฿) via **Surat Thani** (9-10hr., 277฿). Private **A/C mini-vans** leave from the office opposite the Merlin Hotel and opposite the Savoy Hotel for **Hat Yai** (4hr., every hr. 6am-5pm, 150฿).

ORIENTATION AND PRACTICAL INFORMATION. The **border crossing** (see below) is at the end of **Asia 18 Rd.,** a broad avenue running parallel to the train tracks. Heading north, the **Tourist Information Center** (☎612 126; open daily 8:30am-4:30pm; offers free map) and **tourist police** (☎612 008; **emergency** ☎1155; open 24hr.) are in the same building on the right just after passport control. **Motorcycle taxis** wait just past the TAT (around town 20฿); **bicycle rickshaws** (40฿) may cost less on busier streets. Opposite the train station, **Charoenkhet Rd.** runs perpendicular to Asia 18 Rd. into the heart of Sungai Kolok. The **police station** (☎611 070) is here, opposite the **Narathiwat Immigration Office,** 70 Charoenkhet Rd. (☎611 231; open M-F 8:30am-4:30pm), and **Thai Farmer's Bank,** 1/6 Vorakamin Rd. (☎611 578; **24hr. ATM;** open M-F 8:30am-3:30pm). For **medical services** (☎615 161), you can find doctors at Saitong 6 Rd. The **post office** is on On Prachawiwat Rd. (☎611 141. *Poste Restante.* Open M-F 8:30am-4:30pm, Sa-Su 9am-noon.) **Postal code:** 96120.

ACCOMMODATIONS AND FOOD. There is no reason to spend a night in Sungai Kolok unless transportation forces you. **Savoy Hotel,** 34 Charoenkhet Rd., has a Chinese restaurant. (Open daily 7am-noon.) Its rooms have fans and bearable bathrooms. Get a room off the street to avoid traffic noise. (☎611 093. Singles with bath 130฿; doubles with bath 150฿. Reception 4am-midnight.)

Sungai Kolok's daily **market** spreads out behind Asia 18 Rd. before the sun gets out of bed. At night, **food vendors** along Shern Maroar Rd. sell local specialties. Those who want to sit while they eat can try the vendors along Vorakamin Rd., starting at the Thai Farmers Bank (fried vegetables on rice 20-25฿). **Siam Restaurant,** 2-4 Shern Maroar Rd., cooks up several extravagantly garnished seafood dishes for 60-100฿. (Open daily 10:30am-9pm.)

BORDER CROSSING: SUNGAI KOLOK/RANTAU PANJANG. The Thailand/Malaysia border, on Asia 18 Rd. near the Sungai Kolok River, is open daily from 5am to 9pm Thai time (1hr. behind Malaysian time). Thai buses do not cross through to Malaysia, nor do trains on the east coast.

Those crossing over into Malaysia can take a share-taxi (RM5 per person; price doubles after dark) or bus #29 (RM2.70, every hr. until 6:15pm) from Rantau Panjang to **Kota Bharu** (p. 418). Those crossing into Thailand have their choice of trains and buses from Sungai Kolok to **Hat Yai** (p. 775) and beyond.

Transportation on both sides of the border is most abundant in the morning. If you are arriving from Malaysia and plan to cash traveler's checks for Thai baht, try to arrive on a weekday before 3:30pm. If you're crossing in the other direction, go to Thai Farmers Bank to exchange any leftover baht for Malaysian ringgit. Most banks in Kota Bharu are closed on Fridays.

CHUMPHON ☎077

For many travelers, Chumphon is a transit town en route to the tropical trinity of Ko Tao, Ko Phangan, and Ko Samui and a gateway, both culturally and geographically, to the south. Though the town's center (the only part visitors see) borders on repulsive, the area surrounding Chumphon boasts 222km of white beaches, tranquil islands, coral reefs, caves, and waterfalls among its graces. Travelers in town for a day waiting for a ferry would be wise to catch the first *songthaew* they can to the beaches and out of the hot, dirty town.

TRANSPORTATION

Trains: Chumphon Railway Station (☎511 103), at the west end of Krumluang Chumphon Rd. Luggage storage 10฿ per day. Listed fares are 2nd-class and 3rd-class. To: **Bangkok** (rapid 7½hr.; 4 per day 7:20pm-12:40am; 142฿, 500฿); **Phetchaburi** (5hr.; 10 per day; 112฿, 58฿); **Sungai Kolok** (10½hr.; 8:40 and 11:00pm; 150฿, 334฿); **Surat Thani** (3hr.; 10 per day; 58฿, 34฿).

Buses: Tha Tapoa Rd. Terminal (☎502 725), opposite Tha Tapoa Hotel, runs A/C and non-A/C buses to **Bangkok** (8hr., every hr. 6am-2pm and 10pm, A/C only 211฿) and **Phuket** (6hr.; 4:30am, 4:30, 10pm; with A/C 196฿). Most buses to Bangkok stop in **Hua Hin** (5hr., 126฿). Orange buses to **Surat Thani** leave from across the street, next to Tha Tapao Hotel (3hr.; every 30-60min. 5:30-11am, 4:30pm; 65฿ with A/C 102฿).

Boats: 3 boats leave daily to **Ko Tao. Express boats** (2½hr., 7:30am, 300-400฿) and **speedboats** (1½hr., 7:30am, 400฿) leave from piers at **Hat Sai Ree,** 10km outside town. **Midnight boats** ("slow boats") leave at midnight from a different pier (6hr., 200฿). Ask your guest house owner for the exact location. Tourist agencies selling tickets usually offer transportation to the pier for free. *Songthaew* (20฿) leave until 6pm for **Hat Sai Ree** from Pracha-Uthit Rd. at bottom of the "V." To visit **Ko Maphraw** (Coconut Island), contact a tourist office 15 days in advance for official tours.

Rentals: Infinity Travel Service rents motorcycles (150฿ per day) and cars (1000฿ per day). The **Chumphon Cabana Resort** (☎560 245, ext. 7) and **SMC Travel Center,** 69/20 Tha Tapoa Rd. (☎504 442), rent diving equipment. Both open daily 9am-8pm.

THAILAND

ORIENTATION AND PRACTICAL INFORMATION

The main roads of Chumphon, 498km south of Bangkok, follow a grid system. **Krumluang Rd.** runs east from the train station, forming the northern edge of the town. The long **Poraminthra Manka Rd.** marks the southern limit; look here for the **hospital, post office,** and **tourist information office.** The **bus station** and several travel agencies lie along **Tha Tapoa Rd.,** running north-south through the western part of the city. Parallel to Tha Tapoa Rd. and one block east is hotel- and eatery-studded **Sala Daeng Rd.** "V"-shaped **Pracha-Uthit Rd.** straddles the **city center;** the **day market** and *songthaew* to Ko Tao-bound ferries and Hat Thung Wua Laen are on this road.

Tourist Office: Commercial tourist agencies sell boat tickets and arrange tours on Tha Tapoa Rd. near the bus station. **Infinity Travel Services,** 68/2 Tha Tapoa Rd. (☎501 937), provides more general services and can arrange scuba diving on Ko Tao. Open daily 7am-11pm.

Currency Exchange: Bangkok Bank, 111/1-2 Sala Daeng Rd. (☎511 446). **24hr. ATM.** Open M-F 8:30am-3:30pm. Pick up extra cash for later since Ko Tao has no ATMs.

Emergency: ☎191.

Police: ☎511 300. On Sala Daeng Rd., about 50m north of the intersection with Krumluang Rd. Little English spoken. **Open 24hr.**

Pharmacy: 188/38 Sala Daeng Rd., opposite the Sri Chumphon Hotel. Open daily 7am-9pm.

Medical Services: Virajsilp Hospital (☎503 238), at the south end of Tha Tapoa Rd., a 5min. walk from the bus station. Some English spoken. No credit cards. Open 24hr.

Telephones: Chumphon Telecommunication Office (☎511 351), 1km down Poraminthra Manka Rd. from the GPO, beneath the red radio tower. International telephone/fax. Open daily 8am-8pm. Several tourist offices and guest houses also have international telephone service.

Internet Access: The **Freshmart** convenience store, at the back of the Suriwong Chumphon Hotel, has a dozen computers in addition to aisles of junk food. 30-40฿ per hr. Open daily 7am-2am. Also at Infinity Travel. 1฿ per min.

Post Office: GPO, 192 Poraminthra Manka Rd. (☎511 041), southeast of town, about 100m past the tourist office. *Poste Restante*. Open M-F 8:30am-4:30pm, Sa 9am-noon. **Postal code:** 86000.

ACCOMMODATIONS

Chumphon has a surprisingly good selection of budget accommodations, and for the price of most guest houses, you can upgrade to a hotel. Most hotels and guest houses cluster near the bus station, either on Tha Tapoa Rd., Sala Daeng Rd., or in the alleyways connecting the two.

Sri Chumphon Hotel, 127/22-24 Sala Daeng Rd. (☎570 536). Off the backpacker trail, but who cares? Spacious rooms come with luxuries like TVs, private baths, and hot water, all at unheard of prices. Pillows are extra firm. Tea and coffee downstairs. Singles/doubles with fan 250฿, with A/C 350฿.

Mayazes Resthouse, 111/35-36 Soi Bangkok Bank, Sala Daeng Rd. (☎504 452). Turn left from the bus station onto Tha Tapoa Rd., then take the 1st right onto the alleyway. Conveniently close to bus station. Rooms are tidy and cozy. Clean, common bathrooms have hot water. Free water, tea, coffee, and fruit. Ring doorbell id after hours. Singles 200฿, with A/C 280฿; doubles 250฿/350฿.

New Chumphon Guest House (Miao House), (☎502 900), on a side street to the left off Krumluang Rd., 600m from the railway station. One of the cheapest options in town. Close to night market. Clean, simple rooms in Thai-style houses with shared baths. Comfortable place to relax downstairs. Annex with more rooms about 100m away. Singles and doubles 120-180฿.

FOOD

For Chumphon's finest victuals, head to the markets. The **main market** offers the renowned *gluay lep meu* (fingernail bananas), in addition to the wide selection of stomach-churning meats. (Open daily 5am-5pm.) The small **night market** is on Krumluang Chumphon Rd. between Pracha-Uthit and Poraminthra Manka. Find more mouth-watering options at the dozens of cheap, makeshift restaurants on **Sala Daeng Rd.** A **bakery** on the corner of Sala Daeng and Pracha-Uthit Rd. sells great pastries. (Open daily 6am-5pm.) Twenty meters down at the **Tiw Restaurant,** brothers O and Noom serve tasty food late into the night. (Rice and curry dishes 20-40฿. Open daily noon-6am.) **Thara Coffeehouse,** in Thatapao Hotel across from the bus station, offers Western and Thai dishes from 35฿. (Open daily 6:30am-1am.)

DAYTRIPS FROM CHUMPHON

Trek to the beach and visit the soothing **Rab Ro Caves** and the **Ka Po Waterfalls,** 30km from Chumphon. Tourist agencies and guest houses arrange daytrips to Hat Thung Wua Laen, Rab Ro Caves, and Ka Po waterfalls for 600-800฿.

HAT THUNG WUA LAEN

In Chumphon, yellow songthaew *to Hat Thung Wua Laen (sometimes called Cabana Beach) leave from the market along Pracha-Uthit Rd. in front of 7-11 and stop at Chumphon Cabana Resort at the south end of the beach. To return to Chumphon, walk 1km to the main road and take a passing* songthaew *or take Cabana Beach Resort's shuttle from its office on Tha Tapoa Rd. near the bus station directly to its resort on the beach. It's usually free, but they may charge 50฿ (8am, 2, 6, and 7pm, returning 7:30am, noon, and 5:30pm).*

The area's premier beach, Hat Thung Wua Laen, is 16km north of Chumphon. The 2km long beach remains pristine, thanks to rules forbidding further development and very few foreigners bothering to make the trek.

Concrete bungalows and restaurants line Mu 8, the road running the length of the beach. A 20min. walk from the taxi drop-off overlooks an empty stretch of sand. At the north end, **Seabeach Bungalows,** 42 Mu 8, is covered in bougainvillea. (☎560 115. Doubles with bath 300฿; bungalows with bath and fan 400฿, with A/C 600฿; quads with bath and A/C 600฿.) **The View Restaurant,** 13/2 Mu 8, has savory seafood plates

THAILAND

SPIT OR SWALLOW? Chumphon herbalists consider swallows' nests an all-natural Viagra. Although all nests work, the white ones are most powerful and sell for up to 70,000฿ per kilo. Harvesting nests, permitted for three months per year, is difficult, dangerous work, and people have shot each other over the scraps. After harvesting, the nests are torn into strips, rinsed in cold water for a day, made into a soup, and sold by the bowl. Why do the nests pack such kick? Perhaps because swallows can stay up (in the air, that is) all day. Most believe, however, that it's a combination of the bird's saliva and the "love nest" itself that provides that special something for your special something.

(50-70฿) served by terminally upbeat young women and new bungalows across the road with amenities like TVs and phones. (☎560 214. Bungalows 400฿, with A/C 600-700฿, with A/C and hot water 800-900฿.) **Clean Wave Resort,** next to the View, has small, hotel-like rooms. Their restaurant serves the gamut of Thai food for 60-100฿. (☎560 151. 300฿, with A/C 600฿, with hot water 700฿.)

Off the shores of Hat Thung Wua Laen are **Ko Ngam Yai** and **Ko Ngam Noi,** which are prized for their swallow's nests, coral reefs, and soaring cliffs. They are seldom visited but well worth the trip. Chartering a boat is expensive; it's best to book with an organized tour. Ask at the Chumphon Cabana Resort or their office in town.

SURAT THANI ☎077

Many travelers know the provincial capital of Surat Thani as just a stopover en route to points south. The increasing prevalence of joint bus, train, and boat tickets to the mainland means that few stay here long. The outlying areas, however, have famous monks and monkeys.

TRANSPORTATION

Flights: Thai Airways, 3/27-8 Karoonrat Rd. (☎273 710), flies daily to **Bangkok** (12:30am and 7:15pm, 1815฿). More destinations accessible from Ko Samui's airport.

Trains: Railway station (☎311 213), 13km from Surat Thani in Phun Phin. Orange bus #3 runs between the local bus terminal and the station; catch it anywhere on Talaat Mai Rd. (every 5min., 10฿). Listed fares are for 3rd- and 2nd-class tickets. Trains to: **Bangkok** (11hr.; 10 per day 10:25am-midnight; 147฿, 508฿); **Butterworth, Malaysia** (11hr., 2:50am, 2nd-class 800฿); **Chumphon** (3hr.; 10 per day 10:25am-midnight; 78฿, 178฿); **Hat Yai** (6hr.; 5 per day 9:20am-1:20am; 120฿, 306฿); **Sungai Kolok** (10hr.; 1:20, 3, 4am; 231฿); **Trang** (5hr.; 6, 8am; 115฿).

Buses: Bus travel in and out of Surat Thani is needlessly complicated. Tour and travel agencies try to lure you to **private buses,** which cost 50-100฿ more than public buses but take less time. Average prices for private buses and minibuses to: **Hat Yai** (5hr.; every hr. 6:30am-5pm; 150฿, minibus 180฿); **Krabi** (3hr.; every hr. 6:30am-5:30pm; 120฿, minibus 150฿); **Penang, Malaysia** (6hr.; every hr. 6am-5pm; minibus 450฿); **Phuket** (3hr.; every 8am-5pm; 100฿, minibus 250฿). For scam-free travel, head to one of Surat Thani's three bus stations which serve the same destinations with cheaper, albeit much slower buses. The **local bus terminal,** Talaat Kaset 1, serves **Chumphon** and **Surat Thani Province** with frequent buses to the railway station. The **regular bus terminal** Talaat Kaset 2 (☎272 341), behind Thai Tani Hotel next to the market, has orange buses departing for **Hat Yai, Krabi, Phuket,** and other southern destinations (roughly every 30min. 6am-5pm). Buses to **Bangkok** depart frequently from the **New Bus Station,** about 10min. outside town on the railway station bus.

Boats: Ferries depart from several points around town. **Samui Tours** offers buses (1hr.; 7 per day 6:15am-4:30pm; 45฿, with A/C 65฿) to the Donsak Car Port, where **Raja Car Ferry** goes to **Ko Phangan** (5hr., 120฿) and **Ko Samui** (2hr., every 2hr. 6am-6pm, 55฿). **Songserm Travel Center** operates a **daily express boat** leaving from the pier in town to **Ko Phangan** (4hr., 7:30am, 205฿) and **Ko Samui** (3hr.; 7:30, 8am, 2pm;

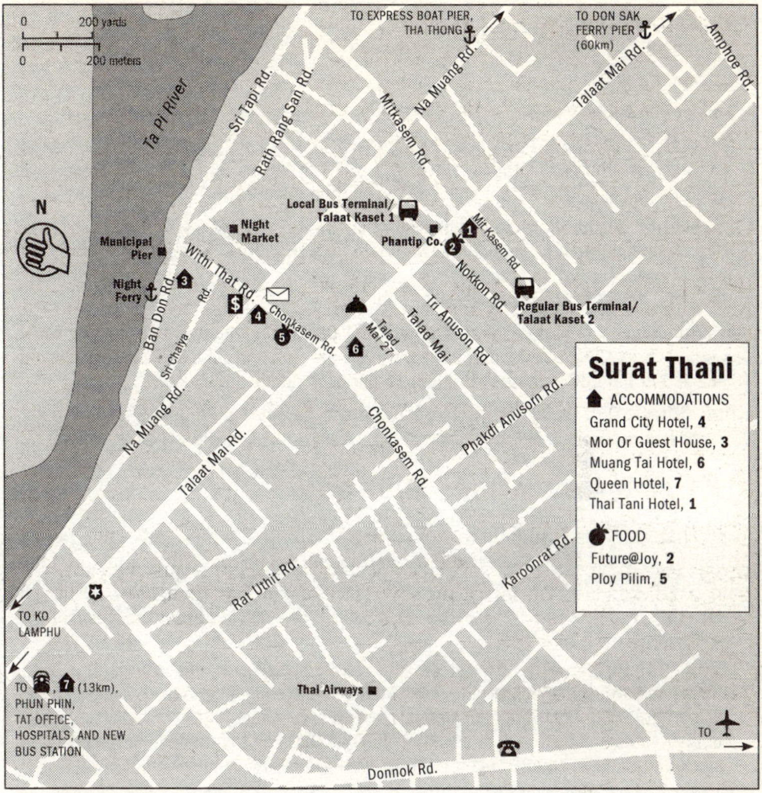

150฿); ticket includes transportation to the pier. The same company operates a night **boat** which sets off from the Surat Thani pier at 11pm for: **Ko Phangan** (6hr., 200฿); **Ko Samui** (6hr., 150฿); **Ko Tao** (7hr., 400฿). Buying from an agent will cost an added 50-100฿ surcharge.

Local Transportation: Few tourists stray from the bus-train-ferry station triangle, which is well-served by the railway station bus. For off-the-beaten-track travel, take a **motorcycle taxi** (20-40฿), **songthaew** (10฿), or **tuk-tuk** (7-10฿ within downtown).

ORIENTATION AND PRACTICAL INFORMATION

Trains arrive at **Phun Phin Railway Station,** 13km from Surat Thani. Phun Phin and Surat Thani are connected by **Talaat Mai Rd.,** which enters Surat Thani from the southwest and passes the **tourist, police,** and **post offices.** Local buses leave from two separate **markets,** each a block from Talaat Mai Rd. Ferries depart from the town pier on **Ban Don Rd.,** which runs along the banks of the mighty **Ta Pi River.** Most budget accommodations and travel agencies operate a few blocks from the pier.

Tourist Office: TAT, 5 Talaat Mai Rd. (☎288 817). A 20min. walk on Talaat Mai Rd. from the town center, but good info and maps. Open daily 8:30am-4:30pm.

Travel Agencies: Agencies touting everything from day trips to bus and train tickets abound near the pier and on Talaat Mai Rd. between the two markets.

Currency Exchange: Surat Thani's exchange rates are better than those on the islands. Banks line Na Muang Rd. Usually open M-F 8:30am-3:30pm. **Bangkok Bank,** 195-7 Na Muang Rd. (☎273 927), has a booth in front. Open daily 8:30am-5pm. **24hr. ATMs.**

Markets: Talaat Kaset 1 and **2,** near the bus station. The **night market** sprawls between Na Muang Rd. and Talaat Lang Rd. by the Tapi River.

Emergency: ☎191.

Police: 188 Na Muang Rd. (☎272 095). Little English spoken. **Open 24hr.**

Hospitals: Surat Thani Provincial Hospital (☎284 700), 1km past TAT on the road to privately-run **Phun Phin Taksin Hospital** (☎273 239), on Talaat Mai Rd. Both have English-speaking staff, accept credit cards, and are **open 24hr.**

Telephones: Surat Thani Telecommunication Center (☎283 050), on Donnok Rd., 2km from most hotels. Walk down Talaat Mai Rd. toward the TAT from the intersection with Chonkasem Rd. and turn left onto Donnok Rd.; it's 20min. down on the left under the radio tower. **HCD.** Open daily 8am-10pm.

Internet Access: Expensive Internet access available around the pier area (2฿ per min.). Cheaper access can be found near the Muang Tai Hotel on Chonkasem Rd. (20฿ per hr.) and at the **ECC** (25฿ first 15 min., 1฿ per each additional minute).

Post Offices: GPO (☎272 013), near the corner of Talaat Mai Rd. and Chonkasem Rd. *Poste Restante.* Open M-F 8:30am-4:30pm, Sa-Su 9am-noon. **Postal code:** 84000.

ACCOMMODATIONS AND FOOD

Surat Thani has several good accommodation options, which make it a rather refreshing change. Most good establishments can be found within a few blocks' radius of the pier or in the area around the markets. Ignore touts trying to push you onto a *tuk-tuk* to take you to your hotel; unless you're arriving by train or long-distance bus, it's just a short walk.

Muang Tai Hotel, 390-2 Talaat Mai Rd. (☎273 586), at the intersection with Chonkasem Rd. The best option in town. Rooms are averaged-sized but come with creature comforts like TVs, wood furnishings, phones, and private baths. At night, the cheerful staff gathers in the lobby to watch bootlegged DVDs and grab a bite in the adjacent snack bar. Singles/doubles with fan 200฿, with A/C 300฿.

Thai Tani Hotel, 442/306-308 Talaat Kaset 2 (☎272 977), off Talaat Mai Rd. between the two markets. Reception on 3rd fl. The run-down external facade hides a surprisingly clean and popular establishment. Hallways are depressingly long and cavernous, but rooms are standard. Singles 240฿, with A/C 320฿; 2 beds 260฿/380฿.

Grand City Hotel, 428/7-10 Na Muang Rd. (☎272 560), at the corner of Chonkasem Rd. Clean rooms in a prime location. Singles/doubles with squat toilets 200฿, with A/C, hot water, and TV 350฿; 2 beds with fan 280฿, with A/C 500฿.

Mor Or Guest House, 136-8 Ban Don Rd. (☎210 268), right across from the pier. Proximity to the ferry makes it a popular spot for stranded backpackers. Sauna-like rooms with clean, common showers and toilets. Internet 2฿ per min. Cafe/restaurant. Singles and doubles 150฿.

Queen Hotel, on the street heading away directly opposite the railway station in Phun Phin, 100m down. Convenient for those on early or late trains. Rooms are clean but small and could use a good coat of paint. A bevy of tourist services are available in the lobby downstairs. Internet 2฿ per min. Singles 200฿; doubles 250฿/400฿.

Talaat Kaset has stalls displaying curries, meats, and vegetables ladled over rice. Before sailing away, passengers can stock up on provisions at the **food stalls** and **night market** by the night-boat pier. For a variety of Thai dishes and seafood, try the **Ploy Pilim Restaurant,** 100 Chonkasem Rd., 30m behind the post office on bottom floor of Tapee Hotel. (Dishes 40-50฿. Open daily 8am-11pm.) **Future@Joy,** across from the Thai Tani Hotel, has a huge selection of Thai and Western dishes (70-80฿) with Internet (2฿ per min.) and offers a little rest after the hassle of finding a ferry. (Open daily 8am-9:30pm.)

SIGHTS

Visit the areas around Surat Thani as a daytrip via *songthaew*. Enormous **oysters** are bred around the Kadaeh and Ta Tong Rivers. If you're interested in how they're raised and harvested, catch a bus to **Kanchanadit** (15km from Surat Thani) and hire a longtail boat (100-150฿), or contact **Kiang Lay Oyster Farm** (☎255 242) for information. For more active distractions, observe primate pedagogy at the **Monkey Training College.** Monkeys learn to do tricks like collecting gigantic coconuts and bringing them to their trainer from the river. Local travel agents usually have better deals for larger groups. (☎227 351. 1-3 people 300฿, 4-10 people 700฿.) To go on your own, catch a *songthaew* (6฿) on Talaat Mai Rd. on the Phanthip Co. side of the street. Ask to be let off at *Rong Rian Sawn Ling*. Take a motorcycle taxi the rest of the way (20฿) or hike the 2km.

DAYTRIPS FROM SURAT THANI

CHAIYA

The best way to visit the sights is to take a Chumphon-bound bus from Surat Thani's local market bus station, get off at Suan Mokkha, and catch a north-bound songthaew *to Wat Phra That. From there, it's a 15min. walk to town and to Surat Thani-bound buses and* songthaew.

A pleasant escape from the cultural vacuum of the islands is the town of Chaiya, 40km north of Surat Thani. The town boasts several wats, museums, and ruins that together mark its status as an important city-state in the southern Gulf Coast. **Wat Phra Borom That Chaiya,** known as Wat Phra That, is a 1200-year-old pagoda sheltering Buddhist relics and surrounded by 174 Buddha images. Unlike most Thai temples, this one is consecrated to Mahayana Buddhism, the religion of the ancient Sumatran Srivijaya Empire. Next door, the small but interesting **National Museum** houses artifacts dating from Chaiya's heyday. (☎431 090. Open W-Su 9am-4pm. 30฿.) Situated in a forest along Hwy. 41, **Wat Suan Mokkha Phalaram** (Suan Mok) is more a working monastery than a tourist attraction. A daytrip may not bestow enlightenment but will certainly allow a glimpse of the beautiful paths and art collections. As if to combat the indulgent lifestyles of nearby islands, Suan Mok urges restraint in all its attendees—from cigarette smoking to mosquito slapping. Anyone can attend meditation retreats held by resident monks. Retreats start on the last day of each month and run to the 11th day of the following month. It's not possible or necessary to reserve a spot; you need only show up a few days before the end of the month. (☎431 552. 1200฿ covers food, accommodations, and expenses for the 12-day retreat.)

KHAO SOK NATIONAL PARK

Many Surat Thani travel agencies and private guest houses that cluster near the park's entrance arrange excursions into the park. Otherwise, take a Phuket- or Takuapa-bound orange public bus from Surat Thani's southern market (every 30min. 6am-5pm) and direct the driver to Khao Sok, roughly 60km (1½hr.) away.

Nestled in the mountain ridge separating the east and west coasts of peninsular Thailand, splendid Khao Sok National Park is a relic of the country's geologic past. The 160 million-year-old rain forest (some date it as old as 380 million years) covers roughly 650sq. km., mostly comprised of jungle-covered foothills and protruding limestone formations. Its unique geography and generous rainfall allow it to sustain a remarkable ecosystem, home to hundreds of wildlife species, including tigers, panthers, bears, gibbons, elephants, guars, and languars. The park's jewel is doubtlessly the native flora, which includes dozens of species of orchids and ferns. Most spectacular is the **Bua Phut,** a lotus flower that can grow up to 80cm. The **park headquarters** near the entrance dispenses trail maps and arranges guided hikes to some of the park's waterfalls and caves.

PHANG-NGA ☎076

While Phang-Nga Province is rich in natural beauty and cultural attractions, its capital, the small mainland town of Phang-Nga, has not been so blessed. Hot, sticky, and devoid of any worthwhile sights, the city has only two mentionable assets: a friendly population and proximity to some of the most spectacular scenery on the Thai-Malay Peninsula. Understandably, many visit the area around Phang-Nga as a side trip from Phuket (or even Krabi), bypassing Phang-Nga Town altogether. Still, with less tourist traffic and cheaper tour services, Phang-Nga attracts budget travelers who spend a night or two here before heading out to explore the wonders of the bay and province areas.

TRANSPORTATION. The bus station is on **Phetkasem Hwy.** near the center of town. **Buses** run to: **Bangkok** (13hr., 5pm, 225฿; A/C 2, 4:30, 5, 8pm; 326-625฿); **Hat Yai** (6hr., every hr. 8am-2pm, A/C 196฿); **Ko Samui** (6½hr., 11:30am, A/C and ferry 230฿); **Krabi** (1½hr.; every 30min. 9:30am-9:30pm; 40฿, A/C 59฿); **Phuket** (1½hr.; every hr. 9am-9pm; 50฿, A/C 65฿); **Surat Thani** (2½hr., 5 per day 6:30am-2:20pm, 70฿; A/C 9:30am, 11pm; 130฿); **Trang** (4½hr., every hr. 7:30am-8:30pm, A/C 151฿). Blue **songthaew** run along the highway from the bus station to points around town (10฿) and the pier (15฿). **Motorcycle taxis** cost about 20฿ around town.

THAILAND

PRACTICAL INFORMATION. The unregistered **travel agencies** near the bus station provide most tourist services. These agencies are less professional than those offering tours from Phuket and Krabi but also about 200-400฿ cheaper (day tours 200-500฿; overnight tours to Phang-Nga Bay 500฿). **Sayan Tours,** next to the bus terminal, is one of the more established tour operators. (☎430 348. Open daily 8am-6pm.) Other services include: **Thai Farmers Bank,** 126 Phetkasem Hwy., across the street from the bus station, with a **24hr. ATM** (open M-F 8:30am-3:30pm); a **police station,** 193 Phetkasem Hwy. (☎412 075), 500m to the left of the bus station; **Phang-Nga General Hospital,** 436 Phetkasem Hwy., 2km to the left of the bus station (☎412 034; **open 24hr.;** English spoken; no credit cards); and a **post office** on Phetkasem Hwy. (☎412 171; *Poste Restante;* open M-F 8:30am-4:30pm, Sa-Su 9am-noon) with international phone (open daily 8:30am-4:30pm). **Postal code:** 82000.

ACCOMMODATIONS AND FOOD. The new kid in town is the centrally located and antiseptically clean **Phang-Nga Guest House** on Phetkasem Hwy. immediately to the right of the bus station. The spotless new rooms and common baths pass the white glove finger test with flying colors. (☎411 358. Continental breakfast 50฿. Singles 200฿; doubles with bath and A/C 350฿.) A bit farther from town is the **Luk Muang Hotel,** 1/2 Phetkasem Hwy. Exit to the right of the bus station and walk about 10min. past the temple and "Have a Good Trip" sign. Friendly and family-run, the hotel offers comfortable, airy rooms, some with TVs and phones. (☎411 512. Singles 200฿; doubles 250฿.) **Thawisuk Hotel,** 79 Phetkasem Hwy. is located in a seemingly ancient building. The hallways aren't great, but the rooms are cozy with the extra bonus of wooden floors. The clean baths have Western toilets. (☎412 100. Singles/doubles 150฿, with bath 200฿.)

Phang-Nga has a few good dining options near the bus station. The best restaurant around, **Duang Seafood,** 122 Phetkasem Hwy, next to Thai Farmers Bank, serves shrimp fried rice and hot-and-sour seafood soup. (Dishes 50-100฿. Open daily 9am-10:30pm.) Bismilla, 247 Phetkasem Hwy., has wonderful Thai lemon soups. (Open daily 7am-11pm.) The **day market,** off Phetkasem Hwy., to the right of the bus station, sells fruit. **Night markets** set up near the post office on Phetkasem Hwy. and along Riverside Rim Kong Rd. (Open daily 4:30pm-midnight.)

DAYTRIPS FROM PHANG-NGA: PHANG-NGA BAY NATIONAL PARK. Travelers don't come to see Phang-Nga Town; they come to see Phang-Nga Province. With its majestic limestone formations and stunning Phang-Nga Bay, the province offers the rugged beauty sorely missing from built-up tourist resorts like Phuket and Krabi. Unfortunately, travelers without a car (and, for that matter, a boat) find the province highly inaccessible. Rather than attempt to go it alone, join one of the day tours or overnight stays offered by many travel agencies (from Phang-Nga 200-500฿; from Phuket 450-650฿).

The province's real attraction, Phang-Nga Bay National Park stretches over 400 sq. km, encompassing more than 120 postcard-perfect limestone islands. Though the bay's status as a national park has aided in its conservation, responsible eco-tourism is critical to prevent damage to the islands. Use the old maxim: see as it is, leave as it was. Most tourists make a beeline to the park's twin jewels, beautiful **Ko Khao Ping Gan** and its satellite, **Ko Tapu,** better known as "James Bond Island" since the 1962 Bond flick, *The Man With The Golden Gun,* was filmed here. While the image of the thin limestone rock that is Ko Tapu (literally, "Nail Island") slicing into the bay is quite striking, be prepared to throw elbows at shell-vendors and tourists to stake a prime photo-taking spot. If it gets too crowded, head to Ko Khao Ping Gan where a small pier juts into the bay for more spectacular panoramas. If you have more time, be sure to paddle through the **Tam Lod Grotto,** a sea-level open-ended cave dripping with stalactites. **Ko Khien** displays drawings of boats and animals over 300 years old on the mountain's edge. Songthaew run from the Phang-Nga Bus Station to the pier (15฿), where longtail boats are chartered (600฿ for a few hours). Though more expensive than longtail boat tours, kayaking tours allow more flexibility and time to explore the park.

THAILAND

NEAR PHANG-NGA

KO PANYI AND THE MUSLIM FISHING VILLAGE. Though technically part of the Phang-Nga Bay National Park, Ko Panyi is worth a separate visit. About 250 years ago, Muslim fishermen from Indonesia settled on the island, constructing homes and businesses on stilts jutting into the water. Almost three centuries later, the Muslim Fishing Village is alive and well, though nowadays it seems to cater more to tourists than to fish. Other than the prominent town mosque, there's not much to see in the village per se; the real fascination is ambling down the rickety, suspended streets to watch the town inhabitants—some 200 of them in all—go about their daily chores in the most unusual of settings. Overnight stays are recommended, as the village assumes a different character after daytrippers return to the mainland. It's possible to arrange a room with the locals or book an overnight stay through a travel agency for 500-650฿.

WAT SUWANNAKUHA. A popular stop for most tourist groups, this pleasant Buddhist temple consists of several caves, the largest of which measures 40m long and houses an impressive 15m long reclining Buddha. The temple (and its resident monkeys) are best seen late in the afternoon when tourist buses have returned to Phuket. (8km outside Phang-Nga, off Phang-Nga Koke Kloy Rd. 10฿.)

KO SAMUI

Thailand's third largest island has come a long way since its "discovery" by backpackers in the 1970s. Once the country's largest exporter of coconuts, the island now thrives on a far more lucrative business: tourists. Thousands of travelers rush to Ko Samui's luscious beaches, which run the gamut from loud, shop-crammed Hat Chaweng and Hat Lamai to quiet, tropical enclaves like Hat Bangrak and Hat Choeng Mon. Those looking for a range of entertainment, swimming, and sunbathing options will not be disappointed; those looking for a deserted coconut island most certainly will be.

TRANSPORTATION

Some short-term travelers arrive to Ko Samui by **plane,** but most come by **boat** via the transportation hub of **Surat Thani.**

THE VIEW FROM ABOVE

The lowdown: An island of extremes: from parties to paradise.
Gateway city: Surat Thani.
Nearby islands: Ko Phangan, Ko Tao.
Beaches: Ao Thongsai, Ao Yai Noi, Hat Bangrak (Big Buddha Beach), Hat Bo Phut, Hat Chaweng, Hat Choeng Mon, Hat Lamai, Hat Mae Nam, Laem Thongson, Na Thon.
Highlights: Genitalia-shaped "Grandmother and Grandfather Rocks," Hat Bangrak's 15m golden "Big Buddha," breathtaking Ang Thong Marine National Park, and party central Hat Chaweng.

Flights: Samui Airport is between Hat Chaweng and Big Buddha Beach (Hat Bangrak). **Bangkok Airways,** 17211 Na Thon Rd. (☎420 133), in Na Thon, flies daily to: **Bangkok** (every hr. 6:30am-7:30pm, 3150฿); **Phuket** (9:50, 10:10am, 3:10pm, 1530฿); **Singapore** (8am, 4000฿). Book tickets at Bangkok Airways or other tourist services on the island.

Trains and buses: Most travel agents can book joint boat/train or boat/bus tickets to the mainland. Prices vary slightly from agent to agent. Tickets to **Bangkok** (16hr.; A/C bus 280฿, sleeper train 700฿) and **Kuala Lumpur** (22hr., A/C bus 800฿).

Boats: Songserm Travel Center runs an **express boat** to **Tha Thong Pier,** 5km northeast of Surat Thani (2hr., 7:30am, 150฿) and a **night boat** to **Ko Samui** (6hr., 11pm, 150฿). The **Raja Car Ferry** leaves **Donsak Pier,** 60km east of Surat Thani on the mainland, for a pier 10km south of **Na Thon** on Ko Samui (1½hr., 7 per day 8am-6pm, 45฿). *Songthaew* run from this pier to the major beaches. Inquire at the Ko Samui Tour Office in Surat Thani. **Ferries** to Ko Samui's **Big Buddha Beach** (Hat Bangrak) run from **Hat Rin** on Ko Phangan (1½hr.; 9:30, 11:40am, 2:30pm; 100฿) and **Ko Tao** (3hr.; 10:30am, 2:30pm; 345฿). From Ko Samui, boats go to: **Hat Rin** (30min., 10:30am, 1, 4pm; 400฿); **Ko Phangan** (express boat 1hr.; 9, 11am, noon, 5:30, 7:30pm; 95฿); **Ko Tao** (express boat 3hr.); **Surat Thani** (2½hr., 2pm, 150฿). An **auto-ferry** (every 2hr. 6am-5pm, 80฿) leaves from a pier 7km south of Na Thon and arrives at Surat Thani's Donsak Pier.

Local Transportation: Clearly labeled **songthaew** congregate near the pier and circle the island frequently from 5am-6pm. From Na Thon to: **Hat Bangrak** (Big Buddha Beach; 25฿); **Hat Bo Phut** (20฿); **Hat Chaweng** (35฿); **Hat Lamai** (30฿); **Hat Mae Nam** (15฿). Listed prices are official fares, but actual rates charged tend to be 15-25฿ higher. Speedy **motorcycle taxis** also circle the island, providing a faster but more expensive alternative to *songthaew*. From Na Thon to: **Hat Bo Phut** (150฿); **Hat Chaweng** (200฿); **Hat Mae Nam** (100฿). A/C yellow **metered taxis** are the most expensive way to get around, charging 50-100฿ more than *songthaews* and motorcycle taxis.

Rentals: Motorcycles 150฿ per day; jeeps 800฿ per day, with insurance 1000-2000฿. Accidents involving *farang* on motorcycles are extremely common; request a helmet.

ORIENTATION AND PRACTICAL INFORMATION

Oval-shaped Ko Samui is encircled by one road **(Rte. 4169),** making getting around fairly easy but somewhat time consuming since the island is quite large. From **Na Thon,** the island's transportation hub and service center, going clockwise, Rte. 4169 runs through Ban Thong Po (Km46), Hat Mae Nam (Km36), Ban Tha Po (Km13), Ban Sa Ket (Km6), and Ban Lipa (Km3). At Km33, Rte. 4169 forks, forming **Rte. 4171,** which circles the island's northeastern peninsula, including Hat Bo Phut, Hat Bangrak (Big Buddha Beach), Hat Choeng Mon, and Hat Chaweng, the island's biggest city. At Km22, Rte. 4169 skirts Ko Samui's second most popular beach, Hat Lamai. *Songthaew* circulate Rte. 4169, Hat Chaweng, and Hat Lamai; elsewhere, you will have to take a taxi. In general, Na Thon, Hat Chaeng, and Hat Lamai are the liveliest areas and offer the most services, while Hat Mae Nam, Hat Bo Phut, and Hat Choeng Mon are quiet and more relaxed.

Tourist Office: TAT (☎/fax 420 504), on Na Thon Rd., in a cluster of new buildings behind the post office. Moderately helpful but free maps and brochures are available in businesses all over the island. Open daily 8:30am-4:30pm.

Travel Agencies: Hundreds of establishments all over Na Thon, Hat Chaweng, and Hat Lamai sell boat/bus/train ticket combinations and arrange Ang Thon Marine Park tours, fishing trips, and elephant treks. In Na Thon, agencies line Na Thon Rd. near the pier. **Songserm Travel Center** (☎421 316), opposite the pier on Na Thon Rd. operates the ferry service. Open daily 5am-5pm.

Immigration Office: 2km south of Na Thon at the intersection of Rte. 4167 and Rte. 4172. Visa extensions 555฿. Open M-F 8:30am-noon and 1-4:30pm.

Currency Exchange: Dozens of banks offering the best rates for currency exchange, credit card advances, and **ATMs** line the main roads of Na Thon, Hat Chaweng, and Hat Lamai. Generally open M-F 8:30am-3:30pm.

Markets: The market on **Thaweerat Pakdee Rd.** in Na Thon has fresh produce. Touristy trinket shops line the streets of most beaches, particularly Hat Chaweng.

Emergency: ☎191.

Tourist Police: ☎421 441. On Na Thon Rd. in Na Thon, 400m south of the pier. English spoken. **Open 24hr.**

Police: ☎421 095. On Thaweerat Pakdee Rd. in Na Thon. Other beaches have smaller offices or booths: Hat Chaweng (☎422 067), Hat Lamai (☎424 068), and Hat Bo Phut (☎425 071). All **open 24hr.**

Medical Services: The island has three main hospitals: **Bandon International Hospital** in Hat Bo Phut (☎425 071); **Government Hospital** in Na Thon (☎421 230); **Samui International Hospital** in Hat Chaweng (☎425 012). Smaller nursing stations can be found in Na Thon, Hat Chaweng, and Hat Lamai. All have English-speaking staff and accept credit cards. **Open 24hr.**

Telephones: GPO, 2nd fl. International calls, fax, and cheap email. Open daily 7am-10pm. Travel agencies around the island offer pricier international phone service.

Internet Access: Cheapest access at the **Telephone Office** at GPO (30฿ per hr.) Most travel agencies in Hat Chaweng and Hat Lamai provide pricier access (2฿ per min.).

Post Offices: GPO (☎421 130), on Na Thon Rd. 50m left of the pier parking lot. *Poste Restante.* Open M-F 8:30am-4:30pm, Sa-Su 9am-noon. Licensed, private branches along Rte. 4169. **Postal code:** 84140.

THAILAND

ACCOMMODATIONS, FOOD, AND BEACHES

Budget accommodations on Ko Samui are surprisingly sub par, given the high number of budget travelers. Expect to pay double what you would on the mainland. In general, accommodations at the smaller beaches (Hat Mae Nam, Hat Bo Phut, etc.) are a better value than the ones on the more popular beaches. The following accommodation and food options are listed by beach.

NA THON. Na Thon is Ko Samui's waiting room for visitors killing time until the next ferry. Cheaper communications and souvenirs make it a nice place to spend a rainy afternoon, but unless there's an early ferry to catch or the last *songthaew* has skipped town, there's little reason to spend the night. **Palace Hotel,** 152 Cholvitee Rd., 100m on the right as you exit the pier, has giant rooms with sea views. (☎421 079. Doubles 400฿, with A/C 550฿; twins 450฿/600฿; triples with A/C 750฿.) **Sea View Guest House,** 67/15 Thaweerat Pakdee Rd., opposite the Shell gas station, has modest-sized rooms with showers and peeling paint. Regrettably, the hotel has no sea view. (☎420 298. Doubles with shower 200-400฿, with bath 300฿, with A/C 400฿.) On the waterfront, food carts sell fruit, meat-on-sticks, noodles, and sandwiches. Popular **Ruangthong Bakery,** opposite the pier, serves breads, pastries, and Thai dishes for 40฿. It's a great place to grab a quick meal, cup of coffee, or snack before the ferry ride. (Open daily 7am-7pm.)

HAT MAE NAM. The first major beach on the circuit north of Na Thon stretches from Km39 to Km35 along Rte. 4169, 20min. by motorbike. Tranquillity zealots look no further; tiny Hat Mae Nam has six restaurants to Hat Chaweng's 600 and no tourist bars. Hat Mae Nam's beach is rockier than Hat Chaweng's or Hat

Lamai's, but it's still clean, white, and peaceful. About 1km past the police station, **Friendly Bungalow** has beachside huts with baths and mosquito nets. (☎425 484. Laundry service and motorbike rental. Wooden huts 500฿, 200฿ per night for 3 nights or more; bungalows with Western toilets 600/300฿.) Off the same road is **Rainbow Bungalow,** also with nets and hammocks. (☎425 425. Laundry service and motorbike rental. Doubles 150-500฿.)

HAT BO PHUT. Although smaller than Hat Mae Nam, neighboring Hat Bo Phut has a wider beach, more upscale bungalows, and a more familial atmosphere. To reach **Ziggy Stardust,** the best hotel in the area, take the paved road off Rte. 4169 near Km34. The extensive gardens outside have a rainforest feel. The beachfront bar/restaurant features fabulous homemade yogurt. (☎425 173. Bar/restaurant open daily 7:30am-10pm. Doubles with fan in high season 400฿, with A/C 1200฿; in low season 300฿/1000฿.)

HAT BANGRAK (BIG BUDDHA BEACH). Bungalows abound between Km2 and Km4 of Rte. 4171, 40min. by motorbike from Na Thon. The path leads to Bangrak Port and Samui Airport and eventually becomes the road near Hat Chaweng. Though the area is lively, the rocky, boat-filled beach is not conducive to swimming, and the bungalows are small. **Kinnaree Resort,** at Km3 off Rte. 4171, is a villa among flower gardens, cooing doves, and beach views. (☎245 111. Motorbikes rental. Singles/doubles 200/250฿, with hot shower and A/C 600฿.)

THAILAND

LAEM THONGSON, AO THONGSAI, HAT CHOENG MON, AO YAI NOI. The northeast cape wraps around the island's best views. Beaches are down dirt roads off the mountain highway connecting northern Hat Chaweng to Rte. 4171. Motorbikes can access Laem Thongson via 3km of treacherous dirt roads. Solitude-seekers should follow the signs 2km down to **Samui Thongson Resort,** on the tip of the promontory. (Singles/doubles 300฿; twins 500฿.)

North of Ao Yai Noi, bordering Ao Thongsai, and 4km north of Hat Chaweng, Hat Chaoeng Mon's serene beaches make it worth visiting, especially if Hat Chaweng's crowds annoy you. At the **Imperial Boat House Hotel,** guests bunk in small arks. **Choeng Mon Bungalow** has stilt houses with baths. (☎425 372. In high season singles/doubles 250฿, with A/C and hot water 500฿; in low season 200฿/400฿.)

HAT CHAWENG. The biggest and brashest of Ko Samui's beaches, Hat Chaweng roars 5km over the east coast. As the sunbathing and party capital of the island, the beach is a loud, happy combination of good sand, cheap booze, clean waters, and loud music. Even if you don't want to swim, people-watching provides hours of entertainment. Hat Chaweng's main road, **Chaweng Rd.,** is parallel to the beach and connected to Rte. 4169 via three access roads; most services can be found there.

Budget accommodations in Hat Chaweng are scarce and fill up quickly. The few places that cater to budget travelers cluster in the middle of the beach, near the turnoff for the lagoon and the Thai boxing center. The fastest way to find lodging is to start with **Charlie's Huts,** which caters almost exclusively to backpackers. The wooden bungalows have thatched roofs, bamboo walls, and mosquito nets. (☎230 283. Electricity runs 6pm-9am. Movies 6pm in the restaurant. Doubles 200฿, with bath 300฿.) Next door, the more upscale **Silver Sands** resort has a few budget bungalows close to the water. The large ones have private baths but are not in particularly good shape. (Bungalows starting from 200฿.) **Matlang Resort,** 15411 Chaweng Rd., in North Chaweng near the end of the cape, is a quiet hideaway from the main drag. (☎/fax 422 172. Singles/doubles with bath and fan 300-350฿, with A/C 800฿ in high season, 650฿ in low season.) Other accommodations include **Lotus Bungalow,** 60/1 Chaweng Rd., Central Chaweng (☎230 891) and **Suneast Bungalow,** 159 Chaweng Rd., Central Chaweng (☎422 115).

Budget accommodations on Chaweng may be scarce, but budget food is not. Inexpensive food stalls cramming the road by the Green Mango serve pizzas, sandwiches, and Thai favorites to drunken revelers. Some top-end establishments line Chaweng Rd. **La Taverna** on the road circling to the Green Mango cooks the best Italian on the beach; feast on good pizzas (120-200฿) and pastas (150฿). **The Deck Restaurant** (☎230 898), before the Green Mango as you approach from Na Thon, has great food (including vegan and vegetarian options), music, and three levels of cushions to enjoy them on.

HAT LAMAI. Hat Lamai is second to Hat Chaweng in terms of nightlife and beauty but has a more family-friendly environment, good body surfing, and fewer crowds. Most tourist services can be found in South Lamai on the road running parallel to the beach, while the best budget accommodations are in North Lamai. Though the area has a less spectacular beach, the significantly lower prices compensate. **New Hut,** the unofficial backpacker central, is the best and cheapest. Bungalows are clean but small. The cheaper ones are nothing more than a mattress with a triangular straw roof. (☎230 439. Bungalows 100-150฿, with bath 200-250฿.) Just to the south, **Lamai Resort** has more expensive, sturdier bungalows. (Bungalows with bath 200-400฿.)

Though more centrally located, South Lamai has fewer budget options; most establishments are solidly mid-range. The centrally-located **Utopia Resort** has well-groomed gardens and more upscale clientele. The clean bungalows and rooms have private baths. (Bungalows 500฿, with A/C 1000฿.) The friendly Italian owners of the **Sun Splash Hotel,** two spots down, keep their rooms in good shape. All bungalows have baths. (☎418 021. Bungalows with fan 400-500฿, with A/C 900-1000฿.)

Most bungalows serve standard meals until 10pm and let more expensive restaurants and pubs along the main drag pick up the slack late at night. The **Will Wait Bakery** in the center of Lamai Beach Rd. is a perennial island favorite, serving a standard menu of Thai and Western favorites. (Open daily 8am-11pm.) The **market** at Ban Hua Thanon sells fruit and munchies. (Open until sunset.)

SIGHTS

Ko Samui has a few sights and cultural attractions to keep you mildly entertained if you get too burned by the sun. Most are located off Rte. 4169; you'll have to take a taxi or walk. Travel agencies also offer day tours of the island for around 1000฿.

GRANDMOTHER AND GRANDFATHER ROCKS (HIN TA AND HIN YAI. According to an old Samui legend, an elderly couple was en route to the mainland to procure a wife for their son when, lo and behold, a fierce storm pummeled the ship and killed the two seafarers. Their bodies washed ashore, and their respective genitals were somehow petrified in the shapes of "Grandfather Rock" and "Grandmother Rock," a set of unusual, if slightly distasteful, natural formations. The rest of their bodies, however, curiously escaped being immortalized in stone.

LAMAI CULTURAL HALL. Located where Rte. 4169 takes a sharp right turn at Km20, Lamai Cultural Hall's museum holds a small but interesting collection of phonographs, pottery, and weaponry. *(Open daily 6am-6pm. Free.)*

THE BIG BUDDHA. Ko Samui's most prominent landmark, the golden "Big Buddha" is off Rte. 4171 on Ko Fan Mountain on the island's northeast corner. Serenely overlooking nearby Hat Bangrak (Big Buddha Beach) and Ko Phangan, the 15m statue was built in 1972 as a place for both islanders and *farang* to worship.

WAT KUNARAM. Rather sensational as far as wats go, this temple, off Rte. 4169 in the island's southeast corner, is known for the body of a **mummified monk** who died in 1973 but somehow evaded decomposition via complex pre-death meditation.

BAN LAMAI CULTURAL CENTER. The mildly interesting center displays traditional agricultural practices in an attempt to show what the island was like before tourists began outnumbering coconuts.

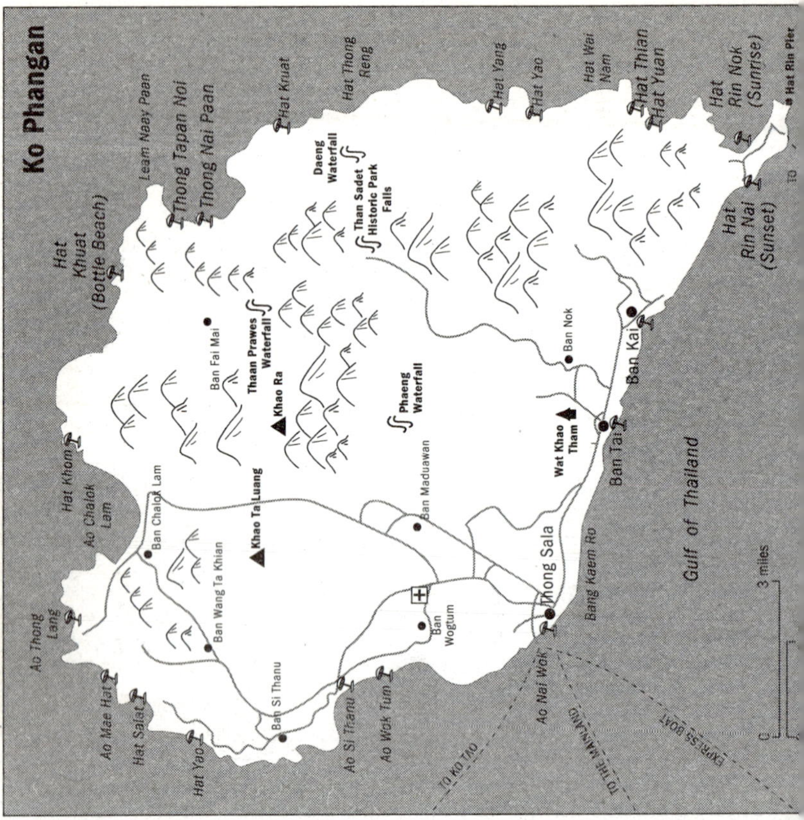
Ko Phangan
Hat Khuat (Bottle Beach)
Laem Naay Paan
Thong Tapan Noi
Thong Nai Paan
Hat Kruat
Hat Thong Reng
Daeng Waterfall
Than Sadet Historic Park Falls
Hat Yang
Hat Yao
Hat Wai Nam
Hat Thian
Hat Yuan
Hat Rin Nok (Sunrise)
Hat Rin Pier
Hat Rin Nai (Sunset)
Ban Fai Mai
Thaan Prawes Waterfall
Khao Ra
Phaeng Waterfall
Ban Nok
Ban Kai
Wat Khao Tham
Ban Tai
Hat Khom
Ao Chalok Lam
Ban Chalok Lam
Khao Ta Luang
Ban Maduawan
Thong Sala
Bang Kaem Ro
Gulf of Thailand
3 miles
Ao Thong Lang
Ban Wang Ta Khian
Ban Wogtum
Ao Mae Hat
Hat Salat
Ban Si Thanu
Ao Si Thanu
Ao Wok Tum
Ao Nai Wok
Hat Yao
TO KO TAO
TO THE MAINLAND
EXPRESS BOAT

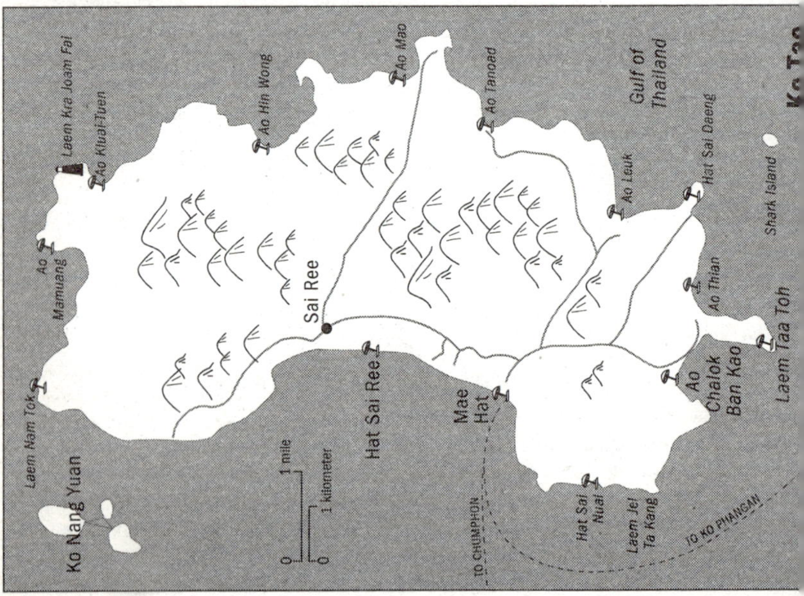
Laem Kra Joam Fai
Ao Kluai Tuen
Ao Hin Wong
Ao Mao
Ao Tanoad
Gulf of Thailand
Ao Mamuang
Ao Leuk
Hat Sai Daeng
Shark Island
Sai Ree
Ao Thian
Laem Nam Tok
Hat Sai Ree
Mae Hat
Ao Chalok Ban Kao
Laem Taa Toh
Ko Nang Yuan
1 mile
1 kilometer
Hat Sai Nual
Laem Jel Ta Kang
TO CHUMPHON
TO KO PHANGAN
Ko Tao

Ko Samui
Gulf of Thailand
Na Thon
Ban Thong Po
Ban Tai
Ban Bo Phut
Ban Chaweng
Ban Lamai
Ban Hua Thanon
Ban Thurian
Ban Saket
Ban Li Pa Noi
Thong Yang
Ferry Pier
Ban Bang Kao
Ban Thong Krut
Ban Phang Ka
Ban Plai Laem
Hat Chaweng
Hat Lamai
Hat Mae Nam
Hat Bo Phut
Hat Bangrak (Big Buddha Beach)
Big Buddha Pier
Buffalo Fighting Field
Hin Lat Waterfall
Na Muang Waterfall
Snake Farm
Butterfly Garden
Grandmother and Grandfather Rocks
Lamai Cultural Hall
View Point
Ao Chaweng Yai
Ao Bang Po
Ao Na Kai
Ao Bang Kao
Ao Thong Krut
Ao Phang Ka
Ao Taling Ngam
Ao Nai Sai
Ao Thong Yang
Ao San Ti
Ao Laem Din
Laem Yai
Laem Na Phra Lan
Laem Sai
Laem Son
Laem Set
Laem Chon Khram
Laem Hin Khom
Wat Laem Saw
Ko Mat Lang
TO KO PHANGAN
TO SURAT THANI
VEHICLE/PASSENGER FERRY TO DON SAK
TO THONG SALA & MAE HAT
4169
4170
4171
4173
5 miles
5 kilometers

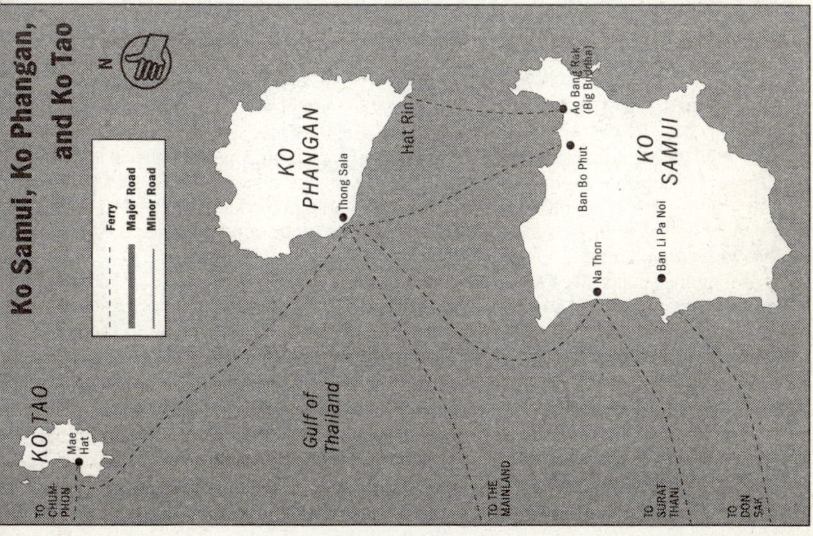
Ko Samui, Ko Phangan, and Ko Tao
Ferry
Major Road
Minor Road
N
KO TAO
Mae Hat
KO PHANGAN
Thong Sala
Hat Rin
KO SAMUI
Ao Bang Rak (Big Buddha)
Ban Bo Phut
Na Thon
Ban Li Pa Noi
Gulf of Thailand
TO CHUMPHON
TO THE MAINLAND
TO SURAT THANI
TO DON SAK

WATERFALLS. Ko Samui boasts several impressive waterfalls scattered around the interior of the island. Two-tiered **Hin Lad Waterfall,** 3km south of Na Thon, is the most accessible though not the most beautiful. **Namnang Waterfall,** 11km south of Na Thon, is more impressive and offers opportunities for hiking through the leafy, mountainous heart of the island. *(Both are best reached by taxi from Na Thon, though many travel agencies offer waterfall and trekking trips.)*

SAMUI SNAKE FARM. This gimmicky complex, on Rte. 4170 in the island's southeast corner, features snakes indigenous to Samui. The snake farmers also offer potentially exciting but undoubtedly absurd events like centipede and scorpion fighting shows. *(☎423 247. Shows daily 11am and 2pm. Open M-F 8:30am-4pm, Sa-Su 8:30am-noon. 150฿.)*

SAMUI BUTTERFLY GARDEN. One of Samui's most popular non-beach attractions, the Butterfly Garden maintains over 24 species of southern Thai butterflies in addition to less spectacular (and less popular) species of insects and moths. *(Off Rte. 4170, opposite Central Samui Village. ☎424 020. Open daily 9am-6pm. 120฿, children 60฿.)*

THE SAMUI AQUARIUM. Thailand's only privately-owned aquarium features fish native to the Gulf of Thailand as well as such treats as sharks and turtles. The adjacent tiger farm houses several displaced Bengal tigers. *(Off Rte. 4170, south of Lamai Beach near Ban Han and the Butterfly Garden. ☎423 247.)*

THAILAND

NIGHTLIFE

With dozens of pubs and girlie bars, Hat Chaweng is Samui's nightlife capital. The mega-pub **Green Mango** is a massive complex that draws a raging, young drink-and-dance crowd. The mood picks up at around 11pm and doesn't die until 4am. (Beers 100฿. Cocktails 120-150฿.) The famous **Reggae Pub** attracts an older, mellower crowd. More like an entertainment center than a "pub," this pub comes complete with a tacky souvenir shop. Sunday nights attract party-lovers to the "get-bombed-at-Reggae" drinking contest. To get there, follow the signs to the boxing stadium across the lagoon.

Hat Lamai has fewer nighttime options than Hat Chaweng, but bars and strip joints are popping up by the dozen. **Bauhaus Pub, Bistro and Disco,** south of the bar area, is *the* hot spot for Lamai's young and restless. The Saturday Gin and Vodka party offers half-price cocktails. (Most drinks 30-100฿. Open daily 9pm-4am.)

DAYTRIP FROM KO SAMUI

ANG THONG MARINE NATIONAL PARK. Made infamous as the setting for Alex Garland's *The Beach*, Ang Thong Marine National Park is a breathtaking collection of over 40 limestone islands about 60km north of Ko Samui. Most visit the islands as a three- or four-hour drive from Samui. Travel agencies all over the island arrange tours to the park, most offering a boat-ride-and-bad-lunch combo (600฿) or a more worthwhile kayaking option (1800฿), which gives more opportunities to explore the craggy island inlets.

Among the islands are **Ko Mae Ko** (Mother Island), popular for saltwater lake **Thalay Nai** (Lake Crater); **Ko Sam Sao** (Tripod Island), famous for its huge rock arch and fantastic snorkeling; and **Ko Wua Talap** (Sleeping Cow Island), home to the **park office. Ko Lak** and similar limestone formations tower 400m above the water. Dolphins prance in the water around the longtail boats that sail near **Ko Thai Plao.** The waters at **Hat Chan Charat** (Moonlight Beach) are as good for diving as Ko Tao's. Visit the park on your own by chartering a boat or arranging transportation with the tour ferry operator. If you stay on the island, the park office rents several modest bungalows starting at 400฿; camping is free.

KO PHANGAN ☎077

Divers check out Ko Tao, and sunbathers bake in Ko Samui, but the hard-core partiers go wild in Ko Phangan, especially by the light of the full moon when the revelry runs all night and litters Hat Rin with bottles, cigarette butts, and passed-out English lads. Even when the moon isn't full, there's something about the island that draws in both the relaxed beach aficionados and the ardent ravers. Maybe it's the laid-back beachers. Maybe it's the gushing waterfalls. Maybe it's the throbbing nightlife. One thing is sure, though; Ko Phangan is the island of choice for backpackers in Southern Thailand. Welcome home, party animals.

THE VIEW FROM ABOVE

The lowdown: Sun-soaked beaches by day, drunken tourist-drenched beaches by night.
Gateway cities: Ko Tao/Chumphon, Ko Samui/Surat Thani.
Nearby islands: Ko Samui, Ko Tao.
Beaches: Bottle Beach (Hat Khuat), Hat Rin Nai, Hat Rin Nok, Thong Sala, Thong Nai Paan, Thong Tapan Noi.
Highlights: Hat Rin Nok's wild full moon parties, soothing Bottle Beach, and Than Sadet Historical Park's refreshing waterfalls.

TRANSPORTATION

Ferries: To get to Ko Phangan, you must go through either Ko Tao/Chumphon or Ko Samui/Surat Thani. From **Ko Tao,** ferries leave from **Mae Hat's southern pier** (5 per day 9:30am-2:30pm, 180-350฿). From **Ko Samui,** boats leave from **Big Buddha Pier** for **Hat Rin** (100฿) and from **Na Thon** for **Thong Sala** (9, 11am, 5:30pm; 95฿). You can also head to Ko Phangan directly from **Surat Thani** via the **Donsak Car Port** (10am, 1, 6pm) or the **town pier** (7:30am, 205฿; 11pm, 400฿). Ferries leaving Ko Phangan depart from **Hat Rin** and **Thong Sala.** From the pier at Hat Rin Nai, boats go to **Ko Samui's Big Buddha Beach** (1½hr., 9:30, 11:40am, 2:30pm; 100฿) and at 12:40pm to **Hat Tian** (50฿), **Than Sadet** (80฿), and **Thong Nai Paan** (100฿). From the main pier at Thong Sala, boats go to: **Ko Samui** (1hr.; 12:30, 6:30pm; 105฿); **Ko Tao** (2hr.; 8, 10am, 12:30; 250฿); **Surat Thani** (night boat 7hr., 10pm, 400฿; express boat 4hr., 12:30pm, 205฿).

Local Transportation: Songthaew meet ferries at the pier and run from Thong Sala to the island's major beaches. To: **Ban Kai** (30฿); **Ban Tai** (20฿); **Chalok Lam** (40฿); **Hat Rin** (50฿); **Hat Yow** (50฿); **Thong Nai Paan** (80฿). In Hat Rin Nai, *songthaew* wait across from the police booth and go to **Thong Sala** (min. 3 passengers, 50฿).

Rentals: Motorcycles are available for rent around the pier and market in Thong Sala and in several guest houses in Hat Rin Nai (150฿ per day with passport deposit).

ORIENTATION AND PRACTICAL INFORMATION

Ko Phangan is 100km northeast of Surat Thani and 12km north of Ko Samui. Boats arrive at the island's main city and port of call, **Thong Sala,** where most services are located. From the pier, a paved road runs 10km southeast to the party beaches of **Hat Rin,** which is split into **Hat Rin Nai** to the west and **Hat Rin Nok** to the east. A partially paved road makes its way 10km northward to **Chalok Lam Bay,** a departure point for boats heading to lovely **Bottle Beach.** A bumpy dirt road also connects Thong Sala to the northeastern beaches of **Thong Nai Paan** and **Thong Tapan Noi,** and other dirt trails stretch to more remote coves. More so than other islands, Ko Phangan rewards those who explore the far corners of the island. The amusingly titled *V. Hongsombud Guide Map of Koh Pha-Ngam & Koh Tao* (50฿) is useful.

Travel Agencies: Songserm Travel Center (☎377 046), on the left side of the main road in Nathon. Boat and A/C bus packages to: **Bangkok** (350฿); **Krabi** (290฿); **Phuket** (290฿). Open daily 8am-5pm.

Currency Exchange: Several exchange booths line the street leading from the main pier in Thong Sala. **Krung Thai Bank,** about 100m down the road on the right, has the island's sole **ATM.** Open for exchange M-F 8:30am-4:30pm. In Hat Rin, your best option is the **Siam City Bank** branch on a side street near the middle of Haadrin Rd. Exchange rates here are slightly more expensive than in Thong Sala. Open daily 9:30am-4:30pm.

Markets: Bovy Supermarket (☎377 231), in Thong Sala about 20m from the end of the pier on the right. An eclectic mix of junk food and knick-knacks. Open daily 8:30-midnight. For fresh fruit and cheap rubber sandals, try the morning market farther down. Open daily until evening.

Emergency: ☎191.

Police: Main office (☎377 114), 2km north of Thong Sala on the road to Ao Chalak Lam. English spoken. Open 24hr. A small, phone-less **police booth** operates at Hat Rin off Haadrin Rd., opposite the school. Some English spoken. Both **open 24hr.**

Medical Services: Koh Pha-Ngan Hospital (☎377 034), 3km north of Thong Sala. English spoken. No credit cards. **Open 24hr.** In Hat Rin, **private nursing stations** provide basic medical services. For serious medical attention, take a boat to Ko Samui.

Internet Access: The cheapest access providers dot the road stemming from Thong Salas's main pier (1฿ per min). More expensive providers in Hat Rin (2฿ per min.).

Post Office: GPO (☎377 118), in Thong Sala. From the end of the pier, walk down the main road, take the first right, and follow the road until it ends and turn left; the post office is on the right. *Poste Restante.* In Hat Rin, a private licensed branch (☎375 204) on the southern road to connecting Hat Rin Nok and Hat Rin Nai functions as a tourist and telephone office. Open daily 9am-midnight. **Postal code:** 84280.

THAILAND

ACCOMMODATIONS, FOOD, AND BEACHES

Most travelers to Ko Phangan head immediately to the southern coast and the beaches of Hat Rin. Those looking for more attractive, secluded beaches should head north to lovely Bottle Beach or quiet Thong Tapan. Accommodation prices and availability rise and fall with lunar tides. The island fills to maximum capacity in the days surrounding the full moon. If you plan to be there for the party, arrive a few days early to score accommodations or be prepared to sleep on the beach. Lunar fluctuations aside, prices jump about 100-200฿ during high season, especially on the Hat Rin beaches. The following accommodations and food options are listed by beach.

GET MOONED, THAI STYLE Every month on the full moon, backpackers and 20-something tourists from all over Thailand drop what they're doing and hop on the next boat to Ko Phangan to partake in the island's legendary lunar festivities. Originally a modest affair (first hosted by Paradise Bungalows in 1989), the party has mushroomed into a massive all-night beach rave, complete with strobe lights, imported Euro-DJs, and illicit substances galore. More people may mean more fun, but it also means more headaches. Some tips to survive the full moon madness:

Accommodations. If you want to stay on Ko Phangan the night of the full moon, arrive a few days early to secure a spot or even earlier if you want to stay on Hat Rin. Otherwise, stay at either Ko Tao or Ko Samui and take advantage of special "Full Moon Party boats" that make round-trips to Phangan on full moon nights. (Keep in mind, however, that the rocking boats are known to be unkind to over-boozed stomachs.)

Safety. Full moon night is big for theft. Keep all your valuables securely locked or in a money belt on your person. Don't leave any important items unlocked in your bungalow or in obvious hiding places such as under your pillow or mattress.

Drugs. Despite stiff penalties imposed by the Thai government, *farang* still flock to Phangan to partake in a thriving drug culture, which crescendos with the lunar cycle. Before taking that next joint or tab, be aware that Thai police, both in uniform and undercover, are out in extra numbers on full moon night and won't look kindly on your extravagance. Also, an increasing number of travelers have been reportedly drugged or tranquilized and then robbed. *Let's Go* urges you to "just say no."

BOTTLE BEACH (HAT KHUAT). This gorgeous beach lulls those who intend to stay for a few days into spending weeks and or months instead. To get here, take a *songthaew* from Thong Sala to **Ao Chalok Lam Bay,** 10km away (20min., 100฿). The bay is the departure point for boats to Bottle Beach. (9:30am, 3, 6pm; return 8am, 1, 5pm; 50฿.) It's also possible to walk the 4km from Ao Chalok Lam to Bottle Beach.

Once on Bottle Beach, your options are limited to four bungalow operations: **Bottle Beach Bungalows 1, 2,** and **3,** and **Smile Bungalows,** all of which are owned by the same family. (Common ☎01 229 4762.) Bottle Beach 1, in the middle of the beach, is the cheapest, with bathroom-less bungalows hidden from the beach starting at 100฿. Bottle Beach 3 and Smile Bungalows at the far end of the beach have bungalows with private baths and hammocks starting at 250฿. The bungalows at the former sit right on the beach but fill up quickly, while the ones at the latter are farther from the beach. All have friendly staff and similar facilities. **OD Bungalow,** situated on a cliff, has great views. (All rooms with squat toilets 100-150฿.)

THONG SALA. Thong Sala is a lifeline for the island, boasting the cheapest email, most tourist services, and an aggressive barrage of *songthaew* drivers waiting at the pier. Staying here usually denotes an early ferry departure or an inability to get accommodation elsewhere, but some comfortable rooms lie close to the pier. **Sea Mew,** on the waterfront and visible from the pier, has a great staff. Enjoy the restaurant decorated with Christmas lights and the cable TV. (Singles with fan 200-250฿.) Across from the post office, the multi-storied **Poonum Patana** has large, passably clean rooms and tiled private baths. (☎377 089. Singles/doubles 200฿, with A/C 500฿.) The **Corner Kitchen** is opposite Poonum Patana and serves Thai, European, and Chinese cuisine.

THAILAND

HAT RIN NOK (EAST). Accommodation-wise, Hat Rin Nok, brims with over-priced and flimsily constructed bungalows. Your best bet is to start at the southern end of the beach with **Paradise Bungalows,** the proud host of the first Full Moon Party in 1989. The bamboo bungalows have balconies and are a bit removed from all the action. (☎375 245. Bungalows 200-250฿.) Toward the center of the beach, things get louder and more crowded, especially at night. **Sun Rise Bungalows,** in the middle of the beach, has breezy bamboo cottages with large beds. (☎375 145. Bungalows 250฿, with bath 300฿.) **Ali Baba's Restaurant,** on the left when coming from Hat Rin pier, has clean and simple rooms on its second floor. (☎375 054. Singles with fan, locking windows, and outside bath 150฿.) At the beach's northern end, **Tommy's Resort** is an old favorite with some of the cheapest beds on the island, but it's starting to show its age. At night, brace yourself for pulsing techno from the beachside bar. (☎01 926 0515. Bungalows 150฿, with bath 250-600฿, depending on proximity to beach.)

Restaurants representing half a dozen nationalities line Haadrin Rd. and the dirt alleys stemming from it. In the middle of the road connecting the south ends of both Hat Rin beaches, **Niras Beach Kitchen and Bakery** caters to health spa types and sweet tooths. (Kitchen open daily 8am-10pm. Bakery open 24hr. Raisin nut scone 20฿. Hummus sandwich on homemade bread 50฿.) Nearby **Chicken Corner** has the best chicken breast sandwiches (40฿), and consequently, the longest lines. **Sao's Kitchen,** behind Tommy's Resort, dishes out tofu-based vegetarian food to reclining customers under low lights. (☎375 166. Open daily 8:30am-10:30pm. Vegetable curries 40฿. Pumpkin soup with coconut milk 40฿.)

Songthaew from Thong Sala drop off passengers at Hat Rin Nok's quieter west side twin, Hat Rin Nai, a five-minute walk. The two beaches are connected by several dusty roads, all of which intersect Haadrin Rd., the area's main artery, which runs parallel to the beach. In this area you can find most basic services in addition to shops peddling rave gear and hippie paraphernalia.

HAT RIN NAI (WEST). Though separated by a mere 100m, Hat Rin Nai is far from its throbbing, and marijuana mist-enveloped eastern neighbor, Hat Rin Nok. The strip of muddy sand at Hat Rin Nai is hardly attractive, but the beach does have its perks—a good choice of bungalows, pretty sunsets, and a locations that's close enough to take advantage of Hat Rin Nok's nightlife but distant enough to provide a quiet retreat.

Budget bungalows lie at the northern end of the beach, a 15min. walk from the Hat Rin Pier. **Sooksom Bungalow,** past a rocky outcropping at the north end of the beach, has simple, wooden huts and a vegetarian-friendly restaurant. (☎375 230. Bungalows 100฿, with bath 300-350฿.) A bit farther north, **Phangan Buri Resort's** concrete bungalows and tiled patios are more expensive but cleaner and prettier. (☎375 330. Bungalows 200฿, with bath 350-400฿.)

THONG TAPAN NOI AND THONG NAI PAAN. With beautiful, clear water and a relaxed atmosphere, these twin beaches offer ample reward for those who endure the hour-long *songthaew* ride from Thong Sala or the boat ride from Hat Rin. *Songthaew* stop first at Thong Tapan Noi, the more populated of the two, known for good swimming and snorkeling. Near the *songthaew* drop-off, the popular **Star Huts** is the largest operator on the beach and teems with long-termer guests. (☎299 055. Bungalows 150-200฿, with bath 350-400฿.) Younger backpackers frequent **Honey Bungalows** farther north from the beach. The thatched-roof huts propped on concrete blocks aren't as nice, but the atmosphere is friendly and social. (Bungalows 150-250฿.) At the very north end of the beach, a 15min. walk from the *songthaew* drop-off, **Pong Bungalow** is deservedly popular for its lively bar and its less popular library. Bungalows 150-180฿, with bath 250-300฿.) Most take their meals at bungalow restaurants, though many recommend **Banglangon Vegetarian Restaurant,** halfway up the beach, known for its pizza.

The east beach, Thong Nai Paan, is longer, less populated, and somewhat less tidy than Thong Tapan Noi. Ask the *songthaew* driver to let you off here or make the 30min. walk from Thong Tapan Noi yourself. At the end of the road to Thong Nai Paan's easternmost point, **Nice Beach Bungalows** has bright, white-washed rooms with mosquito nets and high ceilings. (200-1600฿, depending on season and A/C.) In the middle of Thong Nai Paan beach is **Pen's Bungalow,** which has clean, white, wooden bungalows with peaceful porches with hammocks. (☎229 004. Bungalows 100-150฿, with bath 200-300฿.) Everyone's happy at **Baan Panburi,** where each bungalow has a hole-free mosquito net. (☎238 599. Singles with fan 300-800฿.)

SIGHTS

Second to full moons and beaches, **waterfalls** are Ko Phangan's major attractions. The most famous stretches of river run through **Than Sadet Historical Park,** a good daytrip from the beach. Kings Rama V, VII, and IX all walked along its bathtub-sized waterfalls and cascades, leaving their initials as seals of inspection. Longtail boats from Hat Rin (50฿) drop off passengers at the mouth of the river. From here they make the 2-3km trek to the park by following the parallel road to the north.

The Sanctuary is a backpacker's spa that comes highly recommended by Ko Phangan's long-term vacationers. Noted for its seclusion, clean facilities, attentive staff and free evening meditations, many are happy to pay 60฿ for a dorm bed and splurge on yoga classes (150฿), oil massages (400฿), and 10-day fasts (singles/doubles with bath 200-1000฿). A longtail boat from Hat Rin will take you there (50฿).

NIGHTLIFE

Hat Rin Nok (see p. 797) is the stuff of legends. Each month under the full moon, thousands gather on this strip of sand. Bodies gyrate to the latest imported mixes, minds dance to the beat of illicit substances, and stomachs and bladders empty themselves gratefully into the ocean. Even when the moon isn't full, don't come here for a quiet, beautiful beach. Hat Rin Nok is loud, brash, dirty, and proud of it.

KO TAO

☎077

Ko Tao has become Southeast Asia's largest dive-training site. Scuba neophytes come for the cheap certification courses, veterans for the clear gulf waters and quality dive sites, and non-divers for the snorkeling and secluded, sun-baked coves, many of which can be reached only by boat or a long hike. With no airport or luxury hotels and few paved roads, Ko Tao is underdeveloped compared to its island siblings and, despite its popularity, remains a laid-back paradise for scuba enthusiasts.

THE VIEW FROM ABOVE

The lowdown: Southeast Asia's biggest dive site.
Gateway cities: Chumphon, Ko Phangan, Surat Thani.
Nearby islands: Ko Nang Yuan.
Beaches: Ao Chalok Ban Kao, Ao Hin Wong, Ao Leuk, Ao Tanoad, Ao Thian, Hat Sai Daeng, Hat Sai Ree, Laem Taa Toh, Mae Hat.
Highlights: Candle-lit dinners on laid-back Hat Sai Ree, fantastic snorkeling off Ko Nang Yuan, and scuba diving from just about anywhere on the island.

TRANSPORTATION

Boats leave for Ko Tao from **Chumphon** (express boat 2½hr., 7:30am, 400฿; speedboat 1½hr., 7:30am, 400฿; midnight boat 6hr., 200฿). From **Ko Phangan,** boats head to Ko Tao from Thong Sala (2hr., 12:30pm, 250฿). A direct boat leaves from **Surat Thani** (7hr., 11pm, 400฿). Ferries leave Ko Tao from **Mae Hat** to **Chumphon** (slow boat 5hr., 10am, 200฿; speedboat 2hr., 10:30am, 400฿; express boat 3hr., 3pm, 450฿) and **Ko Phangan** (slow boat 4hr., 9:30am, 180฿; speedboat 1½hr.; 9:30am, 3pm; 350฿; express boat 1½hr.; 10:30am, 2:30pm; 250฿).

Hell-bent **motorcycles** and **pickup truck-taxis** go anywhere accessible by the island's few paved roads (30-60฿). Many bungalows and shops rent motorcycles for 150฿ per day and a passport deposit.

ORIENTATION AND PRACTICAL INFORMATION

Boats arrive at **Mae Hat** (Mother Beach), where most services and travel agencies are located. Facing the island from the pier, a paved road heads left over a small hill to **Hat Sai Ree,** Ko Tao's most popular beach and the heart of the backpacking and scuba scene. The paved road uphill from the pier eventually bends right, leading to **Ao Chalok Ban Kao,** the main southern beach, and, 500m farther, **Ao Thian.** A pickup truck-taxi or motorbike from Mae Hut to either beach costs about 30฿.

Dirt roads connect Mae Hat to more remote beaches, including **Ao Hin Wong** (the east coast); **Ao Leuk,** a fantastic snorkeling destination; **Ao Ta-Note;** and **Hat Sai Daeng** (in the island's southeast corner). With the exception of the 20min. walk from Mae Hat to Hat Sai Ree, the island is fairly difficult to explore by foot during the day; by night, it's almost impossible. Taxis go most places but can be hard to flag down in remote corners of the island. The *Visitors' Guide Map of Koh Pha-Ngam & Koh Tao* (70฿), sold at shops across the island, is a good reference.

Travel Agencies: Ko Tao has no official tourist office; information and tickets are instead provided by private agencies lining the roads around the pier in Mae Hat and on the main road in Hat Sai Ree. All offer similar services and prices. The omnipotent **Mr. J** (☎456 066) claims to provide any type of service, from scoring visa extensions to arranging emergency loans. Find him and his knick-knack shop on the hill just north of the pier, a 10min. walk from Mae Hat toward Hat Sai Ree. Open daily 7am-10pm.

Currency Exchange: Krung Thai Bank Booth, on the left off the pier in Mae Hat, has mainland exchange rates. Generally open daily 9am-3pm. Many bungalows and all dive shops accept credit cards.

Markets: The **Mae Hat pier area** is called the **talat (market).** Buy fruit, postcards, clothes, and snorkel gear.

Police: ☎456 260. A 10min. walk north of the pier on the hill heading toward Hat Sai Ree opposite the school. Some English spoken. **Open 24hr.**

Medical Services: There is **no doctor on the island;** in an emergency, get on the first boat to Chumphon or Ko Samui. Boats are infrequent because of tide variations, so instant medical attention may not be available. **Nursing stations** are scattered around Ao Chalok, Hat Sai Ree, and Mae Hat, offering basic service for ear and eye irritations, wound dressing, and pregnancy/STD tests. Dive shops recommend the **Chintana Nursing Unit** at the top of the hill directly in front of the pier. Open daily 8am-8pm.

Telephones: Nearly all travel agencies and bungalows offer international phone service. About 80฿ per min.

Internet Access: It's impossible to walk 2 steps without passing an Internet facility in Mae Hat or Hat Sai Ree. Prices don't vary. 2฿ per min.

Post Office: A privately licensed post office (☎456 122) sits 20m uphill from the pier. *Poste Restante*. Open daily 8am-10pm. **Postal Code:** 84280.

ACCOMMODATIONS, FOOD, AND BEACHES

Finding good budget accommodations in Mae Hat can be a tricky business, particularly if you're here on a non-scuba agenda. Prices tend to be high, and, to make matters worse, the island seems particularly susceptible to low season/high season fluctuations. Prices listed reflect high season rates; in the low season, you may be able to knock off 100-150฿. The following accommodation and food options are listed by beach.

MAE HAT. Mae Hat is the food, fuel, and equipment center of Ko Tao. Despite its "metropolitan" status within the island community, this low-key beach is a haven for travelers. Besides that, though there's little reason to linger; you'll find better beaches and better vibes elsewhere on the island. Should an early morning ferry keep you on Mae Hat, budget accommodations cluster just south of the pier. Just before the Sensi Resort, the dive-oriented **Kallapangha Resort** has friendly management and cheerfully-painted bungalows, complete with swinging hammocks. (☎456 058. Bungalows 200-1000฿, depending on size and proximity to beach.) More bungalows hide north of the pier on the hill between Mae Hat and Hat Sai Ree, a 15min. walk from the pier. Though hardly beautiful, the area is closer to the beaches and dive shops of Hat Sai Ree. Jack-of-all-trades **Mr. J** owns several sparkling new bungalows just behind his store across from the school. (Rooms with private baths and new fixtures 400฿.)

Even though Mae Hat may not be the best place to stay, it's one of the better places to eat. In the morning, *farang* feast on fresh pastries and bread (20-30฿) at the **Swiss Bakery,** past the post office. (Open daily 6:30am-6:30pm.) On the other side of the street, the aptly-named **Farango** serves pasta (90-120฿) and pizza (150-230฿) after dark. (Open noon-3pm and 6-10pm.) **Yang's,** opposite Farango, has fried noodle chicken (40฿) and breakfast omelets (30฿), among other cheap Thai eats. (Open daily 6am-10pm.)

HAT SAI REE. Backpackers and divers congregate in the bungalows along this 2km beach, which is Ko Tao's busiest bit of sand. Despite its popularity, the beach is laid back; candle-lit dinners fade into easy-going nightlife, and by day even the palm trees are too relaxed to stand straight up. Most accommodations on the beach cater to divers, and prices are generally higher than elsewhere on the island; however, there are some exceptions. To get to the relatively inexpensive **Pranee's Bungalows,** head to the northern side of Hat Sai Ree, a 20min. walk on the sand from the start of the beach. With plywood walls and simple, private baths, the bungalows are fairly standard, but the service is friendly, and the clientele relaxed. (☎456 080. 400-500฿.) A good bet in the center of the beach is the popular **Sai Ree Cottage,** just past Scuba Junction. Their wooden bungalows get points for cleanliness as does the happenin' beachside restaurant which boasts an extensive menu of inexpensive Thai dishes, milkshakes, and cocktails. (☎01 229 4952. Bungalows 350-600฿, depending on size and proximity to the beach.) Two others to try are the **Ko Tao Cabana Resort,** before Sai Ree Cottage, and **AC Resort,** farther south (rooms from 300฿). Closer to Mae Hat, **Viewcliff Bungalows** has immaculate rooms. (Singles 350฿; doubles 600฿.)

For culinary offerings, Hat Sai Ree is second-best to Mae Hat. Most bungalows along the beach have good restaurants, ideal for quick in-between-dive meals and for evening pre-party drinks. At **La Matta Restaurant** in the middle of the beach, five Italians serve up homemade everything—sauces, noodles, bread, and cakes. Fine Italian and French wines are also available. (Open daily 7am-3pm and 6-11pm.) The **Lotus Restaurant,** past Sai Ree Cottage at the northern end of the beach, is one of the island's few restaurants specializing in Thai cuisine (dishes 60-100฿). In the evening, divers put away their gear, and sunbathers slather on aloe vera in preparation for nights passed drinking by the beach. **AC Bar,** at the south end of the beach, draws partiers from all over the island with its theme nights. Farther north, the **Venus Bar** induces dizziness with its large screen showing trippy videos.

NORTH OF HAT SAI REE. Bungalows beyond Hat Sai Ree can be reached by taxi (40฿) or foot, a 3-4km hike north of the pier. **CFT Bungalow,** the northernmost bungalow at the end of the road, offers spectacular views of Ko Nang Yuan. Walk five minutes from where the taxi drops you off or take a boat. A bridge from the pier leads to hillside huts with outdoor showers (100฿). Two rooms higher on the hill are spacious and breezy (300฿). South of Hat Sai Ree (east of Mae Hat), **Ao Leuk** is great for year-round **snorkeling.** Follow the main road from Mae Hat past Farango and follow signs to Ao Leuk Rd; it's a 500m slide down a dusty road. **Ao Leuk Bungalows** is nestled there with simple accommodations. (☎229 3070. Rooms 150-300฿. Restaurant open 7am-10pm.)

Further north from Ao Leuk is **Ao Ta-Note,** famous for off-the-beach snorkeling and more rugged beaches. Long-term vacationers recommend meals at **Mountain Reef,** one of the last set of bungalows to get full, due to its remote location. (☎01 956 8876. Basic singles with shower and fan 250฿; bigger rooms 350฿.) **Diamond Beach Resort,** nearby, has a mellow staff and cheaper rooms. (Singles with outside bath/shower 150฿, with private bath 250-450฿.)

THAILAND

AO CHALOK BAN KAO. Chalok Ban Kao Bay is carved out of the island's south end, 3km from Mae Hat (45min. by foot, 50฿ taxi ride). The beach supports a dense concentration of bungalows, dive shops, and restaurants but somehow manages to seem less crowded than Hat Sai Ree, probably because the beach is, well, just nicer. Most bungalows are affiliated with dive shops, but non-divers seek happy refuge in the new **JP Resort,** smack in the center of the beach. Its cliffside bungalows are new and squeaky clean with nice bay-views and private baths. Internet access (2฿ per min.) and a relaxed restaurant round out this newcomer. (☎456 099. 300-400฿.) **Sunshine Bungalows** is also conveniently located but features less glamorous plywood bungalows with private baths (350฿).

AO THIAN. A walk uphill south from Ao Chalok leads to a fork in the dirt road. The left path leads downhill to the small but stunning **Ao Thian Bay,** home to little more than a smattering of bungalows, snack bars, and sun worshipers. The **snorkeling** here is some of the best on the island (equipment rental 50฿). The closest thing to a real accommodation is **Rocky Resort** on the bay's east end. It also doubles as the beach's only restaurant. (Bungalows 300-500฿.)

LAEM TAA TOH. This lovely cape juts into the gulf, separating Ao Chalok from Ao Thian. To get here, follow the dirt road uphill from Ao Chalok, taking the right path leading uphill at the fork. Besides spectacular views, the cape is home to the **Taa Toh Lagoon Dive Resort,** on Taa Toh Beach halfway around the cape, which has simple bungalows among the weather-beaten boulders rimming the sand. Many guests are divers-in-training at the resort's **scuba school.** (☎377 792. Bungalows 300-500฿.) On the way up, stop at **New Heaven Restaurant,** which has a delicious menu and near-celestial views of Ao Thian. (Dishes 50-100฿. Open daily 8am-10pm.)

ACTIVITIES

Scuba diving is popular year-round in Ko Tao, although late September through December often brings heavy rains and choppy waters. The island also has a unique tide; September to May is high water season and better for snorkeling, while May to September is low water season and better for basking on the beach. Ko Tao has over 20 dive sites. **Chumphon Pinnacle,** where a granite tower rises 14m above the surface, is a favorite for deep dives. **Southwest Pinnacle** and **Shark Island** are known for gorgeous coral and leopard sharks. **Green Rock** and **Sail Rock** on the way to Ko Phangan are famous for rock "swim-throughs." Closer to Ko Tao, **Hin Wong Pinnacle** and **Ko Nang Yuan** (see **Daytrips from Ko Tao,** below) have coral and fish in shallow waters suitable for snorkeling.

Scuba prices are standardized, so friendliness and professionalism, not price, make a good dive shop. Four types of classes are available. Beginners can choose from the four-day **open-water certification course** (7800฿) or the supervised one-day **"discover scuba" dives** (1600฿, with the option of additional dives for 800฿). Certified divers can hone their skills with the two-day **advanced open-water course** (6600฿) or tag along with any dive class on a one-day **"fun dive"** (one dive 800฿, 700฿ each for 2-5 dives, 600฿ each for 6-9 dives, 500฿ each for 10 or more dives). Bring your own equipment for a 15% discount. Prices include accommodation in affiliated bungalows for the duration of the course. If you choose to stay on your own in non-affiliated lodging, however, prices drop by only 150฿, which means you'll almost certainly lose money during the high season. Snorkelers can also take advantage of the dive scene by tagging along on shallower dives for around 50฿.

The following is an abbreviated list of dive shop operations. The Internet can be a good way to familiarize yourself with the various options, but be sure to talk to the staff and patrons about teaching and equipment before committing. The larger shops have representative offices on Mae Hat.

Asia Divers (☎377 754; www.asiadivers-kontao.com).

Ban's Diving Resort (☎456 061; www.ban-diving-resort-kon-tao-thailand-scuba-idc-divemaster.com).

Big Blue Diving Center (☎377 750; www.bigbluediving.com).

Buddha View Dive Resort (☎456 074; www.buddhaview-diving.com).

Scuba Junction (456 164; www.scuba-junction.com).

Sunshine Divers (☎456 061; www.sunshine-divers.com).

Taa Toh Lagoon Dive Resort (☎456 192; www.taatohdivers.com).

DAYTRIP FROM KO TAO

KO NANG YUAN

Longtail boat taxis go to Ko Nang Yuan from just south of the Mae Hat's (20min., 100฿). Try negotiating with the driver to have him come pick you up later in the day. A ferry departs from Mae Hat once per day (10:30am, 50฿).

About 2km off Ko Tao's northwest coast, lovely Ko Nang Yuan is actually three separate islets connected by a three-pronged stretch of white sand. The beach, the only one of its kind in the world, not only makes a good photo-op, but its **snorkeling** is among the Ko Tao's best. The island is best visited as a daytrip from Ko Tao, since the island's only accommodation, **Koh Nangyuan Dive Resort,** is expensive. (☎01 299 5212. Rooms 1500-3500฿.) The resort's restaurant is accordingly expensive (dishes 200฿). If you bring your own food and drink, be clandestine; the monopolizing resort attempts to "forbid" travelers from bringing their own ailments to the island.

PHUKET

☎076

A tropical playground of international stature, Phuket (FOO-ket, not "Fuck It") is best compared to other Eden-cum-tourist-meccas. Thailand's biggest island in the Andaman Sea, Phuket draws tourists looking for anything but a cultural or solitary experience. Most visitors arrive by plane and are swiftly shepherded into A/C taxis, which deposit them at five-star luxury resorts. Here they frolic and play for a week or two, safely avoiding almost everything having to do with, god forbid, Thailand. Consequently, for the budget traveler, Phuket can be an icky, over-touristed experience. Prices tend to be higher than on other islands, and the beaches more crowded. Backpackers relax on beaches like Hat Kamala and Hat Karon by day and revel with randy Romeos cruising the discos in legendary nightlife hub Hat Patong by night. The mantra is simple: give up your dreams of idyllic seclusion for a few nights, soak up a raucous good time with fellow vacationing tourists, and, in your own way, make the most of the "Jewel of the South."

THE VIEW FROM ABOVE

The lowdown: Thailand's biggest and most-touristed island. The Sarasin Bridge connects it to Phang-Nga on the mainland.
Gateway city: Phuket Town.
Nearby island groups: Racha, Similan.
Beaches: Hat Ao Bang Tao, Hat Chalong, Hat Kamala, Hat Karon, Hat Kata, Hat Nai Yang, Hat Patong, Hat Rawai, Hat Surin, Sing Cape.
Highlights: Great snorkeling and diving around Hat Karon and Hat Kata, gorgeous Hat Surin, legendary nightlife hub Hat Patong, and Phuket Town's Vegetarian Festival (late Sept. or Oct.).

TRANSPORTATION

Flights: Phuket International Airport, 28km outside of Phuket Town on Rte. 4026. Taxis and *tuk-tuks* cruise between the beaches and airport (taxi from airport to Phuket Town 300฿). **Bangkok Airways,** 158/2-3 Yao Warat Rd. (☎225 033; open daily 8am-5pm) and **Thai Airways,** 78/1 Ranong Rd., across from the local bus station (☎211 195; open daily 8am-5pm), run most domestic and international flights. To: **Bangkok** (every hr. 8am-8pm, 2570฿); **Hat Yai** (12:50am, 1180฿); **Ko Samui** (daily 11:15am, 4:20pm; 1560฿; M, W, F, Su 11:10am; 1480฿); **Kuala Lumpur** (daily, 3730฿); **Penang** (Tu, F, Su 12:30pm; 2230฿); **Singapore** (4 per day, 6085฿).

Buses: Intercity bus station (☎211 480), off Phang-Nga Rd. in eastern Phuket Town, behind a shopping plaza. TAT office has a good, free bus schedule. A/C and non-A/C buses to: **Bangkok** (14hr., 19 per day 6am-7pm, 278-755฿); **Hat Yai** (7hr., 12 per day, 150-270฿); **Khao Sok National Park** (7:30, 9am); **Krabi** (4hr., 22 per day, 65-117฿); **Phang-Nga** (2½hr., 5 per day 10:10am-4:30pm, 36฿); **Surat Thani** (5hr., 14 per day, 104-180฿); **Trang** (6hr., 20 per day 6am-6:30pm, 105-189฿).

Boats: Boats to **Ko Phi Phi** depart from Tonsai Bay (9am, 2:30pm; 350-450฿). Tickets are cheaper in Ko Phi Phi—buy your return ticket there.

Local Transportation: Local bus station on Ranong Rd. in Phuket Town, near the market. Labeled **songthaew** (every 30min. 7am-5pm) to: **Hat Kamala** (25฿); **Hat Karon** (20฿); **Hat Kata** (20฿); **Hat Patong** (15฿); **Hat Rawai** (20฿); **Hat Nai Yang** (30฿); **Hat Surin** (20฿); **Tuk-tuk** to: **Hat Kamala** (250฿); **Hat Kata** (150฿); **Hat Nai Yang** (300฿); **Hat Patong** (15฿); **Hat Rawai** (100฿); **Hat Surin** (250฿). Within Phuket Town *tuk-tuk* charge 10-20฿; rates are negotiable to other points on the island and go up after 5pm.

Rentals: Motorcycles (150-200฿ per day) and **jeeps** (600-1000฿ per day) are available for rent all over the island. All vehicles are uninsured, and accident rates for foreigners are alarmingly high. TAT does not recommend renting a motorcycle.

ORIENTATION

Getting around Phuket is not particularly complicated, but given the island's size (570sq. km), traveling takes time. Phuket is connected to the mainland by **Rte. 402,** the island's main north-south artery. Bordering the Andaman Sea, the west coast is lined with beaches, the province's pride and joy. The northern beaches, especially **Hat Kamala, Hat Surin,** and **Sing Cape** are quieter and prettier, while south of Kamala, party central **Hat Patong** has a sensory overload of tacky bars, cabaret shows, and gimmicky tourist stalls. Further south are the gentle duo of **Hat Karon** and **Hat Kata,** while a few smaller, less attractive beaches fringe the island's southwestern tip. Phuket's bleak and muddy eastern coast is filled with mangroves, prawn farms, and bobbing boats. On the island's southeast corner, **Phuket Town,** the island's lifeline, offers financial, postal, and telecommunications services in addition to a bevy of good, authentic, budget restaurants. It's not glamorous, but it's a decent base for exploring the rest of the island.

PRACTICAL INFORMATION

Tourist Office: TAT, 73-75 Phuket Rd. (☎212 213), in Phuket Town, northwest of the clock-tower and hidden among furniture stores. Helpful staff provides maps, bus schedules, and accommodation lists. Open daily 8:30am-4:30pm.

Travel Agencies: Tour operators are a dime a dozen in Hat Karon, Hat Kata, Hat Patong, and Phuket Town. Most can arrange tours to Phang-Nga Bay and nearby islands (450-650฿) and bus or ferry transportation to Krabi and Ko Phi Phi. The agency in the **On On Hotel** (see **Accommodations,** p. 806) is reportedly one of the cheapest.

Currency Exchange: In Phuket Town, a slew of banks are on Phang-Nga Rd. in front of the On On Hotel, and several more are one block down on Rat Sada Rd. **Thai Farmers Bank,** 14 Phang-Nga Rd. (☎217 125). Open daily 8:30am-5pm. **24hr. ATM.** Currency exchange booths and ATMs abound on the larger beaches, especially Hat Karon, Hat Kata, and Hat Patong.

Medical Services: Phuket has some of Thailand's finest hospitals outside Bangkok. **Bangkok Phuket Hospital** 21 Hong Yok-H-Thit Rd. (☎254 421), on the northwest side of Phuket Town. **Phuket International Hospital,** 44 Chalerm Prakiat Rd. (☎249 400), on the way to the airport. Credit cards accepted. English spoken. Both **open 24hr.**

Emergency: ☎199.

Tourist Police: 81-83 Satun Rd. (☎335 015), northwest corner of Phuket Town. English spoken. **Open 24hr.** Smaller booths on major beaches.

Police: ☎212 115. Little English spoken. Contact TAT or tourist police first.

Telephones: Phuket Telecommunication Center, 112/2 Phang-Nga Rd. (☎216 861), in the building under the radio tower. International phone/fax and Internet. Cheaper than services provided by travel agencies. Open daily 8am-midnight.

Internet Access: Cheapest at the Telecommunications Center (see **Telephones,** above). Purchase of a 100฿ Internet card is required to begin service. 30฿ per hr. Travel agencies and guest houses charge 1-2฿ more per min.

Post Offices: GPO, 12/16 Montri Rd. (☎211 020), on the corner with Talang Rd. *Poste Restante.* Open M-F 8:30am-4:30pm, Sa-Su 9am-noon. **Postal code:** 83000.

PHUKET TOWN ☎076

Lacking the glamour of its beachside siblings, Phuket Town is about as close as one can get to an "authentic" Thailand on the Island. Though tourist dollars have started to trickle in as more tourists venture here from the island's more alluring beaches, the town still retains its original Sino-Portuguese character. Despite the scant entertainment options, Phuket Town has enough budget hotels and restaurants to remain a popular springboard for exploring the rest of the island.

ORIENTATION

Phuket Town is small and walkable. The island's **intercity bus terminal** is one block north of the main road, **Phang-Nga Rd.,** which runs west from the station to the **On On Hotel** and many banks. Past the Telecommunications Center (distinguished by its clock tower), Phang-Nga Rd. intersects **Phuket Rd.,** which runs south past **TAT** and

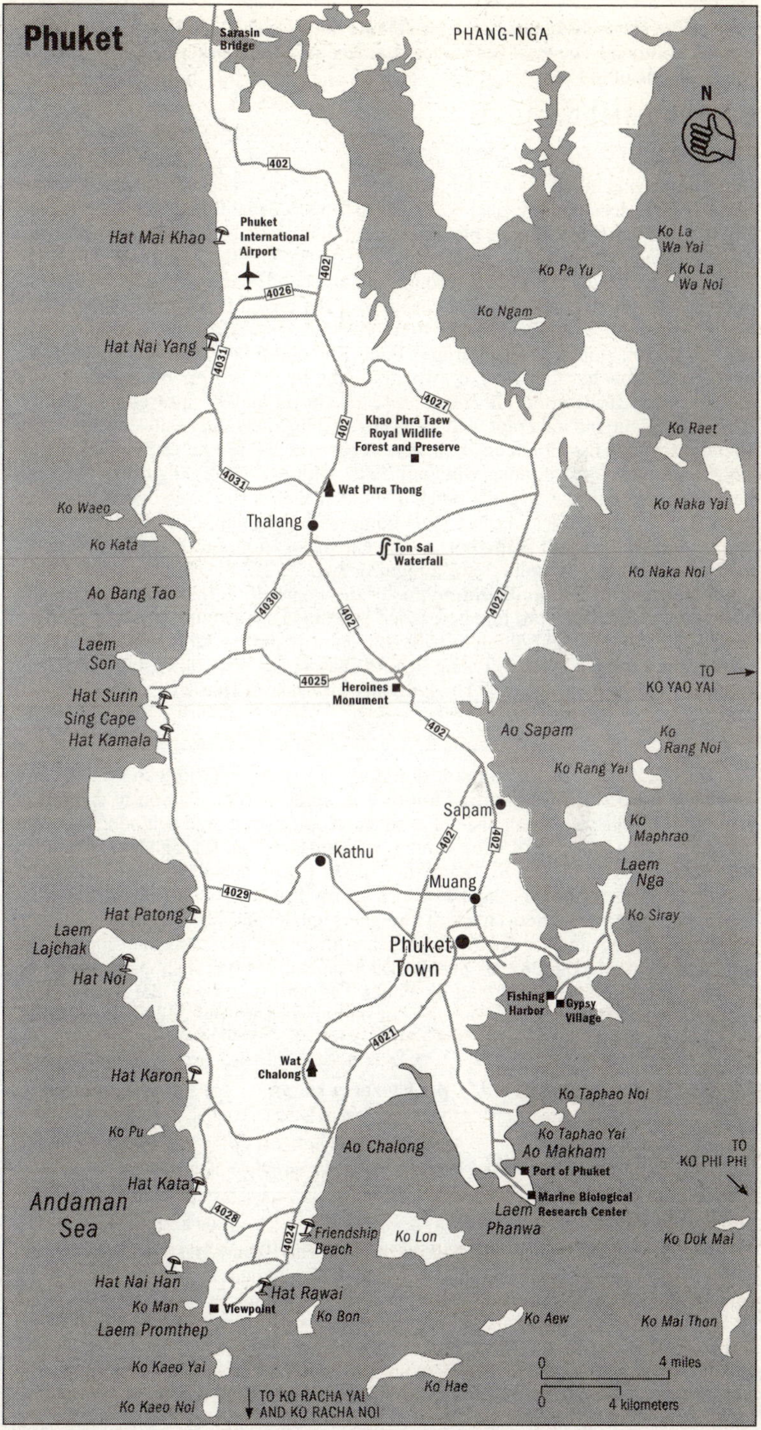
Phuket
Sarasin Bridge
PHANG-NGA
N
402
Phuket International Airport
Hat Mai Khao
402
4026
Ko La Wa Yai
Ko La Wa Noi
Ko Pa Yu
Ko Ngam
Hat Nai Yang
4031
4027
402
Khao Phra Taew Royal Wildlife Forest and Preserve
Ko Raet
4031
Wat Phra Thong
Ko Waeo
Thalang
Ko Naka Yai
Ko Kata
Ton Sai Waterfall
Ko Naka Noi
Ao Bang Tao
4030
402
4027
Laem Son
TO KO YAO YAI
4025
Heroines Monument
Hat Surin
Sing Cape
Hat Kamala
402
Ao Sapam
Ko Rang Noi
Ko Rang Yai
Sapam
Ko Maphrao
402
402
Kathu
Laem Nga
Muang
4029
Ko Siray
Hat Patong
Laem Lajchak
Phuket Town
Hat Noi
Fishing Harbor
Gypsy Village
4021
Wat Chalong
Hat Karon
Ko Taphao Noi
Ko Pu
Ko Taphao Yai
Ao Chalong
Ao Makham
TO KO PHI PHI
Port of Phuket
Hat Kata
Marine Biological Research Center
Andaman Sea
4028
Laem Phanwa
Friendship Beach
Ko Lon
Ko Dok Mai
4024
Hat Nai Han
Hat Rawai
Ko Man
Viewpoint
Ko Bon
Ko Aew
Ko Mai Thon
Laem Promthep
Ko Kaeo Yai
0
4 miles
Ko Hae
TO KO RACHA YAI AND KO RACHA NOI
0
4 kilometers
Ko Kaeo Noi

THAILAND

Navamindra Memorial Square to the **Clock Tower Rotary,** a main landmark in the southern part of town. The **local bus station** is adjacent to the market on **Ranong Rd.,** on the west side of town.

ACCOMMODATIONS

Phuket Town has the best selection of budget accommodations on the island, but that's not saying much. By and large, heavy demand translates into the unwelcome duo of high prices and low quality. To get to the **Suk Sabai Hotel,** 82/9 Thep Kasatri Rd. follow Phuket Rd. several blocks north until it becomes Thep Kasatri Rd. Turn onto the small alleyway just before the Ford dealership; the hotel is at the end of the alleyway. It's quite a walk, but rooms are quiet and spacious rooms. (☎212 287. Singles 180฿; doubles 250฿.) The cheapest of the bunch is the rather dilapidated but architecturally significant **On On Hotel,** 19 Phang-Nga Rd., a 15min. walk west of the bus station, opposite Thai Farmers Bank. The oldest hotel in town, On On has a devoted backpacker following, drawn, no doubt, by the low prices and the hotel's cameo in the Hollywood hit *The Beach.* The hotel may be interesting, but the rooms are plain and unkempt, and walls are so thin you could easily converse with friends staying a few doors down. Internet access is 25฿ per hr. (☎211 154. Singles 120฿, with bath 180฿; doubles with bath 250฿, with A/C 360฿.) Slightly out of "budget" range is luxurious **Imperial Hotel,** 51 Phuket Rd., at the intersection with Ratsada Rd. The fully decked out rooms come with A/C, cable TV, hairdryers, hot water, and wall-to-wall carpeting. A convenient location and friendly staff make this the ideal place to splurge for a night or two. (☎212 311. Singles 650฿.) **Nana Chart Mansion,** 41/34 Montri Rd. opposite the Pearl Hotel, has new, crisp-white sheets and a pleasant staff that isn't jaded by Phuket's constant stream of tourists. (☎230 041, ext. 3. Singles/doubles with cold shower 250฿, with hot shower and TV 350฿.) The **Pengmen Hotel,** 69 Phang-Nga Rd., has a restaurant downstairs and clean rooms in a great location. (☎211 186. Rooms with shared Thai-style bath 120฿.)

THAILAND

FOOD

Phuket is famous for its culinary delights, like *tao sor* (Chinese crepes) and *kanohm jin Phuket* (breakfast noodles in spicy curry). The daily **market** on Ranong Rd. sells aisle upon aisle of produce, tropical fruit, and seafood. The **night market** is at the junction of Tilok Uthit 1 and Ong Sim Phai Rd. **Chinese Mae Porn Restaurant,** on Phang-Na Rd. near the On On Hotel, serves some of the most scrumptious dishes on the island. Portions are on the skimpy side, but oh, the taste! The neighborly atmosphere caters to foreigners and locals alike. (Delicious chicken with cashew nuts and various seafood dishes 80-100฿. Open daily 9am-10pm.) The expensive but excellent **Ka Jok See,** 26 Takuapa Rd., is several shops south of the Ratsada Rd. intersection, hidden by plants. The staff treats you like royalty. Thai dishes run 80-380฿. Try the *tom yum* or *goong-sarong* for 150฿ each. Reservations recommended. (Open Tu-Su 6-11pm.)

THIS AIN'T BAYWATCH. Phuket is known for dangerous, sometimes fatal, ocean currents during the rainy season. Exercise caution in the water, especially at high tide. If you're caught in a current, signal distress by waving one arm (wave two arms for serious distress) and try to stay afloat until help arrives.

HAT PATONG

If Bangkok's infamous Patpong ever had an heir, Hat Patong is it. On Phuket's west coast, Hat Patong is the island's nightlife and entertainment center. An intoxicating mix of themed bars, strip shows, Thai boxing, and gimmicky souvenir stalls won't disappoint if you're in the mood to party into the wee hours of the morning. Hat Patong and its not-so-forbidden pleasures are best experienced after dark; during the day, there's not much to do except buzz around the shops or attempt a dip in the beach, which is sadly one of the dirtiest and most crowded on the island.

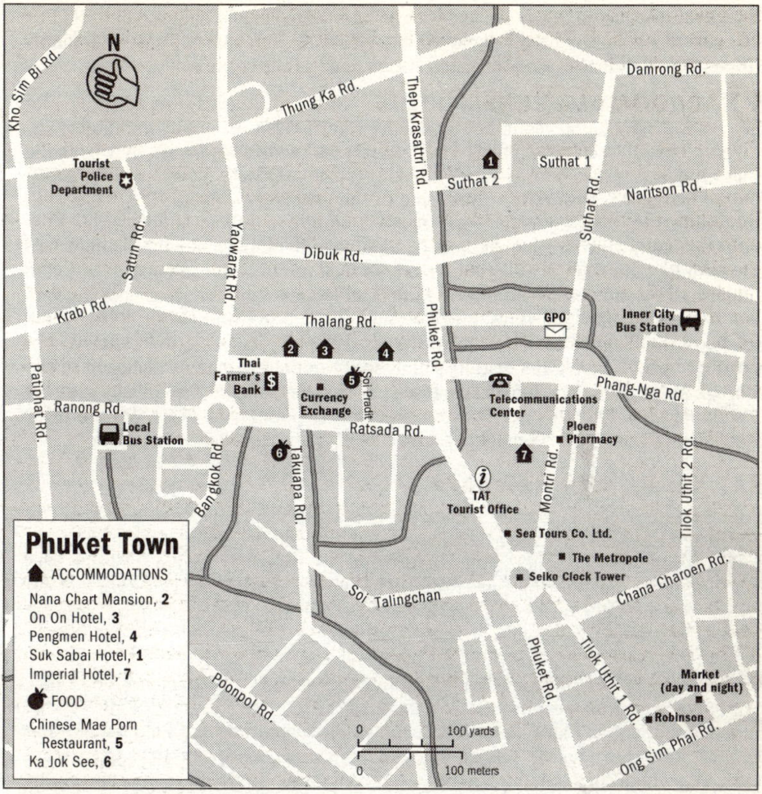

ORIENTATION. ""Patong" is defined by two roads that run parallel to the 3km long beach. Closest to the water is **Thaweewong Rd.,** full of expensive seafood restaurants, outdoor bars, and souvenir stalls. One block east, **Song Roi Pee Rd.** (known as **Rat-U-Thit Rd.** north of the Bangla Rd. intersection) offers more restaurants and Hat Patong's few budget hotels. Phuket's raciest bars cluster in alleyways off **Bangla Rd.,** which connects Rat-U-Thit and Thaweewong Rd.

ACCOMMODATIONS AND FOOD. Accommodations in Hat Patong are Phuket's most expensive—stay here only if you plan to do some serious late-night partying or have extra baht to burn. Partiers without rooms will have to fork over 200-300฿ for a taxi back to Phuket Town. The cheapest places to stay are on Rat-U-Thit Rd. on the north side of the beach. Popular with backpackers is the friendly **PS2 Bungalow,** 21 Rat-U-Thit Rd., a 15min. walk from the Bangla Rd. intersection. The large, squeaky-clean bungalows are decked-out with windows and microfridges. (☎342 207. Singles/doubles 600-800฿ in high season, 400-600฿ in low season, with A/C and TV 900-1500฿.) Closer to the beach, rooms usually get more expensive and a lot noisier. An exception is the **Chanathip Guest House,** 53/7 Rat-U-Thit Rd., which has bright, comfortable rooms with TV, hot water, and fridges. (☎294 087. Singles/doubles 600฿, with A/C 800฿.) For clean and simple rooms, try **Shamrock Park Inn,** 29 Ratuthit Rd. (☎340 991. Fan rooms 400฿.)

Like everything on Hat Patong, food is generally expensive. The **market** by Chanathip Guest House on Rat-U-Thit Rd. has the cheapest meals. Nearly every restaurant claims to specialize in European and American food. To minimize the risk of an unpleasant surprise, stick to the basics: pizza, pastas, and sandwiches. (Avoid

"Mexican" food at all costs. You'll thank us later.) **The Pizzeria Hut,** on Song Roi Pee Rd., one block south of the Bangla Rd. intersection, serves tasty brick-oven pizzas (100-200฿) in a shaded outdoor patio. (Open daily 11am-11pm.)

ENTERTAINMENT AND NIGHTLIFE. No beach knows how to party like Hat Patong. Night after night, hot-blooded Western lads turn out by the thousands, eager to chat up the pretty, young Thai "waitresses" who smile seductively from the bars on every corner. For pre-party boozing, head to **Molly Malone's Irish Pub,** 68 Thaweewong Rd., toward the south side of the beach underneath KFC. Thai waitstaff aside, you'd swear you'd been teleported straight to Ireland. Guinness and Kilkenny beer on tap, live Irish music, and "traditional pub grub" round out this slick bar. (Open daily 11am-2am.) Once you're ready to pick up (or be picked up), head to the center of the action on the streets off Bangla and Sawatdirak Rd. Dozens of gay venues with names like "Hot Boys" and "Connect Bar" cluster on Rat-U-Thit Rd., while the reknowed **Simon Cabaret,** 8 Sirirat Rd. (☎342 011/5), has a hilarious transvestite extravaganza (7, 9pm). Hat Patong's club scene definitely takes a backseat to the more popular girlie bars. **The Banana Disco,** on Thaweewong Rd. two blocks south of the Bangla Rd. intersection, features two wildly popular levels: a ground floor lounge/restaurant (open 7pm-2am) and an upper floor disco (open 9pm-2am).

THAILAND

HAT KARON AND HAT KATA

Popular with backpackers and package tourists alike, the adjacent beaches of Hat Karon and Hat Kata have the best balance of good nightlife, plentiful dining options, and nice sand. Perhaps most importantly, they are blessfully free of the girlie bars that dominate neighboring Hat Patong. Though Hat Karon and Hat Kata can get crowded, especially the area around Hat Kata's Club Med Beach, the duo is still one of the most pleasant getaways on the island.

ORIENTATION. Hat Karon and Hat Kata are actually three separate beaches. To the north, luxury resorts dot 3km long Hat Karon. To the south, a hilly, rocky cape separates Hat Karon from Hat Kata, which is split into **Hat Kata Noi** and **Hat Kata Yai.** Hat Kata's budget restaurants and hotels are generously sprinkled around **Taina Rd.,** which runs uphill from the beachfront **Patak Rd.** South of the cape, a gargantuan **Club Med** monopolizes the handsome northern half of Hat Kata. Crossing another rocky cape leads to Hat Kata Noi, the most solitary beach of the three.

ACCOMMODATIONS AND FOOD. Most budget accommodations cluster on **Taina Rd.** on the cape separating Hat Karon from Hat Kata. Unfortunately, they're not on the beach. One of the best budget hotels on the island is the Scandinavian-themed **Little Mermaid Guest House** on Taina Rd. near the highway intersection. The four-story multicolored building has rooms with private bathrooms, hot water, phones, and optional fridges and TVs (both 50฿). Two restaurants, three bars, a pool table, a swimming pool and Internet access (2฿ per min.) are provided for general use. (☎330 730. Singles/doubles 345฿, with A/C 445฿.) In the same neighborhood, the small, family-run **Rose Inn** on Taina Rd., closer to the beach has simple, clean rooms. The staff speaks little English. (☎330 582. Singles/doubles 400฿, with A/C 650฿.) Another option is the **Lucky Guest House,** 110/44 Mu 4 Taina Rd., a few meters away from the Rose Inn. It's clean and empty during the off-season, but those "lucky" enough to stay here will have to put up with the rather crotchety staff. (☎330 572. Singles/doubles with bath 350-450฿.)

Both Hat Karon and Hat Kata have a good selection of budget restaurants on **Taipan Rd. The Kwong Seafood Shop** on Taipan Rd. is a no-frills, no-nonsense place to get a good, fast, cheap bite to eat. (Chicken and beef dishes 50-70฿. Seafood dishes 200฿. Open daily 9am-midnight.) At the **Dive Cafe,** 111/25-26 Taina Rd., about one block from the water on the left, divers and beachgoers devour the house specialty, *kai manao* (lemon chicken), for 120฿. (Open daily 9am-11pm.)

ACTIVITIES. For those with the cash, Hat Karon and Hat Kata are perfect for exploring some of the world's best **snorkeling** and **diving** around the Similan and

Racha Islands. Head to PADI-certified **Siam Diving Center,** 121/9 Patak Rd., opposite Dino Park Mini-Golf. Four-day diver certification courses cost 6700฿ for one dive and 8900฿ for two dives, including transport, equipment, and food. Without the course, prices run 1900฿ for one dive and 2400฿ for two dives. Equipment rental is about 700฿ per day. (☎330 967. Open M-Sa 11am-8pm.) **Hat Kata Center's** bar scene offers rowdy excitement after a long day in the sun, while **Dino Park Mini-Golf** provides more innocent fun. (Golf open daily 10am-midnight. 200฿, children 180฿.)

HAT SURIN, HAT NAI YANG, AND AO BANG TAO

Once known to harbor the most beautiful beaches on Phuket, the island's northwestern shore has exploded with luxury resorts over the past decade. Beautiful **Hat Surin** is no exception, but there are some cheaper guest houses closer to the highway. **Tiw-Too Guest House,** 13/11 Srisoonthorn Rd., a 10min. walk from the beach, has exceptionally clean rooms, TVs, refrigerators, and sweet owners—it's easy to feel at home. (☎270 240. Singles with A/C 500฿.) On the southern end of Surin Beach, **Diver's Place** is a beachfront pub with a friendly expat crowd. Diver, who's saved over 90 people over the years, is a good person to ask about the surf. (Beers 60฿.)

With your own food, a towel, and a book, attractive **Ao Bang Tao** makes a nice daytrip, especially between May and July when heavy rains haven't hit yet but crowds have skedaddled. Ao Bang Tao is dominated by two resorts that monopolize access to the water. Squeezed between the two beaches on the road from Surin to Ao Bang Tao is **Bangtao Lagoon Bungalows,** with compact, comfortable huts with a blue patina and marble floors. Ask the bus driver from Phuket Town to drop you off here or you may never find it. (☎324 260. Singles/doubles 400-600฿.)

The National Park of **Hat Nai Yang,** 13km of coconut and rubber trees on the northeastern tip of the island, has kept private developers at bay, although condominium vultures still stalk the park boundaries. In the rainy season, Hat Nai Yang has Phuket's most dangerous rip tides. The **visitors' office** is near the entrance. (☎327 407 or 328 226. Open daily 8:30am-4:30pm.) The only accommodations here are park bungalows on the beach, and popular among Thai vacationers (300-600฿).

HAT KAMALA

Escape to quiet **Hat Kamala** on the way to Hat Surin from Phuket Town (*songthaew* 20฿). There are no luxury hotels, and the beaches are decent. To get to the spotless rooms of **Malinee House,** 74/7 Mu 3, follow the beach road from the south end of the beach until it curves inland; the restaurant/guest house is on the right. An Internet cafe is below. (☎324 094. Singles/doubles in high season 650฿, with A/C 950฿; in low season 350/500฿; cable TV 100฿ extra.)

HAT RAWAI AND AO CHALONG

Squished into the southeastern tip of Phuket Island, Hat Rawai caters mostly to locals, who come here to take a break from fishing and driving duties. The beach's narrow strip of sand and muddy water render it quite unappealing; try its more attractive neighbor **Hat Nai Han.** Both slow down during rainy season. At Hat Rawai, the **Pornmae Bungalows,** 58/1 Wisas Rd., inside the hair salon opposite the central part of the beach, has new, simple rooms with fridges. (☎/fax 381 300. Singles/doubles 300-400฿.)

Pretty Ao Chalong, north of Hat Rawai on the island's southeastern side, is the largest bay on the island. Because of its size and shallow, muddy waters, the bay is primarily used for docking and is unsuitable for swimming. It's a good place to stay if you are involved with or want to learn more about the active Andaman Sea yachting culture. A good place to meet other sailors is **Friendship Beach,** 27/1 Soi Mittrapap, about 2km north of Hat Rawai towards Phuket Town on the southern side of the bay, across from the Phuket Shell Museum. Friendly and relaxed, it has bungalows, a restaurant, Sunday jam sessions, a pool table, cable TV, and Internet (1฿ per min.). The kitchen serves good Thai and Western food. (Spanish omelette 100฿. Bungalows 600฿ high season, 350฿ low season. Open daily 7am-11pm).

KRABI

☎075

The hyped-up town of Krabi is little more than a necessary transit point. Travelers stop by for a few hours while waiting for the ferry to Ko Phi Phi or longtail boat to Hat Rai Lay, killing time by checking email and mingling with other travelers. Though Krabi does offer some accommodation and a side trip to Wat Tham Sua, there's little reason to linger before moving on to the nearby islands and beaches.

THE VIEW FROM ABOVE

The lowdown: A not-so-happening town near some very happening islands.
Gateway cities: Ko Lanta, Krabi, Phuket Town, Trang.
Nearby islands: Ko Phi Phi Don, Ko Phi Phi Ley.
Beaches: Ao Nang, Ao Lo Dalam, Hat Hin Kohn, Hat Phra Nang, Hat Rai Lay, Hat Yao (Long Beach).
Highlights: Rai Lay's limestone cliffs, Phra Nang's Princess Cave, and beautiful Ko Phi Phi Ley, the filming site of *The Beach*.

TRANSPORTATION

Buses: The **bus station** (☎611 804) is 5km outside town. Red *songthaew* run between the bus station and town (every 15min., 7฿). Buses to: **Bangkok** (14hr., 4 per day 7am-7pm, 486-710฿); **Hat Yai** (5hr., every hr. 9am-3:20pm, 173฿); **Phuket** (5hr., every hr. 9am-5pm, 117฿); **Satun** (5hr., 11am and 1pm, with A/C 175฿); **Surat Thani** (4½hr.; every hr. 9:30am-1:30pm; 80฿; A/C 3½hr.; 7, 8, 9, 11:40am, 1pm; 120฿); **Trang** (2½hr., every 2hr. 9am-5pm, 90฿). Private travel agents operate **A/C minivans** to various towns in Thailand and Malaysia.

Ferries: Longtail boats leave from **Chao Fah Pier** on Kongka Rd. for **Hat Rai Lay** (30min., 8am-5pm, 70฿). From the same pier, **express boats** go to **Ko Lanta** (high season only; 2½hr.; 10:30am, 1:30pm; 200฿) and **Ko Phi Phi** (1½hr.; 10am, 2pm; 150฿). Service is irregular during low season. Tourist offices have up-to-date boat schedules.

Local Transportation: Songthaew waiting opposite the City Hotel by the market go to **Ao Nang** (30฿, 50฿ after 5pm), the **Shell Cemetery** (30฿), **Wat Tham Sua** (10฿), and other places near Krabi.

ORIENTATION AND PRACTICAL INFORMATION

Central Krabi is fairly compact and easily navigable by foot. **Utarakit Rd.,** the city's main street, runs parallel to the **Krabi River** and is home to the **post office, telecommunications office, banks, travel agencies,** and **TAT office.** Parallel and one block over, **Maharat Rd.** has shops and cheap eateries. Boats to Hat Rai Lay, Ko Phi Phi, and Ko Lanta leave from **Chao Fah Pier** on **Kongka Rd.,** which branches off Utarakit Rd. and runs along the river.

Tourist Offices: TAT (☎612 740), on Utarakit Rd. Good maps. Open Nov.-May daily 8:30am-4:30pm; closed June-Oct.

Tours: For a small town, Krabi has an obscene number of travel agencies. For boat tickets, go to **PP Family** on Chao Fah Pier, (☎612 463), the company that operates most ferry services from Krabi. Open daily 8am-9pm.

Currency Exchange: Several banks line Utarakit Rd. **Thai Farmers Bank,** 199/201 Utarakit Rd. **24hr. ATM.** Exchange booth open daily 8:30am-4pm.

Markets: A large market sets up across from the City Hotel on Sukhon Rd.

Emergency: ☎191.

Police: ☎611 222. 500m past the post office. Little English spoken.

Medical Service: The **town hospital** (☎611 227), on Utarakit Rd., 2km from town. Some English spoken. No credit cards. **Open 24hr.**

Telephones: Krabi Telecommunications Office (☎612 729), on Utarakit Rd., 5min. past the hospital. Open daily 7am-midnight.

Internet Access: All along Utarakit Rd. in cafes and guest houses (1฿ per min.).

Post Office: 190 Utarakit Rd. (☎611 050), on top of the hill on the left. *Poste Restante.* Open M-F 8:30am-4:30pm, Sa 9am-noon. **Postal code:** 81000.

ACCOMMODATIONS AND FOOD

Krabi has a good selection of budget accommodations, most of which lie one block from the pier along **Utarakit Rd.** Prices below represent high season rates; in the low season rates may be 100-200฿ cheaper.

Chan-Cha-Lay Guest House, 55 Utarakit Rd. (☎620 952), on the slope uphill. The recently-opened guest house is already one of the hippest digs in town, with ultra-clean, bright rooms with showers. Popular restaurant and friendly staff to boot. Singles 200฿; doubles 250฿.

Grand Tower Hotel, 9 Chaofa Rd. (☎621 456), at the intersection with Utarakit Rd. A multiple story hotel, it's not your typical guest house, but it's popular for those waiting for the next ferry. Plain, cheap rooms with double mattresses. Singles 150฿, with bath 300฿, with A/C 500฿; doubles with bath 400฿, with A/C 700฿.

City Hotel, 15/2-3 Sukhon Rd. (☎621 280), between Utarakit Rd. and Maharat Rd. in the heart of downtown. Off the main backpacker drag. Spacious, well-furnished rooms, all with cable TV and phone. Singles/doubles with fan 400฿, with A/C 600-650฿.

Siboya Guest House, 69 Utarakit Rd. (☎611 258). The set up is a bit messy, but the modestly-sized, cheap rooms are cozy with funky, fresh decor. Singles/doubles 170฿.

Pan Guest House, 182 Utarakit Rd. (☎612 555), next to the post office. Cheapest place in town—and it shows. Plain plywood huts are little more than four walls, a ceiling, and a bed. A lovely garden surrounds the huts. Singles/doubles 150฿, with bath 300฿.

Several *farang*-friendly restaurants and cheap food stalls with everything from Thai food to grilled cheese cluster on **Kongka Rd.,** just north of the pier. For a memorable experience, try **Ruenmai Thai** on Maharat Rd., 2km from town past the hospital. This huge outdoor restaurant has tables dispersed amidst jungle-like vegetation. For 60฿, try the blissful coconut cream prawn soup with *pak mieng* or edible ferns with fish. (Open daily 10am-10pm.) Hang out with locals at the **Muslim Restaurant,** 110 Praksa-Uthit Rd., a morning meeting spot for *roti* and coffee (20฿).

THAILAND

SIGHTS

Krabi's most impressive sights is **Wat Tham Sua,** 9km outside town. A working monastery of monks, nuns, and tourists, the wat is best known for its **Tiger Cave.** Legend has it that a large tiger once lived here, and its footsteps don the wat's entrance (donation requested). Outside, stairs by the rear of the monastery lead 30-45min. up the mountain to a pair of **Buddha's footprints.** *Songthaew* from the Sukon St. market drop you off at an access road 2km from the wat (15min., 10฿.) Otherwise, walk or take a motorcycle taxi (5min., 10฿) to the entrance.

NEAR KRABI

The world-renowned beaches near Krabi are some of Thailand's most beautiful and popular, so if you're planning on staying at Ao Nang or Hat Rai Lay, it's best to bypass Krabi and head straight for the beaches. Locals heartily embrace the arrival of sun- and sand-lovers, mostly for their wallets. A regional festival in November even celebrates the coming of a prosperous tourist season.

HAT RAI LAY AND HAT PHRA NANG ☎075

With spectacular limestone cliffs dropping onto sand beaches and luminous, turquoise waters, Hat Rai Lay has become a haven for both climbers and beach lovers. It has developed into a climbing mecca of sorts, and climbing schools all over the beach welcome rookies and veterans. For those who prefer their feet on the ground, Hat Rai Lay also offers hiking trails, a mellow nightlife, and pretty beaches, while Hat Phra Nang's caves provide hours of audacious exploring.

ORIENTATION. Hat Rai Lay is actually two beaches, **Hat Rai Lay East** and **Hat Rai Lay West,** which occupy opposite sides of a jutting peninsula. The only way to get to Hat Rai Lay is by **longtail boat** docking at Hat Rai Lay East from Ao Nang (40฿) or Krabi (70฿). This side of the peninsula has some budget accommodations, climbing schools, mangrove trees, and the heart-stopping duo of Hat Rai Lay East and **Hat Phra Nang.** To get to Hat Phra Nang from Hat Rai Lay East, with your back to the boats, turn left and walk to the end of the beach; a dirt path to your right snakes to the limestone cliffs and crystal waters of Hat Phra Nang. Hat Rai Lay West can be reached easily by cutting through Sand Sea Bungalow or Rai Lay Bay Bungalows.

ACCOMMODATIONS AND FOOD. Finding good deals on Hat Rai Lay can be more difficult than scaling its toughest climb. Prices listed reflect high season (Nov.-May) rates. De facto segregation keeps backpackers on Hat Rai Lay East. **Ya-Ya Bungalow,** the most popular among budget travelers, has the best off-beach location and a lively restaurant. (☎622 593. Singles with bath 450฿; doubles with bath 550-750฿.) On the northern end of Hat Rai Lay East, **Viewpoint Bungalow** has the only Internet access on the beach and modern bungalows with enormous windows that put the "view" in Viewpoint. (☎01 228 4115. Singles with bath 400฿; doubles 500-800฿.) **Diamond Bungalow** has the cheapest accommodations on the island. (Singles/doubles 350฿, with bath 500฿, with A/C 1200-1500฿).

Hat Rai Lay West has more upscale accommodations. **Rai Lay Village** (☎612 476) charges twice as much as Hat Rai Lay East bungalows for nicer bathrooms and landscaping. Next door, **Rai Lay Bay Bungalows** has a great beachside bar (Carlsberg 60฿) and A/C rooms with fridges and enormous baths. (☎01 622 330. Singles/doubles 1200-1600฿, depending on season.) Extremely expensive **Dusit Rayavadee Resort** dominates Hat Phra Nang. It's much more practical to find cheaper accommodation on Hat Rai Lay East and daytrip it to Hat Phra Nang.

After a hard day of climbing, many travelers flock to **Coco Restaurant** on the northern part of Hat Rai Lay East for tasty Thai dishes, including chicken wrapped in steamed leaves (60฿). **Cholay Pancakes,** in a booth outside Ya-Ya Bungalow, serves delicious *roti* (light bread) for 15-30฿. (Open daily 9am-midnight.)

SIGHTS AND ENTERTAINMENT. The Rai Lay beaches and environs have become the rock climbing capital of Southeast Asia, and several rock climbing schools have popped up to meet the demand. Prices are the same everywhere. **Krabi Rock Climbing** on Hat Rai Lay East is well-known for its friendly staff. (☎676 0642. Half-day course 800฿, 1-day course 1800฿, 3-day course 5000฿. **Hot Rock Climbing** (☎01 677 3727), next to CoCo Restaurant on Hat Rai Lay East, is also popular. Don't let inexperience intimidate you—tons of others are first-timers too.

Adventure closer to sea-level awaits you on Hat Phra Nang. Extending beyond the water, dagger-like stalagmites protect **Princess Cave,** which can be explored by land or sea with a flashlight. About halfway down the dirt path to Hat Phra Nang from Hat Rai Lay East, another dirt path leads to a few mountain viewpoints and a lagoon best visited at high tide. Bring sturdy footwear, expendable clothing (especially during the wet season), and companions for the challenging climb to the top. Closer to East Rai Lay Beach, a hidden path leads to the popular and appropriately named **Diamond Cave,** whose walls sparkle with the precious stone.

Nights on Hat Rai Lay bring together opposite tourist factions: beach bums and hard-core climbing/hiking/diving types. Everyone achieves equal party status under the moon, relaxing at **Yaya's Bar, Last Bar,** or the **beachfront,** where fire dancers sometimes light up the beach to pulsing music.

AO NANG

Ao Nang's accessibility by car gives it a completely different atmosphere than either secluded Rai Lay or Phrang Nga. With brightly colored shops and beachfront hotels, it has a very pleasant holiday feel. The bustle dies out past the Phra Nang Inn. From here, you can walk down a dirt road into forested seclusion. Alternately, rent a bike as an escape and zoom your way through rice paddies, villages, and the ubiquitous waving kids.

On the road that runs past the beach, there are moneychangers, a **minimarket,** restaurants, and **tour offices.** For **police,** dial ☎611 222 (**emergency** ☎191). White *songthaew* from Krabi to Ao Nang (and Hat Noppharat Thara) leave from Pattana Rd. opposite the New Hotel (every 15min. or when full, 20฿).

Sea Canoe Krabi (☎612 740), near Gift's Bungalows, offers half-day (500-800฿) and full-day (800-1200฿) self-paddled trips along the coast as well as rental equipment. A guided trip including meals, fruit, and water costs 1200-1600฿. Rent **mountain bikes** (30฿ per hr.) at **Ao Nang Adventure Travel and Tour** on the corner before the main shops coming from Krabi. Ask for a map. **Nosy Parker's Elephant Trekking and River Camp** (☎637 464) offers elephant treks (700฿) and half-day tours (1600฿).

Blue Bayou, in the quiet outskirts of town, has kayak rentals (200฿ per 2hr.) and a volleyball court. The restaurant serves Thai and Western cuisine. (☎637 148. Single/double bungalows in high season with fan 350-500฿, with A/C 750฿; in low season 200-400/500฿.) If you happen to hit Ao Nang in the low season, fabulous rates abound. One such steal is **For You House,** 245/11-12 Moo 2, which has hotel-style rooms with A/C, minibar, satellite TV, and hot showers. Get off the *songthaew* at Henry's Collection and walk behind it. (☎637. High season 600฿, low season 300฿.) Other cheap places are in the same row as For You.

Last Cafe, at the end of Ao Nang Beach, after the road becomes a dirt trail, is only open in the high season (muesli with fruit and yogurt 30฿; omelettes 40฿; Thai noodle soup 30฿; open daily 6:30am-midnight). The ideally situated **Poda Restaurant,** in Felix Phra Nang Inn, in the circular building, is an alternative to bungalow basics. The green curry soup with shrimp is exceptional. (Open daily 7am-10pm.) **Azzurra Ristorante-Pizzeria** cooks homemade pasta, fresh bread, and focaccia (80฿) with cheese, tomatoes, and lettuce. (Open daily 7am-11pm.)

KO PHI PHI DON ☎075

The secret is out. Beautiful Ko Phi Phi Don—once an un-touristed island dotted with swaying palms, shimmering turquoise waters, and isolated spits of sand—is now *the* destination for backpackers in southern Thailand. Paradoxically, it was the filming of *The Beach* on nearby Ko Phi Phi Ley that helped transform the once ignored island into a hub of backpacker activity. Instead of the peace and solace promised by the film, however, travelers will find street after street of restaurants, travel agencies, and guest houses. Yes, the beaches are beautiful, but, to be sure, none of them is *The Beach.* It's too late for that.

NO MORE, WE PROMISE. *Let's Go* promises not to mention *The Beach* again in its coverage of Ko Phi Phi Don and Ko Phi Phi Ley to respect the wishes of travelers as sick of the reference as we are. Yes, *The Beach* was filmed here. Please get over it–we have.

TRANSPORTATION

To get to Ko Phi Phi Don (generally known as Ko Phi Phi), go through either **Ko Lanta, Krabi,** or **Phuket.** Ferries depart regularly from Ko Phi Phi to the above destinations, except during the low season, when ferry service may be irregular. From **Ton Sai Pier,** boats head to: **Ko Lanta** (2hr.; 11:30am, 2pm; 200฿); **Krabi** (1½hr.; 9am, 1:30pm; 200฿); **Phuket** (1½hr.; 9am, 2:30pm; 250฿). Boats to uninhabited **Ko Phi Phi Ley** depart from the pier and can also be hired independently from Ao Thon Sai travel agencies. Hire **longtail boats** for more remote beaches.

ORIENTATION AND PRACTICAL INFORMATION

Shaped like a lop-sided dumbbell, Ko Phi Phi is small and devoid of vehicular traffic; it's easy to walk the entire island. The main port of call is pretty **Ao Thon Sai Bay,** nestled in the narrow part of the island, where travelers come to check email and make travel plans. On the other side of the island, beautiful **Ao Lo Dalam** has several bungalows. Smaller, less developed beaches ring the island's outer peninsulas, the most popular of which is **Hat Yao (Long Beach),** east of Ao Thon Sai.

Travel Agencies: The **TAT** office in Krabi serves Ko Phi Phi. **Ao Thon Sai travel agencies** arrange trips to Ko Phi Phi Ley and boat/train/bus combos to Bangkok and Malaysia.

Currency Exchange: For best rates, get cash before heading to Ko Phi Phi. The **Siam Commercial Bank** in Ao Thon Sai exchanges cash and gives credit card advances. Open daily 9:30am-7:30pm. Travel agents have poor rates.

Emergency: ☎191.

Tourist Police: Straight off the pier in Ao Thon Sai. Provides some tourist information. English spoken. Erratic hours. **Police booth** past the Chao Khao Lodge in Ao Thon Sai.

Medical Services: Pi Pi Hospital (☎622 151), in Ao Thon Sai, to the left of the pier. Basic medical services. Some English spoken. Open daily 8:30am-noon and 1-4:30pm.

Telephones: Private travel agencies in Ao Thon Sai offer expensive connections.

Internet Access: Plentiful all over Ao Thon Sai. Type fast–it's expensive. 3฿ per min.

THAILAND

ACCOMMODATIONS

Ko Phi Phi's bungalows are plentiful but fluctuate in price and quality between high and low seasons. Generally, rooms are cheaper around the pier and isolated beaches. It pays to explore the outer rims of the island, where fewer mainstream backpackers venture. Accommodations are listed by beach.

AO LO DALAM AND AO THON SAI. The best place for thrifty travelers is Ao Thon Sai's pier area, where loads of fly-by-night travel agencies offer cheap accommodations. It's far from the beach but conveniently located to shops and restaurants. Popular on the island, **Charlie Resort** has clean bungalows on beachfront property. Bungalows in the back are a bit noisier (600-1000฿). **Chong Khao Lodge,** between the pier and Ao Lo Dalam Bay, has plain plywood bungalows with crusty squat toilets and spigots scattered amidst litter and clucking chickens. The restaurant shows flicks. It's one of the cheapest on the island—hence, a backpacker favorite. (Singles 200฿; doubles 300-400฿.) Across from Ao Thon Sai, Ao Lo Dalam's handsome crescent-shaped bay is good for swimming and sunbathing.

HAT HIN KOHN. Just southeast of Ao Thon Sai, a path by a rocky hill leads to flat Hat Hin Kohn, a long stretch of sand generously sprinkled with bungalows. The water and sand conditions are decent but far from the island's best. **Andaman Guest House** has rows of new rooms that are plain but fairly clean. (Singles/doubles 500-600฿.) The staff are eager to recruit backpackers from the similarly-named but more professional **Andaman Resort** at the end of the beach. Clean, white bungalows occupy a quiet spot by the island's sole primary school. (Singles/doubles 850฿.)

HAT YAO (LONG BEACH). Known commonly as Long Beach, Hat Yao's good mix of budget accommodations complement its pleasant beach conditions. Several walk here from Ao Thon Sai by continuing past Hat Kin Kohn through some rocky jungle, but the 30-45min. walk is a bit tedious. Longtail boats (40฿) from Ao Thon Sai's pier are more convenient. The most wallet-friendly accommodation is the friendly, ex-pat run **Long Beach Resort,** offering little more than four walls surrounding a bed, but at least it's with a smile. (☎612 217. Singles/doubles 150-350฿.)

FOOD AND ENTERTAINMENT

Homesick tourists munch on faux Italian, Mexican, and Swedish fare in restaurants all over the island. Take your pick. The **Lemongrass Restaurant** off the main drag in Ao Thon Sai is one of the only places to get good Thai food. (Rice dishes 60฿. Curries 70-80฿. Open daily 9am-11pm.) By night, Ao Thon Sai transforms into a surprising hotbed of nightlife activity. Backpackers wander about, mingling more as alcohol makes the world seem gentler. The self-explanatory **Rolling Stoned Bar** reigns over the party scene, spewing chill music and good times until sunrise. The similarly-themed **Reggae Bar** has a large dance floor and a Thai boxing ring featuring nightly matches (starting around 10pm).

DAYTRIP FROM KO PHI PHI: KO PHI PHI LEY

Four years ago, they filmed a movie on Ko Phi Phi Ley. Struggling to cope with the post-Hollywood success tourist demand, the island has since become the battleground between corporate filmmakers and environmental groups, which claim that the island's delicate environment has been irreversibly damaged by the planting of coconut palms and beach digging that occurred during filming. Politics aside, the real reason to visit the island is for the natural beauty that made it such a spectacular backdrop in the first place.

Getting to Ko Phi Phi Ley from Ko Phi Phi Don usually involves some sort of organized tour activity. Plenty of Ao Thon Sai agencies arrange daytrips to the island, individual longtail boat tours around the island cost less. Tours generally include a stop at famous **Ao Maya,** the location of the filming, as well as a look at the prehistoric paintings in the **Viking Cave** in the northeast point of the island.

KO LANTA

Two hours by boat from Krabi, Ko Lanta is actually closer to Trang (see below). Krabi, however, holds a monopoly on transport and tours for now. Boats from Krabi go to Ko Lanta's **Ban Saa Laadaan Pier** daily during the high season (2½hr., 10:30am and 1:30pm, returns 8am, 150฿). Boats also leave from Ko Phi Phi for Ko Lanta (1½hr., 10am-1pm, 150฿). Otherwise, minivans depart year-round from Krabi and connect by ferry to Ko Lanta (2hr.; 11am, 1, 4pm; 150฿).

Ko Lanta is an ideal escape from tourist-plagued Ko Phi Phi. Low season makes the island a ghost town, ideal for those seeking cheap solitude. **Golden Bay Cottages** offers comfortable, spacious accommodations with huge price swings depending on the season. (In high season cottages with fan 800฿, with A/C 1500฿; in low season 100฿, 300-600฿.) **Khlong Dao Beach** and **Long Beach** are the main beaches in the north; **Kantiang Bay** and **Khlong Jak Bay** greet travelers headed south.

INLAND

The **Khao Nawe Choochee Lowland Forest** is one of the last remaining forests of its kind in Thailand. Among the 290-plus bird species that nest in the forest is *Pitta gurneyi*, a brightly colored, ground-dwelling bird of which only 150 remain. The **Thung Tieo Nature Trail,** a 2.7km path, eases through some of Thailand's most lush and undisturbed slices of nature. Bring your swimming gear and hop into the natural pool or hot spring for relaxation. To get to the trail motorbike from Krabi or take a *songthaew* to **Khlong Thom. Mr. Koyou** at the **Krabi Bird Club,** 24 Phetkasem Rd., will haul tourists around in his pickup truck (300฿). Contact him by calling the park's tourist office (☎622 124); TAT officials can also track him down. If hiring a motorcycle taxi from Khlong Thom (100฿), arrange return transport.

VIETNAM

DONG

US$1 = 15,043.00Đ	10,000Đ = US$0.67
CDN$1 = 9736.57Đ	10,000Đ = CDN$1.03
EURO€1 = 13,697.90Đ	10,000Đ = EURO€0.73
UK£1 = 21,841.40Đ	10,000Đ = UK£0.46
IR£1 = 17,385.10Đ	10,000Đ = IR£0.58
AUS$1 = 7971.24Đ	10,000Đ = AUS$1.26
NZ$1 = 6629.92Đ	10,000Đ = NZ$1.52
ZAR1 = 1804.28Đ	10,000Đ = ZAR5.57

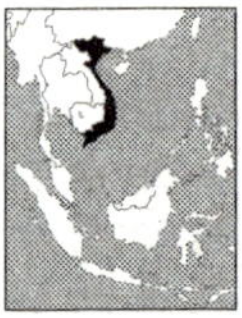

PHONE CODE **Country Code:** 84. **International dialing prefix:** 00.

Whether drifting along the slow-moving Mekong or battling the rush of motorbikes in Hanoi, travelers are surrounded by Vietnam's hardworking and friendly people. Vietnam prides itself on its unique heritage and strong survival instinct; after centuries of invasion and forcible influence by the Chinese, French, and Japanese, Vietnamese culture is anything but simple. Its history of struggle against imperialism and desire for independence has created a culture unique from its Southeast Asian neighbors. Vietnamese soil has hosted over a dozen wars, and 25 years after the Second Indochina War, Vietnam slowly opened its doors with a self-confidence borne from its earlier sacrifices. For the visitor, understanding the nuances of Vietnamese culture is not easy. The endless chain of cookie-cutter mini-hotels and utilitarian state-run establishments adds a certain sense of monotony. Tourist cafes whisk visitors around on sputtering minibuses, usually providing only spoon-fed doses of local color and recurrent run-ins with fellow travelers. A truer taste of contemporary Vietnam hides in alley-way eateries, *bia hoi* stalls, and amid the plastic furniture of streetside cafes. Few experiences rival the spontaneous smile and wave inviting one in for a glass of Bia Hanoi (a local beer) or the sound of the busy street markets coming to life. Those who search for this Vietnamese essence will most definitely be rewarded with a glimpse of a society that's proud of its past but has its eyes locked firmly on the future.

FACTS AND FIGURES

Official Name: Socialist Republic of Vietnam.
Government: One-party rule by the Vietnamese Communist Party.
Capital: Hanoi.
Land Area: 330,363 sq. km
Geography: Borders China, Laos, and Cambodia. River systems: Red River in the north, Mekong River in the south.
Climate: Rainy (low season) May-Oct., dry (high season) Nov.-Apr.
Population: 81,022,000.
Major Cities: Đà Nẵng, Hồ Chí Minh City.
Religion: Mahayana Buddhism, Catholicism, Taoism, Islam, Hoa Hao, Cao Dai.
Average Income Per Capita: US$320.
Major Exports: Textiles, petroleum, rice, coffee, agricultural products.

LIFE AND TIMES

THE PEOPLE OF VIETNAM

Ethnic Vietnamese (also called **Kinh**) constitute 90% of the population. The **Chinese** (Hoa), concentrated in the urban south, are the largest minority. **Chàm, Khmer,** and other **hill tribes** inhabit the northern and central regions. Vietnam War's heavy death tolls dramatically shifted the demographics of Vietnam; today, two-thirds of Vietnam's population is under the age of 25.

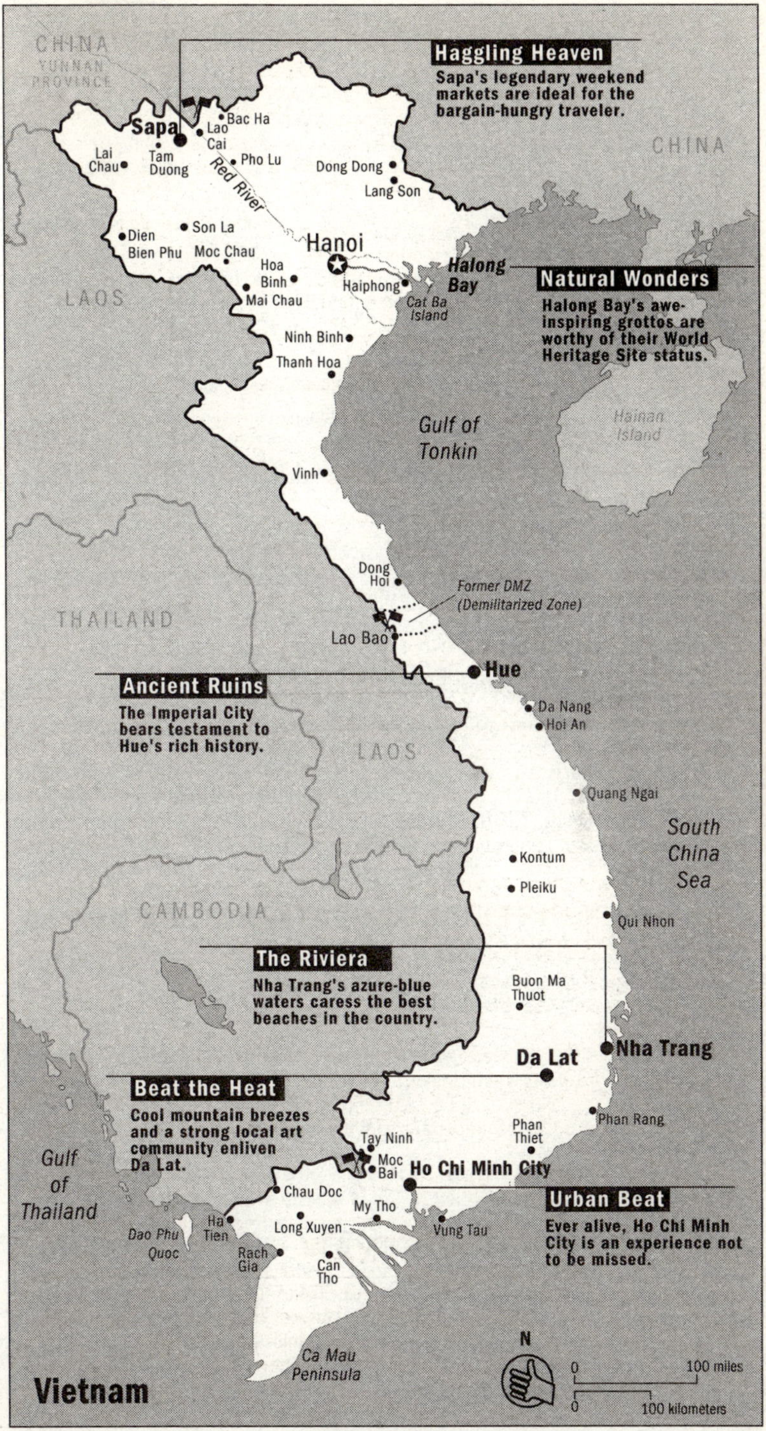

Haggling Heaven
Sapa's legendary weekend markets are ideal for the bargain-hungry traveler.
Natural Wonders
Halong Bay's awe-inspiring grottos are worthy of their World Heritage Site status.
Ancient Ruins
The Imperial City bears testament to Hue's rich history.
The Riviera
Nha Trang's azure-blue waters caress the best beaches in the country.
Beat the Heat
Cool mountain breezes and a strong local art community enliven Da Lat.
Urban Beat
Ever alive, Ho Chi Minh City is an experience not to be missed.
CHINA
YUNNAN PROVINCE
CHINA
Sapa
Bac Ha
Lao Cai
Lai Chau
Tam Duong
Pho Lu
Red River
Dong Dong
Lang Son
Dien Bien Phu
Son La
Moc Chau
Hanoi
Hoa Binh
Mai Chau
Halong Bay
Haiphong
Cat Ba Island
LAOS
Ninh Binh
Thanh Hoa
Gulf of Tonkin
Hainan Island
Vinh
Dong Hoi
Former DMZ (Demilitarized Zone)
THAILAND
Lao Bao
Hue
Da Nang
Hoi An
LAOS
Quang Ngai
South China Sea
Kontum
Pleiku
Qui Nhon
CAMBODIA
Buon Ma Thuot
Nha Trang
Da Lat
Phan Rang
Phan Thiet
Tay Ninh
Moc Bai
Ho Chi Minh City
Gulf of Thailand
Chau Doc
My Tho
Ha Tien
Long Xuyen
Vung Tau
Dao Phu Quoc
Rach Gia
Can Tho
Ca Mau Peninsula
N
0
100 miles
0
100 kilometers
Vietnam

VIETNAM

HIGHLIGHTS OF VIETNAM

CULTURAL HERITAGE. Hanoi (p. 826) is a 1000-year-old city steeped in history and tradition. Hill tribe cultures are the chief attractions of **Mai Châu** (p. 854) and **Sapa** (p. 846) in the northwest. The **Perfume Pagoda** (p. 838) ranks as one of the region's most unique shrines. Gentle **Huế** (p. 859) stewards an array of palaces and tombs. **Hội An's** (p. 877) ornate Chinese architecture is some of the best-preserved in Southeast Asia.

URBAN BEAT. Hồ Chí Minh City (p. 888) flaunts a vibrant market culture, colonial architecture, and extravagant nightlife.

BEACHES. Nha Trang (p. 881), "the Vietnamese Riviera," features infamous pleasure cruises and fine food. **Phú Quốc Island** (p. 910) remains tourist-free...for now.

NATURAL WONDERS. Treks in the northwest around **Sapa** (p. 846) or the rugged **Central Highlands** (p. 877) rival the best that Thailand has to offer. **Hạ Long Bay's** (p. 842) cool green waters and over 3000 islets capture a calm beauty.

HANGING OUT. Đà Lạt (p. 884) boasts cool vibes, an eclectic avant garde scene, and friendly locals. The livin' is easy on the Mekong in **Cần Thơ** (p. 900) and **Châu Đốc** (p. 905). Remote **Hà Tiên** (p. 908) is likely the most mellow town on earth.

Long, long ago A serpent and a fairy made a little love and did a little dance

11BC Chinese armies capture Nam Việt,

40AD Trưng sisters defeat Han

939 Đại Việt established

1009 Lý Thái Tổ establishes the Lý Dynasty

12c Lý invade Champa to the south, loses Champa to Trần; Trần loses Champa to Chinese

13-14c Chinese Ming Dynasty gains control, destroys all things Vietnamese

HISTORY

PREHISTORY

—Green eggs and Hùng

According to legend, the Vietnamese descended from the union of a sea serpent named Lạc Long Quân and Âu Cơ, an immortal fairy. Âu Cơ laid 100 eggs, 50 of which she took with her to the mountains, leaving the other 50 in the lowlands with Lạc Long Quân. The descendants were the Hùng kings, who founded the Văn Lang Kingdom in 2789 BC and are considered the first incarnation of modern-day Vietnam.

CHINESE OCCUPATION (111 BC–1600S AD)

—Can we please be our own country now, Mr. Chairman? Please?

The Chinese began their quest to acquire Vietnam in the 2nd century BC when Han armies captured Nam Việt. Power shifted back and forth until 939 AD, when Ngô Quyền defeated the Chinese army and founded the independent state of **Đại Việt.**

THE LØ-TR<N PERIOD (1009–1400)

Đại Việt was ruled by the **Lý Dynasty,** which established its capital at Thăng Long (Hanoi). During their reign, Chinese influence further waned, and young scholars mirrored former Vietnamese heros. The Lý kings invaded the kingdom of **Champa,** but their victory was short-lived, as Trần rulers from farther south claimed central Vietnam. The Trần, however, also soon lost what they had just won, and the country fell back under Chinese control, who tried to eradicate all vestiges of Vietnamese civilization and enslaved the population.

THE L^ DYNASTY (1428–1776)

In 1428, Lê Lợi, a Thanh Hóa aristocrat, and Nguyễn Trãi, a brilliant military strategist, drove out the Chinese and founded the Lê Dynasty, which instituted a highly centralized state founded upon Confucian principles. The 37-year reign of **Lê Thánh Tông** marked the apex of the territorial expansion of Đại Việt. The long struggle with Champa for supremacy of the central coast ended in 1471, when the Việt sacked the Chàm capital.

CIVIL WAR AND THE TÂY S£N REBELLION (1788–1802)

Modern-day Vietnam was briefly unified under Đại Việt when **Nguyễn Huệ** and his brothers capitalized on widespread peasant discontent to spark the **Tây So'n Rebellion,** which swept the Nguyễn and Trịnh lords. After crushing a Chinese army dispatched to prop up the last of the Lê Dynasty rulers, Nguyễn Huệ declared himself emperor, taking the name Quang Trung. Hope for independence lasted only briefly as **Nguyễn Anh,** later named Gia Long, took over the throne and reinstated Chinese culture through a retrenchment of Confucian values.

CONTACT WITH THE WEST AND COLONIALISM (1863–1925)

–Actually, can we have the Chinese back?

The first Westerners to visit Vietnam were the Portuguese, who established a trading center at Faifo (Hội An). Missionaries and Jesuits, never far behind, began proselytizing in northern and central Vietnam. Among them was Alexander de Rhodes, a Portuguese priest who devised a system of transliterating the Vietnamese language into Latin characters, an early version of today's quốc ngữ (national language) script.

The Portuguese presence didn't last long, however, and the next encounter with the West occurred almost 300 years later. France's interest in Indochina lay in trade, natural resources, and a chance to compete with Britain's rapidly expanding Asian empire. The fateful decision to colonize Vietnam was finally made by Napoleon III in 1857 in response to the execution of some French missionaries. By 1867 the French had seized the entire Mekong Delta region, and by the mid-1880s, the French took the entire country and divided it into three administrative units: Cochinchina (the Mekong Delta region), Annam (the center), and Tonkin (the north). Only Cochinchina was an official colony; Annam and Tonkin, along with Laos and Cambodia, were ruled as protectorates.

The French *mission civilistrice,* as they euphemistically dubbed their colonial endeavor, was anything but civil. Landless tenancy skyrocketed in the south as ownership became concentrated in the hands of wealthy landlords. In Annam and Tonkin, traditionally much poorer than southern Vietnam, peasants were forced to work on rubber plantations. Apologists for the colonial regime claimed that the French made great strides in the areas of medicine and education. In reality, only one doctor was available for every 50,000 Vietnamese, and educational reforms were largely cosmetic. Literacy rates actually declined during the colonial period, and only an estimated 10% of all school-age children received education.

1428
Lê Dynasty defeats Ming, establishes Confucian state

1471
Lê Thánh Tông sacks Thăng Long and defeats the Champas

1460-97
Đai Việt expands

17c
Nguyễn Huệ unites all of Đai Việt

1790
Nguyễn Anh comes to power; brings back Chinese influences

1857
French ships sail into Vietnam

1867-80
French gain control of entire Mekong Delta and then entire country

19c
French landlords exploit Vietnamese

1920s
Resistance movements grow

1930
Hồ Chí Minh establishes Indochinese Communist Party

1941
Vietnam Independence League formed

1941
Japanese annex Indochina, place Vietnamese government in charge

1944
Việt Minh leads August Revolution

1945
Vietnam gains independence

1945
First Indochina War

1954
French defeated at Điện Biên Phủ

1955
Geneva Convention, division of Vietnam

Late 1950s
Ngô Đình Diệm rules South Vietnam

Early 1960s
US involvement increases as North Vietnam allies with USSR

1963
Diệm assassinated

1964-66
North Vietnam supports NLF infiltration into the south

1965
US officially enters Second Indochina War; bombs the north

1968
NLF forces launch Tet Offensive

1972
Christmas bombings

1973
Paris Peace Accords finally end war

1975
North Vietnamese enter Saigon, form Socialist Republic of Vietnam

NATIONALISM AND THE REVOLUTIONARY MOVEMENT (1920–45)

–Parties of the "right" kind: the rise of communism.

By the 1920s, a new generation of young Vietnamese, steeped in the tradition of the French Revolution and the writings of Locke and Rousseau, assumed control of a rising nationalist movement. In 1930, **Hồ Chí Minh** founded the **Indochinese Communist Party (ICP),** which helped instigate a series of violent uprisings in the central provinces of Nghệ An and Hà Tĩnh; both were brutally suppressed by the French. In the early 40s, the communists shifted from a platform of class struggle to a more moderate approach that emphasized independence; the **Vietnam Independence League (Việt Minh)** was established in 1941. That same year, the Japanese gained permission to occupy Indochina militarily, hastily deposing the French and placing an ill-prepared Vietnamese government in charge.

THE FIRST INDOCHINA WAR AND ITS AFTERMATH (1946–65)

–Independence, partition and war: three decades of bad news begin.

Power struggles began with the largely peaceful August Revolution, in which the Việt Minh forces occupied most of the country. The culmination of the Việt Minh anti-colonial movement occurred on September 2, 1945, when Hồ Chí Minh read Vietnam's **Declaration of Independence** in Hanoi's Ba Đình Square. The French were not content to watch their empire slip away, however, and in October they drove the Việt Minh out of south Vietnam. After a year of failed negotiations, the First Indochina War officially began. For most of the bloody eight-year struggle, Việt Minh forces dominated the mountainous regions along the Lao and Chinese borders, while the French controlled the Red River Delta and the major population centers. In the spring of 1954, Việt Minh forces defeated the French at **Điện Biên Phủ,** an isolated valley in the northwest. Humiliated, the French agreed to begin a peace process.

At the Geneva Convention, both sides agreed to an interim compromise and partitioned Vietnam along the 17th Parallel. Plans were drawn up calling for national elections to reunify the country two years after the treaty. In the meantime, the communists gained control of the north, and a coalition of non-communists came to power in the south. The Republic of Vietnam (South Vietnam) became an American client-state ruled by the dictatorial Catholic Ngô Đình Diệm, who refused to hold the elections agreed upon at the Geneva Convention. In fall 1963, Diệm's own generals assassinated him in a coup and General Nguyễn Văn Thiệu seized power. The Democratic Republic of Vietnam (DRV) in the north sought to build a socialist state, carrying out a disastrous land reform campaign in the late 1950s. Hanoi maintained good relations with both the USSR and China, and received military and economic aid from both.

In the early 1960s, things began to heat up as the north gave support to the popular National Liberation Front of South Vietnam (NLF)—guerrilla forces in the South. The NLF was modeled on the Việt Minh, with front organizations accommodating women, students, and peasants. The fighting arm of the NLF, known as the Việt Cộng (pejorative slang meaning Vietnamese Communist), with military aid from the DRV (in the north), marched down the Hồ Chí Minh Trail through Laos and Cambodia into southern Vietnam. The US, viewing the accelerated wave of Việt Cộng violence through a Cold War anti-communist lens, began to increase its presence in the south.

1976
War continues, conflict with the Khmer Rouge

1979
Foreign relations weaken after a brief war with China

1986
"Renewal" reforms sweep the country

1990
Vietnamese forces leave Cambodia

1995
Relations with US normalized; Vietnam joins ASEAN

THE SECOND INDOCHINA WAR (1965–75)

–The new sibling rivalry: Vietnamese and Jane Fonda take on Big Brother.

Known in Vietnam as the "American War," the Second Indochina War marked the pinnacle of destruction and violence on Vietnamese soil. The US officially entered the war in 1965, when President Lyndon Johnson approved regular bombings of North Vietnam and deployed American troops to the south. By 1968, half a million US troops were fighting in South Vietnam. During the first part of 1968, NLF forces launched the **Tet Offensive,** during which they attacked more than 100 cities and military bases over the course of the Vietnamese New Year (early February). Although a military defeat, the bloody offensive was a propaganda victory for Hanoi and fueled American dissatisfaction with the war. The US stepped up bombing campaigns against the north, culminating in the 1972 **Christmas bombings,** an attempt to force the Vietnamese to come to the negotiating table. Without popular support to sustain the conflict, the US terminated active participation in the war with the **1973 Paris Peace Accords.** On April 30, 1975, North Vietnamese tanks rolled into Saigon and reunited the country under communist rule.

THE SOCIALIST REPUBLIC OF VIETNAM (1975–98)

–Uncle Ho becomes a lot like Chairman Ho.

The decade following the end of the war was one of the darkest in modern Vietnamese history. More than one-seventh of the population had been wounded or killed in the war, and millions were left homeless. Immediately after the established the **Socialist Republic of Vietnam (SRV),** the Vietnamese began a protracted war with the Khmer Rouge in Cambodia. Worsening relations with Beijing climaxed in a brief but destructive border war with China in 1979. South Vietnam's once prodigious agricultural production declined precipitously. In the north, conditions approached famine. Crippled by a US-led embargo, the SRV became dependent on aid from the former Soviet Union.

In 1986, at the historic **8th Party Congress,** the Communist Party approved sweeping economic reforms, dubbed **Đổi Mới (Renewal).** Frightened by events in the former Soviet Union and by the Tiananmen Square pro-democracy uprising in China, the Vietnamese Politburo sought to grant the Vietnamese economic freedom while maintaining a tight grip on political power. Since Đổi Mới, Hanoi has pursued a foreign policy aimed at reintegrating the country into regional and global affairs. Vietnam's withdrawal from Cambodia in 1990 cleared the way for better relations with its Southeast Asian neighbors. On July 11, 1995, Vietnam normalized relations with the US and joined the Association of Southeast Asian Nations (ASEAN) 17 days later.

VIETNAM TODAY

Vietnam stands at a crossroad. While the first 10 years of Đổi Mới have brought impressive results, talk of "the next Asian Tiger" now appears to have been grossly premature. The government has been reluctant to push economic reforms too far, especially in the wake of the region's recent economic crisis. While the January 1998 Politburo reshuffle brought two pro-reform officials to power—President Trần Đức Lương and Prime Minister Phan Văn Khải—conservative elements within the Politburo (led by the military) have succeeded in keeping reforms in check. A series of demonstrations in Thái Bình and Đồng Nai provinces over local government corruption prompted President Lương to call for the elimination of "immoral and incapable officials." The response is part of a nationwide effort to reduce corruption, rife within government and businesses.

In November 2000, US President Bill Clinton visited Hanoi, the first trip a US president has made to a reunified Vietnam. The US began crafting new relations to its former adversary when President Clinton lifted the trade embargo from Vietnam in 1994. Two years later, the US embassy in Hanoi reopened, and diplomatic relations slowly resumed. Even with other foreign investors taking interest in Vietnam, the average income remains only about US$1 a day. Several human rights activists in Vietnam currently push for democracy.

CULTURE AND CUSTOMS

BROS, BAGUETTES, AND BOW-WOWS

The Vietnamese tremendously value family and derive cultural beliefs and attitudes from it. In conversation with locals, be attentive to family details, injuring about one's spouses, children, parents, and grandparents. Vietnamese dogs are man's best meal, not man's best friend. Dog lovers should avoid *thit cho* (dog meat), served in restaurants mainly in the north, which is thought to remedy colds and flu. Certain meats that are considered delicacies (indicated by higher prices) are often endangered species. Thankfully, though, Vietnamese bread is safe—the baguettes, influenced by the colonial era, are perhaps the only positive element the French left behind.

HUMAN RIGHTS

While Hanoi's human rights record is desultory, there are signs that the political climate is changing—on the Communist Party's terms. The leadership's candid response to the Thái Bình incident is emblematic of a new willingness to address sticky issues. Large-scale prisoner absolution in 1998, including the early release of Professor Doan Viet Hoat, a prominent pro-democracy demonstrator, was a small step toward human rights protection. However, the same laws under which Doan Viet Hoat and other peaceful political protestors were arrested still exist. Open letters to the Politburo calling for political reform have also been tacitly tolerated. Some human rights groups have aligned themselves with Buddhism, calling to help the people, the country, and education. However, in creating a better Vietnam, such groups remain intent on keeping out foreign powers, mimicking a long history of similar struggle with foreign counterparts. Human rights supporters also call for the US trade agreement with Vietnam to follow with the implementation of the Universal Declaration of Human Rights.

BISEXUAL, GAY, AND LESBIAN TRAVELERS

Homosexuality is not openly discussed in Vietnam, though major cities like Hồ Chí Minh City and Hanoi have a small but growing gay nightlife. The importance of the family in Vietnamese society, however, means that most gay men remain closeted, so the gay community stays underground. Public displays of affection are frowned upon for both heterosexuals and homosexuals, while displays of affection between the same-sex are far more acceptable.

PINK INK. *The Men of Vietnam*, by Douglas Thompson, is the first comprehensive account of Vietnamese gay subculture. Utopia-Asia (*www.utopia-asia.com*) also offers tips for gay travelers in Vietnam.

ARTS AND RECREATION

ART

Pre-modern Vietnamese art was a reflection of traditional Chinese styles. During the colonial period, painting was heavily influenced by French impressionism, and a generation of Vietnamese artists was trained at the Indochina College of Art. Following independence, art in the Democratic Republic of Vietnam mirrored Soviet Socialist realism. Today, Vietnam's artistic scene is centered in Hanoi, but traditional **folk art** (including weaving, musical instrument construction, and wood figure carving) is found in all regions. The Hindu kingdom of Champa produced many sculptures, some examples of which are at the Chàm Museum in Đà Nẵng (see **Sights,** p. 868).

DANCE AND DRAMA

Vietnam has many traditional music genres, especially **folk music** and **theater/opera,** that remain popular today. Folk songs *(dân ca)* originated in the countryside and were sung at festivals and in the fields. One common style, the **quan họ** tradition of Bắc Ninh Province north of Hanoi, was sung in a call and response fashion between young men and women as an important element in courtship.

Musical theater is also characterized by regional variation. Most famous in the north is **hát chèo,** which combines singing, acting, and dancing. Today, traditional music troupes occasionally stage performances in theaters in Hanoi. More popular in the central and southern Vietnam are **hát tuồng** and **cải lương** (reformed opera). Tuồng was influenced by Chinese opera in plot, costumes, and instrumentation. More popular during the colonial and post-colonial periods is *cải lương*, which combines elements of *tuồng* with Western musical traditions.

A third popular genre is **múa rối nước** (water puppetry), which originated in the north. Wooden puppets cavort across the surface of a shallow pool, acting out fairy tales. A team of puppeteers, standing knee-deep in water behind a screen, manipulate the puppets with rods.

LITERATURE

Literature is Vietnam's most treasured legacy of the pre-modern period. Early literature was written in classical Chinese and the *nôm* demotic script. During the 17th and 18th centuries, one of Vietnam's greatest *nôm* writers, including poet **Hồ Xuân Hương,** was famous for her innuendo-laden poems about the lives of court women. **Nguyễn Du** is recognized as Vietnam's greatest writer, based on **Truyện Kiều** (Tale of Kieu), an epic in verse about the tragic life of an aristocratic woman. Vietnamese of all ages and class backgrounds can recite passages from the epic. When the French occupied Vietnam, they sought to curtail Chinese influence by banning Chinese and instituting the *quốc ngữ* script. Literature written in the vernacular flourished by the 1920s and 30s and played a significant role in the nationalist struggle by highlighting the injustices of the colonial regime.

OUTDOORS

With an endless coastline in the west, rugged mountains in the north and the lazy Mekong Delta in the south, Vietnam has a plethora of outdoors. **Trekking** opportunities abound near the villages of Sapa, mixing glimpses of indigenous communities in stunning landscapes. **Divers, beach-bummers swimmers,** and **snorkelers** head to the blue waters off Nha Trang or Đà Nẵng along the western coast.

ADDITIONAL SOURCES

A Bright, Shining Lie: John Paul Vann and America in Vietnam, by Neil Sheehan (1988). Winner of the National Book Award. By a correspondent who covered the war, a scathing indictment of America's involvement in Vietnam.

Vietnam: A History, by Stanley Karnow (1983). A straight-forward modern Vietnamese history, focusing on the Second Indochina War. Winner of the Pulitzer Prize.

The Sorrow of War, by Bảo Ninh (1994). A moving novel about love and war in the North; a must-read for anyone familiar with American Vietnam War literature. Written by a North Vietnamese veteran.

ON THE WEB

Vietnam News (www.vietnamnews.net). This comprehensive website updates its news daily, with current events, and also include links to history and culture.

Nam Viet (www.namviet.net). A great source of information on anything from current events to traditional art and Vietnamese recipes.

ESSENTIALS

VIETNAM

VISAS

All travelers must obtain a one-month single-entry tourist visa at any Vietnamese consulate or embassy. Be ready to specify the exact port of entry and departure; **you will be denied passage if you try to cross at a border point not specified on your visa.** You can change the point of departure for a small fee through the Foreign Affairs Ministry in Hanoi or Saigon. Visas are available from the Vietnamese embassy in **Bangkok** (2050¼, 2- to 3-day processing), **Phnom Penh** (single-entry visa US$35, double-entry US$90; 3-day processing), and **Vientiane** (US$50, 5-day processing), but it has been reported that visas obtained in Thailand have been denied despite having the correct point of entry stamped. One-month **extensions** can be arranged by tour agencies all over Vietnam.

MONEY

The Vietnamese **đồng (Đ)** comes in denominations of 200, 500, 1000, 2000, 5000, 10,000, 20,000, and 50,000Đ. US dollars are widely accepted in accommodations and restaurants in larger towns, where prices are frequently quoted in dollars. However, for other expenses, paying in đồng allows more room to bargain. *Let's Go* lists prices according to the currency cited by the establishments. Many establishments list prices in US$ but accept đồng as well. Credit cards are generally accepted at expensive restaurants and hotels, travel agencies, and some stores. Banks regularly give credit card cash advances in dollars. **Tipping** is not necessary but is appreciated and occasionally expected at some touristy establishments. At more expensive restaurants and hotels, a 10% service charge is added. **Bargaining** should always be done in đồng.

GETTING THERE

BY PLANE. Vietnam has two **international airports:** Nội Bài International Airport in Hanoi (p. 826) and Tân Sơn Nhất International Airport in Hồ Chí Minh City (p. 889). **Don't lose your baggage claim tickets**—you won't be allowed to take your luggage out of the airport without them. **Vietnam Airlines** (www.vietnamair.com) runs the most flights to these airports.

BY LAND. Refer to the table on p. 825 for overland border crossings to Vietnam.

BORDER CROSSINGS. On your visa application, be sure to specify the correct point of entry and exit (see **Visas,** above).

LAOS. There is a crossing open from **Đà Nẵng/Huế** (p. 859) through **Lao Bảo** to **Savannakhet** (p. 357). It's rumored that the border crossing at **Điện Biên Phủ** will open soon; check with embassies for the latest details.

CHINA. Borders are open from **Đồng Đăng,** near Lạng Sơn (p. 844), to **Pingxiang** (Guangxi Province) and from **Lào Cai** (p. 846) to **Hekou** (Yunnan province). From there, trains run to **Nanning** and **Kunming,** respectively.

CAMBODIA. The border at **Mộc Bài** (p. 890) provides a cheap way to get between Vietnam and Cambodia. Agents in Hồ Chí Minh City arrange bus transport via Svay Rieng, Cambodia to **Phnom Penh** (p. 69).

GETTING AROUND

BY PLANE. If you can afford it, travel by plane is the fastest and most comfortable way to get from one end of the country to the other. **Vietnam Airlines** has extensive domestic connections from hubs in Hồ Chí Minh City and Hanoi.

BY TRAIN. Trains exist in Vietnam, but solely for the joy of existing. They move no faster than 50km per hour and require patience. Tracks that once extended throughout the country were destroyed during the Vietnam War. Passengers should retain their tickets, lest they be charged a fee upon disembarking. A journey on the "**Unification Express**" from Hanoi to HCMC or vice versa is a scenic way to visit most of Vietnam's major cities and offers much more contact with local culture than travel by tourist minibuses.

BY BUS. Vietnam's public bus system is the cheapest way to travel off the beaten path. Buses go everywhere, and foreign faces are rare. To avoid getting stuck with ridiculous "tourist prices," try to learn numbers and phrases for "how much is it to..." and "no, it is..." (See **Appendix,** p. 912) Buses are not, however, for the impatient, faint of heart, or claustrophobic. Expect to be packed in with bikes, fruits, vegetables, and sweating commuters. The rides tend to be exciting, loud, dusty, and tiring. In general, it's much public bus travel is easier in southern Vietnam than northern Vietnam.

BY MINIBUS. Many backpackers use minibuses operated by budget travel cafes based in Hồ Chí Minh City and Hanoi. Minibuses reduce the headaches of public transportation and are surprisingly cheaper for most routes. The downside is that they limit your contact with locals as well as the places you can visit, since many of the destinations *Let's Go* lists lie off the well-trodden minibus path.

HOME SWEET SCAM. In any major city, you'll likely be surrounded by *cyclo* and motorbike drivers. They'll attempt to bring you to a hotel that is paying them a commission instead of wherever it is that you want to go. Be adamant about your intended accommodation and quoted price. It's a good idea to write down your destination (with accent marks) and the fare before you negotiate.

BY BICYCLE OR MOTORCYCLE. Despite safety risks, traveling by motorbike is a good alternative for getting from city to city without having to rely on nightmarish public transportation. Foreigners are legally allowed to operate engines of 100cc and under without a license. Travelers can flag down motos (called "*xe ôm,*" literally "hugging bike," because the passenger hugs the driver to stay on) for intercity travel. Bicycles are readily available for rent, but helmets aren't; bring your own if you plan on doing some serious cycling. Vietnamese drivers tend to be much more attuned to cyclists than drivers in the West; ride defensively, signal clearly, and avoid highways.

KEEPING IN TOUCH

The Vietnamese **postal service** is reliable when letters are sent to or from major cities, although letters to most Western countries can take anywhere from 10 days to three weeks to arrive. All overseas packages must be processed through customs before they can be received. **Poste Restante** is available in Đà Lạt, Đà Nẵng, Hanoi, Hồ Chí Minh City, and Nha Trang and but isn't always reliable. **Long-distance calls** placed from Vietnam can cost an arm and a leg. **Collect calls** aren't possible from private phones. **International phonecards,** such as those issued by AT&T and MCI, can be used for no fee, but rarely work. **Home Country Direct (HCD)** service is available in Hanoi, Hồ Chí Minh City, Hội An, and Đà Nẵng. For **HCD** numbers from Vietnam, refer to the table on the inside back cover of this book.

NORTHERN VIETNAM

Vietnamese civilization came of age in the northern half of the country over two millennia before civilization flourished in the south. Due to Chinese influence, northern Vietnamese maintain Confucian reserve and a dedicated work ethic. They are further affected by the legacy of over 40 years of socialism and 30 years of war. In addition to the contrast with unfettered capitalism in the south, the ethnic diversity in the northwest in particular lends the region its distinct flavors. As the north's population elevates itself out of hardship and poverty, the region's sights are becoming more popular with foreign visitors. Using Hanoi as a base, travelers can make excursions east to the coast, north to the mountains, or south to the Red River Delta.

VIETNAM

HANOI (HÀ NỘI) ☎4

The idea of Hanoi evokes images of a stern, austere bastion of Vietnamese communism, ravaged by war and closed to the world. Visitors to the capital, however, will be surprised to find themselves in one of the most charming cities of Southeast Asia. This ancient city of lakes with its Chinese architecture, majestic French colonial buildings, and tree-lined lanes, extends a reserved but genuine friendliness that is the essence of the North Vietnamese. Less cosmopolitan than its southern rival Ho Chi Minh City, Hanoi is the kinder and gentler antidote to its southern counterpart. There is less traffic, fewer after-hours temptations, and fewer sky-scrapers; the almost overnight transformation, however, of the infamous "Hanoi Hilton" prison into the Hanoi Tower Commercial Center is surely an omen for things to come. Hammers and sickles still adorn the cityscape, but the Doi Moi "Renovation" policies are slowly taking effect.

INTERCITY TRANSPORTATION

BY PLANE

Flights into Hanoi land at **Nội Bài International Airport,** 35km north of the city. There's a 25,000Đ domestic departure tax and a US$12 tax for international flights. The white Nội Bài Transport Co-op booth right outside the airport runs **taxis** to (US$10) and from (US$7.50) town. Most travelers split the fare with one or two others, so ask around. **Minibuses** run US$2 (20,000Đ if you purchase tickets on board), though they're mostly reserved for locals. Where you get dropped off depends on the whim of your latest friend, the hotel commission hound. The more disinterested you seem in your choice of hostel, the more likely it is that you will get a better value. Vietnam Airlines minibuses also run between the airport and city every hour (40 min., US$4), stopping at the Vietnam Airlines office near the train station. To head back to the airport, call ☎886 56 15 to arrange for pick-up.

Hanoi

ACCOMMODATIONS
- Lotus Guest House, **22**
- Trang An Hotel, **9**

SERVICES
- Alliance Francaise, **30**
- Foreign Book Center, **15**
- International SOS Hanoi Clinic and UK Embassy, **20**
- National Library, **14**
- Pharmacy, **11**
- Vietnam Airlines Office, **29**

NIGHTLIFE
- Apocalypse Now, **31**
- New Century Night Club, **12**
- Relax Bar, **27**

FOOD
- Al Fresco's Bar and Grille, **19**
- Com Chay Nang Tam Vegetarian Restaurant, **28**
- Indochine Restaurant, **13**

SIGHTS
- 19/12 Market, **23**
- Army Museum, **7**
- Fansland, **25**
- Museum of Fine Arts, **8**
- Hoa Lo Prison/Hanoi Towers, **24**
- Ho Chi Minh Mausoleum, **4**
- History Museum, **17**
- Ho Chi Minh's House, **3**
- Ho Chi Minh Museum, **6**
- National Circus, **32**
- One Pillar Pagoda, **5**
- Opera House, **18**
- Presidential Palace, **2**
- Quan Su Pagoda, **26**
- Quan Thanh Pagoda, **1**
- Revolutionary Museum, **16**
- Temple of Literature/Royal College, **10**
- Women's Museum, **21**

THE WIND BENEATH MY WINGS...					
DESTINATION	**FREQUENCY**	**PRICE**	**DESTINATION**	**FREQUENCY**	**PRICE**
Bangkok	1 per day	US$175	**Hue**	3 per week	US$75
Da Nang	1 per day	US$75	**Kuala Lumpur**	1 per day	US$250
Ho Chi Minh City	2 per day	US$130	**Manila**	2 per week	US$280
Hong Kong	1 per day	US$272	**Nha Trang**	1 per day	US$100

Several airlines operate domestic and international flights from Hanoi. **Cathay Pacific Airways,** 49 Hai Bà Trưng (☎826 72 98); **China Airlines,** 18 Trần Hưng Đạo (☎824 26 88); **Lao Aviation,** 40 Quang Trung (☎826 65 38); **Malaysia Airlines,** 15 Ngô Quyền (☎826 88 20); **Pacific Airlines,** 100 Lê Duẩn (☎518 15 03); **Singapore Airlines,** 17 Ngô Quyền (☎826 88 88); **Thai Airways,** 44B Lý Thường Kiệt (☎826 68 93); and **Vietnam Airlines,** 1 Quang Trung (ằ825 08 88), at the intersection with Trang Thi.

> **!** Keep your baggage tags or you won't be allowed to claim your bags. **Keep your stamped white or green immigration card with your passport at all times;** you'll need it to leave the country.

BY TRAIN

Hanoi Railway Station (Ga Hà Nội): Trains are the safest and most comfortable mode of domestic transport. Travelers arriving in Hanoi from Lang Son, Lào Cai, and southern Vietnam disembark at **Hanoi Railway Station,** 120 Lê Duẩn (☎825 39 49), at the west end of Trần Hưng Đạo, a 10min. cyclo ride from the city center (5000-10,000Đ). Purchase tickets in đồng from the special booking window for foreigners in the main building (open 7-12:30am and 1-8:45pm); a booth beside the tourist window exchanges foreign currency. Buy tickets several days in advance for special events like the Saturday market in Sapa. **Save your ticket or you will be forced to pay again upon arrival.** Fares vary by speed. Prices listed are for soft seats. To: **Đà Nẵng** (18hr., with A/C 376,000-523,000Đ); **Hồ Chí Minh City** (32hr., 8am-10:50pm); **Huế** (15-16hr., with A/C 329,000-457,000Đ); **Nha Trang** (32hr., with A/C 673,000-940,000Đ); **Ninh Bình** (2½hr., 54,000-60,000Đ); **Sapa** via **Lao Cai** (9hr., F 9pm); **Vinh** (7hr., 135,000-150,000Đ).

Other Departure Points: On the opposite side of the tracks from the main station (accessible via Trần Quý Cáp), daily trains to **Lạng Sơn** (7½hr., 10pm; 9hr., 5:40am; 78,000Đ) and **Lào Cai** (10hr., 5:15am and 9:45pm, 137,000Đ). Trains to **Hải Phòng** (2½hr.; 8:20, 9:55am, 2:55, 5:10pm; 56,000-60,000Đ) leave from **Long Biên Station** across the Red River (motorcycle taxi 10,000Đ).

BY BUS

Using public buses requires patience for overcrowded, jostling rides that leave only when full, regardless of quoted departure time. In true Vietnamese style, the prices below are approximations. Always buy your ticket at the station; on board, the collector may demand an inflated fare.

Gia Lâm Bus Station: 2km across the Red River on the left. To: **Hải Phòng** (2½hr., roughly every hr. 6am-4:30pm, 38,000Đ); **Hạ Long City** (3hr., 5am-4pm, 45,000Đ); and **Lạng Sơn** (5hr., every hr. from 7am, 35,000Đ). Moto to the station (10,000Đ). Buses to **Hải Phòng** can also be caught on Trần Quang Khải, the highway to the bridge over the Red River.

Southern Bus Station (Bến Xe Nam Hà Nội): On Đường Giải Phóng, the extension of Lê Duẩn, 5km south of the train station. For all destinations south of Hanoi. To **Ninh Bình** (2½hr., every 2hr., 30,000Đ).

Sơn La Bus Station: 5km south of Hanoi on Nguyễn Trãi, the extension of Tôn Đức Thắng. Daily buses to **Sơn La** (4am and noon, 60,000Đ). To get to **Mai Châu,** ask to get off at **Tòng Đậu.**

Kim Mã Bus Station: On Nguyễn Thái Học. To **Lào Cai** (20hr., 5am, 70,000Đ) and **Sơn La** (8hr., 5:30am, 55,000Đ).

VIETNAM

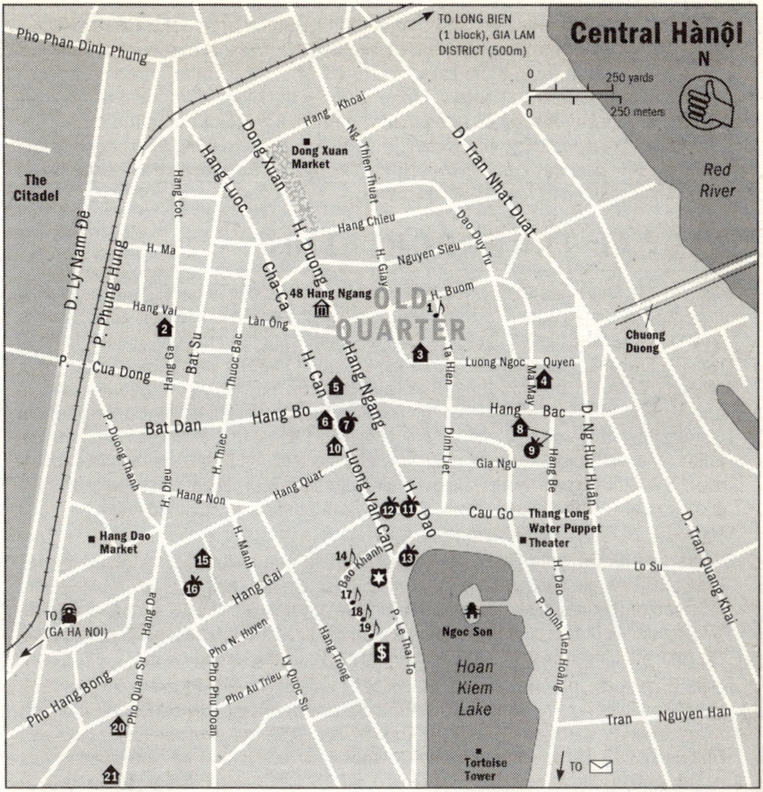

Central Hànội

ACCOMMODATIONS

- A Dong Hotel, **3**
- Anh Dao Hotel, **4**
- Especen No. 8 Hotel, **10**
- Green Hotel, **21**
- Manh Sung Internet Guest House, **15**
- Phu Hoa Hotel Guest House, **6**
- Prince II Hotel, **20**
- Thanh An Hotel, **2**
- Thuy Loi Hotel, **8**
- Youth Hotel, **5**

NIGHTLIFE

- Dong Khoi, **19**
- Le Maquis Bar, **1**
- Funky Monkey Bar, **14**
- Golden Cock Bar, **17**
- Polite Pub, **18**

FOOD

- Cafe Giang, **11**
- Cyclo Bar and Restaurant, **16**
- Little Hanoi, **12**
- Pho Chua Ngot Eatery, **7**
- Tandoor Restaurant, **9**
- Thuy Ta Cafe, **13**

Tourist buses: More comfortable and reliable, albeit more expensive. An established bus line departs daily at 6:30pm from **Sinh Cafe,** 18 Luong Van Can (☎828 75 72) to: **Dong Ha** (13¼hr., US$10); **Hue** (15¼hr., US$10) via **Ninh Binh** (2¼hr., US$4); **Quang Binh** (11hr., US$9); and **Vinh** (6¼hr., US$8). A popular **open ticket** to **Ho Chi Minh City** (US$23) via **Da Nang, Dalat, Hoi An,** and **Nha Trang** lets you get off at any of these towns and then jump back on the bus to the next destination southward at your leisure.

ORIENTATION

Hanoi divides into seven districts (quận): **Hoàn Kiếm** (the Old Quarter), **Hai Bà Trưng** to the south, **Ba Đình** and **Đống Đa** to the west, **Cầu Giấy** and **Thanh Xuân** to the far southwest, and **Tây Hồ** in the north. Most streets in Vietnam are called "đường," though Hanoi still uses the word "phố" and, in the Old Quarter, "hàng." Downtown

Hanoi is small but disorganized; a good map is helpful. Large color maps (10,000-25,000Đ) are available from guest houses, bookstores, the international post office, and hawkers around **Hoàn Kiếm Lake,** the heart of central Hanoi. A backpacker's heaven of shops, cafes, and hotels, Hoàn Kiếm is the oldest and most interesting district. The one-way **Đường Lê Duẩn** leads south to **Bẩy Mẫu Lake** in the more residential **Hai Bà Trưng** district, and west (down Khâm Tiên) to **Đống Đa's** pagodas and small lakes. Farther north, up Đường Hùng Vương, the **Ba Đình district** hosts the **Hồ Chí Minh Mausoleum** and **Temple of Literature.**

LOCAL TRANSPORTATION

Bicycles (Xe Đạp) and Motorcycles (Xe Máy): Hanoi traffic is hectic and challenging even for the most capable drivers. Still, driving is a convenience that many think is worth the woe. Most hotels, guest houses, and rental shops in the Old Quarter, north of Hoàn Kiếm Lake, rent **mopeds** (US$5 per day) and **motorcycles** (US$8-10 per day). **Memory Cafe,** 33 Bis Trần Hưng Đạo (☎826 58 54), by the Ngô Quyền intersection has mopeds and the irresistible Honda Dreams. Though it might make you feel like your grandmother, the extra safety of a moped might just be worth it. If you can't resist temptation for a motorbike, however, renting a helmet is required by law. Be prepared to fork over 1000-2000Đ each time you park your motorbike. **Bicycles** are less glamorous but sufficient for getting around town. Rent them from most accommodations or rental shops for 10,000-15,000Đ per day.

Cyclos and Motorcycle Taxis (Xe Ôm): Abundant and cheap three-wheeled **cyclos** (pedicabs) are the bastard children of rickshaws, tricycles, and bicycles. Banned from most major thoroughfares, but a must for any traveler, with chatty drivers and slow, winding routes. Agree on a price beforehand (10,000-15,000Đ per hr.). Hire **motorcycle taxis** for longer rides (2000-3000Đ per km, 10,000Đ around town).

Taxis: Everywhere in Hanoi. Lines form outside the Vietnam Airlines office, the train station, and major hotels. **Hanoi Taxi** (☎853 52 52) or **Huong Luo Taxi** (☎825 25 25) will pick you up curbside (7000Đ per km). Insist that the driver use the meter. **Airport Taxi** (☎873 33 33) runs to and from the airport (40,000Đ). **Renting** cars is uncommon but an option. **Especen,** 79E Hàng Trống, ☎826 68 56. US$35 per day in town or US$50 per 200km outside Hanoi. Open daily 9am-5pm.

PRACTICAL INFORMATION

TOURIST AND FINANCIAL SERVICES

Tourist Offices: Hanoi Toserco, 8 To Hien Thanh (☎978 00 04), and **Vietnam Tourism,** 5 Ba Trieu (☎829 41 30), are useless state-run travel agencies that will try to book you on expensive package tours. Best avoided.

Tours: Tourist cafes organize cheap package tours, which provide a hassle-free way to see Northern Vietnam. Services and prices vary slightly, but quality can vary considerably. Standard packages include: **Hạ Long Bay** (1 night US$18-35, 2 nights including **Cát Bà Island** US$28-53); **Hoa Lư-Tam Cốc** (daytrip US$20); **Mai Châu** (1 night US$20-25); **Perfume Pagoda** (daytrip US$12-16); **Sapa** (3 nights including **Bắc Hà** US$32-70). Some established tourist cafes are: **Green Bamboo Cafe,** 42 Nhà Chung (☎826 87 52); **Queen Cafe,** 65 Hàng Bạc (☎826 08 60); **TF Handspan Cafe,** 116 Hàng Bạc (☎828 19 96), branch at 18 Bảo Khánh (☎828 99 31). Most tourist cafes also arrange **visas** to China (1 month US$25-30) and Laos (1 month US$60) and 30-day Vietnam **visa extensions** (US$25-35).

Embassies: Australia, 8 Dao Tan (☎831 77 55), behind Hanoi-Daewoo Hotel. Open M-F 8:30am-4:50pm. **Cambodia,** 71 Trần Hưng Đạo (☎942 47 88). Visa US$20, 1-day processing. Bring a photo. Open M-F 8-11:30am and 2-5pm. **Canada,** 31 Hùng Vương (☎823 55 00). **China,** 46 Hoàng Diệu (☎845 37 36). For visas, go to the consulate (☎823 55 69) on Trần Phú. Visa US$27, 5-day processing; US$47, 2-day processing. Bring 2 photos. Open M-F 8:30-11am. **France,** 57 Trần Hưng Đạo (☎825 27 19). Open M-F 8:30am-noon and 2-6pm. **Indonesia,** 50 Ngô Quyền (☎825 33 53). **Laos,** 22 Trần

Bình Trọng (☎942 45 76). Visa US$60, 1- to 3-day processing. Bring a photo. Open M-F 8am-noon and 1-4pm. **Malaysia,** Fortuna Hotel, GB Lang Ha (☎831 34 00). **Myanmar,** block A3 Vạn Phúc (☎845 33 69). **New Zealand,** 32 Hàng Bài (☎824 1481). **Philippines,** 27B Trần Hưng Đạo (☎943 79 48). **Singapore,** 41-43 Trần Phú (☎823 39 66). **Thailand,** 63-65 Hoàng Diệu (☎823 50 92). **UK,** 31 Hai Bà Trưng (☎825 25 10). Open daily 8:30am-4:30pm. **US,** 7 Láng Hạ (☎772 15 00). Open 8am-5pm. Cheaper visa services to Cambodia, Laos, and Thailand also available in tourist cafes and certain hotels (see **Tours,** above).

Immigration Office: 40A Hàng Bài (☎826 62 00). Best avoided. Refuses service to foreigners. Tourist agencies or embassies can resolve most visa difficulties.

Currency Exchange: Vietcombank, Sun Red River Building, 23 Phan Chu Trinh (☎934 31 37). Best exchange rates in Hanoi. Open M-F 8am-4:30pm, Sa 9am-3pm for currency exchange. **ANZ Bank,** 14 Lê Thái Tổ (☎825 81 90), on the west bank of Hoàn Kiếm Lake. Hanoi's only **24hr. ATM.** Both banks exchange and issue traveler's checks and offer MC/V cash advances.

LOCAL SERVICES

Local Publications: The Guide, published monthly with the *Vietnam Economic Times,* provides useful information on events, hotels, shops, and local services (13,000Đ). **Hanoi Pathfinder** has a similar monthly listing with a map, although it only lists businesses that advertise. Available free at most Western restaurants and guest houses.

English-Language Bookstore: Foreign Book Center, 2nd fl. 44 Tráng Tiền (☎829 15 76). Chinese, English, French, Korean, Japanese, Lao, and Russian books. Open M-F 8am-9pm, Sa-Su 8am-10pm. **Hanoi Book Distribution,** 17 Ngo Quyen (å824 16 16), has maps and a few English-language staples, but no guidebooks. Open daily 8am-7:30pm. **Thăng Long Bookshop,** 55 Tràng Tiền (☎825 70 43), has Western newspapers, paperbacks, and phrasebooks. Open daily 8am-7pm. You can also find European periodicals and literature at **Alliance Francaise,** 42 Yết Kiên (☎942 29 70). Open M-Sa 8am-7:30pm.

Library: National Library of Vietnam (Thư Viện Quốc Gia), 31 Tràng Thi (☎825 53 97). A good mix of English magazines on the 2nd fl. Dress modestly. Open daily 8am-6pm.

EMERGENCY AND COMMUNICATIONS

Emergency: ☎115. **Police** ☎113.

Police: Hoàn Kiếm District Headquarters, 2 Lê Thái Tổ (☎825 41 08), on the northwest corner of Hoàn Kiếm Lake. Don't expect knights in shining armor.

Pharmacy: Nguyễn Luận, 3 Tràng Thi (☎826 86 44), just south of Hoàn Kiếm Lake. Open daily 8am-noon and 2-6pm. The **24hr. pharmacy** at 14 Phu Doan (☎825 59 34) is small but well-stocked.

Medical Services: International SOS Clinic, 31 Hai Bà Trung (☎934 06 66). From south of Hoàn Kiếm Lake, walk 1 block down Bà Triệu. Large office sign post. **24hr. emergency care.** US$74 per consultation, $50 for dental, $15 for vaccine. Medivac service available. **Hanoi French Hospital**, 1 Phuong Mai (☎570 07 40). Expat doctors provide **24hr.** emergency care. US$25-30 per consultation. **Hanoi Family Medical Practice**, 1A Van Phuc 109-112 Kim Ma (☎843 07 48; emergency ☎09 040 19 19).

Telephones: Telephone office, 75B Đinh Tiên Hoàng (☎825 52 36), next to the international post office. International calls (4400Đ). Fax and AT&T/MCI card calls are free but don't always work. Open daily in summer 6am-10pm; in winter 6am-9:30pm. **Branch office,** 66 Lương Văn Can (å826 29 99). Open daily 6am-9pm. **Information** å1080. **Directory** ☎1080. **International Operator (collect calls):** ☎110 (only available from post office).

Internet Access: Most tourist cafes, especially those concentrated on Hàng Bac, offer Internet access for 100-300Đ per min.

Post Offices: International Post Office, 6 Đinh Tiên Hoàng, is a large Stalinist-looking building east of Hoàn Kiếm Lake. *Poste Restante.* Open daily in summer 7am-9pm; in winter 7am-8:30pm.

Express Mail: FedEx, 6B Dinh Le (☎826 49 25). **DHL,** 778 Làng (☎775 39 99). English spoken.

ACCOMMODATIONS

Most tourists stay in the **Old Quarter.** Combating a current dip, the hotel industry has reduced its prices, so finding a cheap place to stay is easy. Plan ahead during the high season when the best hotels are packed. Most accommodations charge by the room, not by the number of people. Get cozy and get cheap. In case you've forgotten that you're in a communist bureaucracy, your hotel owner will request your passport and papers so he can register you with the local police.

THE OLD QUARTER (KHU PHỐ CỔ)

Hàng Bè and **Hàng Bac** streets are still the center of backpacking universe in Hanoi, but the streets to the north and west offer better and quieter alternatives.

Thủy Lợi Hotel, 24 Hàng Bè (☎824 22 52). The most pleasant option on the busy street. Amazingly, doesn't pester guests to sign up for tours. Clean, quiet, and friendly staff. Tandoori Indian restaurant downstairs. Dorms US$3-4; rooms with A/C US$8; gargantuan "big room" US$15.

Mạnh Sung Internet Guest House, 2 Tam Thương St. (☎826 72 01), down a small alley off Hàng Bông near Hàng Gai Market. Organizes tours. Friendly feel in an English-speaking household. Spotless rooms with private bath. Doubles US$8, with A/C US$10.

Á Đông Hotel, 46 Lương Ngọc Quyến (☎825 69 48). At the end of Hàng Bē, turn left on Hàng Bac, take the 1st right on Mà Mây, and turn left on Lương Ngọc Quyến. It's the 1st hotel on the right. Outstanding rooms. Tranquil courtyard. Staff serves local cuisine. Singles with TV, A/C, and fridge US$8; doubles US$12-16.

Especen No. 8, 30 Lương Văn Can (☎824 59 23). At the intersection with Hàng Quạt. Singles with fan and shared bath from US$5; doubles US$10. V accepted.

Anh Đào Hotel, 37 Ma May (☎828 19 94; camellia@hn.vnn.vn). A real gem. 31 spotless wooden-furnitured rooms run by a highly professional team. 30min. free Internet each day. Free laundry for deluxe guests. Includes breakfast buffet (7-10am). All rooms have A/C and satellite TV. Large doubles US$10; deluxe US$15. MC/V.

Youth Hotel, 33 Luong Van Can (☎828 58 22). Centrally located; 50m to Hoàn Kiếm Lake. Popular with younger crowds. Internet 200Đ per min. in a buzzing backpacker cafe. Connected to Sinh Cafe for tour booking. Rooms US$8-20.

Thanh An Hotel, 46 Hang Ga (☎826 71 91)., in the northwest part of the Old Quarter. Attentive service by the French-speaking Mr. Nguyễn and his daughter. Rooms facing the back of the hotel can be a bit dark. Homey rooms US$10.

Phú Hoa Hotel Guest House, 16 Lương Văn Can (☎828 51 73). Inexpensive, airy rooms in the center of town. Shared bathroom. Once you've got the room key, don't expect much else. Doubles US$5-7.

VIETNAM

ELSEWHERE IN HANOI

Lotus Guest House, 42V Lý Thường Kiệt (☎/fax 826 86 42). Walking south from the lake on Bà Triệu, turn right at intersection with Lý Thường Kiệt; it's 2 blocks down on the right. Informal, cozy, and popular. Food (5000-25,000Đ), laundry, and tours. Dorms US$4; singles US$6-8; doubles with fan US$8, with A/C US$10-15.

Tràng An Hotel, 46 Hàng Cháo (☎/fax 823 28 37). About 1km from the lake, cross the Điện Biên Phủ intersection from Tràng Thi to Nguyễn Thái Học, turn left onto Tôn Đức Thắng just past the Temple of Literature, then take the 1st right onto Hàng Cháo; it's on the left. Twins with A/C, TV, and huge private bath from US$10.

Green Hotel, 50 (☎824 97 38) and 32 (☎828 77 28) Quán Sú. Basically the same hotel a few doors apart. Modern rooms at 50 Quán Sú with fans and shared baths run US$8, and doubles with beautiful bathtubs cost US$20. 32 Quán Sú rents bikes ($1 per day) and motorbikes ($5 per day). Internet 300Đ per min. Dorms US$3.

Prince II Hotel, 24 Quán Sú (å828 94 65). A handsome joint. Rooms with bathtub, desk, and balconies if you're lucky. Small breakfast included. Doubles US$15-25. MC/V.

FOOD

Culinary delights in the capital city cater to all palates and budgets. Backpackers can easily find the usual spaghetti and pancake fares in the Old Quarter, but the most rewarding experiences are to be had at the numerous street stalls at the markets. All of them serve basic *phở* (noodles) or *cōm* (rice) dishes, and plenty of pure vegetarian options.

FOOD STALL HEAVEN. Vendors set up all day long in the **Dong Xuan Market,** north of Hoàn Kiếm Lake, on **Hãng Bong** street between the lake and main train station, and in the block behind the Vietnam Airlines office at **Tran Binh Trong** and **Tran Hung Dao**. Over 30 seafood eateries beckon your patronage along **Thuy Khue** south of **Ho Tay** (West Lake). It's a 10min. walk directly north from the mausoleum. **Pho Mai Hac De,** in the south part of the city, serves cheap, authentic Vietnamese food. To get there, head south from Hoàn Kiếm Lake on Bà Triệu for seven blocks, turn left on Tran Nhan Tong and right on Mai Hac De. Gorge on fruit at the **19/12 Market** and cool off with drinks like *mïa da* (pressed sugar cane with ice) or *che* (sweet bean drink). *Bia hơi* shops set up in the evening on Phan Chu Trinh, three blocks south of the Opera House.

Cafe Giang, 7 Hang Gai. Open since 1945, this is arguably the most famous coffee shop among the locals, and for good reason. The unique egg coffee (2500Đ), a shot of espresso with sugar and a beaten egg, is an absolute can't-miss. Artists, students, and local eclectics sit in this tiny, dark cafe whose grimy walls simply add to the charm. Open daily 6am-noon and 3-9pm.

Cyclo Bar and Restaurant, 38 Duòng Thành. Duòng Thành intersects Hàng Gai as it becomes Hàng Bông; the restaurant is 100m down on the left. Good variety of Vietnamese and Western food. Excellent beer. Cyclo chairs and a nice garden add to the ambience. Set lunch menu 50,000Đ. *A la carte* 40,000-60,000Đ. Open daily 11am-midnight.

Co'm Chay Nàng Tấm Vegetarian Restaurant, 79A Trần Hưng Đạo, between Quang Trung and Quán Sứ intersections. Buddhist eatery. Come early for lunch, since it gets crowded. Most entrees 30,000-50,000Đ. Open daily 11am-1:30pm and 5-10pm.

Tandoor Restaurant, 24 Hàng Bè. From Đinh Tiên Hoàng on the eastern shore of Hoàn Kiếm Lake, walk up Hàng Dầu, which becomes Hàng Bè; it's on the left past the intersection with Gia Ngư. Delicious *naan* and good vegetarian selections. North Indian dishes 40,000-70,000Đ. Open daily 8am-10:30pm.

Phỏ Chua Ngot, 26 Lượng Van Can. A brightly lit local dive that serves only two specialties: sweet and sour noodle (10,000Đ per bowl) and fried dumplings (5000Đ). Open 9am-9pm or later.

Little Hanoi, 21 Hang Gai, a block from the lake. A favorite meeting point for Westerners. Quiche, shakes, and a good selection of dessert cakes run 25,000-50,000Đ. Open daily 7:30am-11pm.

Al Fresco's Cafe, Bar and Grille, 23 Hai Ba Trung, two blocks south of the main GPO. Big portions of pizza and buffalo wings. A local expat hangout. It's claim to fame: since 1996, 37 tons of ribs have been sold here. An annual rib-eating contest is held in Nov. Entrees $4.50-7. Open daily 9am-11pm.

Indochine Vietnamese Restaurant, 16 Nam Ngu. High quality local specialties with impeccable service. The house spring rolls have achieved crispy fried yet unoily perfection. Entrees start at US$3. Open daily 11am-late.

Thuỷ Ta Cafe, 1 Le Thai To. The tasty French cakes, Italian ice creams, and Vietnamese coffee are a bit pricey, but a good seat overlooking the Ngoc Son Temple is priceless. Cakes start at 20,000Đ per piece. Open daily 6am-11pm.

SIGHTS

Concentrated in Hoàn Kiếm and Ba Đình, most of Hanoi's sights can be reached by foot or bicycle. Hanoi has a fascinating mixture of old and new, juxtaposing tradi-

A MINI-KEG A DAY... Though most *bia hơi* (draft beer) stands fall short of Munich *Biergartens*, the enthusiasm and passion with which the Vietnamese quaff their delicious beer rivals that of malt-drinkers anywhere in the world. Every morning, beer is delivered fresh in mini-keg beer bombs; there are no added preservatives and reduced chances of hangovers should you imbibe too liberally. Be warned; while Vietnamese beer may not have as much body as many international beers, it certainly has a kick. Moreover, it's tastier than the other national favorite, *mua loi* (rice vodka), which will send you rolling under the table without ceremony. The Vietnamese celebrate their traditional booze with plenty of drinking games. If you're playing "50/50," they'll make you drink half the beer that's in your glass, so don't get caught with a whole glass. *"Tram Phan Tram"* means "bottoms up," the global slogan for draining your glass. Many Vietnamese are extraordinarily fond of the word "cheers" so expect to hear it twice for every sip you take.

Almost every city or region has its own local brew: in Hanoi, try Bia Hanoi or Halida; in Huế, drink Hú đá; in HCMC, don't miss 333 or Bia Saigon. Haiphong brews Bia Haiphong, and even tiny Sơn La brews its own Bia Son Dong. Locals everywhere insist their city's beer is Vietnam's best—and we all know that the only way to know for sure is careful, empirical research. To find a good beer stall, look for peanut shells on the floor or a crowd. You'll find that good *bia hơi* is a social equalizer: doctors and lawyers swig elbow-to-elbow with cyclo drivers and shoeshine boys. Get to your stall early and grab a handful of peanuts in the shell *(lạc)* or dried squid *(mực)*. As they say, *Tram Phan Tram* and let the night begin.

tional Vietnamese and French colonial designs with 1930s art deco, 1970s communist looks, and modern skyscrapers, each style symbolizing a different epoch in Vietnam's troubled history.

VIETNAM

HOÀN KIẾM DISTRICT

OLD QUARTER. North of Hoàn Kiếm Lake and west of the Hanoi Citadel, this labyrinthine neighborhood stretches to Long Biên Bridge, which was continually bombed and repaired during the war. Many streets *(hàng)* take their names from the goods sold there. **Hàng Bạc** (Silver St.) is lined with gold and silver shops, and **Hàng Thiếc** (Tin St.) is home to metalworkers. Since merchants used to be taxed by the length of their storefronts, houses are thin structures that extend deep into the middle of the block. A typical house is 3m wide and 50-60m long, and families build upward when they add on. After hitting the shops, check out the museum at **48 Hàng Ngang,** where Hồ Chí Minh drafted the Declaration of Independence in 1945. *(Open daily 8-11am and 1-4:30pm. Free.)* The winding **Nguyễn Quang Bịch** hosts a mix of typical Old Quarter and 1900s French-style houses painted bright yellow and green. Rather than trying to find specific sights, just wander about, and you'll probably find what you're looking for. Though the Old Quarter is well-touristed, foreigners are still viewed with (polite) bewilderment.

HOÀN KIẾM LAKE (HỒ HOÀN KIẾM). The lake takes its name from a 15th-century legend of a magic turtle who loaned a sacred sword to Lê Lợi, the nobleman who led the Vietnamese against the invading Ming army. Paddling in the lake following the victory, the newly crowned emperor encountered the turtle, who demanded the sword back. The **Tortoise Tower** on a tiny island in the lake's center commemorates the event. Several mammoth turtles still live in the lake and occasionally surface, a heralded event that locals believe is a sign that one of the country's leaders will die soon. Around the lake, Vietnamese couples sit on tiny stone benches holding hands during the weekends, and timid gay men sit in search of conversation, usually avoiding their more obvious counterparts. Should a Westerner attempt to do the same, they'll be assaulted by dozens of kids selling postcards and T-shirts.

NGỌC SƠN TEMPLE (ĐỀN NGỌC SƠN). Generations have added more and more frills to this shrine since its construction during the Trần Dynasty (1225-1400). Last renovated in 1865, this Chinese-style temple is located on a wooded island in Hoàm Kiêm lake and is dedicated primarily to Văn Xương, the god of literature. Thirteenth century hero Trần Hưng Đạo, and the physician La To are also honored. The entrance to the temple is through **Tam Quan** (Three Passage) gate on the northeast shore on Dinh Tiên Hoàng. Behind the **Hall of the Cult,** the sanctuary to **Văn Xương** offers a beautiful view of the lake. *(Open daily 8am-6pm. 12,000Đ.)*

HỎA LÒ PRISON. Nicknamed the "Hanoi Hilton," Hỏa Lò Prison held American POWs during the Vietnam War and Vietnamese revolutionaries under French rule. The towering Hanoi Towers, which hold offices, a five-star hotel and a shopping center, now occupies most of the sight. A portion of the old prison, preserved on Phố Hỏa Lò off Hai Bà Trưng just before the skyscraper, is now a small, self-explanatory museum. *(A few blocks past the intersection of Quang Trung and Hai Bà Trưng, walking away from the lake. Open Tu-Su 8-11:30am and 1-4:30pm. 10,000Đ.)*

QUÁN SỨ PAGODA (CHÙA QUÁN SỨ). The official center of Buddhism in Hanoi, this site served as a guest house for visiting Buddhist ambassadors. The structure as it stands today was completed in 1942. Inside are several depictions of the Buddha. Be extremely respectful in dress and manners. *(73 Quán Sứ, a block south of the prison between Lý Thường Kiệt and Trần Hưng Đạo. Open Tu-Su 8:30-11am and 1-4pm.)*

OTHER SIGHTS. The French-built **Opera House (Nhà Hát Lớn),** constructed in 1911, majestically stands guard over the main traffic circle facing east over Pho Trang Tien and remains one of the finest examples of colonial architecture in the country (see **Entertainment,** p. 837). Both the **Revolutionary Museum (Bảo Tàng Cách Mạng)** and the **History Museum (Bảo Tàng Lịch Sử)** are just a short walk behind the Opera House. The former is a visual lesson in communist historiography that retells the history of Vietnam's struggle against foreign aggression. *(25 Tông Đản. Open Tu-F, Su 8-11:30am and 1:30-4pm, Sa 8-11:30am. Free.)* At the latter, don't miss the Đông Sơn bronze drums and ceramics or the Khmer and Champa artifacts. *(Open M-W and F-Su 8:15-11:45am and 1:30-5pm. Curator guide 10,000Đ. Admission 10,000Đ.)* The **Women's Museum,** 42 Lý Thường Kiêt balances the macho-er museums by detailing the "she" story with pictures and words. *(Open Tu-Su 8am-4pm. 10,000Đ.)*

BA ĐÌNH DISTRICT

The area around **Ba Đình Square,** site of Hồ Chí Minh's delivery of Vietnam's Declaration of Independence in 1945, contains the principle sights west of Hoàn Kiếm Lake. The most convenient route to get here is via Điện Biên Phủ. Along the way is a small park with a massive **statue of Lenin.** Catch a game of soccer or badminton in the early morning or evening.

HANOI CITADEL. Inside its gates is the **Army Museum (Bảo Tàng Quân Đội),** which details the exploits of the People's Army of Vietnam. Highlights include a light-and-sound diorama of Điện Biên Phủ Valley and the tank that crashed through the gates of the Presidential Palace in Saigon in April 1975. Next door is the 31m **Hanoi Flag Staff,** built in 1812 under the Nguyễn Dynasty. *(Museum, 28A Điện Biên Phủ. Open Tu-Su 7:30-10:30am and 1:30-4:30pm. 10,000Đ; cameras 2000Đ.)*

HỒ CHÍ MINH MAUSOLEUM (LĂNG HỒ CHÍ MINH). Poor Hồ Chí Minh couldn't escape his well-preserved fate despite his wish to be cremated. Completed in 1975, the granite structure serves as a receiving stand for officials and party leaders and continues the Communist tradition of building glass sarcophagi to attract pilgrims. *(Up Điện Biên Phủ, away from the Army Museum, west of the lake. Open Tu-Th, Sa-Su 8am-11am and 1:30pm-4pm. Closed briefly every Nov. for the make-up artist, eh, embalmer to touch up a bit. Free. Be certain to wear respectable attire—no shorts, short skirts, or tank tops. No bags or cameras allowed; stash them at the visitors entrance at the south end of the square.)*

PRESIDENTIAL PALACE. The former residence of the Governor General of French Indochina, this beautiful colonial structure has served as a state guest house since

1954, when the Viet-Minh defeated the French. Hồ Chí Minh believed the building should belong to the people and chose to live in an electrician's hut on the grounds. In 1958, he moved into a simple house on stilts near a carp pond, which remained his residence until 1969. His personal area upstairs has been carefully preserved. *(North of the mausoleum. Open daily 8am-5:30pm. 5000Đ.)*

HỒ CHÍ MINH'S STILTED HOUSE. A beautifully preserved ex-residence of Uncle Hồ was built near the Presidential Palace so he would feel more "with the people." It's probably the best example of ethnic Thai architecture in Hanoi proper. *(West of the Palace. Same hours and prices.)*

HỒ CHÍ MINH MUSEUM (BẢO TÀNG HỒ CHÍ MINH). If you visit one museum in Hanoi, this should be it. It chronicles his life and times through a series of bizarre displays that blend Socialist Realism and postmodernism. Musicians in the concert hall play traditional Vietnamese music. *(From Ba Đình Square, head south on Hùng Vương for 3 blocks and turn left on Nguyễn Thái Học. Open Tu-Su 8-11am and 1:30-4pm. 5000Đ, but often not collected.)*

ONE PILLAR PAGODA (CHÙA MỘT CỘT). One of the few structures remaining from old Thăng Long, the pagoda is dedicated to Quan Âm, the goddess of mercy. Emperor Lý Thánh Tông built the pagoda after dreaming that the goddess, sitting on a lotus flower, gave him a boy. Soon afterward, a son was born to him. The pagoda was thus built to resemble a lotus plant. The French destroyed the pagoda on their way out of Hanoi in 1954, but the communist government rebuilt it entirely. *(South of the palace, behind the mausoleum.)*

TEMPLE OF LITERATURE (VĂN MIẾU)/ROYAL COLLEGE (QUỐC TỬ GIÁM). To enter, head to the south entrance of the Four Pillars, allegedly built in 1070 during the reign of Emperor Lý Thánh Tông to honor scholars and literary men. Dedicated to Khổng Tử (Confucius), the college was founded to educate the children of court mandarins. Though in a busy part of town, the temple has a feeling of calm retreat. The succession of open courts is established by a series of gates, symbolic of the academic experience. The first set is the Gates of Talent and Virtue. The next set heading north honors letters and leads to one of the 82 Tortoise Stelae on which the names of 1306 successful examination candidates are inscribed. Next is the Gate of Synthesis and the sanctuary, housing statues of Confucius and his four greatest disciples. *(At the intersection of Tôn Đức Thắng and Nguyễn Thái Học, 2km west of Hoàn Kiếm Lake. Open in summer Tu-Su 7:30am-6pm, in winter 8am-5pm. 12,000Đ.)*

OTHER SIGHTS. West Lake (Hồ Tây) is 500 hectares of green-brown water north of the mausoleum. **Đường Thanh Niên,** between West Lake and Trúc Bạch Lake, is a venue for fruit and drink vendors and a hangout spot for young lovers at sunset (see **Food**, p. 833). A statue on the shore commemorates the downing of the American fighter with US Senator John McCain during the Vietnam War. For a scenic walk from West Lake to the Old Quarter, take tree-lined **Phố Phan Đình Phùng,** which parallels the north wall of the citadel. At the intersection of Phố Quán Thánh and Đường Thanh Niên is **Quán Thánh Pagoda (Đền Quán Thánh),** built by Emperor Lý Thái Tổ during the 11th century. On a bit of land jutting into West Lake near the north end of Đường Thanh Niên is **Trần Quốc Pagoda (Chùa Trần Quốc),** built during the Lê dynasty. Spend a relaxing day at **Lenin Park (Công Viên Lenin),** the largest in Hanoi, 1km south of the train station on Lê Duẩn. To get to the **Air Force Museum,** go 1km further south from Lenin Park on Lê Duẩn, take a right on Trường Chinh, and walk down 1km further; the museum is on the left. *(Open Tu-Su 8am-noon and 1-4pm. Free.)* The **Museum of Fine Arts (Bảo Tàng Mỹ Thuật),** one block over from the Hồ Chí Minh Museum, features premodern and modern art. *(66 Nguyễn Thái Học. Open Tu-Su 9:15am-5pm. 10,000Đ.)*

MARKETS

In the olden days, each of the Old Quarter's 36 streets had its own specialty trade. **Hàng Dầu** specializes in cheap shoes (many of them exported to Europe) while its continuation, **Hàng Bê,** makes funeral stones. Best known are the silk shops on **Hàng Gai Luong Vàn Can,** which sell ready-made and tailored clothing of varying quality. **Hàng Quạt** peddles colorful funeral flags and religious objects; **Hàng Mã** sells paper products, including votives burned for ancestors; **Lãn Ông** exudes the sweet scent of medicinal herbs; and **Hàng Ðào** sells clothing.

Chợ' Ðồng Xuân (Dong Xuan Market) is in the northern part of the Old Quarter, off the extension of Hàng Ðào. **Chợ' Hôm** (Hôm Market), on Phố Huế, the extension of Hàng Bài, burgeons six blocks south of Hoàn Kiếm Lake. (Open daily 6:30am-7pm.) **19/12 Market** takes up the block between Hai Bà Trưng and Lý Thường Kiệt, west of Quang Trung. Produce at the entrance tends to be more expensive than at the stands within. (Open 6am-6pm.)

ENTERTAINMENT

For the more culturally-minded, Hanoi offers several non-party options. A definite must-see is the **Thăng Long Water Puppet Theatre,** 57B Ðinh Tiên Hoàng, up the street two blocks north of the GPO on Hoàn Kiếm Lake. The troupe has performed in folk art festivals worldwide, and the theater is packed nightly with tourists; the show is innovative and the craftmanship is superb. (☎824 51 17. Shows nightly at 8pm. 1½-2hr. Tickets 20,000-40,000Ð.) To rub shoulders with well-heeled Hanoians, try the **Hanoi Opera House,** 1 Trang Tien, also home to the **Vietnam National Symphony Orchestra.** The newly renovated architecture and primly manicured courtyards alone are worth the 80,000-150,000Ð tickets. Call the **Vietnam Opera & Ballet Theater,** 18 Nui Truc (☎869 45 63), for additional cultural events. **August Cinema,** 45 Hang Bai (☎825 39 11), and **Fansland,** 84 Lý Thủờng Kĩit (☎825 74 84), next to the Saigon Hotel, show Western films regularly. French films are available most nights (except Monday) at **Alliance Francaise,** 42 Yet Kein (☎942 29 70), near the train station. To see amazing human contortions by pubescent boys and girls (if that's your thing), spend an evening at the **Vietnam National Circus** in Lenin Park. Animal lovers stay away. (☎822 02 77. Shows W-Su 8pm.)

NIGHTLIFE

Slap on your dancing shoes, because entertainment in Hanoi is all about bars, nightclubs, and karaoke bars.

Apocalypse Now, 5C Hòa Mã (☎971 27 83). Run by the brother of its namesake in HCMC. Large and hip. Caters to the well-to-do of all nationalities and ages and the "working girls" who like them. Army motif. Music ranges from Britney Spears to the B-52s. Beer 25,000Ð. Open daily 7:30pm-4am. Best after 11pm.

New Century Night Club, 10 Trang Thi St. (☎928 52 85). Disco of the moment. Young local hipsters grooving to Euro-techno. Bright lights, loud speakers, and a mind-boggling contrast from the serene National Library across the street. 40,000Ð ticket includes one drink. Open daily 7pm-2am.

Le Maquis Bar, 2A Ta Hien St. (☎828 25 98). From Hoãn Kièm Lake, go north on Hàng Dão; take a right on Hàng Buom and the 1st right on Ta Hiềm. Try this bar for a taste delicious cocktails and French expat life. A tiny grotto-like bar with odd metal chairs, this place is also known as the home of the Minsk Club. Open daily noon-midnight.

Golden Cock Bar, 5 Ngõ Bảo Khán (☎825 04 99). Commonly referred to as the GC, Hanoi's only gay bar is also one of the most comfortable drinking holes for all persuasions, which explains its large straight male (local and foreign) following. Low key. Lesbians are once again rendered invisible. Pool table. Happy hour 5-11pm. Open daily 5pm-whenever.

Polite Pub, 5 Bảo Khánh (☎825 09 59). Right next to the GC, this bar exudes heterosexuality, albeit politely. Frequented by expatriates for after-hour drinks. Sports on TV, darts, and pool table. Happy hour 5-8pm. Open daily 4pm-whenever.

Ðông Khôi, 7 Bảo Khánh (☎828 98 81). In the same neighborhood as the GC and Polite Pub but completely different. A friendly, well-lit pool hall. At 20,000Ð per hour, you can drink, relax, and think about the music that isn't blasting in your ear. About an 80/20 locals/foreigners mix.

Relax Bar, 60 Lý Thuong Kiet (☎942 44 09). An open air charmer with a bonsai fountain in the middle and a banana thatch roof on top. It's a bit out of the way, and the crowds (mostly older expats) are cliquish. Beer 15,000Đ. Open daily 9am-2am.

Funky Monkey Bar, 15b Hãng Hãnh (☎928 61 13). Self-advertised as having "cool muzik," but you be the judge. Snacks and pizza served to chatty backpackers in a small blue room. Longest happy hour in town from 1am-8pm.

DAYTRIP FROM HANOI

CHÙA HƯƠNG (PERFUME PAGODA)

Set in lush rice paddies studded with jagged limestone karsts like the ones found in Halong Bay, the Perfume Pagoda is a center of Buddhism in Vietnam. The shrine derives its name from the huge grotto in the Hương Tích Mountains (Mountain of the Fragrant Traces) in which it peacefully resides. Though the Perfume Pagoda itself is disappointing, the complex of temples at the bottom of the mountain, known as **Thiên Trù Pagodas,** are serene and beautiful. Destroyed during the French war, the pagoda area, once home to over 100 temples, was partly rebuilt in 1968 but still has just seven temples. For one month after the Lunar New Year, thousands of Buddhist pilgrims flock to the temple during the **Perfume Pagoda Festival** (Lễ Hội Chùa Hương), a spectacle worth experiencing. A typical tour to the Perfume Pagoda from Hanoi includes road transport, a boat ride, and the 3-4km hike to the main temple. An option for solo travelers is taking a public bus to Hà Dōng (30 min, 5000-7000Đ) and catching another bus to Yèn Vỹ village. Arrange transportation from a tourist cafe in Hanoi. The size of the crowds at tour operators is inversely proportional to the price. (US$12-16 includes transport, lunch, and admission.)

HAIPHONG (HẢI PHÒNG) ☎31

A quiet city of wide, shady avenues and crumbling colonial buildings, Haiphong offers travelers a calmer and more laid-back version of Hanoi. Built by the French in the early 1900s, its trees and public parks were meant to resemble quiet towns in the south of France. Haiphong, however, has a darker history. Because of its key role as a conduit for Soviet aid to northern Vietnam during the Vietnam War, Haiphong suffered severe US bombing and, at times, it seems like it has yet to recover. New industries trying to stimulate this revival have changed the face of the Haiphong that the French imagined, making it an industrial center that drives most travelers toward the beaches and parks of nearby Cát Bà Island. Remnants of the city's old pace, however, still remain hidden in its food-laden alleyways, away from the inevitable forces of change.

TRANSPORTATION

Flights: Cát Bi Airport (☎728 209), 7km southwest of the town center. Take a taxi (50,000Đ), motorcycle taxi (US$5), or cyclo (15,000-20,000Đ) from the town center. To **HCMC** via **Hanoi** (2hr., daily at noon, 1,900,000Đ). **Vietnam Airlines,** 30 Trần Phú (☎847 137). Open M-Sa 8-11:30am and 1:30-4:20pm.

Trains: Haiphong Railway Station, 75 Lương Khánh Thiện (☎846 433), at the end of Phạm Ngũ Lão. Trains to **Hanoi Central Station** (2hr.; 1 per day 6:10pm; soft seat 56,000Đ, hard seat 52,000Đ) and **Hanoi Long Bien Station** (2hr.; 6:20, 10:40am, 2, 4:10, 6:45pm; same prices).

Buses: Tam Bạc Bus Station, opposite the Steel Market. Buses to **Hanoi** (2Ă-3hr.; every 15min. from 5:30am-7pm, every 30min. after 7pm; 25,000Đ). Buses also go to **Hạ Long City** (2¾hr.; 6, 8:30, 11am, 1:30, 4pm; 50,000Đ).

Ferries: Pier on Bến Bính Rd. on the Cấm River. From the west end of Điện Biên Phủ, head north toward the port. To **Cát Bà** (slow boat 3hr.; 6:30am, 1pm; 70,000Đ; under the "Bến Tàu Khách Haiphong" sign; hydrofoil 1 hr., 10:30am, 90,000Đ). Buy tickets one day in advance or at the booth before boarding. Times change frequently.

Local Transportation: Cyclos should get you anywhere in the city for 5,000-10,000Đ. **Haiphong Taxi** (☎822 991) charges 6000Đ per km; ask the driver to use the meter.

ORIENTATION AND PRACTICAL INFORMATION

On the Red River Delta 103km east of Hanoi on **Hwy. 5**, Haiphong has a compactly populated center flanked by industrial zones. After crossing the **Lạc Long Bridge**, Hwy. 5 becomes **Điện Biên Phủ**, Haiphong's main drag, and runs past many hotels. A block east of the Lac Long Bridge, Điện Biên Phủ intersects **Hoàng Văn Thụ**, the second-largest street in town. **Trần Hưng Đạo, Trần Phú,** and **Lư'ơng Khánh Thiện** run diagonally between Điện Biên Phủ and Hoàng Văn Thụ. This area, called "Center" is home to the **train station,** a park, and **Tam Bac Lake.** From the **Municipal Theater**, at the intersection of Trần Hưng Đạo and Hoàng Văn Thụ, **Quang Trung** runs along Tam Bac Lake before ending at the **Tam Bac bus station** and **steel market.**

Tourist Office: Haiphong Tourist Company, 57 Điện Biên Phủ (☎745 432). Open M-Sa 7-11:30am and 1:30-5pm. **Branch office,** 15 Lê Đại Hành (☎822 516), next to Hotel du Commerce at Điện Biên Phủ intersection.

Currency Exchange: Vietcombank, 11 Hoàng Diệu (☎842 658). Heading east on Điện Biên Phủ, turn left onto Minh Khai; it's at the end on the left. Open M-Sa 7:30-11:30am and 1:30-4pm. **No ATM.**

Emergency: Police ☎113. **Ambulance** ☎115.

Pharmacy: Hoàng Lê Pharmacy, 63 Điện Biên Phủ (☎841 605). Well-stocked. Open M-Sa 8am-7pm, Su 8am-2pm.

Medical Services: Việt-Tiệp Friendship Hospital, 1 Nhà Thương (☎700 436).

Telephones: Inside the GPO. International phone/fax. Open 6:30am-10pm.

Internet: In hotels and tour agencies around town.

Post Office: GPO, 5 Nguyễn Tri Phương (☎842 563), at intersection with Hoàng Văn Thụ. *Poste Restante.* Open daily 7am-10pm. **DHL** inside GPO.

ACCOMMODATIONS AND FOOD

Most hotels are on **Điện Biên Phủ,** and rooms are pricey. For better options, try **Cát Bà Island** (p. 841).

Điện Biên Hotel, 135 Điện Biên Phủ (☎745 553). Gorgeous old colonial mansion around a shady central courtyard. Friendly owners. Rooms are spacious and clean. US$8, with A/C US$10.

Thắng Nam Hotel, 55 Điện Biên Phủ (☎842 820). As long as you're paying Haiphong's hotel prices, you might as well get your money's worth. Clean rooms with A/C, TV, phone, and balcony overlooking tennis court US$13-15.

Bến Bính Hotel, 6 Đúong Bến Bính (☎842 260), 100m east of the ferry dock. Colonial mansion facade offers standard rooms. Convenient location opposite the pier is worth the extra đong. Doubles with bath and A/C US$15-25.

Food stalls crowd the corner of **Điện Biên Phủ** and **Minh Khai,** and **Trần Hưng Đạo** is full of cheap eateries. The **Ga Market** on Lương Khanh Thien is known for giant seafood dishes. For a slightly classier dinning experience, try the restaurants on Hoàng Văn Thụ between Điện Biên Phủ and Trần Hưng Đạo. **Quang Minh Hotel Restaurant,** 20 Minh Khai, halfway down the block from the intersection with Điện Biên Phủ, serves a variety of Vietnamese and Western dishes for 30,000-100,000Đ. (Open daily 8:30am-11:30pm.)

VIETNAM

SIGHTS

MUNICIPAL THEATER (CITY SQUARE THEATRE). The recently-renovated Municipal Theater is proof of Hanoi's French architectural influence. It was built using materials imported from France in the style of the Hanoi Opera House. The square in front of the theater was the site of a bloody four-day standoff between French forces and Việt-Minh revolutionaries in November 1946. *(At the intersection of Quang Trung/Trần Hưng Đạo and Hoàng Văn Thụ. Ticket prices vary.)*

NGHÈ TEMPLE. The colorful temple and its large courtyard commemorate Lê Chân, a leader of the Trung sisters' insurrection against the Chinese before founding An Biên Village, Haiphong's predecessor. The Vietnamese celebrate Lê Chân's birth and death at the temple on the eighth day of the second lunar month and the twenty-fifth day of the twelfth lunar month, respectively. Special offerings are made at the shrine. *(51 Ngõ Nghè. Best reached by cyclo. Open daily 6am-9pm.)*

DƯ HÀNG PAGODA. Dư Hàng Pagoda on Chùa Hàng, with a beautiful Chinese-style garden and a multitude of little inner courtyards, exudes a calm thoughtfulness. Built during the Trần dynasty (1225-1400), the pagoda was restored earlier this century. The monks can be callous to visitors because of the families who come here to discuss their problems at the two meeting-houses in the temple. *(Open daily 5-11:30am and 1:30-6pm.)*

ĐỒ SƠN BEACH. The beach attracts tourists from all over Vietnam and is cleaned regularly in a government-led effort to boost the local economy. Đồ Sơn boasts Vietnam's lone (foreigners-only) casino. *(20km southeast of Haiphong. Motorcycle taxi, 30,000Đ, is best. Buses depart to Đồ Sơn daily from Haiphong's bus stations when full. Open noon to early morning.)*

OTHER SIGHTS. Pagoda-like **Flower Stalls,** built in 1944, dot the squares near Tam Bac Lake with vibrant colors. Farther west, hawker shops overflowing with miscellany flank **Quang Trung** and its side streets. At the east end of Quang Trung on the site of old rice markets is the modern behemoth known as **Chợ' Sắt (Steel Market).** History buffs should stop by the **Hàng Kênh Communal House** (Đình Hàng Kênh), 1.5km south on Hàng Kênh. Remnants of imperial Vietnam adorn all objects and surfaces within this Chinese-style compound. On an altar stands a statue of Ngô Quyền, the liberator and king. *(Open M-Sa 8am-5pm. 5000Đ.)* Also check out the **Navy Museum,** 38 Điện Biên Phư, where a graceful French edifice contains some poignant remnants of the city's battles with foreigners. *(Open Tu-Su 8am-5pm. 10,000Đ.)*

NIGHTLIFE

Despite being a port city, Haiphong has a pretty quiet nightlife. Locals take walks along Ho Tam Bac or sit in bars and cafes, including **Dilman** on 84 Điện Biên Phủ (juices 3,000Đ, beer 10,000Đ) and **Dat Cang,** 28 Quang Trung, near the theater (cocktails 35,000Đ). Good bars include **Maxim's,** 51B Điện Biên Phủ, which has live music until late every night plus cocktails (30,000-40,000Đ) and light dishes (20,000-50,000Đ). Other happening places are the plush **Piano Bar** inside the Huu Nghi Hotel, 60 Điện Biên Phủ (☎823 314), which has a great view and live music on weekends, and its cousin the **Saigon Disco,** 31 Điện Biên Phủ, the only place to dance in town. (Admission 20,000-40,000Đ. Open daily until 2am.)

CÁT BÀ ISLAND

Cát Bà Island National Park, 50km east of Haiphong, is the site of a recent tourist boom, as backpackers and Vietnamese vacationers have descended in huge numbers on its 350 sq. km. The island is an impressive array of limestone mountains overgrown with jungle and ringed by fine sand beaches, but is also fertile enough to support rice, maize, and lychee plantations. Guides and locals are quick to point out that Cát Bà is not just a larger version Ha Long Bay; despite the horde of tourists, especially in July and August, Cát Bà is the ideal place to go on rigorous hikes, boat excursions into Halong Bay, or simply to relax on the beach.

TRANSPORTATION. This little paradise is most easily reached from Haiphong (see **Transportation,** p. 843). **Ferries** run to **Haiphong** (slow boat 3hr.; daily 5:45am, 1pm; 70,000Đ; hydrofoil 1hr.; daily 9am, 3:30pm; 90,000Đ) and **Ha Long** (4hr., 1 per day 5:45am, 80,000Đ). Otherwise, hitch onto a tour (US$10). Public **buses** run from Cát Bà town to the National Park entrance. Bus drivers assume any foreigners to be part of an organized tour and usually don't charge anything. The official fare starts from 500Đ. Alternatively, hire a **motorcycle** (US$8 per day) or charter a **boat** (US$15 for 4 hr.).

PRACTICAL INFORMATION. The main ferry dock at Cát Bà town is the center of the island's universe. The **GPO**—with **telephone** booths—is directly across the street. (Open M-F 7am-10pm, Sa-Su 9:30am-9pm.) Hotels line the main drag for about 400m to either side. The closest swimming beach is 200m to your right, while to your left is the highway to the National Park. **Vãng Bac,** a pharmacy that doubles as a **foreign exchange** counter, is 500m down from the dock on this road. (☎888 308. Open 9am-11pm.)

ACCOMMODATIONS AND FOOD. Since the introduction of electricity in 1998, hotels and restaurants have sprung up like mushrooms. Most line Cát Bà's main drag and offer similar services including tours of the island and the bay, rooms with A/C and sea views, motorbike and boat rentals. The **Quang Duc Family Hotel,** located directly across from the dock, has professional English-speaking tour service. (☎888 231. Balcony rooms US$12-15.) Next door, the **Vân Anh Guest House** offers similar rooms but no tour service. (☎888 201. Doubles US$15 and up.)

> **BOOK AHEAD.** In the high season call from Hanoi or Haiphong to book ahead or try the tourist cafes; some hotels have permanent contracts with tourist cafes like Sinh and Queens Cafe and refuse service to walk-ins.

Since most visitors eat inferior hotel food as part of their deal, the restaurants have fewer foreigners than most tourist sites. The restaurants sell good seafood and the local specialty, crab. **Jane's Garden Coffee Bar & Restaurant** (☎888 840) and **Hữu Dũng Restaurant,** both on the side street, are worth a trip.

Nightlife can be found on the main drag that runs along the water. Beer and refreshment stalls on the dock have outdoor seatings and an almost Riviera-like ambience. Towards the Park is the best bar in town, the Vietnamese-Kiwi owned **Flightless Bird Cafe** (☎888 517), which has darts, movies, and book exchange. Avoid the "karaoke lounge" or you'll get more than cheesy singalongs. The two discotheques, perched on the hill behind the GPO are refreshingly not-so-seedy. Follow the neon signs for **Cát Bà** (☎888 789) and next-door **Sóng Xanh Disco.** (☎888 637. No cover. **Tiger beer only 10,000Đ.**) Try them if you ever wondered how Public Enemy can blend with Canto-pop in a remix that features Celine Dion.

SIGHTS. In order to visit the island at your own pace, rent a motorbike with a driver (US$5-6) from a hotel or restaurant. Otherwise, join up with a tour and ride around in their minibus (US$5-6). Apart from the bay itself, Cát Bà's main attraction is its lush **National Park,** 17km from the pier. (15,000-25,000Đ depending on length of trek. Guides US$5-6 per half-day.) The park hosts a botanical garden, fields of lychee trees, and around 60 animal species. It's an ideal place to go on short hikes (2hr. up a very steep hill) or more demanding hikes (5-6hr. up six hills), though trails are sometimes poorly defined and can be treacherous during the rainy season. On the road to the park is **Trung Trang Cave** (the "army hospital cave"), one of the centers of Vietnamese troops and coordination in the north during the war (15,000Đ). The local veteran organization has its members as guides.

Another 15km past the park, surrounded by rice and maize fields, lies the town of **Phu Long.** The town proper is bland, and the cave that lies 2km upriver, with its cement paths and neon overhead lights, would make a true spelunker scoff. (Open daily 8am-7pm. 15,000Đ.) The journey itself, up and down rocky hills, past small creeks and unexplored beaches (by motorbike), however, is worth the effort. **Boats** can also be hired at the end of the main drag (40,000Đ). Boat owners offer tours of the coastline. Check with hotels for other half-or full-day tours.

If any movement at all sounds unappealing, loll in the warm water at **Cat Co Beach,** accessible via the road over the hill at the edge of Cát Bà town (toll 7,000Đ). To escape Cat Co's crowds, sneak up the stairs at the back to nearly deserted **Cat Co II Beach** or visit **Bai Beo** beach, on the other side of the island, where local fishermen go. Another popular option is the **Monkey Island** (45 min. from Cát Bà by boat, toll 7000Đ). Most backpackers organize afternoon trips among themselves so ask around. (40,000-50,000Đ per person for a 4 hr. trip for a group of 15.)

HALONG BAY (VỊNH HẠ LONG) ☎33

Halong Bay, featured in films such as *Indochine*, stretches from Haiphong in the south to Halong City in the north and around 10mi. out to sea. With its 1968 limestone islands and 23 grottoes, this marvel of nature is now protected by UNESCO. According to legend, Halong ("Dragon Descending") Bay was formed when a dragon spat out divine pearls that formed a barrier against an invading Chinese fleet. Once the enemy had been turned back, the dragon settled in the bay and its scales converted into rocky islets.

At first glance, Halong City is an impersonal town full of identical mini-hotels, outrageous prices, and pushy locals. Most Westerners readily dismiss the place as tacky and offensive but to judge Halong City by that yardstick alone misses the point. The reality of Vietnam today is places like Halong City, where a drive for development and a liberalizing economy are re-defining Vietnamese society. In the past decade, local authorities have courted regional investment in hotels and recreation facilities, making Halong City into a top tourist getaway for northern Vietnamese and southern Chinese. The bay is most effectively and inexpensively reached by a tour from Hanoi. It's also possible to skip Halong City altogether and explore the bay from Cát Bà Island via Haiphong.

TRANSPORTATION

Buses depart from Bãi Cháy Bus Station, 600m south of the pier on Bãi Cháy Rd., to: **Hanoi** (4-5hr., every 20-30min. 4:50am-5pm, 35,000Đ); **HCMC** (W, Th, Su 7:30am; 225,000Đ); **Vinh** (7-8hr., 6:30am, 55,000Đ). **Minibuses** leave from across the street to **Hảiphòng** (2½hr., 6am-5pm, 18,000Đ) and **Hanoi** (4hr., 6am-5pm, from 80,000Đ). **Ferries** leave from Bãi Cháy to Hòn Gai (every 10min. until 10pm, then every 30min.; 500Đ). The Hòn Gai pier (Bến Tàu Hòn Gai), 1.5km down Lê Thánh Tông from the pier, at the end of the road to the right at the first small traffic circle, has ferries to **Cát Bà Island** (2½hr., Sa-Su 7am, 70,000Đ) and **Hảiphòng** (2½hr.; 6, 8:30, 11am, 4pm; 50,000Đ). A better option is to take the **Tourist Hydrofoil.** It runs to Cát Bà (daily 7:30am-8:10am, return 4:15pm-4:55pm; 90,000Đ) and to the Chinese border town of **Mong Cai** (3hr., 7am and 1pm, US$12).

ORIENTATION AND PRACTICAL INFORMATION

Bãi Cháy and **Hòn Gai** are the west and east halves of **Halong City** which lies 165km east of Hanoi and 55km northeast of Haiphong. Tourist-oriented **Bãi Cháy** is across a strait from the more industrial **Hòn Gai. Hạ Long,** the main road in Bãi Cháy, runs northeast, passing the only beach accessible without a boat. The heart of Ha Long City is an easy 1km stroll from the **pier.** The **Royal Amusement Park, GPO,** restaurant row, and Vườn Đào street are clustered together. All chartered boats to the grottoes leave from a pier another 2½ km down from the center. **Halong Tourist Company,** 1 Halong Rd., just south of the pier to Hòn Gai, organizes 4hr. boat trips (US$27) and gives useful information. (☎846 272. Open M-Sa 7:30-11:30am and 1-5pm.) **Commercial Bank of Quảng Ninh,** on Halong Rd. down the road from Halong Tourist Company, changes major currencies and traveler's checks. (☎825 297. Open M-Sa 8-11am and 1-5pm.)

In **emergencies,** call ☎825 486. **Quảng Ninh Provincial Hospital,** 651 Lê Thánh Tông, is 1km beyond the Hòn Gai GPO on the road that forks to the right. The director of the hospital, Mr. Hanh, speaks English. (☎825 490. US$50 per visit.) **Internet access** can be found at Hái Yên Hotel, 57 Vườn Đào (☎846 125; open 6am-midnight; 500Đ per min.), **Emotion Cyber Cafe** (☎847 354; 500Đ per min.), and various tourist agencies. The **Halong City Post Office,** at Vườn Đào intersection, has **phones;** you must purchase a phone card (100,000Đ) first. (☎846 201. Open daily 6:30am-9:30pm.)

VIETNAM

ACCOMMODATIONS

To catch a sight like no other, veer off to the left from the GPO and walk 400m up the hill on Vườn Đào. **Minihotels** line this street with a vengeance—over 75 on this small hill alone. All ask US$8-15 depending on amenities that include two beds, A/C, and hot showers. Enjoy making your choice.

Khách San Vân Anh (☎847 618) across from the ferry dock, on top of 100 steps with a commanding view of the Bay. From the public bus station, turn left and follow the sign 50m away. A/C doubles 180,000Đ.

Thùy Dường Hotel (☎846 137) and **Hong Minh Hotel** (☎846 264), next door. Facing the GPO, walk 100m along the water on Ha Long Rd. Their views, cleanliness, and location away from karaoke bars are their forte. Thùy Dường Hotel doubles 200,000Đ; Hong Minh Hotel doubles US$15, with view US$20.

Nhà Nghỉ Sơn Hà, 63 Lê Thánh Tông (☎826 553), in Hòn Gai, 400m down from the dock to Bãi Cháy on the left. The owner of this family-run, charming, and cheap hotel speaks excellent English. Doubles US$8-10.

FOOD

Seafood is the specialty in Halong Bay but it doesn't come cheaply. **Restaurant Row** around the GPO is the culinary epicenter for tourists. Live lobster, crabs, fish, and clams await customers in water tanks outside each eatery. Most come boiled, steamed, fried, and souped, respectively; just ask the chef for more options. (Seafood entrees 30,000-180,000Đ.) In this lot, **Phướng Oanh** (☎846 145) is recommended for its menu titled "To our dear backpacker customers" and their cheap prices. The further you walk away from the row, the cheaper the food, though only marginally. **Cafe Halon** (☎847 715) across from the dock has a more extensive English menu.

SIGHTS

Travelers from all over come to explore beautiful Halong Bay. Of the 1500 plus limestone grottoes protruding from the sea, over 150 caves have been identified so far, and at least 50 of them are blessed with multi-colored illumination for the tourists' benefit. Private boats are necessary, however, to explore the obscure grottoes, because packaged boat tours only stop at a select few. The favorite stop is the **Heavenly Palace Grotto** and the **Dau Go Grotto** (grotto of the Wooden Stakes). The former is so named because of the varying shape of mineral formations that resemble a den of heavenly creatures, while legend has it that the latter hid shipbuilding wood for the Vietnamese during their conflicts with the Chinese at the turn of the millennium. As the most visited cave (the two are adjoined on the same island), their splendor is somewhat mired by the harsh neon lighting and concrete paths that make it look like a Disney attraction. Another site is the **Virgin Grotto,** named for a stalagmite figure that resembles a young maiden pining after her lost love. All grottoes require the purchase of tickets (10,000-20,000Đ, included if you are booked on a boat tour from Hanoi or Ha Long City).

The easiest way to see Halong Bay is via a tour booked in Hanoi. The most popular agencies are **TF Hanspan,** 116 Pho Hang Bac (☎828 1996) and its sister organization **Kangaroo Cafe,** 18 Pho Bao Khanh (☎828 9931). Three-day trips, including Cát Bà, cost US$50-60 (all inclusive). Cheaper tours are run by **Queen and Sinh Cafes** (see **By Bus,** p. 828). Tours are also available on-site; fear not, the touts will find you. The quality of these tours is impossible to ascertain. (4hr. trip, US$30 for 4 people.) Groups can charter boats at Halong Tourism or at the **Bãi Cháy Travel Wharf,** 4km south of the ferry on Halong Rd. (20-person boat US$6-10 per hr.). All tours include a US$3 surcharge for foreigners. Tours from Cát Bà Island are possible, though these tend to focus less on exploring caves than swimming in coves. Don't expect killer surf at gorgeous **Bãi Cháy Beach.** The limestone islands that majestically rise from the water simply flatten the waves.

ENTERTAINMENT

In the daytime, the beachfront rents jet skis (US$15 per 15 min.), parasailing gear (US$100 per hr.), and a variety of aqua paraphernalia. At night, the same area boasts **Oh La La Bar** with assorted live music (from Tchaikovsky to the Titanic theme song) played in bamboo-decorated bliss. (Beer from 10,000Đ. Open daily 2pm-midnight.) The nearby **Disco 2000** blasts the latest Chinese pop. (US$3 includes one drink. Half-price drinks and no cover for ladies Su-Th. Cockfighting 100,000Đ, show/slaughter times vary.)

The waterfront **Royal Amusement Park** with jet skis, fake sand, and carnival games in the daytime turns into food stalls, live music and fancy pubs at night. The young (or young at heart), kitsch, and anthropologically-astute travelers should not miss this place. All others should keep an open mind, get ear plugs at night and quit whining.

LẠNG SƠ'N ☎25

During the last 2000 years, the pass at Lạng Sơ'n has seen many uninvited crossings by invading Chinese armies. In 1979, Chinese troops razed Lạng Sơ'n as part of Deng Xiaoping's effort to "teach the Vietnamese a lesson." Ironically, Lạng Sơ'n's sole attraction now is Đồng Đăng, one of two legal places in Vietnam to enter China. Travelers should follow the lead of the many big-rig trunks—just pass on through.

BORDER CROSSING: ĐONG ĐANG/PINGXIANG. North of Lạng Sơn at the north terminus of Rte. 1 lies the tiny border town of Đồng Đăng. The border is past 2 checkpoints, 3km beyond Đồng Đăng at the Hữu Nghị (Friendship) Crossing. To enter China, your **visa** must have a Đồng Đăng **exit stamp.** Tourist cafes in Hanoi can procure Chinese visas (US$132) and can change the exit stamp on Vietnamese visas (US$30). At **Pingxiang,** in Guangxi Province, there are rail and bus connections to Nanning. Travelers have found Chinese customs here low-key, quick, and easy.

TRANSPORTATION. Buses drop people at the **Ngộ Quyền bus station** on Ngộ Quyền, left off Trần Đăng Ninh after the intersection, unless they have to transfer buses on route from Hanoi, in which case they terminate at the **Lạng Sơn Bus Station** off **Lê Lợi.** Buses run from the Ngộ Quyền Bus Station to Động Đăng on the Chinese border (20-30min., 8am, 20,000Đ) and Hanoi (5-6hr., 10-15 buses per day 6am-midnight, leave when full, 35,000Đ; 6am and 1:30pm buses for foreigners only). Most people return to Hanoi by **minibus,** which ply the streets looking for passengers (5hr., roughly 60,000-80,000Đ for foreigners). Smaller minibuses run to the border (20min., up to 50,000Đ for foreigners), and taxis can be hired in front of the Kim Sơn Hotel off **Đường Minh Khai** (20,000-30,000Đ). **Trains** from the Lang Son Station (☎873 452), at the far end of Lê Lợi, leave for **Hanoi** (regular trains 10½hr.; 10am; express trains 7-8hr., 6:30am and 2pm; 70,000Đ for soft seat). Tickets for the M1 train to **Beijing,** leaving from Đồng Đăng Train Station every Tuesday and Friday at 8am, and should be booked in Hanoi.

PRACTICAL INFORMATION. Lạng Sơn is 130km north of Hanoi on Rte. 1. The town's main drag, **Trần Đăng Ninh,** heads north to Đồng Đăng. In the southern part of town, **Đường Lê Lợi** branches east from Trần Đăng Ninh, passes the **post office,** and terminates at the **train station.** Just 100m south of the intersection, Trần Đăng Ninh crosses a **river** and continues on to the **bank.** Follow Trần Đăng Ninh south over the bridge and around the curve and then take the first left to get to the **Đầu Tư Bank,** 2 Hoàng Văn Thụ, which exchanges currency but not traveler's checks. (☎870 033. Open daily 7am-11:30pm.) There is a **pharmacy** at 52A Trần Đăng Ninh, 50m north of the Lê Lợi intersection. (☎870 878. Open daily 8am-9pm.) The **hospital** is west of town. The **GPO,** 49 Lê Lợi, 100m from the Trần Đăng Ninh intersection, has an **international telephone.** (☎870 047. Open daily 6am-10pm.)

ACCOMMODATIONS AND FOOD. Kim Sòn Hotel, 3 Minh Khai, is well-situated near the new bus station and has decent rooms. (☎870 378. Doubles US$8-10.) The cheapest deal in town is **Kỳ Lừa Hotel,** 208 Trần Đăng Ninh. (☎870 020. Large doubles/triples with bathtub, TV, and phone, 100,000-120,000Đ.) Slightly fancier is the **Ngọc Mai Hotel,** 25 Lê Lợi, near the train station, which is modern and clean. (☎871 837. Doubles US$15-20.)

In the evenings a large **market** sets up on Lê Lợi and spills down along the riverside; Trần Đăng Ninh and Lê Lợi host the usual **phở** shops (full meals 10,000-20,000Đ). Providing a bit of a break from the routine, **Vân Anh Restaurant,** on Lê Lợi 100m past the post office on the right as you come from Trần Đăng Ninh, serves just about everything from civet to rabbit, at very affordable prices. (Most entrees under 30,000Đ. Open daily 7am-11pm.) Also good and affordable is the **Minh Quang Restaurant,** 45 Ngộ Quyền, serving excellent beef dishes (15,000-20,000Đ).

SIGHTS. A motorcycle taxi can transport travelers to the mountains 2-3km west of town to the **Tam Thanh Cave** (5000Đ) and **Nhị Thanh Cave** (10,000Đ). An opening at the back of the cave allows visitors to see the surrounding countryside and mountains—a fine photo-op. (Both caves open daily 7am-7pm. 10,000Đ each.)

NORTHWEST VIETNAM

The remote Hoàng Liên Sơn Mountains of northwest Vietnam present some of the most challenging—and rewarding—travel opportunities in mainland Southeast Asia. The physical beauty of the region is breathtaking, and the ethnic diversity of the highland population is reminiscent of northern Laos, with whom the peoples of this region share close cultural and linguistic bonds. Travel is arduous when navigating windy roads with constant ascent and descent; of course it doesn't help that the government has scarcely improved roads since colonial times. Travelers with limited time can get a superficial taste of the region with a trip (easily organized in Hanoi) to highly touristed Sapa or Mai Châu. Otherwise, those braving the entire circuit of Mai Châu, Sơn La, Điện Biên Phủ, Lai Châu, and easy-going Sapa and Bắc Hà will get more than kitschy embroideries and encounters with prepubescent tourist-hound veterans. The loop can be done by public bus, by motorbike, or for the athletic (and masochistic), by bicycle.

LÀO CAI ☎20

Lào Cai is one of two border crossings into Yunnan province, China, and the chief point of access to Sapa and Bắc Hà. Despite blossoming trade between China and Vietnam, Lào Cai is really just a boring little town. Most travelers hardly pause before speeding north into China, south to Hanoi, or directly into the mountains.

VIETNAM

TRANSPORTATION. Most travelers arrive in Lào Cai by **train** from Hanoi or China. Train ticket stubs are collected at the gate on arrival; don't lose them. Trains run to Hanoi (10hr.; 10:10am and 6:45pm; 125,000Đ hard seat, 207,500Đ soft sleeper).

Plenty of transfer options to Sapa await at Lào Cai train station to take you to their guest houses in Sapa. Some guest houses have **minibuses** (25,000Đ per person); you are not obliged to stay at the assigned address, only to look. An official from Hanoi Tourism also has a makeshift desk selling 25,000Đ Sapa bus tickets redeemable at most private vans outside the station. Purchase direct from drivers outside, however, and you'll likely pay only 15,000Đ. **Cheaper tickets are likely to be fraudulent.** Other modes of Sapa-bound transport include a **motorcycle taxi** (2hr. on bumpy road, 50,000Đ), **taxi** (150,000Đ or less), or **public buses** at the bus station (2hr.; around 6, 9am, 1, 4pm; 25,000Đ).

Buses also depart to: **Bac Ha** (4hr.), Hanoi, and **Lai Chau** (8hr., 6:30am every other day in summer, 4500Đ).

ORIENTATION AND ACCOMMODATIONS. Lào Cai suffers from poor urban planning; the three reasons for its existence are inconveniently far apart. The **Lào Cai train station** lies over 2km away from the customs building (open daily 7:30am-4pm), which also houses the **currency exchange office** (US dollars, Đong, Chinese yuan; open daily 7am-3pm). The **bus station** sits somewhere between the train and customs, but on the opposite side of the river. Luckily, all these sites are more or less along one straight line on **Phố Nguyen Hue.** Motorcycle taxis take passengers from one end to the other for 5000-10,000Đ depending on how tired and desperate one looks. For those arriving at odd hours, there are hotels clustered around the customs building, along with eateries and a post office. The **Sông Hông Guest House** is your best bet; it has all the amenities in a clean environment. (☎830 004. With A/C US$10.)

SAPA ☎20

The hills around Sapa are alive—with the sound of tourists and the vendors who love them. Once a remote hill station, Sapa is now the premiere spot for weekend package tours to view tribal minorities on display. The famed Saturday market has become a freak show, where everyone (including grubby backpackers) becomes a caricature for others in an amusing arena of mutual—and communal—bewilder-

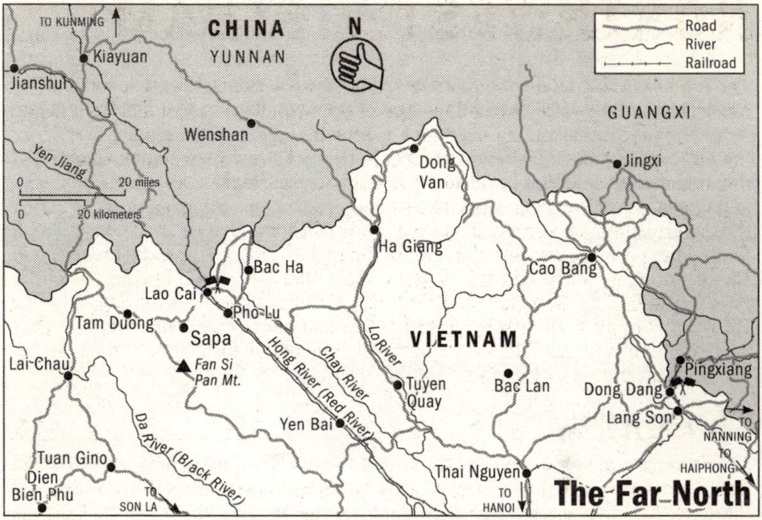

ment. For that reason, more visitors are choosing to come mid-week to see Sapa's true idyllic beauty. Guided walks to nearby villages and Vietnam's highest peak, the Fan Si Pan, can be easily organized. The marginalized communities of Sapa have little but a history of deprivation and an unyielding pride—something tourists should remember before losing their patience in front of an aggressive hawker.

VIETNAM

TRANSPORTATION

Buses: Tourist minibuses to **Lào Cai** leave from the large square in front of the church (1½hr., every hr. from 6am, 25,000Đ). Buy tickets at the post office or in any of the tourist cafes a day in advance. **Public buses** (2hr., 9am and noon, 20,000Đ), as well as **jeeps, sedans,** and **minibuses** (2hr., leave when full, no more than 20,000Đ) leave for Lào Cai from the church. Other transportation to Lào Cai can be secured through your hotel. The public bus to **Lai Châu** (8hr., 45,000Đ for Vietnamese, more for foreigners) must be flagged down on Hwy. 4; facing the main post office, walk left down the road out of town 1km and wait at the traffic triangle. Start waiting at 7am, but the bus may come as late as 11am. **Demand a ticket with Lai Châu written on it.** Buses also run to **Tam Duong** (hourly 6am-2pm, 15,000Đ) where buses can be caught to Lai Châu and then Hanoi. Since the bus to Lai Châu has no official price, travelers can pay what they ask. Bring a trusted Vietnamese friend (often from the guest house) to purchase a ticket before boarding.

Local Transportation: Minibuses (at the church) can usually take you to hotels.

Rentals: Many hotels rent *minsks*, old Russian motorcycles (US$1.50 per hr., US$8 per day), and jeeps with drivers (from US$30 per day).

ORIENTATION AND PRACTICAL INFORMATION

Sapa has one of those rare geographical layouts that is hard to describe in words and even confusing on a map. Upon arrival, however, it only takes a few minutes to get your bearings. From the church at the town center, it takes no more than 10-15min. to reach anywhere in town. Facing the church, the **GPO** and **Friendly Cafe** are one block to your left, a stairway 100m to your right leads to the **market** and the **mainstreet,** and a lone **phone booth** stands diagonally across the football field up on the hill.

Tours: Friendly Cafe in the Viet Hung Hotel offers treks around Sapa (1-day trek, US$7-20 depending on group size), as well as trips up Fan Si Pan Mountain (3-5 days, US$25). **Meeting Cafe** (☎871 881), a few doors down, has similar service plus motorbike rental (US$10/20,000Đ per day with petrol). A branch of Hanoi's **Green Bamboo Cafe** (☎871 556), on the main road below the market. The manager, Hung, serves travelers well.

Currency Exchange: The bank won't change currency. Most guest houses change US$ and traveler's checks at low to decent rates (5-7ổ commission).

Hospital: ☎871 237, 1km down the road, to the right of the Viet Hung Hotel.

Telephones: Cash calls available at the GPO. US$2.35-2.70 for the 1st min. to Asia, US/Canada and Europe; under US$0.50 per min. thereafter. Faxes costs US$3-4 per page.

Internet Access: Available at most hotels and guest houses for 1000-2000Đ per min.

Post Offices: GPO (☎871 292). Facing the church, go left on the road leading back to Lào Cai. Open in summer daily 7am-9:30pm; in winter 7:30am-8pm. *Poste Restante.* A branch (☎871 247) is on the main street below the market. Little English spoken.

ACCOMMODATIONS

Most rooms in Sapa run on both a seasonal and weekly price schedule. During the weekend market in high season (May-July for Vietnamese tourists, July-October for foreigners), hotels charge what they want. On the off days, however, it's a buyers market: bargain hard. Also look for hot water, mosquito net, fireplace (crucial for the winter) and to pamper yourself, a room with a view. As new hotel construction shows no sign of fatigue, "promotional deals" also help to deflate cost.

Phượng Hoàng Guest House (☎871 515), past the Auberge, 200m towards the remote end. Unobstructed view of Fan Si Pan. No constructions nearby: just you, a lush view, and a TV at a great price. With view, balcony, and two large beds US$7; less pleasant but adequate alternatives for US$5.

Minh Quang Hotel (☎871 449), 50m down from Phượng Hoàng. New, bright palatial-looking building. Not yet backpacker central. Everything you need for US$8 per room.

Queen Hotel (☎871 301), on the main road around the bend below the market, next to Auberge. Ask for Room 403 or 503 for a deluxe experience with leather seats and bednets made from wedding gown lace. Fastest Internet in town (1000Đ per min.). Rooms with hot water US$4-10.

Auberge Dang Trung Hotel (☎871 243). Walk down the stairs toward the market, make the 1st left onto the main street and follow the bend 200m down. An old-time favorite in a stylish French villa. Views from cheaper rooms have been obstructed by new construction, but high-end ones with fireplace are unaffected. Relax by the bonsai garden. French, English speaking staff. Internet access. Same rates all year. Rooms US$6-15.

Twilight Guest House (☎871 601), down the stairs and across the market. The rooms are standard but the view is unparalleled. Room with view US$5.

Càt Càt Guest House (☎871 387), opposite the Twilight Guest House. If you crave wild parties and hordes of beer guzzling backpackers, the perennial favorite Càt Càt is for you. Internet access, great tourist info. Rooms US$4-15.

Cầu Mây Guest House (☎871 293). Head up the slope and make the first left. Rooms are sparse though hot water and satellite TV are guaranteed to work. Located in an attractive villa with vegetable gardens in front. Away from usual tourist hangouts. Run by an earnest non-English speaking manager, Ms. Vương. Rooms US$8 or 112,000Đ.

FOOD

Local culinary delights aim to please all. Meat eaters can taste venison, frog legs, and wild boars; vegetarians snack on tofu and special Sapa mushrooms (similar to shiitake mushrooms). Fruits such as plums and apricots grow in abundance. **Stalls** in the market and around town serve *phở*, rice dishes, and grilled corn. Sapa Wine, though neither wine nor a product of Sapa, is the choice spirit for chilly evenings.

Mimosa Restaurant, on the main street around the corner from Auberge. Favorite tourist spot in a secluded setting. Excellent lemon grass frog legs. Open daily 7am-11pm.

Camellia Restaurant, across the market, on the right before Cát Cát Guest House. Some of the best food in Sapa. Chicken curry 10,000Đ. Excellent beef dishes 10,000Đ. Open daily 6am-midnight.

Thanh Ngoc, near the GPO, has basic Vietnamese fare with an English menu. Entrees 40,000Đ and up. Open late. **The Gecko,** next door, is an upscale European choice with an atmosphere to match. Open late.

Auberge Dang Trung Restaurant, on the Auberge, has terrace seating with fine views. Slightly pricier, but worth it. Novels to read, swap, or buy. Huge vegetarian plate 15,000Đ. Banana shake 3000Đ. Open daily 7am-10pm.

Chapa Cafe, 50m from Auberge. Typical backpacker's stable: muesli, pancakes, etc. Full dinner menu as well. Open daily 7am-11pm.

SIGHTS

Fan Si Pan Mountain (3143m), across the valley, is Vietnam's highest peak and a popular expedition for those willing to brave its deceptively steep slopes. A competent guide and provisions are necessary for the three- to five-day trip to the summit and back. All guest houses can arrange tours complete with sleeping bags, tents, and rain gear. Comparison shop; prices vary according to the size of the group and the time of year. Expect to pay at least US$40 per person from a reputable source, such as the Green Bamboo, Friendly Cafe, or Càt Càt.

Thác Bac Waterfall, 7km from Sapa on the road to Lai Chau, with its 500m drop and staircase to the top, is also worth a photo, though maybe not for the 5000Đ fee. Instead, walk, or better yet ride a motorbike, for a few more kilometers and experience the breathtaking **Tram Ton Pass** on the route to Lai Châu.

MARKETS

Sapa's main attraction is its **market.** On Saturday afternoons and Sunday mornings, mountain tribal groups come to sell their goods—colorful shirts, musical instruments, and silver jewelry—to travelers. The number of traders has dropped recently, but the market remains a colorful sight.

The market began as a "Love Market" by the Daos where friends from near and far villages came to meet, sing, impress, and entertain each other. Unfortunately, with tourists filming their every move, the event ceased. If you see the "Love Market" advertised now, it's for the fleeting kind you have to pay for.

For weekdays visitors, there are still plenty of trinket sellers. The second floor of **Chợ Sa Pa,** the town market, is their gathering spot. To get away from the sales pitches, the **Photography Gallery of Vietnamese Countryside,** across the park from the GPO, is run by the aloof artist Kim Minh (prints US$2-70 depending on size, add 40,000Đ for frame).

DAYTRIPS FROM SAPA

Shorter hikes through ethnic villages, past waterfalls and green rice fields, rival Fan Si Pan and transcend Sapa's commercialism. Though it's possible to hike solo, guides are available for US$8-10.

The round-trip to three villages around Sapa takes 4-8hr., and makes for a relaxing and pleasant walk. From Sapa, head out of town past the Auberge Restaurant. Pay the 5000Đ "entrance fee." About 7km into the hike, a bridge appears far below the road. After a series of waterfalls and just behind a Hmong homestead, a steep trail leads downhill toward the river and across a footbridge to the Hmong village of **Lao Chai.** From here, the river downstream leads to the Giay village of **Ta Van,** just past a second bridge. Backtrack across this bridge to return to the main road. From here, it's about 2hr. back to town or 1½hr. on to the Dao village of **Giang Ta Chai.** The village is across the river on the left at the fork. Prehistoric etchings adorn rocks along the road. The path crosses a small waterfall on the way.

To get to villages from another directions, cross the market, head downhill past Cát Cát guest house, and follow the path northwest along the valley. (5000Đ entrance fee.) You'll see the remains of a French villa built in the 1930s. About 10min. farther, a small path splits off to the left. The main path leads to the Hmong village of **Sin Chai** after 5km; the left path leads to **Cát Cát,** another Hmong village, less than 1km away. Deeper in the valley is an old hydroelectric power station and **San Sa Ho waterfall,** which is visible from town.

BẮC HÀ ☎20

Bắc Hà, 110km northeast of Sapa, recently came into the crosshairs of Hanoi's tourist cafes, which tout it as an "alternative to Sapa." Once a mountain hamlet of hill tribe traders and old wooden homes, the village is changing fast. Tourist cafes offer daytrips to Bắc Hà's huge, colorful Sunday hill tribe market every Sunday for about US$10 per person. Since few travelers attempt to visit Bắc Hà on their own, from Monday through Saturday Bắc Hà really does become an "alternative" for those wishing to encounter north Vietnam's ethnic minorities and mountain scenery free from the influence of the tourist industry.

Bắc Hà's **Sunday market** (open 7am-2pm) is still genuine: Hmong come from all around to buy clothes and accessories. The market is also known for its food stalls, which serve cheap dishes. Arrive early for the freshest food. Live animals, fruit and vegetables are sold there. The countryside surrounding Bắc Hà beckons hikers. You can also hire a motorcycle taxi (50,000Đ per day) to **Coc Ly** 18km away, which has a **waterfall** (Thác Coc Ly) and a large **suspension bridge** (Cầu Treo Coc Ly) built over the Chay River by local hill tribes. Those in town should not miss a motorcycle trip to the **Saturday morning market** in Can Cau, 13km away (50,000Đ each way).

Bắc Hà has one main road with several smaller side streets. **Buses** (until Oct. 2000, when a new bus station will be built at the south end of town) drop people off on the main road in front of the **post office** (☎880 280; open daily 7am-8pm) and leave from a lot across the street to **Lào Cai** (2-4hr.; 6am, 12:30, 7pm; 40,000Đ), **Hanoi** (10-14hr., Tu 5am, 70,000-80,000Đ), and **Pho Lu,** on the train line between Lao Cai and Hanoi (1hr; 7am, noon, 1pm; 20,000-30,000Đ). **Motorcycle taxis** wait in front of the bus lot. There is no direct public transportation to Sapa. The road intersecting the main road next to the post office leads to Bắc Hà's gigantic market. A **pharmacy** is 60m uphill from the post office on the right. (☎880 365. Open daily 8am-noon and 1:30-5pm.) About 75m farther down the road, a paved road branches left and leads past the Sao Mai Hotel to the **hospital** (☎880 263).

The largest and most modern accommodation by far is **Sao Mai Hotel,** 150m along the road that branches to the left 150m up the main road from the post office. Most rooms have great views of the surrounding peaks. The restaurant and bar (entrees 10,000-20000Đ) are connected to Hanoi's Sinh Cafe and organize tours. (☎880 288. Doubles with TV, fridge, and hot water US$8-20.) The **Dang Khoa Hotel,** on the main road on the left 75m up from the post office, is the cheapest in town. (☎880 289. Singles US$5-8; doubles US$10-15.) The slightly friendlier **Suoi Hoa Hotel,** opposite the market, has impeccable, though small, rooms. (☎880 370. Doubles with shower US$8-12.) Bắc Hà is renowned for its **small plums** *(quả mận)*, a definite must-try. Locals dip them in salt and eat them when they are still green and bitter. **Xuân Về,** opposite the Sao Mai Hotel, has an English menu. (☎880 352. Omelette 8000Đ. Spring rolls 10,000Đ. Open daily 6am-11pm.)

ĐIỆN BIÊN PHỦ ☎23

Điện Biên Phủ, an ugly but historically significant town, is easy to miss. Off the backpacker ant-trail, it holds a sacred place in the lore of the Vietnamese Revolution as the site of the French defeat in 1954 at the hands of Hồ Chí Minh's Việt Minh. Điện Biên Phủ remains one of the best-known symbols in Vietnam for the collapse of European colonialism. The town is currently booming with construction to accommodate its new status as the capital of Lai Châu Province. For military history buffs, the tanks and bunkers scattered through the corn fields make a stop here worthwhile. For those travelers heading farther north, readily available bus schedules make a stop in Điện Biên Phủ a requirement.

TRANSPORTATION. **Buses** run to: **Hanoi** (20-30hr.; 4:30, 8:30, 10:30am; 95,000Đ) via Sơn La and Tong Dau (Mai Châu); **Sơ'n La** (6-7hr.; 4:45am, noon; 38,000Đ for tourists); and **Lai Châu** (5-6hr., every hr. 6-11am and 1:30pm, 25,000Đ or more for tourists). Buy tickets before boarding. The **airstrip** runs parallel to Hwy. 12 and the **terminal** is on the left, 1km north of the bus station on the road to Lai Châu. Flights are available to **Hanoi** (W, F, Su 12:55pm; 660,000Đ) and **HCMC** (Tu, F-Sa; 1,250,000Đ). The government plans to open the border to Laos for foreigners by March 2001. Flights will be available to Vientiane. Buy tickets at the **Vietnam Airlines office** in the airport hotel on Phuong Thanh Binh, left off the main street, between the bus station and the Bế Văn Đàn intersection on Hwy. 12. (☎824 692. Open M-Sa 7:30-10am and 2-4pm.)

ORIENTATION AND PRACTICAL INFORMATION. Over 450km northwest of Hanoi and 34km from the Lao border, Điện Biên Phủ is in the Mường Thanh Valley. The **bus station** is west of town on **Highway 12,** which continues northwest to Lai Châu. As Hwy. 12 heads east from the bus station, it bridges the **Nam Yum River** after 300m and intersects **Dư'ờng Mư'ờng Thanh,** the town's main street, which bends left toward the rest of town and on to Laos (34km), the hospital, post office, Điện Biên Phủ Museum, and most of the military sights. The **Bank for Investment and Development of Vietnam,** on Dường Mường Thanh, halfway to the post office, exchanges foreign cash. (☎825 774. Open M-F 7-11am and 2-5pm, Sa 7-11am.) A **hospital** (☎825 463) is on Hoang Van Thai, off the main street to the left. From the bridge, turn left onto the main street, and a **pharmacy** is 75m ahead on the right. (☎824 377. Open daily 6:30-11am and 1:30-7pm.) The **GPO** is on the same street to the right, south of the bridge. It has *Poste Restante* and an **international telephone office.** (☎825 833. Open daily 6:30am-9pm.)

ACCOMMODATIONS AND FOOD. The nicest hotel in town is on the right off the main road coming from Sơn La: **Muong Thanh Hotel,** 25 Phuong Him Lam on the road from Hanoi before the bridge, has a swimming pool, ping-pong, massage parlor and large rooms. (☎826 719. Doubles with A/C and bath US$12-20.) Cheaper and still friendly is the **Binh Long Hotel,** on Muong Thanh 200m from the Hwy. 12 intersection, has immaculate rooms with hot showers. (☎824 345. Doubles US$10, with A/C US$12.) Another decent option is **Phuong Hayền Mini-hotel,** on Rte. 8 off the main road after the bridge, whose large glass windows offer views of the mountains surrounding Điện Biên Phủ. (☎824 460. Doubles with A/C and bath US$10-12.) Opposite the bus station, the **Mây Hồng Hotel** is the cheapest option. (☎826 300. Singles/doubles with bath and hot shower 85,000-130,000Đ.)

Rice and *phở* can be bought along **Muong Thanh;** stalls past the GPO offer a wider selection of eats, and **Bế Văn Đàn,** the second street on the right after the bridge, has little restaurants serving dog (*cho*) meat. The **market** next to the bridge features a wide selection of produce. Fresh crab makes an exotic snack (1500Đ). Two restaurants are worth mentioning: **Ngoc Mai** (☎825 932), on Hoang Van No, left off Rte. 279, serves excellent spring rolls and entrees (8000-15,000Đ). **Lien Tuoi Restaurant,** on Hoang Van Thai near the hospital, serves quality Vietnamese dishes for 15,000-30,000Đ. To get there, follow the left branch of Hoang Van Thai; it's 200m down on the right.

SIGHTS. Điện Biên Phủ's main draw is its history. For travelers who come to Điện Biên Phủ by bus, it is not difficult to imagine why the French reckoned the valley too remote to be threatened by the Việt Minh. To get a sense of its geographic remoteness, see the **road from Sơn La** as it winds through the majestic mountains of Pa Đin park for 34km. The key to the Việt Minh victory was their ability to drag artillery to the ridges ringing Điện Biên Phủ Valley. On May 6, 1954, the French lowered the *tricoleur* and hoisted another flag—the white one; a day later, negotiations began in Geneva.

Điện Biên Phủ is now a memorial to the Vietnamese victory. Though the museum (a large yellowish compound 1km down Duong Muong Thanh) is closed for renovation, there are plenty of other testaments to the historic events of 1954. Opposite the museum, 60m toward Hwy. 12, is **Al Hill,** scene of fierce fighting. A large Vietnamese cemetery opposite the museum, next to Al Hill, has become a popular pilgrimage destination for Vietnamese tourists, more numerous than foreigners. (Open daily 7am-7pm.)

From the hill, head 500m back toward town and turn left onto Be Vam Dam that crosses a small bridge to the battlefield after 50m. After the bridge, turn left; 50m up the road on the right lies **Colonel Christian de Castries' command bunker.** (Open M-Sa 8-10:30am and 2-4:30pm. 5000Đ.) Ask to be let into the **French cemetery** (Nghĩa Trang Pháp) up the road. The roads in this area are littered with the remains of (genuine) French mortars and tanks in fields of red roses.

LAI CHÂU ☎23

VIETNAM

The landscapes between Sapa and Điện Biên Phủ, a succession of majestic mountains, ethnic villages, and gorgeous rice fields, are superb. The relatively long distance, however (300km), forces the traveler to stop in two insignificant and unappealing towns: Lai Châu (Phong Tho) and Tam Đuong. **Buses** leave from a lot marked by a sign labeled "Bến Xe Thị Xã Lai Châu" 3km toward Điện Biên Phủ from Lai Châu proper. To: **Hanoi** (18-30hr., 6am, 90,000Đ) via **Điện Biên Phủ** (5-6hr.; 4, 5, 8, 9, 11am; 25,000Đ); and **Lào Cai** (10-14hr., 6am, 45,000Đ) via **Sapa** (8-11hr., 45,000Đ). The Lai Châu **GPO,** at the far end of town toward Sapa, has *Poste Restante* and international phones. (☎852 301. Open daily 7am-9pm.)

The nicest and cheapest of the town's hotels is **Nâm Lay Hotel,** at the far end of town toward Sapa, which has rooms with balconies. (☎876 622. Doubles with fan 60,000-80,000Đ.) **Lan Anh Hotel** is a large white building 3km from the bus station in central Lai Châu; it offers basic fan rooms. (☎23 852 370. Singles/doubles US$8-10.) **Song Da Hotel,** on the main road at the entrance of town, offers similar rooms for similar prices. Locals invite travelers to stay in their homes, usually for around 40,000Đ; they often provide dinner for 25,000Đ.

The small town of **Tam Duong,** where many buses also stop, lies 120km down the road and 80km before Sapa. The bus station is on the main street, to the right if you're coming from Điện Biên Phủ. **Buses** run to Sapa via Lào Cai (2hr.; 6, 7, 11am; 25,000Đ); to **Hanoi** (12-14hr., 5am, 100,000Đ); and to Điện Biên Phủ via Lai Chau (4-6hr.; 6, 11am; 40,000Đ). The town has two nice hotels. **Tam Đuong Hotel,** on the left off the main street, is modern. (☎875 288. Doubles 100,000-120,000Đ.) **Phuong Thanh Mini-hotel,** on the right farther down the main street, has comfortable rooms and gorgeous views of the valley. (☎875 235. Doubles US$8-12.) **Phuong Thanh Restaurant,** opposite Tam Đuong Hotel, serves good food for 10,000-20,000Đ. Tam Đuong is also a base for hikers and tours of villages organized by **Phuong Thanh Hotel,** which provides English-speaking guides and rents cars, motorbikes, and bicycles.

SƠN LA ☎22

Travelers who don't know where to look may feel their experience in Sơn La resembles that of the political prisoners incarcerated here by the French: surrounded by natural beauty, but trapped in an uninteresting town. Like the revolutionaries who escaped in 1936, there's hope for you, too. Sơn La is surrounded by Black Thài hill tribes, its original settlers, whose villages are ripe for exploration. Caves and hot springs within easy reach make Sơn La a worthy stop, despite the town's decrepit look.

TRANSPORTATION AND PRACTICAL INFORMATION. Sơn La is 320km west of Hanoi and two-thirds of the way from the capital to Điện Biên Phủ on **Route 6. Cau Trang Rd.**, which runs west toward Điện Biên Phủ, and **Trường Chinh Rd.**, which runs south to Hanoi, meet to form the center of Sơn La. Buses stop at the terminal on Trường Chinh, 50m north of this intersection. Approaching the intersection from the bus station, the road to the right crosses a small bridge over the Nam La River. It continues straight as **Điện Biên Rd.**, eventually becoming Rte. 6, while **Tô Hiệu Rd.** branches to the right after the bridge, passing the post office before becoming **Rte. 12.** From the bus station, **buses** and **minibuses** leave to **Hanoi** (8hr.; 8 per day; large buses 4:30, 5am; minibuses 6, 7, 8am; 60,000Đ) and **Điện Biên Phủ** (6hr.; 5:30am, noon; 54,000Đ). Occasional buses plying the Hanoi-Điện Biên Phủ route can be hailed as they cross the bridge. Buses also run to **Lai Chau** (6hr., every hr. from 5am, 60,000Đ) and **boat trips** can be arranged by Khach San Cony Doan (2 days; overnight stay at Man (black Thài) village; US$70 including accommodation and food). The largest **pharmacy** in town is **Hai Anh Sau Phu Bien,** 37Đ. Điện Biên, just across the bridge. (☎852 905. Open daily 6:30am-10pm.) The **hospital** (☎852 325) is 2.5km down Tô Hiệu on the right. A large **market** sits 1km down from the Trường Chinh/Can Trang intersection off Trường Chinh, and sells fresh fruit, meat and vegetables as well as clothes and all kinds of goods. (Open daily 6am-6pm.) The **GPO,** 200m down Tô Hiệu, has an **international telephone office.** (☎852 421. Open daily 6am-9pm.)

ACCOMMODATIONS AND FOOD. Your best bet is the **Union Hotel** (Nhà Khách Công Đoàn). Turn right from the bus station, cross the bridge on the right, turn right onto Tô Hiệu, and proceed 300m past the GPO; turn left at the blue sign. The staff speaks English and provides a free guidebook for guests. (☎852 244. Doubles with fan US$10, with A/C US$15-25.) **Hoa Hong Hotel,** 79 Precinct Quyet Thang, is also very good; it's massive, modern, and clean with a stunning view through large glass walls onto surrounding mountains. (☎852 615. Doubles with bath, TV, and A/C US$10-15.) Cheapest is the **People's Committee Guest House,** 400m up Đ. Điện Biên from the bridge. (☎852 080. Dorms US$5; private rooms from US$10.)

Tiệm Ăn Restaurant, 158 Tô Hiệu, on the right just before the GPO from the bridge, has an English menu. (Entrees 30,000-60,000Đ. Open daily 7am-8pm.) For a local specialty, head 500m up Điện Biên Rd. from the bridge; as the road curves past the Tô Hiệu Monument, look for a sign on the left reading **Thịt Dê.** The name means "goat meat," which the cook will whip up in a kebab for 25,000Đ. (Open daily 10am-8pm.) **Long Phuong Restaurant** serves local specialties from the forests (pheasant, rabbit, and quail) for 30,000-50,000Đ. The local brew, Bia Sơn Dương, is on tap all over town. Though less tasty than Bia Hanoi, it has some kick to it and will make up for the lack of nightlife in town.

SIGHTS. The **French prison** (Nhà Tù Cũ Của Pháp) is a monument to French oppression of the Việt Minh in the 1930s and 1940s. To get to the prison, head toward Điện Biên Phủ on Đ. Điện Biên for 500m. Along the way, **Tô Hiệu Monument** stands on the left, dedicated to the favorite son of Sơn La. Roughly 75m beyond the monument, take the first right and follow it to the top. The museum is the yellow building on the right before the radio tower; the entrance to the prison is down a path to the right. Ask the museum attendant to open the exhibit inside the prison. The left wing of the reconstructed prison building has a photo-exhibit of the prison's history, and the main yellow building—where the guards used to stay—now hosts a **cultural museum** containing some artifacts of local ethnic minorities and a photo history of the prison. (Monument and museum open daily 7-11:30am and 1:30-5pm. 10,000Đ.)

Ask at the Công Đoàn Guest House to hire a guide to visit the **hill-tribe villages** around Sơn La. The **Tam Tong Caves** are 3km toward Điện Biên Phủ on Hwy. 12; a local guide costs 10,000Đ at the caves. If visiting alone, make sure to take a flashlight. A motorcycle costs 20,000Đ to the **hot springs** (Suối Nước Nóng), 7km south of town. The springs are worth the detour only in the winter, when their temperature reaches 25 degrees C.

MAI CHÂU ☎18

Surrounded by steep mountains, tiny Mai Châu is a slow-paced paradise of rice paddies. Just outside town, Bản Làc, one of the many Thài ethnic minority villages scattered throughout the valley, allows visitors to step into Thài life by spending nights in stilt-houses, eating home-cooked meals, and observing rural Thài and Vietnamese culture. Many stay a few days to explore the hills and villages and to get a true taste of Black and White Thài lifestyles.

TRANSPORTATION AND PRACTICAL INFORMATION. Mai Châu is 140km west of Hanoi and 6km from Tòng Đậu, which lies on Rte. 6 roughly half way to Sơn La. The entire town stretches along 1½km of Rte. 15A, from the **post office** at the end of town closest to Tòng Đậu to the **Mai Châu Guest House** at the opposite end of town. About halfway between the two is the **market** and, on the other side of the street, the **bus station.** There are daily buses to **Hòa Bình** (2-3hr.; 6am, noon; 20,000Đ), from which travelers can catch buses to **Hanoi** (3-4hr.; 6:30, 7:30am; 30,000-40,000Đ). **Motorcycle taxis** gather near the market; take one to **Tòng Đậu** (10,000-20,000Đ) to reach buses traveling to **Sơn La** or **Hanoi.** Locals can tell you when to expect buses (as early as 6:30am). There is **no formal currency exchange** in Mai Châu, but some residents will change dollars into đồng. A **pharmacy** is on the main road 100m past the market toward Mai Châu Guest House. (☎867 129. Open daily 7am-4pm.) Another 200m in the same direction on the main road is a **hospital.** (☎867 244. Open daily 7-11am and 2-5pm.) The **post office** is 500m from the market toward Tòng Đậu, and has **international telephone** and **fax** at exorbitant rates but no calling card access. (☎867 100. Open daily 7am-9pm.)

VIETNAM

ACCOMMODATIONS AND FOOD. Mai Châu's accommodations are its primary attraction. The **Mai Châu Guest House** is a large modern building by the lake at the end of town farthest from Tòng Đậu, and has large rooms and a balcony with views of surrounding rice paddies. (☎867 262. Singles/doubles 70,000-100,000Đ.) For a friendlier atmosphere, accommodations are available in nearby **Bản Lác,** 1km from Mai Châu (take the road branching to the right) and a White Thài village. It has been set aside by the government as a place where tourists can stay overnight without a special permit. Thài houses are built on stilts and consist of one large main room and a kitchen. For 10,000-15,000Đ, the Bàn Lác families prepare traditional Thài meals. Visitors sleep on a mat on the floor in the main room; mosquito nets are provided. One night usually costs around 50,000Đ. The nicest views are available from the guest house at the entrance of the village (☎867 255), which contains a modern bathroom and shower and charges the same price as families.

The other options for food are the **phở' shops** in Mai Châu proper and the market that sells fresh fruit, vegetables, and meat in the morning. Heading toward the post office from the market, the *phở'* shop at the bend in the road before the bridge has an English-speaking proprietor. (*Phở'* 8000Đ. Open daily 7am-9pm.)

SIGHTS. The area around Mai Châu is teeming with Thài, Hmong, and Mường villages, as well as thrilling scenery; dayhikes down any of the roads that branch out from town are the best means of exploration. More extensive treks require a guide and are best booked through a tourist cafe in Hanoi. These often involve long hikes through several villages, occasionally with an overnight stay or a boat trip on the nearby reservoir. A stay in Bản Lác is a staple of these tours (US$30 for a 2-day/1-night trip booked in Hanoi). Past Mai Châu heading toward Sơn La, La Linh and Yen Chau are two nice villages to visit.

The area around Mộc Châu on the way to Sơn La is one of the most densely populated in the northwest. Mainly inhabited by Thài and Hmong people, it offers beautiful hilly landscapes, waterfalls, and hot springs. Though an insignificant town in itself, Mộc Châu—with its three hotels and two guest houses—can be used as a convenient base to explore the surrounding countryside.

NINH BÌNH ☎30

Someday perhaps travelers will wise up and notice that Ninh Bình more than just a place to stop for breakfast on the way to Hanoi from Huè or vice versa. Dramatic scenery, historic intrigues, religious pilgrimage sites, and an endangered animal sanctuary to boot within 50 km, the area deserves to be explored. Day-tours from Hanoi (2hr. drive each way) are simply too hurried to indulge in the environ's serenity. navigating the nearer sights to town is best done by bikes when weather cooperates. Poverty-stricken Ninh Binh town itself is a forgettable collection of concrete buildings. Those passing through during harvest season (June and Oct.) will see what hard agricultural work really is. But it has some of the best backpackers' accommodation in Vietnam. Intense (and hilarious) rivalry among the few choices has kept prices reasonable and quality high.

TRANSPORTATION. The **bus station** is on **Lê Đại Hành** opposite the bridge. **Buses** leave for: **Hanoi** (2½-3hr., 11 per day 6:40am-3:30pm, 12,000Đ); **HCMC** (45hr., 6:30 and 8am, 135,000Đ); **Hải Phòng** (6hr., 5:45am, 18,000Đ); and **Kim Sơn** (Phát Diệm Church; 50min., 13 per day 5:30am-5pm, 4500Đ; return from Kim Sơn 4pm). Additional buses can be caught anywhere along Tram Hund Dao between 5pm and 6pm but must be waved down (prices are at least double the quoted ones for foreigners). An easier option are **tourist buses** to **Hanoi** (US$4) and **Huế** (US$12) which run daily at 7am; seats can be booked at any Hotel (see below), but the best seats are usually taken since these are part of the open tour tickets from either ends. The **train station** lies at the end of Đường Hoàng Hoa Thám. Walk up the street from the station to **Lê Đại Hành,** turn left, and walk 100m or so to reach the bridge. Trains go to **Hanoi** (2-3½hr., 9 per day at all hours, 49,000Đ soft seat) and to **Vinh** (3½-4½hr. 76,000Đ soft seat) **Huế** (10-12hr., 9 per day, 197,000Đ soft seat), which continues to **HCMC** (30-40hr., 524,000Đ soft seat). Buy tickets to the south several days in advance, preferably in Hanoi. Tickets to Hanoi can be purchased in Ninh Bình a day ahead. Time and prices are posted on the bulletin outside of main entrance.

ORIENTATION AND PRACTICAL INFORMATION. Ninh Bình lies 93km south of Hanoi on Highway 1A. Most of the town lies along the highway **(Đường Trần Hưng Đạo). Đường Lê Đại Hành,** which runs parallel to **Trần Hưng Đạo** along a narrow river until the two intersect at a **bridge** at the south end of town, is the town's second main street and leads to Hồ Chí Minh City.

Near the bridge, Đường Hải Thượng Lãn Ông intersects **Trần Hưng Đạo** next to the radio tower at the west edge of town; 1km down Tran Phu at the far end is the **hospital** (☎871 030). From the bridge, follow **Trần Hưng Đạo** past the next two intersecting streets and on the right is a **pharmacy,** 12B Trần Hưng Đạo, which is well-stocked and has a German-speaking owner. (☎871 766. Open daily 7am-9pm.) Look for the blue "Apothekel Parmicist" sign. Hotels will exchange đồng for dollars, but to exchange traveler's checks, head up **Trần Hưng Đạo** from the bridge past the Star Hotel. On the right is the brand new **Industrial and Commercial Bank of Vietnam,** 1 Lương Văn Tuý, in a large yellow building. (☎872 675. Open M-Sa 7-11am and 1-4:30pm.) The **telephone office** (with fax) is inside the **GPO,** which is two buildings to the right of the radio tower and near the bridge, on **Trần Hưng Đạo;** look for the red Bưu Điện sign. (☎871 104. Open weekdays 6am-10pm, weekends 7am-9pm.) **Internet access** is available at most hotels listed below for 4-500Đ per min. Cyber cafe's have yet to invade the town.

ACCOMMODATIONS AND FOOD. Mr. De at **Thuy Anh Hotel,** 55 Truong Han Sieu, off Trân Hưng Đạo in the center of town, leads the quality hotel rat-race. Trained as an electrician in Bulgaria for 8 years, he is worldly, attentive, and definitely has a hygiene-obsession with daily spot checks on his room service staff. All staff are trained as mini-De in attitudes and service. Full tourist service offered include (as in most other hotels) full-day tour US$14, motorbike rental US$5, and Internet 500Đ per min. The Roof-Top restaurant is quiet and pleasant with ordinary local fares. A/C Doubles with bath from US$10-25. A few outside toilet tiny rooms US$7. **Thanh Thuy's Guest House,** 128 Lê Hồng Phong, (☎871 811) can definitely give Mr. De a run for his money. The German and English speaking owners have cheap clean fan singles US$3-8 and A/C doubles US$10. This is also the only place to rent sturdy Japanese mountain bike for 13,000Đ per day, or 8000Đ for Chinese-made models. Internet 400Đ per min. If coming by train, **Queen Hotel**, 21 Hoang Hoa Tham (☎871 874; fax 871 200) 150m directly outside of the station has adequate but darker rooms from US$3-15. Services are somewhat less attentive than the other two, but then most hotels are. The tree-shaded pedestrian-only street in front of Queen Hotel to the train station has good **Phở** and **Còm** shops. But go to the intersection of Tran Hung Đao and Van Giang, 5m cross the street outside of Thuy Anh Hotel, for famed local **miện lúón,** or eel in vermicelli noodle soup, if the 10,000Đ bowl is too exotic, wash it down at the bonsai courtyard of Café Sơn a few doors down with a mango shake (6000Đ).

SIGHTS. Ninh Bình's rice fields become otherworldly in the **Tam Cốc Cave** area, 8km south of town. From **Trần Hưng Đạo,** cross the bridge and turn right at the traffic circle. After several kilometers, a small bridge appears on the right under a blue sign. Cross the bridge and follow the road to the water through rice fields. The mountains have earned the area the nickname "Halong Bay without water," a moniker borne out by the limestone karst which dot the area. A booth at the water sells tickets for seats on bamboo skiffs to Tam Cốc Cave. (40,000Đ, plus 3000-5000Đ tip for the driver. Open daily 6am-5pm.) Trips last about three hours: they pass by spectacular cliffs and through three low-hanging caves, tiny farming communities, graveyards, and intricate rock formations. But rather than an open water, the 4-person boat has only one water-highway to tread and traffic jam is a frequent occurrence, giving peddlers-entrepreneurs a chance to pitch their embroidery to a captive audience. Visitors can leave the boat at Thanh boat stop and, after a short walk, discover the thirteenth-century Thai Vi Temple. The **Bích Động Pagoda,** farther down the road, dates back to 1428 and features beautiful temple buildings, a grotto, and a path up the mountainside with fantastic views of the cliffs and surrounding farmlands. They are especially beautiful during harvest season in June, when the fields resemble a yellow sea. Some residential nuns speak English, but only good enough to (justifiably) ask for tips for renovation. (Open daily 7am-5pm. 30,000Đ plus 3-5000Đ for tips.)

Hoa Lư, the capital of Đại Cồ Việt, the first independent Việt state following the millennium of Chinese rule, lies 12km north of town in a valley ringed with volcanic peaks. It was chosen for its geographic location, virtually impregnable to attack, and served as capital from AD 938 until Lý Công Uẩn, founder of the Lý dynasty, moved the capital to Thăng Long (modern-day Hanoi) in 1011. Nothing remains of the citadel. Two temples dating from the 17th century commemorate Đinh Bộ Lĩnh (Đinh Tiên Hoàng), the first Vietnamese king to declare himself emperor, and Lê Hoàn, founder of the short-lived early Lê dynasty. The site is still used for occasional village and/or religious festivities, which explains the perfectly manicured lotus pond and incessant indoor incense burning as tribute. (Open daily 7am-5pm. 30,000Đ for foreigners.) Visitors may also climb the 265 steps up the nearby mountainside to sample yet another splendid view of the surrounding country. Highly aggressive water/soda/postcards selling children proliferate in this vicinity.

The center of Vietnamese Catholicism is the **Phát Diệm Cathedral,** one of the 30 or so churches in this area once colonized by French Jesuits. The edifice blends Chinese (pagodas on the rooftops and bell-tower, Buddhist lotuses carved on the walls of the Stone Chapel) and Western (neo-Romanesque columns and rectangular structure) styles. Thousands of Vietnamese Catholics visit every year, from Ninh Bình diocese (140,000 Catholics) and elsewhere. To get there, cross the bridge from Trần Hưng Đạo and continue on the road ahead; follow the signs when the road forks. After 28km, across a small river, a bridge appears over the canal on the left. From here, any local can point you to the church. The church (sometimes called Nhà Thờ Đá, "Stone Church") is accessible by public bus from Ninh Bình to Kim Sơn. Built from 1875 to 1899 by the Vietnamese Father Sáu, it was nearly destroyed in 1972 by American bombs, but was quickly repaired. Mass is held daily at 5am and 5:30pm. though curious onlookers - more Vietnamese than foreigners—should be present at visiting hours only. (Open daily 7:30-11:30am and 2:30-5pm.)

Nature-lovers may escape to the **Cúc Phương National Park** 45km north of town. The park is an excellent daytrip, offering hikes and wildlife. If possible, the Endangered Primate Rescue Center provides a much appreciated antidote to caged bears in **Chó** Ninh Binh. This is a research, not tourist, facility, some travel agency can make discreet arrangement. Ask around. The park can be reached by motorbike, but the most convenient way to get there is aboard a guided organized tour from Ninh Binh or Hanoi for about US$15 per day (Open daily 7am-5pm).

VINH ☎038

Historically a poor region, Vinh. capital of Nghệ An province, is home to the first communist rebellion, the Xô Viết Nghệ Tĩnh uprisings, and has bred numerous Party leaders, including Hố Chi Minh, born here in 1880. today, this unappealing highway town attracts only die-hard tourists coming on a pilgrimage to Uncle Hố's birth village. Accommodations and food leave much to be desired, but those searching for an unromanticized glimpse of poor industrial Vietnam will find it in Vinh.

TRANSPORTATION. Vietnam Airline flies M.W.Sa 12:10pm to Da Nang (1hr;700,000Đ) and onward to Ban Me Thuot (3½hr) and Ho Chi Minh City (5hr;1.7milĐ)Vinh, marked by wide boulevards, is equidistant from Hanoi and Huế. Hwy. 1 rolls in from the north becoming **Lê Lợi** and then **Quang Trung** (near the bus station) before breaking east at a four-street intersection. From here, it departs toward Huế (south) as **Trần Phú.** The **bus station** (☎844 127), on Lê Lợi, sends early risers to **Hanoi** (6hr., every 30-50min. 5-10am, 31,000Đ); **Huế** (10hr., 5am, 42,500Đ); **Hai Phong** (7½hr., 5am 43,000Đ); **HCMC** (5am; 156,000Đ) and **Đà Nẵng** (12hr., 5am, 55,000Đ). The **train station** (☎824 924) is northwest of the bus station. To get there, turn left from the bus station on Lê Lợi until Phan Boi Chàn and make another left for 1km. Train; 8 trains all day to the south. **Huế** (7-9hrs; 89,000Đ soft seat); **HCMC** (27-33hrs; 365,000Đ soft seat); **Hanoi** (4½-6½hrs; 74,000Đ soft seat). Cash-starved foreigners should hit the **Vietcombank,** 6 Nguyễn Sỹ Sách, off Lê Lợi though English speakers are few and far between. (☎842 304. V, MC advance. Open M-Sa 7:30-11:30am and 1:30-4:30pm.) A **market** looms near the town center. At the four-street intersection where Quang Trung meets Trần Phú, continue straight rather than turning left. The **post office** is at 2 Nguyễn Thị Minh Khai (☎833 711. Open daily 7:30am-9:30pm.)

ACCOMMODATIONS AND FOOD. **Phú Nguyên Hải Hotel and Restaurant** 81 Lê Lợi (☎848 429 ctpnh@h.n.vnn.vn) is a gaudy pink building conveniently located next to the bus station. Fully equipped A/C Doubles start at US$20 (but can be bargained down). Don't miss the roof top restaurant. No meal is complete without stewed eel and banana (20,000Đ), roasted weasel with false dog meat (40,000Đ) and sauteéd porcupine with cinnamon leaf (seasonal prices). No, really. A few doors down is the **Hồng Ngọc Hotel 1,** 99 Lê Lợi. Front rooms, sparkling tile floors and wall-sized windows if and when the renovation finishes by August. A/C doubles US$10 and up. Across the highway is **Hồng Ngoc 2,** a more cabin-like arrangement hidden behind a restaurant. Similar offerings though the food is less adventurous than its neighbor. All rooms have A/C, TV, and fridges. (Singles/doubles 120,000; larger rooms 140,000Đ; grandiose rooms with glass wall 160,000Đ.)

SIGHTS. Party members from across the country pay homage to Hồ Chí Minh at his maternal and paternal villages, known collectively as **Làng Sen** or **Làng Kim Liên** (Lotus Village). Hồ spent his formative years (5-10 years old) in a modest thatched house. The attached museum pays tribute to the leader and his cause, displaying personal artifacts from his life. (Open M-Sa 6:30-11am and 2-5pm. Free.) Not far from Làng Sen is a museum commemorating one of Hồ's heroes, the anti-colonial activist **Phan Bội Châu.** The family altar of laureate **Nguyễn Du (Đền Nguyễn Du),** author of the *Tale of Kieu*, is also in Vinh. All above sites exude a forced grandeur of the subjects in shabbily maintained environments. Due to a dearth of foreign visitors, sometimes we exotic aliens become the most interesting display, particularly with children. Taxi hire for a full day trip from hotels start at US$20 per day. The undeveloped **Cửa Lò** beaches, some of the most pristine sand north of Nha Trang, are about 20km from Vinh, though price inflation from water to rooms are worse than other similar resort towns.

NEAR VINH

PHONG NHA CAVES

The Phong Nha Caves are one of Central Vietnam's most interesting natural landmarks, or at least the tourism authorities think so. The attraction consists of large caverns—illuminated with Christmas lights—through which visitors float through on boats. If you liked Đà Lạt's Lake of Sighs, you'll love Phong Nha. A visit to the

VIETNAM

ON THE TRAIL WITH HỒ CHÍ MINH: 30 YEARS OF BUDGET TRAVEL The Vietnamese have a saying: "a day on the road is a day of wisdom." The mysterious, charismatic Hồ Chí Minh spent thirty years globetrotting in search of adventure, wisdom, and a way to deliver his country from French colonialism. In 1912, at 22, the man born Nguyễn Tất Thành left Vietnam after being rejected by a prestigious colonial school. Assuming the name Nguyễn Văn Ba (his fourth alias), he explored North Africa, Spain, New York, and Boston. Two years later, he worked as an apprentice to a renowned pastry chef in London. He hung out with Irish nationalists, Fabian socialists, and migrant workers from China and India. Following WWI, the "patriot," now known as Nguyễn Ái Quốc, hopped the Channel to the Paris of Picasso and Hemingway and engaged himself in politics, joining the anti-colonial crowd of Vietnamese expatriates. During these years, he wrote political tracts, letters of petition, pamphlets, and newspaper articles.

Weary of French sophism, Hồ headed for Moscow in 1924. There he was recruited by the Comintern and founded the Revolutionary Youth League to train Vietnamese activists. He hoped Southeast Asian communism would follow the success in China, which he visited the next year, changing his name to Wang. However, the splintered Vietnamese struggle and adverse political climate slowed his plans. From China he went to Hong Kong, where he was able to consolidate the leaders of other independence movements under the newly formed Indochinese Communist Party (ICP) in 1930. But an informer tipped off the French, and Hồ was thrown in jail for two years before he was diagnosed with tuberculosis. Medical transfers found him back in Moscow, but he returned to China after the Japanese invasion of Manchuria. In the spring of 1941, he and his revolutionaries made their way along a jungle trail into Vietnam, where he finally renamed himself Hồ Chí Minh, "he who enlightens." His travels culminated in Ba Đình Square, where he delivered his historic Vietnamese Declaration of Independence following the expulsion of the Japanese on September 2, 1945.

caves is best launched from **Đồng Hới,** 50km southeast of the caves (70km north of the DMZ). Hwy. 1 parts the small but spread-out town, first under the alias Quang Trung in the south, later becoming Lý Thường Kiệt at its intersection with Trần Hưng Đạo, the major east-west street. The **tourist office,** on the second floor of the **Đồng Hới Hotel,** 50 Quang Trung, provides information, tickets, and rentals. (☎822 669. Open daily 7-11am and 1:30-5pm. Moto with driver 100,000Đ, 12-person minibus 450,000Đ. Entrance ticket 60,000Đ. Boat into caves 40,000Đ.) Huế tourist agencies also offer tours to the caves and the main sights of the DMZ (2 days, includes bus, accommodation, meals, guide, and a boat through the cave, 390,000Đ).

There is no interprovince bus station in **Đồng Hới,** but buses rumbling through on Hwy. 1 can be flagged down (**Hanoi** 70,000Đ; **Huế** 25,000Đ). The **train station** lies 3km west of town. From Trần Hưng Đạo, trains rumble to **Hanoi** (14hr., 5 per day, 202,000-412,000Đ); **HCMC** (30hr., 5 per day, 452,000-937,000Đ); and **Huế** (3hr., 1pm, 72,000-139,000Đ). Exchange currency at **Vietinde Bank,** 3 Nguyễn Trãi St. (Open M-Sa 7-11:30am and 1:30-4pm.) Nguyễn Trãi St., a small road off Quang Trung and next to a bridge, is marked by a sign for the Phương Đông Hotel. The **Đồng Hới Hotel,** 50 Quang Trung, has lackluster fan-cooled chambers and pricey A/C rooms. (Singles 60,000Đ; doubles 70,000Đ, with A/C and TV 150,000Đ; triples with A/C and TV 200,000Đ.) Clean A/C rooms at the **Mỹ Ngọc Travel Hotel,** 5 Lý Thường Kiệt, opposite the post office, are prone to price reductions. (☎822 074. Bargain for 125,000Đ; lower floor rooms 180,000Đ.)

CENTRAL VIETNAM

Hardscrabble poverty is the norm in Central Vietnam, particularly in the provinces north of Huế. But hardship has bred heroism: Hồ Chí Minh and dozens of other figures in Vietnamese history hail from the region. Nowhere is the tragedy of modern Vietnamese history more palpable. The most intense fighting of the Vietnam War occurred here, in the remote Central Highlands. Today the Highlands offer some of the most exciting travel in Southeast Asia. The imperial city at Huế and the Chinese trading city at Hội An are two of Vietnam's most arresting sights. The beaches of Nha Trang and Phan Thiết are easily tops in the country, and no trip is complete without a few days in cool, misty Đà Lạt. Independent travel here isn't easy, but with stamina and flexibility, it can be the highlight of a trip to Vietnam.

HUẾ ☎54

As Vietnam's spiritual, artistic, and cultural center, Huế has an incredible concentration of sights and ruins. In the 19th century, under the rule of the Nguyễn Dynasty, Huế reached preeminence as the seat of Vietnam's first united court. Home rule was short-lived, however, as French ships blockaded and prepared to attack the city in 1833. Recognizing the might of the French, the emperor relented, and Vietnam became a French protectorate. Though the colonial administration did much to protect the Huế's treasures and preserve its historic integrity, it eventually became a combat zone during the war with the US. During the 1968 Tet Offensive, the Citadel was captured by both sides as fighting raged in the Imperial City.

TRANSPORTATION

Flights: Phú Bài Airport, 15km south of the city off Hwy. 1. Taxis (88,000-110,000Đ) and Vietnam Airlines airport buses (25,000Đ) run between the airport and city center. **Vietnam Airlines,** 7 Nguyễn Tri Phương St. (☎846 320), in Thuận Hóa Hotel. Open daily 7-11am and 1:30-4:30pm. To **Hanoi** and **HCMC** (both 1,000,000Đ).

Trains: Huế Railway Station (☎822 175), at the southwest end of Lê Lợi over the small bridge that spans the canal. Trains to: **Đà Nẵng** (3hr.; 6am, 1pm; 32,000Đ); **Hanoi** (13-16hr., 8 per day 10am-11:30pm, 244,000-746,000Đ); **HCMC** (20-25hr., 7 per day 2:30am-3pm, 362,000-1,120,000Đ) via **Nha Trang** (15-17hr., 223,000-681,000Đ). Purchase tickets 3 days in advance.

Buses: Most hotels book **minibuses** to: **Đà Nẵng** (3hr.; 8am, 1pm; US$3); **Hanoi** (16hr., 6am, US$7); **HCMC** (20hr., 5:30am, US$18); **Hội An** (4hr.; 8am, 1pm; US$3); **Nha Trang** (16hr., 5:30am, US$10); **Lao Bảo** (4hr., 6am, US$11); **Savannakhet, Laos** (6pm, 9pm; US$18). Huế has three bus stations:

An Hòa Bus Station (☎822 716), outside the Citadel at the northwest corner off Hwy. 1, 2km from town center. Buses go north to: **Đồng Hới** (5hr.; 5, 6, 7am; 25,000Đ); **Hanoi** (1 day, 4am, 150,000Đ); **Khe Sanh** (5½hr., 5am, 40,000Đ); **Vinh** (11hr., 5am, 70,000Đ). To get to **Lao B=o**, catch a bus to **Đ®ng Ha** (6:15am) and transfer to a bus bound for the border.

An Cựu Bus Station (☎823 817), on Hùng V™£ng, 1km southeast of the Perfume River past the traffic circle on the left. Primarily serves southern destinations. Buses to: **Buôn Ma Thuột** (18hr., 6am, 87,000Đ); **Đà Lạt** (20hr., 6am, 100,000Đ); **Đà Nẵng** (3hr., every 50min. 5am-3:30pm, 15,000Đ); **HCMC** (30hr., 6am, 108,000Đ).

Đông Ba Bus Station (☎823 055), on Tr<n H™ng Đảo, on the Citadel side of the Perfume River. Buses to **Thuận An Beach** (20min., every 30min. 7am-3pm, 8000Đ).

Local Transportation: Cyclos swarm. 10,000Đ per ride. Bargain. **Motos** are often cheaper. 3000-7000Đ per ride, 10,000-15,000Đ per hr.

Taxis: ATC Taxi (☎833 333). Unmetered rides to just about anywhere.

Boats: Tourist Boat Pier, 5 Lê Lợi. 1-day tour up Perfume River to **Thiên Mụ Pagoda** and the **Royal Tombs** or to **Thuận An Beach** (8am-5pm, 10-person boat US$15). The acclaimed **Folk Songs of Huế** boat tour and performance leaves every night (1Ăhr., 7pm, 6 people US$25).

Rentals: Hotels and outfits on Hùng Vương rent **bicycles** (7000-8000Đ per day) and **motorcycles** (50,000-110,000Đ per day). **DMZ Tours** (see **Orientation and Practical Information: Tourist Offices,** p. 860) rents **cars** with drivers (US$35 per day).

ORIENTATION AND PRACTICAL INFORMATION

Over 16km inland from the South China Sea, Huế is bisected by the **Perfume River (Sông Hương).** The ancient **Citadel,** which fails to keep armies of tourists from penetrating to the Imperial City and the Royal Palace of the Nguyễn Dynasty within, is on the northwest bank. The **Flagpole of Huế,** which marks the front gate of the Royal Palace and the Imperial City, is inside the Citadel. Across the river on the southeast side, **New Huế** has most hotels, restaurants, and services. On the Citadel side, **Lê Duẩn/Trần Hưng Đạo** runs between the river and the Citadel wall. On the southeast bank of the Perfume River, **Lê Lợi,** the main tourist strip, runs parallel to the water. **Hùng Vương,** the other major tourist drag, starts at the **Tràng Tiền Bridge,** crosses Lê Lợi, and heads southeast to **Hwy. 1.** Farther upstream (southwest), **Phú Xuân Bridge** spans the river between Lê Lợi and Lê Duẩn.

Tourist Offices: Nearly all tour agencies offer identical services and prices (1-day tours US$8; half-day Perfume River tour US$2). Most guest houses also book tours. **DMZ Tour Office Center,** 26 Lê Lợi (☎825 242). Day on the Perfume River with lunch US$20. Tour with breakfast US$15. Open daily 6am-10pm. **Huang Giang,** 17 Lê Lợi (☎832 221). Books tours and helps with visa problems. Open daily 6am-10pm.

Currency Exchange: Vietcombank, 46 Hùng Vương (☎846 058). 3% commission on MC/V cash advances. Cashes traveler's checks (US$2.50 per check). No ATM. Open M-F 7:30-11:30am and 1-4:30pm.

Market: Đông Ba Market, Huế's largest, sprawls on the Citadel side of the Perfume River at the far northeast end of Trần Hưng Đạo. Open daily 6am-7:30pm.

Pharmacy: Tuấn Hà, 5 Hoàng Hoa Thám (☎821 319), opposite the post office and Victoria bank. Open daily 6am-8pm. Another is at 37 Bến Nghé (☎832 079), off of Nguyễn Tri Phương. Open daily noon-11pm.

Medical Services: Huế City Hospital, 16 Lê Lợi (☎822 325, ext. 2247). Emergency entrance on Nguyèn Huy Tá.

Internet: High Net, 14 Hùng Vương (☎829 004). A/C. Open daily 7am-11:30pm. **MQV Computer,** 6A Phạm Ngũ Lão (☎847 052). 300Đ per min. Generally open 24hr.

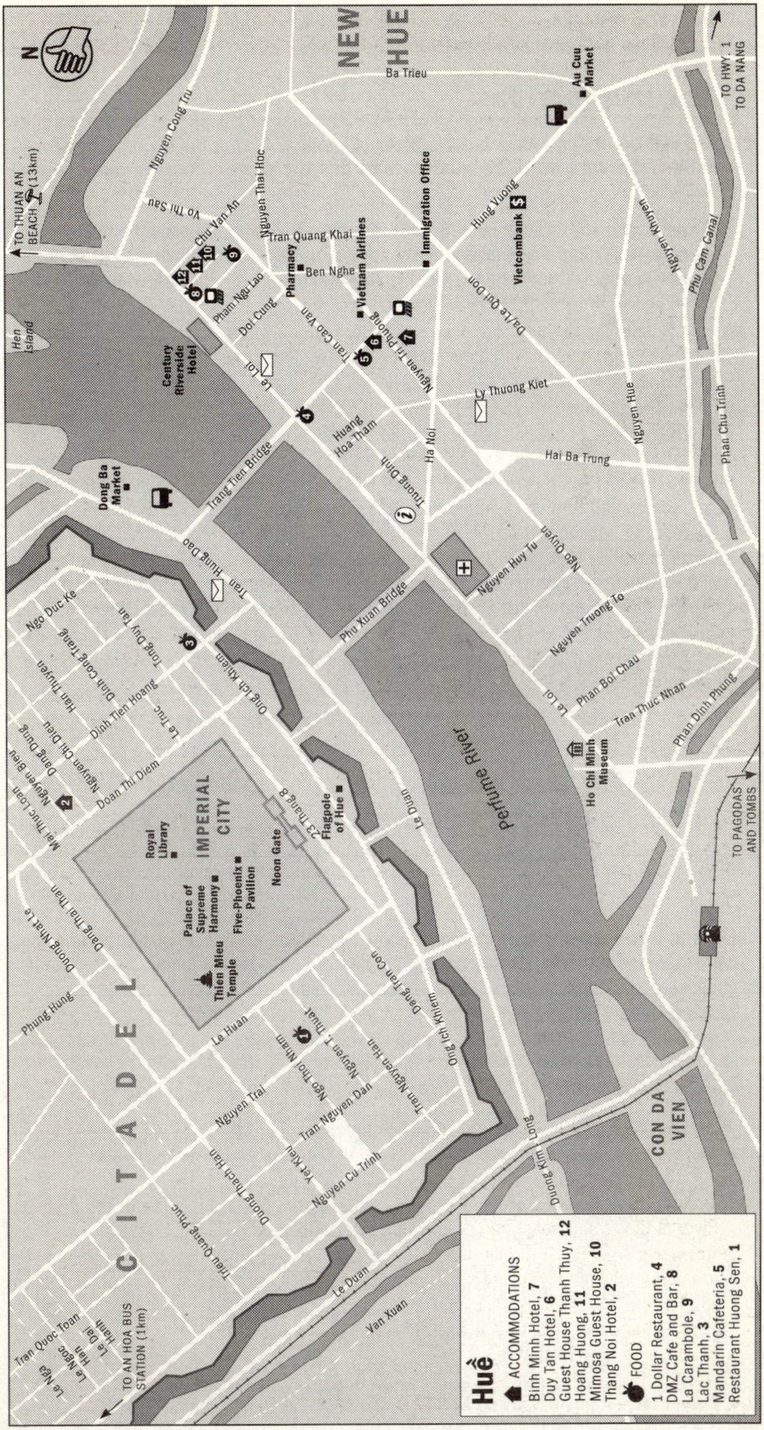
Huê
ACCOMMODATIONS
Binh Minh Hotel, 7
Duy Tan Hotel, 6
Guest House Thanh Thuy, 12
Hoang Huong, 11
Mimosa Guest House, 10
Thang Noi Hotel, 2
FOOD
1 Dollar Restaurant, 4
DMZ Cafe and Bar, 8
La Carambole, 9
Lac Thanh, 3
Mandarin Cafeteria, 5
Restaurant Huong Sen, 1
N
TO THUAN AN BEACH (13km)
NEW HUE
Ba Trieu
Au Cuu Market
TO HWY. 1 TO DA NANG
Nguyen Cong Tru
Vo Thi Sau
Chu Van An
Nguyen Thai Hoc
Tran Quang Khai
Ben Nghe
Pharmacy
Immigration Office
Vietnam Airlines
Hung Vuong
Vietcombank
Dong Da
Doi Cung
Pham Ngu Lao
Le Loi
Tran Cao Van
Nguyen Tri Phuong
Hen Island
Century Riverside Hotel
Ly Thuong Kiet
Nguyen Truong To
Phu Cam Canal
Nguyen Hue
Hai Ba Trung
Phan Chu Trinh
Ha Noi
Truong Dinh
Hoang Hoa Tham
Trang Tien Bridge
Dong Ba Market
Tran Hung Dao
Phu Xuan Bridge
Nguyen Huy Tu
Ngo Quyen
Phan Boi Chau
Tran Thuc Nhan
Phan Dinh Phung
Ho Chi Minh Museum
TO PAGODAS AND TOMBS
Perfume River
Le Duan
Ong Ich Khiem
Flagpole of Hue
23 Thang 8
Noon Gate
IMPERIAL CITY
Royal Library
Palace of Supreme Harmony
Five-Phoenix Pavilion
Thien Mieu Temple
Ngo Duc Ke
Tong Duy Tan
Dinh Cong Trang
Han Thuyen
Dinh Tien Hoang
Le Truc
Nguyen Chi Dieu
Dang Dung
Nguyen Bieu
Doan Thi Diem
Mai Thuc Loan
Dang Thai Than
Duong Nhat Le
Phung Hung
CITADEL
Le Huan
Nguyen Trai
Ngo Thoi Nham
Nguyen T. Thuat
Dang Tran Con
Tran Nguyen Han
Tran Nguyen Dan
Yet Kieu
Nguyen Cu Trinh
Duong Thach Han
Trieu Quang Phuc
Duong Kim Long
CON DA VIEN
Van Xuan
Tran Quoc Toan
Le Ngoc Han
Le Nga
Le Dai Hanh
TO AN HOA BUS STATION (1km)

VIETNAM

Post Office/Telephones: Mini-post offices abound in tourist centers. **GPO,** 14B Lý Thường Kiệt, 1 block southwest of Húng Vương. *Poste Restante.* Open daily 7am-9pm.

ACCOMMODATIONS

The alley at 46 Lê Lợi has a dense cluster of quality, affordable accommodations. Elsewhere, bargain until the quality matches the price. Most establishments arrange tours.

Hoàng Hương, 46/2 Lê Lợi (☎828 509), down a small alley opposite the Century Riverside Hotel. Cheap and friendly. Accommodating owner isn't pushy about tours. All rooms have bath. Dorms among the household laundry US$3; rooms with fan and 2 beds US$4-5; doubles with A/C US$6-10.

Guest House Thanh Thủy, 46/4 Lê Lợi (☎824 585). More lavish than its next-door neighbor. Front rooms have balconies. Discounts for long stays. Rooms US$5-8, with A/C and bath US$6-12.

Mimosa Guest House, 46/6 Lê Lợi (☎828 068), in the alley. Lovely rooms tucked away from the bustle. 2nd-fl. terrace is ideal for breakfast (US$1). Doubles US$8, with A/C US$10-12.

Duy Tan Hotel, 12 Hùng Vương (☎825 001), is a monster building behind the Mandarin Café. Rooms are surprisingly quiet despite the location. Dorms US$3; doubles with A/C US$8-12; quads rooms US$12-18.

Binh Minh Hotel, 12 Nguyễn Tri Phương (☎825 526). Large rooms with satellite TV, full-service restaurant, library, and overeager staff that pushes guests to book tours and rent motorcycles. Rooms US$5-8, with A/C from US$12, with breakfast US$15-17.

Thàng Nội Hotel, 3 Dang Dung (☎522 478), next to the Forbidden City in the old town. A worthy upscale choice with ornate Chinese furniture. Small outdoor swimming pool is heaven on a hot day. Room US$15-30.

FOOD

Huế's food is arguably the best in Vietnam. Scores of touristy eateries on **Hùng Vương** and **Lê Lợi** entice patrons with greasy dishes. Venture farther for more authentic victuals. Try *bánh nam* (shrimp and pork with sticky rice in a banana leaf) or *nem lựi* (grilled pork and greens in rice paper with peanut sauce), usually called the "Huế pancake" on menus. For a break from the grease, head to **30 Bèn Nghè,** across from Binh Minh II Hotel, for fresh juices and desserts (1500-3000Đ).

1 Dollar Restaurant, 30 Lê Lợi, in the fancy Saigon Morin Hotel. Unique selections and superb service. Try the meat cooked in medicinal broth. Nightly buffet inside a lovely courtyard 70,000Đ. All dishes US$1. Open daily 6am-11pm.

Mandarin Cafeteria, 12 Hùng Vương. A veritable Huế institution for backpackers. Owner Mr. Cuu is an amateur photographer. His ironic snapshots, devoid of the usual postcard sentimentality, decorate the walls. Books Sinh Café tours. Exquisite rice dishes and omelettes 10,000Đ. Open daily 7am-11pm.

Lạc Thạnh, 6A Đinh Tiên Hoàng, through the easternmost gate on the Citadel's front side. Famous for the deaf and mute owner who takes orders by every other means. Sizeable serving of *nem lựi* 12,000Đ. Open daily 7am-11pm.

La Carambole, 11A Dhạm Ngu Lão. Decent European and Vietnamese fare in large portions. Bamboo decor and uniformed hostesses haven't inflated prices too badly. Most entreés 20,000-50,000Đ. Open daily until 10pm.

Restaurant Hương Sen, 42 Nguyễn Trãi, inside the Citadel. Heading southwest on Lê Duẩn, turn right on Nguyễn Trãi and enter the last gate on the southwest side. Delicious food, prompt service, and an inviting atmosphere. Most dishes 20,000-40,000Đ. Steamed freshwater eel 30,000Đ. Open daily 7am-10pm.

DMZ Café and Bar, 44 Lê Lợi. An unpretentious hangout with free pool, cheap beer, and a lively crowd by 11pm. Tiger beer 12,000Đ. Food served 10am-8pm; bar open late.

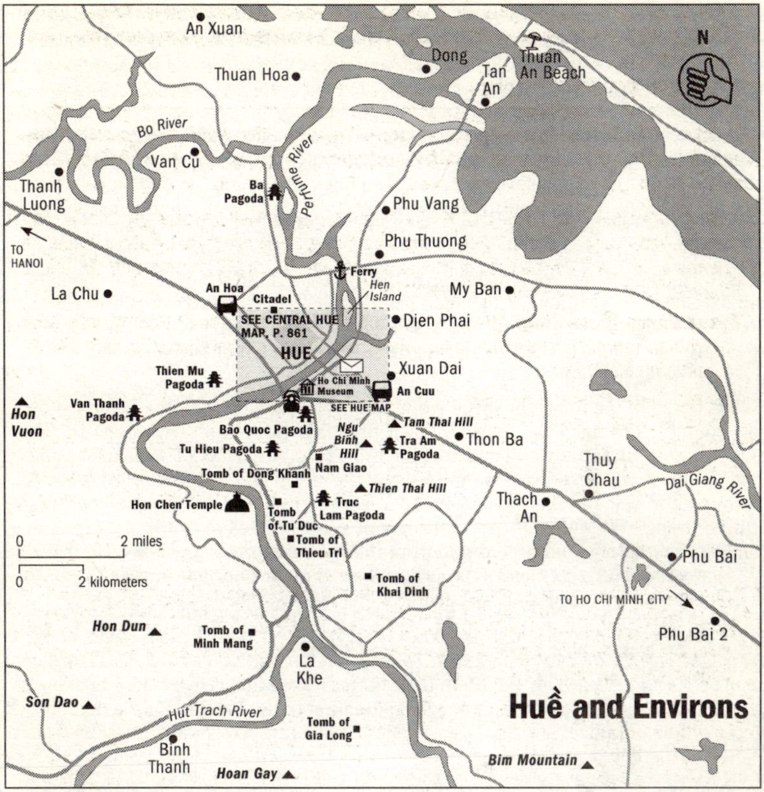

Huề and Environs

SIGHTS

The ancient Citadel, Imperial City, and Royal Tombs dominate the tourist landscape of Huế. All are pricey; only some are worth it. Pay admission in đong to avoid higher rates. Renting a bike and spreading the sights over two days is a safe and leisurely way to explore the monuments and find hidden gems along the way.

THE CITADEL

Emperor Gia Long, founder of the Nguyễn Dynasty, began building the Citadel in 1805. **Emperor Minh Mạng** completed the fortification by reinforcing the wall with brick and expanding the moat to its current size at 4m deep and 23m wide. Today, the massive square is 10km across with four gates on its front side along the Perfume River and two on each of the other three sides. Within the Citadel lie the remnants of the **Imperial City.**

FLAGPOLE OF HUẾ AND PAVILION OF EDICTS. The 47m **Flagpole of Huế** stands between the central front gates just inside the Citadel. The tallest pole in Vietnam, it has been rebuilt several times since its construction in 1807. The **Pavilion of Edicts** is just off Hwy. 1, opposite the pole and outside the Citadel. Built in 1810, the square was used by Emperor Gia Long to announce the successful national exam candidates and declare important edicts.

IMPERIAL CITY. The red and saffron **Noon Gate (Ngọ Môn),** the grand entrance to the Imperial City, is opposite the flagpole. The city was modeled on the much larger Forbidden City of Beijing's Qing Dynasty. Built in 1833, the **Five-Phoenix Pavilion,**

which sits atop the gate, served as a viewing platform from which the emperor could observe ceremonies. Behind it, the **Palace of Supreme Harmony** once housed the emperor's throne. The different heights of the courts in front of the throne corresponded to the status of the mandarins (the court's intellectual elite), with military leaders on the right and civil leaders on the left.

The **Forbidden Purple City,** the formerly walled-in residence of the royal family, is in line with the Imperial City and Citadel. Elaborate inscriptions explain what would be here if it hadn't been so heavily bombed. The **Royal Library,** on the right side as you face north, is one of the few structures still intact. West of the city are the residences of the Queen Mother and Great Queen Mother. In the west corner of the Imperial City is **Thiên Miếu Temple,** dedicated to Gia Long and his successors. The **Nine Dynastic Urns** by the temple represent members of the dynasty. These structures are undergoing extensive renovations with funds from UNESCO, which has declared Huế a World Heritage Site. (Imperial City open daily 6:30am-5:30pm. 55,000Đ. English-speaking tour guides US$5; hire them in the office to the left of the entrance.)

ROYAL TOMBS

Huế is home to the tombs of seven emperors of the Nguyễn Dynasty. Designed by the emperors themselves, each tomb represents the expressive spirit of the emperor as well as the architecture of the time; most are a mix of Vietnamese and French styles. A few kilometers southwest of the city center, the tombs are accessible by motorcycle or bike. Most visitors, however, opt for a US$2 dragon boat trip, which, though charming, throws all sorts of sales pitches at tourists. For some tombs the additional motorbike ride from the river may cost upwards of 50,000Đ. An access road connects most of the sights. (Tombs open daily 6am-sunset.)

VIETNAM

ROYAL ARENA AND TOMB OF TỰ ĐỨC. The Royal Arena was built in 1830 to stage duels between elephants and tigers. (*From Lê Lợi, head west toward the train station. Across the small bridge, turn right on Bùi Thị Xuân, continue for 3km, and turn left; the arena is 100m down on the right.)* Nearby is the tomb of Tự Đức, whose indecisive rule was one of the factors causing the Nguyễn's quick capitulation to the French. This is the tomb to see if time or budget are tight. *(2km south of the Royal Arena on the access road; take the 2nd left. 55,000Đ.)*

TOMBS OF ĐỒNG KHÁNH AND THIỆU TRỊ. The less-visited tomb of Đồng Khánh is dedicated to the late emperor and contains portraits of many of his nine wives as well as one of himself. *(500m from the tomb of Tự Đức. 22,000Đ.)* One kilometer down the gravel access road is the tomb of Thiệu Trị. *(22,000Đ.)*

TOMB OF MINH MANG AND TEMPLE OF MINH LẦU. Built from 1841-43, the tomb of Minh Mạng has the greatest architectural balance and poise of all the tombs. Three sets of stairs lead to a steel pavilion that bears Minh Mạng's eulogy, composed by Thiệu Trị. Three large courtyards are at the bottom of the pavilion. *(Boats take passengers to the tomb for 50,00Đ). Head 2km south on the access road until you see the boats.)* The Minh Lầu Temple houses an altar to the king's prosperity and longevity. Over a stone bridge is the tomb proper; look for a dirt mound. (*Opposite the courtyards at the tomb of Minh Mạng. 55,000Đ.)*

TOMBS OF GIA LONG AND KHĂI ĐỊNH. Built from 1814-20, this rarely-visited mausoleum has a courtyard surrounded by a lotus pond. *(Several kilometers from the tomb of Minh Mạng. Follow the access road southeast through Minh Mạng Village to a tributary of the Perfume River. Cross the river on a ferry for 10,000Đ round-trip and then take the dirt path to the tomb.)* After 11 years of construction, the tomb of Khải Định was finally completed in 1931. The last of the tombs to be built, it pays tribute to European architectural influence. At the top, a large altar houses a gilded statue of Khải Định, making it the only tomb with a visual representation of the emperor. *(From the tomb of Gia Long, head toward the ferry dock and backtrack across the Perfume River. Turn left up the access road and right after 200m. 55,000Đ.)*

NAM GIAO ALTAR AND BĂO QUỐC PAGODA. The Nam Giao Altar is a giant open-air monument where the Nguyễn emperors performed Confucian rituals. Its three levels represent Heaven, Earth, and Man. *(From the tomb of Khải Định, head north up the access road until it terminates near the altar.)* Before returning to the city, stop at the **Bảo Quốc Pagoda.** Built in 1670, this pagoda sits atop stairs in a quiet sanctuary. Its altar is flanked by classrooms where monks have taught for 50 years. *(Heading toward the city center, head north on Phan Bội Châu, take a left on Điện Biên Phủ and a right just after the train tracks.)*

OTHER SIGHTS

THIÊN MỤ PAGODA. On a high hill overlooking the Perfume River, the pagoda is dedicated to a legendary 16th-century woman who declared that a time of great prosperity would come if a Buddhist pagoda were built on the site. Lord Nguyễn Hoàng heard her decree and built the pagoda in 1601. The first monk to immolate himself publicly in Saigon during Ngô Đình Diệm's presidency came from this pagoda; his car is on display. Past the seven-story pagoda is an active monastery. Monks chant periodically in the well-manicured wooden temple behind the golden Buddha statue; tourists stream though constantly at a decidedly less spiritual pace. *(3km southwest of the Citadel. An easy and enjoyable riverside bike ride. Head west on Lê Duẩn and continue across the train tracks to Kim Long.)*

DAYTRIPS FROM HUÊ

THUẬN AN BEACH

Head northeast on Lê Lợi/Thuận An until it branches off the Perfume River, 3km north of the post office. The road follows a stream 10km to the beach, past the Huda Beer Factory. Take a motorbike (1hr.; park it before the road ends as parking there costs an exorbitant 6000Đ), hop on a boat from the pier (1½hr., US$12), or flag down a bus (7am-3pm, 8000Đ) from the station in Đông Hà near the market by the east corner of the Citadel.

Thuận An Beach, 13km from Huế, is the perfect place to kick back between long days of sightseeing. The beach is empty on weekdays but receives a flood of visitors on the weekends. Thuận An has a floating restaurant with basic dishes and rents umbrella-shelters for beachgoers—agree on a price beforehand.

THE DEMILITARIZED ZONE (DMZ)

Touring solo requires at least 2 days, a good motorcycle, and an excellent map. Although you can find guides in Đồng Hới and Đông Hà (halfway to Đồng Hới from Huế), the easiest and most reliable way to tour is from Huế. DMZ Tours and other agencies offer US$8-11 tours that include breakfast and A/C transport (tours leave at 6am and return at 7pm).

ON THE BEATEN TRACK. As per the guidelines of the Geneva Accords of 1954, Vietnam was divided at the 17th parallel that runs through the DMZ. **Live mines and undetonated shells still litter the area.** Be careful and stick to well-established paths.

HIỀN LƯƠNG BRIDGE AND VĨNH MỘC TUNNELS. The Bến Hải River follows the 17th parallel. Spanning the river, **Hiền Lương Bridge,** 59km north of Huế, was one of the first targets destroyed by the US. North of the river, winding roads lead to the Vĩnh Mộc Tunnels, the DMZ's most interesting sight. Built in 1966, Vĩnh Mộc has walkways 1.5m tall and 1.2m wide, a maternity ward, and a deep freshwater spring and offers more breathing room than the Củ Chi tunnels in Tây Ninh.

ĐÔNG HÀ AND FARTHER WEST. Đông Hà is 22km south of the 17th parallel. On Hwy. 1 (called Lê Duẩn here), the **bus station** runs public buses to **Đà Nẵng** (4½hr., 8am, 50,000Đ) and **Huế** (2hr., every hr. 7am-6pm, 20,000Đ). Next door, the **Quảng Trị Tourist Company** operates from the **Đông Hà Hotel.** (Tourist office ☎053 852 292. Guide with car US$15-20 per day. Open M-Sa 7-11am and 1:30-5pm. Hotel ☎053 852 927. Singles with shared bath US$6, with A/C US$8; doubles with shared bath US$8/10; triples with shared bath US$19.)

From Đông Hà, Rte. 9 runs 60km west to Laos and was one of the principal highways the Americans used for artillery and troop transport. About 15km west on the highway is **Cam Lộ,** where a road heads north to both **Con Thien Firebase,** the site of a fierce 1968 battle that served as a diversion for the Tet offensive, and **Trường Sơn National Cemetery,** a memorial to the tens of thousands of soldiers who died on the Hồ Chí Minh Trail. Five kilometers west of Cam Lộ, an unpaved road turns left off Rte. 9 to the old US base at **Camp Carroll.** The **rockpile,** which stands another 7km west on Rte. 9, was thought by US Marines to be an unassailable helicopter landing pad until it was stormed by Việt Minh commandos. Another 20km west toward Khe Sanh is **Dakrong Bridge,** built from 1975-76 with the assistance of the Cubans. The **Khe Sanh Combat Base** is 10km from the bridge toward Khe Sanh. Amazingly, all the military intrigues are little more than wild weeds and arable land. Except for an occasional cow detonating landmines while grazing, your average tourist needs a good guide and a better imagination to reconstruct history.

ĐÀ NẴNG ☎511

In the 19th century, Đà Nẵng replaced nearby Hội An as Central Vietnam's principal port. Later the city received steady foreign traffic, albeit largely unwanted, first in the form of French colonialists and then with the US Marines, who splashed ashore in 1965. Today the tables have turned, and while thousands of tourists flock to Hội An, Đà Nẵng is content to carry on with business as usual, easily accommodating the few backpackers who swing through. Although the city doesn't beckon, it does provide: beer and snack stalls line the riverside, and ice cream parlors, pagodas, and churches dot the city and its environs, while the Chàm Museum is the best of its kind in the country.

TRANSPORTATION

Flights: Đà Nẵng International Airport (☎827 286), 4km from town, is a misnomer—there are no international flights. **Vietnam Airlines,** 35 Trần Phú (☎811 111). Open daily 7:30-11am and 1:30-5:30pm. Flights to: **Buôn Ma Thuột** (M, W, Sa 2:10pm; 550,000Đ); **Hanoi** (2 per day, 1,000,000Đ); **HCMC** (2 per day, 1,000,000Đ); **Nha Trang** (Tu, Th-F, Su 10:20am; 550,000Đ); **Pleiku** (M, Th, Sa 10:10pm; 550,000Đ); **Vinh** (M, W, Sa 10:20am; 700,000Đ).

Trains: Đà Nẵng Railway Station (Ga Đà Nẵng), 4 Hải Phòng (☎823 810). To **Hanoi** (15-22hr.; 8:30am, 12:45, 1:45, 7pm; 297,000-857,000Đ) and **HCMC** (17-23hr.; 6:15, 10:45am, 12:20, 5:50pm; 349,000-1,011,000Đ). Ticket office open daily 6am-5pm.

Buses: There are 2 bus stations in Đà Nẵng:

Interprovince bus station, 33 Đi_n Bi^n Ph© (☎821 265), 2km west of town. Buses to: **Đà Lắt** (19hr., 5am, 175,000Đ); **Hanoi** (1 day; 5, 7am; 220,000Đ); **HCMC** (1 day, every hr. 4:30am-12pm, 200,000Đ); **Hu** (3hr., every 30min. 6am-4pm, 35,000Đ); **Nha Trang** (13hr., 6am, 125,000Đ); **Qu=ng Ngãi** (5hr., every hr. 6am-4pm, 50,000Đ); **Savannakhet, Laos** (19hr., 8pm, 300,000Đ).

Intraprovince bus station, 29 Đi_n Bi^n Ph© (☎823 715). Sends **tiny buses** to **Hÿi An** (10,000-20,000Đ).

Full-sized public buses make the same trip to: **Hÿi An** from well-marked stops all over town; there's one outside the Đà N{ng Cathedral (20,000Đ). **A/C tourist minibuses** can be booked at most hotels to: **Hanoi** (1 day, 2pm, US$10); **HCMC** (1 day, 5:30am, US$17); **Hÿi An** (1hr.; 7, 9am, 2pm; US$3); **Hu** (3hr.; 7, 9am, 2pm; US$3); **Nha Trang** (10-12hr., 5:30am, US$7); **Savanna-keht, Laos** (6, 9pm; US$18).

Local Transportation: Motorbike and **cyclo** drivers will gladly take you to: the **airport** (8000Đ); the **bus station** (7000Đ); **China Beach** (30,000Đ); **Lan Co Beach** (100,000Đ); **Marble Mountains** (30,000Đ). Metered **taxis** to the airport 30,000Đ.

Rentals: Most hotels rent **motorcycles** (US$7 per day) and **bicycles** (15,000Đ per day).

ORIENTATION AND PRACTICAL INFORMATION

Almost at the center of Vietnam, 750km south of Hanoi and 990km north of HCMC, Đà Nẵng is bounded in the east by the **Hàn River** and in the north by **Đà Nẵng Bay.**

Bạch Đằng, the main boulevard, runs north along the river's west bank. One block inland, **Trần Phú** runs south, and three blocks inland, **Lê Lợi/Phan Chu Trinh** is the major north-south artery. These three streets are intersected by **Điện Biên Phủ/Lý Thái Tổ/Hùng Vương,** the busy east-west road that spurs off Hwy. 1 and bisects the city. A few blocks north, **Lê Duẩn** ends in a bridge across the river. The city's southern boundary, **Nguyễn Văn Trỗi,** runs east over the Hàn River and toward the Marble Mountains, China Beach, and Hội An.

Tourist Office: Most hotels offer basic tour services. **An Phu Tourist,** 147 Lê Lợi (☎818 366) has the best reputation. Mr. An speaks excellent English.

Consulates: Laos, 16 Trần Quý Cáp (☎821 208). Issues tourist visas to cross the border at Lao Bảo; 1-day processing. Open M-F 8-11:30am and 2-4:30pm.

Currency Exchange: Vietcombank, 140 Lê Lợi (☎823 503). Cashes traveler's checks and gives credit card cash advances. No ATM. Open M-Sa 7:30-11am and 1-4pm.

Markets: Chợ Hàn spills out around the river at the intersection of Hùng Vương and Trần Phú. Open daily 6am-8pm. Massive **Chợ Cồn** hulks at the corner of Hùng Vương and Ông Ích Khiêm. Open daily 6:30am-6:30pm.

Pharmacies: 237 Nguyễn Chí Thanh (☎834 787). Open daily 7am-4:30pm.

Police: 1 Nguyễn Thị Minh Khai (☎828 371).

Medical Services: Central Đà Nẵng Hospital, 74 Hải Phòng (☎ 821 483), 1 block north of Lê Duẩn. Has a Foreign Relations Affairs Office affiliated with AEA International.

Internet Access: Most restaurants listed (see **Food and Nightlife,** p. 868) have Internet access. 500-800Đ per min. **Đà Nẵng Information Technology Center,** 59 Trần Phù

(☎893 119), has faster connections and more computers. 500Đ per min. Open daily 7am-5pm.

Post Offices: GPO, 60 Bạch Đằng, north of the Hùng Vương intersection. **Foreign Services Post Office,** 64 Bạch Đằng (☎821 327). International phone/fax. *Poste Restante.* Open daily 6am-10pm.

ACCOMMODATIONS

Budget travelers usually bypass Đà Nẵng, so dirt cheap dorm beds are hard to find. Low-end accommodations are spread out and difficult to reach with a backpack.

Binh Dương Hotel, 30-32 Tran Phu (☎821 930). Exceedingly friendly owner and fully-equipped rooms with A/C and satellite TV. Car for hire to nearby sights. Breakfast included. Doubles from US$12.

Thuận An Mini Hotel, 14 Bạch Đằng (☎820 527), at the quiet northern end of the road. Motorbike rental US$7 per day. Basic fan-cooled doubles US$8, with hot water, telephone, and A/C US$10-15.

Nhà Khách 34, 34 Bạch Đằng (☎822 732). Not as bad as it looks. Check the karaoke bar next door if staff isn't at the reception desk. Doubles with A/C, TV, fridge, hot water, and passably-clean bath US$8; quads with A/C and hot water US$10.

Hoa Sen (Lotus) Hotel, 105 Hùng Vương (☎245 05). Sparkling clean rooms and a lobby full of cryptic aphorisms. A bit far from the water. Singles with A/C and phone US$12; doubles US$13.

FOOD AND NIGHTLIFE

Most food options lean toward the utilitarian. For after-dinner treats, however, Đà Nẵng residents have gone ice cream crazy. Ice cream parlors cluster near the Đà Nẵng Cathedral on Trần Phú and Quang Trung. Evening strolls along the river on Bach Dang are peaceful and pleasant as long as you don't mind rats milling about.

Miền Trung, 1B Bạch Đằng. Riverfront views from the balcony. Popular for local weddings and parties. The chef has never met a bottle of cooking oil he didn't like; grease floats on generous and tasty dishes. Entrees 20,000-50,000Đ. Open daily 7:30am-9:30pm.

Christie's, north of the market. An expat haunt with English book exchange and Internet access (800Đ per min.). Prices are inversely proportional to the amount of food, though quality is passable. Pizza 50,000-80,000Đ. Open daily 10am-midnight.

Liên Café, 20 Dong Da (☎895 422). A *bona fide* backpacker cheapie eatery. Serves the usual pancakes as well as providing tours and rental info. Breakfast under 12,000Đ. Open daily 6:30am-10pm.

VIP Club, 17 Quang Trung, isn't just the only nightclub in town, but it's open later than the competition. Small but loud, hip young locals shake it alongside aging foreigners aspiring to be hip young locals. (☎823 295. Beer 25,000Đ. Open daily 8pm-2am.)

SIGHTS

The small but celebrated **Chàm Museum,** 2 Tieu La, on the south end of town past where Trần Phú and Bạch Đằng merge, is the premier exhibition of Chàm sculpture. The open-air galleries showcase sandstone sculptures dating from the 4th to 16th century, organized by their recovery location, including Mỹ Sơn. (☎821 951. Open daily 7am-6pm. 20,000Đ.)

The Theravada **Tam Bảo Pagoda,** 253 Phan Chu Trinh, lies southwest of the Chàm Museum. Built in 1953, this towering combination of French, Chinese, and Chàm architectural styles has five tiers which represent the steps to heaven. Mr. Tung, the genial custodian, loves to practice his English with visitors. The light-pink **Đà Nẵng Cathedral,** near 158 Trần Phú, is a more grandiose house of worship. Called the "rooster cathedral" for its steepletop weathercock, this church was built in 1923 to serve the French Catholic community. (Open to visitors daily 8-10am and 2-5pm. Mass daily 5am and 5pm; Su 5, 6:30am and 4:30pm.) Đà Nẵng's **Cao Đài Temple,** 63 Hải Phòng, is farther north opposite the Central Hospital. Built in 1956, the temple serves 10,000 locals, sports the "all-seeing" eye, and is the largest such temple outside Tây Ninh. (Services daily 5:30, 11am, 5:30, and 11pm.)

DAYTRIPS FROM ĐÀ NANG

MARBLE MOUNTAINS (NGŨ HÀNH SƠN)

17km north of Hội An and 12km south of Đà Nẵng. Motos and cyclos *make the trip for 30,000Đ. All tourist buses stop here for an hour. Open daily 7am-6pm. 20,000Đ.*

The Marble Mountains are named after the five fundamental elements: the thin Metal Mountain, the subtle Wood Mountain, the double-peaked Fire Mountain, and the no-adjective-getting Earth Mountain. Limestone and marble quarries cluster around the foot of **Water Mountain** (Ngon Thủy Sơn), the main tourist attraction, with grand temples, eerie grottos, and idols hewn from the rock. In the 1960s, the mountain served as a base for the NLF.

From the right-hand entrance, stairs lead past a white Buddha to the **Linh Ứng Pagoda.** The **Tàng Chôn Cave,** in the back, contains a shrine flanked by a Chàm sculpture and a square stone platform on which, according to legend, fairies and gods played checkers. The Buddha behind the shrine is fabulous. Moving on up, the "Simply Stunning Sea View," **Vọng Hải Đài,** really isn't so stunning. For a grander panorama of China Beach from the mountain's highest accessible point, ascend **Động Vân Thông,** the "Way to Heaven." Back on the path, the **Tam Thái Pagoda** sports some beautiful bas reliefs and sits in front of the unspectacular **Linh Nham Cave.** To the pagoda's right, a stone Quan Am is carved from **Oa Nghiêm Cave,** but the best sight lies behind it: the light that penetrates the **Huyền Không Cave** through overgrown, overhead holes, semi-illuminating the cave. Four warrior statues at the cavern's entrance, dating from Minh Mạng's time, protect it from evil spirits. Near the left stairwell, a path leads past two small pagodas to **Vọng Giang Đài,** the perfect place to take in the "Five-Mountain View."

CHINA BEACH

Just east of the Marble Mountains. Motos and cyclos *make the trip for 30,000Đ.*

Famous for its role as landing spot for US troops during the war, China Beach makes a great daytrip from Đà Nẵng or Hội An. You'll find few foreigners here and even fewer Vietnamese, though the **Non Nước Resort Hotel** complex hopes to lure another wave of invaders. (☎836 216. Doubles US$10). Just a hop, skip, and jump away, the clean, wide, white beach stretches to both horizons.

HỘI AN ☎51

From the 16th to the 19th centuries, Hội An (known to Europeans as "Faifo") was a bustling port frequented by Chinese, Japanese, and European merchants. As the river began to silt up in the 19th century, the French chose nearby Đà Nẵng, with its superior port, as the next commercial center. Hội An remained a backwater town until the tourism floodgates swung open with a vengeance. Merchants' mansions, ornate Chinese assembly halls, and a laid back charm—not to mention over 100 inexpensive quality tailor shops—win the hearts of travelers. A government-sponsored celebration every month on full and new moon evenings closes off the town center to motorized traffic and allows pedestrians to meander amidst thousands of glowing multicolored lanterns.

TRANSPORTATION

Buses: Public bus station, 84 Huỳnh Thúc Kháng (☎861 284), 400m west of town. Tiny open-air trucks (2hr., every hr. 5am-4pm, 10,000Đ) and full-size red-and-white buses run to **Đà Nẵng** (via **Marble Mountain** or **China Beach,** 1hr., every hr. 5:30am-5:30pm,

20,000Đ) from less than 1km northwest of town at the intersection of Nhi Trung and Lê Hồng Phong. For **Nha Trang** and **Quảng Ngãi,** head to Hwy. 1, about 10km away, and play the flagging game. **Tourist minibuses** are available at any hotel to: **Đà Nẵng** (1hr.; 2, 8am; US$3); **Huế** (3hr.; 2, 8am; US$3); **Nha Trang** (10hr.; 6am, 8pm; US$7-12).

Rentals: Most hotels and travel agencies rent **cars** with drivers (from US$20 per day), **motorbikes** (US$5 per day including petrol) and **bicycles** (4000-7000Đ per day). Freelance operations are at the east end of Trần Phú and across the Cẩm Nam Bridge.

ORIENTATION AND PRACTICAL INFORMATION

Hội An is 25km south of Đà Nẵng and 102km north of Quảng Ngãi. Most public buses let out passengers at the side of **Hwy. 1;** from here, it's a 10km, 10,000Đ motorbike ride east to Hội An via **Huỳnh Thúc Kháng.** Just before town, the street breaks into three branches. **Phan Đình Phung** marks the north edge of town, eventually becoming **Trần Hưng Đạo,** home to the **post office** and Hội An Hotel. The middle branch is **Phan Chu Trinh.** The last branch, **Nguyễn Thị Minh Khai,** heads southeast toward the **Japanese Covered Bridge** and the river. After the bridge it becomes **Trần Phú,** the town's most sight-packed road. One block south, **Bạch Đằng** hugs the Thu Bon River. The major north-south streets, from west to east, are **Nhị Trưng, Lê Lợi, Nguyễn Huệ,** and **Hoàng Diệu.** Small **maps** are available at most hotels.

Tourist Offices: An Phu Tourist Company, 29 Phan Đình Phung (☎862 627). Open tickets, English-speaking guides (2hr., US$3), currency exchange, bus and plane tickets, and Internet access (300Đ per min.). Open daily 8am-10pm. **Sinh Cafe,** 61A Phan Chu Trinh (☎861 818), in Cafe Do Re Mi. Popular bus tours. Open daily 5:30am-11pm.

Currency Exchange: Vietcom Bank, 4 Hoàng Diệu (☎862 675). Currency exchange window cashes traveler's checks. MC/V cash advances. Open M-Sa 7:30am-7pm.

Markets: Near the intersection of Nguyễn Huệ and Trần Phú. Open daily 6am-7:30pm.

Bookstore: King Books, 83 Trần Phú. Best selection in town. Open daily 9am-10pm. **Foreign Book Exchange,** 48 Lê Lợi. Good and cheap. Large German and French sections. Open daily 9am-10pm.

Police: 8 Hoàng Diệu (☎861 204).

Pharmacy: 65 Lê Lợi (☎862 470), close to the water. Open daily 7am-10pm.

Medical Services: Local **hospital,** 4 Trần Hưng Đạo (☎861 218), diagonal from the GPO.

Internet Access: Outlets proliferating by the day. 300Đ per min. **Banana Split Cafe** and **Thùy Dương I Hotel** have the fastest connections. Why not try a Hội An special—a cyber-tailor shop?

Post Office/Telephones: GPO, 4B Trần Hưng Đạo (☎861 480). International phonecalls. *Poste Restante.* Open daily 6am-9:30pm.

ACCOMMODATIONS

The high volume of tourists inflates hotel prices. The prices listed below reflect peak months (July-Aug. and Dec.-Feb.). In the off season, bargaining can cut the price by almost half.

Huy Hoàng Mini Hotel, 73 Phan Bội Châu (☎861 453). Spotless waterfront property with French architecture and superb service invokes the romance of yesteryears—without the soaring price tags. Singles/doubles US$7-12, with A/C US$12-15.

Thùy Dương 2, 68 Huynh Thuc Khang (☎861 394), between the bus station and the Cao Đai Pagoda on the western outskirts of town. Thùy Dương Mini Hotel's quieter sibling. Slightly cheaper and bigger rooms.

Thùy Dương Mini Hotel, 11 Lê Lợi (☎861 574). On a happening strip. Tourist service galore in the lobby. Windowless doubles US$7-12.

Phố Hội 1 Mini Hotel, 7/2 Trần Phú (☎861 633), in the alley. As good a choice as any for "cheap livin," Hội An-style. Bare but clean with A/C, bathrooms, hot water, and balconies. Singles US$10; doubles US$15; large quad US$20.

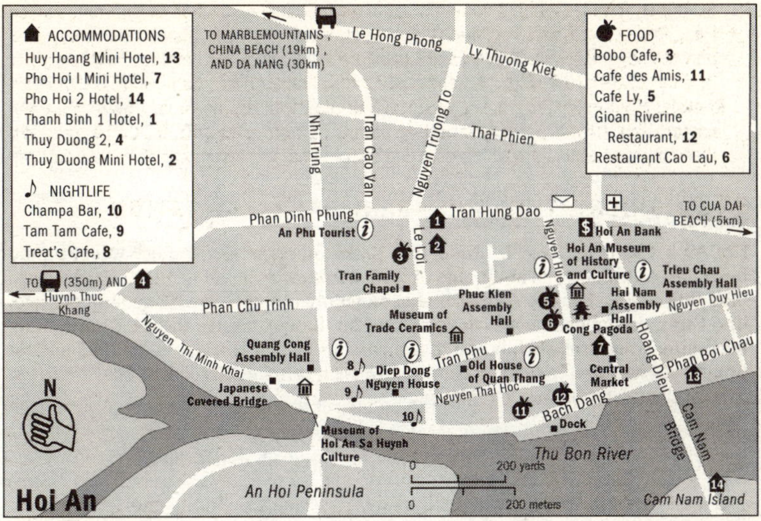

Phố Hội 2, Câm Nam (☎862 628), across the Câm Nam Bridge. Cheapies from US$8 to spacious digs with river views at US$25.

Thanh Binh 1 Hotel, 1 Lê Lợi (☎861 740). More affordable but cramped. Rooms US$8, with A/C US$10-12.

FOOD

Hội An's local culinary specialties are its true attractions. Try *cao lầu,* thick rich noodles in a tasty soup, or white roses, an appetizer of steamed shrimp in rice paper. *Hoành thánh,* fried wonton, are special because only two families in town hold the key to making the secret noodle dough. For dessert, try *bánh ít,* sugary rice and beans in a banana leaf. **Đ Nguyen Hue** is the tiny block near the Japanese Covered Bridge that turns into a local eatery strip from early evening until late.

Bobo Cafe, 18 Lê Lợi, facing Thuy Dương 1 Hotel. A long-time favorite among backpackers. Vegetarian versions of local specialties.

Cafe Ly, 22 Nguyễn Huệ. Excellent *cao lầu* (800Đ), white roses (15,000Đ), and fried wonton (18,000Đ) are among Mrs. Ly and Belgian hubby René's top offerings. Open daily 7am-10pm.

Cafe des Amis, 11 Bạch Đằng, on the river near the market. 14 splendid menus, seafood or vegetarian, US$3. Open daily 8am-11:30pm.

Restaurant Cao Lầu, 42 Trần Phú. Full of locals getting their daily *cao lầu* fix (5000Đ). Milk coffee 3000Đ. Open daily 6am-8pm.

Gioan Riverine Restaurant, 78A Bach Đang. Yet to be overrun by foreigners. Generous portions of seafood delicacies. Fixed price menu 30,000-50,000Đ.

SIGHTS

Hoi An's official sights hold less interest for most travelers than the narrow streets of town. The most beautiful sights demand an **entry ticket** (50,000Đ), available from 7am-6pm at **Hội An Tourist Offices:** 12 Phan Chu Trinh (☎862 715), 5 Hoàng Diệu (☎861 114), 37 Trần Phú (☎862 118), 78 Lê Lơi (861 982), and 19 Nhị Trưng (☎861 984). Each ticket provides access to the Japanese Covered Bridge or the Công Pagoda, your choice of one old house, one assembly hall, one museum, and one additional sight. Government **tour guides** have a sweeping knowledge of local history (free for groups over 10; 50,000Đ per 2hr. tour for smaller groups).

OLD HOUSES

TRẦN FAMILY CHAPEL. Devoted to ancestor worship, the Trần Family Chapel contains Chinese-style roof beams, crabshell designs, and coconut-sheathed ironwood columns. The Trầns, who live next door, explain their heritage and serve refreshments to guests. On the family altar rests a group of boxes, each one containing a small personal object from a patriarch leader and a wooden tablet listing his accomplishments. In the garden behind the sanctuary, a newborn baby's umbilical cord and placenta are buried as a token of family remembrance. *(At the corner of Lê Lợi and Phan Chu Trinh. Open daily 7am-6pm.)*

TRƯƠNG FAMILY CHAPEL. For a less polished (but free) family-worshipping house, head to the Trương Family Chapel. First constructed in 1840 and rebuilt in 1897, this edifice honors a family that came from Fukien, China, 10 generations ago. The central altar honors the family's first three generations, the left altar honors generations four through six, and the right altar awaits those next in line. The best time to visit is after 5pm when guide Trương Tri is home. *(69/1 Phan Chu Trinh.)*

OTHER HOUSES. The 200-year-old **Old House of Phùng Hưng** shelters eight people of the 8th generation. *(4 Nguyễn Thị Minh Khai, just west of the Japanese Covered Bridge. Open daily 7am-6pm.)* The **Old House of Tấn Ký** boasts an illustrious commercial history, a trap door, wood-wrought furniture, and memorabilia for sale. *(101 Nguyễn Thái Học. Open daily 8am-5:30pm.)* Built by a Chinese captain in the late 18th century, the **Old House of Quân Thắng** is said to be the oldest in Hội An. The house's 7th-generation owner, Diệp Bảo Hùng, encourages guests to drop in after 6pm, when entrance is free. *(77 Trần Phú. Open daily 7am-9pm.)* For an offbeat choice, check out the **Diệp Đồng Nguyễn House,** which has the largest collection of antiques in the province. The owner speaks Chinese but no English. *(40 Nguyễn Thái Học. Free.)*

ASSEMBLY HALLS

When Chinese merchants came to Hội An centuries ago, they formed congregations *(bang)* according to native region. The halls follow similar patterns and purposes: four open chambers surround a courtyard, providing an ornate environment for meeting peers, worshipping gods, and honoring ancestors.

PHÚC KIẾN ASSEMBLY HALL. Hội An's oldest, largest, most colorful, and most complex structure, this hall was first constructed in 1697 by Fukienese immigrants who began building the main existing elements in 1757. Just past the pink columns of the Red Phoenix Gate, look down to see the symbol for longevity surrounded by the five bats of happiness. The first courtyard contains stonework with a statue called "Carp Contemplating the Moon." Above the inner archway, the five bats frame the phrase "The Goddess Will Give Her Fellow Man Favor." The aforementioned deity is Thánh Mẫu, Holy Mother, Protectress of Sailors, and Goddess of the Sea. Just inside the main building, a mural depicts Thánh Mẫu preparing to rescue a ship from a wipe-out-caliber wave. The main altar upholds the congregation's ancestors; a smaller one to the right honors the God of Prosperity. *(46 Trần Phú. Open daily 7am-6pm.)*

QUẢNG CÔNG ASSEMBLY HALL. This hall serves the families of Cantonese merchants who arrived in the 17th century, built the hall in the 18th century, renovated it in 1885, and built the courtyard's colorful dragon fountain just five years ago. A large bas-relief mural at the entrance depicts a red-faced Quan Công, a military hero from the 3rd century whose morality was high enough to earn him deification. The main sanctuary houses a 3D image of Quan Công with the Goddess of Mercy and God of Prosperity on either side. *(176 Trần Phú. Open daily 6am-6pm.)*

TRIỀU CHÂU ASSEMBLY HALL. Intricate wood carvings lure visitors to this 150-year-old hall. Inside the sanctuary, a first-century Han emperor sits surrounded by tiny figures carved and painted on wooden panels. *(157 Nguyễn Duy Hiệu, the east extension of Trần Phú. Open daily 7am-5pm. Free, despite what the entrance ticket says.)*

HẢI NAM ASSEMBLY HALL. For a glimpse of amazing woodwork, go to the Hải Nam Assembly Hall. This congregation came from the island of Hainan near the coast of North Vietnam. In 1851, 108 of their merchant sailors were wrongfully killed by local mandarins, who in turn were executed by the emperor. The assembly hall was built in the sailors' memory. *(10 Trần Phú. Open daily 6-11am and 2-5pm.)*

MUSEUMS

HỘI AN MUSEUM OF HISTORY AND CULTURE. This 300-year-old museum (which used to be a Quan Âm Pagoda) provides a decent overview of the town's history. Today, its secular displays trace local civilization through the early Sa Huỳnh culture, Champa Empire, and Đại Việt era. *(7 Nguyễn Huệ, around the corner from and connected to the Công Pagoda. Open daily 7am-6pm.)*

MUSEUM OF TRADE CERAMICS. The museum's less-than-eye-opening displays—including a map of ocean routes, a model of a trading ship, and a 17th-century Japanese painting of Faifo—introduce Western visitors to the maritime global network. *(80 Trần Phú. Open daily 7am-6pm.)*

MUSEUM OF HỘI AN SA HUỲNH CULTURE. This museum displays remnants of the Sa Huỳnh civilization, first unearthed around Hội An in 1993. Like Oc Eo in the south and Đông Sơn in the north, the details of this prehistoric, pre-Champa culture remain elusive. There's a free war and revolution museum upstairs. *(159 Trần Phú, opposite the Quảng Công Assembly Hall. Open daily 6am-6pm.)*

OTHER SIGHTS

JAPANESE COVERED BRIDGE. The pink Japanese Covered Bridge, Hội An's most famous symbol, is known locally as Chùa Cầu ("Pagoda Bridge"). Japanese traders built it in the early 17th century. The stone piles on the bridge were meant to be driven into the heart of a monster, whose pesky tail supposedly caused earthquakes in Japan.

CÔNG PAGODA. The Công Pagoda honors Quan Công, a general of the Han Dynasty during the 2nd and 3rd centuries. The 346-year-old temple has the distinction of housing the largest statue of a god in Hội An. *(24 Trần Phú. Opens into the Museum of History and Culture. Open daily 7am-6pm.)*

ENTERTAINMENT AND NIGHTLIFE

For those bent on liver destruction, rice whiskey (see **A Mini-keg a Day**, p. 834) flows on the corner of Lê Lợi and Trần Phú until 4am most days; most other bars are packed until 2am.

Treat's Cafe, 158 Trần Phú. In an elegant two-story building. Mostly Western crowd alternates between drinking cheap beer (10,000Đ), shooting pool/darts, and bantering with those pesky but charming sales kids. Open daily until 1am.

Tam Tam Cafe, 110 Nguyễn Thái Học, 1 block toward the river from Trần Phú. The early evening is quiet as diners sip French wine and enjoy expensive Western cuisine (Australian steaks US$9). The more raucous crowd doesn't leave until 2am. Big BGI draft 10,000Đ. Happy hour 8:30-10:30pm.

Champa Bar, 75 Nguyễn Thái Hoc. Calmer than frantic Tam Tam. Large drinks, Western music, and 2 pool tables. Doubles as a traditional art performance center with sporadic folk music and dancing shows. Tall Tiger beer 16,000Đ. Open daily 5pm-2am.

SHOPPING

In a region renowned for its tailors and dressmakers, Hội An's *couture* scene shines. Rare is the visitor who explores the town without having an article of clothing custom-made. While those oblivious to quality can find US$20 suits, a good suit should cost (depending on the fabric and your bargaining skills) about US$40, a shirt US$6, and a pair of silk pajamas US$10—all made according to the shopper's specifications within a day. Shops are concentrated on Lê Lợi; most have old fashion magazines and pattern books to aid the designing process. The **cloth market,** on Trần Phú near Hóang Dieu, is also worth a look, though seamstresses there tend to be more aggressive. With so many choices, selecting a tailor can be daunting. Most places offer great value and quality, but talk to the dressmakers, look at their previous work, and ask other customers' opinions. **Son Ca,** 127 Tràn Phú, is run by a retired husband and wife team and are more keen on practicing English and French than pushing sales. Another solid but unremarkable option is **Thu Thủy,** 60 Lê Loi. Architecture lovers should ask to see its showroom in the back, which has exquisite handcarved wood beams.

While linings might cost extra, double-stitching, which prevents fraying, should not: you'll have to ask though. Also remember that you can always take off the extra inch; you can never add one. "Chinese silk," "Japanese silk," and "Vietnamese silk" mean different things to different people, but when all's said and done, real silk burns in a flame, while synthetics melt away; ask for a small sample and test the fabric yourself with a lighter.

DAYTRIPS FROM HỹI AN

CUA DAI BEACH

5km east of town on Trần Hưng Đạo.

Although Cua Dai Beach today may be quiet and relaxed (not to mention free), for up to 10 years after liberation, this served as the departure point for many fleeing refugee "boat people" embarking upon a 10-day passage to the Philippines. In town on Bạch Đằng, boat tours depart from near the market between 7am and 10pm. Independent operators charge 30,000Đ per hour; Hội An Tourist's tours are more expensive but better planned. The **Ceramics Village (Làng Gốm),** where brick kilns fire the products that locals create by hand, is the first stop. Note the apostrophe placement in **"Carpenter's Village" (Làng Mộc)**—only one family here does carpentry.

MỸ SƠN

50km south of Hội An. Minibus tours allow two hours at the ruins (8am, return by 2pm; US$3). Alternatively, hire a motorbike driver (US$5-6 round-trip) or get detailed directions and risk the confusing and rocky roads on your own. Ruins open daily 6:30am-4:30pm. Visitors must purchase a 50,000Đ ticket, take a brief bus ride around a hill, and proceed 300m on foot. English-speaking guides cost an extra 30,000Đ (up to 4 people) or 50,000Đ (5 or more), but are rarely available on the spot.

The earliest artifacts from the ruins date from the 4th century, though more permanent temples were not built until the 7th century. From the 7th to the 13th centuries, over 70 towers were built. Today, the ruins are organized into groups A-H. The path from the entrance leads directly to the C group, of which the C1 *kalan* (main tower) is most prominent. The broad, rectangular D1 and D2 were once *mandapas* (meditation chambers) for the Bs and Cs, respectively. Now they house a motley assortment of sculpture, as the cream of the crop were carted off to Đà Nẵng's Chàm Museum (see p. 868). The A1 tower, once the most spectacular testament to Chàm artistry, is now a sad perimeter of stone, with a restored *yoni* open to the sky. Despite the alphabetized grouping, there is little written description at the sights. A visit to the Chàm Museum beforehand adds more history and texture to this important pilgrim site.

QUẢNG NGÃI ☎55

An unremarkable provincial capital between Hội An and Qui Nhơn, Quảng Ngãi is the launching spot for visits to the remains of Sơn Mỹ Village, site of the Mỹ Lai Massacre. Though differing only in scale and circumstance from countless other events in the war, the massacre has come to symbolize the inhumanity of the war. The area's sobering history is a lesson in humility for visitors from the West.

TRANSPORTATION. Near the 200 block, **Lê Thánh Tôn** branches east to the **bus station** (☎822 895). Buses run to: **Buôn Ma Thuột** (16hr., 5:30am, 116,000Đ); **Đà Lạt** (18hr., 4am, 62,000Đ); **HCMC** (1 day, 6am, 110,000Đ); **Hội An/Đà Nẵng** (3-4hr., approx.

every hr. 5am-8am, 18,000Đ); **Kontum** (12hr., 5am, 40,000Đ); **Nha Trang** (10hr., 5am, 45,000Đ); **Pleiku** (10hr., 5am, 35,000Đ); **Qui Nho'n** (4hr., 5am-noon, 18,000Đ). The new Hwy. 1 bypass means that flagging buses from in front of the Petro-Song Tra Hotel, on the north side of town, is more productive. The **train station** (Ga Quảng Ngãi; ☎ 820 272) is 3km west of town off Hùng Vương past the GPO. Trains go to all major stops in either direction on the **Reunification Express,** including **Hanoi** (24-35hr.; 5:30am; hard seat US$25, soft sleeper US$56) and **HCMC** (20-30hr.; 9:30am, 2pm; hard seat US$21, soft sleeper US$46).

ORIENTATION AND PRACTICAL INFORMATION. Quảng Ngãi is 210km north of Qui Nhơn, 102km south of Hội An, and 117km south of Đà Nẵng. Hwy. 1 used to run north-south through town as **Quảng Trung.** Most of Quảng Ngãi's services are on **Hùng Vu'o'ng,** which cuts east-west across Quảng Trung, 2km north of the bus station. **Quảng Ngãi Tourist Company** (Công Ty Du lịch Quảng Ngãi), 310 Quảng Trung, is 100m from Hùng Vương. (☎829 829. Open M-Sa 7-11am and 1:30-5pm.) The **Foreign Currency Transaction Department,** 89 Hùng Vương, cashes traveler's checks at a 2.5ổ commission. (☎822 626. Open M-Sa 7-11:30am and 1:30-4:30pm.) A large **market** is east of Quảng Trung at 30 Nguyễn Nghiêm. (Open daily 6am-8pm.) The **hospital** is on Hùng Vương, 2km west of Quảng Trung. (☎822 888. Some English spoken.) The **post office,** 80 Phan Đình Phùng at Hùng Vương, has **international phones.** (☎822 930. Open daily 6:30am-9pm.)

ACCOMMODATIONS AND FOOD. **Kim Thanh Hotel,** 19 Hùng Vương, is your best bet for clean bathrooms and a friendly, English-speaking staff. (☎823 471. Small singles with lots of light US$7; clean doubles with A/C US$12.) **Vietnam Hotel,** 41 Hung Vương (☎823 610), offers similar amenities in a more run-down building. **Dồng Hư'ng Hotel,** 497 Quảng Trung, 500m south of Hing Vương, has clean rooms and a chatty staff. (☎821 704. Doubles US$6-8, with A/C and hot water US$10, with tub and fridge US$13.) If you're feeling the munchies, head for **Bông Hồng,** 243 Nguyễn Nghiêm, where *cơm gà* (a local chicken and rice concoction) with soup is 7000Đ. (Open daily 7am-11pm.) **Mimosa Com Vietnam,** 21 Hùng Vương, serves superb grilled beef for 18,000Đ. (Open daily 5am-10pm.)

VIETNAM

SIGHTS. Quảng Ngãi's most arresting sights lie along the road to Sơn Mỹ, beginning 1km north of Hùng Vương, over the bridge and to the east. Just past the sign that marks the turn-off, a dirt road runs up the top of **Triên An Hill.** American, Australian, and South Korean soldiers were based here during the Vietnam War. A monument to **Huỳnh Thúc Kháng,** an important figure in the anti-colonial movement, overlooks the area below. Colorful **Triên An Pagoda** stands nearby.

The **So'n Mỹ Memorial,** site of the 1968 **Mỹ Lai** massacre, sits amid peaceful rice fields 12km farther east along the road. Only one of the surrounding hamlets is called Mỹ Lai, but the US armed forces used this to refer to all four hamlets of Sơn Mỹ village. On the morning of March 16, 1968, Charlie Company, frustrated by losses it had incurred from an enemy it hadn't been able to distinguish from civilians, swept through the area, killing everyone in sight. Within four hours, they killed 504 villagers, many of them children and elders. The world didn't learn the truth until 18 months later. After lengthy investigations, just one low-ranking officer, Lieutenant William Calley, was court-martialed, only to be granted a pardon from President Nixon. The memorial to Sơn Mỹ's victims was established in 1976 at the site of the gruesome massacre.

The worthwhile **museum** has an inscription over the entrance that is loosely translated as, "Always remember the hating heart of the US invaders." Inside, photographs and personal belongings of the victims are displayed, with a list of all 504 victims' names and their ages. (Open daily 7am-5pm. 10,000Đ.)

Biển Khé Ky An, a small, pretty beach, is 5km beyond Sơn Mỹ. The road to the beach (which passes several shrimp farms) can be quite rough and windy. It's best undertaken on a moto. Most motos are stationed outside the swanky Petro-Song Tra Hotel. Round-trip ride with waiting time starts at 60,000Đ; add 20,000-30,000Đ more for beach lovers heading to the ocean.

QUI NHƠN ☎56

This charmless seaport town is the capital of Binh Dinh Province, but its current decrepit state masquerades a once glorious historical past. In the 18th century, the Tây Sơn brothers led the great Tây Sơn Rebellion, ending two centuries of division between the North and South. This region, the Tây Sơn District, was also home to Vietnam's most famous modern poet, **Xuân Diệu** (1916-1985), but contemporary Qui Nhơn has no remnants to show for its history. As locals await a Nha Trang-style boom, travelers settle for gray hotels and semi-precious sand.

TRANSPORTATION. The most hassle-free way to get to Qui Nhơn is by any A/C tourist bus cafe in Hội An or Nha Trang; arrange drop off and return dates. Otherwise, the **airport** is 34km out of town; to get there, catch a shuttle bus (2:10pm, 25,000Đ) at 32 Lý Thường Kiệt. **Vietnam Airlines,** 2 Lý Thường Kiệt (☎823 125; open M-Sa 7-11:30am and 1:30-4:30pm), flies to **Đa Năng** (M, W, Sa 3pm; 450,000Đ) and **HCMC** (Tu, Th-F, Su 4:40pm; 750,000Đ). For **trains,** ignore the cargo transport station at Qui Nhơn and head to **Ga Diêu Trì** (☎833 255), 10km outside the city (15,000Đ by motorcycle taxi). Tickets and schedules are at **Ga Qui Nho'n** on Lý Thường Kiệt. (☎822 036. Open M-Sa 7am-4:30pm.) Trains go to: **Đà Nẵng** (6hr., 7:55am, 68,000-246,000Đ); **Hanoi** (22hr., 7:55am, 246,000-884,000Đ); **HCMC** (12½hr., 5:25am, 142,000-508,000Đ); **Huế** (8½hr., 7:55am, 92,000-328,000Đ); and **Nha Trang** (4½hr., 5:25am, 50,000-176,000Đ). The **bus station,** at 543 Trân Hùng-Dao, runs buses to: **Buôn Ma Thuột** (10hr., 96,000Đ); **HCMC** (15hr., 176,000Đ); **Huế** (12hr., 6am, 110,000Đ) via **Đà Nẵng**; **Nha Trang** (8hr., 60,000Đ); and **Pleiku** (5hr., 40,000Đ). All buses depart between 5 and 6:30am. For more frequent journeys on crowded buses, go to Hwy. 1, 10km west of town, and flag away.

ORIENTATION AND PRACTICAL INFORMATION. Qui Nhơn is on a triangular peninsula 220km north of Nha Trang, 210km south of Quảng Ngãi, 150km east of Pleiku, and 12km east of Hwy. 1. **Hwy. 19** runs east into town as **Trần Llúg Đạo** from its intersection with Hwy. 1 and eventually reaches **Quảng Trung Park.** From here **Phan Bội Châu** runs east, **Lê Hồng Phong** heads southeast, and **Lý Thư'ờng Kiệt** curves southwest.

Binh Dinh Tourist Company, 236 Phan Bội Châu, is unusually helpful. (☎822 329. Open daily 7am-5pm.) **Bình Định General Hospital** (☎822 330) is at 106 Nguyễn Huệ. **Nhà Thuốc Thanh So'n pharmacy** is at 473 Trần Hưng Đạo. (☎821 097. Open daily 7am-10pm.) **Vietcombank** is at 152 Lê Lợi. (☎822 266. Open M-F 7-11am and 1-4pm, Sa 8am-12pm.) The **market** is on 1 Tháng 4 between Phan Bội Châu and Tăng Bạt Hổ. The **police** are at 247 Lê Hồng Phong (☎822 583). Internet access is available at **Quang Vũ Computer** in front of the Thanh Binh Hotel. (☎813 458. 500Đ per min. Open 24hr. except dinnertime.) The **GPO,** 197 Phan Bội Châu, provides **international phones.** (☎821 441. Open daily 6:30am-9pm.)

ACCOMMODATIONS AND FOOD. Accommodations tend be uninspiring yet chock-full of services. Many are south of the bus station on Lê Hong Phòng. **Movies Hotel,** 236 Phan Bội Châu, overlooks the central park and has clean, modern rooms. (☎822 876. Doubles with satellite TV movies US$10-15.) **Hòa Bình (Peace) Hotel,** 355 Trần Hưng Đạo, has four floors of sea-green rooms; the real green sea is just a block away. (☎822 900. Doubles US$8, with A/C $12-15.)

Away from the city center and beach, a large bowl of spicy rice soup with meat (*cháo*) and a tall glass of sugarcane juice or ice milk costs 5000Đ, check out the corner of Phân Boi Chán and Mai Xuan Thương, two blocks from the water. **Quê Hư'o'ng 2,** 185 Le Hong Phong St., is good, clean fun. ("Browned-rolling froggy" 15,000Đ. Open daily 8am-9pm.) **Thu Hông,** 189 Tăng Bạt Hố, is another solid choice that whips up a truly fine do-it-yourself hot pot with squid for 15,000Đ. (Open daily 8am-10pm.)

SIGHTS. Qui Nhơn's **public beach** is busy and interesting. Standing in front of a bad paint job called the Qui Nhon Hotel, the **Xiem Riep-Ratanakiri Zoo** is on the left at

2B Nguyễn Hué. To the right, a fascinating 6km walk goes past fishing communities and beaches to the **Leper Hospital.** The **Long Khánh Pagoda** is downtown on Trần Cao Vân, between Phan Bội Châu and Tăng Bạt Hổ. A huge teal Buddha greets visitors from atop a lotus; the main golden Buddha sits indoors with a *bodhi* tree behind him. (Open M-Sa 8-11am and 2-5pm.)

DAYTRIP FROM QUI NHON: BÌNH ĐỊNH. Bình Định is the birthplace of revered poet **Xuân Diệu.** A museum has been set up in the village of Túng Giản (approximately 23km north) at the late great's former home. (Open daily 7:30-11am.) **Hồ Núi Một** (Lake First Mountain) and the dam that created it are off Hwy. 19 30km west of town; look for the small sign and head south. Surrounded by hills, the tranquil lake is perfect for contemplation and romance. Boatmen will take a four-seat boat to a waterfall upriver (US$10). **Tháp Bánh ít,** the Cake Towers, sit on a hill near the crossroads of Hwy. 1 and Hwy. 19, 19km from town. Once a sizeable Chàm temple complex, these 11th-century ruins now sit amidst arid scrub.

CENTRAL HIGHLANDS

Most foreigners, if they're familiar with the Central Highlands at all, heard about them 30 years ago when the region saw some of the bloodiest combat of the Vietnam War. Today, veterans return on remembrance tours, but the region's beauty and native cultures are its main attractions. Of Vietnam's 54 **minorities,** many make their homes here: Mnong and Edeh reside near Buôn Ma Thuột, while the Bahnar, Jarai, and Sodang live around Pleiku and Kontum. In each region, the **tourist offices** wield varying amounts of control. In Pleiku, tourist officials monitor travelers' every move and make them pay for it. Kontum tourist officials require guides, but since it's hard to find a Kontum tourist official, the rule is not strictly enforced. Buôn Ma Thuột officials stick to recommendations and forego the required guide and entry fees. As most attractions are far from the region's principal towns and many require expensive guides, solo travelers find budget travel near-impossible. Groups can split guide fees.

TRANSPORTATION

Two main routes lead into the highlands from **Highway 1** on the coast. **Highway 26** begins 30km north of Nha Trang and leads to **Buôn Ma Thuột,** capital of **Daklak Province. Highway 19** starts near Qui Nhơn and leads to **Pleiku,** capital of **Gialai Province.** Highland cities are connected by **Highway 14,** which spans almost 200km from Buôn Ma Thuột north to Pleiku and an additional 50km up to **Kontum,** capital of **Kontum Province.** Until other highways are improved, these remain the only viable arteries. You can't get directly from Buôn Ma Thuột to Đà Lạt, and you have to backtrack through Pleiku to go from Kontum to the coast.

PLEIKU ☎59

Come in a group, bring wads of cash, or consider pushing on to more budget-friendly locales. Even more than its northern and southern neighbors, Pleiku is a lousy locale for cheap travel. In-town attractions are nonexistent and hill-tribe villages are distant. The tourist office gloats and distributes pictures of wealthy tourists doing things that look like fun. Most budgeteers don't hang around for long.

TRANSPORTATION. Pleiku's **airport** (☎825 097) is 7km east of town off Lê Lợi. The **Vietnam Airlines office** is at 55 Quang Trung. (☎824 680. Open daily 7:30-11am and 1:30-5:30pm.) Flights go to: **Đà Nẵng** (M, Th, Sa 8:35am; 270,000Đ); **Hanoi** via Đà Nẵng (M, Th, Sa 8:35am; 770,000Đ); and **HCMC** (M, Th, Sa 11:55am; 400,000Đ). The **Gia Lai bus station** (☎824 117) is out of town on Hùng Vương. Local rates, quoted as follows, are elusive. Buses go to: **Buôn Ma Thuột** (4½hr., 6:30am, 20,000Đ); **Đà Nẵng** (14hr., 6:30am, 49,000Đ); **Hanoi** (45hr.; 6:30, 8:30am; 134,000Đ); **HCMC** (24hr., 7am, 90,000Đ); **Huế** (17½hr., 6:30am, 62,000Đ); **Quảng Ngãi** (9hr.; 6:30, 7am; 34,000Đ); and **Qui Nho'n** (4hr., every hr. 6am-5pm, 20,000Đ). Minibuses (2hr., 10,000Đ) and motorcycles (1hr., 25,000Đ) leave all day for **Kontum** from Lê Lợi, opposite the Pleiku Hotel.

ORIENTATION AND PRACTICAL INFORMATION. Pleiku is 48km south of Kontum, 168km west of Qui Nhơn, and 190km north of Buôn Ma Thuột. Đ. **Hùng Vu'o'ng** leads to Pleiku from the bus station; **Lê Lọ'i** and **Trần Hu'ng Đạo** branch off to the right, crossing Quang Trung before meeting at the northeast corner of town.

Gialai Tourist, 215 Hùng Vương, at Lê Lợi, dampens enthusiasm, organizes tours, and distributes **maps.** (☎824 891. Open M-Sa 7-11am and 1-4:30pm.) **Vietcombank,** 12 Trần Hưng Đạo, one block from the GPO, cashes traveler's checks and issues credit-card cash advances. (☎828 593. Open M-Sa 7-11am and 1-4:30pm.) For **police services,** contact the **Immigration Office,** on the west end of Trần Phú. (☎869 180. Open M-Sa 7:30-11am and 1:30-5pm.) The **hospital** is at 64 Trần Hưng Đạo (☎824 125; English spoken). Get on the **Internet** in an office around the back of the community center at Hùng Vúóng and Lê Lai, two blocks east of Trần Llúng Đạo; ask around until someone lets you in (500Đ per min.). The **GPO** and its **international phones** are at the corner of Trần Hưng Đạo and Hùng Vương. (Open daily 6am-10pm.)

ACCOMMODATIONS AND FOOD. Thanh Lịch Hotel, 86 Nguyễn Văn Trỗi, off Quang Trung, offers good value and fine service. (☎824 674. Singles with fan and hot water US$7; doubles US$10; rooms with A/C US$20.) If Mondrian had worked in tan and white sculpture, he'd have designed the **Pleiku Hotel,** 124 Lê Lợi. Rooms are spacious and soulless, with hot water, and satellite TV. (☎824 628. Doubles US$11; larger rooms with refrigerator US$26-37.) **Húng Long,** 44 Trồn Húng Đạo, is generously endowed with tourists and locals scarfing up Vietnamese tasties. (Cuttlefish pressed with lotus root 18,000Đ. Open daily 7am-10pm.)

VIETNAM

SIGHTS. The Jarai village **Plei Mrong,** 35km north of Pleiku, is famed for its gravesite wood carvings. About 35km east of town on the way to Qui Nhơn, a small track on the left leads to **Dektu,** a Bahnar village of 200. Unlike most Bahnar communities, this one never converted to Catholicism. When someone dies, the family kills a buffalo and erects a *rong*-shaped grave. The family pays its respects every month by placing food and wine into a hole over the buried body. A moto and guide to both costs US$32.

KONTUM ☎60

Kontum province borders Cambodia and Laos, which gave it considerable strategic significance during the Vietnam War. In 1972, despite US and South Vietnamese boasts to the contrary, DRV forces took and retained the South Vietnamese Army base at nearby Đak Tô. Today, Kontum provides some of the region's most stunning scenery and well-integrated village networks.

TRANSPORTATION AND PRACTICAL INFORMATION. Kontum is 48km north of Pleiku, 228km north of Buôn Ma Thuột, and 216km northwest of Qui Nhơn. The streets form a grid. **Highway 14** rolls north from Pleiku, passing over a small bridge and becoming **Phan Đình Phùng. Lê Hồng Phong** and **Trần Phú** are the other major north-south roads. **Nguyễn Huệ** runs eastward along the Dakbla River at the bottom end of town, paralleled to the north by **Trần Hưng Đạo, Phan Chu Trinh,** and **Bà Triệu.**

The interprovince **bus station** is opposite the Dakbla Hotel. The ticket office won't serve foreigners; the bus driver is the man to talk to. Buses go to: **Buôn Ma**

Thuột (8hr., 7am, 26,000Đ); **Đà Nẵng** (14hr., 6:30am, 56,000Đ); **HCMC** (24hr., 7am, 98,000Đ); **Huế** (17hr., 7am, 73,000Đ); **Qui Nho'n** (7hr., 7am, 25,000Đ); **Quảng Ngãi** (12hr., 7am, 40,000Đ). Minibuses leave all day for **Pleiku** (2hr., 6500Đ).

Kontum Tourist handles tours, permits, and transportation from its Dakbla Hotel office at 2 Phan Đình Phùng. (☎863 336. Free maps. Guide and driver to Đak Tô US$25. Open daily 7-11am and 1-5pm.) **Agribank,** 1 Trần Phú at Nguyễn Huệ, handles **currency exchange.** (☎862 164. Open M-Sa 7-11am and 1-4:30pm.) The **market** is at the corner of Trần Hưng Đạo and Lê Hồng Phong. (Open daily 5am-7pm.) The **police** are at 90 Phan Chu Trinh (**emergency** ☎ 862 459). **Lâm Vy Pharmacy** is at 40 Phan Đình Phùng. (☎862 379. Open daily 7am-6pm.) The **hospital** (☎862 572) is at 224 Bà Triệu. The **GPO,** under the giant radio tower, at Lê Hồng Phong and Bà Triệu, offers fax and **international phones.** (☎862 500. Open daily 7am-9pm.)

ACCOMMODATIONS AND FOOD. The **Dakbla Hotel II** is tucked away inside the administrative-looking building at 163 Nguyễn Huệ, overlooking the bus station. Its new rooms include satellite TV and spotless bathrooms. (☎863 335. US$11, with hot water and A/C US$16.) **Khách Sạn Ngọc Linh,** 12 Phan Đình Phùng, has bright, clean rooms. (☎864 560. 4-bed dorms US$5; doubles with A/C US$12-15; triples with A/C US$15-18.) At **Phòng Ngủ Bình Dân,** 43 Lê Hồng Phong (☎862 706), barren doubles are 40,000Đ. **Food stalls,** serving fruit shakes and rice dishes (7000Đ), line **Lê Hồng Phong** toward the market. **Quán Ăn Dakbla,** 168 Nguyễn Huệ, near Dakbla Hotel, is adorned with etchings and weapons. The sauteed frog (*ếch xào;* 30,000Đ) isn't on the English menu, but should be.

SIGHTS. Unlike the highland cities, many of Kontum's **Bahnar villages** lie near the center of town. A **rong house** stands on the east side, at the intersection of Nguyễn Huệ and Lữ Tự Trọng. Next door, the **Montagnard Church** combines Catholic symbolism with local artistry. (Open daily 5am-6pm. Daily mass 5am, also Su 6 and 7am.)

Continuing east on Nguyễn Huệ, one passes through heavily populated **Kon Klor.** The road then butts into Trần Húng Đạo; a right turn leads to a suspension bridge over the Kon Klor River: across the bridge is **Kon Klor 2.** Taking the first left, then the first right, will lead to a winding dirt road which leads to a dammed **lake,** at the bottom of a series of small hills, where local hill tribes work and paddle.

Back in town, a **Vietnam War-era airstrip** (for civilian aircraft) stretches to the horizon off Bà Triệu. During the early morning, this lengthy strip of asphalt entertains Kontum youth and provides picturesque sunrises and sunsets. The rambling, colonial-style **Kontum Diocese Seminary** crouches behind wire fence and orchards at 56 Trần Hưng Đạo. It was closed by the Vietnamese government following the war but is now open to the public. (Open daily 7-11am and 2-5pm.)

DAYTRIP FROM KONTUM: ĐAK TÔ. Đak Tô, 40km north of Kontum on Hwy. 14, was a strategic region during the Vietnam War, valued for its proximity to the Lao and Cambodian borders. **Skull hill,** the site of a clash between DRV and RVN forces in the spring of 1972, stands on the road to Đak Tô, 17km from Kontum. By overtaking the hill, communists severed the land route to Kontum. The location of the bloody attack is marked by a concrete shrine and three piles of stones where locals burn incense. A right turn after the post office in the village of Đak Tô leads to a Chinese-made anti-aircraft gun, a Russian-made DRV tank, and remnants of a US reconnaissance helicopter.

Atop a plateau, 1km left and beyond the monument at the center of Đak Tô, was the site of a South Vietnamese/American base, marked by a large concrete facade bearing the heading, "*Di Tích Lịch Sử Chiến Thắng Đak Tô-Tân Cảnh*" ("Site of the Đak Tô-Tân Cảnh Victory"). On April 24, 1972, following a five-hour barrage and assault, DRV forces wrested control of the Đak Tô base from the South Vietnamese army and their US advisors.

The remains of a **US airbase** (Phượng Hoàng) are farther down the road, 4.5km from town on the left. **Pak Đri,** a Sedang minority village accessible by a hanging bridge, is a few kilometers down the road.

BUÔN MA THUỘT ☎50

This capital of the Đak Lak region was developed in 1899 by the French colonial Companie d'Agriculture d'Asie for the production of coffee and rubber, which grow well in the fertile red soil. On March 10, 1975, tank treads were planted here as the North Vietnamese Army swept BMT, signaling the inception of their Hồ Chí Minh campaign and the beginning of the end for the South Vietnamese Army. Today in BMT, rubber is still stripped, coffee still grows, and the first tank to arrive on "Liberation Day" sits at the town's center. Those visitors not impressed by the best coffee in Vietnam linger only long enough to visit the local villages.

TRANSPORTATION. Buôn Ma Thuột Airport (☎862 248) is 13km northeast of town via Hwy. 14. The **Vietnam Airlines Booking Office** is at 67 Nguyễn Tất Thanh (☎855 055), just before the bus station. Flights go to: **Đà Nẵng** (M, W, Sa 8:05am; 1,550,000Đ); **Hanoi** via **Đà Nẵng** (Tu, Th, Sa 8:10am; 1,000,000Đ); and **HCMC** (M, W, Sa 4:05pm; Tu, F, Su 4:15pm; 650,000Đ). Reserve early. Buses leave the station at 71 Nguyễn Tất Thanh (☎852 603) for: **Đà Lạt** (11hr., 6am, 56,000Đ); **Đà Nẵng** (19hr., every hr. 7am-1:30pm, 80,000Đ); **HCMC** (9hr., every hr. 7am-7pm, 91,000Đ); **Huế** (25hr., 6am, 70,000Đ); **Kontum** (7hr., 6am, 35,000Đ); **Lak** (2hr., leave when full, 10,000Đ); **Nha Trang** (8½hr., 6am, 28,000Đ); **Pleiku** (5hr., 6am, 28,000Đ); **Quảng Ngãi** (16hr., 6am, 48,000Đ); and **Qui Nho'n** (11hr., 6am, 34,000Đ). **Motorbike rentals** can be arranged by most hotels (100,000Đ per day). Moto drivers ask 80,000Đ round-trip to Lak Lake or Dray Sap Falls, or 15,000Đ per hour.

ORIENTATION AND PRACTICAL INFORMATION. Buôn Ma Thuột is 190km south of Pleiku, 180km northwest of Nha Trang, and 350km northeast of HCMC. The big tank is a navigational godsend. The turret, in its current position, could easily lob shots down Nguyễn Tất Thanh (Hwy. 14) toward the bus station, 2km away. The back left corner of the tank points down Nơ Trang Long, which runs west past the market. Heading from the tank down this street, the first three rights, entailing the heart of BMT, are Hai Bà Trưng, Lý Thướng Kiệt, and Y Jŭt.

Daklaktourist, 3 Phan Chu Trinh, by the tank's front left corner, has info on tours and hill tribes. (☎852 108. Cars to Lak Lake US$50; guide US$15 per day; **maps** 10,000Đ. Open daily 7-11am and 1:30-5pm.) **Vietcombank,** 121-3 Y Jŭt, exchanges travelers' checks and offers V and MC advances. (☎855 037. Open M-Sa 7:30-11am and 1:30-4:30pm). The **Đak Lak General Hospital** is at 2 Mai Hắc Đế (☎852 662), by way of Lê Duẩn (Độc Lập). The **GPO,** 4 Lê Duẩn, 150m south of the tank, has fax and **international phones.** (☎852 612. Open daily 7am-9pm.)

ACCOMMODATIONS AND FOOD. Government-run hotels are woefully overpriced; bargain vigorously. The private **White Horse Hotel,** 54 Hai Bà Trung, rents remarkable rooms with satellite TV, hygienic hot-water bath, and A/C. (☎853 963. Singles US$34; doubles US$38; highly bargainable.) **Khách Sạn San Bay Buôn Ma Thuột** (Buôn Ma Thuột Airport Hotel), 67 Nguyễn Tất Thanh, above the booking office, offers laundry service (3000-5000Đ per piece) and cheap rooms. (☎856 266. Singles with A/C, TV, fridge, and hot water US$12; doubles US$17.) **Khách Sạn 43,** 51 Lỳ Thường Kiệt, is as close as BMT gets to "cheap." (☎853 921. Rooms with 2 beds, fan, and somewhat grimy shared bath US$6 for 1 person, $8 for 2; with bath US$10.) **Ban Mê Hotel** is farther afield, 1km past the bus station, 9 Nguyễn Tất Thanh. (☎851 001. Singles US$6-12; doubles with A/C US$20-25.)

For a filling meal, try **Bò Né Bốn Triệu,** 33 Hai Bà Trưng. Ask for *bò né* (10,000Đ), the breakfast specialty: eggs, beef, scallions, and a pork-ball on a sizzling cow-shaped plate. (Open daily 6am-10pm.) **Phongdinh Quán,** opposite the Vietcombank, can be forgiven for its excessive use of bamboo furniture only because the food's so good. (Fish-sauce fried chicken 25,000Đ. Open daily 8am-11pm.)

SIGHTS. Two small museums highlight local hill-tribe culture and explain the history of the tank. The **Museum of National Cultures (Bảo tàng Văn hóa Dân tộc),** 4 Nguyễn Du (☎850 426), on the corner of Lê Duẩn, in the former Bảo Đại Palace, houses a cross-section of tools, instruments, weapons, and traditional dresses. The **Revolutionary Museum (Bảo tàng Cách Mạng),** 1 Lê Duẩn, houses Hồ Chí Minh paraphernalia and a presentation on the liberation of BMT, along with a comic attempt to display indigenous wildlife. (☎852 527. Both museums open M-Sa 7:30-11am and 1:30-5pm. 10,000Đ.)

The immaculate Edeh village of **Buôn Akŏ Dhong,** amid 50 acres of lucrative coffee fields, offers a conveniently close view of village life, even though it's the most affluent neighborhood in town.

The **Dray Sap Falls,** 29km southwest of town, make for a wild daytrip. A path descends into rainforest, complete with strangler figs, pungent flowers, and hanging vines. Dray Sap III are the first falls you see. When the water level is low, a river crossing leads to Dray Sap I and II. (Open dawn-dusk. 5000Đ.)

At **Yokdon National Park** (☎050 789 149), 37km northwest of town by way of **Phan Boi Chau,** elephants replace Soviet trucks as the chief mode of transport (2-3 people US$20 per hr.). The 60,000 hectares between Cambodia and the Serepok river constitute Vietnam's largest wildlife preserve. Accommodations are available (doubles with fan 100,000Đ). **Ban Đon,** a small hill-tribe village (a mix of Jarai, Mnong, and Edeh), 4km beyond the park, boasts a long history of elephant-taming. The tomb of **Khonsonuk,** a legendary elephant snatcher, stands nearby. One-day treks around the lake and the surrounding countryside can be arranged (1-5 people US$10).

Lak Lake, 56km south of Buôn Ma Thuột, is accessible by a straight shot along Hwy. 27. Or, if coming from Nha Trang, take a shortcut from Hwy. 26; turn left at the Shell station and the white statue to reach the lake. A Mnong community lives by the water, growing rice and raising livestock beneath elevated longhouses. Visitors enjoy touring by elephant (1½hr., 2 people US$30, in a special longhouse US$5 per person). The memorable aspects of Lak Lake—children playing soccer, boats on the water, description-defying dawns and dusks—are free.

NHA TRANG ☎58

Nha Trang is Vietnam's oasis. With high green hills falling away to white sand and turquoise waters, the "Vietnamese Riviera" has yet to turn into holiday-resort hell. Budget accommodations, street-side *pho* stalls, and inexpensive snorkeling and diving opportunities still abound in the "City of the Blue Sea."

TRANSPORTATION

Flights: Nha Trang Airport (☎823 798), 1km south of town, off Trần Phú. Book tickets at **Vietnam Airlines,** 91 Nguyễn Thiện Thuật (☎826 768), 2 blocks off the beach's south end. Open daily 7:30-11am and 2-4:30pm. To: **Đà Nẵng** (Sa-Tu, Th 2pm; 550,000Đ); **Hanoi** (daily 10am, 1,450,000Đ); **HCMC** (3 per day, 650,000Đ).

Trains: Train station (Ga Nha Trang), 17 Thái Nguyên. Open daily 7-11am and 2-4:30pm. To **HCMC** (7-10hr., frequent, 150,000-450,000Đ). Northbound trains leave 3 times per day for: **Đà Nẵng** (10-12hr., 188,000-571,000Đ); **Hanoi** (26-34hr., 497,000-1,547,100Đ); **Huế** (13-16hr., 209,000-681,000Đ).

Buses: Provincial bus station at **Nội Tỉnh Station,** 2 Tháng 4. Most travelers use long-distance terminal at **Liên Tỉnh Station,** 58 23 Tháng 10 (☎822 397), 500m west of the train station. Buses to: **Buôn Ma Thuột** (6-7hr., daily 5am, 63,000Đ); **Đà Lạt** (6hr., every 45min. 5-11am, 75,000Đ); **Đà Nẵng** (14hr., 1 per day, 168,000Đ); **HCMC** (12hr.; 7 per day 5:30am-6:30pm; 120,000Đ) via **Phan Thiết** (6hr., 80,000Đ); **Huế** (15hr., daily 5am, 155,000Đ); **Pleiku** (7hr.; Tu, Sa; 126,000Đ); **Quảng Ngãi** (8hr., 1 per day, 129,000Đ); **Qui Nho'n** (6hr., 1 per day, 78,000Đ). Buses can also be flagged down on the highway. Remember to bargain. Faster private **minibuses** leave from many hotels. To: **Buôn Ma Thuột** (US$6); **Đà Lạt** (US$7); **Hội An** (US$12); **HCMC** (US$11).

Rentals: Most hotels rent **motorcycles** (80,000-100,000Đ per day) and **bicycles** (8000-10,000Đ per day).

ORIENTATION AND PRACTICAL INFORMATION

Nha Trang lies 450km northeast of HCMC and 175km northeast of Đà Lạt. Two-lane **Trần Phú** runs north-south along the length of the 6km beach. **Hùng Vư'ơng,** a block inland, becomes **Trần Hưng Đạo** and then **Pasteur** on its way northward. **Lê Thánh Tôn** shoots northwest from Trần Phú's memorial tower, hits a six-way intersection and becomes **Thái Nguyên,** which continues west as **23 Tháng 10** past the **train station** and passes the **bus station.** Near the northern end of Trần Phú, **Yersin** heads inland toward another six-way hub; from here, **Quang Trung** runs north and continues out of town as **2 Tháng 4. Lê Lợi** runs west from Trần Phú's north end to the town **market.**

Travel Agencies: Agents line Biêt Thú and Trần Hùng Đạo. **Sinh Cafe,** 10 Biêt Thú (☎811 981), handles "open-tour" bus ticketing (see p. 890). **Hanh Cafe,** 5A Tran Hung Dao (☎829 015). Both open daily 7am-9:30pm.

Currency Exchange: Vietcombank, 17 Quang Trung (☎824 093). MC/V cash advances. No ATM. Open M-F 7:30-11am and 1:30-4pm. Most hotels and tourist offices exchange cash and traveler's cheques at punishing rates.

Markets: Chợ' Đàm, west of the post office (take Lê Lợ'i) at the end of Trư'ng Nư'. Known for its dried squids. Central gazebo sells tourist-oriented handicrafts.

Emergency: ☎115.

Pharmacy: Nhà Thuốc Tây, 42 Lê Thánh Tôn (☎825 753). Open daily 6am-10pm.

Medical Services: Khánh Hòa General Hospital, 94 Yersin St. (☎822 168), at the intersection with Quang Trung. Some English and French spoken. **Open 24hr.**

Internet Access: At most tourist agencies. 300Đ per hr.

Post Offices: GPO, 4 Lê Lợ'i (☎829 657). *Poste Restante.* Open daily 6:30am-10pm.

ACCOMMODATIONS

Mini-hotels line **Trần Phú.** Quality and services improve as you move inland.

Thanh Binh Mini-Hotel, 84 Trần Phú (☎825 203), on the south end of the beach. Small family-run guest house. Clean rooms. TV. Doubles US$7, with A/C US$10.

Phú Quý Mini Hotel, 54 Hùng Vư'ơng (☎810 609), near the intersection with Nguyễn Thị Minh Khai. 1 block from the beach. Friendly owners. Rooftop terrace. Doubles US$7, with A/C US$10; beautiful rooms with fridge, TV, and balcony $12.

Minh Thành Hotel, 10C Đinh Tiên Hoàng (☎827 281), 3 blocks from the beach between Lý Tự' Trọng and Nguyễn Chánh. Outgoing staff manages clean rooms. Rooms US$5-8, with A/C US$10.

Hà Hư'ơng Hotel, 26 Nguyễn Trư'ng Trực (☎512 069), off Tô Hiến Thành, 2 blocks south of Lê Thánh Tôn. Large, airy hotel recently refurbished and renamed. Slightly removed from the beach. Doubles with TV, phone US$8; with A/C US$10.

Post Hotel, 2 Lê Lọi (☎821 250), right on the beach. Designed in retro post office style. Rooms US$12-30.

FOOD

Nem nướng, grilled pork and vegetables rolled into rice paper and dipped in fish sauce, is a regional specialty not to be missed. A *nem nướng* district sits near Đàm Market around Lê Lợi. Head to Nguyễn Thiện Thuat for sumptuous local eateries, especially at **Pho Hanoi** at the Nguyễn Thị Minh Khai and Nguyễn Thiện Thuat intersection.

Tandoori Cafe, 34 Hùng Vư'ơng, between Lê Thánh Tôn and Nguyễn Thị Minh Khai. Elegant Indian restaurant with book exchange. Banana *lassi* 7000Đ. Curries 23,000-30,000Đ. Open daily 7am-11pm.

Ninh Hòa, 16A Lãn Ông, past the east end of Hoàng Văn Thụ. Large servings of delicious *nem nướng* 8000Đ. Open daily 7am-11pm.

Red Star, 14B Biệt Thú, next to Sinh Cafe. Table-top grill-it-yourself dishes 20,000Đ. Open daily 8am-midnight.

Bảo Đại Villa (☎590 147), at the southern end of Trần Phú. Affordable restaurant in unaffordable holiday resort overlooking the sea. Dishes from 15,000Đ. Reservations recommended.

SIGHTS AND SAND

Nha Trang is pancake flat and all the sights can be easily covered on bicycle. The city's most splendid attraction is its **public beach.** Ample sand and azure water run the length of town, with enough beach chairs and roving vendors offering everything from fresh mangoes and English books to oil massages. Cushions and beach umbrellas start at 10,000Đ per day. For a more remote seaside experience, pedal north on 2 Tháng 4 to the beaches of **Hòn Chồng.** After crossing the two harbor bridges, turn right onto Nguyễn Đình Chiểu and left before the fishery university. Besides its beach, Hòn Chồng's most striking sight is the yellow boulders that form part of the shore. (Open daily 7am-5pm. 4000Đ.)

The **Po Nagar Chàm Towers,** or **Tháp Bà,** are just north of the Xóm Bóng Bridge and south of Hòn Chồng. The temple is a fascinating example of the appropriation of one faith's deity (the Hindu goddess Po-negar) by Mahayana Buddhists. From the entrance, a brief ascent leads from the former *mandapa* (meditation hall) to the towers. A sculpture of Shiva marks the entrance to the north tower. Buddhists place offerings before Po-negar's image and the *linga* in the smaller towers. (Open daily 6am-6pm. 4000Đ.)

South of Lê Lợi on Trần Phú, the yellow Pasteur Institute houses the **Yersin Museum.** Alexandre Yersin, a Swiss-born French doctor remains one of the most revered Europeans in Vietnam. Artifacts include the microscope he used to discover the black plague bacillus. (Open M-Sa 8-11am and 2-4:30pm. 25,000Đ.)

The **Long So'n Pagoda,** Nha Trang's postcard picture of choice, stands at the west end of Yersin. The pagoda is dedicated to the Buddhists who gave their lives protesting the US-supported Diệm regime and is most renowned for its 9m high hilltop white Buddha statue overlooking a commanding view of the city.

ENTERTAINMENT

Boat tours (US$7) are big business in Nha Trang. The leader of the pack is the infamous cigarette-toting attitude diva ắ**Mama Hanh,** whose personal history makes Madonna look tame. After being picked up at 9am, touring several islands, snorkeling, gorging on seafood and fruit, and indulging in a "floating bar," satiated travelers are brought home by Mama at 5pm. Life preservers become increasingly handy as intoxication is the norm by late afternoon. Buy tickets at **T.M. Brothers,** 22 Trần Hùng Đao (☎814 556). Similar tours are offered by **Mỹ Á,** 10 Hùng Vương (☎826 195), and **Mama Linh,** 01 Húng Vương (☎826 693).

The **Blue Diving Club,** opposite 40 Trần Phú at Coconut Cove Resort, offers several diving and snorkelling options. (☎825 390. 2 dives US$60; PADI open-water course US$320.) The **Vietnam Scuba Diving Center,** 58 Trần Phú (☎811 375), offers a similar two-dive daytrip for US$40-50 for certified divers, and US$30 for beginners. Snorkeling is US$10 at both places.

NIGHTLIFE

Outside HCMC it's difficult to find a city that hits the taps as hard as Nha Trang. Unfortunately, the criminal elements also target foreigners as hard as they do in HCMC. Women are reportedly less enthusiastic than men for bars, and safe spaces for gays and lesbians are still non-existent. Foreigners mingle late into the night on the beach; locals favor inland *bia ho'i* joints.

Nha Trang Sailing Club, 72-74 Trần Phú (☎826 528). Plenty of wicker, beach, and cocktails (40,000-70,000Đ). Laid-back by day, increasingly crowded at night. Bia Sai Gon 15,000Đ. Big bottle of Tiger 25,000Đ. Open daily 7am-2am.

The Rainbow Bar, 55 Trần Phú, north of the sailing club under the ferris wheel. Similar to other clubs along the beach, but more intimate. Beer 18,000Đ. Cocktails 40,000-45,000Đ. Happy hour 8:30-11:30pm. Open until 3am and beyond.

ĐÀ LẠT ☎63

Forget everything you know about Vietnam—Đà Lạt is different. The mountainous city's flourishing artistic community, easygoing atmosphere, and the "Da Lat Eiffel" have led it to be named "Le Petit Paris." Doctor/adventurer Alexandre Yersin was smitten by the alpine climate during a 1892 highland expedition; following his suggestion to build a city, the French displaced ethnic Vietnamese communities and established Đà Lạt in the early 1910s. Đà Lạt's appeal hasn't been limited to Frenchmen; the "Honeymoon City" also has a proud history of domestic tourism, and, for once, Vietnamese couples outnumber the backpacker hordes.

TRANSPORTATION

Flights: Đức Trọng Airport, 30km south of the city. **Vietnam Airlines** booking office in Hotel Hàng Khôi, 40 Hồ Tùng Mậu (☎822 895). Daily flights via **HCMC** (50min., 2pm, 450,000Đ) to: **Đà Nẵng** (850,000Đ); **Hanoi** (1,450,000Đ); **Huế** (1,450,000Đ).

Buses: Tourist minibuses, booked and boarded at any hotel, go to **Nha Trang** via **Phan Rang** (6hr., 8am, US$6) and **HCMC** (7hr., 8am, US$7). **Public bus station** (☎822

077), 3 Tháng 4. Doesn't sell tickets to foreigners, but you can wait outside, hop aboard, and bargain. Local buses to: **Buôn Ma Thuột** (10hr., 1 per day, 63,000Đ); **Đà Nẵng** (15hr., 1 per day, 105,000Đ); **HCMC** (6hr., frequent, 50,000Đ); **Huế** (26hr., 1 per day, 120,000Đ); **Nha Trang** (7hr., 3 per day, 42,000Đ) via **Phan Rang** (3hr., 21,000Đ); **Quảng Ngãi** (8½hr., 3 per day, 96,000Đ).

Rentals: Motorbike (US$5-8 per day) and **bicycle** (US$2 per day) rentals are cheapest at hotels.

ORIENTATION AND PRACTICAL INFORMATION

The capital of Lâm Đồng Province, Đà Lạt is 300km north of HCMC on **Hwy. 20.** The **market area,** just west of **Lake Xuân Hư'o'ng,** forms the town center. To the left of the market, steps lead up to **Hòa Bình Square,** dominated by the 3/4 Cinema. **Tru'o'ng Công Đinh** leads from the cinema into **Phan Đình Phùng,** which runs roughly north-south; most of Đà Lạt's hotels and restaurants line these roads. **Trần Phú** runs east-west along the south side of town, from which **3 Tháng 4** runs out of the city.

Tours: Dalat Holidays, at the corner of Trương Cong Dinh and Phan Dính Phưng. Outdoor adventure tours. Sturdy mountain bikes for rent. Open daily 8am-8pm.

Currency Exchange: Incombank, 46 Hòa Bình (☎824 929). Traveler's checks cashed. MC/V advances. Open M-Sa 7-11:30am and 1-4:30pm.

Markets: Chợ' Đà Lạt, in the town center. Open daily 4am-1am, the market converts into a cheap food stall and bargain heaven.

Emergency: ☎115. **Police** ☎113. **Fire** ☎114.

Police: 19 Trần Phú (☎822 468).

Pharmacies: Medimpex, 34 Hòa Bình Square (☎822 570). Open daily 7am-9pm. **Ladopan,** 34 Khu Haa Binh (☎825 702). Open daily 7am-10pm.

Internet Access: Việt Hưng Internet Cafe, 7 Nguyễn Chí Thanh, toward the lake from the bank. 200Đ per min. Open daily 8am-11pm.

Post Office: GPO, 14-16 Trần Phú (☎822 003), under the Đà Lạt Eiffel. Fax/telex/international phonecalls. *Poste Restante.* Open daily 6:30am-9pm. **Branch** at 178 Phan Đing Phùng. Open daily 7am-9pm.

ACCOMMODATIONS

Many hotels in Đà Lạt have restrictions on housing foreign guests, which explains the "available to foreigners" sign on some of them. But establishments long-frequented by budget travelers are clean, affordable, and invariably friendly.

Hòa Bình (Peace) Hotel, 64 Trương Công Định (☎822 787), and 67 Trương Công Định (☎822 982). Former is impersonal while latter is smaller and family-run. Singles US$4; doubles US$6.

Như My Minihotel, 3 Bùi Thị Xuân (☎827 069). French- and English-speaking owners. Spotless rooms. Singles US$4; doubles US$8; triples US$10.

Mimosa Hotel, 170 Phan Đình Phùng (☎822 656). The orange facade is far from new, but rooms have matured well. Far from town center. Singles US$6; doubles US$8.

Lâm So'n Hotel, 5 Hải Thượng (☎822 362). From Hòa Bình Square, head down 3 Tháng 2, take a right onto Hài Thượng; it's uphill on the left. High wooden ceilings, pink stucco, and an eager staff. Doubles US$8, with TV US$10, with balcony US$15.

FOOD

Đà Lạt's alpine environs supply cartloads of fruits and vegetables and an array of forest critters from deer to porcupine. The cheapest eats are in the **market** area, close to the steps, where a bowl of *hủ tiếu* soup and all-you-can-drink hot tea costs 5000Đ. Affordable restaurants line **Phan Đình Phùng,** arm-in-arm with the budget hotels.

Stop N' Go, 2A Lý Tự Trọng. Walk length of Phan Bội Châu away from cinema area; take hairpin left turn onto Lữ Tự Trọng; it's uphill on right. A cafe and art gallery owned by

VIETNAM

local poet/artist/ex-mayor Duy Việt. Croissant 3000Đ. Coffee 5000Đ. Open daily 7am-7:30pm.

Bành Bèo, 20A Nguyền Chí Thanh. Heading from the cinema, it's past the bank. Named after its speciality: rice cakes with pork rinds, sprinkled with shrimp powder (3000Đ). Open daily 6am-6pm.

Điệu Thảo Vegetarian Rice Shop, 142B Phan Đình Phùng. Friendly hole-in-the-wall serving veggie standards. Boiled morning glories 2000Đ. The cryptic "rice" option for 12,000Đ is the way to go (essentially, it buys the farm). Open daily 5am-10pm.

Đông Á Restaurant, 82 Phan Đình Phùng, between the Hòa Bình and Cao Nguyên Hotels. Wild beasts (35,000-45,000Đ) dot the menu; Western tourists fill the booths. *Cơm* dishes 8000-14,000Đ. Open daily 8am-10pm.

SIGHTS

Linh Sơn Pagoda, Đà Lạt's largest, lies between the north ends of Phan Đình Phùng and Nguyễn Văn Trỗi, a short walk from the market area. Inside the central sanctum is a uniquely human *Thích Ca* (Gautama Buddha). Adjacent alcoves contain two golden guardians with dragons in their bellies. (Open daily 7am-6pm.) Man-made **Lake Xuân Hương** curves away from the downtown center. At its northeast corner, Đà Lạt's magnificent **Flower Garden** grows at the intersection of Bà Huyện Thanh Quan and Phù Đổng Thiên Vương. (Open daily 7am-6pm. 8000Đ.) Đà Lạt's historic **train station,** 1 Nguyễn Trãi, is east of the lake. You can peek at the old trains for 4000Đ or ride them 8km to the village of **Trại Mát** (1hr., 8am and 2pm, round-trip 55,000Đ). There, the **Linh Phước Pagoda,** 120 Tự Phước (☎825 410), features a colorful dragon around the courtyard fountain. (Pagoda open daily 6am-7pm; train station closes at 5pm.)

The **Governor General's Residence,** 12 Trần Hưng Đạo, is surrounded by European gardens. (☎822 092. Open daily 7am-4:30pm. 10,000Đ.) The **Palace of Emperor Bảo Đại (Dinh III)** is 2km southwest of Lake Xuân Hương, on Triệu Việt Vương at the end of Lê Hồng Phong. The royal family lived here from the building's completion in 1938, even after the playboy Bảo Đại's 1945 abdication under Việt Minh pressure. (Open daily 7am-8pm. 5000Đ.)

The **Hang Nga Tree House Hotel** (also called **Cobweb Mansion** and **Crazy House**), siting in riotous splendor at 3 Huỳnh Thúc Kháng (☎822 070) near Lê Hồng Phong, is both art piece and accommodation. Two enormous concrete trees tower over a fanciful sculpture garden. The trees contain nine nature-themed and well-appointed chambers. The building was sculpted by local architect Hang Nga, daughter of former president Trơng Chinh. (Tours 5000Đ.) Just north of Crazy House at 2 Thiệm Mỹ is **Lâm Tỳ Ny Pagoda.** Here, **Viễn Thức,** popularly known as the crazy monk, has established a tranquil one-man art gallery. Viễn Thức may let you take a peek between 7am and 7:30pm. Inside the **Nhà Thờ' Chính Tòa Đà Lạt** (Đà Lạt Cathedral), on Trần Phú near the post office, an intricate series of stained-glass windows will entrance even non-believers. (Daily mass 5:15am, 5:15pm; Su mass 5:15, 6:30, and 7:15am.)

DAYTRIPS FROM ĐÀ LẢT

WATERFALLS. Đà Lạt's waterfalls are popular with domestic tourists. **Cam Ly Falls** are accurately labeled "Toilet Falls." Prenn Falls, west of town, is a much more scenic tourist trap. *(Open daily 5:30am-6pm. 5000Đ.)* **Đa Tanla Falls,** 5km south of town, is surprisingly pristine. *(Open daily 6am-5pm. 4000Đ.)* More remote cascades to the south on Hwy. 20 include **Lien Khuong Falls** (30km), **Gougah Falls** (40km), and Pongour Falls (55km). All falls but Pongour dry up during the winter months. Honeymooners and hikers may want to enter the **Thung Lũng Tình Yêu** (Valley of Love), 6km north of the city, featuring rolling hills, views of Lang Bian Mountain, swarms of tourists, and the nationally famous "Đà Lạt Cowboys," whose American cowboy get-ups complete the tourist-trap atmosphere. *(Open daily 6am-6pm. 4000Đ.)* The love-

VIETNAM

lorn might consider sulking off instead to the **Hồ Than Thở'** (Lake of Sighs), 6km east of town off Hồ Xuân Hương. The fetid man-made reservoir hardly lives up to the name. *(Open daily 6am-6pm. 8000Đ.)*

K'LONG VILLAGE. The K'ho, Chil, Ma, Lat, and Churu highland minorities live and work around Đà Lạt. **K'long Village** (Chicken Village), has received much tourist attention, though the colorful shops seem only weakly connected to the actual village, whose 700 impoverished K'ho residents wear worn Western clothes. Aside from the giant concrete chicken, there's nothing very funny about this place, founded 22 years ago as a permanent home for K'ho nomads. *(18km south of town.)*

LANG BIAN MOUNTAIN. The touristed Lat village at the foot of Lang Bian Mountain. For permit-free frolicking, consider Lake Dankia and Ankroet Falls, 20km north of town behind Lang Bian. *(12km north of Đà Lạt. Dalat tourist guide US$10. Entry fee US$4, goes toward village education programs.)*

PHAN THIẾT ☎62

Four hours northeast of Hồ Chí Minh City on Hwy. 1, Phan Thiết (pop. 192,000) has slumbered as a tourist destination while Vũng Tàu has captured the weekend crowd. Surrounding Bình Thuận Province is home to a stunning set of landscapes and scenic, uncrowded beaches. In town, paths line the banks of the Cà Ty River's green waters, making the city a pleasant stop on a central Vietnam itinerary.

VIETNAM

TRANSPORTATION AND PRACTICAL INFORMATION. Phan Thiết is 198km northeast of Hồ Chí Minh City, 247km south of Đà Lạt, and 250km southwest of Nha Trang. A **bus station** on Trần Hưng Đạo, northeast of town, offers frequent service to **HCMC** (4hr., 31,000Đ), and rare service to **Đà Lạt** (8hr., 27,500Đ) and **Nha Trang** (approximately 6hr., 30,000Đ). Buses run more frequently to **Phan Rang** (3hr., 16,500Đ), where transfers can be made to Đà Lạt or Nha Trang.

Trần Hưng Đạo, Phan Thiết's main drag, runs from the direction of HCMC northeast toward Nha Trang, crossing the southernmost of three bridges spanning the **Cà Ty River.** Just west of town, **Trần Phú** branches north off Trần Hưng Đạo and heads into town, passing the market (where it is part of a seven-street intersection) and crosses the river at the north bridge. **Võ Thị Sáu** fronts the Nha Trang side of the river, while Trưng Trắc does the same on the HCMC bank.

A friendly **tourist office,** Công Ty Du lịch Bình Thuận, 82 Trưng Trắc, lies near the southernmost bridge. (☎821 394. Maps 10,000Đ. Motorcycle rental 10,000Đ per hr. Open M-Sa 8-11:30am and 2-5pm.) **Vietincom Bank** is across the river (as you head toward Nha Trang), at the intersection of Trần Hưng Đạo and Nguyễn Tất Thành. (☎828 078. Cashes traveler's checks. MC/V advances. Open daily 7-11am and 1:30-4:30pm.) Access to the town's **market** is at the seven-street junction. **Pharmacie Hồng Hưng,** 240 Trần Hưng Đạo, has an English-speaking proprietor. (☎821 501. Open daily 6am-9pm.) The **general hospital** (☎821 733) is across the river, 1km northwest of town on Hải Thượng Lãn Ông. The **post office,** 2 Nguyễn Văn Cừ, opposite the market, at the seven-street intersection, has an **international phone.** (☎817 971. Open daily 6am-9:30pm.)

ACCOMMODATIONS AND FOOD. Those sojourning in Phan Thiết for the scenery should head north to the outlying beaches (for accommodations, see **Beaches,** below). Travelers in transit will find cheap options on **Trần Hưng Đao** near the bus station. Beachside and close to town, the **Cong Doan Hotel,** 314 Vo T. Sau, has great location, fan-cooled rooms, and a smattering of insects for protein. (☎821 395. 3-bed rooms 100,000-150,000Đ). Generic, benign US$7 rooms can be had at most of the look-alike mini-hotels on Trần Hưng Đao; exceptional service lifts **Mini Hotel 99A** above the crowd. (Clean rooms with hot water and fan 100,000Đ, with A/

C 120,000Đ.) **Nhà Trọ Hồng Ngọc** is notable among cheaper options for its keenness on lodging foreigners. (Small fan room with clean shared Western bath 50,000Đ.)

Lẫu Bò Hồng, 94 Trần Hưng Đdao, serves *lẫubò*, a mix-your-own, simmer-your-own beef soup with tangy dipping sauce, to crowds of locals (70,000Đ feeds 4). **Nam Thạnh Lầu,** 50 Nguyễn Thị Minh Khai, facing the small park before the center bridge, teems with seafood delights. (Grilled shrimp 20,000Đ. Open daily 6:30am-9pm.)

SIGHTS. **Chùa Ông** (Ông Pagoda), on the north end of Trần Phú, is composed of two smaller temples, Chùa Ông (Grandfather's) on the right and Chùa Bà (Grandmother's) on the left. (Open daily 7am-6pm.)

A large pink **statue of Hồ Chí Minh** keeps vigilant watch over town (north of Chùa Ông, at the west end of the river park, on Trần Phú). Hồ Chí Minh, then known as Nguyễn Tất Thành, taught at the Đức Thành school in Phan Thiết in 1911. The **Hồ Chí Minh Museum,** in an ornate building fronting the statue, chronicles his time in Phan Thiết as well as his later years. (☎821 276. Open daily 7:30-11:30am and 2-4:30pm.) Nguyễn Tất Thành supposedly spent his days reading and teaching in the **garden** across the street. (Open daily 7-11am and 1-5pm.)

Though unremarkable compared to the beaches farther from town, the **local beach,** northeast of the river (Nha Trang side), between Nguyễn Tất Thành and Võ Thị Sáu, does provide respectable sand for local beach bathers.

BEACHES. Most of the out-of-town sights are northeast along Thủ Khoa Huân (Trần Hưng Đạo's right fork after it splits north of town). Moto drivers in Phan Thiết will sally to road's end and back for 70,000Đ. Two **Chàm towers** stand atop rolling hills 7km north of town. Continuing northeast, the road returns to the sea, coming upon **Địa Ông,** 9km from town. Once the site of a rock carved to resemble Địa Ông (Genie of the Earth), it has been replaced by a small Buddhist shrine. The beach at this spot is a mix of sand, rock, and at times crashing surf. Those seeking untrammeled beach access will find tranquility and a pricey menu at **Vườn Nhỏ** (Small Garden), 11km northeast of Phan Thiết. The compound is run by a Vietnamese-Swiss couple. (☎847 012. Breakfast included. US$7 per room.) **Suối Tiên** (Fairy Stream) cuts through the sand dunes 18km east of Phan Thiết. A pleasant stroll along the small path lining the 2km of stream gives a taste of the dunes. Though **Mũi Né** gets plenty of attention, the small town and the adjoining beach are dirty affairs. Skip the muck and head past town to gorgeous **Khu Nghỉ Mát Bãi Sau** (☎848 505). The center's bungalows are simple but clean (2 people 75,000Đ).

SOUTHERN VIETNAM

Approaching from the north, rocky outcroppings and jagged hills grind to a halt, smoothing into rivers and plains. Distinct in geography and personality from its central and northern brethren, southern Vietnam speeds forward on the momentum of governmental reform. The price gap closes, Việt Cộng pith helmets are replaced by baseball caps, and when people speak of "The City" (Thành Phố), they mean Hồ Chí Minh. For the land-weary, waterways replace asphalt and gravel, leading to floating markets and distant fields. Whether in a small Delta village, on a distant tropical island, or in the nation's largest city, southern hearts and minds are open and ready to welcome all comers.

HỒ CHÍ MINH CITY (HCMC) ☎8

After their tanks stormed the Independence Palace on April 30, 1975, ending 30 years of continuous warfare, the North Vietnamese renamed Saigon, Vietnam's capitalist dynamo for some 350 years, after their socialist hero, Hồ Chí Minh. The

French transformed Saigon from a dank citadel to a thriving port with broad boulevards and monumental hotels. During the Vietnam War, Saigon worked and played, while South Vietnam burned. After a depressing flirt with socialism, Hồ Chí Minh City (HCMC) today races with the speed of the thousands of Honda Dreams that zip down its roads. However, this emerging capitalism hasn't overtaken the city; dearer to the hearts of Saigonese than a fat profit is a good time, and no one parties as hard as they do. Removed neighborhoods hide amazing temples, makeshift markets, and charming guest houses, all welcome respites from the city's dizziness. Hồ Chí Minh might be turning in his tomb, but the locals aren't fazed—after all, everyone calls it Saigon anyway.

INTERCITY TRANSPORTATION

BY PLANE

International flights arrive at **Tân So'n Nhất International Airport** (☎844 63 21), 4km north of the city center. **Taxis** (US$6) and **motos** (US$2-3) run into the city. The international departure tax is US$10; domestic is 20,000Đ.

FLY LIKE AN EAGLE...

DESTINATION	FREQUENCY	PRICE	DESTINATION	FREQUENCY	PRICE
Bangkok	2 per day	US$165	**Manila**	4 per week	$247
Da Lat	1 per day	$34	**Nha Trang**	2 per day	$149
Da Nang	2 per day	$74	**Phu Quoc Island**	1 per day	$51
Hai Phong	1 per day	$140	**Phnom Penh**	3 per day	$75
Hanoi	7 per day	$140	**Singapore**	4 per day	$242
Hong Kong	2 per day	$300	**Siem Reap**	3 per day	$100
Kuala Lumpur	2 per day	$160	**Vientiane**	1 per day	$190

Major airlines that serve HCMC are: **Lao Aviation,** 93 Pasteur, next to the Lao embassy (☎822 69 90; open M-F 8:30-11:30am and 2:30-4:30pm); **MAS,** 132-134 Đồng Khởi, in the Continental Hotel (☎829 25 29; open M-F 9am-noon and 1:30-5pm, Sa 9am-noon); **Singapore Airlines,** 29 Lê Duẩn, in the Saigon Tower (☎823 15 88; open M-F 8am-4pm, Sa 8am-noon); **Thai Airlines,** 65 Nguyễn Du. (☎822 33 65; open M-F 8am-4:30pm, Sa 8am-noon); and **Vietnam Airlines,** 116 Nguyễn Hue, next to City Hall (☎ 823 06 96; open M-Sa 7:30am-4:30pm, Su 8am-noon).

BY TRAIN

The railway station, **Ga Sài Gòn,** is on 1 Nguyễn Thông (☎844 39 52), off Cách Mạng Tháng Tám in District 3. Guest houses and travel agencies assist with bookings. Purchase tickets at the **Vietnam Railway Union,** 136 Ham Nghi (open daily 8-11:30am and 1:30-4pm), or from the **Saigon Railway Tourist Services Co.,** 275C Pham Ngũ Lâo. (☎ 836 76 40. Open daily 7:30am-4:30pm.) Tickets may also be purchased at counters #4, 5, and 7-11 in the train station. An **express train** departs nightly for **Hanoi** (32hr., 9pm, 691,000-1,854,000Đ) via (from south to north): **Nha Trang** (7hr., 202,000-352,000Đ); **Đà Nẵng** (16½hr., 442,000-1,011,000Đ); **Huế** (19½hr., 489,000-1,120,000Đ).

BY BUS

HCMC has four major bus stations that serve domestic destinations.

Miền Đông Station: ☎899 40 56. In Bình Thạnh District 4km north of District 1. **Minibuses** and **buses** go north to: **Đà Lạt** (6hr., 9am, 32,000-46,000Đ); **Da Nang** (24hr., 102,000-117,000Đ); **Hai Phong** (50hr., 193,000Đ); **Hanoi** (48hr.; 10am, 4pm; 182,000Đ); **Hội An** (22hr., 9am, 101,000Đ); **Huế** (30hr., 6:30am, 112,500Đ); **Kon**

OPEN TOUR BUSES. The easiest and most popular way to see Vietnam over land is on the **Open Tour Buses** run by Sinh Cafe and Kim's Cafe (See **Tours,** p. 891). Large, 24- or 45-seat A/C buses traverse the country from HCMC to Hanoi, allowing passengers to stop-over in **Đà Lạt, Nha Trang, Hội An,** and **Huế.** You can stay in each destination for as long as you wish; just confirm your ticket at the local representative the day before departure.

Tum (22hr., 9am, 100,000Đ); **Nha Trang** (9hr., 9am, 47,000-63,000Đ); **Phan Thiết** (4hr., every hr., 20,000Đ); **Pleiku** (20hr., 7am, 66,000-100,000Đ); **Vũng Tàu** (4½hr., every hr., 19,000Đ).

Miền Tây Station: 137 Hung Vương (☎ 875 29 53), 12km west of the city center in Bình Chánh District. Buses go south to: **Bến Tre** (2hr., 8 per day 7am-4pm, 13,000Đ); **Cần Thơ'** (5hr., 10 per day 4am-5pm, 21,000Đ); **Châu Đốc** (1hr., 14 per day 4am-8pm, 32,500Đ); **Hà Tiên** (9½hr., 3 per day 4am-5pm, 42,000Đ); **Long Xuyên** (4¼hr., 7 per day 4am-11pm, 32,000Đ); **Rạch Giá** (5¼hr., 8 per day 4am-5pm, 38,500Đ); **Sa Đéc** (4hr., 3 per day 4am-11pm, 17,500Đ); **Sóc Trăng** (4hr., 8 per day 4am-11pm, 32,000Đ).

Other stations: Chợ' Lớ'n Station, 86 Trang Tử, 2 blocks north of Bình Tây Market. Buses to **Mỹ Tho** (2hr., every 30min. 6am-6pm, 9,000Đ). **Tân Bình Station,** 8 Cách Mạng Tháng Tám, in Tân Bình District. Buses to **Tây Ninh** (4hr., every 20min. 6am-8pm). Minibuses also leave Ham Nghi for **Vũng Tàu** (2Ăhr., 30,000Đ).

VIETNAM

BY BOAT

Hydrofoils leave from the pier on Tôn Đức Thắng to **Cần Thơ'** (4hr., 7:30am, US$24) and **Vũng Tàu** (1hr., 10 per day 6:30am-4:30pm, US$10). The ticket office is open daily 6:30am-5pm.

BORDER CROSSING: MOC BÀI/PHNOM PENH. Travelers going from HCMC to Phnom Penh, Cambodia, must through the border crossing at Mộc Bài. Public bus service to the crossing point is frequently disrupted due to poor road conditions on both sides of the border. The cheapest option is the **Sinh Cafe-Capitol Guest House tour bus** (9hr., 8:30am, US$6) which departs from Sinh Café (see **Tour and Travel Agencies,** p. 891) in HCMC and Capitol Guest house in Phnom Penh (see **Phnom Penh: Accommodations,** p. 74). Public buses leave from 147 Nguyen Du (W-Su 6am, US$20.) Alternatively, taxis (2hr., US$20-24) or motos (2hr., US$8-10) will pick you up at your accommodation and drive you to the border. Once across the border, taxis go to Phnom Penh (4hr., US$25-30).

ORIENTATION

HCMC is carved into 12 numbered districts, five named districts, and five named suburban districts. Districts are preceded by a "Q" for *quận*, and some street names are preceded by a "Đ" for *đường*. Most visitors spend the majority of their time in **District 1** (Quận một), which hugs the west bank of the **Saigon River** and contains the city's burgeoning commercial and tourist industries. The latter are concentrated on **Phạm Ngũ Lão,** which runs east to **Bến Thành Market. District 4** (Quận bốn), home to several museums and pagodas, lies south of District 1 across the Bến Nghé Canal. **District 5** (Quận năm), **District 6** (Quận sáu), which includes Chinatown and numerous pagodas, and **Chợ' Lớ'n** (also known as Chợ Bình Tây), are directly west of District 1. **District 3** (Quận ba), home to the **train station** (Ga Sài Gòn), is bound by Nguyễn Thị Minh Khai in the north and Hai Bà Trưng in the northwest. The **airport** lies far northwest in the **Tân Bình District.**

LOCAL TRANSPORTATION

Buses: The basically non-existent city bus system is useful only to get to major bus terminals. Buses go from Ben Thành Market (every 15min. 5am-7pm) to: **airport** (2000Đ); **Chợ' Lớ'n Station** (2000Đ); **Miền Đông Station** (3000Đ); **Miền Tây Station** (4000Đ); **Tân Bình Station** (3000Đ).

Cyclos and Motorcycles: Moto-taxis or **cyclos** US$1 per hr. Cyclos are banned from some major streets, near the palace, and along Saigon River. **Sinh Cafe** (see **Tours,** below) rents **motorcycles** (US$5 per day) and **bicycles** (US$2 per day).

Taxi: For pick-up, call **Vina Taxi** (☎842 28 88) or **Saigon Taxi** (☎842 42 42). 6000Đ for the 1st km, 1000Đ each additional km.

PRACTICAL INFORMATION

TOURIST, FINANCIAL, AND LOCAL SERVICES

Tours: Sinh Cafe, 246-8 Đề Thám (☎836 73 38). Open daily 7am-11pm. **Kim Cafe,** 270 Đề Thám (☎836 98 59). Open daily 7am-10pm. Both cafes run A/C bus tours to the **Củ Chi Tunnels, Cao Đài Temple** (1 day, US$4), and the **Mekong Delta** (1-3 days, US$7-30). Airline tickets, visas, heaps of info, and **Open Tour Buses** from HCMC to Hanoi (see **Open Tour Buses,** p. 890). Government-run **Saigontourist,** 49 Le Thánh Tôn (☎ 829 89 14), offers transport from the Mekong Delta to Phnom Penh and arranges visa extensions. Open daily 7am-10pm.

Consulates: Australia, 5th fl. Landmark Bldg., 5B Tôn Đức Thắng (☎829 60 35, emergency ☎090 82 469). Open M-F 9am-noon and 1:30-5pm. **Cambodia,** 41 Phùng Khắc Khoan (☎829 27 51). 1-month single-entry visa US$30; same-day processing. Open M-F 7:30-11am and 2-5pm, Sa 7:30-11:30am. **Canada,** 235 Đồng Khởi, suite 1002 (☎824 50 25). Consular services M-F 8-10am. Open 8:30am-5pm. **China,** 39 Nguyễn Thị Minh Khai (☎824 24 57). 1-month visa; 1-4 day processing. Consular services M-F 9am-noon. **Laos,** 93 Pasteur St. (☎829 76 67). 2-month visas US$65; same-day processing. Open M-F 8:30-11:30am and 2:30-4:30pm. **New Zealand,** 5th fl. YOCO Bldg., 41 Nguyễn Thị Minh Khai (☎822 69 07). Open M-F 8:30am-noon and 1-5pm. **Thailand,** 77 Trần Quốc Thảo, District 3 (☎836 76 37). 2-month visa; 2-day processing. Open daily 8:30-11:30am and 1:30-4:30pm. **UK,** 25 Lê Duẩn (☎829 84 33), next to Saigon Tower building. Open M-F 8:30am-noon and 1:30-5pm. **US,** 4 Lê Duẩn St., District 1 (24hr. ☎822 94 33). Open M-F 8-11am and 2-4pm.

Currency Exchange: Gold shops have the best rates. Travel agencies are the most popular but offer lower rates. Count your money on the premises. **HSBC,** 235 Dồng Khôi (☎829 22 88). MC/V cash advances. **24hr. ATM.** Open M-Th 8:30am-4:30pm, F 8:30am-5pm. **ANZ Night and Day Bank,** 11 Cong Trường Mê Linh, behind the Dao Monument. **24 hr. ATM.**

English-Language Bookstore: Lệ Duẩn (☎822 95 50), near the US consulate. Diverse selection of new and used books, dictionaries, and stationery. Open daily 8am-9:30pm. **Bookstore,** 267 Đe Thám. Used books in English, French, and Japanese as well as new and used travel guides. Open daily 8am-9pm.

EMERGENCY AND COMMUNICATIONS

Emergency: ☎115. **Police:** ☎113. **Fire:** ☎114.

Police: District 1 Police Office, 73 Yersin St. (☎839 92 50). **Open 24hr.**

Pharmacy: 183 Chuyên Bán Lế (☎836 04 25), near the intersection with Cồng Quynh. Some English spoken. Open daily 7:30am-11pm.

Medical Services: OSCAT/AEA International Clinic, 65 Nguyễn Du (☎829 85 20), inside the Han Nam office building west of intersection with Đồng Khởi. English, French, Russian, and Japanese spoken. Consultations US$55-65. **Open 24hr.** AmEx/MC/V.

Telephones: Murderously expensive international calls at upper-end hotels and at GPO. **Directory assistance ☎108.**

Internet access: Cheapest access on Đề Thám. 150Đ per min. Rates change frequently, so read the signs. Try upstairs at the **Star City Restaurant,** 204 Đề Thám, where dining further lowers the 100Đ per min.

Post Offices: GPO, 2 Công Xã Paris, next to the Notre Dame Cathedral. Open M-Sa 6am-10pm. International calling card and collect calls. *Poste Restante.* **Branch,** 227 Phạm Ngũ Laõ. Open daily 7am-11pm.

ACCOMMODATIONS

The cheapest rooms in HCMC are located in District 1 on **Phạm Ngũ Lão,** one block south on **Bùi Viện,** and on Đe Thám, the road that connects them. For more peace and quiet, head to **Cộ Giang,** two blocks south of Trần Hung Dao. **Chợ' Ló'n** has some budget spots, but the area is better known for brothels and thieves. Upscale neighborhoods have some classier digs down alleys in houses posting *"phòng thue"* (room for rent).

AROUND PHAM NGU LÃO

Hotel 64, 64 Bùi Viện (☎836 50 73). The city's best value, bar none. Very popular. Free breakfast and dinner; constant supply of tea, coffee, and bananas. Rooms with fan US$8, with A/C US$10, with A/C, satellite TV, and minibar US$16.

Hong Hoa Hotel, 185/28 Phạm Ngũ Lão (å836 19 15), on a small side street off Phạm Ngũ Lao by a mini-mart. Family-run hotel in ideal location—at the center of the action *sans* the noise. Free 2hr. Internet for guests. Satellite TV. Rooms $12-16. MC/V.

Room for Rent 70, 70 Bùi Viện (☎836 95 69), near the intersection with Đề Thám. Clean and simple rooms are pretty in pink paint. Motorbikes US$5 per day. Bicycles US$1.50 per day. One meal included. Rooms with fan US$8, with A/C US$10, with A/C and cable TV US$15.

Vinh Guest House (Le Le 2 Hotel), 269 Đề Thám (☎836 87 87), across the street from Kim's Cafe. Spacious, clean rooms complemented by great service. Private bath, minibar, and TV. Rooms with fan US$7-8, with A/C US$10-15. MC/V.

Quyen Thanh Hotel, 212 Đề Thám (☎836 85 70), at the intersection with Bùi Viện. Five stories of rooms, all with pleasant terraces. With 24hr. security, the gift shop downstairs poses more threat to your money belt than do neighborhood crooks. Rooms with a fan US$9, with A/C US$10. AmEX/MC/V.

Hotel 265, 265 Đề Thám (☎836 75 12). Regular rooms are nothing to write home about, but four-bed dorms are a good value for those on a tight budget. Dorms with fan US$3; singles with fan US$7, with A/C US$9; doubles US$8/10.

Dung Hotel, 185/6 Phạm Ngũ Lão (☎836 10 67), down an alley marked by a mini-mart, 30m from the intersection with Nguyễn Thái Học. Ideal location just off the main strip. Rooms couldn't be any cleaner. Don't fault it for it's name—it's pronounced "yoom." Rooms with fan US$8, with A/C US$12.

ELSEWHERE IN DISTRICT 1

Miss Lợi's Rooming House, 178/20 Cô Giang (☎836 79 73), down an alley between Cô Bắc and Cô Giang. Bright, freshly-painted rooms. Patio areas, TV room, and pool table make a great social atmosphere. Good for long-term stays. Breakfast included. Singles with fan US$7, with A/C US$8; doubles with fan US$8, with bath US$10.

Ngọc Huệ, 171/22 Cô Bắc (☎836 00 89), down the alley from Miss Lợi's. 26 average-sized rooms have minifridges, desks, and fabulous roof-top terraces. Internet 200Đ per min. Motorbike rental US$5 per day. Bicycles 10,000Đ per day. Breakfast and family-style Su dinner included. Tourist visa extensions. Singles with fan US$6, with A/C US$8; doubles US$8/10.

IT'S A DOG'S LIFE HCMC has whole markets devoted to selling live animals. A menagerie of caged puppies, birds, mice, roosters, and fish unfolds between Lê Hồng Phong and Vinh Vien at the southeastern edge of District 10. Commonly called "the Pet Market" (*Chợ Bán Chim Thú*), it's the place to go to get a new best friend or, if you change your mind, just dinner. Though it boasts a large selection of leashes and doggie treats, most of the cute canines won't ever need them.

Hotel 127, 127 Công Quynh (☎836 87 61). Prettier but less successful than its older sibling Hotel 64. Same friendly staff and same free breakfasts, dinners, coffee, and bananas included. Singles with fan US$10, with A/C US$12; doubles US$15/20.

Kim Loan Guest House, 171 Cô Bắc (☎836 83 51), in the alley with Miss Lợi's and Ngọc Huệ. Clean rooms with big windows and new appliances. Internet 200Đ per min. Breakfast included. Singles with fan US$6, with A/C US$9.

FOOD

Market stalls, sidewalk stands, and *cơm bình dân* eateries provide meager ambience, but the food is unbeatable. (*Phở* soups 5000-7000Đ. Beer 8000Đ. *Cơm* dishes 9000Đ.) Along **Phạm Ngũ Lão** and **Đề Thám,** tourist cafes serve decent food—banana pancakes, pizza, salads—to a mostly Western crowd. The best of the lot are **Kim's**

Cafe and **Sinh Cafe,** both on Đề Thám. Some slightly more expensive restaurants occupy side streets off Đong Khởi, between the Continental Hotel and the river.

AROUND PHAM NGU LÃO

The Original Bodhi Tree, 175/4 Phạm Ngũ Lão (☎837 19 10), in an alley marked by a Kodak shop–it's the first Bodhi Tree restaurant on the right. Vegetarian food good enough to tempt the most avid carnivores. Best breakfast in town 5000-8000Đ. Appetizers 6000-9000Đ. Entrees 5000-15,000Đ. Open daily 7am-10pm.

Phở Hoà Pasteur, 260C Pasteur Rd., in District 3 opposite the Pasteur Institute. Long regarded as the best *phở* in the city. Bowl of chicken or beef *phở* 13,000-15,000Đ. Open daily 6am-midnight.

Allez-Boo, 187 Phạm Ngũ Lão (☎837 35 05), at the intersection with Đề Thám. Best known for it's late-night rowdiness, but daytime diners enjoy quality dishes and tranquil atmosphere. Slightly more upscale than nearby tourist cafes. Breakfast 6000-1000Đ. Appetizers 8000-12,000Đ. Entrees 10,000-30,000Đ. Open daily 6:30am-midnight.

Tín Nghĩa, 9 Trần Hưng Đạo, at the Phạm Ngũ Lão intersection opposite BP Station. Simple vegetarian menu. Picky eaters are in luck–accommodating owners speak good English. Dishes 6000-1000Đ. Open 24hr.

Phở 2000, 1-3 Phan Chu Trinh (☎822 27 88), at the intersection with the Ben Thành Market. Introducing *phở*–21st-century style. The brainchild of Vietnamese-American businessmen, this place is modern, clean, and hi-tech. Fruit shakes 6000-10,000Đ. Northern-style *phở* prepared without MSG or sugar 14,000Đ. Open 24hr.

ELSEWHERE IN HCMC

Indian Heritage, 12 Thái Văn Lung, (☎823 46 87), at the intersection with Lê Thánh Tôn. Quality Indian food in Vietnam? Who knew? Free delivery in District 1. Veggie buffet 45,000Đ. Buffet open daily noon-2pm, restaurant open daily noon-2pm and 6-10pm.

La Fourchette, 9 Ngo Duc Ke (☎829 81 43), off Đong Khởi. Favorite of French expats who add authenticity to bistro decor. Pricey, but treat yourself. Appetizers 60,000-130,000Đ. Entrees 80,000-155,000Đ. Desserts 35,000-55,000Đ. Open daily noon-3pm and 7-10pm.

Ciao Cafe, 72 Nguyễn Huệ (☎825 12 03). A cheery, Italian cafe in the heart of the Đong Khởi area. Perfect for those nights when you just can't eat another bowl of *phở*. Italian *gelatto* 15,000-25,000Đ. Pizzas 28,000-44,000Đ. Open daily 7am-11:30pm.

Quán 13, 13 Ngô Đức Kế, near the intersection with Đong Khởi, near the Trận Hưng Đao Monument. Solid Vietnamese cuisine. 10 delicious spring rolls for 10,000Đ. Appetizers 12,000-47,000Đ. Entrees 24,000-75,000Đ. Open daily 7am-11:30pm.

Givral Patisserie, 2A Lê Lợi (☎829 27 47), at the intersection with Đồng Khởi, opposite the Continental Hotel. Pricey adjoining restaurant. Mouthwatering pastries 5000-8000Đ. Open daily 6am-10pm.

SIGHTS

Most of HCMC's major sights can be seen in one or two days. Major historical sights are concentrated in District 1; popular pagodas are in **District 5 (Chợ Lớn).** One way to cover all the sights is by following a horseshoe path starting at the zoo in the northeast and ending at Chợ Lớn in the southeast. The Pagodas generally stay open later than historical sites and museums.

WAR REMNANTS MUSEUM. Formerly known as the American War Crimes Museum, this six-room museum exhibits vivid, sometimes gruesome war memories, including photographs of the My Lai Massacre and bottled fetuses deformed by Agent Orange. Stick around for an engrossing exhibit on war photographers who died in the line of duty. *(28 Võ Văn Tần, District 3, 1 block north of the palace. ☎930 63 25. Open daily 7:30-11:45am and 1:30-4:45pm. 10,000Đ.)*

REUNIFICATION PALACE. What better symbol of the last 150 years Southern Vietnamese history than the city's palace, the former residence of South Vietnam's presidents. Behind the palace's simple, boxy exterior is a complex and violent history. It

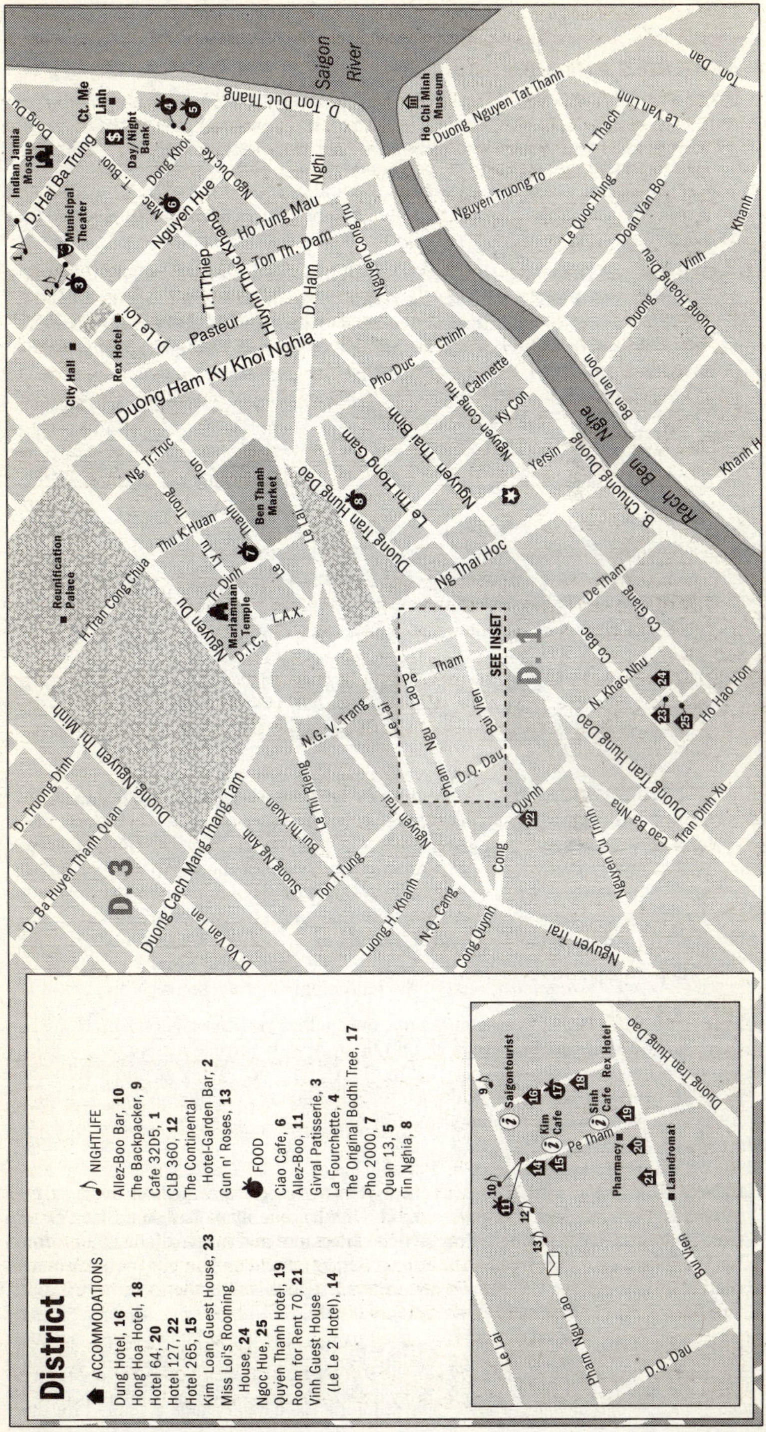
District I
ACCOMMODATIONS
Dung Hotel, 16
Hong Hoa Hotel, 18
Hotel 64, 20
Hotel 127, 22
Hotel 265, 15
Kim Loan Guest House, 23
Miss Loi's Rooming House, 24
Ngoc Hue, 25
Quyen Thanh Hotel, 19
Room for Rent 70, 21
Vinh Guest House (Le Le 2 Hotel), 14
NIGHTLIFE
Allez-Boo Bar, 10
The Backpacker, 9
Cafe 32D5, 1
CLB 360, 12
The Continental Hotel-Garden Bar, 2
Gun n' Roses, 13
FOOD
Ciao Cafe, 6
Allez-Boo, 11
Givral Patisserie, 3
La Fourchette, 4
The Original Bodhi Tree, 17
Pho 2000, 7
Quan 13, 5
Tin Nghia, 8
Reunification Palace
City Hall
Rex Hotel
Municipal Theater
Indian Jamia Mosque
Day/Night Bank
Ben Thanh Market
Mariamman Temple
Ho Chi Minh Museum
Saigon River
Rach Ben Nghe
SEE INSET
D. 1
D. 3
Saigontourist
Kim Cafe
Sinh Cafe
Pharmacy
Laundromat

VIETNAM

was built by the French in 1868 as a home for the Governor General of Indochina. When the French left in 1954, however, US-backed Ngô Đình Diệm changed its name from Reunification Palace to Independence Palace. In 1962, Diệm's own troops tried to assassinate him but ended up destroying the palace instead. A new mansion was completed in 1966 only to be bombed again in 1975 by a disloyal Vietnamese Air Force pilot. Once-rebuilt, twice-bombed, and thrice-christened, today's Reunification Palace remains frozen in its 1975 state. Multi-lingual guides lead tourists through ornate but run-down chambers and underground war rooms, concluding with a rooftop view of the city and an unintelligible film. *(Entrance on Nguyễn Đu, a few blocks west of the cathedral. Open daily 7:30am-11am and 1-4pm. 15,000Đ.)*

MUSEUM OF VIETNAMESE HISTORY. Highlights include ancient Hindu sculptures from the Mekong region and a room dedicated to comparative Buddha images. A must see for Southeast Asian art connoisseurs; for everyone else, it's optional. *(2 Nguyễn Bỉnh Khiêm, next to the zoo. Open M-Sa 8-11:30am and 1:30-4:30pm, Su 8:30am-4:30pm. 10,000Đ.)*

OTHER MUSEUMS. The following museums further explore the war. The **Revolutionary Museum** documents the liberation of the South. The murals, displays, and photographs make it very user-friendly and a big hit with children. *(2 Lê Duẩn. Open daily 8am-4pm.)* A **monument** at 29 Lê Duẩn commemorates the site of the pre-1975 US embassy, which was torn down in 1998. To learn more about Hồ Chí Minh, check out **Hồ Chí Minh Museum,** which displays a map documenting all the countries Uncle Hồ visited as a young man. *(1 Nguyễn Tất Thành, across the Bến Nghè Canal. Open Tu-Th 7:30-11:30am and 1:30-4:30pm, F 1:30-4:30pm, Sa-Su 1:30-9pm. Free music performances daily at 8am and 2:30pm.)*

ZOO AND BOTANICAL GARDEN. Founded in 1864, these gardens are Vietnam's largest. Once inside, turn right to see the **Temple of King Hùng.** This mythical ruler is worshipped as the father of ancient Vietnam, and his altar is accompanied by a display on human prehistory in the region. *(Entrance at the corner of Nguyễn Bỉnh Khiêm and Lê Duẩn. Concerts Sa-Su 6-10pm. Both open 7am-9pm. Adults 8000Đ, children 4000Đ; concerts 12,000Đ.)*

ARCHITECTURAL SIGHTS. In the center of District 1 where Lê Lợi approaches its intersection with Nguyễn Huệ, lies an area filled with pre-liberation opulence. The **Rex Hotel,** though not much of a sight today, served as an American business center throughout the 1960s and boasts a panoramic view of the city from its **Rooftop Garden** (for an exorbitant price). Next door, the yellow colonial-style **City Hall** (not open to foreigners) faces Nguyễn Huệ. and hides a pretty garden inside. The simple pink and white **Municipal Theater,** stands at the end of Lê Lợi, near Hai Bà Trưng. Graham Greene fans will want to visit the **Continental Hotel,** the setting of his novel *A Quiet American*, next to the Municipal Theater (see **Nightlife,** below).

RELIGIOUS SIGHTS. If time constraints only allow you to visit one of HCMC's pagodas, the **Jade Emperor Pagoda** should be it. A wide terrace leads past a turtle-filled pond into the main sanctuary where the Goddess of Mercy gestures with her numerous arms. Behind these Buddhist images is an area devoted to Taoist deities, centered on Ngọc Hoàng, the Jade Emperor and father of all kings. *(73 Mai Thị Lưu, at the northern end of District 1. Open daily 6am-5:30pm.)* Built in 1880, the **Notre Dame Cathedral** is a twin-spired miniature of its Parisian sister. *(On a pleasant square near the intersection of Lê Duẩn and Đồng Khởi. Open M-F 7-11am and 3-4pm; mass 5:30am and 5pm, Su mass 5:30am-6:30pm, 9am mass in French.)* The **Mariamman Hindu Temple** ("Black Lady Temple") has an unassuming entrance that opens into a surprisingly tacky interior; it's looks like a cross between a traditional Hindu temple and an 80s rockstar mansion. From 1975-89, the communist government used this building to store rice, but the temple's religious function has since resumed. *(45 Trương Định, southwest of the Reunification Palace. Open daily 7am-7pm.)* Built in 1935, the **Indian Jamia Muslim Mosque** conducts services for a practicing Muslim community of Chàm, Vietnamese, and Indian followers. (*66 Đông Du, 1 block south of the Lê Lợi. Open daily sunrise-sunset. Shorts, short skirts, and tank-tops not allowed.*) The stunning **Thiên Hậu Pagoda** is named for the goddess of the sea. Its rich ornamentation includes wooden carvings from China and gilded statues of King Hậu. *(710 Nguyễn Trãi, District 4. Open daily 6am-5:30pm.)*

NIGHTLIFE

Locals rave about HCMC's legendary, and backpackers who venture beyond District 1 will whole-heartedly agree. Downtown, on and around **Nguyễn Huệ** and **Đồng Khởi**, near the Rex Hotel are plenty of joints with solid nocturnal activity. The intersection of **Nguyễn Thiện Thuột** and **Nguyễn Đình Chiểu** in District 3 is a local cruising strip where locals and travelers munch on cheap food and sip plastic cups of *bia hơi* into the night. Near Đe Tham, **Phạm Ngũ Lão** also hosts several popular Western bars. near Nguyễn Thai Hoc

Allez-Boo Bar, 187 Phạm Ngũ Lão, at the intersection with Đe Tham. The largest, most popular bar in the backpacker ghetto. Beer 10,000-35,000Đ. Cocktails 30,000-45,000Đ. Open daily 6:30am-2am.

The Backpacker, 169 Phạm Ngũ Lão. Another popular spot with the 20-something foreign crowd. Clientele flock to the pool table in back. Beer 10,000-22,000Đ. Cocktails 20,000-60,0000Đ. Open daily 6pm-3am.

The Continental Hotel-Garden Bar, 132-134 Dổng Khởi, at the corner with Lê Lợi, near the municipal center. The Azur Bar of Graham Greene fame may be gone, but it's atmosphere still lingers. A great place to start the night. Beer 16,000-19,000Đ. Cocktails 40,000Đ. Open daily 6pm-midnight.

CLB 360, 215 Phạm Ngũ Lão. European patrons sip European beers while watching European football. Damn, it's good to be in Vietnam. Beer 10,000-30,000Đ. Cocktails 25,000-40,000Đ. Open daily noon-2am.

Guns n' Roses, 207 Phạm Ngũ Lão. Axel would be proud—nothing but Gn'R all night long. More Use Your Illusion II than The Spaghetti Incident, thankfully. Beer 10,000-15,000Đ. Cocktails 44,000Đ. Open daily 5pm-5am.

Cafe 32D5, 74/2 Hai Bà Trung, behind the Municipal Center. Pleasant cafe by day, a lean, mean, party-generating machine by night. Coffees 15,000-28,000Đ. Beer 28,000Đ. Cocktails 32,000-40,000Đ. Open daily 7:30am-6pm.

DAYTRIPS FROM HCMC

CỦ CHI TUNNELS

Tourist cafes set up cheap, easy trips to the tunnels. Daytrips to the tunnels depart from Sinh Cafe and Kim Cafe (8:30am, return 2pm; tunnel entrance fee US$5). Visitors can climb down into the actual tunnels from 30-150m, depending their degree of claustrophobia. Wear shoes with good traction and breathable clothing.

Few sights capture the tenacity and ingenuity of the Vietnamese guerrillas better than the Củ Chi Tunnels. The Việt Minh constructed the first tunnels during the war against the French in the 1940s. During the early 1960s, the National Liberation Front (NLF, Việt Cộng) greatly expanded the tunnel complex; at one point, the network of underground passageways stretched from Củ Chi to the Cambodian border. The tunnels were a base for commando raids and infiltrations into HCMC and enabled the NLF to surprise the increasingly frustrated American forces with wily defense maneuvers. The area around Củ Chi, known as the "Iron Triangle," is one of the most bombed pieces of real estate on earth.

CAO ĐÀI TEMPLE

Tourist cafes in Đe Tham offer combined one-day tours to the temple and Củ Chi Tunnels (8:30am, return7pm; US$4, tunnel entrance fee US$9).

A religion not known for its artistic subtlety or taste, Caodaism (see **Here's Looking at Chieu,** below) has a large and unique **main temple.** Its double-tower design features bright and gaudy colors. White-robed congregationers usher visitors to an observation balcony, which provides a bird's-eye view of the prayer ceremony (6am, noon, 6pm, and midnight). Situated near the capital of Tây Ninh Province, 100km from HCMC, many travelers feel it's not worth the long trek.

HERE'S LOOKING AT CHIEU In 1919 on Phu Quoc Island, a huge, bright, disembodied eye floated before Ngo Van Chieu as he lay in his hammock. The eye, a divine sign that initiated a series of heart-to-heart talks between God and Ngo, became the symbol of Caodaism, a mongrel religion that Ngo founded from his communications with the Cao Dai (High Palace). In his first chats with the colonial bureaucrat and occult enthusiast Chieu, God expressed deep frustration that humanity had been ignoring his prophets. Over the years, he said, he had sent—to name only a few—Jesus, Gautama, Victor Hugo, Joan of Arc, Louis Pasteur, Shakespeare, Rene Descartes, Lenin, Madonna, and Lao Tse as agents of the gospel. Frustrated with discord and rivalry among religions, God chose Chieu to act as a prophet for a rainbow coalition, including Buddhism, Taoism, Confucianism, Islam, Hinduism, and Christianity. Caodaism stresses love for one another and the belief that God resides within each of us; its saints include persons who have guided, inspired, and instilled ideals of truth and beauty in others. The new faith has spread quickly and now includes two million adherents. Le Van Trung, a rich and debauched Mandarin converted overnight to a life of virtue, and soon became the first Caodai pope.

NAM CÁT TIÊN NATIONAL PARK

Off Hwy. 20, approximately 150km from HCMC. Minibuses leave from Miền Đông Station to Phương Lâm (3hr., 15,000Đ). From here, moto-drivers cover the final 20km to a river ferry crossing (25,000Đ). Take the ferry across the river to the park headquarters to get an entrance permit.

Nam Cát Tiên National Park is a research center where rangers collect information on wildlife, including elephants, tigers, bears, and rhinos. "Visitor Information" consists of a map on the wall of park headquarters. **Jeeps** (60,000-200,000Đ per day) are the most popular means of transport. Hikers have the driver drop them off in the park, arrange a pickup time, and head into the forest. The lack of marked trails make guides (100,000Đ per day) worthwhile.

For **overnight stays,** head to park headquarters where there are small A/C compounds. (Singles with A/C 100,000Đ; doubles with A/C 150,000Đ; triples with fans 150,000Đ.) For a unique experience, camp on a sand dune along the banks of the Mekong River tributaries that ring the park (10,000Đ per person; tents 30,000-80,000Đ). The **canteen** in the park headquarters sells meals (breakfast 5000Đ, lunch/dinner 15,000Đ), canned food, and drinks.

VŨNG TÀU ☎64

For over a century, Saigonese have flocked to Vũng Tàu to escape the grind of their urban existence. Today, the scope has been widened to include Hanoi school teachers and beach-hungry Mekong Delta families. Few foreigners mean that the beach-going tourist is greeted with curiosity and warmth. Vũng Tàu's beaches are its *raison d'etre.* **Bãi Đầu** lies in an alcove northwest of town, **Bãi Tru'ó'c** hosts a stretch of sand west of the city center, rocky **Bãi Dú'a** hugs the southwest coast, and **Bãi Sau,** a long pristine expanse of beach, lies to the east.

Buses arrive at **Vũng Tàu Station,** 50 Nam Kỳ Khởi Nghĩa (☎852 777), and go to **HCMC** (2½hr., every hr. 5am-7pm, 24,000Đ), **Mỹ Tho** (27,000Đ), and just about everywhere else. Most guest houses rent **bicycles** (10,000-20,000Đ per day), and the Palace Hotel, 11 Nguyễn Trãi, rents **motorcycles** (US$7 per day).

Chợ' Mó'i, the largest market in town, is on Nam Kỳ Khởi Nghĩa, north of the bus station. (Open daily 5am-5pm.) For all money matters, try **Vietcombank,** 27-29 Trần Hưng Đạo. (☎852 309. MC/V cash advances. Open M-F 7-11:30am and 1-4pm; no transactions Th afternoon.) **Lê Lợi Hospital,** 22 Lê Lợi (☎832 667) operates a small clinic. **Nhà Sách Kiến Thức,** 58 Xô Viết Nghệ Tĩnh, sells maps of Vũng Tàu. (Open daily 8am-noon and 2-9pm.) **Internet access** is in the center of town at **Dich Vu Internet,** 32 Bacu. (500Đ per min. Open daily 8-11am and 2-9pm.) The **post office,** 45 Lê Hồng Phong, dominates the Xô Viết Nghệ Tĩnh intersection. (24hr. international phones/fax, telegram, FedEx, and DHL. Open daily 7am-8pm.)

Accommodations tend to be expensive. A strip of *nhà trọ* (guest houses) on **Thùy Vân** offers easy access to Vũng Tàu's most popular beach, Bãi Sau, though most guest house cater solely to Vietnamese. A hearty exception is **29 Thùy Vân.** (☎853 481. Western breakfast US$1. Singles with bath US$5, with A/C US$10.) **Bimexico,** on Thùy Vân at the north end of Bãi Sau, offers rustic A-frames. (☎859 916. 130,000Đ, with A/C 140,000Đ.) **Bãi Dứa Restaurant,** 22 Hạ Long, cooks tasty sea vittles. (Steamed shrimp with beer 30,000Đ. ☎856 281. Open daily 6am-10pm.) **Cửu Long,** 57 Thùy Vân next to Bãi Sau, serves flavorful fare. (Fried rice with chicken 15,000Đ. ☎854 018. Open daily 8am-11pm.)

MEKONG DELTA

What the rest of the world calls the Mekong Delta, the Vietnamese call *đồng bằng sông Cửu Long* (River of the Nine-Headed Dragon), a reference to the Mekong River's nine principal tributaries. As the river fans out on its final push to the sea, it forms dozens of tributaries and canals, flattening the landscape and sustaining a vibrant agriculture-based waterfront lifestyle. Agriculture dominates the region's lifestyle and creates a more leisurely pace than nearby Ho Chi Minh City—a characteristic of which delta residents are proud. Inhabitants of the region also take pride as the world's third largest rice exporter. Relatively new to the region, the Vietnamese only began large-scale immigration to the Mekong in the early 19th century, displacing large numbers of ethnic Khmers. With a close proximity to Cambodia and a history of dislike and distrust between the two countries, ethnic tension still exists. However, travelers still enjoy the calm pace of life on the river, the diligent yet slow character of the small fishing villages, and some of the area's best beaches.

MỸ THO ☎73

With its proximity to Hồ Chí Minh City, Mỹ Tho serves as a traveler's gateway to the Mekong Delta. Budget hotel and restaurant options number less-than-stellar few, though some laudable but more expensive rooms exist. While the attractions consist primarily of river islands and waterside markets, Mỹ Tho can be either a convenient excursion or a pleasant introductory stopover on an extended quest to take in the delta life.

TRANSPORTATION AND PRACTICAL INFORMATION. Mỹ Tho, 70km south of HCMC, is the capital of Tiền Giang Province. The **bus station** (☎875 274) lies on **Đường ấp Bắc,** which runs into town from the north. Most buses depart between 4-8am, although buses to Hồ Chí Minh City and Căn Thó run frequently from morning until early evening. **Buses** to: **Cần Thơ'** (4hr., 14,500Đ); **Châu Đốc** (6hr., 25,500Đ); **HCMC** (1½hr., every 30min., 9000Đ); **Tây Ninh** (4hr., 19,000Đ); **Vũng Tàu** (4hr., 22,000Đ). Ask about buses to **Long Xuyên** and **Sa Đéc,** as they often need to be combined with a short motorbike ride from a nearby town. **Nam Kỳ Khởi Nghĩa,** a north-south thoroughfare, intersects Đường ấp Bắc, running to the Tiền River. A left turn at the end of Nam Kỳ Khởi Nghĩa is **Đuong 30/4,** becoming **Trưng Trắc,** which leads along the Bao Dinh River, past restaurants, hotels, and the **market.**

Services in Mỹ Tho include: **Tiền Giang Tourist Office,** 8 Đuong 30/4, which operates **boat tours** (☎873 477; 2-5hr. US$20 first person, each additional person US$1.50; open daily 7:30am-5pm); a bank, **Ngân Hàng Công Thương Việt Nam,** 15B Nam Kỳ Khởi Nghĩa (☎873 026, open M-Sa 7:15 -11am and 1:30-4:30pm, MC/V cash advances); **Mỹ Tho Commercial Service Center,** at the corner of Lê Lợi and Lê Đại Hành, is a large indoor market (open daily 7am-7pm); **internet** access is available at 16 Ấ'p Bă'c at the northwest corner of the intersection with Nam Kỳ Khới Nghia (open 7:30am-9:30pm, 500Đ per min.); **General Hospital,** 2 Hùng Vương (☎872 359 or 872 360, **24hr.** service); and the **GPO,** 59 Đuong 30/4 (☎873 214, **fax** and **international telephones**, open daily 6am-9pm).

ACCOMMODATIONS AND FOOD. The few tourist hotels sit primarily on Đuong 30/4. **Rạng Đông Hotel,** 25 Đuong 30/4, has rooms equipped with TV, A/C, and bath. (☎874 400. 2-3 person rooms 100,000Đ, with hot water 150,000Đ.) **Công Đoàn**

Hotel, 61 Đuong 30/4, next to the post office, offers clean rooms that open to outdoor terraces and have ensuite bathrooms. (☎874 324. Triple with A/C 160,000Đ; quad with fan 120,000Đ.) At the end of Đuong 30/4, **Huớng Dưo'ng Hotel**, 33 Trưng Trắc, has cheaper but less modern options. (☎872 011. Triple with fan and bathroom 90,000Đ.)

Mỹ Tho's famous noodle soup, *Hủ tiếu Mỹ Tho* is cooked up in small food stalls all over town. **Chí Thành Quăn,** 279 Tét Maù Thân, a short walk inland from Đuong 30/4, is recommended for its good food and clean, bright interior. (Fried noodles with beef 15,000Đ. Open daily 9am-9pm.) **Thuân Kiều,** 47 Nam Ky Khởi Nghia, two blocks from the river, is popular with town residents for its friendly atmosphere. (Salty chicken with fried rice, served with *longans* 15,000Đ. Open daily 7am-9pm.)

SIGHTS. Boat tours to the nearby islands typically include a visit to canals, fruit orchards, bee farms, a coconut candy factory, and the **Temple of the Coconut Monk** on Phoenix Island. The temple was home to the French-educated Coconut Monk who preached a fusion of Buddhism and Christianity and ate nothing but coconuts for three years. Boat operators cluster on the tourist pier at the intersection of Đuong 30/4 and Lê Lợi (2-5 hr., US$4 per hr.) Trips conducted by the tourist office are reasonably priced for groups (see **Practical Information,** above). About 1km east of town over the Nguyễn Trãi Bridge (off Trưng Trắc) stands **Vĩnh Tràng Pagoda,** a large temple surrounded by fountains, gardens, and knick-knacks for sale. (Open daily Apr.-July 7am-9pm; daily Aug.-Mar. 7, 11am and 1-7pm.)

The **Đồng Tâm Snake Farm (Trại Rắn Đống Tam)** sits 7km west of **Mỹ Tho,** past the **Foster's/BGI Beer Plant.** Motorcycle drivers will round-trip it for 20,000Đ. Here, caged cobras are milked for their venom, which is used in a snake-bite antidote and pain-killing ointments. In addition, hundreds of bears, monkeys, and birds are on display in an archaic zoo. (Open daily 7am-5pm. 15,000Đ.)

SA ĐÉC ☎67

Sa Đéc's main attractions are its gardens on the outskirts of town, the **Flower Village,** Làng Hoa. Ideal for a relaxing stroll, the gardens make Sa Đéc a worthwhile destination. A lack of reasonably-priced accommodation makes it a great option for a quick daytrip. The Flower Village is a pleasant 15 min. walk north of town on the river's east bank. From the metal bridge off of Hùng Vương, turn left and continue for 2km along the bank until you get to the phone box and the bridge over the tributary; then turn right. **Vườ'ng Hồng Tư Tôn (Tư Tôn's Garden),** one of the area's lushest gardens, lies within the village. (☎861 685. Open early morning to late evening.) The garden is one of the many nurseries that form the life-bestowing phloem of the entire region's decorative flower industry; they bloom brightest from Nov.-Dec. In the town of Sa Đéc itself, **Bửu Quang Pagoda,** 461 Hùng Vương, greets visitors with six-tusked elephants and a chubby Buddha. More elephants await upstairs, with a pictoral history of the Buddha's life. The 164-year-old **Phướ'c Hưng Pagoda,** marked by a Lady Buddha, sits next door. Photographs ring the sanctuary, where dead devotees are remembered. (Both open daily 6am-9pm.)

Ask at the bus station in Mỹ Tho about buses to Sa Đéc, as they often have to be combined with a short motorbike ride. From HCMC, Sa Đéc is a four-hour bus ride (3 per day, 17,5000Đ), or can be arranged in combination with a tour from most guest houses. Foreigners are prohibited from most budget hotels. If you're planing on staying the night, one affordable option is the **Sa Đéc Hotel,** at the end of the road. (*108/5A Hùng Vu'ờng. ☎861 430. Rooms with fan and 2 beds US$8; 4 beds US$14; A/C suite with 2 beds, living room and hot water US$18.*) Close to Sa Đéc Hotel, **Thuỷ,** has both breakfast and lunch/dinner menus. Delicious grilled fish with rice 15,000Đ. (*439 Hùng Vu'ờng. ☎861 644. Open daily 7am-9pm.*)

CẦN THƠ ☎71

Cosmopolitan without the noise or grime, Cần Thơ (pop. 400,000) is the capital of Cần Thơ Province and the unofficial capital of the delta region. As the most popular

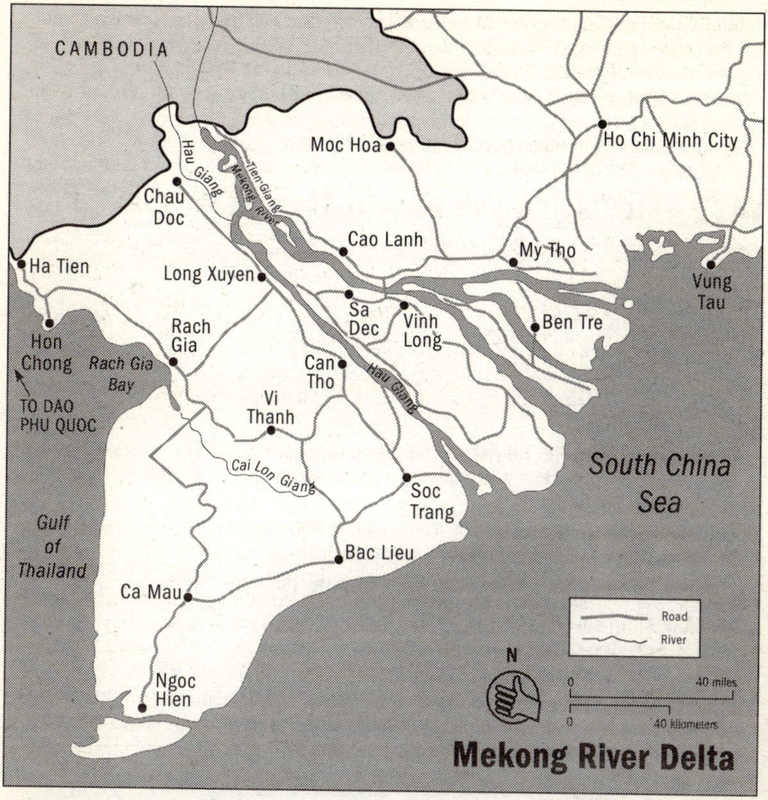

VIETNAM

BULLS AND BEARS ON BOATS Most tourists visit the floating markets of the Mekong Delta, but few take time to see the true dynamo of the delta economy: the floating stock market. In a hard-to-find canal south of Mỹ Tho known to the tourist industry as "Dau," the market features over 3000 local companies (such as Fong's Noodle Stand and Greasy Machine Parts by Vin) traded by short Asian men in red and yellow ties, starched shirts, and small boats. The market is open daily from 4am to 11am; hire a guide at the Mỹ Tho pier to explain the frantic gesticulations and the way the brokers' lips seem to continue moving long after they've finished yelling. Perhaps with a long enough stay, you too could join in the trades.

destination in the delta, the best place to experience the city is from its most vital perspective—the water. Travelers hire boats to visit floating markets or bob through tiny canals bordering quiet villages, rice paddies, and fruit orchards.

TRANSPORTATION

Buses: The **bus station** (☎821 462), is northwest of town on Nguyễn Trãi. Daily buses to: **Châu Đốc** (4hr., continuously 6am-5pm, 13,500Đ); **Hà Tiên** (8hr., 3:40 and 4:20am, 22,500Đ); **HCMC** (3½hr., 5am-6pm, 21,000Đ); **Long Xuyên** (2hr., every hr. 6am-4:30pm, 8000Đ); **Mỹ Tho** (2hr., 10am, 14,500Đ); **Rạch Giá** (4hr., every 45min. 3am-4pm, 13,000Đ); **Sóc Trăng** (1½hr., every 30min. 4:30am-5pm, 8000Đ); **Vũng Tàu** (8hr., 4am, 35,500Đ).

Minibuses: (☎829 476). Run at all hours from near the Hậu Giang ferry crossing, about 3km northeast of the city on Trần Phú. To: **HCMC** (33,000Đ); **Vũng Tàu** (35,500Đ); **Mỹ Tho** (14,500Đ); **Đà Lạt** (54,500Đ).

Rentals: Motorcycles available from most hotels (US$5-7 per day). **Mr. Trí,** 44 Võ Thị Sáu (☎822 219), on the street north of and parallel to Hòa Bình, is an excellent source for information concerning trips in and around Cần Thơ.

ORIENTATION AND PRACTICAL INFORMATION

Cần Thơ is 140km southwest of HCMC, at the confluence of the Hậu Giang and Cần Thơ Rivers. One kilometer from the bus station, **Nguyễn Trãi** leads into the city, curving to form **Hòa Bình,** the city's main thoroughfare. At its north end lie the **bank** and the **post office**. East toward the Hâu Gàng River are parallel streets **Đồng Khởi** and **Phan Dinh Phùng**, and along the riverbank, **Hai Bà Trưng** passes restaurants and a silver statue of Hồ Chí Minh before ending at the market. **Châu Văn Liêm** links Hai Bà Trưng with Hòa Bình. Budget hotels lie along **Châu Văn Liêm** between **Phan Đình Phùng** and **Đồng Khởi.**

Tourist Office: Can Tho Tourist, 20 Hai Bà Trưng (☎821 852). Sells poster-size maps (11,000Đ). 3hr. boat tour with guide for a group of up to 20 for 250,000Đ. Open daily 7-11am and 1-4:30pm.

Currency Exchange: Vietcombank, 7 Hòa Bình (☎820 445). MC/V cash advances with a 3% fee. Open M-F 7:30-10:45am and 1-4:30pm.

Markets: The newly installed market lies north of Nguyễn Trai.

Emergency: ☎115. **Police** ☎113. **Fire** ☎114.

Medical Services: Cần Tho' General Hospital, 4 Châu Văn Liêm (☎821 288), on corner of Hòa Bình. **Pharmacy** at front entrance. Open daily 7-11am and 1-5pm.

Internet Access: Phúc Thái, 161 Ly Tú Trong (☎832 789). From the Hau Giặng River, it's approximately 1km after Châu Vân Liệm changes to Ly Tú Trong, on the left. 200Đ per min.; discounts for delays. Open daily 8-11am.

Post Office/Telephones: 2 Hòa Bình (☎820 077). **International phones** and **fax.** Open daily 6am-8pm.

VIETNAM

ACCOMMODATIONS

Hotels cluster along **Hai Bà Trưng** north of the Hồ Chí Minh statue, along **Châu Văn Liêm,** and on smaller **Ngô Đức Kế,** one block south of Châu Văn Liêm. Use caution when hiring transport from the bus station to hotels. Motodrivers operate with hotels who pay them commission for bringing in business. To subsidize this commission, the hotel inflates prices. Choose a hotel in advance and be firm when telling the driver where to go.

Hien Van Tran, 118/10 Phan Đình Phùng (☎812 718). English-speaking owners treat guests like long-lost family. Nose-flute serenades included. Rooms with fans and shared bath US$4, with A/C US$8.

Hậu Giang B Hotel, 27 Châu Văn Liêm (☎821 950). Not to be confused with more upscale Hậu Giang Hotel. Popular with the Sinh Cafe herd. Ascend the bizarre, colored spiral stairwell to spacious doubles with hot water and fan US$10, with A/C US$15.

Nhà Khách Sô, 3 Hòa Bình (☎822 176), at the north end of the road. Bright rooms. Doubles with fan and cold shower US$8, with A/C and hot shower US$15.

Phan Trung, 9 Lê Thánh Tôn (☎824 477), one block from the riverbank. A central, convenient location. Double with fan and shared bath 50,000Đ, ensuite with fan 60,000-70,000Đ, with A/C 100,000-150,000Đ.

Phong Nhâ Hotel, 75 Châu Vân Liệm (☎821 615). Little English spoken, but convenient location with livable rooms at payable prices. Fan-cooled rooms with bath and cold water: single 50,000Đ; double 60,000Đ, with A/C 150,000Đ; triple 100,000 Đ.

FOOD

Cần Thơ specialties include *lẩu* (seafood vegetable soup) and *canh chua* (sour fish soup). Students munch on local delicacies along **Đề Thám,** east of Hòa Bình. Cheap restaurants line **Nam Kỳ Khởi Nghĩa** east of Điện Biên Phủ. Bakeries are on the north end of **Đồng Khởi** before its intersection with Hòa Bình. Hai Bà Trưng's riverside chowhouses bask in the glow of neon billboards. Popular with travelers, the stall at **49 Nam Kỳ Khởi Nghĩa,** serves baguettes with assorted fillings.

Tiệm Cơm Nam Đô, 10 Điện Biên Phủ, 20m south of its intersection with Nam Kỳ Khởi Nghĩa. Food cooked outside, eaten inside. Crispy fried shrimp 15,000Đ. Frog with rice and noodles 20,000Đ. Open daily 10am-10pm.

Thien Hoa Restaurant, 26 Hai Bà Trưng, on the river. Very popular. Have a bite of stir-fried snake (40,000Đ). Open daily 9am-2pm and 5-11pm.

Phở Oanh, 98 Ly Tú Trong. Fast service is not the only great aspect about this eatery. It also serves up tasty dishes in a bright, breezy atmosphere. Open daily 6am-11pm.

Lò Bánh Sài Gòn, 15 Đồng Khởi. Near the intersection with Hòa Bình. Pastries vie for attention in front of this standout bakery. *Bơ đường* (butter sugar) 2000Đ. Oversized eclairs 2000Đ. Open daily 5am-10pm.

SIGHTS

A trip through the tiny canals that spiderweb Cần Thơ is a highlight of the area. A typical tour includes fruit tasting and a visit to a **floating market.** The four main floating markets lie progressively farther from Cần Thơ. **Cái Răng** (7km, 3-4hr. round-trip) lies under a nearby bridge; **Phong Điền** (18km, 4-5hr. round-trip) sits in a four-river confluence; **Trà Ôn's** five-river market (20km, 6hr. round-trip) is the most popular with foreigners; and **Phụng Hiệp** (33km, 8hr. round-trip) is a bustling market (open daily 4 to 11am). Independent boats line Hai Bà Trưng's riverside at dawn to help catch the sublime sunrise (10,000Đ per hr.).

Cần Thơ's wide, clean boulevards, back alleys, and manicured riverfront are well suited for aimless strolling. Those who need more direction in their sightseeing can visit the **Muniransyarama Pagoda,** 36 Hòa Bình, a Theravada Buddhist temple patronized by Cần Thơ's Khmer population. Khmers come here to pray, offer food to the monks, and listen to the resident 80-year-old master. Some of the monks speak English and enjoy talking with tourists. (Open 6am-10:30pm.)

The **Hồ Chí Minh Museum (Bảo Tàng Hồ Chí Minh),** 6 Hòa Bình, is the large white structure next to the post office. (☎822 173. Open Tu and Th-Sa 8-11am and 2-4pm, Su 8-11am and 7-9pm.) The **Ninth Military Section Museum** is next door. Each of the 12 provinces has its own gallery commemorating local victories. Expect some bafflement, as all displays are in Vietnamese.

ENTERTAINMENT AND NIGHTLIFE

Cần Thơ has more options for nightlife than its delta neighbors, but the variety falls short of what you find in Hồ Chí Minh City. For a drink among locals head to one of the restaurants in town, offering traditional *bia hơi* and karaoke.

Cửa Hàng Bia Sài Gòn, 78 Nguyễn Trãi, under Công Ty Liên Doanh Bia Saigon sign. Cần Thơ's "Labor Bar." Locals will wave you in; smiles will bid you adieu. *Bia hơi* 4500Đ per liter, gentler drinks only slightly more expensive. Open daily 8am-10pm.

New Music Club, 63 Phan Dinh Phùng. A popular hangout where local students and teenagers dance the night away. Cover 20,000Đ. Open daily 9pm-midnight.

DAYTRIPS FROM C<N TH£

VU'Ò'N CÒ (GARDEN OF THE STORKS)

The journey is treacherous but can be painless and enjoyable when booked with a tour. Visit the tourist office or ask your guest house owner for more information. On your own, the easiest method is to catch a bus or moto for Sóc Trăng (40,000Đ) and ask to be let off at Trà Quít (a village 48km southeast of Cần Thơ; it has been renamed Xã Thuận Hòa, but most Vietnamese still know it by its old name). At the beginning of the market (coming from the direction of Cần Thơ), a path leads left to a small tributary where a boat and driver can be hired for the trip to the garden (50min. round-trip plus 1hr. in the garden 60-100,000Đ per boat. Entry to garden 2000Đ.) Another option is to hire a moto for about US$10, but be prepared for a long, bumpy trip.

Some 45km southeast of Cần Thơ, in a dense jungle 6km off the main road, hides Vườn Cò (Garden of the Storks), a breeding ground for thousands of *cò trắng* (white storks) and *cò cộc* (short storks). Storks interact freely with visitors, and with locals who sometimes climb the trees to capture the stork chicks with 6m long poles. The best time to visit the garden is in the afternoon, when the male stork returns from gathering food, but there is always stork activity.

SÓC TRĂNG

Buses from Cần Thơ to Sóc Trăng (hourly., 7000Đ); Moto drivers from Cần Thơ US$10.

Temple-crazy Sóc Trăng, 62km southeast of Cần Thơ, is the capital of Sóc Trăng province, where the local Khmer have erected numerous monuments to Buddha. **Buu Son Tu,** commonly known as **Chua Dat Set (Clay Pagoda),** sits about 1km east of the Sóc Trăng river and the town center on Đ. Mậu Thân 68. The indoor menagerie includes life-size clay statues of lions, tigers, and elephants. Several of the dozens of Buddha figures are adorned with carnival-style flashing lights. A pair of candles, originally 2½m tall, burn for four years before they are spent. Ngo Kim Giang, the resident monk, is fluent in French and eagerly entertains his many visitors. **Im Som Rong Pagoda,** east of the Clay Pagoda and to the left down a dirt road, is an open-air temple with a large Buddha on center stage. **Chùa Do'i,** the aptly-named **Bat Pagoda** awaits 4km west of town down a dirt road off Đ. Lê Hồng Phong. Thousands of fruit bats, with wing spans of up to 1½m, hang in the surrounding trees by day and pillage local orchards by night. They're most active around 6pm. The site also features a collection of rare five-toed pigs. Farmers bring such animals to the temple, since locals say that it's unlucky to eat them.

Local accommodations includes the **Kháng Hung Hotel,** which offers doubles for US$8, with A/C US$16. Across the road from the bus station, **Phong Lan II,** 133 Nguyễn Chí Thanh (☎821 757) has doubles with fan US$8; with A/C US$14-16.

LONG XUYÊN ☎76

While not the most magnetic of delta destinations, the cheerful town with its friendly inhabitants admirably serves as a transit point. The Hậu Giang River and Long Xuyên's gargantuan market are the major attraction of the city. Though like most other Vietnamese markets, Long Xuyên's people dedicate their time to cultivating some of the best fish, rice, and fruit.

TRANSPORTATION. Long Xuyên lies 140km southwest of **HCMC** and 50km northwest of Cần Thơ. The **bus station,** 144 Trần Hưng Đạo (☎841 125), has daily buses to: **Cần Thơ** (1½hr., 10,000Đ); **Châu Đốc** (approx. 1½hr., 10,000Đ. Ask your hotel proprietor where to catch it.); **Hà Tiên** (3½hr., 19,000Đ); **HCMC** (4½hr., 27,000Đ); **Rạch Sôi** (9000Đ). Buses to **HCMC** also wait before crossing the Hậu Giang at a stop near the ferry at the east end of Lý Thái Tổ. **Minibuses** go from the Bình Khánh bus station, 3km north of the town center, to **Châu Doc** (2 hr., 6400Đ). The Long Xuyên long-distance **ferry terminal** (☎854 846) is on the small road to the right of the Duy Tân Bridge at the north end of Hai Bà Trưng.

ORIENTATION AND PRACTICAL INFORMATION. From the bus station, **Trần Hưng Đạo** runs 1km north past a traffic circle to reach the **Catholic church,** a useful landmark. **Nguyễn Huệ** leads east from the church to the Hậu Giang River. **Hai Bà Trưng,** another street with a green median, intersects Nguyễn Huệ on its way north to the Duy Tân Bridge. One block east from the church, **Hùng Vương** runs south, passing the **Vietcombank,** 1 Hùng Vương. (☎841 813. Open M-F 7:30-11am and 1:30-4:30pm.) **Internet** access is at Lan Vy Internet, 48 Nguyễn Thi Minh Khai. (☎847 848. 4000Đ per min., 20,000Đ per hour.) A **pharmacy** is at 34-36 Ngô Gia Tự, near intersection with Lương Văn Cư. (☎841 558. Open M-F 7am-5pm, Sa 7am-noon.) The **immigration office is** at 12 Hùng Vương. (☎843 261. Open daily 7:30-10:30am and 1:30-4:30pm.) Behind the church, there is a **post office** at 11-13 Ngô Gia Tự, on the corner of Lương Văn Cư. (☎841 755. Open 6am-10pm. **International phone** and **fax.**) If desperate, a 24hr. **post office,** 106 Tràn Hưng Dao, north from the church (hire a moto) and has **international phone** and **fax.**

ACCOMMODATIONS AND FOOD. Rooms are available at the **Thoại Chau 2 Hotel,** near the traffic circle. (☎843 096. Singles with fan and hot water 70,000Đ; A/C doubles 120,000Đ.) Next door, the **An Long Hotel,** 281 Trán Hưng Đao, has less value than its neighbor. (☎843 298. Doubles with fan 60-70,000Đ, with A/C, TV, and hot water 150,000Đ.) The **Thái Bình 2 Hotel,** 4 Nguyễn Huệ, has comfortable rooms. (☎847 078. Doubles with fan 70,000Đ, with A/C 120,000Đ. Ask about the options for more expensive rooms.)

Long Xuyên's dining scene lacks the variety of other delta towns. For cheap meals there are several restaurants along **Nguyễn Trãi** between the traffic circle and the intersection with Hai Bà Trưng. One of the best and cheapest eateries, **Hồng Phát,** 242/4 Lương Văn Cư, is just off Nguyễn Trãi. (Open daily 8am-10pm.) The market at the end of Nguyễn Huệ has numerous food stalls.

SIGHTS. Long Xuyên's most exciting sight is the busy **riverside market** which spans several blocks north and south of Nguyễn Huệ, at the east end of the river; trading continues around the clock. A few large barns are devoted to clothing and raw textiles. For those with a spiritual bent, Long Xuyên's **Catholic church** offers peace, but not quiet, as it lies at the confluence of three main roads. Its thin walls do little to block the noise of traffic. (Mass M-Sa 4:30am and 6pm, Su 5am, 4, and 6pm; children's baptisms 7am.) Visitors may visit from 4am-6pm; ask the guard at the gate to unlock the doors. For a tour of Long Xuyên's **river-home community,** small boats for hire are at the landing on the end of Nguyễn Huệ (20,000Đ).

CHĂU ĐỐC ☎76

Twenty years ago, this remote border town fell victim to Khmer Rouge terror tactics. Today, the shrine to Lady Buddha at nearby Sam Mountain has made Châu Đốc a pilgrimage site, especially on Buddha's birthday (usually in late April). Boat trips on the Hậu Giang, attractive colonial style architecture, and a bustling riverside market beckon travelers back to the charming town center, keeping those few travelers who stick around long enough feeling right at home.

TRANSPORTATION. The **bus station** is 2km southeast of town at the intersection of Hwy. 91 and Lê Lợi. Buses leave for: **Cần Thơ'** (3½hr., 15,000Đ); **Hà Tiên** (6hr., 30,000Đ); **HCMC** (7hr., 32,000Đ); **Long Xuyên** (1½hr., 8000Đ); **Mỹ Tho** (6hr., 25,500Đ); **Rạch Giá** (2hr., 15,000Đ); **Tây Ninh** (9hr., 42,000Đ); **Vũng Tàu** (9hr., 43,000Đ). **Buses** to **HCMC** also depart from 58/60 Nguyễn Hữu Cảnh. (☎867 786. 5hr., every 2hr. 7am-11pm, 54,000Đ.) **Ferries** depart from the pier at the west end of the market, near the intersection of Thượng Đăng Lễ and Trần Hưng Đạo. An early morning boat heads to **Hà Tiên** in slow motion (every other day, 12hr., 70,000Đ); inquire at 86 Trần Hưng Đạo, 500m west of the market near an unmarked jetty. **Moto** drivers also ply the picturesque but bumpy dirt track to Hà Tiên (3hr., 100,000Đ).

ORIENTATION AND PRACTICAL INFORMATION. Châu Đốc is 170km southwest of HCMC, 95km northwest of Cần Thơ, and 7km southeast of the Cambodian border. The town's grid-like street layout makes navigating the central area relatively easy. **Đường Lê Lợi/Gia Long/Trần Hưng Đạo** run the length of the town along the shore; east of the market it is Lê Lợi, in the market Gia Long, and west of the market Trần Hưng Đạo. **Bạch Đằng, Nguyễn Hữu Cảnh,** and **Chi Lăng** are the central arteries, beginning at the river, continuing southwest to the public park and a temple. Central Châu Đốc is dominated by the **market,** which spreads from Nguyễn Hữu Cảnh in the east to Thượng Đăng Lễ in the west, and south from the river to Phan Văn Vàng.

The **ICB,** 7 Nguyễn Hữu Cảnh, at the corner with Phan Văn Vàng, changes cash but not traveler's checks; there are no **ATM** or cash advances currently in Châu Đốc. (☎866 259. Open M-F 7-11am and 1-4pm.) A **pharmacy,** 3B Lê Loi, lies a block east of the market. (☎ 866 769. Open daily 7am-9:30pm.) The **General Provincial Hospital,** 5 Lê Lợi, has English-speaking staff. (☎867 184. Open daily 5-7am, 10:30am-2pm, and 4-10pm.) **Internet** access is available at Nhât Kha, 40 Thương Dăng Lễ. (Open daily 7am-9pm). The **GPO,** 73 Lê Lợi, at the intersection with Nguyễn Hữu Cảnh just east of the market, has **international phones.** (☎866 191. Open daily 6am-10pm.)

ACCOMMODATIONS AND FOOD. The newest addition to the Châu Đốc hotel scene is **Hotel Vĩnh Phướ'c,** 12-14 Quang Trung, just off Bạch Dằng near the market, featuring comfortable rooms. (☎866 242. Singles with fan 80,000Đ; doubles with A/C 120,000Đ, with balcony 160,000Đ.) **Khách Sạn Ngọc Phú,** 17 Đôc Phủ Thu, one block west of Bạch Dằng, offers similar but slightly smaller rooms. (☎866 484. Doubles with fan 70,000Đ, with A/C 140,000Đ.) At **Khách Sạn 44,** 44 Đôc Phủ Thu, opposite the Ngọ Phú, rooms are cheap. (☎866 540. Singles with fan and squat toilet 50,000Đ, with flush toilet 70,000Đ; doubles 90,000Đ.) Slightly more upscale **Hàng Châu II,** 10 Nguyễn Văn Thoại, offers some luxuries. (☎868 891. All rooms doubles with A/C, fridge, satellite TV 170,000Đ.)

Makeshift restaurants lie at the entrance to the market at Chi Lăng and Bạch Đằng. They serve up *bò khô* (dry beef), a local specialty. If eating in a large tent doesn't catch your fancy, consider **Tiệm Cơm 88,** 88 Đốc Phủ Thu, where the cooks grill up crab (30,000Đ) and other river delicacies. (Open daily 10am-10pm.)

BORDER CROSSING. Alternatively, those traveling in the Mekong Delta region can now cross to Cambodia by boat from **Châu Dốc** (1¼hr., 1 per day) to the border, and on to **Prey Veng** (1¼hr.); from Prey Veng, it's a short bus trip to Phnom Penh (3hr.). The trip can be arranged only through Saigontourist (see **Tour and Travel Agencies**, p. 891) in HCMC and costs US$15. For information on travel from Phnom Penh to Mộc Bài, see p. 890.

SIGHTS. About 5km southwest of town stands **Sam Mountain** (Núi Sam), the region's prime pilgrimage site, featuring the **Temple of Bà Chúa Xứ** ("Lady Ruling the Region"). Inside, the Lady's image has received throngs of devotees and tourists since the early 19th century. The temple overflows with visitors at the end of the fourth lunar month (around April 26), when the faithful come to thank *Bà* for the gifts of the last year or pray for better luck in the year to come. On the other side of the road, the **Tây An Pagoda** sits at the foot of the mountain. The **tomb of Thoại Ngọc Hầu,** a retainer of Emperor Gia Long, is next door.

The **Chau Phu Temple,** opposite the post office within the market on the east edge, is dedicated to local hero Nguyễn Hữu Cảnh, who vanquished the Khmers almost 300 years ago. This colorful *đình* (meeting house) contains a stairwell of central images, flanked by ornate wooden columns. (Open daily 7am-7pm.) Across the street, at the wooden jetty, hire a rowboat to explore the Hậu Giang River (20,000Đ per hr.) Highlights include **floating houses** with self-contained **fish farms,** the local **fish sauce factory,** and the **Chàm communities,** famous for their weaving.

RẠCH GIA ☎77

Travelers in Rạch Giá are en route to Phú Quốc Island or Hà Tiên. Hangers-on in this busy little city will encounter a mixed bag, but those who can avoid the seedier side enjoy the friendly locals, colorful waterways, and delicious seafood.

TRANSPORTATION. The airport in Rạch Sởi has flights to HCMC (1 stop, 600,00Đ) and Dương Đông (35min., 450,000Đ); check with Vietnam Airlines (HCMC ☎823 08 96; www.vietnamairlines.com) for departure times. The **Rạch So'i Station** (☎864 086) is 7km south on Nguyễn Trung Trực. Buses run to: **Cần Tho'** (4hr., 13,500Đ); **Châu Đốc** (5hr., 15,000Đ); **HCMC** (6hr., 33,000Đ); and **Long Xuyên** (3hr., 9000Đ). **Evening minibuses** to **HCMC** (8pm, 7hr., 50,000Đ) leave from stand 10 on Mâu Thân (☎862 261). The **Provincial Bus Station** (☎862 274) on the corner of Đại Lội and Mâu has buses to **Hòn Chông** (4hr.) and **Hà Tiên** (4hr.). The **ferry** to **Phú Quốc Island** (6-8hr., 59,000Đ) leaves between 9 and 10am, from the pier at the end of Nguyễn Công Trư. Tickets go on sale at 3pm the day before, but you can take the chance of purchasing one by 7:30am on the day of departure.

ORIENTATION AND PRACTICAL INFORMATION. Rạch Giá straddles two branches of the Mekong River 200km from HCMC and 70km from Cần Thơ. Busy **Nguyễn Trung Trực** runs northwest, crosses the first tributary (becoming **Lê Lợi**), and ends in front of the statue. With your back to the statue, **Duy Tân** runs to your left; head left on Duy Tân, and the first right will be **Ly Tự Trọng.** Two blocks farther east, **Trần Phú** also crosses both tributaries, changing names both times (becoming **Đại Lộ** 30-4 to the northwest and Ngô Quyền to the southeast). From the GPO, **Nguyễn Công Trứ** runs westward along the northwestern tributary to the ferry pier. Heading northwest on Đại Lộ, the second road to the right after the bridge is Mâu Thân, a busy thoroughfare that heads towards Hà Tiên.

Services in Rạch Giá include: **Kiên Giang Tourist,** 12 Ly Tự Trọng, opposite Thanh Bình Hotel (☎862 081. Open M-Sa 7am-5pm. Map of the city, province, and Hà Tiện 15,000Đ); the **GPO,** 2 Tu Duc (☎862 551. Open 6:30am-10pm. **International phones.**); the **Vietcombank,** 1 Huỳnh Mẫn Đạt, next door to the GPO (☎863 178. Open M-F 7-11am and 1-5pm); the **General Hospital,** 46 Lê Lợi (☎863 325), before the bridge (on the south side of the island), on the right; and many **pharmacies** around the city center. (Open daily 6am-6pm.)

ACCOMMODATIONS AND FOOD. Indistinguishable *khách sạn* dominate the budget scene. Most are in the city center and charge 50-70,000Đ for a double with fan, and up to 120,000Đ with A/C. **Binh Minh,** 44 Phạm Hồng Thái, has clean, bright rooms that distinguish it from the rest (☎862 154. All rooms have baths. 2-person with fan 90,000Đ, with A/C 110,000-120,000Đ; 3-person 150,000Đ.) Down the road, **Tô Châu Hotel,** 16 Lê Lợi, near the Nguyễn Trung Trực statue, offers A/C bliss. (☎863 718. All rooms with bath. Doubles 120,000-140,000Đ; 3-person 150,000Đ.) **Nhà Trọ Kim Ngân,** 36 Võ Thị Sáu, is a clean and friendly guest house that provides great value for money. To get there from the town center, follow Trâ'n Phú, turn right onto Trân Quốc Tuấn, then right onto Võ Thị Sáu. (☎863 118. Doubles with fan and outside bath 50,000Đ.) Those hoping to save money should head to the *nhà tro* (guest house) area near the pier. Beware that this option is not for the faint-hearted, nor the very tall, as low ceilings could pose discomfort. **Xuâ't Ha'i,** under the Hem 38 sign has an English-speaking staff. (☎863 942. Doubles 30,000Đ.) Up the road, **Nha Tro Xuân Mai** has cheaper rooms and cleaner bathrooms, but no English is spoken. (☎868 437. Singles 20,000Đ; doubles 30,000Đ.)

There are not many restaurant options in Rạch Gía. An exception is the bizarrely-named Kien Giang Aquatic Foodstuffs Store, at the right immediately after crossing the bridge toward the statue. Enjoy grilling your own seafood at a personal burner on the table as you sit next to the canal. (Octopus, okra, and pineapple 10,000Đ. Draught beer 2000Đ. Open daily 8am-10pm.) Trường Cafe, 181 Tran Phu, is a simple, popular cafe with food cooked out front and eaten inside. (Pork ribs and rice run 8000Đ. Open daily 6am-6pm.)

SIGHTS. Rạch Giá has few sights of interest for the visitor—the list consists of just two temples. **Nguyễn Trung Trực Temple** is in the town center on Nguyễn Công Trứ facing the canal, 500m from the post office. It honors a local hero for whom it is named, who led a daring raid in the 1860s against the French warship *Esperance*. He was later captured and executed. (Open daily 6am-9pm.) Outside, machete-wielding women chop up plant parts for the **traditional medicine clinic.** An array of dried stems and leaves covers every sun-exposed surface in sight.

Phật Lớn Pagoda (Chùa Phật Lớn), 2km north of the post office on Quang Trung, is a Theravada Buddhist temple serving Rạch Giá's Cambodian population, surrounded by lush gardens. A beautiful series of paintings that chronicle the Buddha's life encircle the sanctuary. (Open daily 4am-5:30pm.)

HÀ TIÊN ☎77

Tucked into the far southwest corner of Vietnam, picturesque Hà Tiên is sweet relief at the end of a delta tour. This small coastal town is surrounded by gorgeous turquoise water and thriving farmland irrigated by Mekong tributaries fanning out into the sea. Hà Tiên fell into Vietnamese hands in 1708 when Mạc Cửu, a Chinese governor appointed by the Khmer, shifted his allegiance to the Nguyễn Lords in Huế. Tensions ignited when the Khmer Rouge massacred 130 villagers in 1978. Stability has since returned to the region, and the ethnically mixed population draws a peaceful livelihood from fishing and farming.

TRANSPORTATION. The **bus station** (☎852 560) is southeast of town, across the Tô Châu River. Buses run daily to: **HCMC** (8hr.; 8pm, 9pm; 42,000Đ; buy tickets in advance); **Long Xuyên** (7hr., 19,000Đ); and **Rạch Giá** (3½hr., 11,500Đ). The 100km, 4hr. trip to **Châu Đốc** necessitates hiring a moto-driver (usually US$12-15). From the bus station, a pontoon bridge (toll with bike 500Đ, with moto 1000Đ) leads to Hà Tiên's busiest thoroughfare, **Trần Hầu,** which runs parallel to the river and runs west into town past accommodations, cafes, restaurants, and the **market** (open daily 5am-7pm). **Ferries** to **Phú Quốc Island** are presently limited to Vietnamese only; foreigners must depart from Rach Giá (see p. 907).

VIETNAM

ORIENTATION AND PRACTICAL INFORMATION. Hà Tiên is 240km from HCMC, 90km from Rạch Giá, and 7km from the Cambodian border. Hà Tiên's main road, **Trần Hầu,** runs west from the pontoon bridge through the market, terminating at the intersection with **Phương Thành,** which runs north to the Cambodian border.

A branch of **Kiên Giang Tourist** is at the reception desk in the Đông Hồ Hotel; after crossing the bridge into town, it's across the street. **Tô Châu Hotel** next door rents **bicycles** (20,000Đ per day). There is no formal exchange **bank** in Hà Tiên. There are several **pharmacies** on Trần Hầu in the market vicinity. (Open daily roughly 6am-10pm.) To get to the **police** station, go right after the bridge, and left on Tô Châu. The **General Hospital** is at the far (north) end of Bach Dắng, at the intersection with Mạc Cửu. The **post office** is next to the police station. (☎852 190. Open daily 6:30am-8:30pm. **Fax** and **international phone.**)

ACCOMMODATIONS AND FOOD. Hà Tiên is popular in the dry season, with swarms of minibuses invading this serene spot which only recently acquired daytime electricity. The **Hải Vân Hotel,** 646A Đ. Lam Sơn, one block off Trần Hầu, has very comfortable rooms and an accommodating staff. (☎852 872. All rooms have bath and satellite TV. Doubles with fan 70,000Đ, with A/C 120,000-150,000Đ.) **Đông Hồ Hotel,** across the bridge on Trần Hầu, has a great, albeit noisy location. (☎852 141. Rooms with bath: double with fan 70,000Đ; 4-person share 120,000Đ. Rooms with A/C, hot water, TV, fridge: double 120,000Đ; 4-person share 150,000Đ.) **Hà Tiện Hotel,** 38 Trần Hầu, on the corner of Phương Thàng, has a wide selection of rooms at lower prices. (☎851 563. Rooms with bath and fan: 3-person share 70,000Đ; 4-person share 100,000Đ; 5-person share 150,000Đ. Doubles with A/C 100,000Đ.) **Thanh Xuân Room for Rent,** 952A Bạch Đằng, on the road just west of the bridge, is a clean guest house; if you're in need of a quick trim, it doubles as a barber shop. (☎852 318. Fan doubles 60,000Đ, with A/C 100,000Đ.)

Ultra-cheap cafes selling *hủ tiếu* soup, *phở*, and rice dishes line Trần Hầu west of the pontoon bridge. **Tiệm Co'm Hu'o'ng Biển,** 30m west of the bridge on Trần Hầu, specializes in shrimp dishes called *tôm chiên bột.* (Open daily 6am-8pm.) One block over on Bach Dáng, **Quán Cóm Phó Tiní,** has cheap meat dishes (5000Đ).

SIGHTS. Some of the most pleasant sightseeing in Hà Tiên can be done by bike around the countryside. The **tomb of Mạc Cửu,** erected by Emperor Gia Long in 1809, is well worth a visit. Reaching the tomb requires a brief ascent of **Núi Lăng (Hill of Tombs)**—a hill 2km northwest of the town center whose slope is home to over 40 tombs. To reach Mạc Cửu, head away from town on Phương Thành, past the church and turn left down the dirt path, and left again at its end. The pagoda's entrance is 50m down on the right. Turning right on the initial dirt path leads to **Phú Dung Pagoda,** another small temple. From the top of the hill, you will see Hà Tiên and the outlying islands.

About 3km north of town on Phương Thành, a wide, tree-covered shaft of gray rock thrusts skyward. This is the entrance to **Thạch Động (Stone Cave),** marked by a roadside gray fist in memory of 130 Vietnamese slaughtered by the Khmer Rouge in 1978. From the temple, there are stunning views of geometrically arranged rice fields, nearby Cambodia, and the Gulf of Thailand. (1000Đ. Open until dusk.)

Bãi Mũi Nai (Deer's Nose Beach), a strip of black sand flanked by thickly forested hills and a strip of snake stands, is popular with locals and their inner tubes (1500Đ). To reach the beach, continue down the road past Thạch Động, take the first left, and continue 3km; an entrance is on the right. Stunning views of the area abound, though the water is a bit murky.

Hà Tiên also boasts some in-town attractions. The region is known for its **tortoise shell** (*đồi mồi*) carvings. Visitors might also catch wind of Hà Tiên's famous **four-headed coconut tree** (Dùa Bốn Ngon) on **Lâm Văn Quang.** To find it, follow Trần Hầu west until it almost turns back on itself. Head toward the church, turning left onto Lâm Văn Quang. The tree is in a yard on the right, 300m down the road.

VIETNAM

DAYTRIPS FROM HÀ TIEN: BEACHES AT HÒN CHONG. Twenty kilometers south of Hà Tiên (65km north of Rạch Giá), a feeder road branches off at the town of Bà Hòn, leading 15km southward to **Hòn Chông.** This peninsula harbors the most seductive beaches in the delta. The shore stretches east for several kilometers before ending inside a crowded touristy park called **Hòn Phụ Tử (Father and Son Islet).** Entry to the park is a meager 1000Đ. If you don't want to spend the money or join the crowds, beaches on the road before the park are just as inviting. Moto drivers will do a day long round-trip from Hà Tiên for 80,000Đ. **Nhà Trọ Huong Bien,** on the left 100m before the park entrance, is a simple guest house with beaches and miles of horizon. (☎854 537. All rooms with squat toilet 50,000Đ.) About 1km before the park, **Bình An Hotel** offers more modern amenities. (☎854 332. Doubles with fan and bathroom 60,000Đ; 5-person rooms 100,000Đ. Luxury doubles with A/C 100,000-160,000Đ; 5-person 120,000Đ.) Also backtracking 1km from the park is **Hòn Trẹm** boasting luxury beachfront cabins. (☎854 331. All rooms are doubles with bath, A/C, fridge, and satellite TV 140,000Đ.) **Green Hill Hotel** offers rooms atop a beach-surveying bluff. (☎854 369. Doubles with bath, hot water, fridge, TV, and fan US$10, with A/C US$15.)

Cheap *cơm bình dân* (6000-8000Đ) is at several stands around the park. Inside the park, rows of souvenir stands pave the way to **Chùa Hang (Cave Pagoda),** a temple built into caves on the adjacent hillside. Islands of fluted gray stone lie offshore, including the double crags of **Hòn Phụ Tử,** said to resemble a father and son awaiting a faraway mother. At the far end of the beach, boat tours go for 5000Đ, and kayaks rent for 10,000Đ per 15min. For a bite to eat in the park, head to **Hồng Ngọc,** which is on the right when heading towards the temple. The fluent French-speaking owner enthusiastically welcomes patrons.

PHÚ QUỐC ISLAND

Phú Quốc Island, closer to Cambodia than Vietnam, has throughout its history been claimed and reclaimed by Thai, Khmer, and Vietnamese. Now, the island is claimed by Star Cruise Lines and an ever-increasing number of resort owners. With major development schemes planned, like hydroelectric power and paved roads, the commercialization of this sleepy island will only grow. For now, there are still hidden coves, secluded and dramatic landscapes for every solitude-seeking slacker, but the island's idyllic air is dissipating fast—so get it while it's hot.

THE VIEW FROM ABOVE

Gateway cities: Duong Dong, the island's largest urban spread, to the west, and An Thoi, to the south.
Beaches: Bai Tam (Long Beach), Bai Dan, Han Yen, and Bai Sao.
Highlights: Trying the world-renowned fish sauce. You know you love it.

TRANSPORTATION. **Vietnam Airlines** (☎846 086) flies to **HCMC** from Dương Dông (M-Th, Su 11am; 700,000Đ) and to **Rạch Sỏ'i** (M-Th, Su 8am; 60,000Đ). Purchase tickets at least 5 days in advance. **Ferries** connect Rạch Giá with **An Thớ'i** (6-8hr., 9am, 60,000Đ) and **Hà Tiên.** A 45min., 20,000Đ moto ride goes the rest of the distance to Dương Đông. Ferries run from Hàm Ninh to Hà Tiên daily (5hr., 9:30am, 30,000Đ); foreigners are prohibited from travel between Hà Tiên and Hàm Ninh.

ORIENTATION. Phú Quốc Island (48km long) is 302km southwest of HCMC, 90km west of Rạch Giá, 50km west of Hà Tiên, and at its northwest tip just 7km from Cambodia. The major points of entry are by ferry from Rạch Giá to **An Thớ'i** on the island's southern tip, and by plane from HCMC or Rạch Sởi to **Du'o'ng Đông** in the west. Dương Đông is the largest town on the island and most travelers stay nearby. Smaller villages in the mountainous east and the flatter west are connected by a series of sandy paths. Dương Đông is in central Phú Quốc on its west coast, 28km north of An Thới, and 23km south of **Bãi Tho'm.**

VIETNAM

DƯƠNG ĐÔNG ☎77

With the start of weekly visits from behemoth boats of Star Cruise Lines, life in Dương Đông has assumed a 7-day periodicity. Every Saturday at 12:30pm, the entire town turns to its harbor to greet its tanned, relaxed, and above all moneyed guests with open arms and sticky fingers. The other six days of the week, the new, nearby, and very posh Saigon-Phú Quốc Resort seems an anomaly, and the town goes lazily about its coastal existence.

TRANSPORTATION AND PRACTICAL INFORMATION. The town's major road begins before the airport and heads west into town where it crosses **Nguyễn Trung Trực** bridge, ending where it intersects with **Dâng Bach Dằng,** which runs to the coast. Two blocks up from the intersection, **30 Tháng 4** leads eastward out of town, along the Dương Đâng River, passing the post office (see below) and the hospital (☎846 074).

Kiên Giang Tourist is not helpful—hotel proprietors are more useful. (☎846 318. Open M-Sa 7-11:30am and 1:30-5pm.) **Buses** run sporadically between **An Thớ'i** and Dương Đông (8000Đ). The **market** is on the embankment next to the Nguyễn Trung Trực bridge. (Open daily 5am-6pm.) A **pharmacy** is on Nguyễn Trung Trực, 50m away from the market, towards the airport (☎848 121. Open daily 7am-9pm.) The **hospital** is 1km from town. Currently, the cheapest **Internet** access is at Dịch Vụ Vi Tính, Húng Vương, Khu Phô's. (1000Đ per min. Open daily 7am-5pm.) The **post office** is the place to send **faxes** and make **international phone calls.** (☎846 040. Open daily 7am-9pm.)

ACCOMMODATIONS AND FOOD. Travelers usually stay on the beach near Dương Đông, although inland options are either brimming with amenities or are dirt-cheap. The Tropicana Resort, 3½ km from Dương Đông, is a bit pricier than other options, but the luxurious bungalows are worth the price. The shaded beachside bar and restaurant chairs is open to all. (☎847 127. Internet 2000Đ per min. 2-person rooms US$15; 2-person bungalows US$25-35.) Kim Linh Hotel, 500 km from the Tropicana, offers beach access and a restaurant, along with helpful travel advice and island tours. The architecture is not much to write home about, though the English-speaking staff is helpful. (☎846 611. All rooms with fan. Doubles with outside bath 80,000Đ, with bath 100,000Đ; 3-person room 120,000Đ.) To get to the Hu'o'ng Bien Hotel, take the first right after the post office (heading toward the hospital); it's 500m down on a road to the right. It has a beachfront location and proximity to the town center, but its budget doubles are a bit run-down. (☎847 133. Doubles with fan 120,000Đ, with A/C 180,000Đ.)

Most hotels are in Dương Đông. **Hư'o'ng Toán,** on Nguyễn Thái Bình, the first road to the right from the airport, heading out of town. Secure, clean doubles in a quiet atmosphere, but no English spoken. (☎846 792. Without bath 40,000Đ, with bath 60,000Đ.) **Hotel Mini Hồng Hạnh,** opposite the airport, has a beautiful courtyard and rooms with fridge, TV, and private bath. (☎846 187. Rooms with fan 80,000Đ, with A/C 180,000Đ. Bikes 30,000Đ per day; moto rentals 100,000Đ.)

An Thới is redolent with success, as the world producer of the delectable fish sauce, *nước mắm*. For delicious seafood head to **Lê Giang,** 289 Khu Phô Trần Hưng, or the baked fish with rice (20,000Đ), or other local delicacies. (Open daily 5am-10pm.) **Quán An Hạ,** 100m on the right heading away from the airport toward Nguyễn Trung Trực bridge in Dương Đông, features seafood goodies for 10,000Đ. (Open daily 6am-9pm.) To find **Le Giang,** turn right on the dirt road after the post office (heading out of town toward the hospital); it's on the left. Tasty meals are served steaming hot for under 10,000Đ.

BEACHES. Phú Quốc Island boasts a stunning landscape, and in many cases, an empty one. Most beaches are only accessible by sandy paths removed from main roads, making it possible to claim a patch of sand all to yourself. Travelers can hire a moto driver for the journey and set a return time, or hire their own moto for about 100,000Đ per day from most hotels.

Bai Tam (Long Beach) stretches from Dương Đông to An Thới on the west coast, offering kilometers of convenient access. A short trip east of Dương Đông through pepper groves leads to the local bathing area of choice, **Suối Đá Bán,** a river with a series of waterfalls and clear freshwater. The small village of **Cửa Cạn** is some 11km northwest of Dương Đông. About 15m of water separates the mainland from a sand bar. Access to the northwest parts of the island is **officially prohibited** to foreigners due to its proximity to Cambodia, but beaches to the north and northeast remain open.

The east coast of Phú Quốc Island houses coves and inlets and the island's most renowned beaches. **Bãi Đần** is an isolated inlet with a white-sand beach. South of Bãi Đần is **Han Yến,** a rocky stretch of coast home to tidal pools and magnificent *ốc* (seashells). **Bãi Sao,** a protected cove where rickety wooden piers jut into calm sea, lies farther south (moto 25,000Đ).

Hòn Tho'm is an island off Phú Quốc's south coast. (Boats can be rented at the pier to make the 1 hr. trip.)

APPENDIX

COUNTRY CODES

Australia	61	Malaysia	60
Brunei	673	Myanmar	95
Cambodia	855	N. Zealand	64
Canada	1	Philippines	63
Hong Kong	852	Singapore	65
Indonesia	62	South Africa	27
Ireland	353	Thailand	66
Laos	856	UK	44

MEASUREMENTS

1 millimeter (mm) = 0.04 inches (in.)	1 inch = 25mm
1 meter (m) = 1.09 yards (yd.)	1 yard = 0.92m
1 meter (m) = 3.28 feet (ft.)	1 foot = 0.305m
1 kilometer (km) = 0.625 miles (mi.)	1 mile = 1.6km
1 hectare = 2.7 acres	1 acre = 0.37 hectare
1 gram (g) = 0.04 ounces (oz.)	1 ounce = 28.5g
1 kilogram (kg) = 2.2 pounds (lb.)	1 pound = 0.45kg
1 liter = 1.057 U.S. quarts (qt.)	1 U.S. quart = 0.94 liters

LANGUAGES

Languages in Southeast Asia are without exception extremely different from English. Even gifted learners won't be able to pick up more than the barest rudiments of Thai during a short trip, although the rewards of making an effort—however small—to learn local languages are great.

PRONUNCIATION KEY

TONES: Thai, Lao, Burmese and Vietnamese are tonal languages; word meanings are partially determined by intonation and pitch. Five tones in Thai and Lao are neutral, low, high, falling, rising (the phrasebook doesn't distinguish between high- and low-falling tones in Lao). Neutral tones (unmarked) are spoken in a level voice in middle of speaker's vocal range. Low (à) and high tones (acute accent: á) are spoken in level pitch, come from bottom and top of speaker's range respectively. Falling tones (â) begin high and end low, as in the English pronunciation of "Hey!" Rising tone (ä) begins low and ends high, as in the English interrogative "What?" Six Vietnamese tones are neutral, high (á), low (à), stopped (ă), rising-falling (ã), broken (ạ).

VOWELS: Vowels are very roughly pronounced as in English, except "eu" sound in Thai and Lao, which corresponds to vowel sound in the French "bleu."

CONSONANTS: Consonants are pronounced (very roughly) as in English. Exceptions: in Bahasa Indonesia and Bahasa Malayu, "c" is pronounced "ch" as in "cherry." In Vietnamese, "d" is pronounced "z" as in "Zulu" in North, or "y" as in "yankee" in South, while "đ" and "Đ" are pronounced "d" as in "delta." "X" and "x" are pronounced "s" as in "sierra"; "s" and "S" pronounced "sh" as in "shovel"; "ph" pronounced "f" as in "foxtrot." "Th" is usually pronounced as in "tango."

HOLIDAYS AND FESTIVALS

Dates listed below are based on the 2002 lunar calendar.

HOLIDAYS/FESTIVALS	DATE	COUNTRIES
Pathet Lao Day	Jan 6	Laos
National Day	Jan 7	Cambodia
City Festival	Jan 5-29	Hong Kong
Thaipusam Festival	Jan 31	Singapore
Buon Magha Puja	Feb 6	Laos
Hong Kong Arts Festival	Feb 10- Mar 10	Hong Kong
Day of the Burmese Union	Feb 12	Myanmar
Chinese New Year	Feb 12	Cambodia, Hong Kong, Malaysia, Singapore
Tet, Vietnamese New Year	Feb 13-15	Vietnam
People's Power Day	Feb 22	Philippines
National Day	Feb 23	Brunei
Id al-Adha	Mar 6	Brunei, Indonesia, Malaysia
Women's Day parade	Mar 8	Laos
Balinese Saka New Year	Mar 26	Indonesia
Islamic New Year	Mar 15	Brunei, Indonesia, Malaysia
Prophet Muhammad's birthday	May 25	Brunei, Indonesia, Malaysia
Thingyan, Burmese New Year	Apr	Myanmar
Buon Pimai, Lao New Year	Apr	Laos
Royal Ploughin Ceremony and agrarian festival	Apr-May	Cambodia
Songkran	Apr 13-15	Thailand
Traditional Khmer New Year	Apr 13-15	Cambodia
Kartini Day	Apr 21	Indonesia
Reunification Day	Apr 30	Vietnam
Buon Visaka Bucha	May	Laos
Ho Chi Minh's birthday	May 19	Vietnam
Birth of Buddha	May 19	Hong Kong
King's Birthday	June 1	Malaysia
Dragon Boat Festival	June 6	Hong Kong
Manila Day	June 24	Philippines
SAR establishment day	July 1	Hong Kong
H.M. the Sultan and the Yang Di-Pertuan Negara Brunei Darassalam birthday	July 15	Brunei
Indonesian Independence Day	Aug 17	Indonesia
National Day	Aug 31	Malaysia
National Day	Oct 1	Hong Kong
Day of Liberation from the French	Oct 12	Laos
Prachum Ben	Oct 11-13	Cambodia
King Sihanouk's birthday	Oct 31	Cambodia
That Luang Festival	Nov	Laos
All Saint's Day	Nov 1	Philippines
Diwali	Nov 4	Malaysia, Singapore
Start of Ramadan	Nov 6	Brunei
King's birthday	Dec 5	Thailand
Id al-Fitr	Dec 6	Brunei, Indonesia, Malaysia
Christmas	Dec 25	All
Rizal Day	Dec 30	Philippines

ENGLISH	THAI//LAO	BURMESE
1	nèung // neung	ti
2	säwng // säwng	hni
3	sähm // sähm	thoun
4	sèe // see	le
5	hâh // hâh	nga
6	hòk // hók	chau
7	jèt // jét	khun ni
8	pàet // pâet	shi
9	gâo // kâo	ko
10	sìp // síp	tahse
11	sìp-èt // síp-ét	she
12	sìp-säwng // síp-säwng	seh-hni
20	yêe-sìp // sáo	hna se
30	sähm-sìp // sähm-síp	thoun ze
40	sèe-sìp // see-síp	lei ze
50	hâh-sìp // häh-síp	nga ze
100	róy // hâwy	taya
1000	pun // pán	taya fahse
Hello	sàwatdee // sábài-dèe	mingala ba
Goodbye	sawàtdee // pai jao	thwabi
Yes / No	<n/a> / mâi // ya / baw	hou ke / hin in
Thank you	khàwp khun // khâwp jài	kye zui tin ba de
Excuse me	khäw tôht // khäw thôt	(m) khin mya, (f) shin
Please repeat	pôod ìk khráng sâi maï // kálunaa wâo mai beng duu	pyan pyaw ba oun
How are you?	ben yahng ngai // sábài-dèe baw	nei kaun ye la
Fine/well.	sabai-dee // sábài-dee	nei kaun ba de
Help!	chûay dûay // suay dae	lai kya ba oun
Doctor	mäw // mäw	hsaya wun
Police	tham ruat // tham ploh	ye sa khan
Hospital	rohng paiahban // hóhng mäw	hsei youn
Toilet	sûam // sûam	ein tha
Where is . . . ?	. . . yòo têe näi // . . . yôo säi	. . . bema shi th a le
To the right	khwä meu // lîaw khwaa	nya be cho
To the left	saí meu // lîaw sâai	be be cho
Straight ahead	throng bai // pai seu seu	te da thwai
How much?	tâo rài // tao dài	da be lan le
Bus	rót meh // lót meh	ba saka
Train	rót fai // lot duan	mi ya tha
Plane	krêuang bin // héua bìn	lei yin byan
Car	rót yon // lot	twei
Taxi	rót táek-sêe // thâek sée	a hnga ka
Open (hours)	bèrd (gee mohng) // butk	pwin deh
Close (hours)	bìt (gee mohng) // baowk	pei deh
Restaurant	ráhn ah-hän // lán ah-han	sa than hsain
Guest House	bâhn pák // häw hap khäek	e yei tha
Market	thah làt // thah làt	zei
Bank	tanahkhan // thanáhkháhn	ban
Post Office	praisanee // pài-sá-née	sa dai
Yesterday	mêua wahn née // mêu wáhn nêe	manei ga
Today	wan née // mêu nêe	dinei
Tomorrow	prûng née // mêu eun	ne hpan

KHMER	VIETNAMESE	MALAY/INDONESIAN
mouy	một	satu
pee	hai	dua
bei	ba	tiga
boun	bốn	empat
bram	nâm	lima
bram-mouy	sáu	eman
bram-pee	bảy	tujuh
bram-bei	tám	delapan
bram-boun	chín	sembilan
duop	mười	sepuluh
duop-mouy	mười m t	sebelas
duop-pee	mười hai	duabelas
maphei	hai mươi	duapuluh
samseb	ba mươi	tigapuluh
sairseb	bốn mươi	empatpuluh
hahseb	năm mươi	limapuluh
mouy-rouy	một trăm	seratus
mouy-paun	một ngàn	seribu
suas dei	Chào ông (to males) Chào bà (to females)	selamat pagi (morning) selamat siang (afternoon) selamat sore (evening) selamat malam (night)
lia soon hao-i	Chào ông/Chào bà	selamat tinggal (to one staying)/ selamat jalan (to one going)
baht (males), chaat (females) / te	Dạ / Không	ya / tidak
aw kohn	Cám ơn	terima kasih
sohm toh	Xin lỗi	ma'af
sohm niyaymdawng tiat	Làm ơn nhắc lại	ma'af, sekali lagi
niak sohk sabah-ay tay	ần/aẩ	Apa kabar?
khnyohm sohk sabah-ay	ần/aẩ	baik
juay khnyohm pawng	Cứu với	Tolong!
kroo paet	bác sĩ	dokter
po'leez	cảnh sát	polisi
mun'ti peyt	bệnh viện	rumah sakit
bawng-kohn	buồng tắm	kamar kecil
. . . neuv ai nah	ở đâu	Di mana . . . ?
bawt chweng	rẽ trái	ke kanan
bawt sdam	rẽ phải	ke kiri
teuv trawng	đi thẳng	terus menerus
nee tlay pohnmahn	Giá bao nhiêu	Berapa?
lahn chnual	xe buýt	bas (Mal.)/bis (Ind.)
roht plirng	xe lửa	kereta api
yohn haw	máy bay	kapal terbang
laht	xe ô tô	mobil
tahk see	tắc xi	taksi
wia baok maong pohnmaan	giờ mở cửa	jam buka
wia buht maong pohnmaan	giờ đóng cửa	jam tutup
restoorahn	tiệm ăn	rumah makan
oh-tail	nhà khách	wisma
psah	chợ	pasar
thniakia	ngân hàng	bank
praisuhnee	bưu điện	pejebat pos (Mal.) kantor pos (Ind.)
m'sool mein	hôm qua	kemarin
thngay nee	hôm nay	hari ini
thngay saik	ngày mai	besok

APPENDIX

CLIMATE

High and low tourist seasons roughly correspond with rainy and dry seasons in Southeast Asia. There is no uniform seasonal pattern for the region; see the Facts and Figures section in each chapter for country-specific variations. Keep in mind that the monsoon is rarely an impediment for travel in the region, except for in rural Laos and Cambodia. Generally, rainfall peaks from May to September north of Singapore (including the Philippines), and between December to March south and east of Singapore (including Indonesia). To roughly convert Celsius to Fahrenheit, double the Celsius and add 30.

Temperature and Precipitation by City

City	January			April			July			October		
	High (F/C)	Low (F/C)	Rain (in)	High (F/C)	Low (F/C)	Rain (in)	High (F/C)	Low (F/C)	Rain (in)	High (F/C)	Low (F/C)	Rain (in)
Bali	90/32	76/25	13.9	91/33	76/24	3.5	87/31	74/23	2.1	90/32	76/24	3.6
Bangkok	91/33	71/22	0.4	96/36	80/27	2.4	92/33	78/26	5.7	91/33	78/25	7.2
Bandar Seri Begawan	87/30	74/23	11.7	88/31	77/25	6.9	90/32	77/25	8.8	88/31	76/24	11.9
Hanoi	70/21	54/13	0.9	79/26	68/20	4.0	90/32	82/28	10.2	85/29	74/23	5.9
Hong Kong	68/20	59/15	1.2	79/26	71/22	5.6	90/32	82/28	14.4	85/29	76/25	4.8
Jakarta	90/32	75/24	13.1	93/34	75/24	8.3	93/34	72/22	3.4	95/35	74/23	6.3
Kuala Lumpur	91/33	74/23	6.5	93/34	76/24	10.6	92/33	74/24	5.2	91/33	75/24	10.3
Manila	88/31	71/22	0.7	96/35	76/24	1.0	91/33	77/25	17.7	90/32	76/24	7.2
Phnom Penh	74/23	62/17	0.2	84/29	75/24	3.3	82/28	77/25	10.5	80/27	74/23	3.4
Phuket	90/32	73/23	1.8	93/34	77/25	6.1	88/31	78/25	10.2	88/31	76/24	14.3
Singapore	87/30	77/25	6.5	91/33	79/26	10.6	89/32	80/27	5.2	89/32	79/26	10.3
Vientiane	82/28	58/15	0.4	91/33	74/23	3.6	88/31	78/25	9.9	88/31	70/21	3.4
Yangon	91/33	67/19	3.5	101/38	78/25	3.6	87/30	78/25	3.5	90/32	79/26	2.9

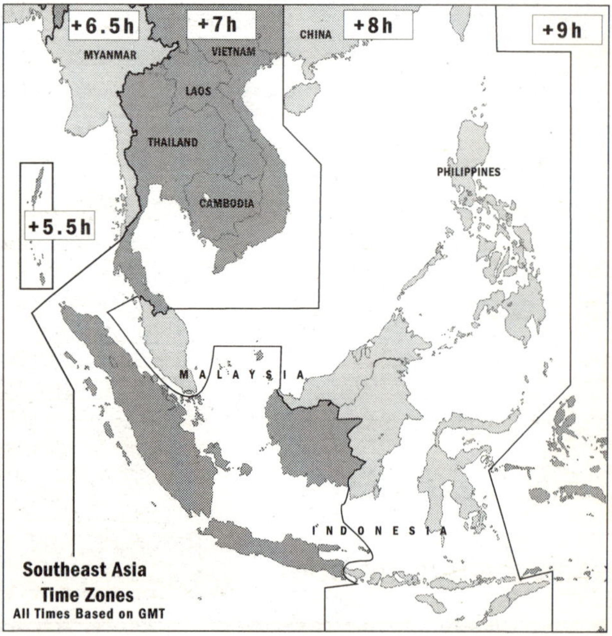

Southeast Asia Time Zones
All Times Based on GMT

INDEX

INDEX

C

D

E

F

G

H

INDEX

V

W

X

Y

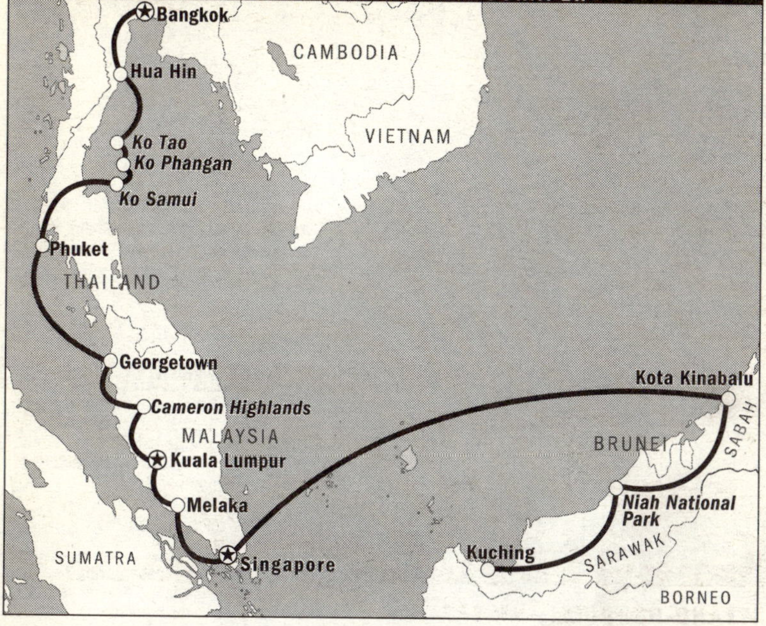

Travel Cheep.
Visit StudentUniverse for real deals on student and faculty airline tickets, rail passes, and hostel memberships.
StudentUniverse.com
Real Travel Deals
800.272.9676

Sheep Tickets.
Visit StudentUniverse.com for real deals on student travel anywhere.
StudentUniverse.com
Real Travel Deals
800.272.9676

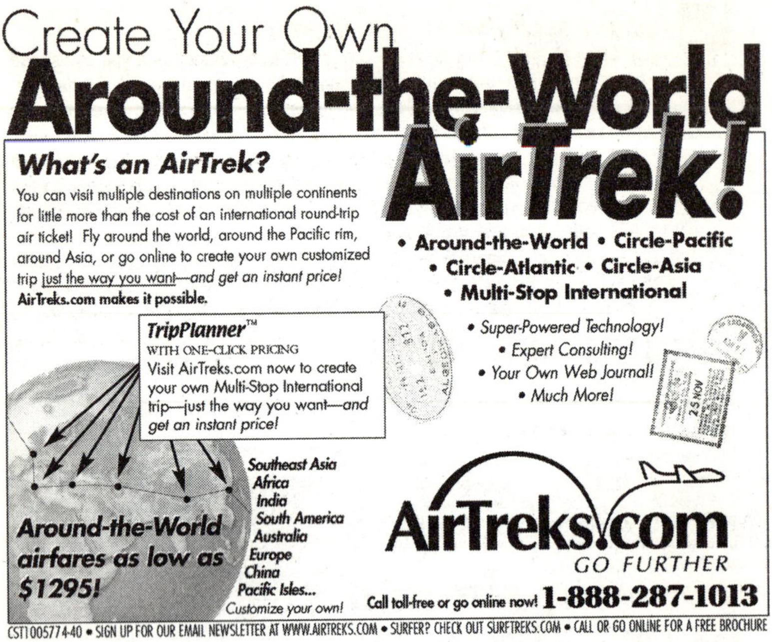

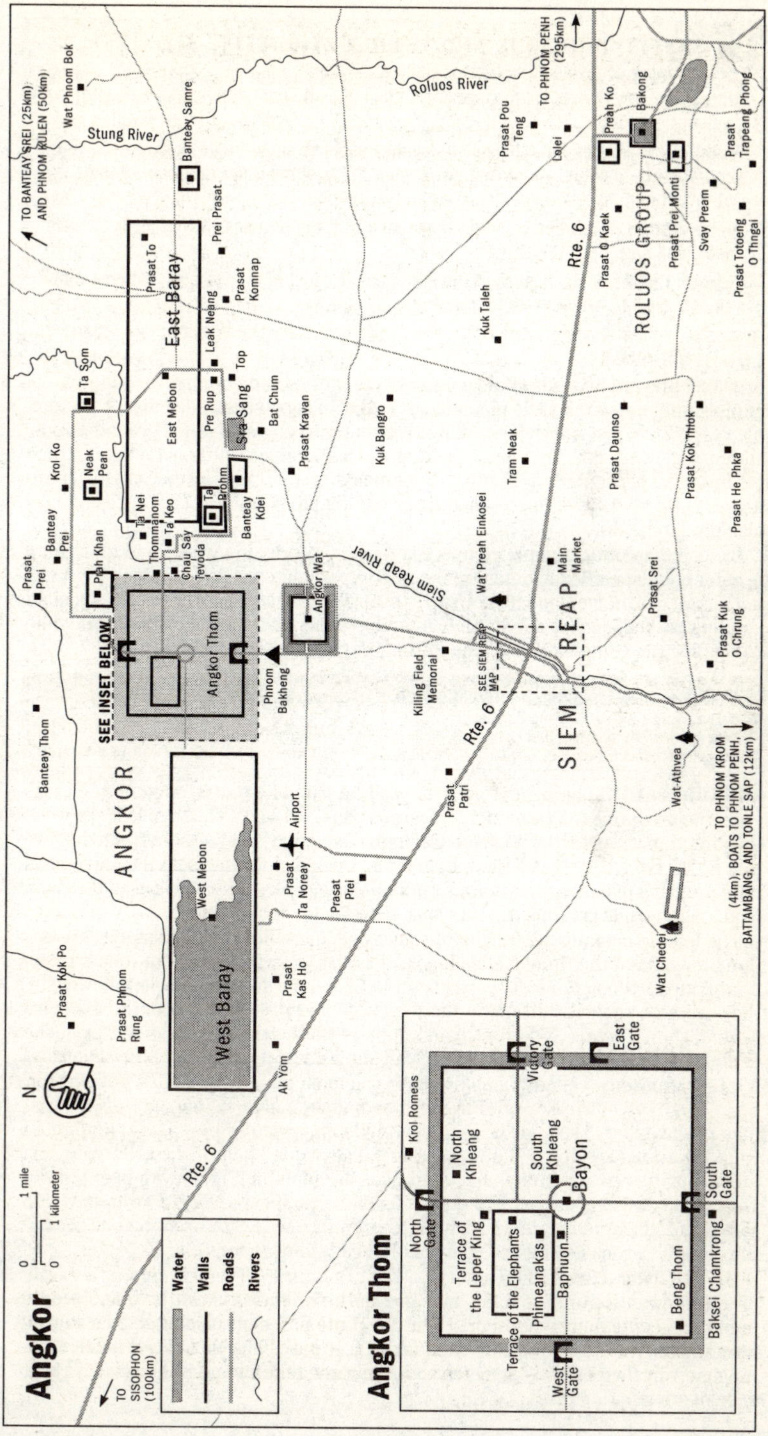
Angkor
0 1 mile
0 1 kilometer
N
Water
Walls
Roads
Rivers
TO SISOPHON (100km)
TO BANTEAY SREI (25km) AND PHNOM KULEN (50km)
TO PHNOM PENH (295km)
TO PHNOM KROM (4km), BOATS TO PHNOM PENH, BATTAMBANG, AND TONLE SAP (12km)
ANGKOR
SEE INSET BELOW
SEE SIEM REAP MAP
SIEM REAP
ROLUOS GROUP
Rte. 6
Stung River
Roluos River
Siem Reap River
Wat Phnom Bok
Banteay Samre
Prasat To
Prei Prasat
East Baray
Prasat Komnap
Leak Neang
Ta Som
East Mebon
Pre Rup
Top
Sra Sang
Bat Chum
Krol Ko
Neak Pean
Ta Prohm
Banteay Kdei
Prasat Kravan
Kuk Bangro
Ta Nei
Thommanom
Ta Keo
Chau Say Tevoda
Banteay Prei
Prasat Prei
Preah Khan
Angkor Thom
Angkor Wat
Phnom Bakheng
Wat Preah Einkosei
Main Market
Killing Field Memorial
Banteay Thom
West Baray
West Mebon
Airport
Prasat Ta Noreay
Prasat Prei
Prasat Patri
Prasat Kas Ho
Ak Yom
Prasat Kok Po
Prasat Phnom Rung
Kuk Taleh
Tram Neak
Prasat Daunso
Prasat Pou Teng
Lolei
Preah Ko
Bakong
Prasat Ó Kaek
Prasat Prei Monti
Svay Pream
Prasat Trapeang Phong
Prasat Totoeng O Thngai
Prasat Kok Thlok
Prasat He Phka
Prasat Srei
Prasat Kuk O Chrung
Wat Athvea
Wat Chedei
Angkor Thom
North Gate
Krol Romeas
North Khleang
South Khleang
Victory Gate
East Gate
Terrace of the Leper King
Terrace of the Elephants
Phimeanakas
Baphuon
Bayon
South Gate
Beng Thom
Baksei Chamkrong
West Gate

CAMBODIA

Hong Kong City Center and Kowloon Peninsula
ACCOMMODATIONS
Chungking Mansions, 3
Mirador Mansions, 2
Victoria Hostel, 1
YMCA, 4
HUNG HOM
TO WONDERFUL WORLD OF WHAMPOA (100m) AND HUNG HOM FERRYS (150m)
TO NORTH POINT
Cross Harbour Tunnel
Coliseum
Hung Hom (Kowloon) Station
Salisbury Rd.
Hong Chong Rd.
Chatham Rd. N.
Chi Man St.
Yuk Choi Rd.
Hong Kong Polytechnic University
Cheong Wan Rd.
Science Museum Rd.
Hong Kong Tourist Association
Tsim Sha Tsui West Ferry Pier
Mody Rd.
TSIM SHA TSUI EAST
Hong Kong Science Museum
Hong Kong Museum of History
Chatham Rd. S.
Austin Av.
Wylie Rd.
Queen Elizabeth Hospital
Gascoigne Rd.
Princess Margaret Rd.
New World Centre
Promenade
Salisbury Rd.
Hong Kong Space Museum
Hong Kong Museum of Art
Peninsula Hotel
China Travel Service
Granville Rd.
Cameron Rd.
Kimberley Rd.
Observatory Rd.
Hillwood Rd.
Austin Rd.
Tak Shing St.
American Express
Nathan Rd.
JORDAN
Hanoi Rd.
Mody Rd.
Hart Av.
Cornwall Av.
Humphreys Av.
Carnarvon Rd.
Minden Av.
Lock Rd.
Hankow Rd.
Ashley Rd.
Peking Rd.
Middle Rd.
Kowloon Park Dr.
Haiphong Rd.
TSIM SHA TSUI
Kowloon Mosque and Islamic Centre
TSIM SHA TSUI
Hong Kong Cultural Centre
Clock Tower
Star House
Star Ferry Concourse
Canton Rd.
Harbour City
China Hong Kong City
Ocean Terminal
CENTRAL-TSIM SHA TSUI FERRY
China Ferry Terminal
KOWLOON
Bowring St.
Austin Rd.
Jordan Rd.
Woosung St.
Parkes St.
Temple St.
Kansu St.
Shanghai St.
Ning Po St.
Nanking St.
Battery St.
Saigon St.
Canton Rd.
Ferry St.
Public Square St.
Tin Hau Temple
Tung Kun St.
Jordan Rd.
Jordan Rd. Ferry Terminal
KOWLOON STATION
TO MACAU AND CHINA
Western Harbour Crossing
TO TSING YI AND TSUEN WAN
TO CHEUNG CHAU AND PENG CHAU
TO LAMMA ISLAND
TO TUEN MUN, TUNG CHAU WAN, AND TAI O
TO MACAU
HK Macau Ferry Terminal
Pier 1

FALL/WINTER 2001 • FREE
student Travels
WORK, STUDY, TRAVEL ABROAD
CZECH IT OUT!
Exploring Prague and Other Pleasures in the Czech Republic
BOSTON
Weekend Wandering in Beantown
INSIDE
Your International Student Identity Card (ISIC) Application
PLUS
-Cuba
-Australia
Bedazzled By BRAZIL
Boundless Attractions From Beautiful Beaches to Spectacular Festivals to Lush Jungles

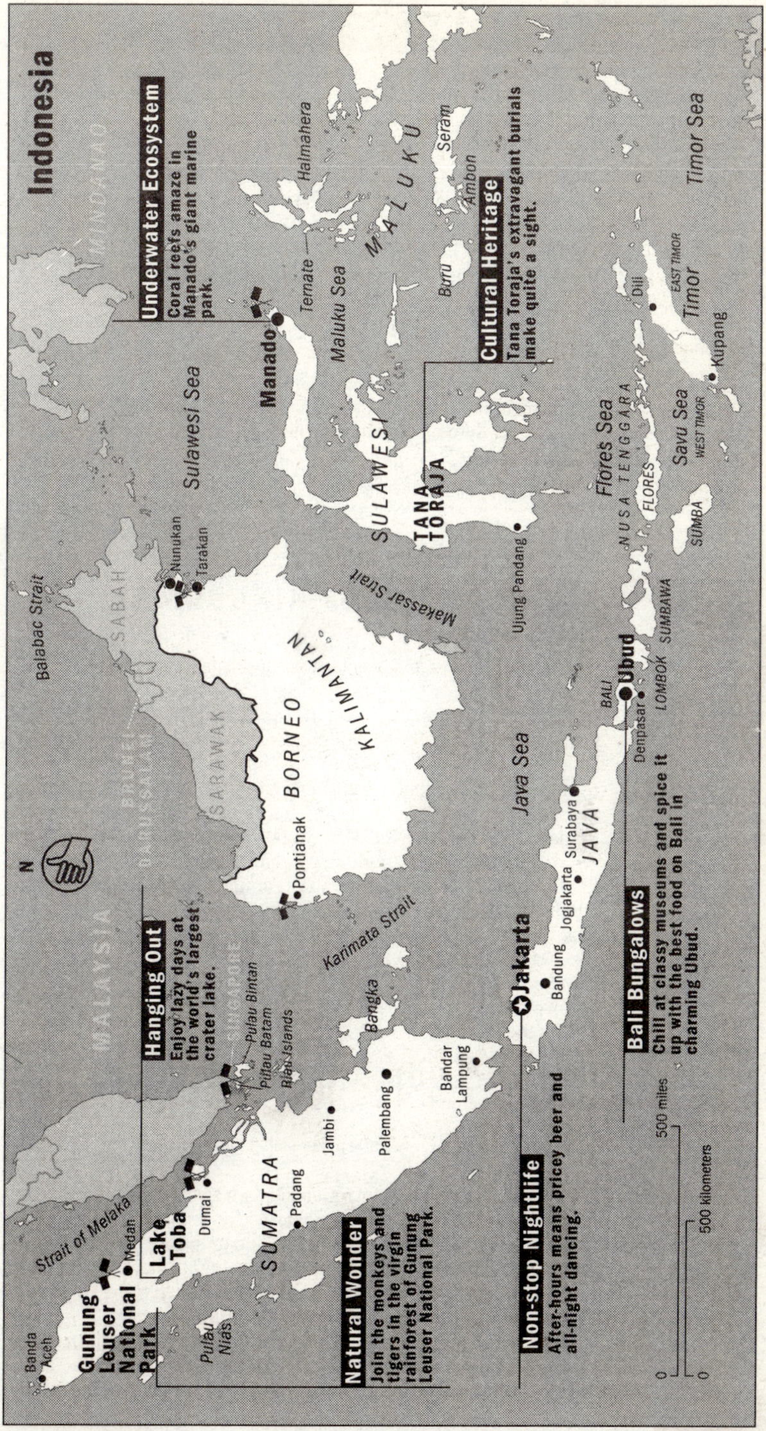
Indonesia
Underwater Ecosystem
Coral reefs amaze in Manado's giant marine park.
Cultural Heritage
Tana Toraja's extravagant burials make quite a sight.
Hanging Out
Enjoy lazy days at the world's largest crater lake.
Natural Wonder
Join the monkeys and tigers in the virgin rainforest of Gunung Leuser National Park.
Non-stop Nightlife
After-hours means pricey beer and all-night dancing.
Bali Bungalows
Chill at classy museums and spice it up with the best food on Bali in charming Ubud.
MINDANAO
Halmahera
Ternate
Seram
Ambon
Buru
MALUKU
Maluku Sea
Manado
Sulawesi Sea
SULAWESI
TANA TORAJA
Ujung Pandang
Makassar Strait
Flores Sea
NUSA TENGGARA
FLORES
SUMBA
SUMBAWA
LOMBOK
BALI
Ubud
Denpasar
Savu Sea
WEST TIMOR
EAST TIMOR
Dili
Timor
Kupang
Timor Sea
Balabac Strait
SABAH
Nunukan
Tarakan
BRUNEI DARUSSALAM
SARAWAK
BORNEO
KALIMANTAN
Pontianak
MALAYSIA
SINGAPORE
Pulau Bintan
Pulau Batam
Riau Islands
Karimata Strait
Bangka
Java Sea
Surabaya
JAVA
Jogjakarta
Bandung
Jakarta
Bandar Lampung
Palembang
Jambi
SUMATRA
Padang
Dumai
Medan
Lake Toba
Strait of Melaka
Banda Aceh
Gunung Leuser National Park
Pulau Nias
N
0
500 miles
0
500 kilometers

INDONESIA

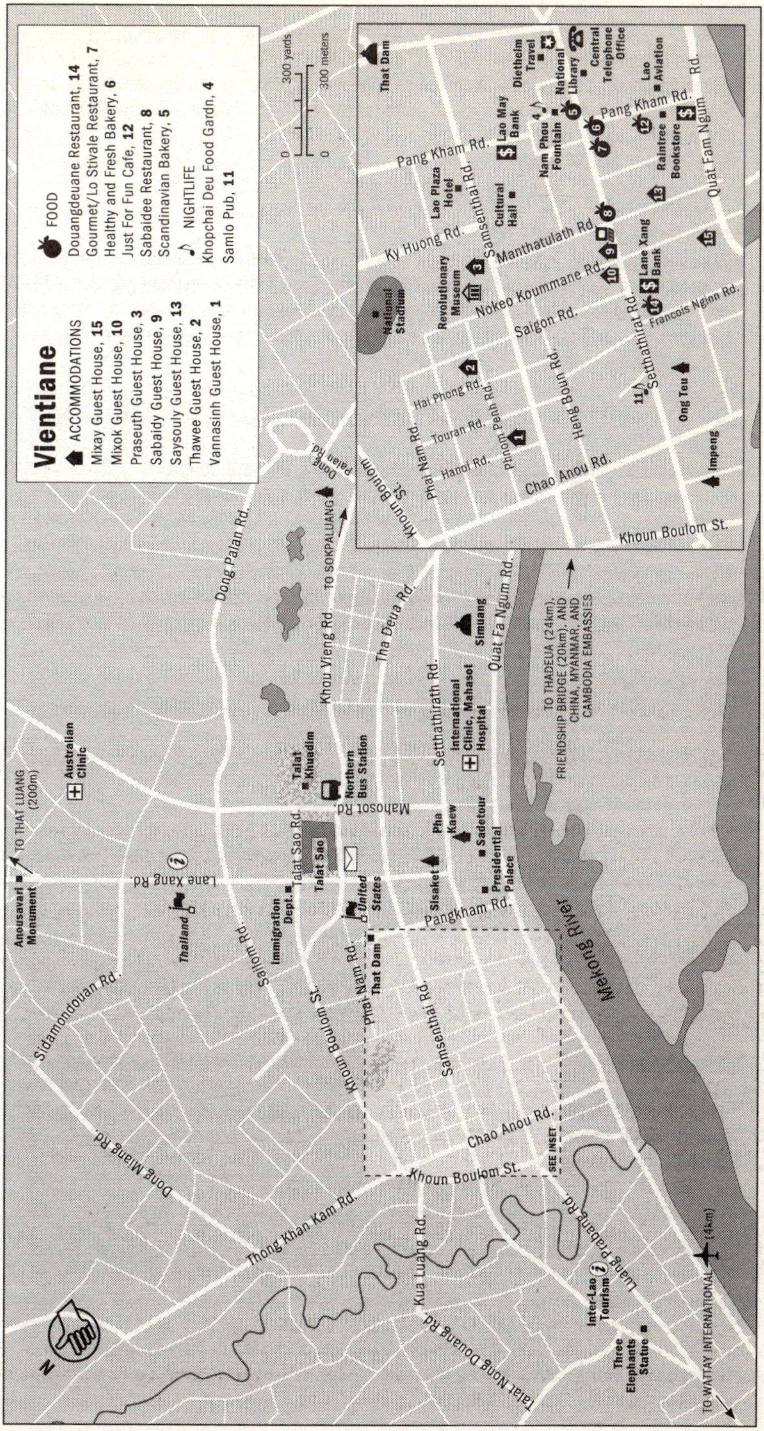
Vientiane
ACCOMMODATIONS
Mixay Guest House, 15
Mixok Guest House, 10
Praseuth Guest House, 3
Sabaidy Guest House, 9
Saysouly Guest House, 13
Thawee Guest House, 2
Vannasinh Guest House, 1
FOOD
Douangdeuane Restaurant, 14
Gourmet/Lo Stivale Restaurant, 7
Healthy and Fresh Bakery, 6
Just For Fun Cafe, 12
Sabaidee Restaurant, 8
Scandinavian Bakery, 5
NIGHTLIFE
Khopchai Deu Food Gardn, 4
Samlo Pub, 11
300 yards
300 meters
That Dam
National Stadium
Revolutionary Museum
Lao Plaza Hotel
Cultural Hall
Lao May Bank
Dietheim Travel
National Library
Central Telephone Office
Nam Phou Fountain
Lao Aviation
Raintree Bookstore
Lane Xang Bank
Ong Teu
Impeng
Pang Kham Rd.
Ky Huong Rd.
Samsenthai Rd.
Manthatulath Rd.
Nokeo Koummane Rd.
Saigon Rd.
Francois Nginn Rd.
Setthathirat Rd.
Quai Fam Ngum Rd.
Heng Boun Rd.
Hai Phong Rd.
Touran Rd.
Hanoi Rd.
Phnom Penh Rd.
Phai Nam Rd.
Chao Anou Rd.
Khoun Boulom St.
Dong Palan Rd.
TO SOKPALUANG
Khou Vieng Rd.
Tha Deua Rd.
Setthathirath Rd.
Simuang
International Clinic, Mahasot Hospital
Quai Fa Ngum Rd.
TO THADEUA (24km), FRIENDSHIP BRIDGE (20km), AND CHINA, MYANMAR, AND CAMBODIA EMBASSIES
TO THAT LUANG (200m)
Australian Clinic
Anousavari Monument
Lane Xang Rd.
Talat Khuadim
Northern Bus Station
Mahosot Rd.
Talat Sao Rd.
Talat Sao
Immigration Dept.
Thailand
United States
Sisaket
Pha Kaew
Sadetour
Presidential Palace
Pangkham Rd.
Mekong River
Salom Rd.
Sidamondouan Rd.
Khoun Boulom St.
Phai Nam Rd.
That Dam
Samsenthai Rd.
Chao Anou Rd.
SEE INSET
Dong Miang Rd.
Thong Khan Kam Rd.
Kua Luang Rd.
Luang Prabang Rd.
Inter-Lao Tourism
(4km)
Talat Nong Douang Rd.
Three Elephants Statue
TO WATTAY INTERNATIONAL
N

LAOS

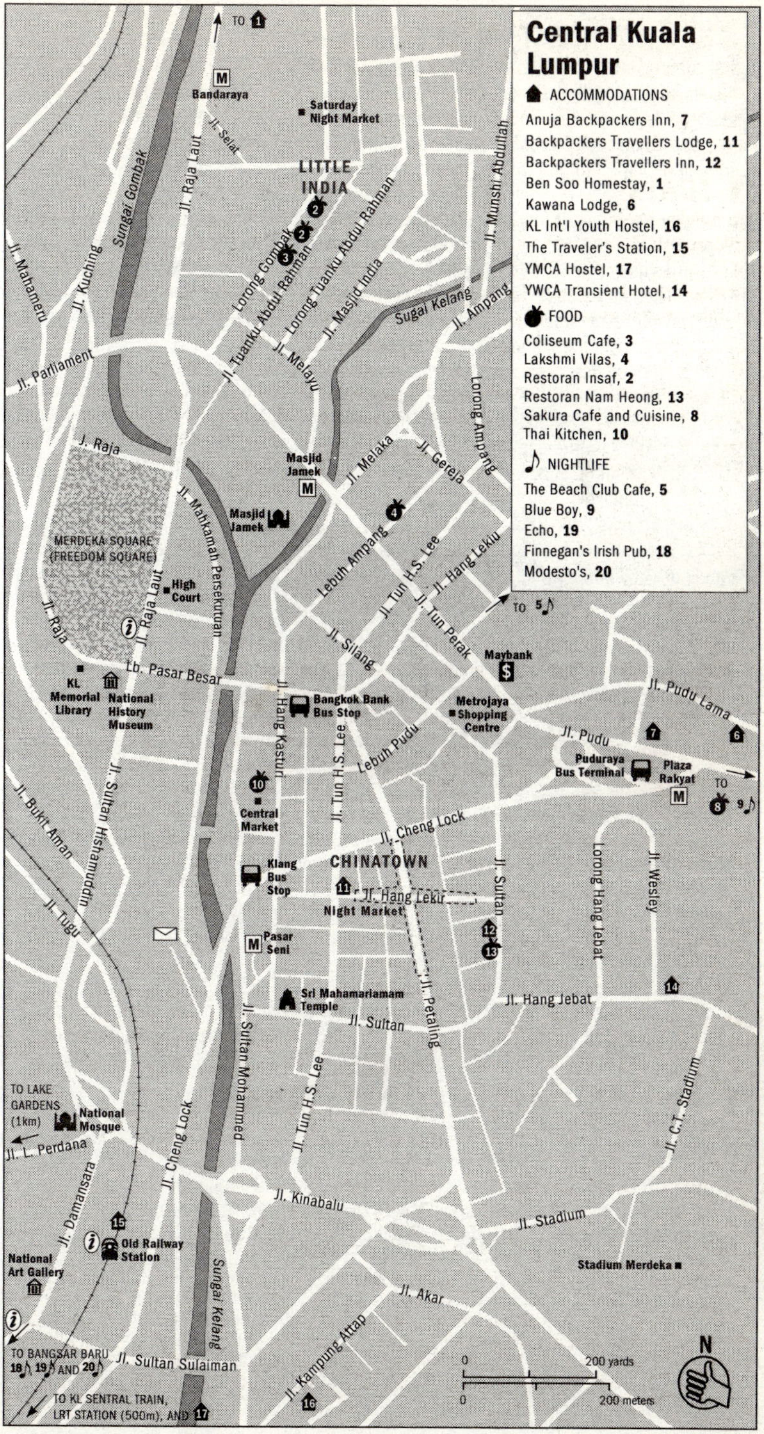
Central Kuala Lumpur
ACCOMMODATIONS
Anuja Backpackers Inn, 7
Backpackers Travellers Lodge, 11
Backpackers Travellers Inn, 12
Ben Soo Homestay, 1
Kawana Lodge, 6
KL Int'l Youth Hostel, 16
The Traveler's Station, 15
YMCA Hostel, 17
YWCA Transient Hotel, 14
FOOD
Coliseum Cafe, 3
Lakshmi Vilas, 4
Restoran Insaf, 2
Restoran Nam Heong, 13
Sakura Cafe and Cuisine, 8
Thai Kitchen, 10
NIGHTLIFE
The Beach Club Cafe, 5
Blue Boy, 9
Echo, 19
Finnegan's Irish Pub, 18
Modesto's, 20
TO 1
Bandaraya
Saturday Night Market
LITTLE INDIA
Jl. Selat
Jl. Raja Laut
Sungai Gombak
Jl. Kuching
Jl. Mahameru
Lorong Gombak
Jl. Tuanku Abdul Rahman
Lorong Tuanku Abdul Rahman
Jl. Masjid India
Jl. Munshi Abdullah
Sugai Kelang
Jl. Ampang
Jl. Parliament
Jl. Melayu
Lorong Ampang
J. Raja
Masjid Jamek
Jl. Melaka
Jl. Gereja
Jl. Mahkamah Persekutuan
MERDEKA SQUARE (FREEDOM SQUARE)
High Court
Lebuh Ampang
Jl. Tun H.S. Lee
Jl. Hang Lekiu
Jl. Tun Perak
TO 5
Jl. Raja
Jl. Raja Laut
Jl. Silang
Maybank
Lb. Pasar Besar
KL Memorial Library
National History Museum
Jl. Hang Kasturi
Bangkok Bank Bus Stop
Metrojaya Shopping Centre
Jl. Pudu Lama
Jl. Pudu
Lebuh Pudu
Puduraya Bus Terminal
Plaza Rakyat
TO 8 9
Central Market
Jl. Sultan Hishamuddin
Jl. Bukit Aman
Jl. Cheng Lock
CHINATOWN
Klang Bus Stop
Jl. Hang Lekir
Night Market
Jl. Sultan
Lorong Hang Jebat
Jl. Wesley
Jl. Tugu
Pasar Seni
Sri Mahamariamam Temple
Jl. Petaling
Jl. Hang Jebat
Jl. Sultan
Jl. Sultan Mohammed
Jl. Tun H.S. Lee
Jl. C.T. Stadium
TO LAKE GARDENS (1km)
National Mosque
Jl. L. Perdana
Jl. Cheng Lock
Jl. Kinabalu
Jl. Stadium
Jl. Damansara
Old Railway Station
National Art Gallery
Sungai Kelang
Stadium Merdeka
Jl. Akar
Jl. Kampung Attap
TO BANGSAR BARU 18 19 AND 20
Jl. Sultan Sulaiman
TO KL SENTRAL TRAIN, LRT STATION (500m), AND 17
0 200 yards
0 200 meters
N

MALAYSIA

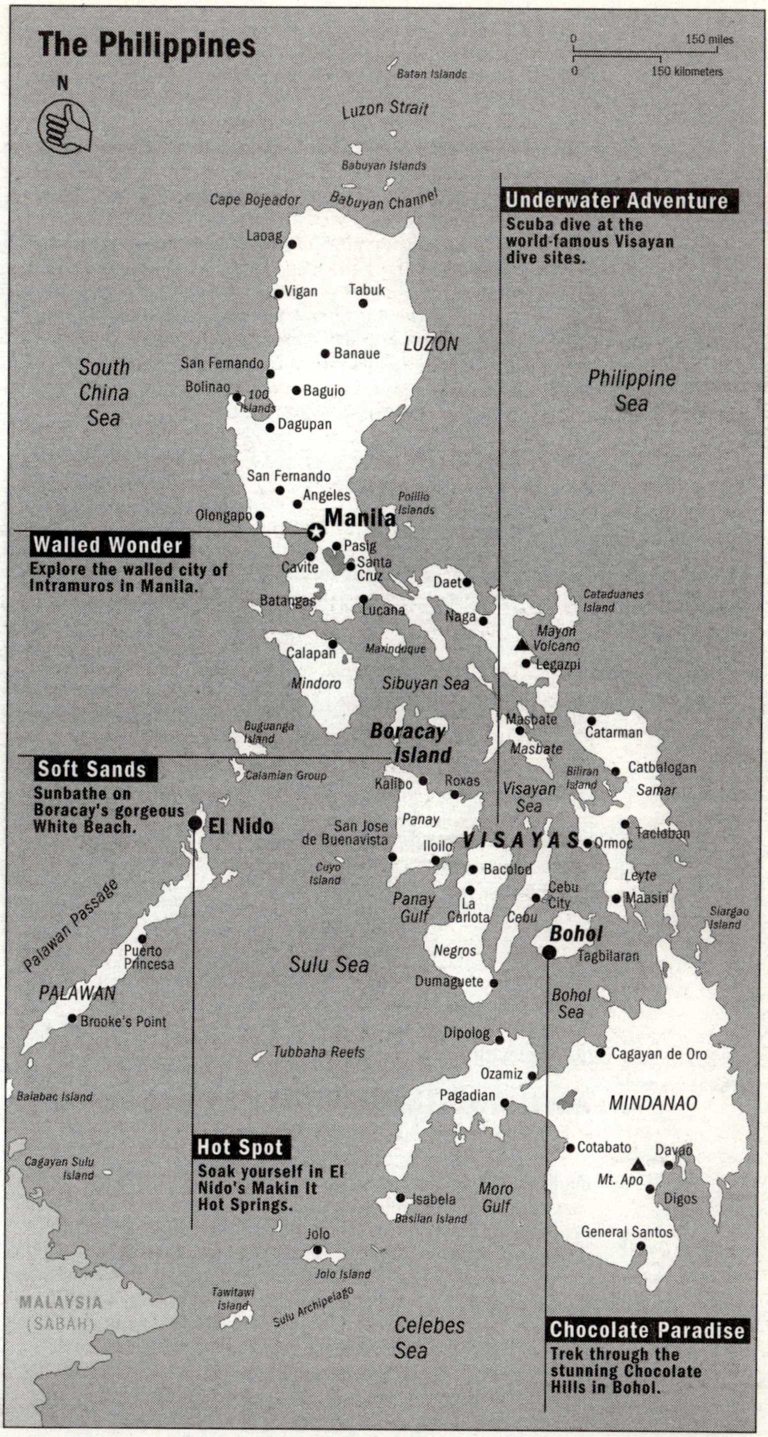
The Philippines
N
0 150 miles
0 150 kilometers
Batan Islands
Luzon Strait
Babuyan Islands
Cape Bojeador
Babuyan Channel
Laoag
Vigan
Tabuk
Banaue
LUZON
San Fernando
Bolinao
100 Islands
Baguio
Dagupan
South China Sea
San Fernando
Angeles
Olongapo
Manila
Polillo Islands
Pasig
Cavite
Santa Cruz
Batangas
Lucena
Daet
Naga
Catanduanes Island
Mayon Volcano
Legazpi
Calapan
Marinduque
Mindoro
Sibuyan Sea
Busuanga Island
Calamian Group
Boracay Island
Masbate
Masbate
Catarman
Kalibo
Roxas
Biliran Island
Catbalogan
Samar
Visayan Sea
Panay
San Jose de Buenavista
Iloilo
VISAYAS
Ormoc
Tacloban
Cuyo Island
Bacolod
Leyte
Cebu City
Maasin
Siargao Island
Panay Gulf
La Carlota
Cebu
Bohol
Tagbilaran
Negros
Dumaguete
Bohol Sea
Philippine Sea
El Nido
Palawan Passage
Puerto Princesa
PALAWAN
Brooke's Point
Sulu Sea
Tubbaha Reefs
Dipolog
Cagayan de Oro
Ozamiz
Pagadian
MINDANAO
Balabac Island
Cotabato
Davao
Mt. Apo
Digos
Cagayan Sulu Island
Isabela
Basilan Island
Moro Gulf
General Santos
Jolo
Jolo Island
Tawitawi Island
Sulu Archipelago
MALAYSIA (SABAH)
Celebes Sea
Underwater Adventure
Scuba dive at the world-famous Visayan dive sites.
Walled Wonder
Explore the walled city of Intramuros in Manila.
Soft Sands
Sunbathe on Boracay's gorgeous White Beach.
Hot Spot
Soak yourself in El Nido's Makin It Hot Springs.
Chocolate Paradise
Trek through the stunning Chocolate Hills in Bohol.

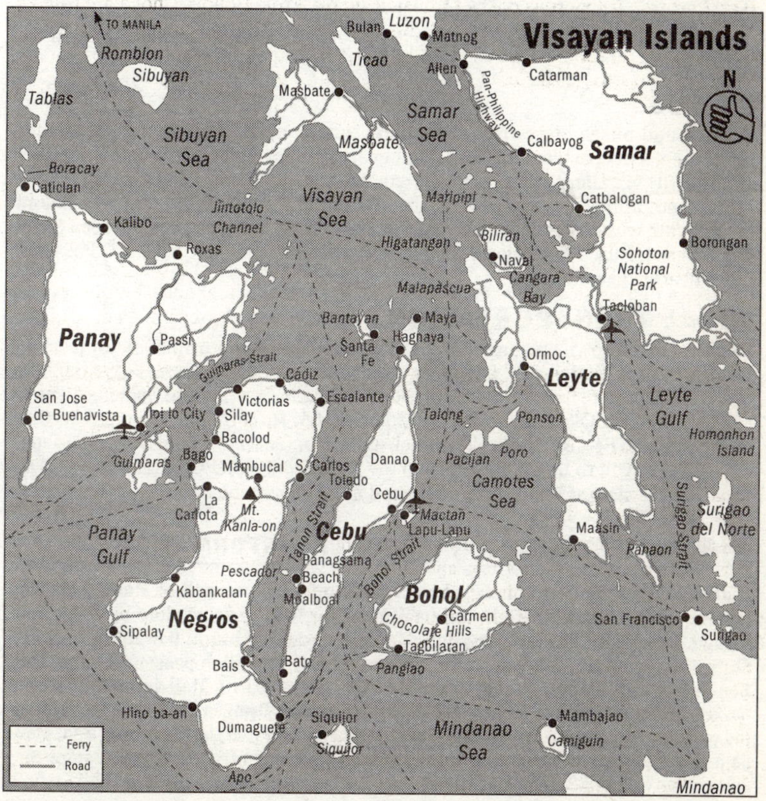

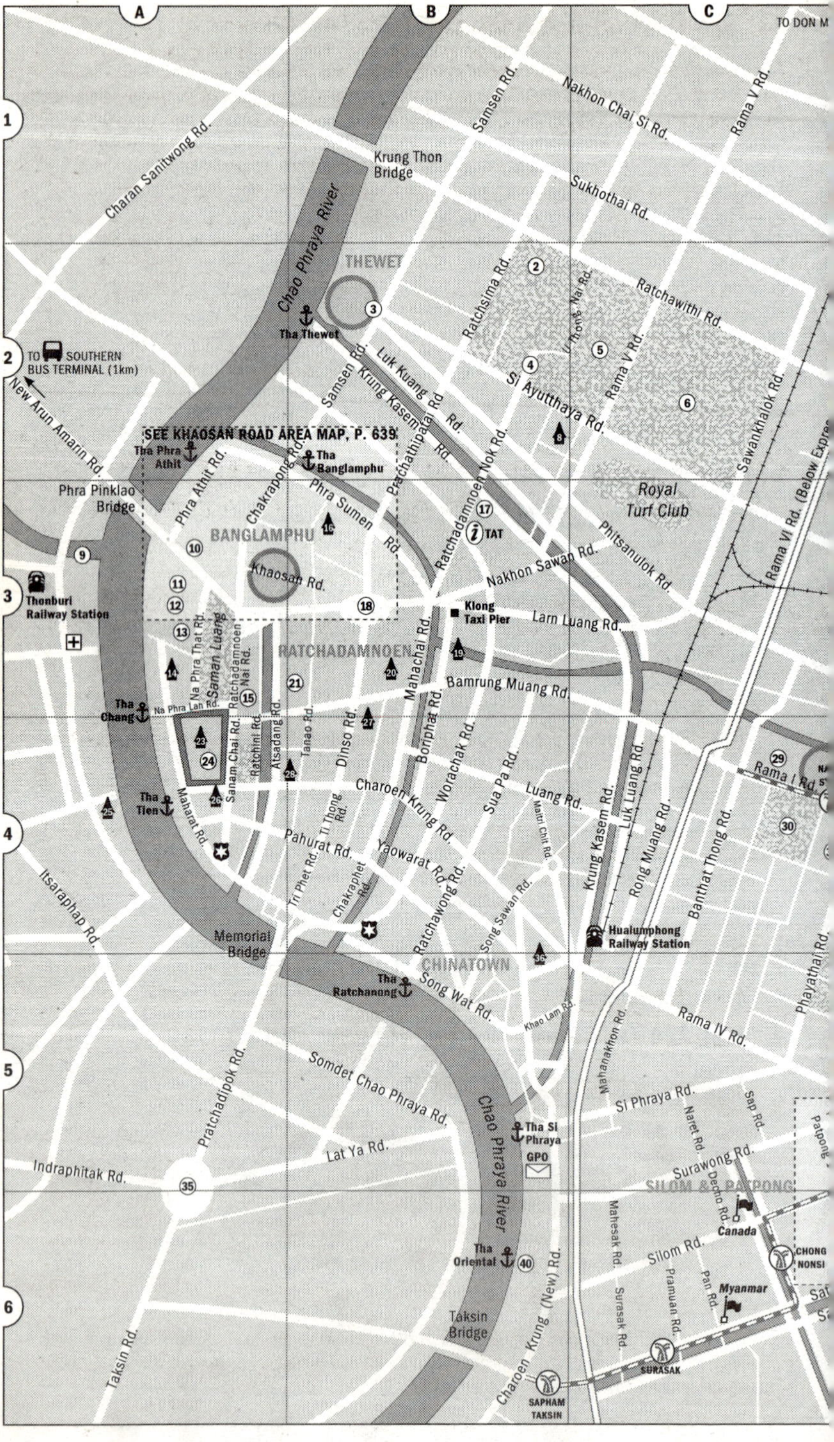

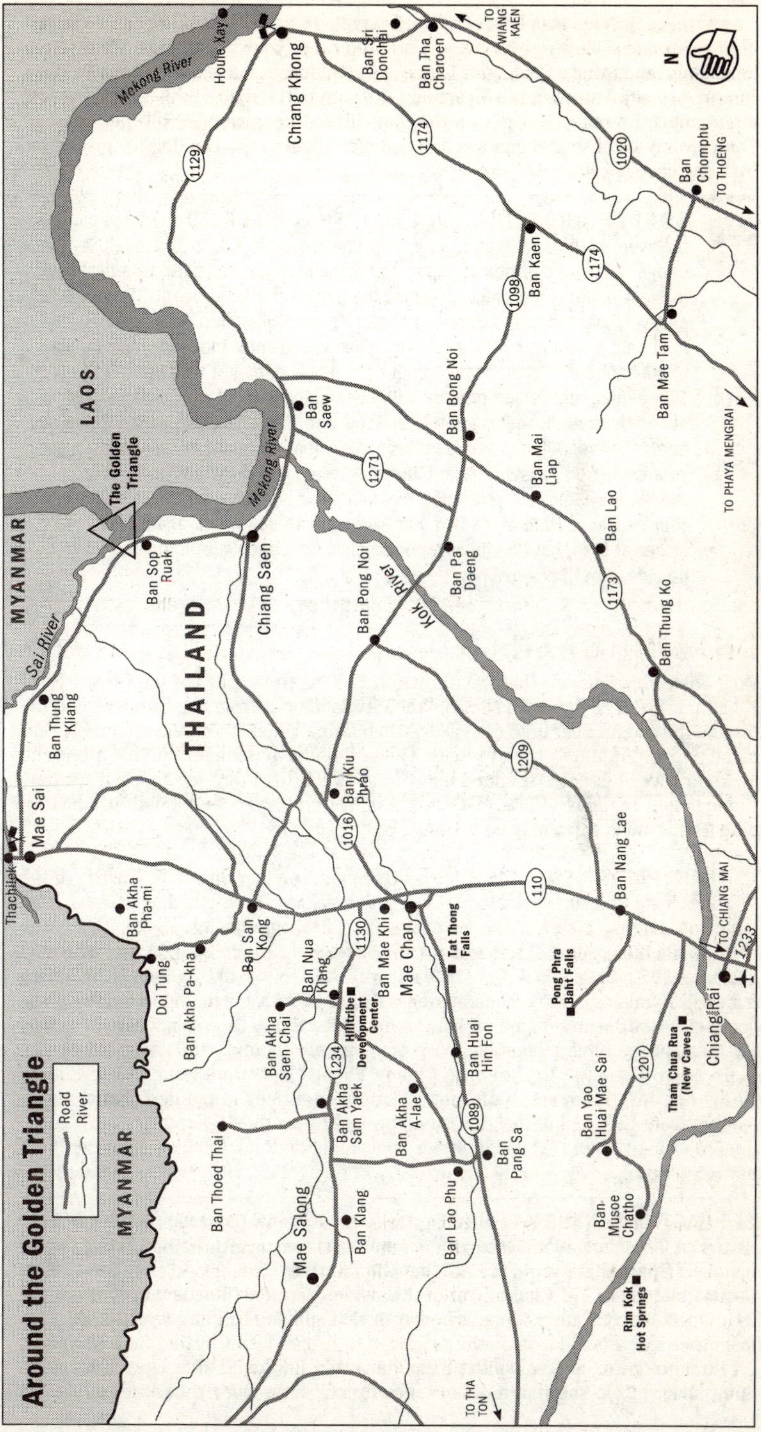
Around the Golden Triangle
Road
River
MYANMAR
LAOS
THAILAND
MYANMAR
Mekong River
Sai River
Kok River
Mekong River
The Golden Triangle
Houie Xay
Chiang Khong
Ban Sri Donchai
Ban Tha Charoen
TO WIANG KAEN
N
1129
1174
1020
Ban Chomphu
TO THOENG
Ban Kaen
1098
1174
Ban Mae Tam
TO PHAYA MENGRAI
Ban Saew
Ban Bong Noi
1271
Ban Mai Liap
Ban Lao
Ban Sop Ruak
Chiang Saen
Ban Pong Noi
Ban Pa Daeng
1173
Ban Thung Ko
Ban Thung Kliang
1209
Ban Kiu Phrao
Mae Sai
Thachilek
1016
Ban Nang Lae
110
TO CHIANG MAI
1233
Ban Akha Pha-mi
Ban San Kong
1130
Ban Mae Khi
Mae Chan
Tat Thong Falls
Doi Tung
Ban Akha Pa-kha
Ban Nua Klang
Hilltribe Development Center
Pong Phra Baht Falls
Chiang Rai
Ban Akha Saen Chai
1234
Ban Huai Hin Fon
Tham Chua Rua (New Caves)
1207
Ban Akha Sam Yaek
Ban Akha A-lae
1089
Ban Yao Huai Mae Sai
Ban Thoed Thai
Ban Pang Sa
Ban Lao Phu
Mae Salong
Ban Klang
Ban Musoe Chatho
Rim Kok Hot Springs
TO THA TON

Ko Samui
Gulf of Thailand
Laem Yai
Ao Bang Po
Ban Thong Po
Ban Tai
4169
Laem Na Phra Lan
Hat Mae Nam
Laem Sai
Hat Bo Phut
Ban Bo Phut
Hat Bangrak (Big Buddha Beach)
Big Buddha Pier
4171
Ban Plai Laem
Ao Thong Sai
Hat Choeng Mon
Laem Son
Ko Mat Lang
Ao Chaweng Yai
Hat Chaweng
Ban Chaweng
Buffalo Fighting Field
View Point
Lamai Cultural Hall
Ban Lamai
Hat Lamai
Grandmother and Grandfather Rocks
Ban Hua Thanon
Ao Na Kai
Laem Set
Butterfly Garden
Ban Bang Kao
Ao Bang Kao
4170
Ban Thurian
Na Muang Waterfall
4173
Ban Thong Krut
Ao Thong Krut
Wat Laem Saw
Snake Farm
Ban Phang Ka
Ao Phang Ka
Laem Hin Khom
Ao Taling Ngam
Ao Nai Sai
Ban Saket
Ban Li Pa Noi
Hin Lat Waterfall
Na Thon
Ao Laem Din
Ao San Ti
Laem Chon Khram
Thong Yang
Ferry Pier
Ao Thong Yang
Vehicle/Passenger Ferry to Don Sak
To Surat Thani
To Ko Phangan
Speed Boats to Thong Sala & Mae Hat
5 miles
5 kilometers

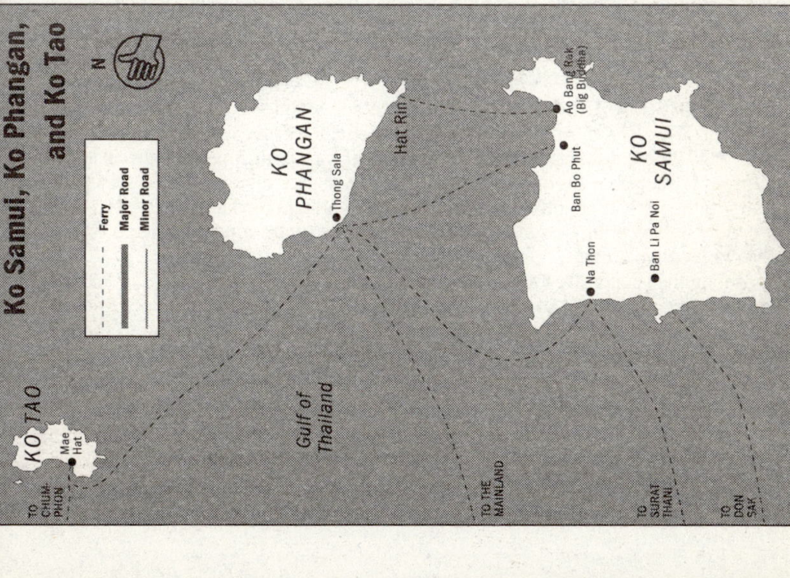
Ko Samui, Ko Phangan, and Ko Tao
Ferry
Major Road
Minor Road
N
Ko Tao
Mae Hat
To Chumphon
Ko Phangan
Thong Sala
Hat Rin
Gulf of Thailand
To the Mainland
Ao Bang Rak (Big Buddha)
Ban Bo Phut
Ko Samui
Na Thon
Ban Li Pa Noi
To Surat Thani
To Don Sak

It's Your World...

MCI

www.mci.com/worldphone

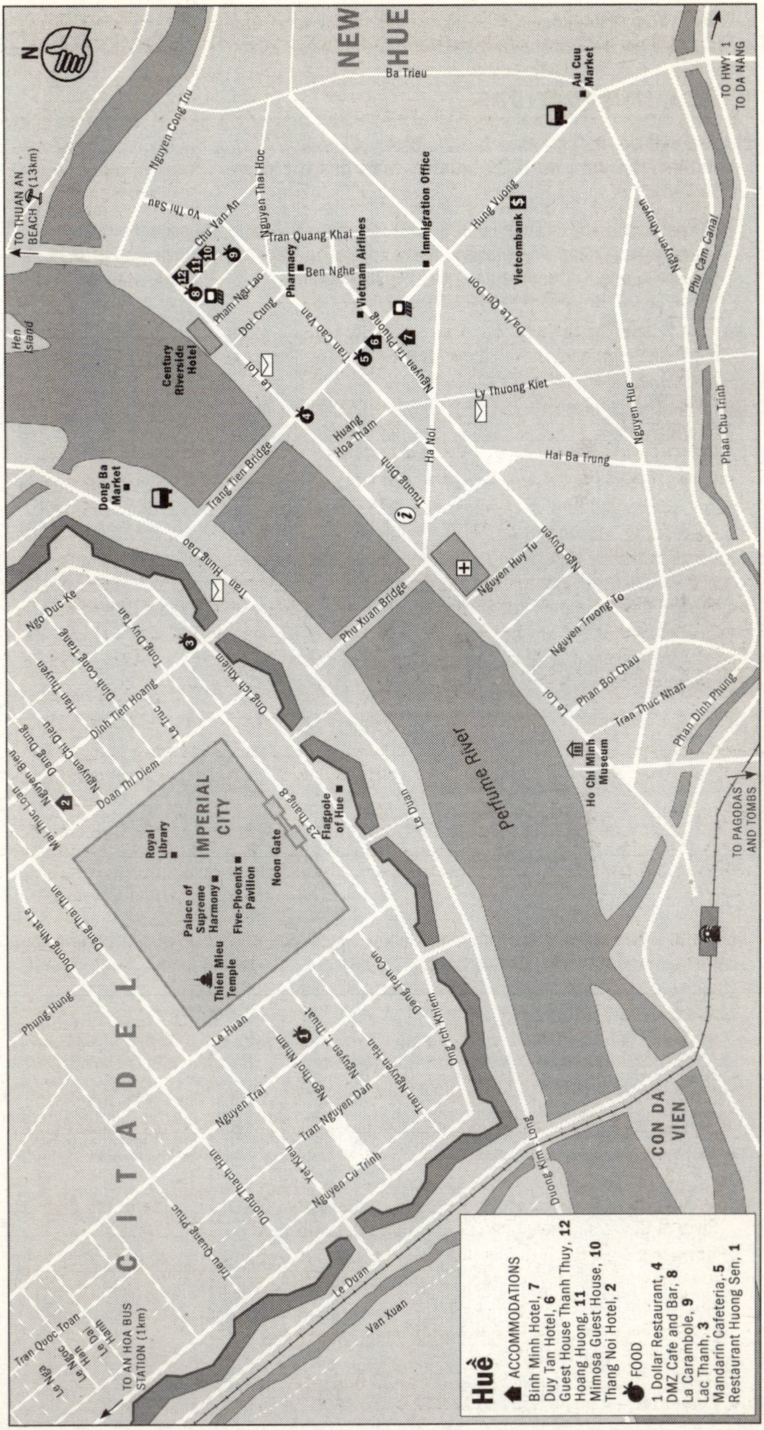
Huế
ACCOMMODATIONS
Binh Minh Hotel, 7
Duy Tan Hotel, 6
Guest House Thanh Thuy, 12
Hoang Huong, 11
Mimosa Guest House, 10
Thang Noi Hotel, 2
FOOD
1 Dollar Restaurant, 4
DMZ Cafe and Bar, 8
La Carambole, 9
Lac Thanh, 3
Mandarin Cafeteria, 5
Restaurant Huong Sen, 1
N
TO THUAN AN BEACH (13km)
NEW HUE
Ba Trieu
Au Cuu Market
TO HWY. 1 TO DA NANG
Nguyen Cong Tru
Vo Thi Sau
Nguyen Thai Hoc
Chu Van An
Tran Quang Khai
Ben Nghe
Pharmacy
Vietnam Airlines
Immigration Office
Hung Vuong
Vietcombank
Pham Ngu Lao
Doi Cung
Century Riverside Hotel
Hen Island
Le Loi
Tran Cao Van
Nguyen Tri Phuong
Da Le Qui Don
Ly Thuong Kiet
Nguyen Khuyen
Phu Cam Canal
Huang Hoa Tham
Ha Noi
Hai Ba Trung
Nguyen Hue
Phan Chu Trinh
Trang Tien Bridge
Dong Ba Market
Truong Dinh
Tran Hung Dao
Nguyen Huy Tu
Ngo Quyen
Phu Xuan Bridge
Nguyen Truong To
Phan Boi Chau
Tran Thuc Nhan
Phan Dinh Phung
Ho Chi Minh Museum
TO PAGODAS AND TOMBS
Ngo Duc Ke
Tong Duy Tan
Dinh Cong Trang
Han Thuyen
Dinh Tien Hoang
Le Truc
Ong Ich Khiem
Nguyen Chi Dieu
Dang Dung
Nguyen Bieu
Doan Thi Diem
Mai Thuc Loan
IMPERIAL CITY
Royal Library
Palace of Supreme Harmony
Five-Phoenix Pavilion
Noon Gate
23 Thang 8
Flagpole of Hue
Thien Mieu Temple
Perfume River
Le Duan
Dang Thai Than
Duong Nhat Le
Phung Hung
Le Huan
Dang Tran Con
Ngo Thoi Nham
Nguyen T. Thuat
Han
Tran Nguyen Han
Nguyen Trai
Tran Nguyen Dan
Duong Thach Han
Yet Kieu
Nguyen Cu Trinh
Trieu Quang Phuc
Duong Kim Long
CON DA VIEN
CITADEL
Van Xuan
Tran Quoc Toan
Le Nga
Le Ngoc Han
Le Dai Hanh
TO AN HOA BUS STATION (1km)

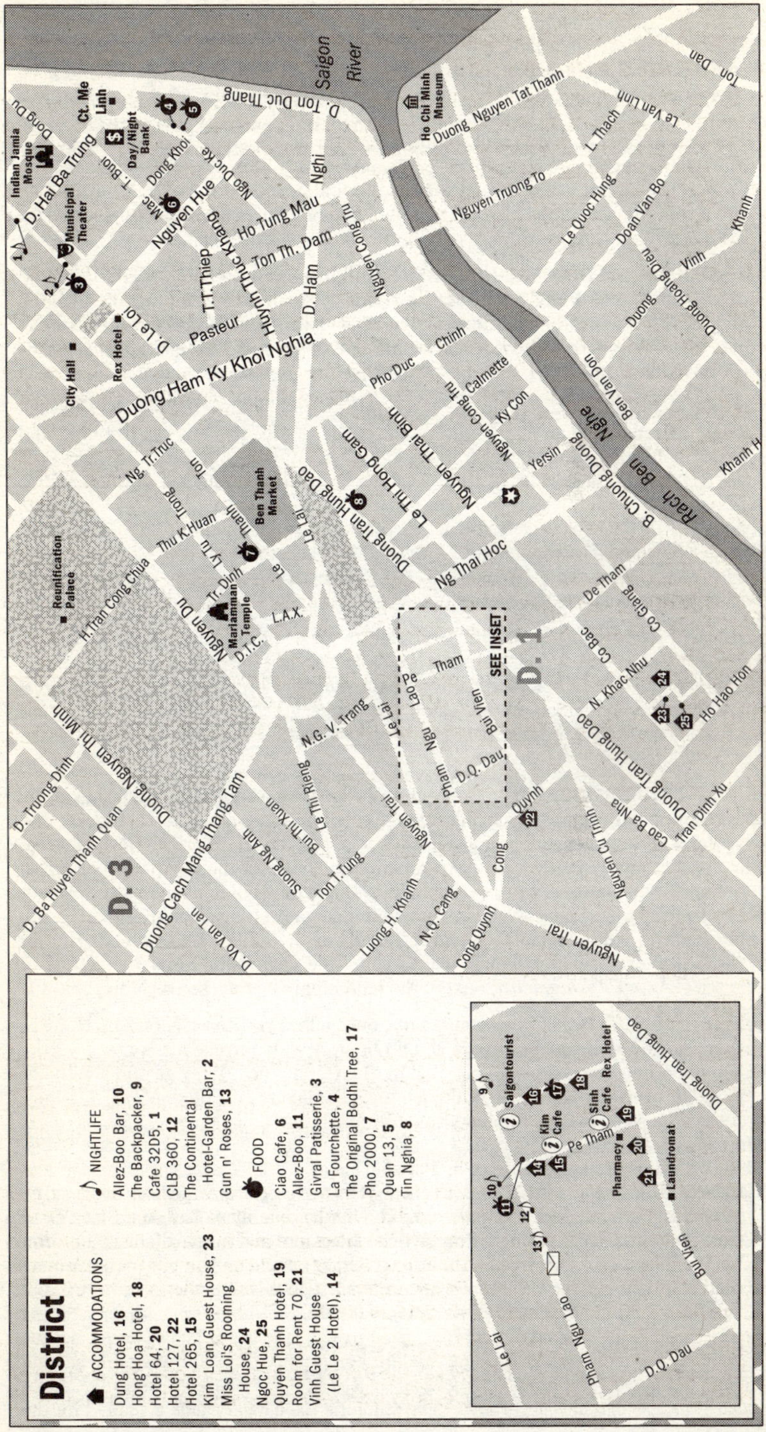
District I
ACCOMMODATIONS
Dung Hotel, 16
Hong Hoa Hotel, 18
Hotel 64, 20
Hotel 127, 22
Hotel 265, 15
Kim Loan Guest House, 23
Miss Loi's Rooming House, 24
Ngoc Hue, 25
Quyen Thanh Hotel, 19
Room for Rent 70, 21
Vinh Guest House (Le Le 2 Hotel), 14
NIGHTLIFE
Allez-Boo Bar, 10
The Backpacker, 9
Cafe 32D5, 1
CLB 360, 12
The Continental Hotel-Garden Bar, 2
Gun n' Roses, 13
FOOD
Ciao Cafe, 6
Allez-Boo, 11
Givral Patisserie, 3
La Fourchette, 4
The Original Bodhi Tree, 17
Pho 2000, 7
Quan 13, 5
Tin Nghia, 8
Saigontourist
Kim Cafe
Sinh Cafe
Rex Hotel
Pharmacy
Laundromat
Pe Tham
Pham Ngu Lao
Le Lai
Bui Vien
D.Q. Dau
Duong Tran Hung Dao
D. 3
D. 1
SEE INSET
Saigon River
Reunification Palace
City Hall
Rex Hotel
Municipal Theater
Indian Jamia Mosque
Day/Night Bank
Ho Chi Minh Museum
Ben Thanh Market
Mariamman Temple
Rach Ben Nghe
Duong Ham Ky Khoi Nghia
Duong Nguyen Thi Minh
Duong Cach Mang Thang Tam
D. Ton Duc Thang
D. Hai Ba Trung
Nguyen Hue
Duong Nguyen Tat Thanh
Duong Tran Hung Dao
Nguyen Thai Binh
Le Thi Hong Gam
Ng Thai Hoc
B. Chuong Duong
Nguyen Trai
Cong Quynh

E

F

G

H

INDEX